FOUNDATIONS OF ACCOUNTING

Edited by
RICHARD P. BRIEF
New York University

A GARLAND SERIES

Accountants' Index

A Bibliography of Accounting Literature to December, 1920

In two volumes
Volume 1
A - E

GARLAND PUBLISHING, INC.

NEW YORK & LONDON 1988

For a list of Garland's publications in accounting, see the final pages of volume II

Reproduced from a copy in the American Institute of Certified Public Accountants

Library of Congress Cataloging in Publication Data

Accountants' index : a bibliography of accounting literature to December, 1920.
p. cm. — (Foundations of accounting)
Reprint. Originally published: New York : American Institute of Accountants, 1921.
Contents: v. 1. A-E — v. 2. F-Z.
ISBN 0-8240-6140-3 (alk. paper)
1. Accounting—Bibliography. 2. Accounting—History—Bibliography. I. American Institute of Accountants. II. Series.
Z7164.C81A22 1988
[HF5635]
016.657—dc 19 88-16489

Design by Renata Gomes

The volumes in this series are printed on acid-free, 250-year-life paper.

Printed in the United States of America

ACCOUNTANTS' INDEX

A BIBLIOGRAPHY OF ACCOUNTING LITERATURE TO DECEMBER, 1920

AMERICAN INSTITUTE OF ACCOUNTANTS
1921

THOMAS E. GEISTWEIT
318 WEST 39TH STREET, NEW YORK

Table of Contents

	Page
Reference books, accounting and allied subjects	1
General literature	1566
Directory	1567

INTRODUCTORY NOTE

There are many books and articles on accounting and allied subjects. The growth of this literature has been especially rapid during the last five years.

The mission of this book is to record and to index in ready reference form this widely scattered material. No attempt has been made to include publications written in foreign languages.

References will be found to the known English literature on the subject of accounting in print in 1912 and published since that year to and including December 31, 1920.

Supplements will be issued at intervals, depending on the amount of published data.

Names of authors, subjects and titles are arranged in a single alphabet with information as to publisher, place of publication, date and number of pages. In analytical or title references, trade information will be found under author entry or, where author is missing, under title entry.

To find books on a certain subject look for that subject as in an encyclopedia, and to find books by a certain author look for that author.

For example, "Interpretations of accounting classifications" by the "Interstate commerce commission" may be found either under the subject, "Railroads—Accounting," or under the author, "United States—Interstate commerce commission."

LOUISE S. MILTIMORE,
Librarian.

135 Cedar Street, New York.
January, 1921.

ACCOUNTANTS' INDEX

A B C automatic balancing charts. Thornton, J. 1901.

A B C of balance sheet making. Layman, A.

A B C of bookkeeping. Dicksee, L. R. 1908.

A B C of bookkeeping. Wells, W. H. 1912.

A B C of cost engineering. Denham, Robert S. 1919.

A B C of loose-leaf bookkeeping. Sweetland, C. A. 1906.

A B C of the foreign exchanges. Clare, George. 1915

A B C of the personal income tax law. State of New York, June 1919. Travis, E. M. 1919.

A B C D series of bookkeeping exercise books. Thornton, J.

A. R. A. section v. 1, purchases and stores, first annual meeting. *Railway age,* June 15, 1920, p. 1813-22. *Railway review,* June 26, 1920, p. 1083-93.

ABBOT, JACK
Depreciation of lighting plants. *Mississippi electrical association, Report of 2nd annual convention,* June 1910, p. 37-9.

ABBOTT, C. A. E.
Advantage of combining theory and practice in banking. *Accountant,* Dec. 30, 1899, p. 1249-52.
Taking of accounts in chambers. *Accountant,* April 18, 1908, p. 575-8.

ABBOTT, C. E.
Flat rate versus meters. *Engineering and contracting,* Sept. 10, 1919, p. 294. *Waterworks association journal,* Jan. 1920, p. 132-6.

ABBOTT, C. T. and H. F. PORTER
Making your cost system tell the truth. *Factory,* Nov. 1917, p. 708-9.

ABBOTT, F. M.
Function of state and municipal accounting. City hall, Feb. 1912, p. 171-4.

ABBOTT, FRANK SHARP
Factors' acts. *Accountant,* April 18, 1885.
Taxation of land values. *Accountant,* March 21, 1908, p. 397-407.

ABBOTT, H. R.
Costs and methods of building large sewers. *Engineering review,* April 25, 1914, p. 473-5
Methods and cost of constructing large brick and concrete sewers in Chicago, with notes on the cost keeping system employed. *Engineering and contracting,* Feb. 11, 1914, p. 201-5.

ABELL, H. C.
Difficult problems which public utility commissions are endeavoring to solve. *Journal of electricity, power and gas,* Jan. 30, 1909, p. 81.

ABELL, O. J.
Labor classified on a skill-wages basis by Ford Motor co. *Iron age,* Jan. 1, 1914, p. 48-51. *Scientific American supplement,* Feb. 7, 1914, p. 86-8.
Making of men, motor cars and profits of the Ford motor company. *Iron age,* Jan. 7, 1915, p. 33-41.
Making the Ford motor car. *Iron age,* June 13, 1912, p. 1454-1460.
Packard motor car company's productive system; records, time, studies etc. *Iron age,* June 19, 1913, p. 1473-6.

ABENDROTH, HARRY G.
Overhead charges in valuation; a discussion of the elements that must be considered in the appraisal of public utilities; percentages as worked out in the experience of the Milwaukee electric railway and light co. *Aera,* Nov. 1914, p. 354. *Electric railway journal,* June 27, 1914, p. 1434-7.

ABERDEEN and depreciation. *Municipal journal* (London), Oct. 23, 1903, p. 943.

ABILITY guaranteed.
Journal of accountancy, Feb. 1916, p. 138-40.

ABOLITION of the trial balance together with twelve studies in book-keeping and accounting. Detroit, Michigan. The Book-keeper publishing company, c1906. 168p.

ABOUT bond issues. Robinson, J. W.

ABSENCES—how to reduce them. *Factory,* Aug. 1918, p. 231-3.

ABSOLUTE and theoretical depreciation. *Scientific American Supplement,* Dec. 9, 1911, p. 374.

ABSTRACT bookkeeping. *Accountant,* March 14, 21, 1891, p. 198-201, 220-2.

ABSTRACT of address before the Boston city club, Oct. 24th, 1907. Chase, H. S.

ABSTRACT of opinion by the Wisconsin commission upon its investigation into rates, rules and regulations of lighting and power companies in Milwaukee. *Electrical world,* Aug. 31, 1912, p. 439-40.

ABSTRACT of the census of manufactures. United States Bureau of census.

ABSTRACT of the twelfth census, 1900. United States. Bureau of census. 1902.

ABSTRACTS of paper at 10th annual convention of Railway store-keepers assn., Chicago, 1913. *Railway age,* May 23, 1913, p. 1134-45. *Railway age* (Mech. ed.) June 1913, p. 297-

ABUSE of the audit in selling securities. Smith, Alexander.

ACCEPTABILITY of commercial paper. *American institute of accountants, Yearbook.* 1915, p. 214-6.

ACCEPTANCES

AMERICAN EXCHANGE NATIONAL BANK. Acceptances; their importance as a means of increasing and simplifying domestic and foreign commerce. Ed. 2, revised. New York, Exchange national bank, 1918. 79p.

AVERY, W. G. Acceptances in retail business. *Journal of accountancy,* Feb. 1919, p. 120-4.

CHEMICAL NATIONAL BANK OF NEW YORK. Bankers acceptances and trade acceptances. New York, Chemical national bank of New York, c1917. 24p.

GREELEY, HAROLD DUDLEY. Notes and trade acceptances. (In his *Theory of accounts.* 1920. p. 294-305).

GUARANTY TRUST COMPANY OF NEW YORK. Acceptances. New York, Guaranty trust company of New York, c1917. 72p.

IRVING NATIONAL BANK. Trade acceptance progress, addresses and discussion by American bankers and business men at open trade acceptance meetings under the auspices of New York credit men's association and American trade acceptance council. New York, Irving national bank, 1917. 108p.

KNIFFIN, WILLIAM HENRY. Commercial paper, acceptances and the analysis of credit statements; a practical treatise on commercial paper, with particular reference to the processes by which the credit risk is determined where such instruments are purchased as a bank investment. New York, Bankers publishing co. 1918. 162p.

LANGTRY, H. Trade acceptance. *Canadian chartered accountant,* July 1918, p. 38-9.

MECHANICS AND METALS NATIONAL BANK. Acceptances: their purpose and advantages. New York. Mechanics and metals national bank, c1918. 50p.

PIERSON, LEWIS E. Survey of trade acceptance progress; an address before the annual trade convention of the American trade acceptance council, New York, December 2, 1920. New York, Irving national bank, c1920. 18p.

WALTON, SEYMOUR. Bank acceptances. *Journal of accountancy,* July 1916, p. 63-4.

WALTON, SEYMOUR. Trade acceptances. *Journal of accountancy,* July 1916, p. 58-62.

ACCIDENT INSURANCE

See Insurance—Accidents.

ACCIDENTS

ASHE, SIDNEY WHITMORE. Organization in accient prevention. New York, McGraw-Hill book co. 1917. 130 p.

CHARLTON, D. E. Utilization of mine-accident reports. *Engineering and mining journal,* Nov. 30, 1918, p. 945-8.

COLE, ROLAND. Complete record of accidents in manufacturing plants; this article describes and shows the proper forms for conducting with accuracy a department necessary in all factories where workmen are liable to injury. *Business man's magazine,* Dec. 1907, p. 76-7.

DAVIS, G. H. Accident blanks in New Orleans. *Street railway journal,* Feb. 1898.

FAY, A. H. Careful records reduce mine accidents. *Coal age,* Sept. 12, 1918, p. 503-4. Excerpts. *Engineering and mining journal,* Oct. 19, 1918, p. 699-701.

FAY, A. H. Mine accidents and uniform record: with discussion. *Pan American scientific congress, Proceedings,* 1915, v.8, p. 494-520

FORMS for use in recording compensation. *Coal age,* Sept. 12, 1918, p. 506-8.

MATTHEWS, CLARENCE D. Records of employes injured; in large factories where accidents of some sort are of daily occurrence, and of which a record should be kept, this system will be found invaluable. *Business man's magazine,* April 1907, p. 118-122.

MINE accident record. *Coal age,* Dec. 30, March 3, 1917, April 14, 1917.

MINE—accident statistics and prevention. *Engineering and mining journal,* March 11, 1916, p. 467-8.

NEW accident report forms. *Railway age gazette,* Aug. 13, 1915, p. 272-3.

OREGON. STATE INDUSTRIAL ACCIDENT COMMISSION. Financial report: Comparative statement: Report on examination and audit; Supplementary balance sheet. 1919-1920. 4 pamphlets.

SIZER, R. W. E. Knowing what accidents cost. *Factory,* Feb. 1917, p. 182-4.

STANDARDIZATION of mine accident reports and statistics. *Engineering and mining journal,* June 29, 1918, p. 1165.

TILLSON, B. F. Recording of accidents, and safety measures employed by the New Jersey zinc co. *Engineering gand mining journal,* April 7, 1917, p. 627-34.

UNITED STATES. BUREAU OF LABOR STATISTICS. Proceedings of the sixth annual meeting of the International association of industrial accident boards and commissions held at Toronto, Canada, Sept. 23-26, 1919. Washington, Government printing office, 1920. 424p.

WEST, T. D. Card notation to help in the reduction of accidents. *American industries,* Feb. 1914, p. 24-6.

WEST, T. D. Recording memoranda on accident prevention. *American industries,* Dec. 1913, p. 19-20.

ACCOMPLISHMENTS of the military railways. Sullivan, W. W. 1919.

ACCOMPTANT'S oracle. Thompson, Wardhaugh. 1777.

ACCOMPTS for landed men. Snell, Charles. 1710.

ACCOUNT analysis in commercial banks. Thompson, H. C.

ACCOUNT book for executors and administrators. Newman, J. T. 1904.

ACCOUNT books for missions, etc. Specially ruled account books for charities missions, and nursing institutions are also supplied. London, Scientific press.

ACCOUNT-KEEPING in principle and practice. Lisle, George and W. A. Middleton. 1911.

ACCOUNT numbers for distribution of costs. Oregon. State highway commission.

ACCOUNTANCY

See also Accountants: Accounting.

ACCOUNTANCY and economics. *Journal of accountancy,* June, 1908, p. 140.

ACCOUNTANCY and economics. *Journal of accountancy,* Jan. 1909, p. 237-9.

ACCOUNTANCY and its future. *Accountant,* Oct. 31, 1896, p. 898-9.

ACCOUNTANCY and law compared. *Journal of accountancy,* May, 1919, p. 364-6.

ACCOUNTANCY as a commodity. *Journal of accountancy,* March, 1913, p. 187-8.

ACCOUNTANCY—*(Continued)*
ACCOUNTANCY as a profession. *Accountant,* Dec. 7, 14, 1912, p. 709-10, 736-9.
ACCOUNTANCY defined. *Journal of accountancy,* Aug. 1914, p. 127-8.
ACCOUNTING papers before the economic association. *Journal of accountancy,* Feb. 1909, p. 321-3.
AMERICAN economic association. Accountancy—discussions. *American economic association. Papers and discussions,* April, 1911, p. 145-53.
AMERICAN economic association. Accounting: round table discussion. *American economic association. Papers and discussions,* April, 1909, p. 59-104.
AMERICAN economic association. *Journal of accountancy,* Jan. 1909, p. 240-1.
As others see us. *Accountant,* May 11, 1907. *Incorporated accountants' journal,* May, 1907. *Journal of accountancy,* June, 1907, p. 158-61.
BARBER, JARVIS W. Notes on present position of accountancy. London, Gee & co. 1896.
BARBER, JARVIS W. Some notes on the profession of accountancy. *Accountant,* Oct. 17, 1896, p. 841-6.
BASIS of success. *Journal of accountancy,* March, 1911, p. 207.
BETTER accounting needed. *Wall street journal,* July 14, 1909. *Journal of accountancy,* Aug. 1909, p. 303.
BINDLOSS, R. H. Accountancy and auditing. *Incorporated accountants'' journal,* Jan. 1912, p. 100-3.
BINDLOSS, R. H. Accountancy from without. *Accountant,* Oct. 11, 1913, p. 479-91. *Incorporated accountants' journal,* Nov. 1913, p. 36-44.
BLACKLOCK, FRANK. Legal accounting and commercial bookkeeping. *Accountant,* Aug. 20, 1898, p. 803-5.
BLACKLOCK, FRANK. Suggestions to those who enter the profession of accountancy. *Business,* Nov. 1897-March, 1898, p. 337, 370; 37-8, 106-7, 173-4.
BRANFORD, VICTOR V. On the correlation of economics and accountancy. *Accountant,* May 25, June 1, 1901, p. 620-8, 642-8.
BREAKING in. *Journal of accountancy.* Aug. 1920, p. 135-8.
BROWN, RICHARD. Accountant. (In Lisle, George. *Encyclopaedia of accounting.* v.1. p. 12-7.)
BROWN, WILLIAM. Address. *Accountant,* Oct. 1, 1904, p. 342-7.
CARTER, ERIC M. Outlook of accountancy. *Accountant,* April 28, June 9, 1906, p. 530-6, 717-21.
CHALMERS, ANTHONY WIGHAM. Address. *Accountant,* March 10, 17, 1883.
CHOICE of a profession. *Journal of accountancy,* April, 1912, p. 291-3.
CHOICE of a profession—accountancy. *Accountant,* Sept. 20, 1890, p. 499-500.
CLEVELAND, FREDERICK ALBERT. Accountancy as a profession; reprinted from the *Financier,* Aug. 1, 1904. New York, 1904. 11 p.
CLEVELAND, FREDERICK A. Appraisements and accountancy. *Auditor,* 1905, p. 125, 153.
CLEVELAND, FREDERICK A. Dr. Cleveland's response: correspondence. *Journal of accountancy,* Dec. 1906, p. 156-7.
CLEVELAND, FREDERICK A. Scope of the profession of accountancy. *Journal of accountancy.* Nov. 1905, p. 40-56.
CLEVELAND, FREDERICK A. What may accountancy teach economics. *Journal of accountancy,* Oct. 1906, p. 401-19.
COBBLER and last. *Journal of accountancy,* Nov. 1920, p. 361-4.
COLE, WILLIAM M. Rise of accountancy. *Journal of accountancy,* Feb. 1909, p. 295-6.
COMINS, CHARLES. General principles. *Accountant,* Nov. 26, 1898, p. 1144-50.
COMMON sense and accountancy. *Accountant,* March 8, 15, 1913, p. 332-3, 380-2.
CONSULTING practice among accountants. *Journal of accountancy,* Dec. 1905, p. 141-2.
COOKE, SILAS. Accountancy and auditing. *Accountant,* June 6, 1885.
COOLEY, MORGAN L. Successful accountancy. *Accountant,* Nov. 13, 1909, p. 598-600. *Journal of accountancy,* Feb. 1909, p. 297-302.
COOPER, JOHN ALEXANDER. Evolution of the accountant. *New York accountants' and bookkeeper's journal,* March, 1904, p. 65-9.
DAKIN, EDWARD. Economics and accountancy. *Incorporated accountants' journal,* July, 1920, p. 212-4.
DICKINSON, ARTHUR LOWES. Profession of the public accountant. *Accountant,* May 27, 1905, p. 650-8. *Auditor,* 1905, p. 165, 185.
DICKINSON, ARTHUR LOWES. Some special points in accountancy practice. *Accountant,* April 22, 1905, p. 495-504. *Auditor,* 1905, p. 105, 130, 158.
DICKSEE, LAWRENCE ROBERT. Student's guide to accountancy. Gee & co. 1897. 110 p.
EDWARDS, GEORGE. Address to students. *Canadian chartered accountant,* April, 1913, p. 261-8.
ENGLISH v. American practice. *Accountant,* May 11, 1907, p. 660-2. *Incorporated accountants' journal,* 1906-7, p. 192. *Journal of accountancy,* April 1907, p. 388-93.
ENGLISH vs. American practice. *Journal of accountancy,* June 1907, p. 139-40.
ESPRIT de corps. *Journal of accountancy,* June 1912, p. 433-5.
FELLS, JOHN MANGER. Accountancy of tomorrow. *Incorporated accountants' journal,* 1910-11, p. 69-74.
FELLS, JOHN MANGER. New accountancy. *Incorporated accountants' journal,* 1906-7, p. 195.
FINDLAY, JAMES. Accounting past and present *South African accountant,* June, Sept. 1917, p. 11-4, 53-7.
FOR the good of the profession. *Journal of accountancy,* May, June, 1913, p 354-6, 472.
FOSTER, A. J. War time accountancy, *Accountant,* Feb. 16, 1918, p. 150-5.
FOX, WILLIAM HENRY. Present and future of accountancy. London, Gee & co. 1887. *Accountant,* 1887, p. 249.
FOX, WILLIAM HENRY. Present and future of accountancy, April 18, 1908, p. 564-8.
FREEMAN, C. E. "Jobs": correspondence, *Journal of accountancy,* Feb. 1916, p. 157.
FRENCH, ROBERT DUNCAN. Theory and practice of accountancy. *Incorporated accountants' journal,* 1899-1900, p. 148.
GARRISON, ELISHA ELY. Currency-banking and accountancy. *Journal of accountancy,* Aug. 1910. p. 286-8.
GORDON, JOHN. Address. *Accountant,* Oct. 18, 1913, p. 513-7, 533-8.
GORDON, JOHN. Speaking in general, and its relation to accountancy in particular. *Accountant,* Jan. 28, 1893, p. 83-93.
GORDON, WILLIAM. General counting-house and man of business. Ed. 2. Edinburgh, 1770.
GOWER, WILLIAM B. Advisory accountancy. *Journal of accountancy,* Oct. 1920, p. 262-70.
GREELEY, HAROLD DUDLEY. New reciprocity of accountancy and law. *Journal of accountancy,* Sept. 1908, p. 317-28.
GREEN, ARTUR E. Thoughts on accountancy. *Incorporated accountants' journal,* Dec, 1912, p. 63-6.

ACCOUNTANCY—*(Continued)*

GREIG, JAMES B. How the profession may serve the community. *Accountant,* June 26, 1897, p. 639-43.

GROWTH of accountancy. *Accountant,* Aug. 18, 1917, p. 134-5. *Journal of accountancy,* April 1917, p. 283-6.

GUIDE to the accountancy profession. Ed. 2 revised, London, Gee & co.

GUNDRY, WILLIAM H. Accountancy. *Accountant,* July 18, 1903, p. 931-3.

GUNDRY, WILLIAM H. Underlying principles of accountancy and their application in law. *Accountant,* Sept. 3, 1904, p. 239-41.

HAMILTON, W. R. Accountancy in its relation to some economic problems. *Accountant,* May 16, July 25, 1908, p. 716-21; 92-3.

HARDCASTLE, JOSEPH. On the dignity of the accountancy profession. *New York accountants and bookkeepers journal,* April, 1904, p. 104-5.

HARMOOD-BANNER, JOHN S. Theory and practice. *Accountant,* Dec. 8, 1900, p. 1117-9.

HASKINS, CHARLES WALDO. Address by the president, New York state society of certified public accountants. *Accountant,* Aug. 18, 1900, p. 756-60.

HASKINS, CHARLES WALDO. Economics and pedagogy. *Accountant,* Nov. 3, 1900, p. 983-4.

HASKINS, CHARLES WALDO. Growing need of the higher accountancy; an address delivered at the annual dinner of the Pennsylvania institute of certified public accountants, April 15, 1901. 14 p. (In his *Business education and accountancy.* c1904. p. 110-25.) *Accountant,* Aug. 3, 1901, p. 869-71. *Commerce, accounts and finance,* April 20, 1901, p. 5-7.

HASKINS, CHARLES WALDO. Possibilities of the profession of accountancy as a moral and educational force. (In his *Business education and accountancy.* c1904. p. 90-109.)

HASKINS, CHARLES WALDO. Progress of professional accountancy; an address at the regular meeting of the Institute of accounts, June 27, 1901. Philadelphia, American academy of political and social science, 1901. 17 p. *Accountant,* July 5, 1902, p. 680-4. *Commerce, accounts and finance,* July, 1901, p. 19-21.

HEMINGWAY, WILFRID H. Few observations on legislation for the accountancy profession and some other matters. *Australasian accountant and secretary,* Dec. 1, 1919, p. 18-21.

HENRY, W. E. Accountancy and efficiency. *Engineering magazine,* June 1912, p. 436.

HEUSHELWOOD, J. J. HADEN. Is accountancy being overdone? *Australasian accountant and secretary,* May, 1920, p. 138-40.

HEWITT, W. J. Hints to students on book-keeping and accountancy. *Associated accountants journal,* 1910, p. 197.

HICKSON, J. B. Accountancy. *Pubilc accountant,* 1908, p. 173.

HIGH SCHOOL ASSOCIATION OF NEW YORK CITY. Accountancy and the business professions. New York, High school teachers association, 1910.

INCOME tax and the accountancy profession. *Accountant,* Oct. 16, 1915, p. 445-7, 449-50.

JOBS: correspondence. *Journal of accountancy,* April, 1916, p. 308.

KINLEY, DAVID. Field of accountancy. *Accountant,* Sept. 1, 1906, p. 243-6. *Journal of accountancy,* July, 1906, p. 187-93.

KIRBY, HORACE WOODBURN. Accountancy a profession. *Accountant,* Oct. 12, 1907, p. 457-65.

KLEIN, JOSEPH JEROME. Accountancy and the business professions. New York, Students aid commitee of the high school teachers association of New York city, 1910. 16 p.

KLEIN, JOSEPH JEROME. Accountancy, the youngest of the professions. New York, National business institute, 1912. 8 p. Title from cover.

LAIRD, THOMAS PATRICK. Development of accountancy in relation to commerce. *Accountants magazine,* Nov. 1919, p. 458-71.

LAKEMAN, JAMES. Accountancy in its relation to finance. *Accountant,* June 18, July 9, 1892, p. 491-5, 537.

LANHAM, HERBERT S. Accountancy as a close profession—some comparisons and suggestions. *Accountant,* Jan. 21, March 4, 1905, p. 83-90, 242-5.

LE ROSSIGNOL, JAMES EDWARD. Relation between accountancy and economics, a paper to be presented at the annual meeting of the American association of public accountants, October 19, 20, 21, 1909. 10 p. *American institute of accountants, Yearbook,* 1909, p. 127-41. *Journal of accountancy,* Dec. 1909, p. 81-8.

LIGHTBAND, R. M. Present and future of the accountancy profession. *Accountant,* Dec. 4, 1920, p. 605-11.

MCNEILL, J. H. Accountancy and insurance. *Incorporated accountants journal,* Aug. 1913, p. 279-83.

MARSHALL, HENRY CALDER. Questions that arise in practice. *Accountant,* June 1, 1895, p. 493-9.

MATHER, JOHN. Influence of the accountancy profession in the commercial sphere. *Accountant,* Oct. 22, Nov. 5, 1898, p. 999-1006, 1053-6. *Business,* Dec. 1898, p. 756-60.

MEADE, E. D. Profession of public accounting. *New York accountants and bookkeepers journal,* June 1904, p. 164-5.

MEADE, EDWARD SHERWOOD. Opportunity of the accountant: an address delivered before the New York state society of certified public accountants, March 14, 1904. 10 p.

MOLE, A. C. Students epitome of accountancy and book-keeping. London, 1908.

MORGAN, HENRY. Some general points of interest to accountants. *Incorporated accountants journal,* Dec. 1915, p. 64-7.

MURRAY, ADAM. Progress of accountancy and the duties which come within the scope of an accountant's practice. *Accountant,* Dec. 24, 31, 1881.

NAIRNE, W. H. Address. *Accountant,* Nov. 23, 1889, p. 626-30.

NAIRNE, W. H. Present position of accountancy in view of recent legal decisions. *Accountant,* March 21, 1896, p. 228-43.

NEAL, THEODORE. Economics and accountancy. *Accountant,* Dec. 15, 1888, p. 815-7.

NELSON, C. HEWETSON. Future of the accountancy profession. *Accountant,* Oct. 24, 31, 1903, p. 1289-99, 1309-12. *Incorporated accountants' journal,* 1903-4, p. 27.

NELSON, CHARLES HEWETSON. Modern accountancy and its relation to commerce. *Accountant,* Nov. 30, 1912, p. 685-91.

NELSON, GODFREY N. Accounting as a skilled profession. *Journal of accountancy,* July, 1906, p. 201.

OUTLOOK of accountancy. *Journal of accountancy,* June, 1906, p. 138-41.

PEAT, WILLIAM BARCLAY. Address: London students' society dinner, 1907. *Accountant,* Dec. 14, 1907, p. 745-8.

PEAT, WILLIAM BARCLAY. Speech at Liverpool chartered accountants' dinner, 1907, *Accountant,* Dec. 7, 1907, p. 705-8.

ACCOUNTANCY—*(Continued)*

PIXLEY, FRANCIS W. Accountancy. London, Sir Isaac Pitman and sons. 315 p.

PIXLEY, FRANCIS W. Profession of a chartered accountant, and other lectures. London, Swan, Sonnenschein & co. 1897. 272 p.

PIXLEY, FRANCIS W. Profession of accountancy. London, Swan, Sonnenschein & co. 1897.

POINTS of interest to accountants. *Accountant,* Jan. 27, Feb. 3, 10, 17, 24, April 7, 1900. p. 93-5, 121-3, 153-5, 176-7, 201-2, 325-7.

POWERS, LE GRAND. New world movement. *Government accountant,* Sept. 1910, p. 185-92.

PRESIDENT PLENDER'S address. *Journal of accountancy,* Nov. 1910, p. 58-61.

PROFESSION—not a business. *Journal of accountancy,* Oct. 1920, p. 271-3.

PROFESSIONAL organization among the technicians of the office. *Accountant,* June 23, 1917, p. 593-5.

RECKITT, ERNEST. Possibilities of the profession. *Auditor,* 1905, p. 137.

RECOLLECTION of an old accountant. *Accountant,* Sept. 5, 1914, p. 268-72. *Canadian chartered accountant,* Oct. 1914, p. 134-41.

REID, J. L. Accountants, a needed profession. *North American review,* v. 159, p. 510.

RICHARDSON, GEORGE H. Combines and accountancy organization. *Accountant,* Oct. 20, 1900, p. 933-6.

ROBERTS, W. H. Systems and system making; and system failures. *Auditor,* 1905. p. 71. 109.

ROBERTSON, JAMES A. Business of an accountant. *Accountant,* Jan. 26, 1895, p. 86-92.

ROSS, F. A. Growth and effect of branch offices. *Journal of accountancy,* Oct. 1920, p. 252-61.

ROWE, C. V. Charlatanism in the profession of accountancy. *Journal of accountancy,* Oct. 1913, p. 301-5.

RYAN, THOMAS P. Accountant in world affairs. *American institute of accountants, Yearbook,* 1907, p. 159-65. *Journal of accountancy.* Dec. 1907, p. 107-13.

SCOPE of accountancy. *Journal of accountancy,* June 1915, p. 456-8.

SOME points in accountancy practice. *Accountant,* May 18, 1901, p. 573-6.

STERRETT, JOSEPH E. Present position and probable development of accountancy as a profession. *Journal of accountancy,* Feb. 1909, p. 265-73. *American economic association, Papers and discussions,* 1909, p. 85-96.

STERRETT, JOSEPH E. Profession of accountancy. *Annals of the American academy of political and social science,* July 1906, p. 16-27.

THEORY and practice in accounting. *Journal of accountancy,* Oct. 1909, p. 449-52.

TREVOR, CHARLES ROBERT. Accountancy prospects. *Accountant,* Nov. 1, 1884.

ULLRICH, WILLIAM A. Educate the business public; correspondence. *Journal of accountancy,* July 1908, p. 213.

VALUE of the profession of accountancy to business men. *Australasian accountant and secretary,* July 1920, p. 199-200.

VANNAIS, GEORGE L. Accounting profession. *Electric railway journal,* Oct. 16, 1920, p. 769.

VOLLUM, CHARLES N. New conception of accountancy. *Accountant,* May 19, 1906, p. 645-7. *Journal of accountancy,* April 1906, p. 475-8.

WALTON, SEYMOUR. Accountancy in relation to business organization and management. *National educational association, Proceedings,* 1912, p. 1069-75.

WALTON, SEYMOUR. "Jobs." *Journal of accountancy,* March 1916, p. 231.

WANTED: a bill of particulars. *Journal of accountancy,* Sept. 1915, p. 216-7.

WEBSTER, NORMAN E. Prerequisites for accountancy practice. *Journal of accountancy,* Sept. 1908, p. 338-9.

WELD, L. D. H. Method of reasoning in economics: correspondence. *Journal of accountancy,* Dec. 1906, p. 154-6.

WELTON, T. A. On some subjects of inquiry open to accountants. *Accountant,* Oct. 17, 1896, p. 853-5.

WHAT the profession offers. *Australasian accountant and secretary,* Jan. 1, 1920, p. 32-3.

WHINNEY, FREDERICK. Address. *Accountant,* 1887, p. 386.

WHINNEY, FREDERICK. Address: London students' society. *Accountant,* May 12, 1883.

WITTY, RICHARD A. How to become a qualified accountant. London, Sir Issac Pitman and sons. 126p.

WORD to those who would be accountants. *Journal of accountancy,* Jan. 1920, p. 53-6.

YARWOOD, F. N. Random notes. *Accountant,* Sept. 6, 1899, p. 954-8.

Australia

ACCOUNTANCY in Australia. *Accountant,* Nov. 18, 1899, Oct. 4, 1913, p. 1135-9; 432-4.

ACCOUNTANCY in New South Wales. *Accountant,* June 26, 1915, June 23, 1917, p. 831-2, 578-80. *Public accountant,* Sept. 1917, p. 49-52, 53-5.

ACCOUNTANCY in New South Wales; select committee's report on the profession of public accountants. *Accountant,* Sept. 4, 11, 18, 1915, p. 282-90, 306-14, 341-6.

ACCOUNTANCY in Tasmania. *Federal accountant,* Oct. 1917, p. 127-30.

ACCOUNTANTS bill for New South Wales. *Accounting and commerce,* Nov. 1915, p. 179-81.

DRAFT bill for registration of accountants in Victoria. *South African accountant and auditor,* Sept. 1916, p. 183-6.

LIGHTBAND, R. M. Present and future of the accountancy profession. *Australasian accountant and secretary,* Aug. 1920, p. 261-6.

NEW SOUTH WALES public accountants' bill. *Incorporated accountants' journal,* Dec. 1915, p. 55-6.

PROPOSED accountancy bill. *Federal accountant,* July 1916, July, Oct. 1917, p. 72-3, 88-92, 130-2.

SOCIETY of incorporated accountants and auditors. Registration of accountants. *Incorporated accountants' journal,* July 1916, p. 226-8.

TITLE 'Chartered accountant' in Australia. *Public accountant,* 1905-6, p. 72; 1906-7, p. 102.

Belgium

ACCOUNTANCY in Belgium. *Accountant,* Oct. 1910, p. 510.

Brazil

BOOKKEEPING in Brazil. *Accounting and commerce,* May 1916, p. 27-8.

Canada

EDWARDS, GEORGE. Accountancy in Canada. *Accountant,* Jan. 1, 1916, p. 25-31. *American institute of accountants, Yearbook,* 1915, p. 122-37. *Journal of accountancy,* Nov. 1915, p. 334-48.

FISK, A. K. Uniformity among provincial societies, as to by-laws, examinations and certificates, legislation. (In *Dominion association of chartered accountants, Yearbook,* 1910.

ACCOUNTANCY—Canada—*(Continued)*

Hyde, John. Address. *Federation of societies of public accountants in the United States of America. Official record of the Congress of accountants held at the World's fair, Saint Louis,* September 26th, 27th and 28th, 1904, p. 83-91.

President's message. *Canadian chartered accountant,* Jan. 1912, p. 133-4.

Chile

Kirkcaldie, W. J. Accountants in Chile. *Accountants' magazine,* May 1904, p. 241-6.

China

Chinese certified accountants. *Incorporated accountants' journal,* April 1919, p. 128.

Fischer, Emil S. Accountant in China. *Accounting and commerce,* Dec. 1915, p. 204-6.

Fischer, Emil S. Accountant in the Orient. (In his *China.* 1916. p. 10-5). *Accountant,* March 4, 1916, p. 288-90. *American institute of accountants, Yearbook,* 1915, p. 105-9. *Journal of accountancy,* Nov. 1915, p. 356-60.

Hall, Ray Ovid. Chinese books of accounts. *Accountant,* Oct. 14, 1916, p. 332-5.

Education

See Education.

Egypt

Accountancy interests in Egypt. *Accountant,* July 6, 1918, p. 1-2.

England

Accountants' bill. *Accountant,* April 15, 1899, p. 430-3.

Accountants' bill no. 2. *Accountant,* Oct. 16, 1909, p. 465-7, 487-90.

Accountants' (England) registration bill. *Accountants' magazine,* June 1909, p. 326-32.

Accountants' (no. 2) bill. *Accountant,* Aug. 1, 1896, p. 657-9.

Baird, John. Legislation for the profession. *Accountant,* June 26, 1897, p. 643-51.

Bill for registration of accountants in England and Wales. *Journal of accountancy,* July 1909, p. 214-5.

Brown, Richard. Recent proposed legislation relating to the profession. *Accountant,* July 28, 1894, p. 669-72.

Chartered accountant students' society of London. Mock parliamentary debate on professional accountants' bill. *Accountant,* Jan. 20, 1912, p. 89-93.

Chartered accountants' bill. *Accountant,* March 18, May 20, 1893, March 2, 1895, Jan. 9, 1897, p. 244-6, 474-5, 213-5; 49-52.

Claridge, William. Registration for the profession. *Accountant,* April 25, 1908, p. 611-3.

Cooper, E. B. Chancery practice as affecting accountancy. *Incorporated accountants' journal,* 1895-6, p. 10.

Dicksee, Lawrence R. Student's guide to accountancy. Ed. 2. London, Gee & co. 1907. 48p.

English registration bill. *Journal of accountancy,* July 1909, p. 209-10.

Hall, W. G. Legislation for the profession. *Associated accountants' journal,* 1910, p. 29.

Hall, W. G. Our association and legislation for the profession. *Associated accountants' journal,* 1908, p. 36.

Institute of chartered accountants in England and Wales. Draft of a bill to provide for the registration of professional accountants in England and Wales; and for other relative purposes. *Accountant,* May 1, 1909, p. 600-6.

Leeds and District chartered accountants students' association. Inter-debate with Chartered accountants students' society of Kingston-upon-Hall. *Accountant,* March 21, 1908, p. 394-6.

Legislation for the profession. *Accountant,* 1, 29, 1909, p. 585-8, 753-6.

London chartered accountant students society. Joint debate on registration with Nottingham students. *Accountant,* Dec. 14, 1907, p. 734-44.

Manchester society of chartered accountants and Manchester students society. Present position of acountancy in view of recent legal decisions. *Accountant,* March 21, 1896, p. 228-43.

Martin, James. Legislation for the profession. *Accountant,* Oct. 13, 1906, p. 416-22. *Incorporated accountants' journal,* 1906-7, p. 30.

Notes and outline of "an act to improve the standing and qualification of accountants, and to regulate the mode of their admission to practice in the United Kingdom." *Accountant,* Feb. 25, 1893, p. 172-5.

Price, Harry L. Case for the statutory registration of accountants. *Accountant,* Dec. 27, 1902, p. 1369-72. *Incorporated accountants' journal,* 1902-3, p. 2.

Professional accounants bill. *Accountant,* March 17, 1900, June 19, Oct. 2, 1909, March 18, April 8, 15, 1911, p. 275-7, 849-52, 416-23, 448-57, 551-5, 592-3.

Professional accountants' bill; introduced in the House of Lords on 8th March, 1911. *Accountants' magazine,* April 1911, p. 195-214.

Professional accountants' bill: report of the committee of the council of the Central association of accountants. *Associated accountants' journal,* 1909, p. 159.

Public accountants and auditors bill. *Accountant,* Sept. 21, 1912, p. 368-70, 386-9.

Public accountants' bill; a bill to amend the law relating to accountants. *Accountant,* April 4, 1896, p. 273.

Rayner, W. G. Position and progress of the accountancy profession. *Accountant,* Oct. 13, 1906, p. 413-6. *Incorporated accountants' journal,* 1906-7, p. 28.

Registered accountants. *Accountant,* March 11, 1911, p. 405-7.

Registration for the profession. *Accountant,* March 7, 14, 1908, July 16, 1910, p. 37, 309-11, 347-9; 69-73.

Registration of public accountants; text of the bill. *Accountant,* June 23, 1894, p. 573.

Regulation of accountancy. *Accountant,* Nov. 16, 1907, p. 599-601.

Regulation of the accountancy profession by act of parliament. *Accountant,* Feb. 22, 1908, p. 241-3.

Reminiscences of the profession in pre-institute days. *Accountant,* Nov. 7, 1914, p. 521-4.

Ethics

See Professional ethics.

France

Accountancy in France. *Accountants magazine,* 1910, p. 246.

Accountants in France. *Accountant,* Jan. 31, 1891, p. 85-7.

Company reform and the accountant profession in France. *Accountants' magazine,* 1907, p. 347.

"Expert-comptable" in France. *Accountant,* Jan. 7, 1911, p. 7-9.

Finlay, Albert A. Accountancy in Paris. *Accountants' magazine,* July 1904, p. 361-7.

French accountants and company law. *Accountants' magazine,* Nov. 1902, p. 492-6.

French bookkeeping. *Accounting and commerce,* Feb. 1917, p. 242.

French view of accountancy. *Accountant,* Feb. 25, 1893, p. 166-8.

ACCOUNTANCY—GERMANY—*(Continued)*

Germany

MATHER, JOHN. Some notes on German balance sheets. *Accountant,* Feb. 11, 1888, p. 84-9.

History

ANTIQUITY of bookkeeping. *Accountant,* May 18, 1901, p. 579.

BARNARD, FRANCIS PIERREPONT. Casting-counter and the counting board; a chapter in the history of numismatics and early arithmetic. Oxford university press, 1917. 358p.

BECKMAN, JOHN. History of inventories, discoveries and origins. 2v. London, 1846.

BRAMBILLA, G. Storia della regioneria Italiana. *Accountants magazine,* 1902, p. 541.

BROWN, RICHARD. History of accounting and accountants. Edinburgh, T. C. and E. C. Jack, 1905. 459p.

CLASSICAL and mediaeval bookkeeping. *Accountant,* June 6, 1891, p. 426-8.

COX, J. CHARLES. Household books of Sir Miles Stapleton, bart., 1656-1705. *Ancestor,* 1902, no. 2, p. 17-39 no. 3 p. 132-62.

DALTON, W. E. Address; the progress of accountancy in the 19th century. *Accountant,* July 27, 1901, p. 856-60.

ELDRIDGE, H. J. Evolution of bookkeeping from early times to the present day. *Accountant,* Jan. 10, 1920, p. 61-3.

ELDRIDGE, H. J. History of bookkeeping and the growth of the accountancy professions. *Associated accountants' journal,* v. 4, p. 177, 283.

FOSTER, BENJAMIN FRANKLIN. Origin and progress of bookkeeping; comprising an account of . . . works on this subject published from 1543-1852, with remarks, critical and historical. London, C. H. Law, 1852. 54p.

GEORGE, M. DOROTHY. Notes on the origin of the declared accounts. *English historical review,* Jan. 1916, p. 41-58.

HASKINS, CHARLES WALDO. Accountancy; a paper read before the Massachusetts society of public accountants at Boston, July 14, 1900. 15p. *Accountant,* Nov. 10, 1900, p. 1010-4.

HASKINS, CHARLES WALDO. Accountancy, its past and its present; an address delivered before the New York chapter of the Institute of accounts, January 25, 1900. 24p.

HASKINS, CHARLES WALDO. History of accountancy. (In his *Business education and accountancy.* c1904. p. 138-217). *Accountant,* June 15, 1901, p. 699-705. Abstract. *Commerce, accounts and finance,* Jan. 5, 1901, p. 3-6.

HASKINS, CHARLES WALDO. President's address, New York state society of certified public accountants. *Accountant,* June 16, 1900, p. 557-63, 567.

HEAPS, JOHN WILLIAM. Antiquity of bookkeeping; an historical sketch. London, Gee & co. 27p. *Accountant,* Feb. 12-26, 1898, p. 187-90, 215-7, 243-6.

"HISTORY" of accountancy, compiled from the pages of Accountants' notes 1901-1918. *Associated accountants' journal,* Sept.-Dec. 1919, p. 85-95.

HISTORY of accountants and accountancy. *Accountant,* Oct. 28-Dec. 23, 1911, Feb. 10-March 2, 9, 1912, p. 560-2, 597-600, 640-2, 670-1, 712-4, 748-50, 780-2, 823-4, 855-7, 901-3; 6-8, 44-6, 80-2, 124-6, 200-1, 259-61, 308-11, 340-2, 379-82.

IMPEY, ROBERT LEVITT. Address [on the history of bookkeeping etc.] *Accountant,* 1886, p. 678.

KESTER, ROY B. History and development of accounting. (In his *Accounting theory and practice.* 1918, p. 1-11).

KHEIL, CHARLES PETER. Bookkeeping exhibition in Genoa. *Accountant,* Oct. 1, 1892, p. 734-7.

MACKENZIE, R. W. B. Bookkeeping in commerce. *Public accountant,* Jan. Feb. 1919, p. 172-4, 200-9.

MARSDEN, N. View of accounts in the thirteenth century. *Acountant,* April 18, 1891, p. 304-5.

MARTIN, JAMES. Evolution of accountancy. *Accountant,* Oct. 14, 1899, p. 1030-1. *Incorporated accountants' journal,* 1899-1900, p. 22.

MULLER, JEAN PAUL. Accounting, auditing, bookkeeping and statistics; a historical sketch. *Government accountant,* 1910, v. 3, p. 431-45.

OLD exchequer tally. *Accountant,* Feb. 17, 1912, p. 261-4.

OLD world account book. *Accountant,* June 21, 1890, p. 330-1.

PURSER, L. C. Roman account books. *Hermathena,* v. 6, no. 13, p. 209.

REMARKABLE set of accounts. *Accountant,* May 2, 1891, p. 326-7.

ROW-FOGO, JOHN. History of bookkeeping. *Accountants' magazine,* June 1898, p. 328.

STRANG, J. LOGAN. Accounting in Babylon. *Accountants' magazine,* March 1920, p. 166-8.

TEICHMANN, MAX. Sketch of accountancy. *Journal of accountancy,* June 1912, p. 420-30.

Two pathfinders. Journal of accountancy, May 1909, p. 42-3.

WILDMAN, JOHN RAYMOND. Part which accounting has played in the development of modern industry; a paper read before the American electric railway accountants' association. 9p.

WITTY, RICHARD A. Brief history of accounting and rise of the accountancy profession. (In his *How to become a qualified accountant.* p. 11-9).

WOOLF, ARTHUR H. Short history of accountants and accountancy; with a bibliography compiled by Cosmo Gordon. London, Gee and co. 1912. 254p.

WORTHINGTON, BERESFORD. Professional accountants; an historical sketch. London, Gee & co. 1895. 127p.

YOUNG, JOHN P. Accounting in antiquity. *American institute of accountants, Yearbook,* 1911, p. 153-65. *Journal of accountancy,* Nov. 1911, p. 513-25.

Holland

HOGEWEG, G. P. J. Accountancy in Holland. *Journal of accountancy,* Feb. 1908, p. 308-11.

NOTES from Holland. *Accountant,* Sept. 24, 1904, p. 314-5.

VAN DIEN, E. Public accountants in Holland. *Federation of societies of public accountants in the United States of America, Official record of the Congress of accountants held at the World's fair, Saint Louis,* September 26th, 27th and 28th, 1904, p. 203-5.

India

ACCOUNTANCY in the East. *Incorporated accountants' journal,* April 1919, p. 125-6.

ACCOUNTANCY profession in India. *Accountant,* March 5, May 7, 1910, p. 323-6, 620-2.

CECIL, GEORGE. Accountant in India. *Accountant,* Sept. 21, 28, Oct. 12, 1901, p. 1027-8, 1040, 1095-6.

CECIL, GEORGE. Anglo-Indian accountant, his social life. *Accountants' magazine,* 1903, p. 26.

CECIL, GEORGE. "Bazaar" accountant. *Accountants' magazine,* Feb. 1910, p. 112-6.

CECIL, GEORGE. Christmas amusements of the Anglo-Indian accountant. *Accountants' magazine,* 1905, p. 29.

CECIL, GEORGE. Hindu accountant: his work and play. *Accountants' magazine,* Aug. 1901, p. 430-8.

ACCOUNTANCY—INDIA—*(Continued)*

CECIL, GEORGE. India: the Parsee accountant. *Accountants' magazine,* March 1901, p. 143-6.

INDIAN method of double entry. *Accountant,* June 23, 1894, p. 556-7.

OUTLOOK for the accountant in India. *Accountant,* May 11, 1907, p. 636-9.

SOCIETY of professional accountants, Bombay. *Accountants magazine,* Nov. 1917, p. 459-60.

Ireland

MUIR, ARTHUR HENRY. Notes on accountancy in Ireland. *Accountants' magazine,* April 1905, p. 225-7.

Italy

HISTORY of accounting in Italy. *Accountants' magazine,* Dec. 1902, p. 541-58.

ROYAL academy of accountants of Bologna. *Accountant,* April 18, 1914, p. 552-3.

Japan

ACCOUNTANCY in Japan. *Accountant,* Jan. 13, 1917, p. 27-8.

ACCOUNTANCY in the East. *Accountant,* July 14, 1917, p. 22-4.

ACCOUNTANTS in Japan. *Accountants' magazine,* April 1916, p. 186-8.

CHARTERED accountants for Japan. *Accountant,* Feb. 26, 1916, p. 253-5, 237-41.

JAPAN society of accounting. *Accountants' magazine,* June 1917, p. 291-2. *Public accountant,* April 1917, p. 223.

Law

See also names of various countries under Accountancy.

ACCOUNTANCY in the States. *Accountant,* April 1, 1899, p. 376-7.

ACCOUNTANCY in the States: legislature of Pennsylvania. *Accountant,* April 15, 1899. p. 433.

ACCOUNTANCY legislation. *Journal of accountancy,* March 1916, p. 206-10.

C. P. A. laws. *Journal of accountancy,* June, July, Oct. Nov. 1913, p. 468-71; 65-77, 328-32, 408-9.

C. P. A. legislation. *Journal of accountancy,* March 1909, p. 400-1.

C. P. A. requirements. *Journal of accountancy,* Oct. 1909, p. 459-60.

CERTIFICATE by legislation. *Journal of accountancy,* Aug. 1915, p. 139.

CERTIFIED public accountant laws. *Journal of accountancy,* Nov. 1914, p. 375-6.

CHASE, WILLIAM ARTHUR. Record-Herald's editorial: correspondence. *Journal of accountancy,* Sept. 1909, p. 384-5.

DRAFT of a model C. P. A. act to create a state board of accountancy and to prescribe its powers and duties to provide for the examination of and issuance of certificates to qualified accountants and to provide a penalty for violation of this act. *American institute of accountants, Yearbook,* 1906, 1907, 1908, p. 66-9 218-20, 353-5.

DRAFT of a standard C. P. A. law; an act to create a state board of accountancy and prescribe its duties and powers; to provide for the examination of and issuance of certificates to qualified applicants with the designation of certified public accountant and to provide the penalty for violations of the provisions thereof; approved September 1916, by the Institute of acountants in the United States of America. 4p.

DRAFT of a model C. P. A. law to regulate the profession of public accounting (under the state university plan of operation). *American institute of accountants, Yearbook,* 1906, 1907, 1908, p. 63-5, 215-7, 350-2.

EXTRACTS from letters from attorneys, bankers, merchants, manufacturers, etc., of the State of Ohio endorsing proposed bill for the regulation of the practice of public accountants. Columbus Ohio, 1906.

FEDERATION OF SOCIETIES OF PUBLIC ACCOUNTANTS IN THE UNITED STATES OF AMERICA. Model C. P. A. bill, the state board of accountancy bill. 10p.

FEDERATION OF SOCIETIES OF PUBLIC ACCOUNTANTS IN THE UNITED STATES OF AMERICA. Model C. P. A. bill, the university bill. 7p.

FEDERATION OF SOCIETIES OF PUBLIC ACCOUNTANTS IN THE UNITED STATES OF AMERICA. Report of the legislative committee, October 17, 1905. *Journal of accountancy,* Nov. 1905, p. 84-5.

FOSTER, WILLIAM H. Thinks all should be examined: correspondence. *Journal of accountancy,* Feb. 1906, p. 326-7.

GOODLOE, J. S. M. Should the practice of public accounting be limited to certified public accountants? *Accountant,* Jan. 27, 1906, p. 116-8. *Journal of accountancy,* Dec. 1905, p. 106-111.

JAMES, FRANCIS B. Proposed bill to establish an Ohio state board of accountancy for the regulation of the profession of public accounting. Columbus, Ohio state board of commerce; Ohio state society of public accountants, 1905, 24p.

JAMES, FRANCIS B. Third draft of proposed bill to establish an Ohio state board of accountancy for the regulation of the profession of public accounting. Columbus, Ohio state board of commerce; Ohio state society of public accountants, 1905. 42p.

LEGISLATION for accountants in the states. *Accountant,* May 23, 1896, p. 427.

MAINE. Board of accountancy. Circular of information for intending applicants for certificates. 8p.

MODEL C. P. A. bills. *New York accountants' and bookkeepers' journal,* Feb. Aug.-Sept. 1904, p. 47-9, 239-40.

MONOPOLISTIC trend among certified accountants: Chicago Record-Herald, June 15, 1909. *Journal of accountancy,* July 1909, p. 223-4.

NEW YORK C. P. A. degree. *Journal of accountancy,* Dec. 1908, p. 133-5.

NEW C. P. A. legislation. Journal of accountancy, May 1915, p. 362-4.

POLITICAL influence upon C. P. A. laws. *Journal of accountancy,* July 1916, p. 52-3.

PRACTICAL experience decried: correspondence. *Journal of accountancy,* June 1917, p. 473-4.

SMITH, ROY. State supervision over accounting methods. *Journal of accountancy,* June Aug. Oct. 1909, p. 77-84, 173-81, 250-8, 419-31.

SPREAD and effect of accountancy legislation. *Journal of accountancy* June 1913, p. 444-8.

STANDARD C. P. A. law; an act to create a state board of accountancy, and prescribe its duties and powers to provide for the examination of and issuance of certificates to qualified applicants, with the designation of certified public accountant; and to provide the penalty for violations of the provisions thereof. *American institute of accountants, Yearbook,* 1916, p. 102-5. *Journal of accountancy,* Jan. 1917, p. 46-9.

STATES that regulate the practice of accountancy. *Journal of accountancy,* April 1906, p. 520-1.

SYNOPSIS of the statutory requirement for the practice of certified public accounting thruout the United States. (In New York state university. *Certified public accountants,* June 1918. p. 13-26).

THREE recent C. P. A. bills. *Journal of accountancy,* June 1909, p. 138-9.

UNIFORM accounting legislation. *Journal of accountancy,* March 1910, p. 373-4.

UNIFORMITY and reciprocity. *Journal of accountancy,* April 1911, p. 458.

ACCOUNTANCY—LAW—*(Continued)*

WALTON, SEYMOUR. National accounting standard. *Journal of accountancy,* June 1916, p. 464-6.

WHAT is a certified public accountant? *Journal of accountancy,* July 1920, p. 54-7. *Accountant,* Dec. 4, 1920, p. 611-2.

WHERE legislation is not needed. *Journal of accountancy* Feb. 1917, p. 129-31.

WILKINSON, GEORGE. Brief history of the movement to secure legal recognition of the public accountant in the United States of America. *Accountant,* June 13, 1903, p. 781-2.

WILKINSON, GEORGE. C. P. A. movement; a historical sketch made up to date (1903) to secure state legislation recognizing the profession of the public accountants in the United States. New York, Wilkinson, Reckitt Williams and co. 22p.

WILKINSON, GEORGE. C. P. A. movement and the future of the profession of the public accountant in the United States of America. *Accountant,* Oct. 22, 1904, p. 464-71. *Federation of societies of public accountants in the United States of America. Official record of the Congress of accountants held at the World's fair, Saint Louis,* September 26th, 27th and 28th, 1904. p. 91-119. *Incorporated accountants' journal,* 1904-5, p. 30, 51, 63.

———— **Alabama**

ALABAMA C. P. A. law. *Journal of accountancy,* Oct. 1919, p. 317-9.

ALABAMA STATE BOARD OF ACCOUNTANCY. Rules and regulations, adopted May 26, 1919. 11p.

———— **Arizona**

ARIZONA C. P. A. law. *Journal of accountancy,* July, 1919, p. 77-80.

———— **Arkansas**

ARKANSAS. *American institute of accountants, Yearbook,* 1915, 1916, p. 243-6, 135-8.

ARKANSAS. STATE BOARD OF ACCOUNTANCY. Act regulating the practice of public accounting passed by the 40th general assembly of Arkansas 1915. 14p.

ARKANSAS. STATE BOARD OF ACCOUNTANCCY. Applications. 2 forms.

ARKANSAS C. P. A. law. *Journal of accountancy,* April 1915, p. 300-3.

———— **California**

CALIFORNIA. *American institute of accountants, Yearbook,* 1907-1915, p. 190-1, 320-1, 298-9, 210-1, 174-5, 237-8, 307-9, 257-9, 247-9, 139-41.

CALIFORNIA accountants' bill. *Journal of accountancy,* Aug. 1911, p. 301.

CALIFORNIA reciprocity clause. *Journal of accountancy,* Aug. 1913, p. 150.

———— **Colorado**

C. P. A. law in Colorado. *Journal of accountancy,* April 1907, p. 495.

COLORADO. *American institute of accountants, Yearbook,* 1907-1916, p. 208-1, 338-41, 316-9, 228-31, 193-6, 256-9, 309-12, 259-62, 249-52, 141-4.

COLORADO. Rules of examination for C. P. A. certificate. 5p.

———— **Connecticut**

CONNECTICUT. C. P. A. law in Connecticut. *Journal of accountancy,* Aug. 1907, p. 271.

CONNECTICUT. *American institute of accountants, Yearbook.* 1907-1916, p. 211-3, 341-3, 319-21, 231-3, 196-8, 259-61, 312-4, 262-4, 252-4, 144-6.

CONNECTICUT. STATE BOARD OF ACCOUNTANCY. Law of the state of Connecticut relative to the board of accountancy and rules for the examination of applicants for certificates as certified public accountants. Connecticut Board of accountancy. 8p.

———— **Delaware**

DELAWARE. *American institute of accountants, Yearbook.* 1913-1916, p. 314-7, 264-7, 254-7, 146-9.

———— **District of Columbia**

ACCOUNTANCY legislation. *Journal of accountancy,* March 1916, p. 206-10.

C. P. A. bill in District of Columbia. *Journal of accountancy,* Feb. 1909, p. 328.

DISTRICT of Columbia. *Journal of accountancy,* March 1909, p. 400.

———— **Florida**

FLORIDA. *American institute of accountants, Yearbook,* 1907-1916. p. 201-3, 331-2, 309-10, 221-2, 185-7, 248-50, 317-9, 267-9, 257-9, 149-51.

FLORIDA. STATE BOARD OF ACCOUNTANCY. Rules. 6 typewritten pages.

———— **Georgia**

GEORGIA. *American institute of accountants, Yearbook,* 1908-1916, p. 343-4, 321-2, 233-4, 198-9, 261-2, 319-21, 269-71, 259-60, 151-2.

GEORGIA. Rules of examination for C. P. A. certificate; application. 4p.

———— **Idaho**

DEFENBACH, BYRON. Accountancy in Idaho. *Journal of accountancy,* Jan. 1916, p. 50-1.

IDAHO. *American institute of accountants, Yearbook,* 1917, p. 243-5.

IDAHO. Laws and regulations governing the practice of certified public accountants in Idaho. 8p.

IDAHO C. P. A. law. *Journal of accountancy,* April 1917, p. 286-7.

———— **Illinois**

ILLINOIS. *American institute of accountants, Yearbook,* 1907-1916, p. 192-3, 321-3, 299-301, 211-3, 176-7, 239-40, 321-3, 271-3, 261-2, 153-4.

SETBACK in Illinois. *Journal of accountancy,* June 1907, p. 140-1.

WALTON, SEYMOUR. Correspondence. *Journal of accountancy,* June 1907, p. 157.

———— **Indiana**

FINNEY, H. A. Indiana examinations. *Journal of accountancy,* Dec. 1920, p. 469.

INDIANA. *American institute of accountants, Yearbook,* 1915, 1916, p. 263-4, 155-6.

INDIANA. *Journal of accountancy,* March 1909, p. 400.

INDIANA. STATE BOARD OF ACCOUNTS. Public accounting law. 22p.

INDIANA C. P. A. law. *Journal of accountancy,* April, 1915, p. 304-5.

———— **Iowa**

IOWA. *American institute of accountants, Yearbook,* 1915, 1916, p. 265-8, 157-60.

IOWA C. P. A. law. *Journal of accountancy,* May 1915, p. 369-72.

———— **Kansas**

KANSAS. *American institute of accountants, Yearbook,* 1915, 1916, p. 268-71, 160-3).

KANSAS C. P. A. law. *Journal of accountancy,* May 1915, p. 372-4.

———— **Kentucky**

ACCOUNTANCY legislation—Kentucky. *Journal of accountancy,* March 1916, p. 210-4.

KENTUCKY. *American institute of accountants, Yearbook,* 1916, p. 163-7.

KENTUCKY C. P. A. law. *Journal of accountancy,* April 1916, p. 320.

———— **Louisiana**

AMENDMENT of Louisiana law. *Journal of accountancy,* Sept. 1912, p. 217-8.

ACCOUNTANCY—LAW—*(Continued)*

LOUISIANA. *American institute of accountants, Yearbook,* 1908-1916, p. 345-7, 323-5, 235-7, 200-2, 263-6, 323-5, 273-5, 271-3, 167-9.

LOUISIANA C. P. A. law. *Journal of accountancy,* July 1908, p. 206-7.

———. **Maine**

MAINE. *American institute of accountants, Yearbook,* 1913-1916, p. 325-8, 275-8, 273-6, 169-72.

MAINE C. P. A. law. *Journal of accountancy,* Oct. 1913, p. 330-2.

———. **Maryland**

MARYLAND. *American institute of accountants, Yearbook,* 1907-1916, p. 188-9, 318-9, 296-7, 208-9, 172-4, 235-7, 328-30, 278-80, 276-8, 172-6.

MARYLAND C. P. A. law amended. *Journal of accountancy,* May 1914, p. 399.

NEW C. P. A. law of Maryland. *Journal of accountancy,* June 1916, p. 446-9.

———. **Massachusetts**

MASSACHUSETTS. *American institute of accountants, Yearbook,* 1909-1916, p. 327-8, 239-40, 204-5, 269-70, 330-2, 280-2, 278-80, 176-7.

MASSACHUSETTS C. P. A. bill. *Journal of accountancy,* Feb. 1907, Feb. April, July 1909. p. 335-6, 327-8, 504 ; 219.

THREE recent C. P. A. bills. *Journal of accountancy,* June 1909, p. 138-9.

———. **Michigan**

MICHIGAN. *American institute of accountants, Yearbook,* 1907-1916, p. 198-200, 328 30, 306-8, 218-20, 183-5, 246-8, 332-5, 282-5, 280-3, 178-81, 245-8.

MICHIGAN. STATE BOARD OF ACCOUNTANCY. Rules. 1p.

MICHIGAN C. P. A. law amended. *Journal of accountancy,* June 1913. p. 477.

———. **Minnesota**

C. P. A. bill in Minnesota. *Journal of accountancy,* May 1909, p. 76.

DURAND, E. DANA. Progress toward absurdity. *Journal of accountancy,* April 1915, p. 297-9.

MINNESOTA. *American institute of accountants, Yearbook,* 1909-1916, p. 328-31, 240-4, 205-9, 271-4, 335-8, 285-8, 284-7, 181-4.

MINNESOTA. Rules for the examination of applicants for certificate as certified public accountant, amended August 29, 1914. 7p.

MINNESOTA. *Journal of accountancy,* April 1907, March 1909, p. 495, 400.

MINNESOTA C. P. A. act. *Journal of accountancy,* Oct. 1909, p. 454.

PROGRESS toward absurdity. *Journal of accountancy.* March, April, 1915, p. 209-10. 297-9.

THREE recent C. P. A. bills. *Journal of accountancy,* June 1909, p. 138-9.

———. **Mississpipi**

MISSISSIPPI. C. P. A. law (official text) ; Chapter 211, House bill no. 117. 3 typewritten pages.

———. **Missouri**

MISSOURI. *American institute of accountants, Yearbook,* 1909-1916, p. 331-4, 244-7, 209-13, 275-8, 338-42, 289-92, 287-90, 184-7.

MISSOURI. *Journal of accountancy,* March, April 1909, p. 401, 504.

PRACTICE requirements in Missouri. *Journal of accountancy,* April 1916, p. 309-11.

PUBLIC accountant's need. *Journal of accountancy,* April 1909, p. 481.

———. **Montana**

MONTANA UNIVERSITY. Committee on accountancy. Act to regulate the practice of the profession of public accounting, and repealing the Chapter 39, acts of the eleventh legislative assembly of the state of Montana entitled "an act to regulate the practice of the profession of public accountancy". 1919. 8p.

MONTANA. *American institute of accountants, Yearbook.* 1909-1916, p. 334-6, 248-50, 213-6, 279-81, 342-4, 292-5, 291-3, 188-90.

MONTANA. *Journal of accountancy,* March 1909, p. 400.

———. **Nebraska**

NEBRASKA. STATE BOARD OF EXAMINERS OF PUBLIC ACCOUNTANTS. Rules. 1p.

NEBRASKA. *American institute of accountants Yearbook,* 1909-1916, p. 337, 251-2, 216-7, 282-3, 344-5, 295-6, 293-4, 190-1.

NEBRASKA. *Journal of accountants,* July 1909, p. 215.

———. **Nevada**

NEVADA. *American institute of accountants, Yearbook,* 1913-1917, p. 346-7, 296-8, 295-6, 192-3, 248-50.

NEVADA C. P. A. law. *Journal of accountancy,* Oct. 1913, p. 328-9.

———. **New Hampshire**

NEW HAMPSHIRE. *American institute of accountants, Yearbook,* 1917, p. 250-2.

NEW HAMPSHIRE. OFFICE OF BANK COMMISSIONERS. Rules : application. 4p.

———. **New Jersey**

DU BOIS, FRANK G. Attack on the New Jersey law : correspondence. *Journal of accountancy,* March 1906, p. 417-8.

NEW JERSEY. *American institute of accountants, Yearbook,* 1907-1916, p. 196-8, 325-8, 303-6, 215-8, 180-2, 243-5, 348-50, 298-301, 247-9, 194-6.

NEW JERSEY C. P. A. bill. *Accountant,* May 14, 1904, p. 657-8.

NEW JERSEY clears the way. *Journal of accountancy,* Sept. 1910, p. 375-6.

NEW JERSEY state board ; change of rules. *Journal of accountancy,* Sept. 1910, p. 379-81.

———. **New York**

BILL aiming to end bogus tax experts favorably reported ; measure provides for personal responsibility ; under term only individual can make report. *New York tribune,* May 11, 1920.

C. P. A. legislation in New York. *Journal of accountancy,* July 1910, p. 216.

C. P. A. syllabi. *Journal of accountancy,* May 1911, p. 61-3.

CERTIFIED public accountant in New York ; editorial. *Journal of accountancy,* Jan. 1913, p. 57-8.

CERTIFIED public accountants in New York. *Journal of accountancy,* Jan. 1913, p. 53-6. Editorial, p. 57-8.

EXPERIENCED requirements depreciated ; correspondence. *Journal of accountancy,* June 1918, p. 478.

LONG step forward and upward. *Journal of accountancy,* Dec. 1913, p. 357-9.

NEW legislation in New York state. *Journal of accountancy,* Dec. 1911, p. 617-21.

NEW YORK. *American institute of accountants, Yearbook,* 1907-1916, p. 185-6, 315-6, 293-4, 205-6, 169-70, 231-4, 351-2, 301-3, 200-301, 196-8.

NEW YORK STATE. UNIVERSITY. Certified public accountants, law, rules and information, June 1916. 25p. (Handbook 14).

NEW YORK C. P. A. degree. *Journal of accountancy,* Dec. 1908, p. 133-5.

NEW YORK C. P. A. law amended. *Journal of accountancy,* June 1913, p. 471.

NEW YORK reciprocity clause. *Journal of accountancy,* June 1913, p. 448.

ACCOUNTANCY—LAW—(Continued)
NEW YORK state C. P. A. *Journal of accountancy,* June 1910, p. 154-60.
PROPOSED legislation in New York. *Journal of accountancy,* March 1914, p. 210.
REGENTS' rules in New York. *Journal of accountancy,* Nov. 1910, p. 70.
UNIFORMITY and reciprocity. *Journal of accountancy,* April 1911, p. 458.
VIOLATIONS of the C. P. A. law. *Accountant,* April 25, 1908, p. 588-90.
WILKINSON, GEORGE. Certified public accountant degree in the state of New York. *Canadian chartered accountant,* April 1912, p. 200-2.

———. **North Carolina**
NORTH CAROLINA. *American institute of accountants, Yearbook,* 1913-1916, p. 353-6, 303-6, 302-5, 199-202.

———. **North Dakota**
NORTH DAKOTA. *American institute of accountants, Yearbook,* 1913-1916, p. 356-7, 306-7, 305-6, 202-3.

———. **Ohio**
C. P. A. law in Ohio. *Journal of accountancy,* May 1908, p. 69.
EXTRACTS from report of the secretary of the Ohio state board of accountancy. *Journal of accountancy,* March 1910, p. 375-7.
OHIO. *American institute of accountants Yearbook,* 1908-1916, p. 347-9, 325-6, 237-9, 202-4, 266-8, 357-9, 307-9, 306-8, 203-5.
OHIO. *Journal of* accountancy, Feb. 1908, p. 320-1.
OHIO bill amended. *Journal of accountancy,* Jan. 1906, p. 235-6.
PROPOSED C. P. A. law for Ohio. *Journal of accountancy,* Dec. 1905, p. 166-8.
REVISED Ohio bill. *Journal of accountancy,* May 1906, p. 69-71.
THIRD draft of Ohio bill. *Journal of accountancy,* Feb. 1906, p. 324.

———. **Oklahoma**
OKLAHOMA. *American institute of accountants Yearbook,* 1917, p. 252-6.
OKLAHOMA. *Journal of accountancy,* March 1909, p. 401.
OKLAHOMA C. P. A. law. *Journal of accountancy,* May 1917, p. 368-73.

———. **Oregon**
OREGON. STATE BOARD OF ACCOUNTANCY. Law regulating the practice of public accounting, rules governing examination of candidates, and other information for C. P. A. Portland, 1919.
OREGON. *American institute of accountants, Yearbook,* 1913-1916. p. 359-61, 309-11, 308-10, 205-7.
OREGON. *Journal of accountancy,* Nov. 1908, April 1913, p. 57,310.

———. **Pennsylvania**
NEW C. P. A. requirements in Pennsylvania. *Journal of accountancy,* Jan. 1907, p. 249-54.
PENNSYLVANIA. *American institute of accountants, Yearbook,* 1907-1916, p. 187-8, 317-8, 295-6, 207-8, 171-2, 234-5, 362-3, 312-5, 310-2, 207-9.
PENNSYLVANIA. STATE BOARD OF EXAMINERS OF PUBLIC ACCOUNTANTS. Information for candidates for C. P. A. examination. 15p.

———. **Rhode Island**
PROPOSED law in Rhode Island. *Journal of accountancy,* April 1906, p. 518-9.
RHODE ISLAND. *American institute of accountants, Yearbook,* 1907-1916, p. 203-6, 333-6, 311-4, 223-6, 187-90, 250-4, 363-6, 313-6, 312-5, 209-12.
RHODE ISLAND enacts a C. P. A. law. *Journal of accountancy,* May 1906, p. 66-8.

———. **South Carolina**
SOUTH CAROLINA. *American institute of accountants, Yearbook,* 1915, 1916, p. 315-9, 212-6.
SOUTH CAROLINA C. P. A. law. *Journal of accountancy,* April 1915, p. 306-9.

———. **South Dakota**
SOUTH DAKOTA. *American institute of accountants, Yearbook,* 1917, p. 257-60.
SOUTH DAKOTA. Laws relative to the board of accountancy and certified public accountants. Pierre, South Dakota, 1917. 8p.
SOUTH DAKOTA C. P. A. law. *Journal of accountancy,* July 1917, p. 72-5.

———. **Tennessee**
C. P. A. legislation—Tennessee. *Journal of accountancy,* April 1913, p. 301-4.
PIKE, F. W. Tennessee C. P. A. *Journal of accountancy,* April 1913, p. 307-8.
TENNESSEE. *American institute of accountants, Yearbook,* 1913-1916, p. 367-70, 317-20, 319-22, 216-9.
TENNESSEE STATE BOARD OF ACCOUNTANCY. Laws and rules of the Tennessee state board of accountancy. Nashville, 1913.
TENNESSEE. *Journal of accountancy,* March 1909, p. 401.

———. **Texas**
TEXAS. *American institute of accountants, Yearbook,* 1915, 1916, p. 323-8, 220-5.
TEXAS. *Journal of accountancy,* March 1909, p. 401.
TEXAS. Statutory requirement. 1p.
TEXAS C. P. A. law. *Journal of accountancy,* May, June 1915, p. 375-80, 488.

———. **Utah**
SWAN, DOUGLAS A. Correspondence. *Journal of accountancy,* June 1907, p. 156.
UTAH. *American institute of accountants, Yearbook,* 1907-1916, p. 206-8, 336-8, 314-6, 226-8, 191-3, 254-6, 370-2, 320-2, 328-30, 225-7.
UTAH. *Journal of accountancy,* June 1907, p. 166.

———. **Vermont**
VERMONT. *American institute of accountants, Yearbook,* 1913-1916, p. 372-3, 322-4, 330-1, 227-9.
VERMONT C. P. A. law; an act to provide for the registration of public accountants. *Journal of accountancy,* Nov. 1913, p. 408-9.

———. **Virginia**
C. P. A. law of state of Virginia. *Journal of accountancy,* Nov. 1910, p. 67-9.
STATE board of accountancy established in Virginia. *Journal of accountancy,* May 1910, p. 57-9.
VIRGINIA. *American institute of accountants, Yearbook,* 1910-1916, p. 252-4, 217-20, 283-0, 374-7, 324-7, 332-5, 229-32.
VIRGINIA. *Journal of accountancy,* March 1909, p. 401.
VIRGINIA C. P. A. law. *Journal of account*ancy, July 1910, p. 218.

———. **Washington**
WASHINGTON. *American institute of accountants, Yearbook,* 1907-1916. p. 194-5, 323-5, 301-3, 213-5, 178-80, 241-2, 377-9, 327-9, 335-7, 232-4.
WHO are opposed in Washington. *Journal of accountancy,* March 1909, p. 404.

———. **West Virginia**
WEST VIRGINIA. *American institute of accountants, Yearbook,* 1911-1916. p. 220-2, 286-7, 379-81, 329-31, 337-9, 234-6.

ACCOUNTANCY—LAW—(Continued)

WEST VIRGINIA. *Journal of accountancy,* March 1909, p. 400.

WEST VIRGINIA. Requirements for admission to the examination for certified public accountants. 1 typewritten page.

WEST VIRGINIA C. P. A. bill. *Journal of accountancy,* Feb. 1909, p. 327.

———— **Wisconsin**

C. P. A. bill. *Journal of accountancy,* July 1907, p. 218.

THREE recent C. P. A. bills. *Journal of accountancy,* June 1909, p. 138-9.

WISCONSIN. *American institute of accountants, Yearbook,* 1913-1916. p. 381-5, 331-5, 339-44, 326-41.

WISCONSIN. *Journal of accountancy,* March 1909, p. 400.

WISCONSIN. STATE BOARD OF ACCOUNTANCY. Laws relative to the state board of accountancy and certified public accountants. Madison, Wisconsin, July 1913.

————, **Wyoming**

WYOMING. *American institute of accountants, Yearbook,* 1912, 1913, 1914, 1915, 1916, p. 288-90, 386-8, 336-8, 244-6, 241-3.

Mexico

HORNADAY, W. O. Boleto system of accounts: this method may look hard to the reader, but it works without friction in the ranches and mines of Mexico, where residents resent errors in harsh terms. *Business man's magazine,* Sept. 1907, p. 100-2.

SWEETLAND, CHARLES A. Audit in Mexico. *Business man's magazine,* June 1910, p. 544-7.

New Zealand

ACCOUNTNCY in New Zealand. *Accountant,* Nov. 13, 1909, May 20, 1911, Sept. 26, 1914. p. 585-8; 773-5; 334-6.

ACCOUNTANCY in other countries. *Journal of accountancy,* Feb. 1908, p. 316-7.

AUSTIN, H. H. Legislation for the profession, with particular reference to the New Zealand act of 1908, *Public accountant,* 1909, p. 111, 119.

NEW ZEALAND accountants' bill. *Accountant,* Aug. 18, 1906, p. 187-95.

NEW ZEALAND accountants' bill, 1907. *Accountant,* Sept. 7. 1907, p. 316-24. *Public accountant,* 1906-7, p. 189.

NEW ZEALAND society of accountants act, 1908. *Accountant,* Nov. 21, 1908, p. 626-32.

Norway

ACCOUNTANCY in Norway. *Accountant,* Oct. 7, 1911, p. 445-6.

Philippine Islands

ACCOUNTANCY in Manila. *Accountant,* Sept. 5, 1914, p. 250-3.

Scotland

ACCOUNTANTS (Scotland) bill. *Accountant,* April 4, 1896, May 21, 1898, p. 274-5, 541-4.

BOOK-KEEPING and accountancy: Scotch practice in 17th and 18th centuries: from the Glasgow herald. *Accountant,* March 25, 1905, p. 356-60.

CERTIFIED accountants; a bill to amend the law relating to accountants practising in Scotland. *Accountant,* Nov. 26, 1892, p. 904-6.

HOWDEN, JAMES. Retrospect. *Accountant,* July 21, 1894, p. 646-52.

PROFESSION in Scotland, the corporation of account. lim., and the Scottish societies of chartered accountants, the use of the initials M. C. A. *Accountant,* Nov. 21, 28, 1903, p. 1433-48, 1475-6.

Societies

See Accountants societies.

Union of South Africa

ACCOUNTANCY in Cape Town. *Journal of accountancy,* March 1909, p. 403.

ACCOUNTANCY in South Africa. *Journal of accountancy,* Jan. 1909, p. 241.

ACCOUNTANCY in the Transvaal. *Accountant,* Aug. 17-31, 1912, p. 208-10, 246-8, 275-7.

ACT to provide for the registration of accountants in Natal. *Accountant,* Feb. 12, 1910, p. 254-7, 229-31.

CAPE COLONY. *Journal of accountancy,* May 1909, p. 44.

DOUGLAS, J. Profession in South Africa; a plea for federation. *South African accountants' journal,* v.2, p. 56.

LEGISLATIVE council (Transvaal) accountants private draft ordinance. *Accountant,* Sept. 24, 1904, p. 318-22, 296-9.

NATAL accountants' act, 1909. *Accountant,* Feb. 12, 1910, p. 229-31, 254-7. *Incorporated accountants' journal,* 1909-10, p. 100, 121.

ORDINANCES of the Transvaal, 1904. *Incorporated accountants' journal,* 1904-5, p. 8.

REGISTRATION of accountants in South Africa. *Accountant,* April 27, 1912, p. 666-7.

UNION accountants' bill. *Accountant,* Nov. 2, 1912, p. 537-41, 566-72.

UNION accountants—proposed registration bill. *Accountant,* Feb. 1 ,1913, p. 163-7.

UNION accountants' registration bill; meeting of Cape society of accountants. *Incorporated accountants' journal,* Nov. Dec. 1912, Jan. May 1913, p. 34-40, 59-60, 99-104, 183-4.

United States

See also Accountancy—Law.

ACCOUNTANCY in the States. *Accountant,* Sept. 12, Nov. 21, 1896, Jan. 9, 1897, April 2, 1898, April 1, 1899, p. 744-5, 951-2, 52-5, 376-7, 349-50, 367-9.

ACCOUNTANCY in the United States. *Incorporated accountants' journal,* Feb. 1914, p. 126-7.

ACCOUNTANCY in the United States of America. *Public accountant,* Dec. 1916, Jan. 1917, p. 134-40, 164-8.

ACCOUNTS and the public service. *Journal of accountancy,* June 1910, p. 134-5.

BLACKLOCK, FRANK. Profession of accountancy viewed from an American standpoint. *Accountant,* Jan. 6, Feb. 3, 17, March 10, 1900, p. 13-4, 143, 194, 253.

BRIGHT prospects of accountancy. *Journal of accountancy,* Dec. 1913, p. 459-60.

CANNON, JAMES G. Banker and the certified public accountant. *Journal of accountancy,* Nov. 1908, p. 1-6.

CHASE, WILLIAM ARTHUR. Mr. Cannon's address. *Journal of accountancy,* Jan. 1909, p. 192-9.

CHASE, WILLIAM ARTHUR. Profession of a certified public accountant. *Journal of accountancy,* July 1906, p. 194-200.

CONGRESS of accountants at St. Louis. *Accountant,* Dec. 10, 17, 24, 1904, 704-6, 737-41, 761-4.

COOPER, JOHN ALEX. Federal relations; advancement and regulations of the profession. *Journal of accountancy,* Jan. 1913, p. 1-9.

COOPER, JOHN ALEX. Public accountants in the states. *Accountant,* Oct. 17, 1903, p. 1251-3.

CO-OPERATION and progress. *Journal of accountancy,* Nov. 1911, p. 542-4.

DUBOIS, CHARLES G. Accounting conditions and prospects. *American institute of accountants, Yearbook,* 1914, p. 97-116. *Canadian chartered accountant,* April 1915, p. 321-33. *Journal of accountancy,* Oct. 1914, p. 245-59.

EARLY days of accountancy. *Journal of accountancy,* Oct. 1913, p. 310-1.

ACCOUNTANCY—United States—(Continued)

English comment on Mr. Sells' address. *Journal of accountancy,* Feb. 1907, p. 316.

Federal registration of accountants. *Journal of accountancy,* April 1920, p. 301-2.

Genuine service. *Journal of accountancy,* April 1919, p. 2701.

Hands across the Atlantic. *Journal of accountancy,* April 1914, p. 297-8.

Kittredge, A. O. Accountancy in the States. *Accountant,* Nov. 21, 1896, p. 965-7.

Masters, J. Edward. Accounting profession in the United States. *Accountant,* Dec. 11, 1915, p. 724-7. *American institute of accountants, Yearbook,* 1915, p. 138-44. *Journal of accountancy,* Nov. 1915, p. 349-55.

National aspects of public accountancy. *Journal of accountancy,* Jan. 1915, p. 46-50.

Profession in the States. *Accountant,* Nov. 7, 1891, p. 782.

Prospects for young accountants. *Journal of accountancy,* Sept. 1908, p. 351-4.

Rand, Waldron H. Growth of the profession. *Journal of accountancy,* June 1919, p. 412-9.

Reckitt, Ernest. Accountancy as a profession. *Accountant,* Sept. 3, 1904, p. 238-9.

Registration of accountants. *Journal of accountancy,* March 1917, p. 185-9.

Scope of accountancy. *Journal of accountancy,* June, Nov. 1915, p. 456-8, 369.

Sells, Elijah W. Accountant of 1917. *Accountant,* Aug. 20, 1908, p. 249-50. *Journal of accountancy,* Feb. 1907, p. 297-9.

Sells, Elijah W. Accounting profession: its demands and its future; delivered before the College of business administration of Boston university on the evening of Wednesday, September 20, 1915. 14p. *Journal of accountancy,* Nov. 1915, p. 325-33.

Sells, Elijah W. Inaugural address; delivered at the annual meeting of the American association of public accountants. *Journal of accountancy,* Nov. 1906, p. 39-41.

Seifert, C. A. Attorney's suggestions; correspondence. *Journal of accountancy,* Sept. 1910, p. 385-6.

Sterrett, James E. Address. *Federation of societies of public accountants in the United States of America, Official record of the Congress of accountants held at the World's fair, Saint Louis,* September 26th, 27th and 28th, 1904, p. 23-33. *Accountant,* Oct. 15, 1904, p. 388-94. *Incorporated accountants' journal,* 1904-5, p. 28.

Sterrett, James E. Congress of accountants at the World's fair; opening address. *New York accountants' and bookkeepers' journal,* Nov. 1904, p. 285-7, 289-94.

Sterrett, James E. Progress of the accounting profession. *Journal of accountancy,* Nov. 1909, p. 11-6.

Sphere of the public accountant. *Journal of accountancy,* Jan. 1912, p. 51-2.

Stockwell, Herbert G. Broader field for certified pubilc accountants. *Journal of accountancy,* Jan. 1912, p. 21-4.

Teichmann, Max. Correspondence. *Journal of accountancy,* May 1908, p. 72.

Trustworthiness of American accountants. *Journal of accountancy,* Oct. 1909, p. 452-3.

Trustworthy accounting. *Journal of accountancy,* July 1909, p. 224-5.

Twenty-five years of progress. *Journal of accountancy,* Oct. 1912, p. 322-5.

What the profession offers. 3p. *Journal of accountancy,* June 1919, p. 437-40.

Whitcomb, W. D. Will we cooperate or must we incorporate? *American institute of accountants, Yearbook,* 1915, p. 86-92. *Journal of accountancy,* Oct. 1915, p. 276-82.

Wilkinson, George. Accounting profession in the United States. *Journal of accountancy,* Sept. 1910, p. 339-47.

Wilkinson, George. Address. *Journal of accountancy,* Feb. 1909, p. 331-2.

Wilkinson, George. C. P. A. movement, and the future if the profession of the pubilc acountant in the United States of America. *Federation of societies of public accountants in the United States of America, Official record of the Congress of accountants held at the world's fair,* September 26th, 27th, and 28th, 1904, p. 91-119. *Accountant,* Oct. 22, 1904, p. 464-71. *Incorporated accountants' journal,* 1904-5, p. 30, 51, 63.

Wilkinson, George. Certified accountancy is still an open field; George Wilkinson denies that a big monopoly exists; from the *Journal of commerce and commercial bulletin,* Jan. 11, 1909, p. 11-5. Bound with: Cannon, James G. Certified accountants have a big monopoly.

Wilkinson, George. New York state society of certified public accountants and its stand regarding chartered accountants. *Accountant,* May 11, 1912, p. 738-40. *Canadian chartered accountant,* April 1912, p. 183-7.

Wilkinson, George. Public accountant in Chicago. *Accountant,* April 8, 1899, p. 395.

Wilkinson, George. Organization of accountancy in the United States. *Incorporated accountants' journal,* 1909-10, p. 276.

Wilkinson, George. Public accountants in the States. *Accountant,* Dec. 12, 1903, p. 1508-10.

Wright, Walter C. National aspects of public accountancy. *Journal of accountancy,* March 1915, p. 243.

Wright, Walter C. National status of accountancy: correspondence *Journal of accountancy,* July 1915, p .78.

ACCOUNTANCY. Bates, Arthur. **1906.**

ACCOUNTANCY. Bennett, R. J.

ACCOUNTANCY. Haskins, C. W.

ACCOUNTANCY. Pixley, F. W.

ACCOUNTANCY. (In Downing, Augustus S. *Higher education.* 1920. p. 173-5).

ACCOUNTANCY and economics. *Journal of accountancy,* June 1908. Jan. 1909, p. 140, 237-9.

ACCOUNTANCY and its future. *Accountant,* Oct. 31, 1896, p. 898-9.

ACCOUNTANCY and law compared. *Journal of accountancy,* May 1919, p. 364-6.

ACCOUNTANCY and machinery. *Accountant,* Oct. 31, 1914, Jan. 2-Feb. 6, May 22, July 31, Aug. 21, 28, Sept 11, 18, Oct. 9, Nov. 6, Dec. 11, 18, 1915. March 11-25. April 22, 1916, p. 488-90, 3-6, 40-3, 74-7, 107-10, 143-6, 183-5, 666-70, 123-4, 205-9, 233-5, 293-6, 328-31, 416-8, 543-8, 697-700, 732-6, 293-7, 318-21, 343-50, 448-54.

ACCOUNTANCY and the business professions. Klein, J. J. 1910.

ACCOUNTANCY and the New Zealand expeditionary force. *Accounting and commerce,* Dec. 1918, p. 203-5.

ACCOUNTANCY and the universities. *Accountant,* Jan. 11, 1913, p. 41-4.

ACCOUNTANCY as a commodity. *Journal of accountancy,* March 1913, p. 187-8.

ACCOUNTANCY as a profession. *Accountant,* Dec. 7, 14, 1912, p. 709-10, 736-9.

ACCOUNTANCY as a profession. Cleveland, F. A. 1904.

ACCOUNTANCY defined. *Journal of accountancy,* Aug. 1914, p. 127-8.

ACCOUNTANCY—discussion. *American economic association bulletin,* April 1911, p. 145-53.

ACCOUNTANCY, economy and efficiency in a city department. Force, H. D.

ACCOUNTANCY education. Gilman, S. W.

ACCOUNTANCY education. Peloubet, M. R.

ACCOUNTANCY education. Robinson, M. H.

ACCOUNTANCY education in New Zealand. *Accountant,* Sept. 6, 1913, p. 300-1.

ACCOUNTANCY education in Pennsylvania. Carlson, John C.

ACCOUNTANCY education should be held to a uniform standard. Sells, E. W.

ACCOUNTANCY examinations. *Journal of accountancy,* Jan. 1916, p. 56.

ACCOUNTANCY in Australia. *Accountant,* Nov. 18, 1899, Oct. 4, 1913, p. 1135-9; 432-4.

ACCOUNTANCY in Australia: company auditors—extended powers under the new act. *Accountant,* March 13, 1897, p. 298-9.

ACCOUNTANCY in Belgium. *Accountant,* Oct. 8, 1910, p. 510.

ACCOUNTANCY in Canada. Edwards, George.

ACCOUNTANCY in Cape Town. *Journal of accountancy,* March 1909, p. 403.

ACCOUNTANCY in France. *Accountants' magazine,* 1910, p. 246.

ACCOUNTANCY in Holland. Hogeweg, G. P. J.

ACCOUNTANCY in Japan. *Accountant,* Jan. 13, 1917, p. 27-8.

ACCOUNTANCY in Manila. *Accountant,* Sept. 5, 1914, p. 250-3.

ACCOUNTANCY in New South Wales. *Accountant,* June 26, 1915, June 23, 1917, p. 831-2, 578-80. *Public accountant,* Sept. 1917, p. 49-52, 53-5.

ACCOUNTANCY in New South Wales; select committee's report on the profession of public accountants. *Accountant,* Sept. 4-18, 1915, p. 282-90, 306-14, 341-6.

ACCOUNTANCY in New Zealand. *Accountant,* Nov. 13, 1909, May 20, 1911, Sept. 26, 1914, p. 585-8; 773-5; 334-6.

ACCOUNTANCY in Norway. *Accountant,* Oct. 7, 1911, p. 445-6.

ACCOUNTANCY in other countries. *Journal of accountancy,* Feb. 1908, p. 316-7.

ACCOUNTANCY in Queen's university. *Journal of accountancy,* Feb. 1911, p. 296.

ACCOUNTANCY in relation to business organization and management. Walton, Seymour. 1912.

ACCOUNTANCY in Scotland and women. *Accountant,* May 13, 1916, p. 545-7.

ACCOUNTANCY in South Africa. *Journal of accountancy,* Jan. 1909, p. 241.

ACCOUNTANCY in Tasmania. *Federal accountant,* Oct. 1917, p. 127-30.

ACCOUNTANCY in the East. *Accountant,* July 14, 1917, p. 22-4.

ACCOUNTANCY in the East. *Incorporated accountants' journal.* April 1919, p. 125-6.

ACCOUNTANCY in the States. *Accountant,* Sept. 12, Nov. 21, 1896, Jan. 9, 1897, April 2, 1898, April 1, 1899, p. 741-5, 951-2, 52-5, 349-50, 367-9, 376-7.

ACCOUNTANCY in the States; legislature of Pennsylvania. *Accountant,* April 15, 1899, p. 433.

ACCOUNTANCY in the Transvaal. *Accountant,* Aug. 17-31, 1912, p. 208-10, 246-8, 275-7.

ACCOUNTANCY in the United States. *Incorporated accountants' journal,* Feb. 1914, p. 126-7.

ACCOUNTANCY in the United States of America. *Public accountant,* Dec. 1916, Jan. 1917, p. 134-40, 164-8.

ACCOUNTANCY in the University of Minnesota. *Journal of accountancy,* Feb. 1908, p. 319-20.

ACCOUNTANCY INSTITUTE OF LOS ANGELES. Catalogue. Los Angeles, Educational department, Y. M. C. A. 1909.

ACCOUNTANCY interests in Egypt. *Accountant,* July 6, 1918, p. 1-2.

ACCOUNTANCY, its past and present. Haskins, Charles Waldo.

ACCOUNTANCY laboratory. Montgomery, R. H.

ACCOUNTANCY lectures in London. *Journal of accountancy,* Oct. 1909, p. 471.

ACCOUNTANCY legislation. *Journal of accountancy,* March 1916, p. 206-10.

ACCOUNTANCY LIBRARY ASSOCIATION. Catalogue of accountancy library at recitation rooms of the School of commerce, accounts and finance, Denver, Colorado. Ed. 2. 1910. 63p.

ACCOUNTANCY methods; hire purchase. *Associated accountants journal,* 1911, p. 225.

ACCOUNTANCY of investment. Sprague, C. E.

ACCOUNTANCY problems discussed. *Australasian accountant and secretary,* Jan. March, June-Aug. Nov. 1920, p. 31, 102-3, 182, 228-30, 268, 367.

ACCOUNTANCY problems with solutions. Greendlinger, Leo. 1910-1911.

ACCOUNTANCY profession for women. *Accountant,* Nov. 16, 1912, Feb. 15, 1913, p. 618-20, 207-9. *Canadian chartered accountant,* Jan. 1913, p. 180-2, 202-3.

ACCOUNTANCY profession in India. *Accountant,* March 5, May 7, 1910, p. 323-6, 620-2,

ACCOUNTANCY recognized by Columbia University. *Journal of accountancy,* May, 1914, p. 401.

ACCOUNTANCY the profession of business administration. *Journal of accountancy,* Aug. 1906, p. 288-9.

ACCOUNTANCY, the youngest of the professions. Klein, J. J. 1912.

ACCOUNTANCY training for lawyers. Greeley, H. D.

ACCOUNTANT. Dodson, James. 1750.

ACCOUNTANT. Pow, J. K. 1850.

ACCOUNTANT; a weekly organ of accountancy. 34 Moorgate St., London, E. C. 2.

ACCOUNTANT and bookkeeper's manual of comercial calculations reduced to their utmost simplicity. Ernst, Henry.

ACCOUNTANT and geometrician. Donn, Benjamin. 1765.

ACCOUNTANT as adviser to the manufacturer. Smart, A. R.

ACCOUNTANT as an expert witness. Bacon, C. F.

ACCOUNTANT containing essays on bookkeeping by single and double entry. Donn, Benjamin. 1778.

ACCOUNTANT for public schools and academies. Powers, M. R. 1877.

ACCOUNTANT in the Orient. Fischer, E. S.

ACCOUNTANT lecturers' association. *Incorporated accountants' journal,* Dec. 1915, p. 63.

ACCOUNTANT of 1917. Sells, E. W.

ACCOUNTANT societies in Great Britain. *Journal of accountancy,* Jan. 1910, p. 218-9.

ACCOUNTANTS

See also Accountants' societies.

ACCOUNTANCY the profession of business administration. *Journal of accountancy,* Aug. 1906, p. 288-9.

ACCOUNTANTS and the press. *Journal of accountancy,* Dec. 1915, p. 451-2.

ACCOUNTANTS and the war. *Journal of accountancy,* Aug. 1917, p. 112-9.

ACCOUNTANTS as corporation officers. *Journal of accountancy,* May 1906, p. 53-4.

ACCOUNTANTS as receivers and trustees. *Journal of accountancy,* Dec. 1910, p. 153.

ACCOUNTANTS' great responsibility. *Journal of accountancy,* Jan. 1918, p. 47-9.

ACCOUNTANTS in war time. *Journal of accountancy,* Dec. 1914, p. 464.

ACCOUNTANTS' services in war time. *Journal of accountancy,* May 1917, p. 364-8.

ACTION by incorporated accountant for wrongful dismissal. *Incorporated accountants' journal,* March 1916, p. 125-6.

AMERICAN accountants aiding Mexican government. *Journal of accountancy,* Aug. 1917, p. 159.

BANNER, G. Relations between accountants and their clients. *Accountant,* June 2, 1883.

BINNIE, ANDREW. Chartered accountants in some administrative capacities. *Accountant,* May 24, 1913, p. 804-11.

BOOKKEEPER as a human being. *World's work,* June 1905, v. 10, p. 6324-6.

CALDICOTT, O. H. Chartered accountants as experts in commerce and manufactures. *Accountant,* May 1897, p. 524-9.

CHARTERED accountants in New York. *Journal of accountancy,* March 1910, p. 377.

CANNON, JAMES G. Certified accountants have a big monopoly; from the *Journal of commerce and commercial bulletin,* Oct. 23, 1908. 10p.

CHARTERED accountant a rare exotic. *Journal of accountancy,* Jan. 1910, p. 222-3.

CLASS exemption not required. *Journal of accountancy,* Feb. 1918, p. 124-5.

COLLATERAL employment of accountants. *Journal of accountancy,* April 1906, p. 504-6.

COLORADO to employ certified acountants. *Journal of accountancy,* March 1911, p. 381.

COOPER, JOHN A. Higher accounting and certified public accountants. *Business man's magazine,* 1904, v. 16, no. 10, p. 103-10.

COOPER, JOHN A. Obligations of a public accountant. *Journal of accountancy,* April 1909, p. 484-5.

COST accountants wanted for signal corps. *Journal of accountancy,* Feb. 1918, p. 160.

CREW, ALBERT. What is an accountant? *Accountant,* July 17, 1920, p. 52-3.

DAVIES, W. SANDERS. Professional accountants not detectives. *Business,* Jan. 1898, p. 33-4.

DEFINITION needed. *Journal of accountancy,* April 1918, p. 266-7.

DEFINITION of public accountant. *Journal of accountancy,* Sept. 1908, p. 356-7.

DEMAND for certified public accountants. *Journal of accountancy,* Sept. 1910, p. 368-71.

DICKINSON, A. LOWES. Relation between the accountant and the banker. *Journal of accountancy,* May 1909, p. 55-7.

DISTRIBUTION of personnel. *Journal of accountancy,* Aug. 1918, p. 109-10.

DRURY, HORATIO N. Your market value. New York, Pace & Pace, 1916. 35p.

EIGHT-dollar-a-day accountants. *Journal of accountancy,* Aug. 1915, p. 138.

ENGLISH and Scottish chartered accountants. *Accountants' magazine,* Jan. 1907, p. 1-9.

EXEMPTION for accountants. *Journal of accountancy,* Sept. 1918, p. 212-5.

FIT and the unfit. *Journal of accountancy,* July 1914, p. 54-5.

"FOREIGN" practitioners. *Accountant,* July 19, 26, Aug. 23, Sept. 6, 1902, p. 723-5, 739-40, 821-2, 869-71.

FORGAN, DAVID R. Relations between bankers and accountants. *American institute of accountants, Yearbook,* 1912. p. 215-22. *Journal of accountancy,* Oct. 1912, p. 291-3.

GOOD word from a foreigner. *Journal of accountancy,* Oct. 1909, p. 465.

HAMILTON, GEORGE W. Plea for the cost accountant. *Industrial management,* June 1918, p. 446.

HOPSON, H. C. Accountants and engineers. *Journal of accountancy,* Nov. 1915, p. 397-9.

HORN, A. J. What an accountant should be. *Accountant,* Nov. 21, 1896, p. 967-8.

HOW best to serve. *Journal of accountancy,* July 1918, p. 38-40.

HUNTER, JOEL. Business and the public accountant. (In his *Thinking in figures.* c1916. p. 82-91.)

HURLBURT, H. M. Compensations of junior accountants: correspondence. *Journal of accountancy,* Sept. 1916, p. 238-9.

IF an accountant audited "Life." *Journal of accountancy,* Feb. 1911, p. 295-6.

INDISPENSIBLE accountant. *Journal of accountancy,* Sept. 1920, p. 186-8.

IS there an accountant type? *Journal of accountancy,* Oct. 1907, p. 470.

ACCOUNTANTS—*(Continued)*

Jack Horner, C. P. A. *Journal of accountancy,* April 1913, p. 261 2.

Joplin, J. Porter. Relationship of the professional public accountant to the world of commerce. *Canadian chartered accountant,* Jan. 1917, p. 171-5.

Kauffman, J. H. Certified public accountant and the people. *Journal of accountancy,* Nov. 1910, p. 53-7.

Kellock, H. Business diagnosticians. Moody's *magazine,* Aug. 1907, p. 272-3.

Knoeppel, Charles E. and Harold Butt. Relation between the accountant and the efficiency engineer. *Journal of accountancy,* Feb. 1916, p. 101-13.

Leavitt, T. H. Professional accountant; what he is and what he does. *Accountant,* Sept. 12, 1896, p. 751-5.

Lescher, H. Chartered accountants and public life. *Accountant,* May 25, 1889, p. 282-3.

Limperg, Thomas. Accountants (abroad). (In Lisle, George. *Encyclopaedia of accounting.* v. 1, p. 17-9.)

Listings. *Journal of accountancy,* May 1918, p. 368-70.

Lord, James Henry. Accountants and clients. *Incorporated accountants' journal,* 1903-4, p. 91.

Love, Henry D. Accountants and the public. *Journal of accountancy,* Dec. 1914, p. 489-92.

M'Candlish, John M. Accountants and actuaries. *Accountant,* Oct. 5, 12, 1889, p. 518-20, 528-31.

Matheson, George C. Accountants and accounting. *Accountant,* Sept. 18, 1897, p. 896-8.

May, I. A. Junior accountants neglecting opportunities. *Electric railway journal,* Aug. 14, 1920, p. 320.

Meats, T. Wheeler. Making of an English accountant. *Commerce, accounts and finance,* Aug. 1902, p. 10-8.

Moorhouse, Eli. Mission of the certified accountant. *Journal of accountancy,* April 1912, p. 266-71.

Morse, P. Regulation of big business through the employment of certified public accountants. Chicago, La Salle extension university, 1912.

Moxey, Edward P. What an accountant should know. *Commerce, accounts and finance,* Jan. 1902, p. 10-3.

Moxon, Thomas B. Suggestions for the consideration of accountants. *Incorporated accountants' journal,* 1891-2, p. 22.

Musaus, William P. What is a certified public accountant? *Journal of accountancy,* Dec. 1915, p. 438-50.

Need for definition. *Journal of accountancy,* Aug. 1918, p. 111-2.

Oates, Lewis A. Definition needed; correspondence. *Journal of accountancy,* June 1918, p. 477-8.

Outside accountants. *Accountant,* Nov. 24, 1906, June 15, 1907, Dec. 25, 1909, p. 617-20, 797-9; 773-5.

Perennial pressure. *Journal of accountancy,* April 1916, p. 281-2.

Pixley, F. W. Accountancy and its practitioners: chartered accountants. (In his *Accountancy.* Ed. 2. p. 13-47).

Pixley, F. W. Chartered accountants and the development of the limited liability companies acts. *Accountant,* Oct. 29, 1904, p. 502-11.

Pogson, P. W. What the accountant does for his clients. *Moody's magazine,* Sept. 1908, p. 201-2.

Pow, J. K. Accountant. Gilpin, 1850.

Problem of the accountant's assistant. *Journal of accountancy,* Aug. 1906, p. 283-6.

Prospects for young accountants. *Journal of accountancy,* Sept. 1908, p. 351-4.

Public accountant and publicity. *Journal of accountancy,* Dec. 1905, p. 136-7.

Rand, Waldron H. Certified public accountants; a paper read before the certified public accountants of Massachusetts incorporated. 14p. Cover reads: What is a certified public accountant? *Journal of accountancy,* Jan. 1915, p. 14-20.

Rand, Waldron H. Concerning criticism; a word to the younger public accountant. *Journal of accountancy,* Nov. 1919, p. 336-9.

Rand, Waldron H. Effects of self-assertion, a word to younger public acountants. *Journal of accountancy,* June 1918, p. 444-6. *South African accountant,* March 1919, p. 305.

Recruiting difficulties. *Journal of accountancy,* March 1916, p. 214-6.

Recruits wanted. *Journal of accountancy,* Feb. April, July, 1916, p. 136-8, 312-5; 77-8.

Release urgently needed. *Journal of accountancy,* April 1919, p. 268-70.

Richardson, C. F. Liability of public accountants to serve on juries. *Accountant,* Dec. 30, 1876.

Right of fiscal court to select accountants. *Journal of accountancy,* March 1914, p. 208-9.

Roberts, George E. Public accountant and the banker. *Journal of accountancy,* Dec. 1907, p. 114-8.

Ryan, Thomas P. Accountant in world affairs. *American institute of accountants, Yearbook,* 1907, p. 159-65. *Journal of accountancy,* Dec. 1907, p. 107-13.

Ryan, Thomas P. Essential qualifications for the public accountant. *Accountant,* June 9, 1906, p. 730-4.

Sammis, L. W. Big money for wizards in figures. *Colliers,* Jan. 8, 1916, p. 66-7.

Scott, G. A. Legal position of auditors and accountants. *Incorporated accountants' Journal,* 1909-10, p. 155, 169, 173.

Sears, Francis B. Mission of the public accountant. *Journal of accountancy,* Oct. 1913, p. 291-300. *American institute of accountants, Yearbook,* 1913, p. 136-62.

Shortage of accountants. *Journal of accountancy,* Nov. 1918, p. 397.

Sir James Martin. *Journal of accountancy,* Aug. 1919, p. 129-30.

Slander refuted. *Journal of accountancy,* Jan. 1914, p. 50-1.

Strachan, Thomas Young. Accountant and the actuary. *Accountant,* April 21, 1888, p. 244-8.

Strachan, Thomas Young. Chartered accountants. *Accountant,* Sept. 23, 30, 1882.

Suffern, Edward L. Accountant as financial advisor. *Moody's magazine,* June 1910, p. 437-44.

Suffern, Edward L. Accountant; what he is, what he does, and the place he occupies in the new economics of business. *Canadian chartered accountant,* Oct. 1912, p. 112-7.

Suffern, Edward L. Contribution of the accountant in support of the commission on industrial relations. *Journal of accountancy,* June 1912, p. 401-4.

Trustworthiness of American accountants. *Journal of accountancy,* Oct. 1909, p. 452-4.

Tipson, Frederick S. Relation of the auditor to the bookkeeper. *New York accountants' and bookkeepers' journal,* May 1903, p. 41-3.

Types of Manchester men; accountants. *Accountant,* May 3, 1890, p. 230-1.

Walton, Seymour. Recruits wanted. *Journal of accountancy,* May 1916, p. 389-91.

Walton, Seymour. Relation of the commercial lawyer to the certified public accountant. *Journal of accountancy,* Jan. 1909, p. 205-13.

Warn, C. E. Economic status of the public accountant. Dallas, Texas, C. E. Warn.

ACCOUNTANTS—*(Continued)*

WATERS, C. C. Public accountants and industrial preparedness. *Journal of accountancy,* June 1917, p. 445-9.

WELL won honor. *Journal of accountancy,* July 1916, p. 50-1.

WHAT constitutes an accountant. *Government accountant,* Jan. 1911, p. 407-9.

WISDOM of Chicago. *Journal of accountancy.* June, 1913, p. 470.

Duties and responsibilities

See also Negligence.

ACCOUNTANTS' liabilities. *Accountant,* Feb. 1, 1919, p. 73-4.

ACCOUNTANTS' risks. *Incorporated accountants' journal,* June 1913, p. 211-2.

ANDERSON, HENRY C. Ethics of accounting. *Accountants' magazine,* April 1901, p. 192-8. *Commerce, accounts and finance,* April 13, 1901, p. 3-5.

BLACKBURN, HENRY GASKELL. Inaugural address. *Accountant,* April 26, 1890, p. 213-5.

BLACKLOCK, FRANK. Rights and duties of public accountants from an American view. *Accountant,* Oct. 8, 1898, p. 950-1.

CALDICOTT, J. Qualifications and duties of accountants. London, Letts, son and co. 1875.

CHARTERED accountants and their duties. *Accountant,* Jan. 22, 1916, p. 124-6. *Public accountant,* March 1916, p. 195-7.

DICKINSON, ARTHUR LOWES. Duties and responsibilities of the public accountant. (In his *Accounting practice and procedure.* 1917. p. 212-48. *Accountant,* July 26, 1902, p. 745-51. *Commerce, accounts and finance,* April 1902, p. 23-7.

FIELDS, JAMES L. Evolution and development of the public accountant: his duties and responsibilities. *New York accountants' and bookkeepers' journal,* May, June, July 1904, p. 134-6, 270-4, 202-5.

GARNETT, J. P. Address [on the work of a chartered accountant]. *Accountant,* Oct. 14, 1911, p. 488-9.

GLASS, WILLIAM J. Accountant's business. *Accountant,* May 13, 1905, p. 606-10.

GORDON, JOHN. Difficulties and responsibilities of the profession. *Accountant,* Oct. 20, 1900, p. 917-22. *Incorporated accountants journal,* 1900-1, p. 24.

GOURLAY, JOHN. Talk about accountants' work. *Accountant,* Jan. 11, 1890, p. 17-21.

HOLDING the accountant responsible. *Journal of accountancy,* July 1919, p. 39-42.

JOHNSTON, J. G. Accountant's equipment; a practical essay on the functions and education of an accountant. *Accountants' magazine,* 1902, p. 331.

JOPLIN, J. PORTER. Growing responsibilities of the public accountant. *Journal of accountancy,* July 1919, p. 9-15.

LEYSHON, R. Duties and qualifications of an accountant. *Accountant,* Dec. 4, 1920, p. 623-4.

LIABILITIES of accountants. *Accountant,* Dec. 21, 1918, p. 325-7.

MASTERS, J. E. Qualifications and responsibilities of public accountants. *Accounting and commerce,* March 1917, p. 274-8. *Journal of accountancy,* Dec. 1916, p. 433-42.

MOXEY, EDWARD P. What an accountant should know; the accountant's work, wherein it differs from that of his brethren, clerk, bookkeeper, auditor. *Business man's magazine,* 1904, v. 16, no. 11, p. 91-6.

PIXLEY, FRANCIS W. Official duties of chartered accountants. *Accountant,* May 16, 23, 1891, p. 380-4, 392-8.

PROVINCE of the public accountant. *Moody's magazine,* Sept. 1908-May 1909.

REYNOLDS, W. B. and F. W. THORNTON. Duties of the junior accountant. New York, American institute of accountants, 1918. 102p. *Journal of accountancy,* Sept.-Nov. 1917, p. 161-92, 289-92, 365-72.

REYNOLDS, W. B. and F. W. THORNTON. Duties of the junior accountant. Ed. 2. New York, American institute of accountants, 1919. 107p.

RICHARDSON, C. F. Liability of public accountant to serve on juries. *Accountant,* Dec. 30, 1876.

SCOTT, G. A. Legal position of auditors and accountants. *Incorporated accountants' journal,* 1909-10, p. 155, 169, 173.

SECRETARIAL duties of accountants. *Incorporated accountants' journal,* 1891-2, p. 43, 74, 104.

SELKIRK, JAMES L. Some notes on the nature and scope of the work of a professional accountant. *Accountant,* Sept. 14, 1901, p. 997-1000. *Incorporated accountants' journal,* 1901-2, p. 19.

SELKIRK, JAMES L. Work of the professional accountant. *Commerce, accounts and finance,* Oct. 1912, p. 11-3.

WILLIAMSON, ALFRED E. A. Liability of accountants. *South African accountants' journal,* v. 2, p. 67.

WITTY, RICHARD A. How to become a qualified accountant. London, Sir Isaac Pitman and sons. 126p.

YARWOOD, F. N. Public accountant's work and duties. *Accountant,* March 11, 1899, p. 285-92.

States

ARKANSAS. State board of accountancy. List of C. P. A. certificates issued, September 25, 1919. 1 typewriten page.

COLORADO. State board of accountancy. List of certificates granted, October 1st, 1919. 1 typewritten page.

CONNECTICUT. Society of certified public accountants. Roster, 1919. 2p.

DELAWARE. State board of accountancy. List of C. P. A. certificates issued, 1919. 1 typewritten page.

FLORIDA. State board of accountancy. List of C. P. A. certificates issued, 1919. 1 typewritten page.

GEORGIA. State board of accountancy. List of C. P. A. certificates issued, September 1, 1919. 4 typewritten pages.

IDAHO. Certified public accountants. 1 typewritten page.

ILLINOIS university. Board of examiners in accountancy. List of C. P. A. certificates issued. 2 typewritten pages.

INDIANA. Certified public accountants, 1919. 12 typewritten pages.

LOUISIANA. State board of accountancy. List of C. P. A. certificates issued. 1 typewritten page.

MAINE. List of certified public accountants. 1 typewritten page.

MASSACHUSETTS. Bank commissioner. List of certified public accountants, April 1, 1919. 10p.

MASSACHUSETTS C. P. A. examinations. *Journal of accountancy.* Feb. 1915, p. 163.

MINNESOTA. State board of accountancy. Record of C. P. A. certificates issued October 2, 1918. 4 typewritten pages.

NEBRASKA. List of C. P. A. certificates issued. 1 typewritten page.

NEW HAMPSHIRE. List of C. P. A. certificates issued. 4 typewritten pages.

NEW JERSEY Society of certified public accountants. List of members. 3p.

NEW YORK C. P. A. certificates issued. *Journal of accountancy,* Nov. 1914, p. 405.

NEW YORK. Certified public accountants of the state of New York, June 1920. 28p.

NEW YORK state society of certified public accountants. Certified public accountants of the State of New York, December 31, 1916. 24p.

ACCOUNTANTS—STATES—*(Continued)*
NORTH CAROLINA. List of certified public accountants holding certificates, Sept. 1st, 1919. 2 typewritten pages.
NORTH DAKOTA. State board of accountancy. List of C. P. A. certificates granted, 1919. 1 typewritten page.
OKLAHOMA. Certified public accountants, 1919. 2 typewritten pages.
RHODE ISLAND. State board of accountancy. List of C. P. A. certificates issued, 1919. 1 typewritten page.
SOUTH CAROLINA. Board of examiners of public accountants. List of certificates issued. 2 typewritten pages.
TEXAS. State board of public accountancy. Official list of certified public acountants registered December 15, 1918. 8p.
VIRGINIA. State board of accountancy. List of certificates issued since the enactment of C. P. A. legislation. 1 typewritten page.
WASHINGTON. *Journal of accountancy,* Nov. Dec. 1905, Feb. 1906, April 1907, p. 75, 160, 347, 496.
WASHINGTON. State board of accountancy. List of holders of certificates issued, Oct. 1, 1919. 1 typewritten page.
WISCONSIN. Official register of certified public accountants. 3 typewritten pages.

ACCOUNTANTS (abroad). Limperg, Thomas.

ACCOUNTANTS' accounts. *Accountdnt,* March 7, April 4, 1914, p. 332-3, 484-6.

ACCOUNTANTS' accounts. Fox, W. H.

ACCOUNTANT'S advertising. *Accounting and commerce,* Sept. 1920, p. 127.

ACCOUNTANT'S advertising. *Journal of accountancy,* April 1910, p. 459-60. *Accountant,* April 17, 1909, Jan. 7, 1911, p. 521-3, 5-7.

ACCOUNTANT'S and bookkeeper's vade-mecum. Whatley, G. E. S. 1893.

ACCOUNTANTS and commission. *Journal of accountancy,* March 1906, p. 412-3.

ACCOUNTANTS and distinctive initials. *Accountant,* July 15-29, 1905, p. 61-3, 103-4, 127-8.

ACCOUNTANTS and engineers. Hopson, H. C.

ACCOUNTANTS and life insurance. *Journal of accountancy,* Dec. 1905, p. 142-4.

ACCOUNTANTS and profit sharing. *Accountant,* April 13, June 1, 1918, p. 290-2, 398-400.

ACCOUNTANTS and receiverships. Barrows, W. P.

ACCOUNTANTS and receiverships. *Journal of accountancy,* May 1916, p. 366-8.

ACCOUNTANTS and solicitors' diary. Edinburgh and London, George Waterston and sons.

ACCOUNTANTS and street railways. Walton, Seymour.

ACCOUNTANTS and the food administration. Stockwell, H. G.

ACCOUNTANTS and the press. *Journal of accountancy,* Dec. 1915, p. 451-2.

ACCOUNTANTS and the public. Love, H. D.

ACCOUNTANTS and the use of English. Philbrick, A. L.

ACCOUNTANTS and the war. *Journal of accountancy,* Aug. 1917, p. 112-9.

ACCOUNTANTS as corporation officers. *Journal of accountancy,* May 1906, p. 53-4.

ACCOUNTANTS as receivers and trustees. *Journal of accountancy,* Dec. 1910, p. 153.

ACCOUNTANT'S assistant. Beckett, Thomas. 1901.

ACCOUNTANTS' association. Report of standing committee on a "Standard system of street railway accounting." *Street railway review,* 1904, p. 840-1.

ACCOUNTANTS' association proceedings. *Electric railway journal,* Oct. 16, 1920, p. 835-7.

ACCOUNTANTS' bill. *Accountant,* April 15, 1899, p. 430-3.

ACCOUNTANTS bill for New South Wales. *Accounting and commerce,* Nov. 1915, p. 179-81.

ACCOUNTANTS bill, no 2. *Accountant,* Oct. 16, 1909, p. 465-7, 487-90.

ACCOUNTANTS' bit in the American expeditionary forces. Halloway, C. B.

ACCOUNTANTS' certificates. *Accountant,* Nov. 1, 8, 15, 1890, Aug. 26, 1893, Sept. 15, 22, Oct. 6, 20, Nov. 10, 1894, Jan 19, Feb. 16, 1895, p. 593-4, 610-11, 621-3, 734-5, 792-3, 815-6, 864-6, 909-11, 983-5; 50-1, 146-8.

ACCOUNTANTS' certificates as to profits. *Accountant,* Sept. 3, 17, Nov. 26, 1898, p. 835-7, 873-5, 1131.

ACCOUNTANTS' charges. (In Lisle, George, *Encyclopaedia of accounting,* v. 1, p. 20.) *Accountant,* July 31, Sept. 4, 1915, p. 145-7, 263-4.

ACCOUNTANTS' claim for fees. *Accountant,* May 22, 1920, p. 600-6.

ACCOUNTANTS' code. London, Gee and co. ltd. 5/ per dozen. Abroad 5/3 per dozen.

ACCOUNTANT'S companion. Seally, John. 1773.

ACCOUNTANTS' compendium. Dawson, S. S. 1898.

ACCOUNTANTS confer with insurance commissioners. *Journal of accountancy,* Aug. 1906, p. 290-3.

ACCOUNTANTS' diary: annual. London, Gee & co.

ACCOUNTANTS' digest. Wardhaugh, J. B.

ACCOUNTANTS' directory and who's who, 1920. Perine, Rita and Leonard Bickwit.

ACCOUNTANTS' directory for 1877. London, 1877.

ACCOUNTANTS' (England) registration bill. *Accountants' magazine,* June 1909, p. 326-32.

ACCOUNTANTS' great responsibility. *Journal of accountancy,* Jan. 1918, p. 47-9.

ACCOUNTANTS' guide. Merchant, F. R. 1915.

ACCOUNTANT'S guide and commercial instructor. London, Hall, 1844.

ACCOUNTANTS' guide for executors, administrators, assignees, receivers and trustees. Gottsberger, Francis. c1902.

ACCOUNTANT'S handbook of interest and decimal calculations consignment and joint accounts. Millar, R. C.

ACCOUNTANTS in France. *Accountant,* Jan. 31, 1891, p. 85-7.

ACCOUNTANTS in Japan. *Accountants' magazine,* April 1916, p. 186-8.

ACCOUNTANTS in war time. *Journal of accountancy,* Dec. 1914, p. 464.

ACCOUNTANTS investigations. *Accountant,* June 18, 25, 1904, p. 793-5, 821-4.

ACCOUNTANTS' liabilities. *Accountant,* Feb. 1, 1919, p. 73-4.

ACCOUNTANTS' library. 51v. London, Gee & co. 1901-1909.

ACCOUNTANT'S lien. *Accountants' magazine,* 1910, p. 248.

ACCOUNTANTS' lien. *Accountant,* May 4 1901, Dec. 10, 1910, p. 516-9, 800-2.

ACCOUNTANT'S lien in company liquidation. *Accountant,* May 28, 1910, p. 751-3.

ACCOUNTANTS' LIENS
See Liens.

ACCOUNTANTS' magazine; a monthly journal for business men. Edinburgh and London, William Blackwood & sons.

ACCOUNTANTS' manual; being the questions set at the Institute of chartered accountants' examinations, 1884 to date. London, Gee & co. 1894 to date.

ACCOUNTANTS (no. 2) bill. *Accountant,* Aug. 1, 1896, p. 657-9.

ACCOUNTANT'S OFFICE

Bartle, C. Few points on policy and office organization for the public accountant. *Public accountant,* Aug. 1918, p. 42-9.
Best system of arranging letters and papers in chartered accountants' offices. *Accountant,* March 9, 23, April 6, 1895, p. 239-40, 284-8, 326-8.
Branch office ethics. *Journal of accountancy,* Sept. 1919, p. 212-6.
Goodwill of an accountant's practice. *Accountant,* April 2, 1910, p. 455-8.
Partnership agreement. New York, American institute of accountants. 8p.
Ross, F. A. Growth and effect of branch offices. *Journal of accountancy,* Oct. 1920, p. 252-61.
Temple, Herbert M. Contractual relations between clients and accountants. *Journal of accountancy,* Oct. 1915, p. 291-6.
Suggestions for professional conduct. *American institute of accountants, Special bulletin,* no. 2. March 1920, p. 1-6. Haskins and Sells, Bulletin, Jan. 15, 1919.
Van de Linde, Gerard. Chartered accountant's office. *Accountant,* Dec. 9, 1893, p. 1034-44.
Wildman, John R. Supervising the work of the accounting staff. *Journal of accountancy,* Oct. 1920, p. 245-51.

Accounting

Accountants' accounts. *Accountant,* March 7, April 4, 1914, p. 332-3, 484-6.
Accountants' time accounts. *Accountant,* Sept. 24, 1910, p. 396-8.
Accounts of professional men. *Accountant,* March 12, 19, 26, April 2, 1898, p. 271-3, 301-2, 323-7, 345-8.
Brown, H. Hay. Office organization; system of bookkeeping suitable for accountants. *Accountants' magazine,* July 1900, p. 396-9.
Fox, W. H. Accountants' accounts; bookkeeping for accountants, with forms and specimen entries. London, Gee & Co. 1888.
Hazlehurst, H. W. Accountants' time book and clients ledger, combined. London, Gee & co. 40, 100p.
Jenkinson, Mark Webster. Accounts of professional men. *Accountant,* March 23, 1907, p. 398-401.
Knight, R. J. Professional accountants' accounts. *Accountant,* Jan. 4, 11, 1919, p. 13-6, 27-30.
Pixley, Francis W. Chartered accountants. (In his *Accountancy,* Ed. 2. p. 88-9.)
Thorburn, James. Accounts of professional men. *Accountant,* Dec. 4, 1897, p. 1148-53.
Wright, Walter C. Office and accounting system for the accounting profession. Chicago, LaSalle extension university, 1917. 21p.
Wright, Walter C. Office system for the accounting profession. *Accountant,* Sept. 3, 1910, p. 315-21. *Journal of accountancy,* June 1910, p. 101-12.

Cost accounting

Fox, W. H. Principles of percentages of cost as applied to various businesses. *Accountant,* Jan. 19, 1907, p. 86-96.
Simple costing system for an accountant's office. *Accountant,* March 2, 1918, p. 192-3.

ACCOUNTANT'S own book. Ross, W. P. 1848.

ACCOUNTANT'S pocket diary and reference book. French, R. D. 1913.

ACCOUNTANT'S pocket diary and reference book. London, Gee & co.

ACCOUNTANT'S practical guide. Wicks, J. H. 1802.

ACCOUNTANT'S preliminary examination course. Lynch, H. F.

ACCOUNTANTS' ready reckoner. Barton, T. S.

ACCOUNTANTS' record, nos. 1-3, 1907. All published.

ACCOUNTANT'S relation to inventory. Magee H. C.

ACCOUNTANT'S report. Goodloe, J. S. M.

ACCOUNTANTS' report submitting the outlines and demonstration of a plan for stating the annual report of the controller of the city of New York. New York. Department of finance.

ACCOUNTANTS' reports for prospectuses. *Incorporated accountants' journal,* 1899-1900. p. 82.

ACCOUNTANT'S right to retain documents. *Accountant,* Feb. 18, 1911, p. 257-9.

ACCOUNTANT'S roundtable. *Journal of accountancy,* Oct. 1910, p. 464.

ACCOUNTANTS' services in war time. *Journal of accountancy,* May 1917, p. 364-8.

ACCOUNTANTS' risks. *Incorporated accountants' journal,* June 1913, p. 211-2.

ACCOUNTANTS (Scotland) bill. *Accountant,* April 4, 1896, May 21, 1898, p. 274-5, 541-4.

ACCOUNTANTS' SOCIETIES

ABILITY guaranteed. *Journal of accountancy,* Feb. 1916, p. 138-40.
ACCOUNTANT—lecturers' association. *Incorporated accountants' journal,* Dec. 1915, p. 63.
ACCOUNTANT societies in Great Britain. *Journal of accountancy,* Jan. 1910, p. 218-9.
ACCOUNTANTS' diary, 1915 to date. London, Gee & co.
See Index under Accountants' societies.
ACCOUNTANTS' directory and who's who, 1920. New York, Forty-fifth street press, c1920. 628 p.
AMALGAMATION of American societies of accountants. *Accountant,* June 17, 1899, p. 660.
CANADA. *Journal of accountancy,* May 1909, p. 76.
DINGWALL, THOMAS. How best to make a chartered accountant students' society popular and useful. *Accountant,* Jan. 25, 1908, p. 126.
EDWARDS, GEORGE. Organization: its objects and their attainment. *Dominion association of chartered accountants, Yearbook,* 1910, p. 275. *Journal of accountancy,* Aug. 1910, p. 275-85.
HEMINGWAY, WILFRED H. Value of an accountants' society to its members. *Australasian accountant and secretary,* June 1920, p. 165-6.
IMPORTANCE and utility of students' societies. *Accountant,* June 21, July 12, 1902, p. 629-31, 693-6.
JOPLIN, J. PORTER. Advantages of society and association affiliations. *Journal of accountancy,* May 1915, p. 325-33.
KESTER, R. B. Organizations of accountants. (In his *Accounting theory and practice.* 1918. p. 9-11.)
L. S. C. A. LTD. *Accountant,* July 17, 1920, p. 58-61.
ORGANIZATION of the profession. *Canadian chartered accountant,* Oct. 1917, p. 110-2.
RECIPROCAL relations. *Canadian chartered accountant,* July 1912, p. 38-9.
RECKITT, ERNEST. Benefits that accrue from societies of accountants and book-keepers. *Business man's magazine,* March 1905, p. 600-5.
REPORT of committee on uniformity of standards amongst provincial societies. *Canadian chartered accountant,* July 1912, p. 27-32.
RETCHFORD, ALFRED WILLIAM. Students' societies—their work and object. *Accountant,* May 12, 1900, p. 457-62.
SMITH, H. MEREDITH and GEORGE C. MCDONALD. Uniformity of standards among provincial societies. *Canadian chartered accountant,* July 1911, p. 46-53.
TURNER, F. C. S. Uniformity of standards among provincial societies; admission and standards of examination. *Canadian chartered accountant,* Jan. 1912, p. 113-4.
UNFORTUNATE departure. *Canadian chartered accountant,* April 1913, p. 277-8.
WILKINSON, GEORGE. Advantages of organization to the accountant. *Journal of accountancy,* May 1908, p. 45-56.
WILKINSON, GEORGE. Organization; the advantages of organization to the accountant; inaugural lecture delivered to the Philadelphia institute of accounts, 24 April, 1908. 18 p.
WORKING unions of accountants [students' societies]. *Accountant,* Oct. 3, 10, 1903, p. 1177-9, 1209-11.

Accountants' roundtable

ACCOUNTANTS' roundtable. *Journal of accountancy,* Oct. 1910, p. 464.

Agriculture

See Agriculture—Societies.

American association of public accountants

See American institute of accountants.

American association of university instructors in accounting.

AMERICAN association of university instructors in accounting. Papers and proceedings: annual 1916 to date.
AMERICAN association of university instructors in accounting. *Journal of accountancy,* Feb. 1918, Dec. 1920, p. 155-6, 478.

American electric railway accountants' association.

See American electric railway association.

American institute of accountants

AMERICAN association of public accountants. *Journal of accountancy,* Nov. 1905, Feb. March, Aug. Oct. Nov. 1906, May, June, Oct.-Dec. 1907, March, May, July, Sept. Nov. Dec. 1908, May, Sept. Nov. Dec. 1909, July-Dec. 1910, May, Aug. Nov. 1911, May, Sept. Oct. Dec. 1912, May, Aug.-Oct. 1913, May, Aug.-Oct. 1914, May, July Sept. Oct. 1915, May, Aug.-Oct. 1916, v. 1, p. 76-98, 324, 424-45; v. 2, p. 300, 471-3; v. 3, p. 38, 58-100; v. 4, p. 46-7, 65-84, 165, 469-70, 477-9; v. 5, p. 57-8, 62-5, 134-6, 137-88, 403-4; v. 6, 62-5, 208-10, 357; v. 7, p. 41-2, 49-51, 140-84; v. 8, p. 45-6, 368-72; v. 9, p. 48-50, 138-40; v. 10, p. 213-4, 373-4, 371-2, 377-9, 465-6; v. 11, p. 63-4, 137-8, 141-2; v. 12, p. 64-7, 295, 297-8, 545-6; v. 13, p. 365-9; v. 14, p. 235-7, 334-40; v. 15, p. 365-9; v. 16, p. 120-1, 253, 306-7, 312-8; v. 17, p. 375-7; v. 18, p. 124-5, 211-3, 298-9, 300-4; v. 19, p. 365-8; v. 20, p. 38-9, 221-3, 297-8, 302-6; v. 21, p. 369-73; v. 22, p. 126-7, 240, 296-302.
AMERICAN association of public accountants. *Accountant,* Feb. 12, 1898, p. 193-4.
AMERICAN association of public accountants' conferences. *Accountant,* Jan. 9, 16, 23, 1909, p. 39-41, 71-4, 109-12.
AMERICAN association of public accountants' golf club. *Journal of accountancy,* Dec. 1906, p. 177.
AMERICAN association yearbook. *Journal of accountancy,* Jan. 1910, p. 223.
AMERICAN association's committee on business and accounting methods of the United States government. *Journal of accountancy,* June 1906, p. 142-6.
AMERICAN INSTITUTE OF ACCOUNTANTS. Alphabetical list of members.
See also *Yearbooks.*
AMERICAN INSTITUTE OF ACCOUNTANTS. American accountants' golf and tennis club, 1906.
AMERICAN INSTITUTE OF ACCOUNTANTS. Bulletin, Dec. 15, 1916, to date.
AMERICAN INSTITUTE OF ACCOUNTANTS. Chicago association of commerce cordially invites Institute of public accountants of the United States to meet in the city of Chicago.
AMERICAN INSTITUTE OF ACCOUNTANTS. Constitution and by-laws.
See also *Yearbooks.*

ACCOUNTANTS' SOCIETIES—AMERICAN INSTITUTE OF ACCOUNTANTS—*(Continued)*

AMERICAN INSTITUTE OF ACCOUNTANTS.. Geographical list of members.
See also *Yearbooks.*

AMERICAN INSTITUTE OF ACCOUNTANTS. New York meeting, October 20, 1910, Hotel Astor—Father Knickerbocker invites William Penn to attend the meeting. 2 p.

AMERICAN INSTITUTE OF ACCOUNTANTS. Nineteen-nineteen annual meeting, Cincinnati, Ohio: Clippings from newspapers.

AMERICAN INSTITUTE OF ACCOUNTANTS. Officers, trustees and members.
See also *Yearbooks.*

AMERICAN INSTITUTE OF ACCOUNTANTS. Proceedings.
See also *Yearbooks.*

AMERICAN INSTITUTE OF ACCOUNTANTS. Report by committee on by-laws and proposed amended constitution and by-laws, Sept. 1910.

AMERICAN INSTITUTE OF ACCOUNTANTS. Report of committees, 1907.

AMERICAN INSTITUTE OF ACCOUNTANTS. Report of special committee on endowment. 12p.

AMERICAN INSTITUTE OF ACCOUNTANTS. Report of special committee on form of organization of association, February 21, 1916.

AMERICAN INSTITUTE OF ACCOUNTANTS. Report of the committee on administration of endowment, January 15, 1918. 3 p.

AMERICAN INSTITUTE OF ACCOUNTANTS. Reports and exhibits at Columbus, Ohio, October, 1906.

AMERICAN INSTITUTE OF ACCOUNTANTS. Sung by the A. A. P. A. glee club at the banquet of the American association of public accountants at Annapolis, September 17, 1914.

AMERICAN INSTITUTE OF ACCOUNTANTS. Yearbook, 1905 to date.

AMERICAN INSTITUTE OF ACCOUNTANTS. *Journal of accountancy,* Jan. May, Oct. Nov. 1917, May, Oct. 1918, May, Oct. 1919, May Oct. 1920, p. 43, 374-8, 299-306, 411-2, 371-2, 296-303, 290-6, 368-71, 364-6, 273-86.

ASSOCIATION'S responsibility. *Journal of accountancy,* May 1911, p. 60-1.

BOARD of examiners. *Journal of accountancy,* Nov. Dec. 1916, p. 387, 451-4.

DAVIES, W. SANDERS. Address. *Accountant,* Dec. 8, 1917, p. 454-5.

DAVIES, W. SANDERS. American institute of accountants, report of the president. *Journal of accountancy,* Oct. 1917, Oct. 1918, p. 241-6, 241-3.

EXECUTIVE officer for the American association of public accountants. *Journal of accountancy,* Oct. 1910, p. 458-9.

GETTING the state societies into touch. *Journal of accountancy,* Feb. 1906, p. 330-1.

IN recognition of Mr. Roberts' services. *Journal of accountancy,* March 1906, p. 419.

INSTITUTE of accountants in the United States of America. *Canadian chartered accountant,* Oct. 1916, p. 124-34. *Journal of accountancy,* Oct. 1916, p. 288-95, 303-6.

JOPLIN, J. PORTER. Report of the president. *Journal of accountancy,* Oct. 1915, Oct. 1920, p. 241-5, 241-4.

MONTGOMERY, ROBERT H. President's address. *Journal of accountancy,* Oct. 1913, p. 265-7.

MONTGOMERY, ROBERT H. Report of the president. *Journal of accountancy,* Oct. 1914, p. 241-4.

NEW "association of accountants." *Journal of accountancy,* July 1908, p. 204-5.

OLD and new are both first-class. *Journal of accountancy,* Nov. 1905, p. 62.

RAND, WALDRON H. Report of the president. *Journal of accountancy,* Oct. 1919, Oct. 1920, p. 241-5, 24-4.

RECORD of the American institute of accountants. *Journal of accountancy,* Oct. 1917, p. 293-6.

REGIONAL meetings. *Journal of accountancy,* Dec. 1920. p. 439-41.

STERRETT, JOSEPH E. American association's year. *American institute of accountants, Yearbook,* 1910, p. 140-7. *Journal of accountancy,* Jan. 1911, p. 179-85.

SUCCESS of the endowment fund. *Journal of accountancy,* Oct. 1917, p. 296-8.

SUFFERN, EDWARD L. President's address. *Journal of accountancy,* Nov. 1911, Oct. 1912, p. 505-12, 254-8.

TWENTY-FIVE years of progress. *Journal of accountancy,* Oct. 1912, p. 322-5.

VOLLUM, C. N. Shall we organize a national association of certified public accountants? *American institute of accountants, Yearbook,* 1907, p. 152-8. *Journal of accountancy,* Dec. 1907, p. 100-6.

WINKE, C. H. Correspondence. *Journal of accountancy,* Feb. 1908, p. 323.

Association of accountants in Montreal

REPORTS and accounts.
See index of *Canadian chartered accountant.*

Association of accountants of Australia (incorporated)

REPORTS and accounts.
See also Index of the *Accountant; Australasian accountant and secretary.*

Association of American government accountants

ASSOCIATION and its official organ. *Government accountant,* May 1907, p. 1-8.

ASSOCIATION of American government accountants. Constitution. *Government accountant,* May 1907, p. 45-52.

MEETING of government accountants. *Journal of accountancy,* July 1910, p. 226.

WEBSTER, N. E. Association of government accountants: correspondence. *Journal of accountancy,* April 1907, p. 491-2.

Australasian corporation of public accountants

AUSTRALASIAN corporation of public accountants. Annual report.
See also Index of the *Accountant.*

AUSTRALASIAN corporation of public accountants. *Public accountant,* Sept. 1904, to date, v. 4, no. 1.

BRENTNALL, T. Presidential address on the formation and early history of the Australasian corporation of public accountants. *Public accountant,* 1911, p. 202.

YARWOOD, F. N. Address. *Accountant,* Nov. 15, 1913, p. 722-27.

Australian institute of cost accountants

AUSTRALIAN institute of cost accountants. *Australasian accountant and secretary,* Nov. 1920, p. 345-6.

Belfast society of chartered accountants

REPORTS and accounts
See Index of the *Accountant.*

Birmingham and district society of chartered accountants

REPORTS and accounts
See Index of the *Accountant.*

Birmingham and Midland society of chartered accountants.

REPORTS and accounts
See Index of the *Accountant.*

Birmingham chartered accountant students' society

CARTER, E. Address, 1882. *Accountant,* Oct. 14, 21, 1882.

DICKSEE, L. R. Address: annual dinner, 1904. *Accountant,* Nov. 19, 1904, p. 626-31.

EDWARDS, A. Address, 1889. *Accountant,* Nov. 23, 1889, p. 623-5.

ACCOUNTANTS' SOCIETIES — BIRMINGHAM CHARTERED ACCOUNTANT STUDENTS' SOCIETY—*(Continued)*

GUTHRIE, E. Address: annual dinner, 1899. *Accountant*, Nov. 4, 1899, p. 1087-91.

HARMOOD-BANNER, J. S. Address: annual dinner, 1900. *Accountant*, Dec. 8. 1900, p. 1117-20.

HEATON, J. H. Address, 1907. *Accountant*, June 8, 1907, p. 782-4.

IMPEY, R. L. Address, 1886. *Accountant*, 1886, p. 678.

KEMP, C. F. Address, 1903. *Accountant*, Nov. 21, 1903, p. 1426, 31.

KNOX, G. W. Address, 1898. *Accountant*, Jan. 21, 1899, p. 83-9.

PIXLEY, F. W. Address, 1901. *Accountant*, Nov. 30, 1901, p. 1303-7.

SAFFERY, J. J. Address, 1892. *Accountant*, March 5, 1892, p. 211-16.

SLOCOMBE, J. Address, 1888. *Accountant*, Nov. 17, 1888, p. 756-8.

SMITH, H. S. Address, 1885. *Accountant*, Oct. 31, 1885.

WADE, J. M. Address, 1902. *Accountant*, Dec. 13, 1902, p. 1302-8.

Bristol chartered accountants students' society

CLARKE, EDWARD GUSTAVUS. Address, 1883. *Accountant*, Oct. 6, 1883.

HAM, H. H. Address, 1899. *Accountant*, Nov. 25, 1899, p. 1150-3.

JENKINS, F. A. Address, 1885. *Accountant*, Nov. 21, 1885.

SMITH, C. Address, 1900. *Accountant*, Oct. 27, 1900, p. 957-8.

Bristol society of chartered accuntants

BRISTOL society of chartered accountants. Reports and accounts.
See Index of the *Accountant*.

ACCOUNTANT'S diary: annual. London, Gee & co.

C. P. A.

STATUS of state societies. *Journal of accountancy*, Nov. 1916, p. 385-6.

TRI-STATE meeting, Richmond. *Journal of accountancy*, May 1915, June, 1916, p. 364, 463.

WILKINSON, GEORGE. C. P. A. movement and the future of the profession of the public accountant in the United States of America; with discussion. *Federation of societies of public accountants in the United States of America. Official record of the congress of accountants held at the World's fair*, September 26, 27 and 28, 1904, p. 91-119. *Accountant*, Oct. 22, 1904, p. 464-71. *Incorporated accountants' journal*, 1904-5, p. 30, 51, 63.

WILKINSON, GEORGE. Interchange of membership between state societies in the United States of America. *Canadian chartered accountant*, Jan. 1912, p. 117-20.

——— **Alabama**

ALABAMA accountants organize. *Journal of accountancy*, June, 1911, Sept. 1911, p. 154, 381.

ALABAMA society of certified public accountants. *Journal of accountancy*, Nov. 1919, p. 399.

ALABAMA state association of public accountants. *Journal of accounting*, July, 1912, April, 1913, p. 57, 310.

——— **California**

ASSOCIATED certified public accountants of California (incorporated). By-laws with list of officers and members, 1906. 28 p.

CALIFORNIA. *Journal of accountancy*, Nov. 1905, Feb. 1906, April 1907, July 1909, p. 70, 343, 496, 213.

CALIFORNIA association of auditors and accountants of public utilities. *Journal of accountancy*, Jan. 1913, p. 74-5.

CALIFORNIA societies consolidated. *Journal of accountancy*, Aug. 1913, p. 149.

CALIFORNIA state society of certified public accountants. *Journal of accountancy*, July, 1917. p. 78.

CALIFORNIA state society of certified public accountants, Los Angeles chapter. *Journal of accountancy*, March 1915, July 1916, July 1918, July 1919, June 1920, p. 244, 80, 80, 80, 479.

OAKLAND association of accountants and bookkeepers. *Journal of accountancy*, Dec. 1906, p. 164.

UNION of Californian societies. *Journal of accountancy*, Sept. 1913, p. 232-3.

——— **Colorado**

COLORADO. *Journal of accountancy*, June, 1907, April, Nov. 1908, Aug. 1909, p. 166, 481-3, 57, 311.

COLORADO society elects. *Journal of accountancy*, Oct. 1911, p. 463.

COLORADO society of certified public accountants. *Journal of accountancy*, Oct. 1909, July 1912, Nov. 1914, Oct. 1915, Oct. 1916, Dec. 1917, p. 476, 57, 406, 324, 312, 491.

COLORADO to employ certified accountants. *Journal of accountancy*, March 1911, p. 381.

RULES adopted governing the work of Colorado accountants. *Journal of accountancy*, March 1908, p. 408.

——— **Connecticut**

CONNECTICUT SOCIETY OF CERTIFIED PUBLIC ACCOUNTANTS. Roster, 1919. 3 p.

CONNECTICUT society of certified public accountants. *Journal of accountancy*, May 1912, Jan. 1913, June 1916, Dec. 1917, May 1920, p. 387, 74, 449, 491, 400.

CONNECTICUT society of public accountants. *Journal of accountancy*, June, 1909, p. 137.

——— **Delaware**

DELAWARE society of certified public accountants. *Journal of accountancy*, April, 1915, April 1917, May 1918, May 1919, July 1920, p. 324, 318, 400, 400, 68.

——— **Georgia**

GEORGIA. *Journal of accountancy*, June 1907. p. 166.

GEORGIA association of public accountants. *Journal of accountancy*, Oct. 1908, p. 447.

GEORGIA society of certified public accountants. *Journal of accountancy*, Jan. Apr. 1913, May 1914, July 1915, July 1916, p. 74, 304, 401, 79, 80.

——— **Illinois**

ANNUAL meeting of Illinois society. *Journal of accountancy*, May 1906, p. 68.

ILLINOIS society. *Journal of accountancy*, Dec. 1906, p. 174-5.

ILLINOIS. *Journal of accountancy*, Nov. 1905, June 1907, Jan. 1908, p. 70-2, 165, 253.

ILLINOIS SOCIETY OF CERTIFIED PUBLIC ACCOUNTANTS. Report of special committee on draft constitution and by-laws for proposed Institute of accountants in the United States of America, July 29, 1916. 27 p.

ILLINOIS SOCIETY OF CERTIFIED PUBLIC ACCOUNTANTS. Yearbook, annual.

ILLINOIS society of certified public accountants. *Journal of accountancy*. Nov. 1915, Feb. 1918, Nov. 1920, p. 400, 156, 400.

MEETINGS of Illinois society. *Journal of accountancy*, Jan. 1910, p. 226.

——— **Iowa**

IOWA society of certified public accountants. *Journal of accountancy*, Oct. 1915, p. 324.

IOWA society of public accountants. *Journal of accountancy*, Jan. 1915, p. 83.

——— **Kansas**

KANSAS city accountants organize. *Journal of accountancy*, Jan. 1910, p. 227.

ACCOUNTANTS' SOCIETIES—C. P. A.—*(Continued)*

——— **Kentucky**

KENTUCKY. *Journal of accountancy.* Feb. 1906, Nov. 1908, Feb. 1909, p. 344, 51, 326-7.

KENTUCKY society of public accountants. *Journal of accountancy,* July 1913, p. 77.

——— **Louisiana**

ASSOCIATED accountants of New Orleans. *Journal of accountancy,* June 1907, July 1913, p. 164, 79.

ASSOCIATED accountants of New Orleans celebrate. *Journal of accountancy,* July 1906, p. 230-1.

CHARTERED accountants of Louisiana. *Journal of accountancy,* Aug. 1906, p. 301.

SOCIETY of Louisiana certified public accountants. *Journal of accountancy,* Sept. 1913, Sept. 1914, Nov. 1918, p. 259, 239, 400.

STATE C. P. A. society in Louisiana. *Journal of accountancy,* Feb. 1911, p. 302.

——— **Maryland**

MARYLAND. *Journal of accountancy,* July 1908, July 1909. p. 211, 225.

MARYLAND association of certified public accountants. *Journal of accountancy.* July 1906, Nov. 1909, July 1912, Aug. 1913, July 1915, July 1916, July 1917, Aug. 1919. p. 232, 49, 74, 149, 79, 79, 78, 160.

MARYLAND notes. *Journal of accountancy,* April 1906, p. 523.

——— **Massachusetts**

BANQUET of Massachusetts society. *Journal of accountancy,* May 1907. p. 86.

CERTIFIED accountants of Massachusetts, Inc. *Journal of accountancy,* June 1912, p. 454.

CERTIFIED public accountants of Massachusetts, Inc. *Journal of accountancy,* June 1914, April, July 1915, June 1916, June 1917, June 1918, June, July 1919, June 1920, p. 482, 324, 79, 477, 469, 480, 479, 80, 479.

I. P. A.'s in Massachusetts *Journal of accountancy,* June 1906, p. 157.

INCORPORATED public accountants of Massachusetts. *Journal of accountancy,* Aug. 1908, p. 293.

MASSACHUSETTS. *Journal of accountancy.* Nov. 1905, June 1907, Aug. 1908, July 1909, p. 72-3, 165-293, 219.

MASSACHUSETTS society. *Journal of accountancy.* Dec. 1906, Feb. 1907, p. 164, 333-4.

——— **Michigan**

MICHIGAN. *Journal of accountancy.* April Nov. 1907, April 1908, March, Sept. 1909, p. 496, 69, 483, 399, 388.

MICHIGAN association elects officers. *Journal of accountancy.* Oct. 1910, p. 464-5.

MICHIGAN association of certified public accountants. *Journal of accountancy,* July 1912, Jan. 1913, Feb. 1914, Dec. 1915, p. 57, 73, 164, 480.

MICHIGAN society. *Journal of accountancy,* March 1907, p. 334.

——— **Minnesota**

MINNESOTA. *Journal of accountancy.* Nov. 1905, April 1907, March 1909, p. 73, 495, 400.

MINNESOTA society. *Journal of accountancy,* Jan. 1907, p. 260.

MINNESOTA society of public accountants. *Journal of accountancy,* Dec. 1906, Oct. 1908, Nov. 1914, 1916. p. 175, 447, 406, 312.

——— **Mississippi**

CERTIFIED accountants' association of Mississippi. *Journal of accountancy,* Sept. 1920, p. 238.

——— **Missouri**

ANNUAL meeting of the Missouri society. *Journal of accountancy,* Aug. 1906, p. 300.

KANSAS city chapter, Missouri society. *Journal of accountancy,* July 1916, p. 79.

MISSOURI. *Journal of accountancy,* Dec. 1905, Feb. 1906, Dec. 1908, March 1909, p. 160, 345, 138, 401.

MISSOURI society elects officers. *Journal of accountancy,* Sept. 1911, p. 391.

MISSOURI society of certified public accountants. *Journal of accountancy,* Aug. 1913, July 1914, Aug. 1915, Oct. 1915, July 1916, Aug. 1917, Aug. 1918, July 1919, July 1920, p. 161, 82, 164, 312, 79, 159, 156, 80, 68.

ST. LOUIS chapter Missouri society. *Journal of accountancy,* July 1912, July 1913, p. 75, 79.

——— **Montana**

ASSOCIATION of certified public accountants of Montana. *Journal of accountancy.* Oct. 1915, p. 324.

MONTANA. *Journal of accountancy,* Dec. 1908, March 1909, p. 138-9, 400.

MONTANA society of certified public accountants. *Journal of accountancy,* Aug. 1920, p. 160.

MONTANA state society of public accountants. *Journal of accountancy,* Feb. 1912, Aug. 1913, p. 142, 149.

——— **New Jersey**

ANNUAL meeting of New Jersey society. *Journal of accountancy,* March 1910, p. 389.

FALL meeting of New Jersey certified public accountants. *Journal of accountancy,* Oct. 1906, p. 473-6.

MEETING of New Jersey society. *Journal of accountancy,* March 1906. p. 423.

NEW JERSEY. *Journal of accountancy,* Nov. 1905, Feb. 1906, Jan.-March, May 1908, March, May 1909. p. 73, 346, 223, 321-2, 407, 65, 397-8, 46.

NEW JERSEY accountants and bookkeepers. *Journal of accountancy,* May 1906, p. 158.

NEW JERSEY association of accountants and bookkeepers. *Journal of accountancy,* Aug. 1906, p. 302.

NEW JERSEY society. *Journal of accountancy.* March 1907, p. 415.

SOCIETY OF CERTIFIED PUBLIC ACCOUNTANTS OF THE STATE OF NEW JERSEY. List of members, revised to July 1, 1919. 4 p.

SOCIETY of certified public accountants of the state of New Jersey. *Journal of accountancy.* March, June 1912, Dec. 1913, March 1914, March 1916, p. 235, 381, 488, 243, 239.

——— **New York**

ANDRADE, C. Status of foreign lawyers in New York: correspondence. *Journal of accountancy,* March 1906, p. 415.

ANNUAL meeting of New York state society. *Journal of accountancy,* June 1906, p. 158.

BACON, CLEVELAND. Advantages of your society to accountants and bookkeepers. *New York accountants' and bookkeepers' journal,* Feb. March 1903, p. 3-5, 21-3.

BANQUET of New York state society. *Journal of accountancy,* May 1907, p. 85.

C. P. A. banquet, New York state society at the Waldorf Astoria. *Accountant,* April 12, 1902, p. 401-2.

CHASE, W. A. New York's standard not the highest: correspondence. *Journal of accountancy,* Feb. 1906, p. 325-6.

FOR juniors and students. *Journal of accountancy,* Feb. 1909, p. 323-4.

MONTGOMERY, ROBERT H. Other side of questions; correspondence. *Journal of accountancy,* Jan. 1906, p. 246-7.

MOYER, M. S. Student wants protection against admission by waiver: correspondence. *Journal of accountancy,* Jan. 1906, p. 247-9.

ACCOUNTANTS' SOCIETIES—C. P. A.—*(Continued)*

NEW YORK. *Journal of accountancy.* Nov. 1905, Feb. 1906, March, Aug. Nov. Dec. 1908, Feb. March, May 1909, June 1909, p. 74, 345-6, 405-7, 283, 57, 136-8, 325-6, 397 76, 135-7.

NEW YORK accountants & bookkeepers. *Journal of accounting.* June 1906, p. 157-8.

NEW YORK society. *Journal of accountancy,* Jan. 1907, p. 259-60.

NEW YORK society discusses corporation tax. *Journal of accountancy,* Jan. 1910, p. 226.

NEW YORK society of accountants and bookkeepers. *Journal of accountancy,* Nov. Dec. 1905-April, July-Sept. Dec. 1906, Jan. 1907, p. 62, 165, 252, 327-8, 418-9, 506, 231, 301-2, 394, 164, 254-5.

NEW YORK society suspends member. *Journal of accountancy,* July 1916, p. 78.

NEW YORK state society. *Journal of accountancy,* July 1907, p. 245-6.

NEW YORK state society elects first honorary member. *Journal of accountancy,* May 1907, p. 85.

NEW YORK state society meeting. *Journal of accountancy,* May 1908, p. 80.

NEW YORK STATE SOCIETY OF CERTIFIED PUBLIC ACCOUNTANTS. Yearbook, 1911 to date.

NEW YORK state society of certified public accountants. *Journal of accountancy,* July 1906, July, 1907, June, Aug. 1912, June, 1913, June 1914, June 1915, June 1916, July 1917 p. 229-30, 245, 454, 150, 471, 159-60, 482, 488, 449, 78, 479.

NEW YORK state society; the proposed amendment to admit outsiders is discussed and rejected. *Journal of accountancy,* Jan. 1906, p. 239-45. *Accountant,* Feb. 10, 1906, p. 185-9.

OFFICERS of the New York state society *Journal of acountancy,* July 1910, p 217.

OPPOSED to outside members at present. *Journal of accountancy,* Dec. 1905, p. 144-6.

OUTSIDE accountants in New York. *Journal of accountancy,* Dec. 1905, p. 138-9.

——— **North Carolina**

NORTH CAROLINA society of public accountants. *Journal of accountancy,* Feb. 1920, p. 160 .

——— **Ohio**

ANNUAL meeting of Ohio society. *Journal of accountancy,* Sept. 1906, p. 393.

OHIO. *Journal of accountancy,* Nov. 1905, p. 74-5.

OHIO society. *Journal of accountancy,* July 1907, July 1908, p. 238, 211.

OHIO society of certified public accountants. *Journal of accountancy,* Jan. 1913, Oct.-Dec. 1915, Sept. 1917, p. 74, 324, 459, 237.

OHIO state society of certified public accountants. *Journal of accountancy,* Dec. 1911, p. 612.

——— **Oregon**

OREGON. *Journal of accountancy,* Nov. 1908, p. 57.

OREGON society of public accountants. *Journal accountancy,* Oct. 1913, p. 336.

OREGON state society of certified public accountants. *Journal of accountancy,* July 1914, Aug. 1916, Dec. 1917, Sept. 1920, p. 82, 160, 491, 238.

OREGON state society of public accountants. *Journal of accountancy.* Nov. 1909, Nov. 1912, p. 49, 428.

——— **Pennsylvania**

ANNUAL dinner of the Pennsylvania institute of certified public accountants. *Journal of accountancy,* July 1906, p. 227-9.

PENNSYLVANIA. *Journal of accountancy,* Nov. Dec. 1905, May, Nov. 1907, May, Dec. 1908, p. 75, 160, 59, 67, 65, 138.

PENNSYLVANIA institute. *Journal of accountancy,* June 1906, p. 157.

PENNSYLVANIA INSTITUTE OF CERTIFIED PUBLIC ACCOUNTANTS. Charter and by-laws. 16p.

PENNSYLVANIA INSTITUTE OF CERTIFIED PUBLIC ACCOUNTANTS. List of officers, committees and members, C. P. A. act, etc. 1912. 27p.

PENNSYLVANIA institute of certified public accountants. *Journal of accountancy,* Nov. 1906, July 1912, June 1913, May, June 1914, May 1915, June 1916, Aug. 1918, Sept. 1920, p. 54, 74-5, 478, 400, 483, 380, 449, 156, 238.

PENNSYLVANIA institute of certified public accountants' special meeting Feb. 21, 1919. *Canadian chartered accountant,* July 1919, p. 31-2.

PENNSYLVANIA state society. *Journal of accountancy,* Feb. 1907, p. 333.

PITTSBURGH branch—Pennsylvania institute. *Journal of accountancy,* May 1914, p. 400.

——— **Rhode Island**

INDIFFERENCE worse than opposition. *Journal of accountancy,* April 1906, p. 524.

RHODE ISLAND. *Journal of accountancy,* Feb. 1906, June 1909, p. 347, 137.

RHODE ISLAND society of certified public accountants. *Journal of accountancy,* June 1913, July 1916, p. 478, 80.

WOONSOCKET accountants and bookkeepers. *Journal of accountancy,* June 1906, p. 154.

——— **South Dakota**

SOUTH DAKOTA INSTITUTE OF PUBLIC ACCOUNTANTS. By-laws. 7p.

SOUTH DAKOTA society of public accountants. *Journal of accountancy,* June 1917, p. 474.

——— **Tennessee**

TENNESSEE society of certified public accountants. *Journal of accountancy,* Sept. 1914, p. 238.

TENNESSEE society of public accountants. *Journal of accountancy,* Sept. 1913, p. 259.

——— **Texas**

TEXAS accountants organize. *Journal of accountancy,* July 1911, p. 216.

TEXAS state society of public accountants. *Journal of accountancy,* Dec. 1911, May 1915, p. 612, 397.

——— **Utah**

UTAH association of certified accountants. *Journal of accountancy,* Aug. 1920, p. 160.

——— **Virginia**

VIRGINIA SOCIETY OF PUBLIC ACCOUNTANTS, INCORPORATED. Constitution and by-laws, 1913. 13p.

VIRGINIA accountants meet. *Journal of accountancy,* Jan. 1911, p. 222.

VIRGINIA'S new society. *Journal of accountancy,* Jan. 1910, p. 226-7.

VIRGINIA SOCIETY OF PUBLIC ACCOUNTANTS. List of members, June 1, 1920. 4p.

——— **Washington**

WASHINGTON. *Journal of accountancy,* Nov. 1905, p. 75.

WASHINGTON society of certified public accountants. *Journal of accountancy,* Nov. 1912, Dec. 1914, Dec. 1915, Oct. 1916, p. 429, 470, 480, 313.

——— **West Virginia**

WEST VIRGINIA accountants organize. *Coal age,* Feb. 19, 1920, p. 356.

WEST VIRGINIA association of certified public accountants. *Journal of accountancy,* Nov. 1920, p. 380.

——— **Wisconsin**

ANNUAL banquet of Milwaukee accountants. *Journal of accountancy,* July 1910, p. 217.

ACCOUNTANTS' SOCIETIES—C. P. A.—*(Continued)*

WISCONSIN society of certified public accountants. Constitution and by-laws. 9 typewritten pages.
WISCONSIN association of public accountants. *Journal of accountancy,* June 1912, p. 448.
WISCONSIN society of certified public accountants. *Journal of accountancy,* Oct. 1915, Dec. 1917, p. 312, 491.

Canadian society of cost accountants

CANADIAN society of cost accountants. *Canadian chartered accountant,* July, Oct. 1920, p. 31-4, 116-9.

Central association of accountants

CENTRAL ASSOCIATION OF ACCOUNTANTS. Journal of accountancy and the Central association of accountants; supplement to the Associated accountants journal, September 1908. 16p.
CENTRAL ASSOCIATION OF ACCOUNTANTS. Prospectus, American centre, 2p.
CENTRAL ASSOCIATION OF ACCOUNTANTS. Yearbook; annual.
CENTRAL association of accountants. *Journal of accountancy,* May, Sept 1908, p. 66-7, 356.
MCCRACKEN, W. G. Central association of accountants: correspondence. *Journal of accountancy,* July 1908, p. 212-3.
NEW "association of accountants." *Journal of accountancy,* July 1908, p. 204-5.

Central electric railway accountants' association

See Central electric railway accountants' association.

Centro de contadores y caligrafos publicos

ESTATUTOS del centro de contadores y caligrafos publicos, fundado en el Rosario de Santa Fe el 18 de Diciembre de 1900. 21p.

Chartered accountants of Scotland

CHARTERED ACCOUNTANTS OF SCOTLAND. *Official directory,* 1898 to date.
CHARTERED ACCOUNTANTS OF SCOTLAND. Report and accounts, 1915 to date.
See also index of the *Accountants' magazine.*
CHARTERED ACCOUNTANTS OF SCOTLAND. Summary of rules for admission and syllabus of examinations by general examining board, February 1919. 5p.
JUBILEE of the chartered accountant; an article from The Scotsman. *Accountant,* April 16, 1904, p. 506-8.
TRAINING of Scottish chartered accountants. *Accountants' magazine,* Dec. 1909, p. 542-6.

Chartered institute of secretaries

REPORTS and accounts.
See Index of the *Accountant.*

Cost association of the paper industry

See Cost association of the paper industry.

Dominion association of chartered accountants

ANNUAL meeting D. A. C. A., 1913. *Canadian chartered accountant,* July 1911, July 1912, July 913, p. 36-46, 80-99, 69-83.
ANNUAL meeting of the Dominion association. *Journal of accountancy,* Aug. 1911, p. 312.
CANADIAN accountants' association. *Canadian chartered accountant,* April 1913, p. 274-6.
CANADIAN journal for accountants; report of a committee at the annual meeting of the Dominion association of chartered accountants, Toronto, July 14 and 15, 1900. *Journal of accountancy,* Sept. 1910, p. 382-4.
CHARTERED accountants active in Winnipeg. *Journal of accountancy,* Feb. 1910, p. 285.
DOMINION association of chartered accountants' report of committee on uniformity of standards, presented at the annual meeting held in Toronto, Sept. 14-16, 1920. *Canadian chartered accountant,* Oct. 1920, p. 96-101.
DOMINION association of chartered accountants. *Journal of accountancy,* Aug. 1910, June, July, Oct. 1913, July Aug. Oct. 1914, Aug. 1917, p. 293-5, 298-9, 327-8, 307, 478, 72, 151, 78-9, 152.
DOMINION ASSOCIATION OF CHARTERED ACCOUNTANTS. Official list of members.
See also index of *Canadian chartered accountant.*
DOMINION convention postponed. *Journal of accountancy.* Sept. 1914, p. 238.
FEDERATION of chartered accountants in Canada. *Journal of accountancy,* Aug. 1909, p. 304-5.
HENDERSON, W. A. Address. *Accountant,* Sept. 27, 1913, p. 412-13.
HYDE, JOHN. President's address. *Canadian chartered accountant,* Oct. 1918, p. 93-103.
PRESIDENT'S address. *Canadian chartered accountant,* July 1912, p. 81-91.
PROCEEDINGS of the 12th annual and special general meeting of the Dominion association of chartered accountants, Halifax, N. S. March 20th, 1915. *Canadian chartered accountant,* April 1915, p. 280-96.
SHAW, ALFRED. Address. *Accountant,* Feb. 5, 1916, p. 182-3.

Federal institute of accountants (incorporated)

REPORTS and accounts.
See Index of the *Accountant; Australasian accountant and secretary; Federal Accountant.*

Federation of societies of public accountants in the United States

CONVENTION of accountants, U. S. A. *Accountant,* Nov. 15, 1902, p. 186-8.
FEDERATION OF SOCIETIES OF PUBLIC ACCOUNTANTS IN THE UNITED STATES OF AMERICA. Bulletin, 1903, 1904.
FEDERATION OF SOCIETIES OF PUBLIC ACCOUNTANTS IN THE UNITED STATES OF AMERICA. Official record of the proceedings of the congress of accountants held at the World's Fair, Saint Louis, September 26th, 27th and 28th, 1904. 231p.
SCOPE and purpose of the Federation of societies of public accountants in the United States. *New York accountants' and bookkeepers' journal,* June 1904, p. 179-83.

Hull chartered accountants students' society

LOCKING, W. R. Address, 1900. *Accountant,* Feb. 3, 1900, p. 138-41.

Incorporated accountants students' society, Victoria

REPORTS and accounts.
See Index of the *Accountant.*

Incorporated institute of accountants, Commonwealth of Australia

REPORTS and accounts.
See also Index of the *Incorporated accountants' journal.*

Incorporated institute of accountants in South Australia

REPORTS and accounts.
See also Index of the *Accountant.*

Incorporated institute of accountants of New Zealand

HUDSON, W. B. Address. *Accountant,* Nov. 15, 1913, p. 716-9.
REPORTS and accounts.
See also Index of Accounting and commerce.

Incorporated institute of accountants, Victoria

REPORTS and accounts.
See also Index of the *Accountant.*

ACCOUNTANTS' SOCIETIES — INCORPORATED INSTITUTE OF ACCOUNTS.—(*Continued*)

Institute of accountants and actuaries in Glasgow

REPORTS and accounts.
See also Index of the *Accountants' magazine.*

Institute of accountants and auditors of the Province of Quebec

INSTITUTE of accountants and auditors of Que bec. *Journal of accounting,* May 1914, p. 401.

Institute of accountants and auditors of Western Australia (incorporated)

INSTITUTE OF ACCOUNTANTS AND AUDITORS OF WESTERN AUSTRALIA (Inc.). Memorandum and articles of association and by-laws. 1901. 76p.

REPORTS and accounts.
See also Index of the *Accountant.*

Institute of accountants in South Australia (in corporated)

REPORTS and accounts.
See also Index of the *Accountant.*

Institute of accounts

INSTITUTE of accounts. *Journal of accountancy,* Nov. Dec. 1905. Jan.-April, June July, Dec. 1906. Jan. 1907. p. 61-2. 164,-5 258, 328, 423, 524, 156, 231, 164, 255.

Institute of actuaries

INSTITUTES of actuaries. *Accountant,* Feb 1901, p. 169-71.

Institute of chartered accountants

BENNETT, E. JAMES. Is the institute of chartered accountants doing its duty? *Canadian chartered accountant,* Jan. 1914, p. 182-3

CARTER, ROGER N. Is it desirable that further legal recognition should be given to the Institute of chartered accountants, and if so what form should it take? *Accountant,* April 14, 1894, p. 338-40.

INSTITUTE OF CHARTERED ACCOUNTANTS. Objects of institution; affiliations; advantages, classification. San Francisco. 2p.

Institute of chartered accountants in Australasia

INSTITUTE of accountants in Australia. Convention of accountants—the formation of an Australasian institute. *Accountant,* Aug. 22, 1903, p. 1062-72.

Institute of chartered accountants in England and Wales

BARBER, JARVIS W. Address. *Accountant* May 10, 1913, p. 717-19.

COOPER, E. Address, 1900. *Accountant,* May 5, 1900, p. 430-34.

COOPER, E. Address, 1901. *Accountant,* May 4, 1901, p. 531-8.

DELOITTE, W. W. Address: Birmingham pro vincial meeting, 1888. *Accountant,* Oct. 27 1888, p. 686-98.

DELOITTE, W. W. Address, 1889. *Accountant* May 4, 1889, p. 236-9.

FISHER, W. N. Address, 1902. *Accountant,* May 10, 1902, p. 504-10.

GANE, J. Address, 1906. *Accountant,* May 5, 1906, p. 568-76.

GIBSON, A. H. Address. *Accountant,* May 5, 1917, p. 442-4.

GRIFFITHS, J. G. Address, 1898. *Accountant* May 7, 1898, p. 475-80.

GRIFFITHS, J. G. Address, 1899. *Accountant,* May 6, 1899, p. 511-18.

GRIFFITHS, J. G. Address: Birmingham pro vincial meeting, 1901. *Accountant,* Oct. 19 1901, p. 1106-15.

GRIFFITHS, J. G. Manchester provincia meeting, 1898. *Accountant,* Oct. 22, 1898 p. 982-90.

HARMOOD-BANNER, J. S. Address, 1905. *Accountant,* May 6, 1905, p. 556-65.

HARMOOD-BANNER, J. S. Address: Liverpool provincial meeting, 1904. *Accountant,* April 16, 1904, p. 488-91.

INSTITUTE OF CHARTERED ACCOUNTANTS IN ENGLAND AND WALES. List of members, annual.

INSTITUTE OF CHARTERED ACCOUNTANTS IN ENGLAND AND WALES. Report and accounts.
See also Index of the *Accountant.*

JAMES, ALFRED AUGUSTUS. Address, 1903. *Accountant,* May 9, 1903, p. 617-30.

KEMP, C. F. Addresss, 1895. *Accountant,* May 4, 1895, p. 410-14.

KEMP, C. F. Address, 1896. *Accountant,* May 9, 1896, p. 393-7.

KEMP, C. F. Address: Liverpool provincial meeting, 1894. *Accountant,* Oct. 27, 1894, p. 932-38.

KIRBY, H. WOODBURN. Address. *Accountant,* Oct. 18, 1913, p. 533-8.

KIRBY, H. WOODBURN. Address. *Accountant,* May 9, 1914, p. 698-702.

KIRBY, H. WOODBURN. Address. *Accountant,* May 8, 1915, p. 611-4.

KIRBY, WOODBURN. Address. *Accountant,* May 6, 1916, p. 523-6.

KNOX, G. W. Address, 1897. *Accountant,* May 8, 1897, p. 479-82.

KNOX, G. W. Address: Sheffield provincial meeting, 1896. *Accountant,* Oct. 17, 1896, p. 833-8.

MILES, A. O. Address, 1909. *Accountant,* May 8, 1909, p. 638-54.

MILES, A. O. Address, 1910. *Accountant,* May 7, 1910, p. 642-8.

PEAT, WILLIAM B. Address. *Accountant,* May 5, 1917, p. 448-51.

PEAT, W. B. Address, 1907. *Accountant,* May 4, 1907, p. 602-11.

PEAT, W. B. Address: Newcastle-upon-Tyne provincial meeting, 1907. *Accountant,* Oct. 12, 1907, p. 446-57.

PEAT, W. B. Address, 1908. *Accountant,* May 9, 1908, p. 680-9.

PIXLEY, F. W. Address, 1904. *Accountant,* May 7, 1904, p. 601-11.

PLENDER, W. Address: Sheffield provincial meeting, 1910. *Accountant,* Oct. 8, 1910, p. 474-81. *Public accountant,* 1911, p. 9.

PLENDER, W. Address, 1911. *Accountant,* May 6, 1911, p. 720-4.

PLENDER, W. Address, 1912. *Accountant,* May 4, 1912, p. 686-92.

SAFFERY, J. J. Address: Newcastle provincial meeting, 1890. *Accountant,* Oct. 11, 1890, p. 533-43.

SAFFERY, J. J. Address, 1890. *Accountant,* May 10, 1890, p. 248-55.

SAFFERY, J. J. Address, 1891. *Accountant,* May 9, 1891, p. 358-61.

WADE, CHARLES H. "Institute of chartered accountants in England and Wales". *Accountant,* April 7, 1888, p. 209-13.

WATERHOUSE, E. Address, 1893. *Accountant,* May 13, 1893, p. 445-55.

WATERHOUSE, E. Address, 1894. *Accountant,* May 5, 1894, p. 401-9.

WELTON, T. A. Address, 1892. *Accountant,* May 7, 1892, p. 382-4.

WHINNEY, F. Address: Manchester provincial meeting, 1886. *Accountant,* 1886, p. 595.

WHINNEY, F. Address, 1884. *Accountant,* May 10, 1884.

WHINNEY, F. Address, 1885. *Accountant,* May 9, 1885.

WHINNEY, F. Address, 1886. *Accountant,* 1886, p. 274.

WHINNEY, F. Address, 1887. *Accountant,* 1887, p. 269.

WHINNEY, F. Address, 1888. *Accountant,* May 5, 1888, p. 285-87.

ACCOUNTANTS' SOCIETIES—INSTITUTE OF CHARTERED ACCOUNTANTS IN ENGLALND AND WALES—*(Continued)*

WHINNEY, F. Address at the meeting to celebrate the Jubilee of H. M. the Queen, London, 1887. *Accountant,* 1887, p. 386.
YOUNG, F. J. Address. *Accountant,* May 4, 1918, p. 344-6.
YOUNG, F. J. Address. *Accountant,* May 10, 1919, p. 395-8.

Institute of chartered accountants in Ireland

INSTITUTE OF CHARTERED ACCOUNTANTS IN IRELAND. Year-book; annual.
INSTITUTE OF CHARTERED ACCOUNTANTS IN IRELAND. Accounts and reports.
See Index of the *Accountant.*

Institute of chartered accountants in South Africa

INSTITUTE of chartered accountants in South Africa. *Accountant,* June 18, 1904, p. 809-12.

Institute of chartered accountants of Alberta

INSTITUTE of chartered accountants of Alberta. Reports.
See index of *Canadian chartered accountant.*

Institute of chartered accountants of British Columbia

ACT to incorporate the Institute of accountants of British Columbia. *Accountant,* Dec. 16, 1905, p. 311-12.
INSTITUTE OF CHARTERED ACCOUNTANTS OF BRITISH COLUMBIA. Year-book; annual.
INSTITUTE of chartered accountants of British Columbia. *Journal of accountancy,* Sept. 1913, p. 259.
REPORTS.
See index of *Canadian chartered accountant.*

Institute of chartered accountants of Manitoba

INSTITUTE of chartered accountants of Manitoba. *Journal of accountancy,* Aug. 1914, p. 155.
REPORTS.
See index of *Canadian chartered accountant.*

Institute of chartered accountants of Nova Scotia

INSTITUTE OF CHARTERED ACCOUNTANTS OF NOVA SCOTIA. By-laws and act of incorporation, incorporated 30 March 1900. Council, 1919. 28p.
REPORTS.
See index of the *Canadian chartered accountant*

Institute of chartered accountants of Ontario

CANADA. *Journal of accountancy.* May 1909. p. 76.
MACPHERSON, F. H. Canadian situation: correspondence. *Journal of accountancy,* Aug. 1909, p. 306-7.
INSTITUTE OF CHARTERED ACCOUNTANTS OF ONTARIO. Library rules and catalogue. 1920. 22p.
INSTITUTE OF CHARTERED ACCOUNTANTS OF ONTARIO. Year-book; annual.
REPORTS.
See index of the *Canadian chartered accountant.*

Institute of chartered accountants of Saskatchewan

INSTITUTE OF CHARTERED ACCOUNTANTS OF SASKATCHEWAN. Year-book; annual.
REPORTS.
See index of the *Canadian chartered accountant.*

Institute of incorporated accountants of New South Wales

REPORTS and accounts.
See also index of the *Accountant.*

ROWTON, JOHN. Institute of accountants—its scope and possibilities. *Australasian accountant and secretary,* Oct. 1919, p. 19-21.

Institute of municipal treasurers and accountants (incorporated)

ALLCOCK, JOHN. Address. *Accountant,* July 19, 1913, p. 90-6.
PATON, R. Address. *Accountant,* July 20, 1912, p. 96-103.
REPORTS and accounts.
See also index of the *Accountant; Incorporated accountants journal.*
WINTER, F. Address. *Accountant,* July 18, 1914, p. 95-9.

International association of accountants

INTERNATIONAL association of accounts. *Journal of accountancy,* Feb. 1911, p. 294.

Leeds and district society of chartered accountants

BLACKBURN, H. G. Address, 1890. *Accountant,* April 26, 1890, p. 213-15.
GORDON, J. Address, 1906. *Accountant,* Jan. 5, 1907, p. 17-19.
REPORTS.
See also index of the *Accountant.*

Leicester society of chartered accountants

REPORTS and accounts.
See also index of the *Accountant.*

Liverpool chartered accountants students' society

BLEASE, W. Address, 1905. *Accountant,* Nov. 25, 1905, p. 615-21.
CHALMERS, ANTHONY WIGHAM. Address, 1883. *Accountant,* March 10, 17, 1883.

Liverpool society of chartered accountants

DAWSON, SIDNEY S. Address. *Accountant,* Dec. 21, 1912, p. 781-5.
REPORTS and accounts.
See Index of the *Accountant.*

London association of accountants

LONDON ASSOCIATION OF ACCOUNTANTS, LIMITED. Qualifications for membership, regulations regarding examinations, 1918.
LONDON ASSOCIATION OF ACCOUNTANTS. Diary; articles of association etc., 1914. London, 1914. 264p.

London chartered accountants students' society

COOPER, ERNEST. Address. *Accountant,* Dec. 14, 1912, p. 750-4.
GRIFFITHS, J. G. Address, 1885. *Accountant,* Dec. 26, 1885.
PLENDER, WILLIAM. Address, 1913. *Accountant,* April 26, 1913, p. 623-4.
PLENDER, WILLIAM. Address, 1914. *Accountant,* April 25, 1914, p. 617-8.
PLENDER, WILLIAM. Address, 1915. *Accountant,* May 8, 1915, p. 627-8.
PLENDER, WILLIAM. Address, 1916. *Accountant,* May 13, 1916, p. 559-60.
PLENDER, WILLIAM. Address, 1917. *Accountant,* July 7, 1917, p. 13-4.
PLENDER, WILLIAM. Address, 1918. *Accountant,* Dec. 14, 1918, p. 323.
REPORTS and accounts.
See index of the *Accountant.*
WHINNEY, F. Inaugural address, 1883. *Accountant,* May 12, 1883.

Manchester chartered accountants students' society

BEARDSALL, FRANCIS EMANUEL MOORE. Address, 1887. *Accountant,* 1887, p. 637.
BOARDMAN, J. Address, 1886. *Accountant,* 1886, p. 695.
BREWIS, ARTHUR STEPHEN. Address, 1910. *Accountant,* March 12, 1910, p. 368-75.
BRODERICK, L Address, 1892. *Accountant,* Oct. 8, 1892, p. 754-8.
BRUTTON, R. Address, 1893. *Accountant,* Dec. 23, 1893, p. 1077-9.

ACCOUNTANTS' SOCIETIES — MANCHESTER CHARTERED ACCOUNTANTS STUDENTS' SOCIETY—*(Continued)*
CARSE, J. A. Address, 1895. *Accountant* Oct. 26, 1895, p. 852-8.
GILLIES, A. A. Address, 1898. *Accountant* Oct. 8, 1898, p. 946-950
GREGORY, T. Address, 1898. *Accountant,* Feb 19, 1898, p. 207-15.
GUTHRIE, E. Address, 1885. *Accountant* Nov 7, 1885.
HALLIDAY, J. E. Address, 1888. *Accountant* Nov. 17, 1888, p. 758-61.
LITTON, J. G. Address, 1896. *Accountant* Oct. 24, 1896, p. 883-5.
MURRAY, A. Inaugural address, 1883. *Accountant,* Feb. 17, 24, 1883.
NAIRNE, W. H. Address, 1889. *Accountant* Nov. 23, 1889, p. 626-30.
PLUMPTON, T. Address, 1894. *Accountant* Oct. 13, 1894, p. 896-900.
POWNALL, ALFRED H. Address, 1890. *Accountant,* Apr. 18, 1891, p. 300-4.
REPORTS and accounts.
See also index of the *Accountant.*
SCOTT, F. Address, 1900. *Accountant,* Oct 13, 1900, p. 893-6.
WALKDEN, MARTIN L. Address, 1891. *Accountant,* Nov. 21, 1892, p. 820-4.

Manchester society of chartered accountants
REPORTS and accounts.
See also index of the *Accountant.*
WOMERSLEY, F. Address. *Accountant,* Nov 30, 1912, p. 691.

National association of controllers and accounting officers
See also National association of controllers and accounting officers.
COMPTROLLER'S and accounting officers in convention. *Journal of accountancy,* July 1910 p. 215-6.
COMPTROLLER'S association to admit fisca officers as delegates. *Journal of accountancy,* Nov. 1909, p. 64.

National society of certified public accountants in the United States
NATIONAL society of certified public accountants in the United States. *Accountant,* Oct. 30, 1897, p. 1016-9.

New Zealand accountants and auditors' association
REPORTS and accounts.
See also Index of the *Accounting and commerce.*

New Zealand society of accountants
NEW ZEALAND SOCIETY OF ACCOUNTANTS. Qualification for membership; syllabus of preliminary commercial and professional examinations; lectures on accountancy at the university colleges; syllabus of examination for bookkeepers. 1919.
REPORTS and accounts.
See also Index of the *Accountant.*

Northern chartered accountants students' society
ARMSTRONG, J. H. Address, 1905. *Accountant,* Oct. 14, 1905, p. 428-31, 500-2.
BOWDEN, T. Address, 1904. *Accountant,* Feb. 25, 1905, p. 226-29, 302-4.
MARTIN, T. C. Address, 1907. *Accountant* Dec. 7, 1907, p. 698-702.
SQUANCE, F. C. Address, 1906. *Accountant,* Jan. 26, 1907, p. 117-22.

Northern institute of chartered accountants
REPORTS and accounts.
See also index of *Accountant.*

Nottingham society of chartered accountants
LEMAN, T. C. Address. *Accountant,* Feb. 17, 1917, p. 168-72.
NOTTINGHAM society of chartered accountants: catalogue of the library, 1907.
REPORTS and accounts.
See also index of the *Accountant.*

Queensland institute of accountants (incorporated)
REPORTS and accounts.
See also index of the *Accountant; Australasian accountant and secretary.*

Railway accounting officers' association
See Railroads—Societies; Railway accounting officers association.

Rhodesia society of accountants
RHODESIA society of accountants. Registration of accountants in Southern Rhodesia. *Incorporated acountants' journal,* June, 1918, p. 172.

Sheffield society of chartered accountants
REPORTS and accounts.
See also index of the *Accountant.*

Sheffield chartered accountants students' society
BEST, J. W. Address, 1902. *Accountant,* Oct. 25, 1902, p. 1084-7.
CAMM, W. H. Address, 1889. *Accountant,* Mar. 9, 1889, p. 126-8.
EVANS, R. J. Address, 1888. *Accountant,* Nov. 24, 1888, p. 770-2.
FRANKLIN, G. Address, 1890. *Accountant,* Nov. 8, 1890, p. 618-19.
REPORTS and accounts.
See index of the *Accountant.*
SHORT, S. Address, 1883. *Accountant,* Oct. 20, 1883.
WATSON, A. T. Address, 1885. *Accountant,* Nov. 21, 1885.

Society of accountants in Aberdeen
SOCIETY of accountants in Aberdeen.
See Index of the *Accountant's magazine.*

Society of accountants in Cape Colony
SOCIETY OF ACCOUNTANTS IN CAPE COLONY. Year-book; annual to date.

Society of accountants in Edinburgh
SOCIETY OF ACCOUNTANTS IN EDINBURGH. Charter of incorporation, rules and regulations and by-laws, 1909. 29p.
SOCIETY of accountants in Edinburgh.
See Index of the *Accountants' magazine.*

Society of incorporated accountants and auditors
BRITISH society of incorporated accountants and auditors. *Journal of accountancy,* July 1906, Aug. 1908, June 1912, July, Nov. 1913, June, July, Dec. 1914, June, July, Dec. 1915, July 1916, July 1917, Aug. 1918, July 1919, p. 230; 247; 455; 77, 416, 483; 83, 494, 486; 79, 480, 79; 78; 156; 80.
GREEN, ARTHUR. Address. *Accountant,* May 31, 1913, p. 839-43.
KEVANS, E. Address. *Accountant,* Oct. 5, 1912, p. 451-2.
MARTIN, J. Incorporated accountants in the British empire. *Incorporated accountants' journal,* 1904-5, p. 178.
NELSON, CHARLES HEWETSON. Address, 1913. *Accountant,* Oct. 11, 1913, p. 476-9.
NELSON, CHARLES HEWETSON. Address, 1914. *Accountant,* May 30, 1914, p. 803-6.
NELSON, CHARLES HEWETSON. Address, 1915. *Accountant,* May 22, 1915, p. 693-9.
NELSON, CHARLES HEWETSON. Address, 1916. *Accountant,* May 27, 1916, p. 606-10.
REPORTS and accounts.
See also index of the *Accountant; Incorporated accountants' journal.*
SOCIETY of incorporated accountants. *Accountant,* Oct. 7, 14, Nov. 4, 11, 1911, p. 441, 479-81, 595-7, 638-40.

ACCOUNTANTS' SOCIETIES—SOCIETY OF INCORPORATED ACCOUNTANTS AND AUDITORS—*(Continued)*

SOCIETY OF INCORPORATED ACCOUNTANTS AND AUDITORS. Proceedings at conference held in London, Oct. 4, 5 and 6, 1906. 138p.
SOCIETY OF INCORPORATED ACCOUNTANTS AND AUDITORS. Results of examination, 1917, to date.
SOCIETY OF INCORPORATED ACCOUNTANTS AND AUDITORS. Year-book, 1895, to date. 441, 479-81, 595-7, 638-40.
SOCIETY of incorporated accountants and auditors. *Journal of accountancy,* July 1920, p. 68.
WOODINGTON, A. E. Address, 1917. *Accountant,* May 26, 1917, p. 510-13.
WOODINGTON, ARTHUR E. Address, 1918. *Accountant,* May 25, 1918, p. 392-7.
WOODINGTON, A. E. Address, 1919 *Accountant,* May 24, 1919, p. 448-50.

Society of public accountants of New South Wales

ACCOUNTANCY in New South Wales. *Accountant,* June 26, 1915, June 23, 1917. p. 831-2, 578-80. *Public accountant,* Sept. 1917, p. 49-52, 53-5.

South Wales and Monmouthshire society of chartered accountants

REPORTS and accounts.
See also index of the *Accountant.*

Sydney institute of public accountants

SYDNEY INSTITUTE OF PUBLIC ACCOUNTANTS. Paper read at conference, January 1901, seventh annual report and accounts and list of members, catalogue of library books.

Transvaal society of accountants

BYE-LAWS. *Accountant,* June 10, 1905, p. 717-23. *Incorporated accountants' journal,* 1904-5, p. 215.
TRANSVAAL SOCIETY OF ACCOUNTANTS. Yearbook; annual.

Wellington accountants students' society

REPORTS and accounts.
See also index of the *Accountant.*

ACCOUNTANTS: their duties and responsibilities. *Accountant,* May 5, 12, 19, 26, June 2, 9, 16, 23, 30, July 14, 21, 28, 1883.

ACCOUNTANTS: their duties and responsibilities: auditing articles. *Accountant,* Jan. 6. 13, 20, 27, Feb 3, 10, 17, 24, Mar. 3, 10, 17, 24, 31, April 7, 14, 21, 28, Nov. 4, 11, 18, 25, Dec. 2, 9, 16, 23, 30, 1882.

ACCOUNTANTS: their duties and responsibilities: bookkeeping articles. *Accountant,* Aug. 5, 12, 19, 26, Sept. 2, 9, 16, 23, 30, Oct. 14, 21, 28, Nov. 4, 11, 18, 25, Dec. 2, 9, 16, 23, 30, 1882.

ACCOUNTANTS: their duties and responsibilities: chancery practice. *Accountant,* May 5, 12, 19, 26, June 2, 9, 16, 23, 30, July 14, 21, 28, Aug. 4, 11, 18, Sept. 1, 22, 29, 1883.

ACCOUNTANTS: their duties and responsibilities: executors and administrators. *Accountant,* July 28, Aug. 4, 11, 18, Sept. 1, 22, 29, 1883.

ACCOUNTANTS: their duties and responsibilities: mercantile law. *Accountant,* Sept. 29, Oct. 6, 13, Nov. 10, 24, Dec. 15, 22, 29, 1883, Jan. 5, 12, 1884.

ACCOUNTANTS' time accounts. *Accountant,* Sept. 24, 1910, p. 396-8.

ACCOUNTANTS' time book and clients ledger, combined. Hazlehurst, H. W.

ACCOUNTANTS who advertise. *Journal of accountancy,* Dec. 1909, p. 160.

ACCOUNTING

See also Accountants: Auditing and Auditors; Balance sheets; Balancing; Bookkeeping; Cost and factory accounting; subdivision Accounting under various headings, e. g., Gas-Accounting; also name of various accounts, e. g., Accounts payable.

ACCOUNTANTS' library. 51v. London, Gee & Co. 1901-1909.
ACCOUNTING and office methods by F. N. Doubleday, W. E. Wilson and others. Chicago, A. W. Shaw Co. 1913. 45p. (Business man's library, v. 10.)
ACCOUNTING and office methods; organizing the office, accounting principles and systems, office work and record keeping. Chicago, A. W. Shaw co. 1914. 200p. (Students' business book series). Also issued as v. 9 of the Library of business practice.
ACCOUNTING methods. *Electrical world,* June 7, 1913, p. 1235-8.
ALLEN, GEORGE. Science of accounts made clear and simple. Raleigh, N. C., George Allen, 1909.
——— Same. High school ed. Raleigh, N. C., George Allen, 1909. 136p.
ANDERSEN, A. E. Complete accounting course. 3 pts. New York, The Ronald press company, 1919-20. Pt. 3 to be issued later.
APPLETON, WILL. Balance day procedure. *Accounting and commerce,* March 1916, p. 281-3.
AREVALO, ALBERTO. A puntes de contabilidad general. Rosario, 1919. 63p.
As others see us. *Journal of accountancy,* June 1907, p. 158-61.
AYRES, MILAN V. Accounting versus statistics. *Electric railway journal,* May 3, 1913, p. 803-5.
BAKER, JAMES WILLIAM. 20th century bookkeeping and accounting; a treatise on modern bookkeeping, accounting and business customs, as illustrated in the Business transactions which accompany this text; 8th ed. for use in all schools that teach bookkeeping and accounting. Knoxville, Tenn., Southwestern publishing co. 1918. 308p.
——— Same. Ed. 10. Cincinnati, Southwestern publishing co. 1920.
BARTON, A. E. Australasian advanced accountancy. Ed. 3. Wellington accountancy publications, 1915.
BASSETT, WILLIAM R. Accounting as an aid to business profits. New York, A. W. Shaw co. c1918. 316p.
BATLIBOI, J. R. Advanced accounts. 56, Esplanade Road, Fort, Bombay. 512p.
BELDING, ALBERT G. Accounts and accounting practice. New York, American book co. c1918. 224p.
BENNETT, GEORGE E. Constructive accounting; a manual of system building. New York, The Ronald press company, 1920. (Business acounting, v. 2.)
BENNETT, ROBERT JOSEPH. Accountancy; special course in accounting, auditing and practice, designed to prepare candidates for examinations for certified public accountants. Ed. 2. Philadelphia, Bennett accountancy institute, 1913.
For sale only to persons taking courses with Bennett accountancy institute.
BENTLEY, HARRY CLARK. Science of accounts; a presentation of the underlying principles of modern accounting; designed as a work of reference for accountants, and a text book for advanced students of accountancy. New York, The Ronald press co. 1911. 392p.
BENTLEY, HARRY CLARK. Standardization of accounting forms and methods. *Accountant,* Sept. 14, 1912, p. 333-8, 351-6. *Journal of accountancy,* Feb. March, May, Sept.

ACCOUNTING—*(Continued)*
1912, p. 109-21, 161-81, 315-38, 389-400; 19-20, 99-106, 169-87. *Correspondence,* Aug. 1912, p. 146-8.

BETTER business accounting system. *Better business,* Dec. 1918, p. 42-3.

BLUE, FRED. O. Uniform public accounting and state supervision thereof. *National tax association, Proceedings,* 1916, p. 332-5.

BOOTH, W. E. Accounting and accounts. *Public accountant,* 1909, p. 126, 158.

BRANFORD, VICTOR V. Accounting in its relation to economics. (In Lisle, George. *Encyclopaedia of accounting.* v. 1, p. 24-50.

BRAY, W. REGINALD. Things that matter in accounts. *Business organization and management,* Oct. 1920, p. 88-90.

BRISCOE, W. R. B. Accountant in relation to legal proceedings. *Incorporated acountants' journal,* April 1914, p. 204-8.

BROAKER, FRANK. Technique of accountics. Lessons 1-20. New York, 1904.

BROWN, WILLIAM M. Importance of proper accounting. *Telephony,* Nov. 3, 1917.

CAMPBELL, THOMAS FINDLEY. Campbell's actual accounting; the apprenticeship in business; the modern method of instruction in elementary and advanced accounting, business forms and business customs. Bobbs-Merrill co. 1912. 135p.

CARR, EBENEZER. Method as relating to accounting and auditing. *Incorporated accountants' journal,* 1905-6, p. 69.

CARTER, ROGER NEAL. Advanced accounts; a manual of advanced bookkeeping and accountancy for accountants, bookkeepers and and business men. London, Sir Isaac Pitman and sons. 980p.

CHAPMAN, CLOWRY. Legal aspects of modern correspondence and accounting systems. *Business world,* Dec. 1905.

CHAPMAN, RICHARD M. Use of documents in accounting. *Business,* Jan. 1898, p. 30-3.

CHAPMAN, S. J. Accounting in relation to economic problems. *Accountant,* Nov. 21, 1914, p. 619-23. *Canadian chartered accountant,* Jan. 1915, p. 238-46.

CHURCH, A. H. Practical principles of rational management. *Engineering magazine,* April, May 1913, p. 24-33, 166-73.

CLARK, N. M. A-B-C of accounting. *System,* Aug. 1913, p. 162-8.

CLARK, N. M. Less time out for accounting. *System,* Nov. 1913, p. 532-5.

CLEVELAND, FREDERICK A. Relation of finance to accounting. *Rand McNally Bankers' monthly,* v. 23, p. 491-505.

COLE, WILLIAM MORSE. Accounting and auditing. Minneapolis, Cree publishing co. 1910.

COLE, WILLIAM MORSE. Accounts; their construction and interpretation for business men and students of affairs. Revised and enlarged edition. Boston, Houghton, Mifflin co. c1915. 445p.

COLE, WILLIAM MORSE. Bookkeeping, accounting and auditing. Chicago, Washington, institute. c1914, 479p. (International business library.)

COLLABORATION with the Federal trade commission. *Federal reserve bulletin,* Jan. 1, 1917, p. 21-3.

COOPER, F. T. Relations of accounting to law. *Accountants' magazine,* Jan. 1913, p. 9-29.

COTTON, GEORGE M. Modern accounting and small undertakings. Business organization and management, May 1920, p. 147-9.

COX, HENRY C. Advanced and analytical accounting. New York, The Ronald press company. 1920. 459p. (Business accounting. v. 4.)

CRAWFORD, J. M. Cleveland accountant, a work designed for experienced bookkeepers on opening and closing the books of joint stock companies, also a complete manual of forms for organizing and managing all kinds of companies and associations, including partnership settlements and partnership changes; auditors, their duties and responsibilities, also points on higher and expert accounting and a practical treatise on banking. Cleveland, Author, 1898. 390p.

CULVER, A. I. Administrative accounting. *Incorporated accountants' journal,* 1902-3, p. 230.

CUTFORTH, ARTHUR E. Early stages of preparation for the accountancy papers of the intermediate. London, Gee & co. 1906. 100p.

CUTFORTH, ARTHUR E. Organization of an accountant's department. *Accountant,* May 10, 1913, p. 729-35.

DAVAR, SOHRAB. Davar's "ad-referendum" of accounting. London, Gee & co. 1903.

DAVEY, FREDERICK. Students' catechism on bookkeeping, accounting and banking; with exercises and examination questions. Ed. 2. ILondon, Butterworth & co. 1917. 478p.

DAWSON, SIDNEY S. and R. C. DE ZOUCHE. Accounting. London, Sir Isaac Pitman & sons.

DAY, CLARENCE MUNRO. Accounting practice. New York, D. Appleton & co. 1915. 318p.

DENNIS, WILLIAM HENRY. Practical accounting. Ed. 2. New York, Leslie J. Thompkins, 1907.

——— Same. Ed. 4. 1910.

DICKINSON, ARTHUR. LOWES. Accounting practice and procedure. New York, The Ronald press co. 1917. 315p.

DICKINSON, ARTHUR LOWES. Accounting practice and procedure. (In Cyclopaedia of commerce, accountancy, business and administration. 1910. v. 7, p. 239-80.)

DICKINSON, ARTHUR LOWES. Accounting practice and procedure; a paper to be presented at the annual meeting of the American association of public acountants, Atlantic City, New Jersey, October 20-23, 1908. 47p. *American institute of accounts, Yearbook,* 1908, p. 188-254. *Accountant,* Dec. 12, 1908, p. 740-58. *Journal of accountancy,* Oct.-Dec. 1908, p. 415-25; 7-18, 96-110. *Incorporated accountants' journal,* 1908-9, p. 51.

DICKINSON, ARTHUR LOWES. Special points in accountancy practice. *Business world,* April, May 1905, p. 157-61, 233-6.

DICKSEE, LAWRENCE ROBERT. Advanced accounting; with an appendix on the law relating to accounts by J. E. G. de Montmorency. Ed. 4. London, Gee & co. 1911. 520p.

——— Same. Ed. 5. London, Gee & Co. 1916. 517p.

DICKSEE, LAWRENCE ROBERT. Importance of accurate and adequate acounting. *Accountant,* Feb. 4, 1905, p. 146-51.

DICKSEE, LAWRENCE ROBERT. Modern accountancy methods in relation to business efficiency. *Accountant,* Nov. 14, 1914, p. 581-6.

DICKSEE, LAWRENCE ROBERT and H. E. BLAIN. Balancing books and audit. (In their *Office organization and management.* 1917. p. 205-26.)

DICKSEE, LAWRENCE ROBERT and H. E. BLAIN. Finance-banking accounts-loans, overdrafts, mortgages, debentures, bills of exchange, etc. (In their *Office organization and management.* 1917. p. 176-87.)

DOBSON, A. Designing of accounting systems. *Accountant,* April 10, 1920, p. 424-30.

DOWLER, FRANK AND E. M. HARRIS. Auditing, accounting and banking; a manual for accountants, advanced bookkeeping students and business men. London, Sir Isaac Pitman & sons. 319p.

DUNCAN, JOHN C. Definition of accounting. *American economic association, Papers and discussions,* April 1909, p. 75-84. *Journal of accountancy,* Feb. 1909, p. 274-81.

DUNN, HOMER A. Accounting inconsistencies and fallacies; an address delivered before

ACCOUNTING—*(Continued)*
the 1916 convention of the American electric railway association. 15p. *Accountant,* Dec. 23, 1916, p. 599-603. *American electric railway accountants association, Proceedings,* 1916. *Electric railway journal,* Oct. 14, 1916.

DUXBURY, NATHANIEL. Abbreviated methods in accountancy. *Accountant,* Oct. 10, 1914, p. 407-11.

EATON, ABIJAH H. Eaton and Burnett revised and improved bookkeeping, corporation, voucher and cost accounting embracing all modern and scientific methods used in business. Baltimore, Eaton and Burnett business college, inc. 1917. 261p.

EDDIS, WILTON C. Text-book for the use of manufacturers, merchants, accountants, and bookkeepers. Toronto, 1912. 199p.

ELDRIDGE, HERBERT JAMES. Accounting: practical methods and useful statistics. *Associated accountants' journal,* 1908, p. 173.

ELWELL, F. H. Laboratory manual; elements of accounting. Madison, Wis., Parker co. 1920.

ENGLISH v. American practice. *Accountant,* May 11, 1907, p. 660-2. *Incorporated accountants'* journal, 1906-7, p. 192. *Journal of accountancy,* March 1907, p. 388-93.

ENGLISH vs. American practice again. *Journal of accountancy,* June 1907, p. 139-40.

ESQUERRÉ, PAUL JOSEPH. Applied theory of accounts. New York, The Ronald press co. 1917. 519p.

FISHER, R. V. Accounts and records that get facts quickly. *System,* Nov. 1915, p. 536-9.

FOOTE, ALLEN RIPLEY. Correct accounting a fundamental basis for regulation and taxation; a paper to be presented at the annual meeting of the American association of public accountants, Denver, Colorado, October 19, 20, 21, 1909. 15p. *American institute of accountants, Yearbook.* 1909, p. 142-58. *Journal of accountancy,* Nov. 1909, p. 17-28.

FORMS and precedents for accountants. 2v. Edinburgh, W. Green & son, 1906.

FOSTER, A. J. Common sense of accountancy. *Accountant,* May 24, 1913, p. 799-804.

GALLOWAY, LEE. Organization of the accounting department. (In his *Office management.* 1918. p. 419-44.)

GANTT, H. L. Efficiency and democracy. *Journal of American society of mechanical engineers,* Jan. 1919, p. 43. Suggestions in regard to accounting systems.

GARRISON, ELISHA ELY. Accounting every business man should know. New York, Doubleday Page & co. 1910. 188p.

GAY, EDWIN F. Uniform accounting systems. *American institute of accountants, Yearbook,* 1913, p. 81-101. *Journal of accountancy,* Oct. 1913, p. 268-79.

GILL, PHILIP J. "Concise" audit and accounting memorandum book. Scranton, Scranton book co. c1912.

GILMAN, STEPHEN. Principles of accounting. Chicago, La Salle extension university, 1917. 415p.

GOODYEAR, LLOYD ERNEST. Principles of accountancy. Cedar Rapids, Iowa, Goodyear-Marshall publishing co. c1913. 190p. (American bookkeeping series).

GOODYEAR, SAMUEL HORATIO. Goodyear's advanced accounting. Cedar Rapids, Goodyear-Marshall publishing co. 1909. 114p.

GOODYEAR, SAMUEL HORATIO. Progressive business accounting. Cedar Rapids, Iowa, Goodyear-Marshall publishing co.

GOODYEAR, SAMUEL HORATIO. Standard accounting. Cedar Rapids, Goodyear-Marsnall publishing co.

GOODYEAR, SAMUEL HORATIO. Theory of accounts. Cedar Rapids, Goodyear-Marshall publishing co. 1902.

GOODYEAR, SAMUEL HORATIO AND LLOYD E. GOODYEAR. Higher accounting. Cedar Rapids, Goodyear-Marshall publishing co. 1907.
In six pamphlet editions as follows: Commission accounting; Real estate and insurance; Practical banking; Corporation and factory accounting; Railway accounting; Wholesale accounting.

GOODYEAR, SAMUEL HORATIO AND LLOYD E. GOODYEAR. Teacher's reference book to Goodyear's higher accounting. Cedar Rapids, Goodyear-Marshall publishing company. 121p.

GRANT, H. D. One place for every account: how income and expenses are classified and handled with the least amount of labor. *System,* March 1914, p. 293-6.

GREELEY, HAROLD DUDLEY, ed. Business accounting. 5v. New York, The Ronald press company, 1920. (Not sold separately.)
Contents: v.1 Theory of accounts, by Harold Dudley Greeley; v.2, Constructive accounting, by George E. Bennett; v.3 Cost accounting, by DeWitt Carl Eggleston; v.4 Advanced and analytical acounting, by Harry C. Cox; v.5 Illustrative accounting problems, by Charles F. Rittenhouse and Harold Dudley Greeley. Reading guide and general index, by Arthur H. Rosenkampff and Gould L. Harris.

GREELEY, HAROLD DUDLEY. Theory of accounts. New York, The Ronald press company, 1920. 442p. (Business accounting, v.1)

GRAVES, R. H. Why it is easy to steal half a million dollars. *Harpers world,* June 1, 1907, p. 802.

GREENDLINGER, LEO. Accounting theory and practice. Chicago, DeBower-Elliott co. c1910. 513p. (Modern business, v.3).

GREENDLINGER, LEO. Financial and business statements. New York, Alexander Hamilton institute, c1917. 329p. (Modern business, v.22).

GREIG, W. M. Explanation of Greig's accounting. Aberdeen, 1913.

GRIFFITH, JAMES B. Single proprietors' and partners' accounts. Chicago, American school of correspondence, 1909.

GRIFFITH, JAMES B. Theory of accounts. 2v. Chicago, American school of correspondence, 1909. (In *Cyclopedia of commerce, accountancy, business administration.* 1910. v.4. p. 11-116).

GUTHRIE, E. Some controversial points in accounts. *Accountant,* Oct. 22, 1898, p. 990-9. *Business,* Jan. 1900, p. 34-9.

HAMILTON, WILLIAM R. How to criticise accounts. *Accountant,* March 17, April 14, 1906, p. 343-51, 453-5.

HARDCASTLE, JOSEPH. Adjustment and regulating of entries and accounts. *Business world,* Jan. 1902, p. 28-30.

HARDCASTLE, JOSEPH. Business statistics—statistical accounting. *Business,* Jan. Feb. 1900, p. 28-32, 87-91.

HARDCASTLE, JOSEPH. Negative accounts. *Business,* April 1899, p. 242-5.

HARDCASTLE, JOSEPH. Old and new. *Business,* May-Sept. 1899, p. 299-301, 361-4, 427-33, 490-6, 569-72.

HARDCASTLE, JOSEPH. Proprietor's business. *New York accountants' and bookkeepers' journal,* April 1903, p. 35-7.

HARDCASTLE, JOSEPH. Purpose in accounts. *Business,* Feb. March, 1899, p. 179-82.

HARDCASTLE, JOSEPH. Sparks from an accountant''s anvil. *Business,* Jan.-June, Nov. 1896-Feb. 1897, p. 35-7, 90-1, 139-40, 185-6, 229-30, 273-6, 477-8, 510, 15-6, 48-9.

HARDCASTLE, JOSEPH. Statement of affairs and deficiency accounts. *Business world,* March 1902, p. 124-6.

HARDCASTLE, JOSEPH. Talks on accounts. *The office,* Aug. Sept. Dec. 1890, p. 227-8, 251-2, 325-6.

ACCOUNTING—*(Continued)*

HARDCASTLE, JOSEPH. Theories of accounts. *Business*, March-June 1897, p. 80-1, 112-3, 141-2, 173-4.

HATFIELD, HENRY RAND. Modern accounting, its principles and some of its problems. New York, D. Appleton & co. 1916. 367p.

HATFIELD, HENRY RAND. Some neglected phases of accounting. *Electric railway journal*, Oct. 16, 1915, p. 799-802.

HAYWARD, WILLIAM R. Keeping account of money. (In his *Money, what it is and how to use it*. c1917. p. 35-53).

HEITMANN, HENRY. Course in the theory and practice of higher accounting, prepared for students of Eastman's College. Poughkeepsie, Eastman College, 1910, 240p.

HERTZ, JOSEPH EMMETT. Secrets of accounting: a practical treatise on how to conduct general audits and ascertain working capital. Portland, Me., J. E. Hertz, 1913. 37p.

HILL, HENRY WOOD. Art of digesting and tabulating accounts and returns. London, Longmans, Green & co. 1879.

HINE, CHARLES DELANO. Fallacies of accounting. (In his *Modern organization*. 1912. p. 59-70). *Engineering magazine*, April 1912, p. 44-8.

HODGE, ALBERT CLAIRE AND J. O. MCKINSEY. Principles of accounting. Chicago, University of Chicago press. 1920. 389p.

HOHENSTEIN, C. V. Principles of accounting. *Business man's magazine*, July, Aug. 1909, p. 56-64, 160-70.

HOLMAN'S NATIONAL SCHOOL OF ACCOUNTANCY, INC. Lectures. 2v. Portland. Holman's national school of accountancy, c1915-6.

HUMPHREYS, ALEXANDER C. Accountancy. (In his *Lecture notes on some of the business features of engineering practice*. p. 168-257).

HUNTER, JOEL. Thinking in figures: commerce, finance and accounts, business systems and short cuts. Atlanta, Joel Hunter, c1916. 234p.

HURLEY, EDWARD NASH. Working with the business man. *System*. Dec. 1915, p. 657-61.

HYANS, EDWARD M. Theory of accounts for accountant students. New York, Universal business institute. 1909. 208p.

HYDE, F. W. Day of exact accounting. *Journal of the American bankers association*, April 1919, p. 531-3.

IN these Utopian days. *Journal of accountancy*, Aug. 1915, p. 127-33.

INTERNATIONAL accountants' manual; or, Twentieth century bookkeeping and business practice. Detroit. The business man's publishing co. 1910. 383p.

INTERNATIONAL library of technology v. 132. Scranton, Pa., International textbook co.

JENKINS, SAMUEL H. Adaptability an essential in accounting. *Business*, Oct. 1895, p. 364-5.

JENKINSON, MARK WEBSTER. Book-keeping and accounting. London, E. Arnold, 1910. 624p.

JENKINSON, MARK WEBSTER. Method in accounting and audit. *Accountant*, Dec. 26, 1903, p. 1567-76.

JENKINSON, MARK WEBSTER. Some debatable matters in accounting and audit. *Accountant*, March 20, 1909, p. 406-16. *Incorporated accountants' journal*, 1898-9, p. 192.

JOHNSON, GEORGE. Bookkeeping and accounts. London, Effingham Wilson, 1917.

JOHNSON, JOSEPH FRENCH. Relation of economics to higher accounting; address delivered before the New York state society of certified public acountants, December 12, 1901. 15p. *Commerce, accounts and finance*, Feb. 1902, p. 6-9.

JONES, CHARLES. Companion to the Solicitor's clerk, embracing magisterial and criminal law, licensing, bankruptcy accounts, bookkeeping, trust accounts, etc. London, 1895.

———— Same. Ed. 3, entitled *The solicitor's clerk, part* 2. London, 1902.

———— Same. Ed. 4. London, 1905.

———— Same. Ed. 5. London, 1910.

KENT, WILLIAM. Investigating an indusrty: accounting and sales department. *Industrial engineering*, May, 1913, p. 208-11.

KESTER, ROY BERNARD. Accounting theory and practice. 2v. New York, The Ronald press co. 1918. 607+796p.

KITTREDGE, A. O. AND J. F. BROWN. Self-proving accounting system; with special application to the instalment business. New York, Self-proving account book co. 1897.

KLEIN, JOSEPH JEROME. Bookkeeping and accounting. New York, D. Appleton & co. 1917. 453p. (College of the City of New York series in commerce, civics and technology).

KLEIN, JOSEPH JEROME. Bookkeeping and accounting; advanced course. New York, D. Appleton & co. 1918.

KLEIN, JOSEPH JEROME. Bookkeeping and accounting, introductory cource. New York, D. Appleton & co. 1918. 226 p. (College of the city of New York series in commerce, civics and technology).

KLEIN, JOSEPH JEROME. Elements of accounting, theory and practice. New York, D. Appleton & co. 1916. 422p.

KOCH, WILLIAM E. What standarized accounting practice means. *American industries*, Feb. 1919, p. 17.

KRIBBEN, B. D. Contact of commercial law and accounting. *American institute of accounts, Yearbook*, 1917, p. 105-10. *Journal of accountancy*, Oct. 1917, p. 283-8.

LAFRENTZ, F. W. Economic aspects of accounting and auditing. *Accountant*, June 9, 1906, p. 734-7. *Journal of accountancy*, April 1906, p. 479-86. *Science*, April 20, 1906, p. 615-6.

LASALLE, EXTENSION UNIVERSITY, CHICAGO. Higher accountancy. Chicago, La Salle extension university, 1918.

LEFFINGWELL, WILLLIAM HENRY. Getting more from the accounting department. (In his *Scientific office management*. 1917. p. 116-23).

LEJEUNE, CAPEL ELLIS. Accounting systems; a pamphlet. Ed. 2. New York, C. E. Le Jeune, 1894. 31p.

LETHERT, HENRY M. What your books should tell you. *Australasian accountant and secretary*, Dec. 1, 1919, p. 10-2.

LISLE, GEORGE. Accounting in theory and practice; a textbook for the use of accountants, solicitors, bookkeepers, investors and business men. Edinburgh, William Green & sons, 1900. 426p.

LISLE, GEORGE AND W. A. MIDDLETON. Account-keeping in principle and practice. Edinburgh, William Green & sons, 1911. 242p.

LITTLETON, A. CHARLES. Introduction to elementary accounting. Cincinnati, South-western publishing company, 1919.

LOGAN, JAMES. Importance of scientific accounting. *Journal of accountancy*, Aug. 1908, p. 276-9.

LYONS, JAMES A. AND OLIVER SAXTON SMITH. Lyons' bookkeeping and accounting. Chicago, Lyons & Carnahan, c1920. 240p.

LYONS, JAMES A. AND WALLACE H. WHIGHAM. Modern accountant. 3pts. Chicago, J. A. Lyons & co.

MACAFEE, W. A. How to schedule accounting work. *100%*, v. 10, no. 1, p. 68.

MCCLUNG, ROBERT GARNDNER. Theory of debit and credit in accounting. Boston, Morgan, Mills & co. 1913. 16p.

MACDONALD, JAMES B. Continental system of accounting (an elementary paper). *South African accountant's journal*, v. 2, p. 26.

MACDONALD, JAMES B. Physical quantities

ACCOUNTING—*(Continued)*
in accounts. *Accountants' magazine,* Aug. 1906, p. 448-52.
MacFarland, George Arthur and Irving David Rossheim. First year in bookkeeping and accounting. New York, D. Appleton and co. 1913. 227p.
McFarland, John J. S. Keeping accounts independent. *Business man's magazine,* Sept. 1907, p. 59-66.
McIntosh, Robert James. Reference book of accounts for manufacturing and mercantile companies. Ed. 2. Toledo, Ohio, R. J. McIntosh co. c1914. 299p.
Mackay, Donald Ross. Some notes on American methods of accounting. *Accountant,* April 1, May 27, 1905, p. 389-95, 641-3.
McKinsey, J. O. Accounting as an administrative aid. *Journal of political economy,* Nov. 1919, p. 759-81.
Madden, John Thomas. Accounting practice and auditing. New York, Alexander Hamilton institute, c1917. 338p. (Modern business, v. 21).
Mambert, S. B. Dwindling cash and growing book profits. *Annalist,* Dec. 31, 1917.
Manning, Anthony B. Advantages of uniform accounting. *Journal of accountancy,* Aug. 1919, p. 113-20. *Cost association of the paper industry, Headquarters bulletin to members,* no. 3, p. 3-9.
Matheson, G. C. Accountants and accounting. *Accountant,* Sept. 18, 1897, p. 896-8.
Merchant, F. R. Accountants' guide. Bombay, 1915.
Millar, Robert Cockburn. Accountants' hand book of interest and decimal calculations consignment and joint accounts. London, Simpkin, Marshall & co., 1889.
Mitchell, Thomas Warner. Accounting principles. New York, Alexander Hamilton institute, c1918. 396p. (Modern business, v.9).
Moffet, Louis Burdell. Manual of bookkeeping and accounting. Ed. 8. Philadelphia, Pierce school, 1908. 175p.
Moore, John Henry and G. W. Miner. Ac counting and business practice. Boston, Ginn & co. 1903. 400p.
Moore, John Henry and G. W. Miner. Accounting and business practice; corporation accounting and banking. Boston, Ginn & co. 1903.
Moore, John Henry and G. W. Miner. Accounting and business practice; shorter course. Boston, Ginn & co. 1903.
Moore, K. Violet. First book on principles of accounts. London, Edward Arnold, 1911. 64p.
Morrison, J. C. Simplified accounting. *Inland printer,* June, 1914, p. 433-4.
Moxey, Edward P. and others. Practical accounting methods; a description of systems appropriate to various kinds of business. New York, Key publishing co. 502p.
Mueller, E. J. How much do we owe? *System,* April 1915, p. 521-2.
Muir, James. Chat about accounting. *Accountant,* Jan. 30, 1892, p. 103-8.
Muller, F. A. Accounting and its progress. *Commonwealth accountant,* June-Sept. 1906.
Mullin, W. J. Keeping tab on sales and profits. *System,* Sept. 1913, p. 290-3.
Nearing, S. If wage earners kept accounts like business concerns. *Survey,* March 13, 1915, p. 655.
Need of common sense accounting. *Worlds work,* June 1906, p. 7685-6.
Newcomb, Ridgley. Modern office practice. *Iron trade review,* Sept. 17, 1908.
Nixon, Alfred. Longmans studies and questions in bookkeeping and advance accounts, (banking and exchange); with notes and answers. London, Longmans, Green & co. 1898.
Nixon, Alfred. Worked studies and questions in theory and practice of bookkeeping and advanced accounts. London, Longmans, Green & co. 1900. 254p.
Nixon, Alfred and J. H. Stagg. Accounting and banking. New York, Longmans, Green & co. 1912. 501p.
Pace, Homer St. Clair. Theory and practice of accounts; applied economics and organization. New York, Pace & Pace. (For sale only to students enrolled for course of instructions.)
Parsons, C. C. Business administration the principle of business organization and system and the actual methods of business operation and management. Chicago, System co. 1909.
Passano, Edward B. Measuring efficiency on a profit basis. *Iron trade review,* March 20, 1913, p. 682-4.
Paton, Ernest Andrew and R. A. Stevenson. Principles of accounting. Ann Arbor, George Wahr, 1917. 373p.
——— Same. Revised ed. New York, Macmillan co. 1918. 685p.
Pegler, Ernest Charles. Preparation of comparative and interim accounts. London, H. Foulks Lynch & co. 1913. 16p. *Accountant,* Jan. 11, 1913, p. 57-62.
Pentlarge, Theodore. Accountant's experiences. *New York accountants' and bookkeepers' journal,* April 1903, p. 30-3.
Pepper, Edmund. Business man's guide in preparing his trading account, profit and loss account, balance sheet, and capital account. Sheffield and London, 1903.
Pixley, Francis William. Accountancy: constructive and recording accountancy. Ed.2. London, Sir Isaac Pitman & sons. 315p.
Pogson, A. H. Common mistakees in accounting. *World's work,* Oct. 1905, p. 6785-6.
Potter, M. H. Details of production department. *Iron trade review,* May 29, 1919, p. 1410-2.
Pridie, G. Roby. Presentation of final accounts. *Incorporated accountants journal,* Nov. 1920, p. 27-30.
Public accounting as a safeguard to the credit system. *Journal of accountancy,* April 1910, p. 451-2.
Questions for accountants. *Hunt's merchants' magazine,* v. 11, p. 192-446.
Racine, Samuel Frederick. Accounting principles. Seattle, Western institute of accountancy, commerce and finance, c1913. 208p. (Accounting students' series).
——— Same. 1917. 320p.
Reitell, Charles. Standard accounting through price control. *Journal of accountancy,* May 1918, p. 360-5.
Rightor, C. E. Recent progress in budget making and accounting. *National municipal review,* Nov. 1917, p. 707-19.
Rittenhouse, Charles Forest. Elements of accounts for individuals, professional men and institutions. New York, McGraw-Hill book co. 1918. 264p.
Rittenhouse, Charles Forest and P. F. Clapp. Acounting theory and practice—unit 1. New York, McGraw-Hill book co. 1918. 165p.
Rittenhouse, Charles Forest and P. F. Clapp. Accounting theory and practice—unit 2. New York, McGraw-Hill book co. 1918. 56p.
Rittenhouse, Charles Forest and P. F. Clapp. Notes on accounting theory and practice. New York, Associated press, 1917. 85p.
Robertson, C. H. D. Constructive accounting. *Business organisation and management,* June, July 1920, p. 251-4, 385-91.
Robinson, Maurice H. Accounting in its relation to economics. *Journal of accountancy,* Feb. 1909, p. 282-94.

ACCOUNTING—*(Continued)*

Rogers, W. S. Cost keeping and accounting. *Business,* Dec. 1898, p. 760-2. *New York railroad club, Proceedings,* Sept. 15, 1898, p. 4-27. Extract. *Railroad gazette,* Nov. 4, 1898, p. 792.

Rowe, Harry M. Bookkeeping and accountancy; complete text presenting the art of bookkeeping in accordance with the principles of modern accountancy. Baltimore, The H. M. Rowe co. c1911. 264p.

Rowe, Harry M. Bookkeeping and accountancy: key. 4v. Baltimore, The H. M. Rowe co. c1910.

Russel, Thomas Herbert and William J. Jackman. Bookkeeping, accounting and auditing. Chicago, Whitman publishing co. 1916. 416p.

Sackett, Gordon. Accounting: correspondence. *Journal of accountancy,* Aug. 1917, p. 157-8.

Sakolski, A. M. Federal corporation tax and modern accounting practice. *Yale review,* Feb. 1910, p. 372-89.

Saliers, Earl A. Accounts in theory and practice; principles. New York, McGraw-Hill book company, 1920. 301p.

Saving labor in the accounting department. *Railway age gazette,* June 22, 1917.

Scovell, Clinton H. Importance of sound accounting in credit relations . *Journal of accountancy,* Nov. 1912, p. 365-80.

Severance, D. N. Rapid calculation and accountants' assistant. Atlanta, Ga., D. N. Severance, 1907.

Shaw, G. W. Less labor in accounting; a receiving and distribution record system. *System,* Feb. 1914, p. 192-5.

Sherwood, John F. Public accounting and auditing, correlating the subjects accounting, auditing, and commercial law. Cincinnati, Southwestern publishing co. 1920. 258p.

Shinn, Eugene. Proper record forms for every business. *World's work,* Jan. 1906, p. 7129-30.

Soule, George. Higher accounting. *Accountant,* Sept. 22, 1894, p. 825-30.

Soule, George. Soule's new science and practice of accounts. Ed. 7. New Orleans, George Soule, 1903. 749p.

Spencer, Enos. Art of modern bookkeeping and accounting. Ed.4. Louisville, Ky. Enos Spencer, 1911. 444p.

Spicer, Ernest Evan and E. C. Pegler. Bookkeeping and accounts. London, H. Foulks Lynch & co.
——— Same. Ed. 2. London, 1910. 424p.
——— Same. Ed. 3. London, 1914. 442p.
——— Same. Ed. 4. London, 1919. 444p.

Spicer, Ernest Evan and E. C. Pegler. Examination note book for accountant students. Ed.3. London, H. Foulks Lynch & co. 1914. 183p.

Spicer, Ernest Evan and E. C. Pegler. Practical bookkeeping and commercial knowledge. London, H. Foulks Lynch & co. 1912. 342p.

Sprague, Charles Ezra. Line-by-line accounts. *Business,* Jan. 1896, p. 29-31.

Sprague, Charles Ezra. Outlay and income. *The office,* Nov. 1889, p. 207-8.

Sprague, Charles Ezra. Philosophy of accounts. Ed.4. New York, The Ronald press co. 1918. 161p. *Journal of accountancy,* Jan.-Nov. 1907, Jan. 1908, p. 181-88, 261-75, 364-75, 449-61; 33-45, 122-30, 198-210, 287 97, 363-8, 432-50; 23-40, 205-10.

Standardisation of accounts. *Accountant,* Oct. 17, 24, 1903, p. 1249-51, 1273-8.

Standardized accounting system. *Journal of electricity,* Aug. 15, 1919, p. 168-70.

Staub, E. Elmer. Designing of accounting systems. *Journal of accountancy,* Dec. 1915, p. 430-7.

Steele, F. R. Carnegie. Development of systems of control. *Journal of accountancy,* Oct. 1913, p. 280-90. *American institute of accountants, Yearbook,* 1913, p. 102-18.

Stephens, John Rittenhouse. Principles of accounting. Kansas City, Mo., J. R. Stephens, 1909.

Stephenson, F. J. Credit man and better accounting. National association of credit men bulletin, Jan. 1917, p. 10-4.

Sub-division, saving and safety. *Horseless age,* Dec. 16, 1914, p. 869-70.

Sweeney, J. E. New standard accounting system. *Electrical review,* March 29, 1919, p. 508-9.

Tabloid systems for salesmanship, accounting, etc. ed. by E. H. Beach. Detroit, Bookkeeper publishing co. 1906. 208p.

Tanner-Gilman schools, inc. Higher accountancy. 2v. Chicago, Tanner-Gilman schools, inc. c1917.

Taylor, Ellsworth. Modern methods and the business specialist. *Iron age,* July 15, 1909.

Technique in accounting. *Journal of accountancy,* May 1906, p. 54-5.

Thorne, William W. Abolition of the trial balance together with 12 studies in bookkeeping and accounting. Detroit. Mich., Business man's publishing co. 1906.

"Triple" account system. *Accountant,* Jan. 11, 1913, p. 45-7.

Two pathfinders. *Journal of accountancy,* May 1909, p. 42-3.

Uniform accounting. *Canadian chartered accountant,* July 1917, p. 5-33. *Journal of accountancy,* June 1917, p. 401-33.

Uniform accounting methods necessary; what a balance sheet means and the correct way to make one. *National wholesale grocers' bul.* November 1917, January 1918, p. 37-8, 38-40, 47-50.

Uniform accounts. *Federal reserve bulletin,* April 1, 1917, p. 270-84.

Vannais Accounting Institute, inc. Accounting. Hartford, Vannais accounting institute, inc. 1918.

Walton, Seymour. Errors of principle. *Accountant,* Oct. 28, 1905, p. 487-92.

Walton, Seymour. Red-tape versus common sense. *Journal of accountancy,* June 1915, p. 474-8.

Walton, Seymour. Students' department. *Journal of accountancy,* Jan. 1914 to date.

Walton school of commerce, Chicago. Advanced accounting. 2v. Chicago, Seymour Walton, c1912.
——— Same. c1918-1920.

Whatley, G. E. Stuart. Accountant's and bookkeeper's vade-mecum; a series of short and concise articles upon capital and revenue expenditure revenue accounts, depreciation, reserve and sinking funds, adjustment of partnership accounts, joint stock companies' accounts, tabular bookkeeping and other matters not generally dealt with in extant works on bookkeeping, together with useful forms and directions. London, Gee & co. 1893. 159p.

Whitcomb, W. D. Uniform accounting needed to satisfy public. *Oregon voter,* Dec. 4, 1920, p. 20-5.

Wardhaugh, J. B. Accountant's digest. London, W. Green, 1912.

Webster, N. E. Set-off; an accounting as well as a legal procedure. *Government accountant,* 1909, v.3, p. 249-61.

Where do the pennies in your dollar go? *American gas engineering journal,* Oct. 12, 1918, p. 343-6. *System,* Oct. 1918, p. 493.

Why accounts should be classified. 100%, Sept. 1918, p. 66.

Wilcox, F. N. Wilcox system of accounts. *Business world,* May 1905, p. 220-1.

Wildman, John Raymond. Place which ac-

ACCOUNTING—(Continued)

counting should occupy in any scheme of national preparedness; a paper read before the American economic association at Co lumbus, Ohio, December 29th, 1916. 8p. *American economic review*, March 1917, sup. 224-8.

WILDMAN, JOHN RAYMOND. Principles of accounting. New York, The William G. Hewitt press, 1914. 360p.

WILLIAMS, SYDNEY E. Law of account. London, Stevens & Sons, 1899.

WILLIAMSON, J. GILMOUR. Counting-house and factory organization; a practical manual of modern methods applied to the counting house and factory. London, Sir Isaac Pitman & sons, 1909. 163p.

WILLIS, HENRY PARKER. Accounting theory and practice. Chicago, LaSalle extension university, 1910.

WITTER, CHARLES A. Business and accounts for public schools and home use. Ed. 6, revised and enlarged. Redlands, Cal., C. A. Witter, 1910. 112p.

WOLFF, ARTHUR. Practical accounting. New York, Universal business institute, 1908. Not for sale.

WRIGHT, ALLAN W. Theory and practice. *Journal of accountancy*, June 1914, p. 431-4.

ZUMSTEIN, H. C. Applied accountancy. *Australasian accountant and secretary*, Jan. 1, 1920, p. 21-4.

Encyclopaedias, dictionaries, etc.

AMERICAN business and accounting encyclopaedia, a standard reference book for accountants and business men, profusely illustrated with hundreds of special forms and tables, compiled by E. H. Beach and W. W. Thorne, commercial law department by A. E. Rouech. Ed.7. Detroit, The Bookkeeper publishing company, c1901. 1090p.

CYCLOPEDIA of commerce, accountancy, business administration. 10v. Chicago, American school of correspondence, 1910.

CYCLOPEDIA of practical accounting. 4v. Chicago, American technical society, 1912.

DAWSON, SIDNEY STANLEY. Accountant's compendium. London, Gee & co. 1898. 431p.

LISLE, GEORGE. Encyclopaedia of accounting. 6v. Edinburgh, William Green & sons, 1903.

PORTERS, R. J. Pitman's dictionary of bookkeeping: a book of reference on all matters concerning bookkeeping and accountancy for students, teachers and practitioners. London, Sir Isaac Pitman and sons. 777p.

SPEAR, RAYMOND H. ed. Commercial world encyclopedia of accounting for bookkeepers, accountants, auditors and business men. Ed.2 2v. Detroit, Commercial world publishing co. 1911.

Problems

See also Examinations.

ACCOUNTANCY problems discussed. *Australasian accountant and secretary*, Jan., March 31, 1920, p. 31, 102-3.

ADVANCED bookkeeping and accounts. *Canadian chartered accountant*, Oct. 1914, p. 148-54.

BENNETT, ROBERT JOSEPH. Bookkeeping and accounting exercises. 2v. Chicago, American book co. 1912.

BENNETT, ROBERT JOSEPH. Key to Bookkeeping and accounting exercises. 2v. Chicago, American book co. 1912.

COLE, WILLIAM MORSE. Problems in the principles of accounting. Cambridge, Harvard university press, 1915. 102p.

COOPER, D. Criticism of department of practical accounting. *Journal of accountancy*, July 1912, p. 70-3.

COOPER, D. Problem department. *Canadian chartered accountant*, Oct. 1911, Jan. April, July, Oct. 1912, April, July 1913, Jan. 1914, p. 78-82, 149-54, 223-9, 48-54, 137-41, 288-97, 54-62, 203-6.

DENNIS, WILLIAM HENBY AND LEO GREENDLINGER. Graded accounting problems. 3v. New York, New York university school of commerce, accounts and finance, 1909.

DICKSEE, L. R. Miscellaneous questions on accounting. (In his *Advanced accounting*. 1916. p. 527-64).

ESQUERRÉ, PAUL-JOSEPH. Practical problems. (In his *Applied theory of accounts*. 1917. p. 521-75).

ESQUERRÉ, JAUL-JOSEPH. Problems involving the application of the theory of accounts; prepared or selected for use in connection with the applied theory of accounts. New York, The Ronald press co., 1915. 69p.

FISCHER, A. Questions for journal contributors: correspondence. *Journal of accountancy*, Aug. 1914, p. 152.

GERHART, L. Question of inventory: correspondence. *Journal of accountancy*, Nov. 1914, p. 395-6.

GILES, ALEX T. Question of depreciation charge: correspondence. *Journal of accountancy*, April 1913, p. 309.

GREENWOOD, WILLIAM J. Bookkeeping and accountancy exercises for accountant students. Manchester, W. J. Greenwood, 1904. 389p.

HARDCASTLE, JOSEPH. Problem in executor's accounts. *Journal of accountancy*, Aug. 1906, p. 311-4.

JENSEN, WILHELM. Cost of prison-made goods: correspondence. *Journal of accountancy*, Sept. 1913, p. 254.

JOHNSON, GEORGE. Pitman's book-keeping and accountancy problems. London, Sir Isaac Pitman and sons, 1914. 116p.

KESTER, ROY BERNARD.. Problems and practice data for elements of accounting. New York, Columbia university book store, 1916. 75p.

KLEIN, JOSEPH JEROME. Student's hand book of accounting: solutions to questions in theory of accounts, practical accounting and auditing contained in Elements of accounting, for the use of teachers, students, and practising accountants. New York, D. Appleton & co. 1915. 136p.

NIXON, ALFRED. Worked studies and questions in theory and practice of bookkeeping and advanced accounts. London, Longmans, Green & co. 1900. 254p.

PATON, W. A. AND R. A. STEVENSON. Problems and exercises in accounting. Ed.3, revised and enlarged. Ann Arbor, George Wahr, 1920. 195p.

POINT in practical accounting. *Journal of accountancy*, May 1906, p. 72.

PROBLEM in employers' obligation: correspondence. *Journal of accountancy*, March 1912, p. 237-8.

QUESTION box. *Australasian accountant and secretary*, Feb. 1920, p. 65-7.

RACINE, SAMUEL FREDERICK. Guide to the study of accounting. Seattle, Western institute of accountancy, commerce and finance, 1914. 76p. (Accounting students' series).

———— Same. 1916. 91p.

RACINE, SAMUEL FREDERICK. Practical problems, graded, series "A". Seattle, Western institute of accountancy, commerce and finance, c1916.

RITTENHOUSE, CHARLES FOREST AND PHILLIP FRANCIS CLAPP. Exercises in accounting. New York, Association press, 1917. 117p.

RITTENHOUSE, CHARLES F. AND HAROLD DUDLEY GREELEY. Illustrative accounting problems. New York, The Ronald press company, 1920. 413p. (Business accounting, v.5).

RORER, WILLIAM W. Problem in practical accounting. *Journal of accountancy*, Jan. 1906, p. 265-73.

ACCOUNTING—PROBLEMS—*(Continued)*
SCOTT, G. G. Waste sales account: correspondence. *Journal of accountancy,* Jan. 1913, p. 73.
SHANNAN, CHARLES R. Bank vs. sureties: correspondence. *Journal of accountancy,* Nov. 1913, p. 415.
SHORT account system: correspondence. *Journal of accountancy,* March 1915, p. 243.
STOCKWELL, HERBERT G. Problem in practical accounting. *Journal of accountancy,* April 1906, p. 543-5.
ULMAN, STEPHEN A. Problem in practical accounting. *Journal of accountancy,* Feb. 1906, p. 349-52.
WALTON, SEYMOUR. Practical problem. *Journal of accountancy,* Dec. 1915, p. 465-8.
WALTON, SEYMOUR. Problem. *Journal of accountancy,* Oct. 1914, p. 325-332.
WILDMAN, JOHN R. Department of practical accounting. *Journal of accountancy,* Jan.-Dec. 1913, p. 58-65, 144-51, 224-35, 295-304, 370-81, 436-444, 58-63, 133-43, 226-34, 327-333, 407-16, 494-500; 65-71, 128-33, 189-97, 264-72. 357-64, 449-58. 54-63, 124-31, 234-44, 319-26, 375-83, 461-7. Correspondence. Criticism of department of practical accounting. *Journal of accountancy,* July 1912, p. 70-2.
WILDMAN, JOHN RAYMOND. Elementary accounting problems. New York, The William G. Hewitt press, 1914. 218p.
WILDMAN, JOHN RAYMOND. Introduction to accounting. Ed.4. New York, The William G. Hewitt press, 1915. 65p.
WOLFF, ARTHUR. Practical accounting; problems for accountant students. New York, University business institute, 1905. 66p.

Law
DE MONTMORENCY, J. E. G. Law relating to accounts. (In Dicksee, Lawrence Robert. *Advanced accounting,* 1916. p. 497-524).
SMITH, ROY. State supervision over accounting methods. *Journal of accountancy,* June-Aug. Oct. 1990, p. 77-84, 173-81, 250-8. 419-31.
STATE supervision of public accounting in Minnesota. *Minnesota academy of social science, Papers and proceedings,* 1910.

ACCOUNTING. *Electrical review and western electrician,* Oct. 3, 1914, p. 671-2.

ACCOUNTING. Sackett, George.

ACCOUNTING and auditing. Cole, W. N. 1910.

ACCOUNTING and auditing as related to credits. Thomas, H. I.

ACCOUNTING and banking. Nixon, Alfred, and J. H. Stagg. 1912.

ACCOUNTING and business practice. Moore, John Henry, and G. W. Miner. 1903.

ACCOUNTING and business secrets. Bender, G. D. 1919.

ACCOUNTING and commerce; the official organ of the New Zealand society of accountants; a monthly magazine for business men. Wellington, New Zealand, Accountancy and educational publications.

ACCOUNTING and cost methods for contractors. *Engineering and contracting,* Sept. 1, 1909, pt. 1.

ACCOUNTING and costs; finding bank costs —how to check profit leaks—simple cost systems that pay—making every account profitable—tested ways to reduce costs. Chicago, A. W. Shaw company, c1918. 225p.

ACCOUNTING and engineering show results. *Coal age,* July 15, 1916, p. 104-6.

ACCOUNTING and investments. Saliers, E. A.

ACCOUNTING and office methods by F. N. Doubleday, W. E. Wilson and others. Chicago, A. W. Shaw co. 1913. 45p. (Business man's library, v. 10.)

ACCOUNTING and office methods, organizing the office, accounting principles and systems, office work and record keeping. Chicago, A. W. Shaw co. 1914. 200 p. (Students' business book series). Also issued as v. 9 of the Library of business practice.

ACCOUNTING and reporting methods of the state of New York. Blackly, Frederick Frank. 1916.

ACCOUNTING and reporting methods of the state of New York. Bureau of municipal research.

ACCOUNTING and supervision. *Railway age gazette,* Aug. 4, 1911, p. 243-4.

ACCOUNTING as a basis for and a measure of efficiency in business. Nau, C. H.

ACCOUNTING as a skilled profession. Nelson, G. M.

ACCOUNTING as an administrative aid. McKinsey, J. O.

ACCOUNTING as an aid to business profits. Bassett, W. R. c1918.

ACCOUNTING as related to the prevention and discovery of fraud. Leavitt, T. H. 1896.

ACCOUNTING at College of the city of New York. *Journal of accountancy,* July, 1917, p. 79.

ACCOUNTING at your own price. *Journal of accountancy,* July, 1910, p. 218-9.

ACCOUNTING between life tenants and remaindermen. Vierling, Frederick.

ACCOUNTING charges. Colley, F. G.

ACCOUNTING charts. (In *Cyclopedia of commerce, accountancy, business administration,* 1910. v. 4, p. 309-23.)

ACCOUNTING circular no. 12d, December 5, 1910. United States. Interstate commerce commission.

ACCOUNTING circular of the Interstate commerce commission. *Electric railway review,* Feb. 29, 1908, p. 266.

ACCOUNTING conditions and prospects. Dubois, C. G.

ACCOUNTING control for company store and commissary. Field, W. P.

ACCOUNTING definitions. *Journal of accountancy,* April, 1909, p. 479-80.

ACCOUNTING department, classification of disbursements. Louisville and Nashville railroad company. 1907.

ACCOUNTING department of the public service railway. *Electric railway journal,* Atlantic city convention section, Oct. 7, 1911, p. 627-35.

ACCOUNTING department war problems. *Railway age gazette,* Dec. 28, 1917, p 1182-3.

ACCOUNTING depreciation. *Railroad age gazette,* July 3, 1908, p. 415.

ACCOUNTING errors in corporation tax bill. *Journal of accountancy,* July, 1909, p. 212-3.

ACCOUNTING every business man should know. Garrison, E. E. 1910.

ACCOUNTING features of public utility valuations. Wade, E. B.

ACCOUNTING for a cast iron pipe foundry. Fischer, A. K.

ACCOUNTING for a magazine publishing business. Buettner, L. A.

ACCOUNTING for a professional institute. Leffler, E. E.

ACCOUNTING for abandoned property. *Electric railway journal,* Feb. 10, 1912, p. 247.

ACCOUNTING for an export house. Shmerler, Maxwell.

ACCOUNTING for building and loan associations *Business man's magazine,* Feb. 1907, p 106-8.

ACCOUNTING for cantonment construction. West, W. H.

ACCOUNTING for cement packages. Wilson, Gordon.

ACCOUNTING for clubs, hotels, and societies. Smeeton, Cecil B.

ACCOUNTING for commission in relief in Belgium. Mapes, L. D.

ACCOUNTING for contractors. Grant, H. D. 1920.

ACCOUNTING for cost of naval vessels under cost-plus-profit contracts. Farquhar, F. P.

ACCOUNTING for department stores. Detroit, Bookkeeper publishing co. 1900. 56 p.

ACCOUNTING for depreciation *Electric railway journal,* Mar. 7, 1914, p. 507.

ACCOUNTING for depreciation. *Electrical world,* Jan. 23, 1915, p. 213-4.

ACCOUNTING for depreciation as prescribed by the interstate commerce commission. *Electric railway review,* July 13, 1907, p. 32.

ACCOUNTING for depreciation of equipment. *Railway age,* July 12, 1907, p. 36.

ACCOUNTING for food preserving companies. Barth, R. E.

ACCOUNTING for grain cars in transit. *Busi-man's magazine,* Dec. 1911, p. 532-3.

ACCOUNTING for income in eleemosynary institutions. Mitchell, P. D.

ACCOUNTING for interest and taxes. *Journal of the American water works association,* March, 1918, p. 40-3.

ACCOUNTING for liberty loan subscriptions. Jones, A. F.

ACCOUNTING for modern corporations. Lybrand, W. M., and others.

ACCOUNTING for music sellers. Bell, Elliot.

ACCOUNTING for ordnance property of the United States army overseas. Sparrow, R. G. 1918.

ACCOUNTING for power in Chicago. *Electric railway journal,* May 16, 23, June 6, 1914.

ACCOUNTING for property and expenses of interstate carriers under the decision of the Supreme court of the United States in the Minnesota rate case. Stone, Henry L. 1913.

ACCOUNTING for proprietary preparations. Devlin, J. H.

ACCOUNTING for railroad construction. Hofford, G. M.

ACCOUNTING [for railways in the United States.] *Times* (London), June 28, 1912, p. 27-8.

ACCOUNTING for receiverships. Freeman, H. C.

ACCOUNTING for rents. *Electric railway journal,* Nov. 13, Dec. 25, 1915, p. 978-9, 1260.

ACCOUNTING for replacement of plant retired from service. *National electric light association, Accounting sessions, Papers, reports and discussions,* 1913. p. 216.

ACCOUNTING for retail jewellers. Foster, Herbert. 1908.

ACCOUNTING for retail shoe stores. Ahlberg, T. J.

ACCOUNTING for retail trades. Wood, Dennis. 1910.

ACCOUNTING for the agricultural machinery industry. Wright, W. R.

ACCOUNTING for the gardener. *Market growers' journal,* Mar. 1, 1919, p. 199.

ACCOUNTING for the handling of scrap metals. Hamilton, F. A.

ACCOUNTING for the import division of a department store. Magee, H. C.

ACCOUNTING for the liberty loan subscriptions. Jones, Arthur F.

ACCOUNTING for the liberty loans. Chase, H. S.

ACCOUNTING for the publishing and printing business. Detroit, Business man's publishing co.

ACCOUNTING for the retail shoe business. *Business man's magazine,* July 1907, p. 112-18.

ACCOUNTING forms for state institutions, Michigan. Finance department. 1914.

ACCOUNTING forms of sheet metal shop. *Metal work,* Nov. 13, 1914, p. 647.

ACCOUNTING forms of the highway department of Milwaukee County, Wisconsin. *Good roads,* July 28, 1917, p. 39-43.

ACCOUNTING in antiquity. Young, J. P.

ACCOUNTING in its relation to economics. Branford, V. V.

ACCOUNTING in its relation to economics. Robinson, M. H.

ACCOUNTING in Philadelphia for power plant and sub-station maintenance and operating costs. *Electric railway journal,* June 11, 1910, p. 1020-1.

ACCOUNTING in the furniture and wood working industries. Timken, Frank H. c1915.

ACCOUNTING in the interior department. *Reclamation record,* Aug. 1917, 1 p.

ACCOUNTING in the peanut industry. Taylor, W. S.

ACCOUNTING in theory and practice. Lisle, George, 1900.

ACCOUNTING in waterworks department of small cities. *Engineering and contracting,* Feb. 28, 1912, p. 244.

ACCOUNTING in world affairs. Ryan, T. P.

ACCOUNTING inconsistencies and fallacies. Dunn, H. A. 1916.

ACCOUNTING information needed by members of the general assembly; accounting needs of heads of departments and boards in charge of state institutions. (In Frazer, George E. *Report on the accounts of the State of Illinois prepared for the efficiency and economy committee,* 1914, p. 40-8, 54-8.)

ACCOUNTING literature. Greendlinger, Leo.

ACCOUNTING—material store expenses; Railway storekeepers' association committee report. *Railway age gazette,* May 21, 1915, p 1043-4. (Mechanical edition), June, 1915 p. 287.

ACCOUNTING matters. *Electric railway journal,* June 6, 1914, p. 1273-4.

ACCOUNTING measures to meet business depression. Saliers, E. A.

ACCOUNTING methods. *Electrical world,* June 7, 1913, 1235-8.

ACCOUNTING methods as applied to Detroit electric properties. Bowers, E. J. 1911.

ACCOUNTANCY methods discussed by N. E. L. A. *Electrical world,* June 12, 1915, p. 1531-2. 1904, v. 16, no. 7, p. 57-63.

ACCOUNTING methods for mercantile corporation. Battin, W. S.

ACCOUNTING methods for receiverships. *Business digest,* Oct. 17, 1917, p. 117-8.

ACCOUNTING methods for the lumber business. *Business man's magazine,* Detroit, 1904, v. 16, no 7, p. 57-63.

ACCOUNTING methods in the paper manufacturing industry. *Business man's magazine,* 1906, v. 18, no. 11, p. 98-104.

ACCOUNTING methods of a holding company. Young, P. S. 1908.

ACCOUNTING methods of Illinois traction system. *Electric railway journal,* July 29, 1911, p. 184-9.

ACCOUNTING methods of the city of Chicago. Haskins & Sells.

ACCOUNTING methods of the city of Chicago; report by Haskins & Sells, certified public accountants, New York. *Accountant,* July 6, 1901, p. 787-9.

ACCOUNTING methods on board of United States men-of-war. *Business man's magazine,* Sept. 1905, p. 430-9.

ACCOUNTING methods: progress toward uniform accounts. *Electrical world,* June 7, 1913.

ACCOUNTING notes, completing New Yorks' new accounting system. *Notes and events,* Jan. 1913, p. 125-6.

ACCOUNTING of depreciation by electric railways. Wallis, R. N.

ACCOUNTING of commission for relief in Belgium. Mapes, L. D.

ACCOUNTING of industrial enterprises. Lybrand, W. M.

ACCOUNTING of interest and discount on notes. Bauer, John.

ACCOUNTING of interline waybills for the guaranty period. *Railway review,* Sept. 4, 1920, p. 372.

ACCOUNTING of machine coal. *Coal age,* July 15-29, Aug. 12, 1916, p. 122, 156-7, 195, 278.

ACCOUNTING of materials. *Coal age,* Aug. 29, Oct. 17, Nov. 21, 1918, Jan. 9, 1919, p. 417, 754-5, 956-8, 66.

ACCOUNTING officers association annual meeting Atlantic city. *Railway age,* May 21, 1920, p. 1457-65

ACCOUNTING officers to co-operate with railroad administration. *Railway age gazette,* Nov. 1, 1918, p. 776-7.

ACCOUNTING papers before the economic association. *Journal of accountancy,* Feb. 1909, p. 321-3.

ACCOUNTING parties and auditors—auditor and bookkeeper. *Accountant.* Feb. 6, March 6, 1909, p. 188-93, 327-9.

ACCOUNTING practice. Day, C. M. 1915.

ACCOUNTING, practice and auditing. Madden, J. T. 1917.

ACCOUNTING practice and procedure. Dickinson, A. L.

ACCOUNTING principles. Mitchell, T. W. 1918.

ACCOUNTING principles. Racine, S. F. 1917.

ACCOUNTING problems in the cane sugar industry. Keyes, J. Brooks.

ACCOUNTING procedure for machine shops. New York city. Department of water supply, gas and electricity.

ACCOUNTING procedure for state universities. Castenholz, William B.

ACCOUNTING profession. Sells, E. W.

ACCOUNTING profession in the United States. Masters, J. E.

ACCOUNTING profession in the United States. Wilkinson, George.

ACCOUNTING publications in the New York library. *Journal of accountancy,* Aug. 1911, p. 296.

ACCOUNTING records for country creameries. Humphrey, John Regester and G. A. Nahstoll. 1917.

ACCOUNTING records for heating work. *Metal work,* April 3, 1914, p. 492-3.

ACCOUNTING records for hospitals. *Business man's magazine,* Dec. 1906, Jan. 1907, p. 65-9, 61-70.

ACCOUNTING; report of committee. *Railway age gazette,* Jan. 31, 1919, p. 287-9.

ACCOUNTING rules and classifications of railways. China. Ministry of communications. 1920.

ACCOUNTING series, circular no. 12c, September 1, 1909. United States. Interstate commerce commission.

ACCOUNTING session. Freeman, W. E. 1915.

ACCOUNTING sessions of N. E. L. A. *Electrical world,* May 29, 1920, p. 1255-6. *Electrical review,* May 22, 1920, p. 873-4.

ACCOUNTING system for a jobbing shop. *Metal work,* October 2, 1914, p. 465.

ACCOUNTING system for a municipal hospital. Eggleston, D. C.

ACCOUNTING system for a small city. Mendenhall, William.

ACCOUNTING system for class C telephone companies. *Telephony,* Dec. 12, 1914, pt. 1.

ACCOUNTING system for coal mines. *Coal age,* Sept. 20, 1913, p. 414.

ACCOUNTING system for contractors. *Electrical review and western electrician,* Jan. 23, 1915, p. 152.

ACCOUNTING system for dealers. *Horseless age,* May 1, 1916, p. 343-5.

ACCOUNTING system for law firms. Wright, W. C.

ACCOUNTING system for office buildings. Wasserman, Edwin.

ACCOUNTING system for printing concerns Jobson, W. P.

ACCOUNTING system for small lighting companies. *Electrical world,* Aug. 23, 1913, p. 380-1.

ACCOUNTING system for the United States Indian service by Victor G. Croissant and others. 1917.

ACCOUNTING system of an ice company. Bluim, J. M. 1911.

ACCOUNTING system of New York department of water supply. Stander, L. E.

ACCOUNTING system of the Maryland state roads commission. *Engineering and contracting,* April 16, 1913, p. 449-51.

ACCOUNTING system of the Milwaukee county, Wis., Highway dept. *Good roads,* May 12, 1917, p. 286.

ACCOUNTING system of the United States from 1789 to 1910. United States. President's commission on economy and efficiency. 1911.

ACCOUNTING systems. Lejeune, C. E. 1894.

ACCOUNTING systems for retail merchants. Hunter, Joel.

ACCOUNTING systems for small mines. *Mining and scientific press,* 1916, v. 112, p. 400.

ACCOUNTING systems for the wholesale grocery and hardware business. Detroit, Business man's publishing co.

ACCOUNTING systems in army camps. Holmes, E. J.

ACCOUNTING TERMINOLOGY.
See Terminology.

ACCOUNTING terminology. *California taxpayers journal,* Feb. 1919, p. 18-20.

ACCOUNTING terminology. Anyon, J. T.

ACCOUNTING terminology. Walton, Seymour.

ACCOUNTING terminology. *Journal of accountancy,* April, June, 1910, p. 459, 135-6.

ACCOUNTING terminology: from a special report of the Bureau of census on financial statistics of cities, 1907, transmitted February 11, 1910. *Government accountant,* May-Oct. 1910, p. 27-32, 65-77, 119-26, 161-8, 205-14, 252-7.

ACCOUNTING theory and practice. Greendlinger, Leo. c1910.

ACCOUNTING theory and practice. Willis, H. P. 1910.

ACCOUNTING theory and practice—units 1 and 2. Rittenhouse, C. F., and P. F. Clapp. 1918.

ACCOUNTING treatment of overhead construction costs in public utilities. Andersen, Delany & company. 1917.

ACCOUNTING under federal control. *Railway age gazette,* April 12, 1918, p. 970.

ACCOUNTING versus statistics. *Electric railway journal,* May 3, 1913, p. 803.

ACCOUNTS.
See Name of various accounts.

ACCOUNTS and accounting practice. Belding, A. G. c1918.

ACCOUNTS and engineers. Hopson, H. C.

ACCOUNTS and the public service. *Journal of accountancy,* June 1910, p. 134-5.

ACCOUNTS for fraternal beneficiary societies. Speakman, F. M.

ACCOUNTS for income tax purposes. *Accountant,* Oct. 26, 1907, p. 523-4.

ACCOUNTS for material on engineering construction. Allen, L. H.

ACCOUNTS for the manufacture of wood veneer. Jordan, H. C.

ACCOUNTS in theory and practice; principles. Saliers, E. A. 1920.

ACCOUNTS of a city. Chapman, Richard M. 1917.

ACCOUNTS of a "holding" corporation. *Business man's magazine*, Sept. 1906, p. 86-8.

ACCOUNTS of a mine. *Monthly journal of the chamber of mines*, West Australia, Feb. 1914.

ACCOUNTS of a motorcab company: reprinted from articles in the *Accountant*. London, Gee & co. 1911. 46p. *Accountant*, Aug. 26-Sept. 16, 1911, p. 259-64, 285-90, 309-14, 338-42.

ACCOUNTS of a paper box factory. Shannon, T. J.

ACCOUNTS of charge and discharge. *Accountants' magazine*, 1907, p. 549.

ACCOUNTS of controlled establishments. *Incorporated accountants' journal*. Feb. 1916, p. 98-9.

ACCOUNTS of engineers and contractors. Narlian, C. A. H.

ACCOUNTS of executors, administrators and trustees. Phillips, W. B. 1913.

ACCOUNTS of executors and testamentary trustees. Hardcastle, Joseph. 1903.

ACCOUNTS of executors and trustees. Chandler, P. W. 1906.

ACCOUNTS of gas undertakings. Field, J. W.

ACCOUNTS of gold mining and exploration companies. Donald, T. 1901.

ACCOUNTS of holding companies. Heinke, L. H.

ACCOUNTS of holding companies. Lybrand, W. M.

ACCOUNTS of instalment furniture dealers. Greenfield, H. G.

ACCOUNTS of local authorities. London, 1907. 2 v. 440 p.

ACCOUNTS of local authorities. *Accountant*, Nov. 18, 1905, Aug. 3-24, 1907, p. 560-2, 129-31, 165-7, 193-5, 225-6.

ACCOUNTS of medical men. *Accountant*, Sept. 7, 14, 28, 1895, p. 709-10, 727-9, 765-7.

ACCOUNTS of mineral water businesses. *Accountant*, Oct. 14, 1899, p. 1024-5.

ACCOUNTS of parish councils notice of audit; statutory financial statement. *Accountant*, June 13, 1896, p. 497.

ACCOUNTS of pianoforte dealers on the hire-purchase system. *Accountant*, Nov. 10, 1900, p. 989-91.

ACCOUNTS of professional men. *Accountant*, Feb. 5-19, March 12, April 2, 1898, p. 144-7, 171-3, 199-202, 271-3, 301-2, 423-7, 345-8.

ACCOUNTS of the distribution of the estates of deceased persons (1) liability of the real and personal estates for the payment of debts, legacies, &c.; (2) intestates' estates act of 1890. *Accountant*, June 11, 18, July 2, 16, 1910, p. 819-23, 853-7, 7-9, 75-8.

ACCOUNTS of the London tube railways. *Electrician* (London), 1907, p. 123-4.

ACCOUNTS of trustees, liquidators and receivers. Dawson, S. S., and H. R. Graves.

ACCOUNTS of voluntary schools. *Incorporated accountants' journal*, 1901-2, p. 48.

ACCOUNTS PAYABLE.

See also Accounting: Bookkeeping.

BAER, W. E. Up-to-date treatment of accounts payable. *Business man's magazine*, Sept. 1909, p. 268-71.

CONOVER, H. J. Standard voucher check and handling accounts payable, with minimum office labor. *Business man's magazine*, March, 1910, p. 251-5.

EGGLESTON, DEWITT CARL. Doing away with the ledger. *Business man's magazine*, Dec., 1910, p. 569-72.

STONE, S. E. Creditors' accounts. *Accountant*, Nov. 27, 1920, p. 591.

ACCOUNTS prescribed by New York public service commission, second district. *Electric railway journal*, Nov. 14, 1908, p. 3173.

ACCOUNTS RECEIVABLE.

See also Accounting: Bookkeeping.

MANN, H. W. Accounts receivable. *Business*, Nov. 1898, p. 692-3.

STEVENS, E. O. Verification of the accounts receivable. *Pace student*, Nov. 1918, p. 3.

WALTON, SEYMOUR. Accounts receivable discounted. *Journal of accountancy*, Dec. 1915, p. 469-70.

WALTON, SEYMOUR. Statement tickler. *Journal of accountancy*, March, 1917, p. 197.

ACCOUNTS with church members. *Business man's magazine*, April, 1907, p. 144-6.

ACCREDITED accountants. *Journal of accountancy*, June, 1915, p. 460-1.

ACCRUALS.

See also Accounting.

CADWALLADER, W. E. Accrual accounting records required in the interest of accuracy and ethics. *Journal of the American bankers' association*, Sept. 1919, p. 140-2.

ACCRUED interest receivable and payable. Jefferson, H. M. 1918.

ACCURATE costing. *Mechanical world*, Dec. 4, 1914.

ACCURATE costing in engineering. *Engineering review*, Jan. 15, 1919, p. 187-8.

ACCURATE stock records maintain plant efficiency. *Automotive industries*, July 22, 1920, p. 172-4.

ACCURATE stores record. *Business man's magazine*, June, 1911, p. 582.

ACCURATE time and material records. *Business man's magazine*, Jan. 1911, p. 100.

ACHATZ, R. V.

Determination of unit prices of material for purposes of valuation of plant. *Engineering and contracting*, May 13, 1914, p. 562-3.

ACIDS

UNITED STATES. Tariff commission. Acids of paragraph 1, and related materials pro-

ACIDS—*(Continued)*
vided for in the Tariff act of 1913. Washington, Government printing office, 1920. 85p. (Tariff information series, no. 13.)

ACKERMAN, E. L., and L. F. MERRITT
Graphical analysis of manufacturing costs. *American industries,* July, 1919, p. 20-1.

ACKLEY, F. S.
How the General electric co. keeps track of its advertising space. *Printers' ink,* v. cii, no. 9, p. 25.

ACT and extracts from the unrevised Hansard follow: 7-8 George V. Chap. 28; an act to authorize the levying of a war tax upon certain incomes; assented to 20th September, 1917. *Canadian chartered accountant,* Jan. 1918, p. 177-218.

ACT concerning sinking funds and sinking fund commissions. New Jersey. 1917.

ACT regulating the practice of public accounting passed by the 40th general assembly of Arkansas, 1915. Arkansas, State board of accountancy.

ACT to amend the business profits war tax act 1916; assented to 24th May, 1918. *Canadian chartered accountant,* July, 1918, p. 42-3.

ACT to amend the companies act; assented to 24th May, 1918. *Canadian chartered accountant,* July, 1918, p. 44-5.

ACT to amend the income war tax act, 1917; assented to 24th May, 1918. *Canadian chartered accountant,* July 1918, p. 46-8.

ACT to amend the tax law, in relation to imposing taxes upon and with respect to incomes, March 28, 1919. New York state. Senate.

ACT to authorize the levying of a war tax upon certain incomes: Assented to 20th Sept. 1917. 11p.

ACT to authorize the levying of a war tax on certain incomes, passed May 16, 1918. St. Johns, Newfoundland, J. W. Withers, 1918. 24p.

ACT to incorporate the Institute of accountants of British Columbia. *Accountant,* Dec. 16, 1905, p. 311-12.

ACT to provide for the registration of accountants in Natal. *Accountant,* Feb. 12, 1910, p. 254-7, 229-31.

ACTION against accountants for negligence. *Incorporated accountants' journal,* Jan. 1919, p. 71-7.

ACTION by incorporated accountant for wrongful dismissal. *Incorporated accountants' journal,* March 1916, p. 125-6.

ACTION on proposed scales of class rate. *Railway age,* Nov. 15, 1918, p. 857. *Railway review,* Nov. 23, 1918, p. 740-1.

ACTIVE-room system of rates. *Electrical world,* April 1, 1916, p. 774-5.

ACTS concerning municipal and county accounts and finances. New Jersey. 1918.

ACTS relating to the income tax. Dowell, Stephen. 1919.

ACTS to prevent fraud in the sale and disposition of stocks, bonds or other securities sold or offered for sale within the State of Minnesota. Minnesota. State securities commission. 1919.

ACTUAL accounting. Campbell, T. F. 1912.

ACTUAL business practice. Massey, R. W. 1891.

ACTUAL construction cost of industrial substation. *Electrical world,* Oct. 19, 1918, p. 747.

ACTUAL construction cost of medium size station. *Eectrical world,* April 20, 1918, p 830.

ACTUAL cost of building 97 miles of oil-macadam road in Los Angeles county, California. *Engineering and contracting,* Feb. 28, 1912. p. 227.

ACTUAL problem in serial bonds. Kerzie, F. L.

ACTUAL railroad contingencies and what they cost. *Engineering record,* June 19, 1915, p. 774.

ACTUARIAL SCIENCE
See also Insurance.
ACTARIAL science. *Journal of accountancy,* Aug. 1918, p. 108-9.
ACTUARIAL SOCIETY OF AMERICA. Recommendations of the educational committee. New York, Actuarial society of America, 1918. 40p.
CAMPBELL, A. M. Actuarial science and its use to the accountant. *Accountant,* June 8, 1907, p. 787-90.
DICKSEE. L. R. Actuarial valuations and accounts. (In his *Advance accounting.* 1916. p. 441-2.)
FINNEY, H. A. Introduction to actuarial science. New York, *American institute of accountants.* c1920. 101p. *Journal of accountancy,* Nov. Dec. 1919, p. 321-52, 435-50.
GLEN, NINIAN. Actuarial science; an elementary manual. Glasgow, John Smith & son, 1912. 96 p.
KENCHINGTON, C. W. Elements of actuarial science. *Accountant,* Jan. 24, 1914, p. 110-4.
INSTITUTE OF ACTUARIES. Text-book of the principles of interest, life annuities, and assurances, and their practical application; new edition revised by Ralph Todhunter. London. Charles & Edwin Layton, 1915. Pt. 1 Interest (including annuities-certain).
KIDSON, HERBERT. Reversions, life interests and life policies. *Accountant,* Nov. 5, 1904. Jan. 21, 1905, p. 572-6; 73-5.
M'CANDLISH, JOHN M. Accountants and actuaries. *Accountant,* Oct. 5, 12, 1889, p. 518-20, 528-31.
SMITH, J. B. Responsibilities of actuaries. *Accountant,* Nov. 25, 1905, p. 618-21.
STRACHAN, THOMAS YOUNG. Accountant and the actuary. *Accountant,* April 21, 1888, p. 244-8.
TINNER, THOMAS. Actuarial calculation for accountants. *Incorporated accountants' journal,* 1899-1900, p. 190.

ACTUARIAL science; an elementary manual. Glen, Ninian. 1912.

ACTUARIAL SOCIETY OF AMERICA.
Recommendations of the educational committee. New York, Actuarial society of America, 1918. 40 p.

ACTUARIAL SOCIETY OF AMERICA—*(Continued)*

REGULATIONS regarding the use of the library. September, 1919. 8 p.

ACWORTH, WILLIAM MITCHELL

British railways: their accounts and statistics: with discussion. *Journal of the Royal statistical society*, 1912, p. 687-743.
Chinese railway accounts. *Economic journal*, March, 1916, p. 120-1.
Commission control on its trial. *Railway age*, October 2, 1914, p. 611-2.
Elements of railway economics. Oxford, The Clarendon press, 1905. 159 p.
English railway accounts and statistics. *Journal of the Royal statistical society*, Dec. 1902, p. 613-52.
Railroad accounting in America vs. England. *North American review*, March, 1910, p. 330-9.
Railways and the traders. London, 1891. 378 p.
Report no 2 (Great Britain) on the question of statistics (subject xiv for discussion at the 8th session of the railway congress). *International railway congress association Bulletin*, Eng. edition, Jan. 1910, p. 3-10. *International railway congress association, Proceedings, 8th session*, 1910, p. 87-94.
Simplification of rate schedules. *Railway age* April 3, 1914, p. 772.

ADAM, J. REID

Modern office equipment. *Accountant*, Jan. 4, 1913, p. 21-6.

ADAMS, ALTON D.

Valuation of water works. *Municipal journal*, June 20, 1913, p. 942.
Value of water. *Municipal engineering*, Aug., 1909, p. 77. Editorial. Value of water and water power. *Municipal engineering*, Aug. 1909, p. 102.

ADAMS, E. A. R.

Formation of rate basis. *Accountant*, July 17, 1897, p. 707-9, 737-43.

ADAMS, HENRY CARTER

Administrative supervision of railways under the twentieth section of the act to regulate commerce. *Quarterly journal of economics*, May, 1908, p. 264-83.
American railway accounting; a commentary. New York, Henry Holt & co. 1918. 465 p
Government supervision of railway accounts *Electric railway review*, Jan. 11, 1908, p. 43. *Government accountant*, Dec. 1907, p. 361-71. *International railway congress, Bulletin*, May, 1908, p. 595-603. Abstract. *Railway age*, Dec. 1907, p. 884-6.
Problems of budgetary reform. *Journal of politcal economy*, Oct. 1919, p. 621-38.
Railway accounting in its relation to the twentieth section of the act to regulate commerce; a paper to be presented at the annual meeting of the American association of public accountants, Atlantic city, N. J., October 20-23, 1908. 15 p. *Accountant*, Dec. 5, 1908, p. 691-9. *American institute of accountants, Yearbook*, 1908, p. 146-87. *Journal of accountancy*, Oct. 1908, p. 381-93.
Report on interstate accounting system. *Electric railway journal*, Aug. 7, 1909, p. 218.
Service of a bureau of railway statistics and accounts in the solution of the railway question. (In *National convention of railroad commissioners, Proceedings*, 1893, p. 44-56.) Abstract. Publicity of accounts as a means of controlling railroads. *Railroad gazette*, April 28, 1893, p. 315-6.
Uniform accounting for public institutions. *Mich. state tax association, Proceedings*, 1918, p. 18-38.
Valuations of public service utilities. *Quarterly of American economic association*, April, 1910, p. 184-95.

ADAMS, MASON T.

System of mine accounts. *Columbia university school of mines quarterly*, Jan. 1913. v. 34, p. 137-48. Abstract. *Mining and engineering world*, April, 1913, p. 659-63.

ADAMS, ROMANZO

Essentials to orderly progress in tax reform. *National tax association, Bulletin*, Nov. 1920, p. 42-3.

ADAMS, T. S.

Valuation of railway property for purposes of taxation. *Journal of political economy*, Jan. 1915, p. 1-16.

ADAMS, WILLIAM

Bookkeeping. New York, Collins & brother.
Uniform electric rates based on costs. *Electrical world*, June 26, July 17, 1915, p. 1666-7; 124-5.

ADAMS, WILLIAM JAMES

Up-to-date regents' questions in bookkeeping. Syracuse, C. W. Bardeen, 1919. 49 p.

ADAMSON, J. E.

Concentration as a quality of mind and a habit of life. *S. African accountants' journal*, v. 1, p. 103.

ADAMSON, N. E.

Production betterment by time studies. *Iron age*, April 4, 1912, p. 835-8.
Time study observations—different methods of discovering faults in machine operation and manual labor. *Iron age*, Nov. 16, 1911, p. 1090-2.

ADAMSON, TILDEN

Preparation of estimates and the formulation of the budget; the New York city method. *Annals of the American academy of political and social science*, Nov. 1915, p. 113-276.

ADAPTATION in simpler form of the needs of smaller cities of the scientific but too elaborate systems of municipal accounting developed in the big cities. Farwell, F. M.

ADDIE, A. S.

Perpetual inventory. Chicago, Inland trade press co. 1914.

ADDING MACHINES.

See Calculating machines; Mechanical devices—Calculating machines.

ADDINSELL, WILLIAM ARTHUR

New system of cost taking in trade. *Accountant*, May 20, 1899, p. 577-81.

ADDISON, JOSEPH

Solicitors' accounts and clients' moneys. *Accountant*, Dec. 14, 1907, p. 753-4.

ADDITIONAL increases allowed in western rate case. *Railway review*, Jan. 1, 1916, p. 3-4.

ADDITIONS to the list of increased fare cities. *Aera*, Sept. 1918, p. 125.

ADDRESS before the conference upon uniform legislation at Washington, D. C., Jan. 19, 1910. Chase, H. S.

ADDRESS on railway accounting and the preparation of young men for the accounting profession. Plant, A. H. 1910.

ADDRESS on municipal accounts and reports before the Wonolancet club, Concord, New Hampshire, Feb. 17, 1909. Chase. H. S.

ADDRESS on reform in municipal accounting. Haskins, C. W.

ADDRESSES and discussions at the conference on scientific management held October 12, 13, 14, 1911. Dartmouth college. 1912.

ADDRESSES and reports given at the cost accounting session, ninth annual meeting. Chicago, Ill., June 27, 28, 29, 1916. National gas engine association. 1916.

ADDRESSES delivered before the World's railway commerce congress, Chicago. World's Columbian auxiliary of the World's Columbian exposition. 1893.

ADDRESSING the pay envelop and filling it. *Factory,* April, 1918, p. 635.

ADEQUATE depreciation rates should be established. *Railway age gazette,* Feb. 21, 1919, p. 427-8.

ADEQUATE return reason for rate order injunction. *Gas age,* Feb. 15, 1919, p. 186-7.

ADGIE, WILLIAM

Modern bookkeeping and accounts, in three parts: part 1, elementary: part 2; intermediate; part 3, advanced. 3 vols. London, The Macmillan co. 1901-2.
——— Same. Ed. 2. London, 1904. 378 p.
——— Same. 3 v. London, 1912.

ADJUSTABLE reach logging trailer. *American lumberman,* May 10, 1919, p. 63.

ADJUSTING fares and rates. *Oregon voter,* Jan. 18, 1919, p. 177.

ADJUSTMENT of financial relations between local authorities. *Incorporated accountants' journal,* 1910-11, p. 296.

ADJUSTMENT of fire losses. Reed, P. B.

ADJUSTMENT of partners' accounts. *Accountants' magazine,* May, July, 1911. p. 256-60, 346-51.

ADJUSTMENT of partnership accounts. Greendlinger, Leo.

ADJUSTMENT of trust accounts. *Accountant,* Dec. 13, 1913, p. 859-60.

ADJUSTMENTS

See also Accounting.

TEBBS, HERBERT. Few remarks to students on adjustment and reconciliation accounts; the use of percentages in illustrating results; the importance of methods in displaying accounts, etc., etc. *Accountant,* May 29, 1897, p. 541-6.

ADJUSTMENTS through elimination. Freeman, Charles E. 1911.

ADKINSON, HENRY M.

Commonsense of mine management. *Engineering and mining journal,* Dec. 8, 1917, p. 991-3.

ADLING, VAN VLIET

Devising a cost system for the farmer. *Business man's magazine,* June, 1910, p. 523-32.

ADMINISTRATION EXPENSES

See also Accounting.

HATHAWAY, C. E. Administrative expense. *Business man's magazine,* April, 1907, p. 130-4.

ADMINISTRATION of industrial enterprises with special reference to factory practice. Jones, E. D. 1917.

ADMINISTRATION of insolvent estates. *Accountant,* June 22, 29, July 6, 13, 20, 27, Aug. 10, 24, Sept. 14, 21, 1878.

ADMINISTRATION of municipal finances. *Journal of accountancy,* Jan. 1913, p. 196-8.

ADMINISTRATION of public debts. Mason, H. A.

ADMINISTRATION of the income tax acts. Isaacs, C. E.

ADMINISTRATION of the income tax acts. *Accountant,* March 4, 1911, p. 354-9. *Incorporated accountants' journal,* 1910-11, p. 134, 45.

ADMINISTRATION of the Ohio public accounting law. Tracey, J. T.

ADMINISTRATION of workshops, public and private. Metcalfe, Henry, 1885.

ADMINISTRATIVE and industrial organization. Griffith, James.

ADMINISTRATIVE organization of the American smelting and refining company. Wright, A. W.

ADMINISTRATIVE purchase and general description of the new system of accounting and reporting installed in the city of New York. New York city. Department of finance. 1909.

ADMINISTRATIVE purpose of the accounting methods and procedure which have been installed in the departments. United States. President's commission on economy and efficiency. 1913.

ADMINISTRATORS.

See Executors and trustees.

ADMINISTRATOR'S account book. Kuhn, R. K.

ADMISSION of proofs in bankruptcy. *Accountant,* Jan. 13, 1905, p. 36-8.

ADMISSION of women confirmed. *Incorporated accountants' journal,* Dec. 1918, p. 45.

ADMISSION of women into the profession. *Accountant,* Jan. 23, 1915, p. 127-9.

ADOPTION of by-laws. Conyngton, Thomas.

AD-REFERENDUM of accounting. Davar, S. R. 1903.

ADSIT, CHARLES G., and W. P. HAMMOND

Construction elements of the Tallulah Falls development. *American institute of electrical engineers, Proceedings,* Oct. 1915, p. 2497-546. Abstract. *Electrical world,* Oct. 23, 1915, p. 916-8.

ADULTS and high school studies. *Journal of accountancy,* April, 1909, p. 477-9.

ADVANCE in freight rates necessary. *Railway and engineering review,* May 31, 1913, p. 496.

ADVANCE in rates. *Railway age,* May 31, 1918, p. 1310.

ADVANCED accounting. Dicksee, L. R, 1916.

ADVANCED accounting. Goodyear, S. H. 1909.

ADVANCED accounting. 2 v. Walton school of commerce, Chicago. c1912.

ADVANCED accounts. Batliboi, J. R.

ADVANCED accounts. Carter, R. N.

ADVANCED and analytical accounting. Cox, H. C. 1920.

ADVANCED book-keeping. Grierson, Walter. 1908.

ADVANCED bookkeeping. Maclean, J. D. 1882.

ADVANCED bookkeeping and accounts. *Canadian chartered accountant,* Oct. 1914, p. 148-54.

ADVANCED bookkeeping and banking. New York, American book company.

ADVANCED examination papers in bookkeeping with notes by J. Thornton. London, Macmillan co. 1899. 32 p.

ADVANCED rate hearing reaches its end. *Railway review,* July 10, 1920, p. 60-2.

ADVANCED thought on accounts. Caldwyn, W. B. ?1894.

ADVANTAGES of a job cost system. Holme, A. L. 1911.

ADVANTAGES of an independent continuous audit. Moorhouse, Eli.

ADVANTAGES of an independent railway audit to the investor. Cleveland, Frederick A.

ADVANTAGES of electric vehicles in municipal truck haulage. *Electrical world,* Jan. 3, 1914, p. 45-6.

ADVANTAGES of machine billing in railroad offices. *Railway review,* Jan. 3, 1920, p. 11-2.

ADVANTAGES of mathematical training to an accountant. *Journal of accountancy,* June, 1910, p. 137-8.

ADVANTAGES of mathematical training to an accountant. Perrine, LeRoy.

ADVANTAGES of organization to the accountant. Wilkinson, George.

ADVANTAGES of society and association affiliations. Joplin, J. P.

ADVANTAGES of the cost plus form of contract. *Engineering and contracting,* Oct. 22, 1919, p. 467-71.

ADVANTAGES of uniform accounting. Manning, A. D.

ADVERTISERS want better retail accounting. *Printers' ink,* Sept. 26, 1918, p. 122.

ADVERTISING

See also Professional ethics.

ACKLEY, F. S. How the General electric co. keeps track of its advertising space. *Printers' ink,* v.cii, no. 9, p. 25.

AMERICAN business and accounting encyclopaedia; comp. by E. H. Beach and W. W. Thorne. Detroit, Bookkeeper publishing co. 1901. Advertising, p. 49-66.

BRISCOE, NORRIS ARTHUR. Principles of advertising. (In his *Economics of business.* 1913. p. 260-306).

CLARK, F. Accurate accountancy in connection with advertising. *Business organization and management,* Nov. 1920, p. 192-4.

CORPORATIONS and advertising. *Journal of accountancy,* Sept. 1911, p. 374-7.

DEBOWER, HERBERT FRANCIS. Advertising principles. New York, Alexander Hamilton institute, c1918. 330p. (Modern business, v.6).

DICKSEE, LAWRENCE ROBERT and H. E. BLAIN. Advertising. (In their *Office organisation and management.* 1917. p. 126-33).

DUNN, ARTHUR. Scientific selling and advertising. Ed. 4. New York, Industrial publishing company, 1920. 119p.

FINNEGAN, JOSEPH A. Handling inquiries. *Business man's magazine,* Dec. 1908, p. 499-503.

GALLOWAY, LEE. Advertising department and its work. (In his *Office management,* 1918, p. 396-418).

GOODWILL and advertising. *Accountant,* Feb. 28, 1914, p. 287-90, 319-20.

GRIFFITH, JAMES B. Advertising and sales organization. (In *Cyclopaedia of commerce, accountancy, business administration,* 1910, v.1, p. 61-124).

HEMINGWAY, W. H. Ad. club of Victoria; uberrimae fidei in advertising. *Australasian accountant and secretary,* April 1920, p. 115-8.

KASTOR, E. H. Advertising. Chicago, La Salle extension university, 1918. 317p.

KEEP tab on advertising returns. *Business man's magazine,* March 1911, p. 291.

LEFFINGWELL, WILLIAM HENRY. Office side of advertising and sales. (In his *Scientific office management.* 1917. p. 104-9).

MCBRIDE, RAYMOND. Reaching the purse of the public in modern business. *Business man's magazine,* Dec. 1907, p. 83-7.

MARTIN, MAC. Advertising campaigns. New York, Alexander Hamilton institute, c1918. 338p. (Modern business, v. 13).

MORGAN, R. A. My plan of records; an effective record and filing system for the advertising department. *System,* October 1914, p. 436-7.

MORRISON, J. C. Sliding scale of advertising costs. *Inland printer,* Dec. 1913, p. 433-6.

PARSONS, CARL COPELAND. Advertising department records. (In his *Office organization and management.* 1918. p. 207-20).

RECORD of advertising returns. *Business man's magazine,* Sept. 1911, p. 259.

SALES promotion by mail; how to sell and how to advertise; a handbook of business building with numerous illustrative diagrams. New York, G. Putnam's sons, c1916. 359p.

SALVESEN, EDGAR C. Advertising and asset on the balance sheet. *Journal of accountancy,* March 1914, p. 203-6.

SCOTT, J. Law of advertising. *Accountants' magazine,* May 1909, p. 256-62.

ADVERTISING—(Continued)

SEE, GEORGE. Newspaper advertising distribution; correspondence. *Journal of accountancy,* Dec. 1911, p. 622-3.
SELLS, ELIJAH W. Advertising as a business asset; an address at the meeting of the Advertising club of St. Louis, April 18, 1916. 14p. *Accountant,* July 8, 1916, p. 40-2. *Accounting and commerce,* June 1916, p. 64-7. *Journal of accountancy,* June 1916, p. 424-30.
SELLS, ELIJAH W. Publicity of financial affairs of corporations; should advertising expenditures be charged as an investment or as an expense; an address delivered before the convention of associated advertising club of America, Boston, August 2, 1911. 11p.
SELLS, ELIJAH W. Should advertising expenditures be charged as an investment or as an expense? *Journal of accountancy,* Sept. 1911, p. 346-51.

Bibliographies

Advertising. Special libraries, April 1916, p. 61-76.

ADVERTISING. *Journal of accountancy,* Feb. 1920, 127-30.

ADVERTISING. *Canadian chartered accountant,* Oct. 1914, p. 103-6.

ADVERTISING. *Special libraries,* April 1916, p. 61-76.

ADVERTISING. Kastor, E. H. 1918.

ADVERTISING AGENCIES

Accounting

FARRAR, GEORGE. Accounting methods for advertising agencies. *Business man's magazine,* 1906, v.18, no. 9, p. 112-28.
GARDNER, H. E. System for an advertising agency. *System,* Oct. 1903, p. 238-42.
WEIDNER, H.-C. H. Advertising agency's system. *Business man's magazine,* Oct. 1909, p. 366-7.
WHALLEY (Miss). System of accountancy in an advertising business. *Accounting and commerce,* Aug. 1917, p. 107.

Auditing

MONTGOMERY, ROBERT H. Advertising agencies. (In his *Auditing theory and practice.* 1916. p. 742-3).

ADVERTISING an asset on the balance sheet. Salvesen, E. C.

ADVERTISING and sales organization. Griffith, J. B.

ADVERTISING as a business asset. Sells, E. W.

ADVERTISING campaigns. Martin, Mac. c1918.

ADVERTISING ETHICS.

See Professional ethics.

ADVERTISING goods figure in national hardware questionnaire. *Printers' ink,* Feb. 15, 1917, p. 133-5.

ADVERTISING principles. De Bower, Herbert Francis. 1918.

ADVICE to examinees. *Canadian chartered accountant,* Jan. 1913. p. 187-90.

ADVISING salesmen of goods out of stock. *Business man's magazine,* Dec. 1911, p. 537.

ADVISORY accountancy. Gower, W. B.

AERONAUTICS, MILITARY

UNITED STATES. WAR DEPARTMENT AIR SERVICE. DIVISION OF MILITARY AERONAUTICS Instructions to field auditors. 61 typewritten pages and forms.

AEROPLANES

Time study of aircraft operations. *Automotive industries,* May 30, 1918, p. 1036.

Cost accounting

ALLOCATION of timber materials from the view point of costing. *Accountant,* Aug. 17, 1918, p. 82-3.
HART, C. H. Airplane cost finding. *Industrial management,* Sept. 1918, p. 208.

AETERS, GEORGE C.

Engineering accounts. *New York accountants' and bookkeepers' journal,* April, May 1904, p. 97-103, 136-40.

AFTER-acquired property of bankrupts. *Accountant,* April 21, Dec. 22, 1906, p. 512-4, 781-2.

AGAINST departmental reforms. *Journal of accountancy,* May 1914, p. 371-4.

AGE limit in pension benefits. *Railway age,* May 2, 1913, p. 980.

AGENCIES

See also Advertising agencies: Employment agencies; Mercantile agencies; Lumber agencies.

ISING, HAROLD ERNEST. For the superintendent of agencies. *Business man's magazine,* Dec. 1908, p. 472.

Accounting

AGENTS record system. *Business man's magazine,* Jan. 1905, p. 106-7.
AMERICAN business and accounting encyclopaedia; comp. by E. H. Beach and W. W. Thorne. Detroit Bookkeeper publishing co. 1901. Agents' accounts, v.1, p. 68-75.
BENNETT, GEORGE E. Agencies and branches. (In his *Constructive accounting.* 1920. p. 373-88).
DICKINSON, A. L. Agency and commission. (In his *Accounting practice and procedure.* 1917. p. 59).
KESTER, R. B. Agency and branch differentiated; agency accounts. (In his *Accounting theory and practice.* 1918. v.2. p. 522, 525-6).
MCCALL, J. H. Accounts and audit of the English agency of a foreign company. *Incorporated accountants' journal,* Nov. 1912, p. 41-4.
NIXON, ALFRED and J. H. STAGG. Departments, agency and branch accounts. (In their *Accounting and banking.* 1912. p. 149-55).
SALES agency accounts: correspondence. *Journal of accountancy,* July 1913, p. 81-5.

Auditing

MCCALL, J. H. Accounts and audit of the English agency of a foreign company. *Incorporated accountants' journal,* Nov. 1912. p. 41-4.

AGENCY

See also Commercial law; Contracts.

ALEXANDER, G. G. Law of agency. *Incorporated accountants' journal,* 1891-2, p. 69.
ATKINSON, C. J. F. Law of agency. *Accountant,* April 25, 1891, p. 321-3.
BARRETT, LEONARD, F. C. A. Some points relating to the law of agency. *Incorporated accountants' journal,* July 1912, p. 263-5.

AGENCY—*(Continued)*

Corpus juris; being a complete and systematic statement of the whole body of the law as embodied in and developed by all reported decisions; ed. by William Mack and W. J. Hale. New York, American law book co.

DORSET, S. S. Law of principal and agent. *Incorporated accountants' journal,* 1902-3, p. 132.

ELLIOTT, G. Mercantile law (principal and agent). *Accountant,* Jan. 14, 21, 1888.

GLOAG, W. M. Law of agency. *Accountants' magazine,* May, Aug. 1907, p. 266-78, 299-311, 356-8, 438-51.

GRIERSON, A. Principal and agent. *Accountant,* 1887, p. 234.

KERSHAW, J. F. Principal and agent. *Accountant,* Nov. 11, 1899, p. 1105-11.

LINDLEY, TINSLEY. Notes on principal and agent. *Accountant,* June 22, 1907, p. 845-9.

PREVENTION of corruption act and agency fees. *Acountant,* Dec. 29, 1906, p. 787-90.

THOMSON, A. Agency. *Public accountant,* 1904-5, p. 61.

WHITE, HOWARD E. Agency. (In Humphreys, A. C. *Lecture notes on some of the business features of engineering practice.* p. 411-9).

WHITFIELD, L. Law relating to principal and agent. *Public accountant,* 1905-6, p. 31.

AGENCY plan on the St. Louis and San Francisco. *Railway age,* Mar. 20, 1914, p. 671-4.

AGENTS' record system. *Business man's magazine,* Jan. 1905, p. 106-7.

AGENTS requisition for stationery. *Railway age gazette,* Feb. 16, 1912, p. 286.

AGG, T. R.

Surface oiling of city streets. *Municipal journal,* May 13, 1915, p. 653-4.

AGGER, EUGENE EWALD

Organized banking. New York, Henry Holt & co. 1918. 385p.

AGGREGATES of polls, property, taxes, etc., as assessed April 1, 1919. Massachusetts, 1919.

AGNEW, WILLIAM FISCHER. Treatise on the statute of frauds. London, 1876.

AGREEMENTS.

See Contracts.

AGREEMENTS between practitioners and clerks. *Accountant,* Sept. 25, Nov. 6, 1909, p. 368-70, 561-5.

AGRICULTURAL bookkeeping instructor. Mann, J. D. 1914.

AGRICULTURAL DEPARTMENTS

HATHAWAY, W. A. Organization and business methods of the division of agriculture in the bureau of the census. *Government accountant,* May 1911, p. 3-14.

WANLASS, WILLIAM L. United States department of agriculture; a study in administration. Baltimore, The Johns Hopkins press, 1920. 131p. (Johns Hopkins university studies in historical and political science).

AGRICULTURAL economics. Nowise, E. G. 1916.

AGRICULTURAL MACHINERY

RUSSELL, H. A. Keeping records of finished products. *Iron age,* July 13, 1916, p. 70-3.

RUSSELL, H. A. Keeping track of work in process. *Iron age,* July 6, 1916, p. 6-9.

RUSSELL, H. A. Production methods of a large agricultural implement factory. *Iron age,* June 29, July 6, 13, 1916.

UNITED STATES. BUREAU OF CORPORATIONS. Farm machinery trade associations. Washington, Government printing office. 1915. 368p.

UNITED STATES. BUREAU OF CORPORATIONS. International harvester co. Washington. Government printing office, 1913. 384p.

UNITED STATES. FEDERAL TRADE COMMISSION. Report on the causes of high prices of farm implements, May 4, 1920. Washington, Government printing office, 1920. 713p.

Accounting

AMERICAN business and accounting encyclopaedia; comp. by E. H. Black and W. W. Thorne. Detroit, Bookkeeper publishing co. 1901. Agricultural implements' business accounting, p. 80-1.

GREENFIELD, L. L. Special loose leaf system of bookkeeping in the agricultural implement business. *Business man's magazine,* May 1909, p. 461-2.

GRIFFITH, J. B. System of factory records. *Business man's magazine,* Aug. 1905, p. 257-69.

WOODS, LEONARD R. Accounting methods in agricultural implement business. *Business man's magazine,* Oct. 1908, p. 295-302.

WRIGHT, WILLIAM ROLLAND. Accounting for the agricultural machinery industry. *Journal of accountancy,* June 1920, p. 435-51.

Cost accounting

BERTSCHI, E. R. Cost system for an agricultural implement business. *Business man's magazine,* 1904, v.17, p. 249-50.

WHARTON, T. F. Uniform cost accounting system for manufacturers of implements and other farm operating equipment. Chicago, National implement and vehicle association, 1916, 26p.

Costs

UNITED STATES. BUREAU OF CORPORATIONS. Cost of production. (In its *International harvester co.* 1913. p. 256-78).

UNITED STATES. BUREAU OF CORPORATIONS. Farm machinery trade associations. Washington. Government printing office, 1915. 368p.

AGRICULTURE

See also Agricultural machinery; Creameries; Dairying; Fruit; Livestock; Poultry; also names of special products, e.g. Cotton.

CATHCART, CHARLES S. Commercial feeding stuffs and registrations for 1917 New Brunswick, 1917. 100p. (New Jersey agricultural experiment stations, bulletin 311).

GUILD, ALEXANDER. Management of agricultural estate. *Accountant,* March 13,-April 17, 1897, p. 299-300, 322-3, 378-80, 402-4, 418-20.

MOOREHOUSE, L. A. and others. Farm practice in growing sugar beets for three districts in Utah and Idaho, 1914-1915. Washington, Government printing office, 1918. (United States Department of agriculture, bulletin no. 693). 44p.

UNITED STATES. Department of agriculture. Yearbook, 1919. Washington. Government printing office, 1920. 790p.

WILLARD, REX E. Farm management study of cotton farms of Ellis County, Texas. Washington, Government printing office, 1918. 54p. (United States. Department of agriculture, bulletin no. 659).

Accounting

AIKENS, D. System of book-keeping suitable

AGRICULTURE—Accounting—*(Continued)*
for the farmer. *Journal of the department of agriculture,* (South Australia) Dec. 1917, p. 431-6.
Allison, J. Farmers' income tax. *Accountant,* April 14, May 3, 17, 24, 1919, p. 325-6. 369-70, 421-3, 440-1.
Allred, C. E. This book helps the farmer keep books. *Banker-farmer,* Dec. 1917, p. 10.
American business and accounting encyclopaedia; comp. by E. H. Beach and W. W. Thorne. Detroit Bookkeeper publishing co. Plantation business accounting p. 883.
Angle, P. E. Business methods and farm accounts. *Ontario agricultural and experimental union. Report.* 1915, p. 77-81.
Atkeson, T. Clark. Bookkeeping for farmers to which is added the Stockbridge system of accounts. New York, Orange Judd co.
Balancing the farm ledger. *Agricultural digest,* March 1918, p. 872.
Baldwin, F. C. Keeping of farm records. *Jersey bulletin and dairy world,* Sept. 24, 1919, p. 1816.
Baldwin, P. M. Farm accounting and the income tax. *Conservation* (Ottawa). March 1920, p. 11. *Journal of agriculture* (Quebec), April 1920, p. 218.
Balfour, John. Concise farmer's account book. 1898.
Ball, James Stuart. Value of records to the farmer. Washington, Government printing office, 1917. 17p. (United States. Department of agriculture, year book separate no. 735). *United States agricultural year book,* 1917, p. 153-67. Condensed. *Agricultural gazette of Canada,* Dec. 1919, p. 1096-1100.
Banks: get these account sheets. *Banker-farmer,* Nov. 1918, p. 16.
Barrows, H. P. Farm records and accounts. Washington, United States relations service, 1917. 10p. (Doc. 38).
Bates, H. S. Newman-Bates system of farm bookkeeping. Ottawa, Canada, H. S. Bates, 1918.
Beasley, J. Farm account book. Longman, 1847.
Beaty, John Y. Complete farm accounts. *System on the farm,* March 1919, p. 143-50.
Beaty, John Y. How I figure my farm profits. *System on the farm,* Oct. 1920, p. 215-20.
Bexell, John Andrew. Business side of farming; farm records. Cornwallis, Oregon agricultural college press, 1909. 70p.
Bexell, John Andrew. Farm accounting and business methods. Springfield, Home correspondence school, 1911.
Bexell, John Andrew. Farm records. Corvallis, Oregon agricultural college, 1909. 71p.
Bexell, John Andrew. Farm statistics and standardized accounts. *National educational association.* 1915, p. 925-30.
Bexell, John Andrew and Frank G. Nichols. Principles of bookkeeping and farm accounts. New York, American book co. c1913. 184p.
Bexell, John A. and Frank G. Nichols. Teacher's reference book to accompany principles of bookkeeping and farm accounts. Chicago, American book co. 1914, 104p.
Book of the farm. 2v. Edinburgh, 1855.
Book-keeping for farmers. Edinburgh, William Green & son, 1916. 44p.
Boss, Andrew and Frank W. Peck. Farm records and accounts. St. Paul, Webb publishing, 1914, 116p.
Brown, George F. Simple accounting of a small Adirondack farm. *Business man's magazine,* May 1909, p. 434-46.
Brown, Richard. Farm accounts. *Accountants' magazine,* Dec. 1898, p. 562-83.
Brown, William. Farmer's annual account book. Ed. 5. 1897.
Buffum, D. Farm accounts as they should be kept. *Country life,* June 1916, p. 84.
Burroughs, M. W. Income tax for farmers, together with a simple form of book-keeping specially adapted for farmers. London, Iliffe & sons. 1918. 36p.
Campbell, G. H. Smith comes through. *Hoard's dairyman,* March 22, 1918, p. 369.
Card, Fred W. Farm management, including business accounts, suggestions for watching markets, time to market various products, adaption to local conditions, etc. New York. Doubleday, Page & co. 1912. 270p.
Carlisle, Charles A. Keeping books on the farm. *Leslie's weekly,* Nov. 21, 1912, p. 530, 537.
Cavert, W. L. When is farming profitable. *Breeder's gazette,* May 27, 1920, p. 1472.
Champlin, Manley. Lessons in field management. Brookings, S. D., South Dakota state college, 1917.
Cook, W. A. Card system for simplifying farm records. *System on the farm,* July 1917, p. 180-1.
Dagger, G. N. Useful farm records and accounts. Ohio agricultural extension bureau, v. 12, no. 4, 1916-17. 12p.
Demaree, F. H. Farm bookkeeping. *Farm engineering,* Aug. Sept. 1917, p. 9, 13.
Demaree, F. H. Farm bookkeeping; how to get an accurate estimate of profits. *Farm engineering,* Dec. 1917, p. 11.
Demaree, F. H. Simple method of keeping farm records. *Farm engineering,* Jan. 1916, p. 131-2.
Dixon, M. and H. W. Hawthorne. Method of analyzing the farm business. *Farmers' bulletin,* 1139, 1920, p. 1-40.
Does it pay to keep farm accounts. *Ohio Judd farmer,* Sept. 25, 1920, p. 1394.
Doty, L. E. How I avoid unprofitable crops. *System on the farm,* July 1920, p. 22-3.
Dowsley, W. G. Farmer's account book; a simple and concise system of account keeping. London, Sir Isaac Pitman & sons, 1911.
Duncan, C. S. Mercantile and agricultural economics. *Journal of political economy,* Oct. 1918, p. 769-806.
East of Fife agricultural society. Farmers' cash book. Cupar-Fife, A. Westwood & son, 1916.
Ellsworth, H. W. Industrial farm bookkeeping. Mont Vale, N. J. Ellsworth co.
Engberg, R. C. What does the record say? *Successful farmer,* April 1920, p. 10.
Eve, H. Tristm. Simple farm accounts. Journal Bath and west and southern co. society, London, 1905, ser. 4, v.15, p. 77-88.
Eveleigh, F. W. Anton. Taxation of farmers: some observations and suggestions. *South African accountant,* Sept. 1918, p. 206-11.
Extensive work thru income tax. *Cornell countryman,* June 1918, p. 521-2.
Farm account book; being a plain and concise method of keeping farm accounts . . . published by direction of the Commission of national education in Ireland. Dublin, 1853.
Farm accounting. *Business man's magazine,* July 1906, p. 94-6.
Farm accounting. *Michigan agricultural experiment quarterly bulletin,* Feb. 1920, p. 109-12.
Farm accounting for the income tax. *Country gentlemen,* March 23, 1918, p. 40.
Farm accounting in theory and practice. *Progressive farms,* Jan. 18, 1919, p. 111.
Farm book-keeping. *Agricultural gazette of Canada,* July 1917, p. 578-81.

AGRICULTURE—ACCOUNTING—*(Continued)*

FARM bookkeeping problems. *Progressive farmer,* Nov. 24, 1917, p. 1231.

FARM management club at North Lake. *Banker-farmer,* Jan. 1918, p. 2-4.

FARMER who keeps books. *American co-operative journal,* Dec. 1917, p. 168.

FARMERS account books. London, Simpkin, Marshall, Hamilton, Kent & co. 1868.

FARMERS' bookkeeping. *Accountant,* Sept. 22, 29, Oct. 6, 13, 20, 27, Nov. 3, 17, 1883.

FARMERS' bookkeeping for income tax. *Agricultural diary,* March 1918, p. 891.

FARMERS' experience meeting; experiences in keeping farm books and records. *Progressive farmer,* Dec. 27, 1919, p. 2145.

FARMERS' experience meetings; keeping farm accounts. *Progressive farmer,* Nov. 16, 1918, p. 1252.

FARQUHARSON, A. Rural accountant; or A practical system of farmers' book-keep- Edinburg, 1811.

FERGUSON, GEORGE A. Farmers and bookkeeping. *Accountant,* Feb. 26, 1916, p. 255-9.

FINLAY, W. B. Income tax law and farm accounting methods. *Journal of accountancy,* July 1914, p. 47-51.

FRANCIS, SIDNEY. Farmers', graziers', agricultural students' surveyors', land agents' auctioneers', etc., tables and memoranda. Ed. 5. New York, D. Van Nostrand co.

FRANCIS, SIDNEY. Tables, memoranda, etc. for farmers, surveyors etc. with a new system of farm bookkeeping. Ed. 4. London, 1898.

FRENCH, S. Farmers balance sheet. *Country life,* April 1, 1911, p. 576.

FULCHER, ———. Bookkeeping for farmers. London, Simpkin, Marshall, Hamilton, Kent & co. 1854.

FULTON, LEVI S. and G. W. EASTMAN. Practical system of bookkeeping by single and double entry, containing forms of books and practical exercises; adapted to the use of the farmer. Ed. 7. New York, A. S. Barner & co. 1853. 296p.

FUNK, WARREN CLEMMER. Farm household accounts. Washington, Government printing office, 1918. 11p. (United States. Department of agriculture, farmers' bulletin 964).

FUNK, WARREN CLEMMER. What the farm contributes directly to the farmer's living. Washington, Government printing office, 1914. 21p. (United States department of agriculture, farmer's bulletin 635).

GENTLEMAN'S auditor; or a new and easie method for keeping accompts of gentlemen's estates; with the manner of auditing and stating the accompts. London, 1707.

GLOVER, J. N. Keeping farm accounts and records. *Hoard's dairyman,* Jan. 24, 1919, p. 22.

GODDARD, C. P. Practical system of farm bookkeeping. Boston, Massachusetts state board of agriculture, 1915. 19p. (Massachusetts agricultural circular no. 39).

GODDARD, C. P. Some experiences in farm accounting. Massachusetts state board of agriculture, Annual report, 1914, p. 124-41.

GOODYEAR, LLOYD E. Farm accounting for the practical farmer. Cedar Rapids, Goodyear-Marshall publishing co. 36p.

GREAT BRITAIN. AGRICULTURE AND FISHERIES BOARD. Leaflet 240, Farm book-keeping. Feb. 1911. 8p.

GREEN, JOHN. Worcestershire farmer's account book. London. 1911.

GREEN, R. M. Cost and price tendencies on the farm. *Missouri agricultural experiment circular* 97, 1920. p. 1-8.

GREEN, ROY MONROE and DILLER CLEMENT WOOD. How to keep farm accounts. Columbia, University of Missouri, College of agriculture, 1918. 28p. (Agric. exper. station, circular 84).

GREEN, SAMUEL. Practical accountant; or Farmer's and mechanicks' best method of book-keeping . . . designed as a companion to Daboll's arithmetic. (In *Daboll, N. Schoolmaster's assistant.* Utica, 1832, p. 21).

GUNNER, W. Farm accounts. Corporate treasurers' and accountants' institute proceedings, 1887, p. 17.

HACKETT, P. Management plan that makes 17% a year for me. *System on the farm,* Mar. 1917, p. 11-14.

HAMMET, C. I. Farm records that reduce costs. *System on the farm,* Aug. 1917, p. 215-18.

HARMON, R. L. If there had been accounting. *Nonpartisan leader,* Sept. 6, 1917, p. 8.

HARRIS, B. F. Simple farm account system. *Banker-farmer,* Feb. 1918, p. 16.

HATCH, KIRK LESTER and JOHN ADAM HASELWOOD. Elementary agriculture and practical arithmetic. Chicago, Row, Peterson & co. 1907.

HAYS, W. M., A. BOSS, A. D. WILSON and T. COOPER. Farm management investigations in the United States. Washington, April 15, 1912. (United States Department of agriculture, Bureau of plant industry, bulletin no. 236).

HEIDENREICH, R. Value of a farm record. *Swine world,* July 5, 1919, p. 46.

HOBERT, J. Simple records that helped our farm. *System on the farm,* Jan. 1919, p. 13-4.

HOFINS, P. H. How accurate records helped in establishing a pure bred business. *System on the farm,* Mar. 1918, p. 85-8.

HOWELL, H. G. Farm accounts, profits and costs. *Journal of the Ministry of agriculture* (Australia), May 1920, p. 162-71.

HUNGERFORD, D. Instructions in farm accounting. *Georgia agricultural college extension bulletin* 194, 1919, p. 1-36.

HUNTER, JOEL. Farm accounts. (In his *Thinking in figures.* c1916. p. 143-52). *Journal of accountancy,* March 1913, p. 166-73.

HURRELL'S farm labour book. Ed. 19. London, Simpkin, Marshall, Hamilton, Kent & co. 1868.

IMPROVED system of farm bookkeeping; by the author of British Husbandry. London, 1851.

INGLIS, WILLIAM. Farm bookkeeping. London and Edinburgh, 1865?

——— Same. New ed. Edinburgh, W. & R. Chambers, 1873.

IRELAND. DEPARTMENT OF AGRICULTURAL AND TECHNICAL INSTRUCTION. Farmers account book, Dublin, Browne & Nolan.

JACKSON, W. Why farmers should keep a farm record. *Purdue agriculturist,* Dec. 1919, p. 134.

JAMIESON, JOHN. Easy introduction to book-keeping in four short sets [also] farm book-keeping, etc. Glasgow, 1835.

JEMMETT, A. Estate and farm bookkeeping. London, Simpkin, Marshall, Hamilton, Kent & co. 1878.

JEMMETT, A. Farm book. London, Simpkin, Marshall, Hamilton, Kent & co. 1868.

JOHNSON, E. C. and P. E. MCNALL. How Kansas bankers are bringing better business to the farm. *Banker-Farmer* (Champaign, Ill.), May 1916, p. 14-5.

JONES, J. J. How I know my farm income. *System on the farm,* Sept. 1918, p. 98-9.

JONES, M. D. Farm accounts. *Maine agricultural extension bulletin* 128, 1920. 8p.

KEEP farm accounts. *Weekly news letter,* March 13, 1918, p. 4.

KEEPING farm accounts and records. *Progressive farm,* Sept. 15, 1917, p. 963.

AGRICULTURE—ACCOUNTING—*(Continued)*

KERR, WILLIAM HORACE and G. A. NAHSTOLL. Co-operative organization business methods. Washington, Government printing office, 1915. 24p. (United States. Department of agriculture, bulletin no. 178).

KERSEY, H. W. Simple method of book-keeping for farmers, market gardeners and dairymen. London, Headley brothers, 1907. 64p.

KIRKPATRICK, C. D. Farm bookkeeping. *Wallaces' farmer,* Dec. 12, 1919, p. 2461.

LAMB, HENRY GRANT. Farm bookkeeping. New York, The Thomas press, 1908. 69p.

LISET, A. Amphithalami; or the Accomptants closet. London, 1660, 1684.

MCCLELLAND, C. K. Bookkeeping for farmers. *Progressive farmer,* Dec. 27, 1919, p. 2142.

MACDONALD, D. G. and JAMES GRANT. Simple system of bookkeeping for farmers and smallholders, with model statement of accounts and balance sheet. Edinburgh, W. & R. Chambers, [1918.] 72p.

MAKING poor land pay. *System on the farm,* Nov. 1917, p. 323-6.

MAKING shorter work of records and accounts. *System on the farm,* Oct. 1918, p. 160.

MANN, JASPER DALBON. Agricultural bookkeeping instructor. Galena, Ohio, J. D. Mann, 1914. 55p.

MARQUIS, J. C. Farming without guesswork. *Country gentleman,* Dec. 22, 1917, p. 2010-11.

MATTERN, J. R. System that spells success. *Country life,* Jan. 1916, p. 43.

MAYLAND, E. Work in North Dakota. *Dakota farmer,* Mar. 1, 1919, p. 422.

MEATS, THOMAS WHEELER. Agriculture accounts (including income tax as relating to agriculture). London, Gee & co. 1911, 114p. (*Accountants' library,* v. 4).

MILLER, H. P. Keep farm business records. *Ohio farmer,* Jan. 24, 1920, p. 131.

MILLER, R. N. Farm accounts. *Western Washington Agricultural experiment station bulletin,* July 1918, p. 46-8.

MUNRO, I. Guide to farm book keeping. Edinburgh, Nicol, 1821.

NEWMAN-BATES system of farm bookkeeping. 102 Bank st., Ottawa, H. S. Bates.

NICHOLS, J. L. and others. Farmers' manual and complete account book. Springfield, Mass. J. L. Nichols.

NORTH, ROGER. Gentleman accomptant; or, An essay to unfold the mystery of accompts, by way of debtor and creditor, etc. by a Person of honour. London, 1714.

NOWISE, E. G. Agricultural economics: a selection in which economic principles are applied to the practice of agriculture. Chicago, University of Chicago press, 1916. 896p.

OMISSIONS in agricultural accounting. *Hoard's dairyman,* Jan. 14, 1916, p. 823.

ORWIN, CHARLES STEWART. Farm accounts. Cambridge university press, 1914. 209p.

OSTRANDER, W. A. Farming as a business. *South Dakota agricultural extension,* 1918, p. 1-30.

OTIS, DANIEL HENRY. Farm accounts simplified; a simplified system of farm accounts that requires no posting, the minimum of descriptions and additions and sufficiently itemized to determine the cost of production. New York, Orange Judd co. 1915. 42p.

OTIS, DANIEL HENRY. How banks can cooperate with farmers in keeping farm accounts. *Banker-farmer,* May 1916, p. 12.

OTIS, DANIEL HENRY. Review of Wisconsin farm management demonstration. *Hoard's dairyman,* Dec. 1917, p. 762-3.

PARK, A. D. Farm book-keeping. *Journal of agriculture of New Zealand,* Dec. 1919, p. 374-7.

PARK, A. D. Interest and depreciation charges in farm accounts. *Journal of agriculture of New Zealand,* April 1919, p. 206-7.

PARKER, J. M. Bookkeeping for the householder and farmer. *Country life,* March, 1909, v.15, p. 526.

PEET, J. B. Farm accounts. *Journal Board of agriculture,* Sept. 1909. *Economic Bulletin,* Dec. 1909, p. 415.

PERKINS, C. O. and F. Farmer's accountant; adapted to the practical farmer. Boston, J. E. Farwell & co. 1867. 55p.

PHILLIPS, THOMAS D. Farm inventory. *Ohio farms,* Jan. 27, 1917, p. 107.

PIXLEY, FRANCIS W. Landed proprietors. (In his *Accountancy.* Ed. 2. p. 98-9, 274-6.

PLANTATION teacher and farm instruction, regulation, record, inventory and account book. Richmond, Va., J. W. Randolph.

POE, C. Corn field bookkeeping for Hilltop farm. *Progressive farmer,* Dec. 27, 1919, p. 2153.

PRICE, W. M. Farm book-keeping and accounts. Glasgow, Scottish agricultural publishing co.

PROGRESSIVE farmer. Farmer's account book. Birmingham, Ala, Progressive farmer, 1918, 32p.

RECORDS and accounts. *System on the farm,* Sept. 1918, p. 106.

RECORDS and accounts. *System on the farm,* Jan.-July 1919, p. 48, 120, 192, 244, 330, 400.

RECORDS farmers should keep. *Progressive farmer,* Nov. 16, 1918, p. 1256.

REID, WALTER A. Book-keeping for farmers. *Accountants' magazine,* Dec. 1920, p. 663-9.

REVIEW of Wisconsin farm management demonstration. *Hoard's dairyman,* Dec. 1917, p. 762-3.

ROBERTS, ISAAC PHILLIPS. Bookkeeping for the householder and farmer. *Country life,* March 1909, p. 526.

ROBERTS, ISAAC PHILLIPS. Farmer's business handbook, a manual of simple farm accounts and of brief advice on rural law. New York, Macmillan co., 1903, 300p.

ROBERTSON, L. Farm records and accounts. *Purdue agriculturist,* Jan. 1919, p. 152-3.

ROBERTSON, L. S. Farm records and the income tax. *Purdue agriculturist,* April 1918, p. 426.

RONALDSON, PETER. Farm bookkeeping. (In Lisle, George. *Encyclopaedia of accounting.* v.2. p. 480-517).

ROOKE, GEORGE C. and THOMAS GRANT. Farm bookkeeping and accounts. Regina, Sask. Canada, Prairie farm and home, 1914. 89p.

ROYAL agricultural society journal. pt. 2. 1883.

SANDERS, ———. Book-keeping for farmers. London, Simpkin, Marshall, Hamilton, Kent & co. 1854.

SAXBY, C. J. Farmers' labour and account book. New York, D. Van Nostrand co.

SCHOENFELD, W. A. Farm accounting. Univ. of Texas, Extension department, Public welfare division, 1915.

SCOTT, J. Farmer's account book. London, Longman's, Green & co. 1863.

SCOVILL, HIRAM THOMPSON. Farm accounting. New York, D. Appleton & co. 1918. 429p.

SIMPLE system of farm accounting. *Successful farmer,* Jan. 1920, p. 148.

SIMPLE system of farm book-keeping. *Journal of agriculture* (Quebec), Feb. 1919, p. 132.

SLOMAN, L. A. Accounts for a general farm. *Country gentleman,* Dec. 23, 1911, p. 12.

SLOMAN, L. A. Diversified farm accounting. Boston, Wright & Potter printing co. 1914, 14 p. (Mass. agricultural board circular 29). *Massachusetts, Board of agriculture, Annual report,* 1914.

SMITH, A. W. Farm bookkeeping. *Journal*

AGRICULTURE—ACCOUNTING—*(Continued)*
of the department of agriculture of South Australia, Feb. 1919, p. 594-5.

SMITH, CHESTER WILLIAM and S. MILES THOMAS. Farm accounts. Philadelphia, Laurel book co. 1913. 82p.

SMITH, CLINTON D. Suggestions on farm accounts. Lansing, Mich., Agricultural experiment station special bulletin, no. 9. 12p.

SMITH, E. L. Farm accounting problem. *Scientific American*, Nov. 30, 1918, p. 436.

SNELL, CHARLES. Accompts for landed men: or, A plain and easie form which they may observe in keeping accompts of their estates. London, 1710.

SOULE, GEORGE. Plantation or farm business. (In his *New science and practice of accounts*. 1903. p. 301-7).

SPILLMAN, WILLIAM JASPER. Formulae for calculating interest on farm equipment. Washington, Government printing office, 1915. 4p. (United States. Department of agriculture, circular no. 53).

STATE finances; farm number (v.1 no. 11) Albany, New York state comptroller's office, Feb. 1918, p. 3-5.

STEINER, HARRY LEE. How to keep farm accounts. Ed. 3. Toledo, Steiner & co. 1909. 152p.

STEWART, G. H. Value of farm book-keeping. *Agricultural journal of British Columbia*, June 1920, p. 102.

STRACHAN, J. Concise system of farm bookkeeping. Edinburgh, 1854.

TABER, R. F. Farmers keeping accounts. *Ohio farmer*, June 14, 1919, p. 911.

TABER, R. F. To keep farm books; Ohio college and bankers unit. *Banker-farmer*, Dec. 1918, p. 11.

TAYLOR, C. C. Farm accounting. *Idaho extension circular* 21, 1920. 4p.

TAYLOR, HERBERT and J. O. PEET. Principles and practice of book-keeping for the farm, garden, dairy and estate. London, Simpkin, Marshall, Hamilton, Kent & co. 1912. 265p.

TENANT farmers' income tax and accounts. *Accountant*, July 20, 27, 1918, p. 42-4, 52-4.

THOMPSON, A. W. Text-book of the principles and practice of bookkeeping and estate-office work. London, G. Bell & sons.

——— Same. Ed. 3, enlarged by F. C. McClellan, London. 1901.

——— Same. Ed. 5. London. 1910.

THOMSON, EDWARD HERRMANN. Farm bookkeeping. Washington, Government printing office, 1915. 37p. (United States. Department of agriculture, farmers' bulletin 511).

THOMSON, EDWARD HERRMANN. Farm bookkeeping. *Farmers' bulletin*, 1912, p. 1-37.

THOMSON, EDWARD HERRMANN. Farm diary: a business record and account book; prepared by the World book company after the plan outlined by E. H. Thomson, with an introduction by W. J. Spillman, Yonkers-on-Hudson. New York, World book co. 1918. 410p.

THOMSON, EDWARD HERRMANN. Use of a diary for farm accounts. Washington, Government printing office, 1917. 19p. (United State. Department of agriculture, farmers' bulletin 782).

THOMSON, EDWARD HERRMANN and H. M. DIXON. Method of analyzing the farm business. Washington, Government printing office, 1918. 28p. (United States. Department of agriculture, farmers' bulletin 661).

TIPTON, C. S. Method of keeping farm accounts. *Orange Judd farmer*, Dec. 13, 1919, p. 912.

UMMEL, J. R. Farm accounts, their significance and importance. *Reclamation record*, May 1917, p. 238-9.

UNITED STATES. FEDERAL BOARD FOR VOCATIONAL EDUCATION. Bookkeeping; farm receipts and expenditures in single entry. Washington, Government printing office. 1919. 23p. (Rehabilitation monograph joint ser. 62).

VALUE of farm bookkeeping and cost accounting. *Journal Board of agriculture*, Oct. 1919, p. 708-12.

VYE, JOHN. Farm accounts. St. Paul, J. A. Vye, 1906. 141p.

WARREN, ———. Farmers account book. Ed. 22. London, Simpkin, Marshall, Hamilton, Kent & co. 1868.

WARREN, GEORGE FREDERICK. Farm management. New York, The Macmillan co. 1913. 590p.

WENZ, A. No need of settling up. *Dakota farmer*, Mar. 15, 1919, p. 528.

WHEELER, J. R. Farmer's books and the banker—a great chance for cooperation. *Banker-farmer*, May 1916, p. 11.

WHELPLEY, CORYDON SAMUEL. Money maker for farmers. Kingsville, Ohio, Big Maple truck co. 1906.

WILSON, JAMES. Notes on landed estate accounts. *Accountant*, June 19, 1909, p. 872-83.

WOOD, J. Farm accounts. *Accountant*, June 19, 1920, p. 713-5.

WOOD, J. Farmers' accounts. London, Gee & co. *Accountant*, Nov. 16, 23, 30, 1918, p. 264-6, 275-6, 290-2.

WOOD, W. S. Are you making money? *Country gentleman*, Feb. 22, 1919, p. 66.

WOODMAN, JOHNSON M. Bookkeeping for farmers and estate owners. Crosby Lockwood and son, 1893.

WOODMAN, JOHNSON M. Yearly farm account book. Ed. 2. London, Crosby Lockwood & son, 1897.

WOODMAN, JOHNSON M. Farm accounts and matters relating thereto. *Accountant*, Nov. 27, 1897, p. 1121-7.

WORKABLE plan for keeping farm accounts. *Dairy farmer*, Sept. 1, 1920, p. 739.

WRAY, G. E. System on the farm. *Business man's magazine*, Sept. 1910, p. 283-6.

WYLLIE, JAMES. Farm valuations for bookkeeping purposes. *Journal of the board of agriculture* (London), March 1916, p. 1215-28.

Auditing

CUTFORTH, A. E. Landed estate. (In his *Audits*. 1914. p. 75-6).

METHOD for supporting financial records. *Journal of Home Economics*, March 1916, p. 130-2.

NECESSITY of having the books audited at least once a year. *Co-operative manager and farmer*, Jan. 1919, p. 42-3.

PIXLEY, FRANCIS W. Landed estates. (In his *Auditors, their duties and responsibilities*. 1910, p. 503-4.

SPICER, ERNEST EVAN and ERNEST C. PEGLER. Landed estate. (In their *Audit programmes*. 1919. p. 62-3).

SPICER, ERNEST EVAN and ERNEST C. PEGLER. Landed estates. (In their *Practical auditing*. 1914. p. 489-90).

Bibliography

UNITED STATES. Superintendent of documents. Farm management, farm accounts, credits, marketing, homes and statistics. Washingington, Government printing office, 1918. 17p. (Price list 68)

Cost accounting

ADLING, VAN VLIET. Devising a cost system for the farmer. *Business man's magazine*, June 1910, p. 523-32.

ANALYZING farm business. *Weekly news letter*, Jan. 31, 1917, p. 2.

BENEDICT, M. R. Cost of production to the farmer. *Dakota farmer*, Aug. 15, 1920, p. 1438.

AGRICULTURE—Cost Accounting — *(Continued)*

Bonner, Joseph Claybaugh. Farm cost system arranged for the farmer. Toledo, Bonner & co. c1915. 58p.

Burritt, M. C. Farm cost accounting made easy. *Power,* Jan. Feb. March, April, 1916, p. 14, 14, 24, 30.

Butler, T. Cost keeping and the farm business. *Progressive farmer,* Aug. 11, 1917, p. 855.

Calvert, W. L. How to figure the profits from investments in farm equipment. Minnesota farmers' institute annual, 1916, p. 46-8.

Carrigan, C. W. Cutting operating expenses by knowing costs. *System on the farm,* April 1918, p. 125-8.

Chandler, A. E. Farm cost accounting. *Hoard's dairyman,* Feb. 11, 1916, p. 91.

Committee gives plan for finding production costs. *Weekly news letter,* Mar. 26, 1919, p. 15-6.

Connor, L. G. Farm management and farm profits in irrigated land in the Provo area (Utah Lake valley), U. S. A. *International review of science and practice of agriculture,* Sept. 1918, p. 1095-1103.

Cook, W. A. Card system for simplifying farm records. *System on the farm,* July 1917, p. 180-1.

Cost of production to be studied in large way. *Weekly news letter,* June 18, 1919, p. 1.

Cost of things. *Hoard's dairyman,* Feb. 1, 1918, p. 45.

Crissey, F. Getting together in Iowa. *Country gentleman,* Dec. 15, 1917, p. 1974-5.

Currier, E. L. Labor charge in farm cost accounting. *Hoard's dairyman,* Nov. 2, 1917, p. 494.

Davenport, H. J. Farm products and cost accounting. *Journal of political economy,* May 1919, p. 354-61.

Davis, John H. Keeping separate crop accounts. *Progressive farmer,* Feb. 26, 1916, p. 300.

Demarest, H. P. Short cut to knowing crop costs. *System on the farm,* Mar. 1917, p. 21-2.

Difficulties of farm cost accounting. *Progressive farmer,* Dec. 14, 1918, p. 1363.

Falconer, J. I. Ascertaining cost of production. *Ohio farmer,* Oct. 2, 1920, p. 394.

Farm accounts: cost of production. *Journal of the Board of agriculture* (London), Feb. 1917, p. 1077-80.

Foster, L. F. Farm costing. *Journal of the board of agriculture* (London), May 1918, p. 153-65.

Geil, G. J. Costing of the produce of the land. *Accounting and commerce,* Feb.-July, 1920, p. 253-5, 280-3, 10-12, 36-8, 62, 85-8.

Hackett, P. Management plan that makes 17% a year for me. *System on the farm,* March 1917, p. 11-4.

Handschin, W. F. Economic problems of the farmer. *Ohio Judd farmer,* Feb. 1920, p. 345.

Importance of cost accounting system. *Hoard's dairyman,* Feb. 13, 1920, p. 224.

Johnson, E. C. and P. E. McNall. How Kansas bankers are bringing better business to the farm. *Banker-farmer,* May 1916, p. 14-5.

Jones, E. P. Easy way of keeping track of labor. *System on the farm,* Sept. 1917, p. 251.

Keane, John. Determination of farm costs. *Journal of the board of agriculture,* Dec. 1919, p. 891-906.

Keep farm accounts. *Journal of agriculture* (Quebec), Aug. 1918, p. 32.

Kidder, A. F. What is your labor income? *Progressive farms,* Jan. 13, 1917, p. 51.

Kirkpatrick, Charles. How cost accounts increase my profits. *System on the farm,* April 1920, p. 225-6.

Kirkpatrick, Charles D. Overhead charges on the farm. *Wallaces' farmer,* March 22, 1918, p. 542.

Ladd, Carl Edwin. Cost accounts on some New York farms. *Cornell agricultural experiment station bulletin* no. 377, 1916, p. 773-815. *Cornell agricultural experiment station, Report,* 1916, p. 773-815. Excerpt, *New York agricultural department bulletin.* Sept. 1916, p. 2781-3.

Ladd, Carl Edwin. System of farm cost accounting. Washington, Government printing office, 1915. 15p. (United States. Department of agriculture, farmers' bulletin 572).

Lee, L. W. Cost system on Ashtabula co. farms. *Ohio farms,* March 11, 1916, p. 395.

Libbert, M. S. Cost accounting. *Purdue agriculturist,* Nov. 1916, p. 30-1.

Main, F. W. Costs as a basis for prices. *American fertilizer,* May 8, 1920, p. 114.

Making poor land pay. *System on the farm,* Nov. 1917, p. 323-6.

Marenghi, E. Method of determining the cost of production of agricultural products. *International review of science and agriculture,* Jan. 1917, p. 147-8.

Marquis, J. C. Joker in cost of production. *Country gentlemen,* Feb. 28, 1920, p. 32.

Martin, O. R. Cost of producing farm crops. *Journal of accountancy,* April 1915, p. 245-59.

Mendum, S. W. Do we want cost of production. *Hoard's dairyman,* Feb. 13, 1920, p. 169.

Mattern, J. R. System that spells success. *Country life,* Jan. 1916, p. 43.

Mercantile and agricultural economics. *Journal of political economy,* Oct. 1918, p. 769.

Method for finding cost of production on farms recommended in report by committee of experts. *Official bulletin,* March 18, 1919, p. 1-2. *North Dakota banker,* April 1919, p. 8-9.

Miller, H. P. Farm cost accounting. *Ohio farmer,* Jan. 25, 1919, p. 111.

Mitchell, E. B. How I learn what a job costs. *System on the farm,* Oct. 1919, p. 224-5.

Montgomery, C. W. Cost accounting. *National stock management and farmer,* Feb. 2, 1919, p. 1161.

Montgomery, C. W. Guesses in cost accounting. *National stock management and farmer,* May 15, 1920, p. 234.

More about uniform accounting. *American cooperative journal,* Sept. 1916, p. 68.

Old problem again. *Hoard's dairyman,* Nov. 9, 1917, p. 538.

Orwin, Charles Stewart. Determination of farming costs. Oxford, Clarendon press, 1917. 144p. Bibliography p. 121-42.

Oskison, J. M. Farming on a business basis. *System,* April, 1913, p. 379-83.

Otis, D. H. and R. V. Gunn. Sources of farm profits and their relative importance. *Hoard's dairyman,* June 30, 1916, p. 900. Abstract. *International review of science and practice of agriculture,* Aug. 7, no. 11; 1663-7, Nov. 1916.

Park, A. D. Costing for farmers. *South African accountant,* March 1920, p. 422-3.

Park, A. D. Farm costing. *Journal of agriculture of New Zealand,* Sept. 1919, p. 148-51.

Plan for finding cost of agricultural production reported to Secretary Houston. *Commercial and financial chronicle,* March 22, 1919, p. 1119.

Randall, B. G. Farm cost keeping system. *Wallaces' farm,* April 7, 1916, p. 571.

Rice, S. J. Cost production on the farm. *Wallaces' farm,* Feb. 18, 1916, p. 270.

AGRICULTURE—Cost Accounting — *(Continued)*

Roberts, H. P. What it costs to run the tractor. *Progressive farmer,* July 12, 1919, p. 1142.

Rockwell, F. F. Accounting the cost of farming. *Country life,* May 1917, p. 70-2.

Ross, H. and P. G. Gilder. Basis of cost in wheat production. *Agricultural gazette of New South Wales,* Dec. 1917, p. 869-80.

Ryan, J. E. My experience with cost accounting. *Farm engineering,* April 1917, p. 10.

Stanley, H. V. Keeping records to lower production costs. *System on the farm,* Nov. 1917, p. 337-8.

Taylor, H. C. Cost accounts on the farm. *Journal of agriculture of Quebec,* April 1920, p. XVII.

Thomson, E. H. Farm cost accounting; essential farm records and their interpretation. *Journal of accountancy,* Dec. 1915, p. 401-20.

Tweddle, A. B. Farm cost accounting. *Agricultural gazette of Canada,* May 1918, p. 504-5.

Valentine, J. A. Farm management. *American economic review,* March 1913, sup. 102-11.

Value of farm book-keeping and cost accounting. *Journal of board of agriculture,* Oct. 1919, p. 708-12.

Wenz, A. Experience meeting on what it costs. *Dakota farmer,* Jan. 15, 1920, p. 106.

What does it cost? *Wallace's farmer,* May 28, 1920, p. 1489.

White, G. G. Farm cost accounting. Winnipeg, 1916. 51p. (Manitoba agricultural college bulletin no. 21).

Willard, R. E. What does a study of cost production reveal? *Dakota farmer,* June 15, 1920, p. 1202-3.

Williams, R. How we study our records in cutting expense bills. *System on the farm,* Dec. 1917, p. 362-4.

Wyllie, J. Determination of the cost of production of farm crops. *Journal of the board of agriculture,* July 1917, p. 403-16.

Wyllie, J. Profit and loss sharing in agriculture. *Journal of the Ministry of Agriculture,* June 1920, p. 254-61.

Yerkes, Arnold Phipps. Cost of harvesting wheat by different methods. Washington, Government printing office, 1918. 22p. (United States. Department of agriculture, bulletin no. 627).

Zenders, F. A. Cost system on a Missouri farm. *Collier's,* April 8, 1916, p. 26.

Costs

Cooper, P. Checking a crop loss. *System on the farm,* March 1918, p. 90.

Cooper, T. P., F. W. Peck and A. Boss. Labor requirements of crop production. *Minnesota agricultural experiment station bulletin,* 1916. p. 1-55.

Cost of producing crops on the college farms in 1915; tabulation. (In *Report* 1916, p. 10-11. Ontario agricultural department, Toronto, Canada, 1917).

Cost of producing wheat. *Commercial and financial chronicle,* June 26, 1920, p. 2623.

Davenport, E. High cost of bumper crops. *Country gentleman,* Feb. 16, 1918, p. 3-4.

Fertilizers and production costs. *Kimball's dairy farmer,* Feb. 1, 1918, p. 88.

Johnson, O. M. and A. J. Dadisman. Amount and cost of labor required for growing crops in West Virginia. West Virginia agricultural experiment bulletin, 1916, p. 1-11.

Mowry, H. H. Machinery cost of farm operations in western New York. *United States department of agriculture bulletin,* no. 338, Jan. 18, 1916. 24p.

Orwin, Charles Stewart. Determination of farming costs, Oxford, Clarendon press, 1917. 144p.

Thompson, A. L. Cost of crop production. *New York agricultural department bulletin,* Aug. 1916, p. 2251-7.

Thorne, C. E. High cost of low crop yields. *Ohio agricultural experiment station bulletin,* June 1917, p. 181-7.

Credit

Corn exchange national bank. Philadelphia. Complete text and analysis of the Federal farm loan act, approved July 17, 1916. Philadelphia, Corn exchange national bank, 1916. 40p.

Dworak, E. A. comp. Corey and McKenzie complete accounting system and record for national farm loan associations. 1407 Harney St., Omaha, Nebraska, Corey and McKenzie printing company, 1917. 49p.

Guaranty trust company of New York. Digest of the Federal farm loan act (rural credits bill). New York, Guaranty trust company of New York, 1916. 16p.

Thompson, Carl William. Costs and sources of farm mortgage loans in the United States. Washington, Government printing office, 1916. 16p. (United States. Department of agriculture, bulletin no. 384).

Truesdell, Leon E. and C. W. Thompson. Amortization methods for farm mortgage loans. Washington, Government printing office, 1916. 12p. (United States. Department of agriculture, circular no 60).

United States. Federal farm loan bureau. Amendments to the Federal farm loan act, with comments and notes by the farm loan board. Washington, Government printing office, 1920. 8p. (Circular no. 11).

United States. Federal farm loan bureau. Farm loan primer; with definitions, rulings and regulations of the Federal farm loan board to June 1, 1917. Ed. 4. Washington, Government printing office, 1917. 22p.

United States. Federal farm loan board. Farm loan primer, here you will find in brief form answers to the questions most frequently asked about the Federal farm loan. Washington, Government printing office, 1920. 13p. (Circular no. 5 revised).

United States. Federal farm loan bureau. Federal farm loan act, with amendment approved January 18, 1918. Washington, Government printing office, 1920. 29p. (Circular no. 4, revised)

United States. Federal farm loan bureau. How farmers may form a national farm loan association. Washington, Government printing office, 1919. 8p. (Circular no 2)

United States. Federal farm loan bureau. Improved farm mortgage; a story illustrating the practical application of the Federal farm loan act, January 2, 1919. Washington, Government printing office, 1919. 8p. (Circular no. 3, revised)

United States. Federal farm loan bureau. Killing off mortgages; a description of the methods of amortization and their benefits to borrowers. Washington, Government printing office, 1920. 16p. (Circular no. 7, revised).

United States. Federal farm loan bureau. National farm loan associations; organization, management, powers, and limitations, June 1920. Washington, Government printing office, 1920. 4p. (Circular no 1, revised)

United States. Federal farm loan bureau. Rulings and regulations of the Federal farm loan board of June 1, 1920; in matters pertaining to the Federal farm loan act. Washington, Government printing office, 1920. 14p. (Circular no. 10).

Walton, Seymour. Farm loans. *Journal of accountancy,* Sept. 1916, p. 222-4.

AGRICULTURE—CREDIT—*(Continued)*

WALTON, SEYMOUR. Federal land banks. *Journal of accountancy,* Sept. 1916, p. 224-8.

UNITED STATES. TREASURY DEPARTMENT. Federal land bank, general report. 6 forms.

Inventories

ALLRED, C. E. Farm business inventory. Tennessee university, College of agriculture, Division of extension, form 37, 1918, p. 1-31.

ENGBERB, R. C. Annual farm inventory. *Successful farmer,* Jan. 1920, p. 5.

FARM inventories. *Ohio farmer,* Feb. 14, 1920, p. 255.

LUTTS, F. M. What have you got? *Ohio farmer,* Sept. 14, 1918, p. 239.

PEACOCK, W. M. Value of inventories on rented farms. *Rural New York,* Dec. 29, 1917, p. 1462.

PHILLIPS, T. D. Farm inventory. *Ohio farmer,* Jan. 27, 1917, p. 107

WILLIAMS, H F. Farm inventory. Nebraska agricultural extension bulletin, 41:1-10, 1917.

Reports

UNITED STATES. SECRETARY OF AGRICULTURE. Annual report. Washington, Government printing office.

UNITED STATES. Industrial commissions. Reports. v.10, 11. Washington, Government printing office, 1900-1901.

Societies

AUDITING association formed at Aberdeen, S. D. *Cooperative manager and farmer,* Feb. 1917, p. 60.

FARM bookkeeping circle suggested. *Hoard's diary,* Jan. 4, 1918, p. 842.

NORTH DAKOTA COOPERATIVE AUDITING CIRCLE. By-laws. *Cooperative manager and farmer,* July 1917, p. 32-4.

Statistics

UNITED STATES. DEPARTMENT OF AGRICULTURE. Yearbook. Washington, Government printing office.

UNITED STATES. DEPARTMENT OF COMMERCE. Butter, cheese and condensed milk. Washington, Government printing office, 1917.

Valuation

REEP, S. N. Factors of farm appraisal. *Hoard's dairyman,* June 28, 1918, p. 958.

WYLLIE, J. Farm valuations for bookkeeping purposes. *Journal board of agriculture,* March 1916, p. 1215-28.

AGRICULTURE accounts (including income tax as relating to agriculture, Meats, T. W. 1911.

AHLBERG, T. J.

Accounting for retail shoe stores. *Journal of accountancy,* Aug. 1920, p. 97-105.

AHRENS, C. R., R. D. LONG and A. G. SHAVER

Signal and supply department. *Railway review,* July 24, 1915, p. 120-4.

AHSUIOLH, N. H.

Piece work and bonus systems in the boiler shop. *Railway age* (Mech. ed.), May 1915, p. 240-2.

AIDS for merchant mechanics in office work. *Metal work,* April 14, 1916, p. 380-1, 520.

AIDS in estimating concrete costs. *Coal age,* March 10, 1917, p,. 422.

AIDS to brass foundry management. *Foundry,* April 1913, p. 162-3.

AIKEN, ALEXANDER

Economic position of the Transvaal. *South African accountant's journal,* v.1, p. 50.

Note issues and currency. *South African accountant,* Sept. 1918, p. 196-9.

Notes on the audit of a gold mining company's accounts. *South African accountants' Journal,* v.2. p. 35.

AIKENS, D.

System of bookkeeping suitable for the farmer. *Journal of the department of agriculture,* South Australia, Dec. 1917, p. 431-6.

AINSLEY, T. L.

How to keep ship's accounts and to calculate exchange at foreign ports. 1897.

AINSWORTH, J. C.

Accounting for all road expenditures and need of authority to enforce. *Commonwealth review,* Jan. 1917, v. 2, p. 299-403.

AIR, A. W.

Remarks on railway records. *Accountant,* Jan. 13, 1912, p. 53-62.

AIREY, F. S.

Land values (finance (1909-10) act, 1910). *Incorporated accountants' journal,* 1910-11, p. 45.

AIRPLANES.

See Aeroplanes.

AITCHISON, C. B.

Compensatory scale of rates. *Railway review,* Oct. 25, 1919, p. 602-3.

AITCHISON, CRAIGIE M.

Auditing of public accounts. *Accountant,* May 29, 1909, p. 776-84.

AITKEN, HENRY

Ranking of secure creditors. *Accountants' magazine,* April 1910, p. 214-24.

ALABAMA. RAILROAD COMMISSION

Book of instructions for the guidance of carriers in making annual reports to the railroad commission of the state of Alabama. Washington, 1889. 27p.

Classification of operating expenses as prescribed by the Railroad commission. Washington, 1889. 27p.

ALABAMA STATE BOARD OF ACCOUNTANCY

Rules and regulations, adopted May 26, 1919. 11p.

ALABAMA accountants organize. *Journal of accountancy,* June, Sept. 1911, p. 154, 381.

ALABAMA C. P. A. law. *Journal of accountancy,* Oct. 1919, p. 3179.

ALABAMA society of certified public accountants. *Journal of accountancy,* Nov. 1919, p. 399.

ALABAMA state association of public accountants. *Journal of accountancy,* July 1912, April 1913, p. 57, 310.

ALBAN, FREDERICK JOHN

Income tax. *Incorporated accountants' journal,* April 1913. p. 168-77.

Income tax as affecting local authorities. *Accountant,* July 6, 13, 1912, p. 19-30, 51-61. *Incorporated accountants' journal,* April,

ALBAN, FREDERICK JOHN—*(Continued)*
July, Aug. 1912, April 1913, p. 189-90, 269-76, 298-303, 168-77.
Preparation for examinations. *Accountant,* March 30, April 6, 13, 1912, p. 510-20, 549-58, 586-9.
Some phases of municipal accountancy. *Accountant,* April 24, 1909, p. 571-80.
Some points on municipal revenue accounts, capital accounts and balance sheets. *Accountant,* Sept. 3, 1910, p. 309-15. *Incorporated accountants journal,* 1909-10, p. 241.
Waterwork department. (In Bateson, William, ed. *Pitman's municipal office organisation and management.* p. 421-35).

ALBERD, C. E.
Farm business inventory. *Tennessee agricultural extension form,* 1918, p. 1-3.

ALBERGER, W. R.
Reduction in power cost affected by the use of coasting recorders. *Electric railway journal,* Sept. 18, 1915, p. 520-1.

ALBERTSON, R. B.
Washington utility commission overruled. *American municipalities,* July 1913, p. 106-8.

ALCOHOL
M'Intosh, John Geddes. Industrial alcohol, the production, and the use of alcohol for industrial purposes and for use as an illuminant and as a source of motive power. London, Scott, Greenwood & son, 1907. 252p.

Stockkeeping
Fleischer, O. H. Always ready for the revenue officers' inspection. *Business man's magazine,* Nov. 1907, p. 58-9.

ALCORN, EDGAR G.
About bookkeeping in banks. *Business man's magazine,* April-Aug. 1907, p. 85-92, 77-82, 63-8, 75-80, 53-61.
Alcorn system of modern bank bookkeeping and accounting. 3v. Columbus. American text book co. 1918. 132+92+48p.
Average book. *Bankers magazine,* Nov. 1912, p. 519-22.
Balancing pass-books. *Bankers magazine,* Dec. 1912, p. 669-77.
Bookkeeping in building and loan associations. *Business man's magazine,* Sept. 1910, p. 272-8.
Building and loan associations; their organization, management and methods. *Business man's magazine,* Aug. 1910, p. 181-88.
Different methods of keeping the certificates of deposit account. *Bankers magazine,* Jan. 1911, p. 45-8.
Duties and liabilities of bank directors; including instruction with regard to directors' meetings, the discount committee, the auditing committee, official bank reports and indemnity bonds. Ed. 3, revised. Indianapolis, United States bank note co. c1915. 167p.
Five books in one. *Bankers magazine,* April 1910, p. 573-6.
How some banks keep a record of the liability of their customers. *Business man's magazine,* Jan. 1912, p. 86-8.
How to handle coupon notes. *Business man's magazine,* April 1912, p. 320.
Keeping a record of open and closed accounts. *Bankers magazine,* Dec. 1910, p. 809-13.
Opening a new ledger. *Bankers magazine,* Dec. 1911, p. 711-16.
Value of the liability ledger. *Bankers magazine,* Jan. 1913, p. 11-5.

ALDCROFT, W. H.
Evolution of a life assurance fund. *Accountant,* Jan. 23, 1897, p. 109-16.

ALDERSON, G. F.
Comparison of horse and motor-truck hauling in Pennsylvania. *Engineering news,* Feb. 15, 1917, 283-4.

ALDERSON, M. W.
Keeping account of supplies. *Mining and scientific press,* 1907, v.95, p. 274, 340.

ALDRICH currency reform system analysed. New York, Fourth National bank, 1911.

ALDRIDGE, B. H. MOORING
Easy method of keeping rent and interest accounts. London, 1899.

ALEXANDER, A. G.
Costs with fewest clerks. *System,* May 1915, p. 543-6.

ALEXANDER, CHARLES B.
Need for a budget system in the United States. *Annals of the American academy of political and social science,* July 1918, p. 144-8.

ALEXANDER, G. G.
Law of agency. *Incorporated accountants' journal,* 1891-2, p. 69.

ALEXANDER, GEORGE
"Simplex" system of hotel book keeping. London, 1895.

ALEXANDER, H.
Uniform accounts. *Railway age,* June 5, 1879, p. 268, 273-4.

ALEXANDER, J. H.
New method of keeping accounts. *Bankers magazine,* v.15, p. 337.

ALEXANDER, JOHN S.
New international decimal money system. *Accountant,* Dec. 2, 9, 1916, p. 524-9, 550-5.

ALEXANDER, M. W.
Employee representation in industrial plants. *Electrical world,* Jan. 17, 1920, p. 121-2.
Practical experience with profit sharing in industrial establishments. *Iron age,* July 22, 1920, p. 205.

ALEXANDER, WILLIAM
Interesting facts about annuities. *American magazine,* Feb. 1919, p. 130-2.

ALEXANDER, HAMILTON INSTITUTE.
On actual manufacturing costs. New York. Alexander Hamilton institute, c1912, 18p.

ALGEBRA
Milne, William J. High school algebra. New York, American book company. c1906. 391p.
Sprague, Charles E. Algebra of accounts. *The Office,* May, July, Aug. 1889, p. 91-2. 122-3, 144-5.

ALL about bookkeeping. London, Ward, Lock & co. 1877-78.

ALL San Francisco's consumers on meter basis. *Municipal journal,* Sept. 28, 1918, p. 253.

ALLAN, A., and W. HARDIE
Manual of bookkeeping by double entry. Ed. 2. Edinburgh, 1893.

ALLAN, A. S.
Card system of time recording and its application to cost taking in the boot and shoe industries. *Accountant,* 1903, p. 294, 417.

ALLAN, JOHN
Income tax law and practice. *Accountants' magazine,* March 1905, p. 153-71.
Income tax with special reference to recent legislation. *Accountants' magazine,* Aug. 1913, p. 476-502.

ALLCOCK, HARRY
British decimal coinage. *Accountant,* Jan. 18, 1919, p. 49-50.
Decimal system of coinage weights and measures. *Accountant,* July 7, 14, 1917, p. 15-20, 30-7.
Few notes on the payment out of borrowed money of wages of permanent workmen. *Accountant,* July 27, 1907, p. 123-5.
Local taxation and municipal accounts. *Accountant,* Oct. 3, 1908, p. 402-49.
Municipal accounts. London, Gee & co. 1903. 190p. (Accountants' library, v. 21).
Municipal insurance. *Accountant,* Aug. 2, 1902, p. 765-7.
Municipal revenues &c., and their control. *Accountant,* Sept. 10, 1898, p. 864-6.
National and local finance. *Accountant,* Nov. 29, Dec. 13, 1913, p. 783-8, 857-8. *Incorporated Accountant's Journal,* Dec. 1913, p. 82-5.
Notes on sinking funds for redemption of loans. *Accountant,* Sept. 14, 1901, p. 987-8.
Problems of municipal finance. *Accountant,* Dec. 3, 1910, p. 787-8.

ALLCOCK, JOHN
Address. *Accountant,* July 19, 1913, p. 90-6.
Allowance for depreciation: Cardiff tramways and electric light. *Accountant,* Dec. 28, 1907, Jan. 11, 1908, p. 787-9, 64-5. *Incorporated accountants' journal,* 1907-8, p. 80.
Depreciation of Cardiff electric tramway and lighting undertakings. *Electric railway review,* Jan. 4, 1908, p. 16.
Depreciation of tramway and electrical plant; report of Cardiff accounts. *Incorporated accountants' journal,* 1907-8, p. 80.
Housing finance. *Incorporated accountants' journal,* Jan. 1920, p. 79-82.
Local taxation and municipal accounts. *Accountant,* Oct. 3, 1908, p. 402-49. *Incorporated accountants journal,* 1908-9, p. 17.
Municipal insurance. *Incorporated accountants journal,* 1901-2, p. 240.
Municipal accounts. London, Gee & co. 1903. 190p. (Accountant's library, v.21).
Municipal revenues &c., and their control. *Accountant,* Sept. 10, 1898, p. 864-6.
Notes on sinking funds for redemption of loans. *Accountant,* Sept. 14, 1901, p. 987-8.
Sinking funds for redemption of loans. *Incorporated accountants journal,* 1900-1, p. 228.
Taxation and local rating. *Incorporated accountants' journal,* 1910-11, p. 120.
Track depreciation at Cardiff. *Tramway and railway world,* Jan. 6, 1910, p. 30.

ALLEN, A. S.
Card system of time recording and its application to cost taking in the boot and shoe industries. *Accountant,* Feb. 28, March 28, 1902, p. 294-302, 417-9.

ALLEN, A. W.
Cost of automobile transportation for the highway engineer. *Engineering and contracting,* Oct. 4, 1916, p. 304.
Statement of working costs. *Mining and scientific press,* 1912, v. 104, p. 204-6.

ALLEN, ALBERT F.
Operating statistics for street railways. *Journal of accountancy,* July 1907, p. 211-15.

ALLEN, ALEXANDER.
See Hardie, William, joint author

ALLEN, ASHLEY T.
Vouchers and voucher records. *New York accountants' and bookkeepers' journal,* Sept. 1903, p. 109-15.

ALLEN, C. A.
Methods and economics in mining. *American institute of mining engineers, Bulletin,* Aug. 1914, p. 2137-45, 2154-63.

ALLEN, C. F., AND OTHERS
Discussion of cost-plus and other forms of contracts. *Journal of the Boston society of civil engineers,* Jan. 1920, p. 1-39.

ALLEN, CLARENCE E.
Notes on publishers' bookkeeping. *Accountant,* Feb. 6, 1897, p. 156-61.
Publishers' accounts; including a consideration of copyright and the valuation of literary property. London, Gee & co. 1897. 127p.

ALLEN, CLIFFORD VAN
Full cost of freight movement. *Railway age gazette,* Jan. 26, 1912, p. 141.

ALLEN, DANIEL A.
Perpetual inventory for the wholesale hardware business. *Business man's magazine,* June 1908, p. 508-9.
Pricing material returned for credit. *Business man's magazine,* Dec. 1909, p. 574-6.
Simplifying the sales ledger. *Business man's magazine,* Sept. Oct. 1910, p. 265-8, 379-83.
System for making customers' statements posting and footing the ledger by the same operation. *Business man's magazine,* Oct. 1908, p. 321-23.

ALLEN, F. A.
Necessity for and method of providing depreciation in the case of (1) a manufacturing company (2) a trading company. *Accountant,* May 14, 1910, p. 694-7.

ALLEN, FRANKLIN
Professional ethics. *American institute of accountants, Yearbook,* 1907. p. 149-51. *Journal of accountancy,* Dec. 1907, p. 97-9.

ALLEN, FREDERICK JAMES
Shoe industry. Boston, Vocation bureau of Boston, c1916. 327p.

ALLEN, G. T. H.
Costing in relation to selling. *Accountant,* July 19, 1919, p. 58-61.

ALLEN, GEORGE
Science of accounts made clear and simple. Raleigh, N. C., George Allen, 1909.
——— Same. High school ed. Raleigh, N. C., George Allen, 1909. 136p.

ALLEN, GEORGE E.

Balance sheet system of accounting. *Commerce, accounts and finance,* Aug. Sept. Nov. Dec. 1901, Feb. June 1902, p. 3-4, 3-4, 12-3, 11-4, 9-10, 7.

ALLEN, JOHN

Income tax law and practice. *Accountants' magazine,* March 1905, p. 153-71.

ALLEN JOHN E.

Co-operative accounts. *Accountant,* Sept. 26, 1891, p. 680-7.
Income tax scale. *Accountant,* Jan. 8, 1918, p. 412-3.

ALLEN, LESLIE H.

Accounts for material on engineering construction. *Journal of accountancy,* May 1915, p. 352-8.
Comparative cost of concrete and mill buildings. *Concrete,* Oct. 1916, p. 135-6.
Cost accounting and its importance on construction work. *Contract record,* Sept. 23, 1914.
Cost accounting for the contractor. *Journal of accountancy,* March 1917, p. 177-84. Condensed. *Engineering news-record,* Feb. 17, 1917, p. 270-1. *Engineering and contracting,* Feb. 21, 1917, 192-3. Abstract. *Concrete,* March 1917, p. 97-8.
Cost accounting on construction work—detailed description of an efficient system. *Engineering and contracting,* April 8, 22, 1914, v. 41, p. 404-10, 403-465.
Cost accounting on construction work, with a description of the system used by the Aberthaw construction company. *Journal of the Boston Society of civil engineers,* March 1914, p. 133-77. Discussion, Oct. 1914, p. 455-79.
Discussion of the quantity system of estimating. *Engineering and contracting,* June 10, 1914, p. 658-62.
Methods of selling houses to employees. *Industrial management.* Dec. 1, 1920, p. 427-32.
Payroll distribution on construction work. *Journal of accountancy,* July 1914, p. 38-46.

ALLEN, R. C.

Valuation of mines for taxation purposes. *Michigan state conference on taxation, Proceedings,* 1915, p. 14-24.

ALLEN, R. H.

Operating costs at a small Mexican mine. *Engineering and mining journal,* June 26, 1915, p. 1122-4.

ALLEN, SIDNEY E.

Accounts of local authorities. London, Gee & co. 60p.
Diagrammatic presentment of the accounts of local authorities. London, Gee & co. 1912. 60p.
Notes on local and imperial taxation. *Accountant,* Sept. 4, 1920, p. 238-42.

ALLEN, W. H.

See Ralph, G. G., joint author.

ALLEN, WALTER S.

Accounts of grantees of municipal franchises. *National municipal league, Proceedings,* 1899, p. 162-68.

ALLEN, WILLIAM H.

Better business methods for cities. *American review of reviews,* Feb. 1908, p. 195-200.
Budget as an instrument of financial control. *Government accountant,* 1908, v. 2, p. 192-200.
Comparison of recent bids for various types of paving in the New York navy yard. *Engineering news-record,* March 27, 1913, p. 629-30.
How to overtake the grafter by municipal accounting. *National municipal league, Proceedings,* 1910, p. 497-512.
Ready helps in state budget making. *National tax association bulletin,* May 1916, p. 91-3.
Wanted—one thousand efficient accountants for municipal research. *Journal of accountancy,* July 1908, p. 187-93.

ALLES, A. A.

Have you a danger line in your cost estimates. *Automotive industries,* Nov. 27, 1919, p. 1067-9.

ALLING, N. D.

Chief clerk. *Journal of the American bankers association,* June 1912, p. 775-81.

ALLINGHAM, HENRY W.

Determination of standards in scientific management. *Accountant,* April 26, 1919, p. 345-52. *Australasian accountant and secretary,* Feb. 1920, p. 62-5.

ALLISON, J.

Farmers' income tax. *Accountant,* April 14, May 3, 17, 24, 1919, p. 325-6, 369-70, 421-3, 440-1.
Multiple shop accounts. *Accountant,* Aug. 5, 1911, p. 185-95.

ALLISON, JAMES E.

Criticism of theoretical depreciation. *Utilities magazine,* Jan. 1916, p. 124-6.
Depreciation of public service properties. *Annals of the American academy of political and social science,* May, 1914, p. 198-213.
Ethical and economic elements in public service valuation. *Quarterly journal of economics,* Nov. 1912, p. 998.
Rate of return. *Stone and Webster public service journal, Boston,* 1915, v. 16, p. 277-89.
Should public service properties be depreciated to obtain fair value in rate or regulation cases? St. Louis, 1912, 50p. *Stone and Webster public service journal,* Feb. 1913.
Theoretical depreciation. *Telephone engineer,* Nov. 1917.
Valuation of the physical property of a telephone plant. *Telephony,* Dec. 27, 1913.

ALLISON, LEROY W.

Accounting at Pasadena plant. *Power,* Sept. 19, 1916, p. 413-4.
Accounting system for both large and small water works properties. *Engineering and contracting,* Jan. 14, 1914, p. 77-80.
• Accounting system for electric companies. *Power,* Nov. 11, 1913, p. 697-700.
Complete accounting system for both large and small water works properties. *Engineering and contracting,* Jan. 14, 1914, v. 41, p. 77-80.
Cost of electric dredging for land reclamation, San Diego, California. *Engineering and contracting,* August 4, 1915, p. 95-6.
Standard meter rates. *Power,* Feb. 3-17, 1920, p. 183-4, 218-9.

ALLOCATING expenses; railways have a hard task in the apportionment of operating costs between passenger and freight service—a theoretical road to revenue increase. *Annalist,* Sept. 14, 1914, p. 246-7.

ALLOCATION of timber materials from the view point of costing. *Accountant,* Aug. 17, 1918, p. 82-3.

ALLOWANCE for depreciation on gas plant for income tax purposes. *Accountant,* Dec. 4, 1909, p. 700-2, 673-6.

ALLOWANCE for maintenance to cover depreciation. *Light railway and tramway journal* (London), July 2, 1909, p. 29.

ALLOWANCE for obsolescence upheld in franchise tax case. *Electric railway journal,* Dec. 10, 1910, p. 1154.

ALLOWANCES.

See Returned purchases, allowances; etc.

ALLOWANCES for depreciation in the pipe system of the Los Angeles waterworks. *Engineering news,* May 4, 1899, p. 283.

ALLOWANCES for depreciation of plant and machinery. *Accountant,* Nov. 13, 1909, p. 604-5.

ALLOWANCES to short lines of railroads serving industries. *Railway reviews,* Nov. 14, 1914, p. 602-3.

ALLPORT, J. H.

See Garnsey, C., joint author.

ALLRED, C. E.

Farm business inventory. *Tennessee agriculture extension,* form 317, 1918, p. 1-31.

This book helps the farmer keep books. *Banker-farmer,* Dec. 1917, p. 10.

ALMANACS

WHITAKER, JOSEPH. Almanack for the year of our Lord 1918; containing an account of the astronomical and other phenomena; a vast amount of information respecting the government finances, population, commerce and general statistics of the various nations of the world with special reference to the British empire. 12 Warwick Lane, London, E. C. 973p.

WORLD almanac and encyclopedia; annual. New York, Press publishing co.

ALMERT, HAROLD

Need of valuation of public utility company properties. *Public service,* Sept. 1913, p. 83.

ALPHABET values in the ledger. Cooper, John Alexander.

ALPHABETICAL double entry bookkeeping. Broadbridge, 1883.

ALPHABETICAL list of representative items chargeable to operating expenses of carriers by water. United States. Interstate commerce commission. 1917.

ALT, H. L.

School power plant. *Brickbuilder,* April 1916, p. 99-101.

ALVORD, C.

Premium plan of paying for labor. *Journal of Worcester polytechnic institute,* Jan. 1911, p. 75-86.

ALVORD, JOHN W.

Appellate court of the state of New York and the question of allowances for paving over mains in valuation work. *Journal of the American waterworks association,* Sept. 1915, p. 465-92. Abstract. Discussion of the question of allowances for paving over mains in valuation work. *Engineering and contracting,* June 16, 1915, p. 532.

Depreciation. *Engineering record,* June 15, 1912, p. 670.

Depreciation. *American water works association, Proceedings,* 1903, p. 473, 523.

Depreciation of public utility properties as affecting their valuation and fair return. *American society civil engineers, Proceedings,* Nov. 1913, p. 2045-60. *American society of civil engineers, Transactions,* Dec. 1914, p. 788.

Depreciation of waterworks. *Fire and water engineering,* Aug. 22, Sept. 12, 1903, p. 104, 144. *American waterworks association, Proceedings,* 1903, p. 473, 523.

Financial questions in water works valuation. *Proceedings of the American waterworks association,* 1902, p. 142. Abstracts. *Engineering record,* July 12, 1902, p. 30. *Engineering news,* June 19, 1902, p. 509.

Fixing utility valuations. *Public service,* Oct. 1918.

Fundamental principles of public utility valuation. *American society of civil engineers, Transactions,* 1916, p. 117. *Proceedings of the American society of civil engineers,* Oct. 1914, p. 2389-2435.

Influence of recent events on utility valuation procedure. *Municipal engineering,* Dec. 1918, p. 210-2.

Necessary elements for water works valuation. *Engineering news,* Mar. 10, 1910, p. 286.

Notes on going value and methods for its computation. *Proceedings of the American water works association,* 1909, p. 184. Abstract. *Engineering and contracting,* Aug. 4, 1909, p. 95.

Principles of valuation. *Engineering record,* Dec. 19, 1914, p. 677.

See also Metcalf, Leonard, joint author.

ALVORD, JOHN W. and J. H. GANDOLPO.

Papers on public utility valuation: abstracts. *Electric railway journal,* Dec. 5, 1914, p. 1252.

ALWYN-SCHMIDT, L. W.

Better results by better management: some financial problems of the sugar factory. *Sugar magazine,* Sept. 1919.

Economics of the power house. *Power plant engineering,* Dec. 1, 1918, p. 949-52.

Effects of increased use upon machine depreciation. *Industrial management,* April 1920, p. 313-4.

Effect of machine depreciation upon cost of dye making. *Color trade journal,* April 1920, p. 103-6.

Equipment and maintenance factors in cost accounting during transition period. *American machinist,* Feb. 20, 1919, p. 366-8.

Getting more out of existing plant. *American gas engineering journal,* March 6, 1920, p. 177-9.

Problem of overhead in the repair shop. *Machinery,* Aug. 1920, p. 1161-2.

Rapid rise in the cost of equipment—an important factor in rubber production cost accounting. *India rubber world,* March 1920, p. 342-4.

AMALGAMATION of American societies of accountants. *Accountant,* June 17, 1899, p. 660.

AMALGAMATIONS.

See Consolidations; Trusts.

AMBERG, E. J.
Overhead, contact systems, construction and costs. *Proceedings of the American institute of electrical engineers,* June 1915, p. 1255-66. Abstract. *Electric railway journal,* July 10, 1915, p. 56.

AMBROSE, JOHN EDWARD
Competent mine management and contracts. *Coal age,* Aug. 19, 1916, p. 294-5.

AMEND the corporation tax law. *Journal of accountancy,* Sept. 1909, June 1911, p. 362-4, 129-130.

AMENDMENT of Louisiana law. *Journal of accountancy,* Sept. 1912, p. 217-8.

AMENDMENT of Ohio non-par value law. *Corporation journal,* May 1920, p. 187.

AMENDMENT of the West Virginia corporation law so as to permit the issuance of non-par-value stock. *Corporation journal,* May 1920, p. 187.

AMENDMENT of the companies acts. *Incorporated accountants' journal,* 1904-5, 1905-6, 1906-7, p. 123, 254, 89, 96.

AMENDMENTS to the non-par value law of Maryland. *Corporation journal,* May 1920, p. 187.

AMERICAN ACADEMY OF POLITICAL AND SOCIAL SCIENCE
Efficiency in city government. Philadelphia, 1912.
Government regulation of water transportation. Philadelphia, American academy of political and social science, 1914, 306p. (Annals v. 55, whole no. 144).

AMERICA as a field for investment. *Accountant,* July 23, 1892, p. 585-7.

AMERICAN accountant. Sandy, W. C. 1894.

AMERICAN accountants aiding Mexican government. *Journal of accountancy,* Aug. 1917, p. 159.

AMERICAN accountants' examinations. *Accountant,* May 1, 1909, p. 588-90. *Journal of accountancy,* June 1909, p. 132-4.

AMERICAN accountants manual, v. 1. Broaker, Frank. c1897.

AMERICAN association and business education. *Journal of accountancy,* Dec. 1906, p. 139-41.

AMERICAN association committee on the business and acounting methods of the United States government. *Journal of accountancy,* June 1906, p. 142-6.

AMERICAN ASSOCIATION OF PARK SUPERINTENDENTS.
Proceedings, 1916.

AMERICAN ASSOCIATION OF PUBLIC ACCOUNTANTS.
See American institute of accountants.

AMERICAN association of public accountants. *Accountant,* Feb. 12, 1898, p. 193-4.

AMERICAN association of public accountants. *Journal of accountancy,* Nov. 1905, Feb. March, Aug. Oct. Nov. 1906, May, June, Oct.-Dec. 1907, March, May, July, Sept. Nov. Dec., 1908, May, Sept. Nov. Dec. 1909, July-Dec. 1910, May, Aug. Nov. 1911, May, Sept. Oct. Dec 1912, May, Aug.-Oct. 1913, May, Aug.-Oct. 1914, May, July, Sept. Oct. 1915, May. Aug.-Oct. 1916 v. 1, p. 76-98, 324, 424-45; v. 2, p. 300, 471-3; v. 3, p. 38, 58-100; v. 4, p. 46-7, 65-84, 165, 469-70, 477-9; v. 5, p. 57-8, 62-5, 134-6, 137-88, 403-4; v. 6, 62-5, 208-10, 357; v. 7, p. 51-2, 49-51, 140-84; v. 8, p. 45-6, 368-72; v. 9, p. 48-50, 138-40; v. 10, p. 213-4, 373-4, 371-2, 377-9, 465-6; v. 11, p. 63-4, 137-8, 141-2; v. 12, p. 64-7, 295, 297-8, 545-6; v. 13, p. 365-9; v. 14, p. 235-7, 334-40; v. 15 p. 365-9; v. 16, p. 120-1, 253, 306-7, 312-8; v. 17, p. 375-7; v. 18, p. 124-5, 211-3, 298-9, 300-4; v. 19, p. 365-8; v. 20, p. 38-9, 221-3, 297-8, 302-6; v. 21, p. 369-73; v. 22, p. 126-7, 240, 296-302.

AMERICAN association of public accountants' conference. *Accountant,* Jan. 9-23, 1909, p. 39-41, 71-4, 109-12.

AMERICAN association of public accountants golf club. *Journal of accountancy,* Dec. 1906, p. 177.

AMERICAN association of public accountants. movement to secure an executive officer. *Journal of accountancy,* Sept. 1910, p. 377-9.

AMERICAN association of public accountants report of the committee upon standard schedules for uniform reports on municipal industries and public service companies. *Accountant,* Feb. 9, 1907, p. 186-97.

AMERICAN ASSOCIATION OF UNIVERSITY INSTRUCTORS IN ACCOUNTING.
Papers and proceedings, annual. 1916 to date.

AMERICAN association of university instructors in accounting. *Journal of accountancy,* Feb. 1918, Dec. 1920, p. 155-6, 478.

AMERICAN association yearbook. *Journal of accountancy,* Jan. 1910, p. 223.

AMERICAN association's year. Sterrett, J. E.

AMERICAN AUDIT COMPANY, NEW YORK
Recommendations relative to a general system of accounts for the city of Baltimore. (Baltimore, 1909). 48p.
Explanation of the numerical system of the American bankers' association. Chicago, Continental and commercial national bank, 1911.

AMERICAN audit note book. Cooley, M. L. 1909.

AMERICAN BANKERS' ASSOCIATION
Forms for national and state banks. New York. American bankers association, 1913. 124 numbers.
Forms for saving banks and savings departments in commercial banks and trust companies. New York, American bankers association, 1914, 118 numbers.
Trust company section. Forms for trust companies, selected by a committee of the Trust company section, American bankers association, from forms in use by trust companies of the United States. New York, Anthony Stumpf publishing company, 1910. 140p.

AMERICAN bookkeeping series. Goodyear, L. E. c1913.

AMERICAN business and accounting encyclopaedia, a standard reference book for accountants and business men, profusely illustrated with hundreds of special forms and tables, compiled by E. H. Beach and W. W. Thorne; commercial law department by A. E. Rouech. Ed. 7. Detroit, The Bookkeeper publishing company, c1901. 1090p.

AMERICAN business law. Sullivan, J. J. 1917.

AMERICAN business manual. Montgomery, R. H. 1911.

AMERICAN CAN COMPANY.

Plan of cost accounting for general line factories. New York, 1909. 100p. (Private publication.)

AMERICAN company law: the Federal corporation bill. *Accountant,* April 9, 1910, p. 486-90.

AMERICAN company shop committee plans. Bureau of industrial research. 1919.

AMERICAN CO-OPERATIVE CONVENTION.

How to start a cooperative wholesale, being the report of the committee on wholesale of the second American co-operative convention. New York, The co-operative league of America, 1920. 8p.

AMERICAN corporations. Sullivan, J. J. 1916.

AMERICAN dictionary of the English language. Lyons, Daniel. 1908.

AMERICAN ECONOMIC ASSOCIATION

Accountancy: discussion. *American economic association, Papers and discussions.* April 1911, p. 145-53.

Accounting: round table discussion. *American economic association, Papers and discussions,* April 1909, p. 59-104.

Forms of municipal records. *American economic association, Proceedings,* 1910. Milwaukee, 1910, p. 290-320.

Committee on uniform municipal accounts and statistics. Report. *American economic association, Papers and proceedings.* 1900, p. 254-62. Appendix I-II, p. 263-80. Condensed. *Engineering news,* June 14, July 5, 1900.

Committee on uniform municipal accounts and statistics. Report. *American economic association. Papers and proceedings,* 1901, p. 351-53. Discussion, p. 354-68.

AMERICAN economic association. *Journal of accountancy,* Jan. 1909, p. 240-1.

AMERICAN economic association discussion on valuations and rate making. *Electric railway journal* Jan. 3, 1914, p. 36-8.

AMERICAN economic review. Ithaca, N. Y. American economic associations.

AMERICAN electric railway accountants and engineering associations: report of joint committees on engineering accounting. *Electric railway journal,* Oct. 17, 1913, p. 852.

AMERICAN ELECTRIC RAILWAY ACCOUNTANTS' ASSOCIATION

Bibliography on valuation of public utilities to December 23rd, 1915. New York, American electric railway association. 61+72p.

Maintenance and depreciation; abstracts from commissions' decisions and engineers' reports, including a bibliography. New York. American electric railway association, Dec. 1, 1919. 43p.

Proceedings. 8 W. 40th Street, New York, American electric railway association.

[Proceedings and abstracts of addresses given at the mid-year meeting at Chicago, Feb. 4, 1916.] *Electric railway journal,* Feb. 5, 1916, p. 244-72. Principles of railway valuation by N. T. Guernsey; rate of return on railway capital by J. D. Mortimer; Uncertainty of utility valuation by T. S. Williams: Elements of utility valuation, by T. S. Williams; Elements of utility valuation, by George Weston; What constitutes utility value by P. J. Kealy.

Report of the committee on cost of passenger transportation service. *American electric railway association, Proceedings,* 1914, p. 207-12.

Report of the committee on fares and transfers. *American electric railway transportation and traffic association, Proceedings,* 1914, p. 367-94. *Electric railway journal,* Oct. 16, 1913, p. 811.

Report of the committee on interline accounting. *American electric railway association, Proceedings,* 1909, 1911, 1913, p. 52-8, 69-89, 221-44.

Report of the joint committee on engineering accounting. In its *Proceedings,* 1912, p. 141-89, 160-80.

Report of the joint committee on express and freight accounting. (In its *Proceedings,* 1911, p. 140-52.

——— **Bureau of Information**

Collection of articles on motor bus and jitney costs. American electric railway association, 1919. 31p.

Comparison of the capitalization of electric railways with their valuation as determined by public service commissions or other public authority. New York, American electric railway association, Dec. 3, 1919, 9p.

Effect of increased rates of fare on operating revenue, on passengers carried and on number of transfers issued. New York, American electric railway association, Jan. 28, 1920, Feb. 16, 1920. 83p.

Elements that enter into the determination of the fair value of a public utility: extracts from decisions of courts and public service commissions. American electric railway association, Feb. 10, 1919, 28p.

Methods of interurban companies in increasing fares. New York, American electric railway association, Jan. 1, 1920. 29p.

Rate of return and valuation on electric railways based on decisions of public utility commissions. New York. American electric railway association, Dec. 1, 1919. 21p.

AMERICAN electric railway accountants' association annual meeting October 9-12. *Electric railway journal,* Oct. 14, 1916, p. 814-20.

AMERICAN electric railway accountants' association, convention, Atlantic city, Oct. 7-8. *Electric railway journal,* Oct. 11, 1919, sup. 85-6.

AMERICAN electric railway accountants' association; meeting at Atlantic city, Tuesday, October 14, 1913. *Electric railway journal,* Oct. 15, 1913, 761-3.

AMERICAN electric railway accounting association: papers at final session of Atlantic City convention. *Electric railway journal,* Oct. 18, 1913, p. 893-9.

AMERICAN electric railway accounting association; proceedings at Atlantic City convention, October 17. *Electric railway journal,* Oct. 18, 1913, p. 900-1.

AMERICAN electric railway accounting asciation; report of committee on education. *Electric railway journal,* Oct. 15, 1913, p. 769.

AMERICAN electric railway association; accountants' papers and proceedings. *Electric railway journal,* October 9, 1913, p. 736-44.

AMERICAN ELECTRIC RAILWAY TRANSPORTATION AND TRAFFIC ASSOCIATION.

Proceedings 1919, containing a complete report of the twelfth annual convention held at Young's million dollar pier, Atantic city, N. J., October 6, 7, 8 and 9, 1919. New York, American electric railway association, 1919. 238p.

Report of the commission on fares and transfers. (In its *Proceedings,* 1914, p. 367-94). *Electric railway journal,* Oct. 16, 1913, p. 811.

AMERICAN excess profits duty. *Accountant,* April 20, 1918, p. 309-10.

AMERICAN EXCHANGE NATIONAL BANK.

Acceptances; their importance as a means of increasing and simplifying domestic and foreign commerce. Ed. 2, revised. New York, Exchange national bank, 1918. 79p.

War tax law, 1917. New York, John H. Eggers co. 1917.

AMERICAN foundrymen's association committee recommends universal cost keeping system. *Foundry,* Nov. 1915, p. 451-4.

AMERICAN GAS INSTITUTE.

Report of committee on a uniform system of accounts for gas companies. New York, American gas institute, c1914. 128p.

AMERICAN HOME ECONOMICS ASSOCIATION

Report of the committee on uniform acocunting in institutions. *Journal of home economics,* 1912, p. 448-459.

Thrift by household and weekly cash record forms, 1916. Baltimore, American home economics association 1916.

AMERICAN INSTITUTE OF ACCOUNTANTS

American accountants golf and tennis club, 1906.

Bulletin, Dec. 15, 1916 to date.

Chicago association of commerce cordially invites Institute of public accountants of the United States to meet in the City of Chicago.

Definitions. 5 typewritten pages.

Examinations, June 1917. *American institute of accountants, yearbook,* 1917, p. 154-72. *Journal of accountancy,* July 1917, p. 1-20.

Examinations, Nov. 1917. *Journal of accountancy,* Dec. 1917, p. 413-23.

Examinations, May 1918. *Journal of accountancy,* Dec. 1920, p. 401-19.

Examinations, Nov. 1918. *Journal of accountancy,* Dec. 1918, p. 401-11.

Examinations, May 1919. *Journal of accountancy,* July 1919, p. 1-20.

Examinations, Nov. 1919. *Journal of accountancy,* Dec. 1919, p. 401-12.

Examinations, May 1920. *Journal of accountancy,* June 1920, p. 401-15.

Examinations, Nov. 1920. *Journal of accountancy,* Dec. 1920, p. 401-19.

Executive officer for the American association of public accountants; reprinted from the September number of the *Journal of accountancy,* 1910.

Library and bureau of information special bulletin, no. 1, January 1920 to date.

Library catalogue, January 1919. New York, American institute of accountants, c1919. 237p.

Memorandum on certain proposals for federal taxation legislation, July 19, 1917. 9p.

New York meeting, October 20, 1910, Hotel Astor—Father Knickerbocker invites William Penn to attend the meeting. 2p.

Nineteen nineteen annual meeting, Cincinnati, Ohio: clippings from newspapers.

Report by committee on by-laws and proposed amended constitution and by-laws, Sept. 1910.

Report of committee on accounting terminology. *American institute of accountants, Yearbook,* 1909, 1913, 1915, p. 159-91, 176-226, 160-2.

Report of committee on administration of endowment January 15, 1918. 3p.

Report of committee on education. *American institute of accountants, Yearbook,* 1913, 1914, 1915, 1916, 1917, 1919, p. 232-57, 191-21, 165-98, 73-95, 177-216, 106-8.

Report of committees. 1907.

Report of special committee on endowment. 12p.

Report of special committee on form of organization of association. Feb. 21, 1916.

Report of special committee on interest in relation to cost. *American institute of accountants, Yearbook,* 1918, p. 110-2.

Report of the committee on standard schedules for uniform reports upon municipal industries and public service corporations; annual meeting at Atlantic City, N. J., October 20-22, 1908. 15p. *Journal of accountancy,* May, Oct. 1909, p. 47-54, 455. *Accountant,* Feb. 9, 1907, p. 186-97.

Reports and exhibits at Columbus, Ohio, October 1906.

Rules of professional conduct including amendments and additions prepared by the committee on professional ethics and approved by the council prior to September 30, 1919. 2p.

Rules of professional conduct prepared by the committee on professional ethics and approved by the council April 9, 1917. 1p.

Special library planned for accountants. Library journal, Nov. 1917, p. 893.

Sung by the A. A. P. A. glee club at the banquet of the American association of public accountants at Annapolis, September 17, 1914.

Yearbook, 1905 to date.

AMERICAN institute of accountants. *Journal of accountancy,* Jan. May, Oct. Nov. 1917, May ,Oct. 1918, May, Oct 1919, May, Oct. 1920, p. 43, 374-8, 299-306, 411-2, 371-2, 296-303, 290-6, 368-71, 364-6, 273-86.

AMERICAN law relating to income and principal. Hawes, E. A. 1905.

AMERICAN LUMBERMAN.

Bookkeeping systems for a retail lumber business. Chicago, American lumberman, 1910-1911. 52p.

AMERICAN MALLEABLE CASTINGS ASSOCIATION.

Uniform cost accounting methods; by Robert E. Belt; adopted by the American malleable castings association, November 14, 1917. 22p.+forms.

AMERICAN manual for accountants. Eddis, W. C.

AMERICAN mine accounting. Charlton, W. H. 1913.

AMERICAN munitions 1917-1918. Crowell, Benedict. 1919.

AMERICAN national banking. Rowe, Harry N. 1895.

AMERICAN notions on depreciation. *Electrical review* (London), May 10, 1907, p. 757.

AMERICAN petroleum industry. Bacon, R. F. and W. A. Hamor. 1916.

AMERICAN railroad economics. Sakolski, Aaran Morton. 1913.

AMERICAN railway accounting. Adams, H. C. 1918.

AMERICAN railway accounting. London, 1897. 8p. *Statist (London)*, Feb. 13, 20, 1897. Editorial. *Railway age*, March 19, April 2, 9, 1897, p. 221-2, 272-3, 295.
Reply. *Railway age*, March 19, 1897, p. 226-7.

AMERICAN RAILWAY ASSOCIATION

Special committee on relations with Interstate commerce commission. Depreciation in steam railway accounting. *Electric railway journal*, Aug. 1908, p. 748-9.

AMERICAN RAILWAY, BRIDGE AND BUILDING ASSOCIATION

Cost of structures: report of committees. (In its *Proceedings of the 25th annual convention*, 1915, p. 181-205). Abstract. *Railway gazette*, Oct. 22, 1915, p. 760.

AMERICAN RAILWAY ENGINEERING AND MAINTENANCE OF WAY ASSOCIATION.

Manual of recommended practice for railway engineering and maintenance of way. Ed. of 1905. Chicago, 1905. 175p.

AMERICAN RAILWAY ENGINEERING ASSOCIATION

Manual of the American railway engineering association of 1915. Chicago, Ill., American engineering association, 1916. 680p.

Report of committee XI—on records and accounts. (In its *Proceedings of the 13th-18th annual conventions*, 1912-1918.) Also in its Bulletin.

Manual of recommended practice for railway engineering and maintenance of way, containing the definitions, specifications and principles of practice adopted and recommended. Chicago, American railway enneering and maintenance of way association, 1907. 291p.

AMERICAN railway problems in the light of European experience. Vrooman, Carl S. 1910.

AMERICAN SCHOOL OF CORRESPONDENCE

Cyclopedia of practical accounting. 4v. Chicago, American technical society, 1912.

Cyclopedia of commerce, accountancy, business administration. 10v. Chicago, American school of correspondence. 1910.

AMERICAN SOCIETY OF CIVIL ENGINEERS

Bibliography on valuation of public utilities to December 23, 1915. New York, American electric railway association, 1916.

AMERICAN society of civil engineers valuation report. *Electric railway journal*, Jan. 13, 1917, p. 72-5.

AMERICAN SOCIETY OF MECHANICAL ENGINEERS. Yearbook.

AMERICAN SOCIETY OF MUNICIPAL IMPROVEMENTS. COMMITTEE ON MUNICIPAL DATA.

Report. *American society of municipal improvements. Proceedings*, 1898, p. 188-206.

Report by Charles Carroll Brown. *American society of municipal improvements. Proceedings*, 1902.

Report of the special committee on uniformity in municipal accounting on national statistics. *American society of municipal improvement. Proceedings*, 1901, p. 35-9. appendix, A-H, p. 40-81.

AMERICAN standard bookkeeping. Curtis, C. C.

AMERICAN STREET AND INTERURBAN RAILWAY ACCOUNTANTS ASSOCIATION.

Report of the committee on standard classification of accounts and form of report. (In its *Proceedings*, 1908, p. 113-22, 1909, v. 2, p. 58-72.)

AMERICAN street railway investments; published annually by the publishers of the Electric railway journal. New York, McGraw-Hill book co.

AMERICAN system of bookkeeping adopted to the commerce of the United States and its domestic and foreign relations. Bennett, James.

AMERICAN system of practical book-keeping, Bennette, James.

AMERICAN system of practical bookkeeping, adapted to the commerce of India. Cooke, C. N. 1840.

AMERICAN TELEPHONE AND TELEGRAPH COMPANY, NEW YORK

Circular no. 6. New York, 1910.

Catalogue accounting library. v.1. New York, American telephone and telegraph co. 1914. 75p.

Comparative summary of laws relating to the regulation of telephone and telegraph companies by commissions in force November 1, 1913. Boston, 1914. 710p.

Standard telephone accounts; accounting circular no. 6. *Government accountant*, Oct.-Dec. 1910, Jan.-March 1911, p. 231-41, 286-300, 332-44, 400-6, 446-59, 501-7.

AMERICAN telephone gets many favorable decisions. *Wall street journal*, Jan. 27, 1917.

AMERICAN transportation question. Dunn, S. O. 1912.

AMERICAN transportation system. Rankin, G. A. 1909.

AMERICAN UNITARIAN ASSOCIATION.

Report on church finances and accounting. May 25, 1915. 41p.

AMERICAN WAREHOUSEMEN'S ASSOCIATION.

Proceedings: 1919.

AMERICAN WATER WORKS ASSOCIATION

Final report of committee on depreciation. *Journal of the American water works association*, Sept. 1917, p. 1-38.

Report of the commission on tabulation of water rates and other information of inter-

AMERICAN WATER WORKS ASSOCIATION —(Continued)
est to water companies. Baltimore, American water works association, 1914, 337p. Abstract. *Journal of the American waterworks association,* June 1914, p. 231-7.

AMERICAN water works association committee on depreciation; final report. *Journal of the American water works association,* sup. Sept. 1917, p. 1-38.

AMERICAN year book, 1914. New York, D. Appleton and co., 1915. 862p.

AMMONIA
VINCENT, CAMILLE. Ammonia and its compounds, their manufacture and uses. London, Scott, Greenwood and son, 1901. 114p.

AMMONIA and its compounds. Vicent, Camille. 1901.

AMORTIZATION
AMORTIZATION of bonds. *Bankers magazine,* Nov. 1910, p. 648-54.
ANALYSIS of amortization. *Journal of the American bankers association,* May 1919, p. 614.
CARDULLO, F. E. Capital costs in a manufacturing business. *Iron age,* May 21, 1914, p. 1278-80. *Metal work,* June 5, 1914, p. 745-7.
CHANDLER, ALFRED D. Amortization. *American economic review,* Dec. 1913.
ERICKSON, H. Amortization and other special charges. *Electrical review and western electrician,* Aug. 8, 1914, p. 283.
GUARANTY TRUST COMPANY OF NEW YORK. Amortization. New York. Guaranty trust co. 1917. 16p.
GUARANTY TRUST COMPANY OF NEW YORK. Some notes on amortization of interest to executors and trustees. New York, Guaranty trust co. 12p.
INGALLS, RALPH. Amortization from the economic standpoint. *Commercial and financial chronicle,* American bankers' convention section, Dec. 13, 1919, p. 224-5.
PULLEYN, JOHN J. Differences among amortization methods. *Journal of the American bankers association,* June 1919, p. 658-9. *Economic world,* June 28, 1919, p. 917-8.
PULLEYN, JOHN J. Effective amortization plan. *Journal of the American bankers' association,* May 1919, p. 592-3.
TARBELL, T. F. Amortization of securities in the accounting of insurance companies. *Economic world,* May 22, 1920, p. 741-3.
VINAL, EUGENE R. Amortization. (In his *Mathematics for the accountant.* 1920. p. 93-100).
WALTON, SEYMOUR. Amortizing discount on instalment contracts. *Journal of accountancy,* June 1920, p. 470-8.
WALTON, SEYMOUR. Amortizing serial bonds. *Journal of accountancy,* Dec. 1919, p. 470-1.
WALTON, SEYMOUR. Simple amortization method. *Journal of accountancy,* Dec. 1916, p. 477-82.
WOLFE, S. H. Suggestion for a modified form of amortization with a brief memorandum of the applicability of that principle to the bonds of the miscellaneous companies. *Economic world,* Nov. 4, 1916, p. 600-3.

AMORTIZATION. Sprague, C. E. 1908.

AMORTIZATION and inventory values regulations promulgated. *American industries,* June 1919, p. 42-3.

AMORTIZATION methods for farm mortgage loans. Truesdell, L. E. and C. W. Thompson. 1916.

AMORTIZATION of bond incomes. *Bankers magazine,* Mar. 1915, p. 335-7.

AMORTIZATION of bonds. *Bankers magazine,* Nov. 1910, p. 648-54.

AMORTIZATION rule of the New York public service commission of the second district. *Electrical world,* Nov. 11, 1909, p. 1162.

AMOUNT of maintenance and depreciation charges. *Electric railway review,* Feb. 23, 1907, p. 244.

AMPHITHALAMI. Liset, Abraham.

AMRATH, J. W.
Shall we have a supreme tribunal? Correspondence. *Journal of accountancy,* July 1909, p. 217-9.

AMSDON, DAN
Cost profits and rate of turnover. *System,* Jan.-Feb. 1915, p. 21, 143.
How I keep up with rising costs. *System,* Jan. 1915, p. 19-28.

AMSDON, EDWARD
Amsdon's complete system of bookkeeping for brewers, malters, wine and spirit merchants, mineral water manufacturers. London, Spottiswoode & co. 1906.
Amsdon's guide to brewers' book-keeping. London, 1881.

AMUSEMENTS
Bentley, Harry C. General ledger accounts of amusement enterprises operating at pleasure resorts, etc. (In his *Science of accounts.* 1913. p. 337-47).

ANALYSIS of a bank account. Bordwell, G F. 1911.

ANALYSIS of a newspaper editorial by President Rea of the Pennsylvania railroad. *Railway reviews,* July 21, 1917, p. 86-8.

ANALYSIS of amortization. *Journal of the American bankers' association,* May 1919, p. 614.

ANALYSIS of bookkeeping. Jones, T.

ANALYSIS of borrowers' statements. Post, William.

ANALYSIS of consumption by small lighting customers. *Electrical world,* June 22, 1918, p. 1326.

ANALYSIS of cost of electric drive in a foundry. *Electrical world,* Sept. 13, 1913, p. 537.

ANALYSIS of cost records. *Power plant engineering,* Jan. 1, 1920, p. 47-9.

ANALYSIS of costs and rates. *Gas age,* Sept. 1, 1914, p. 208.

ANALYSIS of costs in a refrigerating plant. *Electrical world,* Jan. 18, 1913, p. 148-9.

ANALYSIS of costs to operate isolated plants; report of subcommittee of the power sales bureau of the N. E. L. A.; with table. *Electrical world,* May 26, 1917, p. 1020-1.

ANALYSIS of examination results. *Journal of accountancy,* Feb. 1918, p. 121-4.

ANALYSIS of expenditures at Iowa state institutions. *U. S. Bureau of Education bulletin* no. 19, 1916, p. 184-95.

ANALYSIS of expenses among the several branches of railway service. *Electric railway journal,* Nov. 8, 1913, p. 1015.

ANALYSIS of factory work. *Iron age,* Nov. 16, 1911, p. 1074-6.

ANALYSIS of financial statements. Havener, Paul.

ANALYSIS of financial statements. Wilson, R. P. and H. J. Carpenter.

ANALYSIS of incandescent lighting costs for a year. *Electrical world,* Oct. 11, 1919, p. 800.

ANALYSIS of incandescent lighting costs for a year. *Electrical world,* Feb. 21, 1920, p. 424.

ANALYSIS of increased building costs. *American lumberman,* May 8, 1920, p. 1.

ANALYSIS of kilowatt hour costs of combination system. *Electrical world,* August 2, 1913, p. 238.

ANALYSIS of motor-service and heating costs in a jewelry factory; Codding-Heilborn Co., North Attleboro, Mass. *Electrical world,* June 21, 1913, p. 1369-70.

ANALYSIS of municipal gas accounts, 1908-1909. *Gas world,* London, Jan. 1910. 2 large sheets.

ANALYSIS of revenues and expenses from Ada rate case. *Telephony,* February 3, 1912, p. 147-9.

ANALYSIS of selling price of flour. Justin, W. H. c1917.

ANALYSIS of street-lighting costs. *Electrical world,* Sept. 25, 1920, p. 637.

ANALYSIS of the appraisal of the railways of Minnesota with comments on the same. *Engineering and contracting,* March 3, 1909, p. 172.

ANALYSIS of the appropriation ordinance on county budget. Hendren, Gilbert and others.

ANALYSIS of the estimated saving in a proposed change from 0.6 to 0.3 per cent ruling grade on a typical 130-mile division. *Engineering record,* October 4, 1913, p. 375-6.

ANALYSIS of the funds of the New York (circulation department) Brooklyn and Queens borough public libraries. New York city. Board of estimate and apportionment. 1916.

ANALYSIS of the laws affecting municipal and county finances and taxation. Pierson, A. N. 1918.

ANALYSIS of the premises adopted and methods used in determining the cost to reproduce new, together with the depreciation thereon of the physical property of the metropolitan system and the Kansas City and Westport Belt railway of Kansas City, Mo. *Engineering and contracting,* May 28, 1913, p. 617-20.

ANALYSIS of the science of accounts. Geer, G. P. 1883.

ANALYZING bank accounts. *Pace student,* Feb. 1918.

ANALYZING farm business. *Weekly news letter,* Jan. 31, 1917, p. 2.

ANALYZING maintenance costs: connection between the cost of steam and electric equipment maintenance. *Electrical world,* Sept. 25, Oct. 9, 1920, p. 613-6, 739.

ANALYZING the expense for power. *Factory,* April 1913, p. 684.

ANATOMY of a railroad report. Woodlock, Thomas F. 1895.

ANATOMY of a railroad report and ton mile cost. Woodlock, T. F. c1900.

ANCIENT duble-entry bookkeeping. Geijsbeek, J. B. c1914.

ANCIENT form of articles of association [of the Darien company, 1696]. *Accountants' magazine,* 1903, p. 248.

ANDERSEN, A. E.

Complete accounting course. 3 pts. New York, The Ronald press company, 1919-20. pt. 3 to be issued later.

ANDERSEN, DELANY & COMPANY.

Accounting treatment of overhead construction costs in public utilities. Chicago, Andersen, DeLany & co. c1917. 23p.

ANDERSON, A. C.

Digest on railway accounts; being a short explanation of the accounts of a railway company, based upon note made during a study of J. Alfred Fisher's well-known work, Railway accounts and finance from an accountant's standpoint. London, Gee & co. 1908. 93p.

ANDERSON, A. E.

Behind the figures. *System,* Jan. 1913, p. 3-12.

Modern accounting methods. *Telephony,* Sept. 8, 1917.

ANDERSON, ARTHUR and ERIC L. KOHLER.

1918 revenue law. Chicago. Northwestern university, February 15, 1919.

ANDERSON, E.

Book-keeping for post exchanges. *Journal of the military service institute,* v.15, p. 1168.

ANDERSON, F. E.

Audit of share transfers. *Incorporated accountants' journal,* Sept. 1912, p. 313-6.

ANDERSON, G. W.

How to get rid of the reproduction cost theory. *Utilities magazine,* 1916, v.1, no. 3, p. 28-36.

ANDERSON, H. D.

Handling accident reserves. *Electric railway journal,* May 20, 1916, p. 955-6.

ANDERSON, HENRY C.

Construction period. *Canadian engineer,* May 27, 1920, p. 506-7. *Engineering and contracting,* June 16, 1920, p. 694-5. *Mechanical engineering,* Oct. 1920, p. 560-1.

Ethics of accountancy. *Accountants' magazine,* April 1901, p. 192-8. *Commerce, accounts and finance,* April 13, 1901, p. 3-5.

Hotel bookkeeping. *Accountants' magazine,* April 1904, p. 212-19. *Business man's magazine,* June 1905, p. 1169-73.

ANDERSON, J. F.
Accounting system for the real estate business. *Business man's magazine,* Dec. 1910, p. 576-580.

ANDERSON, J. M.
Manufacture of beds and bedding. *Business man's magazine,* Oct. 1907, p. 43-6.

ANDERSON, J. M.
Openpit steam shovel costs. *Engineering and mining journal,* Jan. 27, 1917, p. 183-4.

ANDERSON, J. W.
Brown's ships accounts and Captains letter writer; also how to calculate exchange at foreign ports. 1907.

ANDERSON, JAMES B.
Vouchers and vouching. *Accountants' magazine,* July 1911, p. 337-45.

ANDERSON, LESLIE
Estate agents' accounts. *Accounting and commerce,* Dec. 1916, p. 213-6. *Incorporated accountants' journal,* March 1917, p. 132-4.

ANDERSON, N. L.
Danish income taxes. *Commerce reports,* no. 77, April 2, 1918, p. 26-7.

ANDERSON, THOMAS KERR
Title to goods in bankruptcy. *Accountant,* April 25, 1908, p. 602-11.

ANDERSON, W. F.
Estimating and building costs. *American architect,* June 12, 1918, p. 798-800.
Methods of office accounting for achitects. *American architect,* March 27, 1918, p. 369-76.

ANDERSON, W. H. P.
Manufacturing costs. *Accountant,* Nov. 4, 1905, p. 513-24.

ANDERSON, W. P.
Cost keeping for reinforced concrete buildings. *Engineering magazine,* April 1913, p. 34-49.
Cost of concrete buildings. *Machinery,* July 1916, p. 978-9.

ANDERSON, DE LANY & COMPANY
Accounting treatment of overhead construction costs in public utilities. Chicago, Anderson, De Lany & co. c1917. 23p.

ANDRADE, C.
Status of foreign lawyers in New York: correspondence. *Journal of accountancy,* March 1906, p. 415.

ANDRADE, E.
Manufacturing costs accounts, their use and treatment. *Accountant,* Feb. 11, 1899, p. 168.

ANDRAS, H. W.
Accountants and life assurance. *Accountant,* Feb. 5, 12, 1898, p. 159-63, 183-7.

ANDRES, G. E.
Comparative foundry cost records. *Foundry,* May, Dec. 1911, p. 93-7, 133-7.
Comparative records of all foundry costs. *Iron trade review,* May 18, 1911.
Comparative records of foundry operations. *Iron trade review,* Dec. 14, 1911, p. 1053-7.

ANDREW, WILLIAM
Distillery accounts. *Accountants' magazine,* May 1903, p. 252-64.

ANDREWS, B. F. Comp.
Registration and student records for smaller colleges. Washington, Government printing office. 1916. United States Bureau of education bulletins, 1916, 33:1-67p.

ANDREWS, BENJAMIN RICHARDS
Family account books. *Journal of home economics,* Oct. 1916, p. 545-51.
Survey of your household finances. New York, Teachers' college, Columbia university, 1914. 10c.

ANDREWS, H. L.
Motor buses or trackless trolleys. *General electric review,* April 1920, p. 331-4. Abstract. *Scientific American monthly,* June 1920, p. 565-6.

ANDREWS, H. P.
Standardization of cost-keeping methods for shipyards. *Pacific shipping,* Feb. 1918.

ANDREWS, WILLIAM E.
Accounting offices—their proper administration. *Government accountant,* May 1907, p. 35-42.

ANGERT, EUGENE H.
Proper distribution of interest on bonds between life tenants and remaindermen. *Journal of accountancy,* Aug. 1906, p. 259-74.

ANGLE, P. E.
Business methods and farm accounts. *Ontario agricultural and experimental union. Report,* 1915, p. 77-81.

ANN ARBOR (Mich.) rates system. *Gas age,* Oct. 1, 1918, p. 310.

ANN ARBOR R. R. loses in Michigan rate case. *Railway reviews,* March 11, 1916, p. 361-2.

ANNABLE, H. C.
Card payroll system arranged for department store. *Business man's magazine,* March 1908, p. 265-6.
System for indexing magazine articles and newspaper clippings. 1p.

ANNAN, WILLIAM
Apportionment; a plea for consistency. *Accountants' magazine,* March 1904, p. 164-73.
Cash sales and departmental accounts. *Accountants' magazine,* June 1906, p. 313-21.
Some notes for students on trading and cost accounts. *Accountants' magazine,* Feb. 1919, p. 82-92. *Public accountant,* June 1919, p. 354-64. *South African accountant,* March 1919, p. 298-301.
Trust accounts. (In *Lisle, George. Encyclopaedia of accounting.* v.6. p. 308-37).

ANNELLS, G. R.
Status of an auditor. *Accountant,* Aug. 22, 1908, p. 218-20.

ANNETT, C. B. and C. F. CUNNINGHAM
Textile cost accounting; its purpose and application. *Journal of the American society of mechanical engineers,* Jan. 1914, p. 16-20.

ANNUAL banquet of Milwaukee accountants. *Journal of accountancy,* July 1910, p. 217.

ANNUAL cost of locomotive upkeep. *Engineering,* Feb. 19, May 7, 1915, p. 187, 453-4.

ANNUAL dinner of the Pennsylvania institute of certified public accountants. *Journal of accountancy,* July 1906, p. 227-9.

ANNUAL magazine subject-index, 1915-1917. Faxon, F. W. 1916-1918.

ANNUAL meeting D. A. C. A. 1913. *Canadian chartered accountant,* July 1911, July 1912, July 1913, p. 36-46, 80-88, 69-83.

ANNUAL meeting of C. E. E. A. accountants. *Electric railway journal,* Dec. 19, 1914, p. 1334-7.

ANNUAL meeting of Dominion association. *Journal of accountancy,* Aug. 1911, p. 312.

ANNUAL meeting of New Jersey society. *Journal of accountancy,* March 1910, p. 389.

ANNUAL meeting of New York state society. *Journal of accountancy,* June 1906, p. 158.

ANNUAL meeting of Ohio society. *Journal of accountancy,* Sept. 1906, p. 393.

ANNUAL meeting of the Illinois society. *Journal of accountancy,* May 1906, p. 68.

ANNUAL meeting of the Missouri society. *Journal of accountancy,* Aug. 1906, p. 300.

ANNUAL report of committee on economics of the electric service. *American institute of electrical engineers, Proceedings,* July, 1917, p. 600-1.

ANNUAL report of the Nevada consolidated copper co. for 1916. *Engineering and mining journal,* May 19, 1917, p. 884-6.

ANNUAL return prescribed by the chief registrar for societies carrying on industries and trades under the industrial and provident societies act 1893. Pixley, Francis W.

ANNUAL statement of the trade of the United Kingdom with foreign countries and British possessions 1917 compared with the four preceding years. Great Britain. Statistical office of the customs and excise department. 1915.

ANNUAL value. *Accountant,* Dec. 10, 17, 24, 31, 1910, p. 793, 833, 881, 913.

ANNUITIES

- ALEXANDER, WILLIAM. Interesting facts about annuities. *American magazine,* Feb. 1919, p. 130-2.
- ANNUITIES free of income tax. *Accountant,* March 16, May 11, 1918, p. 224-7, 354-5.
- BENNETT, ROBERT J. Annuities and bond discount. *Journal of accountancy,* June, July 1915, p. 405-24, 1-20.
- COX, HENRY C. Sinking funds and annuities. (In his Advanced and analytical accounting. 1920. p. 143-64).
- FATKIN, THOMAS. Interest, annuities, and insurance. *Accountant,* Jan. 27, 1900, p. 104-11.
- GILLETTE, HALBERT P. Present worth of annuity. (In his *Handbook of cost data for contractors and engineers.* 1910. p. 14-6).
- GLEN, NINIAN. Acturial science; an elementary manual. Glasgow, John Smith and son, 1912. 96p.
- INSTITUTE OF ACTUARIES. Text book of the principles of interest, life assurances, and their practical application; new edition revised by Ralph Todhunter. London, Charles & Edwin Layton, 1915.
- INWOOD, WILLIAM. Inwood's tables of interest and mortality for the purchasing of estates and valuation of properties; thirtieth edition revised and extended by William Schooling; with logarithms of natural number and Thoman's logarithmic interest and annuity tables. London, Crosby Lockwood and son, 1913. 320p.
- JACOBSSON, GUSTAVE. Annuity problems made easy. *Business man's magazine,* Oct. 1911, p. 357-8.
- JACOBSSON, GUSTAVE. Loans repayable by special terminable annuities. *Canadian chartered accountant,* April 1916, p. 308-10.
- KESTER, ROY B. Formulas for annuities. (In his *Accounting theory and practice.* 1918. v.2, p. 272).
- KING, GEORGE C. Theory of finance; a short treatise on the doctrine of interest and annuities-certain. Ed. 3. London, Charles & Edwin Layton, 1898. 94p.
- LEAKE, P. D. Annuity or sinking fund theory of measurement of depreciation of plant. *Accountant,* July 3, 1915, p. 18-25. *Electrician* (London), March 26, 1915.
- LING, GEORGE H. Annuities and their relation to certain financial problems. *Canadian chartered accountant,* April 1917, p. 261-70.
- LITTLE, ARTHUR S. Tyranny of the engraver. *Journal of accountancy,* Sept. 1915, April 1916, p. 186-202, 307-8.
- PRICE, E. E. Interest and annuities. *Accountant,* Nov. 28, 1885.
- PENDER, HAROLD. Interest, annuities and sinking fund. (In his *Handbook for electrical engineers.* c1914. p. 830).
- RACINE, SAMUEL FREDERICK. Annuity studies. Seattle, Western institute of accountancy, commerce and finance, c1919. 21p.
- ROBERTSON, W. A. Annuities. (In Lisle, George. *Encyclopaedia of accounting,* v.1. p. 63-72).
- ROBERTSON, W. A. Interest and annuities—certain. (In *Lisle, George. Encyclopadia of accounting.* v.3. p. 357-431).
- SPICER, ERNEST EVAN. Reserves, annuities and sinking funds. Ed. 2. London, H. Foulks Lynch & co. 1911. 28p. (In Feather, J. Stuart, ed. *Joint transactions,* 1911, p. 75-91). *Accountant,* April 29, 1911, p. 678-84.
- SPIES, OTTO A. Annuities and bond discount. *Journal of accountancy,* Sept. 1915, p. 203-15.
- SPRAGUE, CHARLES EZRA. Annuities. (In his *Accountancy of investment.* 1914. p. 53-71, 183-90).
- VINAL, EUGENE R. Annuities: amount and present worth. (In his *Mathematics for the accountant.* 1920. p. 60-74).
- WALTON, SEYMOUR. Annuities. *Journal of accountancy,* Oct. 1916, p. 316.
- WALTON, SEYMOUR. Present worth of an annuity. *Journal of accountancy,* April 1920, p. 314.

ANNUITIES. Robertson, W. A.

ANNUITIES. Walton, Seymour.

ANNUITIES and bond discount. Spies, O. A.

ANNUITIES and bond discounts. Bennett, R. J.

ANNUITIES free of income tax. *Accountant,* March 16, May 11, 1918, p. 224-7, 354-5.

ANNUITY fund of religious organizations. Ross, T.

ANNUITY studies. Racine, S. F. c1919.

ANOTHER Connecticut fare increase. *Electric railway journal,* Oct. 20, 1917, p. 738.

ANOTHER device for encouraging power saving. *Electric railway journal,* April 28, 1917, p. 788-9.

ANOTHER fallacy in bond values. Little, A. S.

ANOTHER fare increase for Massachusetts; Milford and Uxbridge street railway. *Electric railway journal,* Aug. 18, 1917, p. 261.

ANOTHER Massachusetts fare increase; 6 cent fare to the Norfolk Bristol street railway. *Electric railway journal,* Aug. 28, 1915, p. 354-5.

ANOTHER Massachusetts fare increase; the Blue Hill street railway. *Electric railway journal,* Aug. 7, 1915, p. 226-8.

ANOTHER six cent fare granted. *Electric railway journal,* Sept. 25, 1915, p. 628-31.

ANOTHER step in San Francisco ten-year water rate suit. *Engineering news-record,* Aug. 8, 1918, p. 291-2.

ANOTHER Third avenue chapter. *Electric railway journal,* Feb. 10, 1912, p. 230.

ANOTHER $23,500,000 added to express service cost: director general McAdoo disregards suggestion made by Interstate commerce commission for keeping rates down and orders advance company asked. *Greater New York,* November 25, 1918, p. 7-8.

ANOTHER view of New York examinations: correspondence. *Journal of accountancy,* Nov. 1912, p. 421-2.

ANOTHER way to prevent strikes. *Outlook,* Sept. 27, 1916, p. 175-6.

ANSWER to report of Arthur C. King on electric rates of Union gas and electric co., Cincinnati, Ohio. King, A. C.

ANSWERS to additional exercises in bookkeeping. London, Sir Isaac Pitman & sons, 1912. 54p.

ANSWERS to income tax problems. *Domestic engineering,* Feb. 1, 1919, p. 223-4.

ANSWERS to the Commission's questions 42 to 45. *Railway age,* May 15, 1914, p. 1073-4.

ANTE-audit. Carlill, J. A. 1900.

ANTE-DATING

WALTON, SEYMOUR. Ante-dating. *Journal of accountancy,* Aug. 1914, p. 150-1.

ANTHONY, C. C.

What does it cost to stop a tonnage train *Railway age,* May 2, 1919, p. 1105-7.

ANTHRACITE coal decision. *Journal of political economy,* Oct. 1915, p. 840-2.

ANTHRACITE coal rates reduced in Pennsylvania. *Railway age,* Dec. 25, 1914, p. 1196.

ANTI-CONFUSION business methods. Sweetland, C. A. 1905.

ANTI-EFFICIENCY appropriation legislation. *American industries,* April 1918, p. 13.

ANTIQUATED personal property tax. *Journal of accountancy,* July 1910, p. 209-10.

ANTIQUITY of bookkeeping. *Accountant,* May 18, 1901, p. 579.

ANVILS

Cost accounting

EGGLESTON, DEWITT CARL. Cost of manufacture of one 450 pound wrought iron horseshoe anvil. (In his *Problems in cost accounting.* 1918. p. 178-9).

ANYON, JAMES T.

Accounting terminology. *Journal of accountancy,* Oct. 1910, p. 435-8.
Safeguarding bank loans. *Journal of accountancy,* Dec. 1910, p. 97-107.
Sinking funds and reserve accounts. *Journal of accountancy,* Jan. 1909, p. 185-91.

APARTMENT HOUSES

Accounting

AUSTIN, F. A. System of bookkeeping in apartment house operation. *Real estate magazine,* May & June 1914.
JOSEPH, LEON. Records for owners of flat buildings or apartment houses. *Business man's magazine,* Jan. 1909, p. 84-7.

APEDAILE, J. LEONARD

Depreciation. *Canadian chartered accountant,* April 1916, 297-308.
Management of a manufacturing concern or a plea for the manufacturer. *Canadian chartered accountant,* Oct. 1915, p. 132-47.

APITZ, J. W.

Question of partners drawings and dividends: correspondence. *Journal of accountancy,* Jan. 1913, p. 72-3.

APPEAL for an advance in rates. *Railway age,* March 30, 1917, p. 686.

APPEAL of the specialization of the railway accounts. *Japan financial and economic monthly,* April 1908, p. 5-6.

APPEL, R.

Reducing time out through graphic charts. *Factory,* Sept. 1917, p. 349.

APPELBY, W., and others

System of bookkeeping specially arranged for industrial and provident [co-operative] societies. Manchester, 1896.

APPELLATE court of the state of New York and the question of allowances for paving over mains in valuation work; with discussion by John W. Alvord; some aspects of water works valuation by R. E. Heilman. *American waterworks association journal,* Sept. 1915, p. 465-92, 538-43.

APPENDIX to bookkeeping. Maclean, J. D. 1895.

APPLEBY, C. T.

See Poppleton, G. G., joint author.

APPLEGATE, C. E.

Distribution of expense to departments. *National retail dry goods association, Report and digest of the proceedings, first annual convention controllers' congress,* 1920, p. 14-18, 26, 30.

APPLES.
See Fruit.

APPLETON, WILL
Balance day procedure. *Accounting and commerce,* March 1916, p. 281-3.

APPLICATION for increase of revenues in southern classification territory. United States. Interstate commerce commission. 1920.

APPLICATION of business methods to construction work. *Engineering and contracting,* Oct. 22, 1913, p. 474-6.

APPLICATION of efficiency principles. Shepard, G. H. 1917.

APPLICATION of increased freight rates in Illinois. *Railway age,* Aug. 20, 1920, p. 315-6.

APPLICATION of overhead expense. *Metal work,* April 14, 1916, p. 511.

APPLICATION of sinking funds in exercise of borrowing powers. *Accountant,* July 10, 17, 1909, p. 55-63, 90-5.

APPLICATION of sorting and tabulating machines to the inventory of transmission and distribution systems. National electric light association, Accounting sessions, Papers, reports, and discussions, 1914.

APPLICATION of the eastern roads for increased rates. *Railway review,* Oct. 20, Nov. 10, 24, 1917, p. 484, 571-5, 627-9

APPLICATION of the railroads for an increase of freight rates. *Economic world,* March 31, 1917, p. 445.

APPLICATION to a municipality of modern methods of accounting and reporting. *Annals of the American academy of political and social science,* May 1912, p. 64-8.

APPLIED methods of scientific management. Parkhurst, F. A. 1917.

APPLIED motion study. Gilbreth, F. B., and L. M. Gilbreth. 1917.

APPLIED theory of accounts. Esquerre, P. J. 1917.

APPLIGARTH, E. M.
Uniform system of accounting: floor measurements; computing profits. *Building and building management,* Aug. 9, 1920, p. 33-6.

APPLYING efficiency standards in central station accounting. Miller, H. C.

APPLYING methods of scientific management to coal mines. *Coal age,* July 4, 1914, p. 3.

APPLYING system in the office. *Electric railway journal,* Aug. 18, 1917, p. 276.

APPOINTMENT and remuneration of auditors. *Accountant,* Feb. 17, 1912, p. 253-6.

APPOINTMENT of company auditors. *Accountant,* Feb. 20, 1915, 238-41.

APPOINTMENT of first auditor to a company. *Accountant,* Jan. 14, 28, 1899, p. 35-8, 101-2.

APPORTIONMENT
See also Capital; Executors and trustees.

Annan, William. Apportionment: a plea for consistency. *Acountants' magazine,* March 1904, p. 164-73.
Apportionment; causalties. *Accountants' magazine,* 1909, p. 5.
Apportionment of capital and income in financial companies. *Accountant,* Aug 25, 1900, p. 761-4.
Carter, R. N. Apportionments. (In his *Advanced accounts.* p. 38-9).
Cudworth, Alfred James. Apportionment. *Accountant,* 1887, p. 343.
Dudbridge, Sidney. Apportionment between capital and income. *Incorporated accountants' journal,* Jan. 1912, p 104-7.
Hill, Daniel. Apportionment of expenses as between capital and revenue. *Accountant,* Jan. 2, 1909, p. 27-30.
Lisle, George. Apportionment. (In his *Accounting in theory and practice.* 1900. p. 152-74).
MacIntyre, W. A. D. and David Allan Hay. Theory and practice of apportionment. *Accountants' magazine,* June 1915, p. 302-17.
Mead, Charles Walter. Apportionment. *Accountant,* June 5, 1897, p. 565-70.
Ranking, D. Fearon De L'Hoste. Apportionment. (In his *Handbook of executorship law and accounts.* 1915. p. 189-229).
Sharpe, R. S. Some points on apportionment. *Accountants' magazine,* June 1903, p. 308-28.
Tebbs, Herbert Louis. Apportionment. (In Lisle, George. *Encyclopaedia of accounting.* v.1. p. 92-126).
Tebbs, Herbert Louis. Apportionment between capital and income. *Incorporated accountants' journal,* 1902-3, p. 101.

APPORTIONMENT between life tenant and remainderman. *Trust companies,* May 1912, p. 401; Nov.-Dec. 1914, p. 426, 514; Sept. 1917, p. 198.

APPORTIONMENT: casualties. *Accountants' magazine,* 1909, p. 5.

APPORTIONMENT of capital and income in financial companies. *Accountant,* Aug. 25, 1900, p. 761-4.

APPORTIONMENT of dividends as between life tenant and remainderman. *Trust companies,* Dec. 1914, p. 514.

APPORTIONMENT of dividends between life tenant and remainderman. *Trust companies,* May 1912, p. 401.

APPORTIONMENT of dividend by trustees as between life tenant and remainderman. *Trust companies,* Nov. 1914, p. 426.

APPORTIONMENT of dividends on death. *Accountant,* Aug. 19, 1902, p. 735-6.

APPORTIONMENT of establishment charges during construction. *Accountant,* Aug. 18, 1900, p. 745-7.

APPORTIONMENT of expense items. *Horseless age,* Mar. 17, 1915, p. 367-8.

APPORTIONMENT of expenses to suburban traffic. *Railway age gazette,* Jan. 16, 1914, p. 124.

APPORTIONMENT of income in trust accounts. *Accountant,* 1887, p. 186, 201, 215, 229.

APPORTIONMENT of partnership profits. *Accountant,* Dec. 20, 1902, p. 1321-4.

APPORTIONMENT of profits of building and loan associations. Scott, G. G.

APPORTIONMENT of railroad revenues from ticket sales and other resources. *Official bulletin,* July 5, 1918, p. 20.

APPORTIONMENT of the cost of anthracite coal between domestic and steam sizes. Meade, E. S.

APPRAISAL of city real estate. *Engineering and contracting,* Feb. 24, 1915, p. 167.

APPRAISAL of intangible values in public utilities. *Electrical world,* Oct. 26, 1912, p. 866-7.

APPRAISAL of Memphis street railway. *Electric railway journal,* July 10, 1920, p. 120-1.

APPRAISAL of public service properties as a basis for the regulation of rates. *Proceedings of the American society of civil engineers,* Sept. 1912.

APPRAISAL of street lighting service. *Engineering record,* July 27, 1912, p. 104.

APPRAISAL of the Chicago telephone co. and a comparison with the results of the three similar appraisals. *Engineering and contracting,* Sept. 13, 1911, p. 269.

APPRAISAL of the city lines of the Detroit united railway. *Electric railway journal,* May 17, 1913, p. 897-8.

APPRAISAL of the Gloucester waterworks. *Engineering record,* Aug. 19, 1898, p. 264. Aug. 10, 1901, p. 121.

APPRAISAL of the Madison gas and electric co. *Engineering and contracting,* June 28, 1911, p. 747.

APPRAISAL of the New York surface systems. *Electric railway journal,* June 20, 1908, p. 111.

APPRAISAL of the Pere Marquette lines in Michigan. *Railway age gazette,* Feb. 26, 1915, p. 376.

APPRAISAL of the physical properties of railroads of Minnesota. *Railway and engineering review,* Mar. 13, 1909.

APPRAISAL of the Quincy water works. *Engineering record,* July 23, 1904, p. 118.

APPRAISAL of the railways of New Jersey and progress in other states. *Engineering and contracting,* June 21, 1911, p. 701.

APPRAISAL of the Seattle telephone companies by the railroad commission of Washington. *Engineering and contracting,* May 3, 1911, p. 520-4.

APPRAISAL of the Third avenue street railroad systems, New York city. *Engineering and contracting,* June 7, 1911, p. 666.

APPRAISAL of water rights. *Engineering and contracting,* April 17, 1912, p. 429-32.

APPRAISAL of water works properties with special reference to the reproduction method. *Engineering and contracting,* April 9, 1913, p. 420-1. *Engineering news,* April 3, 1913, p. 677. *Engineering record,* May 10, 1913, p. 532.

APPRAISAL report of Pere Marquette railroad fills ten large boxes. *Engineering record,* Feb. 13, 1915, p. 200-2.

APPRAISAL value of the railway in five states and the probable cost of reproducing all railways in America. *Engineering and contracting,* Aug. 3, 1910, p. 89.

APPRAISALS.

See Valuation.

APPRAISALS and their relation to accounts. Hawkins, L. G.

APPRAISALS of Ohio public utilities. *Electric railway journal,* Oct. 24, 1914, p. 962-4.

APPRAISED value of the electric street railways of Detroit, Mich. *Engineering and contracting,* July 6, 1910.

APPRAISING abandoned railroad property. *Engineering record,* Nov. 7, 1914, p. 502.

APPRECIATION

Appreciation of assets and dividends. *Accountant,* July 21, 1900, p. 668-71.

Appreciation of building. *Business man's magazine,* June 1908, p. 532-3.

Burton, Francis George. Appreciation of municipal assets. *Accountant,* March 9, 23, 1907, p. 327-36, 375-7.

Dicksee, L. R. Appreciation. (In his *Advanced accounting.* 1916. p.12-3).

Herr, John P. Appreciation of assets—when is it legitimate? *Journal of accountancy,* Nov. 1906, p. 1-13.

Hubbard, H. Supreme court on appreciation in value as an element in "invested capital." *Economic world,* Sept. 21, 1918, p. 413-4. *Wall street journal,* Sept. 18, 1918.

Kester, Roy B. Appreciation. (In his *Accounting theory and practice.* 1918. v.2, p. 206-9, 304-5.

Maltbie, Milo F. Proper treatment of appreciation of land. *Utilities magazine,* 1916, v.1, no. 3, p. 96-7.

Paton, W. A. Depreciation, appreciation, and productive capacity. *Journal of accountancy,* July 1920, p. 1-11.

Paton, W. A. and R. A. Stevenson. Appreciation and depreciation. (In their *Principles of accounting.* 1918. p. 238-43).

Racine, S. F. Appreciation from outside sources. (In his *Accounting principles.* 1917. p. 125-6).

Walton, Seymour. Increase in market price of fixed assets. *Journal of accountancy,* Nov. 1918. p. 392-3.

Walton, Seymour. Increase in stumpage value. *Journal of accountancy,* Jan. 1919, p. 77-8.

Walton, Seymour. Increased value of fixed assets. *Journal of accountancy,* Aug. 1918, p. 153.

Walton, Seymour. Writing up land value. *Journal of accountancy,* April 1920, p. 308.

APPRECIATION as a factor in business building. *Electrical review and western electrician,* Nov. 18, 1916, p. 905.

APPRECIATION of assets and dividends. *Accountant,* July 21, 1900, p. 668-71.

APPRECIATION of assets—when is it legitimate. Herr, J. P.

APPRECIATION of building. *Business man's magazine,* June 1908, p. 532-3.

APPRECIATION of land values in valuation of public utilities. *Municipal engineering,* Dec. 1913, p. 533.

APPRECIATION of the New York C. P. A. examinations. Colley, F. G.

APPRENTICES time-entertainer accomptantly. Dafforne, Richard. 1670.

APPROACHING standardization. *Journal of accountancy,* Aug. 1919, p. 126-9.

APPROPRIATION OF PAYMENTS

Appropriation of payments. *Incorporated accountants' journal,* 1905-6, p. 182.

Hislop, James. Law of appropriation of payments. *Accountant,* June 20, 1885.

APPROPRIATION of payments. *Incorporated accountants' journal,* 1905-6, p. 182.

APPROVAL of demand rates by public service commissions. *Electrical review and western electrician,* Nov. 14, 1914, p. 960-1.

APPROVED methods for the preparation of balance sheet statements. United States. Federal reserve board. 1918.

APPROXIMATE cost of stopping a train. *Railway age,* March 22, 1918, p. 708.

APPROXIMATE value placed on physical property of Brooklyn transit system. *Electric railway journal,* Dec. 25, 1909, Jan. 22, Feb. 5, 1910, p. 1261, 156, 248.

AQUEDUCTS

Cost accounting

Organization and cost-keeping on the Los Angeles aqueduct. *Engineering record,* Oct. 15, 1910.

ARBITRATION AND AWARD

Arbitration. *Accountant,* 1886, p. 198.

Arbitrations. *Accountant,* Jan. 26-Feb. 9, March 8, 22, April 5, 12, 26, Aug. 30-Oct. 11, 1884.

Arbitrators' decisions. *Accountant,* April 12, 1913, p. 538-9.

Ball, William Valentine. Law of arbitrations and awards. *Incorporated accountants' journal,* 1903-4, p. 239.

Barber, Jarvis William. Arbitrations and award. *Accountant,* Nov. 16, 1907, p. 611-6.

Cariss, Astrup. On arbitration ; and on forms of balance sheets. *Accountant,* April 14, 1883.

Commercial arbitration. *Incorporated accountants' journal,* Aug. 1912, p. 283-6.

Corpus juris: being a complete and systematic statement of the whole body of the law as embodied in and developed by all reported decisions; ed. by William Mack and W. J. Hale. New York, American law book co.

Defects in procedure: arbitrations in reconstructions. *Accountant,* Aug. 31-Sept. 21, Nov. 9-23, 1901, p. 940-2, 961-4, 979-81, 1008-9, 1203-5, 1231-5, 1231-2, 1264-6.

Effect on an award based on the existence of a trade custom. *Accountant,* Jan. 16, 1909, p. 94-6.

Future of arbitration. *Accountant,* April 6, 1912, p. 529-32.

Hart, Dudley Frank. Arbitrations and awards. *Accountant,* June 24, 1893, p. 595-9.

Lamond, R. P. Settlement of traders' claims by arbitration. *Accountant,* April 21, 1894, p. 360-4.

M'Ilraith, John R. Arbitration. (In Lisle, George, *Encyclopaedia of accounting.* v.1 p. 127-33).

Miller, P. L. Law of arbitration in Scotland. *Accountant,* Aug. 31, 1912, p. 294-304.

Nelson, Walter. Some notes on arbitration procedure. *Accountants' magazine,* March 1918, p. 87-105.

Owen, William Henry. Law of arbitration. *Accountant,* June 7, 1902, p. 592-7.

Parfitt, James John. Brief outline of arbitration law. *Accountant,* Jan. 29, 1898, p. 132-5.

Pearson, Frank Shakespeare. Arbitration and awards. *Incorporated accountants' journal,* 1900-1, p. 156.

Pixley, Francis William. Arbitrations. (In *Four lectures delivered to the Institute of chartered accountants in England and Wales during the years 1894 and 1895,* p. 93-122.)

Ranking, D. Fearon, de l'Hoste. Arbitration. *Accountant,* Feb. 11, March 11, 1905, p. 168-80, 271-3.

Rhodes, George. Arbitration and awards. *Incorporated accountants' journal,* 1907-8, p. 268.

Robertson, D. Claude. Arbitration and awards. *Accountant,* Oct. 9, 1915, p. 432-40.

Shaw, William. Law of arbitration. *Accountant,* Jan. 4, 1902. p. 23-8. *Accountants' magazine,* Dec. 1901, p. 518-35.

Singleton, John Edward. Arbitration and awards. *Accountant,* May. 28, 1910, p. 761-8.

Slater, Joshua. Arbitrations and awards. *Accountant,* Nov. 10, 17, 1883.

Smith, John Hudson. Arbitration. *Accountant,* 1886, p. 198.

Stevens, Thomas Moffitt. Arbitration and award. *Accountant,* March 23, April 6, 1895, p. 277-84, 320-6.

Stevens, Thomas Moffit. Outline of the law of arbitrations. *Accountant,* Aug. 23, 1890, p. 449-52.

Taylor, William. Powers and duties of arbitrators. *Accountant,* Jan. 15, 1910, p. 87-94.

Trevor, Charles Robinson. Arbitrations. *Accountant,* May 11, 1889, p. 252-6.

Yates, Charles U. Arbitration. *Accountant,* 1886, p. 25.

ARBITRARY depreciation requirement. *Railway world,* Feb. 16, 1912, p. 141.

ARBITRATED result in Cleveland. *Electric railway journal,* June 28, 1913, p. 1134.

ARBITRATION. *Accountant,* 1886, p. 198.

ARBITRATION of operating expense charges in Cleveland. *Electric railway journal,* May 24, 1913, p. 925.

ARBITRATIONS. *Accountant,* Jan. 26-Feb. 9, March 8, 22. April 5, 12, 26, Aug. 30-Oct. 11, 1884.

ARBITRATIONS. Pixley, Francis William.

ARBITRATORS' decisions. *Accountant,* April 12, 1913, p. 538-9.

ARC lamps show low-outage record at Detroit. *Electrical world,* March 4, 1916, p. 546.

ARCH, W. H.

Bookkeeping in verse. London, Effingham Wilson, 1914.

ARCHER, JOHN P.

Examiner's impressions. *Journal of accountancy,* Oct. 1918, p. 247-9.

ARCHITECTS

Accounting

AMERICAN business and accounting encyclopaedia; comp. by E. H. Beach and W. W. Thorne. Detroit, Bookkeeper publishing co. 1901. Architects' accounting—v.1, p. 101-2.
ANDERSON, W. F. Methods of office accounting for architects. *American architect,* March 27, 1918, p. 369-76.
DAVIDSON, JAMES. Architects' accounts. *Incorporated accountants' journal,* 1903-4, p. 93.
HOLLIS, TILTON & PORTE. Proposed general accounting and cost system for the Michigan society of architects. *Architectural forum,* Jan. 1919, p. 13-21.
JOSEPH, LEON. System for achitect's office. *Business man's magazine,* June 1907, p. 75-80.
LEVIE, GEORGE ELDER. Architect's book-keeping, accounts and office management. *Accountants' magazine,* Dec. 1900, p. 576-89.
MARSHALL, HENRY CALDER. Accounts for architects. *Accountant,* March 12, 1898, p. 284-91.
PIXLEY, FRANCIS W. Architects. (In his *Accountancy.* Ed.2. p. 93-4).
VAN ARSDALL, H. P. Organization, management and an accounting system for an architect's office. *American architect,* Aug. 11, 1920, p. 179-87.

Auditing

DICKSEE, LAWRENCE ROBERT. Architects. (In his *Auditing.* Authorized American edition. p. 165-6).
MONTGOMERY, ROBERT H. Architects. (In his *Auditing theory and practice.* 1916. p. 728-30).

ARDREY, R. L.

Report on St. Paul arouses champion. *Chicago record-herald,* March 10, 1914.

ARE examinations worth while? *Accountant,* Nov. 16, 1918, p .271-2.

ARE higher fares getting the results? *Electric railway journal,* Jan. 25, 1919, p. 186-9.

ARE railroads concealing profits? *Journal of commerce,* Aug. 9, 1910.

ARE railway and public utility companies entitled to dividends upon unearned increments in value. *Engineering and contracting,* June 16, 1920, p. 671-2.

ARE these charges true? Well-known financial writer claims that all audits are not what they ought to be. *Canadian chartered accountant,* July 1914, p. 42-4.

ARE you getting enough turnover? *Pacific coast merchant,* April 20, 1918, p. 7.

ARE your finances sometimes short? *Metal work,* Nov. 30, 1917, p. 653.

AREVALO, ALBERTO

Apuntes de contabilidad general. Rosario, 1919. 63p.

——— **and HIRAM G. GALOGERO**

La partida doble pro el metodo logismo grafico. Buenos Aires, Cabaut and cia, 1918. 97p.

ARGALL, P. H.

Metallurgical accounts. *Mining and scientific press,* Nov. 1906, v.93, p. 573-6.

ARGUMENT on bituminous coal rates east. *Railway review,* February 28, 1914, p. 320-1.

ARGUMENTS against the higher railroad rates *Journal of political economy,* June 1914, p. 582-4.

ARGUMENTS for higher railroad rates. *Journal of political economy,* Jan. 1914, p. 85-7.

ARGUMENTS in transcontinental rate case. *Railway age,* April 13, 1917, p. 794-5.

ARGUMENTS of Mr. Brandeis and Mr. Brownell. *Railway age,* Nov. 13, 1914, p. 895-902.

ARITHMETIC

BROWN, W. On wrinkles. *Accountant,* Dec. 3, 1904, p. 693-9.
MOORE, JOHN H. and GEORGE K. MINER. Practical business arithmetic. Boston, Ginn and company, c1915. 460p.
SCHOOLING, WILLIAM. Dodges in arithmetic. *Accountant,* Nov. 11, 1899, p. 1111-2.

ARITHMETIC and book-keeping. Brown, Thomas and Vincent E. Collinge. 1916.

ARITHMETIC of railroad operation. *Railway review,* Mar. 1-8, 1919, p. 316-18, 355-7.

ARITHMETICK and bookkeeping. Malcolm, A. 1718.

ARIZONA. COMMISSION OF STATE INSTITUTIONS

Forms.

——— **CORPORATION COMMISSION.**

Incorporation laws of Arizona relating to corporations in general and foreign corporations, amended 1919. Phoenix, July 15, 1917. 32p.

——— **EXAMINER**

Annual report transmitted to the governor December 23, 1918. 169p.

——— **STATE TAX COMMISSION**

General taxation and revenue laws of the state of Arizona, March 1918. 150p.

ARIZONA, C. P. A. law. *Journal of accountancy,* July 1919, p. 77-80.

ARKANSAS. COMMITTEE APPOINTED TO AUDIT THE STATE DEPARTMENTS AND INSTITUTIONS

Report on the office of the auditor of the state of Arkansas. *Arkansas gazette,* June 13, 1915.

——— **SECRETARY OF STATE**

Articles of agreement and incorporation. Little Rock, Arkansas.

——— **STATE BOARD OF ACCOUNTANCY**

Act regulating the practice of public accounting passed by the 40th general assembly of Arkansas, 1915. 14p.
Applications. 2 forms.
List of C. P. A. certificates issued, September 25, 1919. 1 typewritten page.

ARKANSAS.. *American institute of accountants, Yearbook,* 1915, 1916, p. 243-6, 135-8.

ARKANSAS. C. P. A. law. *Journal of accountancy,* April 1915, p. 300-3.

ARKLEY, A. K.

Business methods of a lumber company. *Business man's magazine,* Detroit, 1904, v.17, p. 849-855.

Keeping track of income and outgo. *Business man's magazine,* March 1912, p. 246-252.

ARMIES

"Cost plus" form of contract used on cantonment work, including a schedule of equipment rental rates. *Engineering and contracting,* Nov. 28, 1917, p. 448-51.

How progress is recorded on army construction jobs. *Engineering news,* May 23, 1918, p. 993-4.

United States. War Department. Board of review of construction. Report to the assistant secretary of war, August 31, 1919. Washington, Government printing office, 1920. 381p.

United States. War Department. Construction division. National army cantonments, plans and photographs, June 1918; a compilation of plans of the sixteen national army cantonments, together with photographs showing typical buildings and their construction selected from progress photographs sent from the various cantonments. Construction division, War Department, 1918. 94 plates.

Accounting

Anderson, E. Book-keeping for post exchanges. *Journal of the military service institute,* v.15, p. 1168.

Business man of the army. *Journal of accountancy,* Dec. 1905, p. 112-7.

Carlock, Floyd D. Manual for post exchanges. Menasha, Wis., George Banta publishing co. c1917. 193p.

Creighton, W. M. Mode of keeping the accounts of a regimental pay office. Abergavenny, 1884.

Holloway, C. B. Accountants' bit in the American expeditionary forces. *Journal of accountancy,* Oct. 1918, p. 244-6.

Holloway, C. B. Carrying on with the accountants in the American expeditionary forces. *Journal of accountancy,* Dec. 1918, p. 412-6.

Holmes, E. J. Accounting systems in army camps. *Journal of accountancy,* Dec. 1918, p. 429-35.

Meal tickets for use of drafted men en route to camps. *Federal reserve bulletin,* Oct. 1918, p. 938.

Redway, G. W. How to check a pay list: letters to a young officer on soldiers' settlements and paymasters' advances. London, 1901.

Sparrow, Robert G. Accounting for ordnance property of the United States army overseas, June 19, 1918 to Dec. 16, 1918. 49 typewritten pages.

Todd, Campbell. Guide to keeping company accounts in the new armies; revised to 31st August 1918. London, Gale & Polden. 83p.

West, William H. Accounting for cantonment construction. *Journal of accountancy,* Nov. 1918, p. 321-6.

Cost accounting

Grimwood, J. Costing in relation to government control, efficiency and economy. *Accountant,* March 29, April 5, 12, 1919, p. 257-62, 279-87, 305-10. *Incorporated accountants' journal,* March-May 1919, p. 114-20, 133-8, 156-61.

Pinkerton, C. W. Cost accounting system of construction division, U. S. army. *Engineering and contracting,* May 21, 1919, p. 548-51.

Costs

Cost of housing soldiers at cantonments averages $214.92. *Engineering news,* March 21, 1918, p. 569.

Fuller, George W. Estimated and actual cost of the army camps. *Engineering and contracting,* June 26, 1918, p. 629-30.

ARMITAGE, HERBERT C.

Model tool stores. *Engineering and industrial management,* June 12, 26, July 10, 24, 1919, p. 615-7, 35-7, 99-101, 551-3.

Wages and bonus system. *Engineering and industrial management,* Dec. 4, 1919, Jan. 1, 15, Feb. 5, March 11, 1920, p. 714-6; 18-20, 66-9, 163-5, 323-5.

ARMITAGE, P.

Depletion of mineral deposits and the federal income tax. *Engineering and mining journal,* April 26, 1919, p. 750-2.

ARMITAGE, SMITH G.

Incidence of taxation. *Accountant,* Aug. 24, Sept. 21, 1907, p. 244-52, 363-4.

ARMOUR, J. O.

Some lessions learned in selling $525,000,000 a year. *System,* Mar. 1917, p. 227-33.

ARMOUR, S. B.

Rating of machinery. *Accountants' magazine,* 1902, p. 364.

ARMSTRONG, AUGUSTUS

Double entry bookkeeping up to date. New York, Armstrong & co. 1915. 64p.

ARMSTRONG, C. W.

Valuation of assets. *Accounting and commerce,* Sept. 1917, p. 142-4.

ARMSTRONG, CHARLES H.

Depreciation and kindred matters. *Journal of gas lighting,* April 28, 1908, p. 223-7.

ARMSTRONG, F. K.

Actual cost of a contract. *Domesitc engineering,* Dec. 22, 1917, p. 497-8.

ARMSTRONG, G. M. S. comp.

Pulp paper power. New York, Joseph H. Wallace & co. c1909.

ARMSTRONG, GEORGE W.

Cost accounting; the key to cost control. *Railway mechanical engineering,* June 1920, p. 374-9.

General machine tool efficiency. *Railway age* (Mech. ed.), May 1914, p. 255-8.

ARMSTRONG, JOHN HOBART

Address, 1905. *Accountant,* Oct. 14, 1905, p. 428-31, 500-2.

Depreciation reserves. *Accountant,* Aug. 8, 1903, p. 1014-21.

Finite differences. (In Lisle, George. *Encyclopaedia of accounting.* v.3. p. 16-26).

Integral calculus. (In Lisle, George. *Encyclopaedia of accounting.* v.3. p. 352-7).

ARMSTRONG, N. B.

Method of raising overhead expense. *Metal work,* Aug. 11, 1916, p. 179, 80.

ARMSTRONG, R. D.

Connersville sliding scale. *National municipal review,* Oct. 1919, p. 562-6.

ARMSTRONG, ROBERT D.

Regulation of bond discount. *Journal of accountancy,* July 1920, p. 18-35.

ARMSTRONG, RONALD
Comptometer. *Accountant,* July 5, 1919, p. 9-12.
Death duties. *Incorporated accountants' journal,* 1900-1, p. 186.
Law of partnership. *Incorporated accountants' journal,* 1901-2, p. 220.

ARNOIS, A.
Cost of operating a vacuum ash-handling system. *Power,* Sept. 9, 1914, p. 354.

ARNOLD, BION J.
Approximate value placed on physical property of Brooklyn transit company. *Electric railway journal,* Dec. 25, 1909, p. 1261.
Depreciating overhead charges; supplementary note and glossary of terms. *Electric railway journal,* Mar. 11, 1916, p. 498-9.
Foundation principles of utility valuation. New York American electric railway association, 1916.
Foundation principles of utility valuation with special application to plans for resettlement. *Aera,* Oct. 1915, p. 189-223. *Electric railway journal,* Oct. 9, 16, 1915, p. 713-9, 803-6. *Engineering news,* Oct. 28, 1915, p. 859.
Reply on accounting procedure. *Electric railway journal,* May 23, 1914, p. 1152.
Valuation of the Brooklyn rapid transit system. *Electric railway journal,* July 22, 1910, p. 156.

——— and GEORGE W. WESTON
Valuation of the property of the Chicago consolidated traction co. *Engineering news,* Sept. 1, 1910, p. 241.

ARNOLD, C. E.
Cost and extraction in the selection of a mining method. *Bulletin of the American institute of mining engineers,* Sept. 1916, p. 1519-22.

ARNOLD, H. F. W.
Cost of handling material with motor versus horse-drawn equipment. *Engineering magazine,* Oct. 1915. p. 28-32.

ARNOLD, HORACE L.
Complete cost keeper together with an exposition of the advantages of account keeping by cards instead of books. *Engineering magazine,* 1912.
Complete cost keeper. *Engineering magazine,* 1907, p. 408.
Cost-finding methods for moderate sized shops. *Engineering magazine,* Dec. 1902-April 1903, p. 385-95, 577-89, 714-28, 870-8.
Expense account of machine shop. *Engineering magazine,* Dec. 1902, p. 365-72.
Expense account of the machine shop. *Engineering magazine,* Dec. 1900.
Factory manager and accountant; some examples of the latest American factory practice. New York, Engineering magazine, 1903, 431p.
Factory record and tracing system. *American machinist,* May 22, 1913, p. 851-4.
Pratt's record scroll. *American machinist,* Sept. 17, 1903.
Purchase by the organized factory. *Engineering magazine,* June 1903, p. 399-408.
Stores method of the Pond Machine tool works. *Engineering magazine,* March 1905, p. 919-41.
Work in progress record. *American machinist,* April 23, 1903.

——— and F. L. FAUROTE
Ford methods and the Ford shops. New York, Engineering magazine, 1915. *Engineering magazine,* April-Oct., Dec. 1914, June 1915, p. 1-26, 179-203, 331-58, 507-32, 667-92, 857-86; 33-60, 338-66, 524-50, 704-21, 859-76; 67-87, 184-201, 372-93.

——— and others
Cost finding from moderate sized shops. *Engineering magazine,* December 1902, April 1903. p. 385-95, 577-80, 714-78, 870-8, 89-98.

ARRANGEMENTS between companies and their creditors and contributors. *Accountant,* July 6, 13, 20, 27, 1912, p. 6-10, 41-2, 80-3, 112-3.

ARREARS of preference dividends. *Accountant,* Aug. 23, 1902, p. 822-3.

ARRIAN system of book-keeping. Farr, J. W. 1894.

ARSENALS.
See Ordnance.

ART of accounts. Hall, M. P. 1898.

ART of budget-making. *Journal of accountancy,* Nov. 1907, p. 60-1.

ART of collecting. Cassell, R. J. 1910.

ART of digesting and tabulating accounts and returns. Hill, H. W. 1879.

ART of modern bookkeeping and accountancy. Spencer, Enos. 1911.

ARTER, JOHN JAMES BEDNEY
Brewery accounts. *Accountant,* May 15, 1897, p. 496-504.
Treatment and form of brewers' accounts. Birmingham, 1892.

ARTHUR, B. E.
Behind the scenes with five state budgets. *National municipal review,* May 1920, p. 279-88.

ARTHUR, JOSEPH
Daily work of a cost clerk. *Accountant,* Feb. 8, 1913, p. 197-9.

ARTICLED CLERKS
AGREEMENTS between practicioners and clerks. *Accountant,* Sept. 25, Nov. 6, 1909, p. 368-70, 561-5.
EDUCATION of the articled clerk. *Accountant,* Aug. 12, 19, Sept. 23, 1911, p. 197-200, 231-4, 369-71.
RIGHT to take articled clerk. *Accountant,* Jan. 8, 1910, p. 41-3.
VAN DE LINDE, GERARD. Articled clerk. *Accountant,* Nov. 23, 30, 1895, p. 946-52, 969-76.

ARTICLES of partnerships. *Accountant,* Aug. 27, Sept. 3, 1892, p. 649-50, 661-3.

ARTICULATION account. *Journal of accountancy,* June 1907, p. 143.

ATTINGSTALL, WILLIAM
Cost data in small water works systems. *Municipal engineering,* Oct. 1919, p. 184.

AS England sees our rate case; a British railway authority reviews the recent denial of a rate increase, advancing points in support of railways position which are pertinent to the renewal of their plea. *New York Times annalist,* N. Y. 1914, p. 262.

AS others see us. *Accountant,* May 11, 1907. *Incorporated accountants' journal,* May 1907. *Journal of accountancy,* June 1907.

AS others see us. *Journal of accountancy,* Jan. 1911, p. 215-7.

AS the government interprets railroad depreciation. *Engineering record,* June 17, 1916, p. 794-5.

ASCERTAINING parts costs. *Business man's magazine,* Aug. 1911, p. 160.

ASCERTAINING the status of an industry. *Iron age,* February 24, 1916, p. 471-2.

ASCERTAINMENT of value and profits from books of accounts. McKenna, J. A. 1915.

ASCH, N.

Silicates in chemistry and commerce, including the exposition of a hexite and pentite theory and of a stereo-chemical theory of general application: translated with critical notes and some additions by Alfred B. Searle. London, Constable & company, 1913. 456p.

ASH HANDLING

Costs

ARNOIS, A. Cost of operating a vacuum ash-handling system. *Power,* Sept. 9, 1914, p. 354.
MILLER, R. H. Cost of handling ashes with steam vacuum system. *Power,* June 15, 1915. p. 820.
RELATIVE costs of handling ashes manually and mechanically. *Electrical review,* June 21, 1919, p. 1047.
RICKER, W. W. Cost of operating a vacuum ash-handling system. *Power,* Sept. 15, 1914, p. 388-9.
SANDSTROM, C. O. Cost of operating a vacuum ash-handling system. *Power,* July 7, 1914, p. 21-2.
SANDSTROM, C. O. AND R. H. MILLER. Cost of operating vacuum ash-handling systems. *Power,* March 23, 1915, p. 412.

ASHBY, E. G.

Cost accounting as a branch of accounting, and the work of accountants. *Metallurgical and chemical engineering,* Sept. 1914, p. 549-50.

ASHBY, WILLIAM SILAS

See Haworth, Smith Gordon, joint author.

ASHE, SYDNEY WHITMORE

Organization in accident prevention. New York, McGraw-Hill book co. 1917. 130p.

ASHE, W. W.

Cost of logging large and small timber. *Forestry quarterly,* Sept. 1916, p. 441-52.

ASHFORD, J.

Stores arrangement as a factor in shop management. *Engineering magazine,* October, November 1904, p. 98-100, 177-98.

ASHLEY, GEORGE S.

Modern hotel and its management. *Business man's magazine,* Jan. 1908, p. 49-60.

ASHLEY, H. W.

Public policy and legal regulation of central-station charges. *Engineering magazine,* Jan. 1914, p. 545-6.
Public service electric rates. *Practical engineer,* Sept. 1, 1914, p. 877-9.
Theories of electric current rate schedules. *Engineering magazine,* Oct. 1914, p. 86-8.

ASHBY, L. E.

Formula for costs. *System,* Jan. 1915, p. 92-3.

ASHLEY, PERCY

Local authorities and their work. *Accountant,* Sept. 8, Oct. 20, 1906, p. 269-723 453-5.

ASHLEY, W. J.

Statistical measurement of profit. *Accountant,* Jan. 28, 1911, p. 141-51. *Economic journal,* Dec. 1910.

ASHMAN, WILLIAM N.

Preparation of accounts for the court. *Business,* June 1895, p. 234-9

ASHMEAD, ALFRED ERNEST

Trustees under deeds of arrangement. *Accountant,* Jan. 22, June 4, 1898, p. 102-6, 573-6.

ASHMEAD, EDWARD

"Cost book" memories: some reasons for the Cornish mining decline in late years, and hopes for its revival. *Accountant,* June 29, 1901, p. 762.

ASHTON, A. J.

Recent commercial legislation: bankruptcy. *Incorporated accountants' journal,* 1890-1, p. 169.
Recent commercial legislation: commercial law. *Incorporated accountants' journal,* 1890-1, p. 171.
Recent commercial legislation: partnership. *Incorporated accountants' journal,* 1890-1, p. 169.

ASHWORTH, HENRY M.

Some safe guards against fraud. *Accountant,* July 4, 1885.
Some safe guards against fraud and errors. Rochdale, E. Wrigley & sons, 1885.

ASKE, ROBERT WILLIAM

Deeds of arrangement with creditors. *Accountant,* Dec. 21, 1901, Jan. 4, 1902, p. 1387-96, 4-5.

ASKWITH, J. S.

Compendium of coal control accounting. Cromwell House, Surrey St., Strand, London, W.C.2. Commercial compendium co. 256p.

ASMAN, H. R.

Drudgery taken out of lumber figuring. *American lumberman,* Sept. 20, 1919, p. 51.

ASPHALT

BUTLER, M. R. How a contractor equipped his asphalt plant to dispense with two men and lower cost of asphalt. *Municipal engineering,* June 1919, p. 206.

Costs

COST of asphalt repairs. *Municipal engineering,* May 1913, 387-91.
COST of operating municipal asphalt plant of District of Columbia. *Engineering and contracting,* June 6, 1917, p. 512.
COST of operating municipal asphalt plant of Los Angeles. *Engineering and contracting,* March 7, 1917, p. 239.
INVESTIGATION of municipal asphalt plants. *Engineering record,* Feb. 8, 1913.
OPERATING cost, municipal asphalt plant of the District of Columbia. *Engineering news,* April 17, 1919, p. 764.
OPERATION costs at Los Angeles asphalt plant. *Engineering review,* Oct. 28, 1916, p. 523.

ASPHALT—Costs—*(Continued)*
Operation costs of municipal asphalt plant of the city of Portland, Oregon. *Engineering news-record*, June 19, 1919, p 1200-1.

ASPHALT block pavements on sand. *Municipal journal*, November 22, 1917, p. 509. 509.

ASPHALT maintenance costs in Columbus. *Enginering news*, Aug. 26, 1920, p. 423.

ASPHALT pavements laid in 1916 and proposed for 1917; descriptions of pavements as laid, cost per square yard and total cost; tabulation. *Municipal engineering*, February 1917, p. 63-5.

ASPINWALL, C. A.
Overhead on packing labor. *Bulletin of the American warehousemen's association*, Nov. 1920, p. 367.

ASPRAY, NEVILLE
Loose-leaf books. *Accountant*, Oct. 20, 1917, p. 311-4.

ASSAYING
See Mining and Metallurgy.

ASSEMBLING of disbursing officers' checks and vouchers and the verification of their balances in the offices of the auditors of the treasury department. United States. Treasury Department. 1907.

ASSESSMENT of mines. *Engineering and mining journal*, Nov. 22, 1913, p. 969.

ASSESSMENT of real estate. Purdy, Lawson.

ASSESSMENTS on stock of corporations organized under the laws of California. *Journal of accountancy*, Feb. 1913, p. 117-21.

ASSETS
Blackwell, Philip H. Verification of assets. *Accountant*, May 27, 1911, p. 818-23.

Current
Fedde, A. S. Mis-stated current assets. *Journal of accountancy*, June, 1917, p. 440-4.
Rogers, C. S. Arrangement of current assets, correspondence. *Journal of accountancy*, May, 1912, p. 388.

Intangible
Intangible values in balance sheets. *Journal of accountancy*, Aug. 1916, p. 122-5.

Quick
Walton, Seymour. Quick assets. *Journal of accountancy*, July, 1917, p. 65-6.

Wasting
Carter, Eric M. Income tax reform; particularly in regard to profits and wasting assets. *Accountant*, Dec. 31, 1904, p. 799-808.
Depreciation and wasting assets. *Canadian chartered accountant*, Jan. 1914, p. 184-5
Wasting assets. *Accountant*, Feb. 13, 1909, p. 220-2.

ASSIGNMENT of accounts receivable. *Bankers magazine*, Dec.., 1914, p. 654.

ASSIGNMENT of valuation of facilities to more than one state. *Engineering and contracting*, June 25, 1913, p. 726.

ASSOCIATED accountants of New Orleans. *Journal of accountancy*, July, 1913, p. 79.

ASSOCIATED accounts of New Orleans. *Journal of accountancy*, July 1906, June 1907, p. 230-1, 164.

ASSOCIATED ADVERTISING CLUBS OF THE WORLD
Business record systems book of instructions for retail hardware dealers. Indianapolis, Associated advertising clubs of the world, c1917. 46 p.
Business record systems book of instructions for retail jewelry merchants; a simplified system of retail records that provide day-to-day information to facilitate the conduct of business. Indianapolis, Associated advertising clubs of the world, c1916. 52 p.
Business record systems book of instructions for retail shoe merchants, a simplified system of retail records that provide day-to-day information to facilitate the conduct of business. Indianapolis, Associated advertising clubs of the world, c1916. 46 p.

ASSOCIATED CERTIFIED PUBLIC ACCOUNTANTS OF CALIFORNIA (INCORPORATED)
By-laws with list of officers and members, 1906. 28 p.

ASSOCIATION and its official organ. *Government accountant*, May 1907, p. 1-8.

ASSOCIATION OF AMERICAN GOVERNMENT ACCOUNTANTS.
Constitution. *Government accountant*, May, 1907, p. 45-52.

ASSOCIATION OF AMERICAN PORTLAND CEMENT MANUFACTURERS, PHILADELPHIA.
Cost accounting. Philadelphia, Association of American Portland Cement manufacturers. 41 p.

ASSOCIATION OF AMERICAN RAILWAY ACCOUNTING OFFICERS.
See Railway accounting officers' association.

ASSOCIATION of certified public accountants of Montana. *Journal of accountancy*, Oct. 1915, p. 324.

ASSOCIATION OF CHAMBER OF COMMERCE OF SOUTH AFRICA.
Paper in bookkeeping and accountancy, 1916. *South African accountant and auditor*, Dec. 1916, p. 228-33, 235-6.

ASSOCIATION OF CHAMBERS OF COMMERCE.
Bankruptcy bill. *Incorporated accountants' journal*, April, 1917, p. 171-2.
Debate on the bankruptcy bill. *Accountant*, April 13, 1912, p. 590-2.

ASSOCIATION OF CITY AUDITORS OF THE STATE OF OHIO.
Proceedings, 1903.

ASSOCIATION OF RAILWAY EXECUTIVES.
Remedial railroad legislation, 1919.

ASSOCIATION OF TRANSPORTATION AND CAR ACCOUNTING OFFICERS.
Circular no. 21-25 (1906) 50-56 (1907), 60, 63-66 (1908), 92 (1909), 101-105, 107-108 (1910). New York, 1906-10.
Proceedings, 1-4, 1904-07.

ASSOCIATION of transportation and car accounting officers. *Railway age gazette,* Dec. 25, 1914, p. 1192.

ASSOCIATIONS

See Societies, clubs, etc.

ASSOCIATION'S responsibility. *Journal of accountancy,* May, 1911, p. 60-1.

ASSURANCE companies act, 1909. *Accountant,* Sept. 10, 17, Oct. 1, 1910, p. 345-52, 383-7, 439-42.

ASTLE, WILFRED G.

Checking losses in the storeroom. *Iron trade review,* Jan. 27 1916, p. 235-9.
Cost keeping system for plumbing and heating contractors. *Domestic engineering,* Dec. 15, 1917, p. 448-51.
Efficiency in the stores department. *Electric railway journal,* Oct. 30, 1915, p. 906-10.
Functions of the purchasing agent. *Iron trade review,* Dec. 27, 1917, p. 1381-4.
Handling stores according to the cash-control idea. *Electrical review and western electrician,* Dec. 4, 1915, p. 1012-5.
Plugging leaks in the stock room. *Textile world,* July 31, 1920, p. 663.
Storeroom organization and management; mnemonic symbolizing. *Iron age,* Aug. 26, 1915, p. 457-60. *Metal work,* Sept. 10, 1915, p. 332-4.
Tested plans that add to an employee's income. *Industrial management,* Aug. 1917, p. 632-8.

ASTON, W. S.

Some notes on auditing. *Accountants' magazine,* Dec. 1903, p. 556-75.

ASYLUM account keeping. Bryning, R. 1890.

ASYLUMS

See Institutions.

ATKESON, T. CLARK

Bookkeeping for farmers, to which is added the Stockbridge system of accounts. New York, Orange Judd co. 1892. 40p.

ATKIN, FRANCIS

Bookkeeping made easy: or, How to open a set of books by double entry. London, [1886].

ATKINS, PAUL M.

Reading executive policies in factory cost figures. *Factory,* Dec. 15, 1920, p. 1874-7.

ATKINS, ROBERT

Cost records and profits. *Journal of accountancy,* Sept. 1917, p. 239-40.
Peace time cost problems. *Financial world,* Sept. 8, 1919, p. 9.

ATKINSON, ARTHUR S.

Construction and depreciation. *Electric traction weekly,* July 17, 1909, p. 919.
Reducing the cost of depreciation on electric railways. *Street railway bulletin,* Feb. 1907, p. 80.
Insurance. *Accountant,* Feb. 11, 1911, p. 237-47.

ATKINSON, CHARLES JOSHUA FEARNSIDE

Law of agency. *Accountant,* April 25, 1891, p. 321-3.

ATKINSON, GEORGE J.

Duties of trustees. *Incorporated accountants' journal,* 1905-6, p. 139.

ATKINSON, HENRY

Economical production and prevention of waste. *Accountant,* May 1, 1920, p. 521-4.
Incentives to efficiency under scientific management. *Accountant,* July 26, Aug. 2, 1919, p. 94-6, 105-12.

ATKINSON, MEREDITH

Some principles of the credit system. *Accountant,* Oct. 30, 1920, p. 470-6.

ATLANTA company gives reasons why increase is asked for in advertisement. *American gas engineering journal,* Nov. 30, 1918, p. 515-17.

ATLANTIC CITY, NEW JERSEY COMMISSIONERS.

Report on an examination of the books and accounts of the City of Atlantic City, Jan. 1, 1912, to July 16, 1912, inclusive, and changes installed in the system of accounting as at Sept. 1, 1912. Philadelphia, E. P. Moxey and co. 1912. *American society of municipal improvements, Proceedings,* 1912, p. 52-3.

ATLANTIC COAST SHIPBUILDERS' ASSOCIATION.

Cost accounting in shipbuilding report of the uniform methods of cost accounting adopted June 4, 1919. 30 Church street, New York, 1919. 132 p.

ATLASES

DOUBLEDAY, PAGE & COMPANY. Geographical manual and new atlas; ed. by C. O. S. Mawson. New York, Doubleday, Page & co. 1918. 392 p.

ATTACK on the shop committee plan. *Industrial management,* Aug. 1919, p. 162-3.

ATTELL, J.

Filing leases and agreements. *Business man's magazine,* Sept. 1907, p. 122-24.

ATTEMPT to standardize valuation terms. *Engineering news,* Oct. 26, 1916, p. 787-8.

ATTENBERG, HENRY N.

Internal revenue accounting in the cigar business. *Business man's magazine,* June 15, 1901, p. 705-6.

ATTERBURY, W. W.

Increased rates to offset increased expenses. *Railway age,* Aug. 31, 1917, p. 394.

ATTFIELD, J. H.

See Bogle, John W. Stewart, joint author.

ATTITUDE of central stations on rates. *Electrical world,* Sept. 7, Nov. 2, Dec. 7, 1918, p. 445-6, 832-3, 1075-6.

ATTITUDE of organized labor. Golden, John.

ATTLEE, THOMAS MORRIS ENGLAND

Colliery accounts. *Accountant,* Dec. 19, 1885.
Some notes on bankruptcy and deeds of arrangement. *Accountant,* June 22, 1901, p. 728-34.

ATTORNEYS.

See Lawyers.

ATWOOD, ALBERT WILLIAM
Exchanges and speculation. New York, Alexander Hamilton institute, c1918. 334 p. (Modern business, v. 20.)

AUBRY, V. G.
Lessons to be learned by keeping records. *New Jersey agricultural exp. hints to poultry men,* Feb. 1919, v. 7, 4 p.

AUCTIONEERS
DUTCH auctions. *Accountant,* April 30, 1910, p. 589-92.

Accounting
AMERICAN business and accounting encyclopaedia; comp. by E. H. Beach and W. W. Thorne. Detroit, Bookkeeper publishing co. 1901. Auctioneers' accounts, v. 1, p. 151-2.
DICKSEE, LAWRENCE ROBERT. Auctioneers' accounts. London, Gee & co. 1901. 79p. (Accountants' library, v. 2.)
DICKSEE, LAWRENCE ROBERT. Auctioneers' accounts. (In Lisle, George. *Encyclopaedia of accounting.* v. 1. p. 157-63.)
FARR, C. Auctioneers' system of book-keeping. *Accountant,* Aug. 25, 1888, p. 542-5.
LISLE, GEORGE. Hide, skin and tallow auctioneering. (In his *Encyclopaedia of accounting.* v. 3. p. 248-71.)
PIXLEY, FRANCIS W. Auctioneers. (In his *Accountancy.* Ed. 2. p. 96-7.)
RUBERY, JOHN EVANS. Auctioneers' book and accounts. London, Simpson, Low, Marston and co. 1900.

Auditing

SPICER, ERNEST EVAN and ERNEST C. PEGLER. Estate agents, auctioneers, surveyors, &c. (In their *Practical auditing,* 1914. p. 480-1.)

AUCTIONEERS' accounts. Dicksee, L. R. 1901.

AUCTIONEERS' book and accounts. Rubery J. E. 1900.

AUDIT COMPANIES
ACCREDITED accountants. *Journal of accountancy,* June, 1915, p. 460-1.
OPPOSED to all accounting corporations. *Journal of accountancy,* March, 1906, p. 415-6.
SHORROCK, E. G. Firms or corporations. *Auditor,* 1905, p. 128.
TOUCHING appeal. *Journal of accountancy,* Nov. 1916, p. 387.
Two kinds of auditing companies. *Journal of accountancy,* Feb. 1906, p. 320-1.

AUDIT memoranda. Binnie, Andrew.

AUDIT note book [a specimen]. London. [?1894.]

AUDIT of a public limited company. Jenkinson, M. W. 1913.

AUDIT of banks of discounts and deposits. Moyer, M. S.

AUDIT of building societies accounts. *Accountant,* Oct. 15, 22, Nov. 5, 19, Dec. 3, 10, 1892, p. 765-7, 785-7, 791, 832-3, 869-71, 913-5, 941-3.

AUDIT of co-operative societies accounts. *Accountant,* July 25, Sept. 5, 12, 19, 1896, p. 627-9, 721-2, 743-4, 762-3.

AUDIT of county councils' accounts. *Accountant,* April 9, 1892, p. 297-8, 307-11.

AUDIT of electric lighting companies accounts. *Accountant,* June 27, July 4, 1908, p. 919-20, 1-4.

AUDIT of insurance accounts. Wilkinson, George. 1905.

AUDIT of local authorities' accounts. *Accountant,* Dec. 22, 1906, Sept. 7, 14, 21, Nov. 2, 1907, p. 755-8, 778-9, 297-9, 327-9, 359-61, 543-5.

AUDIT of local authorities' accounts. *Accountant,* Jan. 28, April 22, 1911, p. 132-5, 617-21, 646-8.

AUDIT of local authorities' accounts; the systems in New South Wales. *Accountant,* Feb. 17, April 13, 1912, p. 275-7, 565-9, 597-600.

AUDIT of municipal accounts. *Accountant,* Jan. 19, 1901, p. 73-5.

AUDIT of municipal accounts. *Accountant,* July 8, 1911, p. 33-6.

AUDIT of municipal accounts; abstract. *Accountant,* Feb. 28, 1920, p. 247-9.

AUDIT of partnership accounts. Jenkinson, Mark Webster. 1914.

AUDIT of private companies acts. *Accountant,* Dec. 5, 1908, p. 669-71.

AUDIT of private limited companies' accounts. *Accountant,* Aug. 6, Oct. 15, 1898, p. 768-70, 953-6.

AUDIT of railroad accounts. *Law review and quarterly journal,* v. 11, p. 292.

AUDIT of railway accounts. *Accountant,* Sept 19, 26, Oct. 3, 10, 17, 24, 1891, p. 659-61, 675-7, 691-3, 706-8, 723-5, 739-41.

AUDIT of savings banks accounts. *Accountant,* Aug. 24, 1889, p. 444-6.

AUDIT of the accounts of land development companies, particularly as applied to colonial condition. *Accountant,* March 11, 1916, p. 297-9.

AUDIT of the accounts of tramway undertakings and tramway finance companies, Great Britain. *Electrical review* (London), Sept. 24, Oct. 1, 1901.

AUDIT of the books of the city of Birmingham, Ala., for the fourteen months ending June 30, 1907, and the new system of municipal accounting. Beck, H. C. 1907.

AUDIT of the city of Montgomery, Alabama, October 1, 1910, to July 1, 1911, and a new system of municipal accounting. Standard audit company, Atlanta. 1911.

AUDIT of the public service accounts. *Public service* (Los Angeles), Dec. 1918, p. 1-4.

AUDIT of trust accounts. *Accountant,* Nov. 14, 1914, p. 555-7.

AUDIT of trust accounts under the Public trustee act, 1906. Pegler, E. E. 1911.

AUDIT of war charities accounts. *Accountant,* Oct. 16, 1915, p. 447-9.

AUDIT of war savings associations. *Incorporated accountants' journal,* Nov. 1916, p. 30.

AUDIT programmes. Spicer, E. E., and E. C. Pegler. 1919.

AUDIT record book. *Accountants' magazine,* 1901, p. 248.

AUDIT system of a trust company. *Accountants' journal,* 1906-7, p. 83.

AUDIT working papers. Bell, W. H.

AUDITED and found correct. *Accountant,* April 7, 1888, p. 213-4.

AUDITING

See Auditing and auditors.

AUDITING. *Accountant,* April 30, 1910, p. 594

AUDITING. Dicksee, L. R.

AUDITING, accounting and banking. Dowler, Frank, and E. M. Harris.

AUDITING AND AUDITORS

See also Accounting; Investigations; also subdivision Auditing under various headings, e. g. Railroads—Auditing.

ACCOUNTANTS; their duties and responsibilities: auditing articles. *Accountant,* Jan. 6, 13, 20, 27, Feb. 3, 10, 17, 24, Mar. 3, 10, 17, 24, 31, April 7, 14, 21, 28, May 5, 1883.

ACCOUNTING parties and auditors—auditor and bookkeeper. *Accountant,* Feb. 6, March 6, 1909, p. 188-93, 327-9.

AMERICAN business accounting encyclopaedia; comp. by E. H. Beach and W. W. Thorne. Detroit, Bookkeeper publishing co. 1901. Auditing, p. 125-51.

ANNELLS, G. R. Status of an auditor. *Accountant,* Aug. 22, 1908, p. 218-20.

APPOINTMENT and remuneration of auditors. *Accountant,* Feb. 17, 1912, p. 253-6.

ARE these charges true? a well-known financial writer claims that all audits are not what they ought to be. *Canadian chartered accountant,* July 1914, p. 42-4.

ASTON, WILLIAM SMEDLEY. Some notes on auditing. *Accountants' magazine,* Dec. 1903, p. 556-75.

AUDIT note book [a specimen]. London. [?1894]

AUDIT record book. *Accountants magazine,* 1901, p. 248.

AUDITING. *Accountant,* April 30, 1910, p. 594.

AUDITING balance sheets. *Canadian chartered accountant,* April 1912, p. 208.

AUDITING in Australia. *Accountant,* April 2, 1898, p. 369. *Public accountant,* 1908, p. 11.

AUDITING in Ireland. *Accountant,* April 22, 1911, p. 640-4.

AUDITING in Japan. *Accountant,* Aug. 28, 1909, p. 253-6.

AUDITING in relation to "unearned income." *Accountant,* March 19, 1910, p. 398-9.

AUDITING under the local government act, 1906 (N. S. W.) *Public accountant,* 1908, p. 181; 1909, p. 2, 59.

AUDITOR-BOOKKEEPER. *Accountant,* Feb. 15, 1908, p. 205-8.

AUDITORS and accounts. *Accountant,* Jan. 14, 21, Feb. 4, 1893, p. 25, 45, 50, 103.

AUDITORS and auditing; a straight talk on "opinions." *Accountant,* Aug. 17, 1912, p. 233-7.

AUDITORS and secret commissions. *Accountant,* Jan. 31, 1914, p. 135-7.

AUDITORS and shareholders. *Accountant,* Jan. 27, 1912, p. 120.

AUDITORS and stocktaking. *Accountant,* Jan. 13, Feb. 10, April 20, 1912, Feb. 1, 1913, p. 42-4, 193-7, 600-2, 139-43, 161-3. *Incorporated accountants' journal,* Feb. 1912, p. 116-7.

AUDITORS and summarized balance sheets. *Accountant,* April 6, 1901, p. 413-6.

AUDITORS and their duties. *Accountant,* July 29, 1893, p. 679-83.

AUDITORS' contracts. *Incorporated accountants' journal,* June 1912, p. 227-8.

AUDITORS duties and responsibilities. *Incorporated accountants' journal,* Sept. 1918, p. 232-3, 234-40.

AUDITORS, duties and responsibilities. *Incorporated accountants' journal,* June 1920, p. 192-4.

AUDITOR'S duty in relation to "fictitious transactions." *Incorporated accountants' journal,* Aug. 1920, p. 219-20.

AUDITORS in India. *Accountant,* June 20, 1914, p. 873-6, 894-7.

AUDITOR'S legal liability. *Journal of accountancy,* July 1912, p. 53-7.

AUDITORS of causes, etc., acts of Scotland. London, Longman, 1846.

AUDITORS' qualifications; House of Lords select committee; re Hightown gas and electricity bill, May 5th, 1914. *Incorporated accountants' journal,* June, 1914, p. 257-9.

AUDITORS' qualifications; important decision of select committee of the House of Lords re Whitwell and District gas bill, March 19, 1914 *Incorporated accountants' journal,* April 1914, p. 189-203.

AUDITOR'S relation to the appraiser and others. *Journal of accountancy,* Dec. 1910, p. 138-41.

AUDITOR'S standing in England and America; what are we going to do about it? *Canadian chartered accountant,* April 1914, p. 237-43.

AUDITORS v. directors. *Accountant,* Dec. 7, 14, 1907, Jan. 4, 1908, March 20, Dec. 25, 1909, p. 689-90, 724-6; 3-4, 389-93, 769-72.

AUTHORITY and responsibility of the auditor. *Journal of accountancy,* May 1912, p. 360-4.

BAILEY, LAWRENCE. Duties and responsibilities of auditors in relation to stocktaking. *Incorporated accountants' journal,* April 1912, p. 186-8.

BAINBRIDGE, J. P. Depreciation, and an auditor's responsibility in connection therewith. *Accountant,* Sept. 22, 1906, p. 334-7. *Incorporated accountants' journal,* 1906-7, p. 12.

BALANCE sheet audits. *Accountant,* Dec. 28, 1918, p. 337-9.

BATCHELOR, J. B. Verification and value of book debts for the purpose of a balance sheet. *Accountant,* Jan. 12, 1901, p. 51-3.

BECAUSE unaudited. *Journal of accountancy,* Feb. 1915, p. 141-2.

BECK, HERBERT. Value of auditing to the business man. Philadelphia. American academy of political and social science, 1903. Annals of the American academy of political and social science, Nov. 1903, p. 433-4.

BELL, ALBERT and others. Duties of an auditor. *Accountant,* Feb. 18, 1911, p. 277.

BELL, WILLIAM H. Audit working papers. *Journal of accountancy,* Aug. 1919, p. 104-12.

BENINGTON, HAROLD. Limitations. *Accounting and commerce,* May 1916, p. 35-40. *Accountant,* Sept. 30, 1916, p. 287-91. *Canadian chartered accountant,* April 1917, p. 289-98. *Journal of accountancy,* May 1916, p. 333-43.

BERGMAN, NATHANIEL B. Verification of inventories during an audit. *Journal of accountancy,* Sept. 1911, p. 352-6.

BHALLA, K. C. Auditors, their duties and responsibilities. Calcutta, 1913.

BINDLOSS, ROBERT HUGH. Accountancy and auditing. *Incorporated acountants' journal,* Jan. 1912, p. 100-3.

BINNIE, ANDREWS. Audit memoranda. London, Gee & co. 1910.

BIRD, CYRIL F. Duty and responsibility of auditors with regard to the item "Stock-in-trade" on a balance sheet. (In Chase, W. A. *Auditing and cost accounting.* 1917. p. 266-78.)

BLACKWELL, PHILIP H. Verification of assets. (In Feather, J. Stuart, ed. *Joint transactions.* 1911. p. 111-25.) *Accountant,* May 27, 1911, p. 818-23.

AUDITING AND AUDITORS—*(Continued)*

Bourne, J. H. Auditing. *Accountant,* 1887, p. 330.

Bradford chartered accountants students' association debate—the duties of an auditor. *Accountant,* Feb. 18, 1911, p. 277-81.

Brewer, Andrew Herbert. Auditing. *Incorporated accountants' journal,* 1909-10, p. 158.

Bridge, G. H. Auditors' responsibilities in respect to the verification of stock-in-trade. *Incorporated accountants' journal,* Oct. 1912, p. 10-4.

Bristol chartered accountants students' society. Auditors and certificates to stock. *Accountant,* April 26, May 31, 1902, p. 447-54, 562-3.

Bristol society of chartered accountants. Discussion on the responsibilities of auditors. *Accountant,* March 4, 1911, p. 352-4.

Burton, Francis G. Limitations of auditors. *Accountant,* May 10, 1913, p. 735-41.

Caldicott, Oswald Holt. Auditor's duty in respect of depreciation. *Accountant,* Jan. 25, 1896, p. 74-6.

Caldicott, Oswald Holt. Chartered accountants as experts in commerce and manufactures. *Accountant,* May 22, 1897, p. 524-9.

Caldicott, Oswald Holt. Specialization for accountants. *Accountant,* April 22, 1905, p. 490-5.

Carlill, John Albert. Ante-audit; being the auditor's instructions to the employer's bookkeeping staff. London, Gee & Co. 1900.

Carr, Ebenezer. Duties and responsibilities of auditors. *Accountant,* Sept. 14, 1901, p. 990-7. *Commerce, accounts and finance,* March 1902, p. 11-5. *Incorporated accountants journal,* 1901-2, p. 11.

Carr, Ebenezer. Method as relating to accounting and auditing. *Incorporated accountants journal,* 1905-6, p. 69.

Carter, Eric M. Criticism of the opinions of some chartered accountants on the routine work of an audit. *Acountant,* Jan. 6, 1894, p. 13-22.

Castenholz, William Curtis. Auditing procedure. Chicago, LaSalle extension university, 1918. 342p.

Cavell, Arthur Silvester. Auditors and certificates as to stock. *Accountant,* April 26, May 31, 1902, p. 447, 562.

Chadwick, David. Duties of a professional auditor: with discussion. *Accountant,* Sept. 29, Nov. 3, 1883.

Charlton, F. F. More important differences in the duties and responsibilities arising in the following audits—1, single trader; 2, partnership; 3, public company. *Accountants' magazine,* Dec. 1908, p. 543-59.

Chartered accountants and their duties. *Accountant,* Jan. 22, 1916, p. 124-6. *Public accountant,* March 1916, p. 195-7.

Chase, William Arthur. Auditing and cost accounting. Chicago, La Salle extension university, 1917. 493p.

Chase, William Arthur. Legal liability of auditors. (In his *Auditing and cost accounting.* 1917. p. 352-65.) *Accountant,* June 26, 1915, p. 846-51.

Child, Percy. Paper on some of the bookkeeping questions set at the June examinations. *Accountant,* Dec. 31, 1898, p. 1264-71.

Claim against an auditor for alleged negligence. *Accounting and commerce,* Sept. 1918, p. 134-8.

Claridge, William. Checking of bank interest. *Accountant,* March 7, 1908, p. 326. *Incorporated accountants' journal,* 1907-8, p. 1151.

Cleveland, Frederick A. Relation of auditing to public control. *Annals of the American academy of political and social science,* Nov. 1905, p. 665-80.

Clinch, S. H. Some points in the completion of an audit. *Accountant,* May 23, 1914, p. 765-70. *Incorporated accountants' journal,* April 1913, p. 164-8.

Cobbler and last. *Journal of accountancy,* Nov. 1920, p. 361-4.

Cocke, Hugh Golding. Summary of the principal legal decisions affecting auditors; a paper read before the Chartered accountant student society of London on Wednesday, February 20th, 1907. London, Gee & co. 1907. 39p. *Accountant,* May 18, 1907, p. 678-90.

Cole, William Morse. Accounting and auditing. Minneapolis. Cree publishing co, 1910.

Cole, William Morse. Auditing. (In his *Accounts, their construction and interpretation.* c1915. p. 362-5.)

Cole, William Morse. Auditing. (In his *Bookkeeping, accounting and auditing.* c1914. p. 397-449).

Colley, F. G. Working papers. *Journal of accountancy,* July 1916, p. 43-9.

Collins, Charles W. Problem of an independent national audit. *Journal of political economy,* Jan. 1920, p. 37-45.

Cooke, G. C. Audit of cash transactions. *Accounting and commerce,* Aug. 1916, p. 117-9.

Cooke, Silas. Accountancy and auditing. *Accountant,* June 6, 1885.

Cooley, Morgan. American audit note book. New York, Accountancy publishing co. 1909.

Cooley, Morgan L. Close of an audit. *Accountant,* July 17, 1909, p. 96-8. *Journal of accountancy,* May 1909, p. 33-9.

Cooper, F. T. Liability of an auditor. *Accountants' magazine,* July 1909, p. 351-65.

Crewdson, Ernest. Codification of an audit. *Accountant,* Feb. 22, 1902, p. 214-20.

Criminal liabilities of auditors. *Accountant,* Nov. 24, Dec. 1, 15, 1900, p. 1045-54, 1069-73, 1133-5.

Cutforth, Arthur Edwin. Audits. London, Gee & co. 1914. 238p.

Dangerfield, Athelstan. Reports on accounts. *Accountant,* July 25, 1896, p. 633-9.

Davie, P. Essay to set forth, in full and minute detail instructions to be given to assistant by senior on all checking (other than vouching) and other considerations involved in a complete audit up to the trial balance, including the checking of the arithmetic, &c., of subsidiary books and stocks, and in all respects describing even the most elementary aspects of the checking. *Accountant,* Oct. 3, 1914, p. 375-81.

Davies, Bertram C. Business system, and internal check in relation to the audit. *Accountant,* May 15, 1915, p. 648-52.

Day, Clarence Munro. Methods of working. (In his *Accounting practice.* 1915. p. 3-76.

Defective audits and fraud. *Accountant,* Jan. 23, 30, 1909, p. 112-4, 153-7, 1910, p. 428.

DePaula, Frederick R. M. Few notes on auditing. *Accountant,* June 15, 1912, p. 899-906.

DePaula, Frederick R. M. Principles of auditing; a practical manual for students and their practitioners. London, Sir Isaac Pitman & sons. 207p.

DePaula, Frederick R. M. Some further notes on auditing. *Accountant,* March 22, 1913, p. 442-51.

Dickinson, Arthur Lowes. Duties and responsibilties of the public accountant in respect of audit. (In his *Accounting practice and procedure.* 1917. p. 231-40.)

Dickinson, Arthur Lowes. Duties of the public accountant. *Business world,* April 1902, p. 169-70.

Dicksee, Lawrence Robert. Auditing. (In Lisle, George. *Encyclopaedia of accounting.* v. 1. p. 163-93.)

AUDITING AND AUDITORS—*(Continued)*

DICKSEE, LAWRENCE ROBERT. Auditing; a practical manual for auditors. Ed. 2, revised and enlarged. London, Gee & co. 1895. 577p.

——— Same. Ed. 10. London, Gee & co. 1915. 975p.

DICKSEE, LAWRENCE ROBERT. Auditing; a practical manual for auditors; ed. by Robert H. Montgomery. Authorized American edition. New York, R. H. Montgomery, 1909. 385p.

——— Same. Authorized American edition, revised and enlarged. New York, The Ronald press co. 1909. 586p.

DICKSEE, LAWRENCE ROBERT. Liabilities of auditors under the companies acts. *Accountant,* May 14, 1898, p. 500-11, 597.

DILLON, A. Continuous audit, public accounts. London, A. Brown, 1880.

DIRECTORS and auditors. *Accountant,* June 12, Dec. 25, 1909, p. 819-22, 769-72.

DIRECTORS v. auditors. *Accountant,* Jan. 13, 20, 24, 29, April 20, July 6, Aug. 31, Dec. 28, 1894, Jan. 27, April 21, 1900, March 15, April 19, 1902, July 8, 15, 22, 1905, Jan. 13, 1906, p. 29-31, 53-6 173-4, 839-42, 349-52, 589-92, 693-5, 1045-2, 95, 365, 276-9, 407-9, 33-5, 65-7, 104-6, 34-6.

DODD, ARTHUR F. Powers and duties of auditors under section 113 of the companies (consolidation) act, 1908. *Accountant,* Sept. 25, 1909, p. 380-9.

DODD, ARTHUR F. Professional auditors. *Accountant,* March 1, 1913, p. 320-6.

DODD, ARTHUR F. Some suggestions as to the discovery and prevention of defalcations and an auditor's point of view. *Accountant,* May 30, 1903, p. 723-31, 855.

DOHERTY, JAMES L. Law relating to auditors and masters in Mass. Boston, Little Brown & co. 1906.

DOWLER, FRANK and E. M. HARRIS. Auditing, accounting and banking; a manual for accountants advanced bookkeeping students and business men. London, Sir Isaac Pitman & sons. 319p.

DRUMMOND, ARTHUR. On the mode of conducting an audit. *Acountant,* May 2, 16, 1891, p. 341-3, 377-9.

DUGUID, CHARLES. Rights and duties of auditors. *Accountant,* Oct. 22, Dec. 17, 1910, Jan. 21, 1911, Feb. 17, March 9, 1912, p. 570, 837, 865, 84, 119, 301, 373. *Incorporated accountants' journal,* 1910-11, p. 36, 53, 62, 79, 92, 124. Editorial. *Journal of accountancy,* Dec. 1910, p. 143-5.

DUNCAN, NATHANIEL B. Verification of inventories during an audit. *Journal of accountancy,* Sept. 1911, p. 352-6.

DUTIES and liabilities of auditors. *Accountant,* Oct. 22, Nov. 12, 1910, Dec. 2, 6, 1911, Jan. 20, 1912, p. 547-5, 637-9, 741-4, 813-8, 73-7.

DUTIES and responsibilities of auditors. *Accountant,* Sept. 30, 30, Nov. 18, Dec. 16, 16, 1899, p. 980-1, 990-3, 1121-2, 1203-6, 1223-4.

DUTIES and responsibilities of auditors. *Business,* April 1895, p. 159-60.

DUTIES of auditors. *Accountant,* May 18, 1912, p. 745.

DUTIES of auditors. *Accountant,* Jan. 8, 1916, Feb. 2, 1918, p. 36-8, 89-92.

DUTIES of auditors: a symposium. *Accountant,* March 28, 1896, p. 259-62. *Business,* Feb. 1896, p. 87-9.

DUTIES of auditors; limits of responsibility; clearer definition needed. *Accountant,* May 18, 1912, p. 780-1.

DUTIES of auditors under the companies act, 1900. *Accountant,* Dec. 15, 22, 29, 1900, p. 1135-8, 1157-60, 1185-7.

DUXBURY, NATHANIEL. Scope of the audit. *Accountant,* Feb. 5, 1916, p. 177-81. *Incorporated accountants' journal,* Jan. 1916, p. 78-81. *South African accountant and auditor,* Sept. Dec. 1916, p. 191-3, 207-9.

EASTON, JAMES MARSHALL. Liabilities of auditors of companies with special reference to the Companies act, 1900. *Accountant,* April 27, 1901, p. 501-6, 895.

EDDIS, WELTON C. Auditing. *Accountant,* Feb. 1899, p. 231-7.

ELGAR, WILLIAM DANIEL and others. Surprise visits of auditors. *Incorporated accountants journal,* 1900-1, p. 96.

EVANS, HARRY E. Student's auditing. London, Longmans, Green & co. 1914. 204p.

EWING, R. O. and company. Incomplete audits: correspondence. *Journal of accountancy,* Sept. 1913, p. 254-5.

EWING, R. O. and company. Importance of comments on reports: correspondence. *Journal of accountancy,* May 1913, p. 391-3.

FEDERAL reserve board and audits. *Journal of accountancy,* June 1917, p. 452-4.

FIELD, CHARLES and others. Partial audits. *Incorporated accountants journal,* 1906-7, p. 297.

FINCHAM, R. F. W. Statutes and statutory regulations affecting company auditors. *Accountant,* Dec. 16, 1899, p. 1211-22.

FORNEY, E. J. Practical auditing by totals. *Bookkeeper,* 1903, v. 16, no. 6, p. 61-5.

FORNEY, E. J . What is essential in an audit. *Business man's magazine,* 1904, v. 16, no. 10, p. 86-8.

FREE audits for needy charities. *Survey,* June 10, 1916, p. 290.

GENT, JOHN H. Some notes on the close of an audit. *Incorporated accountants' journal,* Oct. 1914, p. 19-21.

GIBSON, ARTHUR HENRY. Auditors. *Accountant,* Oct. 13, 1894, p. 901-6.

GILES, S. E. Verification of assets and liabilities. *Incorporated accountants' journal,* Oct. 1913, p. 15-9.

GILL, PHILIP J. "Concise" audit and accounting memorandum book. Scranton, Scranton book co. c1912.

GLASGOW CHARTERED ACCOUNTANTS STUDENTS' SOCIETY. Can an audit be such as to effectually prevent fraud? *Accountant,* March 1, 1902, p. 241-4.

GOODLOE, J. S. M. Accountant's report from the standpoint of the several parties at interest. New York state society of public accountants, 1915. *Accountant,* Oct. 2, 1915, p. 402-8. *Canadian chartered accountant,* Jan. 1916, p. 199-212. *Journal of accountancy,* Aug. 1915, p. 91-103.

GOODYEAR, LLOYD EARNEST. Principles of accountancy. Cedar Rapids, Iowa, Goodyear-Marshall publishing co. c1913. 190p. (American bookkeeping series.)

GOVERNMENT audit. *Accountant,* June 3, 1916, p. 643-4.

GRANT, GEORGE W. Auditing balance sheets. *Canadian chartered accountant,* Oct. 1912, p. 111-12.

GRANT, J. A. Cash book; its purpose, character, and need of exhaustive verification by the auditor. *Accountant,* Aug. 12, 1916, p. 134-9. *Canadian chartered accountant,* April 1916, p. 252-63.

GRAVES, HARRY ROBERT. Some audit memoranda. *Accountant,* April 18, May 16, 1903, p. 522-7, 648-50.

GREGORY, THEODORE. Responsibilities of auditors. *Accountant,* Oct. 27, 1894, p. 956-63.

GRIFFIN, J. L. Verification of assets. *Accounting and commerce,* April, May, June 1919, p. 14-16, 37-9, 59-63.

GROVER, P. H. Side issues in auditing work. *Business,* Feb. 1899, p. 114-5.

HALDANE, HERBERT W. Examination of securities. *Accountant,* Jan. 15, 1910, p. 95-102. *Accountants' magazine,* Jan. 1910, p. 14-32.

HAMILTON, W. R. Some notes on the prep-

AUDITING AND AUDITORS—*(Continued)*
aration and audit of a balance sheet. *Accountant,* Jan. 7, 1911, p. 20-7.
HARVEY, BALDWIN SYDNEY. Limits which a chartered accountant should place on his duties and responsibilities as an auditor. *Accountant,* April 3, 1897, p. 372-5.
HAY, GEORGE H. How to check a bank passbook at the rate of 300 cheques per hour. *Accountant,* May 2, 1908, p. 630-2.
HENDERSON, W. H. Auditing. *Accountant,* Sept. 13, 1919, p. 225-9. *Canadian chartered accountant,* Oct. 1920, p. 102-15.
HERTZ, JOSEPH EMMETT. Secrets of accounting: a practical treatise on how to conduct general audits and ascertain working capital. Portland, Me. J. E. Hertz. 1913. 37p.
HICKOX, E. BASKERVILLE. Conduct of an audit, with notes on special cases. *Incorporated accountants' journal,* Nov. 1911, p. 37-42.
How to audit: a manual of instruction. New York, McArdle press, c1919. 112p.
HULL, ERNEST. Value of an audit. *Accountant,* March 20, 1897, p. 312-3.
HUTTON, GEORGE JOHNSTON. On auditing commercial and company books. *Accountant,* Oct. 26, Nov. 2, 9, 28, 1889, p. 562-4, 574-80, 592-3, 613-5.
IMPORTANCE of comments on reports. *Journal of accountancy,* May 1913 p. 391-3.
INDEPENDENT audits. *Journal of accountancy,* Sept. 1909, p. 382. *Wall street journal,* Aug. 7, 1909.
JENKINSON, MARK WEBSTER. Audit of manufacturing concerns. *Accountant,* Feb. 13, 1909, p. 232-47.
JENKINSON, MARK WEBSTER. Audit of various businesses. *Accountant,* April 4, 1914, p. 495-506.
JENKINSON, MARK WEBSTER. Method in accounting and audit. *Accountant,* Dec. 26, 1903, p. 1567-76.
JENKINSON, MARK WEBSTER. Some debatable matters in accounting and audit. *Accountant,* March 20, 1909, p. 406-16. *Incorporated accountants journal,* 1908-9, p. 192.
JENKINSON, MARK WEBSTER. Some notes on the audit of different businesses. London, Gee & co. 1913. 40p. *Accountant,* April 19, 1913, p. 579-93.
JONES, WARREN JOHN. Auditing. *Accountant,* May 24, 31, 1884.
JUDD, HAROLD G. and others. Can an audit be such as to effectually prevent fraud? *Accountant,* March 1, 1902, p. 241.
KEISTER, D. A. Auditors and auditing. *Business,* March, April, May, June 1896, p. 141-2, 192, 235-6, 279-80.
KIRKCALDIE, W. I. Auditing in the desert of Tarapaca. *Accountant,* Jan. 27, 1906, p. 118-9.
KLEIN, JOSEPH J. Auditing. (In his *Elements of accounting.* 1916. p. 322-56.)
LAFRENTZ, F. W. Economic aspects of accounting and auditing. *Accountant,* June 9, 1906, p. 734. *Journal of accountancy,* April 1906, p. 479. *Science,* April 20, 1906, p. 615-6.
LEGAL liability of auditors. *Accountant,* July 23, 30, 1904, Feb. 12, 1910, p. 92-4, 102, 116-8, 225-9. *Journal of accountancy,* March 1910, p. 380-1.
LEWIS, J. SLATER. Commercial organization of factories. London, 1896. 540p.
LIABILITIES of auditors. *Accountant,* Jan. 5, 12, 26, Feb. 22, 1901, Jan. 3, 10, 17, April 25, 1914, p. 6-9, 40-2, 102-4, 133-5, 3-6, 35-7, 64-6, 590-601.
LIABILITIES of auditors—insurance policies. *Accountant,* Feb. 22, 1908, p. 237-40.
LIABILITIES of auditors the Kingston cotton mill case. *Accountant,* Jan. 4, 11, 1896, p. 3-6, 23-6.
LIABILITY of auditors. *Accountant,* Feb. 17, 24, March 3, 17, 24, 1900, June 29, 1907, p. 173-6, 198-201, 217-20, 261-3, 281-4, 861-3.
LIABILITY of auditors for negligence. *Accountant,* March 11, 1911, p. 390-5.
LISLE, GEORGE. Duties and responsibilities of an auditor. (In his *Accounting theory and practice,* 1900, p. 348-50.)
LOCAL government act (Australia); regulations as to audit. *Public accountant,* 1906-7, p. 115.
LYNN, JOHN R. Classification and certification of profits. *Accountant,* May 13, 1916, p. 564-5. *Journal of accountancy,* April 1916, p. 255-60.
McDOUGALL, J. L. Quarter of a century's audit. *Canadian magazine,* May 1903, p. 67-73.
MACKENZIE, W. R. Verification and treatment of inventories in audits and examinations of manufacturing and trading concerns. *Journal of accountancy,* Dec. 1909, p. 114-22. *American institute of accountants, Yearbook,* 1909, p. 273-89.
MADDEN, JOHN THOMAS. Accounting practice and auditing. New York, Alexander Hamilton institute, c1917. 338p. (Modern business, v. 21.)
MARSH, H. Duty and responsibility of auditors with regard to "stock-in-trade." *Accountant,* March 16, 1912, p. 448-9.
MARSHALL, HENRY CALDER. Questions that arise in practice. *Accountant,* June 1, 1895, p. 493-9.
MEELBOOM, J. A. Audit note book and how to keep it. *Accountant,* June 24, 1893, p. 593-4.
MELLORS, T. G. Uniformity of practice in the certificates and the "requirements" of auditors under the companies act, 1900, and in the report to shareholders. *Accountant,* Dec. 14, 1901, Jan. 4, 1902, p. 1362-4, 2-4.
METHOD of supporting financial records. *Journal of home economics,* March 1916, p. 130-1.
MILBURNE, R. J. Necessity of a manual on auditing. *Accountant,* June 18, 25, 1881.
MILLER, ROBERT FERGUSON. Professional auditors: some aspects of their qualifications and work. *Accountant,* Feb. 1, April 11, 1908, p. 151-9, 505-7.
MOERAN, EDWARD H. Auditor's responsibility in regard to verification of inventories. *Journal of accountancy,* March 1918, p. 176-86.
MONTGOMERY, ROBERT H. Auditing. Chicago, American school of correspondence, 1909. (In *Cyclopaedia of commerce, accountancy, business administration.* 1910. v. 6. p. 11-204.)
MONTGOMERY, ROBERT H. Auditing, theory and practice. New York, The Ronald press co. 1916. 542p.
——— Same. 1916. 889p.
MONTGOMERY, ROBERT H. Co-operation between auditors and bookkeepers. *Business man's magazine,* Nov. 1908, p. 361-5.
MONTGOMERY, ROBERT HESTER. Work of the auditor. *Accountant,* May 5, 1906, p. 582-6. *Journal of accountancy,* April 1906, p. 492-500.
MOORHOUSE, ELI. Advantages of an independent continuous audit. *Journal of accountancy,* June 1910, p. 95-100.
MORGAN, H. Procedure in the complete audit of the accounts of a commercial firm. *Commerce, accounts and finance,* Nov. 1902, p. 7-11. *Incorporated accountants journal,* 1901-2, p. 163.
MOSS, A. G. Value of an audited statement. *Journal of accountancy,* Dec. 1914, p. 455-9.
MOSS, WILLIAM. Auditors' requirements, certificates and reports under the companies act, 1900. *Accountant,* Feb. 21, March 7, 1903, p. 269-73, 313-5.

AUDITING AND AUDITORS—*(Continued)*

MOSS, WILLIAM. Some contested points in auditing practice. *Accountant,* March 18, April 15, 1899, p. 308, 412.

MORULL, JOHN. Auditing for accountant students. New York, Universal business institute, 1908. 140p.

NECESSITY of having the books audited at least once a year. *Cooperative management and farmer,* Jan. 1919, p. 42-3.

NORTON, F. W. Three practical points for auditors. *Business man's magazine,* Dec. 1910, p. 573-5.

NORTON, GEORGE PEPLER. Audit of a manufacturer's accounts. *Accountant,* Nov. 8, 15, 1890, p. 619-20, 628-33.

OFFICIAL audits. *Accountant,* Jan. 27, 1917, p. 73-7.

OFFICIAL audits in New Zealand: companies accounts audit. *Accountant,* Nov. 28, 1896, p. 981-2.

ON auditors and accounts. *Accountant,* Jan. 14, 21, Feb. 4, 1893, p. 25-6, 45-6, 50-1, 103-4.

PARFITT, JAMES JOHN. Present legal position of auditors, their rights and responsibilities. *Accountant,* Feb. 2, March 2, 1907, p. 150-6, 266-70.

PARTIAL audits. *Accountant,* July 27, 1907, p. 104.

PARTON, JOHN. Merchandise inventories and the auditors responsibility therefor. *Accountant,* Nov. 17, 1917, p. 385-8. *Canadian chartered accountant,* Oct. 1917, p. 93-100.

PARTRIDGE, ALBERT HENRY. Principles governing the selection of the work to be performed on a partial audit. *Accountant,* Feb. 21, 1903, p. 266-9.

PATERSON, JOHN. Notes on auditing. *Accountant,* Feb. 6, 1897, p. 161-5.

PATON, WILLIAM ANDREW and R. A. STEVENSON. Auditing. (In their *Principles of accounting.* 1918. p. 642-9.)

PEGLER, ERNEST C. Auditor's duty in relation to stock-in-trade. London, H. Foulks Lynch & co. 20p. *Accountant,* May 1, 1915, p. 575-82.

PEGLER, ERNEST CHARLES. Principles of auditing. London, H. Foulks Lynch & co.

PEGLER, ERNEST C. Principles of auditing. *Accountant,* Feb. 14, 1914, p. 224-32.

PITT, GEORGE STANHOPE. Main issues of auditing. *Incorporated accountants' journal,* Feb. 1920, p. 101-4.

PIXLEY, FRANCIS WILLIAM. Auditing. *Accountant,* May 26, 1883.

PIXLEY, FRANCIS WILLIAM. Auditing. *Accountant,* 1887, p. 676, 686.

PIXLEY, FRANCIS WILLIAM. Auditors; their duties and responsibilities under the companies acts, partnership acts, and acts relating to executors and trustees and to private audits. Ed. 10. London, Henry Good & son, 1910. 658p.

PIXLEY, FRANCIS WILLIAM. Consulting accountants. *Accountant,* April 17, 1915, p. 504-9, 489-91.

PIXLEY, FRANCIS WILLIAM. Investigation of the accounts of commercial undertakings previous to their conversion into public companies. *Accountant,* March 8, 15, 1890, p. 120-4, 134-6.

PLUMPTON, THOMAS. Practice of auditing commercial accounts. *Accountant,* April 5, 12, 1890, p. 169-72, 184-8.

POWERS and duties of auditors. *Accountant,* Feb. 17, 1912, p. 256-8. *Incorporated accountants' journal,* March 1912, p. 139-41.

PRESIDENT PLENDER on the duties of an auditor. *Journal of accountancy,* Nov. 1910, p. 65-6.

PRICE, HARRY LLOYD. Auditor's duties and responsibilities. *Accountant,* July 18, 1896, p. 611-5. *Incorporated accountants' journal,* 1895-6, p. 111.

PROFESSIONAL auditing of financial institutions. *Journal of accountancy,* March 1910, p. 379.

QUALIFICATIONS of auditors. *Accountant,* May 16, 1916, p. 741-3.

RACINE, SAMUEL FREDERICK. Guide to the study of auditing; arranged in question form to accompany Auditing, theory and practice, by Robert H. Montgomery. Seattle, Western institute of accountancy, commerce and finance, 1914. 63p. (Accounting students' series.)

———— Same. Ed. 2, revised and enlarged. Seattle, Western institute of accountancy, commerce and finance, 1916. 74p. (Accounting students' series.)

RENN, GEORGP BENTON. Practical auditing; a working manual for auditors describing in complete detail the method of conducting a commercial audit and indicating in proper order the successive steps of procedure, with a treatise on auditing. Ed. 3, revised and enlarged. Chicago, George B. Renn, c1907. 130p.

REQUIREMENTS of auditors. *Accountant,* Jan. 18, 1902, p. 58-60.

RESOLUTIONS of Minnesota state bankers' association. *Journal of accountancy,* July 1910, p. 214.

RESPONSIBILITIES of auditors. *Accountant,* April 1, 1882, Jan. 5, 12, 19, 1895, p. 6, 27, 49.

RESPONSIBILITIES of auditors. *Accountant,* June 11, 1892, p. 477-81.

RESPONSIBILITIES of auditors in respect of prior accounts. *Accountant,* Aug. 31, 1901, p. 937-40.

RESPONSIBILITY of accountants and auditors. *Accounting and commerce,* April 1919, p. 12-3.

RESPONSIBILITY of auditors. *Journal of accountancy,* Nov. 1912, p. 422-6.

RESPONSIBILITY of auditors: correspondence. *Journal of accounting,* July 1912, p. 73.

RESPONSIBILITY of auditors: People vs. Green, 5 Daly 194 N. Y.: Smith vs. London assurance co., 109 appellate division, 882 N. Y.

RETCHFORD, ALFRED WILLIAM. Other methods of proving ledgers and accounts than by detail checking. *Accountant,* Aug. 13, 1892, p. 628-31.

REYNOLDS, W. B. and F. W. THORNTON. Duties of the junior accountant. New York, American institute of accountants, 1918. 102p. *Journal of accountancy,* Sept. Oct. Nov. 1917, p. 161-92, 289-92, 365-72.

REYNOLDS, W. B. and F. W. THORNTON. Duties of the junior accountant. Ed. 2. New York, American institute of accountants, 1919. 107p.

RIGHTS and duties of auditors. *Accountant,* Feb. 3, 24, March 9, 1912, p. 153-8, 301-5, 373-5.

RINTOUL, PETER. Treatment in the accounts of joint stock companies of depreciation in value of assets arising from their employment, and the duties of an auditor relating thereto. *Accountant,* April 4, 1908, p. 496-503.

ROBERTS, L. A. Duty of an auditor: correspondence. *Journal of accountancy,* July 1913, p. 80.

ROBERTSON, WILLIAM. Nature and extent of an auditor's responsibility. *Accountant,* June 26, 1897, p. 632-6.

ROSS, J. MUNN. Law relating to audits and auditors. *Accountant,* Jan. 5, 1895, p. 19-24.

RUCKSTELL, JOHN R. Limited audit. *Accountant,* Oct. 7, 1916, p. 314-6. *Incorporated accountants' journal,* Dec. 1918, p. 54-6. *Journal of accountancy,* Sept. 1916, p. 190-5.

AUDITING AND AUDITORS—*(Continued)*

RULES for the election of vestrymen and auditors in London. *Acountant,* Nov. 24, 1894, p. 1043-7.

RUSSELL, THOMAS HERBERT and WILLIAM J. JACKMAN. Bookkeeping, accounting and auditing. Chicago, Whitman publishing co. 1916. 416p.

SCOPE of an audit. *Canadian chartered accountant,* Oct. 1919, p. 107-10. *Public accountant,* March 1919, p. 247-50.

SCOTT, GEORGE ALEXANDER. Legal position of auditors and accountants. *Incorporated accountants journal,* 1909-10, p. 155, 169, 173.

SEATREE, W. ERNEST. Relation of the auditor to valuation of inventories. *Accountant,* Dec. 26, 1914, May 29, 1915, p. 795-9, 725-9. *Journal of accountancy,* Sept. Nov. 1914, p. 196-205, 333-41.

SHEFFIELD CHARTERED ACCOUNTANTS STUDENTS' SOCIETY. Some notes on the preparation and audit of a balance sheet. *Accountant,* Feb. 19, 1916, p. 231-3.

SHERWOOD, JOHN F. Public accounting and auditing; correlating the subjects accounting, auditing and commercial law. Cincinnati, Southwestern publishing co. 1920. 258p.

SHORE, H. W. Comments upon internal check and audit. *Accounting and commerce,* Aug. 1917, p. 104-6.

SHOULD an auditor give advice. *Australasian accountant and secretary,* March 1920, p. 75-6.

SISSON, JAMES ARNOTT. Auditing. *Accountant,* 1887, p. 125, 169.

SLOCOMBE, JOSEPH. Auditing. *Accountant,* Dec. 9, 16, 1882.

SMITH, ALEXANDER. Abuse of the audit in selling securities. *Journal of accountancy,* Oct. 1912, p. 243-53. *American institute of accountants, Yearbook,* 1912, p. 169-79.

SMITH, WALTER JAMES. Audit; its responsibilities and possibilities. *Accountant,* Oct. 14, 1899, p. 1031-2. *Incorporated accountants' journal,* 1899-1900, p. 29.

SOULE, GEORGE. Soule's manual on auditing; suggestions to auditors, receivers and liquidators, and points on higher and expert accounting. Ed. 3. New Orleans, 1894.

SPEAR, RAYMOND HERBERT. Scientific auditing. Detroit, Commercial world publishing co. c1912. 63p.

SPICER, ERNEST EVAN. Auditors' duties. *Canadian chartered accountant,* April 1920, p. 276.

SPICER, ERNEST EVAN. Internal check in relation to a manufacturer's business. Ed. 2. London, H. Foulks Lynch & co. 1911. 36p. *Accountant,* March 28, May 2, 1908, p. 434-43, 621-4.

SPICER, ERNEST EVAN and ERNEST C. PEGLER. Audit programmes: being an outline of the principle points involved in some special kinds of audits. London, H. Foulks Lynch & co. 1919. 107p.

SPICER, ERNEST EVAN and E. C. PEGLER. Practical auditing. Ed. 2. London, H. Foulks Lynch & co. 1914. 776p.

SQUIERS, JOSEPH. Points on fraud and deficiencies in audit practice. *Accountant,* Jan. 14, Feb. 25, 1905, p. 45-53, 213-5.

STACEY, WALTER EDWIN. Auditing. *Accountant,* 1887, p. 345.

STAUB, WALTER A. Interrelation of financial and operating data. *Journal of accountancy,* Jan. 1914, p. 1-12.

STAUB, WALTER A. Mode of conducting an audit. *Accountant,* Oct. 22, 1904, p. 453-8. *Business world,* Jan. Feb. 1905, p. 30-2, 80-2. *Federation of societies of public accountants in the United States of America, Official record of the Congress of accountants held at the World's fair, Saint Louis,* September 26th, 27th and 28th, 1904, p. 206-14. *New York accountants' and bookkeepers' journal,* Nov. 1904, p. 277-84.

STEPHENS, HENRY JAMES BONDFIELD. Duties of an auditor in relation to the valuation of assets. *Incorporated accountants' journal,* 1893-4, p. 46.

STEWART, R. Auditing accounts. Groombridge. 1854.

STRACHAN, WILLIAM. Auditing in war time. *Incorporated accountants' journal,* Aug. 1917, p. 228-31.

SUFFERN, EDWARD L. Responsibility of the accountant. *Journal of accountancy,* March 1914, p. 197-202.

TANNER-GILMAN schools, inc. External auditing: C. P. A. coaching. Chicago, Tanner-Gilman schools, inc. c1908-1919.

THOMPSON, G. SEYMOUR. Balance sheet audits. *Accountant,* Jan. 25, 1919, p. 55-7.

TOVEY, PHILIP. Auditor's report—duties and responsibilities of auditors—typical examples. (In his *Balance sheets, how to read and understand them.* p. 64-71.)

TREVOR, CHARLES ROBINSON. Auditing. *Accountant,* Dec. 7, 1889, p. 658-63.

TYNDALL, W. B. Auditing mortgages. *Business,* Feb. 1896, p. 81-6.

UNCOMPLETED audits. *Accountant,* Jan. 13, 1917, p. 25-7.

UNIFORM accounting. *Canadian chartered accountant,* July 1917, p. 5-33. *Journal of accountancy,* June 1917, p. 401-33.

UNITED STATES. FEDERAE RESERVE BOARD. Approved methods for the preparation of balance sheet statements; a tentative proposal submitted for the consideration of banks, bankers, and banking associations; merchants, manufacturers and associations of manufacturers; auditors, accountants, and associations of accountants; reprinted from Federal reserve bulletin, April, 1917. Washington, Government printing office, 1918. 25p. Same as Uniform accounting.

UNITED STATES. FEDERAL RESERVE BOARD. Uniform accounting. *Accountant,* Oct. 13, 1917, p. 282-92.

UNITED STATES. FEDERAL RESERVE BOARD. Uniform accounting; a tentative proposal submitted for the consideration of banks, bankers, and banking associations; merchants, manufacturers, and associations of manufacturers; auditors, accountants, and associations of accountants: reprinted from Federal reserve bulletin, April 1917. Washington, Government printing office, 1917. 25p. Same as Approved methods for the preparation of balance sheet statements.

UNIVERSITY of Minnesota (abstract of an address by J. Gordon Steele on "Auditing and the duties and responsibilties of a public accountant and auditor") *Journal of accountancy,* July 1908, p. 219.

USE and limitation of detail checking. *Incorporated accountants' journal,* Dec. 1912, p. 60-2.

VALUE of an audit. *Accountant,* Jan. 27, Feb. 3, March 10, 31, 1894, Jan. 27, 1912, p. 77-8, 103-5, 213-4, 281-2, 147-8.

VALUE of audited statements. *Bulletin of the New York credit men's association,* Nov. 1, 1919. *Journal of accountancy,* Dec. 1919, p. 454-5.

VALUE of "outside audits." *Journal of accountancy,* April 1912, p. 289-91.

VAN DE LINDE, GERARD. Audit of banks and mercantile firms (with or without branches at home or abroad). *Accountant,* Dec. 11, 18, 25, 1897, p. 1184-8, 1202-12, 1221-8.

VAN DE LINDE, GERARD. Bookkeeping and other papers. London, Blades, East & Blades.

VAN DE LINDE, GERARD. Preparation and audit of income and expenditure accounts. *Accountant,* April 25, May 2, 1885.

AUDITING AND AUDITORS—*(Continued)*
VICTORIAN audit commissioners and Melbourne university accounts. *Incorporated accountants journal,* 1901-2, p. 256; 1902-3, p. 58.
VINCENT, JOSEPH WALTER. Methods by which the existence and value of the debtors and creditors on a balance sheet may be verified. *Accountant,* March 30, 1901, p. 399-405.
VIVIAN, G. W. Book debts, and the auditor's duties with regard thereto. *Accountant,* April 15, 1911, p. 602-5.
WADE, JOHN MERRETT. Auditor's duties. *Accountant,* June 23, 1894, p. 574-6.
WALBANK, JOHN ARTHUR. Auditing essays, and other matters, being hints, etc., for examination and other purposes. Newcastle-upon-Tyne, Northern accountancy coaching classes, 1910. 88p.
WALKDEN, MARTIN LUTHER and others. Auditing. *Accountant,* 1887, p. 63, 192.
WALTON, SEYMOUR. Errors of principle. *Accountant,* Oct. 28, 1905, p. 487-92. *Auditor,* 1905, p. 172, 192.
WALTON, SEYMOUR. Suspected defalcation—duty of auditor. *Journal of accountancy,* April, 1915, p. 419-20.
WALTON, SEYMOUR. Vouchers: distribution of expenses. *Journal of accountancy,* Nov. 1918, p. 395-6.
WARDHAUGH, JOHN B. Legal limitations of an auditor's duties and responsibilities. *Accountants' magazine,* Aug. 1909, p. 429-53.
WEBSTER, G. COLIN. Concise forms of procedure (a) on undertaking the audit of a manufacturing concern (b) on the appointment of a trustee under an assignment deed (c) on preparing administration accounts for the executors of a deceased person's estate. *Accountant,* May 18, 25, 1901, p. 590-6, 614-8.
WHAT *is* a partial audit. *Accountant,* May 26, 1906, July 27, 1907, p. 655-7, 104-6.
WHAT is an auditor. *Accountant,* July 8, 15, 15, 22, Aug. 5, 19, Sept. 9, 1899, p. 739, 741-4, 760-1, 794, 825-7, 877-8, 927-31.
WHINNEY, FREDERICK. Audits and certificates. *Accountant,* Nov. 28, 1891, May 14, 1892, p. 836-42, 404-11.
WHITE, EDMUND D. Books and accounts of manufacturing companies and their audit. *Accountant,* Jan. 10, 17, 1885.
WHITEHILL, ROBERT. Cost and productiou accounts and their audit. *Accountant,* Dec. 15, 1894, p. 1097-1113.
WHITING, GRAFTON. Payroll audit, the duties of the auditor. *Journal of accountancy,* April 1920, p. 260-5.
WIHL, OSCAR MORRIS. Auditors and their liabilities. *Incorporated accountants journal,* 1897-8, p. 187.
WILDMAN, JOHN RAYMOND. Auditing studies. New York, The William G. Hewitt press, 1917. 26p.
WILDMAN, JOHN RAYMOND. Principles of auditing. New York, The William G. Hewitt press, 1916. 196p.
WILKINSON, GEORGE. How to begin an audit. *Accountant,* April 13, 1907, p. 495-9. *Journal of accountancy,* March 1907, p. 376-85.
WILLIAMSON, J. G. Auditors. (In his *Counting house and factory organization.* 1909. p. 143-4.)
WILSON, P. MCCANDLISH. Checks that can be applied by an auditor examining stock sheets. *Accountant,* Dec. 20, 1919, p. 532-5.
WITTY, RICHARD ALFRED and others. Verification of cash and securities. *Incorporated accountants journal,* 1902-3, p. 271.
WOODBURY, ARTHUR K. Physical appraisal in relation to accountancy. *Journal of accountancy,* Dec. 1910, p. 108-18.
WOODINGTON, A. E. Value of an audit. *Accountant,* Oct. 11, 1913, p. 491-500. *Incorporated accountants' journal,* Nov. 1913, p. 45-51.
WOOLLEY, CHARLES. Duties of auditors. *Accountant,* July 29, 1899, p. 822-3.

AUDITING and cost accounting. Chase, William Arthur. 1917.

AUDITING and cost accounting business administration. LaSalle extension university. 1910.

AUDITING association formed at Aberdeen, S. D. *Cooperative manager and farmer,* Feb. 1917, p. 60.

AUDITING balance sheets. *Canadian chartered accountant,* April 1912, p. 208.

AUDITING conductor's collection on interurban railways. Forse, W. H. 1907.

AUDITING essays and other matters. Walbank, J. A. 1910.

AUDITING features of the mining industry. Hooker, J. C.

AUDITING for accountant students. Moull, John. 1908.

AUDITING in Australia. *Accountant,* April 2, 1898, p. 369. *Public accountant,* 1908, p. 11.

AUDITING in Ireland. *Accountant,* April 22, 1911, p. 640-4.

AUDITING in Japan. *Accountant,* Aug. 28, 1909, p. 253-6.

AUDITING in relation to unearned income." *Accountant,* March 19, 1910, p. 398-9.

AUDITING insurance accounts. Wilkinson, George. 1912.

AUDITING of bank accounts. *Accountant,* Jan. 18, Feb. 15, Mar. 1, May 10, May 17, June 14, 1879.

AUDITING of Glasgow corporation accounts. *Accountant,* Jan. 16, 23, 1904, Aug. 24, 1907, p. 89-91, 99-100, 130-2, 227-9.

AUDITING procedure. Castenholz, William Burtis. 1918.

AUDITING studies. Wildman, J. R.

AUDITING theory and practice. Montgomery, R. H. 1916.

AUDITING the companies act, 1907. *Accountant,* Aug. 15, 22, 29, 1908, p. 177-9, 208-10, 238-40.

AUDITING under the local government act, 1906 (N. S. W.). *Public accountant,* 1908, p. 181; 1909, p. 2, 59.

AUDITOR-bookkeeper. *Accountant,* Feb. 15, 1908, p. 205-8.

AUDITOR; published monthly by the Illinois society of certified public accountants, 1905.

AUDITORS.

See Auditing and auditors.

AUDITORS. Pixley, F. W. 1910.

AUDITORS and accounts. *Accountant,* Jan. 14, 21, Feb. 4, 1893, p .25, 45, 50, 103.

AUDITORS and auditing; a straight talk on "opinions." *Accountant,* Aug. 17, 1912, p. 233-7.

AUDITORS and directors' fees. *Accountant,* Nov. 16, 1918, p. 263-4.

AUDITORS and friendly societies. *Incorporated accountants' journal,* 1890-1, p. 151.

AUDITORS and prospectuses. *Accountant,* March 24, 1906, p. 362-3.

AUDITORS and secret commissions. *Accountant,* Jan. 31, 1914, p. 135-7.

AUDITORS and shareholders. *Accountant,* Jan. 27, 1912, p. 120-3.

AUDITORS and stocktaking. *Accountant,* Jan. 13, Feb. 10, April 20, 1912, Feb. 1, 1913, p. 42-4, 193-7, 600-2, 139-43, 161-3. *Incorporated accountants' journal,* Feb. 1912, p. 116-7.

AUDITORS and summarised balance sheets. *Accountant,* April 6, 1901, p. 413-6.

AUDITORS and their duties. *Accountant,* July 29, 1893, p. 679-83.

AUDITORS' certificates. *Journal of accountancy,* Dec. 1919, p. 456-7.

AUDITOR'S certificate and report in terms of companies' act, 1900. *Accountant,* Feb. 2, 1901, p. 140-1.

AUDITOR'S certificate and report in terms of the companies' act, 1900. *Accountant,* May 2, 1903, p. 568-70.

AUDITOR'S certificate as to amount of profits. *Public accountant,* Sept. 1918, p. 59-60.

AUDITOR'S certificate in relation to stock-in-trade. *Incorporated accountants' journal,* 1895-6, p. 68.

AUDITOR'S certificates. *Accountant,* July 4, 1891, p. 507, Sept. 19, Oct. 31, 1908, p. 317-9, 509-11. *Journal of accountancy,* Dec. 1919, p. 456-7. *Accountaint,* July 4, 1891, p. 507.

AUDITORS' certificates and reports. *Accountant,* July 19, 1902, p. 721-3.

AUDITORS' certificates and reports. *Accountant,* March 2, 1907, p. 273-5.

AUDITORS' contracts. *Incorporated accountants' journal,* June, 1912, p. 227-8.

AUDITORS duties and responsibilities. *Incorporated accountants' journal,* Sept. 1918, p. 232-3, 234-40.

AUDITOR'S duties and responsibilities. *Incorporated accountants' journal,* June 1920, p. 179-80, 192-4.

AUDITOR'S duty in relation to "fictitious transactions." *Incorporated accountants' journal,* Aug. 1920, p. 219-20.

AUDITOR'S duty in relation to stock-in-trade. Pegler, Ernest C.

AUDITORS financial mirror and record. Bartley, R. M. 1862.

AUDITORS' handbook; friendly society accounts, how they should be kept and audited. Pinhorn, A. 1896.

AUDITORS in India. *Accountant,* June 20, 1914, p. 873-6, 894-7.

AUDITORS insurance. *Accountant,* Sept. 21, Oct. 26, 1912, p. 365-8, 511-13.

AUDITOR'S legal liability. *Journal of accountancy,* July, 1912, p. 53-7.

AUDITORS of causes, &c., acts of Scotland London, Longman, 1846.

AUDITORS' qualifications; House of Lords select committee; re Hightown gas and electricity bill, May 5th, 1914. *Incorporated accountants' journal,* June, 1914, p. 257-9.

AUDITORS' qualifications; important decision of select committee of the House of Lords re Whitwell and District gas bill, March 19th, 1914. *Incorporated accountants' journal,* April, 1914, p. 189-203.

AUDITOR'S relation to the appraiser and others. *Journal of accountancy,* Dec. 1910, p. 138-41.

AUDITOR'S responsibility in regard to verification of inventory. Moeran, E. H.

AUDITOR'S standing in England and America; what are we going to do about it? *Canadian chartered accountant,* April, 1914, p. 237-43.

AUDITORS, their duties and responsibilities. Bhalla, K. C. 1913.

AUDITORS under the Indian companies act. *Incorporated accountants' journal,* April, 1914, p. 188.

AUDITORS v. directors. *Accountant,* Dec. 7, 14, 1907, Jan. 4, 1908, March 20, Dec. 25, 1909, p. 689-90, 724-6, 3-4, 389-93, 769-72.

AUDITS. Cutforth, A. E. 1914.

AULD, G. P.

Navy yard accounting. *United States naval institute, Proceedings,* Sept.-Oct. 1915.

AUSTIN, F. A.

System of book-keeping in apartment house operation. *Real estate magazine,* May and June, 1914.

AUSTIN, H. H.

Legislation for the profession, with particular reference to the New Zealand act of 1908. *Public accountant,* 1909, p. 111, 119.

AUSTIN, HERBERT

General value of cost control and organization in the factory. *Accountant,* June 19, 1920, p. 721-4.

AUSTIN, JAMES VALENTINE

Law of bankruptcy. *Accountant,* Jan. 18, Feb. 15, 1902, p. 69-79, 178-80.
Municipal government. *Accountant,* Dec. 24, 1904, p. 775-9.

AUSTIN, R. J.

Accounting at your own price: correspondence. *Journal of accountancy,* July, 1910, p. 218-9.

AUSTIN, TEXAS

Annual report of commissioner Haynes showing the receipts and disbursements for the year 1917. *Austin American,* April 15, 1918.

AUSTIN, TEXAS—*(Continued)*

Purchasing agent (blank form for); bid on estimated supplies needed by Texas state charitable and eleemosynary institutions for twelve months beginning September 1, 1915. Austin, State purchasing agent, 1916.

AUSTRALASIAN accountant and secretary Aberdeen House, 528-30 Collins St. Melbourne, Australia.

AUSTRALASIAN advanced accountancy. Barton, A. E. 1915.

AUSTRALIA

Federal income tax acts, 1915-1918; incorporation of the amending provisions of the income tax assessment act of 1918 in the consolidated income tax assessment acts of 1915 and 1916, together with the taxing acts of 1915, 1916, 1917, 1918, regulations to date and rules of high court and official instructions for making returns of income, incorporated and indexed by F. L. V. Coffey. Sydney, Butterworth and co. 1918. 114 p.

Income tax assessment; war time profits tax assessment, 1917-20. 12 pamphlets.

Ready reckoner; federal income tax, for the purpose of assisting the department and taxpayers to readily ascertain the amounts of and the average rate of tax payable under the federal income tax act of 1918, compiled under the authority of the commonwealth treasurer, W. A. Watt. Melbourne, Albert J. Mullett, 1919. 124 p.

State of New South Wales. Income tax acts, 1912-1919, complete to April, 1920. [Sydney], 1919.

State of New South Wales. Taxation, 1898-1917. 6 pamphlets.

State of Queensland. Taxation. 1892-1920. 15 pamphlets.

State of South Australia. Taxation, 1884-1917. 6 pamphlets.

State of Tasmania. Taxation, 1910-1919. 14 pamphlets.

State of Victoria. Taxation, 1915-1919. 3 pamphlets.

State of Western Australia. Taxation, 1902-1918. 8 pamphlets.

War-time profits tax, a guide to the requirements of the Act, concisely explaining the law under each heading, arranged in alphabetical order of subjects for facility of reference. Ed. 2. Melbourne, Albert J. Mullett, 1917. 192 p.

——— **FEDERAL INCOME TAX DEPARTMENT**

Depreciation. *Accountant*, Oct. 4, 1916, Oct. 13, 1917, p. 327, 277-9. *Accounting and commerce*, June, 1916, June, 1917, p. 53, 55-7. *Federal accountant*, July, 1916, July, 1917, p. 77-8, 93-9. *Public accountant*, June, 1916, Jan. 1917, 249-50, 145-52.

AUSTRALIA amending her income tax law. *Economic world*, June 15, 1918, p. 846.

AUSTRALIAN CORPORATION OF PUBLIC ACCOUNTANTS.

Public accountant, Sept. 1904, to date, v. 4, no. 1.

AUSTRALIAN institute of cost accountants. *Australasian accountant and secretary*, Nov. 1920, p. 345-6.

AUSTRALIAN mining companies' accounts. Godden, Danvers, and W. N. Robertson. 1902.

AUTHORITY and responsibility of the auditor. *Journal of accountancy*, May 1912, p. 360-4

AUTHORITY of commissions in regard to depreciation accounting. *Electrical world*, Sept. 22, 1917, p. 591.

AUTHORS

Ising, Harold Ernest. For the author's guidance. *Business man's magazine*, Oct. 1907, p. 77.

Weidner, H. C. H. Keeping track of submitted manuscript. *Business man's magazine*, June 1909, p. 577.

AUTO-trolley-car shows big saving in operating costs. *Electric railway journal*, Aug. 10, 1918, p. 248.

AUTOMATIC accounting. McCormack, C. T. 1917.

AUTOMATIC adjusting rate in Indiana. *Gas age*, May 15, 1918, p. 473-4.

AUTOMATIC fare collector and change-making machine. *Electric railway journal*, Nov. 20, 1915, p. 1047-8.

AUTOMATIC follow-up system. *Foundry*, Dec. 1908.

AUTOMATIC inventory for hosiery mill; permanent record of goods in process—forms used. *Textile world*, June 7, Aug. 23, Dec. 13, 1919, March 20, 1920, p. 3505, 1055, 3363, 2153.

AUTOMATIC rating of workmen. *Iron age*, April 3, 1913, p. 811-2.

AUTOMATIC self auditing system of mercantile bookkeeping. Neely, J. A. 1916.

AUTOMOBILE INDUSTRY

Abel, O. J. Making the Ford motor car. *Iron age*, June 13, 1912, p. 1454-60.

Arnold, H. L. and F. L. Faurote. Ford methods and the Ford shops. New York, Engineering magazine, 1915. *Engineering magazine*, April-Oct. Dec. 1914, June, 1915, p. 1-26, 179-203, 331-58, 507-32, 667-92, 857-86; 33-60, 338-66, 524-50, 704-21, 859-76; 67-87, 184-201, 372-93.

Emmet, Boris. Labor turnover and employment policies of a large motor vehicle manufacturing establishment; from the *Monthly review* (October, 1918) of the Bureau of labor statistics, U. S. Department of labor, p. 837-54.

Prentiss, F. S. Making motor trucks in the White plant, Cleveland. *Iron age*, Aug. 17, 1916, p. 344-9.

Standard name for every part of a car recommended by the standard committee of the Society of automobile engineers. *Motor world*, July 5, 1916, p. 19-22.

Accounting

Baer, W. E. Office accounting system for an automobile body co. *Business man's magazine*, July 1910, p. 88-93.

Auditing

Castenholz, William B. Automobile manufacturers. (In his *Auditing procedure*. 1918. p. 275-8.)

AUTOMOBILE INDUSTRY—*(Continued)*

Cost accounting

AUTOMOBILE tire factory. *American institute of accountants, Special bulletin,* No. 1, Jan. 1920, p. 3-5.

KLAXON factory system seen in detail. *Automobile,* May 22, 1913, p. 1066-9.

MILLS, JAMES COOKE. Short cuts to cost finding. *Business man's magazine,* July, 1910. p. 73-82.

MITCHELL, A. Z. Automobile factory accounting. *Business man's magazine,* July 1910, p. 73-82.

MITCHELL, ARTHUR. Cost accounting in an automobile factory. *Business man's magazine,* Sept. 1906, p. 65-75.

MOTOR truck. *American institute of accountants, Special bulletin,* no. 5, Sept. 1920, p. 5-7.

RIDGWAY, A. CLIFFORD. System of costing for motor car manufacturers, etc. (In his *Cost accounts in principle and practice,* p. 70-80.)

VALPERCE, C. G. Cost accounting system of the Ceveland motor co. *Business man's magazine,* Nov. 1908, p. 409-13.

Stores systems

CADILLAC stock room methods. *Machinery,* Feb. 1920, p. 501-2.

How the Ford Motor company takes inventory. *Factory,* Nov. 1916, p. 521-5.

LUCAS, C. L. Production methods from the locomobile factory: machine fixtures and a stock system that facilitates the manufacture of a high grade motor car. *Machinery,* Nov. 1914, p. 177-80.

NEW shop accounting system. *Automotive industries,* April 17, 1919, p. 859.

SCHIPPER, J. E. System based on skeleton of forms. *Automobile,* March 26, 1914, p. 686-9.

SPEEDING up the stock room; the parts service department stock room of the Buick motor company, New York. *Horseless age,* Feb. 1, 1918, p. 36-7.

STUDEBAKER employees at home in any branch standardized system permits man from one branch to locate any part in another branch in two minutes. *Motor world,* July 5, 1916, p. 35-8.

AUTOMOBILE INSURANCE.

See Insurance—Automobile.

AUTOMOBILE insurance. *American institute of accountants, Special bulletin,* no. 4, July 1920, p. 8.

AUTOMOBILE profitable to plumber. *Metal work,* Nov. 30, 1917, p. 653.

AUTOMOBILE SERVICE STATIONS

CAR record joins master sheet. *Motor age,* Sept. 18, 1919, p. 20-1.

CHARTS divide work and place responsibility. *Motor age,* Nov. 6, 1919, p. 32-3.

FORD service system. *Automobile,* Feb. 13, 1913, p. 470-3.

HERRICK, K. Only three forms used in service station. *Motor age,* Jan. 8, 1920, p. 36-7.

HERRICK, K. Selling service. *Motor age,* Sept. 25, Oct. 2, 9, 16, 1919, p. 7-11, 11-15, 10-12, 24-5.

KEEPING track of tires: sales records and other forms. *Automobile,* June 26, 1913, p. 1034-5.

KNOW how your business stands: charting your records. *Motor age,* Aug. 12, 1920, p. 7-9.

MAKING profits by recording every sale. *Horseless age,* May 15, 1918, p. 22-4.

MASTER sheet; repair operations analyzed to give basis for estimating. *Motor age,* Nov. 6, 1919, p. 37.

SHOP forms to better your service. *Motor age,* July 15, 1920, p. 12-3.

SIMPLE service record system. *Motor age,* Nov. 6, 1919, p. 35.

SKINNER, H. C. Repair contracts. *Motor age,* Oct. 16, 1919, p. 26-7.

SKINNER, H. C. Service records. *Motor age,* Oct. 9, 1919, p. 47.

SKINNER, H. C. System and efficiency in the service station. *Motor age,* Sept. 18, 25, 1919, p. 7-11, 24-6.

STANDARDIZED tags for service stations and garages. *Motor age,* June 26, 1919, p. 23.

Two forms only in this service system. *Motor age,* March 25, 1920, p. 18-9.

Stock keeping

FAHNESTOCK, M. Simple parts stock system. *Horseless age,* April 1, 1917, p. 45.

SIMPLIFIED stock system. *Automobile,* July 3, 1913, p. 26-7.

SKINNER, H. C. Stockroom. *Motor age,* Oct. 2, 1919, p. 23-6.

SKINNER, H. C. Stockroom system. *Motor age,* Oct. 23, 1919, p. 31-2.

AUTOMOBILE tire factory. *American institute of accountants, Special bulletin,* No. 1, Jan. 1920, p. 3-5.

AUTOMOBILE TIRES

See Tires.

AUTOMOBILE TRADE

How to run a retail automobile business at a profit; plans and methods for cutting down expense and increasing sales—cost figures that help point out chances to make better profits. Chicago, A. W. Shaw co. c1918. 218p.

MAKING profits by recording every sale. *Horseless age,* May 15, 1918, p. 22-4.

SALES room work forms. *Automobile,* Aug. 7, 1913, p. 240-1.

Accounting

ACCOUNTING system for dealers. *Horseless age,* May 1, 1916, p. 343-5.

How to run a retail automobile business at a profit; plans and methods for cutting down expense and increasing sales—cost figures that help point out chances to make better profits. Chicago, A. W. Shaw co. c1918. 218p.

McCORMACK, CHARLES THOMAS. Automobile accounting. Fort Worth, Texas, C. T. McCormack, 1917. 16p.

MOTOR world publishing company. Motor world simplified system of accounting; a complete description of the system with instructions for installation and operation. New York, Motor world publishing co. Nov. 1915-Jan. 1916. 36p.

REMSEN, A. H. Should dealers' parts accounts be standardized? *Horseless age,* July 21, 1915, p. 69.

SALES book. *Horseless age,* July 15, 1914, p. 90-1.

SIMPLIFIED system of accounting for auto dealers and garagemen. *Motor world,* Sept. 13, 1916, p. 18-21, 40.

WALTON, SEYMOUR. Second-hand automobiles account. *Journal of accountancy,* July 1917, p. 62.

Auditing

AUTOMOBILE dealers and agents. (In *How to audit.* 1919. p. 81-2.)

MONTGOMERY, ROBERT H. Automobile dealers. (In his *Auditing theory and practice.* 1916. p. 626-8.)

AUTOMOBILE TRADE—*(Continued)*

Costs

How to run a retail automobile business at a profit; plans and methods for cutting down expense and increasing sales—cost figures that help point out chances to make better profits. Chicago, A. W. Shaw co. c1918. 218p.

AUTOMOBILES

See also Automobile industry; Automobile trade; Automobile service stations; Garages; Motor buses.

BULLARD, J. E. Keeping auto service records. *Gas age,* July 15, 1919, p. 80.

CHARTING motor truck performance. *Textile world,* June 1, 1918, p. 5901. Condensed. *Engineering and contracting,* June 19, 1918, sup. 34.

CONVENIENT system of motor maintenance and repair record cards. *Electrical world,* June 7, 1913, p. 1266-7.

DELIVERY record. *American lumberman,* Dec. 14, 1918, p. 29.

DEVICE for recording the movements of motor trucks. *Municipal engineering,* Oct. 1918, p. 105. *Concrete,* Nov. 1918, p. 170.

DOUTHWAITE, W. W. Steam wagon transport trade. *Business organisation and management,* Dec. 1919-Jan. 1920, p. 55-60; 59-70.

ELECTRIC vehicle department of the Rochester railway and light company—results of experience in the operation of electric vehicles —system of inspection and forms of report. *Electrical world,* April 6, 1912, p. 743-4.

FRADUS, J. 6-form system for keeping track of truck work. *Engineering and contracting,* Jan. 7, 1920, p. 18-9.

INSPECTION report blanks. *Automobile,* May 8, 1913, p. 986-7.

FISHLEIGH, W. T. Value of a used car. *Horseless age,* June 1, 1916, p. 416-7.

MECHANICAL bookkeeper for the careful motorist. *Scientific American,* Aug. 11, 1917, p. 104.

MOTOR truck operation records in Chicago. *Municipal journal,* Sept. 27, 1917, p. 306-7.

OHMER truck auditor. *Motor age,* Sept. 2, 1920, p. 30-1.

TRUCK running time record. *Good roads,* June 7, 1919, p. 249.

Cost accounting

CADLE, C. L. Keeping account of trucking costs. *Electric railway journal,* Oct. 19, 1918, p. 698-9.

COST keeping system for warehouse trucks. *Automobile,* May 1, 1913, p. 942-3.

COST keeping system of Seattle street and sewer department for motor truck operation. *Engineering and contracting,* Aug. 7, 1918, p. 154-5.

COST system for any make of truck. *Domestic engineering,* April 19, 1919, p. 104-5.

CURBING waste in motor trucking. *Iron trade review,* April 18, 1918, p. 976-8.

DICKENS, CHARLES A. Motor truck operation and accounting. *Municipal engineering,* Aug. Oct. 1915-Sept. Nov. 1917-Jan. June, Sept.-Feb. Aug. 1919, Oct. Dec. 1918, p. 46-9, 130-6, sup. 25, sup. 23+, sup. 23+, sup. 23+, sup. 23+, sup 23+, sup. 23+, sup23+, 51; sup. 23+, sup. 23+, sup. 23+, sup. 23+, sup. 23+, sup. 23+, 52: sup. 49+, sup. 83+, sup. 145+, sup. 213+, sup. 277+, sup. 223+, 53: sup. 21+, sup. 21+, sup. 21+, sup. 27+, sup. 27+, sup. 27+; 54: sup. 15+; 55: sup. 13+, sup. 13+, sup. 12+, sup. 12+, sup. 20+, sup. 20+, sup. 20+, sup. 20+, sup. 18+, sup. 18+.

DRIVERS and garage clerks keep contractor's motor truck costs. *Engineering news,* Sept. 26, 1918, p. 589-90.

FIRESTONE SHIP BY TRUCK BUREAU. Relation of costs to motor truck transportation. Firestone Park, Akron, O. Firestone tire and rubber company, 1920. 15p. (Bulletin no. 5).

FORM showing performance and cost record with which one company keeps track of the efficiency of its power wagons and their drivers. *System,* Oct. 1912, p. 406.

GOODING, F. E. Getting at your trucking costs. *Factory,* May 1916, p. 464-5.

GOODRICH COMPANY, THE B. F. (Akron, O.) Motor truck expense records, 1915. 13 forms.

HEINLY, B. A. Operating cost records show comparative economy of 65 motor vehicles in Los Angeles water department. *Engineering record,* June 3, 1916, p. 728-32.

How it works; the commercial vehicles standard cost system for motor trucks and how it works is shown on this chart. *Commercial vehicle,* June 15, 1916, supplement.

HUSSON, J. Items that must be considered in calculating cost of truck operation. *Engineering and contracting,* June 4, 1919, p. 597.

IOWA. STATE COLLEGE OF AGRICULTURE AND MECHANIC ARTS. ENGINEERING EXTENSION DEPARTMENT. Cost keeping system for the automobile. Ames, 1915. 15p. (Bulletin no. 7).

JEWETT, C. C. How we keep motor truck costs. *Factory,* March 1917, p. 322-3.

KEEPING costs on the motor truck. *Factory,* Sept. 1918, p. 496.

KEEPING score of the motor truck. *Scientific American,* Aug. 17, 1918, p. 134. Condensed. *Literary digest,* Oct. 5, 1918, p. 23-4.

KENNEDY, WILLIAM P. AND OTHERS. Electric vehicle cost accounting discussed at N. E. L. A. convention: relation between electric vehicle and central station also considered at 5-day conclave, June 7-11, at San Francisco. *Commercial vehicle,* July 1, 1915, p. 12-3.

LIGHT delivery cost-record system and cost figures obtained by its use by South Bend owners. *Automobile,* April 10, 1913, p. 814-6.

LOCOMOBILE truck system devised for vehicle users' cost keeping. *Automobile,* May 15, 1913, p. 1030-3.

LYON brewery, New York city—complete records of full truck-operating cost. *Automobile,* Feb. 27, 1913, p. 550-1.

MERITHEW, S. S. Cost accounting routing and dispatching; economical motor truck operation depends upon a proper analysis of a complete accounting system. (In Fenn, F. W. and J. D. Eggleston. *Farm market.* 1920. p. 8-11).

MOTOR truck operation and accounting. *Municipal engineering,* Jan. March-Sept. 1920, sup. 18, sup. 18, sup 18, sup 18, sup. 18, sup. 18, sup. 10, sup. 10.

NATIONAL AUTOMOBILE CHAMBER OF COMMERCE. Organization of a rural motor express line. New York, National motor truck committee of the National automobile chamber of commerce.

NATIONAL standard truck cost system. *Good roads,* Oct. 5, 1918, p. 134-5.

NATIONAL standard truck cost system unanimously adopted March 9th. *Business digest,* April, May 22, 1918, p. 126-35, 683-5. *100%,* April 1918, p. 126-35.

NEW YORK CITY. DEPARTMENT OF WATER SUPPLY GAS AND ELECTRICITY. Standard procedure and forms relating to the cost of operation and maintenance of motor vehicles. 1913. 11p. (Bureau of economy and efficiency bulletin 5).

NEW YORK Edison company's truck system. *Automobile,* July 17-24, 1913, p. 122-4, 160-1.

AUTOMOBILES — Cost Accounting — *(Continued)*

New York telephone company. [Forms used in compiling statistics relative to the operation of automobiles]. 1915. 21 forms.

Norton, S. V. Standard system for motor operating costs. *Engineering and contracting,* Feb. 6, June 19, 1918, sup. 24+, sup. 28+. Excerpts. *Electrical review,* Feb. 16, 1918, p. 304.

One-form motor truck cost system. *Factory,* Nov. 1917, p. 738.

Osier, C. A. Seattle keeps accurate records of auto trucks and automobile operations. *Engineering news,* April 4, 1918, p. 655-6.

Simple and accurate cost keeping system for motor truck operation. *Engineering and contracting,* July 3, 1918, sup. 36.

Some unique cost record cards. *Comercial car journal,* Oct. 15, 1911.

Spillman, H. C. Suggestions on operating power trucks: forms for keeping cost and the use which should be made of the records. *Iron age,* April 23, 1914, p. 1012-4.

Stuart, J. B. Automobile cost accounting. *Farm engineering,* Oct. 1916, p. 60.

Truck cost records. *Power plant engineering,* Aug. 15, 1920, p. 804-6.

Two-form standard cost system for motor trucks. *Commercial vehicle,* June 1, 15, 1916, p. 5-10, 22-4.

Van Harlingen, J. M. Holding down motor truck costs. *System,* Sept. 1915, p. 317-9.

Welsh, J. A. Monthly report sheet gives accurate accounting of repairs, runs and miscellaneous maintenance costs of motor tire apparatus. *Municipal engineering,* Oct. 1915, p. 150-2.

Weysz, H. W. Increasing the efficiency of trucks. *Automobile,* July 10, 1913, p. 68-70.

Cost of operation

Adjustable reach logging trailer. *American lumberman,* May 10, 1919, p. 63.

Advantages of electric vehicles in municipal truck haulage. *Electrical world,* Jan. 3, 1914, p. 45-6.

Alderson, G. F. Comparison of horse and motor-truck hauling in Pennsylvania. *Engineering news-record,* Feb. 15, 1917, p. 283-4.

Allen, A. W. Cost of automobile transportation for the highway engineer. *Engineering and contracting,* Oct. 4, 1916, p. 304.

Arnold, H. F. W. Cost of handling material with motor versus horse-drawn equipment. *Engineering magazine,* Oct. 1915, p. 28-32.

Automobile profitable to plumber. *Metal work,* Nov. 30, 1917, p. 653.

Automobiles facilitate survey work. *Engineering news-record,* July 5, 1917, p. 36-7.

Automobiles run on four cents a mile in supervising road work. *Engineering work,* April 8, 1916, p. 484.

Automobiles save 32 cents per mile in road supervision. *Automobile,* March 2, 1916, p. 408.

Availability of motor trucks for mines. *Engineering and mining journal,* Oct. 18, 1913, p. 731-4.

Average annual cost of maintaining and operating electric vehicles averaging 10,000 miles per year. *Electrical world,* May 11, 1918, p. 990.

Avey, D. M. Motor trucks aid war time steel production. *Iron trade review,* April 11, 1918, p. 907-12.

Baker, C. W. Relative economy of freight transport by railway and by motor truck. *Engineering news-record,* July 10, 1919, p. 56-62.

Banham, W. J. L. Comparison of short-haul truck and rail shipments; abstracts. *Engineering news-record,* May 8, 1919, p. 903-4. *Engineering and contracting,* May 7, 1919, p. 498.

Barnett, R. C. Ton-mile cost of motor truck haulage. *Good roads,* March 2, 1918, p. 129.

Bartlett, E. J. Where and why electric trucks are economical. *Electrical review and western electrician,* March 14, 1914, p. 543-4.

Blaise, J. E. What motor trucks have saved for a brewer. *Scientific American,* Feb. 22, 1913, p. 182.

Blaksell, J. I. Operating costs of government owned motor trucks in postal service. *Engineering and contracting,* April 17, 1918, sup. 26.

Boyle, M. W. Long-distance motor-truck haulage costs in Ohio. *Engineering news-record,* April 10, 1919, p. 717.

Brewer, Robert W. A. Running costs of motor vehicles. *Mechanical engineering,* March 12, 1915.

Bryan, E. N. Cost data for auto trucks. *Engineering record,* Feb. 13, 1915, p. 211-2.

Bryan, E. N. Underestimating the cost of motor trucking. *Engineering and contracting,* March 10, 1915, p. 210.

Bullard, J. E. Costs of operating gas company motor vehicles. *Gas age,* March 15, 1919, p. 314-6.

Cadle, C. L. Keeping account of trucking costs. *Electric railway journal,* Oct. 19, 1918, p. 698-9.

Cadle, C. L. Operating cost of motor trucks. *Engineering and contracting,* Nov. 20, 1918, p. 492.

Carpenter, C. V. Cost of operating a Ford car in county road supervision. *Engineering and contracting,* May 3, 1916, p. 414.

Central station saving with electric trucks. *Electrical world,* Nov. 8, 1913, p. 957.

Chamberlain, R. E. Efficiency of the motor truck in terms of cost per ton-mile. *Good roads,* Feb. 23, 1918, p. 111-2. *Engineering and contracting,* March 6, 1918, sup. 30, 32. Abstract. *Municipal journal,* March 2, 1918, p. 186.

Chicago auto truck service reduces hauling charges. *Engineering record,* Sept. 4, 1915, p. 299-300.

Chicago efficiency bureau estimates that electric trucks would save $15,775 yearly. *Automobile,* Dec. 18, 1913, p. 1158-9.

Clapp, W. H. Motor trucks in southern California; economics and costs. *Journal of the society of mechanical engineers,* Oct. 1916, p. 791-5. *Engineering and contracting,* Oct. 18, 1916, p. 343-7. Condensed. *Concrete,* Nov. 1916, p. 144-7.

Cleveland, John A. Electric truck about 50 per cent cheaper than horse and wagon. *Automobile,* Jan. 16, 1913, p. 236.

Commercial car expenses small. *Commercial car journal,* May 15, 1912, p. 54-5.

Commercial electric truck operating costs. *Electrical world,* Feb. 27, 1915, p. 567.

Commercial-truck cost comparison. *Electrical world,* Sept. 6, 1913, p. 484.

Comparative cost of automobiles and horses. *Municipal journal,* Aug. 28, 1913.

Comparative cost of horse-drawn and electric vehicles in delivery service. *Electrical world,* June 14, 1913, p. 1315.

Comparative costs of electric and gasoline vehicles. *Electrical review and western electrician,* April 22, 1916, p. 705-6.

Comparative data on cost of operating gas and electric cars. *Electrical review ana western electrician,* June 30, 1917, p. 1097-8.

Comparative haulage costs by trucks and horse drawn vehicles. *Engineering and contracting,* April 17, 1918, sup. 30.

Comparative operating expenses of horse, electric and gasoline commercial vehicles. *Electrical world,* May 3, 1913, p. 936-7.

Compares automobile and team costs for project and irrigation managers. *Engineering news-record,* Aug. 2, 1917, p. 228.

AUTOMOBILES — COST OF OPERATION — *(Continued)*

COMPARISON of motor trucks with horses. *Domestic engineering,* May 10, 1913, p. 146-8.

COST and charges of motor truck service. *Railway review,* Dec. 7, 1918, p. 805-10.

COST data for horse-drawn and electric trucks. *Engineering record,* April 19, 1913, p. 429-30.

COST of automobile and motor truck operation at San Diego, Cal. *Engineering and contracting,* April 17, 1918, sup. 26.

COST of commercial electric vehicle operation; gives average costs for a great diversity of industries operating in widely separated localities. *Electrical world,* Oct. 17, 1917, p. 765.

COST of hauling and spreading gravel with motor trucks. *Engineering and contracting,* Jan. 3, 1917, p. 23.

COST of hauling in Chicago. *Engineering record,* July 11, 1914, p. 49.

COST of hauling paving materials with motor truck. *Engineering and contracting,* Jan. 2, 1918, p. 32.

COST of motor-car service for field parties on surveys. *Engineering news-record,* Sept. 13, 1917, p. 518.

COST of motor truck haulage in road construction. *Engineering and contracting,* March 3, 1920, p. 251-2.

COST of motor truck hauling on Catskill aqueduct tunnel, New York. *Municipal and county engineering,* Dec. 1913, p. 565-70.

COST of motor truck operation. *Progressive farmer,* July 12, 1919, p. 1144.

COST of motor truck operation for refuse collection. *Engineering and contracting,* July 2, 1919, p. 11-3.

COST of motor trucking. *System,* July 1916, p. 109.

COST of motor-trucking by Chicago water works in 1914. *Engineering and contracting,* Sept. 1, 1915, p. 162.

COST of operating a Ford car for three years. *Engineering and contracting,* Aug. 9, 1916, p. 124.

COST of operating 541 motor trucks. *Engineering and contracting,* May 1, 1918, sup. 29.

COST of operating motor truck. *Engineering and contracting,* April 4, 1917, p. 316.

COST of operating motor trucks. *Municipal and county engineering,* May 1913, p. 444-6.

COST of operating motor trucks. *Iron trade review,* Feb. 15, 1912, p. 401.

COST of operating motor trucks in Seattle. *Municipal journal,* March 8, 1917, p. 340.

COST of up-keep of horse-drawn vehicles against electric vehicles. *Journal of the American society of mechanical engineers,* April 1913.

COWAN, D. R. AND F. C. HART. Motor transportation in rural Ontario. *Canadian engineer,* Sept. 2, 1920, p. 309-10.

CRYAN, GEORGE H. Cutting transportation costs with motor trucks. *Paper,* July 21, 1920, p. 23-4.

COSTS of electric delivery for ice-cream manufacturers. *Electrical review and western electrician,* May 5, 1917, p. 749.

CULSHAW, WILLIAM. Motors for municipalities—the economic aspect. *Accountant,* July 26, 1913, p. 139-43.

CURTISS, W. M. Trucking costs. *Engineering record,* Feb. 7, 1914, p. 166. *Industrial engineering,* March 1914, p. 132.

DANA, RICHARD T. Automobiles. (In his *Handbook of construction plant.* 1914. p. 34-56).

DATA on storage-battery haulage by railroads. *Electrical world,* Jan. 17, 1920, p. 167.

DELIVERY costs. *American lumberman,* Jan. 12, 1918, p. 55.

DELIVERY costs with electric trucks. *Electrical world,* March 2, 1912, p. 482.

DRIVERS and garage clerks keep contractor's motor truck costs. *Engineering news-record,* Sept. 26, 1918, p. 589-90.

DRY goods delivery by electric vehicles in winter. *Electrical world,* March 28, 1914, p. 712.

DUTTON, L. R. Commercial motor delivery, costs and results. *Progressive age,* Nov. 15, 1911, p. 958-68.

DUTTON, L. R. Motor delivery. *Progressive age,* June 1, 1911, p. 464-6.

ECONOMIC operation of Smith form-a-truck in public service work. *Engineering and contracting,* Jan. 2, 1918, p. 32.

ECONOMICS effected by electric refuse trucks. *Electrical review and western electrician,* June 9, 1917, p. 976. *Municipal journal,* July 12, 1917, p. 32.

ECONOMY of industrial electric trucks. *Electrical world,* June 23, 1917, p. 1196-9.

ECONOMY of motor trucks. *Engineering record,* Jan. 10, 1914, p. 42.

ECONOMY of motor trucks for haulage. *Building age,* Oct. 1917, p. 580.

ECONOMY of the electric truck for delivering coal-unit costs compared. *Electrical world,* Nov. 6, 1915, p. 1038.

EDWARDS, THOMAS H. Motor truck lessens cost of maintaining gravel roads in Alabama. *Engineering record,* July 15, 1916, p. 73-4.

ELECTRIC commercial vehicle versus the horse. *Electrical review and western electrician,* Aug. 8, 1914, p. 290.

ELECTRIC truck saves $800 a year on horse equipment. *Electrical review and western electrician,* May 26, 1917, p. 897. *Electrical world,* June 2, 1917, p. 1068.

ELECTRIC trucks show economy in San Francisco delivery work; daily averages for December 1915. *Electrical review,* Aug. 18, 1917, p. 286.

ELECTRIC-VEHICLE research at the Massachusetts Institute of Technology—special department established to determine comparative costs of operating electric, gasoline, and horse vehicles. *Electrical world,* April 6, 1912, p. 740-3.

ELECTRIC vehicles for meat delivery. *Electrical world,* Aug. 16, 1913, p. 320.

ELECTRICS in express service. *Good roads,* Oct. 1, 1919, p. 168.

FIGURING the cost of haulage by motor trucks. *Engineering and contracting,* Feb. 6, 1918, sup. 22.

FULTON, R. E. Motor truck freight and operating costs. *Municipal and county engineering,* Aug. 1919, sup. 30. *Textile world,* Sept. 6, 1919, p. 1393.

GAMBLE, G. M. Road traction by petrol, steam, and electric motor vehicles. *Engineer,* Feb. 25, 1916, p. 182.

GARBAGE collection studies in Chicago justify continued use of horses. *Engineering record,* July 10, 1915, p. 52-3.

GOODING, FRANK E. Getting at your trucking costs. *Factory,* May 1916, p. 464-5.

GREELEY, SAMUEL A. Extent and cost of use of motor trucks in municipal refuse collection service. *Engineering and contracting,* Oct. 13, 1915, p. 286-7.

HANDLING coal with an electric truck. *Electrical world,* Aug. 4, 1917, p. 209.

HARDENBURG, W. E. Truck transportation of laborers and material. *Municipal journal* March 29, 1919, p. 229-30.

HARGREAVES, R. C. Applying the motor truck to the ice business. *Sibley journal of engineering,* Dec. 1915, p. 90-3.

HARLINGEN, J. M. Holding down motor truck costs. *System,* Sept. 1915, p. 317-9.

HAULING brick wih commercial cars most satisfactory. *Commercial car journal,* May 15, 1912, p. 38-9.

HAULING wood electrically. *Electrical review,* Sept. 14, 1918, p. 426.

AUTOMOBILES — Cost of operation — *(Continued)*

Heinly, B. A. Motor vehicles in water-works service at Los Angeles. *Engineering news-record,* May 6, 1915, p. 861-3.

Heinly, B. A. Operating cost records show comparative economy of 65 motor vehicles at Los Angeles water department. *Engineering record,* June 3, 1916, p. 728-32.

Hilder, J. C. Motor truck operating costs. *Independent,* June 16, 1917, p. 524.

Horne, R. W. Complete average operating costs of trucks. *Engineering news-record,* Sept. 20, 1917, p. 569.

Horne, R. W. Operating cost of motor trucks. *Engineering and contracting,* March 6, 1918, sup. 26.

Horse living versus horse power. *Scientific management,* June 28, 1913, p. 574.

Horses vs. motor trucks in refuse collection. *Municipal journal,* Aug. 16-23, 1919, p. 110-1, 119-20.

How load and mileage influence truck costs; chart. *Factory,* March 1917, p. 317.

How one company reduces delivery costs. *American lumberman,* Jan. 12, 1918, p. 55.

Hutchinson, R. William. Economy of motor trucks in engineering and contracting. *Concrete cement age,* April 1913, p. 194-5.

Hutchinson, R. William. Efficiency to and from the shop. *Industrial management,* Jan. 1917, p. 481-92.

Improved management and reduction of construction and operation costs, following introduction of automobiles in the San Francisco Gas distribution department, information from a paper by D. S. Keppelmann before the Pacific coast gas assn. *Engineering and contracting,* Nov. 12, 1913.

Irrigation company gives automobile costs| *Engineering news-record,* May 31, 1917, p. 439. Discussion. Harrison, J. L. *Engineering news-record,* July 12, 1917, p. 82.

James, E. W. Accurate detailed cost data on use of automobiles in road supervision. *Engineering and contracting,* March 1, 1916, p. 221-2.

Jones, Richard A. Auto truck in ash collection. *Municipal journal,* Dec. 21, 1916, p. 784.

Kennedy, William P. Operating cost of commercial electric vehicles. *Electrical world,* May 22, 1915, p. 1316-22. Discussion. *Electrical world,* June 12, 1915, p. 1532.

LaSchum, E. E. Electric truck operating costs. *Textile world,* Oct. 4, 1919, p. 2009.

LaSchum, E. E. Electric trucks and transportation. [Operating data of American railway express co.] *Electrical review,* June 7, 1919, p. 931-3.

Light delivery cost. *Automobile,* April 10, 1913, p. 814-6.

Light delivery van costs. *Electrical review,* Oct. 12, 1918, p. 587.

Lipsner, B. B. Methods of reducing maintenance cost. *100%,* v.10, No. 1, p. 138.

Lohmeyer, H. B. Reducing and recording tire costs. *100%,* Nov. 1917, p. 141.

Long experience in delivery van working: fifty-six light motor trucks replace about 450 horses. *Commercial car journal,* May 15, 1912, p. 42-3.

McBride, W. G. Motor truck operation at Mammoth Collins mines, Schultz, Arizona. *Bulletin of the American Institute of mining engineers,* July 1916, p. 1253-6. Condensed. Records of motor truck mine haulage costs. *Engineering and contracting,* Aug. 16, 1916, p. 161. Excerpt. Long distance haulage with motor trucks. *Engineering news-record,* Aug. 10, 1916, p. 271. Excerpt. *Engineering and mining journal,* Oct. 14, 1916, p. 709.

Maintenance cost of municipal automobiles. *Engineering and contracting,* Dec. 6, 1916, p. 496-7.

Maloney, J. E. Operating costs of tractor, trucks and sand screen and loader in road maintenance. *Engineering and contracting,* Jan. 1, 1919, p. 19-20.

Marshall, A. J. Electric truck operating costs. *Electrical review,* June 8, 1918, p. 958. *Good roads,* Aug. 10, 1918, p. 53.

Masury, A. F. Cost of operating motor trucks in road maintenance with methods of upkeep. *Engineering and contracting,* June 17, 1914, p. 702-4.

Maxwell, W. D. Automobile transportation for county engineers. *Engineering and contracting,* March 22, 1916, p. 283-4.

Mechanical traction in road and street work. *Good roads,* May 2, 1914, p. 264-8.

Metz, W. R. Cost of upkeep of horse-drawn vehicles against electric vehicles. *Journal of the society of mechanical engineers,* April 1913, p. 577-91. Discussion. *Journal of the society of mechanical engineers,* Aug. 1913, p. 1247-57.

Motor cars for field work, meter setting and repairs, Milwaukee water works. *Engineering and contracting,* May 31, 1916, p. 504.

Motor truck and trailer costs. *Engineering record,* Nov. 28, 1914, p. 588-9.

Motor truck cost charts-tables prepared by leading motor truck manufactures. *Scientific management,* Jan. 6, 1912, p. 22.

Motor truck costs much higher than generally assumed. *Engineering news-record,* Feb. 27, 1919, p. 438-9. Discussion. E. N. Bryan. *Engineering news-record,* April 17, 1919, p. 786.

Motor truck operation records in Chicago. *Municipal journal,* Sept. 27, 1917, p. 306-7.

Motor truck practice of Georgia railway and power company. *Electric railway journal,* July 28, 1917, p. 152-3.

Motor truck reduces cost of hauling road and bridge material. *Engineering and contracting,* Dec. 5, 1917, sup. 30.

Motor truck service successful in New York City park departments. *Engineering and contracting,* June 14, 1916, p. 550.

Motor truck vs. teams for local hauling around the mine. *Coal age,* Dec. 15, 1917, p. 1006-7.

Motor trucks and business efficiency. *Metal work,* Jan. 1, 1915, p. 50-2.

Motor trucks in Portland, Oregon. *Municipal journal,* Sept. 6, 1917, p. 228-9.

Motor trucks in railway maintenance work. *Engineering and contracting,* Feb. 18, 1920, p. 179.

Motor trucks in Seattle in railway and lighting service. *Electric railway journal,* July 7, 1917, p. 24-5.

Motor trucks on city work in Lansing, Michigan, pay for themselves in less than a year. *Engineering and contracting,* Dec. 5, 1917, sup. 30.

Motor trucks save $14,800 in hauling 16,000 cu.yd. of earth. *Engineering and contracting,* Dec. 5, 1917, sup. 36.

Motor vehicle operating costs of water department of Pasadena, Cal. *Engineering and contracting,* Feb. 6, 1918, sup. 26.

Motor vehicles; costs of operation. *Municipal journal,* Aug. 2, 1917, p. 103.

Nebraska studies truck operation. *Automotive industries,* July 31, 1919, p. 237.

New York city. Department of water supply, gas and electricity. Standard procedure and forms relating to the cost of operation and maintenance of motor vehicles. 1913. 11p. (Bureau of economics and efficiency bulletin no. 5).

Newark foundrymen's association hears speakers on relative merits of electric, gasoline and horse-drawn trucks. *Iron age,* Oct. 16, 1913, p. 852-3.

Ogden, C. E. Cost of electric-truck operation. *Electrical review and western electrician,* April 15, 1916, p. 678.

AUTOMOBILES — COST OF OPERATION — *(Continued)*

OPERATING cost data for industrial trucks on piers and transfers. *Electrical world,* Feb. 7, 1920, p. 328-9.

OPERATING cost data of electric vehicles. *Electrical world,* April 6, 1912, p. 756-7.

OPERATING cost of a five-ton electric vehicle. *Electrical review and western electrician,* Sept. 11, 1915, p. 470.

OPERATING cost of 10 teams as the hauling equivalent of one 5-ton or 7-ton truck. *Concrete,* Dec. 1916, p. 177.

OPERATING cost of the motor truck. *Iron age,* May 9, 1912, p. 1143-4.

OPERATING cost of truck and trailer. *Engineering and contracting,* June 4, 1919, p. 590.

OPERATING costs for commercial electric vehicles: investigation undertaken by the Electrical world. *Electrical world,* Oct. 3-17, 1914, p. 664-5, 719-20, 765.

OPERATING costs for trucks. *Electrical world,* April 7, 1917, p. 658.

OPERATING costs of a two-ton electric truck. *Electrical review,* March 16, 1918, p. 478.

OPERATING costs of government owned motor trucks in postal service. *Engineering and contracting,* April 17, 1918, sup. 26.

OPERATING costs of industrial electric trucks. *Electrical review and western electrician,* Nov. 6, 1915, p. 872.

OPERATING costs of motor truck in delivering sand and gravel. *Engineering and contracting,* March 21, 1917, p. 278.

OPERATING costs of two Cincinnati factories in comparison with horse drawn vehicles. *Iron age,* July 22, 1915, p. 223. Condensed. *Industrial engineering and engineering digest,* Sept. 1915, p. 104.

OPERATING expenses of electric delivery truck. *Electrical world,* May 12, 1917, p. 928.

OPPORTUNITY for the sale of electrics; specific advantages for various industries. *Electrical review and western electrician,* Oct. 16, 1915, p. 703-9.

PEARCE, S. L. Costs of the operation of electric vehicles in municipal service. *Engineering and contracting,* July 31, 1918, p. 107-8.

PERRY, H. W. Disinterested suggestions on motor truck costs. *Scientific management,* March 29, 1913, p. 294.

PERRY, H. W. Light and heavy car costs compared. *Scientific management,* Jan. 6, 1912, p. 24.

PERRY, H. W. Motor trucks and the high cost of living. *Horseless age,* Jan. 7, 1914, p. 44-5. Condensed. *Municipal engineering,* Feb. 1914, p. 165-6.

PERRY, H. W. Teams and motor trucks compared. *Scientific American,* Jan. 18, 1913, p. 66.

PHILADELPHIA'S new ash trucks. *Municipal journal,* Nov. 30, 1918, p. 426-7.

PIEPMEIER, B. H. Cost of operating trucks on highway maintenance in Illinois. *Engineering news-record,* May 29, 1919, p. 1074. *Concrete,* July 1919, p. 28-9.

PIEPMEIER, B. H. Operating cost of small trucks in maintaining state aid roads in Illinois. *Engineering and contracting,* March 6, 1918, p. 243.

PORTER, E. A. Small automobile opens up new opportunities in government stream gaging work. *Engineering record,* April 17, 1915, p. 490-1.

REFUSE collection and disposal in Hampstead. *Municipal journal,* Aug. 23, 1919, p. 124.

REFUSE collection in Chicago. *Municipal journal,* Jan. 8, 1914, p. 35-9.

REID, R. C. Cost of gasoline truck service. *Scientific American,* Feb. 22, 1913, p. 182.

RICE, C. S. Motor truck utility in the metal industry: economics effected. *Iron trade review,* Jan. 1, 1914, p. 59-62.

RITCHIE, JAMES. Cost estimates of horse and motor trucks. *Scientific American,* Jan. 18, 1913, p. 70-1.

ROOT, W. H. Motor truck hauling in Black Hawk county, Iowa. *Good roads,* Oct. 5, 1918, p. 133-4.

RUNNING cost of two ton electric refuse van. *Accountant,* Sept. 9, 1916, p. 212-3.

RUNNING your truck at least cost. *Iron trade review,* July 2, 1914, p. 33-6.

RUPRECHT, L. Cost of operating motor trucks; charts for conveniently determining trucking economy. *Engineering magazine,* Oct. 1912, p. 118-20.

SAVING in cost of garbage collection at Saskatoon, Canada, by use of motor trucks. *Engineering and contracting,* Feb. 6, 1918, sup. 26.

SAVINGS through electric vehicle operation at Wichita, Kansas. *Electrical world,* Dec. 26, 1914, p. 1253.

SCOTT, F. P. Motor trucks cheaper than teams on hauling gravel. *Engineering news-record,* May 16, 1918, p. 958-9.

SEVENTY thousand miles at 3½ cents per mile. *Automobile,* April 13, 1916, p. 687.

SHEETS, F. F. Cost data on operation of small maintenance trucks. *Engineering and contracting,* July 4, 1917, p. 6-7.

SHOP and equipment of Kuiken Bros., inc., Fairlawn, N.J. *Building age,* July 1917, p. 371.

SHOP equipment and motor trucking costs, meter division of Milwaukee water works. *Engineering and contracting,* April 14, 1915, p. 334-5.

SIEMINSKI, HENRY. Use of electric vehicles in laundry service. *Electrical review and western electrician,* Oct. 21, 1916, p. 721-2. Condensed. *Electrical world,* Oct. 21, 1916, p. 817-8.

SLADE, A. J. AND R. D. DUMONT. Electric vehicles in municipal service; data on economy effected. *Electrical review and western electrician,* Dc. 4, 1915, p. 1045-6. Abstract. *Municipal journal,* Dec. 23, 1915, p. 948-9.

SMART, F. W. Use of motor vehicles in haulage of materials on the highways gives detail costs of motor lorries. *Surveyor,* July 2, 1915.

SOME notes on the development of motor trucks for contractors' service, with data concerning operating cost. *Engineering and contracting,* Feb. 7, 1912, p. 152-5.

STONE, C. E. Operating costs for 3½ ton truck. *Engineering and contracting,* Aug. 6, 1919, p. 173.

STUDY of motor trucks. *Electrical world,* April 6, 1912, p. 719.

SUMMARY of cost of five weeks' operation of 100 electric vehicles, showing a total cost per car per day (exclusive of interest and depreciation) of $1.03. *Commercial car journal,* May 15, 1912, p. 37.

SUTHERLAND, D. A. Economy of heavy motor trucking for Lynn, Mass., water works. *Engineering and contracting,* Nov. 24, 1915, p. 416.

SYKES, F. W. Cost of operating municipal Edison electric motor tipping trucks, New Castle, England. *Engineering and contracting,* July 31, 1918, p. 110.

TABULATION of the costs of using electric truck. *Electrical world,* June 1, 1918, p. 1144.

TARRANT, S. C. Graphic record of auto costs. *Gas age,* Dec. 15, 1916, p. 657-8.

TERRY, JOHN. Working costs of municipal motor ash trucks at Nottingham, England. *Engineering and contracting,* July 31, 1918, p. 103.

THOMPSON, H. F. Comparisons between horse, gasoline and electric delivery costs; summary of electric vehicle study by Massachusetts institute. *Electrical review and western electrician,* Nov. 6, 1915, p. 874.

AUTOMOBILES — Cost of operation — *(Continued)*

Time saving on furnace installations. *Metal work,* April 10, 1914, p. 521.
Trucks save 86.6 per cent in heavy work. *Automobile,* June 5, 1913, p. 1172-4.
Using the ton-mile as a basis for cost figures. *Building age,* March 1918, p. 172-3.
Utilization of the motor truck in highway work. *Good roads,* May 1, 1915, p. 171-9.
Vestal, A. G. Running a car one year; what it cost two persons, for operation accessories and kindred expenses. *Motor age,* July 11, 1918, p. 26-7.
Ware, Charles A. Electric commercial vehicle vs. the horse. *Electrical review and western electrician,* Aug. 1, 1914, p. 254.
Wayland, E. B. Cost of hauling fruit by motor trucks. *American fruit grower,* Oct. 1919, p. 16.
Weller, R. C. Comparison of electric and hand trucks in freight house service. *Railway age,* Dec. 19, 1913, p. 1153.
Weysz, H. W. Increasing the efficiency of trucks. *Automobile,* July 10, 1913, p. 68-70.
What does it cost to operate motor trucks? *Paper,* Sept. 15, 1920, p. 26.
What it costs to operate an industrial electric truck. *Electrical world,* April 1, 1916, p. 775.
What it costs to operate trucks of the May lumber co. *American lumberman,* Nov. 8, 1919, p. 55.
What motor trucks cost to operate. *American lumberman,* March 2, 1918, p. 58.
Whitehead, G. B. Cost of hauling gravel with motor truck . *Engineering and contracting,* June 2, 1920, p. 623.
Whitlock, W. L. Auto truck for track repairs. *Electric railway journal,* July 17, 1920, p. 134-5. *Engineering and contracting,* Sept. 15, 1920, p. 250.
Why I bought a motor truck for my plumbing and heating business. *Domestic engineering,* Aug. 5, 1916, p. 192-4.
Williams, Charles P. Comparative cost of operating automobiles and teams on irrigation project. *Engineering and contracting,* Oct. 10, 1917, p. 291-2.
Year's operating costs of an electric emergency wagon. *Electric railway journal,* May 23, 1914, p. 1157.
Young, George F. Motor trucks operated on long hauls over bad roads in the West. *Engineering record,* April 22, 1916, p. 557-8.

Rates

Brown, T. Rates for cross country trucking. *Good roads,* Jan. 16, 1920, p. 307-8.

AUTOMOBILES facilitate state survey work. *Engineering news-record,* July 5, 1917, p. 36-7.

AUTOMOBILES run on four cents a mile in supervising road work. *Engineering work,* April 8, 1916, p. 484.

AUTOMOBILES save 32 cents per mile in road supervision. *Automobile,* March 2, 1916, p. 408.

AVAILABILITY of motor trucks for mines. *Engineering and mining journal,* Oct. 18, 1913, p. 731-4.

AVERAGE annual cost of maintaining and operating electric vehicles averaging 10,000 miles per year. *Electrical world,* May 11, 1918, p. 990.

AVERAGE cost of laying water mains in the District of Columbia. *Engineering and contracting,* April 11, 1917, p. 349.

AVERAGE cost of 1 mile of 16 ft. pavement of six different types in New York state as of Jan. 1, 1920. *Good roads,* May 12, 1920, p. 247.

AVERAGE costs of sewer construction and material for the past 15 years, Washington, D. C. *Engineering and contracting,* April 11, 1917, p. 361.

AVERAGE DUE DATE

Carter, R. N. Average due date. (In his *Advanced accounts,* p. 138-41.)
Dicksee, L. R. Average due date. (In his *Advanced accountancy.* 1916. p. 83-4.)
Lisle, George. Average due date. (In his *Accounting theory and practice.* 1900. p. 354-6.)
Spicer, E. E. and E. C. Pegler. Average date. (In their *Book-keeping and accounts.* 1914. p. 74-5.)
Spicer, E. E. and E. C. Pegler. Average date. (In their *Practical bookkeeping and commercial knowledge.* 1912. p. 167.

AVERAGE freight car capacity, average load, and cost of maintenance per ton mile on thirty-three systems for year ended June 30, 1916. *Railway review,* June 9, 1917, p. 801.

AVERAGE freight rate per ton-mile on railroads in important countries. *Economic world,* July 21, 1917, p. 87.

AVERAGE hardware costs, percentage to sales. *System,* March 1915, p. 314.

AVERAGE interest yield problems. *Accountant,* Jan. 18, 1919, p. 49.

AVERAGE life in track of express ties. *Railway age gazette,* March 23, 1911, p. 636-7.

AVERAGE life of street pavements in American cities. *Engineering and contracting,* Dec. 10, 1913, p. 670-1.

AVERAGE light and power rates. *Public service regulations,* March 1913, p. 134.

AVERAGE monthly prices of leading iron and steel products, 1908-1919. *Iron trade review,* Jan. 1, 1920, p. 128.

AVERAGE rates for electricity in thirty-six large American cities. *Electrical world,* March 16, 1912, p. 595-6.

AVERAGES.

Bowley, A. L. Averages. (In Lisle, George. *Encyclopaedia of acounting.* v 1. p. 195-202.)
Cost accounts and average prices *Accountant,* Feb. 11, 1911, p. 211-4. *Journal of accountancy,* March 1911, p. 375-6.
Cost accounts, average prices: correspondence. *Journal of accountancy,* March 1911, p. 380-1.
Hardcastle, Joseph. Units of use; averaging accounts; current interest on accounts; current and adjusting accounts for interest. *Business,* Oct.-Dec. 1899, p. 626-9, 691-5, 756-60.
Walton, Seymour. Averages. *Journal of accountancy,* July 1914, p. 70-2.
Walton, Seymour. Averages again. *Journal of accountancy,* Dec. 1914, p. 471-7.
Walton, Seymour. Averaging cost of material. *Journal of accountancy,* March 1916, p. 234-5.
Walton, Seymour. Averaging cost of sales. *Journal of accountancy,* May 1917, p. 397-8.

AVERAGES—*(Continued)*
WALTON, SEYMOUR. Averaging cost. *Journal of accountancy,* Feb. 1920, p. 159.
WALTON, SEYMOUR. Averaging costs. *Journal of accountancy,* July 1915, p. 67-70.
WALTON, SEYMOUR. Averaging overhead expense. *Journal of accountancy,* July 1914, p. 72-4.
WALTON, SEYMOUR. Deceptive averaging, again. *Journal of acountancy,* Sept. 1919, p. 237-8.

AVERAGES. Bowley, A. L.

AVERAGING account sales. Grant, H. D.

AVERAY, W. G.

Acceptances in retail business. *Journal of accountancy,* Feb. 1919, p. 120-4.

AVEY, D. M.

Applying the premium plan to a pattern shop. *Foundry,* March 1919, p. 95-9.
Motor trucks aid war time steel production. *Iron trade review,* April 11, 1918, p. 907-12.

AVOIDANCE of settlements under 13 Eliz. C. 5; an article from "The solicitors' journal." *Accountant,* Oct. 5, 1907, p. 423-5.

AVON exercise books for bookkeeping ledger. Pitman, Isaac.

AWAKENING of business. Hurley, E. N. 1916.

AWARDS

See Arbitration and award.

AXIOMS concerning manufacturing costs: discussion of paper by H. R. Towne. *Engineering and contracting,* Dec. 11, 1912, p. 650-2. *Journal of the American society of mechanical engineers,* April 1913, p. 655-62.

AXLES

Accounting
AXLE manufacturing. (In *International accountants' manual,* 1910, paragraph 452.)

AYERS, A. R.

Organization maintenance. *Railway age,* Feb. 1, 1918, p. 257-8. *Railway mechanical engineer,* April 1918, p. 210-1.

AYLING, CHARLES L.

Purchased power and the street railway. *Electric railway journal,* Jan. 3, 1914, p. 9-10.

AYRES, E. F.

Cost keeping system Oregon state highway commission. *Enginering and contracting,* Nov. 3, 1915, p. 349-50.

AYRES, MILAN V.

Accounting versus statistics. *Electric railway journal,* May 3, 1913, p. 803-5.

AYRES, W. J.

Time-saving purchase record. *System,* June 1907, p. 635-7.

AYROUT, LOUTFI-YOUSSEF

Audit departments of the English, French, Italian, Swiss and Egyptian railways. *International railway congress association, Bulletin,* English ed., Sept. 1897, p. 1251-79.

B. J. ARNOLD states principles of utility valuation. *Engineering news,* Oct. 28, 1915, p. 859.

BABBAGE, HENRY P.

Bitter cry of the rate payers; its remedy: an intelligible system of accounts, with full publicity and a government audit. *Accountant,* Nov. 3, 1906, p. 543-52.
Corporation accounts; preliminary draft of an act to regulate the accounts and audit. *Accountant,* Oct. 11, 18 Nov. 15, 1902, p. 1026-31, 1049-50, 1183-5.

BABBITT, H. E.

Illinois—administration of municipal waterworks. *University of Illinois bulletin,* Jan. 15, 1917, p. 89-99.

BABCOCK, C. E. P.; J. A. UNDERWATER

Asphalt repair records kept and methods followed at Buffalo; abstracts. *Engineering news-record,* October 10, 1918, p. 664-5. *Municipal engineering,* October 1918, p. 148-9. *Engineering and contracting,* November 6, 1918, p. 446, 448.

BABCOCK, D. P.

Ultimate costs of bituminous and water-bound macadams nearly equal in New York. *Engineering news-record,* July 11, 1918, p. 87-90.

BABCOCK, GEORGE D.

Fixing individual wage rates on facts. *Iron age,* June 8, 1916, p. 1375-9.

——— **AND REGINALD TRAUTSCHOLD.**

Taylor system in Franklin management, application and results. New York, Engineering magazine co. 1917. 245p. (Industrial management library.)

BABCOCK, LOUIS L.

Accidents to employees and liability therefor. (In Humphreys, A. C. *Lecture notes on some of the business features of engineering practice,* p. 456-72).

BABCOCK, STEPHEN E.

Municipal acquirements of private water company plants, as illustrated by the Syracuse, N. Y., water company condemnation by the city. *Proceedings of the American waterworks association,* 1893, p. 85. Abstract. Municipal acquirement of the plant of the Syracuse water co. *Engineering news,* Sept. 14, 1893, p. 207.

BACHE, JULES S.

Release business from the slavery of taxation: address at Economic club, New York city, November 29, 1920. 16p.

BACHELDER, F. J.

Procedure in Chicago elevated valuation. *Electric railway journal,* Mar. 3, 1917, p. 386-8.

BACHMAN, E. P. AND R. BOWMAN

Gary public schools; costs, school year 1915-1916. New York, General education board, 1918.

BACK to single entry. Hall, R. O.

BACKENHUS, R. E.

Card system records cost of engineering. *Engineering record,* Oct. 21, 1916, p. 502-3.

BACKENHUS, R. E.—*(Continued)*

Cost records of drafting and engineering. *Engineer and contracting,* Nov. 29, 1916, p. 472-4.

BACKERT, A. O.

How to estimate selling prices of castings. *Foundry,* Nov. 1914, p. 449-52. Excerpt. *Iron age,* Oct. 22, 1914, p. 933.

BACON, CLEVELAND F.

Accountant as an expert witness. *Accountant,* Feb. 3, 1906, p. 155-8. *Journal of accountancy,* Dec. 1905, p. 99-105.
Advantages of your society to accountants and bookkeepers. *New York accountants and bookkeepers' journal,* March 1903, p. 21-3.

BACON, RAYMOND FOSS AND WILLIAM ALLEN HAMOR

American petroleum industry, with special chapters by F. G. Clapp, Roswell H. Johnson, J. P. Cappeau, and L. G. Huntley. 2v. New York. McGraw-Hill book company. 1916. 963p.

BAD DEBTS.

See Losses; Reserves and sinking funds —Reserves.

BAD FEATURES OF CONTRACT WORK. Shorrock, E. G.

BADGER, ARTHUR

Chat about money. *Accountant,* March 30, 1889, p. 164-72.
Land tax and its redemption. *Accountant,* July 7, 1894, p. 608.
Manufacturer's trading account; its divisions and departments as applied to any one of the following business (1) electro plate (2) cutlery including saw, steel and, file trades (3) rolling mills. *Accountant,* June 25, 1892, p. 508-19.

BADGER, C. F.

Collection tickler for the financial man's guidance. *Business man's magazine,* Feb. 1908, p. 205-6.

BADGER, H. R. RALPH

Work of valuation of electric railway property. *Electric traction weekly,* Feb. 19, 1910, p. 197.

BAER, W. E.

Manifold manufacturing forms. *Business man's magazine,* Aug. 1906, p. 76-8.
Office accounting system for an automobile body co. *Business man's magazine,* July 1910, p. 88-93.
Up-to-date treatment of accounts payable. *Business man's magazine,* Sept. 1909, p. 268-71.

BAGG, C. B.

No part of funds used in Montreal pension plan obtained from employees. *American gas engineering journal,* Sept. 7, 1918, p. 223-4.

BAGG, F. A.

Life of railway physical property from the engineering standpoint. *Electric railway journal,* Dec. 9, 1911, p. 1205-6. Discussion. Dec. 9, 1911, p. 1210.

BAGOT, E.

Accounting for branch stores. *Business man's magazine,* 1904, v. 16, p. 104-5.

BAGSHAW, J. F. G.

Bank balance sheets and how to prepare them. London, J. F. G. Bagshaw, 1909. 15p.

BAILEY, A. R.

Valuation of track special work. *Electric railway journal,* May 12, 1917, p. 876-7.

BAILEY, GUY W. AND HORACE F. GRAHAM.

Report on uniform town accounting under the provisions of no. 199 of the acts of 1915. Montpelier, Vermont, Secretary of state, 1916.

BAILEY, H.

Chart for determining power costs. *Power,* June 5, 1917, p. 762-3.

BAILEY, H. R.

See Wood, Thomas, joint author.

BAILEY, J.

Operating costs of hydraulic vs. electric elevators. *Power,* May 6, 1913, p. 644.

BAILEY, J. T. H.

Conversion of irredeemable securities of local authorities. *Accountant,* July 27, 1895. p. 636-9.
Life assurance accounts. *Incorporated accountants' journal,* 1891-2, p. 100.

BAILEY, JOHN HENRY.

Police super annuation funds. *Accountant,* Aug. 6, 20, 1904, July 30, 1910, p. 149-55, 208, 144-6. *Incorporated accountants' journal,* 1909-10, p. 254.

BAILEY, LAWRENCE.

Duties and responsibilities of auditors in re lation to stocktaking. *Incorporated accountants' journal,* April 1912, p. 186-8.

BAILEY, W. E.

Organization; an address delivered before the Association of American railway accounting officers at its twenty-eighth annual meeting. Detroit, Michigan, June 28 and 29, 1916. 10p.

BAILEY, WALTER.

Railway accounts, old and new. *Jubilee of railway news* (London), 1914, p. 78-86.

BAILLET, HENRY F.

Overhead expense and percentage methods; a lecture on the cost of doing business, explaining how to find it and what to do with it when found, with practical examples of its use taken from actual business experiences. New York, David Williams co. 1915. 128p.
Overhead expenses from a new angle. *Metal work,* March 29, 1918, p. 423-4.
Overhead expense in combination shops. *Metal work,* Jan. 7, 1916, p. 5-6.

BAILLIE, MURRAY GLADWIN.

Some notes on stock exchange securities. *Accountant,* April 8, May 27, 1905, p. 425-35, 644-5.

BAILMENTS

Caporn, Arthur C. Law of bailments as effecting accountants. *Incorporated accountants' journal,* May 1913, p. 192-6.
Corpus juris; being a complete and systematic statement of the whole body of the law as embodied in and developed by all reported decisions; ed. by William Mack and W. J. Hale. New York, American law book co.

BAILY, JAMES THOMAS HERBERT

Life assurance accounts. *Incorporated ac countants' journal,* 1891-2, p. 100.

BAIN, J. B. AND R. J. POSSON

Requirements and cost of producing market milk in northwestern Indiana. Washington, Government printing office, 1920. 31p. (United States. Department of agriculture, bulletin no. 858).

BAINBRIDGE, C. N.

Costs of bridges for grade-crossing elimination. *Engineering record,* June 19, 1915, p. 770.
Study of grade crossing elimination in cities. *Journal of the western society of engineers,* October 1915, p. 639-51. Excerpt. *Engineering record,* June 19, 1915, p. 770.

BAINBRIDGE, J. P.

Depreciation, and an auditor's responsibility in connection therewith. *Accountant,* Sept. 22, 1906, p. 334-7. *Incorporated accountants' journal,* 1906-7, p. 12.

BAIRD, J. W.

Municipal accounting in Louisville. *Annals of the American academy of political and social science,* Nov. 1906, p. 459-62.
See also Chase, H. S., joint author.

BAIRD, JOHN

Legislation for the profession. *Accountant,* June 26, 1897, p. 643-51.
Remarks on the laws of succession and devolution of property in Scotland and England. *Accountant,* Feb. 17, 24, 1894, p. 167-71, 190-2.

BAIRD, W. P.

Routine of billing and receiving department *American gas light journal,* Nov. 29, 1915, p. 340-3, 346-7.

BAIRD, WILLIAM RAIMOND

Patents and patent law. (In Humphreys, A. C. *Lecture notes on some of the business features of engineering practice.* p. 420-43).

BAKER, C. A.

Load-factor, output and cost; abstract. *Electrical world,* July 3, 1915, p. 20.

BAKER, C. M.

Cost of chlorine treatment of water supplies. *Engineering and contracting,* April 10, 1918, p. 373.

BAKER, CHARLES W.

Elimination of idleness by systematic study. *Engineering news-record,* Sept. 1918, p. 450-1.
Relative economy of freight transport by railway and by motor truck. *Engineering news-record,* July 10, 1919, p. 56-62.

BAKER, E. A.

Basic principles that should underlie cost finding plans. *Americas,* Aug. 1919, p. 9-16.
Control of manufacturing costs. *Americas,* Jan. 1918, p. 16-8.
Underlying principles in purchasing and handling materials and supplies. *Americas,* Jan. 1920, p. 28-32.

BAKER, E. R.

Municipal balance sheet. *Business man's magazine,* May, 1905, p. 1046-9.

BAKER, EDWIN RICE

Municipal balance sheet. *Business man's magazine,* May 1905, p. 1046-8.

BAKER, GEORGE A.

Duties of trustees and official receivers in bankruptcy. (In Feather, J. Stuart. *Joint transactions.* 1911. p. 288-313). *Accountant,* Dec. 30, 1911, p. 909-19.
Legal personal representatives; their duties and liabilities. *Accountant,* Dec. 6, 1913, p. 832-41.
Some notes on bills of sale. *Accountant,* Jan. 24, 1914, p. 115-27.

BAKER, J. E.

Valuation of terminal lands. *Journal of accountancy,* Aug. 1909, p. 237-49.

BAKER, JAMES WILLIAM

Reference book; 20th century bookkeeping and office practice. Ed.7. Knoxville, Tenn., Southwestern publishing co. 1909.
20th century bookkeeping and accounting; a treatise on modern bookkeeping, accounting and business customs as illustrated in the "business transactions" which accompany this work; the only system of bookkeeping in which the transactions, as well as the business papers that illustrate them, are identical with those in the business world for use in all schools that teach bookkeeping and accounting. Cincinnati. Southwestern publishing company, 1912. 304p.

BAKER, JOHN

Shipping accounts. *Accountant,* June 30, 1894, p. 589-94.
Some methods of regulating wages. *Accountant,* Aug. 9, 1919, p. 133-6.

BAKER, JOHN A.

Building the Tough-Oakes mill. *Engineering and mining journal,* Nov. 27-Dec. 4, 1915, p. 869-74, 915-18.

BAKER, M. N.

Bibliography of uniform municipal accounting. *National municipal league, Proceedings,* 1902, p. 327-9.
Progress towards uniform municipal statistics in the United States. *Engineering news,* July 5, 1900, p. 12-14.
Uniform accounting a prerequisite to national municipal statistics. *Engineering news,* June 14, 1900, p. 393-4.
Uniform accounting and national municipal statistics. *American society of municipal improvements. Proceedings,* Milwaukee, 1900. p. 68-71. Discussion. p. 72-3. *City governments,* Sept. 1900, p. 61-2. *Municipal engineering,* Sept. 1900, p. 210-11. *Public policy,* Sept. 15, 1900, p. 168-9.
Uniform municipal accounting. *National municipal league. Proceedings,* 1900, p. 239-42. *Public policy,* Sept. 29, 1900, p. 196-8.

BAKER, M. N.—*(Continued)*

Uniform municipal accounts and reports. *Public policy,* Sept. 22, 1900, p. 183-4. *Municipal engineering,* Nov. 1900, p. 336-7.

What has been done towards uniform accounts for street railway electric and gas lighting, and water works systems. *National municipal league, Proceedings,* 1903, p. 296-7.

BAKER, N. D.

Employes advisory plan of the arsenals. *Industrial management,* Nov. 1919, p. 400-2.

Franchises—inclusion of franchise values in amount of investment for calculating rate of return for Detroit united railway. *Electric railway journal,* Jan. 29, 1910, p. 203.

BAKER, W. C. M.

Labor-saving system of accounts. Columbus. W. C. M. Baker. 1878.

BAKERIES

New Jersey bakery installation cuts fuel cost of 1000 loaves from $6.95 with coal to $3.27 with gas. *American gas engineering journal,* May 19, 1917, p. 502.

Accounting

American business and accounting encyclopaedia; comp. by E. H. Beach and W. W. Thorne. Detroit, Bookkeeper publishing co. 1901. Bakery accounting, v. 1, p. 162-3.

Bakery, retail. *International accountants' manual,* 1910, paragraph 482.

Brocklehurst, G. R. Bookkeeping for bakers, grocers, drapers, dairymen, butchers, co-operative societies, etc. Gainsborough, 1892.

Horndrup, N. A. Practical accounting in a retail bakery business. *Business man's magazine,* Jan. 1909, p. 87-90.

Meggison, F. Bakers' accounts, containing a system of bookkeeping for bakers, together with chapters on income tax, branch shops and bake-house accounts. London, Gee & co. 1908. 114p. (Accountants' library, v. 50).

Thorne, W. W. Accounting records of a bakery business. *Business man's magazine,* Jan. 1907, p. 83-7.

Wernig, C. E. Principles of bakery accounting. (In William Hood Dunwoody industrial institute. *Proceedings of the 2d short course for bakers.* 1920. p. 150-5).

Cost accounting

Eggleston, DeWitt Carl. Cost of manufacture of 1,000 pounds of ginger snaps; cost of producing and selling bread. (In his *Problems in cost accounting.* 1918. p. 176-7, 247-9).

Estes, L. V. Unit cost accounting for control; a system for the industrial executive. *Industrial management,* Nov. 1919, p. 359-63.

Kent, William. Cost accounts for a bakery. (In his *Bookkeeping and cost accounting for factories.* 1918. p. 206).

Wihlfahrt, Julius E. Treatise on increasing bakery efficiency specimens for figuring costs, expenses and results. New York, The Fleischmann company, c1917. 19p. +forms.

Depreciation.

See Depreciation, depletion and obso lescence—Bakeries.

BAKERS' accounts. Meggison, F. 1908.

BAKEWELL, W. B.

Computing savings interest on a uniform basis; method adopted by the associated savings banks of San Francisco suggests a simple way of overcoming some of the difficulties that are now encountered. *Bankers monthly,* Dec. 1920, p. 25-63.

BALANCE of trade. *Journal of accountancy,* Nov. 1910, p. 61-2.

BALANCE sheet audits. *Accountant,* Dec. 28, 1918, p. 337-9.

BALANCE sheet audits of stock brokers' accounts. Smith, H. M.

BALANCE sheet: correspondence. *Journal of accountancy,* July 1911, p. 217.

BALANCE sheet valuations. Page, E. D.

BALANCE sheet values. *Accountant,* Jan. 11, 1908, Dec. 4, 1909, Jan. 15, 22, Feb. 5, 1910, p. 42-3, 676-7, 699; 75-7, 115-7, 185-8.

BALANCE sheet values and reserve funds. Hamilton, W. R.

BALANCE SHEETS

See also Accounting.

Allen, George E. Balance sheet system of accounting. *Commerce, accounts and finance,* Aug. Sept. Nov. Dec. 1901, Feb. June 1902, p. 3-4, 3-4, 12-3, 11-4, 9-10, 7- .

Auditors and summarized balance sheets. *Accountant,* April 6, 1901, p. 413-6.

Balance sheet: correspondence. *Journal of accountancy,* July 1911, p. 217.

Balance sheet values. *Accountant,* Jan. 11, 1908, Dec. 4, 1909, Jan. 15, 22, Feb. 5, 1910, p. 42-3, 676-7, 699; 75-7, 115-7, 185-8.

Balance sheets and credits. *Canadian chartered accountant,* Jan. 1919, p. 230-1.

Batchelor, John Bennett. Verification and value of book debts for the purpose of a balance sheet. *Accountant,* Jan. 12, 1901, p. 51-3.

Bird, Cyril F. Duty and responsibility of auditors with regard to the item "Stock-in-trade" on a balance sheet. (In Chase, W. A. *Auditing and cost accounting.* 1917. p. 266-78). *Accountant,* Dec. 8, 1906, p. 705-9.

Brown, Richard. Form of revenue accounts and balance sheets and the use of percentages in connection therewith. *Accountants' magazine,* March 1904, p. 145-64. *South African accountant,* Dec. 1917, March 1918, p. 133-6.

Brutton, Richard. Study of a balance sheet with special reference to reserves and reserve funds. *Accountant,* Jan. 12, 1895, p. 39-43.

Cariss, Astrup. On arbitration: and on forms of balance sheets. *Accountant,* April 14, 1883.

Carter, Eric M. What is an annual balance sheet. *Accountant,* Oct. 22, 1910, p. 560-6.

Chase, Harvey S. Budgets and balance sheets. *National municipal league, Proceedings,* 1910, p. 214-29. *Journal of accountancy,* Dec. 1910, p. 81-96.

Cole, W. M. General characteristics and the interpretation of balance sheets. (In his *Accounts, their construction and interpretations.* c1917. p.109-40).

Cox, Henry C. Balance sheet. (In his *Advanced and analytical accounting.* 1920. p. 279-93).

Criticism of a balance sheet. *Canadian chartered accountant,* July 1920, p. 18-21.

Cropper, L. Cuthbert. Some notes on balance sheets. *Accountant,* April 19, 1919, p. 326-32. *Canadian chartered accountant,* July 1919, p. 6-20.

Dawson, Sidney S. Balance sheets. *Accountant,* Feb. 3, 1900, p. 131-8, 361,

BALANCE SHEETS—*(Continued)*

DEXTER, EDWARD. Some remarks on the verification of the items in a balance sheet. *Accountant,* March 28, April 4, 1903, p. 433-40, 454-6.

DICKSEE, LAWRENCE ROBERT. Forms of accounts and balance sheets. *Accountant,* Nov. 11, 18, 1893, p. 954-9, 973-81.

DICKSEE, LAWRENCE ROBERT. Publishing balance sheets and accounts. *Accountant,* Nov. 20, 1920, p. 561-4.

DOUBLE account balance sheet. *Business man's magazine,* April 1909, p. 377.

ELGAR, WILLIAM DANIEL and others. Stating of a balance sheet. *Incorporated accountants' journal,* 1900-1, p. 192.

FEDERAL reserve board and audits. *Journal of accountancy,* June 1917, p. 452-4.

FILING of balance sheets. *Accountant,* March 27, April 3, 1909, p. 421-4, 457-9. 1912. v. 1. p. 748.

FINCHAM, RUPERT F. W. Amalgamation of head office and branch balance sheets; with special reference to the elimination of internal branch balances. *Accountant,* Nov. 30, Dec. 7, 1901, p. 1307-14, 1336-43.

FORM of balance sheets. *Accountant,* Oct. 20, 1917, p. 293-5.

GREELEY, HORACE DUDLEY. Balance sheet. (In his *Theory of accounts.* 1920. p. 116-28).

HAMILTON, WILLIAM ROBERT. Balance sheet values and reserve funds. (In Feather, J. Stuart, ed. *Joint transactions.* 1911. p. 92-110.)

HAMILTON, WILLIAM ROBERT. Balance sheet values and reserve funds. *Accountant,* May 6, 1911, p. 730-7.

HAMILTON, WILLIAM ROBERT. Some notes on the preparation and audit of a balance sheet. *Accountant,* Jan. 7, 1911, p. 20-7.

HAWNT, F. M. Plea for greater detail ln balance sheets of limited companies. *Incorporated accountants' journal,* Dec. 1914, p. 64-6.

HEBREW balance sheet. *Accountant,* Jan. 4, 1902, p. 13-4.

HILLER, AUGUST. How to make up a balance sheet. *Business man's magazine,* Nov. 1910, p. 488-90.

HODGE, A. C. Designation of proprietary interests in the balance sheet. *Journal of political economy,* Jan. 1920, p. 77-80.

HOW to understand the balance sheet and other periodical statements by a chartered accountant. Ed. 2. London, Jordan & sons, 1905. 102p.

INTANGIBLE values in balance sheets. *Journal of accountancy,* Aug. 1916, p. 122-5.

JACKSON, WILLIAM LEACH. Balance sheets. *Accountant,* June 9, 1883.

JENKINSON, MARK WEBSTER. Composition and criticism of a balance sheet. *Accountant,* April 11, June 27, 1908, p. 520-32, 917-9.

JOBSON, ALEXANDER. Criticism of balance sheets. *Australasian accountant and secretary,* Nov. 1919, p. 24-8.

KEEN, FRANK N. Balance sheet of a limited company. *Accountant,* April 16, 1898, p. 399-409

KERR, DAVID S. How to read a balance sheet. *Canadian chartered accountant,* April 1913, p. 270-1.

KITTREDGE, A. O. Balance sheet. *Commerce, accounts and finance,* Dec. 1901, p. 3-7.

LAYMAN, A. A. B. C. of balance sheet making. Huddersfield, 1915.

LISLE, GEORGE. Balance sheets. (In his *Encyclopaedia of accounting.* v.1. p. 203-16).

MACDONALD, JAMES B. Balance sheets and balance-accounts. *Accountants' magazine,* Nov. 1898, p. 504-14. *Business,* March 1899, p. 182-6.

MACKENZIE, V. ST. CLAIR. Modern balance sheet and analysis of company finance; with historical chapters by A. Pulbrook. London, Effingham Wilson. 1908.

MANN, HENRY W. How to make up a balance sheet. *Business man's magazine,* Aug. 1911, p. 153-6.

MANN, HENRY W. Theoretical building of the balance sheet. *Business world,* Sept. 1905. p. 473-6.

MATHER, JOHN. Some notes on German balance sheets. *Accountant,* Feb. 11, 1888, p. 84-9.

MINIMUM prices and balance sheets. *Accountant,* Dec. 25, 1915, p. 765-8.

MINING company. *American institute of accountants, Special bulletin,* no. 2, no. 4, March 1920, July 1920, p. 7-8, 3-5.

MONTGOMERY, ROBERT H. Influence of the war on balance sheets. *Journal of accountancy,* July 1919, p. 1-8.

MURRAY, ADAM. Erroneous and objectionable entries in balance-sheets. *Accountant,* March 7, 1885.

NOONE, JOHN. Study of industrial corporation balance sheets. *Journal of accountancy,* Aug. Sept. 1910, p. 241-55, 348-67.

NOTES on balance-sheets. *Incorporated accountants' journal,* 1897-8, p. 18, 34, 50, 66.

PAGE, EDWARD D. Balance sheet valuations. *Accountant,* June 17, 1916, p. 685-90. *Accounting and commerce,* April 1916, p. 8-14. *Canadian chartered accountant,* Jan. 1917, p. 189-200. *Journal of accountancy,* April 1916, p. 241-54.

PIXLEY, FRANCIS WILLIAM. Balance sheet. (In his *Accountancy.* Ed. 2. p. 221-61, 278-83).

PIXLEY, FRANCIS WILLIAM. How to read a balance sheet of a commercial concern (a) from the point of view of a financial expert, dealing in this connection with "Working capital," "Fixed capital", and the gauging of the position of a company from its certified balance sheet (b) from an auditor's point of view, in respect of clear stating. *Accountant,* Oct. 27, Nov. 24, 1906, p. 511-24, 620-3.

PIXLEY, FRANCIS WILLIAM. How to read a balance sheet of a commercial concern. (In Chase, W. A. *Auditing and cost accounting.* 1917. p. 279-315).

PIXLEY on balance sheets. *Journal of accountancy,* April 1907, p. 473-5.

ROBERTS, WILLIAM H. Proper form of balance sheet. *American institute of accountants, Yearbook,* 1910, p. 148-70. *Journal of accountancy,* Nov. 1910, p. 10-16.

SCOTT, GEORGE G. Treasury stock and its relation to other balance sheet factors. *Journal of accountancy,* April 1917, p. 259-63.

SHACKELL, R. H. Valuation of assets for statement on balance sheets of companies. *Accountant,* Jan. 18, 1913, p. 90-7.

SHEFFIELD CHARTERED ACCOUNTANTS STUDENTS' SOCIETY. Some notes on the preparation and audit of a balance sheet. *Accountant,* Feb. 19, 1916, p. 231-3.

SIGNED balance sheets and auditors liabilities. *Accountant,* March 19, April 2, 1910 p. 393-5, 481-4.

SINGLE entry balance sheets. *Accountant,* 1887, p. 202.

SPICER, E. E. and E. C. PEGLER. Balance sheet. (In their *Practical bookkeeping and commercial knowledge.* 1912. p. 49-50, 74-5, 208-9, 211-3.

STOCKWELL, HERBERT GRANT. Net worth and the balance sheet. New York, The Ronald press co. 1912. 206p.

STRACHAN, WILLIAM. Critical examination of profit and loss accounts and balance sheets. *Incorporated accountants' journal,* 1907-8, p. 181.

BALANCE SHEETS—*(Continued)*

STRACHAN, WILLIAM. Some remarks on balance sheets and profit and loss accounts. *Incorporated accountants' journal,* 1902-3, p. 172.

STRONG, W. L. Monthly balance sheet. *Business man's magazine,* April 1905, p. 758-9.

SWANSON, G. Evoluation of a municipal balance sheet depreciation. *Accountant,* June 22, 1901, p. 735-7.

TOVEY, PHILIP. Balance sheets; how to read and understand them; a guide for investors, business men, commercial students, etc. London, Sir Isaac Pitman & sons. 77p.

UNIFORM accounting. *Canadian chartered accountant,* July 1917, p. 5-33. *Journal of accountancy,* June 1917, p. 401-33.

UNIFORM balance sheets in Australia. *Accountant,* June 4, 1910, p. 798-9.

UNITED STATES. FEDERAL RESERVE BOARD. Approved methods for the preparation of balance sheet statements; a tentative proposal submitted for the consideration of banks, bankers and banking associations; merchants, manufacturers and associations of manufacturers; auditors, accountants and associations of accountants; reprinted from Federal reserve bulletin, April 1917. Washington, Government printing office, 1918. 25p.

Same as Uniform accounting.

UNITED STATES. FEDERAL RESERVE BOARD. Uniform accounting; a tentative proposal submitted for the consideration of banks, bankers, and banking associations; merchants, manufacturers and associations of manufacturers, auditors, accountants and association of accountants; reprinted from the Federal reserve bulletin, April 1917. Washington, Government printing office, 1917. 25p.

Same as Approved methods for the preparation of balance sheet statements.

UNITED STATES. FEDERAL RESERVE BOARD. Uniform accounting. *Accountant,* Oct. 13, 1917, p. 282-92.

VALUE of assets in balance sheets. *Incorporated accountants' journal,* 1909-10, p. 99.

VALUES of assets in balance sheets. *Journal of accountancy,* April 1910, p. 458-9.

VIGEON, HARRY. Balance sheets. *Accountant,* Jan. 7, 1899, p. 27-32.

VINCENT, JOSEPH WALTER. Methods by which the existence and value of the debtors and creditors on a balance sheet may be verified. *Accountant,* March 30, 1901, p. 399-405.

WALMSLEY, F. Depreciation in relation to balance sheets. *Incorporated accountants' journal,* 1893-4, p. 8.

WALTON, SEYMOUR. Notes in a balance-sheet. *Journal of accountancy,* Aug. 1919. p. 154-5.

WELTON, THOMAS A. Suggestion as to the regulation of balance sheets. *Accountant,* Jan. 19, 1907, p. 96-8.

WILKINSON, R. H. E. Balance sheets. *Accountant,* Aug. 1, 1914, p. 159-61.

BALANCE sheets. Lisle, George.

BALANCE sheets. Tovey, Philip.

BALANCE sheets and credits. *Canadian chartered accountant,* Jan. 1919, p. 230-1.

BALANCE, TRIAL.

See Trial balance.

BALANCING

See also Accounting; Trial balance.

BELL, WILLIAM T. Sectional balancing. *Accountant,* Dec. 12, 1903, p. 1529-32.

DUXBURY, NATHANIEL. Sectional balancing. *Incorporated accountants' journal,* 1910-11, p. 209.

ELIMINATING pencil balances. *Business man's magazine,* April 1911, p. 395.

ERRORS in balancing; a concise hand-book dealing with the more usual causes of differences in trial balances, and the method of their detection; based on articles which have appeared in the Accountant. Ed. 3. London, Gee & co. 1912. 31p.

ERRORS in balancing. *Accountant,* March 7, April 4, 18, 25, 1896, p. 178-9, 218-20, 247-8, 267-8, 308-9, 332-3.

GRANT, HARRIS D. Advantage of ledger proof over trial balance. *Business man's magazine,* Feb. 1906, p. 180-2.

GRIFFITHS, J. P. Sectional balancing. *Incorporated accountants' journal,* Feb. 1913, p. 117-8.

HAAS, E. H. Daily business record and trial balance. New York, 1894.

LISLE, GEORGE and W. A. MIDDLETON. Balancing methods. (In their *Account-keeping in principle and practice.* 1911. p. 76-92).

MILLAR, THOMAS JOHN. Check numbers and other aids to balancing books of account. Edinburgh, 1907.

MOSS, C. A. Balancing and self-balancing ledgers. London, 1913.

NORTON, GEORGE PEPLER. Balancing for expert book-keepers. London, Simpkin, Marshall, Hamilton, Kent & co. 1894. 61p.

PENDER, CHARLES. Key to balancing. Dublin, Sealy, Bryers and Walker. 1909. 92p.

PITT, F. S. Up-to-date methods of balancing. *Incorporated accountants' journal,* Feb. 1914, p. 134-7.

RAMSON, AUBREY. Self-balancing devices. *New York accountants' and bookkeepers' journal,* March 1904, p. 77-9.

SCOTT, BENJAMIN. Principles of bookkeeping and balancing. Birmingham, 1879.

SHARP, JAMES R. Yesterday's and to-day's balances. *Business man's magazine,* June 1908, p. 512.

SMITH, C. N. Yesterday's and to-day's balances for commercial houses. *Business man's magazine,* March 1908, p. 255-6.

SPICER, E. E. and E. C. PEGLER. Sectional balancing or self-balancing ledgers. (In their *Book-keeping and accounts.* 1914. p. 226-30).

SWEETLAND, C. A. Improvements in balancing. *System,* Dec. 1905.

THORNTON, J. A. B. C. automatic balancing charts; supplement to bookkeeping for business men. London, The Macmillan co. 1901.

WEBBER, HENRY JOHN. Bookkeeper's companion: bookkeeping simplified; the principles of posting and balancing shown by a diagram, etc. London, [?1897].

BALANCING and self-balancing ledgers. Moss, C. A. 1913.

BALANCING for expert bookkeepers. Norton, G. P. 1894.

BALANCING the farm ledger. *Agricultural digest,* March 1918, p. 872.

BALANCING value as well as quantity. *Factory,* Jan. 1917, p. 58.

BALCH, C. F.

Stores keeping in railway work. *Engineering magazine,* Oct. 1905, p. 123-4.

BALCH, GEORGE T.

General classification of railway realties, rights and plant, designed to facilitate the work of taking an active inventory of such property; applies to the property of the Erie railway company, New York, Lange, Little & co., printers, 1875. 41p.

BALCH, JOHN.

How the cost accountant works in the paper industry. *Paper,* June 30, 1920, p. 14.
Proper duties of the cost accountant. *Paper industry.* Nov. 1920. p. 1182-3

BALDWIN, D. C.

Budget procedure of English and French cities. *Annals of the American academy of political and social science,* Nov. 1915, p. 204-10.

BALDWIN, F. C.

Keeping of farm records. *Jersey bulletin and dairy world,* Sept. 24, 1919, p. 1816.

BALDWIN, G. P.

Commercial statistics and their value to the executive. *General electric review,* Aug 1920, p. 648-52.

BALDWIN, HENRY DE FOREST

Discussion on the valuation of waterworks special franchises with an illustrative example. *Engineering and contracting,* Dec. 24, 1913, p. 707-9.
It shows how ignorance results in oppression. *Journal of accountancy,* July 1910, p. 165-9.
On the valuation of water works' special franchises. *Proceedings of the Ameircan waterworks association,* 1913, p. 9.

BALDWIN, P. M.

Farm accounting and the income tax. *Conservation* (Ottawa), March 1920, p. 11. *Journal of agriculture* (Quebec), April 1920, p. 218.

BALDWIN, R. L.

Unit costs for use in public utility appraisals. *Engineering news,* Sept. 11, 1919, p. 514-6.

BALDWIN, R. N.

Use of municipal ownership to abolish trans-Mississippi freight and passenger tolls at St. Louis. *National municipal review,* July 1915, p. 468-72.

BALDWIN, W. M.

Trust company audits; the advisability of a trust company maintaining an auditing department rather than have periodical audits from the outside. *Commercial and financial chronicle,* Bankers convention section, Oct. 15, 1910, p. 180-2.

BALDWIN REGISTER COMPANY

Principles of the Baldwin automatic business register. Berea, O., Baldwin register co. 1917. 22, 10p.

BALE, GEORGE R.

Modern iron foundry practice. London, 1905.

BALFOUR, H. N.

Accounting for betterments and replacements *Electric railway journal,* April 22, 1916, p. 770-1.

BALFOUR, JOHN

Concise farmers account book. 1898.

BALFOUR, WILLIAM A. A.

Power of a company with reference to purchasing its own shares. *Accountant,* Aug. 25, 1894, p. 744-8.

BALL, A. P.

Profit-sharing plan for executives. *Industrial management,* April, 1919. p. 296-8.

BALL, CHARLES E.

Brokerage questions and problems. New York, Universal business institute, inc. c1910. 55p.

BALL, JAMES STUART

Value of records to the farmer. Washington, Government printing office, 1917. 17p. (United States. Department of agriculture, year book separate no. 735). Condensed. *United States agricultural yearbook,* 1917, p. 153-67.

BALL, KATHARINE E. AND MIRIAM E. WEST.

Household arithmetic. Philadelphia. J. B. Lippincott co. 1910. 271p.

BALL, SARAH B. comp.

1600 business books; arranged by authors, by titles and by subjects; 2d ed., revised and enlarged to 2100 titles by L. H. Morley and S. H. Powell. New York, The H. W. Wilson co. 1917. 232p.

BALL, W. J.

Bookkeeping for electrical contractors. *Electrical world,* May 23, 1914, p. 1188.

BALL, WILLIAM VALENTINE

Law of arbitrations and awards. *Incorporated accountants' journal,* 1903-4, p. 239.

BALLANTINE, N. D.

Fallacies in figuring cost of freight car repairs. *Railway age gazette,* Jan. 26, 1912, p. 141.
Value of a freight locomotive from transportation standpoint. *Railway review,* March 1, 1915, p. 596-9. *Railway age,* April 23, 1915, p. 885-8.

BALLANTYNE, JAMES

Law and customs relating to marine insurance contracts. *Incorporated accountants journal,* 1897-8, p. 41.

BALLARD, E. H.

Comparing costs of steel making. Foundry, Sept. 1, 1920, p. 697-8.

BALLARD, F. W.

Power plant supervision and accounting. *Engineer.* June 1, 1905.

BALLARD, R. H.

Can profit sharing with employees be successfully worked out? *American gas engineering journal,* Dec. 8, 1917, p. 517-19.

BALLINGER, WALTER F.

Complete building transaction record. 3p,

BALMFORD, JOHN A.

Account-keeping by loose-leaf methods. *Accountant,* Aug. 3, 1902, p. 148-56.

BALTES, F. W.

Basis for estimating on printing. *Inland printer,* Nov. 1913, p. 286-7.

BALTIMORE BUREAU OF STATE AND MUNICIPAL RESEARCH

City of Baltimore balance sheets, 1911, 1912, general accounts, 1912. Baltimore, 1913. 13p. (Report no. 4).

——— **DEPARTMENT OF CITY ENGINEER**

Records and forms used in the municipal garage. 1915. 14 forms.

BALTIMORE *Journal of accountancy,* Dec. 1909, p. 142.

BALTIMORE costs mount. *Electric railway journal,* Aug. 3, 1918, p. 210.

BALTIMORE gas and electric rate decision. *Public service regulations,* March 1913, p. 141-7.

BALTIMORE pension system. *Electric railway journal,* Jan. 23, 1915, p. 172-3.

BALZARI, R. A. AND OTHERS.

Electricity in the development of oil lands. *Journal of electricity,* April 15, 1920, p. 373-7.

BAMMON, F. C.

Analysis of cost keeping as applied to municipal management of street cleaning. *American journal of public health,* Aug. 1914, p. 674-78.

BANCKER, J. W.

Records and reports of work. *Annals of the American academy of political and social science.* May 1916, p. 252-72.

BANCO MODELO DE LA ESCUELA SUPERIOR NACION AL DE COMMERCIO DEL ROSARIO.

Estatutos; reformados y aprobados por la Asamblea general ordinaria de accionistas relaizada el dia 30 de agosto de 1918. Argentine, 1919. 12v.

BANCROFT, B. M.

Apportioning the cost of power. *Paper,* Oct. 16, 1918, p. 13-14.

BANCROFT, F. J.

Rating of water undertakings. *Transactions of the British association of waterworks engineers,* 1900, p. 26. *Journal of gas lighting,* July 3, 1900, p. 24.

BANCROFT, WILFRED

New factory cost accounting system. *American machinist,* July 24, 1902, 1048-52.

BANE, W. F.

Practicable form of voucher-check. *Business man's magazine,* July 1906, p. 93-4.

BANGOR gas company submits new schedule of rates. *American gas engineering journal,* Aug. 31, 1918, p. 212.

BANGS, J. E.

Requirements as to acceptance of corporate trusts and bond certification. *Trust companies,* Dec. 1914, p. 501-3.

BANHAM, W. J. L.

Comparison of short-haul truck and rail shipments; abstracts. *Engineering news-record,* May 8, 1919, p. 903-4. *Engineering and contracting,* May 7, 1919, p. 498.

BANK account. Wallace, William.

BANK accounting. Goodyear, L. E. 1906.

BANK accounting. *Bookkeeper,* 1903, v. 16, no. 6, p. 82-94.

BANK ACCOUNTS

KESTER, R. B. (In his *Accounting theory and practice.* 1918. p. 194-8, 293-5).
LEMASTER, ELLIS. Treatment of bank account: correspondence. *Journal of accountancy,* Nov. 1915, p. 399-400.
LISLE, GEORGE *and* W. A. MIDDLETON. Banking transactions. (In their *Account-keeping in principle and practice.* 1911. p. 23-7).
MCINTOSH, R. J. Reconciliation of bank account. (In his *Reference book of accounts for manufacturing and mercantile companies.* c1914. p. 35-6).
NEFF, A. C. Old and new methods of keeping the cash and bank accounts. *Accountant,* Jan. 28, 1899, p. 117-20.
RACINE, S. F. Reconciliation of bank pass book and bank account. (In his *Accounting principles,* 1917. 1917. p. 247-9).
RITTENHOUSE, C. F. Banking practice. (In his *Elements of accounts for individuals, professional men and institutions.* 1918. p. 44-8.
SPICER, E. E. and E. C. PEGLER. Bank reconciliation statement. (In their *Book-keeping and accounts.* 1914. p. 31-2).
TREATMENT of bank account. *Journal of accountancy,* Dec. 1915, p. 473-4.
WALTON, SEYMOUR. Bank accounts on the ledger. *Journal of accountancy,* Nov. 1915, p. 394-6.
WALTON, SEYMOUR. Treatment of bank account. *Journal of accountancy,* Dec. 1915, p. 471-2.

BANK and public holidays throughout the world. Guaranty trust company of New York.

BANK and the treasury. Cleveland, F. A. 1905.

BANK audit or government inspection. *Canadian chartered accountant,* April 1913, p. 271-3.

BANK audit or inspection compulsory from outside: is it justifiable or expedient? *Canadian chartered accountant,* July 1911, p. 24-8.

BANK audits. *Canadian chartered accountant,* April 1913, p. 250-4.

BANK audits and balance sheets. *Accountant,* Aug. 23, 1913, p. 237-9.

BANK audits in Australia. *Accountant,* March 28, May 30, 1908, p. 416-8, 775-8.

BANK balance sheets. *Accountant,* Jan. 18, 1913, p. 77-9.

BANK balance sheets and how to prepare them. Bagshaw, J. F. G. 1909.

BANK bookkeeping. *The Office,* Oct. 1890, p. 274-5.

BANK bookkeeping. M'Kie, David. 1907.

BANK bookkeeping. Musselman, De Lafayette.

BANK book-keeping. Packard, S. S.

BANK bookkeeping. Sweetland, C. A. 1909.

BANK bookkeeping and accounts. Meelboom, J. A. 1901.

BANK columns in cash books. *Accountant,* June 20, 1885.

BANK defalcations—how they may be prevented or guarded against. *Trust companies,* Feb. 1914, p. 132-4.

BANK examinations. Ross, A. A.

BANK examinations. *Journal of accountancy,* Jan. 1906, p. 215-22.

BANK examinations in Canada. *Journal of accountancy,* May 1909, p. 40-2.

BANK examinations in New Jersey. *Journal of accountancy,* June 1911, p. 154.

BANK law and taxation digest. Harrison, Milton W. 1918.

BANK loans under the new conditions. Colley, F. G.

BANK OF AMERICA. BOARD OF DIRECTORS. Profitt sharing plan. New York, Bank of America, 1920. 1p.

BANK organization management and accounts. Davis, J. F.

BANK pass book bugbear. *Business man's magazine,* Sept. 1908, p. 231-3.

BANK vs. sureties. Shannon, C. R.

BANKER and the certified public accountant. Cannon, J. G.

BANKERS acceptances and trade acceptances. Chemical national bank of New York. c1917.

BANKERS and certified public accountants. Chase, W. A.

BANKERS and merchants perpetual maturity guide. New York, Bankers publishing company.

BANKERS and our gold reserves. *Accountant,* Jan. 26, 1907, p. 130-2.

BANKER'S credit manual. Wall, Alexander. c1919.

BANKERS' directory and list of attorneys. Rand, McNally & co.

BANKERS favor supervision of reports. *Journal of accountancy,* Oct. 1910, p. 464.

"BANKER'S" forms and the Negotiable instruments law annotated. Chapin, Heman Gerald. 1918.

BANKERS TRUST COMPANY.

Ownership certificates and information at the source. New York, Bankers trust co. June 29, 1918. 36p.

Personal income tax record book. New York, Bankers trust company, 1918. 26p.

State of New York tax on investments. New York, Bankers trust company, 1918. 16p.

Trust department records used by Bankers trust company, New York. New York, Bankers trust company, 1911. 53p.

BANKING.
See Banks and banking.

BANKING. Foster, Major Bronson. 1918.

BANKING accounts. *Economic review,* Oct. 18, 1913, p. 767-8.

BANKING and bank accounting. Morton, D. W. 1917.

BANKING and bank note currency. Roberts, G. E.

BANKING by mail. Cleveland, Cleveland trust co. 12p.

BANKING evolution. Salem, C. H.

BANKING forms. New York, Banking law journal, 1918. 96p.

BANKING law journal: devoted to banking, finance and law. Postal telegraph building, New York city.

BANKING with the government. *Journal of accountancy,* Dec. 1917, p. 455-6.

BANKRUPTCY

Accounting

BANKRUPTCY estate book. [?1889]

BENTLEY, H. C. Proceeding in bankruptcy. (In his *Science of accounts.* 913. p. 275-84).

CARTER, R. N. Bankruptcy statement of affairs, deficiency account, trustees' account. (In his *Advanced accounts.* p. 737-60).

COLE, WILLIAM MORSE. Bankruptcy. (In his *Accounts, their construction and interterpretation.* c1915. p. 354-62).

COLES, ARTHUR. Liquidation accounts—compulsory winding up. (In his *Company accounts.* p. 277-301).

COX, HENRY C. Statement of affairs and deficiency statements. (In his *Advanced and analytical accounting.* 1920. p. 319-29).

DAWSON, SIDNEY S. Trustees' accounts under bankruptcy deeds of arrangement, England. (In Lisle, George. *Encyclopaedia of accounting.* v. 6. p. 337-50).

DICKSEE, LAWRENCE R. Bankruptcy and insolvency accounts. (In his *Advanced accounting.* 1916. p. 163-80).

GRAVES, H. R. Accounts of trustees in bankruptcy. *Accountant,* Nov. 11, 1905, p. 540-5.

KANZLER, HUGO. Books of accounts in bankruptcy proceedings. *New York accountants' and bookkeepers' journal,* March 1904, p. 79-80.

KESTER, R. B. Accounts and reports in bankruptcy proceedings. (In his *Accounting theory and practice.* 1918. v. 2. p. 620-54).

KLEIN, J. J. Statement of affairs and deficiency account. (In his *Elements of accounting.* 1916. p. 258-75).

LISLE, GEORGE. Statement of affairs of a bankrupt. (In his *Accounting theory and practice.* 1900. p. 83-95).

MCEWEN, D. Handy guide and instruction for the preparation of a debtor's statement of affairs in bankruptcy. London, 1893.

BANKRUPTCY—ACCOUNTING—*(Continued)*

NIXON, ALFRED AND J. H. STAGG. Bankruptcy. (In their *Accounting and banking*. 1912. p. 320-33).

PARTRIDGE, ALBERT HENRY. Preparation of a statement of affairs in bankruptcy. *Accountant,* April 6, May 14, 1904, p. 461-9, 626-7.

PATON, WILLIAM ANDREW and R. A. STEVENSON. Statement of insolvency. (In their *Principles of accounting*. 1918. p. 599-605).

POPPLETON, G. G. and C. T. APPLEBY. Estate and record book for use in insolvency cases.

PORTERS, R. J. Statement of affairs (bankruptcy): Trustee in bankruptcy. (In his *Pitman's dictionary of bookkeeping*. p. 693-712. 742-5).

PRIESTLEY, HERBERT. Bankrupts' accounts, N. S. Wales: the preparation of a bankrupt's statement of affairs and supplementary accounts under the N. S. W. Bankruptcy act of 1887, etc. 1894.

SPICER, ERNEST EVAN AND ERNEST C. PEGLER. Bankruptcy. (In their *Bookkeeping and accounts*. 1914. p. 317-28).

SPICER, E. E. and E. C. PEGLER. Bankruptcy. (In their *Practical bookkeeping and commercial knowledge*. 1912. p. 193-201).

Australia

PARKER, W. A. Order and disposition clauses of the bankruptcy act. *Public accountant,* 1906-7, p. 163.

WEIR, J. L. B. Bankruptcy. *Public accountant,* May 1919, p. 323-31.

Canada

GRUNDY, H. P. Federal bankruptcy act; reasons given before Canadian credit men's trust association why there should be a Dominion bankruptcy act—suggestions as to its scope and provisions. *Canadian chartered accountant,* April 1917, p. 282-4.

MCMASTER, A. C. Bankruptcy act. *Canadian chartered accountant,* April 1913, p. 236-41.

MARTIN, N. L. New bankruptcy act. *Canadian chartered accountant,* July 1918, p. 24-30.

NEW bankruptcy act. *Canadian chartered accountant,* Oct. 1919, July 1920, p. 117-20, 22-6.

WADE, OSLER. Insolvency, including assignments and winding-up proceedings under the Dominion and Ontario winding-up acts. *Canadian chartered accountant,* Jan. 1920, p. 167-86.

England

ADMISSION of proofs in bankruptcy. *Accountant,* Jan. 13, 1906, p. 36-8.

AFTER-ACQUIRED property of bankrupts. *Accountant,* April 21, Dec. 22, 1906, p. 512-4, 781-2.

ANDERSON, THOMAS KERR. Title to goods in bankruptcy. *Accountant,* April 25, 1908, p. 602-11.

ASHTON, A. J. Recent commercial legislation: bankruptcy. *Incorporated accountants' journal,* 1890-1, p. 175.

ASSOCIATION OF CHAMBERS OF COMMERCE. Bankruptcy bill. *Incorporated accountants' journal,* April 1917, p. 171-2.

ASSOCIATION OF CHAMBERS OF COMMERCE. Debate on the bankruptcy bill. *Accountant,* April 13, 1912, p. 590-2.

ATTLEE, THOMAS M. E. Some notes on bankruptcy and deeds of arrangement. *Accountant,* June 22, 1901, p. 728-34.

AUSTIN, JAMES VALENTINE. Law of bankruptcy. *Accountant,* Jan. 18, Feb. 15, 1902, p. 69-79, 178-80.

AVOIDANCE of settlements under 13 Eliz. C. 5: an article from *"The solicitors' journal."* *Accountant,* Oct. 5, 1907, p. 423-5.

BAKER, GEORGE. Duties of trustees and official receivers in bankruptcy. *Accountant,* Dec. 30, 1911, p. 909-19.

BAKER, GEORGE A. Duties of trustees and official receivers in bankruptcy. (In Feather, J. Stuart, ed. Joint transactions. 1911. p. 288-313).

BANKRUPTCY act and private arrangements. *Accountant,* June 22, 29, July 1889, p. 342-3, 354-5, 367-8.

BANKRUPTCY acts, 1883 to 1913; draft general rules. *Accountant,* Feb. 21, 1914, p. 265-71.

BANKRUPTCY (administration order) rules, 1914. *Accountant,* Feb. 14, 1914, p. 232-7.

BANKRUPTCY and deeds of arrangement act, 1913. *Accountant,* Sept. 6, Oct. 4, 11, 18, Dec. 20, 1913, p. 309-20, 429-32, 464-6, 518-21. 896-9. *Incorporated accountants' journal,* Sept. 1913, p. 293-300.

BANKRUPTCY bill. *Accountant,* Jan. 6, 13. 20, Aug. 7, 1912, p. 4-6, 24-31, 40-2, 77-80, 222-30. *Incorporated accountants' journal,* Jan. June-Sept. 1912, April 1913, p. 89-94, 240-1, 261-6, 296-7, 307-8, 157-8.

BANKRUPTCY fees order. *Incorporated accountants' journal,* May 1920, p. 171-3.

BANKRUPTCY law. *Accountants' diary; annual. Incorporated accountants' journal,* June-Sept. 1912, April 1913, p. 240-1, 261-6, 296-7, 307-8, 157-8.

BANKRUPTCY law reform. *Accountant,* Dec. 2, 1911, p. 745-7.

BANKRUPTCY reform. *Accountant,* March 23, April 13, May 25, 1907, p. 373-5, 409-12, 466, 705-8.

BINNEY, JOSEPH. Some consideration on the law of bankruptcy. *Accountant,* April 13, 1912, p. 583-6.

BIRMINGHAM Chamber of Commerce: memorandum of evidence to be submitted to the Bankruptcy law amendment committee. *Accountant,* Aug. 18, 1906, p. 182-7.

BOURNER, ARTHUR CHARLES. Costs in bankruptcy. *Accountant.* Nov. 25, 1893, Feb. 3. 1894, p. 1004-8, 113-6.

BOWLER, HERBERT W. Work of a trustee in bankruptcy. *Accountant,* July 2, 1904, p. 13-20.

BRACKENBURY, CHARLES ERNEST. Some changes in bankruptcy law. *Accountant,* Feb. 20, 1909, p. 272-6.

BUCHANAN, HUGH R. Ranking in bankruptcy. *Accountants' magazine,* April 1920, p. 236-53.

BULLOCK, T. Costs in bankruptcy. *Accountant,* Jan. 6, 1894, p. 11-3.

CALDICOTT, O. H. Germs of insolvency. *Accountant,* Nov. 3, 1888, p. 707-12.

CARR, G. A. BUXTON. Disclaimers in bankruptcy. *Incorporated accountants' journal,* 1902-3, p. 83.

CLEAVE, JOHN K. F. Comparison of landlord's rights in bankruptcy and winding up. *Incorporated accountants' journal,* 1898-9, p. 230.

CLOUGH, WALTER OWEN. Bankruptcy law amendment bill. *Incorporated accountants' journal,* 1890-1, p. 86.

CLOUGH, WALTER O. Bankruptcy legislation: a review; Bankruptcy act, 1883, its working etc. *Incorporated accountants' journal,* 1889-90, p. 63.

COLEY, ALFRED H. Doctrine of reputed ownership in bankruptcy. *Accountant,* March 7, 1903, p. 328-34.

COLLIE, REGINALD. Notes on the comparative costs of winding-up bankrupt estates in Scotland and in England. *Accountants' magazine,* June 1897, p. 373-8.

COLLINS, ARTHUR. Few points in bankruptcy. *Accountant,* Jan. 16, 1909, p. 85-94.

COSTS in bankruptcy. *Accountant,* Jan. 16, 1915, p. 70-4.

CROOM-JOHNSON, R. P. Bankruptcy and deeds of arrangement act, 1913. *Incorporated accountants' journal* Oct. 1914, p. 15-8.

BANKRUPTCY—ENGLAND—*(Continued)*

CROOM-JOHNSON, R. P. Preferential payments in bankruptcy and winding-up. *Incorporated accountants' journal,* 1908-9, p. 262.

DAVIES, DAVID P. Deeds of arrangement act, 1914. *Accountant,* Jan. 16, 1915, p. 87.

DAVIES, DAVID P. Some points in bankruptcy practice. *Accountant,* Sept. 8, 15, 1900, p. 799-803, 821-5.

DAVIES, R. C. Trustees in bankruptcy. *Accountant,* March 2, 1912, p. 360-6.

DAWSON, SIDNEY S. Bankruptcy (England). (In Lisle, George. *Encyclopaedia of accounting.* v. 1. p. 268-329).

DAWSON, SIDNEY S. Interest in respect of proof of debt. *Accountant,* Oct. 23, 1909, p. 505-8.

DAWSON, SIDNEY S. Rights of billholders under bankruptcy administration; the rule in ex parte Waring v. Scotch law. *Accountant,* June 6, 1896, p. 476-8.

DAWSON, SIDNEY S. Some points in bankruptcy of interest to municipal officers. *Accountant,* Sept. 4, 1915, p. 277-80.

DEEDS of arrangement act, 1914. *Accountant,* Sept. 19, 1914, p. 324-9.

DICKINSON, WALTER S. Property of a bankrupt. *Accountant,* March 7, 1903, p. 334-9.

DISALLOWANCE of taxed costs in a bankruptcy. *Incorporated accountants' journal,* Jan. 1915, p. 76-7.

DOBSON, ALFRED. Bankruptcy bill. *Accountant,* May 18, 1912, p. 762-7.

DODDS, NORMAN R. Rights and duties of a trustee in bankruptcy. *Accountant,* Nov. 28, 1908, p. 660-3.

DOWDALL, H. CHALONER. Bankruptcy bill. *Accountant,* June 1, 1912, p. 847-50.

DRAFT rules under the deeds of arrangement acts, 1887 to 1913. *Incorporated accountants' journal,* March 1914, p. 172-8.

EAVES, WILLIAM. Bankruptcy and deeds of arrangement act, 1913. *Incorporated accountants' journal,* Dec. 1913, p. 76-8.

EDWARDS, ALLEN. Bankruptcy reform. *Accountant,* Feb. 2, 23, March 30, 1907, p. 156-60, 253-8, 417-25.

EDWARDS, ALLEN. Some professional views upon bankruptcy and private arrangements. *Accountant,* Dec. 20, 27, 1890, p. 696-9, 705-8.

EDWARDS, ALLEN. Suggested reforms in bankruptcy law and administration. *Accountant,* Dec. 7, 14, 1895, p. 987-93, 1010-5.

EDWARDS, G. W. Privilege under the bankruptcy acts. *Accountant,* Oct. 15, 1898, p 969-73.

EDWARDS, G. W. Question of privilege as between solicitor and client under the Bankruptcy acts. *Accountant,* Oct. 15, 1898, p. 969-73.

EHRHARDT, ALBERT. Alterations in the law of bankruptcy effected by the Bankruptcy act, 1890. *Accountant,* May 30, 1891, p. 417-20.

ENGLISH and Scottish bankruptcy. *Accountant,* July 4, 11, 25, 1914, p. 6-8, 37-8, 110-1.

ENGLISH and Scottish bankruptcy law. *Accountant,* May 30 June 27, 1914, p. 788 90, 817-20, 850-3, 878-80, 910-3.

FARR, W. E. Steps heading to a petition in bankruptcy. *Incorporated accountants' journal,* 1902-3, p. 227.

FERGUSON, JOHN A. Proceedings after sequestration order. *Public accountant,* May 1916, p. 234-42.

FLEMING, D. P. Question in bankruptcy arising out of the relationship of husband and wife. *Accountant,* May 2, 1908, p. 642-7.

FORD, T. Insolvencies. *Accountant,* Feb. 27, 1892, p. 189-95,

GATEY, J. Fraudulent preferences in bankruptcy and in winding-up of companies. *Incorporated accountants' journal,* 1895-6, (July).

GIBSON, JOHN GRANT. Effect of modern bankruptcy legislation on insolvency throughout the country. *Incorporated accountants' journal,* 1900-1, p. 150.

GIBSON, JOHN GRANT. Present system of administering the estates of insolvent persons. *Accountant,* Sept. 18, 25, Oct. 9, 1897, p. 884-9, 908-12, 935-7.

GIBSON, JOHN GRANT. Some criticized points in bankruptcy, law and their suggested amendments. *Accountant,* March 14, 1908, p. 365-73.

GIBSON, JOHN GRANT. Status of an undischarged bankrupt. *Incorporated accountants' journal,* 1905-6, p. 111.

GOURLAY, T. Some general principles in bankruptcy of special interest for trustees. *Accountant,* April 4, 1908, p. 468-78.

GRAINGER, W. H. Bankruptcy and deeds of arrangement act, 1913. *Incorporated accountants' journal,* Feb. 1914, p. 138-41.

GRIERSON, ALBERT. Deeds of arrangement. *Accountant,* Jan. 30, 1897, April 20, May 25, 1901, p. 136-42, 472-82, 604-5.

GROVE, FRANCIS G. M. Duties of a trustee in bankruptcy. *Accountant,* Jan. 27, 1894, p. 89-93.

HIBBERT, WILLIAM NEMBHARD. Fraudulent preferences. *Accountant,* Dec. 17, 1904, p. 756-8.

HISTORY and present practice of disclaimer in bankruptcy. *Accountant,* May 17, 24, June 14, 21, 28, July 26, Aug. 2, 9, 23, 30, Sept. 20, Oct. 4, 11, 1902, p. 537-8, 557-9, 624-6, 650-1, 665-8, 754-5, 773-4, 792-3, 846-8, 865-8, 952-4, 1005-7, 1032-3.

HODGE, JAMES R. Some bankruptcy experiences. *Accountant,* March 10, 1900, p. 258-60. *Accountants' magazine,* Aug. 1900, p. 477-85.

HUMPHREYS, E. WYNNE. Administration of bankrupt estates. *Accountant,* June 22, 1912, p. 933-6.

INGALL, WHATLEY W. Avert insolvencies—a suggestion. *Accountant,* Oct. 21, 1911, p. 539-40.

JACOBS, BERTRAM. Doctrine of "relation back" in bankruptcy. *Accountant,* June 6 ,1914, p. 828-34.

JACOBS, HERBERT. After-acquired property. *Accountant,* June 2, 1900, p. 519-23.

JACOBS, HERBERT. Bankruptcy and deeds of arrangement act, 1913. *Accountant,* May 9, 1914, p. 712-7.

JACOBS, HERBERT. Disclaimer by trustee in bankruptcy. *Accountant,* Feb. 10, 1900, p. 162-5.

JACOBS, HERBERT. Secured creditors in bankruptcy and winding-up. *Accountant,* May 13, 1905, p. 596-600.

JACQUES, C. A. Principles of the law of bankruptcy. *Accountant,* Feb. 18, 1893, p. 156-63.

JENKINSON, MARK WEBSTER. Some notes on bankruptcy. London, Gee & co. 1915. 95p.

JOHNSON, ELLIS. Proofs in bankruptcy. *Accountant,* Jan. 18, March 21, 1908, p. 90-8, 385-6.

JOHNSON ELLIS. Property available for payment of debts: Relation back of trustees title. *Accountant,* Jan. 9, 1909, p. 50-8.

JOLLY, WILLIAM A. Bankruptcy: the avoidance of voluntary settlements. *Accountant,* Oct. 26, 1895, p. 862-3.

KEOGH, GEORGE DARRELL. Order and disposition clause of the Bankruptcy act. *Incorporated accountants' journal,* 1900-1, p. 129.

LIABILITY of trustees under deeds of assignment. *Accountant,* Nov. 20, 1909, p. 609-12.

BANKRUPTCY—England—(Continued)

Marriage settlements and subsequent bankruptcy. *Accountant,* April 25, 1908, p. 585-7.

Married women and bankruptcy. *Accountant,* Dec. 19, 1908, p. 769-70.

Minton-Senhouse, Robert Metcalfe. Admission of proofs of debt in bankruptcy. *Incorporated accountants' journal,* 1895-6, p. 32.

Myers, John. Some notes as to the rights and duties of trustee in bankruptcy with regard to proofs. *Accountant,* Aug. 30, 1913, p. 280-90.

Partridge, Albert Henry. Compositions and schemes of arrangements in bankruptcy. *Accountant,* Jan. 1907, p. 14-7.

Pearson, Frank Shakespeare. Administration of debtors' estates. *Accountant,* Oct. 31, 1896, p. 904-8.

Pearson, Frank Shakespeare. Deeds of assignment with creditors. *Incorporated accountants' journal,* March 1912, p. 158-60.

Plowman, Percival C. Admission of proofs in bankruptcy. *Accountant,* June 22, 1895, p. 554-8.

Potter, J. Proofs of debts in bankruptcy. *Incorporated accountants' journal,* 1909-10, p. 237.

Potter, John. Proposed new bankruptcy act. *Accountant,* May 11, 1912, p. 733-8.

Price, Harry L. Bankruptcy reform. *Accountant,* Oct. 13, 1906, p. 430-7. *Incorporated accountants' journal,* 1906-7, p. 40

Price, Harry L. English bankruptcy procedure. *Accountant,* June 29, 1907, p. 886-95.

Price, H. L. Some financial and commercial aspects of trade insolvency. *Incorporated accountants' journal,* 1905-6, p. 185, 181.

Private examinations in bankruptcy. *Accountant,* Nov. 2, Dec. 28, 1889, p. 565-7, 699-700.

Pybus, R. Officialism, with special reference to bankruptcy. *Accountant,* Oct. 15, 1892, p. 778-82.

Randle, William. Bankruptcy acts, 1883 and 1890. *Accountant,* June 17, 1893, p. 569-78.

Ranking, D. F. de l'Hoste. Position of a trustee with regard to the property of the bankrupt. *Incorporated accountants' journal,* Dec. 1916, p. 61-5.

Ringwood, Richard. Secured creditors in bankruptcy. *Accountant,* April 25, 1896, p. 339-41.

Rogers, S. Some points of difference between the bankruptcy acts and the companies acts, with especial reference to winding-up. *Accountant,* July 6, 13, 1889, p. 371-5, 384-5.

Secured creditors in bankruptcy. *Accountant,* Dec. 11, 1909, p. 708-9, 735-7.

Sharp, Luke Jesson. Bankruptcy. *Accountant,* May 30, June 6, 1896, p. 448-51, 466-9.

Society of incorporated accountants and auditors. Bankruptcy bill: report of the parliamentary committee of the council. *Incorporated accountants' journal,* May 1912. p. 198-200.

Special managers in bankruptcy. *Accountant,* April 8, 1911, p. 539-40.

Spicer, Ernest Evan and Ernest C. Pegler. Bankruptcy, and arrangements with creditors. (In their *Practical bookkeeping and commercial knowledge.* 1912. p. 193-202).

Statham, Arnold. Legal duties of accountants in the administration of assets. *Incorporated accountants' journal,* 1889-90, p. 48.

Statutory rules and orders 1914 bankruptcy, England. *Incorporated accountants' journal,* May 1914, p. 245-8.

Statutory rules and orders, 1914; deeds of arrangement, England. *Accountant,* April 18, 25, 1914, p. 582-96, 624-30.

Stevens, Thomas Moffitt. Administration of partners' estates in bankruptcy. *Accountant,* July 8, 1899, p. 721-6.

Stevens, Thomas Moffitt. Bankruptcy law, with special reference to recent legislation. *Accountant,* Nov. 22, 29, 1890, p. 645-8, 656-9.

Stevens, Thomas Moffitt. Deeds of arrangements. *Accountant* Sept. 17, 1892, p. 701-7.

Strachan, W. Practical points in bankruptcy practice. *Incorporated accountants' journal,* Feb. 1916, p. 110-3.

Stuart, John. On the realization of estates in bankruptcy. *Accountant,* Aug. 18 1894, p. 720-4.

Sudgen, Robert J. Law of reputed ownership. *Accountant,* March 21, 1908, p. 396-7.

Tebbs, Herbert L. Fraudulent preference in bankruptcy. *Incorporated accountants' journal,* May 1916, p. 174-7.

Tebbs, Herbert L. Law relating to preferential debts and the rights of judgment creditors, and landlords with respect to rent, in bankruptcy, winding-up and receiverships. *Incorporated accountants' journal,* July 1913, p. 249.

Time table of some of the principal matters in connection with bankruptcy and deeds of arrangement. *Accountant,* Dec. 17, 1898, p. 1226-30.

Transfer of fixtures on bankruptcy and disclaimers. *Incorporated accountants' journal,* 1895-6, p. 118.

Trickett, Wilfred R. L. Contractual capacity of married women and the application to them of the bankruptcy laws. *Accountant,* June 27, 1908, p. 929-33.

Turner, Edward F. Reputed ownership. *Accountant,* July 15, 1893, p. 642-6.

Turner, Edward F. State turned solicitor. *Accountant,* Oct. 22, 1892, p. 798-801.

Welton, Thomas A. Some gossip concerning failures. *Accountant,* Nov. 3, 1888, p. 712-7.

Whinney, F. Recent legislation. *Accountant,* Oct. 11, 1890, p. 554-7.

Willis, Frederick C. Realisation and distribution of an estate in bankruptcy. *Incorporated accountants' journal,* 1892-3, p. 46.

Willson, W. R. Origin and development of the office of trustee in bankruptcy. *Accountant,* Aug. 21, 1900, p. 373-7.

Wollett, Charles. Bankruptcy acts 1883 and 1890. *Incorporated accountants' journal,* 1893-4, p. 112.

Woollett, C. Different acts of bankruptcy upon which a petition can be filed. *Incorporated accountants' journal,* 1897-8, p. 57.

Wreford, Herbert F. Winding-up of a bankrupt's estate. *Incorporated accountants' journal,* 1895-6, p. 146.

Wright, J. J. Bankruptcy, ancient and modern. *Incorporated accountants' journal,* Jan. 1912, p. 108-11.

Yates, Charles U. Comparison between English and foreign bankruptcy codes. *Accountant,* 1886, p. 228.

Ireland

Kevans, Edward. Irish bankruptcy law. (In Lisle, George. *Encyclopaedia of accounting.* v. 3. p. 469-90).

Robb, J. H. Some suggested amendments in Irish bankruptcy law. *Accountant,* Feb. 27, 1909, p. 312-9.

New Zealand

Bankruptcy laws. *Accounting and commerce,* Aug. 1915, p. 97-100.

Scotland

Aitken, Henry. Ranking of secured creditors. *Accountants' magazine,* April 1910, p. 214-24.

BANKRUPTCY—SCOTLAND—*(Continued)*

BANKRUPTCY law of Scotland and its administration. *Accountant,* Aug. 20, 27, 20, 1910, p. 248-54, 285-92, 223-5.

BANKRUPTCY reform in Scotland. *Accountant,* July 7, 1906, Dec. 7, 1907, p. 25-7, 719-20.

BANKRUPTCY (Scotland) consolidation bill. *Accountants' magazine,* Aug. 1913, p. 512-22.

BROWN, RICHARD. Comparative legislation in bankruptcy. *Accountants' magazine,* Jan. 1900, p. 6-33.

BRUNTON, WILLIAM. Trust deeds in Scottish bankruptcies. *Accountant,* June 6, 1903, p. 753-62.

BURNS, JOHN. Ancestor's creditors. *Accountants' magazine,* July 1916, p. 322-4.

COLLIE, R. Comparison of the working of the English and Scottish bankruptcy laws. *Accountant,* Sept. 8, 1894, p. 777-88.

COLLIE, R. Notes on the comparative costs of winding-up bankrupt estates in Scotland and in England. *Accountants' magazine,* June 1897, p. 373-8.

CRAWFORD, DAVID. Trustee in bankruptcy, his rights and duties. *Accountants' magazine,* Jan.-March 1915, p. 9-26, 98-115, 150-66.

CULLEN, W. J. Bankruptcy (Scotland). (In Lisle, George. *Encyclopaedia of accounting.* v. 1. p. 329-62).

EAST of Scotland bankruptcy reform association. *Accountant* June 15, 1907, p. 827-30.

ENGLISH and Scottish bankruptcy. *Accountant,* July 4, 11, 25, 1914, p. 6-8, 37-8, 110-1.

ENGLISH and Scottish bankruptcy law. *Accountant,* May 30-June 27, 1914, p. 788-90, 817-20, 850-3, 878-80, 910-3.

FLEMING, W. A. Report of the Departmental committee on Scottish bankruptcy law. *Accountants' magazine,* July 1910, p. 342-5.

FYFE, T. A. Bankruptcy reform. *Accountant,* Dec. 24, 1910, p. 905-10.

GORDON, JOHN COOK. Composition settlements in bankruptcy in Scotland. *Accountant,* Nov. 19, 26, 1892, p. 878-80, 906-9.

GOWANS, JOHN STUART. Trust deeds and deeds of arrangement [in Scotland]. *Accountant,* June 3, 1911, p. 868-75. *Accountants' magazine,* March 1911, p. 125-43.

INGRAM, WILLIAM. Bankruptcy reform in Scotland. *Incorporated accountants' journal,* 1908-9, p. 115.

MCFARLAN, ROBERT. Winding up of a sequestrated estate. *Accountants' magazine,* Feb.-March 1910, p. 95-112, 150-68.

MORTON, W. KINSBURGH. Bankruptcy reform. *Accountants' magazine,* Feb. 1907, p. 95-115.

MORTON, W. KINSBURGH. Bankruptcy reform—private arrangement. *Accountants' magazine,* April 1907, p. 214-27.

Union of South Africa

DANSIE, CROWN. Insolvency law of the colony. *Accountant,* Sept. 30, 1899, p. 997-1000.

GIBSON, HARRY. Some notes on the insolvency law of Cape Colony. *South African accountants' journal,* v. 1, p. 97.

KERR, JOHN G. Insolvency reform (Transvaal). *South African accountants' journal,* vol. 1, p. 43-95.

MACDONALD, JAMES B. Outline of bankruptcy law in the Transvaal. *Accountants' magazine,* March 1905, p. 145-52.

NATHAN, M. General view of the Transvaal insolvency law. *South African accountants' journal,* vol. 1, p. 119.

REPORT of committee appointed to inquire into the bankruptcy law of Scotland and its administration. *Accountant,* Aug. 20, 27, 1910, p. 223-5, 248-54, 261-3, 285-92.

RUTHERFORD, A. C. Sketch of the development of the law of bankruptcy in Scotland. *Accountant,* Feb. 20, 1909, p. 280-4.

RUTHERFORD, A. C. Suggested amendments on the bankruptcy (Scotland) acts. *Accountant,* June 25, 1898, p. 660-4.

WATT, JAMES. Some points in ranking. *Accountants' magazine,* Jan. 1907, p. 13-33.

WILSON, JOHN. Minor commercial insolvencies. *Accountant,* Jan. 2, 1898, p. 113-4.

WINSHIP, THOMAS. Deeds of assignment in Natal. *South African accountants' journal,* v. 1, p. 145.

United States

BANKRUPTCY law in the States. *Accountant,* Jan. 14, 1911, p. 40-2, 59-62.

COLLIER, WILLIAM MILLER. Law and practice in bankruptcy under the national Bankruptcy act of 1898; fourth edition by William H. Hotchkiss; eleventh edition with amendments of statutes and rules, and all decisions to June 1, 1917, including amendments to Bankruptcy act of February 5, 1903, June 15, 1906, June 25, 1910, and March 2, 1917, by Frank G. Gilbert. Albany, Matthew Bender & co. 1917. 1671p.

CORPUS juris; being a complete and systematic statement of the whole body of the law as embodied in and developed by all reported decisions; ed. by William Mack and W. J. Hale. New York, American law book co.

GERSTENBERG, CHARLES W. Law of bankruptcy; a text for business men and students of business, with copies of the National bankruptcy act, general orders of the Supreme court and the official forms, with problems. New York, Prentice-Hall, Inc. c1917. 187p.

GERSTENBERG, CHARLES W. Law of bankruptcy; answers to problems to accompany the Law of bankruptcy, a text for business men and students of business, with copies of the National bankruptcy act, general orders of the Supreme court and the official forms, with problems. New York, Prentice-Hall, inc. c1917. 68p.

HAGERTY, JAMES EDWARD. Bankruptcy legislation. (In his *Mercantile credit.* 1913. p. 247-356).

HUNTER, RICHARD. Law and practice in bankruptcy. *Journal of accountancy,* Sept. 1906, p. 358-87.

LOUGH, WILLIAM HENRY. Insolvency and receivership. (In his *Business finance.* 1917. p. 573-92).

MEYER, CHARLES A. Mercantile credits and collections. New York. The Macmillan company, 1919. 302p.

MEYER, CHARLES A. United States bankruptcy law. (In his *Mercantile credits and collections.* 1917. p. 179-54).

PRENDERGAST, WILLIAM AMBROSE. Bankruptcy act. (In his *Credit and its uses.* 1916. p. 297-322).

SULLIVAN, JOHN JAMES. Dissolution of corporations. (In his *American corporations.* 1916. p. 255-81).

SWARTZ, H. R. Recent bankruptcy legislation. *Journal of accountancy,* Nov. 1910, p. 35-52.

WAHLSTAD, PETER P. and W. S. JOHNSON. Bankruptcy. (In their *Credit and the credit man.* 1918. p. 238-61).

BANKRUPTCY act and private arrangements. *Accountant,* June 22, 29, July 1889, p. 342-3, 354-5, 367-8.

BANRUPTCY acts, 1883 to 1913; draft general rules. *Accountant,* Feb. 21, 1914, p. 265-71.

BANKRUPTCY (administration order) rules, 1914. *Accountant,* Feb. 14, 1914, p. 232-7.

BANKRUPTCY and deeds of arrangement act, 1913. *Accountant,* Sept. 6, Oct. 4, 11, 18, Dec. 20, 1913, p. 309-20, 429-32, 464-6, 518-21, 896-9. *Incorporated accountants' journal,* Sept. 1913, p. 293-300.

BANKRUPTCY bill. *Accountant,* Jan. 6, 13, 20, Aug. 7, 1912, p. 4-6, 24-31, 40-2, 77-80, 222-30. *Incorporated accountants' journal,* Jan. June-Sept. 1912, April 1913, p. 89-94, 240-1, 261-6, 296-7, 307-8, 157-8.

BANKRUPTCY estate book. [?1889]

BANKRUPTCY fees order. *Incorporated accountants' journal,* May 1920, p. 171-3.

BANKRUPTCY law. *Accountants' diary;* annual. London, Gee & co. *Incorporated accountants' journal,* June-Sept. 1912, April 1913, p. 240-1, 261-6, 296-7, 307-8, 157-8.

BANKRUPTCY law in the states. *Accountant,* Jan. 14, 1911, p. 40-2, 59-62.

BANKRUPTCY law of Scotland and its administration. *Accountant,* Aug. 20, 27, 20, 1910, p. 248-54, 285-92, 223-5.

BANKRUPTCY law reform. *Accountant,* Dec. 2, 1911, p. 745-7.

BANKRUPTCY laws. *Accounting and commerce,* Aug. 1915, p. 97-100.

BANKRUPTCY reform. *Accountant,* March 23, April 13, May 25, 1907, p. 373-5, 409-12, 466, 705-8.

BANKRUPTCY reform in Scotland. *Accountant,* July 7, 1906, Dec. 7, 1907, p. 25-7, 719-20.

BANKRUPTCY (Scotland) consolidation bill. *Accountants' magazine,* Aug. 1913, p. 512-22.

BANKRUPTS' accounts, N. S. Wales. Priestley, H. 1894.

BANKS, ALEXANDER SCOTT.

Operations of the grain corporation. *Journal of accountancy,* June 1919, p. 420-26.

BANKS, MARY

Municipal accounting; list of publications issued in the United States since Jan. 1, 1900 (not including articles in periodicals). *National municipal review,* April, 1914, p. 449-53.

BANKS AND BANKING

See also Building and loan associations; credit; Finance; Foreign exchange; Money; Stock exchange; Tables.

ABBOTT, C. A. E. Advantage of combining theory and practice in banking. *Accountant,* Dec. 30, 1899, p. 1249-52.

AGGER, EUGENE EWALD. Organized banking. New York, Henry Holt & co. 1918. 385p.

ALDRICH currency reform system analysed. New York, Fourth national bank, 1911.

ANYON, J. T. Safeguarding bank loans. *Journal of accountancy,* Dec. 1910, p. 97-107.

BANKERS and our gold reserves. *Accountant,* Jan. 26, 1907, p. 130-2.

BANKING by mail. Cleveland, Cleveland trust co. 12p.

BARHAM, F. F. Banking. *Accountant,* Feb. 18, 1888, p. 104-8.

BARTON, JOHN S. Bank of England, the bank reserve the bank rate and foreign exchanges. *Accountant,* Sept. 1, 1906, p. 236-43.

BOARDMAN, J. Banking. *Accountant,* Feb. 23, March 1, 1884.

BOARDMAN, J. Banking. *Accountant,* 1886, p. 256.

BRYAN, WILLIAM JENNINGS. Government should issue notes and guarantee bank deposits. *Journal of accountancy,* March 1908, p. 366-79.

BUTCHART, J. R. Money, credit and banking. *Accountant,* June 23, 30, 1917, p. 589-93, 606-10. *Acounting and commerce,* April, May, June 1917, p. 14-8, 36-44, 63-5.

CANNON, JAMES G. Banker and the certified public accountant. *Journal of accountancy,* Nov. 1908, p. 1-6.

CARNEGIE, ANDREW. Worst banking system in the world. *Journal of accountancy,* March 1908, p. 357-61.

CARY, R. H. Foreign banking. (In Lisle, George. *Encyclopaedia of accounting.* v.3. p. 53-88).

CECIL, G. Banking in India: the rate of interest allowed. *Accountants' magazine,* 1904, p. 89.

CHAPIN, HEMAN GERALD. "Banker's" forms and the Negotiable instruments law annotated. Ed.5. New York, Bankers encyclopaedia co. c1918. 133p.

CHASE, WILLIAM ARTHUR. Bankers and certified public accountants. *Journal of accountancy,* Aug. 1908, p. 242-7.

CLARK, ARCHIBALD B. High bank rate. *Accountants' magazine,* April 1907, p. 201-13.

CLEVELAND, FREDERICK A. Financial reports of national banks as a means of public control: reprinted from the *Annals of the American academy of political and social science* for July 1904. 21p.

CLEVELAND, FREDERICK A. Relation of the public accountant to the banker. *New York accountants' and bookkeepers' journal,* Nov. 1903, p. 171-3.

CLEWS, HENRY. Business education and commercial and banking methods. *Accountant,* Sept. 16, 1905, p. 305-11.

CONANT, CHARLES A. Functions of centralized banking. *Bankers magazine,* Oct. 1914, p. 388-98.

CURRENCY and banking problem. *Journal of accountancy,* Aug. 1910, p. 289-91.

DAVEY, FREDERICK. Students' catechism on book-keeping, accounting and banking, with exercises and examination questions. Ed.2. London. Butterworth & co. 1917. 478p.

DAVIS, CLEMENT H. Dangers of a federal note issue. *Accountant,* Oct. 1, 1910, p. 443-5.

DICKINSON, ARTHUR LOWES. Relations between the accountant and the banker. *Journal of accountancy,* May 1909, p. 55-7.

DOUGLAS, R. A. Banking facilities for importers. *Accounting and commerce,* May 1918, p. 43-6.

DOUTHWAIT, WILLIAM. Notes on banking. *Accountant,* Nov. 24, 1900, p. 1059-63.

DUNBAR, CHARLES FRANKLIN. Theory and history of banking. Ed.3, enlarged. New York, G. P. Putnam's sons, 1917. 297p.

EASTON, H. T. Practical banking. *Incorporated accountants journal,* 1905-6, p. 241.

EBERSOLE, J. F. Cattle loan banks. *Journal of political economy,* June 1914, p. 577-80.

FISK, HARVEY E. Banks and banking system. (In his *Dominion of Canada.* 1920. p. 43-63).

FORGAN, DAVID R. Relation between bankers and accountants. *American institute of accountants, Yearbook,* 1912, p. 215-22. *Journal of accountancy,* Oct. 1912, p. 291-3.

FORM of trust agreement to prevent overcertification. *Bankers magazine,* Jan. 1912, p. 36.

FOWLER, WILLIAM. Banking reserves. *Accountant,* April 14, 1900, p. 358-9.

GARDNER, JAMES P. Bank clerk and his work. *Business man's magazine,* Jan-June 1909, p. 44-7, 141-6, 250-3, 339-43, 447-8, 564-5.

BANKS AND BANKING—*(Continued)*

GARRISON, ELISHA ELY. Currency—banking and accountancy. *Journal of accountancy,* Aug. 1910, p. 286-8

GOTTLIEB, LOUIS ROSS. Money, prices, credit and banking. *American economic review,* Sept. 1920, p. 652-61.

GRAINGER, WILFRED H. Banking notes. *Accountant,* Oct. 9, 1920, p. 390-4.

GUARANTY TRUST COMPANY OF NEW YORK. How business with foreign countries is financed. New York, Guaranty trust company of New York, 1919. 55p.

HASKINS, CHARLES WALDO. Scope of banking education; an address before the New York chapter American institute of bank clerks, Nov. 21, 1901. 11p.

HENDERSON, J. M. Joint stock companies act, 1862-1900, in relation to banking. *Accountant,* Feb. 3, 1906, p. 147-55.

HIGGINS, AMES. Advantages of bank combination. *Journal of accountancy,* Jan. 1906, p. 194-204.

HISTORY law and practice of banking. *Accountant,* April 12, 19, 26, May 3, 17, 24, 31, June 7, 14, 21, 28, July 5, 12, 19, 26, Aug. 2, 9, 16, 23, 1913, p. 536-8, 569-71, 609-10, 654-5, 751-3, 786-8, 821-3, 863-5, 898-9, 930-1, 961-3, 7-9, 33-5, 82-4, 123-4, 150-1, 179-81, 208-9, 239-41.

HOLDSWORTH, JOHN THOM. Money and banking. New York, D. Appleton & co. 1917. 511p.

HULL, WALTER HENRY. Practical problems in banking and currency. New York, The Macmillan co. 1907. 596p.

HUNTER, JOEL. Banking and finance. (In his *Thinking in figures.* c1916. p. 23-33).

IMMOBILITY of capital in the United States. *Journal of accountancy,* Feb. 1911, p. 289-91.

INDIAN banks. *Accountant,* Nov. 8, 15, 1913, p. 665-6, 687-91, 697-8.

INDIA'S banking requirements. *Accountant,* Aug. 9, 1913, p. 193-6

JACOBS, H. Collecting banker. *Incorporated accountnts journal,* 1908-9, p. 106.

JOHNSON, JOSEPH FRENCH. Schemes for currency reform. *Journal of accountancy,* Jan. 1908, p. 224-35.

KERR, ANDREW W. Bank of England weekly accounts. *Accountants' magazine,* 1902, p. 531.

KERR, ANDREW W. Characteristics of banking systems. *Accountants' magazine,* Jan. 1899, p. 15-35.

M'NEIL, ALLAN. Banking outlook. *Accountants' magazine,* June 1907, p. 254-67.

MAHAFFY, JAMES PENTLAND. Banking in ancient times. *Accountant,* April 1, 1899, p. 366-7.

MAZENGARB, C. R. Some notes on bank guarantees. *Accounting and commerce,* Aug. 1917, p. 108-10.

MIXTER, CHARLES W. Measures for banking reform. *Journal of accountancy,* April, June, July 1908, p. 463-76, 123-32, 194-203.

MOURANT, H. P. Functions of banks. *Accounting and commerce,* May-July 1920, p. 46-8, 70-1, 93-5.

MOXON, T. B. Banking notes. *Accountant,* 1887, p. 725.

NICHOLS, T. B. Collateral loans. *Journal of the American bankers association,* Feb. 1912, p. 513-7.

OUR currency problem. *Journal of accountancy,* April 1909, p. 480-1.

POWNALL, GEORGE *H.* Services of banking to trade. *Accountant,* Jan. 16, 1892, p. 60-70.

PRICE, T. Bank of England return and foreign exchanges. *Incorporated accountants' journal,* 1906-7, p. 151.

RAND, MCNALLY & CO. Bankers' directory and list of attorneys. Chicago, Rand, McNally & co.

ROBERTS, GEORGE E. Banking and bank note currency. *Journal of accountancy,* March 1909, p. 368-83.

ROBERTS, GEORGE E. Public accountant and the banker. *Journal of accountancy,* Dec. 1907, p 114-8.

SALIERS, EARL A. Bank loans under the new conditions: correspondence. *Journal of accountancy,* Jan. 1915,, p. 80-1.

SMITH, STANLEY G. Bankers and their relation to the money market. *Accountant,* May 26, 1906, p. 664-72.

STEAD, F. R. Everyday banking transactions. *Accountant,* March 14, 1914, p. 375-83.

SYKES, ERNEST. "Adventurous" banking. *Accountant,* April 8, 1916, p. 409-12.

SYKES, ERNEST. Banking. (In Lisle, George. *Encyclopaedia of accounting.* v.1. p. 231-68).

THOMPSON, HARWELL, CLOUD. Account analysis in commerical banks. *Journal of accountancy,* Sept. 1913, p. 210-29.

To use public accountants; comptroller may require banks to get certificate. *Journal of accountancy,* Oct. 1910, p. 471.

UNCLAIMED bank deposits. *Accountants' magazine,* Aug. 1897, p. 505-14.

VANDERHOOF, HERBERT. Story of banking by mail. Cleveland, Cleveland trust co. c1907. 34p.

VON HAAST, H. F. Banker and customer. *Accounting and commerce,* May-Dec. 1920, p. 43-5, 69, 95-6, 118-9, 143-4, 189-92.

WALKER, W. H. History and causes of the bank crises in Newfoundland and the Isle of Man. *Accountant,* Aug. 15, 1903, p. 1042-8. *Accountants' magazine,* April 1902, p. 210-26.

WALTON, SEYMOUR. Rediscounting by banks. *Journal of accountancy,* July 1916, p. 62.

WELTON, THOMAS A. Some notes and comments on banking matters. *Accountant,* Dec. 19, 1891, p. 893-904.

WHAT the comptroller would save. *Journal of accountancy,* June 1916, p. 441-3.

WHITE, HORACE. Money and banking; illustrated by American history; revised and continued to the year 1914. Boston, Ginn & co. c1911 541p.

WITHERS, HARTLEY. "Strong as the bank of England". *Canadian chartered accountant,* Oct. 1914, p. 94-6.

Accounting

ADVANCED bookkeeping and banking. New York, American book company.

ALCORN, EDGAR G. About bookkeeping in banks. *Business man's magazine,* April-Aug. 1907, p. 85-92, 77-82, 63-8, 75-80, 53-61.

ALCORN, EDGAR G. Alcorn system of modern bank bookkeeping and accounting. 3v. Columbus, American text book co. 1918. 132+92+48p.

ALCORN, EDGAR G. Average book. *Bankers magazine,* Nov. 1912, p. 519-22.

ALCORN, EDGAR G. Balancing pass-books. *Bankers magazine,* Dec. 1912, p. 669-77.

ALCORN, EDGAR G. Different methods of keeping the certificates of deposit account. *Bankers magazine,* Jan. 1911, p. 45-8.

ALCORN, EDGAR G. Five books in one. *Bankers magazine,* April 1910, p. 573-6.

ALCORN, EDGAR G. How some banks keep a record of the liability of their customers. *Business man's magazine,* Jan. 1912, p. 86-8.

ALCORN, EDGAR G. How to handle coupon notes. *Business man's magazine,* April 1912, p. 320.

ALCORN, EDGAR G. Keeping a record of open and closed accounts. *Bankers magazine,* Dec. 1910, p. 809-13.

ALCORN, EDGAR G. Opening a new ledger. *Bankers magazine,* Dec. 1911, p. 711-6.

ALCORN, EDGAR G. Value of the liability ledger. *Bankers magazine,* Jan. 1913, p. 11-5.

ALEXANDER, J. H. New methods of keeping accounts. *Bankers magazine.* v.15, p. 337.

BANKS AND BANKING—ACCOUNTING—*(Continued)*

AMERICAN BANKERS ASSOCIATION. Explanation of the numerical system of the American bankers' association. Chicago, Continental and commercial national bank, 1911.

AMERICAN BANKERS ASSOCIATION. Forms for national and state banks. New York, American bankers association. 1913. 124 numb.

AMERICAN business and accounting encyclopaedia. Detroit, Book-keeper publishing co. 1901. Bank accounting, v.1, p. 175-242.

ANALYZING bank accounts. *Pace student,* Feb. 1918.

ASSIGNMENT of accounts receivable. *Bankers magazine,* Dec. 1914, p. 654.

BAGSHAW, J. F. G. Bank balance sheets and how to prepare them. London, J. F. G. Bagshaw, 1909. 15p.

BAKEWELL, W B. Computing savings interest on a uniform basis: method adopted by the associated savings banks of San Francisco suggests a simple way of overcoming some of the difficulties that are now encountered. *Bankers monthly,* Dec. 1920, p. 25-63.

BANK accounting. *Bookkeeper,* 1903, v.16, no. 6, p. 82-94.

BANK audits and balance sheets. *Accountant,* Aug. 23, 1913, p. 237-9.

BANK balance sheets. *Accountant,* Jan. 18, 1913, p. 77-9.

BANK bookkeeping. *The office,* Oct. 1890, p. 274-5.

BANK pass book bugbear. *Business man's magazine,* Sept. 1908, p. 231-3.

BANKERS and merchants perpetual maturity guide. New York, Bankers publishing company.

BANKING accounts. *Economic review,* Oct. 18, 1913, p. 767-8.

BANKING forms. New York, *Banking law journal,* 1918. 96p.

BARRETT, ALBERT REED. Modern banking methods and practical bank bookkeeping; illustrated with over two hundred forms of bank books, records and blanks. Ed. 5. New York, Bankers publishing co. 1907. 325p.

BATCHELOR, A. Banker's balance sheet. *Incorporated accountants' journal,* 1893-4, p. 16.

BEERBOWER, C. W. Checking and savings accounts. *Bankers magazine,* March 1914, p. 297-302.

BEERBOWER, C. W. Simple card system for handling collections. *Bankers magazine,* June 1912, p. 771-3.

BEERBOWER, C. W. Unit tellers' system. *Bankers magazine,* June 1913, p. 692-6.

BELCHER, F. PERCY. Bank bookkeeping. *Accountant,* Nov. 27, 1909, p. 657-67.

BENGER, T. H. Banking accounts. *Incorporated accountants' journal,* 1902-3, p. 267.

BENNETT, GEORGE E. Bank depositors ledger. (In his *Constructive accounting.* 1920. p. 253).

BENTLLEY, HARRY C. General ledger accounts of national banks. (In his *Science of accounts.* 1913. p. 311-5).

BLACKLOCK, J. H. Bank clerk. *The office,* Sept. 1890, p. 238-9.

BLOMFIELD, F. C. Making the deposit account pay. *Business man's magazine,* Dec. 1911, p. 538-42.

BLUM, A. S. Rules and regulations for the guidance of employees of safe deposit department. *Trust companies,* May, 1915, p. 456-8.

BOARDMAN, J. Bookkeeping and banking. London, Gee & co. 1886.

BOOKKEEPING in banks. *Business man's magazine,* Sept. 1907, p. 130-2.

BOOKS of account as evidence. *Bankers magazine,* Aug. 1915, p. 196-8.

BORDWELL, GEORGE O. Analysis of a bank account. San Francisco, Coast banker publisher, 1911. 18p.

BORDWELL, GEORGE O. Modern banking methods as applied to the tellers and bookkeepers. San Francisco, Hicks-Judd company, c1913. 122p.

BRECKENRIDGE, T. S. Use of card ledgers in a country bank. *Business man's magazine,* June 1907, p. 130-4.

BROAKER, F. Accounts, the safeguard of a business. *Bankers magazine,* Dec. 1909, p. 983-8.

BURKHOLDER, T. E. Modern bank accounting. *Southern banker,* Feb. 1906.

CANNON, JAMES G. Uniform statement blanks and credit department; address delivered Sept. 7, 1898. New York, J. S. Babcock, 1899. 17p.

CARTER, R. N. Bank book-keeping and accounts. (In his *Advanced accounts.* p. 937-60).

CHAMBERS, R. E. Statement system of balancing depositors' accounts. *Bankers magazine,* Feb. 1913, p. 152-5.

CHECKING of bank interest. *Accountant,* Feb. 29, 1908, p. 275-7.

CENTRAL bank issue. *Journal of accountancy,* Nov. 1909, p. 45-7.

CHRISHOLM, G. D. Suggestions towards a system of records in connection with advances. *Institute of bankers journal* (London) 1911, v.32, p. 301-6.

CLARIDGE, W. Checking of bank interest. *Accountant,* March 7, 1908, p. 326. *Incorporated accountants journal,* 1907-8, p. 151.

CLEMENTS, DAVID M. Selling the Northwest. *Bankers' monthly,* March 1918, p. 14.

COCKE, HUGH G. Bank balance sheets; under the Indian companies act, 1913. *Accountant,* April 21, 1917, p. 391-6.

COFFIN, GEORGE M. Administration and bookkeeping of a national bank. *Business,* Oct. 1898, p. 630-4.

COLE, WILLIAM MORSE. Some general principles illustrated in bank accounting. (In his *Accounts, their construction and interpretation.* c1915. p. 249-54).

COLLATERAL register for a bank. *Business man's magazine,* Oct. 1911, p. 342-3.

CONCERNED about Yankee morality. *Journal of accountancy,* Nov. 1905, p. 60-1.

COOK, J. B. How your bank account is protected. *Business man's magazine,* June, 1912, p. 502-5.

COOK, J. B. National bank earnings. *Journal of accountancy,* Sept. 1910, p. 334-8, Editorial, Dec. 1910, p. 146.

COWLRICK, A. S. Bank bookkeeping and methods of internal check. *Accountant,* Jan. 31, 1914, p. 156-66.

CREDIT forms—prepared by the committee on credit blanks, American bankers association. *Journal of the American bankers association,* May, 1910.

CROCK, H. R. Reducing errors in the accounting routine; how a St. Louis bank met the labor problem caused by the war and made the work easier for the new women bookkeepers. *Bankers' monthly,* Chicago, v. 35, no. 7, p. 18.

CROWELL, NORMAN H. Checking up the bank's records. *Business man's magazine,* Feb. 1912, p. 178-9.

CUTFORTH, A. E. Bank. (In his *Audits.* 1914. p. 87-8).

DAILY balances in several banks. *Business man's magazine,* April 1911, p. 393-4.

DAVEY, F. Students' catechism on book-keeping, accounting and banking; with exercises and examination questions. Ed.2. London, Butterworth & co. [1917] 478p.

DAVIESS circuit court. T. A. Pedley as receiver of the Owensboro Savings Bank and trust company. Plaintiff vs. inequity action no. 9306 Owensboro savings bank and trust company etc., defendents exhibit A and B showing notes and bills and real estate notes. 17p.+34p.

BANKS AND BANKING—ACCOUNTING—*(Continued)*

DAVIS, J. F. Bank organization management and accounts London, Sir Isaac Pitman and sons. 157p.

DETECTION of fraud—by manipulation of the adding machine slips bank examiners were fooled. *Commercial and financial chronicle,* July 23, 1910, p. 192.

DICKINSON, A. L. Banking. (In his *Accounting practice and procedure.* 1917. p. 60-1).

DICKINSON, ARTHUR LOWES Form of statement for national banks. (In his *Accounting practice and procedure.* 1917. p. 288-9).

DODGE, J. MORRELL. Keeping your assets at the 100% mark. *Bankers' monthly,* Nov. 1917, p. 11.

DOING an old thing in a new way: the maturity guide saves time and work. *Bankers magazine,* Nov. 1910, p. 663-5.

DOWLER, FRANK AND E. M. HARRIS. Auditing, accounting and banking; a manual for accountants, advanced bookkeeping students and business men. London. Sir Isaac Pitman & sons, 319p.

DUNBAR, CHARLES FRANKLIN. Banking operations and accounts. (In his *Theory and history of banking.* 1917 p. 22-42).

EASTON, HARVEY TUCKER. English bank bookkeeping; with an introduction on the theory and practice of accountants. London, Effingham Wilson, 1910. 208p.

EASTON, HARVEY TUCKER. Practice of banking, with special reference to bookkeeping. *Accountant,* July 15, 22, 1899, p. 751-9, 778-88.

EASTON, HARVEY TUCKER. Work of a bank; an elementary text-book for bank officials. London, Effingham Wilson, 1916. 150p.

EKIRCK, A. A. Ideal teller's cash-sheet—how it worked in a small bank. *Bankers magazine,* Aug. 1909, p. 213-4.

ESQUERRÉ, P. J. Bank balance sheet. (In his *Applied theory of accounts.* 1917. p. 418-21).

ETHICS of accounting. *Bankers magazine,* v. 62, p. 730.

FISKE, AMOS KIDDER. Bookkeeping of the bank. (In his *Modern bank.* 1916. p. 169-85).

FORM of trust agreement to prevent over-certification. *Bankers magazine,* Jan. 1912, p. 36.

GAIL, HARRY E. Safekeeping of bonds as a business getter. *Bankers' monthly,* Feb. 1919, p. 8.

GARDNER, JAMES P. Bank clerk and his work. *Business man's magazine,* Jan.-June, 1909, p. 44-7, 141-6, 250-3, 339-40, 447-8, 564-5.

GARDNER, JAMES P. New form for use in the analysis of an account offering items for discount. *Bankers' magazine,* May 1912, p. 661-2.

GARDNER, LYMAN S. Keeping in touch with the bank's loans. *Business man's magazine,* Dec 1910, p. 560-1.

GOODYEAR, LLOYD EARNEST. Bank accounting. Cedar Rapids, Goodyear-Marshall publishing co. 1906. 68p.

GOODYEAR, SAMUEL HORATIO. Practical banking. Cedar Rapids, Goodyear-Marshall publishing co.

GRAHAM, E. J. To detect excessive loans in banks. *Journal of commerce,* Aug. 10, 1910, p. 4.

GUARANTY trust company of New York. How to figure interest returns on securities. New York, Guaranty trust company of New York, 1917.

GUARANTY trust company of New York. Safe keeping of securities. New York, Guaranty trust company of New York, 1918. 54p.

HANDLING a bank's transit items. *Business man's magazine,* July 1911, p. 72-3.

HOW a small bank handles its payments. *Business man's magazine,* Feb. 1911, p. 180.

HOW are you handling customers' accounts? *Bankers' monthly,* Feb. 1919, p. 28.

HOW to treat "arrival of goods" drafts. *Business man's magazine,* Sept. 1911, p. 242.

HUBBARD, CLARENCE T. Handling only the accounts that change. *System,* Dec. 1914, p. 651-4.

HUBBARD, CLARENCE T. Practical card system for bank and trust company bookkeeping. *Trust companies,* Mar. 1915, p. 241-4.

HUBBARD, CLARENCE T. Statement system for banks and trust companies. *Trust companies,* May, 1915, p. 453-5.

HUGHES, THOMAS R. Checking bank balances. *New York accountants' and bookkeepers' journal,* Feb. 1903, p. 11.

HUTCHINSON, A. J. Bank statements. *Accounting and commerce,* Nov. 1916, p. 190-1.

HYDE, F. W. Day of exact accounting. *Journal of the American bankers association,* April 1919, p. 531-3.

INDIVIDUAL bookkeeping for banks. *Business man's magazine,* Aug. 1908, p. 132-4.

INNOVATION in bank balance sheets. *American industries,* Aug. 1918, p. 7-8.

INTEREST accrued receivable and unearned discount. *Bankers magazine,* v. 96, no. 6, p. 673.

INTERNATIONAL CORRESPONDENCE SCHOOLS. Bank accounting. (In their *I. C. S. reference library.* c1915, 279, Section 40, p. 1-3, 10, 19, 24).

JACKSON, GEORGE. Practical system of bookkeeping, including bank acounts; revised by H. T. Easton. Ed.24. London, Effingham Wilson, 1901. 152p.

JEFFERSON, HOWARD MCNAYR Accrued interest receivable and payable; an accurate daily statement. Ed.2. New York, Bankers publishing company, 1918 93p. (Bank department series, 2).

JEFFERSON, HOWARD MCNAYR. Interest accrued receivable and unearned discount. *Bankers' magazine,* May 1918, p. 554.

KLEIN, F. L. Danger of excessive bank credits. *Journal of commerce,* Aug. 10, 1910, p. 4.

KNIFFIN, WILLIAM HENRY. Bank as an accounting machine. (In his *Practical work of a bank.* 1917. p. 249-318).

KNIFFIN, WILLIAM HENRY. Passing of the deposit ledger. *Bankers' magazine,* Aug. 1908, p. 201-8.

KNIFFIN, WILLIAM HENRY. Receiving deposits. *Bankers magazine,* Nov. 1909, p. 729-37.

KNIFFIN, WILLIAM HENRY. Trial balance and the adding machine. *Bankers magazine,* June 1908, p. 840-7

LAMPMAN, R. W. Trust and loan company accounts. *Canadian chartered accountant,* July 1913, p. 14-21.

LARASH, C. J. Check settlement system designed for big business. *Bankers magazine,* Oct. 1911, p. 437-43.

LARASH, C. J. Triplicate collection system. *Bankers magazine,* Oct. 1912, p 370-1.

LAWTON, WILLARD H. Liberty loan accounting for small banks. *Journal of accountancy,* Aug. 1918, p. 93-7. *Trust companies,* Aug. 1918, p. 156-8.

LERSNER, V. A. Methods of handling deposits and withdrawals in banks of varying size. *Bankers magazine,* Nov. 1912, p. 537-41.

LEWIS, ABRAHAM. Error-proof method of keeping a bank account. New York, Lewis systems company, 1913. 23p.

LEWIS, E. M. E. Method of recording branch statistics. *Institute of bankers journal,* v. 32, p. 191-3.

LOWRIE, W. Convenience, principles and method of keeping accounts with bankers; with tables adapted to the calculating of interest accounts, etc 1805.

MCCORMICK, W. System of records for a safe deposit company. *Business man's magazine,* April 1900, p. 355-7.

BANKS AND BANKING—ACCOUNTING—*(Continued)*

MACHINERY in banks. *Bankers magazine,* April 1916, p. 543-6

M'KIE, DAVID. Bank bookkeeping. Ed. 2. Edinburgh, Andrew Baxendine, 1907. 99p. *Accountants' magazine,* March, April, May, June 1900, p. 135-54, 221-45, 286-310, 353-79.

——— Same. Ed. 4, revised by F. H Alland. Edinburgh, A. Baxendine, 1918. 101p.

MAKING it easy to get new bank customers. *Business digest,* July 17, 1918, p. 90-1.

MARSH, C. C. Theory and practice of bank bookkeeping arranged in accordance with the principles of double entry. New York, D. Appleton & co ? 1866.

MARTIN, W. McC. Modern banking and trust company methods. *Banking law jorunal,* May-July, 1918, p. 363, 427, 510.

MEELBOON, JOHN ADAM. Bank bookkeeping and accounts. London, Gee & co. 1901. 135p. (Acountants' library, v.1).

MERRY J. TATE. How the passbook has been superseded in the case of large accounts. *Accountant,* May 6, 1916, p. 536-8. *South African accountant and auditor,* Sept. 1916, p. 171-2.

MESERVEY, A. B. Manual of book-keeping and banking. Boston, Johnson, Blagden and McTurnan, 1900.

METHOD of supporting financial records. *Journal of home economics,* March 1916, p. 130-1.

MINER, GEORGE W. Bookkeeping; banking. Boston, Ginn and company, 1913.

MINER, GEORGE W. Teachers' reference book to be used with Bookkeeping; banking. Boston, Ginn and company, 1913.

MITCHELL, S. R. What does an accountant's certified statement represent? *Bankers magazine,* June 1916, p. 749-56.

MODE of public accounting. *Bankers magazine,* v. 37, p. 531.

MOODIE, JOHN. Notes on a banker's accounts. *Accountant,* April 15, 1905, p. 461-4.

MOORE, JOHN H. AND GEORGE W. MINER. Banks and banking. (In their *Accounting and business practice.* 1903. p . 293-393).

MOREHOUSE, W. R. New account teller ana the new account department. *Bankers magazine,* March 1913, p. 333-6.

MORTON, DAVIS WALTER. Banking and bank accounting; an advanced set on the individual business practice plan. Chicago, Lyons & Carnahan, 1917 112p.

MOSHER, W. K. Preparing for the comptroller's call. *Bankers magazine,* June 1911, p. 740-3.

MOWAT, WILLIAM G. Some weak places in bank bookkeeping and admiinstration and their remedies. *Business,* Feb. 1899, p. 113-4.

MOXEY, EDWARD P. Bank accounting. *Bookkeeper.* 1903, v.16, no. 3, p. 130-6.

MOXEY, EDWARD P. AND OTHERS. Bank accounting. (In their *Practical accounting methods.* p. 108-134).

MOYER, ALFRED H. Handling the accounts of a deposit vault. *Business man's magazine,* May, 1911, p 486-90.

MURRAY, R. Bank bookkeeping by machinery. *Trust companies,* June, 1916, p. 34-6.

MUSSELMAN, DE LAFAYETTE. Bank bookkeeping with memoranda of several days banking transaction to be written by the student; containing chapters on banking laws, bank organizations, definition of terms, forms of instruments, the clearing house books of accounts, ruled forms, etc. Quincy, Ill., D. L. Musselman. 234p.

NEAL, E. V. Modern banking and bank accounting. New York, Williams and Rogers, 1900.

NEAL, E. VIRGIL AND JOHN H. MOORE. Modern illustrative banking. Boston, American book company, 1904.

NEW method of keeping accounts. *Bankers magazine,* v. 15, p. 261.

NEW style customer's statement sheet for banks and trust companies. *Trust companies,* Dec. 1912, p. 472-3.

NIXON, ALFRED AND J. H. STAGG. Accounting and banking. New York, Longmans Green & co. 1912. 501p.

NO trial balance for thirty-nine years: Lippitt vs Ashley, Windsor Locks, Conn. *Bankers magazine,* Dec. 1915, p. 789-800.

OLMSTEAD, R. Y. Statement system of balancing accounts. *Bankers magazine,* April 1913, p. 451.

PACAUD, F. Practical work of a bank. *Bankers magazine,* March 1912, p. 333-41.

PACKARD, SILAS SADLER. Bank book-keeping. New York, S. S. Packard, c1897. 88p.

PADON, T. C. Method of handling loans and discounts as used by the Continental bank and trust company, Shreveport, La. *Bankers magazine,* May 1913, p. 565-8.

PALGRAVE, R. H. INGLIS. Bank balance sheets. *Accountant,* Feb. 23, April 27, 1907, p. 251-3, 565-73.

PARKINS, T. C. Bank booking. *Accountant,* Jan. 31, Feb. 7, 1891, p. 102-4, 115-22.

PARRISH, R B. Handling accounts in a small bank. *Bankers magazine,* Nov. 1909, p. 725-8.

PASSING of the pass book. *Accountant,* Dec. 25, 1915, p. 768-70.

PATTEN, CLAUDIUS BUCHANAN. Methods and machinery of practical banking. Ed 13. New York, Bankers publishing co. 1908. 515p.

PATTERSON, STUART H. What the items of a bank statement mean. New York, Guaranty trust company of New York, c1920 11p.

PENDER, WILLIAM F. Labor saving bank register. *Busines man's magazine,* April 1912, p. 328-9.

PHILLIPS, ELROY M. New plan for proving receiving tellers. *Business man's magazine,* Feb., April 1910, p. 180-5, 342-8.

PIXLEY, FRANCIS W. Banks. (In his *Accountancy,* Ed.2. p. 126-9).

POST, WILLIAM. Analysis of borrowers' statements. *Journal of accountancy,* Jan. 1906, p. 181-93.

POTTS, W. W. Liability ledger. *Bankers magazine,* April 1912, p. 518-21.

POWERS, ORVILLE M. Practical bank bookkeeping. Chicago, J. A. Lyons.

PRODUCTION of bank's books as evidence. *Journal of the American bankers association,* Dec. 1918, p. 331.

PROVIDING for accrued interest. *Business man's magazine,* June 1911, p. 579.

RAPID method of handling dividend checks. *Business man's magazine,* Oct. 1911, p. 343-4.

RECKITT, E. Commercial balance sheet from the bankers' standpoint. *Bankers magazine,* Jan. 1909, p. 23-39.

RECORDING cashier's checks. *Business man's magazine,* June 1911, p. 581-2.

REGAN, JOSEPH M. Getting the spotlight on your accounts. *Bankers' monthly,* Jan 1918, p. 14.

REIHL, CHARLES W. Helping the teller. *Bankers magazine,* May 1908, p. 725-7.

REIHL, CHARLES W. Important addition to the collection department. *Bankers magazine,* Oct. 1909, p. 515-7.

REIHL, CHARLES W. Most important book in the bank, the general ledger. *Bankers magazine,* March 1908, p. 347-52.

REIHL, CHARLES W. Numerical system for the transit department and acounts current. *Bankers magazine,* Sept. 1909, p. 354-9.

REST account of a Canadian bank. *Canadian chartered accountant,* April 1912, p. 210

REVENUE accounting. *National municipal review,* Jan. 1913, sup. 17-21.

REYNOLDS, G. M. Rediscounts and book credits. *Commercial and financial chronicle,* Bankers section, Dec. 2, 1911, p. 152-6.

BANKS AND BANKING—ACCOUNTING—*(Continued)*

RHOADES, JOHN H. Ambiguous bookkeeping and bank reports. *Moody*, Nov. 1912, p. 342-4.

RITTENHOUSE, C. F. Banking practice. (In his *Elements of accounts for individuals, professional men and institutions.* 1918. p. 44-8).

ROSENDALE, WILLIAM M. Loan department methods. *Bankers magazine*, Feb. 1909, p. 250-54.

ROWE, HARRY M. America national banking. Baltimore, H. M. Rowe co. c1895.

SALADE, ROBERT P. System for the collection department of a bank. *Business man's magazine*, May 1910, p. 475-6.

SCHUMACKER, CHARLES P. How to find outstanding drafts. *Bankers magazine*, Sept. 1910, p. 324-5.

SCHUMACKER, CHARLES P. Sub-total. *Bankers magazine*, Sept. 1912, p. 245-7.

SCHUMACKER, CHARLES P. Sub-totals in the bookkeeper's work. *Bankers magazine*, Dec. 1912, p. 679-83.

SELLE, E. H. Collection department in the country bank. *Bankers magazine*, March 1911, p. 350-1.

SHARP, G. G. Bank of England coupons; a suggestion for simplifying collection. *Accountant*, Jan. 27, 1917, p. 94.

SHARP, G. G. Coupon collection; the interior working of a bank. *Accountant*, March 24, 1917, p. 274-9.

SHAW, A. W. COMPANY. Accounting and costs; how to check profit leaks; simple cost systems that pay; making every account profitable; tested ways to reduce costs. Chicago, A. W. Shaw co. 1918. 225p.

SHERMAN, GEORGE N. System that proves itself. *System*, Oct. 1904, p. 335-9.

SINGEWALD, H. E. Recording of stock transfers and registrations. *Trust companies*, July, 1913, p. 7-10.

SMITH, ARTHUR W. Bank accounts and their audit. *Accountants' magazine*, Aug. 1898, July 1899, p. 450-4, 405-9. *Business*, July 1898, April 1899, p. 436-7, 247-8.

SNYDER, F. B. Credit department. *Journal of the American bankers association*, July, 1911, p. 41-7.

SOULÉ, GEORGE. Banking. (In his *New science and practice of accounts.* 1903. p. 430-83).

STANDARDIZED statement. Blank form used by the Liberty National bank of New York for standardizing information for its credit department. *Bankers magazine*, May, 1916, p. 638.

STATISTICAL analysis of bank operations. *Business digest*, Aug. 28, 1918, p. 281.

STRAUB, EDWARD G. Keeping the accounts of an investment banker. *Business man's magazine*, April 1908, p. 361-3.

SUPPLY and expenses department of branch banking. *Business man's magazine*, Dec. 1907, p. 71-6.

SWEETLAND, CHARLES A. Bank bookkeeping. (In *Cyclopedia of commerce, accountancy, business administration.* 1910. v.7. p. 11-144).

SWEETLAND, CHARLES A. Bank bookkeeping; a working handbook of bookkeeping and accounting methods used in modern banks; including departmental organization and the duties of officers and clerks. Chicago, American technical society, 1914. 140p.

SWEETLAND, CHARLES A. Bank bookkeeping; instruction paper. 2v. Chicago, American school of correspondence, 1909.

SYSTEM for handling collateral. *Business man's magazine*, Dec. 1911, p. 534-5.

SYSTEM for the daily balance. *Bankers magazine*, June 1908, p. 853-5.

SYSTEM of accounts for receivers of national banks. Rochester, Lawyers cooperative publishing co. 1904.

THOMPSON, H. C. Account analysis in commercial banks. *Journal of accountancy*, Sept. 1913, p. 210-29.

THORBURN, J. Some points in mercantile and banking accounts. *Accountant*, July 8, 1893, p. 624-9.

THULIN, FREDERICK. Scientific analysis of accounts. *Bankers magazine*, Aug. 1913, p. 157-61.

TICKNER, GEORGE L. Day's business—how to analyze it. *Bankers' monthly*, Jan. 1918, p. 9.

UNITED STATES FEDERAL RESERVE BOARD. Circular no. 7; system of accounting for banks. Washington, Government printing office, 1914. 47p.

UNITED STATES NATIONAL BANK, DENVER, COLORADO. How we handle interest earned but not collected and interest collected but not earned. Denver, Colorado, United States national bank, 1918 11p.

VAN DE LINDE, GERARD. Bookkeeping and other papers. London, Blades, East & Blades, 1904. 460p.

VAN RIPER, W. M. How one bank prevents little leaks. *Business man's magazine*, March 1911, p. 286-8.

WADSWORTH, P. C. Bicentral banking system. *Bankers magazine*, Nov. 1910, p. 725-30.

WALL, ALEXANDER. Banker's credit manual; a complete survey of the credit department—its obligations and its opportunities, how to sysematize the work, stabilize operations, and facilitate investigations; together with schemes for comparative analysis and many approved forms reproduced in facsimile. Indianapolis, Bobbs-Merrill company, c1919. 247p.

WALLACE, WILLIAM. Bank account. (In Lisle, George. *Encyclopaedia of accounting.* v.1. p. 216-7).

WARREN, GRAY. Cash on hand. *Bankers magazine*, June 1909, p. 943-7.

WARREN, GRAY. Method of keeping records of exchange transactions. *Bankers' magazine*, Sept. 1911, p. 313-8.

WHITE, MERCER V. Simple method of handling bank pass book. *Business man's magazine*, May 1908, p. 420-1.

WHITE, MERCER V. Suggestion for paying tellers. *Business man's magazine*, April 1908, p. 363-5.

WHITLOCK, J. P. Handling incoming dividends. *Bankers' magazine*, Nov. 1910, p. 661-3.

WILEY, ALBERT J. Card system for the safe deposit department of a bank or trust company. *Business man's magazine*, Sept. 1909, p. 262-3.

WILLIAMS, F. H. Method of proving the semi-annual trial balance. *Bankers magazine*, Feb. 1916, p. 202-5.

WOLFF, HENRY. Village banks, or, Agricultural credit societies; with model rules and account sheets; a pamphlet. London, 1894.

WOODWARD, W. H. Simplifying the work of the receiving teller's department. *Trust companies*, Nov. 1913, p. 382-5.

Auditing

AUDITING of bank accounts. *Accountant*, Jan. 18, Feb. 15, Mar. 1, May 10, May 17, June 14, 1879.

BANK audit or government inspection. *Canadian chartered accountant*, April 1913, p. 271-3.

BANK audit or inspection compulsory from outside: is it justifyable or expedient? *Canadian chartered accountant*, July 1911, p. 24-8.

BANK audits. *Canadian chartered accountant*, April 1913, p. 250-4.

BANK audits and balance sheets. *Accountant*, Aug. 23, 1913, p. 237-9.

BANKS AND BANKING — Auditing — *(Continued)*

Bank audits in Australia. *Accountant,* March 28, May 30, 1908, p. 416-8, 775-8.

Bank examination in New Jersey. *Journal of accountancy,* June 1911, p. 154.

Bank examinations. *Journal of accountancy.* Jan. 1906, p. 215-22.

Bank examinations in Canada. *Journal of accountancy,* May 1909, p. 40-2.

Bank examinations in New Jersey. *Journal of accountancy,* June 1911, p. 154.

Bank's risk in cashing checks. *Banking law journal,* Mar. 1911, p. 193.

Broderick, J. A. Examination of the foreign exchange departments in state banks and trust companies. *Journal of commerce,* Aug. 2, 1911, p. 5.

Brown, Vere. Chartered accountant and the banker. *Canadian chartered accountant,* Jan. 1914, p. 136-43.

Canadian bank auditors. *Canadian chartered accountant,* Jan. 1913, p. 199-202.

Canadian bank audits. *Journal of accountancy,* Jan. Oct. 1913 ,p. 61-4, 309-10.

Castenholz, W. B. National and federal reserve banks. (In his *Auditing procedure.* 1918. p. 211-5).

Chapin, A. B. Efficiency of supervision of banks. *Commercial and financial chronicle* (Bankers' section), Dec. 2, 1911, p. 228-32.

Chapman, Joseph. National bank examinations. (In Hull, Walter Henry. *Practical problems in banking and currency.* 1907, p. 97-105).

Company audits: foreign branches. *Auditor,* 1890-1, p. 186, 201.

Cook, J. B. How your bank account is protected. *Business man's magazine,* June 1912, p. 502-505.

Crowell, Norman H. Checking up the banks records. *Business man's magazine,* Feb. 1912, p. 178-9.

Cutforth, A. E. Bank. (In his *Audits.* 1914. p. 58-60).

Detection of fraud—by manipulation of the adding machine slips bank examiners were fooled. *Commercial and financial chronicle,* July 23, 1910, p. 192.

Dicksee, Lawrence Robert. Banks. (In his *Auditing.* Authorized American edition. p. 114-21).

Economical bank examinations. *Bankers magazine,* Mar. 1912, p. 341.

Fisher, Walter N. Few suggestions on a bank audit. *Accountant,* Jan. 7, 14, 1888, p. 10, 18.

Gibson, A. H. Auditors. *Bankers magazine,* (London), v. 58, p. 481.

Graham, E. J. To detect excessive loans in banks. *Journal of commerce,* Aug. 10, 1910, p. 4.

Handling of bank audits. *Canadian chartered accountant,* Jan. 1914, p. 183-4.

Hanna, C. A. Examination of the foreign exchange department in banks. *Journal of commerce,* July 26, 1911, p. 3.

Hardt, W. M. Value of clearing house examinations in establishing the solvency of banks. *Commercial and financial chroni-* Nov. 20, 1920, p. 160-1. *Journal of the American bankers association,* Nov. 1920, p. 351-3.

Hay, George H. How to check a bank pass book at the rates of 300 cheques per hour. *Accountant,* May 2, 1908, p. 630-2.

Hohlfelder, F. Of what value is an audit? *Bankers' magazine,* Aug. 1909, p. 211-2.

Improvement in national bank examination. *Journal of accountancy,* Jan. 1906, p. 236-7.

Jenkinson, Mark Webster. Banks. (In his *Some notes on the audit of different businesses,* 1913, p. 7-12). *Accountant,* April 19, 1913, p. 580-3.

Keister, D. A. Bank examinations. (In his *Corporation accounting and auditing.* 1909. p. 195-9).

Kniffin, William Henry. Bank examinations and audit. (In his *Practical work of a bank.* 1917. p. 349-70).

Meyer, Charles H. Fourteen years of clearing house bank examinations in Chicago; originator of the system. *Commercial and financial chronicle,* American bankers' convention section, Nov. 20, 1920, p. 161-3. *Journal of the American bankers' association,* Nov. 1920, p. 353-8.

Mills, James Cooke. Perpetual audit for banks. *Business man's magazine,* Nov. 1910, p. 476-80.

Montgomery, R. H. National and state banks. (In his *Auditing theory and practice.* 1916. p. 531-47).

Moyer, Melbourne S. Audit of banks of discount and deposits. *Journal of accountancy,* April, May, Aug. 1912, p. 261-5, 355-9, 107-112.

Neville, Charles. Verification of depositors' accounts in banks. *Journal of accountancy,* Feb. 1915, p. 137-8 .

Pixley, Francis W. Banks. (In his *Auditors, their duties and responsibilities.* 1910. p. 489-91).

Public accountants and banks. *Journal of accountancy,* Jan. 1906, p. 250-1.

Ramos, F. L. Meaning of a bank audit, its purpose, methods and errors to be avoided. *Journal of the American bankers' association,* Jan. 1916, p. 639-41.

Reihl, C. W. Bank audits; are they beneficial or of any practical value? *Bankers' magazine,* Feb. 1907, p. 221-6.

Reihl, C. W. Bank examinations analyzed. *Bankers' magazine,* May, 1910, p. 734-8.

Renn, George B. Auditing banks. (In his *Practical auditing.* c1907. p. 121-6).

Report of committee on auditing at convention of the American bankers' association. *Banking law journal,* Nov. 1910, p. 994-8.

Riddell, Alex F. Audit of banks. *Canadian chartered accountant,* Oct. 1911, p. 64-7.

Resolutions of Minnesota state bankers' association. *Journal of accounting,* July 1910, p. 214.

Ross, Adam A. Bank examinations. *Accountant,* Feb. 17, 1906, p. 220-3. *Journal of accountancy,* Jan. 1906, p. 215-22.

Selection of bank auditors. *Canadian chartered accountant,* Oct. 1913, p. 115-7.

Shareholders audits. *Accountant,* April 5, 1913, p. 483-6.

Smith, Arthur W. Bank accounts and their audit. *Accountants' magazine,* Aug. 1898, July 1899, p. 450-4, 405-9. *Business,* July 1898, April 1899, p. 436-7, 247-8.

Spicer, Ernest Evan and Ernest C. Pegler. Bank. (In their *Audit programmes.* 1919 p. 9-10).

Spicer, Ernest Evan and Ernest C. Pegler. Banks. (In their *Practical auditing.* 1914, p. 464-7).

Stocks, J. Sudgen. Some notes for the audit of bank accounts. *Accountant,* May 2, 1891, p. 337-41.

Suggestions drafted by Mr. Murray, comptroller of the currency, to be forwarded to the directors for the use of the examining committees in conducting examinations of national banks. *Commercial and financial chronicle,* July 20, 1912, p. 151.

Thomson, W. Garth. Canadian bank audits. *Canadian chartered accountant,* April 1916, p. 264-74.

Thulin, F. Procedure in a bank audit. *Journal of accountancy,* Sept. 1918, p. 191-211.

Van de Linde, Gerard. Audit of banks and mercantile firms (with or without branches at home or abroad). *Accountant,* Dec. 11, 18, 25, 1897, p. 1184-8. 1202-12, 1221-8.

BANKS AND BANKING — AUDITING — *(Continued)*

WALTON, SEYMOUR. Bank audits. *Auditor,* 1905, p. 215.

WALTON, SEYMOUR. Bank audits. *Accountant,* Nov. 17, 24, 1883, Feb. 9, 23, 1884.

WALTON, SEYMOUR. Bank audits. (In Hull, Walter Henry. *Practical problems in banking and currency.* 1907. p. 56-62).

WADSWORTH, P. C. Bicentral banking system. *Bankers magazine,* Nov. 1910, p. 725-30.

WELTON, T. A. Bank auditing. *Accountant,* Oct. 18, 1884.

WHINNEY, F. Bank auditing. *Accountant,* Feb. 19, 1898, p. 218-21.

WHINNEY, F. Cornish bank, bank auditing. *Accountant,* Feb. 19, 1898, p. 218-21.

Cost accounting

ACCOUNTING and costs; finding bank costs—how to check profit leaks—simple cost systems that pay—making every account profitable—tested ways to reduce costs. Chicago, A. W. Shaw company, c1918. 225p.

BLOMFIELD, F. C. Making the deposit account pay. *Business man's magazine,* Dec. 1911, p. 538-42.

BULKLEY, W. A. Cost accounting in banks: administration expenses, how to arrive at a unit of cost. *Banking law journal,* Dec. 1910, p. 1065-9.

BULKLEY, W. A. Plan of bank cost accounting; a method of calculating administration expenses in banks by arriving at the unit of cost that will determine the value of an active account. *Bankers home magazine,* Feb. 1911, p. 37-41.

COST accounting in banks; symposium conducted at the Rochester Convention of the American institute of banking, how institute experts clarified one of the most complicated of subjects. *Journal of the American bankers' association,* Dec. 1911, p. 385-98.

ENSELL, E. H. Cost accounting. *Banking law journal,* Dec. 1911, p. 1049-53.

FIGURING the cost of handling items. *Bankers' monthly,* Oct. 1918, p. 49.

GROVE, CHARLES C. Statistical cost analysis in a bank. *Bankers' magazine,* April, June 1919, p. 427-33, 689-98.

KNIFFIN, WILLIAM HENRY. Cost accounting and analysis of accounts. (In his *Practical work of a bank.* 1917. p. 537-68).

LEE, JAMES S. Cutting out 2800 losing accounts. *Bankers' monthly,* June 1919, p. 32.

LEWIS, J. FRANKLIN. Classifying the costs in your bank. *Bankers' monthly,* May 1919, p. 24.

LEWIS, J. FRANKLIN. $30,000 account that lost $468. *Bankers' monthly,* March 1919, p. 12.

REGAN, JOSEPH M. Analyzing accounts to make them pay. *Bankers' monthly,* Nov 1917, p. 14.

REGAN, JOSEPH M. Finding profit and loss. *Bankers' monthly,* Dec. 1917, p. 11.

REGAN, JOSEPH M. Getting the most for your money. *Bankers' monthly,* Oct. 1917, p. 11.

ROBINSON, C. O. Profit vs. losses in accounts. *Burroughs clearing house,* Nov. 1917, p. 22.

SIMPLE cost system for banks. *Journal of accountancy,* Oct. 1906, p. 480.

THOMAS, FRANK W. Cost accounting in a bank. Ed. 2, Toledo, Ohio, F. W. Thomas, 1910. 52p.

WILSON, JOHN F. Cost of handling checking accounts. *Bankers' magazine,* Sept. 1906.

WOODWORTH, R. L. Dividing the costs in a small bank. *Bankers' monthly,* April, 1919, p. 11.

Costs

WHAT it costs to run a bank; a report by the Bureau of business standards. Chicago, A. W. Shaw co. c1916. 55p.

Depreciation.

See Depreciation, depletion and obsolescence—Banks.

Directors

ALCORN, EDGAR GREENVILLE. Duties and liabilities of bank directors; including instruction with regard to directors' meetings, the discount committee, the auditing committee, official bank reports and indemnity bonds. Ed. 3, revised. Indianapolis, United States bank note co. c1915. 167p.

Failures and defalcations

BANK defalcations—how they may be prevented or guarded against. *Trust companies,* Feb. 1914, p. 132-4. 194-204.

MOXEY, EDWARD PRESTON. Causes, methods and prevention of bank defalcation. *Journal of accountancy,* Jan. 1906, p. 223-32.

RAWLINGS, EDWARD. Bank defalcations. *Accountant,* Sept. 19, 1896, p. 769-70.

Finance

HOWARD, EARL DEAN. Profits on bank deposits. *Journal of accountancy,* Jan. 1906, p. 205-14.

PATTERSON, S. H. Guaranty's budget system. *Guaranty news,* Dec. 1918, p. 339-40.

PROFITS on cash deposits. *Journal of accountancy,* Jan. 1906, p. 234-5.

History

CONANT, CHARLES ARTHUR. History of modern banks of issue; with an acount of the economic crisis of the nineteenth century and the crisis of 1907. Ed.4, revised and enlarged. New York, G. P. Putnam's sons, c1909. 751p.

SABIN, CHARLES H. Banking evolution. New York, Guaranty trust company of New York, Sept .25, 1918. 5p.

Law

BARROW, WALTER. Some notes on banking law. *Accountant,* June 17, 1899, p. 662-8.

CONWAY, THOMAS AND E. M. PATTERSON. Operation of the new bank act. Philadelphia, J. B. Lippincott co. c1914, 431p.

DICKINSON, ARTHUR LOWES. Sections relating to shareholders' audit in the Canadian bank Oct. 1913. (In his *Accounting practice and procedure.* 1917. p. 272-9).

FISK, A. K. Banking and bills of exchange. *Canadian chartered accountant,* April 1912, p. 172-80.

FLETCHER, HENRY. Illegality of limited partnerships as bankers. *Journal of accountancy,* Nov. 1909, p. 6-10.

FURTHER, recognition of the C. P. A. in Massachusetts. *Journal of accountancy,* Sept. 1910, p. 386.

HARRISON, MILTON W Bank law and taxation digest New York, Bankers publishing co. 1918. 108p.

RHODE ISLAND banking law. *Journal of accountancy,* Aug. 1910, p. 296-7.

RHODE Island's recognition of the certified public accountant. *Journal of accountancy,* Aug. 1910, p. 292-3.

SELECTION of bank auditors. *Canadian chartered accountant,* Oct. 1913, p. 115-7.

STEVENS, T. M. Points on banking law. *Accountant,* Aug. 14, 1897, p. 794-800.

UNITED STATES CONGRESS. National bank act as amended; the Federal reserve act and other laws relating to national banks, 1920. Washington, Government printing office, 1920.

Management

AGGER, EUGENE EWALD. Organized banking. New York, Henry Holt & co. 1918. 385p.

BANKS AND BANKING—MANAGEMENT—(Continued)

ALLING, N. D. Chief clerk. *Journal of the American bankers association,* June 1912, p. 775-81.

BARKER, J. M. W. Adoption of time and labour saving devices with a view to the economical work of a bank. *Institute of bankers journal* (London) 1914, v.35, p. 598-615.

BLUIM, ARTHUR S. Rules and regulations for the guidance of employees of safe deposit department. *Trust companies,* May 1915, p. 456-8.

BRANCH banks, its origin, forms, administration, operation and examination. *Banking law journal,* May and June 1912.

CLEVELAND, FREDERICK ALBERT. Bank and the treasury. New York, Longmans, Green & co. 1905. 326p.

CRAMER, J. ARTHUR. Filing department. New York, Bankers publishing co. 1917. 110p.

DAVIS, J. F. Bank organisation management and accounts. London, Sir Isaac Pitman and sons. 157p.

DJORUP, CHRISTIAN. Modern foreign exchange department and its function. *Bankers magazine,* Aug. 1912, p. 150-5.

ENSELL, E. H. Bank service pensions. *Bankers magazine,* Nov. 1912, p. 498-505.

FISKE, AMOS KIDDER. Modern bank; a description of its functions and methods and a brief account of the development and present system of banking. New York, D. Appleton & co. 1916. 348p.

FOSTER, MAJOR BRONSON. Banking. New York, Alexander Hamilton institute, c1918. 348p. (Modern business, v.16).

14 better banking methods. *System,* Feb. 1918, p. 280-6.

GARDNER, A. V. Modern machinery of banking. *Trust companies,* Dec. 1915, p. 547-52.

HARRIS, RALPH SCOTT. Practical banking, with a survey of the Federal reserve act. Boston, Houghton, Mifflin co. c1915. 309p.

HAZLEWOOD, C. B. Transit department and bank relations. *Bankers magazine,* Jan. 1913, p. 17-20.

HUBBARD, CLARENCE T. Statement system for banks and trust companies. *Trust companies,* May 1915, p. 453-5.

JESS, STODDARD. System of uniting the work of receiving and paying tellers, as used in the first national bank at Los Angeles. *American bankers association, Proceedings, 36th annual convention,* 1910, p. 701-6.

KNIFFEN, WILLIAM HENRY. Practical work of a bank; a treatise of practical banking which aims to show the fundamental principles of money; the practical work of a bank in detail, and particularly credit in its relation to banking operations. Ed. 3, revised. New York, Bankers publishing co. 1917. 600p.

OF interest to bankers. *Business man's magazine,* Dec. 1906, p. 78-80.

PATTEN, CLAUDIUS BUCHANAN. Methods and machinery of practical banking. Ed. 13. New York, Bankers publishing co. 1908. 515p.

PRIEST, H. M. Clearing-house inspection of credits. *Bankers magazine,* June 1913, p. 697-8.

RAE, GEORGE. Country banker; his clients, cares and work. New York, Charles Scribner's sons. 1886. 320p.

——— New ed. New York, Scribner, 1920. 324p.

ROBINSON, HAROLD A. Organization of a foreign department. *Bankers magazine,* Sept. 1917, p. 383-90.

SALADE, ROBERT P. System for the collection department of a bank. *Business man's magazine,* May 1910, p. 475-6.

SAVING kinks for the bank clerk. *Business man's magazine,* July 1911, p. 69.

SNYDER, F. B. Credit department. *Journal of the American bankers association,* July 1911, p. 41-7.

WHITE, M. V. Installing a signature card index; in a bank having 15,000 accounts. *Business man's magazine,* Feb. 1909, p. 160-1.

WOODWARD, W. H. Simplifying the work of the receiving tellers department. *Trust companies,* Nov. 1913, p. 382-5.

Reports

NEW YORK STATE. SUPERINTENDENT OF BANKS. Annual report of banks of deposit and discount. Albany, Superintendent of banks.

NEW YORK STATE. SUPERINTENDENT OF BANKS. Annual report relative to saving and loan associations, land bank of the state of New York and credit unions. Albany, Superintendent of banks.

NEW YORK STATE. SUPERINTENDENT OF BANKS. Annual report relative to savings banks, trust companies, investment companies, safe deposit companies, personal loan companies and personal loan brokers. Albany, Superintendent of banks.

REPORTS of various companies

UNITED STATES. COMPTROLLER OF CURRENCY. Annual report. Washington, Government printing office.

BANKS AND BANKING, CLEARING HOUSES.

BARRETT, ALBERT R. Clearing-house. (In his *Modern banking methods.* 1907. p. 245-79).

CANNON, JAMES GRAHAM. Clearing houses. Washington, Government printing office, 1910. 335p.

CAWCROFT, ERNEST. Widening sphere of clearing houses. *Business man's magazine,* July 1910, p. 35-40.

KNIFFIN, WILLIAM HENRY. Clearings and clearing-houses. (In his *Practical work of a bank.* 1917. p. 145-63).

M'NEIL, ALLAN. Clearing house. (In Lisle, George. *Encyclopaedia of accounting.* v.2. p. 87-94).

MOORE, JOHN H. and GEORGE W. MINER. Clearing house. (In their *Accounting and business practice.* 1903. p. 374-83).

PATTEN, CLAUDIUS BUCHANAN. Clearing house system. (In his *Methods and machinery of practical banking.* 1908. p. 349-64).

WHITE, HORACE. Clearing-house system. (In his *Money and banking illustrated by American history.* c1911. p. 216-31).

Accounting

AMERICAN business and accounting encyclopaedia; comp. by E. H. Beach and W. W. Thorne. Detroit, Bookkeeper publishing co. 1901. Clearing house, v.2, p. 320-5.

NAISH, H. W. Clearing house system. *Accountant,* April 17, 1920, p. 459-65.

TODMAN, FREDERICK SIMSON. Clearing house sheet. (In his *Brokerage accounts.* 1916. p. 67-76.

Auditing

JONES, BRECKENRIDGE. Clearing house bank examination system. *Commercial and financial chronicle,* American bankers convention section, Sept. 18, 1915, p. 161-5.

ST. LOUIS CLEARING HOUSE ASSOCIATION. Clearing house bank examinations. 1910. 11p.

BANKS AND BANKING, FEDERAL RESERVE BANKS.

CONANT, CHARLES ARTHUR. History of modern banks of issue; with an account of the economic crisis of the nineteenth century and the crisis of 1907. Ed. 4, revised and enlarged. New York, G. P. Putnam's sons, c1909. 751p.

BANKS AND BANKING—FEDERAL RESERVE BANKS—*(Continued)*

GUARANTY TRUST COMPANY OF NEW YORK. Foreign financing under the Edge act; approved December 24, 1919. New York. Guaranty trust company of New York, c1919. 40p.

HARRIS, RALPH SCOTT. Practical banking, with a survey of the Federal reserve act. New York, Houghton, Mifflin co. c1915. 309p.

MECHANICS AND METALS NATIONAL BANK. Edge export finance act as approved December 24, 1919, and the McLean-Pratt act as approved September 17, 1919. New York, 1920. 18p.

PEPLE, CHARLES A. Statements of borrowers from the viewpoint of the Federal reserve bank. *Journal of accountancy,* June 1916, p. 410-23.

SNYDER, FREAS B. Federal reserve banks and the reserve agent. *Journal of accountancy,* July 1915, p. 28-33.

UNITED STATES. FEDERAL RESERVE BOARD. Federal reserve bulletin; monthly. Washington, Government printing office.

UNITED STATES. FEDERAL RESERVE BOARD. Federal reserve inter-district collection system; changes in list of banks upon which items will be received by Federal reserve banks for collection and credit; monthly. Washington, Government printing office.

WILLIS, HENRY PARKER. Federal reserve; a study of the banking system of the United States. New York, Doubleday, Page & co. 1917. 342p.

Accounting

ENSELL, E. H. Reconcilement of accounts; system in vogue in large reserve banks. *Bankers magazine,* Jan. 1912, p. 17-9.

Auditing

CASTENHOLZ, WILLIAM B. National and federal reserve banks. (In his *Auditing procedure.* 1918. p. 211-5).

Cost accounting

ENSELL, E. H. Cost accounting—application of the scientific principles in a large reserve bank—comparative study of the different methods used in analyzing an account. *Bank law journal,* Jan. 1912, p. 70-4.

ENSELL, E. H. Outline of cost of an account in a large reserve bank. *Bankers magazine,* March 1911, p. 347-9.

Law

BILL enacted permitting Federal reserve banks to have 100% surplus. *Commercial and financial chronicle,* March 8, 1919, p. 918-9.

COLLEY, F. G. Bank loans under the new conditions; borrowers' certified statement as a basis for national currency. *Journal of accountancy,* Dec. 1914, p. 418-26.

GUARANTY TRUST COMPANY OF NEW YORK. Digest of the Federal reserve act (including amendments to June 21, 1917). New York, Guaranty trust company of New York, 1917. 47p.

HAMLIN, CHARLES S. Federal reserve act. *Journal of accountancy,* Nov. 1916, p. 329-37.

UNITED STATES. CONGRESS. Hearings before the Committee on banking and currency on S. 2472, a bill to amend the act approved December 23, 1913, known as the Federal reserve act. Washington, Government printing office. 1919. 28p.

UNITED STATES. CONGRESS. National bank act as amended; the Federal reserve act and other laws relating to national banks, 1920. Washington, Government printing office, 1920.

Reports

UNITED STATES. Federal reserve board. Annual report. Washington, Government printing office.

BANKS AND BANKING, LAND BANKS.

See Agriculture—Credit.

BANKS AND BANKING, NATIONAL BANKS.

See Banks and banking.

BANKS AND BANKING, SAVINGS BANKS

BECKETT, FRED J. Municipal savings banks; a practical and profitable scheme. *Accountant,* July 8, 1905, p. 39-41.

CARGILL, ALEXANDER. Savings banks. (In Lisle, George. *Encyclopaedia of accounting.* v. 6. p. 31-6).

HILTON, J. P. Municipal savings banks. *Accountant,* March 17, 1917, p. 261-3.

HOWDEN, JOHN M. Trustee savings banks. *Accountants' magazine,* July 1907, p. 368-74

POSTAL savings bank question. *Journal of accountancy,* June 1909, p. 124-8.

RORIE, T. H. B. Progress of trustee savings banks in 1906. *Accountants magazine,* 1908, p. 149.

TRUSTEE savings banks. *Accountant,* March 16, 1918, p 241. *Incorporated accountants' journal,* March 1918, p 116.

WATSON, T. W. M. Trustee savings banks. *Accountant,* June 18, 25, 1904, p. 812-20, 841-7.

WOODWORTH, L. D. Savings department forms and suggestions for operating a savings department in a national bank. *Journal of the American bankers association,* March 1920, p. 514-8.

Accounting

AMERICAN BANKERS ASSOCIATION. Forms for savings banks and savings departments in commercial banks and trust companies. New York, American bankers association, 1914 11? numb.

AMERICAN business and accounting encyclopaedia; comp. by E. H Beach and W. W. Thorne. Detroit, Bookkeeper publishing co. 1901. Card indexes and ledgers for savings banks. v. 4, p. 1106-8.

BATCHELOR, A. Banker's balance sheet. *Incorporated accountants journal,* 1893-4, p. 16.

BENTLEY, HARRY C. General ledger accounts of savings banks. (In his *Science of accounts.* 1913. p. 316-23).

BOND valuations of savings banks. *Journal of accountancy,* June 1906, p. 159-60.

ENTRY in pass book not an admission. *Banking law journal,* Aug. 1910, p. 710-2.

HALLETT, WALTER E. Investment value as a basis for savings bank accounting. *Moody,* Feb. 1913, p. 97-102.

HALLETT, WALTER E. Savings banks trial balances. *Commerce, accounts and finance,* Aug. 1902, p. 22-3.

JOHNSON, T. J. New and attractive methods for savings banks. *Business man's magazine,* Jan. 1908, p. 71-3.

JOHNSTON, A. W. Savings bank bookkeeping; a reply to Rhoades' article. *Moody,* Dec. 1912, p. 507-8.

KNIFFIN, W. H. Figuring intetrest in the savings bank. *Bankers magazine,* Nov. 1907, p. 699-702.

KNIFFIN, W. H. Figuring interest in the savings banks. *Bankers magazine,* June 1911, p. 719-28.

KNIFFIN, W. H. Figuring interest in the sav- and its practical work. New York, Bankers publishing co. 1912. 551p.

McCAFFREY, W. T. Handling interest payments on bonds and mortgages. *Bankers' magazine,* July 1911, p. 16-24.

BANKS AND BANKING—SAVINGS BANKS—ACCOUNTING—(Continued)

MIDGELEY, FRANK W. Savings bank bookkeeping. *Moody,* April 1913, p. 310-2.
PEPLE, CHARLES A. Handling savings accounts. *Business man's magazine,* Aug. 1906, p. 71-5.
RHODES, J. H. Savings bank accounting—investment values or present cost vs. market values. *Commercial and financial chronicle,* May 23, 1914, p. 1579.
ROBERTS, H. A. Methods of figuring interest in a savings bank. *Business man's magazine,* March 1908, p. 277-80.
ROWE, D. D. Loan records in detail. *Business man's magazine,* Nov. 1905, p. 882-6.
STARROCK, J. Savings banks system of accounts. London, Longmans, 1844.
SWEETLAND, CHARLES A. Savings banks. (In his *Bank bookkeeping.* 1910. p. 104-22).
USE of card ledgers in a country savings bank. *Business man's magazine,* Jan. 1907, p. 49-51.
WILLIAMS, FRANK H. Short cuts and time-savers in savings bank work. *Bankers magazine,* May, 1915, p. 594-7.

Auditing

AUDIT of savings banks accounts. *Accountant,* Aug. 24, 1889, p. 444-6.
BISHOP, GEORGE L. Savings bank audits. *Journal of accountancy,* Feb. 1914, p. 97-114.
CASTENHOLZ, WILLIAM B. Savings banks. (In his *Auditing procedure.* 1918. p. 217-18).
KNIFFIN, WILLIAM HENRY. Savings bank audits. (In his *Savings bank and its practical work.* 1912. p. 428-41).
KNIFFIN, WILLIAM HENRY. Savings bank audits. *Bankers magazine,* Sept. 1911, p. 307-13.
MONTGOMERY, ROBERT H. Savings banks. (In his *Auditing theory and practice.* 1916. p. 547-550).
NOVEL method of audit. *Journal of accountancy,* March 1907, p. 393-4.
PERINE, EDWARD T. Independent audit of a savings bank. *Bankers magazine,* Dec. 1907, p. 861-8.
PIXLEY, FRANCIS W. Savings banks. (In his *Auditors, their duties and responsibilities.* 1910. p. 491-2).
PROPER audit of a savings bank. *Banking law journal,* July, 1911, p. 601-3.
SAVINGS bank audits. *Bankers magazine,* Nov. 1908, p. 732-4.
SAVINGS bank examinations. *Journal of accountancy,* March 1911, p. 376.
SPICER, ERNEST EVAN and ERNEST C. PEGLER. Trustee savings bank. (In their *Audit programmes.* 1919. p. 102-103).
SPICER, ERNEST EVAN and ERNEST C. PEGLER. Trustee savings banks. (In their *Practical auditing.* 1914. p. 518-19).

Law

TRUSTEE savings banks. *Accountant,* March 16, 1918, p. 241. *Incorporated accountants' journal,* March 1918, p. 116.

Management

KNIFFIN, WILLIAM HENRY. Saving bank and its practical work. New York, Bankers publishing co. 1912. 551p.
WILLIAMS, FRANK H. Short cuts and time-savers in savings bank work. *Bankers magazine,* May 1915, p. 594-7.

BANKS AND BANKING, SCHOOL SAVINGS BANKS.

BANCO modelo de la escuela superior nacion al de commercio del Rosario. Estatutos; reformados y aprobados por la Asamblea general ordinaria de accionistas realizada el dia 30 de agosto de 1918. Rosario Argentine, 1919. 12p.
SAVINGS bank of Public school No. 14, 225 East 27th Street, New York. 1p.
WOODWORTH, LEO DAY. School savings banking. *Journal of the American bankers association,* Dec. 1920, p. 412-22.

Accounting

KNIFFIN, WILLIAM HENRY. School savings banks. (In his *Savings bank and its practical work.* 1912. p. 497-515).
PRATT, LEE S. Teaching boys the science of banking *Business man's magazine,* July 1910, p. 30-5.

BANKS AND BANKING, STATE BANKS.

ILLINOIS. AUDITOR'S OFFICE. Pointers, suggestions and model by-laws relating to the organization of a state bank, under the laws of Illinois; also rulings of the auditor's office and opinions of the attorney general. Ed. 2. 1917. 52p.

Auditing

CASTENHOLZ, WILLIAM B. State banks. (In his *Auditng procedure.* 1918. p. 215-6).
MONTGOMERY, ROBERT H. National and state banks. (In his *Auditing theory and practice.* 1916. p. 531-47).

BANKS AND BANKING, TRUST COMPANIES.

BANGS, J. E. Requirements as to acceptance of corporate trusts and bond certification. *Trust companies.* Dec. 1914, p. 501-3.
CUSHING, HARRY A. Services rendered by trust companies under voting trust agreements. *Trust companies,* Feb. 1916, p. 170-2.
ELEMENTS of a valid trust. *Trust companies,* Sept. 1913, p. 181.
JUDD, ORRIN R. Discretion and powers of trustees in the matter of investments. *Trust companies,* Sept. 1913, p. 160-2.
JUDD, ORRIN R. Economical and profitable administration of small personal trusts. ..*Trust companies,* Mar. 1916, p. 249-50.
LIABILITY of trust company for depreciation of trust securities. *Banking law journal,* Oct. 1914, p. 743-4, 728-9.
MCKINNEY, F. C. Legal duties and principles governing corporate trusteeships—responsibilities of trust companies as trustee under mortgage deed of trust. *Trust companies,* July 1911, p. 3-9.
PAINE, WILLIS S. Duties of trustees of financial corporations. *Accountant,* Dec. 1, 1900, p. 1091-3.
POTTS, W. W. How trust departments of trust companies located in smaller cities may be rendered profitable. *Trust companies,* Aug. 1911, p. 84-8.
PROPER compensation to trustees under mortgages securing bond issues—recent decision by Delaware court of Chancery. *Trust companies,* Oct. 1915, p. 336-8.
SCHEDULE of transfer and registrar charges based on scientific cost analysis. *Trust companies,* Sept. 1920, p. 248.
SHEPPARD, R. L. Scale of charges made by trust companies for specific and variable fiduciary services. *Trust companies,* Aug. 1915, p. 103-10.
SHEPPARD, R. L. Standard schedule of charges for various kinds of trust company service. *Trust companies,* Dec. 1916, p. 537-54.
STANDARD requirements governing equipment trust indentures: defining the duties and obligations of trust companies as trustees. *Trust companies,* Nov. 1914, p. 401-4.
UNITED STATES MORTGAGE AND TRUST COMPANY. Trust companies of the United States: annual. New York, United States mortgage and trust company.
WHY trust companies as trustees should be represented on bondholders' protective committees. *Trust companies,* Dec. 1914, p. 475-6.

BANKS AND BANKING, TRUST COMPANIES —(Continued)

Accounting

AMERICAN BANKERS ASSOCIATION. Forms for savings banks and savings departments in commercial banks and trust companies American bankers association, 1914.

AMERICAN BANKERS ASSOCIATION. TRUST COMPANY SECTION. Forms for trust companies, selected by a committee of the Trust company section, American bankers association, from forms in use by trust companies of the United States. New York, Anthony Stumpf publishing company, 1910. 140p.

AMERICAN business and accounting encyclopaedia; comp by E. H. Beach and W. W. Thorne. Detroit, Bookkeeper publishing co. 1901. Trust company accounting, p. 1047-9.

BANKERS TRUST COMPANY, NEW YORK. Trust department records used by Bankers trust company, New York. New York, Bankers trust company, 1911. 53p.

BENTON, M. E. Revised system of bookkeeping for the trust department. *Trust companies*, Feb. 1914, p. 111-7.

BOND records of a trust company. *Business man's magazine*, Aug. 1906, p. 93-8.

CHARLESWORTH, A. Remarks upon the accounts of trust companies and their audit. *Accountant*, 1894, p. 331-8.

CLEVELAND, A. W. Trust companies, their books, accounts and audit. Sydney institute of public accountants conference, 1901. *Bookkeeper*, 1902, v. 14, no. 7, p. 73-8.

HAMMETT, CHARLES E. Trust accounting; a new plan of standardized trust department accounting and procedure and suggestions for the use of bookkeeping machines and commercial photography in departmental operations. *Journal of the American bankers association*, Dec. 1919, p. 294-6.

HERRICK, CLAY. Trust companies—books, records and forms for the trust department. *Bankers' magazine*, Dec. 1905, Jan., Feb. 1906.

HOLCOMBE, H. R. Accounting methods in the savings fund department of a trust company. *Business man's magazine*, Nov. 1905, p. 851-6.

HOSACK, F. A. Ingenious mechanical aids in promoting efficiency in trust company accounting methods. *Trust companies*, Feb. 1915, p. 149-53.

HUBBARD, C. T. Practical card system for bank and trust company bookkeeping. *Trust companies*, March 1915, p. 241-4.

HERRICK, CLAY. Forms and records. (In his *Trust companies*. 1909. p. 172-368).

HUMMEL, A. Operation of an up-to-date coupon department of a trust company. *Trust companies*, June 1911, p. 15-18.

HUMPHREY, H. M. Practical systems of accounting for trust companies. Detroit, Burroughs adding machine company, c1904, 4p. *Trust companies*, Jan. 1905.

JONES, A. W. Transfer department of a well equipped trust company. *Trust companies*, Dec. 1914, p. 505-6.

LAMPMANN, R. W. Trust and loan company accounts. *Canadian chartered accountant*, July 1913, p. 14-21.

LARAWAY, B. R. Complete records of a trust company. *System*, 1904, v. 6, no. 6, p. 550-6.

MURRAY, R. Bank bookkeeping by machinery as applied to various departments of a trust company. *Trust companies*, June, 1916, p. 34-6.

NEW style customer's statement sheet for banks and trust companies. *Trust companies*, Dec. 1912, p. 472-3.

RAPID method of handling dividend checks. *Business man's magazine*, Oct. 1911, p. 343-4

ROWE, D. D. Loan records in detail. *Business man's magazine*, Nov. 1905, p. 882-6.

RUSSELL, J. A. Successful system of trust department accounting by machine. *Trust companies*, Dec. 1919, p. 577-80.

TURNER, H. L. Stock records and methods of a transfer agent. *Trust companies*, May, July. 1911.

WOODWARD, W. H. Improved system of bookkeeping for banking departments of trust companies. *Trust companies*, 1913, v. 17, p. 462-4.

Auditing

AUDIT system of a trust company. *Accountants' journal*, 1906-7, p. 83.

BALDWIN, W. M. Trust company audits; the advisability of a trust company maintaining an auditing department rather than have periodical audits from the outside. *Commercial and financial chronicle*. Bankers convention section, Oct. 15, 1910, p. 180-2.

BOTHMANN, THEODORE. Audit system of a trust company. *Business world*, March 1908, p. 202, 210.

BRODERICK, J. A. Examinations of the foreign exchange departments in state banks and trust companies. *Journal of commerce*, Aug. 2, 1911, p. 5.

CASTENHOLZ, WILLIAM B. Trust companies. (In his *Auditing procedure*. 1918. p. 218-9).

CHARLESWORTH, A. Remarks upon the accounts of trust companies and their audit. *Accountant*, April 14, 1894, p. 331-8.

CUTFORTH, A. E. Finance company (also trust company). (In his *Audits*. 1914. p. 71-2).

DICKSEE, LAWRENCE ROBERT. Trust companies (In his *Auditing*. Authorized American edition. p. 121).

JARVIS, E. C. and others. Audit of trust companies, the trust department and the banking department. *Business man's magazine*, 1904, v. 16, no. 7, p. 105-21.

JENKINSON, MARK WEBSTER. Some notes on the audit of different businesses. *Accountant*, April 19, 1913, p. 590-2.

JENKINSON, MARK WEBSTER. Trust and finance companies. (In his *Some notes on the audit of different businesses*. 1913. p. 35).

MADISON, T. E. Accounting fundamentals for trust companies; classification of accounts for various departments. *Trust companies*. Sept. 1919, p. 228-30.

MONTGOMERY, ROBERT H. Trust companies. (In his *Auditing theory and practice*. 1916. p. 550-2).

SPICER, ERNEST EVAN and ERNEST C. PEGLER. Trust and finance companies. (In their *Audit programmes*. 1919. p. 100-101).

SPICER, ERNEST EVAN and ERNEST C. PEGLER. Trust and finance companies. (In their *Practical auditing*. 1914. p. 515-8)

WILLIAMS, H. D. Trust company audits and examinations. *Journal of accountancy*, Sept.-Dec. 1912, p. 211-6, 304-7, 389-400, 446-65.

Failures and defalcations

REAL estate trust failure and the duty of bank directors. *Journal of accountancy*, Oct. 1906, p. 454-8.

Management

BURKE, J. I. How trust companies handle and solve income tax problems. *Trust companies*, Feb. 1914, p. 129-30.

BURRAGE, FRANCIS J. Proper safeguards in the conduct of the transfer department. *Trust companies*, Jan. 1915, p. 34-8.

EFFICIENT banking and trust company methods. *Trust companies*, Oct. 1911, p. 244-7.

EFFICIENCY departments as a new development in trust company organization. *Trust companies*, Aug. 1913, p. 99-100

GRIFFENHAGEN, E. O. Efficiency ratings, promotions, removals, pensions and other essentials of a complete employment plan for a modern trust company. *Trust companies*, Dec. 1919, p. 572-5.

BANKS AND BANKING, TRUST COMPANIES —MANAGEMENT—*(Continued)*

HAINES, EDWIN IRVINE. Building a banking business; how a trust company has increased its profits by progressive advertising methods. *Business man's magazine,* Nov. 1911, p. 444-5.

HERRICK, CLAY. Trust companies; their organization, growth and management. New York, Bankers publishing co. 1909. 481p.

HUMMEL, ARTHUR. Operation of up-to-date coupon department of a trust company. *Trust companies,* June 1916, p. 15-8.

JONES, B. W. Recording and collecting coupons under income tax law. *Trust companies,* March 1914, p. 219.

JONES, A. W. Transfer department of a well equipped trust company. *Trust companies,* Dec. 1914, p. 505-6.

KIRKBRIDE, FRANKLIN BUTLER and J. E. STERRETT. Modern trust company; its functions and organization. Ed. 4, revised. New York, The Macmillan co. 1913. 319p

——— and HENRY PARKER WILLIS. Modern trust company; its functions and organization; an outline of fiduciary banking. Ed. 5, enlarged and revised. New York, The Macmillan co. 1920. 549p.

LEAF, E. M. Internal organization of trust companies. *Journal of the American bankers association,* July 1920, p. 7-12.

MODERN trust deposit system. *Trust companies,* June 1913, p. 417-8.

PRACTICAL suggestions for increasing the efficiency of trust company employees. *Trust companies,* Sept. 1912, p 242-4.

SHERMAN, F. T. System of safe guarding securities held by trust companies as custodian. *Trust companies,* Feb. 1916, p. 163-9.

WOODWARD, WALTER H. Up-to-date transit and collection department facilities *Trust companies,* Sept. 1914, p. 198-201.

BANKS: get these account sheets. *Banker farmer,* Nov. 1918, p. 16.

BANKS of the United States vs. voucher checks. *Business man's magazine,* April 1907, p. 136-8.

BANK'S risk in cashing checks. *Banking law journal,* Mar. 1911, p. 193.

BANNER, GEORGE

Relations between accountants and their clients. *Accountant,* June 2, 188[illegible]

BANNER year in accounting progress. *Electric railway journal,* Jan. 3, 1915, p. 9-10.

BANNING, K.

More sales with less stock: stockkeeping methods. *System,* March 1914, p. 326-9.

Short cuts in executive work: ingenious devices to save time and effort. *System,* June 1913, p. 602-9.

BANNISTER, J. C.

How buildings were appraised in revaluation of real property of Los Angeles. *Engineering record,* April 8, 1916, p. 472-5.

BANQUET of Massachusetts society. *Journal of accountancy,* May 1907. p. 86.

BANQUET of New York state society. *Journal of accountancy,* May 1907, p. 85.

BANTA, C. W.

How the public accountant helps modern business. *Bankers monthly,* Dec. 1920, p. 28-9, 88.

BARBER, ALBERT DUNCAN.

Colliery accounts. *Accountant,* April 21, 1906, p. 500-6.

Recent financial legislation in some of its bearings on professional accountancy. *Accountant,* Oct. 8, 1910, p. 487-95.

BARBER, EDGAR M.

Contribution to the history of commercial education; an address delivered at the annual meeting of the Eastern commercial teachers' association held at Brooklyn, N. Y., April 1903. 23p.

BARBER, JARVIS WILLIAM

Address. *Accountant,* May 10, 1913, p. 717-19.

Arbitrations and award. *Accountant,* Nov. 16, 1907, p. 611-6.

Bills of exchange and foreign exchanges. *Accountant,* Dec. 14, 1901, p. 1365-71.

Notes on present position of accountancy. London, Gee & co. 1896.

Some notes on the profession of accounting. *Accountant,* Oct. 17, 1896, p. 841-6.

BARBER, ROBERT NODES

Works accounting. *Accountant,* April 3, 1909, p. 470-8.

BARBOUR, CHARLES S.

Plating costs. *Metal industries,* May 1914, p. 211.

BARBOUR, DAVID.

Indian courage and paper currency act, 1893. *Accountant,* Nov. 25, 1893, p. 998-1004.

BARBOUR, GEORGE H.

Stock and cost records of the Michigan stove company. *Business man's magazine,* July 1907, p. 66-71.

BARBOUR, I. W.

Cost of engineering on highway work. *Engineering and contracting,* February 7, 1917, p. 143-4.

BARBOUR, PERCY E.

Cost of an ounce of gold. *Engineering and mining journal,* July 10, 1915, p. 49-50.

Employes' representation plans in American industries. *Engineering and contracting,* March 10, 1920, p. 276-8.

BARCROFT, FREDERICK T.

Report and appraisal of the Detroit united railway (city lines), Detroit, Michigan, Oct. 1, 1909. Detroit, 1910. Abstract. Appraisal value of the electric street railways of Detroit. *Engineering and contracting,* July 6, 13, 1910, p. 16, 35. Editorial. Noteworthy article on electric street railway appraisal. *Engineering and contracting,* July 6, 1910, p. 1.

BARDEEN, CHARLES WILLIAM

Dime and question books of bookkeeping. Syracuse, New York, C. W. Bardeen, 1888.

BARDSLEY, JAMES HICKEY

Other methods of proving ledgers and accounts than by detail checking. *Accountant,* Aug. 13, 1892, p. 631-5.

BARDSLEY, JOHN BURTON

Hints to students in devising systems of engineers' cost accounts. *Accountant,* Oct. 18, 25, 1902, p. 1053-61, 1087-98.

Protection against, and detection of, fraud in cash accounts. *Accountant,* Aug. 11, 1900, p. 738-43.

BARGES

See Ships and shipping.

BARHAM, F. F.

Banking, *Accountant,* Feb. 18, 1888, p. 104-8.

BARHAM, HAROLD EDMUND

Vouching in the conduct of audits of the accounts of joint stock companies. *Accountant,* June 2, July 14, 1906, p. 698-705, 33-5.

BARKER, FORREST F.

Capitalization and depreciation in municipal plants. *Inter-nation,* April 1907, p. 76.

BARKER, HARRY

How to appraise water rights. *Engineering news,* June 22, 1916, p. 1179-82.
Making depreciation discussion understood. *Utilities magazine,* Jan. 1, 1916, p. 131.
Public utility rates; a discussion of the principles and practice underlying charges for water, gas, electricity, communication and transportation services. New York, McGraw-Hill book co. 1917. 387p.
Side lights on depreciation problems of utilities. *Engineering news,* Dec. 21-28, 1916, p. 1167-9, 1212.

BARKER, J. HEATON

Card ledgers and card index systems. *Accountant,* Sept. 24, 1904, p. 315-8.

BARKER, J. M. W.

Adoption of time and labor saving devices with a view of the economical work of a bank. *Institute of bankers journal* (London), 1914, v. 35, p. 598-615.

BARKER, JOHN S.

Profit sharing plan of the Baker manufacturing co. *Wisconsin engineer,* March 1919, p. 193-201.

BARKER, P.

Cost of coal and oil as fuel. *Engineering and mining journal,* July 8, 1916, p. 93-4. *Power,* May 30, 1916, 765-7.

BARLOW, H. G.

System in the order and shipping department. *Business man's magazine,* Sept. 1905, p. 548-52.

BARNARD, FLORENCE.

Prosperity book. Boston, Small Maynard & co. 1919. 128p.

BARNARD, FRANCIS PIERREPONT

Costing-counter and the counting board; a chapter in the history of numismathics and early arithmetic. Oxford university press, 1919, 358p.

BARNES, C.

Industrial peace. *Engineer,* Jan. 12, 1917, p. 35-6.

BARNES, FREDERICK ASA

Cost keeping and management. *Cornell civil engineer,* 1915, p. 434-45.

BARNES, F. E.

Curves of building cost increases used in valuation work. *Engineering news,* Oct. 7, 1920, p. 702.

BARNES, G. N.

Unemployment, production, high prices and world competition. *Accountant,* Oct. 9, 1920, p. 384-8.

BARNES, H. EDGAR

Law governing promoters. *Journal of accountancy,* July 1908, p. 177-86

BARNES, J. P.

What economies can be profitably effected in the mechanical department. *Electric railway journal,* March 16, 1912, p. 426.
Value of cost accounting. *Aera,* Sept. 1913, p. 128-32.

BARNES, J. R. AND ALEXANDER SHARPLES

Bookkeeping for commercial classes; elementary. London, Macmillan & co. 1914. 242p.
Elementary bookkeeping for commercial classes. London, Macmillan & co. 228p
Key to the exercises in bookkeeping for commercial classes. London, Macmillan & co. 1916.

BARNES, R. Y.

Abridged edition of the new improved universal system of book-keeping, etc. London, 1869.
————. Same. Another ed. London, 1872.
New and improved universal system of bookkeeping. Ed. 3. London, 1871.
————. Same. London, 1872.
————. Same. London, 1874.
————. Same. London, 1875.
————. Same. London, 1877.

BARNES, W. C. AND J. T. JARDINE

Meat situation in the United States pt. 2, livestock production in the eleven far western range states. *United States agricultural report,* 1916, p. 26-43.

BARNETT, HAROLD DARRACOTT MORRIS

Receivers in partnership (including the limited partnership bill). *Accountant,* June 20, 1908, p. 900-4.

BARNETT, M.

Plea for profit sharing. National metal trades association, 1913.

BARNETT, R. C.

Cost of a bad road. *Good roads,* n.s. August 31, 1918, p. 77-8.
Economic highway transportation. *Good roads,* May 11, 1918, p. 241-5.
Ton-mile cost of motor truck haulage. *Good roads,* n.s., March 2, 1918, p. 129.

BARNETT, SAMUEL

Life insurance accounting. Louisville, Ky., Insurance field, 112p.

BARNUM, M. K.

Life and maintenance of all-steel cars. *Railway age gazette,* March 4, 1916, p. 389-94.

BARR, A. W.

Theatre accounts. *Incorporated accountants' journal,* 1897-8, p. 106.

BARRATT, NORRIS STANLEY

Book-keepers and commercial law; address. May 12, 1913, before the Book-keepers' beneficial association of Philadelphia. Philadelphia, 1913. 24p.

BARRELS.

See Coopers.

BARRETT, ALFRED REED
Modern banking methods and practical bookkeeping; illustrated with over two hundred forms of bank book, records and blanks. Ed.5, New York, Bankers publishing co. 1907. 325p.

BARRETT, D. O.
Comprehensive stock record form. *Iron age,* December 1918, p. 1386.
Cost system for a medium size foundry. Iron *age,* Oct. 3, 1918, p. 810-3.

BARRETT, GEORGE E.
How to investigate securities. *Journal of accountancy,* May 1907, p. 23-32.

BARRETT, GEORGE K.
How to fan out your space charges. *Factory,* Jan. 1919, p. 51-3.

BARRETT, GEORGE L.
Calculation of depreciation. *Electrical engineering,* Nov. 1914, p. 449.

BARRETT, R. S.
Proposed Argentine income tax. *Commerce reports,* no. 266, Nov. 12, 1918, p. 586-7.

BARRETT-LENNARD, F. C. A.
Some points relating to the law of agency. *Incorporated accountants journal,* July 1912, p. 263-5.

BARRETT combined adding. listing and computing machine. *Industrial management,* May 1917, sup. 1-2.

BARROW, WALTER
Some notes on banking law. *Accountant,* June 17, 1899, p. 662-8.

BARROWS, GEORGE E.
Making industrial valuation for tax purposes. *Engineering news,* July 26, 1917, p. 164-6.

BARROWS, H. K.
Cost of hydroelectric development; abstracts. *Electrical world,* March 1, 1919, p. 413-7. *Engineering and contracting,* March 12, 1919, p, 271-3. *Power,* April 8, 1919, p. 544-6.
First cost of steam plants using small-sized units. *Electrical world,* April 5, 1919, p. 689.

BARROWS, H. P.
Farm records and accounts. Washington, United States relations service, 1917. 10p. (Doc. 38)

BARROWS, O. C.
Foundry accounting and methods of estimating cost of castings. *Iron trade review,* April 16, 1903.

BARROWS, W. P.
Accountants and receiverships. *Journal of accountancy,* May 1916, p. 366-7.
Receivers and public accountants. *Journal of accountancy,* Jan. 1916, p. 1-15.

BARSTOW, W. S.
Fuel costs in Public utilities. *Gas age,* March 1, 1917, p. 237.

BARTER, JOHN
How to learn bookkeeping without a master. London, Simpkin, Marshall, Hamilton, Kent & co. 1899. 32p.

BARTH, C. G.
Scientific management in a brass foundry. *Foundry,* Aug. 1916, p. 319-20.
Time studies for rate setting as originated by Dr. F. W. Taylor. *American machinist,* Feb. 1, 1917, p. 177-8.

BARTH, RAYMOND E.
Accounting for food preserving companies. *Journal of accountancy,* Feb. 1920, p. 91-7.

BARTHMAIER, FRANK J.
Manufacture of shot guns. *Business man's magazine,* Dec. 1909, p. 560-5.

BARTHOLOMEW, H. S.
Cost plans for associations. *Textile world,* May 1, 1920, p. 3245.

BARTHOLOMEW, WALLACE EDGAR
Bookkeeping exercises. 2v. New York, Gregg publishing co. c1919.
Fundamental aims in the teaching of bookkeeping. Albany, University of the state of New York, 1916, 8p. *National educational association, Papers and proceedings.* 1916. p. 362-5.
Key to Bartholomew's bookkeeping exercises, pt. 1. New York, Gregg publishing company, 1920. 218p.

BARTINE, O. H.
Building of the hospital; with segregated costs of the construction of twenty-two hospitals. *Heating and ventilating,* July 1916, p. 33-7. Excerpts. *Engineering and contracting,* July 26, 1916, p. 82.

BARTLE, A. C.
Executorship accounts. *Accountant,* Oct. 21, 28, Nov. 4, 1916, p. 361-7, 384-90, 411-6.
Hints to students and examinees. *Accountant,* Sept. 15, 22, 1917, p. 207-11, 226-32.

BARTLE, C.
Accounting system for a coal mining company. *Public accountant,* May 1919, p. 304-16.
Few points on policy and office organisation for the public accountant. *Public accountant,* Aug. 1918, p. 42-9.
Goodwill: its treatment in accounts. *Accountant,* March 15, 1919, p. 213-20.
Goodwill: with special reference to its treatment in partnership accounts. *Accountant,* June 13, 1914, p. 863-72.
Hints to students and examinees. *Accountant,* Oct. 30, Nov. 6, 13, 1915, p. 533-9, 564-6, 589-95. *Public accountant,* July, Sept. 1915, p. 12-20, 69-76.

BARTLEET, LEWIS
Legal rights and liabilities of everyday life. *Accountant,* Feb. 29, 1908, p. 284-90.

BARTLETT, E. J.
Where and why electric trucks are economical. *Electrical review and western electrician,* March 14, 1914. p. 543-4.

BARTLETT, JOHN
Familiar quotations; a collection of passages, phrases and proverbs traced to their sources in ancient and modern literature. Ed.10. Boston, Little, Brown & co. 1916. 1454p.

BARTLETT, RICHARD WILSON
Checking of coal royalty accounts. *Accountant,* June 18, 1910, p. 869-75. *Incorporated accountants' journal,* 1909-10, p. 210.

BARTLETT, ROBERT MONTGOMERY

Auditor's financial mirror and record; a new system of keeping county, state and government accounts. Cincinnati, 1862.

BARTON, ALBERT E.

Australasian advanced accountancy. Ed.3. Wellington. Accountancy publications, 1915.

Suggested amendments of the New South Wales companies act. *Public accountant,* 1909, p. 39.

BARTON, E. C.

Metric system. *Accountant,* Feb. 3, 1917, p. 118-20.

BARTON, JOHN S.

Bank of England, the bank reserve the bank rate and foreign exchanges. *Accountant,* Sept. 1, 1906, p. 236-43.

Finance act, 1916. *Accounting and commerce,* July 1917, p. 80-1.

BARTON, T. S.

Accountants' ready reckoner. London, Simpkin, Marshall, Hamilton, Kent & co. 1868.

BARWICK, THOMAS

Systems for the engineer and contractor. *Heating and ventilating,* Nov. Dec. 1914, Jan. 1915, p. 27-34, 15-21, 18-22.

BASE electric rates on the cost of coal. *Electrical world,* July 9, 1917, p. 1128.

BASING depreciation on par value. *Electric railway journal,* June 19, 1915, p. 1143.

BASING fares on frequency of use. *Aera,* April 1919, p. 865-6.

BASING rates upon cost of service. *Electrical review and western electrician,* Jan. 9, 1915, p. 61-2.

BASIS of Portland (Me.) rates. *Electric railway journal,* Aug. 17, 1918, p. 310.

BASIS of quality of paper. Little, Arthur D. 1910.

BASIS of stock valuation. *Incorporated accountants' journal,* May, 1919, p. 146-7

BASIS of success. *Journal of accountancy,* March 1911, p. 207.

BASIS of valuation as between interstate and intrastate business. *Railway age gazette,* Feb. 12, 1909, p. 319.

BASSETT, E. M.

Railroad taxes and plans for ascertaining a fair valuation of railway properties. *Electric railway journal,* Nov. 11, 1911, p. 1026-7.

BASSETT, WILLIAM R.

Accounting. *American machinist,* Oct. 14, 1920. Abstract. *Factory,* Dec. 1, 1920, p. 1720.

Accounting as an aid to business profits. New York, A. W. Shaw co. c1918. 316p.

Charging materials to get true manufacturing costs. *Factory,* April 1918, p. 644-7.

Developing pride and interest in the job. *Factory,* April 1919, p. 693-6.

Fitting the wage to the work. *Factory,* Aug. 1918, p. 236-8.

Handling factory costs. *Factory,* January 1919, p. 138 +.

How to find what your factory is worth. *Factory,* May 1918, p. 850-1.

Modern production methods. *American machinist,* May 6, 1920, p. 1003-8.

Other side of profit sharing. *System,* Aug. 1919, p. 310-9.

Trends in management. *Factory,* June 15, 1920, p. 1905-7.

Uniform cost accounting. *American machinist* Dec. 11, 1919, p. 991-3.

What is good will worth? *System,* April, 1918, p. 556-8.

When competitors stop guessing. *System,* April 1920, p. 736-8.

——— **AND W. T. FITZPATRICK**

Group economy bonus that increased production 26 per cent. *Factory,* March 15, 1920, p. 817-9.

——— **AND S. R. GORDON**

Cost system that guides policies. *Factory,* Jan. 1920, p. 43-8.

BASTABLE, C. F.

On some economic effects of war. *Accountants' magazine,* 1900, p. 399.

BATCHELDER, JACOB

National accountant. Boston, Jewett & co.

BATCHELLER, W. T.

Cost of fuel for steam-electric stations. *Journal of electricity,* May 15, 1919, p. 470-2.

BATCHELOR, ARTHUR

Banker's balance sheet. *Incorporated accountants' journal,* 1893-4, p. 16.

BATCHELOR, JOHN BENNETT

Debentures. *Accountant,* April 2, 1904, p. 422-7.

Verification and value of book debts for the purpose of a balance sheet. *Accountant,* Jan. 12, 1901, p. 51-3.

BATEMAN, C. T. TALLENT.

See Tallent-Bateman, Charles Tallent.

BATES, A.

Accountancy; a treatise on the keeping of accounts, specially Salvation army accounts. London, 1906.

BATES, CHARLES A.

Scratching the surface from the troubles of the publishers. *Inland printer,* Feb. 1917, p. 638.

BATES, H.

Maintaining a continuous property inventory. *Electric railway journal,* Jan. 20, 1917, p. 115-16.

BATES, H. S.

Newman-Bates system of farm bookkeeping. Ottawa, Canada, H. S. Bates, 1918.

BATES, L.

Two form report of progress contractor and his cost reports. *System,* Mar. 1914, p. 311-4.

BATES, O.

Railway valuation and rate making. *Railway review,* Mar. 14, 1914, p. 397-405.

BATESON, H. D.

Amendments to the companies acts. *Accountant,* Oct. 31, 1896, p. 906.

BATESON, WILLIAM

Finances of Cardiff. *Accountant,* Oct. 21, 1905, p. 462-4.

BATESON, WILLIAM—*(Continued)*

Local rates. *Accountant,* July 16, 1904, p. 78-83. *Incorporated accountants' journal,* 1903-4, p. 234.

Municipal accounts. *Accountant.* Aug. 13, 20, 1904, p. 169-76, 195-200. *Incorporated accountants' journal,* 1903-4, p. 189.

Pitman's municipal office organisation and management; a comprehensive manual of information and direction on matters connected with the work of officials of municipalities. London, Sir Isaac Pitman and sons. 483p.

BATH, Maine, acquires properties of Maine water company at less than reproduction cost. *Engineering and contracting,* March 15, 1916, p. 250.

BATHS

Accounting

FARNSWORTH, PERCY. Baths and wash houses. (In Bateson, William, ed. *Pitman's municipal office organisation and management.* p. 284-92).

BATLIBOI, J. R.

Advanced accounts. 56, Esplanade Road, Fort, Bombay. 512p.

BATT, F.

Appraisal of gas property for rate making. *Gas age,* Dec. 15, 1919, p. 538-41.

BATTELLE, GEORGE I.

Method of contract payments based on cost. *Engineering news,* Aug. 29, 1912.

BATTEN, EDWARD

Home and foreign trade as affected by tariff. *Accountants' magazine,* Nov. 1915, p. 475-87.

BATTERSBY, THOMAS

Perfect double entry book-keeper (abridged) and the perfect prime cost and profit demonstrator for iron and brass founders, machinists, engineers, shipbuilders, manufacturers, etc. Manchester, 1878.

BATTIN, WILLIAM F.

Accounting methods for mercantile corporations. *Journal of accountancy,* July, Aug. 1912, p. 30-52, 117-27.

BAUER, JOHN

Accounting of interest and discount on notes. *Journal of accountancy,* April, May 1913, p. 248-58, 341-50.

Allowance for working capital in a rate case. *Political science quarterly,* Sept. 1916, p. 413-29.

Bases of valuation in the control of return on public utility investments. *American economic review,* Sept. 1916, p. 568-88.

Control of street railway rates fixed by local franchises in the state of New York. *American economic review,* Sept. 1918, p. 650-3.

Cost versus value of service in rate making. *Electrical word,* Aug. 31-Sept. 7, 1918, p. 388-9, 443-4.

Depreciation and rate control a question of justice. *Quarterly journal of economics,* May 1915, p. 651-9.

Depreciation formula of the American society of civil engineers. *Journal of accountancy,* Aug. 1915, p. 104-11. Discussion. *Utilities magazine,* Jan. 1, 1916 p. 127-30.

Federal valuation of railroads in relation to a definite policy of national railway control. 16p. *American economic review,* March 1918, sup. 113-40.

Fixing depreciation requirements under the public service commission's law of New York. *American economic review,* Sept. 1918, p. 647-50. *Public service,* Oct. 1918.

Going value in connection with a physical appraisal in a rate case. *Political science quarterly,* Sept. 1916, p. 463-75.

Idea of capitalisation as applied to public service corporations. *Accountant,* Aug. 19, 1916, p. 155-8. *Journal of accountancy,* July 1916, p. 1-9.

Physical valuation and guaranteed return on railway investments. *Magazine of Wall street,* Oct. 18, 1919, p. 1098-101.

Pitfalls in regulating depreciation. *Electric railway journal,* Aug. 24, 1918, p. 326-8. Discussion. L. L. G. Benedict. *Electric railway journal,* Sept. 14, 1918, p. 465-6.

Renewal costs and business profits in relation to rising prices. *Journal of accountancy,* Dec. 1919, p. 413-19.

Rents in public utility accounting. *Journal of accountancy,* July 1915, p. 21-7.

Returns on public service properties. *Political science quarterly,* March 1915, p. 106-33.

Valuation of public service properties. *Political science quarterly,* June 1915, p. 254-76.

BAUGH, FREDERICK HENRY

Grain export calculation tables for wheat, corn, rye, oats, barley, peas, and oil cake. Baltimore, John Hinrichs cable code company, 1920. 104p.

Principles and practice of cost accounting for accountants, manufacturers, mechanical engineers, teachers and students. Baltimore, F. H. Baugh, 1915. 194p.

——— **AND W. C. SCHMEISSER**

Estate accounting. *Trust companies,* Sept. 1912, p. 245-7.

Theory and practice of estate accounting for accountants, lawyers, executors, administrators and trustees. Baltimore, M. Curlander, 1910.

——— Same. Baltimore, M. Curlander, 1917. 321p.

BAUM, F. G.

Best control of public utilities. *American Institute of electrical engineers, Proceedings,* Jan. 1915, p. 1-23. Abstract. *Electrical world,* Jan. 23, 1915, p. 258-9. Discussion. *American institute of electrical engineers, Proceedings,* Jan. 1916, p. 58-70.

Class rates for light and power systems or territories. *American institute of electrical engineers, Proceedings,* April 1915, p. 485-505. Abstract. *Electrical world,* July 10, 1915, p. 67. Discussion. *American institute of electrical engineers, Proceedings,* Jan. March, 1916, p. 58-70, p. 398-400.

Economic proportion of hydroelectric and steam power. *Electrical review,* Sept. 21, 1918, p. 450-1.

BAUM, FRED H. J.

Accounting methods for the furniture manufacturing business. *Business man's magazine,* June 1909, p. 509-17.

BAUMAN, F. C.

First year's operation of Washington's municipal garbage reduction works. *Engineering news,* May 6, 1920, p. 908-11.

BAVARIAN report on steam versus electric operating costs. *Electric railway journal,* April 11, 1914, p. 811.

BAVIN, T. R.
Suretyship and guarantee. *Public accountant,* 1905-6, p. 56.

BAXTER, C. H.
Observations on the appraisal of iron mines of Michigan. *Engineering and mining journal,* March 6, 1915, p. 439-40.

BAXTER, R. M.
Buying only the sizes that will sell; a retail stockkeeping chart. *System,* January 1913, p. 90-1.

BAXTER, W. M.
Operating capacity of single truck divisions. *Railway age,* April 17, 1914, p. 869-71.

BAY state asks 10-cent city fare. *Electric railway journal,* Oct. 19, 1918, p. 707.

BAY state company says last word. *Electric railway journal,* July 29, 1916, p. 189-90.

BAY state loses 6 cent fare case. *Electric railway journal,* Sept. 2, 1916, p. 412.

BAY state opens fare case. *Electric railway journal,* Nov. 13, 1915, p. 1006-7.

BAY state opens mileage rate case. *Electric railway journal,* Nov. 24, 1917, p. 942-3.

BAY state rate case. *Electric railway journal,* Dec. 4, 1915, p. 1121-3. *Public utility reports,* annotated, 1916F, p. 336-9.

BAY state street railway valuation. *Electric railway journal,* Dec. 4, 1915, p. 1121-3.

BAY state substations. *Electric railway journal,* Jan. 22, 1916, p. 164-5

BAY state system wants a 10 cent unit. *Aera,* Oct. 1918, p. 242-3.

BAY state way organization. *Electric railway journal,* Aug. 7, 1915, p. 229.

BAY state zone case closed. *Electric railway journal,* May 11, 1918, p. 937-8.

BAYER, HENRY G.
Metric system in all its details compared with the American weights and measures, twenty-eight tables of equivalents, the thermometers, illustrations. New York, Henry G. Bayer, c1912. 94p.

BAYLEY, J. ERNEST
Drapery business organisation, management and accounts. London, Sir Isaac Pitman & sons. 291p.

BAYNE, C. W.
Cutting out inefficiency at the start. *Business man's magazine,* Feb. 1912, p. 158-61.

BEACH, E. H. AND W. W. THORNE, COMP.
American business and accounting encyclopaedia. Detroit, Bookkeeper publishing co. 1901.

BEACH, O. M.
Tables of interest and discount containing two sets of tables for interest at 3, 3½, 4, 4½, 5, 6, 7, 8, 9, and 10 per cent, one set computed for days, 365 to the year, the other for months and days, 30 days a month, 360 to the year. New York, Samuel Hall, 1892.

BEAL, CARL H.
Classification of undeveloped oil land for purposes of valuation. *Economic geology,* June 1920, p. 315-27.
Decline and ultimate production of oil wells, with notes on the valuation of oil properties. Washington, Government printing office, 1919. 215p. (United States. Bureau of mines bulletin 177; Petroleum technology 51).
Essential factors in valuation of oil properties. *Bulletin of the American institute of mines,* Sept. 1919, sup. 2219-27.
Valuation of speculative, deferred and wasting assets. *Engineering and contracting,* Jan. 21, 1920, p. 77-80.

BEALE, WILLIAM PHIPSON
Judicial dicta and legislative restrictions on the payment of dividends out of revenue. *Accountant,* Dec. 1, 1900, Jan. 26, 1901, p. 1083-91, p. 104-7.

BEAMAN, R. J.
Uniform accounting and cost records as applied to mining. *Coal age,* 1915-16, v.8. p. 1053-4; v.9, p. 20.
Coal mine accounting. *Coal mining review,* 1916, v.4, no. 23, p. 4.

BEAN, B. C.
Cost of production: the principles of the science of costs, with illustrative examples by cost experts for various lines of manufacturing industry. Enlarged edition. Chicago, The system company, 1905. 198p.

BEARD, CHARLES A.
Budgetary provisions of the New York constitution. *Annals of the American academy of political and social science,* Nov. 1915, p. 64-8.

BEARD, J. R.
Design of high pressure distributing systems. *Journal of the Institute of electrical engineers,* Jan. 1, 1916, p. 125-41.

BEARD, J. T.
Conference on standardization of mining reports. *Coal age,* March 11, 1916, p. 457-8.

BEARD, PHILIP LEO
Law of partnership. *Accountant,* April 1, 1911, p. 520-4.
Partnership law. *Incorporated accountants' journal,* March 1913, p. 148-51.
Partnership law—relations of partners to one another. *Accountant,* May 17, 1913, p. 767-72.

BEARD, W. D.
Ascertain your daily profits. *Business man's magazine,* May 1911, p. 491-3.
Convenient ledger sheet. *Business man's magazine,* Nov. 1910, p. 486-7.

BEARDSALL, FRANCIS EMANUEL MOORE
Accounts of joint stock companies. *Accountant,* 1887, p. 217.
Address, 1887. *Accountant,* 1887, p. 637.

BEARDSLEE, F. D.
Central-station sales department organization and work. *Electrical review and western electrician,* Dec. 5, 1914, p. 1073-9.

BEARDSLEY, H. M.
Accounting for four departments. *Street railway revue,* Oct. 1905.

BEARING fruit. *Journal of accountancy*, Feb. 1916, p. 140-1.

BEASLEY, J.

Farm account book. Longman, 1847.

BEATTY, CHARLES

Practical guide to the death duties and to the preparation of death-duty accounts. London, 1911.

BEATTY, I. J.

Lincoln motor production plan. *Factory*, July 1, 1920, p. 38-41.

BEATY, JOHN Y.

Complete farm accounts. *System on the farm*, March 1919, p. 143-50.

How I figure my farm profits. *System on the farm*, Oct. 1920, p. 215-20.

BEAUCHAMP, J. W.

Tariffs for domestic electricity service. *Electrician*, July 2, 1920, p. 37-9.

BEAUDIN, J. A. A.

Piece work system as applied to specific routine operations a happy innovation. *American gas engineering journal*, Aug. 23, 1919, p. 163-5.

Piece work system of payment for meter readers. *Municipal engineering*, Jan. 1920, p. 40. *Engineering and contracting*, Feb. 11, 1920, p. 159-60.

BEAUMONT, H.

Accounting system for law offices. *Case and comment*, Feb. 1918.

BEAUMONT, JOHN WILLIAM FISHER

Mortgages. *Incorporated accountants' journal*, 1902-3, p. 37.

BEAVIS and Jack's bookkeeping. London, Houlston & sons, 1871.

BECAUSE unaudited. *Journal of accountancy*, Feb. 1915, p. 141-2.

BECHTEL, A. E.

Cost of earth work of the second unit of the Dodson North canal, Milk river project, Matal, Montana. *Engineering and contracting*, September 20, 1916, p. 266-7.

Cost of structures of the second unit of the Dodson north canal, Milk river irrigation project, Malta, Mont. *Engineering and contracting*, August 9, 1916, p. 126-9.

BECK, A. C.

Accounting system for the real estate business. *Business man's magazine*, May 1910, p. 453-8.

BECK, HERBERT

Theory and practise. *Journal of accountancy*, July 1917, p. 21-7.

Value of auditing to the business man. Philadelphia, American academy of political and social science, 1903. *Annals of the American academy of political and social science*, Nov. 1903, p. 433-4.

BECK, HOWARD C.

Audit of the books of the city of Birmingham, Ala., for the 14 months ending June 30, 1907, and the new system of municipal accounting. Birmingham, Dispatch printing co., 1907. 128p.

Capital accounts of a city. National association of comptrollers and accounting officers. *Proceedings*. 1911. p. 78-82.

BECK, PETER

How I keep up with rising costs. *System*, May 1916, p. 535-9.

Why the retail coal dealer should employ a modern accounting system. *Cooperative management and farmer*, Aug. 1918, p. 94-5.

BECKER, CHARLES E.

Taking care of dental stock. *Business man's magazine*, Oct. 1907, p. 106-22.

BECKER, GEORGE J.

System of bookkeeping. Philadelphia, E. H. Butler & co.

BECKETT, FREDERICK J.

Municipal savings banks; a practical and profitable scheme. *Accountant*, July 8, 1908, p. 39-41.

BECKETT, J.

Elementary education in relation to local rating. *Accountant*, July 1, 1911, p. 15-20.

Elementary education in relation to local taxations and finance. *Accountant*, July 30, 1904, p. 124-31.

Memorandum on the basis of grants by the state to local authorities in aid of elementary education. *Accountant*, Sept. 7, 1912, p. 321-8.

BECKETT, THOMAS

Accountant's assistant; an index to the accountancy lectures and leading articles reported in "The Accountant," "The Accountant's Journal" and the transactions of the various students' societies and other periodicals during the last 30 years of the nineteeth century, to which is added a list of the principal treaties now in use on each of the 117 subjects. London, Gee & co. 1901. 141p.

BECKFORD, J. S. V.

Card systems and diagrams, keeping tract of stock, factory management. *American machinist*, April 14, 1904.

BECKFORD, W. C.

Rates for electric service. *Electrical review and western electrician*, June 10, 1916, p. 1073-5.

BECKMAN, JOHN

History of inventories, discoveries and origins. 2v. London, 1846.

BEDDING

Accounting

ANDERSON, J. M. Manufacture of beds and bedding. *Business man's magazine*, Oct. 1907, p. 43-6.

CLARK, EARL S. Cost and accounting records. *Business man's magazine*, July, Aug. 1907, p. 64-70, 61-6.

BEDDOE, E. E.

Block system of bookkeeping for real estate. *The Office*, Sept. 1889, p. 165-7.

BEDDOW, W. W.

Coal company organization. *Coal age*, April 27, 1918, p. 778-80.

BEDE, GRIDLEY

Valuation of railroads. *Railway and engineering review*, Oct. 18, 1913, p. 978-9.

BEDFORD, EDWARD H.

Intermediate (solicitors) examination guide

BEDFORD, EDWARD H.—*(Continued)*
to book-keeping; the examinations questions with answers. Ed. 2. London, Stevens & sons, 1875.

BEDFORD, H. D.
War finance. *Accounting and commerce,* Oct. Nov. Dec. 1915, p. 161-3, 177-9, 200-2.

BEDFORD, R. H. AND W. HAGUE
Drilling costs at the North star. *Engineering and mining journal,* Sept. 5, 1914, p. 439.

BEDS.
See Furniture.

BEE, G. E.
Accounting and business procedure as applied to the construction of large irrigation projects. *Engineering and contracting,* Mar. 22, 1916, p. 269-74.

BEEBE, A. H.
Appraisal values. *Buildings and building management,* Jan. 12, 1920, p. 18-20.

BEEBY, W. S. M.
Partnership law. *Accountant,* Jan. 10, 1914, p. 52-4.

BEECH, FRANKLIN
Dyeing of cotton fabrics; a practical handbook for the dyer and student. Second revised edition. London, Scott, Greenwood and son, 1917. 267p.
Dyeing of woolen fabrics. London, Scott, Greenwood and son, 1902. 237p.

BEECHAM, W. E.
Terminal car record. *Railway age gazette,* Dec. 15, 1911, p. 1213-4. *St. Louis railway club, official proceedings,* Oct. 13, 1911, p. 81-110.

BEECHING, C. L. T. AND J. A. SMART
Grocery business organization and management; with chapters on buying a business, grocer's office work and bookkeeping and a model set of grocer's accounts. London, Isaac Pitman & sons. 164p.

BEEDLE E. W.
Publishing trades and the fright rate advance. *Inland printer,* Sept. 1913, p. 858-9.

BEELER, J. A.
Comparative costs of subway and surface lines in Boston; report to the Massachusetts public service commission. *Electric railway journal,* Feb. 16, 1918, p. 313.

BEEMAN, C. V.
Cost and selling prices for merchant tailors. St. Louis, C. V. Beeman, 1916. $5.

BEERBOWER, C. W.
Checking and savings accounts. *Bankers magazine,* Mar. 1914, p. 297-302.
Convenient form of voucher check. *Business man's magazine,* July 1905, p. 96-7.
Simple card system for handling collections. *Bankers magazine,* June 1912, p. 771-3.
Unit tellers system. *Bankers magazine,* June, 1913, p. 692-6.

BEES

Accounting
MILLER, A. C. Why apiary records? *American bee journal,* Sept. 1920, p. 309-10.
PARKS, C. R. Beekeepers' bookkeeping. *Gleanings in bee culture,* May 1918, p. 278.

Costs
MILLER, A. C. Costs of production. *Gleanings,* April 1920, p. 212-3.
PARKS, C. R. Lowering the cost of bee-keeping. *System on the farm,* March 1920, p. 204.

BEET SUGAR.
See Sugar.

BEET-SUGAR industry in the United States. Towsend, C. O. 1918.

BEEUWKES, R.
St. Paul electrification results. *Electric railway journal,* July 31, 1920, p. 227-30. *Railway age,* Aug. 6, 1920, p. 235-8. *Journal of the American institute of electrical engineers* Sept. 1920. p. 813-8. *Journal of electricity, power and gas,* Aug. 1, 1920, p. 117-8.

BEFORE providing for depreciation. *Incorporated accountants' journal,* Feb. 1914, p. 127-8.

BEGG, F. FAITHFULL
Excess profits duty. *Incorporated accountants' journal,* May 1917, p. 167-9.
Limited liability company reform. *Accountants' magazine,* Dec. 1897, p. 631-52. *Accountant,* Nov. 13, 1897, p. 1076-80.

BEGGS, JOHN I.
Depreciation in gas plants. *American gas light journal,* July 6, 1908, p. 5.
Maintenance of plant. *Progressive age,* July 15, 1908, p. 427.

BEGINNINGS bookkeeping. Hunter, J. 1886.

BEGINNINGS in bookkeeping for commercial schools. Hunter, John. 1898.

BELCHER, F. PERCY
Bank bookkeeping. *Accountant,* Nov. 27, 1909, p. 657-67.

BELDEN, CHARLES P.
System for purchasing. *System,* Oct. 1903, p. 265-7.

BELDING, ALBERT G.
Accounts and accounting practice. New York, American book co. c1918. 224p.

BELFIELD, A. MILLER
System in a patent law office. *System,* Nov. 1903, p. 321-3.

BELL, ALBERT AND OTHERS
Duties of an auditor. *Accountant,* Feb. 18, 1911, p. 277.

BELL, E. D.
Executorship accounts in relation to rural properties. *Accounting and commerce,* Nov. Dec. 1916, p. 180-8, 201-10.

BELL, ELLIOT
Accounting for music sellers. Reading, Petty & sons, 1907, 31p.
"Moveable-leaf system" applied to commercial bookkeeping. Reading, Petty & sons, 1908. 188p.

BELL, FINLEY F.
Illinois budget. *Annals of the American academy of political and social science,* Nov. 1915, p. 73-84.

BELL, FREDERICK ADDISON

Annual investigation of an underwriter's accounts as required by the committee of Lloyd's. *Accountant,* March 27, 1915, p. 415-24.

BELL, G.

Examination bookkeeping. Edinburgh, W. & R. Chambers, 1889.

BELL, HUGH

Trade after the war. *Accountants' magazine,* Feb. March 1917, p. 55-66, 98-126.

BELL, JOHN

Bookkeeping examination questions. Edinburgh, W. & R. Chambers, 1867.
Chambers's examinations book-keeping, with civil service and other papers fully solved. London and Edinburgh, 1908.

BELL, K. K.

Records salesmen like. *System,* Feb. 1916, p. 198-201.

BELL, LAWRENCE BRUCE

Depreciation and valuation. *Accountants' magazine,* Jan. 1904, p. 23-30.
History of the income tax. *Accountants' magazine,* Nov., Dec. 1910, p. 466-79, 519-30.
Study in depreciation. *Electrical world,* Aug. 23, 1913, p. 379.

BELL, R. L.

Costs of monolithic brick road construction *Engineering and contracting,* November 10, 1915, p. 369.

BELL, ROBERT R.

Commercial bookkeeping simplified for beginners. London, Simpkin, Marshall, Hamilton, Kent & co. 1918.

BELL, SPURGEON

Report on accounting administration for correctional institutions. Illinois, Efficiency and economy committee, 1914. 91p.
Fixed costs and market price. *Quarterly journal of economics,* May 1918, p. 507-24.

BELL, STOUGHTON

Cambridge, Mass., system of real estate assessment. *National tax association bulletin,* May 1918, p. 196-8.

BELL, WILLIAM H.

Audit working papers. *Journal of accountancy,* Aug. 1919, p. 104-12.
Corporation organization and accounting. *Journal of accountancy,* Aug. Sept. 1918, p. 98-107, 169-90.

BELL, WILLIAM T.

Profit sharing. *Accountant,* March 15, 1903, p. 393-403.
Sectional balancing. *Accountant,* Dec. 12, 1903, p. 1529-32.

BELLEVILLE, F. E.

What economics can be profitably effected in the accounting department? *Electric railway journal,* March 16, 1912, p. 429.

BELLINGER, L. F.

Duties of the naval civil engineer and their system of keeping cost accounts. *Cornell civil engineer,* April, 1908.

BELLS asbestos co. ltd. *Economist,* April 3, 1909, p. 736.

BELOIT utility decision by railroad commission of Wisconsin. *American gas light journal,* Sept. 11, 1911, p. 162.

BELSER, F. C.

Cost accounting. *Barrel and box,* May 1917. p. 32.
Cost accounting for fertilizer manufacturers. *Journal of accountancy,* March 1915, p. 165-81. *American fertilizer,* July 25, 1914, p. 77-85.
Elements of cost accounting. *Accountant,* Jan. 19, 1918, p. 57-61. *Australasian accountant and secretary,* April 1920. p. 122-7. *Journal of accountancy,* Nov. 1917, p. 325-41. *Public accountant,* March 1918, 218-32.
Rapid calculation of compound interest processes. *Journal of accountancy,* April 1919, p. 241-8.

BELT, ROBERT E.

Foundry cost accounting, practice and procedure. Cleveland, Ohio, Penton publishing co. c1919. 271p.
Importation of true cost. *Accountant,* Aug. 26, 1916, p. 177-80. *Journal of accountancy,* July 1916, p. 28-34.
Uniform cost accounting methods; adopted by the American malleable castings association November 14, 1917. 22p. + forms.

——— **AND R. W. GARDNER**

Cost accounting for manufacturers. *Railway review,* Aug. 12, 1916, p. 222-3.

BELTING

BELT-cost estimating chart. *Engineering and mining journal,* Jan. 27, 1917, p. 188-9. *Coal age,* Mar. 3, 1917, p. 382.

Cost accounting

CARROLL, WILLIAM F. Cost keeping in the leather belting industry. Philadelphia, Leather belting exchange, 1916. 29p.

BELTON, RUSSELL

Stock-in-hand; modes of taking; pricing and verification. *Accountant,* Jan. 12, 1901, p. 50-1.

BELTS.

See Belting; Link belts.

BEMENT, A.

See Ewen, John M., joint author.

BEMENT, C. E.

Methods of figuring costs. *Engineering record,* January 21, 1905.

BEMIS, EDWARD W.

Accounting side of rate making. *Electric railway journal,* Nov. 1, 1913, p. 978-9. *National association of railway commissioners, Proceedings.* 1913. p. 309-27.
Answer of the Chicago telephone company to the report of E. W. Bemis, submitted to the committee on gas, oil and electric light. Chicago, November 21, 1912. 31p.
Control of municipal accounting and statistics in Great Britain. *National municipal league. Proceedings,* 1901. p. 278-81.
Original cost as the chief basis for fair value. *Utilities magazine,* 1916, v. 1, no. 3, p. 36-42.
Progress in municipal accounting reform *Public policy,* Aug. 10, 1901, p. 92-3.
Re: progress of the engineering and accounting work on the Peoples gas light and coke company to date. *Chicago city council journal,* Aug. 2, 1918, p. 746-52.

BEMIS, EDWARD W.—*(Continued)*

Report on the investigation of the Chicago telephone company submitted to the committee on gas, oil and electric light. Chicago, October 25, 1912, paper, 127p.

Report upon the price of gas in Chicago, for the Chicago council committee on gas oil and electric light. Chicago, The Henry O. Shepard co. 1911. 31p.

Street railway settlement in Cleveland. *Quarterly journal of economics,* Aug. 1908.

Testimony on depreciation before Nebraska commission re the consolidation of the properties of the Lincoln traction company. *Electric railway journal,* March 12, 1910, p. 441.

Treatment of land in rate cases. *National municipal review,* Oct. 1914, p. 741-5.

BENDER, GEORGE D.

Accounting and business secrets; a ready reference book of accounting principles, forms, charts, rules, tables, outlines, and other information for business men, executives, office managers, accountants, bookkeepers and clerks. Seattle, G. D. Bender, 1919. 64p.

BENDER, H. C.

Results of fare increase in Spokane. *Electric railway journal,* Feb. 28, 1920, p. 433-4.

BENEDICT, GEORGE H.

Know the cost. *Inland printer,* Feb. 1914, p. 698-701.

BENEDICT, L. L. G.

Depreciation of public service property. *Gas age,* Dec. 1, 1917, p. 502-6.

BENEDICT, M. R.

Cost of production to the farmer. *Dakota farmer,* Aug. 15, 1920, p. 1438.

BENEFITS of governmental regulation of monopolies. *Journal of accountancy,* Nov. 1915, p. 367-8.

BENGER, THOMAS HAROLD

Banking accounts. *Incorporated accountants' journal,* 1902-3, p. 267.

BENHAM, W. J. L.

Comparison of short haul truck and rail shipments; abstracts. *Engineering news,* May 8, 1919, p. 903-4. *Engineering and contracting,* May 7, 1919, p. 498.

BENINGTON, HAROLD

Detection of frauds. Chicago, LaSalle extension university, c1917. 32p.

Frauds in accounts. London, Gee & co. 1904. 92p. (*Accountants' library,* v. 30).

Limitations. *Accountant,* Sept. 30, 1916, p. 287-91. *Accounting and commerce,* May 1916, p. 35-40. *Canadian chartered accountant,* April 1917, p. 289-98. *Journal of accountancy,* May 1916, p. 333-43.

BENJAMIN, G. A.

Cost of plowing with tractor outfits. *Engineering and contracting,* June 19, 1918, p. 616-17.

BENN, E. J. P.

Should wages be lowered? *Accountant,* July 31, 1920, p. 123-5.

BENNETT, C. J.

System in road management. *Engineering record,* November 14, 1914, 533-4.

BENNETT, CHARLES ALAN

Some provisions of the companies act, 1907. *Accountant,* March 6, 1909, p. 342-7.

BENNETT, E. JAMES

Is the Institute of chartered accountants doing its duty? *Canadian chartered accountant,* Jan. 1914, p. 182-3.

Revision of the dominion companies act. *Canadian chartered accountant,* April 1913, p. 255-8.

BENNETT, E. L.

Basis of rate making. *Minnesota municipalities,* Oct. 1918, p. 136-9. *New Jersey municipalities,* Jan. 1919, p. 9-10.

BENNETT, GEORGE E.

Constructive accounting; a manual of system building. New York, The Ronald press company, 1920. (Business accounting, v. 2).

BENNETT, J. H.

Computing cost of mix. *New York produce review,* May 14, 1919, p. 72.

BENNETT, JAMES ARLINGTON

American system of practical bookkeeping adapted to the commerce of the United States in its domestic and foreign relations; comprehending all the modern improvements in the practical art, and exemplified in one set of books kept by double entry; embracing five different methods of keeping a journal; designed for the use of schools, academies, and counting houses, to which are added forms of the most approved auxiliary books with a chart exhibiting at one view the final balance of the ledger and blanks for practice. New York, A. Paul, 1820.

———— Same. Ed. 12. New York, Collins & Hanway, 1829. Ed. 31. New York, Ivson & Phinney, 1855. 160p.

BENNETT, R. W.

Accounting system for factory, repair shop and sales department. *Business man's magazine,* May 1905, p. 972-7.

BENNETT, ROBERT JOSEPH

Accountancy: special course in accounting, auditing and practice, designed to prepare candidates for examinations for certified public accountants. Ed. 2. Philadelphia, Bennett accountancy institute. 1913. For sale only to persons taking courses with Bennett accountancy institute.

Accounting system for a factory, repair shop and sales department. *Business man's magazine,* May 1905, p. 972-7.

Annuities and bond discount. *Journal of accountancy,* June, July, Sept. 1915, p. 405-24, 1-20, 203-15.

Audit of a building and loan association. *American building association news,* Dec. 1912. *Journal of accountancy,* July 1912, p. 1-18.

Bookkeeping and accounting exercises. 2 parts and key. New York, American book co. 1912.

Key to bookkeeping and accounting exercises. 2 v. Chicago, American book co. 1912.

Vital importance of knowing costs. *Philadelphia chamber of commerce journal,* Jan. 1917, p. 8-10.

———— **AND FREDERICK W. MORTON**

C. P. A. questions and answers. Detroit, *International accountants' society,* 1914. 310p.

C. P. A. questions and answers. *Business man's magazine,* Sept.-Nov. 1909, Jan. May,

BENNETT, ROBERT JOSEPH AND FREDERICK W. MORTON—*(Continued)*

July-Dec. 1910, Jan.-Dec. 1911, Jan.-June 1912, p. 275-80, 373-6. 481-3, 71-4, 186-9, 278-81, 371-8, 465-72, 93-7, 189-90, 279-82, 384-8, 81-6, 583-7, 93-6, 196-207, 302-6, 397-402, 499-501, 595-7, 74-8, 161-3, 253-6, 353-6, 451-5, 545-9, 93-6, 180-4, 263-9, 346-8, 425-30, 514-16.

Corporation accounting. New York, The Ronald press co. 1917. 563p.

Educational training of an accountant. *Journal of accountancy,* March 1912, p. 182-93.

Pennsylvania C. P. A. examinations for 1912 with answers and solutions; reprinted from the *Journal of accountancy,* New York, of March, April and May, 1913. Philadelphia, R. J. Bennett. 72p.

Pennsylvania C. P. A. examinations of November 1912. *Journal of accountancy,* March, April, 1913, p. 198-230, 273-301.

Reorganization through receivership. *Journal of accountancy,* May 1916, p. 354-62.

Vital importance of knowing costs. *Accounting and commerce,* Sept. 1917, p. 137-41. *Accountant,* Aug. 25, 1917, p. 148-50. *Canadian chartered accountant,* July 1917, 34-42. *Public accountant,* Nov. 1917, p. 122-32. *Philadelphia chamber of commerce journal,* Jan. 1917, p. 8-10.

BENNETT, S. H.

Reducing the operating ratio. *Electric railway journal,* Oct. 10, 1914, p. 764-5.

BENNETT, W. A.

Method of keeping a graphic cost progress record on sewer construction. *Engineering and contracting,* Jan. 19, 1916, p. 64-5.

BENNETT, WILLIAM JOHN

Railway accounts. *Incorporated accountants' journal,* 1906-7, p. 126.

BENSON, A. S.

Fire insurance. *South African accountants journal,* v. 1, p. 26.

BENTHAM, JEREMY

On public account keeping. London, 1830. 13p.

BENTHAM, SAMUEL

Financial reform scrutinized, in a letter to Sir Henry Parnell. London, J. Hatchard & son, 1830. 82p.

BENTLEY, ARTHUR

Defects of title 2 of the federal revenue act of October 3, 1917; viewed from the accounting standpoint. *Journal of accountancy,* Feb. 1918, p. 81-90.

BENTLEY, HARRY CLARK

C. P. A. auditing questions to January 1, 1914, comprising all the available examination questions in auditing that have been set by C. P. A. examining boards up to and including December 31, 1913. New York, Ronald press company, 1914. 247p. Correspondence, Aug. 1912, p. 146-8.

Problem in the distribution of expense burden. *Journal of accountancy,* July, Sept. 1913, p. 25-50, 175-209.

Science of accounts; a presentation of the underlying principles of modern accounting; designed as a work of reference for accountants, and a text book for advanced students of accountancy. New York, The Ronald press co. 1911. 392p.

Science of accounts—author's reply to critic: correspondence. *Journal of accountancy,* June 1912, p. 449-52.

Standardization of accounting forms and methods. *Accountant,* Sept. 14, 1912, p. 333-8, 351-6. *Journal of accountancy,* Feb. March, May, June, July, Aug. Sept. 1912, p. 109-121, 161-81, 315-38, 389-400, 19-29, 99-106, 169-87.

When year ends on Sunday: correspondence. *Journal of accountancy,* Aug. 1912, p. 146.

BENTON, A. A.

Federal reserve discounts and requirements as to certain financial statements. *Trust companies,* Oct. 1915.

BENTON, A. C.

Budget system of expense control. *National retail dry goods association, Report and digest of the proceedings, first annual convention controllers' congress,* 1920. p. 35-7, 47.

Retail expense accounting. (In *Cost accounting addresses.* 1920. p. 17-22).

BENTON, CHARLES WILLIAM

Practical bookkeeping. Valparaiso, Ind., M. E. Bogarte book co. 1910. 222p.

BENTON, J. E.

Commission valuation for rate purposes. *Electric railway journal,* Oct. 14, 1916, p. 782-6.

BENTON, M. E.

Revised system of bookkeeping for the trust department. *Trust companies,* Feb. 1914, p. 111-7.

BENYON, RICHARD

Drapery and drapers' accounts. London, Sir Isaac Pitman and sons. 1909. 274p.

BERG, WALTER G.

Classification of maintenance-of-way expenses. *Railway age,* Mar. 20, 1903.

Distinction between repairs and improvements and a proposed classification of railroad maintenance of way expenses. *American railway engineering and maintenance-of-way association, Bulletin,* March 1903, p. 46-85. *Proceedings,* 1904, p. 305-45. *Engineering record,* April 4, 1903.

BERGEN, F.

Public service gas co. rate case. *Aera,* Jan. 1913, p. 465.

BERGENGREN, E.

Auditing department of a great electric railroad company. *Business man's magazine,* Jan. 1905, p. 59-65.

BERGENGREN, R. W.

Record system of a street railway company. *Business man's magazine,* March 1906.

BERGLAND, A.

Valuation of railroads in the state of Washington. *Journal of political economy,* April 1913, p. 332-4.

BERGMAN, NATHANIEL B.

Verification of inventories during an audit. *Journal of accountancy,* Sept. 1911, p. 352-6.

BERNARD, G.

"Line and column" system of bookkeeping [by] double entry, etc. Manchester, 1894.

BERNARD, M.

Cost data on special work renewals. *Electric railway journal,* July 21, August 18, Sept.

BERNARD, M.—*(Continued)*
8, 29, October 27, Nov. 10, 24, Dec. 8, 1917, p. 108, 279, 406, 588, 781, 871, 957, 1043.
Derailments reduced by investigation, classification and study of causes. *Electric railway journal,* June 16, 1917, p. 1101.

BERNDT, IRVING A.
Costs, their compilation and use in management. Chicago, H. P. Gould company, c1920. 235p.

BERNHARD, E. W.
Simple cost keeping system. *American machinist,* April 4, 1912.

BERNHARD, JOHN H.
Development of inland water transportation. *Engineering record,* September 11, 1915, p. 332-4.

BERNHARDT, M.
Date number index and bill book; showing bills received and bills paid, with several new features, concerning a new system of indexing the bills and stock and simplifying bookkeeping. New Brighton, N. Y. M. Bernhardt, 1916. 10p.

BERNHEIM, OSCAR G.
Accounting and manufacturing systems for a Portland cement business. *Business man's magazine,* 1904, v. 17, p. 829-35.

BERRIDGE, ARTHUR
Treatment of interest on manufacturing investment. *Journal of accountancy,* July 1913, p. 22-4.

BERRY, A. W.
Law of partnership and private limited companies. *Incorporated accountants' journal,* Aug. 1912, p. 292-5.

BERRY, C. J.
Inventory records that follow cost changes. *Factory,* June 1916, p. 576-7.

BERRY, FRED.
Public health department. (In Bateson, William, ed. *Pitman's municipal office organization and management.* p. 156-209).

BERRY, GORDON
Directors of limited liability companies. *Accounting and commerce,* Nov. 1919. p. 190-2.

BERRY, OSCAR
Deeds of arrangement; draft of a bill to amend the law. *Accountant,* Oct. 28, 1893, p. 904-9.

BERTOYA, O.
Organization in non-ferrous foundries. *Metal industry* (London), March 19, 1920, p. 225-9.

BERTSCHI, E. R.
Cost system for an agricultural implement business. *Business man's magazine,* 1904; v. 17, p. 249-50.

BEST, A. E.
Recovery of income tax. *Incorporated accountants' journal,* April 1914, p. 209-14.

BEST, B. G.
Cost keeping and its value to the average contractor. *Concrete,* Feb. 1920, p. 87-93.

BEST, JOHN WILLIAM
Address, 1902. *Accountant,* Oct. 25, 1902, p. 1084-7.
Cost accounts with special reference to those of an engineer and iron-founder. Ed. 2. London, Gee & co. 1911. 128p.
Cost accounts of an engineer and ironfounder. *Accountant,* Feb. 23, March 2, 9, 1901, p. 246-54, 273-80, 304-12.
Payment of dividend out of capital. *Accountant,* Dec. 5, 19, 1885.

BEST accounting method for railway fuel. *Railway age gazette,* Nov. 1909, p. 861-3.

BEST system of arranging letters and papers in chartered accountants' offices. *Accountant,* March 9, 23, April 6, 1895, 239-40,

BETHKE, WILLIAM
Business organization and management. Chicago, LaSalle extension university, 1918. 24p.

BETHLEHEM plan of employee representation. *Iron age,* Oct. 24, 1918, p. 1020-2. Abstract. *Iron trade review,* Oct. 24, 1918, 872-3.

BETHLEHEM steel company's bonus distribution. *Railway review,* March 31, 1917, p. 468.

BETTENDORF, J. W.
Freight rates and business activity. *Railway age,* April 2, 1915, p. 750.

BETTER accounting needed. *Wall street journal,* July 14, 1909. *Journal of accountancy,* Aug. 1909, p. 303.

BETTER business accounting system. *Better business,* Dec. 1918, p. 42-3.

BETTER business methods. *Engineering magazine,* June 1916, p. 432.

BETTER day's work. Burroughs adding machine company. c1908.

BETTER method for handling invoices. *Railway age gazette,* Sept. 7, 1917, p. 425.

BETTER store system and department accounting. Jackson, H. A. 1914.

BETTER work through bonus plans.*Factory,* Jan. March 1, April 15, July 1—Aug. 15, 1920, p. 220, 298, 1258; 88, 450, 642.

BETTS, PHILANDER
Effect of recent decisions on the work of inventory and appraisal. *American institute of electrical engineers, Proceedings,* Nov. 1916, p. 1539-44. Excerpts. *Electric railway journal,* Nov. 18, 1916, p. 1052-3.
Recent decisions and inventories. *Electric railway journal,* November 18, 1916, p. 1052-3.
Stock dividends, why and when justified. *Electric railway journal,* Oct. 10, 1914, p. 725-8.

BETZ, LOUIS
Discussion on municipal accounting. *Federation of societies of public accountants in the United States of America. Official record of the Congress of accountants held at the World's fair, St. Louis,* September 26th, 27th and 28th, 1904, p. 76-7.
Receipt and disbursement method of municipal accounting. *National association of comptrollers and accounting officers. Proceedings,* 1906. p. 109-12.

BEVAN, T. H.

Glasgow, Scotland—Increase in gas and electric rates. *Commerce reports no.* 273, Nov. 21, 1917, p. 717.

BEVIS, D. C.

How a contractor handles state highway work. *Municipal engineering,* April 1916, p. 167-8.

BEXELL, JOHN ANDREW

Business side of farming; farm records. Cornwallis, Oregon agricultural college press, 1909. 70p.
Farm accounting and business methods. Springfield, Home correspondence school, 1911.
Farm records. Cornwallis. Oregon agricultural college, 1909. 71p.
Farm statistics and standardized accounts. *National educational association,* 1915, p. 925-30.

See also Lemon, E. B., joint author.

——— AND W. H. KERR

Business practice and accounts for cooperative stores. Washington, Government printing office, 1916. 56p. (United States. Department of agriculture, bulletin no. 381).

——— HECTER MacPHERSON AND W. H. KERR.

Survey or typical co-operative stores in the United States. Washington, Government printing office, 1916. 32p. (United States. Department of agriculture, bulletin no. 394).

——— AND F. G. NICHOLS

Principles of bookkeeping and farm accounts. New York, American book co. c1913. 184p.
Teacher's reference book to accompany Principles of bookkeeping and farm accounts. Chicago, American book co. 1914. 104p.

BEYER, O. S.

Factors in the selection of locomotives in relation to the economics of railway operation. *Journal of the American society of mechanical engineers,* Jan. 1913, p. 1-24.
Standard practice cards on the Erie. *Railway age gazette,* May 17, 1912, p. 1108-1111

BEYLAND, E. H. H.

Plate glass manufacture. *Business man's magazine,* March 1909, p. 260.

BEYMER, W. D.

Southeastern accounting conference. Paper prepared and read by W. D. Beymer. Subjects: audits and auditors. Efficiency auditing. 1913. 7p.
Waybilling. *Pilot,* Dec. 1914. p. 371-3.

BEYNON, R.

Drapery and drapers' accounts. London, Sir Isaac Pitman and sons, 1909. 274p. $1.

BHALLA, K. C.

Auditors, their duties and responsibilities. Calcutta, 1913.

BIBBINS, J. R.

Economic limit of passenger haul. *Electric railway journal,* Oct. 3, 1914, p. 619-20.
Rational valuation—a comparative study. *Mechanical engineering,* Oct. 1920, p. 549-53.

BIBLE

Holy Bible. Oxford university press. 1087 + 324p.

BIBLIOGRAPHERS, INDEXES, CATALOGUES, ETC.

See also subdivision Bibliographies under various headings, e. g. Real Estate—Bibliographies.

ACCOUNTANCY INSTITUTE OF LOS ANGELES. Catalogue. Los Angeles, Educational department, Y. M. C. A. 1909.

ACCOUNTANCY LIBRARY ASSOCIATION. Catalogue of accountancy library at recitation rooms of the School of commerce, accounts and finance, Denver, Colorado. Ed. 2. 1910. 63p.

AMERICAN INSTITUTE OF ACCOUNTANTS. Library catalogue January 1919. New York, American institute of accountants, c1919. 237p.

AMERICAN INSTITUTE OF ACCOUNTANTS. Report of the committee on education. *American institute of accountants, Yearbook,* 1919, p. 106-8.

AMERICAN TELEPHONE AND TELEGRAPH CO. NEW YORK. Catalogue accounting library. v.1. New York, American telephone and telegraph co. 1914. 75p.

BALL, SARAH B. comp. 1600 business books; arranged by authors, by titles and by subjects; 2d ed., revised and enlarged to 2100 titles by L. H. Morley and S. H. Powell. New York, The H. W. Wilson co. 1917. 232p.

BARRETT, GEORGE E. Current magazine articles. *Journal of accountancy,* Feb.-May, July-Aug., Oct. 1907, Feb. April-Aug. Nov. 1908, p. 319-21, 406-9, 486-8; 60-2, 231-5, 315-8, 471-4, 329-32, 487-91; 70-1, 139-41, 217-9, 290-3.

BECKETT, THOMAS. Accountant's assistant; an index to the accountancy lectures and leading articles reported in "The Accountant," "The Accountant's Journal" and the transactions of the various students' societies and other periodicals during the last 30 years of the nineteenth century, to which is added a list of the principal treaties now in use on each of the 117 subjects. London, Gee & co. 1901. 141p.

BROWN, RICHARD. Bibliography of bookkeeping. (In his *History of accounting and accountants.* 1905. p. 343-60). *Accountants' magazine,* Nov. 1897, April 1898, May 1901, p. 568-73, 220-3, 240-8.

BROWN, RICHARD. Bookkeeping-bibliography. (In Lisle, George. *Encyclopaedia of accounting.* v.1. p. 493-6).

CLELAND, ETHEL, COMP. Five hundred business books. Washington, D. C., American library association, Library war service, 1919. 72p.

——— Same, with an introduction by John Cotton Dana. Ed. 3, revised by Jessica Hopkins. Chicago, American library association, 1920. 62p.

COWING, HERBERT L. One thousand technical books; a selected list with annotations emphasizing especially elementary practical books. Washington, American library association, Library war service, 1919, 123p.

CUMULATED book index; author, title and subject catalog in one alphabet of books published during 1918-June 1919 to date. New York, The H. W. Wilson co.

DANA, JOHN C. Books on accounting. *Nation's business,* June 1919, p. 78.

FAXON, FREDERICK WINTHROP. Annual magazine subject-index 1915-1917; a subject index to a selected list of American and English periodicals and society publications. Boston, The Boston book co. 1916-1918.

GORDON, COSMO. Bibligraphy. (In Woolf, Arthur H. *Short history of accountants and accountancy.* 1912. p. 197-239.)

GREENDLINGER, LEO. Accounting literature. *Journal of accountancy,* Feb., April 1908, p. 300-7, 450-62.

BIBLIOGRAPHIES, INDEXES, CATALOGUES, ETC.—*(Continued)*

Industrial arts index; subject index to a selected list of engineering and trade periodicals for 1913 to date. New York, The H. W. Wilson co.

Institute of chartered accountants in England and Wales. Library catalogue, printed for the institute by T. and A. Constable, 1913. 963p.

Institute of chartered accountants of Ontario. Library rules and catalogue. 1920. 22p.

Johnson, Mildred Noé. Brief selected list of books in accountancy for the use of small public and private libraries. 1 typewritten page. *Public libraries,* June 1918, p. 268.

Journal of accountancy index, vols. 1-16 inclusive, November 1905-December 1913. New York, The Ronald press company, c1914. 153p.

Library of congress. Division of bibliography. List of bibliographies on accounting. 3 typewritten pages.

Meyer, H. H. B. Select list of reference on scientific management and efficiency. *Special libraries,* May 1913, p. 72-109.

New department. *Journal of accountancy,* Feb. 1907, p. 302-3.

New York. Public service commission for the first district. New York city, library. List of uniform systems of accounts formulated by companies, associations and state commissions. *Special libraries,* April 1913, p. 56-67.

Office libraries. *Accountant,* Jan. 26, 1918, p. 65-7.

Oregon agricultural college. School of commerce. Bibliography on accounting. 1917. 16p.

Paton, William Andrew and R. A. Stevenson. Selected bibliography. (In their *Principles of accounting.* 1918. p. 675-6).

Pennsylvania state board of examiners of public accountants. *Journal of accountancy,* Aug. 1913, p. 156-8.

Periodical literature. *Journal of accountancy,* Jan. Feb. April, May, 1906, p. 274-6, 353-6, 547-8; 79-80.

Public affairs information service. Bulletin of the Public affairs information service, a cooperative clearing house of public affairs information, 1915 to date. New York, The H. W. Wilson co.

Reader's guide to periodical literature; author and subject index to a selected list of periodicals, 1915 to date. New York, The H. W. Wilson co.

Scovell, Wellington and company, comp. Selected professional and business books. Boston, Scovell, Wellington & co. c1918. 21p.

United States. Library of congress. Division of documents. Monthly list of state publications. Washington, Government printing office.

United States. Superintendent of documents. Monthly catalogue, United States public documents. Washington, Government printing office.

United States catalogue; books in print January 1, 1912; ed. by M. E. Potter. Ed.3. New York, The H. W. Wilson co. 1912. 2837p.

United States catalogue supplement; books in print 1912-1917. New York, The H. W. Wilson co. 1918. 2298p.

University of Illinois library. Selected list of bibliographies on accounting prepared in April, 1918. 2 typewritten pages.

BIBLIOGRAPHY of copper-zone fare system. *Aera,* June 1917, p. 1279-81.

BIBLIOGRAPHY on accounting. Oregon agricultural college. School of commerce. 1917.

BIBLIOGRAPHY on valuation of public utilities to December 23, 1915. American electric railway association.

BICKERSTAFF, H.

Dictionary of bookkeeping: terms and definitions. Percival. 1890.

BICKFORD, A. E. CHRON

Report of committee on municipal accounting with discussion. *Minnesota municipalities,* April 1918, p. 54-8.

BICKLEY, E. H.

Records that match the man to the job. *Factory,* July 1918, p. 28-30.

BICKWIT, LEONARD.

See Perine, Rita, joint editor.

BICYCLES

Accounting

American business and accounting encyclopaedia; comp. by E. H. Beach and W. W. Thorne. Detroit, Bookkeeper publishing co. 1901. Stock of completed bicycles, v.4. p. 1091-2.

Cost accounting

Wakefield, F. W. Cost accounting methods for bicycle manufacturing. *Business man's magazine,* Jan. 1908, p. 105-8.

BID on estimated supplies needed by Texas state charitable and eleemosynary institutions for twelve months beginning September 1, 1915. Austin, Texas. State purchasing agent. 1916.

BIDDING prices on public work, June-August, 1917, *Engineering and contracting,* August 29, 1917, p. 177-82.

BIDEZ, M. H.

Executive and accounting systems for a steam laundry. *Business man's magazine,* Feb. 1905, p. 320-5.

BIERCK, ALBERT B.

Effect of electrification on the accounting methods of a steam railway. *Railway and engineering review,* Oct. 17, 1908, p. 841-2.

Railroad accounting. *Business,* Feb.-May 1895, p. 73, 113-4, 153-4, 193-5.

BIG business and monopoly. *Journal of accountancy,* Dec. 1911, p. 609-11.

BIG raise in water rates at Detroit, Michigan. *Municipal journal,* March 22, 1917, p. 419.

BIG war-time rate increase for Jersey utilities. *Municipal journal,* March 23, 1918, p. 248-9.

BIGELOW, CARLE M.

Accumulation of costs in woodworking. *Industrial management,* June 1920, p. 480-2.

Establishing basic rates saves time study work. *Industrial management,* Jan. 1917, p. 17-22.

Installing management methods in the woodworking industry. *Industrial management,* July-Dec. 1919, p. 1-8, 124-33, 185-95, 295-305, 388-91, 470-7.

BIGGAR, O. M.

Cost system for lawyers; the unique method by which one firm of attorneys keeps record of the time and money spent on each client. *System,* May, 1912, p. 493-7.

BIGGER, EDWARD CLARENCE.
See Bishop, William George, joint author.

BIGGEST thing in profit sharing. *Literary digest,* Aug. 21, 1920, p. 16.

BIGGS, CHARLES H. W.
Depreciation of plant and works under municipal and company management. *Accountant,* Jan. 17, 1903, p. 91-7. *Society of engineers, Transactions,* 1902, p. 271-300.

BIGNOLD, H. B.
Federal Australian land tax. *Public accountant,* 1911, p. 63, 88, 115, 138.

BILDERBECK, G. L.
Economics of brick and macadam pavements. *Engineering news,* April 30, 1914, p. 975-6.

BILGER, H. E.
Comparative costs of brick and concrete roads in Illinois. *Engineering news,* April 1, 1915, p. 633.
Price and cost of a road. *Municipal engineering,* May 1915, p. 266-8.

BILKAM, GEORGE
Machine shop cost estimating. *American machinist,* v. 30, no. 22.

BILL aiming to end bogus tax experts favorably reported; measure provides for personal responsibility; under terms only individual can make report. *New York Tribune,* May 11, 1920.

BILL BOOKS
See also Accounting: Bookkeeping
BILL books. *Accountant,* July 18, 1885.

BILL enacted permitting Federal reserve banks to have 100% surplus. *Commercial and financial chronicle,* March 8, 1919, p. 918-9.

BILL for physical valuation. *Railway and engineering review,* Feb. 22, 1912, p. 169.

BILL for physical valuation of railways. *Railway age gazette,* April 5, 1912, p. 811.

BILL for registration of accountants in England and Wales. *Journal of accountancy,* July 1909, p. 214-5.

BILL passed by New York legislature increasing tax on corporations. *Commercial and financial chronicle,* May 3, 1919, p. 1780-1.

BILL to increase the revenue and for other purposes. *Journal of accountancy,* Aug. 1916, p. 128-46.

BILLING
ADVANTAGES of machine billing in railroad offices. *Raiway review,* Jan. 3, 1920, p. 11-2.
BILLING by machine makes large saving. *Electrical world,* Feb. 2, 1918, p. 259-60.
BILLING plan that hastens collections. *Electrical world,* Sept. 14, 1918, p. 497-8.
COMBINATION gas and electrical billing. *Electrical world,* May 2, 1918, p. 468.
DUPLICATE form of power and light bill. *Electrical review,* Aug. 3, 1918, p. 178.
HOUSTON bill saves lots of trouble. *Electrical world,* Sept. 7, 1918, p. 449.
METHOD of handling billing in city of 70.000. *Electrical world,* July 13, 1918, p. 68-9.
POSTAL cards for billing used by Oklahoma properties. *Electrical world,* Aug. 6, 1918, p. 730.
RUBBER stamps save expense in billing. *Electrical world,* March 16, 1918, p. 572.
RUSSELL, GEORGE C. Billing and order recording. (In *Cyclopedia of commerce, accountancy, business administration.* 1910. v.5. p. 235-301).
SAVE time in billing. *Business man's magazine,* May 1911, p. 490.
SHARP, L. B. Charging and billing system. *Business man's magazine,* May 1907, p. 122-6.
USING bill form with two detachable slips. *Electrical world,* April 13, 1918, p. 781.

BILLING and collecting systems of small companies. *Electrical review and western electrician,* July 31, 1915, p. 184-6.

BILLING and record system of the New York Edison company. *Electrical world,* Sept. 2, 1911, p. 573-4.

BILLING by machine makes large saving. *Electrical world,* Feb. 2, 1918, p. 259-60.

BILLING plan that hastens collections. *Electrical world,* Sept. 14, 1918, p. 497-8.

BILLINGS, J. D.
COST accounting in the manufacture of silk threads. *Business man's magazine,* Dec. 1908, p. 484-6.

BILLINGSLEY, M. P.
SERVICE-AT-COST bibliography; selected list of references on a subject of great interest to electric railway men. *Aera,* Nov. 1919, p, 494-501.

BILLS OF EXCHANGE.
See Negotiable instruments.

BILLS of exchange. Wallace, William.

BILLS OF LADING
FEDERAL bill of lading act. *Banking law journal,* Sept. 1916, p. 701-7.
WALTON, SEYMOUR. Bills of lading. *Journal of accountancy,* Aug. 1916, p. 147-52.

BILLS OF SALE
BAKER, GEORGE A. Some notes on bills of sale. *Accountant,* Jan. 24, 1914, p. 115-27.
BILLS of sale. *Accountant,* Oct. 18, Nov. 1, 15, 29, Dec. 6, 27, 1884.
BILLS of sale acts. *Accountant,* April 18, 25, 1885.
CARR, GEORGE ARTHUR BUXTON. Law of bills of sale. *Incorporated accountants' journal,* 1895-6, p. 46.
CORPUS juris; being a complete and systematic statement of the whole body of the law as embodied in and developed by all reported decisions; ed. by Wiliam Mack and W. J. Hale. New York, American law book co.
EVANS, FRANK. Bills of sale. *Accountant,* 1886, p. 475, 485, 500, 511.
JACOBS, BERTRAM. Bills of sale. *Accountant,* April 10, 1915, p. 477-81.
LIENS and bills of sale. *Incorporated accountants' journal,* 1905-6, p. 40.
LINDLEY, TINSLEY. Bills of sale. *Accountant,* March 16, 1907, p. 359-65.
LINDLEY, TINSLEY. Bills of sale. *Accountant,* May 15, 1920, p. 569-73.
LYDE, H. W. Sale of goods act, 1893. *Accountant,* Feb. 7, 1914, p. 190-5.
PARKER, W. A. Bills of sale. *Public accountant,* 1905-6, p. 77.
STATUTORY form of bills of sale. *Accountant,* Aug. 15, 1885, 1886, p. 427, 438.

BILLS of sale. *Accountant,* Oct. 18, Nov. 1, 15, 29, Dec. 6, 27, 1884.

BILLS of sale acts. *Accountant,* April 18, 25,1885.

BILLS PAYABLE

See also **Accounting.**

SUPPLEMENTARY record of bills payable. *Business man's magazine,* Sept. 1911, p. 243.

WALTON, SEYMOUR. Notes or bills payable. *Journal of accountancy,* Nov. 1919, p. 398-9.

BILLS RECEIVABLE

See also Accounting.

COPY of query addressed to the institute's solicitor regarding the acceptance of bills receivable as payment for stock, etc. re Manitoba stock companies act; opinion re bills receivable, etc. *Canadian chartered accountant,* Jan. 1913, p. 30-2.

PROPER method of keeping bills receivable records. *Business man's magazine,* Sept. 1910, p. 270-1.

BIN-TAG system provides perpetual inventory. *Electrical railway journal,* August 19, 1916, p. 323-4.

BINCKLEY, GEORGE S.

Why appraisal is not valuation. *Engineering record,* Oct. 23, 1915, p. 515-7.

BINDLOSS, ROBERT HUGH

Accountancy and auditing. *Incorporated accountants' journal,* Jan. 1912, p. 100-3.

Accountancy from without. *Accountant,* Oct. 11, 1913, p. 479-91. *Incorporated accountants' journal,* Nov. 1913, p. 36-44.

Private companies (a) the advantages of a private company (b) the conversion of a business into a private company. *Incorporated accountants' journal,* 1910-11, p. 101.

BINGHAM, C. A.

Municipal cost data. *American city,* April, 1912, p. 651-2.

BINNEY, JOSEPH

Some consideration on the law of bankruptcy. *Accountant,* April 13, 1912, p. 583-6.

BINNIE, ANDREW

Audit memoranda. London, Gee & co. 1910.

Chartered accountant in some administrative capacities. *Accountant,* May 24, 1913, p. 804-11.

Loose leaves from a note book. *Accountant,* March 6, 1915, p. 322-30.

Some legal decisions and legislative enactments from a chartered accountant's point of view. *Accountant,* April 29, 1916, p. 487.

BIOGRAPHICAL DICTIONARIES

Who's who in America; a biographical dictionary of notable living men and women of the United States, v. 10, 1918-1919; ed. by Albert Nelson Marquis. Chicago, A. N. Marquis & co. 3296p.

THOMAS, JOSEPH. Universal pronouncing dictionary of biography and mythology. Ed. 4, revised. 2v. Philadelphia, J. B. Lippincott co. c1915. 1278 + 250p.

BIRD, CYRIL F.

Advantages to a trader of keeping proper books of account, and the evils arising through failure to do so. *Accountant,* Dec. 30, 1904, p. 690-3.

Duty and responsibility of auditors with regard to the item "stock-in-trade" on a balance sheet. (In Chase, W. A. *Auditing and cost accounting.* 1917. p. 266-78). *Accountant,* Dec. 8, 1906, p. 705-9.

BIRD, WILLIAM W.

Foundry cost and accounting system. *Journal of the American society of mechanical engineers,* May 1918, p. 370-3. *Foundry,* June, 1918, p. 256-8. Discussion. *Journal of the American society of mechanical engineers,* Aug. 1910, p. 681-4.

BIRDSEYE, C. F.

College bookkeeping and accounting. *American college,* Oct. 1905, p. 15-24.

BIRKS, W. J.

Trust accounts. (In Feather, J. Stuart, ed. *Joint transactions.* 1911. p. 314-22). *Accountant,* Jan. 6, 1912, p. 15-8.

BIRMINGHAM, Ala., water rate agreement. *Engineering news,* March 18, 1915, p. 552-3.

BIRMINGHAM Chamber of commerce: memorandum of evidence to be submitted to the Bankruptcy law amendment committee. *Accountant,* Aug. 18, 1906, p. 182-7.

BIRMINGHAM CHARTERED ACCOUNTANTS STUDENTS' SOCIETY.

DEBATE—"That it is injudicious to invest a reserve fund in the business creating it." *Accountant,* Sept. 14, 1895, p. 732-5.

DEBATE: That the sum for death charges should be included in the valuation of finished stock. *Accountant,* Dec. 8, 1894, p. 1080-4.

BISCHOFF, J. M.

Development of a unit cost system. *Association of engineering societies,* Sept. 1914, p. 165-70.

BISCUITS AND CRACKERS

Cost accounting

ESTES, L. V. Unit cost accounting for control. *Industrial management,* Nov. 1919, p. 259-63.

BISHOP, E. J.

Accounting for cities of less than the first class. *Minnesota municipalities,* Aug. 1919, p. 114-8.

BISHOP, GEORGE L.

Savings bank audits. *Journal of accountancy,* Feb. 1914, p. 97-114.

BISHOP, H. G.

Order book and cost record [for job work]. Schenectady, H. G. Bishop.

BISHOP, WILLIAM GEORGE

Industry sidings on government owned roads in Europe: laws in Germany, France and Italy. *Railway review,* January 31, 1914, p. 178-9.

Short course in business training for normal schools, high schools, common schools, teachers and independent students. Lincoln, Nebraska, University publishing co. 1911.

——— **AND EDWARD C. BIGGER**

Introductory bookkeeping and business practice. Ed. 3 revised. Lincoln, Nebraska, Lincoln business college, 1910. 168p.

BISHOP calculating recorder. *Engineering magazine,* April 1915, p. 3.

BISNI, K. N.

See Manji, D. E. joint author.

BISSELL, G. W.
Depreciation of electrical properties. *Electrical age,* June 1906, p. 459.

BITTING, C. R.
Preparation of data in connection with rate cases. *Electric railway journal,* Oct. 11, 1919, sup. 29-30.
Separation of costs in a combined steam heating and electric plant, H. W. Meyer cases. *Electric railway journal,* Oct. 11, 1919, sup. 29-30.

BITUMINOUS costs and realizations in middle Appalachian field. *Coal age,* July 29, 1920, p. 257-8.

BLACK, A. C.
Law of evidence. *Accountants' magazine,* July 1920, p. 428-40.

BLACK, C. N.
Address at midyear banquet of A. E. R. A. *Electric railway journal,* Jan. 31, 1914, p. 234-7.
Planning department system. *Industrial management,* September 1919, p. 225-9.

BLACK, R. P.
Actual economy in railway management. *Railway age gazette,* May 17, 1912, p. 1111-12.

BLACKADDER, R. J.
Depreciation of investments and plant. *Accountant,* April 19, 1913, p. 578.

BLACKBOROW, HAROLD S.
Brewery accounts and their audit. *Accountant,* April 22, 29, 1899, p. 448-53, 474-81.

BLACKBURN, HENRY GASKELL
Inaugural address. *Accountant,* April 26, 1890, p. 213-5.

BLACKFORD, F.
Cost of growing tobacco. *Ohio farmer,* Aug. 16, 1919, p. 162.
537.

BLACKLOCK, FRANK
Conversion of individual enterprises into corporations. *Accountant,* Sept. 25, Oct. 9, 1897, p. 912-3, 946-7. *Business,* March-Oct. 1897, p. 204-6, 236-7, 278-9, 311-2, 79, 111, 143, 175.
Industrial plants. *Accountant,* Oct. 29, 1898, p. 1050-1.
Legal accounting and commercial bookkeeping. *Accountant,* Aug. 20, 1898, p. 803-5.
Profession of accountancy, viewed from an American standpoint. *Accountant,* Jan. 6, Feb. 3, 17, March 10, 1900, p. 13-4, 143, 194, 253.
Rights and duties of public accountants from an American view. *Acountant,* Oct. 8, 1898, p. 950-1.
Suggestions to a young accountant on adjusting a fire loss. *Accountant,* June 18, 1898, p. 633-4. *Business,* May 1898, p. 295-7.
Suggestions to those who would enter the profession of accountancy. *Business,* Nov. 1897, March 1898, p. 337; 370; 37-8, 106-7, 173-4.

BLACKLOCK, JOHN H.
Bank clerk. *The office,* Sept. 1890, p. 238-9.
Municipal accounting. *Bookkeeper,* Nov. 1899, p. 27-8.
Uniform municipal accounting. *Nation,* Feb. 6, 1902, p. 110.
Uniform municipal reports. *Baltimore journal of commerce,* Feb. 15, 1902, p. 1, 4. *Public policy,* March 8, 1902, p. 150-1.

BLACKLY, FREDERICK FRANK
Accounting and reporting methods of the State of New York. New York, 1916. Thesis—Columbia university. 1916. Pts. 1-2 of Municipal research, no. 74, June 1916.

BLACKMER, ERNEST A.
Notes receivable record. *Business man's magazine,* Oct. 1907, p. 81-2.

BLACKSMITH SHOPS
Cost accounting
ELBOURNE, E. T. Smithy. (In his *Factory administration and accounts.* 1918. p. 463-4).
EVANS, HOLDEN A. Blacksmith shop. (In his *Cost keeping and scientific management.* 1911. p. 208-22).
HONECKER, CHARLES A. Valuable suggestions on a shop accounting system. *Business man's magazine,* Dec. 1907, p. 95-104.
KENT, WILLIAM. Distribution of burden in minor departments blacksmith shop. (In his *Bookkeeping and cost accounting for factories.* 1918. p. 70).

BLACKWELL, PHILIP H.
Verification of assets. (In Feather, J. Stuart, ed. *Joint transactions.* 1911. p. 111-25). *Accountant,* May 27, 1911, p. 818-23.

BLADEE, H. G.
Actual figures of existing street railways. *Aera,* Dec. 1912, p. 392.

BLAIN, H. E.
See Dicksee, Lawrence Robert, joint author.

BLAIR, A.
General principles governing the law of contract. *Accounting and commerce,* Dec. 1915, Jan. Feb. March 1916, p. 206-8, 226-8, 255-6, 268-72.

BLAIR, J. C.
Organizing an office. *Canadian chartered accountant,* April 1919, p. 334.
Organizing and standardizing an office. *Accounting and commerce,* Dec. 1917, Jan. 1918, p. 212-6, 229-34.

BLAIR, P. W.
How to obtain the accurate cost in manufacturing brass goods. *Metal industry,* Jan. 1917, p. 10-1.
Increasing the efficiency of a brass manufacturing plant. *Metal industries,* Jan. 1913, p. 13-4.
Installing a cost system in a brass manufacturing plant. *Metal industry,* Feb. 1918, p. 67-8.
Ordering tools and supplies in the factory. *Machinery,* May 1915, p. 745.

BLAIR, W. P.
Records of street and road repairs. *Municipal engineering,* April 1916, 137.

BLAISDELL, B. H.
Bonus plan reduces coal consumption at Manila, P. I. *Electric railway journal,* Feb. 16, 1918, p. 308-11.
Bonus system for power houses; result of nearly three years trial by the Manila electric railway and light company. *Aera,* Feb. 1918, p. 659-67.

BLAISDELL, B. H.—*(Continued)*
Kilowatt-hour and the coal required to produce it. *Electric railway journal,* March 16, 1918, p. 525-6.

BLAISE, J. E.
What motor trucks have saved for a brewer. *Scientific American,* Feb. 22, 1913, p. 182.

BLAKE, A. F.
Alinement chart for the evaluation of coal. *Journal of industrial and engineering chemistry,* August 1918, p. 627-9.
Graphic chart for the evaluation of coal. *Journal of industrial and engineering chemistry,* Dec. 1916, p. 1140-2.

BLAKE, E. M.
Cost data an the work of improving the Neponset river in Massachusetts. *Engineering and contracting,* January 10, 1915, p. 34-6.

BLAKE, HAROLD T.
Examinations notes on book-keeping and accountancy. London, Pitman, about 58p.

BLAKE, J. P.
Detailed cost accounting. *System,* Oct. 1904, p. 330-4.
Keeping detailed records of stock on hand. *System,* Nov. 1904, p. 426-9.

BLAKEBOROUGH, H. A.
Light and power rates. *Canadian municipal journal,* Jan. 1917, p. 22-3.

BLAKEMAN, S. R.
Selection, installation and test of a 1,000,000 gallon motor driven centrifugal pump. *Journal of the American water works association,* June 1916, p. 96-106.

BLAKEMORE, W. G
See Elgar, W. D., joint author.

BLAKSELL, J. I.
Operating costs of government owned motor trucks in postal service. *Engineering and contracting,* April 17, 1918, sup. 26.

BLANCHARD, A.
Convenient inspection record system. *Electric railway journal,* Dec. 30, 1916, p. 1352.
See also Westervelt, J. W., joint author.

BLANCHARD, A. H.
Method and costs of constructing pitchmac pavement. *Engineering and contracting,* June 5, 1918, p. 575-6.

BLANCHARD, ISAAC H.
Actual costs in printing and how to discover and reckon them. *Business man's magazine,* 1901, v. 14, no. 2, p. 89-99.
Finding the work that pays: how to charge each job with its proper ratio of wages, machine time and overhead expense. *System* Feb. 1913, p. 154-7.

BLANDFORD, E. W. E.
Licensing trade accounts. *Incorporated accountants' journal,* 1900-1, p. 58.

——— **AND OTHERS.**
Auditors certificates. *Incorporated accountant's journal,* 1898-9, p. 140.

BLANK forms—some interesting blank forms of small interurban railway company. *Electric railway journal,* May 28, 1910, 956-7.

BLANK forms to be used by railroads in reporting to the interstate commerce commission: form (a) large roads, form (b) small roads, form (c) switching and terminal companies, form (d) outside operations, (e) lessor companies.

BLANKET supplement authorized for rate advance. *Railway age,* Aug. 13, 1920, p. 287-9.

BLASTING
Costs
CHAMBER blasting methods and costs. *Engineering and contracting,* Sept. 18, 1918, p. 279-83.
COST of quarry blasting. *Municipal engineering,* Oct. 1916, p. 144.
COSTS of blasting drainage ditches. *Engineering record,* Mar. 31, 1917, p. 511.
METHOD and cost of clearing cut over land with powder. *Engineering and contracting,* Dec. 19, 1917, p. 505-7.
RUSSELL, S. R. Reducing quarry costs. *Concrete,* Oct. 1916, sup. 41.

BLAUVELT, M. P.
Railroad accounting under government supervision. *Journal of accountancy,* June 1908, p. 81-92. Abstract. *Railway age gazette,* May 15, 1908.

BLAUVELT, W. S.
Application of the index number of commodity prices in adjustments of gas rates a way out of a vicious cycle. *American gas engineering journal,* Oct. 11, 1919, p. 313-4.

BLEACHERY forms and records. *Textile world,* Aug. 31, 1918, p. 941.

BLEACHING
Bleachery form and records. *Textile world* Aug. 31, 1918, p. 941.
Costs
WOLLASTON, T. RONALD. Power and heat costs in bleach and dye works. *Journal of the British association of managers of textile works,* 1914-15, p. 111-20.

BLEAKLY, E. G. C.
Camden's view of the New Jersey zone plan. *Electric railway journal,* Oct. 11, 1919, sup. 126-7.

BLEASE, W.
Address, 1905. *Accountant,* Nov. 25, 1905, p. 615-21.

BLEASE, WALTER
Clearing house arrangements of the Liverpool cotton association. *Accountant,* Oct. 29, 1904, p. 514-9.
Executorship accounts. *Accountant,* 1883, p. 593.
Executorship accounts. *Accountant,* Sept. 15, 22, 1888, p. 593-5, 598-9.

BLINN, E. S.
Distribution of costs on street paving construction. *Municipal engineering,* September 1918, p. 96.

BLINN, T. W.
Daily work-train report. *Electric railway journal,* Sept. 25, 1915, p. 636.

BLISS, F. H.
Bliss system of bookkeeping and office practice: handbook. Saginaw, Michigan, The F. H. Bliss publishing company, 1920. 188p.

BLISS, GEORGE H.

Organization of irrigation operating and maintenance force and its training. *Engineering and contracting,* May 6, 1914, p. 535-7.

BLOCK, JOSEPH LUCIEN

Crude petroleum business. *Business man's magazine,* July, Aug. 1907, p. 49-61, 77-9. Abstract. *Journal of accountancy,* July 1907, p. 233-4.

BLOCK number system. *Machinery* (London), Oct. 2, 1919, p. 7-9.

BLOEDEL Donovan shop committee organization. *Timberman,* March 1920, p. 35.

BLOG, L.

Defense of the piece rate method of wage payment. *Industrial management,* Oct. 1919, p. 325-7. Excerpts. *Engineering and contracting,* April 14, 1920, p. 443-4.

BLOMEYER, E. C.

Accounts with electric light subscribers. *System,* Jan. 1906.

System for a telephone company; keeping track of material and supplies used and on hand. *Business man's magazine,* 1906, v. 18, no. 9, p. 94-6.

BLOMFIELD, F. C.

Making the deposit account pay. *Business man's magazine,* Dec. 1911, p. 538-42.

BLUE, F. K.

Practical application of the self-adjusting standard for rate fixing. *Journal of electricity,* April 26, 1913.

BLUE, F. S.

See Bookman, Clarence Munroe, joint author.

BLUE, FRED. O.

Uniform public accounting and state supervision thereof. *National tax association. Proceedings,* 1916, p. 332-5.

BLUIM, J. M.

Accounting system of an ice company. Cleveland, J. M. Bluim. 1911. 104p.

Systems of accounting. *Ice and refrigeration,* 1906, v. 30, p. 167-8.

BLUM, A. S.

Rules and regulations for the guidance of employees of safe deposit department. *Trust companies,* May, 1915, p. 456-8.

BLUNDEN, G. H.

Income tax. *Accountant,* Aug. 28, 1897, p. 823.

BLUNT, JOHN E.

Reorganizations and railroad bonds. *Railroad review,* Nov. 13, 1915, p. 633-4.

BLYTH, ROBERT

War scares and commercial dislocations. *Accountant,* Jan. 28, 1919, p. 126-8.

BOAG, GEORGE L.

Manual of railway statistics. London, Railway gazette, 1912. 185p.

BOAG, HAROLD

Allowances for exceptional depreciation in the assessment of excess profits duty. *Accountant,* Feb. 23, 1918, p. 162-3.

Business capital in excess profits duty computations. *Business organization and management,* Sept. Oct. 1920, p. 605-11; 91-6.

BOARD of examiners. *Journal of accountancy,* Nov. Dec. 1916, p. 387, 451-4.

BOARDING HOUSES

Accounting

Soulé, George. Bookkeeping for hotels and boarding houses. (In his *New science and practice of accounts.* 1903. p. 318-23).

BOARDMAN, JAMES

Address, 1886. *Accountant,* 1886, p. 695.

Banking. *Accountant,* Feb. 23, March 1, 1884.

Banking. *Accountant,* 1886, p. 256.

Bookkeeping and banking. London, Gee & co. 1886.

Notes on the formation of companies. *Accountant,* 1887, p. 206.

BOARDMAN, W.

System of bookkeeping. 1802.

BOATS.

See Shipbuilding; Ships and shipping.

BOBER, W. C.

Graphic planning of payroll procedure. *Industrial management,* Nov. 1920, p. 336-7.

BODDINGTON, A. LESTER

Foreign exchanges; the part they play in international commerce. *Accountant,* Jan. 29, 1916, p. 146-50.

BOERICKE, W. F.

Rise in cost of zinc mining in Wisconsin. *Engineering and mining journal.* Mar. 29, 1919, p. 564-6.

BOES, F. C.

Valuation of steam railroads. *Engineering record,* Nov. 8, 1913, p. 533.

BOGLE, ARTEMIS MELVIN

Comprehensive bookkeeping. New York, The Macmillan co. 1905.

Everyday bookkeeping. New York, The Macmillan co. 1917. 126p.

Teachers manual to accompany "Comprehensive bookkeeping." The Macmillan co. 1908.

BOGLE, J. D. S.

Writing off of depreciation on the wasting assets of a joint stock company. *Accountant,* Dec. 21, 1889, p. 691-6.

BOGLE, STEWART AND J. H. ATTFIELD

M'Dougall's bookkeeping for elementary schools. London and Edinburgh, 1895-6.

BOHEIM, OTTO A.

Accounting system for a bottling works. *Business man's magazine,* July 1908, p. 43-51.

BOHMANN, H. P.

Block system of handling water consumers' accounts at Milwaukee, Wis. *Engineering and contracting,* June 11, 1919, p. 636.

BOILER and engine-room record sheets. *Power,* Sept. 16, 1919, p. 46-53.

BOILER log sheet for oil-fired boilers. *Electrical review,* April 20, 1918, p. 688.

BOILER PLANTS

Boiler log sheet for oil-fired boilers. *Electrical review,* April 20, 1918, p. 688.

BOILER PLANTS—*(Continued)*

HOUGH, B. K. Coal accounting in the boiler room. *Power,* April 15, 1919, p. 586.

BOILER-ROOM bonus that satisfies the men. *Electrical world,* Feb. 8, 1919, p. 274.

BOILERS

Cost accounting

ARNOLD, H. L. Cost finding methods for moderate sized shops. *Engineering magazine,* Dec. 1902—April 1903, p. —385-95, 577-89, 714-28, 870-8.

ARNOLD, HORACE LUCIEN. Cost finding system of the Bigelow Company of New Haven, Conn. (In his *Factory manager and accountant.* 1903. p. 101-112).

CONNELLY, W. C. Shop costs of boiler and plate work. *Iron age,* Sept. 18, 1913 p. 614-5.

HONECKER, CHARLES A. Valuable suggestions on a shop accounting system. *Business man's magazine,* Dec. 1907, p. 95-104.

KNOWLTON, H. S. Cost-stores system of a boiler manufacturing plant. *Engineering magazine,* Oct. 1906, p. 45-57.

LABOR cost keeping in a boiler shop. *Iron age,* Aug. 17, 1916, p. 342-3. *Cassier's engineering monthly,* Dec. 1916.

Costs

DAW, CARL S. Suggestion for overloaded boiler plants. *Engineering magazine,* June 1909, p. 406-16.

LATHROP, J. C. Cost of rapid erection of six 1000-hp. boilers. *Power,* Nov. 17, 1914, p. 705-7.

BOISOT, E. K.

What factors determine the market value of bonds; with discussion. (In *National association of comptrollers and accounting officers. Proceedings.* 1917. p. 34-42).

BOLEMANN, H. P.

Operating expenditures of Milwaukee (Wis.) water works. *Engineering and contracting,* Aug. 8, 1917, p. 117.

BOLEN, N. W.

Some features of electric railway departmental organization. *Electric railway journal,* Feb. 21, 1914, p. 415-6.

BOLINGER, C. D.

Monotype accounting problems. *Inland printer,* July 1915, p. 473-5.

BOLTON, JAMES CHARLES

First audit of a joint stock company's accounts. *Accountant,* Dec. 12, 1885.

Marine insurance. *Accountant,* May 16, 1885.

Merchants' accounts. *Accountant,* May 17, 1884.

BOLTON, REGINALD PELHAM

Building for profit; principles governing the economic improvement of real estate. New York, The De Vinne press, 1911. 124p.

BOLTS AND NUTS

Cost accounting

BOLTS and nuts. *American institute of accountants, Special bulletin,* no. 6, Nov. 1920, p. 3-4.

EGGLESTON, DEWITT CARL. Cost of manufacture of 500 ½ inch hexagon head stove bolts. (In his *Problems in cost accounting.* 1918. p. 180-1).

Depreciation

See Depreciation, depletion and obsolescence—Bolts.

BOLTS and nuts. *American institute of accountants. Special bulletin,* No. 6, Nov. 1920, p. 3-4.

BOMER, CHARLES F.

Iron mine accounting. *Journal of accountancy,* Sept. 1920, p. 180-5.

BONBRIGHT, J. C.

Basis of railroad capitalization. *Political science quarterly,* March 1920, p. 30-53.

Depreciation and rate control. *Quarterly journal of economics,* May 1918, p. 546-8.

BOND, C. O.

See Klumpp, J. B., joint author.

BOND BROKERS.

See Brokers.

BOND issues—for road improvements. *Engineering and contracting,* Nov. 6, 1912, p. 514.

BOND PRINTING.

See Printing

BOND records of a trust company. *Business man's magazine,* Aug. 1906, p. 93-8.

BOND valuations of savings banks. *Journal of accountancy,* June 1906, p. 159-60.

BOND value calculations simplified. *Canadian chartered accountant,* Oct. 1915, p. 149.

BOND values from another point of view. Little, A. S.

BONDHOLDERS reorganization plans for an irrigation district. Geijsbeek, J. B.

BONDS

See also Investments and securities

AMORTIZATION of bond incomes. *Bankers magazine,* Mar. 1915, p. 335-7.

ANGERT, EUGENE H. Proper distribution of interest on bonds between life tenants and remaindermen. *Journal of accountancy,* Aug. 1906, p. 259-74.

BENNETT, GEORGE E. Coupon books. (In his *Constructive accounting.* 1920. p. 187-8).

BENTLEY, H. C. Bonds. (In his *Science of Accounts.* 1913. p. 182-3).

BOISOT, E. K. What factors determine the market value of bonds; with discussion. (*National association of comptrollers and accounting officers. Proceedings,* 1917, p. 34-42).

BOND issues—for road improvements. *Engineering and contracting,* Nov. 6, 1912, p. 514.

BOND value calculations simplified. *Canadian chartered accountant,* Oct. 1915, p. 149.

BONDS and the rate of interest. *Journal of accountancy,* July 1910, p. 210-2.

BONDS which are and bonds which are not tax exempt. *Chronicle,* Nov. 1913—April 1914.

BRADT, S. E. Efficient methods of promoting highway bond issues. *Good roads,* March 29, 1919, p. 139-40. Condensed. *Engineering news,* March 20, 1929, p. 573-4.

CALCULATING premiums on bonds. *Municipal journal,* April 1, 1915, p. 426.

CHAMBERLAIN, LAWRENCE. Principles of bond investment. Ed. 7. New York, Henry Holt & co. 551p.

CHASE, HARVEY STUART. Governmental sinking funds, serial bonds and depreciation reserves; read at the annual meeting of the Dominion association of chartered accountants at Montreal, September 18th to 20th, 1918. 18p. *Accountant,* March 1, 1919.

BONDS—*(Continued)*
p. 162-8. *Canadian chartered accountant,* Oct. 1918, p. 142-65. *Journal of accountancy,* Oct. 1918, p. 253-68. *National association of comp. and accounting officers, proceedings,* June 1918. 64-74p.

CONRAD, CHARLES. Bonds for government industrial plants. *Journal of accountancy,* Oct. 1911, p. 401-9.

COX, HENRY C. Bonds and bond investments; accounting for bonds. (In his *Advanced and analytical accounting.* 1920. p. 121-42).

DICKINSON, ARTHUR L. Bonds. (In his *Accounting practice and procedure.* 1917. p. 116-7, 133-43).

DICKINSON, ARTHUR L. Duties and responsibilities of the public accountant with regard to new issues of stocks and bonds. *Journal of accountancy,* Nov. 1905, p. 16-27.

ESQUERRÉ, P. J. Corporation-stock securities, bonded debt. (In his *Applied theory of accounts.* 1917. p. 34-8, 336-45).

FERRIN, A. W. Principles of bond investment. *Moody's magazine,* Feb. 1915.

FINNEY, H. A. Effective rate on serial bonds *Journal of accountancy,* Nov. 1920, p. 385-400.

FOGARTY, JAMES F. Accounting treatment of bond discount. *Electric railway journal,* Oct. 15, 1914, p. 871.

GEIJSBEEK, J. B. Bondholders' reorganization plan for an irrigation district. *Journal of accountancy,* July 1914, p. 30-7.

GEIJSBEEK, J. B. Future of irrigation bonds; correspondence. *Journal of accountancy,* Jan. 1911, p. 223.

GOLD suply and the bond market. *Journal of accountancy,* Jan. 1906, p. 237-8.

GREENDLINGER, LEO. Bonded debt. (In his *Financial and business statements.* c1917. p. 180-3).

GREENWOOD, W. J. How to make money in foreign exchange and foreign bonds. New York, Financial books company, 1920. 129p.

HALLETT, WALTER E. Some aspects of the bond problem. *Journal of accountancy,* Oct. 1906, p. 442-9.

HARDIE, W. D. L. Bond value calculations simplified. *Accountant,* Sept. 11, 1915, p. 314-9. *Canadian chartered accountant,* July 1915, p. 6-19.

HESS, R. H. Irrigation bonds. *Journal of accountancy,* Oct. 1910, p. 426-34.

HILL, DANIEL. Book debts. *Accountant,* Jan. 28, 1899, p. 110-13

HILTON, WILLIAM P. Bonus capital stock and bonds. *Journal of accountancy,* June 1915, p. 425-36.

HUEBNER, S. S. Bonds and the bond market. *Annals of the American academy of political and social science,* March 1920, v. 88, no. 177. 223p.

JONES, ARTHUR F. Accountant's relation to timber bond issues. *Annals of the American academy of political and social science,* May 1912, sup. 51-8.

JONES, EDWARD DAVID. Bonds. (In his *Investment.* c1918. p. 80-126).

KERZIE, F. L. Actual problem in serial bonds. *Journal of accountancy,* Feb. 1917, p. 119-28.

KESTER, ROY B. Bonds. (In his *Accounting theory and practice.* 1918. v. 2. p. 356-76)

KILLAM, S. D Bond schedules for the amortization of a premium or accumulation of a discount *Canadian chartered accountant,* April 1920, p. 231-7.

LAWTON, WILLARD H. Treatment of unissued stock and bonds. *Journal of accountancy,* April 1917, p. 241-53.

LITTLE, ARTHUR S. Another fallacy in bond values. *Journal of accountancy,* March 1908, p. 386-97.

LITTLE, ARTHUR S. Bond values from another point of view. *Journal of accountancy,* Sept. 1908, p. 329-37.

LITTLE, ARTHUR S. Brothers all. *Journal of accountancy,* May 1916, p. 344-53.

LITTLE, ARTHUR S. Computation of coupon values. *Journal of accountancy,* April 1920, p. 283-98.

MCCARTNEY, G. Housing problem in Wellington; how it might be financed by co-operative borrowing. *Accounting and commerce,* Nov. 1918, p. 170-2.

MCINTOSH, R. S. Bonds. (In his *Reference book of accounts for manufacturing and mercantile companies.* c1914. p. 36-7, 80-1).

MACMILLAN, H. P. Bonds of caution in liquidations. *Accountants' magazine,* 1901, p. 479.

MACPHERSON, F. H. Sinking fund principle and practice. *Journal of accountancy,* Aug. 1912, p. 113-6.

MARR, WILLIAM W. Operation of proposed bond issue plan for state roads of Illinois. *Engineering news,* Dec. 13, 1917, p. 1129.

MAY, GEORGE O. Premiums and discounts. *Journal of accountancy,* Nov. 1906, p. 32-3.

MAY, GEORGE O. Proper treatment of premiums and discounts on bonds. *Journal of accountancy,* July, 1906, p. 174-86.

MITCHELL, WLATER K. What the borrower owes. *Journal of accountancy,* Feb. 1916, p. 156.

MOTT, HOWARD S. Course of bond prices; a comparison, with civil war conditions. New York, Irving national bank, 1918. 15p.

MUHLEMAN, M. L. Municipal bonds and municipal credit. *Banking law journal,* Aug. 1911, p. 639-44.

PATON, W. A. and R. A. STEVENSON. Mortgages and bonds. (In their *Principles of accounting,* 1918. p. 322-7).

RACINE, S F. Bonds issued for constructive purposes. (In his *Accounting principles.* 1917. p. 119-20).

RECORDING bond investments. *Bankers' magazine,* May 1917, p. 533-4.

ROBINSON, J. WATTS. About bond values. *Journal of accountancy,* Nov. 1907, p. 9-12.

ROLLINS, MONTGOMERY. Principles upon which tables of bond values are based. *Journal of accountancy,* Nov. 1907, p. 4-9.

SANDERSON, KENNETH. Bonds of caution in executries, curatories, etc. *Accountants' magazine,* 1901, p. 163.

SPIES, OTTO A. Present worth of future coupon payments. *Journal of accountancy,* March 1917, p. 171-6.

SPRAGUE, CHARLES EZRA. Amortization: guide to the ready computation o f the investment value of bonds. New York, C. E. Sprague, 1908. 22p.

SPRAGUE, CHARLES EZRA. Bonds. (In his *Accountancy of investment.* 1914. p. 75-122-148-66, 196-211, 228-70).

SPRAGUE, CHARLES EZRA. Fallacy in bond values. *Journal of accountancy,* Nov. 1907, p. 1-4.

SPRAGUE, CHARLES EZRA. Premiums and discounts. *Journal of accountancy,* Aug. 1906, p. 294-6.

SPRAGUE, CHARLES EZRA. Stock value of a bond. *Accountant,* Sept. 12, 1908, p. 314-5. *Journal of accountancy,* July 1908, p. 174-6

STANDARD STATISTICS COMPANY INC., NEW YORK. Status of bonds under the federal income tax. 1918 ed. New York Standard statistics co. inc. c1918. 197p.

STANDARD STATISTICS COMPANY INC., NEW YORK. Status of bonds under the federal income tax. 1920 ed. New York, Standard statistics company, inc. c1920. 244p.

SYMPOSIUM on bond values. *Journal of accountancy,* Nov. 1907, p. 1-12.

THOMAS, EDWARD S. Determination of income rate on unusual serial bonds. *Journal of accountancy,* Aug. 1917, p. 105-11.

VINAL, EUGENE R. Valuation of bonds. (In his *Mathematics for the accountant.* 1920, p. 101-22).

BONDS—(Continued)

Walton, Seymour. Amortizing serial bonds. *Journal of accountancy,* Dec. 1919, p. 470-1.

Walton, Seymour. Bond interest. *Journal of accountancy,* July 1915, p. 65-6.

Walton, Seymour. Bond sale—construction contract. *Journal of accountancy,* Sept. 1916, p. 228.

Walton, Seymour. Bond tables. *Journal of accountancy,* Oct. 1916, p. 319-22.

Walton, Seymour. Bonds and sinking funds. *Journal of accountancy,* Dec. 1918, p. 468-72.

Walton, Seymour. Premium or discount on bonds in sinking fund. *Journal of accountancy,* May 1915, p. 390-2.

Walton, Seymour. Redeeming bonds "out of earnings". *Journal of accountancy,* April 1917, p. 314-5.

Walton, Seymour. Sinking fund or serial bond plan. *Journal of accountancy,* May 1919, p. 384-5.

Webster, George R. Methods of writing off discount on bonds. *Journal of accountancy.* Sept. 1913. p. 169-74.

What New York might save by adopting serial bond method for loans. *Commercial and financial chronicle,* Aug. 1, 1914, p. 304-5.

Wildman, J. R. Secondary income group. (In his *Principles of accounting.* 1914. p. 228-30).

Wright, Walter C. What the borrower owes: correspondence. *Journal of accountancy,* Feb. 1916, p. 157.

Discounts.

See Discounts—Bonds.

Tables.

See Tables.

BONDS and sinking funds. Walton, Seymour.

BONDS and the rate of interest. *Journal of accountancy,* July 1910, p. 210-2.

BONDS' egg record and poultry account book. Middletown, N. Y., Bonds press, 1914.

BONDS exempt or exemptible from the personal property tax under the mortgage tax law of the state of New York. Guaranty trust company of New York. 1917.

BONDS for government industrial plants. Conard, Charles.

BONDS which are and bonds which are not tax-exempt. *Commercial and financial chronicle,* Nov. 1913, April 1914.

BONERSMITH, J. E.

Small steam shovel work in road grading, contra costa county, California; with cost data. *Engineering and contracting,* July 19, 1916, p. 59-60.

BONN, BENJAMIN

Accountant and geometrician; containing the doctrine of circulating decimals, logarithms, book-keeping, and the plane geometry. London, 1765.

BONNELL, GEORGE M.

Simple accounting system for sales in carload lots. *Business man's magazine,* Dec. 1907, p. 87-8.

BONNER, F. A.

Is intercolonial's failure due to low rates? *Railway age,* December 15, 1916, p. 1081-4.

BONNER, H. R.

Graphic method for presenting comparative cost analysis. *Quarterly publication of the American statistical association,* Sept. 1920, p. 277-8.

BONNER, JOSEPH CLAYBAUGH

Farm cost system arranged for the farmer. Toledo, Bonner & co. c1915. 58p.

BONSALL, R. F.

Handling of customes' orders. New York, National electric light association, 1911. 11p.

BONSON settlement trust; specimen of form of account employed by the public trustees in rendering a statement of trust to beneficiaries.

BONUS and income tax. *American institute of accounts, Special bulletin,* No. 1, 3, Jan. May, 1920, p. 7, 8.

BONUS capital stock and bonds. Hilton, W. P.

BONUS for motor truck drivers. *Engineering and contracting,* Aug. 1, 1917, p. 87

BONUS plan as amended, April 1, 1919. General motors corporation.

BONUS plan for salaried employees. Goodwin, J. P.

BONUS, profit-sharing and pension. *Journal of accountancy,* Nov. 1911, p. 541-2.

BONUS—profit sharing—pensions. Rand, Waldron H.

BONUS shares. *Accountant,* Nov. 2, 1912, p. 541-.2

BONUS shares. *Accountant,* July 3, 1920, p. 22.

BONUS STOCK.

See Stock—Bonus.

BONUS system for mechanics. *Motor age,* March 18, 1920, p. 13.

BONUS system in coal mining. *Coal age,* Nov. 11, Dec. 2-16, 30-Jan. 6, 27, Feb. 10, 24, 1917. p. 815-16, 939-40, 977-8, 1019-20, 1099; 30, 202-3, 289, 370-1.

BONUS system increased number of meters read by 50 per cent. *Electrical world,* June 26, 1920, p. 1488. *Engineering and contracting,* July 14, 1920, p. 46.

BONUS system on the Santa Fe. *Railway age gazette,* Dec. 17, 1909, p. 1192-3.

BONUS system started in St. Louis. *Electric railway journal,* Oct. 6, Nov. 10, 1917, p. 622-3, 864.

BONUS system stimulates Ohio operating men. *Electrical world,* June 30, 1917, p. 1260.

BONUS SYSTEMS

See Bonuses; Wages and fees—Bonus.

BONUSES

Bonus and income tax. *American institute of accountants, Special bulletin,* No. 1, 3, Jan. May, 1920, p. 7, 8.

BONUSES to policemen. *Municipal Journal,* Nov. 16, 1916, p. 600-1.

BOOK KEEPER.

See Bookkeeper.

BOOK of instructions for the guidance of carriers in making annual reports to the Board of railroad and warehouse commissioners. Minnesota. Railroad and warehouse commission. 1889.

BOOK of the farm. 2v. Edinburgh. 1855.

BOOK-PAPER industry. United States. Federal trade commission. 1917.

BOOK REVIEWS

Accountants' diary for 1911, no. IV. London, Gee & co. *Journal of accountancy,* April 1911, p. 464.

Accountnants' manual. London, Gee & co. *Journal of accountancy,* April 1911, p. 463.

Accounting system for Chalmers distributers. Chalmers motor company. *Journal of accountancy,* July 1916, p. 72-3.

Accounts of hospitals and other charitable institutions. *Journal of accountancy,* March 1909, p. 409.

Acme corporation record. Acme publishing co. 246p. *Journal of accountancy,* Oct. 1908, p. 443.

Allen, Nellie B. Industrial studies, United States. New York, Ginn & co. 1910. *Journal of accountancy,* April 1911, p. 463.

American academy of political and social science. Bonds and the bond market. Philadelphia, American academy of political and social science, March number. $1.25. *Journal of accountancy,* Dec. 1920, p. 475-6.

American association of public accountants, Yearbook 1914. New York, The Ronald press co. 355p. *Journal of accountancy,* Jan. 1915, p. 76.

American association of public accountants, Yearbook 1915. New York, The Ronald press co. 363p. *Journal of accountancy,* Jan. 1916, p. 80.

American institute of accountants. Library catalogue. New York, Jan. 1919. 237p. *Journal of accountancy,* July 1919, p. 69-70.

Arnold, Horace Lucien and Fay Leone Faurot. Ford methods and the Ford shops. Engineering magazine company. *Journal of accountancy,* April 1916, p. 316-7.

Auerbach, Louis J. Electrical contracting. New York, McGraw publishing company. 155p. *Journal of accountancy,* Nov. 1908, p. 70.

Bailey, L. H. State and the farmer. New York, MacMillan company. 1908. 176p. *Journal of accountancy,* Nov. 1908, p. 71.

Baker, James W. Twentieth century bookkeeping and accounting complete. Cincinnati, Southwestern publishing co. 1912. 304p. *Journal of accountancy,* Dec. 1912, p. 504.

Baker, James W. Twentieth century bookkeeping and office practice. Ed. 8, revised. Southwestern publishing co. 1910. *Journal of accountancy,* July 1912, p. 64-5.

Bardeen, C. W. Manual of common school law. Syracuse, N. Y., Author. 470p. *Journa of accountancy,* July 1910, p. 225-6.

Barker, Arthur H. Management of engineer ing workshops. London, Technical publishing co. *Journal of accountancy,* Aug. 1911, Jan. 1912, p. 303-4, 70-1.

Basset, William R. Accounting as an aid to business profits. Chicago, A. W. Shaw company, 1919. 316p. *Journal of accountancy,* July 1919, p. 72-3.

Baugh and Schmeisser. Estate accounting. Baltimore, M. Curlander. *Journal of accountancy,* May 1910, p. 60-1.

Baugh, Frederick H. Grain export calculation tables. Baltimore, The John Hinrichs cable code company. $15. *Journal of accountancy,* Dec. 1920, p. 477.

Baugh, Frederick H. Principles and practice of cost accounting. Baltimore, Author. *Journal of accountancy,* June 1916, p. 480.

Bayer, Henry G. Metric system. New York, 1914. *Journal of accountancy,* Jan. 1915, p. 74.

Beach, E. H. ed. Tools of business: an encyclopedia of office equipment and labor saving devices. Detroit, Mich., Bookkeeper publishing company. 211p. *Journal of accountancy,* Feb. 1906, p. 333-4.

Belding, Albert G. Accountants and accounting practice. American book co. *Journal of accountancy,* July 1915, p. 75-6.

Belding, Albert G. Commercial correspondence. ' American book co. 150p. *Journal of accountancy,* March 1909, p. 411-2.

Bell, William O. Practical short methods in rapid calculation. Kansas City, Mo. Burton publishing co. *Journal of accountancy,* Sept. 1916, p. 235.

Bennett, John W. Roosevelt and the republic. New York, Broadway publishing company, 1908. 424p. *Journal of accountancy,* Sept. 1909, p. 386-7.

Bennett, R. J. Corporation accounting. New York, The Ronald press co. *Journal of accountancy,* April 1917, p. 319-20.

Bentley, H. C. C. P. A. auditing questions. New York, The Ronald press company, 1914. *Journal of accountancy,* Dec. 1914, p. 483.

Bentley, Harry C. Corporate finance and ac counting. New York, 1908, 525p. *Journal of accountancy,* May 1908, p. 68-9.

Bentley, Harry C. Science of accounts. New York, The Ronald press company. 1911. 390p. *Journal of accountancy,* March 1912, p. 239-40. Correspondence. Science of accounts—author's reply to critic. *Journal of accountancy,* June 1912, p. 449-52.

Bexell, J. A. Business side of farming: farm records. Oregon agricultural college press, 1909. *Journal of accountancy,* Nov. 1911, p. 547-8.

Bexell, J. A. and F. G. Nichols. Principles of bookkeeping and farm accounts. American book company, 1913. 176p. *Journal of accountancy,* March 1914, p. 244.

Binnie, Andrew. Audit memoranda. London, Gee & company, 1910. 12p. *Journal of accountancy,* Sept. 1910, p. 388.

Bithell, J. Handbook of German commercial correspondence. Longmans, Green & company, 1908. 228p. *Journal of accountancy,* Jan. 1909, p.247.

Blanton, Ben H. Credit, its principles and practice. New York, The Ronald press company. *Journal of accountancy,* July 1915, p. 73-4.

Bogart, Ernest Ludlow. Economic history of the United States. New York, 1907. 522p. *Journal of accountancy,* April 1908, p. 484.

Bolce, Harold. New internationalism. New York, D. Appleton & co. 1907. 309p. *Journal of accountancy,* April 1907, p. 484-5.

Bolles, Albert S. Money, banking and finance. New York, American book company. 335p. *Journal of accountancy,* Jan. 1909, p. 245-6.

Book of American municipalities. Chicago, Municipal information bureau, 1910. *Journal of accountancy,* May 1910, p. 63.

Booth, Mary H. Character in handwriting. Philadelphia, John C. Winston company, 1910. *Journal of accountancy,* Jan. 1912, p. 71.

Brandeis, Louis D. Scientific management. New York, Engineering magazine, 1910. *Journal of accountancy,* May 1911, p. 69-74.

Brinton, Willard C. Graphic methods for presenting facts. New York, The Engineering magazine company, 1914. *Journal of accountancy,* Jan. 1915, p. 72-3.

Brisco, Morris A. Economic policy of Robert Walpole. New York, Columbia university press, 1907. *Journal of accountancy,* Nov. 1908, p. 70-1.

Brockway, W. B. Electric railway accounting. New York. *Journal of accountancy,* Dec. 1906, Sept. 1908, p. 172-3, 359.

BOOK REVIEWS—*(Continued)*

Brown, Richard. History of accounting and accountants. Edinburgh, T. C. & E. C. Jack, 1905. *Journal of accountancy,* Jan. 1906, p. 253-5.

Bullock, Charles J. Selected readings in economics. New York, Ginn & company 1907. *Journal of accountancy,* Oct. 1907, p. 475-6.

Bullock, Charles J. Selected readings in public finance. Boston and New York, Ginn & company. 1906. 654p. *Journal of accountancy,* April 1906, p. 508-9.

Bunnell, Sterling H. Cost-keeping for manufacturing plants. New York, D. Appleton & company. 1911. *Journal of accountancy,* Aug. 1911, p. 306.

Callender, Guy Stevens. Selections from the economic history of the United States 1765-1860, with introductory essays. Ginn & company. 1909. 819p. *Journal of accountancy,* Dec. 1909, p. 147.

Carpenter, Charles U. Profit making management. New York, 1908. 150p. *Journal of accountancy,* Sept. 1908, p. 359.

Casson, Herbert N. History of the telephone A. C. McClurg & company. 1910. 315p. *Journal of accountancy,* July 1911, p. 218.

Casson, Herbert N. Romance of the reaper. New York, Doubleday, Page and company, 1908. *Journal of accountancy,* Aug. 1908, p. 289.

Castenholz, William B. Auditing procedure. Chicago, LaSalle extension university. *Journal of accountancy,* May 1919, p. 398.

Channing, Edward and Marion Florence Lansing. Story of the Great Lakes. New York, The Macmillan company, 1909. 398p. *Journal of accountancy,* Sept. 1909, p. 387-8.

Chantrey, W. H. Theatre accounts. London, Gee & company. (Accountants' library, v.5). *Journal of accountancy,* July 1915, p. 76.

Charlton, W. H. American mine accounting. McGraw-Hill book company, 1913. 367p *Journal of accountancy,* Feb. 1913, p. 140.

Cherinston, Paul Terry. Advertising as a business force. New York, Doubleday, Page & company, 1913. 569p. *Journal of accountancy,* Sept. 1913, p. 263.

Church, A. Hamilton. Manufacturing costs and accounts. New York, McGraw-Hill book company, 1917. *Journal of accountancy,* June 1917, p. 475-7.

Church A. Hamilton. Production factors in cost accounting and works management. New York, Engineering magazine, 1910. *Journal of accountancy,* May 1911, p. 69-74.

Church, A. Hamilton. Proper distribution of expense burden. New York, The Engineering magazine, 1908. 116p. *Journal of accountancy,* Oct. 1908, p. 444

Church, A. Hamilton. Science and practice of management. New York, The engineering magazine company, 1914. *Journal of accountancy,* Dec. 1914, p. 484-6.

Clapp, John Mantle. Language for men of affairs; v. 1, Talking business. New York, The Ronald press company. *Journal of accountancy,* Sept. 1920, p. 235.

Clarke, J. Maurice, Walton H. Hamilton and Harold G. Moulton. Readings in the economics of war. University of Chicago press. *Journal of accountancy,* May 1919, p. 398.

Cleveland, Frederick A. Bank and the treasury. New York, Longmans, Green & co. 1905. *Journal of accountancy,* Nov. 1905, p. 67-9.

Cleveland, Frederick A. Municipal administration and accounting New York, Longmans, Green & company. *Journal of accountancy,* July 1909, Dec. 1909, p. 220-1; 143-4.

Cleveland, Frederick A. and Fred Wilbur Powell. Railroad finance. New York, D. Appleton and company, 1913 463p. *Journal of accountancy,* Aug. 1913, p. 166-7.

Cleveland, Frederick A. and Fred Wilbur Powell. Railroad promotion and capitalization in the United States. New York, Longmans, Green & co. 1909. 368p. *Journal of accountancy,* Aug. 1909, p. 309.

Clews, Henry. Speeches and essays. New York, Irving publishing company. 456p. *Journal of accountancy,* March 1911, p. 382-5.

Cody, Sherwin. Geographical reference list. Chicago, 1909. *Journal of accountancy,* Jan. 1910, p. 230

Cody, Sherwin. How to do business by letter. Yonkers, N. Y., World book company, 1918. *Journal of accountancy,* Sept. 1918, p. 238.

Cody, Sherwin. Success in letter writing. Chicago, A. C. McClurg company, 1906, 224p. *Journal of accountancy,* March 1907, p. 404.

Cole, William Morse. Accounts, their construction and interpretation. Boston, Houghton, Mifflin & company, 1908. 343p. *Journal of accountancy,* Jan. 1909, p. 244-5.

Cole, William Morse. Accounts, their construction and interpretation. Boston, Houghton, Mifflin & co. 1915. *Journal of accountancy,* Sept. 1915, p. 242-3.

Cole, William Morse. Cost accounting for institutions. New York, The Ronald press company, 1913. *Journal of accountancy,* Feb. 1915, p. 159-60.

Cole, Wiliam Morse. Problems in the principles of accounting. Harvard university press. *Journal of acountancy,* Aug. 1915, p. 160-1.

Collins, Charles Wallace. National budget system. New York, Macmillan company. *Journal of accountancy,* Dec. 1917, p. 487-8.

Collver, Clinton. How to analyze industrial securities. New York, Moody's investors service. *Journal of accountancy,* July 1918, p. 77-8.

Collver, Clinton. How to analyze industrial securities. New York, Moody's investors service. *Journal of accountancy,* Dec. 1919, p. 478-9.

Comparative statement of trust companies in the state of New York: compiled from the annual reports of the superintendent of banks, 1894 to 1904. New York, George W. Young & company. *Journal of accountancy,* May 1906, p. 59-60.

Conant, Charles A. Principles of money and banking. 2v. New York, Harper & brothers, 1905. 437+488p. *Journal of accountancy,* Feb. 1906, p. 332-3.

Conyngton, Thomas. Business law. 2v. New York, The Ronald press company. 870p. *Journal of accountancy,* Dec. 1920, p. 473-4.

Conyngton, Thomas. Corporate organization and management. New York, Ronald press company. 760p. *Journal of accountancy,* Jan. 1918, p. 79.

Conyngton, Thomas. Partnership relations. New York, 1906. *Journal of accountancy,* May 1906, p. 58-9.

Cooper, Francis. Financing an enterprise. 2v. 500p. *Journal of accountancy,* Jan. 1907, p. 258.

Cooper, F. Financing an enterprise. New York, The Ronald press co. *Journal of accountancy,* Aug. 1915, p. 159-60.

Cost and wage rate book. New York, Special purpose book company, 1919. *Journal of accountancy,* Dec. 1920, p. 476-7.

Cotton movement and fluctuation. New York, Latham, Alexander and company. *Journal of accountancy,* June 1908, p. 137-8.

Currency problem and the present financial situation: a series of addresses delivered at Columbia university, 1907-8. 170p. *Journal of accountancy,* April 1908, p. 485-6.

Cutforth, A. E. Audits. London, 1908, 151p. *Journal of accountancy,* May 1908, p. 68.

BOOK REVIEWS—*(Continued)*

CUTFORTH, A. E. Audits. Ed.2. London, Gee & co. 1910. *Journal of accountancy,* April 1911, p. 464-5.

CUTFORTH, A. E. Treatment of fluctuating currency in accounts. London, Gee & company, 1910. *Journal of accountancy,* Aug. 1910, p. 304.

CYCLOPEDIA of commerce, accountancy, business administration. 10v. Chicago, American school of correspondence, 1910. *Journal of accountancy,* March, June 1910, p. 382-4, 141-2.

DAGGETT, STUART. Railroad reorganization. Boston and New York, Houghton, Mifflin & company, 1908. 482p. *Journal of accountancy,* July 1908, p. 214-5.

DAVIS, JOHN P. Engineering office systems and methods. New York, McGraw-Hill book company, 1915. *Journal of accountancy,* July 1915, p. 72-3.

DAWSON, SIDNEY STANLEY. Accountants' compendium. Ed.3. London, 1908. 630p. *Journal of accountancy,* Aug. 1908, p. 288.

DAWSON, SIDNEY STANLEY. Accountants' compendium. Ed.4. London, Gee & company, 1911. 749p. *Journal of accountancy,* July 1912, p. 64.

DAY, CLARENCE. Accounting practice. New York, D. Appleton company, 1908. 318p. *Journal of accountancy,* Oct. 1908, p. 443.

DAY, CHARLES. Industrial plants, their arrangement and construction. New York, Engineering magazine, 1911. *Journal of accountancy,* May 1911, p. 74-5.

DELAND, LORIN F. Imagination in business. New York & London, Harper & brothers, 1909. 170p. *Journal of accountancy,* Feb. 1910, p. 302-3.

DEWEESE, TRUMAN A. Practical publicity Philadelphia, George W. Jacobs & company. *Journal of accountancy,* July 1909, p. 221.

DEWEESE, TRUMAN A. Principles of practical publicity, being a treatise on "the art of advertising". Buffalo, Matthews-Northrup works, 1906. *Journal of accountancy.* Nov. 1906, p. 55-6.

DEWSNUP, ERNEST RITSON. Railway organization and working. Chicago, University of Chicago press, 1906. 498p. *Journal of accountancy,* Nov. 1906, p. 56-7.

DICKINSON, ARTHUR LOWES. Accounting, practice and procedure. New York, Ronald press company, 1914. *Journal of accountancy,* Dec. 1914, p. 480-2.

DICKSEE, LAWRENCE R. Auditing. Ed. 9 London, Gee & co. 1912. 1016p. *Journal of accountancy,* Aug. 1912, p. 154.

DICKSEE, LAWRENCE R. Auditing. Ed.10. revised and enlarged. London, Gee & company. *Journal of accountancy,* Aug. 1915, p. 156-7.

DICKSEE, LAWRENCE R. Bookkeeping for accountant students. Ed.7. London, Gee & company, 1913. *Journal of accountancy,* June 1914, p. 475.

DICKSEE, LAWRENCE R. Business organization. London & New York, Longmans, Green & company, 1910. *Journal of accountancy,* Nov. 1910, p. 71-2.

DICKSEE, LAWRENCE R. Depreciation, reserves and reserve funds. Ed.3. 1912. 70p. *Journal of accountancy,* July 1913, p. 87-8.

DICKSEE, LAWRENCE R. Dicksee's auditing. 2nd American edition. New York, Ronald press company, 1910. *Journal of accountancy,* April 1910, p. 461-2.

DICKSEE, LAWRENCE R. Dicksee's auditing; a practical manual for auditors. New York, Robert H. Montgomery, 1905. 359p. *Journal of accountancy,* Nov. 1905, p. 63-5.

DICKSEE, LAWRENCE R. Hotel accounts. Ed.2. London, Gee & co. 1912. *Journal of accountancy,* Jan. 1913, p. 76-7.

DICKSEE, LAWRENCE R. Mines accounting and management. London, Gee & company, 1914. *Journal of accountancy,* April 1914, p. 322.

DICKSEE, LAWRENCE R. Office machinery. London, Gee & company. *Journal of accountancy,* Aug. 1917, p. 155-6.

DICKSEE, LAWRENCE R. Office machinery and appliances. London, Gee & company. *Journal of accountancy,* April 1919, p. 320.

DICKSEE, LAWRENCE R. "Solicitors' accounts". London, Gee & company. *Journal of accountancy,* Aug. 1910, p. 303-4.

DICKSEE, LAWRENCE R. and H. E. BLAIN. Office organization and management including secretarial work. London, Sir Isaac Pitman & sons, 1908. *Journal of accountancy,* Feb. 1910, p. 303-5.

DIEMER, HUGO. Factory organization and administration. New York, McGraw-Hill book company, 1910. *Journal of accountancy,* Sept. 1911, p. 382-7.

DIEMER, HUGO. Factory organization and administration Ed.2. New York, Ronald press company, 1914. *Journal of accountancy,* Nov. 1914, p. 403-4.

DRAPER, GEORGE OTIS. More—a study of financial conditions now prevalent. Boston, Little, Brown & company, 1908. *Journal of accountancy,* Feb. 1911, p. 306-8.

DRURY, HORACE B. Scientific management. New York, Longmans, Green & company. *Journal of accountancy,* July 1916, p. 71-2.

DUNCAN, C. S. Commercial research. New York, The Macmillan company. *Journal of accountancy,* March 1920, p. 239-40.

DUNCAN, JOHN C. Principles of industrial management. New York, D. Appleton & company, 1911. *Journal of accountancy,* Oct. 1911, p. 456-60.

EDWARDS, H. M. Electric light accounts and their significance. New York, McGraw-Hill book company, 1914. *Journal of accountancy,* June 1914, p. 474.

ELY, RICHARD T. and GEORGE RAY WICKER. Elementary principles of economics, together with a short sketch of economic history. New York, Macmillan company, 1905. 388p. *Journal of accountancy,* June 1906, p. 156.

EMERSON, HARRINGTON. Efficiency as a basis for operation and wages. New York, Engineering magazine, 1909. *Journal of accountancy,* Dec. 1909, p. 145-7.

EMERSON, HARRINGTON. Efficiency as a basis for operation and wages. Ed.3, revised and enlarged New York, Engineering magazine, 1912. *Journal of accountancy,* April 1912, p. 305-7.

EMERSON, HARRINGTON. Twelve principles of efficiency. New York, Engineering magazine, 1912. *Journal of accountancy,* April 1912, p. 305-7.

EMERY, BENJAMIN F. Ethics and principles of salesmanship. Philadelphia, 1905. 131p. *Journal of accountancy,* Feb. 1908, p. 328.

ENGINEERING index annual for 1913. New York, Engineering magazine company, 1914. *Journal of accountancy,* June 1914, p. 476.

ERRORS in balancing. Ed. 3. London, Gee & company, 1912. *Journal of accountancy,* Jan. 1913, p. 76.

ESDALE, M. How property is valued. London, Cable printing and publishing co., 1909. *Journal of accountancy,* Feb. 1912, p. 153-4.

ESQUERRÉ, PAUL-JOSEPH. Applied theory of accounts. New York, Ronald press company *Journal of accountancy,* April 1916, p. 317.

FAGAN, JAMES O. Labor and the railroads. Boston, Houghton, Mifflin company, 1909. 164p. *Journal of accountancy,* Dec. 1910, p. 147.

FAIRLIE, JOHN H. Essays on municipal administration. Macmillan company, 1908. *Journal of accountancy,* Aug. 1908, p. 287-8.

FIELD, CLINTON C. Retail buying. New York. Harper & brothers. *Journal of accountancy,* Aug. 1917, p. 323.

BOOK REVIEWS—*(Continued)*

FILLEBROWN, C. B. A. B. C. of taxation. New York, Doubleday, Page and company, 1909, 229p. *Journal of accountancy,* March 1910, p. 384-5.

FINLAY, JAMES RALPH. Cost of mining. New York, McGraw-Hill book co. 1909. *Journal of accountancy,* Jan. 1910, p. 229-30.

FISHER, IRVING. Nature of capital and income. New York, Macmillan company, 1906. *Journal of accountancy,* Feb. 1907, p. 318.

FISK, JAMES W. Retail selling. New York, Harper brothers, 1916. *Journal of accountancy,* Nov. 1916, p. 407.

FORSE, WILLIAM H., jr. Electric railway auditing and accounting. New York, McGraw publishing company, 1908. 157p. *Journal of acountancy,* Jan. 1909, p. 247.

FORTY-SIXTH annual report of the city of Burlington, Vermont for the year 1910. *Journal of accountancy,* Aug. 1911, p. 302. 3.

FOSTER, HORATIO A. Engineering valuation of public utilities and factories. New York, D. Van Nostrand company, 1912. 345p. *Journal of accountancy,* Aug. 1912, p. 153-4.

FRANK, ROBERT J. Science of organization and business development. *Journal of accountancy,* Dec. 1909, p. 145.

FRAUD in accounts. *Journal of accountancy,* July 1910, p. 222.

FROST, THOMAS GOLD. Incorporation and organization of corporations. Ed.4. Boston, Little, Brown and company, 1913. 926p. *Journal of accountancy,* Aug. 1913, p. 165-6.

GAMBLE, WILLIAM. Straight talks on business. Philadelphia, 1907. 230p. *Journal of accountancy,* Feb. 1908, p. 328.

GANTT, H. L. Work, wages and profits. New York, Engineering magazine. 1910. *Journal of accountancy,* May 1911, p. 69-74.

GARDNER, EDWARD HALL. Effective business letters. New York, Ronald press company. *Journal of accountancy,* Aug. 1915, p. 157-9.

GARDNER, E. H. New collection methods. New York, Ronald press company. 467p. *Journal of accountancy,* Oct. 1919, Dec. 1920, p. 315, 474-5.

GARRISON, ELISHA ELY. Accounting every business man should know. New York, Doubleday, Page & co. 1909. 188p. *Journal of accountancy,* Aug. 1910, p. 305.

GEIJSBEEK, JOHN B. Ancient double-entry bookkeeping. New York, Ronald press company, 1914. *Journal of accountancy,* Nov. 1914, p. 404-5.

GILBERT, JAMES HENRY. Trade and currency in early Oregon. New York, Columbia university press, 1907. *Journal of accountancy,* June 1909, p. 140-1.

GILBRETH'S field system. New York, Myron C. Clark publishing company. New York, 1908. 194p. *Journal of accountancy,* Jan. 1908, p. 256.

GILMAN, STEPHEN. Principles of accounting. LaSalle extension university, 1916. *Journal of accountancy,* Oct. 1916, p. 326-7.

GOING, CHARLES BUXTON. Methods of the Santa Fe. Engineering magazine, May 1909. *Journal of acountancy,* June 1911, p. 141.

GOING, CHARLES BUXTON. Principles of industrial engineering. New York, McGraw-Hill book company, 1911. *Journal of accountancy,* Sept. 1911, p. 382-7.

GOODYEAR, LLOYD E. Principles of accountancy. Iowa, Goodyear Marshall publishing co. 1913. *Journal of accountancy,* Jan. 1915, p. 74-5.

GOULD, GEORGE M. Righthandedness and lefthandedness. Philadelphia, J. B. Lippincott co. 1908. *Journal of accountancy,* Feb. 1912, p. 154-5.

GREENDLINGER, LEO. Accountancy problems with solutions. New York, University accountancy publishing co. 325p. *Journal of accountancy,* April 1909, p. 488-9.

GREENDLINGER, LEO. Accounting problems with solutions. v. 11. New York, Business book bureau. *Journal of accountancy,* Jan. 1912, p. 66-8.

GREGORY, H. E., A. G. KELLER and A. L. BISHOP. Physical and commercial geography. New York, Ginn and company, 1910 469p. *Journal of accountancy,* Nov. 1910, p. 73.

GRUNSKY, CARL EWALD. Valuation, depreciation and the rate-base. New York, John Wiley & sons. 387p. *Journal of accountancy,* July 1917, p. 477-8.

GUIDE to reading in social ethics and allied subjects. Cambridge, Harvard university, 1910. *Journal of accountancy,* April 1912, p. 307-8.

HAINES, HENRY S. Restrictive railway legislation. New York, The Macmillan company, 1905. 355p. *Journal of accountancy,* March 1906, p. 422-3.

HALSEY, N. W. & co. Most satisfactory bonds. New York, Author, 1911. *Journal of accountancy,* June 1911, p. 143.

HAMILTON, W. R. Principles of modern bookkeeping. London, Gee & company, 1912. 144p. *Journal of accountancy,* Sept. 1912, p. 239.

HANUS, PAUL H. Beginnings in industrial education. Boston and New York, Houghton Mifflin company, 1908. 209p. *Journal of accountancy,* April 1909, p. 490-1.

HARRISON, RICHARD COMPTON. New York corporations; a manual of New York corporation law. New York, 1906. 430p. *Journal of accountancy,* Jan. 1907, p. 258.

HARTNESS, JAMES. Human factor in works management. New York, McGraw-Hill book company, 1912. 159p. *Journal of accountancy,* Sept. 1912, p. 238.

HARVARD bureau of business research. Bulletin no. 10. *Journal of accountancy,* July 1918, p. 73-7.

HARVEY, RICHARD SELDON. Rights of the minority stockholders. New York, Baker, Voorhis & company, 1909. *Journal of accountancy,* Oct. 1909, p. 466.

HATFIELD, HENRY RAND. Modern accounting. D. Appleton & co. 1909. *Journal of accountancy,* Sept. 1910, p. 387.

HAUER, DANIEL J. Modern management applied to construction. New York, McGraw Hill book company, inc. *Journal of accountancy,* May 1919, p. 399.

HAWKINS, L. WHITTEN. Cost accounts. Ed.3. London, Gee & company. 120p. *Journal of accounting,* Feb. 1913, p. 140.

HAYES, HAMMOND V. Public utilities: their fair present value and return. D. Van Nostrand co. *Journal of accountancy,* July 1915, p. 71-2.

HAYWARD, WILLIAM R. Money: what it is and how to use it. Boston, Houghton, Mifflin company. *Journal of accountancy,* Aug. 1917, p. 156.

HEITMANN, HENRY. Course in the theory and practice of higher accounting. Poughkeepsie & New York, Eastman college, 1910. *Journal of accountancy,* Jan. 1911, p. 224-5.

HENDRICK, BURTON J. Story of life insurance, New York, McClure, Phillips & co. 1907. 296p. *Journal of accountancy,* June 1907, p. 152-3.

HIGINBOTHAM, HARLOW W. Making of a merchant. 1906. 210p. *Journal of accountancy,* Dec. 1906, p. 171-2.

HINE, CHARLES DELANE. Modern organization. New York, Engineering magazine company, 1912. *Journal of accountancy,* Jan. 1913, p. 76.

HIRSCH, ADOLPH. Science of commercial bookkeeping. New York, J. S. Ogilvie publishing co. *Journal of accountancy,* June 1911, p. 142.

HODGE, ALBERT CLAIRE and JAMES OSCAR MCKINSEY. Principles of accounting. Chicago. University of Chicago press. 389p. *Journal of accountancy,* Dec. 1920, p. 471-2.

BOOK REVIEWS—*(Continued)*

HOLLANDER, JACOB H. Studies in American trade unionism. New York, Henry Holt & company, 1906. 380p. *Journal of accountancy,* July 1906, p. 223-6.

HOLLISTER, HORACE EDWARD. Practical garage accounting. Rockford, The garage systems company, 1916. *Journal of accountancy,* Oct. 1916, p. 327.

HOLT, BYRON W. COMP. Gold supply and prosperity. New York, The Moody corporation, 1907. 257p. *Journal of accountancy,* April 1907, p. 485.

HOLT, HAMILTON. Commercialism and journalism. Houghton, Mifflin company, 1909. 105p. *Journal of accountancy,* March 1910, p. 385.

HOOPER, WILLIAM E. Railroad accounting. New York, D. Appleton and company, 1915. *Journal of accountancy,* May 1915, p. 401-3.

HOOVER, HERBERT C. Principles of mining. New York, E. M. Hill publishing company, 1909. 200p. *Journal of accountancy,* Nov. 1909, p. 59-60.

HOTCHKISS, WILLARD EUGENE.. Higher education and business standards. Boston and New York, Houghton, Mifflin company. *Journal of accountancy,* Aug. 1918, p. 158-9.

HOUGH, B. OLNEY. Elementary lessons in exporting and exporters' gazetteer. New York, Johnston export publishing company, 1909. *Journal of accountancy,* Nov. 1910, p. 72-3.

How to audit. New York, The McArdle press. *Journal of accountancy,* Dec. 1920, p. 478.

How to calculate progressive transfer tax. *Journal of accountancy,* June 1911, p. 143.

How to successfully conduct a mail-order business. Kansas City, Mo., Advertisers' magazine. *Journal of accountancy,* April 1910, p. 464.

How to write letters that win. Chicago, System company, 1909. *Journal of accountancy,* Feb. 1910, p. 305.

HOWARD, EARL DEAN. Cause and extent of the recent industrial progress of Germany. Houghton, Mifflin & company, 1907. 147p. *Journal of accountancy,* Feb. 1908, p. 326-7.

HOWE, FREDERIC C. Confessions of a monopolist. Chicago, Public publishing company, 1906. 157p. *Journal of accountancy,* March 1907, p. 404-5.

HUDDERS, E. R. Indexing and filing. New York, Ronald press company. *Journal of accountancy,* April 1916, p. 318.

HUNTER, JOEL. General information on the Georgia C. P. A. examinations and typical questions. *Journal of accountancy,* Feb. 1913, p. 141.

HURLEY, EDWARD N. Awakening of business. New York, Doubleday, Page and company. *Journal of accountancy,* Feb. 1917, p. 160.

IGNATUS, MILTON B. Financing of public service corporations. New York, Ronald press company. *Journal of accountancy,* Feb. 1919, p. 159-60.

INCORPORATED accountants' year-book for 1920. *Journal of accountancy,* Dec. 1920, p. 477.

INCORPORATED students telephone. London, H. Foulks Lynch & company. *Journal of accountancy,* Sept. 1910, p. 388.

INTERSTATE commerce commission's uniform system of accounts for class "C" telephone companies— objections as set forth in the brief submitted by the Wisconsin railroad commission. *Journal of accountancy,* May 1915, p. 398-401.

INVENTOR'S pocket library. Washington, Engineer searching co. 1910 . *Journal of accountancy,* Sept. 1910, p. 388.

ISAACS, C. E. Surtax. London, Gee & company, 1910. 20p. *Journal of accountancy,* Sept. 1910, p. 388.

JOHNSON, EMORY R. American railroad transportation. Ed 2, revised. New York, D. Appleton & company, 1908. 434p. *Journal of accountancy,* March 1909, p. 410.

JOHNSON, EMORY R. Bonds as investment securities. Philadelphia, Pa., 1907. 235p. *Journal of accountancy,* Nov. 1907, p. 71-2.

JOHNSON, EMORY R. Elements of transportation. New York and London, D. Appleton & company, 1909. 360p. *Journal of accountancy,* Nov. 1909, p. 58.

JOHNSON, EMORY R. Ocean and inland water transportation. New York, D. Appleton & co. 1906. 385p. *Journal of accountancy,* July 1906, p. 221-3.

JOHNSON, GEORGE. Electric lighting accounts. London, Gee & company. 171p. (The accountants' library, v.29) *Journal of accountancy,* June 1914, p. 476.

JOHNSON, JOSEPH FRENCH. Money and currency. Ed. 5, revised. New York, Ginn and company, 1915. *Journal of accountancy,* Aug. 1915, p. 155-6.

JOHNSON, JOSEPH FRENCH. Money and currency in relation to industry, prices, and the rate of interest. Ginn and company, 1906. 398p. *Journal of accountancy,* May 1906, p. 56-8.

JOINT transactions of the chartered accountants' students societies, 1911. London, Gee & company, 1912. *Journal of accountancy,* Sept. 1912, p. 238-9.

JONES, EDWARD D. Business administration. its models in war, statecraft and science. New York, The Engineering magazine company, 1914. 275p. *Journal of accountancy,* July 1914, p. 84.

KELLOGG, JAMES L. Shell-fish industries. Henry Holt & company, 1910. *Journal of accountancy,* July 1910, p. 224-5.

KENNAN, K. K. Income taxation. Milwaukee, Wis., Burdick and Allen, 1910. *Journal of accountancy,* Nov. 1911, p. 548-9.

KENT, WILLIAM. Bookkeeping and cost accounting for factories. New York, John Wiley & sons. *Journal of accountancy,* Aug. 1918, p. 157-8.

KESTER, ROY B. Accounting theory and practice; a first year text. New York, The Ronald press company. *Journal of accountancy,* Dec. 1917, p. 488-90.

KIRKBRIDE, F. B. and J. E. STERRETT. Modern trust company: its functions and organization. New York, Macmillan company. 309p. *Journal of accountancy,* Jan. 1906, p. 255-8.

KLEIN, JOSEPH J. Bookkeeping and accounting. New York, D. Appleton and company. *Journal of accountancy,* March 1918, p. 238.

KLEIN, JOSEPH J. Elements of accounting. New York, D. Appleton and company, 1913. 422p. *Journal of accountancy,* Aug. 1913, p. 167.

KNIFFIN, W. H. Savings bank and its practical worth. Bankers publishing company, 1913. 551p. *Journal of accountancy,* Aug. 1913, p. 263-4.

KNOOP, DOUGLASS. American business enterprise. Gartside, University of Manchester, 1907. Reports on commerce and industry. *Journal of accountancy,* Feb. 1908, p. 327-8.

KOHN, AUGUST. Cotton mills of South Carolina: republished from the News and courier, Charleston, S. C., issued by South Carolina department of agriculture, commerce and immigration, 1907. 228p. *Journal of accountancy,* July 1908, p. 215-6.

LAKIN-SMITH, H. Printers' accounts. London, Gee & co. (Accountant's library). *Journal of accountancy,* May 1917, p. 400.

LARSEN, CARL W. Milk production cost accounts; principles and methods. New York, Columbia university press. *Journal of accountancy,* Jan. 1917, p. 80.

LAUGHLIN, J. LAURENCE. Industrial America; Berlin lectures of 1906. New York, 1906. *Journal of accountancy,* Dec. 1906, p. 165-71.

LAWS, C. R. Manual for the collection of commercial paper. 1908. 41p. *Journal of accountancy,* Oct. 1908, p. 444

LEE, JAMES MELVIN. Language for men of affairs: v.2, Business writing. New York,

BOOK REVIEWS—*(Continued)*

The Ronald press company. *Journal of accountancy*, Sept. 1920, p. 235.

LEROY-BEAULIEU, PIERRE. United States in the twentieth century. Authorized translation. New York, Funk and Wagnalls co. 1906. *Journal of accountancy*, April 1906, p. 509-510.

LEVY, HERMAN. Steel industry in the Untied States. Berlin, Julius Springer, 1905. 364p. *Journal of accountancy*, April 1906, p. 507-8.

LINCOLN, EDMUND EARLE. Results of municipal electric lighting in Massachusetts. New York and Boston, Houghton, Mifflin company. 484p. *Journal of accountancy*, July 1919, p. 70.

LINCOLN, JONATHAN THAYER. City of the dinner-pail. Boston and New York, Houghton, Mifflin company, 1909. *Journal of accountancy*, Jan. 1911, p. 225-6.

LINDGREN, CHARLES. New salesmanship. Chicago, Laird & Lee. 1909. 190p. *Journal of accountancy*, April 1910, p. 464-5.

LIPPMAN, FREDERICK L. Creating capital. Boston and New York, Houghton, Mifflin company. *Journal of accountancy*, Aug. 1918, p. 158.

LITTLE, ARTHUR S. Annual bond tables; a table of value for bonds, stocks, or notes, having a fixed time to run of one to thirty years and bearing interest payable annually, showing prices at which they will yield 3.5%, 3.6%, 3.7%—6% compounded semi-annually. *Journal of accountancy*, July 1907, p.228-9.

LITTLE, ARTHUR S. Bond values: a table for bonds, notes, etc., running from 1½ months to 20 years and bearing interest at the rate of 4%, 4½%, 5%, and 6%, showing approximate prices at which they will yield 10½%, 11%, 11½% and 20%. St. Louis. *Journal of accountancy*, Sept. 1908, p. 361-2.

LITTLE, ARTHUR S. Odd rate bond value formulae. St. Louis, Author. *Journal of accountancy*, Dec. 1919, p. 476-7.

LOUGH, WILLIAM. Business finance. New York, Ronald press company. *Journal of accountancy*, Aug. 1917, p. 153-5.

LUCE, ROBERT. Writing for the press. Boston, Clipping bureau press. 302p. *Journal of accountancy*, May 1909, p. 412.

LYON, LEVERETT S. Survey of commercial education in the public high schools of the United States. Chicago, University of Chicago press. *Journal of accountancy*, March 1920, p. 239.

LYON, W. H. Capitalization; a book on corporation finance. Boston, Houghton, Mifflin company, 1912. 296p. *Journal of accountancy*, July 1915, p. 86-7.

LYONS, J. A. & CO. Modern accountant. Chicago. *Journal of accountancy*, March 1911, p. 385.

LYONS, J. A. & CO. Wholesale accounting. Chicago. *Journal of accountancy*, June 1911, p. 141-2.

MCCLUNG, ROBERT GARDNER. Theory of debit and credit in accounting. Boston, Morgan, Mills and company, 1913. 16p. *Journal of accountancy*, Jan. 1914, p. 80.

MCINTOSH, ROBERT J. Reference book of accounts for manufacturing and mercantile companies. Ohio, Robert J. McIntosh and company. *Journal of accountancy*, Feb. 1916, p. 158-9

MCPHERSON, LOGAN G. Working of the railroads. New York, Henry Holt and company, 1907. 273p. *Journal of accountancy*, July 1908, p. 214.

MACFARLAND, G. A. and I. D. ROSSHEIM. First year in bookkeeping and accounting. D. Appleton & company, 1913. 224p. *Journal of accountancy*, Jan. 1914, p. 81-2.

MACHEN, ARTHUR W. Federal corporation tax law. Boston, Little, Brown and company, 1910. *Journal of accountancy*, Dec. 1910, p. 148-9.

MACKENZIE, M. A. Interest and bond values. Toronto, University press, 1912. 94 +10p. *Journal of accountancy*, May 1913, p. 396.

MACLEAN, A. H. Insurance agents accounts. London, Gee & co. 1911. *Journal of accountancy*, Aug. 1911, p. 305.

MACQUAID, CRAIG. St. Louis securities; a history and statement of condition of the principal financial institutions, traction and industrial companies of St. Louis. 1906. 107p. *Journal of accountancy*, Dec. 1906, p. 173.

MALONE, FRANK. Malone's mathematical dexterities. 1906. 164p. *Journal of accountancy*, Feb. 1907, p. 317.

MANN AND JUDD. Colliery accounts. London, Gee & co. 107p. *Journal of accountancy*, Oct. 1909, p. 467-8.

MANUAL of statistics; stock exchange hand book. New York, Manual of statistics company. 1907. 1064p. *Journal of accountancy*, Oct. 1907, p. 475.

MARCOSSON, ISAAC F. How to invest savings. Philadelphia, Henry Altemus company, 1907. 120p. *Journal of acccountancy*, Feb. 1908, p. 328.

MASON, B. B., FRANK ROBOTKA and A. V. SWARTHOUT. System of bookkeeping for grain elevators, Bulletin no. 811. United States Department of agriculture. *Journal of accountancy*, March 1920, p. 240.

MEGGISON, F. Bankers' accounts. London, Gee & co. 1908. 114p. *Journal of accountancy*, Sept. 1908, p. 360.

MEYER, CHARLES A. Mercantile credits and collections. New York, Macmillan co. *Journal of accountancy*, Dec. 1919, p. 478.

MEYER, HUGO R. Government regulation of railway rates. New York, Macmillan co. 1905. 486p. *Journal of accountancy*, Dec. 1905, p. 148-9.

MINER AND ELWELL. Principles of bookkeeping. Boston, Ginn and co. 270p. *Journal of accountancy*, June 1918, p. 480.

MONTGOMERY, ROBERT H. Auditing theory and practice. New York, Ronald press company, 1912. 720p. *Journal of accountancy*, Oct. 1912, p. 341-5.

MONTGOMERY, ROBERT H. Auditing theory and practice. New York, Ronald press company, 1916. 900p. *Journal of accountancy*, June 1916, p. 478-80.

MONTGOMERY, ROBERT H. Income tax procedure, 1917. New York, Ronald press company. *Journal of accountancy*, Jan. 1917, p. 157-60.

MONTGOMERY, ROBERT H. Income tax procedure, 1918. New York, The Ronald press company. *Journal of accountancy*, April 1918, p. 157-9.

MONTGOMERY, ROBERT H. Income tax procedure, 1919. New York, The Ronald press company. *Journal of accountancy*, May 1919, p. 395-6.

MONTGOMERY, ROBERT H. Income tax procedure, 1920; Excess profit tax procedure, 1920; a review by Harold Dudley Greeley. 2v. New York, The Ronald press company. *Journal of accountancy*, March, 1920, p. 237-8.

MOODY, JOHN. Part of Wall street investing. New York, The Moody corporation, 1906. 167p. *Journal of accountancy*, June 1906, p. 155.

MOODY, JOHN. How to invest money wisely. New York, John Moody, 1912. 177p. *Journal of accountancy*, Sept. 1913, p. 262-3.

MOORE, J. H. Moore's new commercial arithmetic. American book co. 1907. *Journal of accountancy*, July 1908, p. 215.

MORSE, PERLEY. A. B. C. of the government of the United States. New York, Perley Morse and company. *Journal of accountancy*, Sept. 1916, p. 235.

MOXEY, EDWARD P. Principles of factory cost keeping. New York, The Ronald press co. 1913. 102p. *Journal of accountancy*, June 1914, p. 475.

BOOK REVIEWS—*(Continued)*

MUCKLOW, WALTER. Real estate accounts New York, Ronald press co. *Journal of accountancy,* Dec. 1917, p. 485-7.

MULHALL, JOHN F. J. Quasi-public corporation accounting and management; an exposition of accounting forms and methods for quasi-public corporations. Boston, Corporation publishing co. 1905. *Journal of accountancy,* Sept. 1907, p. 394.

MUNDY, FLOYD W. ed. Earning power of railroads. New York, 1907. *Journal of accountancy,* Aug. 1908, p. 288-9.

MURRAY, ADAM and ROGER N. CARTER. Guide to income tax practice. Ed. 7. London, Gee & company, 1915. *Journal of accountancy,* Sept. 1915, p. 243-4.

NELSON, S. A. Bond buyers' dictionary. New York, S. A. Nelson and company, 1907. 174p. *Journal of accountancy,* Oct. 1907, p. 475.

NELSON, S. A. Consolidated stock exchange of New York. New York, A. B. Benesch company, 1907. *Journal of accountancy,* April 1908, p. 486.

NEW ZEALAND accountants' and auditors' association. Seventh annual report; presented at eighth ordinary meeting, held at Wellington, February 22, 1906. *Journal of accountancy,* Sept. 1906, p. 400.

NICHOLAS, FRANCIS C. Mining investments and how to judge them. New York, Moody's magazine book department, 1907, *Journal of accountancy,* Feb. 1912, p. 152.

NICHOLSON, J. LEE. Factory organization and costs. *Journal of accountancy,* July 1909, p. 222.

NICHOLSON, C. H. Nicholson's three figure method of rapid addition. New York, Author, 1910. *Journal of accountancy,* April 1910, p. 462.

NICHOLSON, J. LEE and J. F. D. ROHRBACH Cost accounting. New York, Ronald press co. *Journal of accountancy,* April 1919, p 318.

NICHOLSON, JOHN. Income tax as applied to persons. *Journal of accountancy,* June 1914, p. 477.

NIXON, ALFRED. Accounting and banking New York, Longmans, Green and company, 1907. 472p. *Journal of accountancy,* Nov. 1908, p. 69-70.

NORTH, S. N. D. ed. American year book. D. Appleton & company, 1911. *Journal of accountancy,* Aug. 1911, p. 305-6.

NORTHCOTT, W. C. ed. Joint transactions of the chartered accountant students' societies, 1909. London, Gee & company, 1910. *Journal of accountancy,* July 1910, p 222-4.

OPDYCKE, JOHN B. English of commerce New York, Charles Scribner's sons company. *Journal of accountancy,* Sept. 1920, p. 237-8

OSBORN, HENRY FAIRFIELD. Age of mammals. New York, Macmillan co. 1910. *Journa of accountancy,* Dec. 1910, p. 147-8.

OSBORN, HERBERT. Economic zoology. New York, The Macmillan co. 1908. 490p. *Journal of accountancy,* June 1909, p. 141-2

OVERLAND, M. V. Classified corporation laws of all states; a manual of statutory corporation law. New York. 458p. *Journal of accountancy,* Jan. 1907, p. 257-8.

PAINE, WILLIS S. Failed savings banks. Ed. 2. New York, The Financier, 1906. 170p. *Journal of accountancy,* June 1906, p. 156.

PARKHURST, FREDERIC A. Predetermination of prices. New York, John Wiley & sons. 104p. *Journal of accountancy,* Sept. 1916, p. 235-7.

PARSONS, CARL C. Business administration Chicago, System company, 1909. *Journa of accountancy,* May 1910, p. 64-5.

PARSONS, HENRY GRISCOM. Children's gardens for pleasure, health and education. New York, Sturgis & Walton co. 1910. *Journal of accountancy,* Sept. 1911, p. 387.

PARSONS, THEOPHILUS. Laws of business; with forms and directions for all transactions and abstracts of the laws of all the states and territories on various topics. New revised edition. Hartford, S. S. Scranton co. New York. The accountancy publishing company, 1906. 867p. *Journal of accountancy,* June 1906, p. 155-6.

PATON, WM. ANDREW and RUSSELL ALGER STEVENSON. Principles of accounting. New York, Macmillan company. 685p. *Journal of accountancy,* July 1919, p. 71-2.

PAXSON, FREDERICK LOGAN. Last American frontier. Macmillan company, 1910. *Journal of accountancy,* July 1911, p. 218-9.

PEARN, SINCLAIR and FRANK PEARN. Workshop costs, engineers and manufacturers. Ed. 2. Manchester, England, Technical publishing co. 1905. *Journal of accountancy,* Aug. 1911, p. 306-9.

PENNSYLVANIA STATE BOARD OF EXAMINERS OF PUBLIC ACCOUNTANTS. Examination questions, 1899 to 1907. Philadelphia, 1908. 158p. *Journal of accountancy,* June 1908, p. 138.

PERRIGO, OSCAR F. Modern machine shop, construction equipment and management. New York, Norman W. Henley publishing co. 1906. *Journal of accountancy,* May 1911, p. 75-6.

PERSON, HARLOW STAFFORD. Industrial education; a system of training for men entering upon trade and commerce. Boston and New York, Houghton, Mifflin & co. 1907. 86p. *Journal of accountancy,* Nov. 1907, p. 70-1.

PIXLEY, FRANCIS W. Accountancy. London, 1908. 311p. *Journal of accountancy,* Sept. 1908, p. 359-60.

PIXLEY, FRANCIS W. How to read the balance sheet of a commercial concern. Ed. 3. London, Gee & company. *Journal of accountancy,* Aug. 1911, p. 305.

PIXLEY, FRANCIS W. How to read the balance sheet of a commercial concern. Ed. 3, London, Gee & company, 1913. 64p. *Journal of accountancy,* Aug. 1913, p. 168.

PLAYER, PRESTON. Hydro-electric developments. New York, McGraw publishing company, 1908. *Journal of accountancy,* Jan. 1910, p. 230.

PLEHN, CARL C. Government finance in the United States. Chicago, A. C. McClurg and company, 1915. *Journal of accountancy,* Dec. 1915, p. 478-9.

POCKET tax law for business men. New York, New York tax reform association, 1906. 32p. *Journal of accountancy,* Feb. 1907, p. 317.

PRENDERGAST, WILLIAM. Credit and its uses. New York, D. Appleton & company, 1906. 361p. *Journal of accountancy,* Jan. 1907, p. 256-7.

PRINDLE, EDWIN J. Patents as a factor in manufacturing. New York. *Engineering magazine,* 1908. 134p. *Journal of accountancy,* April 1909, p. 489-90.

PROCEEDINGS of Minnesota educational association, 1908. 336p. *Journal of accountancy,* Aug. 1908, p. 287.

RACINE, SAMUEL F. Guide to the study of auditing. Seattle, Washington, The western institute of accountancy, commerce and finance. 1914. 63p. *Journal of accountancy,* June 1914, p. 477.

RAHILL, J. J. Corporation accountancy and corporation law of corporate organization and management, accounting in theory and practice. Fresno, California, 1906. *Journal of accountancy,* Sept. 1906, p. 395-7.

RANKING, E. F. DEL'HOSTE, E. E. SPICER AND E. C. PEGLER. Partnership law. London, H. Foulks Lynch and company, 1911. *Journal of accountancy,* Aug. 1911, p. 304-5.

RAYMOND, WILLIAM G. What is fair? New York, John Wiley and sons, inc. *Journal of accountancy,* June 1918, p. 479-80.

BOOK REVIEWS—*(Continued)*

RENN, GEORGE B. Practical auditing: a working manual for auditors. Chicago, New York, Accountancy publishing co. 1906. 31p. *Journal of accountancy*, Feb. 1906, p. 335.

RENN, GEORGE B. Practical auditing: a working manual for auditors. Ed. 2. Chicago, Ill., 1907. *Journal of accountancy*, Jan. 1908, p. 254.

REPORT of the auditor for the Philippine Islands. 1914. *Journal of accountancy*, Feb. 1916, p. 159-60.

RICHARDSON, A. P. ed. Influence of accountants' certificates on commercial credit. American association of public accountants, 1913. 99p. *Journal of accountancy*, Sept. 1913, p. 260-2.

RIPLEY, WILLIAM Z. Railway problems. New York. 686p. *Journal of accountancy*, July 1907, p. 229.

RIPLEY, WILLIAM Z. "Trusts, pools and corporations." Boston, Ginn & co. 1905. 473p. *Journal of accountancy*, Dec. 1905, p. 149-51.

RISQUE, F. W. Loose leaf books and systems for general business. St. Louis, R. P. Studley & co. 1907. *Journal of accountancy*, Oct. 1907, p. 476.

RITTENHOUSE, CHARLES F. New modern illustrative bookkeeping. New York, American book company. 152p. *Journal of accountancy*, May 1919, p. 397.

RITTENHOUSE, CHARLES F. New modern illustrative bookkeeping, introductory course. New York, American book company. 152p. *Journal of accountancy*, Oct. 1919, p. 315-6.

ROLLINS, MONTGOMERY. 5½% bond values. Boston, Mass., Author. 1911. *Journal of accountancy*, Jan. 1912, p. 71-2.

ROLLINS, MONTGOMERY. Money and investments; a reference book for the use of those desiring information in the handling of money or the investment thereof. Boston, Dana Estes and company, London, Gay & Bird, 1907. 436p. *Journal of accountancy*, Jan. 1908, p. 254-5.

ROLLINS, MONTGOMERY. Tables of bond values. Ed. 19. Boston, Mass., The financial publishing co. 1912. *Journal of accountancy*, Dec. 1912, p. 504.

ROWE, L. S. Problems of city government. New York, D. Appleton & co. 1908. *Journal of accountancy*, Nov. 1909, p. 58-9.

RUSTON, JOHN E. Decedents' estates. New York, Erle Whitfield, 1910. *Journal of accountancy*, Feb. 1911, p. 304.

SALIERS, EARL A. Accounts in theory and practice. New York, McGraw-Hill book company. 300p. *Journal of accountancy*, Dec. 1920, p. 471-2.

SCHOCH, PRKE and MURRAY GROSS. Elements of business. New York, American book company. 216p. *Journal of accountancy*, May 1919, p. 397-8.

SCHREFFLER, ROBERT B. Department store statistics with the aid of the slide rule. Chicago, Author. 1915. *Journal of accountancy*, March 1916, p. 239.

SCHULZE, J. WILLIAM. Office administration. New York, McGraw-Hill book company. 295p. *Journal of accountancy*, June 1919, p. 478.

SCOVELL, CLINTON H. Cost accounting and burden application. New York, D. Appleton and company, 1916. *Journal of accountancy*, May 1917, p. 399-400.

SCOVILLE, HIRAM T. Farm accounting. New York, D. Appleton and co. 430p. *Journal of accountancy*, June 1918, p. 479.

SECRIST, HORACE. Introduction to statistical methods. New York, The Macmillan company. *Journal of accountancy*, Sept. 1918, p. 238.

SECRIST, HORACE. Statistics in business. New York, McGraw-Hill book company. *Journal of accountancy*, Dec. 1920, p. 476.

SELIGMAN, EDWIN R. A. Income tax. New York, The Macmillan co. 1911. *Journal of accountancy*, Dec. 1911, p. 624-5.

SELIGMAN, EDWIN R. A. Principles of economics; with special reference to American conditions. New York, Longmans, Green & co. 1905. *Journal of accountancy*, Sept. 1906, p. 397-9.

SEVENTH annual report. New Zealand accountants' and auditors association. Presented at eighth ordinary meeting held at Wellington, Feb. 22, 1906. *Journal of accountancy*, Sept. 1906, p. 400.

SIMONS, CHARLES C. Commercial law simplified. Detroit, Business man's publishing company. 508p. *Journal of accountancy*, Sept. 1909, p. 386.

SKINNER, E. B. Mathematical theory of investment. Boston, Ginn & co. 1913. 245p. *Journal of accountancy*, July 1914, p. 84.

SKINNER, E. N. AND H. R. PLATE. Mining costs of the world. McGraw-Hill book company. *Journal of accountancy*, Aug. 1915, p. 161.

SLIPPY, J. C. Telephone appraisal practice. Pittsburgh, 1915. *Journal of accountancy*, Dec. 1915, p. 475-6.

SMITH, J. RUSSELL. Ocean carrier. New York, G. P. Putnam's sons and company. *Railroad age gazette*, 1908. 344p. *Journal of accountancy*, March 1909, p. 410-1.

SMITH, ROLLIN E. Wheat fields and markets of the world. St. Louis, Modern Miller co. 1908. *Journal of accountancy*, May 1910, p. 61-3.

SNYDER, CARL. American railways as investments; a detailed and comparative analysis of all the leading railways, from the investor's point of view; with an introductory chapter on the methods of estimating railway values. New York, Moody corporation. *Journal of accountancy*, Sept. 1907, p. 395-8.

SPARGO, JOHN. Social democracy explained. New York, Harper and brothers. *Journal of accountancy*, July 1918, p. 78-9.

SPARGO, JOHN. Spiritual significance of modern socialism. New York, B. W. Huebsh, 1908. *Journal of accountancy*, Jan. 1909, p. 246-7.

SPARLING, SAMUEL E. Introduction to business organization. New York, The Macmillan co. 1906. 374p. *Journal of accountancy*, July 1907, p. 230.

SPENCER, EDWARD W. Manual of commercial law. Indianapolis, Bobbs Merrill company. 685p. *Journal of accountancy*, Dec. 1912, p. 504.

SPICER, ERNEST EVAN. Accounts of an executor. London, H. Foulks Lynch & co. *Journal of accountancy*, April 1916, p. 319.

SPICER, ERNEST EVAN. Bookkeeping and accounts. London, H. Foulks Lynch & co. 1908. 399p. *Journal of accountancy*, March 1909, p. 409-10.

SPICER, ERNEST EVAN. Dissolution, amalgamation and reconstruction accounts. Ed. 2. London, H. Foulks Lynch & co. *Journal of accountancy*, April 1916, p. 319.

SPICER, ERNEST E. Divisible profits and dividends. London, H. Foulks Lynch and company, 1912. *Journal of accountancy*, July 1912, p. 64.

SPICER, ERNEST E. Exportation of British capital. London, Gee & co. 1912. *Journal of accountancy*, July 1912, p. 64.

SPICER, E. E. AND E. C. PEGLER. Audit programmes. London, H. Foulks Lynch & co. 1910. *Journal of accountancy*, Feb. 1911, p. 305-6.

SPICER, ERNEST E. and E. C. PEGLER. De mortuis nil nisis bona. London, H. Foulks. Lynch and co. 1914. *Journal of accountancy*, June 1914, p. 476-7.

SPRAGUE, CHARLES E. Accountancy of investment: including a treatise on compound interest, annuities, amortization, and the valuation of securities. New York, New

BOOK REVIEWS—*(Continued)*

York university school of commerce, accounts and finance. 1905. *Journal of accountancy,* Nov. 1905, p. 66-7.

SPRAGUE, CHARLES E. Amortization. New York, 1908. 22p. *Journal of accountancy,* Aug. 1909, p. 308-9.

SPRAGUE, CHARLES E. Extended bond tables. New York, 1905. *Journal of accountancy,* Nov. 1905, p. 67.

SPRAGUE, CHARLES E. Exetended bond tables. Ed. 4. New York, Ronald press company, 1915. *Journal of accountancy,* Dec. 1915, p. 475.

SPRAGUE, CHARLES E. Philosophy of accounts. New York, Author, 1908. 161p. *Journal of accountancy,* Nov. 1908, p. 67-9.

SPRAGUE, CHARLES E. Problems and studies in the accountancy of investment. New York, 1906. 64p. *Journal of accountancy,* Sept. 1906, p. 395.

SPRAGUE, CHARLES E. Table of factors for computing twelve-place logarithms. *Journal of accountancy,* July 1909, p. 221.

SPRAGUE, CHARLES E. Tables of compound interest, discount, annuities, sinking funds and other computations. Part 3 of The accountancy of investment. New York. 1907. 32p. *Journal of accountancy,* Feb. 1907, p. 317.

SPRAGUE, CHARLES E. Twelve-place logarithms and their use in interest calculations. *Journal of accountancy,* June 1910, p. 139-41.

SPRINGER, DURAND W. Michigan C. P. A. manual. Ann Arbor, Michigan state board of accountancy, 1915. *Journal of accountancy,* March 1916, p. 239.

STAUB, WALTER A. Income tax guide. New York, Lybrand, Ross bros. and Montgomery, 1913. *Journal of accountancy,* Jan. 1914, p. 81.

STEPANEK, W. H. Business methods in a hardware store. Cedar Rapids, Iowa, Author, 1908. *Journal of accountancy,* Feb. 1911, p. 308.

STEVENS, HORACE J. Copper hand book, v. 10. Houghton, Mich., Horace J. Stevens. 1911. *Journal of accountancy,* Feb. 1912. p. 152-3.

STEWART, R. S. and F. C. EBBELS. Rubber companies accounts. London, Gee and co. *Journal of accountancy,* July 1917, p. 479-80.

STRACHAN, W. Cost accounts. Ed. 3, with appendix of forms. London, Stevens and Haynes. 110p. *Journal of accountancy,* Oct. 1909, p. 466-7.

STRAYER, PAUL MOORE. Reconstruction of the church. New York, Macmillan co. 1915. *Journal of accountancy,* Dec. 1915, p. 477-8.

STRYKER, H. M. Advertisers hand book. Chicago, Trade journal advertiser, 1909. *Journal of accountancy,* April 1910, p. 463-4.

SUFFERN & SON. Railroad operating costs. New York. 82p. *Journal of accountancy,* May 1912, p. 386-7.

SULLIVAN, JOHN J. American business law. New York and London, D. Appleton and co. 1909. *Journal of accountancy,* Nov. 1909, p. 57.

SULLIVAN, JOHN J. Pennsylvania business law; a practical handbook for business men and lawyers. New York, Accountancy publishing co. 700p. *Journal of accountancy,* Oct. 1906, p. 478-80.

TAINTER, C. W. Analysis earnings, United States steel corporation. Boston, Author, 1909. *Journal of accountancy,* April 1911. p. 462.

TAUSSIG, F. W. Inventors and money-makers. New York, Macmillan company, 1915. *Journal of accountancy,* Dec. 1915, p. 478.

TAYLOR, FREDERICK WINSLOW. Principles of scientific management. New York, Harper and brothers, 1911. *Journal of accountancy,* May 1912, p. 385-6.

THORNE, WILLIAM V. S. Hospital accounting and statistics. New York, E. P. Dutton and company. *Journal of accountancy,* July 1919, p. 70-1.

THORNE, WILLIAM V. S. Hospital accounting and statistics. New York, E. P. Dutton and company. *Journal of accountancy,* Jan. 1917, p. 80.

THORNTON, FRANK W. Brewery accounts. New York, Ronald press co. 1913. *Journal of accountancy,* April 1916, p. 318-9.

TREAT, PAYSON JACKSON. National land system, 1785-1820. New York, E. B. Treat & co. 1910. *Journal of accountancy,* Dec. 1911, p. 625-6.

TWYFORD, H. B. Storing, its economic aspects and proper methods. New York, D. Van Nostrand company. *Journal of accountancy,* May 1919, p. 398-9.

U. S. reclamation service manual. vol. 2, accounting. *Journal of accountancy,* April 1919, p. 319-20.

UNCKLESS, LESLIE. How to find manufacturing costs and selling costs. Detroit, Mich., Modern methods, 1909. *Journal of accountancy,* Aug. 1911, p. 309-10.

UNITED STATES. Bureau of the census. Census statistics of cities: statistics of cities having a population of over 30,000, 1905. Washington, D. C., Department of commerce and labor. 372p. *Journal of accountancy,* April 1908, p. 484-5.

UNITED STATES MORTGAGE AND TRUST COMPANY. Trust companies of the United States. *Journal of accountancy,* Feb. 1911, p. 304-5.

VAN CLEVE, CHARLES M. Principles by double-entry bookkeeping. New York, Author, 1913, 210p. *Journal of accountancy,* Aug. 1913, p. 163-4.

VAN CLEVE, CHARLES M. Theory of double entry bookkeeping. New York, 1907, 59p. *Journal of accountancy,* May 1908, p. 69.

VAN DE LINDE, GERARD. Reminiscences. London, Gee & co. *Journal of accountancy,* Aug. 1918, p. 160.

VANDERLIP, FRANK A. Business and education. New York. Duffield and company 1907. 563p. *Journal of accountancy,* June 1907, p. 151-2.

VAN DEVENTER, J. H. Machine shop management. McGraw-Hill book co. *Journal of accountancy,* July 1915, p. 74-5.

VINAL, EUGENE R. Mathematics for the accountant. New York, The Biddle publishing company. 175p. *Journal of accountancy,* Dec. 1920, p. 472-3.

WALBANK, JOHN A. Builders' accounts. Ed. 3. London, Gee & co. 1913. 96p. *Journal of accountancy,* May 1913, p. 395.

WALLACE, DAVID. Simple mine accounting. New York, Hill publishing co. 1908. 63p. *Journal of accountancy,* June 1908, p. 138.

WARD, ROBERT DECOURCY. Climate. New York, G. P. Putnam's sons, 1908. *Journal of accountancy,* June 1908, p. 137.

WARNE, FRANK JULIAN. Coal mine workers: a study in labor orgainzation. New York, Longmans, Green & co., 1905. *Journal of accountancy,* Feb. 1906, p. 334-5.

WARREN, WALDO PONDRAY. Thoughts on business. Chicago, Forbes and co. 1907. 237p. *Journal of accountancy,* Nov. 1907, p. 71.

WEBB, WALTER LORING. Economics of railroad construction. New York, John Wiley and sons, 1906. 339p. *Journal of accountancy,* June 1907, p. 152.

WEBB'S comparisons simplified, or How to select the best life insurance company; a book of comparisons compiled from sworn statements to the insurance departments. January 1, 1906. 147p. *Journal of accountancy,* Dec. 1906, p. 171.

WEBNER, FRANK E. Factory costs. New York, Ronald press co. 611p. *Journal of accountancy,* Jan. 1912, p. 68-70.

WEISS, W. F. Public accountant: a vital factor in management and control of business and affairs. New York, 1905. *Journal of accountancy,* Feb. 1906, p. 334.

BOOK REVIEWS—*(Continued)*

WELLS, H. G. Future in America. Harpers. 1906. 259p. *Journal of accountancy,* Jan. 1908, p. 255-6.

WHATLEY, G. E. STUART. Accountants' and bookkeepers' vade-mecum. Ed. 2, by Roger N. Carter. London, Gee & co. 1913. 224p. *Journal of accountancy,* Aug. 1913, p. 167-8.

WHEELER, G. W. Bookkeeping for beginners. London, Gee & co. 1912. 39p. *Journal of accountancy,* Sept. 1912, p. 239.

WHITTEN, ROBERT H. Valuation of public service corporations. New York, The Banks law publishing co. 1912. 798p. *Journal of accountancy,* Aug. 1912, p. 151-2.

WILDMAN, JOHN RAYMOND. Principles of auditing. New York, William G. Hewitt press. *Journal of accountancy,* July 1916, p. 70-1.

WILLS, H. P. Our Philippine problem; a study of American colonial policy. New York, Henry Holt & co. 1905. 479p. *Journal of accountancy,* March 1906, p. 421-2.

WILSON, L. C. Corrosion of iron. New York, Engineering magazine co. 1915. *Journal of accountancy,* Dec. 1915, p. 478.

WITT, HAROLD TANSLEY. Club accounts and their control. London, Gee & co. 1913. *Journal of accountancy,* Jan. 1914, p. 80.

WOOD, WILLIAM ALLEN. Modern business corporations. Indianapolis, The Bobbs-Merrill co. 1906. 358p. *Journal of accountancy,* March 1907, p. 405.

WOODS, CLINTON E. Unified accounting methods for industrials. New York, The Ronald press company. *Journal of accountancy,* July 1917, p. 478-9.

WOODSON, E. R. ed. R. A. O. A. nineteen-twenty synopsis. Washington, Railway accounting officers' association. *Journal of accountancy,* Dec. 1920, p. 477.

WOOLF, A. H. Stock exchange past and present. London, Gee & co. 121p. *Journal of accountancy,* June 1914, p. 475.

WOOLF, C. H. Short history of accountants and accountancy. London, Gee & co. 1912. 284p. *Journal of accountancy,* April 1913, p. 311.

YOUNG, T. E. Insurance; a practical exposition for students and business men. Revised ed. New York, Sir Isaac Pitman & sons, 1907. 146p. *Journal of accountancy,* April 1908, p. 485.

ZARTMAN, LESTER W. Investments of life insurance companies. New York, Henry Holt & co. 1906. *Journal of accountancy,* March 1907, p. 403-4.

BOOK TRADE

Cost accounting

MULLIN, WILLIAM J. How my business got well. *System,* May 1918, p. 740.

STOBBS, JOHN W. Cost keeping in the book trade. *Accountant,* Sept. 1, 1917, p. 157-8, 167-8.

BOOKBINDING

Costs

COST of pamphlet binding. *Inland printer,* Feb. 1914, p. 740-1.

DANIELS, B. Cost of folding. *Inland printer,* Oct. 1914, p. 93-4.

DANIELS, B. Little study in binding prices. *Inland printer,* May 1916, p. 235.

HUGHMARK, A. H. Bookbinding labor-cost. *Inland printer,* Sept. 1915, p. 805-8.

PORTE, R. T. Costs of bindery operations. *Inland printer,* Jan.-Dec. 1918, p. 474-6, 617-20, 746-9; 36-9, 173-6, 313-5, 447-9, 586-9, 707-9; 47-8, 196-7, 295-6.

BOOKKEEPER and accountant civil service examination instruction. Wolff, Mark. 1918.

BOOKKEEPER as a human being. *World's work,* June 1905, v. 10, p. 6324-6.

BOOKKEEPERS.

See Accountants.

BOOK-KEEPERS and commercial law. Barratt, N. S. 1913.

BOOKKEEPERS and mechanical appliances. *Accounting and commerce,* Feb. 1920, p. 256-7.

BOOK-KEEPER'S assistant. (In *Fisher's ten cent hand-books*). New York, A. J. Fisher.

BOOKKEEPER'S companion. Lyle, T. A. 1881.

BOOK-KEEPER'S companion. Webber, H. J. 1897.

BOOKKEEPER'S compendium. Robertson, P. W.

BOOKKEEPER'S guide. Cowan, T. W. 1885.

BOOKKEEPER'S handbook. International correspondence schools. 1910.

BOOKKEEPING.

See also Accounting: various headings: e. g. Balance sheets; also subdivision Accounting under various headings, e. g. Gas-Accounting.

ABOLITION of the trial balance together with twelve studies in book-keeping and accounting. Detroit, Michigan, The Book-keeper publishing company, c1906. 168p.

ACCOUNTANTS guide and commercial instructor. London, Hall 1844.

ACCOUNTANTS: their duties and responsibilities: book-keeping articles. *Accountant,* Aug. 5, 12, 19, 26, Sept. 2, 9, 16, 23, 30, Oct. 14, 21, 28, Nov. 4, 11, 18, 25, Dec. 2, 9, 16, 23, 30, 1882.

ACCOUNTING and office methods; organizing the office, accounting principles and systems, office work and record keeping. Chicago, A. W. Shaw co. 1914. 200p. (Students' business book series). Also issued as v.9 of the Library of business practice.

ADAMS, WILLIAM. Bookkeeping. New York, Collins & brother.

ADGIE, WILLIAM. Modern book-keeping and accounts. in 3 parts; part 1 elementary; part 2, intermediate; part 3, advanced. 3 vols. London The Macmillan co. 1901-2.

——— Same. Ed. 2. London, 1904. 378p.

——— Same. 3v. London, 1912.

ADVANCED bookkeeping and accounts. *Canadian chartered accountant,* Oct. 1914, p. 148-54.

ADVANCED bookkeeping and banking. New York, American book company.

ALDRIDGE, E. H. MOORING. Easy method of keeping rent and interest accounts. London, 1899.

ALL about bookkeeping. London, Ward, Lock & co. 1877-78.

ALLEN, GEORGE. Science of accounts made clear and simple. Raleigh, N. C., George Allen, 1909.

——— Same. High school ed. Raleigh, N. C., George Allen, 1909.

ANSWERS to additional exercises in book-keeping. London, Sir Isaac Pitman & sons, 1912. 54p.

ARCH, W. H. Bookkeeping in verse. London, Effingham Wilson, 1914.

AREVALO, ALBERTO AND HIRAM G. GALOGERO. La partida doble pro el metodo logismográfico. Buenos Aires, Cabaut and cia, 1918. 97p.

BOOKKEEPING—*(Continued)*

ARMSTRONG, AUGUSTUS. Double entry bookkeeping up to date. New York, Armstrong & co. 1915. 64p.

ATKIN, FRANCIS. Book-keeping made easy: or, How to open a set of books by double entry. London, [? 1886].

BAKER, JAMES WILLIAM. Reference book: 20th century bookkeeping and office practice. Ed. 7. Knoxville, Tenn., Southwestern publishing co. 1909.

BAKER, JAMES W. 20th century bookkeeping and accounting; a treatise on modern bookkeeping, accounting and business customs as illustrated in the "Business transactions" which accompany this work; the only system of bookkeeping in which the transaction, as well as the business papers that illustrate them, are identical with those in the business world; for use in all schools that teach bookkeeping and accounting. Cincinnati, Southwestern publishing company, 1912. 304p.

——— Same. Ed. 10. Cincinnati. Southwestern publishing co. 1920. 308p.

BAKER, W. C. M. 1878. Labor-saving system of accounts. Columbus, W. C. M. Baker.

BALDWIN REGISTER COMPANY. Principles of the Baldwin automatic business register. Berea, O., Baldwin register co. 1917. 22, 10p.

BARDEEN, CHARLES WILLIAM. Dime and question books of bookkeeping. Syracuse, C. W. Bardeen, 1888.

BARNES, J. R. AND ALEXANDER SHARPLES. Book-keeping for commercial classes: elementary. London. Macmillan & co. 1914. 242p.

BARNES, J. R. and ALEXANDER SHARPLES. Elementary bookkeeping for commercial classes. London, Macmillan & co. 228p.

BARNES, J. R. and ALEXANDER SHARPLES. Key to the exercises in book-keeping for commercial classes. London, Macmillan & co. 1916.

BARNES, R. Y. Abridged edition of the new improved universal system of book-keeping, etc. London, 1869.

——— Same. Another ed. London, 1872.

BARNES, R. Y. New and improved universal system of book-keeping. Ed. 3. London, 1871.

——— Same. London, 1872.
——— Same. London, 1874.
——— Same. London, 1875.
——— Same. London, 1877.

BARRATT, NORRIS STANLEY. Book-keepers and commercial law; address, May 12, 1913, before the Book-keepers' beneficial association of Philadelphia. Philadelphia, 1913. 24p.

BARTER, JOHN. How to learn bookkeeping without a master. London, Simpkin, Marshall, Hamilton, Kent & co. 1899. 32p.

BARTHOLOMEW, WALLACE EDGAR. Bookkeeping exercises. 2v. New York, Gregg publishing co. c1919

BARTON, T. S. Accountants' ready reckoner. London, Simpkin, Marshall, Hamilton, Kent & co. 1868.

BATCHELDER, JACOB. National accountant. Boston, Jewett & co.

BATTERSBY, THOMAS. Perfect double entry book-keeper (abridged) and the perfect prime cost and profit demonstrator for iron and brass founders, machinists, engineers, shipbuilders, manufacturers, etc. 1878. Manchester, 1878.

BEAVIS and Jack's bookkeeping. London, Houlston & sons, 1871.

BECKER, GEORGE J. System of bookkeeping. Philadelphia, E. H. Butler & co.

BEDFORD, EDWARD HENSLOWE. Intermediate [solicitors'] examination guide to book-keeping; the examination questions with the answers. Ed.2. London, Stevens & sons, 1875.

BELL, G. Examination bookkeeping. Edinburgh, W. & R. Chambers, 1889.

BELL, JOHN. Chamber's examination bookkeeping, with civil service and other papers fully solved. London and Edinburgh, W. & R. Chambers, 1908.

BELL, ROBERT R. Commercial book-keeping simplified for beginners. London, Simpkins, Marshall, Hamilton, Kent & co. 1918.

BENDER, GEORGE DEWITT. Accounting and business secrets; a ready reference book of accounting principles, forms, charts, rules, tables, outlines and other information for business men, executives, office managers, accountants, bookkeepers and clerks. Seattle, G. D. Bender, 1919. 64p.

BENNETT, JAMES. American system of bookkeeping adopted to the commerce of the United States and its domestic and foreign relations. . . New York, A. Paul, 1820.

——— Same. Ed. 12. New York, Collins & Hanway, 1829.

BENNETT, JAMES ARLINGTON. American system of practical book-keeping adapted to the commerce of the United States in its domestic and foreign relations, comprehending all the modern improvements in the practical art and exemplified in one set of books kept by double entry; embracing five different methods of keeping a journal, designed for the use of schools, academies and counting houses, to which are added forms of the most approved auxiliary books with a chart exhibiting at one view the final balance of the leger and blanks for practice. Ed.31. New York, Ivison & Phinney, 1855. 160p.

BENNETT, ROBERT JOSEPH. Bookkeeping and accounting exercises. 2v. New York, American book co. 1912. 96 + 112p.

BENNETT, ROBERT JOSEPH. Key to Bookkeeping and accounting exercises. 2v. New York, American book co. 1912.

BENTON, CHARLES WILLIAM. Practical bookkeeping. Valparaiso, Ind., M. E. Bogarte book co. 1910. 222p.

BERNARD, GEORGE. Line and column system of bookkeeping [by] double entry, etc. Manchester, 1894.

BERNHARDT, MARTIN. Date number index system and bill book; showing bills received and bills paid, with several new features, combining a new system of indexing the bills and stock and simplifying bookkeeping. New Brighton, N. Y., M. Bernhardt, 1916. 10p.

BEXELL, JOHN ANDREW and FREDERICK GEORGE NICHOLS. Principles of bookkeeping and farm accounts. Chicago, American book co. 1913. 184p.

BEXELL, JOHN ANDREW and FREDERICK GEORGE NICHOLAS. Teacher's reference book to accompany Principles of bookkeeping and farm accounts. Chicago, American book co. 1914. 104p.

BICKERSTAFF, H. Dictionary of bookkeeping: terms and definitions. Percival, 1890.

BISHOP, WILLIAM GEORGE. Short course in business training for normal schools, high schools, common schools, teachers and independent students. Lincoln, Nebraska, University publishing co. 1911.

BISHOP, WILLIAM GEORGE and EDWARD CLARENCE BIGGER. Introductory bookkeeping and business practice. Ed. 3, revised. Lincoln, Nebraska, Lincoln business college, 1910. 168p.

BLISS, F. H. Bliss system of bookkeeping and office practice; handbook. Saginaw, Mich., F. H. Bliss co. 1912. 154p.

BOOKKEEPING—*(Continued)*

BOARDMAN, W. System of book-keeping. 1802.

BOGLE, ARTEMAS MELVIN. Comprehensive bookkeeping. New York, The Macmillan co. 1905.

BOGLE, ARTEMAS MELVIN. Everyday bookkeeping. New York. The Macmillan co. 1917. 126p.

BOGLE, ARTEMUS MELVIN. Teachers manual to accompany Comprehensive bookkeeping. New York, The Macmillan co. 1908.

BOGLE, JOHN DOUGLAS STEWART and J. H. ATTFIELD. M'Dougall's bookkeeping for elementary schools. London and Edinburgh, 1895-6.

BOOKKEEPER as a human being. *World's work*, June 1905, v.10, p. 6324-6.

BOOK-KEEPER'S assistant. (In *Fisher's ten cent hand-books.* New York, A. J. Fisher.)

BOOKKEEPING. London, Cassell & co. 1860.

BOOKKEEPING; an elementary treatise. Browne & Nolan.

BOOKKEEPING and business practice: complete course. New York, American book company.

BOOKKEEPING and business practice: introductory course. New York, American book company.

BOOKKEEPING by single entry. Scratchard, 1817.

BOOK-KEEPING (elementary) by double entry for evening continuation schools (elementary stage), and day schools (specific subject—two stages). London, Simpkins, 1898. 112p. (Waddington & Jackman series).

BOOKKEEPING for every business. Kent. 1865.

BOOK-KEEPING made easy. New York, Hurst & co.

BOOKKEEPING manual for booksellers and publishers. London, Simpkin, Marshall, Hamilton, Kent & co. 1849.

BOOKKEEPING terms and definitions. Rivingtons.

BOOKEEPING transactions. London, W. & R. Chambers.

BOOKKEEPING, with some chapters on business usages, by "Hugh" [? 1897].

BOOKKEEPING without ledgers. *Accountant*, Jan. 11, 1919, p. 17-9.

BOOKMAN, CLARENCE MONROE and F. S. BLUE. First steps in bookkeeping; a practical introduction to bookkeeping, containing an abundance of drill work in arithmetic, arranged to accompany Bookman's Business arithmetic or any other modern arithmetic in eighth or ninth grade work. 806 Neave bldg., Cincinnati, Ohio, C. M. Bookman, 1917. 86p.

BOOTH, BENJAMIN. Complete system of bookkeeping by an improved mode of double entry, etc. London, 1789.

BOOTH, W. E. On accounts. *Public accountant*, 1904-5, p. 90; 1906-7, p. 22.

BOULTER, G. H. Course of bookkeeping by double and single entry. London, Simpkin, Marshall, Hamilton, Kent & Co. 1860.

BOULTER, GEORGE H. Principles of balancing, by single and double entry, including partnerships by each method. Ed.3. London, [? circa 1860].

BRACKENBURY, BEATRICE. Book-keeping for beginners. London, Longmans-Greene & co. 1908. 142p.

BRAMWELL, JOHN. Sectional double-entry bookkeeping; an illustrative treatise on the fundamental principles, designed for home study, class work or text reference; complete in fifteen portfolio sections. 407 4th avenue, New York, O. H. Labarre, 1913.

BREWER, E. C. Bookkeeping by single or double entry. London, Jarrold and sons.

BREWER, E. C. Entire systsem of book-keeping by double entry. London, Jarrold & sons, 1850.

BREWER, E. C. Entire new system of book-keeping by single entry. London, Simpkin, Marshall, Hamilton, Kent & co. 1846.

——— Same. Ed. 10. London, ?1869.

——— Same. Ed. 12. London, Jarrold & sons London, ?1885.

BREWER, E. C. Key to entire new system of bookkeeping by single entry. Ed. 7. London, 1857.

BRIERLY, JOHN THOMAS. Bookkeeping at a glance, or, How to become an expert bookkeeper. New York, Excelsior publishing house, 1893.

BRIERLY, JOHN THOMAS. Book-keeping at a glance; a simple and concise method of practical book-keeping. New York, Nourse co. 1920. 135p.

BROADBRIDGE ——— Alphabetical double entry bookkeeping. London, Simpkin, Marshall, Hamilton, Kent & co. 1883.

BROCKLEHURST, G. R. Bookkeeping for bakers, grocers, drapers, dairymen, butchers, co-operative societies, etc. Gainsborough, 1892.

BRODIE, ALEXANDER. New and easy method of book-keeping. London, 1722.

BROWN, D. J. A. First guide to elementary practical book-keeping; ed. by Jenkins. London, Longmans, Green & co. 1899. 66p.

BROWN, IRA SMITH. Typewriter bookkeeping. New York, Underwood typewriter co. 1909. gratis.

BROWN, THOMAS and VINCENT E. COLLINGE. Arithmetic and bookkeeping. pt. 1. London, Sir Isaac Pitman & sons, 1916. 117p.

BROWNE, T. R. First bookkeeping course. Brooklyn, Browne's Brooklyn business college, 1900.

BRYANT, HENRY BENJAMIN and H. D. STRATTON. Common school bookkeeping. New York, American book co.

BRYANT, HENRY BENJAMIN and H. D. STRATTON. National book-keeper. New York. Ivison, Phiny & co.

BRYANT, HENRY B. and H. D. STRATTON. New counting-house book-keeping. New York. Ivison, Bakeman, Taylor & co. 1879.

BRYANT, HENRY BENJAMIN AND H. D. STRATTON. New high school bookkeeping. New York, American book co.

BRYANT, HENRY BENJAMIN, H. D. STRATTON and S. S. PACKARD. Bryant & Stratton's counting-house bookkeeping. New York. Ivison, Plinney, Blakeman & co., 1861, 1863, 1866. 375p.

BRYANT, HENRY BENJAMIN, H. D. STRATTON and S. S. PACKARD. High school book-keeping. New York, Ivison, Blakeman, Taylor & co. 1860.

BRYANT, HENRY W. Practical bookkeeping. Chicago, Bryant and Stratton business college, 1907, 1910.

BRYANT, JOHN C. Bryant's bookkeeping: a treatise on the science of accounts, elementary and practical. Ed. 5. Buffalo, J. C. Bryant, 1877.

BRYANT, JOHN C. Commercial bookkeeping. New York, W. C. Bryant & co. 1885.

BRYANT, JOHN C. Common school book-keeping. New York, W. C. Bryant & co. 1885.

BRYANT, JOHN C. Counting-house book-keeping. New York, W. C. Bryant & co. 1885.

BRYANT, JOHN C. New counting-house bookkeeping; with manufacturing and modern banking. New York, J. C. Bryant.

BRYANT, JOHN C. New elementary bookkeeping. Buffalo, J. C. Bryant.

BRYANT, JOHN C. New standard commercial book-keeping, theoretical and practical, containing a thorough elucidation of the principles of double and single entry. Buffalo, J. C. Bryant, 1887. 160p.

BRYANT, JOHN C. New standard practical and progressive bookkeeping, double and single entry. Buffalo, N. Y., J. C. Bryant, 1911. 223p. (Counting house ed.)

BOOKKEEPING—*(Continued)*

BRYANT AND STRATTON BUSINESS COLLEGE. Theory and practice of book-keeping and accounting as taught and practiced in the School of commerce; comp. and arranged for sole use of this school, 1902, by A. S. Hubbard and others; rev. and enl. 1910, by T. B. Stowell and others. Providence, R. I., Bryant and Stratton business college, 1910. 125p.

BRYCE, J. Bookkeeping. London, Longmans, Green & co. 1860.

——— Same. New ed. London, Collins sons & co. 1873, 1884.

BUCHANAN, C. Practical book-keeping. Edinburgh, 1806.

BUCHANAN, WILLIAM. Journal dictionary and bookkeepers' proof book, based on laws and principles of commercial science. Cleveland, W. D. Browning, 1905.

BUCKLIN, J. N. Double entry bookkeeping. Troy, New York, 1833.

BUSINESS bookkeeping simply explained. South African accountant and auditor, June, Sept. 1916.

BUSINESS short cuts in accounting, bookkeeping, card indexing, advertising, correspondence, management. Detroit. Bookkeeper publishing co. 1904.

BUSINESS standard bookkeeping. Cowperthwait, 1887.

BUTZ, R. H. How to change from single-entry to double-entry bookkeeping. Domestic engineering, Jan. 11, 1919, p. 85-6.

BUXTON, WILLIAM O. Bookkeeping. London, Sir Isaac Pitman & sons, 1915. 158p.

BUXTON, WILLIAM O. Pitman's advanced bookkeeping. London, Sir Isaac Pitman and sons, 1918. 298p.

BUXTON, WILLIAM O. Simplified bookkeeping. London, Sir Isaac Pitman & sons, 294p.

BYRNE, HENRY EDWARD. Practical bookkeeping. Ed. 5. Tyler, Texas, Byrne publishing co. 1905.

CALDECOTT, J. Practical guide for retail tradesmen and others to bookkeeping by double entry. London, 1851, 1855.

CALDER MARSHALL, SON & IBOTSON. Bookkeeping. London, 1907.

CALDICOTT, OSWALD HOLT. Poetry of accounts. *Accountant,* 1887. p. 622.

CALLAWAY, WILLIAM DALE. From school to counting-house; an explanation of the elementary principles of double-entry bookkeeping. London, T. Nelson & sons, 1910. 160p.

CAMPBELL, THOMAS FINDLEY. Business practice for twenty lessons in bookkeeping. Indianapolis, Ind., Bobbs-Merrill co. 1915.

CAMPBELL, THOMAS FINDLEY. Campbell's actual accounting; the apprenticeship in business; the modern method of instruction in elementary and advanced accounting, business forms and business customs. Indianapolis, Ind., Bobbs-Merrill co. 1911. 135p.

CARISS, A Double entry bookkeeping. London, Effingham Wilson, 1884.

CARLILL, JOHN ALBERT. Ante-audit: being the auditor's instructions to the employer's bookkeeping staff. London, [?1901].

CARLILL, JOHN ALBERT. Principles of bookkeeping. London, Gee & co. 1896. 116p.

CARTER, EDWARD HAROLD. How to open a set of books. Birmingham, 1883. Accountant, Nov. 3, 10, 17, 24, 1883.

CARTER, F. HAYNE. Practical book-keeping, adapted to commercial and judicial accounting, with sets of books and forms of accounts. Ed. 2. Edinburgh, Simpkin, Marshall, Hamilton, Kent & co. 1874.

——— Same. Ed. 4. Edinburgh, 1878.

——— Same. Ed. 5. Edinburgh, 1886.

——— Same. Ed. 5, revised and corrected. Edinburgh, John Menzies & co. 1885. 241p.

——— Same. Ed. 6. Edinburgh, 1890.

CARY, R .H. Elementary book-keeping by double-entry for evening continuation schools and day schools; key. 2v. London, Simpkin, Marshall, Hamilton, Kent & co. 1898. 130p.

CARY, R. H. Up-to-date examples in bookkeeping. 2v. Bolton and London, 1901.

CASEY, CHARLES C. Economy of knowing. *Country life,* Sept. 15, 1911, p. 36.

CASH book bookkeeping. Council of education, National society, 1867.

CASTLE, W. H. Single entry bookkeeping. Accountant, June 26, 1920, p. 735-8.

CATON, M. J. Counting house book-keeping. Syracuse, N. Y., C. W Bardeen, 1905.

CAYLEY, ARTHUR. Principles of bookkeeping by double entry. New York, G. P. Putnam's sons.

CHAMBERS' bookkeeping. London, W. & R. Chambers, 1895.

CHAMBERS' modern bookkeeping. London, W. & R. Chambers, 1908.

CHAPLIN, J. G. Three principles of bookkeeping: the theory and practice of accounts. London, Sampson Low & co. 1887.

CHAPMAN, THOMAS. Chapman's introduction to business. London, 1774.

CHATTERIS, HENRY. Tradesman's manual: a simple method of book-keeping. London, 1843.

CHILD, F. W. Value of bookkeeping. *Engineering magazine,* vol. 1, p. 599-604.

CHILD, PERCY. Book-keeping and accounts. London, R. E. Thomas & co. 1891.

——— Same. London, 1899.

——— Same. London, 1905.

CHILDS, C. W. Essentials of bookkeeping for public schools; single and double entry. San Francisco, Bancroft & co. 1888.

CHRISTIAN BROTHERS. Bookkeeping by double and single entry. Ed. 5. Dublin, 1889.

CIVIL service book-keeping: bookkeeping no mystery; by an experienced book-keeper. London, Crosby, Lockwood & son, 1870, 1872, 1874, 1883.

CLARE, MARTIN. Youth's introduction to trade and business. Ed. 5. London, 1740.

——— Same. Ed. 7. London, 1751.

——— Same. Ed. 8. London, 1758

——— Same. Ed. 9, revised by B. Webb. London, 1764.

——— Same. Ed. 10, revised by B. Webb. London, 1769.

——— Same. Ed. 11, corrected by J. Good. London, 1782.

——— Same. Ed. 12. London, 1791.

CLARK, GEORGE E. Practical instruction in bookkeeping. London, 1907.

CLARK, N. M. A-B-C of accounting. *System.* Aug. 1913. p. 162-8.

CLARK, N. M. Less time out for accounting. *System,* Nov. 1913, p. 532-5.

CLARKE, GEORGE F Bookkeeping for technical classes and schools. London, Gee & co. 110p.

CLARKE, GEORGE F. Double entry bookkeeping for technical classes and schools. London, Gee & co., 1898. 108p.

CLEARY, P. ROGER. Study and practice of business bookkeeping and accounting. Ypsilanti, Mich., Cleary publishing co. 1907.

COFFIN'S exercises in bookkeeping. Greenfield, Mass., A. Phelps.

——— Same. Key. Greenfield, Mass., A. Phelps.

COLE, WILLIAM MORSE. Bookkeeping, accounting and auditing. Chicago, Washington institute, c1914. 479p. (International business library).

COLE, WILLIAM MORSE. Single entry. (In his *Accounts their construction and interpretation.* c1915. p. 410-1).

COLINSON, ROBERT. Idea rationaria, or The perfect accomptant, necessary for all merchants and trafficquers; Containing the true forme of bookkeeping, according to the Ital-

BOOKKEEPING—*(Continued)*
ian methode: Wherein is first, The Introduction to the forme, 244 Querries and Answers, with instructions how to Ballance the leger, two Waste-books transported in two journals, out of which are transported 2 legers both ballanced. After which followes A moneth-book, invoys-book, factor-book, specie or cash book; instructions how to keep a book of petty-charges or pocket-book. Edinburgh, Printed by David Lindsay, Mr. James Kniblo, Josua van Solingen and John Colmar, in the year 1683.

COLLIER, JAMES. Bookkeeping. London, Relfe bros. 1884.

COLLINS, JOHN. Introduction to Merchants accounts, containing five distinct questions or accounts. 1. An easie question to enter beginners, with instructions to post, stated two several ways, upon several suppositions. 2. A question of a merchant, adventuring a stock or cargazoon with the purser or supra-cargo of a ship, who sells the adventure and furnisheth returns, stated two several ways. 3. A question of factorage or goods received by consignation, and returns shipp'd off, with an analysis thereto belonging. 4. A question of a ship's fraightment, with instructions to keep ship-accounts. 5. A question of double exchanges. Compiled by John Collins student in the mathematicks, late professor of Writing, merchants accounts, &c. And may serve as an appendix to the Merchant's mirrour, lately re-printed. The second edition. London, printed by James Flesher for Thomas Clark, at the South-entrance of the Royal Exchange, 1664. [See Malynes Consuetudo, vel lex mercatoria, 1656.]

——— Same. Another edition; containing seven distinct questions or accompts. [1 to 5 as above]. 6. An easie partable accompt between three dyers. 7. A controversal partable accompt between three turkey merchants. By John Collins, Fellow of the Royal Society. London, William Godbid, 1675.

COLLINS, JOHN. Perfect method of merchants-accompts demonstrated. London, Printed for Thomas Horne, at the South entrance of the Royal exchange, 1697.
This is really another edition of An introduction to merchants accounts.

COLT, JOHN CALDWELL. Science of double entry bookkeeping. Ed. 45. New York, Lamport. Blakeman & Law, 1853. 188p.

COMBINED ms. book for bookkeeping. New York, Sir Isaac Pitman & sons. 96p.

COMER, GEORGE N. Bookkeeping. Boston, Tappan, Whittemore & Mason.

COMER, GEORGE N. Bookkeeping by double entry. N. N. & H. Whittemore.

COMMERCIAL bookkeeping in four languages. Ed. 15. London, Crosby, Lockwood & son, 1879.

COMMERCIAL correspondence schools. Practical bookkeeping. Rochester, Commercial correspondence schools.

COMMERCIAL instructor, and accountant's guide [by R. C.] London, [?circa 1842].

COMPLEAT compting-house companion; by a society of merchants and traders. London, 1763.

COMPLEAT English tradesman. Ed. 2. London, 1727.

COMPLEAT tradesman. London, 1720.

COMPLETE practical bookkeeping; a text-book on modern methods of accounting; including an appendix of useful information and helpful hints for bookkeepers and office men; fully illustrated by forms of books furnished by merchants, bankers and manufacturers. Cleveland, Practical text-book company, 1906 (c1898). 308p.

COMPLETE business register. New York, H. W. Pamphilon.

CONSTABLE, JOHN. Book-keeping taught by examples of complete annual accounts. London, Stewart, 1875, 1884.

COOKE, CHARLES N. American system of practical book-keeping, adapted to the commerce of India, etc. Calcutta, 1840.

COOKE, JOHN. Compting-house assistant; or, Book-keeping made easie: being a complete treatise on merchants accompts, etc. Ed. 2. London, 1764.

COPELAND, T. E. Everybody's guide to book-keeping. London, Brindley & Howe, 1914. 97p.

CORY, ISAAC PRESTON. Practical treatise on accounts, mercantile, partnership, solicitor's, private, steward's, receiver's, executor's, trustee's, etc., etc. London, 1839.

——— Same. Ed. 2. London, 1839.

CORY, ISAAC PRESTON. Practical treatise on accounts, mercantile, private and official; exhibiting the manner in which the method of double entry may be applied to government; with proposal for the introduction of a uniform and centralized system of accounts in all the public offices. London, William Pickering, 1840. 184 + 65p.

CORY, J. P. Bookkeeping. London, William Pickering, 1839.

CORY, J. P. Practical accounts. London, William Pickering, 1839.

COTHEAL, WILLIAM. New method of keeping accounts. New York, 1860.

COUNTING-HOUSE manual and introduction to business: practical book-keeping, by Calculator. London, 1843.

COWAN, T. W. Bookkeeper's guide. Ed. 6. London, Houlston & sons, 1885.

CRELLIN, PHILIP. Bookkeeping and commercial terms. London, Whittaker, 1892.

CRELLIN, PHILIP. Bookkeeping for teachers and pupils, with accounts in illustration, exercises, etc. London, 1892.

CRITTENDEN, S. W. Elementary treatise on bookkeeping by single and double entry. Philadelphia, W. S. Fortescue & co. 1852.

CRITTENDEN, S. W. Inductive and practical treatise on book-keeping by single and double entry . . . containing nine sets of books . . . also a set of steamboat books, etc. Philadelphia, 1850.

——— Same. Counting house edition. Philadelphia, W. S. Fortescue & co. 1870, 1878.

——— Same; including key to high school edition. Philadelphia, W. S. Fortescue & co. 1870.

——— Same. High school edition. Philadelphia, W. S. Fortescue & co. 1870.

CRITTENDEN, S. W. Inductive and practical treatise on book-keeping for high-schools and academies. Philadelphia, 1854.

CRITTENDEN, S. W. Key to an elementary treatise on book-keeping by single and double entry. Philadelphia, E. C. & J. Biddle, 1853. 60p.

CRITTENDEN, S. W. Key to the counting-house and high-school editions of Crittenden's book-keeping. Philadelphia, 1853.

CRITTENDEN, S W. Single entry book-keeping explained in five sets of books. Enlarged edition. Philadelphia. W. S. Fortescue & co. 1878.

CRITTENDEN, S. W. Treatise on bookkeeping by single and double entry. Philadelphia, E. C. & J. Biddle.

CRITTENDEN, S. W. Treatise on book-keeping by single and double entry; abridged for the use of schools. Philadelphia, E. C. & J. Biddle.

CRITTENDEN, S. W. Treatise on single entry book-keeping. Philadelphia. W. S. Fortesque & co. 1854.

CRITTENDEN AND GROSBECK. Bookkeeping. Philadelphia, 1870.

BOOKKEEPING—*(Continued)*

CRONHELM, F. W. Double entry by single: a new method of book-keeping. London, Longmans, Green & Co. 1818.

CROPPER, LIONEL CUTHBERT. Bookkeeping and accounts: a text-book for students London, McDonald & Evans, 1910. 760p.

——— Same. Ed. 11. London, Gee & co. 900p.

CROPPER, LIONEL CUTHBERT. Elementary book-keeping: a text book for beginners London, Macdonald and Evans, 1910. 284p.

——— Same. New ed. London, Macdonald and Evans, 1916. 105p.

CROPPER, LIONEL CUTHBERT. Key to Book keeping and accounts. London, Macdonald and Evans. 1918. 736p.

CROPPER, LIONEL CUTHBERT. Primer of book-keeping: a first course for students. Adelphi, England, Macdonald & Evans, 1911 160p.

CROXTON, OSCAR C. Short cuts to practica bookkeeping. Heath Springs, S. C., O. C Croxton, 1907.

CUMMINS, C. Bookkeeping; key. London, Simpkin, Marshall, Hamilton, Kent & co 1887-9.

CUMMINS, C. Bookkeeping: suggestions on editing of accounts. London, Simpkin, Marshall, Hamilton, Kent & co. 1893.

CURTISS, C. C. American standard bookkeeping. High school edition. New York American book co. 1903, 1906.

CURTISS, C. C. Key to American standard book-keeping High school edition. New York, American book co. 1906.

CURTISS, C. C. Manual of bookkeeping. New York, American book co.

CURTISS, C. C. New common school book-keeping and blanks. St. Paul, D. D. Merrill co. 1886.

CUSACK, JAMES. Double-entry book-keeping; a complete treatise on its theory and practice. London, Methuen & co. 1911. 414p.

DAFFORNE, RICHARD. Apprentices time-entertainer accomptantly: or, A methodical means to obtain the exquisite art of accomptantship: Digested into Three parts, as is exemplified upon the next leaf. By Richard Dafforne, authour of the Merchants-mirrour. Very requisite to be exervicsed by all such as profess the Teaching of the said art. Now reviewed, and in several places rectified, the Waste-books altered, and composed after the usual method of merchants: Augmented with 85 instances; and at the end of each book is added a trial ballance: Likewise how to draw out accompts of sales, accompt currant, and invoices for him we serve in commission. Also, the form of a book for charges of merchandize, which is at the end of the first Waste-book; by the use of which all the particular charges paid in the cash book are at the months end collected into one sum and so carried into the Journal. By John Dafforne Accomptant, and teacher of the said famous and never-dying art of accomptanship, in English or Dutch: Resident in More-Fields near Long-Alley in Neptune Court. Who likewise rectifieth books of accompts abroad or at home, whether in proper, factorage, or company. The third edition. London, W. Godbid, 1670.

DAFFORNE, RICHARD. English merchants companion: or, An entertainment for the young merchants, their servants. Digested into three parts. Wherein the perfect method of merchants book-keeping, and other matters relating to traffick, is compleatly demonstrated. Being the most exact work of this nature, extant. To which is annexed, directions for accomptants, and other persons, who enter themselves into the service of the Honourable Companies of Merchants of England, trading into the East Indies: shewing them how to begin, prosecute, and compleatly finish their several functions and offices. Entred by way of debitor and creditor. The fourth edition, carefully corrected and augmented. London, Printed for Tho. Horne, at the South-entrance of the Royal exchange in Cornhil, 1700.

DAFFORNE, RICHARD. Merchants' mirrour: or Directions for the Perfect ordering and keeping of his accounts; Framed by way of debitor and creditor after the (so tearmed) Italian-manner: containing 250 rare questions, with their answers, in forme of a dialogue. As likewise, A waste-booke, with a compleat iournall, and leager thereunto appertaining; unto the which I haue annexed two other Waste-bookes for exercise of the studious: and at the end of each is entered the briefe contents of the Leagers accounts arising from thence. And also, A moneth booke, very requisite for merchants, and commodious for all other science-lovers of this famous art. Compiled by Richard Dafforne of Northampton, accountant, and teacher of the same, after an exquisite method, in the English and Dutch language. At the end, addressed to the art-inspiring youth are foure tables of principall and simple interest, etc.; by his son, John Dafforne. London, R. Young, 1636.

——— Same. Ed. 2, corrected and amended [Same title, with 3 mottoes in Dutch.] London, Printed by J. L. for Nicolas Bourn, at the South entrance of the Royall-Exchange, 1651.

——— Same. Ed. 3, corrected and amended [Same title, with 3 mottoes in Dutch.] London, Printed by R. H. and J. G. for Nicholas Bourn, at the south-entrance of the Royall Exchange, 1660. [See Malynes Consuetudo, vel Lex Mercatoria, 1656.]

——— Same. [Same title as the 3rd.] London. Printed by Miles Flesher, for Robert Horne, at the south entrance of the Royal Exchange, 1684. [See Malynes Consuetudo, vel lex mercatoria, 1686.]

DANDO, JOSEPH. Practical book-keeping. Philadelphia, Author, 1842.

DARBY, WILLIS W. and ALPHONSO RAGLAND. Practical bookkeeping. Dallas, Texas, Darby and Ragland, 1905.

DAVAR, SOHRAB R. Davar's ad-referendum of accounting. London, Gee & co. 1903.

DAVEY, FREDERICK. Students' catechism on bookkeeping, accounting and banking; with exercises and examination questions. Ed. 2. London, Butterworth & co. 1917. 478p.

DAVIDSON, A. Introductory lessons in book-keeping: short commercial calculations and invoices. London, 1892.

reference to iegalised systems. *Accountant,*

DAWSON, SIDNEY STANLEY. British and foreign methods of bookkeeping, with special Oct. 29, 1904. p. 531-40.

DAY, B. H. Book-keeping without a master. New York, Dick & Fitzgerald.

DAY, WILLIAM GEORGE. Elementary bookkeeping. London, Gee & co. 1901. 48p.

DEIGHAN, P. Complete treatise on book-keeping, rational and practical, wherein the invention of debtors and creditors are clearly pointed out, etc. 2 vols. in 1. London, 1807.

DE LAY, DANIEL WASHINGTON. Manual of book-keeping. Mattoon, Ill., Gazette printing co. 1907.

DELL, B. Double entry bookkeeping. London, Webster & co. 1850.

DELP, JOSEPH DANIEL. Comprehensive modernized rapid calculator. Springfield, Mo., J. D. Delp 1910.

DENMAM, J. S. Book-keeping for the people; practical system of accounts. New York, Baker & Taylor co. 1887.

BOOKKEEPING—*(Continued)*

DETROIT SCHOOL OF ACCOUNTS AND COMMERCE. Book-keeping. 6 v. in 1. Detroit, Mich., F. W. Morton, 1914. 96p.

DEWHIRST, JOHN MARK. Elements of book-keeping. Galesburg, Ill. Wagoner printing co. 1910.

DICKINSON, WALTER S. Method and arrangement in accounts. Accountant, Feb. 15, 1902, p. 188-94.

DICKSEE, LAWRENCE ROBERT. A B C of bookkeeping. London, Longmans-Green & co. 1908.

DICKSEE, LAWRENCE ROBERT. Bookkeeping. London, Gee & co.

DICKSEE, LAWRENCE ROBERT. Bookkeeping exercises for accountant students. Ed. 3. London, Gee & co. 1910. 99p.

DICKSEE, LAWRENCE ROBERT. Bookkeeping for accountant students. 3 v. London, Gee & co. 1893.

——— Same. Ed. 3. London, 1910. 99p.

——— Same. Ed. 7. London, Gee & co. 1914. 300p.

DICKSEE, LAWRENCE ROBERT. Bookkeeping: its adaptability to the requirements of every class of undertaking. (In *Lisle, George. Encyclopaedia of accounting.* v.1. p. 496-501).

DICKSEE, LAWRENCE ROBERT. Forms of accounts and balance sheets. *Accountant,* Nov. 11, 18, 1893, p. 954-9, 973-81.

DICKSEE, LAWRENCE ROBERT. Nature and limitations and accounts. *Accountant,* April 4, 1903, p. 469-74.

DICKSON, N. Books of bookkeeping. London, Longmans, Green & co. 1863.

DILWORTH, THOMAS. Young book-keeper's assistant: showing in the most plain and easy manner the Italian way of stating debtor and creditor, etc. Ed. 7. London, 1777.

——— Same. Ed. 8. London, 1781.

——— Same. Ed. 9. London, 1784.

——— Same. Ed. 12. London, 1793.

——— Same. Ed. 13. London, 1798.

——— Same. New ed. London, 1810.

——— Same. New ed. York, 1828.

——— Same. New ed. London, 1856.

——— Same. New ed. London, 1870.

DIMELOW, JAMES. Bookkeeping. London, Collins, sons & co. 1876.

DIMELOW, JAMES. Practical bookkeeping. London, Collins, sons & co. 1882.

DODSON, JAMES. Accountant: or, The method of book-keeping. London, 1750.

DOHERTY, J. J. Book-keeping. Dublin, Sullivan, 1897.

DOHERTY, J. J. Text-book of book-keeping. London, Simpkin, Marshall, Hamilton, Kent & co. 1912. 86p.

DOHERTY, J. J. Text-book of book-keeping, pt. 1, Ed. 44. Dublin, Ireland, Alex. Thom. 1917. 91p.

DONLEY, D. R. Preventing loss from charge accounts. *Metal work,* Mar. 9, 1917, p. 338. *Domestic engineering,* Mar. 10, 1917, p. 362-3. *Electrical review and western electrician,* Mar. 17, 1917, p. 457.

DONN, BENJAMIN. Accountant and geometrician; containing the doctrine of circulating decimals, logarithms, book-keeping, and plane geometry. London, 1765.

DONN, BENJAMIN. Accountant, containing essays on book-keeping by single and double entry. Ed. 2. London, 1778.

DOUBLE entry bookkeeping. *Hunt's merchants' magazine,* v. 1, p. 256.

DOWLING, DANIEL. Complete system of Italian book-keeping according to the modern method. Ed. 2. Dublin, 1770.

——— Same. Ed. 3. Dublin, 1775.

DRAUGHON, JOHN FRANKLIN. Draughon's progressive bookkeeping and business manual. Nashville, Tenn., Draughon text-book co. 1917. 216p.

DREW, W. A. Practical book-keeping. New edition. Chicago, George Sherwood & co. 1876.

Duff, C. P. and others. Common school bookkeeping. New York, American book co.

DUFF, PETER. North American accountant, embracing single and double entry bookkeeping for the use of schools. New York, Harper & brothers, 1855.

——— Same. School edition. New York, Harper & brother.

DUFF, PETER. Duff's book-keeping by single and double entry. Ed. 20. New York, Harper & brothers, 1868.

——— Same. Ed. 20, enlarged and revised. New York, Harper & brothers, 1882. 398p.

DYER, S. Common-sense method of double entry bookkeeping on first principles, as suggested by De Morgan. London, G. Philip & son, 1897. 140+166p.

DYSON, C. E. Bookkeeping. New ed. London Warne & co. 1889.

EASTMAN, GEORGE. Book-keeping by single and double entry. New York, A. S. Barnes & co. 1851.

EASY introduction to book-keeping . . . for the improvement of young accountants. Anon. 1776.

EASY-to-keep account book. Nashville, Tenn., Southern publishing association.

EATON, ABIJAH H. Eaton and Burnett revised and improved bookkeeping, corporation, voucher and cost accounting embracing all modern and scientific methods used in business. Baltimore, Eaton & Burnett business college, inc. 1917. 261p.

EATON, SEYMOUR. Business forms, customs and accounts for schools. New York, American book co. 1895.

EDDIS, WILTON C. Text-book for the use of manufacturers, merchants, accountants, and bookkeepers. Toronto, 1912. 199p.

EDWARDS, GEORGE. Books of account. *Accountant,* June 3, 24, 1899, p. 617-21, 672-4.

EDWARDS, J. Bookkeeping; double entry simplified. London, Relfe bros.

——— Same; key. London, Relfe bros. 1871.

EDWARDS, J. Double entry bookkeeping. London, Relfe bros. 1842.

EDWARDS, J. Key to single entry bookkeeping. London, Relfe bros. 1856.

EDWARDS, J. Single entry bookkeeping. London, Relfe bros.

ELEMENTS de comptabilite financiere a l' usage du levant publies par un groupe de professeurs. Novelle edition. Constantinople, Procure des Freres Maristes. (Enclos St. Benoit) 343p.

ELEMENTS of book-keeping, for schools; printed and published by direction of the Commissioners of National Education, Ireland. Dublin, 1850, 1859, 1863, 1870, 1872, 1882.

ELLIS, CARLOS BENT. Practical bookkeeping. Boston, Allyn & Bacon, 1908.

ELLIS, CARLOS BENT. Reference book for use with Ellis's practical bookkeeping. Boston, Allyn & Bacon, 1908.

ELLIS, F. W. Bookkeeping. Infield, 1883.

ELLIS PUBLISHING CO. Business directions used in connection with Ellis industrial bookkeeping. Battle Creek, Mich., Ellis publishing co. 1912. 75p.

ELLIS PUBLISHING CO. Cabinet manual. Battle Creek, Mich., Ellis publishing co.

ELLIS PUBLISHING CO. Guide to accompany the Ellis tablet method of teaching bookkeeping, elementary course. Battle Creek, Mich., Ellis publishing co. 1919. 93p.

ELLIS PUBLISHING CO. Guide to Ellis system of actual business training. Battle Creek, Mich., Ellis publishing co.

BOOKKEEPING—*(Continued)*

ELLIS PUBLISHING CO. Student's guide to accompany the Ellis cabinet system of teaching bookkeeping and business practice. Revised ed. Battle Creek, Mich., Ellis publishing co. 1910.

ELLIS PUBLISHING CO. Student's guide to accompany the Ellis tablet method of teaching bookkeeping and business practice; complete course. Battle Creek, Mich., Ellis publishing co. 1910.

——— Same; elementary course. Battle Creek, Mich., Ellis publishing co. 1910.

ELLIS PUBLISHING COMPANY. Student's tablet of transactions (elementary course); the tablet method of teaching bookkeeping and business training. Battle Creek, Mich., Ellis publishing company, 1919. 109p.

ELLIS PUBLISHING CO. Tablet method of teaching bookkeeping. Battle Creek, Mich., Ellis publishing co.

ELLSWORTH, H. W. Book-keeping and business manual, single and double entry. 2 parts. New York, Taintor bros., Merril & co.

ELLSWORTH, H. W. Single and double entry bookkeeping manual. Mont Vale, N. J., Ellsworth co. 1868.

ELLSWORTH, H. W. Steps or shorter course bookkeeping (single and double entry). Mont Vale, Ellsworth co.

ELWORTHY, W. R. and C. C. CAMPLING. Bookkeeping for traders, manufacturers, and companies. Ed. 3. London, Jordon & sons, 1904. 224p.

ENCYCLOPAEDIA Britannica, a dictionary of arts; science, literature and general information. Ed. 11. Cambridge, University press, 1910.

Bookkeeping, v. 4, p. 225-30.

ERNST, HENRY. Accountant and book-keeper's manual of commercial calculations reduced to their utmost simplicity. New York, Harper & bros.

ESSAY on the elements of book-keeping; by a merchant. 1861.

FAIRBAINE, L. System of double entry bookkeeping. Boston, W. J. Reynolds & co.

FAIRBANKS, L. Science and practice of bookkeeping by double and single entry. Philadelphia, Sower, Potts & co.

FALL, F. A. Efficient book-keeping. *Musician.* March, 1916, p. 144-5.

FARR, J. W. Farrian system of book-keeping. Downs, Kansas book co. 1894.

FAURE, GABRIEL. Comptabilite generale. Douziene edition. Paris, Masson et cie, 1919. 308p.

FEAST, HENRY. Bookkeeping simplified: a method (with examples) of keeping books by double entry, applicable to any business, and complying with the Bankruptcy act, 1883. London, 1883.

——— Same. New ed. London [? 1900].

FERNEYHOUGH, M. P. Chart of bookkeeping. Hanley, Wood Mitchell and co.

FIELD, MILLARD LINCOLN. Outlines of bookkeeping. Topeka, Kansas, Crane & co.

FIELDHOUSE, ARTHUR. Bookkeeping mss; ledger: journal. London, Simpkin, Marshall & co. 1918. 48p.

FIELDHOUSE, ARTHUR. Key to Student's commercial book-keeping accountancy and banking. London, Simpkin, Marshall, Hamilton, Kent & co. 1908. 372p.

FIELDHOUSE, ARTHUR. Key to Student's elementary commercial book-keeping. London, Simpkin, Marshall, Hamilton, Kent & co. 1919. 421p.

FIELDHOUSE, ARTHUR. Student's advanced commercial bookkeeping. Ed. 22. London, Simpkin-Marshall & co. 1918. 749p.

FIELDHOUSE, ARTHUR. Student's business methods or commercial practice. London, Simpkin, Marshall, Hamilton, Kent & co. 1906. 214p.

——— Same. Ed. 2. 1906. 214p.

——— Same. Ed. 3. 1908. 264p.

——— Same. Ed. 4. 1909. 314p.

FIELDHOUSE, ARTHUR. Students' commercial bookkeeping; comprising principles and practice of double entry as applied to modern business; course of training for all examinations. Leeds, 1898, 1899, 1900, 1902, 1903, 1904, 1906, 1907, 1909, 1910, 1912.

FIELDHOUSE, ARTHUR. Student's complete commercial bookkeeping. Ed. 9, revised and enlarged. London, Simpkin, Marshall, Hamilton, Kent & co.

——— Same. Ed. 11. London, 1907. 490p.

——— Same. Ed. 14. London, 1910. 786p.

——— Same. Ed. 20. London, 1914. 914p.

——— Same. Ed. 22. London, 1917. 967p.

FIELDHOUSE, ARTHUR. Student's elementary commercial bookkeeping. Ed. 10, enlarged. London, Simpkin, Marshall, Hamilton, Kent & co.

——— Same. Ed. 19. London, 1914. 356p.

——— Same. Ed. 21. London, 1917. 362p.

FIELDHOUSE, ARTHUR. Student's elementary commercial book-keeping: key. Ed. 2. London, Simpkin-Marshall & co. 1914. 414p.

FIELDHOUSE, ARTHUR and EDWIN WILSON. Key to Students' advanced commercial book-keeping. London, Simpkin, Marshall, Hamilton, Kent & co. 1910. 436p.

——— Same. Ed. 4. London, 1917. 545p.

FIELDHOUSE, ARTHUR and EDWIN WILSON. Key to the Student's elementary book-keeping. London, Simpkin, Marshall, Hamilton, Kent & co. 1909. 310p.

FIELDHOUSE, ARTHUR and EDWIN WILSON. Student's advanced book-keeping. Ed. 11. London, Simpkin, Marshall, Hamilton, Kent & co. 1907. 490p.

FINDLATER, J. Bookkeeping. London, Simpkin. Marshall, Hamilton Kent & co. 1868.

FINDLATER, J. Bookkeeping. London, Simpexplained. Ed. 3. Edinburgh, Oliver and Boyd, 1900. 72p.

FINDLAY, JAMES. Bookkeeping simplified. London, Gee & co. 1901. 76p.

FIRST lessons in bookkeeping. Chicago, O. M. Powers, 1896.

FIRST series of examples in bookkeeping by double entry: by a professional accountant. 1880.

FISHER, GEORGE. Instructor: or, Young man's best companion; containing, spelling, reading, writing and arithmetic . . . Instructions to write variety of hands . . . Also merchants accompts, and a short and easy method of shop and book-keeping, etc. Ed. 23. London, 1779.

——— Same. Ed. 30. London, 1810.

FLEMING, R. Double entry in one lesson. New York, Sir Isaac Pitman & sons, 1908.

FLETCHER, EDWARD H. Method and form in book-keeping and accounts. *Accountant,* 1886, p. 338, 361, 377. Revised. *Accountant,* April 13, 1889, p. 195-200.

FLINT, GEORGE. Short and easy book-keeping: double entry. New ed. London, Effingham Wilson, 1892.

——— Same. New ed., revised by S. W. Flint. London, [? 1896].

FOLSOM, E. G. Logic of accounts: exposition of theory and practice of double entry bookkeeping. New York, A. S. Barnes & Co. 1872.

FORBES, CHARLES. System of practical short cuts in bookkeeping. Australasian accountant and secretary, Feb. 1920, p. 56-9.

FORM of accounts. *Accountant,* June 20, 1908, March 26, April 9, 1910, p. 888-90; 425-8, 484-6.

FOSTER, BENJAMIN FRANKLIN. Bookkeeping by double entry. Boston, James French.

FOSTER, BENJAMIN FRANKLIN. Bookkeeping by single entry. Boston, James French.

BOOKKEEPING—*(Continued)*

FOSTER, BENJAMIN FRANKLIN. Concise treatise on commercial book-keeping. Boston, Perkins & Marwin, 1836. 171p.

FOSTER, BENJAMIN FRANKLIN. Counting-house manual. Boston, Benjamin Perkins & co.

FOSTER, BENJAMIN FRANKLIN. Double entry elucidated. London, 1843.

——— Same. Ed. 3. London, 1847.

——— Same. Ed. 4. London, 1849.

——— Same. Ed. 5. London, 1852.

——— Same. Ed. 7. London, 1857.

——— Same. Ed. 7. London, 1858.

——— Same. Ed. 12. London, 1881.

——— Same. Ed. 13. London, 1884.

FOSTER, BENJAMIN FRANKLIN. Origin and progress of bookkeeping; comprising an account of . . . works on this subject published from 1843-1852, with remarks, critical and historical. London, C. H. Law, 1852.

FOSTER, BENJAMIN FRANKLIN. Theory and practice of book-keeping, illustrated and simplified. London, 1840.

FOSTER, W. Universal bookkeeping. Groombridge, 1886.

FREDERICK, O. D. Intercommunic business practice. National educational association, Proceedings, 1912, p. 1092-3.

FREEMAN, CHARLES E. Adjustments through elimination; including a detailed explanation of why trial balance totals vary. Indianapolis, Ind., C. E. Freeman, 1911.

FREESE, JOHN HENRY. Commercial class-book; or young merchant's compendium, London, 1849.

FRENCH, CHARLES. Practical bookkeeping. Boston, Beale publishing co. 1891.

FRY, DANBY P. Exemplification of the general order for accounts issued by the Poor law board in 1867. London, 1867.

FULTON, JOHN W. British Indian bookkeeping; a new system of double entry. London, 1800.

FULTON, L. S. and GEORGE W. EASTMAN. Bookkeeping. New York, A. S. Barnes & co.

FULTON, L. S. and GEORGE W. EASTMAN. Practical system of book-keeping by single and double entry. Troy, N. Y. H. B. Nims & co. 1876.

FUNDAMENTAL BASIS OF ACCOUNTS. *Accountant,* April 23, June 11, 18, July 2, 23, 1910, p. 557-60, 814-7, 849-52; 1-4, 105-7.

GALBRAITH, JOSEPH A. Reasons for adopting double entry in keeping the [Trinity] college [Dublin] accounts. [?Dublin], 1883.

GASKELL, G. A. Gaskell's compendium of forms, educational, social and commercial, embracing a self-teaching course in penmanship and bookkeeping. . . St. Louis, R. S. Peale and co, 1882. 536p.

——— Same. New and revised ed. by L. T. Palmer. Chicago, Fort Dearborn publishing co. 1894. 934p.

GAY, GEORGE E. Business bookkeeping. Boston, Ginn & co.

GEER, GEORGE F. Analysis of the science of accounts. Springfield & Holyoke, Mass., C. W. Bryan, 1883. 294p.

GEIJSBEEK, JOHN BART. Ancient double-entry bookkeeping; Lucas Pacioli's treatise (A. D. 1494—the earliest known writer on bookkeeping) reproduced and tr. with reproductions, notes and abstracts from Manzoni, Pietra, Mainardi, Ympyn, Stevin and Dafforne. Denver, John B. Geijsbeek, c1914. 180p.

GENTLEMANS auditor: or A new and easie method for keeping accompts of Gentlemens estates; with the manner of auditing and stating the accompts. etc. by T. R. London, 1707.

GEORGE, S. Guide to book-keeping by single and double entry. Calcutta, 1893.

GIBBS, HENRY. Double entry bookkeeping. London, Simpkin, Marshall, Hamilton, Kent & co. 1877.

GILBERT, A. L. Business book-keeping; a new and logical exposition. Milwaukee.

GILBERT, A. L. Manual of business bookkeeping. Revised ed. Milwaukee. C. N. Caspar, 1895.

GILBERT, A. L. Modern business bookkeeping. Indianapolis, Ind., Bobbs-Merrill co. 1902, 1903.

GILBERT, A. L. Twenty lessons in bookkeeping. Indianapolis, Bobbs-Merrill co. 1915.

GILL, W. Accountants' sheet (the young). London, Simpkin, Marshall, Hamilton, Kent & co. 1860.

GOETSCHE, H. C. Importance of good bookkeeping. *Inland printer,* Dec. 1917, p. 379.

GOLDSMITH, B. and W. J. RENVILLE. System of double entry book-keeping. New York, Sheldon & co.

GOODACRE, ROBERT. Treatise on book-keeping. London, Craddock, 1811.

——— Same. Ed. 2. London, 1818.

GOODMAN, ———. Bookkeeping. Nashville, Tenn., Wheeler, Osborn and Duckworth manufacturing co. 1884.

GOODSPEED, E. J. Karanis accounts. *Classical philology,* Oct. 1908, p. 428-34.

GOODWIN, JOSEPH HENRY. Goodwin's improved book-keeping and business manual. New York, J. H. Goodwin, 1881.

——— Same. Ed. 28. New York, J. H. Goodwin, 1913. 301p.

GOODWIN, JOSEPH HENRY. Goodwin's practical bookkeeping. New York, Popular publishing co.

GOODWIN, JOSEPH HENRY. Practical instruction for business men. New York, J. H. Goodwin, 1906-7.

GOODWIN, PHILIP C. Bookkeeping self-taught. Chicago, Frederick J. Drake & co. 1903.

GOODYEAR, LLOYD EARNEST. American bookkeeping series. 3 units. Cedar Rapids, Iowa, Goodyear-Marshall publishing co. c1913.

GOODYEAR, LLOYD EARNEST. Principles of accountancy. Cedar Rapids, Iowa, Goodyear-Marshall publishing co. c1913. 190p. (American bookkeeping series).

GOODYEAR, LLOYD EARNEST. Principles, rules and definitions for bookkeeping. Ed. 6, revised. Cedar Rapids, Iowa, Goodyear-Marshall publishing co. 1918. 232p.

GOODYEAR, LLOYD EARNEST. Progressive business accounting. Waterloo, Iowa, Waterloo systems co. 1910.

GOODYEAR, LLOYD EARNEST AND OTHERS. Goodyear's secretarial bookkeeping. Cedar Rapids, Goodyear-Marshall publishing co. 1919. 104p.

GOODYEAR, SAMUEL HORATIO. Community business practice; text and equipment complete course. Cedar Rapids, Iowa, Goodyear-Marshall publishing co.

GOODYEAR, SAMUEL HORATIO. Intercommunication business practice, text and equipment. Cedar Rapids, Iowa, Goodyear-Marshall publishing co.

GOODYEAR, SAMUEL HORATIO. Theory of accounts, containing a complete exhibit of the principles of bookkeeping for use in business colleges and other commercial schools. Cedar Rapids, Iowa, Samuel H. Goodyear, 1890. 228p.

GOODYEAR, SAMUEL HORATIO. Progressive business accounting. Cedar Rapids, Iowa, Goodyear-Marshall publishing co.

GOODYEAR, SAMUEL HORATIO and L. E. GOODYEAR. Higher accounting. Cedar Rapids, Iowa, Goodyear-Marshall publishing co. 1908. In six pamphlet editions as follows: Commission accounting; Real estate and insurance; Practical banking; Corporation

BOOKKEEPING—*(Continued)*
and factory accounting; Wholesale accounting.

GOODYEAR, SAMUEL HORATIO and CARL C. Marshall. Modern inductive bookkeeping; with business practice by office and tablet methods. 2v. Cedar Rapids, Iowa, Goodyear-Marshall publishing co. 1908.

GORDON, WILLIAM. General counting-house, and man of business. Ed. 2. Edinburgh, 1770.

GORDON, WILLIAM. Universal accountant, and complete merchant. 2 vols. Ed. 2. Edinburgh, 1765.

——— Same. Ed. 4. Edinburgh, 1777.

GRANT, H. D. One place for every account: how income and expenses are classified and handled with the least amount of labor. *System*, March 1914, p. 293-6.

GRAPHIC bookkeeping exercises. 2 books. 3d. London, William Collins, sons & co.

GRAY, J. Single entry bookkeeping and arithmetic. London, Simpkin, Marshall, Hamilton, Kent & co. 1855.

GREELEY, HAROLD DUDLEY. Bookkeeping. (In his Theory of accounts. 1920. p. 38-45, 377-84.)

GREENWOOD, WILLIAM J. Bookkeeping and accountancy exercises for accountant students. Manchester, W. J. Greenwood, 1904. 389p.

GREENWOOD, WILLIAM J. Bookkeeping and office routine. Part I, elementary; part II, intermediate. Manchester, John Heywood, [? 1900]. 522p.

GREENWOOD, WILLIAM J. Bookkeeping for beginners. Manchester, [? 1906]. 64p.

GREENWOOD, WILLIAM J. Bookkeeping made easy; single and double entry. Manchester, John Heywood, 1903.

——— Same. Ed. 2. Manchester, 1894.

——— Same. Ed. 5, with exercises, key, etc. Manchester, 1898.

——— Same. Ed. 8, enlarged. Manchester, 1903. 304p.

——— Same. Ed. 9, enlarged. Manchester, 1912. 478p.

GREGORY, W. P. Gregory's practical bookkeeping. Revised ed. Easton, Pa. M. J. Riegel, 1884.

GREIG, WILLIAM M. Greig's index figure system. Aberdeen, 1913.

GREY, J. Single entry bookkeeping. London, Simpkin, Marshall, Hamilton, Kent & co. 1865.

GRIERSON, WALTER. Advanced book-keeping for commercial and accountancy classes London, Blackie & son. 1908. 232p.

GRIERSON, WALTER. Practical bookkeeping for commercial classes. London, Blackie & son, 1902. 132p.

GRIFFITH, JAMES BRAY. Practical bookkeeping; a working handbook of elementary bookkeeping and approved modern methods of accounting, including single proprietorship, partnership, wholesale, commission, storage, and brokerage accounts. Ed. 3. Chicago, American technical society, 1918. 255p. (American accountants' library.)

GRIFFITH, JAMES BRAY. Single entry book keeping—comparative statements; instruction paper. Chicago, American school of correspondence, 1909.

GRIFFITH, JAMES BRAY. Single entry bookkeeping, trial balance and comparative statements. (In Cyclopedia of commerce accountancy, business administration. 1910. v.5. p. 91-161).

GROESBECK, JOHN. Practical bookkeeping School edition. Philadelphia, Eldredge & bro. 1878.

GROESBECK, JOHN. Practical bookkeeping single and double entry. Philadelphia, Eldredge & bro. 1875.

GUTHRIE, EDWIN. Some controversial points in accounts. *Accountant*, Oct. 22, 1898, p. 990-9. *Business*, Jan. 1900, p. 34-9.

GUTHRIE, EDWIN. Want of uniformity in the modes of stating accounts, etc. Accountant, Oct. 28, 1882.

GUY, JOSEPH. Guy's complete treatise of book-keeping by single entry. London, Cradock, 1839.

HAAS, E. H. Daily business record and trial balance. New York, 1894.

HADDON, JAMES. Bookkeeping. New York, D. Van Nostrand co.

HADDON, JAMES. Commercial bookkeeping. Ed. 15 [of Rudimentary bookkeeping]. London, 1879.

——— Same. Ed. 18. London, 1904.

HADDON, JAMES. Commercial phraseology bookkeeping and arithmetic. Weale, 1851.

HADDON, JAMES. Rudimentary book-keeping. London, 1851.

——— Same. Ed. 5. London, 1861.

HALE, M. Bookkeeping system. London, Stevens & sons, 1884.

HALE, MATTHEW. Short treatise touching sheriffs accompts. London, 1716.

HALL, JOSEPH CASTLE. Principles of bookkeeping practically explained, with charts illustrating the science of "double entry" at a glance. London, 1885.

——— Same. Ed. 2. London, 1890.

——— Same. Ed. 3. London, H. Good & son, 1899.

HALL, MARSHALL PARKER. Art of accounts; an elementary treatise on bookkeeping and the nature and use of money. New York, Silver Burdett & co. 1898.

——— Same. Ed. 2. New York, Silver Burdett & co. 1913. 86p.

HALL, MARSHALL PARKER. Bookkeeping blanks, 5 books. New York, Silver, Burdett & co.

HALL, RAY OVID. Back to single entry. *Accounting*, Sept. 23, 1916. p. 264-7. *Journal of accountancy*, Sept. 1916, p. 196-204.

HALL, RAY OVID. Chinese books of accounts. *Accountant*, Oct. 14, 1916, p. 332-5.

HAMILTON, ROBERT. Introduction to merchandize; containing a complete system of arithmetic, a system of algebra, book-keeping in various forms; an account of the trade of Great Britain, and the laws and practices which merchants are chiefly interested in. v. 2. Edinburgh, J. Balfour & co. 1779.

HAMILTON, ROBERT. Short system of arithmetic and book-keeping. Ed. 5. Edinburgh, 1802.

HAMILTON, ROBERT GEORGE CROOKSHANK and JOHN BALL. Bookkeeping. Ed. 3. Oxford, Clarendon press, 1869.

——— Same. New ed. Oxford, 1874.

——— Same. New ed. Oxford, 1876.

——— Same. New ed. Oxford, 1879.

——— Same. New ed. Oxford, 1882.

——— Same. New ed. Oxford, 1885.

——— Same. New ed. Oxford, 1890.

——— Same. New ed. Oxford, 1896.

——— Same. New ed. Oxford, 1904.

HAMILTON, ROBERT GEORGE CROOKSHANK and JOHN BALL. Elementary bookkeeping. Oxford, Clarendon press, 1896.

HAMILTON, WILLIAM ROBERT. Double-entry in theory and practice. *Accountant*, March 18, 1911, p. 429-37.

HAMILTON, WILLIAM ROBERT. Principles of modern bookkeeping. London, Gee & co. 1913. 152p.

HANAFORD, LYMAN B. and J. W. PAYSON. Bookkeeping by single and double entry. Boston, Crosby and Ainsworth, 1867. 140p.

HANCOCK, ———. Concise system of bookkeeping. Ed. 6. London, [? 1856].

HANCOCK, W. J. Bookkeeping by double entry. Ed. 2. Dublin, 1883.

BOOKKEEPING—*(Continued)*

HANSON, F. I. Teacher's handbook of commercial subjects. Syracuse, N. Y., C. W. Bardeen, 1906.

HARCASTLE, JOSEPH. Single entry. *Accountant*, July 21, 1906, p. 76-81. *Journal of accountancy*, July 1906, p. 202-15.

HARDIE, WILLIAM and ALEXANDER ALLEN. Bookkeeping by double entry. Ed. 2. Edinburgh, William Green & sons, 1893.

HARLOW, EDWARD. Book-keeping (double entry): modern business transactions; for colleges and schools. London, Simpkin, Marshall, Hamilton, Kent & co. 1892.

HARRIS, H. A. How I plan books to control details. *System*, Sept. 1914, p. 305-9.

HARRIS, H. A. Indexing income and outlay. *System*, April 1914, p. 424-7.

HARRIS, NICHOLAS. Complete system of practical bookkeeping exemplified in six sets of books; journalized daily, weekly, and monthly; by single and double entry; applicable to all kinds of business, both individual and partnership concerns, accompanied with the various forms of bills, mercantile letters, etc. in daily use in the counting room; an interest and time table; also a series of concise rules for performing various computations in business, designed for the counting-house and schools. Hartford, Brown and Parsons, 1845. 230p.

HARRIS, NICHOLAS. First lessons in bookkeeping. Hartford, Brown & Parsons.

HASWELL, CHARLES H. Bookkeeping by double entry explained and illustrated in a complete record of mercantile and financial transactions. New York, D. Appleton & co.

HATCHARD, WILLIAM A. Book-keeping. New York, Sir Isaac Pitman & sons, 1911.

HATTON, EDWARD. The merchant's magazine: or, Trades man's treasury, containing I. Arithmetick . . . . adorn'd with curious coppercuts of the chief tables and titles; II. Merchants accompts . . . III. Bookkeeping . . . IV. Maxims concerning bills of exchange . . . V. The Port of letters to and from foreign countries . . . VI. An account of the commodities produced by all countries . . . VII. A merchant or trader's dictionary . . . VIII. Precedents of merchants writings, etc. Ed. 3. London, 1699.

——— Same. Ed. 5. London, 1707.

——— Same. Ed. 7. London, 1719.

——— Same. Ed. 8. London, 1726.

——— Same. Ed. 9. London, 1734.

HATTON, LINIUS MONROE and JOSEPH A. PROWINSKY. H. and P. practical bookkeeping. Tampa, Fla., Tampa business college publishing co. 1917. 47p.

HAWKINS, LESLIE WHITTEN. Bookkeeping: the principles and practice of double entry, with exercises, key and appendix of forms. London, H. Good, 1905. 190p.

HAYES, PRYOR LEE. Bookkeeping teacher. Springfield, Mo. International bookkeeping Institute, 1917. 126p.

HAYES, RICHARD. Gentleman's complete bookkeeper. London, 1741.

HENDERSON, A. G. Book-keeping by single and double entry. London, Hamilton, 1841, 1847.

HENDERSON, JAMES A. Evolution of double-entry bookkeeping. *Canadian chartered accountant*, April 1912, p. 194-9.

HENDRYX, F. H. Compendium of bookkeeping and business forms for self instruction. Hendryx, 1892.

HEWITT, W. J. Hints to students on bookkeeping and accountancy. *Associated accountants journal*, 1910, p. 197.

HIGHER accounting; modern bookkeeping. *Accountant*, Sept. 22, 1894, p. 825.

HILL, H. W. Digesting and tabulating accounts. London, Longmans, Green & co. 1882.

HIRSCH, ADOLPH. Science of commercial bookkeeping. New York, A. Hirsch, 1903.

——— Same. New York, J. S. Ogilvie publishing co. 1910.

HITCHCOCK, E. Bookkeeping. 2v. Boston, B. B. Mussey & co.

HITCHCOCK, I. I. Bookkeeping; journal and ledger. Boston, Nichols & Hall, 1825.

HITCHCOCK, I. IRVINE. Key to Hitchcock's new method of teaching book-keeping. Philadelphia, 1826. 56p.

HODGE, ARTHUR. Letters belonging to a system of book-keeping and accounts. London, 1812.

HOFFMAN, GEORGE LAWRENCE. Simplified bookkeeping. Pittsburgh, George L. Hoffman co. 1916. 58p.

HOFFMAN, JOHN V. Bookkeeping: as it is practised in large business houses. Baltimore, J. V. Hoffman, 1899.

HOLAH, ERNEST. Double entry: or, The principle of perfect book-keeping. London, Effingham Wilson, 1883, 1886, 1903.

HOLBROOK, ——— and ———, ROHRER. Complete counting-house book-keeping. Lebanon, Ohio, C. K. Hamilton & co. 1888.

HOLBROOK, ——— and ———, ROHRER. Condensed counting house and school bookkeeping. Lebanon, Ohio, C. K. Hamilton & co. 1888.

HOLBROOK, ——— and ———, ROHRER. Primary book-keeping. Lebanon, Ohio, C. K. Hamilton & co. 1888.

HOLBROOK, ——— and ———, ROHRER. Science of keeping accounts. Lebanon, Ohio, C. K. Hamilton & co. 1888.

HOOKLAND, SEIBERT S. Inductive bookkeeping and business practice. Philadelphia, Hookland & Hayward, 1904.

HOOPER, W. E. Book-keeping for beginners. London, 1913.

HOW to teach bookkeeping. London, Sir Isaac Pitman & sons.

HOWATT, J. Practical book keeping abridged. London, Simpkin, Marshall, Hamilton, Kent & co. 1842.

HOWE, GEORGE ALONZO. Hints and helps to bookkeepers. Marshalltown, Ia., G. A. Howe, 1905. 39p.

HUMPHRYS, I. H. Principles of bookkeeping explained. London, Sir Isaac Pitman & sons, 1918. 114p.

HUNTER, ALEXANDER T. "Unispect" system of book-keeping. Edinburgh, Gordon Wilson, 1905.

HUNTER, J. Beginnings bookkeeping. London, Longmans, Green & co. 1886.

HUNTER, JOHN. Beginnings in bookkeeping for commercial schools. London, 1898.

HUNTER, JOHN. Bookkeeping instructor; key London, Longmans, Green & co. 1886.

HUNTER, JOHN. Double entry bookkeeping for the civil service. London, Longmans, Green & co. 1878.

HUNTER, JOHN. Key to Double entry bookkeeping. London, Longmans, Green & co. 1871.

HUNTER, JOHN. Practical compendium of accounts. London, 1866.

——— Same. Ed. 2. London, King, 1867.

HUNTER, JOHN. Progressive exercises in bookkeeping by double entry. London, Longmans, Green & co. 1864, 1876.

HUNTER, JOHN. Self instruction in bookkeeping. London, Longmans, Green & co. 1871. 112p.

HUNTER, JOHN. Supplementary bookkeeping by double entry. London, 1883.

HUNTINGTON, J. H. True art of bookkeeping. J. H. Huntington, 1850.

HUTCHISON, CALVIN G. and WALTER S. PARKER. Elementary principles of single entry bookkeeping. [? Boston], Ware, 1884.

BOOKKEEPING—*(Continued)*

HUTCHINSON, CALVIN G. and WALTER S. PARKER. Single and double entry bookkeeping. [? Boston], Ware, 1884.

HUTTON, CHARLES. Complete treatise on practical arithmetic and bookkeeping. Ed. 11. London, 1801.

——— Same. New ed. by A. Ingram. Hanwick, 1811.

——— Same. Ed. 19, by Maynard. London, Whittaker & co. 1842.

HUTTON, CHARLES. Complete treatise on practical book-keeping; edited by A. Ingram. New ed. by J. Trotter. Edinburgh, 1840.

——— Same. New ed. Edinburgh, 1858.

HUTTON, CHARLES. Ruled books for bookkeeping. London, Simpkin, Marshall, Hamilton, Kent & co. 1851.

IMPEY, ROBERT LEVITT. Bookkeeping. *Accountant,* Nov. 25, 1882.

INGERSON, CARLOS I. Normal method in double entry bookkeeping. Chicago, Interstate book co. 1901, 1902.

INGLIS, WILLIAM. Chambers's book-keeping by single and double entry. London, W. & R. Chambers, 1855. 150p.

——— Same. London, 1882.

——— Same. London, 1884.

——— Same. London, 1893.

——— Same. London, 1908.

INGLIS, WILLIAM. Single entry bookkeeping. Orr, 1849.

——— Same. Edinburgh, W. & R. Chambers, 1866.

INTERNATIONAL accountants' manual; or, Twentieth century bookkeeping and business practice. Detroit, Mich., Business man's publishing co. 1910. 384p.

INTERNATIONAL correspondence schools. Bookkeeper's handbook. Scranton, Pa., International textbook co. 1910.

——— Same. Ed. 2. Scranton, International text-book co. 1920. 302p.

INTERNATIONAL library of technology. v. 59. Scranton, Pa., International textbook co.

IRESON, FRANK. Textbook of bookkeeping. London, Macmillan & co. 1900. 332p.

ISBISTER, A. K. Elements of book-keeping by single and double entry. New ed. London, Longman, 1853, 1854, 1856, 1897.

JACKSON, G. Double-entry book-keeping. London, Effingham Wilson, 1855.

JACKSON, GEORGE. Jackson's complete system of bookkeeping, both by single and double entry, etc.; [ed.] by M. Trotter. Dublin, [? 1830].

——— Same. New ed. Belfast, 1833.

——— Same. Another ed. Dublin, 1860.

JACKSON, GEORGE. New check journal upon the principle of double entry. Ed. 5. London, 1836.

——— Same. Ed. 6. London, 1841.

——— Same. Ed. 7. London, 1849.

——— Same. Ed. 8. London, 1856.

——— Same. Ed. 10. London, 1861.

——— Same. Ed. 12. London, 1863.

——— Same. Ed. 13. London, [? 1868].

——— Same. Ed. 14. London, [? 1875].

——— Same. Ed. 15. London, [? 1880].

——— Same. Ed. 17. London, [? 1882].

JACKSON, GEORGE. Practical system of bookkeeping, including bank accounts; revised by H. T. Easton. Ed. 24. London, Effingham Wilson, 1901. 152p.

JACKSON, THOMAS CHALICE. Junior bookkeeping. Cambridge, England, W. B. Clive.

JACKSON, THOMAS CHALICE. Key to practical bookkeeping. London, W. B. Clive.

JACKSON, THOMAS CHALICE. Practical lessons in bookkeeping. London, W. B. Clive, 1899. 380p.

——— Same. London, 1903. 778p.

——— Same. Ed. 3. London, 1904. 408p.

——— Same. London, University Tutorial press, 1912. 367p.

JACKSON, THOMAS CHALICE. Preceptors' bookkeeping. London, W. B. Clive, 1901. 182p.

JACKSON, WILLIAM. Bookkeeping in the true Italian form of debtor and creditor by way of double entry; or Practical bookkeeping, exemplified from the precepts of the late ingenious M. Dowling with the addition of computations in exchange and tables showing the proportion of weights and measures of the principal cities in Europe bear to each other. New York, M. Dermut and Thompson, 1804. 288p.

JAMIESON, JOHN. Easy introduction to bookkeeping, in four short sets, [also] farm book-keeping, etc. Glasgow, 1835.

JENKINS, B. G. Book-keeping for bar students. London, 1908.

JENKINSON, MARK WEBSTER. Book-keeping and accounting. London, Edward Arnold, 1910. 624p.

JENKINSON, MARK WEBSTER. Elements of book-keeping. London, Edward Arnold, 1907. 624p.

JENKS, MAURICE. Exact explanation of the theory of double entry bookkeeping; the advantages of double entry bookkeeping over single. *Accountant,* May 28, 1892, p. 446-8.

JENNINGS, WILLIAM. Jenning's book-keeping. Ed. 3. Dublin, J. Cumming, 1812. 181p.

JOERRES, LUDWIG. New and compendiores method of calculating the equation of payments, with systematic application of it to accounts current. Philadelphia, H. L. Lipman, 1843.

JOHNSON, GEORGE. Bookkeeping and accounts. London, Effingham Wilson, 1917.

JOHNSON, GEORGE. Pitman's book-keeping and accountancy problems. London, Sir Isaac Pitman & sons, 1914. 116p.

JOHNSON, GEORGE. Practical bookkeeping. London, Sir Isaac Pitman & sons, 1917. 432p.

JOHNSON, J. W. Fundamental principles of double entry book-keeping. *Business,* April 1895, p. 156-8.

JOHNSON, T. R. Text-book on bookkeeping; double entry made easy. Montreal, Canada, Dawson bros., 1879.

JOHNSTON, J. G. Forms of account books for various classes of business. London, Gee & co. 94p.

JONES, CHARLES. Companion to the Solicitor's clerk, embracing magisterial and criminal law, licensing, bankruptcy, accounts, bookkeeping, trust accounts, etc. London, 1895.

——— Same. Ed. 3, entitled The Solicitors clerk, part 2. London, 1902.

——— Same. Ed. 4. London, 1905.

——— Same. Ed. 5. London, 1910.

JONES, EDWARD THOMAS. Bookkeeping for schools. E. T. Jones, 1840.

JONES, EDWARD THOMAS. Jones's English system of book-keeping. Bristol, 1796.

JONES, EDWARD THOMAS. Jones's English systems of bookkeeping by single and double entry. Ed. 16. London, Theodore Jones & co. 107p.

JONES, EDWARD THOMAS. Science of bookkeeping, exemplified in Jones's English systems of single and double entry. London, author, 1831.

——— Same. Ed. 5. London, 1837.

——— Same. Another ed. with title page slightly altered. London, 1837.

——— Same. Ed. 6. [edited] by his sons. London, 1839.

——— Same. Ed. 9. [ed.] by his son, T. Jones, London, 1847.

BOOKKEEPING—*(Continued)*
——— Same. Ed. 11. [edited] by T. Jones. London.
——— Same. Ed. 15. [edited] by T. Jones. London.
——— Same. Ed. 16. [edited] by T. Jones. London.
JONES, EDWIN. Jones's test ledger: a plan for epitomizing the results of the working of a business, periodically; also, the key ledger, illustrating the mode of using the above. London, [?1868].
JONES, JOHN. Six questions in company accompts, published in the year 1730 by Mr. John Jones, late writing-master and accomptant in Bristol, as exercises for his rules in bookkeeping. *Accountants' magazine*, Nov. Dec. 1910; p. 483-6, 531-3.
JONES, SAMUEL MASTERMAN. Young man's study and commercial hints . . . including set of books by single and double entry. Birmingham, 1842.
JONES, T. Analysis of bookkeeping. *Hunt's merchants' magazine*, v.7. p. 513.
JONES, T. Book-keeping and accountantship; double entry. New York, John Wiley & sons.
JONES, T. Book-keeping; elementary and practical. New York, John Wiley & sons.
JONES, T. Double entry and single entry bookkeeping. Ed. 17. T. Jones, 1877.
JONES, THEODORE. Jones's English system of bookkeeping by single or double entry. Bristol, England, 1796.
JONES, THEODORE. Jones's English system of book-keeping for schools. London, Cassell & co.
——— Same. London, [?1883].
——— Same. London, [?1889].
JONES, THEODORE. Jones's English system of bookkeeping for the million. London, Cassell & co.
——— Same. Ed. 2. London, [?1882].
JONES, THOMAS. Principles and practice of bookkeeping. New York, Wiley and Putnam, 1841. 160p.
KAIN, GEORGE JAMES. Kain's solicitors' bookkeeping by double entry, on the triple column system. Ed. 6. London, Waterloo bros. & Layton, 1858.
——— Same. Ed. 10. London, 1887.
——— Same. Ed. 11., revised by H. Brown. London, 1895.
——— Same. Ed. 12., revised by H. Brown. London, 1902.
KATTE, STEPHEN. New method of keeping books by double entry. Ed. 2. London, Snow, 1839, 1843.
KEEFE, JOHN. Civil service book-keeping. New ed. London, Murray, 1904.
KELLER, JOSEPH B. Students' guide to bookkeeping. 2v. Salt Lake City, Utah, Skelton publishing co. 1902.
KELLY, P. Elements of book-keeping, both by single and double entry. London, Johnson, 1801.
——— Same. Ed. 2. London, 1802.
——— Same. Ed. 3. London, 1805.
——— Same. Ed. 4. London, 1811.
——— Same. Ed. 5. London, 1815.
——— Same. Ed. 6. London, 1819.
——— Same. Ed. 7. London, 1821.
——— Same. Ed. 8. London, 1824.
——— Same. Ed. 9. London, 1828.
——— Same. Ed. 10. London, 1833.
——— Same. Ed. 11. London, 1839.
——— Same. Ed. 12. London, Longman, 1847.
KENT, WILLIAM. Bookkeeping and cost accounting for factories. New York, John Wiley & sons, 1918. 261p.
KING, THOMAS. Exact guide to book-keeping by way of debtor and creditor. London, **1717.**
KING, THOMAS. Expert King's double entry book-keeping manual: business pointers and the secret of success. New York, Thomas King, 1906.
KIRTON, C. H. Book-keeping teachers' manual. London, Sir Isaac Pitman & sons, 1919. 239p.
KITCHINER, WILLIAM. Housekeeper's ledger. London, [circa 1820].
KITTREDGE, A. O. Bookkeeping adaptations and expedients. *Business*, Nov. 1895, p. 395-8.
KITTREDGE, A. O. and J. F. BROWN. Self-proving accounting system; with special application to the instalment business. New York Self-proving account book co. 1897.
KLEIN, JOSEPH JEROME. Bookkeeping and accounting. New York, D. Appleton & co. 1917. 435p. (College of the city of New York series in commerce, civics and technology).
KLEIN, JOSEPH JEROME. Bookkeeping and accounting; advanced course. New York, D. Appleton & co. 1918.
KLEIN, JOSEPH JEROME. Bookkeeping and accounting: introductory course. New York, D. Appleton & co. 1918. 226p. (College of the city of New York series in commerce, civics and technology).
KNOLLYS, G. Ledgers and literature; essays on the romance of bookkeeping, etc. London, 1907.
KNOX, JAMES. Bookkeeping in its simplest and most useful form. London, 1859.
KREPP, FREDERICK CHARLES. Statistical bookkeeping: being a simplification and abbreviation of the common system by double entry, etc. London, Longman, 1858.
LAMBERT, JOHN. Perpetual balance: or, Bookkeeping by double entry upon an improved principle. London, 1812.
LANGFORD, R. Merchants' accounts; or, Bookkeeping according to the Italian method of double entry. London, 1822.
——— Same. Another ed. London, 1824.
——— Same. Another ed. London, 1826.
——— Same. Another ed. London, 1828.
——— Same. Another ed. London, 1830.
——— Same. Another ed. London, 1835.
——— Same. Another ed. London, 1843.
——— Same. Another ed. London, 1853.
LASSEN, CLAUDIUS. Commercial guide: systematic bookkeeping by single and double entry; with the system taught in Heriot-Watt college, Edinburgh. Edinburgh and Glasgow, 1891.
LAWS of bookkeeping; part 1, single entry; by an accountant. 1873.
LAYMAN, A. A. B. C. of a cash book; a first guide to cash book-keeping, told in story form, simply illustrated for children and beginners. London, Simpkin, Marshall, Hamilton, Kent & co. 1916. 64p.
LEGG, R. Handbook of errors in accounts. London, Longmans, Green & co. 1858.
LEMOWITZ, NATHAN H. Bookkeeping made easy. New York, E. J. Clode, 1919. 193p.
L'ESTRANGE, J. E. Bookkeeping, single and double entry for use in schools and for self instruction. London, Simpkin, Marshall, Hamilton, Kent & co. 1897. 176p.
LETHERT, H. M. If your books could talk. *System*, Feb. 1919, p. 216-7.
LEVIE, GEORGE ELDER. Modern practical bookkeeping. Huddersfield, 1910.
LEVIE, GEORGE ELDER. Modern book-keeping for beginners. Huddersfield, 1910.
LEVIE, GEORGE ELDER. Modern practical book-keeping. Complete ed. Huddersfield, 1910. 644p.
LEVIE, GEORGE ELDER. Practical bookkeeping. Part 1, elementary. Huddersfield, 1909. 192p.

BOOKKEEPING—*(Continued)*

LEWIS, JAMES HENRY. Quick and easy method of teaching book-keeping. New ed. London, [? 1840.]

——— Same. Ed .14. London, [? circa 1860.]

LISET, ABRAHAM. Amphithalami, or, The accomptants closet, being an abbridgment of merchants-accounts kept by debitors and creditors; exactly and accurately showing how to order, state and keep accounts either of a public farm or private estate into a single book, without a memorial and journal, or annal, whereby calculation may be made at pleasure of the advance or arrear, gain and loss, of the whole stock and architecture. A new method, illustrated and inlarged with necessary instructions and inferences of the essential parts of traffick, as also of denomination, valuation and reduction of moneys, weights and measures of divers climates of the world. Very useful and convenient for Lords, knights, gentlemen, commissioners, treasurers, comptrollers, auditors, farmers, merchants, factors, stewards, and all degress of men. Digested into two parts. The first whereof is called Litera A [and the second Littera B, which has a second, slightly different, title-page]. Invented and composed by Abraham Liset, Gentleman. London, James Flesher, 1660.

——— Same. Another edition with the same title-page differently set up; but printed for Robert Horne, 1684.

LISLE, GEORGE. Bookkeeping. (In his *Encyclopaedia of accounting.* v.1. p. 406-93).

LISLE, GEORGE. Elementary bookkeeping in theory and practice, with examples, exercises [and] solutions. London, 1894.

LITCHFIELD, ———. Bookkeeping. Kent, 1860.

LITTLE, ———. Bookkeeping. London, Seeley & co. 1865.

LITTLE, ROBERT. Principles of double-entry bookkeeping explained and illustrated. London, Simpkin, Marshall, Hamilton, Kent & co. 1903. 58p.

LOCKYEAR, M. H. Introductory course; Lockyear's bookkeeping. New York, Gregg publishing co. 1911. 105p.

LOGAN, J. School and examination book keeping: treatise on double entry system suitable for schools, self-taught students public examination preparation; containing questions, exercises, examination papers, outline keys. London, Longmans, Green & co. 1902. 174p.

LOOMIS, L. C. Home book-keeping. New York, J. W. Schermerhorn & co. 1867.

LORRAIN, W. Bookkeeping by double entry etc. Hawick, 1807.

LOWELL, DANIEL W. Treatise upon the theory and practice of bookkeeping by double entry as it obtains in the first commercial houses of the world: containing full and plain explanations, new illustrations and a copious glossary of commercial words and customs; the whole designed to afford to the merchant, the clerk, and the student at the academy an explanation of how business is done, and a knowledge of double entry book-keeping without a master. Auburn, Daniel W. Lowell, 1852. 144p.

LOWRIE, WILLIAM. Convenience, principles and method of keeping accounts with bankers, with tables adapted to the calculating of interest accounts, etc. Sheffield, 1805.

——— Same. Ed. 2. London, 1809.

LUCKCOCK, JAMES. Practical English book keeping, for schools, apprentices and tradesmen, etc. London, ? 1801.

LYLE, T. A. Bookkeeper's companion; bookkeeping simplified. Philadelphia, J. G. Beidleman. 1884.

LYNAUGH, MATTHEW EDMUND and CLYDE O. THOMPSON. Practice exercises in bookkeeping. New York, American book co. 1920. 144p.

LYONS, JAMES A. and WALTER L. READ. Bookkeeping from vouchers. Chicago, J. A. Lyons & co. 1909.

LYONS, JAMES A. and WALTER L. READ. Lyons' bookkeeping pts. 1 and 2. Chicago, Lyons and Carnahan, 1913. 216p.

LYONS, JAMES A. and WALTER L. READ. Modern accountant, revised. Chicago, J. A. Lyons & co. 1911. 168p.

LYONS, JAMES A. and OLIVER SAXTON SMITH. Lyons' bookkeeping and accounting. Chicago, Lyons & Carnahan, c1920. 240p.

LYTE, ELEPHALET ORAM. Practical bookkeeping. Philadelphia, Pa. C. Sower co. 1906. 224p.

M'ALLEN, J. E. B. Principles of book-keeping by double entry; with examples and examination papers. London, Methuen & co. 1899. 150p.

MCCLURE, E. L. Equipoise bookkeeping by mechanism. *Overland,* April 1916, p. 395-8.

MACDONALD, JAMES B. Continental system of accounting (an elementary paper). *South African accountants' journal,* v. 2, p. 26.

MACDOUGAL, DUNCAN. Bookkeeping. London, A. Hall, 1847.

MACDOUGAL, DUNCAN. Complete system of book-keeping. Ed. 7. London, Simpkin, Marshall, Hamilton, Kent & co. 1869.

——— Same. Ed. 9. Manchester, 1881.

MACFARLAND, GEORGE ARTHUR and I. D. ROSSHEIM. First year in bookkeeping and accounting. New York, D. Appleton & co. 1913. 227p.

MACGHIE, ALEXANDER. Principles of book-keeping explained. Edinburgh, 1718.

MCGREGOR, P. Treatise on bookkeeping by single and double entry. New York, M. H. Newman & co. 1850.

MCKEE, JAMES. How to post the ledger. New York, Sir Isaac Pitman & sons.

M'KEE, JAMES. Pitman's book-keeping diagrams. London, Sir Isaac Pitman & sons, 1908. 36p.

MCKINNEY, W. S. Bookkeeping fundamentals. National educational association, Proceedings, 1911. p. 829-33.

MACLAREN, J. Improved bookkeeping. London, Bell, 1842.

MACLAREN, J. Practical improved book-keeping. London, Simpkin, Marshall, Hamilton, Kent & co. 1851.

MACLAREN'S ruled books for bookkeeping. London, Simpkin, Marshall, Hamilton, Kent & co. 1851.

MCLAUGHLIN, D. Bookkeeping by double entry. New York, Davis & Trumbell, 1847.

MACLEAN, H. S. High school book-keeping single and double entry. Toronto, 1890.

MACLEAN, JOHN DALZIEL. Advanced bookkeeping. London, Collins, sons & co. 1882.

MACLEAN, JOHN DALZIEL. Appendix to bookkeeping: examination papers. London, Simpkin, Marshall, Hamilton, Kent & co. 1895.

MACLEAN, JOHN DALZIEL. Bookkeeping as a specific subject. London, Simpkins, Marshall, Hamilton, Kent & co. 1892.

MACLEAN, JOHN DALZIEL. Book-keeping for the classroom and counting house. Ed. 6. London, Collins, sons & co. 1875.

——— Same. Ed. 7. London [? 1889].

MACLEAN, JOHN DALZIEL. Counting-house and examination bookkeeping. London, Simpkin, Marshall, Hamilton, Kent & co. 1891.

BOOKKEEPING—*(Continued)*

MACLEAN, JOHN DALZIEL. Introduction to counting-house and examination bookkeeping, with examination papers, and an appendix on government bookkeeping. London, 1892.

MACLEAN, JOHN DALZIEL. Key to Book-keeping for the classroom and counting-house. Ed. 6. London and Glasgoe, 1887.

——— Same. London, Simpkin, Marshall, Hamilton, Kent & co. 1893.

MAINARDI, MATTEO. La scrittura mercantile. Bologna, 1632.

MAIR, JOHN. Book-keeping methodiz'd: or, A methodical treatise of merchant-accompts, according to the Italian form, wherein the theory of the art is fully explained, and reduced to practice, by variety of suitable examples in all the branches of trade. Ed. 4. Edinburgh, W. Sands, A. Kincaid and A. Donaldson, 1752. 288p.

MAIR, JOHN. Bookkeeping moderniz'd: or, Merchant-accounts by double entry, according to the Italian form, wherein the theory of the art is clearly explained, and reduced to practice, in copious sets of books, exhibiting all the varieties that usually occur in real business, to which is added a large appendix. Ed. 6. Edinburgh, Bell & Bradfute and William Creech, 1793. 620p.

MALCOLM, ALEXANDER. New treatise of arithmetick and book-keeping. Edinburgh, 1718.

MALCOLM, ALEXANDER. Treatise of book-keeping, or Merchants accounts. London, 1731.

——— Same. Ed. 2. London, 1743.

MALYNES, GERARD. Consuetudo, Vel Lex Mercatoria, or The Ancient law-merchant. Diuded into three parts: According to the essentiall parts of trafficke. Necessarie for all statesmen, iudges, magistrates, temporall and ciuile lawyers, mint-men, merchants, marriners, and all others negotiating in all places of the world. London, Adam Islip, 1622.

——— Same. Ed. 2. London, Adam Islip, 1629.

——— Same. 3rd, but the first containing the additional matter at end. Whereunto is annexed the Merchants mirrour. London, Adam Islip, 1636.

——— Same. 3rd edn. [which contains additional matter, but ? 5th of Lex mercatoria] Whereunto are annexed the following tracts, viz. I. The collection of sea laws. II. Advice concerning bills of exchange. by John Marius. III. The merchants mirrour by R. Dafforne. IV. An introduction to merchants accompts by John Collins. V. The accountants closet by Abraham Liset. The Third edition, Wherein are inserted the three tracts following, never before printed in any former impression. I. The jurisdiction of the admiralty of England asserted by Pichard Zouch. II. The ancient sea laws of Oleron, Wisby, and the Hanse-Towns, still in force. Rendered into English for the use of navigators by G. Miege, Gent. III. The sovereignty of the British seas proved by Sir John Burroughs. London, Printed for T. Basset, at the George in Fleetstreet; R. Chiswell, at the Rose and Crown in St. Paul's Church-yard; T. Horne at the South Entrance of the Royal Exchange, and E. Smith, at the Bible under the Piazza, 1686.

——— Same. 4th of Lex mercatoria, and 2nd containing the additional matter; containing the above and also, Advice concerning bills of exchange by John Marius. Together with a collection of all sea-laws. . . Whereunto is annexed, The Merchants mirrour by Richard Dafforne. To which is added a Introduction to merchants accounts, compiled by Iohn Collings. London, William Hunt, 1656.

MANKATO COMMERCIAL COLLEGE. Business directions used in connection with Brandrup & Nettleton system of teaching bookkeeping and business practice; a direct didactic method of presenting mercantile, manufacturing and corporation bookkeeping and business methods. Mankato, Minn., Mankato commercial college, 1914. 65p.

MANKATO COMMERCIAL COLLEGE. Student's guide to accompany Brandrup & Nettleton system of teaching bookkeeping and business practice. Mankato, Minn., Mankato commercial college, 1914. 255p.

MANLY, HENRY. Principles of book-keeping by double entry. London, 1864.

——— Same. Ed. 2. London, E. Stamford, 1868.

——— Same. Ed. 3. London, 1872.

——— Same. Ed. 4. London, 1875.

——— Same. Ed. 5. London, 1877.

——— Same. Ed. 8. London, 1894.

MANNING, R. H. Book-keeping by single and double entry simplified for common schools. New York, D. Appleton & co. 1886.

MARSH, ALFRED T. Book-keeping; guide to young beginners. London, A. H. Stockwell, 1919.

MARSH, CHRISTOPHER COLUMBUS. Bookkeeping. New York. J. C. Riker.

MARSH, CHRISTOPHER COLUMBUS. Bookkeeping in Spanish. New York. D. Appleton & co.

MARSH, CHRISTOPHER COLUMBUS. Course of practice in single-entry bookkeeping. New York, D. Appleton & co. 1859. 142p.

MARSH, CHRISTOPHER COLUMBUS. Lecture on the study of book-keeping, with the balance sheet, being an easy introduction to double entry book-keeping. New York, C. Shepard, 1837. 38p.

MARSH, C. C. Science of double entry bookkeeping, simplified by the application of an infallible rule for journalizing; calculated to insure a complete knowledge of the theory and practice of accounts; being a series of well selected mercantile transactions so arranged as to form a complete course of practice and instruction; designed for the use of schools and counting-houses in the United States; including numerous examples of mercantile calculations, and an original diagram showing the relation between the account books. Enlarged and improved, 1858. New York, D. Appleton and company, 1875 (c1858). 235p.

MARSHALL, (CALDER), SON AND IBBOTSON. Bookkeeping. New York, Cassell & co. 1907. 390p.

MARSHALL, CARL CORAN. Bookkeeping and business training. Cedar Rapids, Ia., Goodyear-Marshall publishing co. 1910.

MARSHALL, CARL CORAN. Double entry drills. Cedar Rapids, Ia., Goodyear-Marshall publishing co.

MARSHALL, J. W. Books and bookkeeping. *Accountant*, Feb. 11, 1893, p. 132-6.

MARTIN, JAMES. Book-keeping in its relation to commerce. *Incorporated accountants' journal*, 1902, p. 143.

MARTINNANT, C. W. P. Bookkeeping at a glance. London, Jarrold & sons.

MARTINNANT, C. W. P. Synopsis of the principles of book-keeping and posting by double entry. London, Jarrold & sons, 1902.

MASSEY, ROBERT W. Actual business practice, Boston, Beale publishing co. 1891.

BOOKKEEPING—*(Continued)*

MASSEY, ROBERT W. Bookkeeping and business practice. [8th rev. ed.] Birmingham, Ala Massey business college co.. 1912. 204 p.

MASSEY, ROBERT W. Bookkeeping and business practice. [8th rev. ed.] Birmingham, Ala., Columbus, Ga., T. Gilbert, 1902.

MATHER, W. Youngman's companion; or, Arithmetick made easy; containing plain directions ...to attain to read and write true English ...a short and easy method of shop and book-keeping, merchants-accompts, etc. Ed. 17. London, 1747.

MATHESON, J. Theory and practice of bookkeeping. Baldwin, 1818.

MAYHEW, IRA. Eclectic complete bookkeeping. Cincinnati, Van Antwerp, Bragg & co. 1884.

——— Same. New York, American book co.

MAYHEW, IRA. Eclectic key to Complete bookkeeping. Cincinnati, Van Antwerp, Bragg & co. 1884.

MAYHEW, IRA. Practical system of bookkeeping by single and double entry. New York, Cady & Burgess, 1851, 1855.

MAYHEW, IRA. Standard book-keeping. Boston, Silver, Burdett & co.

——— Same. Chicago, J. C. Buckbee & co. 1889.

MAYHEW, IRA. University book-keeping and treatise on business and accounts. Boston, Silver, Burdett & co. 1867.

MAYNE, DEXTER DWIGHT. Office methods and practical bookkeeping. Chicago, J. A. Lyons & co. 1900.

MEDHURST, JOHN T. Bookkeeping by double entry, theoretical, practical and for examination purposes. London, G. Bell & co. 1898. 130 p.

MELCHIOR, ROGER LOGAN. Hints in bookkeeping. Toledo, R. L. Melchior, 1915. 60p.

MELLIS, JOHN. Briefe instruction and manner how to keepe bookes of accompts after the order of debitor and creditor, & as well for proper accompts partible, &c. By the three bookes named the Memoriall iournall and leager, and of other necessaries, appertaining to a good and diligent marchant. The which of all other reckoninges is most lawdable: for this treatise well and sufficiently knowen, all other wayes and maner may be the easier & sooner discerned, learned and knowen. London, Iohn Windet, 1588.

MERCES, F. A. D. New and simple system of bookkeeping by double entry. London, 1906.

MEREDITH, ARTHUR JOHN. Meservey's new bookkeeping and manual of business forms. Boston, Johnson, Blagden & McTurnan, 1912. 276p.

MESERVEY, A. B. Double entry bookkeeping. Boston, Johnson, Blagden & McTurnan, 1889.

MESERVEY, A. B. Key to bookkeeping. Boston, Johnson, Blagden & McTurnan, 1879.

MESERVEY, A. B. Manual of bookkeeping and banking. Boston, Johnson, Blagden & McTurnan, 1900.

MESERVEY, A. B. Single and double entry bookkeeping. Boston, Johnson, Blagden & McTurnan, 1878.

MESERVEY, A. B. Single entry bookkeeping. Boston, Johnson, Blagden & McTurnan, 1882.

METTENHEIMER, H. J. Safety book-keeping exposition of bookkeeper's frauds. Cincinnati, Robert Clarke & co. 1875.

MICHOD, C. J. Bookkeeping: a manual for the use of schools in India. Calcutta, 1890.

MILLAR, THOMAS JOHN. Business management through directly recorded statistics; a new method. *Accountants' magazine,* April 1918, p. 146-70.

MILLAR, THOMAS JOHN. Classification of business fact v. double-entry of business fact as a main consideration in bookkeeping. *Accountants' magazine,* Feb. 1916, p. 78-94.

MILLAR, THOMAS JOHN. Limits and limitations in business record keeping. *Accountants' magazine,* Jan. 1919, p. 19-24.

MILLAR, THOMAS JOHN. Management bookkeeping for the manufacturer, wholesaler and retailer. London, Charles and Edwin Layton, 1910. 132p.

MILLAR, THOMAS JOHN. Methods of stating accounts with particular reference to trust accounts. London, Gee & co. 1908. *Accountant,* May 16, July 25, 1908, p. 725-32; 89-92.

MILLAR, THOMAS JOHN. Notes on the principles of bookkeeping and modern methods applied to lawyers' transactions. Edinburgh, George Waterston & sons, 1906.

MILLER, O. L. Abridged edition of Miller's system of bookkeeping and business. Ed. 2. Seattle, O. L. Miller, 1907.

MILLS, J. C. Saving time on running accounts. *System,* July 1913, p. 93-4.

MILTON, J. Practical bookkeeping. J. Milton, 1851.

MINCK, O. R. F. Text book of double entry book-keeping, with exercises and key. London, Simpkin, Marshall, Hamilton, Kent & co. 1893.

MINER, GEORGE WASHINGTON. Bookkeeping; complete course. New York, Ginn & co. c1912. 334p. (Moore and Miner series).

MINER, GEORGE WASHINGTON. Bookkeeping, intermediate and advanced courses. Boston, Ginn & co. 1912. 218p. (Moore and Miner series).

MINER, GEORGE WASHINGTON. Bookkeeping; introductory course. Boston, Ginn & co. 1912. 126p. (Moore and Miner series).

MINER, GEORGE WASHINGTON. Bookkeeping; introductory course and intermediate course. Boston, Ginn & co. 1912. 248p.

MINER, GEORGE WASHINGTON and FAYETTE HERBERT ELWELL. Principles of bookkeeping; advance course. Boston, Ginn & co. 1918. 365+500p. (Miner and Elwell series).

MINER, GEORGE WASHINGTON and FAYETTE HERBERT ELWELL. Principles of bookkeeping; brief course, illustrating the direct method of closing the ledger. Boston, Ginn & co. 1918. 192p. (Miner and Elwell series) Published with slight alterations under title: Principles of bookkeeping; first course.

MINER, GEORGE WASHINGTON and FAYETTE HERBERT ELWELL. Principles of bookkeeping; combined course. Boston, Ginn & company, c1918. 416p. (Miner and Elwell series).

MINER, GEORGE WASHINGTON and FAYETTE HERBERT ELWELL. Principles of bookkeeping; complete course. Boston, Ginn & company, c1918. 416p. (Miner and Elwell series).

MINER, GEORGE WASHINGTON and FAYETTE HERBERT ELWELL. Principles of bookkeeping; corporation and voucher accounting. Boston, Ginn & co. c1918. 417 + 500p. (Miner and Elwell series).

MINER, GEORGE WASHINGTON and FAYETTE HERBEPT ELWELL. Principles of bookkeeping; intermediate and advanced courses. Boston, Ginn & co. 1918. 167 + 416p. (Miner and Elwell series). Published also, with slight alterations, as chapters 14-32 of the authors' Principles of bookkeeping; combined course.

MINER, GEORGE WASHINGTON and FAYETTE HERBERT ELWELL. Principles of bookkeeping; intermediate course. Boston, Ginn & co., 1918. 257 + 368p. (Miner and Elwell series).

MINER, GEORGE WASHINGTON and FAYETTE HERBERT ELWELL, Principles of bookkeep-

BOOKKEEPING—*(Continued)*

ing; introductory course; illustrating the journal methods of closing the ledger. Boston, Ginn & co. 256p. (Miner & Elwell series). Published with slight alterations under title: Principles of bookkeeping, elementary course.

MINER, GEORGE WASHINGTON and FAYETTE HERBERT ELWELL. Principles of bookkeeping, single entry set. Boston, Ginn & co. 1918. 10p. (Miner and Elwell series).

MINTON, R. Bookkeeping, single entry. Bennett, 1857.

MITCHELL, F. J. Bookkeeping simplified. London, Sir Isaac Pitman & sons. 1895.

MITCHELL, F. J. Notes and hints on bookkeeping. Ed. 5, edited by G. T. Barton. G. T. Barton, 1918.

MITCHELL, THOMAS WARNER. Fundamentals of bookkeeping. (In his *Accounting principles.* c1918. p. 37-74).

MITCHELL, WILLIAM. New and complete system of book-keeping by an improved method of double entry. Philadelphia, Bioren & Madan, 1796. 454p.

MODERN accountant. Chicago, J. A. Lyons & co.

MODERN business bookkeeping. Indianapolis, Bobbs-Merrill co.

MOFFETT, LOUIS BURDELLE. Manual of bookkeeping and accounting. Ed. 8. Philadelphia, Peirce school, 1908. 175p.

MOLE, ALBERT CHARLES. Students' epitome of accountancy and bookkeeping. London, 1908.

MOLLESON, JAMES ALEXANDER. Books and book-keeping. *Accountant,* Sept. 28, 1889, p. 505-7.

MONTEAGE, STEPHEN. Debtor and creditor made easie: or, A short instruction for the attaining the right use of accounts. After the best method used by merchants. Fitted to the trades or wayes of dealing in these several capacities: Viz. The youth or young scholar, The husband-man or farmer, The country gentleman, the retailing shop-keeper, The Handicrafts-man, The Merchant. The second edition with amendments. To which is added A Maiden scholars advice trained up in this learning: Which the author recommends to be read and practised in the first place. London, Printed by John Richardson for Ben. Billingsley at the Printing Press in Cornhil, 1682.

——— Same. Third edition with amendments. 1690.

——— Same. Another edition. To which is added, instructions for rent gatherers, &c. London, Printed by T. W. for Benj. Billingsley at the Printing Press at the Royal exchange in Cornhill, 1708.

——— Same. Instructions for rent gatherers accompts, &c. made easie. By the author of the book, entituled, debtor and creditor. London, Printed by J. Richardson for Benj. Billingsley, at the Printing Press in Cornhil, 1683.

——— Same. Another edition. 1708. (Bound with the 1708 edition of Debtor and creditors.

MONTEITH, A. W. Bookkeeping. Kent, 1872.

MONTGOMERIE, A. Bookkeeping. London, Simpkin, Marshall, Hamilton, Kent & co. 1882.

MONTGOMERY, JAMES L. Modern book-keeping and business practice. New York, Maynard, Merrill & co. 1906.

MONTGOMERY, JAMES L. Modern bookkeeping: single and double entry. New York, Maynard, Merrill & co. 1897.

MONTGOMERY, ROBERT HIESTER, ED. American business manual; a complete guide to modern systems and practice. 3v. New York, P. F. Collier & son, 1911.

MOODY's bookkeeping. Philadelphia, J. B. Lippincott & co.

MOORE, JOHN HENRY and G. W. MINER. Accounting and business practice. Boston, Ginn & co. 1903. 400p.

MOORE, JOHN HENRY and G. W. MINER. Accounting and business practice; corporation accounting and banking. Boston, Ginn & co. 1903.

MOORE, JOHN HENRY and G. W. MINER. Accounting and business practice; shorter course. Boston, Ginn & co. 1903.

MOORE, K. V. First book on principles of accounts. London, E. Arnold, 1911. 64p.

MORGAN, EDWIN. System of bookkeeping. London, Longman, 1831.

MORRISON, C. Complete system of practical book-keeping; by single entry, double entry in present practice, and a new method of double entry by single, etc. Ed. 3. Glasgow, 1823.

——— Same. Ed. 5. Edinburgh, 1834.
——— Same. Ed. 6. London, 1838.
——— Same. Ed. 7. London, 1843.
——— Same. Ed. 8. London, 1849.
——— Same. Ed. 9. London, 1862.

MORRISON, C. Introduction to book-keeping; comprising inland and foreign trade; arranged by single entry, Italian method of double entry, and by the present practice of the counting-house, etc. Ed. 2. London and Glasgow, 1819.

MORRISON, C. System of practical bookkeeping, etc. Ed. 3, Glasgow 1822, ed. 4, Edinburgh 1828.

MORRISON, C. Young lady's guide to practical arithmetic and book-keeping. Glasgow, 1820.

MORRISON, JAMES. Complete guide to practical book-keeping, by single and double entry, etc. Dublin, 1843. [This is really another edition of The mercantile teacher's assistant.]

MORRISON, JAMES. Complete system of merchants' accounts. Edinburgh, 1808.

MORRISON, JAMES. Complete treatise on practical book-keeping, etc. Ed. 3, with dissertation on the business of the counting-house, etc. London, 1820.

MORRISON, JAMES. Elements of book-keeping, by single and double entry. Ed. 2. London, Longman, 1813.

——— Same. Ed. 2. 1814.
——— Same. Ed. 3. London, 1818.
——— Same. New ed. London, 1825.

MORRISON, JAMES. General system of mercantile book-keeping. London, 1830.

MORRISON, JAMES. Mercantile teacher's assistant; or, A guide to practical book-keeping, etc. Dublin, 1829.

——— Same. Another ed., entitled A complete guide to practical bookkeeping, etc. Dublin, 1843.

MORRISON, JAMES. Practical bookkeeping, etc. Ed. 3. Leeds, 1802.

——— Same. New ed. London, Griffin, 1862.

MORRISON, JAMES. Queries on book-keeping. Leeds, 1818.

MORTON, FREDERICK W. Book-keeping in six lessons. Detroit, Press of Richmond & Backus co. 1914. 94p.

MULL, EDWARD EVERETT. Sixty lessons in business arithmetic. New York, J. J. Little co. 1898. 84p.

MUNRO, ANDREW. Book-keeping down to date. London, Effingham Wilson, 1907. 410p.

——— Same. Ed. 2. London, 1905. 214p.
——— Same. Ed. 3. London, 1907. 224p.
——— Same. Ed. 4, revised and enlarged. London, 1907. 410p.

——— Same. Ed. 4. London, 1910. 432p.

MUNRO, ANDREW. Book-keeping down-to-date. Elementary ed. London, Effingham Wilson, 1908. 140p.

BOOKKEEPING—(*Continued*)

MUNRO, ANDREW. Book-keeping down to date including accountancy and banking. Ed. 5. London, Effingham Wilson, 1911. 751p.

MUNRO, ANDREW. Elementary book-keeping for schools. London, Effingham Wilson.

MUNRO, ANDREW. Elementary book-keeping for day and evening schools and commercial classes. Ed. 2. London, Effingham Wilson, 1910. 156p.

MUNRO, ANDREW. Key to Munro's book-keeping down-to-date. London, Effingham Wilson, 1910. 100p.

——— Same. London, 1912. 410p.

MURRAY, DAVID. Bookkeeping and accountancy; Scotch practice in 17th and 18th centuries: a paper from the Glasgow herald. *Accountant,* March 25, 1905, p. 356-60.

MURRAY, GEORGE STANLEY. Elements of accounts. University city, St. Louis, Mo., Peoples university, 1907. 92p.

MURRAY, P. Graduated exercises and examination papers in book-keeping for national, intermediate and private schools, business colleges, and civil service academies. London, G. Bell & sons, 1900. 232p.

MURRAY, W. B. New system of bookkeeping. *Business,* Sept. 1899, p. 573-6.

MUSSELMAN, DELAFAYETTE. High school bookkeeping. Quincy, Ill. DeLafayette Musselman.

MUSSELMAN DELAFAYETTE. Musselman's bookkeeping for business colleges. Quincy, Ill., DeLafayette Musselman, 1909. 111p.

MUSSELMAN, DELAFAYETTE. Musselman's complete bookkeeping. Quincy, Ill. DeLafayette Musselman, 1911. 143p.

MUSSELMAN, DELAFAYETTE. Practical bookkeeping. Quincy, Ill., DeLafayette Musselman.

MUZZY, LEWIS C. Logic of bookkeeping. *Business,* July 1899, p. 440-3.

NAGEL, C. N. Bookkeeping principles. London, Relfe bros. 1889.

NEAL, E. VIRGIL and C. T. CRAGIN. Modern illustrative bookkeeping; designed as a textbook for all schools giving a course in business training; advanced course; script illustrations by E. C. Mills. New York, American book company, c1900. 272p.

NEELY, JOHN ALEXANDER. Neely's automatic self auditing system of mercantile bookkeeping. Anderson, N. C., John A. Neely, 1916. 14p.

NELSON, J. Double entry bookkeeping. London, Simpkin, Marshall, Hamilton, Kent & co. 1871.

NELSON, RICHARD. Nelson's new book-keeping; a text-book for schools and colleges and a book of reference for accountants. Ed. 4. Cincinnati, The Cincinnati & Springfield publishing co. 1890 (c1885). 351p.

NELSON, ROBERT. Bookkeeping. Louisville, Ky., J. P. Morton & co. 1870.

NEW and simple system of bookkeeping for Indian currency. London, Effingham Wilson.

NEW complete accountant. Chicago, J. A. Lyons & co. 1908.

NEW standard commercial bookkeeping, theoretical and practical, containing a thorough elucidation of the principles of double and single entry. Buffalo, J. C. Bryant, 1887. 160p.

NEW York question book in bookkeeping with answers. Syracuse, N. Y., C. W. Bardeen.

NEWBY, ———. Book-keeping exercises. pts. 1-3. New York. Potter Ainsworth & co. 1886.

NEY, FRED J. Bookkeeping simplified. New York, Sir Isaac Pitman & sons, 1911. 336p.

NICHOL, J. D. Bookkeeping. Central school dep., 1878.

NICHOLAS, A. Young accomptant's debtor and creditor, etc. Ed. 2. London, 1713.

NICHOLS, FREDERICK GEORGE. Elementary bookkeeping; exercises for class drill. Rochester, N. Y., Scranton and Wetmore co. 1918. 115p.

NIXON, ALFRED. Bookkeeping exercises. London, Longmans, Green and co. 1898.

NIXON, ALFRED. First lessons and exercises in practical book-keeping. Manchester, 1900.

NIXON, ALFRED. Longmans' advanced bookkeeping. London, Longmans, Green & co. 1894, 1908.

NIXON, ALFRED. Longmans' elementary bookkeeping. London, Longmans, Green & co. 1893.

NIXON, ALFRED. Longmans' studies and questions in bookkeeping and advanced accounts (banking and exchange); with notes and answers. London, Longmans, Green & co. 1898.

NIXON, ALFRED. Worked studies and questions in theory and practice of bookkeeping and advanced accounts. London, Longmans, Green & co. 1900. 254p.

NIXON, JAMES. Rudiments of bookkeeping. New York, Mason & brother. 1854.

NORTH, ROGER. Gentleman accomptant; or, An essay to unfold the mystery of accompts, by way of debtor and creditor, etc.; by a person of Honour. London, 1714.

NORTON, GEORGE PEPLER. Bookkeeping. London, Hamilton Adams & co. 1889.

NOTLEY, A. F. Commercial bookkeeping. London, Bemrose & sons, 1885.

NUTTERHEIMER, H. J. Safety bookkeeping. Cincinnati, 1880.

O'GORMAN, DANIEL. O'Gorman's new and comprehensive system of self-instructing bookkeeping. Newcastle-upon-Tyne, 1850.

O'GORMAN, DANIEL. Original and comprehensive system of self-instructing book-keeping. New ed. Manchester, 1857.

OLD Dutch account book.

OLDHAM, WALTER DEANE and WILLIAM EDWARD HOLLAND. Practical book-keeping; part 1, elementary; part 2, advanced. London, Allman & son, 1901. 226p.

ORR, WILLIAM B. Dominion accountant: or New method of teaching the Irish national book-keeping. Toronto, 1872.

PACIOLI, LUCAS. Summa de arithmetica geometria, proportioni et proportionalita. Venice, 1494. 225 + 76p.

PACKARD, SILAS SADLER. Complete course of business training: instruction in bookkeeping, arithmetic, commercial law and correspondence. New ed. New York, S. S. Packard, 1876.

PACKARD, SILAS SADLER. Method of teaching bookkeeping. New York, S. S. Packard.

PACKARD, SILAS SADLER. Packard's new manual of bookkeeping and correspondence. New York, S. S. Packard, 1884. 158p.

PACKARD, SILAS SADLER and H. B. BRYANT. New Bryant and Stratton counting-house bookkeeping; embracing theory and practice of accounts. New York, Ivison, Blakeman, Taylor & co. 1878.

PALMER, J. H. Common school book-keeping. New York, Farmer Brace & co.

PALMER, J. H. Elements of bookkeeping; embracing single and double entry. New York, Sheldon & co. 1878.

PALMER, J. H. First lessons in bookkeeping. New York, D. Appleton & co.

PALMER, J. H. Lesson in bookkeeping. Jacksonville, Ill., J. H. Palmer, 1885.

PALMER, J. H. Practical bookkeeping. New York, Sheldon & co.

PALMER, J. W. Bookkeeping. London, Knight & co. 1899.

PAPPS, THOMAS. Improved system of bookkeeping. London, F. Hodgson, 1818.

PARTRIDGE, ALBERT HENRY. Is the compulsory adoption of a stereotyped form of accounts

BOOKKEEPING—*(Continued)*
possible and desirable? *Accountant,* July 4, Aug. 22, 1903, p. 871-5, 1050-2.
PATON, WILLIAM ANDREW. Theory of the double entry system. *Canadian chartered accountant,* April 1919, p. 300-15. *Journal of accountancy,* Jan. 1917, p. 7-26.
PEABODY, LORENZO J. Road to independence and wealth; cont. novel system of petty cash accounting. Boston, L. J. Peabody, 1899.
PEPPER, EDMOND. Business man's guide in preparing his trading account, profit and loss account, balance sheet and capital account. Sheffield and London, 1903.
PERCIVAL, RAYMOND. Tradesman's complete book-keeper. London, 1834.
——— Same. Ed. 12. London.
PERCIVAL, RAYMOND. Tradesman's true friend; or, Every man his own book-keeper. New ed. London, [? 1836.]
PERRY, WILLIAM. Man of business, and gentleman's assistant: containing . . . arithmetic . . . book-keeping by single and double entry. Edinburgh, 1774.
——— Same. Ed. 3. 1777.
PHILLIPS, CHARLES. Concise check-system of double entry book-keeping for small businesses; with examples applied to the dairy trade. [? London, 1895.]
PIETRA, DON ANGELO. Indrizzo de gli economi Mantua 1586.
PINNOCK, GEORGE. First steps to knowledge: bookkeeping; single entry. London, 1860.
PITMAN, SIR ISAAC. Additional exercise in bookkeeping. Nos. 1 and 2. London, Sir Isaac Pitman and sons, ltd. 56p.
PITMAN, SIR ISAAC. Advanced bookkeeping. London, Sir Isaac Pitman and sons, 1900. 190p.
PITMAN, SIR ISAAC. Answers to additional exercises in bookkeeping. New York, Sir Isaac Pitman & sons, 1912. 54p.
PITMAN, SIR ISAAC. Avon exercise books for bookkeeping ledger. New York, Sir Isaac Pitman & sons.
PITMAN, SIR ISAAC. Book-keeping test cards, elementary, intermediate, advanced. London, Sir Isaac Pitman & sons, 1904.
PITMAN, SIR ISAAC. Business bookkeeping transactions. London, Sir Isaac Pitman & sons, 1899, 1908.
PITMAN, SIR ISAAC. Commercial book-keeping. Enlarged ed. London, Sir Isaac Pitman & sons, 1910. 424p.
PITMAN, SIR ISAAC. Complete bookkeeping; a text book for private students and public classes, with questions, specimen papers and lists of business terms and abbreviations. Enl. ed. London, Sir Isaac Pitman & sons, 1904. 372p.
——— Same. London, 1908. 432p.
PITMAN, SIR ISAAC. Easy exercises for primer of bookkeeping. New York, Sir Isaac Pitman and sons. 48p.
PITMAN, SIR ISAAC. Key to Pitman's bookkeeping primer. London, Sir Isaac Pitman & sons, 1900.
PITMAN, SIR ISAAC. Key to Pitman's bookkeeping simplified. London, Sir Isaac Pitman & sons, 1912.
PITMAN, SIR ISAAC. Key to Pitman's complete bookkeeping. New York, Sir Isaac Pitman & sons. 213p.
PITMAN, SIR ISAAC. Pitman's book-keeping simplified; a guide to the principles and practice of double entry book-keeping, with exercises in partnership and departmental accounts. Revised edition. London, Sir Isaac Pitman & sons, 1900. 240p.
——— Same. London, 1908. 264p.
PITMAN, SIR ISAAC. Pitman's book-keeping simplified, chapters on reserves and the formation of joint stock companies by W. O. Buxton. London, Sir Isaac Pitman & sons, 1912. 294p.
PITMAN, SIR ISAAC. Pitman's combined manuscript book for bookkeeping. New York, Sir Isaac Pitman & sons, 1912.
PITMAN, SIR ISAAC. Pitman's primer of bookkeeping. New York, Sir Isaac Pitman & sons, 1912. 148p.
PITMAN, SIR ISAAC. Pitman's simplified bookkeeping: answers to exercises in Pitman's book-keeping simplified. New and revised edition. London, Sir Isaac Pitman & sons, 1908. 74p.
PIXLEY, FRANCIS WILLIAM. Recording branch of accountancy or book-keeping. (In his *Accountancy.* Ed. 2. p. 48-60).
PIXLEY, FRANCIS WILLIAM and JOHN WILSON. Bookkeeping. London, George Allen and company.
POCOCK, BERNARD G. Bookkeeping and modern methods of accountancy. *Accountant,* Aug. 6, 1910, p. 169-73.
PORRIT, H. W. and WILLIAM NICKLIN. How to teach book-keeping; practical guide for private tutor and commercial master in day and evening schools. London, Sir Isaac Pitman & sons, 1905. 180p.
PORRITT, H. W. and WILLIAM NICKLIN. Pitman's bookkeeping annual. New York, Sir Isaac Pitman & sons, 1910. 220p.
PORRITT, H. W. and WILLIAM NICKLIN. Pitmans full course in bookkeeping. New York, Sir Isaac Pitman, 1913. 540p.
PORRITT, H. W. and WILLIAM NICKLIN. Pitman's higher bookkeeping and accounts. London, Sir Isaac Pitman and sons, 1911. 308p.
PORTERS, R. J. Pitman's dictionary of bookkeeping: a book of reference on all matters concerning bookkeeping and accountancy for students, teachers and practitioners. London, Sir Isaac Pitman and sons. 777p.
POTTER, S. A. and W. P. HAMMOND. System of practical book-keeping by single and double entry. Common school ed. New York. A. Potter & co.
——— Same. High school edition. New York, A. Potter & co.
POW, J. K. Double entry book-keeping. Gilpin, 1850.
POWER, MICHAEL. Book-keeping no bugbear, or Double entry simplified, in opposition to the insufficiency of the present practice. London, Rivington, 1813, 1815.
POWERS, LEGRAND. Analytical and statistical bookkeeping. *Government accountant,* 1907, v. 1, p. 53-71.
POWERS, M. R. Accountant for public schools and academies. St. Louis, C. R. Barnes, 1877.
POWERS, M. R. and M. R. JOHNSON. Complete accountant, Chicago, W. B. Keen, Cooke & co. 1874.
POWERS, ORVILLE M. Complete accountant. Counting house ed. Chicago, J. A. Lyons.
POWERS, ORVILLE, M. First lessons in bookkeeping. Chicago, J. A. Lyons.
POWERS, ORVILLE M. Single entry bookkeeping for the grades. Chicago, J. A. Lyons.
POWERS, ORVILLE M. Theory of bookkeeping. Chicago, Metropolitan text book co. 1913. 125p.
PRACTICE book in business forms aid bookkeeping. New York, D. C. Heath and co. 1898.
PRACTICAL bookkeeping. Rochester, Commercial correspondence schools.
PRESENTING the theory of double entry bookkeeping. *The office,* June, July 1889, p. 105-7, 127-9.
PRESTON, LYMAN. District-school bookkeeping. New York, R. B. Collins.
PRESTON, LYMAN. Preston's treatise on bookkeeping by double and single entry. New edition. New York, Collins & bro. 1867.

BOOKKEEPING—*(Continued)*

PRESTON, LYMAN. Preston's treatise on bookkeeping: or, Arbitrary rules made plain: in two parts, adapted to the use of academies and common schools, with varied examples; accompanied with detailed explanations: the first part being designed for the use of mechanics of all classes; the second, arranged more particularly for the instruction of young men who contemplate the pursuit of mercantile business, showing the method of keeping accounts by double entry: embracing a variety of useful instruction relative to different kinds of business. New York, R. & G. S. Wood, c1831. 184p.

PRICE, ISAAC. Questions in advanced bookkeeping for drill, test and review. New York, Hinds, Hayden and Eldridge, 1918. 80p. (Progressive series regents question and answer books).

——— Same, with answers. New York, Hinds, Hayden and Eldridge, 1918. 107 + 210p. (Progressive series; regents question and answer books).

PRICE, ISAAC. Questions in elementary bookkeeping for drill, test and review. New York, Hinds, Hayden and Eldridge, 1918. 107 + 220p. (Progressive series; regents question and answer books).

PROGRESS of bookkeeping. *Dublin review,* v. 19, p. 433.

PULLEN, PHILIP. Book-keeping improved: or, A certain method for the detection and prevention of errors, superseding the process of calling the books over. London, 1803.

PURCELL, H. E. One cure for national waste; instruction in simple bookkeping forms or budget-making. *School and society,* Dec. 9, 1916, p. 899-900.

PURKIS, H. W. Students guide to bookkeeping. 1872.

QUIN, MATTHEW. Quin's rudiments of bookkeeping; comprised in six plain cases, and attainable in as many days, without the help of a teacher; calculated for persons of either sex, grown to maturity; with an essay on the fit manner of initiating youth to temperance and moral rectitude; by an easy arithmetical scale. London, 1776.

——— Same. Ed. 3. London, 1779.

RACINE, SAMUEL F. Syllabus of bookkeeping. Seattle, The Western institute of accountancy, commerce and finance, c1918-1920. 86p.

RADFORD, GEORGE. On book-keeping. London, 1910.

RAIM'S commercial bookkeeping. Roworth, 1882.

REYNOLDS, GEORGE. Introduction to bookkeeping. London, Hurst 1829.

REYNOLDS, GEORGE. Scholar's introduction to merchants' accounts. Ed. 2. London, 1831.

REYNOLDS, W. Systems of book-keeping by double entry. London, 1828.

RICE, THOMAS A. Practical bookkeeping. Ed. 2, enlarged. St. Louis, T. A. Rice, 1879.

RICHARDS, W. M. Matters of the counting house. London, Gee & co. 1899.

RICHMOND, WELLINGTON HARRISON. Comprehensive system of book-keeping, by double entry, adapted to the business transactions of merchants and mechanics; with lectures on the science of book-keeping, etc. Montreal, 1846.

RISQUE, FERDINAND WILLIAM. Loose leaf books and systems for general business. St. Louis, Studley & co. 1907. 174p.

RITTENHOUSE, CHARLES FOREST. New modern illustrative bookkeeping; introductory course. New York, American book co. c1918. 152p.

ROBERTSON, POWHATAN WYNDHAM. Bookkeeper's compendium; or, Bookkeeping in a nutshell. Philadelphia, Hinds, Noble and Eldridge.

ROBERTSON, POWHATAN WYNDHAM. Bookkeeping and science of accounts. Philadelphia, Hinds, Noble and Eldridge.

ROBINSON, JAMES. Compend of bookkeeping by single entry. Boston, C. Stimpson.

ROE, RICHARD. Introduction to book-keeping. London, Harvey 1825.

ROHRER, L. Lectures on book-keeping; for teachers. St. Louis, W. J. Gilbert, 1875.

ROHRER, L. Primary bookkeeping. St. Louis, W. J. Gilbert, 1875.

ROHRER, L. School edition book-keeping. St. Louis, W. J. Gilbert, 1873.

ROOSE, RICHARD. Essay to make a compleat accomptant: in two parts; I. A treatise of book-keeping according to the true Italian method, etc.; II. The solution of 18 questions in company accompts, etc. London, ?1760.

ROSS, W. P. Accountant's own book. Philadelphia, Author, 1848.

ROSS, W. P. Bookkeeping. Philadelphia, C. Desilver.

ROSS, W. P. Double entry bookkeeping. Philadelphia, Zieber & co. 1847.

ROUTLEY, JOHN. Business book-keeping. London, Sir Isaac Pitman & sons, 1919.

ROWE, HARRY MARC. Bookkeeping and accountancy; complete text presenting the art of bookkeeping in accordance with the principles of modern accountancy. Baltimore, The H. M. Rowe co. c1911. 264p.

ROWE, HARRY MARC. Business bookkeeping and practice. Baltimore, H. M. Rowe co.

ROWE, HENRY MARC. Commercial and industrial bookkeeping: an educational method of teaching the principles and laws of accounts; as derived from the established customs, practices and usages of business and the most progressive and labor saving systems of bookkeeping as practiced in all lines of commerce and industry using all the business papers, documents and vouchers required in the transaction of business as contained in the various sets that accompany this reference book. Baltimore, Sadler-Rowe company, 1899. 96p.

ROWE, HARRY MARC. Junior arithmetic—bookkeeping for junior high schools, advanced grades, and such other schools as desire to give an intensely practical training course in the arithmetic of bookkeeping and in the bookkeeping of everyday business affairs that is graded to suit elementary students. 2 pts. Baltimore, H. M. Rowe, co. 1918.

ROYALL, JOHN PRICE. Manual of the elements of bookkeeping. Kirtley, 1884.

RUIZ, ANTONIO L. Nociones de teneduria de libros, parte primera Teoria de la contabilidad mercantil; libro de texto o de referencia para el curso práctico de contabilidad por el método objetivo. Guadalajara. Talleres tipograficos. Libreria font. 1919. 124p.

RUSSELL, THOMAS HERBERT and WILLIAM J. JACKMAN. Bookkeeping, accounting and auditing. Chicago, Whitman publishing co. 1916. 416p.

SADLER, W. H. and R. M. ROWE. Sadler's business bookkeeping and practice; school edition; a new work that presents an old subject in a new way, presenting the theory of accounts by the inductive method and illustrating the principles of bookkeeping and the best practice of experienced bookkeepers in modern accounting. Baltimore, W. H. Sadler, c1894. 92p.

——— Same. Ed. 10. Baltimore, W. H. Sadler, 1897. 18p.

SANDY, W. C. American accountant; a new and practical treatise on double entry bookkeeping. New York, University publishing company, 1904. 118p.

BOOKKEEPING—*(Continued)*

SARLL, ANDREW. Double entry bookkeeping in theory and practice; with examination papers. Ed. 15. London, 1899.

SARLL, ANDREW. Modern bookkeeping in theory and practice. London, 1907.

SARLL, ANDREW. Practical bookkeeping (new code bookkeeping) London.

SARLL, ANDREW. Principles of practical bookkeeping; with exercises, examination papers and key. London, 1881.

——— Same. Enlarged ed. London, 1890.

——— Same. Ed. 15. London, 1903.

SAWYER, JOHN. Practical book-keeping for all businesses, with stock-books especially adapted to the tanning trade. London, Effingham Wilson, 1895.

SCHOOL and examination bookkeeping. London, Longmans, Green & co. 1902.

SCHREFFLER, R. B. I know now why I keep books. *System,* Feb. 1917, p. 195-201.

SCRIBNER, W. M. Bookkeeping exercises; tablet form. New York, American book co.

SCHWARTZ, GEORGE W. Office routine and bookkeeping. New York, American book co.

SCHWARTZ, LEON. Pocket journalizer. Manticoke, Pa., Journalizer co. 1915. 28p.

SCOTT, BENJAMIN. Principles of bookkeeping and balancing. Birmingham, 1879.

SCOTT, ROBERT. New century book-keeping for business people. Glasgow, W. & R. Holmes, 1901. 110p.

SCOTT, ROBERT. Scott's book-keeping chart for business people. Glasgow, David Robertson & co. 1908.

SCOTT'S new bookkeeping guide. Glasgow, David Robertson & co. 1919.

SCOULLER, JOHN. Practical book-keeping. Ed. 6. London, Simpkin, Marshall, Hamilton, Kent & co. 1904. 108p.

SCOULLER, JOHN. Practical book-keeper and accountant's guide. London, Simpkin, Marshall, Hamilton, Kent & co. 1905. 228p.

SCRIBNER, W. M. Bookkeeping exercises: tablet form, single entry. Boston, American book co.

SCRIBNER, WILLIAM M. Scribner's common school book-keeping exercises. New York, Potter, Knight Ainsworth & co. 1887.

SCRUTON, JAMES. Practical counting-house. Glasgow, 1777.

SEALLY, JOHN. Accountant's companion: or Schoolmaster's new assistant to practical arithmetic . . . with a course of book-keeping by single entry. London, 1773.

SEAVY, MANSON. Practical business bookkeeping. New York. D. C. Heath and co. 1893.

SEDGER, J. Introduction to merchants' accounts. Part 1 and 2. London, 1807-1808.

SEDGER, J. Sedger's rudiments of book-keeping. London, 1777.

SEEBOHM, BENJAMIN. Theory of bookkeeping. London, Effingham Wilson, 1892.

SHARP, P. G. Bookkeeping and machine application. *Accountant,* Nov. 8, 1919, p. 399. *Australasian accountant* and *secretary,* Dec. 1, 1919, p. 21-2.

SHAW, JOHN. Book-keeping epitomized: a compendium of Mair's Merchants-accompts. Leeds, 1794.

SHAW, JUDSON WADE. Business forms and elementary book-keeping. Boston, D. C. Heath & Co., 1893.

SHAW, JUDSON WADE. Busy man's bookkeeping. New York, D. C. Heath and co.

SHAW, JUDSON WADE. Elementary bookkeeping. New York, D. C. Heath and co.

SHEAFFER, WILLIAM ADAM. Metropolitan system of bookkeeping. Chicago, Metropolitan text book co. 1914. 246p.

SHEFFIELD AND NORTHERN CHARTERED ACCOUNTANTS STUDENTS' SOCIETIES. Joint debate—Would legislation to compel traders to keep proper books, open to government inspection be desirable? *Accountant,* Jan. 28, March 11, 1905, p. 111-9, 269-71.

SHEPHERD, R. Bookkeeping. Preston, 1755.

SHERIFF, DANIEL. Improved principles of single-entry book-keeping. London, Longmans, 1862.

——— Same. Another ed. London, 1880.

SHERIFF, DANIEL. Whole science of double-entry book-keeping. Ed. 2. London, 1852.

——— Same, undated with title-page slightly altered.

——— Same. 1858.

——— Same. Ed. 3. London, 1882.

SHINN, E. Proper record forms for every business. World's work, Jan. 1906, p. 7129-30.

SHORT notes on Mr. Webster's set of books annexed to the Compleat compting house. 1747.

SIMPLE, P. Second thoughts on double entry bookkeeping. London, Simpkin, Marshall, Hamilton, Kent & co. 1872.

SKERRY, G. E. Practical notes on book-keeping and accountancy. London, Simpkin, Marshall, Hamilton, Kent & co. 1910.

SKERRY, G. E. Practical papers in bookkeeping. London, Civil service press, 1918. 68p.

SKERRY, G. E. Practical papers in book-keeping adapted to the requirements of candidates for all public examinations and commercial life. London, Simpkin, Marshall, Hamilton, Kent & co. 1910. 228p.

SKERRY, G. E. and ERNEST JONES. Practical papers in civil service bookkeeping. London, 1886.

SMITH, FREDERICK W. Confound that boy! A manual of book-keeping and office routine. George Newnes, 1898. 118p.

SMITH, HENRY H. Book-keeping and commercial practice. London, Sir Isaac Pitman and sons, 1916. 148p.

SMITH, J. C. National accountant. Philadelphia. J. B. Lippincott and co.

SMITH, STANLEY GEORGE. Book-keeping in 1793. *Accountant,* Feb. 14, 1903, p. 226-8.

SMITH, T. Commercial bookkeeping and arithmetic hints. London, Simpkin, Marshall, Hamilton, Kent & co. 1841.

SMITH, T. Double entry bookkeeping. London, Simpkin, Marshall, Hamilton, Kent & co. 1840.

SMITH, T. Practical bookkeeping. London, Simpkin, Marshall, Hamilton, Kent & co. 1851.

SMITH, WILLIAM and E. MARTIN. Bookkeeping by single and double entry simplified and adapted to use of common schools. New York, A. S. Barnes & co. 1859.

SMYTHE, LILLIAN C. Old account book. *Cornhill magazine,* v. 87, p. 551. *Electic magazine,* v. 141, p. 47. *Littell's living age,* v. 237, p. 506.

SNAILUM, W. W. Studies in bookkeeping. Cambridge, Harvard university press, 1900.

SNELL, CHARLES. Accompts for landed-men: or, A plain and easie form which they may observe in keeping accompts of their estates. London, ?1710.

SNYDER, C. and E. L. THURSTON. Universal system of practical bookkeeping. New York, American Book co. 1902.

SNYDER, WILLIAM THOMAS. Brief exposition of the fundamental principles of bookkeeping and a complete guide to corporation bookkeeping. Charlottsville, Va., William Thomas Snyder, 1907.

SOMMER, M. M. Practical guide to double entry bookkeeping in tabular form, etc. Newark, Martin R. Dennis & co. 1876.

SOULÉ, GEORGE. Higher accounting. *Accountant,* Sept. 22, 1894, p. 825-30.

SPENCER, ENOS. Art of modern bookkeeping and accounting. Ed. 4. Louisville, Ky., Enos Spencer, 1911. 444p.

BOOKKEEPING—*(Continued)*

SPENCER, ENOS. Disciplinary value of bookkeeping as a study. *National educational association, Proceedings,* 1903, p. 741-6.

SPENCER, ENOS and J. W. DRYE. Bookkeeping and business calculation; arranged for bookkeepers, business students and pupils preparing for commercial training. Louisville, Ky., Enos Spencer, 1918. 48p.

SPENCERIAN business college bookkeeping. Revised edition. Milwaukee, C. N. Caspar, 1887.

SPICER, ERNEST EVAN and ERNEST C. PEGLER. Bookkeeping and accounts. London, H. Foulks Lynch & co.
——— Same. Ed. 2. 1910. 424p.
——— Same. Ed. 3. 1914. 442p.
——— Same. Ed. 4. 1919. 444p.

SPICER, ERNEST EVAN and ERNEST C. PEGLER. Elementary book-keeping. Oxford, Oxford university press, 1914. 380p.
——— Same. Ed. 2. Oxford, 1918. 366p.

SPICER, ERNEST EVAN and E. C. PEGLER. Practical bookkeeping and commercial knowledge. London, H. Foulks Lynch & co. 1912. 342p.

SPRAGUE, LEVI L. Student's guide: theoretical and actual business departments of Wyoming college of business; rev. by Willis L. Dean. Kingston, Pa., Willis L. Dean, 1912. 1911.

STANDARD bookkeeping. New York, Silver Burdett and co.

STEPHENS, C. E. and HENRY THOMAS LOOMIS. Complete practical bookkeeping; journal or ledger method. Cleveland, Ohio, Practical text book co. 1898.

STEPHENS, HUSTCRAFT. Italian book-keeping reduced into an art: being an entire new, and compleat system of accompts in general; with a preface by J. Weir. Dublin, 1737.
——— Same. Another ed. Dublin, 1754.

STEPHENS, JOHN RITTENHOUSE. Principles of accounting. Kansas city, Mo., John R. Stephens, 1909.

STEPHENSON, J. and A. J. BOWLER. Text-book of elementary book-keeping. London, Normal press, 1910.

STEVENS, C. E. and HENRY THOMAS LOOMIS. Progressive bookkeeping. Cleveland, Ohio, Practical text book, 1908.

STEVENSON, W. Bookkeeping by double entry. Edinburgh, 1762.

STEWART, ———. Civil service bookkeeping. Stewart, 1886.

STRAYER, S. IRVING. Modern bookkeeping. Baltimore, Modern text book co.

STRAYER, S. IRVING and H. WINFIELD WRIGHT. Modern bookkeeping, accounting and business practice. Philadelphia, Modern text book co. 1918. 258p.

STREETER, T. E. Elements of practical bookkeeping. London, Gee & co. 1896. 70p.

STUART, ALEXANDER MOODY. Bookkeeping; observations and suggestions. Edinburgh, 1894.

SWEET, JAMES S. Business practice bookkeeping; a thorough treatise on modern and practical methods of accounting. Santa Rosa, Cal., J. S. Sweet publishing co. 1913. 192p.

SWILL, A. Double entry bookkeeping. London, Gill, 1885.

SYSTEM of whole numbers. London, Effingham Wilson, 1871.

TANNER, HENRY T. Modern bookkeeping and practical business instructor. Akron, Ohio, Saalfield publishing co. 1907.

TAYLOR, E. Book-keeping. Madden, 1850.

TAYLOR, HERBERT WALTER. Elementary double-entry book-keeping. London, Simpkin, Marshall, Hamilton, Kent & co. 1898.

TAYLOR, WILLIAM. Complete system of practical arithmetic; with various branches in the mathematics . . . to which is added bookkeeping, by single and double entry, etc. Birmingham, 1783.

THOMAS, S. Economist: or Housekeeper's accompts made easy, after the Italian method: the like not extant. (In *Webster, Wiliam. Essay on book-keeping.* 1779).

THOMAS, S. A. Bookkeeping; single entry. New Haven, Conn., H. H. Peck.

THOMAS, S. A. Bookkeeping; double entry. New Haven, Conn., H. H. Peck.

THOMPSON, JNO. G. Old account book. *Journal of political economy,* v. 10, p. 614-8.

THOMPSON, WARDHAUGH. Accomptant's oracle; or, Key to science being a treatise of common arithmetic: in two volumes; vol. 1 [as above]; vol. 2, a compleat practical system of book-keeping, etc. York, 1777.

THOMSON, ———. Bookkeeping principles and practice. London, Bell, 1887.

THOMSON, A. W. Text-book of the principles and practice of bookkeeping and estate-office work. New York, G. Bell and sons.
——— Same. Ed. 3, enlarged by F. C. McClellan. London, 1901.
——— Same. Ed. 5. London, 1910.

THOMSON, J. ROWAN. Single-entry book-keeping. *Accountants' magazine,* Feb. 1912, p. 92-100.

THOREAU, P. New course of book-keeping. Law, 1815.

THORNE, WILLIAM W. Abolition of the trial balance together with 12 studies in bookkeeping and accounting. Detroit, Mich., Business man's publishing co. 1906.

THORNE, WILLIAM W. Twentieth century book-keeping and business practice. Detroit, Mich., Business man's publishing co. 1904.

THORNTON, ———. Every man his own accountant. London, Simpkin, Marshall, Hamilton, Kent & co. 1889.

THORNTON, F. OLIVER. Bookkeeping for evening classes. London, Macmillan & co. 412p.

THORNTON, F. OLIVER. Key to bookkeeping for evening classes. London, Macmillan & co. 1916.

THORNTON, JOHN. A B C D series of bookkeeping exercise books. London, Macmillan & co. 1901.

THORNTON, JOHN. Bookkeeping for elementary schools. London, Macmillan & co.

THORNTON, JOHN. Book-keeping primer; 14 introductory lessons. London, Macmillan & co. 1879, 1883.

THORNTON, JOHN. Easy exercises in bookkeeping; also key. London, Macmillan & co. 1909.

THORNTON, JOHN. First lessons in bookkeeping. London, Macmillan & co. 1883.
——— Same. [? Ed. 6.] London, 1889.
——— Same. [Ed. 13.] London, 1894.
——— Same. [Ed. 14.] London, 1896.
——— Same. [?Ed. 15.] London, 1002.

THORNTON, JOHN. Manual of bookkeeping for the use of students. London, Macmillan & co. 1895.
——— Same. New ed. London, 1907.
——— Same. New and revised ed. London, 1912. 554p.

THORNTON, JOHN. Primer of bookkeeping; also key. London, Macmillan & co. 1890, 1892.

THORNTON, JOHN. What is bookkeeping? *Business,* Aug. 1895, p. 299-301.

THORNTON, JOHN and S. W. THORNTON. Bookkeeping for business men. London, Macmillan & co. 1900, 1901, 1902.

THOUGHTS on double entry and balance sheets. London, 1869.

TINLING, JAMES ALEXANDER. Schoolmaster's diary and account book: Tinling's system for private schools. Eastbourne, 1901.

BOOKKEEPING—*(Continued)*

TOLMIE, DAVID. Book-keeping; a learner's guide to its theory and practice. London, Sir Isaac Pitman & sons, 1890.
——— Same. Ed. 3. London, 1911.
TOLMIE, DAVID. Elementary bookkeeping. Glasgow, Blackie & son, 1885.
TRELEVEN, JOHN EDWARD. Bookkeeping in the high school. Austin, University of Texas, 1916. 53p.
TREVOR, CHARLES ROBINSON. Book-keeping. *Accountant,* Mar. 17, 24, 1883.
TREVOR, CHARLES ROBINSON. Practical book-keeping; the ledger, the journal, and trial balance. *Accountant,* March 24, 1894, p. 267-78.
TUCK, HENRY. Manual of book-keeping; by an experienced clerk. Ed. 6. London, Bell, 1849, 1853, 1856.
TUFFS, EDWARD J. Expense books for solicitors, auctioneers, accountants, etc. London, Gee & co.
TURNER, FREDERICK W. Elementary bookkeeping. London, James Nisbet & co. 1918. 144p.
TURNER, R. [Book-keeping in the] Italian method, by debtor and creditor; in which the theory of that art is not only elucidated, but the practice made easy and familiar, by the addition of a set of books. First American edition from the third English ed. Boston, I. Thomas and E. T. Andrews, 1794. 24p.
TUSHAK, GERALD. Modern method of bookkeeping. *New York accountants' and bookkeepers' journal,* Nov. 1903, 161-5.
TYRANNY of the bookbinder. *Journal of accountancy,* July 1907, p. 216-7.
UNITED STATES. FEDERAL TRADE COMMISSION. Helpful activities to strengthen American business. Washington, Government printing office, 1916. 4p.
UNIVERSITY bookkeeping and treatise on business and accounts. New York, Silver-Burdett and co.
VAN CLEVE, CHARLES MCKINSTRY. Principles of double entry bookkeeping. New York, James Kempster printing co. 1913.
VAN CLEVE, CHARLES MCKINSTRY. Principles of double-entry bookkeeping. tr. by Shigeo Nakamura. (Japanese).
VAN CLEVE, CHARLES MCKINSTRY. Principles of double entry: correspondence. *Journal of accountancy,* Aug. 1914, p. 153-5.
VAN CLEVE, CHARLES MCKINSTRY. Theory of double entry bookkeeping. Brooklyn, C. M. Van Cleve, 1907.
——— Same. New York, James Kempster, 1913. 210p.
VAN DE LINDE, GERARD. Bookkeeping. Ed. 2. London, Gee & co. 1891.
——— Same. Ed. 3. London, Gee & co. 1891.
Accountant. Nov. 7-Dec. 12, 1891, Jan. 9, 30, Feb. 6, 13, 1892, p. 783-8, 796-804, 842-4, 857-64, 881-4; 39-47, 109-12, 124-32, 150-2.
VAN DE LINDE, GERARD. Bookkeeping and other papers. London, Blades, East & Blades, 1904. 460p.
Contents.
1. Bookkeeping in four parts.
2. A merchant's office.
3. A merchant's accounts.
4. Company works.
5. Collieries.
6. Secretarial.
7. Audit of banks and mercantile firms.

VAN VLISSINGEN, A. One-man business: a complete record for five minutes work a day. *System,* April 1917, p. 438-40.
VAUGHAN, L. BRENT. Complete courses in bookkeeping, double and single entry. Chicago, Civil service publishing co. 1912. 91p.
VAUTRO, P. C. L. New system of book-keeping. London, Salva, 1828.
VERNON, G. F. CARR. Key to book-keeping as required by the civil service commissioners, etc. London, [? 1895.]
VERNON, JOHN. Compleat compting-house; or, The young lad taken from the Writing school, and fully instructed, by way of dialogue, in all the mysteries of a merchant, from his first understanding of plain arithmetick, to the highest pitch of trade: whereby the Master is saved much labour, and the lad is led by the hand to all his work and business; which to Youth is accounted troublesome, but will here seem pleasant. A work very necessary for all that are concerned in keeping accompts, of what quality soever. By John Vernon. London, Printed by J. D. for Benj. Billingsley, at the Printing-press in Cornhil, 1678.
——— Same. Ed. 3. 1698.
——— Same. Ed. 5. 1722.
WADLEY, T. M. Single entry book-keeping. *South African accountant,* June, Sept. 1917, p. 38-40, 79-80.
WAGGONER, D. B. Book-keeping simplified; double entry system explained. Philadelphia, D. B. Waggoner & co. 1874.
WAINWRIGHT, H. S. and others. Book-keeping and commercial practice; v. 1, for first year students. London. Macmillan & co. 1916. 85p.
WAKEFORD, JAMES.. Modern bookkeeping. London, T. S. Clark, 1907. 232p.
WALKER, H. D. Bookkeeping for the million: by single entry. Philadelphia, Claxton, Remsen & Haffelfinger, 1869.
WALKINGHAME, FRANCIS. Short treatise upon book-keeping, by single entry. [See Walkinghame's Tutor's assistant.] London, 1817.
WALKINGHAME, FRANCIS. Tutor's assistant, Ed. 14. London, 1776.
——— Same. Derby, 1818.
——— Same. Ed. 62. London, 1823.
WALLACE, ———. Pocket guide to commercial book-keeping. Glasgow, 1849.
——— Same. Another ed. Glasgow, 1856.
WALLACE, R. Commercial bookkeeping. London, Hall, 1850.
WALMSLEY, JOHN. Elements of the theory and practice of book-keeping, based upon the principles of correlative double entry. London, 1905.
WALSH, W. H. Bookkeeping transactions, set II.; Peter Brown and Smith Robinson; adapted to Chambers' bookkeeping. London and Edinburgh, 1893.
WALTON, SEYMOUR. Test by double entry. *Journal of accountancy.* Feb. 1916, p. 154-5.
WATSON, E. L. Watson's improved system for detecting and locating errors in posting and taking off trial balances. New York, E. L. Watson, 1888. 48p.
WEBBER, HENRY JOHN. Book-keeper's companion: book-keeping simplified: the principles of posting and balancing shown by a diagram, etc. London [? 1897.]
WEBER, FRED CHARLES. Bookkeeping and accountancy; arranged for use in the classes of high schools, intermediate schools and private commercial schools. Ed. 5. 8145 Spring Street, Los Angeles, Cal., Pacific sales and duplicating co. 1916. 205p.
WEBER, FRED CHARLES. Introductory bookkeeping; arranged for the use in the classes of the commercial department of the Los Angeles polytechnic high school. Los Angeles, Cal., F. C. Weber, 1907.

BOOKKEEPING—*(Continued)*

WEBSTER, J. E. and HARRY HUGHES. Elementary book-keeping. Leeds, S. Grant, 1899. 78p.

——— Same. Ed. 2. Exeter, 1906.

WEBSTER, WILLIAM. Essay on book-keeping according to the true Italian method of debtor and creditor, by double entry, etc.

——— Same. Ed. 2. London, 1721.

——— Same. Ed. 3. London, 1726.

——— Same. Ed. 7. London, 1740.

——— Same. Ed 8. London, 1744.

——— Same. Ed. 9. London, 1747.

——— Same. Ed. 10. London, 1749.

——— Same, 15th ed., corrected by E. Webster. London, 1772.

——— Same. Another edn., revised by S. Thomas. Newcastle, 1779.

WEBSTER, WILLIAM. Short notes on Mr. Webster's set of books annexed to the compleat compting-house. Dublin, 1747.

WELLS, CHARLES R. Practice system of business training. 2 courses. New York, American book co.

WELLS, CHARLES R. Practice system of business training and bookkeeping. Rochester, Williams & Roger, c1896. 136p.

WELLS, W. HENRY. A B C of book-keeping. London, Drane's ltd. 1912. 88p.

WENLOCK, RANKIN. Key to public school modern book-keeping. London, J. M. Dent and sons, 1912.

WENLOCK, RANKIN. Public school modern book-keeping. London, J. M. Dent and sons, 1910. 192p.

WESTERVELT, J. W., A. BLANCHARD, J. W. WESTERVELT and D. HOSKINS. Canadian standard bookkeeping. Toronto, 1901.

WESTON, WILLIAM. Complete merchant's clerk: or, British and American compting-house; in two parts. Part 1 contains a system of bookkeeping . . . as practiced by the merchants of Great Britain . . . Part II contains book-keeping in factory, as used in Barbadoes, Nevis, etc. London, 1754.

WHATLEY, G. E. STUART. General book-keeping for trades, merchants, business and professional men. London, Simpkin, Marshall, Hamilton, Kent & co. 1894.

WHEELER, GEORGE W. Book-keeping for beginners. London, Gee and co. 45p.

WHIGHAM, WALLACE H. and OLIVER D. FREDERICK. Bookkeeping and business practice; book one. Boston, D. C. Heath & co. c1910. 142p.

WHINYATES, JOHN W. Bookkeeping without a master. Chicago, M. A. Donahue and co.

WHITEHILL, ROBERT. Some notes on matters of opinion in connection with accounts. *Accountant,* July 1, 1899, p. 702-10.

WHY double-entry is scientific. *Accountant,* April 14, 1900, p. 353-5.

WIBLER, H. J. Bookkeeper's companion: bookkeeping simplified: the principles of posting and balancing . . . shown by a diagram, etc. [? 1897].

WICKS, JOHN H. Accountant's practical guide. 1802.

WICKS, JOHN H. Book-keeping reformed. Egham, 1797.

WIGHTMAN, WILLIAM W. COMP. Student's guide to the principles of bookkeeping. Battle Creek, Mich., Ellis publishing co. 1909. 116p.

——— Same, in chart form. Ed. 2. Battle Creek, Mich., Ellis publishing co. 1909. 38p.

WILLETT, JACOB. Bookkeeping. Poughkeepsie, P. Potter, 1830.

WILLIAMS, LOUIS L. and FERNANDO E. ROGERS. First lessons in bookkeeping. Rochester, Williams & Rogers, 1892.

WILLIAMS, LOUIS L. and FERNANDO E. ROGERS. Key to Supplementary exercises in bookkeeping. New York, American book co. 1913. 28p.

WILLIAMS, LOUIS L. and FERNANDO E. ROGERS. New complete bookkeeping. New York, American book co. 1907.

WILLIAMS, LOUIS L. and FERNANDO E. ROGERS. New introductive bookkeeping. New York, American book co.

WILLIAMS, LOUIS L. and FERNANDO E. ROGERS. New theoretical and practical complete bookkeeping, by double and single entry. Rochester, Williams & Rogers, 1894.

WILLIAMS, LOUIS L. and FERNANDO E. ROGERS. Supplementary exercises in bookkeeping. New York, American book co. 1908.

WILSON, G. A. Treatise on bookkeeping. Philadelphia, Lindsay & Blakiston.

WILSON, GEORGE. Practical bookkeeping. Sherwood, 1823.

WILSON, M. MITCHELL. Field-glass view of bookkeeping. Indianapolis, M. M. Wilson. 20p.

WINCHESTER, G. W. System of bookkeeping, double and single entry. Hartford, H. H. Hawley & co.

WING, WILLIAM. Book-keeping and the journal. *Accountant,* May 11, 1889, p. 248-52.

WITTER, CHARLES A. Witter's business and accounts for public schools and home use. Ed. 6, revised and enlarged. Redlands, Cal., C. A. Witter, 1910. 112p.

WOOD, WILLIAM. Book-keeping familiarised. Birmingham. ?1777.

WOOLLEY, EDWARD M. Saving half an office payroll. *System,* Sept. 1913, p. 238-45.

WOOLLEY, S. R. Woolley's practical bookkeeping. Detroit, T. Nourse, 1883.

WREFORD, FRANCIS and WALTER S. MCGREGOR. Bookkeeping by double entry, with exercises and examination papers; in three parts. London, Moffatt and Paige, 1891.

WRIGHT, HENRY C. Manual of book-keeping: containing rules and definitions together with business transactions for practice in single or double entry. Brooklyn, A. C. Huene & brothers, 1884. 73p.

WRIGHT, PRINCE ALBERT. Book-keeping simplified. New York, P. A. Wright and co. 1901. 368p.

——— Same. 1881. 15p.

WRIGHT, WILLIAM. National system of bookkeeping. Philadelphia, Claxton, Remsen & Hafflefinger; J. B. Lippincott & co. 1866.

WRIGHT, WILLIAM. National system of bookkeeping; containing the elements, practice and science . . . in which the true principles are exemplified in seven sets of books kept by double entry. Rev. ed. New York, W. Wright, 1875. 167p.

YALDWYN, W. BUTLER. Advanced thought on accounts. Sydney, 1895.

YALDWYN, W. Butler Re accounts. Sydney, 1895.

YALDWYN, W. BUTLER. Single entry bookkeeping: the simplest and shortest system. Sydney, [? 1894.]

Bibliographies.

See Bibliographies, indexes, catalogues, etc.

Card and loose leaf—

ARNOLD, HORACE, LUCIAN. Complete cost keeper; together with an exposition of the advantages of account keeping by cards instead of books. New York, *Engineering magazine,* 1912.

ASPRAY, NEVILLE. Loose-leaf books. *Accountant,* Oct. 20, 1917, p. 311-4.

BALMFORD, JOHN A. Account-keeping by loose-leaf methods. *Accountant,* Aug. 3, 1912, p. 148-56.

BOOKKEEPING—CARD AND LOOSE LEAF—*(Continued)*

BARKER, J. HEATON. Card ledgers and card index systems. *Accountant*, Sept. 24, 1904. p. 315-8.

BELL, ELLIOT. "Movable-leaf system" applied to commercial bookkeeping. Reading, Petty & sons, 1908. 188p.

BENNETT, GEORGE E. Loose-leaf and bound records. (In his *Constructive accounting*. 1920. p. 60-8).

CARD and loose-leaf ledgers. *Accountant*, Oct. 15, 1904, p. 377-9.

CARTER, R. N. Loose leaf and card ledgers; slip system of bookkeeping. In his *Advanced accounts*. p. 15-9).

CLARK, NEIL M. Efficiency in loose leaf accounting. *System* (London), 1914, v. 26, p. 489-95.

COLE, WILLIAM MORSE. Loose leaf systems. (In his *Accounts, their construction and interpretation*. c1915. p. 413-4).

COTTON, GEORGE M. Card journal and its uses. *Business organization and management*, Sept. 1920, p. 637-41).

DICKINSON, ARTHUR LOWES. Loose-leaf records. In his *Accounting practice and procedure*. 1917. p. 22-3).

DICKSEE, LAWRENCE ROBERT. Bookkeeping without books. In his *Advanced accounting*. 1916. p. 236-52).

DICKSEE, LAWRENCE ROBERT. Loose-leaf systems. *Accountant*, Nov. 11, 1911, p. 652-6. *Incorporated accountants' journal*, 1910-11, p. 198.

DICKSEE, LAWRENCE ROBERT and H. E. BLAIN. Card systems, loose leaf ledgers. (In his *Office organisation and management*. 1917. p. 20, 58-9, 130-2, 154, 21-3).

DOYLE, NORMAN. Uses and limitations of the card, loose-leaf ledgers, and slip systems, in relation to matters of account. *Accountant*, Nov. 9, 1907, p. 581-9.

EDWARDS, ALLEN. Card and loose leaf ledger systems and their adaptability to the jewellery trades. *Accountant*, June 16, 1906, p. 756-65.

EGGELSTON, DEWITT CARL. Doing away with the ledger. *Business man's magazine*, Dec. 1910, p. 569-72.

GARDNER, HERBERT.. Loose-leaf and card methods. *Accountant*, Nov. 21, 1914, p. 618-9.

HALL, H. L. Loose leaf methods. *Business man's magazine*, Jan. 1906.

HEANEY, H. Card ledgers. *Accountant*, Nov. 12, 1904, Jan. 28, 1905, p. 599-605; 101-3.

HOLLIS, W. P. Transformation in bookkeeping: "Contab's" loose leaf system of accounts, etc. Cambridge, England, W. Heffer & sons, ltd. 1917. 36p.

KESTER, ROY B. Card and loose leaf ledgers. (In his *Accounting theory and practice*. 1918. p. 267).

KLEIN, JOSEPH J. Card ledgers, loose-leaf books and devices. (In his *Elements of accounting*. 1916. p. 79-81, 307).

LESLIE, WILLIAM. Loose-leaf and card ledgers. *Accountant*, May 2, 1908. p. 648-52.

LISLE, GEORGE. Card and loose sheet system of keeping ledger accounts. (In his *Accounting in theory and practice*. 1900. p. 114-7).

LOOG, SIDNEY. Loose leaf records vs. bound books. *Business man's magazine*, Aug. 1908, p. 133-6.

LOOSE leaf methods. *Accountant*, Nov. 17, 1917, p. 373-5.

LOOSE-LEAF revolution in bookkeeping. *World's work*, Nov. 1906, p. 8248-9.

MOORE, R. H. Card or loose-sheet system. *Accountant*, Feb. 22, 1896, p. 156. *Business*, Jan. 1896, p. 37-8.

MUELLER, E. J. File instead of a journal. *System*, May 1914, p. 541-2.

NESBITT-EVANS, E. Card ledgers. *Accountant*, March 5, 19, 1904, p. 320-4, 353-4.

NEW idea for indexing loose leaf ledgers. *Business man's magazine*, Jan. 1911, p. 99.

NIEMANN, OSCAR. Practicability of card ledgers as compared with loose leaf ledgers. *Business man's magazine*, April 1910, p. 366-7.

NEW idea for indexing loose leaf ledgers. *Business man's magazine*, Jan. 1911, p. 99.

NIXON, ALFRED and J. H. STAGG. Card and slip ledger accounts. (In their *Accounting and banking*. 1912. p. 313-9).

ONE card for order and ledger account. *Business man's magazine*, Sept. 1911, p. 247.

PARKER, GEORGE. Workshop records; a review and comparison of existing methods with special reference to the use of cards and files instead of books. *Accountant*, Sept. 6, 13, 1902, p. 886-96, 909-19. *New England coast institute of engineers and shipbuilders, Transactions*, July 1902.

PECULIAR Texas loose leaf regulations. *Office appliances*, Feb. 1917, p. 12-3.

PORTERS, R. J. Loose leaf ledgers (card ledgers). (In his *Pitman's dictionary of book-keeping*. p. 538-9).

PRATT, E. A. Loose leaf journal. *Business man's magazine*, Dec. 1905, p. 1118-20.

PRICE, EDWARD EBENEZER. Bookkeeping on the slip and card systems. *Accountant*, March, 10, April 7, 1906, p. 300-3, 424-6.

PRICE, EDWARD EBENEZER. Ledger posting on the slip system. *Accountant*, March 8, 29, 1902, p. 256-66, 331-3.

PRITCHARD, JOHN CASSIN. Pritchard's up-to-date book-keeping on the card index and loose leaf plan. London, 1907.

PRIZER, H. A. Loose leaf leads in modern accounting. *Office appliances*. May 1917, p. 23-4.

PURBRICK, E. L. Loose leaf system of accounting. *Commonwealth accountant*, Nov. Dec. 1906, Jan. Feb. 1907.

REINHARDT, WILLIAM P. Public accountants and loose leaf. *Office appliances*, May 1917, p. 25.

RIGBY, ERNEST. Up-to-date systems. *Business organisation and management*, June 1920, p. 286-8.

RISQUE, FERDINAND WILLIAM. Loose leaf books and systems for general business. St. Louis, Studley co. 1907. 174p.

ROBBINS, ELLIOTT D. Card ledgers. (In *Lisle, George, Encyclopaedia of accounting*. v. 4. p. 91-5). *Incorporated accountants' journal*, 1902-3, p. 219.

"SLIP" or card bookkeeping. *Accountant*, Oct. 25, Nov. 8, 22, Dec. 13, 20, 27, 1902, Jan. 17, 1903, p. 1069-72, 1136-8, 1198-9, 1291-3, 1324-6, 1351-4; 76-7.

SLIP system of bookkeeping. *Accounting and commerce*, Sept. 1916, p. 124-6.

SPICER, ERNEST EVAN and ERNEST C. PEGLER. Loose leaf and card ledgers. (In their *Book-keeping and accounts*. 1914. p. 366-8, 402).

SWEETLAND, CHARLES A. A B C of loose-leaf bookkeeping. St. Louis, Charles A. Sweetland, 1906.

STONE, JOSEPH E. Loose leaf accounting. *Business organisation and management*, Nov. 1920, p. 160-2.

SWEETLAND, CHARLES A. Anti-confusion business methods. St. Louis, Charles A. Sweetland, 1905.

SWEETLAND, CHARLES A. Science of loose-leaf bookkeeping and accounting. St. Louis, 1902. 239p.

SWEETLAND, CHARLES A. Use of loose leaf books. Chicago, 1905.

BOOKKEEPING—CARD AND LOOSE LEAF—(*Continued)*

THORNE, W. W. Card and loose leaf ledgers. *Business man's magazine,* July 1909, p. 67-8.

USES and limitations of the card and loose-leaf ledgers, and slip systems in relation to matters of account. *Accountant,* Oct. 17, 1908, p. 472-9.

VAWTER, WILLIAM A. Origin and development of loose leaf. *Office appliances,* May 1917, p. 16-9.

WALTON, SEYMOUR. Loose leaf books. *Journal of accountancy,* Jan. 1916, p. 73-4.

WEBNER, FRANK E. Loose sheet ledger systems. *Commerce, accounts and finance,* March 30, 1901, p. 2-8.

WILLIAMS, LEONARD PASCOE. Loose-sheet and card system in bookkeeping. *Accountant,* April 30, 1904, p. 561-6.

WILLIAMSON, J. G. Loose-leaf ledgers. (In his *Counting house and factory organization.* 1909. p. 27-8).

WILSON, JOHN. Cards v. ledgers (the card system of bookkeeping). *Accountant,* April 30, 1904, p. 566-8.

Columnar and tabular—

ABSTRACT bookkeeping. *Accountant,* March 14, 21, 1891, p. 198-201, 220-2.

CARTER, R. N. Tabular system of book-keeping. (In his *Advanced accounts.* p. 896-908).

CHASE, CHARLES DYER. Columnar bookkeeping. *Business,* Oct. Nov. 1895. p. 366-8, 402-3.

COLE, WILLIAM MORSE. Columnar books, tabular ledger. (In his *Accounts, their construction and interpretation.* c1915. p. 62-3, 74, 75, 382, 383, 59, 393-4.

COLLIN, THOMAS WATSON. Columnar system of bookkeeping. *Accountant,* March 23, May 11, 1901, p. 374-6, 545-8.

DICKSEE, LAWRENCE R. Tabular bookkeeping. In his *Advanced accounting.* 1916. p. 45-54).

ELDRIDGE, ARTHUR. Kains commercial bookkeeping: columnar system. London, 1882.

GILMAN, STEPHEN. Columnar journal and ledger. (In his *Principles of accounting.* 1917. p. 55-61, 88-9).

HATFIELD, HENRY RAND. Columnar records. (In his *Modern accounting.* 1916. p. 343-5).

JOSEPH, LEON. Flexibility of columnar books. *Business man's magazine,* Nov. 1909, p. 465-7.

KESTER, ROY B. Columnar books, tabular ledger. (In his *Accounting theory and practice.* 1918. p. 152-3, 336-7, 403-11, 429- 263-7).

KITTREDGE, A. O. Columnar. *Business,* June, July, 1895, p. 239-40, 269-72.

LISLE, GEORGE. Columnar cash book. (In his *Accounting theory and practice.* 1900. p. 32-4).

LISLE, GEORGE and W. A. MIDDLETON. Columnar cash book. (In his *Account-keeping in principle and practice.* 1911. p. 46-8).

MOULL, JOHN. Columnar ledger. *Business,* May 1896, p. 231-5.

NIXON, ALFRED and J. H. STAGG. Tabular ledgers and accounts. (In his *Accounting and banking.* 1912. p. 305-19).

PORTERS, R. J. Tabular or columnar bookkeeping. (In his *Pitman's dictionary of book-keeping.* p. 719-22).

SOMMER, M. M. Practical guide to double entry bookkeeping in tabular form, etc. Newark, Martin R. Dennis & company, 1876.

SPICER, ERNEST EVAN and E. C. PEGLER. Columnar and tabular books. (In their *Book-keeping and accounts.* 1914. p. 32-3, 39-40, 361-6).

SPRAGUE, CHARLES E. Tabular bookkeeping. *The office,* Sept. 1890, p. 240-1.

TABULAR bookkeeping. (In *Lisle, George, Encyclopaedia of Accounting.* v. 6. p. 205-9).

WHATLEY, G. E. STUART. Tabular bookkeeping. (In his *Accountant's and bookkeeper's vade-mecum.* 1893. p. 98-102).

Examinations.

See Examinations.

History.

See Accounting-History.

Loose leaf.

See Bookkeeping Card and loose leaf.

Tabular.

See Bookkeeping-Columnar and tabular.

Teaching.

See Education.

BOOKKEEPING. London, Cassell & co. 1860.

BOOK-KEEPING. Detroit school of accounts and commerce. 1914.

BOOKKEEPING. United States. Federal board for vocational education. 1919.

BOOKKEEPING a lá Maître d'École. Wells, H. G.

BOOKKEEPING, accounting and auditing. Cole, William Morse. 1914.

BOOKKEEPING, accounting and auditing. Russell, T. H. and W. J. Jackman. 1916.

BOOKKEEPING, accounts and calculations, relating to hire-purchase wagon trade and colliery royalties and wayleaves. Johnson, George. 1901.

BOOKKEEPING adaptations and expedients. Kittredge, A. O.

BOOK-KEEPING adapted to the business of a corn merchant.

BOOKKEEPING; an elementary treatise. Browne & Nolan.

BOOKKEEPING and accountancy. Murray, David.

BOOKKEEPING and accountancy. Rowe, H. M. c1911.

BOOKKEEPING and accountancy. Weber, F. C. 1916.

BOOKKEPING and accountancy exercises for accountant students. Greenwood, W. J. 1904.

BOOKKEEPING and accountancy. Scotch practice in 17th and 18th centuries; from the Glasgow herald. *Accountant,* March 25, 1905, p. 356-60.

BOOKKEEPING and accountantship. Jones, T.

BOOK-KEEPING and accounting. Jenkinson, M. W. 1910.

BOOKKEEPING and accounting. Klein, J. J. 1917.

BOOKKEEPING and accounting exercises. Bennett, R. J. 1912.

BOOK-KEEPING and accounts. Child, Percy. 1891.

BOOKKEEPING and accounts. Cropper, L. C.

BOOKKEEPING and accounts. Johnson, George. 1917.

BOOKKEEPING and accounts. Spicer, E. E. and E. C. Pegler.

BOOKKEEPING and accounts for county councils. Lisle, G. 1890.

BOOKKEEPING and banking. Boardman, J. 1886.

BOOKKEEPING and business calculation. Spencer, Enos and J. W. Drye. 1918.

BOOK-KEEPING and business manual, single and double entry. Ellsworth, H. W.

BOOKKEEPING and business practice. Massey, R. W. 1902.

BOOKKEEPING and business practice. Whigham, W. H. and O. D. Frederick.

BOOKKEEPING and business practice: complete course. New York American book company.

BOOKKEEPING and business practice. introductory course. New York, American book company.

BOOKKEEPING and business training. Marshall, C. C.

BOOK-KEEPING and commercial practice. Smith, H. H. 1916.

BOOK-KEEPING and commercial practice. Wainwright, H. S. and others.

BOOKKEEPING and commercial terms. Crellin, Philip. 1892.

BOOKKEEPING and cost accounting for factories. Kent, William. 1918.

BOOKKEEPING and machine application. Sharp, P. G.

BOOKKEEPING and modern methods of accountancy. Pocock, B. G.

BOOK-KEEPING and office routine. Greenwood, W. J. ?1900.

BOOKKEEPING and other papers. Van de Linde, Gerard.

BOOKKEEPING and science of accounts. Robertson, P. W.

BOOKKEEPING as a specific subject. Maclean, J. D. 1892.

BOOK-KEEPING at a glance. Brieror, J. T.

BOOKKEEPING at a glance. Martinnant, C. W. P.

BOOK-KEEPING; banking. Miner, G. W. 1913.

BOOKKEEPING blanks, 5 books. Hall, M. P.

BOOK-KEEPING by double and single entry. Christian brothers.

BOOKKEEPING by double entry. Hancock, W. J. 1883.

BOOKKEEPING by double entry. Hardie, William and Alexander, Allen.

BOOKKEEPING by double entry, etc. Lorrain, W. 1807.

BOOKKEEPING by double entry. McLaughlin, D. 1847.

BOOKKEEPING by double entry. Medhurst, J. 1898.

BOOKKEEPING by double entry explained and illustrated in a complete record of mercantile and financial transactions. Haswell, C. H.

BOOKKEEPING by doube entry, theoretical. Medhurst, J. T. 1898.

BOOKKEEPING by double entry, with exercises and examination papers. Wreford, Francis and W. S. McGregor. 1891.

BOOK-KEEPING by Ingram. Hutton, C. 1845.

BOOKKEEPING by machinery. Thompson, E. W. 1906.

BOOK-KEEPING by single and double entry. Eastman, George. 1851.

BOOKKEEPING by single and double entry. Hanaford, L. B. and J. W. Payson. 1867.

BOOK-KEEPING by single and double entry. Henderson, A. G. 1841.

BOOKKEEPING by single and double entry simplified and adapted to use of common schools. Smith, William and E. Martin. 1859.

BOOK-KEEPING by single and double entry simplified for common schools. Manning, R. H. 1886.

BOOK-KEEPING by single and double entry. Duff, P. 1882.

BOOKKEEPING by single entry. Foster, B. F.

BOOKKEEPING by single entry. Scratchard, 1817.

BOOK-KEEPING by single or double entry. Brewer, E. C.

BOOK-KEEPING chart for business people. Scott, Robert. 1908.

BOOKKEEPING; commission and general merchandise. Miner, G. W. 1914.

BOOK-KEEPING diagrams. McKee, James. 1908.

BOOK-KEEPING (double entry). Harlow, Edward. 1892.

BOOK-KEEPING down to data. Munro, Andrew.

BOOKKEEPING (elementary) by double entry for evening continuation schools (elementary stage), and day schools (specific subject—two stages. London, Simpkins, 1898, 112p. (Waddington & Jackman series).

BOOK-KEEPING epitomized. Shaw, John. 1794.

BOOK-KEEPING examination papers for 1910. Royal society of arts. 1910.

BOOK-KEEPING examination papers for 1910, with fully worked answers compiled by H. W. Porrit and W. Nicklin. London, Sir Isaac Pitman & sons, 1910. 39p.

BOOKKEEPING examination questions. Bell, J. 1867.

BOOKKEEPING examiner, junior and senior. Thornton, J.

BOOKKEEPING exercises. Bartholomew, W. E. c1919.

BOOKKEEPING exercises. Dicksee, L. R. 1910.

BOOK-KEEPING exercises. Newby, ———. 1886.

BOOKKEEPING exercises. Scribner, W. M.

BOOKKEEPING exercises for accountant students. Dicksee, L. R. 1893.

BOOK-KEEPING familiarized. Wood, William. ?1777.

BOOKKEEPING for accountant students. Dicksee, L. R. 1893.

BOOKKEEPING for an installment business. *Business,* March 1895, p. 116-9.

BOOKKEEPING for bakers, grocers, drapers, dairymen, butchers, co-operative societies, etc. Brocklehurst, G. R. 1892.

BOOK-KEEPING for bar students. Jenkins, B. G. 1908.

BOOK-KEEPING for beginners. Brackenbury, Beatrice. 1908.

BOOK-KEEPING for beginners. Greenwood, W. J. ?1906.

BOOK-KEEPING for beginners. Hooper, W. E. 1913.

BOOK-KEEPING for beginners. Wheeler, G. W.

BOOKKEEPING for business. Musselman, D. L. 1909.

BOOKKEEPING for business men. Thornton, J. and S. W. Thornton.

BOOK-KEEPING for commercial classes. Barnes, J. R. and A. Sharples. 1914.

BOOKKEEPING for company secretaries. Dicksee, L. R. 1908.

BOOKKEEPING for dentists. White, Frank. 1910.

BOOKKEEPING for doctors. *Collier's,* April 9, 1910, v. 45: p. 34.

BOOKKEEPING for elementary schools. Thornton, J.

BOOKKEEPING for evening classes. Thornton, F. O.

BOOKKEEPING for every business. Kent. 1865.

BOOKKEEPING for executors and trustees. Hawkins, L. W. 1906.

BOOK-KEEPING for farmers. Edinburgh, W. Green. 1916. 44p.

BOOKKEEPING for farmers. Atkeson, J. C. 1892.

BOOKKEEPING for farmers. Sanders, ———. 1854.

BOOKKEEPING for farmers. *Accountants' journal,* 1909-10, p. 299.

BOOKKEEPING for farmers and estate owners. Woodman, J. M. 1902.

BOOKKEEPING for gas works. Sandell, Charles. 1904.

BOOK-KEEPING for groceries. *Australasian accountant and secretary,* July 1919, p. 25-8.

BOOKKEEPING for job printing. *Business,* April 1894, p. 149-50.

BOOK-KEEPING for joint stock companies. Hoskins, David. 1901.

BOOK-KEEPING for laundries. Smith, W. F. and E. F. Jones.

BOOK-KEEPING for parish priests. Kaib, B. J. 1910.

BOOKKEEPING for printers. *Accountant,* May 16, 23, 30, June 6, 13, 1896, p. 416-8, 437-8, 451-3, 475-6, 484-5.

BOOKKEEPING for public institutions. Palmer, James William.

BOOKKEEPING for retail grocers and other tradesmen. Jenkinson, Mark Webster. 1905.

BOOKKEEPING for retail stores. Dean, W. F. 1900.

BOOKKEEPING for retailers. Porritt, H. W. and W. Nicklin. 1909.

BOOKKEEPING for schools. Jones, E. T. 1840.

BOOKKEEPING for solicitors. Hawkins, L. W. 1906.

BOOKKEEPING for solicitors. Woodman, J. M.

BOOKKEEPING for spirit dealers. London, Simpkin, Marshall, Hamilton, Kent & co. 1854.

BOOKKEEPING for teachers and pupils, with accounts in illustration, exercises, etc. Crellin, Philip. 1892.

BOOK-KEEPING for technical classes in schools. Clarke, G. F.

BOOK-KEEPING for terminating building societies. Lees, John. 1895.

BOOKKEEPING for the million. Jones, Theodore.

BOOKKEEPING for the million. Walker, H. D. 1869.

BOOK-KEEPING for the people. Denman, J. S. 1887.

BOOKKEEPING for the plumber. Cosgrove, John J.

BOOKKEEPING for the plumber. Ryan, G. W.

BOOKKEEPING for the tanning trade. Sawyer, Joseph. 1862.

BOOKKEEPING for traders, manufacturers and companies. Elworthy, W. R. and C. C. Campling.

BOOKKEEPING for weekly newspapers. Richardson, G. H.

BOOKKEEPING. for wholesale and retail traders. London, 187.

BOOKKEEPING for wine, spirits and beer retailers and the bar department of hotels etc. Glasgow, Henderson, S. Y. 1900.

BOOKKEEPING frauds and methods for their detection. Craig, A. T.

BOOKKEEPING from vouchers. Lyons, J. A. and W. L. Read. 1909.

BOOKKEEPING fundamentals. McKinney, W. S.

BOOK-KEEPING improved. Pullen, Philip. 1803.

BOOKKEEPING in banks. *Business man's magazine,* Sept. 1907, p. 130-2.

BOOKKEEPING in Brazil. *Accounting and commerce,* May 1916, p. 27-8.

BOOKKEEPING in double entry explained. Findlater, J. 1900.

BOOK-KEEPING in its relation to commerce. Martin, James.

BOOKKEEPING in its simplest and most useful form. Knox, James. 1859.

BOOK-KEEPING in 1793. Smith, S. G.

BOOKKEEPING in nurseries. *The office,* Jan. 1889, p. 12.

BOOK-KEEPING in six lessons. Morton, Frederick W. 1914.

BOOKKEEPING in Spanish. Marsh, C. C.

BOOKKEEPING in the high school. Treleven, J. E. 1916.

BOOK-KEEPING in the Italian method, by debtor and creditor. Turner, R. 1794.

BOOKKEEPING in the tailoring trade. *Accountant,* April 24, 1897, p. 434-5.

BOOKKEEPING in the true Italian form of debtor and creditor by way of double entry. Jackson, William. 1804.

BOOKKEEPING in verse. Arch, W. H.

BOOKKEEPING instructor. Hunter, J. 1886.

BOOKKEEPING, intermediate and advanced courses. Miner, G. W. 1912.

BOOKKEEPING MACHINES
See mechanical devices—Calculating machines.

BOOKKEEPING made easy. New York, Hurst & co.

BOOKKEEPING made easy. E. J. Larby.

BOOK-KEEPING made easy. Atkin, Francis.

BOOKKEEPING made easy. Greenwood, W. J. 1903.

BOOKKEEPING made easy. Lemowitz, N. H. 1919.

BOOKKEEPING manual for booksellers and publishers. London, Simpkin, Marshall, Hamilton, Kent & co. 1849.

BOOKKEEPING methodiz'd. Mair, John.

BOOK-KEEPING no bugbear, or double entry simplified, in opposition to the insufficiency of the present practice. Power, Michael.

BOOKKEEPING no mystery, by an experienced bookkeeper. Lockwood, 1883. Ed. 4.

BOOKKEEPING no mystery (civil service bookkeeping). Lockwood, 1874.

BOOKKEEPING on Alaska government railways. *Railway age gazette,* April 24, 1914, p. 929-30.

BOOKKEEPING outlines. (Private publication. Ellis publishing co. 1909. 56p.)

BOOK-KEEPING primer. Thornton, J.

BOOKKEEPING principles. Nagel, C. N. 1889.

BOOKKEEPING principles and practice. Thomson.

BOOKKEEPING. Question XIV, 7th session, International railway congress. *International railway congress bulletin* (Eng. ed.), Dec. 1905, p. 1823-54.

BOOKKEEPING self-taught. Goodwin, P. C. 1903.

BOOKKEEPING simplified. Feast, Henry. 1883.

BOOKKEEPING simplified. Findlay, James. 1901.

BOOKKEEPING simplified. Mitchell, F. J. 1895.

BOOKKEEPING simplified. Ney, F. J. 1911.

BOOK-KEEPING simplified. Waggoner, D. B. 1874.

BOOK-KEEPING simplified. Wright, P. A.

BOOKKEEPING simplified. Revised edition. London, Sir Isaac Pitman & sons. 1900. 240p.

BOOKKEEPING, single and double entry for use in schools and for self-instruction. L'Estrange, J. E. 1897.

BOOK-KEEPING. sixteen figures papers set at the society's examinations during 1886-99, Cary, R. H. 1899.

BOOK-KEEPING specially adopted to public companies. Fitzpatrick, James. 1910.

BOOKKEEPING system. Hale, M. 1884.

BOOKKEEPING system. MacDougal, ——— 1869.

BOOKKEEPING system. O'Gorman, D.

BOOKKEEPING system for Delco-light dealers. Funkhouser, R. D. c1919.

BOOKKEEPING system for solicitors. MacKenzie, 1858.

BOOKKEEPING systems for retail lumber business. *American lumberman.* 1910-1911.

BOOKKEEPING taught by examples. Constable, J. 1875.

BOOKKEEPING teacher. Hayes, P. L. 1917.

BOOK-KEEPING teachers' manual. Kirton, C. H. 1919.

BOOKKEEPING terms and definitions. Rivingtons.

BOOKKEEPING test cards; elementary, intermediate and advanced. New York, Sir Isaac Pitman & sons. per set 1/6

BOOKKEEPING transactions. London, W. & R. Chambers.

BOOKKEEPING transactions. Walsh, W. H. 1893.

BOOKKEEPING: wholesale and retail traders' manual. 1856.

BOOKKEEPING, with some chapters on business usages, by "Hugh" [? 1897]

BOOK-KEEPING without a master. Day, B. H.

BOOKKEEPING without a master. Whinyates, J. W.

BOOKKEEPING without ledgers. *Accountant,* Jan. 11, 1919, p. 17-9.

BOOKMAN, C. M. AND F. S. BLUE
First steps in bookkeeping; a practical introduction to bookkeeping containing an abundance of drill work in arithmetic, arranged to accompany Bookman's business arithmetic or any other modern arithmetic in eighth or ninth grade work. 806 Neaue bldg., Cincinnati, Ohio, C. M. Bookman, 1917. 86p.

BOOKS
See also Printing; Publishing
Jenkins, L. H. Book manufacturing business. *Business man's magazine,* June 1905, p. 1163-8.

Accounting
Maupin, B. F. Manufacturing system for book publishers. *Business man's magazine,* Oct. 1909, p. 368-71.

Auditing
Montgomery, Robert H. Publishers of books. (In his *Auditing theory and practice.* 1916. p. 592-6).

BOOKS and accounts of charitable institutions. *Accountant,* Sept. 8, 15, 29, 1888, p. 571-2, 586-7, 615-6.

BOOKS and accounts of cotton manufacturers. *Accountant,* June 23, 30, July 14, 21, 1888, p. 395-7, 410-2, 442-3, 457-8.

BOOKS and bookkeeping. Marshall, J. W.

BOOKS and book-keeping. Molleson, J. A.

BOOKS of account. Edwards, George.

BOOKS of account as evidence. *Bankers magazine,* Aug. 1915, p. 196-8.

BOOKS of bookkeeping. Dickson, N.

BOOT and shoe costings. Headley, L. C. 1908.

BOOTH, BENJAMIN
Complete system of book-keeping by an improved mode of double entry, etc. London, 1789.

BOOTH, JOHN
Mortgages: the duties and powers of a receiver. *Accountant,* Feb. 23, 1889, p. 94-6.

BOOTH, W. E.
Accounting and accounts. *Public accountant,* 1909, p. 126, 158.
On accounts. *Public accountant,* 1904-5, p. 90; 1906-7, p. 22.
On accounts: partnerships. *Public accountant,* 1909, p. 191.

BOOTH, W. H.
Sinking fund charges. *Tramway and railway world,* April 9, 1903, p. 349.
System in charging. *Power,* April 1, 1913, p. 474-5.

BOOTS.
See Shoes.

BORAH, WILLIAM E.
Income tax sound in law and economics. *Journal of accountancy,* May 1910, p. 26-42.

BORDEN, J. A.
New awakening in cost finding. *Inland printer,* Feb. 1917, p. 677-8.

BORDON, S. W.
Coupon purchase plan for lamp renewals. *Electrical world,* April 29, 1916, p. 990-2.

BORDWELL, GEORGE O.
Analysis of a bank account. San Francisco, Coast banker publisher, 1911. 18p.
Modern banking methods as applied to the tellers and bookkeepers. San Francisco, Hicks-Judd company, c1913. 122p.

BORGET, A. J.
Records the buyer needs. *System,* April 1914, p. 404-7.

BORHEK, R. J.
Cost of hydraulic sand and gravel mining. *Engineering and contracting,* June 30, 1915, p. 573-4.

BORKENHAGEN, J. J.
Lay-out and piece rate card system; forms that assist in efficient shop management. *Machinery,* December 1918, p. 327-9.

BORLAND, WILLIAM P.
Budget system for the United States. *Congressional record,* Dec. 11, 1918, p. 343-7.

BORNHOLT, O. C.
Continuous manufacturing by placing machines in accordance with sequence of operation. *Journal, American society mechanical engineers,* November, 1913, p. 1669-78. *Iron age,* December 4, 1913, p. 1276-7. Condensed. *Iron trade review,* December 18, 1913, p. 1102-3.

BOROUGH and township audit ordinance (Natal), 1916. *Incorporated accountants' journal,* Oct. 1916, p. 6-7.

BOROUGHS.
See Municipal.

BORTIN, H.
National valuation convention urged, concerted action should be taken to make appraisal of railways economical intelligent and just. *Railway age gazette,* April 11, 1913, p. 836.

BOSHER, LEWIS H.
Controlling accounts in cost accounting. *Journal of accountancy,* June 1912, p. 405-19.

BOSLEY, W. B. AND C. E. GRUNSKY
Depreciation as an element for consideration on the appraisals of public service properties. *American society of civil engineers, Proceedings,* Aug. 1915.

BOSS, A.
See Hays, W. M., joint author.

BOSS, ANDREW FRANK AND FRANK W. PECK.
Farm records and accounts. St. Paul, Webb publishing, 1914. 116p.

BOSTON and Northern half—fare case—special points of interest in connection with the argument of the company as presented to the supreme court of Massachusetts. *Electric railway journal,* July 13, 1912, p. 54-5.

BOSTON consolidated files schedule of manufacturing costs. *American gas engineering journal,* Oct. 6, 1917, p. 313.

BOSTON Edison service annuities. *Electrical world,* May 24, 1913, p. 1074-5.

BOSTON lighting contract considered by commission: data on cost of street lighting presented by Edison electric illuminating company of Boston. *Electrical world, and western electrician,* April 29, 1916, p. 747.

BOSTON, Mass., underground construction costs. *Electrical review, and western electrician,* March 3, 1917, p. 357.

BOSWORTH, R. L.
Simple collection scheme. *Business man's magazine,* Oct. 1917, p. 83-4.

BOSWORTH, ROBINSON
Standards for tuberculosis sanatoriums; location—importance of considering the individual patient—standard of efficiency—necessity of central authority—value of sanatorium records—the records used in Minnesota. *Modern hospital,* Feb. 1919, p. 97-106.

BOTH, CHARLES
Silk manufacturers' accounts. *Business,* March 1896, p. 1379.

BOTH sides of the Priestman plan. *Factory,* March 15, 1920, p. 814-5.

BOTH Washington railways find cost and wage burdens more than present fares will stand. *Electric railway journal,* Sept. 21, 1918, p. 526.

BOTHMANN, THEODORE
Audit system of a trust company. *Business, world,* March 1906, p. 202, 210.

BOTTLING

Accounting
Boheim, Otto A. Accounting system for a bottling works. *Business man's magazine,* July 1908, p. 43-51.
Bottling works. *International accountants' manual,* 1910, paragraph 480.
Horndrup, N. A. Keeping track of bottled goods. *Business man's magazine,* May 1912, p. 416-20.
Koeller, A. H. Special accounting system for breweries with a bottling department. *Bookkeeper,* 1903, v.16, no. 6, p. 37-44.
Lanham, Herbert. Brewers' and bottlers' accounts; with a chapter on the licensing act, 1904 by W. C. Northcott. London, Gee & co. 1906. 191p. (Accountants' library, v.44).
Schirmer, C. F. G. Bottlers bookkeeping system. *National bottler's gazette,* Nov. 5, 1920, p. 92-6.
Wall, Raymond J. Bottle and case accounting. *National bottler's gazette,* Nov. 5, 1920, p. 98-101.
Wall, Raymond J. Columnar books for bottlers. *National bottler's gazette,* Dec. 5, 1920, p. 200-10.

BOTTOMLEY, LEONARD
Points in company formation. *Accountant.* Dec. 17, 1898, p. 1219-25.

BOUCHER, GEORGE HERBERT
Faults in the companies acts and their remedies. *Accountant,* April 28, 1906, p. 537-42.
Mercantile law. *Accountant,* June 27, 1914, p. 925-8.

BOUCHEROT, P.
Charging for electrical energy according to the consumer's power factor; abstract. *Electrical world,* March 9, 1918, p. 623.

BOUGHTON, JUDSON H.
Commercial depreciation in electric plants. *Public service,* July 1908, p. 7.

BOULTER, GEORGE H.
Course of bookkeeping by double and single entry. London, 1857.
Principles of balancing by single and double entry, including partnerships by each method. Ed. 3. London, [circa 1860].

BOUNDY, F. P.
Some incidental factory accounts and their treatment. *Public accountant* 1906-7, p. 235.

BOURKE, R. W.
Property accounting; with discussion *National association of comptrollers and accounting owcers Proceedings.* 1917, p. 43-63.

BOURKE, RAYMOND W.
Property accounting in the City of New York. *Journal of accountancy,* Nov. 1917, p. 342-54.

BOURLIER, E. B.
Accounting system for roofink business. *Metal work,* Jan. 1, 1915, p. 39-42.

BOURNE, JOHN HOWE
Auditing. *Accountant,* 1887, p. 330.
Goodwill. *Accountant,* Sept. 22, 1888, p. 604-5.
Some notes on companies and their accounts. *Accountant,* Dec. 10, 1898, p. 1197-1202.

BOURNER, ARTHUR CHARLES
Costs in bankruptcy. *Accountant,* Nov. 25, 1893, Feb. 3, 1894, p. 1004-8, 113-6.

BOUTON, A. W.
Neglected charges interfere with success. *Metal work,* July 25, 1919, p. 105-6.

BOUVIER, JOHN
Bouvier's law dictionary and concise encyclopedia. Ed. 3, revised. 3v. Kansas City, Vermont law book co. 1914. 3504p.

BOWDEN, C. M.
Depreciation of ships. *Accounting and commerce,* Nov. 1915, p. 187-8.
Exchange rates and the cost of living. *Accounting and commerce,* Oct. 1919, p. 153-5. *Australasian accountant and secretary,* March 1920, p. 95-7.

BOWDEN, C. M.—*(Continued)*

Some notes on bank exchange in relation to New Zealand trade. *Accounting and commerce,* Oct. 1917, p. 154-8.

BOWDEN, J. H.

Standardization of tariffs. *Electrical review and western electrician,* July 18, 1915, p. 117-20.

BOWDEN, J. HORACE AND FRED F. TATE

Adequate depreciation of capital expenditure by municipal electricity undertakings. *Electrical review,* London, June 21, 28, 1907, p. 1021, 1064.

BOWDEN, THOMAS

Address, 1904. *Accountant,* Feb. 25, 1905, p. 226-29, 302-4.

Presidential address: North chartered accountants students' society. *Accountant,* Feb. 25, 1905, p. 226-9.

BOWEN, DAVID

Taxation rating and valuation of mines *Colliery guardian,* March 1, 1918.

BOWEN, H. P.

See Palmer, C. H., joint author.

BOWERMAN, C. W.

Some industrial problems. *Accountant,* Aug. 23, 1919, p. 174-7.

BOWERS, E. J.

Accounting methods as applied to Detroit electric properties. National electric light association, 1911, 16p.

Collection of bills. National electric light association, 1911. 13p.

BOWERS, GEORGE W.

Approximate weights of square strips—specific gravity 1.00, approximate weights of sheets —specific gravity 1.00, approximate weight of cylinders—specific gravity 1.00, approximate weights of discs 1-64 inch thick. New York, John Wiley & sons, c1917. 4p.

BOWERS, H M.

Construction details on the Marin water and power project. *Journal of electricity,* July 1, 1919, p. 22-3.

BOWERS, M. A.

Proper method for the keeping of church records. *Business man's magazine,* May 1908, p. 435-7.

BOWKER, WILLIAM R.

Depreciation and permanent renewal fund. *Street railway bulletin,* May 1907, p. 298.

BOWLER, HERBERT W.

Work of a trustee in bankruptcy. *Accountant,* July 2, 1904, p. 13-20.

BOWLES, B.

Executors and executorship accounts. *Associated accountants' journal,* 1912, p. 257.

BOWLES, J. D.

Cost of electric service for a town of 750. *Electrical world,* July 31, 1915, p. 254.

BOWLES, OLIVER

Blasting costs in American quarries. *Engineering and contracting,* Jan. 15, 1919, p. 56-7.

Limestone quarry methods and quarry costs. *Concrete,* May 1919, sup. 55-6.

Rock quarrying for cement manufacture. Washington, Government printing office, 1918. 160p. (Bureau of mines bulletin 160, mineral technology 22).

Sandstone quarrying in the United States. Washington, Government printing office, 1917. 143p. (United States. Bureau of mines. Bulletin 124. Mineral technology 17).

Technology of marble quarrying. Washington, Government printing office, 1916. 174p. (United States. Bureau of mines, bulletin 106; mineral technology 13).

BOWLEY, A.

Averages. (In Lisle, George. *Encyclopaedia of accounting.* v.1. p. 195-202).

Diagrams. (In Lisle, George. *Encyclopaedia of accounting.* v.2. p. 377-87).

Elementary manual of statistics. London, MacDonald and Evans, 1915. 220p.

BOWMAN, J. F.

Testing out material in the factory. *Business man's magazine,* April 1912, p. 337-8.

BOWMAN, R.

See Bachmann, F. R., joint author.

BOWMAN, T. P.

Employing a bookkeeper. *Motor age,* Oct. 31, 1918, p. 10-1.

Over the top in service and repairs: bookkeeping and accounting system. *Motor age,* Aug. 29, 1918, p. 10-11.

BOWMAN, WILLIAM L.

Architect in cost plus contracts. *Brickbuilders,* Sept. 1914, p. 223-5.

BOWSER, J. T.

Comparison of maintenance of way costs on a mileage basis. *Railway age,* August 21, 1914, p. 337-8.

Discussion of labor appropriations. *Railway maintenance engineer,* April 1918, p. 135-7.

Distribution of labor and material. *Railway maintenance engineer,* Jan. 1918, p. 18-20.

Importance of miscellaneous reports. *Railway maintenance engineer,* June 1918, p. 201-2.

Keeping accurate records of materials. *Railway maintenance engineer,* March 1918, p. 105-7.

Preparation of special reports. *Railway maintenance engineer,* May 1918, p. 168-70.

Preparing maintenance of way reports. *Railway maintenance engineer,* Dec. 1917, p. 381-4.

Supervisor's familiarity with reports. *Railway maintenance engineer,* July 1918, p. 243-4.

BOWSTEAD, WILLIAM

Mortgage. (In Lisle, George. *Encyclopaedia of accounting.* v.5. p. 134-55).

Sale of goods. (In Lisle, George. *Encyclopaedia of accounting.* v.6. p. 1-14).

Trust and trustee England. (In Lisle, George. *Encyclopaedia of accounting.* v.6. p. 262-92).

BOXES, PACKING CASES, ETC.

See also Paper boxes.

Accounting.

MILLS, JAMES COOKE. Handling yard and mill orders. *Business man's magazine,* May 1912, p. 412-15.

OLDENBERG, WILLIAM. Devised for manufacturers. *Business man's magazine,* Oct. 1907, p. 63-5.

Cost accounting

JORDAN, JOHN P. and GOULD L. HARRIS. Wood box industry. (In their *Cost accounting.* 1920. p. 31-3, 145-6).

BOXES, PACKING CASES ETC.—COST ACCOUNTING—(*Continued*)

MOZINGO, F. P. Cost accounting and system accounts for the manufacture of cigar boxes and dovetail packing boxes. *Business man's magazine,* Sept. 1909, p. 252-7.

BOYCE, E. A.

System for keeping costs in a foundry. *Iron age,* March 6, 1913, p. 601-5.

BOYCE, W. H.

Complete records help to offset the rising cost of labor and material. *Electric railway journal,* Sept 16, 1916, p. 478-80.

BOYD, EDWARD BROWNRIGG

Marine insurance and accounts. *Incorporated accountants' S.S.L. transactions,* 1907, p. 110.

BOYD, H. H.

Costing in relation to scientific management. *Accountant,* July 12, 1919, p. 33-40.

BOYD, J. H.

Costing in relation to scientific management. *Electrician,* Aug. 28, 1919, p. 171-2.

BOYD, N. G. E.

Accounting methods for brick manufacturing business. *Business man's magazine,* Aug. 1905, p. 270-8.

BOYD, R. P.

Cost accounting system for convict and hired labor forces used in Alabama. *Engineering and contracting,* June 24, 1914, v.41, p. 734-5.

Cost keeping in road work. *Good roads,* May 2, 1914, p. 258

Cost of accounting system for contract, convict and hired labor forces used in Alabama. *Engineering and contracting,* June 24, 1914, p. 734-5.

BOYD, S. H.

Federal income tax: a discussion. *American institute of accountants, Yearbook.* 1914. p. 122-33.

BOYD, W. G. E.

Accounting methods for brick manufacturing business. *Business man's magazine,* Aug. 1905, p. 270-8.

BOYD, WILLIAM

Agreements and conferences in their relation to ocean rates. *Annals of the American academy of political and social science,* Sept. 1914, p. 194-204.

BOYKIN, ROBERT M.

Reclamation pumping a profitable power load of North Coast power company. *Electrical review and western electrician,* June 2, 1917, p. 936-7.

BOYLAN, M. R.

Collecting and auditing receipts of prepayment cars. *American street and interurban railway accountants association, Proceedings,* 1910, p. 155-80.

BOYLE, A. R. M.

Some phases of capital stock. *Journal of accountancy,* July 1919, p. 74-6.

BOYLE, C.

Methods and organisation in business. *Commonwealth accountant,* May 1907.

BOYLE, J. E.

Some debatable questions in farmers' elevators. *Co-operative manager and farmer,* Feb. 1917, p. 26.

BOYLE, M. W.

Long-distance motor-truck haulage costs in Ohio. *Engineering news-record,* April 10, 1919, p. 717.

BOYNTON, C. M.

Concrete pavement costs. *Municipal engineering,* September 1913, p. 243.

BOYNTON, R. H.

City engineer's records in Frankford, Ind. *Municipal engineering,* Aug. 1915, p. 78-9. *Engineering and contracting,* Sept. 1, 1915, p. 165-6.

BRABOOK, N. W.

Building societies and their accounts. *Accountant,* 1886, p. 165, 174.

BRABOOK, EDWARD.

Friendly societies. *Accountant,* Jan. 27, 1912, p. 137-42.

BRACE, CHARLES

Accounting methods of a great New York daily. *Business man's magazine,* May 1905, p. 947-53.

BRACE, LAMONT

Cold storage accounting. *Ice and refrigerator,* Jan. 1906, p. 11.

Cold storage accounting. *Ice and refrigeration,* v.30, 1906, p. 1-3, 43-5, 83-5, 261-2, 291-3.

BRACE, W. O.

Easily-applied common sense cost system: the method of distributing direct and indirect foundry costs. *Foundry,* Feb.-May, 1913, p. 43-6, 97-100, 152-7, 207-8.

BRACKENBURY, BEATRICE

Bookkeeping for beginners. London, Longmans-Greene & co. 1908. 142p.

BRACKENBURY, CHARLES ERNEST

Some changes in bankruptcy law. *Accountant,* Feb. 20, 1909, p. 272-6.

BRACKETT, G. S.

Comparative costs of operating. *Colliery,* Oct. 1915, p. 132-4.

Efficiency in coal mining. *Colliery,* June 1915, 588-92.

BRADBROOK, EDWARD

Life assurance accounts. *Incorporated accountants' journal,* Sept. 1917, p. 251-7.

BRADDOCK, J. H.

Some suggestions for preparing a budget exhibit. *Annals of the American society of political and social science,* May, Nov. 1916, p. 113-276, 148-61.

BRADDON, H. Y.

Modern world of credit. *Accountant,* March 11, 1916, p. 308-15.

BRADEN, WILLIAM

Conditions and costs of mining at the Braden copper mines, Chile. *Engineering and contracting,* Oct. 27, 1909, p. 349.

BRADFORD, EDITH FLEMING
Household accounts. Ithaca, 1916. 41 & 71p. (New York state. College of agriculture, Cornell reading course for the farm house, Lesson 110).

BRADFORD, H. C.
How opticians records should be kept and filed. *Business man's magazine,* April 1908, p. 349-51.

BRADFORD, WILLIAM A.
Efficient time-keeping system. *Domestic engineering,* November 24, 1917, p. 307-8.
Profit and the cost of doing business. *Metal work,* Sept. 14, 1917, p. 320-1.
Uniform percentage system of adding profit. *Metal work,* July 13, 1917, p. 50-1.

BRADFORD chartered accountants students' association debate the duties of an auditor. *Accountant,* Feb. 18, 1911, p. 277-81.

BRADLEY, FRANCIS ERNEST
Reduction of capital. *Accountant,* Feb. 22, 1913, p. 266-72.
Some aspects of the companies act. 1900; with especial reference to the duties of auditors and company secretaries. *Accountant,* Jan. 5, 1901, p. 23-35.

BRADLEE, HENRY G.
Actual figures of existing street railways. *Aera,* Dec. 1912, p. 392.
Profitable limit of five-cent street railway fare. *Engineering news,* Jan. 30, 1913, p. 214-5.

BRADLEY, R. A.
Filling in records quickly. *System,* January 1915, p. 103-4.

BRADLEY, V. L.
Railway revenue and the parcel post. *Engineering magazine,* January 1915, p. 593-6.

BRADLEY, W. R.
Storekeeping methods in Roanoke, Va. *Gas age,* February 1, 1917, p. 141.

BRADSHAW, EDWARD
Handling credit accounts in a retail store. *Business man's magazine,* April 1912, p. 325-7.
Increasing sales by personal attention. *Business man's magazine,* May 1912, p. 423-24.

BRADSHAW, THOMAS
Municipal borrowing. *Canadian chartered accountant,* Jan. 1916, p. 192-3.
Some notes on municipal finance. *Canadian chartered accountant,* Oct. 1915, p. 93-106.
Study of a city's sinking funds. *Canadian municipal journal,* Oct. 1916, p. 531-2. *Union of Canadian municipalities. 16th annual convention,* 1916.

BRADT, S. E.
Efficient methods of promoting highway bond issues. *Good roads,* March 29, 1919, p. 139-40. Condensed. *Engineering news,* March 20, 1919, p. 573-4.

BRADY, JAMES E.
Accountancy and investments. *Business world,* Feb. 1902, p. 58-9.

BRADY, JOHN E.
Bank management of estates under the New York statutes. *Banking law journal,* Aug.-Sept. Nov. 1919, p. 599-608, 685-90, 847-54.

BRADY, JOHN T.
Tracing storeroom material. National electric light association, 1911, 12p.

BRAINARD, C. G.
Accounting methods in the poultry business. *Business man's magazine,* 1906, v.18, no. 7, p. 65-73.

BRAINARD, GEORGE C.
Bonus system succeeds in forge shop. *Iron trade review,* July 22, 1920, p. 247-8.

BRAMBILLA, G.
Storia della regioneria Italiana. *Accountants' magazine,* 1902, p. 541.

BRAMBLE, B. E.
Accounting for capital expenditures. *Electric railway journal,* June 15, 1912, p. 1023-4.

BRAMLEY, EDWARD
Death duties. *Accountant,* Jan. 3, Feb 7, 1903, p. 15-9, 187-9.

BRAMWELL, JOHN
Sectional double-entry bookkeeping; an illustrative treatise of the fundamental principles designed for home study, class work or text reference; complete in fifteen part folio sections. 407 4th Ave., New York, O. H. Labarre, 1913.

BRANCH accounts.
See Branches—Accounting.

BRANCH accounts. *Australasian accountant and secretary,* Feb. April 1920, p. 59-62, 84-6, 110-12.

BRANCH banks; its origin, forms, administration, operation and examination. *Banking law journal,* May and June 1912.

BRANCH office ethics. *Journal of accountancy,* Sept. 1919, p. 212-16.

BRANCH store accounting. Strachan, J. R.

BRANCH stores.
See Branches.

BRANCHES
ROSS, F. A. Growth and effect of branch offices. *Journal of accountancy,* Oct. 1920, p. 252-61.

Accounting
AMERICAN business and accounting encyclopaedia; comp. by E. H. Beach and W. W. Thorne. Detroit, Bookkeeper publishing co. 1901. Branch business accounting—v.1, p. 266-7.
BAGOT, E. Accounting for branch stores. *Business man's magazine,* 1904, v.16, p. 104-5.
BAYLEY, J. ERNEST. Branch shops, ledger, accounts, statistics. (In his *Drapery business organisation, management and accounts.* p. 251-88).
BENNETT, GEORGE E. Agencies and branches. (In his *Constructive accounting.* 1920. p. 373-88).
BRANCH accounts. *Australasian accountant and secretary,* Feb.-April 1920, p. 59-62, 84-6, 110-12.
BRANCH bookkeeping. (In Lisle, George. *Encyclopaedia of accounting.* v.1. p. 502-8).
BRANCH stores. *International accountants' manual,* 1910, paragraph 486, 487.
CARTER, R. N. Branch accounts, foreign exchange, foreign branches. (In his *Advanced accounts.* p. 641-736).
CLOSING branch accounts. *Accountant,* April 11, 1914, p. 519-20.
COLES, ARTHUR. Accounts of branch establishments. (In his *Company accounts.* p. 168-82).

BRANCHES—Accounting—(*Continued*)

Dawson, Sidney Stanley. Accounts of branch establishments. *Accountant,* Nov. 13, 1897, p. 1063-71, 1101.

Day, C. M. Branch office accounts. (In his *Accounting practice.* 1915. p. 75-6).

Dicksee, Lawrence R. Branch accounts. (In his *Advanced accounting.* 1916. p. 28-40).

Dicksee, Lawrence R. Foreign currencies and the accounts of foreign branches. *Accountant,* Feb. 27, 1904, p. 281-91.

Dicksee, Lawrence R. and H. E. Blain. Departmental and branch accounts. (In their *Office organisation and management.* 1917. p. 162-75).

Dowler, Frank and E. M. Harris. Branch accounts. (In their *Auditing, accounting and banking.* p. 164-75).

Fincham, R. F. W. Amalgamation of head office and branch balance sheets; with special reference to the elimination of internal branch balances. *Accountant,* Nov. 30, Dec. 7, 1901, p. 1307-14, 1336-43.

Foreign branches. *Australasian accountant and secretary,* Aug. 1920, p. 246-7.

Frotheringham, A. K. Methods for the supervision of branch houses. *Business man's magazine,* Jan. 1908, p. 131-6.

Gray, H. John. Book-keeping for foreign branches. *Accountants' magazine,* June 1916, p. 275-82.

Green, Arthur E. Branch accounts. *Accountant,* Jan. 28, 1911, p. 160-7. *Incorporated accountants journal,* 1910-11, p. 83.

Henderson, E. Branch stores competition. *Business man's magazine,* July 1906, p. 140-4.

Holmes, C. H. Branch accounts. *Accountant,* Sept. 4, 1920, p. 243-5.

Jenkinson, M. Webster. Branch accounts. *Accountant,* March 25, 1905, p. 339-49.

Kester, Roy B. Branch house accounting. (In his *Accounting theory and practice.* 1918. v.2. p. 521-55).

Lisle, George. Accounts of branches. (In his *Accounting theory and practice.* 1900. p. 95-8).

Lisle, George and W. A. Middleton. Branch accounts. (In their *Account keeping in principle and practice.* 1911. p. 101-21).

McCall, J. H. Accounts and audit of the English agency of a foreign company. *Incorporated accountants' journal,* Nov. 1912, p. 41-4.

McIntosh, R. J. Revenues—branches. (In his *Reference book of accounts for manufacturing and mercantile companies.* c1914. p. 97).

Madden, John Thomas. Branch accounts. (In his *Accounting practice and auditing.* 1917. p. 208-30.

Morton, J. T. How to handle branch stores. *System,* Mar. 1912, p. 296-9

Nixon, Alfred and J. H. Stagg. Branch accounts. (In their *Accounting and banking.* 1912. p. 161-78).

Office tact and versatility in branch management; showing methods and plans by which branch managers and their assistants may arrange their work to harmonize with that of the main office and increase their own business. *Business man's magazine,* Feb. 1908, p. 188-90.

Porters, R. J. Branch accounts. (In his *Pitman's dictionary of bookkeeping.* p. 123-53).

Proposition on branch accounts. *Pace student,* June 1916.

Racine, S. F. Branches. (In his *Accounting principles.* 1917. p. 252).

Rahn, W. J. Business system for branch stores. *Business man's magazine,* Oct. 1910, p. 365-72.

Ransom, C. A. How to run a branch store. *System,* Dec. 1911, p. 632-5.

Retail branch accounts. *Accountant,* 1911, p. 775.

Rose, C. A. Branch accounting. *Business man's magazine,* 1904, v.17, p. 457-9.

Rowe, Harry M. Branch accounts. (In his *Bookkeeping and accountancy.* c1911. p. 161-3).

Running a branch, question of policy. *Accounting and commerce,* June 1917, p. 49-50).

Soule, George. Accounts with branch houses. (In his *New science and practice of accounts.* 1903. p. 569-70.)

Spicer, Ernest Evan and Ernest C. Pegler. Branch accounts. (In their *Bookkeeping and accounts.* 1914. p. 235-63).

Strachan, J. R. Branch store accounting. *Journal of accountancy,* July 1909, p. 190-206.

Walton, Seymour. Branch accounts, home office overhead. *Journal of accountancy,* May 1920, p. 398-99.

Walton, Seymour. Inter-branch accounts. *Journal of accountancy,* June 1916, p. 470-3.

Wheeler, G. W. Treatment of branch accounts in a trading concern. *Incorporated accountants' journal,* 1897-8, p. 71

Auditing

Castenholz, William B. Branch accounts. (In his *Auditing procedure.* 1918. p. 256-9).

Company audits; foreign branches. *Auditor,* 1890-1, p. 186-201.

Cutforth, A. E. English company trading or operating abroad. (In his *Audits.* 1914. p. 68-9).

Montgomery, Robert H. Branch accounts. (In his *Auditing theory and practice.* 1916. p. 628-30).

Spicer, Ernest Evan and Ernest C. Pegler. Branch accounts. (In their *Practical auditing.* 1914. p. 467-70).

Watson, William I. Auditing "branch house" of corporations; paper read before the Chicago institute of accounts. *Commerce, accounts and finance,* April 6, 1901, p. 2-5.

Stockkeeping

Walton, Seymour. Stock record at branches. *Journal of accountancy,* Feb. 1920, p. 158-9.

BRANDEIS, LOUIS D.

Brandeis's brief and argument. *Railway age,* May 8, 1914, p. 1014-5.

Brandeis's brief and Willards rebuttal in rate case. *Railway age,* May 8, 1914, p. 1023-6.

New conception of industrial efficiency. *Journal of accountancy,* May 1911, p. 35-43.

Scientific management and railroads. New York, *Engineering magazine co.* 1911. 92p.

BRANDES, J.

Is producer gas a competitor. *Ameican gas light journal,* July 19, 1915, p. 42-3.

BRANDON, H. B.

Joint stock companies. *Incorporated accountants' journal,* Feb. 1915, p. 111-5.

BRANDON (MANITOBA). DEPARTMENT OF PUBLIC FINANCE.

Forms used in the accounting system, 1914. Balance sheet. Bureau of accounts, Forms 1-14. Bureau of revenue, Forms 4-34. Bureau of supplies. Forms 3a-8. Bureau of treasury. Form 3.

BRANFORD, VICTOR V.

Accounting in its relation to economics. (In Lisle, George. *Encyclopaedia of accounting.* v.1. p. 24-50.

On the correlation of economics and accountancy. *Accountant,* May 25, June 1, 1901, p. 620-8, 642-8.

BRANNAN, JOSEPH DODDRIDGE
Negotiable instruments law annotated, with references to the English bills of exchange act and with the cases under the negotiable instruments law and the bills of exchange act and comments thereon, together with comments and criticisms on the Negotiable instruments law by James Barr Ames, Lyman D. Brewster, and Charles L. McKeehan. Ed. 3, revised, re-arranged, enlarged. Cincinnati, The W. H. Anderson company, 1920. 622p.

BRANSON, H.
Punches vs. pencils for daily car-shop reports. *Electric railway journal,* Sept. 9, 1916, p. 454.

BRANTLEY, W. G.
Condition per cent; criticism of engineering board's circular no. 226 with respect to depreciation and depreciation on the Atlanta, Birmingham and Atlantic railroad. Philadelphia, President's conference committee, 1916.

BRASCH, H.
Foreign exchange. *Accounting and commerce,* July 1915, p. 90-3.

BRASS
See also Foundries—Brass.
BLAIR, P. W. Increasing the efficiency of a brass manufacturing plant. *Metal industries,* Jan. 1913, p. 13-14.

Cost accounting
BLAIR, P. W. How to obtain the accurate cost in manufacturing brass goods. *Metal industry,* Jan. 1917, p. 10-1.
BLAIR, P. W. Installing a cost system in a brass manufacturing plant. *Metal industry,* Feb. 1918, p. 67-8.

BRASTER, R. R.
Relation of accounting offices to other members of official family. *Electric railway journal,* June 17, 1916, p. 1136-9.

BRATAGER, S, J.
Cost of coal on the heat value basis. *Railway review,* December 9, 1916, p. 791.

BRAY, THOMAS J.
Investment factor and sales policy. *Iron age,* May 28, 1914, p. 1362-5.
Investment factor in costs. *Iron trade review,* May 28, 1914, p. 967-8. *Iron age,* May 28, 1914, p. 1362-3.

BRAY, W. REGINALD
Approximate monthly accounts. *Business organisation and management,* Sept. 1920, p. 595-8.
Things that matter in accounts. *Business organisation and management,* Oct. 1920, p. 88-90.
Wages and salaries book for insurance tax purposes. *Accountants' magazine,* June 1914, p. 336-7.

BRAZIL
Brazilian federal government regulations for collection of income tax affecting incorporated companies, lenders and others. Rio de Janeiro, Wileman's Brazilian review, 1920.

BREADNER, R. W.
Business profits and income war tax acts. *Canadian chartered accountant,* Oct. 1918, p. 104-23.
Canadian business profits and income war tax accounts. *National tax association,* Bulletin, Jan. 1919, p. 93-7.

BREAKAGE.
See Scrap, waste, etc.

BREAKING in. *Journal of accountancy,* Aug. 1920, p. 135-8.

BREAKING in stock clerks. *Factory,* July 1918, p. 76.

BREAKWATER CONSTRUCTION

Cost accounting
GILLETTE, HALBERT P. and RICHARD T. DANA. Forms for breakwater construction, including quarrying, concrete work and dredging. (Engineering-contracting, Feb. 1906). (In their *Cost keeping and management engineering.* 1916. p. 238-47).

BREAR, CHARLES H.
Some points in the laying of rates. *Accountant,* July 7, 1906, p. 17-22.

BREARLEY, JOHN HENRY
Balance sheet, *Gas light journal,* Nov. 29, 1898.

——— **and BENJAMIN TAYLOR**
Gas companies' book-keeping. Ed. 2. London, Walter King, 1906. 240p.
Useful forms for gas undertakings. Bound with "Gas companies book-keeping. London, W. King, 1906, 28p.

BRECHEEN, THOMAS L.
Relation of a modern adding machine to accountancy in the high school course. *National educational association,* 1912, p. 1079-84.

BRECKENRIDGE, L. P.
Plant records and the importance of keeping them. *Power,* May 14, 1918, p. 711-2.

BRECKENRIDGE, T. S.
Use of card ledgers in a country bank. *Business man's magazine,* June 1907, p. 130-4.

BREED, A. H.
Report of the committee on uniform municipal accounting. League of California municipalities. *Public policy,* Feb. 9, 1901, p. 70-2. *California municipalities,* Dec. 1899, p. 145-48.

BREED, H. E.
Cost and life of New York state highway pavements. *Engineering and contracting,* August 6, 1919, p. 178.
Effect of grades on cost of haulage. *Engineering and contracting,* June 5, 1918, p. 577.
How New York state department paves with brick. *Engineering record,* March 11, 1916. Excerpt Construction costs. *Engineering record,* March 15, 1916, p. 260.
Maintenance costs of New York state roads. *Engineering and contracting,* Mar. 15, 1916, p. 246.
Uniform system for highway statistics and data. *Engineering and contracting,* Sept. 22, 1915, p. 233-6. *Good Roads,* Nov. 6, 1915, p. 257-9.

BREHM, G. C.
Brick and asphalt paving by day labor. *Engineering news-record,* July 1, 1916, p. 1033.
Cost data for asphaltic macadam pavement by day labor. *Municipal engineering,* September, 1916, p. 98.

BREMER, OTTO
Municipal accounting. *Business man's magazine,* Nov. 1905, p. 866-8.

BRENNAN, T. F.
Colliery accounts. *Accountant,* May 2, 1914, p. 660-5.
Double account system. *Accountant,* June 14, 1919, p. 509-15. *Accounting and commerce,* April-June 1920, p. 19-22, 40-2, 65-6.

BRENTNALL, THOMAS
Profits. *Public accountant,* April 1917, p. 224-48.
Presidential address on the formation and early history of the Australasian corporation of public accountants. *Public accountant,* 1911, p. 202.

BREWER, ———
Merchant accounts. London, Jarrold & sons, 1850.

BREWER, ALLEN F.
Comparison of appraisal methods. *Industrial management,* Nov. 1917, p. 172-5.
Costs of preparing valuations for small water companies. *Engineering and contracting,* July 11, 1917, p. 26-7.
Overhead charges as applied to appraisal reports. *Industrial management,* Sept. 1917, p. 861-5.
Overhead charges in power plant construction. *Industrial management,* Sept. 1919, p. 183-4.
Personal element in valuation and appraisal. *Industrial management,* Aug. 1919, p. 104.
Principles of the calculation of straight line depreciation. *Industrial management,* April 1917, p. 49-50.
Rates for annual depreciation. *Industrial management,* April 1918, p. 268.
Reasonable limits of accuracy for valuation of water utility properties. *Engineering and contracting,* Oct. 10, 1917, p. 287-8.
Unit costs for setting water meters. *Engineering news,* Aug. 22, 1918, p. 366.

BREWER, ANDREW HERBERT
Auditing. *Incorporated accountants journal,* 1909-10, p. 158.

BREWER, BERTRAM
Rate revision in municipal works. *Municipal journal,* September 20-7, 1917, p. 285-6, 310. *New England water works association,* March 1918, p. 310.
Water rate revision by municipal works. *Engineering and contracting,* Dec. 12, 1917, p. 497-8.

BREWER, C. B.
Economy and efficiency in the government. *North American review,* Mar. 1912, p. 368-80.

BREWER, E. C.
Bookkeeping by single or double entry. London, Jarrold and sons.
Entire new system of bookkeeping by double entry. Ed. 6. London, Jarrold & sons, 1850.
Entire new system of book-keeping by single entry. Ed. 8. London, Simpkin, Marshall, Hamilton, Kent & co. 1846.
———. Same. Ed. 10. London, [?1869.]
———. Same. Ed. 12. London, Jarrold & sons [?1855]
Key to an entire new system of bookkeeping by single entry. Ed. 7. London [?1857]

BREWER, ROBERT W. A.
Running costs of motor vehicles. *Mechanical engineering,* March 12, 1915.

BREWERIES

Accounting
AMERICAN business and accounting encyclopaedia, comp. by E. H. Beach and W. W. Thorne, Detroit, Bookkeeper publishing co. 1901. Brewery accounting—v.1., p. 269-72.
AMSDON, EDWARD. Amsdon's complete system of book-keeping for brewers, maltsters etc. wine and spirit merchants, mineral water manufacturers etc. London, Spotteswoods & co. 1906.
AMSDON, EDWARD. Amsdon's guide to brewers' book-keeping. London, 1881.
ARTER, JOHN J. B. Brewery accounts. *Accountant,* May 15, 1897, p. 496-504.
ARTER, JOHN J. B. Treatment and form of brewers' accounts. Birmingham, 1892.
BLACKBOROW, HAROLD S. Brewery accounts and their audit. *Accountant,* April 22, 29, 1899, p. 448-53, 474-81.
BREWERIES. *American institute of accounttants, Special bulletin,* No. 2, March 1920. p. 6-7.
BREWERIES. *American institute of accountants, Special bulletin,* no. 5, no. 6, Sept. 1920, Nov. 1920, p. 7-8, 2.
BREWERY. (In *International accountants manual,* 1910, paragraph 142, 144.)
CAMPBELL, C. D. Brewery accounts and accounting books. (In Lisle, George, *Encyclopaedia of accounting,* v.1. p. 508-14.
CLARKE, EDWARD W. Practical treatise on brewery accounts and office management. Chicago, 1898. 181p.
COOK, KENNETH. Brewery accounts. *Accountants' magazine,* Jan. 1906, p. 8-27.
CRAMER, J. F. Book-keeping for breweries. *Bookkeeper,* 1902, v.15, no. 1, p. 73-81.
CUTFORTH, A. E. Brewery company. (In his *Audits.* 1914. p. 89-91).
EDMUNDS, GARNET W. Brewery accounts. *Accountants' magazine,* Nov. 1907, p. 480-501.
GRUNDMANN, OTTO A. Brewery accounting. *Journal of accountancy,* Feb. 1907, p. 285-93.
HARRIS, WILLIAM. Brewers' accounts. Ed. 2. London, Howard & Jones, 1899. 235p.
HILL, DANIEL. Brewery accounts. *Accountant,* Dec. 4, 1897, March 5, 1898, p. 1144-7, 252-4.
INGALL, WHATELY WILLIAM. Financial elements of brewing. London, 1887.
KOEHLER, THEODORE. Brewery accounts. *Brewers journal,* Aug. Nov. 1906.
KOELLER, A. H. Special accounting system for breweries with a bottling department. *Bookkeeper,* 1903, v.16, no. 6, p. 37-44.
LANHAM, HERBERT. Brewers' and bottlers' accounts; with a chapter on the licensing act, 1904 by W. C. Northcott. London, Gee & co. 1906. 191p. (Accountants' library, v.44).
LANHAM, HERBERT. Brewery and bottled beer accounts and audit. *Accountant,* Feb. 10, March 31, 1906, p. 175-85, 389-90.
MOODY, A. F. Easy detail account book for rectifiers and wholesale liquor dealers. Lynn, Mass., T. P. Nichols & son, 1912.
MOXEY, EDWARD P. and others. Brewery accounting. (In their *Practical accounting methods.* p. 135-63).
PIXLEY, FRANCIS W. Brewers. (In his *Accountancy.* Ed. 2, p. 115-7).
SALE records of a retail brewery company. *Accountant,* Oct. 28, 1911, p. 549-60.
SMART, ALLEN R. Brewery accounts. *Business,* April 1898, p. 223-4.
SOME problems in brewery accounts. *Accountant,* Dec. 9, 1905, p. 661-4.
SWEETLAND, CHARLES. Brewers' accounts. Chicago, American school of correspondence, 1909. (In *Cyclopaedia of commerce, ac-*

BREWERIES—ACCOUNTING—*(Continued)*
countancy, business administration. 1910. v.8. p. 11-79).
THORNTON, FRANK WELDON. Brewery accounts. New York, The Ronald press co. 1913, 102p. (Ronald accounting series).
TRADING accounts. *Accountant,* July 26, Aug. 2, 30, Sept. 6, 13, 20, 27, Oct. 4, 11, 25, Nov. 1, 8, 15, 22, 1884.
WALKDEN, C. H. Accounts of a brewery. *Accountant,* June 13, 1891, p. 458-64.
WILKINSON, GEORGE. Brewery accounting. *Business man's magazine,* Nov., Dec. 1908, Jan. 1909, p. 387-95, 490-5, 74-83.

Auditing
BLACKBOROW, HAROLD S. Brewery accounts and their audit. *Accountant,* April 22, 29, 1899, p. 448-53, 474-81.
CASTENHOLZ, WILLIAM R. Breweries. (In his *Auditing procedure.* 1918. p. 252-55).
COMPANY audits: brewery accounts. *Auditor,* 1890-1, p. 144, 167.
CUTFORTH, A. E. Brewery. (In his *Audits.* 1914. p. 60-1.
DICKSEE, LAWRENCE ROBERT. Breweries. (In his *Auditing.* Authorized American edition. p. 96-8).
JENKINSON, MARK WEBSTER. Breweries. (In his *Some notes on the audit of different businesses.* 1913. p. 13-9).
JENKINSON, MARK WEBSTER. Some notes on the audit of different businesses. *Accountant,* April 19, 1913, p. 583-5.
LANHAM, HERBERT. Brewery and bottled beer accounts and audit. *Accountant,* Feb. 10, March 31, 1906, p. 175-85, 389-90.
MONTGOMERY, ROBERT H. Breweries. (In his *Auditing theory and practice.* 1916. p. 602-3).
SPICER, ERNEST EVAN and ERNEST C. PEGLER. Breweries. (In their *Practical auditing.* 1914. p. 470-1).
SPICER, ERNEST EVAN and ERNEST C. PEGLER. Brewery. (In their *Audit programmes.* 1919. p. 13-16).

Cost accounting
FOX, W. H. Principles of percentages of cost as applied to various businesses. *Accountant,* Jan. 19, 1907, p. 86-96.
RIDGWAY, A. CLIFFORD. Single and process cost accounts. (In his *Cost accounts in principle and practice.* p. 59-65).

Depreciation.
See Depreciation, depletion and obsolescence—Breweries.

Stockkeeping
CLASSIFIED statement of stores received, used and on hand. *Business man's magazine,* June 1908, p. 523-4.

BREWERIES *American institution of accountants, Special bulletin,* No. 2, 5, 6, March, Sept., Nov., 1920, p. 6-7, 7-8, 2.

BREWERS' accounts. Harris, William. 1899.

BREWER'S accounts. Sweetland, C. A. 1909.

BREWERS' and bottlers' accounts. Lanham, Herbert. 1906.

BREWERY accounting. Grundmann, O. A.

REWERY accounts. Thornton, Frank Weldon. 1913.

BREWERY accounts and account books. Campbell, C. D.

BREWIS, ARTHUR STEPHEN
Address, 1910. *Accountant,* March 12, 1910, p. 368- 75.

Duties and accounts of trustees. *Accountant,* 1886, p. 320.
Executorship accounts. *Accountant,* April 4, 1885.

BRICK HANDLING

Costs
HASKELL, A. C. Cost of loading bricks into a box car by means of a portable belt conveyor. *Engineering and contracting,* Sept. 15, 1915, p. 204.

BRICK pavements being adapted to country roads. *Engineering news-record,* February 28, 1918, p. 402-3.

BRICK pavements, 1917; tabulation. *Municipal journal,* February 1916, April 20, 1918, p. 138-40, 318-19.

BRICK paving for New York state roads. *Engineering news-record,* April 2, 1914, p. 742-4.

BRICKMAKERS' accounts. Fox, W. H. 1904.

BRICKMAKING

Accounting
BOYD, W. G. E. Accounting methods for brick manufacturing business. *Business man's magazine,* Aug. 1905, p. 270-8.
FOX, WILLIAM HENRY. Brickmakers' accounts. London, Gee & co. 1904. 96p. (Accountants' library, v. 34).
OLSON, NELS. System of accounting for brick manufacturing. *Business man's magazine,* April 1910, p. 358-63.
RUDLAND, ERNEST MARSTON. Brickmaking accounts. *Accountant,* Nov. 23, 1901, p. 1278-85.

Auditing
BRICK company. (In his *Audits.* 1914. p. 61-2).

Cost accounting
EGGLESTON, DEWITT CARL. Costs in the brick manufacturing. (In his *Problems in cost accounting.* 1918. p. 314-7).
EGGLESTON, DEWITT CARL. Process cost system, clay products. (In his *Cost accounting.* 1920. p. 328-48).
HUDSON, F. HOWARD. Cost in brickmaking. *Accountant,* Aug. 17, 1907, p. 210-3.
MATTES, C. F. Simplified system of counting cost. *Brick and clay record,* April 8, 1919, p. 591-4.
MOOREHOUSE, ELI. Cost system that works. *Business man's magazine,* Nov. 1911, p. 448-50.

Depreciation.
See Depreciation, depletion and obsolescence—Brickmaking.

BRIDGE, G. H.
Auditors' responsibilities in respect to the verification of stock-in-trade. *Incorporated accountants' journal,* Oct. 1912, p. 10-4.

BRIDGE, JOSIAH
Rating of electricity supply works. *Accountant,* July 29, Aug. 5, 1905, p. 135-41, 158-62.

BRIDGE cost record used by the Illinois highway commission. *Engineering and contracting,* Aug. 26, 1914, p. 200-3.

BRIDGES, M. H.
Interstate classification of accounts. *Electric railway journal,* April 18, 1914, p. 883.

BRIDGES

Cost accounting

BRIDGE cost record used by the Illinois highway commission. *Engineering and contracting,* August 26, 1914, p. 200-3.

COST-KEEPING system for small bridge and culvert jobs. *Engineering and contracting,* June 27, 1917, p 588-9.

GILLETTE, HALBERT POWERS and RICHARD T. DANA. Cost keeping system of the Kosmos engineering co., New York city. (*Engineering—contracting,* March 13, 1907.) (In their *Cost keeping and management engineering.* 1916. p. 278-83).

SMALL, R. A. Labor cost-keeping system for concrete bridge work. *Engineering and contracting,* Feb. 9, 1916, p. 142-3.

Costs

BAINBRIDGE, C. N. Costs of bridges for grade-crossing elimination. *Engineering record,* June 19, 1915, p. 770.

BAINBRIDGE, C. N. Study of grade crossing elimination in cities. *Journal of the western society of engineers,* Oct. 1915, p. 639-51. Excerpt. *Engineering record,* June 19, 1915, p. 770.

COBB, L. Detailed cost of 113-ft. reinforced concrete through girder bridge built near Douglas, Arizona. *Engineering and contracting,* December 27, 1916, p. 573-6.

COLLECTION and use of construction cost data. *Engineering news record,* Dec. 25, 1913, p. 1305-7.

COMPARATIVE costs of steel and concrete bridges. *Engineering and contracting,* December 27, 1916, p. 572.

CONCRETE arch railway bridge costs less than steel. *Engineering news-record,* February 21, 1918, p. 342-5.

COST of covered wood bridge. *Engineering and contracting,* Sept. 24, 1919, p. 367.

COST of erecting a steel bridge. *Engineering news-record,* March 20, 1913, p. 575-6.

COST of I-beam highway bridges in Boone county, Iowa. *Engineering and contracting,* Aug. 23, 1916, p. 182-3.

COST of railway foot bridges. *Engineer,* August 27-September 17, 1915, p. 197-9, 221-3, 240-2, 266-8.

DAVIDSON, WILLIAM C. Cost and details of construction of a steel highway bridge, McLennan co., Tex. *Engineering and contracting,* Oct. 25, 1916, p. 365-8.

DESIGN, construction and detailed costs of the McKinley Ford bridge, La Salle county, Ill. *Engineering and contracting,* February 24, 1915, p. 179-82.

GANNETT, F. and J. D. CARPENTER. Keep accurate costs on war-time fee contract. *Engineering news-record,* March 20, 1919, p. 571-3.

GILLETTE, HALBERT POWERS. Bridges. (In his *Handbook of cost data for contractors and engineers.* 1910. p. 1471-1744).

HELL GATE arch bridge and its cost. *Engineering and contracting,* November 28, 1917, p. 443-4.

HOWARD, E. E. Construction of the Twelfth street traffic way viaduct, Kansas city, Mo *Engineering and contracting,* October 27, 1915, p. 331-2.

JOHNSON, C. O. Design, construction and detailed labor costs of the substructure of the double leaf trunnion bascule bridge at Chicago avenue, Chicago. *Engineering and contracting,* November 4, 1914, p. 426-33.

LEONARD, GEORGE K. Cost of constructing concrete arch bridge over Platte river in Nebraska. *Engineering and contracting,* Feb. 27, 1918, p. 222-3.

LEONARD, GEORGE K. Methods and cost of erecting the St. Paul, Nebraska, state aid bridge. *Engineering and contracting,* Feb. 28, 1917, p. 207-9.

PETTEE, E. E. Portland bridge. *Journal of the Boston society of civil engineers,* Dec. 1916, p. 508-10.

ROBINSON, E. W. Methods and cost of constructing a 450 ft. reinforced concrete viaduct of the beam and girder type at Fort Worth, Texas. *Engineering and contracting,* April 29, 1914, p. 500-5.

SPRADLING, R. D. Cost of labor and materials used in painting the St. Louis municipal bridge. *Engineering and contracting,* July 15, 1914, p. 65-6.

SPOFFORD, CHARLES M. Apportionment of cost of highway bridges between street railways and cities; with discussion. *Journal of the western society of engineers,* May 1915, p. 405-43.

SPOFFORD, CHARLES M. Cost of highway bridges. *Electric railway journal,* July 10, 1915, p. 53-4.

STEWART, R. W. Design and cost of ornamental arch bridges in Los Angeles. *Engineering record,* Feb. 14, 1914, p. 180-2.

WADDELL, J. A. L. Comparative economics of cantilever and suspension bridges. *Journal of the western society of engineers,* April 1919, p. 210-4.

WEIGHT and cost of bridges: comparison of different types in Buffalo. *Engineering record,* Dec. 6, 1913, p. 640-1.

BRIDGMAN, A. F.

Property returns on public works. *Engineering record,* Dec. 27, 1902.

BRIDGMAN, R. L.

Civic righteousness via percentages. *Atlantic monthly,* Dec. 1908, p. 797-802.

BRIEF analysis of the appropriation ordinance. Indiana. State board of accountants. 1916.

BRIEF exposition of the fundamental principles of bookkeeping. Snyder, W. T. 1905.

BRIEF history of telephone accounting. Du Bois, Charles G.

BRIEF on accounting scheme submitted to public service commission, second district, on behalf of New York state association. *Electric railway review,* May 16, 1908, p. 591.

BRIEF selected list of books in accountancy for the use of small public and private libraries. Johnson, M. N.

BRIEFE instruction and maner how to keepe bookes of accompts after the order of debitor and creditor, & as well for proper accompts partible, &c. Mellis, John. 1588.

BRIERLEY, FREDERICK

Income tax. *Accountant,* May 28, June 4, 1892, p. 449, 464.

BRIERLEY, JOHN T.

Book-keeping at a glance; a simple and concise method of practical book-keeping. New York, Nourse co. 1920. 135p.

Book-keeping at a glance, or How to become an expert bookkeeper. New York, Excelsior publishing house. 1893.

Manufacturing cost accounts; being a manual of instruction for bookkeepers and managers in factory cost acounts. 432 West St., Kensington, Brooklyn, J. T. Brierley, 1913.

BRIGG, WILLIAM ANDERTON

Local bodies. *Accountant,* May 17, 24, 1890, p. 273-6, 284-7.

Our judicial system. *Accountant,* May 21, 1892, p. 421-26.

BRIGGS, W. W.

Proposed divided-type domestic service rate. *Electrical world,* Oct. 28, 1916, p. 850-3.

BRIGHAM, E. F.

Electricity for suburban and country institutions; light, power, cooking, heating and farm work. *Electrical review,* July 21, 1917, p. 89-93.

BRIGHT, G.

See Sykes, W., joint author.

BRIGHT, R. L.

Accounting methods for a navigation company. *Business man's magazine,* July 1908, p. 40-1.

BRIGHT prospect in Minnesota. Temple, H. M.

BRIGHT prospects of accountancy. *Journal of accountancy,* Dec. 1913, p. 459-60.

BRIGHT spot in the industry in Charleston. *Electric railway journal,* Jan. 10, 1920, p. 108-10.

BRIGHTMAN, M. H.

City improvement records on 4x6-inch cards. *Engineering record,* April 8, 1916, p. 488-9. Condensed. *Engineering news,* March 9, 1916, p. 470.

BRINKERHOFF, J. J.

How to examine a fire insurance company. (In Fricke, William A. *Insurance.* 1898. p. 889-911).

BRINKLEY, M. H.

Estimating grading quantities on revaluation. *Engineering and contracting,* May 27, 1914, p. 617-9. *Engineering news,* Jan. 22, 1914, p. 191.

Tables for estimating grading quantities on revaluation. *Engineering and contracting,* May 27, 1914, p. 617.

BRINSMADE, R. B.

Calculation of mine values. *Bulletin of the American institute of mining engineers,* Jan. 1908.

BRINTON, WILLARD COPE.

Graphic methods for presenting facts. New York, Engineering magazine co. 1914. 371p. (Works management library.)

Graphic methods for presenting data. *Engineering magazine,* August 1914-January 1915, p. 651-66, 817-29, 73, 85, 229-41, 396-406, 551-68.

BRION, EDWARD A.

Interstate classification of accounts. *Electric railway journal,* May 2, 1914, p. 980-1.

BRISCO, NORRIS ARTHUR

Economics of business. New York, The Macmillan co. 1913. 390p.

Economics of efficiency. New York, The Macmillan co. 1914. 383p.

BRISCOE, WILLIAM RICHARD BRUNSKILL

Accountant in relation to legal proceedings. *Incorporated accountants' journal,* April 1914, p. 204-8.

Notes on the history of commercial law. *Incorporated accountants journal,* 1892-3, p. 101.

Outlines of company law. *Incorporated accountants' journal,* 1889-90, p. 73.

BRISSENDEN, P. F.

Employment system of the Lake carriers' association. Washington, Government printing office, 1918. 58p. United States. Bureau of labor statistics.

BRISTOL CHARTERED ACCOUNTANTS STUDENTS' SOCIETY.

AUDITORS and certificates to stock. *Accountant,* April 26, May 31, 1902, p. 447-54, 562-3.

BRISTOL SOCIETY OF CHARTERED ACCOUNTANTS

Discussion on the responsibilities of auditors. *Accountant,* March 4, 1911, p. 352-4.

PROBLEMS of municipal finance. *Accountant,* Dec. 28, 1907, p. 798-807.

BRITAIN'S proposals as to valuation of stocks and allowances for wear and tear, depreciation and obsolescence of assets, for purposes of excess profits duty. *Canadian chartered accountant,* Jan. 1918, p. 219-228.

BRITISH and foreign methods of bookkeeping, with special reference to legalised systems. Dawson, Sidney Stanley.

BRITISH decimal coinage. *Australasian accountant and secretary,* June 1919, p. 18-20.

BRITISH decision on valuation of a public service property. *Electrical world,* June 30, 1910, p. 1694.

BRITISH fuel research board recommends charging for gas by beat units. *American gas engineering journal,* May 17, 1919, p. 420-3.

BRITISH Indian bookkeeping. Fulton, J. W. 1800.

BRITISH profit sharing. *Gas age,* Sept. 25, 1920, p. 223.

BRITISH railway reserve fund. *Railway gazette,* March 28, 1919, p. 558.

BRITISH RED CROSS SOCIETY.

Accounts of auxiliary hospitals. *Incorporated accountants' journal,* Aug. 1918, p. 213-4.

BRITISH society of incorporated accountants and auditors. *Journal of accountancy,* July 1906, Aug. 1908, June 1912, July Nov. 1913, June, July, Dec. 1914, June, July, Dec. 1915, July 1916, July 1917, Aug. 1918, July 1919, p. 230; 247; 455; 77; 416, 483; 83, 494, 486; 79, 480, 79; 78; 156; 80.

BRITTAIN, ARNOLD

Law of distress. *Accountant,* July 11, 1914, p. 51-8.

BRITTAIN, HORACE L.

Bureau of municipal research. *Canadian chartered accountant,* April 1915, p. 297-306.

Financial relations of boards of education to municipal governments and cost accounting in education. *National association of comptrollers and accounting officers, Proceedings,* 1914, p. 36-59.

Movement for improved financing and accounting practice in Toronto. *Annals of the American academy of political and social science,* Nov. 1915, p. 211-22.

Municipal accounting and finance. *Canadian chartered accountant,* April 1915, p. 311-18.

What is a city budget? *Canadian chartered accountant,* July 1915, p. 26-49.

BRITTEN, C. D.
Works costing. *Accountant,* March 16, 1912, p. 449-51.

BRITTON, JOHN A.
Accounting under utility regulation. *Gas age,* July 15, 1913, p. 62-4. *Journal of electricity, power and gas,* April 12, 19, 26, 1913.
Depreciation. *Progressive age,* June 15, 1908. p. 379.
Methods of calculating depreciation. *Electric railway journal,* Nov. 7, 1914, p. 1059-60.
Pacific gas rate valuation. *Progerssive age,* April 15, 1912, p. 330-3.

BROACHING MACHINES
Cost accounting
Simonds, H. R. Controlling production and keeping costs in a broaching tool plant. *Iron trade review,* May 4, 1920, p. 697-702.

BROAD, B. G.
Methods of changing the old accounts to the new. *Electric railway journal,* April 24, 1909, p. 779.

BROAD principles enunciated by another order in the Shreveport rate case. *Railway review,* Aug. 19, 1916, p. 253-5.

BROADBRIDGE, ———
Alphabetical double entry bookkeeping. London, Simpkin, Marshall, Hamilton, Kent & co. 1883.

BROADER field for certified public accountants. Stockwell, H. G.

BROAKER, FRANK
Accounts, the safeguard of a business. *Bankers magazine,* Dec. 1909, p. 983-8.
American accountants manual, v. 1: examination questions prepared by the State board of examiners of expert public accountants appointed by the Board of regents of the University of the state of New York; together with answers in concise form, further elucidated by author's comment upon the technique and expression of modern accountancy. New York, Broaker & Chapman, c1897. 210p.
——— Same. New York, Broaker & Chapman, c1915. 210p.
Cost and factory accounts with use of consumption journal. *Accountant,* June 19, 1897, p. 604-5. *Business,* June 1897, p. 179-80.
Teaching of accounting in commercial schools. *Business man's magazine,* 1906, v. 18, no. 9, p. 166-70. *Journal of accountancy,* Feb. 1906, p. 328-30.
Technique of accountics. Lessons 1-20. New York, 1904.

BROCKLEHURST, F. R.
Growth of municipal expenditures. *Manchester statistical society. Transactions,* session, 1905, 1906. London, 1906, p. 1-20.

BROCKLEHURST, G. R.
Bookkeeping for bakers, grocers, drapers, dairymen, butchers, co-operative societies, etc. Gainsborough, 1892.

BROCKUNIER, S. H.
Mining costs at Cordova, Ontario. *Engineering and mining journal,* Jan. 5, 1918, p. 22.
Stamp-mill reports. *Engineering and mining journal,* Dec. 30, 1916, p. 1138.

BROCKWAY, WALTER BELDING
Accounting department of interurban railways. *Street railway journal,* October 4, 1902.
Electric railway accounting; the monthly report, the accounting and the accountant. New York, McGraw-Hill publishing co. 1906. 84p.
ELECTRIC railway auditor, his duties and relation to the organization. *American street and interurban railway accountants association, Proceedings,* 1909, p. 107-20. *Journal of accountancy,* Feb. 1910, p. 253-62.
Reporting a street railway examination. *Journal of accountancy,* May 1907, p. 16-22.
Small company and the new classification of accounts. *Street railway journal,* March 14, 1908.

BRODERICK, J. A.
Examination of the foreign exchange departments in state banks and trust companies. *Journal of commerce,* Aug. 2, 1911, p. 5.

BRODERICK, LONSDALE
Address, 1892. *Accountant,* Oct. 8, 1892, p. 754-8.
Paper on 'A bill to amend the companies' acts, 1862'. *Accountant,* Feb. 13, 1892, p. 146.

BRODIE, ALEX
NEW and easy method of book-keeping. London, 1722.

BROKERAGE.
See Brokers.

BROKERAGE accounts. Todman, F. S. 1916.

BROKERAGE questions and problems. Ball, C. E. c1910.

BROKERS
See also Cotton brokers; Cotton seed oil brokers; Coffee brokers; Produce brokers; Stock exchange.
CECIL, GEORGE. Stockbroking in India. *Accountant,* Sept. 8, 15, 22, 1906, p. 279, 297-8, 337-8.
DAY, JULIUS E. Stock-broker's office organisation, management and accounts. London, Sir Isaac Pitman & sons. 231p.
MORISON, THOMAS B. Stockbrokers' contracts. *Accountants' magazine,* Aug. 1905, p. 423-9.
PEGLER, ERNEST C. Some notes on stock exchange transactions. London, Gee & co., 1912, 15p. *Accountant,* April 27, 1912, p. 652-7. *Incorporated accountants journal.* Nov. 1915, p. 36-7.

Accounting
BALL, CHARLES E. Brokerage questions and problems. New York, Universal business institute, inc. c1910. 55p.
BENNETT, GEORGE E. Stock brokerage. (In his *Constructive accounting.* 1920. p. 415-31).
BUTLER, HENRY G. Cotton, grain and coffee —future contract brokerage business. *Business man's magazine,* 1906, v. 18, no. 8, p. 100-6.
BUTLER, HENRY G. Stock-brokerage bookkeeping. *Business man's magazine,* 1906, v. 18, no. 10, p. 162-170.
CALLAWAY, WILLIAM DALE. Stockbrokers' accounts. London, Gee & co. 1902. 88p. (Accountants' library, v.9).
CARTER, R. N. Stock exchange transactions. (In his *Advanced accounts.* p. 894-96.)
DAVIDSON, D. W. Stock exchange accounts. *Incorporated accountants' journal,* 1906-7, p. 180.
DAY, JULIUS E. Stock broker's office organization, management and accounts. London, Sir Isaac Pitman & sons. 231p.
DOSCH, ARNO. How Wall Street keeps its books. *Business man's magazine,* Sept. 1910, p. 252-58.

BROKERS—ACCOUNTING—*(Continued)*

EGGERS, G. C. Option accounting in the board of trade. *Bookkeeper,* 1902, v.15, no. 6, p. 56-61.

GRIFFITH, J. B. and C. A. SWEETLAND. Trustees', executors' and stock brokers' accounts. Chicago, American school of correspondence, 1909.

How to check your stockbroker's accounts. (In Carr, E. *Investors' bookkeeping.*)

JOHNSON, J. BOLAIN. Stockbrokers' bookkeeping. (In Lisle, George. *Encyclopaedia of accounting.* v.6. p. 142-66).

JOHNSTON, J. G. Forms of accounts for the use of stockbrokers. (In his *Forms of account books,* p. 67-81).

KILLIK, STEPHEN HENRY MOLYNEUX. Stock exchange accounts. London, Effingham Wilson, 1895.

——— Ed. 2. 1908.

KRAMER, FRANK C. Suggestions for a comprehensive system of keeping books as applied to stock and bond brokerage business; with special reference to houses outside of New York city. *Business man's magazine,* 1904, v. 16, no. 10, p. 74-78, no. 11, p. 76-90.

LUDLAM, CHARLES S. Methods of auditing and accounting in a bond house. *Annals of the American academy of political and social science,* Sept. 1907, p. 284-91.

MALLINSON, J. Sharebroker's accountant, &c. London, Simpkin, Marshall, Hamilton, Kent & co. 1843.

MULLARD, THOMAS S. Stock exchange accounts. *Accountant,* June 10, 1899, p. 642-8.

PFENDER, L. D. Stock brokerage book-keeping. *Business man's magazine,* Feb. 1907, p. 78-80.

PFENDER, L. D. Stock brokerage business. *Business man's magazine,* Dec. 1905, p. 1156-62.

PORTER, R. J. Stock exchange transactions. (In his *Pitman's dictionary of bookkeeping.* p. 714-6).

SLOAN, D. NORMAN. System of book-keeping for stockbrokers. *Accountants' magazine,* Nov. 1903, p. 505-14.

SPICER, E. E. and E. C. PEGLER. Stock exchange transactions. (In their *Bookkeeping and accounts.* 1914. p. 368-71).

SPICER, E. E. and E. C. PEGLER. Stock exchange transactions. (In their *Practical bookkeeping and commercial knowledge.* 1912. p. 236-40).

STEVEN, J. ANGUS. Stock exchange practice and accounting. *Accountant,* Dec. 23, 1905, p. 737-47.

SWEETLAND, CHARLES A. Stock brokers' accounts. (In *Cyclopedia of commerce, accountancy, business administration.* 1910. v. 5. p. 195-232).

THOMSON, T. S. Practice of the stock exchange. *Accountants' magazine,* April 1912, p. 180-95.

TODMAN, FREDERICK SIMSON. Brokerage accounts; a treatise on the business of brokerage, its accounting books and records. New York, The Ronald press co. 1916. 388p. (Ronald accounting series).

WALTON, SEYMOUR. Long and short sales. *Journal of accountancy,* June 1916, p. 466-70.

WARNER, ROBERT. Stock exchange bookkeeping. London, Effingham Wilson and co. 1889.

WELLS, EDWARD. Stock exchange transactions in relation to accounts. *Accountant,* June 6, 13, 1896, p. 470-4, 488-92.

WILSON, ——. Sharebroker's and speculator's account book. London, Effingham Wilson, 1845.

Auditing

CASTENHOLZ, WILLIAM B. Bond and stockbrokers, business brokers. (In his *Auditing procedure.* 1918. p. 219-23, 231-3).

DICKSEE, LAWRENCE ROBERT. Stockbrokers. (In his *Auditing.* Authorized American edition. p. 129-31).

HALTER, EDWIN S. Stock brokerage audits. *Journal of accountancy,* Nov. 1918, p. 349-54.

LUDLAM, CHARLES S. Methods of auditing and accounting in a bond house. *Annals of the American academy of political and social science,* Sept. 1907, p. 284-91.

MONTGOMERY, ROBERT H. Stockbrokers. (In his *Auditing theory and practice.* 1916. p. 556-65).

SMITH, HARRY MASON. Balance sheet audit of stock brokers' accounts. *Journal of accountancy,* Jan. 1911, p. 195-204.

SPICER, ERNEST EVAN and ERNEST C. PEGLER. Stockbrokers. (In their *Practical auditing.* 1914. p. 504-9).

SPICER, ERNEST EVAN and ERNEST C. PEGLER. Stockbrokers' accounts. (In their *Audit programmes.* 1919. p. 91-3).

SPICER, ERNEST EVAN and ERNEST C. PEGLER. Stockjobbers. (In their *Practical auditing.* 1914. p. 510-512).

SPICER, ERNEST EVAN and ERNEST C. PEGLER. Stock-jobbers' accounts. (In their *Audit programmes.* 1919. p. 94-6).

TODMAN, FREDERICK SIMSON. Brokerage accounts; a treatise on the business of brokerage, its accounting books and records. New York, The Ronald press co. 38p. (Ronald accounting series.)

BROMFIELD, J. C.

English courts of justice; their functions and powers. *Accountant,* Oct. 16, 1915, p. 464-72.

BROMLEY, CHARLES H.

Aspects of the power situation in New England. *Power,* March 27, 1917, p. 404-9.

Depreciation and how it is applied. *Power,* June 2, 1914, p. 767.

Keeping tabs in the Fifth Avenue building. *Power,* May 2, 1916, p. 614-6.

Oil fuel in New England. *Power,* December 19, 1916, p. 852-4.

Operation at Holtwood. *Power,* May 20, 1919, p. 770-6.

BROMLEY, J. H.

Company law. *Accountant,* June 5, 1920, p. 659-69.

BRONSON, JOHN L.

Depreciation problem. *Cassier's magazine,* July 1905, p. 190-2.

BROOK, C. H.

Audit of small trading concerns in cases where there is practically no internal check. *Accountant,* Aug. 17, 1907, p. 208-10.

BROOKLINE, MASS., BOARD OF SELECTMEN.

Report of the expert accountant appointed by the selectmen to examine the accounts of the town of Brookline when the town was deprived of the services of its regular accountant by the death of Mr. Edward B. Hill, on Feb. 7, 1902. Brookline, C. A. W. Spencer, 1902. 517+504p.

BROOKLYN rate order not accepted. *Electrical world,* Dec. 2, 1916, p. 1093-4.

BROOKMAN, THIRMUTHUS A.

Family expense account, including problems of investment and expenditure. Boston, D. C. Heath & co. 1914.

BROOKS, HENRY W.
Comparative statements. *Street railway review,* March 20, 1903.
Province of the street railway accountant. *Street railway review,* Sept. 20, 1903.

BROOKS, HOWARD KEYES
Brooks' foreign exchange text book; an elementary treatise on foreign exchange and the monetary systems of the world. Chicago, H. K. Brooks, 1906. 239p.

BROOKS, THOMAS BURNLEY
Building societies. *Accountant,* Dec. 22, 1883.
Outline of the practice in relation to the compulsory winding-up of public companies. *Accountant,* 1886, p. 367.

BROPHY, J. P.
Hardships of the cost-plus plan. *Industrial management,* Oct. 1918, p. 320.
Office management. *Machinery,* Nov. 1915, p. 209.

BROSS, E. E.
"For instance, employee representation has": ten results a year's trial of the plan has brought us. *Factory,* Aug. 15, 1920, p. 538-40.

BROSSMANN, CHARLES
PRACTICAL measures for securing greatest economy in public utility plant operation. *Municipal engineering,* Jan. April, July, Sept. Dec. 1918, p. 13-5, 140-2, 29-31, 111-3, 206-8.

BROTHERS all. Little, A. S.

BROWDER, EARL R.
Co-operative accounting. *Co-operative consumer,* March 1918, p. 36-7.
System of accounts for a small consumers' co-operative. New York, Co-operative league of America. 8p.

BROWN, A. HERBERT
Use of percentages. *Accountant,* Sept. 29, 1906, p. 363-7.
Personal status of a liquidator. *Accountants' magazine,* June 1905, p. 301-4.

BROWN, A. L.
How I reduced the cost of marketing. *System on the farm,* July 1917, p. 175-8.

BROWN, A. M.
Standard forms in fire insurance and the work of the Standard forms bureau of the Pacific coast. *Economic world,* April 26, 1919, p. 599-601.

BROWN, A. R.
Model accounts in the Sheriff court, *Edinburgh,* 1910.

BROWN, A. S.
Personal status of a liquidator. *Accountants' magazine,* 1905, p. 301.

BROWN, C. C.
Report of the committee on municipal data. *American society of municipal improvements,* 1900, p. 36-58. *Municipal engineering,* Sept. 1900, p. 174-8.
Uniform municipal accounting. Michigan political science association. Publications, 1904, v.5, no.4, p. 121-28. *Public policy,* March 12, 1904, p. 130-2.
Uniformity in municipal accounting and on national statistics. *American society of municipal improvements. Proceedings,* 1901, p. 35-9.

BROWN, CHARLES H.
Companies' act, 1907. *Accountants' magazine,* July, Aug. 1908, p. 358-80, 439-55.
Finance act, 1907. *Accountants' magazine,* April 1908, p. 210-7.
Importance of inventories in figuring excess profits tax and fire insurance. *Inland printer,* March 1919, p. 681-2.
Judicial factors. *Accountant,* April 13, 1912, p. 592-6.
Limited partnership act, 1907. *Accountants' magazine,* March 1908, p. 152-69.
Values of printing offices. *Inland printer,* Oct. 1915, p. 43-5.

BROWN, D. J. A.
First guide to elementary practical bookkeeping; ed. by J. A. Jenkins. London, Longmans, Green & co. 1899. 66p.

——— **AND EDGAR THOMAS.**
Investment and loan societies' accounts. London, Gee & co. 1908. 109p.

BROWN, D. W.
Freight rates and popular interest. *Railway age,* January 2, 1914, p. 11.

BROWN, E. M.
Stocking and distribution of school supplies, National association of school accounting and business officials of public schools, Report, 1919, p. 6-11.

BROWN, ELMER ELLSWORTH
Opening address; New York university, Graduate school of business administration. September 28, 1920. 14p.
Some educational bearings of accounting. *American institute of accountants. Yearbook.* 1910, p. 125-39
Some educational bearings of accounting; discussion by W. R. Gray, Joseph French Johnson, J. B. Geijsbeek, H. T. Westermann. *Journal of acconutancy,* Jan 1911, p. 165-70.

BROWN, EVERARD
Depreciation of power plant equipment. *Electrical world,* Aug. 3, 1912, p. 268.

BROWN, FRANK
Excess profits tax. *Accountant,* Jan. 15, April 8, 1916, p. 89-91, 405-9. *Federal accountant,* July, Oct. 1916, p. 90-5, 110-4. *Incorporated accountants' journal,* April 1916, p. 147-50. *Public accountant,* June 1916, p. 252-62.
Finance act, 1916—excess profits duty. *Accountant,* July 29, Aug. 12, 1916, p. 101, 139-40.

BROWN, GEORGE F.
Detroit board of education. *Business man's magazine,* July 1905, p. 100-4.
Keeping organization accounts. *Business man's magazine,* Sept. 1907, p. 118-122.
Simple accounting of a small Adirondack farm. *Business man's magazine,* May 1909, p. 434 46.

BROWN, H. B.
Comparative cost of kindling fires in locomotives. *Railway mechanical engineer,* June 1917, p. 332-3.

BROWN, H. G.
Accounting for the storage business. *Business man's magazine,* Dec. 1905, p. 1176-80.
Complete accounting system for a department store. *Business man's magazine,* 1904, v. 17, p. 86-99.

BROWN, H. G.—(*Continued*)
System of accounts for a small mutual insurance company of North Dakota. *Business man's magazine*, 1904, v.17, p. 419-22.

——— **AND OTHERS**
Voucher system. *Business man's magazine*, 1904, v. 16, no. 11, p. 124-46.

BROWN, H. HAY
Office organization; system of book-keeping suitable for accountants. *Accountants' magazine*, July 1900, p. 396-9.

BROWN, HENRY
War and life assurance. *Accountants' magazine*, March 1916, p. 137-41.

BROWN, HENRY GUNNISON
Principle of commerce: a study of the mechanism, the advantages, and the transportation costs of foreign and domestic trade. New York, 1916. 154, 188, 207p.

BROWN, HERBERT D.
Savings and annuity plan proposed for retirement of superannuated civil service employees. *Government accountant*, Oct. Nov. Dec. 1911, Jan. Feb. March, May, June, July 1912, p. 249-63, 317-24, 331-56, 379-401, 462-6, 510-4, 35-8, 51-4, 118-32.

BROWN, I. S.
Typewriter bookkeeping. New York, Underwood typewriter co. 1909. gratis.

BROWN, J. F.
See Kittredge, A. O., joint author.

BROWN, J. F. K.
Continuous face haulage. *Coal age*, Dec. 25, 1915, p. 1063-4.
Cost of reaching the market. *Coal age*, June 1, 1918, p. 1003-5.
Puzzle in mining costs. *Coal age*, Feb. 5, 1916, p. 246-9.

BROWN, NICOL
Organization of gold mining business with specimens of the departmental report books and the account books. Ed. 2. Glasgow, Duncan, Campbell & son, 1903, 220p.
Specimens of working records and account books for gold mining companies. Glasgow, 1896.

BROWN, R. C.
Accounting not a proper function of the railroad storekeeper. *Railroad herald*, Oct. 1919, p. 14-5.
Simplification of mechanical and store accounts. *Railroad herald*, Feb. 1918, p. 46-7.

BROWN, R. D.
Comparative cost study of steam and electric equipment for a 1,500-ton coal mine. *Engineering and contracting*, March 11, 1914, p. 296-7.
Economics of grade revision for underground haulage. *Coal age*, April 21, 1917, p. 706-8.

BROWN, RICHARD
Accountant. (In Lisle, George. *Encyclopaedia of accounting*. v.1. p. 12-7).
Arabic numerals. *Accountants' magazine*, Dec. 1914, p. 584-5.
Bibliography of book-keeping. *Accountant's magazine*, Nov. 1897, April 1898, May 1901, p. 568-73, 220-3, 240-8.
Bookkeeping — bibliography. (In Lisle, George. *Encyclopaedia of accounting*. v. 1, p. 493-6).
Comparative legislation in bankruptcy. *Accountants' magazine*, Jan. 1900, p. 6-33.
Duties of a secretary. *Accountants' magazine*, April 1910, p. 185-94.
Farm accounts. *Accountants' magazine*, Dec. 1898, p. 562-83.
Financial trusts. *Accountant*, April 1, 1893, p. 302-8.
Form of revenue accounts and balance sheets and the use of percentages in connection therewith. *Accountants' magazine*, March 1904, p. 145-64. *South African accountant*, Dec. 1917, March 1918, p. —— 133-6.
History of accounting and accountants. Edinburgh, T. C. and E. C. Jack, 1905. 459p.
Joint stock company code. *Accountant*, Dec. 27, 1902, p. 1360-9.
Life assurance book-keeping. *Accountants' magazine*, April 1908, p. 198-210.
Parish council accounts and their audit. *Accountants' magazine*, Feb. 1897, p. 90-105.
Recent proposed legislation relating to the profession. *Accountant*, July 28, 1894, p. 669-72.
Sketch of the history of the law of debtor and creditor, with special reference to Cessis Bonorum. *Accountant*, June 25, 1898, p. 651-7.

BROWN, T.
Rates for cross country trucking. *Good roads*, Jan. 16, 1920, p. 307-8.

BROWN, THOMAS AND VINCENT E. COLLINGE
Arithmetic and bookkeeping. pt. 1. London, Sir Issac Pitman & sons, [1916.] 117p.

BROWN, VERE
Chartered accountant and the banker. *Canadian chartered accountant*, Jan. 1914, p. 136-43.

BROWN, W. V.
Scientific management: a list of references in the New York public library. *New York (city) public library bulletin*, Jan. Feb. 1917, p. 19-43, 83-136.

BROWN, WILLIAM
Address. *Accountant*, Oct. 1, 1904, p. 342-7.
Dredging and dredging companies in New Zealand. *Accountant*, Feb. 10, 1900, p. 169-72.
Farmers annual account book. Ed. 5. 1897.
Notes on value, credit, money. *Accountant*, Sept. 2, 1905, p. 263-9.
On wrinkles. *Accountant*, Dec. 3, 1904, p. 693-9.

BROWN, WILLIAM ALDEN
Portland cement industry: a practical treatise on the building, equipping and economical running of a Portland cement plant with notes on physical testing. New York, D. Van Nostrand company, 1917. 158p.

BROWN, WILLIAM HENRY TROTTER
Trusts and trustees. *Incorporated accountants' journal*, 1903-4, p. 165.

BROWN, WILLIAM M.
Importance of proper accounting. *Telephony*, Nov. 3, 1917.

BROWN, WILLIAM S.
See Schaeffer, J. J., joint author.

BROWN-WALES CO., BOSTON.
Perpetual inventories. *Business man's magazine*, May 1908, p. 454-5.

BROWNE, BALFOUR.
On some economic effects of war. *Accountants' magazine,* 1900, p. 399.

BROWNE, ERNEST ARTHUR
Goodwill: its ascertainment and treatment in accounts. *Accountant,* Dec. 20, 1902, p. 1339-44.

BROWNE, T. R.
First bookkeeping course. Brooklyn, Browne's Brooklyn business college. 1900.

BROWNING, EARL HARRISON
General stores-keeping department of the Browning engineering co. *Engineering magazine,* June 1905, p. 359-80.

BROWNING, W. B.
Storekeeping—a complete system for maintaining the work of a stockroom that avoids the wastes of surplus material and the losses through delays. *System,* Nov. 1911, p. 551-5.

BROWNLEE, G
C. P. A. problem. *Business man's magazine,* Aug. 1907, p. 116-20.
Cost accounting for cotton goods manufacturing business. *Business man's magazine,* Nov. 1905, p. 863-5.

BROWNLEE, J. W.
Accounting methods for the textile business. *Business man's magazine,* 1904, v.16, no. 8, p. 65-71.

BROWN'S ships accounts and captain's letter writer. Anderson, J. W. 1907.

BRUCE, C. R.
Marine engineering estimates and costs. Glasgow 1911.

BRUCE, E. E.
Record for railway passenger traffic. *Business man's magazine,* May, 1909, p. 462-4.

BRUCE, THOMAS
Government requirements in regard to re-insurancé reserves of fire insurance companies. *Canadian chartered accountant,* July 1914, p. 40-1.

BRUCKE, E. E.
Record for railway passenger traffic. *Business man's magazine,* May 1909, p. 462-4.

BRUERE, HENRY
Budget as an administrative program. *Annals of the American academy of political and social science,* May Nov. 1915, p. 113-276, 176-91.
New city government; a discussion of municipal administration based on a survey of ten commission governed cities. New York, D. Appleton and company, 1919. 438p.

BRUMBY, L. A.
Exchange. *Accountant,* March 13, 1920, p. 310-4.

BRUMMER, LEON
Inception and foundation of the school of commerce, accounts, and finance. *Journal of accountancy,* Feb. 1911, p. 252-55.

BRUNDAGE, H. M.
Accounting for property withdrawn from service. *National electric light association. Bulletin,* May 1920, p. 311-2.

BRUNSWICK consolidated costs. *Engineering and mining journal,* June 24, 1916, p. 1115.

BRUNTON, D. W. AND JOHN A. DAVIS
Cost of tunneling. United States. Bureau of mines bulletin, 1914, p. 192-214. *Engineering and contracting,* June 24, 1914, p. 729-33.

BRUNTON, F. K.
British Columbia copper co. smelter; average daily report for May 1913. *American institute of mining engineers, bulletin,* July 1915, p. 1415-17. Excerpt. *Metallurgical and chemical engineering,* Aug. 1915, p. 509.

BRUNTON, WILLIAM
Trust deeds in Scottish bankruptcies. *Accountant,* June 6, 1903, p. 753-62.

BRUSH, M. C.
Favors six-cent fare instead of zone system. *Electric railway journal,* Feb. 2, 1918, p. 229-30.
Satisfactory service and sound securities. *Aera,* Sept. 1917, p. 86-93.
To eliminate fare increase delays. *Electric railway journal,* Sept. 8, 1917, p. 400.
Zone system impracticable in Boston. *Electric railway journal,* Feb. 16, 1918, p. 324.

BRUSH, W. W.
Trenching machine work. *Journal of the American water works association,* December 1917, p. 521-4.

BRUSH industry. United States. Tariff commission. 1918.

BRUSHES
United States. Tariff commission. Brush industry; commercial and industrial conditions in the United States and in foreign countries—tariff laws affecting brushes, court and treasury decisions. Washington, Government printing office, 1918. 76p.

BRUSTER, R. R.
Relation of accounting officers to other members of official family. *Electric railway journal,* June 17, 1916, p. 1136-9.

BRUTTON, RICHARD
Address. 1893. *Accountant,* Dec. 23, 1893, p. 1077.
Study of a balance sheet with special reference to reserves and reserve funds. *Accountant,* Jan. 12, 1895, p. 39-43.

BRYAN, E. N.
Cost data for auto trucks. *Engineering record,* Feb. 13, 1915, p. 211-12.
Piece work faster than day labor on hand excavation. *Engineering news,* April 10, 1919, p. 727.
Practical cost-keeping for contractors. *Engineering news,* March 12, 1914, p. 565-7.
Underestimating the cost of motor trucking. *Engineering and contracting,* March 10, 1915, p. 210.

BRYAN, JOHN ELEY
Municipal accounts. *Incorporated accountants journal,* 1898-9, p. 45.

BRYAN, WILLIAM H.
Appraisal and depreciation of water-works and similar properties. *Journal of the association of engineering societies,* Dec. 1907, p. 336-81. Depreciation of electric light plants. *Municipality,* March 1908, p. 74. Abstract. Depreciation allowance for vari-

BRYAN, WILLIAM H.—*(Continued)*
ous public service industries. *Engineering news,* Jan. 23, 1908, p. 96.
Depreciation of electric light plans. *Municipality,* March 1908, p. 74.
Depreciation of electric light plants. *Electrical world,* May 13, 1909, p. 1173.
Going value as an element in the appraisal of public utility properties. *Journal of the association of engineering societies,* Oct. 1909, p. 147. Abstract. *Engineering and contracting,* Dec. 22, 1909, p. 549.

BRYAN, WILLIAM JENNINGS
Government should issue notes and guarantee bank deposits. *Journal of accountancy,* March 1908, p. 366-79.

BRYANT, HENRY BENJAMIN AND H. D. STRATTON
Common school bookkeeping. New York, American book co.
National bookkeeper. New York, Ivison, Phiny & co.
New counting house bookkeeping. New York Ivison, Bakeman, Taylor & co. 1879.
New high school bookkeeping. New York, American book co.

——— **AND S. S. PACKARD.**
Bryant & Stratton's counting house bookkeeping. New York, Ivinson, Plinney, Blakeman & co. 1861, 1863, 1866. 375p.
High school bookkeeping. New York, Ivison, Blakeman, Taylor & co. 1860.

BRYANT, HENRY W.
Practical bookkeeping. Chicago, Bryant and Stratton business college, 1907, 1910.

BRYANT, J. M.
Rates for public utility service. *Texas municipalities,* Jan. 1916, p. 3-8.

BRYANT, JOHN C.
Bryant's *bookkeeping;* a treatise on the science of accounts, elementary and practical. Ed. 5. Buffalo, J. C. Bryant, 1877.
Commercial bookkeeping. New York, W. C. Bryant & co. 1885.
Common school bookkeeping. New York, W. C. Bryant & co. 1885.
Counting house book-keeping. New York, W. C. Bryant & co. 1885.
New commercial bookkeeping. New York, J. C. Bryant.
New counting-house book-keeping; with manufacturing and modern banking. New York, J. C. Bryant.
New elementary bookkeeping. Buffalo, J. C. Bryant.
New standard commercial book-keeping theoretical and practical, containing a thorough elucidation of the principles of double and single entry. Buffalo, J. C. Bryant, 1887. 160p.
New standard practical and progressive bookkeeping, double and single entry. Buffalo, John C. Bryant, 1911. 223p. (Counting house ed.)

BRYANT AND STRATTON BUSINESS COLLEGE.
Theory and practice of book-keeping and accounting in the School of commerce; comp. and arranged for sole use of this school, 1902, by A. S. Hubbard and others; rev. and enl. 1910, by T. B. Stowell and others. Providence, R. I., Bryant and Stratton business college, 1910. 125p.

BRYCE, EDWARD A.
System for keeping costs in a foundry. *Iron age,* March 6, 1913.

BRYCE, J.
Bookkeeping. London, Longmans, Green & co. 1860.
——— Same. New ed. London, Collins sons & co. 1873, 1884.

BRYCESON, ALEC J.
Consequential loss insurance. *Accountant,* Aug. 21, 1915, p. 221-32. *Incorporated accountants' journal,* Aug. 1915, p. 259-66.
Loss of profits' insurance, the accountant as assessor. *Accountant,* Oct. 2, 1920, p. 358-60.

BRYERS, F T
Effect on the adjustment of losses through writing down fixed assets to provide for depreciation. *Canadian chartered accountant,* July 1914, p. 4-9.

BRYNING, ROBERT
Asylum account keeping (double entry) 1890.
Asylum accounts. *Incorporated accountants' journal,* 1889-90, p. 76.

BUCH, A. M.
Graphical solution of electric railway problems. *Electric railway journal,* Aug. 12, 1916, p. 281.

BUCHAN, DAVID D.
Administration of judicial factors in Scotland. *Incorporated accountants' journal,* 1904-5, p. 45.
Administrative environment in Scotland. *Incorporated accountants' journal,* 1907-8, p. 131.

BUCHANAN, A. N
Death duties. *Incorporated accountants' journal,* Sept. 1912, p. 316-21.

BUCHANAN, C.
Practical book-keeping. Edinburgh, 1806.

BUCHANAN, R. S.
Security-holders should demand independent audits. *Journal of accountancy,* June 1907, p. 92-7.

BUCHANAN, HUGH R.
Ranking in bankruptcy. *Accountants' magazine,* April 1920, p. 236-53.

BUCHANAN, WILLIAM
Journal dictionary and bookkeepers' proof book based on laws and principles of commercial science. Cleveland, W. D. Browning, 1905.

BUCHER, P.
Bonus system as applied to the collection department of a public utility. *American gas engineering journal,* Aug. 31, 1918, p. 193-7.
Preparation of public utility reports; not literary arrangement, but common sense important. *American gas engineering journal,* Sept. 14, 1918, p. 241-2.

BUCK, A. E.
Coming of centralized purchasing in state governments. *National municipal review supplement,* Feb. 1920, 117-35p.
Present status of the executive budget in the state government. *National municipal review,* Aug. 1919, p. 422-35.

BUCK, A. M.
Graphical solutions of electric railway problems: abstract. *Electric railway journal,* August 12, 1916, p. 281.

BUCK, F.
Simplified system of town highway accounts. *Municipal and county engineering.* 1915. p. 56-7 *Engineering record,* Nov. 14, 1914, p. 534. *New York Highways News,* Dec. 1914, v.1. p. 109.

BUCK, GEORGE S.
County auditor with discussion. (In New York constitutional convention commission, comp. *County government,* 1914, p. 37-45.

BUCK, WILLIAM
Some points in executorship accounts. *Federal accountant,* April, July 1916, p. 57-64, 82-4.

BUCKLAND, FRANK
Money its possibilities and its probabilities. *Accountant,* Oct. 24, 31, 1891, p. 748-52, 759-61.

BUCKLE'S system of household accounts. Clifton, 1904.

BUCKLEY, E. J.
Giving employees a share of the profits; legal decisions. *Metal work,* Sept. 7, 1917, p. 301.
How to make a financial statement; what to include and what not to. *Metal work,* Nov. 14, 1919, p. 587.
Is a profit sharer always a partner? *Metal work,* Dec. 18, 1914, p. 803.

BUCKLEY, H. W.
Federal income tax. *Accountant,* Sept. 18, 1920, p. 301-6.

BUCKLEY, J. E.
See Law, C. L., joint author.

BUCKLEY, JUSTICE
Registration of mortgages. *Incorporated accountants journal,* 1902-3, p. 135.

BUCKLIN, J. N.
Double entry bookkeeping. New York, Troy, 1833.

BUDD, JOHN WREFORD.
Solicitors and accounts. *Accountant,* Nov. 19, 1905, p. 586-9, 557-9.

BUDGET *Accountant,* April 24, 1920, p. 496-9. *Incorporated accountants' journal,* May 1920, p. 162-5.

BUDGET as a means of locating responsibility for waste and inefficiency. Cleveland, F. A. 1912.

BUDGET classifications and rules of procedure for department estimates. Indiana. State board of accounts. 1918.

BUDGET, income tax proposals. *Incorporated accountants' ournal,* Oct. 1915, p. 8-9.

BUDGET making in Illinois. *Survey,* Feb. 15, 1919, p. 701-2.

BUDGET planning in social case work. Winslow, E. A.

BUDGET system in Ohio. Fullington, E. M.

BUDGET systems: a discussion before the New York constitutional convention. *Municipal research,* June 1915, p. 251-447.

BUDGETS
Bennett, George E. Budget. (In his *Constructive accounting.* 1920. p. 316-33).
Benton, A. C. Budget system of expense control. National retail dry goods association, Report and digest of the proceedings, First annual convention controllers' congress, 1920, p. 35-7, 47).
Braddock, J. H. Some suggestions for preparing a budget exhibit. *Annals of the American academy of political and social science,* May, Nov. 1915, p. 113-276, 148-61.
Budget systems: a discussion before the New York constitutional convention. *Municipal research,* June 1915, p. 251-447.
Church, A. Hamilton. Budget. (In his *Manufacturing costs and accounts.* 1917. p. 403, 431-3.)
Cleveland, Frederick A. Budget making and the increased cost of government; with discussion. *American economic review,* March 1916, sup. 50-84.
Duncan, John C. Budget system record of materials. (In his *Principles of industrial management.* 1916. p. 276-7).
Fetherston, John T. Efficiency in relation to budget methods. *Engineering record,* Nov. 9, 1912.
Frederick, J. George. Dollar and the budget idea in business finance research. (In his *Business research and statistics.* 1920. p. 212-20).
Greendlinger, Leo. Private budgets. (In his *Financial and business statements.* c1917. p. 273-88).
Hadley, W. Accounting basis of budgetary procedure. *Annals of the American academy of political and social science,* Nov. 1915, p. 136-9.
Hazard, F. R. Budget making. *Iron age,* Oct 1, 1914, p. 804-5.
Mason, C. P. Preparation of the budget. (*National association of school accounting officers, Report,* 1914, p. 45-58.
Miles, Rufus E. Budget and the legislature. *Annals of the American academy of political and social science.* Nov. 1915, p. 36-46.
Powers, Le Grand. Essential of a good budget from the viewpoint of the statistician. *National association of comptrollers and accounting officers, Proceedings* 1911 p. 47-74.
Public budgets. *Annals of the American academy of political and social science,* Nov. 1915, 324p.
Purcell, H. E. One cure for national waste; instruction in simple bookkeeping forms or budget making. *School and society,* Dec. 9, 1916, p. 899-900.
Rightor. C. E. Recent progress in budget making and accounting. *National municipal review,* Nov. 1917, p. 707-19.
Scovell, Clinton H. Budget system. (In his *Cost accounting and burden application.* 1916. p. 197-204).
Shepard, George H. Budget. (In his *Application of efficiency principles.* 1917. p 220, 289.
Sommer, E. O. Budget as basis for calculating predetermined rates. *Industrial management,* Jan. 1920, p 24-8.
Webner, Frank E. Budget system. (In his *Factory accounting.* 1917. p. 217-21).
Williamson, C. C. Budget reform. *National tax association bulletin,* March 1916, p, 51-3

Bibliographies.
List of references on the budgets of cities. *Special libraries,* March 1915, p. 49-56.
Rider, Harry A. Select list of references on national, state, county and municipal budgets in the United tates. *Annals of the American academy of political and social science.* Nov. 1915, p. 277-87.

BUDGETS—Bibliographies—(*Continued*)

SELECT readings on municipal budgets and balance sheets. *Government accountant*, May 1912, p. 30.

WRIGHT, JOSEPH. Select bibiography on municipal budget-making. *National municipal review*, Jan. 1917.

Counties

CARTWRIGHT, O. G. County budgets and their construction. *Annals of the American academy of political and social science*, Nov. 1915, p. 223-34.

Municipal

ADAMSON, TILDEN. Preparation of estimates and the formulation of the budget; the New York city method. *Annals of the American academy of political and social science*, Nov. 1915, p 113-276.

ART of budget-making. *Journal of accountancy*, Nov. 1907, p. 60-1.

BALDWIN, D. C. Budget procedure of English and French cities. *Annals of the American academy of political and social science*, Nov. 1915, p. 204-10.

BRITTAIN, HORACE L. Movement for improved financing and accounting practice in Toronto. *Annals of the American academy of political and social science*, Nov. 1915, p. 211-22.

BRITTAIN, HORACE L. What is a city budget? *Canadian chartered accountant*, July 1915, p. 26-49.

BRUÉRE, HENRY. Budget as an administrative program. Annals of the American academy of political and social science, May, Nov. 1915, p. 113-276, 176-91.

BRUÉRE, HENRY. Budget-making. (In his *New city government*. 1919. p. 171-204).

CHASE, HARVEY S. Budgets and balance sheets; the practical application of sound accounting principles and methods to municipal bookkeeping; an address before the National municipal league at the Buffalo meeting, November 14-17, 1910. 17p. *National municipal league, Proceedings*, 1910, p. 214-29. *Journal of accountancy*, Dec. 1910, p. 81-96.

CHILDS, WILLIAM T. Annual budget. *Municipal journal*, Oct. 7, 1915, p. 545-7.

CLEVELAND, FREDERICK A. Essentials of a municipal budget. *New Jersey municipalities*, June 1917, p. 15-20.

CUMMIN, G. C. Budget making; with discussion. *City managers association, Proceedings*, 1915, p. 94-105.

EFFICIENCY budget of Chicago. *Municipal engineering*, March 1916, p. 111.

EGGLESTON, DEWITT CARL. Budget making as a means of control. (In his *Municipal accounting*. 1914. p. 44-54).

EGGLESTON, DEWITT CARL. Municipal budget accounts. *Journal of accountancy*, Nov. 1911, p. 481-92.

ELLISON, WILLIAM B. Pressing financial problems: the inordinate growth of budgets and taxes. *Economic world*, Jan. 27, 1917, p 125-6.

FESLER, M. Budget making in Cleveland. *Annals of the American academy of political and social science*, Nov. 1915, p. 264-9.

FOSTER, H. M Municipal supply department; budget standardization. *Municipal engineering*, Oct. 1916, p. 137-8.

GEISER, K. F German municipal budget and its relation to the general government. *Annals of the American academy of political and social science*, Nov. 1915, p. 192-203.

GREENDLINGER, LEO. Municipal budget. (In his *Financial and business statements*. c1917. p. 289-304).

GULICK, L. H Municipal budget standards. *American city*, Sept 1920, p. 309-13.

HADLEY, WILL B. Municipal accounting, reporting and budget making. *Journal of accountancy*, May 1914, p. 355-63.

HERRICK, ANSON. Importance of the municipal budget as a means for the control of expenditures. *Journal of accountancy*, April 1911, p. 414-8.

HORMELL, O. C Budget-making in Brunswick, Maine. *American city* (T and C ed.), June 1916, p. 560-2.

JAMES, H. G Municipal finances; debts, budget and accounting. (In his *Municipal functions*, 1917, p. 323-43.)

LINDSAY, SAMUEL M. City budget as a basis for administration. *American city*, April 1917, p. 381-4. *Economic world*, April 28, 1917, p. 593-4.

LOOMIS, MILTON E. Taxation and the municipal budget. *Annals of the American academy of political and social science*, Nov. 1915, p. 113-24.

MANDEL, ARCH. M. Budgetary procedure under the manager form of city government. *Annals of the American academy of political and social science*, Nov. 1915, p. 163-75.

MERRIAM, CHARLES EDWARD. Budget making in Chicago. *Annals of the American academy of political and social science*, Nov. 1915, p. 270-6.

METZ, HERMAN A. Statistical basis of budget making. Boston, American statistical association publications, 1912, p. 67-83. *Journal of accountancy*, Jan. 1910, p. 161-70.

MUNRO, WILLIAM BENNETT. Municipal budget making. (In his *Principles and methods of municipal administration*. 1916. p. 446-60).

NEW YORK city budget. *Municipal research*, Aug 1917, 154p

NEW YORK city's need for a financial program: one which will include plans for improvements and borrowings *Municipal research*, March 1915, p. 211-39.

NEXT steps in the development of a budget procedure for the city of Greater New York; a report. *Municipal research*, Jan. 1915, p. 5-141.

PHILADELPHIA. CONTROLLER. Municipal financial program—budget making. (In his *Manual of accounting, reporting and business procedure of the city and county of phladelphia*. 1917. p. 164-86).

POWERS, LE GRAND. Classifications of municipal expenditures in budgets and accounts and the purposes which they subserve. *Journal of accountancy*, Feb. 1915, p. 118-36.

POWERS, LE GRAND. Municipal budgets and expenditures. *National municipal league, Proceedings*, 1909, p. 258-72. *Government accountant*, 1910, v. 3, p. 385-96.

RATIONAL budget making. *Municipal journal*, Nov. 4, 1915, 695-7.

RECENT progress in municipal budgets and accounts. *National municipal review*, July, Oct. 1916, p. 403-10, 631-7.

REPORT of committee on municipal budgets to the national association of comptrollers and accounting officers at the sixth annual convention, Buffalo, 1912. *National association of comptrollers and accounting officers, Proceedings*, 1912. p. 66-79.

RIGHTOR, C. E. Recent progress in municipal budgets and accounts. *National municipal review*, July, Oct. 1916, p. 403-10, 631-7.

ROUTH, J W. Humanizing the budget. *National municipal review*, Nov. 1919, p. 598-600.

SANDS, H. R. Efficient budget making. Conference of mayors and other city officials of the state of New York, Proceedings, 1915, p 7-11. *American city* (T and C ed), Sept. 1915, p. 225-8.

SHAFER, C. W. Grand Rapids budget system. *Municipal journal*, July 20, 1916, p 68-70.

TAXATION and the municipal budget, by M. E. Loomis; Sources of revenue, by H. S Swan; Accounting basis of budgetary procedure,

BUDGETS—MUNICIPAL—*(Continued)*

by W. B. Hadley; Unit costs in recreational facilities, by P. T. Beisser; Some suggestions for preparing a budget exhibit; by J. H. Braddock; budgetary procedure under the manager form of city government, by A. M. Mandel; Budget as an administrative program, by Henry Bruere; German municipal budget and its relation to the general government, by K. F. Geiser; Budget produre of English and Franch cities, by D. C. Baldwin; Movement for improved financing and accounting practice in Toronto, by H. L. Brittain; County budgets and their construction, by O. G. Cartwright; Budget making for small cities; by L. D. Upson; Preparation of estimates and the formulation of the budget; the New York city method, by Tilden Adamson; Budget making in Cleveland, by Mayo Fesler; Budget making in Chicago by Charles F. Merriam. *Annals of the American academy of political and social science*, Nov. 1915, p. 113-276.

UPSON, L. D. Budget making for small cities. *Annals of the American academy of political and social science*, Nov. 1915, p. 235-48.

WADE, HERBERT T. Influence for efficiency in municipal administration: the New York budget exhibit of 1910. *Engineering magazine*, Jan. 1911, p 585-604.

WAITE, H. M. and others. Standardization of forms; discussion. *City managers association, Year book* 1917-1918. 1918. p. 24-9.

National

ADAMS, H. C. Problems of budgetary reform. *Journal of political economy*, Oct. 1919, p. 621-38.

ALEXANDER, CHARLES B. Need for a budget system in the United States. *Annals of the American academy of political and social science*, July 1918, p. 144-8.

ALLEN, WILLIAM H. Budget as an instrument of financial control. *Government accountant*, 1908, v. 2, p. 192-200.

BORLAND, WILLIAM P. Budget system for the United States. *Congressional record*, Dec. 11, 1918, p. 343-7.

CHAMBERLAIN, J. P. National budget; another angle. *National municipal review*, Oct. 1919, p. 572-3.

CHAMBERLAIN, J. P. New federal budget plan as embodied in the Good-McCormick bill in Congress. *Economic world*, July 12, 1919, p. 53-5.

CHASE, HARVEY STUART. Executive budget in relation to governmental accounting. Chicago, LaSalle extension university, c1917. 17p.

CHASE, HARVEY STUART. Financial plan, or "Budget" for the national government; an address before the National association of comptrollers and accounting officers at the annual meeting 1914, held at Milwaukee, Wisconsin, June 11th to 13th. 10 typewritten pages. *Journal of accountancy*, July 1914, p. 13-29.

CHASE, HARVEY STUART. National budget; proceedings at a meeting held December 6, 1913, to discuss the "federal income" tax the pending currency bill and the national budget. *Journal of accountancy*, Feb. 1914, p. 85-96.

CHASE, HARVEY STUART. National budget. *National economic league quarterly*, Aug. 1915, p. 5-11.

CHASE, HARVEY STUART. National budget on its "expenditure" side; an address before the Massachusetts society of certified public accountants at Boston, Mass. April 9, 1913. 14p. *Accountant*, Nov. 1, 1913, p. 643-9. *Journal of accountancy*, June 1913. p. 397-411.

CHASE, HARVEY STUART. United States' national budget. *Accountant*, April 11, 1914, p. 539-43.

CLEVELAND, FREDERICK A. Budget as a means of locating responsibility for waste and inefficiency—what the president is trying to do by way of budget making for the national government, New York, 1912. 16p.

CLEVELAND, FREDERICK A. Evolution of the budget idea in the United States. *Annals of the American academy of political and social science*, Nov. 1915, p. 15-35.

CLEVELAND, FREDERICK A. Popular control of government; three schools of opinion in the United States with respect to budget making. *Political science quarterly*, June 1919, p. 237-61.

CLEVELAND, FREDERICK ALBERT. Principles of budget making. (In his *Chapters on munipal administration and accounting*. 1909. p. 67-81).

CLEVELAND, FREDERICK A. Principles of budget making. *Journal of accountancy*, Oct. 1907, p. 456-66.

CLEVELAND, FREDERICK A. What a budget may mean to the administration (In *University of Illinois conference on commercial education and business progress*, 1913, p. 35-50).

CLEVELAND, FREDERICK ALBERT. What is involved in the making of a national budget. *Journal of accountancy*, May 1913, p. 313-28.

COLLINS, CHARLES W. Government thrift through a national budget. *Annals of the American academy of political and social science*, Jan. 1920, p. 65-70.

COLLINS, CHARLES WALLACE. National budget system. New York, The Macmillan company, 1917. 151p.

COMMITTEE on the budget. *Congressional record*, July 31, 1919, p. 3681.

CONGRESS and a budget. *Journal of accountancy*, Dec. 1912, p. 487-93.

DEMAND for a national budget. *Economic world*, March 11, 1916, p. 338-40.

FORD, HENRY JONES. Budget making and the work of the government. *Annals of the American academy of political and social science*, Nov. 1915, p. 1-14.

FREAR, J. A. Need for national budget system. *American industries*, Aug. 1919, p. 19-21.

FREAR, J. A. President's recommendation for a single appropriation committee and the necessity for a budget system for the United States. *Congressional record*, Dec. 15, 1917, p. 389-96.

FRENCH, B. L. National budget. *Congressional record*, Nov. 1, 1919, p. 8341-6.

GLASS, CARTER Budget system. *Federal reserve bulletin*, 1919, p. 937-42.

GOOD, J. W. National budget. *Congressional record*, Jan. 23, 1920, p. 2070-6.

GOOD, J. W. National budgetary system: question of much needed reform now up to U. S. Senate: how the proposed plan would work. *Journal of the American bankers association*, Dec. 1919, p. 287-91.

GOOD versus the McCormich budget bill; a debate and a poll of the research bureaus on the issue, by W. F. H. Willoughby and Gaylord C. Cummin for the Good bill, Charles A. Beard for the McCormich bill. *National municipal review*, April 1920, p 219-33.

GULICK, L. H. Municipal budget standards. *New Jersey municipalities*, Oct. 1920, p. 247-9.

HANSON, ELISHA. Need for a national budget. *Congressional record*, May 1, 1920, p. 6949-54.

HASTINGS, WILLIAM W. Budget system. *Congressional record*, Nov. 7, 1919, p. 8582-5.

INSTITUTE FOR GOVERNMENT RESEARCH. National budget system, the most important of all governmental reconstruction measures. Washington, Institute for government research, 1919. 14p.

BUDGETS—NATIONAL—*(Continued)*

KALAW, M. M. Philippine budget system. *American economic review,* Sept. 1919, p. 632-8.

KENYON, WILLIAM S. National budget system. *Congressional record,* Jan. 9, Oct. 17, 1918, p. 740-1, 12312-8.

MCCORMICK, MEDILL. Calls for drastic measures to remedy budget evils. *Annalist,* Dec. 1, 1919, p. 675-6. *Congressional record,* Dec. 16, 1919, p. 629-31.

MILES, R. E. and others. Expert comment on the Good national budget bill. *National municipal review,* Aug. 1919, p. 406-11.

MILES, R. F. Budget and the legislature. *Annals of the American academy of political and social science,* Nov. 1915, p. 36-46.

MILES, R. E. and others. Expert comment on the Good national budget bill. *National municipal review,* Aug. 1919, p. 406-11.

MORSE, P. Putting the government on a business basis. *Forum,* Dec. 1919, p. 594-600.

NATIONAL budget. *Journal of accountancy,* Feb., March, 1915, p. 142-3, 211.

NATIONAL budget. *Journal of accountancy,* July 1919, p. 42-3.

NEED of a national budget; report of the committee on the national budget of the National chamber of commerce. *Nation's business,* Feb. 1916, p. 66-9.

POWELL, T. R. President's veto of the budget bill. *National municipal review,* Sept. 1920, p. 538-45.

POWERS, LE GRAND Accounting and budgetary control. *Government accountant,* Sept. 1911, p. 212-8. *National association of comptrollers and accounting officers, Proceedings,* 1910, p. 26-31.

POWERS, LE GRAND. Essentials of a good budget; being extracts from an address delivered before the convention of comptrollers and accounting officers in Washington, D. C., June 8-10, 1911. *Government accountant,* July 1911, p. 112-9.

TWEEDALE, ALONZO. Proposed Washington budget. *National municipal league, Proceedings,* 1909, p. 273-83.

UCHIIKE, R. and Y. SAKAMOTO. Japan budget system. *Municipal research,* March 1917, p. 1-44.

UNITED STATES. Congress. H. R. 9783, an act to provide a national budget system and an independent audit of government accounts, and for other purposes, October 22, 1919 12p.
 See also Congressional record, v. 58, no. 126, p. 7559, 7703-7844; v. 58, no. 1278, p. 7846-7849; v. 58, no. 129, p. 7927-7928.

UNITED STATES. Congress. Hearings before the committee on consideration of a national budget, on H. R. 9783; a bill to provide a national budget system and an independent audit of government accounts and for other purposes. Washington, Government printing office, 1920. 195p.

UNITED STATES. President's commission on economy and efficiency. Budget with supporting memoranda and reports. Washington, Government printing office, 1913. 433p.

UNITED STATES. President's commission on economy and efficiency. Message of the president of the United States submitting for the consideration of the congress a budget with supporting memoranda and reports for the fiscal year 1914. Washington, Government printing office, 1913. 433p.

UNITED STATES. President's commission on economy and efficiency. Need for a national budget. Washington, Government printing office, 1912.

WILLOUGHBY, WILLIAM F. Good national budget bill. *National municipal review,* July 1919, p. 360-5.

WILLOUGHBY, WILLIAM F. National government as a holding corporation; the question of subsidiary budgets. *Political science quarterly,* Dec. 1917, p. 505-12.

WILLOUGHBY, WILLIAM F. Unified command of the nation's money. *Nation's business,* Dec. 1918, p. 18-9.

State

ACCOUNTING information needed by members of the general assembly; Accounting needs of heads of departments and boards in charge of state institutions. (In Frazer, George E. *Report on the accounts of the State of Illinois prepared for the efficiency and economy committee,* 1914, p. 40-8, 54-8).

ADAMS, HENRY C. Problems of budgetary reform. *Journal of political economy,* Oct. 1919, p. 621-38.

ALLEN, WILLIAM H. Ready helps in state budget making. *National tax association bulletin,* May 1916, p. 91-3.

ARTHUR, B. E. Behind the scenes with five state budgets. *National municipal review,* May 1920, p. 279-88.

BEARD, CHARLES A. Budgetary provisions of the New York constitution. *Annals of the American academy of political and social science,* Nov. 1915, p. 64-8.

BELL, FINLEY F. Illinois budget. *Annals of the American academy of political and social science,* Nov. 1915, p. 73-84.

BUCK, A. E. Present status of the executive budget in the state government. *National municipal review,* Aug. 1919, p. 422-35.

CHAMBERS, JOHN S. California state board of authorization and the limitation of expenditure law. *National tax association bulletin,* Jan. Feb. 1918, p. 89-93, 115-8.

CHAMBERS, JOHN S. California—state budget. *National tax association bulletin,* Feb. 1918, p. 115-8.

CHASE, HARVEY STUART. Budget amendment of the Maryland constitution. *National municipal review,* May 1917, p 395-8.

CLEVELAND, FREDERICK A. Constitutional provision for a budget. *Academy of political science, Proceedings,* Oct. 1914, p. 141-92.

ELEMENTS of state budget making. *Municipal research,* Dec 1916. 63p.

FAIRLIE, JOHN A. Budget methods in Illinois. *Annals of the American academy of political and social science,* Nov. 1915, p. 85-90.

FULLINGTON, E. M. Budget system in Ohio. *Journal of accountancy,* Feb. 1916, p. 114-24.

HEFFERNAN, W. O. State budget making in Ohio. *Annals of the American academy of political and social science,* Nov. 1915, p. 91-100.

HEINEMAN, D. E. Budget system for Michigan. *National tax association bulletin,* May 1916, p. 109-12.

LOWDEN, F. O. Budget system in Illinois. *Review of reviews,* March 1920, p. 299-300.

LOWRIE, S. GALL. Proper function of the state budget. *Annals of the American academy of political and social science,* Nov. 1915, p 47-63.

NEYLAN, JOHN F. California state budget. *Annals of the American academy of political and social science,* Nov. 1915, p. 69-72.

PENNSYLVANIA. Commission on constitutional amendment and revision. Budget system—recommendations of New York, 1915 convention. Harrisburg, 1920. 2p. (Memorandum and briefs, no. 10).

PENNSYLVANIA. Commission on constitutional amendment and revision. State budget system—constitutional provisions in Massachusetts. Harrisburg, 1919. 45p. (Memorandum and briefs, no. 8).

PENNSYLVANIA. Commission of constitutional amendment and revision. State budget system—preliminary memorandum. Harrisburg, 1919. 4p. (Memoranda and briefs, no. 1).

BUDGETS—State—(*Continued*)

PENNSYLVANIA. Commission of constitutional amendment and revision. State budget system—recommendations of New York state reconstruction commission. Harrisburg, 1919. 41p. (Memorandum and Briefs, no. 7).

PROPER function of the state budget, by S. G. Lowrie; Budgetary provisions of the New York constitution, by Charles A. Beard; California's state budget, by John F. Neylan; Illinois budget, by F. F. Bell; Budget methods in Illinois by John A. Fairlie; State budget making in Ohio, by W. O. Heffernan; Financial administration of the commonwealth of Massachusetts by E. H. Maling. *Annals of the American academy of political and social science,* Nov. 1915, p. 47-112.

PROPOSED budget system for New York state. *Journal of accountancy,* Oct. 1915, p. 299-301.

PROPOSED reforms in state governments, by H. S. Chase; Address on state budgets by J. F. Fort; Maryland, act to propose an amendment to section 52 of article 3, title legislative department, of the constitution of this state, regulating the making of appropriations by the general assembly of Maryland in regular session, and to provide for the submission of said amendment to the qualified voters of this state for adoption or rejection. *National economic league quarterly,* Aug. 1916, p. 5-8, 31-40.

RECENT movement for state budget reform, 1911-1917. *Municipal research,* Nov. 1917. 155p.

SAGE, HENRY M. Making of the state budget; with discussion. (In *New York state. Tax department. Proceedings,* 1919. p. 72-94).

STATE budget. *National economic league quarterly,* Aug. 1916, p. 54-6.

STATE budget: constructive proposals to be submitted to the state constitutional convention, Frederick A. Cleveland; Practical side of budget procedure, by Charles D. Norton. *Municipal research,* Feb. 1915, p. 145-98.

THREE proposed constitutional amendments for control of the purse. *Municipal research,* May 1916, 86p.

BUDGETS and balance sheets. Chase, H. S.

BUEHLER, C. E.

Reducing the auditor's worries: abstract. *Electric railway journal,* April 21, 1917, p. 737.

BUEL, A. W.

Contract keeping in general construction and contract work. *Engineering magazine,* Aug. 1905.

Cost keeping on general contract work. *Engineering news,* March, May, 1905, v.28, p. 971-8, 29, 243-54, 707-18.

Cost system of an engineering works. *Engineering magazine,* v. 28, p. 971.

BUETTNER, L. A.

Accounting for a magazine publishing business. *Journal of acountancy,* July 1920, p. 12-7.

BUFFALO interurban fares can be raised. *Electric railway journal,* May 24, 1919, p. 1027.

BUFFALO, Rochester & Pittsburgh. *Railway age,* Aug. 22, 1913, p. 318-9.

BUFFALO vote on six-cent fare unfavorable. *Electric railway journal,* Aug. 24, 1918, p. 353.

BUFFUM, D.

Farm accounts as they should be kept. *Country life,* June 1916, p. 84.

BUFFUM, F. D.

Foreman keep time and deductions on small scattered jobs. *Engineering record,* Sept. 2, 1916, p. 302.

BUILDERS accounts. Walbank, J. A. 1901.

BUILDERS and contractors' accounts. Ward, Arthur. 1906.

BUILDER'S bookkeeping. Saker, S. 1885-1888.

BUILDERS' stores. *Accountant,* Aug. 1, 1914, p. 140-2.

BUILDING

See also Buildings; Contractors.

CHECKING up a builder's correspondence. *Business man's magazine,* Oct. 1911, p. 341-2.

How progress is recorded on army construction jobs. *Engineering news,* May 23, 1918, p. 993-4.

LAWSON, HOWARD R. Efficiency in the building trade. *Accountant,* Dec. 7, 1918, p. 309-12. *Accounting and commerce,* Feb. 1918, p. 258-64.

WATERBURY, L. A. Checking lists for estimates and building work. *Engineering and contracting,* Oct. 14, 1914, p. 364-6.

Accounting

APPLIGARTH, E. M. Uniform system of accounting: floor measurements; computing profits. *Building and building management,* Aug. 9, 1920, p. 33-6

HASLUCK, PAUL N. Double entry book-keeping for builders. London, Cassell & co. 1906.

HASLUCK, PAUL N. Single entry bookkeeping for builders; nearly 60 examples. London, Cassell & co. 1904. 96p.

HORNE, H. R. System of accounts for builders and contractors. *Incorporated accountants' journal,* July 1914, p. 286-9.

HULL, ERNEST. Accounts of a builder and contractor. *Accountant,* Feb. 9, April 13, 1901, p. 181-8, 444-6

PIXLEY, FRANCIS W. Builders. (In his *Accountancy.* Ed.2. p. 114-5).

SAKER, SYDNEY Builder's bookkeeping. London, Simpkin, Marshall, Hamilton, Kent & co. 1885-1888.

SAKER, SYDNEY. Saker's perfected system of builders' book-keeping. London, Simpkin, Marshall, Hamilton, Kent & co. 1881.

——— Same. Ed.2. London. 1895

WALBANK, JOHN ARTHUR. Builders' accounts. London. Gee & co. 1901. 75p. (Accountants library, v.3).

WALBANK, JOHN ARTHUR. Builders' accounts. (In Lisle, George. *Encyclopaedia of accounting,* v.1. p. 514-9). *Accountant,* May 18, 1907, p. 693-8.

WARD, ARTHUR Builders and contractors' accounts. Ed. 2. London, 1906.

Cost accounting

GILLETTE, HALBERT POWERS and RICHARD T. DANA. Cost keeping blanks for building construction. (In their *Cost keeping and management engineering.* 1916. p. 188-93.)

GILLETTE, HALBERT POWERS and RICHARD T. DANA. Flexible cost keeping system and its application to building construction. (Sam W. Emerson, *Engineering contracting,* June 13, 1906). (In his *Cost keeping and management engineering.* 1916. p. 154-65).

GREEN, H. L. Buildings-factor costs. *Engineering magazine,* Dec. 1914, p. 407-10. *Engineering and contracting,* Feb. 3, 1915, p. 101-2.

HARRIS, H. A. Making costs and bids agree. (In Thompson, C. Bertrand. *How to find factory costs.* c1916. p. 150-83).

BUILDING—COST ACCOUNTING—*(Continued)*

MISCELLANEOUS labor costs of excavation and construction for a manufacturing plant. *Engineering and contracting,* March 12, 1913, p. 287.

PRIOR, J. C. AND H. P. GREEN Keeping the costs of building the government houses. *Engineering news,* Aug. 7, 1919, p. 252-61.

Stores systems

BUILDERS' stores. *Accountant,* Aug. 1, 1914, p. 140-2.

BUILDING a system for the laundry business. *Business man's magazine,* Nov. 1908, p. 367-9.

BUILDING AND LOAN ASSOCIATIONS

ALCORN, EDGAR G. Building and loan associations: their organization, management and methods. *Business man's magazine,* Aug. 1910, p. 181-88.

BROOKS, THOMAS B. Building societies. *Accountant,* Dec. 22, 1883.

BUILDING societies. *Accountant,* 1886, p. 469.

CRAWFORD, L. U. Standard plan of organization. *Business man's magazine,* Feb. 1907, p. 112-6.

EVANS, G. A. Building clubs: their formation and administration. *Incorporated accountants' journal,* 1907-8, p. 263.

JACKSON, WILLIAM LEACH. Building societies and recent legislation. *Accountant,* May 21, 1898, p. 532-7.

MOXEY, EDWARD P. AND OTHERS. Business of a building and loan association. (In their *Practical accounting methods.* p. 7-30).

PROCTOR, A. H. Constitution of building societies. *Accountant,* Feb. 14, 21, 28, 1885.

ROSENTHAL, HENRY S. Building, loan and savings associations; how to organize and successfully conduct them. Ed.3, revised and enlarged. Cincinnati, American building association news co. 1911. 425p.

——— Same Ed.4, revised and enlarged. 1920. 500p.

STEVENS, THOMAS M. Dissolution and winding up of building societies. *Accountant,* Nov. 9, 16, 1895, p. 898-9, 919-24.

WALLACE, DAVID E. Building societies. *Accountant,* May 7, 1910, p. 658-63 *Accountants' magazine,* April 1910, p. 201-14.

WILLIAMSON, ALFRED E. A. Building societies in the Transvaal. *South African accountants' journal,* vol. 1, p. 9.

Accounting

ACCOUNTING for building and loan associations. *Business man's magazine,* Feb. 1907, p. 106-8.

ALCORN, EDGAR C. Bookkeeping in building and loan associations. *Business man's magazine,* Sept. 1910, p. 272-8.

AMERICAN business and accounting encyclopaedia; comp. by E. H. Beach and W. W. Thorne. Detroit, Boookkeeper publishing co. 1901. Building society accounting-v.2, p. 275-83.

BRABOOK, EDWARD W. Building societies and their accounts. *Accountant,* 1886, p. 165, 174.

BUILDING societies' accounts. (In Lisle, George. *Encyclopaedia of accounting.* v.1. p. 521-30).

BUILDING societies acts 1874-94; form of annual account and statement. *Accountant,* Oct. 12, 1895, p. 812-5.

COMSTOCK, H. G. Practical accounting system for building and loan associations. *American building association news,* Nov. 1915.

CRAWFORD, L. U. Accounting for building and loan associations. *Business man's magazine,* Feb. March 1907, p. 108-12, 130-4.

CROUCHER, S. H. Building societies' accounts. *Incorporated accountants' journal,* 1893-4, p. 108.

CUTFORTH, A. E. Building society. (In his *Audits.* 1914. p. 92-7)

DAVIS, EDWARD L. Maturing shares in loan associations. *Business man's magazine,* Nov. 1906, p. 102-6.

DUDLEY, BERNARD. Building societies' accounts. *Accountant,* July 27, 1912, p. 119-30.

EDMONDS, WILLIAM. Building societies' accounts. *Accountant,* Dec. 16, 1893, p. 1055-66.

ELSWORTH, THOMAS Building society accounts and their audit *Accountant,* Feb. 15, 1913, p. 220-32.

FITZGERALD, EDWARD J. Building association accounts. *Business,* Dec. 1895, p. 98-101.

FORM of annual account and statement to be made. *Accountant,* Oct. 12, 1895, p 812-15.

FRANKLIN, GEORGE. Building society accounts. *Accountant,* May 23, 1885.

GOULDING, E. S. Building association accounts. *Commerce, accounts and finance,* Oct. 1901, p. 25-8.

JACKSON, WILLIAM LEACH. Building societies' accounts. *Accountant,* Sept. 16, 1893, p. 787-92.

JACKSON, WILLIAM LEACH. Building societies and recent legislation. *Accountant,* May 21, 1898, p. 532-7.

KEISTER, D. A. Building association accounting. (In his *Corporation accounting and auditing,* 1909, p. 346-73).

LAWRENCE, PAGE. Building and loan association tax records. *Business man's magazine,* April 1908, p. 357-8.

LEES, JOHN F. Bookkeeping for terminating building societies. London, Simpkin, Marshall, Hamilton, Kent & co. 1895.

LOWE, C. J. Building societies accounts. *Accountant,* Feb. 7, 1903, p. 203-14.

MCCALL, J. H. Building societies accounts. *Incorporated accountants' journal,* April 1915, p. 160-4.

MILNE, JAMES. Building societies. *Accountants' magazine,* Nov. 1897, p. 552-67.

MOXEY, EDWARD P. AND OTHERS. Accounting system of a building and loan association. (In their *Practical accounting methods.* p. 31-57).

NIXON, ALFRED AND J. H. STAGG. Building societies. (In their *Accounting and banking.* 1912. p 397-412).

PARSONS, GEORGE C. T. Building societies accounts. *Accountant,* 1887, p. 143, 160, 173.

PIXLEY, FRANCIS W. Building societies. (In his *Accountancy.* Ed.2. p. 123-5).

PIXLEY, FRANCIS W. Form of accounts for building societies prescribed by the chief registrar of friendly societies under Building societies act, 1894. (In his *Auditors, their duties and responsibilities.* 1910. p. 591-6).

ROGERS, JOHN HENRY. Building and land societies; a short account of their formation and development, and a few notes on the accounts and audit. *Accountant,* April 27, 1901, p. 506-9.

ROSENTHAL, HENRY S. Books and blanks. (In his *Building, loan and savings associations.* 1911. p. 336-47).

ROWE, D. D. Loan records in detail. *Business man's magazine,* Nov. 1905, p. 882-6.

SCOTT, GEORGE G. Apportionment of profits of building and loan associations. *Journal of accountancy,* Nov. 1913, p 350-7.

SMITH, WILLIAM COLIN GRANT. Building societies' accounts, specially adapted for permanent societies and societies using interest tables. London, Gee & co. 1903. 104p. Accountants' library, v. 25).

SPENCE, GEORGE WILLIAM. Building societies' accounts: correspondence. *Accountant,* Dec. 3, 1892, Jan. 14, 1893, p. 919-23; 31-2.

BUILDING AND LOAN ASSOCIATIONS—*(Continued)*

Auditing

AUDIT of building societies accounts. *Accountant,* Oct. 15, 22, Nov. 5, 19, Dec. 3, 10, 1892, p. 765-7, 785-7, 791, 832-3, 869-71, 913-5, 941-3

BENNETT, ROBERT JOSEPH. Audit of a building loan association. *American building association news,* Dec. 1912. *Journal of accountancy,* July 1912, p. 1-18.

CASTENHOLZ, WILLIAM B. Building and loan associations. (In his *Auditing procedure,* 1918, p. 224-8).

CUTFORTH, A. E. Building society. (In his *Audits.* 1914. p. 62-3).

DICKSEE, LAWRENCE R. Building and loan associations. (In his *Auditing.* Authorized American edition p. 161-3).

DOWLER, FRANK and E. M. HARRIS. (In their *Auditing, accounting and banking.* p. 19-25).

ELSWORTH, THOMAS. Building society accounts and their audit. *Accountant,* Feb. 15, 1913, p. 220-32.

FAWCETT, ARTHUR. Audit of building societies and prospective interest. *Accountant,* Jan. 11, 18, 25, 1908, p. 45-7, 80-2, 110-2.

GOODWIN, N. Building societies' companion. London, Simpkin, Marshall, Hamilton, Kent and co. 1882

GOULDING, E. S. Audit of building society accounts. *Bookkeeper,* 1901, v. 14, no. 3, p. 25-32. *Incorporated accountants' journal,* 1900-1, p. 207.

JENKINSON, MARK WEBSTER. Some notes on the audit of different businesses. London, Gee & co. 40p. *Accountant,* April 19, 1913, p. 585-7.

KEISTER, D. A. Building association auditing. (In his *Corporation accounting and auditing.* 1909. p. 398-407)

MONTGOMERY, ROBERT H. Building and loan associations. (In his *Auditing theory and practice.* 1916 p. 565-72).

PIXLEY, FRANCIS W. Audit of the accounts of building societies. *Accountant,* May 19, 26, 1894, p. 452-7, 469-74.

PIXLEY, FRANCIS W. Building societies (In his *Auditors, their duties and responsibilities.* 1910. p. 496-7).

ROGERS, JOHN H. Building and land societies; a short account of their formation and development, and a few notes on the accounts and audit. *Accountant,* April 27, 1901, p. 506-9.

ROSENTHAL, HENRY S. Auditing. (In his *Building, loan and savings associations.* 1911. p. 166-21)

SPICER, ERNEST EVAN AND ERNEST C. PEGLER. Building society. (In their *Audit programmes.* 1919. p. 17-9).

SPICER, ERNEST EVAN AND ERNEST C. PEGLER. Building society. (In their *Practical auditing.* 1914. p. 471-3).

BUILDING contracts.
See Contracts.

BUILDING for profit. Bolton, R. P. 1911.

BUILDING, loan and savings associations. Rosenthal, H. S. 1911.

BUILDING societies.
See Building and loan associations.

BUILDING societies. *Accountant* 1886, p. 469.

BUILDING societies accounts. (In Lisle, George. *Encyclopaedia of accounting.* v.1. p. 521-30)

BUILDING societies' accounts, specially adapted for permanent societies and societies using interest tables. Smith, W. C. G. 1903.

BUILDING societies acts 1874-1894; form of annual account and statement. *Accountant,* Oct. 12, 1895, p. 812-5.

BUILDING SUPPLIES

Cost accounting

JORDON, WILLIAM A. Cost system for a retail yard; paper delivered before the National builders supply association, Chicago, Feb. 22, 1911. Wilmington, Del., 1911. 28p.

BUILDING yachts and launches *Business man's magazine,* March 1907, p. 156-62.

BUILDINGS

See also Office buildings.

BENTLEY, HARRY C. Buildings. (In his *Science of accounts.* 1913. p. 141-4).

BOLTON, REGINALD PELHAM. Building for profit; principles governing the economic improvement of real estate. New York, The DeVinne press, 1911. 124p.

CHURCH, A. HAMILTON. Buildings and plant. (In his *Manufacturing costs and accounts.* 1917. p. 191-206).

CHURCH, A. HAMILTON. Buildings. (In his *Production factors in cost accounting and works management.* 1910. p. 83-8).

COX, HENRY C. Buildings; repairs and improvements to buildings. (In his *Advanced and analytical accounting.* 1920. p. 234-7).

DAVIDSON, F. E. Buildings as a factor in production costs. *American architect,* June 11, 1919, p. 810-3.

DICKINSON, ARTHUR LOWES. Building and structures. (In his *Accounting practice and procedure.* 1917. p. 77).

FREEHOLD buildings; leasehold buildings. (In *How to understand the balance sheet and other periodical statements.* p. 63-6).

GILMAN, STEPHEN. Buildings. (In his *Principles of accounting.* 1917. p. 184-6).

GREEN, H. L. Buildings—factor costs. *Engineering magazine,* Dec. 1914, p. 407-10. *Engineering and contracting,* Feb. 3, 1915, p. 101-2.

KESTER, ROY B. Buildings. (In his *Accounting theory and practice.* v.2. 1910. p. 298-302).

KESTER, ROY B. Building expenses and income. (In his *Accounting theory and practice.* 1918. v.2. p. 596-9).

POTTER, M. H. Fixing building factors in costs. *Iron trade review,* July 10, 1919, p. 97-8.

RACINE, SAMUEL F. Land and buildings. (In his *Accounting principles.* 1917. p. 65).

WEBNER, FRANK E. Land values and building space costs. (In his *Factory costs.* 1911. p. 158-68).

WILDMAN, JOHN R. Buildings. (In his *Principles of accounting.* 1914. p. 71-101).

WOODS, CLINTON E. Buildings. (In his *Uniform accounting methods for industrials.* 1917. p. 289-90).

Costs

ALLEN, L. H. Comparative cost of concrete and mill buildings. *Concrete, Oct.* 1916, p. 135-6.

ANALYSIS of increased building costs. *American lumberman,* May 8, 1920, p. 1.

ANDERSON, W. F. Estimating and building costs. *American architect,* June 12, 1918, p. 798-800.

BARKER, HARRY. Probable approximate cost of brick building. (In his *Public utility rates.* 1917. p. 347-51).

BOLTON, REGINALD PELHAM. Building for profit: principles governing the economic improvement of real estate. New York, The DeVinne press, 1911. 124p.

COST of an electric express building. *Electric railway journal,* March 18, 1916, p. 574.

BUILDINGS—Costs—*(Continued)*

Cost of constructing and moving portable camp buildings. *Engineering and contracting*, June 19, 1918, p. 614-15.

Costs of concrete and mill type buildings. *Concrete*, July 1916, p. 25. Condensed. *Engineering and contracting*, July 26, 1916, p. 95.

Crosby, W. W. Building construction costs. *Textile world*, Mar. 1915, p. 577-8.

Davidson, F. E. and T. L. Condron. Cost of factory buildings of timber and of concrete *Engineering news*, Nov. 9, 1916, p. 884-6. *Engineering and contracting*, Nov. 22, 1916, p. 450-2.

Dingman, Charles F. Estimating the cost of mill buildings. *Engineering and contracting*, Sept. 8, 1915, p. 185.

Estimating building costs. *Concrete*, Nov. 1917, p. 137-9.

Estimating building costs. *Concrete*, Feb. 1918, p. 60-1.

Eggleston, DeWitt Carl. Cost per square foot for floor space and cost per kilowatt hour for electricity. (In his *Problems in cost accounting*, 1918, p. 244-7).

Fulton, W. L. Design, construction and detailed labor costs of car shops for Omaha and Council Bluffs street railway co., Omaha, Neb. *Engineering and contracting*, Oct. 6, 1915, p. 264-6.

Gillette, Halbert Powers. Buildings. (In his *Handbook of cost data for contractors and engineers*. 1910. p. 1069-177).

Investigation of building costs. *Building age*, Aug. 1919, p. 276-7.

Killman, W. H. Modern schoolhouse; cubage and cost. *Brick*, May 1915, p. 107-10.

Main, C. T. Approximate costs of mill buildings. *Iron age*, Mar. 3, 1910, p. 506-8.

Mikkelsen, M. A. Building and the cost of construction. *Architectural record*, May 1919, p. 398-403.

Moderate cost brick garage with figures of actual cost. *Building age*, March 1917, p. 131-3.

Muhlhausen, L. Comparative costs of concrete and mill construction. *Engineering news*, Dec. 21, 1916, p. 1193.

Sherman, L. K. Comparative cost of building 1913 and 1919. *Monthly labor review*, Feb. 1920, p. 551-7.

Sherman, L. K. Cost of housing: a comparison of building costs in 1913 and 1919 based on a 6-room dwelling. *American contractor*, Jan. 17, 1920, p. 31-5.

Starrett, T. Cost of building. *Architects and building*, April 1914, p. 131-3.

Thompson, S. E. Unit costs in building construction. *Concrete*, March 1916, p. 129-30. *Engineering and contracting*, Mar. 1, 1916, p. 220-1.

Tyrrell, H. G. Comparative cost of buildings of wood, concrete and steel framing. *Engineering magazine*, June 1912, p. 353-73.

Depreciation.

See Depreciation, depletion and obsolescence—Buildings.

Valuation

Bannister, J. C. How buildings were appraised in revaluation of real property of Los Angeles. *Engineering record*, April 8, 1916, p. 472-5.

Burton, H. J. comp. Valuations and depreciations of city buildings; extracts from opinions of leading authorities; from "convention proceedings", tenth annual convention at Omaha, September 10, 11, 12, and 13, 1917. 127p.

Elbourne, E. T. Buildings and fixed plant valuation. (In his *Factory administration and accounts*. 1918. p. 364-77.

Greendlinger, Leo. Important points in the valuation of buildings and structures. (In his *Financial and business statements*. c1917. p. 107).

Hatfield, H. R. Valuation—buildings. (In his *Modern accounting*. 1918. p. 88-9).

Overstreet, R. H. Valuation of buildings. *Engineering news*, Sept. 11, 1913, p. 516-8.

BULKELEY, W. V. C.

Storehouse methods that reduce labour. *Cassier's Engineering Monthly*, December 1916, p. 403-7. *Electrical railway journal*, July 15, 1916, p. 101-3.

BULKELY, O. E.

Waterworks, management. *American city*, April 1917, p. 405-7.

BULKLEY, W. A.

Cost accounting in banks, administration expenses, how to arrive at a unit of cost. *Banking law journal*, Dec. 1910, p. 1065-9.

Plan of bank cost accounting; a method of calculating administration expenses in banks by arriving at the unit of cost that will determine the value of an active account. *Bankers home magazine*, Feb. 1911, p. 37-41.

BULL, A. J.

Probable effect of the war upon the trade of the world. *Accountant*, Dec. 9, 1916, p. 555-65.

BULL, WILLIAM

How to keep old papers. *Accountant*, June 18, 1910, p. 875-7.

BULLARD, A. W.

Shall improvements made from earnings be capitalized or included in valuation? *Electrical review and western electrician*, Nov. 28, 1914, p. 1049-50.

Valuation and improvements made from earnings. *Journal of political economy*, Jan. 1915, p. 61-4.

BULLARD, J. E.

Costs of operating gas company motor vehicles. *Gas age*, March 15, 1919, p. 314-6.

Flat rate unfair to company and consumer. *American gas light journal*, Nov. 30, 1914, p. 337-9.

Keeping auto service records. *Gas age*, July 15, 1919, p. 80.

BULLIVANT, J. B.

Accountancy in the British navy and system of internal check. *South African accountant*, March 1919, p. 306.

BULLOCK, THOMAS

Costs in bankruptcy. *Accountant*, Jan. 6, 1894, p. 11-3.

BULMAN, H. F.

Cost of producing coal. *Colliery guard*, May 19, 1910.

BUNKER Hill and Sullivan mining and concentrating co. report with unit costs of exploration, mining and milling. *Engineering and mining journal*, Aug. 10, 1918, p. 268-9.

BUNNELL, A. K.

Municipal accounts. *Canadian chartered accountant*, Jan. 1913, p. 174-6.

Municipal accounts and audit. *Municipal world*, Oct. 1914, p. 239-40.

Standards of professional conduct and practice. *Canadian chartered accountant*, Oct. 1911, p. 53-60.

BUNNELL, H.
Expense burden: its incidence and distribution. *Journal of the American society of mechanical engineers,* Dec. 1911.

BUNNELL, STERLING H.
Common errors as to the value of a patent. *Iron age,* Dec. 4, 1913, p. 1310-1.
Cost-keeping for manufacturing plants. New York, D. Appleton & co. 1911. 233p.
Cost-keeping for manufacturing plants. *American economic review,* June 1912, p. 364-6.
Cost keeping for small machine shops. *American machinist,* v. 33, no. 42.
Cost system for a machine shop. *Business man's magazine,* Aug. 1908, p. 137-43.
Distributing the works expense burden—how a factory may be divided by imaginary lines into productive units each to earn its interest and other charges. *Iron age,* Jan. 18, 1912, p. 200-1.
Exact cost of machine work. *Business man's magazine,* Jan. 1912, p. 90-3.
Expense burden, its incidence and distribution. *Iron trade review,* March 14, 1912, p. 605-10. *Journal of the American society of mechanical engineers,* 1911, p. 535.
Finding cost from selling price. *Iron age,* July 2, 1914, p. 20-2. *Metal work,* July 24, 1914, p. 95-6.
Making machines earn their living and correct distribution of costs. *Iron age,* July 27, 1911, p. 194-5.
Proper use of cost keeping system. *Cassier's magazine,* Aug. 1908, p. 300-3.
Recent advances in expense distribution. *Iron age,* May 7, 1914, p. 1136-8. *Metal work,* June 12, 1914, p. 795-7.
Standardizing factory expense and cost. *Iron age,* Nov. 16, 1911, p. 1072-3.
Taking an inventory. *Engineering news record,* January 2, 1908.

BUNTING, HERBERT O.
Departmental payroll. *Business man's magazine,* Aug. 1909, p. 195-6.

BUNTZEL, VICTOR A.
Manufacturing architectural sheet metal ornaments. *Business man's magazine,* Dec. 1906, p. 51-9.

BURBRIDGE, NOEL W.
Character from a business point of view. *Accountant,* Nov. 14, 1914, p. 586-91.

BURCH, A. N.
Methods and costs of concrete lining irrigation materials, Orland project, U. S. reclamation service. *Engineering and contracting,* April 12, 1916, p. 352.

BURCH, S. S.
System of accounts for a mutual fire insurance company. *Business man's magazine,* 1904, v.16, no. 10, p. 111-7.
Wholesale grocery business. *Business man's magazine,* May 1907, p. 96-101.

BURDEN.
See Cost and factory accounting—Overhead.

BURDEN application and measuring the loss from curtailed production. Scovell, Wellington and company. 1916.

BURDEN of prosperity. *Journal of accountancy,* Oct. 1914, p. 296-8.

BURDETT, HENRY
Uniform system of accounts for hospitals and public institutions, orphanages, missionary societies, homes, co-operations, and all classes of institutions with special forms of account, complete sets of books, certain suggested checks upon expenditure, forms of tender, and other aids to economy together with an index of classification whereby every item of expenditure may be dealt with under identical heads by every group of institutions. London, Scientific press, 1903. 103p.

BURDICK, CHARLES E.
Valuation of waterworks properties. *Engineering and contracting,* Oct. 23, 1907, p. 238. *Municipal journal and engineering,* Sept. 11, 1907, p. 302.

BURDICK, D. C.
Depletion and depreciation of coal-mining properties. *Coal age,* July 31, 1919, p. 185-7.

BURDICK, FRANCIS MARION
Essentials of business law. New York, D. Appleton & co. 1903. 285p.

BURDICK, R. H.
Performance of Diesel-engine plants in Texas. *Electrical world,* March 11, 1916, p. 587-92.

BUREAU OF INDUSTRIAL RESEARCH.
AMERICAN company shop committee plans; a digest of twenty plans for employees' representation; through joint committees introduced by American companies. New York, Bureau of industrial research, 1919. 37p.

BUREAU of labor statistics on increased gas rates in American cities. *American gas engineering journal,* July 19, 1919, p. 48.

BUREAU OF MUNICIPAL RESEARCH
Accounting and reporting methods of the state of New York. 1916. 212p. (Municipal research no 74).
Business methods of New York city's Police department critical study and constructive suggestions pertaining to administrative and accounting methods of the Bureau of repairs and supplies. New York, Bureau of municipal research, 1910. 212p.
Business methods of New York city's police department summary of critical study and constructive; suggestions pertaining to administrative and accounting methods of the Bureau of repairs and supplies . . . (New York, 1909). 35.
City and county of Denver survey. 1914.
Collecting water revenues; methods of the Bureau of water register, Manhattan, with suggestions for reorganization. 1909. 223p.
Department of municipal audit and examination; report of an investigation of the office of Commissioners of accounts of New York city . . . 1907. (New York, 1907). 35p.
Handbook of municipal accounting; prepared by the Metz fund from descriptive and critical data collected and constructive recommendations made. New York, D. Appleton & co. 1913. 318p. (Metz fund handbooks of city business methods).
Handbook of talks on municipal accounting and reporting . . . New York, Bureau of municipal research, 1911-12. 23 nos.
Making a municipal budget, functional accounts and operative statistics for the Department of health and Greater New York. . . . 1907. (New York, 1907). 171p.
Making a municipal budget; eperative statistics for the Department of health of Greater New York. 1907. 171p.

BUREAU OF MUNICIPAL RESEARCH—*(Continued)*

Memphis; a critical study of some phases of its municipal government with constructive suggestions for betterment in organization and administrative methods. Memphis, Bureau of municipal research, 1909, 203p.

Modern municipal accounting. *Municipal journal*, Jan. 23, 1913, p. 122-24.

New York city's department of finance, report on present methods with suggestions for reorganization. New York, Bureau of municipal research, 1908. 254p.

Organization and administration of the city government of Atlanta, Ga. (Exclusive of health and educational departments.) Report of a general survey made for the Atlanta chamber of commerce committee on municipal research by Herbert R. Sands, for the New York Bureau of municipal research, November, 1912. Atlanta, (1913?). 64p.

Park question. 2 pts. New York, 1908. Pt. 1. Critical study and constructive suggestions pertaining to administration and accounting methods. 152p. Pt. 2. Same pertaining to revenue and deposits. 124p.

Recent movement for state budget reform, 1911-1917. New York, Bureau of municipal research, 1917. 155p.

St. Louis, a preliminary survey of certain departments of the government of the city of St. Louis. St. Louis, City council, 1910. 416p.

Short talks on municipal accounting and reporting. New York, Bureau of municipal research, 1911-12. 23 nos.

BUREAU OF RAILWAY ECONOMICS.

Comparison of railway freight rates in the United States, the principal countries of Europe, South Australia and South Africa. Washington, D. C., Bureau of railway economics 1915. 131p.

Digest of depreciation charges of 172 roads (with annual operating revenues about $1,000,000) calendar year 1917. Washington, Bureau of railway economics, 1918. 26p.

List of references on railroad accounting. Aug. 12, 1914. 16 typewritten pages.

List of references on railroad accounting. December 31, 1919. 68p.

List of references on valuation of railway. Washington, Bureau of railway economics, 1916. 130p.

List of references on valuation of steam railways. *Bulletin of the American railway engineering association*, Oct. 1916, 154p.

Railway earnings in 1918; railways having annual operating revenues above $1,000,000. Washington, 1919. 16p. (Consecutive no. 136, miscellaneous series no. 32).

———— Same, 1919. Washington, 1920, 18p. (Consecutive no. 150).

Railway stockholders December 31, 1917. Washington, Government printing office, 1919. 13p. (Consecutive no. 140, miscellaneous series no. 33).

Statistics of railways 1906-1916 United States. Washington, 1918. (Consecutive no. 120, miscellaneous series no. 30). 58p.

Summary of railway returns year ending December 31, 1916, railways having annual operating revenues above $1,000,000. Washington, 1917. 23p. (Consecutive no. 114, miscellaneous series no. 29).

Summary of railway returns year ending December 31, 1917, railroads having annual operating revenues above $1,000,000. Washington, 1918. 15p.

BURGE, A. E.

Method of recording depreciation on motor vehicles. *Accounting and commerce*, May 1919, p. 40.

BURGESS, ALFRED

Solicitor's accounts. *Accountant*, May 31, June 7, 1890, p. 293-9, 306-11.

BURGESS, CHARLES W.

Mining costs in the Missouri-Kansas district. *Mining and engineering world*, April 26, 1913.

BURGESS, G. H.

Federal railway-valuation work. *Engineering news*, July 1, 1915, p. 12-14.

How the Delaware and Hudson is handling its valuation fieldwork. *Engineering news*, April 5, 1917, p. 35-9.

What the land appraisers of the Delaware and Hudson company are doing. *Engineering news*, Mar. 14, 1918, p. 503-6.

BURGESS, HENRY JOHN

Executorship accounts. *Incorporated accountants' journal*, 1896-7, p. 18.

Investigations. *Incorporated accountants' journal*, 1903-4, p. 143.

BURGESS, J. L.

Underlying principles and general practices of railway accounting departments. *Railway and engineering review*, Dec. 23, 30, 1905, p. 905-6, 924-5.

BURGESS, P.

Factors which determine water rates. *American city*, Dec. 1912, p. 567.

Study of revenue from sale of water to metered domestic consumer. *Engineering news-record*, June 5, 1919, p. 1116-9.

BURINGTON, P. V.

Electric railway accounting review. *Electric railway journal*, Oct. 9, 1915, p. 720-1.

BURKE, J. I.

How trust companies handle and solve income tax problems. *Trust companies*, Feb. 1914, p. 129-30.

BURKE, R. H.

Light and heavy equipment compared on identical sewer construction. *Engineering news*, January 23, 1919, 183-5.

BURKE, W. H.

Nickel in 1913 and 1919. *Electric railway journal*, Sept. 13, 1919, p. 512-5.

BURKHARD, P. L.

Fallacy of the employees' profit sharing as a reward for labor. *Industrial management*, July 1919, p. 42-5.

BURKHARDT, O. M.

Determining of piecework rates from charts. *American machinist*, Aug. 29, 1918, p. 383-7.

BURKHOLDER, J. L.

Drainage works of the Rio Grande irrigation project. *Engineering news*, Sept. 18, 1919, p. 543-9.

BURKHOLDER, T. E.

Modern bank accounting. *Southern banker*, Feb. 1906.

BURLINGAME, HARDIN J.

Livery accounting. *Business man's magazine*, Dec. 1905, p. 1146-50.

BURLINGAME, L. D.

Safety organization of a machine shop. *Machinery*, November 1915, 203-9.

Stock parts and their routing. *Machinery*, August 1919, p. 1109-14.

BURLINGHAM, L. H.
Time savers for the accounting and the laundry departments; advantages of using an individual pay-roll card-time saver and friction and jealousies obviated—simple method of caring for linen. *Modern hospital,* Jan. 1919. p. 21-4.

BURLINGTON adopts new train audit system. *Railway age gazette,* Jan. 17, 1913, p. 112-3.

BURLINGTON'S construction organization. *Railway age gazette,* July 18, 1913, p. 111-2.

BURNAP, W. J.
Cost of delivery; some Pittsburgh figures and suggestions on effecting economies. *New York produce review,* November 28, 1917.

BURNHAM, M. H.
Modern mine valuation. Philadelphia, J. B. Lippincott company, 1912.

BURNLEY, W. E.
Money. *Incorporated accountants journal,* 1901-2, p. 88.

BURNS AND MCDONNELL
Waterworks appraisals. *Engineering record,* May 15, 1909, p. 616.

BURNS, A. J.
How to figure costs in the electrical contracting business. *Electrical review and western electrician,* May 10, 1913.

BURNS, CLINTON S.
Determination of physical values. *Engineering record,* Sept. 16, 1905, p. 328-9.
Relationship of finance and depreciation. *American municipalities,* June, 1917, p. 77-9.
Valuation of public utilities; deduction of formula for expressing present value. *Municipal journal and engineer,* Nov. 30, 1910, p. 744.
Valuation of sewerage systems. *Engineering and contracting,* Feb. 14, 1917, p. 149-51.
Waterworks appraisements in Missouri and Kansas. *Engineering news,* July 29, 1909, p. 115.

BURNS, J. G.
Accountant and written evidence. *Accountant,* Jan. 20, 1912, p. 103-9.

BURNS, JOHN
Ancestor's creditors. *Accountants' magazine,* July 1916, p. 322-4.
Average rate of income. *Accountants' magazine,* May 1918, p. 187-91.
Decisions on land values duties. *Accountants' magazine,* Aug. 1917, p. 371-5.

BURNS, R. EASTON
Amendments to the business profits war tax act, 1916. *Canadian chartered accountant,* July 1918, p. 35-8.
Income war tax act, 1917: a digest. *Canadian chartered accountant,* Jan. 1918, p. 175-228.
Income war tax act, 1917; amendments and rulings. *Canadian chartered accountant,* July 1918, p. 7-15.
Revenue and receipts: the practical; the application of an economic principle. *Canadian chartered accountant,* July 1916, p. 39-41.

BURR, HENRY A.
Filing engineering clippings. *Engineering record,* Oct. 23, 1915, p. 520.

BURRAGE, FRANCIS J.
Proper safe guards in the conduct of the transfer department. *Trust companies,* Jan. 1915, p. 34-8.

BURRELL, F. L.
Cost data in the bridge department. *Railway age gazette,* Nov. 17, 1911, p. 1012-3.

BURRILL, P. C.
Methods of computing overhead expenses of electrical contractors. *Electrical review,* May 18, 1918, p. 849-50.

BURRITT, ARTHUR WINFIELD AND OTHERS.
Profit sharing; its principles and practice; a collaboration. New York, Harper and brothers, 1918. 328p.

BURRITT, M. C.
Farm cost accounting made easy. *Power,* Jan., Feb., March, April, 1916, p. 14, 14, 24, 30.

BURROUGH, MAURICE W.
Income tax for farmers, together with a simple form of book-keeping specially adapted for farmers. London, Iliffe & sons. 1918. 36p.

BURROUGHS, A. M.
Apportioning indirect production expense. *Metal work,* Feb. 19-26, 1915, p. 284-6, 316-8.
Cutting the costs of keeping a cost system. *Metal work,* May 28, 1915, p. 763.
Final disposition of expense figures. *Metal work,* Mar. 26, 1915, p. 471-2.
Handling material and perpetual inventory. *Metal work,* Jan. 22, 1915, p. 153-4.

BURROUGHS, M. W.
Income tax for farmers, together with a simple form of book-keeping specially adapted for farmers. London, 1918.

BURROUGHS adding and listing machine. *Engineer,* May 3, 1907.

BURROUGHS ADDING MACHINE COMPANY.
Better day's work at a less cost of time, work and worry to the man at the desk. Detroit, Burroughs adding machine co. c1908. 159p.
Cost keeping short cuts; prepared from experiences in many lines of business. Detroit, Burroughs adding machine company, 1911. 190p. Ed. 3. Efficient cost keeping. 1914.
Instruction for operating and using Burroughs adding and listing machines, class three hundred. Ed. 9. Detroit, Mich. Burroughs adding machine co. 1915.

BURROUGHS business practice hand book. Walker, J. C. 1913.

BURROWS, ROLAND
Excess profits duty. *Accountant,* July 1916, p. 14-23. *Incorporated accountants' journal,* June 1916, p. 208-14. *Public accountant,* Aug., Sept. 1916, p. 39-47, 67-9.
Guarantees and indemnities. *Incorporated accountants' journal,* Feb. 1915, p. 108-10.
Some recent points in income tax laws. *Accountant,* July 3, 1920, p. 13-7. *Incorporated accountants' journal,* March 1920, p. 121-5.

BURSK, R. C.
Necessity of cost accounting. *National wholesale grocers' association bulletin,* Dec. 1917, p. 25.

BURT, EDWARD R.
Ethics of employing men: correspondence. *Journal of accountancy,* Aug. 1915, p. 162-3.

BURT, J. C.
How we save half the labor cost. *System,* June 1917, p. 654-5.

BURT v. Dervoe; error to municipal court of Chicago. (52-24893). 5 typewritten pages.

BURTON, ARTHUR S.
Why some cost systems fail to produce desired results. *Journal of accountancy,* April 1910, p. 249-58.

BURTON, C. E.
50 rules for locating and preventing errors in trial balances. Chicago, T. Powner co. 1920.

BURTON, E. L.
Accounts of gas companies. *Incorporated accountants' journal,* 1895-6, p. 82.

BURTON, FRANCIS GEORGE.
Appreciation of municipal assets. *Accountant,* March 9, 23, 1907, p. 327-36, 375-7.
Commercial management of engineering works. Manchester, Engineering scientific publ. co., 1905. 432p.
Cost accounts. *Accountant,* Feb. 24, 1912, p. 324-31. *Incorporated accountants journal,* 1900-1, p. 107, 115.
Economic aspect of municipal and state ownership. *Incorporated accountants' journal,* 1905-6, p. 222.
Engineering estimates and cost accounts. Ed. 2. Manchester, Technical publishing co. 1900. 136p.
Engineering valuation. *Incorporated accountants journal,* 1903-4, p. 87-84.
Engineers' "shipbuilders" accounts. London, Gee & co. 1902. 108p. (Accountants' library, v. 14).
Limitations of auditors. *Accountant,* May 10, 1913, p. 735-41.
Shipbuilders' accounts. (In Lisle, George, *Encyclopaedia of accounting.* v.6. p. 64-79).

BURTON, H. J. comp.
Valuations and depreciations of city buildings. *Building and building management,* Oct. 6, Nov. 3, 1919, p. 30, 31.
Valuations and depreciations of city buildings; extracts from opinions of leading authorities; Hurd, Evers, Zangerle, Bernard, Balton, Reed, Saliers, Kester, Holmes, Grunsky, Leake; from "convention proceedings," tenth annual convention at Omaha, September 10, 11, 12, and 13, 1917. 127p.

BURTON, J. H.
Sinking funds. *Accountant,* Oct. 23, 1920, p. 438-42.

BURTON, THEODORE E.
Regulation of corporations. Chicago, La Salle extension university, 1918. 20p.

BURTON-BROWN, G.
Slide rule. *Scientific American, supplement,* July 20, 1918, p. 43.

BUSBEY, WILLIAM G.
In the matter of the application of the Atchison, Topeka & Santa Fe railway co. (and others) . . . for increases in passenger, baggage and freight rates: statement, brief argument by counsel to the Public service commission . . . 1915. 43p. Before the Public esrvice commission of Missouri.

BUSBY, L. A.
Fares in Chicago, Cleveland and Philadelphia compared. *Electric railway journal,* Oct. 25, 1919, p. 795-6.

BUSES, motor.
See motor buses.

BUSEY, F. L.
Heating ventilating and humidifying costs. *Metal work,* Jan. 9, 1914, p. 102-3.

——— AND W. H. CARRIER
Indirect heating systems with respect to maximum economy and operation. *Heating and ventilating magazine,* March 1913, p. 30-7. *Power,* March 18, 1913, p. 380-2.

BUSH, H. J.
Costing systems in sulphuric acid works. *Chemical age,* July 5, 1919, p. 58-9.

BUSH, H. W.
Report of committee on standard cost records [of the American association of park superintendents]. *Parks and recreation,* Oct. 1917, p. 36-40.

BUSH, S. L.
Cost accounting: how to govern and show expense in a productive department. *Paper,* Oct. 23, 1918, p. 11-13.

BUSHONG, C. R.
Wagon factory cost accounting. *Business man's magazine,* Aug. 1907, p. 122-36.

BUSINESS
Bethke, William. Business organization and management, Chicago, La Salle extension university, 1918. 24p.
Boyle, C. Methods and organisation in business. *Commonwealth accountant,* May 1907.
Brisco, Norris Arthur. Economics of business. New York, The Macmillan co. 1913. 390p.
Burden of prosperity. *Journal of accounting,* Oct. 1914, p. 296-8.
Business situation. *Journal of accountancy,* Oct. 1911, p. 450-2.
Business outlook—a symposium. *Journal of accountancy,* March 1907, p. 337-56, 386-7.
Butler, W. C. Efficiency in business. *Australasian accountant and secretary,* July 1920, p. 224-7.
Causes of business failure. *Journal of accountancy,* Sept. 1914, p. 208-9.
Clapp, John Mantle. Talking business. New York. The Ronald press company. 1920. 526p. (Language for men of affairs, v. 1).
Cooke, H. O. Stafford. Some factors of success in business. *Business organisation and management,* June 1920, p. 269-72.
Cooper, Francis. Financing an enterprise; a manual of information and suggestion for promoters, investors and business men generally. 2 v. New York, The Ronald press co. 1906.
Dicksee, Lawrence Robert. Business methods and the war. *Accountant,* Jan. 30-Feb. 20, 1915, p. 161-8, 200-5, 226-32, 261-8.
Dicksee, Lawrence Robert. Business organization. New York, Longmans, Green & co. 1910. 283p.
Dicksee, Lawrence R. Business organization with special reference to fraud. *Accountant,* Dec. 2, 9, 1911, p. 761-7, 802-8. *Incorporated accountants' journal,* 1910-11. p. 203-238.
Dillon, William. Boston clouds have a copper lining. *Journal of accountancy,* March 1907, p. 342-4.
Duncan, Carson Samuel. Commercial research; an outline of working principles,

BUSINESS—*(Continued)*

New York, The Macmillan company, 1919. 385p.

FERNLEY, THOMAS A. Price maintenance. Philadelphia, Commerce publishing company, c1912. 311p.

FOWLIE, ALEXANDER E. Colorado on a solid basis. *Journal of accountancy,* March 1907, p. 354-5.

FREDERICK, J. GEORGE. Business research and statistics. New York, D. Appleton and company, 1920. 342p.

GARFIELD, JAMES R. Commercial ideals. *Journal of accountancy,* Nov. 1906, p. 14-9.

GERSTENBERG, CHARLES W. and W. S. JOHNSON. Organization and control. New York. Alexander Hamilton institute, c1918. 315p. (Modern business, v.3).

GORE, EDWARD E. Confidence prevails in Illinois. *Journal of accountancy,* March 1907, p. 350-2.

GRIMLEY, BERTRAM. How to sell a business. *Accountant,* July 7, 1900, p. 630-5, 709.

HAMILTON, W. R. Going and a growing concern: how it goes and how it grows; from the counting-house point of view. *Accountant,* Dec. 12, 1914, p. 730-8.

HAMILTON, W. R. Joint stock versus private ownership of businesses; some commercial differences. *Accountant,* May 25, Aug. 10, 1907, p. 720-6, 161-5.

HARDCASTLE, JOSEPH. Accounts. *Business world,* May-Oct. 1906, p. 379-385, 477-80, 554-8, 630-4, 738-40, 850-4.

HARDCASTLE, JOSEPH. Administration and business. *Business world,* April, May 1902, p. 168-9, 216-7.

HEHL, CHARLES L. Trifle pessimistic in Maryland. *Journal of accountancy,* March 1907, p. 345-7.

HOTCHKISS, WILLARD EUGENE. Higher education and business standards. Boston, Houghton, Mifflin company, 1918. 109p.

HOW to finance a business; 202 proved methods of raising capital and using credit. Chicago, A. W. Shaw co. 1912. 128p.

HURLEY, EDWARD NASH. Accurate costs mean fair business. *Iron trade review,* June 21, 1917, p. 1354-5.

HURLEY, EDWARD NASH. Awakening of business. New York, Doubleday, Page & co. 1916. 240p.

IN these Utopian days. *Journal of accountancy,* Aug. 1915, p. 129-33.

JENKS, JEREMIAH WHIPPLE. Business and the government. New York, Alexander Hamilton institute. c1918. 353p. (Modern business, v. 24).

JOHNSON, JOSEPH FRENCH. Business and the man. New York, Alexander Hamilton institute, c1918. 330p. (Modern business, v.1).

LEWIS, ELIAS ST. ELMO. Getting the most out of business; observations of the application of the scientific method to business practice. Ed. 5. New York, The Ronald press co. 1916. 515p.

LOUGH, WILLIAM HENRY. Business finance; a practical study of financial management in private business concerns. New York, The Ronald press co. 1917. 631p.

LOUGH, WILLIAM HENRY. Business outlook; introduction. *Journal of accountancy,* March, 1907, p. 337-40.

LOWREY, D. M. American business man. *Accountant,* Jan. 30, 1904, p. 136-7, 147-51.

ROE, CLIFFORD G. Business organizations. Chicago, LaSalle extension university, 1917. 31p.

SALIERS, EARL A. Accounting measures to meet business depression. *Journal of accountancy,* Jan. 1920, p. 1-9.

SHAW, A. W. COMPANY. Shaw management service; business management series, 6v. New York, A. W. Shaw company.
Contents: v.1. Insurance business growth. v.2. Tackling big problems. v.3. Financing the business. v.4. Picking the right man. v.5. Watching profits. v.6. Getting rid of detail.

SPRINGER, D. W. Michigan inclined to be cautious. *Journal of accountancy,* March 1907, p. 349.

SUFFERN, ERNEST S. Healthy reaction not disaster. *Journal of accountancy,* March 1907, p. 340-1.

TEMPLE, HERBERT M. Bright prospect in Minnesota. *Journal of accountancy,* March 1907, p. 352-4.

UEHLINGER, H. Modern method of building up business service. (In *Cost accounting addresses.* 1920. p. 29-38).

WHY reaction may be expected. *Journal of accountancy,* March 1907, p. 341-2.

WILSON, JOHN. Business methods old and new. *Accountant,* Nov. 30, 1907, p. 676-8.

YOUR house in order. *Oregon voter,* Oct. 23, 1920, p. 2506.

BUSINESS accounting. Greeley, H. D. ed. 1920.

BUSINESS administration. Jones, E. D. 1914.

BUSINESS administration and cost accounts. *Accountant,* Sept. 24, 1910, p. 393-6.

BUSINESS administration the principles of business organization and system and the actual methods of business operation and management. Parsons, C. C. 1909.

BUSINESS and accounts for public schools and and home use. Witter, C. A. 1910.

BUSINESS and the government. Jenks, J. W. c1918.

BUSINESS and the law: correspondence. Kauffman, J. H.

BUSINESS and the man. Johnson, J. F. c1918.

BUSINESS and the universties. *Accountant,* Feb. 1, 8, 1913, p. 136-9, 169-71.

BUSINESS bookkeeping. Gay, G. E.

BUSINESS book-keeping. Gilbert, A. L.

BUSINESS book-keeping. Routley, John. 1919.

BUSINESS bookkeeping and practice. Rowe, H. M.

BUSINESS bookkeeping and practice. Sadler, W. H. and R. M. Rowe.

BUSINESS book-keeping annual. Porrit, H. W. and William Nicklin.

BUSINESS bookkeeping simply explained. *South African accountant and auditor,* June,-Sept. 1916, p. 195-6.

BUSINESS college graduate in the business field. Joplin, J. P.

BUSINESS CORRESPONDENCE.
See Commercial correspondence.

BUSINESS correspondence. McJohnston, Harrison. 1918.

BUSINESS directions used in connection with Brandrup & Nettleton system of teaching bookkeeping and business practice. Mankato commercial college. 1914.

BUSINESS directions used in connection with Ellis industrial bookkeeping. Ellis publishing co. 1912.

BUSINESS education and accountancy. Haskins, C. W. c1904.

BUSINESS efficiency for Pittsburgh. Lybrand, Ross Bros. & Montgomery. 1910.

BUSINESS efficiency for Pittsburgh. Pittsburgh civic commission. 1910.

BUSINESS English and correspondence. Davis, Roy and Clarence H. Lingham. 1919.

BUSINESS enterprises. National association of credit men. Business service department. c1919.

BUSINESS finance. Lough, W. H. 1917.

BUSINESS forms and elementary book-keeping. Shaw, J. W. 1893.

BUSINESS forms, customs and accounts for schools. Eaton, Seymour. 1895.

BUSINESS insurance and its relation to accounting procedure. Richardson, N. Y.

BUSINESS LAW.
See Commercial law.

BUSINESS law. Conyngton, Thomas. 1918.

BUSINESS library, what it is and what it does. Krause, L. B. 1919.

BUSINESS man of the army. *Journal of accountancy,* Dec. 1905, p. 112-17.

BUSINESS management of municipalities. Chase, H. S. 1911.

BUSINESS management through directly recorded statistics. Millar, T. J.

BUSINESS man's guide in preparing his trading account, profit and loss account, balance sheet and capital account. Pepper, Edmund. 1903.

BUSINESS methods in a combination shop. *Metal work,* Aug. 14, 1914, p. 208-10.

BUSINESS methods of New York city's police department. Bureau of municipal research.

BUSINESS methods of the government. *Journal of accountancy,* Feb. 1907, p. 300-1.

BUSINESS of finance. Withers, Hartley. c1918.

BUSINESS of insurance. Dunham, Howard P. comp. 1912.

BUSINESS of life insurance. Dawson, Miles Menander. 1905.

BUSINESS of the household. Taber, C. W. and others. 1918.

BUSINESS organization. Dicksee, L. R. 1910.

BUSINESS organization and management. Bethke, William. 1918.

BUSINESS organizations. Roe, C. G. 1917.

BUSINESS outlook—a symposium. *Journal of accountancy,* March 1907, p. 337-56, 386-7.

BUSINESS outlook. *Journal of accountancy,* Aug. 1908, p. 280-2.

BUSINESS practice and accounts for cooperative stores. Bexell, J. A. and W. H. Kerr.

BUSINESS practice bookkeeping. Sweet, J. S. 1913.

BUSINESS practice for twenty lessons in bookkeeping. Campbell, T. F.

BUSINESS profits war tax act. 1916. *Canadian chartered accountant,* July 1916, p. 7-17.

BUSINESS profits war tax act. *Canadian chartered accountant,* Oct. 1917, p. 135.

BUSINESS profits war tax act and amendments. *Canadian chartered accountant,* Jan. 1919, p. 240-1.

BUSINESS profits war tax: Dominion income tax: income war tax act amended. *Canadian chartered accountant,* Oct. 1920, p. 122-30.

BUSINESS record system for jewellers. Ingersoll, R. H. & bro. c1918.

BUSINESS record systems book of instruction for retail hardware dealers. Associated advertising clubs of the world. c1917.

BUSINESS record systems book of instructions for retail jewelry merchants. Associated advertising clubs of the world. c1916.

BUSINESS record systems book of instructions for retail shoe merchants. Associated advertising clubs of the world. c1916.

BUSINESS research and statistics. Frederick, J. G. 1920.

BUSINESS short cuts in accounting, bookkeeping, card indexing, advertising, correspondence, management. Detroit, Bookkeeper publishing co. 1904.

BUSINESS situation. *Journal of accountancy,* Oct. 1911, p. 450-2.

BUSINESS standard bookkeeping. Cowperthwait. 1187.

BUSINESS statistics. Copeland, M. T. 1917.

BUSINESS statistics. Griffith, James B.

BUSINESS training. Haskins, C W. 1902.

BUSINESS writing. Lee, J. M. 1920.

BUSSE, A. W.
Accounting for the wholesaler. *Business man's magazine,* June 1907, p. 69-74.

BUSY man's bookkeeping. Shaw, J. W.

BUTCHART, J. R.
Money and its purchasing power. *Accountant,* Aug. 30, Sept. 6, 1919, p. 196-200 210-6. *Accounting and commerce,* June 1918, p. 65-72.
Money, credit and banking. *Accountant,* June 23, 30, 1917, p. 589-93, 606-10. *Accounting and commerce,* April, May, June 1917, p. 14-8, 36-44, 63-5.

BUTCHER, W. L.
Mass diagram for power and water supply computations. *Engineering news,* Aug. 24, 1916, p. 376-8.

BUTCHERS

Accounting

BROCKLEHURST, G. R. Bookkeeping for bakers, butchers, etc. Gainsborough, 1892.

BUTLER, E. F.

Table showing percentage to be added to cost to bring 5 per cent net on volume of business for the year. *Domestic engineering,* Mar. 23, 1918, p. 448.

BUTLER, H. M.

Method of ordering and handling stores including disposition of all scrap material. *Electric railway journal,* March 16, 1912, p. 428.

BUTLER, HENRY G.

Cotton, grain and coffee; future contract brokerage business. *Business man's magazine,* 1906, v.18, no. 8, p. 100-6.

Stock brokerage bookkeeping. *Business man's magazine,* 1906, v.18. no. 10, p. 162-70.

BUTLER, M. R.

How a contractor equipped his asphalt plant to dispense with two men and lower cost of asphalt. *Municipal engineering,* June 1919, p. 206.

BUTLER, P.

Important principles involved in valuation. *Railway age gazette,* March 17, 1916, p. 477-81.

Some features of the federal valuation of railroads. *Western railway club, Proceedings,* Dec. 18, 1916.

Valuation of railway property for purposes of rate regulation. *Journal of political economy,* Jan. 1915, p. 17-33.

BUTLER, RALPH STARR

Marketing methods. New York, Alexander Hamilton institute, c1918. 346p. (Modern business, v.5).

BUTLER, T.

Cost keeping and the farm business. *Progressive farmer,* Aug. 11, 1917, p. 855.

BUTLER, W. C.

Efficiency in business. *Accountant,* Feb. 21, 1920, p. 223-5. *Australasian accountant and secretary,* July 1920, p. 224-7.

BUTT, HAROLD.

See Knoeppel, C. E., joint author.

BUTT, WILLIAM E.

Bringing an old water works valuation up-to-date. *Engineering news,* Aug. 28, 1913, p. 408-9.

BUTTER

UNITED STATES. DEPARTMENT OF COMMERCE. Butter, cheese and condensed milk. Washington, Government printing office, 1917.

Accounting

FRASER, J. J. Butter factory accounts. *Accountant,* April 20, 1912, p. 532-3.

BUTTER, cheese and condensed milk. United States. Department of commerce. 1917.

BUTTERFIELD, B. F.

Logic of municipal fund accounts. *Journal of accountancy,* Nov. 1916, p. 379-84.

BUTTERFIELD, WILLIAM T.

Notes on the worsted industry. *Accountant,* Oct. 18, 1913, p. 555-83.

Preparation for examination in bookkeeping, accounts and auditing. *Accountant,* Dec. 22, 1900, p. 1174-9.

BUTTERWORTH, GEORGE R.

Audit of the accounts of municipal corporations. *Accountant,* July 4, 8, 1908. p. 19-22, 63-5.

Income tax in relation to the accounts of local authorities. *Accountant,* Dec. 18, 1920, p. 676-80.

Relationship between rates, local debts, and rateable value. *Accountant,* July 22, 1911, p. 123-7.

BUTTERWORTH, J. F.

Modern methods in industry. *Accountant,* March 6, 1920, p. 276-82.

BUTTERWORTH, WILLIAM C.

Cost and price of gas in a small city. *American gas light journal,* March 22, 1915, p. 180-3.

BUTTON, CYRIL MALLAM

Insurance brokers' accounts. *Incorporated accountants' journal,* 1905-6, p. 260.

BUTTON, HOWARD.

Notes on principles of profit sharing and labor co-partnership. *Accountant,* Oct. 19, 26, Nov. 2, 1918, p. 203-5, 219-22, 236-9.

BUTTON industry. United States. Tariff industry. 1918.

BUTTONS

UNITED STATES. TARIFF COMMISSION. Button industry; tariff legislation, commercial and industrial conditions in the United States and in foreign countries—court and treasury decisions—statements from associations and leading manufacturers. Washington, Government printing office, 1918. 125p. (Tariff information series no. 4).

BUTTS, ISAAC RIDDLER.

Merchants and shipmaster's manual, and shipbuilder's and sailmaker's assistant. Ed. 6. Boston, I. R. Butes & co. 1879. 156p.

BUTZ, R. E.

Systematizing production accounts. *Iron trade review,* Mar. 20, 1919, p. 757-9.

BUTZ, RALPH H

Accounting methods; modern methods of handling notes and principles involved. *Textile world,* Dec. 28, 1918, p. 3251.

Calculating manufacturing costs of silk. *Textile world,* May 31, 1919, p. 3313.

Cost accounting methods for dealers. *Electrical review,* Sept. 8, 1917, p. 425-6.

Depreciating the value of patents. *American industries,* Aug. 1917, p. 20.

Handling accounts in the wool department. *Textile world,* Nov. 4, 1916, p. 4729.

How to change from single-entry to double-entry bookkeeping. *Domestic engineering,* Jan. 11, 1919, p. 85-6.

Installing cost system in a silk mill. *Textile world,* Jan. 13, 1917, p. 821.

Manufacturing expense. *Metal industries,* Dec. 1917, p. 511-2.

Profit-sharing promotes thrift. *Iron trade review,* Aug. 28, 1919, p. 571.

Uses of knitting mill cost accounting system. *Textile world,* Oct. 21, 1916, p. 4531.

When a partner is entitled to a salary. *Domestic engineering,* May 11, 1918, p. 218. *Inland printer,* July 1918, p. 450-1.

Wool carding department accounts. *Textile world,* June 14, 1919, p. 3693.

Wool mill accounts supplies. *Textile world,* March 8, 1919, 1569.

BUXTON, T. W.
Purchasing department accounting. New York, National electric light association, 1911. 26p.

BUXTON, WILLIAM ORRELL
Bookkeeping. London, Sir Isaac Pitman & sons. 158p.
Pitman's advanced bookkeeping. New York. Sir Isaac Pitman and sons. 1918. 298p.
Simplified bookkeeping. New York, Sir Isaac Pitman & sons. 294p.

——— **AND A. F. ROUNDTREE**
Profits in company practice. *Accountant,* April 21, June 9, 1906, p. 506, 510, 721.

BY-PRODUCT installation for power stations; abstract. *Journal of the American society of mechanical engineers,* November 1918. p. 692.

BY-PRODUCTS
BAUGH, FREDERICK H. By-product, waste and scrap. (In his *Principles and practice of cost accounting.* 1915. p. 24-5).
BENTLEY, HARRY C. By-products. (In his *Science of accounts.* 1913. p. 216-7, 240-1).
BY-PRODUCTS and costs. *Accountant,* Sept. 29, 1917, p. 233-6.
CHURCH, A. H. By-products. (In his *Manufacturing costs and accounts.* 1917. p. 93-5).
COLE, WILLIAM MORSE. By-products. (In his *Accounts their construction and interpretation.* c1915. p. 111-2).
EGGLESTON, DEW. C. By-products. (In his *Problems in Cost Accounting.* 1918. p. 55, 56, 65, 193, 206).
GREENDLINGER, LEO. Sales of scrap or residuals. (In his *Financial and business statement.* c1917. p. 52-3).
JORDAN, JOHN P. and GOULD L. HARRIS. By-product costs. (In their *Cost accounting.* 1920. p. 344-50).
KENT, WM. Estimates of cost when the by-product or scrap from one product is used in making another. (In his *Bookkeeping and cost accounting for factories.* 1918. p. 108).
MCINTOSH, ROBERT J. By-products. (In his *Reference book of accounts for manufacturing and mercantile companies.* c1917. p. 189-90).
MEADE, E. S. Apportionment of the cost of anthracite coal between domestic and steam sizes: a symposium. *Journal of accountancy,* May 1906, p. 30-8.
RIDGWAY, A. CLIFFORD. By-products. (In his *Cost accounts.* p. 64-5).
WALTON, SEYMOUR. Vouchers: distribution of expenses. *Journal of accountancy,* Nov. 1918, p. 395-6.
WEBNER, FRANK E. By-products. (In his *Factory accounting.* 1917. p. 225-6, 228-29).

BY-PRODUCTS and costs. *Accountant,* Sept. 29, 1917, p. 233-6.

BYE, R. T.
Social welfare in rate making. *Political science quarterly,* Dec. 1917, p. 522-41.

BYERS, M. L.
Economics of railway operation. New York. London, 1908. 672p. *Accounts and accounting,* pt. 3, p. 96-148.

BYLLESBY, H. M.
Appraisals of public utility properties. *Public service,* Aug. 1911, p. 56-8.
Responsibilities of electrical engineers in making appraisals. *Proceedings of the American institute of electrical engineers,* Sept. 1911, p. 2013-27. *Transactions, American institute of electrical engineers,* 1911, p 1251. Abstract. *Electric railway journal,* July 1, 1911, p. 16-8.

BYRN, EDWARD M.
Mechanical work of the twelfth census. *Scientific American,* April 19, 1902.

BYRNE, H. E.
Container records. *Business man's magazine,* Aug. 1906, p. 126-8.
Practical bookkeeping. Ed. 5. Tyler, Texas. Byrne publishing co. 1905.

BYRNE, JAMES.
Foreclosure of railroad mortgages. (In Stetson, Francis L. and others. *Some legal phases of corporate financing, reorganization and regulation.* 1917. p. 77-152).

BYRNE, THOMAS FRANCIS
Law of contracts. *Accountant,* 1886, p. 211.

C. E. R. A. A. meets at Ottawa Beach. *Electric railway journal,* July 24, 1920, p. 168-70.

C. P. A. auditing questions for January 1, 1914, Bentley, H. C. comp. 1914.

C. P. A. banquet, New York state society at the Waldorf Astoria. *Accountant,* April 12, 1902, p. 401-2.

C. P. A. bill. *Journal of accountancy,* July 1907, p. 218.

C. P. A. bill in District of Columbia. *Journal of accountancy,* Feb. 1909, p. 328.

C. P. A. bill in Minnesota. *Journal of accountancy,* May 1909, p. 76.

C. P. A. degree for $50. *Journal of accountancy,* Jan. 1910, p. 222.

C. P. A. examination, December 13, 1898. *Journal of accountancy,* Dec. 1906, p. 176-7.

C. P. A. examination papers, 1902. *Incorporated accountants' journal,* 1901-2, p. 258.

C. P. A. examination questions. *Journal of accountancy,* May 1906, p. 74-8.

C. P. A. EXAMINATIONS
See Examinations.

C. P. A. examinations. Peter, W. F.

C. P. A. examinations. *Business man's magazine,* Feb. 1909, p. 184-9.

C. P. A. examinations, 1899. *Business,* July 1899, p. 444-7.

C. P. A. examinations and how to pass them. Chase, W. A. 1915.

C. P. A. examinations and how to prepare for them. Tanner, J. B. c1916.

C. P. A. examinations: correspondence. *nal of accountancy,* Nov. 1908, p. 60.

C. P. A. examinations in New York. *Journal of accountancy,* Sept. 1913, p. 230-2.

C. P. A. examining board. Vollum, C. N.

C. P. A. language. *Journal of accountancy,* March 1911, p. 404.

C. P. A. law in Colorado. *Journal of accountancy,* April 1907, p. 495.

C. P. A. law in Connecticut. *Journal of accountancy,* April 1907, p. 495.

C. P A. law in Ohio. *Journal of accountancy,* May 1908, p. 69.

C. P. A. law of state of Virginia. *Journal of accountancy,* Nov. 1910, p. 67-9.

C. P. A. laws. *Journal of accountancy,* June July, Oct. 1913, p. 468-71; 65-77, 328-32, 408-9.

C. P. A. legislation. *Journal of accountancy,* March 1909, p. 400-1.

C. P. A. legislation in New York. *Journal of accountancy,* July 1910, p 216.

C. P. A. legislation—Tennessee. *Journal of accountancy,* April 1913, p. 301-4.

C. P. A. movement and the future of the profession of the public accountant in the United States of America. Wilkinson, George.

C. P. A. problem. *Business man's magazine,* Jan. June 1909, p. 57-60, 518-23.

C. P. A. problems and solutions, 1914. 2v. New York, The Ronald press co. 1915, 346+375p.
v.1. Presenting problems, with solutions, for the following examinations: Pennsylvania, November, 1913; New York, January, 1914; Illinois, May, 1913; Colorado, December, 1913.
v.2. Presenting problems with solutions, for the following examinations: Missouri, December, 1913; Ohio, November, 1913; New York, June 1914; Massachusetts, October, 1914.

C. P. A. problems with solutions, 1915. 2v. New York, The Ronald press co. 1916. 351+361p.
v.1. Presenting problems, with solutions for the following examinations: Wisconsin, April, 1914; Ohio, November, 1914; New York, January, 1915; Pennsylvania, November, 1914.
v.2. Presenting problems, with solutions for the following examinations: Missouri, December, 1914; Illinois, May, 1914; Massachusetts, October, 1915; New York, June, 1915.

C. P. A. problems and solutions. Morey, Lloyd and W. B. Castenholz, 1918.

C. P. A. question department. Greendlinger Leo.

C. P. A. question department: correspondence. *Journal of accountancy,* Nov. 1909, p. 75-80.

C. P. A. questions and answers. Bennett, R. J. and F. W. Morton

C. P. A. requirements. *Journal of accountancy,* Oct. 1909, p. 459-60.

C. P. A. syllabi. *Journal of accountancy,* May 1911, p. 61-3.

C. P. A. versus C. A. *Canadian chartered accountant,* April 1912, p. 206-8.

CABLE COMPANIES
See Telephone and telegraph.

CADILLAC stock-room methods. *Machinery* (New York), Feb. 1920, p. 501-2.

CADLE, C. L.
Keeping account of trucking costs. *Electric railway journal,* Oct. 19, 1918. p. 698-9.
Operating cost of motor trucks. *Engineering and contracting,* Nov. 20, 1918, p. 492.

CADWALLADER, L. L.
Office practice. *American gas light journal,* June 8, 1914, p 355-6.

CADWALLADER, W. E.
Accrual accounting records required in the interest of accuracy and ethics. *Journal of the American bankers association,* Sept. 1919, p. 140-2.

CAFES
See Restaurants, cafes, etc.

CAHOON, JAMES BLAKE
Uniform accounting for gas and electric lighting companies. *Engineering news,* June 14, 1900.
Uniform municipal accounting. *National municipal league. Proceedings,* 1900. *Public policy,* Sept. 29, 1900, p. 197-98.
Uniformity of municipal accounts. *Public policy,* Feb. 9, 1901, p. 68-70.

CAIRNS, WILLIAM
Depreciation and depletion in tax returns. *Journal of accountancy,* Sept. 1919, p. 204-211.

CAISSON excavation cost reduced. *Concrete* July 1917, p. 17.

CALCULAGRAPH *Horseless age,* May 6, 1914, p. 729-30.

CALCULATING machine for weavers' wages. *Textile world,* Aug. 1914, p. 543.

CALCULATING MACHINES
See also Mechanical devices—Calculating machines.

Cost accounting
MANUFACTURE of adding machines. *Engineering production,* Feb. 1920, p. 75-82.

Stockkeeping
PRENTISS, F. L. Stock keeping in adding machine factory; Burroughs adding machine co., Detroit. *Iron age,* Dec. 9, 1915, p. 1347-51.

CALCULATING machines and instruments. Kerr, W. H.

CALCULATING premiums on bonds. *Municipal journal,* April 1, 1915, p. 426.

CALCULATING the cost of knit goods. *Textile world,* Nov. 1915, p. 218-24.

CALCULATING the income tax. *Canadian chartered accountant,* July 1919, p. 52-5.

CALCULATION of continual compound interest. Middleditch, Livingston.

CALCULATIONS for accounts with special reference to Inwood's tables and logarithms. Turner, E. Hartley.

CALDECOTT, J.
Double entry bookkeeping. Piper, 1855.
Practical guide for retail tradesmen and others to bookkeeping by double entry. London, 1851, 1855.

CALDER, JOHN
Prevention of accidents in cotton mills. *Efficiency society journal,* Nov. 1917, p. 599-610.

CALDER, MARSHALL SON AND IBOTSON
Bookkeeping. London, 1907.

CALDERWOOD, J. F.
Street railway accounting. *Street railway journal,* January 3, 1905.

CALDICOTT, J.
Qualifications and duties of accountants. London, Letts, son and co. 1875.

CALDICOTT, O. HOLT
Auditor's duty in respect of depreciation. *Accountant,* Jan. 25, 1896, p. 74-6.
Chartered accountants as experts in commerce and manufactures. *Accountant,* May 22, 1897, p. 524-9.
Executors' and trustees' accounts. *Accountant,* April 28, 1883.
Executorship accounts. Ed.3. London, Gee & co. 1906. 82p.
Executorship accounts. *Accountant,* May 30, 1885.
Executorship accounts. *Accountant,* Nov. 9, 16, 23, 30, Dec. 7, 1889, p. 594-6, 604-12, 630-6, 644-51, 663-8.
Flour mills account. (In Lisle, George. *Encyclopaedia of accounting.* v.3. p. 44-50).
Gas works accounts. (In Lisle, George. *Encyclopaedia of accounting.* v. 3. p. 177-87).
Germs of insolvency. *Accountant,* Nov. 3, 1888, p. 707-12.
Hardware factor accounting. (In Lisle, George. *Encyclopaedia of accounting.* v.3. p. 234-6).
Ironwork accounting (In Lisle, George, *Encyclopaedia of accounting.* v.3. p. 490-1).
Journal. *Accountant,* April 26, 1890, p. 215-8.
Poetry of accounts. *Accountant,* 1887, p. 622.
Specialization for accountants. *Accountant,* April 22, 1905, p. 490-5.

CALDWELL, B. D.
Meeting the problems of the express companies. *Railway age,* Feb. 26, 1915, p. 367-9.

CALDWELL, J. W.
Methods and unit costs used in appraising the water works of Honolulu, Hawaii. *Engineering and contracting,* April 22, 29, 1914, p. 462-5, 499-500.

CALENDAR legislation. *Journal of accountancy,* April 1908, p. 479-81.

CALIFORNIA
Acts permitting the issuance of shares without nominal or par value. Ch. 701 and 713, p. 1. 1917.

—— **CONTROLLER'S DEPARTMENT**
Inheritance tax act of California in effect July 27, 1917, with digest of decision and reprint of former acts; comp. by Robert A. Waring. Sacramento, Califronia. State printing office, 1918.

—— **RAILROAD COMMISSION**
Revised uniform classification of accounts for water corporations effective January 1, 1920, 1919. 57p.
Uniform classification of the accounts for electric corporations adopted Oct. 23, 1912, effective Jan. 1, 1913. San Francisco, California railroad commission, 1912

—— **STATE BOARD OF ACCOUNTANCY.**
Examination questions, June 6-8, 1904.
Information in regard to examinations for certified public accountants. Sacramento, 1918. 23p.

—— **STATE TAX COMMISSION.**
Stock and bond valuation of public utilities in California. 1916.

CALIFORNIA *Journal of accountancy,* Nov. 1905, Feb. 1906, April 1907, July 1909, p. 70, 343, 496, 213.

CALIFORNIA *American institute of accountants, Yearbook,* 1915-1917, p. 190-1, 320-1, 298-9, 210-1, 174-5, 237-8, 307-9, 257-9, 247-9, 139-41.

CALIFORNIA accountants bill. *Journal of accountancy,* Aug. 1911, p. 301.

CALIFORNIA association of auditors and accountants of public utilities. *Journal of accountancy,* Jan. 1913, p. 74-5.

CALIFORNIA charges for natural gas delivered at the limits of the city of Long Beach for consumption therein. *Gas age,* Jan. 1, 1915, p. 33-4.

CALIFORNIA commission. *Electrical world,* June 24, 1916, p. 1492.

CALIFORNIA commission admits that market value will not reproduce land. *Engineering record,* Jan. 15, 1916, p. 76.

CALIFORNIA commission on four valuation questions. *Engineering record,* Dec. 4, 1915, p. 697-8.

CALIFORNIA railroad commission approves rate increase for Pacific electric company. *Electrical world,* Aug. 3, 1918, p. 224.

CALIFORNIA railroad commission decision in application of Southern counties gas company for reasonable rates. *American gas engineering journal,* July 20, 1918, p. 63-5.

CALIFORNIA rate increase will further bond issue. *Electrical world,* Feb. 15, 1919, p. 334.

CALIFORNIA reciprocity clause. *Journal of accountancy,* Aug. 1913, p. 150.

CALIFORNIA societies consolidated. *Journal of accountancy,* Aug. 1913, p. 149.

CALIFORNIA state society of certified public accountants. *Journal of accountancy,* July 1917, p. 78.

CALIFORNIA supreme court has held that where a city has an ordinance fixing the rate for gas the company could not give a lower rate than that fixed by ordinance for prompt payment of bills. *American municipalities,* June 1915, p. 72.

CALIFORNIANS adopt accounting system: phases of depreciation stumpage values. labor and other costs. *American lumberman,* Oct. 5, 1918, p. 41.

CALLAHAN, J. J.
Representative government in a manufacturing plant; Passaic metal ware co. *Machinery,* Nov. 1919, p. 256-8.

CALLAWAY, W. D.
From school to countinghouse; an explanation of the elementary principles of double-entry bookkeeping. London, T. Nelson & sons, 1910. 160p.
Public house accounts. *Accountant,* March 13, 20, 27, April 3, 1909, p. 370-2, 404-5, 434-6, 468-70.
Stockbrokers' accounts. London, Gee & co. 1902. 88p. (Accountant' library, v.9).

CALLS
Stevens, T. M. Calls. *Accountant,* Dec. 23, 1893, p. 1079-87.
Money paid in anticipation of calls on shares. *Accountants' magazine,* 1902. p. 6.

CALVERT, ALFRED
Shipping office organisation, management and accounts; a comprehensive guide to the innumerable details connected with the shipping trade; with numerous forms and facsimiles of shipping documents London, Sir Isaac Pitman & sons. 203p.

CALVERT, J. F.
Depreciating in railway accounting. *Journal of accountancy,* Aug. 1908, p. 229-33.

CALVERT, W. L.
How to figure the profits from investments in farm equipment *Minnesota farmers' institute annual,* 1916, p. 46-8.

CALVERT, W. R.
Land classification, its basis and methods; coal lands. *Economic geology,* 1911, v.6, p. 473-92.

CALVIN, E. A.
Cost of cotton production. *Manufacturers record,* Sept. 19, 1918, p. 78.

CAMBRIDGE, MASS. central station practice. *Electrical world,* April 26, 1913, p. 876-7.

CAMERON, B.
Decreasing accidents through a bonus system. *Electric railway journal,* Feb. 3, 1917, p. 209-10.

CAMERON, D. A.
Foreign exchange. *Canadian chartered accountant,* April 1920, p. 252-60.

CAMMERON, JAMES
Lack of system in manufacturing. *Business world,* Dec. 1905.

CAMM, W. H.
Address, 1889. *Accountant,* Mar. 9, 1889, p. 1268.

CAMMACK, F. R.
See Matheson, K. J., joint author.

CAMP, W. E.
Human factor in task setting. *Industrial management,* Nov. 191ṡ, p. 372-4.

CAMPBELL, A. M.
Acturial science and its use to the accountant. *Accountant,* June 8, 1907, p. 787-90.

CAMPBELL, A. W.
Scientific management in road construction. *Contract record,* June 25, 1919, p. 634-5.

CAMPBELL, C. D.
Brewery accounts and account books. (In Lisle, George. *Encyclopaedia of accounting.* v.1. p. 508-14).
Licensed victuallers' (public-house) accounts. (In Lisle, George. *Encyclopaedia of accounting.* v.4. p. 106-13).

CAMPBELL, COLIN B.
Loose leaf books and card systms as legal evidence. *Business man's magazine,* March 1905, p. 559-61.

CAMPBELL, D. A.
Value of redeemable securities. *Federal accountant,* April 1916, p. 53-4.

CAMPBELL, E. H.
Best and most economical methods of handling a station. *Railway age gazette,* May 24, 1912, p. 1164-7.

CAMPBELL, EDWARD P.
System of freight accounts, reporting, auditing and settlements between railroads, of revenue on through way-bills, with samples of blanks, etc. . . . 1889. (New York 1889). 51p.

CAMPBELL, G. E.
Card records of Los Angeles track work. *Electric railway journal,* Sept. 4, 1915, p. 407-8

CAMPBELL, G. H.
Smith comes through. *Hoard's dairyman,* March 22, 1918, p. 369.

CAMPBELL, J. A.
Representative plan praised. *Iron age,* Feb. 19, 1920, p. 547-8.

CAMPBELL, J. R.
Public accounting: its organisation. *Accountant,* Sept. 30, 1913, p. 381-8.

CAMPBELL, NEIL
Reversions. (In Lisle, George. *Encyclopaedia of accounting.* v.5. p. 488-508).

CAMPBELL, T. COLIN
See Innes, J. W., joint author.

CAMPBELL, THOMAS FINDLEY
Business practice for twenty lessons in book keeping Indianapolis, Ind., Bobbs-Merrill co. 1915.
Campbell's actual accounting; the apprenticeship in business; the modern method of instruction in elementary and advanced accounting, business forms and business customs. Bobbs-Merrill co. 1911. 135p.

CAMPBELL, W. GORDON
Investments. (In Lisle, George. *Encylcopaedia of accounting.* v.3. p. 456-68).
Stock exchange. (In Lisle, George. *Encyclopaedia of accounting.* v.6. p. 129-42).

CAMPLING, C. C.
See Elworthy, W. R., joint author.

CAMPS, Army,
See Armies.

CAN profits be shared? *Accounting and commerce,* Oct. 1917, p. 166-8. *Canadian chartered accountant,* April 1919, p. 281-4.

CAN profits be shared? *American machinist,* Jan. 25, 1917, p. 151-2.

CAN the factory generate its own power cheaper than the central station can supply it? *Industrial engineering,* Nov. 1913, p. 478-80.

CAN the jobbers' small order pay its way? *Electrical world,* April 22, 1916, p. 927-9.

CAN the standard measure of value be improved. *Journal of the Engineering institute of Canada,* Nov. 1919, p. 720-7.

CANADA
Bill 157; business profits tax amendment, 1920, an act to amend the business profits war tax, 1916. *Canadian chartered accountant,* July 1920, p. 42-3.

CANADA—*(Continued)*

BILL 158: income tax amendment, 1920, an act to amend the income war tax act, 1917. *Canadian chartered accountant,* July 1920, p. 35-41.

CHAP. 25; an act to amend the income war tax act, 1917; assented to 24th May, 1918. 3p.

CHAP. 28; an act to authorize the levying of a war tax upon certain incomes; assented to 20th September, 1917 11p.

CHAP. 45; an act to amend the income war tax act, 1917; assented to 7th July, 1919, 11p.

Legislation against trusts and combines in the Dominions. *Accountant,* May 20, 1911, p. 777-9.

Finance

See Finance—Canada.

CANADA. *Journal of accountancy,* May 1909, p. 76.

CANADIAN accountants' association. *Canadian chartered accountant,* April 1913, p. 274-6.

CANADIAN bank auditors. *Canadian chartered accountant,* Jan. 1913, p. 199-202.

CANADIAN bank auditors. *Journal of accountancy,* Jan. Oct. 1913, p. 61-4, 309-10.

CANADIAN chartered accountant; official organ of the Dominion association of chartered accountants. 518 Continental life building, Toronto, Canada.

CANADIAN company law. *Accountant,* Oct. 30, 1909, p. 549-50.

CANADIAN company law; how it differs from English legislation. *Accountant,* Sept. 11, 1909, p. 324-5.

CANADIAN income tax. *Accountant,* March 16, 1918, p. 233.

CANADIAN journal for accountants; report of a committee at the annual meeting of the Dominion association of chartered accountants. Toronto, July 14 and 15, 1900. *Journal of accountancy,* Sept. 1910, p. 382-4.

CANADIAN society of cost accountants. *Canadian chartered accountant,* July Oct. 1920, p. 31-4, 116-9.

CANADIAN standard bookkeeping. Westervelt, J. W. A. Blanchard, J. W. Westervelt and D. Hoskins. 1901

CANAL excavation with electric drag-line scrapers. *Electrical world,* Jan. 29, 1916, p. 255-6.

CANALS

NEW YORK STATE. Collection of data on canals of the state.

Accounting

OAKEY, FRANCIS. Determination of the net profit of the Panama canal. *Journal of accountancy,* Sept. 1914, p. 181-95.

REVISED of general accounts and classified expenditure accounts of the Isthmian commission—effective July 1, 1909. *Government accountant,* Nov. 1909, p. 268-91.

Cost accounting

COST keeping system in use on the Panama canal *Engineering and contracting,* Jan. 7, 1914, p. 64.

ENGINEERS' cost keeping system, New York state barge canal. *Engineering and contracting,* Sept. 7, 1910.

FAURE, A. Cost keeping systems employed on the Panama canal. *Engineering record,* Mar. 25, 1911.

NEW cost accounting system for the Panama canal work. *Engineering and contracting,* Dec. 15, 1909, p. 509.

Costs

COST of the Panama canal as estimated and as built. *Engineering news,* May 28, 1914, p. 1207-9.

ESTIMATED and actual cost of construction at Panama. *Engineering record,* Jan. 25, 1913, p. 86.

RANDOLPH, I. Comparison of estimated with actual unit prices on the Panama canal. *Engineering and contracting,* Mar. 11, 1914, p. 294.

Valuation

HANSEL, CHARLES. Report on revaluation of railroads and canals, New Jersey, 1911. Trenton, 1912. 465p.

CANCE, A. E. and R. H. FERGUSON

Cost of distributing milk in six cities and towns in Massachusetts. *Massachusetts agricultural experiment bulletin.* 173, p. 1-54. 1917. Condensed. *Massachusetts agricultural extension bulletin.* 14, p. 1-8, 1917. Excerpt. *New York produce review,* Dec. 5, 1917. p. 168.

CANDLES

Lamborn, Leebert Lloyd. Modern soaps, candles and glycerin. Ed. 3, New York, D. Van Nostrand company, 1918. 688p.

Depreciation

See Depreciation, depletion and obsolescence—Candles.

CANDY.

See Confectionery.

CANDY manufacturers' accounts. Shenton, W. A.

CANE SUGAR.

See Sugar.

CANE sugar industry. United States. Bureau of foreign and domestic commerce. 1917.

CANNING AND PRESERVING

UNITED STATES. Federal trade commission. Report on canned foods, canned salmon. Washington, Government printing office, 1919. 83p.

UNITED STATES. Federal trade commission. Report on canned foods, general report and canned vegetables and fruits. Washington, Government printing office, 1918. 103p.

Accounting

BARTH, RAYMOND E. Accounting for food preserving companies. *Journal of accountancy,* Feb. 1920, p. 91-7.

MINER, E. J. Salmon industry accounting. *Journal of accountancy,* Nov. 1916, p. 361-78.

NATIONAL CANNERS ASSOCIATION. Classification of accounts, classification B for canners who manufacture one line of canned goods at one factory only. Washington, National canners association, 1917. 33p. (Special bulletin no. 2).

NATIONAL CANNERS ASSOCIATION. Classification of accounts for canners who manufacture two or more lines of canned goods or operate two or more factories, classification A. Washington, National canners association, 1917. 58p. (Special bulletin no. 3).

Cost accounting

EGGLESTON, DEWITT CARL. Cost of manufac-

CANNING AND PRESERVING—COST ACCOUNTING—*(Continued)*

ture of 100 dozen cans of peas. (In his *Problems in cost accounting.* 1918. p. 185-7).

NATIONAL CANNERS ASSOCIATION. Cost accounting committee. Washington, National canners association, 1917. 11p. (*Special bulletin no.* 1).

Costs

UNITED STATES. Federal trade commission. Report on canned foods, canned salmon. Washington, Government printing office, 1919. 83p.

Depreciation.

See Depreciation, depletion and obsolescence—Canning and preserving.

CANNING industry accounting. Halloway, C. B.

CANNON, JAMES G.

Banker and the certified public accountant. Address. *Journal of accountancy,* Feb. 1909, p. 330-1. *Journal of accountancy,* Nov. 1908, p. 1-6.

Certified accountants have a big monopoly; from the *Journal of commerce and commercial bulletin,* Oct. 23, 1908. 10p.

Clearing houses. Wasihngton, Government printing office, 1910. 335p.

Uniform statement blanks and credit department. Address delivered Sept. 7, 1898. New York, J. S. Babcock, 1899. 17p.

CANS

Cost accounting

AMERICAN CAN COMPANY. Plan of cost accounting for general line factories. New York, 1909. 100p. (Private publication).

CANT you work this plan?; wage scale in the Hawaiian sugar industry. *Factory,* Jan. 1917, p. 54.

CANVAS

EVANS, HOLDEN A. Organization of canvas shop and flag shop. (In his *Cost keeping and scientific management.* 1911. p. 227-31).

CAPE Colony. *Journal of accountancy,* May, 1909, p. 44.

CAPITAL

See also Accounting; Dividends; Income; Profits.

BAUER, JOHN. Allowance for working capital in a rate case. *Political science quarterly,* Sept. 1916, p. 413-29.

BAUER, JOHN. Idea of capitalisation as applied to public service corporations. *Accountant,* Aug. 19, 1916, p. 155-8. *Journal of accountancy,* July 1916, p. 1-9.

BOAG, HAROLD. Business capital in excess profits duty computations. *Business organisation and management,* Sept.-Oct. 1920, p. 605-11, 91-6.

BRADLEY, F. E. Reduction of capital. *Accountant,* Feb. 22, 1913, p. 266-72.

CAPITAL. *Accountant.* July 26. 1890. p. 392-5.

CAPITAL and income, economic definitions and their utility. *Incorporated accountants' journal,* Sept. 1910. p. 275.

CAPITAL and income: effect of allocation by trustees. *Accountant,* Sept. 6, 1919, p. 201-2.

CAPITAL and income in company finance. *Accountants' magazine,* Nov. 1917, p. 417-20.

CAPITAL and profits. *Accountant,* Jan. 24, March 7, 1891, p. 65-7, 182-4.

CAPITAL reorganisation. *Accountant,* July 25, 1914, p. 105-8.

CAPITAL reorganisation. *Accountant,* Sept. 28, 1918, p. 157-9.

CAPITAL reorganisation schemes. *Accountant,* June 20, 27, 1914, p. 876-7, 908-10.

CAPITALISATION of reserves. *Accountant,* April 6, 1918, p. 280-1.

CAPITALIZATION on merger decision. *Gas age,* Dec. 1, 1917, p. 516.

CAPITALIZING construction expenditures. *Electrical review and western electrician,* April 28, 1917, p. 690.

CARTER, ROGER N. Capital and income. *Accountant,* Aug. 3, 10, 17, 24, 31, Sept. 7, 14, 1907, p. 135-8, 170-1, 199-200, 230-1, 270-2, 301, 330-1.

CARTER, ROGER N. Capital and revenue in commercial accounts. *Accountant,* Dec. 11, 1909, p. 719-27.

CARTER, ROGER N. Repairs, renewals and depreciation, and discrimination between capital and revenues expenditure. *Accountant,* March 7, 1908, p. 318-23.

CHARLESWORTH, ARTHUR. Some items included in capital expenditure accounts. *Accountant,* May 11, June 1, 1901, p. 560-5, 631-3.

CHRISTIE, J. R. Capital losses in relation to dividends. *Public accountant,* April 1918, p. 243-8.

COBBETT, PITT. Practice of underwriting capital *Incorporated accountants' journal,* 1889-90, p. 52.

COMMON errors in calculating the present worth, or capitalized value, of an annual gain. *Engineering and contracting,* Aug. 6, 1914, p. 121.

CURTIS, J. F. Priority board for capital: federal control for regulation of new security issues recommended. *Financial world,* Nov. 24, 1917, p. 23.

DAWE, WILLIAM H. Depreciation, capital expenditure and redemption of capital. *Accountant,* July 23, 1898, p. 735-43. *Business,* Nov. 1898, p. 677-88. *Incorporated accountants' journal,* 1897-8, p. 170.

DEFINITIONS of capital. *Accountant,* July 26, 1890. p. 393-5.

DEPRECIATION and capital expenditure in mining companies. *Incorporated accountants' journal,* 1897-8, p. 180.

DIRECTORS liability for declaring dividends out of capital. *Corporation journal,* Dec. 31, 1915, p. 94.

DIVIDENDS out of capital. *Accountant,* Aug. 2, 9, 1890, p. 407-8, 419-20.

DOUTHWAITE, WILLIAM. Loanable capital. *Accountant,* May 13, 1905, p. 600-6.

DUDBRIDGE, SIDNEY. Apportionments between capital and income. *Incorporated accountants' journal,* Jan. 1912, p. 104-7.

DUTIES and responsibilities of auditors. *Accountant,* Sept. 14, 1901, p. 990-5. *Incorporated accountants' journal,* 1901-2, p. 11.

FISHER, IRVING. Nature of capital and income. New York, The Macmillan co. 1912. 427p.

GOWER, WILLIAM B. Depreciation and depletion in relation to invested capital. *Journal of accountancy,* Nov. 1919, p. 353-68.

GRAVES, H. R. and others. Can the payment ever be correctly considered as capital expenditure? *Accountant,* Feb. 16, April 13, 1901, p. 223-6, 441-4.

GREELEY, HAROLD DUDLEY. Capital: determination of capital or deficit. (In his *Theory of accounts.* 1920. p. 28-37, 46-53).

GRIFFITHS, J. G. Issue of capital at a premium. *Accountant,* Oct. 8, 22, Nov. 12, 1910, p. 481-7, 545-7, 641-3.

GUTHRIE, EDWIN. Payment of interest on capital during construction of works *Accountant,* 1886, p. 98, 112.

HAMILTON, W. R. Rise and growth of modern industrial capital. *Accountant,* May 21, 1910, p. 723-34.

CAPITAL—*(Continued)*

HAYDON, THOMAS E. Capital and income as between tenant-for-life and remainderman. *Accountant,* May 2, July 4, 1908, p. 636-41, 6-8.

HILL, DANIEL. Apportionment of expenses as between capital and revenue. *Accountant,* Jan. 2, 1909, p. 27-30.

HOLLINS, G. F. Capital accounts. *Accountant,* Sept. 15, 1906, p. 298.

HOPSON, H. C. Construction records and accounts. *Journal of accountancy,* July 1917, p. 33-51.

HORNEMANN, G. A. Capital v. revenue. *Accountant,* Feb. 22, 1919, p. 143-7. *Accounting and commerce,* April-June, 1918, p. 17, 38-42, 62-3.

HOWES, EDWIN A. American law relating to income and principal. Boston, Little, Brown & co. 1905. 104p.

HUBBARD, HARRY. Supreme court on appreciation in value as an element in "invested capital." *Economic world,* Sept. 21, 1918, p. 413-4. *Wall street journal,* Sept. 18, 1918.

IMPROVEMENT out of capital. *Accountant,* Aug. 3, 1907, p. 156-7.

INVESTED capital is hopeless puzzle. *Iron trade review,* Nov. 8, 1917, p. 1012-3.

JACOBS, G. S. Rational basis for determining working capital. *Engineering news,* May 30, 1918, p. 1041-5.

JOHNSON, J. W. Capitalization of joint stock companies. *Canadian chartered accountant,* Jan. 1912, p. 100-5.

KERR, DAVID S. Over-capitalisation, watered stock and estimated profits. *Canadian chartered accountant,* Jan. 1914, p. 178-81.

KIRBY, FERD G. What's your invested capital? How to determine it for federal tax purposes. *Factory,* Dec. 1, 1920, p. 1741.

KNIGHT, F. H. Neglected factors in the problem of normal interest. *Quarterly journal of economics,* Feb. 1916, p. 279-310.

LAWRENCE, P. O. Capital of a company, with special reference to its reduction. *Accountant,* Jan. 21, 1893, p. 61-6.

LEAKE, P. D. Fixed and floating capital. (In his *Depreciation and wasting assets.* 1917. p. 12-22).

LEAKE, P. D. Misuse of the word "capital" in the construction of the income tax acts and the effect of this upon income tax assessments. *Accountant,* May 29, 1909, p. 768-73.

LIPMAN, FREDERICK L. Creating capital; money-making as an aim in business. Boston, Houghton, Mifflin company, 1918. 72p.

MACRAE, H. J. Amortisation of capital expenditure. *Incorporated accountants' journal,* 1906-7, p. 131. *South African accountants' journal,* vol. 1, p. 17.

MACDONALD, JAMES B. Capital and revenue accounts; their origin and nature; the genesis of the double account system. *Accountants' magazine,* Feb. 1907, p. 116-21. *South African accountants' journal,* v. 1, p. 57.

MACDONALD, JAMES B. Treatment of fixed and circulating capital in the accounts of joint-stock companies. *Accountants' magazine,* Feb. 1899, p. 97-107.

MANN, OLAF A. Working capital for rate-making purposes. *Journal of accountancy,* Nov. 1918, p. 340-2.

NEW British regulations prohibiting capital issues except by treasury license. *Official bulletin,* Feb. 26, 1919, p. 2.

NORTON, WILLIAM J. Working capital. *American institute of electrical engineers, Proceedings,* Sept. 1915, p. 2149-58. Discussion. Feb. 1916, p. 247-51.

PAYMENT of dividends out of capital. *Accountant,* March 10, 1888, v. 154-5.

PAYMENT of dividends out of capital. *Accountant,* April 23, 1910, v. 560-1.

PAYMENT of dividends out of capital. *Incorporated accountants' journal,* 1898-9, p. 71, 227.

PAYMENT of dividends out of capital: liability of directors. *Accountant,* March 30, 1901, p. 385-8.

PIXLEY, FRANCIS W. Duties of professional accountants in connection with invested capital both prior to and subsequent to the investment. *Federation of societies of public accountants in the United States of America. Official record of the Congress of accountants held at the World's fair, Saint Louis, September 26th, 27th and 28th, 1904.* p. 122-41. *New York accountants' and bookkeepers' journal,* Dec. 1904, p. 309-14.

"RATIONING of capital" in Sweden. *Americas,* Feb. 1919, p. 24.

REDUCTION of a company's capital. *Accountant,* Oct. 6, 1900, April 6-20, 1907, June 21, 1913, p. 867-70, 439-41, 470-3, 508-11, 925-8.

REDUCTION of a company's capital v. reconstruction. *Accountant,* Aug. 15, 1903, p. 1027-9.

REDUCTION of capital. *Accountant,* July 9, 1904, Sept. 25, 1909, June 1, 1912, June 21, 1913, p. 53-4, 365-7, 821-3, 925-8.

REDUCTION of capital and the powers of majorities. *Incorporated accountants' journal,* 1909-10, p. 251.

REVENUE measure examined; significance to lumber industry of two methods of determining invested capital. *American lumberman,* Nov. 16, 1918, p. 43.

ROBERTSON, JOHN B. Principal and income. *Journal of accountancy,* Sept. 1914, p. 235-8.

RUSK, STEPHEN G. Relation of invested capital to excess profits tax. *Journal of accountancy,* Oct. 1919, p. 273-85.

SAUNDERS, ALBERT F. Capital of a limited company. *Incorporated accountants' journal,* 1908-9, p. 126.

SCHMIDT, A. J. B. "Capital and income"—"capital and revenue." *Accounting and commerce,* July, Aug. 1916, p. 87-90, 113-4. *Journal of accountancy,* Oct. 1915, p. 283-90.

SEAMAN, A. M. Capital of a company limited by shares. *Accounting and commerce,* Dec. 1915, Jan. 1916, p. 202-4, 224-6.

SMITH, HOWARD S. Capital and profits of companies. *Accountant,* Jan. 4, 1890, p. 7-12.

SMITH, WILLIAM C. Dividends and capital. *Accountant,* July 11, 18, 1903, p. 900-6, 933-8. *Accountants' magazine,* Jan. 1902, p. 12-36.

SNOWDEN, ERNEST. What is working capital? *Canadian chartered accountant,* Jan. 1913, p. 177-9. *Incorporated accountants' journal,* March 1913, p. 137-8.

SPICER, E. E. Exportation of British capital. London, Gee & co. 1912. 27p. *Accountant,* March 16, 1912, p. 432-40.

STRACHAN, WILLIAM. Differentiation of capital and income. *Accountant,* Aug. 30, 1902, p. 861-4.

STRACHAN, WILLIAM. Economic and legal differentiation of capital and income. *Accountant,* Feb. 26, 1910, p. 316-8.

STRACHAN, WILLIAM. Return of a company's capital to its shareholders. *Accountant,* Sept. 17, 1910, p. 379-82.

TERRELL, A. àBECKET. Principles which should govern the division of profits and the raising of new capital in partnerships and companies. *Incorporated accountants' journal,* 1889-90, p. 48.

UNCALLED capital. *Accountant,* Sept. 3, 1910, p. 299-302.

WALKER, GEORGE L. Capital: a popular discussion of savings, profits and rights of property ownership from a new viewpoint. Boston, Dukelow & Walker co. c1914. 64p.

CAPITAL—*(Continued)*

WALTON, SEYMOUR. Capital. *Journal of accountancy,* Oct. 1914, p. 319-21.
WALTON, SEYMOUR. Capitalization of income. *Journal of accountancy,* April 1917, p. 306-8.
WALTON, SEYMOUR. Capitalizing extraordinary expenses. *Journal of accountancy.* Aug. 1915. p. 151-2.
WALTON, SEYMOUR. Distinction between net asset and net capital. *Journal of accountancy,* Oct. 1914, p. 319-21.
WALTON, SEYMOUR. Joint venture. *Journal of accountancy.* Feb. 1917. p. 150-1.
WALTON, SEYMOUR. Last word on capital as a liability. *Journal of accountancy,* Dec. 1914, p. 477-9.
WALTON, SEYMOUR. Padding invested capital. *Journal of accountancy,* April 1920, p. 308-9.
WALTON, SEYMOUR. Principal and income. *Journal of accountancy.* May 1914. p. 390-5.
WEISS, W. F. Principal and income. *Journal of accountancy,* May 1914, p. 395-8.
WEISS, WILLIAM F. Principal and income and some court decisions thereon of interest to the accountancy profession and discussion thereon at the January monthly meeting of the New York state society of certified public accountants, January 17, 1907. 47p. *Journal of accountancy,* July-Sept. 1907, p. 167-84, 247-60, 350-62.
WELCH, L. J. S. Differential treatment of capital accounts. *Accountant,* Oct. 4, 1913, p. 447-51.
WHAT is capital? *Accountant,* Dec. 18, 1915, Jan. 15-29, 1916, p. 729-32, 652-62; 82-8, 117-24, 142-5.
WHAT is capital? *Accountant,* June 26, 1920, p. 734.

CAPITAL. *Accountant,* July 26, 1890, p. 392-5.

CAPITAL accounts of a municipality. Fernald, H. B.

CAPITAL and "income"—"capital and revenue." Schmidt, A. J. B.

CAPITAL and income economic definitions and their utility. *Incorporated accountants' journal,* Sept. 1910, p. 275.

CAPITAL and income: effect of allocation by trustees. *Accountant,* Sept. 6, 1919. p. 201-2.

CAPITAL and income in company finance. *Accountants' magazine,* Nov. 1917, p. 417-20.

CAPITAL and profits. *Accountant,* Jan. 24 March 7, 1891, p. 65-7, 182-4.

CAPITAL losses and the companies act, 1900. *Accountant,* May 28, June 4, 18, 1904, p 706-8, 737-40, 798-9.

CAPITAL percentages. *Accountant,* Nov. 8, 1919, p. 391-2.

CAPITAL reorganisation. *Accountant,* July 25 1914, p. 105-8.

CAPITAL reorganization. *Accountant,* Sept. 28, 1918, p. 157-9.

CAPITAL reorganisation schemes. *Accountant,* June 20, 27, 1914, p. 876-7, 908-10.

CAPITAL STOCK
See Stock—Capital.

CAPITAL stock of no par value. Hurdman, Frederick H.

CAPITAL stock premiums. Rowe, C. V.

CAPITAL value of a tramway. *Tramway and railway world,* Nov. 9, 1911.

CAPITALISATION of a company's reserve funds. *Australasian accountant and secretary,* Jan. 1, 1920, p. 11-2.

CAPITALISATION of reserves. *Accountant,* April 6, 1918, p. 280-1.

CAPITALISED losses and goodwill. *Accountant,* June 13, 1914, p. 845-7.

CAPITALIZATION on merger decision. *Gas age,* Dec. 1, 1917, p. 516.

CAPITALIZATION of franchises. *Journal of accountancy,* June 1907, p. 138-9.

CAPITALIZING construction expenditures. *Electrical review and western electrician,* April 28, 1917, p. 690.

CAPITALIZING new business expense. *Electrical world,* Sept. 2, 1911, p. 529.

CAPORN, ARTHUR C.

Law of bailments as affecting accountants. *Incorpoarted accountants' journal,* May 1913, p. 192-6.
LAW of contracts, Dec. 7, 1912, p. 720-8.

CAPORN, FRANCIS M.

Deeds: their origin and use in commercial life. *Accountant,* Oct. 7, 1916, p. 307-13. *Incorporated accountants journal,* Sept. 1916, p. 279-83.

CAR depreciation. *Electric railway journal,* June 16, 1917, p. 1080.

CAR record and trouble board combined. *Electric railway journal,* Oct. 23, 1915, p. 878.

CAR record joins master sheet. *Motor age,* Sept. 18, 1919, p. 20-1.

CAR SHOPS
See Railroads.

CAR WHEELS

Accounting

FOWLER, G. L. Car wheel foundry practice—Canadian pacific railway co. *Railway age gazette,* Oct. 7, 1910, p. 645-55.

CARD, F. S.

Cold storage record for the poultry business. *Business man's magazine,* June 1908, p. 524.
Voucher system for the fish business. *Business man's magazine,* Nov. 1908, p. 383-4.

CARD, F. W.

Farm management, including business accounts suggestions for watching markets, time to market various products, adaptation to local conditions, etc. New York, Doubleday, Page & co. 1912. 270p.

CARD, G. F.

Efficiency hints for shop workers; slide chart for rate setting. *American machinist,* Sept. 26, 1918, p. 573-4.

CARD and loose leaf ledgers. *Accountant,* Oct. 15, 1904, p. 377-9.

CARD index increases efficiency of new business department. *Electric review and western electrician,* May 15, 1915, p. 899-900.

CARD index record and filing systems for engineers and contractors. New York, Engineering news, 1906. 25c.

CARD index system of cost keeping. *American machinist,* Sept. 15, 1898.

CARD record in selling accessories. *Horseless age,* Feb. 17, 1915, p. 229-30.

CARD record tracing system. *American lumberman,* March 23, 1918, p. 31.

CARD system for obtaining life record of gas-filled lamps. *Electrical world,* May 15, 1915, p. 1240.

CARD system for stock recording. *Mechanical world,* January 8, 1915.

CARD system for the newsdealer. *Business man's magazine,* Aug. 1911, p. 157.

CARD SYSTEMS
See Bookkeeping—Card and loose leaf.

CARDBOARD. See Paper, cardboard, etc.

CARDIFF tramways finance. *Electrical engineer,* Dec. 24, 1909, p. 879.

CARDULLO, FOREST E.
Bookkeeping of manufacturing costs; elements of the cost of material, etc. *Iron age,* June 4, 1914, p. 1440-2. *Metal work,* June 19, 1914, p. 820-2.
CAPITAL costs in a manufactuirng business. *Iron age,* May 21, 1914, p. 1278-80. *Metal work,* June 5, 1914, p. 745-7.
DEPRECIATION of factory equipment. *Iron age,* May 14, 1914, p. 1236-7. *Metal work,* May 29, 1914, p. 715-6.
ECONOMICS of a manufacturing business. *Iron age,* May 7, 1914, p. 1172-3. *Metal work,* May 22, 1914, p. 684-5.
INDUSTRIAL betterment. *Machinery,* Nov. 1915, p. 183-4.
LABOR and other costs in manufacturing. *Iron age,* May 28, 1914, p. 1365-7. *Metal work,* June 12, 1914, p. 775-7.

CARE of cash by agents and conductors. Kirkman, Marshall Monroe.

CARE of estates. Hill, F. T. 1901.

CAREERS for women. *Canadian chartered accountant,* Jan. 1916, p. 194-8.

CAREY, A.
Car department organization and efficiency. *Railway age* (Mech. ed.), May 1914, p. 235-6.

CAREY, D.
Overhead cost in contracting. *Engineering and contracting,* Oct. 22, 1919, p. 463-5.
What you should know about overhead expense. *Domestic engineering,* August 2, 1919, p. 204-5. *Metal work,* August 15, 1919, p. 196-8. Condensed. *Engineering and contracting,* Oct. 22, 1919, p. 463-5.

CARGILL, ALEXANDER.
Savings banks. (In Lisle, George. *Encyclopaedia of accounting.* v. 6, p. 31-6).

CARING for depreciation. Saliers, E. A.

CARING for the stock. *Journal of electricity.* Dec. 1, 1919, p. 503-5.

CARINGTON, C. What is a manufacturing cost? *Iron age,* Jan. 11, 1905.

CARISS, ASTRUP
Double entry bookkeeping. London, Effingham Wilson, 1884.
On arbitration; and on forms of balance sheets. *Accountant,* April 14, 1883.

CARISS, T. H.
Marine insurance. *Australasian accountant and secretary,* Nov., Dec. 1919, p. 20-3, 23-7.

CARLETON, F. H.
This method makes pay roll records easy to handle. *Business man's magazine,* Oct. 1908, p. 338-9.

CARLILL, JOHN ALBERT
Ante-audit; being the auditor's instructions to the employer's bookkeeping staff. London, Gee & co. 1900.
Example of Sir Kenneth. *Accountant,* Feb. 1, 8, 1913, p. 136-9, 169-71.
How to prepare for chartered accountant examinations. London, Gee & co. 1908. 23p. *Accountant,* March 31, 1900, p. 311-8.
Principles of bookkeeping, London, Gee & co. 1896. 106p.

CARLISLE, CHARLES A.
Keeping books on the farm. *Leslie's weekly,* Nov. 21, 1912, p. 530, 537.

CARLISLE, F. A.
Removing the distrust of piece work. *Engineering and contracting,* May 21, 1919, p. 555.

CARLISLE, J. N.
ORGANIZATION of a state highway department with discussion. *Good roads,* February 6, 1915, 53-5.
Sub-organization for securing efficient maintenance with discussion. *Good roads,* February 7, 1914, 109-15.

CARLOCK, FLOYD D.
Manual for post exchanges. Menasha, Wis., George Banta publishing co. c1917. 193p.

CARLSON, JOHN C.
Accountancy education in Pennsylvania. *Journal of accountancy,* Jan. 1907, p. 195-7.

CARMAN, E. C.
Defects of physical valuation of railways as a basis for rate making. *Case & comment,* April 1917, p. 880-5.

CARMENT, D. M.
Suretyship insurance. (In Lisle, George. *Encyclopaedia of accounting.* v.6. p. 191-204).

CARMICHAEL, A. W.
Shipbuilding for beginners. Washington, Industrial source department, Emergency fleet corporation, 1918. 25p.

CARMICHAEL, R.
County council accounts. *Accountant,* Jan. 21, 1893, p. 68-74.

CARMONT, JOHN
Responsibility of trustees. *Accountants' magazine,* June 1910, p. 307-14.

CARNAHAN, THOMAS S.
Underground mining methods of Utah copper co. *Bulletin of the American institute of mining engineers,* Jan. 1916, p. 60-3. Condensed. *Engineering and mining journal,* Jan. 29, 1916, p. 218-9.

CARNEGIE, ANDREW.
Worst banking system in the world. *Journal of accountancy,* March 1908, p. 357.

CARNEGIE, DAVID AND SIDNEY C. GLADWYN.
Liquid steel, its manufacture and cost. Ed. 2. New York, Longmans, Greene and co. 1918. 526p.

CARNEGIE FOUNDATION FOR THE ADVANCEMENT OF TEACHING.
Standard forms for financial reports of colleges, universities and technical schools. N. Y., 1910, 37p. (Carnegie foundation for the advance of teaching. Bulletin no. 3).

CARNESS, A. J.
Manual on opening and closing the books of joint stock companies. Ed. 3. Baltimore, 1891.

CAROLINA PUBLIC SERVICE COMMISSION
Classification of accounts. Atlanta, Ga., La Hatte printing company, 1913. 46p.

CARPENTER, A. E.
Trade union accounting. *Journal of accountancy,* Dec. 1913, p. 440-2.

CARPENTER, C. A.
Cost methods of jobbing shops. *Industrial management,* Sept. 1917. p. 888-95.

CARPENTER, C. V.
Cost of operating a Ford car in county road supervision. *Engineering and contracting,* May 3, 1916, p. 414.

CARPENTER, CHARLES U.
Profit making in shop and factory management. New York. Engineering magazine, 1908. 146p. (Works management library).
Stimulating production by wage, stock and cost systems. *Engineering magazine,* Sept. 1907, p. 931-41.

CARPENTER, HARRY J.
See Wilson, R. P., joint author.

CARPENTER, I.
Most excellent instruction for the . . keeping merchants books of accounts by way of debtor and creditor. London, 1632.

CARPENTER, J. A.
Effect of the war upon Tonopah mining. *Engineering and mining journal,* Oct. 5, 1918, p. 601-4.

CARPENTER, J. D.
See Gannett, F., joint author.

CARPENTER, J. T.
Simplest form of voucher system. *System,* 1904, v.6, no. 6, p. 565-8.

CARPENTER, JAMES S.
Contracts by trustees. *Incorporated accountants' journal,* 1907-8, p. 244.
Method of squaring mixed numbers and extracting square roots. *Power,* June 18, 1918, p. 872.

CARPENTER SHOPS
Accounting.
Soulé, George. Carpentry business. (In his *New science and practice of accounts.* 1903. p. 295-300).
Cost accounting.
Honecker, Charles A. Valuable suggestions on a shop accounting system. *Business man's magazine,* Dec. 1907, p. 95-104.
Kent, William. Carpenter, pattern, and paint shop. (In his *Bookkeeping and cost accounting for factories,* 1918, p. 70-1).
Depreciation
See. Depreciation, depletion and obsolescence—Carpenter shops.

CARPETS, RUGS, ETC.
Accounting
Eldridge, William J. On the tapis. *Business man's magazine,* Sept. 1906, p. 79-86.

CARR, EBENEZER
Duties and responsibilities of auditors. *Accountant,* Sept. 14, 1901, p. 990-7. *Commerce, accounts and finance,* March 1902, p. 11-5. *Incorporated accountants journal,* 1901-2, p. 11.
Investors' book-keeping; with examples and full explanations of a simple and efficient system of accounts upon double entry principle and "How to check your stockbrokers' account," by an accountant. London, Effingham Wilson, 1913. 15+36p.
Method as relating to accounting and auditing. *Incorporated accountants journal,* 1905-6, p. 69.

CARR, G. A. BUXTON
Disclaimers in bankruptcy. *Incorporated accountants' journal,* 1902-3, p. 83.
Law of bills of sale. *Incorporated accountants' journal,* 1895-6, p. 46.

CARR, JOHN E.
Systems used in office and factory. *System* Sept. 1903, p. 203-8.

CARR, O. O.
Failures and costs. *Railway review,* March 15, 1919, p. 399-400.

CARRIER, W. H.
See Busey, F. L., joint author.

CARRIER'S brief on federal valuation of the railroads. *Railway review,* Jan. 29, 1916, p. 167-9.

CARRIERS' general suggestions for railroad valuation. *Engineering record,* Sept. 20, 1913, p. 327.

CARRIERS present evidence in rate case. testimony of railway executives. *Railway age,* May 11, 18, 1917, p. 989-97, 1045-9.

CARRIERS submit new plans for adjustment of transcontinental freight rates. *Railway age,* April 9, 1915, p. 785-6.

CARRIERS suggest rates to meet the wage increases. *Railway age,* July 30, 1920, p. 183-4. *Railway review,* July 31, 1920, p. 160-1.

CARRIGAN, C. W.
Cutting operating expenses by knowing costs. *System on the farm,* April 1918, p. 125-8.

CARRINGTON, J. B.
General stores and cost accounts of a municipal body. *Incorporated accountants' journal,* 1908-9, p. 83
Sinking funds. *Incorporated accountants' journal,* June 1914, p. 271-6.

CARROLL, A. W.
Electrically operated contractor's plant for building Kensico dam. *Engineering record,* Jan. 2, 1915, p. 18-20.

CARROLL, HARRY W.
Municipal accounting and its relationship to government. *American institute of accountants, Yearbook,* 1915. p. 110-21. *Journal of accountancy,* Oct. 1915, p. 260-70,

CARROLL, J. B.

Wage payment slide rule. *American machinist,* Feb. 28, 1918, p. 375-6.

CARROLL, J. E.

Methods and results of cost recording on pavement work at St. Paul, Minn. *Engineering and contracting,* Dec. 8, 1915, p. 441-4.

CARROLL, WILLIAM F.

Cost keeping in the leather belting industry. Philadelphia, Leather belting exchange, 1916. 29p.

CARRUTH, CHESTER B. AND H. I. JACOBSON

Cost finding for warehousemen. *Bulletin of the American warehousemen's association,* Nov. 1920, p. 335-42.

CARRUTH, E. K.

Card system of household accounting. *Journal of home economics,* Jan. 1920, p. 37-9.

CARRYING on with the accountants in the American expeditionary forces. Halloway, C. B.

CARSE, JAMES A.

Address, 1895. *Accountant,* Oct. 26, 1895, p. 852-8.

Companies acts. *Accountant,* March 31, April 7, 1883.

Sinking funds in relation to corporation accounts. *Accountant,* Oct. 25, 1890, p. 583.

CARSON, G. E.

Repairing steel cars. *Railway age gazette,* June 12, 1908, p. 59-60.

CARTER, ———

Cost sheets for collieries, iron works, &c. London, Simpkins, Marshall and co. 1890.

CARTER (MISS).

Principles of free trade. *Accounting and commerce,* Nov. 1918, p. 178-80.

CARTER, CHARLES ALBERT

Some criminal offences relating to accounts. *Accountant,* Dec. 17, 1892, p. 970-6.

CARTER, EDWARD

Address, 1882. *Accountant,* Oct. 14, 21, 1882.

CARTER, EDWARD HAROLD

How to open a set of books. Birmingham, 1883. *Accountant,* Nov. 3, 10, 17, 24, 1883.

CARTER, ERIC MACKAY

Books of tables and their use: a paper. *Accountant,* June 20, 1885.

Criticism of the opinions of some chartered accountants on the routine work of an audit. *Accountant,* Jan. 6, 1894, p. 13-22.

Income tax reform, particularly in regard to profits and wasting assets. *Accountant,* Dec. 31, 1904, p. 799-808.

Outlook of accountancy. *Accountant,* April 28, June 9, 1906, p. 530-6, 717-21.

What is an annual balance sheet. *Accountant,* Oct. 22, 1910, p. 560-6.

CARTER, F. HAYNE

Practical bookkeeping, adapted to commercial and judicial accounting, with sets of books and forms of accounts. Ed. 2. Edinburgh, Simpkin, Marshall, Hamilton, Kent & co.

——— Same. Ed. 4. Edinburgh, Simpkin, Marshall, Hamilton, Kent & co. 1878.

——— Same. Ed. 5. London, Simpkin, Marshall, Hamilton, Kent & co. 1886.

——— Same. Ed. 5, revised and corrected. Edinburgh, John Menzies & co. 1885. 241p

——— Same. Ed. 6. London, Simpkin, Marshall, Hamilton, Kent & co. 1890.

Study to determine the most economical motive power for pumping sewage at Lynn, Mass. *Engineering and contracting,* Jan. 7, 1914, p. 14-7.

CARTER, H. K. AND C. A. PORTER

Bookkeeping for small hospitals and allied institutions. *Modern hospital,* March-May, 1918, p. 182-9, 254-60, 341-4.

CARTER, HERBERT K.

See Porter, Charles A., joint author.

CARTER, PHILIP H

Some points in connection with estate accounts. *Accountant,* Jan. 20, 1900, p. 75-80, 345.

Tramway audits. *Accountant,* July 26, 1890, p. 401-4.

CARTER, ROGER NEAL

Advanced accounts: a manual of advanced bookkeeping and accountancy for accountants, bookkeepers and business men. London, Sir Isaac Pitman and sons. 980p.

Appeals for repayment of income tax. *Accountant,* March 29, 1902, p. 341-7.

Capital and income. *Accountant,* Aug. 3, Sept. 14, 1907, p. 135-8, 170-1, 199-200, 230-1, 270-2, 301, 330-1.

Capital and revenue in commercial accounts. *Accountant,* Dec. 11, 1909, p. 719-27.

Executorship accounts. *Incorporated accountants' journal,* 1908-9, p. 172.

Hints to accountancy examinees, with special reference to the accountancy subjects. (In Feather, J. Stuart, ed. *Joint transactions.* 1911, p. 239-67). *Accountant,* Nov. 25, 1911, p. 727-36. *Incorporated accountants' journal,* Dec. 1911, p. 71-8.

Income tax. *Accountant,* March 1, 1902, p. 233-8.

Income tax and super tax. *Accountant,* July 2, 1910, p. 34-5.

Income tax as affecting insurance companies. *Accountant,* April 23, 1904, p. 525-35.

Income tax—some practical points. *Accountant,* Nov. 7, 1903, p 1375-82.

Income tax, with special reference to changes and successions. *Accountant,* April 1, 1911, p. 532-6.

Income tax, with special reference to recent legislation. *Accountant,* Dec. 21, 1907, p. 769-75.

Institute examinations. *Accountant,* March 4, 11, 1911, p. 346-50, 395-403.

Institute examinations: some hints to students. *Accountant,* Nov. 23, 30, Dec. 7, 14, 1907, p. 645-56, 673-4, 697-8, 731-2.

Is it desirable that further legal recognition should be given to the Institute of chartered accountants, and if so what form should it take? *Accountant,* April 14, 1894, p. 338-40.

Notes on the evidence taken by the select committee on income tax, 1906. *Accountant,* Feb. 23, March 2, 1907, p. 240-2, 275-80.

Notes on the report of the departmental committee on income tax. *Accountant,* Dec. 16, 1905, p. 706-13.

Notes on the report of the select committee on income tax. *Accountant,* Dec. 15, 1906, p. 726.

Preparation of profit and loss accounts for income tax purposes. *Accountant,* March 25, 1899, p. 341-8.

Repairs, renewals and depreciation, and discrimination between capital and revenue expenditure. *Accountant,* March 7, 1908, p. 318-23.

CARTER, ROGER NEAL—*(Continued)*
Simplex guide to income tax; its assessment and repayment. 1908.
Some hints to students, with special reference to executorship accounts. *Accountant*, Jan. 16, 1909, p. 82-5.
Some notes on executorship accounts. *Accountant*, Feb. 24, 1900, p. 209-12.
Some notes on income tax. *Accountant*, Nov. 10, 1906, p. 581-6.
Some practical income tax difficulties. *Accountant*, Jan. 1, 1910, p. 16. *Incorporated accountants' journal*, 1909-10, p. 132.
Some suggested changes in income tax law and practice. *Accountant*, Dec. 13, 1902, p. 1308-17.
Student's guide to executorship. Ed. 2. London, Gee & co. 1912. 240p.

CARTER oil company gives workers voice in establishing working conditions. *National petroleum news*, March 10, 1920, p. 49.

CARTHAGE, PHILIP I.
Retail organization and accounting control. New York, D. Appleton and company, 1920. 349p.
See also Murray, Adam, joint author.

CARTING
See Transfer companies.

CARTWRIGHT, H. H.
Land computations for railway valuation. *Engineering news*, June 27, 1918, p. 1232.

CARTWRIGHT, O. G.
County budgets and their construction. *Annals of the American society of political and social science*, Nov. 1915, p. 113-276.

CARUSI, CHARLES F.
Government contracts: before the accounting officers and in the U. S. court court of claims. *Government accountant*, Aug.-Dec. 1910, p. 145-57, 193-204, 242-51, 306-15, 352-60.

CARVER, H. E.
Continuous inventories: their preparation and value. *American institute of electrical engineers, Proceedings*, Nov. 1916, p. 1545-7. Condensed. *Electric railway journal*, Nov. 18, 1916, p. 1053-4.

CARVER, W. S.
Municipal trading. *Incorporated accountants' journal*, 1902-3, p. 252.
Taxation of land values in relation to local rating. *Accountant*, July 1, 1911, p. 15-20. *Incorporated accountants' journal*, 1910-11, p. 285.

CARY, R. H.
Elementary bookkeeping by single entry for evening continuation schools and day schools: key. 2v. London, Simpkin, Marshall, Hamilton, Kent & co. 1898. 130p.
Foreign banking. (In Lisle, George. *Encyclopaedia of accounting*. v. 3. p. 53-88).
Society of arts' bookkeeping; 16 papers set at the society's examinations, during 1886-99; notes and glossary of commercial terms. London, Simpkin, Marshal, Hamilton, Kent & co. 1899. 108p.
Up-to-date examples in bookkeeping. 2v. Boston and London. 1901.

CARY, S.
How my men help me manage. *Factory*, May 1919, p. 917-8.

CASE, CHARLES H.
Standard system of cost accounting adapted to the paper and pulp industry. New York, 1914. 29p

CASE, HIRAM C. COMP.
Handbook of instructions for recording disbursements for school purposes. Albany C. F. Williams & son, 1916. 25p.

CASE against speculation. *Journal of accountancy*, May 1908, p. 57-61.

CASE for higher rates. *Commercial and financial chronicle*, May 17, 1913, p. 1393-4.

CASEY, CHARLES C.
Economy of knowing. *Country life*, Sept. 15, 1911, p. 36.

CASEY, W. E. AND E. WEBER.
Bonus system reduces coal consumption at Denver. *Electric railway journal*, Feb. 8, 1919, p. 266-71. *Engineering and contracting*, May 14, 1919, p. 526-8.

CASH, B. K.
Comparative costs of gas and electricity for illuminating purposes. *American gas light journal*, March 15, 1915, p. 167.

CASH, W.
Gas accounts and finance, with a sketch of the history of the industry. *Accountant*, Oct. 18, 1913, p. 543-55.
Gas companies' accounts. *Accountant*, June 4, July 9, 1904, p. 749-56; 30-2.
Municipal accounts. *Accountant*, Dec. 11, 1920, p. 639-43.

CASH
See also Accounting.
BANK columns in cash books. *Accountant*, June 20, 1885.
BENNETT, GEORGE E. General cash records; petty cash records; miscellaneous cash records. (In his *Constructive accounting*. 1902. p. 89-230).
CASTLEDINE, W. Comprehensive cash book; plain and concise bookkeeping. London, 1902.
DETAIL cash book and journal. *Commerce, accounts and finance*, April 1902, p. 12-4.
DRAUGHON, W. H. How to safeguard the cash accounts. *Business man's magazine*, Aug. 1911, p. 141-3.
GRANT, J. A. Cash book; its purpose, character, and need of exhaustive verification by the auditor. *Accountant*, Aug. 12, 1916, p. 134-9. *Canadian chartered accountant*, April 1916, p. 252-63.
GREELEY, HAROLD DUDLEY. Statement of cash receipts and payments; the cash book; miscellaneous cash matters; illustrative cash book entries. (In his *Theory of accounts*. p. 104-15, 188-97, 215-31, 284-93).
HANDLING the incoming cash. *Business man's magazine*, Oct. 1907, p. 85-7.
HUNTER, JOEL. Petty cash system. (In his *Thinking in figures*. c1916. p. 123-4.
LAYMAN, A. A B C of a cash book; a first guide to cash bookkeeping, told in story form, simply illus. for children and beginners. New York, Simpkin, Marshall, Hamilton, Kent & co. 1916. 64p.
LISLE, GEORGE. Cash book. (In his *Encyclopaedia of accounting*. v.2, p. 19-32).
NEFF, A. C. Old and new methods of keeping the cash and bank accounts. *Accountant*, Jan. 28, 1899, p. 117-20.
PEABODY, LORENZO J. Road to independence and wealth; cont. novel system of petty cash accounting. Boston, L. J. Peabody, 1899.
RISQUE, F. W. Loose leaf covers for cash books aid bookkeepers. *Business man's magazine*, Nov. 1907, p. 114-18.

CASH—*(Continued)*
Saliers, Earl A. Accounting for petty cash payments. (In his *Accounts in theory and practice: principles*. 1920. p. 114-8).
Sutliff, L. S. Combination voucher record and cash book. *Business man's magazine*, Jan. 1906
Walton, Seymour. Imprest system. *Journal of accountancy*, July 1914, p. 66-7.

Discounts
See Discounts—Cash.

CASH book bookkeeping. Council of education. National society, 1867.

CASH book system. *Railway age gazette*, Oct. 3, 1913, p. 606.

CASH books. Lisle, George.

CASH discount ratios. *Dry goods economist*, Aug. 23, 1913.

CASH DISCOUNTS
See Discounts—Cash.

CASH discounts. *Accountant*, Sept. 27, 1890, p. 503-4.

CASH discounts. Conen, A. J.

CASH discounts. Schackman, J. H.

CASH discounts. Wellington, C. O.

CASH REGISTERS

Cost accounting
Cost system of the National cash register company. *Business world*, July 1902, p. 312-7.
Schaeffer, J. J. and William S. Brown. Manufacturing costs; the National cash register company system. *Business*, March 1900, p. 155-6.

CASH statement including bank balances. *Business man's magazine*, June 1911, p. 581.

CASSELL, F.
Debentures of trading companies; report of paper the Law Times. *Accountant*, Feb. 9, 1907. p. 197.

CASSELL, RALPH JOSEPH.
Art of collecting; a statement of the underlying principles and practices of collecting, with suggestions, form of reports, letters, etc., etc., for the collection manager and business man. New York, The Ronald press co. 1916. 261p.

CASSELL'S new French dictionary, French-English and English-French. New York, Funk & Wagnalls co. c1903. 616p.

CASSON, WILLIAM A.
Local authorities' accounts and their audit (England). (In Lisle, George. *Encyclopaedia of accounting*. v.4. p. 180-23.)

CAST-IRON pipe prices, 1900-1919; Philadelphia. *Iron age*, Jan. 1920, p. 55-9.

CASTENHOLZ, WILLIAM B.
Accounting procedure for state universities. *Journal of accountancy*, Feb., March 1916, p. 81-92, 167-75.
Auditing procedure. Chicago, La Salle extension university. 1918. 342p
Is interest on invested capital a cost? *Journal of accountancy*, April 1918, p. 248-54.
See also Morey, Lloyd, joint author.

CASTING-COUNTER and the counting board. Barnard, F. P. 1917.

CASTING of clay works. McDougal, T. G. 1916.

CASTINGS
See Foundries.

CASTLE, HENRY A.
Defects in the accounting systems of the United States Post office department. *Business man's magazine*, 1904, v. 17, p. 1109-20.
Our system of postal accounts. *Business man's magazine*, 1904, v. 16, no. 12, p. 43-9.
Castle, W. H. Single entry bookkeeping. *Accountant*, June 26, 1920, p. 735-8.

CASTLE, W. H.
Single entry bookkeeping. *Accountant*, June 26, 1920, p. 735-8.

CASTLEDINE, W.
Comprehensive cash book.

CASTOR OIL
Shrader, J. H. Castor-oil industry. Washington, Government printing office, 1920. 40p. (United States. Department of agriculture, Bulletin no. 867).

CASWELL, G. L.
Study of costs on small newspapers. *Inland printer*, March 1920, p. 723-5.
Use care in bookkeeping. *Inland printer*, June 1918, p. 369-70.

CASWELL, WILLIAM W.
Value of cost accounting in commercial laboratories. 6p. *Journal of industrial and engineering chemistry*, Jan. 1920, p. 79-81.

CATALOGUE accounting library. American telephone and telegraph co. 1914.

CATALOGUE of accountancy libraries at recitation rooms of the School of commerce, accounts and finance. Accountancy library association, 1910.

CATALOGUES
See Bibliographies, indexes, catalogues, etc.

CATCHING the discounts. *System*, Sept. 1917, p. 420.

CATHCART, CHARLES S
Commercial feeding stuffs and registrations for 1917. New Brunswick, 1917. 100p. (New Jersey. Agricultural experiment stations, Bulletin 311).

CATHLES, A.
Business organisation. *Accountant*, Nov. 20, 1920, p. 552-9.
General principles of costing. *Accountant*, Feb. 28, 1920, p. 249-56.

CATHLES, JOHN
Glimpse at the internal organisation of a railway company. *Accountants' magazine*, May 1899, p. 294-312.

CATION, J. G.
Start teaching accounts. *Industrial arts magazine*, March 1920, p. 122-3.

CATON, M. J.
Counting house book-keeping. Syracuse, C. W. Bardeen, 1905.

CATTLE
See Livestock.

CATTLE industry. *American institute of accountants, Special bulletin*, No. 3, May 1920, p. 3-7.

CAUSES, methods and prevention of bank defalcation. Moxey, E. P.

CAUSES of business failure. *Journal of accountancy*, Sept. 1914, p. 208-9.

CAUSES of increases in operating expenses. *Railway age*, August 9, 1918, p. 245-6.

CAVANAGH, HARRY L
Mail order accounting. *Journal of accountancy*, Dec. 1918, p. 436-440.

CAVELL, ARTHUR SILVESTER
Auditors and certificates as to stock. *Accountant*, April 26, May 31, 1902, p. 447-54, 562.

CAVERT, W. L.
When is farming profitable. *Breeder's gazette*, May 27, 1920, p. 1472.

CAWCROFT, ERNEST.
Widening sphere of clearing houses. *Business man's magazine*, July 1910, p. 35-40.

CAYLEY, ARTHUR
Principles of bookkeeping by double entry. New York, G. P. Putnam's sons.

CECIL, GEORGE
Accountant in India. *Accountant*, Sept. 21, 28, Oct. 12, 1901, p. 1027-8, 1040, 1095-6.
Anglo-Indian accountant: his social life. *Accountants' magazine*, 1903, p. 26.
Banking in India: the rate of interest allowed. *Accountants magazine*, 1904, p. 89.
"Bazaar" accountant. *Accountants' magazine*, Feb. 1910, p. 112-6.
Christmas amusements of the Anglo-Indian accountant. *Accountants magazine*, 1905, p. 29.
Hindu accountant: his work and play. *Accountants' magazine*, Aug. 1901, p. 430-8.
India: the Parsee accountant. *Accountants' magazine*, March 1901, p. 143-6.
Indian government accounts department. *Accountants' magazine*, Dec. 1912, p. 515-9.
Stockbroking in India. *Accountant*, Sept. 8, 15, 22, 1906, p. 279, 297-8, 337-8.

CELLULOID

Cost accounting
Nicholson, J. Lee and John F. D. Rohrbach. Rubber and celluloid manufacturing plants. (In their *Cost accounting*. 1919. p. 31).

CEMENT
Bowles, Oliver. Rock quarrying for cement manufacturer. Washington, Government printing office, 1918. 160p. (Bureau of mines bulletin 160, mineral technology 22). p. 100 Quarry costs. p. 101-5 Blasting records.
Brown, William Alden. Portland cement industry; a practical treatise on the building, equipping and economical running of a Portland cement plant with notes on physical testing. New York, D. Van Nostrand company, 1917. 158p.
Eckel, Edwin C. Portland cement industry from a financial standpoint. New York, Moody's magazine, 1908. 93p.
Meade, Richard K. Portland cement; its composition, raw materials, manufacture, testing and analysis. Ed.2. London, Williams & Norgate, c1911. 512p.
New York city. Commissioners of accounts. Report—comparison between physical tests and chemical analysis of 34 samples of Portland and Rosendale cements. New York, 1900.
United States. Department of commerce. Industrial standards no. 1. Standard specifications and tests for Portland cement. Washington, Government printing office, 1918.

Accounting
Bernheim, Oscar G. Accounting and manufacturing systems for a Portland cement business. *Business man's magazine*, 1904, p. 829-35.
Wilson, Gordon. Accounting for cement packages. *Journal of accountancy*, March 1915, p. 198-205.

Cost accounting
Association of Ameracan Portland cement manufacturers, Philadelphia. Cost accounting. Philadelphia, Association of American Portland cement manufacturers. 41p.
Brown, William Alden. Systematic cost keeping. (In his *Portland cement industry*. 1917. p 88-9).
Cornell, T. B. Cost accounting methods in the Portland cement manufacturing business. *Business man's magazine*, Feb. 1909, p. 163-5.
Eggleston, DeWitt Carl. Examination question, cost accounting in the Portland cement industry. (In his *Problems in cost accounting*. 1918. p. 321-7).
Stradley, Robert O. Timekeeping and payroll system in cement manufacturing plant. *Business man's magazine*, Aug. 1909, p. 180-3.

Costs
Brown, William Alden. Costs and statistics. (In his *Portland cement industry*. 1917. p. 82-108).
Meade, Richard K. Cost of plant and manufacture. (In his *Portland cement*. 1911. p. 247-51).

Depreciation
See Depreciation, depletion and obsolesence—Cement.

CEMENT SACKS.
Cost of cement sacks to the user. *Concrete*, April 1916, p. 181-2.
Cost of cement sacks to the user. *Concrete cement*, Nov. 1914, p. 212-3.
Downey, B. C. Reducing cost of handling cloth bags. *Concrete*, June 1916, p. 250.
Wilson, Gordon. Accounting for cement packages. *Journal of accountancy*, March 1915, p. 198-205.

CEMETERIES

Accounting
American business and accounting encyclopaedia; comp. by E. H. Beach and W. W. Thorne. Detroit, Bookkeeper publishing co. 1901. Cemetery accounting, p. 304.
Eggleston, D. Carl. Municipal cemetery accounts. *Journal of accountancy*, March 1913, p. 174-84.
Farnworth, Percy. Cemeteries and burial. (In Bateson, William, ed. *Pitman's municipal office organisation and management*. p. 278-84).
Robinson, Joseph. Theory and practise: correspondence. *Journal of accountancy*, Dec. 1918, p. 478
Walton, Seymour. Cemetery accounts. *Journal of accountancy*, Aug. 1914, p. 140-2.

CENSUS
Census machines. *The office*, Aug. 1890, p. 219.

CENSUS—*(Continued)*
HANDLING the census returns for the whole United States. *American machinist,* v. 33, no. 18.
SMITH, G. T. BISSET. Census. (In Lisle, George *Encyclopaedia of accounting.* v.2. p. 41-50).
WILLEY, D. A. Machinery of census taking. *Business man's magazine,* Aug. 1910, p. 172-7.

CENSUS machines. *The office,* Aug. 1890, p. 219.

CENSUS of dyes and coal tar chemicals. United States Tariff commission. 1919.

CENSUS of manufacturers, 1914. United States. Bureau of census. 1917.

CENTRAL ASSOCIATION OF ACCOUNTANTS
Final examination questions, December 1919. Central association of accountants. 15p.
Intermediate examination questions. December 1919. Central association of accountants. 10p.
Journal of accountancy and the Central association of accountants; supplement to the *Associated accountants' journal,* September 1908. 16p.
Licentiate examination, December 1909. *Accountant,* April 9, 1910, p. 512-3.
Prospectus, American centre. 2p.
Yearbook, annual.

CENTRAL association of accountants. *Journal of accountancy,* May-Sept., 1908, p. 66-7, 356.

CENTRAL banks issue. *Journal of accountancy,* Nov. 1909, p. 45-7.

CENTRAL electric railway accountants' association: proceedings at annual meeting, December 12-13, 1913. *Electric railway journal,* Dec. 20, 1913, p. 1275-80.

CENTRAL electric railway accountants' association, 27th meeting. *Electric railway journal,* June 19, 1915, p. 1151-4.

CENTRAL electric railway accountants' association, 33d meeting, Fort Wayne, Ind. Feb. 15. *Electric railway journal,* Feb. 22, 1919, p. 372-3.

CENTRAL electric railway accountants' meetings, Toledo, June 24. *Electric railway journal,* June 27, 1914, p. 1444-6.

CENTRAL LOOSE LEAF COMPANY
Millers' log instructions. Benton Harbor, Mich., Central loose leaf co. 1918.

CENTRAL power station rates. *Power,* Sept. 9, 1913, p. 371.

CENTRAL STATION
See Electric light and power companies; Power plants.

CENTRAL station construction—cost data obtained from Tenney central station companies in Massachusetts. *Electrical world,* Sept 27, 1913, p. 639-40.

CENTRAL-STATION costs in Massachusetts. *Electrical review and western electrician,* Feb. 12, 1916, p. 284.

CENTRAL-STATION costs in Nashville show present rates are equitable. *Electrical review and western electrician,* April 14, 1917, p. 628.

CENTRAL station equipment costs. *Electrical world,* April 28, 1917, p. 800.

CENTRAL station investment to serve electric range load. *Electrical world,* Sept. 25, 1915, p. 706.

CENTRAL-STATION labor costs. *Electrical world,* Nov. 16, 1912, p. 1031-2.

CENTRAL station management and finance. Foster, H. A. 1899.

CENTRAL station merchandising costs. *Electrical world,* April 24, 1920, p. 961.

CENTRAL station plant depreciation charge. *Electrical world,* March 16, 1912, p. 581.

CENTRAL-STATION rate bill opposed at Boston. *Electrical world,* Feb. 13, 1915, p. 441.

CENTRAL-STATION rate increases during 1917. *Electrical review,* Jan. 5, 1918, p. 18-24.

CENTRAL-STATION rate making; analysis of and discussion of general theory. *Power,* Aug. 24, 1915, p. 268-70.

CENTRAL-STATION rates in New York and Brooklyn. *Electrical world,* May 19, 1910, p. 1307-8.

CENTRAL station saving with electric trucks. *Electrical world,* Nov. 8, 1913, p. 957.

CENTRAL-STATION unit-cost accounting. *Electrical world,* Dec. 20, 1913, p. 1271-2.

CENTRAL stations and profit sharing; bonus systems advocated in England. *Electrical review,* July 28, 1917, p. 144-5.

CENTRAL stations in Massachusetts reduce manufacturing cost. *Electrical review and western electrician,* June 10, 1916, p. 1072.

CENTRALIZED consumption of anthracite coal. Jefferson, H. M.

CENTRALIZING and systematizing the stores department. *Electric railway journal,* Aug. 25, 1917, p. 319-20.

CENTURY dictionary; an encyclopedic lexicon of the English language. New York, Century company, c1914.

CERTIFICATE by legislation. *Journal of accountancy,* Aug. 1915, p. 139.

CERTIFICATE of profits. *Accounting and commerce,* Sept. 1920, p. 132.

CERTIFICATE qualified. *Journal of accountancy,* Aug. 1913, p. 121-3.

CERTIFICATES
ACCOUNTANTS' certificates as to profits. *Accountant,* Sept. 3, 17, Nov. 26, 1898, p. 835-7, 873-5, 1131.
AUDITED and found correct. *Accountant,* April 7, 1888, p. 213-4.
AUDITORS' certificate. *Journal of accountancy,* Dec. 1919, p. 456-7.
AUDITOR'S certificate and report in terms of the companies' act, 1900. *Accountant,* Feb. 2, 1901, p. 140-1.
AUDITOR'S certificate and report in terms of the companies act, 1900. *Accountant,* May 2, 1903, p. 568-70.
AUDITOR'S certificate as to amount of profits. *Public accountant,* Sept. 1918, p. 59-60.
AUDITOR'S certificate in relation to stock in trade. *Incorporated accountants' journal,* 1895-6, p. 68.
AUDITORS' certificates. *Accountant,* July 4, 1891, p. 507.
AUDITORS' certificates. *Accountant,* Sept. 19, Oct. 31, 1908, p. 317-9, 509-11.
AUDITORS' certificates. *Journal of accountancy,* Dec. 1919, p. 456-7.

CERTIFICATES—*(Continued)*

AUDITORS' certificates and reports. *Accountant* July 19, 1902, p. 721-3.

AUDITORS' certificates and reports. *Accountant,* March 2, 1907, p. 273-5.

AUDITORS' report in terms of section 23 of companies act, 1900. *Accountant,* June 1, 1901, p. 655-6.

BANKERS favor supervision of reports. *Journal of accountancy,* Oct. 1910, p. 464.

BLACKLOCK, FRANK. Industrial plants. *Accountant,* Oct. 29, 1898, p. 1050-1.

BLANDFORD, ERNEST W. E. and others. Auditors' certicates. *Incorporated accountants journal,* 1898-9, p. 140.

BRISTOL chartered accountants students' society. Auditors and certificates to stock. *Accountant,* April 26, May 31, 1902, p. 447-54, 562-3.

CAVELL, ARTHUR S. and others. Auditors and certificates as to stock. *Accountant,* April 26, 1902, p. 447-54.

CERTIFICATE of profits. *Accounting and commerce,* Sept. 1920, p. 132.

CERTIFICATE qualified. *Journal of accountancy,* Aug. 1913, p. 121-3.

CERTIFICATION of borrowers' statements. *Journal of accountancy,* April 1913, p. 305-6.

CERTIFICTION of borrowers' statements. *Journal of accountancy,* June, Aug. Sept. 1914, p. 435-6, 128-9, 209-10.

COLLEY, F. G. Bank loans under the new conditions; borrowers' certified statements as a basis for national currency. *Journal of accountancy,* Dec. 1914, p. 418-26.

COMMERCIAL credits. *Journal of accountancy,* Dec. 1914, p. 460-1.

CO-OPERATION between bankers and accountants. *Journal of accountancy,* July 1913, p. 51-3.

DANGERFIELD, ATHELSTAN. Reports on accounts. *Accountant,* July 25, 1896, p. 633-9.

DICKINSON, ARTHUR LOWES. Duties and responsibilities of the public accountant with regard to new issues of stocks and bonds. *Journal of accountancy* Nov. 1905, p. 16-27.

DODD, ARTHUR F. Auditor's certificate and report. *Accountant,* June 11, July 2, Aug. 20, 1904, p. 776-84; 7-8, 183-6.

DODD, ARTHUR F. Preparation of accountants' certificates for purpose of joint stock company flotations. *Accountant,* April 6, 1907, p. 451-62. Revised. May 14, 1910, p. 698-711.

DUROSE, ARTHUR. Uniformity of practice in the certificate and requirements of auditors under the companies act, 1900, and in the report to shareholders. *Accountant,* May 31, 1902, p 575-7.

EDINBURGH chartered accountants students' society. Auditors' report in terms of section 23 of companies act, 1900. *Accountant,* June 1, 1901, p. 655-6.

FISHER, WALTER N. Presidential address. *Accountant,* Oct. 19, 1901, p. 1106-10, 1112-13, 1115.

FORM of certificate. (In *How to audit.* 1919. p. 52-8).

HANKS, J. W. Certificate qualified: correspondence. *Journal of accounting,* Sept. 1913, p. 258-9.

HARMOOD-BANNER, JOHN S. True meaning of an audit certificate. *Accountant,* Oct. 27, 1894, p. 938-46.

JENKINS, FREDERICK A. Auditor's certificate and report under the act of 1900. *Accountant,* Dec. 30, 1905, Jan. 27, 1906, p. 760-3, 103-5.

LEAKE, PERCY DEWE and others. Auditor's certificates. *Accountant,* 1887, p. 529.

LITTON, JOHN G. Auditors' certificates. *Accountant,* April 26, 1902, p. 443-5.

MACPHERSON, F. H. Corporation accounting and investigations. (In *Cyclopedia of commerce, accountancy, business administration.* 1910. v.6, p. 239).

MACPHERSON, F. H. Corporation accounting and investigations. *Journal of accountancy,* Nov. 1908, p. 19-31.

MADDEN, JOHN THOMAS. Forms of certificates. (In his *Accounting practice and auditing.* c1917. p. 329-31).

MAY, GEORGE O. Qualifications in certificates. *Accountant,* Nov. 13, 1915, p. 595-600. *American institute of accountants. Yearbook,* 1915, p. 93-104. *Accounting and commerce,* June, July 1916, p. 60-71, 82-5. *Canadian chartered accountant,* Jan. 1916, p. 181-91. *Incorporated accountants' journal,* March 1916, p. 133-6. *Journal of accountancy,* Oct. 1915, p. 248-59.

MELLORS, ROBERT G. Uniformity of practice in the certificates and "requirements" of auditors under the companies' act, 1900, and in the report to shareholders. *Accountant,* Dec. 14, 1901, Jan. 4, 1902, p. 1362-4, 2-4.

MINING company. *American institute of accountants,* Special bulletin, No. 2, 4, March July 1920, p. 7-8, 3-5.

MISUSE of accountants' reports. *Journal of accountancy,* April Aug. 1920, p. 299-300, 138-9.

MONKHOUSE, GEORGE BENSON. Certificates. *Accountant,* Oct. 11, Nov. 1-15, 1890, p. 538, 593-4, 610-11, 621-3.

MONTGOMERY, ROBERT H. Certificates and reports. (In his *Auditing theory and practice.* 1916. p. 235-92).

MOSS, WILLIAM. Auditors' requirements, certificates and reports under the companies' act, 1900 *Accountant,* Feb. 21, March 7, 1903, p. 269-73, 313-5.

OPINION of an auditor. *Incorporated accountants' journal,* 1901-2, p. 113.

PIXLEY, FRANCIS W. Auditor's certificate and report. (In his *Auditors, their duties and responsibilities.* 1910. p. 555-70.)

PIXLEY, FRANCIS W. Report and the certificate to be given by auditors under the Companies' act of 1900. *Accountant,* Nov. 3, Dec. 7, 14, 1901, p. 1303-6, 1321-4, 1351-4.

RAILWAY audit certificates. *Accountant,* Feb. 27, 1915, p. 283.

REQUIREMENTS of auditors. *Accountant,* Jan. 18, 1902, p. 58-60.

RICHARDSON, A. P. ed. Influence of accountants' certificates on commercial credit. New York, American association of public accountants, 1913. 99p.

SMITH, CLARE. Chartered accountants and company prospectuses—certificates. *Accountant,* Feb. 4, 1893, p. 111-5.

SOME accountants' certificates. *Accountant,* Sept. 15, 22, Oct. 6, 20, Nov. 10, 1894. Jan 19, Feb 16, 1895, p. 792-3, 815-6, 864-6, 909-11, 983-5, 50-1, 146-8.

SPREAD of reform. *Journal of accountancy,* Nov. 1914, p. 376.

UNITED STATES. Federal reserve board. Form of certificate. (In its *Approved methods for the preparation of balance sheet statements.* 1918. p. 23-4).

VALUE of an accountant's certificate. *Journal of accountancy,* Sept. 1906, p. 389-90.

WHINNEY, FREDERICK. Audits and certificates. *Accountant,* Nov. 28, 1891, p. 836-42. Revised. *Accountant,* May 14, 1892, p. 404-11.

WHITEHILL, ROBERT. Some notes on the responsibilities of chartered accountants with regard to their certificates. *Accountant,* Jan. 2, 1897, p. 14-20.

WORDING of auditors' certificates. *Accountant,* May 19, 1900, p 477-9.

WORDING of auditor's certificate to statutory report. *Accountant,* Dec. 3, 1910, p. 757-9.

CERTIFICATION of administrative examination of accounts. United States. Treasury department. 1906.

CERTIFICATIÓN of borrowers' statements. *Journal of accountancy,* April 1913, p. 305-306.

CERTIFICATION of borrowers' statements. *Journal of accountancy,* June, Aug. Sept. 1914, p. 435-6, 128-9, 209-10.

CERTIFIED accountancy is still an open field Wilkinson, George.

CERTIFIED accountants; a bill to amend the law relating to accountants practising in Scotland. *Accountant,* Nov. 26, 1892, p. 904-6.

CERTIFIED accountants have a big monopoly Cannon, J. G.

CERTIFIED accountants of Massachusetts, inc *Journal of accountancy,* June 1912, p. 454.

CERTIFIED financial statements as a basis for credit. Wildman, J. R.

CERTIFIED public accountant. Rand, W. H

CERTIFIED public accountant and the people Kauffman, J. H.

CERTIFIED public accountant in New York; editorial. *Journal of accountancy,* June 1918, p. 478.

CERTIFIED public accountant laws. *Journal of accountancy,* Nov. 1914, p. 375-6.

CERTIFIED public accountant syllabus. New York state Education department. 1912.

CERTIFIED public accountants.
See Accountancy—Law; Accountants; Examinations.

CERTIFIED public accountants. Rand, W. H.

CERTIFIED public accountants and the people Kaufman, J. H.

CERTIFIED public accountants' examination questions, 1900. *Business,* July 1900, p. 346-8.

CERTIFIED public accountants have a big monopoly. Common, J. R.

CERTIFIED public accountants in New York. *Journal of accountancy,* Jan. 1913, p. 53-6 Editorial. p. 57-8.

CERTIFIED public accountants, laws, rules and information, June 1916. New York state University.

CERTIFIED public accountants of Massachusetts, inc. *Journal of accountancy,* June 1914, April, July 1915, June 1916, June 1917, June 1918, June, July 1919, p. 482, 324, 79, 477, 469, 480, 479, 80.

CERTIFIED PUBLIC ACCOUNTANTS OF NEW JERSEY.
Examination questions, July 1906 to April 1909. *Accountant,* Oct. 15, 1910, p. 528-35, 516-8.

CERTIFIED public accountants of the state of New York. New York. 1920.

CERTIFIED quarterly statement advocated for corporations. Sells, E. W.

CHADDOCK, J B
System of accountings and costs for a plant with eleven departments *Business man's magazine,* Oct. 1909, p. 354-8.

CHADWICK, DAVID
Duties of a professional auditor; with discussion. *Accountant,* Sept. 29, Nov. 3, 1883.

CHADWICK, H. M.
Cost of engineering work for maintenance and operation of large irrigation project. *Engineering and contracting,* Oct. 8, 1919, p. 418-9.

CHADWICK, W. A.
Pass book vs. statements. *Business man's magazine,* June 1908, p. 524-6.

CHAFFEY, J. B.
Cost-plus contract a success. *Engineering news,* March 6, 1919, p. 485.

CHAIN STORES
BUTLER, RALPH STARR. Chain store. (In his *Marketing methods.* 1918. p. 79-92).
How I watch the sales of 11,000 stores (United cigar stores). *System,* May 1916, p. 481-7.
NYSTROM, PAUL H. Chain-store systems. (In his *Economics of retailing.* 1917. p. 216-34).
PHILLIPS, CAMILLUS. Executive systems of the United cigar stores company. *Business man's magazine,* April 1905, p. 724-34.
SWINNEY, JOHN B. Chain store. (In his *Merchandising.* 1918. p. 298-318).

Accounting
ALLISON, J. Multiple shop accounts. *Accountant,* Aug. 5, 1911, p. 185-95.
ELDRIDGE, B. H. B. Stock accounts for multiple shops. *Accountant,* Dec. 12, 1903, p. 1532-5.
HAZELIP, J. Multiple-shop accounts. London, Gee & co. 1903. 114p. (Accountants' library, v. 24).
MULTIPLE-SHOP accounts. *Accountant,* Dec. 31, 1910, p. 918-21.
SWINNEY, JOHN B. Accounting system for store. (In his *Merchandising.* 1918. p. 316-18).
WILSON, P. MCCANDLISH. Accounts and audit of multiple shop companies. *Accountant,* Feb. 7, 1914, p. 195-9.

Auditing
WILSON, P. MCCANDLISH. Accounts and audit of multiple shop companies. *Accountant,* Feb. 7, 1914, p. 185-9.

Statistics
CHANDLER & COMPANY. Chain stores; reprinted from *New York evening post,* April 9, 1919. 19p.

Stockkeeping
ELDRIDGE, B. H. B. Stock accounts for multiple shops. *Accountant,* Dec. 12, 1903, p. 1532-5.
SWINNEY, JOHN B. Stockkeeping system. (In his *Merchandising.* 1918. p. 314-16).

CHAINS

Cost accounting
HILDITCH, F. W. Cost accounting in the chain industry. *Journal of accountancy,* Jan. 1920, p. 10-18.

CHAIRS.
See Furniture.

CHALLENGE of facts and other essays. Sumner, W. G. 1914.

CHALMERS, A. H.
Audit of shipping accounts. *Accountant,* Dec. 11, 1897, p. 1177-82.
Receiver of a trading concern. *Accountant,* May 1, 1915, p. 572-4.

CHALMERS, ANTHONY WIGHAM
Address, 1883. *Accountant*, March 10, 17, 1883.

CHAMBER blasing methods and cost. *Engineering and contracting*, Sept. 18, 1918, p. 279-83.

CHAMBERLAIN, J. P.
New federal budget plan, as embodied in the Good-McCormick bill in Congress. *Economic world*, July 12, 1919, p. 53-5.
National budget; another angle. *National municipal review*, Oct. 1919, p. 572-3.

CHAMBERLAIN, JOHN ALDRICH.
Commercial law. (In Cyclopedia of commerce, accountancy, business administration. 1910. v.3. p. 11-309).
Commercial law; a practical manual covering the fundamental principles of law as applied to business in general; with a special reference to common law affecting the more usual commercial transactions. Chicago, American technical society, 1916. 316p. (American accountants' library).

CHAMBERLAIN, LAWRENCE
Principles of bond investment. Ed. 7. New York, Henry Holt & co. 1917. 551p.

CHAMBERLAIN, R. E.
Efficiency of the motor truck in terms of cost per ton-mile. *Good roads*, n.s. Feb. 23, 1918, p. 111-2 . *Engineering and contracting*, March 6, 1918, sup. 30, 32. Abstract. *Municipal journal*, March 2, 1918, p. 186.

CHAMBERLAIN, WILLIAM
Regulating rates in Iowa. *Electric railway journal*, July 5, 1919, p. 28-9.

CHAMBERS, F. C.
Steam-driven auxiliaries versus auxiliary turbine and motor driven units. *Electric railway journal*, April 14, 1917, p. 684-5. Abstract. *Power*, May 8, 1917, p. 644.

CHAMBERS, JOHN S.
California state board of authorization and the limitation of expenditure law. *National tax association bulletin*, Jan. Feb. 1918. p. 89-93, 115-8.
Inheritance taxes; with discussion. *National tax association, Proceedings*, 1919, p. 273-93.

CHAMBERS, R. E.
Statement system of balancing depositors accounts. *Bankers magazine*, Feb. 1918, p. 152-5.

CHAMBERS OF COMMERCE.
Goodwin, Elliott H. Chamber of commerce of the United States. *American institute of accountants, yearbook*, 1914, p. 117-21.

CHAMBERS'S bookkeeping. London, W. & R. Chambers. 1895.

CHAMBERS'S book-keeping by single and double entry. Inglis, William. 1855.

CHAMBERS'S examination bookkeeping. Bell, J. 1908.

CHAMBERS' modern bookkeeping. London, W. & R. Chambers, 1908.

CHAMPION, R. B.
Graphic charts show progress. *American city*, July 1917, p. 39-41.

CHAMPLAIN, MANLEY
Lessons in field management. Brookings, S. D. South Dakota state college, 1917.

CHAMPNESS, C. H
Form and arrangement of profit and loss accounts. *Accountant*, Nov. 20, 1897, p. 1094-1100.

CHANCE, H. M.
Appraisal of coal land for taxation. *American institute of mining engineers, Bulletin*, July 1914, p. 1461-6. *American institute of mining engineers, Transactions*, 1915, p. 624.
Valuation of coal land. *American institute of mining engineers, Bulletin*, July 1913, p. 1315-41. Discussion. Nov. 1913, p. 2693-2701.

CHANDLER, A. E.
Farm cost accounting. *Hoard's diary*, Feb. 11, 1916, p. 91.

CHANDLER, ALFRED D.
Amortization. *American economic review*. Dec. 1913.

CHANDLER, B. A.
System of cost accounts for a forest tree nursery. *Forestry quarterly*, v.13, 1915, p. 468-71.

CHANDLER, PRETOR WHITTY
Accounts of executors and trustees. *Accountant*, Nov. 7, 1908, p. 566-9, 541-4.
Accounts of executors and trustees, with specimen register, ledger, and accounts for the residuary legatee, next of kin and others. 2v. London, Butterworth & co. 1906.
Guide to trust accounts. London, Butterworth & co. 1907.
———— Same. Ed. 2. Same as Trust accounts, including the history, preparations, investigation and audit thereof.
Trust accounts, including the history, preparation, investigation and audit thereof. London, Butterworth & co. 1910.

CHANDLER, W. H.
Chamber makes vigorous fight against Poindexter amendment. *Current affairs*, June 23, 1919, p. 5.

CHANDLER, WILLIAM HENRY
Express service and rates. Chicago, La Salle extension university, 1914-16. 340p.

CHANDLER AND COMPANY
Chain stores; reprinted from *New York evening post*, April 9, 1919, 19p.

CHANGE in unit fare approved for Massachusetts northeastern street railway. *Electric railway journal*, July 20, 1918, p. 132.

CHANGES in South Africa's income tax. *Commerce reports*, no. 261, Nov. 7, 1917.

CHANGING customs in cash discounts. *Iron age*, May 9, 1912, p. 1169-70.

CHANGING from flat rate service to metered basis in Sacramento, California. *Electrical world*, Jan. 27, 1917, p. 187-8.

CHANGING the date of the trial balance. *Business man's magazine*, July 1911, p. 68-9.

CHANNING, J. PARKE.
Mine accounts. *Business*, Oct. 1897, p. 305-7. *Engineering magazine*, Sept. 1897.

CHANTREY, WILLIAM HERBERT.
Theatre accounts. London. Gee & co, 1902, 83p. (Accountants' library, v.5).

CHANUTE, O.
Cost of railroad freight traffic. Railway pamphlets, law department, Baltimore and Ohio railroad company, 1884-6, p. 1-16.

CHAPIN, A. B.
Efficiency of supervision of banks. *Chronicle* (Bankers' section), Dec. 2, 1911, p. 228-32.

CHAPIN, HEMAN GERALD.
"Banker's" forms and the negotiable instruments law annotated. Ed. 5. New York, Bankers encyclopedia co. c1918. 133p.

CHAPLIN, J. G.
Three principles of book-keeping; the theory and practice of accounts. London, Sampson Low & co. 1887.

CHAPMAN, CLOURY
Legal aspects of modern correspondence and accounting systems. *Business world,* Dec. 1905.

CHAPMAN, J. E.
Mine accounting for small mines. (In Chase, W. A. *Auditing and cost accounting,* 1917. p.366-75). *Bulletin of the American institute of mining engineers,* March 1916, p. 663-9. Abstract. *Mining and scientific press,* 1916, v.112, p. 400.

CHAPMAN, JOHN J.
Printing office cost system. *Business man's magazine,* Feb. 1911, v. 190-1.

CHAPMAN, JOSEPH
National bank examinations. (In Hull, Walter Henry. *Practical problems in banking and currency.* 1907. p. 97-105).

CHAPMAN, RICHARD M
Accounts of a city. (In Chase, W. A. *Auditing and cost accounting.* 1917. p. 203-65). *Government accountant,* Aug. 1909-March 1910, p. 125-8, 198-202, 261; 316-24, 355-9, 397-405, 446-36.
Municipal accounts; paper read at the annual meeting of the American association of public accountants. New York, 1910. 10p. *American institute of accountants, Yearbook,* 1910, p. 171-202. *Journal of accountancy,* Nov. 1910, p. 17-26.
Serial bonds versus sinking fund bonds. *American city,* March 1917. *New Jersey municipalities,* May 1917, p. 10-11, 16.
Serial bonds vs. sinking fund bonds for municipal financing. *Economic world,* March 17, 1917, p. 377-8.
Significance of fund accounting. *Government accountant,* Sept. 1908, p. 201-08.
Use of documents in accounting. *Business,* Jan. 1898, p. 30-3.
See also MacInnes, Duncan, joint author.

CHAPMAN, SAMUEL
American methods of railway accounting. *Accountant,* Jan. 23, 1909, p. 127-41. *Journal of the Royal statistical society,* 1908, p. 619-48.

CHAPMAN, SYDNEY J.
Accounting in relation to economic problems. *Accountant,* Nov. 21, 1914, p. 619-23. *Canadian chartered accountant,* Jan. 1915, p. 238-46.
Faculty of commerce, in relation to accounts. *Accountant,* Feb. 24, March 24, 1906, p. 249-54, 365-7.

CHAPMAN, THOMAS
Chapman's introduction to business. London, 1774.

CHAPPELLE, C. C.
Some problems of rate making. *Public service.* Feb. 1913, p. 57-9.

CHAPTERS on municipal administration and accounting. Cleveland, F. A. 1909.

CHARGE AND DISCHARGE ACCOUNTS.
ACCOUNTS of charge and discharge. *Accountants' magazine,* 1907, p. 549.
LISLE, GEORGE. Charge and discharge accounts. (In his *Encyclopaedia of accounting.* v.2. p. 54-75).
WALTON, SEYMOUR. Charge and discharge. *Journal of accountancy,* April 1920, p. 306.

CHARGE and discharge accounts. Lisle, George.

CHARGE that railroads jiggled the ore adjustment. *Iron trade review,* February 10, 1914, p. 392-3.

CHARGES.
See Wages and fees.

CHARGES for London water. *Engineer,* March 26, 1915, p. 298.

CHARGING for energy. *Electrical world,* April 3, 1915, p. 859.

CHARGING labor and material. *Factory,* Dec. 1917, p. 914.

CHARGING labor and material; how a factory which employs four hundred and fifty workmen keeps its accounts with eleven men. *System,* July 1912, p. 103-5.

CHARITABLE INSTITUTIONS.
See Institutions.

CHARITABLE institutions. Van de Linde, G.

CHARLATANISM in the profession of accountancy. Rowe, C. V.

CHARLATANS of method. *Journal of accountancy,* March 1912, p. 222-3.

CHARLES, F. R.
Using home-made equipment on a small monolithic brick pavement construction job. *Municipal engineering,* April 1918, p. 137-8.

CHARLES A. PROUTY on railway valuation. *Railway world,* Mar. 1914, p. 190.

CHARLES E. HUGHES, referee, allows higher gas rate in Brooklyn. *Municipal journal,* Aug. 24, 1918, p. 154-5.

CHARLESTOWN, S. C. WAYS AND MEANS COMMITTEE.
Method employed in the keeping of accounts, appropriations, etc. City of Charlestown, S. C. n.d. 3p.

CHARLESWORTH, A.
Few points in company law. *Accountant,* 1887, p. 176.
Remarks upon the accounts of trust companies and their audit. *Accountant,* April 14, 1894, p. 331-8.
Some items included in capital expenditure accounts. *Accountant,* May 11, June 1, 1901, p. 560-5, 631-3.
Trust companies and their audit. London, Gee & co. 1894.

CHARLESWORTH, G H
Trustees' investments. *Accountant,* June 9, 1888, p. 369-72.

CHARLETON, A. G.
Mining accounts and cost sheets. *Transactions of the institute of mining and metallurgy,* 1897, v.5, p. 243-313.
Principles and methods of profitably working the mine; office organization, cost-keeping and records of work done. *Engineering magazine,* Jan. 1901.

CHARLOTTESVILLE'S fare increase carried unanimously. *Electric railway journal,* May 25, 1918, p. 1030.

CHARLTON, D. E.
Utilization of mine accident reports. *Engineering and mining journal,* Nov. 30, 1918, p. 945-8.

CHARLTON, F. F.
More important differences in the duties and responsibilities arising in the following audit; 1, single trader, 2, partnership, 3, public company. *Accountants' magazine,* Dec. 1908, p. 543-59.
School board audits. *Accountants' magazine,* May 1911, p. 245-55.

CHARLTON, FRANK TRACY
Education and industrial evolution. New York, The Macmillan co. 1913. 320p.

CHARLTON, WILLIAM HURST.
American mine accounting methods and forms employed by leading mining companies. New York, McGraw-Hill book company, c1912. 367p. (Mining library, v. 8).

CHART for reducing the cost of billing. *Electrical world,* April 7, 1917, p. 660-1.

CHART for use in appraisal of standard machine tools to determine service value. *American machinist,* June 19, 1919, p. 1202.

CHART of bookkeeping. Ferneyhough, M. P.

CHART of organization of the Michigan united railways. *Electric railway journal,* April 29, 1911, p. 738.

CHART of the organiations of the U. S. railroad administration, with a table showing regional limits. *Railway age,* July 5, 1918.

CHART used by Canadian company to determine income at known load factor. *Electrical world,* Aug. 17, 1918, p. 309.

CHARTERED accountant as a rare exotic. *Journal of accountancy,* Jan. 1910, p. 222-3.

CHARTERED accountants advertising. *Journal of accountancy,* Sept. 1911, p. 379-81.

CHARTERED accountants and profit sharing. *Accountant,* March 23, 1918, p. 255-6.

CHARTERED accountants active in Winnipeg. *Journal of accountancy,* Feb. 1910, p. 285.

CHARTERED accountants and profit-sharing. *Accountant,* March 23, 1918, p. 255-6.

CHARTERED accountants and their duties. *Accountant,* Jan. 22, 1916, p. 124-6. *Public accountant,* March 1916, p. 195-7.

CHARTERED accountants' bill. *Accountant,* March 18, May 20, 1893, March 2, 1895, Jan. 9, 1897, p. 244-6, 474-5, 213-5, 49-52.

CHARTERED accountants' charges, and the law relating thereto. Pixley, F. W. 1904.

CHARTERED accountants' fees. *Accountant,* Dec. 7, 1918, p. 301-3.

CHARTERED accountants for Japan. *Accountant,* Feb. 26, 1916, p. 253-5, 237-41.

CHARTERED accountants in New York. *Journal of accountancy,* March 1910, p. 377.

CHARTERED accountants' examination guide and students' help to self-preservation for the intermediate and final examination. Norton, G. P. and H. F. Lynch. 1887.

CHARTERED accountants of Lousiana. *Journal of accountancy,* Aug. 1906, p. 301.

CHARTERED ACCOUNTANTS OF SCOTLAND.
OFFICIAL directory; annual.

———, **GENERAL EXAMINING BOARD.**
REPORT and accounts for 1918. Glasgow, 1919. 4p.
SUMMARY of rules for admission and syllabus of examinations by general examining board, February 1919. 5p.

CHARTERED ACCOUNTANTS STUDENTS' SOCIETY OF LONDON.
Debate on examination questions. *Accountant,* March 7, 1914, p. 338-41.
Depreciation of assets and goodwill of limited companies. *Accountant,* Jan. 9, 1904, p. 44-52.
Discussion of the questions set at the December (1903) examinations. *Accountant,* March 26, 1904, p. 399-404.
Discussion on examination questions. *Accountant,* June 27, 1903, p. 839-43.
Discussion on examination questions. *Accountant,* Oct. 26, 1901, p. 1169-73.
Discussion on examination questions. *Accountant,* July 27, Oct. 26, 1901, p. 849-54, 1169-73.
Discussion on the audit of the accounts of private firms. *Accountant,* Feb. 25, 1893, p. 179-81.
Discussion on (1) the best methods of dealing in companies' accounts with share acquired in exchange for properties sold, underwriting services &c., (2) on the value to be placed on shares unquoted. *Accountant,* Feb. 11, 1899, p. 201-6.
Discussion on the companies act, 1909. *Accountant,* April 11, May 23, 1903, p. 494-501, 680-3.
Discussion on the May examination questions, 1912. *Accountant,* Oct. 19, 1912, p. 491-6.
Income tax. *Accountant,* May 11, 1895, p. 433.
Joint debate: That municipal trading, under the present conditions, is detrimental to the national interests. *Accountant,* June 17, 1905, p. 736-40.
June examination questions discussed. *Accountant,* Nov. 7, 1903, p. 1367-73.
Mock parliamentary debate on professional accountants' bill. *Accountant,* Jan. 20, 1912, p. 89-93.
Profit of companies available for distribution. *Accountant,* Jan. 10, 1891, p. 30-4.
Report of departmental committee on income tax. *Accountant,* Feb. 3, 1906, p. 137-47.

CHARTERED accountants students society of Edinburgh and Glasgow. Chartered accountants students society debate: That trade unions are injurious to the commerce of the country. *Accountant,* Nov. 26, 1910, p. 745-50.

CHARTERED accountants students' society of Edinburgh and the Scots law society debate "That women should be admitted to the legal and accounting professions". *Accountant,* Feb. 25, 1911, p. 319-24.

CHARTING instructions to get better economies. *Electrical world,* May 11, 1918. p. 982-3.

CHARTING motor truck performance. *Textile world,* June 1, 1918, p. 5901. Condensed. *Engineering and contracting,* June 19, 1918, sup. 34.

CHARTS.

See Graphic methods.

CHARTS divide work and place responsibility. *Motor age,* Nov. 6, 1919, p. 32-3.

CHARTS showing fluctuations in iron and steel prices for nineteen years. *Iron trade review,* Jan. 1, 1914, p. 64a.

CHASE, CHARLES DYER.

Columnar bookkeeping. *Business,* Oct. Nov. 1895, p. 366-8, 402-3.

CHASE, CHARLES H.

Advantages of system in the keeping of mine accounts. *Mining science,* 1912, v.66, p. 184-5.

Keeping accounts at the Liberty bell mine, Colorado. *Mining and engineering world,* 1913, v.38, p. 961.

CHASE, HARVEY STUART

Abstract of address before the Boston city club, Oct. 24th, 1907. 2 typewritten pages.

Accounting for the liberty loans. *Accountant,* Feb. 2, 1918, p. 102-5.

Accounting for the liberty loans. the first loan. 11p. *Journal of accountancy,* Jan. 1918, p. 7-16.

Accounting for the liberty loans; the second loan. *Accountant,* Aug. 3, 1918, p. 64-7, *Journal of accountancy,* Feb. 1918, p. 91-100.

Address before the conference upon uniform legislation at Washington, D. C., January 19, 1910. 4p.

Address on municipal accounts and reports; before the Wonolancet club, Concord, New Hampshire, February 17, 1909. 6 typewritten pages.

Audit of uncollected tax accounts, City of Boston. *Public policy,* July 7, 1900, p. 14-6.

Boston's expenses analyzed. *Public policy,* March, 1902, p. 152-5.

Brief history of the movement towards uniform municipal reports and accounts in the United States. *Accountant,* Oct. 15, 1904, p. 394-9. *Federation of societies of public accountants in the United States of America. Official record of the Congress of accountants held at the World's fair, Saint Louis,* September 26th, 27th and 28th, 1904, p. 40-8.

Budget amendment of the Maryland constitution. *National municipal review,* May 1917, p. 395-8.

Budgets and balance sheets. *Journal of accountancy,* Dec. 1910, p. 81-96. *National conference for good city government, Proceedings,* 1910, p. 214-29.

Budgets and balance sheets; the practical application of sound accounting principles and methods to municipal bookkeeping; an address before the National municipal league at the Buffalo meeting, November 14-17, 1910. 17p.

Business management of municipalities. New York, Alexander Hamilton institute, 1913. 21p.

City government by commission. *Journal of accountancy,* Nov. 1907, p. 66-7.

City of Cambridge, report on financial condition of the city with recommendations, January 14, 1908. 15p.

Concerning uniform international financial statements; remarks before the American economic association and the American statistical association at Princeton, N. J., December 30, 1914. 9p.

Cost of maintenance and depreciation of cotton mills; from the transactions, no. 82, of the National association of cotton manufacturers, Boston, Mass., April 24-5, 1907. 8p. *Accountant,* Sept. 21, 1907, p. 370-2, 357-9. *Journal of accountancy,* July 1907, p. 236-8.

Depreciation in water works accounts, with reference to uniform reports. *Journal of the New England water works association,* June 1910, p. 305-31. Abstract. *Engineering and contracting,* June 29, 1910, p. 598. Editorial. Depreciation and sinking fund accounts. *Municipal engineering,* July 1910, p. 26.

Executive budget in relation to governmental accounting. Chicago, LaSalle extension university, c1917. 17p.

Explanation in relation to the new form of the "daily statement" of the United States treasury, July 1, 1913. *Accountant,* Aug. 30, 1913, p. 290-4.

Financial plan, or "Budget" for the national government; an address before the National association of comptrollers and accounting officers at the annual meeting 1914, held at Milwaukee, Wisconsin, June 11th to 13th. 10 typewritten pages. *Journal of accountancy,* July 1914, p. 13-29.

Fundamental necessity; a brief address before the Econmic club of Boston as a part of the discussion upon "Questions relating to a new city charter for Boston," Nov. 30, 1908. 3 typewritten pages.

Governmental sinking funds, serial bonds and depreciation reserves; read at the annual meeting of the Dominion association of chartered accountants at Montreal, September 18th to 20th, 1918. 18p. *Accountant,* March 1, 1919, p. 162-8. *Canadian chartered accountant,* Oct. 1918, p. 142-65. *Journal of accountancy,* Oct. 1918, p. 253-68. *National association of comptrollers and accounting officers, Proceedings,* June 1918, p. 64-74.

Holyoke water power company, petitioners v. city of Holyoke, statistics and computations from the annual reports of the Board of gas and electric light commissioners, the returns of certain companies to the commission and the evidence in the case. Boston, George H. Ellis, 1900. 31p.

Investigation of Boston's municipal printing plant. *Public policy,* April 19, 1902, p. 252-6.

Investigation of Boston's public building department. *Public policy,* May 3, 1902, p. 284-8.

Maintenance and depreciation charges in accounts of public service corporations. *Accountant,* July 6, 1907, p. 18-32. *Journal of accountancy,* May 1907, p. 1-9.

Municipal accounting as the basis for publicity of municipal affairs; before the National municipal league, Pittsburgh meeting, November 17-20, 1908. 8 typewritten pages. *National municipal league, Proceedings,* Pittsburg, 1908, (Philadelphia), 1908, p. 337-47.

Municipal accounting in Boston and Louisville. *Annals of the American academy of political and social science,* 1906, p. 453-62.

Municipal revenues and expenditures in relation to "the control of quasi-public enterprises"; an address before the Massachusetts reform club, February 2, 1906. 18p.

National budget. *National economic league quarterly,* Aug. 1915, p. 5-11.

National budget; an address before the Massachusetts society of certified accountants, Boston, April 9, 1913. 14p. *Journal of accountancy,* Feb. 1914, p. 85-96.

National budget. In Proceedings at a meeting held December 6, 1913, to discuss the "federal income tax" the pending currency bill" and the national budget." p. 11-27.

National budget on its "expenditure" side; an address before the Massachusetts society

CHASE, HARVEY STUART—*(Continued)*
of certified public accountants at Boston, Mass., April 9, 1913. 14p. *Accountant,* Nov. 1, 1913, p. 643-9. *Journal of accountancy,* June 1913, p. 397-411.
National finance. *American institute of accountants. Yearbook,* 1914, p. 153-72. *Journal of accountancy,* Oct. 1914, p. 276-95.
National finances: an address before the American association of public accountants at Washington, D. C., September 16, 1914. 16p. *Canadian chartered accountant,* Jan. 1915, p. 214-31.
Practical application of modern methods of accounting in municipalities. *National association of comptrollers and accounting officers.* 1910. p. 39-58.
Practical application of the schedules of uniform municipal reports and accounts. *National municipal league. Proceedings,* 1904, p. 216-229.
Practical application of uniform accounting to city comptrollers' reports. *League of American municipalities. Proceedings,* 1901, p. 36-40. *Public policy,* Sept. 28, 1901, p. 205-08. *Municipal journal and engineer,* Nov. 1901, p. 218-20.
Progress of uniform municipal accounting in Ohio. *National municipal league. Proceedings,* Detroit, 1903, p. 287,95.
Recent changes in the "net balance" in the United States treasury. *Journal of accountancy,* Jan. 1916, p. 16-23.
Recent development in the United States of the uniform system for comparative municipal reports. *Association of city auditors of the state of Ohio, Proceedings,* 1903, p. 17-29.
Regeneration of municipal governments and the part to be played therein by uniform and comparative accounts and reports. Chicago. Public policy publishing company. 15p. *Public policy,* June 27, 1903, p. 401-4.
Report and recommendations on the examinations of the books of the city departments, together with a statement of the city's debt, Pawtucket, R. I. 1905. 48p.
Report of Boston' street department; municipal ferries a failure. *Public policy,* June 28, 1902, p. 409-12.
Report of expert accountant; accounts of the town of Brookline, Mass. *Public policy,* April 12, 1902, p. 238-40.
Report of expert accountant to mayor and city council, March, 1903. Cambridge.
Report on Boston's tax collection department. *Public policy,* July 5, 1902, p. 9-11.
Report on Boston's treasury department. *Public policy,* July 12, 1902, p. 28-30.
Report of His Excellency, the Governor to the executive council and to the joint committee on ways and means of the general court of Massachusetts concerning the bureau of statistics, municipal debts and revenue deficiencies; April 21, 1911. 16p.
Report on the accounts of the commonwealth of Massachusetts. *Journal of accountancy,* July 1911, p. 206-15.
Report to Dr. Frank J. Goodnow, chairman and the members of the commission on efficiency and economy in the state government of Maryland concerning inefficiency and extravagance in various departments and offices, January 17, 1916. 51p.
Report to selectmen of Farmingham, Mass., upon financial condition of the town. Boston, 1910, 26p.
Report upon books and accounts of Haverhill, 1909. Boston, 1910. 21p.
Report upon the books and accounts of the collector's department of the city of Boston, with special reference to the results of the acts in regard to special assessments for laying out and construction of highways during the past 10 years. Boston, May 8, 1901.
"Secret reserves" in textile manufacturing accounts, together with correct accounting for depreciation. 7 typewritten pages.
Standard and uniform reports for municipally operated utilities—private operations also—suggested form for schedule . . . other interesting features. *Municipal journal and engineer,* 1906, p. 566-70.
Standard and uniform reports from public utilities both municipally operated and privately operated. *Journal of accountancy,* June 1906, p. 81-96. *National municipal league, Proceedings,* 1906, p. 227-43.
Standardized municipal reports. (In Economic club of Boston, Municipal government . . . Two discussions before the Economic club of Boston, January 11, 1907 and January 21, 1908. (Boston,? 1908?) p. 25-32.
Standards of depreciation. *Boston evening transcript,* April 12, 1907.
Summary statement of receipts and expenses of the city of Newton for the year 1900. (In Newton, Mass., Auditing dept. *Annual report of the city auditor* . . . for the year . . . 1900. Together with an appendix containing a summary of the receipts and expenditures of the city arranged according to the uniform system of the National municipal league. Newton, 1901. p. 131-55.)
Teach English economics, history and law. *Journal of accountancy,* Jan. 1907, p. 191-2.
Uniform accounting applied to Boston, Baltimore and other municipalities. *National municipal league, Proceedings,* Boston, 1902. Philadelphia, 1902. p. 307-21.
Uniform accounting for municipalities. *Commerce, accounts and finance,* Dec. 1901, p. 23-5.
Uniform accounting for municipalities: abstract. *Journal of accountancy,* March 1910, p. 373-4.
Uniform municipal accounting; a practical application to city comptrollers' reports—Chicago to have new system of accounts—applied to Newton, Mass.—every city has its own system—difference between municipal and commercial bookkeeping. *Municipal journal and engineer.*
Uniform municipal reports. *Business world,* April, May, June 1905, p. 172-3, 222-3, 292-3.
Uniform public accounting for the state of Massachusetts. (In Heydecker, Edward comp. Proposed public accounting law—state of New York, with explanatory memorandum, uniform public accounting for the state of New York by L. Purdy. Uniform public accounting for the state of Massachusetts by H. Chase. A good recommendation, editorial *Boston Herald.* The regulation of public expenditures, editorial Public poicy. Chicago, Public policy co. 1903).
Uniform public accounting for the state of Massachusetts. *Public policy,* Dec. 20, 1902, p. 394-5.
United States' national budget. *Accountant,* April 11, 1914, p. 539-43.
Utility and methods of a uniform public accounting system for Massachusetts. *Public policy,* Jan. 24, 1903, p. 59-63.
Work of the bureau for uniform municipal reporting, auditing and accounting in the state of Ohio; an address delivered at the meeting of the league of Ohio municipalities, at Dayton, Ohio, February 11, 1903. 11p.
Work of the Ohio bureau of uniform public accounting and auditing. *Public policy,* Mar. 7, 1903, p. 154-8.

——— **AND J. W. BAIRD**
Municipal accounting in Boston and Louisville. *Annals of the American academy of political and social science,* Nov. 1906, p. 453-62.

CHASE, HARVEY STUART AND OTHERS.
Proposed reforms in state government; some questions that may come before the Massachusetts constitutional convention; Proposed state budget for Massachusetts. *National economic league quarterly,* August 1916.

CHASE, HARVEY S. & COMPANY.
Report to Hon. Emerson C. Harrington, comptroller of the treasury concerning the financial conditions of the state of Maryland and also concerning a proposed "state budget," December 15, 1915. 16p.

CHASE, STUART
What is a reasonable profit? *Journal of accountancy,* June 1920, p. 416-34.

CHASE, WILLIAM ARTHUR
Auditing and cost accounting. Chicago, La Salle extension unversity. 1917. 493p.
Bankers and certified public accountants. *Journal of accountancy,* Aug. 1908, p. 242-7.
C. P. A. examinations and how to pass them. Chicago, LaSalle extension university, 1915. 93p.
C. P. A. examinations and how to pass them. *Journal of accountancy,* April-June 1910, p. 401-11, 43-50, 113-9.
Cost units. *American economic association, Papers and proceedings,* April 1911, p. 136-44.
Federal corporation tax law; the absurdity of the law. *Journal of accountancy,* Sept. 1909, p. 347-51.
How to pass examinations; extract. *Accountants' magazine,* May 1910, p. 256-8.
Legal liability of auditors. (In his *Auditing and cost accounting.* 1917. p. 352-65). *Accountant,* June 26, 1915, p. 846-51.
Mr. Cannon's address. *Journal of accountancy,* Jan. 1909, p. 192-9.
New York's standards not the highest: correspondence. *Journal of accountancy,* Feb. 1906, p. 325-6.
Our critics. *Accountant,* Feb. 12. 1910, p. 257-61, 293-7. *Journal of accountancy,* Oct. 1909, p. 432-9.
Profession of a certified public accountant. *Journal of accountancy,* July 1906, p. 194-200.
Record-Herald's editorial: correspondence. *Journal of accountancy,* Sept. 1909, p. 384-5.
Unit costs. (In his *Auditing and cost accounting.* 1917. p. 376-85). *Accountant* July 1, 1911, p. 20-4.

CHASE on the corporation tax. *Journal of accountancy,* Jan. 1910, p. 224-5

CHATBURN, GEORGE R.
Sky-line graphs for pavement data. *Engineering and contracting,* February 7, 1917, p. 138.

CHATHAM, J.
On life premium book-keeping. *Journal of the Institute of actuaries,* 1904, v. 38, p. 619-67.
On the books and forms to be used in scheduling the particulars of the risks of a life assurance company, etc. *Journal of the institute of actuaries,* 1898, v. 32, p. 393.

CHATERIS, HENRY
Tradesman's manual; a simple method of book-keeping. London, 1843.

CHEAP, efficient cost system. *Iron age,* Jan. 2, 1913, p. 62.

CHECK figure systems. *South African accountant,* Sept. 1917, p. 46-8.

CHECK figures. *Accountant,* Oct. 27, 1906, p. 495-7.

CHECK figures. Neff, G. O. 1908.

CHECK figures and how to use them. Greenup, A. H. 1914.

CHECK NUMBERS
CHECK figure systems. *South African accountant,* Sept. 1917, p. 46-8.
CHECK figures. *Accountant,* Oct. 27, 1906, p. 495-7.
DALTON, J. P. Check figure systems. *South African accountant,* June 1917, p. 5-9.
DICKSEE, L. R. Check numbers. (In his *Advance accounting.* 1916. p. 23-4).
GREENUP, ALAN H. Check figures and how to use them; ready reckoner calculated in £ s d, 1d to £10 in detail, £10 to £40,000 every page; calculated in metric .01 to 96000.00 detail; calculated in weights 1 lb. to 1 cwt. in detail, 1 cwt. to 1 ton, 1 ton to 80,000 tons. London, Gee & co. 1914. 28p.
HAY, GEORGE H. Elementary treatise on check figure systems. London, Gee & co. 24p. *Accountant,* Aug. 1-15, 1908, p. 726-9, 154-7, 181-3.
HAY, GEORGE H. Principles of check figure system for accountants and bookkeepers. London, Gee & co. 1908. 155p.
LISLE, GEORGE and W. A. MIDDLETON. Check numbers. (In their *Account-keeping in principle and practice.* 1911. p. 86-94).
MILLAR, T. J. Check numbers and other aids to balancing books of account. Edinburgh, George, Waterston & sons, 1907.
MILLAR, THOMAS JOHN. Check numbers and their use in connection with the new methods of recording business facts. *Accountants' magazine,* Nov. 1918, p. 408-14.
MUIR, ARTHUR HENRY. Check figure systems. *Accountant,* Feb. 5, 1910, p. 208-13. *Accountants' magazine,* Nov. 1909, p. 486-502.
NEFF, GEORGE O. Check figure. Silvane Avenue, Cleveland, G. O. Neff, 1908.
PORTERS, R. J. Check figure systems. (In his *Pitman's dictionary of bookkeeping.* p. 170-3).
RUARK, JAMES FLETCHER. Simplest check figure. *Business man's magazine,* Dec. 1906, p. 110.
SOULE, GEORGE. Thirteen check figure system of proving postings or transfers. (In his *New science and practice of accounts.* 1903. p. 339).
WEBSTER, N. E. Practical use of the check figure 9. *Business man's magazine,* Sept. 1908, p. 225-6.
WILTZINS, E. Illustrations and demonstrations of the discovery of the E. W. check methods, check figures and check figure groups. La Crosse, Wisconsin, E. Wiltzins, 1913.

CHECK numbers and other aids to valuing books of account. Millar, T. J. 1907.

CHECK on overtime work. *Business man's magazine,* Nov. 1911, p. 440-1.

CHECK on possible customers. *Business man's magazine,* March 1912, p. 255.

CHECK system of bookkeeping for gas companies. Hight, Charles. ?1870.

CHECKING
BARDSLEY, JAMES HICKEY. Other methods of proving ledgers and accounts than by detail checking. *Accountant,* Aug. 13, 1892, p. 631-5.
GOLDMAN, HENRY. Multiplex checking systems to be known as the multi-check. Chicago, Office men's record co, 1906,

CHECKING—(*Continued*)

KESTER, R. B. Internal check. (In his *Accounting theory and practice.* 1918. p. 501).

PITT, GEORGE STANHOPE and others. Methods of internal checque. *Incorporated accountants journal,* 1909-10, p. 78.

RACINE, S. F. Internal check. (In his *Accounting principles.* 1917. p. 249-50).

SHORE, H. W. Comments upon internal check and audit. *Accounting and commerce,* Aug. 1917, p. 104-6.

SPICER, ERNEST EVAN. Internal check in relation to a manufacturer's business. Ed. 2. London, H. Faulks Lynch & co. 1911. 36p. *Accountant,* March 28, May 2, 1908, p. 434-43, 621-4.

SPICER, ERNEST EVAN and ERNEST C. PEGLER. Internal checks. (In their *Bookkeeping and accounts.* 1914. p. 387-413).

USE and limitation of detail checking. *Incorporated accountants' journal,* Dec. 1912, p. 60-2.

WILSON, P. MCCANDLISH. Checks that can be applied by an auditor examining stock sheets. *Accountant,* Dec. 20, 1919, p. 532-5. *South African accountant,* March 1920, p. 425-7.

WITTY, RICHARD ALFRED and others. Detail checking. *Incorporated accountants journal,* 1905-6, p. 79.

CHECKING and auditing system used in the Saint Paul Hotel, St. Paul, Minn. National cash register co. c1912. 69p.

CHECKING costs in a woodworking plant. *Business man's magazine,* Nov. 1911, p. 441-2.

CHECKING in-and-out system in mines. *Coal age,* Feb. 3-24, March 10-17, 1917, p. 246, 288-9, 328, 369, 447-8, 486-7.

CHECKING of bank interest. *Accountant,* Feb. 29, 1908, p. 275-7.

CHECKING the use of raw materials. *Factory,* Dec. 1917, p. 1006.

CHECKING 25-cent key deposit losses. *Factory,* June 1917, p. 914.

CHECKING up a builder's correspondence. *Business man's magazine,* Oct. 1911, p. 341-2.

CHECKS

See also Banks and banking; Negotiable instruments.

BANE, W. F. Practicable form of voucher-check. *Business man's magazine,* July 1906, p. 93-4.

BANKS of the United States vs. voucher checks. *Business man's magazine,* April 1907, p. 136-8.

BASSET, W. R. Checks. (In his *Accounting as an aid to business profits.* c1918. p. 85-9).

BEERBOWER, C. W. Convenient form of voucher check. *Business man's magazine,* July 1905, p. 96-7.

CHECKS on cheques; some precautions which the public ought to adopt but neglect to do. *Accountant,* Oct. 13, 1900, p. 901-3.

COHEN, H. Law of cheques. *Incorporated accountants journal,* 1901-2, p. 150.

COMBINED voucher-check and remittance letter. *Business man's magazine,* Feb. 1910, p. 111.

CONOVER, H. J. Standard voucher check and handling accounts payable with minimum office labor. *Business man's magazine,* March 1910, p. 251-5.

DANCE, E. H. Multiple cheques. *Accountant,* March 15, 1919, p. 201-2. *South African accountant,* March 1919, p. 301-2.

DICKINSON, A. L. Outstanding checks. (In his *Accounting practice and procedure.* 1917. p. 119-20).

DOWLER, FRANK and E. M. HARRIS. Cheques. (In their *Auditing, accounting and banking.* p. 242-56).

DUKES, A. T. Voucher checks. *Business man's magazine,* April 1908, p. 365-6.

EDGAR, A. E. Question of receipts. *Business man's magazine,* Sept. 1905, p. 516.

ESQUERRE, P. J. Memorandum checks. (In his *Applied theory of accounts.* 1917. p. 352.

FORGED cheques and passbooks. *Accountant,* April 17, 1909, p. 517.

FORGED cheques; position of banker paying. *Canadian chartered accountant,* April 1920, p. 261-2.

FRANCIS, E. A. Voucher check system which displaces red tape methods. *Business man's magazine,* Jan. 1908, p. 109-110.

FREDERICKS, M. W. Dispense with the stub system. *Business man's magazine,* Sept. 1909, p. 281-3.

FREEMAN, D. W. Voucher check. *Business man's magazine,* Oct. 1908, p. 325.

FROTHERINGHAM, A. K. Voucher checks. *Business man's magazine,* Aug. 1907, p. 108-10.

GRAINGER, W. H. Cheques and bills of exchange. *Incorporated accountants' journal,* 1904-5, p. 114.

HEILMAN, TYSON. Voucher checks. *Business man's magazine,* Oct. 1906, p. 148-52.

HUTCHISON, G. E. Voucher check. *Business man's magazine,* March, Aug. 1907, p. 140-4, 110-114.

KESTER, R. B. Checks. (In his *Accounting theory and practice.* 1918. p. 517-8).

KESTER, ROY B. Voucher check. (In his *Accounting theory and practice.* v. 2. 1918. p. 32-4).

LATEST banking device, multiple bank cheque; depositor can pay all his monthly bills by drawing one cheque. *Canadian chartered accountant,* Oct. 1916, p. 123.

MCCORMACK, H. S. Voucher checks. *Business man's magazine,* Aug. 1907, p. 110.

M'NEIL, ALLAN. Cheque. (In Lisle, George. *Encyclopaedia of accounting.* v. 2. p. 76-87).

MOSELEY, H. Bills of exchange, cheques and promissory notes. *Accountant,* Sept. 11, 1897, p. 865-73.

NELSON, BERT O. Should be less transcribing in the voucher. *Business man's magazine,* Jan. 1908, p. 123.

NEW YORK bad cheque law. *Canadian chartered accountant,* April 1920, p. 272.

NIXON, ALFRED and J. H. STAGG. Cheques. (In their *Accounting and banking.* 1912. p. 260-70).

PAGET, JOHN. Collecting cheques crossed "not negotiable." *Accountant,* Jan. 9, 1915, p. 56-62.

PAGET, JOHN. Payment of cheques. *South African accountant and auditor,* Dec. 1916, p. 211-3.

PATTERSON, D. Cheques. *Accounting and commerce,* Oct. 1917, p. 164-6.

PAYMENT by a banker of fraudulently altered cheques; an article from the *Solicitors' journal. Accountant,* Sept. 15, 1906, p. 309.

PITT-LEWIS, GEORGE. Cheques in settlement. *Accountant,* July 5, 1902, p. 688-90.

SAMPLE voucher check. *Business man's magazine,* July 1907, p. 118.

SEIFERT, C. A. More about voucher checks. *Business man's magazine,* June 1908, p. 515-8.

SMITH, H. W. Bills, notes, cheques and stamps. *Accountant,* 1886, p. 383.

STANDARD voucher check. *Journal of accountancy,* Jan. 1909, p. 242-3.

UNIFORM bank voucher check. *Journal of accountancy,* Feb. 1909, p. 329-30.

CHECKS—(*Continued*)

UNIFORM law relating to cheques. *Accountant,* Aug. 20, 1910, p. 234-9.
VARIAN, EVERETT B. Vouchers. *Business man's magazine,* Nov. 1906, p. 114.
VOUCHER-CHECKS for small businesses. *Business man's magazine,* Dec. 1908, p. 495.
WALTON, SEYMOUR. Cheques and drafts. *Journal of accountancy,* Sept. 1915, p. 230-3.
WALTON, SEYMOUR. Lost cheques. *Journal of accountancy,* March 1916, p. 231-2.
WALTON, SEYMOUR. Negotiable paper. *Journal of accountancy,* July 1915, p. 58-61.

CHECKS on cheques; some precautions which the public ought to adopt but neglect to do. *Accountant,* Oct. 13, 1900, p. 901-3.

CHECKS that can be applied by an auditor examining stock sheets. *Australasian accountant and secretary,* July 1920, p. 220-4.

CHEEL, ERNEST C.

Co-operative accounting. New York, The co-operative league of America. 1920. 16p.

CHEER, E W

Costing for public works contractors. *Accountant,* Feb. 8, 1919, p. 103-7.

CHEESE

See also Dairying.
MATHESON, K. J. and F. R. CAMMACK. Neuchatel and cream cheese; farm manufacture and use. Washington, Government printing office, 1918. 35p. (United States. Department of agriculture farmers' bulletin 960). Cost of manufacture, p. 15-7.

Accounting

FUTURE deliveries—wholesale cheese business. *Business man's magazine,* Dec. 1906, p. 146-8.

Cost accounting

COST of manufacture of cheese. *New York produce review,* July 25, 1917, p. 520.

Costs

PRICE for making. *New York produce review,* April 1919, p. 1058.
SAMMIS, J. L. Cost of cheese factory equipment. *Hoard's diary,* April 16, 1920, p. 825.
SAMMIS, J. L. Cost of making cheese. *Hoard's diary,* March 26, 1920, p. 629.
SAMMIS, J. L. Costs and profits incurred and realized at large and small cheese factories. *New York produce review,* May 28, 1919, p. 196.

Depreciation.

See Depreciation, depletion and obsolescence—Cheese.

CHEETHAM, FREDERICK

DISCUSSION upon income tax. *Accountant,* March 16, 1899, p. 139-42, 145-7.

CHEMICAL NATIONAL BANK OF NEW YORK.

Bankers acceptances and trade acceptances. New York, Chemical national bank of New York, c1917. 24p.

CHEMICAL works. Dyson, S. S. and S. S. Clarkson. 1912.

CHEMICALS

DYSON, S. S. and S. S. CLARKSON. Chemical works, their design, erection and equipment. London, Scott, Greenwood and son, 1912. 207p.
TIME keeping and payroll distribution. *American institute of accountants, Special bulletin,* No. 6. Nov. 1920, p. 6-8).
UNITED STATES. Tariff commission. Census of dyes and coal-tar chemicals. 1917. Washington, Government printing office, 1918.

Cost accounting

BUSH, H. J. Costing systems in sulphuric acid works. *Chemical age,* July 5, 1919, p. 58-9.
CASWELL, WILLIAM W. Value of cost accounting in commercial laboratories. 6p. *Journal of industrial and engineering chemistry,* Jan. 1920, p. 79-81.
COST analysis in chemical manufacture. *Journal of the society of chemical industries.* June 30, 1919, p. 224R-6R.
GARRY, HENRY STANLEY. Factory costs. *Accountant,* July 25, Sept. 12, 1903, p. 954-61, 1103-5.
NICHOLSON, J. LEE and JOHN F. D. ROHRBACH. Chemical manufacturing plants. (In their *Cost accounting.* 1919. p. 31).

Stores systems

HARTFORD, F. D. Storehouses for chemical plants. *Industrial management,* March 1920, p. 196-8.

CHEMIN, R. S.

System for showing and caring for patterns. *American machinist,* July 14, 1904.

CHEMISTRY

LEIGHOU, ROBERT BENJAMIN. Chemistry of materials of the machine and building industries New York, McGraw-Hill book company, inc. 1917. 449p.
LUNGE, GEORGE. Technical chemists' handbook, tables and methods of analysis for manufacturers of inorganic chemical products. Ed.2, revised. New York, D. Van Bostrand company, 1916. 264p.
ROGERS, ALLEN, ed. Industrial chemistry; a manual for the student and manufacturer. Ed.2. New York, D. Van Nostrand company, 1915. 1005p.

CHEMISTRY and the coal-tar dyes. Fay, Irving W. 1919.

CHEMISTRY of essential oils and artificial perfumes. Parry, Ernest J. 1918

CHEMISTRY of materials of the machine and building industries. Leighou, Robert Benjamin, 1917.

CHEMISTS' credit accounts. *Accountant,* Aprli 10, June 5, 1909, p 489-92, 796,7.

CHENERY, C. T.

New gas ordinance in Chicago. *American gas engineering journal,* Aug. 4, 1917, p. 99-102.

CHENEY, C. E.

Cost accounts in the production of architectural iron work. *The office,* June 1889, p. 109-10.

CHEQUES.

See Checks.

CHERRINGTON, FREDERICK B.

Tying the costs into the general accounts. (In Thompson, C. B. How to find factory costs. c1916. p. 102-9).

CHESSMAN, CARLETON A.

College club accounting by double entry system *Business man's magazine,* Feb. 1908, p. 216-8.

CHESTER, J. N.

Service charge—how constituted. *Journal of the American water works association,*

CHESTER, J. N.—(*Continued*)
Sept. 1917, p. 313-25. *Engineering and contracting.* June 13, 1917, p. 542-3. Discussion. *Journal of the American water works asociation,* Sept. 1917, p. 320-5.

CHEVALIER, C. G.
Handling of supplies for an iron and steel plant. *Business man's magazine,* Jan. 1905, p. 79-88.

CHICAGO. CIVIL SERVICE COMMISSION.
Reports on the Bureau of streets. 1913.

——— **CITY COUNCIL COMMITTEE ON REVISION OF ACCOUNTS.**
Letter transmitting report, relating to system of municipal accounts for the city of Chicago, the necessary ordinances, and other data. Chicago, 1901. 63p.

——— **COMMISSION ON CITY EXPENDITURES**
Bureau of street Civil service commission and special assessment; accounting system of the city of Chicago, reports submitted to the Commission on city expenditures, published by the Chicago bureau of public efficiency, December, 1911. (Chicago, 1911). 112p. Special assessment accounting system, report of T. W. Hetak. p. 81-112.

——— **COMPTROLLER.**
Annual reports.
Financial summary, 1916, 1917.

——— **DEPARTMENT OF FINANCE**
Schedule of commodities, services, benefits and claims, alphabetically listed and classified to conform with standard accounts, 1910. 79p.

——— **GAS, OIL AND ELECTRIC LIGHT COMMITTEE**
Report of the committee on gas, oil and electric light, on the investigation of the Commonwealth Edison Company. Chicago, May 1913. Chicago, J. F. Higgins, 1913. 113p.

CHICAGO and Eastern Illinois compensation fixed. *Railway age,* March 26, 1920, p. 1042.

CHICAGO AND NORTHWESTERN RAILWAY COMPANY
Classification of operating revenues as prescribed by the interstate commerce commission, effective July 1, 1907. (Chicago? 1907?) 12p.
Hand book of expenditures to take effect August 1, 1900. Chicago and north western railway company and Fremont, Elkhorn and Missouri valley railroad company . . . Chicago, 1900. 237p.

CHICAGO & Northwestern railway valuation methods. *Engineering news,* Dec. 16, 1915, p. 1160-2.

CHICAGO & Northwestern railway valuation work. *Engineering news,* Oct. 28, 1915, p. 843-5.

CHICAGO asks for square deal on rates; chart. *Gas age,* Sept. 1919, p. 211.

CHICAGO asks seven cents. *Electric railway journal,* Sept. 7, 1918, p. 436.

CHICAGO ASSOCIATION OF COMMERCE. COMMITTEE OF INVESTIGATION ON SMOKE ABATEMENT AND ELECTRIFICATON OF RAILWAY TERMINALS.
SMOKE abatement and electrification of railway terminals in Chicago. Reports. W. F. M. Goss, chief engineer, Chicago, 1915. 1177p. "Statistics of operation, traffic and train movements", p. 547-9. Describing the methods employed by the committee in compiling the statistical facts which have formed the basis for the various studies relating to electrification. Abstract. *Railway review,* Feb. 6, 1916, p. 197-201.

CHICAGO auto truck service reduces hauling charges. *Engineering record,* Sept. 4, 1915, p. 299-300.

CHICAGO city railway material years; describes the handling of material by this company. *Electric railway journal,* Oct. 5, 1912, p. 537-9.

CHICAGO efficiency bureau estimates that electric trucks would save $15,775 yearly. *Automobile,* Dec. 18, 1913, p. 1158-9.

CHICAGO electrification report discussed at New York railroad club. *Electric railway journal,* March 25, 1916, p. 604-5.

CHICAGO elevated railway valuation. *Electric railway journal,* June 22, 1912, p. 1087. Abstracts. Reports of appraisal of the physical properties of the elevated railways of Chicago. *Engineering and contracting,* May 15, 1912. Valuation of the elevated railroads of Chicago. *Engineering record,* May 18, 1912, p. 552. Editorial. *Engineering record,* May 18, 1912, p. 534.

CHICAGO elevated railways valuation. *Electric railway journal,* June 1, 1912, p. 919.

CHICAGO gas rate. *Gas age,* Aug. 1, 1917, p. 100.

CHICAGO hearings in rate advance cases. *Railway age gazette,* September 9, 1910, p. 475-6.

CHICAGO investigation. *Journal of accountancy,* Dec. 1909, p. 136.

CHICAGO, Milwaukee and St. Paul accounting case. Opinion in full of Commissioner Harlan. *Railway age gazette,* Mar. 13, 1914, p. 511-4.

CHICAGO rate hearing. *Telephony,* January 14, 28, 1911.

CHICAGO-reorganization of the department of electricity. *Electrical world,* Aug. 2, 1913, p. 222-3.

CHICAGO riders are now asking higher fares. *Electric railway journal,* Nov. 30, 1918, p. 951.

CHICAGO, ROCK ISLAND AND PACIFIC RAILROAD COMPANY
Classification of disbursement accounts. In effect July 1, 1904. 113p.

CHICAGO terminal—cost of electrification. summary of the items entering into the expenditure for new equipment. *Railway age,* Dec. 17, 1915, p. 1125-8.

CHICAGO traffic, value and finances. *Electric railway journal,* April 14, 1917, p. 686-9.

CHICAGO valuations—agreements to terms by companies. *Electric railway journal,* Dec. 22, 1906, p. 1164

CHICAGO zone valuation committee. *Railway age gazette,* Aug. 25, 1916. p. 325-6.

CHILD, A. P.

How a street railway counts its receipts. *Popular mechanics.* Nov. 1920, p. 676-7.

CHILD, FREDERICK W.

American accountant's view of plant and stock. *Incorporated accountants' journal,* 1903-4, p.97.
Inventory values. *Business,* Jan. 1897, p. 19-20.
System of cost accounts. *Business,* Feb. 1894, p. 56-9.
Value of bookkeeping. *Engineering magazine,* vol. 1, p. 599-604.

CHILD, JOHN T.

Forms for motor sweeper cost keeping. *Public works,* May 15, 1920, p. 417-9.

CHILD, PERCY

Accountant student. *Auditor,* 1890-1, p. 235, 249, 265, 284.
Accounts of executors and trustees. *Accountant,* Nov. 6, 1897, p. 1038-42.
Book-keeping and accounts. London, R. E. Thomas & co. 1891.
————. Same. London, 1899.
————. Same. London, 1905.
Examination notes; accountancy. *Accountant,* Feb. 2, 1895, p. 101-8.
Paper on some of the bookkeeping questions set at the June examinations. *Accountant,* Dec. 31, 1898, p. 1264-71.
Partnership accounts. London, Gee & co. 1896. 71p. (In Lisle, George. *Encyclopaedia of accounting.* v.5. p. 255-74). *Accountant,* May 17, Nov. 15, 1890, Dec. 21, 1895, Jan. 1, 1898, p. 270-3, 633-6, 1035-40, 12-7.
Private accounts. (In Lisle, George. *Encyclopaedia of accounting.* v.5. p. 354-62).

CHILD, R. W.

WHERE a theory fails; depreciation a physical fact. *Stone and Webster public service journal,* June 1911, p. 422-26.

CHILDS, C. H.

System for hotels. *System,* Sept. 1903, p. 189-93.

CHILDS, C. W.

ESSENTIALS of bookkeeping for public schools; single and double entry. San Francisco, Bancroft & co., 1888.

CHILDS, FRANK HALL

Treatise on American business law. 3v. Chicago, Walton school of commerce, 1916. (Walton series). v.1 Elementary law; contracts. v.2. Agency: partnership. v.3. Sales, negotiable instruments. v.4. Property, real and personal.

CHILDS, WILLIAM

Annual budget. *Municipal journal,* Oct. 7, 1915, p. 545-7.

CHILSON, EDWARD NORTON

ORGANIZATION of a purchasing department in railroad systems. *Journal of accountancy,* June 1910, p. 120-30.

CHINA. MINISTRY OF COMMUNICATIONS.

Accounting rules and classifications of railways. Peking, Jan. 1920. Contents: Classification of capital expenditures; Classification of operating revenues; Rules for the treatment of train and locomotive kilometrage; Rules for the treatment of new lines and extensions and of additions to property; Classification of operating expense; Income account, the Profit and loss account, the surplus appropriation account; Classification of operating expenses; Income account, the profit and loss account, the surplus appropriation account; Classification of the general balance sheet, accounts of railways.
Annual report of the (name of railroad) to the Ministry of communications for the year ( ); forms. 137p.
Chinese government railways, summary report on the working result for 1919 with five years comparison. Peking, Ministry of communications, 1920 6p.
Statistics of government railways, for the year ending Dec. 31, 1918. Peking, Ministry of communications, 84p. + tables.

CHINA to adopt income tax. *Commercial and financial chronicle,* Oct. 2, 1920, p. 1322.

CHINESE books of accounts. Hall, R. O.

CHINESE certificated accountants. *Incorporated accountants' journal,* April 1919, p. 128.

CHINESE government railways' accounts. *Railway gazette,* Nov. 17, 1916, p. 538-41.

CHITTICK, JAMES

Silk manufacturing and its problems; being a series of papers on important questions of interest to all those engaged in the manufacture and distribution of silks and other textiles. New York, James Chittick, 1913. 432p.

CHOATE, J. K.

Fare increases. *Aera,* Oct. 1917, p. 197-204.
Pending applications for New York fare increases. *Electric railway journal,* Oct. 13, 1917, p. 664-7.

CHOICE of a profession—accountancy. *Accountant,* Sept. 20, 1890, p. 499-500.

CHORLTON, T.

Status of married women as to property and trading. *Incorporated accountants' journal,* 1889-90, p. 57.

CHRISHOLM, G. D.

Suggestions towards a system of records in connection with advances. *Institute of bankers journal* (London) 1911, v. 32, p. 301-6.

CHRISTIAN, G. A.

Examinations; preparation and working. *Australasian accountant and secretary,* Nov. 1920, p. 352-3.

CHRISTIAN BROTHERS

Bookkeeping by double and single entry. Ed.5. Dublin, 1889.

CHRISTIE, A. G.

Lethbridge municipal power plant. *Power,* April 4, 1916, p. 466.

CHRISTIE, J. R.

Capital losses in relation to dividends. *Public accountant,* April 1918, p. 243-8.

CHUB, J. WILLIAM.

Cost keeping in an English machine tool works. *American machinist,* v. 28, no. 4.

CHURCH, ALEXANDER HAMILTON

Bonus systems and the expense burden. *Engineering magazine,* Nov. 1913, p. 207-16.
Distributing expense burden the analysis based upon the capacity to produce not

CHURCH, ALEXANDER HAMILTON—(*Continued*)
upon the cost of production. *Iron age,* June 1, 1911, p. 1325-6.
Distribution of factory expenses. *Engineering magazine,* v. 21, p. 725-904.
Distribution of the expense burden. *American machinist,* May 25, 1911.
Manufacturing costs and accounts. New York, McGraw-Hill book co. 1917. 452p.
On the inclusion of interest in manufacturing costs. *Journal of acountancy,* April 1913, p. 236-40.
Organization by production factors. *Engineering magazine,* Oct. 1909, April 1910, p. 15-26, 184-94, 361-70, 557-70, 703-15, 863-75; 77-88.
Practical principles of rational management. *Engineering magazine,* April, May 1913, p. 24-33, 166-73.
Premium, piece work, and the expense burden. *Engineering magazine,* Oct. 1913, p. 7-18.
Production factors in cost accounting and works management. New York, *Engineering magazine,* 1910. 187p. (Works management library).
Proper distribution of establishment charges. *Engineering magazine,* July-Dec. 1901, p. 508-17, 725-34, 904-12; 31-40, 231-40, 367-76
Proper distribution of expense burden. New York, *Engineering magazine,* 1908. 144p. (Works management library).
Proper distribution of expense burden. *Engineering magazine,* New York 1908. 116p.
Proper distribution of the factory expense burden. *Engineering magazine,* July-Dec. 1901, p. 507-17, 725-34, 904-12; 31-40, 231-40, 367-76.
Science and practice of management. New York, Engineering co. 1914. 535p. (Works management library).

CHURCH, E. C.
Philosophy of correct purchasing. *Iron age,* May 6, 1915, p. 1008-9.
Systematic purchase and care of mill supplies. *Textile world,* May 1915 p. 207-9.

CHURCH accounting. *Journal of accountancy,* July 1915, p. 39-40.

CHURCH accounts. Dowsley, W. G.

CHURCH accounts, with church members. *Business man's magazine,* April 1907, p. 144-6.

CHURCH and business methods. *Journal of accountancy,* April 1915, p. 294-6.

CHURCH organisation. Marshall, H. C. 1894.

CHURCHES
CHURCH and business methods. *Journal of accountancy,* April 1915, p. 294-6.
LAWRENCE, WILLIAM. Parish finance; paper read at the church congress. Boston, *The church militant,* 1914, 19p.

Accounting
AMERICAN business and accounting encyclopaedia; com. by E. H. Beach and W W. Thorne. Detroit, Bookkeeper publishing co. 1901. Church accounting—v.2, p. 312-3.
AMERICAN unitarian association. Report on church finances and accounting May 25, 1915. 41p.
BOWERS, M. A. Proper method for the keeping of church records. *Business man's magazine,* May 1908, p. 435-7.
CHURCH accounting. *Journal of accountancy,* July 1915, p. 39-40.
CHURCH accounts with church members. *Business man's magazine,* April 1907, p. 144-6.
DOWSLEY, W. G. Church accounts. London, Sir Isaac Pitman & sons. 1911.
FOOTE, MARK. How records of church membership are kept. *System,* Jan. 1906.
FRITZ, JOHN H. Keeping church records. *Business man's magazine,* Oct. 1909, p. 359-61.
KAIB, D. J. Bookkeeping for the parish priests. Milwaukee, M. H. Wiltzius co. (Diedrich-Schafer co) 1910.
KELSEY, ARNOLD R. Improved methods in church, charitable and similar accounts. *Accountant,* June 10, 1916, p. 667-71. *Public accountant,* Feb. 1916, p. 173-81.
LEE, FREDERIC M. Church accounting procedure: correspondence. *Journal of accountancy,* March 1917, p. 238-9.
MARSHALL, HENRY CALDER. Church organisation; accounts and audit; a manual for churchmen and nonconformists. London, Skeffington and son, 1894.
MILLER, H. H. Church accounts. *Accounting and commerce,* April 1917, p. 6-8.
PAROCHIAL cash-book [specimen sheets], designed to facilitate the keeping of accounts of clergymen and church wardens. 1877.
PLANT, WILLIAM P. Accountkeeping of religious corporations. *Business,* April 1896, p. 189-92.
SENIOR, H. C. Financing a church. *Business man's magazine,* March 1910, p. 266-7.
WOODS, J. R. Church financing. *Business man's magazine,* July 1910, p. 97-98.

Auditing
DICKSEE, LAWRENCE R. Churches. (In his *Auditing.* Authorized American edition. p. 159-60).
MARSHALL, H. C. Church organization accounts and audit; a manual for churchmen and nonconformists. 1894.
MONTGOMERY, ROBERT H. Churches. (In *Auditing theory and practice.* 1916. p. 725-6).
SPICER, ERNEST EVAN and ERNEST C. PEGLER. Church. (In their *Audit programmes.* 1919. p. 24-5).
SPICER, ERNEST EVAN and ERNEST C. PEGLER. Churches. (In their *Practical auditing,* 1914. p. 474.

Depreciation
See Depreciation, depletion and obsolescence—Churches.

CHURCHILL, C.
Cost system for shipyards. *International marine engineering,* July-September 1919, p. 486-8, 545-8, 641-3.
How to determine shipyard costs. *Marine review,* Dec. 1919, p. 586-9.

CHURCHILL, F. A.
Design and constructional features of modern brick pavements. *Municipal engineering,* May 1918, p. 184-6.

CHURCHILL, W. L.
Management—the solution of the shipbuilding problem. *Industrial management,* Nov. 1918, p. 361-6.
On what should profits be based? *Industrial management,* Nov. 1919, p. 375-80.
Profiting. *Metal industries.* March 1920, p. 125-7.
Three ways to test cost figures. *System,* Dec. 1916, p. 606-12.

CIGAR BOXES.
See Boxes, packing cases, etc.

CIGAR TRADE
How I watch the sales of a chain of 1100 stores (United cigar stores.) *System,* May 1916, p. 481-7.

CIGAR TRADE—*(Continued)*

PHILLIPS, CAMILLUS. Executive systems of the United Cigar stores company. *Business man's magazine,* April 1905, p. 724-34.

Accounting

ATTENBERG, HENRY N. Internal revenue accounting in the cigar business; an address delivered before the New York society of accountants and bookkeepers. *Accountant,* June 15, 1901, p. 705-6.

CIGARS, wholesale. *International accountants' manual,* 1910, paragraphs 153, 457

DOBBEL, F. W. Retail cigar and tobacco accounting. *Business man's magazine,* 1904, v.16, no. 8, p. 94-9.

CINCINNATI. AUDITOR

Expense classification. 1913. 13p.

Instructions relative to new accounting system. 1913. 4p.

CINCINNATI franchise negotiations. *Electrical world,* July 10, 1915, p. 105.

CINCINNATI purchasing plan. *Municipal jourgineering,* Sept. 1913.

CINCINNATI rate case. *Electrical world, Aug.* 14, 1915, p. 377-8.

CINCINNATI street cleaning. *Municipal journal,* Jan. 14, 1915, p. 38-9.

CINCINNATI street cleaning. *Municipal ennal,* Aug. 3, 1915, p. 125.

CINEMA.

See Moving pictures.

CIRCULAR computer. *Engineering news,* Aug. 27, 1914, p. 451-2.

CIRCULAR no. 7; system of accounting for banks. United States. Federal reserve board.

CIRCULAR no. 45, to electrical corporations and gas corporations. New York state. Public service commission. 1908.

CIRCULAR of information for intending applicants for certificates as certified public accountants. Connecticut State board of accountancy. 1913.

CIRCULAR relating to verifying accounts. United States. Treasury department. 1870.

CIRCULAR with reference to valuation of abandoned property. *Railway review,* Aug. 12, 1916, p. 217-8. Condensed. *Railway age gazette,* Aug. 25, 1916, p. 326.

CIRCULARS on valuation, issued by the President's conference committee on federal valuation of railroads in the United States. *Railway review,* Dec. 25, 1915, p. 815-7.

CIRCULARS to creditors; accountants' liability for libel. *Accountant,* March 19, 1904, p. 356-8.

CITIES. See Municipal.

CITIES favor six-cent fare for Bay state. *Electric railway journal,* June 30, 1917, p. 1188.

CITY accounting in Massachusetts. *Journal of accountancy,* Feb. 1909, p. 324. *Municipal journal,* Feb. 3, 1909, p 173.

CITY auditors; an ancient office. *Incorporated accountants' journal,* Nov. 1920, p. 26.

CITY for the people. Parsons, Frank, 1901.

CITY government by commission. Chase, H. S.

CITY government in the United States. Goodnow, F. J. 1908.

CITY managers short convention program. *Engineering record,* December 9, 1916, p. 711.

CITY of Cambridge, report on financial condition of the city with recommendations. Chase, H. S.

CITY of Clarksburg, West Virginia, handles water at low cost. *American gas engineering journal,* May 19, 1917, p. 503.

CITY of Coventry tramways department; report of general manager and professional auditor as to making provision in the accounts for renewals and other questions of financial policy. *Acountant,* Aug. 16, 1913, p. 205-8, 216-20.

CITY of East Grand Forks, v. J. G. Steele, 121 *Minnesota Reports,* p. 296 and 141. *Northwestern Reporter,* p. 181.

CITY of Woonsocket, R. I. ,report and recommendations on the examination of the books of the city department. Rex, G. M. 1908.

CIVIC LEAGUE OF ST. LOUIS. MUNICIPAL FINANCE AND TAXATION COMMITTEE.

WORK of a municipal efficiency bureau . . . April, 1911 8p.

CIVIC value of hospital records. *Survey.* October 30, 1915, 113p.

CIVIL CITIES and towns. Indiana. State board of accounts. 1917.

CIVIL engineer's pocket-book. Trautwine, John C. c1919.

CIVIL SERVICE

BROWN, HERBERT D. Savings and annuity plan proposed for retirement of super annuated civil service employees. *Government accountant,* Oct. Nov. Dec. 1911, Jan. Feb. March, May, June, July 1912, p. 249-63, 317-24, 331-50, 379-401, 462-6, 510-4, 35-8, 51-4, 118-32.

UNITED STATES. PRESIDENT'S COMMISSION ON ECONOMY AND EFFICEENCY. Message of the president of the United States, retirement from the classified civil service of super annuated employees. Washington, 1912. (62d congress, 2d session, H document no. 732).

CIVIL service book-keeping. Keefe, John, 1904.

CIVIL service book-keeping: bookkeeping no mystery; by an experienced bookkeeper. London, Crosby, Lockwood & son, 1870, 1872, 1874, 1883.

CIVIL service bookkeeping; examinations papers set 1885 to 1896. Keefe, John. 1897.

CIVIL service commission and special assessment. Chicago, Commission on city expenditures. 1911.

CLADER, WILL-A.

Closing books for fiscal year of electrical and gas corporations. *Journal of accountancy,* April 1910, p. 412-8.

Electric utilities accounting. *Journal of accountancy,* May 1917, p. 326-37.

Water utilities accounting. *Journal of accountancy,* Aug. 1919, p. 81-94.

CLAF, M. D.
Receipt for obtaining higher railway revenue; a new railway tariff and ticket system. Basle, 1908. 15p.

CLAFLIN, GEORGE E.
Depreciation accounting for small companies. *National electric light association, Proceedings,* 1909, p. 165-82. Abstract. *Electric railway journal,* June 12, 1909, p. 107.

CLAIM against an auditor for alleged negligence. *Accounting and commerce,* Sept. 1918, p. 134-8.

CLAIM department—public service railway. *Electric railway journal,* Oct. 7, 1911. Atlantic city convention section, p. 636-8.

CLAITOR, J. D.
Promoting the printer. *Inland printer,* April 1914, p. 56-9.

CLANCY, R. J.
Railway rates and railways cost of living. *Railway and engineering review,* Dec. 27, 1913, p. 1201-2.

CLAPHAM, F. T.
Checking of maintenance costs. *Engineer,* April 19, 1918, p. 343.
Depreciation of plant. *Mechanical world,* Oct. 19, 1917, p. 219-20.
Distribution of establishment charges. *Engineer,* Aug. 31, 1917, p. 177-8.
Foundry costs. *Engineer,* Oct. 5, 1917, p. 286-7.
Intensive production establishment charges and selling price. *Engineer,* June 8, 1917, p. 516-7.

CLAPP, EDWIN J.
Railway traffic. New York, Alexander Hamilton institute. c1918. 349p. (Modern business, v. 14).

CLAPP, JOHN MANTLE
Talking business. New York, The Ronald press company, 1920. 526p. (Language for men of affairs.)

CLAPP, P. F.
See Rittenhouse, Charles F., joint author.

CLAPP, W. H.
Automatic rate system is fair to all; a year's experience with a service at cost franchise in Westerville, Ohio. *Electric railway journal,* Aug. 10, 1918, p. 230-1.
Motor trucks in southern California; economics and costs. *Journal of the society of mechanical engineers,* Oct. 1916, p. 791-5. *Engineering and contracting,* Oct. 18, 1916, p. 343-7. Condensed. *Concrete,* Nov. 1916, p. 144-7.

CLAPPERTON, ALEXANDER
Books and accounts of investment companies and their audit. *Accountants' magazine,* Dec. 1905, p. 531-43.

CLARE, GEORGE
A B C of the foreign exchanges; a practical guide. New York, The Macmillan co. 1915. 160p.

CLARE, MARTIN
Youth's introduction to trade and business. Ed. 5. London, 1740.
——— Same. Ed. 7. London, 1751.
——— Same. Ed. 8. London, 1758.
——— Same. Ed. 9, revised by B. Webb, London, 1764.
——— Same. Ed. 10, revised by B. Webb. London, 1769.
——— Same. Ed. 11, corrected by J. Good. London, 1782.
——— Same. Ed. 12, London, 1791.

CLARE, T. H.
Further notes on the registration and collection of local taxation licenses. *Accountant,* Aug. 2, 1913, p. 161-70.
Local authorities and their finance. *Accountant,* April 6, May 18, 1907, p. 445-51, 668-70.
Municipal accounts. *Accountant,* Jan. 25, Feb. 15, 1902, p. 105-13, 175-6.
Registration and collection of local taxation licenses. *Accountant,* Aug. 7, 14, 1909, p. 179-91, 209-16.
Some notes on the valuation proposals contained in the budget. *Accountant,* Sept. 12, 19, 1914, p. 290-4, 317-22.

CLARENBACH, ERNEST
Clarenbach system of hotel accounting; hotel monthly patented room rack-ledger system by John Willy; Clarenbach system of hotel accounting, by Ernest Clarenbach; Specially ruled hotel blank books, by John Willy, Chicago, Hotel monthly. c1907. 46p.

CLARIDGE, WILLIAM
Checking of bank interest. *Accountant,* March 7, 1908, p. 326. *Incorporated accountants journal,* 1907-8, p. 151.
Examinations. *Incorporated accountants' journal,* June 1913, p. 226-9.
President's address. *Incorporated accountants' journal,* June 1900, p. 185-7. *Accountant,* May 29, 1920, p. 644-6.
Profit-sharing schemes. *Incorporated accountants' journal,* 1890-1. p. 185.
Registration for the profession. *Accountant,* April 25, 1908, p. 611-3.

CLARISTIAN, ARNOLD
Treatment of time. *Accountant,* Sept. 11, 1920, p. 271-3.

CLARITY of diction. *Journal of accountancy,* Sept. 1920, p. 188-9.

CLARK, ARCHIBALD B.
Economic situation in Great Britain as affected by the war. *Canadian chartered accountant,* Jan. 1915, p. 202-213.
Foreign exchanges. (In Lisle, George. *Encyclopaedia of accounting.* v. 3. p. 97-109).
Gold-supply, credit and prices. *Accountants' magazine,* April 1899, p. 238-60.
High bank rate. *Accountants' magazine,* April 1907, p. 201-13.
Indian currency question. *Accountants' magazine,* June 1898, May 1899, p. 338-47, 312-32.
National credit and national debts. *Accountants' magazine,* July 1899, p. 410-33.
Our free trade policy and present day problems. *Accountants' magazine,* June 1899, p. 366-83.
Proposed customs union of the British empire. *Accountants magazine,* March 1898, p. 158.
Recent currency proposals. *Accountants magazine,* 1897, p. 613.
Trusts in their economic aspects. *Accountants' magazine,* Nov. 1901, p. 482-90.

CLARK, E. A.
How we keep costs in our 75-man plant. *Factory,* Oct. 1916, p. 405-8.

CLARK, E. E.

Interstate commerce commission and its work. *Railway age gazette,* Sept. 17, 1915, p. 493.
Rule of rate making. *Railway age,* Feb. 6, 1920, p. 420.

CLARK, E. G.

Depreciation in accounts. *South African accountants' journal,* v. 2, p. 9.

CLARK, EARL S.

Cost and accounting records. *Business man's magazine,* July, Aug. 1907, p. 64-70, 61-6.
Practical costs. *Industrial management,* Dec. 1916, Jan. Mar. May 1917, p. 299-305, 529-33, 768-72; 195-8.

CLARK, ERNEST L.

Time and material system. *Business man's magazine,* June 1907, p. 96-112.

CLARK, F.

Accurate accountancy in connection with advertising. *Business organisation and management,* Nov. 1920, p. 192-4.

CLARK, GEORGE A.

Recent development in railroad finance. *Railway age gazette,* June 18, 1915, p. 1418-20.

CLARK, GEORGE

Practical instruction in bookkeeping. London. [1907]

CLARK, GEORGE F.

Double entry bookkeeping for technical classes and schools. London, 1898.

CLARK, HARLOW C.

Advantages of service-at-cost for electric railroads. *Electric railway journal,* June 21, 1919, p. 1219-20.
Cleveland and its "3-cent" fare: "best service" sacrificed in effort to retain low price of riding. *Aera,* Aug. 1917, p. 1-13.
Fare increases in New York. *Electric railway journal,* Jan 3, 1920, p. 32-5.
Fares are seeking higher level; increases made in 1919 indicate readjustment to meet higher operating costs: conditions in all cities having a population of more than 25,000 as they now exist. *Aera,* Feb. 1920, p. 783-814.
Massachusetts cuts loose. *Aera,* June-July 1918, p. 1077-94, 1199-1215.
Public opinion and fare increase. *Aera,* July 1917, p. 1344-51.
Service at cost agreements. *Aera,* June, July, Sept. 1919-Feb. 1920, p. 1039-46, 1161-9, 228-36, 417-21, 504-9, 582-93, 723-8.
Some aspects of public service at cost. *Public service,* Dec. 1918, v. 25, p. 175-8.
Some aspects of service at cost: an examination of seven laws and ordinances adopted to put this system into effect on electric railways. *Aera,* Oct. 1918, p. 203-14.

CLARK, J. B.

Commercial education in the secondary school. *Accountants' magazine,* Feb. 1902, p. 110-20.

CLARK, J. C.

Simplifying the accounting system in the small newspaper and job printing office. *Inland printer,* Nov. 1917, p. 189-92.

CLARK, J. M.

Economic aspects of the new long and short haul clause. *Journal of industrial economics,* February 1914, p. 322-37.
Railroad valuation as a working tool. *Journal of political economy,* April 1920, p. 265-306.
Rates for public utilities. *American economic review,* Sept. 1911, p. 473-87.
Some neglected phases of the rate regulation. *American economic review,* Sept. 1914, p. 565-74.

CLARK, J. R.

Handling factory costs; how a foundry gathers them. *Factory,* June 1918, p. 1202-8.

CLARK, L. M.

Cataloguing equipment insures accuracy. *Electric railway journal,* April 15, 1916, p. 739-40.

CLARK, LINDLEY AND A. P. NORTON.

Decisions of courts affecting labor: 1917. Washington, Government printing office, 1918. 299p. (United States. Bureau of labor statistics, no. 246).

——— AND MARTIN C. FRINCKE.

Decisions of courts and opinions affecting labor, 1918. Washington, Government printing office, 1920. 239p. (United States. Bureau of labor statistics, no. 258).

CLARK, NEIL M.

A-B-C of accounting. *System,* Aug. 1913, p. 162-8.
Efficiency in loose leaf accounting. *System* (London), 1914, v. 26, p. 489-95.
Less time out for accounting. *System,* Nov. 1913, p. 532-5.
More stock in the same place. *System,* February 1914, p. 153-9.
Short cut inventory. *System,* January 1914, p. 92-5.

CLARK, PERCY G.

Hints to accountants, liquidators, and receivers on office and factory control. *Accountant,* Sept. 13, 1913, p. 344-53.

CLARK, PERCY R.

Storekeeping organization in Russia; where means of communication are primitive, truckmen illiterate and storekeepers poorly educated. *Industrial management,* May 1918, p. 368-72.

CLARK, R. J.

Prepayment cars and the accountant. *Electric railway journal,* Oct. 9, 1915, p. 721-2.

CLARK, W.

Data showing reduction in cost of lighting. *Electrical review,* March 8, 1919, p. 391-2.

CLARK, W. C.

See Zimmermann, Erick W., joint author.

CLARK, W. I.

Aiding workers with personal service. *Iron trade review,* March 18, 1920, p. 849-50.

CLARK, WILLIAM J.

Discussion on rates and fares. *Electric railway journal,* Feb. 1, 1913, p. 192-5.
Financial aspect of steam railroad electrification. *General electric review,* Nov. 1914, p. 1023-4.

CIARKE, EDWARD GUSTAVUS

Address, 1883. *Accountant,* Oct. 6, 1883.

CLARKE, EDWARD W.

Contracts—a comparison of cost plus with other forms. *Engineering and contracting,*

CLARKE, EDWARD W.—(*Continued*)
Sept. 3, 1919, p. 283-5. *Canadian engineer,* Jan. 29, 1920, p. 183-4.
Practical treatise on brewery accounts and office management. Chicago, 1898. 181p.

CLARKE, GEORGE F.
Bookkeeping for technical classes and schools. London, Gee & co. 110p.
Double entry bookkeeping for technical classes. London, Gee & co. 1898. 108p.

CLARKE, K. E.
Keeping control of factory clerical methods. *Factory,* Aug. 1916, p. 140-3.

CLARKE, P. H.
Inventories that take care of themselves. *System,* September-October 1915, p. 310-4, 427-31.
One-man business: a dentist's records. *System,* Feb. 1915, p. 214-7.

CLARKE, U. H.
Railway records. *Railway master mechanic,* Mar. 1907, pt. 1.

CLARKSON, J. A.
Medical accounts. *Incorporated accountants' journal,* 1908. p. 166.

CLARKSON, S. S.
See Dyson, S. S., joint author.

CLASS exemption not required. *Journal of accountancy,* Feb. 1918, p. 124-5.

CLASSICAL and mediaeval bookkeeping. *Accountant,* June 6, 1891, p. 426-8.

CLASSIFICATION
BENNETT, GEORGE E. Detailed classification of accounts. (In his *Constructive accounting.* 1920. p. 264-86).
BENTLEY, H. C. Classification, its importance and treatment. (In his *Science of accounts.* 1913. p. 85-94).
BERNDT, IRVING A. Symbols as an aid. (In his *Costs.* c1920. p. 157-60).
COST accounts and classification. *Accountant,* Aug. 12, 1905, p. 178-9.
ESQUERRE, P. J. Classification of accounts. (In his *Applied theory of accounts.* 1917. p. 131-8).
HATHAWAY, H. K. Mnemonic system of classification. *Industrial management,* Sept. 1920, p. 173-84).
HAWKINS, L. WHITTEN. Job numbers. (In his *Cost accounts.* 1912. p. 114-5).
HAWKINS, L WHITTEN. Symbols instead of job numbers. (In his *Cost accounts.* 1912. p. 98-9).
JORDAN, JOHN P. and GOULD L. HARRIS. Orders and symbols. (In his *Cost accounting.* 1920. p. 77-94).
KENT, WILLIAM. Classification, symbols. (In his *Bookkeeping and cost accounting for factories.* 1918. p. 131-5).
KESTER, R. B. Classification of accounts. (In his *Accounting theory and practice.* 1918. p. 246-57).
KESTER, ROY B. Numbered accounts. (In his *Accounting theory and practice.* v. 2. 1918. p. 563-70).
MILLER, T. J. Some notes on classification. *Canadian chartered accountant,* July 1918, p. 16-23.
MNEMONIC symbols show distribution of construction expenditures. *Engineering news,* Nov. 7, 1918, p. 865.
PARKHURST, FREDERIC. Expense symbols. (In his *Predetermination of prices.* 1916. p. 26-9).
PARKHURST, FREDERIC A. Symbols. New York, John Wiley & sons, 1917. 165p.
SCOVELL, CLINTON H. Mnemonic symbols. (In his *Cost accounting and burden application.* p. 38-9).
SMITH, OBERLIN. Nomenclature of machine details. (In Garcke, Emile and J. M. Fells. *Factory accounts.* 1893. p. 150-7).
THOMPSON, C. BERTRAND. System of classification that makes it hard to forget. (In his *How to find factory costs.* c1916. p. 110-27).

CLASSIFICATION and certification of profits. Lynn, J. R.

CLASSIFICATION and forms for water utilities. Indiana. Public service commission. 1913.

CLASSIFICATION, discrimination. Richards, E. G. 1913.

CLASSIFICATION of accounts. Carolina. Public service company. 1913.

CLASSIFICATION of accounts. Milwaukee electric railway and light company. 1910.

CLASSIFICATION of accounts. National canners' association. 1917.

CLASSIFICATION of accounts for additions and betterments. *Railway and engineering review,* Aug. 14, 1909, p. 737-8. Editorial comment. *Railway and engineering review,* Aug. 14, 1909, p. 736.

CLASSIFICATION of accounts for electric railway companies, electric light companies, electric light and power companies, steam heat companies, gas companies. Duffy, C. N. 1910.

CLASSIFICATION of accounts for interstate steam roads. *Electric railway journal,* July 25, 1908, p. 348.

CLASSIFICATION of accounts to be used in accounting to the United States for requisitioned vessels operated for government accounts. United States. Shipping board. Emergency fleet corporation.

CLASSIFICATION of appropriation accounts, together with an index, intended for use throughout the departments and divisions of the city government concerned with the disbursements of appropriation funds. St. Louis. Comptroller's office. 1913.

CLASSIFICATION of business fact v. double-entry of business fact as a main consideration in bookkeeping. Millar, T. J.

CLASSIFICATION of Chinese government railways accounts. *Railway gazette,* London, July 9, 1915, p. 34-5.

CLASSIFICATION of depreciation percentages used at Dusseldorf municipal gas works. *Progressive age,* Aug. 15, 1910, p. 707.

CLASSIFICATION of disbursement accounts. Chicago, Rock Island and Pacific railroad company. 1904.

CLASSIFICATION of disbursement accounts. Pennsylvania railroad company.

CLASSIFICATION of expenditures. Maine central railroad company. 1898.

CLASSIFICATION of expenditures for additions and betterments for steam roads. United States. Interstate commerce commission. 1910.

CLASSIFICATION of expenditures for highway cost accounting. *Good roads,* Nov. 9, 1918, p. 178-9.

CLASSIFICATION of expenditures for road and equipment. United States. Interstate commerce commission. 1907.

CLASSIFICATION of expense accounts. Cook county. Department of finance. 1914.

CLASSIFICATION of freight commodities. Association of American railway accounting officers. 1911.

CLASSIFICATION of income and profit and loss accounts. Tinsley, A. L.

CLASSIFICATION of income, profit and loss and general balance sheet accounts for steam roads, effective on July 1, 1914. United States. Interstate commerce commission.

CLASSIFICATION of inventory for water utilities and the inspection of water work systems by the Wisconsin railroad commission. *Engineering and contracting,* September 3, 1913, p. 257-8.

CLASSIFICATION of investment in pipe lines operating revenues and pipe line operating expenses of carriers by pipe lines; effective on January 1, 1915. United States. Interstate commerce commission.

CLASSIFICATION of investment in road and equipment of steam roads, effective on July 1, 1914. United States. Interstate commerce commission. 1914.

CLASSIFICATION of ledger accounts for creameries. Knapp, George O. Burton B. Mason and A. V. Swarthout. 1920.

CLASSIFICATION of locomotive-miles, car-miles, and train-miles. United States. Interstate commerce commission. 1907.

CLASSIFICATIONS of municipal expenditures in budgets and accounts and the purposes which they subserve. Powers, L. G.

CLASSIFICATION of objects of expenditure with reference to symbols, conforming to recommendations of the President's commission on economy and efficiency. United States. Mint service. 1912.

CLASSIFICATION of operating expenses. United States. Interstate commerce commission.

CLASSIFICATION of operating expenses and construction accounts. Erie railroad company. 1902.

CLASSIFICATION of operating expenses, Harriman lines. *Railway and engineering review,* April 23, 1910, p. 401.

CLASSIFICATION of operating revenue. United States. Interstate commerce commission. 1914.

CLASSIFICATION of operating revenues of carriers by water. United States. Interstate commerce commission. 1910.

CLASSIFICATION of operating revenues of electric railways. United States. Interstate commerce commission. 1908.

CLASSIFICATION of overhead charges. Public service regulation, Feb. 1913, p. 61.

CLASSIFICATION of railway accounts. *Journal of accountancy,* June 1908, p. 136.

CLASSIFICATION of rent items. *Electric railway journal,* Jan. 1, 1916, p. 11-2.

CLASSIFICATION of revenues and expenses for outside operations for steam roads. United States. Interstate commerce commission. 1908.

CLASSIFICATION of revenues and expenses of pipe line companies as prescribed by the Interstate commerce commission. First issue effective on Jan. 1, 1911. Washington, Government printing office, 1910.

CLASSIFICATION of revenue and expenses of sleeping car operations and of other properties for sleeping car companies. United States. Interstate commerce commission. 1912.

CLASSIFICATION of sales department expenses. *Electrical world,* June 22, 1918, p. 1325.

CLASSIFICATION of train miles, locomotive miles and car miles for steam roads. United States. Interstate commerce commission. 1918.

CLASSIFICATION of units involved in construction and additions and betterments. Washington. Railroad commission.

CLASSIFICATIONS and forms for artificial gas utilities. Indiana. Public service commission. 1913.

CLASSIFICATIONS and forms for electric utilities. Indiana. Public service commission. 1915.

CLASSIFICATIONS and forms for water utilities. Indiana. Public service commission. 1913.

CLASSIFIED C. P. A. problems and solutions, 1915. Cox, H. C. 1916.

CLASSIFIED list of prospects. *Business man's magazine,* Dec. 1911, p. 532.

CLASSIFIED statement of stores received, used and on hand. *Business man's magazine,* June 1908, p. 523-4.

CLASSIFIED water works accounts. *Municipal journal,* March 8, 1917, p. 340.

CLASSIFYING the selling expense. *Business man's magazine,* March 1912, p. 256.

CLAUSEN, E. W.

Effect of war-time prices on water-works valuation. *Municipal engineering,* Nov. 1919, p. 239-40.

CLAUSEN, H. P.

Speeding up production for establishing piece work rates. *Engineering magazine,* April 1911, p. 63-8.

CLAUSSEN, O.

Experiences in force account paving in the city of St. Paul, Minn. *Municipal engineering,* August 1918, p. 52-4. Condensed. *Municipal journal,* August 10, 1918, p. 103-5. Excerpts. *Engineering and contracting,* October 2, 1918, p. 322-3.

CLAUTICE, G. J.

Overhead expense. *Metal work,* May 11, 1917, p. 621-2.

CLAY, C.
Piece work as applied to the track department. *Railway engineering and maintenance of way,* Mar. 1913.

CLAYDON, VICTOR R.
Distribution of foundry tonnage burdens. *Engineering magazine,* Sept. Nov. 1909.
Handling of stores and prevention of waste. *Engineering magazine,* June 1910, p. 402-7.
Time keeping and labour distribution in the foundry. *Engineering magazine,* May-July, Sept. 1910, p. 221-9, 402-7, 549-54, 859-64.

CLAYTON, WILLIAM HENRY
Partnership. *Accountant,* 1886, p. 725.

CLEARING house. M'Neil, Allan.

CLEARING house bank examinations. St. Louis clearing house association, 1910. 11p.

CLEARING HOUSES.
See Banks and banking, Clearing houses.

CLEARING houses. Cannon, J. G. 1910.

CLEARING OF LAND
Gillette, Halbert Powers. Handbook of clearing and grubbing; methods and cost. New York, Clark book co., inc. 1917. 241p.
Thompson, Harry and Earl D. Strait. Cost and methods of clearing land in the Lake States. May 16, 1914. 25p. (United States. Department of agriculture, bulletin no. 91).

Costs.
Gillette, Halbert Powers. Handbook of clearing and grubbing; methods and cost. New York, Clark book co., inc. 1917. 241p
Method and cost of clearing cut over land with powder. *Engineering and contracting,* Dec. 19, 1917, p. 505-7.
Thompson, M. J. Cost of stump removal in land clearing. *Engineering and contracting,* June 19, 1918, p. 613.
White, F. M. and E. R. Jones. Methods and costs of stump removal and land clearing. *Engineering and contracting,* May 21, 1919, p. 535-7.

CLEARY, P. ROGER
How to figure profit; a comprehensive reference book for business men, teachers and students. Dept. A., Ypsilanti, Michigan. P. R. Cleary co., 1918. 265p.
Study and practice of business bookkeeping and accounting. Ypsilanti, Mich., Cleary publishing co. 1907.

CLEAVE, JOHN KYRLE FREDERICK
Comparison of landlords rights in bankruptcy and winding up. *Incorporated accountants' journal,* 1898-9, p. 230.
Proposed alterations in company law. *Incorporated accountants' journal,* 1896-7, p. 47.

CLEGG, A.
National insurance developments; big industrial concern's model system. *Business organization and management,* Nov. 1920, p. 195-7.

CLEGG, R. I.
Keeping close track of shop operation. *Iron age,* Nov. 21, 1918, p. 1251-3.

CLELAND, ETHEL, comp.
Five hundred business books. Washington, D. C., American library association, Library war service, 1919. 72p.

———— Same. Ed. 3, revised by Jessica Hopkins. Chicago, American library association, 1920. 62p.

CLEMEN, R. A.
Trend in profit sharing. *Factory,* March 15, 1920, p. 810-1.

CLEMENT, C. E.
Checking systems for a small retail milk dealer. *Hoard's diary,* May 2, 1919, p. 756.

CLEMENT, E. E.
Comparative costs of handling telephone traffic—comparison of traffic cost for manual and auto-manual systems by the inventor of the latter. *Telephony,* May 6, 1911, p. 551-3.

CLEMENTS, DAVID M.
Selling the Northwest. *Banker's monthly,* March 1918, p. 14.

CLEMINSON, C. L. O.
Goodwill. *Accountant,* June 8, 1907, p. 784-5.

CLERK, ALLAN I. M.
First year's company audit. *Incorporated accountants' journal,* 1903-4, p. 134.

———— **AND OTHERS**
Prevention and detection of fraud. *Incorporated accountants' journal,* 1904-5, p. 84.

CLEVELAND, A. W.
Hints to candidates. *Accounting and commerce,* Feb. 1917, p. 262-4.
Trust companies, their books, accounts and audit. Sydney institute of public accountants conference, 1901. *Bookkeeper,* 1902, v. 14, no. 7, p. 73-8.

CLEVELAND, FREDERICK ALBERT
Accountancy as a profession; reprinted from the *Financier,* Aug. 1, 1904. New York, 1904. 11p.
Administrative significance of a municipal balance sheet. *Government accountant,* Sept. 1908, p. 179-91.
Advantages of an independent railway audit to the investor. *Journal of accountancy,* March 1906, p. 386-95.
Appraisements and accountancy. *Auditor.* 1905, p. 125, 153.
Bank and the treasury. New York, Longmans, Green & co. 1905. 326p.
Budget as a means of locating responsibility for waste and inefficiency—what the president is trying to do by way of budget making for the national government. New York, 1912. 16p.
Budget making and the increased cost of government; with discussion. *American economic review,* March 1916, sup. 50-84.
Chapters on municipal administration and accounting. New York, Longmans, Green & co. 1909. 361p.
Chicago accounting reform. *National municipal league. Proceedings,* 1903, p. 268-86.
Constitutional provision for a budget. *Academy of political science, Proceedings,* Oct. 1914, p. 141-92.
Dr. Cleveland's response; correspondence. *Journal of accountancy,* Nov. 1905, p. 40-56.
Efficiency in public management. Read at the first meeting of the Efficiency society held in New York city, March 18 and 19, 1912. 10p.
Essentials of a municipal budget. *New Jersey municipalities,* June 1917, p. 15-20.

CLEVELAND, FREDERICK ALBERT—(*Continued*)

Evolution of the budget idea in the United States. *Annals of the American academy of political and social science*, Nov. 1915, p. 15-35.

Financial management of municipalities. *Public policy*, April 22, 1905, p. 186-92.

Financial reports of national banks as a means of public control; reprinted from the *Annals of the American academy of political and social science for July*, 1904. 21p.

Forms of municipal balance sheets. *National municipal association of comptrollers and accounting officers. Proceedings*, 1911, p. 83-100. *Government accountant*, June, July, 1912, p. 70-83, 109-17.

Funds and their uses; a book describing the methods, instruments and institutions employed in modern financial transactions. Revised edition. New York, D. Appleton & co. 1916. 304p.

Municipal accounting. *Business world*, July 1905, p. 357-61.

Municipal accounts. *Political science quarterly*. Sept. 1904, p. 391-401.

Municipal credit and accounting reform. *Journal of accountancy*, June 1906, p. 109-17.

NOMENCLATURE and phraseology of municipal administration and accounts. *National municipal league, Proceedings*, 1905, p. 235-43.

PHILANTHROPY and accountancy. *National conference of charities and correction, Proceedings*, 1906. p. 198-206.

Popular control of government; three schools of opinion in the United States with respect to budget making. *Political science quarterly*, June 1919, p. 237-61.

Principles of budget making. *Journal of accountancy*, Oct. 1907, p. 456-66.

Relation of auditing to public control. Philadelphia. *Annals of the American academy of political and social science*, Nov. 1905, p. 665-80.

Relation of finance to accounting. *Rand McNally Bankers' monthly*, v. 23, p. 491-505.

Relation of the public accountant to the banker. *New York accountants' and bookkeepers' journal*, Nov. 1903, p. 171-3.

Revenues and expenses as distinguished from receipts and disbursements in municipal accounting. *Accountant*, Oct. 15, 1904, p. 406-10. *Federation of societies of public accountants in the United States of America. Official record of the Congress of accountants held at the World's fair, Saint Louis, September 26th, 27th and 28th, 1904.* p. 60-70. *Incorporated accountants' journal*, 1904-5, p. 72.

Scope of the profession of accountancy. *Journal of accountancy*, Nov. 1905, p. 40-56.

Suggested curriculum for a professional school of accounting. *Journal of accountancy*, Jan. 1907, p. 199-202.

Uses and purpose of a municipal general ledger. *Journal of accountancy*, Oct. 1910, p. 401-25.

What a budget may mean to the administration. (In *University of Illinois; Conference on commercial education and business progress*, 1913, p. 35-50).

What constitutes reasonable uniformity in municipal accounts and reports. *National municipal league, Proceedings*. 1904. p. 203-15. *Engineering record*, 1904, v.49, p. 598-9, 626-7.

What is involved in the making of a national budget. *Journal of accountancy*, May 1913, p. 313-28.

What may accountancy teach economics? *Journal of accountancy*, Oct. 1906, p. 401-9.

What we do not know about the affairs of our cities. *League of American municipalities, Proceedings*, 1908.

——— **AND F. W. POWELL**

Railroad finance. New York, D. Appleton & co. 1912. 462p.

Railroad promotion and capitalization in the United States. New York, Longmans, Green & co. 1909. 368p.

CLEVELAND, JOHN A.

Electric truck about 50 per cent cheaper than horse and wagon. *Automobile*, Jan. 16, 1913, p. 236.

CLEVELAND, OHIO

Continuous audit must be obtained; preliminary reports of auditors prove its value. *Civic affairs*, no. 6, April 1917. 4p.

(Resolution transmitting suggested "application and agreement for the use of "electric current," "explanation of chart showing rate schedule," "conditions," and the rate chart, and providing that rates for electric energy furnished by the department of public utilities, division of light and heat, be fixed in accordance therewith.) *Cleveland city record*, May 19, 1915, p. 540-1.

——— **CHAMBER OF COMMERCE**

Industrial profit sharing and welfare work; a report of the committee on industrial welfare; approved by the board of directors, April 10th, 1916. 85p.

Municipal accounting. Reports, no. 1-3, 1910-13. Cleveland, 1910-13.

Recommendation for the installation of a general ledger in the office of the city auditor. Cleveland, 1910. 6p. (Municipal accounting report, no. 1).

——— **DEPARTMENT OF ACCOUNTS**

Standard code classification of expenditures. (Cleveland, 1914 40p.).

——— Same. 1915. 42p.

CLEVELAND accountant. Crawford, J. N. 1898

CLEVELAND hearing. *Electric railway journal*, May 24, 31, 1913, p. 925, 971.

CLEVELAND municipal electricity rates. *Engineering news*, Aug. 20, 1914, p. 411.

CLEVELAND Ohio city council authorizes higher fare. *Aera*, Aug. 1918, p. 15-6.

CLEVELAND street railway situation. *Municipal engineering*, Oct. 1916, p. 132.

CLEVELAND'S municipal electric light plant. *Municipal journal*, June 24, 1915, p. 869-75.

CLEVELAND'S new municipal electric plant: selling electricity at three-cent maximum rate. *Engineering news-record*, July 30, 1914, p. 258-61.

CLEWELL, C. E.

Automatic helpers for the management. *Factory*, May 1919, p. 939-43.

Cost tables for the installation of shop and office lighting system. *American machinist*, April 19, 1917, p 677-80.

Initial and operating cost of factory lighting. *Electrical world*, Aug. 18, 1917, p. 292-5.

CLEWS, HENRY

Business education and commercial and banking methods. *Accountant*, Sept. 16, 1905, p. 305-11.

No danger in great fortunes. *Journal of accountancy*, Feb. 1907, p. 276-84.

CLIFTON, CHARLES

Rating of waterworks. *Surveyor*, Dec. 15, 1916.

CLINCH, SIDNEY, H.

Some notes on the law relating to companies limited shares. *Accountant,* Nov. 16, 1912, p. 631-7.

Some points in the completion of an audit. *Accountant,* May 23, 1914, p. 765-70. *Incorporated accountants' journal,* April 1913, p. 164-8.

CLINE, E. L.

Depreciation of telephone companies. *Telephony,* July 2, 1910, p. 16.

CLIPPER profit sharing plan nearly doubles both production and wages. *Automobile,* June 4, 1914, p. 1172-3.

CLOAKS.

See Clothing.

CLOCKS.

See Timekeeping.

CLOSE corporation. Conyngton, Thomas.

CLOSE fiscal year on December 31 instead of June 30. Nay, Frank.

CLOSE of an audit. Cooley, M. L.

CLOSING books for fiscal year of electrical and gas corporations. Clader, W. A.

CLOSING branch accounts. *Accountant,* April 11, 1914, p. 519-20.

CLOSING share transfer books. *South African accountant and auditor,* Dec. 1916, p. 213-4.

CLOTH room report. *Textiles,* October, 1917.

CLOTHIER, C. C.

Suggestions on accounting for municipally owned water works. *Engineering and contracting,* June 23, 1915, p. 551.

CLOTHING

EMMET, BORIS. Labor survey of Cleveland cloak industry; from the *Monthly labor review,* (Aug. 1918) of the Bureau of labor statistics, United States department of labor. 24p.

GORDON, M. Factory management in garment trades. *Industrial management,* May-Oct. 1919, p. 345-9, 446-51; 12-16, 140-5, 230-5, 321-4.

INTERNATIONAL association of garment manufacturers; detailed statement of uniform cost accounting plans to be presented at semi-annual convention. *Clothing trade journal,* Dec. 1920, p. 109.

LAW, J. L. Making of a collar. *Accounting and commerce,* Feb. 1916, p. 244-8.

TABLE prepared showing life of soldier's wearing apparel. 1 typewritten page.

Accounting

AMERICAN business and accounting encyclopaedia; comp. by E. H. Beach and W. W. Thorne. Detroit, Bookkeeper publishing co. 1901. Clothing business accounting—v.2. p. 325-6.

CLOTHING manufacturing. *International accountants' manual,* 1910, paragraph 416.

COHEN, P. I. Accounting methods used by manufacturers of ladies garments *Business man's magazine,* 1904, v.16, no 8, p. 72-6.

MANUFACTURE of shirt waists. *Business man's magazine,* Feb. 1907, p. 140-6.

MAYER, ALEXANDER. Controlling your business from the office. *Business man's magazine,* Jan. 1912, p 68-73.

STEEL, L. R. Accounting system for a shirt and overalls manufacturing business. *Business man's magazine,* 1904, v.16, no. 7, p. 53-9.

Cost accounting

EGGLESTON, DEWITT CARL. Garment factory production orders. (In his *Problems in cost accounting.* 1918. p. 18-9).

FRANKEL, PHILIP. Cost finding in the cloak and suit industry; issued under the direction of the National cloak, suit & shirt mfrs assn. Cleveland, Ohio, P. Frankel, 1912. 19p.

NICHOLSON, J. LEE AND JOHN F. D. ROHRBACH. Garment manufacturing plants. (In their *Cost acounting.* 1919. p. 27).

SANDERS, A H. Accounting in the garment trade. *Daily garment news,* Jan. 6, 1920, p. 18.

TOMPKINS, E. Conversion cost of flat cut woolen underwear. *Textile world,* Jan. 22, 1916, p. 835, 837.

UNITED STATES. Bureau of foreign and domestic commerce. Cost finding and accounting conditions. (In its *Men's factory made clothing industry.* 1916. p 219-33).

UNITED STATES. Bureau of foreign and domestic commerce. Simplified cost accounting. (In its *Women's muslin—underwear industry.* 1915. p. 118-24).

UNITED STATES. Bureau of foreign and domestic commerce. Simplified cost accounting. (In its *Shirt and collar industries.* 1916. p. 108-20).

Costs

UNITED STATES. Bureau of foreign and domestic commerce. Men's factory-made clothing industry; report of the cost of production of men's factory-made clothing in the United States. Washington, Government printing office, 1916. (Miscellaneous series, no. 34).

UNITED STATES. Bureau of foreign and domestic commerce Shirt and collar industries; report on the cost of production of men's shirts and collars in the United States. Washington, Government printing office. 1916. 178p. (Miscellaneous series, no. 36).

UNITED STATES. Bureau of foreign and domestic commerce Women's muslin-underwear industry; report of the cost of production of women's muslin-underwear in the United States. Washington, Government printing office, 1915. 184p. (Miscellaneous series, no. 29).

Stockkeeping

GORDON, MACK. Factory management in garment trades; purchasing and storekeeping methods. *Industrial management,* June 1919, p. 446-51.

CLOTHING TRADE

Accounting

CLOTHING, retail. *International accountants' manual,* 1910, paragraph 433.

SCHLESSINGER, MAX. Retail clothing store accounting. *Journal of accountancy,* July 1919, p 25-32.

SHERMAN, THOMAS H. System for the clothier and furnisher. *System,* Sept. 1903, p. 215-20.

WOLF, W. J. Billing and accounting system for the wholesale cloak business. *Business man's magazine,* June 1908, p. 499-502.

CLOUD, J. D.

Financial problems of cities. 1916. 16p.

CLOUGH, J. L.

Model system of bookkeeping for electric lighting companies. *Municipal engineering,* Oct. 1900, p. 251-5.

CLOUGH, WALTER OWEN

Bankruptcy law amendment bill. *Incorporated accountants' journal,* 1890-1, p. 86.
Bankruptcy legislation; a review; bankruptcy act, 1883, its working, etc. *Incorporated accountants' journal,* 1889-90, p. 63.
Deeds of arrangement. *Incorporated accountants' journal,* 1890-1, p. 180.

CLOW, P. F.

Suggestion for the study of municipal finance. *Quarterly journal of economics,* July, 1896, p. 455-66.

CLOWES, J. H.

Efficiency in water revenue collection. *Annals of the American academy of political and social science,* May 1912, p. 86-92.

CLUB accounts and their control. Witt, Harold Tansley. 1913.

CLUBS.

See Societies, clubs, etc.

CLUBS and their management. Pixley, Francis W. 1916.

CLUBS; their formation and management. Pinks, H. V. 1911.

"CLUSTER" street lighting. Yonkers bureau of municipal research. 1920.

COAL

See also Coal trade; Fuel; Mining and metallurgy—Coal.

HOUGH, B. K. Coal accounting in the boiler room. *Power,* April 15, 1919, p. 586.
NICOLLS, WILLIAM JASPER. Coal catechism. Philadelphia, George W. Jacobs & co. c1906. 235p.
POLAKOV, W. N. Chart with which to make various records for coal. *Electrical world,* Nov. 10, 1917, p. 911-2. *Journal of the American society of mechanical engineers,* Jan. 1918, p. 105.

Costs

BARSTOW, W. S. Fuel costs in public utilities. *Gas age,* March 1, 1917, p. 237.
BLAKE, A. F. Alignment chart for the evaluation of coal. *Journal of industrial and engineering chemistry,* August 1918, p. 627-9.
BLAKE, A. F. Graphic chart for the evaluation of coal. *Journal of industrial and engineering chemistry,* Dec. 1916, p. 1140-2.
BRATAGER, S. J. Cost of coal on the heat value basis. *Railway review,* Dec. 9, 1916, p. 791.
BROWN, J. F. K. Cost of reaching the market. *Coal age,* June 1, 1918, p. 1003-5.
COST of coal. *Power,* Dec. 12, 1916, p. 824.
FEARING, F. C. Relative costs of coal and of oil fuels. *Engineering and mining journal,* March 25, 1916, p. 555-6. *Power,* December 14, 1915, p. 826-7.
GRADY, W. H. Cost factors in coal production. *American institute of mechanical engineers' bulletin,* May, July, 1915, p. 1035-72, 1469-70.
SCHOTT, W. H. Simplified method of determining cost of coal per 1000 lbs. of steam. *Electrical world,* Oct. 2, 1915, 754-6. *Power,* Sept. 28, 1915, 456-8. *Engineering and mining journal,* Oct. 16, 1915, p. 636-8.
SCHAPHORST, W. F. Chart for determining the cost of coal on the heat value basis. *Railway review,* Sept. 23, 1916, 422. *Journal of the American society of mechanical engineers,* Dec. 1916, 1036-7.
SMITH, O. AND C. E. LESHER. Cost of coal. *Metallurgical and chemical engineering,* Dec. 1, 1916, p. 63-15. *Economic geology,* Jan. 1917, p. 42-55. Condensed. *American gas light journal,* Dec. 11, 1916, p. 401-3. *Electrical review and western electrician,* Dec. 23, 1916, p. 1083-4. *American industries,* Jan. 1917, p. 15-17. Abridged. *Gas age,* Dec. 15, 1916, p. 655-7.
WALES, R. L. Equivalent cost of coal and oil as fuel. *Engineering and mining journal,* June 30, 1917, p. 1147-8. *Power,* March 13, 1917, p. 347-8.

Depreciation.

See Depreciation, depletion and obsolescence—coal.

Prices

COST data on which changes in coal prices will be based in hands of fuel officials. *Official bulletin,* Feb. 26, 1918, p. 1.
GARNSEY, C., R. A. NORRIS and J. H. ALLPORT. Method of fixing prices of bituminous coal adopted by the United States fuel administration. *Bulletin of the American institute of mining and metallurgical engineers,* Sept. 1918, p. 1411-33. *Coal age,* Oct. 10-17, 1918, p. 685-9, 736-9. Discussion. *Bulletin of the American institute of mining and metallurgical engineers,* Dec. 1918, p. 1766-8.
SKINNER, J. D. Graphic determination of prices. *Coal age,* May 25, 1918, p. 960-2.
SMITH, GEORGE O. AND C. E. LESHER. Analysis of the cost elements in the price of coal in the United States. *Economic world,* Nov. 25, 1916, p. 683-7. Condensed. *Electrical review and western electrician,* Dec. 23, 1917, p. 1083-4

COAL catechism. Nicolls, W. J. 1906.

COAL HANDLING

COAL handling costs reduced by use of automatic truck loader. *Electrical review,* Oct. 20, 1917, p. 701.
ELECTRIC truck reduces cost of coal handling. *Electrical review,* Dec. 28, 1918, p. 1017-8. *Electrical world,* Jan. 11, 1919, p. 86. *Iron trade review,* Jan. 16, 1919, p. 210.
REDUCING costs of coal loading. *Coal age,* July 28, 1917, p. 160.

COAL handling costs reduced by use of automatic truck loader. *Electrical review,* Oct. 20, 1917, p. 701.

COAL mine accounting systems. *Coal age,* Nov. 1, 1913, p. 653.

COAL mine accounting—uniform system for West Virginia mines. *Black diamond,* July 6, 1916.

COAL mine gatehouse—need of a checking system. *Coal age,* December 8, 1917, p. 959. Discussion, Jan. 26, Feb. 2, April 13, 1918, p. 209, 256-7, 74.

COAL rate decisions. *Journal of political economy,* April 1915, p. 389-92.

COAL rates and new business policy. *Electrical world,* August 11, 1917, p. 253-4.

COAL TAR

UNITED STATES. Tariff commission. Census of dyes and coal-tar chemicals 1918. Washington, Government printing office, 1919. 102p. (Tariff information series no. 11).
WARNES, ARTHUR R. Coal tar distillation and working up of tar products. Ed. 2, revised and enlarged. New York, D. Van Nostrand company, 1918. 302p.

COAL tar distillation and working up of tar products. Warnes, Arthur R. 1918.

COAL TRADE

Accounting

AMERICAN business and accounting encyclopedia; comp. by E. H. Beach and W. W. Thorne. Detroit, Bookkeeper publishing co. 1901. Coal business accounting, v.2, p. 328-9.

BECK, PETER. How I keep up with rising cost. *System,* May 1916, p. 535-9.

BECK, PETER. Why the retail coal dealer should employ a modern accounting system. *Cooperative manager and farmer,* Aug. 1918, p. 94-5.

COX, W. E. Cost accounting for retail fuel dealers. Seattle, University of Washington, 1920. 63p.

MCNEIL, J. C. Accounting system for coal companies; a brief description of a system of bookkeeping in which reliance is placed on vouchers and loose-leaf forms. *Coal age,* Sept. 20, 1913.

PASLEY, ROBERT S. Uniform accounting for retail coal and lumber trade. *Journal of accountancy,* Feb. 1920, p. 118-22.

UNITED STATES. Fuel administration. System of accounts for retail coal dealers, November 1, 1917. Washington, Government printing office, 1918. 23p.

COAPMAN, C. W.

How to find costs on repair work. *Factory,* May 1917, p. 656-7.

COAPMAN, JOHN

Printing office cost system. *Business man's magazine,* Feb. 1911, p. 190-1.

COASTING recorders in New York. *Electric railway journal,* Mar. 20, 1915, p. 572-5.

COASTING records as an aid to faster schedules. *Electric railway journal,* Sept. 1, 1917, p. 355-6.

COASTING records of Northern Texas traction company. *Electric railway journal,* June 26, 1915, p. 1198-1200.

COATH, T. HOWARD

Accounting for retailers and trading concerns. *Australasian accountant and secretary,* Oct. 1919, p. 12-5.

COBB, C. M.

Office methods for a small contracting business. *Engineering and contracting,* April 5, 1916, p. 317-21.

COBB, L.

Cost of engineering supervision in road work. *Engineering and contracting,* May 17, 1916, p. 451-2.

Detailed cost of 113-ft. reinforced concrete through girder bridge built near Douglas, Arizona. *Engineering and contracting,* Dec. 27, 1916, p. 573-6.

Detailed cost of surfacing highway with caliche. *Engineering and contracting,* January 3, 1917, p. 5-6.

COBB, WHITFIELD

Cobb's system of dental bookkeeping. Winston-Salem, N. C., W. Cobb, 1914. 20p.

COBBETT, PITT

Practice of underwriting capital. *Incorporated accountants' journal,* 1889-90, p. 52.

COBBLER and last. *Journal of accountancy,* Nov. 1920, p. 361-4.

COBURN, F. G.

How to use statistics in management. *Engineering magazine,* Aug. 1915, p. 717-23.

COCHRAN, J. TULLIS

Golden rules at an examination. *Accountants magazine,* Nov. 1920, p. 584.

Guide to students; how to answer examination questions. *Accountants' magazine,* May 1920, p. 330-4.

See also Wardhaugh, John B., joint author.

COCHRANE, CHARLES H.

For printers and publishers. *Business man's magazine,* Aug. 1907, p. 80-4.

COCKE, HUGH GOLDING

Bank balance sheets; under the Indian companies act, 1913. *Accountant,* April 21, 1917, p. 391-6.

Indian companies act, 1912; correspondence. *Accountant,* Aug. 2, 1913, p. 156-7.

Summary of the principle legal decision affecting auditors; a paper read before the Chartered accountant students society of London on Wednesday, February 20th, 1907. London, Gee & co. 1907. 39p. *Accountant,* May 18, 1907, p. 678-90.

COCKROFT, WILLIAM

Audit of mining companies' accounts. *New York accountants' and bookkeepers' journal,* June, July 1904, p. 161-3, 193-8.

COCKSEY, EDWARD

Law of partnership. *Incorporated accountants' journal,* Oct. 1915, p. 14-7.

COCOANUTS

Cost accounting

EGGLESTON, DEWITT CARL. Raw material report; sales analysis. (In his *Problems in cost accounting.* 1918. p. 53-5, 190-3).

CODE of ethics for lawyers. *Journal of accountancy,* June 1908, p. 134-6.

CODE of special revenue bonds fund accounts, special and trust fund accounts and borough accounts. New York city. Department of finance. 1910.

CODES

ACCOUNTANTS' code. London, Gee and co. 5/- per dozen. Abroad 5/3 per dozen.

BENTLEY, E. L. Bentley's complete phrase code. New York, Allied code company of U. S.

ROLLINS, MONTGOMERY. Fifth Montgomery code, revised and enlarged, especially adapted for use in the banking and investment business, and the only code of convenient size and arrangement for rapid and economical use. London, George Routledge and sons, c1898-1910. 616p.

CODIFICATION of accountancy ethics. *Journal of accountancy,* Dec. 1905, p. 139-41.

CODY, SHERWIN

How to do business by letter. Revised edition. Yonkers-on-Hudson, New York, World book co. 1918. 238p.

COE, H. L.

Organization for munitions manufacture. *Journal of the American society of mechanical engineers* May 1917, p. 374-6. *American machinist,* July 5, 1917, p. 28-30. *Iron age,* May 10, 1917, p. 1134-5. Condensed. *Iron trade review,* May 24, 1917, p. 1126-8. Discussion. *Journal of the American society of mechanical engineers,* July 1917, p. 611-3.

COE, H. W.
See Leisenring, J.

COES, HAROLD V.
Rehabilitation of existing plants as a factor in production costs. *Engineering magazine,* June 1915, p. 357-71.

COUER D'ALENE power-rates case. *Engineering and mining journal,* Oct. 11, 1913, p. 679.

COFFEE BROKERS

Accounting

TODMAN, FREDERICK SIMSON. Coffee brokerage. (In his *Brokerage accounts.* 1916. p. 226).

COFFIN, FREEMAN C.
Financial management of water works. *Journal of the New England waterworks association,* Sept. 1896, p. 63.

COFFIN, GEORGE M.
Administration and bookkeeping of a national bank. *Business,* Oct. 1898, p. 630-4.

COFFIN'S exercises in bookkeeping. Greenfield, Mass., A. Phelps.

COGHLIN, J. P.
How to estimate cost and keep accounts. *Electrical world,* Oct. 9, 1915, p. 818.

COHEN, H.
Law of cheques. *Incorporated accountants journal,* 1901-2, p. 150.

COHEN, P. I.
Accounting methods used by manufacturers of ladies garments. *Business man's magazine,* 1904, v.16, p. 72-6.

COHN, A.
Installing a half-mile sewer system, Gilbert, Minn. *Engineering news,* August 19, 1915, 364-5.

COIN counter at Kansas City. *Electric railway journal,* July 3, 1920, p. 27.

COKE and iron ore freight rate decisions. *Iron age,* June 19, 1913, p. 1478-80.

COKE and iron ore rates. *Iron trade review,* June 19, 1913, p. 1415-6.

COKE rate reduction. *Iron trade review,* July 31, 1913, p. 186.

COKELEY, W. A.
Valuation of railway land. *Railway age gazette,* Oct. 22, 1915, p. 727.

COLBURN, GEORGE L.
Valuation of machine tools. *Machinery,* May 1915, p. 708-9.

COLD STORAGE

Accounting

BRACE, LAMONT. Coal storage accounting. *Ice and refrigeration,* Jan. 1906, p. 11.
BRACE, LAMONT. Coal storage accounting. *Ice and refrigeration,* v. 30, 1906, p. 1-3, 43-5, 83-5, 261-2, 291-3.
CARD, F. S. Cold storage record for the poultry business. *Business man's magazine,* June 1908, p. 524.
GOODWIN, J. H. System for a cold storage business. *Business man's magazine,* March 1910, p. 255-65.
WASHBURN, CARL H. Some accounting methods for the wholesale produce business. *Business man's magazine,* Oct. 1906, p. 106-14.

Cost accounting

NEFF, PETER. Operating cost in cold storage. *Ice and refrigeration,* 1916, v.50, p. 168-71.

Costs

NEWMAN, P. R. Cost of cold storage buildings. *Concrete,* Nov. 1916, p. 163.
TAIT, R. H. AND L. C. NORDMEYER. Comparative installation and operating costs of a combined ice-manufacturing and cold-storage plant. *Power,* Oct. 28, 1913, p. 606-8.

COLDICOTT, W. ed.
Tabular book-keeping for young men's Christian associations. London, National council of Y. M. C. A. *Y. M. C. A. news.*

COLDWELL, O. B.
Cost accounting. *Journal of electricity, power and gas,* Nov. 14, 1914, p. 455.

COLE, A. B.
Electric freight haulage is an economic duty; organization charts. *Electric railway journal,* Jan. 4, 1919, p. 39-48.

COLE, D. W.
Cost of ditches for reclaiming Idaho lands *Engineering news,* April 3, 1919, p. 678-9.

COLE, E. C.
Cause of the small profit in the plumbing business. *Domestic engineering,* June 14, 1913, p. 306-7.

COLE, ROLAND
Complete record of accidents in manufacturing plants. *Business man's magazine,* Dec. 1907, p. 76-7.
How to find freight rates quickly. *Business man's magazine,* May 1908, p. 438-40.
New card system or record for paying bills. *Business man's magazine,* March, 1908.

COLE, WILLIAM MORSE
Accounting and auditing. Minneapolis, Cree publishing co, 1910.
Accounting methods for determining costs and prices. *Bulletin of the American economic association,* April 1911, p. 124-35.
Accounts; their construction and interpretation for business men and students of affairs. Boston, Houghton, Mifflin co. c1908. 345p. ———— Same. Revised and enlarged edition. Boston, Houghton, Mifflin co. c1915. 445p.
Bookkeeping, accounting and auditing. Chicago, Washington institute, c1914. 479p. (International business library).
Cost accounting for institutions. New York, The Ronald press co. 1913. 247p. (Ronald accounting series).
Income statements for institutions. *Journal of accountancy,* Feb. 1913, p. 79-89.
Institution accounting and records. *Journal of home economics,* Nov. 1910, p. 572-81.
Interest on investment in equipment. *Journal of accountancy,* April 1913, p. 232-6.
Problems in the principles of accounting. Cambridge, Harvard university press, 1915. 102p.
Rise of accountancy. *Journal of accountancy,* Feb. 1909, p. 295-6.
Uniform accounting for institutions. *Journal of home economics,* Feb. 1912, p. 39-50.

COLEFAX, A.
Companies' act, 1900. *Accountant,* April 13, 1901, p. 452-64.

COLEMAN, GEORGE S.

Public service commissions. (In Stetson. Francis Lynde and others. *Some legal phases of corporate financing, reorganization and regulation.* 1917. p. 327-46).

COLEMAN, H. L.

Scientific gas rates; abstracts. *Electric review and western electrician,* Oct. 17. 1914, p. 742. *Electrical world,* Oct. 10, 1914, p. 704.

Specific examples of the benefits from scientific rates. *American gas light journal,* December 7, 1914, p. 362-4.

COLEMAN, WILLIAM C.

Evolution of federal regulation of intrastate rates: the Shreveport rate cases. *Harvard law review,* Nov. 1914, p. 34-81.

COLES, ARTHUR

Company accounts; a complete manual for the use of officials in limited companies and advanced students; with a preface by Charles Comins. Ed. 2. London, Sir Isaac Pitman and sons. 340p.

Depreciation and costing. *Business organization and management,* Nov. 1920, p. 131-8.

COLEY, ALFRED H.

Doctrine of reputed ownership in bankruptcy. *Accountant,* March 7, 1903, p. 328-34.

COLINSON, ROBERT

Idea rationaria, or The perfect accomptant, necessary for all merchants and trafficquers: Containing the true forme of book-keeping, according to the Italian methode; Wherein is first, The Introduction to the forme, 244 Querries and Answers, with instructions how to Ballance the leger, two Waste-books transported in two journals, out of which are transported 2 legers both ballanced. After which followes A moneth-book, invoys-book, factor-book, specie or cash book; instructions how to keep a book of petty-charges or pocket-book. Edinburgh, Printed by David Lindsay, Mr. James Kniblo, Josua van Solingen and John Colmar, in the year 1683.

PERFECT accomptant, etc. Edinburgh. 1683.

COLLABORATION with the Federal trade commission. *Federal reserve bulletin,* Jan. 1, 1917, p. 21-3.

COLLARS.

See Clothing.

COLLATERAL employment of accountants. *Journal of accountancy,* April 1906, p. 504-6.

COLLATERAL in kind. *Journal of accountancy,* March 1914, p. 209.

COLLATERAL register for a bank. *Business man's magazine,* Oct. 1911, p. 342-3.

COLLECTING water revenues. Bureau of municipal research, New York. 1909.

COLLECTION and use of construction cost data. *Engineering news-record,* Dec. 25, 1913, p. 1305-7.

COLLECTION OF ACCOUNTS

BADGER, C. F. Collection tickler for the financial man's guidance. *Business man's magazine,* Feb. 1908, p. 205-6.

BASSETT, W. R. Collection. (In his *Accounting as an aid to business profits.* c1918. p. 132-6).

BOSWORTH, R. L. Simple collection scheme. *Business man's magazine,* Oct. 1907, p. 83-4.

CASSELL, RALPH JOSEPH. Art of collecting; a statement of the underlying principles and practices of collecting with suggestions, form of reports, letters, etc., etc. for the collection manager and the business man: New York, The Ronald press co. 1916. 261p.

CHURCH, A. H. Collecting departmental costs. (In his *Manufacturing costs and accounts.* 1917. p. 377-86).

COLLECTION of small accounts. *Accountant,* Dec. 30, 1911, p. 898-901.

ELIMINATING the monthly statement. *Business man's magazine,* July 1911, p. 66-7.

ETTINGER, RICHARD PRENTICE and David E. GOLIEB. Credits and collections. Ed. 2. New York, Prentice-Hall, c1917.

FORBES, C. Efficient method of dealing with overdue accounts. *Accountant,* Nov. 1, 1919, p. 383. *Accounting and commerce,* Nov. 1919, p. 188-9. *Australasian accountant and secretary,* June 1919, p. 234.

FRENCH, D. G. Monthly installment collections. *Business man's magazine,* Oct. 1907. p. 80.

GALLOWAY, LEE. Handling credits, collections, and complaints. (In his *Office management,* 1918, p. 308-23).

HANBY, WILLIAM H. Subscription collections. *Business man's magazine,* June 1908, p. 527.

HEATON, J. A. Collection of book debts in large businesses with special reference to home and foreign branches. *Accountant,* Sept. 21, 1907, p. 374-6.

JONES, EDWARD D. Credit and collection. (In his *Administration of industrial enterprises.* 1911. p. 417-34).

KESTER, R. B. Discounts and collection costs. (In his *Accounting theory and practice.* 1918, v.2. p. 221).

LEFFINGWELL, WILLIAM HENRY. Office side of credits and collections. (In his *Scientific office management.* 1917. p. 152-7).

MEYER, CHARLES A. Mercantile credits and collections. New York, The Macmillan company. 1919. 302p.

NUCKOLS, J. CECIL. Collection department and its workings. *Commerce accounts and finance,* Sept. 1901, p. 21-3.

PARKER, W. B. Collection records simplified. *Domestic engineering,* Aug. 26, 1916, p. 292.

PARKER, W. B. Method of simplifying collection records for the merchandiser. *Electrical review and western electrician,* Mar. 18, 1916, p. 517.

PARSONS, CARL COPELAND. Credits and collections records. (In his *Office organization and management.* 1918. p. 237-45).

PRENDERGAST, WILLIAM AMBROSE. Collections. (In his *Credit and its uses.* 1916. p. 263-94).

SIMPLE and effective collection system. *Business man's magazine,* June 1908, p. 526-7.

VOLKER, C. E. Collecting past due accounts. *Business man's magazine,* Jan. 1908, p. 111-2.

WAHLSTAD, PETER P. AND W. S. JOHNSON. Collection department. (In their *Credit and the credit man.* 1918. p. 286-335).

WATCHING the overdue accounts. *Business man's magazine,* Sept. 1911. p. 241-2.

WEILER, LOUIS H. Simple collection short cut. *Business man's magazine,* Oct. 1907, p. 105.

COLLECTION of bills. Bowers, E. J. 1911.

COLLECTION of freight charges. *Railway age,* April 23, 1920, p. 1249-50.

COLLECTION of revenue and other fiscal affairs. Kirkman, Marshall Monroe. 1906.

COLLECTION of small accounts. *Accountant,* Dec. 30, 1911, p. 898-901.

COLLECTIVE life insurance. *Electric railway journal,* Jan. 10, 1914, p. 56.

COLLECTIVE systems of payment by results. *Engineering and contracting,* July 30, 1919, p. 151-2.

COLLEGES.
See Schools, colleges, etc.

COLLETT, ROBERT
Standard locomotive fuel performance sheet. (In *Proceedings of the 4th convention of the International railway fuel association.* 1912, p. 42-51). Abstract. *Railway age gazette,* May 31, 1912, p. 1195-8. Discussion, p. 52-85.

COLLEY, FREDERICK GEORGE.
Accounting charges. *Journal of accountancy,* April 1913, p. 245-7.
Appreciation of the New York C. P. A. examinations. *Journal of accountancy,* Aug. 1912, p. 148-50.
Bank loans under the new conditions; borrowers' certified statements as a basis for national currency. *Journal of accountancy,* Dec. 1914, p. 418-26.
Depreciation of manufacturing plants. 15p. *Journal of accountancy,* Sept. 1915, p. 165-72.
Public accountant and office organization. *Journal of accountancy,* Sept. 1912, p. 188-91.
Working papers. *Accountant,* July 22, 1916. p. 83-5. *Canadian chartered accountant,* April 1920, p. 267-72. *Journal of accountancy,* July 1916, p. 43-9.

COLLIE, REGINALD
Comparison of the working of the English and Scottish bankruptcy laws. *Accountant,* Sept. 8, 1894, p. 777-88.
Notes on the comparative costs of winding-up bankrupt estates in Scotland and in England. *Accountants' magazine,* June 1897, p. 373-8.

COLLIER, CHARLES A.
Handling of customers' orders. *Electrical world,* March 27, 1920, p. 740-1.

COLLIER, JAMES
Bookkeeping. London, Relfe bros. 1884.

COLLIER, WILLIAM MILLER
Law and practice in bankruptcy under the national Bankruptcy act of 1898; fourth edition by William H. Hotchkiss; eleventh edition with amendments of statutes and rules, and all decisions to June 1, 1917, including amendments to Bankruptcy act of February 5, 1903, June 15, 1906, June 25, 1910 and March 2, 1917, by Frank B. Gilbert. Albany, Matthew Bender & co. 1917. 1671p.

COLLIERIES.
See Mining and metallurgy—Coal.

COLLIERY accounts. Mann, John and H. G. Judd. 1909.

COLLIERY accounts. Van de Linde, Gerard.

COLLIERY bookkeeping. *Accountant,* Sept. 23, 30, Oct. 7, 14, 1893, p. 796-7, 811-3, 832-3, 852-3.

COLLIERY book-keeping and accounts. Monkhouse, Goddard & co.

COLLIERY GUARDIAN COMPANY.
Colliery guardian series of report books and forms. London, 1903. 16p.

COLLIERY guardian series of report books and forms. Colliery guardian company. 1903.

COLLIERY office organisation and accounts. Innes, J. W. and T. Colin. Campbell. 1912.

COLLIN, T. W.
Columnar system of bookkeeping. *Accountant,* March 23, May 11, 1901, p. 374-6, 545-8.
Newspaper accounts. *Accountant,* Jan. 22, 1910, p. 131-5.
Production of a modern newspaper. *Accountant,* Aug. 9, 1913, p. 188-93.

COLLINGE, BRAMWELL
Executors and their accounts. *Acoountant,* Jan. 4, 1913, p. 27-37.

COLLINGE, VINCENT E.
See Brown, Thomas, joint author.

COLLINS, A. FREDERICK
Short cuts in figures to which added many useful tables and formulas written so that he who runs may read. New York, Clode, c1916. 120p.

COLLINS, ARTHUR
Administration of local government finance in England and Wales. *Accountant,* Sept. 10, 1910, p. 352-61. *Incorporated accountants journal,* Oct. 1910, p. 18-25.
Few points in bankruptcy. *Accountant,* Jan. 16, 1909, p. 85-94.
Municipal debt. *Accountant,* July 26, 1913, p. 132-5.
Municipal internal audit. Ed. 2. London, Gee & co. 1913. 169p.
Organization and audit of local authorities accounts. London, Gee & co. 1908.
Rating reform (with special reference to a wider basis for local rates. *Accountant,* July 27, Aug. 3, 1912, p. 130-6, 160-6.
Some notes on local rates. *Accountant,* July 24, 1920, p. 81-8.
Special features of the audit of municipal trading undertakings. *Accountant,* May 31, 1913, p. 848-51.

COLLINS, B. R. T.
Results of twenty-four hour plant test. *Power,* March 10, 1914, p. 330-2.

COLLINS, CHARLES WALLACE
Governmental thrift through a national budget. *Annals of the American academy of political and social science,* Jan. 1920, p. 65-70.
Minnesota rate cases and the fourteenth amendment. *American law review,* Jan. 1914, p. 27-36.
National budget system. New York, The Macmillan company, 1917. 151p.
Problem of an independent national audit. *Journal of political economy,* Jan. 1920, p. 37-45.

COLLINS, E. F.
Relative thermal economy of electric and fuel-fired furnaces; cost tables. *General electric review,* Sept. 1920, p. 768-73.

COLLINS, F. W.
Waste in the management of public utility power plants. *Engineering magazine,* Sept. 1915, p. 888-93. *American gas light journal,* Feb. 14, 1916, p. 108-9.

COLLINS, G. A.
Efficiency engineering applied to mining. *Industrial engineering,* April 1913, p. 1177-8.
Principles of efficiency for mine management. *Mining and engineering world,* April 4, 1914, p. 643-5.
Small company system for handling accounts. *Electrical world,* July 21, 1917, p. 104-5.

COLLINS, GEORGE E.
Alleviation of gold mining conditions. *Engineering and mining journal,* Sept. 28, 1918, p. 581.

COLLINS, GLENVILLE H.
Efficiency-engineering applied to mining. *Transactions of the American Institute of mining engineers,* 1912, v. 43, p. 649-62.

COLLINS, HUBERT E.
Power costs during years 1914 to 1919; summary of records of fourteen representative plants *Industrial management,* June 1920, p. 467-72.

COLLINS, JAMES H.
Through the knothole "How some business men met their war shrinkage" *World's work,* Nov. 1915, p. 568-74.

COLLINS, JAMES R.
Decimal points. *South African accountant and auditor,* Sept., Dec. 1916, p. 187-90, 220-4.

COLLINS, JOHN
Introduction to Merchants accounts, containing five distinct questions or accounts. 1. An easie question to enter beginners, with instructions to post, stated two several ways, upon several suppositions. 2. A question of a merchant, adventuring a stock or cargazoon with the purser or sopracargo of a ship, who sells the adventure and furnisheth returns, stated two several ways. 3. A question of factorage or goods received by consignation, and returns shipp'd off, with an analysis thereto belonging. 4. A question of a ship's fraightment, with instructions to keep ship-accounts. 5. A question of double exchanges. Compiled by John Collins student in the mathematicks, late professor of Writing, merchants accounts, &c. And may serve as an appendix to the Merchant's mirrour, lately re-printed. The second edition. London, printed by James Flesher for Thomas Clark at the South-entrance of the Royal Exchange, 1664. [See Malynes Consuetudo, vel lex mercatoria, 1656.]
——— Same. Another edition; containing seven distinct questions or accompts. [1 to 5 as above]. 6. An easie partable accompt between three dyers. 7. A controversal partable accompt between three turkey merchants. By John Collins, Fellow of the Royal Society. London, William Godbid, 1675.
Perfect method of merchants-accompts demonstrated. By John Collins, accomptant. London, Printed for Thomas Horne, at the South Entrance of the Royal exchange, 1697. This is really another edition of An introduction to merchants accounts.

COLLVER, CLINTON
How to analyze industrial securities. New York, Moody's investors service, 1917. 204p.
How to analyze industrial securities. Ed. 2. New York, Moody's investors service, 1919. 215p.

COLOR checks on steel requisitions. *Factory,* Nov. 1916, p. 544.

COLORADO. BUREAU OF MINES.
Oil shares of Northwestern Colorado. Denver, 1919. 59p.

——— **PUBLIC UTILITIES COMMISSION.**
Uniform system of accounts for electric light and power utilities; first issue effective January 1, 1916. Denver, 1915. 71p.
Uniform system of accounts for gas utilities; first issue effective January 1, 1916. Denver, 1916. 62p.
Uniform system of accounts for water utilities; first issue effective January 1, 1916. Denver, 1916. 71p.

——— **STATE BOARD OF ACCOUNTANCY.**
List of certificates granted. October 1st, 1919. 1 typewritten page.
Rules of examination for C. P. A. certificate. 5p.

COLORADO. *American institute of accountants Yearbook,* 1907-1916, p. 208-11, 338-41, 316-9, 228-31, 193-6, 256-9, 309-12, 259-62, 249-52, 141-4.

COLORADO. *Journal of accountancy,* June 1907, Nov. 1908, Aug. 1909, p. 166, 481-3, 57, 311.

COLORADO C. P. A. examination. *Journal of accountancy,* Aug. 1909, p. 295-6.

COLORADO C. P. A. examination, 1908. Kingwill, J. H.

COLORADO society elects. *Journal of accountancy,* Oct. 1911, p. 463.

COLORADO society of certified public accountants. *Journal of accountancy,* Oct. 1909, July 1912, Nov. 1914, Oct. 1915, Oct. 1916, Dec. 1917, p. 476, 57, 406, 324, 312, 491.

COLORADO TAXPAYERS PROTECTIVE LEAGUE.
Denver; General balance sheet and other financial statements. Denver, Colorado taxpayers protective league, 1915
Manual of accounting and business procedure for the auditor's office of the city and county of Denver. Denver, Colorado taxpayers protective league, 1915. 55p.
Report on business methods, office of city treasurer, August 1915; prepared by Thomas R. Lill. 1915. 9p.
Uniform system of accounts for the city and county of Denver, issue of 1916. Denver, Colorado, taxpayers protective league. Denver, 1915. 81p.

COLORADO to employ certified accountants. *Journal of accountancy,* March 1911, p. 381.

COLQUHOUN, JAMES
Corporation finance. *Accountant,* April 7, 1894, p. 314-9.

COLSON, C.
Railway rates in the United States. *Railway and engineering review,* Feb. 1, 1913, p. 107-8.

COLT, JOHN CALDWELL
Science of double entry bookkeeping. Ed. 45. New York, Lamport, Blakeman & Law, 1883. 188p

COLTERHILL, GEORGE F.
Maintenance costs of primary highways in Washington for two year period. *Municipal engineering,* Aug. 1919, p. 51-6.

COLUMB, J. S.
Bills of exchange, promissory notes and cheques *Accounting and commerce,* Jan.-April 1919, p. 237-40, 260-2, 287-8, 23-4.

COLUMBIA alumni news, May 28, 1920. New York, Columbia university school of business, 1920.

COLUMBIA, Mo., telephone company. *Electrical review and western electrician,* May 22, 1915, p. 955-6.

COLUMBUS system of customers' records. *Electrical world,* Aug. 9-16, 1919, p. 307, 365.

COLUMNAR RECORDS.
See Bookkeeping, Columnar.

COLVER, WILLIAM B.
Asks that federal cost finding be continued. *Record and guide,* Dec. 28, 1918, p. 744-5.
Lessons of war cost finding. *Annals of the American academy of political and social science,* Mar. 1919, p. 300-5.
Standardized accounting systems recommended. *Foundry,* Feb. 1919, p. 85-6.

COLVIN, F. H.
Bonus plan that works. *American machinist,* May 27, 1920, p. 1137-9.
Cost keeping in the small shop. *American machinist,* Sept. 2, 1920, p. 442-3.
Cost of supervision and overhead. *American machinist,* June 26, 1919, p. 1221-5.
Greenfield tap and die corporation plan of industrial representation. *American machinist,* Feb. 26, 1920, p. 447-8.
How bonus works on the Santa Fe. *American machinist,* Jan. 4, 1912, p. 7-11.

COMBINATION gas and electrical billing. *Electric world,* March 2, 1918, p. 468.

COMBINATION power rate for limited hour service. *Electrical world,* Sept. 15, 1917, p. 530.

COMBINATIONS.
See Consolidations.

COMBINED accountants' time book and clients' ledger. Hazlehurst, H. W. 1912.

COMBINED block and room rate for small town. *Electrical world,* June 30, 1917, p. 1265.

COMBINED ledger page and note memorandum. *Business man's magazine,* March 1910, p. 203.

COMBINED ms. book for bookkeeping. New York, Sir Isaac Pitman & sons. 96p.

COMBINED purchase record and voucher form. *Business man's magazine,* Jan. 1912, p. 81-4.

COMBINED steam and gas engine plant of the Fort Pitt hotel, Pittsburgh. *Power,* June 16, 1914, p. 850-1.

COMBINED tool receipt and inventory. *Factory,* Jan. 1918, p. 148.

COMBINED voucher-check and remittance letter. *Business man's magazine,* Feb. 1910, p. 111.

COMBINING brick or granite block with wood paving blocks. *Municipal engineering,* November 1917, p. 181.

COMER, GEORGE N.
BOOKKEEPING. Boston, Tappan, Whittemore & Mason.
Bookkeeping by double entry. N. H. Whittemore.

COMINS, CHARLES
General principles. *Accountant,* Nov. 26, 1898, p. 1144-50.
Newspaper bookkeeping and accounts. New York, Schultz & Comins. 1896.
Receiverships. *Accountant,* March 11, 1905, p. 281-90.

COMMENT on the commission's decision in the Chicago, Milwaukee and St. Paul accounting case. *Commercial and financial chronicle,* Mar. 14, 1914, p. 788-90.

COMMENT on the proposed revision of accounting rules prescribed by the interstate commerce commission. *Annalist,* April 20, 1914, p. 487-8.

COMMERCE
See also Export trade
BALANCE of trade. *Journal of accountancy,* Nov. 1910, p. 61-2.
BELL, HUGH. Trade after the war. *Accountants' magazine,* Feb., March 1917, p. 55-66, 98-126.
BLYTH, ROBERT. War scares and commercial dislocations. *Accountant,* Jan. 28, 1899, p. 126-8.
BULL, A. J. Probable effect of the war upon the trade of the world. *Accountant,* Dec. 9, 1916, p. 555-65.
DAWSON, SIDNEY S. Commerce and commercial education under post war conditions. *Accountant,* Dec. 28, 1918, p. 345-8.
DAY, CLIVE. History of commerce. New York, Longmans, Green & co. 1917. 640p.
GARFIELD, JAMES R. Commercial ideals. *Journal of accountancy,* Nov. 1906, p. 14-9.
GREAT BRITAIN. Committee on commercial and industrial policy. Final report of the committee on commercial and industrial policy after the war. London, His Majesty's stationery office, 1918. 81p.
GREAT BRITAIN. Statistical office of the customs and excise department. Annual statement of the trade of the United Kingdom with foreign countries and British possessions 1917 compared with the four preceding years. 2v. London, His Majesty's stationery office, 1915.
HAGERTY, J. E. Mercantile agencies. *Journal of accountancy,* Aug 1907, p. 261-71.
IRVING NATIONAL BANK. Trading with the far east; how to sell in the Orient, policies, methods, advertising, credits, financing, documents, deliveries. Cleveland, First national bank, trust and saving co. c1919. 24p.
MACFARLANE, J. P. Value of accountancy to commerce. *Australasian accountant and secretary,* Dec. 1, 1919, p. 13-6.
MANCHESTER society of chartered accountants and chartered accountants students' society. Discussion on "the cause of good and bad trade. *Accountant,* April 18, 1903, p. 516-22.
MARRINER, H. J. British commerce and its outlook. *Accounting and commerce,* May, June 1918, p. 46-8, 64-5.
MATHER, JOHN. Influence of accountancy profession in the commercial sphere. *Accountant,* Oct. 22, Nov. 5, 1898, p. 999-1006, 1053-6.
MILLER, THOMAS JOHN. Lectures on British industry and commerce. *Accountant,* Aug. 31, 1907, Aug. 22, 1908, p. 292, 228-32.
NEAL, THEODORE DAVID. Commercial faculty: its limitations and possibilities. *Accountant,* 1902, p. 397.
NELSON, CHARLES HEWETSON. Modern accountancy and its relation to commerce. *Accountant,* Nov. 30, 1912, p. 685-91.
NEW YORK state. Chamber of commerce. Annual report, 1912-to date.
NICHOLSON, J. S. Commercial crises. *Accountants' magazine,* 1902, p. 442-56.

COMMERCE—*(Continued)*

POWNALL, GEORGE H. Services of banking to trade. *Accountant,* Jan. 16, 1892, p. 60-70.

ROBERTSON, J. M. Trade after the war. *Accountants' magazine,* May 1917, p. 207-23.

SPALDING, WILLIAM F. Eastern exchange currency and finance. Ed.2. London, Sir Isaac Pitman and sons, 1918. 385p.

SPICER, ERNEST EVAN. Why a professional accountant should be a free trader. *Accountant,* Dec. 24, 1910, p. 900-2.

THORBURN, M. G. Fiscal policy with special reference to the textile industries. *Accountants' magazine,* 1903, p. 514-8.

UNITED STATES. Bureau of foreign and domestic commerce. Commercial and industrial organizations of the United States, revised to November 1, 1919. Washington, Government printing office, 1920. (Miscellaneous series, no. 99).

UNITED STATES. Bureau of foreign and domestic commerce. Methods of computing values in foreign trade statistics, by J. J. Kral, translator. Washington, Government printing office, 1917. 23p. (Miscellaneous series no. 59).

UNITED STATES. Bureau of foreign and domestic commerce. Monthly summary of foreign commerce of the United States. Washington, Government printing office.

UNITED STATES. Bureau of foreign and domestic commerce. Trade of the United States with the world 1916 and 1917. Washington, Government printing office, 1918. 112p.

UNITED STATES. Bureau of foreign and domestic commerce. Trade of the United States with the world, 1918-1919. Part 1—Imports; imports of merchandising into the United States by countries and principal article during the calendar years 1918 and 1919. Washington, Government printing office, 1920. 103p. (Miscellaneous series, no. 106).

UNITED STATES. Department of commerce. Foreign commerce and navigation of the United States for the calendar year, 1919. Washington, Government printing office, 1920. 577p.

UNITED STATES. Federal trade commission. Decisions; findings, orders, and conference rulings, March 16, 1915 to June 30, 1919. v.1. Washington, Government printing office, 1920. 631p.

WORDING of commercial documents. *Accountant,* June 10, 1911, p. 879, p. 905.

COMMERCE. Ross, P. H. W.

COMMERCE board recommends rate of $1.07 as fair rate for New Bedford gas and Edison light co. *American gas engineering journal,* Aug. 10, 1918, p. 137-8.

COMMERCE commission makes new ruling as to export freight rates on iron and steel articles. *Iron age,* May 6, 1920, p. 1305.

COMMERCIAL and financial chronicle; weekly. New York, William B. Dana co.

COMMERCIAL and industrial bookkeeping. Rowe, H. M. 1899.

COMMERCIAL arbitration. *Incorporated accountants' journal,* Aug. 1912, p. 283-6.

COMMERCIAL bookkeeping. Haddon, James. 1879.

COMMERCIAL bookkeeping. Notley, A. F. 1885.

COMMERCIAL bookkeeping. Wallace, R. 1850.

COMMERCIAL bookkeeping and arithmetic hints. Smith, T. 1841.

COMMERCIAL bookkeeping in four languages. Ed.15. London, Crosby, Lockwood & son, 1879.

COMMERCIAL bookkeeping simplified for beginners, Bell, R. R. 1918.

COMMERCIAL car expenses small. *Commercial car journal,* May 15, 1912, p. 54-5.

COMMERCIAL class-book. Freese, J. H. 1849.

COMMERCIAL CORRESPONDENCE

CODY, SHERWIN. How to do business by letter. Revised edition. Yonkers-on-Hudson, New York, World book co. 1918. 238p.

DAVIS, ROY and CLARENCE H. LINGHAM. Business English and correspondence. Boston, Ginn & company, c1919. 326p.

GARDNER, EDWARD HALL. Effective business letters; their requirements and preparation with specific directions for the various types of letters commonly used in business. Ed.2. New York, The Ronald press co. 1918. 420p.

LEE, JAMES MELVIN. Business writing. New York, The Ronald press company, 1920. 611p. (Language for men of affairs, v.2).

MCJOHNSTON, HARRISON. Business correspondence. New York, Alexander Hamilton institute, c1918. 322p. (Modern business, v.12).

OPDYCKE, JOHN B. English of commerce, with an introduction by Frank Vanderlip. New York, Charles Scribner's sons, c1920. 435p.

COMMERCIAL CORRESPONDENCE SCHOOLS

PRACTICAL bookkeeping, Rochester, Commercial correspondence schools.

COMMERCIAL credit. *Journal of accountancy,* July 1914, p. 55-6.

COMMERCIAL credit. Haggerty, J. E.

COMMERCIAL credits. *Journal of accountancy,* Dec. 1914, p. 460-1.

COMMERCIAL depreciation in electric plants. *Street railway bulletin,* Aug. 1908, p. 431.

COMMERCIAL digest and business forms. McMaster, J. S. 1902.

COMMERCIAL education. *Accountant,* Jan. 17, 24, 1914, p. 61-4, 100-3.

COMMERCIAL education in Scotland. *Accountant,* Sept. 15, 1917, p. 193-5.

COMMERCIAL education in the University of Edinburgh. Nicholson, J. S.

COMMERCIAL electric truck operating costs. *Electrical world,* Feb. 27, 1915, p. 567.

COMMERCIAL engineering. *Mechanical world,* Oct. 2, 1908.

COMMERCIAL guide. Lassen, Claudius. 1891.

COMMERCIAL ideals. Garfield, J. R.

COMMERCIAL instructor, and accountant's guide [by R. C.], London, [?circa 1842]

COMMERCIAL LAW

See also Bankruptcy; Corporations—Law; Negotiable instruments; Probate law and practice; also subdivision Law under various headings, e.g. Accountancy—Law.

ACCOUNTANTS: their duties and responsibilities; mercantile law. *Accountant,* Sept. 29, Oct. 6, 13, Nov. 10, 24, Dec. 15, 22, 29, 1883, Jan. 5, 12, 1884.

COMMERCIAL LAW—*(Continued)*

BARRATT, NORRIS STANLEY. Book-keepers and commercial law; address, May 12, 1913, before the Book-keeepers' beneficial association of Philadelphia, 1913. 24p.

BOUCHER, G. H. Mercantile law. *Accountant,* June 27, 1914, p. 925-8.

BRISCOE, WILLIAM R. B. Notes on the history of commercial law. *Incorporated accountants journal,* 1892-3, p. 101.

BURDICK, FRANCIS MARION. Essentials of business law. New York, D. Appleton & co. 1903. 285p.

CHAMBERLAIN, JOHN ALDRICH. Commercial law. (In *Cyclopedia of commerce, accountancy, business administration.* 1910. v.3. p. 11-309).

CHAMBERLAIN, JOHN ALDRICH. Commercial law; a practical manual covering the fundamental principles of law as applied to business in general; with a special reference to common law affecting the more usual commercial transactions. Chicago, American technical society, 1916. 316p. (American accountants' library).

CHILDS, FRANK HALL. Treatise on American business law. 4v. Chicago, Walton school of commerce, 1916. Walton series). v.1. Elementary law; contracts. v.2. Agency, partnership. v.3. Sales, negotiable instruments. v.4. Property, real and personal.

CONYINGTON, THOMAS. Business law; a working manual of every day law. New York, The Ronald press, 1918. 535p.

——— Same. Ed.2. 2v. New York, The Ronald press company, 1920. 870p.

CRANE, A. C. Books of account from a legal standpoint. *Incorporated accountants journal,* 1901-2, p. 172.

DANN, JOHN. Introduction to the study of mercantile law. *Accountant,* Sept. 8, 1888, p. 578-83.

ELLIOTT, G. Mercantile law (principal and agent). *Accountant,* Jan. 14, 21, 1888 p. 27, 38.

GOODE, J. Mercantile law, treated generally. *Accountant,* May 3, 1884.

GROVER, JOHN MAHAN. Recent judicial decisions of first class importance. *Incorporated accountants journal,* 1895-6, p. 96.

GUEDALLA, HERBERT. Some points in foreign commercial and company law of interest to accountants. *Accountant,* April 2, 1910 p. 465-72.

GUTTERIDGE, H. C. Origin and growth of English commercial law. *Accountant,* Oct. 30, 1920, p. 461-70.

HALL, J. Dip in mercantile law. *Accountant,* April 5, 1902, p. 371-2.

HUFFCUT, ERNEST WILSON. Elements of business law; with illustrative examples and problems, revised by George Gleason Bogert. Boston, Ginn & co. c1917. 319p.

KAPPELE, GEORGE. Mercantile law, with special reference to its practice in Ontario. *Acoountant,* April 29, May 13, 1899, p 481-7, 554-62.

KRIBBEN, B. D. Contact of commercial law and accounting. *American institute of accountants, Yearbook.* 1917. p. 105-10. *Journal of accountancy,* Oct. 1917, p. 283-8.

MCMASTER, JAMES SMITH. Commercial digest and business forms. New York, Commercial book co. 1902. 594p.

PARRY, EDWARD A. On legal reform in commercial centres. *Incorporated accountants journal,* 1891-2, p. 97.

PARSONS, THEOPHILUS. Laws of business for all the states and territories of the Union and the Dominion of Canada, with forms and directions for all transactions; and abstracts of the laws of all the states and territories on various topics. New revised edition. Syracuse, N. Y. Watson Gill, 1898. 864p.

SLATER, J. Mercantile law. *Incorporated accountants' journal,* 1891-2, p. 65.

SPENCER, EDWARD W. Manual of commercial law; containing a clear concise and logical exposition of the rules relating to business transactions and the management of affairs. Ed.2. Indianapolis, The Bobbs-Merrill company, 1920 (c1898-1913). 736p.

STEVENS, T. M. Registration and ownership of ships. *Accountant,* March 10, 17, 1894, p. 224-7, 243-7.

STEVENS, T. M. Some leading cases on mercantile law. *Accountant,* July 3, 1897, p. 662-8.

SULLIVAN, JOHN JAMES. American business law with legal forms. Ed.2. New York, D. Appleton & co. 1917. 433p.

TIPSON, FREDERICK SAMSON. Commercial law. New York, Frederick S. Tipson, c1903. 126p.

YATES, J. M. Law relating to merchant shipping. *Accountant,* July 28, 1894, p. 661-8.

COMMERCIAL management of engineering works. Burton, Francis G. 1905.

COMMERCIAL organization of engineering factories. Spencer, Henry. 1907.

COMMERCIAL organization of factories. Lewis, J. S. 1896.

COMMERCIAL PAPER

See Negotiable instruments.

COMMERCIAL paper, acceptances and the analysis of credit statements. Kniffin, William Henry. 1918.

COMMERCIAL paper and bills of exchange of the world; a review of the general methods observed in discounting commercial paper and bills of exchange throughout the world, with a special reference to bank acceptances, also a brief history of the origin and development of commercial paper. New York, Banking law journal, c1915. 70p.

COMMERCIAL phraseology bookkeeping and arithmetic. Haddon, J. 1851.

COMMERCIAL problem in buildings. Evers, C. C. 1914.

COMMERCIAL research. Duncan, C. S. 1919.

COMMERCIAL truck cost comparison. *Electrical world,* Sept. 6, 1913, p. 484.

COMMERCIAL valuation of railway operating property in the United States. United States. Bureau of census.

COMMERCIAL world encyclopedia of accounting for bookkeeping accountants, auditors and business men. Spear, R. H. 1911.

COMMERCIALISM rebuked. *Journal of accountancy,* July 1916, p. 53-4.

COMMISSARIES

Accounting

FIELD, W. P. Accounting control for company store or commissary. *Journal of accountancy.* Feb. 1919, p. 96-106.

MOZINGO, F. P. Systems of accounting for the hotel and commissary business. *Business man's magazine,* Nov. 1909, p. 452-7.

COMMISSION book-keeping. Packard, S. S.

COMMISSION for relief in Belgium.

See Relief commission.

COMMISSION forbids Chicago terminal charges. *Railway review,* June 26, 1915, p. 858-9.

COMMISSION grants temporary surcharge in Indianapolis, Ind. *Municipal journal,* Sept. 20, 1917, p. 292-3.

COMMISSION MERCHANTS.
See Consignments.

COMMISSION proposes recasting entire inter-mountain rate structure. *Railway review,* March 17, 1917, p. 378-82.

COMMISSION regulation of accounting systems. *Journal of electricity,* May 15, 1920, p. 520-1.

COMMISSION revises water rates in Leavenworth, Kansas. *Engineering news-record,* July 29, 1915, p. 217.

COMMISSION system of accounting compulsory. *Electrical world,* Aug. 11, 1917, p. 273.

COMMISSIONER WOOLLEY on railway rates and cost of living. *Railway age,* Jan. 23, 1920, p. 283-4.

COMMISSIONERS discuss valuation; National association report shows majority favor investment basis or liberal but not peak reproduction cost. *Electric railway journal,* Nov. 20, 1920, p. 1068-9.

COMMISSIONS
- Auditors and secret commission. *Accountant,* Jan. 31, 1914, p. 135-7.
- Bassett, W. R. Salesmen's commissions. (In his *Accounting as an aid to business profits.* c1918. p. 118-21).
- Bennett, George E. Salesmen's commissions. (In his *Constructive accounting.* 1920. p. 340-1).
- Bentley, H. C. Agents' unearned commissions; agents' earned commissions. (In his *Science of accounts.* 1913. p. 160-1).
- Carter, R. N. Commission. (In his *Advanced accounts.* p. 35).
- Excess profits duty and manager's commission. *Incorporated accountants' journal,* April 1919, p. 126-8.
- Hessol, Philip H. Treatment of the commission account: correspondence. *Journal of accountancy,* Aug. 1911, p. 299-300.
- Kester, R. B. Salesmen's commissions and efficiency records. (In his *Accounting theory and practice.* 1918. p. 345-6).
- McIntosh, R. J. Commissions—traveling salesmen. (In his *Reference book of accounts for manufacturing and mercantile companies.* Ed. 2. c1914. p. 140).
- Managers' commission and excess profits duty. *Accountant,* Jan. 20, 1917, p. 56-9. *Incorporated accountants' journal,* Feb. 1917, p. 97-8.
- Mitchell, T. W. Commissions. (In his *Accounting principles.* c1918. p. 183).
- Pixley, F. W. Commission. (In his *Accountancy.* Ed.2. p. 190).
- Racine, S. F. Commission on loans. (In his *Accounting principles.* 1917. p. 198).
- Reid, James William. Secret commissions. *Accountant* 1899, p. 1053.
- Treatment of the commission account. *Journal of accountancy,* June 1911, p. 140.
- Underwriting commission. *Accountant,* Feb. 22, 1913, p. 252-6.
- Walton, Seymour. Calculating commission on net profits. *Journal of accountancy,* May 1919, p. 390-3.
- Walton, Seymour. Commission on sale of capital stock. *Journal of accountancy,* April 1920, p. 309-10.
- Walton, Seymour. Commissions and federal tax. *Journal of accountancy,* Aug. 1916, p. 153-5.
- Wildman, J. R. Selling-expense group. (In his *Principles of accounting.* 1014. p. 216-8.

COMMISSION'S accounting order in re the separation of operating expenses—opinion of the commission. *Railway age gazette,* July 31, 1914, p. 206-8.

COMMISSION'S decision in cement rate case set aside. *Railway review,* March 4, 1916, p. 342-3.

COMMISSION'S decision in Indianapolis rate cases. *Electrical world,* Aug. 31, 1918, p. 416.

COMMISSIONS know costs are high: canvass by banking house. *Electric railway journal,* May 26, 1917, p. 953-4.

COMMISSIONS on government contracts. *Iron age,* July 25, 1918, p. 200-1.

COMMISSIONS' rate authority superior to contract. *Gas age,* July 15, 1919, p. 55-6.

COMMISSIONS without power in New York; Rochester decision of Court of appeals. *Electric railway journal,* April 27, 1918, p. 811-2. *Municipal journal,* May 18, 1918, p. 420-1.

COMMITTEE approves cost plus a fee contract of quartermaster corps. *Engineering and contracting,* May 22, 1918, p. 508-9.

COMMITTEE gives plan for finding production costs. *Weekly news letter,* Mar. 26, 1919, p. 15-6.

COMMITTEE on accounting terminology. *Journal of accountancy,* Jan. 10, 1910, p. 221.

COMMITTEE on the budget. *Congressional record,* July 31, 1919, p. 3681.

COMMITTEE on the organisation of the office of the public trustee final report. *Accountant,* Jan. 10, 1920, p. 41-53.

COMMODITIES clause decision. Gerstenberg, C. W.

COMMODITY rates to the Pacific coast terminals. *Railway age,* Feb. 19, 1915, p. 297-9.

COMMON, JAMES G.
Certified accountants have a big monopoly; from the Journal of commerce and commercial bulletin, Oct. 23, 1908. 10p.

COMMON confusion of the terms, depreciation, repairs. *Engineering and contracting,* June 30, 1909, p. 517.

COMMON errors in calculating the present worth, or capitalized value, of an annual gain. *Engineering and contracting,* Aug. 6, 1914, p. 121.

COMMON fallacy. *Electric review and Western electrician.* Dec. 4, 1915, p. 1015-6.

COMMON school book-keeping. Bryant, H. D. and H. D. Stratton.

COMMON school bookkeeping. Duff, C. P. and others.

COMMON school book-keeping. Palmer, J. H.

COMMON school book-keeping exercises. Scribner, W. M. 1887.

COMMON sense and accountancy. *Accountant,* March 8, 15, 1913, p. 332-3, 380-2.

COMMONSENSE management of an export department. Rose, Stanley Herbert. c1916.

COMMON-SENSE method of double entry bookkeeping on first principles, as suggested by DeMorgan. Dyer, S. 1897.

COMMON STOCK.
See Stock—Common.

COMMONS, JOHN R.
Eighteen months' work of the Milwaukee Bureau of economy and efficiency. Milwaukee, C. H. Kronenberger & co., 1912. 44p. (Milwaukee. Bureau of economy and efficiency. Bulletin no. 19).
Industrial goodwill. New York, McGraw-Hill book company, 1919. 213p.
Physical valuation of public utilities. *Industrics*, Sept. 10, 1908, p. 582-5.
State supervision for cities. *Annals of the American academy of political and social science*, May, 1895, p. 37-53.

——— **AND OTHERS.**
Where the workers own the stock—the Dennison manufacturing company. *Independent*, Sept. 11, 1920, p. 301.

COMMUNICATION addressed to Hon. W. J. Gaynor, mayor . . . by William A. Prendergast, comptroller under date of March 29, 1912 relative to the statute of the installation of expense ledgers in the administrative departments of the city government together with a copy of the report on the same subject presented by the comptroller of the Board of estimate and apportionment, December 13, 1912. New York city. Department of finance. 1912.

COMMUNITY business practice text and equipment. Goodyear, S. H.

COMPACT central station chart to record progress. *Electrical world*, Jan. 12, 1918, p. 101.

COMPACT shop order and cost system. *Business man's magazine*, Dec. 1911, p. 536-7.

COMPANIES.
See Corporations.

COMPANIES. Knox, George Walter.

COMPANIES act.
See accountants' diary; annual.

COMPANIES act amendment act, 1917. *Canadian chartered accountant*, Jan. 1918, p. 229-34.

COMPANIES act, 1907. *Accountant*, July 18, 25, Aug. 18, 1908, p. 4-6, 61-3, 93-5, 122-5, 149-51.

COMPANIES act, 1908. *Accounting and commerce*, April, May 1916, p. 14-7, 43-4.

COMPANIES act, 1913. *Accountant*, Aug. 30, 1913, p. 295.

COMPANIES act, 1913; an act to amend the provisions of the companies (consolidation) act, 1908, with respect to private companies. *Incorporated accountants' journal*, Sept. 1913, p. 293.

COMPANIES act, 1913: its origin and objects. *Accountant*, Feb. 14, 1914, p. 209-13.

COMPANIES acts and cotton mills. *Accountant*. 1886, p. 579, 590, 605, 621, 637, 671, 685.

COMPANIES amendment act 1906. (New South Wales). *Public accountant*, 1908, p. 39.

COMPANIES and the drawing and making, etc., of bills of exchange and promissory notes. *Accountant*, July 3, 10, 17, 24, 31, 1909, p. 6-7, 37-9, 72-4, 108-13, 141-2.

COMPANIES bill, 1907. *Accountant*, Aug. 24, Sept. 14, 1907, p. 253-4, 342-54.

COMPANIES' capital accounts; the Australian v. the English method of treating same in ledger and balance sheet. *Accountant*, May 17, 1913, p. 761-5.

COMPANIES (consolidation) act, 1908. 180p.

COMPANIES (co-partnership) bill. *Accountant*, April 19, 1913, p. 597-9.

COMPANIES (foreign interests) act, 1917. *Incorporated accountants' journal*, July 1917, p. 213.

COMPANIES (particulars as to directors) act, 1917. *Incorporated accountants' journal*, Sept. 1917, p. 246.

COMPANIES secret reserves. *Accountant*, Dec. 1, 1906, p. 681-3.

COMPANIES (winding up); general rules made pursuant to the companies (winding-up) act, 1890, and the judicature act, 1881. *Accountant*, Jan. 23, 30, Feb. 6, 13, 20, 1904, p. 117-29, 151-62, 185-95, 221-33, 256-65.

COMPANIES (winding-up) act 1890 (administration): reports of the inter-departmental committee. *Incorporated accountants' journal*, 1893-4, p. 77.

COMPANIES (winding-up) act, 1890, and the companies (winding-up) rules, 1890 and 1891. *Accountant*, Feb. 21, 1903, p. 275-7.

COMPANION to hotel bookkeeping and drapery accounts. Whatley, G. E. S. 1895.

COMPANION to the Solicitor's clerk, embracing magisterial and criminal law, licensing, bankruptcy accounts, bookkeeping, trust accounts, etc. Jones, Charles.

COMPANY accounting. Mackay, J. D. C. 1911.

COMPANY accounts. Coles, Arthur.

COMPANY accounts. Hallas, E. R.

COMPANY audits. *Accountant*, Feb. 12, 26, 1910, p. 233-5, 299-300.

COMPANY audits: brewery accounts. *Auditor*, 1890-1, p. 144, 167.

COMPANY audits: foreign branches. *Auditor*, 1890-1, p. 186, 201.

COMPANY audits in India. *Accountant*, Aug. 29, 1914, p. 225-7.

COMPANY depreciation. *Accountant*, April 25, 1914, p. 597-9.

COMPANY law amendment. *Accountant*, April 2, 16, May 7, 14, 1898, p. 357-61, 389-94, 484-7, 512-14.

COMPANY law amendment. *Accountant*, Aug. 11, 18, 25, Sept. 1, 8, 1906, p. 145, 169, 204, 225, 253.

COMPANY law amendment. *Accountant*, May 25, June 1, 8, 15, 22, 1918, p. 381-2, 397-8, 409-10, 425-6, 443-4.

COMPANY law amendment committee. *Accountant*, Oct. 5, 12, 19, 1918, p. 182-7, 199-200, 213-5.

COMPANY law amendment committee, report. *Accountant,* July 14, 21, 28, 1906, p. 45-53, 81-90, 106-15.

COMPANY law amendment committee; report of the committee upon the amendment of the law under the companies acts, 1908 to 1917. *Incorporated accountants' journal,* Sept. 1918, p. 241-8.

COMPANY law in Hong-Kong. *Accountant,* April 6, 1912, p. 533-5.

COMPANY law in India. *Accountant,* June 29, Aug. 10, 1912, p. 961-4, 180-2.

COMPANY law in New South Wales. *Accountant,* April 28, 1900, p. 389-92.

COMPANY law in Russia. *Accountant,* April 27, 1901, p. 495-6.

COMPANY law reform. *Accountant,* Nov. 25, 1905, March 23, April 13, April 26, 1907, p 599, 377, 467, 505.

COMPANY laws in the British empire. *Accountant,* Aug. 10, 17, 1907, p. 167-9, 195-7.

COMPANY laws in the British empire; comparative analysis of the company laws of the United Kingdom, India, Canada, Australia, New Zealand and South Africa; with a memorandum prepared for the Imperial conference, 1911, by the directions of the board of trade. *Accountant,* Oct. 7, 14, 21, 28, 1911, p. 464-71, 497-509, 530-6, 581-4.

COMPANY losses prior to incorporation. *Accountant,* July 28, 1906, p. 93.

COMPANY mail handling system, Oregon short line. *Railway review,* May 4, 1918, p. 643.

COMPANY promotion and frauds *Accountant,* Nov. 19, 1898, p. 1101-4, 1122.

COMPANY reform and the accountant profession in France. *Accountants' magazine,* 1907, p. 347.

COMPANY reserves and their investment. *Accountant,* Feb. 21, April 11, May 23, 1914, p. 272-7, 517-9, 755-7.

COMPANY secretary. Fox, W. H. 1903.

COMPANY STORES.
See Commissaries.

COMPANY work. *Accountant,* Sept. 28, Oct. 5, 12, 19, 1889, Aug. 9, 16, 1890, p. 499-502, 510-2, 523-4, 534-6, 417-9, 429-32.

COMPANY'S statutory report. *Accountant,* Dec. 17, 1910, p. 842.

COMPARATIVE cost of automobiles and horses. *Municipal journal,* Aug. 28, 1913.

COMPARATIVE cost of collecting water bills by mail and by collectors at Seattle, Washington. *Engineering and contracting,* July 14, 1915, p. 33.

COMPARATIVE cost of direct and single phase electrification of steam railroads. *Scientific American,* Feb. 22, 1913, p. 170.

COMPARATIVE cost of distillate. *Engineering and mining journal,* June 24, 1916, p. 1115.

COMPARATIVE cost of flame arc and nitrogen filled incandescent lighting for streets. *Electrical world,* March 13, 1915, p. 682.

COMPARATIVE cost of handling earth on flat and air dump cars. *Railway age,* June 18, 1915, p. 1444.

COMPARATIVE cost of hauling from farms to shipping points: tabulation. *American fruit grower,* June, 1919, p. 14.

COMPARATIVE cost of horse-drawn and electric vehicles in delivery service. *Electrical world,* June 14, 1913, p. 1315.

COMPARATIVE cost of maintenance and operation by steam and electric power. *Engineering and contracting,* Nov. 19, 1913, p. 566-9.

COMPARATIVE cost of motive power in ice manufacturing. *Electrical world,* October 11, 1913, p. 755.

COMPARATIVE cost of steam and electric railroad operation. *Chronicle* (Railway section), June 28, 1913, p. 3-4.

COMPARATIVE cost of steel and wooden pole transmission line. *Electrical review,* Jan. 26, 1918, p. 163.

COMPARATIVE cost of street sweeping and sprinkling with mules and with motors. *Municipal engineering,* May 1915, p. 305.

COMPARATIVE costs between high and low pressure gas for lighting. *Gas age,* Sept. 1, 1913, p. 215.

COMPARATIVE costs for concrete and timber factory buildings. *Engineering and contracting,* Nov. 22, 1916, p. 450-2.

COMPARATIVE costs in salt mining. *Coal age,* Mar. 20, 1919, p. 549.

COMPARATIVE costs of belt finishing and hand floating for concrete roads. *Engineering and contracting,* March 7, 1917, p. 242.

COMPARATIVE costs of central-station and oil-engine power. *Electrical world,* Sept. 4, 1920, p. 483-4.

COMPARATIVE costs of different designs for piers. *Engineering record,* June 6, 1914, p. 638.

COMPARATIVE costs of electric and gasoline vehicles. *Electrical review and western electrician,* April 22, 1916, p. 705-6.

COMPARATIVE costs of guard rail and wide fills on highways. *Engineering news-record,* July 8, 1915, p. 79-80.

COMPARATIVE costs of laying 16 and 12-ft. pipe. *Engineering news,* Aug. 12, 1915, p. 318.

COMPARATIVE costs of mine haulage by horses and compressed air. *Engineering and contracting,* Nov. 15, 1916, p. 433-4.

COMPARATIVE costs of motive power in ice manufacturing. *Electrical world,* Oct. 11, 1913, p. 755.

COMPARATIVE costs of Oregon pavements. *Engineering and contracting,* Nov. 7, 1917, p. 368-9.

COMPARATIVE costs of power generated by oil and coal. *Engineering and mining journal,* April 5, 1913, p. 712.

COMPARATIVE costs of steam locomotive vs. electric trucks for use in factory shop transportation. *Engineering magazine,* July 1911, p. 576.

COMPARATIVE costs of steel and concrete bridges. *Engineering and contracting,* Dec. 27, 1916, p. 572.

COMPARATIVE costs of street sprinkling with motor trucks and horse drawn tanks. *Engineering and contracting,* September 5, 1917, p. 192.

COMPARATIVE costs of typesetting by hand, linotype and monotype of 8, 10 and 12 point non-technical text matter. Cambridge. Harvard university, 1916. 54p. 50c (Students reports on business problems no. 2)

COMPARATIVE data based on inquiries addressed to state road officials. *Engineering and contracting,* May 17, 1916, p. 451-2.

COMPARATIVE data on cost of operating gas and electric cars. *Electrical review and western electrician,* June 30, 1917, p. 1097-8.

COMPARATIVE depreciation tables. Dicksee, L. R. 1909.

COMPARATIVE economy of producer gas and steam for pumping station. *Engineering record,* Sept. 6, 1913, p. 262-3.

COMPARATIVE ethics. *Journal of accountancy,* March 1915, p. 210.

COMPARATIVE figures on delivery costs. National retail dry goods association.

COMPARATIVE haulage costs by trucks and horse drawn vehicles. *Engineering and contracting,* April 17, 1918, sup. 30.

COMPARATIVE operating costs of steam shovels and electric shovels. *Engineering and contracting,* March 11, 1914, p. 293-4.

COMPARATIVE operating expenses of horse, electric and gasoline commercial vehicles *Electrical world,* May 3, 1913, p. 936-7.

COMPARATIVE rates for gas in American cities. Los Angeles, Cal. Board of public utilities, Report, 1915, p. 36.

COMPARATIVE study in operation—Virginian and C.C. & O. *Railway age,* April 24, 1914, p. 935-42.

COMPARATIVE study of the four principal methods of appraising the value of public utilities, with special reference to the valuation of the Freeport (Ill.) water works properties. *Engineering and contracting* Oct. 29, 1912, p. 368, 396.

COMPARATIVE theoretical and actual depreciation. Thomas, J. J.

COMPARATIVE values of personal reputation and conferred degrees. Nau, Carl H.

COMPARES automobile and team costs for project and irrigation managers. *Engineering news-record,* Aug. 2, 1917, p. 228.

COMPARISON as to efficiency and cost with motor trucks, tractors and teams use in highway work in two states. *Municipal journal,* August 2, 1917, 105-6.

COMPARISON of actual cost of laying 6-in. cast iron water pipe in 12 and 16 ft. lengths at Council Bluffs, Iowa. *Engineering and contracting,* Sept. 1, 1915, p. 161.

COMPARISON of American and continental rates. *National municipal review,* April 1914, p. 382-4.

COMPARISON of American and continental rates. *National municipal review,* July 2, 1914, p. 459.

COMPARISON of excavation haulage by motor trucks, industrial railways and teams. *Engineering news,* Nov. 28, 1918, p. 993-6.

COMPARISON of monthly operating expenses. *Railway age gazette,* Feb. 9, 1917, p. 215-6.

COMPARISON of motor trucks with horses. *Domestic engineering,* May 10, 1913, p. 146-8.

COMPARISON of rates of tax in United States, Great Britain, Canada, France. United States. Library of congress. Legislative reference division. 1918.

COMPARISON of wage payment methods. *Monthly labor review,* July 1919, p. 149-52.

COMPARISON of workmen's compensation laws of the United States up to December 31, 1917. Hoostadt. Carl. 1918.

COMPEND of bookkeeping by single entry. Robinson, James.

COMPENDIUM of bookkeeping and business forms for self instruction. Hendryx, F. H. 1892.

COMPENDIUM of forms, educational, social and commercial, embracing a self-teaching course in penmanship and bookkeeping. Gaskell, G. A. 1882.

COMPENSATION

See also wages, fees, etc.

KEEN, F. N. Law of compensation. *Accountant,* Feb. 14, 1903, p. 239-49.

SPICER, ERNEST EVAN and ERNEST C. PEGLER. Claims for compensation. (In their *Bookkeeping and accounts.* 1914. p. 349-50).

COMPENSATION to local government officials on abolition of office. *Accountant,* March 23, 1912, p. 464-6.

COMPENSATIONS of junior accountants. Hurlburt, H. M.

COMPETITION

See also Professional ethics.

ROGERS, EDWARD SIDNEY. Good will, trademarks, and unfair trading. Chicago, A. W. Shaw company, c1914. 288p.

COMPETITION among accountants. *Journal of accountancy,* Sept. 1909, p. 364-6.

COMPETITIVE bidding. *Accountant,* Aug. 28, Oct. 9, 1915, Jan. 1, 1916, p. 246-51, 413-5, 1-3. *Canadian chartered accountant,* Jan. 1916, p. 219-20. *Journal of accountancy,* Nov. 1914, Aug., Nov. 1915, p. 396-7, 81-90, 133-6, 365-6.

COMPETITIVE bidding. Hunter, Joel.

COMPETITIVE bidding. Peter W. P.

COMPETITIVE biding. Shorrock, E. G.

COMPETITIVE bidding. Temple, H. M.

COMPETITIVE bidding on a cost plus fee basis. *Architectural forum,* Oct. 1919, p. 142.

COMPILATION of municipal data in America. *Municipal engineering,* Nov. 1898, p. 291-8.

COMPILATION of operating statistics reports. *Railway age,* June 6, 1919, p. 1353-60.

COMPILING tonnage reports by aid of accounting machines. *Railway review,* March 20, 1920, p. 493-4.

COMPLAINTS

ELLIOTT, BERTON. System for reducing complaints. *Business man's magazine,* Dec. 1908, p. 480.

FINNIGAN, J. A. Method of adjusting complaints. *Business man's magazine,* Aug. 1908, p. 122-7.

COMPLEAT compting-house. Vernon, John.

COMPLETE compting-house companion: by a society of merchants and traders. London, 1763.

COMPLEAT compting-house companion; or Young merchant and tradesman's sure guide (including bookkeeping) by a society of merchants and traders. 1763.

COMPLEAT English tradesman. Ed. 2. London, 1727.

COMPLEAT tradesman. London. 1720.

COMPLETE accountant. Powers, M. R. and M. R. Johnson.

COMPLETE accounting course. Anderson, A. E.

COMPLETE accounting system and record for national farm loan associations. Dworak, E. A. comp. 1917.

COMPLETE bond tables to eight places. Sprague, Charles Ezra. 1915.

COMPLETE bookkeeping. Musselman, D. L. 1911.

COMPLETE business register. New York, H. W. Pamphilon.

COMPLETE calculating machine. *Engineering magazine,* April 1916, sup. 5-6.

COMPLETE cost keeper. Arnold, H. L. 1900.

COMPLETE counting-house book-keeping. Holbrook, and Rohrer. 1888.

COMPLETE course of business training. Packard, S. S. 1876.

COMPLETE courses in bookkeeping, double and single entry. Vaughan, L. B.

COMPLETE guide to practical book-keeping, by single and double entry, etc. Morrison, James. 1843.

COMPLETE loose leaf system for elevator accounting. *Co-operative manager and farmer,* July 1918, p. 83.

COMPLETE merchant's clerk. Weston, William. 1754.

COMPLETE practical book-keeping. Stevens, C. H. and H. T. Loomis. 1898.

COMPLETE practical bookkeeping; a textbook on modern methods of accounting; including an appendix of useful information and helpful hints for book-keepers and office men; fully illustrated by forms of books furnished by merchants, bankers, and manufacturers. Cleveland, Practical textbook company, 1906. (1898). 308p.

COMPLETE system for handling sheet music. *Business man's magazine,* Oct. 1909, p. 379-81.

COMPLETE system of book-keeping. Macdougal, Duncan. 1881.

COMPLETE system of book-keeping, both by single and double entry. Jackson, George. ?1830.

COMPLETE system of book-keeping by an improved mode of double entry. Booth, Benjamin. 1789.

COMPLETE system of bookkeeping for brewers, etc. Amsdon, Edward. 1906.

COMPLETE system of Italian book-keeping according to the modern method. Dowling, Daniel. 1770.

COMPLETE system of merchants' accounts. Morrison, James. 1808.

COMPLETE system of practical arithmetic. Taylor, William. 1783.

COMPLETE system of practical book-keeping. Harris, Nicholas. 1854.

COMPLETE system of practical bookkeeping. Morrison, C.

COMPLETE text and analysis of the Federal farm loan act, approved July 17, 1916. Corn exchange national bank, Philadelphia.

COMPLETE treatise on book-keeping, rational and practical, wherein the invention of debtors and creditors are clearly pointed out, etc. Deighan, P. 1807.

COMPLETE treatise on practical arithmetic and bookkeeping. Hutton, Charles. 1801.

COMPLETE treatise on practical book-keeping. Hutton, Charles. 1840.

COMPLETE treatise on practical book-keeping, ing, etc. Morrison, James. 1820.

COMPOSING room management. Kimball, Dorr. 1918.

COMPOUND division ready reckoner for use in making out cost sheets. Wethered, William. 1886.

COMPREHENSIVE bookkeeping. Bogle, A. M. 1905.

COMPREHENSIVE cash book. Castledine, W.

COMPREHENSIVE modernized rapid calculator. Delp, J. D. 1910.

COMPREHENSIVE stock room system adopted by the R. K. LeBlond machine tool company. *Iron age,* Aug. 6, 1914, p. 324-6.

COMPREHENSIVE system of book-keeping, by double entry, adapted to the business transactions of merchants and mechanics. Richmond, W. H. 1846.

COMPROMISE fare increase approved by Massachusetts commission. *Electric railway journal,* June 22, 1918, p. 1210-11.

COMPTANT, A. C.

Joint venture accounts. *New York accountants' and bookkeepers' journal,* Oct. 1904, p. 255-9.

COMPTING-house assistant. Cooke, John. 1764.

COMPTON, R. K.

Baltimore's paving recorded by map and file system. *Engineering news,* Nov. 13, 1919, p. 865-6.

COMPTON, W.
Methods of handling depreciation and investment in lumber accounting. *American lumberman,* July 27, 1918, p. 48-9.
What is cost? *American lumberman,* March 16, 1918, p. 32-33.

COMPTROLLERS and accounting officers in convention. *Journal of accountancy,* July 1910, p. 215-6.

COMPULSORY apprenticeship. Will, John A.

COMPULSORY auditing of municipal accounts. *Journal of accountancy,* June 1907, p. 162-4.

COMPULSORY bookkeeping for traders. *Accountant,* April 11, 18, 1903, p. 485-8, 507-8.

COMPULSORY depreciation charge. *Journal of accountancy,* Dec. 1912, p. 431-6.

COMPUTATION of a rate. *Power,* March 23, 1915, p. 419-20.

COMPUTATION of coupon values. Little, A. S.

COMPUTATION of excess profits and income taxes. *Journal of accountancy,* March 1918, p. 199-202.

COMPUTATION of interest. *Accountant,* Sept. 3, 1892, p. 672-5.

COMPUTATION of interest rates. *Journal of accountancy,* Nov. 1914, p. 393-5.

COMPUTATION of interest rates. Skinner, P. H.

COMPUTING labor turnover; a questionnaire. *Industrial management,* Sept. 1918, p. 239-45.

COMSTOCK, A. F.
Cost analysis of double-course pavement. *Engineering record,* February 5, 1916, p. 171-2.

COMSTOCK, ALZADA
British income tax reform. *American economic review,* Sept. 1920, p. 488-506.
Fiscal aspects of state income taxes. *American economic review,* June 1920, p. 259-71.

COMSTOCK, H. G.
Practical accounting system for building and loan associations. *American building association news,* Nov. 1915.

COMSTOCK, L. K.
Method for a compensated wage by index numbers. *Journal of accountancy,* July 1918, p. 1-22.

COMSTOCK, LAURA
Household accounting. Boston, 1915. 15p. (Mass. agriculture board circular 34). *Massachusetts Board of agriculture, annual report,* 1916, p. 279-92.

COMSTOCK, THEODORE B.
Card system for mine accounts. *Engineering and mining journal,* 1903, v. 76, p. 514-75.

CONAN, A. J.
Order and Commission record for woolen goods brokerage business. *Business man's magazine,* Oct. 1905, p. 696-8.
Real estate installments. *Business man's magazine,* Nov. 1905, p. 886-8.

CONANT, A. F.
Economies in a malleable iron foundry. *Iron age,* Sept. 25, 1919, p. 859-61.

CONANT, C. A.
Relation of railway charges to the supply of money and capital. *Railway and engineering review,* Dec. 20, 1913, p. 1181-3.

CONANT, CHARLES A.
Functions of centralized banking. *Bankers magazine,* Oct. 1914, p. 388-98.
History of modern banks of issue; with an account of the economic crisis of the nineteenth century and the crisis of 1907. Ed. 4, revised and enlarged. New York, G. P. Putnam's sons, c1909. 751p.

CONANT, E. R.
Cost of constructing concrete pavement at Savannah, Ga. *Engineering and contracting,* March 6, 1918, p. 247.
Street cleaning costs at Savannah, Ga. *Engineering and contracting,* November 1, 1916, p. 397.
Street cleaning in Savannah; abstracts. *Municipal journal,* November 23, 1916, p. 635-7. *Municipal engineering,* December, 1916, p. 219-20.

CONARD, CHARLES
Bonds for government industrial plants. *Journal of accountancy,* Oct. 1911, p. 401-9.

CONCENTRATE stocks and turn them rapidly. *Associated advertising,* July 1917, p. 16.

CONCENTRATE treatment and milling costs at Goldfield. *Engineering and mining journal,* Sept. 5, 1914, p. 440.

CONCERNED about Yankee morality. *Journal of accountancy,* Nov. 1905, p. 60-1.

CONCERNING advertising. *Journal of accountancy,* May 1920, p. 362-3.

CONCERNING codes of ethics. *Journal of accountancy,* April 1908, p. 477-8.

CONCERNING contributors. *Journal of accountancy,* Feb. 1918, p. 125.

CONCERNING criticisms. Rand, W. H.

CONCERNING depreciation. *Accountant,* Jan. 1, Dec. 10, 1910, p. 6-9, 796-800.

CONCERNING directors. *Accountant,* Aug. 26, Sept. 2, 9, 1905, p. 231-2, 256-9, 273-5.

CONCERNING our shortcomings: correspondence. *Journal of accountancy,* April 1913, p. 307-10.

CONCERNING Philadelphia's sinking funds. *Citizens' business,* no. 28,, Nov. 29, 1917. 3p.

CONCERNING uniform international financial statements by H. S. Chase; International cooperation for the standardization of statistical work by R. W. Babson. *American statistical association,* March 1915, p. 452-66.

CONCHAR, JOHN
SOME points in executorship law. *Accountant,* Aug. 15, 22, 1914, p. 192-4, 210-6.

"CONCISE" audit and accounting memorandum book. Gill, P. J. c1912.

CONCISE check-system of double entry book-keeping for small businesses. Phillips, Charles.

CONCISE farmer's account book. Balfour, John. 1898.

CONCISE method of keeping the accounts and stock transfers of railroad and other corporate agencies, in the city of New York. Hill, John J. 1858.

CONCISE system of book-keeping. Hancock. ?1856.

CONCISE system of farm bookkeeping. Strachan, J. 1854.

CONCISE treatise on commercial book-keeping. Foster, B. F. 1836.

CONCLUSIONS reached with respect to expenditure accounting and reporting. United States. President's commission on economy and efficiency.

CONCORD, N. H., company shows increased costs from 21 per cent to 285 per cent. *Electrical world,* June 16, 1917, p. 1178.

CONCRETE arch railway bridge costs less than steel. *Engineering news-record,* Feb. 21, 1918, p. 342-5.

CONCRETE buildings cost less than steel. *Concrete,* Dec. 1917, p. 173-4.

CONCRETE CONSTRUCTION

GILLETE, HALBERT POWERS and CHARLES S. HILL. Concrete construction methods and cost. New York, The Myron C. Clark publishing co. 1908. 690p.

KNOWLTON, H. S. Card indexing plant employees. *Power,* Mar. 28, 1916, p. 439.

PROGRESS reports of concrete construction work. *Concrete,* Oct. 1918, p. 131-2.

Cost accounting

ANDERSON, W. P. Cost keeping for reinforced concrete buildings. *Engineering magazine,* April 1913, p. 34-49.

COST keeping methods for concrete construction. *Engineering and contracting,* Nov. 22, 1916, p. 458-60.

GILLETTE, HALBERT P. and RICHARD T. DANA. Forms of breakwater construction, includind quarrying, concrete work and dredging. (In their *Cost keeping and management engineering,* 1916. p. 238-47).

GOULD, H. J. Simple and efficient cost keeping system for concrete construction. *Engineering and contracting,* Aug. 30, 1916, p. 199-202.

JONES, W. N. Construction by day labor in Minneapolis: methods and costs of concrete vaulting over city reservoir. *Engineering record,* April 19, 1913, p. 424-6.

MOWRY, DON E. Cost keeping on concrete construction on the C. B. & Q. *Railway age gazette,* Jan. 15, 1909.

NICHOLL, JOHN S. Scientific cost-keeping system for reinforced concrete. *Engineering magazine,* Jan. 1913, p. 511-25.

TUTTLE, MORTON C. Keeping concrete costs; explains a method of obtaining construction costs during the progress of the work. *Engineering record,* Jan. 4, 1913, p. 9-11.

Costs

AIDS in estimating concrete costs. *Coal age,* March 10, 1917, p. 422.

ALLEN, L. H. Comparative cost of concrete and mill buildings. *Concrete,* Oct. 1916, p. 135-6.

ANDERSON, W. P. Cost of concrete buildings. *Machinery,* July 1916, p. 978-9.

CONCRETE buildings cost less than steel. *Concrete,* Dec. 1917, p. 173-4.

CONCRETE cost computing chart. *Engineering and mining journal,* Dec. 4, 1915, p. 930.

COST of a concrete building, *Building Age,* Aug. 1916, p. 65-6.

COST of a concrete mill building. *Textile world,* Sept. 9, 1916, p. 3901.

COSTS of concrete and mill type buildings. *Concrete,* July 1916, p. 25. *Engineering and contracting,* July 26, 1916, p. 95.

CURRAN, H. T. Cost of mill construction. *Engineering and mining journal,* Aug. 28, 1915, p. 345-7. *Engineering and contracting,* Oct. 6, 1915, p. 266-8.

DAVIDSON, F. E.; T. L. CONDRON. Cost of factory buildings of timber and concrete. *Engineering news,* Nov. 9, 1916, p. 884-6. *Engineering and contracting,* Nov. 22, 1916, p. 450-2.

ECONOMY of concrete over steel. *Concrete,* April 1919, p. 145.

ESTIMATING building costs. *Concrete,* Nov. 1917, p. 137-9.

FERRISS, H. R. Cost of depositing concrete in bags under water. *Engineering and contracting,* Feb. 10, 1915, p. 128.

GAYLES, E. R. Methods and cost of constructing a reinforced concrete storehouse. *Engineering and contracting,* Aug. 23, 1916, p. 172-3.

GILBERT, C. D. Building concrete silos—unit construction with blocks and staves; with cost tables. *Concrete cement,* July 1915, p. 3-6, 37-8.

GILLETTE, HALBERT P. Concrete construction. (In his *Handbook of cost data for contractors and engineers.* 1910. p. 530-64).

HIGGINS, C. H. Tables to find cost of concrete. *Concrete,* April 1917, p. 138-40.

HOOVER, A. P. Concrete cost computing chart. *Engineering news-record,* Oct. 21, 1915, p. 795-6. *Architecture and building* Feb. 1916, p. 21-3.

JONES, W. D. Construction features, plant layout methods and costs of constructing a reinforced concrete warehouse at Los Angeles harbor, California. *Engineering and contracting,* Dec. 27, 1916, p. 578-80.

KIRKPATRICK, R. Z. Methods and cost of constructing reinforced concrete pier shells for Balboa docks. *Engineering and contracting,* Jan. 16, 1918, p. 66-7.

METHODS and cost of constructing a lock guide wall without use of cofferdam. *Engineering and contracting,* May 23, 1917, p. 474-6.

MUHLHAUSEN, L. Comparative costs of concrete and mill construction. *Engineering news-record,* December 21, 1916, p. 1193.

NEWMAN, P. R. Cost of cold storage buildings. *Concrete,* Nov. 1916, p. 163.

OPERATING cost of concrete mixer reduced by electric motor. *Engineering and contracting,* May 2, 1917, p. 413.

POURING 75 all-concrete houses at Phillipsburg, N. J. *Concrete,* Jan. 1919, p. 9-14.

ROBINSON, E. W. Methods and cost of construcing a reinforced concrete building. *Concrete,* Feb. 1916, p. 47-50.

ROBINSON, E. W. Labor costs on a gravity type quay wall. *Concrete,* Feb. 1918, p. 49-51.

Robinson, E. W. Methods and cost of constructing a sewage pumping station. *Concrete,* March 1917, p. 112-14.

SIMS, C. E. Manufacture and use of concrete irrigation pipe. *Concrete,* Feb. 1917, p. 73-4.

THOMPSON, S. E. Unit costs in building construction. *Concrete,* March 1916, p. 129-30. *Engineering and contracting,* March 1, 1916, p. 220-1. Condensed. *Engineering record,* Feb. 26, 1916, p. 277-8.

TUTTLE, M. C. Keeping concrete costs. *Engineering record,* Jan. 4, 1913, p. 9-11.

CONCRETE CONSTRUCTION — Costs — *(Continued)*

Walker, F. R. Detailed cost figures on forms and concrete for floors. *Concrete,* June 1918,, p. 199-203.

What will your building cost? *Concrete,* June 1918, p. 226.

CONCRETE construction methods and cost. Gillette, Halbert Powers and Charles S. Hill. 1908.

CONCRETE cost computing chart. *Engineering and mining journal,* Dec. 4, 1915, p. 930.

CONCRETE PIPE AND TILE

Cost accounting

Shonlau, G. A. Fundamentals of uniform cost accounting system for the concrete pipe and tile industry. *Cement and engineering news,* Oct. 1919, p. 24-6. *Engineering world,* Feb. 15, 1919, p. 58-60.

Costs

Cost of manufacturing pipe. *Engineering and contracting,* Jan. 14, 1920, p. 34.

Helmuth, D. Experience in concrete roof tile manufacture, with costs. *Concrete,* Oct. 1919, p. 160-1.

Sims, Charles E Costs in the manufacture of concrete drain tile. *Concrete,* May 1916, p. 201-2.

CONCRETE STONE

Cost accounting

Constan, J. Cost system for the concrete building block business. *Business man's magazine,* Oct. 1908, p. 303-6.

Corbett, W. E. Keeping costs in a stone plant. *Concrete,* July 1917, p. 20.

CONDENSED classification of operating expenses of steam roads. United States. Interstate commerce commission. 1914.

CONDENSED counting house and school bookkeeping. Holbrook, and Rohrer. 1888.

CONDITIONS in contracting for war material. *Iron age,* June 27, 1918, p. 1656-7.

CONEN, ALEXANDER J.

Cash discounts. *Journal of accountancy,* April 1914, p. 294-6.

Order and commission record for woolen goods brokerage business. *Business man's magazine,* Oct. 1905, p. 696-8.

Real estate instalments. *Business man's magazine,* Nov. 1905, p. 886-8.

CONEY Island gas rates. *Public service regulation,* Sept. 1913, p. 496. *American gas light journal,* Oct. 27, 1913, p. 264.

CONFECTIONERY

United States. Bureau of labor statistics. Wages of candy maker in Philadelphia in 1919. Washington, Government printing office, 1919. (Bulletin of the women in industry service, no. 4).

Accounting

Shenton, William A. Candy manufacturers' accounts. *Journal of accountancy,* Sept. 1919, p. 197-203.

Cost accounting

Gooch, H. S. Dovetailing costs into the books; cost system of a candy factory. *Factory,* June 1916, p. 577-80.

Price, Guerdon W. Cost manual for National confectioners' association of the United States, under supervision of the executive committee. Chicago, National confectioners' association of the United States, 1916. 101p.

Scoville, Clinton H. Candy costs. (In his *Cost accounting and burden application.* 1916. p. 242-56).

Depreciation.

See Depreciation, depletion and obsolescence—Confectionery.

CONFERENCE on proposed rate advance. *Railway age,* April 13, 1917, p. 787-8.

CONFERENCE on scientific management. *Journal of accountancy,* June 1911, p. 134-5.

CONFERENCE on standard accounts with the interstate commerce commission. *Street railway journal,* May 23, 1908, p. 860.

CONFERENCE on valuation. *Electric railway journal,* Nov. 13, 1915, p. 990, 1031. Editorial. Original cost in valuation work. *Electric railway journal,* Nov. 20, 1915, p. 1020.

CONFERENCE on valuation held in Philadelphia, Nov. 10-13, 1915, under the auspices of the utilities bureau, Proceedings. *Utilities magazine,* Jan. 1916. 227p.

CONFERENCE on valuation of public utiities: meeting arranged by the utilities bureau in Philadelphia, November 10 to 12. *Electrical review,* Nov. 20, 1915, p. 939-41.

CONFIDENCE prevails in Illinois. Gore, E. E.

CONFIDENTIAL COMMUNICATION

Geijsbeek, John B. Confidential communication and privileged communication. *Journal of accountancy,* Aug. Sept. 1911, p. 268-86, 361-73.

Privileged communications. *Journal of accountancy,* June 1916, p. 444-5.

CONFIDENTIAL communication and privileged communication. Geijsbeek, J. B.

CONFISCATION defined by the highest authority. *Railway review,* March 13, 1915, p. 353-5.

CONFOUND that boy! Smith, F. W. 1898.

CONFUSION in high places. *Journal of accountancy,* May 1920, p. 359-62.

CONFUSION on costs; integrated and non-integrated producers. *Iron age,* Oct. 11, 1917, p. 889-90.

CONGER, WILLIAM H.

Approved and new system for trust estate accounting. *Trust companies,* June-July 1914, p. 500-11 ; 23-31.

CONGRESS and a budget. *Journal of accountancy,* Dec. 1912, p. 487-93.

CONGRESS of accountants at St. Louis. *Accountant,* Dec. 10-24, 1904, p. 704-6, 737-41, 761-4.

CONKLIN, L. H.

Rates for electric service. *Electrical world,* Dec. 6, 1913, p. 1167.

CONLIN, JOHN A. AND OTHERS

Income and federal tax reports. New York, Prentice-Hall inc. c1918. 704p.

CONNALLY, S. N.

Performance of fuel oil engines in water works service; with cost comparisons. *Municipal engineering,* Sept. 1918, p. 113-4.

CONNECTICUT

Chapter 292, public acts of 1915—part 4—taxation of miscellaneous corporations in effect August 1. 1915. 6p.

Corporations laws, revised August 1, 1919. Hartford, Conn., 1919. 75p.

CONNECTICUT GENERAL ASSEMBLY. JOINT STANDING COMMITTEE ON RAILROADS.

. . Report of the joint standing committee on railroads on the Railroad commissioner's report. Printed by order of the General assembly. Hartford * * * 1883. 16p.

——— **PUBLIC UTILITIES COMMISSION**

Order governing the appraisal, apportionment and distribution of fixed capital of electric companies, issued March 6, 1914. 16p.

Order governing the appraisal, apportionment and distribution of fixed capital of gas companies. Hartford, Public utilities commission, 1914. 13p.

Order governing the appraisal, apportionment and distribution of fixed capital of water companies, issued March 6, 1914 14p.

Report of the . . . (gas and electric light) company. 20p.

Report of the . . . (water) company. 15p.

——— **STATE BOARD OF ACCOUNTANCY**

Circular of information for intending applicants for certificates as certified public accountants, 1913. 8p.

Law of the state of Connecticut relative to the board of accountancy and rules for the examination of applicants for certificates as certified public accountants. Connecticut, Board of accountancy. 8p.

——— **TAX COMMISSIONER**

General laws concerning taxation and taxing officials, part 1, local revenues, 1912-1915, 1917.

Laws concerning local and state revenues passed by the general assembly session of 1917.

CONNECTICUT *American institute of accountants, Yearbook,* 1907-1916, p. 211-3, 341-3, 319-21, 231-3, 196-8, 259-61, 312-4, 262-4, 252-4, 144-6.

CONNECTICUT company goes to zone plan. *Electric railway journal,* Nov. 8, 1919, p. 852-7.

CONNECTICUT fare brief filed. *Electric railway journal,* March 23, 1918, p. 588.

CONNECTICUT six-cent fare is reasonable. *Electric railway journal,* March 30, 1918, p. 620-1.

CONNECTICUT SOCIETY OF CERTIFIED PUBLIC ACCOUNTANTS.

Roster, 1919. 3p.

CONNECTICUT society of certified public accountants. *Journal of accountancy,* May 1912, Jan. 1913, June 1916, Dec. 1917, May 1920, p. 387, 74, 449, 491, 400.

CONNECTICUT society of public accountants. *Journal of accountancy,* June 1909, p. 137.

CONNECTICUT zone system revised. *Electric railway journal,* April 17, 1920, p. 807-11.

CONNELL, WILLIAM H.

Control of highway work by means of planning boards and current states visible records. *American city,* November 1916, p. 519-26.

Functions of the planning boards installed in the bureau of highways and street cleaning, Philadelphia, Pa. *Engineering and contracting,* September 8, 1915, p. 187. *Good roads* n.s., September 11, 1915, p. 168.

Method and cost of constructing concrete service test road at Philadelphia, P. *Engineering and contracting,* April 26, 1916, p. 390-3. Abridged. *Municipal journal,* July 6, 1916, p. 1-13. Abridged. *Concrete,* September 1916, p. 99.

Organization of highway department and the use of planning boards to simplify the operations. *Good roads,* n.s., January 1, 1916, 14-5.

CONNELLY, W. C.

Shop costs of boiler and plate work. *Iron age,* Sept. 18, 1913, p. 614-5.

CONNER, LYMAN L.

Physicians case history card. *System,* Feb. 1906.

CONNETTEE, E. G.

War bonus for electric railways. *Electric railway journal,* Oct. 13, 1917, p. 662-4.

CONNOLLY, P. H.

Method and cost of collecting and incenerating garbage at Racine, Wis. *Engineering and contracting,* September 15, 1915, p. 211-2.

CONNOR, L. G.

Farm management and farm profits in irrigated land in the Provo area (Utah Lake valley), U. S. A. *International review of science and practice of agriculture,* Sept. 1918, p. 1095-1103.

CONNOR, W. N.

Our men know all about our costs. *System,* May 1920, p. 974-5.

CONNORS, J. R.

Eighteen months' work of the Milwaukee Bureau of economy and efficiency. Milwaukee, C. H. Kronenberger & co., 1912. 44p. (Milwaukee, Bureau of economy and effciency. Bulletin no. 19). "Installation of water accounts." p. 36-39.

State supervision for cities. *Annals of the American academy of political and social science,* May, 1895, p. 37-53.

CONOVER, H. J.

Standard voucher check and handling accounts payable with minimum office labor. *Business man's magazine,* March 1910, p. 251-5.

CONRAD CHARLES

Bonds for government industrial plants. *Journal of accountancy,* Oct. 1911, p. 401-9.

Naval accounting. *Government accountant,* 1909, v.3, p. 98-112.

CONSERVATION of effort in purchasing. *Iron age,* May 21, 1914, p. 1255-6.

CONSIGNMENTS

Swinney, John B. Commission merchant and broker. (In his *Merchandising.* 1918. p. 158-71).

Accounting

American business and accounting encyclopaedia; comp. by E. H Beach and W. W. Thorne. Detroit, Bookkeeper publishing co. 1901. Consignment accounts, p. 346-8.

Bennett, George E. Commission merchants' consignment register; sales on consignments (In his *Constructive accounting.* 1920, p. 345-8, 177-80).

CONSIGNMENTS—ACCOUNTING—*(Continued)*
BENTLEY, H. C. Shipment and consignment accounts. (In his *Science of accounts.* 1913. p. 184-7).
CARTER, R. N. Consignments. (In his *Advanced accounts.* p. 150-82).
DICKINSON, A. L. Agency and commission. (In his *Accounting practice and procedure.* 1917. p. 59).
DOWLER, FRANK AND E. M. HARRIS. Consignments and joint accounts. (In their *Accounting auditing and banking.* p. 152-7)
ESQUERRE, PAUL JOSEPH. Consignments. (In his *Applied theory of accounts.* 1917. p. 186-220).
GOODYEAR, SAMUEL HORATIO AND LLOYD E. Higher accounting. Cedar Rapids, Goodyear-Marshall publishing co. 1908.
GRACE, STEPHENSON. System of consignment accounts which I have met with in auditing. *Accountant,* Feb. 4, 1911, p. 191-7.
GRANT, H. D. Averaging account sales. *Accountant,* Sept. 19, 1908, p. 337-9. *Journal of accountancy,* March 1908, p. 380-5.
GRIFFITH, JAMES B. Wholesale, commission, and storage accounts. Chicago, American school of correspondence, 1909. (In *Cyclopaedia of commerce, accountancy, business administration.* 1910 v.5. p. 11-78).
HUBBS, ELWOOD. Commission produce business. *Busines man's magazine,* July 1907, p. 98-112.
JONES, E. W. ERNEST. Consignment accounts. *Australasian accountant and secretary,* June 1920, p. 167-70.
KESTER, ROY B. Consignments. (In his *Accounting theory and practice.* 1918. p. 465-81).
LISLE, GEORGE. Consignment accounts. (In his *Accounting theory and practice.* 1900. p. 131).
LISLE, GEORGE AND W. A. MIDDLETON. Consignment accounts. (In their *Account-keeping in principle and practice.* 1911. p. 121-7).
MCINTOSH, R. J. Consignments to others. (In his *Reference book of accounts for manufacturing and mercantile companies.* Ed.2. c1914. p. 44-5, 105).
MADDEN, JOHN THOMAS. Consignments and joint ventures. (In his *Accounting practice and auditing.* c1917. p. 103-36).
MINER, G. W. Bookkeeping; commission and general merchandise. New York, Ginn & co., 1914.
MORROW, ROBERT C. Keeping track of commissions earned. *Business man's magazine,* Feb. 1912. p. 175.
PACKARD, SILAS SADLER. Commission bookkeeping. New York, S. S. Packard.
PORTERS, R. J. Consignments. (In his *Pitman's dictionary of bookkeeping.* p. 257-74).
POWERS, O. M. Practical sets, presenting commission, lumbering and manufacturing. Chicago, J. A. Lyons.
RITTENHOUSE, C. F. Consignments. (In his *Elements of accounts for individuals, professional men and institutions.* 1918. p. 116-7).
ROW, H. M. Commission accounts. *The office,* July 1890, p. 180-1.
SMITH, WALTER J. Commission salesman's accounts. *Accountant,* May 28, June 25, 1904, p. 721-30, 826-8. *Incorporated accountants journal,* 1896-7, p. 139.
SOULÉ, GEORGE. Commission business. (In his *New science and practice of accounts.* 1903. p. 213-8).
SPICER, E. E. AND E. C. PEGLER. Consignments. (In their *Practical bookkeeping and commercial knowledge.* 1912. p. 164-6).
SPICER, ERNEST EVAN AND ERNEST C. PEGLER. Goods on sale or return, consignment accounts, etc. (In their *Bookeeping and accounts.* 1914. p. 64-78).
WALTON, SEYMOUR. Returned consigned sales. *Journal of accountancy,* Jan. 1917, p. 72.
WILDMAN, JOHN R. Consignments. (In his *Principles of accounting.* 1914. p. 159-68).

CONSOLIDATED accounts. Webster, G. R.

CONSOLIDATED company seeks injunction to prevent officials from enforcing 80 cent rate. *American gas engineering journal,* Jan. 25, 1919, p. 82-4.

CONSOLIDATED gas and the Knoxville water cases. Gerstenberg, C. W.

CONSOLIDATED GAS COMPANY OF NEW YORK.
IN re theoretical depreciation; a discussion of the subject with an analysis of a paper by Weber entitled "Accounting for depreciation presented for the consideration of the Public service commission for the 1st district, State of New York by the Consolidated gas company of New York; prepared by J. E. Allison. St. Louis, Dufton and Skinner, 1917. 155p.

CONSOLIDATED gas company of New York and affiliated companies adopt profit sharing plan. *American gas light journal,* Nov. 27, 1916, p. 365.

CONSOLIDATED Mercury gold mines co. costs. *Engineering and mining journal,* Jan. 4, 1913, p. 23.

CONSOLIDATION of balance sheet and holding companies accounts. Wright, A. W.

CONSOLIDATION of electricity supply in London. *Electrical world,* Sept. 19, 1908, p. 611.

CONSOLIDATIONS
COX, HENRY C. Methods of combinations; consolidated balance sheet and income statement. (In his *Advanced and analytical accounting.* 1920. p. 330-75).
CUTFORTH, ARTHUR E. Amalgamation schemes; from an accountant's point of view. *Accountant,* Jan. 3, 1920, p. 11-24.
DEWING, ARTHUR STONE. Industrial combinations. (In his *Financial policy of corporations,* v.4. p. 23-68).
GERSTENBERG, CHARLES W. AND W. S. JOHNSON. Consolidations, sales and leases. (In their *Organization and control.* c1918. p. 256-77).
KESTER, ROY B. Combinations and consolidations. (In his *Accounting theory and practice.* 1918. v.2. p. 507-20).
SULLIVAN, JOHN JAMES. Consolidation of corporations. (In his *American corporations,* 1916. p. 285-99).

Accounting
BENNETT, ROBERT JOSEPH. Consolidation. (In his *Corporation accounting.* 1917. p. 390-468).
CUTFORTH, ARTHUR E. Accountancy incidental to company amalgamations. *Business organisation and management,* July-Aug. 1920, p. 363-70, ———).
DICKSEE, LAWRENCE ROBERT. Reconstructions and amalgamations. (In his *Advanced accounting.* 1916. p. 205-12).
ESQUERRE, PAUL JOSEPH. Consolidated balance sheet. (In his *Applied theory of accounts.* 1917 p. 447-60).
GEORGE, E. H. Accounts in connection with reconstruction and amalgamation of companies. *Accountant,* Nov. 27, 1920, p. 575-83.
GILMAN, STEPHEN. Consolidated balance sheet. (In his *Principles of accounting.* 1917, p. 399-407).

CONSOLIDATIONS—ACCOUNTING — *(Continued)*

Rehabilitation of existing plants as a factor in production costs. *Engineering magazine,* June 1915, p. 357-71.

GREENDLINGER, LEO. Consolidated income statements; consolidated balance sheets. (In his *Financial and business statements.* c1917. p. 83-99, 237-72).

HEITMAN, HENRY. Conditions of stability of commercial operations and market of industrial and commercial enterprises—trust control and finance. (In his *Course in the theory and practice of higher accounting.* 1910. p. 156-224).

KERR, DAVID S. Consolidated balance sheets. *Accountant,* Nov. 20, 1915, p. 627-30. *Canadian chartered accountant,* Oct. 1915, p. 107-114.

KESTER, ROY B. Consolidated balance sheet and profit and loss summary. (In his *Accounting theory and practice.* 1918. v.2. p. 600-19).

LOESCH, WILLIAM H. Corporation merger accounts. *New York accountants' and bookkeepers' journal,* June 1904, p. 166-70.

PATON, WILLIAM A. AND R. A. STEVENSON. Comparative and consolidated balance sheets (In their *Principles of accounting.* 1918. p. 587-98).

ROBERTS, J. W. Technique of consolidated returns. *Journal of acountancy,* Jan. 1920, p. 43-52.

ROBINSON, JOSEPH. Theory and practise. correspondence. *Journal of accountancy,* Dec. 1918, p. 473-80.

WALTON, SEYMOUR. Bond discount in consolidated balance sheets. *Journal of accountancy,* Aug. 1916, p 155-7.

WALTON, SEYMOUR. Consolidated statements. *Journal of accountancy,* March-June 1918, p. 225-37, 303-20, 384-99, 460-76.

WALTON, SEYMOUR. Inter-company profits. *Journal of accountancy,* Aug. 1916, p 157-60.

WALTON, SEYMOUR. Interdependent variables. *Journal of accountancy,* June 1920, p. 467-70.

WALTON, SEYMOUR. Reply to Joseph Robinson. *Journal of accountancy,* March 1919, p. 235-9.

WEBSTER, GEORGE R. Consolidated accounts. *Journal of accountancy,* Oct. 1919, p. 258-72.

CONSTABLE, JOHN

Bookkeeping taught by examples of complete annual accounts. London, Stewart, 1875, 1884.

CONSTAN, J.

Cost system for the concrete building block business. *Business man's magazine,* Oct. 1908, p. 303-6.

CONSTANS, E. C.

Promoting accounting efficiency. *Telephony,* Aug. 11, 1917.

Simple cost accounting system. *Telephony,* June 8, 1918.

Kinsley, W. W. Underground plant inventories. *Telephony,* April 13, 1918.

Value of a perpetual inventory. *Telephony,* May 4, 1918.

What about your plant values. *Telephony,* Jan. 12, 1918.

CONSTITUTIONAL barrier against fair rates; decision of Public service commission of first district New York. *Electric railway journal,* Jan. 19, 1918, p. 125-8.

CONSTRUCTING a bituminous macadam street. *Municipal journal,* February 24, 1916, p. 274.

CONSTRUCTION and finance of interurban electric railroads. Conway, Thomas.

CONSTRUCTION and maintenance of roads and bridges from July 1, 1913, to December 31, 1914. *United States Agricultural bulletin,* 1915, p. 1-64.

CONSTRUCTION costs for a 10,000 kw. steam plant, Quincy point, Mass. *Electrical world,* Dec. 11, 1915, p. 1312-4.

CONSTRUCTION costs for two 100,000 volt Montana transmission lines. *Electrical world,* Aug. 19, 1916, p. 371.

CONSTRUCTION costs of certain rapid sand filter plants. *Engineering and contracting,* Nov. 8, 1916, p. 409.

CONSTRUCTION costs of substation, high-tension line and street lighting. *Electrical review and western electrician,* Jan. 1, 1916, p. 34.

CONSTRUCTION costs of various types of freight handling wharves. *Engineering and contracting,* Sept. 26, 1917, p. 245-6.

CONSTRUCTION details and cost; tabulation. *Municipal journal,* February 1, March 29, 1917, p. 139-51, 444-5.

CONSTRUCTION details and costs. *Municipal journal,* Feb. 4-11, 1915, p. 133-5, 144-52, 188-92.

CONSTRUCTION details on the Marin water and power project. Bowers, H M.

CONSTRUCTION expenses in the Minnesota rate decision. *Electrical railway journal,* June 21, 1913, p. 1101.

CONSTRUCTION notes and cost data on concrete road work at Chevy Chase, Md. *Concrete cement,* Sept. 1913, p. 100-2.

CONSTRUCTION of agreement to arbitrate as to gas rates; legal decision. *Gas age,* March 15, 1918, p. 275.

CONSTRUCTION records and accounts. Hopson, H. C.

CONSTRUCTIVE accounting. Bennett, G. E. 1920.

CONSUETUDO, Vel lex mercatoria. Malynes, Gerard.

CONSULTING engineers discuss railway valuation. *Electric railway journal,* May 23, 1913, p. 936-7.

CONSULTING practice among accountants. *Journal of accountancy,* Dec. 1905, p. 141-2.

CONSUMERS' accounts and meter department. Glover, A. C.

CONTACT of commercial law and accounting. Kribben, B. D.

CONTAINERS

See also Boxes, packing cases etc.; Cans; Paperboxes.

BENNETT, GEORGE E. Containers. (In his *Constructive accounting.* 1920. p. 183-5).

BYRNE, H. E. Container records. *Business man's magazine,* Aug. 1906, p. 126-8.

Kester, R. B. Carriers and containers—valuation. In his *Accounting theory and practice.* 1918. v.2. p. 293-4).

LESELLE, W. J. How to keep a record of containers loaned to customers. *Business man's magazine,* Oct. 1905, p. 756-60.

WALL, RAYMOND J. Bottle and case accounting. ***National bottler's gazette,* Nov 5, 1920** p. 98-101.

CONTAINERS—*(Continued)*

WALTON, SEYMOUR. Vouchers: distribution of expenses. *Journal of accountancy,* Nov. 1918, p. 395-6.

YOST, C. E. How to keep a record of containers loaned to customers. *Business man's magazine,* Jan. 1906.

Depreciation.

See Depreciation, depletion and obsolescence—Containers.

CONTENTION over depreciation fund in attack on Cincinnati's union gas and electric company lease. *Electrical world,* Juy 5, 1913, p. 6-7.

CONTENTS and mode of stating executors' accounts. Loomis, J. R.

CONTINENTAL combinations. *Journal of accountancy,* April 1914, p. 299-300.

CONTINENTAL system of accounting (an elementary paper). Macdonald, J. B.

CONTINUATION of rate hearing by the I. C. C. *Railway review,* June 5, 1920, p. 927-30.

CONTINUITY of interest. Sprague, C. E.

CONTINUOUS audit. Dillon, A. 1880.

CONTINUOUS audit for Seattle accounts. *Journal of accountancy,* July 1911, p. 225.

CONTINUOUS cost keeping system maintained by Automatic transportation co., Buffalo. *Iron age,* Jan. 2, 1913, p. 88-90.

CONTINUOUS stock-taking. *Australasian accountant and secretary,* March 1920, p. 76-8.

CONTRACT price for mill power based on cost of coal. *Electrical review and western electrician,* November 18, 1916, p. 891-2.

CONTRACT prices on Illinois state aid road work in 1915 and in 1916. *Engineering and contracting,* May 2, 1917, p. 423.

CONTRACT routing system of Detroit Edison company. *Electrical world,* Aug. 24, 1912, p. 407-8.

CONTRACT work; is it professional or profitable? Shorrock, E. G.

CONTRACTOR-dealers adopt standard accounting system. *Electrical review,* April 5, 1919, p. 544-6.

CONTRACTORS

See also Building; Electrical contractors; Engineering.

CARD-INDEX record and filing systems for engineers and contractors. New York, *Engineering news,* 1906.

HILL, GEORGE W. Estimating hints for the contractor. *Electrical review and western electrician,* Jan. 29, 1916.

How to record contract sales. *Business man's magazine,* May 1911, p. 482-3.

HOVER, J. B. Eye on the contracts. *Business man's magazine,* April 1911, p. 377-84.

KEEPING records for the contracting job. *Journal of electricity,* March 1, 1920, p. 216-7.

MODEL record of distribution of construction plant. *Engineering record,* July 29, 1915, p. 218-9.

THOMASSON, THOMAS WELLS. Estimates in the contracting business. *Business man's magazine,* Aug. 1906, p. 128-30.

TUBESING, W. F. How a contractor keeps tab on the job. *Concrete,* Dec. 1917, p. 180-1.

VISIBLE record system for expediting construction contracts. *Engineering and contracting,* July 24, 1918, p. 83-4.

Accounting

ACCOUNTING and cost methods for contractors. *Engineering and contracting,* Sept. 1, 1909. pt. 1.

ACCOUNTING system for contractors. *Electrical review and western electrician,* Jan. 23, 1915, p. 152.

ALLEN, LESLIE H. Accounts for material on engineering construction. *Journal of accountancy,* May 1915, p. 352-8.

APPLICTION of business methods to construction work. *Enginering and contracting,* Oct. 22, 1913, p. 474-6.

BARWICK, T. Systems for the engineer and contractor. *Heating and ventilation,* Nov.-Dec., 1914, Jan. 1915, p. 27-34; 15-21, 18-22.

BENNETT, GEORGE E. Building contractors. (In his *Constructive accounting.* 1920. p. 453-60).

COBB, C. M. Office methods for a small contracting business. *Engineering and contracting,* April 5, 1916, p. 317-21.

CONTRACTORS. (In *International accountants' manual,* 1910, paragraph 389).

CONTRACTORS' tool records kept on two form sheets. *Engineering news-record,* Oct. 2, 1919, p. 675.

FINK, W. A. Loss suffered by many tradesmen. *Metal work,* April 27, 1917, p. 555-6.

FULLER, S. J. Accounting for railway contractors. *Bookkeeper,* 1902, v.15, no. 2, p. 34-41.

GILLETTE, HALBERT P. AND RICHARD T. DANA. Bookkeeping for small contractors. (In their *Cost keeping and management engineering.* 1916 p. 127-51).

GURMUKH, SINGH. Contractors' (works) accounts and bookkeeping. *Ragoon,* 1910.

HENRY, E. S. Contractors' accounts. *Accounting and commerce,* July 1915, p. 81-5.

HORNE, H. R. System of accounts for builders and contractors. *Incorporated accountants' journal,* July 1914, p. 286-9.

HOVER, J. B. Eye on the contracts. *Business man's magazine,* April 1911, p. 377-84.

HOW two contractors keep daily record of job. *Engineering news-record,* Nov. 9, 1916, p. 897.

HULL, ERNEST. Accounts of a builder and contractor. *Accountant,* Feb. 9, April 13, 1901, p. 181-8, 444-6.

LATHROP, B. L. Accounting for the contractor. *Engineering record,* May 20-June 3, 17-July 22, 1916, p. 685, 717-8, 750, 811, 843, 25-6, 57-8, 89-90, 119-20.

LOSSES on contracts. *Accountant,* Feb. 23, 1918, p. 165.

MCCALLUM, GEORGE. Bookkeeping and costing for contractors. *Business man's magazine,* Nov. 1909, p. 467-70.

NARLIAN, C. A. H. Accounts of engineers and contractors. *Journal of accountancy,* Aug. 1920, p. 81-7.

OFFICE system for construction work covering records of plans, progress and cost and book-keeping methods. *Engineering and contracting,* Dec. 17, 1913, p. 683-6.

PORTERS, R. J. Contracts. (In his *Pitman's dictionary of bookkeeping.* p. 275-91).

ROBERTSON, WILLIAM. Contractor's books. *Incorporated accountants' journal,* 1903-4, p. 253.

ROBINSON, JOSEPH. Theory and practice: correspondence. *Journal of accountancy,* Dec. 1918, p. 478-9.

ROSS, T. EDWARD. Contractors' accounts. *Accounting and commerce,* April 1916, p. 20-2. *Journal of accountancy,* March 1916, p. 161-6.

CONTRACTORS—Accounting—*(Continued)*

Slack, John P. The "Gilbreth field system." How a successful contractor has solved the accounting problem. *Business world,* Nov. 1907, p. 10.

Walker, Frank Robold. "Practical" business methods for contractors. Chicago, Frank R. Walker company, c1919. 50p.

Walton, Seymour. Profit on construction. *Journal of accountancy,* May 1917, p. 396-7.

Ward, Arthur. Builders' and contractors' accounts. Ed. 2. London, 1906.

Weatherwax, L. A. Accounting as applied to the general contractor. *Engineering and contracting,* May 21 1919, p. 552. *Concrete,* Oct. 1919, p. 165-6.

Wright, A. H. Accounting forms on construction work. *Public works,* Oct. 9, 1920, p. 338-40.

Wright, Hugh. Contractors' accounts. Chicago, American school of correspondence, 1909. (In *Cyclopedia of commerce, accountancy, business administration.* 1910. v. 9, p. 217-307).

Wright, Hugh. System in business of general building contractor. *Business man's magazine,* May 1908, p. 413-20.

Auditing

Castenholz, William B. Contractors. (In his *Auditing procedure.* 1918. p. 263-7).

Cutforth, A. E. Contractor. (In his *Audits.* 1914. p. 67-8).

Dicksee, Lawrence Robert. Contractors. (In his *Auditing.* Authorized American edition. p. 95-6).

Montgomery, Robert H. Contractors. (In his *Auditing theory and practice.* 1916. p. 733-6).

Spicer, Ernest Evan and Ernest C. Pegler. Contractor. (In their *Audit programmes.* 1919. p. 33-4).

Spicer, Ernest Evan and Ernest C. Pegler. Contractors. (In their *Practical auditing.* 1914. p. 477-9).

Cost accounting

Accounting and cost methods for contractors. *Engineering and contracting,* Sept. 1, 1909.

Allen, Leslie H. Cost accounting and its importance on construction work. *Contract record,* Sept. 23, 1914.

Allen, Leslie H. Cost accounting for the contractor. *Journal of accountancy,* March 1917, p. 177-84. Condensed. *Engineering news-record,* Feb. 17, 1917, p. 270-1. *Engineering and contracting,* Feb. 21, 1917, p. 192-3. Abstract. *Concrete,* March 1917, p. 97-8.

Allen, Leslie H. Cost accounting on construction work—detailed description of an efficient system. *Engineering and contracting,* April 8, 22, 1914, p. 404-10, 465-9.

Allen, Leslie H. Cost accounting on construction work with a description of the system used by the Aberthaw construction company. *Journal of the Boston society of civil engineers,* March-Oct, 1914, p. 133-77, 455-79.

Allen, Leslie H. Payroll distribution on construction work. *Journal of accountancy,* July 1914, p. 38-46.

Bates, L. Two form report of progress: contractor and his cost reports. *System,* March 1914, p. 311-4.

Best, B. G. Cost keeping and its value to the average contractor. *Concrete,* Feb. 1920, p. 87-93.

Bryan, E. N. Practical cost-keeping for contractors. *Engineering news,* March 12, 1914, p. 565-7.

Buel, A. W. Contract keeping in general construction and contract work. *Engineering magazine,* Aug. 1905.

Buel, A. W. Cost keeping on general contract work. *Engineering news,* March-May, Aug. 1905, p. 791-8, 29, 243-54, 707-18.

Carey, Dan. Overhead cost in contracting. *Engineering and contracting,* Oct. 22, 1919, p. 463-5.

Cheer, F. W. Costing for public works contractors. *Accountant,* Feb. 8, 1919, p. 103-7.

Collection and use of construction cost data. *Engineering news-record,* December 25, 1913, p. 1305-7.

Contractors' cost-keeping system. *Electrical world,* March 27, 1915, p. 797-9.

Cost system for contractor or jobber. *Metal work,* April 23, 1915, p. 599-600.

Cowing, John P. Cost keeping in construction and contract work. *Engineering magazine,* Sept. 1905, p. 921-8.

Cunliff, N. Development of a unit cost system; with discussion. *Journal of the association of engineering societies.* Aug. 1914, v. 53, p. 74-101. Discussion, J. M. Bisdoff, Sept. 1914, p. 165-70.

Curran, M. A. Cost keeping discussed before contractors. *Electrical world,* Mar. 3, 1917, p. 433.

Distribution sheets of contractor's accounting system. *Engineering and contracting,* July 21, 1920, p. 60-1.

Duncan, D. B. Cost keeping system for building contractors. *Engineering and contracting,* Sept. 27, 1916, p. 272-3.

Falk, Myron S. System of cost keeping. *American society of civil engineers, Transactions,* Mar 1909. v. 64, p. 401-40.

Fink, W. A. Jobbing and contract cost books. *Domestic engineering,* April 4, 1914, p. 6-7.

Gillette, Halbert P. and Richard T. Dana. Accounting and cost methods for contractors. (Ernest McCullough in *Engineer-contracting,* Sept. 1, 8, 15, 22, 1909). (In their *Cost keeping and management engineering.* 1916. p. 312-39).

Gillette, Halbert Powers and R. T. Dana. Cost keeping and management engineering; a treatise for engineers, contractors and superintendents engaged in the management of engineering construction. New York, Clark book co. 1916. 346p.

Gillette, Halbert Powers and Richard T. Dana. Cost keeping system of the Aberthaw construction co. (Leonard C. Wason, *Engineering-contracting,* Jan 13, 1909, and March 1906). In their *Cost keeping and management engineering.* 1916. p. 193-210).

Government contracts and cost accounting methods. *American industries,* Sept. 1917, p. 19-22.

Harris, H. A. Making a contractor's cost and bids agree. *Metal work,* Sept. 8-29, Oct. 13, 1916, p. 313-5, 407-9, 467-9.

Hauer, Daniel J. Cost keeping and bookkeeping. (In his *Modern management applied to construction.* 1918. p. 117-30).

Hill, G. W. Cost of doing business. *Domestic engineering,* May 8, June 12, 1915, p. 157, 306-7.

Holloway, G. E. Simple cost forms that help your business pay. *Building age,* Aug. 1919, p. 270-1.

Holloway, G. E. Cost system telling what every contractor wants to know. *Building age,* Dec. 1919, p. 392-4.

Holloway, G. E. Why some contractors' profits appear to shrink. *Building age,* Oct. 1919, p. 332-4.

Horne, R. W. Accounting on cost plus contracts. *Engineering and contracting,* Aug. 20, 1919, p. 228-9.

How to handle long time contracts. *Domestic engineering,* Aug. 7, 1920, p. 268-70.

Items which estimators sometimes omit. *Contract record,* June 2, 1920, p. 498-500.

Lathrop, B. L. Field-office accounting; finding costs. *Engineering record,* Aug. 12, 1916, p. 211.

CONTRACTORS — COST ACCOUNTING — *(Continued)*

LIDRAL, J. F. Contractor's salary as an overhead charge. *Engineering and contracting,* Aug. 27, 1919, p. 256-7.

LOW, EMILE. Recording unit costs of contract work. *Engineering news,* Mar. 26, 1903.

MCDILL, R. O. Uniform system of material cost keeping. *Engineering and contracting,* Sept. 4, 1912, p. 279.

MONTGOMERY, C. B. Keeping accurate daily and total cost sheets will pay the contractor. *Engineering record,* April 24, 1915, p. 535-6.

MOORE, DE WITT V. Cost keeping on municipal contract work. *Municipal engineering,* Jan. 1909.

NICHOLSON, J. LEE and JOHN F. D. ROHRBACH. Construction work. (In their *Cost accounting.* 1919. p. 25-6).

PLAN to simplify cost accounts of government contracts. *Commercial and financial chronicle,* June 16, 1917, p. 2408.

PROBLEM in figuring contract work. *Domestic engineering,* June 20, 1914, p. 357-8.

RUSSELL, RICHARD L. Contractors' cost-keeping and organizations. *Proceedings, Brooklyn engineers' club, paper* 97, Jan. 1911.

SCHNITZ, J. L. How costs are kept by A. J. Yawger & co. *Concrete,* June 1920, p. 255-7.

SHIELDS, GEORGE R. Emergency government contracts. *Case and comment,* Nov. 1917, p. 437.

SPICER, ERNEST EVAN and ERNEST C. PEGLER. Contract cost accounts. (In their *Bookkeeping and accounts.* 1914. p. 268-81).

SYSTEM of cost keeping; discussion of Myron S. Falk's paper. *Proceedings of the American society of civil engineers,* May 1909.

THOMASSON, THOMAS WELLS. Estimates in the contracting business. *Business man's magazine,* Aug. 1906, p. 128-30.

WALKER, FRANK RABOLD. Practical cost keeping for contractors; a book giving system of accurate cost keeping and the methods used for adapting it to all classes of construction work. Chicago, Frank R. Walker, 1916. 273p.

——————Same. Ed. 2, revised. Chicago, Frank R. Walker, 1918. 275p.

WALKER, FRANK RABOLD. Practical "standardized" forms for contractors. Chicago, Frank R. Walker.

WALKER, J. C. Guide posts in the contracting business. *Metal work,* April 23, 1915, p. 607-9.

WELLS, F. A. Cost keeping under the cost-plus fixed-fee contract. *Engineering and contracting,* Oct. 15, 1919, p. 447-9. *Concrete,* Dec. 1919, p. 244-7. *Architecture and building,* Jan. 1920, p. 3-6.

Costs

DANA, RICHARD T. Handbook of construction plant; its cost and efficiency. New York, McGraw-Hill book company, inc. 1914. 702p.

GILLETTE, HALBERT POWERS. Handbook of cost data for contractors and engineers; a reference book giving methods of construction and actual costs of materials and labor on numerous engineering works. Ed. 2. McGraw-Hill book co. 1910. 1854p.

Stockkeeping

BUILDERS' stores. *Accountant,* Aug. 1, 1914, p. 140-2.

CONTRACTORS' accounts. Ross, T. E.

CONTRACTORS' accounts. Wright, Hugh.

CONTRACTORS' accounts and book-keeping. Gurnukh Singh. 1910.

CONTRACTORS' cost-keeping system. *Electrical world,* March 27, 1915, p. 797-9.

CONTRACTORS' house wiring estimate sheet. *Electrical world,* Feb. 26, 1916, p. 491-2.

CONTRACTORS' tool records kept on two form sheets. *Engineering news-record,* Oct. 2, 1919, p. 675.

CONTRACTS

ADVANTAGES of the cost plus form of contract. *Engineering and contracting,* Oct. 22, 1919, p. 467-71.

ALLEN, C. F., and others. Discussion of cost-plus and other forms of contracts. *Journal of the Boston society of civil engineers,* Jan. 1920, p. 1-39.

ARMSTRONG, F. K. Actual cost of a contract. *Domestic engineering,* Dec. 22, 1917, p. 497-8.

AUDITORS' contracts. *Incorporated accountants' journal,* June 1912, p. 227-8.

BLAIR, A. General principles governing the law of contract. *Accounting and commerce,* Dec. 1915, Jan. Feb. March 1916, p. 206-8, 226-8, 255-6, 268-72.

BOWMAN, WILLIAM L. Architect in cost plus contracts. *Brickbuilders,* Sept. 1914, p. 223-5.

BROPHY, J. P. Hardships of the cost-plus plan. *Industrial management,* Oct. 1918, p. 320.

BURT *v.* DERVOE; error to municipal court of Chicago (52-24893). 5 typewritten pages.

BYRNE, THOMAS FRANCIS. Law of contracts. *Accountant,* 1886, p. 211.

CAPORN, ARTHUR E. Law of contracts. *Accountant,* Dec. 7, 1912, p. 720-8.

CARPENTER, JAMES SIDNEY. Contracts by trustees. *Incorporated accountants journal,* 1907-8, p. 244.

CARUSI, CHARLES F. Government contracts; before the accounting officers and in the U. S. Court of claims. *Government accountant,* Aug.-Dec. 1910, p. 145-57, 193-204, 242-51, 306-15, 352-60.

CHAFFEY, J. B. Cost-plus contract a success. *Engineering news,* March 6, 1919, p. 485.

CLARKE, E. W. Contracts—a comparison of cost plus with other forms. *Engineering and contracting,* Sept. 3, 1919, p. 283-5. *Canadian engineer,* Jan. 29, 1920, p. 183-4.

COMMISSIONS on government contracts. *Iron age,* July 25, 1918, p. 200-1.

COMMITTEE approves cost plus a fee contract of quartermaster corps. *Engineering and contracting,* May 22, 1918, p. 508-9.

COMPETITIVE bidding on a cost plus fee basis. *Architectural forum,* Oct. 1919, p. 142.

CONDITIONS in contracting for war material. *Iron age,* June 27, 1918, p. 1656-7.

CONTRACTS by correspondence. *Accountant,* Nov. 20, 1920, p. 533-4.

COST plus a fee contract and a suggested sliding scale fee. *Engineering and contracting,* Nov. 7, 1917, p. 360-1.

COST-PLUS-A-FEE contract for public works letting. *Engineering and contracting,* April 24, 1918, p. 417-8.

COST-PLUS-A-FIXED sum contracts. *Municipal journal,* Sept. 20, 1917, p. 287-8.

COST plus contract. *American architect,* March 13, 1918, p. 320.

COST plus contract for municipal work. *Engineering and contracting,* Feb. 13, 1918, p. 178-9.

COST-PLUS contract for unpounding dam at Decatur, Ill. *Engineering and contracting,* Sept. 8, 1920, p. 238.

COST plus contract form of Bent brothers. *Engineering and contracting,* Dec. 24, 1919, p. 728.

COST plus contract forms of Fred T. Ley and co., inc., Hurley-Mason co. and Ferro concrete construction co. *Engineering and contracting,* Dec. 26, 1917, p. 525-8.

COST plus contract forms of Stone & Webster. *Engineering and contracting,* Nov. 28, 1917, p. 444-5.

CONTRACTS—*(Continued)*

COST-PLUS contract incentive to close management. *Engineering news,* May 1, 1919, p. 863.

COST-PLUS contract satisfactory on Boston army base. *Engineering news,* Feb. 12, 1920, p. 326-9.

COST plus contract with minimum fee guarantee. *Engineering and contracting,* Oct. 22, 1919, p. 465.

COST-PLUS contracts. *Journal of accountancy,* Sept. 1918, p. 216-20.

COST plus contracts involving profit sharing between owner, contractor and employees. *Engineering and contracting,* Jan. 7, 1920, p. 20-3.

COST-PLUS contracts; tentative drift of two cost-plus forms of contracts submitted by the committee on contracts. *Bulletin of associated general contractors,* Nov. 1920, p. 21-2.

COST plus fee contract for bridge construction. *Engineering and contracting,* April 23, 1919, p. 408-9.

COST plus fee contract with divided risk for Kansas city, (Mo.) viaduct. *Engineering news,* March 7, 1918, p. 471.

COST plus fee system. *American architect,* Sept. 10, 1919, p. 341-2.

COST plus fixed sum per unit contracts for highway work. *Engineering and contracting,* Sept. 5, 1917, p. 201.

COST plus form of contract used on cantonment work including a schedule of equipment rental rates. *Engineering and contracting,* Nov. 28, 1917, p. 448-51.

COST plus form of government contract explained in correspondence and tables submitted to congress. *Official bulletin,* June 10, 1918, p. 9-13.

COST plus method in contracting. *American architect,* Oct. 15, 1919, p. 503-4.

COST plus percentage contract of Bureau of yards and docks. *Engineering and contracting,* Aug. 29, 1917, p. 174-6. Excerpt. *Industrial management,* Sept. 1917, p. 912-3.

COST-PLUS-PERCENTAGE contracts. *Journal of accountancy,* Jan. 1918, p. 49-53.

COST-PLUS-PROFIT contract is commended by Council of national defense. *Iron age,* March 21, 1918, p. 738-9.

COST-PLUS system severely criticized. *Iron age,* Sept. 27, 1917, p. 728-30.

COST plus ten per cent. *Literary digest,* Jan. 26, 1918, p. 21.

CRANE, J. L. and J. G. KIMMEL. Design features and form of contract for constructing a large earthen water supply dam on cost plus fee basis. *Municipal engineering,* Aug. 1919, p. 86.

DANN, JOHN T. Law of contracts. *Accountant,* Feb. 28, March 7, 1891, p. 178-80, 193-6.

DORR, W. S. Modified cost plus contracts for city use. *Engineering and contracting,* Feb. 18, 1920, p. 178-9.

ESTIMATING and the builder's overhead. *American architect,* Sept. 10, 1919, p. 366.

FARQUHAR, FRANCIS P. Accounting for cost of naval vessels under cost-plus-profit contracts. *Journal of accountancy,* Sept. 1919, p. 180-9.

FARR, WILLIAM EDWARD. Requisites of a contract. *Accountant,* March 24, 1906, p. 374-9.

FEES to be paid contractors according to contract for emergency work, adopted by the Secretary of war. *Metal work,* July 19, 1918, p. 60-1.

FIXING prices for naval contracts discussed in annual report of the secretary of the navy. *Iron age,* Dec. 13, 1917, p. 1420-1.

FORBES, ARTHUR H. First principles of contract. *Accountant,* Sept. 16, 1911, p. 354-7.

FORBES, ARTHUR H. Void, voidable and illegal contracts. *Incorporated accountants' journal,* Nov. 1911, p. 43-7.

FRANKLAND, F. H. Cost-plus-graded-percentage contracts. *Municipal journal,* Sept. 20, 1917, p. 288-9.

FULLER, GEORGE W. Cost plus contracts for water works construction. *Canadian engineer,* June 24, 1920, p. 599-601 *Journal of the American water works association,* Sept. 1920, p. 683-92. *Municipal engineering,* July 1920, p. 34-8. Abridged. *Engineering and contracting,* July 14, 1920, p. 32-4. Excerpts. *Engineering news,* July 8, 1920, p. 78-9.

GANNETT, F. and J. D. CARPENTER. Keep accurate costs on war-time fee contract. *Engineering news,* March 20, 1919, p. 571-3.

GLASCO, P. B. Cost plus contracts. *Engineering and contracting,* Aug. 29, 1918, p. 210-11.

GOODELL, J. M. Government cost plus contracts for emergency building. *Engineering news,* Oct. 11, 1917, p. 687-8.

GOVERNMENT cantonments and outline of form of contract for their construction. *Engineering and contracting,* June 27, 1917, p. 576-7.

GOVERNMENT contracts. *Journal of accountancy,* June 1917, p. 450-2.

GOVERNMENT contracts and cost accounting methods. *American industries,* Sept. 1917, p. 19-22.

GOVERNMENT contracts for war materials. *American industries,* Aug. 1918, p. 320.

GOVERNMENT contracts in U. S. A. *Accountant,* Sept. 20, 1919, p. 249-52.

GRAHAM, A. W. Unit price and cost-plus systems of contracts for public work. *Engineering and contracting,* April 2, 1919, p. 344-5.

HALLOWAY, G. E. Simple cost forms that help your business pay. *Building age,* Aug. 1919, p. 270-1.

HAMMOND, H. D. New contract system which stimulates efficiency gaining favor. *Engineering news,* July 18, 1918, p. 118-20.

HEWITT, H. E. Advantages of cost plus contracts. *Engineering and contracting,* Sept. 25, 1918, p. 312.

HILTON, E. D. Determination of selling price. *Journal of accountancy,* Jan. 1918, p. 27-33.

HORNE, R. W. Accounting on cost plus contracts. *Engineering and contracting,* Aug. 20, 1919, p. 228-9.

INVENTORIES, commitments, and foreign exchange. *American institute of accountants, Special bulletin,* no. 7, Dec. 1920.

LEGARE, T. K. Cost plus fixed sum contract for municipal construction. *Engineering and contracting,* Feb. 13, 1918, p. 181.

LITTELL, I. W. Government policy in cantonment contracts. *Electrical world,* Sept. 8, 1917, p. 470.

MARSHALL, R. C. Activities of the construction division United States army and the form of contract adopted. *Journal of the Boston society of civil engineers,* Sept. 1919, p. 265-99.

MARSHALL, R. C. Cost-plus contracts great lesson of war construction. *Engineering news,* Dec. 26, 1918, p. 1192.

MASSACHUSETTS cost plus profit road contract. *Engineering and contracting,* July 3, 1918, p. 14.

MEETS high contractors' labor and material problem; Massachusetts state highway commission introduce cost plus unit profit contracts. *Engineering news,* July 26, 1917, p. 172-3.

MEYER, CHARLES A. Requirement of each state as to conditional sales contracts. (In his *Mercantile credits and collections.* 1919. p. 255-91).

CONTRACTS—*(Continued)*

MORRISON, C. J. Cost plus basis for war supplies. *American machinist,* May 16, 1918, p. 828.

MORSE, P. Evils of cost plus contracts. *Forum,* Aug. 1918, p. 200-7.

NICHOLSON, J. LEE and JOHN F. D. ROHRBACH. Cost-plus contracts. (In their *Cost accounting.* 1919. p. 487-95).

OHIO uses cost-plus-lump-sum contract for highway maintenance. *Engineering news,* April 10, 1919, p. 734.

PADDING the cost. *Journal of accountancy,* July 1918, p. 40-2.

PAYMENT for estimating. *American architect,* Sept. 24, 1919, p. 427-9.

PLAN to simplify cost accounts of government contracts. *Commercial and financial chronicle,* June 16, 1917, p. 2408.

POTTER, DAVID. Our newest navy; how its cost is being determined. *Journal of accountancy,* May 1919, p. 336-57.

PROPOSED rehearing of supreme court Dick patent case. *Electrical world,* April 6, 1912, p. 720-2.

PROTECTING the owner under a cost-plus building contract. *Architectural forum,* Sept. 1919, p. 103-5.

QUESTION of extra work. *Building age,* April 1918, p. 190.

RANKING, D. F. DE L'HOSTE. Law of contract. *Incorporated accountants' journal,* Sept. 1914, p. 337-41.

REMARKS on contracts. 10 typewritten pages.

REPORT of the Colwyn committee on co-ordination of departmental action in regard to contracts. *Incorporated accountants' journal,* Nov. 1918, p. 27-9.

REVISED schedule of fees on government contracts. *Engineering and contracting,* April 17, 1918, p. 389.

SANDLANDS, PAUL E. Contracts in restraint of trade. (In Feather, J. Stuart. *Joint transactions.* 1911, p. 126-40). *Accountant,* June 10, 1911, p. 894-9.

SANDLANDS, PAUL E. Some examples of the requirements and difficulties in commercial contracts. *Accountant,* Jan. 16, 1915, p. 90-7.

SAVILLE, F. S. Law of contracts. *Accountant,* July 10, 1920, p. 42-5.

SCHIPPER, J. E. Inadequate cost-keeping retarding adjustment. *Automotive industries,* March 13, 1919, p. 561-3.

SEIDMAN, FRANK E. Overhead distribution for cost-plus contracts. *Accountant,* Nov. 23, 1918, p. 283-7. *Journal of accountancy,* March 1918, p. 161-75.

SHEALEY, R. PRESTON. Law of government contracts. New York, The Ronald press company, 1919. 300p.

SHIELDS, GEORGE R. Emergency government contracts. *Case and comment,* Nov. 1917, p. 437.

SPECIAL committee approves emergency contract form of quartermaster corps. *Engineering news,* Mar. 21, 1918, p. 550-1.

STARRETT, W. A. Government's emergency construction contract. *Scientific American,* Sept. 14, 1918, p. 213.

STARRETT, W. A. Operation of the government's building contract system. *Engineering and contracting,* March 27, 1918, p. 325-6.

STREET, A. L. H. Contract not to re-engage in business. *Iron age,* Oct. 16, 1913, p. 850-1.

TEMPLE, HERBERT M. Contractual relations between clients and accountants. *Journal of accountancy,* Oct. 1915, p. 291-6.

TRICKETT, WILFRED R. L. Elements of contracts, with particular reference to fraud and misrepresentation. *Incorporated accountants' journal,* 1903-4, p. 73.

TURNER, H. C. Labor efficiency good on percentage contracts. *Engineering news,* April 24, 1919, p. 815-8.

TYPICAL form of cost plus fixed fee contract. *Heating and ventilating,* Aug. 1920, p. 58-60.

UNIFORM general contract forms: report of committee of American railway engineering association. *Railway age,* Mar. 20, 1913, p. 620-4.

UNITED STATES. Contract for emergency work. 10 typewritten pages.

UNITED STATES. Department of commerce. Uniform contracts and cost accounting definitions and methods; recommendations by Inter-departmental conference consisting of delegates from the departments of war, navy and commerce, the Federal trade commission and the Council of national defense. Washington, Government printing office, 1917. 45p.

UNITED STATES. War department air service. Division of military aeronautics. Instructions to field auditors. 61 typewritten pages and forms.

UNITED STATES shipping board. Emergency fleet corporation. Cost-plus-contracts; cost analyses for wooden ships. 12p.

VALIDITY of agreement not to engage in business. *Iron age,* Aug. 18, 1910, p. 380.

WADDELL, J. A. L. New method of contract letting based on fairness to both owner and contractor. *American architect,* Sept. 24, 1919, p. 434-8.

WALTON, SEYMOUR. Book entries as affecting contracts. *Journal of accountancy,* Jan. 1919, p. 78-80.

WALTON, SEYMOUR. Equipment cost of contracts. *Journal of accountancy,* Oct. 1915, p. 313-5.

WALTON, SEYMOUR. Sales for future delivery. *Journal of accountancy,* Nov. 1916, p. 401.

WAR contracts and cost accounting. *Canadian chartered accountant,* April 1918, p. 278-88. *Journal of accountancy,* Nov. 1917, p. 373-85.

WELLS, A. E. Advantages of the cost-plus-a-fixed-fee contract for building construction. *Municipal engineering,* June 1919, p. 213-4. *Textile world,* July 5, 1919, p. 103.

WELLS, A. E. Cost plus contracts or lump sum? *Concrete,* Sept. 1919, p. 121-3.

WELLS, A. E. How the cost-plus contract safeguards both the owner and contractor. *American architect,* Sept. 3, 1919, p. 309-10. *Building age,* Sept. 1919, p. 307. *Domestic engineering,* Oct. 18, 1919, p. 110-2. *Engineering and contracting,* Sept. 24, 1919, p. 355. *Municipal and county engineering,* Oct. 1919, p. 160-1.

WELLS, F. A. Cost helping under cost-plus-fixed-fee contracts. *Engineering and contracting,* Oct. 15, 1919, p. 447-9.

WELLS, F. A. Protection of owners on cost-plus contracts. *Canadian engineer,* Sept. 25, 1919, p. 323-6.

WHAT is actual cost on a force account job? *Engineering and contracting,* Oct. 10, 1917, p. 203.

WHITE, HOWARD E. Notes on contracts. (In Humphreys, A. C. *Lecture notes on some of the business features of engineering practice.* p. 379-410).

WORKING agreements. *Accountant,* April 12, 1913, p. 540-1.

CONTRACTS by correspondence. *Accountant,* Nov. 20, 1920, p. 533-4.

CONTRACTS in restraint of trade. Sandlands, P. E. 1911.

CONTRACTURAL relation between clients and accountants. Temple, H. M.

CONTRIBUTION of the accountant in support of the commission on industrial relations, Suffern, Edward L.

CONTROL and audit of masonic accounts. *Accountant,* Nov. 13, 20, Dec. 18, 18, 1897, Jan. 29, 1898, p. 1053-5, 1083-5, 1191-3, 1201, 32, 120-1.

CONTROL of industry *Engineering,* Oct. 31, 1919, p. 585-6.

CONTROLLED key adding and calculating machine. *Scientific American,* July 5, 1913, p. 15.

CONTROLLING ACCOUNTS

Staub, Walter A. Controlling accounts. *Journal of accountancy,* Nov. 1909, p. 29-35.
Walton, Seymour. Consolidated controlling account. *Journal of accountancy,* March 1917, p. 192-4.

CONTROLLING accounts. Staub, W. A.

CONTROLLING accounts in cost accounting. Bosher, L. H.

CONTROLLING profits. Herz, E. 1917.

CONTROLLING salesman's expense accounts. *Business man's magazine,* June 1912, p. 507-8.

CONTROLLING time speed. 100%, Nov. 1917, p. 56.

CONTROLLING time spent. 100%, Dec. 1917, p. 49.

CONVENIENCE of the customer; system of the Commonwealth Edison company, Chicago. *Electrical world,* July 1, 1916, p. 15-20.

CONVENIENCE principles and methods of keeping accounts with bankers. Lowrie, William. 1805.

CONVENIENT estimate and proposal sheets. *Electrical world,* Feb. 27, 1915, p. 555-7.

CONVENIENT method for filing apparatus costs and station records. *Electrical world,* Oct. 7, 1916, p. 718.

CONVENIENT operating reports for steam plants. *Electrical world,* June 19, 1915, p. 1623-6.

CONVENIENT production record. *Machinery,* Feb. 1919, p. 501.

CONVENIENT system of motor maintenance and repair record cards. *Electrical world,* June 7, 1913, p. 1266-7.

CONVENTION of accountants— the formation of an Australasian institute. *Accountant,* Aug. 22, 1903, p. 1062-72.

CONVENTION of accountants, U. S. A. *Accountant,* Nov. 15, 1902, p. 186-8.

CONVENTIONS.
See Societies, Clubs, etc.

CONVERSE, C. M.
Office system and forms for the electrical contractor. *Electrical review and western electrician,* July 24, 1915, 150-2.

CONVERSE, P. D.
Problem of the transcontinental rate structure. *Journal of political economy,* March 1918, p. 291-301.

CONVERSIONS.
See Reorganizations.

CONWAY, J. B.
Accumulating graphic record. *American machinist,* Feb. 6, 1919, p. 242.

CONWAY, THOMAS
Commission-made rates are paramount. *Electric railway journal,* Jan. 19, 1918, p. 130-3.
Construction and finances of interurban electric railroads. *Journal of accountancy,* May 1906, p. 1-11.
Effect of passenger traffic upon freight earnings. *Journal of accountancy,* March 1906, p. 396-409.
Effect of six-cent fares upon the volume of traffic. *Electric railway journal,* Aug. 25, 1917, p. 310-2.
Future of electric railway fares. *Aera,* June 1919, p. 1053-66.
Is the zone system the solution? *Electric railway journal,* Nov. 2, 1918, p. 776-8.
Statuts of the higher fare in the state of New York. *Electric railway journal,* June 29, 1918, p 1235-9.
Traffic problems of interurban electric railroads. *Journal of acountancy,* Sept. Oct 1908, Jan. 1909, p. 340-50, 426-34, 214-23.
Up-state New York lines need relief. *Electric railway journal,* June 16, 1917, p. 1092-5.

——— **AND E. M. PATTERSON**
Operation of the New bank act. Philadelphia, J. B. Lippincott co. c1914. 431p.

CONWAY, W. P.
See Williams, W. H., joint author.

CONYNGTON, THOMAS
Adoption of by-laws. *Journal of accountancy,* Feb. 1913, p. 96-105.
Business law; a working manual of everyday law. New York, The Ronald press, 1918. 535p.
———Same. Ed.2. 2v. New York, The ald press, 1920. 870p.
Close corporation. *Journal of accountancy,* July 1906, p. 161-73.
Corporate organization and management; revised by H. Potter. Ed.4. New York, The Ronald press co. 1918. 778p.
Enforcement of by-laws. *Journal of accountancy,* March 1913, p. 157-65.
Manual of corporate management; containing forms, directions, and information for the use of lawyers and corporation officials. New York. The Ronald press co. 1903. 331p.
Nature of by-laws. *Journal of accountancy.* Jan. 1913, p. 10-20
New York C. P. A. examinations of June 1912. *Journal of accountancy,* Nov. 1912, p. 382-8.

COOK, C. L.
Billing and journalizing for department stores. *Business man's magazine,* April 1908, p. 33?-4.

COOK, C. B.
Economics and equity in valuation. *Electric railway journal,* Nov. 15-Dec. 13, 1919.
Employment department. *Business man's magazine,* June 1905, p. 1174-8.
Facts concerning factory management. *Business man's magazine,* Aug. Oct. 1906, p. 100-4, 64-7.
Factory management. Detroit. Book-keeper publishing co. 1906. 215p. *Business man's magazine,* Sept. Nov. 1905, p. 461-70, 841-8.

COOK, E. FULLERTON

Drug store bookkeeping especially adopted to the needs of the retail pharmacist. Ed.2. Philadelphia, College of pharmacy, Philadelphia, E. F. Cook, 1912. 16p. For use of classes in Philadelphia college of pharmacy.

COOK, HARRY WILLIAM

Anomalies of audit. *Accountant,* Aug. 3, 1907, p. 157-8.

COOK, HENRY R. M.

Standardization of school accounting and of school statistics; an address before the National association of school accounting officers, Feb. 25, 1913; reprinted from the *American school board journal.* 22p.

Standardization of school statistics. *Journal of accountancy,* Aug. 1910, p. 256-66.
Use of motor vehicles by gas companies. *Gas age,* Aug. 15, 1913, p. 154-8.

COOK, J. B.

How your bank account is protected. *Business man's magazine,* June 1912, p. 502-505.
National bank earnings. *Journal of accountancy,* Sept. 1910, p. 334-8. Editorial, Dec. 1910, p. 146.

COOK, J. R.

Use of motor vehicles by gas companies. *Gas age,* Aug. 15, 1913, p. 154-8.

COOK, JOHN J.

Personal liability of trustees and judicial factors. *Acountants' magazine,* June 1900, p. 333-53.

COOK, KENNETH

Brewery accounts. *Accountants' magazine,* Jan. 1906, p. 8-27.
New methods of bookkeeping with reference to pawnbrokers. *Accountant,* April 5, 1913, p. 517-9.

COOK, MORRIS LLEWELLYN

Experts in valuation cases. *Utiilties magazine,* v.1, no. 5, p. 19-20.

COOK, P. R.

Cyaniding clayey ore at the Buckhorn gold mine; with tabulation of milling costs. *Bulletin of the American institute of mining engineers,* Sept. 1916, p. 1560.

COOK, W. A.

Card system for simplifying farms records. *System on the farm,* July 1917, p. 180-1.

COOK, WALTER IVIMEY.

See Gill, F. T., joint author.

COOK COUNTY. DEPARTMENT OF FINANCE

Classification of expense accounts; alphabetically listed and classified to conform with standard appropriation accounts. 1914. 43p.

COOKE, CHARLES B.

Economics and equity in valuation. *Electric railway journal,* Nov. 15, 1919, p. 911-4.

COOKE, CHARLES N.

American system of practical bookkeeping adopted to the commerce of India, etc. 1840.

COOKE, E. AND R. S. HILTON

Gas undertakings. (In Bateson, William, ed. *Pitman's municipal office organisation and management.* p. 373-82).

COOKE, EDWARD

Costing as applied to gas undertakings. *Accountant,* Feb. 7, 14, 1920, p. 153-60, 177-95.

COOKE, F. P.

Cost system of a varnish manufacturing plant. *Business man's magazine,* May 1905, p. 960-8.

COOKE, G. C.

Audit of cash transactions. *Accounting and commerce,* Aug. 1916, p. 117-9.
Some notes on station accounts. *Accounting and commerce,* April 1917, p. 8-10.

COOKE, H. O. STAFFORD

Some factors of success in business. *Business organisation and management,* June 1920, p. 269-72.

COOKE, JOHN

Compting-house assistant; or, Book-keeping made easie: being a complete treatise on merchants accompts, etc. Ed.2. London, 1764.

COOKE, M. L.

True cost finding—what it can do for the railroads. *Annals of the American academy of political and social science,* Nov. 1919, p. 205-13. *Industrial management,* Jan. 1919, p. 40-2.

COOKE, SILAS

Accountancy and auditing. *Accountant,* June 6, 1885.
Gas and water accounts. *Accountant,* July 13, 20, 1889, p. 385-7, 396-9.
Municipal accounts. *Accountant,* 1887, p. 163.

COOKSEY, EDWARD

Law of partnership. *Incorporated accountants' journal,* Oct. 1915, p. 14-7.

COOKSON, BENJAMIN

Audit notes on the close of a company's accounts. *Accountant,* April 29, 1893, p. 399-403.

COOLEY, F. B.

Time and wage calculator. *American machinist,* Nov. 8, 1917, p. 819-20.

COOLEY, MORGAN L.

American audit note book. New York, Accountancy publishing company, 1909.
Close of an audit. *Accountant,* July 17, 1909, p. 96-8. *Journal of accountancy,* May 1909, p. 33-9.
Income and profits under the corporation tax; correspondence. *Journal of accountancy,* Oct. 1909, p. 464-5.
Standardization of state and municipal accounting. *Journal of accountancy,* Feb. 1908, p. 273-9.
Successful accountancy. *Accountant,* Nov. 13, 1909, p. 509-600. *Journal of accountancy,* Feb. 1909, p. 297-302.

COOLEY, MORTIMER E.

Appraisal of the Pere Marquet lines in Michigan; abstract of a report to the railroad road commisison. *Railway age gazette,* Feb. 26, 1915, p. 376-7.
Factors determining a reasonable charge for public utility service. *American institute of electrical engineers.* Proceedings, March 1914, p. 453-71. *Journal of the western society of engineers,* Jan. 1914, p. 1-17. Condensed. *Electric railway journal,* Jan. 17, 1914, p. 124-5. Summary. *Electrical world,* Feb. 14, 1914, p. 356-7.

COOLEY, MORTIMER E.—*(Continued)*

Fundamentals of appraisal and valuation. *Electric railway journal,* Oct. 30, 1915, p. 913.

Overhead charges. *American electric railway accountants association,* Proceedings, 1911 p. 169. Abstracts. *Electric railway journal,* Oct. 14, 1911, p. 877-9. *Canadian engineer,* May 9, 1912, p. 630. Discussion. *Electric railway journal,* Oct. 14, 1911, p. 816. Editorial. *Electric railway journal,* Oct. 21, 1911, p. 897.

COOLIDGE, S.

Guaranteeing piece rates. *Industrial management,* May 1919, p. 411.

COOMBS, CARO D. COMP.

Modern magic; a personal and household budget and account book. Boston, Whitcomb & Barrows, c1920.

COOMBS, EDWARD ALFRED

Some notes on municipal finance under the London government act, 1899. *Accountant,* Aug. 17, 1901, p. 908-12.

COOMBS, W. BAYLEY

Manual of solicitors' bookkeeping. London, 1868.

COOPE, HARRY

Treasury accounting system. *Business man's magazine,* Sept. 1907, p. 66-8.

COOPER, D.

Company amalgamations. *Accountant,* Aug. 26, 1911, p. 277-82.

Criticism of department of practical accounting. *Journal of accountancy,* July 1912, p. 70-3.

Hints to examination candidates. *Canadian chartered accountant,* April 1916, April 1918, p. 294-6, 316-18.

Problem department. *Canadian chartered accountant,* Oct. 1911, Jan. April, July, Oct. 1912, April, July, 1913, Jan. 1914, p. 78-82, 149-54, 223-9, 48-54, 137-41, 288-97, 54-62, 203-6.

COOPER, EDWARD BRODIE

Administration of estates of deceased persons. *Incorporated accountants' journal,* 1892-3, p. 67-72.

Chancery practice as affecting accountancy. *Incorporated accountants' journal,* 1895-6 p. 10.

COOPER, ERNEST

Address, 1900. *Accountant,* May 5, 1900, p. 430-34.

Address, 1901. *Accountant,* May 4, 1901, p. 531-38.

Address, 1912. *Accountant,* Dec. 14, 1912, p. 750-4.

Chartered accountants and the profit question. *Accountant,* Nov. 24, Dec. 8, 15, 22, 1894, p. 1033-43, 1089-91, 1119-21, 1073-5.

Chartered acountants as auditors of companies. *Accountant,* 1886, p. 644.

Notes on Mr. Welton's paper on the profit of companies available for distribution. *Accountant,* Jan. 3, 1891, p. 12-5.

Value of use of colour in making and verify ing accounting records. *Accountant,* Oct. 10, 1914, p. 412-3. *Journal of accountancy,* April 1914, p. 290-3.

What is profit of a company. *Accountant,* Nov. 10, 1888, Dec. 21, 1889, p. 740-6, 689-91.

COOPER, F. T.

Liability of an auditor. *Accountants' magazine,* July 1909, p. 351-65.

Relations of accounting to law. *Accountants' magazine,* Jan. 1913, p. 9-29.

COOPER, FRANCIS

Financing an enterprise; a manual of information and suggestion for promoters, investors and business men generally. 2.v. New York, The Ronald pres co. 1906.

COOPER, FRANK SHEWELL

Some recent decisions on company law. *Accountant,* April 16, 1910, p. 539.

COOPER, H. S.

Giving local 100 per cent service. *Electric railway journal,* Nov. 18, 1916, p. 1060-2.

Indexing car equipment data. *Electric railway journal,* Nov. 20, 1915, p. 1040-1.

Public utility rates. *General electric review,* Nov. 1917, p. 840-7.

Rates for electric service. *Electrical world,* Feb. 7, 1914, p. 326.

Series of articles on rates. *Southwestern electrician,* Mar.-July 1914, p. 18, 19, 16, 23.

COOPER, JOHN

Address and discussion. *Incorporated accountants' journal,* 1901-2, p. 130.

COOPER, JOHN ALEXANDER

Alphabet values in the ledger; correspondence. *Journal of accountancy, March* 1906, p. 420.

Education for the accountant. *Journal of accountancy,* Aug. 1908, p. 261-8.

Evolution of the accountant. *New York accountants' and bookkeepers' journal.* March 1904, p. 65-9.

Federal relations; advancement and regulations of the profession. *Journal of accountancy,* Jan. 1913, p. 1-9.

Higher accounting and certified public accountants. *Business man's magazine,* 1904, v.16, no. 10, p. 103-10.

Obligations of a public accountant. *Journal of accountancy,* April 1909, p. 484-5.

Professional ethics. *Journal of accountancy,* Dec. 1907, p. 81-94. *American institute of accountants. Yearbook* 1907, p. 133-146.

Public accountants in the states. *Accountant,* Oct. 17, 1903, p. 1251-3.

Should accountants advertise? *Journal of accountancy,* Aug. 1914, p. 85-94.

Some precepts of professional conduct. *Canadian chartered accountant,* Jan. 1919, p. 238.

COOPER, M. R.

Cost of keeping farm horses and cost of horse labor. Washington, Government printing office, 1917. *United States agricultural bulletin,* 560, 1917, p. 1-22.

COOPER, P.

Checking a crop loss. *System on the farm,* March 1918, p. 90.

COOPER, T.

See Hays, W. M., joint author.

COOPER, T. P., F. W. PECK AND A. BOSS

Labor requirements of crop production. *Minnesota agricultural exp,* 1916, p. 1-55.

COOPERATION

MURPHY, B. E. Co-operation. *Accounting and commerce,* Oct. 1918, p. 146-9.

COOPERATION and profit sharing. *Monthly labor review,* June 1920, p. 117-45.

CO-OPERATION and progress. *Journal of accountancy,* Nov. 1911, p. 542-4.

CO-OPERATION as a trouble-cure in five cafeterias. *Literary digest,* July 10, 1920, p. 82-6.

CO-OPERATION between bankers and accountants. *Journal of accountancy,* July 1913, p. 51-3.

CO-OPERATION in land valuation. *Railway age gazette,* July 20, 1917, p. 104-5.

COOPERATION of executives and men in cost accounting. *Paper,* May 26, 1920, p. 11-2.

CO-OPERATIVE accounting. Cheel, Ernest C.

CO-OPERATIVE auditing. Tetlow, B.

CO-OPERATIVE bookkeeping. *Accounting,* Ma 28, 1892, p. 438-41.

CO-OPERATIVE bookkeeping. Wood, Alfred. 1904.

CO-OPERATIVE electrical contracting. *Electrical world,* September 19, 1914, 586-7.

CO-OPERATIVE elevator of concrete at low cost. *Concrete,* June 1918, p. 195.

CO-OPERATIVE housing by associations of consumers. Co-operative league of America. c1920.

CO-OPERATIVE LEAGUE OF AMERICA.

Co-operative housing by associations of consumers. New York, The Co-operative league of America, c1920. 16p.

How to start and run a co-operative store on the Rochdale plan, compiled from the experiences of the successful European and American co-operative stores. New York, The co-operative league of America, 1920. 30p.

Pamphlets on cooperative stores, eight.

COOPERATIVE organization business methods. Kerr, W. H. and G. A. Nabstoll. 1915.

CO-OPERATIVE plan for Philadelphia carmen. *Electric railway journal,* Sept. 2, 1911, p. 393-4.

COOPERATIVE SOCIETIES.

See Cooperative stores and societies.

CO-OPERATIVE societies' accounts. Sugden, Frederick H. 1902.

COOPERATIVE STORES AND SOCIETIES

See also Retail trade.

American co-operative convention, 1920. How to start a co-operative wholesale being the report of the committee on wholesale of the second American co-operative convention. New York, The co-operative league of America, 1920, 8p.

Bexell, John Andrew, Hector MacPherson and W. H. Kerr. Survey of typical cooperative stores in the United States. Washington, Government printing office, 1916. 32p. (United States. Department of agriculture, bulletin no. 394).

Co-operative league of America. How to start and run a co-operative store on the Rochdale plan, compiled from the experiences of the successful European and American co-operative stores. New York, The co-operative league of America, 1920, 30p.

Co-operative league of America. Pamphlets issued on cooperative stores, eight.

Gerstenberg, Charles W. and W. S. Johnson. Cooperative societies. (In their *Organization and control.* c1918. p. 108-25).

Swinney, John B. Cooperative store. (In his *Merchandising.* 1918, p. 334-48).

Accounting

Allen, John E. Co-operative accounts. *Accountant,* Sept. 26, 1891, p. 680-7.

Bexell, John Andrew and W. H. Kerr. Business practice and accounts for cooperative stores. Washington, Government printing office, 1916. 56p. (United States. Department of agriculture, bulletin no. 381).

Brocklehurst, G. R. Bookkeeping for bakers, grocers, drapers, dairymen, butchers, co-operative societies, etc. Gainsborough, 1892.

Browder, Earl R. Co-operative accounting. *Co-operative consumer,* March 1918 p. 36-7.

Browder, Earl R. System of accounts for a small consumers' cooperative. New York, Cooperative league of America. 8p.

Cheel, Ernest C. Co-operative accounting. New York, The Co-operative league of America, 1920. 16p.

Co-operative bookkeeping. *Accountant,* May 28, 1892, p. 438-41.

Co-operative union limited. System of bookkeeping specially arranged for the use of industrial and provident societies. Manchester, Co-operative union limited, 1904. 130p.

Hines, G., B. Jones and H. Pumphrey. Easy bookkeeping for small co-operative societies. Edinburgh, 1887.

Pixley, Francis W. Annual return prescribed by the chief registrar for societies carrying on industries and trades under the industrial and provident societies act, 1893. (In his *Auditors, their duties and responsibilities.* 1910, p. 616-8).

Smith, W. J. Co-opeative stores accounts. *Incorporated accountants' journal,* 1892-3, p. 107.

Sugden, Frederick H. Co-operative societies' accounts. London, Gee & co. 1902. 114p. (Accountants' library, v.6).

Tetlow, B. Accounting of industrial and provident societies. *Incorporated accountants' journal,* Feb. 1914, p. 130-2.

Walbank, John A. Accounts of a retail co-operative society doing a cash business. *Accountant,* May 14, 21, 1904, p. 641-56, 679-84.

Ward, P. G. Co-operative accounting. (*Co-operative league of America, Report of the proceedings,* 1918, p. 83-9).

Wood, Alfred. Co-operative bookkeeping. Ed. 12. Manchester, Cooperative union limited, [1904]. 388p.

Young, J. Haydn. Co-operative accounts. *Accountants' magazine,* May 1905, p. 260-72.

Auditing

Audit of co-operative societies accounts. *Accountant,* July 25, Sept. 5, 12, 19, 1896, p. 627-9, 721-2, 743-4, 762-3.

Pixley, Francis W. Co-operative stores. (In his *Auditors, their duties and responsibilities.* 1910. p. 503).

Spicer, Ernest Evan and Ernest C. Pegler. Co-operative societies. (In their *Practical auditing.* 1914. p. 479).

Spicer, Ernest Evan and Ernest C. Pegler. Co-operative society. (In their *Audit programmes.* 1919. p. 35-7).

Spicer, Ernest Evan and Ernest C. Pegler. Retail and co-operative stores. (In their *Practical auditing.* 1914. p. 497).

Tetlow, B. Co-operative auditing. Manchester, Co-operative union limited. 349p.

Wood, T. R. J. Milburne and H. R. Bailey. Manual of auditing for industrial and provident co-operative societies. *Accountant.* May 13, 27, 1876.

Wood, T., R. J. Milburne and H. R. Bailey. Bailey. Manual of auditing, with instructions and explanations on filling up the return to the chief registrar of friendly societies; specially arranged for auditors and officers of industrial and provident co-operative societies, Ed. 3. Manchester, 1899.

CO-OPERATIVE UNION LIMITED.
System of bookkeeping specially arranged for the use of industrial and provident societies. Manchester, Co-operative union limited, 1904. 130p.

COOPERS

Cost accounting
BELSER, F. C. Cost accounting. *Barrel and box*, May 1917, p. 32.

Depreciation.
See Depreciation, depletion and obsolescence—Coopers.

CO-PARTNERSHIP and profit-sharing. Williams, Aneurin. 1913.

CO-PARTNERSHIP and profit sharing as a solution for the wages problem. *Engineering magazine*, Sept. 1912, p. 837-45.

COPE, EDWARD A. AND W. H. ROBINS.
Solicitor's office organisation management accounts. London, Sir Isaac Pitman & sons. 166p.

COPELAND, A. E.
Figuring cost on furniture. *Business*, April 1900, p. 217-9.

COPELAND, MELVIN THOMAS
Business statistics. Cambridge. Harvard university press, 1917. 696p. (Harvard business studies).
Cotton manufacturing industry of the United States. Cambridge, Harvard university, 1912. 415p.

COPELAND, T. E.
Everybody's guide to bookkeeping. London, Brindley & Howe, 1914. 97p.

COPLAND, D. B.
University and commercial education. *Federal accountant*, Jan. 1919, p. 38-43.

COPPER.
See Mining and metallurgy—Copper

COPPER costs average 16c; Federal trade commission publishes results of an investigation. *Engineering and mining journal*, Nov. 8, 1919, p. 764-5.

COPPER-zone system approved for Boston & Worcester street railway. *Electric railway journal*, Sept. 29, 1917, p. 577-8.

COPPER-zone system sustained. *Electric railway journal*, June 10, 1916, p. 1089-90.

COPPER zones for Shore line electric railway. *Electric railway journal*, Sept. 11, 1915, p. 443-5.

COPPER zones in Massachusetts. *Electric railway journal*, Sept. 1, 1917, p. 353-4.

COPY of query addressed to the institute solicitor regarding "stock dividends"; opinion re stock dividend. *Canadian chartered accountant*, Jan. 1913, p. 33-4.

COPY of query addressed to the Institute's solicitor regarding the acceptance of bills receivable as payment for stock, etc. re Manitoba stock companies act; opinion re bills receivable, etc. *Canadian chartered accountant*, Jan. 1913, p. 30-2.

COPYRIGHTS.
See Patents, copyrights, etc.

CORBETT, W. E.
Keeping costs in a stone plant. *Concrete*, July 1917, p. 20.

CORDAGE

Cost accounting
EGGLESTON, DEWITT CARL. Cost of manufacturing cordage. (In his *Problems in cost accounting*. 1918. p. 218).

CORDEAL, EARNEST
Cost accounting in the railroad repair shop. *Engineering magazine*, May, 1915, p. 211-7.
Force organization in the railroad repair shop. *Engineering magazine*, July 1913, 538-45.
Scheduling work in the railroad repair shop. *Engineering magazine*, Nov. 1912, p. 191-8.
Wage systems in the railroad repair shop. *Engineering magazine*, April 1915, p. 51-7.

CORDERY, H. S.
Customs work. *Accounting and commerce*, Nov. 1918, p. 187-90.

COREY, C. L.
Determining rates for gas service. *American gas light journal*, Oct. 23, 1911, p. 259. *Public service*, January 1912, p. 25.
Rátes for gas service. *Progressive age*, Oct. 16, 1911, p. 869-73.
Reasonable gas rates and their determination. *Progressive age*, Nov. 15, 1912, p. 964-9.

COREY and McKenzie complete accounting system and record for national farm loan associations. Dworak, E. A. 1917.

CORK municipal school of commerce. *Journal of accountancy*, June 1911, p. 133.

CORLISS, WILLIAM MILLS
Navy yard cost accounting. *Journal of accountancy*, July 1917, p. 28-32.
Some minor phases of municipal accounting. *Business*, Jan. 1915, p. 9-12.

CORMACK, JAMES
Depreciation of ships in relation to assessment for income tax. *Accountants' magazine*, Dec. 1897, p. 620-31.

CORN EXCHANGE NATIONAL BANK, PHILADELPHIA.
Complete text and analysis of the Federal farm loan act, approved July 17, 1916, Philadelphia, Corn exchange national bank, 1916. 40p.

CORN OPTIONS
DODD, ARTHUR F. Corn options and cotton futures; their object and effect upon commercial transactions. *Accountant*, July 6, 13, 1901, p. 779-87, 804-6.

CORNELL, C. D.
Shopkeepers' accounts simplified. London, Sir Isaac Pitman & sons, 1919. 71p.

CORNELL, S.
Working efficiency of rolling steel. *Metallurgical and chemical engineering*, Aug. 15, 1916, p. 177-84.

CORNELL, T. B.
Cost accounting methods in the Portland cement manufacturing business. *Business man's magazine*, Feb. 1909, p. 163-5.

CORNMEY, ARTHUR G.
System in park expenditures. *Municipal journal and engineer*, 1910, v.28, p. 519-23.

CORPORATE management compared with government control. Sells, E. W.

CORPORATE organization and management. Conyngton, Thomas. 1918.

CORPORATE promotions and reorganizations. Dewing, A. S. 1914.

CORPORATION. Evans, J. M. 1897.

CORPORATION accounting. Bennett, R. J. 1917.

CORPORATION accounting. Dudley, G. O.

CORPORATION accounting. Lyons, John. 1908.

CORPORATION accounting and auditing. Keister, D. A. 1901.

CORPORATION accounting and corporation law. Rahill, J. J. 1899.

CORPORATION accounting and investigation. Macpherson, F. H.

CORPORATION accounts. Griffith, J. B. 1909.

CORPORATION accounts and voucher system. Griffith, J. D. 1917.

CORPORATION accounts; preliminary draft of an act to regulate the accounts and audit. *Accountant*, Oct. 11, 18, Nov. 15, 1902, p. 1026-32, 1049-50, 1183-5.

CORPORATION and factory accounting. Goodyear, S. H. and L. E. Goodyear.

CORPORATION and manufacturing accounts. Griffith, J. B.

CORPORATION and voucher accounting. Marshall, C. C. 1907.

CORPORATION book-keeping. Webber, F. C. 1909.

CORPORATION finance. Greene, T. L. 1897.

CORPORATION finance. Lyon, Walter Hastings. 1912.

CORPORATION finance. Mead, Edward Sherwood. 1915.

CORPORATION finance. Walker, W. H. and F. W. Field.

CORPORATION manual. Parker, J. S, ed. 1920.

CORPORATION of accountants, lim., and the Scottish societies of chartered accountants: report of trial. *Accountant*, 1903, p. 1433, 1475, 1479, 1540.

CORPORATION opening entries. *Business man's magazine,* July 1908, p. 72-5.

CORPORATION organization and accounting. Bell, W. H.

CORPORATION reports. *Journal of accountancy,* Oct., Nov., Dec., 1906, Jan., Feb., March, April 1907, p. 460-70, 42-7, 146-53, 238-48, 305-16, 395-402, 476-83.

CORPORATION securities. *Journal of accountancy,* May, June, 1907, p. 49, 141.

CORPORATION stock-book. Williamson law book co.

CORPORATION tax. *Journal of accountancy,* April 1910, p. 449-50.

CORPORATION tax act. *Journal of accountancy,* Sept. 1909, p. 373-7.

CORPORATION tax amendment. *Journal of accountancy,* Oct. 1911, p. 454-5.

CORPORATION tax bill. Suffern, Edward L.

CORPORATION tax correspondence. *Journal of accountancy,* Aug. 1909, p. 300-303.

CORPORATION tax law amendment. *Journal of accountancy,* Feb. 1912, p. 135-7.

CORPORATION tax law and accounting terminology. Pangborn, W. S.

CORPORATION tax law of 1909; a letter to the members of the American association of public accountants together with copies of correspondence with the attorney general, and a copy of the act, September 30, 1909. 25p.

CORPORATION tax letters. *Journal of accountancy,* Sept. 1909, p. 378-82.

CORPORATION tax publicity. *Journal of accountancy,* Feb. 1911, p. 291-3.

CORPORATION tax returns. *Journal of accountancy,* Feb. 1913, p. 134-39.

CORPORATION tax summary. *Journal of accountancy,* Oct. 1909, p. 458.

CORPORATION taxes in Spain. *Journal of conational law,* Oct. 1920, p. 6-7.

CORPORATION TRUST COMPANY.

- BULLETINS series of 1918. The $8,000,000,000 revenue bill. New York, Corporation trust company, c1918.
- INCOME tax service, 1918. New York, Corporation trust company, 1918.
- INCOME tax service, 1919. New York, Corporation trust company, 1919.
- INCOME tax service, 1920. New York, Corporation trust company, 1920.
- NEW YORK state income tax on manufacturing and mercantile corporations. New York, Corporation trust company. 20p.
- NEW YORK state income tax service. New York, Corporation trust company.
- WAR tax service, 1918. New York, Corporation trust company, c1918.
- WAR tax service, 1919. New York, Corporation trust company, 1919.
- WAR tax service, 1920. New York, Corporation trust company, 1920.

CORPORATIONS

See also Liquidations and receiverships.

- ACCOUNTANTS: their duties and responsibilities. *Accountant*, May 5, 12, 19, 26, June 2, 9, 16, 23, 30, July 14, 21, 28, 1883.
- BENTLEY, H. C. Corporation. (In his *Science of accounts.* 1913. p. 31-48).
- BINDLOSS, ROBERT HUGH. Private companies (a) the advantages of a private company (b) the conversion of a business into a private company. *Incorporated accountants' journal,* 1910-11, p. 101.
- BRANDON, H. B. Joint stock companies. *Incorporated accountants' journal,* Feb. 1915, p. 111-5.
- BUXTON, W. O. AND A. F. ROUNTREE. Points in company practice. *Accountant,* April 21, June 9, 1906, p. 506, 510, 721.
- COMPANY losses prior to incorporation. *Accountant,* July 28, 1906, p. 93.
- CONYNGTON, THOMAS. Close corporation. *Journal of accountancy,* July 1906, p. 161-73.
- CORPORATIONS and advertising. *Journal of accountancy,* Sept. 1911, p. 374.
- CORPORATIONS and the common peoples. *Journal of accountancy,* May 1914, p. 367-70.
- CROSS, JOHN ASHTON. Distinctive features of limited liability companies. *Incorporated accountants' journal,* 1902-3, p. 122.

CORPORATIONS—*(Continued)*

CROSS, JOHN ASHTON. Secretary accounts, dividends and auditors. *Incorporated accountants' journal,* 1902-3, p. 176.

CROSS, JOHN ASHTON. Underwriting, making a market allotment, etc. *Incorporated accountants' journal,* 1902-3, p. 148.

DAWSON, S. S. Some points in connection with limited companies. *Accountant,* March 26, 1904, p. 404.

DERUSETT, H. AND OTHERS. Limited companies and private partnerships. *Incorporated accountants' journal,* 1903-4, p. 117.

DEZOUCHE, RICHARD CATON. Private companies and limited partnerships. *Accountant,* March 4, 1911, p. 339-45.

DICKINSON, A. L. What is a constituent company? (In his *Accounting practice and procedure.* 1917. p. 182-3).

DIXON, OWEN. Some of the consequences which result from the incorporation of companies. *Accountant,* Sept. 11, 1920, p. 261-4.

ELGAR, W. D. AND OTHERS. Private companies and income tax. *Incorporated accountants' journal,* 1908-9, p. 227.

FAUSSETT, F. PORTER. Limited companies after the great war. *Accountant,* March 15, 1919, p. 212-3.

FEDERAL incorporation. *Journal of accountancy,* Jan. 1912, p. 55-7.

GERSTENBERG, CHARLES W. AND W. S. JOHNSON. Joint stock companies. (In their *Organization and control.* c1918. p. 90-8).

GREEN, STEWART. Difference in constitution and relative advantages to private firms and limited companies and the matters of account involved by a conversion. *Accountant,* Dec. 1, 1906, p. 667-75.

HAMILTON, WILLIAM R. Joint stock versus private ownership of businesses: some commercial differences. *Accountant,* May 25, Aug. 10, 1907, p. 720-6, 161-5.

JAMIESON, GEORGE AULDJO. Limited liability. *Accountant,* June 16, 23, 1888, p. 383-6, 404-8.

JORDON, HERBERT W. Private companies; their utility and the exemptions they enjoy. *Accountant,* Oct. 24, 1914, p. 475-84.

NEAL, THEODORE D. Joint stock enterprise with limited liability; its relation to, and effect upon, social and industrial progress. *Accountant,* Jan. 14, 1899, p. 50-6.

PARTNERSHIP or company: the advantages of each. *Canadian chartered accountant,* Jan. 1919, p. 227.

PEARSON, FRANK S. Origin of limited liability companies. *Accountant,* Oct. 17, 1914, p. 447-50.

POWELL, G. T. Companies limited by guarantee. *Accountant,* Oct. 21, 1893, p. 886-90.

PRIVATE companies. *Accountant,* May 16, 1908, p. 704.

PRIVATE companies and earned income. *Accountant,* March 14, 1908, p. 349-52.

RIGHTS to corporate name. *Journal of accountancy,* May 1908, p. 74.

RIPLEY, WILLIAM ZEBINA. Trusts, pools and corporations. Boston, Ginn and co. c1905. 477p.

SELLS, ELIJAH W. Should advertising expenditures be charged as an investment or as an expense? *Journal of accountancy,* Sept. 1911, p. 346-51.

STATUS of private companies. *Accountant,* June 4, 1910, Feb. 4, 1911, p. 787, 179.

SYNDICATES as promoters. *Incorporated accountants' journal,* 1899-1900, p. 2.

TAYLOR, H. M. Private traders compared with 'one man' companies, 1869-84. *Accountant,* 1886, p. 291, 305, 323.

WALTON, SEYMOUR. Selling one company to another. *Journal of accountancy,* Aug. 1918, p. 152-3.

Accounting

AMERICAN business and accounting encyclopaedia; comp. by E. H. Beach and W. W. Thorne. Detroit, Bookkeeper publishing co. 1901. Corporation accounting, p. 359-76.

BEARDSALL, FRANCES E. M. Accounts of joint stock companies. *Accountant,* 1887, p. 217.

BELL, WILLIAM H. Corporation organiation and accounting. *Journal of accountancy,* Aug. Sept. 1918, p. 98-107, 169-90.

BENNETT, ROBERT JOSEPH. Corporation accounting. New York, The Ronald press co. 1917. 563p.

BENTLEY, H. C. Corporation. (In his *Science of accounts.* 1913. p. 171-83, 271-4).

BOURNE, JOHN HOWE. Some notes on companies and their accounts. *Accountant,* Dec. 10, 1898, p. 1197-202.

CARNES, A. J. Manual on opening and closing the books of joint stock companies. Baltimore 1891.

CARTER, R. N. Bonus shares, reduction of capital, redemption of debentures. (In his *Advanced accounts.* p. 924-36).

CARTER, R. N. Joint stock companies. (In his *Advanced accounts.* p. 360-5).

CHARLESWORTH, R. Some items included in capital expenditure accounts. *Accountant,* May 11, June 1, 1901, p. 560-5, 631-3.

CHARTERED ACCOUNTANTS STUDENTS' SOCIETY OF LONDON. Discussion on (1) the best method of dealing in companies' accounts with shares acquired in exchange for properties sold, underwriting services &c., (2) on the value to be placed on shares unquoted. *Accountant,* Feb. 11, 1899, p. 201-6.

CLOSING share transfer books. *South African accountant and auditor,* Dec. 1916, p. 213-4.

COLE, W. M. Opening the books of a corporation. (In his *Accounts their construction and interpretation.* c1915. p. 401-7).

COLE, WILLIAM MORSE. Peculiarities of corporation accounts. (In his *Bookkeeping, accounting and auditing.* c1914. p. 213-37).

COLES, ARTHUR. Company accounts; a complete manual for the use of officials in limited companies and advanced students; with a preface by Charles Comins. Ed.2. London, Sir Isaac Pitman and sons. 340p.

COMPANIES' capital accounts; the Australian v. the English method of treating same in ledger and balance sheet. *Accountant,* May 17, 1913, p. 761-5.

COMPANY work. Accountant, Sept. 28-Oct. 19, 1889, Aug. 9, 16, 1890, p. 499-502, 510-2, 523-4, 534-6, 417-9, 429-32.

CORPORATION opening entries. *Business man's magazine,* July 1908, p. 72-5.

CRAWFORD, J. M. Cleveland accountant; a work designed for experienced bookkeepers on opening and closing the books of joint stock companies. Cleveland, 1898.

CUMMINS, CHARLES. Guide to the formation of the accounts of limited liability companies, with forms etc. London, (?) 1894

CUTFORTH, A. E. Promofion of a public limited company; a few notes on the financial and accountancy aspects. *Accountant,* Dec. 5, 12, 1914, p. 690-5, 719-26.

DAVENPORT, HERBERT JOSEPH. Some problems in corporation accounting. *Journal of accountancy,* Oct. 1907, p. 451-5.

DAWSON, SIDNEY S. Accounts of joint stock companies. *Accountant,* Jan. 6, 1900, p. 14-21.

DEZOUCHE, RICHARD CATON. Acquisition of a business by a limited company. *Accountant,* April 23, 1910, p. 571-6.

DICKINSON, ARTHUR LOWES. Profits of a corporation. (In *Cyclopedia of commerce, accountancy, business administration.* 1910. v.6. p. 255-97).

DICKINSON, ARTHUR LOWES. Some special points in corporation accounting. *Accountant,* Oct. 7, 1905, p. 402-10.

DICKINSON, ARTHUR LOWES. Special points in corporation accounting and finance. (In his *Accounting practice and procedure.* 1917. p. 175-89).

CORPORATIONS—ACCOUNTING—*(Continued)*
DICKSEE, LAWRENCE ROBERT. Bookkeeping for company secretaries. Ed.4. London, Gee & co. 1908. 184p.
DICKSEE, LAWRENCE ROBERT. Bookkeeping—with special reference to joint stock companies. *Accountant,* Jan. 23, Feb. 13, 20, 27, March 27, April 10, 1897, p. 116-9, 182-92, 210-4, 235-40, 339-44, 397-401.
DICKSEE, LAWRENCE ROBERT. Company accounts. (In his *Advanced accounting.* 1916. p. 85-107).
DOWLER, FRANK AND E. M. HARRIS. Joint stock companies' accounts. (In their *Auditing, accounting and banking.* p. 190-205).
DUDLEY, GEORGE OSGOOD. Corporation accountting; including exercises in special accounting problems of the large corporation. Saginaw, Michigan, The F. H. Bliss publishing co. 86p.
EATON, ABIJAH H. Corporation accounting. (In his *Eaton and Burnett revised and improved bookkeeping, corporation, voucher and cost accounting embracing all modern and scientific methods used in business.* 1917. p. 178-93).
ELWORTHY, W. R. and C. C. CAMPLING. Bookkeeping for traders, manufacturers and companies. Ed.3. London, Jordon and sons, 1904. 224p.
ESQUERRÉ, PAUL JOSEPH. Corporation. (In his *Applied theory of accounts.* 1917. p. 28-53).
EVANS, J. M. Corporation. London, Shaw & sons, 1897.
FINNEY, H. A. Reserves and surplus. *Journal of accountancy,* Dec. 1920, p. 464-5.
FITZPATRICK, JAMES. Book-keeping specially adopted for public companies. London, Butterworth & co. 1910. 367p.
FORM of company accounts. *Accountant,* March 9, 1907, p. 305-6.
GILMAN, STEPHEN. Corporations. (In his *Principles of accounting.* 1917. p. 295-328).
GLADSTONE, JOSHUA H. Opening of the books of a limited company. *Accountant,* Aug. 1, 1896, p. 654-6.
GOODYEAR, SAMUEL HORATIO and L. E. GOODYEAR. Corporation and factory accounting. Cedar Rapids, Goodyear-Marshall publishing co.
GRAY, J. C. Standardization of shareholders' accounts and auditors' reports and certificates. *Canadian chartered accountant,* Jan. 1919, p. 193-206.
GREELEY, HAROLD DUDLEY. Corporation accounting. (In his *Theory of accounts.* 1920. p. 362-73).
GREEEN, A. E. Duties of accountants in relation to the initiation of a limited company. *Incorporated accountants' journal,* 1891-2, p. 44.
GREENE, THOMAS LYMAN. Corporation accounting. (In his *Corporation finance.* 1897. p. 80-101).
GREENE, THOMAS LYMAN. Corporation accounting. *Business,* Aug. 1897, p. 238-42.
GREENWOOD, GEORGE W. Mortgage bond problem. *Industrial management,* Sept. 1920, p. 199.
GRIFFITH, JAMES B. Corporation accounts and voucher system; a working handbook of approved methods of corporation accounting, with special reference to records of stock issues, manufacturers' accounts and the use of the voucher system. Chicago, American technical society, 1914. 51p. (American accountans' library).
GRIFFITH, JAMES B. Corporation and manufacturing accounts. Chicago, American school of correspondence, 1909. (In *Cyclopedia of commerce, accountancy, business administration.* 1910. v.4. p. 195-270).
HALLAS, E. IRVINE. Company accounts. London, R. Fleming, 1913. 64p.
HARDCASTLE, JOSEPH. Corporation issuing bonds. *Business,* Feb. 1892, p. 26-7.
HATHAWAY, C. E. comp. Laws requiring corporations to prepare accounts and financial statements. New York state, library. Legislative reference sections, Jan. 1919. 4 typewritten pages.
HEATHCOTE, FREDERIC J. Trade accounts. *Accountant,* April 26, May 3, 1884.
HEITMAN, HENRY. .Course in the theory and practice of higher accounting, prepared for students of Eastman college. Poughkeepsie, Eastman college, 1910. 240p.
HONECKER, CHARLES A. Corporation accounting. *Commerce, accounts and finance,* June 1901, p. 11-4.
HONECKER, CHARLES A. Corporation system. *Auditor,* 1905, p. 206.
HOPSON, H. C. Construction records and accounts. *Journal of accountancy,* July 1917, p. 33-51.
HOSKINS, DAVID. Bookkeeping for joint stock companies. Toronto 1901.
HUNTER, JOEL. Corporation bookkeeping and income tax law. (In his *Thinking in figures.* c1916. p. 8-22).
JENKINSON, MARK WEBSTER. Promotion and accounts of a private limited company. London, Gee & co. 1911. 87p. (In Feather, J. Stuart, ed. *Joint transactions.* 1911. p. 1-74. *Accountant,* March 18, 25, April 1, 1911, p. 437-45, 472-80, 512-9.
JENKINSON, MARK WEBSTER. Promotion and accounts of a public limited company. *Accountant,* June 1, 8, 15, 1912, p. 837-46, 872-83, 906-17.
JOHNSON, J. W. Joint stock company bookkeeping, with general and technical information respecting incorporated companies Ed. 9, revised and enlarge Belleville, Ontario business college, 1899. 188p.
——— Same. Ed. 10. Belleville, Canada, 1911.
JONES, EDWARD DAVID. Corporation reports (In his *Investment.* c1918. p. 150-76).
KEISTER, DAVID ARMEL. Corporation accounting and auditing; a practical treatise on higher accounting. Ed.9. Cleveland, Burrows brothers co. 1901. 525p.
KEISTER, DAVID ARMEL. Expert and stock company accounting and auditing. Cleveland, 1894.
KENT, WILLIAM. Report to stockholders of large corporations. (In his *Bookkeeping and cost accounting for factories.* 1918. p 237).
KESTER, ROY B. Corporation. (In his *Accounting theory and practice.* 1918. p 438-64).
KESTER, ROY B. Corporation. (In his *Accounting theory and practice.* 1918. v.2. p. 1-25).
KLEIN, JOSEPH J. Corporation accounting (In his *Elements of accounting.* 1916 p. 115-59).
KLEIN, JOSEPH J. Corporation bookkeeping and accounting. (In his *Bookkeeping and accounting.* 1917. p. 277-358).
LAWTON, WILLARD H. Treatment of unissued stock and bonds. *Journal of accountancy* April 1917, p. 241-53.
LISLE, GEORGE. Joint stock companies' books (In his *Accounting in theory and practice* 1900. p. 233-52).
LISLE, GEORGE and W. A. MIDDLETON. Joint stock companies. (In their *Account-keeping in principle and practice.* 1911. p. 191-206).
LYBRAND, WILLIAM M. Accounting of industrial enterprises. *Accountant,* Dec. 19, 1908 p. 786-99. *American institute of accountants,* Yearbook, 1908, p. 255-311. *Journal of accountancy,* Nov. Dec. 1908, Jan. 1909, p. 32-40, 111-21, 224-36.
LYBRAND, WILLIAM M. and others. Accounting for modern corporations. Chicago, American school of correspondence, 1909.

CORPORATIONS—ACCOUNTING—*(Continued)*

LYONS, J. A. Modern corporation accounting. Chicago, J. A. Lyons & company, c1908. 80p. + forms.

MACDONALD, JAMES B. Treatment of fixed and circulating capital in the accounts of joint-stock companies. *Accountants' magazine*, Feb. 1899, p. 97-107.

MACKAY, J. D. C. Company accounting; formation to balance sheet. Glasgow, 1911.

MACKAY, J. D. C. Formation to balance sheet. Revised and enlarged by R. T. McCutcheon. 86 Hanover street, Edinburgh, H. & J. Pillans & Wilson.

MACPHERSON, F. H. Corporation accounting and investigations. (In *Cyclopedia of commerce, accountancy, business administration*. 1910. v.6. p. 239). *Journal of accountancy*, Nov. 1908, p. 19-31.

MADDEN, JOHN THOMAS. Corporations. (In his *Accounting practice and auditing*. c1917. p. 177-207).

MARSHALL, CARL C. Corporation and voucher accounting. Cedar Rapids, Goodyear-Marshall publishing co. 1907.

MINER, GEORGE WASHINGTON and FAYETTE HERBERT ELWELL. Principles of bookkeeping, corporation and voucher accounting. Boston, Ginn and co. c1918. 417+500p. (Miner and Elwell series)

NIXON, ALFRED and J. H. STAGG. Joint stock companies. (In their *Accounting and banking*. 1912. p. 62-111).

NOONE, JOHN. Study of industrial corporation balance sheets. *Journal of accountancy*, Aug. Sept. 1910, p. 241-55, 348-67.

OPENING entry in corporation account. *Business man's magazine*, Sept. 1909, p. 274-5.

OPENING new company's accounts. *Accountant*, Aug. 2, 1913, p. 148-50.

ORGANIZATION and management of private corporations; or, Notes on corporation bookkeeping. Chicago, Bankers stationery & supply co. 1894.

PATON, WILLIAM A. and R. A. STEVENSON. Corporate proprietorship. (In their *Principles of accounting*. 1918. p. 269-312).

PATTERSON, W. A. Share register. *Accounting and commerce*, July 1917, p. 91-5.

PENTLARGE, THEODORE. How to open the books of a corporation. *New York accountants' and bookkeepers' journal*, Dec. 1903, Jan. 1904, p. 193-6, 6-8.

PITT, GEORGE S. Forms of published accounts of trading concerns and some observations in their audit. *Accountant*, Oct. 3, 1908, p. 389-402. *Incorporated accountants journal*, 1908-9, p. 9.

PIXLEY, FRANCIS W. Company bookkeeping. (In Lisle, George. *Encyclopaedia of accounting*. v.2. p. 195-200).

PIXLEY, FRANCIS W. Constructive branch of accountancy. (In his *Accountancy*. Ed.2. p. 61-82).

PIXLEY, FRANCIS W. Form of balance for limited companies. (In his *Accountancy*. Ed.2. p. 278-83.

PIXLEY, FRANCIS W. Form required to be made annually by every company registered under the companies (consolidation) act. 1908, having a capital divided into shares. (In his *Auditors, their duties and responsibilities*. 1910. p. 622-3).

PIXLEY, F. W. Profession of a chartered accountant. London, Swan, Sonnenschein & co. 1897.

PORTERS, R. J. Company. (In his *Pitman's dictionary of bookkeeping*. p. 186-257).

POTTER, C. B. Opening and closing corporation books. *Business*, May 1900, p. 263-5).

PROBLEM IN JOINT STOCK COMPANY BOOKKEEPING. *Business*, April 1895, p. 158-9.

PULLING, A. Law of joint stock companies' accounts. London, Butterworth & co. 1850.

RACINE, SAMUEL FREDERICK. Graded corporation problems. Seattle, Western institute of accountancy, commerce and finance, c1914.

RADLEY, G. W. Forms for, and the preparation of monthly or other periodic statements of transactions for the use of boards of directors. *Accountant*, Aug. 17, 1901, p. 900-7.

RAHILL, J. J. Corporation accounting and corporation law; a complete exposition of the science of corporation accounting both in theory and practice, with a digest of the corporation laws of all of the states and a valuable treatise on stock exchanges. Fresno, Cal., J. J. Rahill, 1899. 192p.

READ, WILLIAM WALTER. Accounts in connection with the reconstruction of limited companies. *Accountant*, Dec. 8, 1900, Jan. 19, 1901, p. 1120-9; 75.

SALIERS, EARL A. Corporation accounting. (In his *Accounting in theory and practice principles*. 1920. p. 145-89).

SELLS, ELIJAH W. Certified quarterly statements advocated for corporations; reprinted from the American banker, July 11, 1914. 5p.

SNYDER, WILLIAM T. Brief exposition of the fundamental principles of bookkeeping and a complete guide to corporation bookkeeping. Charlottesville, Va., W. T. Snyder. 1907.

SOULE, GEORGE. Corporation and joint stock company bookkeeping. (In his *New science and practice of accounts*. 1903. p. 369-429).

SOULE, GEORGE. Corporation and partnership questions and our answers. (In his *New science and practice of accounts*. 1903. p. 484-558).

SPICER, ERNEST EVAN. Dissolution amalgamation and reconstruction accounts. Ed.2. London, H. Foulks Lynch & co. 1915. 38p.

SPICER, ERNEST EVAN and ERNEST C. PEGLER. Company accounts. (In their *Bookkeeping and accounts*. 1914. p. 151-217).

SPICER, ERNEST EVAN and E. C. PEGLER. Limited companies. (In their *Practical bookkeeping and commercial knowledge*. 1912. p. 113-62).

SWAINSON, G. Journal in relation to corporate bookkeeping. *Incorporated accountants' journal*, 1897-8, p. 52.

THIENEL, ALOIS G. Problem in corporation accounting from the last C. P. A. examination. *New York accountants' and bookkeepers' journal*, Oct. 1903, p. 133-7.

UNIFORM accounting of corporations. *Municipal affairs*, June 1900, p. 418-20.

VAN DE LINDE, GERARD. Bookkeeping and other papers. London, Blades, East & Blades, 1904. 460p.

VAN DE LINDE, GERARD. Company work. *Accountant*, Feb. 16, 23, March 2, 9, 16, 23, 1889. p. 83-7, 96-100, 107-10, 128-32, 143-4, 153-6.

VENDORS' accounts. *Accountant*, Oct. 8, 15, 29, Nov. 5, 12, 1898, p. 939-40, 956-60, 1039-41, 1058-61, 1084-5.

WALTON, SEYMOUR. Carrying stock in other companies. *Journal of accountancy*, Nov. 1918, p. 388-9.

WALTON, SEYMOUR. Corporation accounting. *Journal of accountancy*, Jan. 1916, p. 66-8.

WALTON, SEYMOUR. Problem, corporation accounting. *Journal of accountancy*, April 1916, p. 299-304.

WALTON, SEYMOUR. Securing a creditor. *Journal of accountancy*, Aug. 1915, p. 148.

WALTON, SEYMOUR. Selling one company to another. *Journal of accountancy*, Aug. 1918. p. 152-3.

WALTON, SEYMOUR. Stock sold at a discount; overdrafts of officers. *Journal of accountancy*, March 1916, p. 235-6.

WALTON, SEYMOUR. Valuation of assets bought with treasury stock. *Journal of accountancy*, Oct. 1918, p. 319-20.

WEBER, FRED. CHARLES. Corporation bookkeeping. Los Angeles, Cal. F. C. Weber, 1909. 256p.

CORPORATIONS—ACCOUNTING—*(Continued)*

WELTON, THOMAS A. Company prospectuses and balance sheets. *Accountant,* 1887, p. 223.

WELTON, THOMAS A. On public companies and their accounts. *Accountant,* 1887, p. 500.

WHATLEY, G. E. STUART. Joint stock companies' accounts (In his *Accountants' and bookkeepers' vade-mecum.* 1893. p. 71-97).

WHITE, EDMUND D. Books and accounts of manufacturing companies and their audit. *Accountant,* Jan. 10, 17, 1885.

WHITE, EDMUND D. Great combinations of industrial enterprises and the changes necessitated in the methods of keeping their books, accounts, and cash. *Accountant,* Oct. 12, 1901, p. 1087-94.

WILLIAMSON LAW BOOK CO. Corporation stock book. Williamson. 100p. $2.00. 200p. $3.00

WOOD, WILLIAM ALLEN. Corporation bookkeeping, auditing and accounting. (In his *Modern business corporations including the organization and management of private corporations with financial principles and practices.* 1906. p. 143-82).

Auditing

ANDERSON, F. E. Audit of share transfers. *Incorporated accountants' journal,* Sept. 1912, p. 313-6.

APPOINTMENT and remuneration of auditors. *Accountant,* Feb. 17, 1912, p. 253-6.

APPOINTMENT of company auditors. *Accountant,* Feb. 20, 1915, p. 238-41.

APPOINTMENT of first auditor to a company. *Accountant,* Jan. 14, 28, 1899, p. 35-8, 101-2.

AUDIT of private limited companies' accounts. *Accountant,* Aug. 6, Oct. 15, 1898, p. 768-70, 953-6.

AUDIT of private companies accounts. *Accountant,* Dec. 5, 1908, p. 669-71.

AUDITING under the companies act, 1907. *Accountant,* Aug. 15, 22, 29, 1908, p. 177-9, 208-10, 238-40.

AUDITORS and directors' fees. *Accountant,* Nov. 16, 1918, p. 263-4.

AUDITORS and shareholders. *Accountant,* Jan. 27, 1912, p. 120-3.

BARHAM, H. E. Vouching in the conduct of audits of the accounts of joint stock companies. *Accountant,* June 2, July 14, 1906, p. 698-705; 33-5.

BOLTON, JAMES CHARLES. First audit of a joint stock company's accounts. *Accountant,* Dec. 12, 1885.

BRADLEY, FRANCIS ERNEST. Some aspects of the Companies acts, 1900; with especial reference to the duties of auditors and company secretaries. *Accountant,* Jan. 5, 1901, p. 23-35.

CARNES, A. J. Manual on opening and closing the books of joint stock companies. Ed. 3. Baltimore, 1891.

CHARLTON, F. F. More important differences in the duties and responsibilities arising in the following audits 1, single trader, 2, partnership, 3, public company. *Accountants' magazine,* Dec. 1908, p. 543-59.

CLERK, ALLAN J. M. First year's company audit. *Incorporated accountants' journal,* 1903-4, p. 134.

CLEVELAND, FREDERICK A. Relation of auditing to public control. Philadelphia, American academy of political and social science, 1905, p. 665-80.

COMPANY audits. *Accountant,* Feb. 12, 26, 1910, p. 233-5, 299-300.

COMPANY audits in India. *Accountant,* Aug. 29, 1914, p. 225-7.

COOKSON, BENJAMIN. Audit notes on the close of a company's accounts. *Accountant,* April 29, 1893, p. 399-403.

COOPER, ERNEST. Chartered accountants as auditors of companies. *Accountant,* 1886, p. 644.

CRAWFORD, F. Few notes on special matters affecting auditors, arising during the first year of the existence of a limited company. *Accountant,* April 15, 1911, p. 600-2.

DAY, C. M. First audit of a new corporation. (In his *Accounting practice.* p. 44-5).

DAWE, R. E. Preparation and audit of the statutory report, section 65 of the companies (consolidation) act, 1908, and the matters co-incident thereto. *Accountant,* Feb. 3, 1912, p. 180-5. (In Feather, J. Stuart ed. *Joint transactions,* 1911. p. 359-75).

DEPAULA, F. R. M. Sections of the companies (consolidation) act, 1908, particularly affecting auditors; special points in connection with the audit of companies under the companies acts, 1908 and 1913. (In his *Principles of auditing.* p. 125-63).

DOWLER, FRANK and E. M. HARRIS. Limited company. (In his *Auditing, accounting and banking.* p. 9-19).

DUROSE, ARTHUR. Uniformity of practice in the certificate and requirements of auditors under the companies act, 1900, and in the report to shareholders. *Accountant,* May 31, 1902, p. 575-7.

DUTIES of accountants towards new COMPANIES. *Accountant,* Jan. 7, 1899, p. 7-9, 67-9.

EASTON, J. M. Liabilities of auditors of companies, with special reference to the companies act, 1900. *Accountant,* April 27, 1901, p. 501-6, 895.

ELECTION of auditors. *Journal of accountancy,* Jan. 1918, p. 54-6.

FINCHAM, RUPERT F. M. Statutes and statutory regulations affecting company auditors. *Accountant,* Dec. 16, 1899, p. 1211-22.

GIBSON, ARTHUR HENRY. Status and responsibility of auditors under the companies act, 1900. *Accountant,* Oct. 19, Nov. 16, 1901, p. 1139-50, 1229-31.

GLASGOW CHARTERED ACCOUNTANTS STUDENTS' SOCIETY. Is the auditor of a public company justified in giving an unqualified docquet when he knows of the existence of hidden reserves? *Accountant,* Feb. 6, 1901, p. 227-9.

GLASIER, WILLIAM. Auditing—with special reference to the accounts of joint stock companies. *Accountant,* May 30, 1891, p. 421-4.

GRAY, J. C. Standardization of shareholders' accounts and auditors' reports and certificates. *Canadian chartered accountant,* Jan. 1919, p. 193-206.

GREENE, THOMAS. Examination of corporation accounts by auditors. *Accountant,* Dec. 26, 1896, p. 1070-2. *Business,* April 1897, p. 113-5.

GRIERSON, ALEXANDER. Audit of a joint stock company's accounts. *Accountant,* Oct. 6, 1906, p. 387-93.

GROSCLAUDE, CHARLES. Audit of companies in Great Britain and France. *Accountants' magazine,* Nov. 1906, p. 497-501.

HASKINS, GEORGE F. Notes in connection with the issue and audit of share capital. *Accountant,* Nov. 22, 29, 1902, p. 1210-6, 1442-51.

HOLMES, R. B. Rights and duties of an auditor under the companies acts 1900 and 1907. *Accountant,* May 8, 1909, p. 662-5.

HOUSE of commons and auditors. *Incorporated accountants' journal,* June 1920, p 181-3.

HUTTON, GEORGE JOHNSTON. On auditing commercial and company books. *Accountant* Oct. 26,-Nov. 28, 1889, p. 462-4, 574-80, 592-3, 613-5.

JACKSON, WILLIAM LEACH. Company legislation and the audit. *Accountant,* April 5 May 3, 1902, p. 364-8. 457-9.

JENKINSON, MARK WEBSTER. Audit of a public limited company. London, Gee &

CORPORATIONS—Auditing—*(Continued)*

co. 1913. 58p. *Accountant,* April 5, 12, 1913, p. 501-4, 550-7. *Accountants' magazine,* Nov. Dec. 1913, p. 557-73, 623-60.

Joint stock companies acts and auditors. *Accountant,* Feb. 4, 11, 18, 25, March 4, 11, April 15, May 13, June 10, 1882.

Keister, D. A. Corporation accounting and auditing. Ed. 5. Cleveland, Burrows bros. co. 1897.

Keister, D. A. Expert and stock company accounting and auditing. Cleveland, 1894.

Kennedy, Neil J. D. Relation of auditors to public companies. *Accountants' magazine,* Dec. 1904, p. 534-51.

Levie, George Elder. Share transfer audit. *Accountants' magazine,* May 1916, p. 242-6.

Littleboy, Wilfrid E. Duties of an auditor under the companies acts in regard to checking postings and additions of personal ledgers, day books, and cash books, which have already been balanced by the company's own staff. *Accountant,* July 11, 1908, p. 44-51.

London and Nottingham students societies debates: duties of company auditors. *Accountant,* March 14, 1914, p. 368-75.

Macpherson, F. H. Corporation accounting and investigations. (In *Cyclopedia of commerce, accountancy, business administration.* 1910. v. 6. p. 239). *Journal of accountancy,* Nov. 1908, p. 19-31.

Mellors, T. G. Uniformity of practice in the certificate and the "requirements" of auditors under the companies act, 1900, and in the report to shareholders. *Accountant,* Dec. 14, 1901, Jan. 4, 1902, p. 1362-4; 2-4.

Mr. Charles Duguid on auditors and shareholders. *Journal of accountancy,* Dec. 1910, p. 143-5.

Mitchell, Matthew. Special points arising in the audit of the balance sheet of a limited company formed to acquire a going business. *Accountant,* Dec. 29, 1906, Feb. 2, 9, 1907, p. 803-16, 141-3, 171-3.

Newton, Francis G. Auditing of public companies; some considerations suggested by the Millwall dock scandal. *Accountants' magazine,* Aug. 1899, p. 486-94.

Official audits in New Zealand: companies accounts audit. *Accountant,* Nov. 28, 1896, p. 981-2.

Pegler, Ernest C. Companies act, 1907, from an auditor's point of view. *Accountant,* April 11, 1908, p. 532-44.

Pitt, George Stanhope. Accountants record in a company audit. *Incorporated accountants' journal,* 1907-8, p. 224.

Pitt, George S. Forms of published accounts of trading concerns and some observations in their audit. *Accountant,* Oct. 3, 1908, p. 389-402. *Incorporated accountants' journal,* 1908-9, p. 9.

Pixley, Francis William. Companies act, 1900, from an auditor's point of view. *Accountant,* June 8, 22, 1901, p. 669-79, 713-7.

Pixley, Francis W. Duties of professional accountants in connection with invested capital both prior to and subsequent to the investment. *Accountant,* Oct. 15, 1904, p. 414-26.

Pixley, Francis William. Report and the certificate to be given by auditors under the companies act of 1900. *Accountant,* Nov. 3, Dec. 7, 14, 1901, p. 1303-6, 1321-4, 1351-4.

Renn, George B. First audit of books of corporations. (In his *Practical auditing.* c1907. p. 101-4).

Richardson, C. L. Series of questions submitted to members of the Institute of chartered accountants of Alberta with summary of the answers received and comments thereon prepared by Mr. C. L. Richardson. *Canadian chartered accountant,* Oct. 1914, p. 121-8.

Rooke, A. W. Duties and responsibilities of an auditor to a public company. *Incorporated accountants' journal,* 1894-5, p. 87.

Saffery, Francis J. Companies (consolidation) act, 1908, with particular reference to auditors. *Accountant,* April 24, Aug. 21, 1909, p. 567-71, 221-3.

Schmalz, W. E. Verification of liabilities. *Accountant,* Jan. 8, 1916, p. 52-4.

Smith, Andrew McL. Is the auditor of a public company justified in giving an unqualified docquet when he knows of the existence of hidden reserves? *Accountant,* Feb. 16, 1901, p. 227.

Spicer, Ernest Evan and Ernest C. Pegler. Auditor of a limited company, accounts. (In their *Practical auditing.* 1914. p. 187-407).

Spicer, Ernest Evan and Ernest C. Pegler. Statutory report of limited company. (In their *Audit programmes.* 1919. p. 88-90).

Standard of auditors' qualifications. *Incorporated accountants' journal,* Sept. 1920, p. 240-1.

Standard of auditors' qualifications; important decision of House of commons local legislation committee; Ossett corporation bill, Thursday, April 23rd, 1914. *Incorporated accountants' journal,* May 1914, p. 225-8.

Statham, Arnold. Modern company finance, the duties of auditors. *Accountant,* Nov. 19, 1904, p. 631-6, 618-9.

Swift, Rigby. Rights, duties and liabilities of auditors of public companies. *Incorporated accountants' journal,* 1896-7, p. 106.

Tighe, W. Status of auditors under the [New South Wales] companies acts. *Public accountant,* 1906-7, p. 175.

Wood, William Allen. Corporation bookkeeping, auditing and accounting. (In his *Modern business corporations, including the organization and management of private corporations with financial principles and practices.* 1906. p. 143-82).

Directors

Berry, Gordon. Directors of limited liability companies. *Accounting and commerce,* Nov. 1919, p. 190-2.

Concerning directors. *Accountant,* Aug. 26, Sept. 2, 9, 1905, p. 231-3, 256-9, 273-5.

Directors and restrictive agreements. *Accountant,* Feb. 19, 1910, p. 265-8.

Directors' qualifications. *Accountant,* May 24, 1902, p. 541-3.

Directors v. auditors. *Accountant,* Jan. 13, 20, Feb. 24, Sept. 29, 1894, April 20, July 6, Aug. 31, Dec. 28, 1895, Jan. 27, April 21, 1900, March 15, April 19, 1902, July 8, 15, 22, 1905, Dec. 25, 1909, p. 29-31, 53-6, 173-4, 839-42; 349-52, 589-92, 693-5, 1045-6; 95-7, 365-8; 276-9, 407-9; 33-5, 65-7, 104-6; 769-72.

Fisher, George A. Directors and their responsibilities. *Accountant,* Oct. 21, 1893, p. 883-6.

Hawksley, Bouchier F. Company director. *Accountant,* Oct. 22, Nov. 5, 1910, p. 567-9, 604-6.

Jordan, Herbert W. Registration and publication of directors' names. *Accountant,* Sept. 15, 1917, p. 212-6.

Liability incurred by directors signing cheques. *Accountant,* May 5, 1910, p. 328-9.

Liability of company promoters and directors. *Accountant,* March 23, 1901, p. 353-5.

Pixley, Francis W. Promotors in their relation to directors. *Accountant,* Dec. 16, 1905, p. 717-8, 695-7.

Failures and defalcations

Dewing, Arthur Stone. Failure and reorganization. (In his *Financial policy of corporations.* 1920. v. 5.)

CORPORATIONS—*(Continued)*

Finance

See also Capital; Dividends; Profits.

CUTFORTH, A. E. Promotion of a public limited company; a few notes on the financial and accountancy aspects. *Accountant,* Dec. 5, 12, 1914, p. 690-5, 719-26.

DEWING, ARTHUR STONE. Financial policy of corporations. 5v. New York, The Ronald press company, 1920.
Contents, v. 1. Corporate securities; v. 2. Promotion. v. 3. Administration of income. v. 4. Expansion. v. 5. Failure and reorganization.

DICKINSON, ARTHUR LOWES. Duties and responsibilities of the public accountant with regard to new issues of stocks and bonds. *Journal of accountancy,* Nov. 1905, p. 16-27.

DODD, ARTHUR F. Preparation of accountants' certificates for the purpose of joint stock company flotations. *Accountant,* April 6, 1907, May 14, 1910, p. 451-62, 698-711.

GERSTENBERG, CHARLES W. Materials of corporation finance. Ed. 3, revised. New York city, Prentice-Hall, inc. c1915. 1034p.

GRANT, G. P. Industrial finance. *Canadian chartered accountant,* April 1912, p. 189-94.

GREENE, THOMAS LYMAN. Corporation finance. New York, G. P. Putnam's sons, 1897. 181p.

HASKINS, GEORGE F. Notes in connection with the issue and audit of share capital. *Accountant,* Nov. 22, 29, 1902, p. 1210-6, 1442-51.

INVESTMENT BANKERS' ASSOCIATION OF AMERICA. Courses of study in corporation finance and investment. New York, Doubleday, Page & co. 1917. 170p.

JONES, EDWARD DAVID. Securities of corporations. (In his *Investment.* c1918. p. 127-49).

LOUGH, WILLIAM HENRY. Business finance; a practical study of financial management in private business concerns. New York, The Ronald press co. 1917. 631p.

LYON, WALTER HASTINGS. Corporation finance. Boston, Houghton, Mifflin co. c1912. 327p.

MEADE, EDWARD SHERWOOD. Corporation finance. Revised ed. New York, D. Appleton & co. 1915. 478p.

RECKITT, CHARLES COLEBY. Corporate dividends from an accountants' viewpoint. *Business world,* Jan. Feb. 1902, p. 30-2, 80-3.

SEAMAN, A. M. Capital of a company limited by shares. *Accounting and commerce,* Dec. 1915, Jan. 1916, p. 202-4, 224-6.

SELIGMAN, ISAAC N. Underwriting the sale of corporate securities. *Journal of accountancy,* Sept. 1906, p. 321-30.

SOME recent tendencies in corporate finance. *Journal of accountancy,* June 1912, p. 431-3.

STANDARDISATION of company forms. *Accountant,* March 23, 1912, p. 457-9, 475-83.

STATHAM, ARNOLD. Modern company finance, the duties of auditors. *Accountant,* Nov. 19, 1904, p. 618-9, 631-6.

STETSON, FRANCIS LYNDE AND OTHERS. Some legal phases of corporate financing, reorganization and regulations. New York, The Macmillan co. 1917. 389p.

WALKER, WILLIAM HOMER and F. F. FIELD. Corporation finance. New York, Alexander Hamilton institute, c1918. 346p. (Modern business, v. 11).

WOOD, WILLIAM ALLEN. Capital stock and bonds. (In his *Modern business corporation, including the organization with financial principles and practices.* 1906. p. 109-30).

Government regulation and control

BURTON, THEODORE E. Regulation of corporations. Chicago, La Salle extension university, 1918. 20p.

CREW, ALBERT. Government and control of limited companies. *Accountant,* Nov. 6, 13, 20, 27, 1920, p. 493-4, 517-9, 541-2, 573-4.

GOVERNMENT control of corporations. *Journal of accountancy,* Feb. 1908, p. 312-6.

LAWTON, W. H. Government regulation of securities. *Journal of accountancy,* Sept. 1911, p. 357-60.

MR. SELL'S address. *Journal of accountancy,* Feb. 1908, p. 317-8.

MONTGOMERY, ROBERT H. Federal control of corporations. *American institute of accountants, Yearbook,* 1912, p. 193-214. *Journal of accountancy,* Oct. 1912, p. 272-90.

NEW light on state control of corporations. *Journal of accountancy,* Feb. 1906, p. 321-2.

SELLS, ELIJAH W. Corporate management compared with government control. *Journal of accountancy,* Jan. 1908, p. 236-42. *Incorporated accountants' journal,* 1907-8, p. 129.

STERRETT, J. E. Legislation for the control of corporations. *Journal of accountancy,* Feb. 1910, p. 241-7.

Law

See also Bankruptcy; Commercial law; Taxation; also subdivision Law under various headings e. g. Partnerships—Law.

COMPANY laws in the British empire. *Accountant,* Aug. 10, 17, 1907, p. 167-9, 195-7.

COMPANY laws in the British empire; comparative analysis of the company laws of the United Kingdom, India, Canada, Australia, New Zealand and South Africa with a memorandum prepared for the Imperial conference, 1911, by the directions of the board of trade. *Accountant,* Oct. 7, 14, 21, 28, 1911, p. 464-71, 497-509, 530-6, 581-4.

GREENWOOD, WILLIAM J. Foreign stock exchange practice and company laws of all the chief countries of the world, methods of selling British securities abroad, foreign laws affecting British works and branches established abroad. London, Financial book co. 1911. 272p.

GUEDALLA, HERBERT. Some points in foreign commercial and company law of interest to accountants. *Accountant,* April 2, 1910, p. 465-72.

HUTCHISON, ALFRED. English and foreign company law, particularly relating to companies carrying on business abroad. *Accountant,* April 25, May 2, 1903, p. 547-51, 577-83.

MOODY-STUART, ALEXANDER. Company law on the continent. *Accountant,* Feb. 23, 1895, p. 186-92.

———— **Australia**

ACCOUNTANCY in Australia: company auditors—extended powers under the new act. *Accountant,* March 13, 1897, p. 298-9.

BARTON, A. E. Suggested amendments of the New South Wales companies act. *Public accountant,* 1909, p. 39.

COMPANIES amendment act 1906 (New South Wales). *Public accountant,* 1908, p. 39.

COMPANY law in New South Wales. *Accountant,* April 28, 1900, p. 389.

COMPANY laws in the British empire; comparative analysis of the company laws of the United Kingdom, India, Canada, Australia, New Zealand and South Africa; with a memorandum prepared for the Imperial conference, 1911, by the directors of the board of trade. *Accountant,* Oct. 7, 14, 28, 1911, p. 464-71, 497-509, 530-6, 581-4.

FERGUSON, J. A. Some aspects of company law. *Public accountant,* March 1916, p. 188-91.

GRIFFITHS, P. L. Some aspects of joint stock company law. *Federal accountant,* Oct. 1918, p. 164-8.

NASH, R. L. Private companies [New South Wales]. *Public accountant,* 1906-7, p. 251.

CORPORATIONS—Law—*(Continued)*

——— **Arizona**

Arizona. Corporation commission. Incorporation laws of Arizona relating to corporations in general and foreign corporations, amended 1919. Phoenix, July 15, 1917. 32p.

——— **Arkansas**

Arkansas. Secretary of state. Articles of agreement and incorporation. Little Rock, Arkansas.

——— **California**

Assessments on stock of corporations organized under the laws of California. *Journal of accountancy,* Feb. 1913, p. 117-21.

——— **Canada**

Act to amend the companies act; assented to 24th May, 1918. *Canadian chartered accountant,* July 1918, p. 44-5.

Bennett, E. James. Revision of the dominion companies act. *Canadian chartered accountant,* April 1913, p. 255-8.

Canadian company law; how it differs from English legislation. *Accountant,* Sept. 11, 1909, p. 324-5.

Companies act amendment act, 1917. *Canadian chartered accountant,* Jan. 1918, p. 229-34.

Election of auditors. *Journal of accountancy,* Jan. 1918, p. 54-6.

Harpell, J. J. Canadian company law. *Accountant,* Oct. 30, 1909, p. 549-50.

Hodgins, W. E. Synopsis of the provisions of the companies act relating to the incorporation of joint stock companies and the issue of letters patent and supplementary letters patent, also the act R. S. C. chapter 130 respecting the incorporation of boards of trade with the necessary forms, to which is added a synopsis of the powers granted by letters patent to incorporated companies from 1869-1887. Toronto, Carswell & co. 1888. 303p.

Hoskin, A. E. Joint stock company acts. *Canadian chartered accountant,* Jan. 1912, p. 121-30.

Mulvey, Thomas. Companies' act: with particular reference to the Bonanza case. *Canadian chartered accountant,* Oct. 1918, p. 124-41.

Mulvey, Thomas. Dominion company law; the companies act of the Dominion of Canada and dominion and provincial legislation applicable to companies incorporated under the dominion companies act. Toronto, The Ontario publishing company, 1920. 889p.

Ontario, 9 George V., 1919, chapter 42; an act to amend the loan and trust corporations act. *Canadian chartered accountant,* July 1919, p. 34-41.

——— **China**

Company law in Hong-Kong. *Accountant,* April 6, 1912, p. 533-5.

——— **Connecticut**

Connecticut. Corporation laws, revised August 1, 1919. Hartford, Conn., 1919. 75p.

——— **Delaware**

Delaware. Secretary of state. General corporation laws, passed 1899, amended by the revised statutes of 1915 and further amended by the ninety-fifth, ninety-sixth, and ninety-seventh general assemblies. Wilmington, 1917. 176p.

Parker, John Scott. Where and how; a corporation hand book and comparative digest of the laws of Delaware, Maine, Massachusetts, New Jersey, New York and Pennsylvania, relating to the formation, regulation and taxation of business corporations. Ed. 5, revised. New York, Brown-Green co. c1914. 264p.

United States corporation company. Delaware corporations; a digest of the decisions and the law. Dover, United States Corporation company. c1920. 86p.

——— **Florida**

Florida. Secretary of state. Laws relating to corporations. Tallahassee, 1917. 65p.

——— **France**

French accountants and company law. *Accountants' magazine,* Nov. 1902, p. 492-6.

——— **Great Britain**

Amendment of the companies acts. *Incorporated accountants' journal,* 1904-5, 1905-6, 1906-7, p. 123, 254, 89, 96.

Ashton, A. J. Recent commercial legislation: company law. *Incorporated accountants' journal,* 1890-1, p. 171.

Bateson, H. D. Amendments to the companies act. *Accountant,* Oct. 31, 1896, p. 906.

Begg, F Faithfull. Limited liability company reform. *Accountant,* Nov. 13, 1897, p. 1076-80. *Accountants' magazine,* Dec. 1897. p. 631-52.

Bennett, Charles A. Some provisions of the companies act, 1907. *Accountant,* March 6, 1909, p. 342-7.

Berry, A. W. Law of partnership and private limited companies. *Incorporated accountants' journal,* Aug. 1912, p. 292-5.

Boucher, George Herbert. Faults in the companies acts and their remedies. *Accountant,* April 28, 1906, p. 537-42.

Bradley, F. E. Some aspects of the companies act, 1900, with especial reference to the duties of auditors and company secretaries. *Accountant,* Jan. 5, 1901, p. 23-35.

Briscoe, W. R. B. Outlines of company law. *Incorporated accountants' journal,* 1889-90, p. 73.

Broderick, L. Paper on 'A bill to amend the companies' act, 1862'. *Accountant,* Feb. 13, 1892, p. 146.

Bromley, J. H. Company law. *Accountant,* June 5, 1920, p. 659-69.

Brown, Charles H. Companies act, 1907. *Accountants' magazine,* July, Aug. 1908, p. 358-80, 439-55.

Brown, Richard. Joint stock company code. *Accountant,* Dec. 27, 1902, p. 1360-9.

Carse, J. A. Companies acts. *Accountant,* March 31, April 7, 1883.

Charlesworth, A. Few points in company law. *Accountant,* 1887, p. 176.

Cleave, J. K. F. Proposed alterations in company law. *Incorporated accountants' journal,* 1896-7, p. 47.

Colefax, A. Companies' act, 1900. *Accountant,* April 13, 1901, p. 452-64.

Companies. Accountants' dairy; annual.

Companies act, 1907. *Accountant,* July 4, 18, 25, Aug. 18, 1908, p. 4-6, 61-3, 93-5, 122-5, 149-51.

Companies act 1913. *Accountant,* Aug. 30, 1913, p. 295.

Companies act, 1913; an act to amend the provisions of the companies (consolidation) act, 1908, with respect to private companies. *Incorporated accountants' journal,* Sept. 1913, p. 293.

Companies act 1913: its origin and objects. *Accountant,* Feb. 14, 1914, p. 209-13.

Companies and the drawing and making, etc., of bills of exchange and promissory notes. *Accountant,* July 3, 10, 17, 24, 31, 1909, p. 6-7, 37-9, 72-4, 108-13, 141-2.

Companies bill, 1907. *Accountant,* Aug. 24, Sept. 14, 1907, p. 253-4, 342-54.

Companies (consolidation) act, 1908. 180p.

Companies (foreign interests) act, 1917. *Incorporated accountants' journal,* July, 1917, p. 213.

CORPORATIONS—LAW—*(Continued)*

COMPANIES (particulars as to directors) act, 1917. *Incorporated accountants' journal,* Sept. 1917, p. 246.
COMPANY law amendment. *Accountant,* April 2, 16, May 7, 14, 1898, p. 357-61, 389-94, 484-7, 512-14.
COMPANY law amendment. *Accountant,* Aug. 11, 18, 25, Sept. 1, 8, 1906, p. 145, 169, 204, 225, 253.
COMPANY law amendment. *Accountant,* May 25, June 1, 8, 15, 22, 1918, p. 381-2, 397-8, 409-10, 425-6, 443-4.
COMPANY law amendment committee. *Accountant,* Oct. 5, 12, 19, 1918, p. 182-7, 199-200, 213-5.
COMPANY law amendment committee, report. *Accountant,* July 14, 21, 28, 1906, p. 45-53, 81-90, 106-15.
COMPANY law amendment committee; report of the committee upon the amendment of the law under the companies acts, 1908 to 1917. *Incorporated accountants' journal,* Sept. 1918, p. 241-8
COMPANY law reform. *Accountant,* Nov. 25, 1905, March 23, April 13, April 20, 1907, p. 599, 377, 467, 505.
COOPER, F. S. Some recent decisions on company law. *Accountant,* April 16, 1910, p. 539.
CRISP, F. Shortcomings of the companies acts. *Accountant,* April 29, June 17, 1905, p. 534, 725.
DANGERFIELD, A. Companies' acts: amendment bills, 1900. *Accountant,* June 9, 1900, p. 534.
DAWE, R. E. Preparation and audit of the statutory report, section 65 of the companies (consolidation) act, 1908, and matters coincident thereto. *Accountant,* Feb. 3, 1912, p. 180-5.
DAWSON, SIDNEY S. Companies act, 1900. *Accountant,* Nov. 3, 10, 26, 1904, Jan. 21, 1905, p. 971-5, 998-1005; 70-3.
DAWSON, SIDNEY S. Some observations on the companies act, 1907. *Accountant,* June 20, 1908, p. 890.
DE PAULA, F. R. M. Sections of the companies (consolidation) act, 1908, particularly affecting auditors; special points in connection with the audit of companies under the companies act, 1908 and 1913. (In his *Principles of auditing,* p. 125-63).
DICKINSON, ARTHUR LOWES. Sections of the English law. (In his *Accounting practice and procedure.* 1917. p. 251-71).
ELLERMAN, J. R. Companies acts, 1862-80. *Accountant,* June 30, 1883.
GIBSON, A. H. Companies acts. *Accountant,* Feb. 17, 24, March 3, 1883.
GODDEN, WILLIAM. Company law amendment. *Accountant,* Oct. 16, 1897, p. 968.
GOVER, JOHN MAHAN. Private companies under the companies (consolidation) act of 1908. *Incorporated accountants' journal,* 1908-9, p. 241
HILL, D. Companies' acts: notes upon the draft bill, 1895. *Accountant,* Jan. 4, 1896, p. 12.
HOLMES, CHARLES MORELL. Review of imperial company legislation. *Accountant,* July 10, 1915, p. 45-54.
JACKSON, W. L. Company legislation. *Accountant,* Oct. 22, 1898, p. 1014.
JACKSON, W. L. Company legislation and the audit. *Accountant,* April 5, May 3, 1902, p. 364-8, 457-9.
JENKINSON, MARK WEBSTER. Some changes in the law relating to joint stock companies which might be desirable. *Accountant,* Dec. 25, 1915, p. 785-94.
JOEL, J. EDMUNDSON. Joint stock companies' acts, with special reference to accountancy. *Accountant,* March 12, 1892, p. 228-36.
KEEN, F. N. Faults in the existing law relating to joint stock companies (1862 to 1888) acts and their remedies. *Accountant,* Aug. 16, 1890, p. 437.
MACKELVIE, ALEXANDER. Company law amendment. *Accountants' magazine,* Dec. 1918, p. 457-64.
MACMILLAN, HUGH PATTISON. Further reforms in company law. *Accountant,* June 15, 1907, p. 822-7.
MACMILLAN, HUGH PATTISON. Law of joint-stock companies as amended by the companies act, 1900. *Accountants' magazine,* March, April, May, June 1901, p. 147-62, 198-214, 250-71, 311-27.
MANCHESTER AND SHEFFIELD CHARTERED ACCOUNTANTS STUDENTS' SOCIETIES. Discussion on the companies act, 1900. *Accountant,* April 16, 1904, p. 491-501.
MANSON, EDWARD. Company. (In Lisle, George. *Encyclopaedia of accounting.* v.2. p. 136-77).
MORICE, BEAUMONT. Companies act, 1907. *Accountant,* Feb. 8, 1908, p. 182-4.
NIXON, E. V. Report of the company law amendment committee (Great Britain). *Public accountant,* March 1919, p. 235-7.
PEARSON, FRANK S. Companies act, 1900. *Accountant,* March 30, 1901, p. 406-11.
PEGLER, E. C. Companies act, 1907, from an auditor's point of view. *Accountant,* April 11, 1908, p. 532-44.
PIKE, G. E. Address [on points in company law]. *Incorporated accountants' journal,* 1904, p. 160.
PINCKNEY, E. B. and others. Debate: That the draft [companies] bill is inadequate to meet the requirements of the trading community. *Accountant,* March 14, 1896, p. 210.
PIXLEY, FRANCIS WILLIAM. Chartered accountants and the development of the limited liability companies acts. *Accountant,* Oct. 29, 1904, p. 502-14
PIXLEY, FRANCIS WILLIAM. Companies act, 1900, from an auditor's point of view. *Accountant,* June 8, 22, 1901, p. 669-79, 713-7.
PIXLEY, FRANCIS WILLIAM. Suggestions for a companies bill. *Accountant,* March 5, 12, 1898, p. 259, 280.
POTTER, J. Companies act, 1907, in relation to private companies. *Incorporated accountants' journal,* 1907-8, p. 209.
PRICE, H. L. Proposed reforms in the companies' acts. *Incorporated accountants journal,* 1898-9, p. 38.
PRIVATE limited companies. *Accountant,* July 1, 18, 1896, p. 573-4, 601-3.
PROGRESS of joint stock companies, 1869-84. *Accountant,* 1886, p. 291, 305, 323.
PROSSER, JOHN. Incorporation of trading companies. *Accountants' magazine,* April 1888, p. 224-44.
RANKING, D. F. DE l'HOSTE. Notes on the new Table 'A.' *Incorporated accountants' journal,* 1906-7, p. 104.
REID, JAMES W. Joint stock companies. *Accountant,* Oct. 20, 1906, p. 470-4.
REPORT of the committee on company law amendment. *Accountant,* Nov. 2, 9, 16, 23, 1918, p. 235-6, 251-2, 261-2, 273-4.
REPORT of the company law amendment committee. *Accountant,* July 14, 21, 28, 1906, p. 45, 81, 106.
RIDGWAY, A. CLIFFORD. Private companies. *Accountant,* Dec. 28, 1912, p. 817-23.
ROBERTS, S. Companies act, 1907. *Accountant,* March 14, 1908, p. 359-64.
SAFFERY, FRANCIS JOSEPH. Companies (consolidation) act, 1908, with particular reference to auditors. *Accountant,* April 24, Aug. 21, 1909, p. 567-71, 221-3.
SAFFERY, FRANCIS JOSEPH. Statutory report, section 65 of the Companies (consolidation) act, 1908. *Accountant,* Feb. 3, 1912, p. 180.
SALIENT features of the new draft bill to amend the companies acts, so far as they relate to accountants and auditors. *Accountant,* March 13, 20, 1897, p. 291-2, 313-7.

CORPORATIONS—LAW—*(Continued)*

SHEPHERD, RICHARD ACKINSON. Outlines of company law. *Accountant,* Feb. 10, 17, 24, 1894, p. 133, 161, 185.

SLOAN, D. NORMAN. Companies act—their use and abuse. *Accountant,* March 25, 1911, p. 484-94.

SMITH, CLARE. Salient features of the new draft bill to amend the companies acts, as far as they relate to accountants and auditors. *Accountant,* March 13, 20, 1897, p. 291, 313.

SMITH, CLARE. Suggested amendments in the companies acts. *Accountant,* 1887, p. 374.

SPICER, E. E. and E. C. PEGLER. Table A: a summarized comparison of the most important provisions affecting accounts contained in the original and revised tables. Ed. 2, 1909.

STATHAM, ARNOLD. Companies' act, 1907. *Accountant,* March 7, 1908, p. 323-5.

STATUTORY companies (redeemable stock) act, 1915. *Incorporated accountants' journal,* Aug. 1915, p. 255.

STEVENS, THOMAS M. Company law (with special reference to recent legislation). *Accountant,* Jan. 31, 1891, p. 94.

STEVENS, THOMAS M. Register of a limited company. *Accountant,* Jan. 8, 1898, p. 41-7.

STRACHAN, W. and others. Outstanding features of the new companies act. *Incorporated accountants' journal,* 1907-8, p. 64.

WELTON, T. A. On some possible amendments of the companies acts, 1862 to 1883. *Accountant,* 1887, p. 390, 402, 414, 438, 451.

WELTON, T. A. Some suggestions as to amending the companies acts. *Accountant,* Dec. 3, 10, 1892, p. 936, 952.

WHINNEY, F. Recent legislation. *Accountant,* Oct. 11, 1890, p. 554-7.

WHINNEY, F. Some remarks on the companies' acts. *Accountant,* Oct. 27, 1888, p. 691.

WHITEHOUSE, ERNEST A. Companies acts, with special reference to secretarial work and the act of 1907. *Accountant,* May 1, 1909, p. 606-14.

WING, W. Limited companies. *Accountant,* Jan. 3, 1885.

WOODINGTON, ARTHUR E. Further amendment of the companies act. *Accountant,* Sept. 30, 1905, p. 361-6. *Incorporated accountants' journal,* 1905-6, p. 6.

——— **Idaho**

IDAHO. SECRETARY OF STATE. Corporation laws, revision of laws effective May 8th, 1919. Boise, Idaho, 1919. 142p.

——— **India**

AUDITORS under the Indian companies act. *Incorporated accountants' journal,* April 1914, p. 188.

COCKE, HUGH G. Indian companies act, 1912: correspondence. *Accountant,* Aug. 2, 1913, p. 156-7.

COMPANY law in India. *Accountant,* June 29, Aug. 10, 1912, p. 961-4; 180-2.

INDIA companies act, 1913. *Accountant,* March 14, 21, 28, 1914, p. 360-2, 403-5, 435-8.

——— **Iowa**

IOWA. SECRETARY OF STATE. Corporation laws. Des Moines, Iowa. 1919. 60p.

——— **Ireland**

See Corporations—Law: Great Britain.

——— **Kansas**

KANSAS. SECRETARY OF STATE. Corporation laws of the state of Kansas, supplement 1917 and 1919. Topeka, Kansas, 1915. 504p.

——— **Kentucky**

KENTUCKY. SECRETARY OF STATE. Corporation laws. Frankfort, Kentucky, Jan. 1, 1919. 64p.

——— **Maine**

MAINE. SECRETARY OF STATE. Provisions of law in force relating to the business corporations. Augusta. Maine, 1917. 66p.

PARKER, JOHN SCOTT. Where and how; a corporation hand book and comparative digest of the laws of Delaware, Maine, Massachusetts, New Jersey, New York and Pennsylvania, relating to the formation, regulation and taxation of business corporations. Ed. 5, revised. New York, Brown-Green co. c1914. 264p.

——— **Maryland**

MARYLAND. STATE TAX COMMISSION. Laws of Maryland relating to business corporations. Baltimore, Md., 1919. 82p.

MARYLAND. *Journal of accountancy,* Feb. 1908, p. 321.

——— **Massachusetts**

PARKER, JOHN SCOTT. Where and how; a corporation hand book and comparative digest of the laws of Delaware, Maine, Massachusetts, New Jersey, New York and Pennsylvania, relating to the formation, regulation and taxation of business corporations. Ed. 5, revised. New York, Brown-Greene co. c1914. 264p.

——— **Michigan**

MICHIGAN. SECRETARY OF STATE. Law governing manufacturing and mercantile corporations and corporations for other lawful business, under act no. 232, P. A. of 1903, Lansing, Michigan. 1917. 41p.

MICHIGAN. Secretary of state. Law relating to organization, regulation and conduct of co-operative companies and associations, 1913. Lansing, Mich., 1914. 4p.

——— **Minnesota**

MINNESOTA. Agreement by stockholders giving corporation right to buy their stock is valid. *Corporation journal,* Nov. 1920, p. 267.

MINNESOTA. SECRETARY OF STATE. Laws of the state of Minnesota relating to the business corporations with synopsis of provisions pertaining to other classes of corporations; annotations and forms. 1919 edition. St. Paul, 1919. 82p.

MINNESOTA. STATE SECURITIES COMMISSIONS. Acts to prevent fraud in the sale and dispositions of stocks, bonds or other securities sold or offered for sale within the state of Minnesota, creating State securities commission, chapter 429, laws of 1917 as amended to March 27, 1919. Minneapolis, Minn., 1919. 12p.

——— **Missouri**

MISSOURI. SECRETARY OF STATE. Corporations laws, revised statutes of 1909 and amendatory acts to and including 1917. Jefferson city, Missouri. 297p.

——— **Nebraska**

NEBRASKA. DEPARTMENT OF STATE. Compilation of the laws providing for the organization of miscellaneous corporations and occupation tax on the same. Lincoln, Nebraska, 1915. 809p.

——— **Nevada**

NEVADA. SECRETARY OF STATE. Foreign corporation laws. Carson city, Nevada. 1919. 8p.

NEVADA. SECRETARY OF STATE. General corporation law. Carson city, Nevada, 1919. 39p.

——— **New Hampshire**

NEW HAMPSHIRE. SECRETARY OF STATE. Corporation laws, 1919. Concord. 1919. 55p.

CORPORATIONS—LAW—*(Continued)*

——— **New Jersey**

NEW JERSEY. Corporation may not purchase its own capital stock except from surplus. *Corporation journal,* Oct.-Dec. 1919, p. 63.

NEW JERSEY. DEPARTMENT OF STATE. General corporation act (revision of 1896), including all supplements thereto, to the end of the legislative session of 1917. Trenton, 1917. 133p.

PARKER, JOHN SCOTT. Where and how: a corporation hand book and comparative digest of the laws of Delaware, Maine, Massachusetts, New Jersey, New York and Pennsylvania, relating to the formation, regulation and taxation of business corporations. Ed. 5, revised. New York, Brown-Green co. c1914. 264p.

——— **New Mexico**

NEW MEXICO. STATE CORPORATION COMMISSION. General corporation laws, codification of 1915 (as amended). Santa Fe, New Mexico. 1919. 100p.

——— **New York**

PARKER, JOHN SCOTT. Where and how: a corporation hand book and comparative digest of the laws of Delaware, Maine, Massachusetts, New Jersey, New York and Pennsylvania, relating to the formation, regulation and taxation of business corporations. Ed. 5, revised. New York, Brown-Green co. c1914. 264p.

——— **New Zealand**

COMPANIES act, 1908. *Accounting and commerce,* April, May 1916, p. 14-7, 43-4.

LAMBERT, E. P. Private limited companies. *Accounting and commerce,* April 1917, p. 19-22.

——— **North Carolina**

NORTH CAROLINA. Corporation law, revisal of 1905, Chapter 21, as amended by public laws, 1907-1915. Raleigh, N. C., 1915. 63p.

——— **North Dakota**

NORTH DAKOTA. SECRETARY OF STATE. Corporation laws of the state of North Dakota, general and co-operative, revised to July 1, 1919. Bismark, 1919. 79p.

——— **Oklahoma**

OKLAHOMA. SECRETARY OF STATE. Corporation laws of Oklahoma, together with laws relative to oil and gas pipe lines and laws relative to all partnerships from the revised laws of 1910, session laws of 1911, 1913, 1915 and 1917. Oklahoma city, Oklahoma. 214p.

——— **Oregon**

OREGON. CORPORATION COMMISSIONER. Corporation laws of the state of Oregon, 1917, supplement 1919. Salem, 1917. 138p.

——— **Pennsylvania**

PARKER, JOHN SCOTT. Where and how; a corporation hand book and comparative digest of the laws of Delaware, Maine, Massachusetts, New Jersey, New York and Pennsylvania, relating to the formation, regulation and taxation of business corporations. Ed. 5, revised. New York, Brown-Greene co. c1914. 264p.

——— **Philippine Islands**

PHILIPPINE ISLANDS. (In Parker, John, ed. Corporation manual.)

——— **Porto Rico**

PORTO RICO. (In Parker, John, ed. Corporation manual.)

——— **Rhode Island**

RHODE ISLAND. Corporation laws, 1913. Providence, R. I., 1913. 35p.

——— **Russia**

COMPANY law in Russia. *Accountant,* April 27, 1901, p. 495-6.

RUSSIAN and British-Russian companies. *Accountants' magazine,* 1905, p. 88.

——— **Scotland**

See Corporations—Law, Great Britain.

——— **South Dakota**

SOUTH DAKOTA. SECRETARY OF STATE. Corporation laws, 1919-1920. Pierre, S. D., 1919. 63p.

——— **Union of South Africa**

HARTOG, ADVOCATE. Liquidation of companies in the Transvaal. *South African accountants journal,* v. 2, p. 115.

MULLIGAN, G. A. Company law reform. *South African accountants' journal,* v. 1, p. 60.

PYEMONT, L. O. P. Notes on the Transvaal draft for the incorporation, regulation and winding-up of companies and other associations. *South African accountants' journal,* v. 1, p. 131.

TRANSVAAL winding-up law. *Accountant,* Nov. 14, 1903, p. 1409-10.

——— **United States**

AMERICAN company law: the Federal corporation bill. *Accountant,* April 9, 1910, p. 486-90.

BARNES, H. EDGAR. Law governing promoters. *Journal of accountancy,* July 1908, p. 177-86.

CORPUS juris; being a complete and systematic statement of the whole body of the law as embodied in and developed by all reported decisions; ed. by Wiliam Mack and W. J. Hale. New York, American law book co.

DILL, JAMES B. Statutory and case law applicable to private companies under the general corporation act of New Jersey. New York, Baker, Voorhis & company, 1898.

FOX, W. H. American company law. *Accountant,* Feb. 15, 1908, p. 220-5.

GERSTENBERG, CHARLES W. Special phases of corporation law. *Journal of accountancy,* Oct. 1909, p. 440-8.

GERSTENBERG, CHARLES W. Special phases of corporation law; a comparison of the statutes and decisions of various jurisdictions. *Journal of accountancy,* Sept. 1909, p. 331-46.

GERSTENBERG, CHARLES W. Special phases of corporation law; procedure in corporate meetings. *Journal of accountancy,* Aug. 1909, p. 259-69.

GERSTENBERG, CHARLES W. Special phases of corporation law; the nature of corporations historically considered. *Journal of accountancy,* July 1909, p. 153-67.

HATHAWAY, C. E. COMP. Laws requiring corporations to prepare accounts and financial statements. New York state, Library. Legislative reference sections, Jan. 1919. 4 typewritten pages.

NATIONAL ASSOCIATION OF MANUFACTURERS OF THE UNITED STATES OF AMERICA. State laws affecting corporations. New York, National association of manufacturers of the United States of American, c1918. 20p.

NEW federal incorporation bill. *Journal of accountancy,* Feb. 1910, p. 279-84.

PARKER, JOHN S. ED. Corporation manual; statutory provisions relating to the regulation and taxation of domestic business corporations, and to the admission, regulation and taxation of foreign business corporations in the several states, territories, and districts of the United States, arranged under a uniform classification, the uniform stock transfer act, laws regulating invest-

CORPORATIONS—LAW—*(Continued)*

ment companies, and the sale of corporate stocks and securities and federal and state anti trust laws with forms and precedents, edited by John S. Parker, assisted by J. B. R. Smith and a board of associated editors in the several states. Ed.21 New York, United States corporation company, 1920. 2421p.

PARKER, JOHN SCOTT. Where and how; a corporation hand book and comparative digest of the laws of Delaware, Maine, Massachusetts, New Jersey, New York and Pennsylvania, relating to the formation, regulation and taxation of business corporations. Ed.5, revised. New York, Brown-Green co. c1914. 264p.

PRESIDENT Sterrett on uniform state legislation. *Journal of accountancy,* Dec. 1909, p. 140.

RAHILL, J. J. Corporation accounting and corporation law; a complete exposition of the science of corporation accounting both in theory and practice, with digest of the corporation laws of all the states and a valuable treatise on stock exchange. Fresno, Cal., J. J. Rahill, 1899, 192p.

SEARS, JOHN HAROLD. Trust estates as business companies Detroit, Counselors publishing co. c1912. 387p.

SONNENSCHEIN, BERKSON AND LAUTMANN AND DAVID LEVINSON. Summary and abstract of blue sky laws in force in the various states of the United States. Chicago, T. H. Flood & co. c1918. 54p.

SUPREME COURT DECISION IN MITCHELL CASE: not necessary that increase in value of timberlands be entered on books. *American lumberman,* May 25, 1918, p. 57.

TEXT of the federal incorporation bill; an act to provide for the formation of corporations to engage in inter-state and international trade and commerce; be it enacted by the Senate and House of representatives of the United States of American in Congress assembled *Journal of accountancy,* Feb. 1910, p. 286-99.

UNITED STATES. BUREAU OF CORPORATIONS. Report of the commissioner of corporations on the state laws concerning foreign corporations. Washington, Government printing office, 1915. 238p.

WHITE, FRANK. White on corporations. Ed.5. New York, Baker, Voorhis & co. 1904. 1189p.

——— Utah

CORPORATION laws; extracts from the compiled laws, 1918. Salt Lake city, Utah. 708p.

——— Vermont

VERMONT. General corporation laws. Montpelier, 1918. 30p.

——— Virginia

VIRGINIA. DEPARTMENT OF THE STATE CORPORATION COMMISSION. Methods and costs of obtaining charters in Virginia. Richmond, Va., 1917. 16p.

VIRGINIA. STATE CORPORATION COMMISSION. Corporation law, with all amendments to June 21, 1918. Richmond, Va., 1918. 96p.

——— West Virginia

WEST VIRGINIA. General corporation laws; containing full text of all laws concerning the formation and regulation of all classes of corporations. Charleston, 1915. 403p.

Management

ANCIENT form of association [of the Darien company, 1696]. *Accountants' magazine,* 1903, p. 248

BELL, WILLIAM H. Corporation organization and accounting. *Journal of accountancy,* Aug. Sept. 1918, p. 98-107, 169-90.

BOARDMAN, JAMES. Notes on the formation of companies. *Accountant,* 1887, p. 206.

BOTTOMLEY, LEONARD. Points in company formation. *Accountant,* Dec. 17, 1898, p. 1219-25.

BRISCO, NORRIS ARTHUR. Interior organization. (In his *Economics of business.* 1913. p. 52-74).

COMPANY promotion and frauds. *Accountant,* Nov. 19, 1898, p. 1101-4, 1122.

CONYNGTON, THOMAS. Adoption of by-laws. *Journal of accountancy,* Feb. 1913, p. 96-105.

CONYNGTON, THOMAS. Corporate organization and management; revised by H. Potter. Ed.4. New York, The Ronald press co. 1918. 778p.

CONYNGTON, THOMAS. Enforcement of by-laws. *Journal of accountancy,* March 1913, p. 157-65.

CONYNGTON, THOMAS. Manual of corporate management; containing forms, directions, and information for the use of lawyers and corporation officials. New York, The Ronald press co. 1903. 331p.

CONYNGTON, THOMAS. Nature of by-laws. *Journal of accountancy,* Jan. 1913, p. 10-20.

CREW, ALBERT. Chairman of general meetings of companies. *Accountant,* Feb. 28, March 6, 13, 1920, p. 321-3, 262-3, 294-6.

CREW, ALBERT. Powers of majorities. *Accountant,* June 14, 1919, p. 498-500.

CROSBY, R. H. Corporate organization and management. *Bankers magazine,* June and July 1912.

CROSS, JOHN ASHTON. Articles of association. *Incorporated accountants' journal,* 1902-3, p. 144.

CROSS, JOHN ASHTON. Promotion and formation of a company. *Incorporated accountants' journal,* 1902-3, p. 126.

DEWING, ARTHUR STONE. Corporate promotions and reorganizations. Cambridge, Harvard university press, 1914. 615p. (Harvard economic studies, v. 10).

DICKINSON, WALTER S. Articles of association of a limited company. *Accountant,* April 25, 1903, p. 551-6.

DICKSEE, LAWRENCE ROBERT and H. E. BLAIN. Company work and returns. (In their *Office organization and management.* 1917. p. 227-53).

FARR, WILLIAM E. Memorandum and articles of association. *Accountant,* Sept. 19, 1908, p. 330-5.

FERGUSON, J. A. Company promotion and its responsibilities. *Public accountant,* 1910, p. 123, 139.

GERSTENBERG, CHARLES W. Corporations. (In his *Organization and control.* c1918. p. 126-255)

GERSTENBERG, CHARLES W. Mathematics of cumulative voting. *Journal of accountancy,* Jan. 1910, p. 177-88.

GREEN, ARTHUR EDWARD. Duties of accountants in relation to the initiation of a limited company. *Incorporated accountants' journal,* 1891-2, p. 44.

HEGEMANN, W. German corporation; its organization and powers. *Journal of accountancy,* April 1906, p. 453-64.

HINTS upon company promotion. *Accountant,* Feb. 10, 17, March 3, 1894, p. 126, 149, 194.

JENKINSON, MARK WEBSTER. Promotion and accounts of a private limited company. London, Gee & co 1911. 87p. *Accountant,* March 18, 25, April 1, 1911, p. 437-45, 472-80, 512-9, June 1, 8, 15, 1912, p. 837-46, 872-3, 906-17.

JORDON, HERBERT W. Promotion and flotation of limited companies. *Accountant,* Feb. 22, 1913, p. 272-82.

KEEN, FRANK NOEL. Parliamentary companies. *Accountant,* May 12, June 16, 1906, p. 600-19, 743.

CORPORATIONS—MANAGEMENT—*(Continued)*

LIABILITY of companies in respect of the issue of share certificates and the registration and certification of transfers. *Accountant,* Sept. 7, 14, 21, 28, 1907, p. 302-4, 331-4, 361-3, 386-92.

LORIMER, J. CAMPBELL. Accountants in their relation to public companies. *Accountants' magazine,* April 1899, p. 222-38.

LOUGH, WILLIAM HENRY. Corporation. (In his *Business finance.* 1917. p. 25-63).

MACFIE, JAMES. Formation of a company. *Accountant,* March 7, 1896, p. 190-6.

MR. SELLS' address. *Journal of accountancy,* Feb. 1908, p. 317-8.

MOCK shareholders meeting. *Accountant,* Aug. 28, Oct. 2, 1920, p. 219-22, 344-53.

ORENSTEIN, B. Organization of large commercial and industrial establishments. *Engineering magazine,* Jan. 1913, p. 588-96.

PALMER, GEORGE. Company promoting. *Accountant,* March 19, 1904, p. 373-80.

PILLING, ALFRED. Company work: voting, polls, and proxies. *Accountant,* Dec. 5, 1896, p. 1001-7.

PROCEDURE at board and committee meetings. *Accountant,* June 23, 30, 1900, p. 569-71, 595-7.

PROMOTION on right foundation. *Journal of accountancy,* Jan. 1917, p. 43-5.

PROXIES and company meetings. *Accountant,* Sept. 24, 1898, p. 895-8.

REID, JAMES W. Formation of limited companies. *Accountant,* Oct. 15, 1898, p. 967-9.

REPORTING of company meetings; articles from The Times. *Accountant,* Feb. 18, 1905, p. 200-2.

RORIE, GEORGE. Registration of transfers and other documents produced to a company. *Accountant,* June 13, 20, 27, 1896, p. 498-500, 517-20, 544-8.

ROWE, HARRY M. Corporations. (In his *Bookkeeping and accountancy.* c1911. p. 193-9).

RUSSELL, CHARLES. Company promotion and frauds. *Accountant,* Nov. 12, 19, 1898, p. 1101, 1122.

SELLS, E. W. Corporate management compared with government control. *Incorporated accountants' journal,* 1907-8, p. 129. *Journal of accountancy,* Jan. 1908, p. 236-42.

SPICER, ERNEST EVAN AND ERNEST C. PEGLER. Limited companies. (In their *Practical bookkeeping and commercial knowledge.* 1912. p. 113-62).

STATUTORY meetings and reports. *Accountant,* July 30, 1910, p. 132-5.

SULLIVAN, JOHN JAMES. American corporations; the legal rules governing corporate organization and management with forms and illustrations. New York, D. Appleton & co. 1916. 455p.

TAYLOR, A. E. and F. D. HEAD. Registration of companies; no.2. Articles of association: Prospectus. *Business organisation and management,* Nov. 1919, p. 31-7.

VAN DE LINDE, GERARD. Company work. *Accountant,* Feb. 16, 23, March 2, 9, 23, 1889, p. 83-7, 96-100, 107-10, 127-32, 143-4, 153-6.

VICKERS, WILLIAM. Company registration. *Accountants' magazine,* April 1914, p. 197-215.

WOOD, WILLIAM ALLEN. Modern business corporations including the organization and management of private corporations with financial principles and practices; summaries of decisions of the courts elucidating the law of private business corporations, explanations of the acts of promoters, directors, officers and stockholders of corporations and forms of procedure illustrative of the formations, organization, operation and consolidation of corporations. Ed.2. Indianapolis, The Bobbs-Merrill co. 1906. 600p.

Promoters

LIABILITIES of company promoters and directors. *Accountant,* March 23, 1901, p. 353.

REID, J. W. Honest and dishonest company promoters. *Accountant,* Oct. 19, 1895, p. 836.

Reorganization

BENNETT, ROBERT JOSEPH. Reorganization by agreement. (In his *Corporation accounting.* 1917. p. 469-80).

BENNETT, ROBERT JOSEPH. Reorganization through receivership. *Journal of accountancy,* May 1916, p. 354-62.

CAPITAL losses and the companies act, 1900. *Accountant,* May 28, June 4, 18, 1904, p. 706-8, 737-40, 798-9.

CRAVATH, PAUL D. Reorganization of corporations. (In Stetson, Francis L. and others. *Some legal phases of corporate financing, reorganization and regulation.* 1917. p. 153-234).

DEFECTS in procedure. *Accountant,* Aug. 31, Sept. 7, 14, 21, Nov. 9, 16, 23, 1901, p. 940-2, 961-4, 979-91, 1008-9, 1203-5, 1231-2, 1264-6.

DEWING, ARTHUR STONE. Corporate promotions and reorganizations. Cambridge, Harvard university press, 1914. 615p. (Harvard economic studies, v. 10).

DEWING, ARTHUR STONE. Failure and reorganization. (In his *Financial policy of corporations.* 1920. v.5).

DICKSEE, LAWRENCE ROBERT. Reconstructions and amalgamations. (In his *Advanced accounting.* 1916. p. 205-12.

DIGEST of plan of reorganization, dated May 16, 1911. Pennsylvania coal and coke company. *Commercial and financial chronicle,* May 27, 1911, p. 1439.

DIGEST of plan of reorganization. Robert MacKinnon and co., manufacturers of underwear, Little Falls, New York. *Commercial*

DISSENTIENT shareholder in reconstruction schemes. *Incorporated accountants' journal,* 1907-8, p. 140.

GREENE, THOMAS LYMAN. Corporation reorganizations and receiverships. (In his *Corporation finance.* 1897. p. 146-76).

HOUSTON oil company of Texas—readjustment plan, approved July 28, 1911. *Chronicle,* Aug. 19, 1911, p. 472-3.

INTERNATIONAL CONSTRUCTION COMPANY AND UNION CONSTRUCTION COMPANY. Plan and agreement of readjustment presented in behalf of stock holders by committee of stockholders under stockholders' deposit agreement dated March 13, 1912. 47p.

INTERNATIONAL CONSTRUCTION COMPANY AND UNION CONSTRUCTION COMPANY. Stockholders' deposit agreement dated March 13, 1912. 22p.

JACOBS, HERBERT. Reconstruction in voluntary winding-up. *Accountant,* May 31, 1902, p. 571-5.

LOUGH, WILLIAM HENRY. Reorganization. (In his *Business finance.* 1917. p. 593).

NIXON, ALFRED AND J. H. STAGG. Liquidations reconstructions and amalgamations. (In their *Accounting and banking.* 1912. p. 346-60).

OUTLINE of plan of reorganization dated July 21, 1910, just declared operative. Yankee fuel company (of colorado). *Commercial and financial chronicle,* May 27, 1911, p. 1441.

PAYMENTS for underwriting upon the reconstruction of companies. *Accountant,* Oct. 10, 1903, p. 1213-5, 1235-6.

READ, W. WALTER. Accounts in connection with the reconstruction of limited companies. *Accountant,* Dec. 8, 1900, Jan. 19, 1901, p. 1120-9; 75.

RECONSTRUCTION schemes and dissentient shareholders. *Accountants' magazine,* 1909, p. 1.

RECONSTRUCTION schemes under memorandums of association. *Accountant,* April 18, 1908, p. 549-52.

RECONSTRUCTIONS and dissentients. *Accountant,* March 31, 1906, p. 390-3,

CORPORATIONS — Reorganization — *(Continued)*

Reduction of a company's capital v. reconstruction. *Accountant,* Aug. 15, 1903, p. 1027-9.

Saville, F. S. Company reconstruction. *Accountant,* June 6, 1914, p. 835-7.

Some points in reconstruction. *Accountant,* May 28, 1904, p. 732-3.

Tait, Andrew. Reconstruction of limited liability companies. *Accountants' magazine,* June, July 1912, p. 283-99, 234-49.

Taylor, H. Mead. Reconstruction of liquidating companies. *Incorporated accountants' journal,* 1896-7, p. 156.

Touch, George Alexander. Reconstruction. *Accountant,* March 24, 1905, March 31, 1906, p. 381-8, 412-20.

Reports

Company's statutory report. *Accountant,* Dec. 17, 1910, p. 842.

Corporation reports. *Journal of accountancy,* Oct. 1906-April 1907, p. 460-70; 42-7, 146-53, 238-48, 305-16, 395-402, 476-83.

Mitchell, Thomas Warner. Review of corporation reports. *Journal of accountancy,* May-Sept. 1907, p. 50-9, 144-50, 219-27, 308-14, 380-9.

New field for the Journal of accountancy. *Journal of accountancy,* Sept. 1906, p. 388-9.

Pedley, T. A. Report of the affairs of the J. W. N. Field, corporation to Central trust company, January 31, 1913. Owensboro, Kentucky. 22 typewritten pages.

Reports of American corporations. *Journal of accountancy,* Oct. 1906, p. 458-9.

Reports of special companies.

Secretaries

Bradley, Francis Ernest. Some aspects of the companies act, 1900; with especial reference to the duties of auditors and company secretaries. *Accountant,* Jan. 5, 1901, p. 23-35.

Brown, Richard. Duties of a secretary. *Accountants' magazine,* April 1910, p. 185-94.

Dicksee, Lawrence R. Secretary. (In Lisle, George. *Encyclopaedia of accounting.* v.6. p. 36-62).

Fox, W. H. Company-secretary, containing a full description of the duties of the company-secretary, together with an appendix of forms and precedents. Ed.4. London, Gee & co. 1903. 354p.

——— Same. Ed. 6. 1911.

Jobson, Alexander. Duties of a secretary. *Australasian accountant and secretary,* Jan. 1, 1920, p. 15-21.

Jordon, Herbert W. Status of the secretary and scope of his duties. *Accountant,* Dec. 4, 11, 1915, p. 685-91, 716-24.

Nelson, C. H. Secretarial work. *Incorporated accountants' journal,* 1898-9, p. 11.

Porter, W. Leslie V. Duties and responsibilities of a company secretary. *Accountant,* Sept. 13, 1919, p. 230-6.

Secretarial duties of accountants. *Incorporated accountants' journal,* 1891-2, p. 43, 74, 104.

Secretary. *Auditor,* 1890-1, p. 301, 219, 233, 252, 266, 285, 303.

Secretary's record book, containing all the books for a limited company (as provided by statute) and various special forms. London, 1890.

Van de Linde, Gerard. Secretarial. *Accountant,* Jan. 7, 14, 1893, p. 16-24, 36-41.

Vickery, B. G. Duties of a secretary in connection with a limited company. *Accountant,* May 1, 1920, p. 509-16.

Welsby, Thomas. Duties of a secretary in connection with limited liability companies. *Accountant,* Sept. 17, 24, 1898, p. 887-91, 914-6.

Woodward, H F. Secretarial work. *Accountant,* April 28, 1888, p. 262-6.

Stockholders

Auditors and shareholders. *Accountant,* Jan. 27, 1912, p. 120-3.

Executors as registered shareholders. *Accountant,* Aug. 26, 1899, p. 885-8.

Ferguson, J. A. Can a fully paid shareholder be compelled to subscribe further capital? *Public accountant,* 1909, p. 186.

Liability of stockholder of corporation for debts of corporation is limited—but stockholder has some responsibility in that respect. *Domestic engineering,* Jan. 25, 1919, p. 171-2.

Rights and liabilities of the personal representatives of a deceased shareholder. *Incorporated accountants' journal,* 1910-11, p. 219.

Stockholder's right to inspect books. *Bradstreet's* Dec. 3, 1910, p. 787.

Walkden, M. L. Shareholders' rights. *Accountant,* April 11, 1885.

Welton, T. A. Rights of partners and shareholders interse. *Accountant,* Oct. 29, 1904, p. 526-31.

CORPORATIONS and advertising. *Journal of accountancy,* Sept. 1911, p. 374.

CORPORATIONS and the common people. *Journal of accountancy,* May 1914, p. 367-70.

CORPUS juris; being a complete and systematic statement of the whole body of the law as embodied in and developed by all reported decisions; ed. by William Mack and W. J. Hale. New York, American law book co.

CORRECT accounting. *Coal age,* Jan. 30, March 13, 1919, p. 248, 501-2.

CORRECT accounting a fundamental basis for regulation and taxation. Foote, A. R. 1909.

CORRECT method of figuring overhead expense. *Metal work,* Dec. 10, 1915, p. 733-4.

CORRECT theory of prorating costs in fixing water rates to secure industrial business. *Engineering and contracting,* May 9, 1917, p. 425-6.

CORRECTIONAL INSTITUTIONS.
See Institutions.

CORRESPONDENCE. *Canadian chartered accountant,* Jan. 1916, p. 217-8.

CORRIGAN, E.

What it should cost us to sell. *System,* Oct. 1917, p. 552-4.

CORROSION of iron. Wilson, L. C. 1915.

CORSE, W. M.

Aids to scientific management. *Iron age,* March 13, 1913, p. 638-9.

CORSON, S. C.

Resurfacing water bound macadam. *Municipal journal,* April 1, 1915, p. 422-3.

Street cleaning in Morristown, Pa. *Municipal journal,* February 11, 1915, p. 189.

CORY, C. L.

Determining rates for gas service. *Public service,* January 1912, p. 25. *American gas light journal,* October 23, 1911, p. 259.

Rates for gas service. *Progressive age,* October 16, 1911, p. 869-73.

Reasonable gas rates and their determination. *Progressive age,* November 15, 1912, p. 964-9.

CORY, C. L., W. C. VINCENT AND WILLIAM J. NORTON

Symposium on inventories and appraisal of properties. *Proceedings of the American institute of electrical engineers,* Sept. 1915, p. 2131-58. Discussion. *Proceedings of the American institute of electrical engineers,* Feb. 1916, p. 236-63.

Symposium on inventories and appraisals of properties. *American institute of electrical engineers, Proceedings,* Sept. 1915, p. 2131-63. Abstract. *Electrical review and western electrician,* Sept. 25, 1915, p. 568.

CORY, ISAAC PRESTON

Practical treatise on accounts, mercantile, partnership, solicitor's, private, steward's, receiver's, executors, trustee's, etc. etc. London, 1839.

——— Same. Ed. 2. London, 1839.

Practical treatise on accounts, mercantile, private and official; exhibiting the manner in which the method of double entry may be applied to government; with proposal for the introduction of a uniform and centralized system of accounts in all the public offices. London. William Pickering, 1840. 184 + 65p.

CORY, J. P.

Bookkeeping. London, William Pickering, 1839.

Practical account. London. William Pickering, 1839.

CORY, Z. F.

Executorship. London. William Pickering, 1839.

COSGROVE, F. H.

Unification of municipal accounting. *City hall,* April, 1912, p. 12-16.

COSGROVE, JOHN J.

Bookkeeping for the plumber. Standard sanitary manufacturing co. $.25.

COSMETICS

KOLLER, THEODOR. Cosmetics; a handbook of the manufacture, employment and testing of all cosmetic materials and cosmetic specialties; translated from the German by Charles Salter. Second English edition London, Scott, Greenwood and sons, 1911. 262p.

COSMOS accountant and business self-instructor. Skaggs, E. H. 1899.

COSS, J. L.

Distribution of labor accounts. *Railway age gazette,* Aug. 20, 1915, p. 336.

COSS, J. S.

Car distributee. *Railway age,* July 23, 1915, p. 159.

COST account with numerous pro forma ruling and full explanations showing method of ascertaining cost on a factory where variety of articles are made. Millener C. A. 1901.

COST accountants wanted for signal corps. *Journal of accountancy,* Feb. 1918, p. 160.

COST ACCOUNTING

See Cost and factory accounting.

COST accounting. *Manual training,* April 1917, p. 344-5.

COST accounting. Association of American Portland cement manufacturers.

COST accounting. *Australasian accountant and secretary,* Jan. 1, 1920, p. 24-5.

COST accounting. Belser, F. C. 1917.

COST accounting. Eggleston, D. C. 1920.

COST accounting. Nicholson, J. L. and J. F. D. Rohrback. 1919.

COST accounting. Sells, Elijah W.

COST accounting. Wildman, J. R.

COST accounting—an explanation of principles and a guide to practice. Hawkins, L. Whitten. 1917.

COST accounting and burden application. Scovell, Clinton Homer. 1916.

COST accounting and profit figuring. Vincent, J. P. c1919.

COST accounting by machinery. *American machinist,* Mar. 16, 1911.

COST accounting by machinery as applied to railroad shops. *Southern and south western railway club. Proceedings,* May 14, 1914.

COST accounting committee. National canners association. 1917.

COST accounting; Federal trade commission offers cooperation with manufacturers. *New York produce review,* Sept. 20, 1916, p. 846.

COST accounting for fertilizer manufacturers. Belser, S. C.

COST accounting for institutions. Cole, William Morse. 1913.

COST accounting for municipal work. *Municipal engineering,* March 1917, p. 125-6.

COST accounting for oil producers. Smith, C. G. 1917.

COST accounting for retail fuel dealers. Cox, W. E.

COST accounting for the contractor. Allen, L. H.

COST accounting for the motion picture industry. Holman, W. S.

COST accounting; fundamental to success; basis of prices; future cost accountant; retail expenses; detailed cost accounting; business service. Eighth annual meeting, Chamber of commerce of the United States. April 27-29. 1920.

COST accounting—general accounts. *Bulletin of the American warehousemen's association,* Nov. 1920, p. 365-6.

COST accounting in a bank. Thomas, Frank W. 1910.

COST accounting in banks; symposium conducted at the Rochester convention of the American institute of banking, how institute experts clarified one of the most complicated of subjects. *Journal of the American bankers' association,* Dec. 1911, p. 385-98.

COST accounting in mine haulage. *Coal age,* Nov. 7, Dec. 26, 1918, p. 876-7, 1175.

COST accounting in principle and practice. Ridgway, Arthur Clifford.

COST accounting in shipbuilding. Atlantic coast shipbuilders' association.

COST accounting in the chain industry. Hilditch, F. W.

COST accounting in the engineering department; explains a system worked out for use on the Northern Pacific. *Railway gazette,* London, Dec. 6, 1912.

COST accounting in the implement and vehicle trade. *Iron age,* November 11, 1909, p. 1534-5.

COST accounting in the navy. *Journal of accountancy,* Feb. 1910, p. 300-301.

COST accounting in the "New industrial day." Harrison, G. C. c1920.

COST accounting on construction work with a description of the system used by the Aberthaw construction company. Allen, Leslie H. 1914.

COST accounting on some New York farms. Ladd, C. E. 1916.

COST accounting pathfinder. Goodwin, F. E. 1910.

COST accounting practice with special reference to machine hour rate. Scovell, C. H

COST accounting principles and practice. Jordan, J. P. and G. L. Harris. 1920.

COST accounting problem. Wildman, J. R. 1910.

COST accounting system for sand and gravel producers. *Engineering and contracting,* January 15, 1919, p. 61.

COST accounting system ready. *American lumberman,* Mar. 15, 1919, p. 57-9.

COST accounting theory and practice. Nicholson, J. L. 1917.

COST accounts. *Accountant,* July 28, Aug. 4, 11, 18, Nov. 3, 24, 1894, p. 655-7, 673-5, 687-9, 702-4, 768-70, 1025-6.

COST accounts. Hawkins, Leslie Whitten. 1912.

COST accounts and average prices. *Accountant,* Feb. 11, 1911, p. 211-4. *Journal of accountancy,* March 1911, p. 375-6.

COST accounts and charging out stores. *Accountants' magazine,* March 1903, p. 147-50.

COST accounts and classification. *Accountant,* Aug. 12, 1905, p. 178-9.

COST accounts, average prices: correspondence. *Journal of accountancy,* March 1911, p 380-1.

COST accounts for small manufacturers. Jenkinson, M. W.

COST accounts suitable to jobbing tradesmen. Dicksee, L. R.

COST accounts: the key to economy in manufacture. Strachan, W. 1903.

COST accounts with special references to those of an engineer and ironfounder. Best, John William. 1911.

COST (actual) records are of little value unless analyzed into component elements. *Engineering and contracting,* Dec. 4, 1907, p. 310-11.

COST anaysis engineering. Dana, R. T. and H. P. Gillette.

COST analysis in chemical manufacture. *Journal of the society of chemical industries,* June 30, 1919, p. 224R-6R.

COST analysis of asphaltic concrete pavements. *Engineering news-record,* July 20, 1916, p. 103.

COST and charges of motor truck service. *Railway review,* Dec. 7, 1918, p. 805-10.

COST and cost keeping. Chicago, La Salle extension university, 1910. 20p.

COST and depreciation of steam and hydro-electric installations. *Electrical world,* Dec. 30, 1909, p. 1558.

COST AND FACTORY ACCOUNTING

See also Accounting; sub-division Cost accounting and Costs under various headings, e. g. Bank and banking—Cost accounting.

ABBOTT, C. J. and H. F. PORTER. Making your cost system tell the truth. *Factory,* Nov. 1917, p. 708-9.

ACCURATE costing. *Mechanical world,* Dec. 4, 1914.

ACKERMAN, E. L. and L. F. MERRITT. Graphical analysis of manufacturing costs. *American industries,* July 1919, p. 20-1.

ADDINSELL, WILLIAM ARTHUR. New system of cost-taking in trade. *Accountant,* May 20, 1899, p. 577-81.

ALEXANDER, A. G. Costs with fewest clerks. *System,* May 1915, p. 543-6.

ALLES, A. A. Have you a danger line in your cost estimates. *Automotive industries,* Nov. 27, 1919, p. 1067-9.

ALWYN-SCHMIDT, L. W. Equipment and maintenance factors in cost acounting during transition period. *American machinist,* Feb. 20, 1919, p. 366-8.

AMERICAN business and accounting encyclopaedia: comp. by E. H. Beach and W. W. Thorne. Detroit, Bookkeeper publishing co. 1901. Factory cost accounting, p. 529-60, 560-81.

AMERICAN ECONOMIC ASSOCIATION. Accountancy; discussion. *American economic association, Bulletin.* April 1911, p. 145-53.

AMERICAN SCHOOL OF CORRESPONDENCE. Cost finding by William G. Nichols. Chicago, American school of correspondence, c1909. 45p.

AMERICAN SCHOOL OF CORRESPONDENCE. Factory accounts: a working handbook of departmental organization and methods as applied to factories, with special reference to purchases, stores, labor records, manufacturing orders, general expense distribution and cost accounts. 207p. (American accountants' library.)

AMERICAN SCHOOL OF CORRESPONDENCE. General expense and cost summaries. Instruction paper, prepared by Charles E. Hathaway and James B. Griffith. Chicago, American school of correspondence, c1909. 64p.

ANALYSIS of factory work. *Iron age,* Nov. 16, 1911, p. 1074-6.

ANDERSON, A. E. Behind the figures. *System,* Jan. 1913, p. 3-12.

ANDERSON, W. H. P. Manufacturing costs. *Accountant,* Nov. 4, 1905, p. 513-24.

ANDRADE, ERNEST. Manufacturing cost accounts, their use and treatment. *Accountant,* Feb. 11, 1899, p. 168.

COST AND FACTORY ACCOUNTING—*(Continued)*

ANNAN, WILLIAM. Some notes for students on trading and cost accounts. *Accountants' magazine,* Feb. 1919, p. 82-92. *Public accountant,* June 1919, p. 354-64. *South African accountant,* March 1919, p. 298-301.

ARMSTRONG, GEORGE W. Cost accounting—the key to cost control. *Railway mechanical engineer,* June 1920, p. 374-9.

ARNOLD, HORACE LUCIAN. Complete cost keeper. *Engineering magazine,* 1907, p. 408.

ARNOLD, HORACE LUCIAN. Complete cost keeper; together with an exposition of the advantages of account keeping by cards instead of books. New York, *Engineering magazine,* 1912.

ARNOLD, HORACE LUCIAN. Cost-finding methods for moderate sized shops. *Engineering magazine,* Dec. 1902-April 1903. p. 385-95, 577-89, 714-28, 870-8.

ARNOLD, HORACE LUCIAN. Factory manager and accountant; some examples of the latest American factory practice. New York, *Engineering magazine,* 1903. 431p.

ARNOLD, HORACE LUCIAN. Work in progress record. *American machinist,* April 23, 1903.

ARTHUR, JOSEPH. Daily work of a cost clerk. *Accountant,* Feb. 8, 1913, p. 197-9.

ASCERTAINING parts costs. *Business man's magazine,* Aug. 1911, p. 160.

ASHBY, E. G. Cost accounting as a branch of accounting, and the work of accountants. *Metallurgical and chemical engineering,* Sept. 1914, p. 549-50.

ASHLEY, L. E. Formula for costs. *System,* Jan. 1915, p. 92-3.

ATKINS, PAUL M. Reading executive policies in factory cost figures. *Factory,* Dec. 15, 1920, p. 1874-7.

ATKINS, ROBERT. Cost records and profits: correspondence. *Journal of accountancy,* Sept. 1917, p. 239-40.

ATKINS, ROBERT. Peace time cost problems. *Financial world,* Sept. 8, 1919, p. 9.

AUEL, C. B. Methods of figuring costs. *Electrical journal,* May 1916.

AUSTIN, SIR HERBERT. General value of cost control and organization in the factory. *Accountant,* June 19, 1920, p. 721-4.

AXIOMS concerning manufacturing costs: discussion of paper by H. R. Towne. *Engineering and contracting,* Dec. 11, 1912, p. 650-2. *Journal of the American society of mechanical engineers,* April 1913, p. 655-62.

BAER, W. Manifold manufacturing forms. *Business man's magazine,* Aug. 1908, p. 76-8.

BAKER, E. A. Basic principles that should underlie cost finding plans. *Americas,* Aug. 1919, p. 9-16.

BAKER, E. A. Control of manufacturing costs. *Americas,* Jan. 1918, p. 16-8.

BALCH, JOHN. Proper duties of the cost accountant. *Paper industry,* Nov. 1920, p. 1182-3.

BANCROFT, WILFRED. New factory cost accounting system. *American machinist,* July 24, 1902, p. 1048-52.

BARBER, ROBERT NODES. Works accounting. *Accountant,* April 3, 1909, p. 470-8.

BARNES, FRED ASA. Cost keeping and management. *Cornell civil engineer,* 1915, p. 434-45.

BARRETT, GEORGE K. How to fan out your space charges. *Factory,* Jan. 1919, p. 51-3.

BASSETT, WILLIAM R. Charging materials to get true manufacturing costs. *Factory,* April 1918, p. 644-7.

BASSET, WILLIAM R. Cost system. (In his *Accounting as an aid to business profits.* c1918. p. 210-79.)

BASSET, W. R. Modern production methods: what a cost system can do for you. *American machinist,* Oct. 14, 1920, p. 709-11. Abstract. *Factory,* Dec. 1, 1920, p. 1720.

BASSET, WILLIAM R. and S. R. GORDON. Cost system that guides policies. *Factory,* Jan. 1920, p. 43-8.

BASSET, WILLIAM R. Trends in management. *Factory,* June 15, 1920, p. 1905-7.

BASSET, WILLIAM R. Uniform cost accounting. *American machinist,* Dec. 11, 1919, p. 991-3.

BASSET, WILLIAM R. When competitors stop guessing. *System,* April 1920, p. 736-8.

BATTELLE, GEORGE I. Method of contract payments based on cost. *Engineering news,* Aug. 29, 1912.

BAUER, JOHN. Renewal costs and business profits in relation to rising prices. *Journal of accountancy,* Dec. 1919, p. 413-9.

BAUGH, FREDERICK HENRY. Principles and practice of cost accounting for accountants, manufacturers, mechanical engineers, teachers and students. Baltimore, F. H. Baugh, 1916. 194p.

BEAN, B. C. Cost of production; the principles of the science of costs; with illustrative examples by cost experts for various lines of manufacturing industry. Enlarged edition. Chicago, The System company, 1905. 198p.

BELL, S. Fixed costs and market price. *Quarterly journal of economics,* May 1918, p. 507-24.

BELSER, F. C. Elements of cost accounting. *Accountant,* Jan. 19, 1918, p. 57-61. *Australasian accountant and secretary,* April 1920, p. 122-7. *Journal of accountancy,* Nov. 1917, p. 325-41. *Public accountant,* March 1918, p. 218-32.

BELT, ROBERT E. Importance of true cost. *Accountant,* Aug. 26, 1916, p. 177-80. *Journal of accountancy,* July 1916, p. 28-34.

BELT, ROBERT E. and R. W. GARDINER. Cost accounting for manufacturers. *Railway review,* Aug. 12, 1916, p. 222-3.

BENNETT, GEORGE E. Cost accounts of a manufacturing enterprise. (In his *Constructive accounting.* 1920. p. 461-5.)

BENNETT, ROBERT JOSEPH. Accounting system for factory, repair shop and sales department. *Business man's magazine,* May 1905, p. 972-7.

BENNETT, ROBERT JOSEPH. Vital importance of knowing costs. *Accountant,* Aug. 25, 1917, p. 148-50. *Accounting and commerce,* Sept. 1917, p. 137-41. *Canadian chartered accountant,* July 1917, p. 34-42. *Public accountant,* Nov. 1917, p. 122-32. *Philadelphia chamber of commerce journal,* Jan. 1917, p. 8-10.

BENTLEY, HARRY C. Manufacturing. (In his *Science of accounts.* 1913. p. 191-250.)

BERNDT, IRVING A. Costs, their compilation and use in management. Chicago, H. P. Goulf company, c1920. 235p.

BERNHARD, E. W. Simple cost-keeping system. *American machinist,* April 4, 1912.

BEST, JOHN WILLIAM. Cost accounts with special references to those of an engineer and ironfounder. Ed. 2. London, Gee & co. 1911. 128p.

BETTER business methods. *Engineering magazine, June* 1916, p. 432.

BISCHOFF, J. M. Development of a unit cost system. *Association of engineering societies,* Sept. 1914, p. 165-70.

BISHOP, HENRY GOLD. Order book and cost record [for job work]. Schenectady, H. G. Bishop.

BLAKE, J. P. Detailed cost accounting. *System,* Oct. 1904, p. 330-4.

BLANCHARD, ISAAC H. Finding the work that pays: how to charge each job with its proper ratio of wages, machine time and overhead expense. *System,* Feb. 1913, p. 154-7.

COST AND FACTORY ACCOUNTING—*(Continued)*

BLOCK number system. *Machinery* (London), Oct. 2, 1919, p. 7-9.

BONNER, H. R. Graphic method for presenting comparative cost analysis. *Quarterly publication of the American statistical association,* Sept. 1920, p. 277-88.

BORDEN, J. A. New awakening in cost-finding. *Inland printer,* Feb. 1917, p. 677-8.

BOSHER, LEWIS H. Controlling accounts in cost accounting. *Journal of accountancy,* June 1912, p. 405-19.

BOUNDY, F. P. Some incidental factory accounts and their treatment. *Public accountant,* 1906-7, p. 235.

BOYD, J. H. Costing in relation to scientific management. *Electrician,* Aug. 28, 1919, p. 171-2.

BRAY, T. J. Investment factor in costs. *Iron trade review,* May 28, 1914, p. 967-8. *Iron age,* May 28, 1914, p. 1362-3.

BRIERLEY, JOHN T. Manufacturing cost accounts: being a manual of instruction for bookkeepers and managers in factory cost accounts. Brooklyn, N. Y. 1913. 42p.

BRISCO, NORRIS ARTHUR. Analysis of cost accounting. (In his *Economics of business.* 1913. p. 121-39.)

BRITTEN, C. D. Works costing. *Accountant,* March 16, 1912, p. 449-51.

BROAKER, FRANK. Cost and factory accounts with use of consumption journal. *Accountant,* June 19, 1897, p. 604-5. *Business,* June 1897, p. 179-80.

BUNNELL, STERLING HAIGHT. Cost-keeping for manufacturing plants. New York, D. Appleton & co. 1911. 233p.

BUNNELL, STERLING HAIGHT. Cost-keeping for manufacturing plants. *American economic review,* June 1912, p. 364-6.

BUNNELL, STERLING HAIGHT. Extra cost of machine work. *Business,* Jan. 1912, p. 90-3.

BUNNELL, STERLING HAIGHT. Finding cost p. 20-2. *Metal work,* July 24, 1914, p. 95-6.

BUNNELL STERLING HAIGHT. Proper use of cost-keeping system. *Cassier's magazine,* Aug. 1908, p. 300-3.

BUNNELL, STERLING HAIGHT. Standardizing factory expense and cost. *Iron age,* Nov. 16, 1911, p. 1072-3.

BURROUGHS, A. M. Cutting the costs of keeping a cost system. *Metal work,* May 28, 1915, p. 763.

BURROUGHS, A. M. Final disposition of expense figures. *Metal work,* Mar. 26, 1915, p. 471-2.

BURROUGHS, A. M. Handling material and perpetual inventory. *Metal work,* Jan. 22, 1915, p. 153-4.

BURROUGHS adding machine company. Cost-keeping short cuts; prepared from experiences in many lines of business. Detroit, Burroughs adding machine company, 1911. 190p. Ed. 3. Efficient costkeeping. 1914.

BURSK, R. C. Necessity of cost accounting. *National wholesale grocers' association bulletin,* Dec. 1917, p. 25.

BURTON, AUTHUR S. Why some cost systems fail to produce desired results. *Journal of accountancy,* April 1919, p. 249-58.

BURTON, FRANCIS GEORGE. Cost accounts. *Incorporated accountants' journal,* 1900-1, p. 107, 115.

BURTON, FRANCIS GEORGE. Cost accounts. *Accountant,* Feb. 24, 1912, p. 324-31.

BUSH, S. L. Cost accounting: how to govern and show expense in a productive department. *Paper,* Oct. 23, 1918, p. 11-13.

BUSINESS administration and cost accounts. *Accountant,* Sept. 24, 1910, p. 393-6.

ITZ, R. E. Manufacturing expense. *Metal industries,* Dec. 1917, p. 511-2.

BUTZ, R. E. Systematizing production accounts. *Iron trade review,* Mar. 20, 1919, p. 757-9.

BY-PRODUCTS and costs. *Accountant,* Sept. 29, 1917, p. 233-6.

CAMERON, JAMES. Lack of system in manufacturing. *Business world,* Dec. 1905.

CAN the standard measure of value be improved. *Journal of the Engineering institute of Canada,* Nov. 1919, p. 720-7.

CARD index system of cost keeping. *American machinist,* Sept. 15, 1898.

CARDULLO, FORREST E. Accounting system for industrial plants. *Metal work,* 1914, v. 81, p. 820-2.

CARDULLO, FORREST E. Bookkeeping of manufacturing costs: elements of the cost of material, etc. *Iron age,* June 4, 1914, p. 1440-2. *Metal work,* June 19, 1914, p. 820-2.

CARDULLO, FORREST E. Capital costs in a manufacturing business. *Iron age,* May 21, 1914, p. 1278-80. *Metal work,* June 5, 1914, p. 745-7.

CARDULLO FORREST E. Economics of a manufacturing business. *Iron age,* May 7, 1914, p. 1172-3. *Metal work,* May 22, 1914, p. 684-5.

CARDULLO FORREST E. Labor and other costs in manufacturing. *Iron age,* May 28, 1914, p. 1365-7. *Metal work,* June 12, 1914, p. 775-7.

CARINGTON C. What is a manufacturing cost? *Iron age,* Jan. 1, 1905.

CARPENTER, CHARLES U. Stimulating production by wage, stock and cost systems. *Engineering magazine,* Sept. 1907, p. 931-41.

CARR, JOHN E. Systems used in office and factory. *System,* Sept. 1903, p. 203-8.

CARTER. Cost sheets for collieries, iron works, etc. London, Simpkins, Marshall and co. 1890.

CARTER, ROGER NEAL. Cost accounts. (In his *Advanced accounts,* p. 808-26).

CARTER, ROGER NEAL. Manufacturing accounts, etc. (In his *Advanced accounts,* p. 566-99).

CATHLES, A. General principles of costing. *Accountant,* Feb. 289, 1920, p. 249-56.

CHASE, WILLIAM ARTHUR. Auditing and cost accounting. Chicago, La Salle extension university, 1917. 493p.

CHEAP, efficient cost system. *Iron age,* Jan. 2, 1913, p. 62.

CHERRINGTON, FREDERIC B. Tying the costs into the general accounts. (In Thompson, C. B. *How to find factory costs.* c1916. p. 102-9.)

CHILD, FREDERICK W. System of cost accounts. *Business,* Feb. 1894, p. 56-9.

CHURCH, ALEXANDER HAMILTON. Manufacturing costs and accounts. New York, McGraw-Hill book co. 1917. 452p.

CHURCH, ALEXANDER HAMILTON. Organization by production factors. *Engineering magazine,* Oct. 1909-April 1910, p. 15-26, 184-94, 361-70, 557-70, 703-15, 863-75; 77-88.

CHURCH, ALEXANDER HAMILTON. Production factors in cost accounting and works management. New York, Engineering magazine, 1910. 187p. (Works management library.)

CHURCHILL, W. L. Three ways to test cost figures. *System,* Dec. 1916, p. 606-12.

CLAPHAM, F. F. Checking of maintenance costs. *Engineer,* April 19, 1918, p. 343.

CLARK, E. A. How we keep costs in our 75-man plant. *Factory,* Oct. 1916, p. 405-8.

CLARK, E. S. Practical costs. *Industrial management,* Dec. 1916, Jan. Mar. May 1917, p. 299-305, 529-33, 768-72, 195-8.

CLARK, PERCY G. Hints to accountants, liquidators, and receivers on office and factory control. *Accountant,* Sept. 13, 1913, p. 344.

COST AND FACTORY ACCOUNTING—*(Continued)*

CLEARY, P. ROGER. How to figure profit; a comprehensive reference book for business men, teachers and students. Dept. A, Ypsilante, Michigan. P. R. Cleary co. 1918. 265 p.

COES, HAROLD V. Rehabilitation of existing plants as a factor in production costs. *Engineering magazine,* June 1915, p. 357-71.

COLE, WILLIAM MORSE. Accounting methods for determining costs and prices. *American economic association, Bulletin.* April 1911, p. 124-35.

COLE, WILLIAM MORSE. Determination of costs. (In his *Bookkeeping, accounting and auditing.* c1914. p. 347-73).

COLE, WILLIAM MORSE. General principles of cost accounting. (In his *Accounts, their construction and interpretation.* c1915. p. 141-50, 270-326.)

COLES, ARTHUR. Costing. (In his *Company accounts,* p. 248-63).

COLLINS, JAMES H. Through the knothole, "How some business men get their war shrinkage." *World's work,* Nov. 1915, p. 568-74.

COLVER, WILLIAM B. Asks that federal cost finding be continued. *Record and guide,* Dec. 28, 1918, p. 744-5.

COLVER, WILLIAM B. Lessons of war cost finding. *Annals of the American academy of political and social science,* March 1919, p. 300-5.

COLVER, WILLIAM B. Standardized accounting systems recommended. *Foundry,* Feb. 1919, p. 85-6.

CONNOR, W. N. Our men know all about our costs. *System,* May 1920, p. 974-5.

CONTINUOUS cost keeping system maintained by Automatic transportation co., Buffalo. *Iron age,* Jan. 2, 1913, p. 88-90.

COST accounting. *Australasian accountant and secretary,* Jan., 1920, p. 24-5.

COST accounting; Federal trade commission offers cooperation with manufacturers. *New York produce review,* Sept. 20, 1916, p. 846.

COST accounts. *Accountant,* July 28, Aug. 4, 11, 18, Nov. 3, 24 1894, p. 655-7, 673-5, 687-9, 702-4, 968-70, 1025-6.

COST accounts and average prices. *Accountant,* Feb. 11, 1911, p. 211-4. *Journal of accountancy,* March 1911, p. 375-6, 380-1.

COST accounts and charging out stores. *Accountants' magazine,* 1903, p. 147-50.

COST accounts and classification. *Accountant,* Aug. 12, 1905, p. 178-9.

COST department and payroll budget. *100%.* Aug. 1917, p. 54.

COST department of the future. *American machinist,* May 29, 1919, p. 1025-6.

COST finding and keeping. *American stone trade,* 1915, v. 15, no. 11, p. 15.

COST keeping and wage systems of the Stillwell-Bierce & Smith-Vaile co. *Iron trade review,* June 5, 1902.

COST keeping at the Chicago works of Fraser and Chalmers. *American machinist,* Nov 1, 1900, pt. 1.

COST of cost keeping. *Inland printer,* June 1914, p. 419.

COST of production . . . articles by A. H. Revell, C. W. Norton and others. Chicago, A. W. Shaw. 196p. (Business man's library, v. 3.)

COST records at Pratt and Whitney's. *The office,* April 1890, p. 108-9.

COST system for manufacturers. *Pace student,* Oct. 1916.

COSTING and cost accounting. *Australasian accountant and secretary,* June 1920, p. 153-5.

COSTING and the components of cost. *Incorporated accountants' journal,* March 1919, p. 104-5.

COSTING by sub-orders or by operations, which? *Accountant,* Feb. 21, 1920, p. 202-3.

COSTING questions. *Accountant,* July 24, 1920, p. 89-90.

COSTS and a call for action. *System,* Feb. 1917, p. 222-3.

COSTS and statistics. Chicago, A. W. Shaw.

COSTS keeping prevents poor bidding. *Concrete,* Oct. 1919, p. 163-4.

COTTER, A. D. Manufacturing accounts. *Public accountants,* 1909, p. 171.

COULTER, WALDO S. Cost keeping on public works. *Engineering news,* June 14, 1906.

COX, HENRY C. Statements of a manufacturing business. (In his *Advanced and analytical accounting.* 1920. p. 303-9.)

CRAGGS, G. SOMERVILLE. Manufacturing costs. *Accountant,* June 5, 1915, p. 756-66.

CUDWORTH, ALFRED JAMES. Some notes on cost accounts. *Accountant,* April 18, 1897, p. 312-9.

CULVER, W. W. How Kenyon "got going." *System,* March 1917, p. 244-52.

CUTLER, F. C. Handy cost sheets for new work. *Factory,* Jan. 1912, p. 26-7.

CUTTING factory costs. *System,* Jan.-Feb. 1913, p. 78-81, 214-7.

CUTTING factory costs. *System,* May-Sept. 1914, p. 549-52, 662-4; 105-8, 216-20, 328-32.

DANIELS, B. Cost of cost keeping. *Inland printer,* June 1920, p. 344.

DANIELS, B. Dividing a man. *Inland printer,* July 1914, p. 585-7.

DANIELS, B. How the hour is divided. *Inland printer,* July 1914, p. 583-4.

DANIELS, B. What is the cost per thousand? *Inland printer,* Dec. 1914, p. 393-6.

DAVENPORT, H. J. Cost and its significance. *American economic review,* Dec. 1911, p. 724-52.

DAY, CLARENCE MUNRO. Cost accounting. (In his *Accounting practice.* 1916. p. 89-312.)

DEACON, THOMAS R. Overhead and general costs in manufacturing. *Journal of the engineering institute of Canada,* July 1919, p. 505-6.

DEAN, STUART. Cost keeping in a factory. (In his *Shop and foundry management.* 1913. p. 69-87).

DEAN, STUART. Results of production methods. (In his *Shop and foundry management.* 1913. p. 43-62.)

DECREASED cost month. *Iron age,* May 15, 1913, p. 1187-8.

DEFINITIONS of cost, unit cost, direct and indirect cost, and overhead cost. *Engineering and contracting,* Feb. 28, 1917, p. 196-7.

DENHAM, ROBERT S. A-B-C of cost engineering. Cleveland, Denham cost finding company, c1919. 105p.

DENHAM, ROBERT S. Applying the principles of cost engineering. *Foundry,* July 1918, p. 309.

DENHAM, ROBERT S. Fundamentals of cost and profit calculation; a vigorous discussion of the vital elements of business. Cleveland, Cost engineer publishing co. 1918. 120p.

DETERMINING costs of manufacturing and selling. *Textile world,* Aug. 19, 1916, p. 3639.

DETERMINATION of cost. *Journal of accountancy,* Sept. 1917, p. 215-22.

DETERMING operation costs. *Factory,* Feb. 1917, p. 240.

DICK, J. R. Economics of works costs. *Electrician,* Nov. 29, 1918, p. 643-5.

DICKINSON, A. L. Economic aspect of cost accounts and its application to the accounts of industrial companies. *American economic association. Bulletin,* April 1911, p. 110-23. *Journal of accountancy,* March 1911, p. 325-39.

COST AND FACTORY ACCOUNTING—*(Continued)*

DICKINSON, ARTHUR LOWES. Some theories and problems in cost accounting. (In his *Accounting theory and practice.* 1917. p. 190-211).

DICKSEE, LAWRENCE ROBERT. Cost accounts. (In his *Advanced accounting.* 1916. p. 253-72).

DICKSEE, LAWRENCE ROBERT. Fundamentals of manufacturing costs. London, Gee & co. 1917. 42p. *Accountant,* Sept. 1, 8, 15, 1917, p. 160-1, 175-6, 196-8.

DICKSEE, LAWRENCE ROBERT and H. E. BLAIN. Cost accounts. (In their *Office organization and management.* 1917. p. 153-61).

DIEMER, HUGO. Cost-finding methods under the premium wage system. *Engineering magazine,* v.24, p. 577.

DIEMER, HUGO. Determination of costs. (In his *Industrial organization and management.* 1917. p. 112-64).

DIEMER, HUGO. Factory accounts, cost department. (In his *Factory organisation and administration.* 1914. p. 51-7, 269-91).

DUNGER, RICHARD F. Present need of proper cost finding. 100%, Dec. 1920, p. 76-84.

DO YOU know exactly what your product costs? *Canadian machinery,* July 31, 1919, p. 101-6.

DUNN, J. H. Uniform cost accounting. *Automotive industries,* May 2, 1918, p. 854. Abstract, *Iron age,* April 25, 1918, p. 1082-3.

EATON, ABIJAH H. Manufacturing. (In his *Eaton and Burnett revised and improved bookkeeping, corporation, voucher and cost accounting embracing all modern and scientific methods used in business.* 1917. p. 193-221).

ECONOMICAL interchangeable manufacturing practice. *Machinery,* March 1920, 636-41.

EDDIS, WILTON C. and WILLIAM B. TINDALL. Manufacturers' accounts. Ed. 3, enlarged. Toronto, Canada, The authors, 1904. 199p.

EFFICIENT production of cylindrical work. *Machinery,* Dec. 1912.

EGGLESTON, DEWITT CARL. Cost accounting. New York, The Ronald press company, 1920. 444p. (Business accounting, v.3).

EGGLESTON, DEWITT CARL. For model cost system. *Business man's magazine,* Feb. 1907, p. 84-8.

EGGLESTON, DEWITT CARL. Manager has opinions of his own. *Business man's magazine,* Jan. 1907, p. 98-100.

EGGLESTON, DEWITT CARL. Problems in cost accounting. New York, D. Appleton & co. 1918. 349p. (College of the city of New York series in commerce, civics and technology).

EGGLESTON, DEWITT CARL. Series of articles about factory cost accounting. *Business man's magazine,* Nov. Dec. 1907, Jan. 1908, p. 81-4, 78-82, 95-100.

EGGLESTON, DEWITT CARL. System of factory cost accounting. *Journal of accountancy,* Dec. 1906, p. 115-22.

ELBOURNE, EDWARD T. "All-in" costs. *Engineer,* July 30, 1915, p. 101.

ELBOURNE, EDWARD T. Approximation in factory accounting. *Accounting,* March 20, 1915, p. 388-96.

ELBOURNE, EDWARD T. Costing problem. London. Liberty press [1919].

ELBOURNE, EDWARD T. Factory administration and accounts: a book of reference with tables and specimen forms, for managers, engineers and accountants: with contributions on the General problems of industrial works design by Andrew Home-Morton and Financial accounts by John Maughfling. London, Longmans, Green & co. 1918. 638p.

ELBOURNE, EDWARD T. Functions of factory accounts. *Accountant,* May 3, 1919, p. 361-5.

ELDRIDGE, H. J. Cost accounts. *Journal of associated accountants,* 1910, p. 242.

ELWORTHY, W. R. and CLAUDE C. CAMPLING. Bookkeeping for traders, manufacturers, and companies. London, Jordon and sons, 1904. 224p.

EMERSON, HARRINGTON. Efficiency as a basis for operation and wages. *Engineering magazine,* Nov. 1908, p. 170-8.

EMERSON, HARRINGTON. Efficiency system in operation. *Engineering magazine,* Feb. 1909, p. 815-24.

EMERSON, HARRINGTON. Location and elimination of wastes. *Engineering magazine,* Jan. 1909, p. 676-83.

EMERSON, HARRINGTON. Modern theory of cost accounting. (In his *Efficiency as a basis for operation and wages.* 1914. p. 149-211).

EMERSON, HARRINGTON. Modern theory of cost accounting. *Engineering magazine,* Dec. 1908, p. 336-46.

EMERSON, HARRINGTON. Practising efficiency and knowing costs; a letter to a New England manufacturer. New York, Emerson co. 1912. 12p.

EMERSON, HARRINGTON. Reliable, immediate, adequate, and permanent records. *Engineering magazine,* Jan. 1911, p. 496-506.

ENNIS, WILLIAM DUANE. Principles of accounting. (In his *Works management.* 1911. p. 1-16, 136-47).

ERSKINE, A. R. Going cost systems and monthly closings for industrial corporations. *Journal of accountancy,* July 1909, p. 168-72.

ESTIMATING cost. *American machinist,* 1900, v.23, p. 1231-3.

EVANS, HOLDEN A. Cost keeping and scientific management. New York, McGraw-Hill book co. 1911. 260p.

EVANS, HOLDEN A. Expense accounts and analysis. *American machinist,* Jan. 12, 1911, p. 60-4.

EVANS, HOLDEN A. Importance of accurate costs. *American machinist,* Nov. 10, 1910, p. 876-8.

EVANS, HOLDEN A. Orders, records and expense accounts. *American machinist,* v.33, no. 52.

EVANS, HOLDEN A. Purpose of a cost system. *American machinist,* Nov. 24, 1910, p. 955-7.

EYES opened by systematic cost keeping. *Rock products and building materials,* 1916, v.18, p. 14-5.

FACTORY cost accounting methods. *Utah payroll builder,* Nov. 1918, p. 3-5.

FALCONER, KENNETH. How to make cost records more valuable. *Business man's magazine,* March 1911, p. 292-295.

FALCONER, KENNETH. Work in progress record. *American machinist,* May 28, 1903.

FALK, MYRON S. System of cost keeping. *American society of civil engineers, Transactions,* 1909, v.64, p. 401-40.

FARNHAM, D. T. Cost figures as an index of efficiency. *Industrial management,* Mar. 1919, p. 232-3.

FARNHAM, D. T. How graphic control facilitates the fixing of profits. *Engineering magazine,* Oct. 1916, p. 16-22.

FARNSWORTH, A. W. Estimation of costs. *Engineer,* London, Jan. 19, 1906. *Engineering record,* Feb. 3, 1906.

FARNSWORTH, A. W. Methods of cost estimation. *Engineering magazine,* March 1906, p. 905-7.

FASSETT, E. S. Making factory cost-finding a part of the sales record. *Factory,* Nov. 15, 1920, p. 1569-71.

FELLS, JOHN M. Conference on scientific costing: cost accountancy: its evolution and its trend. *Accountant,* June 28, 1919, p. 548-52.

COST AND FACTORY ACCOUNTING—*(Continued)*

FELLS, JOHN M. Some principles governing the ascertainment of cost. *Business organisation and management,* July 1920, p. 425-30. *Incorporated accountants' journal,* Nov. 1919, p. 31-5.

FERGUSON, WILLIAM BURDER. Estimating the cost of work; with special reference to unstandardized operations, as in jobbing shops or repair work. New York, Engineering magazine co. 1915. 169p. (Works management library).

FIGURING costs and profits. *Metal work,* Dec. 17, 1915, p. 783.

FIGURING the cost of doing business. *Journal of commerce,* Sept. 27, 1911, p. 6.

FISH, E. H. Labor costs and the workman. *Industrial management,* May 1920, p. 412-5.

FISK, A. K. Principles of cost accounting. *Canadian chartered accountant,* Jan. 1914, p. 167-77.

FOREMAN, A. E. Keeping cost data on municipal work carried out by day labor. *Canadian engineer,* Dec. 14, 1916.

FOURTEEN rules for figuring cost and profit. *Metal work,* Sept. 28, 1917, p. 386.

FRANKLIN, BENJAMIN A. Building a cost system. (In his *Experiences in efficiency.* 1918. p. 121-47).

FRANKLIN, BENJAMIN A. Building a cost system. *Engineering magazine,* Dec. 1913, p. 356-64.

FRANKLIN, BENJAMIN A. Cost figures for the executive. *Engineering magazine,* Jan.-March 1912.

FRANKLIN, BENJAMIN A. Cost methods that give the executive control of his business. *Engineering magazine,* Jan.-Aug. 1912, p. 577-85, 793-8, 921-8; 48-56, 192-7, 421-33, 560-6, 703-9.

FRANKLIN, BENJAMIN A. Cost reports for executors as a means of plant control. New York, Engineering magazine co. c1912. 142p.

FRAZER, GEORGE E. Use of cost accounts. *100%,* Aug. 1917, p. 38-40.

FREMONT, E. C. Making payrolls check with costs. *Factory,* April 1918, p. 639-40.

FRIEDLEBEN, THEODORE J. Manufacturing costs. *Business world,* June 1915, p. 286-8.

FUNDAMENTALS of a cost system for manufacturers. *Excerpt in American industries,* Sept. 1916, p. 26-7.

GAINES, M. W. Tabulating-machine cost accounting for factories of diversified product. *Engineering magazine,* Dec. 1905, p 364-73.

GALLIVER, GEORGE A. Figuring costs in sales estimates. *Paper,* April 7, 1920, p. 18.

GANTT, H. L. Basis of manufacturing costs. *Industrial management,* June 1917, p. 369-70.

GANTT, H. L. Effect of idle plant on costs and profits. *Annals of the American academy of political and social science,* Sept. 1915.

GANTT, H. L. Efficiency and democracy. *Journal of the American society of mechanical engineers,* Jan. 1919, p. 43.

GANTT, H. L. Expenses and costs. *Journal of the American society of mechanical engineers,* Dec. 1917, p. 991,2. *American machinist,* Dec. 20, 1917, p. 1100-1. *Iron trade review,* Dec. 20, 1917, p. 1323. Discussion. *Journal of the American society of mechanical engineers,* Feb. 1918, p. 150-2.

GANTT, H. L. Graphical daily balance in manufacture. *American society of mechanical engineers, Transactions.* 1903, v.24, p. 1322-36.

GANTT, H. L. Measurement of efficiency. *Iron trade review,* Dec. 17, 1914, p. 1131-3. *Industrial engineering,* Dec. 1914, p. 463-5. *Iron age,* Dec. 3, 1914, p. 1320-1. *Automobile,* Dec. 17, 1914, p. 1104-5. Condensed. *Railway age* (Mech. ed.), May 1915, p. 249-51. *Metal work,* May 21, 1915, p. 725-6. Abstract. *Engineering magazine,* Jan. 1915, p. 577-80. Abstract with discussion. *Journal of the American society of mechanical engineers,* Jan. 1915, p. 11-3.

GANTT, H. L. Non-productive labor; the fallacy of its use as a measure of efficient operation. *Engineering magazine,* Jan. 1915, p. 577-80.

GANTT, H. L. Practical application of scientific management. *Engineering magazine,* April 1911, p. 1022.

GANTT, H. L. Production and sales. *Engineering magazine,* Jan. 1916, p. 593-600.

GANTT, H. L. Productive capacity a measure of value of an industrial property. *Journal of the American society of mechanical engineers,* Nov. 1916, p. 876-8. *Iron trade review,* Dec. 7, 1916, p. 1146-8. *Gas age,* Jan. 1, 1917, p. 22-3. Condensed. *Iron age,* Dec. 14, 1916, p. 1341-2. Excerpts. *Textile world,* Dec. 2, 1916, p. 33. Discussion. *Journal of the American society of mechanical engineers,* Feb. 1917, p. 135-7.

GANTT, H. L. Relation between production and costs. *Journal of the American society of mechanical engineers,* Aug. 1915, p. 466-8. *American gas light journal,* July 26, 1915, p. 54-5. *Iron age,* July 1, 1915, p. 16-8. *Iron trade review,* Aug. 5, 1915, p. 267-8. *Machinery,* Aug. 1915, p. 1000-2. *Textile world,* Aug. 1915, p. 510-3. *Transactions of the American society of mechanical engineers.* 1915, p. 109-28. Discussion. *Journal of the American society of mechanical engineers,* Aug. 1915, p. 468-75. Abstract of discussion. *Iron age,* July 1, 1915, p. 24-5.

GARCKE, EMILE and J. M. FELLS. Factory accounts; their principle and practice. London, Crosby, Lockwood and son, 1893. 264p.

GARRARD, CHARLES C. Scientific costing. *Journal of the Institute of electrical engineers,* Dec. 1919, p. 57-9.

GARRARD, CHARLES C. Works costs. *Electrical review,* London, Feb. 7, 1911, pt. 1.

GARRISON, ELISHA ELY. Fundamental principles of cost accounting. (In his *Accounting every business man should know.* p. 129-43).

GATHERING cost figures electrically. *Factory,* April 1918, p. 637.

GETTING lot costs at a glance. *Factory,* Oct. 1917, p. 616.

GIBNEY, A. J. Keeping a line on daily expense. *Railway review,* Oct. 9, 1915, p. 468-70.

GILL, JOSEPH. Duties of a factory cost accountant. *Journal of accountancy,* Dec. 1918, p. 441-9. *Public accountant,* June 1919, p. 346-54.

GILLETTE, HALBERT P. Conversion factors in cost keeping as an aid to management. *Engineering and contracting,* Nov. 29, 1916, p. 477-8.

GILLETTE, HALBERT P. Cost keeping as an aid in managing men. *Engineering and contracting,* July 17, 1907.

GILLETTE, HALBERT POWERS and R. T. DANA. Cost keeping and management engineering; a treatise for engineers, contractors and superintendents engaged in the management of engineering construction. New York, Clark book co. 1916. 346p.

GILMAN, S. What the executive should know about costs. *Industrial management,* Aug. 1917, p. 669-75.

COST AND FACTORY ACCOUNTING—*(Continued)*

GLEDHILL, ARTHUR H. Practical costing. 26, Victoria street, S. W. I. London, A. H. Gledhill, 1917. 72p.

GODFREY, JOHN R. Necessity of knowing what things cost. *American machinist,* May 8, 1913, p. 784.

GOODE, GEORGE EDWARD. Methods of ascertaining costs in a factory where variety of articles are made, which mostly pass through several processes in the course of manufacture, and are turned out in large quantities. *Accountant,* June 30, 1900, p. 600-7.

GOODING, F. E. By-products of cost figures. *Factory,* Jan. 1919, p. 46-7.

GOODWIN, A. E. Principles and practice of correct costing. *Accountant,* March 20, 1920, p. 342-7.

GOODWIN, FRANK ELBERT. Cost accounting pathfinder. Ed. 7, St. Louis, Midland publishing co. 1910. 267p.

GOODYEAR, SAMUEL HORATIO and L. E. GOODYEAR. Corporation and factory accounting. Cedar Rapids, Goodyear-Marshall publishing co.

GORMAN, E. Improved cost summary sheet. *Inland printer,* May 1913, p. 230-1.

GOSART, W. J. Standard factory accounting and organisation. *Accountant,* Nov. 22, 1919, p. 437-43.

GOVERNMENT and cost accounting. *Journal of accountancy,* July 1917, p. 79.

GOVERNMENT contracts, and cost accounting methods. *American industries,* Sept. 1917, p. 19-22.

GREAT BRITAIN. DEPARTMENT OF EXPLOSIVES SUPPLY. FACTORY BRANCH. 2d report on costs and efficiencies for H. M. factories controlled by Factories branch, Department of explosives supply, prepared for 17th factories meeting, Sept. 10, 1918. London, H. M. stationery office, 1918, 134p.

GREAT BRITAIN. MINISTRY OF RECONSTRUCTION. Use of costing. London, H. M. stationery office, 1919, 24p. (Reconstruction problems 35)

GREEN, WARREN L. Cost system that safeguards. (In Thompson, C. B. *How to find factory costs.* c1916. p. 142-9).

GREENWOOD, G. W. Burning brick in the lime light. *Industrial management,* March 1920, p. 207-8.

GREENWOOD, G. W. Liquid profits. *Industrial management,* Oct. 1919, p. 287-8.

GREENWOOD, G. W. Simple flexible cost system. *Industrial management,* Aug. 1918, p. 139-40.

GRIFFITH, JAMES B. Corporation and manufacturing accounts. (In *Cyclopedia of commerce, accountancy, business administration.* 1910. v.4. p. 195-270).

GRIFFITH, JAMES B. Cost summaries. (In *Cyclopedia of commerce, accountancy, business administration,* 1910, v.2. p. 165-90).

GUIGNON, F. A. Semi-automatic cost-system. *Industrial management,* Dec. 1917, p. 353-6.

GUNN, J. NEWTON. Cost keeping. *Engineering magazine,* Jan. 1901, p. 703-8.

GUNN, J. NEWTON. Costs. (In Humphreys, A. C. Lecture notes on some of the business features of engineering practice. p. 498-509.)

GUY, J. H. Use and aim of cost accounts. *Engineer,* April 26, 1918, p. 373.

HAGGERTY, H. C. Factory cost system. *Business world,* Feb. 1906, p. 94-9.

HALL, HARRY LOVINAS CEPHAS. Manufacturing cost. Detroit, Mich., Book-keeper publishing co. 1904. 141 p.

HALSEY, F. A. Principles of cost accounting. *American machinist,* June 20, 27, 1901, p. 684-6, 705-8. *Sibley journal of engineering,* April, 1901, p. 275-92.

HAMILTON, G. W. Plea for the cost accountant. *Industrial management,* June, 1918, p. 446.

HAMILTON, WILLIAM ROBERT. Some economic considerations bearing on costing. *Accountant,* Feb. 5, 1910, p. 200-6.

HANEY, LEWIS H. Opportunity cost. *American economic review,* Sept., 1912.

HANDLING factory costs. *Factory,* July, Nov., 1918, Jan.-Mar., May-June. Sept., 1919, p. 180, 942, 138, 322, 550, 1068, 1252; 618, 1390.

HANDLING factory costs. *Factory,* Jan.-Feb. 1, June 1, Sept. 1, Dec. 15, 1920, p. 200, 356, 1748, 740, 1902-3.

HANDLING special job costs. *Factory,* Aug. 1918, p. 264.

HARDCASTLE, JOSEPH. Cost prices. *Business,* Jan., Feb., March, April, May, June, July, Aug., Sept., 1898, p. 28-30, 101-4, 171-3, 221-3, 293-5, 363-7, 434-5, 490-2, 562-4.

HARRIS, H. A. Fewer clerks for cost work. *System,* June, 1914, p. 643-8.

HARRIS, H. A. Making costs and bids agree. (In Thompson, C. B. *How to find factory costs.* c1916. p. 150-83.)

HARRIS, H. A. Making costs and bids agree. *System,* Dec. 1914—Feb., 1915, p. 641-5; 81-6, 195-9.

HARRISON, G. C. Cost accounting in the new industrial day. New York, Engineering magazine co. c1920. 11p. *Industrial management,* Dec. 1919-Jan. 1920, p. 441-4, 13-7.

HARRISON, G. C. Cost accounting to aid production. *Industrial management,* Oct. 1918-June 1919, p. 273-82, 391-8, 456-63; 49-55, 131-9, 218-24, 314-18, 400-4, 483-7.

HARRISON, G. C. Scientific basis for cost accounting. 8 p. *Industrial management,* March 1920, p. 237-42.

HARROW, JAMES E. Cutting factory costs. *Business man's magazine,* Nov. 1910, p. 404-9.

HATFIELD, HENRY RAND. Cost accounts. (In his *Modern accounting.* 1916. p. 293-315.)

HATHAWAY, CHARLES E. General expense. (In *Cyclopedia of commerce, accountancy, business administration.* 1910. v. 2. p. 127-64.)

HATHAWAY, CHARLES E. AND J. G. GRIFFITH. Factory accounts. American school of correspondence, 1913.

HATHAWAY, CHARLES E. AND J. B. GRIFFITH. General expense and cost summaries. Chicago, American school of correspondence, 1909.

HAWKINS, LESLIE WHITTEN. Cost accounting—an explanation of principles and a guide to practice. (In Chase, W. A. *Auditing and cost accounting.* 1917. p. 386-470.)

HAWKINS, LESLIE WHITTEN. Cost accounts; an explanation of principles and a guide to practice. London, Gee & co. 1912. 124 p.

HEITMAN, HENRY. Course in the theory and practice of higher accounting, prepared for students of Eastman college. Poughkeepsie, Eastman college, 1910. 240 p.

HENRY, S. M. Where to charge factory expense. *Factory,* July 1911, p. 25-6, 49-52.

HERRICK, C. L. Combined payroll and cost sheet. *Business man's magazine,* Feb. 1912. p. 161-3.

HESS, HENRY. Manufacturing: costs and dividends. *Engineering magazine,* v. 26, p. 367.

HESS, HENRY. Manufacturing profits and losses. *Engineering magazine,* Sept. 1910, p. 892-8.

HESS, HENRY. Time saving and its relation to profits. *American machinery,* Dec. 16, 1897.

COST AND FACTORY ACCOUNTING—*(Continued)*

HILL, G. W. Must keep close tab on the business. *Electrical review and western electrician,* Feb. 24, 1917, p. 330-3.

HILL, G. W. Setting an intelligent selling price. *Electric review and western electrician,* Feb. 17, 1917, p. 288-9.

HILL, JAMES G. Various systems of computing the costs of manufacture. *New England cotton manufacturers' association, Transactions.* Oct. 1899, p. 132-8.

HILLER, AUGUST. Cost systematizing. *Journal of accountancy,* Dec. 1913, p. 435-9.

HOLLOWAY, G. E. Simple cost forms that help your business pay. *Building age,* Aug. 1919, p. 270-1.

How cost guides the way, 100%, v.11, No. 1, p. 54.

How shall I charge off that war equipment? *Factory,* Nov. 1919, p. 1034-6.

How to schedule accounting work, 100%, v. 10, no. 2, p. 60.

HOWARD, S. E. Interest, rent and normal return on capital investment in their relation to manufacturing costs. *American economic review,* Sept. 1920, p. 546-63.

HOWARD, T. W. Using material costs so they don't deceive. *Factory,* Oct. 15, 1920, p. 1217-8.

HUNTER, J. A. Standardization and net costings. *Textile world,* Jan. 18, 1919, p. 665.

HUNTER, JOEL. Manufacturing corporations. (In his *Thinking in figures.* c1916. p. 40-7).

HURLEY, EDWARD N. Accurate costs mean fair business. *Iron trade review,* June 21, 1917, p. 1354-5.

HURLEY, EDWARD N. Constructive movement for scientific cost acounting. *Electrical world,* Jan. 6, 1917, p. 17-8.

HURLEY, EDWARD N. Cost accounting the machinery of information. *Inland printer,* Feb. 1917, p. 661-2.

HURLEY, EDWARD N. Knowledge of costs as a basis for manufacturing advance. *Electrical world,* Jan. 1, 1916, p. 15-6.

HURLEY, EDWARD N. Trade association and business progress. *Metal work,* Jan. 12, 1917, p. 91-3.

HURLEY, EDWARD N. Trade associations and better business methods. *American fertilizer,* April 1, 1916, p. 21-3.

HUTCHINS, F. LINCOLN. Real problem in costs: correspondence. *Journal of accountancy,* April, Nov. 1906, p. 521-3; p. 48-53.

HUTCHINSON, E. B. Scope of a cost system. Paper, May 21, 1919, p. 32-5.

IGNATIUS, M. B. Relation of statistics and accounts in industrial management. *Industrial management,* Oct. 1918, p. 312-5.

INSTALLING a cost system. *Textile world,* July 1914, p. 401-3.

INTEREST charges and profit, the lack of agreement in determining manufacturing costs; chart showing cost distribution. *Iron age,* Aug. 24, 1911, p. 426-7.

INTERNATIONAL library of technology. v. 133. Scranton, Pa., International text book co.

Is the system of costing necessary for the effective control of industrial undertakings. *Accountant.* April 3, 1920, p. 405-8.

Is it in the cost system? 100%, Dec. 1917, p. 62.

Is your cost system scientific? *Engineering magazine* Aug. 1916, p. 747.

JACKSON, A. C., A. SMITH; H. R. TOWNE. Axioms concerning manufacturing costs. *Journal of the American society of mechanical engineers,* April 1913.

JENKINSON, MARK WEBSTER. Cost accounts for small manufacturers. London, Gee & co. 56p. *Accountant,* March 9, 16, April 27, 1907, p. 315-26, 351-9, 549-51.

JENKINSON, MARK WEBSTER. Costing in national factories. London 1918. *Iron and coal trades review,* Oct. 25, Nov. 8, 1918, p. 455-8 513-6.

JENKINSON, MARK WEBSTER. Costings. *Accountant,* Jan. 18, 1919, p. 44-6.

JENKINSON, MARK WEBSTER. Workers' interest in costing. *Accountant* March 8, 1919, p. 185-95. *Australasian accountant and secretary,* July, Aug. 1919, p. 19-23, 15, *Iron and coal trades review,* Jan. 31, 1919, p. 127-30.

JOHNSON, GEORGE. Balance sheet of a mining and manufacturing company. *Iron and coal trade reviews,* Sept. 1, 1899.

JOHNSON, GEORGE. Pitman's manufacturing bookkeeping and costs. London, Sir Isaac Pitman and sons, 1913. 122p.

JOHNSTON, J. G. Forms of bookkeeping for manufacturing businesses. (In his *Forms of account books,* p. 7-28.)

JONES, EDWARD D. Cost accounting. (In his *Administration of industrial enterprises.* 1917. p. 169-87.)

JONES, JAMES T. Record of gain or loss on output of manufacturing plants. *Business man's magazine,* Dec. 1907, p. 65-91.

JORDAN, JOHN P. and GOULD L. HARRIS. Prevailing types of cost systems. (In their *Cost accounting.* 1920. p. 327-43).

JOYCE, BRYAN POPE. Joyce system of cost keeping, designed for the use of contractors, architects and engineers. P. O. Box 640, Kansas city, B. P. Joyce, 1912. 29p.

JUDSON, CHARLES. Reconciling the cost accounts. *Business man's magazine,* Oct. 1911, p. 350-2.

KEATOR, S. P. Increasing production by frequent cost reports. *Industrial management,* Dec. 1919, p. 481-2.

KEEPING costs. *Engineering record,* Jan. 4, 1913, p. 3.

KENT, WILLIAM. Bookkeeping and cost accounting for factories. New York, John Wiley & sons, 1918. 261p.

KENT, WILLIAM. Making the cost department worth while. *Industrial engineering* Oct. 1914, p. 393-5.

KENT, WILLIAM. New method of determining factory costs. *Cassier's engineering monthly,* Dec. 1916. *Iron age,* Aug. 24, 1916, p. 392-4.

KERR, DAVID S. Cost accounting and its relation to the tariff question. *Canadian chartered accountant,* Jan. 1912, p. 135-6.

KESTER, ROY B. Factory costs. (In his *Accounting theory and practice.* 1918. v. 2. p. 49-59.)

KIMBALL, DEXTER SIMPSON. Cost finding. New York, Alexander Hamilton institute, c1918. 338p. (Modern business, v. 10.)

KIMBALL, DEXTER SIMPSON. Principles of cost keeping. (In his *Principles of industrial organization.* 1913. p. 110-38).

KIRK, R. H. Factory accounting system shown by diagram. *Business man's magazine,* May 1905, p. 969-71.

KLEIN, JOSEPH J. Cost accounts. (In his *Elements of accounting.* 1916. p. 291-321.)

KNOEPPEL, C. E. Cost reduction through cost comparison. *Engineering magazine,* March-May 1907, p. 918-28; 72-82, 239-50.

KNOEPPEL, C. E. Manufacturing costs. (In his *Installing efficiency methods.* 1917. p. 239-58.)

KNOEPPEL, C. E. Philosophy of costs. *Industrial management,* Sept. 1919, p. 179-83.

KNOEPPEL, F. J. Fundamentals of accounting for industrial waste. *Accountant,* Jan. 25, 1919, p. 65-8. *Australasian accountant and secretary,* June 1919, p. 20-3. *Journal of accountancy,* May 1918, p. 351-9,

COST AND FACTORY ACCOUNTING—*(Continued)*

KNOEPPEL, F. J. Industrial accounting. *Journal of accountancy,* June, Dec. 1916, p. 431-40, 16-27, 90-100, 177-86, 245-52, 353-60, 417-32.

KOLLER, W. B. Cost determining. *Iron age,* Oct. 10, 1907.

KONOPAK, L. T. Factory costs. *Journal of accountancy,* Nov. 1920, p. 329-37.

KREPS, J. B. Should the factory show a profit? *Journal of accountancy,* April 1909, p. 470-2.

LA SALLE extension university. Auditing and cost accounting, business administration. La Salle extension university, 1910. 516p.

LANE, H. M. Method of determining selling prices. American society of mechanical engineering, Dec. 1896.

LARBY, E. J. Profiteering in relation to cost accounting: a 20th century hoax, a treatise in non technical terms for you by an accountant specialist. 30 Paternoster Row, London, E. J. Larby, 1919.

LAUER, CONRAD N. Importance of cost-keeping to the manufacturer. *Annals of the American academy of political and social science,* Nov. 1903, p. 459-68.

LEAN, FRANCIS WILLIAM LE BLOUNT. Cost accounts. *Accountant,* March 16, April 20, Sept. 21, 1901, p. 331-45 483-7, 1015-20.

LEAN FRANCIS WILLIAM LE BLOUNT. Factory cost and departmental accounts. *Accountant,* May 1, 1920, p. 516-21.

LEEDS, E. P. Making sure of your profit. *System,* April 1915, p. 426-8.

LEWIS, ELIAS ST. ELMO. Efficient cost keeping; a study of the most efficient applications of cost keeping principles to certain types of management. Ed. 3. Detroit, Burroughs adding machine co. 1915. 256p.

LEWIS, ELIAS ST. ELMO. Efficient management. *American industries,* July 1914, p. 30-1.

LEWIS, J. SLATER. Commercial organisation of factories. London, 1896. 540p.

LIBBERT, M. S. Cost accounting. *Purdue agriculturist,* Nov. 1916, p. 30-1.

LISLE, GEORGE. Manufacturers' accounts, cost accounts. (In his *Accounting in theory and practice.* 1900. p. 252-77.)

LISLE, GEORGE AND W. A. MIDDLETON. Manufacturers' accounting. (In their *Accountkeeping in principle and practice.* 1911. p. 131-66.

LOGAN, JAMES. Importance of scientific accounting. *Journal of accountancy,* Aug. 1908, p. 276-9.

LOGARITHMS applied to cost accounts. *Accountant,* Jan. 9, 1897, p. 36-43.

LOGICAL manufacturing accounts. *Auditor,* 1905, p. 233.

LORD, W. S. Monthly reports that show you how you stand. *Factory,* Aug. 1918, p. 240-3.

LOWE, R. E. Installing a costing system. *Accounting and commerce,* Feb., March, 1917, p. 260-1, 269-72. *Accountant,* July 28, p. 76-80. *Incorporated accountants' journal,* July 1917, p. 215-8.

LUNT, H. JULIUS. Costing and factory organisation. London, Sir Isaac Pitman & sons, 1920, 124p. *Business organisation and management,* Feb.-Aug. 1920, p. 91-5, 60-4, 89-94, 184-91, 305-12, 419-24. ——. In Feb. No. under title: Cost accounts and factory organization.

LYNN, C. E. Finding costs of manufacture. *Iron trade review,* July 3, 1919, p. 23-5.

LYNN, GEORGE B. Bookkeeping in the miniature industries. *New York accountants' and bookkeepers' journal,* March 1904, p. 69-72.

MACATTAMMANY, A. B. Point in cost-finding. *American machinist,* May 29, 1920, p. 1117.

MCCABE, H. B. Work in progress record. *American machinist,* Sept. 22, 1904.

MCCLURE, JOHN. Counting the cost. *Business man's magazine,* Dec. 1910, p. 581-2.

MCCORMACK, H. S. Where do the pennies in your dollar go? *System,* Oct. 1918, p. 497-9.

MCCUNE, M. Cost system. *Metal industries,* July 1913, p. 299-300.

MCHENRY, WILLIAM E. Is your cost system scientific? *Engineering magazine,* Aug. 1916, p. 678-86.

MCHENRY, WILLIAM E. Logical factory costs. *Engineering magazine,* Feb. 1916, p. 733-41.

MCINTOSH, ROBERT J. Accounts for manufacturing companies. (In his *Reference book of accounts for manufacturing and mercantile companies.* Ed.2. c1914. p. 25-145).

MACK, J. Necessity of proper factory cost-accounting methods. *Inland printer,* Oct. 1918, p. 49-51. Condensed. *American industries,* Sept. 1918, p. 17-18.

MCKAY, CHARLES W. Value of manufacturing property. *Machinery,* Feb. 1918, p. 532-3.

MACKENZIE, COSSAR. Factory organisation and costing arrangements. (In Lisle, George. *Encyclopaedia of accounting.* v.2. p. 464-79).

MCKUNE, M. Factory cost accounting. *Metal industries,* n.s., July 1915, p. 286-7.

MACNEILLE, JOHN R. Manufacturing accounting and cost keeping. *Business world,* Nov. Dec. 1906, p. 952-94.

MAIN, FRANK WILBUR. Costs as a basis for prices. (In *Cost accounting addresses,* 1920. p. 5-9.

MAIN, F. W. Costs constitute the only fair basis for fixing prices. *Coal age,* May 27, 1920, p. 1095-6.

MAKING the cost system work smoothly. *Inland printer,* Dec. 1913, p. 420-1.

MAKING the time ticket a job history. *Factory,* April 1918, p. 674.

MANAGEMENT of retail workrooms. *Accountant,* May 12, 1900, p. 468-9.

MANN, JOHN. Cost records of factory accounting. (In Lisle, George. *Encyclopaedia of accounting.* v.2. p. 260-99).

MANN, JOHN. Notes on cost records: a neglected branch of accountancy. *Accountant,* Aug. 29, Sept. 5, 1891, p. 619-21, 631-7.

MANUFACTURERS' accounts. (In Lisle, George. *Encyclopaedia of accounting.* v.5. p. 1-5).

MANUFACTURING cost. Detroit, Business man's publishing co. 1907. 191p.

MANUFACTURING costs. *Canadian chartered accountant,* July 1914, p. 10-20, 45-57.

MARSH, ARTHUR RICHMOND. Income and excess profits taxes and the cost of production. *Economic world,* July 13, 1918.

MARWICK, JAMES. Cost accounts. *Engineering record,* Nov. 17, 1906.

MASON, J. K. How to study factory efficiency. *Engineering magazine,* July 1916, p. 542-7.

MASON, J. K. Synthetic costs. *Cassier's engineering monthly,* Jan. 1917. *Engineering magazine,* Oct. 1916, p. 63-6.

MASON, J. K. Work vs. cost. *Industrial management,* April 1917, p. 62-4.

MATHEWS, P. L. Making a cost profile. *Coal age,* Nov. 4, 1916, p. 751-2.

MAXWELL, F. CROFTON. Scientific presentation of costs. *Accounting and commerce,* Dec. 1919, Jan. 1920, p. 213-5, 235-42.

MENSCH, J. P. Cost accounting. *New York produce review,* Dec. 27, 1916, p. 358.

MILLAR, THOMAS JOHN. Management bookkeeping for the manufacturer, wholesaler and retailer. London, C. and E. Layton, 1910. 114p.

MILLENER, C. A. Cost account with numerous pro forma ruling and full explanations showing method of ascertaining cost on a factory where a variety of articles are made; ed. by R. F. Spence. Toronto, The Hunter Rose co. 1901. 60p.

COST AND FACTORY ACCOUNTING—*(Continued)*

MILLENER, C. A. Evolution of cost accounts. *Business,* July, Aug., Sept., Oct., Nov. 1895, p. 266-9, 302-4, 332-6, 361-2, 399-400.

MILLER, AUGUST. Cost systematizing. *Journal of accountancy,* Dec. 1913, p. 435-9.

MILLER, L. A. Simplicity and accuracy in cost work. *Engineering magazine,* May 1916, p. 256-9.

MILLER, W. M. S. Errors and difficulties in manufacturing costs. *Engineering magazine,* Feb. 1909, p. 825-32.

MILLS, JAMES COOKE. Cutting the cost of finding costs. *Business man's magazine,* Dec. 1911, Jan. 1912, p. 523-30, 74-80.

MILLS, JAMES COOKE. Where do the cost accounts go? *Business man's magazine,* Feb. 1912, p. 170-4.

MILLWORK cost information bureau; Chicago. Standard cost finding system. Chicago, Millwork cost information bureau, 1916.

MINER, GEORGE W. AND FAYETTE H. ELWELL. Revenue accounts and operating statement of a manufacturing business. (In his *Principles of bookkeeping, corporation and voucher accounting.* c1918. p. 441-76.)

MIXTER, G. W. Operating value of cost systems. *Iron age,* Oct. 26, 1916, p. 932-3.

MONTGOMERY, C. W. Cost accounting. *National stockman and farmer,* Feb. 22, 1919, p. 1161.

MORE about uniform accounting. *American cooperative journal,* Sept. 1916, p. 68.

MORRISON, W. F. Scientific costing; lecture. *Accounting and commerce,* Oct. 1920, p 155.

MORSE, P. Cost accounting and labor. *Forum,* July, 1919, p. 60-6.

MOWAT, D. M. Capital charges considered along with current expenses. *Institute of mining engineers, Transactions.* Jan. 1918.

MOXEY, EDWARD PRESTON. Principles of factory cost keeping. New York, The Ronald press co. 1918. 102 p.

MOZINGO, F. P. Essentials of cost accounting in business economy. *Business man's magazine,* Oct. 1910, p. 376-8.

MURRAY, C. E. Operating costs and economies. *Textile world,* June, 1914, p. 374-6.

MUTTON, F. E. How to get the accurate cost. *Accountant,* June 2, 1917, p. 529-30. *Canadian chartered accountant,* April, 1917, p. 299-301. *South African accountant,* Sept. 1917, p. 72-3.

NAU, CARL H. Accounting as a basis for and a measure of efficiency in business. *Journal of accountancy,* March, 1913, p. 143-56.

NECESSITY of rational cost keeping. *Engineering magazine,* April, 1916, p. 120-1.

NEITHERWAY, A. G. Accounting system of a small manufacturing plant. *New York accountants' and bookkeepers' journal,* Aug., Sept., Oct., 1903, p. 98-103, 118-21, 141-3.

NEVILLE, CHARLES. Necessity for cost accounting. Five typewritten pages.

NEVILLE, CHARLES. Uniform cost methods; an address before the Package club, April 12, 1915. 8 p.

NEW commerce division formed to assist various departments in cost accounting. *Official bulletin,* June 18, 1917, p. 8.

NICHOLS, WILLIAM G. Cost finding. Chicago, American school of correspondence, c1909. 43 p. (In *Cyclopedia of commerce, accountancy, business administration.* 1910. v. 8. p. 263-307.)

NICHOLSON, JEROME LEE. Accounting the fundamental of business success. *American fertilizer,* May 8, 1920, p. 68.

NICHOLSON, JEROME LEE. Cost accounting, theory and practice. New York, The Ronald press co. 1917. 341 p. (Ronald accounting series.)

NICHOLSON, JEROME LEE. Fundamental of business success. (In *Cost accounting, addresses.* 1920. p. 1-3.)

NICHOLSON, JEROME LEE. Factory organization and costs. New York, Kohl technical publishing co. 1909. 410 p.

NICHOLSON, JEROME LEE AND J. F. D. ROHRBACH. Cost accounting. New York, The Ronald press co. 1919. 576 p.

NICOL, ALFRED D. Cost accounts. *Accountants' magazine,* Feb.-March, 1920, p. 92-111, 169-83.)

NIXON, ALFRED AND J. H. STAGG. Manufacturing. (In their *Accounting and banking.* 1912. p. 193-217.)

NOLD, S. E. What should a cost system accomplish? *Foundry,* April 1912, p. 127-32.

NOLD, S. E. Why cost systems fail. *American foundrymen's association, Transactions.* 1912. p. 185-7.

NORRIS, E. Formula for dealers' costs. *Metal work,* May 22, 1914, p. 701-2.

NORTON, G. P. Factories. London, Hamilton, Adams and co. 1889.

O'BRIEN, J. Short cut to factory costs. *Factory,* Dec. 1919, p. 1308-10.

OLD problem again. *Hoard's digest,* Nov. 9, 1917, p. 528.

OLDENBERG, WILLIAM. Main office accounts with factory. *Business man's magazine,* May 1905, p. 978-9.

OPEN conferences on cost-finding between industries and government. *American gas engineering journal,* Jan. 18, 1919, p. 46-9. *American machinist,* Jan. 2, 1919, p. 39-41. *Domestic engineering,* Jan. 4, 1919, p. 63.

ORDE, E. L. Works organization, financial organization of factories. *Iron age,* Jan. 18, 1917, p. 192-4.

PAGANINI, P. S. Cost systems in small factories. *Electrical review and western electrician,* Feb. 7, 1914, p. 280-1.

PALMER, W. B. If he knew his costs. *System,* April 1916, p. 346-50.

PALMER, W. B. Simplified cost accounting for manufacturers. Annals of the American academy of political and social science, Sept. 1915, p. 165-73.

PALMER, W. K. Value of published costs. *Electric railway journal,* May 1, 1915, p. 845-6.

PARKER, GEORGE. Review and comparison of existing methods with special reference to the use of cards and files instead of books. *Accountant,* Sept. 6, 13, 1902, p. 886-96, 909-23.

PARKHURST, FREDERICK AUGUSTUS. Predetermination of true costs and relatively true selling prices. New York, John Wiley & sons, 1916, 96 p.

PARSONS, CARL COPELAND. Cost accounting records. (In his *Office organization and management.* 1918. p. 273-84.)

PASLEY, ROBERT S. Educating the executive to appreciate costs. *Journal of accountancy,* Sept. 1917, p. 207-12.

PATCH, D. Cost of cost-keeping cut out by study of office force. *Engineering record,* July 8, 1916, p. 58.

PATON, WILLIAM A. AND R. A. STEVENSON. Cost accounting. (In their *Principles of accounting.* 1918. p. 609-19.)

PATRICK, F. A. How I train men to spend my money. *System,* July 1918, p. 21-4.

PEDDER, STANLEY. Cost accounts: their advantages and their relation to business results. *Accountant,* April 29, 1905, p. 518-30, 727.

PERRIGO, OSCAR E. Cost system for large manufacturing plant. *Iron trade review,* Oct. 1, 1908.

PERRIGO, OSCAR E. General principles of cost accounting. *Iron trade review,* July 2, 1908.

COST AND FACTORY ACCOUNTING—*(Continued)*

PFLUG-FELDER, R. H. What should the selling price be? *Domestic engineering,* Dec. 13, 1913, p. 338-40.

PIEPKORN, J. A. Developing a cost-keeping system. *Electrical review,* May 25, 1918, p. 886.

PIERCE, C. E. Importance of accurate cost figures. *Metal work,* June 30, 1916, p. 890.

PINKERTON, P. W. Need for complete and accurate cost data. *Engineering and contracting,* Aug. 20, 1919, p. 230.

PITT, H. W. Influence of production costs on designing. *Accountant,* Dec. 18, 1920, p. 671-5.

PIXLEY, FRANCIS W. Construction of cost accounts. In his *Accountancy,* Ed. 2. p. 134-53.)

PLAN to simplify cost accounts of government contracts. *Commercial and financial chronicle,* June 16, 1917, p. 2408.

PLUMPTON, THOMAS. Manufacturing costs. *Accountant,* March 26, 1892, p. 267-75.

POLAKOV, W. N. Mastering power production; principles of essential cost and use of standard cost. *Industrial management,* Oct. 1918, p. 321-9.

POMEROY, LEWIS R. Application of scientific accounting to promote industrial efficiency. *Sibley journal of engineering,* June, 1911.

PORTER, H. F. Cost and overhead expense. *Metal work,* July 6, 1917, p. 10-11.

PORTER, H. F. Cost keeping the basis of prosperity. *Engineering magazine,* June, 1916, p. 325-32.

PORTER, H. F. Quotas of expense. *System,* Dec. 1914, p. 595-602.

PORTER, H. F. J. Cost accounts. *American machinist,* v. 30. No. 26.

PORTERS, R. J. Cost accounts. (In his *Pitman's dictionary of bookkeeping.* p. 292-311.)

POTTER, M. H. Arranging industrial cost factors. *Iron trade review,* Aug. 21, 1919, p. 508-10.

POTTER, M. H. Manufacturing cost systems. *Metal industries,* Aug. 1919, p. 366-8.

POTTER, M. H. Summarizing all cost factors. *Iron trade review,* Sept. 4, 1919, p. 630-1.

POWELL, P. R. Cost keeping in small factories. *Engineering magazine,* Oct. 1910, p. 31-7.

PRATT, EDMUND A. Simple form for cost analysis. *Journal of the American society of engineering and contracting,* Sept. 1911.

PREEN, HARVEY. Reorganization and costings. London, Simpkin, Marshall, Hamilton, Kent & co. 1913. 188 p.

PRINCIPLES of cost keeping. *Horseless age,* Sept. 23, 1914, p. 443.

PRIOR, F. S. Where costs end and profits begin. *Domestic engineering,* Sept. 27, 1913, p. 364-7.

PROBERT, EDWARD. Some notes on cost keeping. *Engineering and contracting,* June, 1915.

PROBERT, R. H. Manufacturing cost. *Iron trade review,* Jan. 3, 1907.

PRODUCING costs. (In *American business manual;* ed. by R. H. Montgomery, 1911, v. 2, p. 479-509.)

PUTNAM, E. T. Cost system that watches estimates and prices. *System,* June, 1916, p. 651-3.

PUTTING in a cost system efficiently. *Metal work,* Oct. 9, Nov. 6, 1914, p. 482-4, 607-8.

RAWLINSON, ERNEST BOWMAN. Some notes on cost accounts. *Incorporated accountants journal,* 1910-11, p. 264.

RECKITT, ERNEST. Some principles of cost accounting. *Journal of accountancy,* March 1909, p. 356-67.

REED, W. M. Charging costs to the right job. *System,* April 1913, p. 421-3.

REGULATING costs and profits. *Metal work,* Feb. 25, 1916, p. 280.

REIFSNEIDER, R. L. P. Group method of cost finding. *Cotton,* April 1920, p. 431-4.

RETAINING fee for high-priced workmen. *Industrial engineering,* Nov. 1913, p. 481.

RICH, HERBERT M. Cost system that controls costs. *American machinist,* v. 32, No. 23.

RIDER, JAMES. Cost accounts. *Incorporated accountants' journal,* 1903-4, p. 175, 179.

RIDGWAY, ARTHUR CLIFFORD. Cost accounting in principle and practice. London, Sir Isaac Pitman & sons. 110 p.

RIDGWAY, ARTHUR CLIFFORD. Cost accounts. *Accountant,* Dec. 6, 1919, p. 485-9.

ROBERTS, A. B. Design of a factory system. *Cleveland engineering journal,* Mar. 1911.

ROBERTSON, J. P. Need and value of accurate cost records. Washington (state) university college of forestry, *Forest club annual,* 1918, p. 36-8.

ROBERTSON, WILLIAM. Cost accounts. *Incorporated accountants' journal,* Feb. 1912, March, 1913, p. 133-4, 143-6.

ROBINSON, C. S. Sane selling policy with attention to costs. *Iron age,* May 28, 1914, p. 1364-5.

ROCKWELL, WILLIAM H. Cost system that runs itself. *Factory,* April, 1912, p. 284-5, 309-11.

ROGERS, W. S. Automatic cost distributing and accounting plan. *Iron and coal trades review,* Nov. 10, 1899.

ROGERS, W. S. Cost keeping and accounting. *Business,* Dec. 1898, p. 760-2. *New York railroad club, Proceedings,* Sept. 15, 1898, p. 4-27. Extracts. *Railroad gazette,* Nov. 4, 1898, p. 792.

ROGERS, W. S. Industrial problem. Keene, N. H., 1903. 32p.

ROSENBERGER, CHARLES GRANT. Time keeping and cost system. (Kingston?, N. Y.) c1911. 13 p.

ROSS, GEORGE EDWARD. Cost-keeping and construction accounting adapted to any work consisting of numerous items, departments or divisions on which detailed unit costs are desired. Salem, Oregon, G. E. Ross, c1917. 59 p. Same as Oregon state highway commission—*Manual for cost keeping and accounting.*

ROSS, GEORGE EDWARD. Cost keeping and construction accounting: adapted to any work consisting of numerous items, departments or divisions on which detailed unit costs are desired; all manner of construction enterprises come under this head, such as irrigation, highway, railroad, shipbuilding and municipal improvement: also adaptable to a large variety of manufacturing enterprises. Ed. 2. Salem, Oregon, Ross system co. c1919. 171 p. + forms.

ROWE, HENRY M. Manufacturing accounts: cost accounts. (In his *Bookkeeping and accountancy.* c1911. p. 200-57.)

RUNNELLS, JOHN S. AND J. HUSBAND. What a new system of management did for us. *System,* July 1916, p. 78-87.

RUSSELL, H. A. Cost estimates and estimated costs. *Industrial management,* April, 1918, p. 284-8.

RUTZ, W. A. New system computes factory costs. *Iron trade review,* April 17, 1919, p. 1022-3.

SALADE, ROBERT F. Ascertaining exact cost of manufacturing. *Business man's magazine,* June 1910, p. 566-7.

SALIERS, EARL A. Manufacturing accounting; practice. (In his *Accounting in theory and practice principles.* 1920. p. 251-72.)

COST AND FACTORY ACCOUNTING—*(Continued)*

SCHIPPER, J. E. Inadequate cost keeping retarding adjustment. *Automotive industries,* Mar. 13, 1919, p. 561-3.

SCHLINK, F. J. Expenditure chart for executives. *Industrial management,* Mar. 1918, p. 192.

SCHREIBER, GEORGE I. These records saved a year's rent. *System,* Sept. 1917, p. 340-1.

SCHULTZ, O. F. Necessity of detailed cost accounting to the individual manufacturer. (In *Cost accounting addresses.* 1920. p. 23-8.)

SCHUYLER, M. Profiteering and industrial efficiency. *Public,* July 20, 1918, p. 915-8.

SCIENTIFIC costing conference. *Incorporated accountants' journal,* July, 1919, p. 195-6.

SCIENTIFIC system of costing. *Australasian accountant and secretary,* July 1920, p. 216.

SCOVELL, CLINTON HOMER. Cost accounting and burden application. New York, D. Appleton & co. 1916. 328 p.

SCOVELL, CLINTON HOMER. Cost accounting practice, with special reference to machine hour rate. *Iron trade review,* April 9, 1914, p. 672-6. *Journal of accountancy,* Jan. 1914. p. 13-27.

SCOVELL, CLINTON H. Finding out about factory profits. *Industrial engineering,* June, 1914, p. 246-50.

SCOVELL, CHARLES HOMER. Necessity of rational cost keeping; abstract. *Engineering magazine,* April 1916, p. 120-1.

SCOVELL, CLINTON HOMER. Relation of the cost department to the factory organization. Boston, Clinton H. Scovell and co. 1916. 20 p.

SCOVELL, CLINTON HOMER. What does it cost? *Nation's business,* Sept. 1917, p. 23-5.

SEELEY, F. E. If the cost system does not produce more income than it does, it is incomplete and improper. *American gas engineering journal,* Oct. 18, 1919, p. 354-6.

SELLING and cost keeping ideas from Barberton, Ohio. *Concrete,* Feb. 1916, p. 67-9.

SELLS, ELIJAH W. Cost accounting; an address before the National association of agricultural implement and vehicle manufacturers at Chicago, 29th November, 1909; reprinted from the *Journal of accountancy,* Jan. 1910, 8 p. *Journal of accountancy,* Jan. 1910, p. 171-6.

SENSIBLE cost accounting. *Journal of accounting,* Sept. 1909, p. 384.

SEYMOUR, H. S. Manufacturing costs. *Business world,* May 1902, p. 218-20.

SHEASGREEN, EDWARD E. Profitable wage. What is it? The capitalizing of the human machine. Chicago, Standard cost finding service co. 1914. 156 p.

SHELDON, WALTER S. Uniform cost systems. *Rock products and building materials,* 1916, p. 14.

SHEPARD, GEORGE H. Cost finding. (In his *Application of efficiency principles.* 1917. p. 324-47.)

SHOWELL, ALFRED ERNEST. Cost accounts. *Commerce, accounts and finance,* Sept. 1902, p. 8-12. *Incorporated accountants' journal,* 1901-2, p. 59.

SIEMENS, A. Cost of production. *Engineering magazine,* Jan. 1905, p. 663-5.

SILVESTER, R. F. Cost accounts. *Incorporated accountants' journal,* Oct. 1920, p. 14-8.

SIMPLE system for procuring cost data; gives details of the routine used by the National tool co. *Iron age,* Mar. 27, 1913, p. 757-9.

SIZER, R. W. E. One card for costs. *System,* June 1915, p. 653-4.

SIZER, R. W. E. Saving time in factory office routine. *Factory,* April 1918, p. 641.

SMART, ALLEN R. Accountant as adviser to the manufacturer. *Journal of accountancy,* Feb. 1906, p. 277-282.

SMITH, WILLIAM A. Checking the factory costs. *Engineering and industrial management,* Dec. 18, 1919, p. 786-7.

SOME observations on costing. *Australasian accountant and secretary,* Nov. 1920, p. 343.

SOME principles of accounting affecting cost accounts. *Accountant,* April 18, 1914, p. 563-82.

SOMETHING on the cost of doing business. *Metal worker, plumber and steam fitter,* Sept. 26, 1919, p. 364-7.

SOULE, GEORGE. Cost or factory bookkeeping. (In his *New science and practice of accounts.* 1903. p. 672-75.)

SPENCER, HENRY. Commercial organization of engineering factories. New York, Spon & Chamberlain, 1907.

SPICER, ERNEST EVAN AND ERNEST C. PEGLER. Cost accounts. (In their *Bookkeping and accounts.* 1914. p. 266-94.)

SPIEGEL, J. Importance of cost finding. *Accountant,* Jan. 17, 1920, p. 76-7.

SPIRE, WALTER J. Factory stock and cost keeping system. *School of mines,* April, 1909.

STANDARD cost calculation. *Textile world,* May 26, 1917, p. 3009.

STANDARD cost methods the first step toward price regulation. *American machinist,* Oct. 4, 1917, p. 605-6.

STANDARD cost system for manufacturers. *Engineering review,* Dec. 1916.

STANSBURY, GEORGE T. Simple system of cost accounting. *Business man's magazine,* July, 1908, p. 53-8.

STARKER, C. W. Analyzing manufacturing costs to increase profits. *Industrial management,* Aug. 1917, p. 659-68.

STARKER, C. W. How to find and use barometric costs. *Industrial management,* Aug. 1918, p. 137-9.

STERN, E. Analyzing every-day cost records. *Metal work,* Jan. 5, 1917, p. 42-4.

STERN, E. Do you estimate or guess in bidding? *Metal work,* Jan. 1, 1915, p. 44-5.

STERRETT, JOSEPH E. Cost accounts. *Accountant,* June 25, Aug. 27, Sept. 3, 1904, p. 835-9, 213-6, 229-30.

STEVENS, D. R. Getting figures on costs before they're cold. *Factory,* March, 1918, p. 427-8.

STILSON, C. H. Machine grouping and factory layout as affecting cost data. *Cassier's magazine,* Jan. 1909, p. 380-3.

STRACHAN, W. Cost accounts; the key to economy in manufacture. London, Stevens and Haynes, 1903. 102p.

STURGESS, JOHN. Simple cost system for complex situations. *Engineering magazine,* March, 1909, p. 940-8.

SUTER, J. PAUL. Some reflections on cost accounting. *Journal of accountancy,* Aug. 1919, p. 95-103.

SYSTEM for the business manager. *Business man's magazine,* March, 1907, p. 104-14.

SYSTEM of cost accounts. *Business,* Jan., July, 1892, p. 5-8, 138.

TAPPING, T. Principles of the cost book system practically considered. London, Shaw & sons, 1854.

TAYLOR, ELLSWORTH MILES. Costing as a sign post to efficiency. *Business organization and management,* Oct. 1919, p. 66-9.

TAYLOR, ELLSWORTH MILES. Practical costing methods. *Accountant,* June 21, 1919, p. 529-34.

THAT cost department! Is it prepared for government work? *100%,* Nov. 1917, p. 70.

COST AND FACTORY ACCOUNTING—*(Continued)*

THOMPSON, CLARENCE BERTRAND. How to find factory costs. Chicago, A. W. Shaw co. c1916. 191p.

THOMPSON, CLARENCE BERTRAND. Taking factory costs apart. *System,* Feb. 1913, p. 131-7.

TIMKEN, FRANK HERMANN. General factory accounting. Chicago, Trade periodical co. 1915. 171p.

TOD, FREDERICK. Cost accounts. *Accountants' magazine,* Aug. 1905, p. 439-46.

TOWLER, K. F. Cost accounting. *Stone and Webster's public service journal,* Aug. 1913.

TOWNE, HENRY R. Axioms concerning manufacturing costs. *Journal of the American society of mechanical engineers,* Dec. 1912, p. 1945-57.

TURNING time cards into costs. *Factory,* Nov. 1919, p. 1048-50.

UNCKLESS, LESLIE. How to find manufacturing costs and selling costs. Detroit. Modern methods publishing, 1909. 90 p.

UNIT costs for day before obtained on this job by 8:30 A. M. *Engineering record,* June 19, 1915, p. 785-6.

UNITED STATES. BUREAU OF FOREIGN AND DOMESTIC COMMERCE. Cost finding and accounting conditions. Washington, Government printing office, 1916. p. 219-33. (Miscellaneous series 34.)

UNITED STATES. CHAMBER OF COMMERCE. Fabricated production department. What a cost system should do for you. Washington, Chamber of commerce of the United States, 1920. 7p.

UNITED STATES. DEPARTMENT OF COMMERCE. Uniform contracts and cost accounting definitions and methods; recommendations by Interdepartmental conference consisting of delegates from the departments of war, navy and commerce, the Federal trade commission and the Council of national defense. Washington, Government printing office, 1917. 45p.

UNITED STATES. Federal trade commission. Fundamentals of a cost system for manufacturers. Washington, Government printing office, 1916. 31 p. *Accountant,* April 28, 1917, p. 411-21. *American industries,* Sept. 1916, p. 26-7.

UPTON, A. S. Cost accounts. *South African accountants' journal,* v. 2, p. 40.

VALUE of cost keeping. *Power,* June 10, 1913, p. 827-8.

VAN SCHAICK, B. L. Accounting. *Industrial management,* Dec., 1918, p. 502.

VANCE, F. O. Factory production cost. *Metal industries,* Feb. 1918, p. 77-8.

VEDDER, H. C. M. Cost accounting; an exposition of its theories and principles. *Accountant,* Nov. 11, 1905, p. 545-51.

VINCENT, JOHN P. Cost accountancy and profit figuring; presenting the art and principles of cost figuring from all angles, coupled with practical profit sharing and disposition. Cincinnati, Ohio, John P. Vincent, c1919. 68 p. + forms.

WALTON, SEYMOUR. Averaging costs. *Journal of accountancy,* July 1915, p. 67-70.

WAR contracts and cost accounting. *Canadian chartered accountant,* April 1918, p. 278-88. *Journal of accountancy,* Nov. 1917, p. 373-85.

WATSON, JOHN. How to install a cost system. *Factory,* Sept.-Nov. 1911, p. 158-9, 172-5, 246, 266-9, 325-6.

WATTS, CHARLES J. Cost of production. Muskegon, Mich., Shaw-Walker co. c1902. 64p.

WEATHERALL, H. Engine costs. *Iron and coal trades review,* Feb. 14, 1908.

WEBNER, FRANK ERASTUS. Costs of power and local transport. Chicago, La Salle university, 1917. 27p.

WEBNER, FRANK ERASTUS. Expense: manufacturing and commercial. *Iron trade review,* April 4, 1907.

WEBNER, FRANK ERASTUS. Factory accounting. Chicago, La Salle university, 1917. 345p.

WEBNER, FRANK ERASTUS. Factory costs: a work of reference for cost accountants and factory managers. New York, The Ronald press. 1911. 611p.

WEBNER, FRANK ERASTUS. Obtaining actual knowledge of the cost of production. *Engineering magazine,* May-Oct., 1908, p. 251-6, 345-8, 591-4, 748-51, 837-42; 76-80.

WEBNER, FRANK ERASTUS. Perfect cost system. *Iron trade review,* Sept. 5, 1907.

WEBNER, FRANK ERASTUS. Tool for cutting down costs. *Iron trade review,* July 5, 1906.

WEBNER, FRANK ERASTUS. Treatise on cost finding. *Industrial engineering,* May, 1912 p. 357-62.

WEBNER, FRANK ERASTUS. What constitutes cost of production. *Iron trade review,* Aug. 1, 1907.

WELLS, F. A. Cost keeping under the cost plus fixed fee contracts. *Engineering and contracting,* Oct. 15, 1919, p. 447-9. *Concrete,* Dec. 1919, p. 244-7. *Architect and building,* Jan. 1920, p. 3-6.

WESTFALL, H. D. Study costs first and make prices afterward. *Iron age,* May 28, 1914, p. 1363-4.

WETHERED, WILLIAM. Compound division ready reckoner, for use in making out cost sheets. Ed. 2, Bristol, 1886

WHAT kind of a cost system do you need? *Metal work* Jan 11, 1918, p 78-9,

WHEELER, SCHUYLER SKAATS. New importance of cost keeping read at the first meeting of the Efficiency society, held in New York city March 18 and 19, 1912. 7p.

WHERE do the pennies in your dollar go? *American gas engineering journal,* Oct. 12, 1918, p. 343-6. *System,* Oct. 1918, p. 493.

WHITE, EDMUND DAVID. Books and accounts of manufacturing companies and their audit. *Accountant,* Jan. 10, 17, 1885.

WHITE, LEE HEYER. Duties of a factory cost accountant. *Incorporated accountants' journal,* Oct. 1919, p. 17-9. *Journal of accountancy,* Sept. 1919, p. 190-6.

WHITEHEAD, H. Necessity of maintaining a cost system. *Domestic engineering,* April 13, 1918, p. 54.

WHITEHILL, ROBERT. Cost and production accounts and their uses for the purposes of an audit. *Accountant,* Dec. 15, 1894, p. 1097-1113.

WHITEHORN, W. J. Costing by machinery. 15 Church street, Dorking R. Fleming, 1916.

WHITFIELD, P. E. What to-day's work cost. *System,* July, 1913, p. 80-2.

WIBBER, WILLIAM O. Reducing the costs of engine building by efficiency methods. *Engineering magazine,* Oct. 1910, p. 86-90.

WILDMAN, JOHN R. Cost accounting. *Journal of accountancy,* Nov. 1910-April 1911, p. 1-9, 119-26, 186-94, 267-76, 346-56, 422-38.

WILDMAN, JOHN R. Cost accounting problem. New York, Accountancy publishing co. 1910.

WILDMAN, JOHN RAYMOND. Principles of cost accounting. New York, New York university press co. 1914. 96p.

WILLIAMS, O. W. Fitting the cost department into the plant. *Factory,* July 15, 1920, p. 224-6.

WILLIAMSON, J. GILMOUR. Counting house and factory organization; a practical manual of modern methods applied to the counting house and factory. London, Sir Isaac Pitman and sons, 1909, 163p.

COST AND FACTORY ACCOUNTING—*(Continued)*

WINDER, A. Higher costings. *Cassier's magazine,* Oct. 1907, p. 517-24.

WOLSELEY, FRANCIS V. Cost accounts of primary products. *Public accountant,* 1906-7, p. 67.

WOODBRIDGE, C. K. Keeping records of factory work. *System,* Nov. 1905.

WOODS, CLINTON EDGAR. Accounting of expenses and costs. (In his Organizing a factory. 1905. p. 61-9.)

WOODS, CLINTON EDGAR. Organizing a factory. Chicago, A. W. Shaw co. 1913. 190p. (Business man's library, v.6.)

WOODS, CLINTON EDGAR. Practical cost accounting for accountant students. 2 v. New York, Universal business institute, 1908.

WOODS, CLINTON EDGAR. Reports on industrial organizations systematization and accounting, 3 v. New York, Woods publishing co. 1909.

WOODS, CLINTON EDGAR. Uniform accounting methods for industrials. New York, The Ronald press, 1917. 484p.

WORCESTER, WILLIAM F. Appraising and cost finding. *Concrete age,* April 1919, p. 14-6.

WRIGHT, WALTER C. Depreciation, interest and manufacturing cost. *Journal of accountancy,* Nov. 1915, p. 361-4.

WYETT, A. E. Card check cost system. *Accountant,* Nov. 8, 1919, p. 399-400. *Australasian accountant and secretary,* July 1919, p. 11-2.

ZINN, R. H. Necessity of knowing manufacturing costs. *American industries,* Sept. 1919, p. 20-1.

Apportionment.

See Cost and factory accounting—Distribution.

Burden.

See Cost and factory accounting—Overhead.

Departmental.

DISTRIBUTING factory operating costs—proportioning department expenses and charges in Cincinnati planer company's works. *Iron age,* June 15, 1911, p. 1479-80.

LEAN, F. W. LEBLOUNT. Factory cost and department accounts. *Accountant,* May 1, 1920, p. 516-21.

LUNT, H. JULIUS. Departmental cost keeping for small businesses. *Accountant,* July 6, 13, 20, 1918, p. 3-6, 19-21, 35-7. *South African accountant,* Sept. 1918, p. 228-30.

SIZER, R. W. E. Simple way to handle departmental expenses. *Factory,* Aug. 1917, p. 196-7.

Distribution.

ANALYSIS of cost records. *Power plant engineering,* Jan. 1, 1920, p. 47-9.

BAILLET, HENRY F. Overhead expense and percentage methods; a lecture on the cost of doing business, explaining how to find it and what to do with it when found, with practical examples of its use taken from actual business experience. New York, David Williams co. 1915. 128p.

BENTLEY, H. C. Problem in the distribution of expense burden. *Journal of accountancy,* July, Sept. 1913, p. 25-59, 175-209.

BUNNELL, S. H. Distributing the works expense burden—how a factory may be divided by imaginary lines into productive units each to earn its interest and other charges. *Iron age,* Jan. 18, 1912, p. 200-1.

BUNNELL, S. H. Expense burden: its incidence and distribution. *Iron trade review,* Mar. 14, 1912, p. 605-10. *Journal of the American society of mechanical engineers,* Dec. 1911.

BUNNELL, S. H. Making machines earn thei living and correct distribution of costs. *Iro age,* July 27, 1911, p. 194-5.

BUNNELL, S. H. Recent advances in expens distribution. *Iron age,* May 7, 1914, p. 113 8. *Metal work,* June 12, 1914, p. 795-7.

BURROUGHS, A. M. Apportioning indirect pro duction expense. *Metal work,* Feb. 19-2 1915, p. 284-6, 316-8.

CHURCH, ALEXANDER HAMILTON. Distribut ing expense burden the analysis based upo the capacity to produce not upon the cos of production. *Iron age,* June 1, 1911, p 1325-6.

CHURCH, ALEXANDER HAMILTON. Distributio of factory expense. *Engineering magazin* v. 21, p. 725-904.

CHURCH, ALEXANDER HAMILTON. Distributio of the expense burden. *American machinist* May 25, 1911.

CHURCH, ALEXANDER HAMILTON. Proper dis tribution of expense burden. New York *Engineering magazine,* 1908. 144p. (Work management library).

CHURCH, ALEXANDER HAMILTON. Proper dis tribution of the factory expense burden. *En gineering magazine,* July-Dec. 1901, p. 508 17, 725-34, 904-12; 31-40, 231-40, 367-76.

DISTRIBUTING factory operating costs propor tioning department expenses and charges i Cincinnati planer company's works. *Iro age,* June 15, 1911, p. 1479-80.

DISTRIBUTING general factory expense. 100% v.11, No. 1, p. 64.

ELWELL, F. H. How to find costs by prope distribution of overhead expense. *Paper* May 25, 1920, p. 13-5.

EMERSON, HARRINGTON. Percentage method o determining production costs. *Foundry* Oct. 1904.

EVANS, HOLDEN A. Distribution of indirec costs. *American machinist,* Dec. 22, 191 p. 1158-62.

FALCONER, KENNETH. Distribution of factor expense. *Business man's magazine,* Fel 1911, p. 192-5.

FICKER, NICHOLAS THIEL. Distributing ove head expense. *Engineering magazine,* Jun 1915-Jan. 1916, p. 321-6, 553-9, 690-7, 86 71, 58-64, 254-61, 390-400, 532-9.

FICKER, NICHOLAS THIEL. Manufacturing e pense distribution. *Engineering magazin* June 1915-Jan. 1916, p. 321-6, 553-9, 690- 862-72, 58-64, 254-61, 390-400, 532-9.

FIGURING cost on labor percentage basi *Metal work,* Jan. 1, 1915, p. 12-3.

GILLETTE, H. P. Rational theory of proratin joint or indirect costs. *Engineering an contracting,* Nov. 29, 1916, p. 470-2.

GORMULLY, A. R. Percentage versus tool-rat plans. *Business man's magazine.* Oct. 190 p. 692-4.

GRAY, C. C. Machine hour rates. *Machinis* April 1917, p. 678.

HATHAWAY, C. E. Distribution of manufa turing expense. *Business man's magazin* May 1905, p. 927-31.

KEELY, R. R. Overhead expense distribution with discussion. *Journal of the America society of mechanical engineers,* June 191 p. 983-96. *Industrial engineering,* Jul 1913, p. 301-4. *Iron trade review,* Aug. 2 1913, p. 337-8. Condensed. *Iron age,* Au 7, 1913, p. 298-9.

OLDENBURG, W. Standard and actual cost a justments. *Business man's magazine,* Marc 1905, p. 526-7.

OVERHEAD expense—how it should be equitabl apportioned. *Iron age,* Nov. 30, 1911, 1190-1.

PERRIGO, OSCA8 E. Opportioning overhea charges to flat cost. *Iron trade reviev* Sept. 3, 1908.

POTTER, M. H. Classifying indirect expense *Iron trade* review, Aug. 7, 1919, p. 361-2.

COST AND FACTORY ACCOUNTING—DISTRIBUTION—*(Continued)*

RANSON, C. A. System of cost keeping—how a manufacturer keeps tab on the cost of material and labor and exactly apportions overhead expense in a medium sized plant. *System,* Feb. 1912, p. 212-15.

ROGERS, W. S. Automatic cost distributing and accounting plan. *Iron and coal trades review,* Nov. 10, 1899.

SCOVELL, CLINTON HOMER. Cost accounting practice, with special reference to machine hour rate. *Iron trade review,* April 9, 1914, p. 672-6. *Journal of accountancy,* Jan. 1914, p. 13-27.

SEIDMAN, FRANK E. Overhead distribution for cost-plus contracts. *Accountant,* Nov. 23, 1918, p. 283-7. *Journal of accountancy,* March 1918, p. 161-75.

SHANNAHAN, J. H. K. and F. G. REISL. Time keeping and distribution of cost systems. *Business man's magazine,* April 1908, p. 347-9.

SMITH, G. Distribution of indirect costs by the machine hour method. *Engineering magazine,* June 1909, p. 384-94.

SUCCESSFUL way of distributing maintenance expense. 100%, v.10, No. 5, p. 62.

URIE, JOHN. On cost and its apportionment. *Accountant,* Jan. 11, 1902, p. 50-3.

VANCE, F. O. Percentage versus time method of applying overhead charges. *Metal industries,* Dec. 1915, p. 504-5.

WALTON, SEYMOUR. Averaging overhead expense. *Journal of accountancy,* July 1914, p. 72-9.

WALTON, SEYMOUR. Distribution of overhead. *Journal of accountancy,* Jan. 1920, p. 77-8.

WALTON, SEYMOUR. Vouchers: distribution of expenses. *Journal of accountancy,* Nov. 1918, p. 395-6.

WEBNER, F. E. Expense: man hour distribution. *Iron trade review,* June 13, 1907.

WEBNER, F. E. Machine hour. *Industrial engineering,* April 1909.

WILLIAMS, GEORGE J. One way to absorb expense. *Business man's magazine,* Sept. 1911, p. 233-4.

WRAY, G. E. Proper distribution of machine cost. *Business man's magazine,* July 1909, p. 80-3.

Elements.

See also Accounting; names of various elements of costs, e.g. Materials.

CHASE, WILLIAM ARTHUR. Cost units. *American economic association, Papers and proceedings,* p. 136-44.

CHASE, WILLIAM ARTHUR. Unit costs. (In his *Auditing and cost accounting.* 1917. p. 376-85).

CHASE, WILLIAM ARTHUR. Unit costs. *Accountant,* July 1, 1911, p. 20-4.

EVANS, HOLDEN A. Various elements of cost. *American machinist,* v. 33, no. 49.

HUDDLE, W. J. Analysis of elements of cost of a complete plant unit. *Engineering and contracting,* Aug. 25, 1915, p. 139-40.

Multiple.

GARRY, HENRY STANLEY. Multiple cost accounts. London, Gee & co. 1906. 97p. (Accountants' library, v. 42).

Overhead.

See also Cost and factory accounting—Distribution.

ABENDROTH, HARRY G. Overhead charges in valuation; a discussion of the elements that must be considered in the appraisal of public utilities; percentages as worked out in the experience of the Milwaukee electric railway and light co. *Aera,* Nov. 1914, p. 354. *Electric railway journal,* June 27, 1914, p. 1434-7.

APPLICATION of overhead expense. *Metal work,* April 14, 1916, p. 511.

ARE your finances sometimes short? *Metal work,* Nov. 30, 1917, p. 653.

ARMSTRONG, N. B. Method of raising overhead expenses. *Metal work,* Aug. 11, 1916, p. 179-80.

BAILLET, HENRY F. Overhead expense and percentage methods; a lecture on the cost of doing business, explaining how to find it and what to do with it when found, with practical examples of its use taken from actual business experience. New York, David Williams co. 1915. 128p.

BAILLET, HENRY F. Overhead expense from a new angle. *Metal work,* March 29, 1918, p. 423-4.

BASSETT, WILLIAM R. Handling factory costs. *Factory,* Jan. 1919, p. 138.

BREWER, A. F. Overhead charges as applied to appraisal reports. *Industrial management,* Sept. 1917, p. 861-5.

BUNNELL, S. H. Expense burden: its incidence and distribution. *Journal of the American society of mechanical engineers,* Dec. 1911. *Iron trade review,* March 14, 1912, p. 605-10.

CLAUTICE, G. J. Overhead expense. *Metal work,* May 11, 1917, p. 621-2.

COLVIN, F. H. Cost of supervision and overhead. *American machinist,* June 26, 1919, p. 1221-5.

CORRECT method of figuring overhead expense. *Metal work,* Dec. 10, 1915, p. 733-4.

DEACON, THOMAS R. Overhead and general costs in manufacturing. *Journal of the Engineering institute of Canada,* July 1919, p. 505-6.

DEFINITION of cost, unit cost, direct and indirect cost and overhead cost. *Engineering and contracting,* Feb. 28, 1917, p. 196-7.

EDWARDS, AUGUSTUS. Principles of manufacturing on cost or indirect expenses. *Accountant,* April 12, 1919, p. 297-305.

EVANS, HOLDEN A. Overhead charges and shop output. *American machinist,* July 28, 1910, p. 165-7.

FALLACY of the 30 per cent profit. *Metal work,* Aug. 29, 1919, p. 257-8.

FIGURING overhead on productive labor. *Metal work,* July, 21, 1916, p. 80.

FISH, E. H. What constitutes overhead. *Engineering magazine,* July 1915, p. 488-97.

FURNACE man and the deficiency item. *Metal work,* July, 31, 1914, p. 142.

GILLETTE, H. P. Appraisal of overhead costs. *Electrical world,* July 3, 1915, p. 41-2. *Engineering and contracting,* July 7, 1915, p. 14-18, 1.

GOODWIN, W. L. Putting overhead on a scientific basis. *Electrical review,* Dec. 7, 1918, p. 895-6.

HENRY, B. F. New points in overhead expense. *Metal work,* Nov. 10, 1916, p. 594-5.

HILL, G. W. Cost of doing business. *Domestic engineering,* June 12, 1915, p. 306-7.

INCLUDE overhead expense in wage charge. *Metal work,* Aug. 13, 1920, p. 214.

ITEMS to be considered in figuring overhead expense. *Heating and ventilating magazine,* Sept. 1916, p. 45-6.

JUDD, HAROLD G. Fixed and fluctuating oncost. *Accountants' magazine,* March 1914, p. 134-46.

JUDD, HAROLD G. Some notes on oncost: a troublesome factor in costing. *Accountants' magazine,* Nov. 1911, p. 470-87.

KEALY, P. J. Overhead charges in valuation work. *Electric railway journal,* Oct. 14, 1916, p. 762-7. Excerpt. *Engineering and contracting,* Nov. 15, 1916, p. 432.

KEATOR, S. P. Handling overhead—a plan that avoids red tape. *Factory,* May 1, 1920, p. 1343-6.

COST AND FACTORY ACCOUNTING—OVERHEAD—*(Continued)*

KEEPING track of the overhead expense. *Metal work*, Nov. 2, 1917, p. 539-40.
McGOWAN, A. E. Machine and its overhead. *Inland printer*, April 1918, p. 43-6.
MANN, JOHN. Oncost or expenses. (In Lisle, George. *Encyclopaedia of accounting*. v.5. p. 199).
MANUFACTURING burden obtained monthly; system of the Gilbert and Barker co., Springfield, Mass. *Iron age*, Feb. 6, 1913, p. 356-9.
MELUM, E. E. Talk on overhead expense and peanuts. *Domestic engineering*, Jan. 1, 1916, p. 9-11.
METZLER, F. Calculating operating expense. *American machinist*, July 26, 1917, p. 160.
MILLS, JAMES COOKE. Treating burden in a scientific way. *Business man's magazine*, April 1912, p. 339-43.
NORRIS, E. Formula for dealers' costs. *Metal work*, May 22, 1914, p. 701-2.
NORWOOD, G. E. Pocket freight line. *Business man's magazine*, July 1908, p. 75-6.
ONE way to account for non-productive labor. *Factory*, Jan. 1920, p. 66-7.
OVERHEAD charges to be considered in making up a bid. *Concrete*, April 1916, p. 153.
OVERHEAD expense articles commented upon. *Domestic engineering*, May 16, 1914, p. 196-7.
PAINE, F. B. H. Preliminary and indirect costs. *Stone and Webster's journal*, Sept. 1916. *Telephone engineer*, Dec. 1916.
PERRIGO, OSCAR E. Determining the overhead burden. *Business man's magazine*, Jan. 1909, p. 69-74.
PIEPKORN, JOHN A. Figuring overhead expenses. *Electrical review*, June 15, 1918, p. 1007.
PORTER, H. F. Cost and overhead expense. *Metal work*, July 6, 1917, p. 10-11.
POTTER, M. H. Fixing indirect production charges. *Iron trade review*, May 1, 1919, p. 1148-9.
QUESTION of overhead expense. *Domestic engineering*, June 7, 1919, p. 429-30.
SCOVELL, WELLINGTON AND COMPANY. Burden application and measuring the loss from curtailed production. Boston, Scovell, Wellington and company, 1916. 14p.
SENIOR, H. Cost of supervision and overhead. *American machinist*, Aug. 21, 1919, p. 363-4.
STANWOOD, JAMES B. Natural increase in the ratio of burden to labor. *Wood craft*, May 1911.
STANWOOD, JAMES B. Ratio of burden to labor. Its natural increase in modern manufacturing processes. *Iron age*, April 20, 1911, p. 965-6.
STERN, E. Analyzing every-day cost records. *Metal work*, Jan. 5, 1917, p. 42-4.
THORPE, J. C. What overhead is and how to figure it. *Horseless age*, May 15, 1917, p. 26-7.
TINGLEY, R. H. Overhead charges in valuation. *Railway age*, June 11, 1915, p. 1247-8.
To prevent leaks in overhead costs—the Bullard machine tool company's system of constant vigilance which has decreased the burden materially . *Iron age*, Nov. 23, 1911, p. 1139.
URIE, JOHN. Oncost and its apportionment. *Accountant*, Jan. 11, 1902, p. 50-3.
WALTON, SEYMOUR. Overhead applicable to work in process. *Journal of accountancy*, Jan. 1917, p. 72-4.
WALTON, SEYMOUR. Supplementary overhead. *Journal of accountancy*, Jan. 1917, p. 74-5.
WELLS, F. A. Protection of owners on cost—plus contracts. *Canadian engineer*, Sept. 25, 1919, p. 323-6.

Process.

GARRY, HENRY STANLEY. Process cost accounts. London, Gee & co. 1908. 152p. (Accountants' library, v. 49).
KEEPING costs on work in process. *Factory*, July 1919, p. 74.
THEORY of factory accounting; as applied to a continuous process factory. *Business man's magazine*, April 1909, p. 371-6.

Single.

CUNLIFFE, N. Development of a unit cost system. *Journal of the Association of engineering societies*, Aug. 1914, p. 74-85. *Engineering and contracting*, Oct. 21, 1914, p. 374-6. Discusion. *Journal of the Association of engineering societies*, Aug-Sept. 1914, p. 85-101, 165-70.
ESTES, L. V. Unit cost accounting for control; a system for the industrial executive. *Industrial management*, Nov. 1919, p. 359-63.
ESTES, L. V. Work unit in cost analysis units of product per operator per hour. *Engineering and contracting*, April 21, 1920, p. 465.
MITCHELL, GEORGE ADAM. Single cost accounts. London, Gee & co. 1907. 160p. (Accountants' library, v. 47).
SCIENCE of management—the law of unit cost reports. *Engineering and contracting*, April 17, 1912, p. 428-9.
SLOAN, W. F. Elements to be considered in preparing unit costs. *Telephone*, June 12, 1915.
UNIT costs of work in progress. *Proceedings of the American society of civil engineers*, Aug. 1902.

Terminal

HALLIDAY, H. L. Terminal cost accounts. *Accounting and commerce*, Oct. 1918, p. 156-8.
NISBET, ANDREW GOW. Terminal cost accounts. London, Gee & co. 1906. 53p. (Accountants' library, v. 46).

COST and formula system for the soap manufacturer. *Business man's magazine*, Feb. 1908, p. 218-9.

COST and methods of clearing land in the Lake States. Thompson, Harry and Earl D. Straight. 1914.

COST and selling price for merchant tailors. Beeman, C. V.

COST and the advantages of using electrically melted ferromanganese. *Metallurgical and chemical engineering*, May 1914, p. 295-6. *Scientific American supplement*, July 4, 1914, p. 11.

COST and use of chemicals at purification plant of St. Louis, Mo. *Engineering and contracting*, October 11, 1916, p. 318-19.

COST and value of road materials. *Municipal engineering*, Sept. 1913, p. 223.

COST ASSOCIATION OS THE PAPER INDUSTRY.

Bulletin to members. 18 East 41st St., New York city.

COST association of the paper industry, 5th convention, New York. *Paper*, Oct. 6, 1920, p. 9-11.

COST book companies. *Accountant*, July 25, Aug. 29, Nov. 7, 1885.

COST book companies. McIlraith, J. R.

COST-book system. *Accountant*, June 22, 1895, p. 547-8.

COST comparison of electric and compressed air hoisting for deep mine shafts. *Engineering and contracting*, Jan. 3, 1912, p. 7-11.

COST data. *Railway age gazette,* June 16, 1911. p. 1416.

COST data for horse-drawn and electric trucks. *Engineering record,* April 19, 1913, p. 429-30.

COST data for the section foreman. *Railway age gazette,* Nov. 17, 1911, p. 1002-3.

COST data on installation for lighting city streets, Lincoln, Nebraska. *Electrical world,* June 23, 1917, p. 1211.

COST data on lining two tunnels. *Engineering and contracting,* Jan. 14, 1914, p. 93-4.

COST data on 1,170 square yards of asphaltic macadam by day labor at Waynesboro, Pa. *Engineering and contracting,* October 4, 1916, p. 303.

COST data on 6,600 volt lines. *Electrical world,* July 3, 1915, p. 16.

COST data on street cleaning in Philadelphia, Pa. *Engineering and contracting,* December 6, 1916, September 5, 1917, p. 508, 190. *Municipal journal,* June 28, 1917, p. 844.

COST data on street paving. *Engineering record,* March 1, 1913, p. 243-4.

COST data on the construction of 27 sand clay roads. *Engineering and contracting,* Jan. 17, 1912, p. 69-72.

COST data on which changes in coal prices will be based in hands of fuel officials. *Official bulletin,* Feb. 26, 1918, p. 1.

COST department and payroll budget. 100%, Aug. 1917, p. 54.

COST department of the future. *American machinist,* May 29, 1919, p. 1025-6.

COST estimating on screw machine products. *Iron trade review,* April 17, 1913, p. 909-15.

COST figures from Brookings. *Electrical world,* Feb. 21, 1914, p. 434.

COST figures of a small sewer system. *Engineering news,* February 8, 1917, 242.

COST figures on four concrete roads. *Concrete cement,* May 1913, p. 223-5.

COST finding. Kimball, D. S. c1918.

COST finding. Nichols, W. G. c1909.

COST finding and accounting conditions. United States. Bureau of foreign and domestic commerce. 1916.

COST finding and keeping. *American stone trade,* 1915, v. 15, no. 11, p. 15.

COST finding in cotton card rooms. *Textile world journal,* Feb. 1914, p. 501-3.

COST finding in the cloak and suit industry. Frankel, Philip. 1912.

COST finding in woolen and worsted mills. Dale, S. S.

COST finding. some practical methods for brass, bronze and aluminum foundries. *Metal industry,* March 1917, p. 112-4.

COST finding, some practical methods for cafeterias. Flint, C. H.

COST keeping and construction accounting. Ross, George Edward. 1919.

COST-keeping and construction accounting adapted to any work consisting of numerous items, departments or divisions on which detailed unit costs are desired. Ross, G. E. c1917.

COST keeping and efficiency in engineering. *Canadian engineer,* Toronto, 1916, v. 30, p. 329-32.

COST keeping and efficiency in works of the engineer department. Godfrey, Stuart C. 1916.

COST keeping and management engineering. Gillette, Halbert Powers and R. T. Dana. 1916.

COST keeping and scientific management. Evans, H. A. 1911.

COST keeping and wage systems of the Stillwell-Bierce & Smith-Vaile co. *Iron trade review,* June 5, 1902.

COST keeping at the Chicago works of Fraser and Chalmers. *American machinist,* Nov. 1, 1900, pt. 1.

COST keeping for manufacturing plants. Bunnell, Sterling Haight. 1911.

COST-keeping for railroad shop power. *Railway age gazette,* June 21, 1916, p. 1494-5.

COST keeping for small metal mines. Pickering, J. C. 1919.

COST keeping forms of Oregon state highway commission. *Engineering and contracting,* May 30, 1917, p. 492-5.

COST keeping in the leather belting industry. Carroll, W. F. 1916.

COST keeping in the United States reclamation service. *Engineering news,* April 25, 1907.

COST keeping methods for concrete construction. *Engineering and contracting,* Nov. 22, 1916, p. 458-60.

COST keeping records used in the construction of two dams for irrigation works at Santa Fe, New Mexico. *Engineering and contracting,* November 13, 1912, p. 555.

COST-keeping system for small bridge and culvert jobs. *Engineering and contracting,* June 27, 1917. p. 588-9.

COST keeping system for the automobile. Iowa State college of agriculture and mechanic arts. 1915.

COST keeping system for warehouse trucks. *Automobile,* May 1, 1913, p. 942-3.

COST keeping system for work performed by municipal forces of the Philadelphia bureau of highways. *Engineering and contracting,* March 31, 1915, p. 292-4. Condensed. *Engineering record,* March 20, 1915, p. 360-1.

COST keeping system in use on the Panama canal. *Engineering and contracting,* Jan. 7, 1914, p. 64.

COST keeping system of Seattle street and sewer department for motor truck operation. *Engineering and contracting,* Aug. 7, 1918, p. 154-5.

COST keeping system of the United States reclamation service. *Engineering record,* July 10, 1909.

COST-keeping systems of an Ohio jobbing foundry. *Iron trade review,* Sept. 4, 1902.

COST manual. Stephens, F. J. 1917.

COST manual prepared for national confectioners' association of the United States. Price, G. W. 1916.

COST MARKS
Cost marks. (In Lisle, George. *Encyclopaedia of accounting.* v. 2. p. 259-60).

COST of a box of apples. *Country gentleman,* Aug. 5, 1916, p. 1473.

COST of a concrete building. *Building age,* Aug. 1916, p. 65-6.

COST of a concrete mill building. *Textile world,* Sept. 9, 1916, p. 3901.

COST of a 1,400-k.w. hydro-electric plant. *Engineering and contracting,* June 4, 1913, p. 624-5.

COST of a small central station system. *Electrical world,* Aug. 3, 1912, p. 260.

COST of a 2,900-kw. plant. *Power,* Jan. 4, 1916, p. 18.

COST of acquisition of lands must be included in valuation. *Railway age,* March 12, 1920, p. 786.

COST of an electric express building. *Electric railway journal,* March 18, 1916, p. 574.

COST of an Illinois concrete road. *Engineering and contracting,* February 2, 1916, p. 108.

COST of arc lighting in Crawfordsville, Indiana. *Electrical world,* Dec. 15, 1917, p. 1154.

COST of ash collection at Phiadelphia with motor trucks. *Engineering and contracting,* October 9, 1918, p. 347.

COST of asphalt block pavement in New York state cities. New York state bureau of municipal information of the New York state conference of mayors and other city officials report, January 28, 1919, no. 82, 1p.

COST of asphalt repairs. *Municipal engineering,* May 1913, p. 387-91.

COST of asphaltic concrete pavement with small portable mixer. *Engineering news,* May 27, 1915, p. 1037-8.

COST of asphaltic macadam second hand concrete on sand, redressed granite blocks and modified Topeka pavements [in New York state cities]. New York state bureau of municipal information of the New York state conference of mayors and other city officials report, January 28, 1916, no. 85, 1p.

COST of asphaltic oil treatments at Portland. *Engineering and contracting,* August 2, 1916, p. 111.

COST of auditor. *Oregon voter,* Nov. 24, 1917, p. 257.

COST of automobile and motor truck operation at San Diego, Cal. *Engineering and contracting,* April 17, 1918, sup. 26.

COST of bitulithic pavements in New York state cities. New York state bureau of municipal information of the New York state conference of mayors and other city officials report. January 28, 1916, no. 78, 1p.

COST of bituminous macadam pavements in New York state cities. New York state bureau of municipal information of the New York state conference of mayors and other city officials report, January 28, 1916, no. 79, 1p.

COST of boulevard lighting and street sprinkling and flushing in Grand Rapids, Michigan. *Engineering and contracting,* November 18, 1914, p. 485-6.

COST of brick pavement in New York state cities. New York state bureau of municipal information of the New York state conference of mayors and other city officials report. January 28, 1916, no. 74, 3p.

COST of brick roads in the country. *Scientific American,* July 1, 1916, p. 3.

COST of burning weeds in Oklahoma. *Electric railway journal,* Sept. 20, 1913, p. 465.

COST of bus operation. *Electric railway journal,* Feb. 27, 1915, p. 414-7.

COST of California road work before and during the war. *Engineering and contracting,* April 2, 1919, p. 339-40.

COST of carriage of passengers in ships. *Scientific American,* Sept. 14, 1918, p. 163.

COST of cement sacks to the user. *Concrete,* April 1916, p. 181-2.

COST of cement sacks to the user. *Concrete-cement,* Nov. 1914, p. 212-3.

COST of cleaning. *Municipal journal,* November 23, 1916, p. 637-42.

COST of cleaning various kinds of city pavements. *Engineering news-record,* May 6, 1915, p. 889.

COST of coal. *Power,* Dec. 12, 1916, p. 824.

COST of collection and method of disposal: tabulation. *Municipal journal,* November 11, 1915, 728-30.

COST of commercial electric vehicle operation. *Electrical world,* October 17, 1914, p. 765.

COST of commercial electric vehicle operation; gives average costs for a great diversity of industries operating in widely separated localities. *Electrical world,* Oct. 17, 1917.

COST of concrete pavement in New York state cities. New York state bureau of municipal information of the New York state conference of mayors and other city officials report, January 28, 1916, no. 76, 1p.

COST of concrete pavement in Queen Victoria, Niagara Falls park, Ont. *Engineering and contracting,* December 5, 1917, p. 473.

COST of concrete paving in Savannah. *Municipal journal,* December 22, 1917, p. 599-600.

COST of concrete road in Blairsville township, Illinois. *Engineering and contracting,* June 21, 1916, p. 571.

COST of constructing a short transmission line. *Electrical world,* May 15, 1915, p. 1244.

COST of constructing a turbogenerator power plant transmission line and substructures. *Engineering and contracting,* Mar. 12, 1913, p. 293-4.

COST of constructing and moving portable camp buildings. *Engineering and contracting,* June 19, 1918, p. 614-15.

COST of constructing Beckwith Pass tunnel of Western Pacific Railway. *Engineering and contracting,* Feb. 21, 1917, p. 182.

COST of constructing concrete roads. *Concrete cement,* March 1914, p. 147-8.

COST of constructing grave foundations for roads. *Engineering and contracting,* February 5, 1919, p. 152.

COST of constructing 1-course concrete road in Indiana. *Engineering and contracting,* February 6, 1918, p. 139.

COST of constructing pavements in St. Paul by force account in 1916; table. *Municipal journal,* August 23, 1917, p. 175.

COST of construction. *Engineering record,* February 26, 1916, p. 288-9.

COST of cost keeping. *Inland printer,* June 1914, p. 419.

COST of covered wood bridge. *Engineering and contracting,* Sept. 24, 1919, p. 367.

COST of crosscutting on the Mother Lode. *Engineering and mining journal,* Aug. 11, 1917, p. 248-9.

COST of cyanidization at Nepessing. *Engineering and mining journal,* Feb. 7, 1914, p. 327.

COST of doing things. *Engineering and mining journal,* Feb. 7, 28, March 28, May 9, 1914, p. 327-9, 476, 665-6, 957-8.

COST of drag line excavator operation on drainage construction. *Engineering and contracting,* Feb. 20, 1918, p. 200.

COST of dredging 29,708,465 cubic yards of material with 24 sea-going Hopper dredges during 1912. *Engineering and contracting,* April 30, 1913.

COST of distributing milk in six cities in Massachusetts. *Massachusetts agricultural experiment bulletin,* 173.

COST of dredging in Mississippi river. *Engineering and contracting,* July 21, 1920, p. 74.

COST of drilling with well drilling machines in ore prospecting. *Engineering and contracting,* March 3, 1915, p. 202-3.

COST of electric freight service of Connecticut company discussed at New Haven hearing. *Electric railway journal,* July 28, 1917, p. 142.

COST of electric power; St. Joseph lead. *Engineering and mining journal,* July 1, 1916, p. 8.

COST of electric pumping for irrigation. *Electrical world,* July 10, 1915, p. 68-71. Excerpts. *Engineering record,* August 28, 1915, p. 257-8.

COST of electric shovel work at Cleveland. *Electric railway journal,* Dec. 5, 1914, p. 1261-2. *Electrical review and western electrician,* Jan. 23, 1915, p. 172-3.

COST of electrification of Chicago terminals; summary of the items entering into the expenditure for new equipment. *Railway age,* Dec. 17, 1915, p. 1125-8.

COST of engineering and other items on California roads. *Engineering and contracting,* Jan. 3, 1917, p. 2-3.

COST of equipping a Mesabi underground mine. *Engineering and mining journal,* Sept. 20, 1913, p. 549.

COST of erecting a steel bridge. *Engineering news-record,* March 20, 1913, p. 575-6.

COST of erecting 110,000 volt transmission lines. *Electrical world,* June 7, 1913, p. 1259.

COST of excavating drainage ditches with steam and electric machines. *Engineering record,* Dec. 26, 1914, p. 704-5.

COST of excavating pavement, trenching and steam pipe laying. *Engineering and contracting,* July 19, 1916, p. 62.

COST of explosives. *Engineering and mining journal,* Jan. 4, 1919, p. 12.

COST of explosives and production of gold. *Engineering and mining journal,* Dec. 14, 1918, p. 1039-40.

COST of extensions. *Electrical world,* May 8, 1915, p. 1191.

COST of fast tunnelling. *Engineering and mining journal,* Sept. 5, 1914, p. 439-40.

COST of filter plant operation. *Engineering and contracting,* Dec. 13, 1916, p. 537-8.

COST of freight car maintenance per car; capacity and cost of cars. *Railway and engineering review,* February 1, 1913, p. 99.

COST of freight car maintenance per ton mile. *Railway and engineering review,* April 26-May 17, June 21-July 5, 1913, p. 388-9, 412-3, 436-7, 461, 598-9, 628, 651.

COST of full crew laws. *Railway age,* April 3, 1914, p. 782.

COST of gas in San Francisco; report to the board of supervisors, May 18, 1908. *Public service,* July 1908, p. 20.

COST of good roads. *Municipal engineering,* Aug. 1914, p. 151-2.

COST of good roads in Kansas. *Municipal journal,* September 13, 1917, p. 262.

COST of government built concrete ships. *Concrete,* Aug. 1919, p. 81-3.

COST of granite block pavements in New York state cities. New York state bureau of municipal information of the New York state conference of mayors and other city officials report, January 28, 1916, no. 83.

COST of gravel road in Clay county, Iowa. *Engineering and contracting,* May 17, 1916, p. 469.

COST of handling gravel with Haiss loading machine. *Engineering and contracting,* May 16, 1917, p. 465. *Municipal engineering,* Aug. 1917, p. 81.

COST of harvestig wheat by different methods. Yerkes, A. P. 1918.

COST of hauling in Chicago. *Engineering record,* July 11, 1914, p. 49.

COST of hauling paving materials with motor truck. *Engineering and contracting,* Jan. 2, 1918, p. 32.

COST of heating and ventilating systems. *Heating and ventilating,* Mar. 1915, p. 61-2.

COST of Hetch Hetchy R. R. *Engineering and contracting,* July 16, 1919, p. 83. *Engineering news,* Nov. 14, 1918, p. 890.

COST of high-explosive shells. *Machinery,* June 1916, p. 841.

COST of highways in three states. *Municipal journal,* April 1, 1915, p. 425.

COST of horse maintenance. *Public works,* Feb. 7, 1920, p. 83-4.

COST of housing soldiers at cantonments averages, $214-92. *Engineering news,* March 21, 1918, p. 569.

COST of I-beam highway bridges in Boone county, Iowa. *Engineering and contracting,* Aug. 23, 1916, p. 182-3.

COST of installing four large electric mine pumps. *Coal age,* July 15, 1916, p. 111. Condensed. *Electrical review and western electrician,* Aug. 5, 1916, p. 237. Excerpts. *Power,* Aug. 1, 1916, p. 165.

COST of installing gas services. *Gas age,* June 1, 1918, p. 517-8.

COST of installing luminous-arc ornamental system. *Electrical world,* January 3, 1914, p. 47-8.

COST of installing street lighting cables in Boston. *Electrical world,* May 20, 1916, p. 1165.

COST of irrigation works per acre of land supplied with water. *Engineering and contracting,* June 4, 1913, p. 634-5. *Engineering news-record,* May 15, 1913, p. 1008-9.

COST of keeping farm horses and cost of horse labor. Cooper, M. R.

COST of labor turnover by M. W. Alexander; Determining cost of turnover of labor by Boyd Fisher; Discussion by the members. *United States bureau of labor statistics, bulletin,* no. 227, p. 13-27, 60-73.

COST of labor turnover; symposium. *Industrial management,* Mar. 1919, p. 239-45.

COST of laying iron pipe. *Municipal journal,* Aug. 10, 1918, p. 110-2.

COST of laying water mains. *Municipal journal,* Oct. 4, 1917, p. 328-30.

COST of laying water mains at Hartford, Conn. *Engineering and contracting,* Dec. 11, 1918, p. 551. *Metal work,* May 2, 1919, p. 548.

COST of laying water mains in city streets. *Engineering and contracting,* June 14, 1916, p. 540.

COST of laying water pipe. *Municipal journal,* Sept. 13, 1919, p. 165.

COST of lighting streets at Galesburg, Illinois. *Electrical world,* September 28, 1918, p. 600.

COST of line materials; data prepared by the Amesbury (Mass.) electric light company. *Electrical world,* May 19, 1917, p. 967.

COST of loading ore with steam shovels. *Engineering and contracting,* Feb. 21, 1917, p. 177.

COST of location survey for a short railway line. *Engineering and contracting,* Feb. 18, 1914, p. 232-3.

COST of locomotives for valuation purposes. *Railway age,* Sept. 3, 1920, p. 387-90.

COST of macadam object lesson roads in North Carolina. *Engineering and contracting,* June 16, 1915, p. 544-5.

COST of magnetite-arc lighting in Worcester. *Electrical world,* June 1, 1911, p. 1451-3.

COST of maintaining city owned teams. *Engineering and contracting,* July 2, 1919, p. 21.

COST of maintaining four stokers and furnaces for six years. *Electrical world,* Dec. 16, 1916, p. 1197.

COST of maintaining private sidings. *Railway age,* Feb. 4, 1916, p. 207-8.

COST of maintenance and depreciation of cotton mills. Chase, Harvey Stuart.

COST of maintenance and repair of Connecticut roads. *Engineering news-record,* February 7, 1918, p. 272.

COST of maintenance of equipment; a record of the Waugh draft gear. *Railway review,* Jan. 9, 1915, p. 66-7.

COST of maintenance of horse and motor fire apparatus. *Municipal engineering,* Aug. 1914, p. 140-2.

COST of making gasoine by the Rittman process. *Mining and engineering world,* June 17, 1916.

COST of making steam for buiding heat. *Electrical world,* Feb. 26, 1916, p. 495-7.

COST of manufacture of cheese. *New York produce review,* July 25, 1917, p. 520.

COST of manufactures. Metcalfe, Henry. 1885.

COST of manufacturing concrete pipe. *Engineering and contracting,* Jan. 14, 1920, p. 34.

COST of manufacturing electricity in very large stations. *Engineering record,* September 20, 1913, p. 311.

COST of manufacturing woolen hoisery. *Textile world,* Feb. 19, p. 1141.

COST of material for 660 volt line construction. *Electrical world,* May 17, 1913, p. 1047.

COST of meter installation and testing in Detroit, Mich. *Engineering and contracting,* May 8, 1918, p. 461.

COST of meter maintenance and repair at Chicago. *Engineering and contracting,* November 8, 1916, p. 420.

COST of meter testing and cost of installing meters at Detroit. *Engineering and contracting,* Feb. 12, 1919, p. 175.

COST of mine cars. *Colliery,* July, 1914, p. 751-2.

COST of mining. Finlay, J. R. 1909.

COST of mining in Alaska. *Engineering and mining journal,* Sept. 18, 1915, p. 480-1.

COST of Minnesota state rural highways. *Engineering and contracting,* May 2, 1917, p. 424.

COST of money to California public utilities. *Electric railway journal,* May 16, 1914, p. 1074-6. Condensed. *Electrical world,* May 16, 1914, p. 1087-8.

COST of motor and horse-drawn apparatus. *Municipal journal,* Oct. 8, 1914, p. 518-9.

COST of motor car service for field parties on surveys. *Engineering news-record,* Sept. 13, 1917, p. 518.

COST of motor truck haulage in road construction. *Engineering and contracting,* March 3, 1920, p. 251-2.

COST of motor truck hauling on Catskill aqueduct tunnel, New York. *Municipal and county engineeering,* Dec. 1913, p. 565-70.

COST of motor truck operation. *Progressive farmer,* July 12, 1919, p. 1144.

COST of motor truck operation for refuse collection. *Engineering and contracting,* July 2, 1919, 11-3.

COST of motor trucking. *System,* July 1919. p. 109.

COST of motor-trucking by Chicago water works in 1914. *Engineering and contracting,* Sept. 1, 1915, p. 162.

COST of operating a Ford car for three years. *Engineering and contracting,* Aug. 9, 1916, p. 124.

COST of operating city lighting plant in Detroit. *Electrical world,* April 29, 1916, p. 997.

COST of operating Fitchburg sewerage disposal plant. *Municipal journal,* Jan. 11, 1917, 39-40.

COST of operating 541 motor trucks. *Engineering and contracting,* May 1, 1918, sup. 29.

COST of operating motor truck. *Engineering and contracting,* April 4, 1917, p. 316.

COST of operating motor trucks. *Iron trade review,* Feb. 15, 1912, p. 401.

COST of operating motor trucks in Seattle. *Municipal journal,* March 8, 1917, p. 340.

COST of operating municipal asphalt plant of District of Columbia. *Engineering and contracting,* June 6, 1917, p. 512.

COST of operating municipal asphalt plant of Los Angeles. *Engineering and contracting,* March 7, 1917, p. 239.

COST of operating producer-gas plant. *Electrical world,* May 5, 1917, p. 848.

COST of operation and comparative cost of chemicals for Columbus, Ohio. *Engineering and contracting,* March 14, 1917, p. 247.

COST of operation during war period; increase granted to Chicago company. *American gas engineering journal,* Sept. 14, 1918, p. 255-6.

COST of pamphlet binding. *Inland printer,* Feb. 1914, p. 740-1.

COST of paving with asphaltic concrete on old macadam. *Engineering and contracting,* Nov. 10, 1915, p. 369

COST of prison made goods. Jensen, Wiliam.

COST of producing apples in Hood River valley. Thomson, S. M. and G. H. Miller. 1917.

COST of producing applies in Maine in 1914. Gardner, H. A. 1915.

COST of producing apples in Maine in 1914. Washington, Miller, G. H. and S. M. Thomson. 1918.

COST of producing apples in Wenatchee valley. Washington, Miller, G. H. and S. M. Thomson. 1917.

COST of producing apples in western Colorado. Thomson, S. M. and G. H. Miller. 1917.

COST of producing copper. *Engineering and mining journal,* April 11, 1914, p. 775-6.

COST of producing copper. *Engineering and mining journal,* June 9, Aug. 11, 25, 1917, p. 271-2, 360.

COST of producing crops on the college farms in 1915; tabulation. (In Report 1916, p. 10-11. Ontario agricultural department, Toronto, Canada, 1917).

COST of producing farms crops. Martin, O. R.

COST of producing lead. *Engineering and mining journal,* Dec. 19, 1914, p. 1073-4.

COST of producing wheat. *Commercial and financial chronicle,* June 26, 1920, p. 2623.

COST of production. Bean, B. C. 1905.

COST of production. Watts, C. J. c1902.

COST of production. Wild, J. A. 1909.

COST of production * * * articles by A. H. Revell, C. W. Norton and others. Chicago, A. W. Shaw. 196p. (Business man's library, v. 3).

COST of production in the pottery industry. United States Bureau of foreign and domestic commerce. 1914.

COST of production of apples in the Fayette Valley, Idaho. Thomson, S. M. and G. N. Miller. 1918.

COST of production of malleable iron castings. *Foundry,* Sept. 1910, p. 10.

COST of production to be studied in large way. *Weekly news letter,* June 18, 1919, p. 1.

"**COST** of progress" and the "profit of progress" in the telephone field. *Engineering and contracting,* April 8, 1914, p. 403.

COST of pumping at Louisville, Kentucky. *Engineering and contracting,* July 10, 1918, p. 33.

COST of pumping for irrigation in western Nebraska. *Engineering and contracting,* Feb. 13, 1918, p. 180-1.

COST of pumping plant and of pumping water for irrigation, Minidoka project, U. S. reclamation service. *Engineering and contracting,* Jan. 24, 1912, p. 106-8.

COST of quarry blasting. *Municipal engineering,* Oct. 1916, p. 144.

COST of quarrying and crushing limestone for a road improvement. *Engineering and contracting,* Feb. 5, 1919, p. 154.

COST of railroad construction. *Railway age gazette,* Feb. 21, 1913, p. 344.

COST of railroad transportation, railroad accounts, and governmental regulations of railroad tariffs. *American railway engineering association,* Sept. 1916.

COST of railway construction. *Railway and engineering review,* May 3, 1913, p. 421.

COST of railway foot bridges. *Engineer,* Aug. 27, Sept. 17, 1915, p. 197-9, 221-3, 240-2, 266-8.

COST of raising a calf. *Jersey bulletin and dairy world,* March 3, 1920, p. 481.

COST of rapid sand filtration at Evanston, Ill. *Engineering and contracting,* Mar. 13, 1918, p. 262.

COST of rice production. *California cultivator,* Nov. 13, 1920, p. 657.

COST of road maintenance in Maryland. *Engineering and contracting,* June 17, 1914, p. 706-7.

COST of road resurfacing with tarmac. *Engineering and contracting,* April 30, 1919, p. 471-2.

COST of rocmac at Springfield, Mass. *Engineering and contracting,* September 6, 1916, p. 223.

COST of rural lines and revenue therefrom. *Electrical world,* Oct. 7, 1916, p. 708-10.

COST of selling pipe and supplies. *System,* May, 1915, p. 480.
Engineering and mining journal, Oct. 18,

COST of shaft sinking in Minnesota iron mining. 1913, p. 739-40.

COST of sheet asphalt and brick pavements at Montreal, Quebec. *Engineering and contracting,* May 3, 1916, p. 495.

COST of sheet asphalt pavement at Montreal, Quebec. *Engineering and contracting,* January 3, 1917, p. 22-3.

COST of sheet asphalt pavements in New York state cities. New York state bureau of municipal information of the New York state conference of mayors and other city officials report, January 28, 916, no. 77, 1p.

COST of shells. *Iron age,* Mar. 16, 1916, p 651.

COST of ships. *Marine news,* Dec. 1919, p 90.

COST of single track macadam roads in Kendall county, Illinois. *Engineering and contracting,* March 6, 1918. p. 250.

COST of sinking Brakpan mine shafts. *Engineering and mining journal,* Nov. 22, 1913, p. 980-1.

COST of 66,000 volt transmission line. *Electrical world,* April 10, 1915, p. 904.

COST of sludge removal, Gloversville, N. Y. *Municipal journal,* Feb. 8, 1917, p. 207.

COST of steam-driven compressor plant. *Engineering and mining journal,* Feb. 28, 1914, p. 476-7.

COST of stopping a train. *Literary digest,* June 7, 1919, p. 114-6.

COST of street cleaning at Chicago, Ill. *Engineering and contracting,* September 5, 1917, p. 202.

COST of street cleaning at Oshkosh, Wisconsin. *Municipal journal,* March 15, 1917, p. 384.

COST of street cleaning at St. Paul by patrol system. *Engineering and contracting,* Sept. 3, 1918, p. 246.

COST of street cleaning at St. Paul, Minnesota. *Engineering and contracting,* Aug. 6, 1919, p. 159.

COST of street cleaning at San Diego, Cal. with vacuum cleaners. *Engineering and contracting,* October 3, 1917, p. 277.

COST of street cleaning in St. Paul, Minnesota in 1913. *Engineering and contracting,* July 22, 1914, p. 94-5.

COST of street flushing and squeegee work at St Paul. *Engineering and contracting,* September 4, 1918, p. 246.

COST of street flushing at Rochester, Minnesota. *Engineering and contracting,* Aug. 7, 1918, p. 155.

COST of street lighting in Chicago. *Electrical world,* Aug. 9, 1913, p. 290.

COST of street lighting in the thirteen United States cities. Details of annual operating cost as estimated for Milwaukee's new lights; tabulation. *Electrical review and western electrician,* April 1916, p. 630-1. *Municipal journal,* May 18, 1916, p. 684.

COST of street oiling and street sprinkling at St. Paul. *Engineering and contracting* September 4, 1918, p. 232.

COST of structures; details to be kept in time book. *Railway age gazette,* Oct. 22, 1915, p. 760.

COST of supplies in railway units. *Electric railway journal,* Aug. 22, 1914, p. 338.

COST of surface treatment of macadam roads in Washington (D. C.) parks. *Engineering and contracting,* Jan. 31, 1912, p. 124.

COST of surveying roads in Illinois. *Municipal engineering,* November 1917, p. 181

COST of the Panama canal as estimated and as built. *Engineering news,* May 28, 1914, p. 1207-9.

COST of the Rawley tunnel, Colorado. *Engineering and mining journal,* April 5, 1913 p. 711.

COST of the Rogers Pass tunnel. *Engineering and mining journal,* June 23, 1917, p 112-3.

COST of things. *Hoard's diary,* Feb. 1, 1918 p. 45.

COST of tie tamping with pneumatic tamper *Engineering and contracting,* May 15, 1918 p. 491.

COST of ties. *Electric railway journal,* April 29, 1911, p. 742.

COST of track laying with a track machine *Engineering and contracting,* April 1, 1914 p. 395-6.

COST of transmission lines in New England *Electrical world,* July 17, 1915, p. 135.

COST of trenching for gas mains. *Gas age,* June 15, 1918, p. 564.

COST of 250 and 400 c.p. incandescent lamps overhead suspension. New York state bureau municipal information, report no. 148, May 17, 1916, 1p.

COST of upkeep of horse-drawn vehicles against electric vehicles. *Journal of the American society of mechanical engineers,* April 1913.

COST of upkeep of mine cars. *Coal age, Nov.* 14, 1918, p. 918.

COST of valuation to the New York, New Haven & Hartford railroad. *Railway review,* July 17, 1915, p. 90.

COST of valuation work. *Railway age gazette,* Aug. 8, 1913, p. 242.

COST of various kinds of pavement. *Municipal engineering,* Nov. 1913, p. 448.

COST of various sewage treatment plants in Illinois. *Engineering and contracting,* Feb. 23, 1916, p. 185.

COST of water bound macadam in New York state cities. New York state bureau of municipal information of the New York state conference of mayors and other city officials report, Jan. 28, 1916, no. 75.

COST of water main construction at Fall River, Mass. *Engineering and contracting,* Sept. 11, 1918, p. 26.

COST of water main construction at Los Angeles. *Engineering and contracting,* March 12, 1919, p. 259.

COST of water main construction at Pasadena, Cal. *Engineering and contracting,* Dec. 12, 1917, p. 487.

COST of water main construction at Pasadena, Cal. *Engineering and contracting,* Nov. 13, 1918, p. 446.

COST of wood block pavement in New York state cities. New York state bureau of municipal information of the New York state conference of mayors and other city officials report, January 28, 1916, no. 80, 1p.

COST of woodblock paving on government pier. *Engineering and contracting,* March 28, 1917, p. 312.

COST of wool scouring. *Textile world,* Feb. 15, 1919, p. 1179.

COST of yarn in knitted cloth. *Textile world,* March 20, 1920, p. 2161.

COST per day of an engine and crew in yard service. *Railway review,* Sept. 4, 1915, p. 313.

COST-plus-a-fee contract and a suggested sliding scale fee. *Engineering and contracting,* Nov. 7, 1917, p. 360-1.

COST-plus-a-fee contract for public works letting. *Engineering and contracting,* April 24, 1918, p. 417-8.

COST-plus-a-fixed sum contracts. *Municipal journal,* Sept. 20, 1917, p. 287-8.

COST pus contract. *American architect, March* 13, 1918, p. 320.

COST plus contract for municipal work. *Engineering and contracting,* Feb. 13, 1918, p. 178-9.

COST-plus contract for unpounding dam at Decatur, Ill. *Engineering and contracting,* Sept. 8, 1920, p. 238.

COST plus contract form of Bent brothers. *Engineering and contracting,* Dec. 24, 1919, p. 728.

COST plus contract forms of Fred T. Ley and co., inc. Hurley-Mason co., and Ferro concrete construction co. *Engineering and contracting,* Dec. 28, 1917, p. 525-8.

COST plus contract forms of Stone & Webster. *Engineering and contracting,* Nov. 28, 1917, p. 444-5.

COST plus contract incentive to close management. *Engineering news,* May 1, 1919, p. 863.

COST-plus contract satisfactory on Boston army base. *Engineering news,* Feb. 12, 1920, p. 326-9.

COST plus contract with minimum fee guarantee. *Engineering and contracting,* Oct. 22, 1919, p. 465.

COST-PLUS CONTRACTS.
See Contracts.

COST-plus contracts. *Journal of accountancy* Sept. 1918, p. 216-20.

COST-plus contracts; cost analysis for wooden ships. United States shipping board. Emergency fleet corporation, 1915.

COST plus contracts involving profit sharing between owner, contractor and employees. *Engineering and contracting,* Jan. 7, 1920, p. 20-3.

COST-plus contracts; tentative draft of two cost-plus forms of contracts, submitted by the committee on contracts. *Bulletin of Associated general contractors,* Nov. 1920, p. 21-2.

COST plus fee contract for bridge construction. *Engineering and contracting,* April 23, 1919, p. 408-9.

COST plus fee contract with divided risk for Kansas city, Mo. viaduct. *Engineering news,* Mar. 7, 1918, p. 471.

COST plus fee system. *American architect,* Sept. 10, 1919, p. 341-2.

COST plus fixed sum per unit contracts for highway work. *Engineering and contracting,* Sept. 5, 1917, p. 201.

"**COST** plus" form of contract used on cantonment work including a schedule of equipment rental rates. *Engineering and contracting,* Nov. 28, 1917, p. 448-51.

COST plus form of government contract explained in correspondence and tables submitted to congress. *Official bulletin,* June 10, 1918, p. 9-13.

COST plus method in contracting. *American architect,* Oct. 15, 1919, p. 503-4.

COST plus percentage contract of Bureau of yards and docks. *Engineering and contracting,* Aug. 29, 1917, p. 174-6. Excerpt. *Industrial management,* Sept. 1917, p. 912-3.

COST-plus-percentage contracts. *Journal of accountancy,* Jan. 1918, p. 49-53.

COST-plus-profit contract is commended by Council of national defense. *Iron age,* March 21, 1918, p. 738-9.

COST-plus system severely criticized. *Iron age,* Sept. 27, 1917, p. 728-30.

COST plus ten per cent. *Literary digest,* Jan. 26, 1918, p. 21.

COST record system used for work done by day labor. *Engineering news,* April 8, 1909,.

COST records. *Journal of commerce,* April 25, 1912, p. 2.

COST records and profits. Atkins, Robert.

COST records at Pratt and Whitney's. *The office,* April 1890, p. 108-9.

COST records on appliance installation. Lohmeyer, H. B. 1916.

COST records or factory accounting. Mann, John.

COST reports, coal. United States. Federal trade commission. 1919

COST reports, copper. United States. Federal trade commission. 1919

COST reports for executors as a means of plant control. Franklin, B. A. c1912.

COST sheets for collieries, iron works, &c. Carter, R. N.

COST sheets for dredging company. *Mining and scientific press,* 1913, v. 106, p. **518-9.**

COST statistics. *Accountant,* Dec. 13, **1913, p.** 853-7.

COST summaries. Griffith, J. B.

COST survey plan; report of National retail lumber dealers' association committee. *American lumberman,* September 21, 1918, p. 47-8.

COST system for a retail yard. Jordon, W. A. 1911.

COST systematizing. Miller, August.

COST system for any make of truck. *Domestic engineering,* April 19, 1919, p. 104-5.

COST system for contractor or jobber. *Metal work,* April 25, 1915, p. 599-600.

COST system for manufacturers. *Pace student,* Oct. 1916.

COST system in Chicago plumbing shops. *Metal work,* July 31, 1914, p. 126-7.

COST system in Michigan plumbing shop. *Metal work,* June 26, 1914, p. 859-60.

COST system of Denver sheet metal shop. *Metal work,* Aug. 6, 1915, p. 175-6.

COST system of Michigan sheet metal shop. *Metal work,* June 4, 1915, p. 802-4.

COST system of the National cash register company. *Business world,* July 1902, p. 312-7.

COST theory of rate making. *Electrical world,* Oct. 24, 1914, p. 819.

COSTELLO, LEONARD W. J.
Some legal terms—their meaning and significance. *Incorporated accountants' journal,* 1904-5, p. 89.
Some points on executorship law. *Incorporated accountants' journal,* 1910-11, p. 278.

COSTIMETER *American machinist,* November 29, 1917, p. 961-2. *Machinery,* November 1917, p. 266-7.

COSTIMETER *Industrial management,* February 1918, p. 158.

COSTING and cost accounting. *Australasian accountant and secretary,* June 1920, p. 153-5.

COSTING and the components of cost. *Incorporated accountants' journal,* March 1919, p. 104-5.

COSTING by machinery. Whitehorn, W. J. 1916.

COSTING by sub-orders or by operations, which? *Accountant,* Feb. 21, 1920, p. 202-3.

COSTING in the printing office. *Accountant,* March 6, 1920, p. 282-6.

COSTING problem. Elbourne, E. T.

COSTING questions. *Accountant,* July 24, 1920, p. 89-90.

COSTINGS in government departments; report of the standing committee on the investigation of prices. *Incorporated accountants' journal,* Dec. 1920, p. 57.

COSTLY road: Hudson county boulevard. *Engineering news-record,* May 27, 1915, p. 1049-50.

COSTS
See also Cost and factory accounting.
ALEXANDER, HAMILTON INSTITUTE. On actual manufacturing costs. New York, Alexander Hamilton institute, c1912. 18p.
BRADFORD, W. A. Profit and the cost of doing business. *Metal work,* Sept. 14, 1917, p. 320-1.
CLAPHAM, F. T. Intensive production establishment charges and selling price. *Engineer,* June 8, 1917, p. 516-7.
DEFINITION of "cost" pertaining to contracts. Washington, Government printing office, 1917. 12p.
DOOLITTLE, F. W. Relationship of items of cost under pre-war conditions and to-day. *Electric railway journal,* Oct. 11, 1919, p. 9-11.
HAMILTON, W. R. Cost of production in relation to an increasing output. *Accountants' magazine,* Dec. 1906, p. 526-38.
HAYES, H. V. Original cost versus replacement cost as a basis for rate regulation. *Quarterly journal of economics.* Aug. 1913, p. 616-29. *Railway age,* Sept. 12, 1913, p. 450-2.
MORRISON, C. J. Cost-plus basis for war supplies. *American machinist,* May 31, 1917, p. 937-8, May 16, 1918, p. 828.
NEW WAY OF SELLING: manufacturing cost plus x percentage. *Scientific American supplement,* Sept. 12, 1914, p. 162.
PFLUG-FELDER, R. H. What is the selling price: *Domestic engineering,* October 11, 1913, p. 45-6.
WATKINS, G. P. Third factor in the variation of productivity: the load factor. *American economic review,* Dec. 1915, p. 753-86.
WELD, L. D. H. "Costs" and the tariff board. *Journal of political economy,* May 1912, p. 492-508.
WRIGHT, P. G. Cost of production and price. *Quarterly journal of economics,* May 1919, p. 560-7.

COSTS—*(Continued)*

Statistics

DANA, RICHARD T. Handbook of construction plant; its cost and efficiency. New York. McGraw-Hill book company, inc. 1914. 702p.

GILLETTE, HALBERT POWERS. Handbook of cost data for contractors and engineers; a reference book giving methods of construction and actual costs of materials and labor on numerous engineering works Ed.2. New York, McGraw-Hill book co. 1910. 1854p.

GILLETTE, HALBERT POWERS AND RICHARD TURNER DANA. Handbook of mechanical and electrical cost data; giving shipping weights, capacities outputs, and net prices of machines and apparatus, and detailed costs of installation, maintenance, depreciation and operation, together with many principles and data relating to engineering economics. New York, McGraw-Hill publishing co. 1918. 1739p.

COSTS and a call for action. *System,* Feb. 1917, p. 222-3.

COSTS and cost keeping. Frantzen, Arthur. 1910.

COSTS and sources of farm-mortgage loans in the United States. Thomson, C. W. 1916.

COSTS and statistics. Chicago, A. W. Shaw co.

COSTS at the Nipissing mines, Cobalt. *Engineering and mining journal,* June 9, 1917, p. 1029.

COSTS in a new mill. *Textile world,* Aug. 23, 1919, p. 1059.

COSTS in bankruptcy. *Accountant,* Jan. 16, 1915 p. 70-4.

COSTS in Illinois of concrete road maintenance using portable hearing kettle and auto trucks. *Engineering and contracting,* Feb. 23, 1916, p. 196.

COSTS keeping prevents poor bidding. *Concrete,* Oct. 1919, p. 163-4.

COSTS of blasting drainage ditches. *Engineering record,* March 31, 1917, p. 511.

COSTS of concrete and mill type buildings. *Concrete,* July 1916, p. 25. Condensed. *Engineering and contracting,* July 26, 1916, p. 95.

COSTS of doing business from book stores. *System,* March 1917, p. 260.

COSTS of dredging irrigating ditches. *Engineering news-record,* May 3, 1917, p. 267.

COSTS of electric delivery for ice-cream manufacturers. *Electrical review and western electrician,* May 5, 1917, p. 749.

COSTS of electrical equipment. *Electrical world* Dec. 19, 1914, p. 1204.

COSTS of electrical shovel at Cleveland. *Electrical review and western electrician,* Jan. 23, 1915, p. 172-3.

COSTS of electrical shovel at Cleveland. *Electric railway journal,* Dec. 5, 1914, p. 1261-2.

COSTS of excavation and concrete for Mayfair pumping station, Chicago, Ill. *Engineering and contracting,* October 25, 1916, p. 364.

COSTS of litigation in trust accounts. *Accountant,* Aug. 17, 1918, p. 81-2.

COSTS of power and local transport. Webner, F. E. 1917.

COSTS of production in the sugar industry. United States. Tariff commission. 1919.

COSTS of receiverships. *Corporation journal,* May 31, 1916, p. 183.

COSTS of material for 660 volt line construction. *Electrical world,* May 17, 1913, p. 1047.

COSTS of state and road work in Wisconsin. *Engineering and contracting,* March 7, 1917, p. 230.

COSTS of state roads in California. *Engineering and contracting,* November 7, 1917, p. 379.

COSTS of 12 and 16-ft. length cast iron pipe. *American gas light journal,* Jan. 17, 1916, p. 45.

COSTS of upkeep of mine cars. *Coal age,* Nov. 14, Dec. 26, 1918, March 6, 1919, p. 918, 1174-5; 460-1.

COSTS on four types of pavement in Philadelphia test road. *Engineering news,* Sept. 23, 1920, p. 607-8.

COSTS show further increase. *Foundry,* June 15, 1920, p. 485.

COSTS, their compilation and use in management. Berndt, I. A. c1920.

COTHEAL, WILLIAM

New method of keeping accounts. New York, 1860.

COTTELL, ALBERT

Ore reduction works account. *Accountant,* Aug. 15, 1908, p. 192-7.

COTTER, A. D.

Manufacturing accounts. *Public accountant,* 1909, p. 171.

COTTON, GEORGE M.

Card journal and its uses. *Business organization and management,* Sept. 1920, p. 637-41.

Modern accounting and small undertakings. *Business organization and management,* May 1920, p. 147-9.

COTTON, J. P.

Argument against an official valuation of railroad properties. *American economic association quarterly,* April 1910, p. 253-8.

COTTON, J. S. and others

Meat situation in the United States, pt. 3. Methods and cost of growing beef cattle in the corn belt states. *United States agricultural report,* 111, 1916, p. 1-64. Abstract. *International review of science and practice of agriculture,* June 1917, p. 927-31.

COTTON

GUARANTY TRUST COMPANY OF NEW YORK. Fabric of civilization; a short survey of the cotton industry in the United States. New York, Guaranty trust company of New York, c1919. 62p.

PRATT, EDWARD EWING. Cotton textiles; international trade and merchandising methods; prepared for the Textile club of New York. Washington, Government printing

COTTON—(Continued)

office, 1917. 19p. (United States. Bureau of foreign and domestic commerce, miscellaneous series no. 58).

RAWLINSON, JOSHUA. Silver question as it affects the cotton trade. *Accountant,* Feb. 15, 22, 1890, p. 82-4, 93-5.

STEWART, CHARLES. Cotton: from planter to consumer. *Accountant,* June 22, 1912, p. 936-42.

UNITED STATES. Department of commerce and labor. Cotton tare. Washington, Government printing office, 1912.

Costs

COTTON growers' cost of production. *Pacific rural press,* Jan. 17, 1920, p. 88.

PRELIMINARY report shows cost of growing cotton. *Weekly news letter,* April 7, 1920, p. 1.

TWENTY-EIGHT cents, bulk line cost of growing cotton. *Progressive farmer,* April 10, 1920, p. 791.

COTTON BROKERS

Accounting

BUTLER, HENRY G. Cotton, grain and coffee —future contract brokerage business. *Business man's magazine,* 1906, v. 18, no. 8, p. 100-6.

TODMAN, FREDERICK SIMSON. Cotton brokerage. (In his *Brokerage accounts.* 1916. p. 129-203).

Auditing

TODMAN, FREDERICK SIMSON. Audit of cotton brokerage books. (In his *Brokerage accounts.* 1916. p. 249-54).

COTTON EXCHANGES

BLEASE, WALTER. Clearing house arrangements of the Liverpool cotton association. *Accountant,* Oct. 29, 1904, p. 514-9.

UNITED STATES. Bureau of corporations. Report of the commissioner of corporations on cotton exchanges. 3v. Washington, Government printing office, 1908-9.

COTTON FUTURES

Accounting

DODD, ARTHUR F. Corn options and cotton futures; their object and effect upon commercial transactions. *Accountant,* July 6, 13, 1901, p. 779-87, 804-6.

SOULÉ, GEORGE. Cotton factorage bookkeeping. (In his *New science and practice of accounts.* 1903. p. 344-48).

COTTON growers' cost of production. *Pacific rural press,* Jan. 17, 1920, p. 88.

COTTON MACHINERY

Costs

UNITED STATES. Bureau of foreign and domestic commerce. Cotton-spinning machinery industry; report on the cost of production of cotton-spinning machinery in the United States. Washington, Government printing office, 1916. 99p. (Miscellaneous series, no. 37).

COTTON manufacturers figure 10% depreciation on plant equipment because of the great advance in cost of mill building. *Journal of commerce,* April 15, 1918.

COTTON manufacturing industry of the United States. Copeland, Melvin Thomas. 1912.

COTTON mill accounting. Scott, G. G.

COTTON mill accounts. Hunter, Joel.

COTTON MILLS

CALDER, JOHN. Prevention of accidents in cotton mills. *Efficiency society journal,* Nov. 1917, p. 599-610.

CLOTH room report. *Textiles,* October, 1917.

COMPANIES acts and cotton mills. *Accountant,* 1886, p. 579, 590, 605, 621, 637, 671, 685.

COPELAND, MELVIN THOMAS. Cotton manufacturing industry of the United States.: Cambridge, Harvard university, 1912. 415p.

COTTON mills. *American institute of accountants, Special bulletin,* No. 4, July 1920, p. 7-8.

HUNT, WILLIAM F. Economy in handling material in cotton mills. *Textile world,* May 1914, p. 204-9. Condensed. *Iron age,* May 21, 1914, p. 1272-8.

ROSE, J. T. General business efficiency in connection with cotton mill management. *Textile world,* May 1915, p. 190-3.

SCIENTIFIC management in a cotton weave room. *Textile world,* Aug. 1915, p. 526-8.

SWEENEY, R. P. Systematizing cotton mill. *Business man's magazine,* June 1911, p. 583-89.

SZEPESI, E. Textile mill organization and costs. *Textile world,* Feb. 17, 24, March 10, 24, April 7, 21, May 5, June 2, 30, Aug. 4, Sept. 1, Oct. 27, Nov. 10, Dec. 8, 22, 1917, Jan. 5, 19, Feb. 16, July 6, 1918, v.52: 1403, 1490, 1697, 1872, 2071, 2274, 2569, 3009, 3109, 3531; v.53: 521+, 1738.

TWYFORD, H. B. Purchasing and storing of materials and supplies for cotton mills. *Textile record,* Sept. 1915.

UNITED STATES. BUREAU OF LABOR STATISTICS. Wages and hours of labor in cotton goods manufacturing and finishing, 1916. Washington, Government printing office, 1918. 258p.

UNITED STATES. BUREAU OF LABOR STATISTICS. Wages and hours of labor in cotton goods manufacturing and finishing, 1918. Washington, Government printing office, 1919. 147p. (Bulletin no. 262).

UNITED STATES cotton future act. *Treasury decisions,* Feb. 4, 1915, p. 57-72.

WAGES and hours of labor in the cotton, woolen and silk industries, 1907-14. *United States bureau of labor, bulletin,* 190.

Accounting

BOOKS and accounts of cotton manufacturers. *Accountant,* June 23, 30, July 14, 21, 1888, p. 395-7, 410-2-442-3, 457-8.

COTTON spinners' books and accounts. *Accountant* March 3, 10, 17, 31, April 14, 21, 28, 1888, p. 130-2, 147-9, 162-3, 195-9, 223-4, 238-9, 255).

HAMER, FRANK. Accounts of a cotton spinning mill. *Accountant,* March 18, May 20, 1905, p. 315-20, 615-60.

HUNTER, JOEL. Cotton mill accounts. (In his *Thinking in figures.* c1916. p. 153-69). *Accountant,* May 31, 1913, p. 852-5. *Journal of accountancy,* Aug. 1913, p. 110-9.

KITTREDGE, A. O. Cotton mill accounting. *Commerce, accounts and finance,* April 27, 1901, p. 1, 8-11).

MOSS, WILLIAM. Cotton spinning companies accounts. London, Gee & co. 1905. 147p. (Accountants' library, v. 39).

SCOTT, G. G. Cotton mill accounting. *Journal of accountancy,* April 1912, p. 251-60.

SCOVELL, CLINTON E. Methods of cost and clear accounting essential to efficient mill management. *National association of cotton manufacturers, Transactions,* 1914, p. 234-54.

SOULE, GEORGE. Set of corporation or capital stock books for a cotton factory business. (In his *New science and practice of accounts.* 1903. p. 394-400).

SYSTEMATIZING a cotton mill. *Business man's magazine,* June 1911, p. 583-589.

COTTON MILLS—ACCOUNTING—*(Continued)*

WILSON, RICHARD P. and HARRY J. CARPENTER. Analysis of a cotton mill statement. (In their *Analysis of financial statements.* c1918. p. 32-36).

YOUNG, GEORGE. Accounting for cotton mills. *Commerce, accounts and finance,* Jan., Feb., March 1902, p. 3-7, 3-5, 3-4.

Cost accounting

BROWNLEE, GEORGE. Cost accounting for cotton goods manufacturing business. *Business man's magazine,* Nov. 1905, p. 863-5.

CHASE, HARVEY STUART. Cost of maintenance and depreciation of cotton mills. *Accountant,* Sept. 21, 1907, p. 370-2, 357-9. *Journal of accountancy,* July 1907, p. 236-8.

CHASE, HARVEY STUART. Cost of maintenance and depreciation of cotton mills from the Transactions, no. 82, of the National association of cotton manufacturers, Boston, Mass., April 24, 25, 1907. 8p.

COST finding in cotton card rooms. *Textile world journal,* Feb. 1914, p. 501-3.

COST RECORDS. *Journal of commerce,* April 25, 1912, p. 2.

DAY, CLARENCE MUNRO. Cotton mill cost system. (In his *Accounting practice.* 1915. p. 135-46).

EGGLESTON, DEWITT CARL. Cost of finishing plain cotton cloth. (In his *Problems in cost accounting.* 1918. p. 229-36).

HARDMAN, ARTHUR H. Production costs in cotton spinning mills. Manchester, England, Emmott & co. 1912. 119p.

HARDMAN, ARTHUR H. Yarn and cloth costing in cotton mills. *Business organisation and management,* Jan.-May 1920, p. 27-32, 49-55, 41-8, 57-61, 161-6.

HARRIS, RICHARD. Cost keeping in cotton mills. *Textile world record,* July, 1903, p. 80-4.

MERRILL, W. A. Cost finding for cotton mills. (In Dale, Samuel S. *Cost finding for textile mills.* c1916. p. 2-10.)

MUNROE, S. P. Distribution of overhead in a cotton mill. *Textile world journal,* Jan. 13, 1917, p. 683.

NICHOLS, HENRY WYMAN. Method of determining costs in a cotton mill. New Bedford, E. Anthony & sons, 1915. 115p.

NICHOLS, WILLIAM G. Cost finding. (In *Cyclopedia of commerce, accountancy, business administration.* 1910. v. 8. p. 263-307).

PRACTICAL cost accounting: keeping the costs in a large mill. *Cotton,* Jan. 1920, p. 147-9.

WYCHE, C. A. Treatment of raw stock in cotton mill accounting. *Business man's magazine,* Nov. 1906, p. 150-2.

Costs

CALVIN, E. A. Cost of cotton production. *Manufacturers record,* Sept. 19, 1918, p. 78.

DETAILED costs upon 100 samples of cotton cloth, presents at the tariff board hearing on the cotton schedule. *Journal of commerce,* May 15, 1912, p. 13-4.

MANUFACTURING cost of print cloths. *Textile world,* July 14, 1917, p. 147.

TOD, J. E. Cost of the permanent fireproofing of cotton goods. Boston, National association of cotton manufacturers, 1914. 4p. *Textile world,* Oct. 1914, p. 104.

Depreciation.

See Depreciation, depletion and obsolescence—Cotton mills.

COTTON mills. *American institute of accountants, Special bulletin,* No. 4, July 1920, p. 7-8.

COTTONSEED OIL

Accounting

HAWORTH, SMITH GORDON and WILLIAM SILAS ASHBY. Cotton seed oil mill bookkeeping; illustrating the use of the voucher system. Battle Creek, Mich. Ellis publishing company, 1916. 55p. + forms.

HUNTER, JOEL. Cotton seed oil mill accounts. (In his *Thinking in figures.* c1916. p. 132-42). *Journal of accountancy,* Dec. 1912, p. 478-82.

TODMAN, FREDERICK SIMSON. Cottonseed oil and coffee brokerage. (In his *Brokerage accounts.* 1916. p. 225-6).

Auditing

CASTENHOLZ, WILLIAM H. Oil mills. (In his *Auditing procedure.* 1918. p. 271-4).

Cost accounting

HUNTER, JOEL. Fallacies in seed and crushing costs. (In his *Thinking in figures.* c1916. p. 74-81). *Cotton seed crushers' association, Proceedings,* 1913, p. 46-9.

COTTONSEED oil mill accounts. Hunter, Joel.

COTTON seed oil mill bookkeeping. Haworth, S. G. and W. S. Ashby. 1916.

COTTON spinners' books and accounts. *Accountant,* March 3, 10, 17, 31, April 14, 21, 28, 1888, p. 130-2, 147-9, 162-3, 195-9, 223-4, 238-9, 255).

COTTON spinning companies accounts. Moss, William. 1905.

COTTON-spinning machinery industry. United States. Bureau of foreign and domestic commerce. 1916.

COTTON tare. United States. Department of commerce and labor, 1912.

COTTON textiles. Pratt, Edward Ewing. 1917.

COTTRELL, G. F.

Uniform maintenance cost-records for roads adopted at Washington. *Engineering news-record,* April 4, 1918, p. 660-2.

COULTER, WALDO S.

Cost keeping on public works. *Engineering news,* June 14, 1906.

COULTHARD, R. W.

Evaluating coal properties in Western Canada; a paper presented at a meeting of the International engineering congress at San Francisco, California, Sept. 20-25, 1915. *Canadian mining journal,* Jan. 1, 1916, p. 21-3.

Principle of coal evaluation. *Colliery engineer,* Aug. 1915, p 22.

COUNTIES

LONDON county council works department. *Accountant,* Jan. 11, 18, 1908, p. 40, 78.

Accounting

CARMICHAEL, R. County council accounts. *Accountant,* Jan. 21, 1893, p. 68-74.

COOK COUNTY. Department of finance. Classification of expense accounts; alphabetically listed and classified to conform with standard appropriation accounts. 1914. 43p.

DODSON, F. E. Urban district councils' accounts. Leeds, Elseworth bros. 1908.

EVANS, J. MEREDYTH. Exemplification of a system of accounts for county councils, urban and rural district councils. London, Shaw and sons, 1897.

JONES, W. E. County council accounts. *Accountant,* Dec. 13, 1919, p. 505-9.

KEEN, WILLIAM BROCK. County council accounts. *Accountant,* May 18, June 29, 1895, p. 456-64, 561-4.

COUNTIES—ACCOUNTING—*(Continued)*

LISLE, GEORGE. On the bookkeeping and forms of accounts required by county councils under the local government (Scotland) act 1889. Edinburgh, 1890.

MITCHELL, WALTER K. Uniform accounting system for California counties. *Journal of accountancy,* April 1916, p. 261-74.

OHIO. Bureau of inspection and supervision of public offices. Schedules for uniform county reporting. Financial report. 1914. 25p.

OREGON. Statutes. Law providing for a uniform system of accounting and supervision and inspection of state and county officers. 1913.

PHILADELPHIA. Controller. Manual of accounting, reporting and business procedure of the city and county of Philadelphia, 1917. 218p.

ROCKEFELLER, L. K. County government from the state comptroller's standpoint. *Conference for the study and reform of county government, Proceedings,* 1914. p. 10-8.

SCOTT, GEORGE C. County accounting; uniform system and county budgets. (In *North Carolina university, Bureau of ext. North Carolina club year book,* 1917-1918, p. 80-103.

SMITH, ROY. State administrative supervision over local accounting. *Journal of accountancy,* Nov., Dec. 1909, Jan., Feb. 1910, p. 36-44, 123-31, 211-17, 263-74

SQUANCE, HARRY. County councils and their accounts. *Accountant,* Oct. 11, 1890, p. 548.

Auditing

AUDIT of county councils' accounts. *Accountant,* April 8, 1892, p. 297-8, 307-11.

BUCK, GEORGE S. County auditor: with discussion. New York constitutional convention commission, comp. *County government,* 1915, p. 37-45.

COUNTY auditors; text of the bill to amend the law relating to the audit of county accounts. *Accountant,* July 14, 1894, p. 633-4.

INDIANA. State board of accounts. Uniform system of examination. Indianapolis, State board of accounts, 1915. 56p.

NEW JERSEY county audits. *Journal of accounting,* May 1914, p. 400.

RAWLINGS, A. LEE. County audits. *Journal of accountancy,* Aug. 1916, p. 112-21.

Budgets.

See Budgets—Counties.

Finance

HENDREN, GILBERT and others. Analysis of the appropriation ordinance on county budget. Indianapolis, 1918. 27p.

PIERSON, ARTHUR N. Analysis of the laws affecting municipal and county finances and taxation. Trenton, N. J. Commission for the survey of municipal financing of New Jersey, 1918. 124p.

COUNTING by electricity. *Accountants' magazine,* April 1913, p. 196-9.

COUNTING-house and examination bookkeeping. Maclean, J. D. 1891.

COUNTING-house and factory organisation. Williamson, J. G.

COUNTING-house book-keeping. Bryant, H. B., H. D. Stratton and S. S. Packard.

COUNTING-house book-keeping. Caton, M. J.

COUNTING-house manual. Foster, B. F.

COUNTING house manual, and introduction to business: practical bookkeeping, by calculators. London, 1843.

COUNTING stock at sight. *Factory,* December 1916, p. 736.

COUNTRY banker. Rae, George.

COUNTY, A. J.

Railway accounts and statistics. Chicago, La Salle extension university, 1911. 67p.

Railway accounts and statistics in the United States. *International railway congress, Bulletin,* Eng. ed. June 1910, p. 2986-3024. *Railway library,* 1911, p. 250-62. Abstract. *Railway age gazette,* July 29, 1910, p. 181-3. Copeland, M. T., *Business statistics,* 1917, p. 627-42.

Where the railroads stand in the spring of 1920; an address delivered at the 32d annual meeting of the Railway accounting officers association, Atlantic city, N. J., May 12 and 13, 1920. Washington, Railway accounting officers association, 1920. 16p.

COUNTY auditing. 2 typewritten pages.

COUNTY auditors; text of the bill to amend the law relating to the audit of county accounts. *Accountant,* July 14, 1894, p. 633-4.

COUNTY audits. Rawlings, A. L.

COUNTY finances in North Caroline by M. S. Willard; County accounting; uniform system and county budgets, by George C. Scott. (In *North Carolina university, Bureau of ext. North Carolina club year book,* 1917 1918, p. 80-103).

COUNTY government from the state comptroller's standpoint. Rockefeller, L. K. 1914.

COUNTY highway work in 1916; construction details and costs for hard surface pavements; tabulation. *Municipal journal,* April 5, 1917. p. 485-90.

COUNTY plant produces gravel at cost of 17.4 cents per yard. *Engineering and contracting,* August 1, 1917, p. 86-7.

COUPONS.

See Bonds.

COURSE in the theory and practice of higher accounting. Heitmann, Henry. 1910.

COURSE of bond prices. Mott, H. S. 1918.

COURSE of book-keeping by double and single entry. Boulter, G. H. 1860.

COURSE of easy exercises in bookkeeping. Thornton, John. 1892.

COURSE of electric railway earnings in 1919. *Commercial and financial chronicle,* July 3, 1920, p. 16-20.

COURSE of practice in single entry. Marsh, C. C. 1859.

COURSE of study in corporation finance and investment. Investment bankers' association of America. 1917.

COURSE on electric railway accounting by mail. *Electric railway journal,* May 30, 1914, p. 1214.

COURT of session accountant's fees. *Accountant,* July 31, 1897, p. 763-4.

COURT ruling on the basis for appraisal of a water works plant. *Engineering news,* Jan. 22, 1903, p. 75.

COURT upholds increased fare for Toledo, O. *Municipal journal,* Aug. 31, 1918, p. 176.

COURTELYOU, G. E.
Commercial and financial aspects of gas manufacture. *Scientific American supplement,* April 26, May 3, 1913. p. 266-7, 274-5.

COURTS enjoin state interference with increased rates. *Railway review,* Aug. 28, 1920, p. 322-3.

COVER PAPER MANUFACTURERS ASSOCIATION.
Report of the committee on costs. 1918. 59p.

COVERDALE, W. H.
Railroad franchise values in Texas. *Railroad gazette,* Feb. 12, 1904, p. 115.

COW index of keeping profit. Fraser, W. J.

COWAN, D. R. AND F. C. HART.
Motor transportation in rural Ontario. *Canadian engineer,* Sept. 2, 1920, p. 309-10.

COWAN, DAVID
Administration of workshops; with special reference to oncost: what it should include; its allocations and recovery. *Accountant,* Nov. 16, 1901, p. 1242-56.
Workshop administration, with special reference to tracking work and promptly ascertaining detailed costs, and profits. *Accountant,* Jan. 19, 26, Feb. 2, 9, 1901, p. 85-92, 114-20, 148-55, 188-93, 242.

COWAN, J. D.
Reserves; from the *Journal of accountancy. Canadian chartered accountant,* April 1918, p. 305-11. *Journal of accountancy,* Feb. 1917, p. 99-106. *South African accountant,* Dec. 1918, p. 246-8.

COWAN, T. W.
Bookkeeper's guide. Ed. 6. London, Houlston & sons. 1885.

COWDRICK, E. S.
Successful trial of industrial representation plan; the Colorado fuel and iron company. *Industrial management,* Feb. 1920, p. 123-5.

COWENS, WILLIAM EDWARD
Shop and general establishment charges in engineering works and their relation to costs and estimates. *Engineering gazette,* June 1899.

COWING, HERBERT L. comp.
One thousand technical books; a selected list with annotations emphasizing especially elementary practical books. Washington, American library association, Library war service, 1919. 123p.

COWING, JOHN P.
Cost keeping in construction and contract work. *Engineering magazine,* Sept. 1905, p. 921-8.

COWLRICK, A. S.
Bank bookkeeping and methods of internal check. *Accountant,* Jan. 31, 1914, p. 156-66.

COWPERTHWAITE, J. J.
Income tax law and practice. *Accountants' magazine,* May 1920, p. 299-327.

COX, CYRIL
Dissolution of partnership. *Accountant,* May 30, Aug. 1, 1908, p. 793-9, 121-2.

COX, HAROLD
How to introduce the metric system. *Accountant,* Sept. 7, 1901, p. 974-5.

COX, HENRY CLAY
Advanced and analytical accounting. New York, The Ronald press company, 1920. 459p. (Business accounting, v. 4).
Classified C. P. A. problems and solutions, 1915; covering the more important questions given in the 1915 examinations of the following states: Arkansas, Delaware, Florida, Kansas, Louisiana, Maine, Maryland, Massachusetts, Michigan, Minnesota, Missouri, Nebraska, Nevada, New York, Ohio, Oregon, Pennsylvania, South Carolina, Washington, Wisconsin. New York, The Ronald press co. 1916, 414p.

COX, J. B.
Contact system of the Butte, Anaconda & Pacific railway. *American institute of electrical engineers. Proceedings,* August 1915, p. 1447-76. *General electric review,* August 1915, p. 842-59. Abstract. *Electric railway journal,* July 10, 1915, p. 59-60.
Electrical operation of the Butte, Anaconda & Pacific railway. *American institute of electrical engineers, Proceedings,* Nov. 1914, p. 1729-53. *General electric review,* Nov. 1914, p. 1047-65. Abtract. *Electric railway journal,* Nov. 7, 1914, p. 1050-1.

COX, J. CHARLES.
Household books of Sir Miles Stapleton, bart. 1656-1705. *Ancestor,* 1902, no. 2, p. 17-39, no. 3, p. 132-62.

COX, ROBERT LYNN
In the matter of reporting "Taxes due or accrued," by life insurance companies under the form provided by the convention blanks of 1907. Brief upon the questions involved. New York, Association of life insurance presidents, 1907.

COX, S. R.
Transactions [Mine accounts]. *Institution of mining and metallurgy,* 1899, p. 217-20.

COX, THOMAS
California—methods and costs of obtaining crude petroleum; with discussion. *Pan American scientific congress, Proceedings,* 1915, p. 92-102.

COX, W. E.
Cost accounting for retail fuel dealers. Seattle, University of Washington, 1920. 63p.

CRABB, GEORGE.
English synonyms. Revised ed. New York, Harper and brothers, c1917. 769p. (Centennial edition).

CRACKERS.
See Biscuits and Crackers.

CRAGGS, G. SOMERVILLE.
Manufacturing costs. *Accountant,* June 5, 1915, p. 756-66.

CRAGGS, J. G.
Agreement of trial balances simplified and secured by a new method. *Accountant,* Aug. 8, 15, 1896, p. 674-80, 689-92.
Heavy trial balances made easy. London. 1897.

CRAIG, A. T.
Bookkeeping frauds and methods for their detection. New York, Business publishing co. 1899. 31p.

CRAIG, A. T.—*(Continued)*
Frauds in connection with bookkeeping, and methods to be used for their detection. *Accountant*, Feb. 26, 1898, p. 237-43. *Business*, Sept. 1898, p. 493-501.

CRAIG, J. HAMILTON.
Accounting in connection with exhibition. *Accountants' magazine*, June 1911, p. 291.
Mineral royalties. *Accountants' magazine*, Nov. 1920, p. 599-609.

CRAIGIE, P. G.
Relation of population and food-production. *Accountants' magazine*, May 1910, 258-75.

CRAIGIN, C. T.
See Neal, E. V., joint author.

CRAIN, G. D.
Business hints for contractor and dealer. *Electrical review and western electrician*, April 10, July 31, Sept. 11, Dec. 11, 25, 1915, Jan. 8-15, Sept. 1916, p. 682, 188-9, 475-6, 1065-6, 1148-9, 81-2, 117-8, 249-50.
Business hints for the electrical dealer. *Electrical review and western electrician*, March 11, May 6, June 10, Aug. 26, 1916, 473-4, 816-7, 1084-5; 382-3.
Business hints for dealer and contractor, *Electrical review and western electrician*, Aug. 21, 1915, p. 324-5.
Cost of stock-room leakage and who shall pay. *Electrical world*, December 25, 1915, p. 1422-3.
FIELD and office methods employed by Louisville water co. in checking construction gang payrolls. *Engineering and contracting*, Feb. 3, 1915, p. 102-3.
Handling the depreciation account. *Iron age*, March 5, 1914, p. 616-7.
Keeping tab on stock. *Inland printer*, June 1914, p. 379-81.
Logical system of meter rates. *Municipal engineering*, May 1913, p. 440-1.

CRAKE, JAMES
Executorship accounts. *Accountant*, Jan. 24, 1903, p. 122-5.

CRAM, R. C.
Analysis of track maintenance costs. *Electric railway journal*, March 17, 1917, p. 479-83.
Cutting costs in storage yards. *Electric railway journal*, Dec. 23, 1916, p. 1284-9.
Money-saving factors in the maintenance of special work. *Electric railway journal*, July 20, 1918, p. 103-8.
Way department requires particularly complete organization. *Electric railway journal*, Aug. 17, 1918, p. 272-4.

CRAMER, J. ARTHUR.
Filing department. New York, Bankers publishing co. 1917. 110p.

CRAMER, J. F.
Book-keeping for breweries. *Bookkeeper* 1902, v.15, no. 1, p. 73-81.

CRAMP, WILLIAM AND SONS SHIP AND ENGINE BUILDING COMPANY, Philadelphia.
Classification of accounts. Philadelphia, 1905. 119p. (Private publication)
Classification of hull and machinery accounts. Philadelphia, 1918. 183p. (Private publication)
Ship yard symbol system. Philadelphia, 1905. 136p. (Private publication)

CRANCH, R. G.
Work of the excess profits tax investigator. *Journal of accountancy*, March 1919, p. 161-70.

CRANDALL, B. V.
Terminal cost data. Chicago, Railway educational press, 1919. 104p.

CRANDELL, JOHN CHESTER AND M. F. CRANDELL.
Manual of household accounts, including complete instructions, illustrative figures and forms for actual use covering three years. Boston. Whitcomb & Barrows, 1917. 24p.

CRANDELL, M. F.
See Crandell, John Chester, joint author.

CRANE, A. C.
Books of accounts from a legal standpoint. *Incorporated accountants journal*, 1901-2, p. 172.
Some points affecting deeds of arrangement with creditors. *Incorporated accountants' journal*, 1909-10, p. 37.

CRANE, C. D.
Double and triplex index expiration register. New York, Spectator company.

CRANE, F. S.
Cost record for printers. *Business man's magazine*, March 1907, p. 93-6.

CRANE, J. B.
Use of electric power in the mining of anthracite coal. *Electrical review*, Dec. 21, 1918, p. 976-7. *General electric review*, Feb. 1919, p. 146-8.

CRANE, J. L. AND J. G. KIMMEL
Design features and form of contract for constructing a large earthen water supply dam on cost plus fee basis. *Municipal engineering*, Aug. 1919, p. 86.

CRANE, W. R.
Index of mining and engineering literature, comprising an index of mining, metallurgical, civic, mechanical, electrical and chemical engineering subjects as related to mining and engineering. 2v. New York, J. Wiley and sons, 1909-12.

CRANKSHAW, H. M.
Successful colliery management. *Coal age*, April 7, 1917, 594-600.

CRANKSHAW, N. P.
Internal books of a weaving mill. *Journal of the British association of Manchester textile works*, 1912-13, p. 108-26.

CRAVATH, J. R.
Accounting for depreciation. *Electrical world*, Jan. 23, 1915, p. 213-4.
Rates and by-products. *Electrical world*, April 24, 1915, p. 1029.
Street lighting rates. *Electrical world*, Oct. 5, 1912, p. 722-3.

CRAVATH, PAUL D.
Reorganization of corporations. (In Stetson, Francis L. and others. *Some legal phases of corporate financing, reorganization and regulation.* 1917. p. 153-234).

CRAVEN, EDWARD J. E.
Local taxation and valuation. (In Lisle, George. *Encyclopaedia of accounting.* v.4. p. 332-432).

CRAVEN, J. C.
Methods and cost of meter reading at Terre Haute, Ind. *Engineering and contracting*, April 11, 1917, p. 347-9.

CRAVENS, GEORGE W.

Depreciation and maintenance of electrical equipment. *Electrical review,* April 23, 1910, p. 853-6.

CRAW, GEORGE ROCKHILL

Organization the key to business service. *Business man's magazine,* April 1910, p. 316-22.

CRAWFORD, DAVID.

Trustee in bankruptcy, his rights and duties. *Accountants' magazine,* Jan.-March 1915, p. 9-26, 98-115, 150-66.

CRAWFORD, F

Few notes on special matters affecting auditors arising during the first year of the existence of a limited company. *Accountant,* April 15, 1911, p. 600-2.

CRAWFORD, J. G.

Coal distribution record system. *International railway fuel association, Proceedings,* 1916, p. 257-66. *Railway age gazette,* May 26, 1916, p. 1124-6.

CRAWFORD, J. M.

Cleveland accountant: a work designed for experienced book-keepers on opening and closing the books of joint stock companies, also a complete manual of forms for organizing and managing all kinds of companies, and associations, including partnership settlements and partnership changes; auditors, their duties and responsibilities, also points on higher and expert accounting and practical treatise on banking. Cleveland, Author, 1898. 390p.

CRAWFORD, J. N.

Office building accounting. *Buildings and building management,* Nov. 17, 1919, p. 5-7.

CRAWFORD, J. T.

Construction field books for bituminous macadam highways. *Good roads,* April 1, 1916, p. 164-6

CRAWFORD, JOHN JAY

Negotiable instruments law, from the draft prepared for commissioners on uniformity of laws; the full text of the law as enacted, with copious annotations. Ed.4. New York, Baker, Voorhis & co. 1916. 290p.

CRAWFORD, L. U.

Accounting for building and loan associations. *Business man's magazine,* Feb. March 1907, p. 108-12, 130-4.
Defalcations. *Accounting and commerce,* Sept. 1915, p. 124-8. *Journal of accountancy,* Aug. 1915, p. 112-21.
Standard plan of organization. *Business man's magazine,* Feb. 1907, p. 112-6.

CRAWFURD, MAJOR

Practical scheme for increasing production: the Priestman bonus system. *Accountant,* June 12, 1920, p. 695-8.

CREAMERIES

See also Dairying.

Accounting

AMERICAN business and accounting encyclopaedia; comp. by E. H. Beach and W. W. Thorne. Detroit, Bookkeeper publishing co. 1901. Creamery business accounting—v.2, p. 384-90.
CREAMERY accounting: a modern, complete and simple system. *New York produce review,* Aug. 8, 1917, p. 588.
ELSWORTH, R. H. System for keeping the accounts of a creamery. *Business man's magazine,* May 1908, p. 427-9.
HOLMES, O. W. Creamery records. *Idaho agricultural experiment station, Bulletin 90,* p. 1-19. 1916.
HUMPHREY, JOHN REGESTER and G. A. NAHSTOLL. Accounting records for country creameries. Washington, Government printing office, 1917, 37p. (United States. Department of agriculture, Bulletin no. 559).
KNAPP, GEORGE, BURTON B. MASON and A. V. SWARTHOUT. Classification of ledger accounts for creameries. Washington, Government printing office, 1920. 40p. (United States. Department of agriculture, bulletin, no. 865).
NIEMAN, JOHN F. Creamery bookkeeping. *The office,* Dec. 1889, p. 219-20.
ROBOTKA, F. Marketing business practice in its relation to the dairy industry. *Cooperative manager and farmer,* Feb. 1918, p. 66-8.
TOLSTRUP, G. A. Accounting systems. *Kimball's dairy farmer,* Sept. 1, 1917, p. 585.
TOLSTRUP, G. A. Vermont creameries install new accounting system. *Hoard's dairyman,* Sept. 18, 1917, p. 289.
WASHBURN, CARL H. Accounting methods for wholesale creamery business. *Business man's magazine,* Feb. 1908, p. 184-87.
WHITE, BENJAMIN D. Simple method of keeping creamery records. Washington, Government printing office, 1908.

Costs

BAIN, J. B. and R. J. POSSON. Requirements and cost of producing market milk in northwestern Indiana. Washington, Government printing office, 1920. 31p. (United States. Department of agriculture, bulletin no. 858).
HIBBARD, B. H. and A. HOBSON. Marketing Wisconsin butter. *New York produce review,* Dec. 20, 1916, p. 302, 314.
PRICE for making butter. *New York produce review,* Feb. 9, 1916, p. 610-11.
VITAL question: what is your operating expense per pound of butter manufactured? *New York produce review,* Mar. 7, 1917, p. 746.

CREAMERY accounting: a modern, complete and simple system. *New York produce review,* Aug. 8, 1917, p. 588.

CREATED goodwill. *Accountant,* Oct. 29, Nov. 12, Dec. 3, 1910, p. 577-9, 639-40, 753-7.

CREATING capital. Lipman, F. L. 1918.

CREDIT

See also Agriculture-Credit; Banks and banking; Loans; Negotiable instruments.

ANYON, J. T. Safeguarding bank loans. *Journal of accountancy,* Dec. 1910, p. 97-107.
ATKINSON, MEREDITH. Some principles of the credit system. *Accountant,* Oct. 30, 1920. p. 470-6.
BALANCE sheets and credits. *Canadian chartered accountant,* Jan. 1919, p. 230-1.
BANTA, C. W. How the public accountant helps modern business. *Bankers monthly,* Dec. 1920, p. 28-9, 88.
BRADDON, H. Y. Modern world of credit. *Accountant,* March 11, 1916, p. 308-15.
BUTCHART, J. R. Money, credit and banking. *Accountant,* June 23, 30, 1917, p. 589-93, 606-10. *Accounting and commerce,* April, May, June 1917, p. 14-8, 36-44, 63-5.
COMMERCIAL credits. *Journal of accountancy,* July 1914, p. 55-6.

CREDIT—*(Continued)*

ETTINGER, RICHARD PRENTICE and DAVID E. GOLIEB. Credits and collections. Ed.2. New York, Prentice-Hall, c1917.

FORM of financial statement. *Journal of accountancy*, March April, July 1916, p. 217-8, 275-80; 74-6.

FORMS for uniform credit statements. *Journal of the American bankers association*, Aug. 1917, p. 99-101.

GALLOWAY, LEE. Handling credits, collections, and complaints. (In his *Office management*. 1918. p. 308-23).

GIFFORD, T. J. CARLYLE. Inflation of credit. *Accountants' magazine*, Dec. 1917, p. 474-84.

GIFFORD, T. J. CARLYLE. Inflation of credit and a tax on capital. *Accountants' magazine*, June 1918, p. 229-43. *Public accountant*, Nov. Dec. 1918, p. 136-40, 150-7.

GRIFFITH, JAMES B. Credit organization. (In *Cyclopedia of commerce, accountancy, business administration*. 1910. v.1. p. 127-80).

HAGERTY, JAMES E. Commercial credit. *Journal of accountancy*, April 1907, p. 429-37.

HAGERTY, JAMES E. Credit man. *Journal of accountancy*, June 1907, p. 112-21.

HAGERTY, JAMES E. History of the National credit men's association. *Journal of accountancy*, Nov. 1907, p. 44-56.

HAGERTY, JAMES E. Mercantile credit. New York, Henry Holt & co. 1913. 382p.

HUNTER, JOEL. Public accountant and the credit man. (In his *Thinking in figures*. c1916. p. 92-109). *Journal of accountancy*, July 1914, p. 1-12.

HURDMAN, FREDERICK H. Credits from the viewpoint of a certified public accountant. *Journal of accountancy*, Dec. 1914, p. 435-54. Editorial. Certified statements. *Journal of accountancy*, Nov. 1914, p. 374-5.

JONES, EDWARD D. Credit and collection. (In his *Administration of industrial enterprises*. 1911. p. 417-34).

KESTER, ROY B. Cash and mercantile credits. (In his *Accounting theory and practice*. 1918. v.2. p. 210-24).

KLEIN, JOSEPH J. Development of mercantile instruments of credit in the United States. *Journal of accountancy*, Sept. 1911-March 1912, p. 321-45, 422-49, 526-37, 594-607, 44-50, 122-32, 207-17.

KNIFFIN, WILLIAM HENRY. Bonds as credit instruments. *Banking law journal*, Jan. 1914, p. 53-7.

KNIFFIN, WILLIAM HENRY. Commercial paper, acceptances and the analysis of credit statements; a practical treatise on commercial paper, with particular reference to the processes by which the credit risk is determined where such instruments are purchased as a bank investment. New York, Bankers publishing co. 1918. 162p.

KNIFFIN, WILLIAM HENRY. Essentials in granting credit. (In his *Practical work of a bank*. 1917. p. 371-502).

KNIFFIN, WILLIAM HENRY. Theory and practice of credit. *Bankers magazine*, Nov. 1914, p. 509-12.

LEAMY, R. H. Essential features in a report for credit purposes. *Accountant*, Jan. 25, 1919, p. 68-70. *Accounting and commerce*, Dec. 1918, p. 200-5. *Canadian chartered accountant*, April 1919, p. 321-6. *Journal of accountancy*, Aug. 1918, p. 161-8.

LEFFINGWELL, WILLIAM HENRY. Office side of credits and collections. (In his *Scientific office management*. 1917. p. 152-7).

MASTERS, J. EDWARD. Financial statements as a basis of credit. *Journal of accountancy*, May 1915, p. 334-43.

MATTHEWS, JAMES. Credit conditions in South American countries. *Journal of accountancy*, Dec. 1916, p. 443-50.

MEEK, CHARLES E. Credit granting. *Journal of accountancy* Dec. 1914, p. 427-34.

MEYER, CHARLES A. Mercantile credits and collections. New York, The Macmillan company, 1919. 302p.

MORAWETZ, VICTOR. Evils of excessive credit expansion. *Journal of accountancy*, March 1908, p. 345-56.

MORSE, HAROLD S. Examination, for credit purpose, of a book publishing house. *Accountant*, Feb. 15, 1919, p. 124-8. *Journal of accountancy*, Oct. 1918, p. 278-89. *Public accountant*, Jan. 1919, p. 184-96.

MOSS, A. G. Value of an audited statement. *Journal of accountancy*, Dec. 1914, p. 455-9.

NEWCOMER, W. Analysis of a credit statement. *Investment weekly*, July 7, 1917.

NICHOLSON, J. LEE and J. F. D. ROHRBACH. Return credit records. (In their *Cost accounting*. 1919. p. 283-.
its uses. New York, D. Appleton & co.

PARSONS, CARL COPELAND. Credits and collections records. (In his *Office organization and management*. 1918. p. 237-45).

PRENDERGAST, WILLIAM AMBROSE. Credit and its uses. New York, D. Appleton & co. 1916. 361p.

PUBLIC accounting as a safeguard to the credit system. *Journal of accountancy*, April 1906, p. 465-74.

ROBERTS, WILLIAM H. Credit man and the public accountant. *Journal of accountancy*, April 1906, p. 465-74.

SCOVELL, CLINTON H. Importance of sound accounting in credit relations. *Journal of accountancy*, Nov. 1912, p. 365-79.

SHARER, W. P. Essentials of credit statements and analysis of credits and balances. *Journal of the American bankers association*, April 1917.

SHARER, W. P. Report of committee on credit forms. *Journal of the American bankers' associatian*, Nov. 1917. p. 351-6.

SKINNER, EDWARD M. and STEPHEN GILMAN. Credits. Chicago, La Salle extension university, 1918. 110p.

THOMAS, H. IVOR. Accounting and auditing as related to credits. *Journal of accountancy*, Feb. 1914, p. 115-20.

THULIN, FREDERICK. Mathematics of credit extension. *Journal of accountancy*, April 1919, p. 259-67.

WAHLSTAD, PETER P. and W. S. JOHNSON. Credit and the credit man. New York, Alexander Hamilton institute, c1918. 342p. (Modern business, v.8).

WALL, ALEXANDER. Banker's credit manual; a complete survey of the credit department —its obligations and its opportunities, how to systematize the work, stabilize operations, and facilitate investigations; together with schemes for comparative analysis and many approved forms reproduced in facsimile. Indianapolis, Bobbs-Merrill company, c.1919. 247p.

WALL, ALEXANDER. Study of "credit barometrics"; reprinted from the Federal reserve bulletin, March 1919. 24p.

WALTON, SEYMOUR. Securing a creditor. *Journal of accountancy*, Aug. 1915, p. 148.

WEIR, FRANK. Credit and merchants' clearing-houses. *Accountant*, July 9, 1892, p. 544-6.

WILDMAN, JOHN RAYMOND. Certified financial statements as a basis for credit. *Journal of accountancy*, Sept. 1920, p. 161-8.

CREDIT, DEFERRED
See Deferred credit.

CREDIT and its uses. Prendergast, W. A. 1916.

CREDIT and the credit man. Wahlstad, P. P. and W. S. Johnson. c1918.

CREDIT conditions in South American countries. Matthews, James.

CREDIT due to operating department for power utilization and train movement that reduces consumption of fuel per ton mile. *Railway and engineering review*, Aug. 16, 1913, p. 782-3.

CREDIT forms—prepared by the committee on credit blanks, American bankers association. *Journal of the American bankers association,* May, 1910.

CREDIT from the viewpoint of the certified public accountant. Hurdman, F. H.

CREDIT granting. Meek, C. E.

CREDIT INSURANCE.
See Insurance—Credit.

CREDIT man. Haggerty, J. E.

CREDIT man and the public accountant. Roberts, W. H.

CREDIT of the nations: correspondence. *Journal of accountancy,* Feb. 1919, p. 158.

CREDIT organisation. Griffith, J. B.

CREDIT system of wage payments in Chicago. *Electric railway journal,* Jan. 12, 1918, p. 89-90.

CREDITS. Skinner, E. M. and Stephen Gilman 1918

CREDITS and collections. Ettinger, R. P. and D. E. Golieb. c1917.

CREDITS from the viewpoint of a certified public accountant. Hurdman, F. H.

CREIGHTON, W. M.
Mode of keeping the accounts of a regimental pay office. Abergavenny, 1884.

CREKE, FRANK.
Investigation of public companies' accounts and reports thereon. *Accountant,* Jan. 5, 1889, p. •7-11.

CRELLIN, PHILIP
Bookkeeping and commercial terms. Whittaker. 1892.
Bookkeeping for teachers and pupils, with accounts in illustration, exercises, etc. London, 1892.
Book-keeping for wholesale and retail traders. London 1871.
New manual of book-keeping for wholesale and retail traders. London, 1871.

CRESPOLANI, RICCARDO.
Imposta straordinaria sul partrimonio, manuale pratico per 1 contribuenti. Roma, 1920. 113p.

CREW, ALBERT.
Chairman of general meetings of companies. *Accountant,* Feb. 28, March 6, 13, 1920, p. 231-2, 262-3, 294-6.
Changes in the law and the chief leading cases during the war. *Accountant,* July 12, 19, 26, Aug. 2, 9, 16, 23, 30, Sept. 6, 13, 20, 27, Oct. 4, 11, 18, 25, Nov. 1, 1919, p. 26-8, 50-2, 75-6, 99-100, 122-4, 38-40, 162-4, 186-7, 202-3, 218-20, 239-40, 254, 278-80, 294-6, 318-20, 339, 362-4.
Examinations. *Canadian chartered accountant,* April 1920, p. 273-5.
Government and control of limited companies. *Accountant,* Nov. 6-Dec. 25, 1920, p. 493-4, 517-9, 541-2, 573-4, 621-2, 637-9, 669-70, 689-91.
Law and practice relating to the stamping of commercial documents. *Accountant,* May 15,-Oct. 23, 1920, p. ——, 586-7, 618-9, 651-2, 683-4, 727-8, 706-8, 3-4, 27-8, 512, 74; 6; 100-2; 130-2; 163-4; 178-81; 212-5; 227-30; 250-3; 2858; 317-9; 341-3; 373-5; 405-7; 437-8.
Law and procedure of meetings. *Accountant,* July 25, Aug. 1, 8, 1914, p. 129-33, 154-8, 179-80. *Incorporated accountants' journal,* May 1914, p. 234-43.
Powers of majorities. *Accountant,* June 14, 1919, p. 498-500.
What is an accountant. *Accountant,* July 17, 1920, p. 52-3.

CREWDSON, ERNEST
Amalgamations. *Accountant,* Jan. 26, 1901, p. 126-32. *Accountants' magazine,* Jan. 1901, p. 8-26.
Codification of an audit. *Accountant,* Feb. 22, 1902, p. 214-20.

CRIMINAL liabilities of auditors. *Accountant,* Nov. 24, Dec. 1, 15, 1900, p. 1045-54, 1069-73, 1133-5.

CRISP, FRANK
Shortcomings of the company's acts. *Accountant,* April 29, June 17, 1905, p. 534, 725.

CRISSEY, F.
Getting together in Iowa. *Country gentleman,* Dec. 15, 1917, p. 1974-5.

CRITES, F. C. Suggested organiation for track maintenance. *Railway age,* Dec. 18, 1914, p. 1148.

CRITICAL guide to the incorporated accountant's examinations. Nelson, C. H.

CRITICISM of a balance sheet. *Canadian chartered accountant,* July 1920, p. 18-21.

CRITICISM of department of practical accounting. *Journal of accountancy,* July 1912, p. 70-3.

CRITICISM of local authorities accounts. *Accountant,* Nov. 17, 1906, p. 592-4.

CRITICISM of Seattle lighting department cost data. *Journal of electricity, power and gas.* Aug. 8, 1914, p. 131.

CRITICISM of tentative system of accounts by Central electric railway accountants' association. *Electric railway journal,* March 28, 1914, p. 723-5.

CRITICISM of the proposed undistributed surplus tax by the American institute of accountants. *Economic world,* July 28, 1917. p. 125-6.

CRITICS, not the examiners, are at fault. Geijsbeek, J. B.

CRITTENDEN, ——— AND GROSBECK
Bookkeeping. Philadelphia. 1870.

CRITTENDEN, S. W.
Elementary treatise on bookkeeping by single and double entry. Philadelphia, W. S. Fortescue & co. 1852.
Inductive and practical treatise on bookkeeping by single and double entry . . . containing nine sets of books . . . also a set of steamboat books, etc. Philadelphia, 1850.
Inductive and practical treatise on bookkeeping by single and double entry. Counting house edition. Philadelphia W. S. Fortescue & co. 1870.
——— Including key to high school edition. Philadelphia, W S. Fortescue & co. 1870.
———Same. High school edition. Philadelphia, W. S. Fortescue & co. 1870.
Key to an elementary treatise on book-keeping by single and double entry. Philadelphia, E. C. & J. Biddle, 1853. 60p.

CRITTENDEN, S. W.—*(Continued)*
Key to the counting-house and high-school editions of Crittenden's book-keeping. Philadelphia, 1853.
Single entry book-keeping explained in five sets of books. Enlarged edition. Philadelphia. W. S. Fortescue & co. 1878.
Treatise on book-keeping by single and double entry; abridged for the use of schools. Philadelphia, E. C. & J. Biddle.
Treatise on bookkeeping for single and double entry. Philadelphia, E. C. & J. Biddle.
Treatise on single entry book-keeping. Philadelphia, W. S. Fortescue & co. 1854.

CROAD, H. J.
Depreciation, appreciation, discount, interest and annuity tables. New York Spectator company.

CROCK, H. R.
Reducing errors in the accounting routine; how a St. Louis bank met the labor problem caused by the war and made the work easier for the new women bookkeepers. *Bankers' monthly,* Chicago, v. 35, no. 7, p. 18.

CROCKER, WILLIAM T.
Efficiency in mining. *Colliery,* Feb. 1913, p. 395-6.
Importance of up-to-date mine accounting. *Mining and engineering world,* 1913, v.39, p. 837-8.

CROHURST, H. R.
Cost of installing small water works systems in Massachusetts. *Engineering and contracting,* May 26, 1915, p. 461-5.

CROISSANT, V. G.
Mechanics of construction. Cost keeping. *Government accountant,* March 1908, p. 504-29.

CROMPTON, JAMES.
Municipal finance. *Accountants' magazine,* April 1903, p. 200-21.

CROMPTON and Knowles loom works adopts old age pensions. *Textile world,* July 15, 1916, p. 3188.

CRONHELM, F. W.
Double entry by single: a new method of bookkeeping. London, Longmans, Green & co. 1818.

CRONHOLM, F. N.
Methods and cost of land leveling with tractors. *Engineering and contracting,* June 12, 1918, p. 590-1. Cond. *Engineering news,* Sept. 5, 1918,. p. 438-9.

CROOM-JOHNSON, R. P.
Bankruptcy and deeds of arrangement act, 1913. *Incorporated accountants' journal,* Oct. 1914, p. 15-8.
Preferential payments in bankruptcy and winding up. *Incorporated accountants' journal,* 1908-9, p. 262.

CROPPER, LIONEL CUTHBERT
Bookkeeping and accounts: a text-book for students. London, McDonald & Evans, 1910. 760p.
——— Same. Ed.11. London, Gee & co. 900p.
Elementary bookkeeping: a text book for beginners. London, Macdonald and Evans, 1910. 284p.
——— Same. New ed. London, Macdonald and Evans, 1916. 105p.
Examinations, with special reference to auditing. *Accountant,* Dec. 6, 1902, p. 1270-83.
Key to bookkeeping and accounts. Adelphi, England, Macdonald and Evans, 1918. 736p.
Primer of bookkeeping: a first course for students. Adelphi, England, Macdonald & Evans 1911. 160p.
Some notes on balance sheets. *Accountant,* April 19, 1919, p. 326-32. *Canadian chartered accountant,* July 1919, p. 6-20.

CROSBY, A. F.
Financial control over municipal receipts and expenditures. *National municipal league, Proceedings,* 1899, p. 148-54.

CROSBY, O. T.
Methods of determining the wages of employees. *Electric railway journal,* Aug. 24, 1912, p. 285.
Physical valuations. *American electric railway association. Proceedings,* 1911, p. 368. Abstract. *Electric railway journal,* Oct. 14, 1911, p. 874-6. Editorial. *Stone and Webster public service journal,* Nov. 1911, p. 309.

CROSBY, R. H.
Corporate organization and management. *Bankers magazine,* June and July 1912.

CROSBY, W. W.
Accounting system for road expenditures. *Engineering record,* Dec. 28, 1912.
Building construction costs. *Textile world,* Mar. 1915, p. 577-8.

CROSS, CLEAVELAND R.
Legal principles governing the determination of partnership assets. *Journal of accountancy,* Feb. 1915, p. 97-106.

CROSS, JOHN ASHTON
Articles of association. *Incorporated accountants' journal,* 1902-3. p. 144.
Distinctive feature of limted liability companies. *Incorporated accountants' journal,* 1902-3, p. 122.
Promotion and formation of a company. *Incorporated accountants journal,* 1902-3, p. 126.
Receivers and liquidators. *Incorporated accountants' journal,* 1902-3, p. 180.
Secretary accounts, dividends and auditors. *Incorporated accountants' journal,* 1902-3, p. 176.
Underwriting, making a market allotment, etc. *Incorporated accountants' journal,* 1902-3, p. 148.

CROSS, L. W.
Foreign exchange; the Eastern exchanges. *Business organisation and management,* Nov. 1920, p. 201-5.

CROSS, WILLIAM L.
Cost of mule and locomotives haulage. *Coal age,* March 6, 1919, p. 439-40.

CROSSIN, A. L.
Audit of the accounts of an executor and trustee on behalf of a life tenant. *Accountants' journal,* 1900-1, p. 168.

CROUCHER, S. H.
Building societies' accounts. *Incorporated accountants' journal,* 1893-4, p. 108.

CROWELL, BENEDICT.
America's munitions 1917-1918. Washington, Government printing office, 1919. 592p.
Cost of construction of the Muscle Shoals Nitrate plant. *Electrical world,* Feb. 8, 1919, p. 281.

CROWELL, H. H.

Electric lighting rates and depreciation. *Municipal journal and engineering,* Dec. 18, 1907, p. 698.
Report of an investigation of the electric companies of Detroit with special reference to rates and methods of charging. Sept. 28, 1907. 22p.
Reproduction cost is fair. *Electric railway journal,* March 15, 1919, p. 500-1.

CROWELL, NORMAN H.

Checking up the banks records. *Business man's magazine,* Feb. 1912, p. 178-9.

CROWTHER, GEORGE.

Private arrangements with creditors. *Accountant,* Nov. 10, 1900, p. 1005-7.

CROWTHER, SAMUEL

Just what is the Whitley report? *Factory,* Aug. 1919, p. 269-73.
Wages and profit sharing delusions. *World's work,* Oct. 1919, p. 625-32.

CROXTON, OSCAR C

Short cuts to practical bookkeeping. Heath Springs, S. C., O. C. Croxton. 1907.

CROZIER, WILLIAM

Answers to arguments against the scientific management system in vogue in arsenals. *Iron trade review,* Nov. 19, 1914, p. 965.
Criminal speeding-up system—and some facts. *American industries,* Jan. 1915, p. 30-1.
Labor's interest in administration. *Annals of the American academy of political and social science,* Sept. 1920, p. 153-8.

CRUDGINTON, C. D.

Goodyear industrial republic. *Industrial management,* Feb. 1920, p. 125-6.

CRUICKSHANK, E W

Transpositions. *Accounting and commerce,* Dec. 1917, p. 200-2. *Federal accountant,* Oct. 1917, p. 122-6.

CRUMB, WILLIAM H

Determination of telephone rates for large exchanges. *Journal of the Western society of engineers,* Dec. 1907, p. 781.

CRUMP, FRANK H.

Detachable voucher draft. *Railroad gazette,* Sept. 13, 1907, p. 284-6.
Operating department accounts—the basis of accounting department records. *Railway age gazette,* Aug. 21, 1908, p. 751-2.

CRYAN, GEORGE H.

Cutting transportation costs with motor trucks. *Paper,* July 21, 1920, p. 23-4.

CUBAN stamp tax law; law of July 31st, 1917. 11p.

CUBBERLY, A. H.

Improvements in time study methods. *Industrial management,* Aug. 1919, p. 118-20.

CUBBERLY, E. P.

Costs, funds and accounting. (In his *Public school administration.* 1916. p. 408-22)
Records and reports. (In his *Portland survey,* 1915, p. 421-5.
Records and reports. (In his *Public school administration.* 1916, p. 423-9).

CUDDEBACK, A. W.

Memoranda of office records. *Journal of the American waterworks association,* Dec. 1918, p. 429-33.

CUDWORTH, ALFRED JAMES

Adjustment of partnership accounts. *Accountant,* Jan. 23, 1892, p. 85-90.
Apportionment. *Accountant,* 1887, p. 343.
Some notes on cost accounts. *Accountant,* April 18, 1897, p. 312-9.

CULLEN, W. J.

Bankruptcy (Scotland). (In Lisle, George. *Encyclopaedia of accounting.* v.1. p. 329-62).

CULKINS, W. C

Cincinnati plan explained. *Aera,* Dec. 1918, p. 465-6.

CULKINS, W. C.

Why do car fares differ? *Electric railway journal,* April 3, 1920, p. 710-11.

CULPIN, H.

Premium wages systems. (In Lisle, George. *Encyclopaedia of accounting.* v.5. p. 315-9).
Stock accounts. *Incorporated accountants journal,* 1905-6. p. 172.
Wage systems. *Incorporated accountants journal,* 1902-3, p. 205.

CULSHAW, WILLIAM

Motors for municipalities—the economic aspects. *Accountant,* July 26, 1913, p. 139-43.

CULVER, A. I.

Administrative accounting. *Incorporated accountants' journal,* 1902-3, p. 230.

CULVER, C. H.

System in a factory stock department. *Engineering magazine,* May 1915, p. 174-83.

CULVER, W. W.

How Kenyon got going. *System,* March 1917, p. 244-52.

CULVERTS

Cost accounting

COST keeping system for small bridge and culvert jobs. *Engineering and contracting,* June 27, 1917, p. 588-9.

Costs

JENSAN, JAMES. Cost of constructing concrete culverts under canal in Sevier county, Utah. *Engineering and contracting,* April 23, 1913.
LAMBIE, J. S. Reinforced concrete successful for railroad culverts. *Engineering record,* Jan. 27, 1917, p. 136-7.
MARSHALL, B. G. Costs of installing corrugated iron culverts. *Engineering and contracting,* June 28, 1916, p. 588.
METHODS and cost of constructing a combination corrugated pipe and concrete culvert. *Engineering and contracting,* Jan. 1, 1913.
MONOLITHIC concrete culverts at low cost in New York state. *Concrete,* Feb. 1916, p. 91.

CUMBERLEDGE, E.

Monthly payroll showing unit costs. *Railway age gazette,* Nov. 17, 1911, p. 1011.

CUMMIN, G. C.

Budget making; with discussion. *City managers' association, Proceedings,* 1915, p. 94-105.

CUMMING, E. J.

Finance act, 1917, part 1 (land and income tax). *Accounting and commerce,* Dec. 1917, p. 202-5.
Note on income tax. *Accounting and commerce,* Oct. Nov. Dec. 1915, June 1916, p. 150-2, 174-6, 197-9, 52.

CUMMING, E. J. R.
See Cunningham, H. A., joint author.

CUMMINGS, F. T.
Methods and cost of making a snow survey for irrigation system. *Engineering and contracting,* Aug. 30, 1916, p. 189-92.

CUMMINS, C. LESLIE
Accounts relating to the conversion of a business into a limited company. *Accountant,* May 26, 1900, p. 502-7.

CUMMINS, CHARLES
Book-keeping: suggestions on editing of accounts. London, Simpkin, Marshall, Hamilton, Kent & co. 1893.
Bookkeeping; key. London, Simpkin, Marshall, Hamilton, Kent & co. 1887-9.
Guide to the formation of the accounts of limited liability companies, with forms, etc. London. ?1894.

CUMULATIVE book index; author, title and subject catalog of books and pamphlets published in the United States; monthly. New York, The H. W. Wilson co.

CUNLIFF, N.
Development of a unit cost system. *Journal of the association of engineering societies,* Aug. 1914, p. 74-85. *Engineering and contracting,* Oct. 21, 1914, p. 374-6. Discussion. *Journal of the association of engineering societies,* Aug.-Sept. 1914, p. 85-101, 165-70.

CUNNINGHAM, H. A. AND E. J. R. CUMMING
Land and income tax law and practice; an exposition of the law and practice relating to land tax and income tax in New Zealand. Wellington, N.Z. Accountancy and educational publications. 178p.

CUNNINGHAM, JOHN W.
Asphalt pavement cost with municipal plant. *Engineering news-record,* August 24, 1916, p. 375.

CUNNINGHAM, W.
Back to Adam Smith. *Accountants' magazine,* Jan. 1904, p. 7-22.
Economics of railroad maintenance of way. *Journal of accountancy,* March 1910, p. 358-68.

CUNNINGHAM, W. A.
What did it cost? how the question is answered in one jewelry factory. *Factory,* Aug. 1916, p. 148-51.

CUNNINGHAM, W. M.
Economics of railroad maintenance of way *Journal of accountancy,* March 1910, p. 358-68.

CUNNINGHAM, WILLIAM
Accomplishments of the United States railroad administration in unifying and standardizing the statistics of operation. *Annals of the American academy of political and social science,* Nov. 1919, p. 35-59.
Costs vs. results at a glance—how the vital statistics of railroad operation are charted for the guidance of the management. *System,* Oct. 1912, p. 384-91.
Machine shop costs (with discussion). *Engineers society of western Pennsylvania, Proceedings,* v.22, p. 429-44.
Separation of railroad operating expenses between freight and passenger services. *Quarterly journal of economics,* Feb. 1917, p. 209-40.
Standardizing of operating statistics; scope and purposes of the railroad administration new plan for uniformity in statistical reports. *Railway age,* Jan. 3, 1919, p. 43-8.

CURBING waste in motor trucking. *Iron trade review,* April 18, 1918, p. 976-8.

CURRAN, H. T.
Cost of mill construction. *Engineering and contracting,* Oct. 6, 1915, p. 266-8. *Engineering and mining journal,* Aug. 28, 1915, p. 345-7.

CURRAN, JOHN PHILPOB
Freight rates; studies in rate construction, Chicago, Railway text book publisher co., 1913, 367p.

CURRAN, L. V.
Coal and ash handling at Grundy plant. *Power,* November 14, 1916, p. 695.

CURRAN, M. A.
Cost keeping discussed before contractors. *Electrical world,* Mar. 3, 1917, p. 433.

CURRAN, S. P.
Sense and system in the sales department. *Business man's magazine,* March 1905, p. 554-8.
Subscription manager. *Business man's magazine,* Dec. 1905, p. 1075-9.

CURRENCY
See Money.

CURRENCY and banking problem. *Journal of accountancy,* Aug. 1910, p. 289-91.

CURRENCY—banking and accountancy. Garrison, E. E.

CURRENCY discussion. *Journal of accountancy,* March 1908, p. 399-402.

CURRENT ASSETS
See Assets—Current.

CURRENT comment on corporation tax bill. *Journal of accountancy,* Nov. 1909, p. 51-6.

CURRIE, ARCHIBALD ERNEST.
Solicitor's audits. London, Whitcomb & Tombs, 1915. 83p.

CURRIE, G W.
On prospectuses. *Accountants' magazine,* May 1906, p. 264-70.
Prospects of Canadian land mortgage companies. *Accountants magazine,* 1899, p. 495.

CURRIER, E. L.
Labor charge in farm cost accounting. *Hoard's diary,* Nov. 2, 1917, p. 494.

CURTIS, J. F.
Priority board for capital: federal control for regulation of new security issues recommended. *Financial world,* Nov. 24, 1917, p. 23.
Double entry bookkeeping; a complete treatise

CURTIS, W. M.
Trucking costs. *Engineering record,* Feb. 7, 1914, p. 166. *Industrial engineering,* March 1914, p. 132.

CURTISS, C. C.
American standard bookkeeping. High school ed. New York, American book co. 1903, 1906.

CURTISS, C. C.—*(Continued)*
Key to American standard book-keeping. High school edition. New York, American book co. 1906.
Manual of bookkeeping. New York, American book co.
New common school book-keeping and blanks. St. Paul. D. D. Merrill co. 1886.

CURTISS, W. B.
Depreciation of property. *General electric review,* Dec. 1915, p. 1099-106.

CUSACK, JAMES
on its theory and practice. London, Methuen & co. 1911. 414p.

CUSHING, A. S. B.
Increased cost of line extensions. *Electrical world,* April 20, 1918, p. 832.

CUSHING, GEORGE H.
What does it cost to make steam; the test in buying coal. *Factory,* June 1917, p. 820-2.

CUSHING, H. G. comp.
Rules and regulations of certain states relating to efficiency records. New York state library. Legislative reference section. March 1919. 44 typewitten pages.

CUSHING, HARRY A.
Services rendered by trust companies under voting trust agreements. *Trust companies,* Feb. 1916, p. 170-2.

CUSHING, S. B.
Develop big consumers. *Gas age,* April 10, 1920, p. 327-8. Condensed. *American gas engineering journal,* April 3, 1920, p. 264.

CUSHMAN, JOHN M.
Survey of operating costs in thirteen school buildings. *Heating and ventilating,* Nov. 1916, v. 25-34.

CUSTODY of depreciation funds. *Electrical world,* Jan. 20, 1912, p. 126.

CUSTOM HOUSES
Clark, A. B. Proposed customs union of the British empire. *Accountants' magazine,* 1898, p. 158.
Cordery, H. S. Customs work. *Accounting and commerce,* Nov. 1918, p. 187-90.
Frank, Charles Leo. United States customs service; its organization and administration. *Journal of accountancy,* June 1917, p. 131-7.

Accounting
American business and accounting encyclopedia: comp. by E. H. Beach and W. W. Thorne. Detroit, Bookkeeper publishing co. co. 1901. Custom house accounting, p. 397-406.

CUTFORTH, ARTHUR EDWIN
Accountancy incidental to company amalgamations. *Business organisation and management.* July, Aug. 1920, p. 363-70.
Amalgamation schemes: from an accountant's point of view. *Accountant,* Jan. 3, 1920, p. 11-24.
Audits. London, Gee & co. 1914. 238p.
Can the institute examinations be improved upon? *Accountant,* June 8, 1912, p. 868-72.
Early stages of preparation for the accountancy papers of the intermediate. London, Gee & co. 1906. 100p.
Methods of providing for depreciation. (In his *Audits.* 1914. p. 184-8).
Month before the examinations. London. 1908.
Organiation of an accountant's department. *Accountant,* May 10, 1913, p. 729-35.
Promotion of a public limited company; a few notes on the financial and accountancy aspects. *Accountant,* Dec. 5, 12, 1914, p. 690-5, 719-26.
Treatment of fluctuating currency in accounts. London, Gee & co. 1910. 56p.
Treatment of fluctuating currency in accounts of English companies. *Accountant,* Nov. 19, 1910, p. 690-9.

CUTLER, A. S.
Valuation of railroad property in Minnesota. *Engineers society; University of Minnesota, Year book,* 1908.

CUTLER, F. C.
Handy cost sheets for new work. *Factory,* Jan. 1912, p. 26-7.

CUTTING central station costs. Williams, S. B. 1919.

CUTTING costs in the factory office. *Factory,* Oct. 1918, Feb., June-July, Sept. Nov.-Dec. 1919, p. 728+, 292+, 1226+, 200+, 686. 1088+, 1462+.

CUTTING costs in the factory office; routing forms graphically. *Factory,* July 1919, p. 200.

CUTTING factory costs. *System,* May-Sept. 1914, p. 549-52, 662-4; 105-8, 216-20, 328-32.

CUTTING haulage costs. *Factory,* March 1918, p. 450.

CUTTING out small charges. *System,* Oct. 1917, p. 610.

CYANIDE PLANTS

Accounting
Irwin, D. F. Cyanide plant accounting. *Engineering and mining journal,* May 2, 1914, p. 897-9.

Costs
Cost of cyanidation at Nipissing. *Engineering and mining journal,* Feb. 7, 1914, p. 327.
Cyaniding costs at Douglas Island, Alaska. *Engineering and mining journal,* July 1, 1916, p. 24.
Megraw, H. A. Cost of cyaniding. *Engineering and mining journal,* Mar. 13, 1915, p. 485-7.
Operating costs at the Liberty Bell mill, Teluride, Colo. *Engineering and mining journal,* July 1, 1916, p. 34.

CYANIDING costs at Douglas Island, Alaska. *Engineering and mining journal,* July 1, 1916, p. 24.

CYCLOPEDIA of civil engineering. Chicago, American technical society. 8v.

CYCLOPEDIA of commerce, accountancy, business administration. 10v. Chicago, American school of correspondence, 1910.

CYCLOPEDIA of law and procedure.
See Corpus juris.

CYCLOPEDIA of practical accounting. 4v. Chicago, American technical society. 1912.

CYPHERS, J. F.
Operation of warehouse heating plant of Merck and company, Rahway, N. J. *Heating and ventilating,* Feb. 1916, p. 35.

DABOLL, N.
Schoolmaster's assistant. Utica, 1832.

DADISMAN, A. J.
See Johnson, O. M., joint author.

DAFFORNE, RICHARD
Apprentices time-entertainer accomptantly; or, A methodical means to obtain the exquisite art of accomptantship: Digested into Three parts, as is exemplified upon the next leaf. By Richard Dafforne, authour of the Merchants-mirrour. Very requisite to be exercised by all such as profess the Teaching of the said art. Now reviewed, and in several places rectified, the Waste-books altered, and composed after the usual method of merchants: Augmented with 85 instances; and at the end of each book is added a trial ballance: Likewise how to draw out accompts of sales, accompt currant, and invoices for him we serve in commission. Also the form of a book for charges of merchandize, which is at the end of the first Waste-book; by the use of which all the particular charges paid in the cash book are at the months end collected into one sum and so carried into the Journal. By John Dafforne Accomptant, and teacher of the said famous and never-dying art of accomptantship, in English or Dutch: Resident in More-Fields near Long-Alley in Neptune Court. Who likewise rectifieth books of accompts abroad or at home, whether in proper, factorage, or company. The third edition. London, W. Godbid, 1670.
English merchants companion: or, an entertainment for the young merchants, their servants. Digested into three parts. Wherein the perfect method of merchants book-keeping, and other matters relating to traffick, is compleatly demonstrated. Being the most exact work of this nature, extant. To which is annexed, directions for accomptants, and other persons, who enter themselves into the service of the Honourable Companies of Merchants of England, trading into the East Indies: shewing them how to begin, prosecute, and compleatly finish their several functions and offices. Entred by way of debitor and creditor. By Richard Dafforne, accomptant. The fourth edition, carefully corrected and augmented. London, Printed for Tho. Horne, at the South-entrance of the Royal exchange in Cornhil, 1700.
Merchants' mirrour: or, Directions for the Perfect ordering and keeping of his accounts; Framed by way of debitor and creditor after the (so tearmed) Italian-manner: containing 250 rare questions, with their answers, in forme of a dialogue. As likewise, A waste-booke, with a compleat iournall, and leager thereunto appertaining; unto the which I haue annexed two other Waste-bookes for exercise of the studious: and at the end of each is entered the briefe contents of the Leagers accounts arising from thence. And also, A moneth-booke, very requisite for merchants, and commodious for all other science-lovers of this famous art. Compiled by Richard Dafforne of Northampton, accountant, and teacher of the same, after an exquisite method, in the English, and Dutch language. At the end addressed To the art-inspiring youth are foure tables of principall and simple interest, etc.; by his son, John Dafforne, London, R. Young, 1636.
——— Same. Ed. 2, corrected and amended [Same title, with 3 mottoes in Dutch.] London, Printed by J. L. for Nicolas Bourn, at the South entrance of the Royall-Exchange, 1651.
——— Same. Ed. 3, corrected and amended [Same title, with 3 mottoes in Dutch.] London, Printed by R. H. and J. G. for Nicholas Bourn, at the South-entrance of the Royall Exchange, 1660. [See Malynes Consuetudo, vel Lex Mercatoria, 1656].
——— Same. [Same title as the 3rd.] London, Printed by Miles Flesher, for Robert Horne, at the South entrance of the Royal Exchange, 1684. [See Malynes Consuetudo, vel lex mercatoria, 1686.]

DAFOE, J. W.
Pressing questions of the day. *Canadian chartered accountant,* Jan. 1920, p. 159-62.

DAGGER, G. N.
Useful farm records and accounts. *Ohio agricultural extension bureau,* v. 12, no. 4, 1916-17. 12p.

DAGGETT, G. F.
County highway books and bookkeeping. *American city,* (T & C ed.) April 1919, p. 327-30.

DAGGETT, STUART
Railroad reorganiation. Cambridge, Harvard university press. c1918. 404p.

DAILY balances in several banks. *Business man's magazine,* April 1911, p. 393-4.

DAILY business record and trial balance. Haas, E. H. 1894.

DAILY cost data sheets on concrete road construction. *Engineering record,* May 29, 1915, p. 676.

DAILY report form for steam shovel and dray line excavation work. *Engineering and contracting,* Sept. 20, 1916, p. 265.

DAILY reports, store room accounting and operating records of the Camden suburban railway. *Street railway journal,* Dec. 19. 1903, p. 1052-61.

DAILY statement of transportation expenses on the Chicago, Milwaukee & St. Paul. *Railway age gazette,* Jan. 19, 1912, p. 93-4.

DAILY time and material report systems of railroads. *Railway age gazette,* Sept. 19, 1913, p. 505-8.

DAIRY accounts. Rowland, Frederick. 1904.

DAIRY company accounts. *Accounting and commerce,* Oct. 1915, p. 154-6.

DAIRYING
See also Butter; Cheese.

Accounting
DAIRY company accounts. *Accounting and commerce,* Oct. 1915, p. 154-6.
FRASER, W. J. Cow index of keep and profit. Urbana, University of Illinois.
KERSIE, H. W. Simple method of book-keeping for farmers, market gardeners and dairymen. London, Headley brothers, 1907. 64p.
OLD problem again. *Hoard's dairyman,* Nov. 9, 1917, p. 538.
PHELPS, C. S. Accounts for a dairy farm. *Country gentleman,* Dec. 2, 1911, p. 6.
PHILLIPS, CHARLES. Concise check system of double entry book-keeping for small businesses; with examples applied to the dairy trade. [?London, 1895].
PIXLEY, FRANCIS W. Dairies. (In his *Accountancy,* Ed. 2, p. 106-8).
ROBINSON, F. D. Gathering in the cream. *Business,* Aug. 1913, p. 96-8.
ROSS, H. E. and others. Practical examples in dairy arithmetic. *Cornell agricultural experiment report,* 1916, v. 2, p. 1079-99.

DAIRYING—ACCOUNTING—*(Continued)*

ROWLAND, FREDERICK. Dairy accounts. London, Gee & co. 1904. 114p. (Accountants' library, v. 33).

SCHOLL, FREDERICK W. A. Dairy accounts. *Incorporated accountants journal,* 1900-1, p. 98.

TAYLOR, HERBERT and J. O. PEET. Principles and practice of book-keeping for the farm, garden, dairy and estate. Ed. 2, London, Simpkin, Marshall, Hamilton, Kent & co. 1912. 256p.

Cost accounting

LARSON, CARL WILLIAM. Milk production cost accounts; principles and methods. New York, Columbia university press, 1916, 60p. Biblography, p. 55-60.

MISNER, E. G. Calculating the cost of milk production. *Cornell reading course for the farm,* 142, p. 199-228, 1919.

Costs

PRELIMINARY report of the council of farms and markets of its investigation of the cost of production and distribution of milk in New York state. *Foods and markets,* Sept. 1919, p. 3-18.

Depreciation.

See Depreciation, depletion and obsolescence—Dairying.

DAKIN, EDWARD

Economics and accountancy. *Incorporated accountants' journal,* July 1920, p. 212-4.

DALE, SAMUEL S.

Cost finding for textile mills: cotton, woolen, worsted, hosiery, underwear. Ed. 2. Boston. Textiles. c1916. 32p.

Cost finding in woolen and wosted mills. Boston, Textiles, c1918. 49p.

DAISH, JOHN B.

Proposal to make railway reports reliable and intelligible. Washington, 1907. 4p.

DALGLEISH, L. B.

Transvaal municipal accounts. *South African accountants' journal,* v. 2, p. 70.

DALRYMPLE, JAMES

Glasgow corporation tramways. *Accountant,* March 4, April 8, 1905, p. 255-67, 406-10.

Standardisation of tramway accounts. *Accountant,* Oct. 3, 10, 1903, p. 1191-3, 1231-5.

Tramway accounts. (In Lisle, George. *Encyclopaedia of accounting.* v. 6. p. 225-43).

DALTON, HUGH

Economics: "Causes of increase and decrease of production." *Incorporated accountants' journal,* Dec. 1919, Feb. March, 1920, p. 51-4, 105-8, 117-20.

DALTON, J. P.

Check figure systems. *South African accountant,* June 1917, p. 5-9.
Excess profits duty and the pre-war standard income tax (consolidation) act. 1917. *South African accountant,* March 1918, p. 121-3.

DALTON, W. E.

Address: the progress of accountancy in the 19th century. *Accountant,* July 27, 1901, p. 856-60,

DALTON ADDING MACHINE COMPANY

Dalton table of decimal reciprocals from 1 to 100000. Ed 2. Poplar Bluff, Mo. Dalton adding machine co., 1912. $1.00.

DALY, J. M.

How to secure maximum use of freight cars. *Railway age gazette,* Oct. 11, 1912, p. 686-8.

DALY, RICHARD RYLAND

Income tax. *Accountant,* Jan. 27, 1894, p. 93.
Shipping accounts. London, Gee & co. 1905. 97p. (Accountants' library, v. 40).
Shipping accounts. *Accountant,* July 5-19, 1890, May 23, 1891, Jan. 7, 1899, Dec. 15, 1900, Jan. 19, 1901, p. 363-4, 377-9, 391-2, 398-404, 18-25, 1147-54, 76-8.

DAME, F. L.

Criticism of the proposed accounting system for New York elctric lighting corporations. *Electrical world,* 1908, v. 52, p. 819-22.

DAMS

Accounting

SEARS, S. P. How to lay out fieldwork and keep office records on earth-dam construction. *Engineering news-record,* May 3, 1917, p. 265-7.

Cost accounting

COST keeping records used in the construction of two dams for irrigation works at Santa Fe, New Mexico. *Engineering and contracting,* November 13, 1912, p. 555.
JENSON, J. Method of keeping costs on the Piute irrigation project earth dam. *Engineering and contracting,*. July 19, 1916, p. 56-8.

DANA, E.

Reporting and checking car defects in Boston. *Electric railway journal,* Sept. 9, 1911, 425-6.

DANA, JOHN C.

Books on accounting. *Nation's business,* June 1919, p. 78.

DANA, RICHARD T.

Analysis of trenching methods and costs. *Engineering record,* May 23, Oct. 10-17, 1914, 581-4, 409-10, 432-3.
Costs and methods of sewer trenching. *Engineering record,* Oct. 17, 1914, p. 432-3.
Economic handling of earth by wheel and Fresno scrapers. *Engineering and contracting,* June 3, 1914, p. 629-37.
Handbook of construction plant; its cost and efficiency. New York, McGraw-Hill book company, inc. 1914. 702p.

——— **and H. H. P. GILLETTE**

Cost analysis engineering. *Cyclopedia of commerce, accountancy, business administration.* 1910. v. 2. p. 251-318.
Cost analysis engineering. (In *Cyclopaedia of civil engineering.* v. 3, p. 313-380).
See also Gillette, Halbert Powers, joint author.

DANCE, E. H.

Multiple cheques. *Accountant,* March 15, 1919, p. 201-2. *South African accountant,* March 1919, p. 301-2.

DANDO, JOSEPH

Practical book-keeping. Philadelphia, Author. 1842.

DANFORTH, GEORGE H.

Items affecting cost of structural steel WORK. *Engineering society of western Pennsylvania,* Dec. 1916, p. 744-8. Excerpt. *Iron trade review,* Dec. 21, 1916, p. 1263-4. Abridged. *Engineering and contracting,* May 28, 1917, p. 297-8. Discussion. *Engineering society of western Pennsylvania,* Dec. 1916, p. 749-71.

DANGERFIELD, ATHELSTAN

Companies' acts: amendment bills, 1900. *Accountant,* June 9, 1900, p. 534.
Reports on accounts. *Accountant,* July 25, 1896, p. 633-9.

DANIEL, E. R.

Highway and survey account book. London, Simpkin, Marshall, Hamilton, Kent & co. 1838.

DANIELL, P. J.

Theory of perpetual compound interest. *Associated accountants' journal,* 1909, p. 178.

DANIELS, B.

Bargain printing. *Inland printer,* May 1918, p. 194-5.
Cost of cost keeping. *Inland printer,* June 1920, p. 344.
Cost of folding. *Inland printer,* Oct. 1914, p. 93-4.
Cost of handling stock. *Inland printer,* Oct. 1914, p. 92-3.
Cost of keeping standing matter. *Inland printer,* May 1914, p. 275-6.
Decimal unit. *Inland printer,* November 1916, p. 227-8.
Dividing a man. *Inland printer,* July 1914, p. 585-7.
Effect of volume of printing on cost. *Inland printer,* Oct. 1916, p. 79-80.
Handling paper costs. *Inland printer,* Jan. 1919, p. 406-7.
How the hour is divided. *Inland printer,* July 1914, p. 583-4.
Increasing costs. *Inland printer,* Nov. 1916, p. 226-7.
Intelligent use of the time-clock. *Inland printer,* Jan. 1913, p. 566-7.
Inventory. *Inland printer,* Feb. 1917, p. 658-9.
Job-ticket and the job. *Inland printer,* Jan. 1916, p. 524-7.
Keeping costs on the selling department. *Inland printer,* June 1917, p. 373.
Little study in binding prices. *Inland printer,* May 1916, p. 235.
Making prices on posters. *Inland printer,* Jan. 1916, p. 523-4.
One of the mysteries of binding; difference in cost between a twelve-page and sixteen-page booklet. *Inland printer,* Oct. 1916, p. 78-9.
Payroll and a few other items. *Inland printer,* Nov. 1919, p. 183-4.
Real plant value. *Inland printer,* March 1917, p. 797.
Salesman and the cost system. *Inland printer,* May 1914, p. 273.
Should proofreading be charged? *Inland printer,* Feb. 1917, p. 660.
What is the cost per thousand? *Inland printer,* Dec. 1914, p. 393-6.
What should a cost system cost? *Inland printer,* Oct. 1919, p. 49-50.

DANIELS, F. H.

Costs of coal and fuel oil compared by chart. *Electrical world,* Oct. 9, 1920, p. 739.

DANIELS, N. H.

Relation of investment, earnings and expense in a growing business. *Stone and Webster public service journal,* Aug. 1911.

DANIELS, W. M.

Economic causes as affecting the political history of the United States. *Accountants' magazine,* May 1, 1907, p. 253-66.
Engineers as arbiters of public equity and justice. *Engineering record,* Dec. 5, 1914, p. 623-4.

DANN, JOHN

Introduction to the study of mercantile law. *Accountant,* Sept. 8, 1888, p. 578-83.
Law of contracts. *Acocuntant,* Feb. 28, March 7, 1891, p. 178-80, 193-6.
On money. *Accountant,* Feb. 1, 8, 1890, p. 57-60, 70-1.

DANNERTH, FREDERIC

Glossary of terms used in the rubber industry. *Metallurgical and chemical engineering,* April 1, 1917, p. 380-3.

DANSIE, CROWN

Insolvency law of the colony. *Accountant,* Sept. 30, 1899, p. 997-1000.

DARBISHIRE, JAMES E.

Depreciation of machinery. *Engineering* (London), 1908, p. 562-563.
Repairs and depreciation in manufacturing plants. *Engineering magazine,* Dec. 1908, p. 519-21.
Repairs, renewals, deteriorations and depreciation of workshop plant and machinery. *Accountant,* Jan. 30, 1909, p. 173-9. *Institute of mechanical engineers, Proceedings,* 1908, p. 797.

DARBY, L.

Report of committee on municipal accounting. *American municipalities,* Jan. 1913, p. 101-03.

DARBY, W. W. and ALPHONSO RAGLAND

Practical bookkeeping. Dallas, Tex., Darby and Ragland, 1905.

DARBY, WALTER R.

Uniform system of sinking fund accounts. *New Jersey department of municipal accounts,* Sept. 1918, 18p.

D'ARCY, IRVINE M. M.

Observations of the land and income tax laws. *Public accountant,* 1905-6, p. 11.

DARCY, J. WILLIAM

Accounting methods in the wholesale salt fish business. *Business man's magazine,* 1906, v. 18, p. 47-53.

DARLING, A. G.

Justice of the power-factor rate. *Electrical world,* Sept. 13-27, 1919, p. 586-7, 660-1, 708-10.

DARLINGTON, P. J.

Developing new product and determining shop cost. *Engineering magazine,* April 1908, p. 57-67.

DARRACH, C. G.

Valuation of the properties of public utility corporations. Philadelphia, Bradford press, 1913.

DARTMOUTH COLLEGE

Addresses and discussions at the conference of scientific management held October 12, 13, 14, 1911. Hanover, N. H. The Amos Tuck school of administration and finance, 1912, 388p.

DASPIT, HENRY
Sugar mills and their accounts. *Journal of accountancy,* August, 1914, p. 109-13.

DATA and estimate sheets. *Electrical review and western electrician.* April 4, 1914, p. 673.

DATA concerning the use of ownership certificates required by the United States Treasury department. Hubbell, C. H. 1918.

DATA on cost of mining coal by electricity. *Electrical world,* May 28, 1917, p. 1019.

DATA on cost per customer served. *Electrical world,* July 31, 1920, p. 247.

DATA on depreciation. *Barrel and box,* May, 1917, p. 19.

DATA on electric water-supply pumping for thirty-seven Iowa communities; tabulation. *Electrical world,* Aug. 26, 1916, p. 423.

DATA on storage-battery haulage by railroads. *Electrical world,* Jan. 17, 1920, p. 167.

DATA on the design and cost of concrete piles used in railroad work. *Engineering and contracting,* May 19, 1915, p. 452-3.

DATA useful in estimating the cost of power plants. *Engineering and contracting,* April 23, 1913, p. 460.

DATE number index system and bill book. Bernhardt, Martin.

DATING.
See Ante-dating.

DAVAR, SOHRAB R.
Davar's ad-referendum of accounting. London, Gee & co. 1903.

DAVENPORT, E.
High cost of bumper crops. *Country gentleman,* Feb. 16, 1918, p. 3-4.

DAVENPORT, HERBERT JOSEPH
COST and its significance. *American economic review.* Dec. 1911, p. 724-52.
Economics of enterprise. New York, The Macmillan co. 1916. 544p.
Farm products and cost accounting. *Journal of political economy,* May 1919. p. 354-61.
Some problems in corporation accounting. *Journal of accountancy,* Oct. 1907, p. 451-5.
Stock dividend again. *National tax association bulletin,* Nov. 1918, p. 53-4.

DAVENPORT, JOHN A.
Machine repair records. *Machinery* (London), June 26, 1919, p. 365-7.

DAVENPORT, REGINALD ARTHUR
Railroad traveling auditor's work and methods, theory and practice; treats fully and authoritatively upon the subject of auditing station accounts at stations. San Francisco, R. A. Davenport, c1912, 66p.

DAVEY, FREDERICK
Students' catechism on bookkeeping, accounting and banking; with exercises and examination question. Ed. 2. London, Butterworth & co. 1917. 478p.

DAVIDS, S. H.
Fire insurance: its origin, principle and practice. *Accountant,* June 3, 1905, p. 678-84.

DAVIDSON, A.
Introductory lessons in bookkeeping; short commercial calculations and invoices. London, 1892.
Scottish university accounts. *Accountants' magazine,* Nov. 1902, p. 485-92.

DAVIDSON, D. W.
Stock exchange accounts. *Incorporated accountants' journal,* 1906-7, p. 180.

DAVIDSON, F. E.
Buildings as a factor in production costs. *American architect,* June 11, 1919, p. 810-3.

——— **AND R. L. CONDRON**
Cost of factory buildings of timber and of concrete. *Engineering news,* Nov. 9, 1916, p. 884-6. *Engineering and contracting,* Nov. 22, 1916, p. 450-2.

DAVIDSON, J.
Foundry casting accounts. *Foundry,* Sept. 1904.

DAVIDSON, JAMES
Architects' accounts. *Incorporated accountants' journal,* 1903-4. p. 93.

DAVIDSON, M. V.
What ails you, Mr. Job Printer? *Business man's magazine,* April 1908, p. 351-4.

DAVIDSON, WILLIAM C.
Cost and etails of construction of a steel highway bridge, McLennan co. Tex. *Engineering and contracting,* Oct. 25, 1916, p. 365-8.

DAVIE, P.
Essay to set forth in full and minute detail instructions to be given to assistant by senior on all checking (other than vouching) and other considerations involved in a complete audit up to the trial balance. including the checking of the arithmetic. etc., of subsidiary books and stocks, and in all respects describing even the most elementary aspects of the checking. *Accountant,* Oct. 3, 1914, p. 375-81.
Few words on "fire insurance." *Accountant,* June 8, 1907, p. 785-7.
Mortgages. *Accountant,* April 15, 1911, p. 605-10.

DAVIE, ROBERT M.
War hospital accounts and their audit. *accountants' magazine,* Aug. 1918, p. 353-61.

DAVIES, BERTRAM C.
Business system, and internal check in relation to the audit. *Accountant,* May 15, 1915, p. 648-52.

DAVIES, DAVID PRICE
Deeds of arrangement act, 1914. *Accountant,* Jan. 16, 1915, p. 87.
Some points in bankruptcy practice. *Accountant,* Sept. 8, 15, 1900. p. 799-803, 821-5.

DAVIES, E. P.
Finances of Great Britain and Germany, London, T. Fisher Unwin. 61p.

DAVIES, G. HUMPHREYS
Value of buildings and machinery as a lender's security. *Accountant,* May 25, 1912, p. 809-17.

DAVIES, H. J.
Address before street railway accountants' association of America (1903) convention. Abstract. *Street railway review,* Sept. 20, 1903. p. 724.
Cost of service accounting: possible improvements in Cleveland "service at cost" plan pointed out by secretary-treasurer of company. *Aera,* Nov. 1920, p. 363-6.
Fair interest on investment in public utilities. *Journal of accountancy,* Jan. 1915, p. 34-45. Condensed. *Electric railway journal,* Dec. 12, 1914, p. 1287-9.
Maintenance provisions of Cleveland ordinance. *Electric railway journal,* April 2, 1910, p. 614-5.
Recent legislation affecting electric railway accounting. *Electric railway journal,* July 1, 1911, p. 26-8.
Service-at-cost accounting in Cleveland. *Electric railway journal,* Oct. 16, 1920, p. 765-8.
Some accounting features of the Cleveland railway company's franchise. *American street and interurban railway engineering association, Proceedings,* 1913, p. 488, 495. *Electric railway journal,* Oct. 15, and Dec. 17, 1910.

DAVIES, H. W.
Railroad accounting officer. *Railway age,* May 28, 1915, p. 1112.

DAVIES, JOHN P.
Engineering office systems and methods. New York, McGraw-Hill book co. 1915.

DAVIES, JOHN VIPOND
Approximate costs of rapid-transit structures. *Engineering record,* June 6, 1914. p. 642.
Engineering accounting. *American electric railway accountants association. Proceedings,* 1913, p. 184-204. *American electric railway engineering association, Proceedings,* 1913, p. 488, 495. *Electric railway journal,* Oct. 17, 1913, p. 864.
Methods and cost of shaft sinking at the Astoria tunnel, New York City. *Engineering and contracting,* Sept. 15, 1915, p. 200.

DAVIES, JOSEPH E.
Relations between government and industry. *American institute of accountants, Yearbook.* 1913. p. 119-35.

DAVIES, O. I.
Method of accounting of freight claims. *Electric railway journal,* March 18, 1911, p. 463.

DAVIES, R. C.
Trustees in bankruptcy. *Accountant,* Mar. 2, 1912, p. 360-6.

DAVIES, W. SANDERS
Address. *Accountant,* Dec. 8, 1917, p. 454-5.
American institute of accountants, report of the president. *Journal of accountancy,* Oct. 1917, Oct. 1918, p. 241-6, 24-3.
Depreciation. *Business,* Nov. 1897, p. 338-40.
Fair profit in peace and war. *Fibre containers,* Jan. 1918.
Profesisonal accountants not detectives. *Business,* Jan. 1898, p. 33-4.
Suggestions for assessment of excess profits. *Journal of accountancy,* Jan. 1918, p. 1-6.

DAVIES, WILLIAM E.
Appraisal of city real estate. *Engineering and contracting,* Feb. 24, 1915, p. 167-70.

DAVIESS circuit court. T. A. Pedley as receiver of the Owensboro Savings bank and trust company. Plaintiff vs. inequity action no. 9306 Owensboro Savings Bank and Trust company; etc., Defendants Exhibits A and B showing notes and bills and real estate notes. 17p. + 34p.

DAVIS, A. P.
Comparative cost of public and private irrigation project. *Engineering news-record,* Jan. 1, 1914, p. 47-50.

DAVIS, ALBERT EUGENE
How to find costs in printing. New York, Oswald publishing co. 1914. 120p.

DAVIS, ALFRED EDWARD MAIDLOW
Indian and colonial merchants' accounts. *Accountant,* March 6, 1897, p. 265-70.

DAVIS, CLEMENT H.
Dangers of a federal note issue. *Accountant,* Oct. 1, 1910, p. 443-5.
Income tax and overhead expense; correspondence. *Australasian accountant and secretary,* June 1920, p. 159.

DAVIS, E. F.
Cost of brass melting. *Gas age,* April 26, 1920, p. 367-9.
High pressure brass melting. *Gas age,* June 1920, p. 367-9.

DAVIS, EDWARD DOUGLAS
Foreign exchange tables. E. D. Davis, c1912, 195p.

DAVIS, EDWARD L.
Accounting methods of large lumber selling agencies. *Business man's magazine,* Nov. 1905, p. 827-33.
Maturing shares in loan associations. *Business man's magazine,* Nov. 1906, p. 102-6.

DAVIS, F. H.
Notes on the design of central station records and returns. *Electrical engineer* (London) May 8, 1903.

DAVIS, F. W.
Truck efficiency graphically shown. *Automotive industries,* Jan. 3, 1918, p. 33-6.

DAVIS, FREDERICK W.
Bookkeeping for a retail store. *Business,* April 1899, p. 249-50.
Outline of a cost accounting system for a wooden shipyard. *Journal of accountancy,* Jan. 1919, p. 33-47.

DAVIS, G. H.
Accident blanks in New Orleans. *Street railway journal,* Feb. 1898.
Adjustment of American street car fares; growth of cities makes five-cent rate unprofitable; charges based on production cost; advantages of light equipment; origin of five-cent fare; position of New York commission. *Public service,* Aug. 1911, p. 53.

DAVIS, HAROLD V.
Solicitors' accounts. *Incorporated accountants' journal,* Feb. 1912, p. 125-7.

DAVIS, J. F.
Bank organiation, management and accounts. London, Sir Isaac Pitman and sons. 157p.

DAVIS, J. J.
Getting mill work out on time. *Business man's magazine,* June 1912, p. 488-95.

DAVIS, J. S. and A. A. YOUNG
Depreciation and rate control; controversy. *Quarterly journal of economics,* Feb. 1915, p. 362-400.

DAVIS, JOHN H.

Keeping separate crop accounts. *Progressive farmer,* Feb. 26, 1916, p. 300.

DAVIS, ROY and CLARENCE H. LINGHAM

Business English and corespondence. Boston, Ginn and company. c1919. 326p.

DAVIS, W. G.

Pitman's examination notes on municipal accountancy. London, Sir Isaac Pitman, and sons, 1912. 50p.

DAVIS, WALTER

Card system of accounting. *Engineering and mining journal,* 1906, v. 81, p. 142-3.

DAVOUD, V. Y.

Valuation of public utilities. *Utah society of engineers' journal,* Jan. 1918.

DAWE, R. E.

Preparation and audit of the statutory report, section 65 of the companies (Consolidation) act, 1908, and matters coincident thereto. (In Feather, J. Stuart, ed. *Joint transactions.* 1911. p. 359-75). *Accountant,* Feb. 3, 1912, p. 180-5.

DAWE, WILLIAM HENRY

Depreciation, capital expenditure and redemption of capital. *Accountant,* July 23, 1898, p. 735-43. *Business,* Nov. 1898, p. 677-88. *Incorporated accountants' journal,* 1897-8. p. 170.

Desirability of the adoption of a uniform system in publishing accounts and balance sheets by the gold mining companies of the Witwatersrand. *Incorporated accountants' journal,* 1897-8. p. 3.

Mining accounts. *Accountant,* Sept. 4, 1897, p. 840-6.

DAWSON, CHARLES H.

Bookkeeping for the master plumber. *Domestic engineering,* October 11, 1913, p. 34-8.

DAWSON, J. W.

Change of railroad rates in West Virginia. *Coal age,* Dec. 11, 1915, p. 973-5.

DAWSON, MILES MENANDER

Business of life insurance. New York, A. S. Barnes & co., 1905. 404p.

Cost and profit-and-loss accounting in fire insurance. *Economic world,* Oct. 6, 1917, p. 491-3.

DAWSON, PHILIP

Engineering and electric traction pocketbook. Ed. 2. New York, John Wiley & sons.

DAWSON, SIDNEY STANLEY

Accountants' compendium. London, Gee & co. 1898. 431p.

Accounts of branch establishments. *Accountant,* Nov. 13, 1897, p. 1063-71, 1101

Accounts of joint stock companies. *Accountant,* Jan. 6, 1900, p. 14-21.

Accounts of trustees, liquidators and receivers, London, Gee & co. 1905. 125p. (Accountants' library, v. 41).

Address. *Accountant,* Dec. 21, 1912, p 781-5.

Balance sheets. *Accountant,* Feb. 3, 1900 p. 131-8, 361.

Bankruptcy (England). (In Lisle, George. *Encyclopaedia of accounting.* v. 1. p. 268 329).

British and foreign methods of bookkeeping, with special reference to legalized systems. *Accountant,* Oct. 29, 1904, p. 531-40.

Commerce and commercial education under post war conditions. *Accountant,* Dec 28, 1918, p. 345-8.

Companies act, 1900. *Accountant,* Nov. 26, 1904, p. 669-75.

Depreciation: correspondence. *Accountant,* Aug. 8, 1914, p. 175-8.

Garner v. Murray. *Accountant,* April 2, 1910, p. 462.

Goodwill. (In Lisle, George. *Encyclopaedia of accounting.* v. 3. p. 196-207).

Financial adjustment on the alteration of the boundaries of a local authority. *Accountant,* Sept. 25, 1915, p. 373-83.

Interest in respect of proof of debt. *Accountant,* Oct. 23, 1909, p. 505-8.

Law papers of the Institute examinations and how to prepare for them. *Accountant,* Nov. 1, 1902, p. 1116-23.

Liquidation's accounts. (In Lisle, George. *Encyclopaedia of accounting.* v. 4. p. 157-79).

Liverpool corporation leaseholds, with special reference to the computation of fines for their extension of renewal. *Accountant,* March 29, 1913, p. 469-78.

Mnemonic aids. *Accountant,* Nov. 22, 1902, p. 1206.

Municipal trading from the financial standpoint. *Accountant,* July 23, Aug. 6, 13, 17, 1910, p. 115-22, 157-60, 189-91, 367-71.

Partnership accounts. *Accountant,* Dec. 9, 1899, p. 1190-7.

Post-examination studies of an accountant student. *Accountant,* Nov. 18, 1899, p. 1128-35.

Receivers' accounts. (In Lisle, George. *Encyclopaedia of accounting.* v. 5. p. 479-82).

Reserves and reserve funds. (In Lisle, George. *Encyclopaedia of accounting.* v. 5. p. 482-8).

Reserves and reserve funds. *Accountant,* Feb. 2, 1901, July 27, 1907, p. 155-60, 110-3.

Rights of billholders under bankruptcy administration; the rule in ex parte Waring v. Scotch law. *Accountant,* June 6, 1896, p. 476-8.

Rights of partners inter se. *Accountant,* April 7, June 2, 1906, p. 446-50, 687-8.

Secret reserves. *Accountant,* Nov. 21, 28, 1908, p. 607-9, 643-5.

Some compound interest problems. *Accountant,* Feb. 4, 1911, p. 188-91.

Some observations on the companies act. 1907. *Accountant,* June 20, 1908, p. 890.

Some points in bankruptcy of interest to municipal officers. *Accountant,* Sept. 4, 1915, p. 277-80.

Some points in connection with limited companies. *Accountant,* March 26, 1904, p. 404.

Some points in municipal finance and accounting. *Accountant,* July 25, 1908, p. 101-8.

Stock and cost accounts of a flour miller. *Accountant,* April 3, 1897, p. 369-71.

Trading stock registers. *Accountant,* April 17, 1897, p. 413-5.

Trustees' accounts under bankruptcy and deeds of arrangement, England. (In Lisle, George, *Encyclopaedia of accounting.* v. 6, p. 337-50).

——— **and HARRY ROBERT GRAVES**

Accounts of trustees, liquidators and receivers. London, Gee & co. 1905. 125p. (Accountants' library, v. 41).

——— **and R. C. DE ZOUCHE.**

Partnership accounts. London, Gee and co., 1913, 176p.

DAWSON, WILFRID JOHN

Goodwill. *Accountant,* Jan. 12, 1901, p. 49-54.

DAY, B. H.

Book-keeping without a master. New York, Dick & Fitzgerald.

DAY, CHARLES
Constructive policy for public service corporations. *Engineering magazine,* Jan. 1915, p. 599-603.

DAY, CLARENCE MUNRO
Accounting practice. New York, D. Appleton & co. 1915. 318p.
Silk mill costs. New York, Clarence M. Day, 1912. 70p.

DAY, CLIVE
History of commerce. New York, Longmans, Green & co. 1917. 640p.

DAY, E. E.
Standardization of the construction of statistical tables. *American statistical association quarterly,* March 1920, p. 59-66. 66.

DAY, F.
Telephone plant organization. *Electrical review and western electrician,* Dec. 4, 1915, p. 1028-31.

DAY, JULIUS E.
Stock-broker's office organization, management and accounts. London, Sir Isaac Pitman & sons. 231p.

DAY, WILLIAM GEORGE
Elementary bookkeeping. London, Gee & co. 1901. 48p.

DAY-book, cash book and ledger, combined for municipal councils and for schools. Wilson, A.

DAY BOOKS
READY money day book. *Accountant,* Jan. 4, 1902, p. 7-8.

DAYS
LISLE, GEORGE. Table of days, days as decimals of a year. (In his *Accounting theory and practice.* 1900. p. 369-75).

DAYTON, T. S.
Spending a railroad's money; the sources from which a railroad corporation receives its money, how it is collected, kept safe and paid out, and the men responsible for it. *Railroad man's magazine,* Dec. 1909, p. 447-53.

DEACON, STUART
Reserve funds and undivided profits. *Incorporated accountants' journal,* 1903-4, p 109.

DEACON, THOMAS R.
Overhead and general costs in manufacturing. *Journal of the engineering institute of Canada,* July 1919, p. 505-6.

DEAKIN, RUPERT and P. J. HUMPHREYS
Household accounts. London, 1911.
Rural arithmetic, including household accounts. London, 1911.

DEALERS oppose seasonal coal rates. *Iron trade review,* May 6, 1920, p. 1349.

DEAN, CHARLES W.
When, what and how much to buy; predetermining raw material needs as a function of cost accounting. *Industrial management,* Nov. 1920, p. 362-4.

DEAN, E.
Checking up service. *American gas engineering journal,* Jan. 11, 1919, p. 21-2.

DEAN, EDWARD S.
Graphic methods of estimating core costs. *Iron age,* May 6, 1915, p. 1012.

DEAN, JOHN S.
Shop organization. *Electric journal,* Nov. 1919, p. 506.

DEAN, S.
Adopting piece work and premium systems. *Iron age,* Dec. 5, 1912, p. 1314.
Cost keeping in a pump factory. *Iron age,* April 3, 1913, p. 814-8.
Cutting the cost of power for the factory. *Iron age,* April 17, 1913, p. 936-7.
Duties of the factory superintendent: outlines details of department operation, graphical production of records and their use, etc. *Iron age,* Nov. 21, 1912, p. 1216-8.
Getting the most out of the shop: illustrations of efforts to bring machines to maximum capacity with resultant effect on overhead charges and profit. *Iron age,* January 16, 1913, 200-2.
Making the gray iron foundry pay dividends. *Iron trade review,* Feb. 19, 1914. p. 363-5. *Foundry,* March 1914, p. 94-7. Condensed. *Iron age,* Feb. 12, 1914, p. 432-3.
Production system for a 200-employee plant. *Iron age,* Dec. 19, 1912, p. 1430-3.
Shop and foundry management. New York, David Williams co. 1913. 220p.

DEAN, W. F.
Bookkeeping for retail stores. Stern, 1900.

DEAN, W. R.
Efficiency in the brass foundry. *Metal industries,* Aug. 1915, p. 327-9.

DEANE, E. G.
Block method of top slicing of the Miami copper co. *American institute of mining engineers, Bulletin,* Sept. 1916, p. 1518.

DE ARMOND, I. R.
Planning and controlling production. *Machinery,* Sept. 1919, p. 60-6.

DEATH duties and income tax. *Accountant,* April 27, 1907, p. 545-7.

DEBATE depreciation and land at valuation hearing. *Engineering record,* Feb. 10, 1917, p. 239.

DEBATE first tentative valuaions at Washington. *Engineering record,* Feb. 3, 1917, p. 201-2.

DEBENTURES
AMERICAN business and accounting encyclopaedia. Comp. by E. H. Beach and W. W. Thorne. Detroit, Bookkeeper publishing co. 1901. Accountants and records of debentures, v. 2, p. 414-21.
BACHELOR, J. B. Debentures. *Accountant,* April 2, 1904, p. 422-7.
CARTER, R. N. Debentures. (In his *Advanced accounts.* p. 383-93, 447-8, 928-33).
CASSEL, F. Debentures of trading companies; report of paper from the *Law times. Accountant,* Feb. 9, 1907. p. 197.
DEBENTURES and wasting assets. *Accountant,* July 19, 1909. p. 69.
DICKSEE, L. R. Debentures. (In his *Advance accounting.* 1916. p. 99-100).
DOUGALL, J. J. Some phases of the debenture. *Accountant,* Aug. 8, 1908, p. 163-8. *Incorporated acocuntants' journal,* 1909-10, p. 13.
DUNN, W. L. Debentures. *Accounting and commerce,* Aug. 1918, p. 113-6.
EASTWOOD, T. C. Debentures. *Accountant,* Oct. 3, 1891, p. 699-704.

DEBENTURES—*(Continued)*
EDWARDS, W. R. Debentures. *Accountant,* June 14, 1890, p. 323-7.
FIRST mortgage debentures. (In *How to understand the balance sheet and other periodical statements.* 1905. p. 34-7).
GIBSON, J. GRANT. Debentures or a criticism of floating charges, with especial reference to the report of the company law amendment committee. *Accountant,* April 8, 15, 1911, p. 555-61, 594-600.
HISLOP, C. H. Debentures. *Incorporated accountants' journal,* 1906-7, p. 253.
HOOTON, J. R. Debenture and debenture stock. *Public accountant,* Nov. 1915, p. 104-15.
JORDON, HERBERT W. Debenture: its use and abuse. *Accountant,* Nov. 8, 1913, p. 680-7.
KESTER, R. B. Debenture stock. (In his *Accounting theory and practice.* v. 2. 1918. p. 8-9).
LYDE, H. W. Rights and duties of a debenture holder's receiver. *Accountant,* Feb. 21, 1920, p. 213-7.
MANCHESTER CHARTERED ACCOUNTANT STUDENTS' SOCIETY. Ought the power of trading companies incorporated under the companies acts to issue mortgage debentures constituting a floating charge on all their assets to be limited or regulated by statute, and if so, to what extent and in what manner? *Accountant,* Dec. 10, 1892, p. 949-52.
MOSSOP, L. Law relating to debentures. *Incorporated accountants' journal,* 1904-5, p. 253.
PEPPER, F. H. Debentures. *Accountant,* June 2, 1894, p. 498-503.
PORTERS, R. J. Debentures. (In his *Pitman's dictionary of bookkeeping.* p. 314-23).
POTTER, JOHN. Debentures. *Accountant,* Oct. 26, 1912, p. 526-31.
PREMIUMS on debentures. *Accountant,* Dec. 10, 1910, 802-3.
REDEMPTION of debentures. *Accountant,* Feb. 16, 1901, p. 206-9.
SAMPSON, J. Debentures. *Accountant,* Feb. 24, 1912, p. 318-24.
SILVESTER, T. E. Debentures and their operation. *Accountant,* Dec. 28, 1912, p. 824-30.
SIMMONS, HAROLD SOLOMON. Debentures. *Accountant,* Oct. 23, 1897, p. 988-92.
SIMMONS, HAROLD SOLOMON. Law relating to debentures. *Incorporated accountants' journal,* 1899-1900, p. 85.
SPICER, E. E. and E. C. PEGLER. Mortgages and debentures. (In their *Practical bookkeeping and commercial knowledge.* 1912. p. 142-5).
STRACHAN, W. Debentures and their redemption. *Incorporated accountants' journal,* 1898-9, p. 196.
TRADE CREDITORS V. DEBENTURE-HOLDERS. *Accountant,* March 11, 18, April 1, 1905, p. 273, 304, 376.
TRUSTEES for debenture-holders. *Accountant,* March 22, 1902, p. 305-6.
WALTON, SEYMOUR. Debenture stock. *Journal of accountancy,* Jan. 1917, p. 71-2.
WILLSON, WILLIAM R. Debentures. *Accountant,* Dec. 3, 1898, p. 1172-9.

DEBENTURES. Sampson, J.

DEBENTURES and wasting assets. *Accountant,* July 17, 1909, p. 69.

DEBIT AND CREDIT
See also Accounting.
MCCLUNG, ROBERT GARDNER. Theory of debit and credit in accounting. Boston, Morgan, Mills & co. 1913. 16p.
THORNTON, J. In and out principle of debit and credit. *Business,* July 1896, p. 322-4.

DE BOWER, HERBERT FRANCIS
Advertising principles. New York. Alexander Hamilton institute. c1918. 330p. (Modern business, v. 6).

DEBTOR and creditor made easie. Monteage, Stephen.

DEBTS AND DEBTORS
See also Losses.
BATCHELOR, JOHN BENNETT. Verification and value of book debts for the purpose of a balance sheet. *Accountant,* Jan. 12, 1901, p. 51-3.
BENTLEY, H. C. Loss on bad accounts. (In his *Science of accounts.* 1913. p. 61-2).
BROWN, R. Sketch of the history of the law of debtor and creditor, with special reference to Cessio Bonorum. *Accountant,* June 25, 1898, p. 651-7.
ESQUERRÈ, PAUL JOSEPH. Bonded debt, secured debt. (In his *Applied theory of accounts.* 1917. p. 336-53).
GILMAN, STEPHEN. Debts receivable, bad debts. (In his *Principles of accounting.* 1917. p. 162-5, 251-2).
HASLUCK, LAWRENCE. Fraudulent debtors, *Accountant,* Dec. 15, 1888, p. 817-9.
HEATON, JAMES ASPIN. Collection of book debts in large businesses, with special reference to home and foreign branches. *Accountant,* Sept. 21, 1907, p. 374-6.
HILL, DANIEL. Book debts. *Accountant,* Jan. 28, 1899, p. 110-3.
INCOME TAX PROCEDURE. *South African accountant,* June 1917, p. 2-5.
KESTER, R. B. Debts. (In his *Accounting theory and practice.* 1918. v.2. p. 216-20).
LISLE, GEORGE AND W. A. MIDDLETON. Bad debts and bad debt reserve. (In their *Account-keeping in principle and practice.* 1911. p. 69-71).
MASON, H. A. Administration of public debts. *National association of comptrollers and accounting officers, Proceedings,* 1915, p. 25-31.
OFFICIAL communication from the Transvaal society of accountants, bad and doubtful debs, income tax procedure. *South African accountant,* June 1917, p. 35-6.
PIXLEY, F. M. Bad debts written off. (In his *Accountancy.* Ed.2. p. 195-6).
PORTERS, R. J. Bad debts. (In his *Pitman's dictionary of bookkeeping,* p. 60-73).
RACINE, S. F. Sundry debtors. (In his *Accounting principles.* 1910. p. 258-61).
RALSTON, J. T. Of debts. *Accountant,* Jan. 20, 1900, p. 80-6.
TREATMENT of bad and doubtful debts. *Accountants' magazine,* 1898, p. 272.
VIVIAN, G. W. Book debts, and the auditor's duties with regard thereto. *Accountant,* April 15, 1911, p. 602-5.

DECAMP, W. V.
BONUS system applied to mining. *Engineering and mining journal,* March 9, 1918, p. 461-2.

DECEPTIVE averages. Finney, H. A.

DECIMAL SYSTEMS
ALEXANDER, JOHN S. New International decimal money system. *Accountant,* Dec. 2, 9, 1916, p. 524-9, 550-5
ALLCOCK, HARRY. British decimal coinage. *Accountant,* Jan. 18, 1919, p. 49-50.
ALLCOCK, HARRY. Decimal system of coinage weight and measures. *Accountant,* July 7, 14, 1917, p. 15-20, 30-7.
BRITISH decimal coinage. *Australasian accountant and secretary,* June 1919, p. 18-20.
COLLINS, JAMES R. Decimal points. *South African accountant and auditor,* Sept. 1916, p. 187-90, Dec. 1916, p. 220-4.

DECIMAL SYSTEMS—*(Continued)*

DECIMAL system. *Accountant*, March 28, April 4, 1891, p. 236-8, 254-5.

DOWSON, F. EMERSON. Decimal coinage weights and measures. *Accountant*, April 18, 1891, p. 299-300.

HUGH-JONES, T. Decimal coinage. *Accountant*, Feb. 19, 1910, p. 286-7.

KINNIBURGH, J. WATKINS. Decimal coinage. *Accounting and commerce*, Nov. 1918, p. 184-7, Dec. 1918, p. 207-12.

MCCONNELL, F. R. Decimal system applied to British coinage and weights and measures. *Accountant*, Sept. 16, 1916, p 241-7.

MACKAY, WILLIAM. Some notes on the decimal and the duo-decimal systems. *Accountants' magazine*, Nov. 1918, p. 403-7.

MILLAR, ROBERT COCKBURN. Decimal system. *Accountants' magazine*, Feb. 1906, p. 89-116.

REPORT of the committee appointed to inquire into the adoption of a decimal coinage and metric system of weights and measures. *Accountant*, Nov. 3, 1917, p. 349-50.

ST. CLAIR, R. W. Common-sense denominations; a plea for the immediate adoption of an all-embracing decimal scheme. *Accountant*, Oct. 11, 1902, p. 1033-9.

SMITH, W. A. Decimal coinage. *Incorporated accountants' journal*, 1890-1, p. 141.

TURNBULL, C. Proposed decimal systems of coinage. *Accountant*, Oct. 14, 1916, p. 341-3.

DECIMAL system. *Accountant*, March 28, April 4, 1891, p. 236-8, 254-5.

DECIMAL time system for factories. *American machinist*, v. 28, no. 16.

DECISION against original cost theory; Judge Van Valkenburgh considers present fair value correct basis for rate making. *Electric railway* journal, Nov. 27, 1920. p. 1122-3.

DECISION by Oregon commission with table of costs for different classes of consumers of the Hood river gas and electric company. *Electrical world*, Aug. 21, 1915, p. 431.

DECISION granting the five per cent rate advance: full text of the majority opinion and dissenting opinions of chairman Harlan and commissioner Clements. *Railway age*, Dec. 25, 1914, p. 1173-8.

DECISION in complaint of Trenton, N. J. *American gas light journal*, May 8, 1916, p. 289-92.

DECISION in Des Moines gas case. *Electrical world*, Aug. 31, 1912, p. 436-7.

DECISION in Indianapolis fare case. *Electric railway journal*, Dec. 15, 1917, p. 1095.

DECISION in Kings county case. *Public service regulation*, Jan. 1913, p. 49.

DECISION in Pacific power and light company's rate case. *Electrical world*, Jan. 1, 1916, p. 6-7.

DECISION in Puget Sound electric railway rate case. *Electric railway journal*, May 23, 1914, p. 1174.

DECISION in rate case in Springfield, Mo. *Electrical world*, July 4, 1914, p. 9-10.

DECISION in Rochester fare case. *Electric railway journal*, Feb. 27, 1915, p. 439-40.

DECISION in the Arkansas rate case. *Railway age*, April 16, 1915, p. 824.

DECISION in the case of Stadtlander et al. vs. The New York Edison company. *Utilities magazine*, July 1915, p. 15-27.

DECISION in the express rate cases. *Railway age gazette*, August 8, 1913, p. 233-5.

DECISION in the five per cent rate advance case: abstract of the majority and dissenting opinions. *Railway age*, Aug. 7, 1914, p. 235-42.

DECISION in the Milwaukee fare case. *Electric railway journal*, Aug. 31, 1912, p. 314-23

DECISION in the western rate advance case. *Railway review*, Aug. 14, 1915, p. 208-13.

DECISION in transcontinental rate case. *Railway age*, July 27, 1917, p. 147-51.

DECISION of arbitrator in Cleveland controversy. *Electric railway journal*, Dec. 25, 1909, p. 1237.

DECISION of board of arbitration in the Cleveland case. *Electric railway journal*, June 28, 1913, p. 1159.

DECISION of California commission in Antioch rate case. *Electrical world*, July 18, 1914, p. 119-20.

DECISION of commission upholding rates of fare in Savannah, Ga. *Electric railway journal*, April 20, 1912, p. 663.

DECISION of Court of appeals in the Kings county lighting company case. *Electrical review and western elctrician*, April 11, 1914, p. 729-31.

DECISION of ex-judge Hughes in Brooklyn borough case. *American gas engineering journal*, Aug. 3, 1918, p. 119.

DECISION of Indiana protest against Illinois freight rates. *Railway review*, Oct. 4, 1919, p. 514-5.

DECISION of Judge Westerhover in the Columbus street railway fare cases. *Minnesota municipalities*, Dec. 1918, p. 192-7.

DECISION of Massachusetts commission in Worcester street lighting case. *Electrical world*, July 27, 1912, p. 190-1.

DECISION of the court of appeals in Kings county lighting company case. *Electrical review and western electrician*, April 11, 1914, p. 729.

DECISION of the Interstate commission in the 15 percent rate advance case. *Raiway review*, July 7, 1917, p. 20-30. Abstract, *Engineering and contracting*, July 18, 1917, p. 45.

DECISION of the Interstate commerce commission in the freight rate advance case; commissioner Harlan's dissenting opinion in the freight rate decision. *Economic world*, July 7, 1917, p. 3-5.

DECISION of the Interstate commerce commission in the industrial railways case. *Railway review*, Feb. 7, 1914, p. 221-6.

DECISION of the Interstate commerce commission on the fourth section violations in the Southeast. *Raiway review*, May 23, 1914, p. 758-61.

DECISION of the railroad commission of Wisconsin in the Racine case. *American gas light journal*, March 20, 1911, p. 547.

DECISION of the supreme court as to railway land values. *Engineering and contracting,* July 9, 1913, p. 29.

DECISION of the U. S. Supreme court in the Shreveport rate case. *Railway review,* June 13, 1914, p. 878-80.

DECISION of the Wisconsin railroad commission ordering a revised and reduced schedule of rates for the Beloit water, gas and electric company. *Electrical world,* July 29, 1911, p. 262-3.

DECISION of United States district judge Westerhover in Columbus, Ohio, street railway fare rate case. *New Jersey municipalities,* Oct. 1918, p. 239-42.

DECISION of United States district judge Westerhover in street railway fare case. *City bulletin,* Sept. 28, 1918, p. 309-11.

DECISION of Wisconsin commission: considers the rate of return. *Electric railway journal,* Sept. 10, 1910, p. 404.

DECISION of Wisconsin commission in superior cases. *Electric railway journal,* Nov. 23, 1912, p. 1067.

DECISION on anthracite rates. *Railway review,* Aug. 14-21, 1915, p 215, 250-3.

DECISION on fabrication in transit charges. *Railway review,* Feb. 14, 1914, p. 267.

DECISION on the Cummins amendment. *Railway review,* May 22, 1915, p. 705-7.

DECISION on transportation of railroad fuel. *Railway review,* Aug. 28, 1915, p. 269.

DECISION on westbound transcontinental commodity rates. *Railway and engineering review,* April 5, 1913, p. 318-9.

DECISIONS affecting gas rates. *Gas age,* Sept. 1, 1919, p. 192.

DECISIONS upon questions raised under classification. United States. Interstate commerce commission.

DECKER, F. L.

System of accounting for electrical CONTRACTORS. *Electrical review and western electrician,* Nov. 2, 1912.

DECKER, M. S.

How could nationalization of rate regulation best be accomplished. *Annals of the American academy of political and social science,* March 1918, p. 229-38.

DECLARING dividends out of surplus. *Electric railway journal,* April 3, 1915, p. 657.

DECLINE and ultimate production of oil wells, with notes on the valuation of oil properties. Beal, Carl H. 1919.

DECREASE in electric-railway traffic resulting from increased fare. *Engineering news-record,* Aug. 13, 1914, p. 353.

DECREASED cost month. *Iron age,* May 15, 1913, p. 1187-8

DECREASING cost of water service in Omaha, Nebraska. *Engineering and contracting,* May 17, 1916, p. 456.

DEDRICK, A. E.

Accrued accounts. *Electric railway journal,* Dec. 11, 1915, p. 1169.
Light and power accounting. *Electric railway journal,* Dec. 23, 1916, p. 1300, 1281.

DEDUCTIBILITY of interest charges under federal tax laws. Thulin, Frederick.

DEDUCTIONS for obsolescence justified. *Railway age gazette,* Dec. 2, 1910, p. 1093.

DEDUCTIONS

WALTON, SEYMOUR. Deductions from income. *Journal of acountancy,* June 1916, p. 473-5.

DEEDS

CAPORN, FRANCIS M. Deeds; their origin and use in commercial life. *Accountant,* Oct. 7, 1916, p. 307-13. *Incorporated accountants' journal,* Sept. 1916, p. 279-83.

DEEDS OF ARRANGEMENT

See Bankruptcy; Liquidation and receiverships.

DEEDS of arrangement act, 1914. *Accountant,* Sept. 19, 1914, p. 324-9.

DEEDS of assignment. *Accountant,* Jan. 13, Feb. 3, 10, 1900, p. 31-2, 123-5, 152-3.

DEEDS of assignment and subsequent bankruptcy. *Accountant,* Nov. 5, 1904, April 10, 1909, p. 558-60; 492-3.

DEEDS of inspectorship. *Accountant,* Jan. 11, 1902, p. 30-2.

DEEP wells cost 0.82 cent per 1000 gallons to operate. *Engineering news,* April 26, 1917, p. 212.

DEEMING, HORACE E.

Uniform municipal accounting and home rule. *National municipal league, Proceedings,* 1905, p. 248-51.

DEESON, F. J.

Logarithmic chart in the analysis of railroad operations. *Railway age,* Sept. 19, 1919, p. 570-1.

DEFALCATIONS

See also Fraud.

CRAWFORD, L. U. Defalcations. *Accounting and commerce,* Sept. 1915, p. 124-7. *Journal of accountancy,* Aug. 1915, p. 112-21.
DEFALCATIONS and audits. *Accountant,* Aug. 11, 1917, p. 101-3, 110-6.
DODD, ARTHUR F. Some suggestions as to the discovery and prevention of defalcations and an auditor's point of view. *Accountant,* May 30, 1903, p. 723-31, 855.
GODDARD, F R. Defalcations and how to prevent them. Newcastle on Tyne, Walter Scott, 1887. *Accountant,* 1887, p. 112, 121, 154.
HARRINGTON, W. C. Defalcations: their prevention and detection. *Accountant,* Sept. 15, 1906, p. 304-9.
LEAVITT, H. Defalcations, embezzlement and fraud. *Accountant,* Sept. 27, 1902, p. 970-3.
MOXEY, E. P. Causes, methods and prevention of bank defalcation. *Journal of accountancy,* Jan. 1906, v.1, p. 223-232.
NAGLE, R. H. Defalcations; their prevention and detection. *Accountant,* Aug. 25, 1906, p. 215-21.
NIXON, H. H. Methods employed by defalcating bookkeepers, and some suggestions for the prevention and detection of the same. *Accountant,* Dec. 26, 1903, p. 1578-80.
PATERSON, JOHN. Defalcations. *Accountant,* Aug. 22, 29, 1896, p. 701-4, 718-20.
RAWLINGS, EDWARD. Bank defalcations. *Accountant,* Sept. 19, 1896, p. 769-70.

DEFALCATIONS. Crawford, L. U.

DEFALCATIONS and audits. *Accountant,* Aug. 11, 1917, p. 101-3, 110-6.

DEFAULT in public service discrimination. *Rate research*, Feb. 19, 1913, p. 327-31.

DEFECTIVE audits and fraud. *Accountant*, Jan. 23, 30, 1909, p. 112-4, 152-7.

DEFECTIVE procedure in income tax courts of appeal. *Accountant*, Sept. 12, Oct. 10, 1908, p. 293-4, 433-4.

DEFECTS in procedure. *Accountant*, Aug. 31-Sept. 21, Nov. 9-23, 1901, p. 940-2, 961-4, 979-81, 1008-9, 1203-5, 1231-2, 1264-6.

DEFECTS of financial statement of the city of New York with suggestions for improved forms. Merchants association of New York.

DEFECTS of the financial statements of the City of New York with suggestions for improved forms. Ford, W. C. 1903.

DEFECTS of title 2 of the federal revenue act of October 3, 1917 viewed from the accounting standpoint. Bentley, Arthur.

DEFENBACH, BYRON

Accounting in Idaho. *Journal of accountancy*, Jan. 1916, p. 50-1.

DEFERRED CHARGES

See also Accounting.

KERR, DAVID S. Deferred charges. *Canadian chartered accountant*, July 1915, p. 50-3.

PATTERSON, WILLIAM J. Deferred credits to profit and loss: correspondence. *Journal of accountancy*, Sept. 1912, p. 240-41.

STAUB, WALTER A. Deferred charges to operating. *Journal of accountancy*, Oct. 1909, p. 401-18.

WALTON, SEYMOUR. Deferred debits and credits; differences in nature of deferred items; treatment in the books. *Journal of accountancy*, May 1914, p. 384-8.

WALTON, SEYMOUR. Moving machinery as deferred charge. *Journal of accountancy*, June 1915, p. 480-1.

DEFERRED charges to operating. Staub, W. A.

DEFERRED credits to profit and loss. Patterson, W. J.

DEFICIENCY ACCOUNTS

See also Accounting.

TREVOR, CHARLES R. Statement of affairs and deficiency accounts. *Accountant*, June 17, 1893, p. 565-9.

DEFINITION needed. *Journal of accountancy*, April 1918, p. 266-7.

DEFINITION of accounting. Duncan, J. C.

DEFINITION of "cost" pertaining to contracts. Washington, Government printing office. 1917. 12p.

DEFINITION of public accountant. *Journal of accountancy*, Sept. 1908, p. 356-7.

DEFINITIONS needed. Oates, Lewis A.

DEFINITIONS of capital. *Accountant*, July 26, 1890, p. 393-5.

DEFINITIONS of cost, unit cost, direct and indirect cost, and overhead cost. *Engineering and contracting*, Feb. 28, 1917, p. 196-7.

DE FOREST, H. P.

Is the cost system overdone? *Inland printer*, Dec. 1917, p. 340. Discussion. Dec. 1917, p. 345-7.

DE FRESE, S. E.

Equitable gas rates. *American gas light journal*, June 8, 1914, p. 353-5. *Gas age*, May 15, 1914, p 466-8.

Small minimum charge a producer of unprofitable accounts. *American gas engineering journal*, Nov. 24, 1917, p. 467.

DEGHUEE, JOSEPH

Tables of bond values. New York, George W. Dougherty, c1908.

DEGREE of Bachelor of commerce. *Accountant*, June 7-21, 1902, p. 583-6, 605-7, 633-4.

DEGREES, ETC.

ACCOUNTANTS and distinctive initials. *Accountant*, July 15, 22, 29, 1905, p. 61-3, 103-4, 127-8

C. P. A. versus C. A. *Canadian chartered accountant*, April 1912, p. 206-8.

CONCERNING our short comings; correspondence. *Journal of accountancy*, April 1913, p. 309-10.

CORPORATION of accountants, lim., and the Scottish societies of chartered accountants: report of trial. *Accountant*, Nov. 21, 28, Dec. 5, 19, 1903, p. 1433-8, 1475-6, 1479-81, 1540-2.

FELLOWSHIP degree. *Canadian chartered accountant*, April 1914, p. 274-6.

LONDON society of accountants and auditors. *Journal of accountancy*, June 1907, p. 142.

VALUE of membership in professional societies. *Journal of accountancy*, Sept. 1910, p. 381.

WRIGHT, JAMES. English versus Scottish degrees: correspondence. *Journal of accountancy*, March 1909, p. 407-8.

DE HART, EDWARD LOUIS

LAW of guarantees. *Accountant*, June 20, 27, 1896, p. 509-12, 529-31.

DE HOLDEN-STONE, GEOFFREY

WHAT the road really costs. *Scientific American supplement*, Aug. 3, 1918, p. 70-1.

DEHORITY, W. A.

Result of three years' experience with the Indiana accounting law. Indianapolis, Sentinel printing co., 1912. 33p. *Public officials magazine*, 1912, v.6, no. 4, p. 22-26, no. 5, p. 14-26.

DEIGHAN, P.

Complete treatise on bookkeeping rational and practical; wherein the invention of debtors and creditors are clearly pointed out, etc. 2 vols. in 1. London, 1807.

DEIGHTON, H.

Brass-foundry records and costs. *Engineering magazine*, Oct. 1905, p. 48-56.

Cost system of an engineering works. *Engineering magazine*, April 1905, v.29, p. 40-58.

DEININGER, A. W.

Your lighting bill for 1925. *Scientific American supplement*, Sept. 18, 1915, p. 187.

DEINZER, ALEXANDER T.

Cost accounting in a box factory. *Fibre containers*, Jan. 1918, p. 22-6.

DE KUZELEWSKI, A. R.

Operating diagrams for the executive. *Industrial management*, March 1918, p. 180-2.

DELANO, FREDERIC A.

Arbitrary depreciation charge. *Railroad gazette*, May 15, 1908, p. 681.

DELANO, FREDERICK A.—*(Continued)*
Notes on application of a depreciation charge in railway accounting. *Journal of political economy*, Nov. 1908, p. 585-601. *Railway age*, March 27, 1908, p. 471.
Rates are not based on capitalization. *Journal of accountancy*, Sept. 1907, p. 347-9.
Some phases of the rate advance case. *Railway age*, Jan. 2, 1914, p. 8-9.

DELAWARE
Business corporations under the laws of Delaware; shares without par value. New York, Corporation trust co. 1917. 32p.
Law relating to inheritance tax. 1917.

——— **SECRETARY OF STATE**
General corporation laws passed 1899— amended by the revised statutes of 1915 and further amended by the ninety-fifth, ninety-sixth and ninety-seventh general assemblies. Wilmington, 1917. 176p.

——— **STATE BOARD OF ACCOUNTANCY**
List of certified public accountants. 1919. 1 typewritten page.

——— **STATE TREASURER**
LAW relating to income tax, 1917.

DELAWARE. *American institute of accountants, Yearbook*, 1913-1916, p. 314-7, 264-7, 254-7, 146-9.

DELAWARE society of certified public accountants. *Journal of accountancy*, April 1915, April, 1917, May 1918, May 1919, p. 324, 318, 400, 400.

DE LAY, DANIEL WASHINGTON
Manual of book-keeping. Mattoon, Ill., Gazette printing co. 1907.

DE LEEUW, A. L.
Wage payment; presented at the annual meeting of the American society of mechanical engineers, Dec. 2 to 5, 1919. 16p.

DELIVERY COSTS
See also Automobiles—Cost of operation.
NATIONAL retail dry goods association. Comparative figures on delivery costs compiled by the Bureau of research and information. New York, 2 typewritten pages, with chart.

DELIVERY costs. *American lumberman*, Jan. 12, 1918, p. 55.

DELIVERY costs with electric trucks. *Electrical world*, March 2, 1912, p. 482.

DELIVERY record. *American lumberman*, Dec. 14, 1918, p. 29.

DELIVERY up of documents subject to solicitor's lien. *Accountant*, May 14, 1910, p. 691-3.

DELL, B.
Double entry bookkeeping. London, Webster & co. 1850.

DELLPLAIN, M.
Would remove control of commissions over rates charged industrial users. *American gas engineering journal*, May 1, 1920, p. 339-40. *Gas age*, May 10, 1920, p. 402-4.

DELMAR, ALGERNON
Future contract prices. *Engineering magazine*, Oct. 1913, p. 1-6.
Mine accounts for the superintendent. *Mining and scientific press*, 1908, v.96, p. 454-7.
Mine valuation. *Engineering and mining journal*, May 23, 1908.

DEL MAR, W. A
Methods of figuring depreciation and present values. *Industrial engineering*, Oct. 1914, p. 402-3.

DELOITTE, WILLIAM WELCH
Address: Brrmingham provincial meeting, 1888. *Accountant*, Oct. 27, 1888, p. 686-98.
Address, 1889. *Accountant*, May 4, 1889, p. 236-9.

DELP, JOSEPH DANIEL
Comprehensive modernized rapid calculator, Springfield, Mo., J. D. Delp, 1910.

DELPRAT, G. D.
Technical education. *Australasian accountant and secretary*, June 1919, p. 24-6.

DELUDED old school accountants. *Journal of accountancy*, May 1910, p. 53-7.

DEMAND for a national budget. *Economic world*, March 11, 1916, p. 338-40.

DEMAND for certified public accountants. *Journal of accountancy*, Sept. 1910, p. 368-71.

DEMAREE, F. H.
Farm bookkeeping. *Farm engineering*, Aug. Sept. 1917, p. 9, 13.
Farm bookkeeping: how to get an accurate estimate of profits. *Farm engineering*, Dec. 1917, p. 11.
Simple method of keeping farm records. *Farm engineering*, Jan. 1916, p. 131-2.

DEMAREST, H. P.
Short cut to knowing crop costs. *System on the farm*, March 1917, p. 21-2.

DEMING, H. E.
Government of American cities. New York, G. P. Putnam's sons, 1909. 323p.

DEMING, H. G.
New method for the graphical solution of algebraic equations. *Science*, April 21, 1916, p. 576-80.

DEMOCRACY is the expression of mill spirit. *Textile world*, Feb. 7, 1920, p. 934.

DEMONTMORENCY, J. E. G.
Law relating to accounts. (In Dicksee, Lawrence R. *Advanced accounting*. 1916. p. 497-524).

DE MURALT, C. L.
Electrification of heavy grades; advantages and cost. *Raiway age*, Jan. 17, 1913, p. 107-9.

DENHAM, F. W.
Depreciation of assets and goodwill of limited companies. *Accountant*, May 28, 1898, p. 568.

DENHAM, ROBERT SCUDDER
A-B-C of cost engineering. Cleveland, Denham cost finding company, c1919. 105p.
Applying the principles of cost engineering. *Foundry*, July 1918, p. 309+.
Fundamentals of cost and profit calculation: a vigorous discussion of the vital elements of business. Cleveland, Cost engineer publishing co 1918. 120p.
Manual of cost engineering and estimating for paper box manufacturers. Cleveland, Robert S. Denham, 1917. 316p.

DENISON, H.

Interest on capital as part of production cost. *Journal of accountancy*, Aug. 1913. p. 145-8.

DENIZEN, A. T.

Accounting methods of a furniture manufacturing business. *Business man's magazine*, 1904, v.17, p. 81-6.

DENMAN, J. S.

Book-keeping for the people; practical system of accounts. New York, Baker & Taylor co. 1887.

DENNEHY, JOHN G.

Executorship accounts. *Accountant*, May 3, 1902, p. 473-80.

DENNIS, WILLIAM HENRY

Practical accounting. Ed.2. New York, Leslie J. Thompkins, 1907.
——— Same. Ed.4. 1910.

——— AND LEO GREENDLINGER

Graded accounting problems. 3v. New York, New York university school of commerce, accounts and finance, 1909.

DENNISON, E. H.

Birmingham (England) increases prices of electricity and gas. *Commerce reports*, no. 81, April 6, 1918, p. 82-3.

DENNISON, H. S.

Why I believe in profit sharing. *Factory*, March 1918, p. 424.

DENNISON, JOHN A.

Working costs on mines as practiced on the Rand. *Transactions of the Institution of mining and metallurgy*, 1908, v.18, p. 108-32.

DENNY, G. A.

Cost reduction on the Rand; review by A. C. Key. *Engineering and mining journal*, Sept. 29, 1917, p. 555-6.

DENNY, M.

Comparative carrying capacities and costs of concrete and steel ships. *Engineering and contracting*, June 26, 1918, p. 651.

DENSHAM, FREDERICK W.

Depreciation of assets and goodwill of limited companies *Accountant*, May 28, 1898, p. 567-71.

DENTAL STOCK

BECKER, CHARLES E. Taking care of dental stock. *Business man's magazine*, Oct. 1907, p. 106-22.

DENTISTS

Accounting

BENTLEY, HARRY C. Ledger accounts used in bookkeeping for professional and scientific men. (In his *Science of accounts*. 1913. p. 360-6).
CLARKE, P. H. One-man business: a dentist's records. *System*, Feb. 1915, p. 214-7
COBB, WHITFIELD. Cobb's system of dental bookkeeping. Winston-Salem, N. C., W. Cobb. 1914. 20p.
HARLOW, A. F. One man business. *System*, Aug. 1917, p. 206-7.
JENKINSON, MARK WEBSTER. Accounts of profesional men. *Accountant*, March 23, 1907, p. 397-8.
STONE, C. N. Card ledger for dentists. *Business man's magazine*, April 1910, p. 364-5.
WHITE, FRANK. Book-keeping for dentists. London, Balliere, Tindall & co. 1910. 60p.

Depreciation

See Depreciation, depletion and obsolescence—Dentists.

DENTON, F. W.

Card system for mine supply accounts. *Proceedings of the Lake Superior mining institute*, 1903, v.9. p. 114-8. Condensed, *Mines anud minerals*, 1903, v.24, p. 125-6.
Card system for mine supply accounts. *Engineering and mining journal*, Oct. 1903, p. 471-2.

DENVER advised to purchase its present waterworks. *Engineering record*, Feb. 10, 1917, p. 227-8.

DENVER reclaim agreement. *Railway age gazette*, Feb. 26, 1915, p. 370.

DENVER tramway inaugurates 6 cent fare with extensive publicity. *Electric railway journal*, Oct. 5, 1918, p. 613.

DEPARTMENT of municipal audit and examination. Bureau of municipal research, New York. 1907.

DEPARTMENT of practical accounting. Wildman, J. R.

DEPARTMENT payrolls. *Drygoods economist*, Sept. 27, 1913, 1p.

DEPARTMENT store accounting. *Journal of accountancy*, March 1914, p. 234.

DEPARTMENT store accounting. Magee, H. C.

DEPARTMENT store accounting for a medium sized business. *Business man's magazine*, April 1908, p. 337-344.

DEPARTMENT store accounts. Sweetland, C. A.

DEPARTMENT store auditing. Newell, G. G.

DEPARTMENT store percentages. *American institute of acountants, Special bulletin*, No. 5, Sept. 1920, p. 3-4.

DEPARTMENT store statistics with the aid of the slide rule. 1914. Schreffler, Robert Bruce.

DEPARTMENT STORES

AMSDEN, DAN. Cost, profits and rate of turnover. *System*, Jan. Feb. 1915, p. 21, 143.
ANNABLE, H. C. Card payroll system arranged for department store. *Bnsiness man's magazine*, March 1908, p. 265-6.
DEPARTMENT payrolls. *Dry goods economist*, Sept. 27, 1913.
DEPARTMENT store percentages. *American institute of accountants*, *Special bulletin*, No. 5, Sept. 1920, p. 3-4.
HENDERSON, R. P. Multiple cash registers for department stores. *Busines man's magazine*, Oct 1906, p. 69-73.
LOSSES from bad debts. *System*, June 1915, p. 647.

Furniture	1.94%
Groceries	.47
Clothing	.34
Vehicles and instruments	.33
Hardware	.31
Jewelry	.21
Dry goods	.21
Department stores	.19
Drugs	.19
Shoes	.10
Variety goods	no loss

MOXEY, EDWARD P. and others. Department stores. (In their *Practical accounting methods*. p. 164-74).

DEPARTMENT STORES—*(Continued)*

NYSTROM, PAUL H. Department store. (In his *Economics of retailing.* 1917. p. 195-215).

QUESTION about department store billing. *Business man's magazine,* June 1908, p. 513-14.

RUSSELL, ANDREW P. Keeping tab on rising costs. *System,* Dec. 1914, p. 603-11.

SWINNEY, JOHN B. Department and specialty shop. (In his *Merchandising.* 1918. p. 283-97).

Accounting

ACCOUNTING for department stores. Detroit, Bookkeeper publishing co. 1900. 56p.

AMERICAN business and accounting encyclopaedia: comp. by E. H. Beach and W. W. Thorne. Detroit, Bookkeeper publishing company, 1901. Department—v.2, p. 426-49.

ANNAN, WILLIAM. Cash sales and departmental accounts. *Accountants' magazine,* June 1906, p. 313-21.

ARE you getting enough turnover? *Pacific coast merchant,* April 20, 1918, p. 7.

BROWN, H. G. Complete accounting system for a department store. *Business man's magazine,* 1904, v. 17, p. 86-99.

COOK, C. L. Billing and journalizing for department stores. *Busines man's magazine,* April 1908, p. 333-4.

DEPARTMENT store accounting. *Journal of accountancy,* March 1914, p. 234-6.

DEPARTMENT store accounting for a medium sized business. *Business man's magazine,* April 1908, p. 337-44.

DEPARTMENT stores. (In *International accountants' manual,* 1910, paragraphs, 50, 86, 97, 223, 494).

DEPARTMENTAL accounts and retailers. *Accountant,* Aug. 9, 16, 30, Sept. 6, 1902, p. 779-81, 799-801, 852-5, 871-2.

DEZOUCHE, RACHARD CATON. Analysis of trading results with reference to departments. *Accountants' magazine,* May 1908, p. 266.

GRIFFITH, JAS. B. and W. W. THORNE. Departmentalization of general stores. *Business man's magazine,* May, June 1907, p. 103-8, 49-53.

GROUCH, N. C. Making money by saving money for customers. *System,* June 1918, p. 890-3.

HIGGISON, FRANCIS WALFORD. Best system of accounts and checks for preventing theft of cash or stock in a large retail business with various departments doing both cash and credit trade. *Accountant,* June 14, July 26, 1902, p. 615-21, 737-9.

HILLER, AUGUST. Voucher record for department stores. *Busines man's magazine,* April 1910, p. 349-51.

HUTCHINSON, A. J. Retailers' monthly statements. *Accounting and commerce,* March 1917, p. 273-4.

JACKSON, HARRY A. Better store system and department accounting; a system for departmentizing a store or for department stores. Grinnell, Iowa, H. A. Jackson, c1914. 73p. + forms $1.25.

JACOBS, A. S. Handling cash in a store; how one department store reduced errors by a system that is operated by four forms. *System,* Feb. 1912, p. 166-8.

KESTER, R. B. Department store sales. (In his *Accounting theory and practice.* 1918. p. 343).

LISLE, GEORGE. Departments. (In their *Accounting in theory and practice.* 1900. p. 99-104).

LISLE, GEORGE and W. A. MIDDLETON. Departmental accounts. (In their *Accountkeeping in principle and practice.* 1911. p. 93-101).

LYONS, D. C. Department store accounting. *Accountant,* Feb. 17, 1906, p. 211-20.

LYONS, D. C. Department store accounting. *Business world,* 1904, v.24, p. 441-4, 409-92, 536-7.

MAGEE, HENRY C. Accounting for the import division of a department store. *Journal of accountancy,* June 1918, p. 433-43.

MAGEE, HENRY C. Department store accounting. *Journal of accountancy,* March 1907, p. 357-63.

MAGEE, HENRY C. Department store accounts; financing and controlling a division or department. *Journal of accountancy,* April 1915, p. 268-91.

MOXEY, EDWARD P. and others. Department stores accounting. (In their *Practical accounting methods.* p. 175-201).

RICHARDSON, GEORGE H. Department results and returns for drapers, etc. *Accountant,* Jan. 11, 1902, p. 40-4.

SALIERS, EARL A. Departmental accounting; practice. (In his *Accounting in theory and practice: principles.* 1920, p. 225-47).

SCHNEPFE, CHARLES H. Problem in department store accounting. *Journal of accountancy,* April 1909, p. 473-6.

SCHREFFLER, ROBERT BRUCE. Department store statistics with the aid of the slide rule. Chicago, Robert B. Schreffler, c1914. 140p.

SOLICITING and handling charge accounts for a department store. Nugent's bulletin. 3p.

SOULE, GEORGE. Department bookkeeping (In his *New Science and practice of accounts.* 1903. p. 667-71).

SWEETLAND, CHARLES AUGUSTUS. Department store accounts. (In *Cyclopedia of commerce, accountancy, business administration.* 1910. v.10. p. 11-126.

SWEETLAND, CHARLES AUGUSTUS. Department store accounts. Chicago, American school of correspondence, 1913. 118 + 61p. (American accountants' library).

WALKER, CHARLES A. Departmental accounts. *Public accountant,* 1906-7, p. 8.

WENZEL, J. F. Accounting for a general store; a complete system for recording on five forms, the ordinary business transactions of a small department store or other retail business of moderate size. *System,* Jan. 1912 p. 71-5.

Auditing

CASTENHOLZ, WILLIAM B. Department stores. (In his *Auditing procedure.* 1918. p. 260-3).

MONTGOMERY, ROBERT H. Department stores. (In his *Auditing theory and practice.* 1916. p. 616-25).

NEWELL, GEORGE G. Department store auditing; a practical text book on modern systems and methods of protection in accounting for sales. Chicago, American audit systems co. 1913. 103p.

Cost accounting

MAKING the leaks show up. *System,* Oct. 1917, p. 604.

DEPARTMENTAL ACCOUNTS

See also Cost and factory accounting—Departmental; Department stores.

CARTER, R. N. Departmental accounts. (In his *Advanced accounts,* p. 271-300).

CHADDOCK, J. B. System of accountings and costs for a plant with eleven departments. *Business man's magazine,* Oct. 1909, p. 354-8.

COLES, ARTHUR. Departmental acounts. (In his *Company accounts,* p. 160-7).

DICKSEE, LAWRENCE ROBERT. Departmental accounts. (In his *Advanced accounting.* 1916. p. 40-4).

DICKSEE, LAWRENCE ROBERT and H. E. BLAIN. Departmental and branch acounts. (In their *Office organization and management.* 1917. p. 153-61).

DOWLER, FRANK and E. M. HARRIS. Departmental accounts. (In their *Auditing, accounting and banking.* p. 116-27).

DEPARTMENTAL ACCOUNTS—*(Continued)*
NIXON, ALFRED and J. H. STAGG. Departmental, agency and branch accounts. (In their *Accounting and banking.* 1912. p. 143-9).
PORTERS, R. J. Departmental accounts. (In his *Pitman's dictionary of bookkeeping,* p. 325-8).
SOULÉ, GEORGE. Department book-keeping. (In his *New science and practice of accounts.* Ed. 7. 1903. p. 667-71.
SPICER, ERNEST EVAN and ERNEST C. PEGLER. Departmental accounts. (In their *Bookkeeping and accounts.* 1914. p. 232-5).
WALTON, SEYMOUR. Allocating general expense to departments. *Journal of accountancy,* Sept. 1918, p. 235.

DEPARTMENTAL accounts. *Accountant,* Jan. 19, Feb. 9, 1907, p. 73-7, 173-4.

DEPARTMENTAL accounts and retailers. *Accountant,* Aug. 9, 16, 30, Sept. 6, 1902, p. 779-81, 799-801, 852-5, 871-2.

DEPARTMENTAL committee on railway accounts and statistical returns. *Accountant,* Aug. 21-Sept. 25, 1909, p. 233-7, 269-76, 301-10, 326-34, 350-61, 390-5.

DEPARTMENTAL organization chart. *Electric railway journal,* Feb. 21, 1914, p. 415.

DEPARTMENTAL payroll. *Business man's magazine,* Sept. 1909, p. 271-4.

DEPARTURE in repair shop accounting. *Street railway journal,* May 20, 1906.

DE PAULA, FREDERICK RUDOLF MACKLEY
Audit and investigation of the accounts of executors and trustees. *Accountant,* April 9, 1910, p. 503-7.
Few notes on auditing. *Accountant,* June 15, 1912, p. 899-906.
Principles of auditing; a practical manual for students and practitioners. London, Sir Isaac Pitman & sons. 307p.
Some further notes on auditing. *Accountant,* March 22, 1913, p. 442-51.

DEPLETION
See Depreciation, depletion and obsolescence.

DEPLETION of copper mines in relation to income tax returns. Gower, W. B.

DEPRECIATED value as a basis for rate making; a review of the supreme court decision and some suggestions as to estimating accrued depreciation. *Engineering and contracting,* July 16, 1913, p. 58.

DEPRECIATION
See Depreciation, depletion and obsolescence.

DEPRECIATION. *Accountant,* June 8, 1918, p. 416.

DEPRECIATION. *Accountant,* Nov. 15, 22, 29, Dec. 13, 20, 27, 1884. *Accountant,* Oct. 2, 1915, Feb. 23, 1918, p. 297-8, 166. *Canadian chartered accountant,* April 1915, p. 347. *Electrical review,* June 24, 1910, *Engineer,* April 26, 1918, p. 360. *Engineering,* May 3, 1907, p. 585-6. *Light railway and tramway journal,* April 6, 1906, p. 210. *Michigan investor* (Detroit), March 13, 1909. *Municipal journal,* (London), Sept. 11, 25, Oct. 23, Nov. 13, Dec. 4, 1903, p. 818, 859, 939. 999, 1059. *Public service,* April 1909, p. 122 *Stone and Webster public service journal,* July 1907, p. 16.

DEPRECIATION. *American gas light journal,* Sept. 5, 1910, p. 435.

DEPRECIATION. *American institute of accountants, Special bulletin,* No. 1, 6, Jan. Nov. 1920, p. 6-7, 5.

DEPRECIATION. *Australasian accountant and secretary,* May 1920, p. 137.

DEPRECIATION. *Electric railway journal,* May 21, 1904, p. 760.

DEPRECIATION. *Electric railway journal,* Jan. 25, 1908, p. 104.

DEPRECIATION. *Electric railway review,* Aug. 1906, p. 452.

DEPRECIATION. *Electrical review,* (London), July 5, 1907, p. 2.

DEPRECIATION. *Electrical world,* Nov. 2, 1912, p. 909.

DEPRECIATION. *Electrician,* Aug. 28, 1908, p. 744.

DEPRECIATION. *Electrician,* Aug. 17, 1906, p. 702.

DEPRECIATION. *Electrician,* Feb. 19, 1909, p. 709. *Industrial engineering and engineering digest,* Oct. 1914, p. 402.

DEPRECIATION. *Engineering,* May 3, 1907, p. 585. *Municipal journal* (London) May 24, 1907, June 5, 1908, p. 449, 459.

DEPRECIATION. *Street railway journal,* May 21, 1904, p. 760.

DEPRECIATION. Alvord, J. W. 1912.

DEPRECIATION. Teichmann, Max.

DEPRECIATION. Wilmot, H. W.

DEPRECIATION account of the Kokomo, Marion and Western traction company. *Electric railway journal,* July 22, 1911, p. 156-7.

DEPRECIATION accounting for public utility companies. Seidman, F. E.

DEPRECIATION accounts. *National association of railway commissioners, Proceedings,* 1914, p. 450.

DEPRECIATION allowance for income tax. *Journal of gas lighting,* Nov. 23, 1909, p. 517-8.

DEPRECIATION allowance on equipment for construction work, United States government department. *Engineering news,* Dec. 2, 1909, p. 621-2.

DEPRECIATION allowances. *Accountants' magazine,* Nov. 1920, p. 578.

DEPRECIATION allowances for machinery and plant; Board of inland revenue regulations. *Board of trade journal,* April 25, 1918, p. 493.

DEPRECIATION allowances for plant and machinery: explanation by the board of inland revenue. *Board of trade journal,* Aug. 22, 1918, p. 244.

DEPRECIATION allowances in respect of second-hand steamships. *Accountant,* Aug. 10, 1918, p. 73-5. *Incorporated accountants' journal,* Sept. 1918, p. 249.

DEPRECIATION: American and British views. *Accountant,* Feb. 12, 1910, p. 231-3.

DEPRECIATION and appraisals. *Electrical review and western electrician,* July 22, 1911, p. 155.

DEPRECIATION and appreciation in railroad valuation. *Railway world,* April 1915, p. 303.

DEPRECIATION and capital expenditures in mining companies. *Incorporated accountants' journal,* 1897-8, p. 180.

DEPRECIATION and Chicago valuation figures. *Electric traction weekly,* May 18, 1912, p. 584.

DEPRECIATION and controlled establishments. *Accountant,* Jan. 15, 29, Feb. 12, 1916, p. 62-5, 129-32, 194-6.

DEPRECIATION and deferred maintenance of equipment testimony of D. F. Crawford, before the valuation division of the Interstate commerce commission. *Railway review,* Aug. 11, 1917, p. 176-9.

DEPRECIATION and depletion in relation to income tax returns. Nelson, Gilbert.

DEPRECIATION and depletion in relation to invested capital. Gower, W. B.

DEPRECIATION and depletion in tax returns. Cairns, William.

DEPRECIATION and depreciation reserves. Mann, Olaf A.

DEPRECIATION and finance. *System,* Oct. 1919, p. 786-90.

DEPRECIATION and income tax. *Accountant,* Oct. 24, 1914, p. 453-5.

DEPRECIATION and income tax. *Accounting and commerce,* June 1916, p. 53, Nov. 1917, p. 185-6.

DEPRECIATION and income tax. *Journal of gas lighting,* June 18, 1912, p. 886.

DEPRECIATION and income tax, the case of municipal undertakings. *Journal of gas lighting,* Jan. 7, 1913, p. 48.

DEPRECIATION and interest in manufacturing cost. Wright, W. C.

DEPRECIATION and measurement of expired outlay on plant. *Engineering and mining journal,* March 17, 1917, p. 447.

DEPRECIATION and obsolescence. *Inland printer,* Sept. 1914, p. 891-2.

DEPRECIATION and absolescence. *Light railway and tramway journal,* Sept. 6, 1912, p. 791.

DEPRECIATION and obsolescence as governed by federal income tax regulations, Loomis, Suffern & Fernald. 1918.

DEPRECIATION and obsolescence memorandum by the Board of inland revenue on the subject of allowances for depreciation and obsolescence of plant and machinery, etc. *Incorporated accountants' journal,* Oct. 1918, p. 10-4.

DEPRECIATION and other reserves. Knight, Alfred.

DEPRECIATION and permanent renewal fund. *Street railway bulletin,* May 1907, p. 298.

DEPRECIATION and publicity in Iowa. *Electric railway review,* May 2, 1908, p. 523.

DEPRECIATION and railroad credit. *Railway age gazette,* June 4, 1915, p. 1142.

DEPRECIATION and rates discussed before American gas institute. *Electrical world,* Nov. 7, 1914, p. 893-4.

DEPRECIATION and renewals accounts modified. *Railway age,* Sept. 6, 1907, p. 308.

DEPRECIATION and repairs. *Electrical review and western electrician,* Nov. 28, 1908, p. 807.

DEPRECIATION and reserve accounts. Grant, H. D.

DEPRECIATION and reserve funds in Milwaukee. *Street railway journal,* Sept. 23, 1905, p. 441.

DEPRECIATION and reserve funds of electrical properties. *Electrical world,* May 12, 1910, p. 186-8.

DEPRECIATION and reserves, warning to Newcastle. *Tramway and railway world,* Sept. 6, 1906, p. 258.

DEPRECIATION and sinking funds. *Accountant,* June 13-Aug. 26, 1903, p. 768-9, 797-800, 825-7, 838-9, 862-6, 882-6, 922-4, 943-6, 979-82, 1003-6, 1124-5, 1135-9, 1149-52.

DEPRECIATION and sinking funds. *Municipal engineering,* Jan. 1910, p. 33.

DEPRECIATION and sinking funds in municipal undertakings. *Accountant,* Aug. 20, 27, Sept. 17, Oct. 1, 1904, p. 180-8, 216-8, 271-4, 329-32.

DEPRECIATION and the federal excise tax. *Journal of accountancy,* Nov. 1912, p. 401-404.

DEPRECIATION and valuation. Tassin, J. S.

DEPRECIATION and valuation. Thomas, J. J.

DEPRECIATION and valuation for rate making. Haney, L. H.

DEPRECIATION and value of public utilities. James, C. C.

DEPRECIATION and values. *Municipal journal* (London), April 12, 1907, p. 304.

DEPRECIATION and wasting assets. *Canadian chartered accountant,* Jan. 1914, p. 184-5.

DEPRECIATION and wasting assets and their treatment in computing annual profit and loss. Leake, P. D. 1917.

DEPRECIATION, appreciation and productive capacity. Paton, W. A.

DEPRECIATION as a business cost: to what extent to be reckoned with? *National association of credit men, Bulletin,* v. 20, no. 8, p. 737.

DEPRECIATION as a factor in rates. *Electric railway review,* Nov. 9, 1909, p. 752.

DEPRECIATION as affecting valuation and fair return. *Electrical world,* Feb. 7, 1914, p. 301. *Electric railway journal,* Feb. 14, 1914, p. 370.

DEPRECIATION as an element for consideration in the appraisal of public service properties. *American society of civil engineers. Proceedings.* Jan. April 1915.

DEPRECIATION as applicable to electric railways. *Street railway journal,* Nov. 24, 1906.

DEPRECIATION as applied to valuation; abstract of testimony of W. B. Storey and D F. Crawford. *Railway age gazette,* June 22, 1917, p. 1406.

DEPRECIATION as between tenant-for-life and remainderman. *Incorporated accountants' journal,* July 1912, p. 258-60.

DEPRECIATION at Detroit. *Finance* (Cleveland, O.), Feb. 16, 1907, p. 201.

DEPRECIATION at Sunderland. *Tramway and railway world,* Nov. 12, 1903, p. 478.

DEPRECIATION charges in Kansas city. *Electrical railway journal,* Sept. 17, 1910, p. 424.

DEPRECIATION charges in Ohio. *Electric railway journal,* June 27, 1914, p. 1472.

DEPRECIATION charges of the international traction company. *Electric railway review,* April 18, 1908, p. 472.

DEPRECIATION: correspondence. *Journal of accountancy,* Dec. 1914, p. 492.

DEPRECIATION, DEPLETION AND OBSOLESCENCE

See also Valuation; various headings under Depreciation, depletion and obsolescence.

ABSOLUTE and theoretical depreciation. *Scientific American supplement,* Dec. 9, 1911, p. 374.

ACCOUNTING for depreciation. *Pacific railway journal,* March 7, 1914, p. 507.ffi

ALLEN, F. A. Necessity for and method of providing depreciation in the case of (1) a manufacturing company (2) a trading company. *Accountant,* May 14, 1910, p. 694-7.

ALLISON, JAMES E. Depreciation. *Annals of the American academy of political and social science,* May 1914, p. 198-213.

ALLOWANCES for depreciation of plant and machinery. *Accountant,* Nov. 13, 1909, p. 604-5.

AMERICAN business and accounting encyclopaedia; comp. by E. H. Beach and W. W. Thorne. Detroit, Bookkeeper publishing co. 1901.

APEDAILE, J. LEONARD. Depreciation. *Canadian chartered accountant,* April 1916, p. 297-308.

ARMSTRONG, JOHN H. Depreciation reserves. *Accountant,* Aug. 8, 1903, p. 1014-21.

ARNOLD, B. J. Depreciating overhead charges; supplementary note and glossary of terms. *Electric railway journal,* March 11, 1916, p. 498-9.

AUSTRALIA. *Federal income tax department.* Depreciation. *Accountant,* Oct. 14, 1916, Oct. 13, 1917, p. 327, 277-9. *Accounting and commerce,* June 1916, June 1917, p. 53, 55-7. *Federal accountant,* July 1916, July 1917, p. 77-8, 93-9. *Public accountant,* June 1916, Jan. 1917, p. 249-50, 145-52.

BAINBRIDGE, J. P. Depreciation and an auditor's responsibility in connection therewith. *Accountant,* Sept. 22, 1906, p. 334-7. *Incorporated accountants' journal,* 1906-7, p. 12.

BASING depreciation on par value. *Electric railway journal,* June 19, 1915, p. 1143.

BASSET, WILLIAM R. Charging off depreciation on the right basis. (In his *Accounting as an aid to business profits.* c1918. p. 192-9).

BASSET, WILLIAM R. How to find what your factory is worth. *Factory,* May 1918, p. 850-1.

BAUER, JOHN. Depreciation formula of the American society of civil engineers. *Journal of accountancy,* Aug. 1915, p. 104-11.

BAUGH, FREDERICK H. Principles and practice of cost accounting, for accountants, manufacturers, mechanical engineers, teachers and students. Baltimore, F. H. Baugh, 1915. 194p.
See index under Depreciation.

BEFORE providing for depreciation. *Incorporated accountants' journal,* Feb. 1914, p. 127-8.

BELL, L. B. Depreciation and valuation. *Accountants' magazine,* Jan. 1904, p. 23-30.

BELLS Asbests co. ltd. *Economist,* April 3, 1909, p. 736.
In the chairman's speech at the 12th annual meeting, he refers to the fact that they have written off to revenue about 2000 renewal, expenditure which might have been added to capital, and at the same time deprecate their plant and effects by the usual 10%.

BENNETT, ROBERT JOSEPH. Depreciation. (In his *Corporation accounting.* 1917. p. 327-33).

BENTLEY, HARRY C. Science of accounts. New York, Ronald press company, 1913. 393p.
See index under Depreciation.

BERNDT, IRVING A. Depreciation. (In his *Costs.* c1920. p. 101-6.)

BIGGS, CHARLES H. W. Depreciation of plant and works under municipal and company management. *Accountant,* Jan. 17, 1903, p. 91-7. *Society of engineers, Transactions,* 1902, p. 271-300.

BLACKADDER, R. J. Depreciation of investments and plant. *Accountant,* April 19, 1913. p. 578.

BOAG, HAROLD. Allowances for exceptional depreciation in the assessment of excess profits duty. *Accountant,* Feb. 23, 1918, p. 162-3.

BOGLE, J. D. S. Writing off of depreciation on the wasting assets of a joint stock company. *Accountant,* Dec. 21, 1889, p. 691-6.

BOLTON, REGINALD PELHAM. Building for profit, principles governing the economic improvement of real estate. New York, De Vinne press, 1911. 124p.

BREWER, A. F. Principles of the calculation of a straight line depreciation. *Industrial management,* April 1917, p. 49-50.

BRITTON, J. A. Methods of calculating depreciation. *Electric railway journal,* Nov. 7, 1914, p. 1059-60.

BROMLEY, CHARLES H. Depreciation and how it is applied. *Power,* June 2, 1914, p. 767.

BRONSON, JOHN L. Depreciation problem. *Cassier's magazine,* July 1905, p. 190-2.

BRYERS, F. T. Effect on the adjustment of losses through writing down fixed assets to provide for depreciation. *Canadian chartered accountant,* July 1914, p. 4-9.

BUNNELL, STERLING H. Cost-keeping for manufacturing plants. New York. D. Appleton & co. 1911. 233p.
See index under Depreciation.

BURNS, CLINTON S. Determination of physical values. *Engineering record,* Sept. 16, 1905, p. 328-9.

BURNS, CLINTON S. Relationship of finance and depreciation. *American municipalities,* June 1917, p. 77-9.

CAIRNS, WILLIAM. Depreciation and depletion in tax returns. *Journal of accountancy,* Sept. 1919, p. 204-11.

CALDICOTT, O. HOLT. Auditor's duty in respect of depreciation. *Accountant,* Jan. 25, 1896, p. 74-6.

DEPRECIATION, DEPLETION AND OBSOLESCENCE—*(Continued)*

CARDULLO, FOREST E. Labor and other costs in manufacturing. *Iron age*, May 28, 1914, p. 1365-7. *Metal work*, June 12, 1914, p. 775-7.

CARTER, ROGER N. Advanced accounts. London, Sir Isaac Pitman & sons. 980p.
Plant and machinery 5-10%
Based on diminishing balances, normal conditions and hours of working.
See index under Depreciation.

CARTER, ROGER N. Repairs, renewals, and depreciation, and discrimination between capital and revenue expenditure. *Accountant*, March 7, 1908, p. 318-23.

CASTENHOLZ, WILLIAM B. Auditing procedure. Chicago, La Salle extension university, 1918. 342p.
See index under Depreciation.

CHARTERED ACCOUNTANTS STUDENTS' SOCIETY OF LONDON. Depreciation of assets and goodwill of limited companies. *Accountant*, Jan. 9, 1904, p. 44-52.

CHASE, HARVEY STUART. Governmental sinking funds, serials bonds and depreciation reserves; read at the annual meeting of chartered accountants at Montreal, September 18th to 20th, 1918. 18p. *Accountant*, March 1, 1919, p. 162-8. *Canadian chartered accountant*, Oct. 1918, p. 142-65. *Journal of accounting*, Oct. 1918, p. 258-68. *National association of comptrollers and accounting officers, Proceedings*, June 1918, p. 64-74.

CHASE, HARVEY STUART. Standards of depreciation. *Boston evening transcript*, April 12, 1907.

CHASE, WILLIAM ARTHUR. Auditing and cost accounting. Chicago, La Salle extension university, 1917. 493p.
See index under Depreciation.

CHILD, R. W. Where a theory fails: depreciation a physical fact. *Stone and Webster pubilc service journal*, June 1911 ,p. 422-6.

CHURCH, ALEXANDER HAMILTON. Manufacturing cost and accounts. New York, McGraw-Hill book co. 1917. 452p.
See index under Depreciation.

CLAPHAM, F. T. Depreciation of plant. *Mechanical world*, Oct. 19, 1917, p. 219-20.

CLARK, E. G. Depreciation in accounts. *South African accountants' journal*, v. 2, p. 9.

COLE, WILLIAM MORSE. Depreciation. (In his *Bookkeeping, accounting and auditing*. c1914. p. 263-80.)

COLE, WILLIAM MORSE. General principles of depreciation. (In his *Accounts; their construction and interpretation*. c1915. p. 95-108).

COLES, ARTHUR. Company accounts; a complete manual for the use of officials in limited companies and advanced students; with a preface by Charles Comins. Ed. 2. London, Sir Isaac Pitman & sons. 340p.
See index under Depreciation.

COLES, ARTHUR. Depreciation and costing. *Business organisation* and *management*, Nov. 1920, p. 131-8.

COLLEY, FREDERICK G. Depreciation of manufacturing plants. *Journal of accountancy*, Sept. 1915. p. 165-72.

COMPANY depreciation. *Accountant*, April 25, 1914, p. 597-9.

CONCERNING depreciation. *Accountant*, Jan. 1, Dec. 10, 1910, p. 6-9, 796-800.

CONLIN, JOHN A. AND OTHERS. Income and federal tax reports. New York, Prentice-Hall, inc. c1918. 704p.
See index under Depletion; Depreciation.

COX, HENRY C. Depreciation problems; depreciation on the books. (In his *Advanced and analytical accounting*, 1920. p. 165-88.)

CRAIN, G. D. Handling the depreciation account. *Iron age*, March 5, 1914, p. 616-7.

CRAVATH, JAMES R. Accounting for depreciation. *Electrical world*, Jan. 23, 1915, p. 213-4. Editorial. Accounting for depreciation. *Electrical world*, Jan. 23, 1915, p. 202.

CROAD, H. J. Depreciation, appreciation, discount, interest and annuity tables. New York, Spectator company.

CURTISS, W. B. Depreciation of property. *General electric review*, Dec. 1915, p. 1099-106.

CUSTODY of depreciation funds. *Electrical world*, Jan. 20, 1912, p. 126.

CUTFORTH, ARTHUR E. Methods of providing for depreciation. (In his *Audits*. 1914. p. 184-8.)

DARBISHIRE, JAMES E. Repairs and depreciation in manufacturing plants. *Engineering magazine*, Dec. 1908, p. 519-21.

DAVIES, W. SANDERS. Depreciation. Business, Nov. 1897, p. 338-40.

DAWSON, SIDNEY STANLEY. Depreciation. (In his *Accountant's compendium*. 1898. p. 89.)

DAWSON, SIDNEY STANLEY. Depreciation; correspondence. *Accountant*, Aug. 8, 1914, p. 175-8.

DEDUCTIONS for obsolescence justified. *Railway age gazette*, Dec. 2, 1910, p. 1093.

DEL MAR, W. A. Methods on figuring depreciation and present values. *Industrial engineer*, Oct. 1914, p. 402-3.

DENHAM, ROBERT S. Depreciation. (In his *Fundamentals of cost and profit calculations*. 1918. p. 44, 46, 47.)

DENSHAM, FREDERICK W. Depreciation of assets and goodwill of limited companies. *Accountant*, May 28, 1898. p. 567-71.

DE PAULA, FREDERICK R. M. Principles of auditing: a practical manual for students and practitioners. London, Sir Isaac Pitman and sons. 207p.
See index under Depreciation.

DEPRECIATION. *Accountant*, Nov. 15, 22, 29, Dec. 13, 20, 27, 1884. Oct. 2, 1915. Feb. 23, 1918, p. 397-8, 166. *American institute of accountants. Special bulletin*, no. 6, Nov. 1920, p. 5. *Australasian accountant and secretary*. May 1920, p. 137. *Canadian chartered accountant*, April 1915, p. 347. *Electrical review*, June 24, 1910. *Engineer*, April 26, 1918, p. 360. *Engineering*, May 3, 1907, p. 585-6. *Light railway and tramway journal*, April 6, 1906, p. 210. *Michigan investor (Detroit)*, March 13, 1909. *Municipal journal, (London)*, Sept. 11, 25, Oct. 23, Nov. 13, Dec. 4, 1903, p. 818, 859, 939, 999, 1059. *Public service*, April 1909, p. 122. *Stone and Webster public service journal*, July 1907, p. 16.

DEPRECIATION. (In *International accountants' manual of twentieth century bookkeeping and business practice*. 1910. p. 44.)

DEPRECIATION allowance on equipment for construction work, United States government department. *Engineering news*, Dec. 2, 1909, p. 621-2.

DEPRECIATION allowances for machinery and plant; Board of inland revenue regulations. *Board of trade journal*, April 25, 1918, p. 493.

DEPRECIATION, DEPLETION AND OBSOLESCENCE—*(Continued)*

DEPRECIATION allowances for plant and machinery: explanation by the Board of inland revenue. *Board of trade journal,* Aug. 22, 1918, p. 244.
DEPRECIATION: American and British views. *Accountant,* Feb. 12, 1910, p. 231-3.
DEPRECIATION and appraisals. *Electrical review and western electrician,* July 22, 1911, p. 155.
DEPRECIATION and controlled establishments. Accountant, Jan. 15, 29, Feb. 12, 1916, p. 62-5, 129-32, 194-6.
DEPRECIATION and finance. *System,* Oct. 1919, p. 786-90.
DEPRECIATION and income tax. *Accountant,* Oct. 24, 1914, p. 453-5.
DEPRECIATION and income tax. *Accounting and commerce,* Nov. 1917, p. 185-6.
DEPRECIATION and obsolescence. *Inland printer,* Sept. 1914, p. 891-2.
DEPRECIATION and obsolescence. *Light railway and tramway journal,* Sept. 6, 1912, p. 791.
DEPRECIATION and obsolescence memorandum by the Board of inland revenue on the subject of allowances for depreciation and obsolescence of plant and machinery, etc. *Incorporated accountants' journal,* Oct. 1918, p. 10-4.
DEPRECIATION and sinking funds. *Municipal engineering,* Jan. 1910. p. 33.
DEPRECIATION and the federal excise tax. *Journal of accountancy,* Nov. 1912, p. 401-4.
DEPRECIATION and values. *Municipal journal (London),* April 12, 1907, p. 304.
DEPRECIATION and wasting assets. *Canadian chartered accountant,* Jan. 1914, p. 184-5.
DEPRECIATION as a business cost: to what extent to be reckoned with? *National Association of credit men, bulletin,* v.20, no. 8, p. 737.
DEPRECIATION as between tenant-for-life and remainderman. *Incorporated accountants' journal,* July 1912, p. 258-60.
DEPRECIATION charges in Ohio. *Electric railway journal,* June 27, 1914, p. 1472.
DEPRECIATION: correspondence. *Journal of accountancy,* Dec. 1914, p. 492-3.
DEPRECIATION funds and loan redemption. *Accountant,* July 2, 1910, p. 4-6.
DEPRECIATION in appraisals. *Journal of accountancy,* June 1915, p. 458-60.
DEPRECIATION of controlled plant. *Engineer,* Nov. 10, 1916, p. 419-20.
DEPRECIATION of gold. *Electrical review and western electrician,* Sept. 27, 1913, p. 601.
DEPRECIATION of plant. *Times engineering supplement,* Jan. 26, 1917.
DEPRECIATION of plant and machinery. *Accountant,* Nov. 14, 21, 1908, p. 576-8, 602.4.
DEPRECIATION plan of the Valuation committee of the American society of civil engineers. *Engineering news,* Feb. 12, 1914, p. 350-2.
DEPRECIATION reserve. *Municipal journal and engineer,* Nov. 24, 1909, p. 772-3.
DEPRECIATION with special reference to assessment of income. *Accountants' magazine,* Jan. 1899, p. 13-4.
DICKINSON, ARTHUR LOWES. Depreciation. (In his *Accounting practice and procedure,* 1917. p. 44-5, 167-74).
DICKSEE, LAWRENCE R. Accountant on depreciation. *American gas light journal,* May 20, 1907, p. 847. *Journal of gas lighting,* April 16, 1907, p. 175.
DICKSEE, LAWRENCE ROBERT. Auditing; a practical manual for auditors; ed. by R. H. Montgomery. Authorized American edition, revised and enlarged. New York, Ronald press co. 1909. 586p.
See index under Depreciation.
DICKSEE, LAWRENCE ROBERT. Comparative depreciation tables. Ed. 2. London, Gee & co. 1909. 25p.
DICKSEE, LAWRENCE ROBERT. Advanced accounting; with an appendix on the law relating to accounts by J. E. G. de Montmorency. Ed. 5. London, Gee & co. 1916. 571p.
See index under Depreciation.
DICKSEE, LAWRENCE ROBERT. Depreciation. *Municipal journal (London).* April 19, 26, 1907, p. 323, 355.
DICKSEE, LAWRENCE ROBERT. Depreciation. (In his *Bookkeeping for company secretaries.* 1908. p. 89-90.)
DICKSEE, LAWRENCE ROBERT. Depreciation, reserves and reserve funds. Ed. 3. London, Gee & co. 1912. 80p. Accountants' library, v. 26.)
DICKSEE, LAWRENCE ROBERT and H. E. BLAIN. Depreciation. (In their *Office organization and management.* 1917. p. 213-8).
DIEMER, HUGO. Depreciation. (In his *Factory organization and administration.* 1914. p. 20, 298-301).
DISCUSSION on principles involved in computing the depreciation of plant. *Journal of the Institute of electrical engineers,* March 1917.
DONALDSON, H. F. Depreciation of building and machinery. *Engineering magazine.* April 1911, p. 171-6. *Engineering record,* Feb. 11, 1911, p. 159. *Mechanical engineer,* Feb. 10, 1911, p. 177-80, 202-4.
DOUBTFUL factor in depreciation rates. *Engineering magazine,* Jan. 20, 1911.
DOWLER, FRANK AND E. M. HARRIS. Depreciation. (In their *Auditing, accounting and banking.* p. 141-6).
DREYFUS, E. D. Reckoning with costs of superseded equipment. *Electrical world,* Aug. 5, 1916, p. 272-4.
DUFFY, C. N. Depreciation. *Electric railway journal,* Jan. 29, 1910, p. 184-7. *Electrical world,* Feb. 1, 1908, p. 217-9. *Progressive age,* Sept. 1, 1909, p. 686.
ECONOMIC aspects of depreciation. *Railway review,* Aug. 25, 1917, p. 234-5.
EGGLESTON, DEWITT CARL. Depreciation. (In his *Cost accounting,* 1920, p. 244-52.)
EGGLESTON, DEWITT CARL. Depreciation. (In his *Problems in cost accounting.* 1918. p. 156-71).
ELBOURNE, EDWARD T. Factory administration and accounts; a book of reference with tables and specimen forms, for managers, engineers and accountants, with contributions on the General problems of industrial works design by Andrew Home-Morton; and Financial accounts by John Maughfling. London, Longmans, Green & co. 1918. 638p.
See Index under Depreciation and obsolescence.
ELY, O. Inadequacy of present depreciation accounts. *Railway age,* Sept. 20, 1918, p. 553 6. Discussion. D. J. Kerr. *Railway age,* Nov. 1, 1918, p. 764.
ENNIS, WILLIAM DUANE. Depreciation. (In his *Works management.* 1911. p. 82-99.)
EQUIPMENT for the future. *Cassier's magazine,* Sept. 1912, p. 277-8.

DEPRECIATION, DEPLETION AND OBSOLESCENCE—*(Continued)*

ERICKSON, E. A. Depreciation and measurement of expired outlay on plant. *Engineering and mining journal,* March 3, 17, 1917, p. 370, 447-9.

ERICKSON, HALFORD. As to depreciation accounting; discusses methods of providing for depreciation. *Public service regulation,* June 1914, p. 305-7.

ESQUERRÉ, PAUL JOSEPH. Applied theory of accounts. New York. The Ronald press co. 1917. 519p.
See index under Depreciation.

EVALUATING depreciation. *Electrical world,* Oct. 7, 1911.

EVANS, HOLDEN A. Depreciation. (In his *Cost keeping and scientific management.* 1911. p. 30-6).

EVELEIGH, F. W. ANTON. Income tax guide; an exposition of the income tax (consolidation) act, 1907, including the normal tax, dividend tax, excess profits duty, and the taxation of profits derived from mining, industrial and other sources; including an exact copy of the income tax (consolidation) act. 1917. Cape Town, Accountants book service supply. 166p.
See index under Depreciation.

EXAMPLE of depreciation charges. *Accountant,* March 7, 1908, p. 343-4. *Journal of accountancy,* Jan. 1908, p. 201-4.

EXCESS profits duty: official statement. *Accountant,* July 21, 1917, p. 50-3. *Incorporated accountants' journal,* Aug. 1917, p. 231-3.

FERNALD, HENRY B. Depreciation and obsolescence as governed by federal income tax regulations. *Engineering and mining journal,* April 6, 1918, p. 631-3. *Journal of accountancy,* April 1918, p. 241-7.

FICKER, NICHOLAS T. Distributing overhead expense. *Engineering magazine,* Nov. 1915, p. 254-61.

FICKER, NICHOLAS T. Factor of depreciation. *Business man's magazine,* Oct. 1907, p. 124-8.

FICKER, NICHOLAS T. Shop expense analysis and control. New York, Engineering magazine co. 1917. 236p. (Industrial management library).
See index under Depreciation.

FISH, WILLISTON. Depreciation reserve fund. *Electric railway journal,* Jan. 31, 1920, p. 239-47.

FITTING, R. U. Analysis of the different kinds of depreciation and various methods evolved for computing it. *Electric railway journal,* Sept. 26, 1914, p. 558-62.

FITTING, R. U. Calculating depreciation. *Electric railway journal,* Nov. 21, 1914, p. 1164.

FLOY, HENRY. Absolute and theoretical depreciation; a distinction of much importance in appraisal; abstract. *Engineering record,* Sept. 18, 1911, p. 335.

FORSE, W. H. Depreciation and appreciation. *Electric railway journal,* Dec. 11, 1915, p. 1169-70.

FORSTER, J. W. Sinking funds and their relation to depreciation funds. *Accountant,* July 20, Aug. 3, 1907, p. 86-96, 133-5. *Incorporated accountants' journal,* 1906-7, p. 272.

FORSTER, HORATIO A. Depreciation. (In his *Engineering valuation of public utilities and factories.* 1913. p. 147-218).

FOSTER, HORATIO A. Depreciation as affecting engineered structures. *Engineers club of Philadelphia, Proceedings,* Oct. 1902, p. 330-49.

FOWLE, FRANK F. Depreciation in its relation to appraisals. *Electrical world,* Oct. 6, 1910, p. 796.

FOWLE, FRANK F. Practical discussion of depreciation. *Southern electrician,* June 1911, p. 227.

GARCKE, EMILE and J. M. FELLS. Factory accounts; their principles and practice. London, Crosby, Lockwood and son. 1893. 264p.
See index under Depreciation.

GARRY, HENRY STANLEY. Depreciation of plant and machinery. *Accountant,* June 23, Sept. 15, 1906, p. 785-9, 285-8.

GILL, F. T. and W. W. COOK. Principles involved in computing the depreciation of plant. Woking, England, Gresham press, 1916. 18p. *Accountant,* March 17-April 21, May 19, 1917, p. 263-6, 289-99, 313-23, 340-51, 366-76, 386-91, 473-6. *Journal of the Institute of electrical engineers,* Feb. 1917, p. 137-54. *Surveyor and municipal and county engineer,* Feb. 9, 1917. Abstract. *Electrical world,* March 17, 1917, p. 519-20. *Electric railway journal,* May 12, 1917, p. 865. *Incorporated accountants' journal,* Feb. 1917, p. 110-1. *Public accountant,* June 1917, p. 289-90. Discussion. *Journal of the Institute of electrical engineers,* Feb. 1, March 1, May 1, 1917, p. 154-74, 213-28, 408-10. Excerpt. G. Nicholson. *Electrical world,* July 30, 1917, p. 1267.

GILLETTE, HALBERT P. Depreciation (In his *Handbook of cost data for contractors and engineers.* 1910. p. 34-8).

GILLETTE, HALBERT P. Methods of computing depreciation. *Electrical world,* Dec. 14, 1912, p. 1273-4.

GILLETTE, HALBERT P. Rational method of calculating depreciated value. *Engineering and contracting,* July 14, 1915, p. 23-7.

GILLETTE, HALBERT P. Use of depreciation data. *Public service regulation,* March 1913, p. 120.

GILLETTE, HALBERT P. Use of depreciation data in rate making and appraisal problems. *Engineering and contracting,* Oct. 30, 1912, p. 476-80. *Electrical world,* Nov. 2, 1912, p. 927. *Editorial.* Depreciation. *Electrical world,* Nov. 2, 1912, p. 909.

GILLETTE, HALBERT P. and RICHARD T. DANA. Handbook of mechanical and electrical cost data. New York, McGraw-Hill book co. 1918. 1739p.
See index under Depreciation.

GILMAN, STEPHEN. *Principles of accounting.* Chicago, LaSalle extension university, 1917. 415p.
See index under Depreciation.

GLASGOW INSTITUTE OF ACCOUNTANTS DEBATING SOCIETY. Obligation of a company to provide for depreciation of wasting assets before declaring dividends. *Accountant,* Dec. 14, 1889, p. 676-82.

GLASGOW JURISDICTIONAL SOCIETY AND GLASGOW INSTITUTE OF ACCOUNTANTS' DEBATING SOCIETY. Debate—Is it desirable to amend the law so as to make it compulsory on joint stock companies to provide for substantial depreciation of assets before arriving at profits? *Accountant,* March 18, 1893, p. 254-60.

GOING, CHARLES BUXTON. Depreciation. (In his *Principles of industrial engineering,* 1911. p. 106, 108-9).

DEPRECIATION, DEPLETION AND OBSOLESCENCE—*(Continued)*

GOWER, WILLIAM B. Depreciation and depletion in relation to invested capital. *Journal of accountancy,* Nov. 1919, p. 353-68.

GRANT, HARRIS D. Depreciation and reserve accounts. *Journal of accountancy,* March 1910, p. 352-7.

GREAT BRITAIN. Board of inland revenue. Depreciation rates. (In its Income tax; statement respecting allowances for wear and tear and obsolescence of plant and machinery. 1918. Cd. 9022, p. 4; Cd. 9134, p. 6). *American economic review, Supplement,* Dec. 1920, p. 51. *Journal of accountancy,* Sept. 1920, p. 190-7.

GREELEY, HAROLD DUDLEY. Depreciation. (In his *Theory of accounts.* 1920. p. 315-27).

GREENDLINGER, LEO. Financial and business statements. New York, Alexander Hamilton institute, c1917. 392p. (Modern business, v. 22).
See index under Depreciation.

GREENDLINGER, LEO and JOHN R. LOOMIS. Depreciation. (In their *Accounting problems.* 1910. v. 1. p. 44, 73-4, 77, 90, 204-5, 185-6).

GRUHL, EDWIN. Depreciation estimates. *Aera,* March 1913, p. 644.

GRUNSKY, CARL EWALD and C. E. GRUNSKY, JR. Valuation, depreciation and the rate-base. New York, John Wiley & sons, 1917. 387p.

GUNDRY, WILLIAM HICKLEY. .Depreciation of assets. *Accountant,* Aug. 26, 1905, p. 238-40.

GUTHRIE, EDWIN. Depreciation. (In Lisle, George. *Encyclopaedia of accounting.* v. 2, p. 357-76).

GUTHRIE, EDWIN. Depreciation and sinking funds. *Accountant,* April 21, Sept. 1, 1883.

HALE, ROBERT S. Depreciatiin and reserve. *Rollins magazine,* April 1912, p. 21-5.

HALL, CHARLES O. Sinking funds and depreciation accounts. *New York accountants' and bookkeepers' journal,* Feb. 1904, p. 33-4.

HALL, SAMUEL TAYLOR. Sinking funds and depreciation. *Accountant,* April 23, 1904, p. 540-1.

HATFIELD, HENRY RAND. Modern accounting, its principles and some of its problems. New York, D. Appleton & co. 1916. 367p.
See index under Depreciation.

HAWKINS, L. WHITTEM. Depreciation. (In his *Cost accounts.* 1912. p. 29, 81, 113-4).

HAWKINS, LESTER G. Reconciling depreciation and appraised values of industrial equipment- *Industrial management,* Sept. 1920, p. 207-9.

HAWLEY, W. C. Relation of depreciation to investment. *Journal of the American water works association,* June 1919, p. 305-19.

HELLYER, ARTHUR LEE. Depreciating assets, sinking funds, and kindred subjects. *Accountant,* July 29, Aug. 5, Sept. 16, 1899, p. 809-17, 834-9, 945-50.

HENDERSON, W. H. Auditing. *Canadian chartered accountant,* Oct., 1920, p. 107-9.

HIXSON, L. T. More about sinking funds: not a deduction from income. *Aera,* Feb. 1914, p. 723.

HORSNAILL, W. O. Depreciation and obsolescence in small engineering works. *Electrical engineering* (London), Nov. 26, 1908.

HOW, FRANCIS. Depreciation. *Accountant,* June 20, Sept. 12, 1903, p. 812-7, 1101-3.

HOW to record depreciation. *System,* Aug. 1915, p. 197.

How to understand the balance sheet and other periodical statements, by a chartered accountant. Ed. 2. London, Jordon & sons. 1905. 102p.
See index under Depreciation.

HOXIE, GEORGE L. Custody of depreciation funds. *Electrical world,* Feb. 17, 1912, p. 367.

HUMPHREYS, ALEXANDER C. Depreciation. (In his *Lecture notes on some of the business features of engineering practice.* p. 258-348).

HUMPHREYS, ALEXANDER C. Depreciation. *Progressive age,* Dec. 2, 1907, p. 688-99.

HURD, E. C. *Should depreciation apply?* Public service regulation, Aug. 1913, p. 401.

IMPORTANCE of depreciation allowances. *Engineering record,* June 15, 1907, p. 703.

IMPORTANCE of engineer, financier and accountant computing plant depreciation. *Electrical review and Western electrician,* March 3, 1917, p. 351-2.

INCOME tax; allowances for wear and tear and obsolescence of plant and machinery. *Incorporated accountants' journal,* May 1918, p. 155-7.

INCOME tax and depreciation. *Municipal journal (London),* Aug. 13, 1907, p. 744.

INCOME tax and depreciation allowances. *Accountant,* May 30, 1914, p. 785-8.

INCOME tax and depreciation; shipping industry, paper mills, printing works. *Incorporated accountants' journal,* May 1914, p. 243.

INCOME tax notes. *Accountant,* May 11, Sept. 28, 1918, p. 358-60, 162-6.

INCOME tax notes—depreciation. *Accountants' magazine,* March 1919, p. 128-31.

INTEREST and depreciation. *Accountant,* Aug. 29, Sept. 5, 12, 1908, Feb. 1, 8, 1909, p. 233-5, 263-5, 289-91, 137-9, 169-72.

INTRODUCTORY notes on Leake's register of industrial plant. *Accountant,* June 4, 1910, p. 801-6, 784-7.

IT is a necessitous duty to provide for depreciation. *Electrical world,* April 7, 1917, p. 670.

JACKSON, WILLIAM B. Depreciation estimating. *Steam, April* 1911, p. 103.

JACKSON, J. HUGH. Depreciation policy and true cost. *Journal of accountancy,* June 1920, p. 452-5.

JAMES, C. C. Hen and Erie ferry boat. *Railway age,* April 6, 1917, p. 733-4.

JENKINS, J. B. Some of the absurdities of the straight line method of determining depreciation. *Railway age gazette,* Feb. 25 1916. p. 357-8. *Railway gazette* (London), 1916. v. 24, p. 614-5.

JENKINSON, Mark Webster. Depreciation. *Accountant,* May 17, 1902, p. 528-34.

JENKINSON, MARK WEBSTER. Some principles of accounting affecting cost accounts. *Accountant,* April 18, 1914, p. 573-7.

JIRGAL, JOHN. Accounting for depreciation. *Electric railway journal,* Oct. 25, 1919, p. 799-800.

JIRGAL, JOHN. Actuarial problem. *Journal of the Western society of engineers,* Jan. 5, 1920, p. 15-20. Condensed. *Electric railway journal,* Oct. 25, 1919, p. 799-800. Excerpt. *Engineering and contracting,* May 19, 1920, p. 564-5.

JOHNSON, GEORGE. Depreciation. *Electrical service* (London), June 24, 1920, p. 1048.

JONES, E. D. Investment. New York, Alexander Hamilton institute. c1918. 352p. (Modern business, v. 23).
See index under Depreciation.
Manufacturing companies in general 6%

DEPRECIATION, DEPLETION AND OBSOLESCENCE—*(Continued)*

JORDAN, JOHN P. and GOULD L. HARRIS. Depreciation. (In their *Cost accounting*. 1920. p. 234-5).

KATES, E. J. Actuary theory of depreciation of physical property values. *Railway age gazette*, May 3, 1918, p. 1133-5.

KEALY, PHILIP J. Discussion of depreciation. *Engineering and contracting*, Aug. 18, 1915, p. 118-23.

KEEPING depreciation records. *Engineering record*, July 22, 1905, p. 82.

KEEPING track of depreciation. *Factory*, Aug. 1917, p. 244.

KEISTER, D. A. Depreciation. (In his *Corporation accounting and auditing*. 1909. p. 374-80).

KENT, WILLIAM. Depreciation; inventory valuation; appraisals. (In his *Bookkeeping and cost accountng for factories*. 1918. p. 85-91).

KER, CHARLES. Depreciation. *Accountant*, March 17, 1900, p. 278-80. *Accountants' magazine*, April 1900, p. 196-220.

KESTER, ROY B. Accounting theory and practice. New York. The Ronald press co. 1917. 607p.
See index under Depreciation.

KESTER, ROY B. Accounting theory and practice. v.2. New York, The Ronald press co. 1918. 796p.
See index under Depreciation.

KIMBALL, DEXTER S. Cost finding. c1918. New York, Alexander Hamilton institute. c1918. 338p. (Modern business, v.10).
See index under Depreciation.

KIMBALL, DEXTER S. Principles of industrial organization. New York, McGraw-Hill book company, 1913. 272p.
See index under Depreciation.

KLEIN, JOSEPH J. Depreciation. (In his *Bookkeeping and accounting*. 1917. p. 328-30.)

KLEIN, JOSEPH J. Depreciation. (In his *Elements of accounting*. 1916. p. 184-9).

KLOTZ, R. G. Principles of depreciation accounting. *Industrial management*, Nov. 1916, p. 164-76.

KLOTZ, R. G. Rational plant units for depreciation accounting. *Engineering news record*, Jan. 6, 1916, p. 23-4.

KNIGHT, ALFRED. Depreciation and other reserves. *Journal of accountancy*, Jan. 1908, p. 189-200.

LADELLE, OSCAR GERARD. Calculation of depreciation. *Accountant*, Nov. 29, Dec. 6, 1890, p. 659-60, 669-71.

LAWTON, W. H. Depreciation accounts. *Electrical world*, June 26, 1915, p. 1678-9.

LEAKE, PERCY DEWE. Annuity or sinking fund theory of measurement of depreciation of plant. *Electrician (London)*, March 26, 1915. *Accountant*, July 3, 1915, p. 18-25.

LEAKE, PERCY DEWE. Depreciation. *Accountant*, Dec. 27, 1913, p. 938-47. *Incorporated accountants' journal*, Jan. 1914, p. 111-5.

LEAKE, PERCY DEWE Depreciation: a plea for the study and use of better methods. *Mechanical engineer*, July 27, Aug. 3, 10, 1907, p. 117-21, 147-9, 179-82.

LEAKE, PERCY DEWE. Depreciation and wasting assets and their treatment in computing annual profit and loss. London, Sir Isaac Pitman & sons, 1917. 233p.

LEAKE, PERCY DEWE. Leake's register of industrial plant. London, Hy Good and sons. 15 blank forms+15p.

LEAKE, PERCY DEWE. Need of present accounting for past unexpired capital outlay. *Accountant*, Oct. 12, 1912, p. 470-5.

LEAKE, PERCY DEWE. Question of depreciation and the measurement of expired outlay on productive plant. (In Chase, W. A. *Auditing and cost accounting*. 1917. p. 316-51. *Accountant*, April 20, June 8, 1907, p. 528-41, 771-3.

LISLE, GEORGE. Depreciation. (In his *Accounting in theory and practice*. 1900. p. 137-41).

LISLE, GEORGE and W. A. MIDDLETON. Depreciation. (In his *Account-keeping in principle and practice*. 1911. p. 71-2, 137-41).

LOCAL authorities and depreciation. *Journal of gas lighting*, April 16, 1907, p. 144. *Electrical review (London)*, April 26, 1907, p. 665.

LOEBENSTEIN, JULIAN. Growth and depreciation. *American institute of electrical engineers, Proceedings*, Nov. 1916, p. 1559-77. Excerpt. *Electric railway journal*, Nov. 18, 1816, p. 1057-9.

LOGAN, PATTERSON J. Depreciation. *Municipal journal* (London), Jan. 26, 1906. p. 93.

LOOMIS, SUFFERN & FERNALD. Depreciation and obsolescence, as governed by federal income tax regulations. New York, Loomis, Suffern & Fernald, c1918. 24p.

LORD AVEBURY and depreciation. *Municipal journal* (London), Feb. 8, 1907, p. 112.

LOUGH, WILLIAM H. Reserves. (In his *Business finance*. 1917. p. 423-6).

LOWLES, D. C. Applying depreciation equitably. *Iron trade review*, Dec. 4, 1919, p. 1510-1.

LYONS, F. O. Depreciation: the surveyor's versus the accountant's standpoint. *Economic journal*, Sept. 1910, p. 469-72.

MCCONNELL, I. W. Things promoters ignore. *Stone and Webster public service journal*, Jan. 1916.

MACGIBBON, D. A. Depreciation reserved and the conservation of capital. *Better business*, Jan. 1918, p. 24-5.

MCINTOSH, ROBERT J. Reference book of accounts for manufacturing and mercantile companies. Ed. 2. Toledo, Ohio, R. J. McIntosh co. c1914. 299p.
See index under Depreciation.

MCJILTON, H. E. Depreciation. *Street railway journal*, May 1897, p. 288.

MCKAY, CHARLES W. Depreciation and federal income tax. *Industrial management*, Aug. 1919, p. 148-52.

MCKAY, CHARLES W. Depreciation and its relation to industrial appraisement. *Industrial management*, April 1918, p. 281-3.

MCKAY, CHARLES W. What is your plant worth? *Factory*, Feb. 15, March 1-15, May 15, 1920, p. 451-3, 639-40, 800-2, 1526-8.

DEPRECIATION, DEPLETION AND OBSOLESCENCE—*(Continued)*

MacLeod, F. J. Obsolescence is serious problem. *Electrical railway journal*, Dec. 1, 1917, p. 987-9.

MacLeod, F. J. What depreciation really means. *Aera*, Dec. 1917, p. 397-403.

Macrae, H. J. Depreciation and secret reserves. *South African accountants' journal*, v. 2, p. 24.

Madden, John Thomas. Accounting practice and auditing. New York, Alexander Hamilton institute, c1917. 338p. (Modern business, v.21.)
See index under Depreciation.

Maintenance and depreciation. *Electric railway journal*, March 21, 28, April 11-18, 1914, p. 620, 720, 827, 881.

Maintenance and obsolescence charges. *Engineering record*, May 11, 1907, p. 584.

Mann, Olaf A. Depreciation and depreciation reserves. *Canadian chartered accountant*, April 1917, p. 271-6. *Journal of accountancy*, Feb. 1917, p. 107-13.

Matheson, Ewing. Depreciation of factories, mines and industrial undertakings and their valuation. Ed. 2. New York, Spon & Chamberlain, 1893. 143p.
——— Same. Ed. 4. London, Spon & Chamberlain, 1910.

Matheson, Ewing. Factory depreciation—the problem of correct valuation. (In *Humphreys, A. C. Lecture notes on some of the business features of engineering practice.* p. 53-60). *Cassier's magazine*, 1902, v. 23, p. 140-4.

May, George O. Problem of depreciation. *Journal of accountancy*, Jan. 1915, p. 1-13.

Mead, Edward Sherwood. Corporation finance. Revised ed. New York, D. Appleton & co. 1915. 478p.
See index under Depreciation.

Meade, Richard K. Depreciation and obsolescence. *Journal of industrial and engineering chemistry*, Sept. 1913, p. 762.

Mitchell, Thomas W. Depreciation. (In his *Accounting principles.* c1918. p. 194-5, 297-325).

Montgomery, Harford H. Depreciation of buildings, machinery and plant, in reference to accounts and income tax. *Accountants' magazine*, June 1908, p. 313-31.

Montgomery, Harford H. Montgomery depreciation tables: building, machinery and plant in reference to accounts and income tax; with tables. Belfast, James Moore, 1908.

Montgomery, Robert H. Auditing theory and practice. Ed. 2. New York, The Ronald press co. 1917. 889p.
See index under Depreciation.

Montgomery, Robert H. Income tax procedure, 1919. New York, The Ronald press co. 1919.
——— Same. New York. The Ronald press co. 1920.
See index under Depletion; Depreciation; Obsolescence.

Mulhall, John F. J. Depreciation. In his *Quasi-public corporation accounting and management.* c1905. p. 180-3).

Murray, Adam. Wear and tear and depreciation. *Accountant*, 1887, p. 610-8.

Nash, L. R. Depreciation reserves as affected by property growth. *American economic review*, March 1916, p. 69-89.

Neale, R. E. Depreciation in engineering works. *Mechanical world*, Feb. 7, 1913, p. 67-8.

Nelson, Gilbert. Depreciation and depletion in relation to income tax returns. *Journal of accountancy*, Feb. 1919, p. 111-9.

Nelson, Godfrey N. Income tax law and accounting, 1918. Ed. 2. New York, The Macmillan company, 1918. 364p.
See index under Depletion; Depreciation; Obsolescence.

Nicholson, J. Lee and John F. D. Rohrbach. Depreciation and maintenance. (In their *Cost accounting.* 1919. p. 144-62, 529).

Nicholson, J. Lee. Nicholson on factory organization and costs. New York, Kohl technical publishing co. 1909.
See index under Depletion; Depreciation; Obsolescence.
Whole plant 6%

Niven, John B. Income tax department. *Journal of accountancy*, June 1917, p. 471.

Nixon, Alfred and J. H. Stagg. Depreciation. (In their *Accounting and banking.* 1912. p. 198-200).

Norris, H. M. Depreciation of plant, and its relation to general expense. *Engineering magazine*, Feb.-April 1899, p. 812, 957; 76.
Miscellaneous plant 10%

Not depreciation but retirement; electric railway representatives suggest change of terms. *Electric railway journal*, July 27, 1918, p. 170.

Obsolescence and decrepitude as factors in depreciation. *Municipal engineering*, Aug. 1912, p. 100.

O'Meara, W. A. J. Depreciation. *Electrician* (London), April 8, 1910, p. 1072-5.

Only safe way is to charge it off. *Engineering news record*, May 10, 1917, p. 323.

Our American view of depreciation. *Journal of accountancy*, March 1910, p. 374.

Parton, John. Debatable points. *Canadian chartered accountant*, April 1913, p. 242-9.

Paton, William. Depreciation, appreciation and productive capacity. *Journal of accountancy*, July 1920, p. 1-11.

Paton, William and R. A. Stevenson. Principles of accounting. New York, The Macmillan co. 1918. 685p.
See index under Depreciation.

Pender, Harold. Depreciation. (In his *Handbook for electrical engineers.* c1914. p. 337-41).

Pennell, Walter O. "Present worth" calculations in engineering studies (with discussion). *Journal of the association of engineering societies* (St. Louis), Sept. 1914, v. 53, p. 112-45.

Philadelphia. Controller. Rates of depreciation. (In his *Manual of accounting, reporting and business procedure of the city and county of Philadelphia.* p. 204-10).

Piez, Charles. Depreciation of plants and tools. *American machinist*, April 5, 1917, p. 614-5 *Factory*, April 1917, p. 520.

Piez, Charles. Perpetual inventory and appraisal values: condensed table of standard depreciation rates. *Engineering and contracting*, Jan. 24, 1917, p. 77. *Factory*, Dec. 1916, p. 668-71. *Iron age*, Nov. 30, 1916, Jan. 11, 1917, p. 1227: 138-9. *Iron trade review*, Feb. 22, 1917, p. 477-8.

DEPRECIATION, DEPLETION AND OBSOLESCENCE—*(Continued)*

Condensed. *Journal of the American society of mechanical engineers,* Dec. 1916. p. 965-6. *Iron trade review,* Dec. 7, 1916, p. 1144-6. Kent, William, *Bookkeeping and cost accounting for factories,* 1918, p. 90, Discussion, *Journal of the American society of mechanical engineers,* March 1917, p. 215-7).

PIXLEY, FRANCIS W. Auditors, their duties and responsibilities under the companies acts, partnership acts, and acts relating to executors and trustees and to private audits. Ed. 10. London, Henry Good and son. 658p.
See index under Depreciation.

PIXLEY, FRANCIS W. Depreciation. (In his *Accountancy.* Ed. 2. p. 202-20).

PLANT depreciation. *Iron Age,* March 15, 1917, p. 655-6.

POLLOCK, WALTER W. Specific depreciation as applied to mechanical deterioration. *American machinist,* Oct. 23, 1919, p. 761-2.

POMEROY, L. R. Depreciation or valuation of properties. *Railway age gazette,* Aug. 15, 1913, p. 274-5.

PORTERS, R. J. Depreciation. (In his *Pitman's dictionary of bookkeeping.* p. 330-44).

POWERS, LE GRAND. Depreciation in commercial and governmental business and accounting. *Government accountant,* 1908, v. 2, p. 1-18.

PRACTICAL studies of depreciation. *Power,* April 8, 1913, p. 500.

PRICE, WILLIAM ORPWOOD. Depreciation of fixed assets. *Accountant,* April 8, 1911, p. 562-4.

PRINCIPLES in computing the depreciation of plant. *Electric railway journal,* May 12, 1917, p. 865.

PRINCIPLES involved in computing the depreciation of plant. *Journal of the Institute of electrical engineers,* May 1917.

PROVISION for obsolescence. *Incorporated accountants journal,* Feb. 1915, p. 102-3.

RACINE, SAMUEL F. Depreciation. (In his *Accounting principles.* 1917. p. 131-64).

RANDOLPH, L. S. Ethics of allowances for depreciation. *Engineering magazine,* Aug. 1910, p. 692-6.

RASTALL, ERNEST S. Depreciation reserves and rising prices. *Journal of accountancy,* Feb. 1920, p. 123-6. *Public accountant,* June 30, 1920, p. 372-5.

RATES of depreciation: standards of the Australian government. *Iron age,* April 26, 1917, p. 1017.

RATIONAL method of calculating depreciated value. *Engineering and contracting,* July 14, 1915, p. 24.

RAYMOND, WILLIAM G. Basis of estimating allowance for depreciation. *Engineering news,* July 22, 1920, p. 178-9.

RAYMOND, W. G. Hen and the Erie ferry boat again. *Railway age,* Feb. 23, 1917, p. 301-2.

REED, W. B. Depreciation a very important subject right now. *Cooperative manager and farmer,* Jan. 1919, p. 84.

REID, WALTER A. Depreciation. *Accountants' magazine,* March 1897, p. 156-62. *Business,* Oct. 1897, p. 310-1.

RELATION of depreciation allowance to interest on investment. *Electrical review and Western electrician,* April 25, 1914, p. 805.

RELATION of depreciation to gross earnings. *Engineering and contracting,* Aug. 10, 1910, p. 130.

REMINDER of the unearned decrement. *Nation,* Dec. 21, 1916, p. 580-1.

REPORT of committees of American society of civil engineers on decretion. *American gas engineering journal,* Jan. 27, 1917, p. 102.

REPRODUCTION versus depreciated value. *Electrical review and Western electrician,* March 14, 1914, p. 512.

RESERVES for depreciation. *Electrical world,* July 11, 1914, p. 82.

RICHARDSON, C. L. Series of questions submitted to members of the Institute of chartered accountants of Alberta; with summary of the answers received and comments thereon prepared by Mr. C. L. Richardson. *Canadian chartered accountant,* Oct. 1914, p. 121-8.

RIDGWAY, A. CLIFFORD. Depreciation. (In his *Cost accounts in principle and practice.* p. 39-44).

RINTOUL, PETER. Treatment in the accounts of joint stock companies of depreciation in value of assets arising from their employment, and the duties of an auditor relating thereto. *Accountant,* April 4, 1908, p. 496-503.

RITTENHOUSE, CHARLES F. and P. F. CLAPP. Accounting theory and practice; unit 1. New York, McGraw-Hill book company, 1918. 165p.
See index under Depreciation.

ROWELL, HENRY K. Principles of valuing property, with special reference to industrial enterprises. *Journal of the American society of mechanical engineers,* Sept. 1912, Feb. 1913, p. 1275: 285. Abstract. *Engineering and contracting,* Sept. 18, 1912, p. 312.

SALIERS, EARL A. Caring for depreciation. *Journal of accountancy,* April 1912, p. 241-50.

SALIERS, EARL A. Cost, fair value, and depreciation reserves. *American economic review,* June, 1920, p. 272-82.

SALIERS, EARL A. Depreciation, bad debts, and valuation reserves. (In his *Accounts in theory and practice; principles.* 1920. p. 59-68).

SALIERS, EARL A. Depreciation reserves vs. depreciation funds. *Journal of accountancy,* Nov. 1913, p. 358-65.

SALIERS, EARL A. Depreciation in theory and practice. Chicago, La Salle extension university, 1917, 27p.

SALIERS, EARL A. Principles of depreciation. New York, The Ronald press co. 1916. 200p. (Ronald accounting series).

SANDERS, WILLIAM. Law and practice of excess profits duty. Ed. 2. London, Gee & co. 1918. 276p.
See index under Depreciation. Obsolescence.

SALIERS, EARL A. Selected bibliography. (In his *Principles of depreciation.* 1916. p. 185-8).

SCHOOLING, WILLIAM. Depreciation of investments and plant. *Accountant,* April 5, 1913, p. 495-501.

SCOVELL, CLINTON H. Cost accounting and burden application. New York, D. Appleton and co. 1916. 328p.
See index under Depreciation.

DEPRECIATION, DEPLETION AND OBSOLESCENCE—*(Continued)*

SEALY, ROBERT. Accounting for depreciation. *Electrical world*, Feb. 20, 1915, p. 460-1.

SEALY, ROBERT. Accounting treatment of depreciation. *American electric railway accountants association, Proceedings*, 1914, p. 145. Abstract. *Electric traction*, Oct. 1914, p. 682. Treatment of depreciation. *Federal trade reporter*, Feb. 1, 1915, p. 89. *Electric railway journal*, Oct. 16, 1914, p. 894-5.

SELIGMAN, EDWIN R. A. Income tax; a study of the history, theory and practice of income taxation at home and abroad. New York, The Macmillan co. 1911. 743p.
See index under Depreciation.

SHALL cities establish depreciation funds for all municipal replacements? *American city*, Aug. 1913, p. 106-7.

SHERLEY-PRICE, HENRY. Depreciation of works and machinery: its causes, effects and treatment. London, 1909. 25p.

SLEMP, C. B. Extract from speech . . . in the hearing on the revenue bill before the ways and means committee on June 25, 1918. 1 typewritten p.

SNELLING, W. E. Depreciation. (In his *Income tax and super tax law and cases*. p. 81-7).

SNELLING, W. E. Excess profits (including excess mineral rights) duty and levies under the munitions of war acts; incorporating the provision of the income tax acts made applicable by statute and by regulation, also the regulation of the commissioners of Inland revenue and of the Minister of munitions. Ed. 3. Revised and enlarged. London, Sir Isaac Pitman & sons. 327p.
See index under Depreciation: Obsolescence.

SNELLING, W. E. Income tax and super-tax practice, including a dictionary of income tax specimen returns, etc., for the use of professional and business men, accountants, householders, etc. Ed. 2, revised and enlarged. London, Sir Isaac Pitman & sons. 503p.
See index under Depreciation; Obsolescence.

SOME depreciation rates on buildings, machinery, shafting, belting, furniture and apparatus, tools and dies, moulds, lasts, patterns and drawings used by the Associated mutual fire insurance companies of Boston, Mass., in making appraisals of manufacturing properties. *Utilities magazine*, Jan. 1, 1916, p. 186-7.

SPICER, E. E. and E. C. PEGLER. Depreciation. (In their *Examination note book for accountant students*. 1914. p. 7-9).

SPICER, ERNEST EVAN and ERNEST C. PEGLER. Depreciation of assets. (In their *Practical bookkeeping and commercial knowledge*. 1912. p. 64-71).

SPICER, ERNEST EVAN and ERNEST C. PEGLER. Depreciation, reserves, sinking funds. (In their *Bookkeeping and accounts*. 1914. p. 43-51).

SPICER, ERNEST EVAN and ERNEST C. PEGLER. Excess profits duty and profits of controlled establishments. Ed. 4, revised and enlarged. London, H. Foulks Lynch & co. 1918. 220p.
See index under Depreciation.

SPICER, ERNEST EVAN and ERNEST C. PEGLER. Practical auditing. Ed. 2. London, H. Faulks Lynch & co. 1914. 766p.
See index under Depreciation.

STAMP, J. C. Wasting assets and income tax. *Economic journal*, March 1910, p. 107-13.

STAUB, WALTER A. Deferred charges to operating. *Journal of accountancy*, Oct. 1909, p. 401-18.

STOCKWELL, HERBERT GRANT. Depreciation, renewal and replacement accounts; a paper read at the annual meeting held in Denver, Colorado, October 18-22, 1909, the American association of public accountants. 63p. *American institute of accountants, Yearbook*, 1909, p. 192-272. *Journal of accountancy*, Dec. 1909, Jan. 1910, p. 89-103, 189-210.

STOCKWELL, HERBERT GRANT. Net worth and the balance sheet. New York, The Ronald press co. 1912. 206p.
See index under Depreciation.

STRACHAN, W. AND OTHERS. How to treat renewals and repairs. *Incorporated accountants' journal*, 1899-1900, p. 71.

STRANGWARD, W. O. Depreciation reserves and sinking funds. *Electric railway journal*, July 27, 1912, p. 123-4. *Incorporated accountants' journal*, 1909-10, p. 264.

SWAINSON, GEORGE. Municipal capital accounts: should assets of value be depreciated as the loans are paid off? *Accountant*, June 29, 1895, p. 579-84.

SYSTEMATIC treatment of depreciation. *Accountant*, June 25, July 9, 1910, p. 881-91; 37-9.

TAXES. *American institute of accountants, Special bulletin, no. 1*, Jan. 1920. p. 2-3.

TEICHMANN, MAX. Depreciation. *Accountant*, Jan. 26, 1907, p. 132-4. *Journal of accountancy*, Dec. 1906, p. 101-5.

THOMAS, JOHN J. Comparative, theoretical and actual depreciation talk made at West Baden, Indiana. 9p.

THOMAS, JOHN J. Depreciation and valuation. *Accountant*, Feb. 5, 1916, p. 173-6. *Journal of accountancy*, Jan. 1916, p. 24-33.

THOMPSON, C. BERTRAND. Should interest and depreciation be included? (In his *How to find factory costs*. c1916. p. 55-69).

TIFFANY, H. S. Tiffany's digest of depreciations with the addition of numerous tables, formulas and rules for the use of architects, builders, contractors, machinists and insurance adjustors. Ed. 28. Chicago, H. S. Tiffany & co. c1890. 76p.

TILT, R. R. On the treatment of the depreciation in assets due to an enhanced rate of interest. *Journal of the institute of actuaries*, July 1914.

TINNER, T. AND OTHERS. Depreciation and the various methods of providing for it; a discussion. *Incorporated accountants' journal*, 1903-4, p. 68, 59.

TOVEY, PHILIP. Balance sheets: how to read and understand them; a guide for investors, business men, commercial students, etc. London, Sir Isaac Pitman & sons. 77p.
See index under Depreciation.

TREATMENT of depreciation in connection with the federal corporation tax. *Journal of accountancy*, March 1912, p. 218-22.

TURNER, EDWARD HARTLEY. Depreciation of machinery and plant. *Accountant*, June 16, 1894, p. 546-52.

TURNER, STANLEY H. Depreciation, shall sinking fund periods be extended? *Municipal journal* (London), Sept. 18, 1903, p. 833. Editorial. *Municipal journal* (London), Sept. 11, 1903, p. 818.

TURNER, A. K. Income tax depreciation. *Accountant*, March 4, 1911, p. 361-2.

DEPRECIATION, DEPLETION AND OBSOLESCENCE—*(Continued)*

UNITED STATES. DEPARTMENT OF COMMERCE. Depreciation: depletion. (In its *Uniform contracts and cost accounting, definitions and methods.* 1917. p. 10-1).

VARIOUS depreciation charges. *New York Times,* June 14, 1914.

VICKERMAN, W. P. Depreciation. *Accountant,* Feb. 25, March 25, 1905, p. 229-32, 330-1.

VIGEON, HARRY. Depreciations. *Accountant,* May 29, 1897, p. 552-5. *Business,* Dec. 1895, p. 93-6.

VITAL distinction between "functional depreciation" and "natural depreciation." *Engineering and contracting,* Aug. 6, 1913, p. 141-2.

WALKER, WILLIAM H. and F. W. FIELD. Corporation finance. New York, Alexander Hamilton institute. c1918. 346p. (Modern business, v. 11).
See index under Depreciation.

WALL, ALEXANDER. Depreciation as a business cost: to what extent to be reckoned with: with discussion. *National association of credit men bulletin,* Aug. 1918, p. 737-42.

WALL, ALEXANDER. Depreciation and generalities. (In his *Banker's credit manual.* c1919. p. 225-30).

WALMSLEY, FREDERIC. Depreciation in relation to balance sheets. *Incorporated accountants' journal,* 1893-4, p. 8.

WALTON, SEYMOUR. Depreciation reserve in sale of factory. *Journal of accountancy,* Oct. 1919, p. 313-4.

WALTON, SEYMOUR. Obsolescence as a cause of depreciation. *Journal of accountancy,* Aug. 1915, p. 149-51.

WALTON, SEYMOUR. Sale of depreciated assets. *Journal of accountancy,* Oct. 1914, p. 316-9.

WALTON, SEYMOUR. Sinking funds and depreciation. *Journal of accountancy,* Feb. 1916, p. 150-2.

WAR finance acts of 1914-1917; an annotation reprint of the income tax provisions of the new acts; by the income tax expert of "the Accountant." London, Gee & co. 1918. 187p.
See index under Depreciation, Obsolescence.

WEBNER, FRANK E. Maintenance and depreciation. (In his *Factory costs.* 1911. p. 169-88).

WEBSTER, GEORGE N. Theatrical depreciation; a menace to the public and the investor. 32p. *Journal of the American gas engineers,* Aug. 9, 1919, p. 112-8, 121-2. Abstract. *Electrical world,* Aug. 9, 1919, p. 308.

WHATLEY, G. E. STUART. Depreciation. (In his *Accountant's and bookkeeper's vade-mecum.* 1893. p. 23-32).

WHEN is it profitable to retire an old plant unit? *Engineering and contracting,* Feb. 28, 1917, p. 195-6.

WHITNEY, L. N., "Present value" misleading, real present value cannot be dependent upon depreciation reserve. What is the proper rate of return? *Public service regulation,* June 1914, p. 346.

WILDMAN, JOHN R. Depreciation from a certified accountant's point of view. *Electric railway journal,* April 18, 1914, p. 882-3.

WILDMAN, JOHN R. Principles of accounting. New York, The William G. Hewitt press, 1914. 360p.
See index under Depreciation.

WILKINSON, GEORGE. Depreciation and reserves. *Electric railway review,* April 13, 1907, p. 491. *Incorporated accountants' journal,* 1905-6, p. 53. Editorial. *Electric railway review,* April 13, 1907, p. 481.

WILKINSON, GEORGE. Depreciation of plant. *Accountant,* Aug. 31, Sept. 28, 1901, p. 952-7, 1031-3.

WILKINSON, GEORGE. How to treat depreciation of plant. *Business world,* Jan. 1902, p. 33-5.

WILLIAMSON, J. GILMOUR. Depreciation of assets. (In his *Counting house and factory organisation.* p. 141-3).

WILMOT, H. W. Depreciation. *Journal of accountancy,* Dec. 1909, p. 104-13).

WILSON, ROWLAND. Depreciation. *Mechanical engineer,* March 10, 1911, p. 309.

WINDER, A. Elements of depreciation. *Cassier's magazine,* Feb. 1909, p. 539-40.

WOODBURY, A. K. Physical appraisal in relation to accountancy. *Journal of accountancy,* Dec. 1910, p. 108-18.

WOODINGTON, A. E. Depreciation of assets. *Incorporated accountants' journal,* 1898-9, p. 50.

WOODS, CLINTON E. Unified methods for industrials, New York. The Ronald press, 1917. 484p.
See index under Depreciation.

WORCESTER, WILLIAM F. How the appraiser views depreciation. *Factory,* May 1917, p. 641-3.

WRIGHT, WALTER C. Depreciation, interest and manufacturing cost. *Journal of accountancy,* Nov. 1915, p. 361-4.

Accumulators

ABERDEEN and depreciation. *Municipal journal* (London), Oct. 23, 1903, p. 943.

Accumulators	7½%	Glasgow
	10	Bolton
	5	Aberdeen

AUSTRALIA. FEDERAL INCOME TAX DEPARTMENT. Depreciation allowance. *Accountant,* Oct. 13, 1917, p. 277-9. *Accounting and commerce,* June 30, 1917, p. 55-7. *Federal accountant,* July 1917, p. 83-8. *Public accountant* Jan. 30, 1917, p. 145-52.
Accumulators 7½%
Written down value, repairs allowed.

BOWDEN, J. HORACE and FRED H. TAIT. Adequate depreciation of capital expenditure by municipal electricity undertakings. *Electrical review* (London), June 21, 1907, p. 1021.
Accumulators 5 years

BRYAN, WILLIAM H. Depreciation of electric light plants. *Municipality,* March 1908, p. 74.
Accumulators and arc lamps 10 years

DAWSON PHILIP. Depreciation. (In his *Engineering and electric traction pocketbook.* Ed. 2, p. 1161).

	% on capital cost
Accumulators in central stations	9-11

DEPRECIATION, DEPLETION AND OBSOLESCENCE—ACCUMULATORS—*(Continued)*

ELBOURNE, EDWARD T. Depreciation rates. (In his *Factory administration and accounts.* 1918. p. 376).

	Prov. dep. % Remainder values	Years 10%	5%
Accumulators, Hydraulic	6	37	48

GRUNSKY, CARL EWALD. Probable useful life of various articles. (In his *Valuation, depreciation and the rate base.* 1917. p. 274).

Accumulators	15 years Robt. Hammond. Journal of Institute of electrical engineers, England, April 25, 1907. 15 years T. C. Parsons. Discussion of Mr. Hammonds paper, Journal of Institute Electrical engineers, England, April 25, 1907. 15 years. 10% residual value. Sir Wm. Preece. Report of Bristol corporation, England, 1906.

HAMMOND, ROBERT. Depreciation. *Institute of electrical engineers, Proceedings,* April 25, 1907. *Journal of the Institute of electrical engineers,* 1907, p. 270. Abstracts. *Accountant,* May 18, 1907, p. 675. *Electric railway review,* June 1, 1907, p. 716. *Electrical review* (Chicago), May 25, 1907, p. 828. *Electrical review* (London), May 3, 1907, p. 744. *Electrician,* April 26, 1907, p. 51. *Engineering magazine,* July 1907, p. 636-8. *Engineering record,* June 15, 1907, p. 703. *Municipal journal* (London), May 10, 17, 1907, p. 411, 435. *Progressive age,* July 1, 1907, p. 305. *Street railway bulletin,* June 1907, p. 382. *Tramway and railway world,* June 6, 1907, p. 497.

Accumulators	15 years

JOHNSON, GEORGE. Depreciation. (In his *Electric lighting accounts.* 1903. p. 23-4).

Accumulators	10%

NELSON, BAILIE WALTER. Limitation and application of profits from municipal undertakings. *Accountant,* Aug. 3, 1912, p. 167-71. *Incorporated accountants' journal,* Oct. 1912, p. 15-7.

Accumulators	5%

PIXLEY, FRANCIS W. Electricity lighting companies. (In his *Accountancy.* Ed. 2. p. 218).

Accumulators	10%

YEAMAN, C. H. Depreciation and reserves for antiquation and obsolescence from an engineering standpoint. *Electrical engineering* (London), July 12, 1907, p. 46. *Electrical review* (London), July 12, 1907, p. 44. *Electrician,* July 5, 1907, p. 475.

Accumulators

15 years	R. Hammond
5-7	L. G. B. (Local Government Board)
20	L. C. C.
10	J. F. C. Snell—M. E. A. 1905.

Acetylene gas plant

ELBOURNE, EDWARD T. Depreciation rates. (In his *Factory administration and accounts.* 1918. p. 377).

	Prov. dep. % Remainder values	Years 10%	5%
Acetylene gas plant	10	22	28

Adding machines

See Depreciation, depletion and obsolescence—Calculating machines.

Advertisements

JENKINSON, MARK WEBSTER. Depreciation. *Accountant,* May 17 ,1902, p. 528-34.

Pictorial advertisements and wall posters.

Depreciation according to the extent of reproduction and the probable time that such advertisemnt will be used, ignoring the residual value of the original.

Depreciation should be written off the amount paid for the right to exhibit wall posters in proportion to the time unexpired, but an additional sum must be added to provide for loss of novelty and attractive power.

Agricultural machinery industry

DEPRECIATION rates used by the Fairbanks company. *Annalist,* Sept. 1, 1919, p. 271.

Buildings	4%
Machinery and equipment	10
Office furniture and fixtures	20
Automobiles	33⅓

JONES, EDWARD DAVID. Depreciation. (In his *Investment.* p. 169).

International harvester co.	10%

UNITED STATES. BUREAU OF CORPORATIONS. Depreciation. (In its *International harvester co.* 1913. p. 221-2).

Buildings	2%
Machinery	5

Agriculture

See also Depreciation, depletion, obsolescence—Dairying;—Fruit;—Horses;—Livestock.

ALLISON, J. Farmers' income tax. *Accountant,* April 19, May 3, 17, 24, 1919, p. 325-6, 369-70, 421-3, 440-1.

Boilers	5%
Dyer's machinery	7½
Gas engines	7½
Steam engines	5
Shafting engines	5
Motor wagons	15

DEPRECIATION, DEPLETION AND OBSOLESCENCE—AGRICULTURE—*(Continued)*

AUSTRALIA. FEDERAL INCOME TAX DEPARTMENT. Depreciation allowance. *Accountant,* Oct. 13, 1917, p. 277-9. *Accounting and commerce,* Jan. 30, 1917, p. 55-7. *Federal accountant,* Oct. 13, 1917, p. 93-8. *Public accountant,* Jan. 30, 1917, p. 145-52.
Farming implements and machinery 10%
Written down value, repairs allowed in addition.

BEXELL, J. A. Valuation and depreciation. (In his *Principles of bookkeeping and farm accounts.* c1913. p. 140-2).
Frame buildings 2-5%
Brick buildings 1-3
Machinery and tools 6-10

MEATS, THOMAS WHEELER. Depreciation. (In his *Agriculture accounts.* 1901. p. 15, 17, 23, 44).
Fixed machinery and plant 7½%
Moveable machinery and plant, implements, casks, etc. 10

MONTGOMERY, ROBERT H. Farmers. (In his *Income tax procedure,* 1919, p. 682. ——— Same. 1920, p. 886-7).

ORWIN, C. S. Depreciation of horses, of implements farming costs. (In his *Determination of farming costs.* 1917. p. 40, 65, 14).

PARK, A. D. Interest and depreciation charges in farm accounts. *Journal of agriculture of New Zealand,* April 1919, p. 206-7.

PHILADELPHIA. CONTROLLER. Rates of depreciation. (In his *Manual of accounting, reporting and business procedure of the city and county of Philadelphia.* 1917. p. 205, 210).
Agricultural equipment 12½%
Buildings used for manufacture or horticulture 2
Horticultural improvements 1

SCOVILL, H. T. Depreciation. (In his *Farm accounting.* 1918. p. 151-6).
Equipment 10% diminishing value.
Building 5 " "

THOMSON, EDWARD H. Determining values and depreciation. (In his *Farm bookkeeping.* 1915. p. 12-5).
Building 3%
Machinery 6-10

THOMSON, EDWARD H. and H. M. DIXON. Depreciation of equipment and buildings. (In their *Method of analyzing the farm business.* p. 8).
Buildings
Stone or brick 1%
Frame 3-4
Machinery 7-12

Air chippers

BELT, ROBERT E. Depreciation. (In his *Foundry cost accounting, practice and procedure.* 1919. p. 243).
Air chippers 10%

BELT, ROBERT E. Depreciation. (In his *Uniform cost accounting methods; adopted by the American malleable castings association,* Nov. 14, 1917. p. 20-1).
Air chippers 10%

Air hose

NICHOLSON, J. LEE and JOHN F. D. ROHRBACH. Depreciation. (In their *Cost accounting.* 1919. p. 150).
Air hose 10%

Alternators

AUSTRALIA. FEDERAL INCOME TAX DEPARTMENT. Depreciation allowance. *Accountant,* Oct. 13, 1917, p. 277-9. *Accounting and commerce,* June 30, 1917, p. 55-7. *Federal accountant,* July 1917, p. 93-8. *Public accountant,* Jan. 30, 1917, p. 145-52.
Alternators, dynamos, motor generators, rotary converters 5%
Written down value, repairs allowed.

BAY state rate case. *Electric railway journal,* Dec. 4, 1915, p. 1121-3. *Public utility reports, annotated,* 1916F, p. 336-9.
Alternators 25%

CROWELL, H. H. Electric lighting rates and depreciation. *Municipal journal and engineering,* Dec. 18, 1907, p. 698.
Turbo-alternators Purchased 10 years or more ago 20 years; Modern 25 years

GRUNSKY, CARL EWALD. Probable useful life of various articles. (In his *Valuation depreciation and the rate base.* 1917. p. 278).
Dynamos and alternators 25 years. Robert Hammond. Journal of the Institute of electrical engineers, England, April 25, 1907. 30 years. 8% residual value. Sir William Preece. Report of Bristol corporation, England, 1906.

HAMMOND, ROBERT. Depreciation. *Institute of electrical engineers, Journal,* 1907, p. 270. *Institute of electrical engineers, Proceedings,* April 25, 1907, p. 270-301. Abstracts: *Accountant,* May 18, 1907, p. 675. *Electric railway review,* June 1, 1907, p. 716. *Electrical review* (Chicago), May 25, 1907, p. 828. *Electrical review* (London), May 3, 1907, p. 744. *Electrician* April 26, 1907, p. 51. *Engineering magazine,* July 1907, p. 636-8. *Engineering record,* June 15, 1907, p. 703. *Municipal journal* (London), May 10, 17, 1907, p. 411, 435. *Progressive age,* July 1, 1907, p. 305. *Street railway bulletin,* June 1907, p. 382. *Tramway and railway world,* June 6, 1907, p. 497.
Dynamos and alternators 25 years

LIFE data on power plant equipment used in valuation of Massachusetts property. *Electrical world,* Dec. 4, 1915, p. 1261.
Alternators 25 years

DEPRECIATION, DEPLETION AND OBSOLESCENCE—ALTERNATORS—*(Continued)*

LIFE of plant. *Electrician,* Nov. 8, 1912, p. 182-4.
Dynamos and alternators 30 years
Wm. Preece.

Ammonia concentrators and tanks

BARKER, HARRY. Typical life expectation tables for public utility property. (In his *Public utility rates.* 1917. p. 367-368).
Ammonia concentrators 15 years
Ammonia storage tanks 15 years
Wisconsin railroad commission

FOSTER, HORATIO A. Rates of depreciation. (In his *Engineering valuation of public utilities and factories.* 1913. p. 206).

	Years life
Ammonia concentrators	15
Ammonia storage tanks, wrought iron or steel	15
Tar and ammonia wells	50

GILLETTE, HALBERT P. and RICHARD T. DANA. Depreciation. (In their *Handbook of mechanical and electrical cost* data. 1918. p. 107).
Concentrators ammonia (gas plant) 15 years
Wisconsin railroad commission

GRUNSKY, CARL EWALD. Probable useful life of various articles. (In his *Valuation, depreciation and the rate base.* 1917. p. 274).
Ammonia concentrators and tanks 15 years
Wisconsin railroad commission.
Quoted by H. A. Foster and in published reports.

Amusements

See also Games; Playgrounds; Theaters.

PHILADELPHIA. CONTROLLER. Rates of depreciation. (In his *Manual of accounting, reporting and business procedure of the city and county of Philadelphia.* 1907. p. 209, 210).

Buildings: Churches, auditoriums, exhibition halls, museums, club houses and amusement places	1%
Fixed apparatus, and equipment for outdoor recreation purposes	10
Gymnasium and play-ground equipment of a permanent nature	8⅓
Air guns and other missile throwing apparatus (not internal combustion and targets)	8⅓
Games equipment	8⅓
Special and miscellaneous educational scientific and recreational equipment	8⅓

Andirons

PHILADELPHIA. CONTROLLER. Rates of depreciation. (In his *Manual of accounting, reporting and business procedure of the city and county of Philadelphia.* 1917. p. 205).
Andirons and fenders for open fire places 4%

Angle-benching machines

NICHOLSON, J. LEE and JOHN F. D. ROHRBACH. Depreciation. (In their *Cost accounting.* 1919. p. 149).
Angle-benching machines 6⅔%

Annealing

BELT, ROBERT E. Depreciation. (In his *Foundry cost accounting practice and procedure.* 1919. p. 242).

Annealing ovens and apparatus	7½%
Annealing trucks—steam, air and electric	20

BELT, ROBERT E. Depreciation. (In his *Uniform cost accounting methods; adopted by the American malleable castings association,* Nov. 14, 1917. p. 20-1).

Annealing ovens and apparatus	10%
Annealing trucks	20

ELBOURNE, EDWARD T. Depreciation rates. (In his *Factory administration and accounts.* 1918. p. 377).

	Prov. dep. %	Years	
	Remainder values	10%	5%
Furnaces, annealing hardening and tempering	15	14	18

Annunciators and call systems

PHILADELPHIA. CONTROLLER. Rates of depreciation. (In his *Manual of accounting, reporting and business procedure of the city and county of Philadelphia.* 1917. p. 207-8).
Annunciator and call systems 8⅓%

Anvils

NICHOLSON, J. LEE and JOHN F. D. ROHRBACH. Depreciation. (In their *Cost accounting.* 1919. p. 150).
Anvils 10%

Apartment houses

BOLTON, REGINALD PELHAM. Depreciation of mechanical equipment and power plants. (In his *Building for profit.* 1911. p. 83, 85).
The fixed and motive equipments of a large apartment house. . . The combined equipment has a relative life compared with that of its most durable part which has been assumed to be such material as elevator guides and fixed iron work, of 40%. The fixed equipment has an average of 52.0%. But the motive apparatus is only 21.8%. The effect of the motive apparatus is, therefore, the greatest in reducing the total life of the building. The cost of the entire equipment in this case approximated 20% of the total cost, and if the buildings, upon dissection of its elements, should show, without equipment, a mean relative life of 77%, then the introduction of the equipment reduces the combination to 70%, or, in other

DEPRECIATION, DEPLETION AND OBSOLESCENCE—APARTMENT HOUSES—*(Continued)*

words, the building alone would have a mean life of 57¾ years; but this would be reduced by the effect of the equipment to 52½ years, involving on each one million dollars of total invested value an annual addition to the necessary sinking fund for depreciation of about $7500 a year.

BOLTON, REGINALD PELHAM. Depreciation of the value of buildings. (In his *Building for profit.* 1911. p. 76). Burton, H. J. *Valuations and depreciations of city buildings.* p. 21-2.

Apartment houses — 18-21 years

MONTGOMERY, ROBERT H. Buildings. (In his *Income tax procedure,* 1919. p. 559. ——— Same, 1920, p. 712).

Apartment houses — 3%

NEW YORK city—U. S. district court held that 3 per cent was an adequate allowance for exhaustion, wear and tear on apartment house property in the case of paying tax in excess of the law by the provision of the special income tax law. Hyman Cohen v. U. S. (Press report July 1, 1916).

Aqueducts

See Depreciation, depletion and obsolescence—Conduits.

Arbors

PHILADELPHIA. CONTROLLER. Rates of depreciation. (In his *Manual of accounting, reporting and business procedure of the city and county of Philadelphia.* 1917. p. 210).

Arbors, trellises, pergolas, flag poles, etc. — 5%

Arches

See Depreciation, depletion and obsolescence—Monuments.

Armies

PHILADELPHIA. CONTROLLER. Rates of depreciation. (In his *Manual of accounting, reporting and business procedure of the city and county of Philadelphia.* 1917. p. 209).

Military equipment — 10%

Art galleries

PHILADELPHIA. CONTROLLER. Rates of depreciation. (In his *Manual of accounting, reporting and business procedure of the city and county of Philadelphia.* 1917. p. 208).

Art galleries stock — 2%

Ash cans

PHILADELPHIA. CONTROLLER. Rates of depreciation. (In his *Manual of accounting, reporting and business procedure of the city and county of Philadelphia.* 1917. p. 206.)

Ash cans — 33⅓%

Ash handling

ANLAYSIS of the premises adopted and methods used in determining the cost to reproduce new together with the depreciation thereon of the physical property of the Metropolitan system and the Kansas City and Westport Belt railway of Kansas City, Mo. *Engineering and contracting,* May 28, 1913, p. 617-20.

Coal and ash handling machinery combined	7%
Ash handling machinery	8

BARKER, HARRY. Typical life expectation tables for public utility property. (In his *Public utility rates.* 1917. p. 368-9).

Conveyors.		
Coal or ash	10 years	Wis. R. R. Comm.
Ash or combined coal and ash	5	Author. Averages or approximate figures secured by examination or inquiry.

ELBOURNE, EDWARD T. Depreciation rates. (In his *Factory administration and accounts.* 1918. p. 376).

	Prov. dep. %	Years	
	Remainder values	10%	5%
Ash handling plant	10	22	28

FLOY, HENRY. Depreciation. Floy, Henry, *Depreciation as related to electrical properties. American institute of electrical engineers, Proceedings,* 1911, p. 1267. Floy, Henry, *Valuation of public utility properties,* 1912, p. 168-217. Foster, Horatio R. *Engineering valuation of public utilities and factories,* 1913, p. 194-8. *Engineering & contracting,* Oct. 4, 1911, p. 359-65. *Engineering magazine,* Aug. 1911, p. 837-40.

	Depreciation per cent per year Straight line		
Coal and ash handling machinery	7	Traction val. comm.	Chicago con. tract. co.
	5	Henry Floy	3rd Ave. case, adopted by P. S. C., N. Y.
	10	Wisconsin P. S. C.	

FOSTER, HORATIO A. Rates of depreciation. (In his *Engineering valuation of public utilities and factories.* 1913. p. 205).

	Years life.
Coal and ash conveyors	10

GILLETTE, HALBERT P. and RICHARD T. DANA. Cost of operating a vacuum ash handling system. (In their *Mechanical and electrical cost data.* 1918. p. 376-8).

Ash tank	8%
An inclined tank would be more.	
Ash pipe	40
Depreciation per ton of ashes	12.68c

DEPRECIATION, DEPLETION AND OBSOLESCENCE—ASH HANDLING—*(Continued)*

GILLETTE, HALBERT P. and RICHARD T. DANA. Depreciation. (In their *Handbook of mechanical and electrical cost data.* 1918. p. 108).

Machinery, coal and ash handling

5 years	W. D. Pence, Milwaukee 3c case.
10	Wisconsin R. R. Commission.
14.3	B. J. Arnold, Chicago appraisals 4 cases.
15 20	Traction valuation commission, Chicago consolidated traction co. Union traction co., Case Chicago and union traction co., Stone & Webster.
20	Henry Floy, 3rd Ave. case. N. Y. city.

GRUNSKY, CARL EWALD. Probable useful life of various articles. (In his *Valuation, depreciation and the rate base.* 1917. p. 276).

Coal and ash machinery	10 years Wisconsin railroad commission. Quoted by Henry Floy and in published reports. 10 years. Milwaukee electric railway and lighting co., in the Milwaukee 3c fare case, Aug., 1912. 14 years. Traction valuation commission. Case of the Chicago consolidated traction co. 14.2 years. Bion J. Arnold. Coney Island and Brooklyn figures adopted by Public Service commission of New York. Four Chicago appraisals quoted by H. A. Foster. 15 years. Chicago union traction co. Quoted in Report Wisconsin railroad commission, vol. 10, p. 220. 20 years. Stone and Webster. Figures for Chicago union traction co. case. Report Wisconsin railroad commission, vol. 10, p. 220. 20 years. Henry Floy. Trans. American institute of electrical engineers, June 1911. Third avenue case figures adopted by Public service commission of New York.

NEALE, R. L. Deprecation on engineering works. *Mechanical world,* Feb. 7, 1913, p. 67-8.

Coal and ash machinery	5-10%	10-20 years.

NICHOLSON, J. LEE and JOHN F. D. ROHRBACH. Depreciation. (In their *Cost accounting.* 1919. p. 150).

Coal and ash handling machinery Based on (1) the cost of equipment (2) the life of the equipment (3) on a ten-hour day	8%

PENDER, HAROLD. Depreciation. (In his *Handbook for electrical engineers.* c1914. p. 339-41).

Conveyors—
coal and ash

5 years	Engineer of valuation staff, of Wisconsin railroad commission
15	Chicago union traction co.
20	Recommended by Stone & Webster for the Chicago union traction co.
20%	Engineer of valuation staff of Wisconsin railroad commission.
6.6	Chicago union traction co.
5	Milwaukee electric railway and light co. Cardiff tramways Glasgow tramways Recommended by Stone & Webster for the Chicago union traction co.

VALUATION of the Chicago consolidated traction property. *Electric railway journal,* Dec. 3, 1910, p. 1111-3.

Coal and ash handling machinery	7%

Asphalt

PHILADELPHIA. CONTROLLER. Rates of depreciation. (In his *Manual of accounting, reporting and business procedure of the city and county of Philadelphia.* 1917. p. 205).

Asphalt preparing equipment	10%
Asphalt paving plant and equipment	10

Assaying

See Depreciation, depletion and obsolescence—Mining and metallurgy.

Auditoriums

PHILADELPHIA. CONTROLLER. Rates of depreciation. (In his *Manual of accounting, reporting business procedure of the city and county of Philadelphia.* 1917. p. 210).

Buildings: churches, auditoriums, exhibition halls, museums, club houses and amusement places	1%

Automobiles

ALLISON, J. Farmers' income tax. *Accountant,* April 19, May 3, 17, 24, 1919, p. 325-6, 369-70, 421-3, 440-1.

Motor wagons	15%

DEPRECIATION, DEPLETION AND OBSOLESCENCE—AUTOMOBILES—*(Continued)*

AMERICAN INSTITUTE OF ACCOUNTANTS. Report of the committee on standard schedules for uniform reports upon municipal industries and public service corporations; annual meeting at Atlantic city, N. J., October 20-22, 1908, 15p. *Journal of accounting,* May 1909, p. 47-54.
The knowledge at the command of the Bureau of the census leads to the conclusion that this average life is approximately as follows:
Horses, carriages, automobiles and laboratory fixtures and meters 10 years

AUSTRALIA. FEDERAL INCOME TAX DEPARTMENT. Depreciation allowance. *Accountant,* Oct. 13, 1917, p. 277-9. *Accounting and commerce,* June 30, 1917, p. 55-7. *Federal accountant,* July 1917, p. 93-8. *Public accountant,* Jan. 30, 1917, p. 145-52.
Motor vehicles (used in business and by professional men for hire) 10%
Motor lorries 10
Motor cars 10
Written down value, repairs allowed in addition.

BELT, ROBERT E. Depreciation. (In his *Foundry cost accounting practice and procedure.* 1919. p. 243).
Automobile trucks 20%
Industrial electric trucks and tractors 25
Truck and tractor trailers 15

BELT, ROBERT E. Depreciation. (In his *Uniform cost accounting methods; adopted by the American malleable castings association,* Nov. 14, 1917. p. 20-1).
Automobile trucks 20%

BREWERIES. *American institute of accountants. Special bulletin no. 2, 5,* March, Sept. 1920, p. 6-7, 5, 7-8.

CARTER, R. N. Rates of depreciation. (In his *Advanced accounts.* p. 618).
Carts, vans, motor lorries, etc. 10-15%
Based on diminishing balances, normal conditions and hours of working.

CASTENHOLZ, WILLIAM B. Audit of balance sheet accounts. (In his *Auditing procedure.* 1918. p. 58).
Automobiles
Light delivery 15-20%
Heavy service 20-30

CHASE, HARVEY STUART. Depreciation in water works accounts, with reference to uniform reports. *Journal of the New England waterworks association,* June 1910, p. 305-31. Abstract. *Engineering and contracting,* June 29, 1910, p. 598. Editorial. Depreciation and sinking fund accounts. *Municipal engineering,* July 1910, p. 26.
Horses, carriages, automobiles and laboratory fixtures and meters 10 years

COOK, H. R. Use of motor vehicles by gas companies. *Gas age,* Aug. 15, 1913, p. 154-8.
Light motor cars 5c. per mile
Trucks costing less than $1,000 6
$1,000-$1,500 7
1,500- 2,500 8
2,500 and above 9

DANA, RICHARD T. Automobiles. (In his *Handbook of construction plant.* 1914. p. 34-56).
Medium priced car, say from $1200 to $1800 for a five passenger touring car equipped, is worth at the end of its first year a little less than two thirds of its first cost, if in proper repair, newly painted and usually with two new tires. After the first year the rate of depreciation is a little less, say 25 per cent of the original cost when new.
Depreciation per year 25-40%

DENHAM, ROBERT S. Depreciation. (In his *Manual of cost engineering* and *estimating for paper box manufacturers.* 1917. p. 249)
Motor trucks. 33⅓%

DEPRECIATION and income tax. *Accounting and commerce,* Nov. 1917, p. 185-6.
Motor vehicles used for business purposes 10% on original cost.

DEPRECIATION in motor cars. *Literary digest,* Sept. 27, 1913, p. 531.

DEPRECIATION rates used by the Fairbanks company. *Annalist,* Sept. 1, 1919, p. 271.
Automobiles 33⅓%

DUTTON, L. R. Commercial motor delivery, cost and results. *Progressive age,* Nov. 15, 1911, p. 958-68.

GREAT BRITAIN. BOARD OF INLAND REVENUE. Depreciation rates: (In its *Income tax; statement respecting allowances for wear and tear and obsolescence of plant and machinery.* 1918. Cd. 9022, p. 4; Cd. 9134, p. 6. *American economic review, Supplement,* Dec. 1920, p. 51. *Journal of accountancy,* Sept. 1920, p. 195.
Motor omnibuses 20%
Traction engines, tractors, motor-cars and haulage plants 20
Written down value

HOW rapidly do motor trucks wear? *Journal of commerce,* Aug. 2, 1912, p. 8.
10% on 10,000 miles

INCOME tax notes. *Accountant,* May 11, Sept. 28, 1918, p. 359, 162-6. *Incorporated accountants' journal,* May, Oct. 1918, p. 157, 14.
Written down value 20%
Motor omnibuses
(a) The rate of 20 per cent is to be reconsidered at the expiration of four years commencing with 1916-1917.
(b) This rate does not apply to commercial motor vehicles.

LIGHT motor trucks have a life of eight years. *Commercial car journal,* May 15, 1912, p. 43.

MCINTOSH, ROBERT J. Rates of depreciation. (In his *Reference book of accounts.* Ed. 2. p. 60).
Automobile 15-25%
Based on life.

MONTGOMERY, ROBERT H. Automobiles. (In his *Income tax procedure,* 1919. p. 558.
——— Same, 1920. p. 711-2).
Not less than 20 % per annum

DEPRECIATION, DEPLETION AND OBSOLESCENCE—AUTOMOBILES—*(Continued)*

MONTGOMERY, ROBERT H. Electrical equipment manufacturers. (In his *Income tax procedure,* 1919. p. 563. ——— Same, 1920. p. 716).
Automobiles and other conveyances 25%
Based on gross book values at the end of the preceding year.

MONTGOMERY, ROBERT H. Wagons, automobiles, etc. (In his *Auditing theory and practice.* 1916. p. 426).
15-20% per annum. The most expensive parts such as tires, motors, and bodies, may be replaced, and if charged to operating will leave unprovided for only accrued depreciation and obsolescence.

NICHOLSON, J. LEE and JOHN F. D. ROHRBACH. Depreciation. (In their *Cost accounting.* 1919. p. 151).
Motor trucks, automobiles, stable equipment, motor boats, etc. 25%
Based on (1) the cost of equipment (2) the life of the equipment (3) on a ten-hour day.

NURGE, A. E. Method of recording depreciation on motor vehicles. *Accounting and commerce,* May 1919, p. 40.
Five years should be allowed, and the prime cost of the vehicle should be written off during this period.

PHILADELPHIA. CONTROLLER. Rates of depreciation. (In his *Manual of accounting, reporting and business procedure of the city and county of Philadelphia.* 1917. p. 206).
Motor vehicles and parts, including auto tires 20%

PHILLIPS, A. E. Mileage used as a basis for computing depreciatoin of automobiles and motor trucks. *Engineering record,* Dec. 16, 1916, p. 733.

PIEZ, CHARLES. Perpetual inventory and appraisal values; table of standard depreciation rates. *Engineering and contracting,* Jan. 24, 1917, p. 77. *Factory,* Dec. 1916, p. 668-71. *Iron age,* Nov. 30, 1916, Jan. 11, 1917, p. 1266, 138-9. *Iron trade review,* Feb. 22, 1917, p. 477-8. Condensed. *Journal of the American society of mechanical engineers,* Dec. 1916, p. 965-6. *Iron trade review,* Dec. 7, 1916, p. 1144-6. Kent, William, *Bookkeeping and cost accounting for factories.* 1918. p. 90. Discussion. *Journal of the American society of mechanical engineers,* March 1917, p. 215-7.

	% on cost	% on reducing value
Motor trucks	20	60

PUBLIC utility reports, annotated. Rochester, Lawyers co-operative publishing co. 1915E, p. 1.
Re Auto Livery Co. (D. C.). An auto-livery and taxicab company was ordered to conform its depreciation account to a rate of 19.7 per cent on the cost of property new for motor cabs.

PUBLIC utility reports, annotated. Rochester, Lawyers co-operative publishing co. 1915C, p. 366.
Simms v. Columbia Teleph. Co. (Mo.). A value of $1,784 placed upon an automobile which had been used for three years and which cost but $1,800 was held too high by at least from $1,000 to $1,200.

PUBLIC utility reports, annotated. Rochester, Lawyers co-operative publishing co. 1915B, p. 546.
Re Terminal Taxicab (D. C.). A taxicab company was ordered to conform its depreciation accounts to a rate of 2½ per cent on the cost of property new for "motor cabs."

WHEELER, CHARLES. Calculating depreciation of commercial automobiles. *Society of automotive engineers bulletin,* May 1913.

WIHLFAHRT, JULIUS E. Depreciation. (In his *Treatise on increasing bakery efficiency.* 1917. p. 6).
Autos 40%

Awnings

PHILADELPHIA. CONTROLLER. Rates of depreciation. (In his *Manual of accounting, reporting and business procedure of the city and county of Philadelphia.* 1917. p. 207-8).
Porch shades, awnings, blinds, etc. 20%

Axe factories

TIFFANY, H. S. Frame axe factories. (In his *Digest of depreciations.* c1890. p. 8).
Annually 5% based upon the actual life of the building without any repairs.

Bacon

See Depreciation, depletion and obsolescence—Meat.

Badges

PHILADELPHIA. CONTROLLER. Rates of depreciation. (In his *Manual of accounting, reporting and business procedure of the city and county of Philadelphia.* 1917, p. 209).
Belts, badges, handcuffs 4%

Bakeries

EGGLESTON, DEWITT, CARL. Depreciation. (In his *Problems in cost accounting.* 1918. p. 248).

Building	3%
Oven	10
Mixer	12½
Divider	12½
Rounder	12½
Proofer	12½
Molder	12½
Misc. equipment	20
Wagons	20
Horses	20
Harnesses	20
Automobiles	20

WIHLFAHRT, JULIUS E. Depreciation. (In his *Treatise on increasing bakery efficiency.* 1917. p. 6).

On value of buildings	3%
Shop equipment	7½
Other shop and store equipment	15
Autos	40
Horses, wagons and harness	15
Office furniture and fixtures	10

DEPRECIATION, DEPLETION AND OBSOLESCENCE—*(Continued)*

Balers

DENHAM, ROBERT H. Depreciation. (In his *Manual of cost engineering and estimating for paper box manufactures.* 1917. p. 249).

	Original cost
Balers	10%

Ball mills

NICHOLSON, J. LEE and JOHN F. D. ROHRBACH. Depreciation. (In their *Cost accounting.* 1919. p. 150).

Ball mills	10%

Ballast

GRAY, HENRY L. Necessity of depreciation reserves. *Railway age gazette,* May 27, 1910, p. 1297-8. Editorial. Depreciation reserves. *Railway age gazette,* May 27, 1910, p. 1290. Letters. Depreciation reserves. *Railway age gazette,* July 8, 1910, p. 66.

Ballast	8% annual depreciation.

Banks

BOLTON, REGINALD PELHAM. Depreciation of the value of buildings. (In his *Building for profit.* 1911. p. 76).

Banks and institutions	44-50 years

Barber shops

UNIFORM cost sheet for coal mining companies. *Coal age,* Sept. 18, 1918, p. 545-7.

	Original cost
Barber shop fixtures and barber shop	10%

PHILADELPHIA. CONTROLLER. Rates of depreciation. (In his *Manual of accounting, reporting and business procedure of the city and county of Philadelphia.* 1917. p. 207-8).

Tonsorial equipment	4%

Barns

TIFFANY, H. S. Barns. (In his *Digest of depreciations.* c1890. p. 5).

Brick barns	3%
Frame barns	4
(without good foundations)	4½

Based upon actual life without any repairs.

Barrels

See also Depreciation, depletion and obsolescence—Cooperage

NICHOLSON, J. LEE and JOHN F. D. ROHRBACH. Depreciation. (In their *Cost accounting.* 1919. p. 150).

Barrels	10%

Basins

See also Depreciation, depletion and obsolescence—Reservoirs.

Bath houses

PHILADELPHIA. CONTROLLER. Rates of depreciation. (In his *Manual of accounting, reporting and business procedure of the city and county of Philadelphia.* 1917. p. 209).

Buildings:	
Bath houses	1%

Batons, Clubs, etc.

PHILADLPHIA, CONTROLLER. Rates of depreciation. (In his *Manual of accounting, reporting and business procedure of the city and county of Philadelphia.* 1917. p. 209).

Batons, night sticks, riot clubs, swords, etc.	10%

Batteries

BARKER, HARRY. Typical life expectation tables for public utility property. (In his *Public utility rates.* 1917. p. 368-9).

Storage batteries	15 years	Wisconsin railroad commission

BRYAN, WILLIAM. Appraisal and depreciation of water-works and similar properties. *Journal of the Association of engineering societies,* Dec. 1907, p. 336-81. Depreciation allowance for various public service industries. *Engineering news,* Jan. 23, 1908, p. 96.

	Years
Storage batteries	9-11

BRYAN, WILLIAM H. Depreciation of electric light plants. *Municipality,* March 1908, p. 74.

Material	Life in years	Authority
Storage batteries	9-11	Dawson's "Engineering and electric traction pocket book", in Iowa engineer, July 1906.

CRAVENS, GEORGE W. Depreciation and maintenance of electrical equipment. *Electrical review,* April 23, 1910, p. 853-6. Foster, H. A. *Engineering valuation of public utilities and factories.* 1913. p. 201-2. Montgomery, Robert H. *Auditing theory and practice.* 1916. p. 424. Montgomery, Robert H. *Income tax procedure,* 1919, p. 570. ——— Same, 1920, p. 722-4.

	Light or intermittent service	Heavy or continuous service
Storage batteries	5-6.6%	6.6-10%

6.6%	Chicago union traction co.
10	Milwaukee electric railway & light co.
5	Average English
5	Average Scotch practice.
9-11	Philip Dawson
5	Stone & Webster
5-10	Industrial power plants
6.6	Prof. G. F. Gebhardt
10	Miscellaneous sources

DEPRECIATION, DEPLETION AND OBSOLESCENCE—BATTERIES *(Continued)*

CROWELL, H. H. Electric lighting rates and depreciation. *Municipal journal* and *engineering*, Dec. 18, 1907, p. 698.

	Purchased 10 years or more ago	Modern
Batteries	10 years	15 years

DEPRECIATION of the equipment of an electric plant. *Electrical world*, Dec. 12, 1914, p. 1161.
Storage batteries 4.15%

ELBOURNE, EDWARD T. Depreciation rates. (In his *Factory administration and accounts*. 1918. p. 376).

	Prov. dep. % Remainder values	Years 10%	5%
Batteries, storage	12½	17	22

ENNIS, WILLIAM DUANE. Depreciation. (In his *Works management*. 1911. p. 86).
Storage batteries
15 years life to 0% residual value

FLOY, HENRY. Depreciation. Floy, Henry, *Depreciation as related to electrical properties. American institute of electrical engineers, Proceedings*, 1911, p. 1267. Floy, Henry, *Valuation of public utility properties*, 1912, p. 168-217. Foster, Horatio R. *Engineering valuation of public utilities and factories*, 1913, p. 194-8. *Engineering & Contracting*, Oct. 4, 1911, p. 359-65. *Engineering magazine*, Aug. 1911, p. 837-40.

Storage batteries	5 Henry Floy	3rd Ave. case, adopted by P.S.C.,
	6⅔ Wisconsin R.R.C.	N.Y.
	5 St. Louis R.R.C.	Union Elec. L. & P. Co.

FOSTER, HORATIO A. Methods of calculating depreciation. (In his *Engineering valuation of public utilities and factories*. 1913. p. 169).
Minimum service value of storage batteries 35% of reproduction cost.
Joint engineering department of the Wisconsin commission.

FOSTER, HORATIO A. Rates of depreciation. (In his *Engineering valuation of public utilities and factories*. 1913. p. 200, 205).
Storage batteries 3%
Marwick, Mitchell & co. in the appraisal of a large street railway system.
Storage batteries 10-15 years

GILLETTE, HALBERT P. and RICHARD T. DANA. Depreciation. (In their *Handbook of mechanical and electrical cost data*. 1918. p. 105).

Batteries, storage

Years	
10	Milwaukee electric railway & light co.
10-20	George W. Cravens; Industrial power plants.
15	Wisconsin R. R. Commission.
15-20	Union traction co. Case Chicago and union traction co. Stone & Webster.
20	St. Louis public service commission. Union electric light & power co.
20	Henry Floy, 3rd Ave. case, New York city.
33.3	Marwick, Mitchell & co., appraisal of a large street railway system, Foster, p. 199.

GRAY, HARRY L. Necessity of depreciation reserves. *Railway age gazette*, May 27, 1910, p. 1297-8. Editorial. Depreciation reserves. *Railway age gazette*, May 27, 1910, p. 1290. Letters. Depreciation reserves. *Railway age gazette*, May 27, 1910, p. 66.

	Annual dep.
Storage batteries	15%

GRUNSKY, CARL EWALD. Probable useful life of various articles. (In his *Valuation, depreciation and the rate-base*. 1917. p. 284).

Storage batteries	10 years. Milwaukee electric railway and lighting co., in the Milwaukee 3c. fare case, Aug. 1912.
	10 years. Wisconsin railroad commission. Milwaukee 3c. fare case, Aug. 23, 1912.
	12.5 years. 6% residual value. Pacific gas and electric company. Figures used in rate hearings before Master in Chancery, San Francisco, 1913-4.
	15 years. 5% residual value. Wisconsin railroad commission. Wisconsin telephone co. case, Aug. 3, 1909.
	15 years. Chicago union traction co. Quoted in Report Wisconsin railroad commission, vol. 10, p. 220.
	20 years. Stone & Webster. Figures for Chicago union traction co. case. Report Wisconsin railroad commission, vol. 10, p. 220.
	20 years. St. Louis public service commission. Case of Union electric light and power co.
	20 years. Henry Floy. Trans. American institute of electrical engineers, June, 1911. Third avenue case figures adopted by Public service commission of New York.

DEPRECIATION, DEPLETION AND OBSOLESCENCE —BATTERIES *(Continued)*

KIMBALL, DEXTER S. Estimated life, and factors of depreciation. (In his *Cost accounting.* 1918. p. 190. *Principles of industrial organization.* 1913. p. 163).

	Storage batteries
Probable life of asset in years	10
Ratio of scrap to original value	0.5
Percentage on original cost	9.5
Percentage on diminishing value	26

NICHOLSON, J. LEE and JOHN F. D. ROHRBACH. Depreciation. (In their *Cost accounting.* 1919. p. 147).
Storage batteries 6%
Based on (1) the cost of equipment
(2) the life of the equipment
(3) on a ten-hour day.

PHILADELPHIA. CONTROLLER. Rates of depreciation. (In his *Manual of accounting, reporting and business procedure of the city and county of Philadelphia.* 1917. p. 204).
Dry and storage batteries 10%

PRACTICAL hints on computing telephone depreciation. *Telephony,* April 1, 1911, p. 40⅓
Batteries 18%

Bedding

PHILADELPHIA. CONTROLLER. Rates of depreciation. (In his *Manual of accounting, reporting and business procedure of the city and county of Philadelphia.* 1917. p. 207-8).
Bedding (exclusive of bed linen) 8⅓%

Beds

PHILADELPHIA. CONTROLLER. Rates of depreciation. (In his *Manual of accounting, reporting and business procedure of the city and county of Philadelphia.* 1917. p. 207-8).
Beds and cots (including bed springs) 5½%

Bells

ELBOURNE, EDWARD T. Depreciation rates. (In his *Factory administration and accounts.* 1918. p. 376).

	Prov. dep. %	Years	
	Remainder values	10½	5%
Bells and signals	7½	29	38

Belt cutters

NICHOLSON, J. LEE and JOHN F. ROHRBACH. Depreciation. (In their *Cost accounting.* 1919. p. 149).
Belt cutters 6⅔%

Belt lacing machines

ELBOURNE, EDWARD T. Depreciation rates. (In his *Factory administration and accounts.* 1918. p. 377).

	Prov. dep. %	Years	
	Remainder values	10½	5%
Belt lacing machines	6	37	48

NICHOLSON, J. LEE and JOHN F. D. ROHRBACH. Depreciation. (In their *Cost accounting.* 1919. p. 149).
Belt lacers 6⅔%

Belt-strapping machines

NICHOLSON, J. LEE and J. F. D. ROHRBACH. (In their *Cost accounting.* 1919. p. 150).
Belt-strapping machines 10%

Belting

BARKER, HARRY. Typical life expectation tables for public utility property. (In his *Public utility rates.* 1917. p. 368-9).
Belting 20-25 years. Wis. R. R. Comm.

BREWER, ALLAN F. Rates for annual depreciation. *Industrial management,* April 1918, p. 268.
Belts.—Life of belting is a variable which depends almost entirely on the manner of use and extent of care. Under average conditions eight to ten years would be fair.

BRYAN, WILLIAM. Appraisal and depreciation of water works and similar properties. *Journal of the association of engineering societies,* Dec. 1907, p. 336-81.
Years
Belts 3-4

BRYAN, WILLIAM. Depreciation allowance for various public service industries. *Engineering news,* Jan. 23, 1908, p. 96.
Years
Belts 3-4

BRYAN, WILLIAM H. Depreciation of electric light plants. *Municipality,* March 1908, p. 74.

Material	Life in years	Authority
Belts	3-4	Dawson's "Engineering and Electric traction pocket-book in Iowa Engineer, July 1906.

DAWSON, PHILIP. Depreciation. (In his *Engineering and electric traction pocket-book..* Ed. 2. p. 1161.
% capital cost
Belts 25-30

FLOY, HENRY. Depreciation. Floy, Henry, *Depreciation as related to electrical properties. American institute of electrical engineers. Proceedings,* 1911, p. 1267. Floy, Henry, *Valuation of public utility properties,* 1912, p. 168-217. Foster, Horatio R. *Engineering valuation of public utilities and factories,* 1913, p. 194-8. *Engineering & Contracting,* Oct. 4, 1911, p. 359-65. *Engineering magazine,* Aug. 1911, p. 837-40.

	Depreciation % per year. Straight line.	
Belting	5	Wis. P. S. C.

DEPRECIATION, DEPLETION AND OBSOLESCENCE—BELTING—*(Continued)*

FOSTER, HORATIO A. Rates of deprecitaion. (In his *Engineering valuation of public utilities and factories.* 1913. p. 205). Years life.
Leather belting 20-25

GILLETTE, HALBERT P. and RICHARD T. DANA. Depreciation. (In their *Handbook of mechanical and electrical cost data.* 1918. p. 105).
Belting 20 years Wisconsin R. R. com.

GRUNSKY, CARL EWALD. Probable useful life of various articles. (In his *Valuation, depreciation and the rate base.* 1917. p. 274).

Belting	8 years	Pacific Gas & Electric Company. Figures used in rate hearings before Master in Chancery, San Francisco 1913-14.
	20 years	Wisconsin railroad commission; quoted by Floy and in published reports.
	10-20 years	Wisconsin railroad commission. Milwaukee 3c fare case. Aug. 23, 1912.
with shafting and ropes	15 years	Chicago union traction co. Quoted in Report Wisconsin R. R. commission, Vol. 10, p. 220.
with shafting and ropes	20 years	Stone & Webster. Figures for Chicago Union traction co. case. Report Wisconsin railroad commission, vol. 10, p. 220.
leather	20-25 years	H. A. Foster. "Engineering valuation of public utilities and factories." Van Nostrand, 1912.

KENT, WILLIAM. Depreciation of shafting, etc. (In his *Bookkeeping and cost accounting for factories.* 1918. p. 91).
Main belts wear slowly, while machine belts will always average 50 per cent wear so that, as a rule, the total amount of belting is depreciated 33 1/3 per cent.

KIMBALL, DEXTER S. Estimated life, and factors of depreciation. (In his *Cost finding,* 1918. p. 190. *Principles of industrial organization.* 1913. p. 163.
Belting
Probable life of asset in years 10-25
Percentage on original cost 10-4

MCINTOSH, ROBERT J. Rates of depreciation. (In his *Reference book of accounts.* Ed. 2. p. 60).
Hangers, shafting and belting 10-20%
Based on life.

MONTGOMERY, ROBERT H. Electrical equipment manufacturers. (In his *Income tax procedure,* 1919. p. 563.—Same, 1920, p. 716).
Shafting, pulleys, belting 15%
Based on gross book values at the end of the preceding year.

NEALE, R. E. Depreciation in engineering works. *Mechanical world,* Feb. 7, 1913, p. 67-8.
Belting 5-10% 10-20 years

NICHOLSON, J. LEE and JOHN F. D. ROHRBACH. Depreciation. (In their *Cost accounting.* 1919. p. 150).
Shafting, pulleys, hangers and belting 5%
Belting 7%
Based on (1) the cost of equipment
(2) the life of the equipment
(3) on a ten-hour day.

NORRIS, H. M. Depreciation of plant and its relation to general expense. *Engineering magazine,* April 1899, p. 76.
Belting 15%

PHILADELPHIA. CONTROLLER. Rates of depreciation. (In his *Manual of accounting, reporting and business procedure of the city and county of Philadelphia.* 1917. p. 205).
Shafting, belting, pulleys, gearing, etc. 4%

SOME depreciation rates on buildings, machinery, shafting, belting, furniture and apparatus, tools and dies, moulds, lasts, patterns and drawings used by the Associated mutual fire insurance companies of Boston, Mass., in making appraisals of manufacturing properties. *Utiltiies magazine,* Jan. 1, 1916, p. 186-7.
Main belts wear slowly while machine belts are always in a state of 50 per cent depreciation so we, as a rule, consider 33⅓ per cent a fair average for belting as a whole.

TIFFANY, H. S. Machinery. (In his *Digest of deprcciations.* c1890. p. 12).
Belting:
leather 20%
rubber 30

Belts

PHILADELPHIA. CONTROLLER. Rates of depreciation. (In his *Manual of accounting, reporting and business procedure of the city and county of Philadelphia.* 1917. p. 209).
Belts, badges, handcuffs 4%
Window cleaning safety belts 20%

Benches

BELT, ROBERT E. Depreciation. (In his *Foundry cost accounting practice and procedure.* 1919. p. 242).
Benches 10%

BELT, ROBERT E. Depreciation. (In his *Uniform cost accounting methods; adopted by the American malleable castings association,* Nov. 14, 1917, p. 120-1).
Benches 10%

DEPRECIATION, DEPLETION AND OBSOLESCENCE—BENCHES—*(Continued)*

ELBOURNE, EDWARD T. Depreciation. (In his *Factory administration and accounts.* 1918. p. 376).

	Prov. dep. %		Years
	Remainder values	10%	5%
Benching	10	22	28

NICHOLSON, J. LEE and JOHN F. D. ROHRBACH. Depreciation. (In their *Cost accounting.* 1919. p. 151).
Benches, partitions—permanent 7½%
Benches 8
Based on (1) the cost of equipment
(2) the life of the equipment
(3) on a ten-hour day.

PHILADELPHIA. CONTROLLER. Rates of depreciation. (In his *Manual of accounting, reporting and business procedure of the city and county of Philadelphia.* 1917. p. 207-8).
Benches 5%

Benches (gas plant)

BARKER, HARRY. Typical life expectation tables for public utility property. (In his *Public utility rates.* 1917. p. 368).
Coal-gas benches 25 years Wis. R. R. Com.

FOSTER, HORATIO A. Rates of depreciation. (In his *Engineering valuation of public utilities and factories.* 1913. p. 206).
Years life
Benches 25

GILLETTE, HALBERT P. and RICHARD T. DANA. Depreciation. (In their *Handbook of mechanical and electrical cost data.* 1918. p. 105).
Benches (gas plant) 25 years Wis. R. R. Comm.

GRUNSKY, CARL EWALD. Probable useful life of various articles. (In his *Valuation depreciation and rate base.* 1917. p. 274).
Benches (gas plant) 25 years
Wisconson railroad commission.
Quoted by H. A. Foster and in published reports.

PROSSER, R. W. Depreciation in gas plants. *American gas light journal,* May 26, 1902, p. 767).
Benches 30 years

Bending machines

ELBOURNE, EDWARD T. Depreciation rates. (In his *Factory administration and accounts.* 1918. p. 377).

	Prov. dep. %		Years
	Remainder values	10%	5%
Plate bending machines	6	37	48

NICHOLSON, J. LEE and JOHN F. D. ROHRBACH. Depreciation. (In their *Cost accounting.* 1919. p. 149, 150).
Bending rolls 6⅔%
Bending blocks 10

PHILADELPHIA. CONTROLLER. Rates of depreciation. (In his *Manual of accounting, reporting and business procedure of the city and county of Philadelphia.* 1917. p. 205).
Metal work equipment: Drawing and bending equipment 5%

PIEZ, CHARLES. Perpetual inventory and appraisal values; table of standard depreciation rates. *Engineering and contracting,* Jan. 24, 1917, p. 77. *Factory,* Dec. 1916, p. 668-71. *Iron age,* Nov. 30, 1916, Jan. 11, 1917, p. 1266, 138-9. *Iron trade review,* Feb. 22, 1917, p. 477-8. Condensed. *Journal of the American society of mechanical engineers,* Dec. 1916, p. 965-6. *Iron trade review,* Dec. 7, 1916, p. 1144-6. Discussion. *Journal of the American society of mechanical engineers,* March 1917, p. 215-7.

	% on cost	% on reducing balance
Punch presses, bending rolls, power shears and drop hammers	4.5	10

Bessemer plant

NICHOLSON, J. LEE and JOHN F. D. ROHRBACH. Depreciation. (In their *Cost accounting,* 1919. p. 148).
Bessemer plant 4%

Beveling machines

NICHOLSON, J. LEE and JOHN F. D. ROHRBACH. Depreciation. (In their *Cost accounting.* 1919. p. 149).
Beveling machines 6⅔%

Bicycles

AUSTRALIA. FEDERAL INCOME TAX DEPARTMENT. Depreciation allowance. *Accountant,* Oct. 13, 1917, p. 277-9. *Accounting and commerce,* June 30, 1917, p. 55-7. *Federal accountant,* July 1917, p. 93-8. *Public accountant,* Jan. 30, 1917, p. 145-52.
Bicycles—motor and ordinary 10%
Based on written down value and repairs allowed in addition.

Bill boards

See Depreciation, depletion and obsolescence—Sign boards.

Billiard tables

AUSTRALIA. FEDERAL INCOME TAX DEPARTMENT. Depreciation allowance. *Accountant,* Oct. 13, 1917, p. 277-9. *Accounting and commerce,* June 30, 1917, p. 55-7. *Federal accountant,* July 1917, p. 93-8. *Public accountant,* Jan. 30, 1917, p. 145-52.
Billiard tables 2½%
Based on written down value and repairs allowed in addition.

DEPRECIATION, DEPLETION AND OBSOLESCENCE—*(Continued)*

Binding

GREAT BRITAIN. BOARD OF INLAND REVENUE. Depreciation rates. (In its *Income tax; statement respecting allowances for wear and tear and obsolescence of plant and machinery.* 1918. Cd. 9022, p. 4, Cd. 9134, p. 6). *American economic review, Supplement,* Dec. 1920, p. 51. *Journal of accountancy,* Sept. 1920, p. 194.
  Printing and binding machines 7½%
  Written down value.

OFFICIAL allowances in respect of depreciation of machinery and plant—Board of Inland revenue, Great Britain. *Accountant,* May 16, 1914, p. 736.
  Printing and binding machines 7½%

PHILADELPHIA. CONTROLLER. Rates of depreciation. (In his *Manual of accounting, reporting and business procedure of the city and county of Philadelphia.* 1917. p. 205).
  Printing, binding and lithographing equipment 8⅓%

Bins

ELBOURNE, EDWARD T. Depreciation rates. (In his *Factory administration and accounts.* 1918. p. 376).

	Prov. dep. % Remainder values	Years 10%	5%
Bins	10	22	28

GILLETTE HALBERT P. and RICHARD T. DANA. Depreciation repairs and renewals. (In their *Mechanical and electrical cost data.* 1918. p. 105).
  Bins 10-33.3 years B. J. Arnold, Chicago appraisals. 4 cases.

NICHOLSON, J. LEE and JOHN F. D. ROHRBACH. Depreciation. (In their *Cost accounting.* 1919. p. 146, 148).
  Bins
    concrete and brick 5%
    wood alone 20
  Based on (1) the cost of equipment
    (2) the life of the equipment
    (3) on a ten-hour day.
  Steel work—including...bins 4%
  Cabinets, cases, lockers, bins and boxes 4

Biograph machines

AUSTRALIA. FEDERAL INCOME TAX DEPARTMENT. Depreciation allowance. *Accountant,* Oct. 13, 1917, p. 277-9. *Accounting and commerce,* June 30, 1917, p. 55-7. *Federal accountant,* July 1917, p. 93-8. *Public accountant,* Jan. 30, 1917, p. 145-52.
  Biograph machines 10%
  Based on written down value and repairs allowed in addition.

Blacksmith shops

UNIFORM cost sheet for coal mining companies. *Coal age,* Sept. 19, 1918, p. 545-7.
  Blacksmith shop Original cost
    Wood 8%
    Stone or brick 5

Blast furnaces

See Depreciation, depletion and obsolescence—Stoves, heaters, etc.

Blinds

PHILADELPHIA. CONTROLLER. Rates of depreciation. (In his *Manual of accounting, reporting and business procedure of the city and county of Philadelphia.* 1917. p. 207-8).
  Porch shades, awnings, blinds, etc. 20%

Blowers

BARKER, HARRY. Typical life expectation tables for public utiilty property. (In his *Public utility rates.* 1917. p. 368).
  Blowers 15 years Wis. R. R. Com.

BREWER, ALLEN F. Rates for annual depreciation. *Industrial management,* April 1918, p. 268.

	Estimated life years	Percent annual depreciation
Blowers	20	5

ELBOURNE, EDWARD T. Depreciation rates. (In his *Factory administration and accounts.* 1918. p. 376).

	Prov. dep. % Remainder values	Years 10%	5%
Blowers	7½	29	38

FOSTER, HORATIO A. Rates of depreciation. (In his *Engineering of public utilities and factories.* 1913. p. 206).

	Years life.
Centrifugal blowers	15

GILLETTE, HALBERT P. and RICHARD T. DANA. Depreciation. (In their *Handbook of mechanical and electrical cost data.* 1918. p. 106).
  Blowers, centrifugal (gas plant) 15 years Wis. R. R. Comm.

GRUNSKY, CARL EWALD. Probable useful life of various articles. (In his *Valuation, depreciation and the rate base.* 1917. p. 274).
  Blowers (gas plant) 15 years
  Wisconsin railroad commission. Quoted by H. A. Foster, and in published reports.
  20 years.
  Pacific Gas & Electric Co. Figures used in rate hearings before Master in Chancery, San Francisco, 1913-1914.

DEPRECIATION, DEPLETION AND OBSOLESCENCE—BLOWERS—*(Continued)*

NICHOLSON, J. LEE and JOHN F. D. ROHRBACH. Depreciation. (In their *Cost accounting.* 1919 p. 150).
Blowers 10%

PHILADELPHIA. CONTROLLER. Rates of depreciation. (In his *Manual of accounting, reporting and business procedure of the city and county of Philadelphia.* 1917. p. 205).
Bellows and other hand or foot blowers 10%
Mechanical blowers 10

Boarding houses

AUSTRALIA. FEDERAL INCOME TAX DEPARTMENT. Depreciation. *Accountant,* Oct. 13, 1917, p. 277-9. *Accounting and commerce,* June 30, 1917, p. 55-7. *Federal accountant,* July 1917, p. 93-8. *Public accountant,* Jan. 30, 1917, p. 145-52.
·Plant and furniture used in connection with hotels and boarding houses 7½%
·Based on written down value, repairs allowed in addition.

Boats

See Depreciation, depletion and obsolescence—Ships.

Boiler industry

DEPRECIATION charged against plant by twenty-three boiler makers. *Iron age,* June 22, 1916, p. 1502-3.
Factory building 0-10%
Power equipment 2-25
Machine tools 4-10
Average for buildings 4.19
These figures came out in a discussion on this subject at the annual meeting of the American boilers manufacturers' asso., Cleveland, Ohio, June 19-20.

Boilers

ALLISON, J. Farmers' income tax. *Accountant,* April 14, May 3, 7, 24, 1919, p. 325-6, 369-70, 421-3, 440-1.
Boilers 5%

AMERICAN INSTITUTE OF ACCOUNTANTS. Report of the committee on standard schedules for uniform reports upon municipal industries and public service corporations; annual meeting at Atlantic city, N. J. October 20-22, 1908, 15p. *Journal of accountancy,* May 1909, p. 47-54.
The knowledge at the command of the Bureau of the census leads to the conclusion that this average life is approximately as follows:
Boilers, steam pipes and filtration equipment 20 years

AMERICAN WATER WORKS ASSOCIATION. Final report of committee on depreciation. *Journal of the American waterworks association,* Sept. 1917, p. 1-38.
Boilers 15-30 years

ANALYSIS of the premises adopted and methods used in determining the cost to reproduce new together with the depreciation thereon of the physical property of the Metropolitan system and the Kansas city and Westport Belt railway of Kansas city, Mo. *Engineering and contracting,* May 28, 1913, p. 617-20.
Boilers
Horizontal tubular boilers and settings 8%
Water tube boilers and settings 3½

AUSTRALIA. FEDERAL INCOME TAX DEPARTMENT. Depreciation allowance. *Accountant,* Oct. 13, 1917, p. 277-9. *Accounting and commerce,* June 30, 1917, p. 66-7. *Federal accountant,* July 1917, p. 93-8. *Public accountant,* Jan. 30, 1917, p. 145-52.
Boilers 5%
Written down value, repairs allowed.

BARKER, HARRY. Typical life expectation tables for public utility property. (In his *Public utility rates,* 1917, p. 368-9, 367).

Boilers: fire-tube	10-15 years	Wis. R. R. Com.
Fire-tube	12-16	L. Metcalf
Water-tube	20-30	Wis. R. R. Com.

BAY STATE RATE CASE. *Electric railway journal,* Dec. 4, 1915, p. 1121-3. *Public utility reports, annotated,* 1916F, p. 336-9.

Boilers	Years
Water-tube	25-30
Fire-tube	20

BELT, ROBERT E. Depreciation. (In his *Foundry cost accounting practice and procedure.* 1919. p. 243).
Steam boilers 5%
Waste heat boilers and apparatus 10

BELT, ROBERT E. Depreciation. (In his *Uniform cost accounting methods; adopted by the American malleable castings association,* Nov. 14, 1917. p. 20-1).
Steam boiler, generator, air compressor, steam piping, electric wiring, etc. 7½%

BENTLEY, HARRY C. Depreciation. (In his *Science of accounts.* 1913. p. 146).
Engines and boilers 5% on original cost, refining being charged to repairs.

BOLTON, REGINALD PELHAM. Depreciation of mechanical equipments and power plants. (In his *Building for profit.* 1911. p. 82, 89).

	Physical years.	%	Economic years.
Heating boilers used part of year	28	70.0	22
Highest class pressure steam boilers	22	55.0	17
Drip and drain piping, cheaper class of pressure steam boilers	18	45.0	14

BREWER, ALLAN F. Rates for annual depreciation. *Industrial management,* April 1918, p. 268.

	Years.	%
Boiler-feed injectors	25	4
Boiler flues and breeching	40	2.5
Boilers, steam, horizontal water tube	30	3.33
Boilers, steam, vertical water tube	25	4
Boilers, steam, fire tube	25	4

DEPRECIATION, DEPLETION AND OBSOLESCENCE—BOILERS—*(Continued)*

BREWERIES. *American institute of accountants, Special bulletin, No. 2,* March 1920, p. 6-7.

BRYAN, WILLIAM. Appraisal and depreciation of water-works and similar properties. *Journal of the association of engineering societies,* Dec. 1907, p. 336-81. Depreciation allowance for various public service industries. *Engineering news,* Jan. 23, 1908, p. 96. *Municipality,* March, 1908, p. 74.

	Years.		% straight	
Boilers	6-23	Ave. 15		Average of 32
"			5-7	
"	15			
"	20-30			
"	20			
"	10-12.5			
"	14-15			
"	25			
"	30			
"			8	
"	14.3-25			
"			2.5-4	
"			6	
"	25			

CARTER, R. N. Rates of depreciation. (In his *Advanced accounts.* p. 618).

Boilers:

High pressure	15%
Low pressure	10

Based on diminishing balances, normal conditions and hours of working.

CHASE, HARVEY S. Depreciation in water works accounts, with reference to uniform reports. *Journal of the New England waterworks association,* June 1910, p. 305-31. Abstract. *Engineering and contracting,* June 29, 1910, p. 598. Editorial. Depreciation and sinking fund accounts. *Municipal engineering,* July 1910, p. 26.

Boilers, steam pipes and filtration equipment — 20 years

CLADER, WILL-A. Water utilities accounting. *Journal of accountancy,* Aug. 1919, p. 91-2.

The following rate is used frequently when wear and tear are made good by operating maintenance:

Boilers — 5%

CLAPHAM, F. T. Depreciation of plant. *Mechanical world,* Oct. 19, 1917, p. 219-20.

Steam boilers:

7% depreciation + 3% wear and tear = 10%.

CRAVENS, GEORGE W. Depreciation and maintenance of electrical equipment. *Electrical review,* April 23, 1910, p. 853-6. Foster, Horatio H. *Engineering valuation of public utilities and factories,* 1913, p. 201-2. Montgomery, Robert H. *Auditing theory and practice.* 1916. p. 424. Montgomery, Robert H. *Income tax procedure,* 1919, p. 570.—Same, 1920, p. 723.

Boilers:

3.5-10%	Chicago traction commission.
6.6	Chicago Union traction co.
7.5	Milwaukee electric railway & light co.
6.6-8.5	Wisconsin railroad comm.
5	Average English.
5	Average Scotch practice.
8-10	Philip Dawson.
5	Stone and Webster.
2.5-3.3	Industrial power plants.
4-6.6	Prof. G. F. Gebhardt.
7.5	Miscellaneous sources.

	Light intermittent service.	Heavy or continuous service.
Boilers		
water tube	4-6.6%	5-8.3
fire tube	5-6.6	6.6-10

CROWEL, H. H. Electric lighting rates and depreciation. *Municipal journal and engineering,* Dec 18, 1907, p. 698.

	Purchased 10 years or more ago.	Modern.
Boilers	15 years	20 years

DAWSON, PHILIP. Depreciation. (In his *Engineering and electric traction pocket-book.* Ed. 2 p. 1161).

Boilers, pumps, piping, etc.	15-30 years
	% capital cost.
Boilers	8-10
Boilers and engines	6-10

DENHAM, ROBERT S. Depreciation. (In his *Manual of cost engineering and estimating for paper box manufactures.* 1917. p. 249).

	Original cost.
Boilers	8%

DENSHAM, F. W. Depreciation of assets and goodwill of limited companies. *Accountant,* May 28, 1898, p. 568.

Boilers — 10-15%

DEPRECIATION. *American institute of accountants, Special bulletin, No. 1,* Jan. 1920, p. 6-7.

DEPRECIATION of steam plant. *Electric railway review,* March 31, 1908, p. 360.

Running about 12 hours a day the life of a boiler should be about 20 years or the depreciation 5% per year.

DEPRECIATION of the equipment of an electric plant. *Electrical world,* Dec. 12, 1914, p. 1161

Boilers, piping and generators — 4.7-4.8%

DEPRECIATION, DEPLETION AND OBSOLESCENCE—BOILERS—*(Continued)*

DICKSEE, LAWRENCE R. Machinery. (In his *Auditing. Authorized American edition.* 1909. p. 192).

	Reducing balances.
Boilers	10-15%

DICKSEE, LAWRENCE R. Machinery. (In his *Depreciation, reserves and reserve funds.* 1912. p. 29-37).

Boilers	12½-20%

EDWARDS, C. LEWIS. Electric lighting accounts. *Incorporated accountants' journal,* April 1912, p. 175.

Boilers	5-7½%

ELBOURNE, EDWARD T. Depreciation rates. (In his *Factory administration and accounts.* 1918. p. 376).

	Prov. dep. %	Years	
	Remainder values	10%	5%
Boilers, Lancashire type	7½	29	38
" heating	15	14	18
" water tube	12½	17	22

ENNIS, WILLIAM DUANE. Depreciation. (In his *Works management.* 1911. p. 86).
Water tube boilers 25 years life to 5% residual value.

ESTIMATED life and depreciation of water works plants. *Municipal journal and engineer,* May 6, 1908, p. 558.

	Years.	Straight line.	
Boilers	6-23		Average of 32 boilers, average life 15 years. J. W. Alvord, Am. W. W. Asso. 103.
		5-7	N. S. Hill, Eng. Rec. June 8, 1907.
	15		Prosser, Eng. News vol. XLVII. p. 425.
	20-30		W. Kiersted, Proc. Am. Soc. C. E. 1897.
	20		R. Hammond, Eng. Rec. June 15, 1907.
	10-12.5		Dawson in Iowa Eng. July 1906.
	14-15		Iowa Elec. Asso: in Iowa Eng. July 1906.
	25		B. Williams, Galena, Kans. appraisal in 1905.
	30	8	Chicago city railway: St. railway journal, Dec. 1898.
	14.3-25		William H. Bryan.
		2.5-4	W. H. Rosecrans—Galena, Kans. appraisal in 1905.
		6	B. S. Dodge: Mt. Vernon, Ill. appraisal in 1906.
	25		Chas. B. Burdick: Mt. Vernon, Ill., appraisal in 1906.

FIGURES from the Iola (Kansas) central station. *Electrical world,* Sept. 23, 1909, p. 725.

Boilers	10%

FLOY, HENRY. Depreciation. Floy, Henry, *Depreciation as related to electrical properties. American institute of electrical engineers, Proceedings,* 1911, p. 1267. Floy, Henry, *Valuation of public utility properties,* 1912, p. 168-217. Foster, Horatio R. *Engineering valuation of public utilities and factories,* 1913, p. 194-8. *Engineering & Contracting,* Oct. 4, 1911, p. 359-65. *Engineering magazine,* Aug. 1911, p. 837-40.

	Depreciation per cent per year. Straight line.		
Boilers	3½-4	Traction Val. Comm.	Chgo. Con. Tract. Co.
	10	B. J. Arnold	Coney Island & Brooklyn adopted by P. S. C., N. Y.
(water tube)	5	Henry Floy	3rd Ave., case adopted by P. S. C., N. Y.
(fire tube)	6⅔	Wis. P. S. C.	
(water tube)	5	Wis. P. S. C.	
(fire tube)	10	Arbitrators	Street lighting controversy, Atlanta, Ga., 1899.
	6⅔	St. Louis P. S. C.	Union Elec. L. & P. Co.

FOSTER, HORATIO A. Rates of depreciation. (In his *Engineering valuation of public utilities and factories.* 1913. p. 200, 205.

		Years' life.
Engines, boilers, heaters, conveyors, pumps and auxiliaries	4.5%	
Boilers, fire tube		10-15
" water tube		20-30

GARRY, H. STANLEY. Depreciation of plant and machinery. *Accountant,* June 23, Sept. 15, 1906, p. 785-9, 285-8.

GILLETTE, HALBERT P. and RICHARD T. DANA. Depreciation. (In their *Handbook of mechanical and electrical cost data.* 1918. p. 105).

Boilers

years	
10	B. J. Arnold—Appraisal of the Coney Island & Brooklyn railroad, Feb. 1, 1909.
10-28.6	Chicago traction commission.
11.75-15	W. D. Pence, Milwaukee 3c case.
12-16	Leonard Metcalf, Transactions, American society civil engineers, 1909, p. 24, v. 64.
13.3	Milwaukee electric railway and light co.
15-20	Union traction co., case Chicago and union traction co., Stone & Webster.
22.2	Marwick Mitchell & co., appraisal of a large street railway system, Foster, p. 199.
25-28.6	Traction valuation commission, Chicago consolidated traction co.
28.6	B. J. Arnold, Chicago appraisals 4 cases.
30-40	George W. Cravens, industrial power plants.
fire tube.	
10	Arbitrators, Street lighting controversy, Atlanta, Ga., 1899.
15	St. Louis Public service commission, Union electric light and power co.

DEPRECIATION, DEPLETION AND OBSOLESCENCE—Boilers—*(Continued)*

fire tube, electric light plants.
15-30 Wisconsin railroad commission.
fire tube, water works.
20-25 Wisconsin railroad commission.
water tube,
20 Henry Floy, 3rd Ave. case, New York city.
water tube, water works,
20 Wisconsin railroad commission.
Water tube, water works.
20-25 Wisconsin railroad commission.

Great Britain. Board of inland revenue. Depreciation rates: (In its *Income tax; statement respecting allowances for wear and tear and obsolescence of plant and machinery.* 1918. Cd. 9022, p. 4, Cd. 9134, p. 6). *American economic review,* Supplement, Dec. 1920, p. 51. *Journal of accountancy,* Sept. 1920, p. 194.
Engines, boilers and main shafting 5%
Written down value.

Greendlinger, Leo and John R. Loomis. Depreciation, machinery. (In their *Accounting problems.* 1910. v. 1. p. 204-5).
Boilers 10-15%

Greenland, S. W. Depreciation *Mississippi electric association,* Report of second annual convention, June 1910, p. 32-6.
Life
Boilers 12-20 years

Grunsky, Carl Ewald. Probable useful life of various articles. (In his *Valuation, depreciation and the rate base.* 1917. p. 274).
Boilers
10 years. Bion J. Arnold. Coney Island and Brooklyn figures adopted by Public service commission of New York. Four Chicago appraisals quoted by H. A. Foster.
15 years. Chicago union traction co. Quoted in Report Wisconsin railroad commission, vol. 10, p. 220.
15 years. John W. Alvord in Proceedings American waterworks association, 1903.
15 years. St. Louis public service commission case of Union electric light and power co.
12-16 years. Leonard Metcalf. Transactions American society of civil engineers, 1909.
16.7 years. B. L. Dodge. Mt. Vernon waterworks appraisal, Illinois, 1906.
15-20 years. Wisconsin railroad commission. Milwaukee 3c. fare case. Aug. 23, 1912.
20 years. Stone & Webster. Figures for Chicago union traction co. case. Report Wisconsin railroad commission, vol. 10, p. 220.
20 years. 0% residual value. Pacific gas and electric company. Figures used in rate hearings before Master in Chancery, San Francisco, 1913-4.
20 years. Robt. Hammond. Journal of Institute of electrical engineers, England, April 25, 1907.
10-28 years. Chicago traction commission. Quoted by G. W. Cravens, Electrical review, April 23, 1910.
25 years. Benezette Williams. Galena appraisal Kansas, 1905.
25 years. Charles B. Burdick. Appraisal of Mt. Vernon waterworks, Ill., 1906.
28.57 years. Bion J. Arnold. Coney Island and Brooklyn figures adopted by Public service commission of New York. Four Chicago appraisals quoted by H. A. Foster.
25-30 years. Traction valuation commission. Case of the Chicago consolidated traction co.
30 years. W. Kiersted. Galena, appraisal, Kansas, 1905.
25-40 years. W. H. Rosecrans. Galena appraisals Kansas, 1905.
water-tube 20 years. Floy. Trans. American institute of electrical engineers, June 1911. Third Ave. case figures adopted by Public service Commission of New York.
water-tube 20 years. Wisconsin railroad commission. Quoted by Floy and in published reports.
water-tube 25 years. 5% residual value. Sir Wm. Preece. Report of Bristol Corporation England, 1906.

DEPRECIATION, DEPLETION AND OBSOLESCENCE—BOILERS—*(Continued)*

water-tube	20-30 years. H. A. Foster. "Engineering valuation of public utilities and factories," Van Nostrand, 1912.
fire tube	10 years. Board of Arbitration in street lighting controversy at Atlanta, Georgia, 1899.
fire tube	10-15 years. H. A. Foster. "Engineering valuation of public utilities and factories," Van Nostrand, 1912.
fire tube electric light	16-30 years. Wisconsin railroad commission. Quoted by Henry Floy and in published reports.
fire tube water works	20-25 years. Wisconsin railroad commission. Quoted by Henry Floy and in published reports.
Lancashire	22 years. 3% residual value. Sir Wm. Preece. Report of Bristol corporation, England, 1906.
Boilers and accessories	20 years. San Joaquin Light & Power corporation. Rate hearing before California Railroad Commission. 1915.
Steel breechings	10 years. Bion J. Arnold. Coney Island and Brooklyn figures adopted by Public Service Commission of New York. Four Chicago appraisals quoted by H. A. Foster.
Breechings and connections	10-30 years. Traction valuation commission case of the Chicago consolidated traction co.

GUTHRIE, EDWIN. Depreciation. (In Lisle, George. *Encyclopaedia of accounting.* v. 2. p. 374).
Boilers • 7½-10%

HAMMOND, ROBERT S. Depreciation. *Institute of electrical engineers, Proceedings,* April 25, 1907. *Journal of the Institute of electrical engineers,* 1907, p. 270. Abstracts. *Accountant,* May 18, 1907, p. 675. *Electric railway review,* June 1, 1907, p. 716. *Electrical review* (Chicago), May 25, 1907. p. 828. *Electrical review* (London), May 3, 1907, p. 744. *Electrician,* April 26, 1907, p. 51. *Engineering magazine,* July 1907, p. 636-8. *Engineering record* June 15, 1907, p. 703. *Municipal journal* (London), May 10, 17, 1907, p. 411, 435. *Progressive age,* July 1, 1907, p. 305. *Street railway bulletin,* June 1907, p. 382. *Tramway and railway world,* June 6, 1907, p. 497.
Boilers 20%

HAZLEHURST, J. N. Final report of the committee on depreciation. *Journal of the American waterworks association,* March 1919, p. 85-135.
Boilers 15-30 years

HENDERSON, W. H. Auditing. *Canadian chartered accountant,* Oct. 1920, p. 107-9.
Boilers Varies from. 10 to 20 per cent

INSTALLATIONS, systems and appliances. *Electrical world,* Dec. 7, 1912, p. 1220.

	Hammond	Preece
Boilers	20 years	22-25 years

JENKINSON, MARK WEBSTER. Depreciation. *Accountant,* May 17, 1902, p. 528-34.
Boilers 10-12½%

JOHNSON, GEORGE. Depreciation. (In his *Electric lighting accounts.* 1903. p. 23-4).
Engines and boilers 7½-10%

KERR, WILLIAM HORACE and G. A. NAHSTOLL. Reserve for depreciation. (In their *Cooperative organization business methods.* 1915. p. 13-14).
Boilers 10%

KIMBALL, DEXTER S. Estimated life, and factors of depreciation. (In his *Cost finding.* 1918. p. 190. *Principles of industrial organization.* 1913. p. 163).

	Steam-boiler	Portable engines and boilers
Probable life of asset in years	15-30	10
Ratio of scrap to original value	0.10	0.05
Percentage on original cost	6-3	9.5
Percentage on diminishing value	14-7.5	26

LEAKE, P. D. Record of depreciation. (In his *Depreciation and wasting assets and their treatment in computing annual profit and loss.* 1917. p. 86).
Boilers 8-10%

LIFE data on power plant equipment used in valuation of Massachusetts property. *Electrical world,* Dec. 4, 1915, p. 1261.
Boilers
Water tube 25-30 yeras
Fire 20

LIFE of plant. *Electrician,* Nov. 8, 1912, p. 182-4.
Boilers 20 years R. Hammond
20-25 years Wm. Preece

McINTOSH, ROBERT J. Rates of depreciation. (In his *Reference book of accounts.* Ed. 2. p. 60).
Boilers 4-8%
Based on life.

MANN, JOHN and H. C. JUDD. Depreciation. (In his *Colliery accounts.* 1909. p. 69-75, 92).
Boilers 10-15%
Calculated on the balance as diminished from year to year.

MATHESON, EWING. Plant and machinery. (In his *Depreciation of factories, mines and industrial undertakings and their valuation.* 1893. p. 35-49).
Engines, boilers 7½%

METCALF, LEONARD. Depreciation in waterworks operation and accounting. *Journal of the New England waterworks association,* Dec. 1910, p. 442. Abstracts. *Engineering news,* Nov. 3, 1910, p. 482. Methods of computing depreciation of and reasonable assumptions as to period of useful life of waterworks. *Engineering and contracting,* Nov. 16, 1910, p. 434. Discussion.

DEPRECIATION, DEPLETION AND OBSOLESCENCE—Boilers—*(Continued)*

Methods of making computations for depreciation in public utility plants. *Engineering and contracting,* Dec. 28, 1910, p. 590.
Boilers 12-20 years 8⅓-5% straight line

Metcalf, Leonard. Waterworks valuation and fair rates, in the light of the Maine supreme court decisions in the Waterville and Brunswick cases. *American society of civil engineers, Papers and discussions,* 1908, p. 1101-73. *American society of civil engineers, Transactions,* Sept. 1909, p. 1. Foster, Horatio A. *Engineering valuation of public utilities and factories.* 1913. p. 207. Gillette, Halbert P. *Handbook of cost data for contractors and engineers,* p. 797.

	Useful life	Annual contribution to depreciation account or sinking fund in per cent of cost. At 5% annual rate sinking fund	General approximate results
Boilers	12-16 years	6.2825%-4.2270%	6-4%

Neale, R. E. Depreciation in engineering works. *Mechanical world,* Feb. 7, 1913, p. 67-8.

Old low-pressure boilers	3.5-4%	25-33 years
High-pressure water tube	5	20
High-pressure fire tube	7-10	10-14

Nicholson, J. Lee and John F. D. Rohrbach. Depreciation. (In their *Cost accounting.* 1919. p. 147).
Boilers 5%
Boilers including boiler house equipment such as economizers, feed water heaters, injectors, damper regulators, etc. (does not include feed water pumps) 5½%
Based on (1) the cost of equipment.
(2) the life of the equipment.
(3) on a ten hour day.

Pender, Harold. Depreciation. (In his *Handbook for electrical engineers.* c1914. p. 338).

Boilers, stationary years	
12-15	Engineer of valuation staff, of Wisconsin Railroad commission.
12-20	S. W. Greenland.
15	Chicago union traction co. J. W. Alvord.
20	R. Hammond, Stone & Webster for Chicago Union traction co.
25	W. Preece.
10-8%	P. Dawson.
8.85-6.66	Engineer of valuation staff of Wis. R. R. Comm.
8	Chicago city railways.
7.5	Milwaukee electric railway and light co.
6.66	Chicago union traction co.
5	Cardiff tramways.
	Glasgow tramways.
	Stone & Webster for the Chicago union traction co.

Philadelphia. Controller. Rates of depreciation. (In his *Manual of accounting, reporting and business procedure of the city and county of Philadelphia.* 1917. p. 204).
Steam boilers and generators 5%

Piez, Charles. Perpetual inventory and appraisal values; table of standard depreciation rates. *Engineering and contracting,* Jan. 24, 1917, p. 77. *Factory,* Dec. 1916, p. 668-71. *Iron age,* Nov. 30, 1916, Jan. 11, 1917, p. 1266, 138-9. *Iron trade review,* Feb. 22, 1917, p. 447-8. Condensed. *Journal of the American society of mechanical engineers,* Dec. 1916, p. 965-6. *Iron trade review,* Dec. 7, 1916, p. 1144-6. Kent, William, *Bookkeeping and cost accounting for factories,* 1918. p. 90. Discussion. *Journal of the American society of mechanical engineers,* March 1917, p. 215-7.

	% on cost	% on reducing balance
Boilers, pumps, feed-water heaters and air compressors.	6	15

Pixley, Francis W. Electric lighting companies. (In his *Accountancy.* Ed. 2. p. 218).
Engines and boilers 7½-12%

Porters, R. J. Rates of depreciation generally adopted. (In his *Pitman's dictionary of bookkeeping.* p. 344).
Boiler
High pressure 15%
Low pressure 10
Based on diminishing balances.

Probable lives of water-works elements. *Engineering news,* Oct. 11, 1917, p. 688.
Boilers 15-30 years

Proposed sale of Toronto utilities to the city. *Electrical world,* Oct. 25, 1913, p. 832.
Horizontal tubular boilers 8%
Water tube boilers 3.5

Prosser, R. W. Depreciation in gas plants. *American gas light journal,* May 26, 1902, p. 767.
Boilers 15 years
10% of first cost.

Racine, Samuel F. Machinery. (In his *Accounting principles.* 1917, p. 153).
Boilers 8-15 years.

Roby, J. J. Schedule of plant depreciation. (In his *Treatise on cost accounting as supplied to coal mining.* c1913. p. 14-5).
Boilers and settings
Deduct as salvage before depreciating 10%
Depreciation rate for remainder, fireproof 8

Runyon, F. V. Report on hydro-electric plant for special committee common council, Newark, New Jersey, April 23, 1902, p. 15, 16, 24.
Boilers and steam fitting 10%

Thompson, C. Bertrand. Interest and depreciation. (In his *How to find factory costs.* c1916. p. 64).
Steam engines and boilers are usually depreciated at 5-7½ per cent.

DEPRECIATION, DEPLETION AND OBSOLESCENCE—BOILERS—*(Continued)*

TIFFANY, H. S. Machinery. (In his *Digest of depreciations.* c1890. p. 12).
Boilers 10%

UNIFORM cost sheet for coal mining companies. *Coal age,* Sept. 19, 1918, p. 545-7.
Original cost
Boilers 11%

VALUATION of the Chicago consolidated traction property. *Electric railway journal,* Dec. 3, 1910, p. 1111-3.
Boilers and settings 3½-4%

WEBNER, FRANK E. Depreciation rate. (In his *Factory costs.* 1911. p. 178).
Stationary engine and boiler 7½ the first year and 7½ annually from the diminishing value or its equivalent.

WEEKS, H. E. Abstract of paper on depreciation read before annual meeting of Iowa street and interurban railway association, April 1910. *Electric railway journal,* April 30, 1910, p. 782-3.
Boilers 15 years.

WHATLEY, G. E. STUART. Depreciation. (In his *Accountant's and bookkeeper's vade-mecum.* 1893. p. 26).
Diminishing value
Boiler 10%

WILLIAMSON, J. GILMOUR. Depreciation of assets. (In his *Counting house and factory organisation.* p. 142).
Boilers 10%

WOLFF, MARK. Interpretation of water works accounts. *Journal of the American waterworks association,* June 1916, p. 543, 546.
Boilers, steam pipes, filters 20 years.

YEAMAN, C. H. Depreciation and reserves for antiquation and obsolescence from an engineering standpoint. *Electrical engineering* (London), July 12, 1907, p. 46. *Electrical review* (London), July 12, 1907, p. 44. *Electrician,* July 5, 1907, p. 475.
Boilers

20 years	R. Hammond
15	L. G. B. Local government board
20	L. C. C.
20	J. F. C. Snell (M. E. A. 1905)

Bolts and nuts

ELBOURNE, EDWARD T. Depreciation rates. (In his *Factory administration and accounts.* 1918. p. 377).

	Prov. dep. %	Remainder values	Years
		10%	5%
Bolt and nut machinery	7½	29	38

TIFFANY, H. S. Nut or bolt works. (In his *Digest of depreciations.* c1890. p. 10).
Buildings
Brick 3-3½%
Frame 4-4½%
Based upon actual life without any repairs.

Bonds

BAY state street railway valuation. *Electric railway journal,* Dec. 4, 1915, p. 1121-3.
Track bonding 2.6 annual depreciation per cent divided by investments

DAWSON, PHILIP. Depreciation. (In his *Engineering and electric traction pocket-book.* Ed. 2. p. 1151.
% capital cost.
Bonding 6-10

DEPRECIATION of overhead structures and substations. *Engineering and contracting,* Nov. 19, 1913, p. 567.
Track bonding 4%

FLOY, HENRY. Depreciation. Floy, Henry, *Depreciation as related to electrical properties. American institute of electrical engineers, Proceedings,* 1911, p. 1267. Floy, Henry, *Valuation of public utility properties,* 1912, p. 168-217. Foster, Horatio A. *Engineering valuation of public utilities and factories,* 1913, p. 194-8. *Engineering & Contracting,* Oct. 4, 1911, p. 359-65. *Engineering magazine,* Aug. 1911, p. 837-40.

Bonds	5	Traction val. comm.	Chicago con. tract. co.
	50		
	wearing value	Henry Floy	3rd Ave. case, adopted by P. S. C., N. Y.
	5	Wisc. P. S. C.	

GRAY, HENRY L. Necessity of depreciation reserves. *Railway age gazette,* May 27, 1910, p. 1297-8. Editorial. Depreciation reserves. *Railway age gazette,* May 27, 1910, p. 1290. Letters. Depreciation reserves. *Railway age gazette,* July 8, 1910, p. 66.
Annual dep.
Rail bonds 3%

GRUNSKY, CARL EWALD. Probable useful life of various articles. (In his *Valuation, depreciation and the rate base.* 1917. p. 274).
Bonds 20 years
Traction valuation commission. Case of the Chicago Consolidated traction co.
20 years.
Wisconsin railroad commission. Quoted by Henry Floy and in published reports.

MURRAY, ALEXANDER. Glasgow corporation accounts with special reference to depreciation and sinking funds. *Accountant,* June 13, 1903. p. 782-94. *Royal philosophical society of Glasgow, Proceedings,* 1903.
Bonding of rails 7½%

DEPRECIATION, DEPLETION AND OBSOLESCENCE—Bonds—*(Continued)*

Neale, R. E. Depreciation in engineering works. *Mechanical world,* Feb. 7, 1913, p. 67-8.
Bonds 5-7.5% 13-20 years
Pixley, Francis W. Tramways. (In his *Accountancy.* Ed. 2. p. 218-9).
Rail bonding 7½ to 10%

Bone milling

Australia. Federal income tax department. Depreciation allowance. *Accountant,* Oct. 13, 1917, p. 277-9. *Accounting and commerce,* June 30, 1917, p. 55-7. *Federal accountant,* July 1917, p. 93-8. *Public accountant,* Jan. 30, 1917, p. 145-52.
Bone milling
Steam vat 5%
Cage mills 7½
Bagging machine 5%
Written down value, repairs allowed in addition.

Bookcases

Philadelphia. Controller. Rates of depreciation. (In his *Manual of accounting, reporting and business procedure of the city and county of Philadelphia.* 1917. p. 207-8).
Bookcases 4%

Books

See also Libraries
Montgomery, Robert H. Depreciation, books. (In his *Income tax procedure,* 1919. p. 559. ——Same, 1920. p. 712).
Charge off the total year's purchases.
Tiffany, H. S. Books and stationery. (In his *Digest of depreciations.* c1890. p. 13).
Depreciate annually 20%
Tiffany, H. S. Household furniture. (In his *Digest of depreciations.* c1890. p. 15).

		Furnished houses
Books	10%	20%

Boosters

Elbourne, Edward T. Depreciation rates. (In his *Factory administration and accounts.* 1918. p. 376).

	Prov. dep. %	Years	
	Remainder values	10%	5%
Boosters	7½	29	38

Boring machines

Australia. Federal income tax department. Depreciation allowance. *Accountant,* Oct. 13, 1917, p. 277-9. *Accounting and commerce,* June 30, 1917, p. 55-7. *Federal accountant,* July 1917, p. 93-8. *Public accountant,* Jan. 30, 1917, p. 145-52.
Bores, windmills &c. 7½%
Based on written down value and repairs allowed in addition.
Elbourne, Edward T. Depreciation rates. (In his *Factory administration and accounts.* 1918. p. 377).

	Prov. dep. %	Years	
	Remainder values	10%	5%
Boring machines			
Horizontal	6	37	48
Portable	6	37	48
Boring and turning mills, vertical	6	37	48

Nicholson, J. Lee and J. F. D. Rohrbach. Depreciation. (In their *Cost accounting.* 1919. p. 150, 149).
Boring machines 6⅔%
Wood-boring machines 5%
Based on (1) the cost of equipment
(2) the life of the equipment
(3) on a ten-hour day.
Piez, Charles. Perpetual inventory and appraisal values; table of standard depreciation rates. *Engineering and contracting,* Jan. 24, 1917, p. 77. *Factory,* Dec. 1916, p. 668-71. *Iron age,* Nov. 30, 1916, Jan. 11, 1917, p. 1266, 138-9. *Iron trade review,* Feb. 22, 1917, p. 477-8. Condensed. *Journal of the American society of mechanical engineers,* Dec. 1916, p. 965-6. *Iron Trade review,* Dec. 7, 1916, p. 1144-6. Kent, William. *Bookkeeping and cost accounting for factories.* 1918. p. 90. Discussion. *Journal of the American society of mechanical engineers,* March 1917, p. 215-7.

	% on cost
Machine tool accessories—boring bars, drivers, key seating broaches, etc.	50

Bottles

See Depreciation, depletion and obsolescence—Containers.

Boxes, packing cases, etc.

See also Containers
Data on depreciation. *Barrel and box,* May 1917, p. 19.
A manufacturer of packing cases and box shooks in Massachusetts writes: Regarding this matter of depreciation, you will note that I have placed against the general items a percentage amount, whereas on the sub-items the percentage does not always agree with the general percentage. For instance, on sawmill and woodworking machinery, electrical plant, dynamos, motors, etc., there is a depreciation due to machines becoming obsolete and out of date, rather than due to the fact that they have become worn out, or, in other words, improvements have been made on machines which warrant their being discarded to a certain extent for others.

DEPRECIATION, DEPLETION AND OBSOLESCENCE—*(Continued)*

On buildings, a good brick mill construction type should not depreciate more than 2%, than on the galvanized sheds, if kept painted and in good condition, are considered 5% fair. This depreciation item, however, depends a great deal on the type of building as to the upkeep.

On live stock, it seems much better to revalue rather than to depreciate.

Rolling stock, should consider 15% fair.

On plant tools, also office supplies, books of accounts, etc., are generally considered by us as items of expense.

Regarding motor equipment, would say that we have never had any experience in this line, consequently our advice would not be of any practical value, although we have an idea that 25 to 30% would not be far off.

Finally, on office fixtures, typewriters, etc., 12 to 15% depreciation is fair.

An Illinois box manufacturer answered the questions item by item as shown in the succeeding schedule:

Machinery, 10%.—Engines, boilers saw mills and woodworking machinery; belting—shafting, electrical plant; dynamos—motors, etc., saws, knife cutters, etc.

Buildings, 5%.—Brick, galvanized iron storage yards.

Live Stock, 15%.—Horses, etc.

Rolling Stock, 20%.—Drays, carts, wagons, lorries, traps, harness, etc.

Plant, 10%.—Such as blacksmiths' tools and implements, stevedoring plant, etc.; motor cars, motor lorries, motor bicycles, etc.

Office Furniture, 10%.—Including typewriters and office system appliances.

Stationery.—Books of accounts, etc.

A box manufacturer in Wisconsin wrote that he checked off five per cent for depreciation on machinery, buildings and team accounts, and everything else is maintained at 100 per cent by repair expenses.

The proprietor of a box factory and planing mill in the state of New York comments in the following words upon the schedule: "The federal income tax in Australia has this question down to a finer point than we have, and we are glad to get such a schedule for comparison. We have arbitrarily depreciated machinery 10% per year; buildings which have to be maintained have not been depreciated; stationery, rolling stock and live stock, and plant equipment not of a permanent nature we have always charged to the proper department expense relying upon an appraisal for our permanent fixed values."

A manufacturer at Cleveland, Ohio, reported that he marked off straight ten per cent on all items for depreciation.

A Minnesota maker of packing boxes gave his practice in the following words: "Up to two years ago we never depreciated our stock and buildings yearly but carried an expense account which covered the upkeep of our machinery and buildings in first class repair, and whenever we sold a machine we stood the loss between the cost and what we sold it for. Two years ago the Lloyd-Thomas Co., of your city, appraised our plant and brought everything down to a sound valuation and their depreciations run from 10 to 50%. Of course this is over a period of years and was based on what they considered the goods worth at the time of appraisal."

A lumberman of Saginaw, Mich., after referring to the question of depreciation, continues in the following words: "The writer regrets that he is unable to give you any data on this matter. We have not had a regular standard percentage of depreciation in the past, and when deduction has been made it has been on straight percentage on the total investment. We regret that we cannot give you any figures which would be of any assistance to you in this matter."

A manufacturer of boxes and box shooks, and dealer in lumber in Virginia disposes of the matter of depreciation by saying that his company has no fixed rule covering the matter, but formerly, before the federal income tax was imposed, it was customary to work off from five to ten per cent for depreciation on machinery, according to the conditions of business.

A Pennsylvania manufacturer answered the questions item by item as follows: Machinery, 8%.—Engines, boilers, sawmill and woodworking machinery; belting—shafting, electrical plant; dynamos—motors, etc., saws, knife cutters, etc.

Buildings, 3%.—Brick, galvanized iron storage yards.

Live Stock, 15%.—Horses, etc.

Rolling Stock, 15%.—Drays, carts, wagons, lorries, traps, harness, etc.

Plant, 15%.—Such as blacksmiths' tools and implements, stevedoring plant, etc., motor cars, motor lorries, motor bicycles, etc.

Office Furniture, 10%.—Including typewriters and office system appliances. Stationery, 10%.—Books of account, etc.

Brackets

AUSTRALIA. FEDERAL INCOME TAX DEPARTMENT. Depreciation allowance. *Accountant,* Oct. 13, 1917, p. 277-9. *Accounting and commerce,* June 30, 1917, p. 55-7. *Federal accountant,* July 1917, p. 93-8. *Public accountant,* Jan. 30, 1917, p. 145-52.

Standards, brackets, posts—iron, wood or steel — 2½%

Written down value, repairs allowed.

Brakes

FLOY, HENRY. Depreciation. Floy, Henry, *Depreciation as related to electrical properties. American institute of electrical engineers, Proceedings,* 1911, p. 1267. Floy, Henry, *Valuation of public utility properties,* 1912, p. 168-217. Foster, Horatio R. *Engineering valuation of public utilities and factories,* 1913, p. 194-8. *Engineering & Contracting,* Oct. 4, 1911, p. 359-65. *Engineering magazine,* Aug. 1911, p. 837-40.

	Dep. Per cent per year. Straight line.	
Air brakes	5	Wis. R. R. C.

GILLETTE, HALBERT P. and RICHARD T. DANA. Depreciation. (In their *Handbook of mechanical and electrical cost data.* 1918. p. 105).

Brakes, air
20 years. — Wisconsin R. R. Commission

DEPRECIATION, DEPLETION AND OBSOLESCENCE—BRAKES—*(Continued)*

GRUNSKY, CARL EWALD. Probable useful life of various articles. (In his *Valuation, depreciation and the rate base.* 1917. p. 274).
Air brakes 20 years
Wisconsin railroad commission. Quoted by Floy and by Foster and in published reports.

NEALE, R. E. Depreciation in engineering works. *Mechanical world,* Feb. 7, 1913, p. 67-8.
Air brakes 5% 20 years

Brazing plant

ELBOURNE, EDWARD T. Depreciation rates. (In his *Factory administration and accounts.* 1918. p. 377).

	Prov. dep. % Remainder values	Years 10%	Years 5%
Brazing plant	15	14	18

Breeching and connections

ANALYSIS of the premises adopted and methods used in determining the cost to reproduce new together with the depreciation thereon of the physical property of the Metropolitan system and the Kansas city and Westport Belt railway of Kansas city, Mo. *Engineering and contracting,* May 28, 1913, p. 617-20.
Smoke breeching:
Steel smoke breeching 10%
Brick " " 5

FLOY, HENRY. Depreciation. Floy, Henry. *Depreciation as related to electrical properties. American institute of electrical engineers, Proceedings,* 1911, p. 1267. Floy, Henry, *Valuation of public utility properties,* 1912. p. 168-217. Foster, Horatio A. *Engineering valuation of public utilities and factories,* 1913, p. 194-8. *Engineering & Contracting,* Oct. 4, 1911, p. 359-65. *Engineering magazine,* Aug. 1911, p. 837-40.

	Depreciation per cent per year straight line	
Breeching and connections	3½-10	Traction val. comm. Chicago con. tract. co.

GILLETTE, HALBERT POWERS and RICHARD T. DANA. Depreciation. (In their *Handbook of mechanical and electrical cost data.* 1918. p. 106).
Breechings, steel
10 years B. J. Arnold, Chicago appraisals 4 cases
Breeching & connections
10-28.6 Traction Valuation commission, Chicago consolidated traction co.

PROPOSED sale of Toronto utilities to the city. *Eelctrical world,* Oct. 25, 1913, p. 832.
Steel smoke breeching 10%

VALUATION of the Chicago consolidated traction property. *Electric railway journal,* Dec. 3, 1910, p. 1111-3.
Breeching and connections 3½-10%

Breweries and distilleries

AUSTRALIA. *Federal income tax department.* Depreciation allowance. *Accountant,* Oct. 13, 1917, p. 277-9. *Accounting and commerce,* June 30, 1917, p. 55-7. *Federal accountant,* July 1917, p. 93-8. *Public accountant,* Jan. 30, 1917, p. 145-52.
Breweries
Casks 7½%
Crates 25
Ammonia pipes 10
General plant 5
Wine makers 5
Based on written down value and repairs allowed in addition.

BREWERIES. *American institute of accountants, Special bulletin No. 5, 6.* Sept. Nov. 1920. p. 7-8, 2,

HARRIS, WILLIAM. Depreciation. (In his *Brewers' accounts.* Ed. 2. p. 59, 70, 99).
Casks
(a) In some cases the stock of casks in the brewery and in customers' hands (after writing off all that are consideerd irrecoverable) at the balancing dates is valued at fixed prices, which are usually lower than the actual cost prices.
(b) Write off 10% from the value at the commencement of each year. This is better plan.
(c) Another method is to base the depreciation on the principle that every year's trade should bear the cost of a certain number of new casks, computed on the amount of the trade.
Average life of a cask is 10.31 years.
Horses—revalued at the end of each year and difference written off.
Drays, wagons, etc. The principle of yearly revaluations is frequently adopted, but an annual charge for fair wear and tear should always be insisted on.

LANHAM, HERBERT. Depreciation. In his *Brewers and bottlers' accounts.* p. 126-32).
Plant and machinery 7½-10%
Casks 7½-10
Bottles and stoppers 3% on sales
Horses 10-15
Vehicles and harness 7½

MONTGOMERY, HALFORD. Depreciation of buildings, machinery and plant, in reference to accounts and income tax. *Accountants' magazine,* June 1908, p. 330-1.

DEPRECIATION, DEPLETION AND OBSOLESCENCE—Breweries and Distilleries—*(Continued)*

DISTILLERIES AND BREWERIES.

Average Approx. Safe Life Years.	Sectional Classification.	Description.	Table 3. On original cost or value. Per annum. For Partnership, Flotation, Insurance or Book-keeping. Sectional Rates (per cent).	Table 3. All over Rate (per cent).	Table 4. On diminishing values. Per annum. For Partnership, Flotation, Insurance or Book-keeping. Sectional Rates (per cent).	Table 4. All over Rate (per cent).	Table 5. On diminishing values. Per annum. Maximum so far as can be ascertained. For Income-Tax. Sectional Rates (per cent).	Table 5. All over Rate (per cent).	Remarks.
Cols. 1 2			3 4	5 6	7 8	9 10	11	12	
60-50	Buildings.	I. Buildings—Substantial.	1¾ to 2	1¾ to 2	4⅜ to 5	4⅜ to 5	One-sixth of Government valuation allowed for repairs. No further depreciation allowed.		
50-35	Do.	II. Do. Ordinary do.	2 to 3	2 to 3	5 to 7⅜	5 to 7⅜			
25-10	Do.	III. Do. Wood, iron, &c.	4 to 10	4 to 10	9¾ to 22½	9¾ to 22½			
35-25	Motive power.	I. Steam-engines and boilers, turbines and water-wheels.	3 to 4		7⅜ to 9¾		5		
26-16	Do.	II. Gas or oil engines, electric motors, dynamos.	4 to 6½		9¾ to 15⅜		7½		
35-25	Transmission.	Shafting, gearing, pulleys.	3 to 4		7⅜ to 9¾		5		
27-20	Lighting.	Gas and electric light plant.	3¾ to 5		9⅛ to 12		5		
30-20	Piping.	Steam, gas, water, and air pipes, cocks, valves, &c.	3½ to 5		8½ to 12		5		
25-15	Process plant.	I. Grain cleaning, drying, and grinding plant, elevators, chutes, conveyors, metal vessels, including receivers, backs, mash tuns, pot and patent stills, cooling and refrigerating plants, pumps, yeast plants, malting drums and plant, laboratory plant, hoists, weighing and measuring machines, coopers' carters', and mechanics' fixed tools, trade and office furniture, fixtures, and fittings.	4 to 7	4 to 6	9¾ to 16⅜	9¾ to 14¼	5	5	
10-5	Do.	II. Wooden fixed vessels, receivers, backs, mash tuns, cooling and wash vats, yeast plant, &c.	10 to 20		22½ to 40		10 or B		B or charge renewals to Revenue, and value at 50, 66⅔ or 75 per cent of cost.
12-7	Accessory plant.	Casks, loose tools, and utensils.	8½ to 14		19½ to 30⅛		10 or B		Do. Do.
9-6	Belting & ropes.	Belting and driving ropes.	11 to 17		24½ to 35½		20 or B		Do. Do.
18-13	Haulage plant.	I. Motor engines and waggons, carts, vans, &c. trucks.	5½ to 7½		13⅛ to 17½		10		
14-10	Do.	II. Horses and harness.	7½ to 10		17½ to 22½		20 or B		Do. Do.

DEPRECIATION, DEPLETION AND OBSOLESCENCE — BREWERIES AND DISTILLERIES — *(Continued)*

THORNTON, FRANK W. Depreciation. (In his *Brewery accounts.* 1913. p. 16, 20, 39-43-51-2).

TIFFANY, H. S. Breweries. (In his *Digest of depreciations,* c1890. p. 8).

Building	
Brick or stone	2½-3%
Frame	3½-4

Based upon the actual life without any repairs.

WILKINSON, GEORGE. Depreciation of plant. *Accountant,* Aug. 31, 1901, p. 953-4.

Boilers, furnaces, engines and refrigerating machines, vats, hogsheads, etc.	5%
Beer-kegs	5-15

Brickmaking

TIFFANY, H. S. Fire brick works. (In his *Digest of depreciations.* c1890. p. 9).

Brick or stone	3½%
Frame	5

Based upon the actual life of the building without any repairs.

Bridges

BAGG, F. A. Life of railway physical property from engineering standpoint. *Electric railway journal,* Dec. 9, 1911, p. 1205-6.

	Life, years
Wooden bridges	20
Steel bridges	30 and over
Ashlar concrete bridge masonry	100 and over

BARKER, HARRY. Typical life expectation tables for public utility property. In his *Public utility rates.* 1917. p. 366).

Bridges, steel	20-50 years
wood	10

Author—average or approximate figure secured by examination or enquiry.

BAY state rate case. *Electric railway journal,* Dec. 4, 1915, p. 1121-3. *Public utility reports, annotated,* 1916F, p. 336-9.

Steel bridges over railroads	25 years
Steel bridges over streams	20
Timber bridges over railroads	15
Timber bridges over streams	30

BREWER, ALLAN F. Rates for annual depreciation. *Industrial management,* April 1918, p. 268.

	Years	
Trestles, coal (steel and concrete)	100	1%
Trestles, coal (wood)	75	1.33

BRYAN, WILLIAM. Appraisal and depreciation of waterworks and similar properties. *Journal of the Association of engineering societies,* Dec. 1907, p. 336-81. Depreciation allowance for various public service industries. *Engineering news,* Jan. 23, 1908, p. 96.

	% straight
Bridges	
Iron	5
Masonry	1
Trestle	15-20

DEPRECIATION of overhead structures and substations. *Engineering and contracting,* Nov. 19, 1913, p. 567.

Steel bridges	3%

FOSTER, HORATIO A. Rates of depreciation. (In his *Engineering valuation of public utilities and factories.* 1913. p. 200, 206).

Bridges	2.5%

Marwick, Mitchell & co. in the appraisal of a large street railway system.

	Years' Life
Railway spans and bracket equipment	15-20

GILLETTE, HALBERT POWERS. Railway. (In his *Handbook of cost data for contractors and engineers.* 1910. p. 1317-8).

Howe truss bridges.	5.0 age years
	10.0 annual depreciation per cent.
	50.0 percent condition per cent

GILLETTE, HALBERT POWERS and RICHARD T. DANA. Depreciation. (*In their Handbook of mechanical and electrical cost data.* 1918. p. 105-6).

Bridges	40 years	Marwick, Mitchell & co., appraisal of a large street railway system, Foster, p. 199.
Bridges, Howe truss	16.7 years	H. P. Gillette, Washington Ry. appraisal.

GRAY, HENRY L. Necessity of depreciation reserves. *Railway age gazette,* May 27, 1910, p. 1297-8. Editorial. Depreciation reserves. *Railway age gazette* May 27, 1910, p. 1290. Letters. Depreciation reserves. *Railway age gazette,* July 8, 1910, p. 66.

	Annual dep.
Bridges	
Combination	6%
Howe truss	9
Pile and frame	10

GRUNSKY, CARL EWALD. Probable useful life of various articles. (In his *Valuation, depreciation and the rate base.* 1917. p. 274).

Howe truss R. R.	10 years. H. P. Gillette. Appraisal of Great Northern & Northern Pacific R. R.'s in Washington. Direction of Washington Railroad commission, 1906.
Trestles and wooden bridges.	10 years. California railroad commission—reports 1913-4. Stockton Terminal & Eastern R. R. April 1913.

DEPRECIATION, DEPLETION AND OBSOLESCENCE—BRIDGES—*(Continued)*

NICHOLSON, J. LEE and J. F. D. ROHROCH. Depreciation. (In their *Cost accounting.* 1919. p. 147, 150).
Trestles (not including rails or ties)
Steel 3⅓%
Wood 6⅔
Based on (1) the cost of equipment
(2) the life of the equipment
(3) on a ten-hour day.
Steel work—foot bridges 4%

PHILADELPHIA. CONTROLLER. Rates of depreciation. (In his *Manual of accounting, reporting and business procedure of the city and county of Philadelphia.* 1917. p. 210).
Bridges 1%

PUBLIC utility reports, annotated. Rochester, Lawyers co-operative publishing co. 1915E. p. 602).
Gates v. Bridgeport Toll Bridge Co. (Wis.). An annual allowance of $1,050 for depreciation was made in the case of a toll bridge property, the composite life of which was estimated at twenty-five years, and the present value of which was fixed at $23,831, and this allowance was held to be conservative when consideration was given to the fact that contingencies and losses due to extraordinary causes might occur at any time.

STATISTICS as to the life of steel railway bridges. *Engineering and contracting,* Oct. 7, 1908, p. 227.

Item No.	Name of R. R.	Location of Bridge	When Built	Life years
1	C. M. & St. P.	Rock River	1884	19
2	Wabash	Sangamon River	1885	21
3	C. B. & Q.	Big Rock Creek	1881	22
4	Ill. Cent.	Big Muddy River	1889	13
5	Ill. Cent.	Tennessee River	1888	17
6	C. & N. W.	Kinnikinnic River	1880	19
8	Grand Trunk	Niagara River	1877	19
9	C. R. R. and St. P.	Menominee River	1886	17
10	C. R. R. of N. J.	Newark Bay	1887	17
Average of the above			18.1 years	

TIFFANY, H. S. Frame bridges. (In his *Digest of depreciations.* c1890. p. 8).
Annually 10%

Broaching machines

ELBOURNE, EDWARD T. Depreciation rates. (In his *Factory administration and accounts.* 1918. p. 377)

	Prov. dep. %	Years	
	Remainder values	10%	5%
Broaching machines	6%	37	48

Broaches

PIEZ, CHARLES. Perpetual inventory and appraisal values; table of standard depreciation rates. *Engineering and contracting,* Jan. 24, 1917, p. 77. *Factory,* Dec. 1916, p. 668-71. *Iron age,* Nov. 30, 1916, Jan. 11, 1917, p. 1266, 138-9. *Iron trade review,* Feb. 22, 1917, p. 477-8. Condensed. *Journal of the American society of mechanical engineers,* Dec. 1916, p. 965-6. *Iron trade review,* Dec. 7, 1916, p. 1144-6. Kent, William. *Bookkeeping and cost accounting for factories.* 1918, p. 90. Discussion. *Journal of the American society of mechanical engineers,* March, 1917, p. 215-7.
% on cost
Machine tool accessories—
boring bars, drivers, key seating broaches, etc. 50

Buffing machines

NICHOLSON, J. LEE and JOHN F. D. ROHRBACH. Depreciation. (In their *Cost accounting.* 1919. p. 149).
Buffing machines 6⅔%

Building

See Depreciation, depletion and obsolescence—Contractors.

Buildings

See also Depreciation, depletion and obsolescence—Apartment houses; Barns; Court houses; Dwellings; Portable houses; Office buildings; Prisons; Tenements; Also name of industry, business or trade, under Depreciation, depletion and obsolescence.

BARKER, HARRY. Typical life expectation tables for public utility property. (In his *Public utility rates.* 1917. p. 368-9).

Buildings	Years	
Masonry	75	Wis. R. R. Comm.
Wood—frame or second class	50	Wis. R. R. Comm.

BASSET, WILLIAM R. Charging off depreciation on the right basis. (In his *Accounting as an aid to business profits.* c1918. p. 198). Basset, William R. *How to find what your factory is worth. Factory,* May 1918, p. 850-1.
Mill construction brick bearing walls, wood floors and roof construction 40 years
2. Steel cage, brick curtain walls, reinforced concrete floors: 30 years
3. Brick-bearing walls, steel beams for floors and roofs, timber flooring and roofing: 25 years
4. Reinforced concrete throughout: at least 40 years, and probably more.
5. All timber: 25 years
6. One-story structure, steel or wood frame, galvanized covering: 5 to 10 years
Estimate 2%

BELT, ROBERT E. Depreciation. (In his *Foundry cost accounting practice and procedure.* 1919, p. 241).

DEPRECIATION, DEPLETION AND OBSOLESCENCE—Bridges—*(Continued)*

Buildings:	
Concrete	2½%
Brick—steel frame	3
Brick—wood frame	3½
Sheet iron—steel frame	5
Wood	7½

Belt, Robert E. Depreciation. (In his *Uniform cost accounting methods; adopted by the American malleable castings association,* Nov. 14, 1917. p. 20-1).

Buildings	
Concrete	2½%
Brick	3
Sheet iron	10

Bemis, Edward W. Report on the investigation of the Chicago telephone company submitted to the Committee on gas, oil and electric light. Chicago, October 25, 1912. 127p.

Buildings

Byllesby and Arnold	Years	Salvage	Dep. % of cost
B. Due to age and wear and tear only	60-100	0	1-2
A. Due to all forms of depreciation	30- 60	0	1.5-2
Chicago commission	40	0	1.33
Westinghouse, Church, Kerr & co.	50	0	2.0
E. L. Cline, Telephony, July 2, 1910	50	0	2

Bentley, Harry C. Depreciation. (In his *Science of accounts.* 1913. p. 146).

Building	
Brick and reinforced concrete	2½%
Frame	4

Bogle, J. D. S. Writing off of depreciation on the wasting assets of a joint stock company. *Accountant,* Dec. 21, 1889, p. 691-6.

Bolton, Reginald Pelham. Depreciation of the value of buildings. (In his *Building for profit.* 1911. p. 50-78).

Classification of depreciation deduced from R. M. Hurd's assignments of life.

Construction	Occupancy	Term of Life in years	Rate of fund Proposed in %	Term of Sinking fund @ 3%. in years
Cheap frame	Tenements	10-15	10-5	9-16
Cheap frame	Residences	25-30	3-2	23-31
Better-class frame	Residences	50-75	2-1	31-47
Cheap brick	Tenements	25-30	3-2	23-31
Cheap brick	Residences	35-50	2-1	31-47
Cheap brick	Office buildings	25-30	3-2	23-31
Better-class brick	Residences	50-75	1½-1	37-47
Good brick or stone	Office buildings	75-100	1	47

Note: Sinking-funds bring all the above within 47 years.

RELATIVE LIFE OF THE COMPONENT PARTS OF BUILDINGS

1. Good Frame Construction

Life of most durable part=45-55 or 100%

Years	Materials	Relative to 45 ys. Percent	Relative to 55 ys. Percent	Years	Materials	Relative to 45 ys. Percent	Relative to 55 ys. Percent
45-55	Masonry	100	100	25	Floors and stairs	55	45
45	Exterior brickwork	100	82	30	Hard-wood trim	66	54
44	Brick flues	99	80	33	Plastering	73	60
41	Lumber framing	90	75	20	Hardware	44	36
39	Studding	86	70	30	Tinwork	66	54
33	Mill-work	73	60	20	Exterior ironwork	44	36
33	Sheathing	73	60	9	Decoration and varnish	20	17
27	Exterior ironwork	60	49	6	Exterior paint	13	11
13	Shingles	30	24	18	Fixtures	40	34
	II. Brick and Stone Construction						
	Life of most durable=55-56 years or 100%						
55-66	Most durable part	100	100	27	Flooring and stairs	49	41
53	Exterior brick	96	80	35	Trim	63	53
53	Brick flues	96	80	33	Plastering	60	50
50	Lumber	90	76	20	Hardware	36	30
40	Studding	72	61	30	Ornamental ironwork	54	45
33	Mill-work	60	50	20	Exterior ironwork	36	30
27	Exterior woodwork	49	41	6	Exterior paint	11	9
27	Roofing-slag	49	41	10	Decoration and varnish	18	15
33	Roofing-tile	60	50	20	Fixtures	36	30

LIFE OF THE MOST DURABLE PART

In the cheapest frame construction	40 to 50 years
In good frame construction	45 to 55 years
In brick-stone-wood construction	55 to 66 years
In steel-brick-terra-cotta or stone compound constructions—	66 to 75 years
In reinforced concrete	75 to 90 years
In most massive forms of a single material	90 to 100 years

See also Burton, H. J. comp. valuations and depreciations of city buildings. 1917. p. 20-2.

DEPRECIATION, DEPLETION AND OBSOLESCENCE—Buildings—*(Continued)*

III. Modern Fireproof Construction

Life of most durable part=66-75 years or 100%

Years	Materials	Relative to 66 ys. (Percent)	Relative to 75 ys. (Percent)	Years	Materials	Relative to 66 ys. (Percent)	Relative to 75 ys. (Percent)
66-75	Most durable part	100	100	50	Interior ironwork	76	66
45	Exterior cut stone	68	60	22	Exterior ironwork	33	29
60	Exterior brick	91	80	45	Window mill-work	68	60
60	Exterior terra-cotta	91	80	40	Hard-wood trim	61	53
66	Interior masonry	100	88	9	Glass	14	12
40	Interior cut stones	61	53	9	Interior decoration	14	12
36	Interior marbles	54	48	20	Exterior woodwork	30	26
36	Plastering, plain	54	48	25	Hardware	37	33
30	Plastering, decorative	45	40	20	Sidewalks	30	26
27	Stone flooring	41	36	24	Roof-houses	36	32
24	Wood flooring	36	32	27	Tanks	41	36
30	Stairs and steps	45	40	20	Plumbing fixtures	30	26
27	Roofing-slag	41	36	20	Lighting fixtures	30	26
40	Roofing-tile	61	53	33	Piping	50	44
46	Partition	70	61	20	Elevator	30	26
46	Joinery	70	61	7	Paint	10	9

ECONOMIC EXISTENCE OF BUILDINGS

Type of building	Life in years
"Taxpayer"	12-15
Hotels	15-18
Apartment-houses	18-21
Store buildings	21-25
Tenements and flats	25-27
Office and business buildings	27-33
Lofts and factories	33-37
Residences	37-44
Banks and institutions	44-50

Bowder, J. Horace and Fred F. Tait. Adequate depreciation of capital expenditure by municipal electricity undertakings. *Electrical review* (London), June 21, 1907, p. 1021.

Building permanent	60 years
Building temporary	20

Bryan, William. Appraisal and depreciation of waterworks and similar properties. *Journal of the association of engineering societies,* Dec. 1907, p. 336-81. Depreciation allowance for various public service industries. *Engineering news,* Jan. 23, 1908, p. 96. Depreciation of electric light plans. *Municipality,* March 1908, p. 74.

Material	Life in years.	Depre. % per year Straight	Authority
Buildings Brick		2	Iowa Electrical Association, in Iowa Engineer, July 1906.
"		2	N. S. Hill, Engineering record, June 8, 1901.
"	40		Prosser in Engineering news vol. XLVII. p. 425.
"	25-40		The author.
"		7	W. H. Rosecrans, Galena, Kan., appraisal, 1905.
"	60		Robt. Hammond: Engineering Record, June 15, 1907.
"	50-100		Dawson's "Engineering and Electric traction pocket book in Iowa Engineer, July 1906.
"	25-33-50		Iowa Electrical association, in Iowa Engineer, July 1906.
"	30		Benezette Williams: Galena, Kan., appraisal 1905.
"	30		W. Kiersted, Galena, Kan., appraisal, 1905.
"		5	Chicago City Railway, Street railway journal, Dec. 1898.
"		3.5	B. L. Dodge, Oak Park, Ill.
"	35		Chas. B. Burdick, Chicago: Ap praisal Mt. Vernon, Ill., Water works, 1906.
Wooden		5	N. S. Hill. Engineering record, June 8, 1901.
"		4	W. H. Rosecrans, Galena, Kan., appraisal, 1905.
"	15-30		The author.

Burton, H. J. comp. Valuations and depreciations of city buildings; extracts from opinions of leading authorities Hurd, Evers, Zangerle, Bernard, Bolton, Reed, Montgomery, Saliers, Kester, Holmes, Grunsky, Leake; from "convention proceedings," tenth annual convention at Omaha, September 10, 11, 12, and 13, 1917. 127p. Letter from Henry E. Reed, p. 12-13.

The basis of the system of depreciation herein set forth is that if a building is habitable, it is worth 20 per cent of its cost. The remaining 80 per cent is depreciated at different periods, varying from 35 years in the case of steel skeleton structures to 15 years in the case of poor frames.

DEPRECIATION, DEPLETION AND OBSOLESCENCE—BUILDINGS—*(Continued)*

STRUCTURAL AND ECONOMIC DEPRECIATION.

Years	Steel	Concrete Good	Concrete Fair	Brick Good	Brick Fair	Frame Good	Brick Poor	Frame Fair	Frame Poor
1	3	3	3.5	3.5	4	4	5	5	5.5
2	6	6	7	7	8	8	10	10	11
3	9	9	10.5	10.5	12	12	15	15	16.5
4	12	12	14	14	16	16	20	20	22
5	15	15	17.5	17.5	20	20	25	25	27.5
6	18	18	21	21	24	24	30	30	33
7	21	21	24.5	24.5	28	28	35	35	38.5
8	24	24	28	28	32	32	40	40	44
9	27	27	31.5	31.5	36	36	45	45	49.5
10	30	30	35	35	40	40	50	50	55
11	32	32	38	38	43	43	54	54	60
12	34	34	41	41	46	46	58	58	65
13	36	36	44	44	49	49	62	62	70
14	38	38	47	47	52	52	66	66	75
15	40	40	50	50	55	55	70	70	80
16	42	42	52	52	58	58	72	72	..
17	44	44	54	54	61	61	74	74	..
18	46	46	56	56	64	64	76	76	..
19	48	48	58	58	67	67	78	78	..
20	50	50	60	60	70	70	80	80	..
21	52	52	62	62	72	72	..	..	..
22	54	54	64	64	74	74	..	..	..
23	56	56	66	66	76	76	..	..	..
24	58	58	68	68	80	80	..	..	..
25	60	60	70	70	78	70	..	..	..
26	62	62	72	72	..	..	..	..	..
27	64	64	74	74	..	..	..	..	..
28	66	66	76	76	..	..	..	..	..
29	68	68	78	78	..	..	..	..	..
30	70	70	80	80	..	..	..	..	..
31	72	72	..	..	..	..	..	..	..
32	74	74	..	..	..	..	..	..	..
33	76	76	..	..	..	..	..	..	..
34	78	78	..	..	..	..	..	..	..
35	80	80	..	..	..	..	..	..	..
Av.	2.28½	2.28½	2.67	2.67	3.2	3.2	4.	4.	5.33

BURTON, H. J. Valuations and depreciations of city buildings. *Building and building management,* Oct. 6, Nov. 3, 1919, p. 30, 31.

CARTER, R. N. Rates of depreciation. (In his *Advanced accounts.* p. 618).
Freehold land and buildings 2½-5%
Based on diminishing balances, normal conditions and hours of working.

CONSOLIDATION of electricity supply in London. *Electrical world,* Sept. 19, 1908, p. 611.
Buildings 60 years

COST and depreciation of steam and hydro-electric installations. *Electrical world,* Dec. 30, 1909, p. 1558.
Buildings 25 years
.67% of total cost

CRAVENS, GEORGE M. Depreciation and maintenance of electrical equipment. *Electrical review,* April 23, 1910, p. 853-6. *Foster, H. A. Engineering valuation of public utilities and factories,* 1913, p. 201-2.

Building	
2%	Chicago Union Traction co.
3	Milwaukee electric railway and light co.
2	Wisconsin railroad commission
2.5	Average English
2.5	Average Scotch practice
1-2	Philip Dawson
2	Stone & Webster
1-2	Industrial power plants
2	Professor G. F. Gebhart
2	Miscellaneous sources

DENHAM, ROBERT S. Depreciation. (In his *Manual of cost engineering and estimating for paper box manufactures.* 1917. p. 249).

Buildings	Original cost
Brick	2%
Frame	3

DENSHAM, F. W. Depreciation of assets and goodwill of limited companies. *Accountant,* May 28, 1898, p. 568.
Freehold buildings
1-5% per annum

DEPRECIATION AND INCOME TAX. *Accounting and commerce,* Nov. 1917, p. 185-6.
Premises (not including land).
Wooden 4% on original cost
Brick or stone 2½% on original cost

DEPRECIATION of buildings in relation to the income tax law. *National real estate journal,* Oct. 15, 1914, p. 309-14.

DEPRECIATION, DEPLETION AND OBSOLESCENCE—BUILDINGS—*(Continued)*

DICKSEE, LAWRENCE R. Buildings. (In his *Auditing. Authorized American edition.* 1909. p. 190).
If the instalment plan, 1¼-3 (or even 5) per cent of the original amount may be deducted annually; if the annuity method be used a fixed sum debited to revenue, which, after crediting interest, will write the asset down to zero in from, say, fifty to one hundred and fifty years.

DICKSEE, LAWRENCE R. Depreciation, freeholds. (In his *Depreciation reserves and reserve funds.* 1912. p. 13-17).

DONALDSON, H. F. DEPRECIATION of buildings and machinery. *Engineering magazine,* April 1911, p. 171-6. *Engineering record,* Feb. 11, 1911, p. 159. *Mechanical engineer,* Feb. 10. 1911. p. 177-80. 202-4.

DURATION of life of flooring materials. *Real estate magazine,* May 1914.

Life Table

Marble	100
Tile	100
Paving brick	100
Mosaic	100
Slate	99
Limestone	98
Terrazzo	95
Portland concrete cement	90
Composition flooring	70
Face brick	70
Common brick	60
Cork	50
Maple	50
Oak	50
White pine	45
Yellow pine	40
Linoleum	5
Asphalt	5
Rubber	0

EDWARDS, C. LEWIS. Electric lighting accounts. *Incorporated accountants' journal,* April 1912, p. 175.

Buildings	1½-2%

ELBOURNE, EDWARD T. Depreciation rates. (In his *Factory administration and accounts.* 1918. p. 376-7.

	Prov. dep. % Remainder values	Years 10%	5%
Buildings—substantial brick, reinforced concrete, and steel framed			
When used for ordinary trades e.g. machine shops	2½	91	118
When used for destructive trades, e.g. Smithy	4	56	73
Buildings, Iron, substantial ordinary trades	4	56	73
Destructive trades	7½	29	38
Buildings, Iron, Light	10	22	28
Partitioning, metal	6	37	48
wood	10	22	28
Floor plates	6	37	48

ENNIS, WILLIAM DUANE. Depreciation. (In his *Work management.* 1911. p. 87).

Buildings	
Frame	20 years
Brick	33⅓

ERRONEOUS data on the lives of buildings. *Engineering and contracting,* April 19, 1916, p. 360-1.
"The alleged average lives of buildings published in books and articles are not natural lives, but functional lives. As no explanation accompanies tables of lives of buildings it is commonly but erroneously assumed, that the tables give natural lives."

Table 1. Mean life of buildings—Brick apartment.

Materials	Life relative to 75 yr., percent	Cost relative to total cost of building	Cost of items
Foundations	100	11	$1,100
Masonry	100	16	1,600
Steel	100	11	1,100
Lumber	50	20½	1,025
Ornamental iron	50	2½	125
Plaster	50	10	500
Partitions	50	2	100
Electric wiring	33	3	100
Painting	10	3	30
Plumbing	33	12	400
Heating	33	4	132
Marble and tile	25	5	125
		100	$6,337

$$\frac{6337}{100} = 63.37 \text{ per cent of 75 yr., or a mean life of } 47\tfrac{1}{2} \text{ yr.}$$

DEPRECIATION, DEPLETION AND OBSOLESCENCE—BUILDINGS—*(Continued)*

Table II. gives the estimated natural life of various types of buildings

Class A, fireproof	Years
Good	90
Medium	82.5
Poor	75

ESTIMATED life and depreciation of water works plants. *Municipal journal and engineer*, May 6, 1908, p. 558.

Material	Life in years	Depre. % per year Straight	Authority
Brick		2	Iowa Elec. Asso.; in Iowa Eng., July 1906.
"		2	N. S. Hill, Eng. Rec., June 8, 1901.
"	40		Prosser, Eng. News, Vol. XLVII, p. 425.
"	25-40		William H. Bryan
"		7	W. H. Rosecrans; Galena, Kan., appraisal in 1905.
"	60		R. Hammond; Eng. Rec. June 15, 1907.
"	50-100		Dawson, Iowa Eng. July 1906.
"	25-33-50		Iowa Elec. Asso. Iowa Eng. July 1906.
"	30		B. Williams; Galena, Kan. appraisal in 1905.
"	30		W. Kiersted. Street railway journal, Dec. 1898.
"		5	Chicago City Railway
"		3.5	B. L. Dodge; Mt. Vernon, Ill., appraisal in 1906.
"	35		C. B. Burdick; Mt. Vernon, Ill. appraisal in 1906.
Wooden		5	N. S. Hill,; Eng. Rec. June 8, 1901.
"		4	W. H. Rosecrans; Galena, Kan., app. in 1905.
"	15-30		W. H. Bryan

FICKER, NICHOLAS T. Depreciation. (In his *Shop expense analysis and control*. 1917. p. 84).

	Factories
Buildings	
Modern fireproof steel and tile	3%
Mill construction	7
Steel construction (only partly fireproof)	6
Wooden buildings (or poor construction)	12
Permanent fixtures	
Pertaining to bldgs.	12
Pertaining to power and lighting plants	12
Pertaining to material	12

FIGURES from the Iola (Kans.) central station. *Electrical world*, Sept. 23, 1909, p. 723.
Buildings 5%

FLOY, HENRY. Depreciation. Floy, Henry, *Depreciation as related to electrical properties. American institute of electrical engineers, Proceedings*, 1911, p. 1267. Floy, Henry, *Valuation of public utility properties*, 1912, p. 168-217. Foster, Horatio A. *Engineering valuation of public utilities and factories*, 1913, p. 194-8. *Engineering & Contracting*, Oct. 4, 1911, p. 359-65. *Engineering magazine*, Aug. 1911, p. 837-40.

Buildings	Dep. p. c. per year Straight line		
(Brick)	1½	Traction Val. Comm	
	2	E. G. Connette	Chicago con. tract. co. 3rd Ave. case, adopted by P. S. C., N. Y.
	2-4	Wisc. P. S. C.	Street lighting controversy, Atlanta, Ga., 1899.
(Wood)	2	Arbitrators	
	2	St. Louis P. S. C.	Union elec. L. & P. co.

FOSTER, HORATIO A. Rates of depreciation. (In his *Engineering valuation of public utilities and factories*. 1913. p. 199, 203, 204, 205).

Buildings 2.5%

Marwick, Mitchell & co. in the appraisal of a large street railway system.

Buildings	Years
Fireproof	25-50
Mill construction	25
Second class shops, car barns and power stations	50

Wisconsin commissions

U. S. government allowance for depreciation	% per annum
Brick, occupied by owner	1-1¼
" " " tenant	1¼-1½
Frame, " " owner	2-2½
" " " tenant	2½-3

GILLETTE, HALBERT POWERS and RICHARD DANA. Depreciation. (In their *Handbook of mechanical and electrical cost data*. 1918. p. 106, 171).

Buildings	
33.3 years	Milwaukee electric railway and light co.
40	Marwick, Mitchell & co., appraisal of a large street railway system, Foster, p. 199.
50-100	George W. Cravens. Industrial power plants.
Buildings, brick	
25-50 years	Wisconsin railroad commission.

DEPRECIATION, DEPLETION AND OBSOLESCENCE—BUILDINGS—*(Continued)*

66.6	Traction valuation commission. Chicago consolidated traction co.
Buildings, frame	
20-50 years	Leonard Metcalf, Transactions American society civil engineers, 1909. p. 24. Vol. XLIV.
50 years	Arbitrators, Street lighting controversy, Atlanta, Ga. 1899.
Buildings, masonry	
40-50 years	Leonard Metcalf; Transactions American society civil engineers, 1909. p. 24, vol. 64.
Buildings, misc.	
33.3 years	H. P. Gillette, Everett railway and water co., Jan. 29, 1912.
	H. P. Gillette, Washington railway appraisal.
wood	1½%
reinforced concrete	½

GRAY, HENRY L. Necessity of depreciation reserves. *Railway age gazette,* May 27, 1910, p. 1297-8. Editorial. Depreciation reserves. *Railway age gazette,* May 27, 1910, p. 1290. Letters. Depreciation reserves. *Railway age gazette,* July 8, 1910, p. 66.

Buildings	Annual dep.
Brick	2%
Frame	3

GREENDLINGER, LEO and JOHN R. LOOMIS. Depreciation, buildings. (In their *Accounting problems.* 1910. v.1. p. 204-5).

Buildings	2-5%

GREENLAND, S. W. Depreciation. *Mississippi electric association, Report of second annual convention,* June 1910, p. 32-6).

	Life
Buildings, Brick	50 years

GRUNSKY, CARL EWAL4. Probable useful life of various articles. (In his *Valuation, depreciation and the rate base.* 1917. p. 274, 275-6).

Buildings	25-50 years Wisconsin railroad commission. Quoted by Henry Floy and in published reports.
	50 years St. Louis public service commission. Case of Union electric light and power co.
	50 years E. G. Connette. 3rd Ave. case figures adopted by Public service commission of New York.
wooden, wood frame	20 years Pacific gas and electric company. Figures used in rate hearings before Master in Chancery, San Francisco, 1913-4.
wooden	25 years W. H. Rosecrans. Galena appraisals, Kansas, 1905.
wooden frame	50 years Board of arbitration in street lighting controversy, Atlanta, Georgia, 1899.
corrugated iron	20 years Pacific gas & electric company. Figures used in rate hearings before Master in Chancery, San Francisco, 1913-4. Wooden frame and floor.
corrugated iron	25 years Pacific gas & electric company. Figures used in rate hearings before Master in Chancery, San Francisco, 1913-4. Wooden frame conc. floor.
corrugated iron	30 years Pacific gas & electric company. Figures used in rate hearings before Master in Chancery, San Francisco, 1913-4. Steel frame, wood floor.
corrugated iron	36 years Pacific gas & electric company. Figures used in rate hearings before Master in Chancery, San Francisco, 1913-4. Steel frame, concrete floor.
brick	14 years W. H. Rosecrans. Galena appraisals, Kansas, 1905.
brick	30 years Benezette Williams. Galena appraisal, Kansas, 1905.
brick	30 years W. Kiersted. Galena appraisal, Kansas, 1905.
brick	30 years B. L. Dodge. Mt Vernon water works appraisal, Illinois, 1906.
brick	30 years Pacific gas and electric company. Figures used in rate hearings before Master in Chancery, San Francisco, 1913-4. Corr. roof, steel roof, frame, conc. floor.
brick	30 years Pacific gas and electric company. Figures used in rate hearings before Master in Chancery, San Francisco, 1913-4. Wood R & Wood F

DEPRECIATION, DEPLETION AND OBSOLESCENCE—BUILDINGS—*(Continued)*

brick	36 years Pacific gas & electric company. Figures used in rate hearings before Master in Chancery, San Francisco, 1913-4. Slate roof, wood r-f., and floor.
brick	40 years Pacific gas & electric company. Figures used in rate hearings before Master in Chancery, San Francisco, 1913-4. Corr. r., steel r-f., conc. roof.
brick	50 years Pacific gas & electric company. Figures used in rate hearings before Master in Chancery, San Francisco, 1913-4. Slate r., steel rf., conc. rf.
brick	50 years Pacific gas and electric company. Figures used in rate hearings before Master in Chancery, San Francisco, 1913-4. Rein conc. r., steel rf., conc. f.
brick	35 years Chas. B. Burdick. Appraisal of Mt. Vernon waterworks, Illinois, 1906.
brick	60 years Robt. Hammond. Journal of Institute of electrical engineers, England, April 25, 1907.
brick	66 2/3 years Traction valuation commission. Case of the Chicago consolidated traction co.
brick	80 years. 0% residual value. Sir Wm. Preece. Report of Bristol corporation, England, 1906.
1st class stone and brick	75 years. Wisconsin railroad commission. Quoted by H. A. Foster and in published reports.
2nd class shops, etc.	50 years Wisconsin railroad commission. Quoted by H. A. Foster and in published reports.
fireproof	40 years 0% residual value. Chicago telephone commission. Published 1908.
reinforced concrete	50 years Pacific gas & electric co. Figures used in rate hearings before Master in Chancery, San Francisco, 1913-4. Steel roof, concrete r., and floor.
foundations	100 years. 0% residual value. Sir Wm. Preece. Report of Bristol corporation, England, 1906.

GUTHRIE, EDWIN. Depreciation. (In Lisle, George. *Encyclopaedia of accounting*, v.2. p. 374).

	Diminishing value.
Mill buildings	2½ to 5%
	There is always a residue of value.
Freehold	0-2½%

INSTALLATIONS, systems and appliances. *Electrical world*, Dec. 7, 1912, p. 1220.

	Hammond	Preece
Buildings	60 years	80 years

JENKINSON, MARK WEBSTER. Depreciation. *Accountant*, May 17, 1902, p. 528-34.
2½% off diminishing value.

JOHNSON, GEORGE. Depreciation. (In his *Electric lighting accounts*. 1903. p. 23-4).
Buildings 2½%

JONES, EDWARD DAVID. Depreciation. (In his *Investment*. p. 167).

Buildings	
Brick	1½%
Frame	2

KENT, WILLIAM. Depreciation of buildings. (In his *Bookkeeping and cost accounting for factories*. 1918. p. 91).

KERR, W. H. and G. A. NAHSTOLL. Reserve for depreciation. (In their *Cooperative organization business methods*. 1915. p. 13-14).

Building	
Brick and reinforced	2½%
Frame	5

KESTER, ROY B. Application of depreciation. (In his *Accounting theory and practice*. 1918. v.2. p. 301-2).
1% to 5% constitute a fair average

KIMBALL, DEXTER S. Estimated life and factors of depreciation. (In his *Cost finding*. 1918. p. 190. *Principles of industrial organization*. 1913. p. 163).

	Probable life of assets in years	Ratio of scrap value to original value	Percentage on original cost	Percentage on diminishing value
Buildings				
Brick or steel frame, easy service	40	0.10	2.25	5.5
Severe service	20	0.10	4.5	11
Wooden, easy service	30	0.10	3	7.5
Severe service	15	0.10	6	14

DEPRECIATION, DEPLETION AND OBSOLESCENCE—BUILDINGS—*(Continued)*

LEAKE, P. D. Record of depreciation. (In his *Depreciation and wasting assets and their treatment in computing annual profit and loss.* 1917. p. 86).

Buildings	1-2%

LIFE of plant. *Electrician,* Nov. 8, 1912, p. 182-4.

Buildings	60 years R. Hammond 80 years Wm. Preece

McINTOSH, ROBERT J. Rates of depreciation. (In his *Reference book of accounts.* Ed. 2. p. 60).

Buildings	
Frame	2-5%
Brick and concrete	1-3
Based on life	

MATHESON, EWING. Land and buildings. (In his *Depreciation of factories, mines and industrial undertakings and their valuation.* 1893. p. 30-4).

Buildings	
Wood or iron	4-10%
Brick	5

METCALF, LEONARD. Water-works valuation and fair rates in the light of the Maine supreme court decisions in the Waterville and Brunswick cases. *American society of civil engineers, Papers and discussions,* 1908, p. 1101-73. American society of civil engineers, Transactions, Sept. 1909, p. 1. Foster, Horatio A. *Engineering valuation of public utilities and factories,* 1913. p. 207. Gillette, Halbert P. *Handbook of cost data for contractors and engineers,* p. 797.

	Useful life	Annual contribution to depreciation account or sinking fund in per cent of cost	
		At 5% annual rate sinking fund	General approximate results.
Masonry buildings	40-50 yrs.	0.8278%-0.4777%	1-½%
Wooden buildings	20-50 "	3.0243%-0.4777%	3-1%

MONTGOMERY, HALFORD H. Montgomery depreciation tables; buildings, machinery and plant in reference to accounts and income tax; with tables. Belfast, James Moore, 1908.

MONTGOMERY, ROBERT H. Buildings. (In his *Auditing theory and practice.* 1916. p. 419-21).

U. S government allowance	
Brick buildings	
Owner	1-1¼%
Tenant	1¼-1½
Frame buildings	
Owner	2-2½%
Tenant	2½-3%
Wisconsin Commissions:	Years of life
First-class stone and brick (office buildings)	75
Second-class shops, car barns, and power stations	50
Brick gas-retort houses	30
Frame dwellings	35
Frame stables and coal sheds	20 to 25
Public service commission, New York:	Per cent Per annum
Brick buildings	2
Chicago traction co. Valuation:	
Brick buildings	1½

MONTGOMERY, ROBERT H. Electrical equipment manufacturers. (In his *Income tax procedure,* 1919. p. 563. ——— Same, 1920, p. 716).

Buildings:	
Reinforced concrete	2%
Brick and steel	2
Mill type	3
Brick and joist	5
Wood, sheet iron and stucco	10

Based on gross book values at the end of the preceding year.

MONTGOMERY, ROBERT H. Buildings. (In his *Income tax procedure,* 1919, p. 559-61. ——— Same, 1920. p. 712-3).

Buildings	3%
Brick	
Concrete, brick & steel fireproof structures	2-2½
(unusual strain)	4
In one state	
cement or brick	2-2½
wooden	3-5
National machine tool builders' association	
Brick	3
Frame	5
The primer states	
Frame building	25
Brick "	35
Stone, or steel and concrete	50-100

MOXEY, EDWARD P. Depreciation. (In his *Principles of factory cost keeping.* 1918. p. 75).

MUCKLOW, WALTER. Depreciation. (In his *Real estate accounts.* 1917. p. 313-8).

Buildings	
Frame	5%
Brick, stone or concrete	2½-3

DEPRECIATION, DEPLETION AND OBSOLESCENCE—BUILDINGS—*(Continued)*

MURRAY, ALEXANDER. Glasgow corporation accounts with special reference to depreciation and sinking funds. *Accountant,* June 13, 1903. p. 782-94. *Royal philosophical societ of Glasgow, Proceedings,* 1903.
Buildings including sites 2½%

NEALE, R. E. Depreciation in engineering work. *Mechanical world,* Feb. 7, 1913, p. 67-8.
Brick buildings: Freehold 1.5-4%
25-66 years
Wood buildings 2%
50 years
Low, owing to less important uses to which such buildings are usually put.

NICHOLSON, J. LEE and J. F. D. ROHRBACH. Depreciation. (In their *Cost accounting.* 1919. p. 146, 151, 152).

Fire-proof:	
Concrete	2%
Brick	2½
Brick and concrete floors	2½
Main buildings—brick and concrete	2-2½
Steel frame non-combustible roof, and corrugated iron walls	3
Steel with corrugated sheet iron or steel plate	5
Corrugated iron-steel frame concrete floor	3
Reinforced concrete, or steel and tile	2
Stone, brick, concrete with or without steel, first-class stone and brick	2
Mill or slow-burning buildings-brick, steel and wood, or brick and wood	3
Non-fire-proof:	
Outbuildings	7½
Wood	5
Substantial wooden buildings	5
All-wood structures—well built	5
All-wood structures—cheap material	7½
Steel frame—wooden roof, and corrugated iron walls	5
Steel or corrugated sheet iron with wood	5
Corrugated iron-wood frame and floor	5
Corrugated iron-wood frame, concrete floor	5
Corrugated iron-steel frame, wood floor	5
Concrete block with wooden roofs and floors	5
Partitions	7½%

Benches, partitions—permanent
Based on (1) the cost of equipment
(2) the life of the equipment
(3) on a ten hour day.

Group rates
Buildings:

Reinforced concrete or steel tile	3
Brick and steel-non-combustible roof and concrete floors	3
Brick, steel and wood	3
Brick and wood	3
Steel frame-wooden roof and corrugated iron walls	3
All-wood structures—well built (20 years)	3
Steel frame, non-combustible roof and corrugated iron walls	3
All-wood structures—cheap (20 years)	
Miscellaneous structures	Special
Miscellaneous real estate improvements	"

Based on (1) the cost of equipment
(2) the life of the equipment
(3) on a ten-hour day.

NORRIS, H. M. Depreciation of plant and its relation to general expense. *Engineering Magazine,* April 1899, p. 76.
Buildings of brick and stone subject only to deterioration from ordinary usage, may be written off very gradually, a rate of from one to two per cent. generally being sufficient. But, in the case of a building put to rougher usage, as, for instance, a foundry or smithy, a rate of 4 per cent will be found more appropriate. Buildings of wood and iron require a still higher rate,—five to ten per cent. not being excessive in some cases. As a general rule, however, an average rate of 2 per cent. for a brick or stone machine shop, four per cent. for a brick or stone foundry, six per cent. for ordinary iron buildings, and eight per cent. for wooden buildings, can be taken as fair, where repairs are properly looked after and are paid out of revenue.

PENDER, HAROLD. Depreciation. (In his *Handbook for electrical engineers.* c1914. p. 338).
Buildings, P. H. and S. S.

50 years	Chicago union traction co. Engineer of valuation staff, of Wisconsin railroad comm.
	W. Preece
	S. W. Greenland
	J. Abbott
	Stone & Webster for Chicago union traction co.
60	R .Hammond
2.5%	Cardiff tramways
	Glasgow "
2	Milwaukee electric railway and light co.
	Engineer of valuation staff, of Wisconsin railroad comm.
	Third Ave. railroad (New York city)
	Stone & Webster for Chicago union traction co.

DEPRECIATION, DEPLETION AND OBSOLESCENCE—BUILDINGS—*(Continued)*

Buildings, P. H. and S. S., brick
25-40 years W. H. Bryan
5% Chicago city railways.

PERRY, J. P. H. Materials and methods of construction for industrial buildings. *Engineering magazine,* Aug. 1909, p. 806-16.
Quotes Kidder's handbook.
Mill buildings 1-1½%
Annual sinking fund charge for depreciation of a reinforced concrete factory, mill or warehouse, not more than ½ of 1%

PHILADELPHIA. CONTROLLER. Rates of depreciation. (In his *Manual of accounting, reporting and business procedure of the city and county of Philadelphia.* 1917. p. 209).
Buildings:
Special and miscellaneous
Toilets 4%
Stairways 4

PIEZ, CHARLES. Perpetual inventory and appraisal values; table of standard depreciation rates. *Engineering and contracting,* Jan. 24, 1917, p. 77. *Factory,* Dec. 1916, p. 668-71. *Iron age,* Nov. 30, 1916, Jan. 11, 1917, p. 1227, 1266, 138-9. *Iron trade review,* Feb. 22, 1917, p. 477-8. Condensed. *Journal of the American society of mechanical engineers,* Dec. 1916, p. 965-6. *Iron trade review,* Dec. 7. 1916, p. 1144-6. Kent, William. *Bookkeeping and cost accounting for factories.* 1918. p. 90. Discussion. *Journal of the American society of mechanical engineers,* March 1917, p. 215-7.

	Percent on cost	Percent on reducing balance
Buildings and accessories:		
Reinforced concrete or steel and tile	2	3
Brick and steel with non-combustible roof and concrete floors	2.5	4
Brick, steel and wood	3	5
Brick and wood	3	5
Steel frame, wooden roof and corrugated iron walls	3.5	7
Steel frame, non-combustible roof and corrugated iron walls	3	6
Concrete block, with wooden roofs and floors	3.5	8
All wood structures, well built (20 years)	4.5	10
All wood structures, cheap (20 years)	5	12

PIXLEY, FRANCIS W. Buildings. (In his *Accountancy.* Ed. 2. p. 213).

PORTERS, R. J. Rates of depreciation generally adopted. (In his *Pitman's dictionary of bookkeeping.* p. 344).
Freehold land and buildings 2½-5%
Based on diminishing balances

RACINE, SAMUEL F. Land and appurtenances. (In his *Accounting principles.* p. 150-1).
Buildings
Frame 25-50 years

SOME depreciation rates on buildings, machinery, belting, furniture and apparatus, tools and dies, moulds, lasts, patterns and drawing used by the Associated mutual fire insurance companies of Boston, Mass., in making appraisal of manufacturing properties. *Utilities magazine,* Jan. 1, 1916, p. 186-7.
Depreciation of buildings:

When one is more than three or four years old, has remained plumb, is kept in repair and is of such dimensions that it perfectly answers the purpose for which it is used, we consider that the depreciation does not increase but stands constant at 5 per cent of total new value for a good many years. When, however, a building in good repair is of such dimensions that it is manifestly out of date and unsuited to obtain best results for its occupancy, we increase the depreciation. Naturally a building not kept in repair is depreciated much more heavily.

SPALDING, A. W. Schedule of depreciation to buildings, read before the Northwestern indemnities association, Chicago, Sept. 18, 1879. *St. Louis, Western insurance review,* 1879. 15p.

SPICER, ERNEST EVAN and E. C. PEGLER. Freehold buildings. (In their *Practical auditing.* 1914. p. 139-40).

TIFFANY, H. S. Buildings. (In his *Digest of depreciation.* c1890. p. 5-10).
Based upon the actual life of the building without any repairs.

Brick or stone buildings,—	Single, slate or tin roofs, occupied as stores by owners, depreciate annually	2%
" " " "	Single, slate or tin roofs, occupied as stores by tenants, depreciate annually	2½
" " " "	In blocks, slate or tin roofs, occupied as stores by owners, depreciate annually	2½
" " " "	In blocks, slate or tin roofs, occupied as stores by owners, depreciate annually	3
" " " "	Single, shingle or gravel roofs, occupied as stores by owners, depreciate annually	2½

DEPRECIATION, DEPLETION AND OBSOLESCENCE—BUILDINGS—*(Continued)*

Brick or stone buildings—Single, shingle or gravel roofs, occupied as stores by tenants, depreciate annually 3

" " " " In blocks, shingle or gravel roofs, occupied as stores by owners, depreciate annually 3

" " " " In blocks, shingle or gravel roofs, occupied as stores by tenants, depreciate annually 3½

Note.—Where the buildings have been occupied for wholesale groceries, heavy hardware and similar stocks, the rate should be proportionately increased.

In omnibus blocks, without fire walls, where there are a number of tenants, the rate per cent. of depreciation should be correspondingly increased.

Brick buildings,—Slate or tin roofs, used as Manufacturing Establishments where there is heavy running machinery, especially those used in Planing mills and for the manufacture of sash, doors, and blinds, wagons, hubs, spokes, furniture, chairs, and other wood workers, depreciate yearly to a greater extent than those used for less hazardous purposes, and a fair estimate on these classes would be annually 4 per cent

" " with shingle or gravel roofs, occupied for same purpose as described, depreciate annually 4½% per cent

It is especially noticeable in buildings of this class that sagged floors, cracked walls, etc., are common. Buildings are frequently crowded with a greater weight of machinery than was originally contemplated when the buildings are constructed, and the result is naturally a corresponding increase of depreciation.

Frame buildings—Slate or tin roofs, used as Manufacturing Establishments, where there is heavy running machinery, especially those used as Planing mills and for the manufacture of sash, doors and blinds, wagons, hubs, spokes, furniture, chairs, and other wood workers, depreciate yearly to a greater extent than those used for less hazardous purposes, and a fair estimate on these classes would be annually 5 per cent.

" " with shingle or gravel roofs, occupied for same purposes, depreciate annually 6 per cent

If the buildings were originally built for the purposes for which they are occupied, it would generally follow that they were built extra strong with heavy timbers, having good foundations, and, in such cases, as a rule, the percentages given would be correct; but as is frequently the case, the machinery for manufacturing establishments is placed in buildings that have been designed originally for other purposes, and the natural consequence is that the floors soon settle and become sagged, and the buildings, sustaining, as they are required to, a greater weight and heavier strain than was intended when constructed, become badly racked, and in such cases the depreciation is greatly increased and at least one per cent. should be added to the annual percentages above given.

TIFFANY, H. S. Veneered buildings. (In his *Digest of depreciations.* c1890. p. 11).
Annually 2-3½%
Based upon the actual value of the building without any repairs.

TYRRELL, HENRY GRATTAN. Depreciation. (In his *Engineering of shops and factories.* 1912).
Wooden buildings 1-1½%
Concrete " ½-1

VARIOUS depreciation charges. *New York Times,* June 14, 1914.
Factory buildings 5%

WEBNER, FRANK E. Depreciation rates. (In his *Factory* costs. 1911. p. 165-6).
Wood or iron 4-10%
Stone or concrete 1½-4

WEEKS, H. E. Abstract of paper on depreciation read before annual meeting of Iowa street and Interurban railway association, April 1910. *Electric railway journal,* April 30, 1910, p. 782-3.

Buildings 50 years

WHATLEY, G. E. STUART. Depreciation. (In his *Accountant's and bookkeeper's vade-mecum.* 1893. p. 23-32).
Freehold buildings should be written off at the rate of not more than 5% and not less than 2½% upon diminishing value.

WOODS, CLINTON E. Depreciation, buildings. (In his *Unified accounting methods for industrials.* 1917. p. 64, 289-90).

Buildings 2 to 2½% per annum

WOODWORTH, LEO DAY. How much does a building depreciate? *Buildings and building management.* Dec. 1918. p. 7-8. 42.

YEAMAN, C. H. Depreciation and reserves for antiquation and obsolescence from an engineering standpoint. *Electric review* (London). July 12, 1907. p. 44. *Electrical engineering* (London), July 12, 1907, p. 46. Electrician, July 5, 1907, p. 475.

Buildings

60 years	R. Hammond
30	L. G. B. (Local govt. board)
50	L. C. C.
60	J. F. C. Snell (M. E. A. 1905).

DEPRECIATION, DEPLETION AND OBSOLESCENCE—(Continued)

Bulkheads

GILLETTE, HALBERT POWERS. Railways. (In his *Handbook of cost data for contractors and engineers.* 1910. p. 1317-8).

Cribbing and bulkheading
4.2 years.
10.0 annual dep. per cent.
58.0 present condition per cent.

GILLETTE, HALBERT POWERS and RICHARD T. DANA. Depreciation. (In their *Handbook of mechanical and electrical cost data.* 1918. p. 106).
Bulkheading
10 years — H. P. Gillette. Washington railway appraisal.

PHILADELPHIA. CONTROLLER. Rates of depreciation. (In his *Manual of accounting, reporting and business procedure of the city and county of Philadelphia.* 1917. p. 210).
Bulkheads 2%

Bulldozers

ELBOURNE, EDWARD T. Depreciation rates. (In his *Factory administration and accounts.* 1918. p. 377).

	Prov. dep. %	Years	
	Remainder values.	10%	5%
Bulldozers	7½	29	38

NICHOLSON, J. LEE and JOHN F. D. ROHRBACH. Depreciation. (In their *Cost accounting..* 1919. p. 149).
Bulldozers 6⅔%

Bureaus

PHILADELPHIA. CONTROLLER. Rates of depreciation. (In his *Manual of accounting, reporting and business procedure of the city and county of Philadelphia.* 1917. p. 207-8).
Bureaus and chiffoniers 4%

Butchers

See Depreciation, depletion and obsolescence—Meat trade.

Cabinets

PHILADELPHIA. CONTROLLER. Rates of depreciation. (In his *Manual of accounting, reporting and business procedure of the city and county of Philadelphia.* 1917. p. 207-8).
Cabinets, cases, lockers, bins and boxes 4%

Cables

ANALYSIS of the premises adopted and methods in determining the cost to reproduce new together with the depreciation thereon of the physical property of the Metropolitan system and the Kansas city and Westport Belt railway of Kansas City, Mo. *Engineering and contracting,* May 28, 1913, p. 617-20.

	Years of life.	Depreciation per year.
Weatherproof cables	30	3⅓
Lead cables	35	3
Transmission line material	20	5
Miscellaneous	20	5
Bare copper	100	1
Wiring and cable	3%	
Cable winding machinery	3-5	

APPRAISAL of the Seattle telephone companies by the railroad commission of Washington. *Engineering and contracting,* May 3, 1911, p. 520-4.

	Life.	Salvage.	Annual dep.	Average Life.	Total dep.
Aerial cable	12	30	6.0	5	30.0
Underground cable	20	40	3.0	5	15.0
Submarine cable	10	00	10.0	5	50.0

AUSTRALIA. FEDERAL INCOME TAX DEPARTMENT. Depreciation allowance. *Accountant,* Oct. 13, 1917, p. 277-9. *Accounting and commerce,* June 30, 1917, p. 55-7. *Federal accountant,* July 1917, p. 83-8. *Public accountant,* Jan. 30, 1917, p. 145-52.
Underground wires and cables 2½%
Overhead wires and cables:
Insulated 7½%
Bare Nil
Written down value, repairs allowed.

BARKER, HARRY. Depreciation of electric railway property. (In his *Public utility rates.* 1917. p. 367).

	Years	
Feeders, insulated aerial	10-15	Wis. R. R. Comm.

BARKER, HARRY. Typical life expectation tables for public utility property. (In his *Public utility rates.* 1917. p. 368-9).

Wire, insulated copper line	10-15 years	Wisconsin R. R. Comm.
Lead covered aerial cable	10-15	
Underground cable	20-25	
Telephone cables, lead covered:		
Aerial	12 years	
Underground	20	

DEPRECIATION, DEPLETION AND OBSOLESCENCE—CABLES—*(Continued)*

BAY state rate case. *Electric railway journal,* Dec. 4, 1915, 1121-3. *Public utility reports, annotated,* 1916F, p. 336-9.

Control cable	Life of car
Signals and interlocking apparatus:	
Hand-thrown-signals	10 years
Automatic signals	14
Signal wire	15
Submarine signal cable	10
Underground signal cable	30
Signals and interlocking apparatus	
Overhead feeder	25-30
Underground cable	30
Submarine cable	10
Telephone and signal cable:	
Submarine	10
Underground	30

BEMIS, EDWARD W. Report on the investigation of the Chicago telephone company submitted to the committee on gas, oil and electric light. Chicago, October 25, 1912, paper. 127p.

	Underground cable, main and toll			Underground cable subsidiary			Aerial cable		
	Years.	Salvage.	Dept. % of cost.	Years.	Salvage.	Dep. % of cost.	Years.	Salvage.	Dep. % of cost.
Byllesby and Arnold									
B. Due to age and wear and tear only	50	1-37	1.26-1.98	35	0.39	2.03-2.85	25	2-35	2.60-3.92
A. Due to all forms of depreciation	18	35.2	5.50	14	10.4	7.00	12.5	19.7	8.00
Chicago commission	20	40	3.72	15	40	5.38	15	40	5.38
Westinghouse, Church, Kerr & co.	20	40	3.0	—	40	—	17.5	30	4.0
E. L. Cline, Telephony July 2, 1910	25	40	2.4	20	40	3	15	40	4

BRYAN, WILLIAM. Appraisal and depreciation of water-works and similar properties. *Journal of the Association of engineering societies,* Dec. 1907, p. 336-81. Depreciation allowance for various public service industries. *Engineering news,* Jan. 23, 1908, p. 96.

	Years
Cables, feeder	20-35

BRYAN, WILLIAM H. Depreciation of electric light plants. *Municipality,* March 1908, p. 74.

Material	Life in years	Authority
Cables, feeder	20-35	Dawson's "Engineering and Electric traction pocket book in Iowa Engineer, July 1906.

CLINE, E. L. Depreciation of telephone companies. *Telephony,* July 2, 1910, p. 16.

	Years	Dep.	Salvage
Underground cable	20	2.4	40%
Underground lateral	20	3.0	40
Aerial cable	15	4.0	40
Cable terminals	12	8.33	0

CONSOLIDATION of electricity supply in London. *Electrical world,* Sept. 19, 1908, p. 611.
Cables 30 years

COST and depreciation of steam and hydro-electric installations. *Electrical world,* Dec. 30, 1909, p. 1558.
Cables and heavy wiring 10 years .318% of total cost

CRAVENS, GEORGE W. Depreciation and maintenance of electrical equipment. *Electrical review,* April 23, 1910, p. 853-6. Montgomery, Robert H. *Income tax procedure,* 1919, p. 570. ——— Same, 1920. p. 723. Montgomery, Robert H. *Auditing theory and practice.* 1916. p. 424. Foster, H. A. *Engineering valuation of public utilities and factories.* 1913. p. 201-2.

	Light or intermittent service	Heavy or continuous service
Wires and cables	3-5	4-6.6

2%	Chicago traction comm.
6.6	Chicago union traction comm.
5	Milwaukee electric railway and light co.
2	Wisconsin railroad comm.
5	Average English comm.
3	Average Scotch practice
3-5	Philip Dawson
5	Stone & Webster
4-6.6	Industrial power plants
5	Prof. G. F. Gebhardt.
5	Miscellaneous sources

CROWELL, H. H. Electric lighting rates and depreciation. *Municipal journal and engineering,* Dec. 18, 1907, p. 698.

	Purchased 10 years or more ago	Modern
Sheathed cable	15 years	25 years

DEPRECIATION, DEPLETION AND OBSOLESCENCE—CABLES—*(Continued)*

DAWSON, PHILIP. Depreciation. (In his *Engineering and electric traction pocket-book.* Ed. 2. p. 1161).

		% capital cost
Feeder cables		3-5
Cables	10-20 years	

DEPRECIATION funds in Europe. *Electric railway journal,* May 7, 21, 1904, p. 696, 760.

Underground cables	3% Glasgow

DEPRECIATION statements—Manitoba government telephones. *Manitoba public utilities commission,* 1913, p. 101.

Exchange aerial cable	5%
Exchange u. g. cable	3

EDWARDS, C. LEWIS. Electric lighting accounts. *Incorporated accountants' journal,* April 1912, p. 175.

Mains and cables	5-10%

ELBOURNE, EDWARD T. Depreciation rates. (In his *Factory administration and accounts.* 1918. p. 376).

	Prov. dep. %	Years	
	Remainder values	10%	5%
Cables	6	37	48

ENNIS, WILLIAM DUANE. Depreciation. (In his *Works management.* 1911. p. 86).

Armored cables	35 years life to 15% residual value.

FERNIE, F. Depreciation of underground cables. *Electrical review,* London, April 5, 1907, p. 577.

Creosote—impregnated oak sleepers have an average life of		25 years
beech		30-35
pine		18-20
non-impregnated oak		12-15
beech		2-3
pine		5-7
rubber insulated cable		8 or 9
	Sir Wm. Preece	
Armoured cables	35 years	Residual value 15%
Cables laid solid in wood troughing	40	12%

FLOY, HENRY. Depreciation. Floy, Henry, *Depreciation as related to electrical properties. American institute of electrical engineers, Proceedings,* 1911, p. 1267. Floy, Henry, *Valuation of public utility properties,* 1912, p. 168-217. Foster, Horatio A. *Engineering valuation of public utilities and factories,* 1913, p. 194-8. *Engineering & Contracting,* Oct. 4, 1911, p. 359-65. Engineering magazine, Aug. 1911, p. 837-40.

	Dep. per cent per year Straight line		
Aerial lines	5	St. Louis P.S.C.	Union Elec. L. & P. Co.
Cables			
Underground (high tension	5	Henry Floy	3rd Ave. case, adopted by P.S.C., N. Y.
Underground (low tension)	50 maintenance cost	Henry Floy	3rd Ave. case, adopted by P.S.C., N. Y.
(Aerial lead covered)	6⅔	Wisc. R.R.C.	
(Underground lead covered)	4	Wisc. R.R.C.	
(Underground lead covered	5	St. Louis P.S.C.	Union Elec. L. & P. Co.
Feeder	Dependent on observedwear	Traction val.	Chicago con.
U. P. insulation	6¼	Wisconsin R.R.C.	Chicago con. trac. co.

FOSTER, HORATIO A. Methods of calculating depreciation. (In his *Engineering valuation of public utilities and factories.* 1913. p. 170, 193).

	Minimum service value, per cent of reproduction cost.
Telephone lead-covered cable, both overhead and underground	25

FOSTER, HORATIO A. Rates of depreciation. (In his *Engineering valuation of public utilities and factories.* 1913. p. 200, 203 205, 206).

Feeder cables, overhead	3.0%
Feeder cables leaded in ducts	4.0

Marwick, Mitchell & co. in the appraisal of a large street railway system.

	Years
Cables:	
Aerial exchange	12-15
In buildings	10
Exchange, Main	20-25
Exchange, Subsidiary	13-20
Toll	30
Submarine	10
Cable terminals	10-12
Cable	
Lead covered, aerial	10-15
Lead covered, underground in conduits	20-25
Cables, lead covered, aerial	12
Cables, lead covered, underground	20
Wisconsin commission	

FOSTER, HORATIO A. Rules for depreciating railways and lighting plants in Great Britain. (In his *Engineering valuation of public utilities and factories.* 1913. p. 166).

Cables

DEPRECIATION, DEPLETION AND OBSOLESCENCE—CABLES—*(Continued)*

In addition to repairs, depreciation should be allowed at the rate of 3% per annum on the written down value.

GILLETTE, HALBERT P. and RICHARD T. DANA. Depreciation. (In their *Handbook of mechanical and electrical cost data.* 1918. p. 106, 105).

Cables	
15-25 years	George W. Cravens, Industrial power plants.
20	Milwaukee electric railway and light co.
50	Chicago traction commission.
aerial exchange	
12	Nathan Hayward, The Bell telephone co. of Pennsylvania, Aug. 31, 1912.
aerial exchange loading coils	
20	Nathan Hayward, The Bell telephone co. of Pennsylvania, Aug. 31, 1912.
aerial exchange terminal	
10	Nathan Hayward, The Bell telephone co. of Pennsylvania, Aug. 31, 1912.
aerial lead covered	
12	Wisconsin railroad commission.
15	Wisconsin railroad commission.
aerial toll	
12	Nathan Hayward, The Bell telephone co. of Pennsylvania, Aug. 31, 1912.
feeders	
25	W. D. Pence, Milwaukee 3c. case.
66.6	B. J. Arnold, Chicago appraisals—4 cases.
feeders overhead	
33.3	Marwick, Mitchell & co. appraisal of a large street railway system, Foster, p. 199.
feeder, underground	
25	Marwick, Mitchell & co. appraisal of a large street railway system, Foster, p. 199.
Cable, house	
13	Nathan Hayward, The Bell telephone co. of Pennsylvania, Aug. 31, 1912.
house terminals	
10	Nathan Hayward, The Bell telephone co. of Pennsylvania, Aug. 31, 1912.
submarine	
9	Nathan Hayward, The Bell telephone co. of Pennsylvania, Aug. 31, 1912.
underground (u.g.)	
16.6	H. P. Gillette, Everett railway and water co., Jan. 29, 1916.
u.g. exchange main	
20	Nathan Hayward, The Bell telephone co. of Pennsylvania, Aug. 31, 1912.
u.g. exchange, subsidiary	
13	Nathan Hayward, The Bell telephone co. of Pennsylvania, Aug. 31, 1912.
u.g. exchange loading coils	
20	Nathan Hayward, The Bell telephone co. of Pennsylvania, Aug. 31, 1912.
u.g. exchange terminals	
10	Henry Floy, 3rd Ave. case, N. Y. city.
u.g. high tension	
20	Henry Floy, 3rd Ave. case, N. Y. city.
u.g. lead covered	
20	Wisconsin railroad commission.
	St. Louis public service commission, Union electric light and power co.
25	Wisconsin railroad commission.
u.g. toll	
25	Nathan Hayward, The Bell telephone co. of Pennsylvania, Aug. 31, 1912.
u.g. toll loading coils	
20	Nathan Hayward, The Bell telephone co. of Pennsylvania, Aug. 31, 1912.
u.g. terminals	
10	Nathan Hayward, The Bell telephone co. of Pennsylvania, Aug. 31, 1912.
Aerial lines	
20	St. Louis public service commission, Union electric light and power co.

GRAY, HARRY. Necessity of depreciation reserves. *Railway age gazette,* May 27, 1910, p. 1297-8. Editorial. Depreciation reserves. *Railway age gazette,* May 27, 1910, p. 1290. Letters. Depreciation reserves. *Railway age gazette,* July 8, 1910, p. 66.

	Annual dep.
Covered copper feeder	2%

GREAT BRITAIN. BOARD OF INLAND REVENUE. Depreciation rates: ((In its *Income tax; statement respecting allowances for wear and tear and obsolescence of plant and machinery.* 1918. Cd. 9022, p. 4; Cd. 9134, p. 6). *American economic review,* Dec. 1920, p. 51. *Journal of accountancy,* Sept. 1920, p. 194.

DEPRECIATION, DEPLETION AND OBSOLESCENCE—Cables—*(Continued)*

Electric light undertakings.	
Cables	3%
Tramways	
Cables	3%
Written down value	

Greenland, S. W. Depreciation. *Mississippi electric association, Report of 2nd annual convention,* June 1910, p. 32-6.

	Years life
Feeders	25

Grunsky, Carl Ewald. Probable useful life of various articles. (In his *Valuation, depreciation and the rate base.* 1917. p. 276).

Cables	
Mains	30 years. 15% residual value. T. C. Parsons. Discussion of Mr. Hammond's paper, Journal Institute electric engineers, England, April 25, 1907.
Mains	20 years. Chicago telephone commission. Published 1908.
Armored mains	25 years. Robert Hammond. Journal of Institute of electrical engineers, England, April 25, 1907. Robert Hammond. Journal of Institute of electrical engineers,
Solid mains	20 years. England, April 25, 1907.
Armored	35 years. 15% residual value. Sir Wm. Preece. Report of Bristol corporation, England, 1906.
Cables and feeders	20 years. Milwaukee electric railway and lighting co., in the Milwaukee 3c. fare case, Aug. 1912.
Cables and feeders	15-25 years. Wisconsin railroad commission. Milwaukee 3c. fare case. Aug. 23, 1912.
Main lead-covered	20 years. 26% residual value. Pacific gas & electric company. Figures used in rate hearings before Master in Chancery, San Francisco, 1913-4.
Subsidiary cables	15 years. 40% residual value. Chicago telephone commission. Published 1908.
Aerial	15 years. Chicago telephone commission. Published 1908.
Aerial Lines	20 years. St. Louis public service commission. Case of Union electric light & power co.
Aerial exchange	12-15 years. 30% residual value. Telephone "data". Compiled from practice A. T. & T. Co., Wisconsin R. R. commission and others. Quoted by H. A. Foster.
Aerial lead-covered	10-15 years. H. A. Foster. "Engineering valuation of public utilities and factories", Van Nostrand, 1912.
Aerial lead covered	15 years. Wisconsin railroad commission. Wisconsin telephone co. case, Aug. 3, 1909.
Aerial terminals	12 years. 0% residual value. Chicago telephone commission. Published 1908.
Aerial terminals	10-12 years. Telephone "Data". Compiled from practice. A. T. & T. Co., Wisconsin R. R. commission and others. Quoted by H. A. Foster.
Underground lead covered	20 years. St. Louis public service commission. Case of Union electric light & power co.
Underground lead covered	25 years. Wisconsin railroad commission. Quoted by H. Floy and in published reports.
Underground lead covered	20 years. Wisconsin railroad commission. Quoted by H. A. Foster and in published reports.
Underground main exchange	20-25 years. 40% residual value. Telephone "Data". Compiled from practice. A. T. & T. Co., Wisconsin R. R. commission and others. Quoted by H. A. Foster.
Underground sub-exchange	13-20 years. 40% residual value. Telephone "Data". Compiled from practice. A. T. & T. Co., Wisconsin R. R. commission and others. Quoted by H. A. Foster.
Toll	30 years. 40% residual value. Telephone "Data". Compiled from practice. A. T. & T. Co., Wisconsin R. R. commission and others. Quoted by H. A. Foster.
Submarine	10 years. Telephone "Data". Compiled from practice A. T. & T. Co., Wisconsin R. R. commission and others. Quoted by H. A. Foster.

DEPRECIATION, DEPLETION AND OBSOLESCENCE—Cables—*(Continued)*

Income tax notes. *Accountant.* May 11, Sept. 28, 1918, p. 359, 162-6. *Incorporated accountants' journal,* May, Oct. 1918, p. 157, 14.
Written down value
Cables 3%

Installations, systems and appliances. *Electrical world,* Dec. 7, 1912, p. 1220.
Armored cables 35 years

Institute *of municipal treasurers and accountants* (*incorporated*). Municipal corporations and companies working tramways and light railway, gas, water and electricity undertakings. *Accountant,* June 26, 1909, p. 106-8. Income tax assessment—allowances for depreciation. *Accountant,* Oct. 2, 1909, p. 423-5, 400-2.
Cables—In addition to repairs, depreciation should be allowed at the rate of 3% per annum on the written down value.

Johnson, George. Depreciation. (In his *Electric lighting accounts.* 1903. p. 23-4).
Mains and cables 5%

Life data on power-plant equipment used in valuation of Massachusetts property. *Electrical world,* Dec. 4, 1915, p. 1261.
Cable
Submarine signal 10 years
Submarine telephone 10
Underground telephone 30
Underground signal 30

Life of plant. *Electrician,* Nov. 8, 1912, p. 182-4.
Armoured cables 35 years Sir Wm. Preece.

London tramway depreciation for income tax. *Electric railway journal,* Feb. 12, 1910, p. 274.
3 per cent on written down capital cost of cables.

Metropolitan street railway reorganization plan. *Electric railway journal,* May 20, 1911, p. 876-8.
Life years
Cables 33⅓

Murray, Alexander. Glasgow corporation accounts with special reference to depreciation and sinking funds. *Accountant,* June 13, 1903, p. 782-94. *Royal philosophical society of Glasgow, Proceedings,* 1903.
Ducts, cables, poles rosettes 3%

Neale, R. E. Depreciation in engineering works. *Mechanical world,* Feb. 7, 1913, p. 67-8.

Bare aerial line		
Bare high tension	5-6%	17-20 years
Bare telegraph or phone copper	2-5	20-50
iron	7-12.5	8-14
Cables		
high tension	4-5	20-25
low tension	6.3	15
traction	3	33
(1909) agreement between Inland revenue and certain municipal tramway associations. These allowances generally considered to be insufficient).		
telephone-main	3-3.3	30-33
telephone small	4-5	20-25
telephone aerial	4-6	17-25

Nelson, Bailie Walter. Limitation and application of profits from municipal undertakings. *Accountant,* Aug. 3, 1912, p. 167-71. *Incorporated accountants' journal,* Oct. 1912, p. 15-7.
Mains and cables 2½% per annum

Nicholson, J. Lee and J. F. D. Rohrbach. Depreciation. (In their *Cost accounting.* 1919. p. 148).
Aerial lines 5%
Cables—underground (high tension) 5
Based on (1) the cost of equipment
(2) the life of the equipment
(3) on a ten hour day.

Official allowance in respect of machinery and plant—Board of Inland revenue, Great Britain. *Accountant,* May 16, 1914, p. 737.
Cables in addition to repairs, depreciation should be allowed at the rate of 3 per cent per annum on the written down value.

Pender, Harold. Depreciation. (In his *Handbook for electrical engineers.* c1914. p. 338).
Cables, underground

25 years	Engineer of valuation staff, of Wisconsin railroad commission.
30	R. Hammond
35	W. Preece
2.5%	E. Matheson
4	Milwaukee electric railway and light co.
	Engineer of valuation staff, of Wisconsin railroad commission.
3.06	Glasgow tramways
3	Cardiff tramways
	Third Ave. railroad (New York city).

Pixley, Francis W. Electricity lighting companies. (In his *Accountancy.* Ed. 2. p. 218).
Cables 5% per annum

Pixley, Francis W. Tramways. (In his *Accountancy.* Ed. 2. p. 218-9).
Cables and feeders 2½-5%

Practical hints on computing telephone depreciation. *Telephony,* April 1, 1911, p. 401-3.
Cable 2%
Cable, messenger hangers, labor, etc. 8
Cable terminals 7

DEPRECIATION, DEPLETION AND OBSOLESCENCE—CABLES—*(Continued)*

PROPOSED sale of Toronto utilities to the city. *Electrical world,* Oct. 25, 1913, p. 832.

Weatherproof cables	3.33%
Lead cables	3
Transmission line material	5

PUBLIC utility reports, annotated. Rochester, Lawyers co-operative publishing co. 1919D. p. 359.

	Years	Salvage	Straight line
Company's life table			
Re Pacific teleph & teleg co.			
Exchange aerial cable	10	31.4	6.9%
Exchange underground cable	15	32.0	4.6
Exchange submarine cable	9	10.0	10.0
Toll aerial cable	12	31.4	5.7
Toll underground cable	12	40.0	5.0
Toll submarine cable	9	10.0	10.0
Commission's life table.			
Exchange aerial cable	14	31.4	4.9
Exchange underground cable	17	32.0	4.0
Exchange submarine cable	9	10.0	10.0
Toll aerial cable	14	31.4	4.9
Toll underground cable	12	40.0	5.0
Toll submarine cable	9	10.0	10.0

RUNYAN, F. O. Report in hydro-electric plant for special committee common council, Newark, New Jersey, April 23, 1902, p. 15, 16, 24.

Underground cable	4%
U.G. cable (Distr).	4

SALIERS, EARL A. Analysis of a hydro-electric plant. (In his *Principles of depreciation.* 1916. p. 34-8).

Cables and heavy wiring	10 years

WALSH, T. J. Depreciation on electric light and power plants. *Electrical railway journal,* July 13, 1912, p. 60.

Underground cable	4%

WEEKS, H. E. Abstract of paper on depreciation read before annual meeting of Iowa street and interurban railway association, April 1910. *Electric railway journal,* April 30, 1910, p. 782-3).

Feeder	20 years

Cafes

See Restaurants, cafes, etc.

Calculating machines

NICHOLSON, J. LEE and J. F. D. ROHRBACH. Depreciation. (In their *Cost accounting.* 1919. p. 151).

Typewriters and adding machines 20%

Based on (1) the cost of equipment
(2) the life of the equipment
(3) on a ten-hour day

Call systems

See Depreciation, depletion and obsolescence—Annunciator and call system

Calorimeters

NICHOLSON, J. LEE and JOHN F. D. ROHRBACH. Depreciation. (In their *Cost accounting.* 1919. p. 150).

Calorimeters	10%

Cam-cutting machines

ELBOURNE, EDWARD T. Depreciation rates. (In his *Factory administration and accounts.* 1918. p. 377).

	Prov. dep. %	Years	
	Remainder values	10%	5%
Cam-cutting machines	7½	29	38

Can brakes

NICHOLSON, J. LEE and JOHN F. D. ROHRBACH. Depreciation. (In their *Cost accounting.* 1919. p. 149).

Can brakes	6⅔%

Candles

TIFFANY, H. S. Soap and candle manufactory. (In his *Digest of depreciations.* c1890. p. 10).

Annually	
Brick	3%
Frame	5%

Based upon actual life of the building without any repairs.

Canning and preserving

NATIONAL CANNERS ASSOCIATION. Rates of depreciation. (In its *Standard classification of accounts.* p. 20-1).

Minimum annual rates	
Buildings, brick, stone or cement	2%
Buildings, shingle, gravel or composition roof-wood floor	4
Buildings, frame-any roof-wood floors	4
Sheds, cement floors	10
Machinery—	5
Office furniture and fixtures	

DEPRECIATION, DEPLETION AND OBSOLESCENCE—*(Continued)*

Car barns

BAY state street railway valuation. *Electric railway journal,* Dec. 4, 1915, p. 1121-3.
Shops and car houses 2.6
Annual depreciation per cent, annual depreciation divided by investment.

DEPRECIATION rates used by the Seattle (Wash.) municipal street railway. *Electric railway journal,* June 24, 1916, p. 1185.
Shops and car-houses 2%

FOSTER, HORATIO A. Rates of depreciation. (In his *Engineering valuation of public utilities and factories.* 1913. p. 205).

	Years' life
Second class shops, car barns and power stations	50
	Wisconsin commissions

GILLETTE, HALBERT P. and RICHARD T. DANA. Depreciation. (In their *Handbook of mechanical and electrical cost data.* 1918. p. 106).
Buildings, carhouses
33.3 years H. P. Gillette, Everett railway & water co., Jan. 29, 1912.
Buildings, car barns
50 years Wisconsin R. R. Commission.

PUBLIC utility reports, annotated. Rochester, Lawyers co-operative co. 1918A, p. 914-8.
New York and N. S. traction co.
Shops and car house 2%

PUBLIC utility reports, annotated. Rochester, Lawyers co-operative publishing co. 1918C, p. 534.
Springfield street R. co.
Shops, car houses and equipment 1.92%

Carpenter shops

BELT, ROBERT S. Depreciation. (In his *Foundry cost accounting practice and procedure.* 1919. p. 242).
Carpenter shop equipment 10%

BELT, ROBERT E. Depreciation. (In his *Uniform cost accounting methods; adopted by the American malleable castings association,* Nov. 14, 1917. p. 20-1.
Patterns and carpenter shop equipment 10%

PHILADELPHIA. CONTROLLER. Rates of depreciation. (In his *Manual of accounting, reporting and business procedure of the city and county of Philadelphia.* 1917. p. 205).

Timber working equipment	
Sawing and cutting machinery—	10%
Planing machinery	5
Mitreing and tonguing, grooving, etc. machinery	5
Carpenters' and wood carvers' hand tools	10
Carpenters' work benches	10

Carpet sweepers

PHILADELPHIA. CONTROLLER. Rates of depreciation. (In his *Manual of accounting, reporting and business procedure of the city and county of Philadelphia.* 1917. p. 208).
Carpet sweepers 20%

Carpets, rugs, etc.

PHILADELPHIA. CONTROLLER. Rates of depreciation. (In his *Manual of accounting, reporting and business procedure of the city and county of Philadelphia.* 1917. p. 207-8).
Carpets and rugs 10%

Cars

See Depreciation, depletion and obsolescence—Rolling stock.

Carts

See Depreciation, depletion and obsolescence—Vehicles.

Carvers

NICHOLSON, J. LEE and JOHN F. D. ROHRBACH. Depreciation. (In their *Cost accounting.* 1919. p. 150).
Carvers 5%
Based on (1) the cost of equipment
(2) the life of the equipment.
(3) on a ten-hour day.

Cases

PHILADELPHIA. CONTROLLER. Rates of depreciation. (In his *Manual of accounting, reporting and business procedure of the city and county of Philadelphia.* 1917. p. 207-8).
Cabinets, cases, lockers, bins and boxes 4%

Cash registers

AUSTRALIA. *Federal income tax department.* Depreciation allowance. *Accountant,* Oct. 13, 1917, p. 277-9. *Accounting and commerce,* June 30, 1917, p. 55-7. *Federal accountant,* July 1917, p. 93-8. *Public accountant,* Jan. 30, 1917, p. 145-52.
Cash registers 5%
Based on written down value and repairs allowed in addition.

MONTGOMERY, ROBERT H. Cash registers. (In his *Income tax procedure,* 1919, p. 561. ——— Same, 1920, p. 714).
The average life of a good cash register is from 10 to 20 years, although some are in use today which were sold more than 20 years ago. If an annual rate is to be constant over the expected effective life, not less than 15%.

DEPRECIATION, DEPLETION AND OBSOLESCENCE—*(Continued)*

Casks

See Depreciation, depletion and obsolescence—Containers.

Cement

LEWIS, F. H. Depreciation factor in cost of producing Portland cement. *Journal of the American society of mechanical engineers,* Feb. 1913, p. 257-61.

PHILADELPHIA. CONTROLLER. Rates of depreciation. (In his *Manual of accounting, reporting and business procedure of the city and county of Philadelphia.* 1917. p. 205).

Gypsum and cement working equipment	10%

STRUCKMANN, H. Depreciation and obsolescence in Portland cement plants. *Journal of the American society of mechanical engineers,* Feb. 1913, p. 262-75.

	% of reproduction value
Factory building	5
Factory machinery	12
Power plant equipment	10
Electric light system	7
Railway tracks	7
Quarry rails and equipment	15
Tools and fixtures	10
General construction fences, retaining walls, etc.	7
Waterworks and pipelines	10
Oil storage tanks	7
Dwellings	5

TIFFANY, H. S. Frame cement works. (In his *Digest of depreciations.* c1890. p. 8).
Annually 5%
Based upon the actual life of the building without any repairs.

Centering machines

ELBOURNE, EDWARD T. Depreciation rates. (In his *Factory administration and accounts.* 1918. p. 377).

	Prov. dep. % Remainder values	Years 10%	Years 5%
Centering machines	6	37	48

Chain transmission

ELBOURNE, EDWARD T. Depreciation rates. (In his *Factory administration and accounts.* 1918. p. 376).

	Prov. dep. % Remainder values	Years 10%	Years 5%
Chain transmission	7½	29	38

Chairs

PHILADELPHIA. CONTROLLER. Rates of depreciation. (In his *Manual of accounting, reporting and business procedure of the city and county of Philadelphia.* 1917. p. 207-8).

Chairs	4%

Charging barrows

NICHOLSON, J. LEE and JOHN F. D. ROHRBACH. Depreciation. (In their *Cost accounting.* 1919. p. 148).

Charging barrows	20%

Charging boxes

NICHOLSON, J. LEE and JOHN F. D. ROHRBACH. Depreciation. (In their *Cost accounting.* 1919. p. 148).

Charging boxes	20%

Chases

See Depreciation, depletion and obsolescene—Printing.

Cheese

TIFFANY, H. S. Cheese factories. (In his *Digest of depreciations.* c1890. p. 9).

Brick or stone	2½%
Frame	3½

Based upon the actual life of the building without any repairs.

Chemical industry

AUSTRALIA. FEDERAL INCOME TAX DEPARTMENT. Depreciation allowance. *Accountant,* Oct. 13, 1917, p. 277-9. *Accounting and commerce,* June 30, 1917, p. 55-7. *Federal accountant,* July 1917, p. 93-8. *Public accountant,* Jan. 30, 1917, p. 145-52.

Chemical manufacture	7½%

Written down value repairs allowed in addition.

DEPRECIATION and income tax. *Accounting and commerce,* Nov. 1917, p. 185-6.
Chemical vats, chambers, etc., 10% on reducing value.

MONTGOMERY, ROBERT H. Chemical industry. (In his *Auditing, theory and practice.* 1916. p. 418).

Buildings	1½-2%
Machinery and equipment	15

MONTGOMERY, ROBERT H. Chemical industry. (In his *Income tax procedure,* 1919. p. 561. ——— Same, 1920. p. 714).

Buildings	2½-3%
Machinery and equipment	15

DEPRECIATION, DEPLETION AND OBSOLESCENCE—*(Continued)*

Chills

PIEZ, CHARLES. Perpetual inventory and appraisal values; table of standard depreciation rates. *Engineering and contracting,* Jan. 24, 1917, p. 77. *Factory,* Dec. 1916, p. 668-71. *Iron age,* Nov. 30, 1916, Jan. 11, 1917, p. 1266, 138-9. *Iron trade review,* Feb. 22, 1917, p. 477-8. Condensed. *Journal of the American society of mechanical engineers,* Dec. 1916, p. 965-6. *Iron trade review,* Dec. 7, 1916, p. 1144-6. Kent, William. *Bookkeeping and cost accounting for factories.* 1918. p. 90. Discussion. *Journal of the American society of mechanical engineers,* March 1917, p. 215-7.

	% on cost
Chills, iron and steel flasks and accessories, net additions	50

Chimneys

See Depreciation, depletion and obsolescence—Stacks.

Churches

MUCKLOW, WALTER. Depreciation. (In his *Real estate accounts.* 1917. p. 313-8).
Stone churches 1½%

PHILADELPHIA. CONTROLLER. Rates of depreciation. (In his *Manual of accounting, reporting and business procedure of the city and county of Philadelphia.* 1917. p. 210).
Buildings
Churches, auditoriums, exhibition halls, museums, club houses and amusement places 1%

TIFFANY, H. S. Churches and schoolhouses. (In his *Digest of depreciations.* c1890. p. 7).
Brick or stone 1½-2%
Frame 3-3½
Based upon the actual life of the building without any repairs.

UNIFORM cost sheet for coal mining companies. *Coal age,* Sept. 19, 1918, p. 545-7.
Churches and schools 4% Original cost

Circuits

GILLETTE, HALBERT P. and RICHARD T. DANA. Cost of street lighting in Chicago. (In their *Mechanical and electrical cost data.* 1918. p. 1039).
Circuits 4%

Classifiers

NICHOLSON, J. LEE and JOHN F. D. ROHRBACH. Depreciation. (In their *Cost accounting.* 1919. p. 150).
Classifiers 10%

Clipping machines

PHILADELPHIA. CONTROLLER. Rates of depreciation. (In his *Manual of accounting, reporting and business procedure of the city and county of Philadelphia.* 1917. p. 206).
Curry combs, clipping machines, feed cans, etc. 33⅓%

Clocks

See Depreciation, depletion and obsolescence—Timekeeping.

Clothing

AUSTRALIA. FEDERAL INCOME TAX DEPARTMENT. Depreciation. *Accountant,* Oct. 13, 1917, p. 277-9. *Accounting and commerce,* June 30, 1917, p. 55-7. *Federal accountant,* July 1917, p. 93-8. *Public accountant,* Jan. 30, 1917, p. 145-52.
Clothing, millinery, whiteworker's sewing machines 20%
Other machines 5
Written down value, repairs allowed in addition.

FRANKEL, PHILIP. Depreciation. (In his *Cost finding in the cloak and suit industry.* c1912. p. 16).
Flat rate of 10% a year from value is often used.

TIFFANY, H. S. Clothing. (In his *Digest of depreciations.* c1890. p. 13).

First year	10%
Second "	25
Third "	50

TIFFANY, H. S. Gents furnishing goods. (In his *Digest of depreciations.* c1890. p. 13).
Annually 25%

TIFFANY, H. S. Hats and caps. (In his *Digest of depreciations.* c1890. p. 14).
Annually 12½%

UNITED STATES. BUREAU OF FOREIGN AND DOMESTIC COMMERCE. Unit cost, including depreciation and interest. (In its *Men's factory made clothing industry.* 1916. p. 138).

Clutches

ELBOURNE, EDWARD T. Depreciation rates. (In his *Factory administration and accounts.* 1918. p. 376).

	Prov. dep. %	Years	
	Remainder values	10%	5%
Clutches	7½	29	38

Coal

See also Mining and metallurgy.

DETERIORATION in heating value of coal during storage. *Power,* Jan. 15, 1918, p. 101-2.

STELKENS, M. Depreciation of coal and coke by shipment. *American gas journal,* Aug. 4, 1902. *Engineering magazine,* July 18, 1902.

Coal breakers

TIFFANY, H. S. Coal breakers. (In his *Digest of depreciations.* c1890. p. 8).
Annually 7%

Coal cutters

MANN, JOHN and H. C. JUDD. Depreciation. (In their *Colliery accounts.* 1909. p. 69-75, 92).
Coal cutters 20-30%
Calculated on the balance as diminished from year to year.

DEPRECIATION, DEPLETION AND OBSOLESCENCE—*(Continued)*

Coal handling

ANALYSIS of the premises adopted and methods used in determining the cost to reproduce new together with the depreciation thereon of the physical property of the Metropolitan system and the Kansas city and Westport Belt railway of Kansas city, Mo. *Engineering and contracting,* May 28, 1913, p. 617-20.

Coal and ash handling machinery combined	7%
Coal handling machinery	6%

BARKER, HARRY. Typical life expectation tables for public utility property. (In his *Public utility rates,* 1917, p. 368-91.

Conveyors		
Coal or ash	10 years	Wis. R. R. Com.
Ash or combined coal and ash	5	Author

Average or approximate figures secured by examination or enquiry.

BAY state rate case. *Electric railway journal,* Dec. 4, 1915, p. 1121-3. *Public utility reports, annotated,* 1916F, p. 336-9.

Coal-handling machinery	25 years.

BREWER, ALLAN F. Rates for annual depreciation. *Industrial management,* April 1918, p. 268.

Coal elevator and conveyor	40 years	2.5%

CROWELL, H. H. Electric lighting rates and depreciation. *Municipal journal and engineering,* Dec. 18, 1907, p. 698.

	Purchased 10 years or more ago	Modern
Coal conveyors and trestles	10 years	10

ELBOURNE, EDWARD T. Depreciation rates. (In his *Factory administration and accounts.* 1918. p. 376).

	Prov. dep. % Remainder values	Years 10%	5%
Coal handling plant	10	22	28

FLOY, HENRY. Depreciation. Floy, Henry, *Depreciation as related to electrical properties. American institute of electrical engineers, Proceedings,* 1911, p. 1267. Floy, Henry, *Valuation of public utility properties,* 1912, p. 168-217. Foster, Horatio A. *Engineering valuation of public utilities and factories,* 1913, p. 194-8. *Engineering & Contracting,* Oct. 4, 1911, p. 359-65. *Engineering magazine,* Aug. 1911, p. 837-40.

FLOY, HENRY. *Valuation of public utility properties.* 1912. p. 168-217).

	Depreciation % per year		
Coal and ash handling machinery	7	Traction val. comm.	Chicago con. tract. co.
	5	Henry Floy	3rd Ave. case adopted by P. S. C. N. Y.
	10	Wis. R. R. C.	

FOSTER, HORATIO A. Rates of depreciation. (In his *Engineering valuation of public utilities and factories.* 1913. p. 205).

	Years' life
Coal and ash conveyors	10

GILLETTE, HALBERT P. and RICHARD T. DANA. Depreciation. (In their *Handbook of mechanical and electrical cost data.* 1918. p. 108).

Machinery, coal and ash handling	
5 years	W. D. Pence, Milwaukee 3c case
10	Wisconsin R. R. Commission.
14.3	B. J. Arnold, Chicago appraisals 4 cases. Traction valuation commission, Chicago consolidated traction co.
15-20	Union traction co. case. Chicago and union traction co., Stone and Webster
20	Henry Floy, 3rd Ave. case N. Y. city

GRUNSKY, CARL EWALD. Probable useful life of various articles. (In his *Valuation, depreciation and the rate base.* 1917. p. 276).

Coal and ash machinery
10 years.
Wisconsin railroad commission. Quoted by Henry Floy and in published reports.
10 years.
Milwaukee electric railway and lighting co., in the Milwaukee 3c fare case, Aug., 1912.
14 years.
Traction valuation commission. Case of the Chicago consolidated traction co.
14.2 years.
Bion J. Arnold. Coney Island and Brooklyn figures adopted by public service commission of New York. Four Chicago appraisals quoted by H. A. Foster.
15 years.
Wisconsin railroad commission. Milwaukee 3c fare case. Aug. 23, 1912.
15 years.
Chicago union traction co. Quoted in Report Wisconsin railroad commission, vol. 10, p. 220.
20 years.
Stone & Webster. Figures for Chicago union traction co. case. Report Wisconsin railroad commission, vol. 10, p. 220.
20 years.
Henry Floy. Trans. American Institute of Electrical engineers, June, 1911. Third avenue case figures adopted by Public service commission of New York.

DEPRECIATION, DEPLETION AND OBSOLESCENCE—Coal handling—*(Continued)*

LIFE data on power-plant equipment used in valuation of Massachusetts property. *Electrical world,* Dec. 4, 1915, p. 1261.
Coal handling machinery 25 years

NEALE, R. E. Depreciation in engineering works. *Mechancial world,* Feb. 7, 1913, p. 67-8.
Coal and ash machinery 5-10% 10-20 years

NICHOLSON, J. LEE and JOHN F. D. ROHRBACH. Depreciation. (In their *Cost accounting.* 1919. p. 150).
Coal and ash handling machinery 8%
Based on (1) the cost of equipment
(2) the life of the equipment
(3) on a ten-hour day.

PENDER, HAROLD. Depreciation. (In his *Handbook for electrical engineers.* c1914. p. 339).
Conveyors, coal and ash
5 years Engineer of valuation staff of Wisconsin railroad commission.
15 Chicago union traction co.
20 Recommended by Stone & Webster for the Chicago union traction co.
20% Engineer of valuation staff of Wisconsin railroad commission.
6.6 Chicago union traction co.
5 Milwaukee electric railway and light co.
Cardiff tramways
Glasgow tramways
Stone & Webster for the Chicago union traction co.

PHILADELPHIA. CONTROLLER. Rates of depreciation. (In his *Manual of accounting, reporting and business procedure of the city and county of Philadelphia.* 1917. p. 206).
Coal hoisting apparatus 16⅔%

PROPOSED sale of Toronto utilities to the city. *Electrical world,* Oct. 25, 1913, p. 832.
Coal handling apparatus 6%

RUNYON, F. O. Report on hydro-electric plant for special committee common council, Newark, New Jersey, April 23, 1902, p. 24.
Coal conveyor 5%

VALUATION of the Chicago consolidated traction property. *Electric railway journal,* Dec. 3, 1910, p. 1111-3.
Coal and ash handling machinery 7%

Coke

PHILADELPHIA. CONTROLLER. Rates of depreciation. (In his *Manual of accounting, reporting and business procedure of the city and county of Philadelphia.* 1917. p. 205).
Coke and illuminating gas preparing equipment 10%

STELKENS, M. Depreciation of coal and coke by shipment. *American gas journal,* Aug. 4, 1902. *Engineering magazine,* July 18, 1902.

Coke and ore pockets

NICHOLSON, J. LEE and JOHN F. D. ROHRBACH. Depreciation. (In their *Cost accounting.* 1919. p. 148).
Coke and ore pockets 4%

Cold drawn machinery

NICHOLSON, J. LEE and JOHN F. D. ROHRBACH. Depreciation. (In their *Cost accounting.* 1919. p. 149).
Cold drawn machinery such as benches, roll straightening machines, etc. 5½%

Cold saw-cutting off machines

NICHOLSON, J. LEE and JOHN F. D. ROHRBACH. Depreciation. (In their *Cost accounting.* 1919. p. 149).
Cold saw-cutting off machines 6⅔%

Commercial travellers

AUSTRALIA. FEDERAL INCOME TAX DEPARTMENT. Depreciation allowance. *Accountant,* Oct. 13, 1917, p. 277-9. *Accounting and commerce,* June 30, 1917, p. 55-7. *Federal accountant,* July 1917, p. 93-8. *Public accountant,* Jan. 30, 1917, p. 145-52.
Commercial travellers' outfits—tin sample boxes and leather bags 12½%

Compressor station

GRUNSKY, CARL EWALD. Probable useful life of various articles. (In his *Valuation, depreciation and the rate-base.* 1917. p. 276).
Compressor station, natural gas 10 years. 50% residual value.
California railroad commission.
Midway gas co., et al.

Compressors

ANALYSIS of the premises adopted and methods used in determining the cost to reproduce new together with the deprecciation thereon of the physical property of the Metropolitan system and the Kansas city and Westport belt railway of Kansas city, Mo. *Engineering and contracting,* May 28, 1913, p. 617-20.
Air compressors
Steam driven 5%
Motor " 5

BAY state rate case. *Electric railway journal,* Dec. 4, 1915, p. 1121-3. *Public utility reports, annotated,* 1916F, p. 336-9.
Air-brake compressors 20 years

BELT, ROBERT E. Depreciation. (In his *Foundry cost accounting practice and procedure.* 1919, p. 243.
Air compressors 7½%

DEPRECIATION, DEPLETION AND OBSOLESCENCE—COMPRESSORS—*(Continued)*

BELT, ROBERT E. Depreciation. (In his *Uniform cost accounting methods; adopted by the American malleable castings association*, Nov. 14, 1917. p. 20-1).
Steam boiler, generator, air compressor, steam piping, electric wiring, etc. 7½%

BOLTON, REGINALD PELHAM. Depreciation of mechanical equipments and power plants. (In his *Building for profit*. 1911. p. 82, 89).

	Physical Years	%	Economic Years
Motor driven pumps, compressors, and moderate-speed fans	20	50.0	17

BREWER, ALLAN F. Rates for annual depreciation. *Industrial management*, April 1918, p. 268.
Air compressors 25 years 4%

COMPARATIVE costs between high and low pressure gas for lighting. *Gas age*, Sept. 1, 1913, p. 215.
Compressors 10%

ELBOURNE, EDWARD T. Depreciation rates. (In his *Factory administration and accounts*. 1918. p. 376).

	Prov. dep. % Remainder values	Years 10%	Years 5%
Compressors, air	7½	29	38
centrifugal	7½	29	38

FLOY, HENRY. Depreciation. Floy, Henry, *Depreciation as related to electrical properties. American institute of electrical engineers, Proceedings*, 1911, p. 1267. Floy, Henry, *Valuation of public utility properties*, 1912, p. 168-217. Foster, Horatio A. *Engineering valuation of public utilities and factories*, 1913, p. 194-8. *Engineering & Contracting*, Oct. 4, 1911, p. 359-65. *Engineering magazine*, Aug. 1911, p. 837-40.

	Dep. per cent per year straight line	
Air compressors	4-5	Traction Val. Comm. Chicago Con. Tract co.

GILLETTE, HALBERT P. and RICHARD T. DANA. Depreciation. (In their *Handbook of mechanical and electrical cost data*. 1918. p. 107).
Compressors, air 20-25 years Chicago Traction Valuation Commission. Consolidated Traction co.

GRUNSKY, CARL EWALD. Probable useful life of various articles. (In his *Valuation, depreciation and the rate base*. 1917. p. 274).
Air Compressors 20 years. 5% residual value.
Pacific Gas & Electric Company. Figures used in rate hearings before Master in Chancery, San Francisco, 1913-4.
20-25 years.
Traction valuation commission. Case of the Chicago consolidated traction co.

NEALE, R. E. Depreciation in engineering works. *Mechanical world*, Feb. 7, 1913, p. 67-8.
Air compressors 4-5% 20-25 years

NICHOLSON, J. LEE and JOHN F. D. ROHRBACH. Depreciation. (In their *Cost accounting*. 1919. 148, 150).
Air compressors 5%
Hydraulic forging presses, bending presses, and fluid compressors 6⅔%
Based on (1) the cost of eqipument
(2) the life of the equipment
(3) on a ten-hour day

PIEZ, CHARLES. Perpetual inventory and appraisal values; table of standard depreciation rates. *Engineering and contracting*, Jan. 24, 1917, p. 77. *Factory*, Dec. 1916, p. 668-71. *Iron age*, Nov. 30, 1916, Jan. 11, 1917, p. 1266, 138-9. *Iron trade review*, Feb. 22, 1917, p. 477-8. Condensed. *Journal of the American society of mechanical engineers*, Dec. 1916, p. 965-6. *Iron trade review*, Dec. 7, 1916, p. 1144-6. Kent, William. *Bookkeeping and cost accounting for factories*. 1918. p. 90. Discussion. *Journal of the American society of mechanical engineers*, March 1917, p. 251-7.

	% on cost	% on reducing balance
Boilers, pumps, feed-water heaters and air compressors	6	15

PROPOSED sale of Toronto utilities to the city. *Electrical world*, Oct. 25, 1913, p. 832.
Air compressors 5%

UNIFORM cost sheet for coal mining companies. *Coal age*, Sept. 19, 1918, p. 545-7.
Original cost
Air compressors 8%

VALUATION of the Chicago consolidated traction property. *Electric railway journal*, Dec. 3, 1910, p. 1111-3.
Air compressors 4-5%

Concrete mixers

LIFE of road construction equipment. *Engineering and contracting*, Jan. 3, 1917, p. 3.
Concrete mixers 20% annual depreciation

NICHOLSON, J. LEE and JOHN F. D. ROHRBACH. Depreciation. (In their *Cost accounting*. 1919. p. 150).
Concrete mixers 10%

Condensers

ANALYSIS of the premises adopted and methods used in determining the cost to reproduce new together with the depreciation thereon of the physical property of the Metropolitan system and the Kansas City and Westport Belt railway of Kansas City, Mo. *Engineering and contracting*, May 28, 1913, p. 617-20.
Condensers:

Cast iron surface condensers	5%
Steam driven condensing apparatus	5
Barometric condensers	3½

DEPRECIATION, DEPLETION AND OBSOLESCENCE—CONDENSERS—*(Continued)*

BARKER, HARRY. Typical life expectation tables for public utility property. (In his *Public utility rates.* 1917. p. 368-9).

Condensers	20-30 years	Wisconsin Railroad Commission. Chicago traction val. comm.

BARKER, HARRY. Typical life expectation tables for public utility property. (In his *Public utility rates.* 1917. p. 368).

Scrubbers and condensers	30 years	Wis. R. R. Comm.

BAY state rate case. *Electric railway journal,* Dec. 4, 1915, p. 1121-3. *Public utility reports, annotated.* 1916F. p. 336-9.

	Years
Condensers	20-25

BOLTON, REGINALD PELHAM. Depreciation of mechanical equipments and power plants. (In his *Building for profit.* 1911. p. 82, 89).

	Physical years	%	Economic years
Fan engines, high speed rotary apparatus on large variations of loads, dynamos, motors, high pressure engines, condensers	12	30.0	9

BREWER, ALLAN F. Rates for annual depreciation. *Industrial management,* April 1918, p. 268.

	Years	%
Condensers, jet	30	3.33
Condensers, surface	33.3	3

BRYAN, WILLIAM. Appraisal and depreciation of water-works and similar properties. *Journal of the Association of engineering societies,* Dec. 1907, p. 336-81. Depreciation allowance for various public service industries. *Engineering news,* Jan. 23, 1908, p. 96.

	years	% straight
Condensers	12.5	7-10

BRYAN, WILLIAM H. Depreciation of electric light plants. *Municipality,* March 1908, p. 74.

Material	Life in years	Dep. % per. year Straight	Authority.
Condensers		7-10	N. S. Hill Engineering Record June 8, 1901.
"	12.5		Iowa electrical association, in Iowa Engineer, July, 1906.

CROWELL, H. H. Electric lighting rates and depreciation. *Municipal journal and engineering,* Dec. 18, 1907, p. 698.

	Purchased 10 years or more ago	Modern
Condensers	10 years	15 years

ELBOURNE, EDWARD T. Depreciation rates. (In his *Factory administration and accounts.* 1918. p. 376).

	Prov. dep. % Remainder values	Years 10%	5%
Condensers			
Evaporative	7½	29	38
Jet & surface	7½	29	38

FLOY, HENRY. Depreciation. Floy, Henry, *Depreciation as related to electrical properties. American institute of electrical ngineers, Proceedings,* 1911, p. 1267. Floy, Henry, *Valuation of public utility properties,* 1912, p. 168-217. Foster, Horatio A. *Engineering valuation of public utilities and factories,* 1913, p. 194-8. *Engineering & Contracting,* Oct. 4, 1911, p. 359-65. *Engineering magazine,* Aug. 1911, p. 837-40.

	Depreciation percent per year Straight line		
Condensers	4	Traction Val Comm.	Chicago Con. Tract. Co.
	5	B. J. Arnold	Coney Island & Brooklyn adopted by P. S. C., N. Y.
	5	Henry Floy	3rd Ave. case, adopted by P. S. C., N. Y.
	5	Wisc. R. R. C.	Street lighting controversy, Atlanta, Ga., 1899.
	10	Arbitrators	Street lighting controversy, Atlanta, Ga., 1899.
	6⅔	St. Louis P. S. C.	Union Elec. Light and Power co.

FOSTER, HORATIO A. Rates of depreciation. (In his *Engineering valuation of public utilities and factories.* 1913. p. 205).

	Years' life
Condensers	20-30

GILLETTE, HALBERT P. and RICHARD T. DANA. Depreciation. (In their *Handbook of mechanical and electrical cost data.* 1918. p. 107).

Condensers	
10 years	Arbitrators, Street lighting controversy, Atlanta, Ga. 1899.
15	St. Louis P. S. C. Union electric light & power co.
	Wisconsin railroad commission
20	B. J. Arnold—Appraisal of the Coney Island & Brooklyn railroad, Feb. 1, 1909.
	Henry Floy, 3rd ave. case, New York city.
25	Trac. Val. comm. Chicago consolidated traction co.
gas plant 30	Wisconsin railroad commission.

DEPRECIATION, DEPLETION AND OBSOLESCENCE—CONDENSERS—*(Continued)*

GREENLAND, S. W. Depreciation. *Mississippi electric association, Report of 2nd annual convention,* June 1910, p. 32-6.

Life
Condensers 15 years

GRUNSKY, CARL EWALD. Probable useful life of various articles. (In his *Valuation, depreciation and the rate-base.* 1917. p. 276).

Condensers. 10 years.
Arbitrators. Board of Arbitration in street lighting controversy at Atlanta, Georgia, 1899.
15 years.
St. Louis public service commission. Case of Union electric light and power co.
20 years.
Wisconsin railroad commission. Quoted by Henry Floy and in published reports.
20 years.
Henry Floy. Trans. American institute of electrical engineers, June 1911. Third Avenue case figures adopted by public service commission of New York.

Condensers. 20 years.
Bion J. Arnold. Coney Island and Brooklyn figures adopted by Public service commission of New York.
Four Chicago appraisals quoted by H. A. Foster.
20 years. 0% residual value.
Pacific gas and electric company. Figures used in rate hearings before Master in Chancery, San Francisco, 1913-4.
25 years.
San Joaquin light and power corporation. Rate hearing before California railroad commission, 1915.

old equipment 20 years.
San Joaquin light and power corporation. Rate hearing before California railroad commission, 1915.
25 years.
Traction valuation commission. Case of the Chicago consolidation traction co.

LIFE data on power plant, equipment used in valuation of Massachusetts property. *Electrical world,* Dec. 4, 1915, p. 1261.
Condensers (steam) 20-25 years

NEALE, R. E. Depreciation in engineering works. *Mechanical world,* Feb. 7, 1913, p. 67-8.
Condensers 4-7% 14-25 years.

NICHOLSON, J. LEE and JOHN F. D. ROHRBACH. Depreciation. (In their *Cost accounting.* 1919. p. 147).
Condensers 6%
Based on (1) the cost of equipment
(2) the life of the equipment
(3) on a ten-hour day.

PENDER, HAROLD. Depreciation. (In his *Handbook for electrical engineers,* c1914. p. 339).
Condensers, steam

10-15 years	J. Abbott
12.5	Iowa electric assoc.
15	S. W. Greenland
7-10%	N. S. Hill.

PROSSER, R. W. Depreciation in gas plants. *American gas light journal,* May 26, 1902, p. 767.
Condensers, scrubbers and purifiers 30 years
20% of first cost.

VALUATION of the Chicago consolidated traction property. *Electric railway journal,* Dec. 3, 1910, p. 1111-3.
Condensers 4%

WEEKS, H. E. Abstract of paper on depreciation read before annual meeting of Iowa street and interurban railway association, April 1910. *Electric railway journal,* April 30, 1910, p. 782-3.
Condensers 15 years

Conduits

See also Depreciation, depletion and obsolescence—Pipe

ABERDEEN and depreciation. *Municipal journal* (London), Oct. 23, 1903, p. 943.
Mains and services

2½%	Glasgow
10	Bolton
1½	Aberdeen

AMERICAN INSTITUTE OF ACCOUNTANTS. Report of the committee on standard schedules for uniform reports upon municipal industries and public service corporations; annual meeting at Atlantic city, N. J. October 20-22, 1908. 15p. *Journal of accountancy,* May 1909, p. 47-54.
The knowledge at the command of the Bureau of the census leads to the conclusion that this average life is approximately as follows:
Reservoirs 100 years

AMERICAN WATERWORKS ASSOCIATION. Final report of committee on depreciation. *Journal of the American waterworks association,* Sept. 1917, p. 1-38.

Storage reservoirs and heavy earthen or masonry dams, large masonry conduits and tunnels	75-100 years
Conduits and distribution pipe, cast iron of large diameter	75-125
wrought iron or steel of large diameter	35-75
wood stave of large diameter	30-60

DEPRECIATION, DEPLETION AND OBSOLESCENCE—CONDUITS—*(Continued)*

APPRAISAL of the Seattle telephone companies by the railroad commission of Washington. *Engineering and contracting,* May 3, 1911, p. 520-4.

Conduit	Life	Salvage	Annual dep.	Av. age	Total dep.
clay	50	00	2.0	5	10.0
fibre	30	00	3.5	5	17.5

AUSTRALIA. FEDERAL INCOME TAX DEPARTMENT. Depreciation allowance. *Accountant,* Oct. 31, 1917, p. 277-9. *Accounting and commerce,* June 30, 1917, p. 55-7. *Federal accountant,* July 1917, p. 93-8. *Public accounant,* Jan. 30, 1917, p. 145-52.

Gas main }
Water mains } Repairs and maintenance only allowable.

BARKER, HARRY. Typical life expectation tables for public utility property. (In his *Public utility rates.* 1917. p. 367-369).

	Years	
Conduit	50	Chicago Telephone commission
Mains		
large cast-iron (6 in. and over)	20-40	L. Metcalf
small cast-iron 4 in. and under)	50-75	"
steel	15-50	"
wood	30-50	Wis. R. R. Comm.
Conduits and manholes	30-50	Wis. R. R. Com.
Mains small cast-iron (4 in. and under)	50	"
large cast-iron (6 in. and over)	75	"
small steel or iron (3 in. and under)	20	"
large steel or iron (above 3 in.)	30	"

BARKER, HARRY. Depreciation of electric railway property. (In his *Public utility rates.* 1917. p. 367).

	Years	
Feeder conduit	30-50	Wis. R. R. Comm.

BAY state rate case. *Electric railway journal,* Dec. 4, 1915, p. 1121-3. *Public utility reports, annotated,* 1916F, p. 336-9.

Underground conduits 50 years

BEMIS, EDWARD W. Report on the investigation of the Chicago telephone company submitted to the committee on gas, oil and electric light. Chicago, October 25, 1912, paper. 127p.

	Clay conduit lines		City conduits
	Years	Dep. % of cost	Salvage
Byllesby and Arnold			
B. Due to age and wear and tear only	Indefinite	0.0	0
A. Due to all forms of depreciation	50	2.00	0
Chicago commission,	50	89	0
Westinghouse, Church, Kerr & Co.	50	2.0	0
E. L. Cline, Telephony, July 2, 1910	Unknown	1	0

BOLTON, REGINALD PELHAM. Depreciation of mechanical equipments and power plants. (In his *Building for profit.* 1911. p. 82, 89).

	Physical years	%	Years
Buried vents and ducts when painted	32	80.0	26
Steel plate stacks and smoke-ducts, cold-water piping, electric conduits	30	75.0	24
Exposed and unpainted vents and ducts	24	60.0	19

BOWDEN, J. HORACE and FRED F. TAIT. Adequate depreciation of capital expenditures by municipal electricity undertakings. *Electrical review* (London), June 21, 1907, p. 1021.

Mains	30 years
" ducts	60

BRYAN, WILLIAM. Appraisal and depreciation of waterworks and similar properties. *Journal of the Association of engineering societies,* Dec. 1907, p. 336-81. Depreciation allowance for various public service industries. *Engineering news,* Jan. 23, 1908, p. 96.

Material	% straight
Conduits	3-5

BRYAN, WILLIAM H. Depreciation of electric light plants. *Municipality,* March 1908, p. 74.

	Dep. % per year Straight	Authority
Conduits	3.5	N. S. Hill. Engineering record, June 8, 1901.

CHASE, HARVEY STUART. Depreciation in water works accounts with reference to uniform reports. *Journal of the New England waterworks association,* June 1910, p. 305. Abstract. *Engineering and contracting,* June 29, 1910, p. 598. Editorial. Depreciation and sinking fund accounts. *Municipal engineering,* July 1910, p. 26.

Reservoirs, tunnels and aqueducts 100 years.

CLASSIFICATION of depreciation percentages used at Dusseldorf municipal gas works. *Progressive age,* Aug. 15, 1910, p. 707.

Mains	
Present %	4
Proposed scale %	4
Life, years	56

CLINE, E. L. Depreciation of telephone companies. *Telephony,* July 2, 1910, p. 16.

	Dep.	Salvage
Conduit	1.0%	0

CROWELL, H. H. Electric lighting rates and depreciation. *Municipal journal and engineering,* Dec. 18, 1907, p. 698.

	Purchased 10 years or more ago	Modern
Conduits	30 years	40 years

DEPRECIATION, DEPLETION AND OBSOLESCENCE—CONDUITS—*(Continued)*

DEPRECIATION statements—Manitoba government telephones. *Manitoba public utilities commission, Annual report,* 1913, p. 101.
Exchange u. g. conduit 2%

DURABILITY of steel water mains. *Engineering and contracting.* July 31, 1912, p. 130.

EDWARDS, C. LEWIS. Electric lighting accounts. *Incorporated accountants' journal,* April 1912, p. 175.
Mains and cables 5-10%

FLOY, HENRY. Depreciation. Floy, Henry, *Depreciation as related to electrical properties. American institute of electrical engineers, Proceedings,* 1911, p. 1267. Floy, Henry, *Valuation of public utility properties,* 1912, p. 168-217. Foster, Horatio A. *Engineering valuation of public utilities and factories,* 1913, p. 194-8. *Engineering & Contracting,* Oct. 4, 1911, p. 359-65. *Engineering magazine,* Aug. 1911, p. 837-40.

	Dep. P. C. per year straight line	Henry Floy
Conduits	1	3rd Ave. case adopted by P. S. C., N. Y.
	2	Wis. P. S C.
	2	St. Louis P. S. C.
		Union Elec. Light & P. Co.

FOSTER, HORATIO A. Rates of depreciation. (In his *Engineerring valuation of public utilities and factories.* 1913. p. 200, 203-6).
Conduits and manholes 2.0%
Marwick, Mitchell & co. in the appraisal of a large street railway system.

	Years' life
Cast-iron mains 3″ and 4″	50
" " 6″ and larger	75
wrought-iron and steel mains	
under 3″	20
over 3″	30
Cast-iron mains, including fittings and valves	75-100
Wrought-iron mains and services, galvanized and including valves and fittings	30-50
Cast-iron mains and services, black	25-35
Services to buildings, lead	50-100
Conduit	30-50
Manholes	30-50
Conduits, main: (includes manholes)	
Clay vitrified	50
Concrete	50
Fibre	20
Iron	20
Wood, creosoted	20
Conduits subsidiary	15

GAS companies and depreciation. *Accountant,* Jan. 24, 1903, p. 109-12.
Mains and service pipes 7½%

GILLETTE, HALBERT P. and RICHARD T. DANA. Cost of street lighting in Chicago. (In their *Handbook of mechanical and electrical cost data.* 1918. p. 1039).
Conduits 3%

GILLETTE, HALBERT P. and RICHARD T. DANA. Depreciation. (In their *Handbook of mechanical and electrical cost data.* 1918. p. 107, 108).

Conduits	50 years	Wisconsin railroad commission.
		St. Louis Public service commission, Union electric light & power co.
(includes manholes)	100	Henry Floy 3rd Ave. case, N. Y. City.
	50	Marwick, Mitchell & co. appraisal of a large street railway system ,Foster, p. 199.
u.g.	16.6	H. P. Gillette, Everett railway and water co. Jan. 29, 1912.
u.g., exchange main	50	Nathan Hayward, The Bell telephone co. of Pennsylvania, Aug. 31, 1912.
u.g. exchange subsidiary	15	Nathan Hayward, The Bell telephone co. of Pennsylvania, Aug. 31, 1912.
u.g. toll	50	Nathan Hayward, The Bell telephone co. of Pennsylvania, Aug. 31, 1912.
Gas mains		
cast iron 3 in. and 4 in.	50	Wisconsin railroad commission.
cast iron 6 in. and larger	75	Wisconsin railroad commission.
wrought iron and steel under 3 in.	20	Wisconsin railroad commission.
wrought iron and steel over 3 ins.	30	Wisconsin railroad commission.

GRUNSKY, CARL EWALD. Probable useful life of various articles. (In his *Valuation, depreciation and the rate-base.* 1917. p. 276).

Conduits	50 years.	Wisconsin railroad commission. Milwaukee 3c fare case. Aug. 23, 1912.
	50 years.	St. Louis public service commission. Union Electric L. & P. co.
	100 years.	Henry Floy. Trans. American Institute of electrical engineers, June 1911. Third avenue case figures adopted by Public Service commission of New York.

DEPRECIATION, DEPLETION AND OBSOLESCENCE—Conduits—*(Continued)*

mains	30 years.	15% residual value. T. C. Parsons. Discussion of Mr. Hammond's paper, Journal Institute eleccal engineers ,England, April 25, 1907.
ducts	30 years.	Robt. Hammond. Journal of Institute of electrical engineers, England, April 25, 1907.
"solid" system	30 years.	Robt. Hammond. Journal of Institute of electrical engineers, England, April 25, 1907.
"ducts" system	30 years.	Robt. Hammond. Journal of Institute of electritrical engineers, England, April 25, 1907.
"solid" system in wood	40 years.	12% residual value. Sir Wm. Preece. Report of Bristol corporation, England, 1906.
clay in concrete	50 years.	0% residual value. Chicago telephone commission. Published 1908.
fibre in concrete	20 years.	0% residual value. Chicago telephone commission.
subsidiary	20 years.	0% residual value. Chicago telephone commission.
main-vitrified clay	50 years.	0% residual value. Telephone "Data." Compiled from practice A. T. & T. Co., Wisconsin R. R. commission and others. Quoted by H. A. Foster.
main-concrete	55 years.	0% residual value. Telephone "Data." Compiled from practice A. T. & T. Co., Wisconsin R. R. commission and others. Quoted by H. A. Foster
main-fibre	20 years.	0% residual value. Telephone "Data". Compiled from practice A. T. & T. Co. Wisconsin R. R. commission and others. Quoted by H. A. Foster.
main-iron	20 years.	0% residual value.. Telephone "data". Compiled from practice A. T. & T. Co. Wisconsin R. R. commission and others. Quoted by H. A. Foster.
main-creosoted wood	20 years.	0% residual value.. Telephone "Data". Compiled from practice A. T. & T. Co. Wisconsin R. R. commission and others. Quoted by H. A. Foster.
subsidiary	15 years.	0% residual value.. Telephone "Data". Compiled from practice A. T. & T. Co. Wisconsin R. R. commission and others. Quoted by H. A. Foster.
vitrified tile	50 years.	Pacific gas & electric company. Figures used in rate hearings before Master in Chancery, San Francisco, 1913-4.
vitrified tile and fibre	40 years.	Pacific gas & electric company. Figures used in rate hearings before Master in Chancery, San Francisco, 1913-4.
fibre duct	30 years.	Pacific gas & electric company. Figures used in rate hearings before Master in Chancery, San Francisco, 1913-4.
wrought iron pipe	20 years.	Pacific gas & electric company. Figures used in rate hearings before Master in Chancery, San Francisco, 1913-4.
Edison tube and fittings	20 years.	15% residual value. Pacific gas & electric company. Figures used in rate hearings before Master in Chancery, San Francisco, 1913-4.
paper conduit	25 years.	Pacific gas & electric company. Figures used in rate hearings before Master in Chancery, San Francisco, 1913-4.
wood conduit	25 years.	Pacific gas & electric company. Figures used in rate hearings before Master in Chancery, San Francisco, 1913-4.
w. i. lateral pipes	15 years.	Pacific gas & electric company. Figures used in rate hearings before Master in Chancery, San Francisco, 1913-4.
conduit under tracks	40 years.	Pacific gas & electric company. Figures used in rate hearings before Master in Chancery, San Francisco, 1913-4.
manholes and paving	40 years.	Pacific gas & electric company. Figures used in rate hearings before Master in Chancery, San Francisco, 1913-4.
service holes and paving	40 years.	Pacific gas & electric company. Figures used in rate hearings before Master in Chancery, San Francisco, 1913-4.

DEPRECIATION, DEPLETION AND OBSOLESCENCE—CONDUITS—*(Continued)*

HAMMOND, ROBERT. Depreciation. *Institute of electrical engineers, Proceedings,* April 25, 1907. *Journal of the Institute of electrical engineers,* 1907, p. 270. Abstracts. *Accountant,* May 18, 1907, p. 675. *Electrical railway review,* June 1, 1907, p. 744. *Electrical review* (Chicago), May 25, 1907, p. 828. *Electrical review* (London), May 3, 1907, p. 744. *Electrician,* April 26, 1907, p. 51. *Engineering magazine,* July 1907, p. 636-8. *Engineering record,* June 15, 1907, p. 703. *Municipal journal* (London), May 10, 17, 1907, p. 411, 435. *Progressive age,* July 1, 1907, p. 305. *Street railway bulletin,* June 1907, p. 382. *Tramway and railway world,* June 6, 1907, p. 497.

	years
Armoured	25
Solid system	30
Ducts	30

HAZLEHURST, J. N. Final report of the committee on depreciation. *Journal of the American waterworks association,* March 1919, p. 85-135.

Conduits and distribution pipe of cast iron of large diameter. Cast-iron pipe coated and buried in the ground is a very durable structure. We have little knowledge of its final effective life from a physical point of view. There are some instances of two hundred years' life for uncoated pipe. Largely, we must amortize such durable material, kept clean and well maintained, again by consideration of the possible changes in public need, functional usefulness, and the burden of a reasonable amortization say—75 to 125 years.

Conduits and distribution pipe of wrought iron or steel of large diameter. Thickness of shell and sensitiveness to a greater range of deteriorating influences must of necessity bring the life of wrought iron and steel physically below that of cast iron, and in many cases below functional considerations—35 to 75.

Conduits and distribution pipe of wood stave of large diameter. Ultimate experience somewhat limited, but thought to be about in same class as steel, when well protected and saturated—30 to 60.

Large masonry conduits and tunnels 75 to 150

INSTALLATIONS, systems and appliances. *Electrical world,* Dec. 7, 1912, p. 1220.

	Hammond	Preece
Armored mains	25 years	
Mains laid solid or in ducts	30	40 years

JOHNSON, GEORGE. Depreciation. (In his *Electric lighting accounts.* 1903. p. 23-4).

Mains and cables 5%

LIFE of plant. *Electrician,* Nov. 8, 1912, p. 182-4.

Armoured mains	25 years	
Mains laid "solid" or in ducts	30	R. Hammond
Mains laid "solid"	40	Wm. Preece

METCALF, LEONARD. Depreciation in waterworks operation and accounting. *Journal, New England waterworks association,* Dec. 1910, p. 442. Abstracts. *Engineering news,* Nov. 3, 1910, p. 482. Methods of computing depreciation of and reasonable assumptions as to period of useful life of waterworks. *Engineering and contracting,* Nov. 16, 1910, p. 434.

Masonry conduits 50-100 years 2-1% straight line

METROPOLITAN street railway reorganization plan. *Electric railway journal,* May 20, 1911, p. 876-8.

Ducts 50 years

MURRAY, ALEXANDER. Glasgow corporation accounts with special reference to depreciation and sinking funds. *Accountant,* June 13, 1903, p. 782-94. *Royal philosophical society of Glasgow, Proceedings,* 1903.

Ducts, cables, poles rosettes 3%

NEALE, R. E. Depreciation in engineering works. *Mechanical world,* Feb. 7, 1913, p. 67-8.

Conduits		
Mains	2-3.3%	30-50 years
Small	5-7	14-20

NELSON, BAILIE WALTER. Limitation and application of profits from municipal undertakings. *Accountant,* Aug. 3, 1912, p. 167-71. *Incorporated accountants' journal,* Oct. 1912, p. 15-7.

Mains and cables 2½% per annum

NICHOLSON, J. LEE and J. F. D. ROHRBACH. Depreciation. (In their *Cost accounting.* 1919. p. 147, 148).

Tunnels, underground piping, vaults and general conduits	5%
Conduits	2%
Conduits, manholes and paving	5

Based on (1) the cost of equipment
(2) the life of the equipment
(3) on a ten-hour day.

PENDER, HAROLD. Depreciation. (In his *Handbook for electrical engineers.* c1914. p. 339).

Conduit lines

3.5%	N. S. Hill
3.06	Glasgow tramways
3	Cardiff tramways
	Third Ave. railroad (New York city)
2	Milwaukee electric railway and light co.

PHILADELPHIA. CONTROLLER. Rates of depreciation. (In his *Manual of accounting, reporting and business procedure of the city and county of Philadelphia.* 1917. p. 210).

Conduits	1⅓%
Water mains, etc.	1⅓%

PIEZ, CHARLES. Perpetual inventory and appraisal values; table of standard depreciation rates. *Engineering and contracting,* Jan. 24, 1917, p. 77. *Factory,* Dec. 1916, p. 668-71. *Iron age,* Nov. 30, 1916, Jan. 11, 1917, p. 1266, 138-9. *Iron trade review,* Feb. 22, 1917, p. 477-8. Con-

DEPRECIATION, DEPLETION AND OBSOLESCENCE—CONDUITS—*(Continued)*

densed. *Iron trade review,* Dec. 7, 1916, p. 1144-6. *Journal of the American society of mechanical engineers,* Dec. 1916, p. 965-6. Discussion. *Journal of the American society of mechanical engineers,* March 1917, p. 215-7.

	% on cost	% on reducing balance
Conduits	4.5	10
Switchboards, main wiring and conduits	6	15

PIXLEY, FRANCIS W. Electric lighting companies; tramways. (In his *Accountancy.* Ed. 2. p. 218-9).

Mains	5%
Ducts and manholes	2%

PROBABLE lives of water-works elements. *Engineering news,* Oct. 11, 1917, p. 688.

	Years
Large masonry conduits and tunnels	75-150

PROSSER, R. W. Depreciation in gas plants. *American gas light journal,* May 26, 1902, p. 767.

Cast iron mains	70 years 10% of first cost

PUBLIC utility reports, annotated. Rochester, Lawyers co-operative publishing co. 1919B. p. 750. In re San Joaquin light & power corp. decision no. 5449, application no. 3531, May 28, 1918, the California commission said that it was reasonable to assume a fifteen year life for a gas main.

Re Pacific teleph. & teleg. co. company's life table	Years	Straight line
Exchange underground conduits	28	3.6%
Toll underground conduits	28	3.6
Commission's life table		
Exchange underground conduits	28	5.6
Toll underground conduits	28	5.6

PUBLIC utility reports, annotated. Rochester, Lawyers co-operative publishing co. 1915A. p. 178. Re Janesville water co. The depreciated condition of 4-inch cast-iron water mains was placed at 90 per cent of value new in a valuation of the waterworks property for municipal purchase, it appearing that the life of such mains is between fifty and one hundred years, and that the depreciated condition on an estimated life of one hundred years would be 97 per cent or 98 and 85 per cent on a life of fifty years, the Commission having also given consideration to the fact that there was no immediate prospect of the distribution system of the company becoming inadequate.

Re Janesville water co. (Wis.). In estimating the accrued depreciation of mains of sizes smaller than 4 inches, for the purpose of determining the fair value of a waterworks property for municipal purchase, the depreciation was placed at 50 per cent of condition new, based on an estimated average life of between thirty and forty years.

PUBLIC utility reports, annotated. Rochester, Lawyers co-operative publishing co. 1917D. p. 277. Re Racine water co. (Wis.). The present condition of cast-iron water mains of a distributing system was fixed at 95½ per cent after twenty years' use.

WALSH, T. J. Depreciation on electric light and power plants. *Electric railway journal,* July 13, 1912, p. 60.

Conduit	2%

WOLFF, MARK. Interpretation of water works accounts. *Journal of the American waterworks association,* June 1916, p. 543, 546.

Mains, fire hydrants, standpipes, buildings, masonry	50 years
Reservoirs, aqueducts	100

YEAMAN, C. H. Depreciation and reserves for antiquation and obsolescence from an engineering standpoint. *Electrical engineering* (London), July 12, 1907, p. 46. *Electrical review* (London), July 12, 1907, p. 44. *Electrician,* July 5, 1907, p. 475.

Mains	25-30 years	R. Hammond
	12-15	L.G.B. (Local government board)
Mains	30	
Services	12	J.F.C. Snell
Ducts	60	(M.E.A. 1905).
Solid mains	25	
Cables	15	

Confectioners

AUSTRALIA. FEDERAL INCOME TAX DEPARTMENT. Depreciation allowance. *Accountant,* Oct. 13, 1917, p. 277-9. *Accounting and commerce,* June 30, 1917, p. 55-7. *Federal accountant,* July 1917, p. 93-8. *Public accountant,* Jan. 30, 1917, p. 145-52.

Machinery—Confectioners	5%

Written down value, repairs allowed in addition.

Containers

AUSTRALIA. FEDERAL INCOME TAX DEPARTMENT. Depreciation allowance. *Accountant,* Oct. 13, 1917, p. 277-9. *Accounting and commerce,* June 30, 1917, p. 55-7. *Federal accountant,* July 1917, p. 93-8. *Public accountant,* Jan. 30, 1917, p. 145-52.

Casks	7½%
Crates	25%

Based on written down value and repairs allowed in addition.

BREWERIES. *American institute of accountants, Special bulletin,* No. 2, 5. March, Sept. 1920, p. 6-7, 7-8.

DEPRECIATION, DEPLETION AND OBSOLESCENCE—CONTAINERS—*(Continued)*

CARTER, R. N. Rates of depreciation. (In his *Advanced accounts.* p. 618).
Casks (in breweries, distilleries, oil refineries) 10-20% or re-valued yearly
Based on diminishing balances, normal conditions and hours of working.

HARRIS, WILLIAM. Depreciation. (In his *Brewers' accounts.* Ed. 2. p. 59, 70).
Casks
(a) In some cases the stock of casks in the brewery and in customers' hands (after writing off all that are considered irrecoverable) at the balancing dates is valued at fixed prices, which are usually lower than the actual cost prices.
(b) Write off 10% from the value at the commencement of each year. This is a better plan.
(c) Another method is to base the depreciation on the principle that every year's trade should bear the cost of a certain number of new casks, computed on the amount of the trade.
Average life of a cask is 10.31 years.

JENKINSON, MARK WEBSTER. Depreciation. *Accountant,* May 17, 1902, p. 528-34.
Barrels and bottles
Brewers estimate that about one-tenth of the stock of casks will on the average be lost or become useless during the year and so write off one-tenth of the value at the commencement of the period.
A better method is to base the calculations on the amount of trade done, reckoning about 1½ to 2 per cent on the total barrelage for the year.
Same principle holds good with bottles, although the depreciation is much heavier it being necessary to write off practically the whole of the new bottles bought during the period unless the turnover has increased so as to necessitate a larger stock.

LANHAM, HERBERT. Depreciation. (In his *Brewers' and bottlers' accounts.* p. 126-32).
Casks 7½-10%
Bottles & stoppers 3% on sales

MONTGOMERY, ROBERT H. Containers. (In his *Income tax procedure,* 1919. p. 561-2. ——— Same, 1920. p. 714).
At balancing time an accurate inventory should be taken, if possible, but if not practicable, it will be necessary to make a calculation as to the number required for the normal operation of the business.

PHILADELPHIA. CONTROLLER. Rates of depreciation. (In his *Manual of accounting, reporting and business procedure of the city and county of Philadelphia.* 1917. p. 206).
Milk and other food cans 33⅓%
Demijohns and casks, jars, etc. 10
Cabinets, cases, lockers, bins, boxes 4

PORTERS, R. J. Rates of depreciation generally adopted. (In his *Pitman's dictionary of bookkeeping.* p. 344).
Casks (in breweries; distilleries ,oil refineries) 10-20% or re-valued yearly.
Based on diminishing balances.

WALTON, SEYMOUR. Depreciation on circulating containers. *Journal of accountancy,* Aug. 1918, p. 150-1.

WHATLEY, G. E. STUART. Depreciation. (In his *Accountant's and bookkeeper's vade-mecum.* 1893. p. 27, 28).

	Diminishing value
Casks	10-20%
new stock	10
old stock	20

Bottles would be better treated as Stock, and valued as such at the periodical stocktakings.

WILKINSON, GEORGE. Depreciation of plant. *Accountant,* Aug. 31, 1901, p. 953-4.
Beer-kegs 5-15%

Contractors

GILLETTE, HALBERT POWERS and RICHARD T. DANA. Plant depreciation. (In their *Cost keeping and management engineering.* 1916. p. 139-41).

PHILADELPHIA. CONTROLLER. Rates of depreciation. (In his *Manual of accounting, reporting and business procedure of the city and county of Philadelphia.* p. 206).
Equipment for buildings, repairing and wrecking structures 12½%
Special and miscellaneous production and construction equipment 16⅔

Contracts

MONTGOMERY, ROBERT H. Contracts. (In his *Income tax procedure,* 1920. p. 715).

Controllers

BAY state rate case. *Electric railway journal,* Dec. 4, 1915, p. 1121-3. *Public utility reports, annotated,* 1916F, p. 336-9.
Controllers 25 years

EASTON, WILLIAM H. Depreciation of electrical machinery. *American machinist,* July 19, 1917, p. 101-2.
Controllers—A 10% depreciation estimate can still be used, but it is by no means as conservative as in the case of motors.

Copyrights

See Depreciation, depletion and obsolescence—Patents, copyrights, trademarks, etc.

Costumes

See Depreciation, depletion and obsolescence—Theater.

DEPRECIATION, DEPLETION AND OBSOLESCENCE—*(Continued)*

Cots

See Depreciation, depletion and obsolescence—Beds.

Covering machines

DENHAM, ROBERT S. Depreciation. (In his *Manual of cost engineering and estimating for paper box manufacturers.* 1917. p. 249).
Covering machines 7%

Converters

ANALYSIS of the premises adopted and methods used in determining the cost to reproduce new together with the depreciation thereon of the physical property of the Metropolitan system and the Kansas City and Westport Belt railway of Kansas City, Mo. *Engineering and contracting,* May 28, 1913, p. 617-20.
Rotary converters 5%

AUSTRALIA. FEDERAL INCOME TAX DEPARTMENT. Depreciation allowance. *Accountant,* Oct. 13, 1917, p. 277-9. *Accounting and commerce,* June 30, 1917, p. 145-52. *Federal accountant,* July 1917, p. 93-8. *Public accountant,* Jan. 30, 1917, p. 145-52.
Alternators, dynamos, motor generators, rotary converters 5%
Written down value, repairs allowed.

BARKER, HARRY. Typical life expectation tables for public utility property. (In his *Public utility rates.* 1917. p. 368-9).

Generators, motors and converters		
high speed	15 years	*
slow speed	20	*
new types	20	Wis. R.R. Comm.
old types	15	"
turbine driven	20	"

*Author-average or approximate figures secured by examination or enquiry.

BRYAN, WILLIAM. Appraisal and depreciation of water-works and similar properties. *Journal of the association of engineering societies,* Dec. 1907, p. 336-81. Depreciation allowance for various public-service industries. *Engineering news,* Jan. 23, 1908, p. 96. Bryan, William H. Depreciation of electric light plants. *Municipalty,* March 1908, p. 74.

Converters	Life in years	Authority
stationary	15	Robt. Hammond Eng. Rec. June 15, 1907.
"	15-20	Dawson's Engineering and electric traction pocket book. in Iowa Engineer, July 1906.
	12.5	Iowa Electrcal association, in Iowa Engineer, July 1906.
rotary	10-12.5	Dawson's Engineering and Electric traction pocket book in Iowa Engineer, July 1906.

CRAVENS, GEORGE. Depreciation and maintenance of electrical equipment. *Electrical review,* April 23, ,1910, p. 853-6. *Foster, H. A., Engineering valuation of public utilities and factories,* 1913, p. 201-2.

Rotary converters	
6.6%	Chicago Union Traction co.
5	Milwaukee electric railway and light co.
5	Wisconsin railroad commission.
5	Average English
5	Average Scotch practice
8-10	Philip Dawson
5	Stone & Webster
4-5	Industrial power plants
4	Prof. G. F. Gebhardt
5	Miscellaneous sources

	Light or Intermittent service	Heavy or Continuous service
Rotary converters	3-5%	4-6.6%

ELBOURNE, EDWARD T. Depreciation rates. (In his *Factory administration and accounts.* 1918. p. 376).

	Prov. dep. %	Years	
	Remainder values	10%	5%
Transformers and converters	7½	29	38

GILLETTE, HALBERT P. and RICHARD T. DANA, Depreciation. (In their *Handbook of mechanical and electrical cost data.* 1918. p. 110).

Rotary converters	
20 years	Milwaukee Electric railway and light co.
20-25 years	George W. Cravens, Industrial Power plants.

GRUNSKY, CARL EWALD. Probable useful life of various articles. (In his *Valuation, depreciation and the rate-base.* 1917. p. 274).

Converters	w
static transformers	15 years. Robt. Hammond. Journal of Institute of Electrical engineers, England, April 25, 1907.
rotary	20 years. Robt. Hammond. Journal of Institute of Electrical engineers, England, April 25, 1907.

HAMMOND, ROBERT. Depreciation. *Institute of electrical engineers, Proceedings,* April 25, 1907, p. *Journal of the Institute of electrical engineers,* 1907, p. 270. Abstracts. *Accountant,* May 18, 1907, p. 675. *Electrician,* April 26, 1907, p. 51. *Electrical review* (Chicago), May 25, 1907, p. 828. *Electrical review* (London), May 3, 1907, p. 744. *Electric railway review,* June 1, 1907, p. 716. *Engineering magazine,* July 1907, p. 636-8. *Engineering record,* June 15, 1907, p. 703. *Municipal journal* (London), May 10, 17, 1907, p. 411, 435. *Progressive age,* July 1, 1907, p. 305. *Street railway bulletin,* June 1907, p. 382. *Tramway and railway world,* June 6, 1907, p. 497.
Converters, rotary 20 years

PENDER, HAROLD. Depreciation. (In his *Handbook for electrical engineers.* c1914. p. 339).
Converters, rotary. 10-12.5 years. Philip Dawson.

DEPRECIATION, DEPLETION AND OBSOLESCENCE—CONVERTERS—*(Continued)*

PIEZ, CHARLES. Perpetual inventory and appraisal values; table of standard depreciation rates. *Engineering and contracting,* Jan. 24, 1917, p. 77. *Factory,* Dec. 1916, p. 668-71. *Iron age,* Nov. 30, 1916, Jan. 11, 1917, p. 1266, 138-9. *Iron trade review,* Feb. 22, 1917, p. 477-8. Condensed. *Journal of the American society of mechanical engineers,* Dec. 1916, p. 965-6. *Iron trade review,* Dec. 7, 1916, p. 1144-6. Kent, William, *Bookkeeping and cost accounting for factories,* 1918, p. 90). Discussion. *Journal of the American society of mechanical engineers,* March 1917, p. 215-7).

	% on cost	% on reducing balance
Cupolas, converters, melting furnaces and accessories	5	10

PROPOSED sale of Toronto utilities to the city. *Electrical world,* Oct. 25, 1913, p. 832.
Rotary converters 5%

YEAMAN, C. H. Depreciation and reserves for antiquation and obsolescence from an engineering standpoint. *Electrical engineering* (London), July 12, 1907, p. 46. *Electrical review* (London), July 12, 1907, p. 44. *Electrician,* July 5, 1907, p. 475.
Rotary converters, switches and instruments.

20 years	R. Hammond
15	L. G. B. (Local government board)
20	L. C. C.
20-25	J. F. C. Snell(M. E. A. 1905)

Conveying and hoisting

ANALYSIS of the premises adopted and methods used in determining the cost to reproduce new together with the depreciation thereon of the physical property of the Metropolitan system and the Kansas City and Westport Belt railway of Kansas City, Mo. *Engineering and contracting,* May 28, 1913, p. 617-20.
Traveling cranes 3%

AUSTRALIA. FEDERAL INCOME TAX DEPARTMENT. Depreciation allowance. *Accountant,* Oct. 13, 1917, p. 277-9. *Accounting and commerce,* June 30, 1917, p. 55-7. *Federal accountant,* July 1917, p. 83-8. *Public accountant,* Jan. 30, 1917, p. 145-52.
Machine tools, cranes and all fixed plant 5%
Written down value, repairs allowed.

BELT, ROBERT E. Depreciation. (In his *Foundry cost accounting practice and procedure,* 1919, p. 242).
Traveling cranes 7½%

BELT, ROBERT E. Depreciation. (In his *Uniform cost accounting methods; adopted by the American malleable castings association,* Nov. 14, 1917, p. 20-1.
Crane 10%

BREWER, ALLAN F. Rates for annual depreciation. *Industrial management,* April 1918, p. 268.
Traveling cranes 100 years 1%

COST and depreciation of steam and hydro-electric installations. *Electrical world,* Dec. 30, 1909, p. 1558.
Cranes 15 years 0.060% of total cost

ELBOURNE, EDWARD T. Depreciation rates. (In his *Factory administration and accounts.* 1918. p. 376).

	Prov. dep. % Remainder values	Years 10%	Years 5%
Conveying machinery	7½	29	38
Cranes, jib traveling	7½	29	38
" , Loco. & portable	7½	29	38
Hoists, chain	7½	29	38
" , Pneumatic	12½	17	22
Lifting magnets	15	14	18
Lifts	6	37	48
Runways and trolleys	7½	29	38
Sheerlegs	6	37	48
Stacking machines (packages)	7½	29	38
Transporters	7½	29	38
Winches	7½	29	38

FOSTER, HORATIO A. Rates of depreciation. (In his *Engineering valuation of public utilities and factories.* 1913. p. 200).
Engines, boilers, heaters, conveyors, pumps and auxiliaries 4.5%

GILLETTE, HALBERT P. and RICHARD T. DANA. Depreciation. (In their *Handbook of mechanical and electrical cost data.* 1918. p. 107).

Conveyors	22.2 years	Marwick, Mitchell & Co., Appraisal of a large street railway system, Foster, p. 199.
Cranes	50 years	B. J. Arnold, Chicago appraisals 4 cases.

GRUNSKY, CARL EWALD. Probable useful life of various articles. (In his *Valuation, depreciation and the rate-base.* 1917. p. 277).
Cranes
15 years
Chicago union traction co. Quoted in Report Wisconsin R. R. Commission, Vol. 10, p. 220.
20 years.
Stone & Webster. Figures for Chicago Union Traction Co. Case. Report Wisconsin Railroad Commission, Vol. 10, p. 220.
50 years.
Wisconsin Railroad commission. Milwaukee 3c fare case.
50 years.
Bion J. Arnold. Coney Island and Brooklyn figures adopted by Public service commission of New York. Four Chicago appraisals quoted by H. A. Foster.

DEPRECIATION, DEPLETION AND OBSOLESCENCE—CONVEYING AND HOISTING—*(Continued)*

wooden — 15 years.
Pacific Gas & Electric company. Figures used in rate hearings before Master in Chancery, San Francisco, 1913-4.

steel — same as bldg.
Pacific Gas & Electric company. Figures used in rate hearings before Master in Chancery, San Francisco, 1913-4.

conveyors — 10 years.
Robt. Hammond. Journal of institute of electrical engineers, England, April 25, 1907.

HAMMOND, ROBERT. Depreciation. *Journal of the Institute of electrical engineers,* 1907, p. 270. *Institute of electrical engineers. Proceedings,* April 25, 1907. Abstracts. *Accountant,* May 18, 1907, p. 675. *Electric railway review,* June 1, 1907, p. 716. *Electrician,* April 26, 1907, p. 51. *Electrical review* (Chicago), May 25, 1907, p. 828. *Electrical review* (London), May 3, 1907, p. 744. *Engineering magazine,* July 1907, p. 636-8. *Engineering record,* June 15, 1907, p. 703. *Municipal journal* (London), May 10, 17, 1907, p. 411, 435. *Progressive age,* July 1, 1907, p. 305. *Street railway bulletin,* June 1907, p. 382. *Tramway and railway world,* June 6, 1907, p. 497.

Conveyors — 10 years

LOCK, FRED J. Depreciation. (In his *West African mining accounts.* 1910. p. 88-9).

Headgears (steel) — 5%

NICHOLSON, J. LEE and J. F. D. ROHRBACH. Depreciation. (In their *Cost accounting.* 1918. p. 149, 148, 150).

Car-molds, cinder and hot metal ladle, cars charging buggies, transfer cars, ore cars, scale cars, jack cars, shop and ash cars, core-oven cars. — 10%
Cars—standard gage and narrow gage used by transportation department — 10%
Cars transfers, turntables, car dumpers, car shifters, pig-casting, water sprays, grab buckets, capstans, windlasses, winches, shear poles, snubbing devices, drag-outs, etc. — 8⅓%
Conveyors—coal ash and sand, screw conveyors — 6
Skip and stock hoists — 6
Locomotive cranes, steam and electric, steam shovels — 10
Cranes
  wooden — 6⅔
  electric, hydraulic, steam and hand power; jib and davit, hand hoists, electric hoists, derricks, lifting magnets, and charging machines — 6⅔
  Based on (1) the cost of equipment
  (2) the life of the equipment
  (3) on a ten-hour day.

PENDER, HAROLD. Depreciation. (In his *Handbook for electrical engineers.* c1914. p. 339).

Cranes, traveling
15 years — Chicago Union traction co.
20 — Stone & Webster for the Chicago union traction co.
6.66% — Chicago union traction co.
5 — Milwaukee electric railway and light co.
Cardiff tramways
Glasgow tramways
Stone & Webster for the Chicago union traction co.

PHILADELPHIA. CONTROLLER. Rates of depreciation. (In his *Manual of accounting, reporting and business procedure of the city and county of Philadelphia.* 1917. p. 206).

Derricks, cranes and hoists — 5%
Hand hoisting apparatus — 12½
Coal hoisting apparatus — 16⅔
Bale hooks and other aids to handling of boxes and packages — 5

PIEZ, CHARLES. Perpetual inventory and appraisal values; table of standard depreciation rates. *Engineering and contracting,* Jan. 24, 1917, p. 77. *Factory,* Dec. 1916, p. 668-71. *Iron age,* Nov. 30, 1916, Jan. 11, 1917, p. 1266, 138-9. *Iron trade review,* Feb. 22, 1917, p. 477-8. Condensed. *Journal of the American society of mechanical engineers,* Dec. 1916, p. 965-6. *Iron trade review,* Dec. 7, 1916, p. 1144-6. Kent, William. *Bookkeeping and cost accounting for factories,* 1918, p. 90. Discussion. *Journal of the American society of mechanical engineers,* March 1917, p. 215-7.

	% on cost	% on reducing balance
Machinery, motors, machine tools, traveling cranes, etc.	4.5	10

ROBY, J. J. Schedule of plant depreciation. (In his *Treatise on cost accounting as applied to coal mining.* c1913. p. 14-5).

Ropes and sheaves
  Deduct as salvage before depreciating — 10%
  Depreciation rate for remainder, fireproof — 25
Hoisting engines
  Deduct as salvage before depreciating — 15
  Depreciation rate for remainder, fireproof — 8

SALIERS, EARL A. Analysis of a hydro-electric plant. (In his *Principles of depreciation.* 1916. p. 34-8).

Cranes — 15 years

UNIFORM cost sheet for coal mining companies. *Coal age,* Sept. 19, 1918, p. 545-7.

Hoist engines — Original cost 7%

Cooking

PHILADELPHIA. CONTROLLER. Rates of depreciation. (In his *Manual of accounting, reporting and business procedure of the city and county of Philadelphia.* 1917. p. 205).

Cooking, roasting and baking other than canning — 4%
  See also Household

DEPRECIATION, DEPLETION AND OBSOLESCENCE—*(Continued)*

Cooling beds

NICHOLSON, J. LEE and J. F. D. ROHRBACH. Depreciation. (In their *Cost accounting.* 1919. p. 149.
Cooling beds 5½%

Cooling towers

NICHOLSON, J. LEE and J. F. D. ROHRBACH. Depreciation. (In their *Cost accounting.* 1919. p. 149.

	Prov. dep. % Remainder values	Years 10%	5%
Cooling towers	7½	29	38

Cooperage

TIFFANY, H. S. Cooper shops. (In his *Digest of depreciations.* 1890. p. 8).
Annually
Brick or stone 3-3½%
Frame 4½-5
Based upon the actual life of the building without any repairs.

Copper cased housings

BOLTON, REGINALD PELHAM. Depreciation of mechanical equipment and power plants. (In his *Building for profit.* 1911. p. 82, 89).

	Physical years	%	Economic years
Heating pipe systems used part of the year gas piping	33	82.5	27

Copy holders

PHILADELPHIA. CONTROLLER. Rates of depreciation. (In his *Manual of accounting, reporting and business procedure of the city and county of Philadelphia.* 1917. p. 207-8).
Tabourets, stands, pedestals, copy holders 4%

Cordage

AUSTRALIA. FEDERAL INCOME TAX DEPARTMENT. Depreciation allowance. *Accountant,* Oct. 13, 1917, p. 277-9. *Accounting and commerce,* June 30, 1917, p. 55-7. *Federal accountant,* July, 1917, p. 93-8. *Public accountant,* Jan. 30, 1917, p. 145-52.
Rope and twine up to 5%
Written down value, repairs allowed in addition.

UNIFORM cost sheet for coal mining companies. *Coal age,* Sept. 19, 1918, 545-7.

	Original cost
Incline ropes	33⅓%
Cage ropes	50

Core boxes

MONTGOMERY, ROBERT H. Foundries. (In his *Income tax procedure,* 1919. p. 564. ——— Same, 1920. p. 717).
Flasks, pattern and core boxes 10-20%

NICHOLSON, J. LEE and JOHN F. D. ROHRBACH. Depreciation. (In their *Cost accounting.* 1919. p. 150).
Core box 5%
Based on (1) the cost of equipment
(2) the life of the equipment
(3) on a ten-hour day.

Core ovens and machines

BELT, ROBERT E. Depreciation. (In his *Foundry cost accounting practice and procedure.* 1919. p. 242).
Core ovens and apparatus
steel 7½%
brick 10
Core machines 15

BELT, ROBERT E. Depreciation. (In his *Uniform cost accounting methods; adopted by the American malleable castings association,* Nov. 14, 1917, p. 20-1.
Core ovens and apparatus 7½%
Core machines 15

ELBOURNE, EDWARD T. Depreciation rates. (In his *Factory administration and accounts.* 1918. p. 377).

	Prov. dep. % Remainder values	Years 10%	5%
Stoves, core	15	14	18

NICHOLSON, J. LEE and J. F. D. ROHRBACH. Depreciation. (In their *Cost accounting.* 1919. p. 150).
Core-ramming machines 10%

Cotton mills

CHASE, HARVEY STUART. Cost of maintenance and depreciation of cotton mills; from the Transactions, no. 82 of the National association of cotton manufacturers, Boston, Mass., April 24-25, 1907. 8p. *Accountant,* Sept. 21, 1907, p. 370-2, 357-9. *Journal of accountancy,* July 1907, p. 236-8.

COTTON manufacturers figure 10% depreciation on plant equipment because of the great advance in cost of mill building. *Journal of commerce,* April 15, 1918.

DEPRECIATION, DEPLETION AND OBSOLESCENCE—COTTON MILLS—*(Continued)*

JONES, EDWARD DAVID. Depreciation. (In his *Investment.* p. 167).
Physical property of cotton mills 5.5%

MOSS, WILLIAM. Depreciation. (In his *Cotton-spinning companies accounts.* 1905. p. 32-7).
Building 2½%
Engines, boilers, gearing 5
Machinery 7½

NICHOLS, HENRY WYMAN. Depreciation. (In his *Methods of determining costs in cotton mills.* 1915. p. 60, 62).
Building 2½%
Machinery 4

ROWELL, HENRY K. Principles of valuing industrial properties with special reference to depreciation of cotton mill machinery. *Engineering and contracting,* Sept. 18, 1912, p. 312-5.

TIFFANY, H. S. Cotton mills. (In his *Digest of depreciations.* c1890. p. 8).
Annually
Brick or stone 2-2½%
Frame 3-3½
Based upon the actual life without any repairs.

Couches

PHILADELPHIA. CONTROLLER. Rates of depreciation. (In his *Manual of accounting, reporting and business procedure of the city and county of Philadelphia.* 1917. p. 207-8).
Couches, lounges and settees 8⅓%

Court houses

PHILADELPHIA. CONTROLLER. Rates of depreciation. (In his *Manual of accounting, reporting and business procedure of the city and county of Philadelphia.* 1917. p. 207-8).
Court furniture, etc. 5%

TIFFANY, H. S. Court houses. (In his *Digest of depreciations.* c1890. p. 9).
Buildings
Brick or stone
With jail 3-3½%
without " 2-2½
Frame
with jail 4½-5
without " 3-4½
Based upon the actual life without any repairs.

Cranes

See Depreciation, depletion and obsolescence—Conveying and hoisting machinery.

Crematories

PHILADELPHIA. CONTROLLER. Rates of depreciation. (In his *Manual of accounting, reporting and business procedure in the city and county of Philadelphia.* 1917. p. 209).
Buildings:
Crematories 1%

Cribs

AMERICAN INSTITUTE OF ACCOUNTANTS. Report of the committee on standard schedules for uniform reports upon municipal industries and public service corporations; annual meeting at Atlantic City, N. J., October 20-22, 1908. 15p. *Journal of accountancy,* May, 1909, p. 47-54. The knowledge at the command of the Bureau of the census leads to the conclusion that this average life is approximately as follows:
Cribs 50 years

CHASE, HARVEY STUART. Depreciation in water works accounts, with reference to uniform reports. *Journal of the New England waterworks association,* June 1910, p. 305-31. Abstract. *Engineering and contracting,* June 29, 1910, p. 598. Editorial. Depreciation and sinking fund accounts. *Municipal engineering,* July 1910, p. 26.
Masonry filtration plant, cribs, iron water pipes, intake pipes, fire hydrants, standpipes and buildings 50 years

GILLETTE. HALBERT POWERS. Railways. (In his *Handbook of cost data for contractors and engineers.* 1910. p. 1317-8).
Cribbing and bulkheading
4.2 age years
10.0 annual dep. per cent
58.0 present condition per cent.

GILLETTE, HALBERT POWERS and RICHARD T. DANA. Depreciation. (In their *Handbook of mechanical and electrical cost data.* 1918. p. 107).
Cribbing
10 years H. P. Gillette, Washington railway appraisal.

NICHOLSON, J. LEE and JOHN F. D. ROHRBACH. Depreciation. (In their *Cost accounting.* 1919. p. 148).
Cribs 4%

Crimping machines

NICHOLSON, J. LEE and JOHN F. D. ROHRBACH. Depreciation. (In their *Cost accounting.* 1919. p. 150).
Crimping machines 10%

Cross arms

See Depreciation, depletion and obsolescence—Poles.

DEPRECIATION, DEPLETION AND OBSOLESCENCE—*(Continued)*

Crossings

GILLETTE, HALBERT P. and RICHARD T. DANA. Depreciation. (In their *Handbook of mechanical and electrical cost data.* 1918. p. 107).
Crossings, railroad
12.5 years — H. P. Gillette, Everett Railway & Water co., Jan. 29, 1912.

GRAY, HENRY L. Necessity of depreciation reserves. *Railway age gazette,* May 27, 1910, p. 1297-8. Editorial. Depreciation reserves. *Railway age gazette,* May 27, 1910, p. 1290. Letters. Depreciation reserves. *Railway age gazette,* July 8, 1910, p. 66.

	Annual dep.
Crossings and signs	8%

Crucibles

BELT, ROBERT E. Depreciation. (In his *Foundry cost accounting practice and procedure.* 1919. p. 242).
Crucibles — 7½%

Crushers

LIFE of road construction equipment. *Engineering and contracting,* Jan. 3, 1917, p. 3.
Rock crushers — 20% annual dep.

NICHOLSON, J. LEE and JOHN F. D. ROHRBACH. Depreciation. (In their *Cost accounting.* 1919. p. 150).
Crushers — 10%

Culverts

BAY state rate case. *Electric railway journal,* Dec. 4, 1915, p. 1121-3. *Public utility reports, annotated,* 1916F, p. 336-9.

Timber culverts	20 years
Dry rubble culverts	25
Masonry and concrete structures	75
Vitrified pipe culverts and drains	30
Cast-iron pipe culverts and drains	60

GILLETTE, HALBERT P. and RICHARD T. DANA. Depreciation. (In their *Handbook of mechanical and electrical cost data.* 1918. p. 107).
Culverts, log or timber — 16.7 years — H. P. Gillette, Washington railway appraisal.

GILLETTE, HALBERT POWERS. Railways. (In his *Handbook of cost data for contractors and engineers,* 1910. p. 1317-8).

Culverts	
log	9.4 years
	6.0 annual depreciation per cent
	41.6 present condition per cent
timber	13.0 years
	6.0 annual depreciation per cent
	12.0 present condition per cent.

GRAY, HENRY L. Necessity of depreciation reserves. *Railway age gazette,* May 27, 1910, p. 1297-8. Editorial. Depreciation reserves. *Railway age gazette,* May 27, 1910, p. 1290. Letters. Depreciation reserves. *Railway age gazette,* July 8, 1910, p. 66.

	Annual dep.
Wooden culverts	10%

GRUNSKY, CARL EWALD. Probable useful life of various articles. (In his *Valuation, depreciation and the rate-base.* 1917. p. 277).

Culverts	
cast iron	16 years California railroad commission. Stockton Terminal & Eastern R. R., April 1913.
log and timber	16⅔ years. H. P. Gillette. Appraisal of Great Northern & Northern Pacific R. R.'s in Washington. Direction of Washington Railroad Commission, 1906.

Cupolas

BELT, ROBERT E. Depreciation. (In his *Foundry cost accounting practice and procedure.* 1919. p. 241).
Cupolas and apparatus — 5%

ELBOURNE, EDWARD T. Depreciation. (In his *Factory administration and accounts.* 1918. p. 377).

	Prov. dep. %	Years	
	Remainder values	10%	5%
Cupolas	7½	29	38

Curry combs

PHILADELPHIA. CONTROLLER. Rates of depreciation. (In his *Manual of accounting, reporting and business procedure of the city and county of Philadelphia.* 1917. p. 206).
Curry combs, clipping machines, feed cans, etc. — 33⅓%

Curtains

PHILADELPHIA. CONTROLLER. Rates of depreciation. (In his *Manual of accounting, reporting and business procedure of the city and county of Philadelphia.* 1917. p. 207-8).
Window curtains — 8⅓%

DEPRECIATION, DEPLETION AND OBSOLESCENCE—*(Continued)*

Cutting machines

DENHAM, ROBERT S. Depreciation. (In his *Manual of cost engineering and estimating for paper box manufacturers.* 1917. p. 249).

	Original cost
Cutting machinery	10%
Round and oval cutters	6
Corner cutters	10
S & S corner cutters	10
Sheet cutters	10
Paper cutters	10

ELBOURNE, EDWARD T. Depreciation rates. (In his *Factory administration and accounts.* 1918. p. 377).

	Prov. dep. % Remainder values	Years 10%	Years 5%
Cutting-off machines	6	37	48
Welding and cutting plant	12½	17	22

NICHOLSON, J. LEE and JOHN F. D. ROHRBACH. Depreciation. (In their *Cost accounting.* 1919. p. 149).
Keyway cutters, belt cutters 6⅔%

PHILADELPHIA. CONTROLLER. Rates of depreciation. (In his *Manual of accounting, reporting and business procedure of the city and county of Philadelphia.* 1917. p. 205).
Sewing and cuttings machines 10%

ROBY, J. J. Schedule of plant depreciation. (In his *Treatise on cost accounting as applied to coal mining.* c1913. p. 14-5).
Cutting machines
Deduct as salvage before depreciating 10%
Depreciation rates for remainder, fireproof 8

Dairying

See also Depreciation, depletion and obsolescence—Agriculture;—Livestock.

AUSTRALIA. FEDERAL INCOME TAX DEPARTMENT. Depreciation allowance. *Accountant,* Oct. 13, 1917, p. 277-9. *Accounting and commerce,* June 30, 1917, p. 55-7. *Federal accountant,* July 1917, p. 93-8. *Public accountant,* July 1917, p. 145-52.
Dairy (factory and dairy farm)
Power plant 5%
Other 10
Written down value, repairs allowed in addition.

INCOME tax notes. *Accounting and commerce,* May 1918, p. 34.
Milking machines 5% on original cost for the first year and 5% on the reducing value in subsequent years.

MEATS, THOMAS WHEELER. Depreciation. (In his *Agriculture accounts.* 1901. p. 15, 17, 23, 44).
Dairy utensils 10%

Dampers

BREWER, ALLEN F. Rates for annual depreciation. *Industrial management,* April 1918, p. 268.

	Years	%
Damper regulators	30	3.33

PHILADELPHIA. CONTROLLER. Rates of depreciation. (In his *Manual of accounting, reporting and business procedure of the city and county of Philadelphia.* 1917. p. 205).
Pipes, valves, dampers, etc. 4%

Dams

AMERICAN WATER WORK ASSOCIATION. Final report of committee on depreciation. *Journal of the American waterworks association,* Sept. 1917, p. 1-38.
Storage reservoirs and heavy earthen or masonry dams, large masonry conduits and tunnels 75-100 years

AUSTRALIA. FEDERAL INCOME TAX DEPARTMENT. Depreciation allowance. *Accountant,* Oct. 13, 1917, p. 277-9. *Accounting and commerce,* June 30, 1917, p. 55-7. *Federal accountant,* July 1917, p. 93-8. *Public accountant,* Jan. 30, 1917, p. 145-52.
Dams. Maintenance only allowable.

GILLETTE, HALBERT P. and RICHARD T. DANA. Depreciation. (In their *Handbook of mechanical and electrical cost data.* 1918. p. 107).
Dams 33.3 & 50 years H. P. Gillette, Everett railway and water co. Jan. 29, 1916.

GRUNSKY, CARL EWALD. Probable useful life of various articles. (In his *Valuation, depreciation and the rate-base.* 1917. p. 277).
Dams
earth 100 years. California railroad commission. Cuyamaca Water co. case, March, 1913.
earth and loose rock 50 years. San Joaquin light & power corporation. Rate hearing before California railroad commission, 1915.
concrete. 50 years. San Joaquin light and power corporation. Rate hearing before California railroad commission, 1915.
concrete diverting 100 years California railroad commission. Cuyamaca Water co. case, March, 1913.

HAZLEHURST, J. N. Final report of the committee on depreciation. *Journal of the American water works association,* March 1919, p. 85-135.
Heavy earthen or masonry dams 75-150 years

DEPRECIATION, DEPLETION AND OBSOLESCENCE—DAMS—*(Continued)*

NICHOLSON, J. LEE and JOHN F. D. ROHRBACH. Depreciation. (In their *Cost accounting.* 1919. p. 146).
Dams and waterways 1½%
Based on (1) the cost of equipment
(2) the life of the equipment
(3) on a ten-hour day

PHILADELPHIA. CONTROLLER. Rates of depreciation. (In his *Manual of accounting, reporting and business procedure of the city and county of Philadelphia.* 1917. p. 210).
Dams 2%

PROBABLE lives of water-works elements. *Engineering news,* Oct. 11, 1917, p. 688.

	Years
Heavy earth or masonry dams	75-150

Dentists

AUSTRALIA. FEDERAL INCOME TAX DEPARTMENT. Depreciation allowance. *Accountant,* Oct. 13, 1917, p. 277-9. *Accounting and commerce,* June 30, 1917, p. 55-7. *Federal accountant,* July 1917, p. 93-8. *Public accountant,* Jan. 30, 1917, p. 145-52.
Dentists' instruments (see also x-ray and electro-cardiograph).
Replacement allowable.

Department stores

See Depreciation, depletion and obsolescence—Retail trade.

Derricks

See Depreciation, depletion and obsolescence—Conveying and hoisting.

Designs

See Depreciation, depletion and obsolescence—Patterns, drawings, models, etc.

Desk equipment

PHILADELPHIA. CONTROLLER. Rates of depreciation. (In his *Manual of accounting, reporting and business procedure of the city and county of Philadelphia.* 1917. p. 207-8).
Desk equipment (including receptacles and devices 12½%

Desks

PHILADELPHIA. CONTROLLER. Rates of depreciation. (In his *Manual of accounting, reporting and business procedure of the city and county of Philadelphia.* 1917. p. 207-8).
Desks 4%

Diamond and drill holes

UNIFORM cost sheet for coal mining companies. *Coal age,* Sept. 19, 1918, p. 545-7.

	original cost
Diamond and drill holes	5%

Dictagraphs

PHILADELPHIA. CONTROLLER. Rates of depreciation. (In his *Manual of accounting, reporting and business procedure of the city and county of Philadelphia.* 1917. p. 206).
Dictagraph 6⅔%

Die sinking machines

NICHOLSON, J. LEE and JOHN F. D. ROHRBACH. Depreciation. (In their *Cost accounting.* 1919. p. 149).
Die sinking machines 6⅔%

Dies

PIEZ, CHARLES. Perpetual inventory and appraisal values; table of standard depreciation rates. *Engineering and contracting,* Jan. 24, 1917, p. 77. *Factory,* Dec. 1916, p. 668-71. *Iron age,* Nov. 30, 1916, Jan. 11, 1917, p. 1266, 138-9 *Iron trade review,* Feb. 22, 1917, p. 477-8. Condensed. *Journal of the American society of mechanical engineers,* Dec. 1916, p. 965-6. *Iron trade review,* Dec. 7, 1916, p. 1144-6. Kent, William. *Bookkeeping and cost accounting for factories.* 1918. p. 90. Discussion. *Journal of the American society of mechanical engineers,* March 1917, p. 215-7.

	% on cost
Punches and dies (Standard) net additions	50

WOODS, CLINTON E. Depreciation, dies, jigs, fixtures and gages. (In his *Unified accounting methods for industrials.* 1917. p. 65.
25 to 50% per annum, according to their character and usage.

Disc grinders

NICHOLSON, J. LEE and JOHN F. D. ROHRBACH. Depreciation. (In their *Cost accounting.* 1919. p 150).
Disc grinders 5%
Based on (1) the cost of equipment
(2) the life of the equipment
(3) on a ten hour day.

Display apparatus

PHILADELPHIA. CONTROLLER. Rates of depreciation. (In his *Manual of accounting, reporting and business procedure of the city and county of Philadelphia.* 1917. p. 209).
Display apparatus 5%

Distilleries

See Depreciation, depletion and obsolescence—Breweries and distilleries.

DEPRECIATION, DEPLETION AND OBSOLESCENCE—*(Continued)*

Ditchers

PHILADELPHIA. CONTROLLER. Rates of depreciation. (In his *Manual of accounting, reporting and business procedure of the city and county of Philadelphia.* 1917. p. 206).
Ditchers and dredges 16⅔%

Ditches

GRÜNSKY, CARL EWALD. Probable useful life of various articles. (In his *Valuation, depreciation and the rate-base.* 1917. p. 278).
Ditches 50 years
San Joaquin light & power corporation. Rate hearing before California railroad commission, 1915.
concrete lining 20 years.
San Joaquin light & power corporation. Rate hearing before California railroad commission, 1915.

Divers

AUSTRALIA. FEDERAL INCOME TAX DEPARTMENT. Depreciation allowances. *Accountant,* Oct. 13, 1917, p. 277-9. *Accounting and commerce,* June 30, 1917, p. 55-7. *Federal accountant,* July, 1917, p. 93-8. *Public accountant,* Jan. 30, 1917, p. 145-52.
During gear (diving dresses and air pipes). Replacements allowable.
Helmet and corselet 10%
Pump 7½

Docks

See Depreciation, depletion and obsolescence—Wharves.

Doctors

See Depreciation, depletion and obsolescence—Physicians.

Dovetailing

NICHOLSON, J. LEE and JOHN F. D. ROHRBACH. Depreciation. (In their *Cost accounting.* 1919. p. 150).
Woodworking machinery—dovetailing machines 5%
Based on (1) the cost of equipment
(2) the life of the equipment
(3) on a ten hour day.

Drafting

PHILADELPHIA. CONTROLLER. Rates of depreciation. (In his *Manual of accounting, reporting and business procedure of the city and county of Philadelphia.* 1917. p. 208).
Mechanical drafting devices 10%

Drag-offs

NICHOLSON, J. LEE and JOHN F. D. ROHRBACH. Depreciation. (In their *Cost accounting.* 1919. p. 149).
Mill machinery—drag-offs 5½%

Drag-ons

NICHOLSON, J. LEE and JOHN F. D. ROHRBACH. Depreciation. (In their *Cost accounting.* 1919. p. 149).
Mill machinery—drag-ons 5½%

Drains

BAY state rate case. *Electric railway journal,* Dec. 4, 1915, p. 1121-3. *Public utility reports, annotated,* 1916F, p. 336-9.
Vitrified pipe culverts and drains 30 years
Cast-iron pipe culverts and drains 60
Catch basins 50

GILLETTE, HALBERT POWERS. Railways. (In his *Handbook of cost data for contractors and engineers.* 1910. p. 1317-8).
Box drains 13.0 age years
6.0 annual dep. per cent
12.0 Present condition per cent.

GILLETTE, HALBERT POWERS and RICHARD T. DANA. Depreciation. (In their *Handbook of mechanical and electrical cost data.* 1918. p. 107).
Drains, box 16.7 years H. P. Gillette, Washington ry. appraisal.

Draperies

PHILADELPHIA. CONTROLLER. Rates of depreciation. (In his *Manual of accounting, reporting and business procedure of the city and county of Philadelphia.* 1917. p. 207-8).
Draperies 8⅓%

Draught installation

ELBOURNE, EDWARD T. Depreciation rates. (In his *Factory administration and accounts.* 1918. p. 376).

	Prov. dep. %	Years	
	Remainder values	10%	5%
Draught installation forced and induced	7½	29	38

Draw benches

ELBOURNE, EDWARD T. Depreciation rates. (In his *Factory administration and accounts.* 1918. p. 377).

	Prov. dep. %	Years	
	Remainder values	10%	5%
Draw benches	6	37	48

DEPRECIATION, DEPLETION AND OBSOLESCENCE—*(Continued)*

Drawing

PHILADELPHIA. CONTROLLER. Rates of depreciation. (In his *Manual of accounting, reporting and business procedure of the city and county of Philadelphia.* 1917. p. 205).
Metal work equipment: drawing and bending equipment 5%

Drawings

See Depreciation, depletion and obsolescence—Patterns, drawings, models, etc.

Dredges

DANA, RICHARD T. Dipper dredges. (In his *Handbook of construction plant.* 1914. p. 202).
6% over 100 working days.

PHILADELPHIA CONTROLLER. Rates of depreciation. (In his *Manual of accounting, reporting and business procedure of the city and county of Philadelphia.* 1917. p. 206).

Ditches and dredges	16⅔%
Pipe line and fittings for floating dredges	20
Floating dredges	10

Drilling

CLAPHAM, F. T. Depreciation of plant. *Mechanical world,* Oct. 19, 1917, p. 219-20.
In a constructural steel works, drilling machines, should be depreciated 10%.

ELBOURNE, EDWARD T. Depreciation rates. (In his *Factory administration and accounts.* 1918. p. 377).

	Prov. dep. %	Years	
	Remainder values	10%	5%
Drilling machines			
multi-spindle	7½	29	38
portable	7½	29	38
radical	7½	29	38
sensitive	7½	29	38
vertical	7½	29	38

NICHOLSON, J. LEE and JOHN F. D. ROHRBACH. Depreciation. (In their *Cost accounting.* 1919. p 149).
Drilling and boring machines 6⅔%

PHILADELPHIA. CONTROLLER. Rates of depreciation. (In his *Manual of accounting, reporting and business procedure of the city and county of Philadelphia.* 1917. p. 205).
Metal working equipment, shearing, punching and drilling 5%

UNIFORM cost sheet for coal mining companies. *Coal age,* Sept. 19, 1918, p. 545-7.

	Original cost
Electric drills	20%

Drivers

PIEZ, CHARLES. Perpetual inventory and appraisal values; table of standard depreciation rates. *Engineering and contracting,* Jan. 24, 1917, p. 77. *Factory,* Dec. 1916, p. 668-71. *Iron Age,* Nov. 30, 1916, Jan. 11, 1917, p. 1266, 138-9. *Iron trade review,* Feb. 22, 1917, p. 477-8. Condensed. *Journal of the American society of mechanical engineers,* Dec. 1916, p. 965-6. *Iron trade review,* Dec. 7, 1916, p. 1144-6. Kent, William. *Bookkeeping and cots accounting for factories.* 1918. p. 90. Discussion. *Journal of the American society of mechanical engineers,* March 1917, p. 215-7.

	% of cost
Machine tool accessories, boring bars, drivers, key-seating broaches	50

Driving gear

CARTER, R. N. Rates of depreciation. (In his *Advanced accounts.* p. 618).
Driving gear 5-7½%
Based on diminishing balances, normal conditions and hours of working.

PORTERS, R. J. Rates of depreciation generally adopted. (In his *Pitman's dictionary of bookkeeping.* p. 344).
Driving gear 5-7½%
Based on diminishing balance.

Drop balls

NICHOLSON, J. LEE and JOHN F. D. ROHRBACH. Depreciation. In their *Cost accounting.* 1919. p. 148).
Steel work—drop balls 4%

Drop stamps

ELBOURNE, EDWARD T. Depreciation rates. (In his *Factory administration and accounts.* 1918. 6. 377).

	Prov. dep. %	Years	
	Remainder values	10%	5%
Drop stamps	10	22	28

Drugs

PHILADELPHIA. CONTROLLER. Rates of depreciation. (In his *Manual of accounting, reporting and business procedure of the city and county of Philadelphia.* 1917. p. 206.)
Equipment for distilling and refining; crude drugs, etc. 8⅓%

TIFFANY, H. S. Drugs. (In his *Digest of depreciations.* c1890. p. 13).
Annually 10%

Drums

BOLTON, REGINALD PELHAM. Depreciation of mechanical equipment and power plants. (In his *Building for profit.* 1911. p. 82, 89).

	Economic years	Physical years	%
Interior drums and tanks, hot-water and pneumatic piping	20	25	62.5 original cost

UNIFORM cost sheet for coal mining companies. *Coal age,* Sept. 19, 1918, p. 545-7.
Incline drums and larries 10%

DEPRECIATION, DEPLETION AND OBSOLESCENCE—*(Continued)*

Drydocks

NICHOLSON, J. LEE and JOHN F. D. ROHRBACH. Depreciation. (In their *Cost accounting.* 1919. p. 147).

Dry docks
Basin 2%
Floating 5
Based on (1) the cost of equipment
(2) the life of the equipment
(3) on a ten-hour day.

Ducts

See Depreciation, depletion and obsolescence—Conduits.

Dumb-waiters

BOLTON, REGINALD PELHAM. Depreciation of mechanical equipments and power plants. (In his *Building for profit.* 1911. p. 82, 89).

	Physical years	%	Economic years
Dumb-waiters	22	55.0	18

Dust extracting

BELT, ROBERT E. Depreciation. (In his *Uniform cost accounting methods; adopted by the American malleable castings association,* Nov. 14, 1917, p. 20-1.

Dust arrester 10%

ELBOURNE, EDWARD T. Depreciation rates. (In his *Factory administration and accounts.* 1918. p. 376).

	Prov. dep. % Remainder values	Years 10%	5%
Dust extracting installation	7½	29	38

Dwellings

See also Depreciation, depletion and obsolescence—Apartment houses;—Tenements

BARKER, HARRY. Typical life expectation tables for public utility property. (In his *Public utility rates.* 1917. p. 366).

Dwellings, etc., wood-frame 30 years
Author—average or approximate figures secured by examination or enquiry.

BOLTON, REGINALD PELHAM. Depreciation of the value of buildings. (In his *Building for profit.* 1911. p. 50-78).

Classification of depreciation.
Deduced from R. M. Hurd's assignments of life.

Construction	Occupancy	Term in life	Rate of fund proposed in %	Term of sinking fund @ 3%, in years.
Cheap frame	Residences	25-30	3-2	23-31
Better-class frame	Residences	50-75	2-1	31-47
Cheap brick	Residences	35-50	2-1	31-47
Better-class brick	Residences	50-75	1½-1	37-47

Note: Sinking-funds bring all the above within 47 years.

BURTON, H. J. Valuations and depreciations of city buildings, p. 21-2.

Residences 37 44 years

FOSTER, HORATIO A. Rates of depreciation. (In his *Engineering valuation of public utilities and factories.* 1913. p. 205).

Frame dwellings 35 years Wis. R. R. Comm.

GILLETTE, HALBERT P. and RICHARD T. DANA. Depreciation. (In their *Handbook of mechanical and electrical cost data.* 1918. p. 105).

Buildings, dwellings, frame 35 years Wis. R.R. Comm.

GRUNSKY, CARL EWALD. Probable useful life of various articles. (In his *Valuation, depreciation and the rate base.* 1917. p. 274.)

Frame dwellings
35 years
Wisconsin railroad commission. Quoted by H. A. Foster and in published reports.

NICHOLSON, J. LEE and JOHN F. D. ROHRBACH. Depreciation. (In their *Cost accounting.* 1919. p. 146).

Dwellings—frame 3%
Based on (1) the cost of equipment
(2) the life of the equipment
(3) on a ten-hour day.

PHILADELPHIA CONTROLLER. Rates of depreciation. (In his *Manual of accounting, reporting and business procedure of the city and county of Philadelphia.* 1917. p. 209).

Residences and other living quarters 1⅔%

ROBY, J. J. Schedule of plant depreciation. (In his *Treatise on cost accounting as applied to coal mining.* c1913. p. 14-15).

Dwellings
Deduct as salvage before depreciating 10%
Depreciation rate for remainder, non-fireproof 5
" " " " fireproof 4

STUCKMANN, H. Depreciation and obsolescence in Portland cement plants. *Journal of the American society of mechanical engineers,* Feb. 1913, p. 262-75.

	% of reproductive value.
Dwellings	5

DEPRECIATION, DEPLETION AND OBSOLESCENCE—DWELLINGS—*(Continued)*

TIFFANY, H. S. Dwellings. (In his *Digest of depreciations*. c1890. p. 5.
Dwellings
Brick or stone 1½-2½%
Frame 2½-4½
Based upon the actual life without any repairs.

VARIOUS depreciation charges. *New York Times*, June 14, 1914.
Dwellings 5%

Dyeing

ALWYN-SCHMIDT, L. W. Effect of machine depreciation upon cost of dye making. *Color trade journal*, April 1920. p. 103-6.

AUSTRALIA. FEDERAL INCOME TAX DEPARTMENT. Depreciation allowance. *Accountant*, Oct. 13, 1917, p. 277-9. *Accounting and commerce*, June 30, 1917, p. 55-7. *Federal accountant*, July 1917, p. 93-8. *Public accountant*, June 30, 1917, p. 145-52.
Woolen manufacturing machinery, scouring, carbonising, dyeing 5%

MONTGOMERY, ROBERT H. Textile industries. (In his *Income tax procedure*, 1919. p. 578-9.—Same, 1920. p. 735).
Dyeing and similar machinery subject to acid fumes 5%

STOCKWELL, HERBERT GRANT. Depreciation, renewal and replacement accounts; a paper read at the annual meeting held in Denver, Colorado, October 18-22, 1909, the American association of public accountants. p. 43. *American institute of accountants, Yearbook*, 1909, p. 236.
Dyeing machinery 14 years

Dynamos

AUSTRALIA. FEDERAL INCOME TAX DEPARTMENT. Depreciation allowance. *Accountant*, Oct. 13, 1917, p. 277-9. *Accounting and commerce*, June 30, 1917, p. 55-7. *Federal accountant*, July 1917, p. 93-8. *Public accountant*, Jan. 30, 1917, p. 145-52.
Alternators, dynamos, motor generators, rotary converters 5%
Written down value, repairs allowed.

BENTLEY, HARRY C. Depreciation. (In his *Science of accounts*. 1913. p. 146).
Dynamos 20% on original cost

BRYAN, WILLIAM H. Depreciation of electric light plants. *Municipality*, March 1908, p. 74.
Dynamos 20 years

BOLTON, REGINALD PELHAM. Depreciation of mechanical equipments and power plants. (In his *Building for profit*. 1911. p. 82, 89).

	Physical Years	%	Economic Years
Moderate-speed reciprocating engines, medium-speed rotary apparatus, dynamos and motors	15	37.5	12
Fan engines, high-speed rotary apparatus on large variations of loads, dynamos, motors, high-speed pressure engines, condensers	12	30.0	9

CROWELL, H. H. Electric lighting rates and depreciation. *Municipal journal and engineering*, Dec. 18, 1907, p. 698.

		Purchased 10 years or more ago	Modern
Dynamos	D.C.C.P.	20 years	20 years

DAWSON, PHILIP. Depreciation. (In his *Engineering and electric traction pocket-book*. Ed. 2, New York, John Wiley & sons. p. 1161.)

	% capital to cost
Dynamos and engines belted plants	5-10
	Years
Slow speed dynamos of modern design	15-35

EDWARDS, C. LEWIS. Electric lighting accounts. *Incorporated accountants' journal*, April 1912, p. 175.
Turbines and dynamos 5-7½%

FIGURES from the Iola (Kans.) central station. *Electrical world*, Sept. 23, 1909, p. 723.
Dynamos and alteration 7%

GRUNSKY, CARL EWALD. Probable useful life of various articles. (In his *Valuation, depreciation and the rate-base*. 1917. p. 278).
Electrical machinery, dynamos and alternators — 25 years. Robt. Hammond. Journal of Institute of Electrical Engineers, England, April 25, 1907. 30 years. 8% residual value. Sir Wm. Preece. Report of Bristol Corporation, England, 1906.

HAMMOND, ROBERT. Depreciation. *Journal of the Institute of electrical engineers*, 1907, p. 270. *Institute of electrical engineers, Proceedings*, April 25, 1907. Abstracts. *Accountant*, May 18, 1907, p. 675. *Electric railway review*, June 1, 1907, p. 716. *Electrical review* (Chicago), May 25, 1907, p. 828. *Electrical review* (London), May 3, 1907, p. 744. *Electrician*, April 26, 1907, p. 51. *Engineering magazine*, July 1907, p. 636-8. *Engineering record*, June 15, 1907, p. 703. *Municipal journal* (London), May 10, 17, 1907, p. 411, 435. *Progressive age*, July 1, 1907, p. 305. *Street railway bulletin*, June 1907, p. 382. *Tramway and railway world*, June 6, 1907, p. 497.
Dynamos and alternators 25 years

JOHNSON, GEORGE. Depreciation. (In his *Electric lighting accounts*. 1903. p. 23-4).
Dynamos 7½%

LIFE of plant. *Electrician*, Nov. 8, 1912, p. 182-4.
Dynamos and alternators 30 years
Wm. Preece

MCINTOSH, ROBERT J. Rates of depreciation. (In his *Reference book of accounts*. Ed. 2. p. 60).
Dynamos 5%
Based on lie

DEPRECIATION, DEPLETION AND OBSOLESCENCE—DYNAMOS—*(Continued)*

NICHOLSON, J. LEE and JOHN F. D. ROHRBACH. Depreciation. (In their *Cost accounting.* 1919. p. 147).
Dynamos 5%
Based on (1) the cost of equipment
(2) the life of the equipment
(3) on a ten-hour day.

PHILADELPHIA. CONTROLLER. Rates of depreciation. (In his *Manual of accounting, reporting and business procedure of the city and county of Philadelphia.* 1917. p. 204).
Dynamos and motors 5%

PIEZ, CHARLES. Perpetual inventory and appraisal values; table of standard depreciation rates. *Engineering and contracting,* Jan. 24, 1917 p. 77. *Factory,* Dec. 1916, p. 668-71. *Iron Age;* Nov. 30, 1916, Jan. 11, 1917, p. 1266, 138-9. *Iron trade review,* Feb. 22, 1917, p. 477-8. Condensed. *Journal of the American society of mechanical engineers,* Dec. 1916, p. 965-6. *Iron trade review,* Dec. 7, 1916, p. 1144-6. Kent, William, *Bookkeeping and cost accounting for factories,* 1918, p. 90. Discussion. *Journal of the American society of mechanical engineers,* March, 1917, p. 215-7.

ROBY, J. J. Schedule of plant depreciation. (In his *Treatise on cost accounting as applied to coal mining.* c1913. p. 14-5).
Engines, dynamos and switchboards.
Deduct as salvage before depreciating 20%
Depreciation rate for remainder, fireproof 4

THOMPSON, C. BERTRAND. Interest and depreciation. (In his *How to find facotry costs.* c1916. p. 69).
Dynamos portable engines, motors and electrical equipment could be figured at from 10-15%

	% on cost	% on reducing balance
Engines and dynamos	5	10

PIXLEY, FRANCIS W. Electric lighting companies. (In his *Accountancy.* Ed. 2. p. 218).
Dynamos 7½ per cent per annum

UNIFORM cost sheet for coal mining companies. *Coal age,* Sept. 19, 1918, p. 545-7.

	original cost
Dynamos and engines	8%

Economizers

BREWER, ALLAN F. Rates for annual depreciation. *Industrial management,* April 1918, p. 268.
Fuel economizers 25 years 4%

ELBOURNE, EDWARD T. Depreciation rates. (In his *Factory administration and accounts.* 1918. p. 376).

	Prov. dep. % Remainder values	Years 10%	5%
Economizers, fuel	7½	29	38

GILLETTE, HALBERT POWERS and RICHARD T. DANA. Depreciation. (In their *Handbook of mechanical and electrical cost data.* 1918. p. 107).
Economizers 10-20 years
Bion J. Arnold. Chicago appraisals four cases.

GRUNSKY, CARL EWALD. Probable useful life of various articles. (In his *Valuation, depreciation and the rate-base.* 1917. p. 278).

Economizers	10-20 years	Henry Floy. Four Chicago appraisals. Transactions American institute of electrical engineers June 1911. Third Avenue case figures adopted by Public service commission of New York.
	15	Chicago Union traction co. Quoted in Report Wisconsin R. R. Commission, vol. 10, p. 220.
	20	Stone & Webster. Figures for Chicago Union Traction co. case. Report Wisconsin railroad commission, vol. 10, p. 220.

PENDER, HAROLD. Depreciation. (In his *Handbook for electrical engineers.* c1914. p. 339).
Heaters, economizers and pumps

15 years	Chicago union traction co.
20	Stone & Webster for Chicago union traction co.
7.5%	Milwaukee electric railway and light co.
6.66	Chicago union traction co.
5	Cardiff tramways
	Glasgow tramways
	Stone & Webster for Chicago union traction co.

PHILADELPHIA. CONTROLLER. Rates of depreciation. (In his *Manual of accounting, reporting and business procedure of the city and county of Philadelphia.* 1917. p. 205).
Patent stokers and fuel economizers 5%

Edison tube

CROWELL, H. H. Electric lighting rates and depreciation. *Municipal journal and engineering,* Dec. 18, 1907, p. 698.

	Purchased 10 years or more ago	Modern
Edison tube	25 years	30 years

Ejectors

ELBOURNE, EDWARD T. Depreciation rates. (In his *Factory administration and accounts.* 1918. p. 376).

	Prov. dep. % Remainder values	Years 10%	5%
Ejectors	12½	17	22

DEPRECIATION, DEPLETION AND OBSOLESCENCE—*(Continued)*

Election booths

PHILADELPHIA. CONTROLLER. Rates of depreciation. (In his *Manual of accounting, reporting and business procedure of the city and county of Philadelphia.* 1917. p. 207-8).

Telephone and election booths 5%

Electric and street railroads

See also various headings under Depreciation, depletion and obsolescence.

ACCOUNTING for depreciation as prescribed by the Interstate commerce commission. *Electric railway review,* July 13, 1907, p. 32.

ALLCOCK, JOHN S. Allowance for depreciation: Cardiff tramways and electric light. *Accountant,* Dec. 28, 1907, Jan. 11, 1908, p. 787-9, 64-5. *Incorporated accountants' journal,* 1907-8, p. 80.

ALLCOCK, JOHN S. Depreciation of Cardiff electric tramway and lighting undertakings. *Electric railway review,* Jan. 4, 1908 p. 16.

ALLCOCK, JOHN S. Track depreciation at Cardiff. *Tramway and railway world,* Jan. 6, 1910, p. 30.

ALLOWANCE for maintenance to cover depreciation. Light railway and tramway journal (London), July 2, 1909, p. 29.

ALLOWANCE for obsolescence upheld in franchise tax case. *Electric railway journal,* Dec. 10, 1910, p. 1154.

AMERICAN ELECTRIC RAILWAY ASSOCIATION. COMMITTEE ON VALUATION. Bibliography on valuation of public utilities to December 23, 1915. 61+72p.

AMERICAN ELECTRIC RAILWAY ASSOCIATION. Maintenance and depreciation; abstracts from commission's decisions and engineers' reports, including a bibliography. New York. American electric railway association, Dec. 1, 1919, 43p.

ANALYSIS of the premises adopted and methods used in determining the cost to reproduce new together with the depreciation thereon of the physical property of the Metropolitan system and the Kansas City and Westport Belt railway of Kansas City, Mo. *Engineering and contracting,* May 28, 1913, p. 617-20.

Item	years	Depreciation per year.
Timber structures	25	
Steel structures	33⅓	
Steel trusses	50	
Plate girders	66⅔	
Pole base, cast iron	40	2½
Iron poles	35	3
Box	35	3
Plate	35	3
Tubular	40	2½
Latticed	30	3½
Cedar poles	20	5
Pole brackets	25	4
Cross arms:		
Wood	20	5
Iron	30	3⅓
Weatherproof cables	30	3⅓
Lead cables	35	3
Transmission line material	20	5
Miscellaneous	20	5
Bare copper	100	1

Rates of Depreciation

	Percent
Coal and ash handling machinery combined	7
Coal handling machinery	6
Ash handling machinery	8
Grates and stokers, maximum	25
That is, depreciated 10% per year for 2½ years, no further depreciation being applied if they are in use.	
Boilers	
Horizontal tubular boilers and settings	8
Water tube boilers and settings	3½
Smoke breeching:	
Steel smoke breeching	10
Brick smoke breeching	5
Stacks:	
Self supporting steel stacks	6
Brick or concrete	3
Guyed steel stacks	8
Heaters:	
Open heaters	3
Closed steel heaters	6
Closed cast iron heaters	4
Water softening apparatus:	
All steel apparatus	5
Pumps	5
Air compressors:	
Steam driven air compressors	5
Motor driven air compressors	5
Engines:	
Corliss slow-speed engines	3
Automatic high speed engines	5-8
Steam turbines with generators	4

DEPRECIATION, DEPLETION AND OBSOLESCENCE — ELECTRIC AND STREET RAILROADS — *(Continued)*

Condensers:	
Cast iron surface condensers	5
Steam driven condensing apparatus	5
Barometric condensers	3½
Piping and covering	3½
Generators and transformers:	
Slow-speed generators	4
High-speed generators	5
Transformers	5
Belt driven generators	5
Rotary converters	5
Switchboards and generator leads:	
Switchboards	3
Generator leads	3
Wiring and cable	3
Traveling cranes	3
Miscellaneous plant tools	25% of total
Cable winding machinery	3-5

ANOTHER six cent fare granted. *Electric railway journal,* Sept. 25, 1915, p. 628-31.
From 1902-1915 the yearly expenditures for maintenance and depreciation averaged 22-42% of operating revenue. . .

ARBITRARY depreciation requirement. *Railway world,* Feb. 16, 1912, p. 141.

ARBITRATED result in Cleveland. *Electric railway journal,* June 28, 1913, p. 1134.

ARBITRATION of operating expense charges in Cleveland. *Electric railway journal,* May 24, 1913, p. 925.

ATKINSON, A. C. Construction and depreciation. *Electric traction weekly,* July 17, 1909, p. 919.

ATKINSON, A. S. Reducing the cost of depreciation on electric railways. *Street railway bulletin,* Feb. 1907, p. 80.

BAGG, F. A. Life of railway physical property from engineering standpoint. *Electrical railway journal,* Dec. 9, 1911, p. 1205-6. Discussion, Dec. 9, 1911, p. 1210.

Material:	Life and years.
Ties in open track:	
Cedar	15 to 20
Yellow pine	10 to 15
Treated ties	25 and more
Untreated ties in pavement or concrete	15 to 20
Treated ties	30 and more
Galvanized wire fencing	10
Wooden bridges	20
Steel bridges	30 and over
Ashlar concrete bridge masonry	100 and over
Asphalt pavement	10 to 15
Brick pavement	15 to 25
Yellow pine trolley poles	10 to 15
Chestnut trolley poles	15
Cedar trolley poles	15 to 20
Trolley wire	15-20

BARKER, HARRY. Depreciation of electric railway property. (In his *Public utility rates.* 1917. p. 367).

	Years	Authority*	Control†
Cars	30	B. J. Arnold	Det.
Car bodies, open type	25	Chicago Trac. Val. Comm.	Det.
closed type	20	Chicago Trac. Val. Comm.	Det.
trucks	30	Chicago Trac. Val. Comm.	Det.
motors	5	Wis. R. R. Comm., H. Floy	Det.
misc. elec. equipment	10-15	*	Det.
Feeder conduit	30-50	Wis. R. R. Comm.	Obs.
Feeders, insulated aerial	10-15	" " "	Det.
Overhead construction trolley wire, No. O, 1 min. headway	2	Wis. R. R. Comm.	
Overhead construction, trolley wire, No. 00, 1 min. headway	2½	" " "	Det. Reduced 25% in size
Overhead construction trolley wire, No. OOO, 1 min. headway	3	Wis. R. R. Comm.	
Overhead construction, single-catenary support	15-20	*	Det.
Overhead construction, double-catenary support	20-25	*	Det.
Overhead construction, cross spans and brackets	15-20	Wis. R. R. Comm.	Det.
Poles, cedar in earth	14	Wis. R. R. Comm.	Det.
Wood in concrete	20	" " "	Det.
Iron or steel	40	" " "	Det.
Track, tangent	18	" " "	Det.
curves	5	*	Det.
special work	5	*	Det.
Trestles (see Railways)			

*Where no authority is cited the data are those of the author—average or approximate figures secured by examination or enquiry.

†Probable action limiting service life; deterioration (due to wear and tear and weathering and obsoletion. Where both are cited, both actions have been secured, the first named predominating in a majority of cases.

DEPRECIATION, DEPLETION AND OBSOLESCENCE — ELECTRIC AND STREET RAILROADS — *(Continued)*

BAY state rate case. *Electric railway journal,* Dec. 4, 1915, p. 1121-3. *Public utility reports, annotated,* 1916F, p. 336-9.

Table I—Statement of Lives of Property Used in Computing Annual Depreciation

	Years
Bridges, Culverts and Drains	
Steel bridges over railroads	25
Steel bridges over streams	30
Timber bridges over railroads	15
Timber bridges over streams	20
Timber culverts	20
Dry rubble culverts	25
Masonry and concrete structures	75
Vitrified pipe culverts and drains	30
Cast-iron pipe culverts and drains	60
Catch basins	50
Buildings	
Dependent upon material and type	15-75
Cars and Car Equipment	
Bodies	
D.T. semis	20
S.T. semis	22
D.T. box	25
S.T. box	28
D.T. open	25
S.T. open	30
Express	20
Snow-plows	18-20
Trucks	10-20
Motors	20
Controllers	25
Control cable	Life of car
Air-brake compressors	20
Registers	18
Arc headlights	8
Jacks and saws	25
Distribution system	
Poles	
Iron	40
Cedar	20
Chestnut	16
Hard pine	12
Cross-arms	10
Guys and anchors	16
Miscellaneous work on poles	15
Trolley	2-30
Overhead feeder	25-30
Underground cable	30
Submarine cable	10
Furniture	40
Miscellaneous Equipment	
Horses, automobiles, wagons, etc.	5-10
Paving	
Asphalt and asphaltina	15-20
Bitulithic	12-15
Bituminous macadam	10-18
Water bound macadam	8-15
Concrete and hassam	‡ 12-25
Grouted brick on concrete base	15-25
Wood block on concrete base	20-30
Wood block on bridges	10-20
Plank on bridges	5
Granite	* 20-60
Cobble and cobble mixed	Same as rail
Power Plant Equipment	
Boilers—water tube	25-30
Boilers—fire tube	20
Engines	30-40
Turbo—generators	20
Condensers	20-25
Pumps	12-20
Stokers	15
Heaters	25-30
Coal—handling machinery	25
Piping	25
Generators—d.c.	30-40
Alternators	25
Switchboards and wiring,	Average of generator served
Roadway Machinery and Tools	
Larger pieces of equipment only	15-20
Shop Equipment	
Machine units	15-25
Signals and Interlocking Apparatus	
Hand-thrown signals	10

DEPRECIATION, DEPLETION AND OBSOLESCENCE — Electric and street railroads — *(Continued)*

Automatic signals	14
Signal wire	15
Submarine signal cable	10
Underground signal cable	30
Telephone and Telegraph Lines	
Telephone sets	10
Iron box telephone sets	14
Telephone wire	15
Submarine telephone cable	10
Underground telephone cable	30
Track and Roadway	
Rails, including all fastenings	10-35
Ties	
Paved track—same as rail	10-35
Unpaved track—under good backfill	16
Unpaved track—open to weather	12
Bonds—same as rail to which they are attached	
Special work	6-20
Track and roadway labor—same as rail or special work where labor was incurred	
Grading and ballast—not depreciated.	
Underground conduits	50

‡ Very little near twenty-five years
* Twice life of rail.

Bay state street railway valuation. *Electric railway journal,* Dec. 4, 1915, p. 1121-3.

Table II—Statement of Annual Depreciation Necessary for Each Property

	Annual Depreciation Per Cent. ‡‡
Grading	2.0
Ties	5.6
Rails, rail fastenings and joints	3.5
Special work	5.7
Track and roadway labor	4.4
Paving	3.1
Roadway machinery and tools	4.0
Bridges, trestles and culverts	3.0
Crossings, fences and signs	2.0
Signals and interlocking apparatus	7.2
Telephone and telegraph lines	6.9
Poles and fixtures	5.9
Underground conduits	2.0
Distribution system	3.7
Track bonding	2.6
Shops and car houses	2.3
Stations, miscellaneous buildings	2.3
Wharves and docks	1.3
Park and resort property	3.8
Passenger and combination cars	4.6
Freight, express and mail cars	5.1
Service equipment	5.2
Electric equipment of cars	4.4
Shop equipment	2.8
Furniture	2.4
Miscellaneous equipment	11.0
Power plant buildings	1.8
Substation buildings	1.6
Power plant equipment	3.4
Substation equipment	3.2
Transmission system	3.1
Total	3.90
Composite life in years	22.7

‡‡ Annual depreciation divided by investment.

Bemis, Edward W. Testimony on depreciation before Nebraska commission re the consolidation of the properties of the Lincoln traction company. *Electric railway journal,* March 12, 1910, p. 441.

A plant with an average of 20 years would have to set aside 3 per cent of its investment annually in a five per cent sinking fund to pay the principle at the end of 20 years.

Bowker, William R. Depreciation and permanent renewal fund. *Street railway bulletin,* May 1907, p. 298.

Bryan, William. Appraisal and depreciation of water-works and similar properties. *Journal of the association of engineering societies,* Dec. 1907, p. 336-81. Depreciation allowance for various public service industries. *Engineering news,* Jan. 23, 1908, p. 96.

	years	Percent straight
Trolley line	12.5-25	5

Capital value of a tramway. *Tramway and railway world,* Nov. 9, 1911.

Cardiff tramways finance. *Electrical engineer,* Dec. 24, 1909, p. 879.

Cleveland hearing. *Electric railway journal,* May 24, 31, 1913, p. 925, 971.

Conway, T. Up-state New York lines need relief. *Electric railway journal,* June 16, 1917, p. 1092-5.

Cravens, George W. Depreciation and maintenance of electrical equipment. Foster, H. A. *Engineering valuation of public utilities and factories.* 1913. p. 201-2. *Electrical review,* April 23, 1910, p. 853-6. Montgomery, Robert H. *Auditing theory and practice.* 1916. p. 424. Montgomery, Robert H. *Income tax procedure,* 1919. p. 570. ——— Same, 1920. p. 722-4. See table p. 429.

DEPRECIATION, DEPLETION AND OBSOLESCENCE — ELECTRIC AND STREET RAILROADS — *(Continued)*

TABLE I. PERCENTAGE DEPRECIATION PER ANNUM

	Chicago Traction Commission	Chicago Union Traction Co.	Milwaukee Electric Railway & Light Co.	Wisconsin Railroad Commission	Average English	Average Scotch Practice	Philip Dawson	Stone & Webster	Industrial Power Plants	Prof. G. F. Gebhardt	Miscellaneous Sources
Buildings	..	2	3	2	2.5	2.5	1-2	2	1-2	2	2
Boilers	3.5-10	6.6	7.5	6.6-8.5	5	5	8-10	5	2.5-3.3	4-6.6	7.5
Steam Piping	3.5	6.6	7.5	5	5	5	8-10	5	2.5-3.3	5-8	5
Auxiliaries	5-10	6.6	5	6.6-8.5	5	5	8-10	5	4-6.6	3-5	7.5
Steam Engines	3-10	6.6	5	5-6.6	5	5	4-6	5	2.5-5	4-6.6	5
Steam Turbines	..	..	5	..	5	5	7-9	5	2.5-5	4	4
Belted Generators	5-10	6.6	7.5	5	5	5	5-10	5	6.6	3.3-4	7.5
Direct Connected Generators	5	6.6	7.5	5	5	5	4-8	5	4	3.3-4	5
Wires and Cables	2	6.6	5	2	5	3	3.5	5	4-6.6	5	5
Switchboards, etc.	2	6.6	5	2	7.5	5	8-10	5	2-5	..	5
Rotary Converters	..	6.6	5	5	5	5	8-10	5	4-5	4	5
Transformers	..	6.6	5	5	5	5	5-6	5	3-5	4	5
Motors	5-10	6.6	5	5	5	5	5-8	5	4-6.6	5	5
Storage Batteries	..	6.6	10	..	5	5	9-11	5	5-10	6.6	10
Overhead Systems	..	10-14	7.5	..	..	3	4-8	10-14	5-10	..	10
Cars	..	5-8.5	6-7.5	5-6.6	10	7.5	4-6	5-8.5	..	..	7.5
Trackwork	..	7.75	7.5-12	5	5	8	7-13	7.2	..	..	7.5
Shop equipment	3-10	5	7.5	3.3-10	7.5	7.5	12-15	5	4-10	..	7.5
Supplies and Miscellaneous	5	..	5	..	5	7.5	1.5-2	..	5		5

DEPRECIATION, DEPLETION AND OBSOLESCENCE — ELECTRIC AND STREET RAILROADS — *(Continued)*

Table II.

Percentage Depreciation For Given Service.

Items of Equipment	Light or Intermittent Service	Heavy or Continuous Service
Boilers, Water Tube	4-6.6	5-8.3
" Fire Tube	5-6.6	6.6-10
Piping, Steam and Water	4-5.5	5.5-8.3
Auxiliaries, Steam	3-5	4-6.6
Engines, Steam	4-5	5-6.6
Turbines, Steam	3-4	4-5
Generators, Belted	4-6.6	5-8.3
" Direct Connected	3-5	4-6.6
Wires and Cables	3-5	4-6.6
Switchboards and Instruments	2-5	5-8.3
Rotary Converters	3-5	4-6.6
Transformers	3-5	4-6.6
Motors, A. C. and D. C.	4-6.6	5-8.3
Storage Batteries	5-6.6	6.6-10
Overhead Systems	4-10	8.3-12.5
Cars and Equipments	5-8.3	6.6-10
Track Work, Ballast, etc.	5-8.3	7.5-12.5
Shop Equipment, Tools, etc.	5-10	7.5-15

DALRYMPLE, JAMES. Tramway accounts. (In Lisle, George. *Encyclopaedia of accounting.* v.6. p. 225-43).

Depreciation 3%

DAVIES, H. J. Maintenance provisions of Cleveland ordinance. *Electric railway journal,* April 2, 1910, p. 614-5.

DAWSON, PHILIP. Depreciation. (In his *Engineering and electric traction pocket-book.* Ed.2. p. 1161.)

Approximate rates of depreciation to be allowed in percent of capital cost.

	Percent.		Percent.
Buildings	1	to	2
Turbines	7	"	9
Boilers	8	"	10
Dynamos and engines, belted plants	5	"	10
Belts	25	"	30
Large slow-speed steam engines	4	"	6
Large slow-speed direct driven plants	4	"	8
Stationary transformers	5	"	6
Accumulators in central stations	9	"	11
Trolley line	4	"	8
Feeder cables	3	"	5
Lighting and current meters	8	"	10
Cars	4	"	6
Repair shop and test-room fitting	12	"	15
Motors	5	"	8
Rotary transformers	8	"	10
Boilers and engines	6	"	10
Spare parts	1½	"	2
Track work	7	"	13
Bonding	6	"	10
On remaining capital expenditure incurred	4	"	6

Durability of railroad sleepers

from a report of the United States department of agriculture.

	Years
White oak and chestnut oak	8
Chestnut	8
Black locust	10
Cherry, black walnut, locust	7
Elm	6-7
Red and black oaks	4-5
Ash, beech, and maple	4
Redwood	12
Cypress and red cedar	10
Tamarack	7-8
Longleaf pine	6
Hemlock	4-6
Spruce	5

Approximate Life of various parts of well-installed and maintained plant

	Years
Track	10-15
Overhead line	10-20
Building	Practically indefinite, say 50 years
Slow speed steam engines	20-40
Boilers, pumps, piping, etc.	15-30
Slow speed dynamos of modern design	15-35
Cables	10-20
Tram or railway motors	10-20
Stationary motors	10-35

DEPRECIATION, DEPLETION AND OBSOLESCENCE — ELECTRIC AND STREET RAILROADS — *(Continued)*

DECISION in the Milwaukee fare case. *Electric railway journal,* Aug. 31, 1912, p. 314-23.
DECISION of board of arbitration in the Cleveland case. *Electric railway journal,* June 28, 1913, p. 1159.
DEPRECIATION. *Electric railway review,* Aug. 1906, p. 452. *Electrical review* (London), July 5, 1907, p. 2. *Electrician,* Aug. 28, 1908, p. 744. *Municipal journal* (London), May 24, 1907, June 5, 1908, p. 449, 459.
DEPRECIATION account of the Kokomo, Marion and Western traction company. *Electric railway journal,* July 22, 1911, p. 156-7.

Distributing lines of the electric light department

Wire	2%
Poles	7%
Wire attachments	7%
Guy wires and anchors	2%

DEPRECIATION and Chicago valuation figures. *Electric traction weekly,* May 18, 1912, p. 584.
DEPRECIATION and permanent renewal fund. *Street railway bulletin,* May 1907, p. 298.
DEPRECIATION and publicity in Iowa. *Electric railway review,* May 2, 1908, p. 523.
DEPRECIATION and reserve funds in Milwaukee. *Street railway journal,* Sept. 23, 1905, p. 441.
DEPRECIATION and reserves, warning to Newcastle. *Tramway and railway world,* Sept. 6, 1906, p. 258.
DEPRECIATION and sinking funds. *Accountant,* June 13-Aug. 26, 1903, p. 768-9, 797-800, 825-7, 838-9, 862-6, 882-6, 922-4, 943-6, 979-82, 1003-6, 1124-5, 1135-9, 1149-52.
DEPRECIATION as applicable to electric railways. *Street railway journal,* Nov. 24, 1906.
DEPRECIATION at Sunderland. *Tramway and railway world,* Nov. 12, 1903, p. 478.
DEPRECIATION charges in Kansas city. *Electric railway journal,* Sept. 17, 1910, p. 424.
DEPRECIATION charges of the International traction company. *Electric railway review,* April 18, 1908. p. 472.
DEPRECIATION from a managers point of view. *Stone and Webster public service journal,* Aug. 1907, p. 69-71.
DEPRECIATION fund in St. Louis. *Electric railway journal,* March 12, 1910, p. 433.

In the year 1905 the United Railways company of St. Louis began to set aside 5 per cent of its gross earnings as a depreciation reserve.

DEPRECIATION funds. *United States census bureau.* (In *Special report on street and electric railways.* 1907. p. 165).
DEPRECIATION funds in Europe. *Electric railway journal,* May 7, 1904, p. 696. Editorial. May 21, 1904, p. 760.

The Berlin-Hohenschonhausen Strassenbahn charges off 1½ per cent of the cost of the equipment.

In Brussels the life of the track is estimated at 25 years, that of conduit lines at 15 years and splice-bars at 12 years. The life of the cars is figured at 25 years and the power station for the same length of time. The overhead construction is figured at 25 years except trolley wire which is put at 10 years.

The municipal tramways of Cologne have not yet been in operation long enough to determine the amount to be charged off. The management at present is charging off 8 per cent of the cost of the rolling stock and 1 per cent of the cost of the buildings.

The Czernowitz railway charges 1½% of the track construction, 3% of the rolling stock, ¼% of the buildings, 2½% of the power station equipment, 1½% of the feeder construction, and 2% of the rest of the equipment.

The municipal road in Frankfort charges 5% of the track, 5% of the overhead equipment and 6% of the mechanical and electrical equipment.

The Glasgow municipal tramways charges off £450 per mile of single track per year, 7⅓% of the cost of the rolling stock, 2½% of the buildings, 5% of the power station equipment, 3% of the underground cables, 7½% of the bonds, 3% of the poles and overhead con struction, and 5% of the section boxes, miscellaneous equipment 7½%.

The Leysziger Strassenbahn charges off 2% of the track, 4% of the overhead equipment, 8%of the rolling stock, 1½% of the buildings and 8% of the power station equipment.

In Mannheim the practice is to charge off for the track construction 5%, motor cars 7%, trail cars 5%, building 1%, feeders, 1%, pole line 3½%, rest of the overhead equipment, 8%.

In Remscheid the proportion is track construction 2%, rolling stock 10%, power station equipment 6%, conductor lines 3%, other electrical apparatus 8%.

DEPRECIATION hearings closed at Boston. *Electric railway journal,* May 23, 1914, p. 1152.
DEPRECIATION in Cleveland. *Street railway journal,* April 27, 1907, p. 743.
DEPRECIATION interesting report from Cardiff. *Municipal journal* (London), Dec. 20, 1907, p. 1083.
DEPRECIATION of air-breaking equipments. *Electric railway journal,* March, 30, 1912, p. 505.
DEPRECIATION of Cardiff electric tramway and lighting undertakings. *Electric railway review,* Jan. 4, 1908, p. 16.
DEPRECIATION of Cardiff properties. *Electric railway journal,* Sept. 10, 1910, p. 409.
DEPRECIATION of electric railway equipment. *Electric traction weekly,* July 17, 1907, p. 736.
DEPRECIATION of electric railways. *Electrical review and Western electrician,* July 3, 1909, p. 1. *Wisconsin railroad commission.* Report, 1913. v. 10, p. 215-40.
DEPRECIATION of equipment accounts. *Electric railway journal,* July 4, 1908, p. 193.
DEPRECIATION of overhead structures and substations. *Engineering and contracting,* Nov. 19, 1913, p. 567.

Trolley wire—copper	4%
Trolley wire—steel	5
Feeder wire	1
Poles and fixtures	5
Steel bridges	3
Track bonding	4
High tension line, including copper	2
Substations	3

DEPRECIATION of public utilities properties. *Electric railway journal,* Feb. 1, 1908, p. 169. Editorial. Depreciation. *Electric railway journal,* Jan. 25, 1908, p. 104.

DEPRECIATION, DEPLETION AND OBSOLESCENCE — ELECTRIC AND STREET RAILROADS — *(Continued)*

DEPRECIATION of tramways. *Accountant,* April 29, May 6, July 29, 1893, p. 392-5, 410-2, 671-2.

DEPRECIATION of tramways and light railways. *Light railway and tramway journal* (London), Aug. 6, 1909, p. 80.

DEPRECIATION rates used by the Seattle (Wash.) municipal street railway. *Electric railway journal,* June 24, 1916, p. 1185).

Way and structures:	
Poles and fixtures	10%
Distribution system	10
Shops and car-houses	2
Equipment:	
Cars	5
Fare boxes	8½
Fenders	8½
Freight cars	8½
Service equipment	8½
Electric equipment of cars	8½
Shop equipment	5
Furniture	5

DEPRECIATION reserves of the Milwaukee and St. Louis railways. *Electric railway review,* March 9, 1907, p. 319.

DEPRECIATION, some thoughts on policy and practice. *Municipal journal* (London), Aug. 28, 1903, p. 773.

DISCUSSION on depreciation of equipment. *Electric railway journal,* Dec. 19, 1914, p. 1335-7.

EDWARDS, H. M. Depreciation accounts: their treatment by Interborough rapid transit co. *Electric railway journal,* June 3, Aug. 12, 1911, p. 972, 280. Abstract. *Electrical review,* June 10, 1911, p. 1162.

ELECTRIC railway securities from the investor's standpoint. *American electric railway association, Proceedings,* 1913, p. 217.

ELECTRIC railway system of Milwaukee and Eastern Wisconsin. *Street railway journal,* June 1899, p. 352.

ENNIS, WILLIAM DUANE. Depreciation. (In his *Works management.* 1911. p. 87).
The reports of 13 large street railway companies in 1909 showed the whole depreciation charge to have varied from 0.7 to 13.7 per cent of gross earnings.

EXPENSES for operation renewals and depreciation of Milwaukee city system. *Electric railway journal,* May 22, 1909, p. 955.

FINAL testimony and arguments in the Cleveland case. *Electric railway journal,* May 31, June 14, 1913, p. 971, 1070-6.

FISH, W. Depreciation reserve fund. *Electric railway journal,* Jan. 31, 1920, p. 239-47.

FISH, WILLISTON. Need of depreciation reserves; no good reason why they should not be established by all electric railways. *Aera,* Jan. 1920, p. 699-706.

FLOY, HENRY. Depreciation. (In his *Valuation of public utility properties.* 1912. p. 199).

	Percent of gross revenue expended or appropriated for Maintenance	Depreciation.
Milwaukee companies		
Railway departments	11.3	9.9
United railways company of St. Louis	13.67	10.0
Omaha and Council Bluffs street railway co.	7.00	10.0
Chicago street railways	6.00	8.0
Philadelphia rapid transit co.	Undivided	15

FLOY, HENRY. Depreciation as related to electrical properties. *American institute of electrical engineers, Proceedings,* 1911, p. 1267. Abstracts. *Electric railway journal,* July 1, 1911, p. 214. Absolute and theoretical depreciation. *Engineering record,* Sept. 16, 1911, p. 333. *Scientific American supplement,* Dec. 9, 1911, p. 374. Depreciation; by H. C. D. Nutting. *Electrical world,* Aug. 5, 1911, p. 323-4. *Engineering magazine,* Aug. 1911, p. 837-40.

FOR immediate depreciation accounts. *Electric railway review,* Aug. 17, 1907, p. 182.

FORD, FRANK R. Treatment of depreciation of street railway properties. *Engineering and contracting,* June 15, 1910, p. 560. *Electric railway journal,* Feb. 12, 1910, p. 284.

	Depreciation per cent gross earnings
Baltimore—United Railways & Electric co.	11.9
Milwaukee Electric railway and light co.	10.0
Minneapolis-Twin city R. T. co.	8.5
Buffalo-International Tr. co.	7.7
St. Louis-United Rys.	5.0
Montreal St. Ry.	4.5
Detroit United ry.	4.2
Toronto railway	4.2
Washington ry. & elec. co.	4.0
Washington-capital traction co.	3.8
Boston elevated ry.	1.4
Brooklyn rapid transit co.	.7
Kansas city ry. & lt. co.	13.7

DEPRECIATION, DEPLETION AND OBSOLESCENCE — ELECTRIC AND STREET RAILROADS — *(Continued)*

FORSE, W. H. Depreciation and appreciation. *Electric railway journal,* Dec. 11, 1915, p. 1169-70.

Table II.

Maintenance and Depreciation as Shown in Published Reports of Electric Railways

	Percentage of Gross Operation Revenue		
	Maintenance	Depreciation (and renewals)	Total
Boston Elevated Railway:			
Year ended June 30, 1914	17.1	None	17.1
Year ended June 30, 1913	18.1	None	18.1
Brooklyn Rapid Transit Company:			
Year ended June 30, 1913	16.0		16.0
Year ended June 30, 1912	16.3		16.3
Chicago Railways:			
Year ended Jan. 31, 1914	7.0	8.0 (renewals)	15.0
Year ended Jan. 31, 1913	7.8	8.0 (renewals)	15.8
Interborough Rapid Transit Company:			
Year ended June 30, 1914	Items not shown separately		12.0
Year ended June 30, 1913	Items not shown separately		13.9
Montreal tramways:			
Year ended June 30, 1914	11.6	5.8 renewals	17.4
Philadelphia Rapid Transit Company:			
Year ended June 30, 1914	11.0	Renewals Res. 4.0	15
Year ended June 30, 1913	10.4	Renewals Res. 4.6	15.
("Established policy is to set aside 15 per cent for maintenance and renewals.")			
Terre Haute, Indianapolis & Eastern Traction Company:			
Year ended Dec. 31, 1913	18.0		18.0
Union Traction Company of Indiana:			
Year ended Dec. 31, 1913	18.5	None	18.5
Year ended Dec. 31, 1912	19.7		19.7
United Railways & Electric Company:			
Year ended Dec. 31, 1913	9.8	5.9	15.7
Year ended Dec. 31, 1912	9.8	4.4	14.2
Washington Railway & Electric Company:			
Year ended Dec. 31, 1913	Items not shown separately		16.3
Year ended Dec. 31, 1912	Items not shown separatey		15.9

Table I.

Showing Various Annual Rates Used for Depreciation of Rolling Stock Equipment

Road No.

1—An arbitrary charge of $1,200 per year.
2—4 per cent of original cost less estimated value of salvage.
3—6 cents per car-mile for maintenance and depreciation.
4—3 per cent of the original value.
5—5 per cent of the valuation of equipment.
6—An arbitrary charge of $3,600 per year.
7—3 per cent of record book value.
8—One twenty-fifth of 75 per cent of original cost. (Twenty-five year life; 25 per cent salvage.)
9—Arbitrary deduction from income; $500,000 per year for several years.
10—1 per cent of appraised value.
11—2 per cent of value.
12—3 per cent of cost of equipment.
13—1 per cent of gross value.
14—An arbitrary charge of $2,400 per year.
15—One twenty-fifth of 75 per cent of original cost.
16—5 per cent of value.
17—2 per cent of estimated value.
18—4 per cent of estimated cost less 25 per cent salvage.
19—2½ per cent of present value.
20—Arbitrary charge of $12,000 per year.
21—2 per cent of book value.
22—2½ per cent of inventory value.
23—An arbitrary charge of $1,000 per year.
24—5 per cent of appraised value.
25—6 per cent of gross income.
26—6 per cent of gross earnings for maintenance and depreciation.
27—Arbitrary charge of 4.3 per cent of investment.
28—5 per cent of appraised value less estimated salvage.
29—10 per cent of value.
30—5 per cent of estimated value.
31—2 per cent of book cost including betterments.

FOSTER, HORATIO A. Depreciation. (In his *Engineering valuation of public utilities and factories.* 1913. p. 169-70, 193).

Electric light and railway	Minimum service value, percent of reproduction cost.
Copper wire, waterproof	Weight of copper
Lead-covered cable, underground and overhead	
Poles both wood and iron, anchors and guys	20%
Service transformers	25%
Arc lamps and span equipment	20%
Service and watt meters	80%

DEPRECIATION, DEPLETION AND OBSOLESCENCE — ELECTRIC AND STREET RAILROADS — *(Continued)*

In a lease of the Northern and Western Chicago Street Railroad companies to the Chicago Union Traction company . . . the provision for depreciation recommended by the engineers was equivalent to 5.59% of the original cost in the case of the Northern Chicago lines and 5.68 per cent of the original cost in the case of the Western Chicago lines. The total charge in respect of maintenance and depreciation recommended by them was equivalent to 21.77 per cent and 23.70 per cent of the gross earnings of the North and West side lines respectively.

FOSTER, HORATIO A. Rates of depreciation. (In his *Engineering valuation of public utilities and factories.* 1913. p. 198-9, 205-6).

In the Milwaukee Three-Cent fare case, a number of engineers testified as to rates of depreciation, and these have been tabulated in comparison with rates specified by other engineers and companies. The table follows:

Rates of Depreciation Compared for the Milwaukee Case.

	Cooley-Beegs-Starrett-Pence			Union T. Co. Case	Chicago U. T. Co. Stone & Webster		Officials M. E. R. & L Co.	Arnold Chicago Appraisals Four Cases
Buildings								
Improvements	4&2		2	2	2	2	3	
Track, Main	8	8.5	8		7.75	7.2	7.5	Rl. Wear Sub.-5
Special work				12.5-7	7.75	7.2	12	10 years
Paving	10	8.5	8		10-4	10-4	10	10-25 grt.
Cars, Bodies and trucks	8	6.66	6	6.66-5	5	5	7.5	As shown
Electrical equipment		8.5			8.5-6⅔	8.5-6⅔	6	12-25-30
Electrical distribution	8	8.5	7				7.5	
Poles—iron				2.5	5	5		2.5
Poles—wood				8⅓-6⅔			7.5	
Overhead equipment								20 total
Wiring, etc.					14-10	14-10		
Feeders and cables				4			5	1½
Power plant	8	5						2
Cranes								2
Engines				6.66-5	6.66	5	5	3-5
Boilers				8.5-6⅔	6.66	5	7.5	3½
Stacks								Steel-7 Brick-3
Stokers								25 total
Economizers								5-10
Breechings								10-steel
Pumps								5
Piping and covering				5	6.66	5	7.5	3½
Heating								3
Coal and ash machinery				20	6.66	5	10	7
Generators				5	6.66	5	7.5	5
Switchboards				2	6.66	6	5	2
Storage batteries					6.66	5	10	
Foundations								6
Storage bins								3-10
Shop tools and machinery	8		7	10-3⅓	5	2	7.5	As shown
Furniture and fixtures	8		5				5	As shown
Telephone systems							7.5	
Horses & wagons	10		5					As shown
Miscellaneous								5

The following table shows the rates used by Marwick, Mitchell & Co., in the appraisal of a large street railway system.

Rates of Depreciation, Exclusive of Maintenance Charge.

Office furniture and fixtures	5.0%
Buildings	2.5
Wagons and horses	10.0
Roadway	
Rails in city streets	4.5
country roads	3.5
private right-of-way	3.5
Substructure in city streets	4.5
country roads	7.0
right-of-way	10.00
Special work	9.0

DEPRECIATION, DEPLETION AND OBSOLESCENCE — ELECTRIC AND STREET RAILROADS — *(Continued)*

Paving	
Block	2.5
Asphalt	7.0
Brick, macadam, etc.	4.5
Fences	
Snow	10.0 per cent
Other	5.0
Power House and Substation Equipment	
Boilers, Engines, Heaters, Conveyors, Pumps and auxiliaries	4.5
Rotaries, Transformers, Switchboards, Auxiliaries	
Storage batteries	3.0
Turbines and generators	6.0
Rolling stock	
Cars (including all equipment)	5.0
Utility equipment	5.0
Shop machinery	
Machine tools	5.0
Hand tools	10.0
Line	
Poles—iron	2.0
Poles—wood	7.0
Wire—trolley	5.0
Wire-guard	10.0
Spans with ears, etc.	5.0
Conduits with manholes	2.0
Feeder cables, overhead	3.0
Feeder cables leaded, in ducts	4.0
Transmission lines	2.0
Special work	8.0
Signals, telegraph, etc.	10.0
Bridges	2.5

Electric light and railways	years
Copper wire, weatherproof insulation	10 to 15
Cable, lead covered,aerial	10 to 15
Cable, lead covered, underground, in conduits	20 to 25
Conduit	30 to 50
Manholes	30 to 50
Poles, cedar, in earth	10 to 18
Poles, cedar, in concrete	12 to 20
Poles, iron in concrete	15 to 30
Poles anchor and guys	10 to 20
Cross arms	10 to 15
Service transformers	10 to 15
Fuse boxes	10 to 12
Lightning arresters	10 to 12
Arc lamps and span equipment	10 to 15
Nernst lamps	8 to 10
Service wattmeters	10 to 15
Railway spans and bracket equipment	15 to 20

Trolley wire; life depends on headway; should never be worn to less than 75 per cent of its original size.
0 wire at 1 minute headway, life 2 years.
00 wire at 1 minute headway, life 2½ years.
000 wire at 1 minute headway, life 2 years.

FOSTER, HORATIO A. Rules for depreciating railways and lighting plants in Great Britain. (In his *Engineering valuation of public utilities and factories.* 1913. p. 165-8, 193).
General plant and machinery 5% per annum on written-down value, in addition to the cost of repairs. The Wisconsin Railroad commission has covered the regular plants by giving as the average life of electric railway 18.02 years.

GEARY street municipal railway—allowance for a depreciation sinking fund of 18 per cent of the passenger revenue made by Wm. Dolge, of the Supervisors' finance committee of San Francisco, in estimate of income for the year ending June 30, 1914. *Electric railway journal,* Aug. 23, 1913, p. 315-6.

GILLETTE, HALBERT P. and RICHARD T. DANA. Depreciation. (In their *Handbook of mechanical and electrical cost data.* 1918. p. 107).
Distribution system, elec. ry.

11.75 years	Beggs, Milwaukee 3c. case.
12.5	Prof. M. E. Cooley, Milwaukee 3c. case.
14.25	M. G. Starret, Milwaukee 3c. case.
33.3	H. P. Gillette, Everett railway & water co., Jan. 29, 1912.

GLASGOW and depreciation. *Municipal journal* (London), Sept. 4, 1903, p. 795.

GLASGOW tramways. *Municipal journal,* Aug. 11, 1905, p. 896.

GREAT BRITAIN. BOARD OF INLAND REVENUE. Depreciation rates. (In its *Income tax; statement respecting allowances for wear and tear and obsolescence of plant and machinery.* 1918. Cd. 9022, p. 4; Cd. 9134, p. 6). *American economic review, Supplement,* Dec. 1920, p. 51. *Journal of accountancy,* Sept. 1920, p. 195.

DEPRECIATION, DEPLETION AND OBSOLESCENCE — ELECTRIC AND STREET RAILROADS — *(Continued)*

Tramways

Permanent way	An allowance per mile of track based upon the estimated life of the permanent way
Cables	3%
Cars and rolling stock	7
General plant and machinery, including standards brackets, and work shop tools Written down value	5

GREENLAND, S. W. Depreciation. (In *Mississippi electric association,* Report of 2nd annual convention held June 1910, p. 32-6).

	Life
Ties, white oak	7-9 years
Rails, 70 pounds	30
Poles, chestnut	12
Trolley wire	15
Feeders	25
Car bodies, closed	18
Car equipment, electric	15
Buildings, brick	50
Boilers	12-20
Engines	20
Piping	20
Generators	12-25
Pumps and heaters	15-20
Condensers	15
Switchboards	20
Transformers	10
Paving	10-25
Shop equipment	15
Meters	20

GRUNSKY, CARL EWALD. Probable useful life of various articles. (In his *Valuation, depreciation and the rate base.* 1917. p. 274, 278, 284-5).

Street railway	50 years. Mortimer E. Cooley. Milwaukee 3c. fare case. Report Wisconsin R. R. com., vol. 10. p. 226.
" "	50 years. Milton G. Starrett. Milwaukee 3c. fare case. Report Wisconsin R. R. commission, vol. 10, p. 220.
" "	50 years. Stone & Webster. Figures for Chicago union traction co. case. Report Wisconsin railroad commission, vol. 10. p. 220.
" "	50 years. Chicago union traction co. Quoted in report Wisconsin R. R. commission, vol. 10. p. 220.
" "	35-75 years. Wisconsin railroad commission. Milwaukee 3c. fare case. Aug. 23, 1912.
Power plants	20 years. Chicago union traction co. Quoted in Report Wisconsin R. R. Commission. vol. 10. p. 220.
" "	25 years. Mortimer E. Cooley. Milwaukee 3c. fare case. Report Wisconsin R. R. comm. vol. 10, p. 226.
" "	50 years. Stone & Webster. Figures for Chicago union traction co. case. Report Wisconsin railroad commission, vol. 10, p. 220.
" "	60 years
" "	Wisconsin railroad commission. Milwaukee 3c. fare case. Aug. 23, 1912.
sub station	50 years. 0% residual value. Sir Wm. Preece. Report of Bristol corporation, England, 1906.
" "	50 years. 1% residual value. California railroad commission. Reports 1913-4. Calistoga Electric co. vs. Napa Valley electric co., May 1914.
Distribution system. Street railway	12½ years. Mortimer E. Cooley. Milwaukee 3c. case. Report Wisconsin R. R. com., vol. 10. p. 226.
street railway	14 years. Milton G. Starrett. Milwaukee 3c. fare case. Report Wisconsin R. R. commission, vol. 10. p. 226.
distrib. and trans.	30.03 years. Wisconsin railroad commission. Milwaukee 3c. fare case.
Electric railway	18.02 years. Wisconsin railroad commission. Fon du Lac W. co. case aver. 7 plants.
	18.6 years. Wisconsin railroad commission. Milwaukee 3c. fare case, Aug. 23, 1912.
	19.8 years. Wisconsin railroad commission. Duluth st. ry. co. case.

DEPRECIATION, DEPLETION AND OBSOLESCFNCE — ELECTRIC AND STREET RAILROADS — *(Continued)*

Power plant equipment 12½ years.
Mortimer E. Cooley. Milwaukee 3c fare case. Report Wisconsin R. R. Com., vol. 10, p. 226.
20 years.
Milton G. Starrett. Milwaukee 3c fare case. Report Wisconsin R. R. com. v.10, p. 226.
21.01 years.
Wisconsin railroad commission. Milwaukee 3c fare case. Aug. 23, 1912.

GUTHRIE, EDWIN. Depreciation. (In Lisle, George. *Encyclopaedia of accounting.* v. 2. p. 374-5).

Company tramways, cars horses or electric rails, cars, electric wires	If the property of a company, write off as for a 21 years' lease in equal proportions after taking into account realisable residual value.
Corporation tramways	
Rails	2½-5% diminishing value.
Cars	5-10% diminishing value.
Electric wires	25-33⅓ original value.

HASELMANN, M. Depreciation as applicable to electric railways. *Street railway journal,* Nov. 24, 1906, p. 1003. Discussion. *Street railway journal,* Nov. 5, 1904, p. 830.

HEARING on depreciation of equipment accounts by Interstate commerce commission. *Electric railway journal,* July 4, 1908, p. 236. *Street railway bulletin,* July 1908, p. 390.

HEARINGS on Milwaukee fare case by Wisconsin railroad commission. *Electric railway journal,* Aug. 1, 1908, March 6-April 24, May 22, 1919, p. 395; 419, 464, 499, 554, 640, 683, 729, 766, 955. Editorial, March 13, 27, 1909, p. 452, 536.

HOLFORD, G. W. Depreciation and renewal funds in relation to tramways undertakings. *Electrician,* Sept. 28, 1906, p. 938. *Electric railway review,* Nov. 1906, p. 906. *Electrical engineer* (London), Sept. 28, 1906, p. 441-3. *Light railway and tramway journal* (London), Oct. 5, 1906, p. 294. *Tramway and railway world,* Oct. 4, 1906, p. 363. Abstract. *Street railway journal,* Oct. 6, 1906, p. 529. Editorial. *Electric railway review,* Nov. 1906, p. 887.

How should depreciation be entered on the books. *Street railway review,* Aug. 20, 1904, p. 523.

INCOME tax and depreciation allowances. *Accountant,* May 30, 1914, p. 785-8.

Tramways	Written down value
Cables—all repairs charged against revenue	3%
Cars and other rolling stock	7%

INCOME tax assessment (Great Britain). *Tramway and railway world,* July 17, 1906, p. 66.

INCOME tax notes. *Accountant,* May 11, Sept. 28, 1918, p. 359, 162-6. *Incorporated accountants' journal,* May, Oct. 1918, p. 157, 14.

Tramways	
Permanent way	Written down value. An allowance per mile of track based upon the estimated life of the permanent way.
Cables	3%
Cars and other rolling stock	7%
General plant and machinery, including standards, brackets, and work shop tools	5%

INGLE, W. O. Life of railway physical property from the accounting standpoint. *Electric railway journal,* Dec. 9, 1911, p. 1205.

INQUIRY by public service commission concerning depreciation accounts. *Electric railway journal,* April 30, 1910, p. 793.

INSTITUTE of *municipal treasurers and accountants* (*incorporated*). Municipal corporations and companies working tramway and light railways, gas, water and electricity undertakings. *Accountant,* June 26, Oct. 2, 1909, p. 906-8, 423-5, 400-2. *Incorporated accountants' journal,* 1909, p. 238-40.

Tramways
Permanent Way.—Allowance for maintenance to cover depreciation—Life.
1. The life of the permanent way is to be taken as twelve, fourteen, or sixteen years, according to the traffic thereon. The classification is to be based on the average car mileage per mile of track per annum of the financial year preceding the year of assessment, viz:
(1) Not exceeding 50,000 car miles per mile of track—16 years.
(2) over 50,000 and not exceeding 75,000 car miles per mile of track—14 years.
(3) Over 75,000 and not exceeding 125,000 car miles per mile of track—12 years.
(4) Over 125,000 car miles per mile of track—special consideration.

Cables
11. In addition to repairs, depreciation should be allowed at the rate of 3 per cent per annum on the written down value.

Overhead Equipment, i. e., Trolley Wires and Connections.
No depreciation should be allowed; all expenditure on maintenance and renewals should be charged as working expenses, as and when incurred.

Cars and other rolling stock.
Subject to the ensuing clause expenditure on maintenance and renewals should be treated as working expenses, and allowed in lieu of depreciation.
Depreciation, however, should be allowed in lieu of renewals where the circumstances justify such an allowance, provided that a strict account is kept of all renewals, and that if such renewals are charged to Revenue Account they shall be shown separately in such account and added back in computing the assessable profits.

DEPRECIATION, DEPLETION AND OBSOLESCENCE — ELECTRIC AND STREET RAILROADS — *(Continued)*

The allowance in such case to be 7 per cent. per annum on the written down value. in any case, the annual expenditure on repairs is to be allowed as a deduction in computing the assessable profits.

All other plant and machinery, including standards, brackets, and workshop tools, but excluding loose implements, office furniture, and small· articles which require frequent renewal, should be bulked together and depreciation shall be allowed thereon at the rate of 5 per cent per annum on the written down value, in addition to the cost of repairs.

JACKSON, WILLIAM B. Depreciation problem. *Annals of the American academy of political and social science,* Jan. 1911, p. 31-42. *Canadian engineer,* Feb. 23, 1911, p. 353. *Public service,* Sept 1911, p. 71.

JACKSON, WILLIAM B. Discussion of the depreciation problem with particular reference to electric railways. *Engineering and contracting,* Feb. 8, 1911, p. 176.

JONES, EDWARD DAVID. Depreciation. (In his *Investment.* p. 167).
Physical property of street railways 5.6%

KEALY, P. J. Valuation and accruing depreciation. *Journal of the Western society of engineers,* Jan. 5, 1920, p. 11-4. Condensed. *Electric railway journal,* Sept. 13, 1919, p. 530-1.

KELSAY, G. H. Cost and sale of electric power. *Electric railway review,* Jan. 26, 1907, p. 126. *Street railway journal,* Feb. 2, 1907, p. 207.

KNOWLTON, H. S. Depreciation problem. *Street railway journal,* July 16, 1904, p. 101.

LARGER depreciation fund in St. Louis. *Electric railway journal,* Feb. 11, 1911, p. 247.

LEASEHOLD concessions and depreciation. *Accountant,* May 2, 1908, p. 624-7.

LIFE data on power plant equipment used in valuation of the property of the Bay state street railway of Boston, Massachusetts. *Electrical world,* Dec. 4, 1915, p. 1261.

LIFE of elements in subway property. *Electric railway journal,* April 6, 1912, p. 575.

Copper sheathed car at	30 years
Steel cars	40
Buildings and fixtures	50
Power plant	30
This was assumed upon an age of copper sheathed cars in service	7 years
Steel cars, a portion	6
Smaller number	5½
Buildings and fixtures	7
Power plant equipment	5

LOCAL boards and depreciation and renewal funds. *Accounting and commerce,* Aug. 1920, p. 1178-9.

LOCK, FRED J. Depreciation. (In his *West African mining accounts.* 1910. p. 88-9).
Tramways and sidings 15%

LONDON tramway depreciation allowance for income tax. *Electric railway journal,* Feb. 12, 1910, p. 274.
Three hundred and fifteen pounds per single mile of track for permanent way in the overhead trolley system, 7 per cent on written down capital cost of cars, 3 per cent on written-down capital cost of cables and 5 per cent on written-down capital cost of general plant and machinery.

MACAFEE, JOHN BLAIR. Insurance fund and depreciation reserves. *Street railway review,* May 15, 1905, p. 292.

MCCALL, DONALD. Depreciation. (In his *Tramway bookkeeping and accounts.* 1902. p. 118-24).

MCCLELLAN, WILLIAM. Life of railway physical property. *American electric railway engineering association, Proceedings,* 1913, p. 516. Abstracts. *Electric railway journal,* Oct. 17, 1913, p. 841. Discussion. *American electric railway accountants' association,* Proceedings, 1913, p. 212-20. *Engineering news,* Nov. 13, 1913, p. 972.

MAINTENANCE and depreciation charges of the Chicago union traction company. *Electric railway review,* Feb. 23, 1907, p. 247. Editorial. Amount of maintenance and depreciation charges. *Electric railway review,* Feb. 23, 1907, p. 244.

MANN, JOHN and H. C. JUDD. Depreciation. (In their *Colliery accounts.* 1909. p. 69-75, 92).
Surface railway 7½-10%
Calculated on the balance as diminished from year to year.

MAY reserve fund to renew obsolete equipment. *Electric traction weekly,* Dec. 31, 1910, p. 1473.

METROPOLITAN street railway reorganization plan. *Electric railway journal,* May 20, 1911, p. 876-8.

	Life years
Foundation and excavation	50
Paving in track	14
Train rail in straight track	14
Slot rail	25
Conductor lines	10
Special work and paving	5
Horse track and special work	25
Ducts	50
Cables	33⅓
Power plant and substation	25
Buildings	50
Equipment of buildings	33
Rolling stock, electric	30
" " horse	33⅓
Fixed tools and appliances	20
Incidentals	33⅓

DEPRECIATION, DEPLETION AND OBSOLESCENCE — ELECTRIC AND STREET RAILROADS — *(Continued)*

Office furniture, etc.	20
Floating tools	15
Incidentals	18

MULHALL, JOHN F. J. Depreciation. (In his *Quasi-public corporation accounting and management.* c1905. p. 180-3).

Electric railway	5-8%

MUNICIPAL trading and depreciation. *Accountant,* June 8, July 6, 1901, p. 657-9, 769-71.

Tram lines	8%
Land, buildings, goodwill, etc.	3
Eqiupment, overhead, etc.	5
Cars	10
Tools and machinery	10
Office fittings, etc.	10

MURRAY, ALEXANDER. Glasgow corporation accounts with special reference to depreciation and sinking funds. *Accountant,* June 13, 1903, p. 782-94. *Royal philosophical society,* Glasgow, Proceedings, 1903.

Permanent way £450 per mile of single track.

Bonding of rails	7½%
Ducts, cables, poles, rosettes	3
Buildings, including sites	2½
Power plant	5
Car works plant, cars, sundry equipments, and furniture	7½

NASH, L. R. Tramway's depreciation problem. *Stone and Webster's public service journal,* April 1919.

NEAL, J. H. Where maintenance ends and depreciation begins. *Street railway journal,* Oct. 19, 1907, p. 700-1. *American street and interurban railway accountants association, Proceedings,* 1907, p. 195-202.

NEALE, R. E. Depreciation in engineering works. *Mechanical world,* Feb. 7, 1913, p. 67-8.

Building, land and plant	2.5-5%	20-40 years
Generating plant and machinery	5	20

(1909 agreement between Inland and certain municipal tramway associations. These allowances generally considered to be insufficient.)

Isolating generating plant	7%	14 years
Small workshop equipment	5-10	10-20
General workshop equipment	8-12	8.5-12.5
Seven American electrical supply	8-16	6.3-12.5
On railway companies—mean	10	10

NELSON, BAILIE WALTER. Limitation and application of profits from municipal undertakings. *Accountant,* Aug. 3, 1912, p. 167-71. *Incorporated accountants' journal,* Oct. 1912, p. 15-7.

Scale of depreciation in force in Glasgow tramways undertakings:

On permanent way £440 per mile of single track

On electrical equipment of line	4.3 per cent per annum
On buildings and fixtures	2½ " " " "
On power station and substations' plant	7.4 " " " "
On workshop tools and sundry plant	7½ " " " "
On cars	7½ " " " "
On electrical equipment of cars	8.79 " " " "
On other rolling stock	10.15 " " " "
On miscellaneous equipment	7½ " " " "
On office furniture	7½ " " " "

OFFICIAL allowance in respect of machinery and plant—Board of Inland Revenue, Great Britain. *Accountant,* May 16, 1914, p. 737.

(1)	Not exceeding 50,000 car miles per mile of track	16 years
(2)	Over 50,000 and not exceeding 75,000 car miles per mile of track	14 years
(3)	Over 75,000 and not exceeding 125,000 car miles per mile of tracks	12 years
(4)	Over 125,000 car miles per mile of track—special consideration.	

Cost of renewals, including selts or other paving but excluding concrete foundations; should be taken at £4,400 per mile of single track until the general renewal of the track takes place.

Cables—In addition to repairs depreciation should be allowed at the rate of 3 per cent per annum on the written down value.

Overhead equipment, i. e., trolley wires and connections—no depreciation should be allowed; all expenditure on maintenance and renewals should be charged as working expenses, as and when incurred.

Cars and other rolling stock.

Subject to the ensuing clause expenditure on maintenance and renewals should be treated as working and allowed in lieu of depreciation. Depreciation, however, should be allowed in lieu of renewals where the circumstances justify such an allowance, provided that a strict account is kept of all renewals, and that if such renewals are charged to Revenue Account they shall be shown separately in such account and added back in computing the assessable profits. The allowance in such case should be 7 per cent per annum on the written down value. In any case the annual expenditure on repairs is to be allowed as a deduction in computing the assessable profits.

General plant and machinery—all other plant and machinery including standards, brackets, and workshop tools, but excluding loose implements, office furniture, and small articles which require frequent renewal, should be bulked together and depreciation allowed thereon at the rate of 5 per cent per annum on the written down value, in addition to the cost of repairs.

DEPRECIATION, DEPLETION AND OBSOLESCENCE — ELECTRIC AND STREET RAILROADS — *(Continued)*

OPINIONS of commission in Third avenue case. *Electric railway journal,* Feb. 10, 1912, p. 237.

OSSOSKI, S. Basis of valuation in case of municipal purchase of street railways. *Electric railway journal,* Nov. 12, 1910, p. 999-1000.

PENDER, HAROLD. Depreciation. (In his *Handbook for electrical engineers.* c1914. p. 337).
The Wisconsin commission has decided that 18 years is a fair life for electric railway properties.

PFEIFFER, A .J. J. Tramway depreciation. *Tramway and railway world,* Aug. 4, 1910, p. 61.

PHILADELPHIA CONTROLLER. Rates of depreciation. (In his *Manual of accounting, reporting and business procedure of the city and county of Philadelphia.* 1917. p. 210).
Elevated railways 1%

PIXLEY, FRANCIS W. Tramways. (In his *Accountancy.* Ed. 2. p. 218-9).
Cables and feeders 2½-5%
Ducts and manholes 2
Electrical plant at power station 5
Overhead wires
The cost of the new wires should, as a rule be charged to Revenue, but if it is the practice to charge all this expenditure in connection with the overhead trolley wires to one account, the rate of depreciation should certainly be from 30 to 60% according to whether the service is a frequent one or the reverse.
Poles and rosettes from 21-25%
Rail bonding from 7½ to 10
Rolling stock from 7½-15
Uniform of conductors, etc.
It is better to make this expenditure a direct charge against Revenue; but if this is not done, a depreciation varying from say 33 to 60 per cent should be charged according to the neighbourhood and the appearance the men have to present.

POLICY of English municipal tramways respecting renewals. *Electric railway journal,* Oct. 7, 1911, p. 661-3.

PROPOSED depreciation account in Nebraska. *Electric railway journal,* May 27, 1911, p. 919.

PROPOSED sale of Toronto utilities to the city. *Electrical world,* Oct. 25, 1913, p. 832.
Depreciation percentages used by Messrs. B. J. Arnold and J. W. Moyes in their valuation of the Toronto electric railroads.
Coal handling apparatus 6%
Horizontal tubular boilers 8
Water tube boilers 3.5
Steel smoke breeching 10
Brick and concrete stacks 3
Heaters 3-6
Pumps 5
Air compressors 5
Corliss slow-speed engines 3
Automatic high-speed engines 5-8
Piping 3.5
Generators 4 and 5
Transformers 5
Rotary converters 5
Switchboards and interior wiring 3
Iron poles 2.5-3
Cedar poles 5
Pole brackets 4
Wooden cross-arms 5
Iron cross-arms 3.33
Weatherproof cables 3.33
Lead cables 3
Transmission-line material 5
Grates and stokers 50
(10% a year for 5 years, no further depreciation being figured after that if the apparatus is still in use).

PROTEST by New York railway against commission orders regarding depreciation *Electric railway journal,* April 26, 1913, p. 777.
The New York (N. Y.) Railways has served upon the public Service Commission for the First District a writ of certiorari, issued by the Supreme Court Justice, M. Warley Platzek, to review the action of the commission in requiring the company to set aside 20% of its gross earnings each month for maintenance and depreciation.

PUBLIC utilities reports, annotated. Rochester, Lawyers cooperative publishing co.
See index under Depreciation.

PUBLIC utility reports, annotated. Rochester, Lawyers co-operative publishing co. 1915E. p. 370.
Re Blue Hill Street R. Co. (Mass.). The Massachusetts Commission in estimating the amount of revenue necessary for a street railroad company, did not apply the rule that 20 per cent of operating revenue is the proper proportion, necessary to cover maintenance of way, structures, and equipment and depreciation with average conditions, but allowed a greater percentage where the road was small with relatively low gross earnings and the accrued depreciation was relatively large.

PUBLIC utility reports, annotated. Rochester, Lawyers co-operative publishing co. 1915B. p. 481.
Re Ft. Scott Gas & Electric Co. v. Ft. Scott (Kan.). A reasonable sum to be set aside annually for depreciation upon the property of an electric and street railway company was found to be 4½ per cent of the value of the property, on the assumption that the fund thus created would be invested and the accruing interest compounded annually or at shorter intervals.

DEPRECIATION, DEPLETION AND OBSOLESCENCE — ELECTRIC AND STREET RAILROADS — *(Continued)*

PUBLIC utility reports, annotated. Rochester, Lawyers co-operative publishing co. 1915 E. p. 411.
Re Norfolk & B. Street R. Co. (Mass.). The Massachusetts Commission, in estimating the amount of revenue necessary for a street railroad company, did not apply the rule that 20 per cent of operating revenue is the proper proportion necessary to cover maintenance of way, structures, and equipment and depreciation with average conditions, but allowed a greater percentage where the road was small with relatively low gross earnings and the accrued depreciation was relatively large.

PUBLIC utility reports, annotated. Rochester, Lawyers co-operative publishing co. 1915B. p. 416.
Re Omaha & L. R. Light Co. (Neb.). Upon authorizing an electric railway and light company to issue securities for improvements to its property, the Commission directed the company to set aside annually 7 per cent of the entire amount of outstanding liabilities for maintenance and depreciation reserve funds, in order that the gross assets of the company should be kept to a value approximately equal to the outstanding liabilities.

PUBLIC utility reports, annotated. Rochester, Lawyers co-operative publishing co. 1915B. p. 558.
Re Washington & M. R. Co. (D. C.). An electric railway company was ordered to conform its depreciation accounts to a rate of 3.34 per cent on the cost of property new for "way and structure."

PUBLIC utility reports, annotated. Rochester, Lawyers co-operative publishing co. 1916F. p. 336-9.
See Bay state rate case.

PUBLIC utility reports, annotated. Rochester, Lawyers co-operative publishing co. 1916E, p. 1066.
Re Waupaca Electric Light & R. Co. (Wis.). An electric railway was allowed only 3 per cent of the cost new for depreciation, instead of a normal allowance of 4 or 5 per cent, where it charged certain renewals to maintenance and oprated at capacity only during the summer months.

PUBLIC utility reports, annotated. Rochester, Lawyers co-operative publishing co. 1917A, p. 255.
Re Manchester & N. Street R. Co. (N. H.). An allowance of 1 per cent for the annual depreciation of an interurban railway is not excessive, even though $500 per mile of track is expended for maintenance.

PUBLIC utility reports, annotated. Rochester, Lawyers co-operative publishing co. 1918A, p. 388.
Re Chicago, N. S. & M. R. Co. (Ill.). An annual allowance of $120,000 was made by the Illinois Commission for accruing depreciation of a street railway, the value of which for passenger rate making was fixed at $5,100,000 and in addition thereto, an allowance was made of a sum equal to 3.5 per cent of the cost of all future additions and betterments.

PUBLIC utility reports, annotated. Rochester, Lawyers co-operative publishing co. 1918C, p. 534.
Re Springfield Street R. Co. In the present instance, the company made no similar analysis, but based its allowance on general percentages derived from the Bay State figures, using the combined "sinking-fund", and "straight line" basis, as follows:

	per cent
Road, track, line, etc.	3.17
Rolling stock	3.71
Power stations and equipment	2.31
Shops, car houses, and equipment	1.92

PUBLIC utility reports, annotated. Rochester, Lawyers co-operative publishing co. 1918A, p. 914-18.
Re New York & N. S. traction co.
Statement showing method used in arriving at the average percentage of Depreciation as shown in exhibit No. 42 accrued depreciation of depreciable property. Assuming that the straight-line method of depreciation had been applied throughout the period of operation on the basis of an average depreciation of 3 per cent per year.

Fixed Capital December 31, 1908	Per cent.
Substation equipment	3
Shop tools and machinery	5
Revenue cars	3
Electric equipment of cars	4
Miscellaneous equipment	3
Grading	1
Ties	7
Rails, rail fastening and joints	2
Special work	6
Track laying and surfacing	2
Paving	3
Poles and fixtures (figure shown herein taken as previous to credit of $1,014.30)	5
Distribution system	3
General office buildings and fixtures	2
Shops and car house	2
Average percentage for one year	2.99-100
Fixed Capital Since December 31, 1908	
Grading	1
Ballast	1
Ties	7
Rails, rail fastenings and joints	2
Special work	6
Track laying and surfacing	2
Paving	3

DEPRECIATION, DEPLETION AND OBSOLESCENCE — ELECTRIC AND STREET RAILROADS — *(Continued)*

Bridges, trestles and culverts	4
Crossings, fences, and signs	6
Interlocking and other signal apparatus	2
Telephone and telegraph lines	2
Poles and fixtures	5
Tranmission system	2½
Distribution system	3
Power plant buildings	2
Substation buildings	2
General office ubildings and fixtures	2
Shops and car houses	2
Stations, waiting rooms, and miscellaneous buildings	2
Docks and wharves	5
Furnaces, boilers and accessories	3½
Steam engines	4
Power plant eelctric equipment	3½
Miscellaneous power plant equipment	3
Substation equipment	3
Shop equipment	5
Revenue cars	3
Electric equipment of cars	4
Other rail equipment	3
Miscellaneous equipment	3
Average percentage	3.01-100

	Life in years	Annual Depr. Rate
Organization, franchises, other intangible street railway capital, right of way other street railway land	....	...
Grading, ballast, ties, rails, rail fastenings, and joints, special work, track laying, and surfacing, paving, roadway tools, crossings, fences, and signs	16 2/3	6%
Interlocking and other signal apparatus, telephone and telegraph lines, transmission system, distribution system, dams, canals, pipe lines, shops and car houses, docks and wharves, furnaces, boilers and accessories, steam engines, power plant electric equipment, miscellaneous power plant equipment, sub-station equipment, shop equipment, electric equipment of cars, miscellaneous equipment, poles, and fixtures.	20	5%
Bridges, trestles, and culverts, general office building and fixtures, stations, waiting rooms, and miscellaneous buildings.	25	4%
Revenue cars, other rail equipment	33 1/3	3%
Power plant buildings, substation buildings	50	2

PUBLIC utility reports, annotated. Rochester, Lawyers co-operative publishing co. 1918D, p. 441.

Re United R. Co.

Company	Per Cent of Gross Revenue Expended or Appropriated for Depreciation
United railways company	10.0%
Milwaukee electric railway	9.9
Detroit Edison & subsidiaries	10.25
Omaha & Council Bluffs St. ry. co.	10.9
Chicago street railways	8.0

PUBLIC utility reports, annotated. Rochester, Lawyers co-operative publishing co. 1918E, p. 679, 1.

In Dover S. & R. Co. D-432, Dec. 20, 1917, Commissioner Gunnison, of the New Hampshire Commission, said that a reasonable allowance for depreciation upon street railway property is at least 2 percent.

PUBLIC utility reports, annotated. Rochester, Lawyers co-operative publishing co. 1918E, p. 1.

Milwaukee Electric R. & Light Co. v. Milwaukee (Wis.). The annual allowance for depreciation in determining the reasonableness of electric railway rates was calculated upon a sinking fund basis of from 3 to 4 per cent. interest at that rate to be credited annually to the reserve.

PUBLIC utility reports, annotated. Rochester, Lawyers co-operative publishing co. 1918F, p. 840.

Re Rockford City Traction Co. (Ill.). An annual allowance of $30,000 was made for the depreciation of a street railway company's property, the value of which, including working capital, was fixed at $1,300,000 in a valuation for rate making.

PUBLIC utility reports, annotated. Rochester, Lawyers co-operative publishing co. 1918D, p. 392.

Re United R. Co. (Mo.). An allowance of 10 per cent of the gross revenue of a street railway company for its depreciation reserve was held reasonable.

PUBLIC utility reports, annotated. Rochester, Lawyers co-operative publishing co. 1919A, p. 161, 169.

Re Connecticut Co. (Conn.). There is no good reason for allowing a 5 per cent depreciation upon all of the elements involved in the total investment in an electric railway, if renewals and replacements are charged to gross earnings, especially where the company has never adopted the policy of carrying a substantial dpreciation account.

Re Manitowoc & N. Traction Co. R-2385, Aug. 7, 1918, the Wisconsin Commission said that ordinarily an allowance of 3 per cent upon the depreciable property is an adequate provision for a street and interurban electric railway.

DEPRECIATION, DEPLETION AND OBSOLESCENCE — ELECTRIC AND STREET RAILROADS — *(Continued)*

PUBLIC utility reports, annotated. Rochester, Lawyers co-operative publishing co. 1919D, p. 504.
Re Milwaukee Electric R. & Light Co. v. Milwaukee (Wis.). In determining the allowance for the operating expenses of a street railway company, the Wisconsin Commission computed depreciation of the entire property at the rate of 2.82 pr cent per annum.

PUBLIC utility reports, annotated. Rochester, Lawyers co-operative publishing co. 1919B, p. 750.
Re Missoula Street R. Co. Docket No. 682, Report and Order No. 251, Dec. 4, 1918. the Montana Commission stated that the rate of depreciation of street railway property was probably somewhere between 2.2 per cent and 4 per cent.

PUBLIC utility reports, annotated. Rochester, Lawyers co-operative publishing co. 1919A. p. 755.
Re New York state R. Co. (N. Y.). In construing the propable operating expense account of a street railway company, provision should be made for an adequate depreciation reserve on the basis of 2 per cent. of the flat field costs of track and roadway, electrical construction, and other fixed imprðvements, and 3 per cent of the flat field costs of rolling stock, power houses equipment, shop machinery, and tools and other equipment.

PUBLIC utility reports, annotated. Rochester, Lawyers co-operative publishing co. 1919F, p. 1053.
Re Moore v. Valley R. Co. (Pa). The Pennsylvania Commission made an allowance of $36,976 for the annual depreciation of a traction company's property the present value of which was fixed at $2,350,000.
Re United R. Co. (Mo.). An amount reserved by a street railway company for accruing depreciation which approximates 2.47 per cent, or 2.97 per cent on the estimated values of its property, is not excessive.

PUBLIC utility reports, annotated. Rochester, Lawyers co-operative publishing co. 1919E, p. 1087.
Re Tri-City R. Co. (Ill.). An annual allowance of $60,000 was made for accruing depreciation of a street railroad company's properyt, the fair value of which was fixed at $2,900,000, in a valuation for rate making.

PUBLIC utility reports, annotated. Rochester, Lawyers co-operative publishing co. 1919A, p. 169.
Re Wisconsin R. & Light & P. Co. R-2384, Sesph. 12t 1918, the Wisconsin Commission in an emergency rate stated that an allowance of 3 per cent upon the cost new of the depreciable property was adequate.

PUBLIC utility reports, annotated. Rochester, Lawyers co-operative publishing company, 1920A, p. 361.
Re Milwaukee electric r. & light co. (Wis) Wisconsin commission allowed a rate of 2.82 pr cent for the depreciation of a street railway.

PUBLIC utility reports, annotated. Rochester, Lawyers co-operative publishing company, 1920B, p. 37.
Re Kansas City, C. C. & St. J. R. co. (Mo.). In calculating development cost on the Wisconsin or deficit method, the Missouri commission assumed that 3 per cent on the investment per annum of an electric railway constituted a reasonable allowance for depreciation.

PUBLIC utility reports, annotated. Rochester, Lawyers co-operative publishing company, 1920C. p. 418, 1, 1010, 298
Re Fort Smith light & traction co. (Ark.) An annual allowance of 4½ per cent for accruing depreciation of a property of a street railway company, is reasonable.
Re Nashville R and light co. (Tenn.) An allowance of 3½ percent of the depreciable accruing depreciation of a property of a street railway company, is reasonable. property of a street railway company is a reasonable requirement for the renewal and replacement reserves.
Re Rockfod and L. R. co. (Wis.) In fixing rates for an interurban railway, the Wisconsin commission made an allowance of 3 per cent for annual depreciation.
Re Tutwiler (Tenn.). Tennessee commission made an allowance of 3 per cent of the value of the renewable property for depreciation of a street railway.

PUBLIC utility reports, annotated. Rochester, Lawyers co-operative publishing company, 1920E, p. 517, 350, 908, 640, 474, 833.
Re Hammond, Whiting & East Chicago railway company. Indiana commission made an allowance of 3½ per cent for depreciation of a street and interurban railway system.
Re Houghton county traction. Michigan commission made an allowance of 2 per cent for the depreciation of a street railway rather than the 3 per cent which was claimed by the company.
Re Illinois northern utilities company. Illinois commission made an allowance of $9,000 for the annual depreciation of a street railway company, the entire value of whose property was fixed at $293,900.
Re New York & Stamford railway company. A street railway company should set aside for depreciation a minimum of 2 per cent on the actual cost of its depreciable property.
Re Springfield consolidated railway company. Illinois commission made an allowance of $60,000 for accruing depreciation for a street railway company, the original cost less depreciation of whose property was $1,320,000.
Re Utah light & tsaction company. Utah commission made an allowance of $265,000 for the dẹpreciation of street railway property valued at approximately $8,500,000. Utah commission required the allowance for depreciation to be set upon a sinking fund basis of 5 per cent.

PUBLIC utility reports, annotated. Rochester, Lawyers co-operative publishing company, 1920F, p. 677, 328.
In passing upon the reasonableness of a street railway rates the Pennsylvania commission held that the company was entitled to an allowance of 3 per cent for annual depreciation.
Re Houston electric company v. City of Houston. Statement of rule that deduction must be made for depreciation in determining the present value of utility property. Allowance without exception, of 4½ per cent of the value of the depreciable property of a street railway company for rate making purposes.

RENEWALS as defined by the Board of supervising engineers Chicago traction; general rulings, etc. *Electric railway journal,* March 4, 1911, p. 374-7.

REPORT and proceedings of Incorporated municipal electrical association and of Incorporated association of municipal and county engineers in relation to the income tax and allowance for depreciation (Great Britain). *Light railway and tramway journal* (London), July 2, 1909, p. 14-9, 27-9.

DEPRECIATION, DEPLETION AND OBSOLESCENCE — ELECTRIC AND STREET RAILROADS — *(Continued)*

REPORT of committee on life of railway physical property. *American electric railway accountants' and engineering association, Proceedings,* 1912, p. 189. *Electric railway journal,* Oct. 11, 1912, p. 828-9.

REPORT of joint committee on life of railway physical property. *American electric railway engineering association, Proceedings,* 1913, p. 509-19. Abstract. *Electric railway journal,* Oct. 17, 1913, p. 870.

REPORT of sub-committee on what constitutes maintenance. *American electric railway engineering association, Proceedings,* 1911, p. 342. Abstract. *Electric railway journal,* Oct. 12, 1911, p. 766.

REPORT of the Illinois traction system. *Electric railway journal,* Sept. 3, 1910, p. 353.

REQUEST for lower fares denied by new New Jersey commission. *Electric railway journal,* Nov. 25, 1911, p. 1117.

RESOLUTION on depreciation and publicity. *Street railway journal,* May 9, 1908, p. 789.

ROYSE, DANIEL. Depreciation in electric railway accounting. Iowa street and interurban railway association. Report of the fifth annual convention, 1908, p. 30. Abstract. *Electric railway journal,* April 25, 1908, p. 687.

RULE for treatment of depreciation in Nebraska. *Electric railway journal,* Nov. 4, 1911, p. 990.

RULES on depreciation in Great Britain. *Electric railway journal,* Sept. 25, 1909, p. 476.

SERGEANT, C. S. Problems confronting street railways. *Electric railway journal,* Jan. 1, 1910, p. 6.

SHEFFIELD SOCIETY OF CHARTERED ACCOUNTANTS AND SHEFFIED CHARTERED ACCOUNTANTS STUDENTS' SOCIETY. Question of municipal profits—tramways and depreciation. *Accountant,* March 14, 21, 28, 1903, p. 365-72, 381-4, 419-21.

SILLIMAN, F. Accounting for depreciation of electric railway property. *Electric railway journal,* Dec. 1, 1917, p. 986-7.

SMITH, C. A. Depreciation and sinking funds. *Canadian engineer,* Aug. 3, 1912, p. 299. *Electric railway journal,* July 27, 1912, p. 122-3.

SOME fundamental considerations in depreciation. *Electric railway journal,* Feb. 2, 1907, p. 144.

STRANGWARD, W. O. Depreciation reserves and sinking funds. *Electric railway journal,* July 27, 1912, p. 123-4.

SWAN, GEORGE F. Valuations of Chicago elevated railways. *Electric railway journal,* May 18, 1912, p. 829-32.

TINGLEY, C. L. S. Cost of carrying a passenger. *Street railway accountants association, Proceedings,* 1905, p. 163.

Quotes table of allowances for depreciation from book by Philip Dawson and comments on street railway depreciation.

TRAMWAYS depreciation. *Municipal journal (London),* April 4, 1902, p. 287.

TREATMENT of depreciation accounts by Interborough rapid transit company. *Electric railway journal,* Aug. 12, 1911, p. 280-1.

TREATMENT of depreciation accounts of New York public service commission. *Electric railway journal,* Nov. 20, 1909, p. 1073.

TREATMENT of depreciation and maintneance in Greater New York. *Electric railway journal,* April 6, 1912, p. 539.

TREATMENT of depreciation in Glasgow. *Electric railway journal,* Sept. 3, 1910, p. 362.

Rates of depreciation at present in operation average between 5% and 6% on the gross capital. £440 per mile on street track renewal regarded as a fair rate. Depreciation on buildings 2½%. Improvement in street paving could not possibly be regarded as capital expenditure.

UNDEPRECIATED valuations urged. *Electric railway journal,* Feb. 28, 1920, p. 440-1.

UNIFORM cost sheet for coal mining companies. *Coal age,* Sept. 19, 1918, p. 545-7.

	original cost
Tram roads	20%

UNITED railways company of St. Louis—depreciation rate increased in 1904 from 5% to 6%—it had been 5% since 1905—for 1910 it was further increased as 6% was considered inadequate. *Electric railway journal,* Feb. 11, 1911, p. 247.

VALUATION of the Chicago consolidated traction property. *Electric railway journal,* Dec. 3, 1910, p. 1111-13.

Machinery foundations	(a)		
Coal and ash handling machinery		7%	
Fuel oil handling machinery		4	
Grates and stokers	(b)		
Boilers and settings		3½-4	
Breechings and connections		3½-10	
Stack		3	
Heaters		4-5	
Water purifying apparatus		3	
Pumps		5	
Air compressors		4-5	
Engines		3-5	(c)
Condensers		4	
Piping and covering		4-4½	
Generators		3-8	(c)
Switchboard and generator leads		3	
Miscellaneous items		3-5	

(a) Machinery foundations were depreciated at a percentage determined from the of the apparatus supported.

(b) The fixed parts of stokers depreciated very little and the moving parts and grates very rapidly. As the moving parts are renewed and maintained in good condition, 10% of the wearing value of stokers was depreciated at 20% per year for 2½ years, and 90% of the fixed parts at 5% per year during the life of the machine.

(c) Engines and generators that had been rebuilt or had had extensive repairs credited with the cost of repairs at the time they were made, and this cost was depreciated at the same rate as machines on which repairs were made.

DEPRECIATION, DEPLETION AND OBSOLESCENCE — ELECTRIC AND STREET RAILROADS — *(Continued)*

WALLIS, ROBERT N. Accounting of depreciation by electric railways. *Accountant,* Sept. 21, 1907, p. 376-9. *Journal of accountancy,* May 1907, p. 10-5.

10% of the gross earnings from operation is a reasonable amount certainly not too large.

WALLIS, ROBERT N. Depreciation as applicable to electric railways. *American street and interurban electric accountants' association, Proceedings.* 1906, p. 168-218. Abstract. *Electric railway review,* April 20, 1907, p. 526. Editorial. Maintenance and depreciation. *Electric railway review,* April 20, 1907, p. 513. Discussion. American motions on depreciation. *Electrical review* (London), May 10, 1907, p. 757.

WALLIS, ROBERT N. and M. SCHREIBER. Life of railway physical property. *Electrical railway journal,* Oct. 17, 1913, p. 870-1.

WEEKS, H. E. Abstract of paper on depreciation read before annual meeting of Iowa street and Interurban railway association, April 1910. *Electric railway journal,* April 30, 1910, p. 782-3. *Electric railway journal,* April 30, 1910, p. 779.

The writer advocates capitalization of expenditures due to radical changes in the art. Properties with which he is connected use the following figures for length of life of property.

Ties	7 yrs.	Buildings	50 yrs.
Rails	20 "	Boilers	15 "
Poles	7 "	Generators	15 "
Trolley Wire	14 "	Pumps	15 "
Feeder	20 "	Condensers	15 "
Car bodies	15 "	Shop equipment	15 "
Transformers	7 "	Paving	15 "
Car equipment	10 "		

WESTERN, R. W. Calculating depreciation, London. *Tramway and railway world,* 1908, v. 23, p. 456.

WHITTEN, ROBERT H. Bibliography. (In his *Valuation of public service corporations.* 1914. p. 745).

WHITTEN, ROBERT HARVEY. Valuation of public service corporations; legal and economic phases of valuation for rate making and public purchases. 1914. v. 1, p. 424, 426-7, v. 2, p. 1202-3.

Six per cent allowance in Chicago street railway assessment case, 1902.

Three per cent allowance in Savannah street railway fare case. Georgia railroad commission, 1912.

Twenty per cent gross receipts of street railway prescribed in capitalization case—New York commission 1912.

Wisconsin commission—City of Milwaukee v. The Milwaukee electric railway and light company.

WILSON, P. NEY. Life of way structure as affected by engineering and municipal conditions. *Electric railway journal,* June 26, 1915, p. 1212-3.

YAPP, THOMAS. Interstate commerce classification. *Electric railway journal,* June 20, 1908, p. 124.

Electric industries

JONES, EDWARD DAVID. Depreciation. (In his *Investment.* p. 169).

General electric co. 10%

MONTGOMERY, ROBERT H. Electrical equipment manufacturers. (In his *Income tax procedure,* 1919, p. 563. ——— Same, 1920. p. 716)

Buildings:	
Reinforced concrete	2%
Brick and steel	2
Mill type	3
Brick and joist	5
Wood, sheet iron and stucco	10
Inside piping and wiring	10
Heating and ventilating	10
Water, sewer, and drain pipes (outside of buildings)	10
Piping and electric conductors (outside of buildings)	10
Railway tracks and overhead equipment	4
Machinery and tools—standard	10
Machinery and tools—special	15
Electrical apparatus—standard	6
Electrical equipment—special	15
Foundations for tools and apparatus	10
Ovens and furnaces	15
Shafting, pulleys, and belting	15
Rolling stock	12
Automobiles and other conveyances	25
Special machinery and tools (additions)	33⅓
Patterns (additions)	25
Miscellaneous shop fixtures and equipment	15
Office furniture and appliances	15
Power plant equipment	8

Based on gross book values at the end of the preceding year, except for patterns and tools, which are based on the previous year's additions.

Electric light and power companies

See also various headings under Depreciation, depletion and obsolescence

ABBOT, JACK. Depreciation of lighting plants. *Mississippi electrical association, Report of 2nd annual convention,* June 1910, p. 37-9.

ABERDEEN and depreciation. *Municipal journal* (London), Oct. 23, 1903, p. 943.

DEPRECIATION, DEPLETION AND OBSOLESCENCE—ELECTRIC LIGHT AND POWER COMPANIES—*(Continued)*

	per cent
Glasgow	
Lands	1
Buildings	1
Accumulators	7½
Machinery	5.7½
Mains and services	2½
Meters	6
Electric Instruments	5
Workshop tools	5
Furniture	5
Aberdeen	
Buildings	1
Accumulators	5
Machinery	5
Mains and services	1½
Meters	5
Electric instruments	2½
Bolton	
Accumulators	10
Machinery	6
Mains and services	6
Meters	10
Electric instruments	10
Transformers	6
Motors	10

ALLCOCK, J. Allowance for depreciation: Cardiff tramways and electric light. *Accountant,* Dec. 28, 1907, Jan. 11, 1908, p. 787-9, 64-5. *Incorporated accountants' journal,* 1907-8, p. 80.

ALLCOCK, JOHN S. Depreciation of Cardiff electric tramway and lighting undertakings. *Electric railway review,* Jan. 4, 1908, p. 16.

ALLCOCK, JOHN S. Depreciation of tramway and electrical plant; report of Cardiff accounts. *Incorporated accountants' journal,* 1907-8, p. 80.

AMERICAN ELECTRIC RAILWAY ASSOCIATION. COMMITTEE ON VALUATION. Bibliography on valuation of public utilities to December 23, 1916. 61+72p.

AUSTRALIA. FEDERAL INCOME TAX DEPARTMENT. Depreciation allowance. *Accountant,* Oct. 13, 1917, p. 277-9. *Accounting and commerce,* June 30, 1917, p. 55-7. *Federal accountant,* July 1917, p. 83-8. *Public accountant,* June 30, 1917, p. 145-52.

	Rates
Electrical machinery	
Buildings	Nil.
Chimneys, flues	Nil.
Boilers	5 per cent
Engines, condensers pumps	
Alternators, dynamos, motor-generators, rotary converters	5 per cent
Instruments, testing apparatus, motors, indicator (fixed and portable)	7½ per cent
Switchboards	Repairs only
Machine tools, cranes and all fixed plant	5 per cent
Hand tools and loose plant	Replacements only
Underground wires and cables	2½ per cent
Overhead wires and cables—	
Insulated	7½ per cent
Bare	Nil.
Arc lamps	10 per cent
Standards, brackets, posts—iron, wood or steel	2½ per cent
Transformers (Static)	
Transformer boxes	2½ per cent
Distributing centres—switchgear	Repairs only
Conveyances, (horses, carts, etc.)	10 per cent
Accumulators	7½ per cent
House installations	5 per cent

BARKER, HARRY. Typical life expectation tables for public utility property. (In his *Public utility rates.* 1917. p. 368-9)

Electricity—Supply Works

	Years	Authority*	Control†
Anchors and guys	10-20	Wis. R. R. Comm.	Det.
Arc lamps and hangings	10-15	Wis. R. R. Comm.	Det. and Obs.
		St. Louis P. S. Comm.	Det.
Belting	20-25	Wis. R. R. Comm.	
Boilers, fire-tube	10-15	" " " "	Det.
Boilers, fire-tube	20-30	" " " "	Det.
water-tube	20-30	" " " "	Obs.
Buildings, masonry	75	" " " "	Det. and Obs.
wood-frame or second class	50	*	Obs.
Chimneys and stacks, masonry	30	*	Det.
steel	10		
Condensers	20-30	Wis. R. R. Comm.	
		Chicago Trac. Val. Comm.	Det.
Conduits and manholes	30-50	Wis. R. R. Comm.	Obs.
Conveyors, coal or ash	10	" " " "	Det.
ash or combined coal and ash	5	*	Det.

DEPRECIATION, DEPLETION AND OBSOLESCENCE—ELECTRIC LIGHT AND POWER COMPANIES—*(Continued)*

Cross arms	10-15	Wis. R. R. Comm.	Det.
Engines, gas	10-15	" " " "	Det. and Obs.
steam, high-speed	15-20	" " " "	Det.
steam, slow speed	25-30	" " " "	Det. and Obs.
Feed-water heaters	20-30	" " " "	Det.
Fuse boxes	10-12	" " " "	Det.
Fuel-oil equipment	25	Chicago Trac. Val. Comm.	Det.
Generators, motors and converters			
high speed	15	*	Det.
slow speed	20	*	Obs.
new types	20	Wis. R. R. Comm.	Det.
old types	15	" " " "	Obs.
turbine driven	20	" " " "	Det.
Lightning arresters	15-20	" " " "	Det.
Piping and covering	20-30	" " " "	Obs. and Det.
Poles, cedar in concrete	12-18	" " " "	Det.
Poles, cedar in earth	10-18	" " " "	Det.
iron or steel in concrete	15-30	*	Obs. and Det.
iron or steel in earth	10-15	Wis. R. R. Comm.	Det.
reinforced concrete	50	*	Obs.
Pumps, boiler feed	15-20	Wis. R. R. Comm.	Det.
small centrifugal	20-30	" " " "	Det.
Service boxes	10-12	" " " "	Det.
Shafting	20-40	" " " "	Obs.
Station wiring, etc.	30	" " " "	Obs. and Det.
Stokers	20	Chicago Trac. Val. Comm.	Det.
Storage batteries	15	Wis. R. R. Comm.	Det.
Switchboard instruments and wiring	25-30	" " " "	Obs. and Det.
Switchboards, old types	20-30	" " " "	Obs.
new types	15-20	" " " "	Obs.
Turbines, hydraulic, old types	25-40	Wis. R. R. Comm.	Obs.
new types	30-50	" " " "	Obs.
Steam, large units	20	" " " "	Det. and Obs.
auxiliary units	10-20	*	Det. and Obs.
Transformers, consumers	10-15	Wis. R. R. Comm.	Det.
station and sub-station	20	" " " "	Obs. and Det.
Watt-hour meters (consumer's)	10-15	" " " "	Det.
Wire, insulated copper line	10-15	" " " "	Det.
lead covered aerial cable	10-15	" " " "	Det. and Obs.
underground cable	20-25	" " " "	Obs.

Where no authority is cited the data are those of the author—average or approixmate figures secured by examination or enquiry.

†Probable action limiting service life; deterioration (due to wear and tear and weathering and obsoletion. Where both are cited, both actions have been observed, the first named predominating in a majority of cases.

BELL, L. B. Study in depreciation. *Electrical world,* Aug. 23, 1913, p. 379.

BISSELL, G. W. Depreciation of electrical properties. *Electrical age,* June 1906, p. 459.

BOUGHTON, JUDSON H. Commercial depreciation in electric plants. *Public service,* July 1908, p. 7.

BOWDEN, J. HORACE and FRED F. TATE. Adequate depreciation of capital expenditure by municipal electricity undertakings. *Electrical review,* London, June 21, 28, 1907, p. 1021, 1064.

	Years
Buildings, permanent	60
Buildings, temporary	20
Machinery	20
Mains	30
Mains, ducts	60
Meters	10
Instruments, tools and office furniture	10
Preliminary and extra	10
Accumulators	5

BRYAN, WILLIAM. Appraisal and depreciation of water-works and similar properties. *Journal of the association of engineering societies,* Dec.. 1907, p. 336-81. Depreciation allowance for various public service industries. *Engineering news,* Jan. 23, 1908, p. 96. Depreciation of electric light plants. *Municipality,* March 1908, p. 74.

	Years	% Straight	% Sinking Fund	
Electric light		10		Am. Inst. E. E.
"	12.33	8		N. Y. Edison Co.
			3	English municipal engineers
"		5		Mass. gas & el. com.
"	12.5, 14 16.66, 20	7.5-10 6.4-7.4		Motions made but not adopted

BRYAN, WILLIAM H. Depreciation of electric light plants. *Electrical world,* May 13, 1909, p. 1178.

Hydro-electric plant 2%

CALIFORNIA commission. *Electrical world,* June 24, 1916, p. 1492.

California railroad commission in its decision re the San Joaquin light and power company allowed a 6 per cent sinking fund depreciation annuity.

CENTRAL station plant depreciation charge. *Electrical world,* March 16, 1912, p. 581.

In a report to the city of Duluth giving an estimate for a municipal lighting plant Messrs. Oscar Claussen and Charles L. Pillsbury adopt 5% for the total annual depreciation of the plant. The report states that Mr. H. H. Crowell, engineer of the N. Y. P. S. C. for

DEPRECIATION, DEPLETION AND OBSOLESCENCE—ELECTRIC LIGHT AND POWER COMPANIES—*(Continued)*

the second district in reporting to the city of Detroit on an investigation he made of the Detroit Edison Co., expressed the opinion that a fair depreciation charge on that plant would be 4.834 per cent.

CLAFLIN, GEORGE E. Depreciation accounting for small companies. *National electric light association.* Proceedings, 1909, p. 165-82. Abstract. Electric railway journal, June 12, 1909, p. 1079.

	Percentage of Gross		
	Total Maintenance	Additional Allowance	Total Depreciation
1904	8.10	8.45	16.55
1905	9.35	8.15	17.50
1906	10.90	6.89	17.79
1907	9.56	6.84	16.40
1908	10.01	7.10	17.10

COMMERCIAL depreciation in electric plants. *Street railway bulletin*, Aug. 1908, p. 431.
Allowance should be made for machinery out of date in addition to allowance of 10% for ordinary wear and tear.

CONSOLIDATION of electricity supply in London. *Electrical world*, Sept. 19, 1908, p. 611.

	Years of life
Buildings	60
Plant	25
Cables	30
Meters	10

CONTENTION over depreciation fund in attack on Cincinnati's union gas and electric company lease. *Electrical world*, July 5, 1913, p. 6-7.

COST and depreciation of steam and hydro-electric installations. *Electrical world*, Dec. 30, 1909, p. 1558.

CROWELL, H. H. Electric lighting rates and depreciation. *Municipal journal and engineering*, Dec. 18, 1907, p. 698.

Estimated life of apparatus

	Table no. 1 Years	Table no. 2 Years
Buildings and fixtures	25	50
Stacks—brick	25	20
Boilers	15	20
Coal conveyors and trestles	10	10
Pumps, etc.	15	25
Piping	15	20
Engines	v5	25
Condensers	10	15
Alternators	20	25
Rotaries	15	15
Switchboards and instruments	15	20
Auxiliary apparatus	15	15
Batteries	10	15
Poles	10	12
Line wire	20	25
Arc lamps	10	10
Miscellaneous	10	10
Meters	10	10
Machine shop	10	10
Conduits	30	40
Edison tube	25	30
Sheathed cables	15	25
Towers	20	10
Railway tracks and scales	25	25
Electric plant	10	—
Turbo-alternators	—	25
Dynamos—D.C.C.P.	20	20
Motors D.CC.C.P.	—	20
Transformers	15	20

In this estimate the first column is assumed to apply to apparatus purchased 10 years or more ago, when the design and quality were inferior to that now furnished; the second column to apply to improved modern apparatus.

DEPRECIATION. *Electrician*, Feb. 19, 1909, p. 709. *Industrial engineering and engineering digest*, Oct. 1914, p. 402.

DEPRECIATION and income tax, the case of municipal undertakings. *Journal of gas lighting*, Jan. 7, 1913, p. 48.

DEPRECIATION and repairs. *Electrical review and western electrician*, Nov. 28, 1908, p. 807.

DEPRECIATION and reserve funds of electrical properties. *Electrical world*, May 12, 1910, p. 186-8.

DEPRECIATION, etc., on electricity supply undertakings. *Electrician*, May 25, June 15, 1906, p. 231, 350.

DEPRECIATION in electric lighting. *Municipal journal* (London), Jan. 2, 1903, p. 12.

DEPRECIATION in its relation to appraisals. *Electrical world*, Oct. 6, 1910, p. 796.

DEPRECIATION in municipal lighting plants. *Electrical review*, Oct. 3, 1908, p. 493.

DEPRECIATION: interesting report from Cardiff. *Municipal journal* (London), Dec. 20, 1907, p. 1083.

DEPRECIATION of assets of electric lighting companies. *Accountant*, Nov. 12, 1898, March 8, 1902, p. 246-8, 1083-4.

DEPRECIATION of Cardiff electric tramway and lighting undertakings. *Electric railway review*, Jan. 4, 1908, p. 16.

DEPRECIATION of companies' assets. *Electrician*, May 10, 1907, p. 146.

DEPRECIATION of electric plant. *Kansas public utilities commission Report*, 1913, p. 53.

DEPRECIATION, DEPLETION AND OBSOLESCENCE—ELECTRIC LIGHT AND POWER COMPANIES—*(Continued)*

The depreciation per year was determined by dividing the depreciable values of the property by the average life of the plant. The average life of an electric plant is about 17 years, thus making 5.9 per cent of the rate of depreciation on the depreciable property, or 5.4 per cent on the total physical value, with no interest accumulations. With the fund drawing 2½% interest, 4¾% of cost new of the plant would suffice.

DEPRECIATION of lighting and telephone plants. *Electrical world and engineer,* July 27, 1901.

DEPRECIATION of municipal lighting plants. *Electrical review and western electrician,* Oct. 3, 1908, p. 493.

DEPRECIATION of public utilities. *Canadian chartered accountant,* Oct. 1913, p. 112-3.

DEPRECIATION of the equipment of an electric plant. *Electrical world,* Dec. 12, 1914, p. 1161.

Plant and substation buildings	2%
Boilers, piping and generators	4.7 to 4.8
Electrical equipment	4.5
Storage batteries	4.15
Poles and pole-line equipment	4.4
Wire	3.75
Line transformers	4.5
Customers' meters	4.5

DICKSEE, LAURENCE R. Electric lighting companies. (In his *Auditing.* Authorized American ed. 1909, p. 142).

5% on the total capital expenditure. In the English editions of this work the minimum stated is 4%, but general opinion seems to require a somewhat higher rate in the United States.

DOHERTY, HENRY L. Comments on development and operation of hydro-electric plants. *American institute of electric engineers. Proceedinis,* 1909, p. 1362. Abstract. Cost and depreciation of steam and hydro-electric installation. *Electrical world,* Dec. 30, 1909, p. 1558.

DUFFY, C. N. Depreciation. *Electric railway review,* Jan. 18, 1908, p. 83. *Electrical world,* Feb. 1, 1908, p. 217. *Electrical review* (London), Sept. 4, 1908, p. 374. *Street railway journal,* Feb. 1, 1908, p. 169. Editorial. *Electrical world,* Feb. 1, 1908, p. 207.

	Dep.
Plant	70-80%
Property	2.9-3% per annum should be allowed for dep upon the duplicate value of the entire property, including land and water power.

EDWARDS, CHARLES LEWIS. Electric lighting accounts: correspondence. *Incorporated accountants' journal,* April 1912, p. 175.

	% Dep.
Buildings	1½-2
Boilers	5 -7½
Turbines and dynamos	5 -7½
Machinery	5 -7½.
Mains and cables	5 -10
General installation	7½-10

EDWARDS, HENRY MONROE. Accounting for depreciation; read before the National electric light association at its thirty-fourth convention held at New York city, May 29 to June 2, 1911. New York. National electric light association. 1911. 10p. *Electric railway journal,* June 3, 1911, p. 972.

Method used by the New York Edison co.

EDWARDS, HENRY MONROE. Regulated electric light accounting. National electric light association. Papers, reports and discussions. 1912. Abstract. *Electric railway journal,* June 15, 1912, p. 1029.

ELECTRIC lighting companies and depreciation. *Accountant,* April 11, 1903, p. 490-1.

Company	Amount actually provided out of Revenue for Depreciation, 1902.	Depreciation provision percentage. (Comparing with 2nd column).	
Blackheath and Greenwich	0.51	..	..
Brompton and Kensington	3.17	1.48	1.62
Charing Cross and Strand (West End areas only)	1.47	1.85	0.30
Chelsea	2.5	0.84	Nil
City of London	2.0	..	..
County of London (Metropolitan areas only)	0.36	Nil	Nil
London Electric	0.66	...	...
Kensington and Knightsbridge	3.13	3.02	2.88
Metropolitan	0.58	0.67	1.07
Notting Hill	0.68	0.86	0.57
St. James' and Pall Mall	3.66	3.64	4.19
South London	0.18	..	..
Westminster	3.33	3.45	3.13

ELECTRIC supply companies and depreciation of assets; from the Statist. *Accountant,* Jan. 13, 1900, p. 57-9.

ELECTRICAL engineers and depreciation. *Accountant,* June 25, 1910, p. 891.

ESTIMATING the cost of an electric plant. *Journal of Franklin institute,* May 1908, p. 397.

FERNIE, F. Obsolescence of electric lighting plnat. *Electrical review* (London), Sept. 25, 1908, p. 516.

FIGURES from the Iola (Kans.) central station. *Electrical world,* Sept. 23, 1909, p. 723.

Plant using natural gas for fuel:

Buildings	5%
Engines	7
Boilers	10
Dynamos and alternation	7

DEPRECIATION, DEPLETION AND OBSOLESCENCE—ELECTRIC LIGHT AND POWER COMPANIES—*(Continued)*

Switchboard and accessories	8
Pole lines	12
Wires	2
Arc lamps	20
Transformer	8
Meters in service	15
Motors	10

FISCAL report of Seattle municipal plant. *Electrical world*, July 20, 1912, p. 130-1.

FLOY, HENRY. Depreciation. (In his *Valuation of public utility properties*, 1912, p. 199).

The present laws of Massachusetts provide in respect to municipally owned gas or electric plants, that there shall be included an amount for "depreciation equal to 3 per cent of the cost of the plant exclusive of land and water power appurtenant thereto."

	Per cent of gross revenue expended or appropriated for Maintenance	Depreciation
Milwaukee companies		
Gas, electric light and steam heat departments	6.15	8.12
Union Electric light & power co., St. Louis	4.95	16.0
Suburban electric light & power co.	7.10	10.85
Detroit Edison company and subsidiaries	6.45	10.23

FOSTER, HORATIO A. Methods of calculating depreciation. (In his *Engineering valuation of public utilities and factories*, 1913, p. 169-70, 205-6).

	Minimum service value per cent of reproduction cost Weight of copper
Copper wire, weather proof lead-covered cable, underground and overhead.	
Weight of copper	
Poles both wood and iron, anchors and guys	20%
Service transformers	25
Arc lamps and span equipment	20
Service and watt meters	80

Electric light and railways

	years
Copper wire, weatherproof insulation	10 to 15
Cable, lead covered, aerial	10 to 15
Cable, lead covered, underground, in conduits	20 to 25
Conduit	30 to 50
Manholes	30 to 50
Poles, cedar, in earth	10 to 18
Poles, cedar, in concrete	12 to 20
Poles, iron in concrete	15 to 30
Pole anchors and guys	10 to 20
Cross arms	10 to 15
Service transformers	10 to 15
Fuse boxes	10 to 12
Lightning arresters	10 to 12
Arc lamps and span equipment	10 to 15
Nernst lamps	8 to 10
Service wattmeters	10 to 15
Railway spans and bracket equipment	15 to 20

Trolley wire: life depends on headway; should never be worn to less than 75 per cent of its original size.
No. 0 wire at 1 minute headway, life 2 years.
No. 00 wire at 1 minute headway, life 2½ years.
No. 000 wire at 1 minute headway, life 3 years.

FOSTER, HORATIO A. Rules for depreciating railways and lighting plants in Great Britain.

General plant and machinery 5% per annum on written down value, in addition to the cost of repairs.

In Massachusetts, the Gas and Electric Lighting Commission has established a rate for application to the property owned by Municipal electric light plants . . . 3 per cent depreciation in the cost of all plant, exclusive of land and water power appurtenant thereto.

The Wisconsin Railroad Commission has covered the regular plants by giving as the average life of electric light plants 17.46 years.

GILLETTE, HALBERT P. and RICHARD T. DANA. Depreciation. (In their Handbook of mechanical and electrical cost data, 1918. p. 109, 115-25, 1039).

Rental equipment, electric.

Table II.
Composite Life of Electric Lighting and Power Plant

Class	Life	Cost new, less scrap	Annual per cent of depreciation	Annual fund required to cover depreciation
A	5	$ 210	20.00	$ 42
B	8	7,110	12.50	889
C	10	17,208	10.00	1,721
D	12	26,272	8.33	2,188
E	15	131,550	6.67	8,774

DEPRECIATION, DEPLETION AND OBSOLESCENCE—ELECTRIC LIGHT AND POWER COMPANIES—*(Continued)*

F.............16	32,258	6.25	2,016
G.............20	104,097	5.00	5,205
H.............25	36,116	4.00	1,445
I.............50	14,337	2.00	287
J.............60	1,165	1.67	19
K.............75	21,920	1.33	292
	$392,243		$22,878

$$\text{Average life} = \frac{392{,}243}{22{,}878} = 17.15 \text{ years}$$

15 years

H. P. Gillette, Everett Railway & Water Co., Jan. 29, 1912.

Buildings	1.08%
Steam equipment	4.1
Electrical equipment	4.7
Repair-shop equipment	10
Lamps	6.66
Circuits	4
Conduits	3
Posts	3.5

GILLETTE, HALBERT P. and RICHARD T. DANA. Electric light and power plants. (In their *Handbook of Mechanical and electrical cost data.* 1918. p. 808, 797, 778-9, 746, 759, 771).

GILLETTE, HALBERT P. and RICHARD T. DANA. Hydro-electric plants. (In their *Haodbook of Mechanical and electrical cost data.* 1918. p. 686, 694-5, 702).

p. 686. Depreciation in water-power plants will range from 1½ to 2½% per year, with 2% for a general average and repairs about 1% per year.

p. 695.	Buildings	1%
	Water-wheels	2
	Generators	2
	Pole lines	3
	Other electrical appliances	3

GOODWIN, HAROLD. Practical economies in distribution with their effect on the commercial policy of a central station company. *General electric review,* Dec. 1914, p. 1159-74. National electric light association. *Papers, reports and discussions,* p. 655.

GREAT BRITAIN. BOARD OF INLAND REVENUE. Depreciation rates: (In its *Income tax; statement respecting allowances for wear and tear and obsolescence of plant and machinery.* 1918. Cd. 9022, p. 4; Cd. 9134, p. 6). *American economic review, Supplement,* Dec. 1920, p. 51. *Journal of accountancy,* Sept. 1920, p. 194.

Electric light undertakings.

Cables	3%
Plant and machinery	5
Written down value	

GRUNSKY, CARL EWALD. Probable useful life of various articles. (In his *Valuation, depreciation and the rate-base.* 1917. p. 284).

Systems and plants

electric light and power	17.46 years. Wisconsin railroad commission. Fond du Lac W. Co. case aver. 6 plants.
electric light and power	18 years. Wisconsin railroad commission. Madison gas and electric light co. case, March 8, 1910.
electric light and power	20 years. Mass. G. & E. com.
electric light and power	20-25 years. Wisconsin railroad commission. Jefferson Mun. E. L. & W. plant.
electric light and power	22.0 years. Pacific gas & electric company. Figures used in rate hearings before Master in Chancery, San Francisco, 1913-4.

HAMMOND, ROBERT. Depreciation. *Institute of electrical engineers, Proceedings,* April 25, 1907. p. 270-301. *Journal of the Institute of electrical engineers,* 1907, p. 270. Abstracts. *Electric railway review,* June 1, 1907, p. 716. *Electrical review* (Chicago), May 25, 1907, p. 828. *Electrical review* (London), May 3, 1907, p. 744. *Electrician,* April 26, 1907, p. 51. *Engineering magazine,* July 1907, p. 636-8. *Engineering record,* June 15, 1907, p. 703. *Municipal journal* (London), May 10, 17, 1907, p. 411, 435. *Progressive age,* July 1, 1907, p. 305. *Street railway bulletin,* June 1907, p. 382. *Tramway and railroad world* June 6, 1907, p. 497. Editorials and discussions. *Electrician,* May 3, 1907, p. 100-103. *Engineering record,* June 15, 1907, p. 703. Depreciation of machinery. *Accountant,* May 18, 1907, p. 675.

Land and buildings	60 years
Machinery and plant:	
Boilers	20
Pumps and pipework	25
Conveyors	10
Engines	25
Turbines	20
Dynamos and alternators	25
Motors	20
Tools and sundries	10
Accumulators	15

DEPRECIATION, DEPLETION AND OBSOLESCENCE—ELECTRIC LIGHT AND POWER COMPANIES—*(Continued)*

Transformers, static	15
Converters, rotary	20
Switching apparatus and instruments	20
Meters	10
Mains:	
Armoured	2
Solid system	30
Ducts	30

HAMMOND, ROBERT. Depreciation of electric light plants. *Municipality,* March 1908, p. 69-77, 100.

HOUGHTON, JUDSON H. Commercial depreciation in electric plants. *Public service,* July 1908, p. 7.

INCOME tax appeal. *Electrician,* June 15, 1906, p. 350.
The commissioners of the income tax decided to allow 2% depreciation from the profits of St. Pancras electricity undertaking in respect of mains and plant, but the surveyor of taxes only allowed depreciation on the written down value of mains, etc., plus any additions or extensions. The 2% referred to above is simply in respect of any possible explosion, breakdown or obsolescence of plant.

INCOME tax notes. *Accountant,* May 11, Sept. 28, 1918, p. 359, 162-6. *Incorporated accountants' journal,* May, Oct. 1918, p. 157, 14.
Electric light undertakings.

3%	Written down value	Cables
5	" "	Plant and machinery

INSTALLATIONS, systems and appliances. *Electrical world,* December 7, 1912, p. 1220.
Robt. Hammond in a paper read in 107, estimated the life of

buildings	60 years
boilers	20
engines	25
turbines	20
armored mains	25
mains laid "solid" or in ducts	30

Sir Wm. Preece gave following in 1906:

Buildings	80 years
boilers	22-25
generators	30
engines	25
armored cables	35
mains laid "solid"	40

INSTITUTE *of municipal treasurers and accountants* (*incorporated*). Municipal corporations and companies working tramway and light railways, gas, water and electricity undertakings. *Accountant,* June 26, 1909, p. 906-8. *Incorporated accountants journal,* 1909, p. 238-40. Income tax assessment; allowances for depreciation. *Accountant,* Oct. 2, 1909, p. 423-5, 400-2.
Cables.
In addition to repairs, allowance for depreciation may be granted at the rate of 3% per annum on the written down value.
Plant and machinery
On all other plant, exclusive of loose tools, meters and office furniture, depreciation may be allowed at the rate of 5% per annum on the written down value, in addition to the cost of repairs.
Conduits.
No allowance should be made for depreciation; but annual expenditure on repairs and renewals may be allowed as working expenses, as and when incurred.
Meters, loose tools, and office furniture.
No allowance should be made for depreciation, but annual expenditure on repairs and renewals may be allowed as working expenses, as and when incurred.
Is depreciation as such needed? *Municipal journal* (*London*), July 31, 1903, p. 699.
Relates to West Ham corporation electric lighting plant.

Is depreciation as such needed? *Municipal journal* (London) July 31, 1903, p. 699.

JACKSON, WILLIAM B. Depreciation and reserve funds of electrical properties. *Journal of the Western society of engineers,* Oct. 1910, p. 587-619. Abstracts. *Electric railway journal,* May 21, 1910, p. 903. *Engineering and contracting,* May 25, 1910, p. 487. *Engineering record,* April 30, 1910.

JACKSON, WILLIAM B. Depreciation of electrical properties. *Public service,* June 1910, p. 161-71.

JOHNSON, GEORGE. Depreciation. (In his *Electric lighting accounts.* 1913. p. 23-4).

Buildings	2½%
Meters	7½
Instruments	7½
Accumulators	10½
Engines and boilers	7½-10
Mains and cables	5
Dynamos	7½
Turbines	7½
Transformers	7½-10
Tools	10
Motors	7½

LACKIE, W. W. Electrical engineers and depreciation. *Accountant,* June 25, 1910, p. 891-2.

LEAKE, P. D. Record of depreciation. (In his *Depreciation and wasting assets and their treatment in computing annual profit and loss.* 1917. p. 84-93).

DEPRECIATION, DEPLETION AND OBSOLESCENCE—ELECTRIC LIGHT AND POWER COMPANIES—*(Continued)*

LIFE of plant. *Electrician,* Nov. 8, 1912, p. 182-4.
In 1906 the periods were fixed at 50 years for buildings, 30 years for mains and 20 years for plant.
Mr. Robert Hammond, in a paper read before Institute of electrical engineers in 1907 estimated the life of

Buildings	60 years
Boilers	60
Engines	25
Turbines	20
Armoured mains	25
Mains, laid "solid" or in ducts	30

In 1906 Sir William Preece gave the following figures:

Buildings	80
Boilers	20-25
Dynamos and alternators	30
Engines	25
Armoured cables	35
Mains laid "solid"	40

20-25 years is by no means a limiting period for the life of mains. In regard to generating plant this may have a useful life of 20 years or perhaps more, but it is evident that, owing to expansion or to the introduction of more efficient types of plant, the time during which it may pay to use any item of machinery may be considerably less than 20 years.

LINCOLN, EDMUND EARLE. Results of municipal electric lighting in Massachusetts. Boston, Houghton, Mifflin company, 1918. 484p.
See index under Depreciation.

MANUFACTURERS' light and heat company of Pittsburgh, Pa. *Commercial and financial chronicle,* July 23, 1910, p. 217.

Pipe lines, pipe rigs and lines	6%
Gas regulators and meters	4
Fittings, other materials, telephone lines, boilers, buildings and office furniture	5

MONTANA public service commission allows an annual depreciation allowance of 5 per cent for a small electric plant. *Electrical world,* April 1, 1916, p. 789.

MONTGOMERY, ROBERT H. Electric light and power companies. (In his *Auditing, theory and practice.* 1916. p. 675).
Depreciation in electric light plants is generally understood to be the deterioration in the property, above ordinary repairs, that take place because of age, use, obsolescence or inadequacy.—4-5% on the average cost value.

MULHALL, JOHN F. J. Depreciation. (In his *Quasi-public corporation accounting and management.* c1905. p. 180-3).

Electric light works	5-10%

MUNICIPAL trading and depreciation. *Accountant,* June 8, July 6, 1901, p. 657-9, 769-71.

Machinery, mains and transformers	6%
Accumulators, meters and electrical instruments	10

MURRAY, ALEXANDER. Glasgow corporation accounts with special reference to depreciation and sinking funds. *Accountant,* June 13, 1903, p. 782-94. *Royal philosophical society of Glasgow, Proceedings,* 1903.

NEALE, R. E. Depreciation in engineering works. *Mechanical world,* Feb. 7, 1913, p. 67-8.

Building, land and plant	2.5-5%	20-40 years
Generating plant & machinery	5%	20 years

(1909 agreement between Inland and certain municipal tramway associations. These allowances generally considered to be insufficient).

Isolated generating plant	7%	14 years
Small workshop equipment	5-10	10-20
General workshop equipment	8-12	8.5-12.5
Seven American electrical supply	8-16	6.3-12.5

NELSON, BAILIE WALTER. Limitation and application of profits from municipal undertakings. *Accountant,* Aug. 3, 1912, p. 167-71. *Incorporated accountants' journal,* Oct. 1912, p. 15-7.
Scale of depreciation in force in Glasgow electricity undertaking:

On land and buildings	1 per cent per annum
On machinery and plant, electrical instruments, transformers in consumers' premises, &c.	3½ " " "
On accumulators	5 " " "
On mains and cables	2½ " " "
On meters	4 " " "

OFFICIAL allowance in respect of depreciation of machinery and plant—Board of Inland revenue, Great Britain. *Accountant,* May 16, 1914, p. 735.
Cables—In addition to repairs, allowance for depreciation may be granted at the rate of 3 per cent. per annum on the written down value.
Plant and machinery—On all other plant, exclusive of loose tools, meters, and office furniture, depreciation may be allowed at the rate of 5 per cent. per annum on the written down value in addition to the cost of repairs.
Conduits—No allowance should be made for depreciation: but annual expenditure on repairs and renewals may be allowed as working expenses as and when incurred.
Meters, loose tools, and office furniture—No allowance should be made for depreciation; but annual expenditure on repairs and renewals may be allowed as working expenses, as and when incurred.

PASADENA municipal lighting plant. *Municipal engineering,* June 1913, p. 505.

DEPRECIATION, DEPLETION AND OBSOLESCENCE—ELECTRIC LIGHT AND POWER COMPANIES—*(Continued)*

PENDER, HAROLD. Depreciation. (In his *Handbook for electrical engineers.* c1914. p. 337).
New York first district Public service commission has assumed the life of electric lighting and gas properties as a whole to be about 20 years.
Wisconsin commission has decided that 17½ years is a fair life for electric lighting properties.

PETITION for changes in treatment of depreciation in New York. *Electrical world,* Dec. 9, 1911, p. 1420.

PHILADELPHIA. CONTROLLER. Rates of depreciation. (In his Manual *of accounting, reporting and business procedure of the city and county of Philadelphia.* 1917. p. 210).

Buildings, used solely for the production of heat, light, power or refrigeration	1⅔%

PIEZ, CHARLES. Perpetual inventory and appraisal values; table of standard depreciation rates. *Engineering and contracting,* Jan. 24, 1917, p. 77. *Factory,* Dec. 1916, p. 668-71. *Iron age,* Nov. 30, 1916, Jan. 11, 1917, p. 1266, 138-9. *Iron trade review,* Feb. 22, 1917, p. 477-8. Condensed. *Journal of the American society of mechanical engineers,* Dec. 1916, p. 965-6. *Iron trade review,* Dec. 7, 1916, p. 1144-6. Kent, William. *Bookkeeping and cost accounting for factories.* 1918. p. 90. Discussion. *Journal of the American society of mechanical engineers,* March 1917, p. 215-7.

	% on cost
Departmental wiring and electric fixtures, net additions	60

PIXLEY, FRANCIS W. Electricity lighting companies. (In his *Accountancy.* Ed. 2. p. 218).

Accumulators	10% per annum
Cables	5
Dynamos	7½
Engines and boilers	7½-12
Instruments	7½
Mains	5
Meters	7½-10
Motors	7½
Tools	10-15
Transformers	7½-10
Turbines	7½-10

PUBLIC utility reports, annotated. Rochester, Lawyers co-operative publishing co.
See index under Depreciation.

PUBLIC utility reports, annotated. Rochester, Lawyers co-operative publishing co. 1915A. p. 547,652.
Re Arlington Light, Heat & Power Co. (Neb.). A light, heat, and power company was ordered to set aside annually out of operating income 7 per cent upon an authorized issue of stock as a maintenance and depreciation fund.
Re Rhinelander Power Co. (Wis.). Annual depreciation on a hydraulic-power plant was computed by the Commission at 2.5 per cent for the prupose of comparing operating expenses at such a plant with those of a hypothetical steam plant in order to calculate the saving due to the operation of the water plant.

PUBLIC utility reports, annotated. Rochester, Lawyers co-operative publishing co. 1915B. p. 1, 135, 416, 846.
Charlesworth v. Omro Electric Light Co. (Wis.). An annual allowance of $420 was made for depreciation, out of a total revenue allowance of $4,196 for the operation of an electric light company the plant and business of which were valued at $11,500.
Public Service Commission ex. rel. Seattle v. Seattle Lighting Co. (Wash.). The sum of $548,170 was allowed for accrued depreciation in the valuation of the property of a lighting company for rate making purposes.
Re Omaha & L. R. & Light Co. (Neb.). Upon acthorizing an electric railway and light company to issue securities for improvements to its property, the Commission directed the company to set aside annually 7 per cent of the entire amount of outstanding liabilities for maintenance and depreciation reserve funds, in order that the gross assets of the company should be kept to a value approximately equal to the outstanding liabilities.
Oakland City Electric Light & Power Co. v. Oakland City (Ind.). In estimating the total amount of revenue necessary for the operation of an electric light and power plant, the Commission fixed the annual depreciation allowance at 4 per cent.

PUBLIC utility reports, annotated. Rochester, Lawyers co-operative publishing co. 1915F. p. 747, 913.
Harris v. South Side Gas & Electric Co. (Ariz.). An allowance was made for annual depreciation of an electric plant at a somewhat higher rate than was customary, where the peculiar nature of the plant consisted largely of shortlived equipment and a power plant of such construction as to make obsolescence a controlling factor.
Harris v. South Side Gas & Electric Co. (Ariz.). An allowance of $5,800 was held sufficient for the annual depreciation in electrical propertp having a book cost of $91,-381.93 and a valuation for rate-amking purposes of $124,000.
Bend v. Bend Water, Light & Power Co. (Or.) A water, light and power company was directed to deduct from its operating income 4 per cent of the value new of its depreciable electric property and 3 per cent of the value new of its water property to be set aside each year for depreciation, and accounted for as provided by Par. 17 of the Public Utilities Act. Laws of 1911, chapter 279.

PUBLIC utilities reports, annotated. Rochester, Lawyers co-operative publishing co. 1916A. p. 227, 372, 848, 872.
Bly v. Winslow Electric Light & Power Co. (Ariz.). An annual allowance of 4 per cent of the value of the physical property of an electric utility was held to be sufficient, under the straight-line method, for a depreciation reserve account to provide for replacements.
Taylor v. Northwest Light & Water Co. (Cal.). The weighted average annual rate of depreciation of an electrical utility, based on the straight line formula, was fixed at 6 per cent of the value of the depreciable property.

DEPRECIATION, DEPLETION AND OBSOLESCENCE—ELECTRIC LIGHT AND POWER COMPANIES—*(Continued)*

Re Fennimore (Wis.). An annual allowance of 4½ per cent of the investment in a municipal electric plant was held necessary to provide for accrued and accruing depreciation, in estimating operating expenses.

Re Colorado Springs, Light, Heat & Power Co. (Colo.). An annual allowance of 4.25 per cent of the cost new of electrical property and 2.8 per cent of the cost new of hydroelectric property was made to provide fo depreciation on a straight line basis in fixing rates.

PUBLIC utility reports, annotated. Rochester, Lawyers co-operative publishing co. 1916B. p. 24, 377, 445, 449, 609.

Belleville v. St. Clair County Gas & Eectric Co. (Ill.). An allowance of 4.4% per annum to cover depreciation, obsolescence, inadequacy, etc., was held sufficient in valuing electric light property for rate making.

Philipsburg v. Montana Power Co. (Mont.). An annual depreciation allowance of 5 per cent for a small electric light plant was held to be proper.

Peck v. Indianapolis, Light & Heat Co. (Ind.). Real estate, working capital, exclusive of stores and supplies, and scrap value of an electric light and power company, do not depreciate; and underground conduits, cable mains, tools, stores, and supplies depreciate very slightly.

Peck v. Indianapolis, Light & Heat Co. (Ind.). Future inadequacy is the only justification for any allowance for depreciation of indestructible underground electric conduits.

Peck v. Indianapolis Light & Heat Co. (Ind.). An allowance for depreciation of only 3 per cent of a total present value of $5,250,000 of an electric light and power company was made in estimating expenses, where such value included non depreciable items valued at $950,000 and items that depreciate very slightly valued at $670,000.

Peck v. Indianapolis Light & Heat Co. (Ind.). An allowance of from 10 to 65 per cent for depreciation of office furniture, equipment of stores department, wagons, drays, motor vehicles and other general equipment, was held excessive as compared with one from 10 to 45 per cent, in fixing the reproduction cost of electric property less depreciation.

Re Moore v. Merchants Heat & Light Co. (Ind.). An allowance of only 3 per cent for depreciation was made where it was computed on the whole value of an electric light and power plant, including real estate, going value, working capital, and inventory, although a higher rate should be allowed if computed on only the depreciable part of the plant.

Monahan v. Pacific gas & e. co. (Cal.). An allowance for depreciation of an electric plant was made on the six per cent sinking fund basis in a rate proceedings.

PUBLIC utility reports, annotated. Rochester, Lawyers co-operative publishing co. 1916C. p. 830.

East Bakersfield Improv. Association v. San Joaquin light & power corporation. (Cal.). An electric depreciation annuity was computed on a 6 per cent sinking fund basis.

PUBLIC utility reports, annotated. Rochester, Lawyers co-operative publishing co. 1916D. p. 380, 651, 1076.

Well v. Hullinger. (Ill.). In ascertaining operating expense, an allowance of 4½% of the value of electrical property was held sufficient for annual depreciation.

Austin v. Phillips Electric light & power co. (Me.). An allowance of 5 per cent for depreciation was made in ascertaining the annual net earnings of an electric utility.

La Junta v. Arkansas Valley R. light & power co. (Colo.). The sum of $2,500 was allowed for annual depreciation of an electric plant having a rate making value of $80,000.

PUBLIC utility reports, annotated. Rochester, Lawyers co-operative publishing co. 1916E. p. 375, 879, 1072.

Kauffman v. Hillsboro Light & Power Co. (Wis.). An allowance of 4.6 per cent was made for the annual depreciation of an electric plant, in ascertaining the operating expenses.

Re Grafton County Electric Light & Power Co. (N. H.). An allowances of 3 per cent for annual depreciation was made in finding the accrued depreciation of a hydro-electric plant.

Gish v. Beaver Dam Light & Power Co. (Wis.). April 19, 1916. A depreciation allowance of 4 per cent of the physical valuation of electric property, exclusive of land, was held ample in ascertaining the operating expenses, where some depreciation was charged to maintenance. Year ending July 7, 1916.

In East Dubuque Electric Co. (Ill.). No. 5218, July 13, 1916, an electric utility was ordered to set aside annually 5 per cent of the value of electric transmission lines for a depreciation fund.

PUBLIC utility reports, annotated. Rochester, Lawyers co-operative publishing co. 1916F. p. 752.

Churchill v. Winthrop & W. Light & Power Co. (Me.). Prospective electric consumers were required to guarantee, as a condition of making the extension, an annual amount sufficient to provide for an allowance of only 2 per cent for a depreciation reserve fund of 25 per cent of the cost of the extension, rather than 5 per cent for straight line depreciation, where the company has no generating plant.

PUBLIC utility reports, annotated. Rochester, Lawyers co-operative publishing co. 1917A. p. 439.

Croty v. Tomah Electric & Telephone Co. (Wis.). The composite life of an electric distributing plant was held to be 14.1 years.

PUBLIC utility reports, annotated. Rochester, Lawyers co-operative publishing co. 1917B. p. 1.

Lincoln v. Lincoln Water & Light Co. (Ill.). An annual allowance of $6,000 with an additional annual allowance of 4¼ per cent of the cost of all additions and betterments, together with all earnings of the fund was held to be reasonable for the electric department of a utility

PUBLIC utility reports, annotated. Rochester, Lawyers co-operative publishing co. 1917C. p. 111, 162, 728.

DEPRECIATION, DEPLETION AND OBSOLESCENCE—ELECTRIC LIGHT AND POWER COMPANIES—*(Continued)*

Re Kansas City Electric Co. (Mo.). An annual allowance of 3½ per cent of the rate-making value of an electric utility was made for a depreciation reserve in fixing rates.

Wiseman v. Rupert Electric Co. (Idaho.). An annual allowance of 6 per cent on the value of the depreciable property of an electric distribution company was held sufficient to cover future depreciation.

Canyon City v. Consolidated Electric Light Co. (Or.) An annual allowance of $577.17 per year was ordered set aside for the replacement of units of an electric plant, the value of which was found to be $9,636.

PUBLIC utility reports, annotated. Rochester, Lawyers co-operative publishing co. 1917D. p. 202, 743.

Commercial Club v. Terre Haute, I. & E. traction co. (Ind.). The annual depreciation charge for an electric light and power plant was fixed at 3 per cent.

Murchie v. St. Croix Gaslight co. (Me.). An annual allowance of 5 per cent for depreciation of an electric utility was held efficiently liberal if applied only to the value of physical property, excluding allowances for overheads and working capital.

Murchie v. St. Croix Gaslight co. (Me.) An allowance of 5 per cent for annual depreciation reserve of an electric company was made in fixing rates, the amount being recommended by the Commission experts, not questioned by the utility, and approved by complainants.

PUBLIC utility reports, annotated. Rochester, Lawyers co.operative publishing co. 1918A. p. 325, 592.

Re Hydro electric light co. (Ind.). In the valuation of the property of an electric utility for rate making, the Indiana Commission allowed 3 per cent per annum for accruing depreciation on the depreciable property, including transmission and distribution systems, buildings and miscellaneous structures, plant equipment, general equipment and 12 per cent structural overhead value of such items.

Re Tualatin valley electric co. (Or.). An annual allowance of $900 was made for depreciation of an electric distributing system valued at $15.771.

PUBLIC utility reports, annotated. Rochester, Lawyers co-operative publishing co. 1918C. p. 133.

Re Carrier Mills Utilities Co. (Ill.). An allowance of 4.94 per cent was fixed as a proper amount for annual depreciation of an electric distributing company.

PUBLIC utility reports, annotated. Rochester, Lawyers co-operative publishing co. 1918E. p. 300, 629, 678-9, 679,

Re Princeton v. Princeton Light & Power Co. (Ind.). An annual allowance of 3 per cent of the present physical value of an electric plant exclusive of lands, working capital, materials, and supplies, with 3 per cent on subsequent plan additions, was made for depreciation, in a rate proceedings.

Re Western Colorado Power Co. (Colo.). The sum of $4,000 to be set aside on the 5 per cent sinking fund basis was allowed for annual depreciation of an electric plant having a rate making value of $250,000.

In Desert Power & Water Co. Docket No. 361, Feb. 20, 1918, the Arizona Commission, in considering the amount of depreciation to be allowed for an electrical plant serving in a mining territory said:

"Experience has shown that an annual depreciation charge of from 3 to 4 per cent of the depreciable property is adequate for a plant of this character. We have analyzed this mattr somewhat farther with a view to localizing figures, and, preliminary to the depreciation study, have adopted percentages as follows:

DEPRECIATION PERCENTAGES

Class of Equipment	Annual Depreciation Per cent	Life in years
Buildings	3%	33 1/3
Power lines wood poles and steel fixtures a)	4%	25
Power lines wood poles and wood x-arms (b)	5%	20
Local distributing systems	5%	20
Plant equipment	4%	25
Office equipment	10%	10
Meters	10%	10
Transformers	5%	20

* Note.—The distinction made between the two classes of power lines is derived, not only from the respective classes of pole hardware, but also from consideration of the fact that there is considerable difference in the quality of all the material as well as workmanship.

"We conclude from the foregoing that 4 per cent of the physical property is a reasonable annual charge to the depreciation reserve.

In Re Peru (Ind.) No. 3815, June 1, 1918, a municipal electric plant was ordered to reduce its depreciation charge from 6 percent to 3 percent per annum.

In Shelbyville v. Interstate Public Service Nos. 1811, 2838, April 26, 1918, the Indiana Commission fixed 3 per cent of the value of an electric plant as a proper amount for depreciation.

Re Suburban light & power co. (Colo.). Decision No. 143. Investigation and Suspension Docket No. 12, Nov. 16, 1917. An annual allowance of $336 for accruing depreciation was held unduly low, for an electric utility, the fair value of whose property for rate making purposes was found to be $16,000; and an annual allowance of $400 to be set aside on the sinking fund basis, was ordered.

Re Increased rates (N. J.) Sept. 10, 1917. Average rates of depreciation of 2 per cent for power station buildings; 6.50 per cent for machinery; 2 per cent for substation buildings, 6.35 per cent for machinery; 3.57 per cent for high tension line; 2.44 per cent for signal line; 4.24 per cent for third rail (Including bonding); 5.78 per cent for passenger cars; 6.345 per cent for electric equipment of cars; and 6.05 per cent for trolley construction,—are normal, being based upon average expected life consistent with the usual practice.

DEPRECIATION, DEPLETION AND OBSOLESCENCE—ELECTRIC LIGHT AND POWER COMPANIES—*(Continued)*

In Shelbyville v. Interstate Public Service Co. Nos. 1811, 2838, April 26, 1918, the Indiana Commission fixed 3 per cent of the value of an electric plant as a proper amount for depreciation.

In re Peru (Ind.). No. 3815' June 1, 1918, a municipal electric plant was ordered to reduce its depreciation charge from 6 per cent to 3 per cent per annum.

PUBLIC utility reports, annotated. Rochester, Lawyers co-operative publishing co. 1918F. p. 316, 624, 872.

Re United public service co. (Ind.). An electric company was required to set aside annually 3 per cent of the value of its plant for depreciation less the value fo lands materials and supplies and working capital.

An allowance for annual depreciation amounting to 2½ per cent on the estimated value of the physical properties of an electric company was held not to be too high.

Re Queens Borough gas & electricity co. (N. Y.) An annual allowance for depreciation amounting to 1½ cents per kilowatt hour of electricity generated less actual cost of repairs is excessive, 0.75 per kilowatt hour being adequate.

PUBLIC utility reports, annotated. Rochester, Lawyers co-operative publishing co. 1919A. p. 552, 602.

Wiseman v. Rupert electric co. (Idaho) 552. An annual allowance of 5 per cent of the total value of an electric distributing company'd system for accruing depreciation was held reasonable in a rate proceedings.

Re Cleveland electric illuminating co. (Ohio). 602. An annual allowance of only 3 per cent was made for depreciation of an electric plant in view of the fact that the property had been maintained in a high state of efficiency.

PUBLIC utility reports, annotated. Rochester, Lawyers co-operative publishing co. 1919B. p. 748, 749, 1073,

Re Wabash water & ight co. No. 3826. Nov. 4, 1918, the Indiana commission fixed the proper allowance of annual depreciation at 3 per cent of the value of an electric plant less the value of lands materials, and supplies, and working capital.

In Re La Porte gas & electric co. Nos. 3774-3777, Aug. 10, 1918, the Indiana commission held that the company should set aside annually for depreciation3 per cent of the value of its depreciable electric property.

In Re San Joaquin light & power corporation decision No. 5449, Application No. 3531. May 28, 1918, the California Commission fixed the rate of depreciation of an electric plant on a 6 per cent sinking fund basis.

In Re Northern Indiana gas & electric co. (Ind.). No. 4115, Jan. 11, 1919, a gas utility was ordered to set aside annually beginning at the expiration of the temporary rate period, 1½ per cent of the value of its property other than lands, materials, and supplies for depreciation.

In Re Louisiana light, power & traction co. case no. 1733, Oct. 29, 1918, the Missouri Commission, upon an application for an incrwease in electric rates, held that the company was entitled to an allowance of 5 per cent to cover depreciation and contingencise.

In Re Falls City electric light & power co. U-F-211, P. S. C. Or. Order No. 407, July 11, 1918, it was held by the Oregon Commission that an annual depreciation allowance of $750 was necessary for the replacement of the equipment of an electric utility at the expiration of its service life, valued at $9,298.

In Re Bandon power co. U-F-205, P. S. C. Or. Order No. 406, June 24, 1918, it was held by the Oregon Commission that an annual allowance of $1,850 for an electric company whose fair value was fixed at $33,000 was sufficient to preserve the integrity of the investment.

In Re alliance gas & power formal case no. 721, Dec. 12, 1918, the Ohio commission in valuing the property of an electric plant for rate making, said that inasmuch as the distribution system was all overhead, and that a considerable portion of the power plant consisted of small units an allowance of 5 per cent for depreciation reserve should be made.

Bean v. Belgrade power co. (Me.) 977. A liberal allowance should be made for the depreciation of an electrical plant where its water power is leased and the entire investment may have to be abandoned or sold at a sacrifice before it is all worn out, or a substantial part abandoned and other power provided.

Bean v. Belgrade power co. (Me.) 977. The annual charge for the depreciation of an electrical plant should not be less than 5 per cent, if the entire investment may have to be abandoned before it is all worn out.

PUBLIC utility reports, annotated. Rochester, Lawyers co-operative publishing co. 1919C. p. 436, 515.

Allen v. Boyertown electric co; (Pa.) 436. An electrical company was allowed 4 per cent annually as a reserve for depreciation.

Re Edina light co. (Mo.) 515. An electrical company was held entitled to an annual allowance of 5 per cent for depreciation.

PUBLIC utility reports, annotated. Rochester, Lawyers co-operative publishing co. 1919D. p. 286, 1078.

Re Appalachian power co. (W. Va.). 286. In a valuation for rate making the accrued depreciation on a hydro-electric plant was estimated at the rate of 1½ per cent per year or a total of 7½ per cent for five years.

Re Hinton water. light & supply co. (W. Va.) 467. The West Virginia Commission made an allowance of 3 per cent for the depreciation of an electric plant.

Manchester v. Colonial power & light co. (Vt.) 21. An allowance of 3 per cent for the annual depreciation of the property of an electric distributing company is a reasonable allowance.

PUBLIC utility reports, annotated. Rochester, Lawyers co-operative publishing co. 1919E. p. 339, 494, 1087.

Re Brigham mun, corp. (Utah). 339. In fixing rates for a municipal electric utility which had allowed its plant to depreciate to the extent of 80 per cent, the city was allowed to set aside 5 per cent annually of the cost of the plant for accruing depreciation, and 5 per cent in addition to provide for past depreciation.

DEPRECIATION, DEPLETION AND OBSOLESCENCE—ELECTRIC LIGHT AND POWER COMPANIES—*(Continued)*

Re Monmouth public service co. (Ill.) 494. In a rate proceedings, the Illinois Commission fixed the sum of $13,500 as a reasonable allowance for annual accruing depreciation of anh electric plant, the value of which was fixed at $300,000.

Re Quincy R. co. (Ill.) 391. The Illinois Commission fixed $25,000 as a reasonable allowance for accruing depreciation of an electric plant valued at $1,030,000.

PUBLIC utility reports, annotated. Rochester, Lawyers co-operative publishing co. 1919F. p. 169, 170, 1053.

In Re Municipal utilities (Ind.) no. 4525, April 30, 1919, a municipal electric utility was ordered to set aside annually for depreciation 3.5 per cent of the value of its depreciable property, and rules were provided for investment and accounting for the depreciation fund or reserve.

In Re Cullum electric co. no. 8944, June 17, 1919, the Illinois commission made an allowance of $500 as annual depreciation of an electric plant the value of which was fixed at $13,600.

In Re Empire state r. corp. (N. Y.). Case No. 6787, July 1, 1919, it was held that a depreciation charge of 2 per cent of the actual field costs of way and structures of an interurban railway and 3 per cent on equipment is not excessive.

Re Big Springs electric co. (Utah) 946. An electric company was ordered to set aside at least 3 per cent of its earnings as a depreciation fund.

PUBLIC utility reports, annotated. Rochester, Lawyers co-operative publishing company, 1920C, p. 942, 509-10.

Re Desert power and water co (Ariz.) Arizona commission fied the depreciation of an electric plant at 4 per cent rather than at 5 per cent which had been claimed by the utility.

Re Municipal electric light system (Wis.) U-1591, Oct. 31, 1919 an allowance of 4 per cent was made for annual depreciation of a municipal electric light system where there had been a large expense on account of dams and because of frequent washouts and because consideration was given to a large increase in the capacity of the system.

In re Wisconsin-Minnesota light and power co. U-1512, July 17, 1919, the Wisconsin commission placed the depreciation of an electric plant upon a 3 per cent sinking fund basis.

PUBLIC utility reports, annotated. Rochester, Lawyers co-operative publishing company, 1920D, p. 806, 775.

Re Idaho power co. (Idaho). Idaho commission made an allowance of 4 per cent for the depreciation reserve of an electric plant.

Re Arkansas light & P. co. (Ark.). Arkansas commission made an allowance of 5 per cent for the depreciation of electric property.

PUBLIC utility reports, annotated. Rochester, Lawyers co-operative publishing company, 1920E, p. 311.

Re Rogers light and power company Arkansas commission made an allowance of 5 per cent for the depreciation of the electrical property of a utility.

Wells	8%
Machinery, casing, pressure stations, water stations, horses and vehicles, tools and supplies, and miscellaneous	10%
Labor, hauling, rights of way and damage an annual depreciation of all the amount invested for the year.	

PUBLIC utility reports, annotated. Rochester, Lawyers co-operative publishing company, 1920A. p. 764.

Fargo v. Union light, heat & p. co. (N. D.) In the main 3½ per cent is a sufficient and adequate allowance for depreciation in a valuation rate making for all of the general property of an electric utility, 2½ per cent for that of a gas utility, and 4 per cent for that of a steam heat utility.

PUBLIC utility reports, annotated. Rochester, Lawyers co-operative publishing company, 1920B, p. 891.

Re Cleveland electric illuminating co. (Ohio). Allowance for the depreciation reserve of an electrical plant was fixed at 3 percent.

PUBLIC utility reports, annotated. Rochester, Lawyers co-operative publishing company, 1920F. p. 124.

Re Centralia gas & electric company. An allowance of 4½ per cent for the depreciation of an electric plant is proper.

REPORT by Sir William Preece on probable life of plant at Bristol. *Electrician*, Aug. 17, 1906, p. 704. Editorial. Depreciation. *Electrician*, Aug. 17, 1906, p. 702.

RIPLEY, C. M. Life of building power plants. *American society of heating and ventilating engineers, Transactions*, 1914. p. 98.

RUNYON, F. O. Report on hydro-electric plant for special committee common council, Newark, New Jersey, April 23, 1902. 27p.

HYDRO-ELECTRIC PLANT

Item	Rate of Depreciation Underground transmission lines
Hydraulic constr. excl. of steel pipe line	1%
Steel pipe line	3
Hydro-Power House	2
Turbine units	3
Switchboard	5
Subway	1
Underground cable	4
Dock improvements	10
Power house and stack	3
Boilers & Stm. Fittg.	10
Engines & Generators	5
Aux. Switchbd. & El. Ap.	5

DEPRECIATION, DEPLETION AND OBSOLESCENCE—ELECTRIC LIGHT AND POWER COMPANIES—*(Continued)*

Property (Substa.)	..
Elec. App. (Substa.)	5
U. G. Cable (Distr.)	4
Subway (Distr.)	1
Overhead Constr.	10

The rate of depreciation against the entire plant from the foregoing is 3.96%.

	Aerial transmission lines
Hydraulic constr. excl. of steel pipe line	1%
Steel pipe line	3
Hydro-Power House	3
Turbine units	2
Switchboard	3
Transmission Line	5
Dock Improvements	10
Power House & Stack	10
Boilers & Stm. Fittg.	3
Engines & Generators	10
Aux. Switchbd. & El. Ap.	5
Property (Substa.)	5
Elec. App. (Substa.)	5
U. G. Cable (Distra.)	4
Subway (Distr.)	1
Overhead Constr.	10

The rate of depreciation against the entire plant from the foregoing is 5.98%.

SALIERS, EARL A. Analysis of a hydroelectric plant. (In his *Principles of depreciation.* 1916. p. 34-8).

TABLE II.

LIFETIME OF TRANSMISSION SYSTEM

1. Transmission Line

	Life in years
Right of way	..
Towers	15
Special structures	10
Insulators	10
Copper	25
Installation	..

2. Sub-Stations

Land	..
Buildings	25
Transformers	20
Switches, etc.	10
Installation	..

TABLE III.

LIFETIME OF POWER HOUSE EQUIPMENT

Stop logs, gates and other wood exposed to air and water	5
Flooring, roofings, hardware, and miscellaneous fixtures	15
Tile wainscoating, sewage, plumbing system, metal window frames, etc.	15
Electric light and telephone	10
Switchboard equipment	10
Cables and heavy wiring	10
Cranes	15
Waterwheels	25
Water-wheel governors	10
Generators and transformers	25

PROPOSED STEAM-ELECTRIC PLANT FOR LIGHTING PURPOSES

Item	Rate of Depreciation
Property	..
Power Station & Stack	3%
Sub-stations	3
Dock improvements	10
Coal conveyor	5
Boilers, steam fittg. &c.	10
Turbo-generators	5
Switchbd. & Elec. App.	5
Underground cable	4
Subway	1
Overhead construction	10

The rate of depreciation from the foregoing is approximately 5.46%.

SLAVIN, MATTHEW. Municipal electricity in Pasadena. *Public service,* April 1910, p. 105-8.
Contains extract from Prof. Cory's Report on depreciation as follows:

	Life Years	
Poles, arc lamps and transformers	10	8.5
Steam Plant	13	6.2
Electrical generating machinery	15	5.2
Copper in distributing system	30	2.0
Power Station	15	3.5

SMITH, S. FRED. Depreciation. *Electrical world,* Aug. 26, 1909, p. 489.

STATE public utilities commission of Illinois in an order in the case of the Belleville electric company considers 4.4 per cent per annum to be an equitable and just depreciation allowance. *Electrical world,* Dec. 11, 1915, p. 1339.

DEPRECIATION, DEPLETION AND OBSOLESCENCE—ELECTRIC LIGHT AND POWER COMPANIES—*(Continued)*

STUCKMANN, H. Depreciation and obsolescence in Portland cement plants. *Journal of the American society of mechanical engineers*, Feb. 1913. p. 262-75.
Electric light system % of reproductive value—7

STUDY in central-station finances and operation from Marquette, Mich. *Electrical world*, Feb. 11, 1909, p. 403.

VALUE of Portland company properties. *Electrical world*, Sept. 2, 1916, p. 492.
In the matter of the valuation of the properties in the State of Washington of the Pacific Power & Light company of Portland, Oregon:—"Reduced to a percentage basis, the accountant (P. S. Commission) testified *** return of 7.38 per cent. exclusive of depreciation. With an allowance of 1.55 per cent for depreciation, the minimum allowance suggested at prior hearings, the profit is cut to 5.83 per cent. The company contended that 2.5% depreciation should be allowed, as is done at the Eugene, Ore., municipal plant. With this allowance the returns shrink to 4.88 per cent.

VARIOUS depreciation charges. *New York Times*, June 14, 1914.

Electric light system	7%

WALSH, T. J. Depreciation on electric light and power plants. *Electric railway journal*, July 13, 1912, p. 60.

Power house and substation building	3%
Apparatus	6
Underground cable	4
Conduit "	2
Overhead distribution	6
Steel tower and bare copper transmission lines	3
High-tension transmission lines	3
Additional for maintenance	1

WHITTEN, ROBERT HARVEY. Bibliography. (In his *Valuation of public service corporations*. 1914. p. 739-40).

WHITTEN, ROBERT HARVEY. Valuation of public service corporations; legal and economic phases of valuation for rate making and public purchases. New York, Bankers law publishing co. 1914. v.1, p. 423, 427, 436-7; v.2. p. 1188-9, 1192, 1196-7, 1202-3.
Three per cent depreciation allowance required by Massachusetts statute for municipal lighting plants.
Five per cent allowance in Columbus, Ohio, Electricity rate case, 1906.
Ten per cent allowance in Arkansas electricity rate case,. 1911.
Arizona commission—Hoffman v. Tucson gas, electric light and power co.—3½% should be allowed annually upon the depreciation property.
California commission—Solari v. Tuolumne county electric power and light company—3%.
Commonwealth Edison Co., Chicago, Annual allowance for depreciation on a 3% sinking-fund basis. The annual allowance amounted to 3.63% of the value new.
Nevada Commission—Life of mining camp—City of Ely v. Ely light and power company—5%.
Wisconsin Commission—Superior Commercial Club v. Superior water, light and power company.

Cost of reproduction new Electric department	4.5%
Gas	2
Water	0.8

WILKINSON, GEORGE. Depreciation of plant. *Accountant*, Aug. 31, 1901, p. 953.
Electric light works.
10% per annuam on the cost of the plant.

1st year	10% of the original principal
2nd "	9
3rd "	8.1
7th "	5.314
10th "	3.874.
14th "	2.542

WISCONSIN railroad commission holds that an allowance of 4.5 per cent of the investment in an electric plant is necessary to provide for accrued and accruing depreciation. *Electrical world*, March 25, 1916, p. 734.

WYER, S. S. Rate regulation of electric power. *Cassier's magazine*, Jan. 1909, p. 410.

YEAMAN, C. H. Depreciation and reserves for antiquation and obsolescence from an engineering standpoint. *Electrician*, July 5, 1907, p. 475. *Electrical engineering* (London), July 12, 1907, p. 46. *Electrical review* (London), July 12, 1907, p. 44.

Table of Estimated Life of Electrical Appliances for Loan Purposes

	Mr. Robt. Hammond April, 1907	L.G.B. Local board)	L.C.C.	Mr. J.F.C. Snell, M.E.A. 1905
Land	60		60	100
Buildings	60	30	50	60
Boilers	20	15	20	20
Engines	20-25	15-25	20	25
Elec. Generators	25	20	20	25
Accumulators	15	5-7	20	10
Static transformers	15	15	20	20
Rotary converters, switches and instruments	20	15	20	20-25
Mains	25-30	12-15	Mains 30 Services 12	Ducts 60 Solid mains 25 Cables 15
Meters	10	5	10	15
Arc lamps	10	7-10	Not granted	15

Electrical machinery

See Depreciation, depletion and obsolescence—Machinery, Electrical.

DEPRECIATION, DEPLETION AND OBSOLESCENCE—*(Continued)*

Electro-cardiograph

AUSTRALIA. FEDERAL INCOME TAX DEPARTMENT. Depreciation allowance. *Accountant,* Oct. 13, 1917, p. 277-9. *Accounting and commerce,* June 30, 1917, p. 55-7. *Federal accountant,* July 1917, p. 93-8. *Public accountant,* Jan. 30, 1917, p. 145-52.

Electro-cardiograph 5%

Based on written down value and repairs allowed in addition.

Electrotypes, woodcuts, etc.

DENHAM, ROBERT S. Depreciation. (In his *Manual of cost engineering and estimating for paper box manufacturers.* 1917. p. 249).

Electros 33⅓%

Cuts 33⅓

MONTGOMERY, ROBERT H. Electrotypes, woodcuts, etc. (In his *Income tax procedure,* 1919. p. 563. ——— Same, 1920. p. 716).

Conservative publishers charge almost the entire cost of plates as a direct cost of a first edition, and are careful to revalue the balance of the accounting frequently.

MONTGOMERY, ROBERT H. Printing. (In his *Income tax procedure,* 1919. p. 575. ——— Same, 1920. p. 732).

Type, printers' tools, electrotypes, plates, etc. 10-12%

Elevators

AUSTRALIA. INCOME TAX DEPARTMENT. Depreciation allowance. *Accountant,* Oct. 13, 1917, p. 277-9. *Accounting and commerce,* June 30, 1917, p. 55-7. *Federal accountant,* July 1917, p. 93-8. *Public accountant,* Jan. 30, 1917, p. 145-52.

Lifts and elevators

Electric 7½%

Hydraulic 10

Based on written down value and repairs allowed in addition.

BOLTON, REGINALD PELHAM. Depreciation of mechanical equipments and power plants. (In his *Building for profit.* 1911. p. 82, 89).

	Physical years	%	Economic years
Most durable elements—steel construction, foundations, elevator guides, and overhead framing	40	100.0	30
Dumb-waiters, switchboards, elevator gates, slow-speed elevator engines, shafting and bearings, slow-geared apparatus, elevators intermittently used	22	55.0	18
Slow-speed reciprocating apparatus, such as pumps, elevator reversing gear, platform lifts	17	42.5	15
Elevators in regular use, laundry kitchen, refrigerating electric devices, and other apparatus frequently reversed	16	40.0	14

BOLTON, REGINALD PELHAM. Depreciation of the value of buildings. (In his *Building for profit.* 1911. p. 62).

	Relative to 66 ys. Percent	Relative to 75 ys. Percent
Elevator	30	26

DENHAM, ROBERT S. Depreciation. (In his *Manual of cost engineering and estimating for paper box manufactures.* 1917. p. 249).

original cost

Elevators 8%

NICHOLSON, J. LEE and JOHN F. D. ROHRBACH. Depreciation. (In their *Cost accounting.* 1919. p. 147).

Elevators 5-7½%

Based on (1) the cost of equipment
(2) the life of the equipment
(3) on a ten-hour day.

PHILADELPHIA. CONTROLLER. Rates of depreciation. (In his *Manual of accounting, reporting and business procedure of the city and county of Philadelphia.* 1917. p. 206).

Elevators and accessory apparatus 5%

Embossing

NICHOLSON, J. LEE and JOHN F. D. ROHRBACH. Depreciation. (In their *Cost accounting.* 1919. p. 150).

Woodworking machinery—
Embossing press 5%

Based on (1) the cost of equipment
(2) the life of the equipment
(3) on a ten-hour day.

Emery wheels

BELT, ROBERT E. Depreciation. (In his *Foundry cost accounting practice and procedure.* 1919. p. 242, 243).

Emery wheel stands, drop hammers, lathes, drill presses, air chippers, milling machines etc. with motor, shafting and belting 10%

BELT, ROBERT E. Depreciation. (In his *Uniform cost accounting methods; adopted by the American malleable castings association,* Nov. 14, 1917. p. 20-1.

Emery wheel stand, with motor, shafting and belting 10%

NICHOLSON, J. LEE and JOHN F. D. ROHRBACH. Depreciation. (In their *Cost accounting.* 1919. p. 149).

Emery wheels 6⅔%

Enders

DENHAM, ROBERT S. Depreciation. (In his *Manual of cost engineering and estimating for paper box manufacturers.* 1917. p. 249).

Enders 12%

DEPRECIATION, DEPLETION AND OBSOLESCENCE—*(Continued)*

Engines

See also Depreciation, depletion and obsolescence—Turbines.

ALLISON, J. Farmers' income tax. *Accountant,* April 14, May 3, 17, 24, 1919, p. 325-6, 369-70, 421-3, 440-1.

Engines	
Gas	7½%
Steam	5
Shafting	5

AMERICAN INSTITUTE OF ACCOUNTANTS. Report of the committee on standard schedules for uniform reports upon municipal industries and public service corporations; annual meeting at Atlantic city, N. J. October 20-22, 1908. 15p. *Journal of accountancy,* May 1909, p. 47-54.

The knowledge at the command of the Bureau of the census leads to the conclusion that this average life is approximately as follows:

Engines, pumping machinery and wood pipe	5 years

AMERICAN WATERWORKS ASSOCIATION. Final report of committee on depreciation. *Journal of the American waterworks association,* Sept. 1917, p. 1-38.

	Years
Steam engines	20-40

ANALYSIS of the premises adopted and methods used in determining the cost to reproduce new together with the depreciation thereon of the physical property of the Metropolitan system and the Kansas City and Westport Belt railway of Kansas City, Mo. *Engineering and contracting,* May 28, 1913, p. 617-20.

Engines	
Carliss slow-speed engines	3%
Automatic high speed engines	5-8
Steam turbines with generators	4

BARKER, HARRY. Typical life expectation tables for public utility property. (In his *Public utility rates.* 1917. p. 368-9).

Engines	Years	Wis. R.R. Comm.
Gas	10-15	
Steam, high-speed	15-20	
" slow-speed	25-30	

BAY state rate case. *Electric railway journal,* Dec. 4, 1915, p. 1121-3. *Public utility reports, annotated,* 1916F, p. 336-9.

Engines	30-40 years

BELT, ROBERT E. Depreciation. (In his *Foundry cost accounting practice and procedure.* 1919. p. 243).

Engines, steam and gas	5%

BENTLEY, HARRY C. Depreciation. (In his *Science of accounts.* 1913. p. 146).

Engines and boilers 2½-5% on original cost, relining being charged to repairs.

BOLTON, REGINALD PELHAM. Depreciation of mechanical equipments and power plants. (In his *Building for profit.* 1911. p. 82, 89).

	Physical years	%	Economic years
Dumb-waiters, switchboards, elevator gates, slow-speed elevator engines, shafting and bearings. slow-geared apparatus, elevators intermittently used	22	55.0	18
Moderate-speed reciprocating engines, medium-speed rotary apparatus, dynamos and motors	15	37.5	12
Fan engines, high-speed rotary apparatus on large variations of loads, dynamos, motors, high-pressure engines, condensers	12	30.0	9
High-speed, high-pressure, reciprocating engines and machines on extreme variable loads	10	25.0	7

BREWER, ALLAN F. Rates of annual depreciation. *Industrial management,* April 1918, p. 268.

	Years	%
Engines, condensing, cross compound	30	3.33
Engines, condensing tandem compound	30	3.33
Engines, non-condensing	33.3	3
Engines, reciprocating	33.3	3
•Engines, gas	20	5

BRYAN, WILLIAM. Appraisal and depreciation of water-works and similar properties. *Journal of the engineering societies,* Dec. 1907, p. 336-81. Depreciation allowance for various public-service industries. *Engineering news,* Jan. 23, 1908, p. 96.

	Years	% straight line	
Engines			
Steam		4-6	
"	25		
"	15-25		
"		8	
"	20	5	
Pumping	20-25-30	5	
"		3-10	
"	15		
"	20-30	4.7	
"	25		
"	10		Boiler,
"	3-36 Av. 21.3		feeds,
"	25-30		etc.
"	30		Average of
"		2.5	50
"	30		
Engines and generators			
belted	10-20		
direct connected	12.5-25		

DEPRECIATION, DEPLETION AND OBSOLESCENCE—ENGINES—*(Continued)*

BRYAN, WILLIAM. Depreciation of electric light plants. *Municipality,* March 1908, p. 74.

Material	Life in years	Authority
Engines and generators		
belted	10-20	Dawson's "Engineering and Electric traction pocket
direct connected	12.5-25	book in Iowa Engineer, July 1906.

CARTER, R. N. Rates of depreciation. (In his *Advanced accounts.* p. 618).

Engines
- movable 10
- fixed 7½

Based on diminishing balances, normal conditions and hours of working.

CHASE, HARVEY STUART. Depreication in waterworks accounts with reference to uniform reports. *Journal of the New England waterworks association,* June 1910, p. 305-31. Abstract. *Engineering and contracting,* June 29, 1910, p. 598. Editorial. Depreciation and sinking fund accounts. *Municipal engineering,* July 1910, p. 26.

Engines, pumping machinery and wood pipes 25 years

CLADER, WILL-A. Water utilities accounting. *Journal of accountancy,* Aug. 1919, p. 91-2.

The following rate is used frequently when wear and tear are made good by operating maintenance.

Steam engines 4%

CLAPHAM, F. T. Depreciation of plant. *Mechanical world,* Oct. 19, 1917, p. 219-20.

Engines 3% depreciation + 3% wear and tear = 6%

Gas engines and electric motors should be written down 10% annually. The highest pitch in efficiency and design has not yet been reached and their life should not be estimated beyond 15 years.

CRAVENS, GEORGE W. Depreciation and maintenance of electrical equipment. *Electrical review,* April 23, 1910, p. 853-6. Foster, Horatio A. *Engineering valuation of public utilities and factories,* 1913. p. 201-2. Montgomery, Robert H. *Auditing, theory and practice,* 1916, p. 424. Montgomery, Robert H. *Income tax procedure,* 1919, p. 570. ——— Same, 1920. p. 722-4.

Steam engines	Auxiliaries	
3-10%	5-10%	Chicago traction commission
6.6	6.6	Chicago union traction co.
5	5	Milwaukee electric railway and light co.
5-6.6	6.6-8.5	Wisconsin railroad commission
5	5	Average English
5	5	Average Scotch practice
4-6	8-10	Philip Dawson
5	5	Stone & Webster
2.5-5	4-6.6	Industrial power plants
4-6.6	3-5	Prof. G. F. Gebhardt
5	7.5	Miscellaneous sources

	Light or intermittent service	Heavy or continuous service
Engines, steam	4-5%	5-6.6%
Auxiliaries, steam	3-5%	4-6.6%

CROWELL, H. H. Electric lighting rates and depreciation. *Municipal journal and engineering,* Dec. 18, 1907, p. 698.

	Purchased 10 years or more ago	Modern
Engines	15 years	25 years

DAWSON, PHILLIP. Depreciation. (In his *Engineering and electric traction pocket-book.* Ed.2. p. 1161).

Slow speed steam engines 20-40 years

	% capital cost
Dynamos and engines belted plants	5-10
Large slow-speed steam engines	4-6
Large slow speed direct driven plants	4-8
Boilers and engines	6-10

DENHAM, F. W. Depreciation of assets and goodwill of limited companies. *Accountant,* May 28, 1898, p. 568.

Engines and gear 5%

DENHAM, ROBERT S. Depreciation. (In his *Manual of cost engineering and estimating for paper box manufacturers.* 1917. p. 249).

DEPRECIATION. *American institute of accountants,* Special bulletin, No. 1, Jan. 1920, p. 6-7.

	Original cost
Engines	8%

DEPRECIATION of steam plant. *Electric railway review,* March 31, 1908, p. 360.

Slow speed engine running about 10 hours a day can be setimated on having a life of about 25 years or a depreciation of 4%. High speed engines are much shorter lived and will not average over 15 years or a depreciation of about 7%

DICKSEE, LAWRENCE ROBERT. Depreciation, machinery. (In his *Depreciation, reserves and reserve funds.* 1912. p. 29-37).

Engines 12½%

ELBOURNE, EDWARD T. Depreciation rates. (In his *Factory administration and accounts.* 1918. p. 376).

	Prov. dep. % Remainder values	Years 10%	5%
Engines			
blower and pumping	6	37	48
gas and oil	7½	29	38
portable	7½	29	38
steam	7½	29	38

ENNIS, WILLIAM DUANE. Depreciation. (In his *Works management.* 1911. p. 86).

Steam engines 25 years life to 6% residual value.

DEPRECIATION, DEPLETION AND OBSOLESCENCE—ENGINES—*(Continued)*

FIGURES from the Iola (Kans.) central stations. *Electrical world*, Sept. 23, 1909, p. 723.
Engines 7%

FLOY, HENRY. Depreciation. Floy, Henry, *Depreciation as related to electrical properties. American institute of electrical engineers, Proceedings*, 1911, p. 1267. Floy, Henry, *Valuation of public utility properties*, 1912, p. 168-217. Foster, Horatio R. *Engineering valuation of public utilities and factories*, 1913, p. 194-8. *Engineering & Contracting*, Oct. 4, 1911, p. 359-65. *Engineering magazine*, Aug. 1911, p. 837-40.

	Dep. % per year		
Engines (steam)	3-5	Traction Val. Commission	Chicago Con. Trac. Co.
	5-7½	B. J. Arnold	Coney Island and Brooklyn adopted by P.S.C., N. Y.
	5	Henry Floy	3rd Ave. case, adopted by P.S.C., N. Y.
gas		Wis. P.S.C.	
(steam slow speed)	5	Wis. P.S.C.	
(steam, high speed)	6 2/3	Wis. P.S.C.	
	5	Arbitrators	Street Lighting Controversy, Atlanta, Ga. 1899.
	6 2/3	St. Louis, P.S.C.	Union Elec. light and power co.

FOSTER, HORATIO A. Rates of depreciation. (In his *Engineering valuation of public utilities and factories*. 1913. p. 200, 204).

Engines, boilers, heaters, conveyors, pumps and auxiliaries	4.5%
	Years' life
Gas engines	10-15
Corliss slow-speed engines	25-30
High-speed engines	15-20
Waterworks	
pumping engines, duplex	20-25
triplex	20-30
flywheel	30-40

GARRY, H. STANLEY. Depreciation of plant and machinery. *Accountant*, June 23, Sept. 15, 1906, p. 785-9, 285-8.
Engines 12½%

GILLETTE, HALBERT POWERS and RICHARD T. DANA. Depreciation. (In their *Handbook of mechanical and electrical cost data*. 1918. p. 107, 116-8, 625-6, 669).

Engines	22.2 years	Marwick, Mitchell & co., appraisal of a large street railway system, Foster, p. 199.
gas	15	Wisconsin railroad commission
steam	10-33.3	Chicago traction commission
	13.3-20	B. J. Arnold—Appraisal of the Coney Island and Brooklyn railroad, Feb. 1, 1909.
	15-20	W. D. Pence, Milwaukee 3c case.
		Union traction co., Case Chicago and union traction co., Stone & Webster

TABLE III. USEFUL LIFE OF RECIPROCATING ENGINES AND GENERATORS

	Type of equipment				Time of service		
	Reciprocating engines		Generators				
Company.	No.	Size in h.p.	No.	Size in kw.	Started	Closed	Useful life years
1.	1	Corliss			1906	1911	4½
2.	1	150	2	45	1891	1907	16
	2	200	4	65	1891	1907	16
	1	150	2	50	1893	1909	16
	3	225	6	75	1893	1909	16
	1	1250	2	400	1894	1915	21
	4	600	8	200	1894	1915	21
	5	1200	10	400	1895	1915	20
	1	3500	1	2500	1901	1915	14
	1	Corliss	2	1000	1902	1915	13
	1	5000	1	3500	1902	1915	13
	1	2500	1	1800	1903	1915	12
	4	200	8	80	1888	1894	6
3	High speed		Edison d. c.		1887	1893	6
	Compound		a. c. single phase		1893	1905	12
4			a. c.		1890	1907	16
	5 Allis Chalmers				1904	1915	11
5	Cross comp.				1891	1905	14

Average life, 34 reciprocating engines, 14 years
Average life, 50 generators, 16 years.
Following is the key to names of companies—also the reasons for retiring the various units:

No.	Name	Remarks
1	Nevada California Power Co.	Equipment replaced by turbine plant, larger unit.
2	Commonwealth Edison co., 27th street, North Clark street, Harrison st., Adams st. stations	Entire plants abandoned.
3	Consumers power co. Jackson station	Replaced by a. c. single phase Curtis turbine

DEPRECIATION, DEPLETION AND OBSOLESCENCE—ENGINES—*(Continued)*

4 Union electric light and power co., 10th, 19th and 20th st. stations — Entire plants abandoned, obsolete

5 Indianapolis light & heat co., Kentucky avenue station. — Obsolete, but used for steam heating.

GREAT BRITAIN. BOARD OF INLAND REVENUE. Depreciation rates: *abstract.* (In its *Income tax; statement respecting allowances for wear and tear and obsolescence of plant and machinery.* 1918. Cd. 9022, p. 4; Cd. 9134, p. 6). *American economic review, Supplement,* Dec. 1920, p. 51. *Journal of accountancy,* Sept. 1920, p. 194.

Engines, boilers and main shafting — 5%
Written down value

GREENDLINGER, LEO and JOHN R. LOOMIS. Depreciation, machinery. (In their *Accounting problems,* 1910. v1. p. 204-5).

Engines — 5-7%

GREENLAND, S. W. Depreciation. *Mississippi electric association, Report of 2nd annual convention,* June 1910, p. 32-6.

Life
Engines — 20 years

GRUNSKY, CARL EWALD. Probable useful life of various articles. (In his *Valuation, depreciation and the rate-base.* 1917. p. 278-9).

Machinery

Engines	15 years. St. Louis public service commission. Case of Union electric light and power co.
	20 years. Arbitrators. Board of arbitration in street lighting controversy at Atlanta, Georgia, 1899.
engines and machinery	25 years Robert Hammond. Journal of Institute of electrical engineers, England, April 25, 1907.
	25 years. 6% residual value. Sir William Preece. Report of Bristol corporation, England, 1906.
	10-33⅓ years. Chicago traction commission. Quoted by G. W. Cravens, Electrical review, April 23, 1910.
	13-20 years. Bion J. Arnold. Coney Island and Brooklyn figures adopted by Public service commission of New York. Four Chicago appraisals quoted by H. A. Foster.
	20-33⅓ years. Bion J. Arnold. Four Chicago appraisals quoted by H. A. Foster.
	15-20 years. Wisconsin railroad commission. Milwaukee 3c fare case.
	20-33 years. Traction valuation commission. Case of the Chicago consolidated traction co.
machinery	27 years. 6% residual value. T. C. Parson. Discussion of Mr. Hammond's paper, Journal Institute electric engineers, England, April 25, 1907.
steam	15 years. Chicago union traction co. Quoted in Report Wisconsin railroad commission, vol. 10, p. 220.
steam	20 years. Stone & Webster. Figures for Chicago union traction co. case. Report Wisconsin railroad commission, vol. 10, p. 220.
steam	20 years. Milwaukee electric railway and lighting co., in the Milwaukee 3c fare case, Aug. 1912.
steam	20 years. 5% residual value. Pacific gas and electric company. Henry Floy. Trans. American institute of electrical engineers, June, 1911. Third avenue case figures adopted by Public service commission of New York.
steam	20 years. San Joaquin light and power corporation. Rate hearing before California railroad commission, 1915.
steam	15-25 years. Leonard Metcalf. Transactions American society of civil engineers, 1909.
steam, slow speed	20 years. Wisconsin railroad commission. Quoted by Henry Floy and in published reports.
Corliss slow speed	25-30 years. H. A. Foster. "Engineering valuation of public utilities and factories," Van Nostrand, 1912.
steam, high speed	15 years. Wisconsin railroad commission. Quoted by Henry Floy and in published reports.
gas	10-15 years. H. A. Foster. "Engineering valuation of public utilities and factories, Van Nostrand, 1912.
gas	15 years. Wisconsin railroad commission. Quoted by Henry Floy and in published reports.
steam, high speed	15-20 years. H. A. Foster. "Engineering valuation of public utilities and factories", 1912.

DEPRECIATION, DEPLETION AND OBSOLESCENCE—ENGINES—*(Continued)*

HAMMOND, ROBERT. Depreciation. *Journal of the Institute of electrical engineers,* 1907, p. 270. *Institute of electrical engineers, Proceedings,* April 25, 1907, p. 270-301. Abstracts. *Accountant,* May 18, 1907, p. 675. *Electric railway review,* June 1, 1907, p. 716. *Electrician,* April 26, 1907. p. 51. *Electrical review* (Chicago), May 25, 1907, p. 828. *Electrical review* (London), May 3, 1907, p. 744. *Engineering magazine,* July 1907, p. 636-8. *Engineering record,* June 15, 1907, p. 703. *Municipal journal* (London), May 10, 17, 1907, p. 411, 535. *Progressive age,* July 1, 1907, p. 305. *Street railway bulletin,* June, 1907, p. 382. *Tramway and railway world,* June 6, 1907, p. 497.
Engines 25 years

HAZLEHURST, J. N. Final report of the committee on depreciation. *Journal of the American water works association,* March 1919, p. 85-135.
Steam engines 20-40 years

HENDERSON, W. H. Auditing. *Canadian chartered accountant,* Oct. 1920, p. 107-9.
Engines vary from 5 to 15 per cent.

INSTALLATIONS, systems and appliances. *Electrical world,* Dec. 7, 1912, p. 1220.

	Hammond	Preece
Engines	25 years	25 years

JENKINSON, MARK WEBSTER. Depreciation. *Accountant,* May 17, 1902, p. 528-34.
Engines 5-7½%

JOHNSON, GEORGE. Depreciation. (In his *Electric lighting accounts.* 1903. p. 23-4).
Engines and boilers 7½-10%

KERR, W. H. and G. A. NAHSTOLL. Reserve for depreciation. (In their *Cooperative organization business methods.* 1915. p. 13-4).
Engines 7-12%

KIMBALL, DEXTER S. Estimated life, and factors of depreciation. (In his *Cost finding.* 1918. p. 190).

KIMBALL, DEXTER S. *Principles of industrial organization.* 1913. p. 163.

	Steam engines	Portable engines and boilers	Gas engines
Probable life of asset in years	15-30	10	10-15
Ratio of scrap to original value	0.10	0.05	0.05
Percentage on original cost	6-3	9.5	9.5-6.3
Percentage on diminishing value	14-7.5	26	26-18

LIFE data on power plant equipment used in valuation of Massachusetts property. *Electrical world,* Dec. 4, 1915, p. 1261.
Engines 30-40 years

LIFE of plant. *Electrician,* Nov. 8, 182-4.
Engines 25 years R. Hammond
25 Sir Wm. Preece

LIFE of road construction equipment. *Engineering and contracting,* Jan. 3, 1917, p. 3.
Engines, gas or steam 20% annual depreciation.

MCINTOSH, ROBERT J. Rates of depreciation. (In his *Reference book of accounts.* Ed. 2, p. 60).
Engines 4-6%
Based on life

MANN, JOHN and H. C. JUDD. Depreciation. (In their *Colliery accounts.* 1909. p. 69-75, 92).
Engines and machinery 7½-10%
Calculated on the balance as diminished from year to year.

MATHESON, EWING. Plant and machinery. (In his *Depreciation of factories, mines and industrial undertakings and their valuation.* 1893. p. 35-49).
Engines, boilers 7½%
Portable engines 10-15
Steam engines, steam hammers, etc. (in engineering factories) 5-10

METCALF, LEONARD. Depreciation in waterworks operation and accounting. *Journal of the New England waterworks association,* Dec. 1910, p. 442. Abstracts. *Engineering news,* Nov. 3, 1910, p. 482. Methods of computing depreciation of and reasonable assumptions as to period of useful life of waterworks. *Engineering and contracting,* Nov. 16, 1910, p. 434.
Steam engines 15-25 years 6⅔-4% straight line

METCALF, LEONARD. Water-works valuation and fair rates, in the light of the Maine supreme court decisions in the Waterville and Brunswick cases. *American society of civil engineers, Papers and discussions,* 1908, p. 1101-73. *American society of civil engineers, Transactions,* Sept. 1909, p. 1. Foster, Horatio A., *Engineering valuation of public utilities and factories,* 1913, p. 207. Gillette, Halbert P. *Handbook of cost data for contractors and engineers,* p. 797.

	Useful life	Annual contribution to depreciation account or sinking fund in per cent of cost: At 5% annual rate sinking fund	General approximate results
Steam engines	15-25 years	4.6342%-2.0952%	5-3%

NEALE, R. E. Depreciation in engineering works. *Mechanical world,* Feb. 7, 1913, p. 67-8.

Engines		
Low speed steam	3.5%	20-33 years
High speed steam	6-7.5	13-17
Gas	6.5	15

NICHOLSON, J. LEE and JOHN F. D. ROHRBACH. Depreciation. (In their *Cost accounting.* 1919. p. 147, 148).
Engines 5%
gas and oil 7½
Based on (1) the cost of equipment
(2) the life of the equipment
(3) on a ten-hour day

DEPRECIATION, DEPLETION AND OBSOLESCENCE—ENGINES—*(Continued)*

PENDER, HAROLD. Depreciation. (In his *Handbook for electrical engineers.* c1914. p. 339, 340).
Engines, steam reciprocating

15 years	Chicago union traction co.
15-20	Engineer of valuation staff, of Wisconsin railroad commission
	J. Abbott
20	S. W. Greenland
	Stone & Webster for the Chicago union traction co.
25	Wm. Preece
27	R. Hammond
	T. C. Parsons
10-5%	P. Dawson
6.66	Chicago union traction co.
6.66-5	Engineer of Valuation staff of Wisconsin railroad commission
5	Milwaukee electric railway and light co.
	Cardiff tramways
	Glasgow tramways
	Stone & Webster for Chicago union traction co.
4	Third ave. railroad New York city).
pumping	21.3 years J. W. Alvord

PHILADELPHIA CONTROLLER. Rates of depreciation. (In his *Manual of accounting, reporting and business procedure of the city and county of Philadelphia.* 1917. p. 204).

Steam and other elastic fluid engines	
Steam engines	5%
Internal combustion engines	10
Gasoline engines	10

PIEZ, CHARLES. Perpetual inventory and appraisal values; table of standard depreciation rates. *Engineering and contracting,* Jan. 24, 1917, p. 77. *Factory,* Dec. 1916, p. 668-71. *Iron age,* Nov. 30, 1916, Jan. 11, 1917, p. 1266, 138-9. *Iron trade review,* Feb. 22, 1917, p. 477-8. Condensed. *Iron trade review,* Dec. 7, 1916, p. 1144-6. *Journal of the American society of mechanical engineers,* Dec. 1916, p. 965-6. Kent, William, *Bookkeeping and cost accounting for factories.* 1918. p. 90. Discussion. *Journal of the American society of mechanical engineers,* March 1917, p. 215-7.

	% on cost	% on reducing balance
Engines and dynamos	5	10

PIXLEY, FRANCIS W. Electric lighting companies. (In his *Accountancy.* Ed. 2. p. 218).
Engines and boiler 7½-12%

PORTERS, R. J. Rates of depreciation generally adopted. (In his *Pitman's dictionary of bookkeeping.* p. 344).

Engines	
movable	10%
fixed	7½

Based on diminishing balance

PROBABLE lives of waterworks elements. *Engineering news,* Oct. 11, 1917, p. 688.

	Years
Steam engines	20-40

PROPOSED sale of Toronto utilities to the city. *Electrical world,* Oct. 25, 1913, p. 832.

Corliss slow-speed engines	3%
Automatic high-speed engines	5-8

PROSSER, R. W. Depreciation in gas plants. *American gas light journal,* May 26, 1902, p. 767.
Engines 25 years 20% of first cost

PUBLIC utility reports, annotated. Rochester, Lawyers co-operative publishing co. 1915A. p. 178.
Re Janesville water co. Wis.) In estimating the cost of reproduction for the purpose of obtaining the fair value of a water works property for municipal purchase, allowance of a condition of 50% new of a Sturdevant fan and engine which was secondhand at the time of installation, and which had been in use for eleven years, was held to be ample.

ROBY, J. J. Schedule of plant depreciation. (In his *Treatise on cost accounting as applied to coal mining.* c1913. p. 14-5).

Engines, dynamos and switchboards	
Deduct as salvage before depreciating	20%
Depreciation rate for remainder, fireproof	.4

RUNYON, F. O. Report on hydro-electric plant for special committee common council, Newark, New Jersey, April 23, 1902, p. 15, 16.
Engines and generators 5%

THOMPSON, C. BERTRAND. Interest and depreciation. (In his *How to find factory costs.* c1916. p. 64).
Steam engines and boilers are usually depreciated at 5-7½%
Dynamos, portable engines motors and electrical equipment could be figured at from 10-15

TIFFANY, H. S. Machinery. (In his *Digest of depreciations.* c1890. p. 12).
Engines 5%

UNIFORM cost sheet for coal mining companies. *Coal age,* Sept. 19, 1918, p. 545-7.

	original cost
Dynamos and engines	8%

VALUATION of the Chicago consolidated traction property. *Electric railway journal,* Dec. 3, 1910, p. 1111-3.
Engines 3-5%

WEBNER, FRANK E. Depreciation rates. (In his *Factory costs.* 1911. p. 178).
Stationary engine and boiler
7½ the first year and 7½ annually from the diminishing value or its equivalent.

DEPRECIATION, DEPLETION AND OBSOLESCENCE—ENGINES—*(Continued)*

WHATLEY, G. E. STUART. Depreciation. (In his *Accountant's and bookkeeper's vade-mecum.* 1893. p. 26).

Engines and gear — Diminishing value. 5%

WILLIAMSON, J. GILMOUR. Depreciation of assets. (In his *Counting house and factory organisation.* p. 142).

Engines — 7½%

YEAMAN, C. H. Depreciation and reserves for antiquation and obsolescence from an engineering standpoint. *Electrician,* July 5, 1907, p. 475. *Electrical engineering* (London), July 12, standpoint. *Electrical engineering* (London), July 12, 1907, p. 46. *Electrical review* (London), July 12, 1907, p. 44. *Electrician,* July 5, 1907, p. 475.

Engines	20-25 years	R. Hammond
	15-25 years	L. G. B. (Local govt. board)
	20 years	L. C. C.
	25 years	J. F. C. Snell (M. E. A. 1905)

Engraving

ELBOURNE, EDWARD T. Depreciation rates. (In his *Factory administration and accounts.* 1918. p. 377).

	Prov. dep. %	Years	
	Remainder values	10%	5%
Engraving machines	7½	29	38

PHILADELPHIA. CONTROLLER. Rates of depreciation. (In his *Manual of accounting, reporting and business procedure of the city and county of Philadelphia.* 1917. p. 205).

Metal working equipment, turning, planing, milling, stamping and engraving equipment — 5%

Equipment

See Depreciation, depletion and obsolescence—Machinery and equipment.

Exciters

BREWER, ALLAN F. Rates for annual depreciation. *Industrial management,* April 1918, p. 268.

Exciters — 30 years — 3.33%

Equipment companies

JONES, EDWARD DAVID. Depreciation. (In his *Investment.* p. 167).

Physical property of equipment companies — 8%

Exhaust heads

BOLTON, REGINALD PELHAM. Depreciation of mechanical equipments and power plants. (In his *Building for profit.* 1911. p. 82, 89).

	Physical years	%	Economic years
Exhaust heads, exposed galvanized ironwork, hot-water drums	12	30.0	9

Exhaust systems

BARKER, HARRY. Typical life expectation tables for public utility property. (In his *Public utility rates.* 1917. p. 368).

Exhausters — 25 years — Wis. R.R. Comm.

BELT, ROBERT E. Depreciation. (In his *Foundry cost accounting practice and procedure.* 1919. p. 242).

Exhaust system — 10%

ELBOURNE, EDWARD T. Depreciation rates. (In his *Factory administration and accounts.* 1918. p. 376).

	Prov. dep. %	Years	
	Remainder values	10%	5%
Ventilating and exhausting installation	7½	29	38

FOSTER, HORATIO A. Rates of depreciation. (In his *Engineering valuation of public utilities and factories.* 1913. p. 206).

Exhausters — Years life 25

GILLETTE, HALBERT P. and RICHARD T. DANA. Depreciation. (In their *Handbook of mechanical and electrical cost data.* 1918. p. 107).

Exhausters (gas plant) — 25 years — Wisconsin railroad comm

GRUNSKY, CARL EWALD. Probable useful life of various articles. (In his *Valuation, depreciation and the rate-base.* 1917. p. 279).

Exhausters
gas plant — 25 years — 1c. lb. residual value
Wisconsin railroad commission. Quoted by H. A. Foster and in published reports.

NICHOLSON, J. LEE and JOHN F. D. ROHRBACH. Depreciation. (In their *Cost accounting.* 1918. p. 148, 150).

Exhaust system	7½%
" blower system	7½
Shaving exhaust system	10

Based on (1) the cost of equipment
(2) the life of the equipment
(3) on a ten-hour day

DEPRECIATION, DEPLETION AND OBSOLESCENCE—*(Continued)*

Exhibitions

PHILADELPHIA. CONTROLLER. Rates of depreciation. (In his *Manual of accounting, reporting and business procedure of the city and county of Philadelphia.* 1917. p. 209, 210).

Buildings:

Churches, auditoriums, exhibition halls, museums, club houses and amusement places	1%
Picture exhibitors and accessory apparatus	5

Extractors

GILLETTE, HALBERT P. and RICHARD T. DANA. Depreciation. (In their *Handbook of mechanical and electrical cost data.* 1918. p. 107).

Extractors, tar P. & A. (gas plant) 40 years Wisconsin railroad commission.

NICHOLSON, J. LEE and JOHN F. D. ROHRBACH. Depreciation. (In their *Cost accounting.* 1919 p. 150).

Extractors 10%

Fans

BOLTON, REGINALD PELHAM. Depreciation of mechanical equipments and power plants. (In his *Building for profit.* 1911. p. 82, 89).

	Physical years	%	Economic years
Motor-driven pumps, compressors, and moderate-speed fans	20	50	17

ELBOURNE, EDWARD T. Depreciation rates. (In his *Factory administration and accounts.* 1918. p. 376).

	Prov. dep. %	Years	
	Remainder values	10%	5%
Fans			
Blast	6	37	48
Exhaust and ventilating	6	37	48

NICHOLSON, J. LEE and JOHN F. D. ROHRBACH. Depreciation. (In their *Cost accounting.* 1919. p. 150).

Fans 10%

PHILADELPHIA. CONTROLLER. Rates of depreciation. (In his *Manual of accounting, reporting and business procedure of the city and county of Philadelphia.* 1917. p. 204).

Fans 10%

UNIFORM cost sheet for coal mining companies. *Coal age,* Sept. 19, 1918, p. 545-7.

	Original cost
Fans	5%

Feed cables

See Depreciation, depletion and obsolescence—Cables.

Feed cans

PHILADELPHIA. CONTROLLER. Rates of depreciation. (In his *Manual of accounting, reporting and business procedure of the city and county of Philadelphia.* 1917. p. 206).

Curry combs, clipping machines, feed cans, etc. 33⅓%

Fences

AUSTRALIA. FEDERAL INCOME TAX DEPARTMENT. Depreciation allowance. *Accountant,* Oct. 13. 1917, p. 277-9. *Accounting and commerce,* June 30, 1917, p. 55-7. *Federal accountant,* July 1917, p. 93-8. *Public accountant,* Jan. 30, 1917, p. 145-52.

Fences Nil

BAGG, F. A. Life of railway physical property from engineering standpoint. *Electric railway journal,* Dec. 9, 1911, p. 1205-6.

	Life years
Galvanized wire fencing	10

BELT, ROBERT E. Depreciation. (In his *Foundry cost accounting practice and procedure.* 1919. p. 243).

Fences	
wooden	10%
wire	7½

ELBOURNE, EDWARD T. Depreciation rates. (In his *Factory administration and accounts.* 1918. p. 376).

	Prov. dep. %	Years	
	Remainder values	10%	5%
Fencing	4	56-	73

FOSTER, HORATIO A. Rates of depreciation. (In his *Engineering valuation of public utilities and factories.* 1913. p. 200).

Fences	
Snow	10.0%
Other	5.0

Marwick, Mitchell & co. in the appraisal of a large street railway system.

GILLETTE, HALBERT POWERS. Railways. (In his *Handbook of cost data for contractors and engineers.* 1910. p. 1317-8).

Fences
6.5 age years
7.0 annual depreciation per cent
54.5 Present condition per cent

GILLETTE, HALBERT POWERS and RICHARD T. DANA. Depreciation. (In their *Handbook of mechanical and electrical cost data.* 1918. p. 107).

Fences	
14.3 years	H. P. Gillette. Washington railway appraisal.
20	Marwick, Mitchell & co., appraisal of a large street railway system, Foster, p. 199.
snow	
10	Marwick, Mitchell & co., appraisal of a large street railway system, Foster, p. 199.

DEPRECIATION, DEPLETION AND OBSOLESCENCE—FENCES—(Continued)

GRAY, HENRY L. Necessity of depreciation reserves. *Railway age gazette,* May 27, 1910, p. 1297-8. Editorial. Depreciation reserves. *Railway age gazette,* May 27, 1910, p. 1290. Letters. Depreciation reserves. *Railway age gazette,* July 8, 1910, p. 66.

	Annual dep.
Fences and cattle-guards	8%

GRUNSKY, CARL EWALD. Probable useful life of various articles. (In his *Valuation, depreciation and the rate-base.* 1917. p. 279).

Fences

wooden	12 years	Pacific gas & electric company. Figures and in rate hearings before Master in Chancery, San Francisco, 1913-4.
wire mesh	12 years.	Pacific gas & electric company. Figures used in rate hearings before Master in Chancery, San Francisco, 1913-4.
railroad	14.3 years	H. P. Gillette. Appraisal of Great Northern & Northern Pacific R.R.'s in Washington. Direction of Washington Railroad Commission, 1906.
railroad	15 years.	California railroad commission—Reports 1913-4. Stockton Terminal & Eastern R.R., April, 1913.

NICHOLSON, J. LEE and JOHN F. D. ROHRBACH. Depreciation. (In their *Cost accounting.* 1919. p. 147).

Fences	
wooden	10%
wooden and wire mesh	8⅓

Based on (1) the cost of equipment
(2) the life of the equipment
(3) on a ten-hour day.

PHILADELPHIA. CONTROLLER. Rates of depreciation. (In his *Manual of accounting, reporting and business procedure of the city and county of Philadelphia.* 1917. p. 210).

Fences	4%

PIEZ, CHARLES. Perpetual inventory and appraisal values; table of standard depreciation rates. *Engineering and contracting,* Jan. 24, 1917, p. 77. *Factory,* Dec. 1916, p. 668-71. *Iron age,* Nov. 30, 1916, p. 1266. Condensed. *Iron trade review,* Dec. 7, 1916, p. 1144-6. *Journal of the American society of mechanical engineers,* Dec. 1916, p. 965-6. Discussion. *Journal of the American society of mechanical engineers,* March 1917, p. 215-7. Kent, William. *Bookkeeping and cost accounting for factories.* 1918. p. 90.

	% on cost	% on reducing balance
Miscellaneous real estate improvements: pavements, sidewalks, fences, retaining walls, roadways, tracks, yard drainage, general conduit, tunnels, vaults, etc.	4.5	10

VARIOUS depreciation charges. *New York Times,* June 14, 1914.

General construction, fences, retaining walls, and so on	7%

Fenders

PHILADELPHIA. CONTROLLER. Rates of depreciation. (In his *Manual of accounting, reporting and business procedure of the city and county of Philadelphia.* 1917. p. 205).

Andirons and fenders for open fire places	4%

Fertilizers

RANKIN, W. S. Appraisal and depreciation of fertilizer plants. *American fertilizer,* July 22, 1916, p. 94.

Filing machines

ELBOURNE, EDWARD T. Depreciation rates. (In his *Factory administration and accounts.* 1918. p. 377).

	Prov. dep. % Remainder values	Years 10%	Years 5%
Filing machines	10	22	28

NICHOLSON, J. LEE and JOHN F. D. ROHRBACH. Depreciation. (In their *Cost accounting.* 1919. p. 149).

Saw-setting and filing machines	6⅔%

Films

AUSTRALIA. FEDERAL INCOME TAX DEPARTMENT. Depreciation allowance. *Accountant,* Oct. 13, 1917, p. 277-9. *Accounting and commerce,* June 30, 1917, p. 55-7. *Federal accountant,* July 1917, p. 93-8. *Public accountant,* Jan. 1917, p. 145-52.

Films	20%

Based on written down value and repairs allowed in addition

Filters

AMERICAN INSTITUTE OF ACCOUNTANTS. Report of the committee on standard schedules for uniform reports upon municipal industries and public service corporations; annual meeting at Atlantic city, N. J. October 20-22, 1908, 15p. *Journal of accountancy,* May 1909, p. 47-54.

The knowledge at the command of the Bureau of the census leads to the conclusion that this average life is approximately as follows: masonry of filtration 50 years; boilers, steam pipes and filtration equipment 20 years.

AMERICAN WATERWORKS ASSOCIATION. Final report of committee on depreciation. *Journal of the American waterworks association,* Sept. 1917, p. 1-38.

Filter plants	
Masonry filters	30-50 years
Wood "	15-30

DEPRECIATION, DEPLETION AND OBSOLESCENCE—FILTERS—*(Continued)*

BARKER, HARRY. Typical life expectation tables for public utility property. (In his *Public utility rates.* 1917. p. 367.
Filter beds 30-50 years Wis. R.R. Comm.

BRYAN, WILLIAM. Appraisal and depreciation of waterworks and similar prpoerties. *Journal of the Association of engineering societies,* Dec. 1907, p. 336-81. Depreciation allowance for various public service industries. *Engineering news,* Jan. 23, 1908, p. 96.
Years
Filters, water 15-20

CHASE, HARVEY STUART. Depreciation in water works accounts, with reference to uniform reports. *Journal of the New England waterworks association,* June 1910, p. 305-31. Abstract. *Engineering and contracting,* June 29, 1910, p. 598. Editorial. Depreciation and sinking fund accounts. *Municipal engineering,* July 1910, p. 26.
Masonry of filtration plant, cribs, iron water pipes, intake pipes, fibre hydrants, stand pipes and buildings 50 years
Boilers, steam pipes and filtration equipment 20

CLADER, WILL-A. Water utilities accounting. *Journal of accountancy,* Aug. 1919, p. 91-2.
The following rate is used frequently when wear and tear are made good by operating maintenance.
Filter plants 3%

ESTIMATED life and depreciation of water works plants. *Municipal journal and engineer,* May 6, 1908, p. 558.
Years
Water filters 15-20 William H. Bryan

FOSTER, HORATIO A. Rates of depreciation. (In his *Engineering valuation of public utilities and factories.* 1913. p. 204).
Years' life
Filter beds 30-50

HAZLEHURST, J. N. Final report of the committee on depreciation. *Journal of the American water works association,* March 1919, p. 85-135.
Masonry filters 30-50 years
Wood " 15-30

METCALF, LEONARD. Depreciation in waterworks operation and accounting. *Journal of the New England waterworks association,* Dec. 1910, p. 442. Abstracts. *Engineering news,* Nov. 3, 1910, p. 482. Methods of computing depreciation of and reasonable assumptions as to the period of useful life of waterworks. *Engineering and contracting,* Nov. 16, 1910, p. 434.
Filter plants, permanent construction 25-50 years 4-2% straight line

PHILADELPHIA. CONTROLLER. Rates of depreciation. (In his *Manual of accounting, reporting and business procedure of the city and county of Philadelphia.* 1917. p. 206, 210).
Equipment for distilling and refining of water (filters) etc. 8 1/3%
Filtration beds and galleries 3 1/3%

PROBABLE lives of lives of water-works elements. *Engineering news,* Oct. 11, 1917, p. 688.
Filter plants
masonry 30-50 years
wood 15-3

WOLFF, MARK. Interpretation of waterworks accounts. *Journal of the American waterworks association,* June 1916, p. 543, 546.
Boilers, steam pipes, filters 20 years

Fire apparatus

AUSTRALIA. FEDERAL INCOME TAX DEPARTMENT. Depreciation allowance. *Accountant,* Oct. 13, 1917, p. 277-9. *Accountant and commerce,* June 30, 1917, p. 55-7. *Federal accountant,* July 1917, p. 93-8. *Public accountant,* Jan. 30, 1917, p. 145-52.
Grinnell sprinklers 5%
Based on written down value and repairs allowed in addition.

GRUNSKY, CARL EDWARD. Probable useful life of various articles. (In his *Valuation, depreciation and the rate-base.* 1917. p. 279).
Fire protection apparatus 12 years
Pacific gas and electric company. Figures used in rate hearings before Master in Chancery, San Francisco, 1913-4.

NICHOLSON, J. LEE and JOHN F. D. ROHRBACH. Depreciation. (In their *Cost accounting.* 1919. p. 147).
Fire alarm and fire prevention apparatus 5%
Hose reel and guard houses 15
Based on (1) the cost of equipment
(2) the life of the equipment
(3) on a ten-hour day.

PHILADELPHIA. CONTROLLER. Rates of depreciation. (In his *Manual of accounting, reporting and business procedure of the city and county of Philadelphia.* 1917. p. 208).
Pumping engines and water towers 3⅔%
Chemical engines 4
Hook and ladder trucks 3
Hose carts and other supply wagons 3
Fire hooks, nozzles and other fire fighting implements 4
Hose and reels 20
Hand grenades and other hand fire extinguishers 10
Combination hose and chemical vehicles 5
Miscellaneous fire preventing equipment (fire gongs) 10

ROBY, J. J. Shedule of plant depreciation. (In his *Treatise on cost accounting as applied to coal mining.* c1913. p. 14-5).
Safety appliances, fire extinguishers
Deduct as salvage before depreciating 10%
Depreciation rate for remainder, fireproof 10

DEPRECIATION, DEPLETION AND OBSOLESCENCE—FIRE APPARATUS—*(Continued)*

UNIFORM cost sheet for coal mining companies. *Coal age,* Sept. 19, 1918, p. 545-7.
original cost
Fire equipment 20%

Firearms

PHILADELPHIA. CONTROLLER. Rates of depreciation. (In his *Manual of accounting, reporting and business procedure of the city and county of Philadelphia.* 1917. p. 209).
Air guns and other missile throwing apparatus (not internal combustion) and targets 8⅓%
Rifles, revolvers and other small arms 4

Firing tools

PHILADELPHIA. CONTROLLER. Rates of depreciation. (In his *Manual of accounting, reporting and business procedure of the city and county of Philadelphia.* 1917. p. 205).
Oil cans, firing tools, wrenches, etc. 16⅔%

Fishing

PHILADELPHIA. CONTROLLER. Rates of depreciation. (In his *Manual of accounting, reporting and business procedure of the city and county of Philadelphia.* 1917. p. 205).
Fishing, hunting and trapping equipment 10%

Fixtures

See Depreciation, depletion and obsolescence—Furniture and fixtures.

Flag poles

PHILADELPHIA. CONTROLLER. Rates of depreciation. (In his *Manual of accounting, reporting and business procedure of the city and county of Philadelphia.* 1917. p. 210).
Arbors, trellises, pergolas, flag poles, etc. 5%

Flags

PHILADELPHIA. CONTROLLER. Rates of depreciation. (In his *Manual of accounting, reporting and business procedure of the city and county of Philadelphia.* 1917. p. 207-8).
Flags and covers for flags 20%

Flanging machines

DENHAM, ROBERT S. Depreciation. (In his *Manual of cost engineering and estimating for paper box manufacturers.* 1917. p. 249).
original cost
Flange benders 10%

ELBOURNE, EDWARD T. Depreciation rates. (In his *Factory administration and accounts.* 1918. p. 377).

	Prov. dep. %	Years	
	Remainder values	10%	5%
Flanging machines	6	37	48

NICHOLSON, J. LEE and JOHN F. D. ROHRBACH. Depreciation. (In their *Cost accounting.* 1919. p. 149).
Flanging machines 6⅔%

Flasks

BELT, ROBERT E. Depreciation. (In his *Foundry cost accounting practice and procedure.* 1919. p. 242).
Flasks
Steel 15%
Malleable iron 33⅓
Grey iron 33⅓
Aluminum 20

MONTGOMERY, ROBERT H. Foundries. (In his *Income tax procedure,* 1919. p. 564. ——— Same, 1920. p. 717).
Flasks, patterns and core boxes 10-20%

PIEZ, CHARLES. Perpetual inventory and appraisal values; table of standard depreciation rates. *Engineering and contracting,* Jan. 24, 1917, p. 77. *Factory,* Dec. 1916, p. 668-71. *Iron age,* Nov. 30, 1916, Jan. 11, 1917, p. 1266, 138-9. *Iron trade review,* Feb. 22, 1917, p. 477-8. Condensed. *Journal of the American society of mechanical engineers,* Dec. 1916, p. 965-6. *Iron trade review,* Dec. 7, 1916, p. 1144-6. Kent, William. *Bookkeeping and cost accounting for factories.* 1918. p. 90. Discussion. *Journal of the American society of mechanical engineers,* March, 1917, p. 215-7.
Chills, iron and steel flasks and accessories, net additions 50% on cost

Floating equipment

NICHOLSON, J. LEE and J. F. D. ROHRBACH. Depreciation. (In their *Cost accounting.* 1919 p. 151).
Floating equipment 10%
Based on (1) the cost of equipment
(2) the life of equipment
(3) on a ten-hour day

Floors

See Depreciation, depletion and obsolescence—Buildings.

Flotation machines

NICHOLSON, J. LEE and J. F. D. ROHRBACH. Depreciation. (In their *Cost accounting.* 1919 p. 150).
Flotation machines 10%

DEPRECIATION, DEPLETION AND OBSOLESCENCE—*(Continued)*

Flour mills

AUSTRALIA. FEDERAL INCOME TAX DEPARTMENT. Depreciation allowance. *Accountant,* Oct. 13, 1917, p. 277-9. *Accounting and commerce,* June 30, 1917, p. 55-7. *Federal accountant,* July 1917, p. 93-8. *Public accountant,* Jan. 30, 1917, p. 145-52.

Flour milling

Machinery (other than power) 7½%

Based on written down value and repairs allowed in addition.

DEPRECIATION of machinery in respect of income tax. *Accountants' magazine,* May 1900, p. 259-60.

Engines, boilers and main shafting 5%

Other machinery 7½

Written down value

GREAT BRITAIN. BOARD OF INLAND REVENUE. Depreciation rates: (In its *Income tax; statement respecting allowances for wear and tear and obsolescence of plant and machinery.* 1918. Cd. 9022, p. 4; Cd. 9134, p. 6). *American economic review, Supplement,* Dec. 1920, p. 51. *Journal of accountancy,* Sept. 1920, p. 194.

Flour milling engines, boilers and main shafting 5%

Other machinery 7½

Written down value

INCOME tax notes. *Accountant,* May 11, Sept. 28, 1918, p. 359, 162-6. *Incorporated accountants' journal,* May, Oct. 1918, p. 157, 14.

Flour milling

Other machinery 7½

Engines, boilers and main shafting 5%

Written down value

OFFICIAL allowances in respect of depreciation of machinery and plant Board of Inland revenue, Great Britain. *Accountant,* May 16, 30, 1914, p. 736, 785-8.

Engines, boilers and shafting 5%

Other machinery 7½

As the maximum, calculated on the written-down value.

TIFFANY. H. S. Flour mills. (In his *Digest of depreciations.* c1890. p. 9, 12, 34).

Buildings:	
brick or stone	2-2½%
frame	3-3½
Machinery:	
Flour mills	
1st year	12½
2nd "	8
3rd "	5
4th "	2½
5th "	2
Every year thereafter	2
Mill stones	2
" spindles	1½
Roller mills	3
Hopper stands and shoe	5
Mill curbs	10
Corn mills, portable	8
Smut machines	10
Middlings' purifiers	12
Bolting chests	8
" cloths	20
" screens, wires	5
Hoisting screw, bails, &c	1
Cranes	2
Elevator belting and cups	15
Stock hoppers and spouting	8
Shafting and couplings	1
Iron pulleys	2
Boxes, Babitted	10
Iron gearing	8
Core wheels	8
" cogs, wooden	15
Leather belting	20
Rubber "	30

UNITED STATES. FEDERAL TRADE COMMISSION. Depreciation. (In its *Report on flour milling and jobbing.* 1918. p. 14).

Since the practice of companies regarding depreciation varied so greatly the Commission has included in its cost a uniform charge of 3c. a barrel.

Flues

See Depreciation, depletion and obsolescence—Stacks.

Flumes

GRUNSKY, CHARLES EWALD. Probable useful life of various articles. (In his *Valuation, depreciation and the rate-base.* 1917. p. 279).

Flumes

wooden	30 years California Railroad commission—Reports 1913-2. Cuyamaca Water co. case, March, 1913.
steel	25 years San Joaquin light and power corporation. Rate hearing before California railroad commission, 1915.

DEPRECIATION, DEPLETION AND OBSOLESCENCE—FLUMES—*(Continued)*

concrete 50 years.
San Joaquin light and power corporation. Rate hearing before California railroad commission, 1915.

Flying machines

DENHAM, ROBERT S. Depreciation. (In his *Manual of cost engineering and estimating for paper box manufacturers.* 1917. p. 249).
Flying machines 12%

Foods

PHILADELPHIA. CONTROLLER. Rates of depreciation. (In his *Manual of accounting, reporting and business procedure of the city and county of Philadelphia.* 1917. p. 205).
Food preparing equipment (excluding household utensils):

Slaughtering, butchering and dry-curing equipment	10%
Cooking, roasting and baking other than canning	4

Foot stools

PHILADELPHIA. CONTROLLER. Rates of depreciation. (In his *Manual of accounting, reporting and business procedure of the city and county of Philadelphia.* 1917. p. 207-8).
Foot stools 8⅓%

Foreign branches

RACINE, SAMUEL F. Depreciation and foreign branches. (In his *Accounting principles.* 1917. p. 156-7).

Forging

ELBOURNE, EDWARD T. Depreciation rates. (In his *Factory administration and accounts.* 1918. p. 377).

	Prov. dep. % Remainder values	Years 10%	5%
Smith's forges and hearths	12½	17	22
Forging machines	7½	29	38

NICHOLSON, J. LEE and J. F. D. ROHRBACH. Depreciation. (In their *Cost accounting.* 1919. p. 149, 150).

Forges	10%
Forging and upsetting machines	6⅔

PHILADELPHIA. CONTROLLER. Rates of depreciation. (In his *Manual of accounting, reporting and business procedure of the city and county of Philadelphia.* 1917. p. 204).
Forges 10%

PIEZ, CHARLES. Perpetual inventory and appraisal values; table of standard depreciation rates. *Engineering and contracting,* Jan. 24, 1917, p. 77. *Factory,* Dec. 1916, p. 668-71. *Iron age,* Nov. 30, 1916, Jan. 11, 1917, p. 1266, 138-9. *Iron trade review,* Feb. 22, 1917, p. 477-8. Condensed. *Journal of the American society of mechanical engineers,* Dec. 1916. p. 965-6. *Iron trade review,* Dec. 7, 1916, p. 1144-6. Kent, William. *Bookkeeping and cost accounting for factories.* 1918. p. 90. Discussion. *Journal of the American society of mechanical engineers,* March, 1917, p. 215-7.

	% on cost	% on reducing balance
Annealing and heating furnaces, ovens, forges, etc.	5	10

Foundations

BOLTON, REGINALD PELHAM. Depreciation of mechanical equipments and power plants. (In his *Building for profit.* 1911. p. 82, 89).

	Physical years	%	Economic years
Most durable elements—steel construction, foundations, elevator guides, and overhead framing	40	100.0	30

ELBOURNE, EDWARD T. Depreciation rates. (In his *Factory administration and accounts.* 1918. p. 376).
Foundations for machinery—same as machinery.

FLOY, HENRY. Depreciation. Floy, Henry. Depreciation as related to electrical properties. *American institute of electrical engineers, Proceedings.* 1911. p. 1267. Floy, Henry. *Valuation of public utility properties.* 1912. p. 168-217. Foster, Horatio A. *Engineering valuation of public utility properties.* 1912. p. 168-217. Foster, Horatio A. *Engineering valuation of public utilities and factories,* 1913, p. 194-8. *Engineering and contracting,* Oct. 4, 1911, p. 359-65. *Engineering magazine,* Aug. 1911, p. 437-40.
Foundations. Same as life of apparatus supported. Trac. val. comm. Chicago con trac. co.
Same as life of apparatus supported. Henry Floy. 3rd Ave. case, adopted by P.S.C., N. Y.

FOSTER, HORATIO A. Rates of depreciation. (In his *Engineering valuation of public utilities and factories.* 1913. p. 205, 207).
Foundations for machinery give same life as the machine they support.

GILLETTE, HALBERT P. and RICHARD T. DANA. Depreciation. (In their *Handbook of mechanical and electrical cost data.* 1918. p. 107).
Foundations, machinery, same as life of apparatus supported.
Traction valuation commission. Chicago consolidated traction co.
Henry Floy, 3rd Ave. case.
16.6 years New York city.
Bion J. Arnold. Chicago appraisals. Four cases.

DEPRECIATION, DEPLETION AND OBSOLESCENCE—FOUNDATIONS—*(Continued)*

GRUNSKY, CARL EWALD. Probable useful life of various articles. (In his *Valuation, depreciation and the rate-base.* 1917. p. 279).

Foundations. Same as life of article supported. Traction valuation commission. Case of the Chicago consolidated traction co.

Henry Floy. Trans. American institute of electrical engieners, June 1911. Third avenue case figures adopted by Public service commission of New York.

MONTGOMERY, ROBERT H. Electrical equipment manufacturers. (In his *Income tax procedure,* 1919. p. 563. ——— Same, 1920. p. 716).

Foundations for tools and apparatus	10%

Based on gross book values at the end of the preceding year

VALUATION of the Chicago consolidated traction property. *Electric railway journal,* Dec. 3, 1910, p. 1111-3.

Machinery foundation—life of the apparatus supported.

Foundries

AUSTRALIA. FEDERAL INCOME TAX DEPARTMENT. Depreciation allowance. *Accountant,* Oct. 13, 1917, p. 277-9. *Accounting and commerce,* June 30, 1917, p. 55-7. *Federal accountant,* July 1917, p. 93-8. *Public accountant,* Jan. 30, 1917, p. 145-52.

Foundries	
Furnaces	15%
Patterns	2½
Ladles	10
Other	5

Based on written down value and repairs allowed in addition

BELT, ROBERT E. Depreciation. (In his *Foundry cost accounting, practice and procedure.* c1919. p. 235-48).

	Percent
Buildings:	
Concrete	2½
Brick—steel frame	3
Brick—wood frame	3½
Sheet iron, steel frame	5
Wood	7½
Melting department equipment:	
Cupolas and apparatus	5
Air furnaces and apparatus	7½
Open hearth furnaces and apparatus	10
Electric furnaces and apparatus	10
Crucibles	7½
Sprue mill and slag washer	15
Laboratory equipment	10
Tensile testing machines	5
Traveling cranes	7½
Hand trucks	10
Molding department equipment:	
Flasks—steel	15
Flasks—grey iron	33⅓
Flasks—malleable iron	33⅓
Flasks—aluminum	20
Air molding machines	20
Hand squeezers	15
Benches, tables, racks, etc.	10
Sand mixers	15
Pattern shop equipment	10
Carpenter shop equipment	10
Hand trucks	10
Core department equipment:	
Core ovens and apparatus—steel	7½
Core ovens and apparatus—brick	10
Core machines	15
Oil separators	7½
Sand mixers	15
Benches, tables, racks, trays, etc.	10
Hand trucks	7½
Cleaning department equipment:	
Tumbling barrels, with motor, shafting and belting	15
Sand blast barrels, and tables, with motor, shafting and belting	25
Exhaust system	10
Trimming and inspecting department equipment:	
Benches, scales, trucks	10
Emery wheel stands, with motor, shafting and belting	10
Annealing department equipment:	
Annealing ovens and apparatus	7½
Annealing trucks—steam, air and electric	20
Traveling cranes	7½
Pyrometers	10
Finishing and shipping department equipment:	
Emery wheel stands, drop hammers, lathes, drill presses, air chippers milling machines, etc., with motor, shafing and belting	10
Automobile trucks	20
Sorting tables, trucks, scales, etc.	10

DEPRECIATION, DEPLETION AND OBSOLESCENCE—FOUNDRIES—*(Continued)*

Power plant equipment	
Steam boilers	5
Electric generators and switch boards	7½
Waste heat boilers and apparatus	10
Air compressors	7½
Steam separators	10
Steam piping	5
Electric wiring and fixtures	7½
Engines, steam and gas	5
Heating system, steam	5
Brick stacks	5
Pumps, steam and hydraulic	5
Industrial electric trucks and tractors	25
Truck and tractor trailers	15
Sprinkler system	5
Sewers	2½
Fences—wooden	10
Fences—wire	7½
Office furniture and fixtures	10

In a foundry, there is a long list of smaller equipment consisting of wood flasks, mold jackets and bands, patterns, hand tools, etc., the entire cost of which should be charged directly to current operations and not be charged to capital for the reason that the life of such equipment is so uncertain that it is not safe to charge any part thereof to capital.

BELT, ROBERT E. Depreciation. (In his *Uniform cost accounting methods; adopted by the American malleable castings association,* Nov. 14, 1917, p. 20-1).

	Percent
Buildings:	
Concrete	2½
Brick	3
Sheet iron	10
Melting department equipment:	
Melting furnaces and apparatus	7½
Sprue mill and slag washer	15
Laboratory equipment	10
Crane	10
Molding department equipment	
Hand squeezers	15
Air molding machines	20
Pattern and carpenter shop equipment	10
Core department equipment:	
Core ovens and apparatus	7½
Core machines	15
Sand mixer	20
Benches, racks, trays, trucks	10
Hard iron cleaning department equipment:	
Tumbling barrels, with motor, shafting and belting	15
Sand blast barrels with tables, with motor, shafting and belting	30
Dust arrester	10
Trimming and inspecting department equipment:	
Benches, scales, trucks	10
Emery wheel stands, with motor, shafting and belting	10
Annealing department equipment:	
Annealing ovens and apparatus	10
Annealing trucks	20
Crane	10
Soft iron cleaing department, equipment:	
Tumbling barrels, with motor, shafting and belting	15
Sand blast barrels and tables, motor shafting and belting	30
Dust arrester	10
Finishing and shipping department equipment:	
Emery wheel stands, drop hammers, lathes, drill presses, air chippers, milling machines, threading machines, etc., with motor, shafting and belting	10
Sorting tables, trucks, scales, etc.	10
Automobile trucks	20
Power plant equipment:	
Steam boiler, generator, air compressor, steam piping, electric wiring, etc.	7½
Office furniture and fixtures	10

MONTGOMERY, ROBERT H. Foundries. (In his *Income tax procedure,* 1919. p. 564. —— Same, 1920. p. 717. *Auditing, theory and practice,* 1916, p. 418).

Buildings	2½%	1½%
Equipment	3	3
Flasks, patterns and core boxes	10-20	10-20

TIFFANY, H. S. Foundries. (In his *Digest of depreciations.* c1890. p. 9).

Buildings:	
brick	3%
frame	4½

Based upon the actual life without any repairs.

DEPRECIATION, DEPLETION AND OBSOLESCENCE—*(Continued)*

Frame-setting machines

NICHOLSON, J. LEE and J. F. D. ROHRBACH. Depreciation. (In their *Cost accounting.* 1919. p. 149).

Frame-setting machines 6⅔%

Frames

BOLTON, REGINALD PELHAM. Depreciation of mechanical equipments and power plants. (In his *Building for profit.* 1911. p. 82, 89).

	Physical years	%	Economic years
Most durable elements, steel construction, foundations, elevator guides, and overhead framing	40	100.0	30
Exterior framing, copper-cased housing, etc., heating pipe systems used part of the year, gas piping	33	82.5	27

NICHOLSON, J. LEE and JOHN F. D. ROHRBACH. Depreciation. (In their *Cost accounting.* 1919. p. 146).

Frames, stables and sheds 5%

Franchises

KESTER, ROY B. Depreciation of franchises. (In his *Accounting theory and practice.* 1918. v. 2. p. 328-30).

Freezing

See Depreciation, depletion and obsolescence—Refrigeration.

Fruit

AUSTRALIA. FEDERAL INCOME TAX DEPARTMENT. Depreciation allowance. *Accountant,* Oct. 13, 1917, p. 277-9. *Accounting and commerce,* June 30, 1917, p. 55-7. *Federal accountant,* July 1917, p. 93-8. *Public accountant,* Jan. 30, 1917, p. 145-52.

Fruitgrowers dips, pans, drying trays, spray pumps, etc. 7½%
Written down value, repairs allowed in addition.

PHILADELPHIA. CONTROLLER. Rates of depreciation. (In his *Manual of accounting, reporting and business procedure of the city and county of Philadelphia.* 1912. p. 210).

Building used for manufacture or horticulture 2%
Horticultural improvements 1

Furnaces

See Depreciation, depletion and obsolescence—Stoves, furnaces, etc.

Furniture and fixtures

See also name of various professions, industries and trades and various headings under Depreciation, depletion and obsolescence.

AUSTRALIA. Federal income tax department. Depreciation allowance. *Accountant,* Oct. 13, 1917, p. 277-9. *Accounting and commerce,* June 30, 1917, p. 55-7. *Federal accountant,* July 1917, p. 93-8. *Public accountant,* Jan. 30, 1917, p. 145-52.

Furniture 5%
Business places 5
Doctors', lawyers' and other profession men's consulting rooms 2½
Houses let furnished 7½
Based on written down value and repairs allowed in addition.

BAY state street railway valuation. *Electric railway journal,* Dec. 4, 1915, p. 1121-3.

Furniture 2.4
Annual depreciation per cent, annual depreciation divided by investment.

BELT, ROBERT E. Depreciation. (In his *Foundry cost accounting practice and procedure.* 1919. p. 243).

Office furniture and fixtures 10%

BENTLEY, HARRY C. Depreciation. (In his *Science of accounts.* 1913. p. 146).

Stable equipment, office equipment, store fixtures 5-10%

CARTER, R. N. Rates of depreciation. (In his *Advanced accounts.* p. 618).

Furniture, fixtures and fittings 2½-7½%
Based on diminishing balances, normal conditions and hours of working.

DENSHAM, F. W. Depreciation of assets and goodwill of limited companies. *Accountant,* May 28, 1898, p. 568.

Furniture and fixtures 5-10%

DICKSEE, LAWRENCE R. Landlord's fixtures. (In his *Auditing.* Authorized American edition. 1909. p. 196).

FOSTER, HORATIO A. Rates of depreciation. (In his *Engineering valuation of public utilities and factories.* 1913. p. 199).

Office furniture 5.0%
Marwick, Mitchell & co. in the appraisal of a large street railway system.

GILLETTE, HALBERT POWERS and RICHARD T. DANA. Depreciation. (In their *Handbook of mechanical and electrical cost data.* 1918. p. 107).

Furniture	7 years. Wisconsin railroad commission
Furniture and fixtures	12.5 years. Prof. M. E. Cooley, Milwaukee 3c. case
	20 years. H. P. Gillette, Everett railway and water co., Jan. 29, 1912.
	M. G. Starret, Milwaukee 3c. case
	Marwick, Mitchell & co., appraisal of a large street railway system, Foster, p. 199.

DEPRECIATION, DEPLETION AND OBSOLESCENCE—FURNITURE AND FIXTURES—*(Continued)*

GRUNSKY, CARL EWALD. Probable useful life of various articles. (In his *Valuation, depreciation and the rate-base.* 1917. p. 279).

Furniture and fixtures — 12½ years. Mortimer E. Cooly. Milwaukee 3c. fare case. Report Wisconsin railroad commission, vol. 10, p. 226.
20 years. Milton G. Starrett. Milwaukee 3c. fare case. Report Wisconsin railroad, commission, vol. 10, p. 226.
20 years. Milwaukee electric railway and lighting co. in Milwaukee 3c. fare case, Aug. 1912.
20 years. Wisconsin railroad commission. Milwaukee 3c. fare case. Aug. 23, 1912.

GUTHRIE, EDWIN. Depreciation. (In Lisle, George. *Encyclopaedia of accounting.* v. 2. p. 374).
Furniture and fixtures — 7-12½% on dim. val.
They have always some residue of value.

JENKINSON, MARK WEBSTER. Depreciation. *Accountant,* May 17, 1902, p. 528-34.
Fixtures, fittings, etc. — 5-7½% on dim. val.
Office furniture — 7½-15

JONES, EDWARD DAVID. Depreciation. (In his *Investment.* p. 167).
Furniture and fixtures

KENT, WILLIAM. Depreciation of shafting, etc. (In his *Bookkeeping and cost accounting for factories.* 1918. p. 91).
Furniture and apparatus — 20-50%

KERR, W. H. and G. A. NAHSTOLL. Reserve for depreciation. (In their *Cooperative organization business methods.* 1915. p. 13-14).
Office equipment and fixtures — 10%

KESTER, ROY B. Valuation of furniture and fixtures. (In his *Accounting theory and practice.* 1918. v. 2. p. 291).
Straight line method — 10-20%

MCINTOSH, ROBERT J. Rates of depreciation. (In his *Reference book of accounts.* Ed. 2. p. 60).
Office furniture and fixtures — 10-15%
Factory fixtures — 7½-10
Based on life.

MONTGOMERY, ROBERT H. Electrical equipment manufacturers. (In his *Income tax procedure,* 1919. p. 563).
Office furniture and appliances — 15%
Based on the gross book values at the end of the preceding years.

MONTGOMERY, ROBERT H. Furniture and fixtures. (In his *Income tax procedure,* 1919. p. 564-5. ——— Same, 1920, p. 717).
15% per annum.
Tax commissioner of one of the states has adopted a standard rate of 10% but in exceptional cases allows as much as 25%

MONTGOMERY, ROBERT H. Furniture and fixtures. (In his *Auditing theory and practice.* 1916. p. 425-6).
15 per cent per annum will represent a fair average allowance.

NEALE, R. E. Depreciation in engineering works. *Mechanical world,* Feb. 7, 1913, p. 67-8.
Office furniture and tools — 7.5-10% — 10-13 years

NICHOLSON, J. LEE and JOHN F. D. ROHRBACH. Depreciation. (In their *Cost accounting.* 1919. p. 151).
Factory equipment — 10%
Furniture and fixtures — 10
Miscellaneous equipment—including desks, chairs, typewriters, adding and calculating machines, blue-printing machines, filing cabinets and trucks, shelving partitions, time clocks, time detector systems, telephone, flexotypes, graphotypes, etc. — 10
Based on (1) the cost of equipment
(2) the life of the equipment
(3) on a ten-hour day.

NORRIS, H. M. Depreciation of plant, and its relation to general expense. *Engineering magazine,* April 1899, p. 76.
Office and shop fixtures — 5%

PHILADELPHIA. CONTROLLER. Rates of depreciation. (In his *Manual of accounting, reporting and business procedure of the city and county of Philadelphia.* 1917. p. 207-8).
Chairs, beds and other supports for the body:
Chairs — 4%
Stools — 4
Beds and cots, including bed springs — 5½
Benches — 5
Couches, lounges and settees — 8⅓
Foot stools — 8⅓
Hammocks — 25
Tables, desks and other supports and depositories for commodities:
Tables — 4
Desks — 4
Cupboards, sideboards, counters, shelves — 4
Cabinets, cases, lockers, bins and boxes — 4
Bookcases — 4

DEPRECIATION, DEPLETION AND OBSOLESCENCE—FURNITURE AND FIXTURES—*(Continued)*

Tabourets, stands, pedestals, copy holders	4
Vaults and safes	2
Bureaus and chiffoniers	4
Miscellaneous supports and depositories for commodities:	20
Floor coverings:	
Carpets and rugs	10
Mattings	25
Linoleum	12½
Mats and treads	25
Portiers, wall, window and furniture coverings, draperies and window shades:	
Portiers	6⅔
Wall coverings	8⅓
Window curtains	8⅓
Furniture coverings	16⅔
Draperies	8⅓
Window shades	12½
Window poles	4
Kitchen, dining room and household utensils and crockery	10
Baths, lavatories, toilets and toilet accessories:	
Bath tubs, shower baths and portable baths	3⅓
Lavatories, sinks and fountains	3⅓
Toilets and urinals	3⅓
Plumbing, pipes and other fittings	4
Toilet accessories (hair dryer, toilet paper holder)	4
Bath room fittings	4
Toilet or commode chairs	4
Tonsorial equipment	4
Bedding (exclusive of bed linen)	8⅓
Office, library and store furniture and furnishings not otherwise classified:	
Railings, etc.	5
Office machines and devices	12½
Court furniture, etc.	5
Telephone and election booths	5
Ornamental furnishings, such as jardiniers, vases, and candelbra, statuary	4
Annunciator and call systems	8⅓
Desk equipment (including receptacles and devices)	12½
Store equipment	12½
Equipment for convenience and comfort:	
Porch shades, awnings, blinds, etc.	20
Tents and portable houses	20
Mirrors	10
Equipment for convenience and comfort:	
Flags and covers for flags	20
Window and door screens	20
Gavels	5

PIEZ, CHARLES. Perpetual inventory and appraisal values; table of standard depreciation rates. *Engineering and contracting*, Jan. 24, 1917, p. 77. *Factory*, Dec. 1916, p. 668-71. *Iron age*, Nov. 30. 1916, Jan. 11, 1917, p. 1266, 138-9. *Iron trade review*, Feb. 22, 1917, p. 477-8. Condensed. *Journal of the American society of mechanical engineers*, Dec. 1916, p. 965-6. *Iron trade review*, Dec. 7, 1916, p. 1144-6. Kent, William. *Bookkeeping and cost accounting for factories.* 1918. p. 90. Discussion. *Journal of the American society of merchanical engineers*, March 1917, p. 215-7.

	% on cost	% on reducing balance
Fixtures, furniture and miscellaneous equipment:		
1. Steel shelving, lockers, etc.	5	12
2. Mechanical appliances, net additions	60	
3. Departmental wiring and electric fixtures, net additions	60	
4. Miscellaneous items (wood), net additions	70	

PORTERS, R. J. Rates of depreciation generally adopted. (In his *Pitman's dictionary of bookkeeping*. p. 344).

Furniture, fixtures and fittings 5-7½%
Based on diminishing balances.

ROBY, J. J. Schedule of plant depreciation. (In his *Treatise on cost accounting as applied to coal mining*. c1913. p. 14-5).

Office building—
Furniture and fixtures
Deduct as salvage before depreciating 10%
Depreciation rate for remainder, fireproof 6

SOME depreciation rates on buildings, machinery, shafting, belting, furniture and apparatus, tools and dies, moulds, lasts, patterns and drawings used by the Associated mutual fire insurance companies of Boston, Mass., in making appraisals of manufacturing properties. *Utilities magazine*, Jan. 1, 1916, p. 186-7.

A majority of objects making up the subject of furniture and apparatus are wearing out all the time and we deduct from 20 to 50 per cent.

SPICER, ERNEST EVAN and ERNEST C. PEGLER. Furniture fixtures and fittings. (In their *Practical auditing*. 1914. p. 145-6).

Furniture 5-12½ per cent per annum on the reducing instalment system

TIFFANY, H. S. Furniture and fixtures. (In his *Digest of depreciations*. c1890. p. 11, 13)

Store furniture and fixtures 10%
Furniture 10

DEPRECIATION, DEPLETION AND OBSOLESCENCE—FURNITURE AND FIXTURES—*(Continued)*

VARIOUS depreciation charges. *New York Times,* June 14, 1914.
Tools and fixtures 10%

WHATLEY, G. E. STUART. Depreciation. (In his *Accountant's and bookkeeper's vade-mecum.* 1893. p. 26).
Furniture, fixtures, etc. 7% upon diminishing value.

WILLIAMSON, J. GILMOUR. Depreciation of assets. (In his *Counting-house and factory organisation.* p. 142).
Furniture 7½%

WOODS, CLINTON E. Depreciation. (In his *Unified accounting methods for industrials.* 1917. p. 64-5).
Office furniture and equipment 15-20% per annum

Furniture coverings

PHILADELPHIA. CONTROLLER. Rates of depreciation. (In his *Manual of accounting, reporting and business procedure of the city and county of Philadelphia.* 1917. p. 207-8).
Furniture coverings 16⅔%

Furs

TIFFANY, H. S. Furs. (In his *Digest of depreciations.* c1890. p. 13).
Furs 10%

Fuse boxes

BARKER, HARRY. Typical life expectation tables for public utility property. (In his *Public utility rates.* 1917. p. 368-9).

	Years	
Fuse boxes	10-20	Wisconsin railroad commission

FOSTER, HORATIO A. Rates of depreciation. (In his *Engineering valuation of public utilities and factories.* 1913. p. 206).

	Years' life
Fuse boxes	10-12

Gages

BREWER, ALLEN F. Rates for annual depreciation. *Industrial management,* April 1918, p. 268.
Steam gages 33.3 years 3%

NICHOLSON, J. LEE and JOHN F. D. ROHRBACH. Depreciation. (In their *Cost accounting.* 1919. p. 150).
Gages 10%

WOODS, CLINTON E. Depreciation, dies, jigs, fixtures and gages. (In his *Unified accounting methods for industrials.* 1917. p. 65).
Gages 25 to 50% per annum according to their character and usage.

Galvanising

ELBOURNE, EDWARD T. Depreciation rates. (In his *Factory administration and accounts.* 1918. p. 377).

	Prov. dep. %	Years	
	Remainder values	10%	5%
Galvanising plant	12½	17	22

Games

PHILADELPHIA. CONTROLLER. Rates of depreciation. (In his *Manual of accounting, reporting and business procedure of the city and county of Philadelphia.* 1917. p. 209).
Games equipment 8⅓%

Garages

HOLLISTER, HORACE EDWARD. Depreciation. (In his *Practical garage accounting.* 1916. p. 78-9).
Machinery furniture and fixtures 10%
Small tools and used automobiles 20

PHILADELPHIA. CONTROLLER. Rates of depreciation. (In his *Manual of accounting, reporting and business procedure of the city and county of Philadelphia.* 1917. p. 210).
Garages 4%

Gardens

PHILADELPHIA. CONTROLLER. Rates of depreciation. (In his *Manual of accounting, reporting and business procedure of the city and county of Philadelphia.* 1917. p. 208).
Clipping, trimming, rolling, and watering equipment for lawn and garden:
Trimming lawn mower 12½
Rolling 3
Watering 12½
Lawn and garden tools and implements hose and reels 12½
Snow shovels, ice scrapers and planers 12½

Gas

See also various headings under Depreciation, depletion and obsolescence.

ALLOWANCE for depreciation on gas plant for income tax purposes. *Accountant,* Dec. 4, 1909, p. 700-2, 673-6.

ALWYN-SCHMIDT, W. L. Getting more out of existing plant. *American gas engineering journal,* March 6, 1920, p. 177-9.

AMERICAN ELECTRIC RAILWAY ASSOCIATION. COMMITTEE ON VALUATION. Bibliography on valuation of public utilities to December 23, 1915, 61 + 72p.

ARMSTRONG, CHARLES H. Depreciation and kindred matters. *Journal of gas lighting,* April 28, 1908, p. 223-7.

	Life years	Cost	percent	Annual depreciation £	s.	d.
Gasholder and underground tanks foundations, etc.	100	5,000	1	50	0	0
Buildings generally, roofs, boundary walls, gates, etc.	75	11,000	1⅓	146	13	4

DEPRECIATION, DEPLETION AND OBSOLESCENCE—GAS—*(Continued)*

Gasholders, purifiers, works mains, buildings for sulphate plant, etc.	40	11,300	2½	282	10	0
Stage flooring, bench bracing fittings, etc.	30	3,500	3⅓	116	13	4
Condensers, station meters, governors, distribution chambers, etc.	25	2,000	4	80	0	0
Condenser mains and tank, Livesey washers, exhausters, pumps, boilers, gas engines, electrical plant, locomotive, oxide shed, producer plant, retort-house, machinery, weighing machines, etc.	20	7,000	5	350	0	0
Scrubber-washers, sulphate plant, etc.	15	1,250	6⅔	83	6	8
				1109	3	4

BARKER, HARRY. Typical life expectation tables for public utility property. (In his *Public utility rates*. 1917. p. 368).

	Years	Authority	Control ‡
Gas works			
Blowers	15	Wis. R.R. Comm.	Det.
Ammonia Contractors.	15	" " "	Det.
Ammonia storage tanks	15	" " "	Det.
Coal-gas benches	25	" " "	Det.
Exhausters	25	" " "	Det.
Gas holders	50	" " "	Obs. and Det.
Governors	50	" " "	Det. and Obs.
Mains, small cast-iron (4 in. and under)	50	" " "	Obs.
Mains, large cast-iron (6 in. and over)	75	" " "	Obs.
small steel or iron (3 in. and under)	20	" " "	Det.
large steel or iron (above 3 in.)	30	" " "	Det.
Meter cases, station	50	" " "	Obs.
drums "	20	" " "	Det.
Meters and governors, consumers	25	" " "	Det.
Purifiers	50	" " "	Obs.
Scrubbers and condensers	30	" " "	Det.
Service pipes	20	" " "	Det.
Tar and ammonia wells	50	" " "	Obs.
Extractor	40	" " "	Obs.
Water-gas machines	30	" " "	Det.

‡ Probable action limiting service life; deterioration (due to wear and tear and weathering and obsoletion). Where both are cited, both actions have been observed, the first named predominating in a majority of cases.

BEGGS, JOHN I. Depreciation in gas plants. *American gas light journal,* July 6, 1908, p. 5.

BEGGS, JOHN I. Maintenance of plant. *Progressive age,* July 15, 1908, p. 427.

BRITTON, JOHN A. Depreciation. *Progressive age,* June 15, 1908, p. 379.
In the state of Mass. the Board of gas and electric light commissioners allow annually to the several companies a charge for depreciation approximately 3%, and allow all maintenance and ordinary repair charges in addition thereto, as does the P.S.C. of N.Y.

BRITTON, JOHN A. Pacific gas rate valuation. *Progressive age,* April 15, 1912, p. 330.

CASH, W. Gas accounts and finance. *Accountant,* Oct. 18, 1913, p. 543-55.
The appendix to this article on page 552, shows a form of agreement, accepted by the Board of Inland Revenue "Gas Undertakings other than those owned by municipal or other public authorities—Scheme for determining the income tax allowances to be granted for wear and tear and maintenance." Provisions for depreciation are made in this agreement and the following percentages are given:

Gasholders, including steel or iron, but not brick tanks, on written down value	3%
Meters (ordinary and prepayment), cookers and gas fires, on written down value	10%
Street services and house fittings, allowed as a revenue charge.	

CLASSIFICATION of depreciation percentages used at Dusseldorm municipal gas works. *Progressive age,* Aug. 15, 1910, p. 707.

	Present %	Proposed scale %	Life, years
Gas works building	3	5	44
Gas holders	6	6	37
Retort settings and apparatus	10	7.5	22-29
Railways about works	6	6	37
Mains	4	4	56
Meters	12.5	12.5	17
Average on book value	6.6	..	
Residual value after 33 years	10.6	..	
" " " 23 "		10	

COMPARATIVE costs between high and low pressure gas for lighting. *Gas age,* Sept. 1, 1913, p. 215.

Compressors	10%
Lamps	10
Fixtures	3
Interest on original cost	4

CONSOLIDATED GAS COMPANY OF NEW YORK. In re theoretical depreciation; a discussion of the subject with an analysis of a paper by Weber entitled "Accounting for depreciation" presented for the consideration of the Public service Commission for the 1st district, State of New York by the Consolidated gas company of New York; prepared by J. E. Allison. St. Louis, Dufton & Skinner, 1917. 155p.

DEPRECIATION, DEPLETION AND OBSOLESCENCE—GAS—(Continued)

CONTENTION over depreciation fund in attack on Cincinnati's union gas and electric company lease. *Electrical world,* July 5, 1913, p. 6-7.

DEPRECIATION. (*American gas light journal,* Sept. 5, 1910, p. 435. *Gas accounts.* 1902. p. 62, 63, 66, 67, 85.

DEPRECIATION allowance for income tax. *Journal of gas lighting,* Nov. 23, 1909, p. 517-8.

DEPRECIATION and income tax. *Journal of gas lighting,* June 18, 1912, p. 886.

No depreciation shall be allowed in respect of the plant, machinery, and mains, other than specified hereinafter; but in lieu thereof all expenditure on repairs and renewals is to be charged in the company's accounts for income tax purposes and allowed as working expenses, as and when incurred. All expenditure on extensions and improvements where debited against revenue to be distinguished and excluded from said allowances.

Gas holders:

In addition to repairs, depreciation shall be allowed at the rate of 3% per annum on the written down value. Such value not to include tanks, except where constructed of steel or iron, and in no case is the cost of excavation to be included in the value upon which the depreciation allowance is computed.

Meters ordinary & prepayment, cookers, & gas-fires:

In addition to repairs, allowance for depreciation shall be granted at the rate of 10% per annum on the written down value.

DEPRECIATION and income tax, the case of municipal undertakings. *Journal of gas lighting,* Jan. 7, 1913, p. 48.

DEPRECIATION as a factor in rates. *Electric railway review,* Nov. 9, 1909, p. 752.

DEPRECIATION in gas works. *Progressive age,* Oct. 15, 1912, p. 870-2.

Gas producer plant	3%
Gas mains & distribution	1½
Gas meters	5
Public lighting installation	5
Fixtures and miscellaneous tools, etc.	10

DEPRECIATION used for uniform accounts. *Public service,* May 1907, p. 147.

ELBOURNE, EDWARD T. Depreciation rates. (In his *Factory administration and accounts.* 1918. p. 376).

	Prov. dep. % Remainder values	Years 10%	5%
Gas lighting, high pressure installation	15	14	18
Gas mains, meters, piping and valves	6	37	48
Gas producer plant	7½	29	38

ERICKSON, H. Wisconsin method of depreciation accounting. *Gas age,* Aug. 1, 1914, p. 113-7.

FLOY, HENRY. Depreciation. (In his *Valuation of public utility properties.* 1912. p. 199).

The present laws of Massachusetts provide in respect to municipally owned gas or electric plants that there shall be included an amount for "depreciation equal to 3 per cent of the cost of the plant exclusive of land and water power appurtenant thereto"

	Per cent of gross revenue expended or appropriated for maintenance department	
Milwaukee companies		
Gas, electric light and steam heat department	6.15	8.12

FOSTER, HORATIO A. Methods of calculating depreciation. (In his *Engineering valuation of public utilities and factories.* 1913. p. 170).

	Min. ser. val. of reproduction cost
Gas plant	
Purifiers, old type, according to style and condition	25%
Consumer's meters	70

FOSTER, HORATIO A. Rates of depreciation. (In his *Engineering valuation of public utilities and factories.* 1913. p. 206-7).

Gas plants (Wisconsin Commissions).	
Benches	25%
Scrubbers and condensers	30
P. and A. tar extractors	40
Cast-iron washers	40
Exhausters	25
Purifiers, modern	50
Purifiers, old type, according to size and condition	. .
Cast-iron gas connections, within the plant	50
Station meter cases	50
Station meter drums	20
Ammonia concentrators	15
Ammonia storage tanks, wrought iron or steel	15
Tar and ammonia wells	50
Water gas machines complete	30
Centrifugal blowers	15
Holders	50
Governors	50
Cast-iron mains. 3" and 4"	50
Cast-iron mains. 6" and larger	75
Wrought-iron and steel mains under 3"	20
Wrought-iron and steel mains over 3"	30
Services	20
Consumers' meters	25
Consumers' governors	25
Retort house floors, depending on construction	15-30

Foundation for machinery, same life as machine they support.

DEPRECIATION, DEPLETION AND OBSOLESCENCE—GAS—*(Continued)*

GAS companies and depreciation. *Accountant,* Jan. 24, 1903, p. 109-12.
Buildings and plant 6%
Mains and service pipes 7½
Meters 10

GAS companies and depreciation. *Accountant,* Feb. 10, May 12, 1906, p. 161-3, 591-3.

GAS companies and depreciation. *Accountant,* March 19, 1910, p. 395-7.

GAS undertakings other than those owned by municipal or other authorities. Income tax and wear and tear. *Accountant,* Aug. 9, 1913, p. 181-2.
Written down value
Plant, machinery, and mains—no depreciation but in lieu thereof all expenditure on repairs and renewals is to be charged for income-tax purpose and allowed as working expenses as and when incurred.
Gas holders 3%
Meters 10
Services and fittings none, but in lieu thereof all expenditure is to be allowed as a trading expense as and when incurred.

GAS works and depreciation. *Accountant,* June 6, 1908, p. 819-22.

	years
Gasholders and underground tanks, foundations, etc.	100
Buildings generally, roofs, boundary walls, gates, etc.	75
Gas holders, purifiers, works, mains, buildings for sulphate plant, etc.	40
Stage flooring, bench bracing, fittings, etc.	30
Condensers, meters, governors, distribution chambers, etc.	25
Condensers mains and tanks, Livesey washers, exhausters, pumps, boilers, gas engines, electric plant, locomotive, oxide shed, producer plant, retort house machinery, weighing machinery, weighing machines, etc.	20
Scrubber washers, sulphate plant, etc.	15

GILLETTE, HALBERT P. and RICHARD T. DANA. Depreciation. (In their *Handbook of mechanical and electrical cost data.* 1918. p. 107).
Gas connections, c. i. (within the plant)
50 years Wisconsin railroad commission

GILLETTE, HALBERT P. and RICHARD T. DANA. Internal combustion engines. (In their *Mechanical and electrical cost data.* 1918. p. 626-7).
The fixed charges were apportioned for the steam and gas plants as follows:
depreciation 5%

GREAT BRITAIN. BOARD OF INLAND REVENUE. Depreciation rates. (In its *Income tax; statement respecting allowances for wear and tear and obsolescence of plant and machinery.* 1918. Cd. 9022, p. 4; Cd. 9134, p. 6.) *American economic review, Supplement,* Dec. 1920, p. 51. *Journal of accountancy,* Sept. 1920, p. 194.
Gas undertakings other than those owned by municipal or other public authoriites.
Gas holders 3%
Meters, cookers and gas fires 10
Written down value

GUTHRIE, EDWIN. Depreciation. (In Lisle, George. *Encyclopaedia of accounting.* v. 2. p. 375).
Gas works
Building and gas holders 2½ to 5%
Engines, etc. 5
Retorts, furnaces, etc. 10% on original outlay, plus a renewal fund for term of life chargeable to revenue.

HAYS, V. A. Depreciation of natural gas properties. *Progressive age,* v.30, p. 787-8.

HUMPHREYS, A. C. Depreciation of gas plants. *American gas institute,* 2nd annual report, p. 1-47.

INCOME tax and depreciation. *Journal of gas lighting,* Aug. 15, 1911, p. 281, 433.
Special Commissioners have allowed 2% on the value of gas holders and 5% on all other plant, including stoves and meters.

INCOME tax and depreciation allowances. *Accountant,* May 30, 1914, p. 785-8.

INCOME tax and depreciation; result of negotiation swith Inland revenue authorities; from the *Gas world. Accountant,* June 29, 1912, p. 986-90.

	Written down value
Plant, machinery and mains	none
Gas holders	3%
Meters (ordinary and prepayment) cookers and gas fires	10
Services and fittings	none

INCOME tax assessment; allowances for depreciation. *Accountant,* Oct. 2, 1909, p. 423-5, 400-2.

INCOME tax notes. *Accountant,* Sept. 28, May 11, 1918, p. 162-6, p. 359. *Incorporated accountants' journal,* May, Oct. 1918, p. 157, 14.
Gas undertakings other than those owned by municipal or other public authorities.
Written down value
Gas holders 3%
Meters, cookers, and gas fires 10%

INSTITUTE OF MUNICIPAL TREASURERS AND ACCOUNTANTS (INCORPORATED). Memorandum—depreciation: wear and tear allowances for income tax purpose on machinery and plant used for gas and tramway undertakings. *Accountant,* Jan. 18, 1913, p. 97-100.

INSTITUTE OF MUNICIPAL TREASURERS AND ACCOUNTANTS (INCORPORATED). Municipal corporations and companies working tramway and light railways, gas, water and electricity undertakings. *Accountant,* June 26, 1909, p. 906-8.

JONES, EDWARD DAVID. Depreciation. (In his *Investment,* p. 167).
Physical property of gas companies 3%

KING, ALDERMAN. Corporation gas works accounts. *Accountant,* Aug. 4, 11, 25, Sept. 8, 1888, p. 491-2, 496-7, 521-3, 541-2, 573-6.

DEPRECIATION, DEPLETION AND OBSOLESCENCE—GAS—*(Continued)*

MACK, EDWIN. Depreciation. *American gas light journal,* June 8, 1908, p. 971. *Progressive age,* June 15, 1908, p. 372-5. *Public service,* Aug. 1909, p. 42-5. *Water and gas review,* Aug. 1909, p. 29. Editorial. *Progressive age,* June 15, 1908, p. 362.

MANUFACTURERS LIGHT AND HEAT COMPANY OF PITTSBURGH, PA. Report of committee. *Commercial and financial chronicle,* July 23, 1910, p. 217.

Resolution to write off the following depreciation annually:

Pipe lines, pipe rigs and lines	6%
Gas regulators and meters	4
Fittings, other materials, telephone lines, boilers, buildings, and office furniture	5
Wells	8
Machinery, casing, pressure stations, water stations, horses and vehicles, tools and supplies, and miscellaneous	10%

Labor, hauling, rights of way and damages all written off.

MONTGOMERY, ROBERT H. Gas and oil wells—detailed regulations for determining depletion. (In his *Income tax procedure,* 1919, p. 602-9. ——— Same, 1920. p. 726, 788-9).

MULHALL, JOHN F. J. Depreciation. (In his *Quasi-public corporation accounting and management.* c1905. p. 180-3).

Gas 3-5%

MURRAY, ADAM. Corporation gas works accounts, depreciation and sinking fund. *Accountant,* Aug. 18, 1888, p. 521-3.

NELSON, BAILIE WALTER. Limitation and application of profits from municipal undertakings. *Accountant,* Aug. 3, 1912, p. 167-71. *Incorporated accountants' journal,* Oct. 1912, p. 15-7.

Scale of Depreciation in force in Glasgow gas undertaking:

On gasworks	1½ per cent per annum
On chemical works	3 " "
On pipes	2 " "
On meters	6 " "
On stoves	10 " "

NICHOLSON, J. LEE and J. F. D. ROHRBACH. Depreciation. (In their *Cost accounting.* 1919. p. 148).

Gas plant equipment:

Steel gas producers, piping, etc., including gas washers, gas scrubbers, gasometers, dust catchers, and dust collectors	6⅔%
Brick gas producers	6⅔
Gas supply system	6⅔
Gas plant equipment	6⅔

Based on (1) the cost of equipment
(2) the life of the equipment
(3) on a ten-hour day.

OFFICIAL allowance in respect of depreciation of machinery and plant. Board of Inland Revenue, Great Britain. *Accountant,* May 16, 1914, p. 738-40.

Gasholders	3%
Meters (ordinary and prepayment)	10

Written down value.

PENDER, HAROLD. Depreciation. (In his *Handbook for electrical engineers.* c1914. p. 337).

New York first district Public service commission has assumed the life of electric lighting and gas properties as a whole to be about 20 years.

PHILADELPHIA. CONTROLLER. Rates of depreciation. (In his *Manual of accounting, reporting and business procedure of the city and county of Philadelphia.* 1917. p. 205).

Coke and illuminating gas preparing equipment 10%

PROSSER, R. W. Depreciation in gas plants. *American gas light journal,* May 26, 1902, p. 767.

	Life in years	% of first cost
Buildings & foundations	40	0
Brick tanks	30	0
Gasholders	30	5
Steel tanks & holders	30	10
Benches	30	0
Condensers, scrubbers and purifiers	30	20
Station meters and governors	25	30
Engines	25	20
Boilers	15	10
Steel tanks	30	20
Pumps & piping	15	10
Pipe connections & valves	20	33
Water gas apparatus, including generators, superheaters, washbox, etc.	25	25
Cast iron mains	70	10
Services	25	0
Consumers' meters	30	0

PUBLIC utilities reports, annotated. Rochester, Lawyers co-operative publishing co.

See index under Depreciation.

PUBLIC utilities reports, annotated. Rochester, Lawyers co-operative publishing co. 1915A. p. 226.

El Reno v. El Reno gas & electric co. (Okla.). In an investigation of gas rates, an allowance of the minimum rate of 4 per cent annually for depreciation for purposes of a computation is not to be considered a determination by the Commission of the proper rate.

PUBLIC utilities reports, annotated. Rochester, Lawyers co-operative publishing co. 1915E. p. 197.

Re Southern counties gas co. (Cal.). An allowance of $100 per month for the depreciation of the property of a gas company, while possibly justifiable on a "depreciated value" theory, is too large where the company claims on an investment of $61,914.24, but on the basis of investment a proper depreciation annually should be provided by a sinking fund with interest at 6 per cent, which would result in an annuity not to exceed $486 for seven months.

DEPRECIATION, DEPLETION AND OBSOLESCENCE—GAS—(*Continued*)

PUBLIC utilities reports, annotated. Rochester, Lawyers co-operative publishing co. 1915F. p. 235.
Belleville v. St. Clair County gas & electric co. (Ill.). The Illinois Commission made an allowance of 3 per cent per annum to cover depreciation, obsolescence, inadequacy, etc., in valuing the property of a gas utility for rate making purposes.

PUBLIC utilities reports, annotated. Rochester, Lawyers co-operative publishing co. 1916A. p. 872, 936.
Re Colorado Springs light, heat & power co. (Colo.). An allowance of 3 per cent of the cost new of gas property was made to provide for depreciation on a straight-line basis
Re Broken Bow gas co. (Neb.). An annual allowance of not less than 8 per cent of the capitalized value of a gas plant was held necessary to provide for current repairs or maintenance and depreciation.

PUBLIC utilities reports, annotated. Rochester, Lawyers co-operative publishing co. 1916C. p. 281.
Springfield v. Springfield gas & electric co. (Ill.). An allowance of 1.89 per cent, equal to 6.5 cents a 1,000 feet of gas, was held sufficient for annual depreciation in fixing gas rates.

PUBLIC utilities reports, annotated. Rochester, Lawyers co-operative publishing co. 1916D. p. 740, 825.
West Allis v. West Allis gas co. (Wis.). An allowance of 2 per cent for depreciation was held ample in estimating the cost of artificial gas service.
Hermann v. Newtown gas co. (N. Y. 1st Dist.). An annual allowance of $25,000 for depreciation including contingencies, to be increased $2,500 a year on account of additions, was held adequate for a gas system valued at $1,600,000 some replacements being charged to repair accounts.

PUBLIC utilities reports, annotated. Rochester, Lawyers co-operative publishing co. 1916E. p. 1, 1072, 1073.
Commercial Club v. Citizen's gas & fuel co. (Ind.). An annual allowance of 1½ per cent to provide a depreciation fund was made in fixing gas rates.
In Marshall v. St. Joseph gas co. Cases Nos. 293, 455, and 533, decided November 27, 1915, rehearing finally denied February 23, 1916, the Missouri Commission held that no allowance in a gas rate case need be made from income for a depreciation reserve, but only for surplus and contingencies, where $30,000 has been set aside for depreciation, each year for nine years for a plant valued at $1,620,000, and no renewals and replacements had been charged against the fund. Kennish, Commissioner, said: "In a number of cases this Commission has announced the rule that in a rate-making case, where the utility has been many years in service, there should be set aside from income a sum amply sufficient for renewals and replacements for the ensuing year and for surplus and contingencies, but not for the purpose of building up a large depreciation reserve, upon the theory that the plant would be worn out at some future date, and that a sufficient reserve should then be on hand to reimburse the investor. In this case as realized depreciation (renewals and replacements) was not charged to the sum reserved for that purpose, we need not provide for that out of income, but only for surplus and contingencies.
Palo Alto v. Palo gas co. (1913), Cal. R. C. R. 300. An annual allowance of 7 per cent for depreciation was held too high for an artificial gas transmission system, Palo.

PUBLIC utilities reports, annotated. Rochester, Lawyers co-operative publishing co. 1917A. p. 577.
Re Clarksburg light & heat co. (W. Va.) The depreciation of a natural gas company is more rapid than that of other utilities.
Re Clarksburg light & heat co. (W. Va.) An annual allowance of 10 per cent of the preent value of a natural gas system was held to be sufficient for a depreciation fund, upon taking into consideration the value of the recoverable material, that the life of the utility will be between five and ten years, and that its land, in so far as the drilling of new wells is concerned, will be finally developed within three or four years, when decreased production will have to be met, if met at all by the purchase of gas.

PUBLIC utilities reports, annotated. Rochester, Lawyers co-operative publishing co. 1917B. p. 300, 384.
Re Richmond light, heat and power co., (Ind.). Two per cent was held to be the proper depreciation account to be carried by a natural gas utility.
Murchie v. St. Croix gaslight co. (Me.) An allowance of 1.67 per cent was made for depreciation of a gas system in determining the annual operating expense, the allowance having been adopted by complainants, and not question by the utility.

PUBLIC utilities reports, annotated. Rochester, Lawyers co-operative publishing co. 1917D. p. 426.
Re Osage & O. Co. (Okla.). Depreciation for a natural gas utility was estimated at 10 per cent on the entire physical property where a large portion of the property had already depreciated 50 per cent and other portions of the property do not depreciate at the rate of 10 per cent per annum.

PUBLIC utilities reports, annotated. Rochester, Lawyers co-operative publishing co. 1918A. p. 506.
San Francisco v. Pacific gas & electric co. (Cal.). The depreciation annuity for a gas plant was fixed on the 6 per cent sinking fund basis, rather than on the straight line basis.

PUBLIC utilities reports, annotated. Rochester, Lawyers co-operative publishing co. 1918B. p. 762.
Re Indiana fuel & light co. (Ind.). A proper rate for depreciation of an artificial gas plant was found to be 2 per cent of its present value, less the value of land and materials and supplies.

PUBLIC utilities reports, annotated. Rochester, Lawyers co-operative publishing co. 1918C. p. 193, 224, 475.
Re United fuel gas co. (W. Va.). A natural gas company was held entitled to set aside annually as depreciation reserve, 7 per cent of the value of its production investment, 5 per cent of the value of its transmission investment, and 4 per cent of the value of its distribution and general investment.
Re Light, fuel & power co. (W. Va.). Case nos. 554, 555, Dec. 1, 1917. Annual allowances of 5 and 6 per cent were held sufficient for depreciation of natural gas distributing plants although a higher percentage would be necessary for a producing company.
In Re Valley natural gas co. Decision no. 4485. Application no. 2620, July 27, 1917, the

DEPRECIATION, DEPLETION AND OBSOLESCENCE—GAS—*(Continued)*

California Commission fixed the depreciation annuity at 7 per cent for a natural gas distributing company.

Re West Virginia traction & electric co. (W. Va.) Case no. 568, Oct. 29, 1917. An annual allowance of 8 per cent was made for accruing depreciation of a natural gas plant in a proceedings to determine the reasonableness of natural gas rates.

In Re Vinita gas co. Cause no. 2890, order no. 1335, Sept. 27, 1917, it was held that a larger depreciation reserve must be set up in the case of a natural gas company, whose supply was likely to be exhausted within a few years, than in a case where there was a reasonable assurance of a supply for a longer period of years. It was also held that the fact that the character of the soil caused the rapid deterioration in the pipes should be considered.

PUBLIC utilities reports, annotated. Rochester, Lawyers co-operative publishing co. 1918D. p. 121. p. 121.

Re Monmouth Public service co. (Ill.). An annual allowance of $2,100 equivalent to about 7 cents per 1,000 feet of gas sold, was made for depreciation in fixing rates for a gas system valued at $145,000.

PUBLIC utilities reports, annotated. Rochester, Lawyers co-operative publishing co. 1918E. p. 680, 728.

In People's Power Co. (Ill.) No. 7642, May 14, 1918, it was held that a sum equivalent to 6½ cents per 1,000 cubic feet of gas sold be set aside for annual depreciation.

Central Illinois Public service co. (Ill.). No 7617, May 28, 1918, it was found that a sum equal to 7½ cents per 1,000 cubic feet of gas sold should be set aside to cover accruing depreciation.

In Central Illinois Public service co. (Ill.). No. 7618, May 13, 1918, an application for increased gas rates, the Commission found that a sum equal to 8 cents per 1,000 cubic feet of gas sold should be set aside annually for depreciation.

Seattle v. Seattle lighting co. (Wash.). An annual allowance of 2.18 per cent of the plant value was made to provide for depreciation on a straight line basis, in fixing rates for a gas utility.

PUBLIC utilities reports, annotated. Rochester, Lawyers co-operative publishing co. 1918F. p. 872.

An annual allowance for depreciation amounting to 20 cents per thousand cubic feet of gas generated less actual cost of repairs is excessive, 10 cents per thousand cubic feet being adequate. Re Queens Borough Gas & Electric Co. (N. Y.).

PUBLIC utilities reports, annotated. Rochester, Lawyers co-operative publishing co. 1919B. p. 749, 750, 1073.

In Re La Porte gas & electric co. Nos. 3774-3777, Aug. 10, 1918, the Indiana Commission held that the company should set aside annually for depreciation 2 per cent of the value of its depreciable gas property.

In Re Northern Indiana gas & electric co. (Ind.). No. 4116, Jan. 15, 1919, a gas utility was ordered to set aside annually, beginning at the end of the temporary period for which rates were fixed, 1½ per cent of the value of its property other than lands, materials, and supplies, for depreciation.

Re San Diego Consol. gas & electric co. (Cal.). Decision no. 5158, Application no. 3294. Feb. 25, 1918. A sum of $56,000 computed on the 6 per cent sinking fund basis was allowed for a depreciation annuity for a gas plant with a rate value of $3,102,255.

In Washington water, light & power co. v. Washington, no. 3842, Nov. 4, 1918, the Indiana Commission fixed 2 per cent of the value of the gas plant less the value of lands, materials, supplies, and working capital, as a proper allowance for depreciation.

In Re Southern Illinois light & power co., no. 8068, Oct. 29, 1918, the Illinois Commission held that the gas company operating in Litchfield was entitled to a return of 8 cents per 1,000 cubic feet of gas sold as an allowance for depreciation.

In Re San Joaquin light & power corporation decision. No. 5449. Application no. 3531. May 28, 1918, the California Commission said that it was reasonable to assume a fifteen-year life for a gas main.

In Re Granite City gas light & fuel co. (Ill.) no. 8013, Sept. 18, 1918, the company was allowed for accruing depreciation a sum equal to 7 cents per thousand cubic feet of gas sold.

In Re Central Illinois public service co. (Ill.). No. 7619, July 16, 1918, a gas company was held entitled to an annual allowance for depreciation of 8 cents per thousand cubic feet of gas sold.

Re Northern Indiana gas & electric co. (Ind.), 507. A gas utility was ordered to set aside annually on the expiration of a temporary period for which rates are fixed 1½ per cent of the value of its property other than lands, materials, and supplies, for depreciation.

PUBLIC utilities reports, annotated. Rochester, Lawyers co-operative publishing co. 1919D. p. 645.

Re Utah gas & coke co. (Utah) 645. An allowance of 2 per cent annually of the value of the depreciable property of a gas company was authorized as a depreciation reserve such reserve to make unnecessary the setting up of special reserve accounts hitherto carried by the company on particular items of physical property.

PUBLIC utilities reports, annotated. Rocheser, Lawyers co-operative publishing co. 1919F. p. 169, 170, 1053.

In Re Northern Indiana gas & electrical co. No. 4243, April 10, 1919, the Indiana Commission required a gas company to set aside annually for depreciation 1.5 per cent of the value of this depreciable property.

Re Brazil gas co. (Ind.) 253. A gas utility was ordered to set aside annually, for depreciation, 2 per cent of the value of its depreciable property including future additions, extensions, and improvements.

In Re Fuel gas co (Ind.), No. 4262, Feb. 10, 1919, a natural gas company was allowed 5 per cent of the value of its property annually for depreciation of its mains and depletion of its wells.

PUBLIC utilities reports, annotated. Rochester, Lawyers co-operative publishing company, 1920A, p. 877, 414.

Re Bismarck gas co. (N. D.) In view of the fact that a gas company had set aside no depreciation reserve during the two years of its operation it was allowed to set aside an amount equal to 2¾ per cent of the present value out of the net surplus resulting from increased rates authorized by the commission.

DEPRECIATION, DEPLETION AND OBSOLESCENCE—GAS—*(Continued)*

Re Indiana Fuel and light co. (Ind.). Indiana commission made an allowance of 1½ per cent on the approximate value of the depreciable property of a gas company for annual depreciation.

PUBLIC utilities reports, annotated. Rochester, Lawyers co-operative publishing company, 1920B. p. 726, 149.

Re Freeport gas co. (Ill.). A gas company, the value of whose plant was fixed at $525,000 for rate making purposes, was allowed to set aside annually for accruing depreciation, the sum of $7,020, plus 1½% of all depreciable additions and betterments to the property.

Holland v. McGuire (Mich.). Michigan commission made an allowance of 2 per cent for the annual depreciation of a gas plant.

PUBLIC utilities reports, annotated. Rochester, Lawyers co-operative publishing company, 1920C, p. 510, 960.

In Re Consolidated light & p. co. nos. 6988-A, 6989-A, Oct. 20, 1919, the Illinois commission made an allowance of 1.75 per cent on the fair value of a gas property for depreciation.

Re Lawrenceburg gas co. no. 4650, Sept. 22, 1919, the Indiana commission required a gas plant company to set aside a depreciation allowance of $800 annually, where the present value of the property was fixed at $28,563.

Re Monarch gas co. (Ind.). An allowance of 5 per cent was made for the depreciation of a natural gas plant.

PUBLIC utilities reports, annotated. Rochester, Lawyers co-operative publishing company, 1920D, p. 257, 979, 470, 428.

Hoff v. Elmira water, light & R. co. (N. Y. 2d dist.). New York commission, Second district, made an allowance of 2 per cent for the depreciation of the plant of natural gas distributing company.

Re Illinois northern utilities co. (Ill.). Illinois commission made an allowance equivalent to 7.5 cents per 1000 cubic feet of gas sold for accruing depreciation.

Re Northern Indiana gas & E. co. (Ind.). Indiana commission made an allowance of 1½ per cent for the depreciation of the property of a gas company.

Re Wisconsin-Minnesota light & p. co. (Wis.). Wisconsin commission made an allowance of 2 per cent for the annual depreciation of a gas plant.

PUBLIC utilities reports, annotated. Rochester, Lawyers co-operative publishing company, 1920E, p. 930, 558, 710, 461.

Maires v. Flatbush gas company. New York commission made an allowance of $60,000 for the depreciation of an electric plant, the rate base of which was fixed at $1,300,000.

Milne v. Montpelier & Barre light & power company. Vermont commission made an allowance of .0273 upon the appraised value of the depreciable property of a hydro-electric plant as an allowance for the annual depreciation.

Re Peoples power company. Illinois commission made an allowance of 1.75 per cent of the rate-making value of a gas plant for annual depreciation to which should be added 1.75 per cent of the net betterments to the property in each year.

Re Rockford gas light & coke company. Illinois commission made an allowance of 7 cents per thousand cubic feet for gas sold for accruing depreciation.

PUBLIC utilities reports, annotated. Rochester, Lawyers co-operative publishing company, 1920F, p. 970, 875, 607, 485, 586.

Re Muskegon traction & lighting company. In fixing the rates of a gas company, the Michigan commission made an allowance of 2 per cent of the total value of the depreciable property and an allowance for replacing worn-out, inadequate or obsolete portions of the plant.

Re Peoples natural gas company. Indiana commission made an allowance of 1 per cent for the depreciation of natural gas property, where the company had maintained no depreciation reserve, and the cost of drilling wells to replace exhausted wells was charged directly to operating expenses.

Re Columbus gas light company. The Indiana commission required a gas company to set aside 1½ per cent of the value of the depreciable property as an allowance for depreciation.

Re Consolidated gas company v. Charles D. Newton. In determining the rate base of a gas utility, the court declined to make any allowance for accrued depreciation.

Re Laporte gas and electric company. A gas company was ordered to set aside annually for depreciation 2% of the value of its depreciable gas property.

SAUNDERS, GEORGE B. Utility appraisals. *Electric railway journal*, May 22, 1915, p. 984-5.

SCHACKLETTE, ROYAL. Depreciation: an item in the manufacture and sale of gas. *American gas light journal*, July 8, 1910, p. 106. *Progressive age gazette*, Sept. 15, 1910, p. 814-7.

WHITTEN, ROBERT. Annual depreciation allowance. (In his *Valuation of public service corporations*. v. 2. 1914, p. 428-9, 429, 1197-8, 1198).

One and seven-tenths per cent allowance on sinking fund basis in Cedar Rapids, Iowa, gas rate case, 1909. Two per cent allowance in Chicago gas rate report by W. H. Hagenah, 1911. New Jersey commission—Re rates of the public service gas company—5%. New York commission, second district—In Buffalo gas company v. city of Buffalo—the average life of the whole to be 35 years. Allowance of 5.3 cents per thousand cubic feet sold.

WHITTEN, ROBERT H. Bibliography. (In his *Valuation of public service corporations*. 1914. p. 740-1).

WHITTEN, ROBERT H. Valuation of public service corporations; legal and economic phases of valuation for rate making and public purchase. 2v. New York, Banks law publishing co. 1914. 1500p. See index under Depreciation.

WILSON, ALEXANDER. Inaugural address of the president. *Institute of gas engineering, Transactions*, 1911, p. 51. Abstract. Gas acts; question of depreciation. *Journal of gas lighting*, June 13, 1911, p. 728.

WISCONSIN railroad commission orders a reduction in rates of the Milwaukee gas light company. *Electrical world*, Sept. 6, 1913, p. 466-7.

Depreciation was provided for at the rate of 2.5 per cent on the depreciable property.

Gas holders

BARKER, HARRY. Typical life expectation tables for public utility property. (In his *Public utility rates*. 1917. p. 368).

Gas holders	50 years	Wis. R. R. Comm.

DEPRECIATION, DEPLETION AND OBSOLESCENCE—Gas holders—*(Continued)*

CASH, W. Gas accounts and finance. *Accountant,* Oct. 18, 1913, p. 543-55.
Gas holders, including steel or iron but not brick tanks—3% written down value

CLASSIFICATION of depreciation percentages used at Dusseldorf municipal gas works. *Progressive age,* Aug. 15, 1910, p. 707.
Gas holders
Present % 6
Proposed scale % 6
Life, years 37

FOSTER, HORATIO A. Rates of depreciation. (In his *Engineering valuation of public utilities and factories.* 1913. p. 207). Years' life
Holders 50

GAS undertakings other than those owned by municipal or other authorities income tax and wear and tear. *Accountant,* Aug. 9, 1913, p. 181-2.
Gasholders 3%

GILLETTE, HALBERT P. and RICHARD T. DANA. Depreciation. (In their *Handbook of mechanical and electrical cost data.* 1918. p. 108).
Holders (gas plant) 50 years Wis. R. R. Comm.

GREAT BRITAIN. BOARD OF INLAND REVENUE. Depreciation rates. (In its *Income tax; statement respecting allowances for wear and tear and obsolescence of plant and machinery.* 1918. Cd. 9022, p. 4; Cd. 9134, p. 6). *American economic review,* Supplement, Dec. 1920, p. 51. *Journal of accountancy,* Sept. 1920, p. 194.
Gas undertakings other than those owned by municipal or other public authorities.
Gas holders 3%
Written down value

GRUNSKY, CARL EWALD. Probable useful life of various articles. (In his *Valuation, depreciation and the rate-base.* 1917. p. 279).
Gas holders 50 years
Wisconsin Railroad Commission. Quoted by H. A. Foster and in published reports.

INCOME tax and depreciation. *Journal of gas lighting,* Aug. 1, 15, 1911, p. 281, 433.
Special commissioners (Great Britain) have allowed 2% on the value of gas holders.

INCOME tax and depreciation; results of negotiations with Inland revenue authorities from the Gas world. *Accountant,* June 29, 1912, p. 986-90.
Gas holders 3%

INCOME tax notes. *Accountant,* May 11, Sept. 28, 1918, p. 359, 162-6. *Incorporated accountants' journal,* May, Oct. 1918, p. 157, 14. Written down value
Gas holder 3%

OFFICIAL allowance in respect of depreciation of machinery and plant—Board of Inland revenue, Great Britain. *Accountant,* May 16, 1914, p. 738-40.
Gasholders: In addition to repairs, depreciation should be allowed at the rate of 3 per cent per annum on the written down value. Such value not to include tanks, except where constructed of steel or iron, and in no case is the cost of excavation to be included in the value upon which the depreciation allowance is computed.

PROSSER, R. W. Depreciation in gas plants. *American gas light journal,* May 26, 1902, p. 767.
Gasholders 30 years 5% of first cost

Gas retorts

FOSTER, HORATIO A. Rates of depreciation. (In his *Engineering valuation of public utilities and factories.* 1913. p. 205).
Brick gas retort houses. 30 years' life. Wisconsin railroad commission.

GILLETTE, HALBERT P. and R. T. DANA. Depreciation. (In their *Handbook of mechanical and electrical cost data.* 1918. p. 106).
Buildings, gas retort houses, brick. 30 years, Wisconsin railroad commission.

GRUNSKY, CARL EWALD. Probable life of various articles. (In his *Valuation, depreciation and the rate-base.* 1917. p. 274).
Brick gas retort. 30 years. Wisconsin railroad commission. Quoted by H. A. Foster and in published reports.

WHATLEY, G. E. STUART. Depreciation, blast furnaces, gas retorts, chemical and other similar fixed plant. (In his *Accountant's and bookkeeper's vade-mecum.* 1893. p. 25).

Gas wells

GRUNSKY, CARL EWALD. Probable useful life of various articles. (In his *Valuation, depreciation and the rate-base.* 1917. p. 286).
gas wells— 10 years. 0% residual value.
California railroad commission—Reports 1913-4.
Midway gas co. et. al case.
gas well drilling equip. 10 years. 25% residual value.
California. Railroad Commission. Reports 1913-4.
Midway gas co. et. al case.

NICHOLSON, J. LEE and JOHN F. D. ROHRBACH. Depreciation. (In their *Cost accounting.* 1919. p. 146).
Wells—gas 10%

Gates

METCALF, LEONARD. Water-works valuation and fair rates, in the light of the Maine supreme court decisions in the Waterville and Brunswick cases. *American society of civil engineers,* 1908, p. 1101-73. *American society of civil engineers, Transactions,* Sept. 1909, p. 1. Foster, Horatio A. *Engineering valuation of public utilities and factories,* 1913, p. 207. Gillette, H. P. *Handbook of cost data for contractors and engineers,* p. 797.

	Useful life	Annual contribution to depreciation account or sinking fund in per cent. of cost: At 5% annual rate sinking fund	General approximate results
Gates	**40-50 years**	**0.8278-0.477%**	**1-½%**

DEPRECIATION, DEPLETION AND OBSOLESCENCE—*(Continued)*

Gavels

PHILADELPHIA. CONTROLLER. Rates of depreciation. (In his *Manual of accounting, reporting and business procedure of the city and county of Philadelphia.* 1917. p. 207-8).

Gavels 5%

Gear cases

BRYAN, WILLIAM. Appraisal and depreciation of water-works and similar properties. *Journal of the association of engineering societies,* Dec. 1907, p. 336-81. Depreciation allowance for various public-service industries. *Engineering news,* Jan. 23, 1908, p. 96.

	% straight
Gear cases	20

Gear cutting machines

ELBOURNE, EDWARD T. Depreciation rates. (In his *Factory administration and accounts.* 1918. p. 377.

	Prov. dep. %	years	
	Remainder values	10%	5%
Gear cutting machines			
Hobbing	6	37	48
Milling	6	37	48
Planing	6	37	48

Gearing

ELBOURNE, EDWARD T. Depreciation rates. (In his *Factory administration and accounts.* 1918. p. 376).

	Prov. dep. %	years	
	Remainder values	10%	5%
Gearing, toothed	7½	29	38

PHILADELPHIA. CONTROLLER. Rates of depreciation. (In his *Manual of accounting, reporting and business procedure of the city and county of Philadelphia.* 1917. p. 205).

Shafting, belting, pulleys, gearing, etc. 4%

Generators

AMERICAN WATER WORKS ASSOCIATION. Final report of committee on depreciation. *Journal of the American waterworks association,* Sept. 1917, p. 1-38.

Electric generators and motors 20-30 years

ANALYSIS of the premises adopted and methods used in determining the cost to reproduce new together with the depreciation thereon of the physical property of the Metropolitan system and the Kansas City and Westport Belt railway of Kansas City, Mo. *Engineering and contracting,* May 28. 1913, p. 617-20.

Slow-speed generators 4%
High-speed generators. 5
Belt driven generators 5
Generator leads 3

AUSTRALIA. FEDERAL INCOME TAX DEPARTMENT. Depreciation allowance. *Accountant,* Oct. 13, 1917, p. 277-9. *Accounting and commerce,* June 30, 1917, p. 55-7. *Federal accountant,* July 1917, p. 93-8. *Public accountant,* Jan. 30, 1917, p. 145-52.

Alternators, dynamos, motor-generators, rotary converters 5%
Written down value, repairs allowed.

BARKER, HARRY. Typical life expectation tables for public utility property. (In his *Public utility rates.* 1917. p. 368-9).

Generators, motors and converters.
high speed 15 years.
slow speed 20 "
new types 20 " Wis. R. R. commission.
old types 15 " " " "
turbine driven 20 " " " "

Where no authority is cited the data are those of the author—average or approximate figures secured by examination or enquiry.

BAY state rate case. *Electric railway journal,* Dec. 4, 1915, p. 1121-3. *Public utility reports, annotated,* 1916F, p. 336-9.

	years
Turbo-generators	20
Generators—d. c.	30-40

BELT, ROBERT E. Depreciation. (In his *Foundry cost accounting practice and procedure.* 1919. p. 243).

Electric generators and switch boards 7½%

BELT, ROBERT E. Depreciation. (In his *Uniform cost accounting methods; adopted by the American malleable castings association,* Nov. 14, 1917. 22p. + forms.

Steam boiler, generator, air compressor, steam piping, electric wiring, etc. 7½%

BREWER, ALLAN F. Rates for annual depreciation. *Industrial management,* April 1918, p. 268.

Electric generators (complete) 30 years 3.33%

BRYAN, WILLIAM. Appraisal and depreciation of water-works and similar properties. *Journal of the Association of engineering societies,* Dec. 1907, p. 336-81. Depreciation allowance for various public-service industries. *Engineering news,* Jan. 23, 1908, p. 96.

BRYAN, WILLIAM H. Depreciation of electric light plants. *Municipality,* March 1908, p. 74.

Engines and generators

Material	Life in Years	% Dep. per year Straight	Sinking fund	Authority
Generators				
Belted	10-20			Dawson's Engineering and electric traction pocket-book in Iowa Engineer, July 1906.

DEPRECIATION, DEPLETION AND OBSOLESCENCE—GENERATORS—*(Continued)*

Direct connected	12.5-25		Dawson's Engineering and electric traction pocket-book in Iowa Engineer, July 1906.
Generators	15		The author
"		7-12	N. S. Hill: Engineering record, June 8, 1901.
"	25		Robt. Hammond: Engineering record, June 15, 1907.
"	10-20		Dawson's Engineering and electric traction pocket book in Iowa engineer, July 1906.
"		3	Chicago city railway, Street railway, journal, Dec. 1898.

CLADER, WILL-A. Water utilities accounting. *Journal of accountancy,* Aug. 1919, p. 91-2.
The following rate is used frequently when wear and tear are made good by operating maintenance.

Electric generators and motors	4%

COST and depreciation of steam and hydro-electric installations. *Electrical world,* Dec. 30, 1909, p. 1558.

	years	% of total cost
Generators and transformers	25	.898%

CRAVENS, GEORGE W. Depreciation and maintenance of electrical equipment. *Electrical review,* April 23, 1910, p. 853-6. Foster, H. A. *Engineering valuation of public utilities and factories.* 1913. p. 201-2. Montgomery, Robert H. *Auditing theory and practice.* 1916, p. 424. Montgomery, Robert H. *Income tax procedure.* 1919, p. 570. ——— Same, 1920, p. 723-4.

	Light or intermittent service	Heavy or Continuous service
Generators		
Belted	4-6.6%	5-8.3%
Direct connected	3-5	4-6.6

Belted	Direct connected	Authority
5-10	5	Chicago traction commission
6.6	6.6	Chicago union traction co.
7.5	7.5	Milwaukee electric railway and light co.
5	5	Wisconsin railroad commission
5	5	Average English
5	5	Average Scotch practice
5-10	4-8	Philip Dawson
5	5	Stone & Webster
6.6	4	Industrial power plants
3.3-4	3.3-4	Prof. G. F. Gebhardt
7.5	5	Miscellaneous sources.

DEPRECIATION of the equipment of an electric plant. *Electrical world,* Dec. 12, 1914, p. 1161.

Boilers, piping and generators	4.7-4.8%

ELBOURNE, EDWARD T. Depreciation rates. (In his *Factory administration and accounts.* 1918. p. 376).

	Prov. dep. % Remainder values	years 10%	years 5%
Generators, electric, alternators	7½	29	38
Generators, continuous current (dynamos)	7½	29	38
Generators, turbo	7½	29	38

ENNIS, WILLIAM DUANE. Depreciation. (In his *Works management.* 1911. p. 86).

Electric generators.	30 years life to 8% residual value.

FLOY, HENRY. Depreciation. Floy, Henry. Depreciation as related to electrical properties. *American Institute of electrical engineers, Proceedings,* 1911, p. 1267. Floy, Henry, *Valuation of public utility properties,* 1912, p. 168-217. Foster, H. A. *Engineering valuation of public utilities and factories.* 1913. p. 194-8. *Engineering and contracting,* Oct. 4, 1911, p. 359-65. *Engineering magazine,* Aug. 1911, p. 837-40.

Material	Depreciation percent per year straight line		
Generators	3-8	Trac. val. comm.	Chicago con. trac. co.
	5	B. J. Arnold	Coney Island & Brooklyn adopted by P. S. C., N. Y.
	5	Henry Floy	3rd. Ave. case, adopted by P. S. C., N. Y.
modern type	5	Wisconsin P. S. C.	
obsolete type	6⅔	Wisconsin P. S. C.	
steam turbo	5	Wisconsin P. S. C.	
	10	Arbitrators	Street lighting controversy, Atlanta, Ga. 1899.
	6⅔	St Louis P. S. C.	Union Elec. L. & P. Co.

FOSTER, HORATIO A. Methods of calculating depreciation. (In his *Engineering valuation of public utilities and factories.* 1913. p. 169).

	Minimum service value, % of reproduction cost.	
Electric generators, motors and rotaries	modern type	20
	obsolete type	15

Joint engineering department of the Wisconsin commissions.

DEPRECIATION, DEPLETION AND OBSOLESCENCE—GENERATORS—*(Continued)*

FOSTER, HORATIO A. Rates of depreciation. (In his *Engineering valuation of public utilities and factories.* 1913. p. 200).

Turbines and generators	6%
Marwick, Mitchell & Co. in the appraisal of a large street railway system.	

FOSTER, HORATIO A. Rates of depreciation. (In his *Engineering valuation of public utilities and factories.* 1913. p. 205).

Generators, motors and rotaries	
Modern	20 years
Obsolete	15
Turbo generators	20

GILLETTE, HALBERT P. AND RICHARD T. DANA. Depreciation. (In their *Handbook of mechanical and electrical cost data.* 1918. p. 108, 695).

Generators	12.5-33.3 years Traction valuation commission. Chicago consolidated traction co. 15-20 years Union traction co., case Chicago and union traction co., Stone & Webster 20 years B. J. Arnold—Appraisal of the Coney Island & Brooklyn railroad, Feb. 1, 1909 Henry Floy, 3rd. Av. case, N. Y. city W. D. Pence, Milwaukee, 3c. case B. J. Arnold, Chicago appraisals, 4 cases
belted	10-20 years Chicago traction commission 13.3 years Milwaukee electric railway and light co. 15 years George W. Cravens, Industrial power plants
direct connected	13.3 years Milwaukee electric railway & light Co. 20 years Chicago traction commission 25 years George W. Cravens, Industrial power plants
modern type	20 years Wisconsin railroad commission
obsolete	15 years Wisconsin railroad commission
steam-turbo	15 years St. Louis public service commission, Union electric light and power co. 20 years Wisconsin railroad commission 10 years Arbitrators, street lighting controversy, Atlanta, Ga. 1899
turbo-generators	16.7 years Marwick, Mitchell & co., appraisal of a large street railway system, Foster, p. 199
Hydro-electric plants—generators	2%

GILLETTE, HALBERT P. AND RICHARD T. DANA. Depreciation. (In their *Handbook of mechanical and electrical cost data.* 1918. p. 116-8.)

TABLE III.

Useful Life of Reciprocating Engines and Generators

	Type of equipment				Time of service		
	Reciprocating engines		Generators		Started	Closed	Useful life
Company	No.	Size in h.p.	No.	Size in kw.			years
1	1	Corliss			1906	1911	4½
2	1	150	2	45	1891	1907	16
	2	200	4	65	1891	1907	16
	1	150	2	50	1893	1909	16
	3	225	6	75	1893	1909	16
	1	1250	2	400	1894	1915	21
	4	600	8	200	1894	1915	21
	5	1200	10	400	1895	1915	20
	1	3500	1	2500	1901	1915	14
	1	Corliss	2	1000	1902	1915	13
	1	5000	1	3500	1902	1915	13
	1	2500	1	1800	1903	1915	12
	4	200	8	80	1888	1894	6
3	High speed		Edison d. c.		1887	1893	6
	Compound		a. c. single phase		1893	1905	12
			a. c.		1890	1907	16
	5	Allis Chalmers			1904	1915	11
5	Cross comp.				1891	1905	14

Average life, 50 generators, 16 years.

Average life, 34 reciprocating engines, 14 years

Following is the key to names of companies given. Also the reasons for retiring the various units.

No.	Company name	Remarks,
1	Nevada California power co.	Equipment replaced by turbine plant, larger unit

DEPRECIATION, DEPLETION AND OBSOLESCENCE—GENERATORS—*(Continued)*

2	Commonwealth Edison co. 27th street, North Clark street, Harrison st., Adams st. stations	Entire plants abandoned
3	Consumers power co. Jackson station	Replaced by a.c. single phase Curtis turbine
4	Union electric light & power co. 10th 19th and 20th st. stations	Entire plants abandoned, obsolete
5	Indianapolis light & heat co. Kentucky avenue station	Obsolete, but used for steam heating

GREENLAND, S. W. Depreciation. *Mississippi electric association, Report of second annual convention held June 1910,* p. 32-6.

	Life
Generators	12-25 years.

GRUNSKY, CARL EWALD. Probable useful life of various articles. (In his *Valuation, depreciation and the rate-base.* 1917. p. 278).

Generators	10 years Board of Arbitration in street lighting controversy at Atlanta, Georgia, 1899
	15 years St. Louis public service commission. Case of Union electric light and power co.
	15 years Chicago union traction co. Quoted in report Wisconsin railroad commission, vol. 10, p. 220
	20 years Stone & Webster. Figures for Chicago union traction co. case. Report Wisconsin railroad commission, vol. 10, p. 220
	15-20 years Wisconsin railroad commission. Wilwaukee 3c. case
	20 years. 2c. lb. residual value Pacific gas and electric company. Figures used in rate hearings before Master in Chancery, San Francisco, 1913-4
	20 years Bion J. Arnold. Coney Island & Brooklyn figures adopted by Public service commission of New York. Four Chicago appraisals quoted by H. A. Foster
	20 years Henry Floy. Trans. American Institute of electrical engineers, June 1911. Third Avenue case figures adopted by Public service commission of New York
	20 years San Jcaquin light and power corporation. Rate hearing before California railroad commission, 1915
	13-33 years Traction valuation commission. Case of the Chicago consolidated traction co.
modern types	20 years Wisconsin railroad commission. Quoted by Henry Floy and in published reports
obsolete types	15 years Wisconsin railroad commission Quoted by Henry Floy and in published reports
belted	10-20 years Chicago traction commission. Quoted by G. W. Cravens, *Electrical review,* April 23, 1910
direct conn.	20 years Chicago traction commission. Quoted by G. W. Cravens, *Electrical review,* April 23, 1910
telephone plant	20 years. 20% residual value Wisconsin railroad commission. Wisconsin telephone co. case. Aug. 3, 1909

HAZLEHURST, J. N. Final report of the committee on depreciation. *Journal of the American water works association,* March 1919, p. 85-135.

Electric generators and motors	20-30 years

INSTALLATIONS, systems and appliances. *Electrical world,* Dec. 7, 1912, p. 1220.

	Preece
Generators	30 years

KIMBALL, DEXTER S. Estimated life, and factors of depreciation. (In his *Cost finding.* 1918. p. 190. *Principles of industrial organization.* 1913. p. 163).

	Life in years.	Ratio of scrap to original value.	Percent on original cost.	Percent on diminishing value.
Electric generators	20-30	0.10	4.5-3	11-7-5
Turbo-generators	20-30	0.10	4.5-3	11-7-5

LIFE data on power-plant equipment used in valuation of Massachusetts property. *Electrical world,* Dec. 4, 1915, p. 1261.

Generators (direct current)	30-40 years
Turbo-generators	20

METCALF, LEONARD. Depreciation in waterworks operation and accounting. *Journal, New England waterworks association,* Dec. 1910, p. 442. Abstracts. *Engineering news,* Nov. 3, 1910, p. 482. Methods of computing depreciation of and reasonable assumptions as to period of useful life of waterworks. *Engineering and contracting,* Nov. 16, 1919, p. 434.

	Years.	% straight line.
Electrical generators and motors	20-30	5-3½

DEPRECIATION, DEPLETION AND OBSOLESCENCE—GENERATORS—*(Continued)*

NEALE, R. E. Depreciation in engineering works. *Mecahnical world,* Feb. 7, 1913, p. 67-8.
Generators
old type 6.6% 15 years
low speed modern 3.5 20-33
turbo sets 5-10 10-20

NICHOLSON, J. LEE AND J. F. D. ROHRBACH. Depreciation. (In their *Cost accounting.* 1919. p. 147, 150).
Electric machinery generators 5%
Acetylene generators 10
Based on (1) the cost of equipment
(2) the life of the equipment
(3) on a ten-hour day

PENDER, HAROLD. Depreciation. (In his *Handbook for electrical engineers.* c1914. p. 339).

Generators	Years life	Dep. %	
electric	12-15		S. W. Greeland
	15		Chicago union traction co.
			W. H. Bryan
			J. Abbott.
	20		Engineer of valuation staff of Wisconsin railroad commission.
			Stone & Webster, for Chicago union traction co.
	25		R. Hammond.
			P. Dawson.
		7-12	N. S. Hill.
		6-66	Chicago union traction co.
		5	Milwaukee electric railway & light co.
			Engineer of valuation staff of Wisconsin railroad commission.
			Cardiff tramways.
			Glasgow "
			Stone & Webster for Chicago union traction co.
		3	Chicago city railways.

PHILADELPHIA. CONTROLLER. Rates of depreciation (In his *Manual of accounting, reporting and business procedure of the city and county of Philadelphia.* 1917. p. 204).
Steam boilers and generators 5%

PROBABLE lives of water-works elements. *Engineering news,* Oct. 11, 1917, p. 688.
Electric generators and motors 20-30 years

PROPOSED sale of Toronto securities to the city. *Electrical world,* Oct. 25, 1913, p. 832.
Generators 4 & 5%

RUNYON, F. O. Report on hydro-electric plant for special committee common council, Newark, New Jersey, April 23, 1902. p. 15, 16, 24.
Engines and generators 5%
Turbo-generators 5%

SALIERS, EARL A. Analysis of a hydro-electric plant. (In his *Principles of depreciation.* 1916. p. 34-8).
Generators and transformers 25 years

VALUATION of the Chicago consolidated traction property. *Electric railway journal,* Dec. 3, 1910, p. 1111-3.
Generators 3-8%

WEEKS, H. E. Abstract of paper on depreciation read before annual meeting of Iowa street and interurban railway association, April 1910. *Electric railway journal,* April 30, 1910, p. 782-3.
Generators 15 years

YEAMAN, C. H. Depreciation and reserves for antiquation and obsolescence from an engineering standpoint. *Electrical engineering* (London), July 12, 1907, p. 46. *Electrical review* (London), July 12, 1907, p. 44. *Electrician,* July 5, 1907, p. 475.
Electric generators 25 years
R. Hammond.
20 years
L. G. B. (Local government board).
20 years
L. C. C.
25 years
J. F. C. Snell (M. E. A. 1905).

Glass

TIFFANY, H. S. Glass works. (In his *Digest of depreciations.* c1890. p. 9).
Buildings
brick 3-3½%
frame 4-4½
Based upon the actual life of the building without any repairs.

UNITED STATES. BUREAU OF FOREIGN AND DOMESTIC COMMERCE. Depreciation of plant and equipment. (In its *Glass industry.* 1917. p. 86-93).
One establishment classified its annual depreciation charges as follows:

	Dep. %
Buildings:	
brick	4
frame	4
concrete	2½
Machines and tools:	
ordinary	10
clay mixing, etc.	20
Equipment (blowing rods, etc.)	10
gas producers	10
furniture and fixtures	10
molds	10

DEPRECIATION, DEPLETION AND OBSOLESCENCE—GLASS—*(Continued)*

Establishments manufacturing	Depreciation % of value
Window glass by hand	7.16
Window glass by machine	8.51
Plate glass	8.25
Wire and opalescent glass	3.81
Bottles by hand	3.50
Bottles by machine	5.18
Bottles by hand and machine	7.31
Jars	6.19
Tableware, blown	5.94
Tableware, blown and pressed	8.58
Lighting goods	5.57
Lamp chimneys	4.56
Miscellaneous articles	9.64
Total	6.38

Glue pots

DENHAM, ROBERT S. Depreciation. (In his *Manual of cost engineering and estimating for paper box manufacturers.* 1917. p. 249).
Glue mixers 6%

DENHAM, ROBERT S. Depreciation. (In his *Manual of cost engineering and estimating for paper box manufacturers.* 1917. p. 249).
Glue pots, brushes 6%

NICHOLSON, J. LEE and JOHN F. D. ROHRBACH. Depreciation. (In their *Cost accounting.* 1919. p. 150).
Glue pots 10%

Gluing machines

DENHAM, ROBERT S. Depreciation. (In his *Manual of cost engineering and estimating for paper box manufactures.* 1917. p. 249).
S & S gluing machine 12%

Goodwill

BOGLE, J. D. S. Writing off of depreciation on the wasting assets of a joint stock company. *Accountant,* Dec. 21, 1889, p. 691-6.
CASTENHOLZ, WILLIAM B. Goodwill. (In his *Auditing procedure.* 1918. p. 79-80).
DENSHAW, F. W. Depreciation of assets and goodwill of limited companies. *Accountant,* May 28, 1898, p. 570-1.
DICKSEE, LAWRENCE R. Depreciation. (In his *Advanced accounting.* 1916. p. 224).
DICKSEE, LAWRENCE R. Goodwill. (In his *Auditing.* Authorized American edition. p. 190-1).
ESQUERRE, PAUL-JOSEPH. Depreciation of good-will. (In his *Applied theory of accounts.* 1917. p. 248-9).
GUTHRIE, EDWIN. Depreciation. (In Lisle, George. *Encyclopaedia of accounting.* v. 2. p. 376).
Goodwill: As an annuity or at discretion, divide the purchase money over the number of years of estimated period of value.
JENKINSON, M. WEBSTER. Depreciation. *Accountant,* May 17, 1902, p. 528-34.
KESTER, ROY B. Periodic revaluation of good-will. (In his *Accounting, theory and practice,* 1918. v. 2, p. 337).
MONTGOMERY, ROBERT H. Goodwill. (In his *Auditing, theory and practice.* 1916. p. 427-8).
MONTGOMERY, ROBERT H. Goodwill. (In his *Income tax procedure,* 1919, p. 565. ——— Same, 1920. p. 718).
No claim for depreciation of goodwill, trade-marks or trade-brands should or will be allowed.
RACINE, SAMUEL F. Goodwill. (In his *Accounting principles.* 1917. p. 169.)
SPICER, ERNEST EVAN and ERNEST CHARLES PEGLER. Goodwill. (In their *Practical auditing.* 1914. p. 147-8.)
WEBNER, FRANK E. Depreciation of goodwill. (In his *Factory costs.* 1911. p. 187-8.)
WHATLEY, G. E. STUART. Depreciation. (In his *Accountant's and bookkeeper's vade-mecum.* 1893. p. 28-32.)

Governors

BARKER, HARRY. Typical life expectation tables for public property. (In his *Public utility rates.* 1917. p. 368.)
Governors. 50 years. Wisconsin R. R. commission.
COST and depreciation of steam and hydro-electric installations. *Electrical world,* Dec. 30, 1909, p. 1558.
Water wheel governors 10 years .235% of total cost
FOSTER, HORATIO A. Rates of depreciation. (In his *Engineering valuation of public utilities and factories.* 1913. p. 207).

Governors	years life
gas plant	50
consumers'	25

GILLETTE, HALBERT P. and RICHARD T. DANA. Depreciation. (In their *Handbook of mechanical and electric cost data.* 1918. p. 108).
Governors
Gas (consumer's) 25 years Wisconsin R. R. commission
gas plant 5 years Wisconsin R. R. commission

DEPRECIATION, DEPLETION AND OBSOLESCENCE—GOVERNORS—*(Continued)*

GRUNSKY, CARL EWALD. Probable useful life of various articles. (In his *Valuation, depreciation and the rate-base.* 1917. p. 279.)
Governors
gas plant 50 years.
Wisconsin Railroad Commission. Quoted by H. A. Foster and in published reports.
consumers 25 years.
Wisconsin Railroad Commission. Quoted by H. A. Foster and in published reports.

PROSSER, R. W. Depreciation in gas plants. *American gas light journal,* May 26, 1902, p. 767.
Station meters and governors 25 years 30% of first cost.

SALIERS, EARL E. Analysis of a hydroelectric plant. (In his *Principles of depreciation.* 1916. p. 34-8).
Water-wheel governors 10 years.

Grade crossings

PHILADELPHIA. CONTROLLER. Rates of depreciation. (In his *Manual of accounting, reporting and business procedure of the city and county of Philadelphia.* 1917. p. 210).
Grade crossings (abolition of). 2%

Grading

BAY state street railway valuation. *Electric railway journal,* Dec. 4, 1915, p. 1121-3.
Grading annual depreciation divided by investment 2.0%

GILLETTE, HALBERT POWERS. Railways. (In his *Handbook of cost data for contractors and engineers.* 1910. p. 1317-8).
Grading 10%

LIFE of road construction equipment. *Engineering and contracting,* Jan. 3, 1917, p. 3.
Graders 20% annual depreciation.

PHILADELPHIA. CONTROLLER. Rates of depreciation. (In his *Manual of accounting, reporting and business procedure of the city and county of Philadelphia.* 1917. p. 210).
Filling and terracing, grading 1%

PUBLIC utilities reports annotated. Rochester, lawyers co-operative publishing co. 1918A. p. 917-8.
New York & N. S. traction co. Grading 1%

Grain elevators

GILLETTE, HALBERT P. Railways. (In his *Handbook of cost data for contractors and engineers.* 1910. p. 1317-8).

	age years	annual depreciation	present condition
Grain elevators	7.0	3.0	79.0

GILLETTE, HALBERT P. and RICHARD T. DANA. Depreciation. (In their *Handbook of mechanical and electrical cost data.* 1918. p. 106).
Buildings
grain elevators 33.3 years
H. P. Gillette, Washington railway appraisal

TIFFANY, H. S. Grain elevators. (In his *Digest of depreciations.* c1890. p. 9).
Buildings
brick
Steam power 3½%
Horse " 2½%
frame
Steam power 4½%
Horse " 3½%

Grates and stokers

ANALYSIS of the premises adopted and methods used in determining the cost to reproduce new together with the depreciation thereon of the physical property of the Metropolitan system and the Kansas city and Belt railway of Kansas city, Mo. *Engineering and contracting,* May 28, 1913, p. 617-20.
Grates and stokers, maximum 25%
That is, depreciated 10% per year for 2½ years, no further depreciation being applied if they are in use.

BARKER, HARRY. Typical life expectation tables for public utility property. (In his *Public utility rates.* 1917. p. 368-9).
Stokers 20 years
Chicago traction val. comm.

BAY state rate case. *Electric railway journal,* Dec. 4, 1915, p. 1121-3. *Public utility reports, annotated,* 1916F, p. 336-9.
Stokers 15 years

ELBOURNE, EDWARD T. Depreciation rates. (In his *Factory administration and accounts.* 1918. p. 376).

	Prov. dep. % Remainder values	Years 10%	5%
Stokers, mechanical	12½	17	22

FLOY, HENRY. Depreciation. Floy, Henry. Depreciation as related to electrical properties. *American institute of electrical engineers, Proceedings,* 1911, p. 1267. Floy, Henry. *Valuation of public utility properties.* 1912. p. 168-217. Foster, Horatio A. *Engineering valuation of public utilities and factories.* 1913. p. 194-8. *Engineering and contracting,* Oct. 4, 1911, p. 359-65. *Engineering magazine,* Aug. 1911, p. 837-40.

DEPRECIATION, DEPLETION AND OBSOLESCENCE—GRATES AND STOKERS—*(Continued)*

	% Dep. per year Straight line	
Stokers		
Fixed parts	5	Traction Chicago con. val. comm. trac. co.
Moving parts	20	Traction Chicago con. val. comm. trac. co.

GILLETTE, HALBERT P. and RICHARD T. DANA. Depreciation. (In their *Handbook of mechanical and electrical cost data.* 1918. p. 110).

Stokers:	
	4 years
	B. J. Arnold, Chicago appraisals 4 cases
Moving parts	5 years
	Traction valuation commission, Chicago consolidated traction co.
Fixed parts	20 years
	Traction valuation commission, Chicago consolidated traction co.

GRUNSKY, CARL EWALD. Probable useful life of various articles. (In his *Valuation depreciation and the rate-base.* 1917. p. 283).

Stokers:	
Fixed parts	20 years
	Traction valuation commission. Case of the Chicago consolidated traction co.
Moving parts	5 years
	Traction valuation commission. Case of the Chicago consolidated traction co.

LIFE data on power-plant equipment used in valuation of Massachusetts property. *Electrical world,* Dec. 4, 1915, p. 1261.

Stokers	15 years

NEALE, R. E. Depreciation in engineering works. *Mechanical world,* Feb 7, 1913, p. 67-8.

Machine stokers:		
Stationary parts	5%	20 years
Moving parts	20	5 years

NICHOLSON, J. LEE and JOHN F. D. ROHRBACH. Depreciation. (In their *Cost accounting.* 1919. p. 147).

Stokers	
Fixed parts	5%
Moving parts	20

Based on (1) the cost of equipment
(2) the life of the equipment
(3) on a ten-hour day

PHILADELPHIA. CONTROLLER. Rates of depreciation. (In his *Manual of accounting, reporting and business procedure of the city and county of Philadelphia.* 1917. p. 205).

Patent stokers and fuel economizers	5%

PROPOSED sale of Toronto utilities to the city. *Electrical world,* Oct. 25, 1913, p. 832.

Grates and stokers	50%

VALUATION of the Chicago consolidated traction property. *Electric railway journal,* Dec. 3, 1910, p. 1111-3.

Grates and stokers—the fixed parts of stokers depreciate very little and the moving parts and grates very rapidly. As the moving parts are renewed and maintained in good condition 10% of the wearing value of stokers was depreciated at 20% per year for 2½ years and 90% of the fixed parts at 5% per year during the life of the machine.

Gravestones

PHILADELPHIA. CONTROLLER. Rates of depreciation. (In his *Manual of accounting, reporting and business procedure of the city and county of Philadelphia.* 1917. p. 210).

Monuments, statuary, arches, gravestones	⅕%

Grinding

ELBOURNE, EDWARD T. Depreciation rates. (In his *Factory administration and accounts.* **1918.** p. 377).

	Prov. dep. % Remainder values	years 10%	5%
Grinding & polishing heads	6	37	48
Grinders			
cutter	12½	17	22
cylindrical plain	7½	29	38
disc	7½	29	38
drill	7½	29	38
internal	12½	17	22
saw	7½	29	38
surface	12½	17	22
tool, wet	7½	29	38
universal	7½	29	38

NICHOLSON, J. LEE and JOHN F. D. ROHRBACH. Depreciation. (In their *Cost accounting.* 1919. p. 149, 150).

Tool and surface grinders, saw grinders	6⅔%
Grinding and mixing machines	10 %

DEPRECIATION, DEPLETION AND OBSOLESCENCE—*(Continued)*

Grindstone troughs

ELBOURNE, EDWARD T. Depreciation rates. (In his *Factory administration and accounts.* 1918. p. 377).

	Prov. dep. %	years	
	Remainder values	10%	5%
Grindstone troughs	6	37	48

Grocery trade

HARVARD UNIVERSITY. GRADUATE SCHOOL OF BUSINESS ADMINISTRATION. BUREAU OF BUSINESS RESEARCH. Depreciation of equipment. (In its *Operating expenses in the wholesale grocery business.* 1917. p. 5).

Wholesale grocery business.

Low	0.00
High	0.5
Common	0.1

HARVARD UNIVERSITY. GRADUATE SCHOOL OF BUSINESS ADMINISTRATION. BUREAU OF BUSINESS RESEARCH. Depreciation of store equipment. (In its *Management problems in retail grocery stores.* 1919. p. 43).

Retail grocery stores

Low	0.05
High	0.77
Common	0.3

TIFFANY, H. S. Groceries (wholesale). (In his *Digest of depreciations.* c1890. p. 14).
Annually 5%

Grooving machinery

PHILADELPHIA. CONTROLLER. Rates of depreciation. (In his *Manual of accounting, reporting and business procedure of the city and county of Philadelphia.* 1917. p. 205).
Mitreing and tonguing, grooving, etc., machinery. 5%

Guard houses

NICHOLSON, J. LEE and J. F. D. ROHRBACH. Depreciation. (In their *Cost accounting.* 1919. p. 147).
Hose reel and guard houses 15%

Guards

ELBOURNE, EDWARD T. Depreciation rates. (In his *Factory administration and accounts.* 1918. p. 377).

	Prov. dep. %	years	
	Remainder values	10%	5%
Guards, machinery and belting	10	22	28

Gymnasiums

PHILADELPHIA. CONTROLLER. Rates of depreciation. (In his *Manual of accounting, reporting and busness procedure of the city and county of Philadelphia.* 1917. p. 205).
Gymnasium and playground equipment of a permanent nature 8⅓%

Gypsum

PHILADELPHIA. CONTROLLER. Rates of depreciation. (In his *Manual of accounting, reporting and business procedure of the city and county of Philadelphia.* 1917. p. 205).
Gypsum and cement working equipment 10%

Hammers

BELT, ROBERT E. Depreciation. (In his *Foundry cost accounting practice and procedure.* 1919. p. 243).
Emery wheel stands, drop hammers, lathes, drill presses, air chippers, milling machines, etc. with moter, shafting and belting. 10%

BELT, ROBERT E. Depreciation. (In his *Uniform cost accounting methods; adopted by the American malleable castings association,* Nov. 14, 1917. p. 20-1).

CLAPHAM, F. T. Depreciation of plant. *Mechanical world,* Oct. 19, 1917, p. 219-20.
Pneumatic tools, such as clipping and caulking hammers, drills, and riveting hammers should be written down. 15%

ELBOURNE, EDWARD T. Depreciation rates. (In his *Factory administration and accounts.* 1918. p. 377).

	Prov. dep. %	years	
	Remainder values	10%	5%
Hammers			
belt driven	10	22	28
drop	10	22	28
pneumatic	10	22	28
steam	10	22	28

NICHOLSON, J. LEE AND J. F. D. ROHRBACH. Depreciation. (In their *Cost accounting.* 1919. p. 149, 150).
Punch presses, bending rolls, power shears, and drop hammers 6⅔%
Hammers—Steam, drop or helve 10%
Based on (1) the cost of equipment
(2) the life of the equipment
(3) on a ten-hour day.

PHILADELPHIA. CONTROLLER. Rates of depreciation. (In his *Manual of accounting, reporting and business procedure of the city and county of Philadelphia.* 1917. p. 205).
Metal work equipment.
Hammering, rolling and welding equipment 5%

DEPRECIATION, DEPLETION AND OBSOLESCENCE—HAMMERS—*(Continued)*

PIEZ, CHARLES. Perpetual inventory and appraisal values; table of standard depreciation rates. *Engineering and contracting,* Jan. 24, 1917, p. 77. *Factory,* Dec. 1916. p. 668-71. *Iron age,* Nov. 30, 1916, Jan. 11, 1917, p. 1266, 138-9. *Iron trade review,* Feb. 22, 1917, p. 477-8. Condensed. *Journal of the American society of mechanical engineers,* Dec. 1916, p. 965-6. *Iron trade review,* Dec. 7, 1916, p. 1144-6. Discussion. *Journal of the American society of mechanical engineers,* March 1917, p. 215-7.

	% on cost	% on reducing bal.
Punch presses, bending rolls, power shears and drop hammers	4.5	10

Hammocks

PHILADELPHIA. CONTROLLER. Rates of depreciation. (In his *Manual of accounting, reporting and business procedure of the city and county of Philadelphia.* 1917. p. 207-8.)

Hammocks	25%

Hand trucks

BELT, ROBERT E. Depreciation. (In his *Foundry cost accounting practice and procedure.* 1919. p. 242).

Hand trucks	10%
core	7½%

BELT, ROBERT E. Depreciation. (In his *Uniform cost accounting methods;* adopted by the American malleable castings association, Nov. 14, 1917, p. 20-1).

Trucks	10%

DENHAM, ROBERT S. Depreciation. (In his *Manual of cost engineering and estimating for paper box manufacturers.* 1917. p. 249).

Hand trucks	6%

NICHOLSON, J. LEE and J. F. D. ROHRBACH. Depreciation. (In their *Cost accounting.* 1919. p. 151).

Trucks and moving racks	7½%

Based on (1) the cost of equipment
(2) the life of the equipment
(3) on a ten-hour day

Handcuffs

PHILADELPHIA. CONTROLLER. Rates of depreciation. (In his *Manual of accounting, reporting and business procedure of the city and county of Philadelphia.* 1917. p. 209).

Belts, badges, handcuffs	4%

Hangers

See Depreciation, depletion and obsolescence—Shafting, pulleys, etc.

Hardware

TIFFANY, H. S. Hardware works. (In his *Digest of depreciations.* c1890. p. 9).

Buildings	
brick	3½%
frame	4

Hardware trade

HARVARD UNIVERSITY. GRADUATE SCHOOL OF BUSINESS ADMINISTRATION. BUREAU OF BUSINESS RESEARCH. Depreciation of store equipment. (In its *Operating expenses in retail hardware stores.* 1919. p. 5).

Retail hardware store	% dep.
low	0.04
high	1.61
common	0.3

TIFFANY, H. S. Hardware. (In his *Digest of depreciations.* c1890. p. 14).

Wholesale stock	% annual dep.
without stock	5
with shelf hardware, tools and cutlery, etc.	10

Harness

AUSTRALIA FEDERAL INCOME TAX DEPARTMENT. Depreciation allowance. *Accountant,* Oct. 13, 1917, p. 277-9. *Accounting and commerce,* June 30, 1917, p. 55-7. *Federal accountant,* July 1917, p. 93-8. *Public accountant,* Jan. 30, 1917, p. 145-52.

Harness	10%

Based on written down value and repairs allowed in addition.

BREWERIES. *American institute of accountants, Special bulletin,* no. 5, Sept. 1920, p. 7-8.

DEPRECIATION, ice industry. *American institute of accountants, Special bulletin,* no. 5, Sept. 1920, p. 5.

JENKINSON, M. WEBSTER. Depreciation. *Accountant,* May 17, 1902, p. 528-34.

	1st five yrs.	afterwards
Carts, vehicles, harness, etc.	10%	5%

LANHAM, HERBERT. Depreciation. (In his *Brewers' and bottlers' accounts.* p. 126-32).

Vehicles & harness	7½%

LIFE of road construction equipment. *Engineering and contracting,* Jan. 3, 1917, p. 3.

	Annual depreciation
Wagons and harness	20%

PHILADELPHIA. CONTROLLER. Rates of depreciation. (In his *Manual of accounting, reporting and business procedure of the city and county of Philadelphia.* 1917. p. 206).

Harness and collars	12½%
Saddles	10
Bridles, bits, halters	12½

DEPRECIATION, DEPLETION AND OBSOLESCENCE—HARNESS—*(Continued)*

ROBY, J. J. Schedule of plant depreciation. (In his *Treatise on cost accounting as applied to coal mining.* c1913. p. 14-5).
Livestock and harness 20%

TIFFANY, *H. S.* Harness and saddlery goods. (In his *Digest of depreciations.* c1890. p. 14).
Harness and saddlery goods 10% annual depreciation.

WIHLFAHRT, JULIUS E. Depreciation. (In his *Treatise on increasing bakery efficiency.* 1917. p. 6).
Horses, wagons and harness 15%

Hat factories

MONTGOMERY, ROBERT H. Hat factories. (In his *Income tax procedure,* 1919. p. 565. ——— Same, 1920, p. 718-9).

Buildings	2½%
Equipment	4½
Molds	10-20

MONTGOMERY, ROBERT H. Hat manufacturers. (In his *Auditing theory and practice.* 1916. p. 418).

Buildings	1½%
Equipment	4½
Molds	10-20

Head gates

GRUNSKY, CARL EWALD. Probable useful life of various articles. (In his *Valuation, depreciation and the rate-base.* 1917. p. 280).
Head gates on ditches 30 years
San Joaquin light & power corporation. Rate hearing before California railroad commission, 1915.

Header lines

UNIFORM cost sheet for coal mining companies. *Coal age,* Sept. 19, 1918, p. 545-7.

	Original cost
Header lines	8%

Heaters

See Depreciation, depletion and obsolescence—Stoves, furnaces, etc.

Heating

See also Depreciation, depletion and obsolescence—Stoves, furnaces, etc.

BELT, ROBERT E. Depreciation. (In his *Foundry cost accounting practice and procedure.* 1919. p. 243).
Heating system, steam 5%

BOLTON, REGINALD PELHAM. Depreciation of mechanical equipments and power plants. (In his *Building for profit.* 1919. p. 82, 89).

	Physical years	Physical %	Economic years
Exterior framing, copper-cased housings, etc., heating pipe systems, used part of the year, gas piping	33	82.5	27

ELBOURNE, EDWARD T. Depreciation rates. (In his *Factory administration and accounts.* 1918. p. 377, 376).

	Prov. dep. % Remainder values	years 10%	years 5%
Heating machines	12½	17	22
Heating pipes, radiators and valves	10	22	28

MONTGOMERY, ROBERT H. Electrical equipment manufacturers. (In his *Income tax procedure.* 1919. p. 563. ——— Same, 1920. p. 716).
Heating and ventilating 10%
Based on gross book values at the end of the preceding year.

MULHALL, JOHN F. J. Depreciation. (In his *Quasi-public corporation accounting and management.* c1905. p. 180-3).
Steam heating works 7-10%

NICHOLSON, J. LEE AND J. F. D. ROHRBACH. Depreciation. (In their *Cost accounting.* 1919. p. 147).
Heating and ventilation 5%
Based on (1) the cost of equipment
(2) the life of the equipment
(3) on a ten-hour day

PHILDELPHIA. CONTROLLER. Rates of depreciation. (In his *Manual of accounting, reporting and business procedure of the city and county of Philadelphia.* 1917. p. 210).
Buildings used solely for the production of heat, light, power or refrigeration 1⅔%

PIEZ, CHARLES. Perpetual inventory and appraisal values; table of standard depreciation rates. *Engineering and contracting,* Jan. 24, 1917, p. 77. *Factory,* Dec. 1916, p. 668-71. *Iron age,* Nov. 30, 1916, Jan. 11, 1917, p. 1227, 138-9. *Iron trade review,* Feb. 22, 1917, p. 477-8. Condensed. *Journal of the American society of mechanical engineers,* Dec. 1916, p. 965-6. *Iron trade review,* Dec. 7, 1916, p. 1144-6. Kent, William. *Bookkeeping and cost accounting for factories.* 1918, p. 90. Discussion. *Journal of the American society of mechanical engineers,* March 1917, p. 215-7.

	years	% on cost	% on red. val.
Heating and ventilating system	20	4	7.5

PUBLIC utilities reports, annotated. Rochester, Lawyers co-operative publishing co.
See index under Depreciation.

DEPRECIATION, DEPLETION AND OBSOLESCENCE—HEATING—*(Continued)*

PUBLIC utilities reports, annotated. Rochester, Lawyers co-operative publishing co. 1919F. p. 1053.
Re Merchants heat & light co. (Ind.) 558. In fixing hot water heating rates, an allowance of 4% was made for depreciation.

PUBLIC utilities reports, annotated. Rochester, Lawyers co-operative publishing co. 1915E. p. 502.
Re Peru heating co. (Ind). In fixing the rates for hot water heating service, an allowance of 3 per cent on the total valuation of the utility for straight line depreciation and 2 per cent on the sinking fund basis was held reasonable where it appeared that the life of the distribution system was estimattd at twenty-five years; the plant equipment was estimated to be in 50 per cent condition after thirteen years' use, and the building estimated at 90 per cent condition.

PUBLIC utilities reports, annotated. Rochester, Lawyers co-operative publishing co. 1918F. p. 316.
Re United public service co. (Ind.). An annual allowance of 3 per cent of the value of a heating plant less the value of land, working capital, and material and supplies, was fixed as proper rate of depreciation.

PUBLIC utilities reports, annotated. Rochester, Lawyers co-operative publishing co. 1919B. p. 750.
Re public service commission v. Billings utility co. Docket no. 690, report and order no. 248, Nov. 20, 1918, upon an application of a steam heating utility for an increase in rates, the Montana commission, in allowing for depreciation, included depreciation of 2 per cent on buildings, 10 per cent on pumping equipment, and 5 per cent on other items going to make up the physical part of the plant.

PUBLIC utilities reports, annotated. 1919B. p. 1073.
Re Wisconsin-Minnesota light & P. co. (Wis.). A depreciation of 1.84 per cent on the value of a utility hot water heating plant on the 4 per cent sinking fund basis was held adequate under the evidence.

PUBLIC utilities reports, annotated. Rochester, Lawyers co-operative publishing company, 1920 A, p. 447.
Re Springfield gas & E. co. (Ill.). Illinois commission made an allowance of 2½ per cent for the accruing depreciation of a plant furnishing steam and also hot water heating.

PUBLIC utilities reports, annotated. Rochester, Lawyers co-operative publishing company, 1920C, p. 510.
Re Central heating co. case no. 212, Sept. 24, 1919. The Utah commission fixed the rate of depreciation of the generating equipment of a steam heating plant at 8 per cent per annum and made an allowance of $70 for the depreciation of the building in which the plant was located, and also made an allowance of 5 per cent for the depreciation of the pipe line forming the distributing system fixing a rate at not to exceed 6 per cent per annum on the value of the property considered as a whole.

Heating pockets

NICHOLSON, J. LEE AND J. F. D. ROHRBACH. Depreciation. (In their *Cost accounting.* 1919. p. 148).
Steel work:
Heating pockets 4%

Highways

See Depreciation, depletion and obsolescence—Roads and highways.

Hoisting

See Depreciation, depletion and obsolescence—Conveying and hoisting.

Hop houses

TIFFANY, H. S. Hop houses. (In his *Digest of depreciations.* c1890. p. 9).
Buildings
brick 2%
frame 3%
Based upon the actual life of the building without any repairs.

Horse rugs

AUSTRALIA. FEDERAL INCOME TAX DEPARTMENT. Depreciation allowance. *Accountant*, Oct. 13, 1917, p. 277-9. *Accounting and commerce*, June 30, 1917, p. 55-7. *Federal accountant*, July 1917, p. 93-8. *Public accountant*, Jan. 30, 1917, p. 145-52.
Horse rugs 20%
Based on written down value and repairs allowed in addition.

PHILADELPHIA. CONTROLLER. Rates of depreciation. (In his *Manual of accounting, reporting and business procedure of the city and county of Philadelphia.* 1917. p. 206).
Blankets, robes, covers, weights 16⅔%

Horses

AMERICAN INSTITUTE OF ACCOUNTANTS. Report of the committee on standard schedules for uniform reports upon municipal industries and public service corporations; annual meeting at Atlantic city, N. J. October 20-22, 1908. 15p. *Journal of accountancy*, May 1909, p. 47-54.
The knowledge at the command of the Bureau of the census leads to the conclusion that the average life is approximately as follows:
Horses, carriages, automobiles and laboratory fixtures and meters 10 years

AUSTRALIA. FEDERAL INCOME TAX DEPARTMENT. Depreciation allowance. *Accountant*, Oct. 13, 1917, p. 277-9. *Accounting and commerce*, June 30, 1917, p. 55-7. *Federal accountant*, July 1917, p. 83-8. *Public accountant*, Jan. 30, 1917, p. 145-52.
Conveyances (horses, carts, etc.) 10%
Written down value, repairs allowed.

BEXELL, J. A. Valuation and depreciation. (In his *Principles of book keeping and farm accounts.* c1913. p. 140-2).
Horses above 5 years 10%

DEPRECIATION, DEPLETION AND OBSOLESCENCE—Horses—*(Continued)*

Castenholz, William B. Audit of balance sheet accounts. (In his *Auditing procedure.* 1918. p. 57).
Horses in heavy service give out rapidly and should be depreciated at about 25 percent of cost annually.

Chase, Harvey S. Depreciation in water works accounts, with reference to uniform reports. *Journal of the New England water works association,* June 1910, p. 305-31. Abstract. *Engineering and contracting,* June 29, 1910, p. 598. Editorial. Depreciation and sinking fund accounts. *Municipal engineering,* July 1910, p. 26.
Horses, carriages, automobiles, laboratory fixtures and meters 10 years

Denham, Robert S. Depreciation. (In his *Manual of cost engineering and estimating for paper box manufacturers.* 1917. p. 249).
Horses 20%

Densham, F. W. Depreciation of assets and goodwill of limited companies. *Accountant,* May 28, 1898 ,p. 570.
Horses—Revalued or 15-25% according to the severity of the work to which the horses are subject.

Depreciation, ice industry. *American institute of accountants,* Special bulletin, no. 5, Sept. 1920, p. 5.

Depreciation in value of horses. *Engineering and contracting,* Oct. 17, 1917, p. 319-20.
These data are taken from a bulletin recently issued by the U. S. Department of agriculture which deals with the cost of keeping farm horses and the cost of horse labor. It shows that the average depreciation on 27 farms in Illinois, Ohio, and New York is $4.50 per horse and that depreciation varied from $11.60 per horse in New York to an appreciation of $2.10 per horse in Ohio.

Dicksee, Lawrence R. Depreciation. (In his *Depreciation, reserves and reserve funds,* 1912. p. 40-1.)
Horses 15-25%

Dicksee, Lawrence R. Horses. (In his *Auditing.* Authorized American edition. 1909. p. 191.)
The rate of depreciation will probably vary between fifteen and twenty-five per cent on the starting balance of the account. Until experience has shown the actual rate of depreciation, it will be safer to arrive at the result by a revaluation.

Foster, Horatio A. Rates of depreciation. (In his *Engineering valuation of public utilities and factories.* 1913. p. 199.)
Wagons and horses 10.0%
Marwick, Mitchell & co. in the appraisal of a large street railway system.

Gillette, Halbert P. and Richard T. Dana. Depreciation. (In their *Handbook of mechanical and electrical cost data.* 1918. p. 110.)
Teams and vehicles
5-8 years.
H. P. Gillette, Everett railway & water co., Jan. 29, 1912.
10 years.
Prof. M. E. Cooley, Milwaukee, 3c case. Marwick, Mitchell & co., appraisal of a large street railway system, Foster, p. 199.
20 years.
M. G. Starret, Milwaukee, 3c case.

Greendlinger, Leo and John R. Loomis Depreciation, horses. (In their *Accounting problems.* 1910. v. 1. p. 204-5.)
Horses 15-25%

Jenkinson, M. Webster. Depreciation. *Accountant,* May 17, 1902, p. 528-34.
Horses 15-20%

Lanham, Herbert. Depreciation. (In his *Brewers' and bottlers' accounts.* p. 126-32.)
Horses 10-15%

McIntosh, Robert J. Rates of depreciation. (In his *Reference book of accounts.* Ed.2. p. 60.)
Horses 15-25%
Based on life

Matheson, Ewing. Horses. (In his *Depreciation of factories, mines and industrial undertakings and their valuation.* 1893. p. 48-9.)
Horses 15-25% annual rate of depreciation.

Montgomery, Robert H. Horses. (In his *Auditing theory and practice.* 1916 p. 426.)
Horses 15-25% of the cost.

Montgomery, Robert H. Horses. (In his *Income tax procedure,* 1919. p. 565-6.——— Same, 1920, p. 719.)
Horses 15-25% of the cost.
Periodical revaluations favored by many.

Nicholson, J. Lee and J. F. D. Rohrbach. Depreciation. (In their *Cost accounting.* 1919. p. 151.)
Horses and wagons 12%
Based on (1) cost of equipment
(2) the life of the equipment
(3) on a ten-hour day.

Philadelphia. Controller. Rates of depreciation. (In his *Manual of accounting, reporting and business procedure of the city and county of Philadelphia.* 1917. p. 209.)
Horses 10%

Piez, Charles. Perpetual inventory and appraisal values; tables of standard depreciation rates. *Engineering and contracting,* Jan. 24, 1917, p. 77. *Factory,* Dec. 1916, p. 668-71. *Iron age,* Nov. 30, 1916, Jan. 11, 1917, p. 1266, 138-9. *Iron trade review,* Feb. 22, 1917, p. 477-8. Condensed. *Journal of the American society of mechanical engineers,* Dec. 1916, p. 965-6. *Iron trade review,* Dec. 7, 1916, p. 1144-6. Kent, William. *Bookkeeping and cost accounting for factories,* 1918, p. 90. Discussion. *Journal of the American society of mechanical engineers,* March 1917, p. 215-7.

	% on cost	% on reducing balance
Horses and wagons	12	35

Racine, Samuel F. Horses. (In his *Accounting principles.* 1917. p. 154.)

DEPRECIATION, DEPLETION AND OBSOLESCENCE—Horses—*(Continued)*

SNELLING, W. E. Horses. (In his *Income tax and super-tax practice.* Ed. 2, revised and enlarged. p. 265-6.)

SPICER, E. E. and E. C. PEGLER. Horses. (In their *Practical auditing.* 1914. p. 147).

WIHLFAHRT, JULIUS E. Depreciation. (In his *Treatise on increasing bakery efficiency.* 1917. p. 6.)

Horses, wagons and harness 15%

WOLFF, MARK. Interpretation of water works accounts. *Journal of the American waterworks association,* June 1916, p. 543, 546.

Horses, carriages and motors 10 years

Hospitals

See Depreciation, depletion and obsolescence—Institutions.

Hot beds

NICHOLSON, J. LEE AND J. F. D. ROHRBACH. Depreciation. (In their *Cost accounting.* 1919. p. 149.)

Mill machinery:
Hot beds 5½%

Hotels

AUSTRALIA. FEDERAL INCOME TAX DEPARTMENT. Depreciation allowance. *Accountant,* Oct. 13, 1917, p. 277-9. *Accounting and commerce,* June 30, 1917, p. 55-7. *Federal accountant,* July 1917, p. 93-8. *Public accountant,* Jan. 30, 1917, p. 145-52.

Hotels—crockery and glassware. Replacements and repairs allowable.
Plant and furniture 7½%
Based on written down value and repairs allowed in addition.

BOLTON, REGINALD PELHAM. Depreciation of the value of buildings. (In his *Building for profit.* 1911. p. 76.) Burton, H. J. *Valuations and depreciations of city building.* p. 21-2.

Hotels 15-18 years

DICKSEE, LAWRENCE ROBERT. Depreciation. (In his *Hotel accounts.* 1912. p. 64-5).

Fixtures, furniture, etc. 5-7½-10%

JENKINSON, M. WEBSTER. Depreciation. *Accountant,* May 17, 1902, p. 528-34.

Hotel bedding, linen, plate, cutlery, glass, etc.
(1) charge all renewals to revenue
(2) debit all renewals direct to capital

MONTGOMERY, ROBERT H. Hotels. (In his *Auditing theory and practice.* 1916. p. 741-2.)

Furnishings, such as china, glass, cutlery, silver, linen, etc., may be reappraised at periods when statements are prepared or depreciated at such times at adequate rates. Another good method is to credit regularly a reserve account and charge against the profit and loss account amounts sufficient to cover the estimated actual renewals and depreciation over a period of years, and then to charge all renewals to this reserve account.

NICHOLSON, J. LEE and J. F. D. ROHRBACH. Depreciation. (In their *Cost accounting.* 1919. p. 146.)

Hotels 5%
Based on (1) the cost of equipment
(2) the life of the equipment
(3) on a ten-hour day.

PIXLEY, FRANCIS W. Hotels. (In his *Accountancy.* Ed.2. p. 219.)

Hotels:
Furniture 2½%
Carpets 15-25
Electro plate 10
China and glass 20-30

TIFFANY, H. S. Hotels. (In his *Digest of depreciation.* c1890. p. 7.)

Buildings
brick and stone 2½-3½%
frame 3½-4½
Based upon the actual life without any repairs.

Household

BOLTON, REGINALD PELHAM. Depreciation of mechanical equipments and power plants. (In his *Building for profit.* 1911. p. 82-9.)

	Physical years	Physical %	Economic years
Sanitary fixtures, refrigerating, piping, kitchen fixtures, and valves	20	50.0	16
Elevators in regular use, laundry, kitchen, refrigerating, electric devices, and other apparatus frequently reserved	16	40.0	14

PHILADELPHIA. CONTROLLER. Rates of depreciation. (In his *Manual of accounting, reporting and business procedure of the city and county of Philadelphia.* 1917. p. 207-8.)

Kitchen, dining room and household utensils and crockery 10%

TIFFANY, H. S. Household furniture. (In his *Digest of depreciations.* c1890. p. 15.)

	% annual dep. Household furniture	Furnished houses
Carpets	10	20
Furniture	10	20
Crockery and glassware	25	33⅓
Stoves and cutlery	10	20
Beds and bedding	10	20
Pianos	5	10
Mirrors	5	10
Pictures and paintings	5	10
Books	10	20
Family weaving apparel	50	50
Plated ware	10	20

DEPRECIATION, DEPLETION AND OBSOLESCENCE—*(Continued)*

Humidifiers

UNIFORM cost sheet for coal mining companies. *Coal age,* Sept. 19 1918, p. 545-7.

Humidifier building	original cost.
wood	7%
stone or brick	5
Humidifiers	12½

Hunting

PHILADELPHIA. CONTROLLER. Rates of depreciation. (In his *Manual of accounting, reporting and business procedure of the city and county of Philadelphia.* 1917. p. 205.)

Fishing, hunting and trapping equipment 10%

Hutches

MANN, JOHN AND H. C. JUDD. Depreciation. (In their *Colliery accounts.* 1909. p. 69-75, 92.)

Hutches 15-20%

Calculated on the balance as diminished from year to year.

Hydrants

AMERICAN INSTITUTE OF ACCOUNTANTS. Report of the committee on standard schedules for uniform reports upon municipal industries and public service corporations; annual meeting at Atlantic city, N. J. October 20-22, 1908. 15p. *Journal of accountancy,* May 1909, p. 47-54.

The knowledge at the command of the Bureau of the census leads to the conclusion that this average life is approximately as follows:

Fire hydrants 50 years.

AMERICAN WATERWORKS ASSOCIATION. Final report of committee on depreciation. *Journal of the American water works association,* Sept. 1917, p. 1-38.

Hydrants 30-50 years

BARKER, HARRY. Typical life expectation tables for public utility property. (In his *Public utility rates.* 1917. p. 367.)

	years	
Hydrants	40-50	L. Metcalf

BRYAN, WILLIAM. Appraisal and depreciation of water-works and similar properties. *Journal of the association of engineering societies,* Dec. 1907, p. 336-81. Depreciation allowance for various public service industries. *Engineering news,* Jan. 23, 1908, p. 96.

Hydrants	Years	% Straight
fire	25-35	
fire		2
fire	40	

CHASE, HARVEY S. Depreciation in water works accounts, with reference to uniform reports. *Journal of the New England water works association,* June 1910, p. 305-31. Abstract. *Engineering and contracting,* June 29, 1910, p. 598. Editorial. Depreciation and sinking fund accounts. *Municipal engineering,* July 1910, p. 26.

Masonry of filtration plant, cribs, iron water pipes, intake pipes, fire hydrants, stand pipes and buildings. 50 years.

CLADER, WILL A. Water utilities accounting. *Journal of accountancy,* Aug. 1919, p. 91-2.

The following rate is used frequently when wear and tear are made good by operating maintenance.

Hydrants 2%

ELBOURNE, EDWARD T. Depreciation rates. (In his *Factory administration and accounts.* 1918. p. 376).

	Remainder values	10%	5%
	Prov. dep. %	years	
Fire hydrants, valves and pipes	6	37	48

ESTIMATED life and depeciation of water works plants. *Municipal journal and engineer,* May 6, 1908, p. 558.

Material	Life in years	Straight per year	Authority
Fire hydrants	25-35	2	Wm. H. Bryan Los Angeles, Cal. Engineering news May 4, 1899.
	40		B. Williams Gal, Kans. app. in 1905.

GILLETTE, HALBERT P. and RICHARD T. DANA. Depreciation. (In their *Handbook of mechanical and electrical cost data.* 1918. p. 108).

Hydrants	40-50 years Leonard Metcalf, Transactions, American society civil engineers, 1909, p. 24, vol. 64.
Connections	6.6 years H. P. Gillette, Everett railway & water co., Jan. 29, 1912.

GRUNSKY, CARL EWALD. Probable useful life of various articles. (In his *Valuation, depreciation and the rate-base.* 1917. p. 279).

Fire hydrants	40 years Benezette Williams. Galena appraisal, Kansas, 1905. 40-50 years Leonard Metcalf. Transactions American society of civil Engineers, 1909.

DEPRECIATION, DEPLETION AND OBSOLESCENCE—HYDRANTS—*(Continued)*

HAZLEHURST, J. N. Final report of the committee on depreciation. *Journal of the American water works association,* March 1919, p. 85-135.
Hydrants 30-50 years

METCALF, LEONARD. Depreciation in waterworks operation and accounting. *Journal of the New England waterworks association,* Dec. 1910, p. 442. Abstracts. *Engineering news,* Nov. 3, 1910, p. 482. Methods of computing depreciation of and reasonable assumptions as to period of useful life of waterworks. *Engineering and contracting,* Nov. 16, 1910, p. 434.

	years	striaght line
Hydrants	35-50	3-2%

METCALF, LEONARD. Water-works valuation and fair rate in the light of the Maine supreme court decisions in the Waterville and Brunswick cases. *American society of civil engineers, Transactions,* Sept. 1909, p. 1. *American society of civil engineers, Papers and discussions,* 1908, p. 1101-73. Foster, Horatio A. *Engineering valuation of public utilities and factories,* 1913. p. 207. Gillette, Halbert P. *Handbook of cost data for contractors and engineers.* p. 797.

Material	Life in years	% Dep. per year Sinking fund
Hydrants	40-50	1-½

PROBABLE lives of water-works elements. *Engineering news,* Oct. 11, 1917, p. 688.
Hydrants 30-50 years

WOLFF, MARK. Interpretation of water works accounts. *Journal of the American water works association,* June 1916, p. 543, 546.
Mains, fire hydrants, stand pipes, buildings, masonry 50 years

Hydraulic jacks

NICHOLSON, J. LEE and J. F. D. ROHRBACH. Depreciation. (In their *Cost accounting.* 1919. p. 150).
Hydraulic jacks 10%

Hydraulic plant

ELBOURNE, EDWARD T. Depreciation rates. (In his *Factory administration and accounts.* 1918. p. 377).

	Prov. dep. % Remainder values	Years 10%	5%
Hydraulic machinery	6	37	48

NICHOLSON J. LEE and JOHN F. D. ROHRBACH. Depreciation. (In their *Cost accounting.* 1919. p. 148, 149).

Hydraulic plant equipment	6%
Water lines	5
Pumps	7½
Hydraulic accumulators	5½

Based on (1) the cost of equipment
(2) the life of the equipment
(3) on a ten-hour day

RUNYON, F. D. Report on hydro-electric plant for special committee, common council, Newark, New Jersey. April 23, 1902, p. 15, 16.
Hydraulic construction exclusive of steel pipe line 1%

Hydro-electric plants

See Electric light and power companies.

Ice

AUSTRALIA. *Federal income tax department.* Depreciation allowance. *Accountant,* Oct. 13, 1917, p. 277-9. *Accounting and commerce,* June 30, 1917, p. 55-7. *Federal accountant,* July 1917, p. 93-8. *Public accountant,* Jan. 30, 1917. p. 145-52.
Ice making 5%
Written down value, repairs allowed in addition.

DEPRECIATION, ice industry. *American institute of accountants,* Special bulletin, no. 5, Sept. 1920, p. 5.

PUBLIC utilities reports, annotated. Rochester, Lawyers co-operative publishing co. 1918E. p. 540.
Harbster v. Angelica water & ice co. (Pa.) In the valuation of a water and ice plant for rate making, the average life of the entire plant was found to be fifty-three years and the rate of annual depreciation 0.96 per cent.

TIFFANY, H. S. Ice houses. (In his *Digest of depreciations.* c1890. p. 9).

Buildings	
brick	3%
frame	4

Based upon the actual life without any repairs.

Ice boxes

See Depreciation, depletion and obsolescence—Refrigerators.

Ice scrapers

PHILADELPHIA. CONTROLLER. Rates of depreciation. (In his *Manual of accounting, reporting and business procedure of the city and county of Philadelphia.* 1917. p. 208).
Snow shovels, ice scrapers and planers, etc. 12½%

Inclines

See Depreciation, depletion and obsolescence—Slopes and inclines.

Ingot buggies

NICHOLSON, J. LEE and J. F. D. ROHRBACH. Depreciation. (In their *Cost accounting.* 1919. p. 149).
Ingot buggies 5½%

DEPRECIATION, DEPLETION AND OBSOLESCENCE—*(Continued)*

Injectors

ELBOURNE, EDWARD T. Depreciation rates. (In his *Factory administration and accounts.* 1918. p. 376).

	Prov. dep. % Remainder values	years 10%	5%
Injectors	12½%	17	22

Insect sprayers

PHILADELPHIA. CONTROLLER. Rates of depreciation. (In his *Manual of accounting, reporting and business procedure of the city and county of Philadelphia.* 1917. p. 208).
Insect sprayers 20%

Inspectors

PHILADELPHIA. CONTROLLER. Rates of depreciation. (In his *Manual of accounting, reporting and business procedure of the city and county of Philadelphia.* 1917. p. 209).
Equipment for inspecting supplies (exclusive of construction) work 10%
Inspectors badges 4

Installments

DICKSEE, LAWRENCE R. Depreciation. (In his *Advanced accounting.* 1916. p. 277-80).

GUTHRIE, EDWIN. Depreciation. (In Lisle, George. *Encyclopaedia of accounting.* v.2. p. 357-76).
Plant acquired on hire and purchase system.
By perpetual renewal if a railway company having permanent existence. If a terminable company 5-7½%

JENKINSON, M. WEBSTER. Depreciation. *Accountant,* May 17, 1902, p. 528-34.

OFFICIAL allowance in respect of depreciation of machinery and plant. Board of Inland revenue, Great Britain. *Agccountant,* May 16, 1914, p. 735.

WHATLEY, G. E. STUART. Depreciation—hire purchase system. (In his *Accountant's and bookkeeper's vade-mecum.* 1893. p. 26-7.).

Institutions

AUSTRALIA. Federal income tax department. Depreciation allowance. *Accountant,* Oct. 13, 1917, p. 277-9. *Accounting and commerce,* June 30, 1917, p. 55-7. *Federal accountant,* July 1917, p. 93-8. *Public accountant,* Jan. 30, 1917, p. 145-52.
Hospital furniture 7½
Hospital bedding, lineh, crockery, etc. Replacements allowable
Based on written down value and repairs allowed in addition.

BOLTON, REGINALD PELHAM. Depreciation of the value of buildings. (In his *Building for profit.* 1911. p. 76.).
Banks and institutions. 44-50 years

PHILADELPHIA. CONTROLLER. Rates of depreciation. (In his *Manual of accounting, reporting and business procedure of the city and county of Philadelphia.* 1917. p. 209).
Buildings:
Hospitals, asylums, prisons, etc. 1%
Equipment for handling insane patients 5

TIFFANY, H. S. Asylums and infirmaries. (In his *Digest of depreciations.* c1890. p.8).
Buildings
brick or stone 2½-3%
frame 3½-4
Based upon the actual life without any repairs.

Instrument cases

PHILADELPHIA. CONTROLLER. Rates of depreciation. (In his *Manual of accounting, reporting and business procedure of the city and county of Philadelphia.* 1917. p. 206).
Cases for instruments 3⅓%

Insulators

BRYAN, WILLIAM. Appraisal and depreciation of water works and similar properties. *Journal of the Association of engineering societies,* Dec. 1907, p. 336-81. Depreciation allowance for various public service industries. *Engineering news,* Jan. 23, 1908, p. 96. Depreciation of electric light plants. *Municipality,* March 1908, p. 74.

Insulators	Dep. % per year Straight	Authority
pole line	12	Chicago city railway, Street railway journal, Dec. 1898.
trolley	7	Chicago city railway, Street railway journal, Dec. 1898.

CLINE, E. L. Depreciation of telephone companies. *Telephony,* July 2, 1910, p. 16.

	Years	% Dep.	% Salvage
Insulators	15	3.33	50

COST and depreciation of steam and hydro-electric installations. *Electrical world,* Dec. 30, 1909, p. 1558.
Insulators 10 years .170% of total cost.

SALIERS, EARL H. Analysis of a hydroelectric plant. (In his *Principles of depreciation.* 1916. p. 34-8).
Insulators 10 years

DEPRECIATION, DEPLETION AND OBSOLESCENCE—*(Continued)*

Intensifiers

NICHOLSON, J. LEE and J. F. D. ROHRBACH. Depreciation. (In their *Cost accounting.* 1919. p. 149).
Mill machinery—intensifiers 5%

Investment companies

MONTGOMERY, ROBERT H. Investment companies. (In his *Auditing, theory and practice.* 1916. p. 553-4).
SPICER, ERNEST EVAN and E. C. PEGLER. Trust and finance companies. (In their *Practical auditing.* Edition 2. p. 516.).

Investments

See Investments and securities.

Iron and steel

BOLTON, REGINALD PELHAM. Depreciation of mechanical equipment and power plants. (In his *Building for profit.* 1911. p. 82-89).

	Physical years	%	Economic years
Most durable elements steel construction, foundations, elevator guides, and overhead framing	40	100.0	30

DEPRECIATION of unprotected steel work. *Iron age,* Feb. 2, 1911, p. 306.
FOSTER, H. A. Depreciation as affecting collieries and iron works. *Iron and coal trades review,* Nov. 21, 1902, p. 1303.
GREAT BRITAIN. Board of inland revenue. Depreciation rates: (In its *Income tax; statement respecting allowances for wear and tear and obsolescence of plant and machinery.* 1918. Cd. 9022, p. 4, Cd. 9134, p. 6.) *American economic review,* Supplement, Dec. 1920, p. 51. *Journal of accountancy,* Sept. 1920, p. 195. Income tax notes. *Accountant,* Sept. 28, 1918, p. 162-6. *Incorporated accountant's journal,* May 11, Oct. 1918, p. 358-60, 14.
Steel manufacturers.
Machinery and plant used in the manufacture of steel 15%
Written down value.
Note: The rate of 15 per cent represents 5 per cent for normal wear and tear and 10 per cent for the additional wear and tear arising from war conditions.
JONES, EDWARD DAVID. Depreciation. (In his *Investment.* p. 167).
Physical property of steel companies 7%
United States steel corporation 7
NICHOLSON, J. LEE and J. F. D. ROHRBACH. Depreciation. (In their *Cost accounting.* 1919. p. 148).
Steel work—including air, oil, and water tanks, stand pipes; gas, hot, and cold, blast furnaces and bessemer plant; scrap drops, crane runways (when not included as part of buildings), bins, racks, poles, foot bridges, steel stack, wire screening, drop balls, coke and ore pockets; heating pockets, cribs, skip, hoists, ladle rests, smoke boxes, etc.; plate carriers, etc. 4%
TIFFANY, H. S. Machinery. (In his *Digest of depreciation.* c1890. p. 12).
Machinery 6% annual depreciation
UNITED STATES. BUREAU OF CORPORATIONS. Depreciation and stripping. (In *Report of the commissioner on the steel industry.* 1913. v. 3. p. 36-8).

Iron gratings

PHILADELPHIA. CONTROLLER. Rates of depreciation. (In his *Manual of accounting, reporting and business procedure of the city and county of Philadelphia.* 1917. p. 208).
Iron gratings etc. 2%

Iron stakes

PHILADELPHIA. CONTROLLER. Rates of depreciation. (In his *Manual of accounting, reporting and business procedure of the city and county of Philadelphia.* 1917. p. 208).
Iron stakes used in parks 10%

Irrigation

AUSTRALIA. FEDERAL INCOME TAX DEPARTMENT. Depreciation allowance. *Accountant,* Oct. 13, 1917, p. 277-9. *Accounting and commerce,* June 30, 1917, p. 55-7. *Federal accountant,* July 1917, p. 93-8. *Public accountant,* Jan. 30, 1917, p. 145-52.
Irrigation plant 5%
Based on written down value and repairs allowed in addition.
WHITTEN, ROBERT HARVEY. Annual depreciation allowance. (In his *Valuation of public service corporations.* 1912. p. 430-1).
Three per cent allowance on straight line basis in irrigation rate case, 1911.

Jack shaft

FOSTER, HORATIO A. Rates of depreciation. (In his *Engineering valuation of public utilities and factories.* 1913. p. 205).
Jack shaft 20-40 years' life

Jails

See Depreciation, depletion and obsolescence—Prisons

Jam

AUSTRALIA. FEDERAL INCOME TAX DEPARTMENT. Depreciation allowance, *Accountant,* Oct. 13, 1917, p. 277-9. *Accounting and commerce,* June 30, 1917, p. 55-7. *Federal accountant,* July 1917, p. 93-8. *Public accountant,* Jan. 30, 1917, p. 145-52.
Jam factory plant 5%
Based on written down value and repairs allowed in addition.

DEPRECIATION, DEPLETION AND OBSOLESCENCE—*(Continued)*

Jarring machines

NICHOLSON, J. LEE and J. F. D. ROHRBACH. Depreciation. (In their *Cost accounting.* 1919. p. 150).
Jarring machines 10%

Jewelry trade

EDWARDS, ALLEN. Depreciation. (In his *Jewellers', silversmiths', and kindred traders' accounts.* 1903. p. 144, 57).
Plant, machinery, etc. 5%

Jigs

NORRIS, H. M. Depreciation of plants and its relation to general expense. *Engineering magazine,* April 1899, p. 76.
Special tools, jigs, and fixtures 5%

WOODS, CLINTON E. Depreciation, dies, jigs, fixtures and gages. (In his *Unified accounting methods for industrials.* 1917. p. 65.)
25 to 50% per annum, according to their character and usage.

Jockeys

AUSTRALIA. FEDERAL INCOME TAX DEPARTMENT. Depreciation allowance. *Accountant,* Oct. 13, 1917, p. 277-9. *Accounting and commerce,* June 30, 1917, p. 55-7. *Federal accountant,* July 1917, p. 93-8. *Public accountant,* Jan. 30, 1917, p. 145-52.
Jockeys' accoutrements, saddles whips, boots &c. 20%
Based on written down value and repairs allowed in addition.

Joggling machines

NICHOLSON, J. LEE and JOHN F. D. ROHRBACH. Depreciation. (In their *Cost accounting.* 1919. p. 149).
Joggling machines 6⅔%

Kettles

NICHOLSON, J. LEE and J. F. D. ROHRBACH. Depreciation. (In their *Cost accounting.* 1919. p. 150.).
Fixed kettles and scales 10%

Key-seating machines

ELBOURNE, EDWARD T. Depreciation rates. (In his *Factory administration and accounts.* 1918. p. 377).

	Prov. dep. % Remainder values	years 10%	5%
Key-seating machines	7½	29	38

Kilns

NICHOLSON, J. LEE and J. F. D. ROHRBACH. Depreciation. (In their *Cost accounting.* 1919. p. 148).
Dolomite and lime kilns, rotary nodulizing kilns 6⅔%
Based on (1) The cost of equipment
(2) the life of the equipment
(3) on a ten-hour day.

Kitchens

See Depreciation, depletion and obsolescence—Household

Knit goods

BASSET, W. R. and S. R. GORDON. Cost system that guides policies. *Factory,* Jan. 1920, p. 43-8.

	Rate % Depreciation
Yarn mill machinery	7½%
Knitting machinery	7½
Finishing machinery	7½
Dye & bleach machinery	15
Reinforced concrete building	2
Steel & brick wood-floor building	2½
Brick wall, wood frame and floor building	3
Wood frame building	5

TEXTILE WORLD RECORD. Depreciation. (In its *Kinks on cost finding in knitting mills.* 1910. p. 58-9.).
The allowance on this must be enough to pay for repairs to the building, wear and tear of the machinery and interest say 10% a year.
Allowed for money invested 6%
Wear and tear of machinery, for 10 years 4%

Laboratory and scientific equipment

BELT, ROBERT E. Depreciation. (In his *Foundry cost accounting practice and procedure.* 1919. p. 242).
Laboratory equipment 10%

BELT, ROBERT E. Depreciation. (In his *Uniform cost accounting methods; adopted by the American malleable castings association,* Nov. 14, 1917, p. 20-1).
Laboratory equipment 10%

CLADER, WILL-A. Water utilities accounting. *Journal of accountancy,* Aug. 1919, p. 91-2.
The following rate is used frequently when wear and tear are made good by operating maintenance.
Laboratory equipment 10%

DEPRECIATION, DEPLETION AND OBSOLESCENCE—LABORATORY AND SCIENTIFIC EQUIPMENT—*(Continued)*

NICHOLSON, J. LEE and J. F. D. ROHRBACH. Depreciation. (In their *Cost accounting.* 1919. p. 151).
Laboratory and scientific apparatus 10%
Based on (1) the cost of equipment
(2) the life of the equipment
(3) on a ten-hour day

PHILADELPHIA. CONTROLLER. Rates of depreciation. (In his *Manual of accounting, reporting and business procedure of the city and county of Philadelphia.* 1917. p. 208-9).

	Rate % depreciation
Scientific equipment	
Surgical and medical equipment	5
Measuring instruments and accessories	5
Weighing and metering apparatus	5
Aids to the senses	5
Photographing equipment	10
Mechanical drafting devices	10
Laboratory equipment not classified	5
Special miscellaneous educational, scientific and recreational equipment	8⅓

Lacing machines

DENHAM, ROBERT S. Depreciation. (In his *Manual of cost engineering and estimating for paper box manufacturers.* 1917. p. 249).
S. & S. lacing machines 12%

Ladders

PHILADELPHIA. *Controller.* Rates of depreciation. (In his *Manual of accounting, reporting and business procedure of the city and county of Philadelphia.* 1917. p. 208, 206).

	Rate % Depreciation
Step ladders	12½
Traveling ladders, etc.	20

Ladles

AUSTRALIA. FEDERAL INCOME TAX DEPARTMENT. Depreciation allowance. *Accountant,* Oct. 13, 1917, p. 277-9. *Accounting and commerce,* June 30, 1917, p. 55-7. *Federal accountant,* July 1917, p. 93-8. *Public accountant,* Jan. 30, 1917, p. 145-52.
Ladles 10%
Based on written down value and repairs allowed in addition.

NICHOLSON, J. LEE and J. F. D. ROHRBACH. Depreciation. (In their *Cost accounting.* 1919. p. 148).
Ladle rests 4%
Steel ladles 20

Lamps

See Depreciation, depletion and obsolescence—Lighting.

Lamson tube system

AUSTRALIA. FEDERAL INCOME TAX DEPARTMENT. Depreciation allowance. *Accountant,* Oct. 13, 1917, p. 277-9. *Accounting and commerce,* June 30, 1917, p. 55-7. *Federal accountant,* July 1917, p. 93-8. *Public accountant,* Jan. 30, 1917, p. 145-52.
Lamson tube system 10%
Based on writen down value and repairs allowed in addition.

Land

BRYAN, WILLIAM H. Depreciation of electric light plants. *Municipality,* March 1908, p. 74.

Land—Purchase	years
Under housing of working classes acts	60
Otherwise where act allows	80

DICKSEE, LAWRENCE R. Land. (In his *Auditing.* Authorized American edition. 1909. p. 189).
GUTHRIE, EDWIN. Depreciation. (In Lisle, George, *Encyclopaedia of accounting.* v.2. p.357-76.
KESTER, ROY B. Depreciation or appreciation of land. (In his *Accounting, theory and practice.* 1918. v.2. p. 304-6).
MONTGOMERY, ROBERT H. Land. (In his *Auditing theory and practice.* 1916. p. 418-9).
MONTGOMERY, ROBERT H. Land. (In his *Income tax procedure,* 1919. p. 566-7. — Same, 1920. p. 719).

NEALE, R. E. Depreciation in engineering works. *Mechanical world,* Feb. 7, 1913, p. 67-8.
Land
Freehold ½% 5-100 years.
A highly approximate figure; freehold land in towns often appreciates considerably.
RACINE, SAMUEL F. Land and appurtenances (In his *Accounting principles.* 1917. p. 150-1).
SPICER, E. E. and E. C. PEGLER. Freehold land. (In their *Practical auditing.* 1914. p. 139).
WHATLEY, G. E. STUART. Depreciation—freehold land. (In his *Accountant's and bookkeeper's vade-mecum.* 1893. p. 25).

YEAMAN, C. H. Depreciation and reserves for antiquation and obsolescence from an engineering standpoint. *Electrical engineering* (London), July 12, 1907, p. 46. *Electrical review* (London), July 12, 1907, p. 44. *Electrician,* July 5, 1907, p. 475.
Land 60 years
R. Hammond
60 years
L. C. C.
100 years
Snell (M.E.A. 1905)

DEPRECIATION, DEPLETION AND OBSOLESCENCE—*(Continued)*

Larries

UNIFORM cost sheet for coal mining companies. *Coal age,* Sept. 19, 1918, p. 545-7.
Incline drums and larries — 10% original cost

Lathes

BELT, ROBERT E. Depreciation. (In his *Foundry cost accounting practice and procedure.* 1919. p. 243).
Lathes — 10%

BELT, ROBERT E. Depreciation. (In his *Uniform cost accounting methods; adopted by the American malleable castings association,* Nov. 14, 1917, p. 20-1).
Lathes — 10%

DEPRECIATION. *American institute of accountants,* Special bulletin, no. 1, Jan. 1920, p. 6-7.

ELBOURNE, EDWARD T. Depreciation rates. (In his *Factory administration and accounts.* 1918. p. 377).

Lathes	Prov. dep. % Remainder values	years 10%	years 5%
bench precision	7½	29	38
boring and facing	6	37	48
brass finishers	7½	29	38
capstan	7½	29	38
crankshaft	7½	29	38
engine	6	37	48
hand	6	37	48
pulley	6	37	48
relieving	6	37	48
shaving	7½	29	38
turret, horizontal	7½	29	38
turret, vertical	7½	29	38
wood-working	6	37	48

NICHOLSON, J. LEE and JOHN F. D. ROHRBACH. Depreciation. (In their *Cost accounting.* 1919. p. 149).
Lathes — 6⅔%

Launches

See Depreciation, depletion and obsolescence—Ships.

Laundries

AUSTRALIA. *Federal income tax department.* Depreciation allowance. *Accountant,* Oct. 31, 1917, p. 277-9. *Accounting and commerce,* June 30, 1917, p. 55-7. *Federal accountant,* July 1917, p. 93-8. *Public accountant,* Jan. 30, 1917, p. 145-52.
Laundry plant — 5%
Based on written down value and repairs allowed in addition.

BOLTON, REGINALD PELHAM. Depreciation of mechanical equipments and power plants. (In his *Building for profit.* 1911. p. 82, 89).

	Physical years	%	Economic years
Elevators in regular use, laundry, kitchen, refrigerating, electric devices, and other apparatus frequently reversed	16	40.0	14

LIVESEY, FRANCIS JAMES. Depreciation. (In his *Laundry accounts.* 1905. p. 92-4).
Laundries:
Freehold premises — 2%
Plant and machinery — 10
Horses — re-valuation
Carts and vans — 15
Baskets and hampers — 25

MONTGOMERY, ROBERT H. Laundries. (In his *Auditing theory and practice.* 1916, p. 418).
Buildings—rate is very low.
Equipment—average — 8%

MONTGOMERY, ROBERT H. Laundries. (In his *Income tax procedure,* 1919. p. 567).
Equipment — 8%

PHILADELPHIA. CONTROLLER. Rates of depreciation. (In his *Manual of accounting, reporting and business procedure of the city and county of Philadelphia.* 1917. p. 209).
Laundry equipment — 8⅓%

Lawn mowers

PHILADELPHIA. CONTROLLER. Rates of depreciation. (In his *Manual of accounting, reporting and business procedure of the city and county of Philadelphia.* 1917. p. 209).
Trimming (lawn mower) — 12½%

Lawns

PHILADELPHIA. CONTROLLER. Rates of depreciation. (In his *Manual of accounting, reporting and business procedure of the city and county of Philadelphia.* 1917. p. 209).
Clipping, trimming, rolling, and watering equipment for lawn and garden: — 12½%
Trimming (lawn mower) — 3
Rolling — 12½
Watering — 12½
Lawn and garden tools and implements, hose and reels — 12½
Snow shovels, ice scrapers and planers, etc.

DEPRECIATION, DEPLETION AND OBSOLESCENCE—*(Continued)*

Leaseholds

CARTER, R. N. Rates of depreciation. (In his *Advanced accounts.* p. 618).
Leasehold land and buildings written off over the period of lease.
DENSHAM, F. W. Depreciation of assets and goodwill of limited companies. *Accountant,* May 28, 1898, p. 569.
DICKSEE, LAWRENCE R. Depreciation of leaseholds. (In his *Depreciation reserves and reserve funds.* 1912. p. 18-21).
DICKSEE, LAWRENCE R. Depreciation of leases. (In his *Bookkeeping for company secretaries.* 1908. p. 91-2).
DICKSEE, LAWRENCE R. Leasehold land and premises. (In his *Auditing.* Authorized American edition. 1909. p. 191-2).
GUTHRIE, EDWIN. Depreciation. (In *Lisle, George, Encyclopaedia of accounting.* v.2. p. 357-76).
Building—Leaseholds. As an annuity having regard to interest, or at discretion, equal division of original value by the number of years to run.
JENKINSON, M. WEBSTER. Depreciation. *Accountant,* May 17, 1902, p. 528-34.
KESTER, ROY B. Leaseholds. (In his *Accounting theory and practice.* 1918. v.2. p. 314-5).
MONTGOMERY, ROBERT H. Leaseholds. (In his *Auditing and practice.* 1916. p. 421-2).
MONTGOMERY, ROBERT H. Leaseholds. (In his *Income tax procedure,* 1919. p. 567-8. ——— Same, 1920, p. 720).
NEALE, R. E. Depreciation in engineering works. *Mechanical world,* Feb. 7, 1913, p. 67-8.
In the case of leaseholds buildings, a sinking fund must be established to re-purchase the lease of these, or equivalent buildings and to cover repairs which may be required on giving up lease.
PIXLEY, FRANCIS W. Leases. (In his *Accountancy.* Ed. 2. p. 213-4).
RACINE, SAMUEL F. Leasholds. (In his *Accounting principles.* 1917. p. 151-3).
SPICER, E. E. and E. C. PEGLER. Leasehold land and buildings. (In their *Practical auditing.* 1914. p. 140-3).
WHATLEY, G. E. STUART. Leases. (In his *Accountant's and bookkeeper's vade-mecum.* 1893. p. 24).

Leather

PHILADELPHIA. CONTROLLER. Rates of depreciation. (In his *Manual of accounting, reporting and business procedure of the city and county of Philadelphia.* 1917. p. 205).
Tanners' and leather workers' equipment 3⅓%
TIFFANY, H. S. Leather. (In his *Digest of depreciations.* c1890. p. 15).
Leather depreciates annually 25%

Libraries

AUSTRALIA. FEDERAL INCOME TAX DEPARTMENT. Depreciation allowance. *Accountant,* Oct. 13, 1917, p. 277-9. *Accounting and commerce,* June 30, 1917, p. 55-7. *Federal accountant,* July 1917, p. 93-8. *Public accountant,* Jan. 30, 1917, p. 145-52.
Libraries
professional 1%
circulating (Instead of allowing depreciation, taxpayers may be permitted to deal with their lending stock in a Trading account. This will provide for allowance of replacements without the danger of increases in the stock being debited against income. Where library is kept by a bookseller who does not keep separate record of his lending stock, such stock may be taken into the general trading account. If a taxpayer specially claims depreciation, and does not wish to adopt the trading account system, discretion should be used as to the allowance to be made for depreciation the class of literature and the binding being taken into consideration).
NEW YORK. COMMITTEE ON EDUCATION. Depreciation on books. (In its *Analysis of the funds of the New York (circulating department) Brooklyn and Queens Borough public libraries.* 1916. p. 17).

	Dep. per 1000 circulation
New York public library (Circulation dept).	$10.36
Brooklyn public library	12.47
Queens Borough public library	11.04
Total	$33.87
Average	11.29

The variation in the amount of depreciation per 1,000 circulation is about in proportion to the difference in the average price paid for books in each of the three library systems.
PHILADELPHIA. CONTROLLER. Rates of depreciation. (In his *Manual of accounting, reporting and business procedure of the city and county of Philadelphia.* 1917. p. 209).
Library stock 5%

Licenses

DENSHAM, F. W. Depreciation of assets and goodwill of limited companies. *Accountant,* May 28, 1898, p. 567-71.

Life saving

PHILADELPHIA. CONTROLLER. Rates of depreciation. (In his *Manual of accounting, reporting and business procedure of the city and county of Philadelphia.* 1917. p. 208).

	Rate % of Dep.
Life saving equipment	
Fire life nets, and other equipment	10
Danger signs	50

Lifts

See Depreciation, depletion and obsolescence—Elevators.

Lighters

See Depreciation, depletion and obsolescence—Ships.

DEPRECIATION, DEPLETION AND OBSOLESCENCE—*(Continued)*

Lighting

See also Depreciation, depletion and obsolescence—Electric lighting and power plants;—Gas

AUSTRALIA. FEDERAL INCOME TAX DEPARTMENT. Depreciation allowance. *Accountant,* Oct. 13, 1917, p. 277-9. *Accounting and commerce,* June 30, 1917, p. 55-7. *Federal accountant,* July 1917, p. 83-8. *Public accountant,* Jan. 30, 1917, p. 145-52.

Arc lamps 10%

Written down value, repairs allowed.

BARKER, HARRY. Typical life expectation tables for public utility property. (In his *Public utility rates.* 1917. p. 368-9).

Arc lamps and hangings	10-15 years	Wis. R.R. commission. St. Louis P.S. commission.

BAY state rate case. *Electric railway journal,* Dec. 4, 1915, p. 1121-3. *Public utility reports, annotated,* 1916F, p. 336-9.

Arc headlights 8 years

BOLTON, REGINALD PELHAM. Depreciation of the value of buildings. (In his *Building for profit.* 1911. p. 62).

	Relative to 66 yrs.	Relative to 75 yrs.
	Percent	Percent
Lighting fixtures	30	26

BRYAN, WILLIAM. Appraisal and depreciation of water works and similar properties. *Journal of the association of engineering societies,* Dec. 1907, p. 336-81. Depreciation allowance for various public-service industries. *Engineering news,* Jan. 23, 1908, p. 96.

	years
Arc lamps	8
" "	12 - 15

BRYAN, WILLIAM H. Depreciation of electric light plants. *Municipality,* March 1908, p. 74.

Arc lamps	8 years	Iowa electrical association, in Iowa Engineer, July 1906.
	12-15 years	Author

COMARATIVE costs between high and low pressure gas for lighting. *Gas age,* Sept. 1, 1913, p. 215.

Lamps 10%

CROWELL, H. H. Electric lighting rates and depreciation. *Municipal journal and engineering,* Dec. 18, 1907, p. 698.

	Purchased 10 years or more ago	modern
Arc lamps	10 years	10 years

ELBOURNE, EDWARD T. Depreciation rates. (In his *Factory administration and accounts.* 1918. p. 376).

	Prov. dep. %	years	
	Remainder values	10%	5%
Light, wiring and fittings	7½	29	38

ENNIS, WILLIAM DUANE. Depreciation. (In his *Works management.* 1911. p. 86).

Arc lamps 12 years life to 0% residual value

Lamp posts 40 years life to 0% residual value

FIGURES from the Iola (Kans.) central station. *Electrical world,* Sept. 23, 1909, p. 723.

Arc lamps 20%

FLOY, HENRY. Depreciation. Floy, Henry. *Depreciation as related to electrical properties. American institute of electrical engineers, Proceedings,* 1911, p. 1267. Floy, Henry. *Valuation of public utility properties.* 1912. p. 168-217. Foster, Horatio A. *Engineering, valuation of public utilities and factories.* 1913. p. 194-8. *Engineering and contracting,* Oct. 4, 1911, p. 359-65. *Engineering magazine,* Aug. 1911, p. 837-40.

	Dep. per cent per year Straight line		
Arc lamps	6⅔	Wisconsin P.S.C.	
	15	Arbitrators	Street lighting controversy, Atlanta, Ga. 1899.
	8	St. Louis P.S.C.	Union elec. light and power co.

FOSTER, HORATIO A. Methods of calculating depreciation. (In his *Engineering valuation of public utilities and factories.* 1913. p. 169-70).

Arc lamps and span equipment. Minimum service value 20% of reproduction cost.

FOSTER, HORATIO A. Rates of depreciation. (In his *Engineering valuation of public utilities and factories.* 1913, p. 206).

	Years' life
Arc lamps and span equipment	10-15
Nernst lamps	8-10

GILLETTE, HALBERT P. and RICHARD T. DANA. Cost of street lighting in Chicago. (In their *Mechanical and electrical cost data.* 1918. p. 1039).

Lamps 6.66%

GILLETTE, HALBERT P. and RICHARD T. DANA. Depreciation. (In their *Handbook of mechanical and electrical cost data.* 1918, p. 105),

DEPRECIATION, DEPLETION AND OBSOLESCENCE—LIGHTING—*(Continued)*

Arc lamps — 6.7 years
Arbitrators, street lighting controversy, Atlanta, Ga., 1899.
12.5 years
St. Louis public service commission, Union electric light and power co.
15 years
Wisconsin Railroad commission.

GRUNSKY, CARL EWALD. Probable useful life of various articles. (In his *Valuation, depreciation and the rate base.* 1917. p. 274-80).

Lamps

arc — 6⅔ years.
Arbitrators. Board of Arbitration in street lighting controversy at Atlanta, Georgia, 1899.

arc — 12 years. 5% residual value.
Sir William Preece. Report of Bristol corporation, England, 1906.

arc — 12½ years.
St. Louis public service commission. Case of Union electric light & power co.

arc — 15 years.
Pacific gas & electric company. Figures used in rate hearings before master in chancery, San Francisco, 1913-4.

Nernst — 8-10 years.
H. A. Foster. "Engineering valuation of public utilities and factories," Van Nostrand, 1912.

arc lamp posts — 40 years. 5% residual value.
Sir Wm. Preece. Report of Bristol corporation, England, 1906.

Lighting systems

incandescent street — 15 years
Pacific gas and electric co. Figures used in rate hearings before master in chancery, San Francisco, 1913-4.

arc (commercial & mun.) — 15 years.
Pacific gas and electric company. Figures used in rate hearings before master in chancery, San Francisco, 1913-4.

municipal street — 20 years. 5% residual value.
California railroad commission—Reports 1913-4. Calistoga electric co. vs. Napa valley electric co., May 1914.

lighting protection — 10 years.
Pacific gas and electric company. Figures used in rate hearings before master in chancery, San Francisco, 1913-4.
15 years.
San Joaquin light & power corporation. Rate hearing before California railroad commission, 1915.
15-20 years.
H. A. Foster. "Engineering valuation of public utilities and factories," Van Nostrand, 1912.
10-12 years.
H. A. Foster. "Engineering valuation of public utilities and factories," Van Nostrand, 1912.

NEALE, R. E. Depreciation in engineering works. *Mechanical world,* Feb. 7, 1913, p. 67-8.

Arc lamps — 7-15% — 6-14 years

PENDER, HAROLD. Depreciation.. (In his *Handbook for electrical engineers.* c1914. p. 338.)

Arc lamps — 8 years
Iowa electric association
12-15 years
W. H. Bryan.

PHILADELPHIA. CONTROLLER. Rates of depreciation. (In his *Manual of accounting, reporting and business procedure of the city and county of Philadelphia.* 1917. p. 204, 210).

Lighting equipment	
Interior lighting fixtures	5%
Exterior lighting fixtures (attached to buildings, etc.)	5
Search lights	5
Incandescent lamps and arc lights	33⅓
Portable lights	10
Naptha street lamps and posts	4

ROBY, J. J. Schedule of plant depreciation. (In his *Treatise on cost accounting as applied to coal mining.* c1913. p. 14-5).

Lighting equipment:	
Light wires	
Deduct as salvage before depreciating	20%
Depreciation rate for remainder, fireproof	5
Fixtures and lamps	
Deduct as salvage before depreciating	10%
Depreciation rate for remainder, fireproof	5

SLAVIN, MATTHEW. Municipal electricity in Pasadena. *Public service,* April 1910, p. 105-8.

Poles, arc lamps and transformers — 10 years — 8.5%

YEAMAN, C. H. Depreciation and reserves for antiquation and obsolescence from an engineering standpoint. *Electrician,* July 5, 1907, p. 475. *Electrical engineering,* (London), July 12, 1907, p. 46. *Electrical review,* (London), July 12, 1907, p. 44.

DEPRECIATION, DEPLETION AND OBSOLESCENCE—LIGHTING—*(Continued)*

Arc lamps — 10 years
R. Hammond
7-10 years
L. G. B. (local gov't board).
15 years
J. F. C. Snell, (M.E.A. 1905).

Lightning arresters

BARKER, HARRY. Typical life expectation tables for public utility property. (In his *public utility rates.* 1917. p. 368-9).
Lightning arresters — 15-20 years — Wisconsin R.R. commission

ELBOURNE, EDWARD T. Depreciation. (In his *Factory administration and accounts.* 1918, p. 376).

FOSTER, HORATIO A. Methods of calculating depreciation. (In his *Engineering valuation of public utilities and factories.* 1913. p. 169).

	Minimum service value, percent of reproduction cost.
Lightning arresters, station type	50%

Joint engineering department of the Wisconsin commission.

FOSTER, HORATIO A. Rates of depreciation. (In his *Engineering valuation of public utilities and factories.* 1913. p. 205, 206).

	years' life
Lightning arresters	10-12
station type	15-20

Linen

GREAT BRITAIN. Board of inland revenue. Depreciation rates: abstract. (In its *Income tax; statement respecting allowances for wear and tear and obsolescene of plant and machinery.* 1918. Cd. 9022, p. 4; Cd. 9134, p. 6.) *American economic review,* Supplement, Dec. 1920, p. 51. *Journal of accountancy,* Sept. 1920, p. 194.
Flax spinning and linen weaving (Ireland)
Machinery and plant — 7½%
Written down value
Note: Machinery and plant (except accessory plant such as pirns, pirn cages, spools, belting, driving ropes, damask cards, designs, patterns, models, furniture and fixtures).

INCOME tax notes. *Accountant,* May 11, Sept. 28, 1918, p. 359, 162-6. *Incorporated accountants' journal,* May, Oct. 1918, p. 157, 14.
Flax spinning and linen weaving (Ireland)
Written down value — 7½%
Machinery and plant (except accessory plant such as pirns, pirn cages, spools, belting, driving ropes, damask cards, designs, patterns, models, furniture, and fixtures).

Liners

DENHAM, ROBERT S. Depreciation. (In his *Manual of cost engineering and estimating for paper box manufacturers.* 1917. p. 249).

	original cost
Liners	10%

Linoleum

PHILADELPHIA. CONTROLLER. Rates of depreciation. (In his *Manual of accounting, reporting and business procedure of the city and county of Philadelphia.* 1917. p. 207-8).
Linoleum — 12½%

Liquor

TIFFANY, H. S. Beer. (In his *Digest of depreciations.* c1890. p. 13).
A stock of beer that has been manufactured from one to two months, will totally spoil in ten to fourteen days when removed from the beer vaults to the ordinary summer atmosphere, if not protected by ice. The depreciation would begin actively in seventy-two hours, and after the fourth day would depreciate ten per cent daily. Beer made during the months of January, February and March, if left in the vaults until it is five or six months old, has sufficiently matured, so that it will stand the ordinary climate without protection from ice in shipping, and with proper protection from exposure to the rays of the sun or unusual heat, will remain good until about December next after being manufactured. The life of good beer well cared for and protected is one year, which is the extreme limit. These facts have been procured from one of the largest brewers in the country, and are perfectly reliable.

TIFFANY, H. S. Highwines. (In his *Digest of depreciations.* c1890. p. 15).
One year — 8%

TIFFANY, H. S. Whiskeys. (In his *Digest of depreciations.* c1890. p. 17).

	1st year	2nd year	Succeeding year
Kentucky whiskeys	3%	2%	1%
Chicago whiskeys	4	3	

Quantity decreases, the merchandise is enhanced in value by age.

Lithography

PHILADELPHIA. CONTROLLER. Rates of depreciation. (In his *Manual of accounting, reporting and business procedure of the city and county of Philadelphia.* 1917. p. 205).
Printing, binding and lithographing equipment — 8⅓%

Livestock

See also Depreciation, depletion and obsolescence—Horses.

AUSTRALIA. FEDERAL INCOME TAX DEPARTMENT. Depreciation allowance. *Accountant,* Oct. 13, 1917, p. 277-9. *Accounting and commerce,* June 30, 1917, p. 55-7. *Federal accountant,* July 1917, p. 93-8. *Public accountant,* Jan. 30, 1917, p. 145-52.

DEPRECIATION, DEPLETION AND OBSOLESCENCE—LIVESTOCK—*(Continued)*

Dairy cattle 10%
Station 5%
Based on written down value and repairs allowed in addition.

BEXELL, J. A. Valuation and depreciation. (In his *Principles of bookkeeping and farm accounts.* c1913. p. 140-2).
Milch cows, after 3rd year 8%

BREWERIES. *American institute of accountants, Special bulletin, No. 5,* Sept. 1920, p. 7-8.

LIFE of road construction equipment. *Engineering and Contracting,* Jan. 3, 1917, p. 3.
Mules 10% annual depreciation

PHILADELPHIA. CONTROLLER. Rates of depreciation. (In his *Manual of accounting, reporting and business procedure of the city and county of Philadelphia.* 1917. p. 209).

Beasts of burden:

Horses	10%
Mules	8⅓
Donkeys and burros	8⅓

Produce-yielding animals:

Cows and heifers	12½
Bulls and bull calves	10
Steers	12½
Sheep and goats	20
Swine	20
Poultry	20
Special and miscellaneous live stock	10

ROBY, J. J. Schedule of plant depreciation. (In his *Treatise on cost accounting as applied to coal mining.* c1913. p. 14-5).
Livestock and harness 20%

Lockers

PHILADELPHIA. CONTROLLER. Rates of depreciation. (In his *Manual of accounting, reporting and business procedure of the city and county of Philadelphia.* 1917. p. 207-8).
Cabinets, cases, lockers, bins and boxes 4%

PIEZ, CHARLES. Perpetual inventory and appraisal values; table of standard depreciation rates. *Engineering and contracting,* Jan. 24, 1917, p. 77. *Factory,* Dec. 1916, p. 668-71. *Iron Age,* Nov. 30, 1916, Jan. 11, 1917, p. 1266, 138-9. *Iron trade review,* Feb. 22, 1917, p. 477-8. Condensed. *Iron trade review,* Dec. 7, 916, p. 1144-6. *Journal of the American society of mechanical engineers,* Dec. 1916 p. 985-6. Kent, William, *Bookkeeping and cost accounting for factories,* 1918. p. 90. *Journal of the American society of mechanical engineers,* March 1917, p. 215-7.

	% on cost	% on reducing balance
Lockers	5	12

Locking machines

NICHOLSON, J. LEE and JOHN F. D. ROHRBACH. Depreciation. (In their *Cost accounting.* 1919. p. 150).
Locking machines 10%

Locomotives

BARKER, HARRY. Typical life expectation tables for public utility property. (In his *Public utility rates.* 1917. p. 366).

Locomotives	
freight	15-20 years
passenger	15-20
switching	20

Author: average or approximate figures secured by examination or enquiry.

CARTER, R. N. Rates of depreciation. (In his *Advanced accounts.* p. 618).
Locomotives 10%
Based on diminishing balances, normal conditions and hours of working.

COMMON confusion of the terms, depreciation, repairs. *Engineering and contracting,* June 30, 1909, p. 517.
Locomotive has a true depreciation of less than 5% per annum, but the cost of renewals (of parts) and repairs usually exceeds 15%

DEPRECIATON of equipment. *Engineering and contracting,* Nov. 19, 1913, p. 567-8.

Locomotives:	
steam	3%
electric	2

ELBOURNE, EDWARD T. Depreciation rates. (In his *Factory administration and accounts.* 1918. p. 376).

	Prov. dep. %	years	
	Remainder values	10%	5%
Locomotives	12½	17	22

GILLETTE, HALBERT P. and RICHARD T. DANA. Depreciation. (In their *Handbook of mechanical and electrical cost data.* 1918. p. 108).
Locomotives 28-31 years. Gillette's Handbook of cost data.

GRAY, HENRY L. Necessity of depreciation reserves. *Railway age gazette,* May 27, 1910, p. 1297-8. Editorial. Depreciation reserves. *Railway age gazette,* May 27, 1910, p. 1290. Letters. Depreciation reserves. *Railway age gazette,* July 8, 1910, p. 66.

	Annual dep.
Steam locomotives	3%

LOCK, FRED J. Depreciation. (In his *West African mining accounts.* 1910. p. 88-9).
Light locomotives and rolling stock 12½%

MANN, JOHN and H. C. JUDD. Depreciation. (In his *Colliery accounts.* 1909. p. 69-75, 92).
Locomotives 10-15%
Calculated on the balance as diminished from year to year

DEPRECIATION, DEPLETION AND OBSOLESCENCE—LOCOMOTIVES—*(Continued)*

MATHESON, EWING. Plant and machinery. (In his *Depreciation of factories, mines and industrial undertakings and their valuation.* 1893. p. 35-49).
Contractors' locomotives 20%

MONTGOMERY, ROBERT H. Steam railroads. (In his *Auditing theory and practice.* 1916. p. 652).
Pennsylvania railroad company sets aside for depreciation renewals and obsolescence 3% on freight cars and 4% upon passenger cars and locomotives.

NICHOLSON, J. LEE and J. F. D. ROHRBACH. Depreciation. (In their *Cost accounting.* 1919. p. 151).
Locomotives—steam and electric 6⅔%
Based on (1) the cost of equipment
(2) the life of the equipment
(3) on a ten-hour day.

OBSOLESCENCE and depreciation for locomotives. *Electric railway journal,* June 7, 1913, p. 997.
Steam locomotive was credited with a scrap value of 20 per cent on its original cost and a useful life of twenty-seven years, while to the electric equipment was assigned a scrap value of 30% at the end of thirty-five years of service.

PIEZ, CHARLES. Perpetual inventory and appraisal values: table of standard depreciation rates. *Engineering and contracting,* Jan. 24, 1917, p. 77. *Factory,* Dec. 1916, p. 668-71. *Iron age,* Nov. 30, 1916, p. 1266. Condensed. *Journal of the American society of mechanical engineers,* Dec. 1916, p. 965-6. *Iron trade review,* Dec. 7, 1916, p. 1144-6. Kent, William. *Bookkeeping and cost accounting for factories,* 1918. p. 90. Discussion. *Journal of the American society of mechanical engineers,* March 1917, p. 215-7.

	% on cost	% on reducing balance
Storage battery locomotives (battery renewals to repairs)	10	30

POMEROY, L. R. Depreciation of locomotives and shop equipment. *Railway age gazette,* April 24, 1914, p. 943-6.

PORTERS, R. J. Rates of depreciation generally adopted. (In his *Pitman's dictionary of bookkeeping.* p. 344).
Locomotives 10%
Based on diminishing balances.

PUBLIC utility reports, annotated. Rochester, Lawyers co-operative publishing co. 1915c. p. 711.
Re Manila R. co. (P. I.) A proper and adequate annual rate of depreciation of locomotives, passenger train cars was found by the Philippine Islands public utilities commission to be 3 per cent . . . of their original cost ledger value or purchase price.

ROBY, J. J. Schedule of plant depreciation. (In his *Treatise on cost accounting as applied to coal mining.* c1913. p. 14-5).
Mine locomotives
Electric locomotives, haulage, engines
Deduct as salvage before depreciating 15%
Depreciation rate for remainder, fireproof 8
Ropes and sheaves
Deduct as salvage before depreciating 10
Depreciation rate for remainder, fireproof 25

SERVICEABLE life and average annual cost of British locomotives. *Railway age gazette,* Sept. 10, 1909, p. 449.

UNIFORM cost sheet for coal mining companies. *Coal age,* Sept. 19, 1918, p. 545-7.
original cost
Mine locomotives 10%

WHATLEY, G. E. STUART. Depreciation. (In his *Accountant's and bookkeeper's vade-mecum,* 1893. p. 26).
Diminishing value
Locomotive 10%

WILLIAMSON, J. GILMAN. Depreciation of assets. (In his *Counting house and factory organization.* p. 142).
Locomotives and rolling stock 10%

Lofts

BOLTON, REGINALD PELHAM. Depreciation of the value of buildings. (In his *Building for profit.* 1911. p. 70).
Lofts and factories 33-37 years

Logging

See Depreciation, depletion and obsolescence—Lumber.

Loose tools

See Depreciation, depletion and obsolescence—Tools.

Lubricating equipment

ROBY, J. J. Schedule of plant depreciation. (In his *Treatise on cost accounting as applied to coal mining.* c1913. p. 14-5).
Rate of depreciation for remainder
Lubricating equipment, retainers and measure, fireproof 10

Lumber

ARKLEY, A. K. Keeping track of income and outgo. *Business man's magazine,* March 1912, p. 246-52.
It is safe to say that about 25% of the cost is all that can be realized out of a mill which has cut all its timber and is to be torn down. The buildings are of no value except as second-hand lumber, and the yards and docks are practically worthless. The machinery is only worth from 25% to 50% of its cost, and all of the railroad is only worth the value of the rails figured as second-hand steel.
A good way to figure depreciation is to estimate how many years' run there is of timber,

DEPRECIATION, DEPLETION AND OBSOLESCENCE—LUMBER—*(Continued)*

and figure on receiving 25% of all the cost of the machinery, and nothing at all for the yards and docks after the proposition has outlived its usefulness, which is whenever all the timber has been cut. We will suppose, for instance, that when the plant is completed there is enough timber to keep it running for 10 years. We would take the cost of all the assets represented by the real accounts and charge off for depreciation 7½% of each and every year for ten years. This would leave our accounts showing 25% of the value at the end of the mill's run, which is just about all that could be gotten out of it. However, on dry kilns, buildings, yards and docks we could not expect to get much more than 5% or 10% of the cost, depending entirely on the location of the plant. Therefore it is well to figure depreciation high enough so that at the end of the 10 years these accounts will only show from 5% to 10% of the actual cost.

When once the main part of the building, yards and docks, dry kilns, etc., were finished I would make it a rule never to charge another thing to these accounts, but charge everything to revenue and keep cutting down your assets as far as your books are concerned. This course may seem radical, but no one who has ever operated a mill and finished his timber knows how little can be gotten out of what is left. It may eat up all the profits the first year or the second year, but in the end it will pay.

The account with "Horses" is also one which must be depreciated very heavily, as nothing loses its value so quickly as a horse. I would not hesitate to depreciate this account 25% per year. Also all the small tools in the woods, such as axes, saws, undercutters, marlin spikes, peavies, cant hooks, etc., etc., which are usually charged to Logging equipment, might just as well be considered as of no value whatever and should be charged to "Logging".

CALIFORNIANS adopt accounting system; phases of depreciation, stumpage value, labor and other costs. *American lumberman,* Oct. 5, 1918, p. 41.

COMPTON, W. Methods of handling depreciation and investment in lumber accounting. *American lumberman,* July 27, 1918, p. 48-9.

COST and depreciation of steam and hydro-electric installations. *Electrical world,* Dec. 30, 1909, p. 1558.

Stop logs, gates, and other wood exposed to air and water.
5 years
0.146% of total cost.

GREAT BRITAIN. BOARD OF INLAND REVENUE. Depreciation rates: (In its *Income tax; statement respecting allowances for wear and tear and obsolescence of plant and machinery.* 1918. Cd. 9022, p. 4; Cd. 9134, p. 6). *American economic review, Supplement,* Dec. 1920, p. 51. *Journal of accountancy,* Sept. 1920, p. 195.

Timber merchants, saw millers, and manufacturers of timber goods.	
Engines, boilers and main shafting	
General saw milling plant and machinery	5%
Traction engines, tractors, motor cars and haulage plant	7½
Written down value	20

HOW to run a retail lumber business at a profit; plans, methods and cost figures for cutting down expenses and increasing sales; contributed by nearly 500 dealers in 32 states. Chicapo, A. W. Shaw co. c1917. 223p.

Depreciation. p. 82-4, 91, 95, 113, 166, 34.	
Real estate	10%
Machinery	10
first year	10
second year	9

INCOME tax notes. *Accountant,* May 11, Sept. 28, 1918, p. 359, 162 6. *Incorporated accountants' journal,* May, Oct. 1918, p. 157, 14.

Timber merchants, saw millers, and manufacturers of timber goods.	
Engines, boilers, and main shafting	
General saw milling plant and machinery	5%
Traction engines, tractors, motor-cars, and haulage plant	7%
Written down value	20

JONES, ARTHUR F. Depreciation. (In his *Lumber manufacturing accounts.* 1914. p. 13-14, 52).

LOGGING business. *Business man's magazine,* July 1909, p. 89.

MONTGOMERY, ROBERT H. Depletion—timber lands. (In his *Income tax procedure,* 1919. p. 609-13).

MONTGOMERY, ROBERT H. Lumber industry. (In his *Income tax procedure,* 1919. p. 579. ——— Same, 1920. p. 726-9, 791-4).

MONTGOMERY, ROBERT H. Timber lands. (In his *Auditing theory and practice.* 1916. p. 429).

SALIERS, EARL A. Analysis of hydroelectric plant. (In his *Principles of depreciation.* 1916. p. 34-8).

Stop logs, gates and other wood exposed to air — 5 years

TIFFANY, H. S. Lumber. (In his *Digest of depreciations.* c1890. p. 16).

	Annual % dep.
Ash	10
Hickory	15
Sycamore	25
Beech	12
Poplar	8
Oak (burr and white)	6
Oak (red and black)	12
Cotton wood	12
Walnut	8
Hard maple	6
Soft maple	8
Linn	12
Pine (white or yellow)	5

DEPRECIATION, DEPLETION AND OBSOLESCENCE—*(Continued)*

Machine shops

CROWELL, H. H. Electric lighting rates and depreciation. *Municipal journal and engineer,* Dec. 18, 1907, p. 698.

	Purchased 10 years or more ago	modern
Machines shop	10 years	10 years

DENHAM, ROBERT S. Depreciation. (In his *Manual of cost engineering and estimating for paper box manufacturers.* 1917. p. 249).

Machine shop equipment 10%

DEPRECIATION. *American institute of accountants,* Special bulletin, No. 1, Jan. 1920, p. 6-7.

NORRIS, H. M. Depreciation as an element of machine shop cost keeping. *Engineering magazine,* April 1899.

SPENCER, HENRY. Fixed charges in the machine shop and the depreciation of machine tools. *Engineer* (London), Sept. 27, 1912, p. 321.

On buildings & estates 2½% only is the usual abatement given.

TIFFANY, H. S. Machine shops. (In his *Digest of depreciations.* c1890. p. 10).

Machine shops	Annual % depreciation
brick	3
frame	4

UNIFORM cost sheet for coal mining companies. *Coal age,* Sept. 19, 1918, p. 545-7.

Machine shop	original cost
wood	8%
stone or brick	5

WEST, C. J. Error in figuring depreciation. *Engineering and contracting,* Dec. 8, 1909, p. 506.

Machinery and equipment

See also Depreciation, depletion and obsolescence—Agricultural machinery;—Machinery, electrical; name of various industries and trades and machines.

ALLISON, J. Farmers' income tax. *Accountant,* April 14, May 3, 17, 24, 1919, p. 325-6, 369-70, 421-3, 440-1.

Dyers machinery 7½%

ALLOWANCES for depreciation of plant and machinery. *Accountant.* Nov. 13, 1909, p. 604-5.

ALWYN-SCHMIDT, L. W. Effects of increased use upon machine depreciation. *Industrial management,* April 1920, p. 313-4.

AUSTRALIA. FEDERAL INCOME TAX DEPARTMENT. Depreciation allowance. *Accountant,* Oct. 13, 1917, p. 277-9. *Accounting and commerce,* June 30, 1917, p. 55-7. *Federal accountant,* July 1917, p. 93-8. *Public accountant,* Jan. 30, 1917, p. 145-52.

Ordinary manufacturing 5%

Written down value; repairs allowed in addition.

BARRETT, GEORGE L. Calculation of depreciation. *Electrical engineering,* Nov. 1914, p. 449.

BASSETT, WILLIAM R. Charging off depreciation on the right basis. (In his *Accounting as an aid to business profits.* c1918. p. 199).

Machinery 5%

BENTLEY, HARRY C. Depreciation. (In his *Science of accounts.* 1913. p. 146).

Stationary machinery, hangers, pulleys and shafting 5-10%

BOLTON, REGINALD PELHAM. Depreciation of mechanical equipment and power plants. (In his *Building for profit.* 1911. p. 79-93).

CARDULLO, FOREST E. Depreciation of factory equipment. *Iron age,* May 14, 1914, p. 1236-7. *Metal work,* May 29, 1914, p. 715-6.

CARTER, R. N. Rates of depreciation. (In his *Advanced accounts.* p. 618).

Plant and machinery 5-10%

Based on diminishing balances, normal conditions and hours of working.

CLAPMAN, F. T. Depreciation of plant. *Mechanical world,* Oct. 19, 1917, p. 219-20.

Machinery depreciation 5%, plus 3%, wear and tear, making 8%

In a constructional steelworks, drilling machines should be depreciated 10%, other machine tools constantly at work should bear 8%, and other machines working intermittently 5%. Pneumatic tools, such as chipping and caulking hammers, drills and riveting hammers, should be written down 15%. In the foundry it will be found that 5% will be a fair average depreciation to put on all power-driven machinery.

DARBISHIRE, JAMES E. Depreciation of machinery. *Engineering* (London), 1908, p. 562-3.

DENHAM, F. W. Depreciation of assets and goodwill of limited companies. *Accountant,* May 28, 1898, p. 568.

Machinery	7-12%
Fixed plant	5-7

DEPRECIATION. *American institute of accountants, Special bulletin, No. 1,* Jan. 1920. p. 6-7.

DEPRECIATION allowance for machinery and plant; Board of inland revenue regulations. *Board of trade journal,* April 25, 1918, p. 493.

DEPRECIATION allowances for plant and machinery: explanation by the Board of inland revenue. *Board of trade journal,* Aug. 22, 1918, p. 244.

DEPRECIATION AND INCOME TAX. *Accountant,* Oct. 24, 1914, p. 453-5.

A leading article urging accountants to adopt united action to secure the abolition of the arbitrary 5% rate of depreciation on the written down value of machinery and plant—the rate generally adopted by surveyors of taxes—on the ground that there is no warrant for such a charge; Section 12 of the customs and inland revenue act, 1878, merely authorizing the commissioners to allow such deduction "as they may think just and reasonable."

DEPRECIATION and income tax. *Accounting and commerce,* Nov. 1917, p. 185-6.

Power driven plant and machinery 5% on reducing value.

DEPRECIATION of machinery. *Engineer,* Mar. 8, 1917, p. 211.

The income tax commissioner allows, in normal cases, a rate of depreciation of 5 per cent, and in exceptional cases 7½% on machinery.

"We recommend," say the reporters of the Engineering and shipbuilding committee, "that in ordinary peace time not less than 15% be allowed for depreciation on the decreasing

DEPRECIATION, DEPLETION AND OBSOLESCENCE—MACHINERY AND EQUIPMENT—*(Continued)*

value of machinery and plant and 7½% on the decreasing value of docks, wharves and similar fixed structures and buildings". The committee of the engineering trades recommened 10% for machinery used by day only and 15% ofr that used both night and day.

DEPRECIATION of machinery. *Home study*, July 1906.

DICKSEE, LAWRENCE R. Depreciation, machinery. (In his *Auditing. Authorized American edition.* 1909. p. 192-3).
7½-12½% annually from reducing balances.

DICKSEE, LAWRENCE R. Depreciation, machinery. (In his *Depreciation reserves and reserve funds.* 1912. p. 29-27).

Machinery	7½-10%
Engines and boilers	10-15
Special machinery	10-25

DONALDSON, H. F. Depreciation of buildings and machinery. *Engineering record*, Feb. 11, 1911, p. 159. *Engineering magazine*, April 1911, p. 171-6. *Mechanical engineer*, Feb. 10, 1911, p. 177-80, 202-4.

ELBOURNE, EDWARD T. Depreciation rates. (In his *Factory administration and accounts.* 1918. p. 377).

	Prov. dep. %	years	
	Remainder values	10%	5%
Automatic screw machines, bar	7½	29	38
Automatic screw machines, chucking	7½	29	38

ENNIS, WILLIAM DUANE. Depreciation. (In his *Works management.* 1911. p. 87).
Machinery 10 years

GARRY, HENRY STANLEY. Depreciation of plant and machinery. *Accountant*, June 23, Sept. 15, 1906, p. 785-9, 285-8.
Some authorities place the depreciation on

Prime movers	5
Process plant fixed	2½
Accessory plant	2½

GILLETTE, HALBERT P. and RICHARD T. DANA. Depreciation. (In their *Handbook of mechanical and electrical cost data.* 1918. p. 107).

Equipment	8 years. H. P. Gillette, Everett Railway & water co., Jan. 29, 1912.

GREENLINDER, LEO and JOHN R. LOOMIS. Depreciation, machinery. (In their *Accounting problems.* 1910. v. 1. p. 304-5).
Machinery 7-10%

GRUNSKY, CARL EWALD. Probable useful life of various articles. (In his *Valuation, depreciation and the rate-base.* 1917. p. 280.)

Machinery	27 years. 6% residual value. T. C. Parsons. Discussion of Mr. Hammond's paper, Journal institute electric engineers, England, April 25, 1907.
Engines and machinery	25 years. 6% residual value. Sir Wm. Preece. Report of Bristol corporation, England, 1906.

GUTHRIE, EDWIN. Depreciation. (In Lisle, George. *Encyclopaedia of accounting.* v.2. p. 374).

Engines, boilers and gearing (if treated together)	4-7½% diminishing value.
Moving machinery such as fixed tools in engineering works, spinning and weaving machinery, etc.	5-10% on diminishing value. There is always a residue of value.
Fixed plants such as blast furnaces, chemical plants etc., subject wholly or in part to rapid depreciation and constant repair, and of little ultimate value.	Divide by the number of years upon the assumed life of the business as if it were a lease until reduced to ultimate break-up value.

HARRISON, W. H. What constitutes depreciation of machinery? *American machinist*, Feb. 22, 1917, p. 346.

How to determine the depreciation of factory machines. *System*, April 1912, p. 386.

INCOME tax and depreciation. *Municipal journal* (London), Aug. 13, 1907, p. 744.

JENKINSON, M. WEBSTER. Depreciation. *Accountant*, May 17, 1902, p. 528-34.
Productive machinery 5-10%

JONES, EDWARD DAVID. Depreciation. (In his *Investment.* p. 167).
Tools and machinery 6%
10% per annum for the first two years.

KENT, WILLIAM. Depreciation of machinery. (In his *Bookkeeping and cost accounting for factories.* 1918. p. 91).

KERR, W. H. and G. A. NAHSTOLL. Reserve for depreciation. (In their *Cooperative organization business methods.* 1915. p. 13-14).
Machinery 7-10%

KESTER, ROY B. Estimate of depreciation. (In his *Accounting theory and practice.* 1918. v.2. p. 283-4, 286-7).

Machinery and equipment	Straight line method
Minimum rate	10%
Maximum rate	15-20

DEPRECIATION, DEPLETION AND OBSOLESCENCE—MACHINERY AND EQUIPMENT—*(Continued)*

KIMBALL, DEXTER S. Estimated life and factors of depreciation. (In his *Cost finding.* 1918. p. 190. *Principles of industrial organization.* 1913. p. 163).

	Prob. life of assets in year	Ratio of scrap to original value	% on orig. cost	% on dim. val.
Engine room instruments and gauges	10	0.05	9.5	26

KING, J. A. How machinery depreciates. *System on the farm,* April 1920, p. 223-5.

MCINTOSH, ROBERT J. Rates of depreciation. (In his *Reference book of accounts.* p. 62, 60).
Machinery and machine tools 10%
Dynamos 5
Machinery 7½-15
Based on life

MATHESON, EWING. Plant and machinery. (In his *Depreciation of factories, mines and industrial undertakings and their valuations.* 1893. p. 35-49).
Engineering factories 5-10%
Steam engines, steam hammers etc. (in engineering factories) 5-10

MONTGOMERY, HALFORD H. Montgomery depreciation tables; buildings, machinery and plant in reference to accounts and income tax; with tables. Belfast, James Moore, 1908.

MONTGOMERY, ROBERT H. Machinery and equipment. (In his *Auditing theory and practice,* 1916. p. 422-4).
In addition to charging all repairs and part renewals to operating, from 7½ to 12½% should be written off annually from the original cost to provide for normal depreciation by wear and tear and obsolescence.

MONTGOMERY, ROBERT H. Machinery and equipment. (In his *Income tax procedure,* 1919. p. 569-71. ——— Same, 1926. p. 722-4).
In addition to charging all repairs and part renewals to operating expenses, from 7½ to 12½% should be written off annually from the original cost to provide for normal depreciation.

NICHOLSON, J. LEE and J. F. D. ROHRBACH. Depreciation. (In their *Cost accounting.* 1919. p. 147, 152)
Power machinery 6%
Drop and helve hammers 10%
Group rate
Mechanical equipment of buildings:
Sprinkler system
Heating and ventilating system
Water and sewer piping, and sanitary fixtures
Electric light and power wiring
Elevators
Fire alarm and fire prevention apparatus
Refrigeration system } 6⅔%
Plant power and large equipments:
Boilers, pumps, and feed-water heaters, air compressors
Power piping (steam, water, air gas, and oil
Switchboards, main wiring, and conduits
Turbines, engines, generators, dynamos, transformers
Cupolas, converters, melting furnaces, and accessories
Annealing and heating furnaces, ovens, forges, etc. } 6%
Machinery—exclusive of hammers:
Machinery, motors, 'machine tools, traveling cranes, etc.
Punch presses, bending rolls, power shears
Woodworking machinery
Miscellaneous machinery
Shafting, pulleys, hangers, and belting 6
Based on (1) the cost of equipment
(2) the life of the equipment
(3) on a ten-hour day

NORRIS, H. M. Depreciation of plant and its relation to general expense. *Engineering magazine,* Feb.-April 1899, p. 812, 957; 76.
Standard machinery and tools 8%

NUSSBAUM, F. W. Depreciation of machinery: correspondence. *Journal of accountancy,* June 1915, p. 487-8.

OBSOLESCENCE of machinery; provision of the 1918 act of Great Britain explained by an official statement. *Accountant,* Sept. 28, 1918, p. 162-4.

PHILADELPHIA. CONTROLLER. Rates of depreciation. (In his *Manual of accounting, reporting and business procedure of the city and county of Philadelphia.* 1917. p. 206).
Special and miscellaneous production and construction equipment 16⅔%

PIEZ, CHARLES. Perpetual inventory and appraisal values: table of standar ddepreciation rates. *Engineering and contracting,* Jan. 24, 1917, p. 77. *Factory,* Dec. 1916, p. 668-71. *Iron age,* Nov. 30, 1916, Jan. 11, 1917, p. 1266, 138-9. *Iron trade review,* Feb. 22, 1917, p. 477-8. Condensed. *Iron trade review,* Dec. 7, 1916, p. 1144-6. *Journal of the American society of mechanical engineers.* Dec. 1916, p. 665-6. Kent, William. *Bookkeeping and cost accounting for factories.* 1918. p. 90. Discussion. *Journal of the American society of mechanical engineers,* March 1917, p. 215-7.

PIXLEY, FRANCIS W. Plant and machinery. (In his *Accountancy.* Ed. 2. p. 214-5).

PORTERS, R. J. Rates of depreciation generally adopted. (In his *Pitman's dictionary of bookkeeping.* p. 344).
Plant and machinery 5-10%
Based on diminishing balances.

RACINE, SAMUEL F. Machinery equipment. (In his *Accounting principles.* 1917. p. 153).
Office and factory equipment 10-12½% on decreasing balances,

DEPRECIATION, DEPLETION AND OBSOLESCENCE—MACHINERY AND EQUIPMENT—*(Continued)*

SOME depreciation rates on buildings, machines, shafting, belting furniture and apparatus, tools and dies, moulds, lasts, patterns and drawings used by the Associated mutual fire insurance companies of Boston, Mass., in making appraisals of manufacturing properties. *Utilities magazine,* Jan. 1, 1916, p. 186-7.

Depreciation of machinery:

With machines we vary the depreciation with the class. An engine, or boiler, nearly any textile machine is used year after year with minor repairs until the time comes when it is thrown out altogether to make room for a new one. In such cases we ascertain the age and deduct an annual percentage varying from 2 to 5 per cent according to the average life of the machine, but seldom carry the total depreciation to a figure beyond 50 per cent. As has been stated, we start with the replacing cost new today and our annual deduction is from the net and not the gross. In bookkeeping the practice is usually to deduct the annual percentage from the first cost.

There is a vast number of machines particularly those that are automatic, where the main portion, sometimes as much as 80 per cent of the total value remain for years with practically no wear, while the small moving parts wear out so rapidly that they are constantly being replaced. With these machines we consider that the wearing parts are always in a state of 50 per cent depreciation and so make the figure on the lot, half of the percentage the wearing parts bear to the whole. In the case of a paper machine that is made up of numerous sections and will vary from 50 to 200 feet long and from $15,000 to $125,000, age has very little influence, for, from time to time, whole sections have been removed and replaced, while other parts, one might say, never wear out. Our depreciation in such cases is based entirely on general conditions.

SPICER, E. E. and E. C. PEGLER. Fixed plant and machinery. (In their *Practical auditing,* 1914. p. 143-5).

STANLEY, F A. Scrapping $150,000 worth of special machinery. *American machinist,* Feb. 1, 1917, p. 187-8.

THOMPSON, C. BERTRAND. Interest and depreciation. (In his *How to find factory costs.* c1916. p. 69.)

Ordinary types of machinery last from six or seven to fifteen years and should be depreciated accordingly.

VARIOUS depreciation charges. *New York Times,* June 14, 1914.

Factory machinery	12%

WANS, OSWALD. Comparison of the working costs of the principal prime movers. *Accountant,* Nov. 24, 1917, p. 413.

Prime movers	8%

WEBNER, FRANK E. Depreciation rate. (In his *Factory costs.* 1911. p. 177-9, 299-302).

Average depreciation rate 5-10% per annum

WHATLEY, G. E. STUART. Depreciation. (In his *Accountant's and bookkeeper's vade-mecum.* 1893. p. 26).

Blast furnaces, gas retorts, chemical and other similar fixed plant. Depreciation very rapid.

	Diminishing value	Possible common rate
Motive plants (engines, boilers, gear, etc.)	10	7½%
Boilers, engines and gear	5	
Boilers	10	
Plant and machinery	5-10	

WOODS, CLINTON E. Depreciation. (In his *Unified accounting methods for industrials.* 1917. p. 64-5).

Building equipment	12 to 15%
Machinery and tools	7½ " 10

Machinery, electrical

BOLTON, REGINALD PELHAM. Depreciation of mechanical equipment and power plants. (In his *Building for profit.* 1911. p. 82, 89).

	Physical years	%	Economic years
Elevators in regular use, laundry, kitchen, refrigerating, electric devices, and other apparatus frequently reversed	16	40.0	14

EASTON, W. H. Depreciation of electrical machinery. *American machinist,* July 19, 1917, p. 101-2.

ENNIS, WILLIAM DUANE. Depreciation. (In his *Works management.* 1911. p. 86.

Electrical instruments 12 years life to 0% residual value

GILLETTE, HALBERT P. and RICHARD T. DANA. Depreciation. (In their *Handbook of mechanical and electrical cost data.* 1918. p. 107, 108).

Equipment electrical	11.75 years. Beegs, Milwaukee, 3c case.
Machinery	20-30 years.
electrical	Leonard Metcalf, Transactions, American society civil engineers, 1909, p. 24, vol. 64.

METCALF, LEONARD. Water-works valuation and fair rates, in the light of the Maine supreme court decisions in the Waterville and Brunswick case. *American society of civil engineers. Papers and discussions,* 1908, p. 1101-73. *American society of civil engineers, Transactions,* Sept. 1909, p. 1. Foster, Horatio A. *Engineering valuation of public utilities and factories.* 1913. p. 207. Gillette, Halbert P. *Handbook of cost data for contractors and engineers,* p. 797.

	Useful life years.	Annual contribution to depreciation account or sinking fund in per cent of cost: At 5% annual rate sinking fund.	General approximate results.
Electrical machinery	20-30	3.0243/0-1.5051%	4-2%

DEPRECIATION, DEPLETION AND OBSOLESCENCE—MACHINERY, ELECTRICAL—*(Continued)*

NICHOLSON, J. LEE and J. F. D. ROHRBACH. Depreciation. (In their *Cost accounting*. 1919. p. 147).
Electric plant equipment 6%
Based on (1) the cost of equipment
(2) the life of the equipment
(3) on a ten-hour day

PENDER, HAROLD. Depreciation. (In his *Handbook for electrical engineers*. c1914. p. 339).

Electrical equipment.	Years
	12
	J. I. Beggs
	12-15
	Chicago Union traction co. Stone and Webster for the Chicago union traction co.
	10%
	Cardiff tramways
	8.5%
	J. I. Beggs
	85-6.66
	Chicago union traction co. Stone and Webster for the Chicago union traction co.
	8%
	Chicago city railways
	7.5%
	Milwaukee electric railway and light co.
	Glasgow tramways
Fenders, lights registers, etc.	10%
	Milwaukee electric railway & light co.
	Cardiff tramways
Gear cases	20%
	Chicago city railways
	8%
Trucks only	Chicago city railways

THOMPSON, C. BERTRAND. Interest and depreciation. (In his *How to find factory costs*. c1916. p. 69).
Dynamos, portable engines motors and electrical equipment could be figured at from 10-15%

WOODS, CLINTON E. Depreciation. (In his *Unified accounting methods for industrials*. 1917. p. 64).
Electrical service, outside of lighting, 15 to 20%

Magazines

NICHOLSON, J. LEE and J. F. D. ROHRBACH. Depreciation. (In their *Cost accounting*. 1919. p. 146).
Pine swamp (magazines) 2%
Based on (1) the cost of equipment
(2) the life of the equipment
(3) on a ten-hour day

Magnetic separators

ELBOURNE, EDWARD T. Depreciation rates. In his *Factory administration and accounts*. 1918. p. 377).

	Prov. dep. %	years	
	Remainder values	10%	5%
Magnetic separators	7½	29	38

Mains

See Depreciation, depletion and absolescence—Conduits.

Malthouses

TIFFANY, H. S. Malthouses. (In his *Digest of depreciations*. c1890. p. 10).
Buildings
brick 2½-3%
frame 3½-4
Based upon the actual life without any repairs.

Mandrels

NICHOLSON, J. LEE and JOHN F. D. ROHRBACH. Depreciation. (In their *Cost accounting*. 1919. p. 150).
Mandrels 10%

Manholes

See Depreciation, depletion and obsolescence—Conduits.

Maps

ROBY, J. J. Schedule of plant depreciation. (In his *Treatise on cost accounting as applied to coal mining*. c1913. p. 14-5).
Surveys and maps—original maps, instruments and outfits.
Deduct as salvage before depreciating 10%
Depreciation rate for remainder, fireproof 6

Marking machines

ELBOURNE, EDWARD T. Depreciation rates. (In his *Factory administration and accounts*. 1918. p. 377).

	Prov. dep. %	years	
	Remainder values	10%	5%
Marking machines	6	37	48

DEPRECIATION, DEPLETION AND OBSOLESCENCE—*(Continued)*

Mats

PHILADELPHIA. CONTROLLER. Rates of depreciation. (In his *Manual of accounting, reporting and business procedure of the city and county of Philadelphia.* 1917. p. 207-8).
Mats and treads 25%

Matting

PHILADELPHIA. CONTROLLER. Rates of depreciation. (In his *Manual of accounting, reporting and business procedure of the city and county of Philadelphia.* 1917. p. 207-8).
Matting 25%

Measuring

PHILADELPHIA. CONTROLLER. Rates of depreciation. (In his *Manual of accounting, reporting and business procedure of the city and county of Philadelphia.* 1917. p. 208-9).
Measuring instruments and accessories 5%

Meat trade

See also Depreciation, depletion and obsolescence—Packing.

AUSTRALIA. FEDERAL INCOME TAX DEPARTMENT. Pepreciation allowance. *Accountant,* Oct. 13, 1917, p. 277-9. *Accounting and commerce,* June 30, 1917, p. 55-7. *Federal accountant,* July 1917, p. 93-8. *Public accountant,* Jan. 30, 1917, p. 145-52.
Butcher's plant 5%
Based on written down value and repairs allowed in addition

Mechanical devices

See also Depreciation, depletion and obsolescence—Calculating machines;—Typewriters.

PHILADELPHIA. CONTROLLER. Rates of depreciation. (In his *Manual of accounting, reporting and business procedure of the city and county of Philadelphia.* 1917. p. 207-8).
Office machines and devices 12½%

Metal work

See also Depreciation, depletion and obsolescence—Foundries;—Iron and steel.

AUSTRALIA. FEDERAL INCOME TAX DEPARTMENT. Depreciation allowance. *Accountant,* Oct. 13, 1917, p. 277-9. *Accounting and commerce,* Jan. 30, 1917, p. 55-7. *Federal accountant,* July 1917, p. 93-8. *Public accountant,* Jan. 30, 1917, p. 145-52.
Stamping blocks used for designs of decorative steel and iron work 5%
Advertising samples and designs 2½%
Based on written down value and repairs allowed in addition

ELBOURNE, EDWARD T. Depreciation rates. (In his *Factory administration and accounts.* 1918. p. 377).

	Prov. dep. %	Years	
	Remainder values	10%	5%
Sheet metal working machinery	6	37	48

PHILADELPHIA. CONTROLLER. Rates of depreciation. (In his *Manual of accounting, reporting and business procedure of the city and county of Philadelphia.* 1917. p. 205).

Metal working equipment:	
Turning, planing, milling, stamping and engraving	5%
Shearing, punching and drilling	5
Drawing and bending	5
Hammering, rolling and welding	5
Plumbers' tools and appliances	5
Handtools for metal working	5
Miscellaneous metal working	4

Meters

ABERDEEN and depreciation. *Municipal journal* (London), Oct. 23, 1903, p. 943.
Meters

% Dep.	
6	Glasgow
10	Bolton
5	Aberdeen

AMERICAN INSTITUTE OF ACCOUNTANTS. Report of the committee on standard schedules for uniform reports upon municipal industries and public service corporations; annual meeting at Atlantic city, N. J. October 20-22, 1908. 15p. *Journal of accountancy,* May 1909, p. 47-54.
The knowledge at the command of the Bureau of the census leads to the conclusion that this average life is approximately as follows:
Horses, carriages, automobiles and laboratory fixtures and meters 10 years

AMERICAN WATER WORKS ASSOCIATION. Final report of committee on depreciation. *Journal of the American water works association,* Sept. 1917, p. 1-38.
Meters, water 20-30 years

BARKER, HARRY. Typical life expectation tables for public utility property. (In his *Public utility rates.* 1917. p. 367, 368-9).

Meters	20-30 years L. Metcalf
Meter cases (station)	Wisconsin Railroad commission.
Meter drums "	50 years
Meters and governors	20 years
consumer's	25 years
Watt-hour meters	10-15 years

BOWDEN, J. HORACE and FRED F. TAIT. Adequate depreciation of capital expenditure by municipal electricity undertakings. *Electrical review* (London), June 21, 1917, p. 1021.
Meters 10 years

DEPRECIATION, DEPLETION AND OBSOLESCENCE—Meters—*(Continued)*

Bryan, William. Appraisal and depreciation of water-works and similar properties. *Journal of the association of engineering societies,* Dec. 1907, p. 336-81. Depreciation allowance for various public service industries. *Engineering news,* Jan. 23, 1908, p. 96.

Meters	years	% straight
electric	10	
"	10	
"	10-12.5	
"	10	
water		3
"		2.1
"	20	
"	20	

Bryan, William H. Depreciation of electric light plants. *Municipality,* March 1908, p. 74.

Meters	
electric	10 years Robt. Hammond, *Engineering record,* June 15, 1907.
"	10 years Iowa Electrical Association, in *Iowa Engineer,* July 1906.
"	10-12.5 years Dawson's "Engineering and electric pocket book, in *Iowa Engineer,* July, 1906.
"	10 years The author.

Cash, W. Gas accounts and finance. *Accountant,* Oct. 18, 1913, p. 543-55.
Meters (ordinary and prepayment) cookers and gas fires—10% on written down value.

Chase, Harvey S. Depreciation in water works accounts, with reference to uniform reports. *Journal of New England water works association,* June 1910, p. 305-31. Abstract. *Engineering and contracting,* June 29, 1910, p. 598. Editorial. Depreciation and sinking fund accounts. *Municipal engineering,* July 1910, p. 26.
Horses, carriages, automobiles and laboratory fixtures and meters 10 years

Clader, Will A. Water utilities accounting. *Journal of accountancy,* Aug. 1919, p. 91-2. The following rate is used frequently when wear and tear are made good by operating maintenance.
Meters 4%

Classification of depreciation percentages used at Dusseldorf municipal gas works. *Progressive age,* Aug. 15, 1910, p. 707.

	Years life	Present %	Proposed scale
Meters	17	12.5	12.5

Consolidation of electricity supply in London. *Electrical world,* Sept. 19, 1908, p. 611.
Meters 10 years

Crowell, H. H. Electric lighting rates and depreciation. *Municipal journal and engineering,* Dec. 18, 1907, p. 698.

	Purchased 10 years or more ago	modern
Meters	10 years	10 years

Dawson, Philip. Depreciation. (In his *Engineering and electric traction pocket-book.* Ed. 2. p. 1161).
Lighting and current meters % on capital cost 8-10

Depreciation and income tax. *Journal of gas lighting,* June 18, 1912, p. 886.
Meters (ordinary & prepayment) cookers & gas-fires.
In addition to repairs, allowance for depreciation shall be granted at the rate of 10% per annum on the written down value.

Depreciation in gas works. *Progressive age,* Oct. 15, 1912, p. 870-2.
Gas meters 5%

Depreciation of the equipment of an electric plant. *Electrical world,* Dec. 12, 1914, p. 1161.
Customers' meters 4.5%

Estimated life and depreciation of water works plants. *Municipal journal and engineer,* May 6, 1908, p. 558.

Material	Year life	Dep. % per year straight	Authority
Water meter		3	Los Angeles, Cal. *Engineering news,* May 4, 1899.
" "		2.1	Mobile, Ala. *Engineering news,* April 23, 1903.
" "	20		B. Williams, Galena, Kans. App. in 1905.
" "	20		W. H. Bryan.

Figures from the Iola (Kans.) central station. *Electrical world,* Sept. 23, 1909, p. 723.
Meters in service 15%

Floy, Henry. Depreciation. Floy, Henry. *Depreciation as related to electrical properties, American institute of electrical engineers, Proceedings,* 1911, p. 1267. Floy, Henry. *Valuation of public utility properties.* 1912. p. 168-217. Foster, H. A. *Engineering valuation of public utilities and factories.* 1913. p. 194-8. *Engineering and contracting,* Oct. 4, 1911, p. 359-65. *Engineering magazine,* Aug. 1911, p. 837-40.

Meters	Dep. % per year straight year		
Electric switch board	5	Wisconsin P. S. C.	
Electric service	6⅔	Wisconsin P. S. C.	
Electric	3	St. Louis P. S. S.	Union elec. L. & P. Co.

DEPRECIATION, DEPLETION AND OBSOLESCENCE—METERS—*(Continued)*

FOSTER, HORATIO A. Methods of calculating depreciation. (In his *Engineering valuation of public utilities and factories.* 1913. p. 169-70).

	Min. ser. val. % of rep. cost.
Service and Watt meters	80
Consumers' meters (gas)	70

FOSTER, HORATIO A. Rates of depreciation. (In his *Engineering valuation of public utilities and factories.* 1913. p. 206).

	years' life
Service Watt meters	10-15
Station meter cases	50
Station meter drums	20
Consumers' meters	25
Service Watt meters	10-15

GAS companies and depreciation. *Accountant,* Jan. 24, 1903, p. 109-12.
Meters 10%

GAS undertakings other than those owned by municipal or other authorities income tax and wear and tear. *Accountant,* Aug. 9, 1913, p. 181-2.
Meters 10%

GILLETTE, HALBERT P. and RICHARD T. DANA. Depreciation. (In their *Handbook of mechanical and electrical cost data.* 1918. p. 108).

Meters	
electric service	12.5 years St. Louis public service commission, Union electric light and power company. 15 years H. P. Gillette, Everett railway & water co. Jan. 29, 1912. Wisconsin railroad commission.
eelctric switch board	20 years Wisconsin railroad commission.
gas (consumers)	25 years Wisconsin railroad commission.
Meter cases, station (gas plant)	50 years Wisconsin railroad commission.
Meter drums, station (gas plant)	20 years Wisconsin railroad commission.
water	20 years H. P. Gillette, Everett railway & water co., Jan. 29, 1912. 20-3 years Leonard Metcalf, Transactions, American society civil engineers, 1909, p. 24. vol. 64.

GREAT BRITAIN. BOARD OF INLAND REVENUE. Depreciation rates. (In its *Income tax; statement respecting allowances for wear and tear and obsolescence of plant and machinery.* 1918. Cd. 9022, p. 4; Cd. 9134, p. 6). *American economic review,* Dec. 1920, p. 51. *Journal of accountancy,* Sept. 1920, p. 194.
Gas undertakings other than those owned by municipal or other public authorities.
Meters, cookers and gas fires 10%
Written down value

GREENLAND, S. W. Depreciation. *Mississippi electric association. Report of second annual convention held June* 1910, p. 32-6.
Meters 20 years life

GRUNSKY, CARL EWALD. Probable useful life of various articles. (In his *Valuation, depreciation and rate-base.* 1917. p. 286, 280).

Watt meters service	10-15 years. H. A. Foster. *"Engineering valuation of public utilities and factories,"* Van Nostrand, 1912.
Meters electric	12 years. 2% residual value. Sir Wm. Preece. Report of Bristol corporation, England, 1906.
electric	10 years. Robt. Hammond. *Journal of Institute of electrical engineers,* England. April 25, 1907.
electric	12 years. 5% residual value. T. C. Parsons. Discussion of Mr. Hammond's paper. *Journal of Institute of electric engineers,* England, April 25, 1907.
electric	12.5 years. St. Louis public service commission. Case of Union electric light and power co.
electric	15 years. Pacific gas an delectric company. Figures used in rate hearings before Master in Chancery, San Francisco, 1913-4.
electric	23.6 years. 10% residual value. California railroad commission—Reports 1913-4. Calistoga electric co. vs. Napa valley electric co., May 1914.
electric switchboard	20 years. Wisconsin railroad commission. Quoted by Henry Floy and in published reports.
electric service	15 years. Wisconsin railroad commission. Quoted by Henry Floy and in published reports.
gas-station (drums)	20 years. Wisconsin railroad commission. Quoted by H. A. Foster and in published reports.

DEPRECIATION, DEPLETION AND OBSOLESCENCE—METERS—*(Continued)*

gas-station (cases)	50 years. Wisconsin railroad commission. Quoted by H. A. Foster and in published reports.
gas consumers	25 years. Wisconsin railroad commission. Quoted by H. A. Foster and in published reports.
water	20 years. Benezette Williams. Galena appraisal, Kansas, 1905.
water	20-30 years. Leonard Metcalf. Transactions American society of civil engineers, 1909.
water	50 years. California railroad commission—Reports 1913-4. Cuyamaca water co. case, March, 1913.

HAMMOND, ROBERT. Depreciation. *Institute of electrical engineers, Proceedings,* April 25, 1907, p. 270. *Journal of the Institute of electrical engineers,* 1907, p. 270. Abstracts. *Accountant,* May 18, 1907, p. 675. *Electrical review* (Chicago), May 25, 1907, p. 828. *Electrical review* (London). May 3, 1907. *Electrician,* April 26, 1907, p. 51. *Engineering magazine,* July 1907, p. 636-8. *Engineering record,* June 15, 1907, p. 703. *Municipal journal* (London), May 10, 17, 1907, p. 411, 435. *Progressive age,* July 1, 1907, p. 305. *Street railway bulletin,* June 1907, p. 382. *Tramway and railway world,* June 6, 1907, p. 497.
  Meters 10 years

HAZLEHURST, J. N. Final report of the committee on depreciation. *Journal of the American water works association,* March 1919, p. 85-135.
  Meters 20-30

INCOME tax and depreciation; result of negotiations with Inland revenue authorities; from *Gas world.*
  Meters (ordinary and prepayment) cookers and gas fires 10%

INCOME tax notes. *Accountant,* May 11, Sept. 28, 1918, p. 359, 162. *Incorporated accountants' journal,* May, Oct. 1918, p. 157, 14.
  Meters, cookers and gas fires. Written down value 10%

JOHNSON, GEORGE. Depreciation. (In his *Electric lighting accounts.* 1903. p. 23-4).
  Meters 7½%

MANUFACTURERS' light and heat company of Pittsburgh, Pa. *Commercial and financial chronicle,* July 23, 1910, p. 217.
  Gas regulators and meters 4%

METCALF, LEONARD. Depreciation in waterworks operation and accounting. *Journal of the New England waterworks association,* Dec. 1910, p. 442. Abstracts. Methods of computing depreciation of and reasonable assumptions as to period of useful life of waterworks. *Engineering and contracting,* Nov. 16, 1910, p. 434. *Engineering news,* Nov. 3, 1910, p. 482.

	Years life	% Straight line
Meters	15-25	6⅔-4

METCALF, LEONARD. Water-works valuation and fair rates, in the light of the Maine supreme court decisions in the Waterville and Brunswick cases. *American society of civil engineers, Papers and discussions,* 1918, p. 1101-73. *American society of civil engineers, Transactions,* Sept. 1909, p. 1. Foster, Horatio A. *Engineering valuation of public utilities and factories.* 1913. p. 207. Gillette, Halbert P. *Handbook of cost data for contractors and engineers.* p. 797.

	Useful life	Annual contribution to depreciation account or sinking fund in per cent of cost: At 5% annual rate sinking fund	General approximate results
Meters	20-30 years	3.0243%-1.5051%	3-2%

NEALE, R. E. Depreciation in engineering works. *Mechanical world,* Feb. 7, 1913, p. 67-8.

Meters:		
American figures	5-8%	12.5-20 years
German authority	14	7

NELSON, BAILIE WALTER. Limitation and application of profits from municipal undertakings. *Accountant,* Aug. 3, 1912, p. 167-71. *Incorporated accountants' journal,* Oct. 1912, p. 15-7.

Meters	% per annum
gas	6
electricity	4

NICHOLSON, J. LEE and J. F. D. ROHRBACH. Depreciation. (In their *Cost accounting.* 1919. p. 150).
  Oil meters 10%

OFFICIAL allowance in respect of depreciation of machinery and plant—Board of Inland revenue, Great Britain. *Accountant,* May 16, 1914, p. 738-40.
  Meters (ordinary and prepayment) cookers and gas fires—In addition to repairs, allowance for depeciation should be granted at the rate of 10% per annum on the written down value.

PENDER, HAROLD. Depreciation. (In his *Handbook for electrical engineers.* c1914. p. 339).

Meters	
electric	8-10 years P. Dawson 10-12.5 years R. Hammond 12 years W. Preece 15 years J. Abbott 20 years S. W. Greenland

DEPRECIATION, DEPLETION AND OBSOLESCENCE—METERS—*(Continued)*

PIXLEY, FRANCIS W. Electricity lighting companies. (In his *Accountancy.* Ed. 2. p. 218).
Meters 7½-10%

PROBABLE lives of water-works elements. *Engineering news,* Oct. 11, 1917 p. 688.
Meters 20-30 years

PROSSER, R. W. Depreciation in gas plants. *American gas light journal,* May 26, 1902, p. 767.

	Years	% of first cost
Consumer's meters	30	
Station meters and governors	25	30

PUBLIC utility reports, annotated. Rochester, Lawyers co-operative publishing co. 1918E. p. 436.
Bangor (Wis.). An allowance of 3 per cent on a 4 per cent sinking fund basis is ample for depreciation on water meters.

PUBLIC utility reports, annotated. Rochester, Lawyers' co-operative publishing co. 1918E. p. 678-9.
Desert power & water co. docket no. 361. Feb. 20, 1918.
Meters 10% annual depreciation in 10 years.

YEAMAN, C. H. Depreciation and reserves for antiquation and obsolescence from an engineering standpoint. *Electrical engineering* (London), July 12, 1907, p. 46. *Electrical review* (London), July 12, 1907, p. 44. *Electrician,* July 5, 1907, p. 475.
Meters 10 years
R. Hammond
5 years
L. G. B. (Local government board)
10 years
L. C. C.
15 years
J. F. C. Snell (M. E. A. 1905)

Microscopes

NICHOLSON, J. LEE and JOHN F. D. ROHRBACH. Depreciation. (In their *Cost accounting.* 1919. p. 150).
Microscopes 10%

Military

See Depreciation, depletion, and obsolescence—Armies.

Mill machinery

NICHOLSON, J. LEE and J. F. D. ROHRBACH. Depreciation. (In their *Cost accounting.* 1919. p. 149).
Mill machinery—including roll trains, tables, shears, and intensifiers, cold saws, hotbeds, cooling beds, straightening machines, drag-ons, drag-offs, pushers, ingot buggies, hydraulic accumulators, cold drawn machinery such as draw benches, roll staightening machines, etc., hot saws 5½%

Millinery

AUSTRALIA. FEDERAL INCOME TAX DEPARTMENT. Depreciation allowance. *Accountant,* Oct. 13, 1917, p. 277-9. *Accounting and commerce,* June 30, 1917, p. 55-7. *Federal accountant,* July 1917, p. 93-8. *Public accountant,* Jan. 30, 1917, p. 145-52.
Clothing, millinery, whiteworks sewing machines 20%
Other machines 5
Written down value, repairs allowed in addition.

TIFFANY, H. S. Millinery goods. (In his *Digest of depreciations.* c1890. p. 16).

	% Dep one season
Artificial flowers	50-75
Straw goods	50-75
Laces and ribbon	25-50

Milling machines

BELT, ROBERT E. Depreciation. (In his *Foundry cost accounting practice and procedure.* 1918. p. 243).
Milling machines 10%

BELT, ROBERT E. Depreciation. (In his *Uniform cost accounting methods; adopted by the American malleable castings association,* Nov. 14, 1917, p. 20-1).
Milling machines 10%

ELBOURNE, EDWARD T. Depreciation rates. (In his *Factory administration and accounts.* 1918. p. 377).

	Prov. dep. %	years	
	Remainder values	10%	5%
Milling machines			
circular forming	6	37	48
hand	6	37	48
horizontal, plain & lincoln	6	37	48
universal	6	37	48
vertical & slot	6	37	48

NICHOLSON, J. LEE and J. F. D. ROHRBACH. Depreciation. (In their *Cost accounting.* 1919. p. 149).
Milling machines 6⅔%

PHILADELPHIA. CONTROLLER. Rates of depreciation. (In his *Manual of accounting, reporting and business procedure of the city and county of Philadelphia.* 1917. p. 205).
Metal working equipment
Turning, planing, milling, stamping and engraving equipment 5%

Mine doors

UNIFORM cost sheet for coal mining companies. *Coal age,* Sept. 19, 1918, p. 545-7.
Patent mine doors 20% original cost

DEPRECIATION, DEPLETION AND OBSOLESCENCE—*(Continued)*

Mining and metallurgy

AMERICAN ELECTRIC RAILWAY ASSOCIATION. Committee on valuation. Bibliography on valuation of public utilities to December 23, 1915. 61+72.

ARMITAGE, P. Depletion of mineral deposits and the federal income tax. *Engineering and mining journal,* April 26, 1919, p. 750-2.

AUSTRALIA. FEDERAL INCOME TAX DEPARTMENT. Depreciation allowance. *Accountant,* Oct. 19, 1917, p. 277-9. *Accounting and commerce,* June 30, 1917, p. 55-7. *Federal accountant,* July 1917, p. 93-8. *Public accountant,* Jan. 30, 1917, p. 145-52.

Collieries:
Rolling stock (trucks for carriage of coal) 2½%
Ships in coal mines 7½
Slidings, chutes and shafts if privately owned by taxpayer claiming depreciation. Repairs and maintenance allowed in full.
Furnaces and flues (assay work). Replacements only.
Mining 7½%
Where mining machinery is situated . . . where dust storms are frequent, additional depreciation may be allowed, as is deemed expedient in view of the damage caused by grit and dust getting into the bearings of the machinery.
Written down value, repairs allowed in addition.

BOGLE, J. D. S. Writing off of depreciation on the wasting assets of a joint stock company. *Accountant,* Dec. 21, 1889, p. 691-6.

BROWN, NICOL. Depreciation of plant. (In his *Organization of gold mining business.* 1903. p. 128).
Mining 7½ on original cost

BURDICK, D. C. Depletion and depreciation of coal mining properties. *Coal age,* July 31, 1919, p. 185-7.

CHARLTON, W. H. Depreciation—mining coal and making coke. (In his *American mine accounting.* 1913. p. 272).
Store buildings, fixtures and furniture, and teams and wagons depreciate 10% a year.

DAWE, WILLIAM H. Depreciation, capital expenditure and redemption of capital. *Accountant,* July 23, 1898, p. 735-43. *Business,* Nov. 1898, p. 677-88. *Incorporated accountants' journal,* 1897-8, p. 170.
Buildings 5-20%
Machinery and plant 5-20
Furniture 5-20

DEPRECIATION and capital expenditure in mining companies. *Incorporated accountants' journal,* 1897-8, p. 180.

DEPRECIATION and measurement of expired outlay on plant. *Engineering and mining journal,* Mar. 17, 1917, p. 447.
Pumps
Length of efficient economic life—10 years, equal to 10%

1895	Cap. outlay	Dep.		Net balance of Unexpired cap. outlay.
Pumps	$1,000.00	$50.00	+	$950.00
Motors	6,000.00	600.00	+	5,400.00
Drills	12,000.00	300.00	+	11,700.00
Mill machinery	11,000.00	100.00	+	10,900.00
Hoist	48,000.00	2,000.46	+	45,999.54
Electric trolley	10,000.00	47.00	+	9,953.00
	$88,000.00	$3,097.46		$84,902.54

DEPRECIATION and the federal excise tax. *Journal of accountancy,* Nov. 1912, p. 401-4.

DEPRECIATION of fixed assets in the accounts of gold mining companies. *South African accountant,* Mar. 1918, p. 139-40.

DICKSEE, LAWRENCE R. Mines. (In his *Auditing. Authorized American edition.* 1909. p. 193-4).

EGGLESTON, DEWITT CARL. Depreciation on mines and mining properties. (In his *Problems in cost accounting.* 1918. p. 167-71).

ERICKSON, E. A. Depreciation and measurement of expired outlay on plant. *Engineering and mining journal,* Mar. 17, 1917, p. 447-9.

FINLAY, JAMES RALPH. Cost of mining Lake Superior iron. (In his *Cost of mining.* c1910. p. 91).
6% per annum

FOSTER, H. A. Depreciation as affecting collieries and iron works. *Iron and coal trades review,* Nov. 21, 1902, p. 1303.

GOWER, WILLIAM B. Depletion of copper mines in relation to income tax returns. *Journal of accountancy,* Aug. 1918, p. 81-92.

GUTHRIE, EDWIN. Depreciation. (In Lisle, Geodge. *Encyclopaedia of accounting.* v. 2. p. 375-6).
Mines: As an annuity or at discretion in equal annual division over the estimated life to the business or estimated tonnage of mineral

HOFMAN, H. O. Copper smeltery. (In his *Metallurgy of copper.* 1914. p. 358).
5% of the original cost of plant
5.49% of the original cost will be recovered as salvage.

JENKINSON, M. WEBSTER. Depreciation. *Accountant,* May 17, 1902, p. 528-34.

JOHNSON, GEORGE. Application of different methods of depreciation in mining property. *Colorado guard,* Nov. 10, 1899.

JOHNSON, GEORGE. Systems of recording different methods of depreciation as applied to mining property. *Colorado guard,* Nov. 17, 1899.

JONES, EDWARD DAVID. Depreciation. (In his *Investment.* p. 167).
Physical property of coal companies 7.5%
Copper companies 9

DEPRECIATION, DEPLETION AND OBSOLESCENCE—MINING AND METALLURGY—*(Continued)*

KURTZ, WADE. Depreciation and depletion. (In his *Mine accounting in relation to federal taxes;* address at the American mining congress, St. Louis, Missouri, November 17 to 21, 1919. p. 3-6).

KURTZ, WADE. Mine accounting in relation to federal taxes. *Journal of accountancy,* Jan. 1920, p. 30-42.

LEWIS, ROBERT S. Amortization and depreciation. *Mining and scientific press,* 1916, v. 113, p. 456-58.

LOCK, FRED J. Depreciation. (In his *West African mining accounts.* 1910. p. 88-9).

	Dep. % per annum on cost
Plant and machinery	
Underground pumping plant	12½-5
Light locomotives and rolling stock	12½
Engine, plant	
Electrical plant	10
Boiler plant	
Reduction plant	7½
Workshop plant	
Headgears (steel)	5
Buildings—brick	5
Buildings—timber	15
Tramways and sidings	5
Furniture and instruments	10

MANN, JOHN and H. C. JUDD. Depreciation. (In his *Colliery accounts* 1909. p. 69-75, 92).

	on balance Dep. % per annum
Buildings	2-5
Engines and machinery	7½-10
Boilers	10-15
Surface railway	7½-10
Locomotives	10-15
Screening	5-7½
Washers	5-7½
Coal cutters	20-30
Hutches	15-20
Wagons	7½-10

Calculated on the balance as diminished by depreciation from year to year.

MONTGOMERY, ROBERT H. Mines. (In his *Auditing theory and practice.* 1916. p. 428-9, 605).

MONTGOMERY, ROBERT H. Mines equipment. (In his *Income tax procedure,* 1919. p. 571. ——— Same, 1920. p. 724-7.

Company mining bituminous coal	
Mine equipment	6⅔%
Power houses and machinery	6⅔%
Tipples, inclines and screens	6⅔%
Saw mill	6⅔%
Tenement houses	5
Buildings and other houses	5

MONTGOMERY, ROBERT H. Mines—detailed regulations for determining depletion. (In his *Income tax procedure,* 1919. p. 598-602. ——— Same, 1920. p. 779-81).

PHILADELPHIA. CONTROLLER. Rates of depreciation. (In his *Manual of accounting, reporting and business procedure of the city and county of Philadelphia.* 1917. p. 205).

Mining and quarrying equipment	20%

ROBY, J. J. Example indicating method of computing coal depletion; schedule of plant depreciation. (In his *Treatise on cost accounting as applied to coal mining.* c1913. p. 12-5).

Schedule of Plant Depreciation

Property Division	Kind of property	Property subject to salvage allowance.	Deduct as salvage before deprecia-ting	Depreciation rate for remainder Non-fire proof	fire proof	Re-marks
Real estate	Surfaced land	All	30%			A.
Mining rights	Coal in fee					B.
	Leased coal					C.
Surveys and maps	Original maps, instruments and outfits	Instruments and Outfits	10%		6	D.
General office	Furniture and fixtures	All	20%		6	D.
Organization	Cost of same					D.
Financing	Cost of same					E.
Railroad	Cost of same	Rail only	50%			D.
Openings and hoists	Openings and Shafts					D.
	Ropes and Sheaves	Ropes & Sheaves	10%		25	D.
	Hoisting Engines	Hoisting Engines	15%		8	D.
Tipple Equipment	Structure	Structural steel only	20%	8	5	D.
	Equipment	Steel only	10%		10	D.

DEPRECIATION, DEPLETION AND OBSOLESCENCE—MINING AND METALLURGY—*(Continued)*

Power Plant	Building	Brick & Steel only	10%	6	4	D.
	Pipe, Heaters and Pumps	All	10%		8	D.
	Boilers and Settings	All	10%		8	D.
	Engines, Dynamos, and Switchboards	All	20%		4	D.
Shop and Equipment	Building	Brick & Steel only	10%	6	4	D.
	Equipment	All	10%		6	
Ventilating equipment	Fan Housing	Brick & Steel only	10%	8	5	D.
	Fans and Drive	All	10%		8	D.
Mine Office	Building	Brick & Steel only	10%	5	4	D.
	Furniture and Fixtures	All	10%		6	D.
	Building	Brick & Steel only	10%	6	4	D.
Storehouse	Fixtures	All	10%		6	D.
	Building	Brick & Steel only	10%	6	4	D.
Stable & Live Stock	Fixtures				6	D.
	Live Stock and				6	D.
	Harness				20	
Mine Tracks	Steel Rails and Splices	All	50%		4	D.
	Wood Ties				20	D.
	Steel Ties and Spikes	All	10%		10	D.
	Labor, Main Roads				25	D.
	Wood Rails				100	D.
Electric Wiring	Trolley and Feed Wire	Wire only	50%		6	D.
	Insulators, Switches and Bonds	All	10%		10	D.
	Poles and Supports				10	D.
	Labor on Mains				10	D.
Lighting equipment	Light Wires	All	20%		5	D.
	Fixtures and Lamps	All	10%		5	D.
Mine Locomotives	Electric Locomotives.					
	Haulage, Engines	All	15%		8	D.
	Ropes and Sheaves	All	10%		25	D.
Mining Machines	Cutting Machines	All	10%		8	D.
Mine Cars	Wood cars	All	10%		20	D.
	Steel cars	All	15%		12	D.
Wagons and Tools	Wagons and tools	All	10%		20	D.
Safety Appliances	Safety Appliances,					
	Fire Extinguishers	All	10%		10	D.
Telephone Equipment	Telephones and Telephone Lines	All			10	D.
Dwellings	Dwellings	All	10%	5	4	D.
Store	Building	All	10%	5	4	D.
Lubricating equipment	Retainers and Measure				10	D.
Steel Roof Supports	Steel	All	20%		10	D.
Mine Pumps and Pipe	Pumps and Drive	All	10%		10	D.
	Pipe	All	5%		20	D.
Stone and Dirt Equipment	Special cars and Equipment	All	10%		20	D.

STATE income tax—deduction for ore depreciation. *Corporation journal,* June 30, 1916, p. 207.

STOCKETT, B. H. and H. B. MILLER. Estimation of depreciation on stripping equipment. *Coal age,* Jan. 5, 1918, p. 34.

UNIFORM cost sheet for coal mining companies. *Coal age,* Sept. 19, 1918, p. 545-7.

Synopsis of a report made by the committee on cost of the Winding gulf association. The committee recommended the following depreciation rates based upon original cost:

Structures	
Wooden tipples, complete	8%
Steel tipples, complete	5
Wooden power house (building)	7
Stone or brick power house	5
Machine shop—wood	8
Machine shop—stone or brick	5
Supply house—wood	8
“ “ —stone or brick	5
Blacksmith shop—wood	8
“ “ —stone or brick	5
Stable building—wood	8
“ “ —stone or brick	5
Churches and schools	4
Squire's office and jail	4
Sand houses	4
Post office building	4
Substation—wood	7
“ —stone or brick	5
Humidifier building—wood	7
“ “ —stone or brick	5

DEPRECIATION, DEPLETION AND OBSOLESCENCE—MINING AND METALLURGY—*(Continued)*

Powder house—concrete, stone or brick	10
Wash house—wood	10
" " —stone or brick	5
Fireproof vaults	4
Freight stations	10
All other small buildings	10
Mine development	
Clearing property	5
Creek changes	5
Wagon roads	5
Slopes and shafts	5
Diamond and drill holes	5
Train roads	20
Mine development	10
Equipment	
Dynamos and engines	8
Boilers	11
Pumps, heaters & other power house equipment	8
Header lines	8
Fans	5
Water tanks	7
Railway sidings and approaches	7
Humidifiers	12½
Telephone lines	10
Saw mills	10
Hoists	7
Incline drums and larries	10
Incline ropes	33⅓
Cage ropes	50
Hoist engines	7
Mine telephones	20
Mine pumps	20
Steel rail	10
Mine wagons (cars) wood	20
" " " steel	17
Mine locomotives	10
Mining machinery	20
Electric drills	20
Stable equipment	25
Patent mine doors	20
Copper wire	7
Supply house fixtures	10
Post office equipment & fixtures	7
Fire equipment	20
Air compressors	8
Good roads machinery	10
Shop fixtures and machinery	7
Stationary motors	7
Watchmens' clocks	10
Pipe lines in mines	33⅓
Barber shop fixtures & barber shop	10
Misc. building and fixtures:	
Theater building	6
Theater building fixtures	6
" " & poolroom	20
Store and office buildings—wood	6
" " " " —stone or brick	5
Furniture & fixtures in same	10
Tenement houses	6
Club house furniture	15

WHATLEY, G. E. STUART. Depreciation. (In his *Accountant's and bookkeeper's vade-mecum.* 1893. p. 28-31).

Mirrors

PHILADELPHIA. CONTROLLER. Rates of depreciation. (In his *Manual of accounting, reporting and business procedure of the city and county of Philadelphia.* 1917. p. 207-8).
Mirrors 10%

Mitreing

PHILADELPHIA. CONTROLLER. Rates of depreciation. (In his *Manual of accounting, reporting and business procedure of the city and county of Philadelphia.* 1917. p. 205).
Mitreing and tonguing, grooving, etc., machinery 5%

Mixing

See also Depreciation, depletion and obsolescence—Concrete mixers—Sand grinders and mixers.

NICHOLSON, J. LEE and J. F. D. ROHRBACH. Depreciation. (In their *Cost accounting.* **1919.** p. 150).
Mixing machines 10%

Models

See Depreciation, depletion and obsolescence—Patterns, drawings, models, etc.

Molding

BELT, ROBERT E. Depreciation. (In his *Foundry cost accounting, practice and procedure.* **1919.** p. 242).
Air molding machines 20%

DEPRECIATION, DEPLETION AND OBSOLESCENCE—MOLDING—*(Continued)*

BELT, ROBERT E. Depreciation. (In his *Uniform cost accounting methods;* adopted by the *American malleable castings association,* Nov. 14, 1917, p. 20-1.
Air molding machines 20%

Monumental masons

AUSTRALIA. FEDERAL INCOME TAX DEPARTMENT. Depreciation allowance. *Accountant,* Oct. 13, 1917, p. 277-9. *Accounting and commerce,* June 30, 1917, p. 55-7. *Federal accountant,* July 1917, p. 93-8. *Public accountant,* Jan. 30, 1917, p. 145-52.
Monumental masons 7½%
Written down value repairs allowed in additions.

Monuments

PHILADELPHIA. CONTROLLER. Rates of depreciation. (In his *Manual of accounting, reporting and business procedure of the city and county of Philadelphia.* 1917. p. 210).
Monuments, statuary, arches, gravestones ⅛%

Mop wringers

PHILADELPHIA. CONTROLLER. Rates of depreciation. (In his *Manual of accounting, reporting and business procedure of the city and county of Philadelphia.* 1917. p. 208).
Mop wringers 20%

Mortar mills

ELBOURNE, EDWARD T. Depreciation rates. (In his *Factory administration and accounts.* 1918. p. 377).

	Prov. dep. %	Years	
	Remainder values	10%	5%
Mortar mills	6	37	48

Mortisers

NICHOLSON, J. LEE and J. F. D. ROHRBACH. Depreciation. (In their *Cost accounting.* 1919. p. 150).
Woodworking machinery—mortisers 5%
Based on (1) the cost of equipment
(2) the life of the equipment
(3) on a ten hour day

Motor buses

See Depreciation, depletion and obsolescence—Automobiles.

Motor cycles

AUSTRALIA. FEDERAL INCOME TAX DEPARTMENT. Depreciation allowance. *Accountant,* Oct. 13, 1917, p. 277-9. *Accounting and commerce,* June 30, 1917, p. 55-7. *Federal accountant,* July 1917, p. 93-8. *Public accountant,* Jan. 30, 1917, p. 145-52.
Bicycles—motor and ordinary 10%

Motor repairing

AUSTRALIA. FEDERAL INCOME TAX DEPARTMENT. Depreciation. *Accountant,* Oct. 13, 1917, p. 277-9. *Accounting and commerce,* June 30, 1917, p. 55-7. *Federal accountant,* July 1917, p. 93-8. *Public accountant,* Jan. 30, 1917, p. 145-52.
Motor repairing 10%

Motor trucks

See Depreciation depletion and obsolescence—Automobiles.

Motors

ABERDEEN and depreciation. *Municipal journal* (London), Oct. 23, 1903, p. 943.
Motors 10% Bolton

AMERICAN WATER-WORKS ASSOCIATION. Final report of committee on depreciation. *Journal of the American waterworks association,* Sept. 1917, p. 1-38.
Eelctric generators and motors 20-30 years

AUSTRALIA. FEDERAL INCOME TAX DEPARTMENT. Depreciation allowance. *Accountant,* Oct. 13, 1917, p. 277-9. *Accounting and commerce,* June 30, 1917, p. 55-7. *Federal accountant,* July 1917, p. 83-8. *Public accountant,* Jan. 30 1917 p. 145-52.
Instruments testing apparatus, motors, indicator (fixed and portable) 7½%
Written down value, repairs allowed.

BARKER, HARRY. Typical life expectation tables for public utility property. (In his *Public utility rates.* 1917. p. 368-9).

Generators, motors and converters		
High speed	20 "	*
Slow speed	15 years	*
New types	20 "	Wisconsin railroad commission
Old types	15 "	" " "
Turbine driven	20 "	" " "

* Author—Average or approximate figures secured by examination or inquiry.

BAY state rate case. *Electric railway journal,* Dec. 4, 1915, p. 1121-3. *Public utility reports, annotated,* 1916F, p. 336-9.
Motors 10-20 years

BOLTON, REGINALD PELHAM. Depreciation of mechanical equipments and power plants. (In his *Building for profit.* 1911. p. 82, 89).

	Physical years	%	Economic years
Motor-driven pumps, compressors and moderate-speed fans	20	50.0	17
Moderate-speed reciprocating engines, medium-speed rotary apparatus, dynamos and motors	15	37.5	12
Fan engines, high-speed rotary apparatus on large variations of loads, dynamos, motors, high pressure engines, condensers	12	30.0	9

DEPRECIATION, DEPLETION AND OBSOLESCENCE—MOTORS—*(Continued)*

BRYAN, WILLIAM. Appraisal and depreciation of water-works and similar properties. *Journal of the association of engineering societies,* Dec. 1907, p. 336-81. Depreciation allowance for various public-service industries. *Engineering news,* Jan. 23, 1908, p. 96. Depreciation of electric light plants. *Municipality,* March 1908, p. 74.

Material	Life in years	Dep. % per year Straight	Authority
car	12.5-20		Dawson's "Engineering and electric traction pocket book in *Iowa engineer,* July 1906.
armatures		33	Chicago City Railway, *Street railway journal,* Dec. 1898.
commutators		33	Chicago City Railway, *Street railway journal,* Dec. 1898.
controllers		4	Chicago City Railway, *Street railway journal,* Dec. 1898.
fields		12	Chicago City Railway, *Street railway journal,* Dec. 1898.
pole line	15		The author.

CLADER, WILL A. Water utilities accounting. *Journal of accountancy,* Aug. 1919, p. 91-2.
The following rate is used frequently when wear and tear are made good by operating maintenance.

Electric generators and motors	4%

CLAPHAM, F. T. Depreciation of plant. *Mechanical world,* Oct. 19, 1917, p. 219-20.
Gas engines and electric motors should be written down 10% annually. The highest pitch in efficiency and design has not yet been reached, and their life should not be estimated beyond 15 years.

CRAVENS, GEORGE W. Depreciation and maintenance of electrical equipment. *Electrical review,* April 23, 1910, p. 853-6. Montgomery, Robert H. *Income tax procedure* 1919. p. 570. ——— Same, 1920, p. 722-4. Montgomery, Robert H. *Auditing theory and practice.* 1910. p. 424. Foster, H. A. *Engineering valuation of public utiiities and factories.* 1913. p. 201-2.

	% dep. per annum.	Light or intermittent service	Heavy or continuous service
Motors, A.C. and D.C.		4-6.6%	5-8.3%
Motors.	5-10	Chicago traction commission.	
	6.6	Chicago union traction co.	
	5	Milwaukee electric railway & light co.	
	5	Wisconsin railroad commission.	
	5	Average English.	
	5	Average Scotch practice.	
	5-8	Philip Dawson.	
	5	Stone and Webster.	
	4-6.6	Industrial power plants.	
	5	Prof. G. F. Gebhardt.	
	5	Miscellaneous services.	

CROWELL, H. H. Electric lighting rates and depreciation. *Municipal journal and engineer,* Dec. 18 ,1907, p. 698.

	Modern
Motors—DCCCP	20 years

DAWSON, PHILIP. Depreciation. (In his *Engineering and electric traction pocket-book.* **Ed. 2.** p. 1161).

	Years	% capital cost
Tram or railway motors	10-20	
Stationary motors	10-35	
Motors		5-8

DENHAM, ROBERT S. Depreciation. (In his *Manual of cost engineering and estimating for paper box manufacturers.* 1917. p. 249).

	Original cost
Motors	8%

DEPRECIATION. *American institute of accountants. Special bulletin, No. 1,* Jan. 1920, p. 6-7.

EASTON, WILLIAM H. Depreciation of electrical machinery. *American machinist,* July 19, 1917, p. 101-2.

	Years
Direct-current motors	4-15

ECONOMICAL life of car motors. *Electrical review* (London), Nov. 27, 1908, p. 914.

ELBOURNE, EDWARD T. Depreciation rates. (In his *Factory administration and accounts,* **1918.** p. 376).

	Prov. dep. % Remainder values	Years 10%	5%
Motors			
Electric	7½	29	38
Motor rheostate and switches	7½	29	38
Motor stands	6	37	48

ENNIS, WILLIAM DUANE. Depreciation. (In his *Works management.* 1911. p. 86).
Electric motors — 25 years life to 9% residual value

FIGURES from the Iola (Kans.) central station. *Electrical world,* Sept. 23, 1909, p. 723.
Motors — 10%

FLOY, HENRY. Depreciation. Floy, Henry. Depreciation as related to electrical properties. *American institute of electrical engineering, Proceedings,* 1911, p. 1267. Floy, Henry. *Valua-*

DEPRECIATION, DEPLETION AND OBSOLESCENCE—MOTORS—*(Continued)*

tion of public utility properties. 1912. v. 168-217. Foster, H. A. *Engineering valuation of public utilities and factories.* 1913. p. 194-8. *Engineering and contracting,* Oct. 4, 1911, p. 359-65. *Engineering magazine,* Aug. 1911, p. 837-40.

	Dep. % per year Straight line		
Motors	railway 3⅓	Trac. Val. Comn.	Chicago con. tract. co.
railway	By inspection	B. J. Arnold	Coney Island and Brooklyn, adopted by P. S. C., N. Y.
railway	5	Henry Floy	3rd Ave. case, adopted by P. S. C., N. Y.
railway	5	Wisconsin P. S. C.	
	10	Arbitrators	Street lighting controversy, Atlanta, Ga., 1899.

FOSTER, HORATIO A. Methods of calculating depreciation. (In his *Engineering valuation of public utilities and factories.* 1913. p. 169).

	Minimum service value, % of reproduction Cost Modern type	Obsolete type	
Electric generators Motors and rotaries	20	15	Joint engineering dept. of the Wisconsin Comn.

GILLETTE, HALBERT P. and RICHARD T. DANA. Depreciation. (In their *Handbook of mechanical and electrical cost data.* 1918. p. 108).

Motors	10-20 years. Chicago traction commission.
	15-25 years. George W. Cravens, Industrial power plants.
	20 years. Milwaukee electric railway and light co.
railway	10 years. Arbitrators, Street lighting controversy, Atlanta, Ga. 1899.
	20 years. Wisconsin Railroad commission. Henry Floy, 3rd avenue case, N. Y. City.
	30 years. Traction valuation commission. Chicago consolidated traction company.

GRUNSKY, CARL EWALD. Probable useful life of various articles. (In his *Valuation, depreciation and the rate-base.* 1917. p. 278).

motors	10 years. Arbitrators. Board of arbitration in street lighting controversy at Atlanta, Georgia, 1899.
motors	20 years. Robt. Hammond. Journal of Institute of electrical engineers, England, April 25, 1907.
motors	25 years. 9% residual value. Sir Wm. Preece. Report of Bristol Corporation, England, 1906.
motors	25 years. 9% residual value. T. C. Parsons. Discussion of Mr. Hammond's paper, Journal Institute electric engineers, England, April 25, 1907.
motors	20 years. 2c. lb. Pacific gas & electric company. Figures used in rate hearings before Master in Chancery, San Francisco, 1913-4.
motors, modern types	20 years. H. A. Foster. "Engineering valuation of public utilities and factories," Van Nostrand, 1912.
motors, obsolete	15 years. H. A. Foster. "Engineering Valuation of Public Utilities and Factories," Van Nostrand, 1912.
motors, street railway	20 years. Henry Floy. Trans. American Institute of electrical engineers, June, 1911. Third avenue case figures adopted by Public service commission of New York.
motors, street railway	20 years. Wisconsin railroad commission. Quoted by Henry Floy and in published report.
motors, street railway	30 years. Traction valuation commission. Case of the Chicago consolidated traction co.
motors, small, misc.	20 years. Pacific gas & electric company. Figures used in rate hearings before Master in Chancery, San Francisco, 1913-4.

HAMMOND, ROBERT. Depreciation. *Journal of the Institute of electrical engineers,* 1907, p. 270. *Institute of electrical engineers, Proceedings,* April 25, 1907, p. 270. Abstracts. *Accountant,* May 18, 1907, p. 675. *Electric railway review,* June 1, 1907, p. 716. *Electrical review* (Chicago), May 25, 1907, p. 828. *Electrical review* (London), May 3, 1907, p. 716. *Electrician,* April 26, 1907, p. 51. *Engineering magazine,* July 1907, p. 636-8. *Engineering record,* June 15, 1907, p. 703. *Municipal journal* (London), May 10, 17, 1907, p. 411, 435. *Progressive age,* July 1, 1907, p. 305. *Street railway bulletin,* June 1907, p. 382. *Tramway and railway world,* June 6, 1907, p. 497.

Motors	20 years

DEPRECIATION, DEPLETION AND OBSOLESCENCE—MOTORS—*(Continued)*

HAZLEHURST, J. N. Final report of the committee on depreciation. *Journal of the American water works association,* March 1919, p. 85-135.
Electric generators and motors 20-30 years

JOHNSON, GEORGE. Depreciation. (In his *Electric lighting accounts.* 1903. p. 23-4).
Motors 7½%

KIMBALL, DEXTER S. Estimated life and factors of depreciation. (In his *Cost accounting.* 1918. p. 190. *Principles of industrial organization,* 1913, p. 163).

	Prob. life of assets in years	Ratio of scrap to orig. val.	% on Orig. cost	% on dim. val
Motors				
electric	20	0.10	4.5	11

METCALF, LEONARD. Depreciation in waterworks operation and accounting. *Journal of the New England waterworks association,* Dec. 1910, p. 442. Abstracts. *Engineering news,* Nov. 3, 1910, p. 482. Methods of computing depreciation of and reasonable assumptions as to period of useful life of waterworks. *Engineering and contracting,* Nov. 16, 1910, p. 434.
Electric generators and motors, 20-30 years, 5-3½ straight line

NEALE, R. E. Depreciation in engineering works. *Mechanical world,* Feb. 7, 1913, p. 67-8.

Motors		
ordinary	3.3-5%	20-30 years
traction, etc.	5-10	10-20

NICHOLSON, J. LEE and J. F. D. ROHRBACH. Depreciation. (In their *Cost accounting.* 1919. p. 147.)
Electric machinery—motors 5½%
Electric motors and apparatus 10
Based on (1) the cost of equipment
(2) the life of the equipment
(3) on a ten-hour day

PHILADELPHIA. CONTROLLER. Rates of depreciation. (In his *Manual of accounting, reporting and business procedure of the city and county of Philadelphia.* 1917. p. 204).
Dynamos and motors 5%

PIEZ, CHARLES. Perpetual inventory and appraisal values; table of standard depreciation rates. *Engineering and contracting,* Jan. 24, 1917, p. 77. *Factory,* Dec. 1916, p. 668-71. *Iron age,* Nov. 30, 1916, Jan. 11, 1917, p. 1266, 138-9. *Iron trade review,* Feb. 22, 1917, p. 477-8. Condensed. *Journal of the American society of mechanical engineers,* Dec. 1916, p. 965-6. *Iron trade review,* Dec. 7, 1916, p. 1144-6. Kent, William. *Bookkeeping and cost accounting for factories,* 1918, p. 90. Discussion. *Journal of the American society of mechanical engineers,* March 1917, p. 215-7.

	% on cost	% on reducing balance
Machinery, motors, machine tools, traveling cranes, etc.	4.5	10

PIXLEY, FRANCIS W. Electric lighting companies. (In his *Accountancy.* Ed. 2. p. 218).
Motors 7½%

PROBABLE lives of water-works elements. *Engineering news,* Oct. 11, 1917, p. 688.
Electric generators & motors 20-30 years

THOMPSON, C. BERTRAND. Interest and depreciation. (In his *How to find factory costs.* c1916. p. 69).
Dynamos, portable engines, motors and electrical equipment could be figured at from 10-15%

UNIFORM cost sheet for coal mining companies. *Coal age,* Sept. 19, 1918, p. 545-7.

	Original cost
Stationary motors	7%

Moulding machines

ELBOURNE, EDWARD T. Depreciation rates. (In his *Factory administration and accounts.* 1918. p. 377).

	Prov. dep. %	Years	
	Remainder values	10%	5%
Moulding machines	12½	17	22

NICHOLSON, J. LEE and J. F. D. ROHRBACH. Depreciation. (In their *Cost accounting.* 1919. p. 150).
Moulding machines 10%
Wood working machinery—moulding machines 5%
Based on (1) the cost of equipment
(2) the life of the equipment
(3) on a ten hour day

Moving pictures

See also Depreciation, depletion and obsolescence—Films.

MOVING pictures. *American institute of accountants, Special bulletin,* No. 3, 4, May, July, 1920, p. 1-3; 1-3.

Mud guns

NICHOLSON, J. LEE and J. F. D. ROHRBACH. Depreciation. (In their *Cost accounting.* 1919. p. 150).
Mud guns 10%

Muffles

ELBOURNE, EDWARD T. Depreciation rates. (In his *Factory administration and accounts.* 1918. p. 377).

	Prov. dep. %	Years	
	Remainder values	10%	5%
Muffles	12½	17	22

DEPRECIATION, DEPLETION AND OBSOLESCENCE—*(Continued)*

Museums

PHILADELPHIA. CONTROLLER. Rates of depreciation. (In his *Manual of accounting, reporting and business procedure of the city and county of Philadelphia.* 1917. p. 210).
Buildings:
Churches, auditoriums, exhibition hall, museums, club houses and amusement places 1%

Musical instruments

AUSTRALIA. FEDERAL INCOME TAX DEPARTMENT. Depreciation allowance. *Accountant,* Oct. 13, 1917, p. 277-9. *Accounting and commerce,* June 30, 1917, p. 55-7. *Federal accountant,* July 1919, p. 93-8. *Public accountant,* Jan. 30, 1917, p. 145-52.

Organs (mechanical)	10%
Pianos used by association or others for production of income	5
Pianolas	10

Written down value repairs allowed in addition.

PHILADELPHIA. CONTROLLER. Rates of depreciation. (In his *Manual of accounting, reporting and business procedure of the city and county of Philadelphia.* 1917. p. 209).
Musical instruments and accessories 3⅓%

TIFFANY, H. S. Musical instruments. (In his *Digest of depreciations.* c1890. p. 16).
Musical instruments 5%

Nails

TIFFANY, H. S. Rolling mills and nail works. (In his *Digest of depreciations.* c1890. p. 10).
Buildings:

brick	2½%
frame	4

Necking machines

DENHAM, ROBERT S. Depreciation. (In his *Manual of cost engineering and estimating for paper box manufacturers.* 1917. p. 249).
Necking machines 12%

Newspapers

See also Depreciation, depletion and obsolescence—Printing.

NORTON, BENJAMIN THOMAS and G. T. FEASEY. Depreciation. (In their *Newspaper accounts.* 1895. p. 35-6).

Machinery, in addition to current repairs	10%
Type	20-35
Furniture	10
Fixtures and fittings	10-20

Night sticks

See Depreciation, depletion and obsolescence—Batons, clubs etc.

Notching machines

NICHOLSON, J. LEE and J. F. D. ROHRBACH. Depreciation. (In their *Cost accounting.* 1919. p. 149).
Lathes 6⅔%

Nuts

See Depreciation, depletion and obsolescence—Bolts and nuts.

Office buildings

BARKER, HARRY. Typical life expectation tables for public utility property. (In his *Public utiity rates.* 1917. p. 366).
Buildings:
Office, masonry — 70 years
Average or approximate figures secured by examination or enquiry.

BOLTON, REGINALD PELHAM. Depreciation of mechanical equipments and power plants. (In his *Building for profit.* 1911. p. 85).
In an office building where no power plant is installed, but elevators and heating—boilers are included, we find that the relative life of this equipment is 45.7%. The building without the equipment is 77.0 and the effect of the equipment is to reduce this to 74.7.

BOLTON, REGINALD PELHAM. Depreciation of the value of buildings. (In his *Building for profit.* 1911. p. 50-78, 76).

CLASSIFICATION OF DEPRECIATION.
Deduced from R. M. Hurd's assignments of life.

Construction	Occupancy	Term of life in years	Rate of fund proposed in %	Term of sinking fund @ 3% in years
Good brick or stone	Office buildings	75-100	1	47
Cheap brick	Office buildings	25-30	3-2	23-31

Office and business buildings 27-33 years

BURTON, H. J. Office buildings. (In his *Valuations and depreciations of city buildings.* p. 5-7).

Best authorities	annual depreciation
Structural portion	1.5-2%
Mechanical plant & equipment	7 -10
Combined structure	3.2
Committee	minimum
1-10 years	3%
2-10 "	2.5
Thereafter doubtful	

DEPRECIATION, DEPLETION AND OBSOLESCENCE—OFFICE BUILDINGS—*(Continued)*

Recommended by Mr. Mortimer—Depreciation 8% or 30 and 50 years would have proved inadequate for present economic conditions. Additional allowance of 2% for contingencies.

%	years	years
30	10	30
25	10	30
20	10	30
15	10	
10	10	

FOSTER, HORATIO A. Rates of depreciation. (In his *Engineering valuation of public utilities and factories.* 1913. p. 205).
Buildings: First class stone and brick (office buildings) 75 years, Wisconsin commissions.

GILLETTE, HALBERT P. and RICHARD T. DANA. Depreciation. (In their *Handbook of mechanical and electrical cost data.* 1918. p. 106).
Buildings, office 1st class stone and brick 75 years
Wisconsin Railroad commission

NATIONAL ASSOCIATION OF BUILDING OWNERS AND MANAGERS. Taxation committee. Depreciation of office buildings. *Engineering and contracting,* Dec. 25, 1918, p. 588. Abstract. Woodworth, Leo Day. How much does a building depreciate. *Buildings and building management,* Dec. 1918, p. 7-8, 42.
After much research work it was concluded that the minimum annual depreciation of normal office buildings is 3% of actual building cost for each of the first ten years, 2.5% for the second ten years, 2% for the third ten years, and thereafter doubtful. The report also states: "The best authorities consider that there is a steady and inevitable annual depreciation ranging from 1.5 to 2% for the structural portion of the average modern office building, and from 7 to 10% per annum for the mechanical plant and equipment. This makes the annual depreciation of the combined structure and plant 3.2% per annum.
The obsolescence of the ornamental and finishing work and of the architectural plan, which reduces the competitive earning capacity of the building, should also be allowed, and should be differential from the obsolescence or decadence of the location, which is reflected in the reduced land values.
National association of building owners and managers. Taxation committee. Land valuations and office building valuation, from the annual report, June 23-26, 1920. 24p.
Annual depreciation on any new office building should not be less than 3 per cent on its total cost for the first ten or twenty years. The best authorities consider that there is a steady and inevitable annual depreciation ranging from 1.5 to 2 per cent for the structural portion of the average modern office building and from 7 to 10 per cent per annum for the mechanical plant and equipment. This makes the annual depreciation of the combined structure and plant 3.2 per cent per annum.
Note: In order to show at a glance the comparative life, depreciation and yearly repairs of the different mechanical appliance the following table has been compiled on page 246 of the Commercial problem in building by Cecil C. Evers which is based on R. P. Bolton's figures in his Building for profit and such other information as has been procurable.

	Average life in years	Percent of yearly Repairs	Per cent of average yearly depreciation
Steam boilers, tubular	20	2	5
Hot water boilers, cast iron	30	1	3⅓
Hot air furnaces	10	2	10
Pumps	18	4	5½
Engines	18	2	5½
Gas engines	16	8	6¼
Motors	13	2	7¾
Hydraulic elevator machinery	22½	2-3	4½
Electric " "	18	3-5	5½
Dynamos	18	2	5½
Storage batteries	10	5	10½
Switchboards	20	½	5
Laundry machinery	15	4	8⅔
Refrigerating plants	15	5	6⅔
Steel chimney stacks	28	2	3½
Water pipes	28	½	3½
Steam pipes	30	½	3⅓
Gas pipes	26	....	3½
Electrical wiring	15	....	6⅔
Pipe covering	10	3	10
Arc lamps	5	2	20
Plumbing fixtures	18	1	5½
Radiators	45	1	22-9

Sidewalk lights, about 20 years for the best kind
Exterior plaster, liable to crack, and would need at least one going over during the life of the building
Carpentry work, wood floors, maximum of 20 years
Marble floors, maximum of 20 years
Terrazzo floors, maximum of 20 years
Marble wainscoting, would have to be reset during the life of the building
Roofing and sheet metal work, 15 years
Ornamental iron work, probably life of building, excepting elevator doors, sidewalk elevator doors, iron stairways
Painting, probably long life, but ultimately will crack and peel. The only real permanent paint has been that on a backing of gold leaf.
Glazing, after 40 years loses life and easily fractured when exposed to the sun, from a slight vibration
Hardware, less than 20 years
Vaults, the structural life is very long, but the obsolescence feature is very great

DEPRECIATION, DEPLETION AND OBSOLESCENCE—OFFICE BUILDINGS—*(Continued)*

Electric wires, 20 years, due to expansion and contraction, and the breaking down of insulation, shorts develop.
Electric fixtures, have been obsolete in about 10 years.
Plumbing, 25 years maximum
Water cooling, 15 years
Deep well, 20 years, often loses water in less time
Heating and ventilating, 30 years, but in many cases has lasted 20 years
Window shades, every 10 years

PHILADELPHIA. CONTROLLER. Rates of depreciation. (In his *Manual of accounting, reporting and business procedure of the city and county of Philadelphia.* 1917. p. 209).
Office buildings for administrative purposes 1%

PUBLIC utility reports, annotated. Rochester, Lawyer's co-operative publishing co. 1918A. p. 914-8.
New York & N. S. Traction co. General office buildings and fixtures 2%

ROBY, J. J. Schedule of plant depreciation. (In his *Treatise on cost accounting as applied to coal mining.* c1913. p. 14-5).
Mine office—Building, brick & steel only
Deduct as salvage before depreciating 10%
Depreciation rate for remainder, non-fireproof 5
fireproof 4

UNIFORM cost sheet for coal mining companies. *Coal age,* Sept. 19, 1918, p. 545-7.
Store and office buildings original cost
wood 6%
stone or brick 5
Furniture & fixtures 10
Squire's office and jail 4

WOODWORTH, LEO DAY. How much does a building depreciate. *Buildings and building manageagement,* Dec. 1918, p. 7-8, 42.

Oil cans

NICHOLSON, J. LEE AND JOHN F. D. ROHRBACH. Depreciation. (In their *Cost accounting.* 1919. p. 150).
Oil and powder cans 10%

PHILADELPHIA. CONTROLLER. Rates of depreciation. (In his *Manual of accounting, reporting and business procedure of the city and county of Philadelphia.* 1917. p. 205).
Oil cans, firing tools, wrenches, etc. 16⅔%

Oil equipment

BARKER, HARRY. Typical life expectation tables for public utility property. (In his *Public utility rates.* 1917. p. 368-9).
Fuel-oil equipment 25 years.
Chicago traction valley commission

BELT, ROBERT E. Depreciation. (In his *Foundry cost accounting practice and procedure.* 1919. p. 242).
Oil separators 7½%

ELBOURNE, EDWARD T. Depreciation rates. (In his *Factory administration and accounts.* 1918. p. 376-7).

	Prov. dep. % Remainder values	Years 10%	5%
Petroleum and petrol storage installation	10	22	28
Oil fuel apparatus	12½	17	22
Oil extractors	6	37	48

FLOY, HENRY. Depreciation. Floy, Henry, *Depreciation as related to electrical properties. American institute of electrical engineers, Proceedings,* 1911, p. 1267. Floy, Henry, *Valuation of public utility properties.* 1912. p. 168-217. Foster , H. A. *Engineering valuation of public utilities and factories,* 1913, p. 194-8. *Engineering and contracting,* Oct. 4, 1911, p. 359-65. *Engineering magazine,* Aug. 1911, p. 837-40.

	Dep. % per year straight line		
Fuel oil handling machinery	4	Trac. Cal. Comm.	Chicago con. trac. co.

GILLETTE, HALBERT P. and RICHARD T. DANA. Depreciation. (In their *Handbook of mechanical and electrical cost data.* 1918. p. 108).
Fuel oil handling machinery 25 years.
Traction valuation commission, Chicago consolidated traction co.

GRUNSKY, CARL EWALD. Probable useful life of various articles. (In his *Valuation, depreciation and the rate-base.* 1917. p. 279).
Fuel oil handling apparatus 25 years.
Traction valuation commission. Case of the Chicago consolidated traction co

NICHOLSON, J. LEE and JOHN F. D. ROHRBACH. Depreciation. (In their *Cost accounting.* 1919. p. 148, 150).
Oil and powder cans 10%
Fuel oil system 7½
Oil lines 5
Oil-testing machines 10
Based on (1) the cost of equipment
(2) the life of the equipment
(3) on a ten-hour day

VALUATION of the Chicago consolidated traction property. *Electric railway journal,* Dec. 3, 1910, p. 1111-3.
Fuel oil handling machinery 4%

DEPRECIATION, DEPLETION AND OBSOLESCENCE—*(Continued)*

Oils

AUSTRALIA. FEDERAL INCOME TAX DEPARTMENT. Depreciation allowance. *Accountant,* Oct. 13, 1917. p. 277-9. *Accounting and commerce,* June 30, 1917, p. 55-7. *Federal accountant,* July 1917, p. 93-8. *Public accountant,* Jan. 30, 1917, p. 145-52.

Boiler	5%
Stills (coolers)	2½
Tanks	2½

Written down value, repairs allowed in addition.

BEAL, CARL H. Computing depletion for purposes of taxation. (In his *Decline and ultimate production of oil wells, with notes on the valuation of oil properties.* 1919. p. 97-103).

HENRY, PHILIP W. Depreciation as applied to oil properties. *American institute of mining engineers, Bulletin,* Jan. 1915, p. 23-30. Discussion. May 1915, p. 1148-51. *American institute of mining engineers Transactions,* 1916, p. 560-70.

That for California such average annual percentages should be 4% on cost of oil lands, 7% on cost of field equipment and 10% on cost of individual wells and appurtenances, but that these percentages should be changed in accordance with the development of the characteristics of the property under consideration.

LEWIS, ROBERT S. Amortization and depreciation. *Mining and scientific press,* 1916, v. 113, p. 456-58.

In certain cases a fair depreciation charge would be 4% on the cost of oil lands, 7% on the cost of field equipment, and 10% on the cost of individual wells and appurtenances.

MONTGOMERY, ROBERT H. Gas and oil wells—detailed regulations for determining depletion. (In his *Income tax procedure,* 1919. p. 602-9. ——— Same, 1920, p. 726, 782-91).

PHILADELPHIA. CONTROLLER. Rates of depreciation. (In his *Manual of accounting, reporting and business procedure of the city and county of Philadelphia.* 1917. p. 206).

Equipment for refining petroleum and mineral oils (oil filters)	8⅓%

SMITH, CLARENCE G. Depreciation and depletion. (In his *Cost accounting for oil producers.* 1917. p. 111-7).

TIFFANY, H. S. Oil factories. (In his *Digest of depreciations.* c1890. p. 10).

Buildings	
brick	2%
frame	4

Based upon the actual life without any repairs.

Omnibuses

See Depreciation, depletion and obsolescence—Automobiles.

Ophthalmic surgeon

AUSTRALIA. FEDERAL INCOME TAX DEPARTMENT. Depreciation allowance. *Accountant,* Oct. 13, 1917, p. 277-9. *Accounting and commerce,* June 30, 1917, p. 55-7. *Federal accountant,* July 1917 p. 93-8. *Public accountant* Jan. 30 1917 p. 145-52.

Opthalmic surgeon, regarded as delicate machinery	10%

Written down value, repairs allowed.

Ore pockets

See Depreciation, depletion and obsolescence—Coke and ore pockets.

Organs

See Depreciation, depletion and obsolescence—Musical instruments.

Ornaments

PHILADELPHIA. CONTROLLER. Rates of depreciation. (In his *Manual of accounting, reporting and business procedure of the city and county of Philadelphia.* 1917. p. 207-8).

Ornamental furnishings, such as jardiniers, vases and candelabra, statuary	4%

Overhead systems

BARKER, HARRY. Depreciation of electric railway property. (In his *Public utility rates.* 1917 p. 367).

Overhead construction,

single catenary support	15-20 years*	
double catenary support	20-25	*
cross spans and brackets	15-20	

Wiscon. Railroad commission

*Author—average or approximate figures secured by examination or enquiry.

CRAVENS GEORGE W. Depreciation and maintenance of electrical equipment. *Electrical review,* April 23, 1910. p. 853-6. Foster, H. A. *Engineering valuation of public utilities and factories.* 1913. p. 201-2.

Overhead systems		Light or intermittent service	Heavy or continuous service
	Dep. % per annum	4-10%	8.3-12.5%
Overhead systems	10-14	Chicago union traction co.	
	7.5	Milwaukee electric light and power co.	
	3	Average Scotch practice.	
	4-8	Philip Dawson	
	10-14	Stone and Webster.	
	5-10	Industrial power plants.	
	10	Miscellaneous sources.	

DAWSON, PHILIP. Depreciation. (In his *Engineering and electric traction pocketbook.* Ed.2. p. 1161).

Overhead line	10-20 years

DEPRECIATION, DEPLETION AND OBSOLESCENCE—OVERHEAD SYSTEMS—*(Continued)*

DEPRECIATION funds in Europe. *Electric railway journal*, May 7, 21, 1904, p. 696, 760.
Overhead construction.
Brussels (overhead construction except trolley wire) 25 years
Frankfort 5%
Leipziger Strassenbahn 4

GILLETTE, HALPERT P. AND RICHARD T. DANA. Depreciation. (In their *Handbook of mechanical and electrical cost data.* 1918. p. 108-9).

Overhead equipment (elect. ry.)	5 years. B. J. Arnold, Chicago appraisals—4 cases.
Overhead spans, complete	20 years Marwick, Mitchell & Co., appraisal of a large street railway system, Foster, p. 199.
Overhead special work	12.5 years Marwick, Mitchell & Co., appraisal of a large street railway system, Foster, p. 199.
Overhead, systems	10-20 years. George W. Cravens, Industrial power plants. 13.3 years Milwaukee electric railway & light company.

GRUNSKY, CARL EWALD. Probable useful life of various articles. (In his *Valuation, depreciation and the rate-base.* 1917. p. 285).
Overhead system. 33⅓ years 35% residual value.
California railroad commission—Reports. 1913-4.
Calistoga Electric Co. vs. Napa Valley electric co., May 1914.

INSTITUTE OF MUNICIPAL TREASURERS AND ACCOUNTANTS (INCORPORATED). Municipal corporations and companies working tramways and light railway, gas water and electricity undertakings. *Accountant,* June 26, 1909, p. 906-8. Income tax assessment:—allowances for depreciation. *Accountant,* Oct. 2, 1909, p. 423-5, 400-2.
Overhead equipment, i.e. No depreciation should be allowed; all expenditure on maintenance and renewals should be charged as working expenses, as and when incurred.

LEAKE, P. D. Record of depreciation. (In his *Depreciation and wasting assets and their treatment in computing annual profit and loss.* 1917. p. 86).
Overhead systems 3-8%

MONTGOMERY, ROBERT H. Electrical equipment manufacturers. (In his *Income tax procedure,* 1919. p. 563. ———— Same, 1920. p. 716.)
Railway tracks and overhead equipment 4%
Based on gross book values at the end of the preceding year.

OFFICIAL allowance in respect of machinery and plant—*Board of Inland revenue, Great Britain. Accountant,* May 16, 1914, p. 737.
Overhead equipment i.e. trolley wire and construction and connections—no depreciation should be allowed; all expenditure on maintenance and renewals should be charged as working expenses, as and when incurred.

RUNYON, F. O. Report on hydro-electric plant for special committee common council, Newark, New Jersey, April 23, 1902, p. 15, 16, 24.
Overhead construction 10%

WALSH, T. J. Depreciation on electric light and power plants. *Electric railway journal,* July 13, 1912, p. 60.
Overhead distribution 6%

Oyster fishing

AUSTRALIA. FEDERAL INCOME TAX DEPARTMENT. Depreciation allowance. *Accountant,* Oct. 13, 1917, p. 277-9. *Accounting and commerce,* June 30, 1917, p. 55-7. *Federal accountant,* July 1917, p. 93-8. *Public accountant,* Jan. 30, 1917, p. 145-52.
Oyster fishing and pearl fishing
Lugger 7½%
Diving gear (diving dresses and air pipes) Replacements allowable
Helmet and corselet 10
Pump 7½
Running gear (sails) replacements allowable.
Written down value, repairs allowed in addition.

Packing

AUSTRALIA. FEDERAL INCOME TAX DEPARTMENT. Depreciation allowance. *Accountant,* Oct. 13, 1917, p. 277-9. *Accounting and commerce,* June 30, 1917, p. 55-7. *Federal accountant,* July 1917, p. 93-8. *Public accountant,* Jan. 30, 1917, p. 145-52.
Bacon curing
Fittings (including trading) 5%
Other 10
Meat works 10
Written down value, repairs allowed in addition

PHILADELPHIA. CONTROLLER. Rates of depreciation. (In his *Manual of accounting, reporting and business procedure of the city and county of Philadelphia.* 1917. p. 205).
Slaughtering, butchering and dry-curing equipment 10%

TIFFANY, H. S. Pork houses. (In his *Digest of depreciations.* c1890. p. 10).
Buildings
Brick with privilege of slaughtering etc. 3½%
without " " " " 2½
Frame with " " " " 4
without " " " " 3½
Based upon the actual life without any repairs.

DEPRECIATION, DEPLETION AND OBSOLESCENCE—PACKING—*(Continued)*

TIFFANY, H. S. Pork products. (In his *Digest of depreciations.* c1890. p. 17).

Hams	14%	
Shoulders	16	
Clear ribbed sides	42	
Total	86%	
Lost by cutting	14	
Hams put in sweet pickle will gain in weight by absorption about	6%	
Hams, from sweet pickle to smoke house, in the process of smoking, will lose in weight		10%
Hams, from green to cured, will lose in weight		7
Hams from cured to bacon will lose in weight		6

Paint mills

ELBOURNE, EDWARD T. Depreciation rates. (In his *Factory administration and accounts.* 1918. p. 377).

	Prov. dep. %	years	
	Remainder values	10%	5%
Paint mills	7½	29	38

Paper boxes

DENHAM, ROBERT S. Depreciation. (In his *Manual of cost engineering and estimating for paper box manufacturers.* 1917. p. 249).

Buildings, brick	2%
Buildings, frame	3
Boilers	8
Engines	8
Motors	8
Elevators	8
Power transmission	10
Cutting machinery	10
Scorers	10
Slitters	10
Corner cutters	10
Paper cutters	10
Sheet cutters	10
Slotters	10
S. & S. corner cutters	10
Balers	10
Liners	10
Stayers	10
Wire stitchers	10
Metal edge stayers	10
Flange benders	10
Covering machines	7
Topping machines	7
Thumb holding machines	7
Gumming machine	7
S. & S. wrapping machine	12
S. & S. stencil machine	12
S. &. S. gluing machine	12
S. & S. lacing machine	12
Flying machine	12
Necking machine	12
Quadruple stayer	12%
Enders	12
Hand work equipment	6
Tables	6
Glue pots, brushes	6
Pony covering machine	6
Shears	6
Round and oval cutters	6
Glue mixers	6
Trays	6
Fixtures and utensils	6
Hand trucks	6
Tape winders	6
Machine shop equipment	10
Saws	10
Shelving	25
Printing Dept.	
Platen presses	15
Cylinder presses	10
Bronzing machines	10
Cutting and creasing press	8
Embossing presses	8
Punching presses	8
Type equipment	33⅓
Electros	33⅓
Cuts	33⅓
Delivery Dept.	
Wagons	20
Horses	20
Motor trucks	33⅓

Paper mills

GREAT BRITAIN. BOARD OF INLAND REVENUE. Depreciation rates: (In its *Income tax; statement respecting allowances for wear and tear and obsolescence of plant and machinery.* 1918. Cd. 9022, p. 4; Cd. 9134, p. 6). *American economic review,* Supplement, Dec. 1920, p. 51. *Journal of accountancy,* Sept. 1920, p. 194.

Machinery	written-down value
Working day only	5%
Working day and night	7½

INCOME tax depreciation allowances. *Accountant,* May 30, 1914, p. 785-8.

Machinery	written-down value
Working day only	5%
Working day and night	7½

INCOME tax and depreciation; shipping industry, paper mills, printing works. *Incorporated accountants' journal,* May 1914, p. 243.

Machinery	written-down value
Working day only	5%
Working day and night	7½

INCOME tax notes. *Accountant,* May 11, Sept. 28, 1918, p. 359, 162-6. *Incorporated accountants' journal,* May, Oct. 1918, p. 157, 14.

Machinery	written-down value
Working day only	5%
Working day and night	7½

MONTGOMERY, ROBERT H. Paper industry. (In his *Auditing, theory and practice.* 1916, p. 418).

Buildings very low rate.

Equipment	3-5%

DEPRECIATION, DEPLETION AND OBSOLESCENCE— PAPER MILLS—*(Continued)*

MONTGOMERY, ROBERT H. Paper mills. (In his *Income tax procedure,* 1919. p. 571).

Machinery, day and night 7½%

Machinery, day only 5

Additions to and renewals and replacements of machinery and plant, are charged to capital.

OFFICIAL allowances in respect of depreciation of machinery and plant—Board of Inland revenue, Great Britain. *Accountant,* May 16, 1914, p. 735).

Machinery, running day and night 7½%

Machinery, running by day only 5

as the maximum, calculated on the written-down value.

STOCKWELL, HERBERT GRANT. Depreciation, renewal and replacement accounts; a paper read at the annual meeting held in Denver, Colorado, October 18-22, 1909, the American association of public accountants. p. 43. *American institute of accountants, yearbook,* 1919, p. 236-7.

The American paper and pulp association hopes to take the matter up shortly as an association matter. In the meantime, testimony by individual members of the association before a committee of House of Representativs recently seems to show that they believe that depreciation ought to be set at not less than 5% of the cost of buildings and machinery.

TIFFANY, H. S. Paper mills. (In his *Digest of depreciations.* c1890. p. 10).

Buildings

Brick 2½%

Frame 3½

Based upon the actual life without any repairs.

UNITED STATES. FEDERAL TRADE COMMISSION. Readjustment of depreciation. (In its *Book-paper industry.* 1918. p. 64).

It was found that several of the best managed mills allowed about 5 per cent upon their investment for depreciation, which figure has been adopted by the commission.

UNITED STATES. FEDERAL TRADE COMMISSION. Readjustment of depreeciation. (In its *Report on the news-print paper industry.* 1917. p. 83-4).

The commission's depreciation figures were based on the testimony of expert mill engineers, which was to the effect that 3 per cent on the investment in plant and equipment is sufficient to depreciate the outlay in a modern mill.

WRAPPING PAPER MANUFACTURERS ASSOCIATION. Report of committee on depreciation and pulpwood costs. New York, April 27, 1916. 13 typewritten pages.

Partitions

See Depreciation, depletion and obsolescence—Buildings.

Patents, copyrights, trademarks, etc.

BOGLE, J. D. S. Writing off of depreciation on the wasting assets of a joint stock company. *Accountant,* Dec. 21, 1889, p. 691-6.

BUTZ, RALPH H. Depreciating the value of patents. *American industries,* Aug. 1917, p. 20.

First year 50%

second year 25

third year 20

fourth year 15

fifth year 10

These percentages apply to the original value.

CARTER, R. N. Rates of depreciation. (In his *Advanced accounts.* p. 618).

Patents (life 14 years) 1/14th of original cost each year. There is sometimes, as with trade marks, a residual value in the form of goodwill caused by the trade these things have created.

DENSHAM, F. W. Depreciation of assets and good will of limited companies. *Accountant,* May 28, 1898, p. 569.

DICKSEE, LAWRENCE R. Patents. (In his *Auditing. Authorized American edition.* 1909. p. 194-5).

DICKSEE, LAWRENCE R. Depreciation of other fixed assets. (In his *Depreciation reserves and reserve funds.* 1912. p. 43-6).

GUTHRIE, EDWIN. Depreciation. (In Lisle, George. *Encyclopaedia of accounting.* v. 2. p. 375).

Patents. Divide upon the number of years of the full term of life or shorter estimated period of value.

JENKINSON, M. WEBSTER. Depreciation. *Accountant,* May 17, 1902, p. 528-34.

Patents and copyrights. Cost should be written off within the periol for which the monopoly is held.

KESTER, ROY B. Elements of depreciation on patents. (In his *Accounting, theory and practice.* 1918. v. 2. p. 319-23).

MONTGOMERY, ROBERT H. Patents. (In his *Auditing theory and practice.* 1916. p. 427).

MONTGOMERY, ROBERT H. Patents. (In his *Income tax procedure,* 1919. p. 562. 572-5, sup. 1141. ——— Same, 1920, p. 715, 727-30).

As patents in this country are issued for a term of 17 years, 17 should constitute the maximum number of annual instalments.

Copyrights may be charged off under the same procedure as patents, except that the term is 42 years or 50 years after author's death. As most copyrights diminish rapidly in value, depreciation should not be based on their life. Revaluation of each one is the only satisfactory solution.

PIXLEY, FRANCIS W. Patents, copyrights. (In his *Accountancy.* Ed. 2. p. 216-7).

PORTERS, R. J. Rates of depreciation generally adopted. (In his *Pitman's dictionary of book-keeping.* p. 344).

Patents (life 14 years) 1/14 of cost each year.

Based on diminishing balances.

RACINE, SAMUEL F. Patents. (In his *Accounting principles.* 1917. p. 155-6).

DEPRECIATION, DEPLETION AND OBSOLESCENCE—PATENTS, COPYRIGHTS, TRADE MARKS, ETC. —*(Continued)*

SPICER, E. E. and E. C. PEGLER. Patents. (In their *Practical auditing.* 1914. p. 146-7).
WEBNER, FRANK E. Depreciation patents. (In his *Factory costs.* 1911. p. 187).
WHATLEY, G. E. STUART. Depreciation—patents, trade marks, etc. (In his *Accountant's and Bookkeeper's vade mecum.* 1893. p. 25).
WOODS, CLINTON E. Depreciation, patents. (In his *Unified accounting methods for industrials.* 1917. p. 65).
Patents. According to their life.

Patterns, drawings, models, etc.

AUSTRALIA. FEDERAL INCOME TAX DEPARTMENT. Depreciation allowance. *Accountant,* Oct. 13, 1917, p. 277-9. *Accounting and commerce,* June 30, 1917, p. 55-7. *Federal accountant,* July 1917, p. 93-8. *Public accountant,* Jan. 30, 1917, p. 145-52.
Patterns 2½%
Designs used in connection with stamping decorative steel and iron work 2½%
Based on written down value and repairs allowed in addition.
BELT, ROBERT E. Depreciation. (In his *Foundry cost accounting, practice and procedure.* 1919. p. 242).
Pattern shop equipment 10%
BELT, ROBERT E. *Uniform cost accounting methods; adopted by the American malleable castings association,* Nov. 14, 1917, p. 20-1.
Pattern and carpenter shop equipment 10%
DEPRECIATION. *American institute of accountants. Special bulletin,* No. 1, Jan. 1920, p. 6-7.
DICKSEE, LAWRENCE R. Depreciation of loose tools, etc. (In his *Depreciation reserves and reserve funds.* 1912. p. 39-40).
Moulds, patterns, etc. 25-33⅓% per annum of the reducing annual balance.
DOWLER, FRANK and E. M. HARRIS. Depreciation. (In their *Auditing, accounting and banking,* p. 142).
Patterns of wood or metal 20-33⅓% per annum
GUTHRIE, EDWIN. Depreciation. (In Lisle, George, *Encyclopaedia of accounting.* v. 2. p. 375).
Designs
first year of user 50%
second year of user 30
third year of user 20
Patterns 20-30% diminishing value
HAWKINS, L. WHITTEM. Patterns, designs, moulds, etc. (In his *Cost accounts.* 1912. p. 94).
The 5% which is sometimes considered a sufficient rate of depreciation, is usually wholly inadequate to keep the account within reasonable limits.
JENKINSON, M. WEBSTER. Depreciation. *Accountant,* May 17, 1902, p. 528-34.
Patterns 25%
MCINTOSH, ROBERT J. Rates of depreciation. (In his *Reference book of accounts.* Ed. 2. p. 60).
Patterns 20-33⅓%
Based on life.
MATHESON, EWING. Plant and machinery. (In his *Depreciation of factories, mines and industrial undertakings and their valuation.* 1893. p. 46-7).
MONTGOMERY, ROBERT H. Electrical equipment manufacturers. (In his *Income tax procedure,* 1919. p. 563. ——— Same, 1920. p. 716).
Patterns (additions) 25%
Based on the previous year's additions.
MONTGOMERY, ROBERT H. Foundries. (In his *Auditing, theory and practice.* 1916. p. 418).
Flasks, patterns and core boxes 10-20%
MONTGOMERY, ROBERT H. Patterns, drawings, models, designs, etc. (In his *Income tax procedure,* 1919. p. 573-5, sup. 1142-3. ——— Same, 1920. p. 730-1).
Usually depreciation charges should equal the annual expenditures for new patterns, etc. Wherever feasible the conservative course is to write down the book value to $1.00.
MORRIS, H. M. Depreciation of plant, and its relation to general expense. *Engineering magazine,* April 1899, p. 76.
Standard drawings 10%
" patterns 15
NICHOLSON, J. LEE and J. F. D. ROHRBACH. Depreciation. (In their *Cost accounting.* 1919. p. 151).
Patterns—standard:
Metal, net additions 75%
Wood, net additions 100
Based on (1) cost of equipment
(2) the life of the equipment
(3) on a ten-hour day.
PIEZ, CHARLES. Perpetual inventory and appraisal values; table of standard depreciation rates. *Engineering and contracting,* Jan. 24, 1917, p. 77. *Factory,* Dec. 1916, p. 668-71. *Iron age,* Nov. 30, 1916, Jan. 11, 1917, p. 1266, p. 138-9. *Iron trade review,* Feb. 22, 1917, p. 477-8. Condensed. *Iron trade review,* Dec. 7, 1916, p. 1144-6. *Journal of the American society of mechanical engineers,* Dec. 1916, p. 956-6. Kent, William. *Bookkeeping and cost accounting for factories.* 1918. p. 90. Discussion. *Journal of the American society of mechanical engineers,* March 1917, p. 215-7.
Drawings:
All new standard drawings to be charged to expense.
All drawings required for a particular order or contract to be charged to the job.
Patterns (standard): % on cost
Metal, new additions 75
Wood, net additions 100
All patterns required for a particular order or contract to be charged to the job.
RACINE, SAMUEL F. Patterns, photographic plates, drawings, etc. (In his *Accounting principles.* 1917. p. 154-5).

DEPRECIATION, DEPLETION AND OBSOLESCENCE — PATTERNS, DRAWINGS, MODELS, ETC.— *(Continued)*

THOMPSON, C. BERTRAND. Interest and depreciation. (In his *How to find factory costs.* c1916. p. 69).
Patterns, drawings and sketches.
When made for a specific job or order, they should be charged to that order at once as expense. When they are made for a stock product, their value depends on the probable duration and extent of their usefulness.

WOODS, CLINTON E. Depreciation, patterns. (In his *Unified accounting methods for industrials.* 1917. p. 65).
Patterns, 33⅓ to 100% per annum.
Drawings, according to their character.

Pavements and paving

AVERAGE life of street pavements in American cities. *Engineering and contracting,* Dec. 10, 1913, p. 670-1.

BAGG, F. A. Life of railway physical property from engineering standpoint. *Electric railway journal,* Dec. 9, 1911, p. 1205-6.

	Years
Asphalt pavement	10-15
Brick pavement	15-25

BAY state rate case. *Electric railway journal,* Dec. 4, 1915, p. 1121-3. *Public utility reports, annotated,* 1916F, p. 336-9.

	Years
Paving	
asphalt and asphaltina	15-20
bitulithic	12-15
bituminous macadam	10-18
water bound macadam	8-15
concrete and hassam	12-25
(very little near twenty-five years)	
grouted brick on concrete base	15-25
wood block on concrete base	20-30
wood block on bridges	10-20
plank on bridges	5
granite	20-60
(twice life of rail)	
cobble and cobble mixed	Same as rail

Paving, 3.1 annual depreciation per cent divided by investment.

BOLTON, REGINALD PELHAM. Depreciation of the value of buildings. (In his *Building for profit.* 1911. p. 62).

	Relative to years	
	66	75
Sidewalks	30%	26%

BRYAN, WILLIAM. Appraisal and depreciations of water-works and similar properties. *Journal of the association of engineering societies,* Dec. 1907, p. 336-81. Depreciation allowance for various public-service industries. *Engineering news,* Jan. 23, 1908, p. 96.

	% straight
Paving	
asphalt	7
brick	7
cedar blocks	16
granite	5
macadam	6

FLOY, HENRY. Depreciation. Floy, Henry. Depreciation as related to electrical properties. *American institute of electrical engineers,* Proceedings, 1911, p. 1267. Floy, Henry. *Valuation of public utility properties.* 1912. p. 168-217. Foster, Horatio A. *Engineering valuation of public utilities and factories.* 1913. p. 194-8. *Engineering and contracting,* Oct. 4, 1911, p. 359-65. *Engineering magazine,* Aug. 1911, p. 837-40.

	Dep. % per year straight line		
Paving	50 wearing	B. J. Arnold	Coney Island & Brooklyn, adopted by P. S. C., N. Y.
	50 value	Henry Floy	3rd Ave. case, adopted by P. S. C., N. Y.

FOSTER, HORATIO A. Rates of depreciation. (In his *Engineering valuation of public utilities and factories.* 1913. p. 199-200).

Paving	
block	2.5%
asphalt	7.0
brick, macadam etc.	4.5
tracks in car houses	3.5

GILLETTE, HALBERT P. and RICHARD T. DANA. Depreciation. (In their *Handbook of mechanical and electrical cost data.* 1918. p. 109).

Paving	2 years. Henry Floy, 3rd avenue case, N. Y. city.
	10 years. Prof. M. E. Cooley, Milwaukee, 3c. case.
	10-25 years. Union traction co. Case Chicago and union traction co., Stone & Webster.
	11.7 years. Belogs, Milwaukee 3c. case.

DEPRECIATION, DEPLETION AND OBSOLESCENCE—PAVEMENTS AND PAVING—*(Continued)*

	12.5 years. M. G. Starret, Milwaukee 3c. case.
	20 years. H. P. Gillette, Everett railway & water co., Jan. 29, 1912.
	20 years. Henry Floy, 3rd Avenue case, N. Y. City.
block	40 years. Marwick, Mitchell & co., appraisal of a large street railway system, Foster, p. 199.
brick	22.2 years. Marwick, Mitchell & co., appraisal of a large street railway system, Foster, p. 199.
Tracks in car houses.	28.6 years. Marwick, Mitchell & co., appraisal of a large street railway system, Foster, p. 199.

GRAY, HENRY L. Necessity of depreciation reserves. *Railway age gazette,* May 27, 1910, p. 1297-8. Editorial. Depreciation reserves. *Railway age gazette,* May 27, 1910, p. 1290. Letters. Depreciation reserves. *Railway age gazette,* July 8, 1910, p. 66.
Plank paving, 8% annual depreciation.

GREENLAND, S. W. Depreciation. ***Mississippi electric association, Reports of 2nd annual convention,*** held June 1910, p. 32-6.

	Life
Paving	10-25 years

GRUNSKY, CARL EWALD. Probable useful life of various articles. (In his *Valuation, depreciation and the rate-base.* 1917. p. 280-1).

Paving	10 years. Milwaukee electric railway and lighting co., in the Milwaukee 3c. Fare Case, Aug., 1912.
	10 years. Mortimer E. Cooley. Milwaukee 3c. fare case. Report Wisconsin R. R. com., vol. 10, p. 226.
	12.5 years. Milton G. Starrett Milwaukee 3c. fare case. Report Wisconsin R. R. com., vol. 10, p. 226.
	10-12.5 years. Wisconsin railroad commission. Milwaukee 3c. fare case. Aug. 23, 1912.
	10-26 years. Stone & Webster. Figures for Chicago union traction co. case. Report Wisconsin railroad commission, vol. 10, p. 220.
	10-25 years. Chicago Union traction co. Quoted in report Wisconsin R. R. commission, vol. 10, p. 220.
asphalt	10 years. Chicago union traction co. Quoted in Report Wisconsin R. R. commission, vol. 10, p. 220.
asphalt	10 years. Stone & Webster. Figures for Chicago union traction co. case. Report Wisconsin railroad commission, vol. 10 ,p. 220.
asphalt	12 years. Wisconsin railroad commission. Milwaukee electric railway & lighting co. case, Nov. 25, 1913.
brick	12 years. Wisconsin railroad commission. Milwaukee electric railway & lighting co. case, Nov. 25, 1913.
cobble	25 years. Chicago union traction co. Quoted in Report Wisconsin R. R. commission, vol. 10, p. 220.
cobble	26 years. Stone & Webster. Figures for Chicago union traction co. case. Report Wisconsin railroad commission, vol. 10, p. 220.
creosoted blocks	12 years. Wisconsin railroad commission. Milwaukee electric railway & lighting co. case, Nov. 25, 1913.
granite	16 years. Chicago union traction co. Quoted in Report Wisconsin R. R. commission, vol. 10, p. 220.
granite	16 years. Stone & Webster. Figures for Chicago union traction co. case. Report Wisconsin railroad commission, vol. 10, p. 220.
granite	21 years. Wisconsin Railroad Commission. Milwaukee electric railway & lighting co. case. Nov. 25, 1913.

LIFE of brick pavements. *Engineering and contracting,* June 19, 1912, p. 697-700.

Light traffic	20-50 years
medium	20-40
heavy	8-35

NEALE, R. E. Depreciation in engineering works. *Mechanical world,* Feb. 7, 1913, p. 67-8.

Paving	50%	2 years

DEPRECIATION, DEPLETION AND OBSOLESCENCE—PAVEMENTS AND PAVING—*(Continued)*

NICHOLSON, J. LEE *and* J. F. D. ROHRBACH. Depreciation. (In their *Cost accounting.* 1919. p. 146).
Paving and pavements 4-10%
Roadways and sidewalks 4
Based on (1) the cost of equipmeent.
(2) the life of the equipment.
(3) on a ten-hour day.

PHILADELPHIA. CONTROLLER. Rates of depreciation. (In his *Manual of accounting, reporting and business procedure of the city and county of Philadelphia.* 1917. p. 205, 210).
Asphalt paving plant and equipment 10%
Pavements 4
Sidewalks 2

PIEZ, CHARLES. Perpetual inventory and appraisal values; table of standard depreciation rates. *Engineering and contracting,* Jan. 24, 1917, p. 77. *Factory,* Dec. 1916, p. 668-71. *Iron age,* Nov. 30, 1916, Jan. 11, 1917, p. 1266, 138-9. *Iron trade review,* Feb. 22, 1917, p. 477-8. Condensed. *Iron trade review,* Dec. 7, 1916, p. 1144-6. *Journal of the American society of mechanical engineers,* Dec. 1916, p. 965-6. Kent, William. *Bookkeeping and cost accounting for factories,* 1918. p. 90. Discussion. *Journal of the American society of mechanical engineers,* March 1917, p. 215-7.
Miscellaneous real estate improvements:
Pavements, sidewalks, fences, retaining walls, roadways, tracks, yard drainage, general conduit, tunnels, vaults, etc., 4.5% on cost: 10% on reducing balance.

PUBLIC utility reports, annotated. Rochester, Lawyers co-operative publishing co. 1918A. p. 917-8.
New York & N. S. Traction Co.
Paving 3%

WEEKS, H. E. Abstract of paper on depreciation read before annual meeting of Iowa street and interurban railway association, April 1910. *Electric railway journal,* April 30, 1910, p. 782-3.
Paving 15 years

Pearl fishing

AUSTRALIA. FEDERAL INCOME TAX DEPARTMENT. Depreciation allowance. *Accountant,* Oct. 13, 1917, p. 277-9. *Accounting and commerce,* June 30, 1917, p. 55-7. *Federal accountant,* July 1917, p. 93-8. *Public accountant,* Jan. 30, 1917, p. 145-52.
Oyster fishing and pearl fishing
Lugger 7½%
Diving gear (diving dresses and air pipes). Replacements allowable
Helmet and corselet 10
Pump 7½
Running gear (sails)
Replacements allowable
Written down value, repairs allowed in addition.

Pedestals

PHILADELPHIA. CONTROLLER. Rates of depreciation. (In his *Manual of accounting, reporting and business procedure of the city and county of Philadelphia.* 1917. p. 207-8).
Tabourets, stands, pedestals, copy holders 4%

Pergolas

PHILADELHIA. CONTROLLER. Rates of depreciation. (In his *Manual of accounting, reporting and business procedure of the city and county of Philadelphia.* 1917. p. 210).
Arbors, trellises, pergolas, flag poles, etc. 5%

Petroleum

See Depreciation, depletion and obsolescence—Oils.

Photo engraving

See Depreciation, depletion and obsolescence—Printing.

Photography

PHILADELPHIA. CONTROLLER. Rates of depreciation. (In his *Manual of accounting, reporting and business procedure of the city and county of Philadelphia.* 1917. p. 210).
Photographing equipment 10%

Physicians

AUSTRALIA. FEDERAL INCOME TAX DEPARTMENT. Depreciation allowance. *Accountant,* Oct. 13, 1917, p. 277-9. *Accounting and commerce,* June 30, 1917, p. 55-7. *Federal accountant,* July 1917, p. 93-8. *Public accountant,* Jan. 30, 1917, p. 145-52.
Doctors' instruments. X-ray and electro-cardiograph. Replacements allowable.

MAY, JAMES HENRY. Depreciation. (In his *Medical practitioners' accounts.* 1903. p. 56, 65).

MONTGOMERY, ROBERT H. Doctors. (In his *Auditing, theory and practice.* 1916. p. 730-1).
Horses and carriages or automobiles 15-30%

MONTGOMERY, ROBERT H. Physicians. (In his *Income tax procedure,* 1919. p. 575-6. ——— Same, 1920. p. 732).
Residence, brick construction, on part occupied as offices only 5%
Automobile 20
Books 20
Instruments 25
Office furniture 20
County residence, wood construction on part occupied by offices only 10

DEPRECIATION, DEPLETION AND OBSOLESCENCE—PHYSICIANS—*(Continued)*

NICHOLSON, J. LEE and J. F. D. ROHRBACH. Depreciation. (In their *Cost accounting.* 1919. p. 151).
Surgical instruments 10%
Based on (1) the cost of equipment.
(2) the life of the equipment.
(3) on a ten-hour day.

PHILADELPHIA. CONTROLLER. Rates of depreciation. (In his *Manual of accounting, reporting and business procedure of the city and county of Philadelphia.* 1917. p. 208).
Surgical and medical equipment 5%

Pianolas

See Depreciation, depletion and obsolescence—Musical instruments.

Pianos

See Depreciation, depletion and obsolescence—Musical instruments.

Pickling

ELBOURNE, EDWARD T. Depreciation rates. (In his *Factory administration and accounts.* 1918. p. 377).

	Prov. dep. % Remainder values	Years 10%	5%
Pickling vats	10	28	28

NICHOLSON, J. LEE and J. F. D. ROHRBACH. (In their *Cost accounting.* 1919. p. 150).
Pickling washing machines, electric and acetylene welding machines 10%
Pickling tanks, etc. 20
Based on (1) the cost of equipment.
(2) the life of the equipment.
(3) on a ten-hour day.

Piers

See Depreciation, depletion and obsolescence—Wharves.

Pile drivers

LIFE of road construction equipment. *Engineering and contracting,* Jan. 3, 1917, p. 3.
Pile drivers 20%

Pipe

ALLOWANCES for depreciation in the pipe system of the Los Angeles waterworks. *Engineering news,* May 4, 1899, p. 283.

All the pipe in use was classified by age as being 5 years, over 5 and less than 10, over 10 and less than 15, and over 15 years old, the average age for the latter being taken at 19 years.

(1) Cast-iron pipe in the better soils, 1.25% per annum, which was applied to the mean of the periods in each of the four classified groups.
(2) Cast-iron pipes in the poorer soils, 2% per annum applied as above.
(3) Sheet iron and steel riveted pipes in the better soils, 4% per annum.
(4) Sheet iron and steel riveted pipe in the poorer soils, 6.77% per annum.
(5) Wrought iron standard screw pipe in the better soils, 3.33% per annum.
(6) Same, 5.71% per annum in the poorer soils.
(7) Cement-lined pipe, 2.86% per annum, all of which is classed as laid in the better class of soils, inasmuch as all of that grade of pipe laid in the poorer soils has failed and been abandoned.

We have included in these estimates of depreciation the cost of pipe, lead, gates, laying pipes, taking up and removing pavements, to all of which the rates given have been applied.

For internal depreciation, due to tuberculation, we have estimated as follows:

For all cast-iron pipe 4 ins. in diameter and over, a mean depreciation of 0.6% per annum.

For all cast-iron pipe 3 ins. in diameter, 2% per annum for ten years or under, and 1% per annum over ten years of age.

For 4 in. wrought iron screw pipe, a mean rate of 1.5% per annum of age.

For cement lined pipe, no internal depreciation.

The above rates of internal depreciation have been applied to the values of the pipes after deducting external depreciation.

The average depreciation of service pipe was assumed to have reached 50%; hydrants, 40%, and meters, 60%. Varying rates were used for the portions of the works outside the distributing system.

AMERICAN INSTITUTE OF ACCOUNTANTS. Report of the committee on standard schedules for uniform reports upon municipal industries and public service corporations; annual meeting at Atlantic City, N. J., October 20-22, 1908. 15p. *Journal of accountancy,* May 1909, p. 47-54.

The knowledge at the command of the Bureau of the census leads to the conclusion that this average life is approximately as follows:

Boilers, steam pipes and filtration equipment	20 years
Engines, pumping machinery and wood pipe	5
Masonry of filtration plant, cribs, iron water pipe, intake pipes, fire hydrants, stand pipes, buildings	50

AMERICAN WATERWORKS ASSOCIATION. Final report of committee on depreciation. *Journal of the American water works association,* Sept. 1917, p. 1-38.

Conduits and distribution pipe

Cast iron of large diameter	75-125 years
Wrought iron or steel of large diameter	35-75
Wood stave of large diameter	30-60

DEPRECIATION, DEPLETION AND OBSOLESCENCE—Pipe—*(Continued)*

Distribution pipe of small diameter
Cast iron 30-70, 50-90
Wrought iron & steel mains 25-40
Services
Wrought iron & steel 15-30
Lead 40-80

Analysis of the premises adopted and methods used in determining the cost to reproduce new, together with the depreciation thereon of the, physical property of the Metropolitan system and the Kansas City and Westport Belt railway of Kansas City, Mo. *Engineering and contracting,* May 28, 1913, p. 617-20.
Piping and covering 3½%

Australia. Federal income tax department. Depreciation allowance. *Accountant,* Oct. 13, 1917, p. 277-9. *Accounting and commerce,* June 30, 1917, p. 55-7. *Federal accountant,* July 1917, p. 93-8. *Public accountant,* Jan. 30, 1917, p. 145-52.
Ammonia pipes 10%
Based on written down value and repairs allowed in addition.

Barker, Harry. Typical life expectation tables for public utility property. (In his *Public utility rates.* 1917. p. 347, 368-9).

Service pipes	20 years.	Wisconsin railroad commission.
lead	50-100 years.	Wisconsin railroad commission.
galvanized iron or sheet	30-50 years.	Wisconsin railroad commission.
Suctions and intakes	30-50 years.	Wisconsin railroad commission.
Piping and covering	20-30 years.	Wisconsin railroad commission.

Bay state rate case. *Electric railway journal,* Dec. 4, 1915, p. 1191-3. *Public utility reports, annotated,* 1916F, p. 336-9. Bay state street railway valuation. *Electric railway journal,* Dec. 4, 1915, p. 1121-3.
Piping 25 years

Belt, Robert E. Depreciation. (In his *Foundry cost accounting, practice and procedure.* 1919. p. 243).
Steam piping 5%

Belt, Robert E. Depreciation. (In his *Uniform cost accounting methods; adopted by the American malleable castings association,* Nov. 14, 1917. p. 20-1).
Steam boilers, generators, air compressor, steam piping, electric wiring, etc. 7½%

Bentley, Harry C. Depreciation. (In his *Science of accounts.* 1913. p. 146).
Piping 5%

Bolton, Reginald Pelham. Depreciation of mechanical equipments and power plants. (In his *Building for profit.* 1911. p. 82, 89).

	years Physical	%	years Economic
Exterior framing, copper-cased housings, etc., heating pipe systems used part of the year, gas piping	33	82.5	27
Steel-plate stacks and smoke ducts, cold-water piping, electric conduits	30	75.0	24
Roof-tanks, sanitary piping systems	27	67.5	21
Pressure steam piping and appliances	26	65.0	20
Interior drums and tanks, hot-water and pneumatic piping	25	62.5	..
Sanitary fixtures, refrigerating piping, kitchen fixtures, and valves	20	50.0	16
Drip and drain piping, cheaper class of pressure steam boilers	18	45.0	14

Bolton, Reginald Pelham. Depreciation of the value of buildings. (In his *Building for profit.* 1911. p. 62).

	Relative	Years
Piping	66	75
	50%	44%

Brewer, Allan F. Rates for annual depreciation. *Industrial management,* April 1918, p. 268.
Steam piping and valves 30 years 3.33%

Bryan, William. Appraisal and depreciation of water-works and similar industries. *Journal of the association of engineering societies,* Dec. 1907, p. 336-81. Depreciation allowance for various public-service industries. *Engineering news,* Jan. 23, 1908, p. 96.

Pipe	years	% straight	
cast iron	50-75		
"	68		Los Angeles, Cal.
"		1.25	Do., Good Soil
"		2	Do., Poor Soil
"	20-60		R. Hering
"	25-60		
"	70		
"	Over 50		Gas Mains
"			Pearsons
"		1.14	

DEPRECIATION, DEPLETION AND OBSOLESCENCE—Pipe—*(Continued)*

cast iron	100	1	
"	100		
"	80		
"	75		
service	10		
"		2.5	
"		5	
wrought iron	30		Underground
"	20		
"	15-20		
"		5	
In plant	15		
"	25		
"	14-15		
"	20-30		
"		10	

Chase, Harvey S. Depreciation in water works accounts, with reference to uniform reports. *Journal of the New England water works association*, June 1910, p. 305-31. Abstract. *Engineering and contracting*, June 29, 1910, p. 598. Editorial. Depreciation and sinking fund accounts. *Municipal engineering*, July 1910, p. 26.

Boilers, steam pipes and filtration equipment	20 years
Engines, pumping machinery, and wood pipes	25
Masonry of filtration plant, cribs, iron water pipes, intake pipes, fire hydrants, stand pipes and buildings	50

Clader, Will-A. Water utilities accounting. *Journal of accountancy*, Aug. 1919, p. 91-2.
The following rates are used frequently when wear and tear are made good by operating maintenance.

Cast iron pipe	1%
Wrought iron pipe	2
Wood pipe	2

Cravens, George W. Depreciation and maintenance of electrical equipment. *Electrical review*, April 23, 1910, p. 853-6. Foster, H. A. *Engineering valuation of public utilities and factories*. 1913. p. 201-2. Montgomery, Robert H. *Income tax procedure*, 1919. p. 570. ——— Same, 1920. p. 722-4. Montgomery, Robert H. *Auditing theory and practice*, 1916, p. 424.

	Light intermittent service	Heavy continuous service
Piping, steam and water	4-5.5%	5.5-8.3%

	per annum % dep.	
Steam piping	3.5%	Chicago traction commission
	6.6	Chicago union traction co.
	7.5	Milwaukee electric railway & light co.
	5	Wisconsin railroad commission
	5	Average English
	5	Average Scotch practice.
	8-10	Philip Dawson
	5	Stone and Webster
	2.5-3.3	Industrial power plants
	5-8	Professor G. F. Gebhardt
	5	Miscellaneous sources

Crowell, H. H. Electric lighting rates and depreciation. *Municipal journal and engineer*, Dec. 18, 1907, p. 698.

	Purchased 10 years or more ago	modern
Piping	15 years	20 years.

Dawson, Philip. Depreciation. (In his *Engineering and electric traction pocket-book*. Ed. 2. p. 1161).

Boilers, pumps, piping, etc.	15-30 years.

Depreciation in cast iron pipe. *Municipal engineering*, Sept. 1911, p. 211.
Cast iron will last 50-80 years, wrought iron half as long, both estimates being approximate averages, depending on soil conditions. 50% depreciation in thirty years is a fair allowance, if exact information is lacking.

Depreciation of the equipment of an electric plant. *Electrical world*, Dec. 12, 1914, p. 1161.

Boilers, piping and generators	4.7-4.8%

Elbourne, Edward T. Depreciation rates. (In his *Factory administration and accounts*. 1918. p. 376, 377).

	Prov. dep. % Remainder values	Years 10%	5%
Power plant pipes	7½	29	38
Blast pipe installation	7½	29	38
Hydraulic piping	7½	29	38
Water supply pipes and connections	7½	29	38
Pipe bending machines	6	37	48
Pipe cutting and screwing machines	7½	29	38

Estimated life and depreciation of water works plants. *Municipal journal and engineer*, May 6, 1908, p. 558.

Material	Life in years	Dep. % per year straight	Authority
Cast-iron pipe	50-75		W. H. Bryan.
" " "	68		Los Angeles. Engineering Record, Aug. 28, 1897.

DEPRECIATION, DEPLETION AND OBSOLESCENCE—Pipe—*(Continued)*

cast iron pipe		1.25	Los Angeles, Cal. Good soil. Engineering news, May 4, 1899.
" " "		2	Los Angeles, Cal. Poor soil. Engineering news, May 4, 1899.
" " "	20-60		Rudolph Hering, Proceedings American society of civil engineers, 1897.
" " "	25-60		W. Kiersted; Pro. Am. soc. C. E. 1897.
" " "	70		Gas Mains, Prosser; Engineering news vol. XLVII p. 425.
" " "	Over 50		Pearsons; Pro. Am. soc. C. E. 1897.
" " "		1.14	W. H. Rosecrans, Galena, Kans. app. in 1905.
" " "		1	B. L. Dodge, Mt. Vernon, Ill. app. in 1906.
" " "	100		J. W. Alvord; Pro. Am. W. W. Ass. 1903.
" " "	100		C. B. Burdick; Mt. Vernon, Ill. app. in 1906.
" " "	80		B. Williams, Galena, Kans. app. in 1905.
" " "	75		W. Kiersted, Galena, Kans. app. in 1905.
Service pipe	10		W. H. Bryan
" "		2.5	Los Angeles, Cal. Engineering news, May 4, 1899.
" "		5	B. L. Dodge; Mt. Vernon, Ill., app. in 1906.

Floy, Henry. Depreciation. Floy, Henry. Depreciation as related to electrical properties. *American institute of electrical engineers, Proceedings,* 1911, p. 1267. Floy, Henry. Valuation of public utility properties. 1912. p. 168-217. Foster, Horatio A. *Engineering valuation of public utilities and factories.* 1913. 194-8. *Engineering and contracting,* Oct. 4, 1911, p. 359-65. *Engineering magazine,* Aug. 1911, p. 837-40.

	Dep. % per year —straight		
Piping and covering	4-4½	Traction Val. Comm.	Chicago con. trac. company.
	6	B. J. Arnold	Coney Island & Brooklyn adopted by P. S. C., N. Y.
	5	Henry Floy	3rd Ave. case, adopted by P. S. C., N. Y.
	5	Wisconsin P. S. C.	
	5	Arbitrators	Street lighting controversy, Atlanta, Ga. 1899.
	6⅔	St. Louis, P. S. C.	Union elec. L. & P. Co.

Foster, Horatio A. Methods of calculating depreciation. (In his *Engineering valuation of public utilities and factories.* 1913. p. 169).
Steam plants of all kinds, shafting and pipe covering. Minimum service value 25 per cent of reproduction cost. Joint engineering department of the Wisconsin commissions.

Foster, Horatio A. Rates of depreciation. (In his *Engineering valuation of public utilities and factories.* 1913. p. 204, 205).

Suction piping and intakes	30-50 years
Piping	20-30
Pipe covering	same as pipe

Gas companies and depreciation. *Accountant,* Jan. 24, 1903, p. 109-12.

Mains and service pipes	7½%

Gillette, Halbert Powers. Water-works. (In his *Handbook of cost data for contractors and engineers.* 1910. p. 796-801).
Estimated Depreciation of Water Pipe. Los Angeles, Calif. In estimating the depreciation of water pipes in Los Angeles, Calif., a board of four engineers (Jas. D. Schuyler, A. L. Adams, A. H. Koebig and J. P. Lippincott) adopted the following rates of annual depreciation, for purposes of appraisal of present value:

Cast iron pipe in good soil	1.25%
Cast iron pipe in poor soil	2.00
Sheet iron pipe in good soil	4.00
Sheet iron pipe in poor soil	6.77
Wrought iron pipe in good soil	3.33
Wrought iron pipe in poor soil	5.71

These depreciations were applied to the cost of the pipe in place (including pipe, lead, labor of laying, removing and replacing pavement, etc.). Soils ranging from salty shales and alkaline adobe (clay) to heavy clay were classed as "poor", and the balance as "good". After deducting the above depreciation from the first cost, a further depreciation, called internal depreciation due to tuberculation, was calculated on those depreciated values and deducted therefrom. The annual internal depreciation was estimated as follows:

Cast iron pipe, 4 in. and over	0.6%
Cast iron pipe, 3 in. for less than 10-yrs. of age	2.0
Cast iron pipe, 3 in. for over 10-yrs. of age	1.0
Sheet iron and steel	0.75
Wrought iron, under 4 ins. for less than 10 yrs. of age	2.00
Wrought iron, under 4 ins. for over 10-yrs. of age	1.00
Wrought iron, 4 ins.	1.50

DEPRECIATION, DEPLETION AND OBSOLESCENCE—PIPE—*(Continued)*

GILLETTE, HALBERT T. and RICHARD T. DANA. Depreciation. (In their *Handbook of mechanical and electrical cost data.* 1918. p. 111, 109, 107, 110).

Water supply lines 25-33.3 years. H. P. Gillette, Everett railway & water co., Jan. 29, 1912.

Pipe

- black iron — 10 years. H. P. Gillette, Everett railway & water co., Jan. 29, 1912.
- cast iron small diameter — 20-40 years. Leonard Metcalf, Transactions, American society civil engineers, 1909, p. 24, vol. 64.
- cast iron large diameter — 50-75 years. Leonard Metcalf, Transactions, American society civil engineers, 1909, p. 24, vol. 64.
- galvanized iron — 10 years. H. P. Gillette, Everett railway & water co., Jan. 29, 1912.
- Matheson — 30 years. H. P. Gillette, Everett railway & water co., Jan. 29, 1912.
- screw flange — 20 years. H. P. Gillette, Everett railway & water co., Jan. 29, 1912.
- steel — 25-50 years. Leonard Metcalf, Transactions, American society civil engineers, 1909, p. 24, vol. 64.
- wood stave — 20-30 years Leonard Metcalf, Transactions, American society civil engineers, 1909, p. 24, vol. 64.
- wood — 25 years. H. P. Gillette, Everett railway & water co., Jan. 29, 1912.

Fittings — 20 years. H. P. Gillette, Everett railway & water co., Jan. 29, 1912.

Piping and covering
- 5 years. Henry Floy, 3rd Ave. case, N. Y. city.
- 15 years St. Louis public service commission, Union electric light & power co.
- 15-20 years. Union traction co., case Chicago and union traction co., Stone & Webster.
- 16.6 years. B. J. Arnold—Appraisal of the Coney Island & Brooklyn railroad, Feb. 1, 1909.
- 20 years. Wisconsin railroad commission. W. D. Pence, Milwaukee 3c Case.
- 22.5-25 years. Traction valuation commission, Chicago consolidated traction co.
- 28.6 years. B. J. Arnold, Chicago appraisals, 4 cases.

steam
- 13.3 years Milwaukee electric railway & light co.
- 28.6 years. Chicago traction commission.
- 30-40 years. George W. Cravens, Industrial power plants.

Service connections, water. 20 years. H. P. Gillette. Everett railway & water co., Jan. 29, 1912.

Gas service. 20 years. Wisconsin railroad commission.

GREENLAND, S. W. Depreciation. *Mississippi electric association, Report of 2nd annual convention* held June 1910. p. 32-6.

Piping — 20 years life

GRUNSKY, CARL EWALD. Probable useful life of various articles. (In his *valuation, depreciation and the rate-base.* 1917. p. 280-283).

Water pipe:
- cast iron — 75 years. W. Kiersted. Galena Appraisal, Kansas, 1905.
- cast iron — 80 years. Benezette Williams. Galena Appraisal, Kansas, 1905.
- cast iron — 100 years. Chas. B. Burdick. Appraisal of Mt. Vernon water works, Illinois, 1906.
- cast iron — 100 years. B. L. Dodge. Mt. Vernon Water works appraisal, Illinois, 1906.
- cast iron — 100 years. John W. Alvord in Proceedings American water works Association, 1903.
- cast iron mains — 50-75 years. Leonard Metcalf. Transactions American society of civil engineers, 1909.
- cast iron mains — 100 years. California Railroad commission—Reports 1913-4. San Jose water co. case, May, 1914.
- cast iron small size — 20-40 years. Leonard Metcalf. Transactions American society of civil engineers, 1909.

DEPRECIATION, DEPLETION AND OBSOLESCENCE—Pipe—*(Continued)*

wrought iron	20 years. W. Kiersted. Galena Appraisal, Kansas, 1905.
wrought iron	20 years. B. L. Dodge. Mt. Vernon water works appraisal, Illinois, 1906.
wrought iron services	15-30 years. Leonard Metcalf. Transactions American society of civil engineers, 1909
wrought iron underground	30 years. Williams. Galena Appraisal, Kansas., 1905.
galv. wrought iron incl. fit's	30-50 years. H. A. Foster. "Engineering valuation of public utilities and factories", Van Nostrand, 1912.
black w. iron and services	25-35 years. H. A. Foster. "Engineering valuation of public utilities and factories", Van Nostrand, 1912.
steel pipe	25-50 years. Leonard Metcalf. Transactions American society of civil engineers, 1909
services	20 years. B. L. Dodge. Mt. Vernon water works appraisal, Illinois, 1906.
woodstave	20-30 years. Leonard Metcalf. Transactions American society of civil engineers, 1909
wood-stave	30 years. San Joaquin light & power corporation. Rate hearing before California railroad commission, 1915.
distributing system	16.5 years. California railroad commission—Reports 1913-4. Cuyumaca water co. case, 1913.
power-plant pen stocks	30 years. San Joaquin light & power corporation. Rate hearing before California railroad commission, 1915.
Gas pipe: w. i. & steel under 3 in. diam.	20 years. Wisconsin railroad commission. Quoted by H. A. Foster and in published reports.
w. iron & steel 3 in. and over	30 years. Wisconsin railroad commission. Quoted by H. A. Foster and in published reports.
c. iron mains 3 in. and 4 in. diam.	50 years. Wisconsin railroad commission. Quoted by H. A. Foster and in published reports.
c. iron mains over 6 in.	75 years. Wisconsin railroad commission. Quoted by H. A. Foster and in published reports.
services	20 years. Wisconsin railroad commission. Quoted by H. A. Foster and in published reports.
Miscellaneous: Pipe and covering	15 years. Chicago union traction co. Quoted in Report Wisconsin R. R. Commission, Vol. 10, p. 220.
pipe and covering	17 years. Bion J. Arnold. Coney Island and Brooklyn figures adopted by Public service commission of New York. Four Chicago appraisals quoted by H. A. Foster.
pipe and covering	20 years. Stone & Webster. Figures for Chicago union traction co. case. Report Wisconsin railroad commission, vol. 10, p. 220.
pipe and covering	20 years. Wisconsin R. R. commission. Milwaukee 3c fare case. Aug. 23, 1912.
pipe and covering	20 years. Henry Floy. Transactions American institute of electrical engineers, June, 1911. Third avenue case figures adopted by Public service commission of New York.
pipe and covering	28.5 years. Bion J. Arnold. Coney Island and Brooklyn figures adopted by Public service commission of New York. Four Chicago appraisals quoted by H. A. Foster.
pipe and covering	22-25 years. Traction valuation commission. Case of the Chicago consolidated traction co.
power stations	20 years. Pacific gas & electric company. Figures used in rate hearings before Master in Chancery, San Francisco, 1913-4.

DEPRECIATION, DEPLETION AND OBSOLESCENCE—PIPE—*(Continued)*

Stand pipes
25 years.
W. H. Rosecrans. Galena appraisals, Kansas, 1905.
30 years.
W. Kiersted. Galena appraisals, Kansas, 1905.
40 years.
Benezette, Williams. Galena Appraisals, Kansas, 1905.
25-40 years.
Leonard Metcalf. Transactions American society of civil engineers, 1909.

HAZLEHURST, J. N. Final report of the committee on depreciation. *Journal of the American water works association,* March 1919, p. 85-135.

Conduits and distribution pipe of cast iron of large diameter. Cast-iron pipe coated and buried in the ground is a very durable structure. We have little knowledge of its final effective life from a physical point of view. There are some instances of two hundred years' life for uncoated pipe. Largely we must amortize such durable material, kept clean and well maintained, again by consideration of the possible changes in public need, functional usefulness, and the burden of a reasonable amortization say 75-125 years.

Conduits and distribution pipe of wrought iron or steel of large diameter. Thickness of shell and sensitiveness to a greater range of deteriorating influences must of necessity bring the life of wrought iron and steel physically below that of cast iron, and in many cases below functional considerations 35-75.

Conduits and distribution pipe of wood stave of large diameter. Ultimate experience somewhat limited, but thought to be about in same class as steel, when well protected and saturated 30-60.

Distribution pipe of small diameter.

(a) Cast iron—Limitations of size increase difficulties in interior cleaning and maintenance. Such smaller mains are at times removed in rapidly growing cities to make way for larger pipe. Often, they are only supplemented 30-70.

It should be noted that in slow growing and smaller cities small mains are less liable to be outgrown than in larger cities 50-90.

(b) Wrought iron and steel mains.
Affected by kind of water carried, soil, and coating. Liability of replacement probably greatest influence in shortening useful life. 25-40.

(c) Services.

Wrought iron and steel	15-30
Lead	40-80

Of services, it should be noted that character of water carried, soil, and coating are influential, but changing needs are also important.

HODGMAN, B. B. Prices and depreciation of cast iron pipe. *Journal of the American water works association,* June 1918, p. 145-62.

KENT, WILLIAM. Depreciation of shafting, etc. (In his *Bookeeping and cost accounting for factories.* 1918. p. 91).
Pipe covering and valves show wear, but piping as a whole is seldom depreciated more than 10 per cent.

KIMBALL, DEXTER S. Estimated life and factors of depreciation. (In his *Cost finding.* 1918. p. 190. *Principles of industrial organization,* 1913, p. 163).

	Prob. life of asset in yrs.	Ratio of scrap to orig. val.	% on orig. cost	% on dim.
Steam piping, valves and fittings	10-15	0.05	9.5-6.3	2.6-18

LIFE and economic use of steel water pipe. *Engineering and contracting,* April 17, 1912, p. 444.

LIFE data on power-plant equipment used in valuation of Massachusetts property. *Electrical world,* Dec. 4, 1915, p. 1261.

Piping	25 years

MANUFACTURERS' light and heat company of Pittsburgh, Pa. *Commercial and financial chronicle,* July 23, 1910, p. 217.

Pipe lines, pipe rigs and lines	6%

METCALF, LEONARD. Depreciation in waterworks operation and accounting. *Journal of the New England waterworks association,* Dec. 1910, p. 442. Abstracts. *Engineering news,* Nov. 3, 1910, p. 482. Methods of computing depreciation of and reasonable assumptions as to period of useful life of waterworks. *Engineering and contracting,* Nov. 16, 1910, p. 434.

	Years	Dep. % per yr. straight line
Cast iron pipe large diameter.		
In non-tuberculating waters	60-100	1⅔-1
In tuberculating waters	50-75	2-1⅓
Cast iron pipe, small diam.	30-50	3⅓-2
Steel pipe	25-40	4-2½
Wood stave pipe	20-30	5-3½
Wrought-iron service pipes	15-30	6⅔-3⅓

METCALF, LEONARD. Water-works valuation and fair rates, in the light of the Maine supreme court decisions in the Waterville and Brunswick cases. *American society of civil engineers. Papers and discussions,* 1908, p. 1101-73. *American society of civil engineers, Transactions,* Sept. 1909, p. 1. Foster, Horatio A. *Engineering valuation of public utilities and factories.* 1913, p. 207. Gillette, Halbert P. *Handbook of cost data for contractors and engineers.* p. 797.

Waterworks structures	General limits of useful life years	Annual contribution to depreciation account or sinking fund in percent of cost: At 5 percent annual rate sinking fund percent	General approximate results percent
Cast-iron pipe of large diameter	50-75	0.4777%-0.0383%	¾-¼

DEPRECIATION, DEPLETION AND OBSOLESCENCE—Pipe—*(Continued)*

Cast-iron pipe of small diameter	20-40	3.0243	-0.8278	3-¾
Steel pipe	25-50	2.0952	-0.4777	2-¾
Wood-stave pipe	20-30	3.0243	-1.5051	3-2
Wrought-iron service pipe	15-30	4.6342	-1.5051	5-2

MONTGOMERY, ROBERT H. Electrical equipment manufacturers. (In his *Income tax procedure,* 1919. p. 563. ——— Same, 1920. p. 716).

Piping and electric conductors outside of buildings	10%
Water, sewer and drain pipes (outside of buildings)	10
Inside piping and wiring	10

Based on gross book values at the end of the preceding year.

NEALE, R. E. Depreciation in engineering works. *Mechanical world,* Feb. 7, 1913, p. 67-8.

Piping	4-7%	14-25 years

NELSON, BAILIE WALTER. Limitation and application of profits from municipal undertakings. *Incorporated accountants' journal,* Oct. 1912, p. 15-7.

Pipes (gas)	2% per annum

NICHOLSON, J. LEE and J. F. D. ROHRBACH. Depreciation. (In their *Cost accounting,* 1919, p. 147).

Tunnels, underground piping, vaults, and general conduits	5%
Piping	7½

Based on (1) the cost of equipment
(2) the life of the equipment
(3) on a ten-hour day.

PENDER, HAROLD. Depreciation. (In his *Handbook for electrical engineers.* c1914. p. 339).

Piping	Years	%	
steam	15		Chicago union traction co.
	20		Engineer of valuation staff of Wisconsin railroad commission.
			Stone & Webster, for Chicago union traction co.
	21		S. W. Greenland
	21.3		J. W. Alvord
		6.66	Chicago union traction co.
		5	Milwaukee electric railway and light co.
			Engineer of valuation staff of Wisconsin railroad commission.
			Cardiff tramways
			Glasgow "
			Stone & Webster, for the Chicago union traction co.

PHILADELPHIA. CONTROLLER. Rates of depreciation. (In his *Manual of accounting, reporting and business procedure of the city and county of Philadelphia.* 1917. p. 205).

Pipes, valves, dampers, etc.	4%

PIEZ, CHARLES. Perpetual inventory and appraisal values; table of standard depreciation rates. *Engineering and contracting,* Jan. 24, 1917, p. 77. *Factory,* Dec. 1916, p. 668-71. *Iron age,* Nov. 30, 1916, Jan. 11, 1917, p. 1266, 138-9. *Iron trade review,* Feb. 22, 1917, p. 477-8. Condensed. *Iron trade review,* Dec. 7, 1916, p. 1144-6. *Journal of the American society of mechanical engineers,* Dec. 1916, p. 965-6. Kent, William. *Bookkeeping and cost accounting for factories,* 1918, p. 90. Discussion. *Journal of the American society of mechanical engineers,* March 1917, p. 215-7.

	% on cost	% on reducing balance
Power piping	6	15
Water and sewer piping and sanitary fixtures where separate	4	7.5

PROBABLE lives of water-works elements. *Engineering news,* Oct. 11, 1917, p. 688.

Services, wrought iron & steel	15-30 years
" " iron & lead	40-80
Cast-iron pipe, large	75-125
" " small	30-70
(in slow growing and small cities)	50-90
Wrought-iron or steel pipe, large	30-75
" " " " " small	25-40
Wood-stave pipe, large	30-60

PROPOSED sale of Toronto utilities to the city. *Electrical world,* Oct. 25, 1913, p. 832.

Piping	3.5%

PROSSER, R. W. Depreciation in gas plants. *American gas light journal,* May 26, 1902, p. 767.

	years	% of first cost
Services (gas)	25	
Pumps & piping	15	10
Pipe connections & valves	20	33

PUBLIC utility reports, annotated. Rochester, Lawyers co-operative publishing co. 1917A. p. 577.
Re Clarksburg light & heat co. (W.Va.) In ascertaining the reproduction cost less accrued depreciation of natural gas-pipe lines, a deduction of 33⅓ per cent from their reproduction cost, rather than 25 per cent, was held to be proper in view of the facts that the age of the pipe averaged from six to fourteen years, and that the average life of wrought iron pipe is from twenty to twenty-five years, and of steel pipe from fifteen to twenty years.

RESULTS of questionnaire on life and depreciation of cast iron water pipe in 14 large American cities. *Engineering and contracting,* Dec. 15, 1915, p. 466-7.

ROBY, J. J. Schedule of plant depreciation. (In his *Treatise on cost accounting as applied to coal mining.* c1913. p. 14-5).

Pipe, heaters and pumps.

Deduct as salvage before depreciating	10%
Depreciation rate for remainder, fireproof	8
Deduct as salvage before depreciating	5
Depreciation rate for remainder, fireproof	20

DEPRECIATION, DEPLETION AND OBSOLESCENCE—PIPE—*(Continued)*

RUNYON, F. O. Report on hydro-electric plant for special committee common council, Newark, New Jersey, April 23, 1902. p. 15, 16.
Steel pipe line 3%

SOME depreciation rates on buildings, machinery, shafting, belting, furniture and apparatus, tools and dies, moulds, lasts, patterns and drawing used by the Associated mutual fire insurance companies of Boston, Mass., in making appraisals of manufacturing properties. *Utilities magazine,* Jan. 1, 1916, p. 186-7.
Piping, where exposed to acid fumes disintegrate rapidly, but generally the valves and pipe covering are the only parts that show any appreciable wear. We, therefore seldom allow a depreciation of more than 10% on the whole.

UNIFORM cost sheet for coal mining companies. *Coal age,* Sept. 19, 1918, p. 545-7.
Pipe lines in mines 33⅓% original cost

VALUATION of the Chicago consolidated traction property. *Electric railway journal,* Dec. 3, 1910, p. 1111-3.
Piping and covering 4-4½%

WOLFF, MARK. Interpretation of water works accounts. *Journal of the American water works association,* June 1916, p. 543, 546.
Boilers, steam pipes, filters 20 years

Pipe lines

PUBLIC utility reports, annotated. Rochester, Lawyers co-operative publishing company, 1920C, p. 510.
In Indiana gas transp. co. no. 4727, Dec. 5, 1919, the Indiana commission said that it believed that a depreciation rate of 1.5 per cent of the value of the depreciable property of a gas transportation company was reasonable.

UNITED STATES. FEDERAL TRADE COMMISSION. Depreciation and obsolescence. (In its *Report on pipe line transportation of petroleum.* February 28, 1916. 1916. p. 75-6).
Pipe lines 3% per annum

Pipe threading machines

NICHOLSON, J. LEE and JOHN F. D. ROHRBACH. Depreciation. (In their *Cost accounting.* 1919. p. 149).
Pipe threading machines 6⅔%

Plate carriers

NICHOLSON, J LEE and J. F. D. ROHRBACH. Depreciation. (In their *Cost accounting.* 1919. p. 148).
Plate carriers etc. 4%

Planing

ELBOURNE, EDWARD T. Depreciation rates. (In his *Factory administration and accounts.* 1918. p. 477).

	Prov. dep. %	Years	
	Remainder values	10%	5%
Planing machines			
parallel	6	37	48
rotary	6	37	48

NICHOLSON, J. LEE and JOHN F. D. ROHRBACH. Depreciation. (In their *Cost accounting.* 1919. p. 149).
Planers 6⅔%

PHILADELPHIA. CONTROLLER. Rates of depreciation. (In his *Manual of accounting, reporting and business procedure of the city and county of Philadelphia.* 1917. p. 205).
Metal working equipment.
Turning, planing, milling, stamping and engraving equipment 5%
Timber working equipment.
Planing machinery 5

Playgrounds.

PHILADELPHIA. CONTROLLER. Rates of depreciation. (In his *Manual of accounting, reporting and business procedure of the city and county of Philadelphia.* 1917. p. 209).
Gymnasium and playground equipment of a permanent nature 8⅓%

Plows

AUSTRALIA. FEDERAL INCOME TAX DEPARTMENT. Depreciation allowance. *Accountant,* Oct. 13, 1917, p. 277-9. *Accounting and commerce,* June 30, 1917, p. 55-7. *Federal accountant,* July, 1917, p. 93-8. *Public accountant,* Jan. 30, 1917, p. 145-52.
Steam ploughs 5%
Written down value, repairs allowed in addition.

BAY state rate case. *Electric railway journal,* Dec. 4, 1915, p. 1121-3. *Public utility reports annotated,* 1916F, p. 336-9.
Cars, snow—plows 18-20

LIFE of road construction equipment. *Engineering and contracting,* Jan. 3, 1917, p. 3.
Plows 20% annual depreciation

Plumbing

BOLTON, REGINALD PELHAM. Depreciation of mechanical equipment and power plants. (In his *Building for profit.* 1911. p. 82, 89).

	Physical years	%	Economic years
Roof tanks, sanitary piping systems	27	67.5	21
Sanitary fixtures, refrigerating piping, kitchen fixtures and valves	20	50.0	16

BOLTON, REGINALD PELHAM. Depreciation of the value of buildings. (In his *Building for profit.* 1911. p. 62).

	Relative to 66 ys.	75 ys.
	Percent	
Plumbing fixtures	30	26

DEPRECIATION, DEPLETION AND OBSOLESCENCE—PLUMBING—*(Continued)*

ELBOURNE, EDWARD T. Depreciation rates. (In his *Factory administration and accounts.* 1918. p. 377).

	Prov. dep. %	years	
	Remainder values	10%	5%
Washing appliances	7½	29	38

NICHOLSON, J. LEE and J. F. D. ROHRBACH. Depreciation. (In their *Cost accounting.* 1919. p. 147).

Plumbing
Inside piping, and water and sewer piping 6%
Based on (1) the cost of the equipment
(2) the life of the equipment
(3) on a ten-hour day

PHILADELPHIA. CONTROLLER. Rates of depreciation. (In his *Manual of accounting, reporting and business procedure of the city and county of Philadelphia.* 1917. p. 205, 207-8).

Baths, lavatories, toilets and toilet accessories:	
Bath tubs, shower baths, portable baths	3⅓%
Lavatories, sinks and fountains	3⅓
Toilets and urinals	3⅓
Plumbing, pipes and other fittings	3⅓
Toilet accessories (hair dryer, toilet paper holder)	4
Bath room fittings	4
Toilet or commode chairs	4
Tonsorial equipment	4
Plumbers' tools and appliances	5%

PIEZ, CHARLES Perpetual inventory and appraisal values; table of standard depreciation rates. *Engineering and contracting,* Jan. 24, 1917, p. 77. *Factory,* Dec. 1916, p. 668-71. *Iron age,* Nov. 30, 1916, Jan. 11, 1917, p. 1127, 138-9. *Iron trade review,* Feb. 22, 1917, p. 477-8. Condensed. *Journal of the American society of mechanical engineers,* Dec. 1916, p. 965-6. *Iron trade review,* Dec. 7, 1916, p. 1144-6. Kent, William. *Bookkeeping and cost accounting for factories,* 1918, p. 90. Discussion. *Journal of the American society of mechanical engineers,* March, 1917, p. 215-7.

	% on cost	% on reducing balance
Water and sewer piping and sanitary fixtures (where separate)	4	7.5

Pneumatic cleaners

PHILADELPHIA. CONTROLLER. Rates of depreciation. (In his *Manual of accounting, reporting and business procedure of the city and county of Philadelphia.* 1917. p. 208).

Pneumatic cleaners 20%

Pneumatic plant.

NICHOLSON, J. LEE and J. F. D. ROHRBACH. Depreciation. (In their *Cost accounting.* 1919. p. 148).

Pneumatic plant equipment	
Compressed air system	7½%
Air compressors	5

Based on (1) the cost of equipment
(2) the life of the equipment
(3) on a ten-hour day.

Pointing machines

NICHOLSON, J. LEE and J. F. D. ROHRBACH. Depreciation. (In their *Cost accounting.* 1919. p. 149).

Pointing machines 6⅔%

Poles and pole lines

ANALYSIS of the premises adopted and methods used in determining the cost to reproduce new together with the depreciation thereon of the physical property of the Metropolitan system and the Kansas City and Westport Belt railway of Kansas City, Mo. *Engineering and contracting,* May 28, 1913, p. 617-20.

	Years	Depreciation per year
Pole base, cast iron	40	2½
Iron poles	35	3
box	35	3
plate	35	3
tubular	40	2½
latticed	30	3½
Cedar poles	20	5
Pole brackets	25	4
Cross arms		
Wood	20	5
iron	30	3½

APPRAISAL of the Seattle telephone companies by the railroad commission of Washington. *Engineering and contracting,* May 3, 1911, p. 520-4.

	Life	Salvage	An. dep.	Av. age	Total dep.
Pole lines	12	00	8.5	5	42.5

AUSTRALIA. FEDERAL INCOME TAX DEPARTMENT. Depreciation allowance. *Accountant,* Oct. 13, 1917, p. 277-9. *Accounting and commerce,* June 30, 1917, p. 55-7. *Federal accountant,* July 1917, p. 83-8. *Public accountant,* Jan. 30, 1917, p. 145-52.

Standard brackets, posts-iron, wood or steel 2½%
Written down value, repairs allowed.

DEPRECIATION, DEPLETION AND OBSOLESCENCE—POLES AND POLE LINES—*(Continued)*

BAGG, F. A. Life of railway physical property from engineering standpoint. *Electric railway journal,* Dec. 9, 1911, p. 1205-6.

	Years
Yellow pine trolley poles	10-15
Chestnut trolley poles	15
Cedar trolley poles	15-20

BARKER, HARRY. Depreciation of electric railway property. (In his *Public utility rates.* 1917. p. 367).

Poles	
cedar in earth	14 years. Wisconsin Railroad commission.
wood in concrete	20 years. Wisconsin Railroad commission.
iron or steel	40 years. Wisconsin Railroad commission.

BARKER, HARRY. Typical life expectation tables for public utility property. (In his *Public utility rates,* 1917. p. 369.)

Cross arms	8-10 years. Wisconsin Railroad commission.
Poles, wood in earth	12-15 years. Wisconsin Railroad commission.
Anchors and guys	10-20 years. Wisconsin Railroad commission.
Cross arms	10-15 years
Poles, cedar in concrete	12-18 "
cedar in earth	10-18 "
iron or steel in concrete	15-30 " Author, average or approximate figures secured by examination or inquiry.
iron or steel in earth	10-15 years. Wisconsin Railroad commission.
reinforced concrete	50 years. Author, average or approximate figures secured by examination or inquiry.

BAY state rate case. *Electric railway journal,* Dec. 4, 1915, p. 1121-3. *Public utility reports, annotated,* 1916F, p. 336-9.

Poles and fixtures	
annual depreciation per cent—	
annual depreciation by investment	
Distribution system	5.9%
Poles	Years
iron	40
cedar	20
chestnut	16
hard pine	12
Cross-arms	10
Guys and anchors	16
Miscellaneous work on poles	15
Trolley	2-30

BEMIS, E. W. Report on the investigation of the Chicago telephone company submitted to the committee on gas, oil and electric light. Chicago, October 25, 1912—paper. 127p.

	Poles and years	Cross-arms salvage	Depreciation % of cost
Byllesby and Arnold			
B. Due to age and wear and tear only	18	0	4.16- 5.55
A. Due to all forms of depreciation	10-14	0	6.66
Chicago Commission	10	0	8.73
Westinghouse, Church, Kerr & Co.	15	0	6. 6
E. L. Cline, Telephony, June 2, 1910	10-19	0-20	4.2 -11.25

BRYAN, WILLIAM H. Appraisal and depreciation of water-works and similar properties. *Journal of the association of engineering societies,* Dec. 1907, p. 336-81. Depreciation allowance for various public-service industries. *Engineering news,* Jan. 23, 1908, p. 96.

	Years	%	Straight
Poles			
iron		4	
wooden		8	
cross arms	10-12.5		
Pole line	15		
" "			12-15

BRYAN, WILLIAM H. Depreciation of electric light plants. *Municipality,* March 1908, p. 74.

Pole line

Poles Material	Life in years	Dep. % straight	Authority
Iron		4	Chicago city railway, *Street railway journal,* Dec. 1898.
Wooden		8	Chicago city railway, *Street railway journal,* Dec. 1898.
Cross arms	10-12.5		Iowa electrical association, in *Iowa engineer,* July, 1906.
Storage batteries	9-11		Dawson's "Engineering and electric traction pocket book, in *Iowa engineer,* July, 1906.

DEPRECIATION, DEPLETION AND OBSOLESCENCE—Poles and pole lines—*(Continued)*

Switchboards	10		Iowa electric association, in *Iowa engineer*, July 1906.
Wire, on poles	25		Iowa electrical association, in *Iowa engineer*, July 1906.
Wiring of cars		8	Chicago city railway, *Street railway journal*, Dec. 1898.

Cline, E. L. Depreciation of telephone companies. *Telephony*, July 2, 1910, p. 16.

		Feet	Life	Dep. %	Salvage %
Poles,	cedar	25	10	9.0	10
"	"	30	12	7.08	15
"	"	35	15	5.33	20
"	"	40	17	4.7	20
"	"	45	19	4.21	20
"	"	50	19	4.21	20
"	chestnut	25	8	11.25	10
"	"	30	10	8.5	15
"	"	35	12	6.7	20
"	"	40	13	6.1	20
"	"	45	15	5.3	20
"	"	50	15	5.3	20
cross arms			8	12.5	0

Crowell, H. H. Electric lighting rates and depreciation. *Municipal journal and engineer*, Dec. 18, 1907, p. 698.

	Purchased 10 years or more ago	modern
Poles	10 years	12 years

Depreciation account of the Kokomo, Marion and Western traction company. *Electric railway journal*, July 22, 1911, p. 156-7.

Poles	7%
Wire attachments	7
Guy wires and anchors	2

Depreciation of overhead structures and substations. *Engineering and contracting*, Nov. 19, 1913, p. 567.

Poles and fixtures	5%

Depreciation of the equipment of an electric plant. *Electrical world*, Dec. 12, 1914, p. 1161.

Poles and pole-line equipment	4.4%

Depreciation rates used by the Seattle (Wash.) municipal street railway. *Electric railway journal*, June 24, 1916, p. 1185.

Poles and fixtures	10%

Depreciation statements—Manitoba government telephones. *Manitoba public utilities commission, Annual report*, 1913, p. 101.

Exchange poles lines	6%
Rural pole lines	5
Toll poles lines	5

Figures from the Iola (Kans.) central station. *Electrical world*, Sept. 23, 1909, p. 723.

Pole lines	12%

Floy, Henry. Depreciation. Floy, Henry. Depreciation as related to electrical properties. *American Institute of electrical engineers, Proceedings*, 1911, p. 1267. Floy, Henry. *Valuation of public utility properties*, 1912, p. 168-217. Foster, Horatio A. *Engineering valuation of public utilities and factories*, 1913, p. 194-8. *Engineering magazine*, Aug. 1911, p. 837-40. *Engineering and contracting*, Oct. 4, 1911, p. 359-65.

Straight line	Dep. % per year		
Poles (Steel)	2	Henry Floy	3rd Avenue case, adopted by P. S. C., N. Y.
wood in concrete	5	Wis. P. S. C.	
wood in earth	5½-8⅓	Wis. P. S. C.	
iron	2½	Wis. P. S. C.	
wooden	10	Arbitrators	Street lighting controversy, Atlanta, Ga., 1899.
Cross Arms	8⅓-12½	Wis. P. S. C.	

Foster, Horatio A. Rates of depreciation. (In his *Engineering valuation of public utilities and factories*. 1913. p. 169-93, 203, 205-6).

Poles	
iron	2.0
wood	7.0

Marwick, Mitchell & co. in the appraisal of a large street railway system.

	Years	
Poles, cedar, in earth	10-18	
" " " concrete	12-20	
" iron " "	15-30	
Pole anchors and guys	10-20	
Cross arms	10-15	
Poles	12-15	Wisconsin commissions
Cross arms	8-12	

	Minimum service value per cent of reproduction cost
Poles, both wood and iron, anchors and guys	20%
Telephone poles	20-40

	Years
Poles:	
cedar, 35 feet and under	10-15
cedar, over 35 feet	15-20
chestnut, 35 feet and under	8-12
chestnut, over 35 feet	12-15
pine, creosoted	20
Poles and cross arms, average exchange	10
Poles and cross arms, average toll	15

DEPRECIATION, DEPLETION AND OBSOLESCENCE—POLES AND POLE LINES—*(Continued)*

GILLETTE, HALBERT P. and RICHARD T. DANA. Depreciation. (In their *Handbook of mechanical and electrical cost data.* 1918. p. 109, 1077).

Poles, iron	20 years. Union traction co. Case Chicago and Union traction co., Stone and Webster. 40 years. Wisconsin railroad commission. W. D. Pence, Milwaukee 3c. case. B. J. Arnold, Chicago appraisal, 4 cases. 50 years. Marwick, Mitchell & co., appraisal of a large street railway system, Foster, p. 199.
steel	50 years. Henry Floy, 3rd avenue case, N. Y. city.
telephone	12-15 years. Wisconsin railroad commission.
wood	12-15 years. W. D. Pence, Milwaukee 3c. case. 14.3 years. Marwick, Mitchell & co., appraisal of a large street railway system, Foster, p. 199.
wood in concrete	20 years. Wisconsin railroad commission.
wood in earth	12-18.2 years. Wisconsin railroad commission.
wooden	10 years. Arbitrators, Street lighting controversy, Atlanta, Ga., 1899.
Cross-arms	8-12 years. Wisconsin railroad commission.

GILLETTE, HALBERT P. and RICHARD T. DANA. Hydro-electric plants. (In their *Mechanical and electrical cost data.* 1918. p. 695).

Pole lines	2%

GRAY, HENRY L. Necessity of depreciation reserves. *Railway age gazette,* May 27, 1910, p. 1297-8. Editorial. Depreciation reserves. *Railway age gazette,* May 27, 1910, p. 1290. Letters. Depreciation reserves. *Railway age gazette,* July 8, 1910, p. 66.

	Annual depreciation
Poles and fixtures	8%

GREENLAND, S. W. Depreciation. Mississippi electric association, *Report of Bnd annual convention,* held June 1910, p. 32-6.

	Life
Poles, chestnut	12 years

GRUNSKY, CARL EWALD. Probable useful life of various articles. (In his *Valuation, depreciation and the rate-base.* 1917. p. 282).

Poles	10 years. 0% residual value. Chicago telephone commission. Published 1908.
wooden	10 years. Arbitrators. Board of arbitration in street lighting controversy at Atlanta, Georgia, 1899.
wooden	13⅓ years. Milwaukee electric railway and lighting co., in the Milwaukee 3c. fare case, Aug., 1912.
wooden in earth	12-18 years. Wisconsin railroad commission. Quoted by Henry Floy and in published reports.
wooden in concrete	20 years. Wisconsin railroad commission. Quoted by Henry Floy and in published reports.
cedar	10 years. 1c.-7c. ft. residual value. Pacific gas & electric company. Figures used in rate hearings before Master in Chancery, San Francisco.
cedar with cross arms	12 years. 0% residual value. Wisconsin railroad commission. Wisconsin telephone co. case. Aug. 3, 1909.
cedar under 35′ long	10-15 years. 0% residual value. Telephone "Data." Compiles from practice A. T. & T. Co., Wisconsin R. R. commission and others. Quoted by H. A. Foster.
cedar 35′ long and over	15-20 years. 0% residual value. Telephone "Data." Compiled from practice A. T. & T. Co., Wisconsin R. R. commission and others. Quoted by H. A. Foster.
cedar in earth	10-18 years. H. A. Foster. "Engineering valuation of public utilities and factories," Van Nostrand, 1912.
cedar in concrete	12-20 years. H. A. Foster. "Engineering valuation of public utilities and factories," Van Nostrand, 1912.
chestnut under 35′ long	8-12 years. Telephone "Data." Compiled from practice A. T. & T. Co., Wisconsin R. R. commission and others. Quoted by H. A. Foster.
chestnut 35′ and over	12-15 years. Telephone "Data." Compiled from practice A. T. & T. Co., Wisconsin R. R. commission and others. Quoted by H. A. Foster.

DEPRECIATION, DEPLETION AND OBSOLESCENCE—POLES AND POLE LINES—*(Continued)*

pine creosoted — 20 years.
Telephone "Data." Compiled from practice A. T. & T. Co., Wisconsin R. R. commission and others. Quoted by H. A. Foster.

redwood — 16 years. 6c-25c. ft. residual value.
Pacific gas & electric company. Figures used in rate hearings before Master in Chancery, San Francisco, 1913-4.

telephone — 12-15 years.
Wisconsin railroad commission. Quoted by H. A. Foster and in published reports.

telephone cross arms — 8-12 years.
Wisconsin railroad commission. Quoted by H. A. Foster and in published reports.

average exchange — 10 years. 0% residual value.
Telephone "Data." Compiled from practice A. T. & T. Co., Wisconsin R. R. commission and others. Quoted by H. A. Foster.

average toll — 15 years. 0% residual value.
Telephone "Data." Compiled from practice A. T. & T. Co., Wisconsin R. R. commission and others. Quoted by H. A. Foster.

iron — 20 years.
Chicago union traction co. Quoted in Report Wisconsin R. R. commission, vol. 10, p. 220.

iron — 40 years.
Wisconsin railroad commission. Milwaukee 3c. fare case. Aug. 23, 1912.

iron — 40 years.
Bion J. Arnold. Four appraisals quoted by H. A. Foster.

steel — 50 years.
Henry Floy. Trans. American institute of electrical engineers, June, 1911. Third avenue case figures adopted by Public Service commission of New York.

LIFE data on power-plant equipment used in valuation of Massachusetts property. *Electrical world,* Dec. 4, 1915, p. 1261.

	Years
Poles	
iron	40
cedar	20
chestnut	16
hard pine	12
Cross arms	10
Guys and anchors	16
Miscellaneous work on poles	15

MURRAY, ALEXANDER.. Glasgow corporation accounts with special reference to depreciation and sinking funds. *Accountant,* June 13, 1903, p. 782-94. *Royal philosophical society of Glasgow, Proceedings,* 1903.

Ducts, cables, poles, rosettes — 3%

NEALE, R. E. Depreciation in engineering works. *Mechanical world,* Feb. 7, 1913, p. 67-8.

Poles	%	Years
wood	5-10	10-20
wood cross arms	8-12	8.5-12.5
steel	2-2.5	40-50

NICHOLSON, J. LEE and J. F. D. ROHRBACH. Depreciation. (In their *Cost accounting.* 1919. p. 148).

Poles, etc. — 4%

PENDER, HAROLD. Depreciation. (In his *Handbook for electrical engineers.* c1914. p. 340, 339).

Poles
wooden
12-15 — Engineer of valuation staff, of Wisconsin railroad commission.
8.33-6.66 — Engineer of valuation staff, of Wisconsin railroad commission.
8 — Chicago city railways.
iron
20 — Chicago union traction co. Stone & Webster for Chicago union traction co.
40 — Engineer of valuation staff of Wisconsin railroad commission. W. Preece.
cross-arms, wooden,
10-12.5 years — Iowa electric association.
5% — Chicago union traction co. Stone & Webster for Chicago union traction co.
4 — Chicago city railways.
2.5 — Engineer of valuation staff, of Wisconsin railroad commission.

PIEZ, CHARLES. Perpetual inventory and appraisal values; table of standard depreciation rates. *Engineering and contracting,* Jan. 24, 1917, p. 77. *Factory,* Dec. 1916, p. 668-71. *Iron age,* Nov. 30, 1916, Jan. 11, 1917, p. 1266, 138-9. *Iron trade review,* Feb. 22, 1917, p. 477-8. Condensed. *Journal of the American society of mechanical engineers,* Dec. 1916, p. 965-6. *Iron trade review,* Dec. 7, 1916, p. 1144-6. Kent, William. *Bookkeeping and cost accounting for factories.* 1918, p. 90. Discussion. *Journal of the American society of mechanical engineers,* March 1917, p. 215-7.

	% on cost	% on reducing balance
Power piping	6	15

PIXLEY, FRANCIS W. Tramways. (In his *Accountancy.* Ed. 2. p. 218-9).
Poles and rosettes from 21 to 25%.

PRACTICAL hints on computing telephone depreciation. *Telephone,* April 1, 1911, p. 401-3.

Poles and guys — 6%
cross arms, hardware, insulators, pins, etc. — 7

DEPRECIATION, DEPLETION AND OBSOLESCENCE—Poles and pole lines—*(Continued)*

Proposed sale of Toronto utilities to the city. *Electrical world*, Oct. 25, 1913, p. 832.
Poles
iron 2.5-3%
cedar 5
Pole brackets 4
wooden cross-arms 5
iron cross-arms 3.33

Public utilities reports, annotated. Rochester, Lawyers cooperative publishing co. 1918E. p. 178-9.
Desert power and water co., Docket no. 361, Feb. 20, 1918.
Power lines wood poles and steel fixtures (a) 4% annual depreciation. 25 years.
Power lines wood poles and wood X-arms (b) 5% annual depreciation. 20 years.
The distinction made between the two classes of power lines is derived, not only from the respective classes of pole hardware, but also from consideration of the fact that there is considerable difference in the quality of all the material as well as workmanship.

Public utility reports, annotated. Rochester, Lawyers cooperative publishing co. 1919D. p. 359.
Re Pacific telephone and telegraph co. Company's life table.

	Years	% Salvage	% Straight line
Exchange pole lines	9	10.4	10.0
Toll pole lines	15	2.3	6.5
Commission's life table.			
Exchange pole lines	8	10.4	11.2
Toll pole lines	14	2.3	7.0

Public utility reports, annotated. Rochester, Lawyers co-operative publishing co. 1918A. p. 914-8.
New York & N. S. traction co.
Poles and fixtures 5%

Roby, J. J. Schedule of plant depreciation. (In his *Treatise on cost accounting as applied to coal mining.* c1913. p. 14-5).
Poles and supports 10%

Slavin, Matthew. Municipal electricity in Pasadena. *Public service*, April 1910, p. 105-8.
10 years
Poles, arc lamps and transformers 8.5%

Weeks, H. E. Abstract of paper on depreciation read before annual meeting of Iowa street and interurban railway association, April 1910. *Electric railway journal*, April 30, 1910, p. 782-3.
Poles 7 years

Police

Philadelphia. Controller. Rates of depreciation. (In his *Manual of accounting, reporting and business procedure of the city and county of Philadelphia.* 1917. p. 207-8)
Rifles, revolvers and other small arms 4%
Batons, night sticks, riot clubs, swords, etc. 10
Belts, badges, handcuffs 4
Special and miscellaneous police equipment 4

Polishing

Elbourne, Edward T. Depreciation rates. (In his *Factory administration and accounts.* 1918. p. 377).

	Prov. dep. % Remainder values	years 10%	5%
Grinding & polishing heads	6	37	48
Polishing machinery	6	37	48

Pony covering machine

Denham, Robert S. Depreciation. (In his *Manual of cost engineering and estimating for paper box manufacturers.* 1917. p. 249).
Pony covering machine 6%

Porch shades

Philadelphia. Controller. Rates of depreciation. (In his *Manual of accounting, reporting and business procedure of the city and county of Philadelphia.* 1917. p. 207-8).
Porch shades, awnings, blinds, etc. 20%

Portable houses

Philadelphia. Controller. Rates of depreciation. (In his *Manual of accounting, reporting and business procedure of the city and county of Philadelphia.* 1917. p. 207-8).
Tents and portable houses 20%

Porter bars

Nicholson, J. Lee and J. F. D. Rohrbach. Depreciation. (In their *Cost accounting.* 1919. p. 150).
Porter bars 10%

Portiers

Philadelphia. Controller. Rates of depreciation. (In his *Manual of accounting, reporting and business procedure of the city and county of Philadelphia.* 1917. p. 207-8).
Portiers 6⅔%

Post offices

Uniform cost sheet for coal mining companies. *Coal age*, Sept. 19, 1918, p. 545-7.
Original cost
Post office building 4%
" " equipment and fixtures 7

DEPRECIATION, DEPLETION AND OBSOLESCENCE—*(Continued)*

POSTERS

See Depreciation, depletion and obsolescence—Advertisements.

Posts

GILLETTE, HALBERT P. and RICHARD T. DANA. Cost of street lighting in Chicago. (In their *Handbook of mechanical and electrical cost data.* 1918. p. 1039).

Posts 3.5%

Potteries

TIFFANY, H. S. Potteries. (In his *Digest of depreciations.* c1890. p. 10).

Buildings:
brick 3½%
frame 5

Based upon the actual life without any repairs.

Powder cans

NICHOLSON, J. LEE and JOHN F. D. ROHRBACH. Depreciation. (In their *Cost accounting.* 1919. p. 150).

Oil and powder cans 10%

Powder houses

UNIFORM cost sheet for coal mining companies. *Coal age,* Sept. 19, 1918, p. 545-7.

Powder house original cost
concrete, stone or brick 10%

Power companies

See Depreciation, depletion and obsolescence—Electric light and power companies.

Power plants

See also Depreciation, depletion and obsolescence—Electric light and power companies;—Steam plants.

BARKER, HARRY. Typical life expectation tables for public utility property. (In his *Public utility rates.* 1917. p. 369).

Power plant 8 years, Wisconsin R. R. Commission

BAY state street railway valuation. *Electric railway journal,* Dec. 4, 1915, p. 1121-3.

Power plant buildings 1.8%
" " equipment 3.4

annual depreciation per cent, annual depreciation divided by investment.

BELT, ROBERT E. Depreciation. (In his *Uniform cost accounting methods; adopted by the American malleable castings association,* Nov. 14, 1917. p. 20-1.)

Power plant equipment
Steam boiler, generator, air compressor, steam piping, electric wiring, etc. 7½%
Office furniture and fixtures 10

BEMIS, EDWARD W. Testimony on depreciation before Nebraska commission re the consolidation of the properties of the Lincoln traction company. *Electric railway journal,* March 12, 1910, p. 441.

Power plant and boilers aside from buildings 15-20 years

BREWER, ALLAN F. Depreciation. Rates for annual depreciation. *Industrial management,* April 1918, p. 268.

	Years	%
Power plant buildings, brick and reinforced concrete	150	.66
Power plant buildings, brick	100	1
Power plant buildings, frame (heavy)	66.6	1.5
Power plant buildings, frame (light)	50	2

BROMLEY, C. H. Depreciation and how it is applied. *Power,* June 2, 1914, p. 767.

BROWN, EVERARD. Depreciation of power plant equipment. *Electrical world,* Aug. 3, 1912, p. 268.

Some contend useful life anywhere from 10-25 years, and charge off from 10 down to 4% annually.

COST and depreciation of steam and hydro-electric installations. *Electrical world,* Dec. 30, 1909, p. 1558.

Cost and depreciation of equipment of power house.

TABLE V.

Item	Prop. Cost	Life years	Annual amount for dep. % of total cost.
1. Stop logs, gates and other wood exposed to air and water	0.80	5	0.146
2. Flooring, roofing and hardware, and miscellaneous fixtures	0.80	15	0.472
3. Tile wainscoting, sewage, plumbing system and metal window frames, etc.	2.45	15	0.118
4. Electric light and telephone	0.80	10	0.065
5. Switchboard equipment	4.35	10	.355
6. Cables and heavy wiring	3.90	10	.318
7. Cranes	1.25	15	0.060
8. Water wheels	33.75	25	0.157
9. Water wheel governors	2.90	10	.235
10. Generators and transformers	40.00	25	.898
	100.00		3.423

An annual depreciation of 3.423 per cent represents an equivalent average life of 19 years for the power house equipment.

DEPRECIATION, DEPLETION AND OBSOLESCENCE—POWER PLANTS—*(Continued)*

DENHAM, ROBERT S. Depreciation. (In his *Manual of cost engineering and estimating for paper box manufactures.* 1917. p. 249).
Power transmission 10% original cost

DEPRECIATION. *American institute of accountants, Special bulletin,* No. 1, Jan. 1920, p. 6-7.

DEPRECIATION funds in Europe. *Electric railway journal,* May 7, 21, 1904, p. 696, 760.
Power plant
Brussels 25 years
Czernowitz railway power station equipment 2½%
Glasgow 5
Leipziger Strassenbaln 8
Renischeid 6

FOSTER, HORATIO A. Methods of calculating depreciation. (In his *Engineering valuation of public utilities and factories.* 1913. p. 169, 170, 193).

	Maximum service value % of reproduction cost.
Power plant	
Steam plants of all kinds, shafting and pipe covering	25
Electric generators, modern type	20
Motors and rotaries, obsolete type	15
Static transformers (including regulators and compensators) station type	40
Switchboard and wiring, modern type	45
complete, obsolete type	35
Switchboard instruments, modern type	80
alone, obsolete type	60
Storage batteries	35
Lighting arresters, station type	50

Joint engineering department of the Wisconsin commissions.

	Minimum service value % of reproduction cost.
Telephone power plant, equipment and wire	25

FOSTER, HORATIO A. Rates of depreciation. (In his *Engineering valuation of public utilities and factories.* 1913. p. 200, 205).
Power plant and substation equipment
Engines, boilers, heaters, conveyors, pumps and auxiliaries 4.5%
Rotaries, transformers, switchboards, auxiliaries 4.5
Storage batteries 3.0
Turbines and generators 6.0
Marwick, Mitchell & Co., in the appraisal of a large street railway system.
Second class shops, car barns and power stations, 50 years, Wisconsin commissions.

GEARE, H. W. What the modern power-plant engineer must know. *Power,* Dec. 21, 1915, p. 869.

GILLETTE, HALBERT P. and R. T. DANA. Depreciation. (In their *Handbook of mechanical and electrical cost data.* 1918. p. 106, 107, 109.)

Buildings	33.3 years.
power plant	H. P. Gillette, Everett railway & water co., Jan. 29, 1912.
Power stations	50 years.
	Wisconsin R. R. commission.
Equipment, power plant	20 years.
	H. P. Gillette, Everett railway & water co., Jan. 29, 1912.
Power plant	12.5 years.
	Prof. M. E. Cooley, Milwaukee 3c. case.
	20 years.
	M. G. Starret, Milwaukee 3c. case.
	50 years.
	B. J. Arnold, Chicago appraisals, 4 cases.
Telephone Power plant and wire telephone	8 years. Wisconsin R. R. commission.

GRUNSKY, CARL EWALD. Probable useful life of various articles. (In his *Valuation depreciation and the rate-base.* 1917. p. 282).

Power plant equipment	12½ years.
	Mortimer E. Cooley. Milwaukee 3c. fare case. Report Wisconsin R. R. commission, vol. 10, p. 226.
	20 years.
	Milton G. Starrett. Milwaukee 3c. fare case. Report Wisconsin R. R. commission, vol. 10, p. 226.
	21.01 years.
	Wisconsin railroad commission. Milwaukee 3c. fare case, Aug. 23, 1912.

LIFE data on power-plant equipment used in valuation of Massachusetts property. *Electrical world,* Dec. 4, 1915, p. 1261.

LIFE of elements in subway property. *Electric railway journal,* April 6, 1912, p. 575.
Power plant 30 years.

McINTOSH, ROBERT J. Rates of depreciation. (In his *Reference book of accounts.* Ed. 2, p. 62).
Power plants 5%
Based on life.

MONTGOMERY, ROBERT H. Electrical equipment manufacturers. (In his *Income tax procedure,* 1919. p. 563. ——— Same, 1920. p. 716).
Power plant equipment, 8%.
Based on gross book values at the end of the preceding year.

MONTGOMERY, ROBERT H. Mine equipment. (In his *Income tax procedure,* 1919. p. 571. ——— Same, 1920. p. 724).
Power house and machinery 6 2-3%

DEPRECIATION, DEPLETION AND OBSOLESCENCE—POWER PLANTS—*(Continued)*

MURRAY, ALEXANDER. Glasgow corporation accounts with special reference to depreciation and sinking funds. *Accountant,* June 13, 1903, p. 782-94. *Royal philosophical society of Glasgow, Proceedings,* 1903.
Power plant 5%

NEELY, F. H. Depreciation of power plant equipment. *Power and the engineer,* June 8, 1909, p. 1028.

NELSON, BAILIE WALTER. Limitation and application of profits from municipal undertakings. *Incorporated accountants' journal,* Oct. 1912, p. 15-17.
Power station and substation plant 7.4% per annum.

PARKER, JOHN C. Fixed costs in industrial plants; comments on same, investments, insurance, interest, depreciation, obsolescence, fair profit. *American Institute of electrical engineers, Proceedings,* March 1911, p. 467.

PIXLEY, FRANCIS W. Tramways. (In his *Accountancy.* Ed. 2. p. 218-9).
Electrical plant at power station 5%

PUBLIC utilities reports, annotated. Rochester, Lawyers co-operative publishing co. 1918C. p. 534.
Springfield street railway co. Power stations and equipment 2.31%

PUBLIC utilities reports, annotated. Rochester, Lawyers co-operative publishing co. 1915B. p. 558.
Re Washington & M. R. Co. (D. C.). An electric railway company was ordered to conform its depreciation accounts to a rate of 4.25 per cent on the cost of property new for "power plant equipment."

ROBY, J. J. Schedule of plant depreciation. (In his *Treatise on cost accounting as applied to coal mining.* c1913. p. 14-5).
Power plant.

Building—brick & steel only	
Deduct as salvage before depreciating	10%
Depreciation rate for remainder, non-fireproof	6
fireproof	4
Pipe, heaters and pumps	
Deduct as salvage before depreciating	10
Depreciation rate for remainder, fireproof	8
Boilers and settings	
Deduct as salvage before depreciating	10
Depreciation rate for remainder	8
Deduct as salvage before depreciating	20
Engines, dynamos and switchboards	
Depreciation rate for remainder	4

RUNYON, F. O. Report on hydro-electric plant for special committee common council, Newark, New Jersey, April 23, 1902, p. 15, 16, 24.
Hydro-power house 2%
Power house and stack 3

SALIERS, EARL A. Analysis of a hydro-electric plant. (In his *Principles of depreciation.* 1916. p. 34-8).

LIFETIME OF POWER HOUSE EQUIPMENT

	years
Stop logs, gates and other wood exposed to air and water	5
Flooring, roofing, hardware, and miscellaneous fixtures	15
Tile wainscoting, sewage, plumbing system, metal window frames, etc.	15
Electric light and telephone	10
Switchboard equipment	10
Cables and heavy wiring	10
Cranes	15
Waterwheels	25
Water-wheel governors	10
Generators and transformers	25

SLAVIN, MATTHEW. Municipal electricity in Pasadena. *Public service,* April 1910, p. 105-8.
Power station 15 years 3.5%

STUCKMAN, H. Depreciation and obsolescence in Portland cement plants. *Journal of the American society of mechanical engineers,* Feb. 1913, p. 262-75.
% of reproductive value
Power plant equipment 10

UNIFORM cost sheet for coal mining companies. *Coal age,* Sept. 19, 1918, p. 545-7.

	original cost
Wooden power house (building)	7%
Stone or brick power house	5
Pumps, heaters and other power house equipment	8

VARIOUS depreciation charges. *New York Times,* June 14, 1914.
Power plant equipment 10%

WALSH, T. J. Depreciation on electric light and power plants. *Electric railway journal,* July 13, 1912, p. 60.
Power house and substation building 3%

WOODS, CLINTON E. Depreciation, power plant. (In his *Unified accounting methods for industrials.* 1917. p. 65).
Power plant 10% per annum.

Preserving

See Depreciation, depletion and obsolescence—Canning and preserving.

Presses

BELT, ROBERT E. Depreciation. (In his *Foundry cost accounting practice and procedure.* 1919. p. 243).
Emery wheel stands, drop hammers, lathes, drill presses, air clippers, milling machines, threading machines, etc., with motor shafting and belting 10%

DEPRECIATION, DEPLETION AND OBSOLESCENCE—PRESSES—*(Continued)*

BELT, ROBERT E. Depreciation. (In his *Uniform cost accounting methods; adopted by the American malleable castings association*, Nov. 14, 1917, p. 20-1.)
Emery wheel stands, drop hammers, lathes, drill presses, air clippers, milling machines, threading machines, etc., with motor shafting and belting 10%

ELBOURNE, EDWARD T. Depreciation rates. (In his *Factory administration and accounts.* 1918. p. 377).

	Prov. dep. % Remainder values	years 10%	5%
Presses			
hydraulic	6	37	48
pneumatic	7½	29	38
belt driven	6	37	48

NICHOLSON, J. LEE and J. F. D. ROHRBACH. Depreciation. (In their *cost accounting.* 1919. p. 149-50).
Hydraulic forging presses, bending presses and fluid compressers 6⅔%
Based on (1) the cost of equipment
(2) the life of the equipment
(3) on a ten hour day.
Arbor presses, car wheel presses, punch presses, bending rolls, power shears, and drop hammers 6⅔

PIEZ, CHARLES. Perpetual inventory and appraisal values; table of standard depreciation rates. *Engineering and contracting*, Jan. 24, 1917, p. 77. *Factory*, Dec. 1916, p. 668-71. *Iron age*, Nov. 30, 1916, Jan. 11, 1917, p. 1266, 138-9. *Iron trade review*, Feb. 22, 1917, p. 477-8. Condensed. *Iron trade review*, Dec. 7, 1916, p. 1144-6. *Journal of the American society of mechanical engineers*, Dec. 1916, p. 965-6. Kent, William, *Bookkeeping and cost accounting for factories.* 1918, p. 90. Discussion. *Journal of the American society of mechanical engineers*, March 1917, p. 215-7.

	% on cost	% on reducing
Punch presses, bending rolls, power shears and drop hammers	4.5	10

Printing

AUSTRALIA. Federal income tax department. Depreciation allowance. *Accountant*, Oct. 13, 1917, p. 277-9. *Accounting and commerce*, June 30, 1917, p. 55-7. *Federal accountant*, July 1917, p. 93-8. *Public accountant*, Jan. 30, 1917, p. 145-52.
Photo engraving plant 5%
Written down value repairs allowed in addition.
Printers
manufacturing 7½%
ordinary 7½
Type 7½
Written down value repairs allowed in addition

DAVIS, A. E. Depreciation. (In his *How to find costs in printing.* 1914. p. 93-6).
Plant 10%
Type etc. 25

DENHAM, ROBERT S. Depreciation. (In his *Manual of cost engineering and estimating for paper box manufacturers.* 1917. p. 249).

Printing dept.	Dep. % on original cost
Platen presses	15
Cylinder presses	10
Bronzing machines	10
Cutting and creasing press	8
Embossing presses	8
Punching presses	8
Type equipment	33⅓
Electros	33⅓
Cuts	33⅓

DEPRECIATION allowances. *Accountants' magazine*, Nov. 1920, p. 578.
Board of inland revenue have approved of extra allowances for depreciation of 50 per cent above the normal rates to meet abnormal conditions due to the war. The normal rates on types, 10 per cent, on machinery, 7½ per cent and on fixtures 5 per cent.

DEPRECIATION of printing machinery. *Incorporated accountants' journal*, Sept. 1911, p. 311.

DEPRECIATION on printing plant. *Accountant*, June 27, 1885.

GREAT BRITAIN. BOARD OF INLAND REVENUE. Depreciation rates. (In its *Income tax; statement respecting allowances for wear and tear and obsolescence of plant and machinery.* 1918. cd. 9022, p. 4; ed. 9134, p. 6). *American economic review*, Supplement, Dec. 1920. 51. *Journal of accountancy*, Sept. 1920, p. 194.
Printing
Engines, boilers and shafting 5%
Printing and binding machines 7½
Type 10
Written down value.

HAZELL, W. HOWARD. Cost finding and keeping. *Accountant*, Feb. 8, 1913, p. 183.
10% per annum on the diminishing value of all plant.

INCOME tax and depreciation allowances. *Accountant*, May 30, 1914, p. 785-8.

	Written down value
General plant	5%
Printing and binding machines	7½

INCOME tax and depreciation; shipping industry, paper mills, printing works. *Incorporated accountants' journal*, May 1914, p. 243.
Engines, boilers and shafting 5%
Printing binding machines 7½

DEPRECIATION, DEPLETION AND OBSOLESCENCE—PRINTING—*(Continued)*

INCOME tax notes. *Accountant,* May 11, Sept. 28, 1918, p. 359, 162-6. *Incorporated accountants' journal,* Oct., May, 1918, p. 14, 157.
Written down value
Engines, boilers and shafting 5%
Printing and binding machines 7½
Type 10

MCELROY, CHARLES F. Depreciation of linotype metal. *Inland printer,* May 1913, p. 229-30.

MONTGOMERY, ROBERT H. Electrotypes, woodcuts, etc. (In his *Income tax procedure,* 1919. p. 563. ———— Same, 1920. p. 716).
Conservative publishers charge almost the entire cost of plates as a direct cost of a first edition, and are careful to revalue the balance of the account frequently.

MONTGOMERY, ROBERT H. Printing. (In his *Auditing theory and practice,* 1916, p. 417-8).
Depreciation is about the same as that of the textile industry.
Type, printers' tools, etc. 10-12%

MONTGOMERY, ROBERT H. Printing. (In his *Income tax procedure,* 1919. p. 575. ———— Same, 1920, p. 732).
About the same as that in the textile industry with the exception of type, printers' tools, electrotype, plates etc., on which about 10-12% should be applied annually.
British practice.
Engines, boilers, shafting 5%
Printing and binding machines 7½
Type not exceeding 10

OFFICIAL allowances in respect of depreciation of machinery and plant—Board of Inland revenue, Great Britain. *Accountant,* May 16, 1914, p. 736.
Engines, boilers and shafting 5%
Printing and binding machines 7½
Type 10
Or special arrangement as the maximum, calculated on the written-down value.

PHILADELPHIA. CONTROLLER. Rates of depreciation. (In his *Manual of accounting, reporting and business procedure of the city and county of Philadelphia.* 1917, p. 205).
Printing, binding, and lithographing equipment 8⅓%

PORTER, H. P. Depreciation of printing plants; with discussion. *International cost congress of employing printers of America, Proceedings,* 1909, p. 49-63.

PRINTERS costs; report and recommendations of the special committee of the Federation of master printers and allied trades of the United Kingdom on costs and charges. *Accountant,* March 8, 15, 1913, p. 329-32, 358-66, 411-2.
On costs and charges 10% per annum recommended by the committee.

SMITH, HERBERT LAKIN. Depreciation. (In his *Printers' accounts.* 1903. p. 69-70).
General plant 5-10%
Type 10-15

STOCKWELL, HERBERT GRANT. Depreciation, renewal and replacement accounts; a paper read at the annual meeting held in Denver, Colorado, October 18-22, 1909, the American institute of accountants. p. 63, 44. *American institute of accountants, Yearbook,* 1909, p. 237.
The manager of the Philadelphia printers' board of trade says that the consensus of opinion of the progressive printers who have given the matter consideration is that the depreciation in the composing room is not less than 20 per cent, per annum; the machinery, stands, furniture, etc. 10 per. Many printers, however, do make a flat depreciation chargt of only 10 per cent throughout, and some limit themselves to 5 per cent.

UNITED TYPOTHETAE OF AMERICA. Depreciation. (In their *Standard accounting system for printers.* p. 6, 58).
Type 25%
Machines, furniture, fixtures 10
Machine composition metal—Based on the cost of the metal actually melted.

UNITED TYPOTHETAE OF AMERICA. Depreciation. (In their *Standard cost finding system.* p. 7).
Type 25%
Standard machines 10
Type, stands, chases, stones 10
Building 5

UNITED TYPOTHETAE OF AMERICA. Depreciation. (In their *Treatise on the standard accountancy system for printers.* p. 40).
Type 25%
Hand composition fixtures 10
Machines 10
Machine composition metal
linotype 2
monotype 3

Prisons

PHILADELPHIA. CONTROLLER. Rates of depreciation. (In his *Manual of accounting, reporting and business procedure of the city and county of Philadelphia.* 1917. p. 209).
Buildings:
Hospitals, asylums, prisons, etc. 1%

UNIFORM cost sheet for coal mining companies. *Coal age,* Sept. 19, 1918, p. 545-7.
Squire's office and jail 4% original cost.

Profiting machines

ELBOURNE, EDWARD T. Depreciation rates. (In his *Factory administration and accounts.* 1918. p. 377).

	Prov. dep. %		years
	Remainder values	10%	5%
Profiting machines	6	37	48

DEPRECIATION, DEPLETION AND OBSOLESCENCE—*(Continued)*

Public utilities

ALLISON, JAMES E. Criticism of theoretical depreciation. *Utilities magazine*, Jan. 1916, p. 124-6.

ALLISON, JAMES E. Depreciation of public service properties. *Annals of the American academy of political and social science*, May 1914, p. 198-213.

ALLISON, JAMES E. Should public service properties be depreciated to obtain fair value in rate or regulation cases? St. Louis, 1912. 50p. *Stone and Webster public service journal*, Feb. 1913.

ALVORD, J. W. Depreciation of public utility properties as affecting their valuation and fair return. *American society of civil engineers, Proceedings*, Nov. 1913, p. 2045-60. *American society of civil engineers, Transactions*, Dec. 1914, p. 788.

AMERICAN electric railway association. Committee on valuation. Bibliography on valuation of public utilities December 23, 1915. New York, American electric railway association, 61+ 72p.

AUTHORITY of commissions in regard to depreciation accounting. *Electrical world*, Sept. 22, 1917, p. 591.

BARKER, FORREST F. Capitalization and depreciation in municipal plants. *Inter-nation*, April 1907, p. 76.

BARKER, HARRY. Depreciation as it affects utility rates. (In his *Public utility rates*. 1917. p. 107-33).

BARKER, HARRY. Making depreciation discussion understood. *Utilities magazine*, Jan. 1, 1916, p. 131.

BARKER, HARRY. Side lights on depreciation problems of utilities. *Engineering news*, Dec. 21-28, 1916, p. 1167-9, 1212.

BAUER, JOHN. Depreciation and rate control a question of justice. *Quarterly journal of economics*, May 1915, p. 651-9.

BAUER, JOHN. Discussion. *Utilities magazine*, Jan. 1, 1916, p. 127-30.

BAUER, JOHN. Fixing depreciation requirements under the public service commission's law of New York. *American economic review*, Sept. 1918, p. 647-50. *Public service*, Oct. 1918.

BAUER, JOHN. Pitfalls in regulating depreciation. *Electric railway journal*, Aug. 24, 1918, p. 326-8. Discussion. L. L. G. Benedict. *Electric railway journal*, Sept. 14, 1918, p. 465-6.

BENEDICT, LOUIS L. G. Depreciation of public service property. *Gas age*, Dec. 1, 1917, p. 502-6.

BONBRIGHT, J. C. Depreciation and rate control. *Quarterly journal of economics*, May 1918, p. 546-8.

BOOTH, W. H. Sinking fund charges. *Tramway and railway world*, April 9, 1903, p. 349.

BOSLEY, W. B. and C. E. GRUNSKY. Depreciation as an element for consideration in the appraisal of public service properties. *American society of civil engineers, Proceedings*, Aug. 1915.

BREWER, ALLAN F. Rates for annual depreciation. *Industrial management*, April 1918, p. 268.

BRYAN, WILLIAM. Appraisal and depreciation of water-works and similar properties. *Journal of the association of engineering societies*, Dec. 1907, p. 336-81. Depreciation of electric light plants. *Municipality*, March 1908, p. 74. Depreciation allowance for various public service industries. *Engineering news*, Jan. 23, 1908, p. 96.

BURNS, CLINTON S. Valuation of public utilities; deduction of formula for expressing present value. *Municipal journal and engineer*, Nov. 30, 1910.

	Per cent Straight	Authority	Remarks
Water, gas and elec. light plant (average of 52)	2.784	E.N. 5-7 '03	14th An. Rep., U. S. Com. of Labor.

CHASE, HARVEY S. Maintenance and depreciation charges in accounts of public service corporations. *Accountant*, July 6, 1907, p. 18-32. *Journal of accountancy*, May 1907, p. 1-9.

CHILD, R. W. Where a theory fails. *Stone and Webster public service journal*, June 1911, p. 422-6.

COOLEY, M. E. Factors determining a reasonable charge for public utility service. *American institute of electrical engineers, Proceedings*, March 1914, p. 453-71. *Journal of the Western society of engineers*, Jan. 1914, p. 1-17. Condensed. *Electric railway journal*, Jan. 17, 1914, p. 124-5. Summary. *Electrical world*, Feb. 14, 1914, p. 356-7.

COOPER, H. S. Giving local 100 per cent services. *Electric railway journal*, Nov. 18, 1916, p. 1060-2.

CUSTODY of depreciation funds. *Electrical world*, Jan. 20, 1912, p. 126.

DAVIS, J. S. and A. A. YOUNG. Depreciation and rate control; controversy. *Quarterly journal of economics*, Feb. 1915, p. 362-400

DEPRECIATION and rates discussed before American gas institute. *Electrical world*, Nov. 7, 1914, p. 893-4.

DEPRECIATION and sinking funds in municipal undertakings. *Accountant*, Aug. 20, 27, Sept. 17, Oct. 1, 1904, p. 186-8, 216-8, 271-4, 329-32.

DEPRECIATION as affecting valuation and fair return. *Electrical world*, Feb. 7, 1914, p. 301. *Electric railway journal*, Feb. 14, 1914, p. 370.

DEPRECIATION as an element for consideration in the appraisal of public service properties. *American society of civil engineers, Proceedings*, Jan., April 1915.

DEPRECIATION at Detroit. *Finance (Cleveland, O.)*, Feb. 16, 1907, p. 201.

DEPRECIATION in municipalities. *Accountant*, March 11, 1905, p. 291-2.

DEPRECIATION in public utilities. *Electrical world*, Oct. 2, 1915, p. 743.

DEPRECIATION of municipal undertakings. *Incorporated accountants' journal*, 1900-1, p. 183.

DEPRECIATION of plant and fair rates for public service. *Engineering record*, Feb. 20, 1909, p. 197-8.

DEPRECIATION of public utilities. *Journal of accountancy*, June 1914, p. 437-8. *Municipal journal and engineer*, Feb. 13, 1907, p. 148.

DEPRECIATION; open discussion. *Utilities magazine*, Jan. 1, 1916, p. 132-6.

DEPRECIATION plan of the valuation committee of the American society of civil engineers. *Engineering news*, Feb. 12, 1914, p. 350-2.

DEPRECIATION reserve and the people. *Public service*, July 1908, p. 2.

DICKSEE, LAWRENCE R. Depreciation: with special reference to the accounts of local authorities. *Accountant*, April 13, June 1, 1907, p. 482-92, 733-5.

DISCUSSION on public utility valuation and depreciation. *Electric railway journal*, April 11, 1914, p. 829-30.

DEPRECIATION, DEPLETION AND OBSOLESCENCE—PUBLIC UTILITIES—*(Continued)*

ERICKSON, HALFORD. Depreciation accounting. *Amtrican gas light journal*, Aug. 10, 1914, p. 81-5.

ERICKSON, HALFORD. Depreciation; address delivered before the convention of Central water works association, Detroit, Mich., Sept. 25, 1912. Madison, Democrat printing co., 1912, p. 43. *Utilities magazine*, Philadelphia, 1916, v. 1, p. 112-124.

ERICKSON, HALFORD. Depreciation problems. *American gas institute, Proceedings*, 1914, p. 1582-1682.

ERICKSON, HALFORD. Facts relating to depreciation and rate making. *Electrical review and western electrician*, Jan. 31, 1914, p. 234-8.

ERICKSON, HALFORD. Methods of determining life of public utilities. *Engineering and contracting*, Oct. 23, 1912, p. 448-50.

ERICKSON, HALFORD. Some problems of public utility accounting. *Electric railway journal*, Feb. 7, 1914, p. 306.

ERICKSON, HALFORD and A. C. HUMPHREYS. Depreciation, repair and valuations; abstract and papers. *Electric railway journal*, Oct. 31, 1914, p. 999.

ESHLEMAN, J. M. Reproduction theory. *Utilities magazine*, Jan. 1916.

EXPLICIT directions for public utility accounting. *Electric railway journal*, Feb. 7, 1914, p. 293.

FINDINGS on depreciation of public utility properties. *Commercial and financial chronicle*, Oct. 16, 1915, p. 1233.

FINKLE, F. C. Methods of making computations for depreciation in public utility plants. *Engineering and contracting*, Oct. 12, 1910, p. 590.

FLOY, HENRY. Depreciation. (In his *Valuation of public utility properties*. 1912. p. 168-217).

FOSTER, HORATIO A. Depreciation. (In his *Engineering valuation of public utilities and factories*. 1913. p. 147-218).

GEIJSBEEK, JOHN B. Fair return to public utilities. *Journal of accountancy*, April 1914, p. 245-63.

GILLETTE, HALBERT P. and RICHARD T. DANA. Depreciation repairs and renewals. (In their *Mechanical and electrical cost data*. p. 82-144).

GOETZ, JACOB H. Court decision on depreciation. *Utilities magazine*, Jan.. 1916, p. 102-12.

GRUNSKY, C. E. Depreciation as an element for consideration in the appraisal of public service properties. *American society of civil engineers, Proceedings*, Nov. 1914. Discussion. *American society of civil engineers, Proceedings*, Jan. Feb. March, April, Aug. 1915.

GRUNSKY, CARL EWALD and C. E. GRUNSKY, jr. Valuation, depreciation and the rate-base. New York, John Wiley and sons, 1917. 387p.

H. M. BYLLESBY on depreciation. *Electric railway journal*, April 4, 1914, p. 791.

HALE, R. S Physical valuation of public utilities—depreciation in its relation to investment, earnings and current value. *Engineering magazine*, May 1913, p. 161-5.

HANEY, LEWIS H. Depreciation and valuation for rate making. *Journal of accountancy*, May 1915, p. 344-51.

HARSHMAN, C. C. Obsolescence in appraisals for rate making. *Engineering news*, Nov. 2, 1916, p. 842-3.

HARTMAN, HARLEITH H. Depreciation. (In his *Fair value*. 1920. p. 196-219).

HAYES, HAMMOND VINTON. Depreciation. (In his *Public utilities, their fair present value and return*. 1915. p. 159-203).

HAYES, HAMMOND VINTON. Public utilities; their cost new and depreciation. Ed.2. New York, D. Van Nostrand co. 1916. 262p.
See index under Depreciation.

HEARING of Missouri commission on accounts. *Electrical world*, May 9, 1914, p. 1048-9.

HOLMES, F. L. Depreciation. (In his *Regulation of railroads and public utilities in Wisconsin*. 1915. p. 79-95).

HOW, J. Depreciation as an element in rate making. *American gas light journal*, April 3, 1916, p. 214.

HOXIE, GEORGE L. Custody of depreciation funds. *Electrical world*, Feb. 17, 1912, p. 367.

HUMPHREYS, ALEXANDER C. Depreciation, estimated and actual. *American gas institute, Proceedings*, 1913, pt. 2, p. 505-30. *Engineering and contracting*, Oct. 8, 1913, p. 394. *Institute of gas engineers, Transactions*, 1913, p. 348. *Institute of gas engineers, Transactions* (London), 1913, p. 220-69. *Public service regulation*, Aug. 1913, p. 430-36. *Stevens institute indicator*, Oct. 1913, p. 311-37.

HUMPHREYS, ALEXANDER C. In rate-fixing by commission should "depreciation" be deducted from plant valuation? *American gas institute, Proceedings*, 1914, p. 1557-82.

HUMPHREYS, ALEXANDER C. Public service rate making. *Journal of electricity, power and gas*, Oct. 25, 1915, p. 367. Editorial. Depreciation. *Journal of electricity, power and gas*, Oct. 25, 1913, p. 389.

IDAHO court overrules depreciation deduction. *Engineering record*, Oct. 16, 1915, p. 480-1.

IGNATIUS, MILTON BERGE. Financing of public service corporations. New York, The Ronald press co. 1918. 508p.
See index under Depreciation.

INCOME tax and allowance for depreciation. *Light railway and tramway journal* (London), July 2, 1909, p. 18, 28.

INDIANA commission adopts definite policy as to depreciation funds. *American gas engineering journal*, Aug. 3, 1918, p. 103-4.

JACKSON, DUGALD C. Equitable rate-making by public service companies. *Public service*, Nov. Dec. 1909, p. 145, 139. *Stone and Webster public service journal*, Dec. 1909, p. 104. *Technology quarterly*, Dec. 1918, p. 348.

JAMES, CHARLES C. Depreciation and value of public utilities. *Journal of accountancy*, Dec. 1916, p. 409-16. *Railway age gazette*, Jan. 19, 1917, p. 99-100.

KNOWLTON, DANIEL W. Depreciation as affecting the valuation and assessment of public utilities. *Colorado electric light, power and railway association*, Sept. 23, 1915.

LAWTON, WILLARD HUBBARD. Depreciation, intangible values and rates. *Journal of accountincy*, May 1914, p. 325-54.

LITTLE, A. S. B. and L. L. G. BENEDICT. Depreciation in the valuation of public service property. *Gas age*, Sept. 1, Dec. 1-15, 1917, p. 203, 502, 557.

LOEBENSTEIN, J. Growth and depreciation. *American institute of electrical engineers, Proceedings*, Nov. 1916. p. 1559-77. Excerpts. *Electric railway journal*, Nov. 18, 1916, p. 1057-9.

LOGAN, JAMES PATTERSON. Depreciation in municipal undertakings. *Incorporated accountants' journal*, 1904-5, p. 275.

DEPRECIATION, DEPLETION AND OBSOLESCENCE—PUBLIC UTILITIES—*(Continued)*

MACK, EDWIN S. Depreciation. *American gas light journal,* June 8, 1908, p. 971. *Progressive age,* June 15, 1908, p. 372-5. *Public service,* Aug. 1909, p. 42-5. Editorial. *Progressive age,* June 15, 1908, p. 362.

MANCHESTER SOCIETY OF CHARTERED ACCOUNTANTS AND MANCHESTER CHARTERED ACCOUNTANTS STUDENTS' SOCIETY. Discussion on "municipal accounts, with special reference to sinking funds and depreciation and to the ascertainment of trading profit". *Accountant,* Dec. 10, 1904, p. 714-30, 701.

METHOD of determining depreciation of property adopted by the Illinois state public utilities commission. *Electrical world,* Oct. 2, 1915, p. 776.

METHODS of determining life of public utilities. *Engineering and contracting;* Oct. 23, 1912, p. 448.

METHODS of providing for and recording depreciation. *Engineering and contracting,* Nov. 6, 1912, p. 506-11.

MONTGOMERY, ROBERT H. Importance of uniform practice in determining the profits of public service corporations where municipalities have the power to regulate rates: with discussion. *Federation of societies of public accountants in the United Stats of America, Official record of the Congress of accountants, held at the World's fair, Saint Louis,* September 26th, 27th, and 28th, 1904, p. 143-59. Abstract. *Accountant,* Oct. 22, 1904, p. 458-64.

MONTGOMERY, ROBERT H. Public utilities. (In his *Auditing, theory and practice.* 1916. p. 635).

MUNICIPAL loan purposes and periods in England and the United States. *Engineering news,* Nov. 2, 1905, p. 462.

MUNICIPAL trading and depreciation. *Accountant,* June 8, July 6, 1901, p. 657-9, 769-71.

MUNICIPALITIES and depreciation. *Accountant,* March 29, April 12, 1902, p. 329-31, 376-8.

MURRAY, ALEXANDER. Glasgow corporation accounts, with special reference to depreciation and sinking funds. *Accountant,* June 13, 1903, p. 782-94. *Royal philosophical society of Glasgow, Proceedings,* 1903.

MURRAY, ALEXANDER. Municipal finance, with special reference to the provision and application of sinking and depreciation funds. *Accountant,* March 26, 1910, p. 444-52.

NASH, L. R. Depreciation and rate making. *Electric railway journal,* Sept. 21, 1918, p. 511-3.

NELSON, *BAILIE* WALTER. Limitation and application of profits from municipal undertakings. *Accountant,* Aug. 3, 1912, p. 167-71. *Incorporated accountants' journal,* Oct. 1912, p. 15-7.

OBSOLESCENCE in public utility plants. *Municipal engineering,* March 1912, p. 182.

PLAYER, P. Depreciation. *Public service regulation,* Sept. 1913, p. 463.

PLAYER, P. Depreciation, obsolescence and inadequacy. *Telephone engineer,* Nov. 1913, p. 253.

PROVISION for depreciation by public utility corporations. *Engineering news,* March 25, 1909, p. 328.

PUBLIC service rates and depreciation. *Electrical review and western electrician,* Jan. 14, 1911, p. 67.

PUBLIC utility reports, annotated. Rochester, Lawyers co-operative publishing co.
See index under Depreciation.

PUBLIC utility reports, annotated. Rochester, Lawyers co-operative publishing co. 1915C. p. 525.
Re Arizona Corp. Commission v. Morenci water co. (Ariz.). In computing the rate of depreciation on overheads, it is obviously error to compute it at the same rate that obtains on the physical property.

PUBLIC utility reports, annotated. Rochester, Lawyers co-operative publishing co. 1915E. p. 516.
Re Wester Teleph. Co. (S. D.). The rate of depreciation must be determined after a careful inspection of the property, and must be considered in connection with its use.

PUBLIC utility reports, annotated. Rochester, Lawyers co-operative publishing co. 1916C. p. 925.
Re Chesapeake & P. telph. co. (Md.). An allowance for working capital in a rate valuation was added to the appraisal after the depreciated value of the system was found since working capital does not depreciate.

PUBLIC utility reports, annotated. Rochester, Lawyers co-operative publishing co. 1916B. p. 331.
Re Landon v. Lawrence (Kan.). An allowance was made for the annual depreciation of natural gas property that would amortize the entire investment during the estimated life of the property.

PUBLIC utility reports, annotated. Rochester, Lawyers co-operative publishing co. 1917E. p. 544.

RAYMOND, W. G. Rate making and depreciation. *Public service regulation,* May 1914, p. 297.

RAYMOND, W. G. Rate making for public utilities. *American gas light journal,* April 6, 1914, p. 220-1. *Municipal engineer,* June 1914, p. 520-5.

REPORT of the New York public service commission, second district. *Electric railway journal,* Feb. 18, 1911, p. 301.

RIFENBERICK, K. B. Some illogical theories discussed—wrong use of the element of depreciation in valuations to control rates. *Aera,* Juy 1913, p. 1038.

RIGGS, HENRY EARLE. Valuation of public service corporation property. *American society of civil engineers, Proceedings,* June 1911, p. 1-300.

SALIERS, EARL A. Compulsory depreciation charge. *Journal of accountancy,* Dec. 1912, p. 431-36.

SALIERS, EARL A. Regulations by courts and commissions. (In his *Principles of depreciation.* 1916. p. 66-79).

SEIDMAN, FRANK E. Depreciation accounting for public utilities companies. *Journal of accountancy,* Nov. 1917, p. 355-64.

SPARROW, W. A. Municipal trading undertakings depreciation and allocation of profits. *Incorporated accountants' journal,* July 1913, p. 259-61.

STANDARDIZATION of depreciation for utility commissions. *Gas age,* Jan. 15, 1917, p. 76.

STEARNS, FREDERIC P. Depreciation defined. *Utilities magazine,* Jan. 1, 1916, p. 100-1.

STOCKWELL, HERBERT G. Depreciation, renewal and replacement accounts: a paper read at the annual meeting held in Denver, Colorado, Oct. 18-22, 1909, the American association of public accountants. 63p. *American institute of accountants, Yearbook,* 1909, p. 192-272. *Journal of accountancy,* Dec. 1909, Jan. 1910, p. 89-103, 189-210.

SUPREME court of Idaho defines the allowance to be made for depreciation. *Journal of commerce,* Sept. 25, 1915, p. 3. *Commercial and financial chronicle,* Oct. 16, 1915, p. 1233.
Sept. 25, 1915, p. 3. *Commerce and financial chronicle,* Oct. 16, 1915, p. 1233.

TASSIN, J. S. Depreciation and valuation: correspondence. *Journal of accountancy,* July 1915, p. 77-8.

DEPRECIATION, DEPLETION AND OBSOLESCENCE—PUBLIC UTILITIES—*(Continued)*

THROPP, GEORGE H. Question of depreciation in the valuation of public utility properties. *Journal of the Worcester political institute,* May 1915.

TREATMENT of depreciation. *Public service regulation,* Nov. 1913, p. 617.

TRUST witness. *Municipal journal* (London), July 17, 1903, p. 659.

TURNER, STANLEY HORSFALL. Depreciation and sinking funds in municipal undertakings; reprinted from the Economic journal. *Accountant,* June 11, 1904, p. 785-90.

UTILITIES bureau, conference on valuation, Philadelphia, 1915. *Electric railway journal,* Nov. 20, 1910, p. 1031-2.

VALUATION committee of American society of civil engineers publishers report. *American gas engineering journal,* Jan. 8, 1917, p. 35, 38-41. *Engineering news-record,* Jan. 13, 1917, p. 59-64. Condensed. *Electric railway journal,* Jan. 13, 1917, p. 72-5.

VALUATION of railroad property and other public utilities; report of the American society of civil engineers. *Engineering and contracting,* April 8, 1914, p. 415-20.

WALMSLEY, FREDERICK. Depreciation. *Municipal journal* (London), Oct. 23, 1903, p. 932. Editorial. *Municipal journal* (London), Oct. 23, 1903, p. 939. Criticism. Ourselves or our successors. *Municipal journal* (London), Feb. 1, 1907, p. 84.

WALMSLEY, FREDERIC. Depreciation and sinking funds in municipal undertakings. *Accountant,* Oct. 31, Nov. 14, 1903, p. 1331-43, 1388-90. *Incorporated accountants' journal,* 1903-4, p. 35.

WEBER, A. F. Depreciation and its relation to fair value. *National association of railroad commissioners, Proceedings,* 1913, p. 342. *Electric railway journal,* Nov. 1, 1913, p. 979-80.

WEBER, A. F. Maintenance and depreciation. *Electric railway journal,* April 11, 1914, p. 827.

WEBSTER, GEORGE N. Theoretical depreciation; a menace to the public and the investor. *National electric light association, 42d convention*: Accounting section sessions, 1919, p. 191-217.

WHITTEN, ROBERT H. Bibliography. (In his *Valuation of public service corporations.* 1914. p. 735-9).

WHITTEN, ROBERT HARVEY. Physical depreciation. (In his *Valuation of public service corporations.* 1914. v. 1, 2. p. 329-439, 1112-1205).

WHITTEN, ROBERT H. Depreciation and public service regulation. *Engineering news,* May 8, 1913, p. 942-7.

WISCONSIN commission policy in valuation. *Gas age,* Sept. 1, 1913, p. 210.

WYER, SAMUEL S. Regulation, valuation and depreciation of public utilities. Columbus, Sears and Simpson co. 1913. 313p.

WYNNE-ROBERTS, R. O. Depreciation in relation to municipal works. *Congressional record,* May 13, 1914. *Contract record,* May 13, 1914.

YOUNG, A. A. Depreciation and rate control. *Quarterly journal of economics,* Feb. 1915, p. 362-400.

YOUNG, ALLYN A. Depreciation and rate control. *Quarterly journal of economics,* August 1914, p. 630-62.

Pulleys

See Depreciation, depletion and obsolescence—Shafting, pulleys, etc.

Pulverizers

NICHOLSON, J. LEE and JOHN F. D. ROHRBACH. Depreciation. (In their *Cost accounting.* **1919.** p. 150).

Pulverizers 10%

Pumping

AMERICAN institute of accountants. Report of the committee on standard schedules for uniform reports upon municipal industries and public service corporations; annual meeting at Atlantic city, N. J. October 20-22, 1908. 15p. *Journal of accountancy,* May 1909, p. 47-54.

The knowledge at the command of the Bureau of the census leads to the conclusion that this average life is approximately as follows:

Engines, pumping machinery and wood pipe 5 years

AMERICAN WATER WORKS ASSOCIATION. Final report of committee on depreciation. *Journal of the American water works association,* Sept. 1917, p. 1-38.

	years
Pumping machinery	
high duty large units	30-60
" " small units (say below 6,000,000 gallons per day capacity)	25-50
ordinary direct—acting	20-40
centrifugal, not geared	20-30
" geared	15-25

Boiler feed and auxiliary pumps usually take the life of the units to which they are attached.

Analysis of the premises adopted and methods used in determining the cost to reproduce new, together with the depreciation thereon of the physical property of the Metropolitan system and the Kansas City and Westport Belt railway of Kansas City, Mo. *Engineering and contracting,* May 28, 1913, p. 617-20.

Pumps 5%

AUSTRALIA. FEDERAL INCOME TAX DEPARTMENT. Depreciation allowance. *Accountant,* Oct. 13, 1917, p. 277-9. *Accounting and commerce,* June 30, 1917, p. 55-7. *Federal accountant,* July, 1917, p. 93-8. *Public accountant,* Jan. 30, 1917, p. 145-52.

Pump 7½%

BARKER, HARRY. Typical life expectation tables for public utility property. (In his *Public utility rates.* 1917. p. 368-9, 367).

Pumps	
boiler feed	15-20 years. Wisconsin railroad commission
small centrifugal	20-30 years. Wisconsin railroad commission
Pumps and engines	20-30 years. L. Metcalf.
duplex	20-25 years. Wisconsin railroad commission
triplex	20-30 years. Wisconsin railroad commission
crank and flywheel	30-40 years. Wisconsin railroad commission

DEPRECIATION, DEPLETION AND OBSOLESCENCE—PUMPING—*(Continued)*

BAY state rate case. *Electric railway journal,* Dec. 4, 1915, p. 1121-3. *Public utility reports, annotated,* 1916F, p. 336-9.

	Years
Pumps	12-20

BELT, ROBERT E. Depreciation. (In his *Foundry cost accounting, practice and procedure.* 1919. p. 243).

Pumps, steam and hydraulic	5%

BOLTON, REGINALD PELHAM. Depreciation of mechanical equipments and power plants. (In his *Building for profit.* 1911. p. 82, 89).

	Physical years	%	Economic years
Slow speed reciprocating apparatus, such as pumps elevator reversing gear, platform lifts	17	42.5	15

BREWER, ALLAN F. Rates for annual depreciation. *Industrial management,* April 1918, p. 268.

Pumps	Years	% Annual Dep.
feed-water	30	33.3
duplex compound	33.3	3
triplex	20	5
air	25	4

CHASE, HARVEY S. Depreciation in water works accounts, with reference to uniform reports. *Journal of the New England waterworks association,* June 1910, p. 305-31. Abstract. *Engineering and contracting,* June 29, 1910, p. 598. Editorial. Depreciation and sinking fund accounts. *Municipal engineering,* July 1910, p. 26.

Engines, pumping machinery and wood pipes	25 years

CLADER, WILL-A. Water utilities accounting. *Journal of accountancy,* Aug. 1919, p. 91-2.

The following rate is used frequently when wear and tear are made good by operating maintenance.

Pumping equipment	4%

CROWELL, H. H. Electric lighting rates and depreciation. *Municipal journal and engineer,* Dec. 18, 1907, p. 698.

	Purchased 10 years or more ago	Modern
Pumps, etc.	15 years	25 years

DAWSON, PHILIP. Depreciation. (In his *Engineering and electric traction pocket-book.* Ed.2. p. 1161.)

Boilers, pumps, piping etc.	15-30 years

DEPRECIATION and measurement of expired outlay on plant. *Engineering and mining journal,* March 17, 1917, p. 447.

Pumps	10 years

ELBOURNE, EDWARD T. Depreciation rates. (In his *Factory administration and accounts.* 1918. p. 376).

	Prov. dep. %	Years	
Pumps	Remainder values	10%	5%
air	7½	29	38
centrifugal and turbine	7½	29	38
hydraulic	6	37	48
steam	7½	29	38

ESTIMATED life and depreciation of water works plants. *Municipal journal and engineer,* May 6, 1908, p. 558.

Material	Life in years	% per year Straight	
Pumping engines	20-25-30	5	N. S. Hill, Eng. Rec.
" "	..	3-10	W. H. Bryan Authority June 8, 1901.
" "	15	..	Prosser: Eng. News, vol. XLVII p. 425.
" "	20-30	..	Wynkoop Kiersted: Pro. Am. Sec. C. E. 1897.
" "	..	4.7	W. H. Rosecrans; Gal. Kan. app. in 1905.
" "	25	..	R. Hammond; Eng. Rec. June 15, 1907.
" "	10	..	Boiler feeds. Iowa elec. asso. Iowa Eng. July 1906.
" "	3-36	..	Av. of 50 engines, Av. life 21.3 years. J. W. Alvord Am. W. W. Asso. 1903.
" "	25-30	..	B. Williams: Gal. Kan. appr. in 1905.
" "	30	..	W. Kiersted; Gal. Kans. app. in 1905.
" "	..	2.5	B. L. Dodge, Mt. Vernon, Ill., app. in 1906.
" "	30	..	C. B. Burdick, Mt. Vernon, Ill. appraisal in 1906.

FLOY, HENRY. Depreciation. Floy, Henry. Depreciation as related to electrical properties. *American institute of electrical engineers, Proceedings,* 1911, p. 1267. Floy, Henry. *Valuation of public utility properties.* 1912. p. 168-217. Foster, H. A. *Engineering valuation of public utilities and factories.* 1913. p. 194-8. *Engineering and contracting,* Oct. 4, 1911, p. 359-65. *Engineering magazine,* Aug. 1911, p. 837-40.

DEPRECIATION, DEPLETION AND OBSOLESCENCE—PUMPING—*(Continued)*

	Dep. per year straight line		
Pumps	5	Traction val. comm.	Chicago con. trac. co.
	5	B. J. Arnold	Coney Island & Brooklyn, adopted by P. S. C., N. Y.
	5	Henry Floy	3rd Ave. case, adopted by P. S. C., N. Y.
small steam	6⅔	Wisconsin P. S. C.	
	5	Arbitrators	Street lighting con. Atlanta, Ga. 1899.
	6⅔	St. Louis P. S. C.	Union elec. L. & P. co.

FOSTER, HORATIO A. Rates of depreciation. (In his *Engineering valuation of public utilities and factories.* 1913. p. 200, 205).

Engines, boilers, heaters, conveyors, pumps and auxiliaries	4.5%
Pumps	years
boiler feed	15-20
geared power	20-30
centrifugal	20-30

GILLETTE, HALBERT P. and RICHARD T. DANA. Depreciation. (In their *Handbook of mechanical and electrical cost data.* 1918. p. 106).

Pumps
- 20 years.
  - Traction valuation commission Chicago consolidated traction co.
  - B. J. Arnold—Appraisal of the Coney Island and Brooklyn railroad, Feb. 1, 1909.
  - Henry Floy, 3rd Ave. case, New York city.
  - B. J. Arnold, Chicago appraisals 4 cases.
- 20-25 years.
  - H. P. Gillette, Everett railway and water co., Jan. 29, 1912,

small steam
- 15 years.
  - Wisconsin railroad comission.
  - St. Louis public service commission, Union electric light and power co.
- 20 years.
  - Arbitrators, Street lighting controversy, Atlanta, Ga. 1899.

And auxiliary machinery
- 20-30 years.
  - Leonard Metcalf: Transactions, American society civil engineers, 1909, p. 24, vol. 64.

And auxiliaries
- 22.2 years.
  - Marwick, Mitchell & co. appraisal of a large street railway system, Foster, p. 199.

GREENLAND, S. W. Depreciation. *Mississippi electric association, Report of 2nd annual convention,* June 1910, p. 32-6.

Pumps and heaters — 15-20 years

GRUNSKY, CARL EWALD. Probable useful life of various articles. (In his *Valuation, depreciation and the rate-base.* 1917. p. 282).

Pumps
- 15 years.
  - St. Louis. Public service commission. Case of Union electric light and power co.
- 20 years.
  - Henry Floy. Trans. American institute of electrical engineers, June 1911. Third avenue case figures adopted by public service commission of New York.
- 20 years.
  - Traction valuation commission. Case of the Chicago consolidated traction co.
- 20 years.
  - Bion J. Arnold. Coney Island and Brooklyn figures adopted by Public service commission of New York. Four Chicago appraisal quoted by H. A. Foster.
- 20 years.
  - Bion J. Arnold. Four Chicago appraisals quoted by H. A. Foster.
- 20 years.
  - Arbitrators. Board of arbitration in street lighting controversy at Atlanta, Georgia, 1899.
- 21.3 years.
  - John W. Alvord in Proceedings American waterworks association 1903.
- 22 years.
  - W. H. Rosecrans. Galena appraisals, Kansas, 1905.
- 25 years.
  - Robt. Hammond. Journal of Institute of electrical engineers, England, April 25, 1907.
- 25 years. 6% residual value.
  - Sir. Wm. Preece. Report of Bristol corporation, England, 1906.
- 25-30 years.
  - Benezette Williams. Galena appraisal, Kansas, 1905.
- 30 years.
  - W. Kiersted. Galena appraisal, Kansas, 1905.
- 30 years.
  - Chas. B. Burdick. Appraisal of Mt. Vernon waterworks, Illinois, 1906.
- 40 years.
  - B. L. Dodge. Mt. Vernon water works appraisal, Illinois, 1906.

And auxiliary machinery
- 20-30 years.
  - Leonard Metcalf. Transactions American society of civil engineers, 1909.

DEPRECIATION, DEPLETION AND OBSOLESCENCE—PUMPING—*(Continued)*

And condensers	15-25 years. Wisconsin railroad commission. Milwaukee 3c fare case, Aug. 23, 1912.
small steam	15 years. Wisconsin railroad commission. Quoted by Henry Floy and in published reports.
general service	16 years. 5% residual value. Pacific gas and electric company. Figures used in rate hearings before Master in Chancery, San Francisco, 1913-4.
centrifugal	16 years. 5% residual value. Pacific gas and electric company. Figures used in rate hearings before Master in Chancery, San Francisco, 1913-4.
centrifugal	20-30 years. H. A. Foster. "Engineering valuation of public utilities and factories," Van Nostrand, 1912.
geared power	20-30 years. H. A. Foster. "Engineering valuation of public utilities and factories," Van Nostrand, 1912.
boiler feed	15-20 years. H. A. Foster. "Engineering valuation of public utilities and factories," Van Nostrand, 1912.
oil	16 years. 5% residual value. Pacific gas and electric company. Figures used in rate hearings before Master in Chancery, San Francisco, 1913-4.

HAMMOND, ROBERT. Depreciation. *Institute of electrical engineers, Proceedings,* 1907, p. 270. *Journal of the Institute of electrical engineers, Proceedings,* April 25, 1907, p. 270. Abstracts. *Accountant,* May 18, 1907, p. 675. *Electric railway review,* June 1, 1907, p. 716. *Electrical review* (Chicago), May 25, 1907, p. 828. *Electrical review* (London), May 3, 1907, p. 744. *Electrician,* April 26, 1907, p. 51. *Engineering magazine,* July 1907, p. 636-8. *Engineering record,* June 15, 1907, p. 703. *Municipal journal* (London), May 10, 17, 1907, p. 411, 435. *Progressive age,* July 1, 1907, p. 305. *Street railway bulletin,* June 1907, p. 382. *Tramway and railway world,* June 6, 1907, p. 497.

Pumps and pipe work	25 years

HAZLEHURST, J. N. Final report of the committee on depreciation. *Journal of the American water works association,* March 1919, p. 85-135.

Pumping machinery	Years
High duty units	35-60
High duty small units (say below 6,000,000 gallons per day capacity)	25-50
Ordinary direct-acting	20-40
Centrifugal, not geared	20-30
Centrifugal, geared	15-25

Boiler feed and auxiliary pumps usually take the life of the units to which they are attached.

KIMBALL, DEXTER S. Estimated life, and factors of depreciation. (In his *Cost finding.* 1918. p. 190. *Principles of industrial organization,* 1913, p. 163).

	Boiler-room feed pumps
Probable life of asset in years	20
Ratio of scrap to original value	0.5
Percentage on original cost	4.75
" " diminishing value	14

LIFE data on power-plant equipment used in valuation of Massachusetts property. *Electrical world,* Dec. 4, 1915, p. 1261.

Pumps	12-20 years

LOCK, FRED J. Depreciation. (In his *West African mining accounts.* 1910. p. 88-9).

Underground pumping plant	12½-5%

METCALF, LEONARD. Depreciation in waterworks operation and accounting. *Journal of the New England waterworks association,* Dec. 1910, p. 442. Abstracts. *Engineering news,* Nov. 3, 1910, p. 482. Methods of computing depreciation of and reasonable assumption as to period of useful life of waterworks. *Engineering and contracting,* Nov. 16, 1910, p. 434.
Ordinary pumping machinery, 20-30 years, 5-3½% straight line.

METCALF, LEONARD. Waterworks valuation and fair rates, in the light of the Maine supreme court decisions in the Waterville and Brunswick cases. *American society of civil engineers, Papers and discussions,* 1908, p. 1101-73. *American society of civil engineers, Transactions,* Sept. 1909, p. 1. Foster, Horatio A. *Engineering valuation of public utilities and factories,* 1913. p. 207. Gillette, Halbert P. *Handbook of cost data for contractors and engineers.* p. 797.

	Useful life	Annual contribution to depreciation account or sinking fund in per cent of cost: At 5% annual rate sinking fund	General approximate result
Pumping auxiliary machinery	20-30 years	3.0243%-1.5051%	4-2%

NEALE, R. E. Depreciation in engineering works. *Mechanical world,* Feb. 7, 1913, p. 67-8.

Pumps	5-6.5%	15-20 years

NICHOLSON, J. LEE and JOHN F. D. ROHRBACH. Depreciation. (In their *Cost accounting.* 1919. p. 147, 149).

Pumps Based on (1) the cost of equipment (2) on the life of the equipment (3) on a ten-hour day	5%
Test pumps	6⅔%

DEPRECIATION, DEPLETION AND OBSOLESCENCE—PUMPING—*(Continued)*

PENDER, HAROLD. Depreciation. (In his *Handbook for electrical engineers.* c1914. p. 339).

Heaters, economizers and pumps

15 years.	Chicago union traction co.
20 years.	Stone & Webster for Chicago union traction co.
7.5%	Milwaukee electric railway and light co.
6.66	Chicago union traction co.
5	Cardiff tramways
	Glasgow "
	Stone & Webster for Chicago union traction co.

PHILADELPHIA. CONTROLLER. Rates of depreciation. (In his *Manual of accounting, reporting and business procedure of the city and county of Philadelphia.* 1917. p. 205).

Auxiliary pumps for water and other liquids	4%
Air compressing pumps	4

PIEZ, CHARLES. Perpetual inventory and appraisal values; table of standard depreciation rates. *Engineering and contracting,* Jan. 24, 1917, p. 77. *Factory,* Dec. 1916, p. 668-71. *Iron age,* Nov. 30, 1916, Jan. 11, 1917, p. 1266, 138-9. *Iron trade review,* Feb. 22, 1917, p. 477-8. Condensed. *Iron trade review,* Dec. 7, 1916, p. 1144-6. *Journal of the American society of mechanical engineers,* Dec. 1916, p. 965-6. Kent, William. *Bookkeeping and cost accounting for factories.* 1918. p. 90. Discussion. *Journal of the American society of mechanical engineers,* March 1917, p 215-7.

	% on cost	% on reducing balance
Boilers, pumps, feed-water heaters, and air compressors	6	15
Pumps	6	15

PROPOSED sale of Toronto utilities to the city. *Electrical world,* Oct. 25, 1913, p. 832.

Pumps	5%

PROSSER, R. W. Depreciation in gas plants. *American gas light journal,* May 26, 1902, p. 767.

Pumps and piping	15 years	10% of first cost

PUBLIC utility reports annotated. Rochester, Lawyers co-operative publishing co. 1915A. p. 178.

Re Janesville water co. (Wis.). In estimating the cost of reproduction for the purpose of obtaining the fair value of a waterworks property for municipal purchase, depreciation of pumps to 50 per cent of condition new on a basis of a 40 year life, which included some allowance for obsolescence, was held not to be too great where the pumps had been used for some time.

ROBY, J. J. Schedule of plant depreciation. (In his *Treatise on cost accounting as applied to coal mining.* c1913. p. 14-5).

Pipe, heaters and pumps	
Deduct as salvage before depreciating	10%
Depreciation rate for remainder, fireproof	8
Pumps and drive	
Deduct as salvage before depreciating	10
Depreciation rate for remainder, fireproof	10

UNIFORM cost sheet for coal mining companies. *Coal age,* Sept. 19, 1918, p. 545-7.

	Original cost
Pumps, heaters and other power house equipment	8%
Mine pumps	20

VALUATION of the Chicago consolidated traction property. *Electric railway journal,* Dec. 3, 1910, p. 1111-3.

Pumps	5%

WEEKS, H. E. Abstract of paper on depreciation read before annual meeting of Iowa street and interurban railway association, April 1910, *Electric railway journal,* April 30, 1910, p. 782-3.

Pumps	15 years

WOLFF, MARK. Interpretation of water works accounts. *Journal of the American water works association,* June 1916, p. 543, 546.

	Years	Total % of operating revenue
Pumping machinery and engines	25	
Pumping system		2.00

Punching

ELBOURNE, EDWARD T. Depreciation rates. (In his *Factory administration and accounts.* 1918. p. 377).

	Prov. dep. % Remainder values	Years 10%	Years 5%
Punching machines			
Hydraulic	6	37	48
Belt driven	6	37	48
Punching and shearing machines, steam	6	37	48

NICHOLSON, J. LEE and JOHN F. D. ROHRBACH. Depreciation. (In their *Cost accounting.* 1919. p. 149).

Punches	6⅔%

PHILADELPHIA. CONTROLLER. Rates of depreciation. (In his *Manual of accounting, reporting and business procedure of the city and county of Philadelphia.* 1917. p. 205).

Metal work equipment	
Shearing, punching and drilling equipment	5%
Punches	6⅔%

PIEZ, CHARLES. Perpetual inventory and appraisal values; table of standard depreciation rates. *Engineering and contracting,* Jan. 24, 1917, p. 77. *Factory,* Dec. 1916, p. 668-71. *Iron age,* Nov. 30, 1916, Jan. 11, 1917, p. 1266, 138-9. *Iron trade review,* Feb. 22, 1917, p. 477-8. Condensed. *Iron trade review,* Dec. 7, 1916, p. 1144-6. *Journal of the American society of me-*

DEPRECIATION, DEPLETION AND OBSOLESCENCE—PUNCHING—*(Continued)*

chanical engineers, Dec. 1916, p. 965-6. Kent, William. *Bookkeeping and cost accounting for factories.* 1918. p. 90. Discussion. *Journal of the American society of mechanical engineers,* March 1917, p. 215-7.

	% on cost
Punches and dies (standard) net additions	50

Punts

See Depreciation, depletion and obsolescence—Ships.

Purifiers

BARKER, HARRY. Typical life expectation tables for public utility property. (In his *Public utility rates.* 1917. p. 368).

Purifiers — 50 years — Wisconsin railroad commission

ELBOURNE, EDWARD T. Depreciation rates. (In his *Factory administration and accounts.* 1918. p. 376).

	Prov. dep. %	Years	
	Remainder values	10%	5%
Water purifying and softening apparatus	7½	29	38

FOSTER, HORATIO A. Rates of depreciation. (In his *Engineering valuation of public utilities and factories.* 1913. p. 206).

	Years' life
Purifiers, modern	50
	Minimum service value % reproduction cost
Purifiers, old type, according to style and condition	25

GILLETTE, HALBERT POWERS and RICHARD T. DANA. Depreciation. (In their *Handbook of mechanical and electrical cost data.* 1918. p. 109).

Purifiers, modern (gas plant) — 50 years — Wisconsin railroad commission

GRUNSKY, CARL EWALD. Probable useful life of various articles. (In his *Valuation, depreciation and the rate-base.* 1917. p. 282).

Purifiers — 50 years.

gas-modern — Wisconsin railroad commission. Quoted by H. A. Foster and in published reports.

NICHOLSON, J. LEE and JOHN F. D. ROHRBACH. Depreciation. (In their *Cost accounting.* 1919. p. 147).

Water purifying plant

Based on (1) the cost of equipment.
(2) the life of the equipment.
(3) on a ten-hour day.

PROSSER, R. W. Depreciation in gas plants. *American gas light journal,* May 26, 1902, p. 767.

Condensers, scrubbers and purifiers — 30 years — 20% of first cost

VALUATION of the Chicago consolidated traction property. *Electric railway journal,* Dec. 3, 1910, p. 1111-3.

Water purifying apparatus — 3%

WOLFF, MARK. Interpretation of waterworks accounts. *Journal of the American waterworks association,* June 1916, p. 543, 546.

Purification system — 0.50% of total operating revenues.

Pushers

NICHOLSON, J. LEE and JOHN F. D. ROHRBACH. Depreciation. (In their *Cost accounting.* 1919. p. 149).

Pushers — 5½%

Pyrometers

BELT, ROBERT E. Depreciation. (In his *Foundry cost accounting practice and procedure.* 1919. p. 242).

Pyrometers — 10%

NICHOLSON, J. LEE and JOHN F. D. ROHRBACH. Depreciation. (In their *Cost accounting.* 1919. p. 150).

Pyrometers — 10%

Quadruple stayers

DENHAM, ROBERT S. Depreciation. (In his *Manual of cost engineering and estimating for paper box manufacturers.* 1917. p. 249).

Quadruple stayer — 12%

Quarries and quarrying

AUSTRALIA. Federal income tax department. Depreciation allowance. *Accountant,* Oct. 13, 1917, p. 277-9. *Accounting and commerce,* June 30, 1917, p. 55-7. *Federal accountant,* July 1917, p. 93-8. *Public accountant,* Jan. 30, 1917, p. 145-52.

Quarrying
Written down value, repairs allowed in addition. — 7½%

IBOTSON, JOHN GEORGE PERCY. Depreciation. (In his *Quarry and stone merchants' accounts.* 1904. p. 7, 16, 53, 63).

Buildings	2½%
Plant and machinery	5

PHILADELPHIA. CONTROLLER. Rates of depreciation. (In his *Manual of accounting, reporting and business procedure of the city and county of Philadelphia.* 1917. p. 205).

Mining and quarrying equipment — 20%

DEPRECIATION, DEPLETION AND OBSOLESCENCE—*(Continued)*

Racks

BELT, ROBERT E. Depreciation. (In his *Uniform cost accounting methods; adopted by the American mallable castings association,* Nov. 14, 1917, p. 20-1).
Racks 10%

BELT, ROBERT E. Depreciation. (In his *Foundry cost accounting practice and procedure.* 1919. p. 242).
Racks 10%

ELBOURNE, EDWARD T. Depreciation rates. (In his *Factory administration and accounts.* 1918. p. 377).

	Prov. dep. % Remainder values	years 10%	5%
Racks, hat and coat	12½	17	22
" tool	7½	29	38

NICHOLSON, J. LEE and JOHN F. D. ROHRBACH. Depreciation. (In their *Cost accounting.* 1919. p. 148, 151).
Steel works—racks 4%
Trucks and moving racks 7½

Radiators

ELBOURNE, EDWARD T. Depreciation rates. (In his *Factory administration and accounts.* 1918. p. 376).

	Prov. dep. % Remainder values	years 10%	5%
Heating pipes, radiators and valves	10	22	28

PHILADELPHIA. CONTROLLER. Rates of depreciation. (In his *Manual of accounting, reporting and business procedure of the city and county of Philadelphia.* 1917. p. 205).
Radiators 4%

Radium

AUSTRALIA. FEDERAL INCOME TAX DEPARTMENT. Depreciation allowance. *Accountant,* Oct. 13, 1917, p. 277-9. *Accounting and commerce,* June 30, 1917, p. 55-7. *Federal accountant,* July 1917, p. 93-8. *Public accountant,* Jan. 30, 1917, p. 145-52.
Radium Nil

Railings

PHILADELPHIA. CONTROLLER. Rates of depreciation. (In his *Manual of accounting, reporting and business procedure of the city and county of Philadelphia.* 1917. p. 207-8).
Railings, etc. 5%

Railroads

See also various headings under Depreciation, depletion and obsolescence.

ACCOUNTING depreciation. *Railroad age gazette,* July 3, 1908, p. 415.

ACCOUNTING for depreciation of equipment. *Railway age,* July 12, 1907, p. 36.

ADAMS, HENRY CARTER. Depreciation. (In his *American railway accounting.* 1918. p. 59, 60, 94, 96, 97, 98, 99, 104, 172, 188).

ADEQUATE depreciation rates should be established. *Railway age gazette,* Feb. 21, 1919, p. 427-8. The railroad administration has taken the first step towards standardizing depreciation rates by specifying that 4½ per cent per annum should be used by all equipment placed in service during 1918.

AMERICAN ELECTRIC RAILWAY ASSOCIATION. COMMITTEE ON VALUATION. Bibliography on valuation of public utilities to December 23, 1915. New York, American electric railway association, 61+72p.

AMERICAN RAILWAY ASSOCIATION. SPECIAL COMMITTEE ON RELATIONS WITH INTERSTATE COMMERCE COMMISSION. Depreciation in steam railway accounting. *Electric railway journal,* Aug. 1908, p. 748-9.

As the government interprets railroad depreciation. *Engineering record,* June 17, 1916, p. 794-5.

AUSTRALIA. FEDERAL INCOME TAX DEPARTMENT. Depreciation allowance. *Accountant,* Oct. 13, 1917, p. 277-9. *Accounting and commerce,* June 30, 1917, p. 55-7. *Federal accountant,* July 1917, p. 93-8. *Public accountant,* Jan. 30, 1917, p. 145-52.
Railways—rails, sleepers, points, signals and others apparatus Nil

BARKER, HARRY. Typical life expectation tables for public utility property. (In his *Public utility rates.* 1917. p. 366).

	Year	Authority*	Control
Railways			
Bridges, steel	20-50	*	Obs.
wood	10	*	Det.
Buildings, office, masonry	70	*	Obs.
dwellings, etc., wood frame	30	*	Obs. or Det.
stations, masonry	40	*	Obs.
wood	20	*	Obs.
shops, first class	75	Wis. R. R. Comm.	Obs.
second class	50	Wis. R. R. Comm.	Det.
sheds, wood-frame	20	*	Det.
Cars, freight, wood	10-20	*	Det.
steel	15-30	*	Det.
passenger, wood	20-25	*	Obs.
steel	25-30	*	Det.
dining, parlor and sleeping, wood	15-20	*	Obs.
steel	20-25	*	Obs.
Locomotives, freight	15-20	*	Det. (1,000,000m.)
passenger	15-20	*	Det. (1,000,000m.)
switching	20	*	Det.
Signals	30	*	Obs.

DEPRECIATION, DEPLETION AND OBSOLESCENCE—RAILROADS—*(Continued)*

Track, rail, main-line tangent	2-8	*	Det. and Obs. ##
main-line curve	1-5	*	Det. and Obs. ##
sidings and yards	10-20	*	Det. ##
ties, ordinary light wood	5-10	*	Det.
ordinary hard wood	10-15	*	Det.
Treated and protected	30	*	Det.

* Where no authority is cited the data are those of the author—average or approximate figures secured by examination or enquiry.

Main-line is removed after 5 to 10% reduction of weight, and is used as relayer rail on less important service like sidings and branches. Here it is good for many years of service. The wear on level main-line tangent rail is in the order of 1.3% per year per 100,000,000 tons passage over it. This wear probably increases by an extra 0.1% per 1% grade and by 0.3% extra per 1 degree curvature.

BLAUVELT, M. P. Railroad accounting under government supervision. *Railway age gazette,* May 15, 1908. *Journal of accountancy,* June 1908, p. 81-92.

BRANTLEY, W. G. Condition per cent; criticism of engineering board's circular no. 226 with respect to depreciation and depreciation on the Atlanta, Birmingham and Atlantic railroad. Philadelphia, Presidents' conference committee, 1916.

BUREAU OF RAILWAY ECONOMICS. Digest of depreciation charges of 172 roads (with annual operating revenues about $1,000,000) calendar year 1917. Washington, Bureau of railway economics, 1918. 26p.

CALVERT, J. F. Depreciation in railway accounting. *Journal of accountancy,* Aug. 1908, p. 229-233.

CLASSIFICATION of depreciation percentages used at Dusseldorf municipal gas works. *Progressive age,* Aug. 15, 1910, p. 707.

Railways about works	
Present %	6%
Proposed scale %	6
Life, years	37

CLEVELAND, FREDERICK ALBERT and F. W. POWELL. Depreciation. (In their *Railroad finance.* 1912. p. 89, 94, 130-1, 170-1).

COMMON confusion of the terms depreciation, repairs. *Engineering and contracting,* June 30, 1909, p. 517.

DEBATE depreciation and land at valuation hearing. *Engineering record,* Feb. 10, 1917, p. 239.

DEDUCTIONS for obsolescence justified. *Railway age gazette,* Dec. 2, 1910, p. 1093.

DELANO, F. A. Arbitrary depreciation charge. *Railroad gazette,* May 15, 1908, p. 681.

DELANO, F. A. Notes on application of a depreciation charge in railway accounting. *Journal of political economy,* Nov. 1908, p. 585-601. *Railway age,* March 27, 1908, p. 471.

DEPRECIATED value as a basis for rate making; a review of the supreme court decision and some suggestions as to estimating accrued depreciation. *Engineering and contracting,* July 16, 1913, p. 58.
Discussion of the decision in the Minnesota rate case.

DEPRECIATION accounts. *National association of railway commissioners, Proceedings,* 1914, p. 450.

DEPRECIATION and appreciation in railroad valuation. *Railway world,* April 1915, p. 303.

DEPRECIATION and deferred maintenance of equipment, testimony of D. F. Crawford, before the valuation division of the Interstate commerce commission. *Railway review,* Aug. 11, 1917, p. 176-9.

DEPRECIATION and railroad credit. *Railway age gazette,* June 4, 1915, p. 1142.

DEPRECIATION and renewals accounts modified. *Railway age,* Sept. 6, 1907, p. 308.

DEPRECIATION as applied to valuation; abstract of testimony of W. B. Storey and D. F. Crawford. *Railway age gazette,* June 22, 1917, p. 1406.

DEPRECIATION estimates report to National association of railway commissioners. *Aera,* March 1913, p. 644.

DEPRECIATION funds of the New York, New Haven and Hartford railroad. *Railway age,* Feb. 1, 1907, p. 133.

DEPRECIATION in railway accounting. *Railway age,* May 10, 1907, May 1, 1908, p. 728, 623.

DEPRECIATION in steam railway accounting. *Electric railway journal,* Oct. 3, 1908, p. 748.

DEPRECIATION of equipment. *Engineering and contracting,* Nov. 19, 1913, p. 567-8.

DEPRECIATION of equipment accounts. *Electric railway journal,* July 4, 1908, p. 193.

DISPUTED points in railway valuation. *Railway age gazette,* May 30, 1913, p. 1164.

DUNN, H. A. Depreciation in railway accounting. *Railway age,* May 29, 1908, p. 756.

EATON, JAMES SHIRLEY. *Handbook of railroad expenses.* New York, McGraw-Hill book co. 1913. 559p. See index under Depreciation.

EQUIPMENT account for each car and locomotive. *Railway age gazette,* Nov. 29, 1907, p. 640.

EQUIPMENT, depreciation and renewal on railways. *Engineering and contracting,* Aug. 31, 1910, p. 193.

FOSTER, HORATIO A. Depreciation of railroads. (In his *Engineering valuation of public utilities and factories.* 1913. p. 152-64).

FRANK, LAWRENCE K. Depreciation and confiscation. *Railway age gazette,* July 9, 1915, p. 44.

GAINES, MORRELL WALKER. Billion dollar confiscation. *Railway age gazette,* June 4, 1915, p. 1150-2.

GILLETTE, HALBERT POWERS. Railways. (In his *Handbook of cost data for contractors and engineers.* 1910. p. 1317-8).

	Age, years	Annual dep. %	Pres. condition %
Cribbing and bulkheading	4.2	10.0	58.0
Howe truss bridges	5.0	10.0	50.0
Log culverts	9.4	6.0	41.6
Timber culverts	13.0	6.0	12.0
Box drains	13.0	6.0	12.0
Ties	4.3	12.5	46.3
Rails, track fastenings, etc.	8.0	2.5	80.0
Fences	6.5	7.0	54.5
Transportation dept. bldgs.	3.5	3.0	89.5
Road dept. bldgs.	8.0	3.0	76.0
Roundhouses and shops	5.5	3.0	83.5

DEPRECIATION, DEPLETION AND OBSOLESCENCE—RAILROADS—*(Continued)*

Fuel and water stations	..	..	80.0
Shop tools and machinery	3.5	10.0	65.0
Grain elevators	7.0	3.0	79.0
Docks and wharves	7.0	3.0	79.0
Other buildings	5.0	3.0	85.0
Snow sheds	6.9	4.0	72.4

Fuel stations 3%
Water stations 2½
Equipment 3.6
Grading 10% in value due to the "Seasoning" of the roadbed.

GILLETTE, HALBERT P. and RICHARD T. DANA. Depreciation. (In their *Handbook of mechanical and electrical cost data.* 1918. p. 106).
Buildings, railroad transportation dept.
33.3 years — H. P. Gillette. Washington ry. appraisal.

GLASGOW, W. A. and L. L. G. BENEDICT. Discussion of the theory of depreciation; abstract of brief filed with Interstate commerce commission in Texas Midland railroad case. *Gas age,* May 15, 1918, p. 458-62. Discussion. *Gas age,* June 15, July 15, 1918, p. 543-4, 69-70.

GRAY, HENRY L. Necessity of depreciation reserves. *Railway age gazette,* May 27, 1910, p. 1297-8. Editorial. Depreciation reserves. *Railway age gazette,* May 27, 1910, p. 1290. Letters. Depreciation reserves. *Railway age gazette,* July 8, 1910, p. 66.
A fair average annual allowance for depreciation on steam roads would be—
of the cost of the property subject to depreciation 5½%
" " on electric roads 6½
" " on street railways 5

The following table is used for the State of Washington—

Item	Annual % depreciation
Ballast	8
Ties	15
Rails (main track)	3
Fastenings	5
Frogs and switches	7
Plank paving	8
Track laying	5
Timber tunnel lining	8
Combination bridges	6
Howe truss bridges	9
Pile and frame bridges	10
Wooden culverts	10
Crossings and signs	8
Fences and cattle-guards	8
Telephone and telegraph instruments	6
Poles and fixtures	8
Covered copper feeder	2
Trolley wire	5
Rail bonds	3
Brick buildings	2
Frame buildings	3
Shop machinery	6
Water and fuel stations	4
Roadway tools	10
Interlocking and signal apparatus	7
Sub-station apparatus	5
Furniture and fixtures	3
Storage batteries	15
Passenger cars (steam)	3
Passenger cars (electric)	5
Freight cars (steam)	4
Freight cars (electric)	4
Steam locomotives	3
Electric equipment of cars	5

GRINLING, C. H. Need of a depreciation fund in railway accounts. *Banker's magazine, London,* v. 75, p. 692.

GRUNSKY, CARL EWALD. Probable useful life of various articles. (In his *Valuation, depreciation and the rate-base.* 1917. p. 283, 274).

Station buildings and R. R. structures	10 years	California railroad commission—Reports 1913-4. Stockton Terminal and Eastern R. R., April 1913.
Railroad station	10 years.	California railroad commission. Reports 1913-4. Stockton Terminal and Eastern R. R., April 1913.
railroad	33⅓ years.	H. P. Gillette. Appraisal of Great Northern & Northern Pacific R. R.'s in Washington. Direction of Washington railroad commission, 1906.

HAND, G. C. Depreciation of railroad property. *Railway age gazette,* Dec. 7, 1917, p. 1035-8. Discussion. *Railway age gazette,* Dec. 21, 1917, Jan. 18, March 22, 1918, p. 1116, 150-2, 695-6.

HEARING on depreciation of equipment accounts by Interstate commerce commission. *Electric railway journal,* July 4, 1908, p. 236-7. *Street railway bulletin,* July 1908, p. 390.

HOOPER, WILLIAM EVERETT. *Railroad accounting.* New York, D. Appleton and co. 1915. 461p. See index under Depreciation.

HUDSON, S. M. Depreciation. *Railway age,* Aug. 9, 1907, p. 175.

DEPRECIATION, DEPLETION AND OBSOLESCENCE—RAILROADS—*(Continued)*

HUMPHREYS, A. C. Depreciation and confiscation. *Railway age gazette,* Aug. 20, 1915, p. 311-2.
INCOME tax and depreciation allowances. *Accountant,* May 30, 1914, p. 785-8.
INTERSTATE commerce commission desire information concerning treatment of depreciation accounts. *Railway age,* Feb. 14, 1908, p. 221.
JENKINS, JENKS B. Absurdities of the straight line method of determining depreciation. *Railway age gazette,* Feb. 25, 1916, p. 357-8.
JONAH, F. G. Misapplication of interest, contingencies and engineering items for valuing railroads by cost of replacement method. *Journal of the Association of engineering societies,* Aug. 1913.
JONES, EDWARD DAVID. Depreciation. (In his *Investment.* p. 167).
Physical property of railroads 5%
KATES, E. J. Actuary theory of depreciation of physical property values. *Railway age gazette,* May 3, 1918, p. 1133-5.
LILL, THOMAS R. Treatment of depreciation in railway income statements. *Journal of accountancy,* Jan. 1917, p. 1-6.
MCCARTY, RICHARD J. Depreciation of railroad property. Kansas City, Tiernan-Dart printing co. 1914. Abstract. Railroad property depreciation. *Public service regulation,* Feb. 1914, p. 66.
MAHL, WILLIAM. Equipment depreciation and renewal. *Railroad gazette,* Oct. 1, 1907, p. 418, 406. *Railway age gazette,* March 4, 1910, p. 440-2. Editorial. *Railroad gazette,* Oct. 11, 1907, p. 406. *Railway age gazette,* May 20, 1910, p. 1249.
MAHL, WILLIAM. Railroad equipment depreciation and renewal; an interesting and timely discussion of the ever important problem of depreciation charges as applied to railroads. *Business man's magazine,* May 1908, p. 430-5.
MAY, FRANK. Income account of railways. *Railway age,* April 17, 1908, p. 560.
MAY reserve fund to renew obsolete equipment. *Electric traction weekly,* Dec. 31, 1910, p. 1473.
METHODS of procedure under the Wisconsin utility law, benefits and restrictions of the law. *Engineering and contracting,* Oct. 16, 1912, p. 425.
MEYERS, WILLIAM J. Railway depreciation accounts. *National association of railway commissioners, Proceedings,* 1909, p. 403-12. Abstract. *Electric railway journal,* Dec. 4, 1909, p. 1146-8.
MONTGOMERY, ROBERT H. Steam railroads. (In his *Auditing theory and practice.* 1916. p. 652).
OBJECTIONS to the depreciation charge. *Railroad age gazette,* Oct. 2, 1908, p. 1050-1. Depreciation in steam railway accounting. *Electric railway journal,* Oct. 3, 1908, p. 748. Editorial. Proposed valuation and rates. *Railway age,* March 1, 1907, p. 268.
POMEROY, L. R. Depreciation of locomotives and shop equipment. *Railway age gazette,* April 24, 1914, p. 943-6.
PRICE, WATERHOUSE & COMPANY. Treatment of maintenance and depreciation accounts in the new classification of accounts prescribed for railroads by the Interstate commerce commission, being a reprint of the communications submitted to the Interstate commerce commission. New York, Price, Waterhouse & company, 1908. 27p.
PROPOSED valuation and rates. *Railway age,* March 1, 1907, p. 268.
PUBLIC utility reports, annotated. Rochester, Lawyers co-operative publishing co. 1915C. p. 711.

Re Manila R. co. (P. I.). A proper and adequate annual rate of depreciation of locomotives, passenger train cars, freight train cars, and work equipment cars was found by the Philippine Islands Public utilities commission to be 3 per cent, on steamships 6½ per cent, on steam launches 15 per cent, on wooden motor launches 20 per cent, on steel motor launches 15 per cent, on lighters 20 per cent, on the machinery of the Pandacan slipway and plant 9 per cent; and on the Pandacan slipway 20 per cent of their original cost, ledger value or purchase price.

PUBLIC utility reports, annotated. Rochester, Lawyers co-operative publishing company, 1920F. p. 726.
Re Southern Pacific company. Accrued depreciation must be taken into consideration in valuing railway property for rate making purposes.
QUESTIONS pertaining to depreciation. *Railway age,* Dec. 6, 1907, p. 805.
RAILWAY evaluation and depreciation, Minnesota rate case decision. *Engineering record,* June 21, 1913, p. 687-8.
RATE of depreciation. *Railway age gazette,* March 27, 1914, p. 727.
A leading article dealing with the attitude of the Interstate commerce commission towards rate of depreciation, as reflected in its condemnation of the Chicago, Milwaukee and St. Paul's charge of 1% on its equipment, and also in the Supreme court's decision in the Kansas City Southern abandonment of the property case. The writer of the article seems to think that the commission will eventually prescribe a uniform rate of depreciation on equipment, say, of 3%.
REPORT of committee on life of railway physical property. *American railway accountants' and engineering association, Proceedings,* 1912, p. 189. *Electric railway journal,* Oct. 11, 1912, p. 828-9.

SALIERS, EARL A. Depreciation in valuations. *Journal of accountancy,* Feb. 1913, p. 106-16.
SALIERS, EARL A. Railroad companies. (In his *Principles of depreciation.* 1916. p. 74-7).
SCHREIDER, M. Work of committee on life of railway physical property. *Electrical railway journal,* April 25, 1914, p. 932.
SCHWINN, F. S. Depreciation of railroad property and its relation to valuation. *Railway review,* May 3, 1919, p. 645-7.
SHEPARD, R. B. Depreciation as applied to valuation. *Engineering news record,* Aug. 12, 1916, p. 202.
SHOULD rates be based on depreciated plant values? *Engineering and contracting,* Dec. 3, 1913, p. 621.
SIKES, CHARLES STEVEN. Railway accounting; one of a series of treatises in an interstate commerce and railway traffic course. 2v. Chicago, LaSalle extension university, c1917. 342p.
See Index under Depreciation.

DEPRECIATION, DEPLETION AND OBSOLESCENCE—RAILROADS—*(Continued)*

SOME disputed points in railway. *Railway age gazette*, May 16, 23, 30, June 6, 1913, p. 1056, 1118, 1164, 1208. Criticism. Mr. Loweth on depreciation in valuation (letter): by C. F. Loweth. *Railway age gazette*, June 20, 1913, p. 1536. Editorial. Depreciation in railway valuation. *Railway age gazette*, June 20, 1913, p. 1535.

STONE AND WEBSTER MANAGEMENT ASSOCIATION. Auditing department. Bibliography on the life of railway physical property. *American electric railway accountants association, Proceedings*, 1912, p. 194-230. *American electric railway engineering association, Proceedings*, 1912, p. 524-60.

STOREY, WILLIAM B. Depreciation, testimony before Interstate commerce commission. *Railway review*, Aug. 25, 1917, p. 229-31.

STURGIS, C. I. and W. J. MEYERS. Railway depreciation accounts. *Electric railway journal*, Dec. 18, 1909, p. 1224-5. *National association of railway commissioners, Report*, 1909, p. 392. *Railway age gazette*, April 8, 1910, p. 944-6.

SWAINSON, G. Evolution of a municipal balance sheet depreciation. *Accountant*, June 22, 1901, p. 735-7.

SWINN, F. S. Depreciation of railroad property and its relation to valuation. *Railway review*, May 3, 1919, p. 645-7.

VANDERBLUE, HOMER BEWS. Railroad valuation. Boston, Houghton, Mifflin company, 1917. 222p.
See Index under Depreciation.

VITALIZING an accounting theory. Commerce commission, having long since defined the theory of depreciation in railway equipment, is now seeing that it is reduced to practice. *Annalist*, Aug. 17, 1914, p. 185.

WHATLEY, G. E. STUART, Depreciation. (In his *Accountant's and book keeper's vade-mecum*. 1893. p. 26).

WHITTEN, ROBERT H. Bibliography. (In his *Valuation of public service corporations*. 1914. p. 741-2).

WHITTEN, ROBERT H. Depreciation and public service regulation. *Engineering news*, May 8, 1913, p. 942.

WILGUS, W. J. Appraisal of the Lehigh valley railroad. *Engineering record*, May 30, 1914, p. 613-7.

WILSON, P. N. Life of way structure as affected by engineering and municipal conditions. *Electric railway journal*, June 26, 1915, p. 1212-3.

WILKINSON, GEORGE. Depreciation of plant. *Accountant*, Aug. 31, 1901, p. 956-7.

WILLIAMS, R. PRICE. British railways—the serviceable life and cost of renewals of permanent way of British railways. *Railway age gazette*, March 15, 1910, p. 576-7.

WOODS, CLINTON E. Railroad depreciation. (In his *Unified accounting methods for industrials*. 1917. p. 65).

	% per annum
Railroad	15
Railroad equipment	20

WORTHINGTON, W. A. Accounting for depreciation of equipment. *Railway age*, Aug. 23, 1907, p. 245.

Rebuilding

MONTGOMERY, ROBERT H. Reconstruction, rebuilding, restoration. (In his *Income tax procedure*, 1919. p. 576. ———— Same, 1920. p. 732-3).

Recreation

See Depreciation, depletion and obsolescence—Amusements.

Refrigeration

BOLTON, REGINALD PELHAM. Depreciation of mechanical equipments and power plants. (In his *Building for profit*. 1911. p. 82, 89).

	Physical years	%	Economic years
Sanitary fixtures, refrigerating piping, kitchen fixtures and valves	20	50.0	16
Elevators in regular use, laundry, kitchen refrigerating electric devices, and other apparatus frequently reversed	16	40.0	14

NICHOLSON, J. LEE and J. F. D. ROHRBACH. Depreciation. (In their *Cost accounting*. 1919. p. 147).

Refrigeration	7½%

Based on (1) the cost of equipment
(2) the life of the equipment
(3) on a ten-hour day

PHILADELPHIA. CONTROLLER. Rates of depreciation. (In his *Manual of accounting, reporting and business procedure in the city and county of Philadelphia*. 1917. p. 210, 204).

Buildings used solely for the production of heat, light, power or refrigeration	1⅔%
Refrigerating equipment:	
Freezing equipment	4%
Equipment for cooling other than freezing:	
Refrigerators	10
Ice boxes	10

Registers

BAY STATE RATE CASE. *Electric railway journal*, Dec. 4, 1915, p. 1121-3. *Public utility reports, annotated*, 1916F, p. 336-9.

Registers	20 years.

Repairing

PHILADELPHIA. CONTROLLER. Rates of depreciation. (In his *Manual of accounting, reporting and business procedure of the city and county of Philadelphia*. 1917. p. 206).

Equipment for building, repairing and wrecking structures	12½%

DEPRECIATION, DEPLETION AND OBSOLESCENCE—*(Continued)*

Reservoirs

AMERICAN institute of accountants. Report of the committee on standard schedules for uniform reports upon municipal industries and public service corporations; annual meeting at Atlantic city, N. J. October 20-22, 1908. 15p. *Journal of accountancy,* May 1909, p. 47-54.

The knowledge at the command of the Bureau of the census leads to the conclusion that this average life is approximately as follows:

Reservoirs, tunnels and aqueducts 100 years

AMERICAN WATERWORKS ASSOCIATION. Final report of committee on depreciation. *Journal of the American waterworks association,* Sept. 1917, p. 1-38.

Small distribution reservoirs 50-75%

Storage reservoirs and heavy earthen or masonry dams, large masonry conduits and tunnels 75-100 years

BARKER, HARRY. Typical life expectation tables for public utility property. (In his *Public utility rate.* 1917, p. 367).

	Years	
Reservoirs	50-100	L. Metcalf Wis. R. R. comm.

BRYAN, WILLIAM. Appraisal and depreciation of water-works and similar properties. *Journal of the Association of engineering societies,* Dec. 1907, p. 336-81. Depreciation allowance for various public service industries. *Engineering news,* Jan. 23, 1908, p. 96.

	Years
Reservoirs	50-75
"	40-75
"	100

CHASE, HARVEY STUART. Depreciation in waterworks accounts, with reference to uniform reports. *Journal of the New England waterworks association,* June 1910, p. 305-31. Abstract. *Engineering and contracting,* June 29, 1910, p. 598. Editorial. Depreciation and sinking fund accounts. *Municipal engineering,* July 1910, p. 26.

CLADER, WILL-A. Water utilities accounting. *Journal of accountancy,* Aug. 1919, p. 91-2.

The following rates are used frequently when wear and tear are made good by operating maintenance:

Large reservoirs	1%
Small reservoirs	2

ESTIMATED life and depreciation of water works plants. *Municipal journal and engineer,* May 6, 1908, p. 558.

		Authority
Reservoirs	50-75 years	W. Kiersted: Pro. Am. soc. C. E. 1897.
"	40-75	W. H. Bryan
"	100	C. B. Burdick; Mt. Vernon, Ill., app. in 1906.

FOSTER, HORATIO A. Rates of depreciation. (In his *Engineering valuation of public utilities and factories.* 1913. p. 204).

Reservoirs 50-100 years

GILLETTE, HALBERT P. and RICHARD T. DANA. Depreciation. (In their *Handbook of mechanical and electrical cost data.* 1918. p. 109).

Reservoirs	33.3-50 years	H. P. Gillette, Everett railway and water co., Jan. 29, 1912.
Rservoirs (except where subject to heavy deposit of silt)	50-100 years	Leonard Metcalf, Transactions American society of civil engineers, 1909, p. 24. vol. 64.

GRUNSKY, CARL EWALD. Probable useful life of various articles. (In his *Valuation, depreciation and the rate-base.* 1917. p. 282-3).

Reservoirs	50-100 years	Leonard Metcalf. Transactions American society of civil engineers, 1909.
	100 years	Chas. B. Burdick. Appraisal of Mt. Vernon, waterworks, Illinois, 1906.
earthen	100 years	California railroad commission—Reports 1913-4. Cuyamaca water co. case, March, 1913.

HAZLEHURST, J. N. Final report of the committee on depreciation. *Journal of the American waterworks association,* March 1919, p. 85-135.

Large storage reservoirs, well located	75-150 years
Reservoirs	15-75

METCALF, LEONARD. Depreciation in waterworks operation and accounting. *Journal of the New England waterworks association,* Dec. 1910, p. 442. Abstracts. *Engineering news,* Nov. 3, 1910, p. 482. Methods of computing depreciation of and reasonable assumptions as to period of useful life of waterworks. *Engineering and contracting,* Nov. 16, 1910, p. 434.

Reservoirs	50-100 years	2-1% straight line

METCALF, LEONARD. Water-works valuation and fair rates, in the light of the Maine supreme court decisions in the Waterville and Brunswick cases. *American society of civil engineers, Papers and discussions,* 1908, p. 1101-73. *American society of civil engineers, Transactions,* Sept. 1909, p. 1. Foster, H. A. *Engineering valuation of public utilities and factories.* 1913. p. 207. Gillette, H. P. *Handbook of cost data for contractors and engineers,* 1910, p. 797.

Reservoirs 50-100 years

NICHOLSON, J. LEE and JOHN F. D. ROHRBACH. Depreciation. (In their *Cost accounting.* 1919. p. 149).

Tanks and reservoirs

steel	4½%
wood	8

Based on (1) the cost of equipment
(2) the life of the equipment
(3) on a ten-hour day.

DEPRECIATION, DEPLETION AND OBSOLESCENCE—RESERVOIRS—*(Continued)*

PHILADELPHIA. CONTROLLER. Rates of depreciation. (In his *Manual of accounting, reporting and business procedure of the city and county of Philadelphia.* 1917. p. 210).

Reservoirs, basins, forebays, etc.	3⅓%

PIEZ, CHARLES. Perpetual inventory and appraisal values; table of standard depreciation rates. *Engineering and contracting,* Jan. 24, 1917, p. 77. *Factory,* Dec. 1916, p. 668-71. *Iron age,* Nov. 30, 1916, Jan. 11, 1917, p. 1227, 138-9. *Iron trade review,* Feb. 22, 1917, p. 477-8. Condensed. *Journal of the American society of mechanical engineers,* Dec. 1916, p. 965-6. *Iron trade review,* Dec. 7, 1916, p. 1144-6. Kent, William. *Bookkeeping and cost accounting for factories.* 1918. p. 90. Discussion. *Journal of the American society of mechanical engineers,* March 1917, p. 215-7).

	% on cost	% on reducing balance
Tanks and reservoirs, steel	4.5	10
" " " wood	9	20
(Ten years)		

PROBABLE lives of waterworks elements. *Engineering news,* Oct. 11, 1917, p. 688.

	Years
Large storage reservoirs, well located	75-150
Small distribution reservoirs	50-75

WOLFF, MARK. Interpretation of waterworks accounts. *Journal of the American waterworks association,* June 1916, p. 543, 546.

Reservoirs, aqueducts	100 years

Restaurants, cafes, etc.

AUSTRALIA. FEDERAL INCOME TAX DEPARTMENT. Depreciation allowance. *Accountant,* Oct. 13, 1917, p. 277-9. *Accounting and commerce,* June 30, 1917, p. 55-7. *Federal accountant,* July 1917, p. 93-8. *Public accountant,* Jan. 30, 1917, p. 145-52.

Restaurants
Replacements and repairs allowable.

ELBOURNE, EDWARD T. Depreciation rates. (In his *Factory administration and accounts.* 1918. p. 377).

	Prov. dep. %	Years Remainder values 10%	5%
Mess room appliances	7½	29	38

NICHOLSON, J. LEE and JOHN F. D. ROHRBACH. Depreciation. (In their *Cost accounting.* 1919. p. 151).

Restaurant equipment	10%

Based on (1) the cost of equipment
(2) the life of the equipment
(3) on a ten-hour day

Restoration

See Depreciation, depletion and obsolescence—Rebuilding.

Retail trade

See also Depreciation, depletion and obsolescence—Shoe trade.

MONTGOMERY, ROBERT H. Miscellaneous data for retail and department stores. (In his *Auditing theory and practice.* 1916. p. 622).

	Depreciation and shrinkage %
Jewelry	.95
Retail clothing	1.16
Drugs	.47
Department store	1.61
Furniture	2.14
Mail order	.12
Shoes	.50
Vehicles and implements	.62
Dry goods	1.11
Hardware	.52
Variety	.06
Grocery	.76

Depreciation and shrinkage includes depreciation on all equipment and irregular losses from stock, besides customary shrinkage from perishable goods.

TIFFANY, H. S. Depreciation. (In his *Digest of depreciations.* c1890. p. 13, 16, 17).

Dry goods	12½%
Military, knight templar and other society goods.	30-50
Notions	
Wholesale	12½
Retail	25
Wooden and willow ware	10
Queensware	5

TIFFANY, H. S. Stocks in retail country stores. (In his *Digest of depreciations.* c1890. p. 18).

Boots and shoes—Depreciate annually	15%
Clothing—Depreciates first year	20
" second year	30
Dry goods—Depreciate annually	15
Groceries— " "	10
Hardware—Depreciates annually	15
Hats and caps—Depreciate annualy	20
Laces—Depreciate annually	25
Notions— " "	25
Queensware—Depreciates annually	10
Ribbons—Depreciate annually	25
Soap—Depreciate annually	5
Straw goods—Depreciate annually	50
Woolen and willow ware—Depreciate annually	15
Miscellaneous goods—Depreciate annually	20

DEPRECIATION, DEPLETION AND OBSOLESCENCE—*(Continued)*

Retort plants

CLASSIFICATION of depreciation percentages used at Dusseldorf municipal gas works. *Progressive age,* Aug. 15, 1910, p. 707.

	Present %	Prop. scale %	Life, years
Retort settings and apparatus	10	7.5	22-29

FOSTER, HORATIO A. Rates of depreciation. (In his *Engineering valuation of public utilities and factories.* 1913. p. 207).

Retort house floors, depending on construction 15-30 years

GRUNSKY, CARL EWALD. Probable useful life of various articles. (In his *Valuation, depreciation and the rate-base.* 1917. p. 283).

Retort house floors 15-30 years.
Wisconsin railroad commission. Quoted by H. A. Foster and in published reports.

GUTHRIE, EDWIN. Depreciation. (In Lisle, George. *Encyclopaedia of accounting.* v.2. p. 375).
Gas works
Retorts, furnaces, etc. 10% on original outlay, plus a renewal fund for term of life chargeable to revenue.

INFLUENCE of operating costs upon the economy of retort producers. *Progressive age,* Aug. 1, 1912, p. 660.

For depreciation of the retort plant about 11 to 12 per cent of the original cost will be found to be sufficient for all purposes.
For repairs and general maintenance about ⅔% of the original installation cost should be laid aside.
Building—0.3% of the original installation cost
Horizontal retorts—3% of the original installation cost
Vertical retorts—2% of the original installation cost
Conveying installation 3% of the original installation cost

Buildings, including chimneys and foundations	1.5%
Producer plant including flues, etc., without retorts	4
Retorts, figuring on 1,000 operating days	36.5
Engines, machines and conveying systems	5

Riveters

ELBOURNE, EDWARD T. Depreciation rates. (In his *Factory administration and accounts.* 1918. p. 377).

	Prov. dep. % Remainder values	Years 10%	5%
Riveters			
pneumatic	7½	29	38
hydraulic	7½	29	38
steam	7½	29	38

NICHOLSON, J. LEE and JOHN F. D. ROHRBACH. Depreciation. (In their *Cost accounting.* 1919. p. 149).

Pneumatic riveters 6⅔%

Roads and highways

LIFE of road construction equipment. *Engineering and contracting,* Jan. 3, 1917, p. 3.

Steam shovels	10%
Engines, gas or steam	20
Concrete mixers	20
Rock crushers	20
Pile drivers	20
Graders	20
Plows	20
Wagons and harness	20
Mules	10
Wheelbarrows	50
Concrete carts	50
Fresno scrapers	100
Tents	75

NICHOLSON, J. LEE and JOHN F. D. ROHRBACH. Depreciation. (In their *Cost accounting.* 1919. p. 146).

Roadways and sidewalks 4%
Based on (1) the cost of equipment
(2) the life of the equipment
(3) on a ten-hour day

PHILADELHIA. CONTROLLER. Rates of depreciation. (In his *Manual of accounting, reporting and business procedure of the city and county of Philadelphia.* 1917. p. 210, 206).

Roads	10%
Streets	2
Road making machinery	16⅔

PIEZ, CHARLES. Perpetual inventory and appraisal values; table of standard depreciation rates. *Engineering and contracting,* Jan. 24, 1917, p. 77. *Factory,* Dec. 1916, p. 668-71. *Iron age,* Nov. 30, 1916, Jan. 11, 1917, p. 1266, 138-9. *Iron trade review,* Feb. 22, 1917, p. 477-8. Condensed. *Iron trade review,* Dec. 7, 1916, p. 1144-6. *Journal of the American society of mechanical engineers,* Dec. 1916, p. 965-6. Kent, William. *Bookkeeping and cost accounting for factories.* 1918. p. 90. Discussion. *Journal of the American society of mechanical engineers,* March 1917, p. 215-7.

	% on cost	% on reducing balance
Roadways	4.5	10

UNIFORM cost sheet for coal mining companies. *Coal age,* Sept. 19, 1918, p. 545-7.

	% original cost
Wagon roads	5
Good roads machinery	10

DEPRECIATION, DEPLETION AND OBSOLESCENCE—*(Continued)*

Roll trains

NICHOLSON, J. LEE and JOHN F. D. ROHRBACH. Depreciation. (In their *Cost accounting*. 1919. p. 149).
Roll trains 5½%

Roller feeders

NICHOLSON, J. LEE and JOHN F. D. ROHRBACH. Depreciation. (In their *Cost accounting*. 1919. p. 150).
Roller feeders 10%

Rolling equipment

PHILADELPHIA. CONTROLLER. Rates of depreciation. (In his *Manual of accounting, reporting and business procedure of the city and county of Philadelphia*. 1917. p. 205).
Metal work equipment
Hammering, rolling and welding equipment 5%

Rolling mills

MATHESON, EWING. Rolling mills. (In his *Depreciation of factories, mines and industrial undertakings and their valuation*. 1893. p. 41-2).
For first four years 7½-10-20%

TIFFANY, H. S. Rolling mills and nail works. (In his *Digest of depreciations*. c1890. p. 10).
Buildings
brick 2½%
frame 4
Based upon the actual life without any repairs

Rolling stock

See also Depreciation, depletion and obsolescence—Locomotives.

AUSTRALIA. FEDERAL INCOME TAX DEPARTMENT. Depreciation allowance. *Accountant*, Oct. 13, 1917, p. 277-9. *Accounting and commerce*, June 30, 1917, p. 55-7. *Federal accountant*, July 1917, p. 93-8. *Public accountant*, Jan. 30, 1917, p. 145-52.
Rolling stock used on trai nlines 2½
Written down value, repairs allowed in addition.

BARKER, HARRY. Depreciation of electric railway property. (In his *Public utility rates*. 1917. p. 367).

Cars	30 years. B. J. Arnold.
Car bodies, open type	25 years. Chicago trac. val. comm.
closed type	20 years. Chicago trac. val. comm.
Trucks	30 years. Chicago trac. val. comm.
Motors	5 years. Wisconsin Railroad Commission H. Floy
Misc. elec. equipment	10-15 years. Author—average or approximate figures secured by examination or enquiry.

BARKER HARRY. Typical life expectation tables for public utility property. (In his *Public utility rates*. 1917. p. 366).

Cars, freight, wood	10-20 years
steel	15-30
passenger wood	20-25
steel	25-30
dining, parlor and sleeping,	
wood	15-20
steel	20-25

Author—Average or approximate figures secured by examination or enquiry.

BARNUM, M. K. Life and maintenance of all-steel cars. *Railway age gazette*, March 4, 1916, p. 389-94.
A discussion of the life, rates of depreciation, rebuilding and painting of steel cars.
Conclusions:
(1) The average age of steel gondola and hopper cars will probably be about 16 years.
(2) The depreciation of steel gondola and hopper cars should be calculated at about 5%.

BAY state rate case. *Electric railway journal*, Dec. 4, 1915, p. 1121-3. *Public utility reports, Annotated*, 1916F, p. 336-9.

Cars and car equipment.	Years	% Dep.
Bodies		
D.T. semis	20	
S.T. semis	22	
D.T. box	25	
S.T. box	28	
D.T. open	25	
S.T. open	30	
Express	20	
Snow-plows	18-20	
Trucks	10-20	
Motors	20	
Controllers	25	
Control cable	Life of car	
Air-brake compressers	20	
Registers	18	

DEPRECIATION, DEPLETION AND OBSOLESCENCE—Rolling stock—*(Continued)*

Arc headlights	8	
Jacks and saws	25	
Passenger and combination cars		4.6
Freight, express and mail cars		5.1
Service equipment		5.2
Electric equipment of cars		4.4

Annual depreciation per cent, annual depreciation divided by investment.

Bryan, William. Appraisal and depreciation of water-works and similar properties. *Journal of the association of engineering societies* Dec. 1907, p. 336-81. Depreciation allowance for various public-service industries. *Engineering magazine,* Jan. 23, 1908, p. 96.

	years	% straight
Cars	15-25	
Bodies		7
Motors	12.5-20	
Trucks		8

Car depreciation. *Electric railway journal,* June 16, 1917, p. 1080.
An editorial discussing the question as to what is the life of an electric car.
"The average of eight estimates on car depreciation gleaned at random from utility commission, consulting engineers and operating company reports is 6.8 per cent. This corresponds to a life of approximately 15 years.

Cravens, George W. Depreciation and maintenance of electrical equipment. *Electrical review,* April 23, 1910 p. 853-6. Foster, H. A. *Engineering valuation of public utilities and factories,* 1913. p. 201-2.

	Light or intermittent service	Heavy or continuous service
Cars and equipments	5-8.3%	6.6-10%

Cars	Annual % Dep.	
	5-8.5	Chicago union traction co.
	6-7.5	Milwaukee electric railway & light co.
	5-6.6	Wisconsin railroad commission.
	10	Average English
	7.5	Average Scotch practice
	4.6	Philip Dawson
	5-8.5	Stone and Webster
	7.5	Miscellaneous sources.

Dawson, Philip. Depreciation. (In his *Engineering and electric traction pocket-book.* Ed. 2. p. 1161).

	% capital cost
Cars	4-6

Depreciation funds in Europe. *Electric railway journal,* May 7, 21, 1904, p. 696, 760.

Rolling stock	Years	% of cost
Brussels—cars	25	
Cyernowitz railway		3
Glasgow		7⅓
Leipziger Strassenbahn		8
Mannheim motor cars		7
trail cars		5
Remscheid		10

Depreciation of equipment. *Engineering and contracting,* Nov. 19, 1913, p. 567-8.

Motor cars	2%
Passenger cars released	3
Coal cars released	3
Steel passenger and freight cars	3

Floy, Henry. Depreciation. Floy, Henry. Depreciation as related to electrical properties. *American institute of electrical engineers, Proceedings,* 1911, p. 1267. Floy, Henry. *Valuation of public utility properties.* 1912. p. 168-217. Foster, Horatio A. *Engineering valuation of public utilities and factories.* 1913. p. 194-8. *Engineering and contracting,* Oct. 4, 1911, p. 359-65. *Engineering magazine,* Aug. 1911. p. 837-40.

Property	Dep. % per year straight line	Authority	Remarks
Rolling stock			
Open car bodies	4	Trac. Val. Comm.	Chic. con. tract. co.
Open trailer bodies	4	Trac. Val. Comm.	Chic. con. tract. co.
Closed car bodies	5	Trac. Val. Comm.	Chic. con. tract. co.
Trucks	3⅓	Trac. Val. Comm.	Chic. con. tract. co.
Closed and open cars	5	B. J. Arnold	Coney Island & Brooklyn, adopted by P. S. C., N. Y.
Trucks	5	B. J. Arnold	Coney Island & Brooklyn, adopted by P. S. C., N. Y.
	5	Henry Floy	3rd Ave. case, adopted by P. S. C., N. Y.
Car bodies and equipment	6⅔	Wisconsin P. S. C.	

Foster, Horatio A. Rates of depreciation. (In his *Engineering valuation of public utilities and factories.* 1913. p. 200).

Rolling stock	
cars (including all equipment)	5.0%
utility equipment	5.0

Marwick, Mitchell & Co. in the appraisal of a large street railway system.

Foster, Horatio A. Rules for depreciating railways and lighting plants in Great Britain. 1918, p. 167.
Cars and other rolling stock.
7% per annum on the written-down value.

DEPRECIATION, DEPLETION AND OBSOLESCENCE—ROLLING STOCK—*(Continued)*

GILLETTE, HALBERT P. and RICHARD T. DANA. Depreciation. (In their *Handbook of mechanical and electrical cost data.* 1918. p. 109-10).

Rolling stock, cars electric	13.3-16.7 years. Milwaukee electric railway & light co.
Cars including all equipment	20 years. Marwick, Mitchell & Co., appraisal of a large street railway system, Foster, p. 199.
bodies closed cars	20 years. Traction valuation commission, Chicago consolidated traction co.
cars, bodies open cars	25 years. Traction valuation commission, Chicago consolidated traction co.
bodies open trailer	25 years. Traction valuation commission, Chicago consolidated traction co.
cars, bodies, trucks	12.5 years. Prof. M. E. Cooley, Milwaukee 3c case.
	15 years Beegs, Milwaukee 3c case.
	15-20 years. W. D. Pence, Milwaukee 3c case.
	16.7 years. M. G. Starret, Milwaukee 3c case.
	20 years. Union traction co., case Chicago and Union traction co., Stone & Webster.
car bodies and equipment	15 years. Wisconsin railroad commission.
electrical equipment	3.3-4-8.5 years B. J. Arnold, Chicago appraisals, 4 cases.
equipment electrical	11.75-15 years. Union traction co., case Chicago and Union traction co., Stone & Webster.
trucks	20 years. Henry Floy, 3rd ave. case, N. Y. City.
	30 years. Traction valuation commission, Chicago consolidated traction co.
utility equipment	20 years. Marwick, Mitchell & co., appraisal of a large street railway system, Foster, p. 199.
cars, wooden, freight	27.5 years.

GRAY, HENRY L. Necessity of depreciation reserves. *Railway age gazette,* May 27, 1910, p. 1297-8. Editorial. Depreciation reserves. *Railway age gazette,* May 27, 1910, p. 1290. Letters. Depreciation reserves. *Railway age gazette,* July 8, 1910, p. 66.

Passenger cars (steam)	3%
" " (electric)	5
Freight cars (steam)	4
" " (electric)	4
Electric equipment of cars	5

GREAT BRITAIN. BOARD OF INLAND REVENUE. Depreciation rates: (In its *Income tax; statement respecting allowances for wear and tear and obsolescence of plant and machinery.* 1918. Cd. 9022, p. 4; Cd. 9134, p. 6.) *American economic review,* Supplement, Dec. 1920, p. 51. *Journal of accountancy,* Sept. 1920, p. 195.

Cars, rolling stock and tramways	7%
Railway wagons	5
Written down value.	

Note: The allowance applies to all wagons owned by traders. In case of railway companies the method adopted is to allow the actual cost of renewals year by year.

GREENLINGER, S. W. Depreciation. *Mississippi electric association, Report of 2nd annual convention,* June 1910, p. 32-6.

	Life
Car bodies, closed	18 years
Car equipment, electric	15

GRUNSKY, CARL EWALD. Probable useful life of various articles. (In his *Valuation, depreciation and the rate-base.* 1917. p. 283).

Rolling stock	
Street railway	12.5 years. Mortimer E. Cooley. Milwaukee 3c fare case. Report Wisconsin R. R. Commission, vol. 10, p. 226.
Street railway	16.7 years. Milton G. Starrett. Milwaukee 3c fare case. Report Wisconsin R. R. Commission, vol. 10, p. 226.
Street railway	15-20 years. Wisconsin railroad commission. Milwaukee 3c fare case. Aug. 23, 1912.
Railroad	28 years. H. P. Gillette. Appraisal of Great Northern & Northern Pacific R. R.'s in Washington. Direction of Washington railroad commission.
Railroad locomotives	20-35 years. W. G. Wilgus. Appraisal of Lehigh valley railroad, January, 1914.
Railroad passenger cars	35-40 years. 30-40% residual value. W. G. Wilgus. Appraisal of Lehigh valley railroad, January, 1914.

DEPRECIATION, DEPLETION AND OBSOLESCENCE—ROLLING STOCK—*(Continued)*

Railroad freight cars	30-50 years. 25% residual value. W. G. Wilgus. Appraisal of Lehigh valley railroad, January, 1914.
Street railway cars	30 years. Bion J. Arnold. Coney Island and Brooklyn figures adopted by Public service commission of New York. Four Chicago appraisals quoted by H. A. Foster.
Street railway bodies	15 years. Wisconsin railroad commission. Milwaukee 3c fare case. Aug. 23, 1912.
Stret railway open bodies	25 years. Traction valuation commission. Case of the Chicago consolidated traction co.
Street railway closed bodies	20 years. Traction valuation commission. Case of the Chicago consolidated traction co.
Street ry. bodies and trucks	13.3 years. Milwaukee electric railway and lighting co. in the Milwaukee 3c fare case, Aug. 1912.
Street ry. bodies and trucks	20 years. Chicago union traction co. Quoted in report Wisconsin R. R. commission, vol. 10, p. 220.
Street ry. bodies and trucks	20 years. Stone & Webster. Figures for Chicago union traction co. case. Report Wisconsin railroad commission, vol. 10, p. 220.
Street railway trucks	15-20 years. Wisconsin railroad commission. Milwaukee 3c fare case, Aug. 23, 1912.
Street railway trucks	30 years. Traction valuation commission. Case of the Chicago consolidated traction co.
Street railway trucks	30 years. Bion J. Arnold. Coney Island and Brooklyn figures adopted by Public service commission of New York.
Street railway elec. equipment	10 years. Milwaukee electric railway and lighting co. in the Milwaukee 3c fare case, Aug. 1912.
Street railway elec. equipment	12-15 years. Chicago union traction co. Quoted in Report Wisconsin R. R. commission, vol. 10, p. 220.
Street railway elec. equipment	12-15 years. Stone & Webster. Figures for Chicago union traction co. case. Report Wisconsin railroad commission, vol. 10, p. 220.
Street railway elec. equipment	10-20 years. Wisconsin railroad commission. Milwaukee 3c fare case, Aug. 23, 1912.
St. ry. fenders and fenders	15 years. Wisconsin railroad commission. Milwaukee 3c fare case, Aug. 23, 1912.

GUTHRIE, EDWIN. Depreciation. (In Lisle, George. *Encyclopaedia of accounting.* v. 2, p. 374),

	Diminishing value
Rolling stock	5-10%

HEARING on electric railway mail pay. *Electric railway journal,* Feb. 15, 1913, p. 291.

INCOME tax and depreciation allowance. *Accountant,* May 30, 1914, p. 785-8.

Tramways	Written down value
Cars and other rolling stock	7%

INCOME tax notes. *Accountant,* May 11, Sept. 28, 1918, p. 359, 162-6. *Incorporated accountants' journal,* May, Oct. 1918, p. 157, 14.

Written down value	
Railway wagons	5%
Cars and other rolling stock	7

(a) The allowance applies to all wagons owned by traders.
(b) In the case of railway companies the method adopted is to allow the actual cost of renewals year by year.

INITIAL cost, cost of maintenance and depreciation of wooden passenger cars. *Engineering and contracting,* Sept. 7, 1910, p. 215.

Class of cars	Rate of Dep. per year %
Coaches	3.4
Comb. pass. & bagg. cars	3.25
Chair cars (owned by railroad)	3.7
Sleeping cars (owned by railroad)	3.33
Parlor cars (owned by railroad)	3.4
Tourist cars (owned by railroad)	3.5

DEPRECIATION, DEPLETION AND OBSOLESCENCE—Rolling stock—*(Continued)*

Colonist cars (owned by railroad)	3
Baggage cars	3.5
Express cars	3.7
Dining cars	3.4
Comb. baggage & mail cars	3.5
Postal cars	3.4
Postal storage cars	4

Institute of municipal treasurers and accountants (incorporated). Municipal corporations and companies working tramways and light railway gas, water and electricity undertakings. *Accountant*, June 26, 1909, p. 906-8. Income tax assessment: allowances for depreciation. *Accountant*, Oct. 2, 1909, p. 423-5, 400-2.
Cars and other rolling stock.
Subject to the ensuing clause expenditure on maintenance and renewals should be treated as working expenses and allowed in lieu of depreciation.
Depreciation, however, should be allowed in lieu of renewals where circumstances justify such an allowance * * * 7% per annum on the written down value.

Leake, P. D. Record of depreciation. (In his *Depreciation and wasting assets and their treatment in computing annual profit and loss.* 1917. p. 86).
Cars 4-6%

Life of different parts of car equipment before and after using recording Wattmeters on card at Cape Town. *Journal of the tramways and light railway association*, Sept. 1911, p. 241.

Life of elements in subway property. *Electric railway journal*, April 6, 1912, p. 575.

	Years
Copper-sheathed car at	30
Steel cars	40

Lock, Fred J. Depreciation. (In his *West African mining accounts.* 1910. p. 88-9).
Light locomotives and rolling stock 12½%

London tramway depreciation for income tax. *Electric railway journal*, Feb. 12, 1910, p. 274.
Dep. 7 per cent in written-down capital cost of cars.

Lyn, Samuel. Life of a steel freight car. *Railway age gazette*, Jan. 7, 1916, p. 10-1.
Wooden cars of either the box or gondola type 20 years.

Metropolitan street railway reorganization plan. *Electric railway journal*, May 20, 1911, p. 876-8.

	Years
Rolling stock, electric	30
" " horse	33⅓

Montgomery, Robert H. Electrical equipment manufacturers. (In his *Income tax procedure* 1919. p. 563. ——— Same, 1920. p. 716).
Rolling stock 12%
Based on gross book values at the end of the preceding year.

Montgomery, Robert H. Steam railroads. In his *Auditing theory and practice*, 1916. p. 652).
Pennsylvania railroad company sets aside for depreciation, renewals and obsolescence 3% on freight cars and 4% upon passenger cars and locomotives.

Municipal trading and depreciation. *Accountant*, June 8, July 6, 1901, p. 657-9, 769-71.
Cars 10%

Nay, F. Depreciation of rolling stock equipment. *Railway and engineering review*, Dec. 27, 1913, p. 1205.
Those who advocate depreciation claim that the life of a car or a locomotive may be approximated as 20, 30 or 40 years.

Neale, R. E. Depreciation in engineering works. *Mechanical world*, Feb. 7, 1913, p. 67-8.

Tramways	%	Years
Rolling stock		
American figs. (trucks)	3-5	20-33
(bodies)	3-6	17-33
English figs.	5-75	13-20
General	7	14

(1909 agreement between inland revenue and certain municipal tramway associations. These allowances generally considered to be insufficient.)

Nelson, Bailie Walter. Limitation and depletion of profits from municipal undertakings. *Incorporated accountants' journal*, Oct. 1912, p. 15-7.

On cars	7½%
On electrical equipment of cars	8.79
On other rolling stock	10.15

Obsolescence in cars. *Electric railway journal*, Aug. 17, 1912, p. 239.

Official allowance in respect of machinery and plant—Board of Inland revenue, Great Britain. *Accountant*, May 16, 1914, p. 737.
Cars and other rolling stock.—Subject to the ensuing clause, expenditure on maintenance and renewals should be treated as working and allowed in lieu of depreciation. Depreciation, however, should be allowed in lieu of renewals where the circumstances justify such an allowance, provided that a strict account is in computing the assessable profits.

Pender, Harold. Depreciation. (In his *Handbook for electrical engineers.* c1914. p. 338).

Cars	Years	%	
electric complete	15		Elberfeld railway
	17		Heidelberg railway
Bodies and trucks	15		J. I. Beggs
	15-20		Engineer of valuation staff of Wisconsin railroad commission.
	20		Chicago Union traction co. Stone & Webster for the Chicago Union traction co.
		10	Cardiff tramways
		7.5	Milwaukee electric railway and light co.
		7	Glasgow tramways—Chicago city railways.

DEPRECIATION, DEPLETION AND OBSOLESCENCE—Rolling stock—*(Continued)*

6.66	J. I. Beggs.
6.66-5	Engineer of valuation staff of Wisconsin railroad commission.
5	Chicago union traction co. Third Ave. railroad (New York City) Stone & Webster, Chicago union traction.

Philadelphia. Controller. Rates of depreciation. (In his *Manual of accounting, reporting and business procedure of the city and county of Philadelphia.* 1917. p. 206).
Couplings, fenders, and other mechanical appliances 4%

Pixley, Francis W. Tramways. (In his *Accountancy.* Ed. 2. p. 218-9).
Rolling stock from 7½-15%

Prices for labor and material. *Railway age gazette,* June 17, 1913, p. 1459-60.
Wooden car bodies, 7% per annum upon the yearly depreciated value.
Wooden car bodies with steel center sills, 6% per annum upon the yearly depreciated value.
All steel car bodies, 5% per annum upon the yearly depreciated value.
Tanks or tank cars for handling non-corrosive substances, 4% per annum upon the yearly depreciated value.
Tanks or tank cars for handling corrosive substances, 5% per annum upon the yearly depreciated value.
Trucks other than all metal, 7% per annum upon the yearly depreciated value.
All metal trucks, 5% per annum upon the yearly depreciated value.
Allowance for depreciation in no case to exceed on:
Wooden car bodies, 80% of original value.
Steel underframe or all steel car bodies, 60% of original value.
Trucks other than all metal, 70% of original value.
All metal trucks, 60% of original value.
Wooden car bodies with steel center sills, 70% of original value.

Public utility reports, annotated. Rochester, Lawyers co-operative publishing co. 1915C. p. 711.
Re Manila R. Co. (P.I.) A proper and adequate annual rate of depreciation of locomotives, passenger train cars was found by the Philippine Islands public utilities commission to be 3 per cent * * * of their original cost, ledger value or purchase price.

Public utility reports, annotated. Rochester, Lawyers co-operative publishing co. 1918A.
New York & N. S. traction co.

Revenue cars	3%
Electric equipment of cars	4
Miscellaneous equipment	3

Public utility reports, annotated. Rochester, Lawyers co-operative publishing co. 1918C, p. 534.
Springfield street R. co.
Rolling stock 3.71%

Recording depreciation on rolling stock. *Railway age gazette,* March 17, 1911, p. 512.

Roby, J. J. Schedule of plant depreciation. (In his *Treatise on cost accounting as applied to coal mining.* c1913. p. 14-5).

Mine cars	
wood	
deduct as salvage before depreciating	10%
depreciation rate for remainder, fireproof	20
Steel	
deduct as salvage before depreciating	15
depreciation rate for remainder, fireproof	12
Special cars and equipment	
deduct as salvage before depreciating	10
depreciation rate for remainder, fireproof	20

Rolling stock depreciation. *Street railway journal,* Aug. 17, 1907, p. 240.

Uniform rates of depreciation for the settlement of cars destroyed on foreign roads recommended by a committee of the Master Car Builders' association. *Railway age gazette,* June 15, 1916, p. 1302-1305.

Wooden cars, all classes, except refrigerator cars	5%
All-steel cars, all classes, including steel tanks of tank cars	3
Wooden cars, steel framed, or steel-underframed or both	4
Refrigerator cars, all wood	7
Refrigerator cars, steel framed or steel-underframed, or both	6

Weeks, H. E. Abstract of paper in depreciation read before annual meeting of Iowa street and interurban railway association, April 1910. *Electric railway journal,* April 30, 1910, p. 782-3.

Car bodies	15 years
Car equipment	10

Williamson, J. Gilmour. Depreciation of assets. (In his *Counting house and factory organization.* p. 142).
Locomotives and rolling stock 10%

Roof supports

Roby, J. J. Schedule of plant depreciation. (In his *Treatise on cost accounting as applied to coal mining.* c1913. p. 14-5.

Steel roof supports	
Deduct as salvage before depreciating	20%
Depreciation rate for remainder	10

Rope

See Depreciation, depletion and obsolescence—Cordage

Rotaries

Bolton, Reginald Pelham. Depreciation of mechanical equipments and power plants. In his *Building for profit.* 1911. p. 82, 89).

	Physical years	%	Economic years
Moderate-speed reciprocating engines, medium-speed rotary apparatus, dynamos and motors	15	37.5	12

DEPRECIATION, DEPLETION AND OBSOLESCENCE—ROTARIES—*(Continued)*

Fan engines, high-speed rotary apparatus on large variations of loads, dynamos, motors, high-pressure engines, condensers 12 30.0 9

CROWELL, H. H. Electric lighting and depreciation. *Municipal journal of engineers,* Dec. 18, 1907, p. 698.

	Purchased 10 years or more ago	Modern
Rotaries	15 years	15 years

FOSTER, HORATIO A. Methods of calculating depreciation. (In his *Engineering valuation of public utilities and factories.* 1913. p. 169).

Electric generators	Modern type	20%
Motors and rotaries	Obsolete type	15

Joint engineering department of the Wisconsin commission.

FOSTER, HORATIO A. Rates of depreciation. (In his *Engineering valuation of public utilities and factories.* 1913. p. 200).

Rotaries, transformers, switch-board, auxiliaries 4.5%

Marwick, Mitchell & co. in the appraisal of a large street railway system.

GILLETTE, HALBERT P. and RICHARD T. DANA. Depreciation. (In their *Handbook of mechanical and electrical cost data.* 1918. p. 110).

Rotaries 22.2 years.

Marwick, Mitchell & co. appraisal of a large street railway system, Foster, p. 199.

Roundhouses

GILLETTE, HALBERT POWERS. Railways. (In his *Handbook of cost data for contractors and engineers.* 1912. p. 1317-8).

	Age years	Annual % dep.	Present Cond. %
Roundhouses and shops	5.5	3.0	83.5

GILLETTE, HALBERT P. and RICHARD T. DANA. Depreciation. (In their *Handbook of mechanical and electrical cost data.* 1918. p. 106).

Building, roundhouses, 33.3 years. H. P. Gillette, Washington ry. appraisal.

Rubber

STEWART, R. S. and F. C. EBBELS. Depreciation (In their *Rubber companies' accounts.* 1916. p. 83).

Buildings 12½% on original cost.
Furniture 20.
Machinery 20.
Temporary building written off entirely in 2 years.

TIFFANY, H. S. Rubber goods. (In his *Digest of depreciations.* c1890. p. 17).

10%

Rugs

See Depreciation, depletion and obsolescence—Carpets, rugs, etc.

Safes

AUSTRALIA. FEDERAL INCOME TAX DEPARTMENT. Depreciation allowance. *Accountant,* Oct. 13, 1917, p. 277-9. *Accounting and commerce,* June 30, 1917, p. 55-7. *Federal accountnat,* July 1917, p. 93-8. *Public accountant,* Jan. 30, 1971, p. 145-52.

Safes. No depreciation.

PHILADELPHIA. CONTROLLER. Rates of depreciation. (In his *Manual of accounting, reporting and business procedure of the city and county of Philadelphia.* 1917. p. 207-8).

Vaults and safes 2%

Safety appliances

ROBY, J. J. Schedule of plant depreciation. (In his *Treatise on cost accounting as applied to coal mining.* c1913. p. 14-5).

Safety apliances, fire extinguishers.

Deduct as salvage before depreciating	10%
Depreciation on rate for remainder, fireproof	10

Salesmen

See Depreciation, depreciation and obsolescence—Commercial travellers.

Salt

TIFFANY, H. S. Saltworks. (In his *Digest of depreciations.* c1890. p. 10).

Frame saltworks 4%

Based upon the actual life without any repairs.

Sand blast machinery

BELT, ROBERT E. Depreciation. (In his *Foundry cost accounting practice and procedure.* 1919. p. 242).

Sand blast barrels and tables, with motor, shafting and belting 25%

BELT, ROBERT E. Depreciation. (In his *Uniform cost accounting methods; adopted by the American malleable castings association,* Nov. 14, 1917. p. 20-1).

Sand blast barrels and tables, with motor, shafting and belting 30%

ELBOURNE, EDWARD T. Depreciation rates. (In his *Factory administration and accounts.* 1918. p. 377).

	Prov. dep. % Remainder values 10%	Years	5%
Sand blast apparatus	12½	17	22

NICHOLSON, J. LEE and JOHN F. D. ROHRBACH. Depreciation. (In their *Cost accounting.* 1919. p. 150).

Sand blast machinery 10%

Sand dryers

NICHOLSON, J. LEE and JOHN F. D. ROHRBACH. Depreciation. (In their *Cost accounting.* 1919. p. 150).

Sand dryers 10%

DEPRECIATION, DEPLETION AND OBSOLESCENCE—*(Continued)*

Sand grinders and mixers

BELT, ROBERT E. Depreciation. (In his *Foundry cost accounting practice and procedure.* 1919. p. 242).
Sand mixers 15%

BELT, ROBERT E. Depreciation. (In his *Uniform cost accounting methods; adopted by the American malleable castings association,* Nov. 14, 1917, p. 20-1).
Sand mixer 20%

ELBOURNE, EDWARD T. Depreciation rates. (In his *Factory administration and accounts.* 1918. p. 377).

	Prov. dep. % Remainder values	Years 10%	5%
Sand grinders and mixers	12½	17	22

Sand houses

UNIFORM cost sheet for coal mining companies. *Coal age,* Sept. 19, 1918, p. 545-7.
Sand houses original cost 4%

Sanding machines

NICHOLSON, J. LEE and JOHN F. D. ROHRBACH. Depreciation. (In their *Cost accounting.* 1919. p. 150).
Woodworking machinery, sanding machines 5%

Saw mills

AUSTRALIA. FEDERAL INCOME TAX DEPARTMENT. Depreciation allowance. *Accountant,* Oct. 13, 1917, p. 277-9. *Accounting and commerce,* June 30, 1917, p. 55-7. *Federal accountant,* July 1917, p. 93-8. *Public accountant,* Jan. 30, 1917, p. 145-52.
Saw milling 7½%
Written down value, repairs allowed in addition.

GREAT BRITAIN. BOARD OF INLAND REVENUE. Depreciation rates. (In its *Income tax; statement respecting allowances for wear and tear and obsolescence of plant and machinery.* 1918. Cd. 9022, p. 4; Cd. 9134, p. 6). *American economic review,* Supplement, Dec. 1920, p. 51. *Journal of accountancy,* Sept. 1920, p. 195.
Timber merchants, saw millers, and manufacturers of timber goods.
Engine boilers and main shafting 5%
General saw milling plant machinery 7½
Traction engines, tractors, motor-cars, and haulage plant 20
Written down value.

MONTGOMERY, ROBERT H. Mine equipment. (In his *Income tax procedure,* 1919. p. 571. ——— Same, 1920. p. 724).
Saw mill 6⅔%

TIFFANY, H. S. Frame saw mills. (In his *Digest of depreciations.* c1890, p. 10).
Steam power 3½-4½%
Water power 2½-4½
Based upon the actual life of the building without any repairs.

UNIFORM cost sheet for coal mining companies. *Coal age,* Sept. 19, 1918, p. 545-7.
Saw mills original cost 10%

Saw setting machines

NICHOLSON, J. LEE and JOHN F. D. ROHRBACH. Depreciation. In their *Cost accounting.* 1919. p. 149).
Saw-setting and filing machines 6⅔%

Saw sharpening machines

ELBOURNE, EDWARD T. Depreciation rates. (In his *Factory administration and accounts.* 1918. p. 377).

	Prov. dep. % Remainder values	Years 10%	5%
Saw sharpening machines	7½	29	38

NICHOLSON, J. LEE and JOHN F. D. ROHRBACH. Depreciation. (In their *Cost accounting.* 1919. p. 149).
Saw-setting and filing machines 6⅔%

Saws

DENHAM, ROBERT S. Depreciation. (In his *Manual of cost engineering and estimating for paper box manufacturers.* 1917. p. 249).
Saws 10%

ELBOURNE, EDWARD T. Depreciation rates. (In his *Factory administration and accounts.* 1918. p. 377).

	Prov. dep. % Remainder values	Years 10%	5%
Sawing machines			
Metal, band	7½	29	38
Metal, circular	7½	29	38
Metal, hack	12½	17	22
Wood, band	6	37	48
Wood, circular	6	37	48

NICHOLSON, J. LEE and JOHN F. D. ROHRBACH. Depreciation. (In their *Cost accounting.* 1919. p. 149, 150).
Saw grinders, saw-setting and filing machines 6⅔%
Cold saws, hot saws 5½
Wood cut—off saws 5

DEPRECIATION, DEPLETION AND OBSOLESCENCE—*(Continued)*

Scales

AUSTRALIA. FEDERAL INCOME TAX DEPARTMENT. Depreciation allowance. *Accountant,* Oct. 13, 1917, p. 277-9. *Accounting and commerce,* June 30, 1917, p. 55-7. *Federal accountant,* July 1917, p. 93-8. *Public accountant,* Jan. 30, 1917, p. 145-52.

Scales (platform) 5%

Written down value, repairs allowed in addition.

BELT, ROBERT E. Depreciation. (In his *Foundry cost accounting practice and procedure.* 1919. p. 242).

Scales 10%

BELT, ROBERT E. Depreciation. (In his *Uniform cost accounting methods; adopted by the American malleable castings association,* Nov. 14, 1917, p. 20-1).

Scales 10%

BREWER, ALLAN F. Rates for annual depreciation. *Industrial management,* April 1918, p. 268.

Coal scale 20 years 5%

CROWELL, H. H. Electric lighting rates and depreciation. *Municipal journal and engineer,* Dec. 18, 1907, p. 698.

	Purchased 10 years or more ago	Modern
Railway tracks and scales	25 years	25 years

ELBOURNE, EDWARD T. Depreciation rates. (In his *Factory administration and accounts.* 1918. p. 376).

	Prov. dep. %	Years	
	Remainder values	10%	5%
Weighbridges	7½	29	38

NICHOLSON, J. LEE and JOHN F. D. ROHRBACH. Depreciation. (In their *Cost accounting.* 1919. p. 150).

Fixed kettles and scales 10%
Crane scales 10
Portable scales 10

NICHOLSON, J. LEE and JOHN F. D. ROHRBACH. Depreciation. (In their *Cost accounting.* 1919. p. 150).

Anvils, forges, bending blocks, surface plates, mandrels, porter bars, extractors, track and wagon scales, crane scales, portable scales, oil and powder cans, oil filters, glue pots, barrels, microscopes, pyrometers, calorimeters, storage batteries, air hose 10%

Schools, colleges, etc.

HUTCHINSON, J. HOWARD. Depreciation of buildings and equipment. (In his *School costs and school accounting.* 1914. p. 126, 137).

MARSHALL, HENRY CALDER. Depreciation. (In his *Polytechnic accounts.* 1902. p. 48, 62).

PHILADELPHIA. CONTROLLER. Rates of depreciation. (In its *Manual of accounting, reporting and business procedure of the city and county of Philadelphia.* 1917. p. 209).

Buildings:
School houses 1%
Schoolroom equipment 4%
Special and miscellaneous educational, scientific equipment 8⅓%

TIFFANY, H. S. Academies. (In his *Digest of depreciations.* c1890. p. 8).

Buildings
brick or stone
without dormitories 2½%
with " 3
frame
without " 3½
with " 4

Based upon the actual life of the building without any repairs.

TIFFANY, H. S. Churches and schoolhouses. (In his *Digest of depreciations.* c1890. p. 7).

Buildings
brick or stone 1½-2%
frame 3-3½%

UNIFORM cost sheet for coal mining companies. *Coal age,* Sept. 19, 1918, p. 545-7.

	original cost
Churches and schools	4%

Scorers

DENHAM, ROBERT S. Depreciation. (In his *Manual of cost engineering and estimating for paper box manufacturers.* 1917. p. 249).

	original cost
Scorers	10%

Scrap drops

NICHOLSON, J. LEE and JOHN F. D. ROHRBACH. Depreciation. (In their *Cost accounting.* 1919. p. 148).

Scrap drops 4%

Scrapers

LIFE of road construction equipment. *Engineering and contracting,* Jan. 3, 1917, p. 3.

Fresno scrapers 100% annual depreciation

PHILADELPHIA. CONTROLLER. Rates of depreciation. (In his *Manual of accounting, reporting and business procedure of the city and county of Philadelphia.* 1917. p. 208).

Snow shovels, ice scrapers and planers, etc. 12½%

Screening

ELBOURNE, EDWARD T. Depreciation rates. (In his *Factory administration and accounts.* 1918. p. 377).

	Prov. dep. %	Years	
	Remainder values	10%	5%
Screening machines	12½	17	22

DEPRECIATION, DEPLETION AND OBSOLESCENCE—Screening—*(Continued)*

Mann, John and H. C. Judd. Depreciation. (In their *Colliery accounts.* 1909. p. 69-75, 92).
Screening 5-7½%
Calculated on the balance as diminished from year to year.

Montgomery, Robert H. Mine equipment. (In his *Income tax procedure,* 1919. p. 571. ——— Same, 1920. p. 724).
Tipples, inclines and screens 6⅔%

Nicholson, J. Lee and John F. D. Rohrbach. Depreciation. (In their *Cost accounting.* 1919. p. 150, 148).
Revolving screens 10%
Wire screening 4

Screens

Philadelphia. Controller. Rates of depreciation. (In his *Manual of accounting, reporting and business procedure of the city and county of Philadelphia.* 1917. p. 207-9).
Window and door screens 20%

Scrubbers

Barker, Harry. Typical life expectation tables for public utility property. (In his *Public utility rates.* 1917. p. 368).
Scrubbers and condensers 30 years Wisconsin R. R. commission

Foster, Horatio A. Rates of depreciation. (In his *Engineering valuation of public utilities and factories.* 1913. p. 206).
Scrubbers and condensers 30 years

Gillette, Halbert P. and Richard T. Dana. Depreciation. (In their *Handbook on mechanical and electrical cost data.* 1918. p. 110).
Scrubbers (gas plant) 30 years Wisconsin railroad comm.

Grunsky, Carl Ewald. Probable useful life of various articles. (In his *Valuation, depreciation and the rate-base.* 1917. p. 283).
Scrubbers and condensers 30 years. Wisconsin railroad commission. Quoted by H. A. Foster and in published reports.

Prosser, R. W. Depreciation in gas plants. *American gas light journal,* May 26, 1902, p. 767.
Condensers, scrubbers and purifiers 30 years 20% of first cost

Section boxes

Neale, R. E. Depreciation in engineering works. *Mechanical world,* Feb. 7, 1913, p. 67-8.
Section boxes 5% 20 years.

Separators

Belt, Robert E. Depreciation. (In his *Foundry cost accounting practice and procedure.* 1919. p. 243).
Steam separators 10%

Nicholson, J. Lee and John F. D. Rohrbach. Depreciation. (In their *Cost accounting.* 1919. p. 150).
Magnetic separators 10%

Service boxes

Barker, Harry. Typical life expectation tables for public utility property. (In his *Public utility rates.* 1917. p. 368-9).
Service boxes 10-20 years. Wisconsin R. R. commission.

Services

See also Pipe.

Aberdeen and depreciation. *Municipal journal* (London), Oct. 23, 1903, p. 943.
Mains and services
2½% Glasgow
10 Bolton
1½ Aberdeen

Foster, Horatio A. Rates of depreciation. (In his *Engineering valuation of public utilities and factories.* 1913. p. 207).
Services 20 years

Gillette, Halbert P. and Richard T. Dana. Depreciation. (In their *Handbook of mechanical and electrical cost data.* 1918. p. 110).
Service connections, elect 28.5 years H. P. Gillette, Everett railway and water co., Jan. 29, 1912.

Grunsky, Carl Ewald. Probable useful life of various articles. (In his *Valuation, depreciation and the rate-base.* 1917. p. 283).
Services (electric)
15 years
Pacific gas & electric company. Figures used in rate hearings before Master in Chancery, San Francisco, 1913-4.
20 years.
San Joaquin light and power corporation. Rate hearing before California railroad commission, 1915.
21.6 years. 30% residual value.
Cailfornia railroad commission. Report 1913-4.
Calistoga electric co. vs. Napa valley electric co., May 1914.

Settees

See Depreciation, depletion and obsolescence—Couches, lounges, etc.

DEPRECIATION, DEPLETION AND OBSOLESCENCE—*(Continued)*

Sewerage

PHILADELPHIA. CONTROLLER. Rates of depreciation. (In his *Manual of accounting, reporting and business procedure of the city and county of Philadelphia.* 1917. p. 210).
Sewage and drainage disposal plants 2½%

PUBLIC utility reports, annotated. Rochester, Lawyers co-operative publishing co. 1919D. p. 404.
Wayne title and trust co. v. Wayne sewerage co. (Pa.). The Pennsylvania commission made an allowance for depreciation of approximately 1 per cent upon the agreed valuation of a sewer plant.

WHAT is a proper allowance for depreciation in a sewerage system? *Engineering news*, Nov. 27, 1913, p. 1093.

Sewers

BELT, ROBERT E. Depreciation. (In his *Foundry cost accounting practice and procedure.* 1919. p. 243).
Sewers 2½%

MONTGOMERY, ROBERT H. Electrical equipment manufacturers. (In his *Income tax procedure*, 1919. p. 563. ——— Same, 1920, p. 716).
Water, sewer and drain pipes (outside of buildings) 10%
Based on gross book values at the end of the preceding years.

PHILADELPHIA. CONTROLLER. Rates of depreciation. (In his *Manual of accounting, reporting and business procedure of the city and county of Philadelphia.* 1917. p. 210).
Sewers 1⅓%

Sewing

NICHOLSON, J. LEE and JOHN F. D. ROHRBACH. Depreciation. (In their *Cost accounting.* 1919. p. 150).
Sewing machines 10%

PHILADELPHIA. CONTROLLER. Rates of depreciation. (In his *Manual of accounting, reporting and business procedure of the city and county of Philadelphia.* 1917. p. 205).
Sewing and cutting machinery 10%

Sewing machines

AUSTRALIA. FEDERAL INCOME TAX DEPARTMENT. Depreciation allowance. *Accountant*, Oct. 13, 1917, p. 277-9. *Accounting and commerce*, June 30, 1917, p. 55-7. *Federal accountant*, July 1917, p. 93-8. *Public accountant*, Jan. 30, 1917, p. 145-152.
Sewing machines
Clothing manufacturers' 20%
Millinery " 20
Whiteworkers' " 20
Factories other than book and umbrella
Written down value, repairs allowed in addition.

PHILADELPHIA. CONTROLLER. Rates of depreciation. (In his *Manual of accounting, reporting and business procedure of the city and county of Philadelphia.* 1917. p. 205).
Sewing equipment 10%

Shafting, pulleys, etc.

BARKER, HARRY. Typical life expectation tables for public utility property. (In his *Public utility rates.* 1917. p. 368-9).
Shafting 20-40 years. Wisconsin railroad commission.

BENTLEY, HARRY C. Depreciation. (In his *Science of accounts.* 1913. p. 146).
Stationary machinery, hangers, pulleys and shafting 5-10%

BOLTON, REGINALD PELHAM. Depreciation of mechanical equipments and power plants. (In his *Building for profit.* 1911. p. 82, 89).

	Physical years	%	Economic years
Dumb-waiters, switchboards, elevator gates, slow-speed elevator engines, shafting and bearings, slow geared apparatus, elevators intermittently used	22	55.0	18

CLAPHAM, F. T. Depreciation of plant. *Mechanical world*, Oct. 19, 1917, p. 219-20.
Mill gearing and shafting
3% depreciation + 2½% wear and tear = 5½%.

DEPRECIATION. *American institute of accountants, Special bulletin*, No. 1, Jan. 1920, p. 6-7.

DICKSEE, LAWRENCE R. Depreciation, machinery. (In his *Depreciation reserves and reserve funds.* 1912. p. 29-37).
Shafting 5-7½%

ELBOURNE, EDWARD T. Depreciation rate. (In his *Factory administration and accounts.* 1918. p. 376).

	Prov. dep. %	Years Remainder values 10%	5%
Shafting (including pulleys, bearings and supports)	7½	29	38

FOSTER, HORATIO A. Methods of calculating depreciation. (In his *Engineering valuation of public utilities and factories.* 1913. p. 169).

	Minimum service value per cent of reproduction cost.
Steam plants of all kinds, shafting and pipe covering	25%

Joint engineering department of the Wisconsin commissions.

GREAT BRITAIN. BOARD OF INLAND REVENUE. Depreciation rates: abstract. (In its *Income tax; statement respecting allowances for wear and tear and obsolescence of plant and machinery.* 1918. Cd. 9022, p. 4; Cd. 9134, p. 6). *American economic review*, Supplement, Dec. 1920, p. 51. *Journal of accountancy*, Sept. 1920, p. 195.
Engines, boilers and main shafting 5%
Written down value.

KENT, WILLIAM. Depreciation of shafting, etc. (In his *Bookkeeping and cost accounting for factories.* 1918. p. 91).

DEPRECIATION, DEPLETION AND OBSOLESCENCE—SHAFTING, PULLEYS, ETC.—*(Continued)*

KERR, W. H. and G. A NAHSTOLL. Reserve for depreciation. (In their *Cooperative organization business methods.* 1915. p. 13-4).

KIMBALL, DEXTER S. Estimated life and factors of depreciation. (In his *Cost finding.* 1918. p. 190. *Principles of industrial organization.* 1913. p. 163).

	Prob. life of asset in years.	Ratio of scrap to orig. val.	% on orig. cost.	% on dim. val.
Shafting, hangers, pulleys	20-30	0.05	4.75-3	14-9

McINTOSH, ROBERT J. Rates of depreciation. (In his *Reference book of accounts.* Ed. 2. p. 60).
Hangers, shafting and belting 10-20%
Based on life.

MONTGOMERY, ROBERT H. Electrical equipment manufacturers. (In his *Income tax procedure,* 1919. p. 563. ——— Same, 1920. p. 716).
Shafting, pulleys and belting 15%
Based on gross book values at the end of the preceding year.

NICHOLSON, J. LEE and JOHN F. D. ROHRBACH. Depreciation. (In their *Cost accounting.* 1919. p. 150).
Shafting, pulley, hangers and belting 5%
Based on (1) the cost of equipment
(2) the life of the equipment
(3) on a ten-hour day

NORRIS, H. M. Depreciation of plant and its relation to general expense. *Engineering magazine,* April 1899, p. 76.
Line shafting and accessories 3%

PHILADELPHIA. CONTROLLER. Rates of depreciation. (In his *Manual of accounting, reporting and business procedure of the city and county of Philadelphia.* 1917. p. 205).
Shafting, belting, pulleys, gearing, etc. 4%

SOME depreciation rates on buildings, machinery, shafting, belting, furniture and apparatus, tools and dies, moulds, lasts, patterns and drawings used by the Associated mutual fire insurance companies of Boston, Mass., in taking appraisal of manufacturing properties. *Utilities magazine,* Jan. 1916, p. 186-7.
Shafting shows such slight wear that depreciation is practically never recognized.

Shafts

UNIFORM cost sheet for coal mining companies. *Coal age,* Sept. 19, 1918, p. 545-7.

	original cost.
Slopes and shafts	5%

Shaping machine

ELBOURNE, EDWARD T. Depreciation rates. (In his *Factory administration and accounts.* 1918. p. 377).

	Prov. dep. %	Years	
	Remainder values	10%	5%
Shaping machines	6	37	48

Shearing

AUSTRALIA. FEDERAL INCOME TAX DEPARTMENT. Depreciation allowance. *Accountant,* Oct. 13, 1917, p. 277-9. *Accounting and commerce,* June 30, 1917, p. 55-7. *Federal accountant,* July 1917, p. 93-8. *Public accountant,* Jan. 30, 1919, p. 145-52.
Shearing 7½%
Written down value, repairs allowed in addition.

Shearing machines

ELBOURNE, EDWARD T. Depreciation rates. (In his *Factory administration and accounts.* 1918. p. 377).

	Prov. dep. %	Years	
	Remainder values	10%	5%
Shearing machines, rotary	6	37	48

PHILADELPHIA. CONTROLLER. Rates of depreciation. (In his *Manual of accounting, reporting and business procedure of the city and county of Philadelphia.* 1917. p. 205).
Metal work equipment
Shearing, punching and drilling equipment 5%

Shears

DENHAM, ROBERT S. Depreciation. (In his *Manual of cost engineering and estimating for paper box manufacturers.* 1917. p. 249).
Shears 6%

NICHOLSON, J. LEE and JOHN F. D. ROHRBACH. Depreciation. (In their *Cost accounting.* 1919. p. 149, 150).
Shears 6⅔%
mill machinery 5½
power shears 6⅔
scrap shears 10

PIEZ, CHARLES. Perpetual inventory and appraisal values: table of standard depreciation rates. *Engineering and contracting,* Jan. 24, 1917, p. 77. *Factory,* Dec. 1916, p. 668-71. *Iron age,* Nov. 30, 1916, Jan. 11, 1917, p. 1266, 138-9. *Iron trade review,* Feb. 22, 1917, p. 477-8. Condensed. *Iron trade review,* Dec. 7, 1916, p. 1144-6. *Journal of the American society of mechanical engineers,* Dec. 1916, p. 965-6. Kent, William. *Bookkeeping and cost accounting for factories,* 1918, p. 90. Discussion. *Journal of the American society of mechanical engineers,* March 1917, p. 215-7.

	% on cost.	% on reducing balance.
Punch presses, bending rolls, power shears and drop hammers	4.5	10

DEPRECIATION, DEPLETION AND OBSOLESCENCE—*(Continued)*

Sheds

BARKER, HARRY. Typical life expectation tables for public utility property. (In his *Public utility rates.* 1917. p. 366).
Sheds, wood-frame, 20 years. Author—Average or approximate figures secured by examination or enquiry.

BRYAN, WILLIAM H. Depreciation of electric light plants. *Municipality,* March 1908, p. 74.
Sheds and shelters 10-20 years

FOSTER, HORATIO A. Rates of depreciation. (In his *Engineering valuation of public utilities and factories.* 1913. p. 205).
Years' life
Frame stables and coal sheds 20-25

GILLETTE, HALBERT POWERS. Railways. (In his *Handbook of cost data for contractors and engineers.* 1910. p. 1317-8).
Snowsheds 6.9 age years
4.0 annual depreciation per cent.
72.4 present condition per cent.

GILLETTE, HALBERT P. and RICHARD T. DANA. Depreciation. (In their *Handbook of mechanical and electrical cost data.* 1918. p. 106).
Buildings, snow sheds 25 years.
H. P. Gillette, Washington ry. appraisal.
Buildings, coal sheds and stables, frame 20-25 years.
Wisconsin railroad comm.

GRUNSKY, CARL EWALD. Probable useful life of various articles. (In his *Valuation, depreciation and the rate-base.* 1917. p. 283, 274).
Snowsheds (R.R.) 25 years.
H. P. Gillette. Appraisal of Great Northern and Northern Pacific R.R.'s in Washington. Direction of Washington railroad commission, 1906.
Frame stables and sheds 20-25 years.
Wisconsin railroad commission.
Quoted by Foster and Floy and in published reports.

NICHOLSON, J. LEE and JOHN F. D. ROHRBACH. Depreciation. (In their *Cost accounting.* 1919. p. 146).
Frames, stables and sheds 5%
Based on (1) the cost of equipment
(2) the life of the equipment
(3) on a ten-hour day.

PHILADELPHIA. CONTROLLER. Rates of depreciation. (In his *Manual of accounting, reporting and business procedure of the city and county of Philadelphia.* 1917. p. 210).
Sheds and shelters 2%

Shelving

DENHAM, ROBERT S. Depreciation. (In his *Manual of cost engineering and estimating for paper box manufacturers.* 1917. p. 249).
Shelving 25%

ELBOURNE, EDWARD T. Depreciation rates. (In his *Factory administration and accounts.* 1918. p. 377).

	Prov. dep. %		Years
	Remainder values	10%	5%
Shelving	10	22	28

PIEZ, CHARLES. Perpetual inventory and appraisal values; table of standard depreciation rates. *Engineering and contracting,* Jan. 24, 1917, p. 77. *Factory,* Dec. 1916, p. 668-71. *Iron age,* Nov. 30, 1916, Jan. 11, 1917, p. 1266, 138-9. *Iron trade review,* Feb. 22, 1917, p. 477-8. Condensed. *Iron trade review,* Dec. 7, 1916, p. 1144-6. *Journal of the American society of mechanical engineers,* Dec. 1916, p. 965-6. Kent, William. *Bookkeeping and cost accounting for factories,* 1918, p. 90. Discussion. *Journal of the American society of mechanical engineers,* March 1917, p. 215-7.

	% on cost	% on reducing balance.
Steel shelving, lockers, etc.	5	12

Ship sheds

NICHOLSON, J. LEE and JOHN F. D. ROHRBACH. Depreciation. (In their *Cost accounting.* 1919. p. 147).
Ship sheds 3⅓%
Based on (1) the cost of equipment
(2) the life of the equipment
(3) on a ten-hour day

Shipbuilding

ATLANTIC COAST SHIPBUILDERS' ASSOCIATION. Table of rates of depreciation recommended by committee on depreciation, December 11, 1918. (In its *Cost accounting in shipbuilding.* c1919. p. 48-50, 125-9).
Recommended that the straight-line method of charging off depreciation be adopted. That the normal rates of depreciation be increased to cover overtime depreciation, this increase being at a rate of 6¼% of the normal rate for each hour of overtime; all time in excess of the standard eight-hour day being considered overtime, in this connection. This rate

DEPRECIATION, DEPLETION AND OBSOLESCENCE—SHIPBUILDING—*(Continued)*

of increase corresponds to 100% increase in normal rates when the plant is operated **for** the full 24 hours.

General Classification	Life in Years	Rate of Depreciation, %	Detailed Classification	Life Years	Rate of Depreciation, %
Buildings	25	4	Buildings—		
			Stone, brick, concrete, with or without steel frame and masonry curtain wall buildings	30	3⅓
			Steel with corrugated sheet iron or steel plate	20	5
			Steel or corrugated sheet iron with wood	15	6⅔
			Power plant buildings	20	5
			Wood buildings	10	10
			Piers, bulkheads, wharves and docks	20	5
			Launching ways (fixed structure) wood	10	10
			Concrete	13⅓	7½
			Water tanks and steel stacks	15	6⅔
			Drydocks, basin, masonry or concrete	40	2½
			Wood	25	4
			Concrete and brick bins, fences and miscellaneous concrete and brick structures	20	5
			Wood bins, fences, racks and other wood structures	5	20
Machinery and tools (including foundations)	15	6⅔	Power machinery—		
			Electric generators, switchboards, and power house equipment; boilers and boiler house equipment, including economizers, feed water heaters, injectors, stacks, uptakes, etc.	15	6⅔
			Engines, gas and oil	11¾	8½
			Engines, steam, including pile drivers, hoisting engines, compressors, air pumps vacuum pumps, etc.	10	10
			Pumps, water supply, feed water, fire, etc.	18	5½
			Electric motors and controllers	11¾	8½
			Coal and ash conveyors	20	5
			Shop machinery—		
			Hydraulic forging presses, bending presses and fluid compressors	30	3⅓
			Hammers, steam drop or helve	10	10
			Machine tools, lathes slotters, planers, boring mills, drilling, boring and milling machines	15	6⅔
			Miscellaneous shop machinery and equipment, including small scales, spare parts, etc.	5	20
			Wood working machinery	20	5
			Small tools	10	10
			Cranes, elevators, etc.—		
			Cranes, electric, hydraulic, steam and hand power, jib and davit; hand, electric or air hoists, derricks lifting magnets and charging machines	15	6⅔
			Locomotive cranes, steam and electric	10	10
			Elevators	20	5
			Craneways	25	4
Portable pneumatic, electric and hydraulic tools; portable hand, electric hydraulic or pneumatic hoists and lifting devices; small jib cranes	3	33⅓	Portable pneumatic, electric and hydraulic tools; portable, hand, electric hydraulic or pneumatic hoists and lifting devices; small jib cranes	3	33⅓
			Furnaces and forges—		
			Heating, treating and annealing furnaces, brass foundry melting furnaces, oil furnaces, etc.	10	10
			Blast, furnaces stacks and stoves, soaking pits, open hearth and crucible melting furnaces, cupolas, etc.	25	4
			Formers and drop forge dies	5	20

DEPRECIATION, DEPLETION AND OBSOLESCENCE—SHIPBUILDING—*(Continued)*

Other equipment (trackage, piping, wiring, etc.)	22	4½	Other equipment—		
			Railroad tracks, including rails, ties, ballast, excavation, grading, etc.	22	4½
			Trestles, steel	25	4
			Wood	15	6⅔
			Bridge and retaining walls	33⅓	3
			Marine railways	30	3⅓
			Fire systems and apparatus	5	20
			Piping and wiring; piping for steam and exhaust, air, oil, gas and water lines, pneumatic and hydraulic transmission, electric light and power systems, wiring, feeder and other outside wiring, including poles	16⅔	6
			Heating and ventilating systems, drying apparatus	20	5
			Sanitary and water supply systems, sewers and drainage systems	25	4
			Floating equipment, barges, boats, scows, motor-boats	5	20
			Portable launching ways	5	20
			Floating dry-docks	20	5
			Stable and garage equipment	3	33⅓
			Motor trucks and automobiles	3	33⅓
			Locomotives, steam and electric	15	6⅔
			Cars used by transportation department	10	10
			Scales, large	10	10
			Water purifier	15	6⅔
			Pickling tanks, etc.	3	33⅓
Furniture and fixtures	5	20	Furniture and fixtures—		
			Office equipment, shop, yard, store and tool room fixtures, typewriters, adding machines, etc., lockers, wardrobes, etc.	5	20

Ships

AUSTRALIA. FEDERAL INCOME TAX DEPARTMENT. Depreciation allowance. *Accountant,* Oct. 13, 1917, p. 277-9. *Accounting and commerce,* June 30, 1917, p. 55-7. *Federal accountant,* July 1917, p. 93-8. *Public accountant,* Jan. 30, 1917, p. 145-52.

Launches	6%
Ships	6
Steamers	6
Lugger	7½
Lighters	
wooden for conveyance of gaseous liquor	6%
Coal	10
Constructed of iron or steel	6
Punts	6

Written down value, repairs allowed in addition.

BOGLE, J. D. S. Writing off of depreciation on the wasting assets of a joint stock company. *Accountant,* Dec. 21, 1889, p. 691-6.
Life of a steamer averages about 20 years. 6-7% considered a fair rate.

BOWDEN, C. M. Depreciation of ships. *Accounting and commerce,* Nov. 1915, p. 187-8.
P. & O. company writes off 5%; also carry sums to suspense account.
Houlder Ltd., under debenture trust deed, must provide 5%.
Cunard line provides nearly 5%.
Royal mail S. P. Coy, slightly more than 5%.
English income tax department allows a deduction of 4% giving an estimated life of 25 years.

CARTER, R. N. Rates of depreciation. (In his *Advanced accounts.* p. 618).
Ships (life about 20 years) 5%.
Based on diminishing balances, normal conditions and hours of working.

CORMACK, JAMES. Depreciation of ships in relation to assessment for income tax. *Accountants' magazine,* Dec. 1897, p. 620-31.

DALY, RICHARD RYLAND. Depreciation. (In his *Shipping accounts.* 1905. p. 17, 83, 24).

DENSHAM, F. W. Depreciation of assets and goodwill of limited companies. *Accountant,* May 28, 1898, p. 567-71.
Average life of a ship is about 20 years.

DEPRECIATION allowances in respect of second-hand steamships. *Accountant,* Aug. 10, 1918, p. 73-5. *Incorporated accountants' journal,* Sept. 1918, p. 249.

New Scale of Allowances

Age.		Expectation of life.	Balance of expectation of life after deducting one year for break-up value.	Proportion of Cost after deducting break-up value to be written off each year for depreciation
Over	Under.	Years.	Years.	Proportion.
0	**1**	25	24	1/24
1	**2**	24	23	1/23
2	**3**	23	22	1/22

DEPRECIATION, DEPLETION AND OBSOLESCENCE—Ships—*(Continued)*

3	4	22	21	1/21
4	5	21	20	1/20
5	6	20	19	1/19
6	7	19	18	1/18
7	8	18	17	1/17
8	9	17	16	1/16
9	10	16	15	1/15
10	11	15	14	1/14
11	12	14	13	1/13
12	13	13	12	1/12
13	14	12	11	1/11
14	15	11	10	1/10
15	16	11	10	1/10
16	17	11	10	1/10
17	18	11	10	1/10
18	19	10	9	1/9
19	20	10	9	1/9
20	21	10	9	1/9

Steamships over 21 years to be dealt with by negotiations according to the facts in each case.
1. Income tax.

(a) Depreciation shall be allowed in respect of second-hand steamships purchased during the war or after the war by reference to the price actually paid, and at the rates shown by the table annexed.

(b) Depreciation will continue to be allowed on the scale previously recognized, in respect of second-hand steamships purchased in pre-war years, but the new owner shall be allowed on application to adopt the new scale as from the 6th April 1918, i. e. he shall be allowed as from that date depreciation calculated upon the cost price to him and by reference to the estimated life at the date of purchase.

(c) These arrangements are not to interfere with the existing practice as to new steamships upon which depreciation will continue to be allowed on the cost price at 4% per annum (based upon a presumed life of 25 years, less 1 year break-up value).

(d) An additional 2% per annum on the cost price will be allowed as from the 6th April 1917, during the remaining period of the war, in respect of all steamships whether new or second-hand and whether purchased in pre-war years or during the war.

(e) The yearly depreciation (other than the additional 2% referred to in Clause (d) above on all second-hand steamships purchased during the war, and still owned by the purchaser, will be recalculated as from the date of purchase, and the balance due, if any, allowed, subject to the necessary adjustment in the rate of duty, against any unpaid balance or from the 1918/19 assessment.

2. Excess profits duty.

(a) The allowances for Income tax purposes shall be followed except in those cases where the provisions of Section 47 of the Finance Act, 1916, are applied.

(b) Where Section 47 is applied the purchaser shall be allowed only the depreciation which would have been granted to the vendor if the steamship had not been sold (together with the extra 2% from the 6th April 1917).

(c) In cases falling under 1 (b) (i. e. cases where the new scale is first adopted for 1918/19) such necessary adjustment shall be made as shall ensure that the net profits of the Standard period and of the Accounting periods are calculated on the same basis. That is to say, the same annual amount of depreciation shall be adopted in both the Standard and Accounting periods, except that the additional 2% Depreciation allowed in the Accounting period shall be excluded from the Standard period.

(d) The additional 2% referred to in Clause 1 (d) above is to be regarded for Excess profits duty purposes as an additional wear and tear allowance, and it will not in any way restrict a claim by the owner under Section 40 (3) of the Finance No. 2 act of 1915 in respect of the difference between the purchase price and the assumed post-war value. Such difference is necessarily reduced for the purpose of Section 40 (3) by the wear and tear allowance.

3. General.

(a) These arrangements shall apply only to such changes of ownership as are "genuine". The decision as to whether the amended scale of depreciation is to be applied shall in any case of doubt rest with the Commissioners of Inland revenue.

(b) In no case shall the owner of a steamship be entitled to receive in the aggregate a larger sum of depreciation than the actual cost to him of the steamship, less its break-up value.

(c) The allowance to be made in respect of any steamship purchased, sold, or lost, during the year of assessment shall be a proportional part of the appropriate year's allowance.

Depreciation and income tax. *Accounting and commerce,* Nov. 1917, p. 185-6.

Steamers and launches	6% on reducing value
Sailing vessels and lighters	5%

Depreciation of sailing ships. *Accountant,* Jan. 1, 1916, p. 10.

Sailing ships	3% on cost
Steamships	4

Depreciation written off by the Royal mail packet company. *Economist,* May 16, 1914, p. 1121.
The sum allowed for depreciation now amounts to slightly more than 5% on first cost.

Depreciation written off by the White star line. *Economist,* May 16, 1914, p. 1121.
The company writes off 4% on original first cost and betterments, which is a very low allowance as ships go nowadays.

Dicksee, Lawrence R. Ships. (In his *Auditing, Authorized American ed.* 1909. p. 195).

Gillette, Halbert P. and Richard T. Dana. Life of vessels on the Great Lakes and Tidewater. (In their *Handbook of mechanical and electrical cost data.* 1918. p. 126-8).

DEPRECIATION, DEPLETION AND OBSOLESCENCE—Ships—*(Continued)*

Life in Years

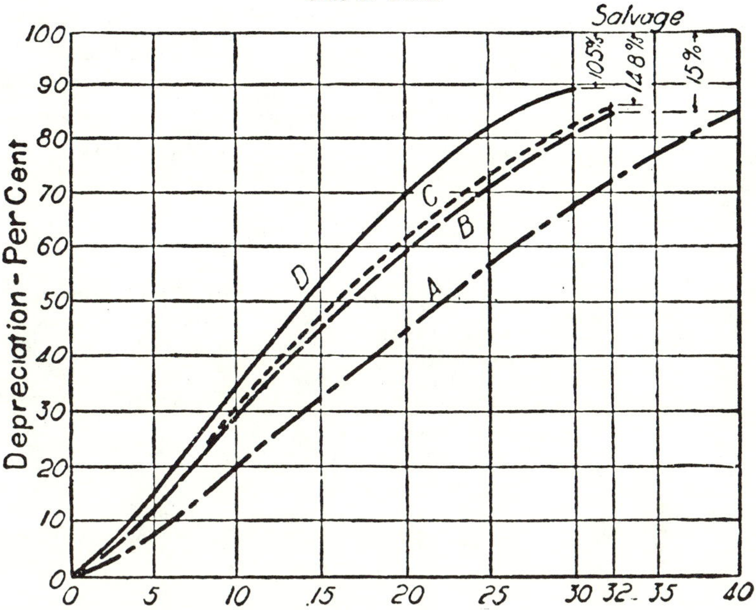

Fig. 1. Depreciation of marine equipment.
A—Steel steam vessels on Great Lakes.
B—Steel steam vessels on tidewater.
C—Steel barges, floats, etc., on tidewater.
D—Wood tugs, barges, etc., on tidewater.

Longevity of scow barges

Dimensions feet	Material	Cost each	Years in service Max.	Min.	Av.	Repairs Max.	Min.	Av.
100x20x4	White pine	$1,600	15	14	15	$1,454	$1,086	$1,283
100x20x4	White pine	768	15	9	12½	1,783	349	1,067
100x20x4	Fir	1,300	22	15	21	2,871	447	2,066
100x20x4	Fir	770	8	6	7¼	681	91	367
100x20x4	Fir	770	8	6	7½	561	134	264
100x20x4	Fir and pine	806	16	13	14¼	1,323	628	1,052
100x20x4¼	Fir	800	17	15	16⅔	881	564	716
110x24x4½	Fir	806	14	12	13	958	661	822
110x24x4½	Fir	790	15	11	14	1,780	517	1,314
120x20x5	Pine with oak bottom	1,400	14	13	13⅓	1,097	802	911

Great Britain. Board of inland revenue. Depreciation rates. (In its *Income tax; statement respecting allowances for wear and tear and obsolescence of plant and machinery.* 1918. Cd. 9022, p. 4; Cd. 9134, p. 6). *American economic review,* Supplement, Dec. 1920, p. 51. *Journal of accountancy,* Sept. 1920, p. 195.

Shipping	
Steamships	4%
Sailing vessels	3
Prime cost	

Note: With regard to ships purchased at second hand at prices in excess of the written down value at the date of purchase, the following arrangements have recently been made:
(a) The allowance is made on the actual cost price of the ship to the owner for the time being without regard to the prime cost to a previous owner.
(b) The rate of depreciation allowable is calculated by reference to the reasonable expectation of the life of the ship at the date of purchase from the previous owner.

Grunsky, Carl Ewald. Probable useful life of various articles. (In his *Valuation, depreciation and the rate-base.* 1917. p. 283).

Steam vessels on Great Lakes	40 years 15% residual value. W. G. Wilgus. Appraisal of Lehigh valley railroad, January, 1914.
on tidewater	32 years. 15% residual value. W. G. Wilgus. Appraisal of Lehigh valley railroad, January, 1914.

Income tax and depreciation: shipping industry, paper mills, printing works. *Incorporated accountants' journal,* May 1914, p. 243.

Steamers	4%
Sailing vessels	3

Computed on original cost price plus subsequent capital expenditure.

DEPRECIATION, DEPLETION AND OBSOLESCENCE—SHIPS—*(Continued)*

INCOME tax notes. *Accountant,* May 11, Sept. 18, 1918, p. 359, 162-6. *Incorporated accountants' journal,* May, Oct. 1918, p. 157, 14.

With regard to ships purchased at second hand at prices in excess of the written down value at the date of purchase, the following arrangements have recently been made:

(a) The allowance is made on actual cost price of the ship to the owner for the time being without regard to the prime cost to a previous owner.

(b) The rate of depreciation allowable is calculated by reference to the reasonable expectation of the life of the ship at the date of purchase from the previous owner.

JACKSON, W. L. Depreciation of shipping. *Accountant,* April 27, May 4, 1899, p. 217-9, 225-6.

JENKINSON, M. WEBSTER. Depreciation. *Accountant,* May 17, 1902, p. 528-34.

MONTGOMERY, ROBERT H. Shipping industry. (In his *Income tax procedure,* 1919. p. 576-8. ———Same, 1920. p. 733-5).

British practice:
Steamers 4%
Sailing vessels 3

On the original cost price of the vessel plus subsequent capital expenditures.
Refrigerators or refrigerating machinery, 6½% on the prime cost.
Oil tank steamers, 5% on prime cost.
Questions to the commissioners with answers are also given.

MONTGOMERY, ROBERT H. Ships. (In his *Auditing theory and practice.* 1916. p. 426-7, 654-5).

Freight boats and ordinary passenger steamers 4%
Boats of high speed and expensive equipment 5

It will be noted that these rates do not mean a life of 25 years and 20 years respectively, but in the former case 16½ years and in the latter case 14 years, based on the investment of the depreciation fund to yield 5 per cent per annum.

NICHOLSON, J. LEE and J. F. D. ROHRBACH. Depreciation. (In their *Cost accounting.* 1919. p. 151).

Motor trucks, automobiles, stable equipment, motor boats, etc. 25%

OFFICIAL allowances in respect of depreciation of machinery and plant—Board of Inland revenue, Great Britain. *Accountant,* May 16, 1914, p. 735.

Steamers 4%
Sailing vessels 3

Computed on original cost price plus subsequent capital expenditure.

PHILADELPHIA. CONTROLLER. Rates of depreciation. (In his *Manual of accounting, reporting and business procedure of the city and county of Philadelphia.* 1917. p. 206).

Fittings specially adapted for equipping boats, etc.
Anchors 5%
Chains, hawsers, lines 5½
Boat hooks, grappling irons, etc. 20
Pipe line and fittings for floating dredges 20
Floating equipment
Steam and gas tugs, launches and yachts 3⅓%
Police and fire boats 3⅓
Ice breakers 3⅓
Row boats, life boats and other small boats 10
Pontoons, scows, etc. 10
Floating dredges 10

PORTERS, R. J. Rates of depreciation generally adopted. (In his *Pitman's dictionary of bookkeeping.* p. 344).

Ships (life about 20 years) 5%
Based on diminishing balances.

PUBLIC utility reports, annotated. Rochester, Lawyers co-operative publishing co. 1915C. p. 711.

Re Manila r. Co. (P.I.). A proper and adequate annual rate of depreciation of locomotive passenger train cars, freight train cars, and work equipment cars was found by the Philippine Islands public utilities commission to be 3 per cent, on steamships 6½ per cent, on steam launches 15 per cent, on wooden motor launches 20 per cent, on steel motor launches 15 per cent, on lighters 20 per cent, on the machinery of the Pandacan slipway and plant 9 per cent; and on the Pandacan slipway 20 per cent, of their original cost ledger value, or purchase price.

PUBLIC utility reports, annotated. Rochester, Lawyers cooperative publishing co. 1915E. p. 66.

Re Twin Falls Commercial Club v. Great Shoshone & T. F. Water Power Co. (Idaho). An allowance of 5 per cent per annum for depreciation was held to be fair and reasonable for a small ferry.

SANDERS, WILLIAM. Depreciation. (In his *Law and practice of excess profits duty.* Ed. 2. 1918. p. 26-31).

SNELLING, W. E. Special provisions regarding shipping and the purchase and sale of ships. (In his *Excess profits (including excess mineral rights) duties and levies under the munitions of war acts.* Ed. 3, revised and enlarged. p. 154-5).

Allowance for depreciation is 4% or 5% on the total cost of the ship.

SPICER, ERNEST EVAN and ERNEST C. PEGLER. Special allowance for depreciation of ships built during the war, and second-hand ships. (In their *Excess profits duty and profits of controlled establishments.* 1918. p. 65-9).

(c) These arrangements are not to interfere with the existing practice as to new steamships upon which depreciation will continue to be allowed on the cost price at 4 per cent per annum (based upon a presumed life of twenty-five years less one year break-up value).

(d) An additional 2 per cent per annum on the cost price will be allowed as from the 6th April, 1917 during the remaining period of the war, in respect of all steamships whether new or second-hand and whether purchased in pre-war years or during the war.

(e) The yearly depreciation (other than the additional 2 per cent referred to in clause (d) above) on all second-hand steamships purchased during the war and still owned by the purchaser, will be re-calculated as from the date of purchase.

WHATLEY, G. E. STUART. Depreciation. (In his *Accountant's and bookkeeper's vade-mecum.* 1893. p. 23-32).

Average life of a ship is assumed to be about 20 years. First-class express liners 5% on original cost. Other vessels 5% on reduced values.

DEPRECIATION, DEPLETION AND OBSOLESCENCE—SHIPS—*(Continued)*

WILLIAMSON, CHARLES. Depreciation. (In his *Fishing industry accounts.* 1903. p. 14).
Trawler 7½% on original cost

Shoe trade

HARVARD UNIVERSITY. GRADUATE SCHOOL OF BUSINESS ADMINISTRATION. Depreciation in the retail shoe business. Cambridge, Harvard university press, 1915. 32p. (Bulletin no. 4).
MONTGOMERY, ROBERT H. Retail shoe stores. (In his *Auditing theory and practice.* 1916. p. 615).
TIFFANY, H. S. Boots and shoes. (In his *Digest of depreciations.* c1890. p. 113).
Shoes 10%

Shoes

AUSTRALIA. FEDERAL INCOME TAX DEPARTMENT. Depreciation allowance. *Accountant,* Oct. 13, 1917. p. 277-9. *Accounting and commerce,* June 30, 1917, p. 55-7. *Federal accountant,* July 1917, p. 93-8. *Public accountant,* Jan. 30, 1917, p. 145-52.
Bootmaking machinery owned by taxpayer 10% leased by taxpayer—generally, installation charges and a premium are paid in addition to an annual rent. The installation charges may be regarded as a "premium" also. Deduction should be allowed under Section 20 (1) of the sinking fund, to recoup the payment of installation and premiums on leased machinery. The lessors of such machines are allowed 10% of depreciation.
Based on written down value and repairs allowed in addition.

Shops

AUSTRALIA. FEDERAL INCOME TAX DEPARTMENT. Depreciation allowance. *Accountant,* Oct. 13, 1917, p. 277-9. *Accounting and commerce,* June 30, 1917, p. 55-7. *Federal accountant,* July 1917, p. 93-8. *Public accountant,* Jan. 30, 1917, p. 145-52.
Shop fittings. Up to 10% according to the circumstances of the case.
BARKER, HARRY. Typical life expectation tables for public utility property. (In his *Public utility rates.* 1917. p. 366).

Shops		
first class	75 years	Wisconsin
second class	50	railroad commission

BAY state street railway valuation. *Electric railway journal,* Dec. 4, 1915, p. 1121-3.

Shops and car houses	2.3 annual depreciation per cent, annual depreciation divided by investment.
Shop equipment	2.8 annual depreciation per cent, annual depreciation divided by investment.

CRAVENS, GEORGE W. Depreciation and maintenance of electrical equipment. *Electrical review,* April 23, 1910, p. 853-6. Montgomery, Robert H. *Income tax procedure,* 1919, p. 570. ——— Same, 1920, p. 722-4. Montgomery, Robert H. *Auditing theory and practice,* 1916, p. 424. Foster, Horatio A. *Engineering valuation of public utilities and factories,* 1913. p. 201-2.
Shop equipment, tools etc.

Light or intermittent service	Heavy or continuous service
5 10%	7.5-15%

	% dep. per annum	
Shop equipment	3-10	Chicago traction commission
	5	Chicago union traction co.
	7.5	Milwaukee electric railway and light co.
	3.3-10	Wisconsin railroad commission
	7.5	Average English
	7.5	Average Scotch practice
	12-15	Philip Dawson
	5	Stone & Webster
	4-10	Industrial power plants
	7.5	Miscellaneous sources

DARBISHIRE, JAMES E. Repairs, renewals, deterioration, and depreciation of workshop, plant and machinery. *Accountant,* Jan. 30, 1909, p. 173-9. *Engineering record,* Oct. 31, 1908, p. 482-4. *Institute of mechanical engineers, Proceedings,* Oct. 16, 1908, p. 797, 812, 879.
DAWSON, PHILIP. Depreciation. (In his *Engineering and electric traction pocket-book.* Ed. 2. p. 1161).

	% capital cost
Repair shop and test-room fittings	12-5

DEPRECIATION rates used by the Seattle (Wash.) municipal street railway. *Electric railway journal,* June 24, 1916, p. 1185.

Shops	2%
Shop equipment	5

FOSTER, HORATIO A. Rates of depreciation. (In his *Engineering valuation of public utilities and factories.* 1913. p. 205).
Second class shops, car barns and power stations. Wisconsin commissions. 50 years' life.
GILLETTE, HALBERT P. Railways. (In his *Handbook of cost data for contractors and engineers.* 1910. p. 1317-18).

	age years	% annual dep.	% present condition
Shop tools and machinery	3.5	10.0	65.0
Roundhouses and shops	5.5	3.0	83.5

GILLETTE, HALBERT P. and R. T. DANA. Cost of street lighting in Chicago. (In their *Handbook of mechanical and electrical cost data.* 1918. p. 1039).
Repair-shop equipment 10%
GILLETTE, HALBERT P. and RICHARD T. DANA. Depreciation. (In their *Handbook of mechanical and electrical cost data.* 1918. p. 106, 107, 108).
Building, shops 33.3 years.
H. P. Gillette, Everett railway and water co., Jan. 29, 1912.
H. P. Gillette, Washington railway appraisal.

DEPRECIATION, DEPLETION AND OBSOLESCENCE—SHOPS—*(Continued)*

Shops, 2nd class — 50 years.
Wisconsin railroad commission

Equipment shop — 10 years.
H. P. Gillette, Everett railway and water co., Jan. 29, 1912.
10-25 years.
George W. Cravens, Industrial power plants.
10-33.3 years.
Chicago traction commision
13.3 years.
Milwaukee electric railway and light co.

Machinery, shop — 10 years.
H. P. Gillette, Washington railway appraisal.
10-30 years.
W. D. Pence, Milwaukee 3c case.
12.5 years.
Prof. M. E. Cooley, Milwaukee 3c case.
14.25 years.
M. G. Starret, Milwaukee 3c case.
20 years.
Marwick, Mitchell & co., appraisal of a large street railway system, Foster, p. 199.
20-50 years.
Union traction co., case Chicago and union traction co., Stone & Webster.

GRAY, HENRY L. Necessity of depreciation reserves. *Railway age gazette,* May 27, 1910, p. 1297-8. Editorial. Depreciation reserves. *Railway age gazette,* May 27, 1910, p. 1290. Letters. Depreciation reserves. *Railway age gazette,* July 8, 1910, p. 66.
Shop machinery 6%

GREENLAND, S. W. Depreciation. *Mississippi electric association, Report of second annual convention,* June 1910, p. 32-6.
Shop equipment 15 years

LOCK, FRED J. Depreciation. (In his *West African accounts.* 1910. p. 88-9).
Workshop plant 7½%

MONTGOMERY, ROBERT H. Electrical equipment manufacturers. (In his *Income tax procedure,* 1919. p. 563. ——— Same, 1920. p. 716).
Miscellaneous shop fixtures and equipment 15%
Based on gross book values at the end of the preceding year.

NEALE, R. E. Depreciation in engineering works. *Mechanical world,* Feb. 7, 1913, p. 67-8 .
Small workshop equipment 5-10% 10-20 years
General workshop equipment 8-10 8.5-12.5

NICHOLSON, J. LEE and J. F. D. ROHRBACH. Depreciation. (In their *Cost accounting.* 1919. p. 150).
Miscellaneous shop equipment:
Anvils, forges, bending blocks, surface plates, mandrels, porter bars, extractors, track and wagon scales, crane scales, portable scales, oil and powder cans, oil filters, glue pots, barrels, microscopes, pyrometers, calorimeters, storage batteries, air hose. 10%
Based on (1) the cost of equipment
(2) the life of the equipment
(3) on a ten-hour day.

PENDER, HAROLD. Depreciation. (In his *Handbook for electrical engineers.* c1914. p. 340).

Tools and machinery (shop)	years	% Dep.	
	10-30		Engineer of valuation staff of Wisconsin railroad commission.
	20		Chicago union traction co. Stone & Webster for the Chicago union traction co.
		10-3.33	Engineer of valuation staff of Wisconsin railroad commission.
		7.5	Milwaukee electric railway and light co. Cardiff tramway. Glasgow tramway
		5	Chicago union traction co. Stone & Webster for the Chicago union traction co.

POMEROY, L. R. Depreciation of locomotives and shop equipment. *Railway age gazette,* April 24, 1914, p. 943-6.

PUBLIC utility reports, annotated. Rochester, Lawyers cooperative publishing co. 1918A. p. 914-8.
New York and N. S. traction co.
Shop tools and machinery 5%

PUBLIC utility reports, annotated. Rochester, Lawyers cooperative publishing co. 1918C. p. 534.
Springfield street R. co.
Shop, car houses and equipment 1.92%

PUBLIC utility reports, annotated. Rochester, Lawyers cooperative publishing co. 1918A. p. 914-8.
New York and N. S. traction co.
Shops and car houses 2%

ROBY, J. J. Schedule of plant depreciation. (In his *Treatise on cost accounting as applied to coal mining.* c1913. p. 14-5).
Shop and equipment
Building, brick and steel only
Deduct as salvage before depreciating 10%
Depreciation rate for remainder, non-fireproof 6
, fireproof 4
Equipment
Deduct as salvage before depreciating 10
Depreciation rate for remainder, fireproof 6

DEPRECIATION, DEPLETION AND OBSOLESCENCE—SHOPS—*(Continued)*

UNIFORM cost sheet for coal mining companies. *Coal age*, Sept. 19, 1918, p. 545-7.
Original cost
Shop fixtures and machinery 7%

WEEKS, H. E. Abstract of paper on depreciation read before annual meeting of Iowa street and interurban railway association, April 1910. *Electric railway journal*, April 30, 1910. p. 782-3.
Shop equipment 15 years

WOODS, CLINTON E. Depreciation. (In his *Unified accounting methods for industrials*. 1917. p. 64-5).
Shop fixtures and fittings 25% per annum

Shovels

LIFE of road construction equipment. *Engineering and contracting*, Jan. 3, 1917, p. 3.
Steam shovel 10% annual dep.

NICHOLSON, J. LEE and JOHN F. D. ROHRBACH. Depreciation. (In their *Cost accounting*. 1919. p. 150.
Locomotive cranes, steam and electric, steam shovels 10%
Based on (1) the cost of equipment
(2) the life of the equipment
(3) on a ten-hour day.

PHILADELPHIA. CONTROLLER. Rates of depreciation. (In his *Manual of accounting, reporting and business procedure of the city and county of Philadelphia*. 1917. p. 208).
Snow shovels, ice scrapers and planers, etc. 12½%

STOCKETT, B. H. and H. B. MILLER. Estimation of depreciation on stripping equipment. *Coal age*, Jan. 5, 1918, p. 34.
Large type shovels—worked single shifts 20 years

Sidewalks

See Depreciation, depletion and obsolescence—Pavements.

Sign boards

AUSTRALIA. FEDERAL INCOME TAX DEPARTMENT. Depreciation allowance. *Accountant*, Oct. 13, 1917, p. 277-9. *Accounting and commerce*, June 30, 1917, p. 55-7. *Federal accountant*, July 1917, p. 93-8. *Public accountant*, Jan. 30, 1917, p. 145-52.
Hoardings. Generally 5% but in special cases allowance may be increased according to circumstances.
Based on written down value and repairs allowed in addition.

ELBOURNE, EDWARD T. Depreciation rates. (In his *Factory administration and accounts*. 1918. p. 376).

	Prov. dep. %	Years	
	Remainder values	10%	5%
Sign boards	15	14	18

Signaling

BARKER, HARRY. Typical life expectation tables for public utility property. (In his *Public utility rates*. 1917. p. 366).
Signals—30 years—Author—Average or approximate figures secured by examination or enquiry.

ELBOURNE, EDWARD T. Depreciation rates. (In his *Factory administration and accounts*. 1918. p. 376).

	Prov. dep. %	Years	
	Remainder values	10%	5%
Bells and signals	7½	29	38

FOSTER, HORATIO A. Depreciation. (In his *Engineering valuation of public utilities and factories*. 1913. p. 200).
Signals, telegraph etc. 10.0%. Marwick, Mitchell & co. in the appraisal of a large street railway system.

GILLETTE, HALBERT P. and R. T. DANA. Depreciation. (In their *Handbook of mechanical and electrical cost data*. 1918. p. 110).
Signal apparatus 10 years.
Marwick, Mitchell & co., appraisal of a large street railway system, Foster, p. 199.
interlocking 20 years.
H. P. Gillette, Everett railway and water co., Jan. 29, 1912.

GRAY, HENRY L. Necessity of depreciation reserves. *Railway age gazette*, May 27, 1910, p. 1297-8. Editorial. Depreciation reserves. *Railway age gazette*, May 27, 1910, p. 1290. Letters. Depreciation reserves. *Railway age gazette*, July 8, 1910, p. 66.
Interlocking and signal apparatus 7%

LIFE data on power-plant equipment used in valuation of Massachusetts property. *Electrical world*, Dec. 4, 1915, p. 1261.
Hand thrown signals 10 years
Automatic signals 14

PHILADELPHIA. CONTROLLER. Rates of depreciation. (In his *Manual of accounting, reporting and business procedure of the city and county of Philadelphia*. 1917. p. 209).
Signal equipment 5%

Signs

AUSTRALIA. FEDERAL INCOME TAX DEPARTMENT. Depreciation allowance. *Accountant*, Oct. 13, 1917, p. 277-9. *Accounting and commerce*, June 30, 1917, p. 55-7. *Federal accountant*, Oct. 13, 1917, p. 277-9. *Public accountant*, Jan. 30, 1917, p. 145-52.
Generally 10% but special circumstances may warrant greater allowance.
Based on written down value and repairs allowed in addition.

GRAY, HENRY L. Necessity of depreciation reserves. *Railway age gazette*, May 27, 1910, p. 1297-8. Editorial. Depreciation reserves. *Railway age gazette*, May 27, 1910, p. 1290. Letters. Depreciation reserves. *Railway age gazette*, July 8, 1910, p. 66.
Crossings and signs 8%

DEPRECIATION, DEPLETION AND OBSOLESCENCE—*(Continued)*

Silk

CHITTICK, JAMES. What to figure for depreciation of plant. (In his *Silk manufacturing and its problems.* 1913. p. 370-8).
Clocks, scales, furniture, shelving, etc. 5%
Regular machinery plant 7½% of the new cost till it stands at 25%, and none thereafter.
Transmission machinery 5
Power plant 10
Buildings 2½
Special equipment. 20% held in reserve till the whole amounts are written off.

Sizers

NICHOLSON, J. LEE and JOHN F. D. ROHRBACH. Depreciation. (In their *Cost accounting.* 1919. p. 150).
Woodworking machinery—sizers 5%
Based on (1) the cost of equipment
(2) the life of the equipment
(3) on a ten-hour day

Slip ways

AUSTRALIA. FEDERAL INCOME TAX DEPARTMENT. Depreciation allowance. *Accountant,* Oct. 13, 1917, p. 277-9. *Accounting and commerce,* June 30, 1917, p. 53-7. *Federal accountant,* July 1917, p. 93-8. *Public accountant,* Jan. 30, 1917, p. 145-52.
Standing ways (patent slip for shipping) 5%
Written down value, repairs allowed in addition

PUBLIC utility reports, annotated. Rochester, Lawyers co-operative publishing co. 1915C. p. 711).
Re Manila R. co. (P.I.) A proper and adequate annual rate of depreciation of . . . the Pandacan slipway and plant 9 per cent and on the Pandacan slipway 20 per cent, of their original cost, ledger value or purchase price.

Slitters

DENHAM, ROBERT S. Depreciation. (In his *Manual of cost engineering and estimating for paper box manufacturers.* 1917. p. 249).

	original cost
Slitters	10%

Slopes and inclines

MONTGOMERY, ROBERT H. Mine equipment. (In his *Income tax procedure,* 1919. p. 571. ——— Same, 1920, p. 724)
Tipples, inclines and screens 6⅔%

UNIFORM cost sheet for coal mining companies. *Coal age,* Sept. 19, 1918, p. 545-7.

	original cost
Slopes and shafts	5%

Slotting machines

DENHAM, ROBERT S. Depreciation. (In his *Manual of cost engineering and estimating for paper box manufacturers.* 1917. p. 249).

	original cost
Slotters	10%

ELBOURNE, EDWARD T. Depreciation rates. (In his *Factory administration and accounts.* 1919. p. 377).

	Prov. dep. %	Years	
	Remainder values	10%	5%
Slotting machines	6	37	48
Portable	6	37	48

NICHOLSON, J. LEE and JOHN F. D. ROHRBACH. Depreciation. (In their *Cost accounting.* 1919. p. 149).
Slotters 6⅔%

Smoke boxes

NICHOLSON, J. LEE and JOHN F. D. ROHRBACH. Depreciation. (In their *Cost accounting.* 1919. p. 148).
Steel work—smoke boxes 4%

Snow sheds

See Depreciation, depletion and obsolescence—Sheds.

Soap

MONTGOMERY, ROBERT H. Soap industry. (In his *Auditing theory and practice.* 1916. p. 418).
About the same as in chemical factories.

MONTGOMERY, ROBERT H. Soap industry. (In his *Income tax procedure,* 1919. p. 578. ——— Same, 1920. p. 735.
About the same as in chemical factories.

TIFFANY, H. S. Soap and candle manufactory. (In his *Digest of depreciations.* c1890. p. 10).
Buildings:
brick 3%
frame 5

Societies, clubs, etc.

PHILADELPHIA. CONTROLLER. Rates of depreciation. (In his *Manual of accounting, reporting and business procedure of the city and county of Philadelphia.* 1917. p. 210).
Buildings:
Churches, auditoriums, exhibition halls, museums, club houses and amusement places 1%

DEPRECIATION, DEPLETION AND OBSOLESCENCE—SOCIETIES, CLUBS, ETC.—*(Continued)*

PIXLEY, FRANCIS. W. Depreciation, clubs. (In his *Clubs and their management.* 1916. p. 126).

Furniture	5%
Upholstery	20
Plate	10
Linen	20
China and glass	30
Ironmongery	20
Books, maps, etc.	5

Off the balance as it existed on the opening date of the year in question.

UNIFORM cost sheet for coal mining companies. *Coal age,* Sept. 19, 1918, p. 545-7.

	original cost
Club house furniture	15%

Soda kettle installation

ELBOURNE, EDWARD T. Depreciation rates. (In his *Factory administration and accounts.* 1918. p. 376).

	Prov. dep. %	Years	
	Remainder values	10%	5%
Soda kettle installation	10	22	28

Sodding

PHILADELPHIA. CONTROLLER. Rates of depreciation. (In his *Manual of accounting, reporting and business procedure of the city and county of Philadelphia.* 1917. p. 210).

Sodding and top soiling	1%

Sprinkler system

BELT, ROBERT E. Depreciation. (In his *Foundry cost accounting practice and procedure.* 1919. p. 243).

Sprinkler system	5%

ELBOURNE, EDWARD T. Depreciation rates. (In his *Factory administration and accounts.* 1918. p. 376).

	Prov. dep. %	Years	
	Remainder values	10%	5%
Sprinkler installation	6	37	48

NICHOLSON, J. LEE and JOHN F. D. ROHRBACH. Depreciation. (In their *Cost accounting.* 1919. p. 147).

Sprinklers	5%

Based on (1) the cost of equipment
(2) the life of the equipment
(3) on a ten-hour day

PIEZ, CHARLES. Perpetual inventory and appraisal values; table of standard depreciation rates. *Engineering and contracting,* Jan. 24, 1917, p. 77. *Factory,* Dec. 1916, p. 668-71. *Iron age,* Nov. 30, 1916, Jan. 11, 1917, p. 1266, 138-9. Condensed. *Iron trade review,* Dec. 7, 1916, p. 1144-6. *Journal of the American society of mechanical engineers,* Dec. 1916, p. 965-6. Kent, William. *Bookkeeping and cost accounting for factories.* 1918. p. 90. Discussion. *Journal of the American society of mechanical engineers,* March 1917, p. 215-7.

	% on cost	% on reducing balance
Sprinkler system (20 years)	4	7.5

Squaring machines

NICHOLSON, J. LEE and JOHN F. D. ROHRBACH. Depreciation. (In their *Cost accounting.* 1919. p. 149).

Squaring machines	6⅔%

Squeezers

BELT, ROBERT E. Depreciation. (In his *Foundry cost accounting practice and procedure.* 1919. p. 242).

Hand squeezers	15%

BELT, ROBERT E. Depreciation. (In his *Uniform cost accounting methods; adopted by the American malleable castings association,* Nov. 14, 1917. p. 20-1).

Hand squeezers	15%

NICHOLSON, J. LEE and JOHN F. D. ROHRBACH. Depreciation. (In their *Cost accounting.* 1919. p. 150).

Squeezers	10%

Stables

AUSTRALIA. FEDERAL INCOME TAX DEPARTMENT. Depreciation allowance. *Accountant,* Oct. 13, 1917, p. 277-9. *Accounting and commerce,* June 30, 1917, p. 55-7. *Federal accountant,* July 1917, p. 93-8. *Public accountant,* Jan. 30, 1917, p. 145-52.

Horse rugs	20%
Stable implements	5

Based on written down value and repairs allowed in addition

BENTLEY, HARRY C. Depreciation. (In his *Science of accounts.* 1913. p. 152).

Stable equipment, office equipment, store fixtures	5-10%

FOSTER, HORATIO A. Rates of depreciation. (In his *Engineering valuation of public utilities and factories.* 1913. p. 205).

	Years' life
Frame stables and coal sheds	20-25

GILLETTE, HALBERT P. and RICHARD T. DANA. Depreciation. (In their *Handbook of mechanical and electrical cost data.* 1918. p. 106).
Buildings, coal sheds and stables, frame—20-25 years—Wisconsin railroad commission.

DEPRECIATION, DEPLETION AND OBSOLESCENCE—STABLES—*(Continued)*

GRUNSKY, CARL EWALD. Probable life of various articles. (In his *Valuation, depreciation and the rate-base.* 1917. p. 274.
Frame stables and sheds, 20-25 years.—Wisconsin railroad commission. Quoted by Foster and Floy and in published reports.
MCINTOSH, ROBERT J. Rates of depreciation. (In his *Reference book of accounts.* Ed. 2. p. 62).
Stable equipment 15%
Based on life
NICHOLSON, J. LEE and J. F. D. ROHRBACH. Depreciation. (In their *Cost accounting.* 1919. p. 146, 151).
Frames, stables and sheds 5%
Based on (1) the cost of equipment
(2) the life of the equipment
(3) on a ten-hour day
Motor trucks, automobiles, stable equipment motor boats, etc. 25%
PHILADELPHIA. CONTROLLER. Rates of depreciation. (In his *Manual of accounting, reporting and business procedure of the city and county of Philadelphia.* 1917. p. 210, 206).
Stables 4%
Harness and collars 12½
Saddles 10
Bridles, bits, halters, chains, boots, pads, spurs 12½
Blankets, robes, covers, weights 16⅔
Curry combs, clipping machines, feed cans, etc. 33⅓
Slings and other equipment for handling sick and injured animals 8⅓
ROBY, J. J. Schedule of plant-depreciation. (In his *Treatise on cost accounting as applied to coal mining.* c1913. p. 14-5).
Stable-building, brick and steel only
Deduct as salvage before depreciating 10%
Depreciation rate for remainder, non-fireproof 6
Fixtures fireproof 4
Depreciation rate for remainder, fireproof 6
TIFFANY, H. S. Livery, hotel, sale and board stables. (In his *Digest of depreciations.* c1890. p. 9).
Buildings
brick 3%
frame 4
Based upon the actual life without any repairs
UNIFORM cost sheet for coal mining companies. *Coal age,* Sept. 19, 1918, p. 545-7.
Stable building original cost
wood 8%
stone or brick 5
Stable equipment 25

Stacks

AMERICAN WATER WORKS ASSOCIATION. Final report of committee on depreciation. *Journal of the American water works association,* Sept. 1917, p. 1-38).
Stacks
masonry 25-50 years
steel 10-25
ANALYSIS of the premises adopted and methods used in determining the cost to reproduce new together with the depreciation thereon of the physical propery of the Metropolitan system and the Kansas City and Westport belt railway of Kansas City, Mo. *Engineering and contracting,* May 28, 1913, p. 617-20.
Stacks:
self supporting steel 6%
brick or concrete 3
guyed steel 8
BARKER, HARRY. Typical life expectation tables for public utility property. (In his *Public utility rates.* 1917. p. 368-9).
Chimneys and stacks
Masonry 30 years. Author. Average or approximate figures
Steel 10 years. secured by examination or enquiry.
BELT, ROBERT E. Depreciation. (In his *Foundry cost accounting practice and procedure.* 1919. p. 243).
Brick stacks 5%
BOLTON, REGINALD PELHAM. Depreciation of mechanical equipments and power plants. (In his *Building for profit.* 1911. p. 82, 89).

	Physical years	%	Economic years
Steel-plate stacks and smoke-ducts, cold-water piping, electric conduits	30	75.0	24

BOLTON, REGINALD PELHAM. Depreciation of the value of buildings. (In his *Building for profit.* 1911. p. 62).

Brick flues	Relative to years		years	
	45	55		
	99%	80%	33	Frame construction
	Relative to years			
	55	66		
	96%	80%	33	Brick and steel construction

BREWER, ALLAN F. Rates for annual depreciation. *Industrial management,* April 1918, p. 268.

	Years	% dep.
Stacks, brick (custodis)	150	.66
Stacks, brick (plain)	100	1
Stacks, steel (plain)	50	2
Stacks, steel (guyed)	30	3.33

DEPRECIATION, DEPLETION AND OBSOLESCENCE—STACKS—*(Continued)*

Stacks (steel)	3 years	Traction val. comm.	Chgo. con. tract. co.
	10 years	B. J. Arnold	Coney Island & Brooklyn adopted by P. S. C., N. Y.

CROWELL, H. H. Electric lighting rates and depreciation. *Municipal journal and engineer,* Dec. 18, 1907, p. 698.

	Purchased 10 years or more ago	Modern
Stacks—brick	25 years	20 years

ELBOURNE, EDWARD T. Depreciation rates. (In his *Factory administration and accounts.* 1918. p. 376).

	Prov. dep. %	Years	
	Remainder values	10%	5%
Chimney shafts, brick	4	56	73
" " , steel	7½	29	38

FLOY, HENRY. Depreciation. Floy, Henry. Depreciation as related to electrical properties. *American institute of electrical engineers, Proceedings,* 1911, p. 1267. Floy, Henry, *Valuation of public utility properties.* 1912. p. 188-93. Foster, H. A. *Engineering valuation of public utilities and factories,* 1913, p. 194-8. *Engineering and contracting,* Oct. 4, 1911, p. 359-65. *Engineering magazine,* Aug. 1911, p. 837-40.

	Dep. % per year straight line		
Stack, steel	10	B. J. Arnold	Coney Island & Brooklyn adopted by P. S. C., N. Y.

GILLETTE, HALBERT P. and RICHARD T. DANA. Depreciation. (In their *Handbook of mechanical and electrical cost data.* 1918. p. 106-7).

Chimney 33.3 years.
Traction valuation commission. Chicago consolidated traction co.
steel 10 years.
B. J. Arnold. Appraisal of the Coney Island and Brooklyn railroad, Feb. 1, 1909.
brick 14.3 years.
B. J. Arnold, Chicago appraisal four cases.
33.3 years.
B. J. Arnold, Chicago appraisals, four cases.

GRUNSKY, CARL EWALD. Probable useful life of various articles. (In his *Valuation, depreciation and the rate-base.* 1917. p. 283).

Stacks
brick 33 years.
Traction valuation commission. Case of the Chicago consolidated traction co.
brick 33.3 years.
Henry Floy. Four Chicago appraisals. Trans. American institute of electrical engineers, June 1911. Third avenue case figures adopted by Public service commission of New York
steel 12 years.
Pacific gas and electric company. Figures used in rate hearings before Master in Chancery, San Francisco, 1913-4.
steel 14.2 years.
Henry Floy. Four Chicago appraisals. Trans. American institute of electrical engineers, June, 1911. Third avenue case figures adopted by Public service commission of New York.

HAZLEHURST, J. N. Final report of the committee on depreciation. *Journal of the American water works association,* March 1919, p. 85-135.

Stacks	
masonry	25-50 years
steel	10-25

NEALE, R. E. Depreciation in engineering works. *Mechanical world,* Feb. 7, 1913, p. 67-8.

Chimneys		
brick	3%	33 years
steel	10	10

NICHOLSON, J. LEE and J. F. D. ROHRBACH. Depreciation. (In their *Cost accounting.* 1919. p. 148, 147).

Stack	
brick	3%
steel	8

Based on (1) the cost of equipment
(2) the life of the equipment
(3) on a ten-hour day.

PHILADELPHIA. CONTROLLER. Rates of depreciation. (In his *Manual of accounting, reporting and business procedure of the city and county of Philadelphia.* 1917. p. 205).
Smoke stacks and chimneys 5%

PROBABLE lives of water works elements. *Engineering news,* Oct. 11, 1917, p. 688.

Stacks	
masonry	25-50 years
steel	10-25

PROPOSED sale of Toronto utilities to the city. *Electrical world,* Oct. 25, 1913, p. 832.
Brick and concrete stacks 3%

VALUATION of the Chicago consolidated traction property. *Electric railway journal,* Dec. 3, 1910, p. 1111-3.
Stack 3%

DEPRECIATION, DEPLETION AND OBSOLESCENCE—*(Continued)*

Stamping

PHILADELPHIA. CONTROLLER. Rates of depreciation. (In his *Manual of accounting, reporting and business procedure of the city and county of Philadelphia.* 1917. p. 205).
Metal working equipment
Turning, planing, milling, stamping and engraving equipment 5%

Standpipes

AMERICAN institute of accountants. Report of the committee on standard schedules for uniform reports upon municipal industries and public service corporations; annual meeting at Atlantic City, N. J., October 20-22, 1908. 15p. *Journal of accountancy*, May 1909, p. 47-54.
The knowledge at the command of the Bureau of the census leads to the conclusion that this average life is approximately as follows:
Standpipes 50 years

AMERICAN WATER WORKS ASSOCIATION. Final report of committee on depreciation. *Journal of the American water works association*, Sept. 1917, p. 1-38.

Standpipes	Years
wrought iron and steel	30-60
reinforced concrete	50-60

BARKER, HARRY. Typical life expectation tables for public utility property. (In his *Public utility rates.* 1917. p. 367).
Standpipes 30-50 years L. Metcalf

BRYAN, WILLIAM. Appraisal and depreciation of water-works and similar properties. *Journal of the association of engineering societies*, Dec. 1907, p. 336-81. Depreciation allowance for various public service industries. *Engineering news*, Jan. 23, 1908, p. 96.

	Years	% straight
Standpipes	25-30	
"		4
"	40	
"	30	

CHASE, HARVEY S. Depreciation in water works accounts, with reference to uniform reports. *Journal of the New England waterworks association*, June 1910, p. 305-31. Abstract. *Engineering and contracting*, June 29, 1910, p. 598. Editorial. Depreciation and sinking fund accounts. *Municipal engineering*, July 1910, p. 26.
Masonry of filtration plant, cribs, iron water pipes, intake pipes, fire hydrants, stand pipes and buildings 50 years

CLADER, WILL-A. Water utilities accounting. *Journal of accountancy*, Aug. 1919, p. 91-2.
The following rates are used frequently when wear and tear are made good by operating maintenance.

Standpipes	
concrete	2%
wood	3

ESTIMATED life and depreciation of water works plants. *Municipal journal and engineer*, May 6, 1908, p. 558.

Material	Life in years	% per year straight	Authority
Standpipes	25-30		Wm. H. Bryan
"		4	W. H. Rosecrans, Galena, Kans. appraisal in 1905.

FOSTER, HORATIO A. Rates of depreciation. (In his *Engineering valuation of public utilities and factories.* 1913. p. 204).
Standpipes 30-50 years

GILLETTE, HALBERT P. and RICHARD T. DANA. Depreciation. (In their *Handbook of mechanical and electrical cost data.* 1918. p. 110).
Standpipe 10 years.
H. P. Gillette, Everett railway and water co., Jan. 29, 1912.
Standpipes 25-40 years.
Leonard Metcalf; Trans. American society civil engineers, 1909, p. 24.

HAZLEHURST, J. N. Final report of the committee on depreciation. *Journal of the American water works association*, March 1919, p. 85-135.

Stand pipes	
wrought iron and steel	30-60 years
reinforced concrete	50-60

METCALF, LEONARD. Depreciation in waterworks operation and accounting. *Journal of the New England waterworks association*, Dec. 1910, p. 442. Abstracts. *Engineering news*, Nov. 3, 1910, p. 482. Methods of computing depreciation of and reasonable assumptions as to period of useful life of waterworks. *Engineering and contracting*, Nov. 16, 1910, p. 434.
Steel standpipes 25-40 years 4-2½% straight line

METCALF, LEONARD. Waterworks valuation and fair rates, in the light of the Maine supreme court decisions in the Waterville and Brunswick cases. *American society of civil engineers, Papers and discussions*, 1908, p. 1101-73. *American society of civil engineers. Transaction*, Sept. 1909. p. 1. Foster, Horatio A. *Engineering valuation of public utilities and factories.* 1913. p. 207. Gillette, Halbert P. *Handbook of cost data for contractors and engineers*, p. 797.

	Useful life	Annual contribution to depreciation account or sinking fund in per cent of cost: At 5% annual rate sinking fund	General approximate results
Standpipes	25-40 years	2.0952%-0.8278%	2-1%

NICHOLSON, J. LEE and JOHN F. D. ROHRBACH. Depreciation. (In their *Cost accounting.* 1919. p. 148).
Standpipes 4%

PHILADELPHIA. CONTROLLER. Rates of depreciation. (In his *Manual of accounting, reporting and business procedure of the city and county of Philadelphia.* 1917. p. 210).
Water towers and stand pipes 4%

DEPRECIATION, DEPLETION AND OBSOLESCENCE—STANDPIPES—*(Continued)*

PROBABLE lives of water works elements. *Engineering news*, Oct. 11, 1917, p. 688.
Standpipes
wrought-iron and steel 30-60 years
reinforced concrete 50-60

WOLFF, MARK. Interpretation of waterworks accounts. *Journal of the American waterworks association*, June 1916, p. 543, 546.
Mains, fire hydrants, stand pipes, buildings, masonry 50 years

Stands

PHILADELPHIA. CONTROLLER. Rates of depreciation. (In his *Manual of accounting, reporting and business procedure of the city and county of Philadelphia*. 1917. p. 207-8).
Tabourets, stands, pedestals, copy holders 4%

Starch

TIFFANY, H. S. Starch factories. (In his *Digest of depreciations*. c1890. p. 11).
Buildings:
brick 3%
frame 5
Based upon the actual life without any repairs.

Stationery

TIFFANY, H. S. Books and stationery. (In his *Digest of depreciations*. c1890. p. 13).
Books and stationery 20%

Stations

BARKER, HARRY. Typical life expectation tables for public utility property. (In his *Public utility rates*. 1917. p. 366).
Stations
masonry 40 years
wood 20
Author-average or approximate figures secured by examination or enquiry.

GILLETTE, HALBERT POWERS. Railways. (In his *Handbook of cost data for contractors and engineers*. 1910. p. 1317-8).
Stations
fuel 3%
water 2½

GILLETTE, HALBERT P. and R. T. DANA. Depreciation. (In their *Handbook of mechanical and electrical cost data*. 1918. p. 106).
Building
Stations, fuel and water 33.3 years.
H. P. Gillette, Washington railway appraisal.
Stations and waiting rooms 33.3 years.
H. P. Gillette, Everett railway and water co., Jan. 29, 1912.

GRAY, HENRY L. Necessity of depreciation reserves. *Railway age gazette*, May 27, 1910, p. 1297-8. Editorial. Depreciation reserves. *Railway age gazette*, May 27, 1910, p. 1290. Letters. Depreciation reserves. *Railway age gazette*, July 8, 1910, p. 66.
Water and fuel stations 4%

UNIFORM cost sheet for coal mining companies. *Coal age*, Sept. 19, 1918, p. 545-7.
Original cost
Freight stations 10%

Statuary

PHILADELPHIA. CONTROLLER. Rates of depreciation. (In his *Manual of accounting, reporting and business procedure of the city and county of Philadelphia*. 1917. p. 210).
Monuments, statuary, arches, gravestones ⅛%

Stayers

DENHAM, ROBERT S. Depreciation. (In his *Manual of cost engineering and estimating for paper box manufactures*. 1917. p. 249).
Original cost
Stayers 10%
metal edge 10

Steam plants

COST and depreciation of steam and hydro-electric installations. *Electrical world*, Dec. 30, 1909, p. 1558.

DEPRECIATION of prime movers. *Electrical review and western electrician*, April 3, 1909, p. 601.

DEPRECIATION of steam plant. *Electric railway review*, March 31, 1908, p. 360.

DOHERTY, HENRY L. Comments on development and operation of hydro-electric plants. *American institute of electrical engineers, Proceedings*, 1909, p. 1362. Abstract. Cost and depreciation of steam and hydro-electric installation. *Electrical world*, Dec. 30, 1909, p. 1558.

FOSTER, HORATIO. A. Methods of calculating depreciation. (In his *Engineering valuation of public utilities and factories*. 1913. p. 169).
Steam plants of all kinds, shafting and pipe covering. Minimum service value, 25% of reproduction cost.

GILLETTE, HALBERT P. and R. T. DANA. Cost of street lighting in Chicago. In their *Mechanical and electrical cost data*. 1918. p. 1039).
Steam equipment 4.1%

GILLETTE, HALBERT P. and RICHARD T. DANA. Internal combustion engines. (In their *Mechanical and electrical cost data*. 1918. p. 626-7).
The fixed charges were apportioned for the steam and gas plants as follows:
Depreciation, 5%.

DEPRECIATION, DEPLETION AND OBSOLESCENCE—STEAM PLANTS—*(Continued)*

GILLETTE, HALBERT P. and RICHARD T. DANA. Steam power. (In their *Mechanical and electrical cost data.* 1918. p. 420, 443, 459, 465, 510).
MAIN, CHARLES T. Depreciation of power plant equipment. *Electrical traction weekly,* May 7, 1908, p. 456.
NICHOLSON, J. LEE and J. F. D. ROHRBACH. Depreciation. (In their *Cost accounting.* 1919. p. 147).
Steam power plant, including boilers and piping 6%
Based on (1) the cost of equipment
(2) the life of the equipment
(3) on a ten-hour day
PUBLIC utility reports, annotated. Rochester, Lawyers co-operative publishing co. 1915A. p. 652).
Re Rhinelander power co. (Wis.). An annual allowance of 3 per cent on the sinking fund basis should be a sufficient charge to the depreciation account for a well built steam power plant.
Re Rhinelander power co. (Wis.). The annual rate of depreciation of steam stations with extensive distribution systems is often 4.5 per cent, computed on the straight line basis.
SLAVIN, MATTHEW. Municipal electricity in Pasadena. *Public service,* April 1910, p. 105-8.
Steam plant 13 years 6.2%

Steam separators and traps

ELBOURNE, EDWARD T. Depreciation rates. (In his *Factory administration and accounts.* 1918. p. 376).

	Prov. dep. %	Years	
	Remainder values	10%	5%
Steam separators and traps	7½	29	38

Steamers

See Depreciation, depletion and obsolescence—Ships.

Steel

See Depreciation, depletion and obsolescence—Foundries; Iron and steel.

Stencil machines

DENHAM, ROBERT S. Depreciation. (In his *Manual of cost engineering and estimating for paper box manufacturers.* 1917. p. 249).
S & S stencil machines 12%

Stereos and blocks

AUSTRALIA. FEDERAL INCOME TAX DEPARTMENT. Depreciation allowance. *Accountant,* Oct. 13, 1917, p. 277-9. *Accounting and commerce,* June 30, 1917, p. 55-7. *Federal accountant,* July 1917, p. 93-8. *Public accountant,* Jan. 30, 1917, p. 145-52.
Stereos and blocks
Replacements allowable
Written down value, repairs allowed in addition.

Stevedoring

AUSTRALIA. FEDERAL INCOME TAX DEPARTMENT. Depreciation allowance. *Accountant,* Oct. 13, 1917, p. 277-9. *Accounting and commerce,* June 30, 1917, p. 55-7. *Federal accountant,* July 1917, p. 93-8. *Public accountant,* Jan. 30, 1917, p. 145-52.
Stevedoring plant—Full repairs and replacement of ropes allowable.

Stills

AUSTRALIA. Federal income tax department. Depreciation allowance. *Accountant,* Oct. 13, 1917, p. 277-9. *Accounting and commerce,* June 30, 1917, p. 55-7. *Federal accountant,* July 1917, p. 93-8. *Public accountant,* Jan. 30, 1917, p. 145-52.
Stills (coolers) 2½%
Written down value, repairs allowed in addition.

Stone

PHILADELPHIA. CONTROLLER. Rates of depreciation. (In his *Manual of accounting, reporting and business procedure of the city and county of Philadelphia.* 1917. p. 205).
Stone crushing and cutting equipment 10%

Stools

PHILADELPHIA. CONTROLLER. Rates of depreciation. (In his *Manual of accounting, reporting and business procedure of the city and county of Philadelphia.* 1917. p. 206-8).
Stools 4%

Storage cells

NEALE, R. E. Depreciation in engineering works. *Mechanical world,* Feb. 7, 1913, p. 67-8.

Storage cells	% Dep.	Years
Central stations	5-6.5	15-20
Substations	6-10	10-17
Traction types	20-30	3.3-5

Storehouses

See Depreciation, depletion and obsolescence—Warehouses.

Stores

BOLTON, REGINALD PELHAM. Depreciation of the value of buildings. (In his *Building for profit.* 1911. p. 76). Burton, H. J. *Valuations and depreciations of city buildings,* p. 21.
Store buildings 21-25 years
BOLTON, REGINALD PELHAM. Depreciation of mechanical equipments and power plants. (In his *Building for profit.* 1911. p. 85).

DEPRECIATION, DEPLETION AND OBSOLESCENCE—STORES—*(Continued)*

In a dry-goods building the investment in the equipment and in a power plant was:

For the fixed equipment, elevators, sprinklers and boilers for heating	20%	of the cost of the building
For the motive apparatus, or generating plant	6	of the cost of the building
The relative life of building alone being	77.00	
The relative life of fixed equipment is	52.00	
Thus the building and fixed equipment average	73.00	
The relative life of the motive plant is, however, only	18.00	
Reducing the average relative life of all to	70.25	
and reducing the mean life of the whole by about	9.00	
and increasing the proportionate sinking fund by about	20.00	

PHILADELPHIA. CONTROLLER. Rates of depreciation. (In his *Manual of accounting, reporting and business procedure of the city and county of Philadelphia.* 1917. p. 210).

Stores 1⅔%

ROBY, J. J. Schedule of plant depreciation. (In his *Treatise on cost accounting as applied to coal mining.* c1913. p. 14-5).

Store, building

Deduct as salvage before depreciating	10%
Depreciation rate for remainder, non-fireproof	5
Depreciation rate for remainder, fireproof	4

TIFFANY, H. S. Frame store buildings. (In his *Digest of depreciations.* c1890. p. 6)

Frame store buildings 3-5%

Based upon the actual life without any repairs.

UNIFORM cost sheet for coal mining companies. *Coal age,* Sept. 19, 1918, p. 545-7.

Store and office buildings	Original cost
wood	6%
stone or brick	5
Furniture and fixtures	10

Stove industry

NATIONAL ASSOCIATION OF STOVE MANUFACTURERS. Depreciation of machinery and buildings: depreciation of patterns. (In their *Cost manual.* p. 42, 39).

Stoves, furnaces, etc.

See also Depreciation, depletion and obsolescence—Annealing.

ANALYSIS of the premises adopted and methods used in determining the cost to reproduce new together with the depreciation thereon of the physical property of the Metropolitan system and the Kansas City and Wesport Belt railway of Kansas City, Mo. *Engineering and contracting,* May 28, 1913, p. 617-20.

Heaters:	
open	3%
closed steel	6
closed cast iron	4

AUSTRALIA. FEDERAL INCOME TAX DEPARTMENT. Depreciation allowance. *Accountant,* Oct. 13, 1917, p. 277-9. *Accounting and commerce,* June 30, 1917, p. 55-7. *Federal accountant,* July 1917, p. 93-8. *Public accountant,* Jan. 30, 1917, p. 145-52.

Furnaces 15%

Based on written down value and repairs allowed in addition.

BARKER, HARRY. Typical life expectation tables for public utility property. (In his *Public utility rates.* 1917. p. 368-9).

Feed-water heaters 20-30 Years Wisconsin railroad commission

BAY state rate case. *Electric railway journal,* Dec. 4, 1915, p. 1121-3. *Public utility reports, annotated,* 1916F, p. 336-9.

Heaters 25-30 years

BELT, ROBERT E. Depreciation. (In his *Foundry cost accounting, practice and procedure.* 1919. p. 241-2).

Air furnaces and apparatus	7½%
Open hearth furnaces and apparatus	10
Electric furnaces and apparatus	10

BELT, ROBERT E. Depreciation. (In his *Uniform cost accounting methods; adopted by the American malleable castings association,* Nov. 14, 1917, p. 20-1).

Melting furnaces and apparatus 7½%

BREWER, ALLAN F. Rates for annual depreciation. *Industrial management,* April 1918, p. 268.

Feed-water heaters		
open tank	30 years	3.33%
horizontal	40	2.5
vertical	40	2.5

BREWERIES. *American institute of accountants, Special bulletin,* No. 2, March, 1920, p. 6-7.

CASH, W. Gas accounts and finance. *Accountant,* Oct. 18, 1913, p. 543-55.

Meters (ordinary and prepayment) cookers and gas fires 10% on written down value.

DEPRECIATION and income tax. *Journal of gas lighting,* June 18, 1912, p. 886.

Meters (ordinary and prepayment) cookers and gas fires. In addition to repairs, allowance for depreciation shall be granted at the rate of 10% per annum on the written down value.

ELBOURNE, EDWARD T. Depreciation rates. (In his *Factory administration and accounts.* 1918. p. 377).

	Prov. dep. % Remainder values	Years 10%	5%
Furnaces, annealing			
hardening and tempering	15	14	18
electric	15	14	18
gas and oil	15	14	18
welding	15	14	18
Heaters, feed water	7½	29	38
Stoves, enamelling and japanning	10	22	28
Oil heaters	7½	29	38

DEPRECIATION, DEPLETION AND OBSOLESCENCE—STOVES, FURNACES, ETC.—*(Continued)*

FLOY, HENRY. Depreciation. Floy, Henry, Depreciation as related to electrical properties. *American institute of electrical engineers, Proceedings,* 1911, p. 1267. Floy, Heny. *Valuation of public utility properties.* 1912. p. 188-93. Foster, Horatio A. *Engineering valuation of public utilities and factories.* 1913. p. 194-8. *Engineering and contracting,* Oct. 4, 1911, p. 359-65. *Engineering magazine,* Aug. 1911, p. 837-40.

	Depreciation % per year Straight line		
Heaters	4-6	Trac. val. comm.	Chic. con. trac. co.
feed water, closed	3⅓	Wisconsin R. R. C.	
feed water, open	3⅓	Wisconsin R. R. C.	

FOSTER, HORATIO A. Rates of depreciation. (In his *Engineering valuation of public utilities and factories.* 1913. p. 200, 205).
Engines, boilers, heaters, conveyors, pumps and auxiliaries 4.5%
Heaters, 20-30 years. Marwick, Mitchell & co. in the appraisal of a large street railway system.

GILLETTE, HALBERT P. and RICHARD T. DANA. Depreciation. (In their *Handbook of mechanical and electrical cost data.* 1918. p. 108).
Heaters 16.7-25 years.
Traction valuation commission. Chicago consolidated traction co.
22.2 years.
Marwick, Mitchell & co. appraisal of a large street railway system, Foster, p. 199.
33.3 years.
B. J. Arnold, Chicago appraisals. 4 cases.
feed water, closed 30 years.
Wisconsin railroad commission.
feed water, open 30 years.
Wisconsin railroad commission.

GREAT BRITAIN. BOARD OF INLAND REVENUE. Depreciation rates: (In its *Income tax; statement respecting allowances for wear and tear and obsolescence of plant and machinery.* 1918. Cd. 9022, p. 4; Cd. 9134, p. 6). *American economic review, Supplement,* Dec. 1920, p. 51. *Journal of accountancy,* Sept. 1920, p. 195.
Gas undertakings other than those owned by municipal or other public authorities.
Meters, cookers and gas fires 10%
Written down value.

GREENLAND, S. W. Depreciation. *Mississippi electric association, Report of 2nd annual convention,* June 1910, p. 32-6.
Pumps and heaters 15-20 years

GRUNSKY, CARL EWALD. Probable useful life of various articles. (In his *Valuation, depreciation and the rate-base.* 1917. p. 280).
Heaters (feed water) 15 years.
Chicago union traction co. Quoted in Report Wisconsin railroad commission, vol. 10, p. 220.
20 years.
Stone & Webster. Figures for Chicago union traction co. case. Report Wisconsin railroad commission, vol. 10, p. 220.
20 years.
Pacific gas and electric company. Figures used in rate hearings before Master in Chancery, San Francisco, 1913-4.
16-25 years.
Traction valuation commission. Case of the Chicago consolidated traction co.
15-30 years.
Wisconsin railroad commission. Milwaukee 3c. fare case. Aug. 23, 1912.
30 years.
Wisconsin railroad commission. Quoted by Henry Floy and in published reports.
33⅓ years.
Bion J. Arnold. Coney Island and Brooklyn figures adopted by Public service commission of New York. Four Chicago appraisals quoted by H. A. Foster.

GUTHRIE, EDWIN. Depreciation. (In Lisle, George. *Encyclopaedia of accounting.* v. 2. p. 375).
Gas works—retorts, furnaces, etc. 10% on original outlay, plus a renewal fund for term of life, chargeable to revenue.

INCOME tax and depreciation: result of negotiations with Inland revenue authorities: from *Gas world. Accountant,* June 29, 1912, p. 986-90.
Meters (ordinary and prepayment) cookers and gas fires 10%

INCOME tax notes. *Accountant,* May 11, Sept. 28, 1918, p. 359, 162-6. *Incorporated accountants' journal,* May, Oct. 1918, p. 157, 14.
Meters, cookers and gas fires 10%

LIFE data on power-plant equipment used in valuation of Massachusetts property. *Electrical world,* Dec. 4, 1915, p. 1261.
Heaters 25-30 years

MATHESON, EWING. Plant and machinery. (In his *Depreciation of factories, mines and industrial undertakings and their valuation.* 1893. p. 35-49).
Blast furnaces 5%

MONTGOMERY, ROBERT H. Electrical equipment manufacturers. (In his *Income tax procedure,* 1919. p. 563. ——— Same, 1920, p. 716).
Ovens and furnaces 15%
Based on gross book values at the end of the preceding year.

NEALE, R. E. Depreciation in engineering works. *Mechanical world,* Feb. 7, 1913, p. 67-8.
Feed heater 3-6% 17-33 years

DEPRECIATION, DEPLETION AND OBSOLESCENCE—STOVES, FURNACES, ETC.—*(Continued)*

NELSON, BAILIE WALTER. Limitation and application of profits from municipal undertakings. *Incorporated accountants' journal,* Oct. 1912, p. 15-7.
Stoves (gas) 10% per annum

NICHOLSON, J. LEE and J. F. D. ROHRBACH. Depreciation. (In their *Cost accounting.* 1919. p. 148, 149).

Steel work	4%
Blast furnace stacks, stoves, soaking pits, open hearth, furnaces, crucible melting furnaces, hot metal mixers, converter vessels, cupolas, open hearth, pre-heaters, cinder runner, slag spouts, etc.	5
Cupolas, converters, melting furnaces and accessories	5
Annealing and heating furnaces, ovens, forges, etc.	5
Furnaces	6
Heating and melting furnaces	6
Puddle furnaces, electric, air, oil and welding furnaces, cooler ovens, drying ovens, etc.	5½

Based on (1) the cost of equipment
(2) the life of the equipment
(3) on a ten-hour day

PENDER, HAROLD. Depreciation. (In his *Handbook for electrical engineers.* c1914. p. 339).

	Years	% Dep.	
Heaters, economizers and pumps			
	15		Chicago union traction co.
	20		Stone & Webster for Chicago union traction co.
		7.5	Milwaukee electric railway and light co.
		6.66	Chicago union traction co.
		5	Cardiff tramways.
			Glasgow "
			Stone & Webster for Chicago union traction co.

PHILADELPHIA. CONTROLLER. Rates of depreciation. (In his *Manual of accounting, reporting and business procedure of the city and county of Philadelphia.* 1917. p. 204).

Incinerators	5%
Hot air furnaces	5
Gas heaters	10
Stoves for heating only	10
Electrical stoves and heaters	10

PIEZ, CHARLES. Perpetual inventory and appraisal values; table of standard depreciation rates. *Engineering and contracting,* Jan. 24, 1917, p. 77. *Factory,* Dec. 1916, p. 668-71. *Iron age,* Nov. 30, 1916, Jan. 11, 1917, p. 1266, 138-9. *Iron trade review,* Feb. 22, 1917, p. 477-8. Condensed. *Journal of the American society of mechanical engineers,* Dec. 1916, p. 965-6. *Iron trade review,* Dec. 7, 1916, p. 1144-6. Kent, William. *Bookkeeping and cost accounting for factories.* 1918. p. 90. Discussion. *Journal of the American society of mechanical engineers,* March 1917, p. 215-7).

	% on cost	% on reducing cost
Boilers, pumps, feed-water heaters and air compressors	6	15
Cupolas, converters, melting furnaces and accessories	5	10

PROPOSED sale of Toronto utilities to the city. *Electrical world,* Oct. 25, 1913, p. 832.
Heaters 3-6%

ROBY, J. J. Schedule of plant depreciation. (In his *Treatise on cost accounting as applied to coal mining.* c1913. p. 14-5).

Pipe, heaters and pumps.	10%
Deduct as salvage before depreciation	8
Depreciation rate for remainder fireproof	

TIFFANY, H. S. Frame blast furnaces. (In his *Digest of depreciations.* c1890. p. 8).
Frame blast furnaces, 5% annual depreciation.

TIFFANY, H. S. Frame iron furnaces. (In his *Digest of depreciations.* c1890. p. 9).
Frame iron furnaces, 4% annual depreciation.

UNIFORM cost sheet for coal mining companies. *Coal age,* Sept. 19, 1918, p. 545-7.
Pumps, heaters and other power house equipment, 8% original cost.

VALUATION of the Chicago consolidated traction property. *Electric railway journal,* Dec. 3, 1910, p. 1111-3.
Heaters 4-5%

WHATLEY, G. E. STUART. Depreciation—blast furnaces, gas retorts, chemical and other similar fixed plant. (In his *Accountant's and bookkeeper's vade-mecum.* 1893. p. 25).

Straightening machines

NICHOLSON, J. LEE and J. F. D. ROHRBACH. Depreciation. (In their *Cost accounting.* 1919. p. 149).

Punches, shears, hydraulic and pneumatic riveters; bending rolls, straightening rolls, straightening press, bull-dozers, juggling machines, flanging machines, frame-setting machines, beveling machines, keel-bending machines, can brakes, etc., forging and upsetting machines	6⅔%
Mill machinery—including roll trains, tables, shears, and intensifiers, cold saws, hot-beds, cooling beds, straightening machines, drag-ons, drag-offs, pushers, ingot buggies, hydraulic accumulators, cold drawn machinery such as draw benches, roll straightening machines, etc., hot saws	5½%

Street railroads

See Depreciation, depletion and obsolescence—Electric and street railroads.

Streets

See Depreciation, depletion and obsolescence—Roads and highways.

DEPRECIATION, DEPLETION AND OBSOLESCENCE—*(Continued)*

Sub-stations

APPRAISAL of the Seattle telephone companies by the railroad commission of Washington. *Engineering and contracting*, May 3, 1911, p. 520-4.

	Life	Salvage	An. dep.	Av. age	Total dep.
Substation apparatus	10	5	9.5	5	47.5

BARKER, HARRY. Typical life expectation tables for public utility property. (In his *Public utility rates*. 1917. p. 319).
Substations (subscribers') 10 years, Wisconsin railroad commission.

BAY state street railway valuation. *Electric railway journal*, Dec. 4, 1915, p. 1121-3.

Substation buildings	1.6%
" equipment	3.2

Annual depreciation per cent, divided by investment.

BEMIS, EDWARD W. Report on the investigation of the Chicago telephone company submitted to the committee on gas, oil and electric light. Chicago, October 25, 1912—paper. 127p.

	Years	Salvage	% of cost
Byllesby and Arnold			
B. Due to age and wear and tear only	20	0	5.0
A. Due to all forms of depreciation	15	10.5	6.67
Chicago commission	10	10	8.73
Westinghouse, Church, Kerr & co.	10	15	8.5
E. L. Cline, Telephony, July 2, 1910	10	..	..

COST and depreciation of steam and hydro-electric installations. *Electrical world*, Dec. 30, 1909, p. 1558.

Depreciation of substation

Item	Prop. cost	life years	Annual amount for dep. in % of total cost
Land	6.0	..	..
Buildings	30.	25	67
Transformers	40	20	1.28
Switches, etc.	16	10	1.29
Installation	8	..	..
	100.		3.24

DEPRECIATION of overhead structures and substations. *Engineering and contracting*, Nov. 19, 1913, p. 567.
Substations 3%

DEPRECIATION statements—Manitoba government telephones. *Manitoba public utilities commission, Annual report*, 1913, p. 101.
Substation equipment, drop and interior wires 8%

FOSTER, HORATIO A. Rates of depreciation. (In his *Engineering valuation of public utilities and factories*. 1913. p. 200).

Power plant and substation equipment	
Engines, boilers, heaters conveyors, pumps and auxiliaries	4.5%
Rotaries, transformers, switchboards, auxiliaries	4.5
Storage batteries	3.0
Turbines and generators	6.0

Marwick, Mitchell & co. in the appraisal of a large street railway system.

GILLETTE, HALBERT P. and R. T. DANA. Depreciation. (In their *Handbook of mechanical and electrical cost data*. 1918. p. 106).
Buildings, sub-station. 33.3 years. H. P. Gillette, Everett railway and water co. Jan. 29, 1912.

GRAY, HENRY L. Necessity of depreciation reserves. *Railway age gazette*, May 27, 1910, p. 1297-8. Editorial. Depreciation reserves. *Railway age gazette*, May 27, 1910, p. 1290. Letters. Depreciation reserves. *Railway age gazette*, July 8, 1910, p. 66.
Sub-station apparatus 5%

GRUNSKY, CARL EWALD. Probable useful life of various articles. (In his *Valuation, depreciation and the rate-base*. 1917. p. 284).

Sub-station equipment
- 20 years
  San Joaquin light & power corporation. Rate hearing before California Railroad Commission, 1915.
- 25 years.
  Sir Wm. Preece. Report of Bristol corporation, England, 1906.
- 50 years.
  California railroad commission—Reports 1913-4. Calistoga electric co. vs. Napa valley electric co., May, 1914.

NICHOLSON, J. LEE and J. F. D. ROHRBACH. Depreciation. (In their *Cost accounting*. 1919. p. 148).
Sub-station equipment 5%
Based on (1) the cost of equipment
(2) the life of the equipment
(3) on a ten-hour day

PUBLIC utility reports, annotated. Rochester, Lawyers co-operative publishing co. 1918A. p. 914-8.
New York & N. S. traction co.
Substation equipment 3%

RUNYON, F. O. Report on hydro-electric plant for special committee common council, Newark, New Jersey, April 23, 1902, p. 15, 16, 24.

Substation	
Elec. ap.	5%
Substation	3

DEPRECIATION, DEPLETION AND OBSOLESCENCE—SUB-STATIONS—*(Continued)*

SALIERS, EARL A. Analysis of a hydro-electric plant. (In his *Principles of depreciation.* 1916. p. 34-8).
Substations
Buildings 25 years
Transformers 20
Switches, etc. 10

UNIFORM cost sheet for coal mining companies. *Coal age,* Sept. 19, 1908, p. 545-7.
Substation Original cost
wood 7%
stone or brick 5

Subways

PHILADELPHIA. CONTROLLER. Rates of depreciation. (In his *Manual of accounting, reporting and business procedure of the city and county of Philadelphia.* 1917. p. 210).
Subways and tunnels 1⅓%

RUNYAN, F. O. Report on hydro-electric plant for special committee common council, Newark, New Jersey, April 23, 1902, p. 15, 16, 24.
Subway 1%
" (distr.) 1

Suds installation

ELBOURNE, EDWARD T. Depreciation rates. (In his *Factory administration and accounts.* 1918. p. 376).

	Prov. dep. %		years
	Remainder values	10%	5%
Suds installation	7½	29	38

Sugar

AUSTRALIA. FEDERAL INCOME TAX DEPARTMENT. Depreciation allowance. *Accountant,* Oct. 13, 1917, p. 277-9. *Accounting and commerce,* June 30, 1917, p. 55-7. *Federal accountant,* July 1917, p. 93-8. *Public accountant,* Jan. 30, 1917, p. 145-52.
Sugar 7½%
" refining 7½
Written down value, repairs allowed in addition.

TIFFANY, H. S. Sugar refineries. (In his *Digest of depreciations.* c1890. p. 11).
Buildings:
brick 2½%
frame 4
Based upon the actual life without any repairs.

UNITED STATES. Federal trade commission. Depreciation. (In its *Report on the beet sugar industry in the United States.* p. 65-9).

Superheaters

BEMIS, E. W. Report on the investigation of the Chicago telephone company submitted to the committee on gas, oil and electric light. Chicago, October 25, 1912—paper. 127p.

	Life	Salvage	Annual Dep. % of cost
Byllesby and Arnold			
B. Due to age and wear and tear only	15-20	0	5.0
A. Due to all forms of depreciation	12-15	10.5	6.67
Chicago commission	8	20	11.25
Westinghouse, Church, Kerr & co.	10	15	....
E. L. Cline, Telephony July 2, 1910	10	20	8

BREWER, ALLEN F. Rates for annual depreciation. *Industrial management,* April 1918, p. 268.
Superheaters . . . . . 30 years 3.33%

ELBOURNE, EDWARD T. Depreciation rates. In his *Factory administration and accounts.* 1918. p. 376).

	Prov. dep. %		years
	Remainder values	10%	5%
Superheaters	12½	17	22

GRUNSKY, CARL EWALD. Probable useful life of various articles. (In his *Valuation, depreciation and the rate-base.* 1917. p. 284).
Superheaters
20 years.
Pacific gas and electric company. Figures used in rate hearings before Master in Chancery, San Francisco. 1913-14.

NICHOLSON, J. LEE and J. F. D. ROHRBACH. Depreciation. (In their *Cost accounting.* 1919. p. 147).
Superheaters 5%
Based on (1) the cost of equipment
(2) the life of the equipment
(3) on a ten-hour day.

Supply houses

See Depreciation, depletion and obsolescence—Warehouses.

Surface plates

NICHOLSON, J. LEE and J. F. D. ROHRBACH. Depreciation. (In their *Cost accounting.* 1919. p. 150).
Surface plates 10%

Surfacers

NICHOLSON, J. LEE and J. F. D. ROHRBACH. Depreciation. (In their *Cost accounting.* 1919. p. 150).
Woodworking machinery—Surfacers 5%
Based on (1) the cost of equipment
(2) the life of the equipment
(3) on a ten-hour day.

DEPRECIATION, DEPLETION AND OBSOLESCENCE—*(Continued)*

Surge tank

GRUNSKY, CARL EWALD. Probable useful life of various articles. (In his *Valuation, depreciation and the rate-base.* 1917. p. 284).
Concrete Surge tank 30 years.
San Joaquin light and power corporation. Rate hearing before California commission. 1915.

Surgeons

See Depreciation, depletion and obsolescence—Physicians.

Surveyors

AUSTRALIA. FEDERAL INCOME TAX DEPARTMENT. Depreciation allowance. *Accountant,* Oct. 13, 1917, p. 277-9. *Accounting and commerce,* June 30, 1917, p. 55-7. *Federal accountant,* July 1917, p. 93-8. *Public accountant,* Jan. 30, 1917, p. 145-52.
Surveyors' instruments; replacements allowable.

ROBY, J. J. Schedule of plant depreciation. (In his *Treatise on cost accounting as applied to coal mining.* c1913. p. 14-5).
Surveys and maps—original maps, instruments and outfits.
Deduct as salvage before depreciating 10%
Depreciation rate for remainder, fireproof 6

Swaging machines

ELBOURNE, EDWARD T. Depreciation rates. (In his *Factory administration and accounts.* 1918. p. 377).

	Prov. dep. %		years
	Remainder values	10%	5%
Swaging machines	10	22	28

Switchboards

ANALYSIS of the premises adopted and methods used in determining the cost to reproduce new together with the depreciation thereon of the physical property of the Metropolitan system and the Kansas City and Westport Belt railway of Kansas City, Mo.
Switchboards and generator leads:
Switchboards 3%
Generator leads 3
Wiring and cable 3

AUSTRALIA. FEDERAL INCOME TAX DEPARTMENT. Depreciation allowance. *Accountant,* Oct. 13, 1917, p. 277-9. *Accounting and commerce,* June 30, 1917, p. 55-7. *Federal accountant,* July 1917, p. 93-8. *Public accountant,* Jan. 30, 1917, p. 145-52.
Switchboards; repairs only.

BARKER, HARRY. Typical life expectation tables for public utility property. (In his *Public utility rates.* 1917. p. 368-9).
Switchboard instruments and wiring 25-30 years
Switchboards
old type 15-20
new type 20-30
Wisconsin Railroad commission

BAY state rate case. *Electric railway journal,* Dec. 4, 1915, p. 1121-3. *Public utility reports, annotated,* 1916F, p. 336-9.
Switchboards and wiring; average of generator served.

BELT, ROBERT E. Depreciation. (In his *Foundry cost accounting practice and procedure.* 1919. p. 243).
Electric generators and switchboards 7½%

BEMIS, EDWARD W. Report on the investigation of the Chicago telephone company submitted to the committee on gas, oil and elecric light. Chicago, October 25, 1912, paper. 127p.

	Private branch boards. Years.	Salvage.	Depreciation % of cost.
Byllesby and Arnold			
B. Due to age and wear and tear only	15-20	0	5.0
A. Due to all forms of depreciation	12-15	10.5	6.67
Chicago commission	8	20	11.25
Westinghouse, Church, Kerr & co.	10	15	—
E. L. Cline, Telephony, July 2, 1910	10	20	8

BOLTON, REGINALD PELHAM. Depreciation of mechanical equipments and power plants. (In his *Building for profit.* 1911. p. 82,89).

	Physical years	%	Economic years.
Dumb-waiters, switchboards, elevator gates, slow-speed elevator engines, shafting and bearings, slow-geared apparatus, elevators intermittently used	22	55.0	18

BRYAN, WILLIAM. Appraisal and depreciation of water?works and similar properties. *Journal of the Association of engineering societies,* Dec. 1907, p. 336-81. Depreciation allowance for various public-service industries. *Engineering news,* Jan. 23, 1908, p. 96.
Switchboards 10 years

BRYAN, WILLIAM H. Depreciation of electric light plants. *Municipality,* March 1908, p. 74.
Switchboards: Life 10 years. Authority. Iowa Electrical association, in *Iowa engineer,* July 1906.

CLINE, E. L. Depreciation of telephone companies. *Telephony,* July 2, 1910, p. 16.

	Years.	% dep.	% salvage.
Switchboards	10	8.0	20

COST and depreciation of steam and hydro-electric installations. *Electrical world,* Dec. 30, 1909, p. 1558.
Switchboard equipment—10 years .355% of total cost.

DEPRECIATION, DEPLETION AND OBSOLESCENCE—SWITCHBOARDS—*(Continued)*

CRAVENS, GEORGE W. Depreciation and maintenance of electrical equipment. *Electrical review*, April 23, 1910, p. 853-6. Montgomery, Robert H. *Auditing theory and practice.* 1916. p. 424. Montgomery, Robert H. *Income tax procedure,* 1919. p. 570. ———— Same, 1920. p. 723-4. Foster, H. A. *Engineering valuation of public utilities and factories.* 1913. p. 201-2.

	Annual % depreciation.	
Switchboards, etc.		
	2	Chicago traction commission.
	6.6	Chicago union traction co.
	5	Milwaukee electric railway and light co.
	2	Wisconsin railroad commission.
	7.5	Average English.
	5	Average Scotch practice.
	8-10	Philip Dawson.
	5	Stone and Webster.
	2-5	Industrial power plants.
	5	Miscellaneous sources.

	Light or intermittent service.	Heavy or continuous service.
Switchboards and instruments	2-5%	5-8.3%

CROWELL, H. H. Electric lighting rates and depreciation. *Municipal journal and engineering,* Dec. 18, 1907, p. 698.

	Purchased 10 years or more ago.	Modern.
Switchboards and instrument	15 years	20 years

ELBOURNE, EDWARD T. Depreciation rates. (In his *Factory administration and accounts.* 1918. p. 376).

	Prov. dep. %	Years	
	Remainder values	10%	5%
Switchboards, distribution boards and fittings	7½	29	38

FIGURES from the Iola (Kans.) central station. *Electrical world,* Sept. 23, 1909, p. 723.

Switchboard and accessories	8%

FLOY, HENRY. Depreciation. (In his *Valuation of public utility properties.* 1912. p. 168-217). Floy, Henry. Depreciation as related to electrical properties. *American institute of electrical engineers, Proceedings,* 1911, p. 1267. Floy, Henry. *Valuation of public utility properties.* 1912. p. 188-93. Foster, Horatio A. *Engineering valuation of public utilities and factories.* 1913. p. 194-8. *Engineering and contracting,* Oct. 4, 1911, p. 359-65. *Engineering magazine,* Aug. 1911, p. 837-40.

	Depreciation % per year straight line		
Switchboard and wiring			
	3	Traction val. comm.	Chicago con. tract. co.
	6	B. J. Arnold	Coney Island & Brooklyn adopted by P. S. C., N. Y.
	5	Henry Floy	3rd Ave. case, adopted by P. S. C., N. Y.
modern type	5	Wisconsin P. S. C.	
obsolete type	6⅔	Wisconsin P. S. C.	
	8	St. Louis P. S. C.	Union elec. L. & P. Co.

FOSTER, HORATIO A. Methods of calculating depreciation. (In his *Engineering valuation of public utilities and factories.* 1913. p. 169).

	Minimum service value, % of reproduction cost	
Switchboard and wiring complete		Joint engineering department of the Wisconsin commission.
modern type	45%	
obsolete "	35	
Switchboard instruments alone		
modern type	80	
obsolete "	60	

	Years
Power plants:	
Switchboards, central office	8-10
Subscribers' station equipment:	
Instruments	8-10
P.B.X.	10

FOSTER, HORATIO A. Rates of depreciation. (In his *Engineering valuation of public utilities and factories.* 1913. p. 200, 203, 205).

Rotaries, transformers, switchboards auxiliaries	4.5%
Marwick, Mitchell & co. in the appraisal of a large street railway system.	

	Years
Switchboard and wiring complete	
modern type	20-30
obsolete "	15-20
Switchboard and instruments	
modern type	20-30
obsolete "	15-20

GILLETTE, HALBERT P. and R. T. DANA. Depreciation. (In their *Handbook of mechanical and electrical cost data.* 1918. p. 110).

DEPRECIATION, DEPLETION AND OBSOLESCENCE—SWITCHBOARDS—*(Continued)*

Switchboards — 15-20 years
Union traction co., case Chicago and Union traction co. Stone & Webster.
20
Milwaukee electric railway and light co.
20-50
George W. Cravens, Industrial power plants.
22.2
Marwick, Mitchell & co. appraisal of a large street railway system; Foster, p. 199.
50
W. D. Pence, Milwaukee 3c case.
B. J. Arnold, Chicago appraisal, 4 cases.
Chicago traction commission.

and wiring — 33.3
Traction valuation commission, Chicago consolidated traction co.
16.7
B. J. Arnold—Appraisal of the Coney Island & Brooklyn railroad, Feb. 1, 1909.
20
Henry Floy, 3rd Ave. case, N. Y. city.

and wiring, modern type — 20
Wisconsin railroad commission.

obsolete type — 15
Wisconsin railroad commission.

GREENLAND, S. W. Depreciation. *Mississippi electric association, Report of 2nd annual convention,* June 1910, p. 32-6.
Switchboards — 20 years

GRUNSKY, CARL EWALD. Probable useful life of various articles. (In his *Valuation, depreciation and the rate-base.* 1917. p. 284).

Switchboards — 12½ years.
St. Louis Public service commission. Case of the Union electric light and power co.
15 years.
Chicago union traction co. Quoted in Report Wisconsin railroad commission, vol. 10, p. 220.
16.7 years.
Bion J. Arnold. Coney Island and Brooklyn figures adopted by Public service commission of New York.
Four Chicago appraisals quoted by H. A. Foster.
20 years.
Stone & Webster. Figures for Chicago union traction co. case. Report Wisconsin railroad commission, vol. 10, p. 220.
20 years.
Milwaukee electric railway and lighting co., in the Milwaukee 3c fare case, Aug. 1912.
20 years.
Henry Floy. Trans. American institute of electrical engineers, June 1911. Third avenue case figures adopted by public service commission of New York.
20 years.
Pacific gas and electric company. Figures used in rate hearings before Master in Chancery, San Francisco, 1913-4.
20 years.
Robt. Hammond. Journal of Institute of electrical engineers, England, April 25, 1907.
15-20 years.
San Joaquin light and power corporation. Rate hearing before California railroad comission, 1915.
15-20 years.
Wisconsin railroad commission. Milwaukee 3c fare case, Aug. 23, 1912.
33.3 years.
Traction valuation commission. Case of the Chicago consolidated traction co.
50 years.
Bion J. Arnold. Coney Island and Brooklyn figures adopted by Public service commission of New York.
Four Chicago appraisals quoted by H. A. Foster.
50 years.
Chicago traction commission. Quoted by G. W. Cravens, *Electrical review,* April 23, 1910.
50 years.
Wisconsin railroad commission.

telephone, central — 8 years. 20% residual value.
Chicago Telephone commission. Published 1908.
8-10 years. 15% residual value.
Telephone "Data". Compiled from practice A. T. & T. Co., Wisconsin railroad commission and others. Quoted by H. A. Foster.
12 years. 20% residual value.
Wisconsin railroad commission. Wisconsin telephone co. case, Aug. 3, 1909.

DEPRECIATION, DEPLETION AND OBSOLESCENCE—SWITCHBOARDS—*(Continued)*

telephone, P.B.X. 8 years. 20% residual value.
Chicago telephone commission. Published 1908.
10 years. 10% residual value.
Telephone "Data". Compiled from practice A. T. & T. Co., Wisconsin railroad commission and others. Quoted by H. A. Foster.
10 years. 15% residual value.
Wisconsin railroad commission. Wisconsin telephone co. case, Aug. 3, 1909.

KIMBALL, DEXTER S. Estimated life and factors of depreciation. (In his *Cost finding.* 1918. p. 190. *Principles of industrial organization.* 1913. p. 163).

	Prob. life of assets in years.	Ratio of scrap to orig. val.	% on orig. cost.	% on dim. val.
Switchboards and instruments	15	0.05	6.3	18

NEALE, R. E. Depreciation in engineering works. *Mechanical world,* Feb. 7, 1913, p. 67-8.

Switchboards		
Power: old type	6.6-8%	12.5-15 years
modern	3-5	20-33
Telephone exchange	10-14	7-10

NICHOLSON, J. LEE and J. F. D. ROHRBACH. Depreciation. (In their *Cost accounting.* 1919. p. 148).
Switchboards
telephone central 5%
telephone P.B.X. 7½
Switchboards and wiring 5
Switchboards, main wiring and conduit 5
Based on (1) the cost of equipment
(2) the life of the equipment
(3) on a ten-hour day.

PENDER, HAROLD. Depreciation. (In his *Handbook for electrical engineers.* c1914. p. 340).
Switchboards, P. H. & S. S. 15 years.
Chicago union traction co.
20 years.
S. W. Greenland.
Stone & Webster for the Chicago union traction co.
50 years.
Engineer of valuation staff, of Wisconsin railroad commission.
7.5 years.
Cardiff tramways.
6.66 years.
Chicago union traction co.
5 years.
Milwaukee electric railway and light co.
Glasgow tramways.
Stone & Webster, for the Chicago union traction co.
2 years.
Engineer of valuation staff, of Wisconsin railroad commission.

PHILADELPHIA. CONTROLLER. Rates of depreciation. (In his *Manual of accounting, reporting and business procedure of the city and county of Philadelphia.* 1917. p. 205).
Switchboards, panel board, and other electrical control apparatus 8⅓%

PIEZ, CHARLES. Perpetual inventory and appraisal values; table of standard depreciation rates. *Engineering and contracting,* Jan. 24, 1917, p. 77. *Factory,* Dec. 1916, p. 668-71. *Iron age,* Nov. 30, 1916, Jan. 11, 1917, p. 1266, 138-9. *Iron trade review,* Feb. 22, 1917, p. 477-8. Condensed. *Iron trade review,* Dec. 7, 1916, p. 1144-6. *Journal of the American society of mechanical enginers,* Dec. 1916, p. 965-6. Kent, William. *Bookkeeping and cost accounting for Factories.* 1918. p. 90. Discussion. *Journal of the American society of mechanical engineers,* March 1917, p. 215-7).

	% on cost.	% on reducing balance.
Switchboards, main wiring and conduit	6	15

PRACTICAL hints on computing telephone depreciation. *Telephony,* April 1, 1911, p. 401-3.
P.B.X. switchboards 7%
Switchboards 7

PROPOSED sale of Toronto utilities to the city. *Electrical world,* Oct. 25, 1913, p. 832.
Switchboards and interior wiring 3%

ROBY, J. J. Schedule of plant depreciation. (In his *Treatise on cost accounting as applied to coal mining.* c1913. p. 14-5).
Engines, dynamos and switchboards.
Deduct as salvage before depreciating 20%
Depreciation rate for remainder, fireproof 4

RUNYON, F. O. Report on hydro-electric plant for special committee common council, Newark, New Jersey, April 23, 1902, p. 15, 16, 24.
Switchboard 5%
Aux. switchbd. & el. ap. 5

SALIERS, EARL A. Analysis of a hydroelectric plant. (In his *Principles of depreciation.* 1916. p. 34-8).
Switchboard equipment 10 years

VALUATION of the Chicago consolidated traction property. *Electric railway journal,* Dec. 3, 1910, p. 1111-3.
Switchboards and generator leads 3%

YEAMAN, C. H. Depreciation and reserves for antiquation and obsolescence from an engineering standpoint. *Electrical engineering* (London), July 12, 1907, p. 4. *Electrical review* (London), July 12, 1907, p. 44. *Electrician,* July 5, 1907, p. 475.

DEPRECIATION, DEPLETION AND OBSOLESCENCE—SWITCHBOARDS—*(Continued)*

Rotary converters, switches and instruments — 20 years.
R. Hammond.
15 years.
L.G.B. (Local government board).
20 years.
L.C.C.
20-25 years.
J. F. C. Snell (M.E.A. 1905).

Switches

BOLTON, REGINALD PELHAM. Depreciation of mechanical equipments and power plants. (In his *Building for profit.* 1911. p. 82, 89).

	Physical years.	%	Economic years.
Electric switches, wiring and connections	15	37.5	11

COST and depreciation of steam and hydro-electric installations. *Electrical world*, Dec. 30, 1909, p. 1558.
Switches, etc., 10 years, 1.29% of total cost.

ELBOURNE, EDWARD T. Depreciation rates. (In his *Factory administration and accounts.* 1918. p. 376).

	Prov. dep. % Remainder values	Years 10%	5%
Motor rheostats and switches	7½	29	38

HAMMOND, ROBERT. Depreciation. *Journal of the Institute of electrical engineers*, 1907, p. 270. *Institute of electrical engineers, Proceedings*, April 25, 1907. Abstracts. *Accountant*, May 18, 1907, p. 675. *Electric railway review*, June 1, 1907, p. 716. *Electrical review* (Chicago), May 25, 1907, p. 828. *Electrical review* (London), May 3, 1907, p. 744. *Electrician*, April 26, 1907, p. 51. *Engineering magazine*, July 1907, p. 636-8. *Engineering record*, June 15, 1907, p. 703. *Municipal journal* (London), May 10, 17, 1907, p. 411, 435. *Progressive age*, July 1, 1907, p. 305. *Street railway bulletin*, June 1907 p. 382. *Tramway and railway world*, June 6, 1907, p. 497.
Switching apparatus and instruments — 20 years

NEALE, R. E. Depreciation in engineering works. *Mechanical world*, Feb. 7, 1913, p. 67-8.
Twine switches, 5-7%, 14-20 years.

Swords

PHILADELPHIA. CONTROLLER. Rates of depreciation. (In his *Manual of accounting, reporting and business procedure of the city and county of Philadelphia.* 1917. p. 209).
Batons, night sticks, riot clubs, swords, etc. — 10%

Tables

See also Depreciation—Billiard tables.

BELT, ROBERT E. Depreciation. (In his *Foundry cost accounting practice and procedure.* 1919. p. 243).
Tables — 10%

BELT, ROBERT E. Depreciation. (In his *Uniform cost accounting methods; adopted by the American malleable castings association*, Nov. 14, 1917, p. 20-1).
Sorting tables — 10%

DENHAM, ROBERT S. Depreciation. (In his *Manual of cost engineering and estimating for paper box manufactures.* 1917. p. 249).
Tables — 6%

NICHOLSON, J. LEE and J. F. D. ROHRBACH. Depreciation. (In their *Cost accounting.* 1919. p. 149).
Mill machinery—including roll trains, tables, shears, and intensifiers, cold saws, hotbeds, cooling beds, straightening machines, drag-ons, drag-offs, pushers, ingot buggies, hydraulic accumulators, cold drawn machinery such as draw benches, roll straightening machines, etc., hot saws 5½%

PHILADELPHIA. CONTROLLER. Rates of depreciation. (In his *Manual of accounting, reporting and business procedure of the city and county of Philadelphia.* 1917. p. 207-8).
Tables — 4%

Tabourets

PHILADELPHIA. CONTROLLER. Rates of depreciation. (In his *Manual of accounting, reporting and business procedure of the city and county of Philadelphia.* 1917. p. 207-8).
Tabourets, stands, pedestals, copy holders — 4%

Tanks

AUSTRALIA. FEDERAL INCOME TAX DEPARTMENT. Depreciation on allowance. *Accountant*, Oct. 13, 1917, p. 277-9. *Accounting and commerce*, June 30, 1917, p. 55-7. *Federal accountant*, July 1917, p. 93-5. *Public accountant*, Jan. 30, 1917, p. 145-52.

Tanks	2½%
Tanks (galvanized iron)	
rain water	5
other "	10
Written down value, repairs allowed in addition.	
Wells and underground tanks	Nil

BOLTON, REGINALD PELHAM. Depreciation of mechanical equipments and power plants. (In his *Building for profit.* 1911. p. 82, 89).

	Physical years.	%	Economic years.
Roof tanks, sanitary piping systems	27	67.5	21
Interior drums and tanks, hot-water and pneumatic piping	25	62.5	

DEPRECIATION, DEPLETION AND OBSOLESCENCE—TANKS—*(Continued)*

BOLTON, REGINALD PELHAM. Depreciation of the value of buildings. (In his *Building for profit.* 1911. p. 62).

	Relative to years	
	66	75
Tanks	41%	36%

BREWER, ALLAN F. Rates for annual depreciation. *Industrial management,* April 1918, p. 268).
Water tower or tanks, 50 years, 2%.

ELBOURNE, EDWARD T. Depreciation rates. (In his *Factory administration and accounts.* 1918. p. 376).

	Prov. dep. %	Years	
	Remainder values	10%	5%
Tanks	10	22	28

GILLETTE, HALBERT P. and R. T. DANA. Depreciation. (In their *Handbook of mechanical and electrical cost data.* 1918. p. 110).
Storage, ammonia, wrought iron or steel tanks, 15 years. Wisconsin railroad commission.

GRUNSKY, CARL EWALD. Probable useful life of various articles. (In his *Valuation, depreciation and the rate-base.* 1917. p. 285).
Tanks
wooden — 12 years.
Pacific gas and electric company. Figures used in rate hearings before Master in Chancery, San Francisco, 1913-4.
steel — 30 years.
Pacific gas and eelctric company. Figures used in rate hearings before Master in Chancery, San Francisco, 1913-4.

NICHOLSON, J. LEE and J. F. D. ROHRBACH. Depreciation. (In their *Cost accounting.* 1919. p. 148, 149).

Steel work—including air, oil, and water tanks	4%
Tanks and reservoirs	
steel	4½%
wood	8

Based on (1) the cost of equipment
(2) the life of the equipment
(3) on a ten-hour day.

PHILADELPHIA. CONTROLLER. Rates of depreciation. (In his *Manual of accounting, reporting and business procedure of the city and county of Philadelphia.* 1917. p. 205).
Tanks — 4%

PIEZ, CHARLES. Perpetual inventory and appraisal values; table of standard depreciation rates. *Engineering and contracting,* Jan. 24, 1917, p. 77. *Factory,* Dec. 1916, p. 668-71. *Iron age,* Nov. 30, 1916, Jan. 11, 1917, p. 1227. 138-9. *Iron trade review,* Feb. 22, 1917, p. 477-8. Condensed. *Iron trade review,* Dec. 7, 1916, p. 1144-6. *Journal of the American society of mechanical engineers* Dec. 1916, p. 965-6. Kent, William. *Bookkeeping and cost accounting for factories.* 1918. p. 90. Discussion. *Journal of the American society of mechanical engineers,* March 1917, p. 215-7.

	% on cost	% on reducing balance
Tanks and reservoirs		
steel	4.5	10
wood (10 years)	9	20

PROSSER, R. W. Depreciation in gas plants. *American gas light journal,* May 26, 1902, p. 767.

Tanks	
brick tanks	30 years
steel tanks	30 years 20% of first cost
Steel tanks and holders	30 years—10% of first cost.

STRUCKMAN, H. Depreciation and obsolescence in Portland cement plants. *Journal of the American society of mechanical engineers,* Feb. 1913, p. 262-75.
Oil storage tanks 7% of reproduction value.

UNIFORM cost sheet for coal mining companies. *Coal age,* Sept. 19, 1918, p. 545-7.
Original cost.
Water tanks — 7%

VARIOUS depreciation charges. *New York Times,* June 14, 1914.
Oil storage tanks — 7%

Tanneries

AUSTRALIA. FEDERAL INCOME TAX DEPARTMENT. Depreciation allowance. *Accountant,* Oct. 13, 1917, p. 277-9. *Accounting and commerce,* June 30, 1917, p. 55-7. *Federal accountant,* July 1917, p. 93-8. *Public accountant,* Jan. 30, 1917, p. 145-52.
Tanneries and wool scourers — 5%
Written down value, repairs allowed in addition.

PHILADELPHIA. CONTROLLER. Rates of depreciation. (In his *Manual of accounting, reporting and business procedure of the city and county of Philadelphia.* 1917. p. 205).
Tanners' and leather workers' equipment — 3⅓%

TIFFANY, H. S. Hides. (In his *Digest of depreciations.* c1890. p. 14, 11).

Rough leather	55%
Sale leather	40
Upper leather	75
Buildings:	
brick	2½-3
frame	3½-4

Based upon the actual life without any repairs.

Tape winders

DENHAM, ROBERT S. Depreciation. (In his *Manual of cost engineering and estimating for paper box manufacturers.* 1917. p. 249).
Tape winders — 6%

DEPRECIATION, DEPLETION AND OBSOLESCENCE—*(Continued)*

Tapping machines

ELBOURNE, EDWARD T. Depreciation rates. (In his *Factory administration and accounts.* **1918.** p. 377).

	Prov. dep. %	Remainder values 10%	Years 5%
Tapping machines	7½	29	38

NICHOLSON, J. LEE and J. F. D. ROHRBACH. Depreciation. (In their *Cost accounting.* **1919.** p. 149).
Tapping machines 6⅔%

Tar

AUSTRALIA. FEDERAL INCOME TAX DEPARTMENT . Depreciation allowance. *Accountant,* Oct. 13, 1917, p. 277-9. *Accounting and commerce,* June 30, 1917, p. 55-7. *Federal accountant,* July 1917, p. 93-8. *Public accountant,* Jan. 30, 1917, p. 145-52.

Tar distillation	
Still	7½%
Boiler	5
Tanks (iron)	12½
" (cement)	2½
Tar barrels	10

Written down value, repairs allowed in addition.

FOSTER, HORATIO A. Rates of depreciation. (In his *Engineering valuation of public utilities and factories.* 1913. p. 206-7).
Tar and ammonia wells 50 years
P. and A. tar extractors 40

GRUNSKY, CARL EWALD. Probable useful life of various articles. (In his *Valuation, depreciation and the rate-base.* 1917. p. 285).
Tar extractors
P. & A. 40 years. Wisconsin railroad commission. Quoted by H. A. Foster and in published reports.

Targets

PHILADELPHIA. CONTROLLER. Rates of depreciation. (In his *Manual of accounting, reporting and business procedure of the city and county of Philadelphia.* 1917. p. 209).
Air guns and other missile throwing apparatus
(Not internal combustion and targets) 8⅓%

Tarpaulins

AUSTRALIA. FEDERAL INCOME TAX DEPARTMENT. Depreciation allowance. *Accountant,* Oct. 13, 1917, p. 277-9. *Accounting and commerce,* June 30, 1917, p. 55-7. *Federal accountant,* July 1917, p. 93-8. *Public accountant,* June 30, 1917, p. 145-52.
Tarpaulins 15%
Written down value, repairs allowed in addition.

Taxicab companies

PUBLIC utility reports, annotated. Rochester, Lawyers co-operative publishing co. 1915B, p. 546.
Re Terminal Taxicab Co. (D. C.). A taxicab company was ordered to conform its depreciation accounts to a rate of 7 per cent on the cost of property new for "office furniture and fixtures, machine shop, tire room, and miscellaneous equipment".
Re Terminal Taxicab Co. (D. C.). A taxicab company was ordered to conform its depreciation accounts to a rate of 3 per cent on the cost of property new for "buildings and electrical equipment of buildings."

PUBLIC utility reports, annotated. Rochester, Lawyers co-operative publishing co. 1915E, p. 1, 6.
Re Auto Livery Co. (D. C.). An auto-delivery and taxicab company was ordered to conform its depreciation account to a rate of 9.3 per cent on the cost of property new for office furniture and fixtures, machine shop, tire room, and miscellaneous equipment.
Re Barnett Taxicab Co. (D. C.). The rate of depreciation for motor cabs was found to be 15.7 per cent and for office furniture and fixtures, machine-shop equipment, and miscellaneous equipment of a taxicab company, 9.5 per cent, such rates to be based on the cost of reproduction new of the property on hand at the time of the valuation and on the orignal cost new in the case of property acquired thereafter.

Telephone and telegraph

See also various headings under Depreciation, depletion and obsolescence.
ALLISON, JAMES E. Theoretical depreciation. *Telephone engineer,* Nov. 1917.
AMERICAN electric railway association. Committee on valuation. Bibliography on valuation of public utilities to Dec. 23, 1915. New York, American electric railway association. 61+72p.
APPRAISAL of the Seattle telephone companies by the railroad commission of Washington. *Engineering and contracting,* May 3, 1911, p. 520-4.

Item	Life	Salvage	An. Dep.	Av. Age	Total Dep.
Pole lines	12	00	8.5	5	42.5
Aerial cable	12	30	6.0	5	30.0
Underground cable	20	40	3.0	5	15.0
Submarine cable	10	00	10.0	5	50.0
Aerial wire, copper	15	40	4.0	5	20.0
Aerial wire, iron	8	00	12.5	5	62.5
Conduit, clay	50	00	2.0	5	10.0
Conduit, fibre	30	00	3.5	5	17.5
Central office equipment	10	10	9.0	5	45.0
Substation apparatus	10	5	9.5	5	47.5
Installation, single	10	5	9.5	5	47.5
Installation, group	20	10	4.5	5	22.5

DEPRECIATION, DEPLETION AND OBSOLESCENCE—TELEPHONE AND TELEGRAPH—*(Continued)*

Drops and block wires	8	10	11.5	5	57.5
Private exchanges	8	15	10.5	5	52.5
Boots, etc.	10	10	9.0	5	45.0
Buildings	20	30	3.5	5	17.5
Tools and vehicles	4	20	20.0	5	100.0
Furniture and fixtures	10	20	8.0	5	40.0

AUSTRALIA. FEDERAL INCOME TAX DEPARTMENT. Depreciation allowance. *Accountant,* Oct. 13, 1917, p. 277-9. *Accounting and commerce,* June 30, 1917, p. 55-7. *Federal accountant,* July 1917, p. 93-8. *Public accountant,* Jan. 30, 1917, p. 145-52.

Telephones and lines owned by taxpayers	5%

Written down value, repairs allowed in addition.

BARKER, HARRY. Typical life expectation tables for public utility property. (In his *Public utility rates.* 1917. p. 369).

	Years	Authority.	Control.
Telephone utilities			
Buildings	40	Chicago Tel. Comm.	Obs.
Cables, lead-covered, aerial	12	Wis. R.R. Comm.	Det. and Obs.
underground	20	" " "	Obs. and Det.
Central exchange equipment	10	" " "	Obs. and Det.
Conduit	50	Chicago Tel. Comm.	Obs.
Cross arms	8-12	Wis. R.R. Comm.	Det.
Furniture and tools	7	" " "	Det.
Poles, wood in earth	12-15	" " "	Det.
Power plant	8	" " "	Det. and Obs.
Private branch exchange equipment	8	Chicago Tel. Comm.	Det. and Obs.
Substations (subscribers')	10	Wis. R.R. Comm.	Det. and Obs.
Wire, copper, line	40	Chicago Tel. Comm.	Obs.
copper, interior	30	" " "	Obs.
galv. iron, line	8-15	Wis. R.R. Comm.	Det. and Obs.

BAY state rate case. *Electric railway journal,* Dec. 4, 1915, p. 1121-3. *Public utility reports, annotated,* 1916F, p. 336-9.

Telephone and telegraph lines

6.9 annual depreciation per cent, annual depreciation divided by investment.

Telephone and telegraph lines.	
Telephone sets	10 years
Iron box telephone sets	14
Telephone wire	15
Submarine telephone cable	10
Underground telephone cable	30

BEMIS, EDWARD W. Report on the investigation of the Chicago telephone company submitted to the committee on gas, oil and electric light. Chicago, October 25, 1912—paper 127p. Answer of the Chicago telephone company to the report of E. W. Bemis, submitted to the committee on gas, oil and electric light. Chicago, November 21, 1912, 31p.

Description	Life Byllesby and Arnold B Due to age and wear and tear only	A Due to all forms of depreciation.	Chicago Commission	Westinghouse, Church, Kerr & Co.	E. L. Cline Telephony, July 2, 1910
	Years	Years	Years	Years	Years
Buildings	60-100	30-60	40	50	50
Central office equipment	25	16⅔	8	15	10
Private branch boards	15-20	12-15	8	10	10
Substation apparatus	20	15	10	10	10
Clay conduit lines	Indefinite	50	50	50	Unknown
Underground cable, main and toll	50	18	20	20	25
Underground cable subsidiary	35	14	15		20
Aerial cable	25	12.5	15	17.5	15
Poles and crossarms	18	10-14	10	15	10-19
Copper wire, long distance and toll lines	25	15	40	40	15
Copper wire exchange lines	20	15	30	20	15

Description	Salvage Byllesby and Arnold b Age and wear only	a All forms of depreciation	Chicago Telephone Commission	Westinghouse, Church, Kerr & Co.	E. L. Cline
Buildings	0	0	0	0	0
Central office equipment } Central battery }	5	12	20	20	20
Private branch boards	0	10.5	20	15	20

DEPRECIATION, DEPLETION AND OBSOLESCENCE—TELEPHONE AND TELEGRAPH—*(Continued)*

Substation apparatus	0	10.5	10	15	
City conduits	0	0	0	0	0
Underground cable main	1-37	35.2	40	40	40
Underground cable subsidiary	0-39	10.4	40	40	40
Aerial cable	2-35	19.7	40	30	40
Poles & crossarms	0	0	0	0	0-20
Copper wire	40	45	70	50	70

CLINE E. L. Depreciation of telephone companies. *Telephony*, July 2, 1910, p. 16.

Exchange Equipment	Years	% dep.	Salvage value
Conduit	Unknown	1.0	0
Underground cable	25	2.4	40%
" lateral	20	3.0	40
Aerial cable	15	4.0	40
Poles, cedar 25 ft.	10	9.0	10
" " 30	12	7.08	15
" " 35	15	5.33	20
" " 40	17	4.7	20
" " 45	19	4.21	20
" " 50	19	4.21	20
" chestnut 25	8	11.25	10
" " 30	10	8.5	15
" " 35	12	6.7	20
" " 40	13	6.1	20
" " 45	15	5.3	20
" " 50	15	5.3	20
Cross arms	8	12.5	0
Copper wire	15	2.0	70
Iron wire	10	10.00	0
Cable terminals	12	8.33	0
Telephones	10	9.0	10
Switchboard	10	8.0	20
Private branch exchange	10	8.0	20
Buildings	50	2.0	0
Insulators	15	3.33	50
Ins. Wire (iron)	12	7.5	10
" " (copper)	12	6.6	20
Messenger	12	8.3	0
Telephone instruments	10	7.0	30
Booths	10	8.0	20

COST and depreciation of steam and hydro-electric installations. *Electrical world*, Dec. 30, 1909, p. 1558.

Electric light & telephone 10 years 0.065% of total cost

"COST of progress" and the "profit of progress" in the telephone field. *Engineering and contracting*, April 8, 1914, p. 403.

CRUMB, WILLIAM H. Determination of telephone rates for large exchanges. *Journal of the Western society of engineers*, Dec. 1907, p. 781.

DEPRECIATION law and practice—recent telephone arbitration: from the Western daily mail. *Accountant*, March 15, 1913, p. 415-8.

DEPRECIATION of lighting and telephone plants. *Electric world and engineer*, July 27, 1901.

DEPRECIATION of plant. Nebraska state railway commission, Annual report, 1913, p. 203-5.

The depreciation of plant * * * is just as real and substantial a charge against revenues as the wages paid to operators or any other employee of the company.

In this case the findings of the various engineers range from 6.01% to 6.54% on reproduction value.

DEPRECIATION of underground conduits, cables and wires. *Electric railway journal*, May 8, 1909, p. 881.

Of the total value of the telephone plants owned by the American telephone and telegraph company and associated companies.

	%
Real estate constitutes	9
Underground conduits and cables	20
Copper wires and aerial cables on poles	18
Pole lines, not including wires	26
Eight million dollars of this represents ownership of rights of way over private property.	
Iron wires	4
Central office and substation equipment	23

As to depreciation of property, real estate is standard and established.

Underground conduits can be classed with real estate, or, rather, with permanent construction on long-term ground rents.

Cables and copper wires have shown very small depreciation and experience has not yet established a definite rate, there is, however, a net scrap value of 40%.

Iron wires have a life of from 8 to 15 years

Pole lines have a life of from 10 to 16

DEPRECIATION statements—Manitoba government telephones. *Manitoba public utilities commission, Anual report*, 1913, p. 101.

Central office equipment	7%
Sub-stations equipment	8
Exchange pole lines	6
Exchange aerial cable	5
Exchange aerial wire	10

DEPRECIATION, DEPLETION AND OBSOLESCENCE—TELEPHONE AND TELEGRAPH—*(Continued)*

Exchange U.G. conduit	2
Exchange U.G. cable	3
Rural pole lines	5
Rural aerial wire	6
Toll poll lines	5
Toll wire, iron	6
Toll wire, copper	2
Sub-station equipment, drop and interior wires	8

ELBOURNE, EDWARD T. Depreciation rates. (In his *Factory administration and accounts.* 1918. p. 376).

	Prov. dep. %	Years Remainder values 10%	5%
Telephone installation	7½	29	38

EXAMPLE of inadequate depreciation. *Public service regulation,* Jan. 1913. p. 2.

FLOY, HENRY. Depreciation. Floy, Henry. Depreciation as related to electrical properties. *American institute of electrical engineering, Proceedings,* 1911, p. 1267. Floy, Henry. *Valuation of public utility properties.* 1912. p. 188-93. Foster, Horatio A. *Engineering valuation of public utilities and factories.* 1913. p. 194-8. *Engineering magazine,* Aug. 1911, p. 837-40. *Engineering and contracting,* Oct. 4, 1911, p. 359-65.

	Dep. % per year—Straight line	
Telephones	10	Wisconsin P. S. C.

FOSTER, HORATIO A. Methods of calculating depreciation. (In his *Engineering valuation of public utilities and factories.* 1913. p. 170, 193).

Telephone equipment	Minimum service value % of reproduction cost.
Power plant and wire	25
Poles	20-40
Iron wire	10
Copper	25
Lead-covered cable, both overhead and underground	25
Subscribers sets	30

The Wisconsin railroad commission has covered the regular plants by giving as the average life of

Telephone plants	11.24 year

FOSTER, HORATIO A. Rates of depreciation. (In his *Engineering valuation of public utilities and factories.* 1913. p. 202, 203, 206).

Chicago telephone commission in 1908 gave the following table of life, depreciation and salvage.

Property	Life in years	Per cent to depreciation account	Per cent salvage	Per cent to reconstruction and insurance
Conduit, main, clay in concrete	50	.89	0	1½
Conduit, main, fiber in concrete	20	3.72	0	1½
Conduit, subsidiary	20	3.72	0	2
Cable, main	20	3.72	..	2
Cable, subsidiary	15	5.38	40	2
Aerial cable	15	5.38	..	3
Poles, including cross arms	10	8.73	0	4½
Aerial strand	12	7.05	0	3½
Aerial cable, terminals	12	7.05	0	3
Aerial wire, copper	15	5.38	70	3
Drop wires	8	11.25	15	4
Subscribers' station instruments	10	8.73	5	2
Private branch exchange switchboards	8	11.28	20	2
Central office switchboards	8	11.25	20	2
Buildings, fireproof	40	1.33	0	1
Teams, tools, furniture, etc.	4	23.92	10	0

Telephone plant, life and depreciation of, from "data" annual depreciation—per cent of first cost in place.

Class of Plant	Life in years	Junk value % of first cost in Place	Without cumulative interest	With 2% interest	With 3% interest	With 6% interest
Buildings:						
Fireproof	25-50	25	3.0-1.5	2.3-0.9	2.1-0.7	1.4-0.25
Mill construction	25	20	3.2	2.8	2.2	1.5
Cables:						
Aerial exchange	12-15	30	5.8-4.7	5.2-4.0	4.9-3.8	4.1-3.0
In buildings	10	30	7	6.4	6.1	5.3
Underground	..	..	..	..	..	..
Exchange, main	20-25	40	3.0-2.4	2.5-1.9	2.2-1.6	1.6-1.1
Exchange, subsidiary	13-20	40	4.6-3.0	4.1-2.5	3,8-2.2	3.2-1.6
Toll	30	40	2.0	1.5	1.3	0.76
Submarine	10	0	10.0	9.1	8.7	7.6
Cable terminals	10-12	0	10.0-8.3	9.1-7.5	8.7-7.0	7.6-5.9
Conduits, main:						
Clay vitrified	50	0	2.0	1.2	0.89	0.34
Concrete	50	0	2.0	1.2	0.89	0.34
Fiber	20	0	5.0	4.1	3.7	2.7
Iron	20	0	5.0	4.1	3.7	2.7

DEPRECIATION, DEPLETION AND OBSOLESCENCE—TELEPHONE AND TELEGRAPH—*(Continued)*

Wood, creosoted	20	0	5.0	4.1	3.7	2.7
Conduits, subsidiary	15	0	6.7	5.8	5.4	4.3
Furniture and fixtures	10	0	10.0	9.1	8.7	7.6
Poles:						
Cedar, 35 feet and under	10-15	0	10.0-6.7	9.1-5.8	8.7-5.4	7.6-4.3
Cedar, over 35 ft.	15-20	0	6.7-5.0	5.8-4.1	5.4-3.7	4.3-2.7
Chestnut, 35 feet and under	8-12	0	12.5-8.3	11.6-7.5	11.2-7.0	10.1-5.9
Chestnut, over 35 feet	12-15	0	8.3-6.7	7.5-5.8	7.0-5.4	5.9-4.3
Pine, creosoted	20	0	5.0	4.1	3.7	2.7
Poles and cross arms, average exchange	10	0	10.0	9.1	8.7	7.6
Poles and cross arms, average toll	15	0	6.7	5.8	5.4	4.3
Power plants:						
Switchboards central office	8-10	15	10.6-8.5	9.9-7.8	9.6-7.4	8.6-6.4
Subscribers' station equipment:						
Instruments	8-10	10	11.2-9.0	10.58-2	10.1-7.9	9.1-6.8
P. B. X. switchboards	10	10	9.0	8.2	7.9	6.8
Tools and teams	5	0	20.0	19.2	18.8	17.7
Wire exchange lines:						
Copper, bare	10-15	40	6.0-4.0	5.5-3.5	5.2-3.2	4.5-2.6
Copper, insulated tw. pr.	10	10	9.0	8.2	7.8	6.8
Iron, bare	8-10	0	12.5-10.0	11.6-9.1	11.2-8.7	10.1-7.6
Wire toll lines:						
Copper, bare	40	40	1.5	1.0	0.8	0.30
Iron, bare	15	0	6.7	5.8	5.4	4.3

Telephone equipment (Wisconsin Commissions)

	Years
Central office equipment including distributing frame	10
Power, plant and wire	8
Poles	12 to 15
Cross arms	8 to 12
Iron wire	8 to 15
Copper wire	20
Weatherproof iron wire	15
Cables, lead covered, aerial	12
Cables, lead covered, underground	20
Subscribers' sets	10
Furniture and tools	7

GEIJSBEEK, JOHN B. & Co. Three elements of plant deterioration, repairs, renewals, depreciation. (In their *Report on the Denver plant of the mountain states telephone and telegraph co.*, January 1914, p. 89-100).

As the engineer estimates the depreciation and renewals to be 5.14%, for the plant in Denver, we can make the following division:

Repairs and maintenance	3.84%
Experienced renewals	3.30
Depreciation to normal value together with accrued renewals	1.84
Total for all three	8.98%

GILLETTE, HALBERT P. and RICHARD T. DANA. Depreciation. (In their *Handbook of mechanical and electrical cost data.* 1918. p. 106, 109, 110, 125).

Buildings, telephone	24 years. Nathan Hayward, The Bell telephone co. of Pennsylvania, Aug. 31, 1912.
Pole lines exchange telephone	10.5 years Nathan Hayward, The Bell telephone co. of Pennsylvania, Aug. 31, 1912.
tool (telephone)	16 years. Nathan Hayward, The Bell telephone co. of Pennsylvania, Aug. 31, 1912.
Telegraph (signal)	10 years Marwick, Mitchell & Co., appraisal of a large street railway system, Foster, p. 199.
Telephone equipment, central office	8.25 years Nathan Hayward, The Bell telephone co. of Pennsylvania, Aug. 31, 1912.
Telephone equipment, sub-station (except installations but including sub-station central office equipment, public brand exchanges booths, and special fittings, sub-license station apparatus.	9 years. Nathan Hayward, The Bell telephone co. of Pennsylvania, Aug. 31, 1912.

DEPRECIATION, DEPLETION AND OBSOLESCENCE—TELEPHONE AND TELEGRAPH—*(Continued)*

Telephone central office equipment including distributing frame. 10 years
Wisconsin railroad commission.

Telephone and telegraph lines 20 years.
H. P. Gillette, Everett railway & water co., **Jan. 29, 1912.**

Telephone subscribers' sets 10 years
Wisconsin railroad commission.

Repair and depreciation costs of telephone company. In the hearing of the Bell telephone company of Pennsylvania, Gillette showed that the average current maintenance and depreciation was 9.46% of the average book valuation of the physical property for a period of 29 years.

GRAY, HENRY L. Necessity of depreciation reserves. *Railway age gazette*, May 27, 1910, p. 1297-8. Editorial. Depreciation reserves. *Railway age gazette*, May 27, 1910, p. 1290. Letters. Depreciation reserves. *Railway age gazette*, July 8, 1910, p. 66.

Telephone and telegraph instruments 6%

GRUNSKY, CARL EWALD. Probable useful life of various articles. (In his *Valuation, depreciation and the rate-base.* 1917. p. 285).

Telephone equipment

street railway 10-12 years.
Wisconsin Railroad Commission. Milwaukee 3c fare case, Aug. 23, 1912.

street railway 13.3 years.
Milwaukee electric railway and lighting co., in the Milwaukee 3c fare case, Aug. 1912.

electric power plants 12 years.
Pacific gas & electric company. Figures used in rate hearings before Master in Chancery, San Francisco, 1913-4.

electric power plant lines 20 years.
San Joaquin light & power corporation. Rate hearing before California railroad commisison, 1915.

electric power plant instruments 20 years.
San Joaquin light & power corporation. Rate hearing before California railroad comimssion, 1915.

electric power plant equipment 8-14 years.
San Joaquin light & power corporation. Rate hearing before California railroad commission, 1915.

farmers line 15 years.
Wisconsin railroad commission. Wautoma & Mt. Morris Tel.

subscribers instruments 8-10 years. 10% residual value.
Telephone "Data." Compiled from practice A. T. & T. Co., Wisconsin R.R. Commission and others. Quoted by H. A. Foster.
10 years. 5% residual value.
Chicago telephone commission. Published 1908.
10 years. 5% residual value.
Wisconsin railroad commission. Wisconsin telephone co. case, Aug. 3, 1909.

telephone drop wires 8 years. 15% residual value.
Chicago telephone commission. Published 1908.

Systems in plants

telephone 10-25 years.
Wisconsin railroad comimssion. Oregon telephone co. case.

telephone 14-15 years.
Wisconsin railroad commission. Various cases in 1912-3.

HURD, E. C. Some factors to be considered in fixing depreciation. *Telephony*, Nov. 6, 1915.

KURTZ, WADE. Depreciation in telephone utilities. *Journal of accountancy*, Feb. 1919, p. 81-95.

LIFE data on power-plant equipment used in valuation of the property of the Bay state street railway of Boston, Massachusetts. *Electrical world*, Dec. 4, 1915, p. 1261.

Telephone sets 10 years
Iron-box telephone sets 14

MONTGOMERY, ROBERT H. Telephone companies. (In his *Auditing theory and practice*, 1916. p. 680-2).

Hard drawn copper wire in toll lines 1.5%
Iron wire in exchange lines 12.5
Composite percentages for complete plants vary from 5%-7% per annum.
Railroad commission of Wisconsin
Large exchange 7
Small exchange 8-10

MULHALL, JOHN F. J. Depreciation. (In his *Quasi-public corporation accounting and management.* c1905. p. 180-3).

Telephone companies 8-12%

NEALE, R. E. Depreciation in engineering works. *Mechanical world*, Feb. 7, 1913, p. 67-8.

Subscribers' 'phone apparatus 9-10% 10-11 years
Over-all 'phone equipment 8 12.5

NICHOLSON, J. LEE and J. F. D. ROHRBACH. Depreciation. (In their *Cost accounting.* 1919. p. 151).

Telephone equipment 7½%
Based on (1) the cost of equipment
(2) the life of the equipment
(3) on a ten-hour day.

DEPRECIATION, DEPLETION AND OBSOLESCENCE—TELEPHONE AND TELEGRAPH—*(Continued)*

PENDER, HAROLD. Depreciation. (In his *Handbook for electrical engineers.* c1914. p. 340).
Telephone system (railways) 7.5% Chicago electric railway & light co.

PHAIR, H. G. Some observations on plant depreciation in the tropics. *Telephony,* Nov. 7, 1914.

PHILADELPHIA. CONTROLLER. Rates of depreciation. (In his *Manual of accounting, reporting and business procedure of the city and county of Philadelphia.* 1917. p. 206).

Telephonic equipment	5%
Telegraphic "	4

PRACTICAL hints on computing telephone depreciation. *Telephony,* April 1, 1911, p. 401-3.
Estimated depreciation, schedule on an illustrative telephone plant.

Poles and guys	6%
Cable	2
Cable, messenger, hangers, labor, etc.	8
Cable terminals	7
Cross arms, hardware, insulators, pins, etc.	7
Line wire, copper	2
Drop wire and fastenings	8.5
Interior wire and fittings	8
Telephones and equipment	6
P.B.X. switchboards	7
Switchboards	7
Terminals, racks and machines	7
Batteries	18
Warehouse stock	3

PUBLIC utilities reports, annotated. Rochester, Lawyers co-operative publishing co.
See index under Depreciation.

PUBLIC utility reports, annotated. Rochester, Lawyers co-operative publishing co. 1915A. p. 64, 359, 562, 1032.

Re Lynch telephone co. (Neb.). A farm telephone company, on an application for an increase in rates, was ordered to set aside a sum amounting approximately to 20 per cent of its gross earnings for current maintenance and depreciation replacements.

Re Clark county telephone co. (Wis.). Provision for interest and depreciation amounting to about 14 per cent of the cost new of a telephone property was allowed by the Commission as reasonable in a rate investigation without definitely fixing the fair value of the apparently excellent condition of the telephone system.

Re Dakota cent. telephone co. (S. D.). An allowance for depreciation of 7 per ecnt of the cost of reproduction of telephone rural party lines was made by the Commission in computing the reasonable expenses to be charged against such lines in a valuation for rate purposes.

Re telephone co. (S. D.). Telephone companies were ordered to establish a just and reasonable schedule of yearly rental rates sufficiently high to pay all legitimate operating and maintenance charges, and set aside not less than 6 per cent, nor more than 8 per cent, of the value of their properties to take care of depreciation.

PUBLIC utility reports, annotated. Rochester, Lawyers co-operative publishing co. 1915B. p. 223, 507.

Re Woonsocket v. Schuler Electric & Telephone Co. (S. D.). In determining the reasonableness of telephone rates, an annual allowance of 7 per cent of the reproduction value of a plant for depreciation was held reasonable.

Re Sabetha mut. telephone co. (Kan.). Six per cent per annum was held to be a fair and reasonable depreciation charge upon the property of a telephone company where the Commission's engineer reported such propertp to be in good general condition.

PUBLIC utility reports, annotated. Rochester, Lawyers co-operative publishing co. 1915C. p. 366.

Re Simms v. Columbia Telephone Co. (Mo.). An allowance of 6½ per cent for annual depreciation and contingencies for a telephone plant including rural and toll lines, was held to be reasonable.

PUBLIC utility reports, annotated. Rochester, Lawyers co-operative publishing co. 1915D. p. 160, 646.

Re People's telephone co. (Neb.). A new telephone company expecting to start operation with a list of 195 subscribers was upon an application for the issuance of securities, directed, prior to the payment of any dividend on the stock issues to set aside out of its operating income as a maintenance and depreciation fund, an amount not less than 8 per cent of the property invested.

Re Ross (Ill.). Five per cent of the gross revenue of a telephone company was ordered set aside for depreciation.

PUBLIC utility reports, annotated. Rochester, Lawyers co-operative publishing co. 1915E. p. 23, 57, 516, 571, 578.

Re Colchester farmers' telephone co. (Ill.). In a proceeding to fix the rates of a telephone company it was held that 5 per cent of the property value should be deducted from the gross revenue annually to provide for depreciation, where no amount had been set aside for this purpose.

Re Monroe independent telephone co. (Neb.). An annual allowance of 6 per cent on the conservative reproduction value of the property of a telephone company was held necessary to cover depreciation.

Re Webster telephone co. (S. D.). In the valuation of a telephone company for rate making purposes, the value of a plant costing $23,541.72, which had been in operation a little over six months, was fixed at $22,750, the depreciation on such a plant beginning at the moment it is installed and put into operation.

Re Webster telephone co. (S. D.). An annual allowance of 6 per cent for depreciation was held adequate for a telephone plant where there was very little probability of depreciation by reason of obsolescence and inadequacy or supersession.

Re Crownover telephone co. (Neb.). An allowance of 9 per cent of the reproduction value of a telephone company was allowed for the purpose of maintenance and depreciation, where the topography of the country and the scarcity of population made the construction of long farm lines necessary.

DEPRECIATION, DEPLETION AND OBSOLESCENCE—TELEPHONE AND TELEGRAPH—*(Continued)*

Re Valparaiso telephone co. (Neb.). Upon granting permission to a telephone company to increase its rates, a company was required to set aside out of its earnings annually an amount equal to 8 per cent upon the reproduction value of its property new, such a sum to be expended for current maintenance and to take care of the depreciation of the plant.

PUBLIC utility reports, annotated. Rochester, Lawyers co-operative publishing co. 1915F. p. 290, 354, 1014.

Re Western telephone co. (Or.). A depreciation annuity of $607 for a consolidated telephone plant, based upon a 4 per cent sinking fund method with annual payments and rests for interest, a composite life of 16.4 years and a present value of $16,800 was held necessary to comply with a statute requiring that the plant shall be kept in a state of efficiency corresponding with the progress of the industry.

Re Lincoln telephone & telegraph co. (Neb.). An allowance for maintenance and depreciation of 8 per cent of the reproduction value of telephone property was made by the Nebraska commission in ascertaining the net operating expense for the purpose of fixing rates.

Re Corona v. Corona home telephone & telegraph co. (Cal.). An allowance was made for depreciation to the amount of 5½% of the value of the physical plant of a telephone company in estimating the operating expenses for rate-making purposes.

PUBLIC utility reports, annotated. Rochester, Lawyers co-operative publishing co. 1916A. p. 364.

Re Remund v. Dakota cent. telephone co. (S. D.). An allowance of 7 per cent for depreciation was held sufficient in estimating the expenses of rural telephone lines.

PUBLIC utility reports, annotated. Rochester, Lawyers co-operative publishing co. 1916B. p. 940.

Re Edwards v. Glen telephone co. (N. Y. 2d Dist.) Accrued depreciation of a telephone 5.8 per cent was made in ascertaining telephone expenses for rate making.

Re Edwards v. Glen telephone co. (N. Y. 2d Dist.) Accrued depreciation of a telephone plant was fixed at the total of 10.5 per cent of the book value each year less actual maintenance charges, in determining an allowance for deficiency in early return, in a rate valuation without deciding that the method was correct.

PUBLIC utility reports, annotated. Rochester, Lawyers co-operative publishing co. 1916C. p. 141, 145, 438, 925, 1020.

Re Long Prairie telephone co. (Minn.). An allowance of 8.938 per cent was made for depreciation in fixing rates for a telephone plant, a part of which was made up of old open-wire construction which would depreciate very rapidly.

Re Lambert v. Northern Idaho & M. power co. (Mont.). Rural telephone depreciation should be charged off at the rate of 10 per cent of original cost for the first year, and at the same rate on the remainder at the end of each succeeding year, provided no prior allowance has been made.

Re Coeur D'Alena v. Interstate utilities co. (Idaho). An annual depreciation of 6.07 per cent under the straight line method was made in ascertaining the net revenue of a telephone company.

Re Chesapeake & P. telephone co. (Md.). Sixteen years was taken as the life expectancy of a telephone system affixing the depreciated value of the rate valuation.

Re Chesapeake & P. telephone co. (Md.). An annual allowance of 6.25 per cent was made for depreciation of a telephone system, to be continued until a depreciation reserve of 20 per cent of the physical property was established.

Re Bogart v. Wisconsin telephone co. (Wis.). In determining cost of telephone service, depreciation was computed on a 2 per cent sinking fund basis upon the cost new of the property less scrap value.

Re Bogart v. Wisconsin telephone co. (Wis.). An allowance for annual depreciation of 4.27 of the cost of reproduction of a telephone exchange on a 2 per cent sinking fund basis, although deemed reasonable by the Wisconsin Commission for the purpose of cost analysis, was declared insufficient as a practical operating expense, the company being held entitled, for that purpose, to not less than 5 per cent of the cost of reproducing the physical property.

PUBLIC utility reports, annotated. Rochester, Lawyers co-operative publishing co. 1916D. p. 572, 603, 631, 781.

Re Lincoln telephone & telegraph co. (Neb.). An allowance of 8 per cent of the value of central office telephone equipment was held sufficient for maintenance and depreciation in estimating exchange operating expenses.

Re Webster telephone co. A depreciation allowance of 7 per cent of the rate-making value of a telephone system was made in estimating its operating expenses.

Re Watertown telephone co. An allowance of 6½ per cent, rather than 6 per cent, was made for annual depreciation of a rural telephone system in a rate case.

Re Roanoke telephone co. (Ill.). Six per cent of the normal value of a telephone plant was held sufficient for depreciation in fixing the operative expenses.

PUBLIC utility reports, annotated. Rochester, Lawyers co-operative publishing co. 1916E. p. 467, 1072, 1073.

Re Cedar County farmers telephone co. (Neb.). An annual maintenance and depreciation allowance of 9 per cent of the reproduction value of physical property was made in a telephone rate case.

Re DeKalb county telephone co. No. 3550, July 13, 1916, the Illinois Commission held that an annual allowance of 2 per cent under the sinking fund method would be set aside as a reserve for telephone depreciation, Yates, commissioner, stating: "This reserve shall be carried in a separate account, which is to be drawn only to cover future accruing depreciation (both physical and functional), and shall receive full credit for all earnings which may accrue, either from interest or otherwise."

Re Allenton Kohlsville telephone co. (Wis.). May 10, 1916. Six and five tenths per cent, rather than 5 per cent, is the property allowance for depreciation in fixing rates for a telephone system having a large amount of overhead rural construction.

Jones v. Connersville telephone co. (Ind.). No. 1179, Aug. 11, 1916, depreciation of telephone plant was fixed at 5 per cent on the physical value of the property less materials and supplies.

Re People's telephone & telegraph co. (Ill.) No. 3844, June 5, 1916, an annual allowance of 6 per cent for depreciation reserve was held fair.

PUBLIC utility reports, annotated. Rochester, Lawyers co-operative publishing co. 1916B. p. 318.

Re Polo Mut. telephone co. (Ill.). Only 7 per cent was allowed for the annual depreciation of a city, rural and toll telephone plant an allowance of 8 per cent being held excessive.

DEPRECIATION, DEPLETION AND OBSOLESCENCE—TELEPHONE AND TELEGRAPH—*(Continued)*

PUBLIC utility reports, annotated. Rochester, Lawyers co-operative publishing co. 1917A. p. 658.
Re Independent telegraph & telephone co. (Ill.). An allowance of 6 per cent, rather than 7.31 per cent, of the reproduction cost new of a telephone system was made for annual depreciation in estimating the operating expenses.

PUBLIC utility reports, annotated. Rochester, Lawyers co-operative publishing co. 1917B. p. 198, 368.
Re Mountain States telephone & telegraph co. (Colo.). In estimating the operating expenses of an interstate telephone company for rate making, the Colorado Commission allowed the company to set aside annually approximately 5.65 per cent of its investment in depreciable property, the exact amount to be determined in each case by the table of lives and salvage values submitted by the engineer for the Commission.
Re Mississippi valley telephone co. (Ill.). An annual depreciation allowance of 6 per cent of the reproduction cost new of a telephone plant was made in a rate valuation, rather than 7.3 per cent claimed by the utility.

PUBLIC utility reports, annotated. Rochester, Lawyers co-operative publishing co. 1917C. p. 507, 647.
Re Sparta v. Monroe county telephone co. (Wis.). The amount to be set aside for depreciation of a telephone system having installed a large amount of comparatively long-lived underground equipment was fixed at 5.5 rather than 7.1 per cent of the cost of reproduction.
Re Portage telephone co. (Wis.). An annual allowance of 5.5 per cent is sufficient to cover accruing depreciation of a telephone plant, a large amount of which is made up of comparatively long-lived equipment

PUBLIC utility reports, annotated. Rochester, Lawyers co-operative publishing co. 1917D. p. 402.
Re Kearney telephone co. (Neb.). In determining the reasonablesness of rates of a consolidated telephone company, 9 per cent of the reproduction cost was held to be a reasonable allowance for both maintenance and depreciation.

PUBLIC utility reports, annotated. Rochester, Lawyers co-operative publishing co. 1917E. p. 540.
Re Tamarack telephone co. (Wis.). The annual depreciation for a small telephone system having 30 village subscribers and 198 rural subscribers should not be less than 6 per cent of the reproduction cost of the property.

PUBLIC utility reports, annotated. Rochester, Lawyers co-operative publishing co. 1917F. p. 161, 209.
Re Estelline telephone & electric co. (S. D.). The annual depreciation allowance for a town telephone exchange line and the rural plant was fixed at 7 per cent for each.
Re Tipton telephone co. (Ind.). The rate of depreciation of a telephone plant was fixed at 4½ per cent of the total valuation of the property.

PUBLIC utility reports, annotated. Rochester, Lawyers co-operative publishing co. 1918A. p. 24.
Re Bradley-Crocker telephone co. (S. D.). An allowance of 7 per cent was made for depreciation of a telephone system operating several exchanges and rural lines.

PUBLIC utility reports, annotated. Rochester, Lawyers co-operative publishing co. 1918B. p. 172.
Re Kewanee Home telephone co. (Ill.). A sufficient annual allowance for a depreciation reserve of a telephone property of the value of $140,000 was held to be $9,116, with an additional allowance, an all additions, of 5.5 per cent of their cost new.

PUBLIC utility reports, annotated. Rochester, Lawyers co-operative publishing co. 1918C. p. 55, 489, 566, 571, 777.
Re Missouri & K. telephone co. (Kan.). An annual allowance of 6.5 per cent of the reproduction cost new of physical property was made for accruing depreciation in a telephone rate case.
Re Home telephone co. (Ind.). An annual allowance of 5 per cent on all physical property exclusive of lands, materials, and supplies is adequate to provide for depreciation of a telephone plant in good condition.
Re Bear River Valley telephone co. (Utah). A telephone utility was directed annually to set aside a reserve based upon 6½ per cent of the value of its property to provide for depreciation, deterioration, and obsolescence in its property and equipment.
Re Missouri & K. telephone co. (Kan.). An annual allowance of $20,000 was made for accruing depreciation, inadequacy, and obsolescence for a telephone plant, in 84.48 per cent condition, having a rate value of $350,000.
Re Northern Indiana & S. M. telephone telegraph & cable co. (Ind.). No. 2773, Feb. 26, 1918, in allowing as a depreciation fund, an amount equal to 5 per cent annually of the physical value of a telephone company's property.
Re Sparta telephone co. (Ill.). No. 5320, Oct. 10, 1917, an allowance of 6 per cent of the cost new of the depreciable property of a telephone company was made for the depreciation reserve in a valuation for rate making.
Re Cass telephone & telegraph co. (Ill.). No. 6840, Dec. 18, 1917. An annual depreciation reserve allowance of 6 per cent of the cost new of a telephone plant, as shown by the Commission's engineers' valuation, was made in ascertaining the utility's expenses for rate making.
Re Mississippi valley telephone co. (Ill.). No. 4663, Sept. 5, 1916. Depreciation was figured at 6 per cent of the reproduction cost new of a telephone system in ascertaining the operating expenses.
Re Star telephone co. No. 3394, Feb. 1, 1918, the Indiana Commission allowed 4 per cent annually to provide for depreciation of a telephone company whose property had not been subjected to depreciation by sleet storms, but was suffering deterioration on sulphur.
Re Battle creek farmers telephone co. (S. D.). Order I-2867, Dec. 18, 1917. Seven per cent of the value of rural telephone plant, consisting almost entirely of outside construction, was allowed for annual depreciation.
Re Walker v. Hermosa telephone co. (S. D.). No. 2925, Feb. 27, 1918, the company was required to set aside as depreciation reserve not less than 7 per cent of the value of its plant.

PUBLIC utility reports, annotated. Rochester, Lawyers co-operative publishing co. 1918E. p. 74, 669, 680, 859.
Re Peoria & Receivers of C. U. telephone co. (Ill.). An annual allowance of $55,000 to cover future and accruing depreciation both physical and functional, of a telephone plant, the fair value of which was found to be $1,100,000, plus an amount equivalent to 5½ per cent of the cost of future additions and betterments, was made in a rate proceedings, con-

DEPRECIATION, DEPLETION AND OBSOLESCENCE—TELEPHONE AND TELEGRAPH—*(Continued)*

sideration having been given, in making this allowance to the extraordinary hazards, such as tornadoes and sleet storms, to which such property is sometimes subjected.

Re Union city telephone co. (Ind.). A 5 per cent annual depreciation rate was held to be proper and adequate in the case of the telephone property under consideration.

Re Littleton & B. mut. telephone co. No. 7736, June 19, 1918, the Illinois Commission held that a sum equal to 6 per cent new of the property should be set aside each year to meet accruing depreciation of a telephone company which was not of the best construction.

Re Shirley telephone co. No. 3803 (Ind.). April 30, 1918, a small telephone company was authorized to set aside 5 per cent of the value of its property annually for depreciation.

Re Dixon home telephone co. (Ill.). No. 6466, April 17, 1918, an annual allowance of $11,714 was made for depreciation of a telephone plant, the fair value of which was found to be $170,000, all net additions to the plant to be similarly provided for in the reserve for depreciation by an annual addition of 5.5 per cent on their cost new.

Re consolidated telephone co. (Ind.). No. 3620, May 25, 1918, in considering the reasonableness of rates of the company's various exchanges it was held that it was entitled to an allowance of 5 per cent for depreciation.

Re Bippus telephone co. (Ind.). No. 3802, April 30, 1918, a rate of 5 per cent was found reasonable in determining the annual rate of depreciation to be allowed a telephone company operating within a sleet storm area.

Re Central Indiana telephone co. (Ind.). An annual allowance of 5 per cent was made for depreciation of a telephone plant, which, it was held, would be ample to provide for every contingency, including extraordinary depreciation due to sleet storm damage, which whenever it occurs should be amortized over a five-year period.

PUBLIC utility reports, annotated. Rochester, Lawyers co-operative publishing co. 1918F. p. 283, 592.

Re Farmers & M. telephone co. (Neb.). An annual allowance of 9 per cent upon the reproduction new value of a telephone plant was allowed for maintenance and depreciation in view of the extraordinary advances in the costs of materials due to war.

Re Coos telephone co. (N. H.). A telephone utility was allowed to annually set aside, for depreciation an amount equal to 7 per cent of the value of the plant.

PUBLIC utility reports, annotated. Rochester, Lawyers co-operative publishing co. 1919A. p. 657, 1057.

Re Lincoln telephone & telegraph co. Application No. 3701, Oct. 1, 1918, Commissioner Wilson of the Nebraska Commission said: "The Commission has always treated maintenance and depreciation (repairs and replacements) together because of the practicability of such treatment by utility companies themselves, the difficulties inherent in separate treatment, and the insuperable obstacles in the way of distinguishing between maintenance and depreciation by regulatory bodies. The Commission has made a number of studies of the cost of maintenance and depreciation of telephone properties which show an average annual expense for the period of time covering the life of such properties of 8 per cent. The percentages during the early years of the property is from 3 to 5 per cent, and in the later years from 9 to 11 per cent, with an average of 8 per cent as indicated." In this case 9 per cent of the book value of the plant was allowed for maintenance and depreciation.

Re Lincoln telephone & Telegraph co. (Neb.). 35. An allowance of 6 per cent for annual depreciation of a telephone plant or of 9 per cent for both maintenance and depreciation was held sufficient notwithstanding material increases in the cost of everything entering into telephone plants.

PUBLIC utility reports, annotated. Rochester, Lawyers co-operative publishing co. 1919B. p. 750, 1073.

Re Farmers telephone co. (Ill.). No. 8297, Oct. 1, 1918, an annual allowance of 7.1 per cent of the reproduction cost of a telephone plant new was authorized for depreciation.

Re Crown point telephone co. No. 4180, Dec. 28, 1918, an application of a telephone company for emergency relief the Indiana Commission said: "The Commission cannct agree that the reasonable expenditures for maintenance and depreciation of this property should be an amount equivalent to approximately 37 per cent of all revenues received, or 11 per cent of the value of the plant. The audit discloses that practically since the 1st day of January, 1913, petitioner has set up out of its operating revenues, as a depreciation reserve, $10,936.10 more than was reasonably necessary or actually expended, to maintain this property in its present state of efficiency. Telephone plants taken as a whole, seldom, if ever, depreciate to a 60 per cent condition, in fact there are but few instances where they reach as low a point as 70 per cent condition. When telephone plants depreciate to 60 per cent condition, their efficiency becomes impaired and they are unable to render a reasonably adequate service. To illustrate: Petitioner's telephone plant was constructed about 1896, and has depreciated approximately 20 per cent in the twenty-two years, as evidenced by the per cent condition shown in the appraisal made by petitioner's engineers. Then, assuming that petitioner's engineers are approximately correct as to the per cent condition of the property, does it not necessarily follow that the large amount heretofore expended in maintenance has been sufficient to keep the property in its 80 per ecnt conditions? In other words, on account of the large expenditures made for maintenance, the property has depreciated less than 1 per cent per year. In making these deductions, we are not unmindful of the fact that the first owners and operators of this property drew small salaries for the services performed, and in some instances none whatever. However, the $10,000 which said owners and operators put into this property, and the labor they performed, either gratuitously or at a small salary, grew until when sold, said property brought $35,600. The Commission is of the opinion that if an amount equal to 2 and 5 per cent of the physical value of the property, as found by the Commission's staff, is allowed, it will be found reasonable and sufficient to take care of reasonable maintenance and depreciation of said property.

Birmingham v. Southern Bell telephone & telegraph co. (Ala.) 791. An annual allowance of 5.5 per cent for the depreciation of a telephone plant in the city of Birmingham was held reasonable.

Re Salem telephone co. (S. D.) 734. An allowance of 7 per cent for the depreciation of a telephone plant is ample and reasonable.

DEPRECIATION, DEPLETION AND OBSOLESCENCE—TELEPHONE AND TELEGRAPH—*(Continued)*

PUBLIC utility reports, annotated. Rochester, Lawyers co-operative publishing co. 1919C. p. 528, 854, 1100.

Re Kearney teleph. co. (Neb.) 528. In view of the increased cost of materials entering into the construction and repair of telephone property, the Nebraska Commission made an allowance of 10 per cent to cover maintenance and depreciation, rather than the normal allowance of 8 or 9 per cent.

Re Fulton telephone co. (Ind.) 854. A telephone utility was authorized to set aside 5 per cent of the value of its depreciable property annually for depreciation.

Re Home telephone co. (Ind.) 209. An allowance of 5 per cent per annum for depreciation of a telephone plant was held reasonable during the period covered by an emergency rate.

PUBLIC utility reports, annotated. Rochester, Lawyers co-operative publishing co. 1919D. p. 909, 359.

Re Theresa union telephone co. (Wis.). 909. In estimating the operating expenses of a telephone company, the Wisconsin Commission reduced the depreciation charged to operating expenses to 6 per cent of the cost of reproduction of the property.

Re Pacific telephone and telegraph co.

Company's Life Table

Item.	Years' life.	% salvage.	% dep. straight line.
Buildings	20	40.0	3.0
Central office equipment	8½	20.0	9.4
Station equipment	..	....	5.6
Exchange pole lines	9	10.4	10.0
Exchange aerial cable	10	31.4	6.9
Exchange aerial wire	8	22.3	9.5
Exchange underground conduits	28	....	3.6
Exchange underground cable	15	32.0	4.6
Exchange submarine cable	9	10.0	10.0
Toll pole lines	15	2.3	6.5
Toll aerial cable	12	31.4	5.7
Toll aerial wire	26	22.3	3.0
Toll underground conduits	28	....	3.6
Toil underground cable	12	40.0	5.0
Toll submarine cable	9	10.0	10.0
Office furniture and fixtures	9	18.6	9.0
Interest during construction	16	....	6.4

Commission's Life Table

Item.	Years' life.	% salvage.	% dep. straight line.
Buildings	20	40.0	3.0
Central office equipment	11	20.0	7.3
Station equipment	..	....	5.6
Exchange pole lines	8	10.4	11.2
Exchange aerial cable	14	31.4	4.9
Exchange aerial wire	11	22.3	7.0
Exchange underground conduits	28	....	5.6
Exchange underground cable	17	32.0	4.0
Exchange submarine cable	9	10.0	10.0
Toll pole lines	14	2.3	7.0
Toll aerial lines	14	31.4	4.9
Toll aerial wire	26	22.3	3.0
Toll underground conduit	28	....	5.6
Toll underground cable	12	40.0	5.0
Toll submarine cable	9	10.0	10.0
Office furniture and fixtures	9	18.6	9.0
Interest during construction	..	....	5.6

The average of these percentages, as applied to the company's property in 1918, is 5.6 per cent of the depreciable property including salvage.

PUBLIC utility reports, annotated. Rochester, Lawyers co-operative publishing co. 1919E. p. 504.

Re Twelve mile telephone co. (Ind.) 504. A telephone company was ordered to set aside for depreciation an amount equal to 5 per cent on the value of the depreciable property

PUBLIC utilities reports, annotated. Rochester, Lawyers co-operative publishing co. 1919F. p. 170-1, 1053.

In the following cases the Indiana Commission made an allowance of 5 per cent for the annual depreciation of telephone plants: Re Flora Teleph. Co. No. 4219, Jan. 21, 1919; Re Knightstown Teleph. Co. No. 4057, March 12, 1919; Re Chalmers Teleph. Co. No. 4284, March 19, 1919; Re Elizaville Co-op. Teleph. Co. No. 4385, April 1, 1919; Re Ladoga Teleph. Co. No. 4235, April 2, 1919; Re Antwerp Teleph. Co. No. 4261, April 3, 1919; Re Home Teleph. Co. No. 4203, April 17, 1919; Re Reddington Twp. Mut. Teleph. Co. No. 4462, April 17, 1919; Re Mt. Summit Rural Teleph. Co. No. 4422, April 24, 1919; Re Pendleton Teleph. Co. No. 4662, Aug. 13, 1919.

Re Kendall Teleph. Exch. U-1496, April 22, 1919, the Wisconsin Commission held that a telephone company should be allowed 6 per cent for depreciation.

Re Conde teleph. co. (S. D.) No. 3519, June 9, 1919, a telephone company was held entitled to an annual allowance of 7 per cent for depreciation.

Re D. & K. teleph. co. Application No. 3813, March 29, 1919, the Nebraska Commission, in permitting an increase in telephone rates, directed that the company set aside 10 per cent of the value of the property for the purpose of maintenance and depreciation to care for unforeseen or emergency situations.

Re Lawrence teleph. co. Application No. 3758, June 13, 1919, an application for an increase in telephone rates, the Nebraska Commission in estimating operating expenses, allowed 10 per cent for depreciation and maintenance.

Re Commercial teleph. & teleg. co. No. 8807, June 17, 1919, the Illinois Commission gave an allowance of $3,000 as the annual depreciation of a telephone plant which was valued at at least $50,000.

DEPRECIATION, DEPLETION AND OBSOLESCENCE—TELEPHONE AND TELEGRAPH—*(Continued)*

Re Portage teleph. co. U-1492, May 8, 1919. It appears that the composite life of the depreciable property is approximately fifteen and one half years.

Re Pierce County Teleph. Co. (Wis.) 92. In determining the reasonableness of telephone rates the Wisconsin Commission computed deprciation on a 3 per cent sinking fund basis.

PUBLIC utility reports, annotated. Rochester, Lawyers co-operative publishing co. 1920A, p. 422.

Re Lafayette telephone co. (Ind.). Indiana Commission made an allowance of 5 per cent on the value of a telephone company's depreciable property for the annual depreciation thereof.

PUBLIC utility reports, annotated. Rochester, Lawyers co-operative publishing co. 1920B. p. 813, 956, 771, 411.

Re Central U. teleph. co. (Ind.). Annual allowance of 5 per cent of the value of the depreciable property of a large telephone plant was held reasonable, although such percentage might be improper in the case of certain exchange on account of varying conditions of plant construction, maintenance, climate, and other factors.

Re Farmers & M. teleph. co. (Neb.). An annual depreciation reserve of 4.3 per cent for a telephone plant is very conservative since depreciation of telephone properties is commonly figured at from 5 to 6 per cent.

Re Nuckolls county independent teleph. co. (Neb.). A telephone company was authorized to set aside 10 per cent of the original cost of its property for maintenance and depreciation.

Re rates and charges of telephone companies. (Ariz.). A telephone company was held justified in setting aside a 6 per cent depreciation reserve.

PUBLIC utility reports, annotated. Rochester, Lawyers co-operative publishing company, 1920C, p. 534, 511, 510, 511, 1019, 510, 614, 511, 1074, 510, 510, 510.

Re Central U. teleph. co. (Ohio). In the case of a large telephone property which has been properly maintained so as to render efficient service, 5.7 per cent is too great an allowance for depreciation.

Re Central Wisconsin teleph. co. U-1638, Nov. 28, 1919 it appeared that the charge to operating expenses for depreciation was varied for three years from about 6.5 per cent to 6.7 of the book value at the end of the year.

Re Citizens teleph. co. No. 4128, March 31, 1919, the Indiana commission made an allowance of 4 per cent for the annual depreciation of a telephone plant.

Re Cumberland teleph. co. U-1660, Nov. 13, 1919 in authorizing an increase in telephone rates, the Wisconsin commission ordered that the company should not pay any dividends except out of its yearly surplus which remains after the depreciation reserve account has been credited and operating expenses charged during the year with an amount equal to at least 6 per cent of the value of the property.

Re Denmark farmers & M. teleph. co. (Wis.) Six per cent of the value of a telephone plant, at the very least, should be set aside every year as a depreciation reserve out of which should be paid all renewal and replacement costs.

Re Eastern Indiana teleph. co. no. 4729, Dec. 1919, a telephone utility was ordered to set aside annually for depreciation 5 per cent of the value of its depreciable property.

Re Intercounty teleph. co. (Wis.) Wisconsin commission generally considers that a telephone company operating a grounded telephone system, serving approximately 371 subscribers over 32 circuits is entitled to earn about 14 per cent to meet its depreciation and interest charges.

Re Public service commission v. Southwestern bell teleph. co. case 2121, Nov. 26, 1919, the Missouri commission made an allowance of 6 per cent per annum for the depreciation of a telephone plant.

Re Reed v. China teleph. co. (Me.) An allowance of $600 was made for the annual depreciation of a telephone plant valued at $20,000.

Re St. Joe teleph. co. no. 4968, Jan. 7, 1920, a telephone utility was ordered to set aside annually for depreciation 5 per cent of the value of its depreciable property.

Re Scott county teleph. co. no. 4269 Oct. 25, 1919, the Indiana commission made an allowance of 5 per cent for the depreciation of a telephone plant.

Re Union city teleph. co. no 4972 Jan. 7 1920' a telephone utility was ordered to set aside annually for depreciation 5 per cent of the value of its depreciable property.

PUBLIC utility reports, annotated. Rochester, Lawyers co-operative publishing company, 1920D, p. 529, 83 59.

Re Baird v. Burleson (N. Y. 2d dist.). A composite percentage of 5.66 per cent for the depreciation of a telephone plant consisting of a group of exchanges having but little underground cable is not unduly high provided the percentage is computed upon the original cost.

Re Fort Wayne v. Home teleph. & teleph. co. (Ind.) Indiana commission fixed an allowance of 5 per cent for the annual depreciation of a telephone plant.

Re Fort Wayne v. Home teleph. & teleg. co. (Ind.) Indiana commission found that from 50 to 60 per cent of a reasonable annual allowance for depreciation of a telephone plant will approximate the amount of currently realized depreciation.

PUBLIC utility reports, annotated. Rochester, Lawyers co-operative publishing company, 1920E, p. 321, 458, 59.

Re Clearwater telephone lines. Idaho commission made an allowance of 6 per cent for the annual depreciation of telephone plant.

Re Farmers independent telephone association. A telephone company was required to set aside an amount of not less than 8 per cent on the book value of the property as a depreciation reserve each year for three years before any dividends were paid where the company had, in the past, failed to provide any depreciation fund.

Re Hanamo telephone company. Missouri commission made an allowance of 7 per cent for the depreciation of the property of a telephone plant.

PUBLIC utility reports, annotated. Rochester, Lawyers co-operative publishing company, 1920F, p. 163, 645, 368, 391.

Re Merchants and farmers telephone company. Indiana commission made an allowance of 5 per cent for the annual depreciation of a telephone plant.

Re Carlson as mayor of Jamestown v. Jamestown Telephone corporation. An allowance of 5 per cent of the book value of the depreciable property of a consolidated telephone company is not unreasonable for annual depreciation.

PUBLIC utility reports, annotated. Rochester, Lawyers co-operative publishing company, 1920F. p. 417, 432.

DEPRECIATION, DEPLETION AND OBSOLESCENCE—TELEPHONE AND TELEGRAPH—*(Continued)*

Re Chesapeake & Potomac telephone company. The policy of the Maryland commission provided that the state wide telephone system should earn a return upon 80 per cent of its plant investment, and create a reserve of not to exceed 20 per cent. Discussion of consideration to be given to deficit in reserves, when deducting full accrued depreciation.

Re Elko county telephone and telegraph company. No separate allowances can be made for depreciation where it appears that depreciation has been and is now being taken care of out of operating expenses, and there is no showing as to what the expenditures for renewals amount to, the amount of the accrued depreciation, the value of the property subject to depreciation, and a segregation of total expenses showing the annual maintenance and renewal expenditures.

Re Union telephone company. The Indiana commission will not make any separate allowance for depreciation for a telephone company, a large part of whose depreciation expenditures had been charged to operation and whose records and accounts are inadequate until the company, through the keeping of proper and adequate accounts, is able to disclose its needs in this respect.

ROBY, J. J. Schedule of plant depreciation. (In his *Treatise on cost accounting as applied to coal mining.* c1913. p. 14-15).

Telephone equipment 10%

SALIERS, EARL A. Analysis of a hydro-electric plant. (In his *Principles of depreciation.* 1916. p. 34-8).

Electric light and telephone 10 years

SMITH, BURKE. Depreciation and replacement of growing telephone plants. *Journal of the Western society of engineers,* Oct. 1912, p. 779. *Telephony,* April 27, 1912, p. 526-8. Abstract. Depreciation and replacement of telephone equipment. *Electrical review and western electrician,* April 27, 1912, p. 790.

Considered as a whole the composite life of telephone plants in very large cities varies from 11 to 14 years.

SPILLMAN, W. J. Determining the mean length of life. *Telephone engineer,* March 1916, p. 135-6.

STATE public utilities commission of Illinois decides in the case of the Colchester Farmers' telephone company that at least 5 per cent of the property value should be deducted for depreciation from the gross revenue annually. *Electrical world,* Dec. 11, 1915, p. 1339.

UNIFORM cost sheet for coal mining companies. *Coal age,* Sept. 19, 1918, p. 545-7.

	% original cost
Mine telephones	20
Telephone lines	10

WHITTEN, ROBERT HARVEY. Valuation of public service corporations; legal and economic phases of valuation for rate making and public purchases. v.1,2, p. 431-3, 433-4, 434-5, 1189-91, 1191-2, 1193-6, 1200-2.

Seven and three-tenths per cent, annual allowance—Massachusetts telephone appraisal for rate purposes 1909—discussion of depreciation.

Seven per cent allowance in Oklahoma telephone rate case, 1911—allowance to cover only current replacement declared inadequate.

Seven per cent allowance in Louisville, Ky. telephone rate case, 1911.

California Commission—San Jose v. The Pacific telephone and telegraph co.—6.5%.

Board of railway commissioners, Canada—6.77%.

Nebraska Commission—Re application of Lincoln's telephone and telegraph co.—6%. 9% to cover both maintenance and depreciation.

Oklahoma commission—Bolen v. pioneer telephone and telegraph company.

WILKINSON, GEORGE. Depreciation of plant. *Accountant,* Aug. 31, 1901, p. 955.

Telephone plants. 10% per annum on the average amount of plant in use throughout the year.

Based on the actual cost of construction.

Telephone booths

APPRAISAL of the Seattle telephone companies of the railroad commission of Washington. *Engineering and contracting,* May 3, 1911, p. 520-4.

	Life	Salvage	An. dep.	Av. age	Total dep.
Booths, etc.	10	10	9.0	5	45.0

CLINE, E. L. Depreciation of telephone companies. *Telephony,* July 2, 1910, p. 16.

	Years	Dep.	Salvage
Booths	10	8.0	20

PHILADELPHIA. CONTROLLER. Rates of depreciation. (In his *Manual of accounting, reporting and business procedure of the city and county of Philadelphia.* 1917. p. 207-8).

Telephone and election booths 5%

Tenements

BOLTON, REGINALD PELHAM. Depreciation of the value of buildings. (In his *Building for profit,* 1911. p. 50-78).

Classification of depreciation deducted from R. M. Hurd's assignments of life

Construction	Occupancy	Term of life in years	Rate of fund proposed in %	Term of sinking fund @ 3%, in years
Cheap frame	Tenements	10-15	10-5	9-16
Cheap brick	Tenements	25-30	3-2	23-31

BURTON, H. J. *Valuations and depreciations of city buildings.* p. 21-2.

Tenements and flats 25-27 years

MONTGOMERY, ROBERT H. Mine equipment. (In his *Income tax procedure,* 1919. p. 571. ———— Same, 1920. p. 724).

Tenement houses 5%

MUCKLOW, WALTER. Depreciation. (In his *Real estate accounts.* 1917. p. 313-8).

Frame tenement 10%

NICHOLSON, J. LEE and JOHN F. D. ROHRBACH. Depreciation. (In their *Cost accounting.* 1919. p. 146).

Tenement houses 5%

Based on (1) the cost of equipment
(2) the life of the equipment
(3) on a ten-hour day.

DEPRECIATION, DEPLETION AND OBSOLESCENCE—TENEMENTS—*(Continued)*

UNIFORM cost sheet for coal mining companies. *Coal age*, Sept. 19, 1918, p. 545-7.

	original cost
Tenement houses	6%

Tenoners

NICHOLSON, J. LEE and JOHN F. D. ROHRBACH. Depreciation. (In his *Cost accounting*. 1919. p. 150).

Woodworking machinery—tenoners	5%

Based on (1) the cost of equipment
(2) the life of the equipment
(3) on a ten-hour day

Tensile testing

BELT, ROBERT E. Depreciation. (In his *Foundry cost accounting practice and procedure*. 1919. p. 242).

Tensile testing machines	5%

Tents

LIFE of road construction equipment. *Engineering and contracting*, Jan. 3, 1917, p. 3.

Tents	75% annual depreciation.

PHILADELPHIA. CONTROLLER. Rates of depreciation. (In his *Manual of accounting, reporting and business procedure of the city and county of Philadelphia*. 1917. p. 207-8).

Tents and portable houses	20%

Terracing

See Depreciation, depletion and obsolescence—Grading.

Testing machines

ELBOURNE, EDWARD T. Depreciation rates. (In his *Factory administration and accounts*. 1918. p. 377).

	Prov. dep. %	Years	
	Remainder values	10%	5%
Testing machines	5	45	58

GRUNSKY, CARL EWALD. Probable useful life of various articles. (In his *Valuation, depreciation and the rate-base*. 1917. p. 285).
Electric testing instruments. 10 years. 20% residual value. California railroad commission. Calistoga electric co. vs. Napa valley electric co., May 1914.

NICHOLSON, J. LEE and J. F. D. ROHRBACH. Depreciation. (In their *Cost accounting*. 1919. p. 150).

Testing apparatus	10%
Testing instruments (electric)	10
Testing machines, oil-testing machines	10%

Based on (1) the cost of equipment
(2) the life of the equipment
(3) on a ten-hour day

Textiles

INCOME tax notes. *Accountant*, May 11, Sept. 28, 1918, p. 359, 162-6. *Incorporated accountants' journal*, May, Oct. 1918, p. 157, 14.
Flax spinning and linen weaving (Ireland)

Written down value	7½%

Machinery and plant (except accessory plant such as pirns, pirn cages, spools, belting, driving ropes, damask cards, designs, patterns, models, furniture, and fixtures).

INCOME tax notes. *Accountant*, Jan. 17, 1920, p. 72.

MONTGOMERY, ROBERT H. Textile industry. (In his *Auditing theory and practice*. 1916. p. 417, 588).

Buildings	3%
Machinery	4

MONTGOMERY, ROBERT H. Textile industry. (In his *Income tax procedure*, 1919. p. 578. ——— Same, 1920. p. 735).

Building	3%
Machinery	6
Woolen and worsted machinery	2-2½
Cotton machinery	3
Dyeing and similar machinery subject to acid fumes	5

NORTON, GEORGE PEPLER. Depreciation. (In his *Textile manufacturers' bookkeeping*. 1894. p. 233-7).

PHILADELPHIA. CONTROLLER. Rates of depreciation. (In his *Manual of accounting, reporting and business procedure of the city and county of Philadelphia*. 1917. p. 205).

Carding, spinning, weaving, knitting, netting and knitting equipment	5%

Theaters

AUSTRALIA. FEDERAL INCOME TAX DEPARTMENT. Depreciation allowance. *Acountant*, Oct. 13, 1917, p. 277-9. *Accounting and commerce*, June 30, 1917, p. 55-7. *Federal accountant*, July 1917, p. 93-8. *Public accountant*, Jan. 30, 1917, p. 145-52.

Costumes—stock of theatrical costumes	20%
Theatre seating accommodation and furniture	7½
Accessories, wigs, costumes &c.	20

Written down value, repairs allowed in addition

CHANTREY, WILLIAM HERBERT. Depreciation. (In his *Theatre accounts*. p. 44-8).

Dresses and scenery	up to 50%
Stock scenery	15-30
Decorations, furniture fixtures	10-15

DEPRECIATION, DEPLETION AND OBSOLESCENCE—THEATERS—*(Continued)*

DICKSEE, LAWRENCE R. Theatrical plant &c. (In his *Auditing. Authorized American edition.* 1909. p. 195-6).
JENKINSON, M. WEBSTER. Depreciation. *Accountant,* May 17, 1902, p. 528-34.
Theatrical plant and appurtenances
Furniture and fixtures 12½-15%
MONTGOMERY, ROBERT H. Costumes, theatrical. (In his *Income tax procedure,* 1919. p. 562. ——— Same, 1920. p. 715).
MONTGOMERY, ROBERT H. Theatrical companies. (In his *Auditing theory and practice.* 1916. p. 747).
The whole cost of an unsuccessful production should be written off forthwith; on the contrary, the copyright of a successful play does not depreciate rapidly in value. In New York the total cost of production is written off against the first year's business. This is obviously the safest practice.
PHILADELPHIA. CONTROLLER. Rates of depreciation. (In his *Manual of accounting, reporting and business procedure of the city and county of Philadelphia.* 1917. p. 209).
Stage equipment 20%
PIXLEY, FRANCIS W. Theatres. (In his *Accountancy.* Ed. 2. p. 219).
Cost of production 30 to 60 per cent if play running at date of balance sheet, and in last period sufficient to bring it to a nominal value. If piece on tour, on arrangement for tour in force, the depreciation need not be so high.
Decorations 15 to 25%
Structural alterations. A rate sufficient to replace all outlay at the date of the expiration of the lease.
UNIFORM cost sheet for coal mining companies. *Coal age,* Sept. 19, 1918, p. 545-7.

	% original cost
Theater building	6
Fixtures and poolroom	20

Thickeners

NICHOLSON, J. LEE and J. F. D. ROHRBACH. Depreciation. (In their *Cost accounting.* 1919. p. 150).
Thickeners 10%

Thread milling machines

ELBOURNE, EDWARD T. Depreciation rates. (In his *Factory administration and accounts.* 1918. p. 377).

	Prov. dep. %	Years	
	Remainder values	10%	5%
Thread milling machines	6	37	48

Thread rolling machines

ELBOURNE, EDWARD T. Depreciation rates. (In his *Factory administration and accounts.* 1918. p. 377).

	Prov. dep. %	Years	
	Remainder values	10%	5%
Thread rolling machines	7½	29	38

Threading machines

BELT, ROBERT E. Depreciation. (In his *Foundry cost accounting, practice and procedure.* 1919. p. 243). Belt, Robert E. *Uniform cost accounting methods; adopted by the American malleable castings association.* Nov. 14, 1917, p. 20-1.
Emery wheel stands, drop hammers, lathes, drill press, air clippers, milling machines, threading machines, etc., with motor shafting and belting, 10%.

Thumb holding machines

DENHAM, ROBERT S. Depreciation. (In his *Manual of cost engineering and estimating for paper box manufacturers.* 1917. p. 249).
Thumb holding machines 7%

Tie rod machines

NICHOLSON, J. LEE and J. F. D. ROHRBACH. Depreciation. (In their *Cost accounting.* 1919. p. 150).
Tie rod machines. 10%

Timber

See Depreciation, depletion and obsolescence—Lumber.

Time keeping

ELBOURNE, EDWARD T. Depreciation rates. (In his *Factory administration and accounts.* 1918. p. 377).

	Prov. dep. %	Years	
	Remainder values	10%	5%
Time recorders and racks	12½	17	22

UNIFORM cost sheet for coal mining companies. *Coal age,* Sept. 19, 1918, p. 545-7.

	Original cost
Watchmen's clocks	10%

Tipples

MONTGOMERY, ROBERT H. Mine equipment. (In his *Income tax procedure,* 1919. p. 571. ——— Same, 1920. p. 724).
Tipples, inclines and screens 6⅔%
ROBY, J. J. Schedule of plant depreciation. (In his *Treatise on cost accounting as applied to coal mining.* c1913. p. 14-5).
Tipple equipment
Structure, structural steel only

DEPRECIATION, DEPLETION AND OBSOLESCENCE—TIPPLES—*(Continued)*

Deduct as salvage before depreciating 20%
Depreciation rate for remainder, non-fireproof 8
Depreciation rate for remainder, fireproof 5
Equipment, steel only
Deduct as salvage before depreciating 10
Depreciation rate for remainder, fireproof 10

UNIFORM cost sheet for coal mining companies. *Coal age,* Sept. 19, 1918, p. 545-7.

% original cost
Wooden tipples, complete 8
Steel tipples, complete 5

Tobacco

PHILADELPHIA. CONTROLLER. Rates of depreciation. (In his *Manual of accounting, reporting and business procedure of the city and county of Philadelphia.* 1917. p. 209).
Tobacco cutters 4%

TIFFANY, H. S. Tobacco. (In his *Digest of depreciations.* c1890. p. 11).
Stemmeries 3%
Prizing or rehandling 3
Houses (no fire heat) 3
Buildings
brick 2½
frame 4
Buildings:
brick 2½-3
frame 3½-4
Based upon the actual life without any repairs.

Tonguing machines

PHILADELPHIA. CONTROLLER. Rates of depreciation. (In his *Manual of accounting, reporting and business procedure of the city and county of Philadelphia.* 1917. p. 205).
Mitreing and tonguing, grooving, etc., machinery 5%

Tool industry

MILLER & FRANKLIN COMPANY. Depreciation. (In their *Uniform cost system for the National machine builders association.* 1912. p. 19).
Machinery 10%
Building
frame 5
brick 3

Tools

ABERDEEN and depreciation. *Municipal journal* (London), Oct. 23, 1903, p. 943.
Workshop tools 5% Glasgow

ANALYSIS of the premises adopted and methods used in determining the cost to reproduce new together with the depreciation thereon of the physical property of the Metropolitan system and the Kansas City and Westport Belt railway of Kansas City, Mo. *Engineering and contracting,* May 28, 1913, p. 617-20.
Miscellaneous plant tools 25% of total

AUSTRALIA. FEDERAL INCOME TAX DEPARTMENT. Depreciation allowance. *Accountant,* Oct. 13, 1917, p. 277-9. *Accounting and commerce,* June 30, 1917, p. 55-7. *Federal accountant,* July 1917, p. 93-8. *Public accountant,* Jan. 30, 1917, p. 145-52.
Electrical machinery
Machine tools, cranes and all fixed plant 5%
Hand tools and loose plant
Replacements only
Tools (loose) 7½
Written down value, repairs allowed in addition.

BASSET, WILLIAM R. Charging off depreciation on the right basis. (In his *Accounting as an aid to business profits.* c1918. p. 199).
Tools 10%

BENTLEY, HARRY C. Small tools. (In his *Science of accounts.* 1913. p. 197).

BURTON, FRANCIS GEORGE. Depreciation. (In his *Engineers' and shipbuilders' accounts.* 1902. p. 44, 45, 46, 47).

CLAPHAM, F. T. Depreciation of plant. *Mechanical world,* Oct. 19, 1917, p. 219-20.
In a constructional steel works, drilling machines should be depreciated 10%, other machine tools constantly at work should bear 8%.
Pneumatic tools, such as clipping and caulking hammers, drills, and riveting hammers, should be written down 15%.

DEPRECIATION. *American institute of accountants, Special bulletin,* No. 1, Jan. 1920, p. 5-6.

DEPRECIATION of machine tools: abstract. *Industrial engineering,* Oct. 1914, p. 409.

DICKSEE, LAWRENCE R. Depreciation of loose tools. (In his *Depreciation reserves and reserve funds.* 1912. p. 38-9).
Loose tools 10%

FOSTER, HORATIO A. Rates of depreciation. (In his *Engineering valuation of public utilities and factories.* 1913. p. 200).
Shop machinery
Machine tools 5.0%
Hand tools 10.0
Marwick, Mitchell & co., in the appraisal of a large street railway system.

GILLETTE, HALBERT P. and R. T. DANA. Depreciation. (In their *Mechanical and electrical cost data.* 1918. p. 110).
Tools 5 years.
H. P. Gillette, Everett railway and water co., Jan. 20, 1916.
7 years.
Wisconsin railroad commission.

DEPRECIATION, DEPLETION AND OBSOLESCENCE—TOOLS—*(Continued)*

roadway 5 years.
H. P. Gillette, Everett railway and water co., Jan. 29, 1916.
10 years.
H. P. Gillette, Washington ry. appraisal.
Marwick, Mitchell & co. appraisal of a large street railway system, Foster, p. 199.
12.5 years.
Prof. M. E. Cooley, Milwaukee 3c. case.
14.25 years.
M. G. Starret, Milwaukee 3c. case.
10-30 years.
W. D. Pence, Milwaukee 3c. case.
20-50 years.
Union traction co. case, Chicago and union traction co. Stone & Webster.

GRAY, HENRY L. Necessity of depreciation reserves. *Railway age gazette,* May 27, 1910, p. 1297-8. Editorial. Depreciation reserves. *Railway age gazette,* May 27, 1910, p. 1290. Letters. Depreciation reserves. *Railway age gazette,* July 8, 1910, p. 66.
Roadway tools 10%

GRUNSKY, CARL EWALD. Probable useful life of various articles. (In his *Valuation, depreciation and the rate-base.* 1917. p. 285).
Tools and shop machinery 5-25 years.
Wisconsin railroad commission. Milwaukee 3c. fare case, Aug. 3, 1909.
12½ years.
Mortimer E. Cooley. Milwaukee 3c. fare case. Report Wisconsin railroad commission, vol. 10, p. 226.
14.2 years.
Milton G. Starret. Milwaukee 3c. fare case. Report Wisconsin railroad commission.
13.3 years.
Milwaukee electric railway and lighting co., in the Milwaukee 3c. fare case, Aug. 1912.
20 years.
Chicago union traction co. Quoted in Report Wisconsin railroad commission, vol. 10, p. 220.
20 years.
Stone & Webster. Figures for Chicago union traction co. case. Report Wisconsin railroad commission, vol. 10, p. 220.
tools, teams and furniture 4 years. 10% residual value.
Chicago telephone commission. Published 1908.
tools and furniture 7 years.
Wisconsin railroad commission. Quoted by H. A. Foster and in published reports.
tools and sundries 10 years. 5% residual value.
Sir Wm. Preece. Report of Bristol corporation, England, 1906.

GUTHRIE, EDWIN. Depreciation. (In Lisle, George. *Encyclopaedia of accounting.* v. 2. p. 374).
Loose tools and utensils.
Are subject to a rate varying according to their nature. They may be treated as stock subject to valuation from year to year.

HAWKINS, L. WHITTEM. Loose tools. (In his *Cost accounts.* 1912. p. 97-8).

JENKINSON, MARK WEBSTER. Depreciation. *Accountant,* May 17, 1902, p. 528-34.
Loose tools 25-33⅓%

JONES, EDWARD DAVID. Depreciation. (In his *Investment.* p. 167).
Tools and machinery 6% (10% per annum for the first two years).

KERR, W. H. and G. A. NAHSTOLL. Reserve for depreciation. (In their *Cooperative organization business methods.* 1915. p. 13-14).
Tools 25%

KESTER, ROY B. Depreciation on hand tools. (In his *Accounting theory and practice.* 1918. v. 2. p. 289).
Method of the inventory valued at cost, and therefore disregarding depreciation is perhaps the best practical way of handling the valuation of tools.

KIMBALL, DEXTER S. Estimated life, and factors of depreciation. (In his *Cost finding.* 1918. p. 190. *Principles of industrial organization.* 1913. p. 163).

	Prob. life of assets in yrs.	Ratio of scrap to original value	% on orig. cost	% on dim. val.
Machine Tools				
heavy	25	0.10	3.6	9
light	15-20	0.10	6-4.5	14-11

MCINTOSH, ROBERT J. Rates of depreciation. (In his *Reference book of accounts.* p. 62).
Machinery and machine tools
Based on life 10%

MATHESON, EWING. Loose plant excluded from average rates. (In his *Depreciation of factories, mines and industrial undertakings and their valuation.* 1893. p. 48).
Machine tools, 50%.
Tools 25%

MONTGOMERY, ROBERT H. Electrical equipment manufacturers. (In his *Income tax procedure,* 1919. p. 563. ——— Same, 1920. p. 716).
Machinery and tools—standard 10%
Machinery and tools—special 15
Special machinery and tools (additions) 33⅓
Based on gross book values at the end of the preceding year, except for patterns and tools, which are based on the previous years' additions.

DEPRECIATION, DEPLETION AND OBSOLESCENCE—TOOLS—*(Continued)*

MONTGOMERY, ROBERT H. Small tools. (In his *Auditing theory and practice.* 1916. p. 425).
Revalue periodically.

MONTGOMERY, ROBERT H. Tools, jigs, dies, etc. (In his *Income tax procedure,* 1919. p. 569-71, 579-80, ——— Same. 1920. p. 724, 736).
In the case of a heavy machine tool the life is usually considered to be from 15 to 20 years, ignoring the question of obsolescence, yet the rate of the National machine tool builders—which is 10 per cent and is for favorable conditions and applies to the total original value and not to a decreasing value—should be given weight.
As a rule the practice of depreciating small tools by means of a percentage cannot be followed satisfactorily. So many tools are used up, lost or stolen, that an inventory should be made periodically and all the tools on hand should be revalued. 25-50% adopted in one state or, as an alternate, the entire cost of replacements. The minimum rate should not be less than 20%.

NEALE, R. E. Depreciation in engineering works. *Mechanical world,* Feb. 7, 1913, p. 67-8.

	% Dep.	Years
Machine tools	7.5-12	8.5-13
specialized	20	5

NICHOLSON, J. LEE and JOHN F. D. ROHRBACH. Depreciation. (In their *Cost accounting.* 1919. p. 149-50, 152-3)
Machine tools:

Lathes, slotters, planers, drilling and boring machines; milling machines, tool and surface grinders, emery wheels, keyway cutters, tapping machines, arbor presses, centering machines, squaring machines, hack saws, notching machines, buffing machines, test pumps, pointing machines, metal band saws, belt lacers, saw grinders, etc., die-sinking machines, trimming presses, etc., belt cutters, pipe threading machines, car wheel presses, saw-setting and filing machines, angle-benching machines, cold saw-cutting machines, etc.	6⅔%
Gun and tool machinery	6
Cartridge machinery	8
Tool and shop machinery	5

Based on (1) the cost of equipment
(2) the life of the equipment
(3) on a ten-hour day.

NICHOLSON, J. LEE and J. F. D. ROHRBACH. Depreciation. (In their *Cost accounting.* 1919. p. 150, 152-3).
Small tools

All small tools of an asset nature	10%

Based on (1) the cost of equipment
(2) the life of the equipment
(3) on a ten-hour day.
Group rates:

Small asset tools, machine tool accessories, boring bars, driver's keyseating broaches, etc. All renewals to repairs	10%

For machines, hand tools, punches and dies, chills, proving ground equipment, gages, chucks, jigs and fixtures, all special.
Based on (1) the cost of equipment
(2) the life of the equipment
(3) on a ten-hour day.

NORRIS, H. M. Depreciation of plant and its relation to general expense. *Engineering magazine,* April 1899, p. 76.

Standard machinery and tools	8%
Special tools, jigs and fixtures	5

NORRIS, H. M. Machine tool depreciation as an element of manufacturing cost. *Engineering magazine,* March 1899, p. 957-68.

PENDER, HAROLD. Depreciation. (In his *Handbook for electrical engineers.* c1914. p. 340).

	Years	% Dep.	
Tools and machinery shop			
	10-30		Engineer of valuation staff of Wisconsin railroad commission.
	20		Chicago union traction co.
			Stone & Webster, for the Chicago union traction co.
		10-3.33	Engineer of the valuation staff of Wisconsin railroad commission.
		7.5	Milwaukee electric railway and light co.
			Cardiff tramway.
			Glasgow "
		5	Chicago union traction co.
			Stone & Webster, for the Chicago union traction co.

PIEZ, CHARLES. Depreciation of plants and tools. *American machinist,* April 5, 1917, p. 614-5. *Factory,* April 1917, p. 520.

PIEZ, CHARLES. Perpetual inventory and appraisal values; table of standard depreciation rates. *Engineering and contracting,* Jan. 24, 1917, p. 77. *Factory,* Dec. 1916, p. 668-71. *Iron age,* Nov. 30, 1916, Jan. 11, 1917, p. 1266, 138-9. *Iron trade review,* Feb. 22, 1917, p. 477-8. Condensed. *Journal of the American society of mechanical engineers,* Dec. 1916, p. 965-6. *Iron trade review,* Dec. 7, 1916, p. 1144-6. Kent, William, *Bookkeeping and cost accounting for factories,* 1918. p. 90. Discussion. *Journal of the American society of mechanical engineers,* March 1917, p. 215-7.

	% on cost	% on reducing balance
Machinery, motors, machine tools, traveling cranes, etc.	4.5	10
Small tools, for machines, net additions	50	
Hand tools, net additions	50	

PIXLEY, FRANCIS W. Electric lighting companies. (In his *Accountancy.* Ed. 2. p. 218).

Tools	10-15%

RACINE, SAMUEL F. Tools. (In his *Accounting principles.* 1917. p. 154).

DEPRECIATION, DEPLETION AND OBSOLESCENCE—Tools—*(Continued)*

Roby, J. J. Schedule of plant depreciation. (In his *Treatise on cost accounting as applied to coal mining.* c1913. p. 14-5).

Wagons and tools	
Deduct as salvage before depreciating	10%
Depreciation rate for remainder fireproof	20

Spencer, Henry. Fixed charges in the machine shop and the depreciation of machine tools. *Engineer* (London), Sept. 27, 1912, p. 321.

Spicer, Ernest Evan and Ernest C. Pegler. Loose plant and tools. (In their *Practical auditing.* 1914. p. 145).

Thompson, C. Bertrand. Interest and depreciation. (In his *How to find factory costs.* c1916. p. 69).

Where the industry can afford it, it is desirable to charge off immediately to expense all small tools and equipment. In some cases, however, as in machine shops, the investment in high-speed steel may be so heavy as to add something permanent to the value of the plant. In this case it is desirable to charge fifty per cent of the investment in tools at once to indirect expense, carrying the other fifty per cent as an asset until scrapped, which is pretty apt to occur within a year or two.

Various depreciation charges. *New York Times*, June 14, 1914.

Tools and fixtures	10%

Whatley, G. E. Stuart. Depreciation. (In his *Accountant's and bookkeeper's vade-mecum,* 1893. p. 27-8).

Loose tools and utensils would be better treated as stock and valued as such at the periodical stocktakings.

Woods, Clinton E. Machinery and tools. (In his *Unified accounting methods for industrials.* 1917. p. 65).

Machinery	7½-10%

Topping machines

Denham, Robert S. Depreciation. (In his *Manual of cost engineering and estimating for paper box manufacturers.* 1917. p. 249).

Topping machines	7%

Towers

Crowell, H. H. Electric lighting rates and depreciation. *Municipal journal and engineer,* Dec. 18, 1907, p. 698.

	Purchased 10 years or more ago	Modern
Towers	20 years	10 years

Elbourne, Edward T. Depreciation rates. (In his *Factory administration and accounts.* 1918. p. 376).

	Prov. dep. %	Years	
	Remainder values	10%	5%
Water towers	7½	29	38

Philadelphia. Controller. Rates of depreciation. (In his *Manual of accounting, reporting and business procedure of the city and county of Philadelphia.* 1917. p. 209).

Water towers and standpipes	4%

Track

Average life in track of express ties. *Railway age gazette,* March 23, 1911, p. 636-7.

	Average years life of track
Central of Georgia. No accurate data; when protected with tie plate	10-12
Charlotte & Western Carolina R. R.	12-14
International & Great Northern	12
Louisiana railway and Navigation Co. Red. yellow and white heart	8
St. Louis and San Francisco, for red and yellow	10-15
Vicksburg, Shreveport & Pacific	12

Bagg, F. A. Life of railway physical property from engineering standpoint. *Electric railway journal,* Dec. 9, 1911, p. 1205-6.

Ties in open track	Life in years
Cedar	15 to 20
Yellow pine	10 to 15
Treated ties	25 and more
Untreated ties in pavement or concrete	15 to 20
Treated ties	30 and more

Barker, Harry. Depreciation of electric railway property. (In his *Public utility rates.* 1917. p. 367).

	Years	Authority
Track		
Tangent	18	Wisconsin railroad commission.
Curves	5	Author—Average or approximate figures secured
Special work	5	by examination or enquiry.

Barker, Harry. Typical life expectation tables for public utility property. (In his *Public utility rates.* 1917. p. 366).

	Years
Track, rail, main-line tangent	2-8
" " main-line curve	1-5
" " sidings and yards	10-20
" " ties, ordinary light wood	5-10
" " ordinary hard wood	10-15
" " treated and protected	30

Author—Average or approximate figures secured by examination or enquiry.

DEPRECIATION, DEPLETION AND OBSOLESCENCE—TRACK—*(Continued)*

BAY state rate case. *Electric railway journal,* Dec. 4, 1915, p. 1121-3. *Public utility reports, annotated,* 1916F, p. 336-9.

	Net % Dep.	Years.
Track and roadway rails, including all fastenings		10-35
Ties		10-35
Paved track, same as rail		16
Unpaved track, under good backfill		12
Unpaved track, open to weather		
Bonds, same as rail to which they are attached		
Special work		6-20
Track and roadway labor, same as rail or special work where labor was incurred		
Grading and ballast	not depreciated	
Ties	5.6	
Rails, rail fastenings and joints	3.5	
Special work	5.7	
Track and roadway labor	4.4	
Roadway machinery and tools	4.0	

Annual depreciation per cent divided by investment.

BEMIS, EDWARD W. Testimony on depreciation before Nebraska commission, re the Consolidation of the properties of the Lincoln traction company. *Electric railway journal,* March 12, 1910, p. 441.

Track 12-18 years

BRYAN, WILLIAM. Appraisal and depreciation of water works and similar properties. *Journal of the Association of engineering societies,* Dec. 1907, p. 336-81. Depreciation allowance for various public service industries. *Engineering news,* Jan. 23, 1908, p. 96.

	% straight	% sinking fund
Ties		7
Track		8-12
"	7-13	
Rails	5.5	
Bonding, track		8
" "	10-16	

CRAVENS, GEORGE W. Depreciation and maintenance of electrical equipment. *Electrical review,* April 23, 1910, p. 853-6. Foster, H. A. *Engineering valuation of public utilities and factories,* 1913, p. 201-2).

	Light or intermittent service	Heavy or continuous service
Track work, ballast, etc.	5-8.3%	7.5-12.5%

Trackwork

7.75	Chicago traction co.
7.5-12	Milwaukee electric railway and light co.
5	Wisconsin railroad commission.
5	Average English.
8	Average Scotch practice.
7-13	Philip Dawson.
7.2	Stone and Webster.
7.5	Miscellaneous sources.

CROWELL, H. H. Electric lighting rates and depreciation. *Municipal journal and engineer,* Dec. 18, 1907, p. 698.

	Purchased 10 years more ago	Modern
Railway tracks and scales	25 years	25 years

DAWSON, PHILIP. Depreciation. (In his *Engineering and electric traction pocket-book.* Ed. 2. p. 1161, 1160).

	Years	% Capital cost
Tracks	10-15	
Track work		7-13

Durability of railroad sleepers, from a report of the United States Department of agriculture.

	Years
White oak and chestnut oak	8
Chestnut	8
Black locust	10
Cherry, black walnut, locust	7
Elm	6-7
Red and black oaks	4-5
Ash, beach and maple	4
Redwood	12
Cypress ,and red cedar	10
Tamarack	7-8
Longleaf pine	6
Hemlock	4-6
Spruce	5

DEPRECIATION funds in Europe. *Electric railway journal,* May 7, 21, 1904, p. 696, 760.

	% Dep.	Years
Track		25
Brussels	1½%	
Czernowitz railway	5	
Frankfort	2	
Leipsiger Strassenbaln	5	
Mannheim	2	
Remscheid		

Glasgow. £4 50 per mile of single track per year.

ELBOURNE, EDWARD T. Depreciation rates. (In his *Factory administration and accounts.* 1918. p. 376).

	Prov. dep %	Years Remainder values 10%	5%
Railway and tramway tracks	4	56	73

DEPRECIATION, DEPLETION AND OBSOLESCENCE—TRACK—*(Continued)*

FLOY, HENRY. Depreciation. Floy, Henry. Depreciation as related to electrical properties. *American institute of electrical engineers, Proceedings,* 1911, p. 1267. Floy, Henry. *Valuation of public utility properties.* 1912. p. 188-93. Foster, H. A. *Engineering valuation of public utilities and factories.* 1913. p. 194-8. *Engineering and contracting,* Oct. 4, 1911, p. 359-65. *Engineering magazine,* Aug. 1911, p. 837-40.

	Dep. % Straight line		
Track, rail joints	5	Tract. val. comm.	Chicago con. tract. co.
Ties	5	Tract. val. comm.	Chicago con. tract. co.
Rails dependent on observed wear		Tract. val. comm.	Chicago con. tract. co.
Special work, dependent on observed wear		Tract. val. comm.	Chicago con. tract. co.
work, wearing value	50 wearing value		
Straight and special		B. J. Arnold	Coney Island and Brooklyn, adopted by P. S. C., N. Y.
Straight and special work, wearing value	50 wearing value	Henry Floy	3rd Avenue case, adopted by P. S. C., N. Y.
Special work	8⅓	Wisconsin P. S. C.	
Straight track	5½	Wisconsin P. S. C.	

FOSTER, HORATIO A. Rates of depreciation. (In his *Engineering valuation of public utilities and factories.* p. 199).

Roadway	
Rails in city streets	4.5%
" " country roads	3.5
" " private right-of-way	3.5
Superstructure in city streets	4.5
" " country roads	7.0
" " private right-of-way	10.0
Special work	9.0

Marwick, Mitchell & co. in the appraisal of a large street railway system.

FOSTER, HORATIO A. Rules for depreciating railways and lighting plants in Great Britain. (In his *Engineering valuation of public utilities and factories.* 1913. p. 165-8).

Permanent way	12, 14 or 16 years
(1) not exceeding 50,000 car miles	16
(2) over 50,000 and not exceeding 75,000	14
(3) over 75,000 and not exceeding 125,000	12
(4) over 125,000	Special consideration

GILLETTE, HALBERT POWERS. Railways. (In his *Handbook of cost data for contractors and engineers.* 1910. p. 1317-8).

	Age years	Annual dep. %	% present cond.
Ties	4.3	12.5	46.3
Rails, track fastenings, etc.	8.0	2.5	80.0

GILLETTE, HALBERT P. and R. T. DANA. Depreciation. (In their *Handbook of mechanical and electrical cost data.* 1918. p. 110-1).

	Years	
Track		
ballast	33.3	H. P. Gillette, Everett railway and water co. Jan. 29, 1912.
bonds	20	Wisconsin railroad commission.
		Traction valuation commission, Chicago consolidated traction co.
fastenings and joints	33.3	H. P. Gillette, Everett railway and water co. Jan. 29, 1912.
fastenings	40	H. P. Gillette, Washington ry. appraisal.
main		
	11.7	Beggs, Milwaukee 3c. case.
	12.5	Prof. M. E. Cooley, Milwaukee 3c. case.
		M. G. Starret, Milwaukee 3c. case.
	12.9-13.9	Union traction co., case Chicago and Union traction co., Stone & Webster.
	13.3	Milwaukee electric railway and light co.
straight	18.2	Wisconsin railroad commission.
rails	33.3	H. P. Gillette, Everett railway and water co., Jan. 29, 1912.
	40	H. P. Gillette, Washington railway appraisal.
rails in city streets	22.2	Marwick, Mitchell & co. appraisal of a large street railway system, Foster, p. 199.
rails in country roads	28.6	Marwick, Mitchell & co. appraisal of a large street railway system, Foster, p. 199.
rails in private right-of-way	28.6	Marwick, Mitchell & co. appraisal of a large street railway system, Foster, p. 199.
rail joints	20	Traction valuation commission, Chicago consolidated traction co.
special work	8.5	Milwaukee electric railway and light co.
	8-14-25	W. D. Pence. Milwaukee 3c. case.
	10	B. J. Arnold, Chicago appraisal, 4 cases.
	11.1	Marwick, Mitchell & co. appraisal of a large street railway system, Foster, p. 199.
	11.75	Wisconsin railroad commission.
	12.9-13-9	Union traction co., Case Chicago and union traction co., Stone & Webster.
	25	H. P. Gillette, Everett railway and water co., Jan. 29, 1912.

DEPRECIATION, DEPLETION AND OBSOLESCENCE—TRACK—*(Continued)*

substructure city streets	22.2	Marwick, Mitchell & co. appraisal of a large street railway system, Foster, p. 199.
country roads	14.3	Marwick, Mitchell & co. appraisal of a large street railway system, Foster, p. 199.
private right-of way	10	Marwick, Mitchell & co. appraisal of a large street railway system, Foster, p. 199.
ties	8	H. P. Gillette, Washington ry. appraisal.
	13.3	H. P. Gillette, Everett railway and water co., Jan. 29, 1912.
	20	Traction valuation commission; Chicago consolidated traction co.

GRAY, HENRY L. Necessity of depreciation reserves. *Railway age gazette,* May 27, 1910. p. 1297-8. Editorial. Depreciation reserves. *Railway age gazette,* May 27, 1910, p. 1290. Letters. Depreciation reserves. *Railway age gazette,* July 8, 1910, p. 66.

	Annual % depreciation
Ties	15
Rails, main track	3
Fastenings	5
Frogs and switches	7
Track laying	5

GREENLAND, S. W. Depreciation. *Mississippi electric association, Report of 2nd annual convention,* June 1910, p. 32-6).

Ties, white oak	7-9 years
Rails, 70 pounds	30

GRUNSKY, CARL EWALD. Probable useful life of various articles. (In his *Valuation, depreciation and the rate-base.* 1916. p. 285-6).

Tracks:

Rails, ties and bonding	12½ years. Wisconsin Railroad Commission. Milwaukee 3c Fare Case, Aug. 23, 1912.
" " " "	12½ years. Mortimer E. Cooley. Milwaukee 3c Fare Case. Report Wisconsin R. R. Com., Vol. 10, p. 226.
" " " "	12½ years. Milton G. Starrett, Milwaukee 3c Fare Case. Report Wisconsin R. R. Commission, Vol. 10, p. 226.
" " " "	12.85 years. Chicago Union Traction Co. Quoted in Report Wisconsin R. R. Commission, Vol. 10, p. 220.
" " " "	13.86 years. Stone & Webster. Figures for Chicago Union Traction Co. Case. Report Wisconsin Railroad Commission, Vol. 10, p. 220.
" " " "	13.33 years. Milwaukee Electric Railway and Lighting Co., in the Milwaukee 3c Fare Case, Aug. 1912.
straight	18 years. Wisconsin Railroad Commission. Quoted by Henry Floy and in published reports.
special work	8.3 years. Milwaukee Electric Railway and Lighting Co., in the Milwaukee 3c Fare Case, Aug., 1912.
" "	10 years. Bion J. Arnold. Coney Island and Brooklyn figures adopted by Public Service Commission of New York. Four Chicago appraisals quoted by H. A. Foster.
" "	12 years. Wisconsin Railroad Commission. Quoted by Henry Floy and in published reports.
" "	12.85 years Chicago Union Traction Co. Quoted in Report Wisconsin R. R. Commission, Vol. 10, p. 220.
" "	13.86 years Stone & Webster. Figures for Chicago Union Traction Co. Case. Report Wisconsin Railroad Commission, Vol. 10, p. 220.
Ties	20 years. Traction Valuation Commission. Case of the Chicago Consolidated Traction Co.
Railroad rails, new	25 years. 26% residual value. California Railroad Commission—Reports 1913-4. Stockton Terminal & Eastern R.R., April 1913.
" " relay	15 years. 48% residual value. California Railroad Commission—Reports 1913-4. Stockton Terminal & Eastern R.R., April 1913.
" " and track fast.	40 years. H. P. Gillette. Appraisal of Great Northern & Northern Pacific R.R.'s in Washington. Direction of Washington Railroad Commission, 1906.
" track fastenings	12½ years. California Railroad Commission. Stockton Terminal & Eastern R.R., April 1913.
" ties	8 years. H. P. Gillette. Appraisal of Great Northern & Northern Pacific R.R.'s in Washington. Direction of Washington Railroad Commission.

DEPRECIATION, DEPLETION AND OBSOLESCENCE—TRACK—*(Continued)*

Railroad ties redwood	16 years. California Railroad Commission. Stockton Terminal & Eastern R.R., April 1913.
" " creosoted	19.35 years. O. Chanute. Houston & Texas Cent. R.R.
Trestles and bridges	10 years. California Railroad Commission. Stockton Terminal & Eastern R.R., April 1913.
Ballast	10 years. California Railroad Commission. Stockton Terminal & Eastern R.R., April 1913.
Frogs and switches	25 years. 36% residual value. California Railroad Commission. Stockton Terminal & Eastern R.R., April 1913.
Cast-iron culverts	16 years. California Railroad Commission. Stockton Terminal & Eastern R.R., April 1913.

GUTHRIE, EDWIN. Depreciation. (In Lisle, George. *Encyclopaedia of accounting.* v.2. p. 374-5).
Rails 2½-5% diminishing value

ISTITUTE OF MUNICIPAL TREASURERS AND ACCOUNTANTS (INCORPORATED). Municipal corporations and companies working tramway and light railways, gas, water and electricity undertakings. *Accountant,* June 26, 1909, p. 906-8. Income tax assessment:—allowances for depreciation. *Accountant,* Oct. 2, 1909, p. 423-5, 400-2.
The life of the permanent way is to be taken as twelve, fourteen, or sixteen years, according to the traffic thereon.
(1) Not exceeding 50,000 car miles per mile of track 16 years
(2) Over 50,000 and not exceeding 75,000 car miles per mile of track 14 years
(3) Over 75,000 and not exceeding 125,000 miles per mile of track 12 years
(4) Over 125,000 car miles per mile of track, special consideration
Cost of renewals, including setts or other paving but excluding concrete foundations, should be taken at £4,400 per mile of single track until the general renewal of track takes place.

LEAKE, P. D. Record of depreciation. (In his *Depreciation and wasting assets and their treatment in computing annual profit and loss.* 1917. p. 86).
Track 7-13%

METROPOLITAN street railway reorganization plan. *Electric railway journal,* May 20, 1911, p. 876-8.

Paving in track	14 years
Train rail in straight track	14
Slot rail	25
Conductor lines	10
Special work and paving	5
Horse track and special work	25

MONTGOMERY, ROBERT H. Electrical equipment manufacturers. (In his *Income tax procedure,* 1919. p. 563. ——— Same, 1920. p. 716).
Railway tracks and overhead equipment 4%
Based on gross book values at the end of the preceding year

MURRAY, ALEXANDER. Glasgow corporation accounts with special reference to depreciation and sinking funds. *Accountant,* June 13, 1903, p. 782-94. *Royal philosophical society of Glasgow, Proceedings,* 1903.
Permanent way £450 per mile of single track

NEALE, R. E. Depreciation in engineering works. *Mechanical world,* Feb. 7, 1913, p. 67-8.
Tramways

Track: straight from	5-6%	17-20 years
to	10-15	6-10
special	10-50	2-10

NELSON, BAILIE WALTER. Limitation and application of profits from municipal undertakings. *Incorporated accountants' journal,* Oct. 1912, p. 15-7.
On permanent way £440 per mile of single track per annum

OFFICIAL allowance in respect of machinery and plant—Board of Inland revenue, Great Britain. *Accountant,* May 16, 1914, p. 737.

(1) not exceeding 50,000 car miles per mile of track	16 years
(2) over 50,000 and not exceeding 75,000 car miles per mile of track	14
(3) over 75,000 and not exceeding 125,000 car miles per mile of track	12
(4) over 125,000 car miles per mile of track—special consideration	

Cost of renewals including setts or other paving but excluding concrete foundations, should be taken at £4,400 per mile of single track until the general renewal of the track takes place

PENDER, HAROLD. Depreciation. (In his *Handbook for electrical engineers.* c1914. p. 340).
Track construction:

Bonding	10-6%	P. Dawson.
	8	Chicago city railways
	7	Chicago city railways
Ties		
Track complete	12	J. I. Beggs
	12.85	Chicago union traction co.
	13.86	Stone & Webster for Chicago union traction co.
	13-7	P. Dawson
	9-8	M. G. Starrett
	8.5	J. I. Beggs
	8	Glasgow tramways
	7.75	Chicago union traction co.
	7.5	Milwaukee electric railway and light co.
	7.2	Stone & Webster for the Chicago union traction co.
	5.5	Chicago city railways
	5	Cardiff tramways

DEPRECIATION, DEPLETION AND OBSOLESCENCE—TRACK—*(Continued)*

PIEZ, CHARLES. Perpetual inventory and appraisal values; table of standard depreciation rates. *Engineering and contracting,* Jan. 24, 1917, p. 77. *Factory,* Dec. 1916, p. 668-71. *Iron age,* Nov. 30, 1916, Jan. 11, 1917, p. 1266, 138-9. *Iron trade review,* Feb. 22, 1917, p. 477-8. Condensed. *Iron trade review,* Dec. 7, 1916, p. 1144-6. *Journal of the American society of mechanical engineers,* Dec. 1916, p. 965-6. *Kent, William. Bookkeeping and cost accounting for factories.* 1918. p. 90. Discussion. *Journal of the American society of mechanical engineers,* March 1917, p. 215-7.

	% on cost	% on reducing balance
Tracks	4.5	10

POLICY of English municipal tramways respecting renewals. *Electric railway journal,* Oct. 7, 1911, p. 661-3.

Rails	15 years

PUBLIC utility reports, annotated. Rochester, Lawyers co-operative publishing co. 1918C. p. 534.

Springfield, Street R. co. road, track, line, etc.	3.17%

ROBY, J. J. Schedule of plant depreciation. (In his *Treatise on cost accounting as applied to coal mining.* c1913. p. 14-5).

Mine tracks	
Steel rails and splices	
Deduct as salvage before depreciating	50%
Depreciation rate for remainder, fireproof	4
Wood ties	
Depreciation rate, fireproof	20
Steel ties and spikes	
Deduct as salvage before depreciating	10
Depreciation rate for remainder, fireproof	10
Labor, main roads	
Depreciation rate	25
Wood rails	
Depreciation rate	100

STUCKMANN, H. Depreciation and obsolescence in Portland cement plants. *Journal of the American society of mechanical engineers,* Feb. 1913, p. 262-75.

	% of reproductive value
Railway tracks	7
Quarry rails and equipment	15

TRACK repairs and renewals. *Light railway and tramway journal,* Nov. 3, 1911.

TREATMENT of depreciation in Glasgow. *Electric railway journal,* Sept. 3, 1910, p. 362.

£440 per mile on street track renewal

UNIFORM cost sheet for coal mining companies. *Coal age,* Sept. 19, 1918, p. 545-7.

	original cost
Steel rail	10%
Railway sidings and approaches	7

VARIOUS depreciation charges. *New York Times,* June 14, 1914.

Railway tracks	7%

WEEKS, H. E. Abstract of paper on depreciation read before annual meeting of Iowa street and interurban railway association, April 1910. *Electric railway journal,* April 30, 1910, p. 782-3.

Ties	7 years
Rails	20

Traction engines

AUSTRALIA. FEDERAL INCOME TAX DEPARTMENT. Depreciation allowance. *Accountant,* Oct. 13, 1917, p. 277-9. *Accounting and commerce,* June 30, 1917, p. 55-7. *Federal accountant,* July 1917, p. 93-8. *Public accountant,* Jan. 30, 1917, p. 145-52.

Traction engines (oil or wood fuel)	7½%

Written down value, repairs allowed in addition.

GREAT BRITAIN. BOARD OF INLAND REVENUE. Depreciation rates: abstract. (In its *Income tax; statement respecting allowances for wear and tear and obsolescence of plant and machinery.* 1918. Cd. 9022, p. 4; Cd. 9134, p. 6. *American economic review,* Supplement, Dec. 1920, p. 51. *Journal of accountancy,* Sept. 1920, p. 195.

Traction engines, tractors, motor-cars and haulage plants	20%

Written down value.

Tractors

BELT, ROBERT E. Depreciation. (In his *Foundry cost accounting practice and procedure.* 1919. p. 243).

Industrial electric trucks and tractors	25%
Truck and tractor trailers	15

GREAT BRITAIN. BOARD OF INLAND REVENUE. Depreciation rates: (In its *Income tax; statement respecting allowances for wear and tear and obsolescence of plant and machinery.* 1918. Cd. 9022, p. 4; Cd. 9134, p. 6). *American economic review, Supplement,* Dec. 1920, p. 51. *Journal of accountancy,* Sept. 1920, p. 195.

Traction engines, tractors, motor-cars, and haulage plant	20%

Written down value.

Trade utensils

AUSTRALIA. FEDERAL INCOME TAX DEPARTMENT. Depreciation allowance. *Accountant,* Oct. 13, 1917, p. 277-9. *Accounting and commerce,* June 30, 1917, p. 55-7. *Federal accountant,* July 1917, p. 93-8. *Public accountant,* Jan. 30, 1917, p. 145-52.

Trade utensils	7½%

Written down value, repairs allowed in addition

Transfer companies

PUBLIC utility reports, annotated. Rochester, Lawyers co-operative publishing co. 1917A. p. 225. Re Union Transfer Co. (D. C.) A baggage transfer company was ordered to conform its depreciation accounts to the following rates of depreciation, based on the cost of reproduction new; land, no depreciation; buildings, 2 per cent; electrical work and other equip-

DEPRECIATION, DEPLETION AND OBSOLESCENCE—TRACK—*(Continued)*

ment, 4.24 per cent; furniture and fixtures, 10.82 per cent; electric trucks, 10 per cent; electric batteries, 40 per cent; garage equipment, 4.58 per cent; wagons, wagon fixtures, busses, buggies, and baggage trucks, 5.50 per cent; horses, 8.19 per cent; harness and harness material, 12.93 per cent.

Transformers

ABERDEEN and depreciation. *Municipal journal (London)*, Oct. 23, 1903, p. 943.
Transformers — 6% — Bolton

ANALYSIS of the premises adopted and methods used in determining the cost to reproduce new together with the depreciation thereon of the physical property of the Metropolitan system and the Kansas City and Westport Belt railway of Kansas City, Mo. *Engineering and contracting*, May 28, 1913, p. 617-20.
Transformers — 5%

AUSTRALIA. FEDERAL INCOME TAX DEPARTMENT. Depreciation allowance. *Accountant*, Oct. 13, 1917, p. 277-9. *Accounting and commerce*, June 30, 1917, p. 55-7. *Federal accountant*, July 1917, p. 93-8. *Public accountant*, June 30, 1917, p. 145-52.
Transformer boxes — 2½%
Written down value, repairs allowed.

BARKER, HARRY. Typical life expectation tables for public utility property. (In his *Public utility rates*. 1917. p. 368-9).

Transformers	
consumers	10-15 years
station and substation	20
	Wisconsin Railroad commission

BRYAN, WILLIAM H. Depreciation of electric light plants. *Municipality*, March 1908, p. 74.
Motor transformers & instruments — 15 years

COST and depreciation of steam and hydro-electric installations. *Electrical world*, Dec. 30, 1909, p. 1558.

	years	% of total cost
Transformers	10	1.29
substation	20	1.28
Generators & transformers	25	.898

CRAVENS, GEORGE W. Depreciation and maintenance of electrical equipment. *Electrical review*, April 23, 1910, p. 853-6. Foster, H. A. *Engineering valuation of public utilities and factories* 1913. p. 201-2.

	Light or intermittent service	Heavy or continuous service
Transformers	3-5%	4-6.6%

	Annual % Dep.	
Transformers	6.6	Chicago union traction co.
	5	Milwaukee electric railway & light co.
	5	Wisconsin railroad commission.
	5	Average English
	5	Average Scotch practice
	5-6	Philip Dawson
	5	Stone and Webster
	3-5	Industrial power plants
	4	Prof. G. F. Gebhardt
	5	Miscellaneous sources

CROWELL, H. H. Electric lighting rates and depreciation. *Municipal journal and engineer*, Dec. 18, 1907, p. 698.

	Purchased 10 years or more age	Modern
Transformers	15 years	20 years.

DAWSON, PHILIP. Depreciation. (In his *Engineering and electric traction pocket-book*. Ed. 2. p. 1161).

	% capital cost
Rotary transformers	8-10
Stationary transformers	5-6

DEPRECIATION of an electric plant. *Electrical world*, Dec. 12, 1914, p. 1161
Line transformers — 4.5%

ELBOURNE, EDWARD T. Depreciation rates. (In his *Factory administration and accounts*. 1918. p. 376).

	Prov. dep. %	years	
	Remainder values	10%	5%
Transformers & converters	7½	29	38

FIGURES from the Iola (Kans.). central station. *Electrical world*, Sept. 23, 1909, p. 723.
Transformer — 8%

FLOY, HENRY. Depreciation. Floy, Henry. Depreciation as related to electrical properties. *American institute of electrical engineers, Proceedings*, 1911, p. 1267. Floy, Henry. *Valuation of public utility properties*. 1912. p. 188-93. Foster, Horatio A. *Engineering valuation of public utilities and factories*. 1913. p. 194-8. *Engineering magazine*, Aug. 1911, p. 837-40. *Engineering and contracting*, Oct. 4, 1911, p. 359-65.

	Dep. % per year Straight line		
Transformers			
station service	5	Wisconsin P.S.C.	
	6⅔	Wisconsin P.S.C.	
	6⅔	St. Louis P.S.C.	Union elec. L.&P. co.

DEPRECIATION, DEPLETION AND OBSOLESCENCE—TRANSFORMERS—*(Continued)*

FOSTER, HORATIO A. Methods of calculating depreciation. (In his *Engineering valuation of public utilities and factories.* 1913. p. 169-70).

Minimum service value, per cent of reproduction cost.

Static transformers, including regulators and compensators, station type 40%
Joint engineering department of the Wisconsin commissions.
Service transformers 25%

FOSTER, HORATIO A. Rates of depreciation. (In his *Engineering valuation of public utilities and factories.* 1913. p. 200, 205, 206).
Rotaries, transformers, switch boards, auxiliaries 4.5%. Marwick, Mitchell & Co. in the appraisal of a large street railway system.
Static transformers, including regulators and compensators, station type 20 years
Service transformers 10-15

GILLETTE, HALBERT P. and R. T. DANA. Depreciation. (In their *Handbook of mechanical and electrical cost data.* 1918. p. 110).
Transformers 20 years.
Milwaukee electric railway & light co.
20-33.3 years.
George W. Cravens, Industrial power plants.
22.2 years.
Marwick, Mitchell & co., appraisal of a large street railway system, Foster, p. 199.
Station service 15 years.
St. Louis public service commission, Union electric light & power co.
15-20 years.
Wisconsin Railroad Commission.
20 years.
H. P. Gillette, Everett railway & water co., Jan. 29, 1912.

GREENLAND, S. W. Depreciation. *Mississippi electric association, Report of 2nd annual convention,* June 1910, p. 32-6.
Transformers 10 years

GRUNSKY, CARL EWALD. Probable useful life of various articles. (In his *Valuation, depreciation and the rate-base.* 1917. p. 286).
Transformers 15 years.
St. Louis public service commission. Case of Union electric light & power co.
16 years.
Wisconsin railroad commission. Quoted by Henry Floy and in published reports.
station service 20 years.
Wisconsin railroad commission. Quoted by Henry Floy and in published reports.
station 25 years.
San Joaquin light & power corporation. Rate hearing before California railroad commission, 1915.
line 20 years. 10% residual value.
California railroad commission—Reports 1913-4. Calistoga electric co. vs. Napa valley electric co., May, 1914.
distribution 20 years. $1.00 kw. residual value.
Pacific gas and electric company. Figures used in rate hearings before Master in Chancery, San Francisco, 1913-4.
power 20 years. $.50 kw. residual value.
Pacific gas and electric company. Figures used in rate hearings before Master in Chancery, San Francisco, 1913-4.
static 15 years.
Robt. Hammond. Journal of the Institute of electrical engineers, England, April 25, 1907.

HAMMOND, ROBERT. Depreciation. *Institute of electrical engineers, Proceedings,* April 25, 1907. *Journal of the Institute of electrical engineers.* 1907. p. 270. Abstracts. *Accountant,* May 18, 1907, p. 675. *Electric railway review,* June 1, 1907, p. 716. *Electrical review* (Chicago), May 25, 1907, p. 828. *Electrical review* (London), May 3, 1907, p. 744. *Electrician,* April 26, 1907, p. 51. *Engineering magazine,* July 1, 1907, p. 636-8. *Engineering record,* June 15, 1907, p. 703. *Municipal journal* (London), May 10, 17, 1907, p. 411, 435. *Progressive age,* July 1, 1907, p. 305. *Street railway bulletin,* June 1907, p. 382. *Tramway and railway world,* June 6, 1907, p. 497.
Transformers, static 15 years

JOHNSON, GEORGE. Depreciation. (In his *Electric lighting accounts.* 1903. p. 23-4).
Transformers 7½-10%

LEAKE, P. D. Record of depreciation. (In his *Depreciation and wasting assets and their treatment in computing annual profit and loss.* 1917. p. 86).
Transformers 5-6%

NEALE, R. E. Depreciation in engineering works. *Mechanical world,* Feb. 7, 1913, p. 67-8.
Transformers 5-6% 17-20 years

NICHOLSON, J. LEE and J. F. D. ROHRBACH. Depreciation. (In their *Cost accounting.* 1919. p. 148).
Transformers—station service 5%
Based on (1) the cost of equipment
(2) the life of the equipment
(3) on a ten-hour day

DEPRECIATION, DEPLETION AND OBSOLESCENCE—TRANSFORMERS—*(Continued)*

PENDER, HAROLD. Depreciation. (In his *Handbook for electrical engineers.* c1914. p. 340).
Transformers, 5-6%
stationary 10 years.
S. W. Greenland.
15-20 years.
J. Abbott.
10 years
R. Hammond.
5-6%
P. Dawson.

PIXLEY, FRANCIS W. Electric lighting companies. (In his *Accountancy.* Ed. 2. p. 218).

PROPOSED sale of Toronto utilities to the city. *Electrical world,* Oct. 25, 1913, p. 832.
Transformers 5%

PUBLIC utility reports, annotated. Rochester, Lawyers co-operative publishing co. 1918E. p. 678-9.
Desert power & water co. docket no. 361, Feb. 20, 1918.
Transformers 20 years 5%
Transformers 7½-10%

PUBLIC utility reports, annotated. Rochester, Lawyers co-operative publishing co. 1918A. p. 914-8.
New York & N. S. Traction Co.
Ties 7%
Rails, rail fastening and joints 2
Special work 6
Track laying and surfacing 2

SALIERS, EARL A. Analysis of a hydro-electric plant. (In his *Principles of depreciation.* 1916. p. 34-8).
Transformers 20 years
Generators and transformers 25

SLAVIN, MATTHEW. Municipal electricity in Pasadena. *Public service,* April 1910, p. 105-8.
Poles, arc lamps and transformers 10 years 8.5%

WEEKS, H. E. Abstract of paper on depreciation read before annual meeting of Iowa street and interurban railway association, April 1910. *Electric railway journal,* April 30, 1910, p. 782-3.
Transformers 7 years

YEAMAN, C. H. Depreciation and reserves for antiquation and obsolescence from an engineering standpoint. *Electrical engineering* (London), July 12, 1907, p. 46. *Electrical review* (London), July 12, 1907, p. 44. *Electrician,* July 5, 1907, p. 475.
Static transformers 15 years.
R. Hammond.
15 years.
L. G. R. (Local gov't boards)
20 years.
L. C. C.
20 years.
J. F. C. Snell (M. E. A. 1905)

Transmission lines

COST and depreciation of steam and hydro-electric installations. *Electrical world,* Dec. 30, 1909, p. 1558.

Transmission System. Table VI.

	Item	Prop. cost	Life years	Annual amt. for dep. in % of total cost
1.	Right of way	45.	..	..
2.	Tamers	18.4	15	.885
3.	Special structures	5.1	10	.415
4.	Insulators	2.1	10	.170
5.	Copper	23.7	25	.530
6.	Installation	5.7	..	..
		100.0		2.000

A 2 per cent depreciation is equivalent to a life of about 26 years for the transmission line.

FOSTER, HORATIO A. Rates of depreciation. (In his *Engineering valuation of public utilities and factories.* 1913. p. 200).
Transmission lines 2.0%
Marwick, Mitchell & co. in the appraisal of a large street railway system.

GILLETTE, HALBERT P. and R. T. DANA. Depreciation. (In their *Handbook of mechanical and electrical cost data.* 1918. p. 111).
Transmission line
material 33.3 years.
H. P. Gillette, Everett railway & water co., Jan. 29, 1912.
50 years.
Marwick, Mitchell & co., appraisal of a large street railway system, Foster, p. 199.

SALIERS, EARL A. Analysis of a hydro-electric plant. (In his *Principles of depreciation.* 1916. 1916. p. 34-8).
Transmission system
Transmission line
Towers 15 years
Special structures 10
Insulators 10
Copper 25

Trapping

See Depreciation, depletion and obsolescence—Hunting.

DEPRECIATION, DEPLETION AND OBSOLESCENCE—*(Continued)*

Traps

PHILADELPHIA. CONTROLLER. Rates of depreciation. (In his *Manual of accounting, reporting and business procedure of the city and county of Philadelphia.* 1917. p. 209).
Vermin traps 5%

Traps, Steam

BREWER, ALLEN F. Rates for annual depreciation. *Industrial management,* April 1918, p. 268
Steam traps 20 years 5%

Trays

BELT, ROBERT E. Depreciation. (In his *Foundry cost accounting, practice and procedure.* c1919. p. 235-48. *Uniform cost accounting methods; adopted by the American malleable castings association,* Nov. 14, 1917, p. 20-1).
Trays 10%

DENHAM, ROBERT S. Depreciation. (In his *Manual of cost engineering and estimating for paper box manufacturers.* 1917. p. 249).
Trays 6%

PHILADELPHIA. CONTROLLER. Rates of depreciation. (In his *Manual of accounting, reporting and business procedure of the city and county of Philadelphia.* 1917. p. 206).
Trays 20%

Trellises

See Depreciation, depletion and obsolescence—Arbors, etc.

Trestles

See Depreciation, depletion and obsolescence—Bridges.

Trucks

See Depreciation, depletion and obsolescence—Automobiles; Hand trucks; Vehicles.

Trunks, etc.

PHILADELPHIA. CONTROLLER. Rates of depreciation. (In his *Manual of accounting, reporting and business procedure of the city and county of Philadelphia.* 1917. p. 206).
Trunks 5½%
Valises 10

Tumbling barrels

BELT, ROBERT E. Depreciation. (In his *Foundry cost accounting practice and procedure.* 1919. p. 242).
Tumbling barrels, with motor, shafting belting 15%

BELT, ROBERT E. Depreciation. (In his *Uniform cost accounting methods; adopted by the American malleable castings association,* Nov. 14, 1917. p. 20-1).
Tumbling barrels, with motor, shafting and belting 15%

ELBOURNE, EDWARD T. Depreciation rates. (In his *Factory administration and accounts.* 1918. p. 377).

	Pro. dep. %	Years	
	Remainder values	10%	5%
Tumbling barrels	12½	17	22

NICHOLSON, J. LEE and J. F. D. ROHRBACH. Depreciation. (In their *Cost accounting.* 1919. p. 150).
Tumbling barrels 10%

Tunnels

AMERICAN WATER WORK ASSOCIATION. Final report of committee on depreciation. *Journal of the American water-works association,* Sept. 1917, p. 1-38.
Storage reservoirs, heavy earthen or masonry dams, large masonry conduits and tunnels 75-100 years

CHASE, HARVEY S. Depreciation in water works accounts, with reference to uniform reports. *Journal of the New England waterworks association,* June 1910, p. 305-31. Abstract. *Engineering and contracting,* June 29, 1910, p. 598. Editorial. Depreciation and sinking fund accounts. *Municipal engineering,* July 1910, p. 26.
Reservoirs, tunnels and aqueducts 100 years

GRAY, HENRY L. Necessity of depreciation reserves. *Railway age gazette,* May 27, 1910, p. 1297-8. Editorial. Depreciation reserves. *Railway age gazette,* May 27, 1910, p. 1290. Letters. Depreciation reserves. *Railway age gazette,* July 8, 1910, p. 66.
Timber tunnel lining 8%

GRUNSKY, CARL EWALD. Probable useful life of various articles. (In his *Valuation, depreciation and the rate-base.* 1917. p. 286).
Tunnels, power plants. 50 years. San Joaquin light & power corporation. Rate hearing before California railroad commission, 1915.

HAZLEHURST, J. N. Final report of the committee on depreciation. *Journal of the American water works association,* March 1919, p. 85-135.
Large masonry conduits and tunnels 75-150 years

NICHOLSON, J. LEE and J. F. D. ROHRBACH. Depreciation. (In their *Cost accounting.* 1919. p. 147).
Tunnels, underground piping, vaults and general conduits 5%
Based on (1) the cost of equipment
(2) the life of the equipment
(3) on a ten-hour day

	% on cost	% on reducing balance
Subway and tunnels		1⅓%

PHILADELPHIA. CONTROLLER. Rates of depreciation. (In his *Manual of accounting, reporting and business procedure of the city and county ot Philadelphia.* 1917. p. 210).

DEPRECIATION, DEPLETION AND OBSOLESCENCE—TUNNELS—*(Continued)*

PIEZ, CHARLES. Perpetual inventory and appraisal values; table of standard depreciation rates. *Engineering and contracting,* Jan. 24, 1917, p. 77. *Factory,* Dec. 1916, p. 668-71. *Iron age,* Nov. 30, 1916, Jan. 11, 1917, p. 1266, 138-9. *Iron trade review,* Feb. 22, 1917, p. 477-8. Condensed. *Iron trade review,* Dec. 7, 1916, p. 1144-6. *Journal of the American society of mechanical engineers,* Dec. 1916, p. 965-6. Kent, William. *Bookkeeping and cost accounting for factories.* 1918. p. 90. Discussion. *Journal of the American society of mechanical engineers,* March 1917, p. 215-7.

	% on cost	% on reducing balance
Tunnels	4.5	10

PROBABLE lives of water-works elements. *Engineering news,* Oct. 11, 1917, p. 688.
Large masonry conduits and tunnels 75-150 years

Turbines

BARKER, HARRY. Typical life expectation tables for public utility property. (In his *Public utility rates.* 1917. p. 368-9).

Turbines		
Hydraulic, old types	25-40 years.	
new types	30-50 years.	
steam, large units	20 years.	
Auxiliary units	10-20 years.	Wisconsin Railroad Commission. Author average or approximate figures secured by examination or enquiry.

BREWER, ALLEN F. Rates for annual depreciation. *Industrial management,* April 1918, p. 268.
Steam turbines 33.3 years 3%

BRYAN, WILLIAM. Appraisal and depreciation of water-works and similar properties. *Journal of the association of engineering societies,* Dec. 1907, p. 336-81. Depreciation allowance for various public-service industries. *Engineering news,* Jan. 23, 1908, p. 96.
Turbines, water 11-14 years

CRAVENS, GEORGE W. Depreciation and maintenance of electrical equipment. *Electrical review,* April 23, 1910, p. 853-6. Foster, H. A. *Engineering valuation of public utilities and factories.* 1913. p. 201-2. Montgomery, Robert H *Income tax procedure,* 1919. p. 570. ——— Same, 1920, p. 723-4. Montgomery, Robert H. *Auditing theory and practice,* 1916. p. 424.

Turbines, steam	% annual depreciation	Light or intermittent 3-4% service	Heavy or continuous 4-5% service
	5	Milwaukee electric railway & light co.	
	5	Average English	
	5	Average Scotch practice	
	7-9	Philip Dawson	
	5	Stone & Webster	
	2.5-5	Industrial power plants	
	4	Prof. G. F. Gebhardt	
	4	Miscellaneous sources	

DAWSON, PHILIP. Depreciation. (In his *Engineering and electric traction pocket-book.* Ed. 2. p. 1161).

	% capital cost
Turbines	7-9

EDWARDS, C. LEWIS. Electric lighting accounts. *Incorporated accountants journal,* April 1912, p. 175.
Turbines and dynamos 5-7½%

ELBOURNE, EDWARD T. Depreciation rates. (In his *Factory administration and accounts.* 1918. p. 376).

Turbines	Pro. dep. % Remainder values	Years 10%	5%
Steam	7½	29	38
Water	7½	29	38

FLOY, HENRY. Depreciation. Floy, Henry. Depreciation as related to electrical properties. *American institute of electrical engineers, Proceedings,* 1911. p. 1267. Floy, Henry. *Valuation of public utility properties.* 1912. p. 188-93. Foster, Horatio A. *Engineering valuation of public utilities and factories.* 1913. p. 194-8. *Engineering and contracting,* Oct. 4, 1911, p. 359-65. *Engineering magazine,* Aug. 1911, p. 837-40.

Turbines	Dep. per year straight line		
steam	5	Wisconsin P. S. C.	
water	3⅓	Wisconsin P. S. C.	
steam	6⅔	St. Louis P. S. C.	Union Elec. L. & P. Co.

FOSTER, HORATIO A. Rates of depreciation. (In his *Engineering valuation of public utilities and factories.* 1913. p. 200).
Turbines and generators 6%
Marwick, Mitchell & co. in the appraisal of a large street railway system.

GILLETTE, HALBERT P. and RICHARD T. DANA. Depreciation. (In their *Handbook of mechanical and electrical cost data.* 1918. p. 111, 117).

Turbines	
steam	20 years. Wisconsin R. R. commission.
	15 years. St. Louis Public Service commission. Union electric light & power co.
	20 years. Milwaukee electric railway & light co.
	20-40 years. George W. Cravens, Industrial power plants.
water	30 years. Wisconsin R. R. commission.

DEPRECIATION, DEPLETION AND OBSOLESCENCE—TURBINES—*(Continued)*

Useful Life of Turbo-Generators.

Company	Capacity of equipment in kws.	Time of service Started	Closed	Useful life years
6	1-4,000	1904	1912	8
	1-4,000	1904	1912	8
	1-4,000	1905	1911	6
	1-4,000	1905	1911	6
	1-4,000	1906	1912	6
7	2-5,000	1903	1909	6
	1-5,000	1904	1909	5
	1-7,500	1904	1909	5
8	1-1,500	1905	1914	9
9	2-2,000	1905	1910	5
	4-5,000	1906	1911	4

Average life, 16 turbines, 6 years.

Following is the key to names of companies given; also the reasons for retiring the various units.

Company No.	Name	Remarks
6	Detroit Edison co., Delroy station.	Entire plant abandoned.
7	Commonwealth Edison co. Fish street station.	Replaced by large unit of same type
8	Consumers power co. Jackson station.	Replaced by 7,500 kw. turbine.
9	Union electric light & power co. Ashley street station.	Replaced by larger units.

GRUNSKY, CARL EWALD. Probable useful life of various articles. (In his *Valuation, depreciation and the rate-base.* 1917. p. 286).

Turbines

steam	15 years. St. Louis Public service commission. Case of Union electric light & power co.
steam	20 years. Wisconsin railroad commission. Quoted by Henry Floy and in published reports.
steam	20 years. Robt. Hammond. Journal of the Institute of electrical engineers, England, April 25, 1907.
steam	30 years. 1c. lb. residual value. Pacific gas & electric company. Figures used in rate hearings before Master in Chancery, San Francisco, 1913-4.
water	30 years. Wisconsin railroad commission. Quoted by Henry Floy and in published reports.
water-type prior 1900	25-40 years. H. A. Foster. "Engineering valuation of public utilities and factories." Van Nostrand, 1912.
water-type after 1900	30-50 years. H. A. Foster. "Engineering valuation of public utilities and factories." Van Nostrand, 1912.
steam	20 years. Milwaukee electric railway and lighting co., in Milwaukee 3c. fare case, Aug., 1912.
steam	15 years. St. Louis public service commission. Case of Union electric light & power co.
steam	20 years. Wisconsin railroad commission. Quoted by Henry Floy and in published reports.
steam	20 years. Robt. Hammond. Journal of Institute of electrical engineers, England, April 25, 1907.
steam	30 years. 1c. lb. residual value. Pacific gas & electric company. Figures used in rate hearings before Master in Chancery, San Francisco, 1913-4.
steam	20 years. Stone & Webster. Figures for Chicago union traction co. case.

HAMMOND, ROBERT. Depreciation. *Institute of electrical engineers, Proceedings,* April 25, 1907, p. 27. *Journal of the Institute of electrical engineers,* 1907, p. 270. Abstracts. *Accountant,* May 18, 1907, p. 675. *Electric railway review,* June 1, 1907, p. 716. *Electrical review (Chicago).* May 25, 1907, p. 828. *Electrical review (London),* May 3, 1907, p. 744. *Electrician,* April 26, 1907, p. 51. *Engineering magazine,* July 1907, p. 636-8. *Engineering record,* June 15, 1907, p. 703. *Municipal journal (London),* May 10, 17, 1907, p. 411, 435. *Progressive age,* July 1, 1907, p. 305. *Street railway bulletin,* June 1907, p. 382. *Tramway and railway world,* June 6, 907, p. 497.

Turbines 20 years

INSTALLATIONS, systems and appliances. *Electrical world,* Dec. 7, 1912, p. 1220.

Turbines 20 years Hammond

JOHNSON, GEORGE. Depreciation. (In his *Electric lighting accounts.* 1903. p. 23-4).

Turbines 7½%

LEAKE, P. D. Record of depreciation. (In his *Depreciation and wasting assets and their treatment in computing annual profit and loss.* 1917. p. 86).

Turbines 7-9%

DEPRECIATION, DEPLETION AND OBSOLESCENCE—Turbines—*(Continued)*

Life of plant. *Electrician,* Nov. 8, 1912, p. 182-4.
Turbines 20 years R. Hammond

Neale, R. E. Depreciation in engineering works. *Mechanical world,* Feb. 7, 1913, p. 67-8.
Turbines
water 3.3% 30 years
steam 5-6.6 15-20

Nicholson, J. Lee and J. F. Rohrbach. Depreciation. (In their *Cost accounting.* 1919. p. 147).
Steam turbines 5%
Based on (1) the cost of equipment
(2) the life of the equipment
(3) on a ten-hour day

Pender, Harold. Depreciation. (In his *Handbook for electrical engineers.* c1914. p. 340).

Turbines	% dep.	20 years.
steam		R. Hammond
	7-9	P. Dawson
water	3.33	Wisconsin railroad commission

Pixley, Francis W. Electric lighting companies. (In his *Accountancy.* Ed. 2. p. 218).
Turbines 7½-10%

Runyon, F. O. Report on hydro-electric plant for special committee common council, Newark, New Jersey, April 23, 1902, p. 15, 16.
Turbine units 3%

Turning

Philadelphia. Controller. Rates of depreciation. (In his *Manual of accounting, reporting and business procedure of the city and county of Philadelphia.* 1917. p. 205).
Metal working equipment. Turning, planing, milling stamping and engraving equipment 5%

Turpentine

Turpentine leases. *American institute of accountants, Special bulletin,* No. 6, Nov. 1920, p. 2-3.

Twine

See Depreciation, depletion and obsolescence—Cordage.

Type

See Depreciation, depletion and obsolescence—Printing.

Typewriters

Australia. Federal income tax department. Depreciation allowance. *Accountant,* Oct. 13, 1917, p. 277-9. *Accounting and commerce,* June 30, 1917, p. 55-7. *Federal accountant,* July, 1917, p. 93-8. *Public accountant,* Jan. 30, 1917, p. 145-52.
Typewriters 10%
Written down value, repairs allowed in addition.

Montgomery, Robert H. Typewriters. (In his *Income tax procedure,* 1919. p. 580. ——— Same, 1920. p. 736-7).
Annual rate of 20% is conservative.

Nicholson, J. Lee and J. F. D. Rohrbach. Depreciation. (In their *Cost accounting.* 1919. p. 151).
Typewriters and adding machines 20%
Based on (1) the cost of equipment
(2) the life of the equipment
(3) on a ten-hour day.

Umbrellas

Australia. Federal income tax department. Depreciation allowance. *Accountant,* Oct. 13, 1917, p. 277-9. *Accounting and commerce,* June 30, 1917, p. 55-7. *Federal accountant,* July 1917, p. 93-8. *Public accountant,* Jan. 30, 1917, p. 145-52.
Umbrella manufacturers
Cutting board 10%
Sewing machines 10
Lathes Nil
Motor 5
Written down value, repairs allowed in addition.

Uniforms

Pixley, Francis W. Tramways. (In his *Accountancy.* Ed. 2. p. 218-9).
Uniform of conductors: It is better to make this expenditure a direct charge against Revenue: but if this is not done a depreciation varying from say 33 to 60 per cent should be charged according to the neighborhood and the appearance the men have to present.

Upsetting machines

Nicholson, J. Lee and J. F. D. Rohrbach. Depreciation. (In their *Cost accounting.* 1919. p. 149).
Upsetting machines 6⅔%

Valises

See Depreciation, depletion and obsolescence—Trunks, valises, etc.

Valves

American water works association. Final report of committee on depreciation. *Journal of the American waterworks association,* Sept. 1917, p. 1-38.
Valves 40-60 years

Barker, Harry. Typical life expectation tables for public utility property. (In his *Public utility rates.* 1917. p. 367).
Valves 40-50 years L. Metcalf

DEPRECIATION, DEPLETION AND OBSOLESCENCE—VALVES—*(Continued)*

BOLTON, REGINALD PELHAM. Depreciation of mechanical equipments and power plants. (In his *Building for profit.* 1911. p. 82, 89).

	Physical years	%	Economic years
Sanitary fixtures, refrigerating piping, kitchen fixtures and valves	20	50.0	16

BRYAN, WILLIAM. Appraisal and depreciation of water-works and similar properties. *Journal of the association of engineering societies,* Dec. 1907, p. 336-81. Depreciation allowance for various public-service industries. *Engineering news,* Jan. 23, 1908, p. 96.

Valves 25-35 years
" 40

CLADER, WILL-A. Water utilities accounting. *Journal of accountancy,* Aug. 1919, p. 91-2.
The following rate is used frequently when wear and tear are made good by operating maintenance.

Valves 2%

GILLETTE, HALBERT P. and R. T. DANA. Depreciation. (In their *Handbook of mechanical and electrical cost data.* 1918. p. 111).

Valves 16.6 years.
H. P. Gillette, Everett railway & water co. Jan. 29, 1912.

gate, water 40-50 years.
Leonard Metcalf, Transactions, American society civil engineers, 1909, p. 24. vol. 64.

HAZLEHURST, J. N. Final report of the committee on depreciation. *Journal of the American water works association,* March 1919, p. 85-135.

Valves 40-60 years

METCALF, LEONARD. Depreciation in waterworks operation and accounting. *Journal of the New England waterworks association,* Dec. 1910, p. 442. Abstracts. *Engineering news,* Nov. 3, 1910, p. 482. Methods of computing depreciation of and reasonable assumptions as to period of useful life of waterworks. *Engineering and contracting,* Nov. 16, 1910, p. 434.

Valves 40-50 years 2½-2% straight line

PHILADELPHIA. CONTROLLER. Rates of depreciation. (In his *Manual of accounting, reporting and business procedure of the city and county of Philadelphia.* 1917. p. 205).

Pipes, valves, dampers, etc. 4%

PROBABLE lives of water-works elements. *Engineering news,* Oct. 11, 1917, p. 688.

Valves 40-60 years

Varnish

STOREY, EUGENE WILFRED. Depreciation. (In his *Monthly cost accounting for varnish plants.* 1917. p. 20-2).

Vaults

NICHOLSON, J. LEE and J. F. D. ROHRBACH. Depreciation. (In their *Cost accounting.* 1919. p. 147).

Tunnels, underground piping, vaults and general conduits 5%
Based on (1) the cost of equipment
(2) the life of the equipment.
(3) on a ten-hour day.

PHILADELPHIA. CONTROLLER. Rates of depreciation. (In his *Manual of accounting, reporting and business procedure of the city and county of Philadelphia.* 1917. p. 207).

Vaults and safes 2%

PIEZ, CHARLES. Perpetual inventory and appraisal values; table of standard depreciation rates. *Engineering and contracting,* Jan. 24, 1917, p. 77. *Factory,* Dec. 1916, p. 668-71. *Iron age,* Nov. 30, 1916, Jan. 11, 1917, p. 1266, 138-9. *Iron trade review,* Feb. 22, 1917, p. 477-8. Condensed. *Iron trade review,* Dec. 7, 1916, p. 1144-6. *Journal of the American society of mechanical engineers,* Dec. 1916, p. 965-6. Kent, William. *Bookkeeping and cost accounting for factories.* 1918. p. 90. Discussion. *Journal of the American society of mechanical engineers,* March 1917, p. 215-7.

	% on cost	% on reducing balance
Vaults	4.5	10

UNIFORM cost sheet for coal mining companies. *Coal age,* Sept. 19, 1918, p. 545-7.

	Original cost
Fireproof vaults	4%

Vehicles

See also Depreciation, depletion and obsolescence—Automobiles.

AMERICAN INSTITUTE OF ACCOUNTANTS. Report of the committee on standard schedules for uniform reports upon municipal industries and public service corporations; annual meeting at Atlantic city, N. J. October 20-22, 1908. 15p. *Journal of accountancy,* May 1909, p. 47-54.
The knowledge at the command of the Bureau of the census leads to the conclusion that this average life is approximately as follows:

Horses, carriages, automobiles and laboratory fixtures and meters 10 years

AUSTRALIA. FEDERAL INCOME TAX DEPARTMENT. Depreciation allowance. *Accountant,* Oct. 13, 1917, p. 277-9. *Accounting and commerce,* June 30, 1917, p. 55-7. *Federal accountant,* July 1917, p. 93-8. *Public accountant,* Jan. 30, 1917, p. 145-52.

Conveyances (horses, carts, etc.) 10%
Buggies, sulkies, drays and wagons (farms and stations) 7½
Carts used by brewers, flour millers, and other tradesmen 10
Based on written down value and repairs made in addition.

BREWERIES. *American institute of accountants, Special bulletin,* No. 5, Sept. 1920, p. 7-8.

CARTER, R. N. Rates of depreciation. (In his *Advanced accounts.* p. 618).

Carts, vans, motor lorries, etc. 10-15%
Wagons (life about 15 years) 7½
Based on diminishing balances, normal conditions and hours of working.

CASTENHOLZ, WILLIAM B. Audit of balance sheet accounts. (In his *Auditing procedure.* 1918. p. 58).

Wagons 10-15%

DEPRECIATION, DEPLETION AND OBSOLESCENCE—Vehicles—*(Continued)*

Chase, Harvey S. Depreciation in water works accounts, with reference to uniform reports. *Journal of the New England water works association*, June 1910, p. 305-31. Abstract. *Engineering and contracting*, June 29, 1910, p. 598. Editorial. Depreciation and sinking fund accounts. *Municipal engineering*, July 1910, p. 26.
Horses, carriages, automobiles and laboratory fixtures and meters 10 years

Denham, Robert S. Depreciation. (In his *Manual of cost engineering and estimating for paper box manufacturers*. 1917. p. 249).
Wagons 20%

Depreciation, ice industry. *American institute of accountants, Special bulletin*, No. 5, Sept. 1920, p. 5.

Foster, Horatio A. Rates of depreciation. (In his *Engineering valuation of public utilities and factories*. 1913. p. 199).
Wagons and horses 10.0%
Marwick, Mitchell & Co. in the appraisal of a large street railway system.

Gillette, Halbert P. and R. T. Dana. Depreciation. (In their *Handbook of mechanical and electrical cost data*. 1918. p. 110).
Teams and vehicles 5-8 years.
H. P. Gillette, Everett railway & water co., Jan. 29, 1912.
10 years.
Prof. M. E. Cooley, Milwaukee 3c case.
system, Foster, p. 199.
Marwick, Mitchell & co., appraisal of a large street railway
20 years.
M. G. Starret, Milwaukee 3c case.

Jenkinson, M. Webster. Depreciation. *Accountant*, May 17, 1902, p. 528-34.
Carts, vehicles, harness, etc.
First five years 10%
Afterwards 5

Lanham, Herbert. Depreciation. (In his *Brewers' and bottlers' accounts*. p. 126-32).
Vehicles and harness 7½%

Life of road construction equipment. *Engineering and contracting*, Jan. 3, 1917, p. 3.
Wagons and harness 20%
Concrete carts 50

McIntosh, Robert J. Rates of depreciation. (In his *Reference book of accounts*. Ed. 2. p. 60).
Wagons 8-10%
Based on life.

Mann, John and H. C. Judd. Depreciation. (In their *Colliery accounts*. 1909. p. 69-75, 92).
Wagons 7½-10%
Calculated on the balance as diminished from year to year.

Montgomery, Robert H. Electrical equipment manufacturers. (In his *Income tax procedure*, 1919. p. 563).
Automobiles and other conveyances 25%
Based on gross book values, at the end of the preceding year.

Montgomery, Robert H. Wagons, automobiles, etc. (In his *Auditing theory and practice*. 1916. p. 426. *Income tax procedure*, 1919. p. 580. ——— Same, 1920, p. 737).
Note: 8-10% provided that all repairs, renewals of parts and maintenance are charged to operating expenses.

Nicholson, J. Lee and J. F. D. Rohrbach. Depreciation. (In their *Cost accounting*. 1919. p. 151).
Horses and wagons 12%
Based on (1) the cost of equipment
(2) the life of the equipment
(3) on a ten-hour day.

Philadelphia. Controller. Rates of depreciation. (In his *Manual of accounting, reporting and business procedure of the city and county of Philadelphia*. 1917. p. 206).
Animal hauled vehicles, sleighs and sleds 5%
Vehicles pushed, pulled or propelled by the occupant 20

Piez, Charles. Perpetual inventory and appraisal values; table of standard depreciation rates. *Engineering and contracting*, Jan. 24, 1917, p. 77. *Factory*, Dec. 1916, p. 668-71. *Iron age*, Nov. 30, 1916, Jan. 11, 1917, p. 1266, 138-9. *Iron trade review*, Feb. 22, 1917, p. 477-8. Condensed. *Iron trade review*, Dec. 7, 1916, p. 1144-6. *Journal of the American society of mechanical engineers*, Dec. 1916, p. 965-6. Kent, William. *Bookkeeping and cost accounting for factories*. 1918. p. 90. Discussion. *Journal of the American society of mechanical engineers*, March, 1917, p. 215-7.

	% on cost.	% on reducing balance.
Horses and wagons	12	35

Porters, R. J. Rates of depreciation generally adopted. (In his *Pitman's dictionary of bookkeeping*. p. 344).
Carts and vans 10-15%
Wagons (life about 15 years) 7½
Based on diminishing balances.

Roby, J. J. Schedule of plant depreciation. (In his *Treatise on cost accounting as applied to coal mining*. c1913. p. 14-5).
Wagons and tools
Deduct as salvage before depreciating. 10%
Depreciation rate for remainder, fireproof 20

Uniform cost sheet of coal mining companies. *Coal age*, Sept. 19, 1918, p. 545-7.
Mine wagons (cars) % original cost.
wood 20
steel 17

Whatley, G. E. Stuart. Depreciation. (In his *Accountant's and bookkeeper's vade-mecum*. 1893. p. 26).
% dim. value.
Wagons 7½

DEPRECIATION, DEPLETION AND OBSOLESCENCE—VEHICLES—*(Continued)*

WIHLFAHRT, JULIUS E. Depreciation. (In his *Treatise on increasing bakery efficiency.* 1917. p. 6).

Horses, wagons and harness	15%

WOLFF, MARK. Interpretation of water works accounts. *Journal of the American waterworks association,* June 1916, p. 543, 546.

Horses, carriages and motors	10 years

Ventilating

ELBOURNE, EDWARD T. Depreciation rates. (In his *Factory administration and accounts.* 1918. p. 376).

	Prov. dep. %	Remainder values 10%	Years 5%
Ventilating and exhausting installation	7½	29	38

MONTGOMERY, ROBERT H. Electrical equipment manufacturers. (In his *Income tax procedure,* 1919. p. 563. ——— Same, 1920. p. 716).

Heating and ventilating	10%

Based on gross book values at the end of the preceding year.

NICHOLSON, J. LEE and J. F. D. ROHRBACH. Depreciation. (In their *Cost accounting.* 1919. p. 147).

Heating and ventilation	5%

Based on (1) the cost of equipment
(2) the life of the equipment
(3) on a ten-hour day.

PHILADELPHIA. CONTROLLER. Rates of depreciation. (In his *Manual of accounting, reporting and business procedure of the city and county of Philadelphia.* 1917. p. 205).

Ventilating equipment	10%

PIEZ, CHARLES. Perpetual inventory and appraisal values; table of standard depreciation rates. *Engineering and contracting,* Jan. 24, 1917, p. 77. *Factory,* Dec. 1916, p. 668-71. *Iron age,* Nov. 30, 1916, Jan. 11, 1917, p. 1227, 138-9. *Iron trade review* Feb. 22, 1917, p. 477-8. Condensed. *Iron trade review,* Dec. 7, 1916, p. 1144-6. *Journal of the American society of mechanical engineers,* Dec. 1916, p. 965-6. Kent, William. *Bookkeeping and cost accounting for factories,* 1918. p. 90. Discussion. *Journal of the American society of mechanical engineers,* March 1917, p. 215-7.

	Years	% on cost	% on reducing balance
Heating and ventilating system	20	4	7.5

ROBY, J. J. Schedule of plant depreciation. (In his *Treatise on cost accounting as applied to coal mining.* c1913. p. 14-15.

Ventilating equipment	
Fan housing brick and steel	
Deduct as salvage before depreciating	10%
Depreciation rate for remainder, non-fireproof	8
Depreciation rate for remainder, fireproof	5
Fans and drive	
Deduct salvage before depreciating	10
Depreciation rate for remainder, fireproof	8

Vents

BOLTON, REGINALD PELHAM. Depreciation of mechanical equipment and power plants. (In his *Building for profit.* 1911. p. 82, 89).

	years	Physical %	Years
Buried vents and ducts when painted	32	80.0	26
Exposed and unpainted vents and ducts	24	60.0	19

Vibrating machines

NICHOLSON, J. LEE and JOHN F. D. ROHRBACH. Depreciation. (In their *Cost accounting.* 1919. p. 150).

Vibrating machines	10%

Wagons

See Depreciation, depletion and obsolescence—Vehicles.

Wall coverings

PHILADELPHIA. CONTROLLER. Rates of depreciation. (In his *Manual of accounting, reporting and business procedure of the city and county of Philadelphia.* 1917. p. 207-8).

Wall coverings	8⅓%

Walls

NICHOLSON, J. LEE and J. F. D. ROHRBACH. Depreciation. (In their *Cost accounting.* 1919. p. 147).

Retaining walls	2-5%

Based on (1) the cost of equipment
(2) the life of the equipment
(3) on a ten-hour day.

PHILADELPHIA. CONTROLLER. Rates of depreciation. (In his *Manual of accounting, reporting and business procedure of the city and county of Philadelphia.* 1917. p. 210).

Dams	2%
Levees, riprap works, embankments along streams and water fronts	2
Intake cribs and structures	2
Retaining walls	2
Bulkheads	2

PIEZ, CHARLES. Perpetual inventory and appraisal values; table of standard depreciation rates. *Engineering and contracting,* Jan. 24, 1917, p. 77. *Factory,* Dec. 1916, p. 668-71. *Iron age,* Nov. 30, 1916, Jan. 11, 1917, p. 1266, 138-9. *Iron trade review,* Feb. 22, 1917, p. 477-8. Con-

DEPRECIATION, DEPLETION AND OBSOLESCENCE—WALLS—*(Continued)*

densed. *Iron trade review,* Dec. 7, 1916, p. 1144-6. *Journal of the American society of mechanical engineers* Dec. 1916, p. 965-6. Kent, William. *Bookkeeping and cost accounting for factories.* 1918. p. 90. Discussion. *Journal of the American society of mechanical engineers,* March 1917, p. 215-7.

Miscellaneous real estate improvements:

	% on costs	% on reducing balance
Pavements, sidewalks, fences, retaining walls, roadways, tracks, yard drainage, general conduit, tunnels, vaults, etc.	4.5	10

VARIOUS depreciation charges. *New York Times,* June 14, 1914.

General construction, fences, retaining walls, and so on 7%

Warehouses

BREWERIES. *American institute of accountants, Special bulletin,* No. 2, 5, March Sept. 1920, p. 6-7, 7-8.

ELBOURNE, EDWARD T. Depreciation rates. (In his *Factory administration and accounts.* 1918. p. 377).

	Prov. dep. %	Remainder values Years 10%	5%
Storage fittings			
Steel	6	37	48
Wood	7½	29	38

FICKER, NICHOLAS T. Depreciation. (In his *Shop expense analysis and control.* 1917 p. 84).

Warehouses

Buildings

modern fireproof steel and tile	3%
mill construction	4
steel construction only partly fireproof	3
wooden buildings of poor construction	8
Permanent fixtures	
pertaining to buildings	8
pertaining to power and lighting plants	8
Pertaining to material	8

PHILADELPHIA. CONTROLLER. Rates of depreciation. (In his *Manual of accounting, reporting and business procedure of the city and county of Philadelphia.* 1917. p. 210, 207-8).

Storehouses	2%
Store equipment	12½

ROBY, J. J. Schedule of plant depreciation. (In his *Treatise on cost accounting as applied to coal mining.* c1913. p. 14-5).

Storehouse

Building, brick and steel only	
Deduct as salvage before depreciating	10%
Depreciation rate for remainder, non-fireproof	6
Depreciation rate for remainder, fireproof	4
Fixtures	
Deduct as salvage before depreciating	10
Depreciation rate for remainder, fireproof	6

TIFFANY, H. S. Hemp warehouses. (In his *Digest of depreciations.* c1890. p. 9).

Buildings	
brick	3%
frame	4

Based upon the actual life without any repairs.

TIFFANY, H. S. Whiskey warehouses. (In his *Digest of depreciations.* c1890. p. 11).

Buildings	
brick	2-2½%
frame	3-3½

Based upon the actual life without any repairs.

UNIFORM cost sheet for coal mining companies. *Coal age,* Sept. 19, 1918, p. 545-7.

Supply house	% original cost
wood	8
stone or brick	5
Fixtures	10

Wash house

UNIFORM cost sheet for coal mining companies. *Coal age,* Sept. 19, 1918, p. 545-7.

Wash house	original cost
wood	10%
stone or brick	5

Washers

BELT, ROBERT E. Depreciation. (In his *Foundry cost accounting practice and procedure.* 1919. p. 242).

Sprue mill and slag washer 15%

BELT, ROBERT E. Depreciation. (In his *Uniform cost accounting methods; adopted by the American malleable castings association,* Nov. 14, 1917, p. 20-1).

Sprue mill and slag washer 15%

FOSTER, HORATIO A. Rates of depreciation. (In his *Engineering valuation of public utilities and factories.* 1913. p. 206).

Cast-iron washers 40 years

GILLETTE, HALBERT P. and RICHARD T. DANA. Depreciation. (In their *Handbook of mechanical and electrical cost data,* 1918. p. 111).

Washers, cast iron (gas plant) 40 years. Wisconsin railroad commission.

GRUNSKY, CARL EWALD. Probable useful life of various articles. (In his *Valuation, depreciation and the rate-base.* 1917. p. 286).

Washers cast iron (gas plant) 40 years. Wisconsin railroad commission. Quoted by H. A. Foster and in published reports.

DEPRECIATION, DEPLETION AND OBSOLESCENCE—WASHERS—*(Continued)*

MANN, JOHN and H. C. JUDD. Depreciation. (In their *Colliery accounts.* 1909. p. 69-75, 92).
Washers 5-7½%
Calculated on the balance as diminished from year to year.

Watchman's system

NICHOLSON, J. LEE and J. F. D. ROHRBACH. Depreciation. (In their *Cost accounting.* 1919. p. 151).
Watchman's system 7½%
Based on (1) the cost of equipment
(2) the life of the equipment
(3) on a ten-hour day.

Water cinder mills

NICHOLSON, J. LEE and J. F. D. ROHRBACH. Depreciation. (In their *Cost accounting.* 1919. p. 150).
Water cinder mills 10%

Water cooling

ELBOURNE, EDWARD T. Depreciation rates. (In his *Factory administration and accounts.* 1918. p. 376).

	Prov. dep. %	Years	
	Remainder values	10%	5%
Water cooling plant	7½	29	38

Water gas machines

BARKER, HARRY. Typical life expectation tables for public utility property. (In his *Public utility rates.* 1917. p. 368).
Water-gas machines, 30 years. Wisconsin railroad commission.
GILLETTE, HALBERT P. and RICHARD T. DANA. Depreciation. (In their *Handbook of mechanical and electrical cost data.* 1918. p. 107).
Gas water machines complete, 30 years. Wisconsin railroad commission.
GRUNSKY, CARL EWALD. Probable useful life of various articles. (In his *Valuation, depreciation and the rate-base.* 1917. p. 286).
Water gas machines, 30 years. Wisconsin railroad commission. Quoted by H. A. Foster and in published reports.
PROSSER, R. W. Depreciation in gas plants. *American gas light journal,* May 26, 1902, p. 767.
Water gas apparatus, including generators, super heaters, washbox etc. 25 years. 25% of first cost.

Water softening

ANALYSIS of the premises adopted and methods used in determining the cost to reproduce new together with the depreciation thereon of the physical property of the Metropolitan system and the Kansas City and Westport Belt railway of Kansas City, Mo. *Engineering and contracting,* May 28, 1913, p. 617-20.
Water softening apparatus all steel 5%

Water wheels

COST and depreciation of steam and hydro-electric installations. *Electrical world,* Dec. 30, 1909, p. 1558.
Water wheels, 25 years, 0.157% of total cost.
ELBOURNE, EDWARD T. Depreciation rates. (In his *Factory administration and accounts.* 1918. p. 376).

	Prov. dep. %	Years	
	Remainder values	10%	5%
Water wheels	6	37	48

FOSTER, HORATIO A. Rates of depreciation. (In his *Engineering valuation of public utilities and factories.* 1913. p. 205).
Turbine water wheels, built
before 1900 25-40 years
after 1900 30-50
GILLETTE, HALBERT P. and R. T. DANA. Hydro-electric plants. (In their *Mechanical and electrical cost data.* 1918. p. 695).
Water wheels 2%
SALIERS, EARL A. Analysis of a hydro-electric plant. (In his *Principles of depreciation.* 1916. p. 34-8).
Water-wheels 25 years

Waterways

NICHOLSON, J. LEE and J. F. D. ROHRBACH. Depreciation. (In their *Cost accounting.* 1919. p. 146).
Dams and waterways 1½%
Based on (1) the cost of equipment
(2) the life of equipment
(3) on a ten-hour day.

Waterworks

ALLOWANCES for depreciation in the pipe system of the Los Angeles waterworks. *Engineering news,* May 4, 1899, p. 283.
Deducted depreciation to the average amount of 29.31%

ALVORD, JOHN W. Depreciation. *Engineering record,* June 15, 1912, p. 670.

ALVORD, JOHN W. Depreciation of waterworks. *American water works association, Proceedings,* 1903., p. 473, 523. *Fire and water engineering,* Aug. 22, Sept. 12 1903, p. 104, 144.
AMERICAN ELECTRIC RAILWAY ASSOCIATION. COMMITTEE ON VALUATION. Bibliography on valuation of public utilities to December 23, 1916. 61+72p.

DEPRECIATION, DEPLETION AND OBSOLESCENCE—WATERWORKS—*(Continued)*

AMERICAN INSTITUTE OF ACCOUNTANTS. Report of the committee on standard schedules for uniform reports upon municipal industries, and public service corporations; annual meeting at Atlantic City, N. J., October 20-22, 1908. 15p. *Journal of accountancy,* May 1909, p. 47-54.

The knowledge at the command of the Bureau of the census leads to the conclusion that this average life is approximately as follows:

	Years
Horses, carriages, automobiles and laboratory fixtures and meters	10
Office furniture and general equipment	15
Boilers, steam pipes and filtration equipment	20
Engines, pumping machinery and wood pipes	5
Masonry of filtration plant, cribs, iron water pipes, intake pipes, fire hydrants, stand pipes, buildings	50
Reservoirs, tunnels and aqueducts	100
Water system as a whole	50

AMERICAN WATER WORKS ASSOCIATION. Final report of committee on depreciation. *Journal of the American water works association,* Sept. 1917, p. 1-38.

	Years
Storage reservoirs and heavy earthen or masonry dams, large masonry conduits and tunnels	75-150
Conduits and distribution pipe of cast iron of large diameter	75-125
Conduits and distribution pipe of wrought iron or steel of large diameter	35-75
Conduits and distribution pipe of wood stave of large diameter	30-60
Distribution pipe of small diameter	
cast iron	30-70, 50-90
wrought iron and steel	25-40
Services	
wrought iron and steel	15-30
lead	40-80
Small distribution reservoirs	50-75
Standpipes	
wrought iron and steel	30-60
reinforced concrete	50-60
Valves	40-60
Hydrants	30-50
Meters	20-30
Pumping machinery	
High duty large units	30-60
High duty small units (say, below 6,000,000 gallons per day capacity)	25-50
Ordinary direct-acting	20-40
Centrifugal, not geared	20-30
Centrifugal, geared	15-25
Boiler feed and auxiliary pumps usually take the life of the units to which they are attached.	
Steam engines	20-40
Boilers	15-30
Electric generators and motors	20-30
Filter plants	
Masonry filters	30-50
Wood filters	15-30
Buildings	
masonry	30-60
wood	20-40
Stacks	
masonry	25-50
steel	10-25

BARKER, HARRY. Typical life expectation tables for public utility property. (In his *Public utility rates.* 1917. p. 367).

Waterworks	Years	Authority	Control*
Buildings, masonry	40-50	L. Metcalf	Obs.
wood-frame	20-50	"	Det.
Boilers, fire-tube	12-16	"	Det.
water-tube	20-30	Wis. R.R. Comm.	Det.
Filter beds	30-50	" " "	Obs.
Hydrants	40-50	L. Metcalf	Det.
Mains, large cast-iron (6 in. and over)	20-40	"	Obs
small cast-iron (4 in. and under)	50-75	"	Obs.
steel	15-50	"	Det.
wood	30-50	Wis. R.R. Comm.	Det.
Meters	20-30	L. Metcalf	Det.
Pumps and engines	20-30	"	Det.
duplex	20-25	Wis. R.R. Comm.	Det.
triplex	20-30	" " "	Det.
crank and flywheel	30-40	" " "	Obs. and Det.
centrifugal	20-30	" " "	Det.
Reservoirs	50-100	L. Metcalf Wis. R.R. Comm.	Obs.
Standpipes	30-50	L. Metcalf	Det.
Service pipes, lead	50-100	Wis. R.R. Comm.	Det. and Obs.
galvanized iron or steel	30-50	" " "	Det.
Suctions and intakes	30-50	" " "	Det. and Obs.

DEPRECIATION, DEPLETION AND OBSOLESCENCE—WATERWORKS—*(Continued)*

Valves	40-50	L. Metcalf	Det.
Wells, driven or drilled	50-75	Wis. R.R. Comm.	Det.
open and lined	75-100	" " "	Obs.

* Probable action limiting service life; deterioration due to wear and tear and weathering and obsoletion. Where both are cited, both actions have been observed, the first named predominating in a majority of cases.

BRYAN, WILLIAM. Appraisal and depreciation of water-works and similar properties. *Journal of the association of engineering societies,* Dec. 1907, p. 336-81. Depreciation allowance for various public-service industries. *Engineering news,* Jan. 23, 1908, p. 96.

	Years	% straight	Sinking fund	
Water works		1.465		Los Angeles, Cal. 29.3% in 20 yr.
"		1.667		Kansas City, Mo. 33.3% in 20 yr.
"		1.1		Tuttle, 22% in 20 yr.
"		.62		Quincy, Ill. 18.7% in 30 yr.
"		2.47		Valparaiso' Ind. 37.1% in 15 yr.
"		.86	1.58	Mobile, Ala., 12% in 14 yr.
"	37.35	1.95	1.49	Washington, Mo. 37.3% in 19 yr.
"	40			C. Palmer
"			1	Court Contra, Costa, Cal.
"	37		1.50	F. C. Coffin
"	31		2	Haverhill, Mass.
"		1.99		Rich Hill, Mo.
"		2.21		Galena, Kan.
"		2.91		Mt. Carmel, Ill.

CHASE, HARVEY S. Depreciation in water works accounts, with reference to uniform reports. *Journal of the New England water works association,* June 1910, p. 305-31. Abstract. *Engineering and contracting,* June 29, 1910, p. 598. Editorial. Depreciation and sinking fund accounts. *Municipal engineer,* July 1910, p. 26.

	Years
Horses, carriages, automobiles and laboratory fixtures and meters	10
Office furniture and general equipment	15
Boilers, steam pipes and filtration equipment	20
Engines, pumping machinery, and wood pipes	25
Masonry of filtration plant, cribs, iron water pipes, intake pipes, fire hydrants, standpipes, and buildings	50
Reservoirs, tunnels, and aqueducts	100
Water system as a whole	50

CLADER, WILL-A. Water utilities accounting. *Journal of accountancy,* Aug. 1919, p. 81-94. The following rates are used frequently when wear and tear are made good by operating maintenance.

Large reservoirs	1%
Small reservoirs	2
Cast iron pipe	1
Wrought iron pipe	2
Wood pipe	2
Standpipes, concrete	2
Standpipes, wood	3
Valves	2
Hydrants	2
Meters	4
Pumping equipment	4
Steam engines	4
Boilers	5
Electric generators and motors	4
Filter plants	3
Buildings	2
Laboratory equipment	10

DEPRECIATION. *Accountant,* June 8, 1918, p. 416.
S. W. Suburban water co. claimed depreciation as follows:

Written down value of meters	10%
Machinery in iron reservoirs	5
Mains	2

DEPRECIATION and income tax, the case of municipal undertakings. *Journal of gas lighting,* Jan. 7, 1913, p. 48.

DEPRECIATION of plant and fair rates for public service. *Engineering record,* Feb. 20, 1909, p. 197.

DISCUSSION of depreciation and a comparison of rates and bookkeeping methods of municipally and privately owned waterworks. *American waterworks association, Proceedings,* 1912, p. 325-47. Abstract. Depreciation by John W. Alvord. *Engineering record,* June 15, 1912, p. 670.

DEPRECIATION, DEPLETION AND OBSOLESCENCE—Waterworks—*(Continued)*

Estimated life and depreciation of waterworks plants. *Municipal journal and engineer,* May 6, 1908, p. 558.

Material	Life in years	Depreciation per cent straight	per year sinking fund	Authority
Entire works		1.465		Los Angeles, Cal. 2.93% in 20 years. Engineering news, May 4, 1899.
” ”		1.667		Kansas City, Mo. 33.3% in 20 years. Wynkoop Kiersted. Proceedings, American society of civil engineers, 1897.
” ”		1.1		22% in 20 years, Tuttle; same as previous.
” ”		0.62		Quincy, Ill, 18.7% in 30 years. Engineering record, July 23, 1904.
” ”		2.47		Valparaiso, Ind. 37.1% in 15 years. Munic. engineering May 1903.
” ”		0.86	1.58	Mobile, Ala.: 12% in 14 yrs. Engineering news, April 23, 1903.
” ”	37.35	1.95	1.49	Washington, Mo.: 37.3% in 19 yrs. Wm. H. Bryan.
” ”	40			C. Palmer, Proceedings. American society of civil engineers, 1897.
” ”			1.00	Court Contra Costa, Cal. Engineering Record, June 1, 1901.
” ”	37		1.50	F. C. Coffin, Proceedings, American society of civil engineers. 1897.
” ”	31		2	Haverhill, Mass.: Proceedings, American society of civil engineers, 1897.
” ”		1.99		Rich Hill, Mo. Wm. H. Bryan.
” ”		2.21		Galena, Kan. Wm. H. Bryan.
” ”		2.91		Mt. Carmel, Ill. Wm. H. Bryan. Average of 32 boilers.
Boilers	6-23			Average life 15 years, J. W. Alvord, American water works association, 1903.
”		5-7		N. S. Hill; Engineering record, June 8, 1907.
”	15			Prosser, Engineering news. vol. XLVII, p. 425.
”	20-30			W. Kiersted; Proceedings American society of civil engineers. 1897.
”	20			R. Hammond; Engineering record, June 15, 1907.
”	10-12.5			Dawson, in Iowa engineer, July 1906.
”	14-15			Iowa electrical association in Iowa engineer, July 1906.
”	25			B. Williams, Galena, Kans. Appraisal in 1905.
”	30	8		Chicago, City Railway: street railway journal, December 1898.
”	14.3-25			Wm. H. Bryan.
”		2.5-4		W. H. Rosecrans—Galena, Kans. Appraisal in 1905.
”		6		B. L. Dodge; Mt. Vernon, Ill. Appraisal in 1906.
”	25			Chas. B. Burdick: Mt. Vernon, Illinois. Appraisal in 1906.
Brick buildings		2		Iowa Electrical Association: in Iowa Engineer, July 1906.
” ”		2		N. S. Hill, Engineering record, June 8, 1901.
” ”	40			Prosser, Engineering News, vol. XLVII, p. 425.
” ”	25-40			Wm. H. Bryan.
” ”		7		W. H. Rosecrans; Galena, Kans., appraisal in 1905.
” ”	60			R. Hammond; Engineering record, June 15, 1917.
” ”	50-100			Dawson; Iowa engineer. July 1906.
” ”	25-33-50			Iowa electrical association, Iowa Engineer, July 1906.
” ”	30			B. Williams; Galena, Kans., appraisal in 1905.
” ”	30			W. Kiersted, Galena Kans., appraisal, 1905.
” ”		5		Chicago city railway, street railway journal, December 1898.
” ”	35			C. B. Burdick; Mt. Vernon, Ill., appraisal in 1906.
” ”		3.5		B. L. Dodge, Mt. Vernon, Ill., appraisal in 1906.

DEPRECIATION, DEPLETION AND OBSOLESCENCE—WATERWORKS—*(Continued)*

Wooden Buildings		5	N. S. Hill, Engineering record, June 8, 1901.
" "		4	W. H. Rosecrans, Galena, Kans., appraisal in 1905.
" "	15-30		W. H. Bryan.
Pumping engines	20-25-30	5	W. H. Bryan.
" "		3-10	N. S. Hill; ;Engineering record, June 8, 1901. •
" "	15		Prosser; Engineering news, vol. XLVII, p. 425.
" "	20-30		Wynkoop Kiersted; Proceedings American society of civil engineers, 1897.
" "		4.7	W. H. Rosecrans; Galena, Kans., appraisal in 1905.
" "	25		R. Hammond; Engineering record, June 15, 1907.
" "	10		Boiler feeds, Iowa Electrical Association. Iowa engineer, July 1906.
" "	3-36		Average of 50 engines, average life 21.3 years. J. W. Alvord. American waterworks association 1903.
" "	25-30		B. Williams; Galena, Kans., appraisal in 1905.
" "	30		W. Kiersted; Galena, Kans., appraisal in 1905.
" "		2.5	B. L. Dodge, Mt. Vernon, Ill. Appraisal in 1906.
" "	30		C. B. Burdick, Mt. Vernon, Ill., appraisal in 1906.
Water filters	15-20		Wm. H. Bryan.
Fire Hydrants	25-35		Wm. H. Bryan.
" "		2	Los Angeles, Cal. Engineering news, May 4, 1899.
" "	40		B. Williams, Galena, Kans., appraisal in 1905.
" "		3	Los Angeles, Cal. Engineering news, May 4, 1899.
" "		2.1	Mobile, Ala.; Engineering news, April 23, 1903.
" "	20		B. Williams; Galena, Kans., appraisal in 1905.
" "	20		W. H. Bryan.
Water meters		3	Los Angeles, Cal. Engineering news, May 4, 1899.
" "		2.1	Mobile, Ala.; Engineering news, April 23, 1903.
" "	20		B. Wililams; Gal. Kans., app. in 1905.
" "	20		W. H. Bryan.
Cast-iron pipe	50-75		W. H. Bryan.
" "	68		Los Angeles, California, Engineering record, August 28, 1897.
" "		1.25	Los Angeles, Cal. Good soil; Engineering news, May 4, 1899.
" "		2	Los Angeles, Cal. Poor soil; Engineering news, May 4, 1899.
" "	20-60		Rudolph Hering; Proceedings, American society civil engineers, 1897.
" "	25-60		W. Kiersted. Proceedings American society of civil engineers, 1897.
" "	70		Gas mains. Prosser, Engineering news, vol. XLVII, p. 425.
" "	Over 50		Pearsons; Proceedings, American society civil engineers, 1897.
" "		1.14	W. H. Rosecrans; Galena, Kans., appraisal in 1905.
" "		1	B. L. Dodge, Mt. Vernon, Ill., appraisal in 1906.
" "	100		J. W. Alvord; Proceedings, American waterworks association, 1903.
" "	100		C. B. Burdick; Mt. Vernon, Ill., appraisal in 1906.
" "	80		B. Williams, Galena, Kans. Appraisal in 1905.
" "	75		W. Kiersted. Galena, Kans. Appraisal in 1905.
Service pipe	10		W. H. Bryan.
" "		2.5	Los Angeles, Cal. Engineering news, May 4, 1899.
" "		5	B. L. Dodge; Mt. Vernon, Ill. Appraisal in 1906.
Reservoirs	50-75		W. Kiersted; Proceedings American society civil engineers, 1897.
"	40-75		W. H. Bryan.

DEPRECIATION, DEPLETION AND OBSOLESCENCE—Waterworks—*(Continued)*

Reservoirs	100		C. B. Burdick; Mt. Vernon, Ill. Appraisal in 1906.
Standpipes	25-30		W. H. Bryan.
"		4	W. H. Rosecrans, Galena, Kans., appraisal in 1905.
"	40		B. Williams; Galena, Kans., appraisal in 1905.
"	30		W. Kiersted, Galena, Kans., appraisal in 1905.

Final report of the American waterworks association committee on depreciation. *Journal of the American waterworks association, supplement,* Sept. 1917, p. 1-38.

Foster, Horatio A. Rates of depreciation. (In his *Engineering valuation of public utilities and factories.* 1913. p. 204).

Waterworks	Years
Wells, driven or drilled	50-75
Wells, large open, stone or brick walled	75-100
Suction piping and intakes	30-50
Stand pipes	30-50
Reservoirs	50-100
Filter beds	30-50
Distribution system, for waterworks.	
Cast-iron mains, including fittings and valves	75-100
Wrought-iron mains and services, galvanized and including valves and fittings	30-50
Cast-iron mains and services black	25-35
Services to buildings, lead	50-100

Gillette, Halbert P. Valuation of water works properties. *Engineering and contracting,* June 2, 1918, p. 486-8.

Gillette, Halbert P. Waterworks valuation and plant depreciation. (In his *Handbook of cost data for contractors and engineers.* 1910. p. 796-801).

Grunsky, Carl Ewald. Probable useful life of various articles. (In his *Valuation, depreciation and the rate-base.* 1917. p. 285, 279).

Systems and plants

Water supply — 50-65 years. Wisconsin railroad commission. Various cases in 1910-1911.

Gates and valves.

water works — 40 years. Benezette Williams. Galena appraisal, Kansas, 1905.

water works — 40-50 years. Leonard Metcalf. Transactions American society of civil engineers, 1909.

Filter beds

water filters — 15-20 years. Wm. H. Bryan. "The Appraisal and depreciation of water works". Journal of association of engineering societies, Dec. 1907.

waterworks — 30-50 years. H. A. Foster. "Engineering valuation of public utilities and factories," Van Nostrand 1912.

Guthrie, Edwin. Depreciation. (In Lisle, George. *Encyclopaedia of accounting.* Vol. 2, p. 375). No depreciation. Kept in perpetual repair out of revenue.

Hawley, W. C. Relation of depreciation to investment. *Public service,* Jan. 1920, p. 25-9.

Hazlehurst, J. N. Final report of the committee on depreciation. *Journal of the American waterworks association,* March 1919, p. 85-135.

Physical. All structures of earth or earth and masonry are very durable and in some cases reservoirs, aqueducts, and dams have lasted thousands of years. Undoubtedly such construction well-maintained is ordinarily good for some hundreds of years, physically often far outliving their functional usefulness.

	Years
Large storage reservoirs, well located	75-150
Heavy earthen or masonry dams	75-150
Large masonry conduits and tunnels	75-150
Conduits and distribution pipe of cast iron of large diameter.	
Cast-iron pipe coated and buried in the ground is a very durable structure. We have little knowledge of its final effective life from a physical point of view. There are some instances of two hundred years' life for uncoated pipe. Largely, we must amortize such durable material, kept clean and well maintained, again by consideration of the possible changes in public need, functional usefulness, and the burden of a reasonable amortization, say	75-125
Conduits and distribution pipe of wrought iron or steel of large diameter.	
Thicknees of shell and sensitiveness to a greater range of deteriorating influences must of necessity bring the life of wrought iron and steel physically below that of cast iron, and in many cases below functional considerations	35-75
Conduits and distribution pipe of wood stave of large diameter.	
Ultimate experience somewhat limited, but thought to be about in same class as steel, when well protected and saturated	30-60
Distribution pipe of small diameter.	
(a) Cast iron—Limitations of size increase difficulties in interior cleaning and maintenance. Such smaller mains are at times removed in rapidly growing cities to make way for larger pipe. Often, they are only supplemented	30-70
It should be noted that in slow growing and smaller cities small mains are less liable to be outgrown than in larger cities	50-90
(b) Wrought iron and steel mains.—Affected by kind of water carried, soil, and coating. Liability of replacement probably greatest influence in shortening useful life.	25-40

DEPRECIATION, DEPLETION AND OBSOLESCENCE—WATERWORKS—*(Continued)*

(c) Services	
wrought iron and steel	15-30
lead	40-80
Of services, it should be noted that character of water carried, soil, and coating are influential, but changing needs are also important.	
Small distribution reservoirs.	
Physically, these structures are very permanent. Changing needs often destroy or impair their usefulness and value; they are often surrounded by growing population and increasing land value, which, in connection with decreasing need, make it desirable to abandon them. They sometimes lose value on account of need for increased head.	50-75
Standpipes.	
Wrought iron and steel	30-60
Reinforced concrete	50-60
Valves	40-60
Hydrants	30-50
Meters	20-30
Pumping machinery.	
High duty units	35-60
High duty small units (say below 6,000,000 gallons per day capacity)	25-50
Ordinary direct-acting	20-40
Centrifugal, not geared	20-30
Centrifugal, geared	15-25
Boiler feed and auxiliary pumps usually take the life of the units to which they are attached.	
Steam engines.	
About the same consideration as above	20-40
Boilers	15-30
Electric generators and motors	20-30
Filter plants.	
Now well standardized. Life should be predicated on general usefulness of station and source, as well as function of the filters themselves.	
Masonry filters	30-50
Wood filters	15-30
Buildings	
Masonry	30-60
Wood	20-40
Stacks	
Masonry	25-50
Steel	10-25

HELWICK, CHARLES W. Depreciation charges. *Engineering record,* May 29, 1909, p. 672.

IDAHO court overrules depreciation deduction. *Engineering record,* Oct. 16, 1915, p. 480-1.

INCOME tax assessment; allowances for depreciation. *Accountant,* Oct. 2, 1909, p. 423-5, 400-2,

INSTITUTE OF MUNICIPAL TREASURERS AND ACCOUNTANTS (INCORPORATED). Municipal corporations and companies working tramway and light railways, gas, water and electricity undertakings. *Accountant,* June 26, 1909, p. 906-8.

METCALF, LEONARD. Depreciation in waterworks operation and accounting. *Journal of the New England waterworks association,* Dec. 1910, p. 442. Abstracts. *Engineering news,* Nov. 3, 1910, p. 482. Methods of computing depreciation of and reasonable assumptions as to period of useful life of waterworks. *Engineering and contracting,* Nov. 16, 1910, p. 434. Discussion. Methods of making computations for depreciation in public utility plants. *Engineering and contracting,* Dec. 28, 1910, p. 590.

Waterworks structures	General limits of useful life years	Straight line methods.
Reservoirs	50-100	2-1
Steel stand-pipes	25-40	4-2½
Masonry buildings	30-50	3⅓-2
Wooden buildings	20-40	5½-2½
Filter plants, permanent construction	25-50	4-2
Pumping machinery, high duty in large units		
Ordinary pumping machinery	20-30	5-3⅓
Steam engines	15-25	6⅔-4
Boilers	12-20	8⅓-5
Electric generators and motors	20-30	5-3⅓
Masonry conduits	50-100	2-1
Cast iron pipe, large diameter		
In non-tuberculating waters	60-100	1⅔-1
In " "	50-75	2-1⅓
Cast iron pipe, small diameter	30-50	3⅓-2
Steel pipe	25-40	4-2½
Wood stave pipe	20-30	5-3½
Wrought-iron service pipes	15-30	6⅔-3⅓
Hydrants	35-50	3-2
Valves	40-50	2½-2
Meters	15-25	6⅔-4

METCALF, LEONARD. Practical checks upon water-works depreciation estimates. *Journal of the American waterworks association,* Sept. 1919, p. 371-93.

METCALF, LEONARD. Water-works valuation and fair rates, in the light of the Maine supreme court decisions in the Waterville and Brunswick cases: *American society of civil engineers, papers and discussions,* 1908, p. 1101-73. *American society of civil engineers, Transactions,* Sept.

DEPRECIATION, DEPLETION AND OBSOLESCENCE—WATERWORKS—*(Continued)*

1909, p. 1. Foster, Horatio A. *Engineering valuation of public utilities and factories,* 1913, p. 207. Gillette, Halbert P. *Handbook of cost data for contractors and engineers.* p. 797.

	Useful life.	Annual contribution to depreciation account or sinking fund in per cent. of cost. At 5% annual rate sinking fund.	General approximate results.
Reservoirs	50-100 years*	0.4777%-0.0383%	½-0%
Standpipes	25-40 "	2.0952%-0.8278%	2-1%
Masonry buildings	40-50 "	0.8278%-0.4777%	1-½%
Wooden buildings	20-50 "	3.0243%-0.4777%	3-1%
Cast-iron pipe of large diameter	50-75 "	0.4777%-0.1322%	¾-¼%
Cast-iron pipe of small diameter	20-40 "	3.0243%-0.8278%	3-¾%
Steel pipe	25-50 "	2.0952%-0.4777%	2-¾%
Wood-stave pipe	20-30 "	3.0243%-1.5051%	3-2%
Wrought-iron service pipe	15-30 "	4.6342%-1.5051%	5-2%
Meters	20-30 "	3.0243%-1.5051%	3-2%
Hydrants	40-50 "	0.8278%-0.4777%	1-½%
Gates	40-50 "	0.8278%-0.4777%	1-½%
Pumping and auxiliary machinery	20-30 "	3.0243%-1.5051%	4-2%
Steam engines	15-27 "	4.6342%-2.0952%	5-3%
Boilers	12-16 "	6.2825%-4.2270%	6-4%
Electrical machinery	20-30 "	3.0243%-1.5051%	4-2%
Average for entire plant (gravity system)			1% to ½%
" " " " (pumping system)			2% to 1½%

*Except where subject to heavy deposit of silt.

METCALF, LEONARD and JOHN W. ALVORD. Going value of waterworks. *American society of civil engineers, Proceedings,* Feb. 1911. *American society of civil engineers, Transactions,* Sept. 1911, p. 334.

MULHALL, JOHN F. J. Depreciation. (In his *Quasi-public corporation accounting and management.* c1905. p. 180-3).

Waterworks 1½-3%

OFFICIAL allowances in respect of depreciation of machinery and plant. Board of Inland revenue, Great Britain. *Accountant,* May 16, 1914, p. 738-9.

No depreciation should be allowed. All expenditure on repairs and renewals, but excluding extensions and improvements is to be charged and allowed as working expenses; as and when incurred.

PROBABLE lives of water-works elements. *Engineering news,* Oct. 11, 1917, p. 688.

	Years.
Large storage reservoirs, well located	75-150
Heavy earth or masonry dams	75-150
Large masonry conduits and tunnels	75-150
Cast-iron pipe, large	75-125
Cast-iron pipe, small	30-70*
Wrought-iron or steel pipe, large	30-75
Wrought-iron or steel pipe, small	25-40
Wood-stave pipe, large	30-60
Services, wrought-iron and steel	15-30
Services, wrought-iron and lead	40-80
Small distribution reservoirs	50-75
Standpipes, wrought-iron and steel	30-60
Standpipes, reinforced-concrete	50-60
Valves	40-60
Hydrants	30-50
Meters	20-30
Pumping machinery, high duty, large units	35-60
Pumping machinery, high duty, small units	25-50
Pumping machinery, ordinary direct-action	25-50
Pumping machinery, centrifugal not geared	20-30
Pumping machinery, centrifugal geared	15-25
Steam engines	20-40
Boilers	15-30
Electric generators and motors	20-30
Filter plants, masonry	30-50
Filter plants, wood	15-30
Buildings, masonry	30-60
Buildings, wood	20-40
Stacks, masonry	25-50
Stacks, steel	10-25

*In slow-growing and small cities, 50-90 years.

PUBLIC utility reports, annotated. Rochester, Lawyers co-operative publishing co.
See index under Depreciation.

PUBLIC utility report, annotated. Rochester, Lawyers co-operative publishing co. 1915C. p. 525, 561.

Re Arizona corp. commission v. Morenci water co. (Ariz.). A rate of 4 per cent of depreciation on the cost of installation of meter services by a water company which the Commission directed the company to install was fixed as fair and equitable.

Re Apple v. Brazil (Ind.). The Indiana Commission fixed the rate of depreciation of a municipal water plant as 1 per cent.

PUBLIC utility reports, annotated. Rochester, Lawyers co-operative publishing co. 1915A. p. 178.

Re Janesville water co. (Wis.). In estimating the cost of reproduction for the purpose of obtaining the fair value of a waterworks property for municipal purchase, allowance of a condition of 50 per cent new of a Sturdevant fan and engine which was secondhand at the time of installation, and which had been in use for eleven years was held to be ample.

DEPRECIATION, DEPLETION AND OBSOLESCENCE—WATERWORKS—*(Continued)*

Re Janesville water co. (Wis.). The Commission placed a present value of $8,000 upon a water works company's reservoir, the cost of reproduction of which was estimated by the Commission's engineers at $9,787, the present value at $6,753, based partly upon obsolescence due to deterioration of ground waters by open storage, the Commission, in fixing such valuation taking into consideration the facts that the reservoir valued was not likely to become inadequate, and that it was of an uneconomical type which could be replaced by modern reservoir for about the same amount as would be required to reproduce the existing reservoir.

PUBLIC utility reports, annotated. Rochester, Lawyers co-operative publishing co. 1915B. p 611.

Re Leavenworth v. Leavenworth city & Ft. L. water co. (Kans.). A reasonable sum to be set aside for the depreciation reserve of a water company was held to be 1 per cent per annum on the assumption that the fund thus created would be properly invested and the accruing interest to be compounded annually or at shorter intervals.

PUBLIC utility reports, annotated. Rochester, Lawyers co-operative publishing co. 1915D. p. 1008.

Re Lake forest v. Lake forest water co. (Ill.). In a proceeding to determine the reasonableness of a waterworks company, an allowance of 1.6 per cent for annual depreciation was held to be ample.

PUBLIC utility reports, annotated. Rochester, Lawyers co-operative publishing co. 1915E. p. 27.

Re Galveston waterworks co. (Ind.). A proper annual depreciation charge for a waterworks plant was found to be 1 per cent of its present value.

PUBLIC utility reports, annotated. Rochester, Lawyers co-operative publishing co. 1915F. p. 445, 913.

Re Sandpoint v. Sandpoint water & light co. (Idaho). An annual allowance of 3 per cent of the value new of the depreciable physical properties owned by a water company was made in a rate making proceeding to cover future depreciation.

Re Bend v. Bend water, light & power co. (Or.). A water, light, and power company was directed to deduct from its operating income 4 per cent of the value new of its depreciable electric property and 3 per cent of the value new of its water property to be set aside each year for depreciation, and accounted for as provided by Par. 17 of the Public utilities act, Laws of 1911, chapter 279.

PUBLIC utility reports, annotated. Rochester, Lawyers co-operative publishing co. 1916E. p. 962, 1073.

Re Thayer v. Beaver valley water co. (Pa.). In fixing water rates, an allowance of $12,000 was made for annual depreciation of a system valued at $985,000.

Re Angola v. Indiana utilities co. (Ind.) No. 937, Aug. 11, 1916. An allowance of 2 per cent of the value of the property of a water utility was made for depreciation, where the property consisted almost entirely of plant equipment, the utility owning but a small part of the distribution system.

Re Los Banos v. West San Joaquin valley water co. (Cal.). Decision No. 2990, Case No. 822, Dec. 22, 1915. A sinking fund allowance of $866.01 was made for depreciation of a water system valued at $42,019 in fixing rates.

Re Los Banos v. West San Joaquin valley water co. (Cal.). Decision No. 2990, Case No. 822, Dec. 22, 1915. A sinking fund allowance of $215 was made for depreciation of a water filter and meters valued new at $5,100 in view of their relatively short life.

Re Plains v. Plains light & water co. Docket no. 527, June 20, 1916, the Montana Commission made the following allowances in a rate proceedings for the annual depreciation of water and electric property: 6⅔ per cent for water aqueduct and mains, water and electric meters, and electric transformers; 10 per cent for water services, electric street lights, and water and electric general office equipment; and 20 per cent for miscellaneous equipment.

PUBLIC utility reports, annotated. Rochester, Lawyers co-operative publishing co. 1916D. p. 725, 894.

Re Charlestown water co. (Va.). An annual allowance of 2 per cent was held sufficient to take care of the depreciation of water plant and provide for upkeep.

Re Mullan waterworks (Idaho). Five per cent of the value of the depreciable property of a water system was taken for the weighted average annual rate of depreciation, based on the straight-line formula, in fixing rates.

PUBLIC utility reports, annotated. Rochester, Lawyers co-operative publishing co. 1916B. p. 180.

Re Commercial club v. Terre Haute waterworks co. A water utility was ordered to carry a depreciation account of .83 of 1 per cent of the value of its property found to be $1,200,000.

PUBLIC utility reports, annotated. Rochester, Lawyers co-operative publishing co. 1916C. p. 406, 788.

Re Thorn v. Montgomery light & water improvement co. (W. Va.). In fixing the operating expenses of a water system, an allowance of 5 per cent was made for depreciation, upkeep, and repairs of a poorly constructed plant having steel mains with a shorter life than cast iron.

Re Cripple Creek water co. (Colo.). An annual allowance of $2,500 for depreciation reserve was held to be sufficient for a water utility valued for rate making at $150,000.

PUBLIC utility reports, annotated. Rochester, Lawyers co-operative publishing co. 1916F. p. 364, 782.

Re Los Banos v. West San Joaquin valley water co. (Cal.). An annual allowance of $94 was made for depreciation of a chlorination plant costing $420, in a water rate proceedings.

Re San Anselmo v. Marin water & power co. (Cal.). The sum of $6,815 is a reasonable allowance in a water rate case for a depreciation annuity, estimated on a 5 per cent sinking fund basis, on a rate making value of $998,430.61.

PUBLIC utility reports, annotated. Rochester, Lawyers co-operative publishing co. 1917A. p. 261, 685, 763.

Re Kent water & light co. (Ohio). An allowance of 1.07 per cent for the annual depreciation of low-pressure and high-pressure systems was made in fixing water rates.

Goldfield consolidated water co. v. Public service commission (Fed.). In determining whether water and sewer rates in a mining town are confiscatory, an annual allowance of 12½ per cent for depreciation based on an assumed exhaustion of the mines in 8 years is too high, where the profits and such allowance would be drawn from patrons using only 4 per cent of the capacity; where nothing has been collected for accrued depreciation although the company was able to fix its own rates; where it does not appear that the

DEPRECIATION, DEPLETION AND OBSOLESCENCE—WATERWORKS—*(Continued)*

supply will not be needed for other purposes on the exhaustion of the present market; where no consideration is given to salvage; and also for the reason that a court will not speculate as to the life of mines.

Re Wood v. La Fargo (Wis.). An allowance of 1½ per cent was made for annual depreciation of municipal waterworks in ascertaining the expenses for rate making.

PUBLIC utility reports, annotated. Rochester, Lawyers co-operative publishing co. 1917B. p. 624, 1.

Re City water co. (Mo.). Accrued depreciation of water mains was estimated, in a rate valuation, on the basis of an assumed life of 100 years, where, on account of favorable conditions, there had been little actual depreciation and the date of necessary renewals by reason of depreciation was remote.

Re City water co. (Mo.). An allowance of 2 per cent on the value of water property was made by the Missouri commission for depreciation surplus and contingencies, in determining the reasonableness of rates.

Re Lincoln v. Lincoln water & light co. (Ill.). An annual allowance of $3,300 plus an annual allowance of 1¼ per cent of the cost of all additions and betterments, together with the earnings of the fund, was held to be reasonable for the water department of a utility.

PUBLIC utility reports, annotated. Rochester, Lawyers co-operative publishing co. 1917C. p. 390, 521, 838.

Re Ben Avon v. Ohio valley water co. (Pa.). The annual allowance for depreciation of a gravity water system was fixed at a sum equal to ¾ of 1 per cent of the fair value of the property.

Re Murray (Cal.). The depreciation annuity of a water system was estimated on the 6 per cent sinking-fund basis on the depreciable property useful in the service, including the investment in additions about to be added to the system.

Re Pekin v. Pekin waterworks co. (Ill.). A water company the fair value of whose property for rate making was fixed at $200,000 including an allowance of $7,000 for working capital, was ordered to set aside, on a specified date, an allowance of $3,000 and thereafter annually to increase this by an amount equivalent to $3,000 plus ¼ per cent of the cost of all additions and betterments, exclusive of all replacements, made upon such property after a specified date, together with all earnings of such sum or sums.

PUBLIC utility reports, annotated. Rochester, Lawyers co-operative publishing co. 1917D. p. 277, 478.

Re Racine water co. (Wis.). Liability of freezing will be given little consideration in ascertaining the depreciation of water mains, where the occasions of freezing have been rare.

Re Racine water co. (Wis.). No depreciation can be allowed for inadequacy of a 24" water pipe which must be augmented by another intake in the future, because of failure originally to lay a 48" intake, where that intake exceeds the present demand and the demand to be expected within a reasonable future time; nor because of failure originally to lay a 36" intake where the investment for a 36" intake compounded, would greatly exceed the cost of a 30" intake which, in connection with the 24" intake, will have a great advantage over one 36" intake.

Re Racine water co. (Wis.). No general rule can be used to measure the depreciable life of cast-iron water mains, as their life is unknown and unknowable, being affected by the character of the soil, the degree of care exercised in laying, the frequency of disturbance by other trenching, the kind of water carried, electrolysis, and other forces.

Re Racine water co. (Wis.). The utility value of a water intake pipe is not to be measured entirely by the reduction in capacity from use, since an intake which has stood the test of years and lost but little in efficiency and has, by experience, been demonstrated to be well conceived, and is known to be laid with engineering skill, has an added value over a new intake which has not been subjected to the test of actual experience.

Re Racine water co. (Wis.). Water mains should be depreciated because of inadequacy from failure to install mains of sufficient capacity to provide for the resaonable future growth of a city, in ascertaining the reproduction cost less depreciation of the system.

Re Racine water co. (Wis.). A water intake pipe cannot be depreciated because of future inadequacy, where it will probably continue indefinitely to be properly used and useful, and the time when it will be discarded or abandoned is pure conjecture.

Re Greensburg v. Westmoreland water co. (Pa.). The sum of $9,000 rather than $12,762 claimed by the utility, was allowed for the annual depreciation of a water system having a rate-making value of $1,100,000, in view of the fact that renewals have been charged to operating expenses and some of them are reflected in an allowance for repairs, and that the rate-making value is less than the figure resulting under the reproduction theory.

PUBLIC utility reports, annotated. Rochester, Lawyers co-operative publishing co. 1917E. p. 147, 556, 750.

Re Hackensack water co. (N. J.). In a waterworks rate valuation, the annual depreciation reserve was computed at the rate of 1.1 per cent upon the cost value of the depreciable property, in each current year.

Re Indianapolis water co. (Ind.). A water utility was authorized to maintain a depreciation fund of 8/10 of 1 per cent of the present value of its property plus 8/10 of 1 per cent of the annual additions thereto where it appeared that the plant was in good physical condition and furnishing efficient service, and that about one fourth of the value of the property was in real estate, which has a tendency to appreciate rather than depreciate.

Re Briggs v. Peaks Island corp. (Me.) An allowance of 2 per cent on the full value of a water plant was made for depreciation and contingencies, including the creation of an adequate fund to meet accidents and possible claims of all sorts.

PUBLIC utility reports, annotated. Rochester, Lawyers co-operative publishing co. 1918B. p. 724, 774, 844.

Edgerton (Wis.). An annual depreciation allowance of 1 per cent of the cost new, excluding materials and supplies, is adequate, for a water company, in a rate-fixing case.

Re Louisiana v. Louisiana water co. In fixing water rates, an annual allowance of 2 per cent of the property value was made for depreciation, surplus, and contingencies of the utility.

DEPRECIATION, DEPLETION AND OBSOLESCENCE—WATERWORKS—*(Continued)*

PUBLIC utility reports, annotated. Rochester, Lawyers co-operative publishing co. 1918C. p. 844, 916.
Montrose v. Consumers water co. (Pa.). An allowance of 2 per cent was fixed for annual depreciation of a water plant.
Guilford water co. (Me.). An allowance approximating ½ of 1 per cent per year for depreciation of a gravity water plant is not unreasonably high.

PUBLIC utility reports, annotated. Rochester, Lawyers co-operative publishing co. 1918D. p. 561.
Re Capital city water co. (Mo.). An annual allowance of 1½ per cent of a water utility's plant value is reasonable for depreciation, surplus, and contingencies.

PUBLIC utility reports, annotated. Rochester, Lawyers co-operative publishing co. 1918E. p. 443, 451, 540, 680, 681, 884.
Re Hagar (Idaho). An annual depreciation allowance of 3 per cent of the value of the plant was made in a water-rate case.
Re Harbster v. Angelica water & ice co. (Pa.). In the valuation of a water and ice plant for rate making, the average life of the entire plant was found to be fifty-three years and the rate of annual depreciation 0.96 per cent.
Re Collingswood sewerage co. April 16, 1918, in estimating the annual amount of depreciation to be set aside for a water plant the New Jersey commission said: "In consideration of the long-lived property in the collection system and real estate, the Board is of the opinion that 1 2/10 per cent of the fixed capital will provide a sufficient appropriation to provide for the annual amortization of capital.
Re Coalinga consolidated water co. (Cal.). Decision No. 4908, Application No. 3204, Nov. 30, 1917. In fixing water rates an allowance of $4,100 was made for annual depreciation of a water system valued at $80,000.
Re Burlington sewerage co. April 16, 1918, the New Jersey commission considered as a fair amount to be appropriated to provide for accruing annual depreciation of a water plant, 1.2 per cent of the value of the total fixed capital.
Re Burlington waterworks, U-841, May 28, 1918, the Wisconsin commission held that a depreciation allowance of 1 per cent from the depreciable property of a small water plant was a sufficient charge to operating expenses.
Re Tualatin Valley electric co. (Or.). P. S. C. Or. Order no. 274, U-F-179, Oct. 5, 1917, an annual allowance of $250 was made for depreciation of a water plant valued at $4,855.
Re Shelbyville v. Interstate public service co. nos. 1811, 2838, April 26, 1918, the Indiana commission in determining the reasonableness of the rates of a water utility, fixed 1 per cent of the value of the property as the proper amount to be set aside as a depreciation fund.
Re Knowlton v. Farmington Village corp. (Me.). An annual allowance was made for the depreciation of a municipal water plant substantially in excess of the rate at which the cost of reproduction new was depreciated, to arrive at present value for rate making.

PUBLIC utility reports, annotated. Rochester, Lawyers co-operative publishing co. 1918F. p. 75, 316.
Water Comrs. (Wis.). An allowance of .8 of 1 per cent of the value of a water plant was made for annual depreciation. United public service co. (Ind.). An annual allowance of 1 per cent of the value of a water plant was fixed for depreciation.

PUBLIC utility reports, annotated. Rochester, Lawyers co-operative publishing co. 1919A. p. 180, 448.
Re Hammond waterworks (Ind.). An annual allowance of 1 per cent upon the depreciable property of a municipal water plant was held reasonable in a proceedings to determine the reasonableness of its rates.
Re Indianapolis water co. (Ind.) A depreciation of .8 of 1 per cent per annum was held sufficient to care of accruing depreciation of a water company's property.

PUBLIC utility reports, annotated. Rochester, Lawyers co-operative publishing co. 1919B. p. 749, 751.
Re Greensburgh water co. no. 3617, Dec. 1918, the Indiana commission said that it fixed 1 per cent of the value of the property less the value of lands, materials, and supplies and working capital, as a proper rate of depreciation for the property of the water company.
Re Washington water, light & power co. v. Washington, no. 3842, Nov. 4, 1918, the Indiana commission fixed 1 per cent of the value of a water plant less the value of lands, materials, supplies, and working capital, as a proper allowance for depreciation.
Re Wabash water & light co. no. 3826, Nov. 4, 1918, the Indiana commission fixed a proper depreciation charge at 1 per cent of the value of a water plant less working capital and the value of lands, materials, and supplies.
Re Newport v. Newport Waterworks, Nos. 4, 15, Nov. 25, 1918, the Rhode Island commission after finding the fair value of the property of a water company exclusive of working capital to be $1,700,000 held that the company should set aside $18,000 annually for depreciation plus 1¼ per cent of the cost of all additions and betterments.
Re Commonwealth water co. Dec. 30, 1918, the New Jersey commission fixed the charge for annual depreciation of a water plant at 1.1 per cent, to be computed on the depreciable property, excluding all intangible value and land.

PUBLIC utility reports, annotated. Rochester, Lawyers co-operative publishing co. 1919C. p. 404.
Re Kane v. Spring water co. (Pa.) 404. A water company the value of whose property for rate making was fixed at $200,000 was allowed $1,708.11 for annual depreciation.

PUBLIC utility reports, annotated. Rochester, Lawyers co-operative publishing co. 1919D. p. 467.
Re Hinton water, light & supply co. (W. Va.) 467. The West Virginia commission made an allowance of 3 per cent for the depreciation of a water plant.

PUBLIC utility reports, annotated. Rochester, Lawyers co-operative publishing co. 1919E. p. 117, 599.
Re Bluffton municipal light & waterworks (Ind.) 117. An annual allowance of 1 per cent of the depreciable value of a municipal water plant was made for depreciation.
Re Independent waterworks co. (Mo.) 599. In fixing the rates of a water company, an annual allowance for depreciation of 1.5 per cent of the estimated reproduction cost new of the property was made.

DEPRECIATION, DEPLETION AND OBSOLESCENCE—WATERWORKS—*(Continued)*

PUBLIC utility reports, annotated. Rochester, Lawyers co-operative publishing co. 1917F. p. 171.
Rt Mt. Holly water co. April 10, 1919, the New Jersey commission made an allowance of 1.6 per cent for the annual depreciation of a water plant.

PUBLIC utility reports, annotated. Rochester, Lawyers co-operative publishing company, 1920B, p. 390, 597.
Re Heckert v. Hegins water co. (Pa.). Pennsylvania commission allowed $300 for the annual depreciation of a water plant valued at $48,000.
Statement that a water plant as a whole is estimated to have a life of 100 years.

PUBLIC utility reports, annotated. Rochester, Lawyers co-operative publishing company, 1920C, p. 745.
Re Roanoke water works co. (Va.) An allowance of 1 per cent on the depreciable property of a water company is a reasonable allowance for depreciation.

PUBLIC utility reports, annotated. Rochester, Lawyers co-operative publishing company, 1920D, p. 775, 1081.
Re Arkansas light & p. co. (Ark.) Arkansas commission made an allowance of 2½ per cent for the depreciation of a water plant.
Re Peaks island corp. v. Itself (Me.) 1038 Maine commission made an allowance of 2 per cent for the depreciation of a water company.

PUBLIC utility reports, annotated. Rochester, Lawyers co-operative publishing company, 1920E, p. 803, 311.
Re Kane v. Spring water company. Pennsylvania commission made an allowance of $2,100 for the depreciation of a water plant of the fair value of $230,000.
Re Rogers light and power company. Arkansas commission made an allowance of 2½ per cent for the depreciation of the property of a water company.

PUBLIC utility reports, annotated. Rochester, Lawyers co-operative publishing company, 1920F, p. 954, 943.
Re Public service commission v. Pacific power and light company. Washington commission fixed an allowance of 4 per cent for the annual depreciation of a water plant where but a small proportion of the distribution system was composed of cast iron pipe the greater portion being of much less durable material.
Re Borough of Verona v. Suburban water company. In computing the return of a water company, the Pennsylvania commission made an allowance for depreciation based on the theory that the present worth of the property, as measured by reproduction cost new less accrued depreciation, must be safeguarded by an allowance which if allowed to accumulate at 4 per cent interest for the remaining life of the property, would result in a sum equal to such present worth.

STRUCKMANN, H. Depreciation and obsolescence in Portland cement plants. *Journal of the American society of mechanical engineers,* Feb. 1913, p. 262-75.

Waterworks and pipelines	10%

USEFUL life of water works units. *Engineering and contracting,* June 13, 1917, p. 541-2.
See American waterworks association. Committee on depreciation. Final report.

VALUATION of public utility properties. *Electrical world,* Feb. 25, March 18, 25, April 15, 29, 1909, p. 509, 692, 740, 928, 1036.

WATERWORKS charges and depreciation at Fargo. *Engineering news,* May 20, 1915, p. 994-5.

WHITTEN, ROBERT H. Bibliography. (In his *Valuation of public service corporations.* 1914., p. 745).

WHITTEN, ROBERT HARVEY. Valuation of public service corporations; legal and economic phases of valuation for rate making and public purchases. New York, Banks law publishing co. v.1. p. 428, 430, 437-8, 438-9, 1204.
One per cent allowance on sinking fund basis in Des Moines, Iowa, water rate case, 1910.
Allowance in San Francisco water rate case, 1911.

Cast iron pipe	1%
Wrought iron pipe	2
Pump engines, flumes and wooden structures	2.5
Boilers	5

Depreciation allowance refused by California Court, San Diego, Cal., water rate case, 1897.
Depreciation allowance refused by Iowa court in 1902 but approved in 1909.
Wisconsin commission—City of Green Bay v. Green Bay water company—2% on sinking-fund basis on the depreciation property.

WINSLOW, W. H. Provision for depreciation by public utility corporations. *Engineering news,* Mar. 4, 1909, p. 251.

WOLFF, MARK. Interpretation of waterworks accounts. *Journal of the American water works association,* June 1916, p. 543, 546.
Following is the estimated life of the various assets used in arriving at the annual depreciation shown in the Income account:

	Years
Horses, carriages and motors	10
Office furniture and general equipment	15
Boilers, steam pipes, filters	20
Pumping machinery and engines	25
Mains, fire hydrants, standpipes, buildings, masonry	50
Reservoirs, aqueducts	100

Depreciation.	Per cent of total operating revenues, $400,000.00
Collecting and storage system	0.50
Purification system	0.50
Pumping system	2.00
Distribution system	6.25
General	0.75
Total depreciation	10.00

Weighbridges
See Depreciation, depletion and obsolescence—Scales, platforms, etc.

DEPRECIATION, DEPLETION AND OBSOLESCENCE—*(Continued)*

Welding

ELBOURNE, EDWARD T. Depreciation rates. (In his *Factory administration and accounts.* 1918. p. 377).

	Prov. dep. % Remainder values	Years 10%	5%
Welding and cutting plant	12½	17	22

NICHOLSON, J. LEE and J. F. D. ROHRBACH. Depreciation. (In their *Cost accounting.* 1919. p. 150).

Welding machines 10%
Pickling washing machines, electric and acetylene welding machines 10
Based on (1) the cost of equipment
(2) the life of the equipment
(3) on a ten-hour day.

PHILADELPHIA. CONTROLLER. Rates of depreciation. (In his *Manual of accounting, reporting and business procedure of the city and county of Philadelphia.* 1917. p. 205).

Metal work equipment
Hammering rolling and welding equipment 5%

Wells

AUSTRALIA. FEDERAL INCOME TAX DEPARTMENT. Depreciation allowance. *Accountant,* Oct. 13, 1917, p. 277-9. *Accounting and commerce,* June 30, 1917, p. 55-7. *Federal accountant,* July 1917, p. 93-8. *Public accountant,* Jan. 30, 1917, p. 145-52.

Wells and underground tanks, Nil.

BARKER, HARRY. Typical life expectation tables for public utility property. (In his *Public utility rates.* 1917. p. 368, 367).

Tar and ammonia wells	50 years. Wisconsin railroad commission
extractor	40 years. Wisconsin railroad commission
Wells, driven or drilled	50-75 years. Wisconsin railroad commission
open and lined	75-100 years. Wisconsin railroad commission

FOSTER, HORATIO A. Rates of depreciation. (In his *Engineering valuation of public utilities and factories.* 1913. p. 204).

Wells, driven or drilled 50-75 years
Wells, large open, stone or brick walled 75-100

GILLETTE, HALBERT P. and R. T. DANA. Depreciation. (In their *Handbook of mechanical and electrical cost data.* 1918. p. 111).

Wells, tar and ammonia, (gas plant), 50 years. H. P. Gillette, Everett railway and water co., Jan. 29, 1912.

GRUNSKY, CARL EWALD. Probable useful life of various articles. (In his *Valuation, depreciation and the rate-base.* 1917. p. 286, 284).

Wells	
water	30 years. San Joaquin light & power corporation. Rate hearing before California railroad commission, 1915.
water driven or drilled	50-75 years. H. A. Foster. "Engineering valuation of public utilities and factories", Van Nostrand, 1912.
water, large open masonry	75-100 years. H. A. Foster. "Engineering valuation of public utilities and factories", Van Nostrand, 1912.
Water well pumps	10 years. San Joaquin light & power corporation. Rate hearing before California railroad commission, 1915.
Pumps and wells at gas plant	30 years. Pacific gas & electric company. Figures used in rate hearings before Master in Chancery, San Francisco, 1913-4.
tar and ammonia	50 years. Wisconsin railroad commission. Quoted by H. A. Foster and in published reports.

MANUFACTURERS' light and heat company of Pittsburgh, Pa. *Commercial and financial chronicle,* July 23, 1910, p. 217.

Wells 8%

NICHOLSON, J. LEE and J. F. D. ROHRBACH. Depreciation. (In their *Cost accounting.* 1919. p. 146).

Wells—gas 10%
Wells—water 3
Based on (1) the cost of equipment
(2) the life of the equipment
(3) on a ten-hour day.

PHILADELPHIA. CONTROLLER. Rates of depreciation. (In his *Manual of accounting, reporting and business procedure of the city and county of Philadelphia.* 1917. p. 210).

Wells 2%

Wharves

ELBOURNE, EDWARD T. Depreciation rates. (In his *Factory administration and accounts.* 1918. p. 376).

	Prov. dep. % Remainder values	Years 10%	5%
Wharves	2½	91	118

DEPRECIATION, DEPLETION AND OBSOLESCENCE—WHARVES—*(Continued)*

GILLETTE, HALBERT POWERS. Railways. (In his *Handbook of cost data for contractors and engineers.* 1910. p. 1317-8).

	Age years	Annual % dep.	% present cond.
Docks and wharves	7.0	3.0	79.0

GILLETTE, HALBERT P. and R. T. DANA. Depreciation. (In their *Handbook of mechanical and electrical cost data.* 1918. p. 107).
Docks, 33.3 years. H. P. Gillette, Washington railway appraisal.

GILLETTE, HALBERT P. and R. T. DANA. Depreciation, repairs and renewals. (In their *Mechanical and electrical cost data.* 1918. p. 107).
Wharves and docks 33.3 years

GRUNSKY, CARL EWALD. Probable useful life of various articles. (In his *Valuation, depreciation and the rate-base.* 1917. p. 286).
Wharves and docks, 33⅓ years. H. P. Gillette. Appraisal of Great Northern & Northern Pacific R.R.'s in Washington. Direction of Washington railroad commission. 1906.

NICHOLSON, J. LEE and J. F. D. ROHRBACH. Depreciation. (In their *Cost accounting.* 1919. p. 147).
Docks, piers and wharves 3⅓%
Based on (1) the cost of equipment
(2) the life of the equipment
(3) on a ten-hour day.

PHILADELPHIA. CONTROLLER. Rates of depreciation. (In his *Manual of accounting, reporting and business procedure of the city and county of Philadelphia.* 1917. p. 210).
Piers 3⅓%
Wharves 2

RUNYON, F. O. Report on hydro-electric plant for special committee common council, Newark, New Jersey, April 23, 1902, p. 15, 16, 24.
Dock improvements 10%

Wheelbarrows

LIFE of road construction equipment. *Engineering and contracting,* Jan. 3, 1917, p. 3.
Wheelbarrows 50%

Whips

PHILADELPHIA. CONTROLLER. Rates of depreciation. (In his *Manual of accounting, reporting and business procedure of the city and county of Philadelphia.* 1917. p. 209).
Punitive and correctional equipment—Whips 20%

Whistles

BREWER, ALLAN F. Rates for annual depreciation. *Industrial management,* April 1918, p. 268.
Steam whistles 40 years 2.5%

Windmills

AUSTRALIA. FEDERAL INCOME TAX DEPARTMENT. Depreciation allowance. *Accountant,* Oct. 13, 1917, p. 277-9. *Accounting and commerce,* June 30, 1917, p. 55-7. *Federal accountant,* July 1917, p. 93-8. *Public accountant,* Jan. 30, 1917, p. 145-52.
Bores, windmills etc. 7½%
Based on written down value and repairs allowed in addition.

Window poles

PHILADELPHIA. CONTROLLER. Rates of depreciation. (In his *Manual of accounting, reporting and business procedure of the city and county of Philadelphia.* 1917. p. 207-8).
Window poles 4%

Window shades

PHILADELPHIA. CONTROLLER. Rates of depreciation. (In his *Manual of accounting, reporting and business procedure of the city and county of Philadelphia.* 1917. p. 207-8).
Window shades 12½%

Wire and wiring

ANALYSIS of the premises adopted and methods used in determining the cost to reproduce new together with the depreciation thereon of the physical property of the Metropolitan system and the Kansas City and Wesport Belt railway of Kansas City, Mo. *Engineering and contracting,* May 28, 1913, p. 617-20.
Wiring and cable 3%

APPRAISAL of the Seattle telephone companies by the railroad commission of Washington. *Engineering and contracting,* May 3, 1911, p. 520-4.
Aerial wire

	Life	Salvage	Annual dep.	Average	Total dep.
copper	15	40	4.0	5	20.0
iron	8	00	12.5	5	62.5

AUSTRALIA. FEDERAL INCOME TAX DEPARTMENT. Depreciation allowance. *Accountant,* Oct. 13, 1917, p. 277-9. *Accounting and commerce,* June 30, 1917, p. 55-7. *Federal accountant,* July 1917, p. 93-8. *Public accountant,* Jan. 30, 1917, p. 145-52.

Underground wires and cables	2½%
Overhead wires and cables	
insulated	7½
bare	Nil
House installations	5

Written down value, repairs allowed.

DEPRECIATION, DEPLETION AND OBSOLESCENCE—WIRE AND WIRING—*(Continued)*

BAGG, F. A. Life of railway physical property from engineering standpoint. *Electric railway journal,* Dec. 9, 1911, p. 1205-6.

Trolley wire 15-20 years

BARKER, HARRY. Depreciation of electric railway property. (In his *Public utility rates.* 1917. p. 367).

Overhead construction trolley wire	Years	Authority
No. 0, 1 min. headway	2	Wis. R. R. comm.
No. 00, 1 min. headway (25% in size)	2½	Wis. R. R. comm.
No. 000, 1 min. headway	3	Wis. R. R. comm.

BARKER, HARRY. Typical life expectation tables for public utility property. (In his *Public utility rates.* 1917. p. 368-9).

Station wiring, etc.	30 years	
Wire, insulated copper line	10-15	
Lead covered aerial cable	10-15	
Underground cable	20-25	
	Wisconsin railroad commission	
Telephone wire, copper, line	40 years	Chic. tel. comm.
copper interior	30	Chic tel. comm.
galvanized iron, line	8-15	Wis. R. R. comm.

BAY state rate case. *Electric railway journal,* Dec. 4, 1915, p. 1121-3. *Public utility reports, annotated,* 1916F, p. 336-9.

Signal wire 15 years
Telephone wire 15

BELT, ROBERT E. Depreciation. (In his *Foundry cost accounting, practice and procedure.* 1919. p. 243).

Electric wiring and fixtures 7½%

BELT, ROBERT E. Depreciation. (In his *Uniform cost accounting methods; adopted by the American malleable castings association,* Nov. 14, 1917, p. 20-1).

Steam boilers, generators, air compressor, steam piping, electric wiring, etc. 7½%

BEMIS, EDWARD W. Report on the investigation of the Chicago telephone company submitted to the committee on gas, oil and electric light. Chicago, October 25, 1912. 127p.

	Copper wire, long distance and toll lines			Copper wire, exchange lines		
	Years	Salvage	%	Years	Salvage	%
Byllesby and Arnold						
B. Due to age and wear and tear only	25	40	2.4	20	40	2.4
A. Due to all forms of depreciation	15	45	6.50	15	45	6.50
Chicago commission	40	70	5.38	30	70	5.38
Westinghouse, Church Kerr & co.	40	50	2.5	20	50	2.5
E. L. Cline, Telephony, July 2, 1910	15	70	2	15	70	2

BOLTON, REGINALD PELHAM. Depreciation of mechanical equipments and power plants. (In his *Building for profit.* 1911. p. 82, 89).

	Physical years	%	Economic years
Electric switches, wiring and connections	15	3.75	11

BRYAN, WILLIAM. Appraisal and depreciation of water-works and similar properties. *Journal of the association of engineering societies,* Dec. 1907, p. 236-81. Depreciation allowance for various public-service industries. *Engineering news,* Jan. 23, 1908, p. 96.

	Years	% straight
Wiring of cars		8
Wire on poles	25	5

BRYAN, WILLIAM H. Depreciation of electric light plants. *Municipality,* March 1908, p. 74.

Material	Life in years	Dep. % per year straight	Authority
Wire on poles	25		Iowa electrical association, in *Iowa engineer,* July 1906.
Wiring of cars		6	Chicago city railway, *Street railway journal,* Dec. 1898.

CLINE, E. L. Depreciation of telephone companies. *Telephony,* July 2, 1910, p. 16.

	Life	% Depreciation	Salvage
Wire			
copper	15	2.0	70
iron	10	10.00	0
ins. (iron)	12	7.5	10
" (copper)	12	6.6	20

COST and depreciation of steam and hydro-electric installations. *Electrical world,* Dec. 30, 1909, p. 1558.

Cables and heavy wiring 10 years .318% of total cost

CRAVENS, GEORGE W. Depreciation and maintenance of electrical equipment. *Electrical review,* April 23, 1910, p. 853-6. Foster, H. A. *Engineering valuation of public utilities and factories.* 1913. p. 201-2. Montgomery, Robert H. *Income tax procedure,* 1919, p. 570. ——— Same, 1920, p. 723-4. Montgomery, Robert H. *Auditing theory and practice,* 1916. p. 424.

	Depreciation Annual %	Light or intermittent service	Heavy or continuous service
Wires and cables		3-5	4-6.6

Wires and cables	2	Chicago traction commission.
	6.6	Chicago union traction co.
	5	Milwaukee electric railway & light co.
	2	Wisconsin railroad commission.
	5	Average English.

DEPRECIATION, DEPLETION AND OBSOLESCENCE—Wire and wiring—*(Continued)*

3	Average Scotch practice.
3.5	Philip Dawson.
5	Stone & Webster.
4-6.6	Industrial power plants.
5	Prof. G. F. Gebhardt.
5	Miscellaneous sources.

Crowell, H. H. Electric lighting rates and depreciation. *Municipal journal and engineering,* Dec. 18, 1907, p. 698.

	Purchased 10 years or more ago	Modern
Line wire	20	25 years

Depreciation account of the Kokomo, Marion and Western traction company. *Electric railway journal,* July 22, 1911, p. 156-7.

Wire	2%

Depreciation funds in Europe. *Electrical railway journal,* May 7, 21, 1904, p. 696, 760.

Trolley wire	
Brussels	10 years

Depreciation of overhead structures and substations. *Engineering and contracting,* Nov. 19, 1913, p. 567.

Trolley wire—copper	4%
Trolley wire—steel	5
Feeder wire	1
High tension line, including copper	2

Depreciation of the equipment of an electric plant. *Electrical world,* Dec. 12, 1914, p. 1161.

Wire	3.75%

Depreciation statements—Manitoba government telephones. *Manitoba public utilities commission, Annual report,* 1913, p. 101.

Exchange aerial wire	10%
Rural aerial wire	6
Toll wire, iron	6
Toll wire, copper	2

Figures from the Iola (Kans.) central station. *Electrical world,* Sept. 23, 1909, p. 723.

Wires	2%

Floy, Henry. Depreciation. Floy, Henry. Depreciation as related to electrical properties. *American institute of electrical engineers, Proceedings.* 1911. p. 1267. Floy, Henry. *Valuation of public utility properties.* 1912. p. 188-93. Foster, Horatio A. *Engineering valuation of public utilities and factories.* 1913. p. 194-8. *Engineering and contracting,* Oct. 4, 1911, p. 359-65. *Engineering magazine,* Aug. 1911, p. 837-40.

Wire	Depreciation per cent per year straight line		
Trolley allowance of 80.5 lbs. per 1,000 ft. for wearing value of No. 1/0 wire		Tract. val. comm.	Chicago con. tract. co.
Trolley allowance of 106.8 for No. 2/0		Tract. val. comm.	Chicago con. tract. co.
From observation		B. J. Arnold	Coney Island & Brooklyn, adopted by P. S. C., N. Y.
W. P. 50 maintenance cost		Henry Floy	3rd Avenue case, adopted by P. S. C., N. Y.
Trolley 1/0 under 1 minute headway	50	Wis. P. S. C.	
Trolley 2/0 under 1 minute headway	40	Wis. P. S. C.	
Trolley 3/0 under 1 minute headway	33⅓	Wis. P. S. C.	
W. P.	6¼	Wis. P. S. C.	
W. P.	7½	Arbitrators	Street lighting con., Atlanta, Ga. 1899.

Foster, Horatio A. Methods of calculating depreciation. (In his *Engineering valuation of public utilities and factories.* 1913. p. 170, 193).

	Minimum service value, per cent of reproduction cost
Telephone—iron wire	10
copper wire	25

Foster, Horatio A. Rates of depreciation. (In his *Engineering valuation of public utilities and factories.* 1913. p. 200, 203, 205, 206).

Wire	
trolley	5.0
guard	10.0
Spans with ears, etc.	5.0

Marwick, Mitchell & co. in the appraisal of a large street railway system.

	Years
Wire exchange lines	
copper, bare	10-15
copper, insulated tw. pr.	10
iron, bare	8-10
Wire toll lines:	
copper, bare	40
iron, bare	15

DEPRECIATION, DEPLETION AND OBSOLESCENCE—WIRE AND WIRING—*(Continued)*

Copper wire, weatherproof insulation	10-15
Trolley wire; life depends on headway; should never be worn to less than 75% of its original size.	
#0 wire at 1 minute headway life	2
#00 wire at 1 minute headway life	2½
#000 wire at 1 minute headway life	3
Iron wire	8-15
copper wire	20
weather proof iron wire	15
Wisconsin commissions	

GILLETTE, HALBERT P. and RICHARD T. DANA. Depreciation. (In their *Handbook of mechanical and electrical cost data.* 1918. p. 111).

Wires	15-25 years. George W. Cravens, Industrial power plants.
	20 years. Milwaukee electric railway & light co.
	50 years. Chicago traction commission.
Wiring	7.1-10 years. Union traction co., Case Chicago and union traction co., Stone & Webster.
copper	20 years. Wisconsin railroad commission.
guard	10 years. Marwick, Mitchell & co., appraisal of a large street railway system, Foster, p. 199.
	8-15 years. Wisconsin railroad commission.
Telephone aerial exchange bare copper	14 years. Nathan Hayward, The Bell telephone co. of Pennsylvania, Aug. 31, 1912.
Telephone aerial exchange, bare iron	8.5 years. Nathan Hayward, The Bell telephone co. of Pennsylvania, Aug. 31, 1912.
Telephone aerial exchange insulated (including drop wire)	6.5 years. Nathan Hayward, The Bell telephone co. of Pennsylvania, Aug. 31, 1912.
Telephone aerial toll, copper	30 years. Nathan Hayward, The Bell telephone co. of Pennsylvania, Aug. 31, 1912.
Telephone aerial toll, iron	15 years. Nathan Hayward, The Bell telephone co. of Pennsylvania, Aug. 31, 1912.
Telephone interior block	8 years Nathan Hayward, The Bell telephone co. of Pennsylvania, Aug. 31, 1912.
Wire, trolley #0—1 min. headway	2 years. Wisconsin railroad commission.
trolley #00—1 min. headway	2.5 years Wisconsin railroad commission.
trolley #000—1 min. headway	3 years. Wisconsin railroad commission.
trolley	20 years. Marwick, Mitchell & co., appraisal of a large street railway system, Foster, p. 199.
weatherproof	13.3 years. Arbitrators, Street lighting controversy, Atlanta, Ga., 1899.
	16 years. Wisconsin railroad commission.
weatherproof, iron	15 years. Wisconsin railroad commission.

GRAY, HENRY L. Necessity of depreciation reserves. *Railway age gazette,* May 27, 1910, p. 1297-8. Editorial. Depreciation reserves. *Railway age gazette,* May 27, 1910, p. 1290. Letters. Depreciation reserves. *Railway age gazette,* July 8, 1910, p. 66.

Trolley wire	5%

GREENLAND, S. W. Depreciation. *Mississippi electric association, Report of 2nd annual convention,* June 1910, p. 32-6.

Trolley wire	15 years

GRUNSKY, CARL EWALD. Probable useful light of various articles. (In his *Valuation, depreciation and the rate-base.* 1917. p. 286-7).

Wire	
aerial	20 years. St. Louis public service commission. Case of Union electric light & power co.
aerial copper	15 years. Chicago telephone commission. Published 1908.

DEPRECIATION, DEPLETION AND OBSOLESCENCE—WIRE AND WIRING—*(Continued)*

bare	25 years. 35% residual value. Pacific gas & electric company. Figures used in rate hearing before Master in Chancery, San Francisco, 1913-4.
insulated	20 years. 15% residual value. Pacific gas & electric company. Figures used in rate hearing before Master in Chancery, San Francisco, 1913-4.
copper, weatherproof	13 years. Arbitrators. Board of Arbitration in street lighting controversy at Atlanta, Georgia, 1899.
copper, weatherproof	16 years. Wisconsin railroad commission. Quoted by Henry Floy and in published reports.
copper, weatherproof	10-15 years. H. A. Foster. "Engineering valuation of public utilities and factories," Van Nostrand, 1912.
2-kv. distribution	15 years. San Joaquin light & power corporation. Rate hearing before California R. R. commission.
4-kv. distribution	15 years. San Joaquin light & power corporation. Rate hearing before California R. R. commission.
10-kv. distribution	20 years. San Joaquin light & power corporation. Rate hearing before California R. R. commission.
telephone, iron	10 years. 0% residual value. Wisconsin railroad commission. Wisconsin telephone co. case. Aug. 3, 1909.
telephone, iron	8-15 years. Wisconsin railroad commission. Quoted by H. A. Foster and in published reports.
telephone, weatherproof iron	15 years. Wisconsin railroad commission. Quoted by H. A. Foster. Wisconsin telephone co. case. Aug. 3, 1909.
telephone, copper	20 years. 75% residual value. Wisconsin railroad commission. Wisconsin telephone co. case. Aug. 3, 1909.
telephone exch., bare copper	10-15 years. 40% residual value. Telephone "data". Compiled from practice A. T. & T. Co., Wisconsin R. R. commission and others. Quoted by H. A. Foster.
telephone exch., insul. copper	10 years. 10% residual value. Telephone "data". Compiled from practice A. T. & T. Co., Wisconsin R. R. commission and others. Quoted by H. A. Foster.
telephone exch., bare iron	8-10 years. 0% residual value. Telephone "data". Compiled from practice A. T. & T. Co., Wisconsin R. R. commission and others. Quoted by H. A. Foster.
telephone toll, bare copper	40 years. 40% residual value. Telephone "data". Compiled from practice A. T. & T. Co., Wisconsin R. R. commission and others. Quoted by H. A. Foster.
telephone distribution	10 years. 15% residual value. Wisconsin railroad commission. Wisconsin telephone co. case. Aug. 3, 1909.
telephone distribution	15 years. 15% residual value. Wisconsin railroad commission. Wisconsin telephone co. case. Aug. 3, 1909.

GUTHRIE, EDWIN. Depreciation. (In Lisle, George, *Encyclopaedia of accounting.* v.2. p. 374-5).

Electric wires	25-33⅓%	original value

KENT, WILLIAM. Depreciation of shafting, etc. (In his *Bookkeeping and cost accounting for factories.* 1918. p. 91).

LIFE data on power-plant equipment used in valuation of Massachusetts property. *Electrical world,* Dec. 4, 1915, p. 1261.

Telephone wire	15 years
Signal wire	15

MONTGOMERY, ROBERT H. Electrical equipment manufacturers. (In his *Income tax procedure,* 1919, p. 563. ——— Same, 1920. p. 716).

Inside piping and wiring	10%

Based on gross book value at the end of the preceding year.

MONTGOMERY, ROBERT H. Telephone companies. (In his *Auditing theory and practice.* 1916. p. 680-2).

Hard drawn copper wire in toll lines	1.5%
Iron wire in exchange lines	12.5

NEALE, R. E. Depreciation in engineering works. *Mechanical world,* Feb. 7, 1913, p. 67-8.

Trolley wire	33.3-50%	2-3 years

DEPRECIATION, DEPLETION AND OBSOLESCENCE—WIRE AND WIRING—*(Continued)*

NICHOLSON, J. LEE and J. F. D. ROHRBACH. Depreciation. (In their *Cost accounting.* 1919. p. 148, 147).

Electric wiring 5%
Electric light and power wiring:
Departmental wiring net additions 6
Inside wiring 5
Based on (1) the cost of equipment
(2) the life of the equipment
(3) on a ten-hour day

PENDER, HAROLD. Depreciation. (In his *Handbook for electrical engineers.* c1914. p. 340).

	% dep.	
Wires. overhead		7-10 years. Chicago union traction co. Stone & Webster for Chicago union traction co.
		12 years. J. I. Beggs.
	14-10	Chicago union traction co. Stone & Webster for Chicago union traction co.
	10	Milwaukee electric railway & light co.
		8.5 years. J. I. Beggs.
Trolley wire	5	Chicago city railways.

PHILADELPHIA. CONTROLLER. Rates of depreciation. (In his *Manual of accounting, reporting and business procedure of the city and county of Philadelphia.* 1917. p. 205, 210).

Wiring 5%
Wiring and necessary supports (including street lamps, signal systems) 4%

PIEZ, CHARLES. Perpetual inventory and appraisal values; table of standard depreciation rates. *Engineering and contracting,* Jan. 24, 1917, p. 77. *Factory,* Dec. 1916, p. 668-71. *Iron age,* Nov. 30, 1916, Jan. 11, 1917, p. 1266, 138-9. *Iron trade review,* Feb. 22, 1917, p. 477-8. Condensed. *Journal of the American society of mechanical engineers,* Dec. 1916, p. 965-6. *Iron trade review,* Dec. 7, 1916, p. 1144-6. Kent, William. *Bookkeeping and cost accounting for factories,* 1918. p. 90. Discussion. *Journal of the American society of mechanical engineers,* March, 1917, p. 215-7.

	% on cost	% on reducing balance
Switchboards, main wiring and conduit	6	15
Departmental wiring and electric fixtures, net additions	60	

PIXLEY, FRANCIS W. Tramways. (In his *Accountancy.* Ed. 2. p. 218-9).

Overhead wires
The cost of the new wires should, as a rule, be charged to Revenue, but it is the practice to charge all this expenditure in connection with the overhead trolley wires to one account, the rate of depreciation should certainly be from 30 to 60% according to whether the service is a frequent one or the reverse.
Poles and rosettes from 21-25%

PRACTICAL hints on computing telephone depreciation. *Telephony,* April 1, 1911, p. 401-3.

Line wire, copper 2%
Drop wire, and fastenings 8.5
Interior wire and fittings 8

PUBLIC utility reports, annotated. Rochester, Lawyers co-operative publishing co. 1919D. p. 359.

Re Pacific telephone & telegraph co.

	Years	Salvage	Straight line
Company's life table.			
Exchange aerial wire	8	22.3	9.5%
Toll aerial wire	26	22.3	3.0
Commission's life table			
Exchange aerial wire	11	22.3	7.0
Toll aerial wire	26	22.3	3.0

ROBY, J. J. Schedule of plant depreciation. (In his *Treatise on cost accounting as applied to coal mining.* c1913. p. 14-5).

Electric wiring
Trolley and feed wire, wire only
Deduct as salvage before depreciating 50%
Depreciation rate for remainder, fireproof 6
Insulators, switches and bonds
Deduct as salvage before depreciating 10
Depreciation rate for remainder, fireproof 10
Poles and supports 10
Labor on mains 10
Light wires
Deduct as salvage before depreciating 20
Depreciation rate for remainder, fireproof 5
Trolley and feed wire
Deduct as salvage before depreciating 50
Depreciation rate for remainder, fireproof 6

SALIERS, EARL A. Analysis of a hydroelectric plant. (In his *Principles of depreciation.* 1916. p. 34-8).

Cables and heavy wiring 10%

SOME depreciation rates on buildings, machinery, shafting, belting, furniture and apparatus, tools and dies, moulds, lasts, patterns, and drawings used by the Associated mutual fire insurance companies of Boston, Mass., in making appraisal of manufacturing properties. *Utilities magazine,* Jan. 1, 1916, p. 186-7.

Electric wiring wears little and the rigid rules of both local authorities and insurance companies compel its being kept pretty well up to date so that the total depreciation is always light.

DEPRECIATION, DEPLETION AND OBSOLESCENCE—WIRE AND WIRING—*(Continued)*

UNIFORM cost sheet for coal mining companies. *Coal age*, Sept. 19, 1918, p. 545-7.

	% original cost
Copper wire	7

WALSH, T. J. Depreciation on electric light and power plants. *Electric railway journal*, July 13, 1912, p. 60.

Steel tower and bare copper transmission lines	3%
High-tension transmission lines	3
Additional for maintenance	1

WEEKS, H. E. Abstract of paper on depreciation read before annual meeting of Iowa street and interurban railway association, April 1910. *Electric railway journal*, April 30, 1910, p. 782-3.

Trolley wire	14 years

Wire stitchers

DENHAM, ROBERT S. Depreciation. (In his *Manual of cost engineering and estimating for paper box manufacturers.* 1917. p. 249).

Wire stitchers	10%

Woodcuts

See Depreciation, depletion and obsolescence—Electrotypes, woodcuts, etc.

Woodwork

ELBOURNE, EDWARD T. Depreciation rates. (In his *Factory administration and accounts.* 1918. p. 377).

	Prov. dep. %		Years
	Remainder values	10%	5%
Woodworking machinery	6	37	48

GREAT BRITAIN. BOARD OF INLAND REVENUE. Depreciation rates: Abstract. (In its *Income tax; statement respecting allowances for wear and tear and obsolescence of plant and machinery.* 1918. Cd. 9022, p. 4; Cd. 9134, p. 6). *American economic review*, Dec. 1920, p. 51. *Journal of accountancy*, Sept. 1920, p. 195.

Timber merchants, saw millers and manufacturers of timber goods.	
Engines, boilers and main shafting	5%
General saw milling plant and machinery	7½
Traction engines, tractors, motor cars and haulage plant	20
Written down value.	

MONTGOMERY, ROBERT H. Wood-working industry. (In his *Auditing theory and practice.* 1916. p. 418. *Income tax procedure*, 1919, p. 580. ——— Same, 1920, p. 737.

Building	2-3%
Equipment	6

NICHOLSON, J. LEE and J. F. D. ROHRBACH. Depreciation. (In their *Cost accounting.* 1919. p. 150).

Woodworking machinery—including band, jig, and rip saws, dovetailing machines, moulding machines, tenoners, mortisers, sixers, wood-boring machines, wood workers, carvers and moulders, sanding machines, surfacers, swing saws, scroll saws, jointers and wood cut-off saws, embossing press, core box, disc grinders 5%

Based on (1) the cost of equipment
(2) the life of the equipment
(3) on a ten-hour day.

PHILADELPHIA. CONTROLLER. Rates of depreciation. (In his *Manual of accounting, reporting and business procedure of the city and county of Philadelphia.* 1917. p. 205).

Timber working equipment	
Sewing and cutting machinery	10%
Planing machinery	5
Mitreing and tonguing, grooving, etc. machinery	5
Carpenters' and wood carvers' hand tools	10
Carpenters' work benches	10

TIFFANY, H. S. Machinery. (In his *Digest of depreciations.* c1890, p. 12).

First year	12½%
Every year thereafter	10

Wool and worsted

AUSTRALIA. FEDERAL INCOME TAX DEPARTMENT. Depreciation allowance. *Accountant*, Oct. 13, 1917, p. 277-9. *Accounting and commerce*, June 30, 1917, p. 55-7. *Federal accountant*, July 1917, p. 93-8. *Public accountant*, Jan. 30, 1917, p. 145-52.

Woolen manufacturing machinery,	
Scouring carbonising, drying	5%
Willey house and carding	5
Spinning	7½
Weaving	7½
Milling and finishing	7½
Engines, boilers	5
Rolling stock, belting shafting and pulley rope drives	5

Pirns, bobbins, shuttles, loose tools, reeds. Replacements only allowable.

Note—These are based on normal working hours. Increase pro rata for overtime work; overtime being over 48 hours per work.

STOCKWELL, HERBERT GRANT. Depreciation, renewal and replacement accounts; a paper read at the annual meeting held in Denver, Colorado, October 18-22, 1909, the American association of public accountants, p. 43. *American institute of accountants, Yearbook*, 1909, p. 236.

Writers on the subject of factory cost have attempted to set up tables of average depreciation of different kinds of buildings and machinery. One of these estimates that on a worsted mill the annual depreciation charge should be based on the average life of the plant as follows:

Buildings	50 years
Wool-combing machinery	14
Worsted spinning machinery	10
Warping and beaming	13
Weaving " "	20
Scouring and finishing machinery	14
Dyeing machinery	14

DEPRECIATION, DEPLETION AND OBSOLESCENCE—WOOL AND WORSTED—*(Continued)*

TIFFANY, H. S. Woolen mills. (In his *Digest of depreciations*. c1890. p. 11).
Buildings:
brick 2-2½%
frame 3-3½
Based upon the actual life without any repairs.

Wool scourers

AUSTRALIA. FEDERAL INCOME TAX DEPARTMENT. Depreciation allowance. *Accountant*, Oct. 13, 1917, p. 277-9. *Accounting and commerce*, June 30, 1917, p. 55-7. *Federal accountant*, July 1917, p. 93-8. *Public accountant*, Jan. 30, 1917, p. 145-52.
Tanners and wool scourers 5%
Written down value, repairs allowed in addition.

Wrapping machines

DENHAM, ROBERT S. Depreciation. (In his *Manual of cost engineering and estimating for paper box manufacturers*. 1917. p. 249).
S. & S. wrapping machines 12%

Wrecking

PHILADELPHIA. CONTROLLER. Rates of depreciation. (In his *Manual of accounting, reporting and business procedure of the city and county of Philadelphia*. 1917. p. 206, 210).
Equipment for building, repairing and wrecking structures 12½%
Razing structures and removing obstructions 1

Wrenches

PHILADELPHIA. CONTROLLER. Rates of depreciation. (In his *Manual of accounting reporting and business procedure of the city and county of Philadelphia*. 1917. p. 205).
Oil cans, firing tools, wrenches, etc. 16⅔%

X-ray

AUSTRALIA. FEDERAL INCOME TAX DEPARTMENT. Depreciation allowance. *Accountant*, Oct. 13, 1917, p. 277-9. *Accounting and commerce*, June 30, 1917, p. 55-7. *Federal accountant*, July 1917, p. 93-8. *Public accountant*, Jan. 30, 1917, p. 145-52.
X-ray and high frequency current plant 7½%
Written down value, repairs allowed in addition

Yard equipment

NICHOLSON, J. LEE and J. F. D. ROHRBACH. Depreciation. (In their *Cost accounting*. 1919. p. 151).
Yard equipment—industrial or shop 7½%
Based on (1) the cost of equipment
(2) the life of the equipment
(3) on a ten-hour day.

DEPRECIATION estimates report to National association of railway commissioners. *Aera*, March 1913, p. 644.

DEPRECIATION, etc., on electricity supply undertakings. *Electrician*, May 25, June 15, 1906, p. 231, 350.

DEPRECIATION formula of the American soiety of civil engineers. Bauer, John.

DEPRECIATION from a managers point of view. *Stone and Webster public service journal*, Aug. 1907, p. 69.

DEPRECIATION fund in St. Louis. *Electric railway journal*, Mar. 12, 1910, p. 433.

DEPRECIATION funds and loan redemption. *Accountant*, July 2, 1910, p. 4-6.

DEPRECIATION funds in Europe. *Electric railway journal*, May 7, 1904, p. 696. Editorial. May 21, 1904, p. 760.

DEPRECIATION funds of the New York, New Haven and Hartford railroad. *Railway age*, Feb. 1, 1907, p. 133.

DEPRECIATION hearings closed at Boston. *Electric railway journal*, May 23, 1914, p. 1152.

DEPRECIATION—ice industry. *American institute of accountants. Special bulletin*. No. 5, Sept. 1920, p. 5.

DEPRECIATION in appraisals. *Journal of accountancy*, June 1915, p. 458-60.

DEPRECIATION in cast iron pipe. *Municipal engineering*, Sept. 1911, p. 211.

DEPRECIATION in Cleveland. *Street railway journal*, April 27, 1907, p. 743.

DEPRECIATION in electric lighting. *Municipal journal* (London), Jan. 2, 1903, p. 12.

DEPRECIATION in gas works. *Progressive age*, Oct. 15, 1912, p. 870-2.

DEPRECIATION in its relation to appraisals. *Electrical world*, Oct. 6, 1910, p. 796.

DEPRECIATION in motor cars. *Literary digest*, Sept. 27, 1913, p. 531.

DEPRECIATION in municipal lighting plants. *Electrical review*, Oct. 3, 1908, p. 493.

DEPRECIATION in municipalities. *Accountant*, March 11, 1905, p. 291-2.

DEPRECIATION in public utilities. *Electrical world*, Oct. 2, 1915, p. 743.

DEPRECIATION in public utilities. Kurtz, Wade. 1919.

DEPRECIATION in railway accounting. Calvert, J. F. 1908.

DEPRECIATION in railway accounting. *Railway age*, May 10, 1907, May 1, 1908, p. 728, 623.

DEPRECIATION in steam railway accounting. *Electric railway journal*, Oct. 3, 1908, p. 748.

DEPRECIATION in telephone utilities. Kurtz, Wade.

DEPRECIATION in the retail shoe business. Harvard university. Graduate school of business administration. Bureau of business research. 1915.

DEPRECIATION in theory and practice. Saliers, Earl Adolphus. 1917.

DEPRECIATION in valuations. Saliers, E. A.

DEPRECIATION in value of horses. *Engineering and contracting,* Oct. 17, 1917, p. 319-20.

DEPRECIATION, intangible values and rates. Lawton, W. H.

DEPRECIATION, interest and manufacturing cost. Wright, W. C.

DEPRECIATION: interesting report from Cardiff. *Municipal journal* (London), Dec. 20 1907, p. 1083.

DEPRECIATION: law and practice—recent telephone arbitration; from the Western daily mail. *Accountant,* March 15, 1913, p 415-8.

DEPRECIATION of air-breaking equipments. *Electric railway journal,* March 30, 1912, p. 505.

DEPRECIATION of assets of electric lighting companies. *Accountant,* Nov. 12, 1898, March 8, 1902, p. 1083-4. p. 246-8.

DEPRECIATION of buildings in relation to the income tax law. *National real estate journal,* Oct. 15, 1914, p. 309-14.

DEPRECIATION of Cardiff electric tramway and lighting undertakings. *Electric railway review,* Jan. 4, 1908, p. 16.

DEPRECIATION of Cardiff properties. *Electric railway journal,* Sept. 10, 1910, p. 409.

DEPRECIATION of companies' assets. *Electrician,* May 10, 1907, p. 146.

DEPRECIATION of controlled plant. *Engineer,* Nov. 10, 1916, p. 419-20.

DEPRECIATION of electric plant—Kansas public utilities commission, Report, 1913, p. 53.

DEPRECIATION of electric railway equipment. *Electric traction weekly.* July 17, 1907, p. 736.

DEPRECIATION of electric railways. *Electrical review and western electrician,* July 3, 1909, p. 1. *Wisconsin railroad commission, Report,* 1913, v.10, p. 215-40.

DEPRECIATION of equipment. *Engineering and contracting,* Nov. 19, 1913, p. 567-8.

DEPRECIATION of equipment accounts. *Electric railway journal,* July 4, 1908, p. 193.

DEPRECIATION of factories, mines and industrial undertakings and their valuation. Matheson, Ewing.

DEPRECIATION of fixed assets in the accounts of gold mining companies. *South African accountant,* March 1918, p. 139-40.

DEPRECIATION of gilt-edged securities. Spicer, Ernest Evan. 1913.

DEPRECIATION of gold. *Electrical review and western electrician,* Sept. 27, 1913, p. 601.

DEPRECIATION of leaseholds and income tax. *Accountant,* Oct. 9, 1909, p. 433-6.

DEPRECIATION of lighting and telephone plants. *Electrical world and engineer,* July 27, 1901.

DEPRECIATION of machine tools; abstract. *Industrial engineering,* Oct. 1914, p. 409.

DEPRECIATION of machinery. *Engineer,* Mar. 8, 1918, p. 211.

DEPRECIATION of machinery. *Home study,* July 1906.

DEPRECIATION of machinery in respect of income tax. *Accountants' magazine,* May 1900, p. 259-60.

DEPRECIATION of manufacturing plants. Colley, F. G.

DEPRECIATION of municipal lighting plants. *Electrical review and western electrician,* Oct. 3, 1908, p. 493.

DEPRECIATION of municipal undertakings. *Incorporated accountants' journal,* 1900-1, p. 183.

DEPRECIATION of office buildings. *Engineering and contracting,* Dec. 25, 1918, p. 588.

DEPRECIATION of overhead structures and substations. *Engineering and contracting,* Nov. 19, 1913, p. 567.

DEPRECIATION of plant. *Times engineering supplement,* Jan. 26, 1917.

DEPRECIATION of plant and fair rates for public service. *Engineering record,* Feb. 20, 1909, p. 197-8.

DEPRECIATION of plant and machinery. *Accountant,* Nov. 14, 21, 1908, p. 576-8, 602-4.

DEPRECIATION of prime movers. *Electrical review and western electrician,* April 3, 1909, p. 601.

DEPRECIATION of printing machinery. *Incorporated accountants' journal,* Sept. 1911, p. 311

DEPRECIATION of public utilities. *Canadian chartered accountant,* Oct. 1913, p. 112-3.

DEPRECIATION of public utilities. *Journal of accountancy,* June 1914, p. 437-8.

DEPRECIATION of public utilities. *Municipal journal and engineer,* Feb. 13, 1907, p. 148.

DEPRECIATION of public utilities properties. *Electric railway journal,* Feb. 1, 1908, p. 169. Editorial. Depreciation. *Electric railway journal,* Jan. 25, 1908, p. 104.

DEPRECIATION of sailing ships. *Accountant,* Jan. 1, 1916, p. 10.

DEPRECIATION of ships. *Accountant,* Aug. 10, 1918, p. 73-5.

DEPRECIATION of steam plant. *Electric railway review,* March 31, 1908, p. 360.

DEPRECIATION of stock-in-trade; its effect on manager's commission. *Accounting and commerce,* April 1915, p. 9-10.

DEPRECIATION of the equipment of an electric plant. *Electrical world,* Dec. 12, 1914, p. 1161.

DEPRECIATION of tramways. *Accountant,* April 29, May 6, July 29, 1893, p. 392-5, 410-2, 671-2.

DEPRECIATION of tramways and light railways. *Light railway and tramway journal* (London), Aug. 6, 1909, p. 80.

DEPRECIATION of underground conduits, cables and wires. *Electric railway journal,* May 8, 1909, p. 881.

DEPRECIATION of unprotected steel work. *Iron age,* Feb. 2, 1911, p. 306.

DEPRECIATION of works and machinery. Sherley-Price, Henry. 1909.

DEPRECIATION on printing plant. *Accountant,* June 27, 1885

DEPRECIATION; open discussion. *Utilities magazine,* Jan. 1, 1916, p. 132-6.

DEPRECIATION plan of the valuation committee of the American society of civil engineers. *Engineering news,* Feb. 12, 1914, p. 350-2.

DEPRECIATION policy and true cost. Jackson, J. H.

DEPRECIATION rates. *Journal of accountancy,* Sept. 1920, p. 190-7.

DEPRECIATION rates used by the Fairbanks company. *Annalist,* Sept. 1, 1919, p. 271.

DEPRECIATION rates used by the Seattle (Wash.) municipal street railway. *Electric railway journal,* June 24, 1916, p. 1185.

DEPRECIATION, renewal and replacement accounts. Stockwell, H. G.

DEPRECIATION reserve. *Municipal journal and engineer,* Nov. 24, 1909, p. 772-3.

DEPRECIATION reserve and the people. *Public service,* July 1908, p. 2.

DEPRECIATION reserves. *Railway age gazette,* May 27, 1910, p. 1290.

DEPRECIATION reserves. *Railway age gazette,* July 8, 1910, p. 66.

DEPRECIATION, reserves and reserve funds. Dicksee, Lawrence R.

DEPRECIATION, reserves and rising prices. Rastall, Ernest S.

DEPRECIATION reserves of the Milwaukee and St. Louis railways. *Electric railway review,* Mar. 9, 1907, p. 319.

DEPRECIATION reserves vs. depreciation fund. Saliers, E. A.

DEPRECIATION, some thoughts on policy and practice. *Municipal journal* (London), Aug. 28, 1903, p. 773.

DEPRECIATION tables. Montgomery, H. H. 1908.

DEPRECIATION used for uniform accounts. *Public service,* May 1907, p. 147.

DEPRECIATION value as a basis for rate making; a review of the supreme court decision and some suggestions as to estimating accrued depreciation. *Engineering and contracting,* July 16, 1913, p. 58.

DEPRECIATION with special reference to assessment of income. *Accountants' magazine,* Jan. 1899, p. 13-4.

DEPRECIATION written off by the Royal mail packet company. *Economist,* May 16, 1914, p. 1121.

DEPRECIATION written off by the White star line. *Economist,* May 16, 1914, p. 1121.

DERBY, L.

Report of committee on municipal accounting. *American municipalities,* Jan. 1913, p. 101-3.

DERBY, RODNEY

Simple system of foundry accounting. *Iron age,* Sept. 20, 1917, p. 682-3.

DE RIGGLES, A. E.

How one cattle company figures its cost. *Breeder's gazette,* April 20, 1916, p. 866.

DE ROODE, A.

Revised pension plan; funding provision upon actuarial calculations for each employee over and above present wage due upon separation from service. *Engineering magazine,* Aug. 1913, p. 728-30.

DERR, H. W.

Routine necessary for granting service. *Electrical world,* Nov. 10, 1917, p. 914-5.

DE RUSSETT, HENRY

Treatment of exchange in Indian accounts. *Incorporated accountants journal,* 1899-1900, p. 7.

——— AND OTHERS

Limited companies and private partnerships. *Incorporated accountants' journal.* 1903-4. p. 117.

DERVOE, WERNER

See Burt v. Dervoe.

DESBOROUGH, W. Office labor-saving machinery and appliances. *Business organisation and management,* Oct. 1919-Feb. 1920, p. 75-80, 93-8, 73-8, 71-6, 79-87.

Tabulating machinery. *Business organisation and management,* June 1920, p. 255-63.

DESCRIPTION and illustrations of a uniform system of accounts designed for the use of private charitable institutions receiving money from the city of New York. Patterson, Teele & Dennis.

DESCRIPTION of the Youngstown sheet and tube company's profit-sharing plan. *Iron trade review,* Aug. 17, 1911, p. 278.

DESEURE, F.

L'impot sur les benefices de guerre; qui doit le payer? Quel en est le montant? Quand faut -il le payer; formalitiés; renseignements divers. Bruxelles, Ferdinand Larcier, 1920, 138p.

DESIGN, construction and detailed costs of the McKinley Ford bridge, La Salle county, Ill. *Engineering and contracting,* Feb. 24, 1915, p. 179-82.

DESIGN, construction and unit costs of the power house for the new smelter of the Arizona copper co., ltd., Clifton, Arizona. *Engineering and contracting,* Sept. 16, 1914, p. 262-5.

DESIGN of railway location. Williams, Clement Clarence. 1917.

DESIGNING of accounting systems. Staub, E. E.

DES MOINES gas company case. *Electrical review and western electrician,* Aug. 21, 1915, p. 329-30.

DES MOINES value fixed; appraisers for city report that fare of 5¾ cents would yield 7 per cent return. *Electric railway journal,* Nov. 20, 1920, p. 1079.

DESPARD, W. P.
Capital in the installment business. *Business man's magazine,* March 1905, p. 523-5.

DESPARD, WALTER H.
Accounting methods for a copper-nickel mine, *Business man's magazine,* 1906, v.18, no. 7, p. 60-3.

DETAIL and description of the new system of accounting for expenditures made operative January 1, 1909. New York city. Department of finance. 1909.

DETAIL cash book and journal. *Commerce, accounts and finance,* April 1902, p. 12-4.

DETAILED cost of a recntly completed concrete road near Aurora, Illinois. *Engineering and contracting,* September 23, 1914, p. 304.

DETAILED cost of bituminous surface treatment work at Philadelphia. *Engineering and contracting,* July 4, 1917, p. 11.

DETAILED cost of bituminous surface treatment work at Philadelphia. *Engineering and contracting,* Dec. 6, 1916, p. 503-4.

DETAILED cost of gravel road maintenance. *Engineering and contracting,* Dec. 6, 1916, p. 504.

DETAILED cost of 13,000-volt line. *Electrical world,* Jan. 15, 1916, p. 155.

DETAILED costs upon 100 samples of cotton cloth presented at the tariff board hearing on the cotton schedule. *Journal of commerce,* May 15, 1912, p. 13-4.

DETAILED description of the new system of accounting for expenditure made operative. Jan. 1, 1909. New York city. Department of finance.

DETAILED statement of the proposed contents of the revised annual report forms for steam railroads for 1918. *Railway age,* Nov. 1, 1918, p. 774-6.

DETAILS of Baltimore's gas rate schedules. *American gas light journal,* Feb. 28, 1916, p. 138-40.

DETAILS of costs at El Tigre *Engineering and mining journal,* Dec. 12, 1914, p. 1047.

DETAILS of Harvester stock distribution. *Iron age,* Sept. 2, 1920, p. 576-7.

DETAILS of practical mining, compiled from the Engineering and mining journal by the editorial staff. New York, McGraw-Hill book company, c1916. 544p. (Mining library, v.5).

DETECTION of fraud—by manipulation of the adding machine slips bank examiners were fooled. *Commercial and financial chronicle,* July 23, 1910, p. 192.

DETECTION of frauds. Benington, Harold. c1917.

DETENTION of books; an accountants' lien. *Incorporated accountants' journal,* March 1914, p. 165.

DETERIORATION in heating value of coal storage. *Power,* Jan. 15, 1918, p. 101-2.

DETERMINATION of cost. *Journal of accountancy,* Sept 1917, p. 215-22.

DETERMINATION of farming costs. Orwin, C. S. 1917.

DETERMINATION of income rates on unusual serial bonds. Thomas, E. S.

DETERMINATION of selling price. Hilton, E. D.

DETERMINATION of the "fair rate of return" on the value of the property of the Madison gas and electric co., two theories of rate making. *Engineering and contracting,* June 21, 1911, p 726.

DETERMINATION of the income rate of investment. Kribben, D. D.

DETERMINATION of the net profits of the Panama Canal. Oakey, Francis.

DETERMINATION of the proper basis for rates and fares. *Electric railway journal,* Dec. 2, 1911, p. 1154-63.

DETERMINING a proper basis for rates and and fares. *Electric railway journal,* Feb. 1, 1913, p. 184.

DETERMINING average fuel costs in combination coal and oil. *Electrical world,* Sept. 25, 1920, p. 640.

DETERMINING costs of manufacturing and selling. *Textile manufacturers,* Oct. 15, 1916, p. 314.

DETERMINING costs of manufacturing and selling. *Textile world,* Aug. 19, 1916, p. 3639.

DETERMINING operation costs. *Factory,* Feb. 1917, p. 240.

DETROIT. BOARD OF EDUCATION
Inventory and audit of the board. Oct. 20, 1917. 199-203p.

DETROIT appraisal. *Electric railway journal,* Aug. 20, 1910, p. 304.

DETROIT Edison changes to bi-monthly billing. *Electrical world,* July 14, 1917, p. 68.

DETROIT production costs at Connors Creek station. *Electrical world,* Sept. 20, 1919, p. 656.

DETROIT SCHOOL OF ACCOUNTS AND COMMERCE.
Book-keeping. 6v. in 1. Detroit, Mich., F. W. Morton. 1914. 96p.

DETROIT united railway files bill of particulars in arbitration, placing reproduction value of property at $24,676,181.75. *Electric railway journal,* April 30, 1910, p. 796.

DEUCHAR, DAVID
Fire insurance. (In Lisle, George. *Encyclopaedia of accounting.* v.3. p. 26-41).
Life assurance. (In Lisle, George. *Encyclopaedia of accounting.* v.4. p. 119-51).

DEUTMAN, E. G.
Roasting and magnetic separation of Wisconsin zinc ores; with cost table. *Engineering and mining journal,* June 28, 1919, p. 1107-11.

DEVELOPMENT and status of the rate raise case. *New Jersey municipalities,* May 1918, p. 133-4.

DEVELOPMENT charges. *Electric railway journal* Sept. 18, 1915, p. 576-7.

DEVELOPMENT COMPANIES
See Real estate.

DEVELOPMENT cost or "going value" of public service companies. *Engineering and contracting,* June 26, July 17, 1912.

DEVELOPMENT of mercantile instruments of credit in the United States. Klein, J. J.

DEVELOPMENT of systems of control. Steele, F. R. C.

DEVELOPMENT of the freight rate hearing regarding the physical valuation of railways. *Engineering and contracting,* Sept. 28, 1910, p. 263.

DEVELOPMENTS in connection with federal valuation. *Railway review,* Nov. 13, 1915, p. 633.

DEVELOPMENTS in federal valuation of the railroads. *Railway review,* March 18, 1916, p. 391-3.

DEVELOPMENTS in railway valuation. *Railway review,* August 1, September 5, 1914, May 15, 1915, Oct. 6, 1917, p. 135-8, 299-300, 653, 429.

DEVELOPMENTS in valuation. *Railway review,* Nov. 18, Dec. 16, 1916, p. 701-3, 818-9, 818-9.

DEVEREUX, H.
Methods and cost in driving the Pine Mountain tunnel. *Engineering and contracting,* Aug. 15, 1917, p. 137-8.

DEVEREUX, W.
System of keeping records of current work in electrical inspection department. *Electrical review and western electrician,* Dec. 18-25, 1915, p. 1122, 1156.

DEVLIN, JOHN H.
Accounting for proprietary preparations. *Journal of accountancy,* July 1920, p. 36-42.

DEVLIN, T.
Why castings cost more. *Foundry,* Feb. 1, 1920, p. 116.

DEWATERING Cobalt lake. *Engineering and mining journal,* Sept. 23, 1916, p. 560.

DEWEY, DAVIS RICH
Financial history of the United States. Ed. 6. New York, Longmans, Green & co. 1918. 550p.

DEWHIRST, JOHN MARK
Elements of bookkeeping, class instruction. Galesburg, Wagoner printing co. 1910.

DEWHURST, M.
Something better than philanthropy profit sharing scheme of the Dennison manufacturing company. *Outlook,* Sept. 1, 1915, p. 48-51.

DEWING, ARTHUR STONE
Corporate promotions and reorganizations. Cambridge, Harvard university press, 1914. 615p. (Harvard economic studies, v.10).
Financial policy of corporations. 5v. New York, The Ronald press company, 1920. Contents: v.1 Corporate securities; v.2 Promotion; v.3 Administration of income; v.4 Expansion; v.5 Failure and reorganization.

DE WOLF, R. D.
Combination rates for steam heating and electric service. *Electrical world,* July 1, 1911, p. 45.
Electric central-station rates. *Engineering magazine,* March 1914, p. 959-61.

DEWSNUP, ERNEST RITSON
Necessity of care in the interpretation of railway statistics used comparatively. *Railway age gazette,* May 13, 1910.
Railway organization and working—a series of lectures delivered before the railway classes of the University of Chicago. Chicago, 1906. 487p.
Railway rate theory and practice in the light of Ripley's railroads. *Political science quarterly,* Sept. 1915, p. 476-509.

DEXTER, EDWARD
Some remarks on the verification of the items in a balance sheet. *Accountant,* March 28, April 4, 1903, p. 433-40, 454-6.

DEZOUCHE, R. C.
Acquisition of a business by a limited company. *Accountant,* April 23, 1910, p. 571-6.
Analysis of trading results with reference to departments. *Accountants' magazine,* May 1908, p. 266.
Miscellaneous points regarding trust estates. *Accountant,* June 21, 1913, p. 939-46.
Partnership losses. *Accountant,* June 20, 1914, p. 889-94.
Private companies and limited partnerships. *Accountant,* March 4, 1911, p. 339-45.
Shipping accounts. *Accountant,* June 21, 1913, p. 947-8.
See also Dawson, Sidney Stanley, joint author.

DIAGRAMMATIC presentment of the accounts of local authorities. Allen, S. E. 1912.

DIAGRAMS for cost of ties. Canadian Pacific railway. *Engineering news,* Aug. 12, 1915, p. 292.

DIAGRAMS showing the need for higher fares. *Electric railway journal,* Jan. 26, 1918, p. 187-8.

DICK, J. R.
Economics of works costs. *Electrician,* Nov. 29, 1918, p. 643-5.

DICKENS, CHARLES A.
Motor truck operation and accounting. *Municipal engineering,* Aug., Oct. 1915—Sept, Nov. 1917—Jan. June, Sept.—Oct. Dec. 1918, Feb.-Aug. 1919, p. 46-9, 130-6, sup. 25, sup 23+, sup 23+, sup 23+, sup. 23+ sup. 23+, sup 23+, sup. 23+. 51: sup. 23+, sup. 23+, sup. 23+, sup. 23+, sup. 23+, sup. 23+, 52: sup. 49+, sup. 83+, sup. 145+, sup. 213+, sup. 277+, sup. 223+; 53: sup. 21+, sup. 21+, sup. 21+, sup. 27+, sup. 27+, sup. 27+; 54: sup. 15+; 55; sup. 13+, sup. 13+, 56; sup. 12+, sup. 12+, sup. 20, sup. 20, sup. 20, sup. 20, 57; sup. 18+, sup. 18+.

DICKENS, O. T., T. S. GRANT, AND K. R. MITCHELL
Decreasing engine terminal delay; prize essays. *Railway mechanical engineer,* Dec. 1917, p. 697-701.

DICKERMAN, J. C.

Comparison of electric light and power rates. *Power,* July 6, 1915, p. 8-15.

Cost of producing illuminating gas in American cities exclusive of returns to capital invested. *Utilities magazine,* July 1915, p. 10-2.

Cost of supplying illuminating gas in the smaller American cities, exclusive of returns to capital invested. *Utilities magazine,* Nov. 1915, p. 19-23.

Lower electric rates in Philadelphia. *American city,* April 1916, p. 341-2.

DICKEY, E. D. V.

Solicitors and house record cards—methods of checking. *American gas light journal,* May 8, 1916, p. 294-5

DICKIE, JAMES M.

Costing and general management in mining. *Accountant,* June 8, 1907, p. 791-4.

Duties of the public accountant. *Business world,* April 1902, p. 169-70.

Economic aspect of cost accounts and its application to the accounting of industrial companies. *Journal of accountancy,* March 1911, p. 325-339. *American economic association, Bulletin.* April 1911. p. 110-23.

Fallacy of including interest and rent as part of manufacturing cost. *Journal of accountancy,* Dec. 1911, Aug. 1913, p. 588-93, 89-98.

DICKINSON, ARTHUR LOWES

Accounting practice and procedure. New York. The Ronald press co. 1917. 315p.

Accountancy practice and procedure. (In *Cyclopedia of commerce, accountancy, business administration.* 1910. v.7. p. 239-80).

Accounting practice and procedure; a paper to be presented at the annual meeting of the American association of public accountants, Atlantic City, New Jersey, October 20-23, 1908. 47p. *American institute of accountants, Yearbook.* 1908, p. 188-254. *Accountant,* Dec. 12, 1908, p. 740-58. *Incorporated accountants' journal,* 1908-9, p. 51. *Journal of accountancy,* Oct.-Dec. 1908, p. 415-25; 7-18, 96-110.

Economic aspect of cost accounts and its application to the accounting of industrial companies. *Journal of accountancy,* March, 1911, p. 325

Duties and responsibilities of the public accountant with regard to new issues of stocks and bonds. *Journal of accountancy,* Nov. 1905, p. 16-27.

Duties and responsibilities of the public accountants. *Accountant,* July 26, 1902. p. 745-51. *Commerce, accounts and finance,* April 1902, p. 23-7.

Fallacy of including interest and rent as part of manufacturing cost. *Journal of accountancy,* Dec. 1911, Aug. 1913, p. 588-93, 89-98.

Interest and sinking funds. *Accountant,* Oct. 10, 1891, p. 715-20.

Life assurance accounts. *Accountant,* 1887, p. 455, 464.

Notes on some problems relating to the accounts of holding companies. *Accountant,* May 19, 1906, p. 647-9. *Journal of accountancy,* April 1906, p. 487-91.

Profession of the public accountant. *Accountant,* May 27, 1905, p. 650-8. *Auditor,* 1905, p. 165, 185.

Profits of a corporation. (In *Cyclopedia of commerce, accountancy, business administration,* 1910, v.6, p. 255-97).

Profits of a corporation; with discussion. *Federation of societies of public accountants in the United States of America, Official record of the Congress of accountants held at the World's fair, Saint Louis, September 26th, 27th and 28th, 1904,* p. 171-203. *Accountant,* Oct. 22, 1904, p. 442-53. *Incorporated accountants journal,* 1904-5, p. 34.

Relation between the accountant and the banker. *Journal of accountancy,* May 1909, p. 55-7.

Some special points in accountancy practice. *Accountant,* April 22, 1905, p. 495-504. *Auditor,* 1905, p. 105, 130, 158.

Some special points in corporation accounting. *Accountant,* Oct. 7, 1905, p. 402-10.

Special points in accountancy practice. *Business world,* April, May 1905, p. 157-61, 233-6.

DICKINSON, R.

Management and employees work out plan of factory conduct. *Printers ink,* Jan. 29, 1920, p. 130.

New business conscience in good business. Printers ink, July 15, 1920, p. 109-10.

DICKINSON, WALTER SIGISMUND

Accounts of a public gas company. *Accountant,* April 12, May 10, 1902, p. 386-96, 491-2.

Articles of association of a limited company. *Accountant,* April 25, 1903, p. 551-6.

Deeds of arrangement. *Accountant,* March 28, 1903, p. 441-7.

Executorship accounts. *Accountant,* March 22, April 12, 1902, p. 313-8, 374-6.

Executorship accounts. *Accountant,* May 23, 1903, p. 696-702.

Method and arrangement in accounts. *Accountant,* Feb. 15, 1902, p. 188-94.

Preparation and study for the institute examinations. *Accountant,* April 30, 1910, p. 606-12.

Property of a bankrupt. *Accountant,* March 7, 1903, p. 334-9.

Vouchers. *Accountant,* Dec. 28, 1901, Jan. 1911, p. 1410-4, 33-5.

DICKINSON, WILMOT AND STERRETT

Uniform classification of accounts and reports for hospitals. St. Louis, Dickinson, Wilmot & Sterrett, 1908.

DICKSEE, LAWRENCE ROBERT

A B C of bookkeeping. London, Longmans-Green & co. 1908.

Accountant on depreciation. *American gas light journal.* May 20, 1907, p. 847. *Journal of gas lighting,* April 16, 1907, p. 175.

Address: annual dinner. 1904. *Accountant,* Nov. 19 1904, p. 626-31.

Advanced accounting: with an appendix on the law relating to accounts by J. E. G. de Montmorency. Ed. 4. London, Gee & co. 1911. 520p.

——— Same. Ed. 5. London, Gee & co. 1916. 571p.

Auctioneers' accounts. London, Gee & co. 1901. 79p. (Accountants' library, v.2).

Auctioneers' accounts. (In Lisle, George. *Encyclopaedia of accounting.* v.1. p. 157-63).

Auditing. (In Lisle, George. *Encyclopaedia of accounting.* v.1. p. 163-93).

Auditing; a practical manual for auditors. Ed.2, revised and enlarged. London, Gee & co. 1895. 579p.

——— Same. Ed.10. London, Gee & co. 1915. 975p.

Auditing; a practical manual for auditors; ed. by Robert H. Montgomery. Authorized American edition. New York, R. H. Montgomery, 1909. 385p.

——— Same. Authorized American edition, revised and enlarged. New York, The Ronald press co. 1909. 586p.

Auditing, with special reference to the accounts of local authorities. *Accountant,* Aug. 13, 1910, p. 201-5.

Bookkeeping. London, Gee & co.

DICKSEE, LAWRENCE ROBERT—*(Continued)*
Bookkeeping for accountant students. 3v. London, Gee & co. 1893.
——— Same. Ed.3. London, 1910. 99p.
——— Same. Ed.7. London, Gee & co. 1914. 300p.
Bookkeeping exercises for accountant students. Ed.3. London, Gee & co. 1910. 99p.
Bookkeeping for company secretaries. Ed.4. London, Gee & co. 1908. 184p.
Bookkeeping: its adaptability to the requirements of every class of undertaking. (In Lisle, George. *Encyclopaedia of accounting,* v.1. p. 496-501).
Bookkeeping—with special reference to joint stock companies. *Accountant,* Jan. 23, Feb. 13-27, March 27, April 10, 1897, p. 116-9, 182-92, 210-4, 235-40, 339-44, 397-401.
Business methods and the war. *Accountant,* Jan. 30-Feb. 20, 1915, p. 161-8, 200-5, 226-32, 261-8.
Business organization. New York, Longmans, Green & co. 1910. 283p.
Business organisation, with special reference to fraud. *Accountant,* Dec. 2, 9, 1911, p. 761-7, 802-8. *Incorporated accountants' journal,* 1910-11, p. 203, 238.
Comparative depreciation tables. Ed.2. London, Gee & co. 1909. 25p.
Cost accounts suitable to jobbing tradesmen. (In Lisle, George. *Encyclopaedia of accounting.* v.2. p. 252-8).
Depreciation. *Municipal journal* (London), April 19, 26, 1907, p. 323, 355.
Depreciation, reserves, and reserve funds. Ed.3. London, Gee & co. 1912. 80p. (Accountants' library, v. 26).
Depreciation: with special reference to the accounts of local authorities. *Accountant,* April 13, June 1, 1907, p. 482-92, 733-5.
Efficient administration; a prime essential to Britain's economic recovery. *Accountant,* Oct. 30, 1920, p. 479-81.
Foreign currencies and the accounts of foreign branches. *Accountant,* Feb. 27, 1904, p. 281-91.
Forms of accounts and balance sheets. *Accountant,* Nov. 11, 18, 1893, p. 954-9, 973-81.
Fundamentals of manufacturing costs. London, Gee & co. 1917. 42p. *Accountant,* Sept. 1-15, 1917, p. 160-1, 175-6, 196-8.
Hotel accounts. London, Gee & co. 905. 76p. (Accountants' library, v.37).
Hotel accounts. *Accountant,* Dec. 21, 1912, p. 795.
Importance of accurate and adequate accounting. *Accountant,* Feb. 4, 1905, p. 146-51.
Investigations: their object and extent. *Accountant,* March 11, 1893, p. 228-34.
Liabilities of auditors under the companies acts. *Accountant,* May 14, 1898, p. 500-11, 597.
Local authorities and depreciation. *Journal of gas lighting,* April 16, 1907, p. 144. *Electrical review* (London), April 26, 1907, p. 665.
Loose-leaf systems. *Accountant,* Nov. 11, 1911, p. 652-6. *Incorporated accountants journal,* 1910-11, p. 198.
Machinery as an aid to accountancy. London. Gee & co. 1916. 19p. *Accountant,* June 10, 1916, p. 660-6. *South African accountant and auditor,* June, Sept. Dec. 1916, p. 173-4, 225-7.
Mine accounting and management. London, Gee & co. 1914. 100p.
Modern accountancy methods in relation to business efficiency. *Accountant,* Nov. 14, 1914, p. 581-6.
Nature and limitations of accounts. *Accountant,* April 4, 1903, p. 469-74.
Office machinery and appliances; a handbook for office managers. Ed.2. London, Gee & co. 1918. 154p.
Profits available for dividend. (In *Four lectures delivered to the Institute of chartered accountants in England and Wales during the years 1894 and 1895.)*
Publishing balance sheets and accounts. *Accountant,* Nov. 20, 1920, p. 561-4.
Secretary. (In Lisle, George. *Encyclopaedia of accounting.* v.6. p. 36-62).
Solicitors' accounts. London, Gee & co. 1902. 84p. (Accountants' library, v. 12).
Some suggestions on stock, accounts and stock-keeping. *Accountant,* May 3, 1913, p. 668-73.
Student's guide to accountancy. London, Gee & co. 1897.
——— Same. Ed. 2. London, Gee & co. 1907. 48p.

——— **AND H. E. BLAIN**
Office organization and management. Ed.4. London, Pitman & sons, 1917. 306p.

——— **AND FRANK TILLYARD**
Goodwill and its treatment in accounts. Ed.3. London, Gee & co. 1906. 168p. *Accountant,* Jan. 9, 1897, p. 40-8.

DICKSON, N.
Books of bookkeeping. London, Longmans, Green & co. 1863.

DICKSON, W. B.
Results of employee representation plan when tested by steel strike. *Mining and metallurgy,* Oct. 1920, p. 17-8.

DICTIONARIES
Cassell's new French dictionary, French-English and English-French. New York, Funk & Wagnalls co. c1903. 616p.
Century dictionary; an encyclopedic lexicon of the English language. New York, Century co. c1914.
Funk & Wagnall's new standard dictionary of the English language. Complete in one volume. New York, Funk & Wagnalls co. 1913. 2916p.
Graham, James and George A. S. Oliver. Foreign traders' dictionary of terms and phrases in English, German, French and Spanish. London, Macmillan and co. 1906. 283p.
Lyons, Daniel. American dictionary of the English language. New York, P. F. Collier & son, c1908. 1016p.
Macdonald, George Robert. Spanish-English and English-Spanish commercial dictionary of the words and terms used in commercial correspondence which are not given in the dictionaries in ordinary use; compound phrases, idiomatic and technical expressions, etc. Philadelphia, David McKay, 644p.

DICTIONARY of bookkeeping. Bickerstaff, H. 1890.

DICTIONARY of English synonyms and synonymous or parallel expressions. Soulé, Richard. 1913.

DIEMER, HUGO
Aids in taking machine shop inventory. *Engineering magazine,* February 1902, p. 747-52.
Cost finding methods for moderate sized shops. *Engineering magazine,* v.24. p. 577-89.
Cost-finding methods under the premium wage system. *Engineering magazine,* v.24, p. 577.
Factory organization and administration. Ed. 2. New York, McGraw-Hill book co. 1914. 378p.
Handling shop orders. *Factory,* May 1918, p. 934.
Industrial management. *Journal of accountancy,* April 1912, p. 272-8.
Industrial organization and management. Chicago, La Salle extension university, 1917. 291p.
Manufacturing organization. Chicago, La Salle extension university, 1917. 18p.

DIES

Cost accounting

ARNOLD, HORACE LUCIEN. Wells brothers company, of Greenfield, Massachusetts. (In his *Factory manager and accountant.* 1903. p. 274-316).

Costs

HERDEGEN, R. T. Die cost as a factor in selling forgings. *American machinist,* July 10, 1919, p. 87-8.

DIESEL engined flour mill. *Power,* Aug. 31, 1920, p. 326.

DIFFERENCES in cost of refuse collection. *Municipal journal,* December 2, 1915, 845-6.

DIFFERENCES of opinion. *Journal of accountancy,* March 1920, p. 214.

DIFFERENTIAL rate schedule increases annual gas consumption by industrial consumers in Baltimore, 55,578,700 cu. ft. *American gas light journal,* Sept. 4, 1916, p. 156-7.

DIFFERING opinions should find expression. *Journal of accountancy,* April 1912, p. 287-9.

DIFFICULT point in the railway valuation law. *Engineering news,* Oct. 23, 1913, p. 829-30.

DIFFICULTIES of farm cost accounting. *Progressive farmer,* Dec. 14, 1918, p. 1363.

DIFFICULTY of valuation. Electric railway *journal,* Oct. 17, 1914, p. 924.

DIGEST of depreciations. Tiffany, H. S. c1890.

DIGEST of plan of reorganization, dated May 16, 1911, Pennsylvannia coal and coke company. *Commercial and financial chronicle,* May 27, 1911, p. 1439.

DIGEST of plan of reorganization, Robert MacKinnon and co., manufacturers of underwear Little Falls, New York. *Chronicle,* July 1, 1911, p. 50.

DIGEST of President Taft's message sent to congress, January 17, 1912, transmitting the first report of his committee on federal efficiency and economy. *Journal of political economy,* Mar. 1912, p. 282-3.

DIGEST of state laws relating to uniform accounting. North Dakota. Tax commission. 1912.

DIGEST of the Federal farm loan act (rural credits bill). Guaranty trust company of New York.

DIGEST of the Federal reserve act (including amendments to June 21, 1917). Guaranty trust company of New York.

DIGEST of the law of trust accounts chiefly in relation to life owner and remainderman. Strachan, W. 1911.

DIGEST of the profit-sharing plan recently adopted by the Pittsburgh trust company. *Trust companies,* Nov. 1919, p. 504.

DIGEST of workmens compensation laws; comp. by committee for accident prevention and workmen's compensation. New York, National association of manufacturers, c1913.

DIGEST on railway accounts. Anderson, A. C. 1908.

DIGESTING and tabulating accounts. Hill, H. W. 1882.

DIGNIFIED business. Robertson, H. R.

DILL, HOWARD A.

Some notes and figures on the valuation of the water works plant at Richmond, Ind. *Engineering-contracting,* March 2, 1910, p. 202.

Valuation of water works system of Richmond, Ind. *Mining and engineering,* June 1910, p. 410.

DILL, JAMES B.

Statutory and case law applicable to private companies under the general corporation act of New Jersey. New York, Baker, Voorhis, & company. 1898.

DILL, S. J.

Efficient employees are an element in costs. *Electrical world,* Aug. 26, 1916, p. 410-1.

DILLER, H. E.

Time study underlies bonus system. *Foundry,* Sept. 1, 1920, p. 682-6.

DILLINGHAM, R. H.

New York C. P. A. examinations. *Journal of accountancy,* Nov. 1913, p. 410-2.

DILLION, T. M.

Valuation of mine plant and depreciation assessment. *Engineering and mining journal,* Dec. 23, 1916, p. 1106.

DILLON, A.

Continuous audit, public accounts. London, A. Brown, 1880.

DILLON, CHARLES

Bookkeeping for a big ranch. *Country gentleman,* Oct. 28, 1911, p. 10.

Bookkeeping for swine. *Country gentleman,* Dec. 30, 1911, p. 13.

DILLON, WILLIAM

Boston clouds have a copper lining. *Journal of accountancy,* March 1907, p. 342-4.

DILWORTH, J. B.

Cost accounting at coal mines. *Coal age,* May 11, 1918, p. 874-6.

Method of calculating sinking funds, and a table of values for ordinary periods and rates of interest. *Transactions of the American institute of mining engineers,* 1910, v.41, p. 533-5.

DILWORTH, THOMAS

Young book-keeper's assistant: showing in the most plain and easy manner the Italian way of stating debtor and creditor, etc. Ed.7. London, 1777.

——— Same. Ed.8. London, 1781.
——— Same. Ed.9. London, 1784.
——— Same. Ed.12. London, 1793.
——— Same. Ed.13. London, 1798.
——— Same. New ed. London, 1810.
——— Same. New ed. York, 1828.
——— Same. New ed. London, 1856.
——— Same. New ed. London, 1870.

DIME and question books of book-keeping. Bardeen, C. W. 1888.

DIME fare asked in Jersey. public service railway loses $1,200,000 in year under 7 cent rate. *Electric railway journal,* Dec. 11, 1920. p.1214.

DIMELOW, JAMES

Bookkeeping. London, Collins, sons & co. 1876.

Practical bookkeeping. London, Collins, sons & co. 1882.

DIMMOCK, W. S.
Accounting system of the Omaha and Council Bluffs railway and bridge company. *Street railway review,* May 15, 1899.
Materials and supplies accounting. *Street railway review,* 1903, p. 970-4.

DINGMAN, CHARLES F.
Estimating the cost of mill buildings. *Engineering and contracting,* Sept. 8, 1915, p. 185.

DINGWALL, THOMAS
Distillery accounting. *Accountant,* Feb. 28, 1903, p. 303-12. *Accountants' magazine,* Feb. 1903, p. 91-116.
How best to make a chartered accountants students' society popular and useful. *Accountant,* Jan. 25, 1908, p. 126.

DINSMERE, W.
Registration of pedigres. *Breeders' gazette,* Nov. 9, 1916, p. 881-2. Abstract. *International review of science and practical agriculture,* Jan. 1917, p. 105-8.

DIRECT legislation and direct nomination. Walker, Joseph.

DIRECT reading time study watch. *Iron age,* Mar. 25, 1915, p. 663.

DIRECTORIES
Accountant's directory for 1877. London, 1877
Directory of directors in the city of New York, 1917-1918. New York, Directory of directors co. 1918. 944p.
Directory of directors in the city of New York, 1919-1920. New York, Directory of directors co. c1919. 1034p.
Perine, Rita and Leonard Bickwit. Accountants' directory and who's who 1920. New York, Forty-fifth street press, c1920. 628p.
Rand, McNally & co. Bankers' directory and list of attorneys, January 1918. Chicago, Rand, McNally & co. c1918. 2111p.
United States. Congress. Official congressional directory for the use of the United States congress.

DIRECTORS and auditors. *Accountant,* June 12, Dec. 25, 1909, p. 819-22, 769-72.

DIRECTORS and restrictive agreements. *Accountant,* Feb. 19, 1910, p. 265-8.

DIRECTORS' liability for declaring dividends out of capital. *Corporation journal,* Dec. 31, 1915, p. 94.

DIRECTORS' qualifications. *Accountant,* May 24, 1902, July 16, 1904, Feb. 6, 1909, p. 541-3, 61-2, 206-7.

DIRECTORS v. auditors. *Accountant,* Jan. 13, 20, Feb. 24, Sept. 29, 1894, April 20, July 6, Aug. 31, Dec. 28, 1895, Jan. 27, April 21, 1900, March 15, April 19, 1902, July 8, 15, 22, 1905, Dec. 25, 1909, p. 29-31, 53-6, 173-4, 839-42; 349-52, 589-92, 693-5, 1045-6; 95-7, 365-8, 276-9, 407-9, 33-5, 65-7, 104-6; 769-72.

DIRECTORY of directors in the city of New York, 1917-1918. New York directory of directors co. 1918. 944p.

DIRECTORY of directors in the city of New York 1919-20. New York, Directory of directors co. c1919. 1034p.

DIRECTS Bell telephone to supply particulars *Canadian official record,* December 10, 1918, p. 2.

DISADVANTAGE of "self-balancing" ledgers; and suggestions thereon. *Accountant,* Aug. 4, 1888, p. 493-4.

DISALLOWANCE of taxed costs in a bankruptcy. *Incorporated accountants' journal,* Jan. 1915, p. 76-7.

DISBROW, A. B.
Mechanical devices for disbursement accounting; report of railway accounting officers' committee. *Railway age gazette,* June 14, 1918, p. 1433-6. *Railway review,* June 22, 1918, p. 924-9.

DISBURSEMENTS
Hughes, James F. Meaning of disbursements: correspondence. *Journal of accountancy,* Nov. 1912, p. 418.

DISBURSEMENTS of railways. Kirkman, Marshall Monroe. 1904.

DISCIPLINARY value of bookkeeping as a study. Spencer, E. 1903.

DISCOUNT HOUSES

Accounting
Pixley, F. W. Discount houses. (In his *Accountancy.* Ed.2. p. 127-9).

Auditing
Pixley, Francis W. Discount houses. (In his *Auditors, their duties and responsibilities.* 1910. p. 492-3).

DISCOUNTS
Bentley, H. C. Accounts relating to interest and discount. (In his *Science of accounts,* 1913. p. 132-7).
Carter, R. N. Discount. (In his *Advanced accounts.* p. 34).
Catching the discounts. *System,* Sept. 1917, p. 420.
Cole, W. M. Treatment of commercial discounts. (In his *Accounts their construction and interpretation.* c1915. p. 340-2).
Esquerre, P. J. Discount and premium accounts. (In his *Applied theory of accounts.* 1917. p. 331-2).
Freight, express and discount. *Business man's magazine,* June 1908, p. 534-5.
Gilman, Stephen. Purchase and sales discounts. (In his *Principles of accounting.* 1917. p. 248-50).
Jackson, J. Hugh. Neglected commercial discounts. *Journal of accountancy,* Nov. 1920, p. 321-8.
Kester, Roy B. Discounts. (In his *Accounting theory and practice.* 1918. p. 298-312).
Lisle, George and W. A. Middleton. Discounts and provision for outstanding discounts. (In their *Account-keeping in principle and practice.* 1911. p. 66-9).
Millar, T. J. Some notes of an investigation into discounts. *Accountants' magazine,* Nov. 1920, p. 585-95.
Mitchell, T. W. Expected discounts on uncollected income. (In his *Accounting principles.* c1918. p. 191).
Paton, W. A. and R. A. Stevenson. Discounts on securities. (In their *Principles of accounting.* 1918. p. 448-50).
Pixley, Francis W. Discounts. (In his *Accountancy,* Ed. 2. p. 127-9).
Quick discount figuring. *American industries,* Nov. 1917, p. 10.
Racine, S. F. Interest and discount. (In his *Accounting principles.* 1917).
Rittenhouse, C. F. Interest and discount. (In his *Elements of accounts for individuals, professional men and institutions.* 1918. p. 29-31).
Scott, G. G. Invoice discounts. *Journal of accountancy,* Dec. 1912, p. 437-45.

DISCOUNTS—*(Continued)*

SPICER, E. E. and E. C. PEGLER. Discounts. (In their *Book-keeping and accounts.* 1914. p. 31).

SPRAGUE, CHARLES EZRA. Discounted values: interest and discount. (In his *Accountancy of investment.* 1914. p. 167-82, 223-7).

THOMPSON, J. P. Checking invoices to gain the discount. *Factory*, Oct. 1916, p. 440.

WALTON, SEYMOUR. Accounts receivable discounted. *Journal of accountancy*, Dec. 1915. p. 469-70.

WALTON, SEYMOUR. Amortizing discount on instalment contracts. *Journal of accountancy*, June 1920, p. 470-8.

WALTON, SEYMOUR. Offsetting discount and premium. *Journal of accountancy*, May 1916, p. 393.

WEBNER, F. E. Discount. (In his *Factory costs.* 1911. p. 205-6).

Bills

WHITE, G. J. Labor saving treatment of bills discounted. *Business man's magazine*, Feb. 1908, p. 207.

Bonds

ARMSTRONG, ROBERT D. Regulation of bond discount. *Journal of accountancy*, July 1920, p. 18-35.

BECK, HERBERT. Theory and practice. *Journal of accountancy*, July 1917, p. 21-7.

BENNETT, R. J. Annuities and bond discount. *Journal of accountancy*, June, July, Sept. 1915, p. 405-24; 1-20, 203-15.

DICKINSON, A. L. Discounts on bonds. (In his *Accounting practice and procedure.* 1917. p. 134, 135, 142).

ESQUERRE, P. J. Premiums and discounts on bond sales. (In his *Applied theory of accounts.* 1917, p. 341-4).

FINNEY, H. A. Effective rate on serial bonds. *Journal of accountancy*, Nov. 1920, p. 385-400.

FOGARTY, JAMES F. Accounting treatment of bond discount. *Electric railway journal*, Oct. 15, 1914, p. 871.

GREENDLINGER, LEO. Bond discount. (In his *Financial and business statements.* c1917, p. 167-70).

KESTER, R. B. Nature of bond discount or premium. (In his *Accounting theory and practice.* 1918. v. 2, p. 226-7, 269-71).

LITTLE, ARTHUR S. Computation of coupon values. *Journal of accountancy*, April 1920. p. 283-98.

LITTLE, ARTHUR S. Tyranny of the engraver. *Journal of accountancy*, Sept. 1915, April 1916, p. 186-202, 307-8.

MAY, GEORGE O. Premium and discounts. *Journal of accountancy*, Nov. 1906, p. 32-3.

MAY, GEORGE O. Proper treatment of premiums and discounts on bonds. *Journal of accountancy*, July 1906, p. 174-86.

SPIES, OTTO A. Annuities and bond discount. *Journal of accountancy*, Sept. 1915, p. 203-15.

SPRAGUE, CHARLES EZRA. Premiums and discounts. *Journal of accountancy*, Aug. 1906, p. 294-6.

WALTON, SEYMOUR. Bond discount. *Journal of accountancy*, Aug. 1918, p. 150.

WALTON, SEYMOUR. Bond discount in consolidated balance sheet. *Journal of accountancy*, Aug. 1916, p. 155-7.

WALTON, SEYMOUR. Discount on bonds redeemed with stock. *Journal of accountancy*, Aug. 1918, p. 151-2.

WALTON, SEYMOUR. Premium or discount on bonds in sinking fund. *Journal of accountancy*, May 1915, p. 390-2.

WALTON, SEYMOUR. Problem. *Journal of accountancy*, Jan. 1917, p. 75-6.

WALTON, SEYMOUR. Theory and practice. *Journal of accountancy*, Aug. 1917, p. 148-51.

WEBSTER, GEORGE R. Methods of writing off discount on bonds. *Journal of accountancy*, Sept. 1913, p. 169-74.

WHAT the borrower owes: correspondence, *Journal of accountancy*, Feb. 1916, p. 156-7.

Cash

CASH discount ratios. *Dry goods economist*, Aug. 23, 1913.

CASH discounts. *Accountant*, Sept. 27, 1890, p. 503-4.

CHANGING customs in cash discounts. *Iron age*, May 9, 1912, p. 1169-70.

COHEN, ALEXANDER J. Cash discounts. *Journal of accountancy*, April 1914, p. 294-6.

ESQUERRE, P. J. Cash discounts. (In his *Applied theory of accounts.* 1917. p. 438).

GREELEY, HAROLD DUDLEY. Trade discounts and cash discounts. (In his *Theory of accounts.* 1920. p. 271-83).

HANSEN, C. Freight and cash discount. *Business man's magazine*, June 1908, p. 533.

HAWKINS, L. W. Cash discounts. (In his *Cost accounts.* 1912. p. 112-3).

KESTER, R. B. Cash discount. (In his *Accounting theory and practice.* 1918. p. 149-51, 156-7, 303-11).

KESTER, R. B. Discounts. (In his *Accounting theory and practice.* 1918. v. 2, p. 44-6, 221).

MACFARLAND, J. J. S. Settlement of notes and cash discount. *Business man's magazine*, June 1908, p. 535-6.

MCINTOSH, R. J. Cash discounts. (In his *Reference book of accounts for manufacturing and mercantile companies.* c1914. p. 98, 108).

MILLAR, T. J. Some notes of an investigation into discounts. *Accountants' magazine*, Nov. 1920, p. 585-95.

MITCHELL, THOMAS WARNER. Relation of cash discounts to goods valuation and to reserves for bad debts. *Journal of accountancy*, May 1912, p. 339-50.

NICHOLSON, J. L. Cash discounts. (In their *Cost accounting.* 1919. p. 21-3).

PARTON, JOHN. Debatable points. *Canadian chartered accountant*, April 1913, p. 242-9.

PATON, W. A. Cash discounts. *Journal of accountancy*, May 1920, p. 335-46.

PATON, WILLIAM ANDREW and R. A. STEVENSON. Treatment of cash discounts. (In their *Principles of accounting.* 1918. p. 653-6).

SCHACKMANN, J. H. Cash discounts. *Journal of accountancy*, Jan. 1918, p. 43-6.

TREATMENT of cash discounts: correspondence. *Journal of accountancy*, Feb. 1915, p. 162-3.

WALTON, SEYMOUR. Cash discount. *Journal of accountancy*, May 1915, p. 385-7.

WALTON, SEYMOUR. Cash discount and prepaid freight. *Journal of accountancy*, Dec. 1915, p. 468.

WALTON, SEYMOUR. Cash discount as a penalty. *Journal of accountancy*, May 1915, p. 387-90.

WALTON, SEYMOUR. Cash discount on capital purchases. *Journal of accountancy*, April 1920, p. 313-4.

WALTON, SEYMOUR. Cash discount on returned goods. *Journal of accountancy*, April 1915, p. 317-9.

WALTON, SEYMOUR. Discounts on capital expenditures. *Journal of accountancy*, May 1920, p. 398.

WELLINGTON, C. OLIVER. Cash discounts. *Journal of accountancy*, Aug. 1912, p. 147-8.

WILDMAN, J. R. Deductions from income group. (In his *Principles of accounting.* 1914. p. 231-2).

Debentures

CARTER, R. N. Discount on debentures. (In his *Advanced accounts.* p. 444-6).

DISCOUNTS—*(Continued)*

Notes

BAUER, JOHN. Accounting of interest and discount on notes. *Journal of accountancy*,

PATON, W. A. Prepaid interest. *Journal of accountancy*, May 1920, p. 346-50.

STOCKWELL, N. G. Notes discounted. (In his *Net worth and the balance sheet*. 1912. p. 172-4).

WALTON, SEYMOUR. Discount on long time notes. *Journal of accountancy*, Jan. 1916, p. 68-9.

Stock

GREENDLINGER, LEO. Discount on the sale of capital stock. (In his *Financial and business statements*. c1917. p. 166-7).

ISSUE of shares at a discount. *Accountant*, Aug. 20, 1904, Feb. 1, 1908, Aug. 20, 1910, p. 210-12, 163-4, 221-3.

ISSUING of shares at a discount. *Incorporated accountants journal*, 1896-7, p. 114.

ISSUING shares and debentures at a discount. *Accountant*, Feb. 1, 1908, Aug. 20, 1910, p. 163-4, 221-3.

KESTER, R. B. Discount on stock. (In his *Accounting theory and practice*. 1918. v. 2, p. 13-4).

KESTER, R. B. Premium on discount on stock. (In his *Accounting theory and practice*. 1918. p. 455-7).

ROBINSON, JOSEPH. Further discussion of discount on capital stock: correspondence. *Journal of accountancy*, Sept. 1918, p. 239-40.

SALE of shares at a discount. *Canadian chartered accountant*, July 1912, p. 11-2.

WALTON, SEYMOUR. Discount on capital stock. *Journal of accountancy*, Nov. 1915, p. 392-4.

WALTON, SEYMOUR. Discount on capital stock. *Journal of accountancy*, Oct. 1919, p. 302-5.

WALTON, SEYMOUR. Discount on stock. *Journal of accountancy*, Sept. 1915, p. 238-41.

WALTON, SEYMOUR. Discount on treasury stock. *Journal of accountancy*, Sept. 1918, p. 234-5.

WALTON, SEYMOUR. Stock sold at a discount. *Journal of accountancy*, March 1916, p. 235-6.

Trade

ESQUERRE, P. J. Trade discounts. (In his *Applied theory of accounts*. 1917. p. 155-6).

GREELEY, HAROLD DUDLEY. Trade discount and cash discount. (In his *Theory of accounts*. 1920. p. 271-83).

HEAPS, JOHN WILLIAM. Trade discounts. *Accountant*, April 27, 1895, p. 381-92.

KESTER, R. B. Trade discount. (In his *Accounting theory and practice*. 1918, p. 299-303).

MILLAR, T. J. Some notes of an investigation into discounts. *Accountants' magazine*, Nov. 1920, p. 585-95.

NICHOLSON, J. L. and J. F. D. ROHRBACH. Trade discounts. (In their *Cost accounting*. 1919. p. 21).

WALTON, SEYMOUR. Trade discount. *Journal of accountancy*, Aug. 1915, p. 148-9.

WILDMAN, J. R. Trade discounts. (In their *Principles of accounting*. 1914. p. 200-1).

DISCOUNTS and turnovers. *System*, Sept. 1915, p. 307-8.

DISCRIMINATION against interstate commerce. *Railway age*, Aug. 18, 1916, p. 270-1.

DISCUSSION at the City club shows that Baltimore's bookkeeping and auditing systems are surpassed by no other municipality in America. *Municipal journal, Baltimore*, Feb. 5, 1915, p. 1-5.

DISCUSSION by mayor, railroad executive and commissioners follows 6-cent fare appeal in New York city. *Electric railway journal*, March 30, 1918, p. 628.

DISCUSSION by railway commissioners on rates and valuation. *Electric railway journal*, December 17, 1910, p. 1192-3.

DISCUSSION in reference to maintenance and depreciation charges in accounts of public service corporations before "The Incorporated public accountants of Massachusetts," April 11, 1907. 32p.

DISCUSSION of accounting in sewer departments. *Engineering and contracting*, Dec. 10, 1913, p. 645.

DISCUSSION of Central west rate situation. *Electrical world*, July 27, 1918, p. 165.

DISCUSSION of cost accounting on construction work. *Journal of the Boston society of civil engineers*, Oct. 1914.

DISCUSSION of depreciation and a comparison of rates and bookkeeping methods of municipally and privately owned waterworks. *American waterworks association, Proceedings*, 1912, p. 325-47. Abstract. Depreciation by John W. Alvord. *Engineering record*, June 15, 1912, p. 670.

DISCUSSION of effect on maintenance of way accounts produced by physical characteristics of location and nature of traffic. *Engineering and contracting*, May 7, 1913, p. 530-3.

DISCUSSION of fare systems. *Electric railway journal*, Sept. 27, 1919, p. 610-2.

DISCUSSION of Milwaukee fare decision. *Electric railway journal*, Jan. 18, 1913, p. 110.

DISCUSSION of public utility valuation matters. *Electrical world*, April 11, 1914, p. 805.

DISCUSSION of reports of sub-committee on administration on present state of industrial management. *Journal of the American society of mechanical engineers*, March 1913, p. 463-4.

DISCUSSION of the elements of water works accounting. *Engineering and contracting*, Dec. 30, 1914, p. 600.

DISCUSSION of the Milwaukee fare decision. *Electric railway journal*, Jan. 18, 1913, p. 110.

DISCUSSION of the valuation of water works special franchises with an illustrative example. *Engineering and contracting*, Dec. 24, 1913, p. 707.

DISCUSSION of water works accounting with a suggested system of accounts. *Engineering and contracting*, March 5, 1913, p. 279-80.

DISCUSSION on class rates for light and power systems or territory (Baum), Deer Park, Md., July 2, 1915. *American institute of electrical engineers, Proceedings*, March 1916, continued from January.

DISCUSSION on depreciation of equipment. *Electrical railway journal*, Dec. 19, 1914. p. 1335-7.

DISCUSSION on principles involved in computing the depreciation of plant. *Journal of the Institute of electrical engineers*, March 1917.

DISCUSSION on public utility valuation and depreciation. *Electric railway journal,* April 11, 1914, p. 829-30.

DISCUSSION on "rates and rate making." *American institute of electrical engineering, Proceedings,* Jan. 1916, p. 71-112.

DISCUSSION on report of the special committee to formulate principles and methods for the valuation of railroad property and other public utilties. *American society of civil engineers, Proceedings,* April, Aug. 1917.

DISCUSSION on rule of Illinois commission covering methods of handling customers' accounts. *Electrical world,* April 6, 1918, p. 729.

DISCUSSION on the Milwaukee fare decision. *Electric railway journal,* Jan. 18, 1913, p. 110-1.

DISCUSSION on the valuation of water works special franchises with an illustrative example. *Engineering and contracting,* Dec. 24, 1913, p. 707.

DISCUSSION on vocational guidance school records. Leavitt, F. M.

DISPATCHING work of engineering department; Denver tramway company. *Electric railway journal,* July 28, 1917, p. 134-40.

DISPENSARIES
See Institutions.

DISPUTED points in railway valuation. *Railway age,* May 16-June 6, 1913, p. 1056, 1118, 1164, 1208.

'DISSENTIENT shareholder' in reconstruction schemes. *Incorporated accountants' journal,* 1907-8, p. 140.

DISSOLUTION, amalgamation and reconstruction accounts. Spicer, E. 1915.

DISTILLING PLANTS
See also Breweries.
Leilich, F. T. Operation and costs of a light effect distilling plant; abstract. *Metallurgical and chemical engineering,* Aug. 15, 1916, p. 213-15.

Accounting
Andrew, William. Distillery accounts. *Accountants' magazine,* May 1903, p. 252-64.
Dingwall, Thomas. Distillery accounting. *Accountant,* Feb. 28, 1903, p. 303-12. *Accountants' magazine,* Feb. 1903, p. 91-116.

DISTINCTION between cost and value. *Electrical world,* March 27, 1915, p. 782.

DISTINCTION between trading (or manufacturing) and profit and loss accounts. *Accountant,* Sept. 13, 20, 1890, p. 469-70, 488-9.

DISTRIBUTING factory operating costs proportioning department expenses and charges in Cincinnati planer company's works. *Iron age,* June 15, 1911, p. 1479-80.

DISTRIBUTING general factory expense. *100%* v. 11, no. 1, p. 64.

DISTRIBUTION department stockroom methods. *Electrical world,* Dec. 30, 1916, p. 1297.

DISTRIBUTION line records. *Electrical world,* Aug. 9, 16, 1913.

DISTRIBUTION of accounts of road construction. *Municipal engineering,* June 1913, p. 524-7.

DISTRIBUTION of additions and betterments. *Railway age,* May 31, 1918, p. 1313-6.

DISTRIBUTION of employees in departments of a central station. *Electrical world,* October 28, 1916, p. 866.

DISTRIBUTION of income taxes to localities: a vagary of the Wisconsin income tax law. *National tax association, Bulletin,* Dec. 1919, p. 73-5.

DISTRIBUTION of personnel. *Journal of accountancy,* Aug. 1918, p. 109-10.

DISTRIBUTION of shop tools. *Railway age* (mech. ed.) August 1914, p. 431-2. Condensed. *Railway age,* July 31, 1914, p. 205.

DISTRIBUTION of urban land values. *Yale review,* Aug. 1902, p. 124.

DISTRIBUTION sheets of contractor's accounting system. *Engineering and contracting,* July 21, 1920, p. 60-1.

DISTRICT auditors and their clerks. *Accountant,* March 25, April 8, 15, 1899, p. 349-51, 403-6, 426-8.

DISTRICT of Columbia. *Journal of accountancy,* March 1909, p. 400.

DISTRICT-school bookeeping. Preston, Lyman

DITCH dug with dynamite at 15 cents per cubic yard. *Engineering record,* Nov. 27, 1915, p. 673.

DIVERSIFIED farm accounting. Sloman, L. A. 1914.

DIVIDEND paid out of capital. *Accountant,* Aug. 10, 1912, p. 177-80.

DIVIDENDS
Apportionment of dividends as between life tenant and remainderman. *Trust companies,* Dec. 1914, p. 514.
Apportionment of dividends between life tenant and remainderman. *Trust companies,* May 1912, p. 401.
Apportionment of dividends by trustees as between life tenant and remaindermen. *Trust companies,* Nov. 1914, p. 426.
Appreciation of assets and dividends. *Accountant,* July 21, 1900, p. 668-71.
Arrears of preference dividends. *Accountant,* Aug. 23, 1902, p. 822-3.
Beale, William Phipson. Judicial ditca and legislative restrictions on the payment of dividends out of revenue. *Accountant,* Dec. 1, 1900, Jan. 26, 1901, p. 1083-91, 104-7.
Bentley, H. C. Dividends. (In his *Science of accounts.* 1913. p. 181-2).
Best, John William. Payment of dividend out of capital. *Accountant,* Dec. 5, 19, 1885.
Betts, Philander. Stock dividends, why and when justified. *Electric railway journal,* Oct. 10, 1914, p. 725-8.
Carter, R. N. Dividends. (In his *Advanced accounts.* p. 438-43).
Christie, J. R. Capital losses in relation to dividends. *Public accountant,* April 1918, p. 243-8.
Confusion in high places. *Journal of accountancy,* May 1920, p. 359-62.
Copy of query addressed to the institute's solicitor regarding "stock dividend" opinion re stock dividend. *Canadian chartered accountant,* Jan. 1913, p. 33-4.

DIVIDENDS—*(Continued)*

COX, HENRY C. Corporate dividends: accounting for dividends. (In his *Advanced and analytical accounting.* 1920. p. 55-94).

DAVENPORT, H. J. Stock dividend again. *National tax association bulletin,* Nov. 1918, p. 53-4.

DECLARING dividends out of surplus. *Electric railway journal,* April 3, 1915, p. 657.

DEWING, ARTHUR STONE. Practical expediency of dividend disbursements. (In his *Financial policy of corporations.* 1920. v. 3. p. 114-24).

DIRECTORS liability for declaring dividends out of capital. *Corporation journal,* Dec. 31, 1915, p. 94.

DIVIDEND paid out of capital. *Accountant,* Aug. 10, 1912, p. 177-80.

DIVIDENDS and profits. *Accountant,* Feb. 1, 8, May 17, 1902, p. 120-1, 152-4, 519-20.

DIVIDENDS and profits prior to incorporation. *Accountant,* Aug. 13, 1904, p. 160-1.

DIVIDENDS as between life tenant and remainderman. *Trust companies,* Dec. 1913, p. 477.

DIVIDENDS on watered stock. *Journal of accountancy,* May 1907, p. 47-8.

DIVIDENDS out of capital. *Accountant,* Aug. 2, 9, 1890, p. 407-8, 419-20.

ESQUERRE, P. J. Dividends payable. (In his *Applied theory of accounts.* 1917. p. 355-62).

EVANS, H. E. Dividends and profits. *Accounting and commerce,* Jan. 1917, p. 221-7.

FAIRCHILD, F. G. Economic nature of the stock dividend. *Bulletin of the National tax association,* April 1918.

FATKIN, THOMAS. Interest, annuities and insurance. *Accountant,* Jan. 27, 1900, p. 104-11.

GUARANTEED dividends. *Accountant,* Feb. 22, 1913, p. 248-50.

KENNEDY, JOHN T. Dividends and the new income tax law. *Journal of accountancy,* Jan. 1917, p. 39-42.

KESTER, R. B. Dividends. (In his *Accounting theory and practice.* 1918. p. 460-1).

KESTER, R. B. Dividends. (In his *Accounting theory and practice.* 1918. v. 2. p. 428-46).

KEYES, J. Brooks. Dividends and the new income tax law. *Journal of accountancy,* March 1917, p. 239-40.

KROHN, THEODORE. Taxation of stock dividends. *Journal of accountancy,* Aug. 1920, p. 94-6.

LAIRD, THOMAS PATRICK. Trust accounts and apportionment of dividends. *Accountants' magazine,* Nov. 1912, p. 452-67.

McINTOSH, R. J. Dividends. (In his *Reference book of accounts for manufacturing and mercantile companies.* c1914. p. 86-8).

MOERAN, EDWARD H. Stock dividends. *Journal of accountancy,* March 1918, p. 239-40.

OBLIGATION of company to provide for depreciation of wasting assets before declaring dividends. *Accountant,* Dec. 14, 1889, p. 676-82.

PAYMENT of dividends in shares. *Accountant,* Aug. 12, 1899, p. 845-8.

PAYMENT of dividends on corporate stock as between life tenant and remainderman. *Trust companies,* Oct. 1914, p. 346-7.

PAYMENT of dividends out of capital. *Accountant,* March 10, 1888, p. 154-5, March 30, 1901, p. 385-8, April 23, 1910, p. 560-1.

PAYMENT of dividends out of capital. *Incorporated accountants' journal* 1898-9, p. 71, 227.

PIXLEY, F. W. Dividends. (In his *Accountancy.* Ed. 2, p. 176-7).

PLEHN, CARL C. Income tax as applied to dividends. *American economic review,* Dec. 1919, p. 771-5.

POWELL, T. R. Judicial debate on the taxability of stock dividends as income: Eisner v. Macomber. *National tax association bulletin,* May 1920, p. 247-56.

POWELL, THOMAS REED. Stock-dividend decision and the corporate nonenty. *National tax association bulletin,* April 1920, p. 201-13.

POWELL, THOMAS REED. Stock dividends, direct taxes and the sixteenth amendment. *Columbia law review,* May 1920, p. 536-49.

PRIESTLEY, HERBERT. Profits and dividends. *Accountant,* Aug. 27, Sept. 3, 1898, April 7, 1906, Feb. 8, 1913, June 21, 1919, p. 822-8, 841-6, 421-4; 172-4, 517-9.

PRIESTLEY, HERBERT. Profits and dividends. *Incorporated accountants' journal* 1897-8, p. 127.

PROFITS and dividends. *Incorporated accountants' journal,* 1895-6, p. 26, 42.

PROFITS available for dividend. *Accountant,* Aug. 4, Sept. 22, Dec. 1, 15, 1917, p. 81-4, 217-9, 417-9, 458-80.

RACINE, S. F. Dividends payable account. (In his *Accounting principles.* 1917. p. 264).

RECKITT, CHARLES COLEBY. Corporate dividends; an address before the Illinois association of public accountants. *Accountant,* Nov. 2, 1901, p. 1192-9.

RECKITT, CHARLES COLEBY. Corporate dividends from an accountant's viewpoint. *Business world,* Jan. Feb. 1902, p. 30-3, 80-3.

ROGERSON, GEORGE. Preparation of dividend sheets. *Business organisation and management,* Oct. 1920, p. 105-6.

SELIGMAN, E. R. A. Are stock dividends income? *American economic review,* Sept. 1919, p. 517-36.

SMITH, WILLIAM. Dividends and capital. *Accountant,* July 11, 18, 1903, p. 900-6, 933-8. *Accountants' magazine,* Jan. 1902, p. 12-36.

SPICER, ERNEST EVAN. Divisible profits and dividends. London, H. Foulks Lynch & co. 30p. *Accountant,* Feb. 3, 1912. p. 170-9.

STOCK dividends, life tenants and remaindermen. *Trust companies,* Feb. 1916, p. 183-4.

STOCK dividends not subject to income tax according to United States supreme court. *Commercial and financial chronicle,* March 13, 1920, p. 1049-50.

UNCLAIMED dividends. (In *How to understand the balance sheet and other periodical statements.* 1905. p. 52-6).

WALTON, SEYMOUR. Dividends of subsidiary companies. *Journal of accountancy,* March 1917, p. 190-1.

WALTON, SEYMOUR. Dividends on treasury stock. *Journal of accountancy,* July 1916, p. 65-6.

WALTON, SEYMOUR. Interest on unpaid cumulative dividends. *Journal of accountancy,* Sept. 1919, p. 236-7.

WALTON, SEYMOUR. Preferred dividends. *Journal of accountancy,* June 1917, p. 461-2.

WALTON, SEYMOUR. Profits and dividends. *Journal of accountancy,* Dec. 1919, p. 461-70.

WALTON, SEYMOUR. Stock dividend-subscription rights. *Journal of accountancy,* July 1917. p. 66-7.

WALTON, SEYMOUR. Stock dividends. *Journal of accountancy,* March April 1917, Aug. 1918, p. 192, 313-4, 155-6.

WALTON, SEYMOUR. Treasury stock, dividends on no par value. *Journal of accountancy,* April 1920, p. 315-7.

WEISS, W. F. Dividends and the new income tax law. *Journal of accountancy,* Nov. 1916, p. 343-52.

WILDMAN, J. R. Secondary-income group. (In his *Principles of accounting.* 1914. p. 226-8).

WOODS, C. E. Dividends. (In his *Uniform accounting methods for industrials.* 1917. p. 309-10).

DIVIDENDS and profits. *Accountant*, Feb. 1, 8, May 17, 1902, p. 120-1, 152-4, 519-20.

DIVIDENDS and profits prior to incorporation. *Accountant*, Aug. 13, 1904, p. 160-1.

DIVIDENDS and the new income tax law. Kennedy, J. T.

DIVIDENDS and the new income tax law. Keyes, J. B.

DIVIDENDS and the new income tax law. Weiss, W. F.

DIVIDENDS as a form of profit-sharing: Doherty public utility organization. *American gas engineering journal*, Aug. 4, 1917, p. 116-17. Excerpts. *Electrical review*, Aug. 11, 1917, p. 225.

DIVIDENDS as between life tenant and remainderman. *Trust companies*, Dec. 1913, p. 477.

DIVIDENDS on watered stock. *Journal of accountancy*, May 1907, p. 47-8.

DIVIDENDS out of capital. *Accountant*, Aug. 2, 9, 1890, p. 407-8, 419-20.

DIVISIBLE profits. *Accountant*, May 25, 1912, p. 785-8.

DIVISIBLE profits and creditors. *Incorporated accountants' journal*, July 1912, p. 260-1.

DIVISIBLE profits and dividends. Spicer, E. E. 1912.

DIVISIBLE profits of companies; a plea for fuller parliamentary recognition of double entry. *Accountant*, April 19, 1902, p. 417-24.

DIVISION of five cent fare in New York state. *Electric railway journal*, June 10, 1911, p. 1027.

DIVISION of freight and passenger expense. *Railroad herald*, Oct. 1914, p. 207-8.

DIVISION of freight and passenger expenses: new and old formulas contrasted and the newest formula applied to the 1914 classification of expenses. *Railway age*, July 24, 1914, p. 153-8.

DIVISION of maintenance of way expense between passenger and freight traffic. *Railway age gazette*, Sept. 11, 1914, p. 458-9.

DIVISION of operating expenses. *Railway and engineering review*, April 12, 1913, p. 345.

DIVISION of partnership profits. *Accountants' magazine*, June 1912, p. 299-302.

DIVISION of profits of a company. *Accountant*, June 15, 1912, p. 891-3.

DIVISION of railway expenses and earnings, and the limitation of accounts in connection therewith. Kirkman, Marshall Monroe. 1886. 1886.

DIVISION of surplus assets. *Accountant*, March 21, 28, April 11, 1891, p. 218-20, 234-6, 275-6.

DIXON, F. H.
How to study a railroad report; address before the Railway man's improvement society, March 15, 1917. *R. M. I. S. journal*, April-May 1917. 2p.
Physical valuation and capitalization. *Railway age*, Jan. 20, 1911.

DIXON, H. M.
See Thomson, Edward Hermann, joint author.

DIXON, M. and H. W. HAWTHORNE.
Method of analyzing the farm business. *Farmers' bulletin*, 1139, 1920, p. 1-10.

DIXON, OWEN
Some of the consequences which result from the incorporation of companies. *Accountant*, Sept. 11, 1920, p. 261-4.

DJORUP, CHRISTIAN
Foreign exchange. *Journal of accountancy*, June 1913, p. 412-26.
Modern foreign exchange department and its function. *Bankers' magazine*, Aug. 1912, p. 150-5.

DO exchange sales pay. Smith, H. Gordon, and Lent D. Upson.

DO you know axactly what your product costs? *Canadian machinery*, July 31, 1919, p. 101-6.

DOANE, S. E.
Fixed charges for fixed expenses. *Public service*, Oct. 1909, p. 105-108.
Handling the small consumer in Europe. *Electrical world*, May 23, 1914, p. 1157-74.

DOBBEL, F. W.
Retail cigar and tobacco accounting. *Business man's magazine*, 1904, v. 16, no. 8, p. 94-9.

DOBBS, S. M.
Journal and journalizing. *Accounting and commerce*, April 1915, p. 6-9.

DOBSON, ALFRED
Bankruptcy bill. *Accountant*, May 18, 1912, p. 762-7.
Designing of accounting systems. *Accountant*, April 10, 1920, p. 424-30.

DOCK capital, expenditure, receipts and management. Galloway, Lee.

DOCKS
See Wharves.

DR. ADAMS and railway accounts. *Far eastern review*, Sept. 1914, p. 115-6.

DOCTORING the currency. *Journal of accountancy*, Dec. 1906, p. 143-5.

DOCTORS.
See Physicians.

DODD, ARTHUR F.
Auditor's certificates and report. *Accountant*, June 11, July 2, Aug. 20, 1904, p. 776-84, 7-8, 183-6.
Corn options and cotton futures: their object and effect upon commercial transactions. *Accountant*, July 6, 13, 1901, p. 779-87, 804-6.
Duties of chartered accountants on the conversion of private concerns into limited companies. *Accountant*, April 26, 1896, p. 346-52.
Elements of profit sharing applied to commercial ventures. *Accountant*, June 10, 1905, p. 706-14.

DODD, ARTHUR F.—*(Continued)*
Fraud in accounts. (In Lisle, George. *Encyclopaedia of accounting.* v. 3. p. 113-49).
Powers and duties of auditors under section 113 of the companies (consolidation) act, 1908. *Accountant,* Sept. 25, 1909, p. 380-9.
Preparation of accountants' certificates for purpose of joint stock company flotations. *Accountant,* April 6, 1907, p. 451-62. Revised, May 14, 1910, p. 698-711.
Professional auditors. *Accountant,* March 1, 1913, p. 320-6.
Railway accounts and their audit. (In Lisle, George. *Encyclopaedia of accounting.* v. 5. p. 423-66).
Railways and their financial records. *Accountant,* Jan. 19, Feb. 9, 1895, p. 60-8, 129-39.
Report of the departmental committee on income tax. *Accountant,* Feb. 3, 1906, p. 37.
Some suggestions as to the discovery and prevention of defalcations and an auditor's point of view. *Accountant,* May 30, 1903, p. 723-31, 855.
Uses of a journal. *Accountant,* Jan. 20, 1894, p. 69-76.

DODD, S. T.
Comparison of the costs of operating steam and electric switching locomotives. *Engineering and contracting,* Dec. 31, 1913, p. 747-8.

DODDS, H. W.
Procedures in state legislatures. Philadelphia, American academy of political and social science, 1918.

DODDS, NORMAN R.
Rights and duties of a trustee in bankruptcy. *Accountant,* Nov. 28, 1908, p. 660-3.

DODGE, J. MORRELL
Keeping your assets at the 100% mark. *Bankers' monthly,* Nov. 1917, p. 11.

DODSON, FREDERICK ERNEST
Urban district councils' accounts. Leeds, Elseworth bros. 1908.

DODSON, JAMES
Accountant: or, the method of bookkeeping. London. 1750.

DOES business or the law need reform? *Journal of accountancy,* March 1910, p. 369-72.

DOES it pay to keep farm accounts. *Ohio Judd farmer,* Sept. 25, 1920, p. 1394.

DOESN'T want exactly a palace. *Journal of accountancy,* March 1909, p. 405.

DOHERTY, HENRY L.
Comments on development and operation of hydro-electric plants. *American institute of electrical engineers, Proceedings,* 1909, p. 1362.
Cost and depreciation of steam and hydro-electric installation. *Electrical world,* Dec. 30, 1909, p. 1558.
Methods of charging for public service. *Public service,* Jan. 1911, p. 9-12.
Present situation will prove in the end the greatest blessing to public utilities. *American gas engineering journal,* Feb. 2, 1918, p. 103-4.
State regulation of lighting enterprises. *American gas light journal,* July 20, 1908, p. 92. Abstract. Doherty on electrical rates and franchises. *Electrical world,* July 25, Aug. 15, 1908, p. 170, 352. Editorial. Valuation of lighting systems. *Electrical world,* Sept. 19, 1908, p. 607.
Three-part rate reduces average rate per thousand from eighty cents to seventy-five cents. *American gas engineering journal,* May 29, 1920, p. 421-2.

DOHERTY, J. J.
Book-keeping. Dublin, Sullivan, 1897.
Text book of bookkeeping. pt. 1. Ed. 44. Dub- Marshall, Hamilton, Kent & co. 1912. 86p.
Text book of bookkeeping. pt. 1, Ed. 44. Dublin, Ireland, Thom; Simpkin, 1917. 91p.

DOHERTY, JAMES L.
Law relating to auditors and masters in Mass. Boston, Little Brown & co. 1906.

DOHERTY—3-part rate. *Gas age,* Jan. 26, 1920, p. 79-80.

DOHR, JAMES L.
Some aspects of flour mill accounting. *Journal of accountancy,* Sept. 1919, p. 161-79.

DOING an old thing in a new way: the maturity guide saves time and work. *Bankers' magazine,* Nov. 1910, p. 663-5.

DOING business on low overhead expense; W. B. Perry electric company of Brooklyn. *Electric world,* Feb. 27, 1915, p. 544-6.

DOLGE, WILLIAM
Antonym in accounting: correspondence. *Journal of accountancy,* April 1910, p. 455.
New municipal report. *Pacific municipalities,* Sept. 1911, p. 71-2.
Origin, development and effect of uniform municipal accounting. *National association of comptrollers and accounting officers, Proceedings,* 1915 and 1916, p. 56-8.
Practical talks on municipal accounting. *Pacific municipalities,* Aug. 31, 1912, p. 398-402.
Side lights on municipal accounting and administration. *Pacific municipalities,* Sept. 1910, p. 45-7.
Value of cost accounts. *Pacific municipalities,* Aug. 1914, p. 405-7.

DOLKART, LEO
Cost systems in electrical contracting. *Western society of engineers journal,* Dec. 1913, p. 969-83.

DOLPH, J. N.
Keeping the cost of tool work. *American machinist,* v. 23, p. 167.

DOMESTIC and foreign exchange. Patterson, E. L. S. c1917.

DOMINION accountant. Orr, W. B. 1872.

DOMINION association convention. *Canadian chartered accountant* Oct. 1920, p. 75-95.

DOMINION association of chartered accountants. *Journal of accountancy,* Aug. 1910, June, July, Oct. 1913, July, Aug. Oct. 1914, Aug. 1917, p. 293-5, 298-9, 3278, 307, 478, 72, 151, 78-9, 152.

DOMINION association of chartered accountants' report of committee on uniformity of standards, presented at the annual meeting, held in Toronto, Sept. 14-16, 1920. *Canadian chartered accountant,* Oct. 1920, p. 96-101.

DOMINION company law. Mulvey, Thomas. 1920.

DOMINION convention postponed. *Journal of accountancy,* Sept. 1914, p. 238.

DOMINION of Canada. Fisk, H. E. 1920.

DOMINION rubber system pension. *Credit men's journal,* May 1918, p. 408-10.

DONALD, R.
Commercial audit of municipal accounts. *Contemporary review,* Nov. 1903, p. 724-7.

DONALD, T.
Accounts of gold mining and exploration companies. London, 1901.

DONALDSON, H. F.
Depreciation of building and machinery. *Engineering magazine,* April 1911, p. 171-6. *Engineering record,* Feb. 11, 1911, p. 159. *Mechanical engineer,* Feb. 10, 1911, p. 177-80, 202-4.

DONALDSON, J. S.
Railway accounting, mental and mechanical. *Association of American railway accounting officers,* 27th Report, 1912, p. 49-97. *Railway age gazette,* Aug. 30, Sept. 6, 1912, p. 392-4, 442-4.

DONALDSON, R. D.
Cost of operating motors in lime plants and quarries. *Electrical world,* August 12, 1916, p. 326.

DONATIONS
Esquerre, P. J. Donation account. (In his *Applied theory of accounts.* 1917. p. 334-5).
Finney, H. A. Contingent stock donation. *Journal of accountancy,* Dec. 1920, p. 469-70.
Jacobsson, Gustave M.A. Practical questions in accounting. *Business man's magazine,* Feb. 1912, p. 185-6.
Kester, R. B. Donated land. (In his *Accounting theory and practice.* 1918. v. 2. p. 308-9).
Kester, R. B. Treasury stock donated. (In his *Accounting theory and practice.* v. 2. 1918. p. 15-6).
McIntosh, R. J. Charities and donations. (In his *Reference book of accounts for manufacturing and mercantile companies.* c1914. p. 136).
Paton, William Andrew and R. A. Stevenson. Stock. (In their *Principles of accounting.* 1918. p. 280-90).
Pixley, Francis W. Donations to charities, etc. (In his *Accountancy.* Ed. 2, p. 195).
Robinson, Joseph. Gratuities. *Journal of accountancy,* Nov. 1918, p. 355-6.
Walton, Seymour. Donated real estate. *Journal of accountancy,* July 1918, p. 68-81.
Walton, Seymour. Donated surplus. *Journal of accountancy,* Dec. 1916, p. 485-6.
Walton, Seymour. Stock donated to cover deficit. *Journal of accoutnancy,* July 1915, p. 61-2.
Wildman, J. R. Administrative-expense group. (In his *Principles of accounting.* 1914. p. 223-4).

DONECKER, H. C.
Organization and functions of a valuation staff. *American electric railway association, Proceedings,* 1914, p. 99-118. Abstract. *Electric railway journal,* Oct. 14, 1914, p. 843.

DONLEY, D. R.
Preventing loss from charge accounts. *Metal work,* Mar. 9, 1917, p. 338. *Domestic engineering,* Mar. 10, 1917, p. 362-3. *Electrical review and western electrician,* Mar. 17, 1917, p. 457.

DONN, BENJAMIN
Accountant and geometrician; containing the doctrine of circulating decimals, logarithms, bookkeeping, etc. London, 1765.
Accountant, containing esays on book-keeping by single and double entry. Ed. 2. London, 1778.

DONOVON, D. J.
Contracts between steamhsip lines and shipping. *Annals of the American academy of political and social science,* September 1914, p. 168-84.

DOOLITTLE, F. W.
Anatomy of the interurban report. *Electric railway journal,* Feb. 10, 1917, p. 242-9.
Collection of traffic data. *Electric railway journal,* July 17, 1915, p. 94-101.
Operating cost and shifts in service. *Electric railway journal,* Aug. 21, 1915, p. 306-8.
Operating costs and shifts in service. *Electric railway journal,* Sept. 4, 1915, p. 400.
Problems of the electric railway industry. *Electric railway journal,* June 3, 1916, p. 1037-8.
Railway operation in Cleveland. *Electric railway journal,* February 19, 1916, p. 359-64.
Relationship of items of cost under pre-war conditions and today. *Electric railway journal,* Oct. 11, 1919, p. 9-11.

DOORS
See Woodwork.

DORR, E. S.
Modified cost plus contracts for city use. *Engineering and contracting,* Feb. 18, 1920, p. 178-9.

DORRANCE, C.
Increased cost of producing anthracite. *Coal mining review,* Feb. 1, 1916, p. 4.

DORSETT, SAMUEL SMITH
Law of principal and agent. *Incorporated accountants' journal,* 1902-3, p. 132.

DOSCH, ARNO
How Wall Street keeps its books. *Business man's magazine,* Sept. 1910, p. 252-8.

DOTY, L. E.
How I avoid unprofitable crops. *System on the farm,* July 1920, p. 22-3.

DOUBLE account balance sheet. *Business man's magazine,* April 1909, p. 377.

DOUBLE ACCOUNT SYSTEM
Brennan, T. F. Double account system. *Accountant,* June 14, 1919, p. 509-15. *Accounting and commerce,* April-June 1920, p. 19-22, 40-2, 65-6.
Carter, R. N. Double account system. (In his *Advanced accounts.* p. 909-23).
Dicksee, Lawrence R. Double-account system. (In his *Advanced accounting.* 1916. p. 157-62).
Dicksee, Lawrence R. Double account system. (In his *Depreciation, reserves and reserve funds.* 1912. p. 67-9).
Lisle, George. Double account form of balance sheet. (In his *Accounting theory and practice.* 1900. p. 79-82).
Nixon, Alfred and J. H. Stagg. Double account system. (In their *Accounting and banking.* 1912. p. 293-304).

DOUBLE ACCOUNT SYSTEM—*(Continued)*
RACINE, S. F. Double account system. (In his *Accounting principles.* 1917. p. 120).
SEAMAN, A. M. Double account system. *Accounting and commerce,* July, Aug. 1916, p. 86-7, 105-8.
SPICER, ERNEST EVAN and ERNEST C. PEGLER. Double account system. (In their *Bookkeeping and accounts.* 1914. p. 295-316).

DOUBLE account system. (In their *Accounting and banking.* 1912. p. 293-304).

DOUBLE entry. Holah, Ernest. 1883, 1886, 1903.

DOUBLE entry and single entry bookkeeping. Jones, T. 1877.

DOUBLE entry bookkeeping. *Hunt's merchant's magazine,* v. 1, p. 256.

DOUBLE entry book-keeping. Bucklin, J. N. 1883.

DOUBLE entry book-keeping. Cariss, A. 1884.

DOUBLE-entry book-keeping. Cusack, James. 1911.

DOUBLE entry bookkeeping. Dell, B. 1850.

DOUBLE entry bookkeeping. Edwards, J. 1842.

DOUBLE entry bookkeeping. Gibbs, Henry. 1877.

DOUBLE-entry book-keeping. Jackson, G. 1855.

DOUBLE entry bookkeeping. Meservey, A. B. 1889.

DOUBLE entry bookkeeping. Nelson, J. 1871.

DOUBLE entry book-keeping. Pow, J. K. 1850.

DOUBLE entry bookkeeping. Ross, W. P.

DOUBLE entry bookkeeping. Smith, T. 1840.

DOUBLE entry bookkeeping. Swill, A. 1885.

DOUBLE entry book-keeping for builders. Hasluck, P. N. 1906.

DOUBLE entry book-keeping for technical classes in schools. Clarke, G. F.

DOUBLE entry bookkeeping for the civil service. Hunter, J. 1878.

DOUBLE entry bookkeeping in theory and practice. Sarll, Andrew. 1899.

DOUBLE entry by single. Cronhelm, F. W. 1818.

DOUBLE entry drills. Marshall, C. C.

DOUBLE entry elucidated. Foster, B. F. 1843.

DOUBLE entry in one lesson. Fleming, R. 1908.

DOUBLE-entry in theory and practice Hamilton, W. R.

DOUBLE entry up to date. Armstrong, Augustus.

DOUBLEDAY, PAGE AND COMPANY.
Geographical manual and new atlas; ed. by C. O. S. Mawson. New York, Doubleday, Page & co. 1918. 392p.

DOUBTFUL factor in depreciation rates. *Engineering magazine,* Jan. 20, 1911.

DOUDS, H. J.
Preliminaries to the financing of electric railway projects. *Electric railway journal,* Aug. 1, 1914, p. 208-10.

DOUGALL, J. J.
Some phases of the debenture. *Accountant,* Aug. 8, 1908, p. 163-8. *Incorporated accountants' journal,* 909-10, p. 13.

DOUGHARTY, HAROLD
Notes on a profit sharing scheme for commercial travellers or buyers. *Accountant,* April 13, 1918, p. 292-3.

DOUGHERTY, G. E.
Decreasing accidents and increasing efficiency. *Coal age,* May 19, 1917, p. 866-7.

DOUGHTON, JOHN
Foundry accounting methods. *Iron age,* Nov. 12, 1908.

DOUGLAS, A. W.
Barometer prices that reflect business prosperity. *Factory,* Jan. 1917, p. 24-5.
Manufacturer's analysis of the railroad problem. *Factory,* March 1917, p. 326-7.
Manufacturer's reflections on textiles, rubber and finance. *Factory,* April 1917, p. 488-9.
Material prices worth thinking about. *Factory,* February 1917, p. 181.

DOUGLAS, H. K.
Goodwill. *Accounting and commerce,* Nov. 1915, p. 184-5.

DOUGLAS, J.
Profession in South Africa; a plea for federation; *South African accountants' journal,* v. 2, p. 56.

DOUGLAS, J. B.
Pensions and profit-sharing. *Progressive age,* Dec. 1, 1911, p. 1000-3.

DOUGLAS, P. H.
Methods of computing labor turnover. *American economic review,* June 1919, p. 402-5.

DOUGLAS, R. A.
Banking facilities for importers. *Accounting and commerce,* May 1918, p. 43-6.

DOUGLAS, THOMAS
Powers, duties and liabilities of executors. *Incorporated accountants' journal,* 1897-8, p. 55.

DOUTHWAITE, WILLIAM
Loanable capital. *Accountant,* May 13, 1905, p. 600-6.
Notes on banking. *Accountant,* Nov. 24, 1900, p. 1059-63.
Steam wagon transport trade. *Business organisation and management,* Dec. 1919, Jan. 1920, p. 55-60, 59-70.

DOVEY, W. R.
Some notes on valuation, with special reference to Mr. Chatham's paper in v. 32. *Journal of the Institute of actuaries,* 1900, v. 34, p. 346.

DOW, A.
Art of rate-making. *Electrical world,* Jan. 2, 1915, p. 17-8.

DOW, E. Y.
Pontchartrain hotel plant records. *Power,* June 23, 1914, p. 877.

DOW, WILLIAM
Laundry accounts. *Accountant,* June 13, 1908, p. 875-84.
Licensed trade accounts and goodwill. *Incorporated accountants' journal,* Jan. 1912, p. 95-7.

DOWD, A. A.
Effect of design on the cost of machining. *Machinery,* Dec. 1914, p. 273-7.
Use and abuse of time studies. *Iron age,* Feb. 4, 1915, p. 300-3.

DOWDALL, H. CHALONER
Bankruptcy bill. *Accountant,* June 1, 1912, p. 847-50.

DOWELL, STEPHEN
Acts relating to the income tax. Eighth edition embodying the income tax act, 1918, with complete notes, references and decisions, by John Edwin Piper. London, Butterworth & co. 1919. 744p.

DOWLER, FRANK and E. M. HARRIS.
Auditing, accounting and banking; a manual for accountants, advanced bookkeeping students and business men. London, Sir Isaac Pitman & sons. 319p.

DOWLING, DANIEL
Complete system of Italian book-keeping according to the modern method. Ed. 2. Dublin. 1770.
——— Same. Ed. 3. Dublin, 1775.

DOWNEY, B. C.
Reducing cost of handling cloth bags. *Concrete,* June, 1916, p. 250.

DOWNING, H. F.
Printing costs. *Pace student,* Aug. 1917.

DOWNING, W. J.
Cost of heating and power plant apparatus. *Power,* Nov. 18, 1913, p. 721-2.
Cost of power plant apparatus. *Engineering and mining journal,* March 21, 1914, p. 620.

DOWNS, W. S.
Form for filing records of construction conditions. *Engineering record,* February 24, 1917, p. 321.

DOWSLEY, W. G.
Church accounts. London, Sir Isaac Pitman & sons. 1911.
Farmers' account book; a simple and concise system of account keeping. London, Sir Isaac Pitman & sons, 1911.
Personal account book; a simple, concise and self-explanatory method of personal or domestic bookkeeping. London, Sir Isaac Pitman and sons, 1911. 106p.

DOWSON, F. EMERSON
Decimal coinage weights and measures. *Accountant,* April 18, 1891, p. 299-300.

DOXSEY, W. S.
Compiling cost data in a naval steel foundry. *Foundry,* April 15, 1919, p. 206-11.

DOYLE, E. P.
Shop methods—a description of the problems met and overcome in adapting a medium sized shop with few special facilities for a great variety of car maintenance work. *Electric railway journal,* Jan. 20, 1912, p. 115-6.

DOYLE, J. J.
Cost of operating the Washington, Baltimore and Annapolis electric railroad. *Engineering and contracting,* Dec. 31, 1913, p. 748-50.

DOYLE, J. S.
Maintenance of coasting recorders. *Electric railway journal,* Jan. 29, 1916, p. 215-6.

DOYLE, NORMAN
Uses and limitations of the card, loose-leaf ledgers, and slip systems, in relation to matters of account. *Accountant,* Nov. 9, 1907, p. 581-9.

DRAFT bill for registration of accountants in Victoria. *South African accountant and auditor,* Sept. 1916, p. 183-6.

DRAFT of a model C. P. A. act to create a state board of accountancy and to prescribe its powers and duties to provide for the examination of and issuance of certificates to qupalified accountants and to provide a penalty for violation of this act. *American institute of accountants, Yearbook,* 1906, 1907, 1908, p. 66-9, 218-20, 353-5.

DRAFT of a model C. P. A. law to regulate the profession of public accounting (under the state university plan of operating). *American institute of accountants, Yearbook,* 1906, 1907, 1908, p. 63-5, 215-7, 350-2.

DRAFT of a standard C. P. A. law; an act to create a state board of accountancy, and prescribe its duties and power; to provide for the examination of and issuance of certificates to qualified applicants, with the designation of certified public accountant and to provide the penalty for violations of the provisions thereof; approved September, 1916, by the Institute of accountants in the United States of America. 4p.

DRAFT rules under the deeds of arrangement acts, 1887 to 1913. *Incorporated accountants' journal,* March 1914, p. 172-8.

DRAFTING
DIEMER, HUGO. Drafting department. (In his *Factory organization and administration.* 1914. p. 149-58).
HAMMOCK, H. Hints for the drafting office *Business man's magazine,* Aug. 1907, p. 95 102.
JONES, FRANKLIN D. and EDWARD K. HAMMOND. Drafting room systems. (In their *Shop management and systems.* 1918. p. 276-98).
JORDAN, JOHN P. and GOULD L. HARRIS. Drafting department. (In their *Cost accounting.* 1920. p. 237).

Cost accounting
BAKENHUS, R. E. Cost records of drafting and engineering. *Engineering and contracting,* Nov. 29, 1916, p. 472-4.

Depreciation
See Depreciation, depletion and obsolescence—Drafting.

DRAFTS
AMERICAN institute of accountants, Special bulletin, No. 6. Nov. 1920, p. 4-5.
WALTON, SEYMOUR. Cheques and drafts. *Journal of accountancy,* Sept. 1915, p. 230-3,

DRAGLINE excavation costs. *Engineering and mining journal,* May 27, 1916, p. 940-1.

DRAINAGE

Accounting

MINDER, E. G. Work of the referee: accounting and efficiency as applied to drainage matters. *Affiliated engineering societies of Minnesota, Bulletin,* July 1917. Abstract. *Engineering news,* March 1, 1917, p. 351.

Costs

BURKHOLDER, H L. Drainage works of the Rio Grande irrigation project. *Engineering news,* Sept. 18, 1919, p. 543-9.

COLE, D. W. Cost of ditches for reclaiming Idaho lands. *Engineering news,* April 3, 1919, p. 678-9.

FERRIS, H. R. Cost of laying tile drain on two jobs. *Engineering and contracting,* Sept. 13, 1916, p. 233.

GODDARD, L. H. and H. O. TIFFANY. Cost of tile drainage; a study of the cost of installing thirty-five mile of tile drains on a farm in Huron county, Ohio *Ohio agricultural experiment station circular* no 147, Sept. 1914, p. 21-44.

OKEY, C. W. Cost of drainage pumping in southern Louisiana. *Engineering news,* Oct. 14, 1915, p. 733-5.

DRAPER CORPORATION.

Textile texts for cotton manufacturers, including special articles on carding, spinning, spooling, warping, dyeing, reeling, twisting and weaving; also genral history mathematical tables, and a description of the patented cotton machinery introduced and sold by Draper company, Hopedale, Mass., Draper corporation, 1917. 360p.

DRAPERS

See Dry goods.

DRAPERS' accounts. Richardson, G. H.

DRAPERS', dressmakers' and milliners' accounts. Richardson, G. H. 1904.

DRAPERY and drapers' accounts. Beynon, R. 1909.

DRAPERY business organization, management and accounts. Bayley, J. E.

DRAUGHON, J. F.

Draughon's progressive bookkeeping and business manual. Nashville, Tenn., Draughon text-book co 1917. 216p.

DRAUGHON, W. H.

How to safeguard the cash account. *Business man's magazine,* Aug. 1911, p. 141-3.

Insurance expense accounting. *Journal of accountancy,* July 1919, p. 16-24.

Pointers in up-to-date business science; looseleaf system in a tobacco warehouse. *Business man's magazine,* Dec. 1906, p. 106-8.

DRAYTON, CHARLES D.

Co-ordination of interstate and intra-state rates. *Traffic world,* Jan. 31, 1920, p. 191-4.

DREAM of scientific management on railroads. Fagan, J. O.

DREDGES

Costs

DANA, RICHARD T. Dredges. (In his *Handbook of construction plant.* 1914. p. 202-31).

Depreciation

See Depreciation, depletion and obsolescence—Dredges.

DREDGING

See also Gold dredging.

RECORDS and cost of work of Dipper dredges operated by the United States engineers in river and harbor improvements. *Engineering and contracting,* Aug. 13, 1913.

Cost accounting

COST sheets for dredging company. *Mining and scientific press,* 1913, v. 106, p. 518-9.

GILLETTE, HALBERT P. and RICHARD T. DANA. Cost keeping blanks for dredging (Engineering-contracting,May 26, 1909.) (In their *Cost kepeing and management engineering,* 1916. p. 225-30).

GILLETTE, HALBERT P. and RICHARD T. DANA. Forms of breakwater construction, including quarrying, concrete work and dredging. (In their *Cost keeping and management engineering.* 1916. p. 238-47).

GILLETTE, HALBERT P. and RICHARD T. DANA. Report card system for dredging work. (Engineerings news, June 13, Aug. 22, 1907). (In their *Cost keeping and management engineering.* 1916 p. 215-20).

GILLETTE, HALBERT P. and RICHARD T. DANA. System for recording costs of dredging and dredge maintenance. (Magee Fisher, Engineering-contracting, Aug. 14, 1907). (In their *Cost keeping and management engineering.* 1916. p. 220-5).

SHAW, A. M. Dredging contractor must keep in close personal touch with work. *Engineering and record,* Dec. 30, 1916, p. 802-3.

Costs

ALLISON, L. R. W. Cost of electric dredging for land reclamation, San Diego, California. *Engineering and contracting,* August 4, 1915, p. 95-6

BLAKE, E. M. Cost data on the work of improving the Neponset river in Massachusetts. *Engineering and contracting,* January 13, 1915, p. 34-6.

COST of dredging in Mississippi river. *Engineering and* contracting, July 21, 1920 p. 74.

COST of dredging irrigating ditches. *Engineering news-record,* May 3, 1917, p. 267.

COST of dredging 29,708,465 cubic yards of material with 24 sea-going Hopper dredges during 1912 *Engineering and contracting,* April 30, 1913.

LIPSEY, T. E. L. Cost of pipe dredging in open Gulf of Mexico. *Engineering and contracting,* July 21, 1920, p. 63-5.

DREFS, A. G.

Shop production—control and accounting systems. *Journal of the Society of automotive engineers,* July 1920, p. 33-8. Condensed. *Automotive industries,* July 1, 1920, p. 22-5.

DRENNAN, K. W.

Life assurance accounts. *Canadian chartered accountant,* Oct. 1915, p 115-31. *Public accountant,* March, April, 1916, p. 198-204, 213-23.

DRESSMAKING

Accounting

RICHARDSON, GEORGE HENRY. Drapers; dressmakers' and milliners' accounts. London, Gee & co. 1904. 132p. (Accountants' library, v. 31).

Cost accounting

FOX, W. H. Principles of percentages of cost as applied to various businesses. *Accountant,* Jan. 19, 1907, p. 86-96.

DREW, W. A.

Practical book-keeping. New edition. Chicago, George Sherwood & co. 1876.

DREYFUS, EDWIN D.

Appraisement of small electric properties. *Electric review and western electrician,* March 6, 13, 1915, p. 433-8, 500-5.

Graphic analyses of managerial problems. *Electrical world,* Oct. 7, 1916, p. 710-2.

Graphic representations of power plant losses. *Power,* May 11, 1915, p 638-9.

Notes on large power rates. *Electrical review and western electrician,* Feb. 28, 1914, p. 419-23.

Reckoning with costs of superseded equipment. *Electrical world,* Aug. 5, 1916, p. 272-4.

DRILL and tool sharpening shop at the Copper Queen mine. *Engineering and mining journal,* June 24, 1916, p. 1103-4.

DRILLING

Cost accounting

GILLETTE, HALBERT P. and RICHARD T. DANA. Blanks for recording work of well drills as used by the Nevada consolidated copper co. (Engineering-contracting, July 3, 1907). (In their *Cost keeping and management engineering.* 1916 p. 283).

GILLETTE, HALBERT P. and RICHARD T. DANA. Cost keeping on rock drill work (Engineering-contracting, Oct 23, 1907). (In their *Cost keeping and management engineering.* 1916. p. 210-5).

GILLETTE, HALBERT P. and RICHARD T. DANA. Forms for recording well-drilling costs. (Engineering-contracting, Nov. 20, 1907). (In their *Cost keeping and management engineering.* 1916. p. 215).

DRIVERS and garage clerks keep contractor's motor truck costs. *Engineering news-record,* Sept. 26, 1918, p. 589-90.

DROGE, W. H.

Cost of asphalt repairs at Fort Wayne, Indiana. *Enginering and contracting,* Feb. 7, 1917, p. 120.

DRUAR, JOHN F.

Rates and rate making. *Journal of the association of enginering societies,* 1907, p. 146.

Rates and rate making. *Journal of the association of engineering societies,* May 1913, p. 221.

DRUCKER, A. P. R.

Teaching bookkeeping by the historical method. *School science and mathematics,* Jan. 1920, p. 70-7.

DRUG store bookkeeping. Cook, E. Fullerton.

DRUG TRADE

Accounting

AMERICAN business and accounting encyclopaedia; comp. by E. H. Beach and W. W. Thorne. Detroit, Bookkeeper publishing co. 1901. Drug business—v.2. p. 473-7.

CHEMISTS' credit accounts. *Accountant* April 10, June 5, 1909, p. 489-92, 796-7.

COOK, E. FULLERTON. Drug store bookkeeping, especially adopted to the needs of the retail pharmacist. Ed.2. Philadelphia college of pharmacy, Philadelphia, E. F. Cook, 1912. 16p. For use of classes in Philadelphia college of pharmacy.

DRUG store. (In *International accountants' manual,* 1910, paragraph 420).

HARVARD university. Graduate school of business administration. Bureau of business research. Operating accounts for retail drug stores. Cambridge, Harvard university press. 1920. (Bulletin no. 16).

HOPKINS, E. C. Office system for wholesaler. *Business man's magazine,* Oct. 1907, p. 52-62.

STILL, J. H. Accounting methods for retail drug business. *Business man's magazine,* Sept. 1906, p. 136-46.

SYSTEM for the prescription department of a retail druggist. *Business man's magazine,* Jan. 1905, p. 105.

WEDDELL, GEORGE. How do I stand? bookkeeping and balancing for retail chemists. Newcastle-on-Tyne, 1891.

WILEY, ALBERT J. System of accounting for a drug store. *Business man's magazine,* Sept. 1909, p. 264-7.

Cost accounting

GOLDBERG, J. A. My fight with rising costs. *System,* Jan. 1917, p. 30-6.

IT pays to know. *System,* Sept. 1917, p. 392.

SCHREIBER, GEORGE I. Because I know my costs. *System,* Jan. 1918, p. 52-4.

DRUGS

See also Chemicals.

Accounting

DEVLIN, JOHN H. Accounting for proprietary preparations. *Journal of accountancy,* July *of accountancy,* July 1920, p. 36-42.

Cost accounting

DAY, CLARENCE MUNRO. Cost system for a drug compounding laboratory and factory. (In his *Accounting practice.* 1915. p 146-51).

MILLS, JAMES COOKE. Find the cost of drug products. *Business man's magazine,* June 1911, p. 569-75.

Depreciation

See Depreciation, depletion and obsolescence—Drugs.

DRUMMOND, ARTHUR

On the mode of conducting an audit. *Accountant,* May 2, 16, 1891, p. 341-3, 377-9

DRUMMOND, R. C. S.

Six-cent fare problem; past and future. *New York state conference of mayors and other city officials Proceedings,* 1918, p. 63-77.

DRURY, A. G.

Determining labor costs of pole line extensions. *Electrical world,* June 29, 1918, p 1376.

Effecting economies by the study of time slips. *Domestic engineering,* May 8, 1920 p. 235-6.

DRURY, HORACE BOOKWALTER

Scientific management; a story and criticism Ed. 2, revised. New York, Longmans, Green & co. 1918. 222p. Columbia university studies in history, economics and public law. v. 65, no. 2).

Scientific management and organized labor *Industrial engineering,* May, 1914, p. 192-3

DRURY, HORATIO N.

Your market value. New York, Pace & Pace [1916]. 35p.

DRY GOODS

NATIONAL retail dry goods association. Report and digest of the proceedings first annual convention controllers' congress. June 7, 8, 9, 1920. Cleveland, Ohio. New York, National retail dry goods association, 1920 48p.

Accounting

BAYLEY, J. ERNEST. Drapery organisation, management and accounts. London, Sir Isaac Pitman & sons. 291p.

BEYNON, R. Drapery and drapers' accounts London, Sir Isaac Pitman and sons, 1909, 274p.

DRY GOODS—ACCOUNTING—*(Continued)*
DRY goods. (In *International accountants' manual,* 1910, paragraphs 478, 479).
DRY goods economist. See Department of accounting and system.
ERNEST & ERNEST. Some accountancy questions and answers. *National retail dry goods association. Accounting department, Bulletin,* 1913, v.2, special, no. 2, p. 2-8.
MANUAL for drapers accounts and allied trades. Royal exchange. Effingham Wilson. 1899.
MODERN methods of accounting in the dry goods business. *The office,* Aug. 1890, p. 216-8.
NATIONAL retail dry goods association. *Accountancy bulletin,* 1912-3.
RICHARDSON, GEORGE HENRY. Drapers' accounts; by a corporate accountant. London, Effingham Wilson, 1898. 92p.
RICHARDSON, GEORGE HENRY. Drapers', dressmakers' and milliners' accounts. London, Gee & co. 1904. 132p. (Accountants' library, v. 31).
RICHARDSON, GEORGE HENRY. Statistical side of bookkeeping; monthly returns for drapers etc. *Accountant,* Nov. 16, 1901, p. 1257-8.

Stockkeeping
TIENKEN, H. ALBERT. Perpetual inventory and record of stock to sell. *Business man's magazine,* July 1908, p. 63-6.

DRY goods delivery by electric vehicles in winter. *Electrical world,* March 28, 1914, p. 712.

DRYE, J. W.
See Spencer, Enos, joint author.

DUBOIS, CHARLES G.
Accounting conditions of prospects. *American institute of accountants, Yearbook,* 1914, p. 97-116. *Canadian chartered accountant,* April 1915, p. 321-33. *Journal of accountancy,* Oct. 1914, p. 245-59.
Brief history of telephone accounting; a lecture delivered to the students of the Amos Tuck school of administration and finance, associated with Dartmouth college, Hanover, N.H., February 10, 1913. 39p. *Accountant,* Nov. 22, 29, 1913, p. 749-61, 788-803.
Standard telephone accounts; a commentary on accounting circular no. 6; a paper read before the Philadelphia telephone society, December 14, 1909. 29p. *Government accountant,* June, July, Aug. 1911, p. 51-63, 127-32, 172-8.

DUBOIS, FRANK G.
Attack on the New Jersey law: correspondence. *Journal of accountancy,* March 1906, p. 417-8.

DUDBRIDGE, SIDNEY
Apportionments between capital and income. *Incorporated accountants' journal,* Jan. 1912, p. 104-7.

DUDGEON, H. A.
Paying the men who deliver the goods. *Factory,* Aug. 15, 1920, p. 535-6.

DUDLEY, BERNARD
Building societies' accounts. *Accountant,* July 27, 1912, p. 119-30.

DUDLEY, GEORGE OSGOOD
Corporation accounting; including exercises in special accounting problems of the large corporation. Saginaw, Michigan, The F. H. Bliss publishing co. 86p.

DUDLEY, W. F.
Work of the freight auditor. (In Dewsnup, Ernest Ritson, ed. *Railway organization and working.* 1906. p. 335-66).

DUE DATES
See Average due dates.

DUE dates for returns and payments of federal and New York state and city taxes for 1921. Guaranty trust company of New York. 1920.

DUER, J. V. B.
Third rail and trolley system of the West Jersey and seashore railroads. *American institute of electrical engineers, Proceedings,* June 1915, v. 34, p. 1237-53. Abstract. *Electric railway journal,* July 10, 1915, p. 58-9.

DUES
See also Societies, clubs etc.
KEEPING track of dues. *System,* Sept. 1917, p. 436.

DUETMAN, E. G.
Roasting and magnetic separation of Wisconsin zinc ores; with cost talks. *Engineering and mining journal,* June 28, 1919, p. 1107-11.

DUETZMAN, L. F.
Bonus system. *Inland printer,* Feb. 1914, p. 741.

DUFF, C. P. AND OTHERS
Common school bookkeeping. New York, American book co.

DUFF, PETER
Duff's book-keeping by single and double entry practically illustrating 'marchants', 'manufacturers', 'private bankers', railroad, and national bank accounts, including all the late improvements in the science, with a copious index. Ed. 20, revised and enlarged. New York, Harper & brothers, 1882.
North American accountant, embracing single and double entry bookkeeping; for the use of schools. New York, Harper & brothers, 1855.
——— School edition. New York, Harper & brothers.

DUFFEY, EDWIN
Work of providing the State of New York with good roads and its cost. *Economic world,* Jan. 1917, p. 45-7.

DUFFEY, P. R.
Boiler and engine-room sheets. *Power,* Sept. 16, 1919. p. 461-3.
Tool room equipment and management. *Railway age* (Mech. ed.), Feb. 1914, p. 87-8.

DUFFY, C. N.
Classification of accounts for: electric railway companies, electric light and power companies, steam heat companies, gas companies, Milwaukee, Jan. 1, 1910, 163p.
Depreciation. *Electrical world,* Feb. 1, 1908, p. 217. *Electric railway review,* Jan. 18, 1908, p. 83. *Electrical review* (London), Sept. 4, 1908, p. 374. *Street railway journal,* Feb. 1, 1908, p. 169. Editorial. *Electrical world,* Feb. 1, 1908, p. 207.
Depreciation. *Electric railway journal,* Jan. 29, 1910, p. 184. *Electrical world,* Feb. 1, 1908, p. 217-9. *Progressive age,* Sept. 1, 1909, p. 686.

DUFFY, C. N.—*(Continued)*

Economics of the Cleveland railway situation as developed in the 1913 arbitration decision. *Electric railway journal*, October 15, 1913, p. 770-3.

Effect of load factor on cost of electric railway passenger service. *Electric railway journal*, Feb. 1, 1913, p. 195-6.

Electric utilities rates of fare and return on investment. *Electric railway journal*, Jan. 20, 1912, p. 103.

Failure of three-cent car fares. *Public service*, Nov. 1913, p. 153.

Milwaukee electric railway and light company's reply to accounting circular. *Electric railway journal*, April 4, 1908, p. 419.

Rate of return of electric railways. *Electric railway journal*, May 14, 1910, p. 871-2.

DUFOUR, F. O.

Federal valuation of railroads. *Stone and Webster journal*, Aug. 1917, p. 93-104.

DUGUID, CHARLES

Rights and duties of auditors. *Accountant*, Oct. 22, Dec. 17, 1910, Jan. 21, 1911, Feb. 17, March 9, 1912, p. 570, 837, 865, 84, 119, 301, 373. *Incorporated accountants' journal*, 1910-11, p. 36, 53, 62, 79, 92, 124. Editorial. *Journal of accountancy* Dec. 1910, p. 143-5

DUKES, A. T.

Voucher checks. *Business man's magazine*, April 1908, p. 365-6.

DULING, J. F.

Office methods in planning and building a new town. *Engineering news*, Jan. 22, 1914, p. 188-90.

DUMAS, L. F.

Cutting wisdom and orchard costs. *Better fruit*, April 1917, p. 42.

DUMONT, R. D.

See Slade, A. J., joint author.

DUNAWAY, J. A.

Some efficiency methods of city administration. *Annals of the American academy of political and social science*, March 1916.

DUNBAR, CHARLES FRANKLIN

Theory and history of banking. Ed.3, enlarged. New York, G. P. Putnam's sons, 1917. 297p.

DUNCAN, CARSON SAMUEL

Commercial research; an outline of working principles. New York, The Macmillan company, 1919. 385p.

Mercantile and agricultural economics. *Journal of political economy*, Oct. 1918, p. 769-806.

DUNCAN, D. B.

Cost keeping system for building contractors. *Engineering and contracting*, Sept. 27, 1916, p. 272-3.

DUNCAN, J. C. D.

Discussion. *American economic association, Bulletin*, April 1911, p. 146-9.

DUNCAN, JAMES

Efficiency. *Journal of accountancy*, May 1911, p. 26-34.

DUNCAN, JOHN C.

Definition of accounting. *Journal of accountancy*, Feb. 1909, p. 274-81.

Methods of determining the efficiency of labor. *Journal of accountancy*, Feb. 1906, p. 301-9.

Principles of industrial management. New York, D. Appleton & co. 1916. 323p.

Priority in educational methods. *Journal of accountancy*, Feb. 1915, p. 161-2.

Property accounting for fire losses. *Journal of accountancy*, April, July, Dec. 1908, p. 442-9, 166-73, 122-32.

Some scientific and educational problems of the accountancy profession. *American institute of accountants, Yearbook*, 1914, p. 134-52. *Journal of accountancy*, Oct. 1914, p. 260-75.

Teacher's view of the examiner's attitude. *Journal of accountancy*, Sept. 1909, p. 356-61.

DUNCAN, NATHANIEL B.

Verification of inventories during an audit. *Journal of accountancy*, Dec. 1910, Sept. 1911, p. 143-5, 352-6.

DUNDERDALE, CHARLES

Responsibilities of trustees. *Accountant*, Sept. 13, 27, 1890, p. 492-3, 510-3.

DUNGAN, W. G.

Weekly progress report for section foremen as a means of increasing efficiency. *Railway age gazette*, July 21, 1911, p. 131-2.

DUNGER, RICHARD F.

Present need of proper cost finding. *100%*. Dec. 1920, p. 76-84.

DUNHAM, A. C.

Comparative values of water power and steam power. *Electrical world*, Jan. 6, 1912, p. 38. Abstract. Value of water power. *Engineering record*, Feb. 17, 1912, p. 181.

DUNHAM, HOWARD P. COMP.

Business of insurance; a text book and reference work covering all lines of insurance. 3v. New York, The Ronald press co. 1912.

DUNLAP, JOHN HOFFMAN

Water works statistics of 38 cities of Iowa with meter rates of 70 cities. University of Iowa, 1915. 52p. (University extension bulletin 8)

DUNN, ARTHUR

Scientific selling and advertising. Ed.4. New York, Industrial publishing company, 1920. 119p.

DUNN, H. H.

Fifty shops given to clerks. *Technical world*, June 1915, p. 444-8.

DUNN, HOMER A.

Accounting inconsistencies and fallacies; an address delivered before the 1916 convention of the American electric railway accountants association. 15p. *Accountant*, Dec. 23, 1916, p. 599-603.

American electric railway accountants' association. Proceedings, 1916, p. 76-83, *Electric railway journal*, Oct. 14, 1916.

Depreciation in railway accounting. *Railway age*, May 29, 1908, p. 756.

Federal taxes on incomes. *American association of university instructors in accounting, Papers and proceedings*, March 1918, p. 11-26.

Information needs of investors for judgment of public utilities; reprinted from the Journal of commerce and commercial bulletin, New York, September 26, 1916. Ed.3. New York, *Journal of commerce and commercial bulletin*, c1916. 15p. *Accountant*, Dec. 30, 1916, p. 616-20.

DUNN, J. H.
Uniform cost accounting. *Automotive industries*, May 2, 1918, p. 854. Abstract, *Iron age*, April 25, 1918, p. 1082-3.

DUNN, RUSSELL L.
Valuation of water power sites. *Journal of electricity, power and gas*, Jan. 10, 1914, p. 39.

DUNN, S. O.
American transportation question. New York, D. Appleton & co. 1912. 290p.
Current railway problems. New York, *Railway age gazette*, 1911.
Railway efficiency in its relation to an advance in freight rates. *Journal of political economy*, Feb. 1915, p. 128-43.
Valuation of public utilities from the railway point of view. *Journal of the western society of engineers*, May, 1914, p. 507-16.
Valuation of railways. *Atlantic*, March 1914, p. 403-16.
Valuation of railways, with special reference to the physical valuation in Minnesota. *Journal of political economy*, April 1909, p. 189-205.

DUNN, THOMAS
Importance of bookkeeping to traders. *Accountant*, June 25, 1898, p. 657-9.

DUNN, W. L.
Co-operation on pay-day. *Accounting and commerce*, Apri 1918, p. 10-12.
Debentures. *Accounting and commerce*, Aug. 1918, p. 113-6.

DUPLICATE form of power and light bill. *Electrical review*, Aug. 3, 1918, p. 178.

DURABILITY of steel water mains. *Engineering and contracting*, July 31, 1912, p. 130.

DURAND, E. D.
Finances of New York city. New York. The Macmillan company. 1898. 397p.
Progress toward absurdity. *Journal of accountancy*, April 1915, p. 297-9.

DURAND, W. L. AND D. FLIEGELMAN
Method of cost finding. *Power*, December 2, 1913, p. 797-8.

DURATION of life of flooring materials. *Real estate magazine*, May 1914.

DURELL, FLETCHER
Fundamental sources of efficiency. Philadelphia, J. B. Lippincott co. 1914. 368p.

DUREN, GEORGE A.
Cost of a mile of road. *Engineering and contracting*, May 7, 1919, p. 485-6.

DURFEE, BRADFORD K.
How to examine a life insurance company. (In Fricke, William A. *Insurance*. 1898. p. 510-2).

DURHAM, E. M.
Comments on the general features embodied in the report of the reproduction cost now of the Atlanta, Birmingham & Atlanta railroad company. President's conference committee. 1916.

DURHAM, H. W.
Comparative costs of pavements. *Engineering and contracting*, February 7, 1917, p. 119.

DURHAM, J. A. ROBERTSON
See Robertson-Durham, J. A.

DUROSE, ARTHUR
Uniformity of practice in the certificate and requirements of auditors under the companies act, 1900, and in the report to shareholders. *Accountant*, May 31, 1902, p. 575-7.

DURRELL, ARTHUR JAMES VAVASOR
Principles and practice of the system of control over parliamentary grants. Portsmouth, Gieves publishing co. 1917. 519p.

DUSENBURY, B. A.
Accounting for wireless service companies. *Pace student*, Aug. 1920.

DUTCH auctions. *Accountant*, April 30, 1910, p. 589-92.

DUTCH view of sinking fund accounts. Hogeweg, G. P. J.

DUTIES and liabilities of auditors. *Accountant*, Oct. 22, Nov. 12, 1910, Dec. 2, 6, 1911, Jan. 20, 1912 p. 547-55 637-9, 741-4, 813-8, 73-7.

DUTIES and liabilities of bank directors. Alcorn, E. G. c1915.

DUTIES and responsibiities of auditors. *Accountant*, Sept. 30, 30, Nov. 18, Dec. 16, 16, 1899, p. 980-1, 990-3, 1121-2, 1203-6, 1223-4.

DUTIES and responsibilities of auditors. *Business*, April 1895, p. 159-60.

DUTIES and responsibilities of auditors. *Incorporated accountants journal*, 1901-2, p. 11. *Accountant*, Sept. 14, 1901, p. 990-5.

DUTIES and responsibilities of the public accountant with regard to new issues of stocks and bonds. Dickinson, A. L.

DUTIES of a factory cost accountant. Gill, Joseph.

DUTIES of a factory cost accountant. White, L. H.

DUTIES of accountants towards new companies *Accountant*, Jan. 7, 1899, p. 7-9, 67-9.

DUTIES of auditors. *Accountant*, May 18, 1912, p. 745.

DUTIES of auditors. *Accountant*, Jan. 8, 1916, Feb. 2, 1918, p. 36-8, 89-92.

DUTIES of auditors; a symposium. *Accountant*, March 28, 1896, p. 259-62. *Business*, Feb. 1896, p. 87-9.

DUTIES of auditors; limits of responsibility —clearer definition needed. *Accountant*, May 18, 1912, p. 780-1.

DUTIES of auditors under the companies act, 1900. *Accountant*, Dec. 15, 22, 29, 1900, p. 1135-8, 1157-60, 1185-7.

DUTIES of receivers and managers. *Accountant*, March 16, 1912, p. 419-20.

DUTIES of the junior accountant. Reynolds, W. B. and F. W. Thornton, 1918.

DUTIES of trustees and official receivers in bankruptcy. Baker, George A.

DUTIES, responsibilities and rightful authority of an accounting officer. *Railroad gazette*, Jan. 19, 1877, p. 25-6.

DUTTON, L. R.

Commercial motor delivery, costs and results. *Progressive age,* Nov. 15, 1911, p. 958-68.

Motor delivery. *Progressive age,* June 1, 1911, p. 464-6.

DUTTON, M. S.

Sterilization by liquid chlorine and hypochlorite of lime. *Journal of the American water works association,* June 1917, p. 228-30. Condensed. *Engineering and contracting,* April 11, 1917, p. 358.

DUTY and responsibility of auditors with regard to the "stock-in-trade" on a balance sheet. Bird, Cyril F. 1917.

DUTY of an auditor. Roberts, L. A.

DUXBURY, NATHANIEL

Abbreviated methods in accountancy. *Accountant,* Oct. 10, 1914, p. 407-11.

Points arising in income tax practice. *Incorporated accountants' journal,* April 1915, p. 152-4.

Scope of the audit. *Accountant,* Feb. 5, 1916, p. 177-81. *Incorporated accountants' journal,* Jan. 1916, p. 78-81. *South African accountant and auditor,* Sept. Dec. 1916, p. 191-3, 207-9.

Sectional balancing. *Incorporated accountants' journal,* 1910-11, p. 209.

Taxation of co-operative societies. *Incorporated accountants' journal,* 1909-10, p. 130.

DWIGHT, EDMUND

Employers' liability and workmen's compensation. (In Humphreys, A. C. *Lecture notes on some of the business features of engineering practice.* p. 444-55).

DWOROK, E. A.

Corey and McKenzie complete accounting system and record for national farm loan associations. 1407 Harney St., Omaha, Nebraska, Corey and McKenzie printing company, 1917. 49p.

DYCHE, WILLIAM A.

Need of business methods in our universities. *Journal of accountancy,* Dec. 1905, p. 122-7.

DYEING

BEECH, FRANKLIN. Dyeing of cotton fabrics; a practical handbook for the dyer and student. Second revised edition. London, Scott, Greenwood and son, 1917. 267p. $3.00.

BEECH, FRANKLIN. Dyeing of woolen fabrics; London, Scott, Greenwood and son, 1902. 237p.

HEERMANN, PAUL. Dyers' materials; an introduction to the examination, valuation and application of the most important substances used in dyeing, printing and bleaching and finishing: translated by Arthur C. Wright. Second English edition, revised and enlarged by H. B. Stocks. London, Scott, Greenwood & son, 1919. 152p.

Costs

MATOS, L. J. Labor cost of dyeing cotton yarns. *Textile world,* Mar. 1915, p. 625-6.

WOLLASTON, T. RONALD. Power and heat costs in bleach and dye works. *Journal of the British association of managers of textile works,* 1914-15, p. 111-20.

DYEING of cotton fabrics. Beech, Franklin. 1917.

DYEING of woolen fabrics. Beech, Franklin. 1902.

DYER, CHARLES EDWIN

Auditors, and the audit of municipal accounts. *Accountant,* June 29, 1895, p. 584-8.

Consolidated rate for all local purposes. *Incorporated accountants journal,* 1906-7, p. 14.

DYER, S.

Common-sense method of double entry bookkeeping on first principles, as suggested by De Morgan. London, G. Philip & son, 1897. 140 + 166p.

DYERS' materials. Heermann, Paul. 1919.

DYES

FAY, IRVING W. Chemistry of the coal-tar dyes. Ed.2, revised and enlarged. New York, D. Van Nostrand company, 1919. 500p.

UNITED STATES. House of representatives. Dyestuffs, hearings before the committee on ways and means, House of representatives on H. R. 2706, a bill to amend an act entitled "An act to increase the revenue, and for other purposes," approved September 8, 1916, and H.R. 6495 a bill to regulate the importation of coal-tar products, to promote the establishment of the manufacture thereof in the United States, and, as incident thereto, to amend the act of September 8, 1916, entitled "An act to increase the revenue, and for other purposes. June, 18-20 and July 14-18, 1919. Washington, Government printing office, 1919. 735p.

UNITED STATES. Tariff commission. Census of dyes and coal-tar chemicals 1917. Washington, Government printing office, 1918 73p. (Tariff—information series no. 6)

UNITED STATES. Tariff commission. Census of dyes and coal-tar chemicals 1918. Washington, Government printing office, 1919. 103p. (Tariff information series no. 11).

UNITED STATES. Tariff commission. Dyes and other coal-tar chemicals; report to congress recommending amendments to title V of act of September 8, 1916. Washington, Government printing office, 1918. 83p.

Cost accounting

EFFECT of machine depreciation upon cost of dye-making. *Color trade journal,* April 1920, p. 103-6.

SCHOELLKOPH, HARTFORD and HANNA CO. Tables showing cost of a coal-tar dye plant designed for a yearly output of three million pounds; depreciation; employees needed, materials required and cost of production. *Journal of industrial and engineering chemistry,* 1917, v.7, p. 708.

DYSON, C. E.

Bookkeeping. New ed. London, Warne & co. 1889.

DYSON, S. S. AND S. S. CLARKSON

Chemical works, their design, erection and equipment. London, Scott, Greenwood and son, 1920. 207p.

EARL, GEORGE G.

Improvement and standardization of procedure in water works management. *Engineering and contracting,* June 30, 1915, p. 569-70.

EARL, W. A.

Employees representation in its relationship to industrial peace—an English experience. *Industrial management,* Sept. 1920, p. 187-8.

EARLY days of accountancy. *Journal of accountancy,* Oct. 1913, p. 310-1.

EARLY rate decision expected. *Railway age,* July 23, 1920, p. 145-6.

EARLY stages of preparations for the accountancy papers of the intermediate examinations. Cutforth, A. E. 1906.

EARNINGS and income of the corporation tax law. Panghorn, W. S.

EARNINGS of ore roads discussed. *Iron trade review*, May 28, 1914, p. 978-9.

EARNSHAW, J. P.
Voluntary liquidation under the companies (consolidation) act 1908, with forms. 1911.

EARTH excavated for less than six cents per yard in district no. 9, Mississippi county, Arkansas. *Engineering record*, Feb. 6, 1915, p. 176.

EARTH handled cheaply in grading Utah roads. *Engineering news-record*, July 6, 1916, p. 28-9.

EAST OF FIFE AGRICULTURAL SOCIETY
Farmers' cash book. Cupar-Fife, A. Westwood & Son, 1916.

EAST of Scotland bankruptcy reform association. *Accountant*, June 15, 1907, p. 827-30.

EASTERN exchange currency and finance. Spalding, William F. 1918.

EASTERN roads rate case. *Railway age*, Oct. 19-26, 1917, p. 691, 756.

EASTMAN, GEORGE
Book-keeping by single and double entry. New York, A. S. Barnes & co. 1851.

EASTMAN, GEORGE W.
See Fulton, L. S., joint author.

EASTMAN, JOSEPH B.
Address delivered at the thirty second annual meeting of the Railway accounting officers association, Atlantic city, May 12, 1920. Washington, Railway accounting officers association, 1920. 13p.

EASTON, EDWARD D.
Outposts of business. *Business man's magazine*, Dec. 1910, p. 503-8.

EASTON H. D.
Daily report forms. *Coal age*, Oct. 20, 1917, p. 660-1.

EASTON, H. T.
English bank book-keeping. London, Effingham Wilson, 1910, 199p.
English bank bookkeeping; with an introduction on the theory and practice of accounts. London, Effingham Wilson, 1910. 208p.
Practical banking. *Incorporated accountants journal*, 1905-6, p. 241.
Practice of banking, with special reference to bookkeeping. *Accountant*. July 15, 22, 1899, p. 751-9, 778-88.
Work of a bank; an elementary text-book for bank officials. London, Effingham Wilson, 1916. 150p.

EASTON, JAMES MARSHALL
Liabilities of auditors of companies, with special reference to the companies act, 1900. *Accountant*, April 27, 1901, p. 501-6, 895.

EASTON, WILLIAM H.
Depreciation of electrical machinery. *American machinist*, July 19, 1917, p. 101-2.

EASTWOOD, THOMAS CROSSLEY
Debentures. *Accountant*, Oct. 3, 1891, p. 699-704.

EASY book-keeping for small cooperative societies. Hines, G., B. Jones and H. Pumphrey.

EASY detail account book for rectifiers and wholesale liquor dealers. Moody, A. F. 1912.

EASY exercises for primer of bookkeeping. Pitman, Isaac.

EASY exercises in bookkeeping. Thornton, J.

EASY introduction to bookkeeping—for the improvement of young accountants. 1776.

EASY introduction to book-keeping, in four short sets, (also) farm book-keeping, etc. Jamieson, John. 1835.

EASY method of keeping rent and agents accounts. Aldridge, E. H. M. 1899.

EASY method of keeping rent and interest accounts. Aldridge, E. H. M.

EASY-TO-KEEP account book. Nashville, Tenn., Southern publishing association.

EATON, ABIJAH H.
Eaton and Burnett revised and improved bookkeeping, corporation, voucher and cost accounting embracing all modern and scientific methods used in business. Baltimore, Eaton & Burnett business college, inc. 1917. 261p.

EATON, HARVEY D.
Maine water districts and appraises. *Journal of the New England water works association*, June 1905, p. 147.

EATON, JAMES SHIRLEY
Auditor and station agent. Cleveland, Ohio. 1898. 11p. *Railway agent and station agent*, July 1898.
Duties of the traveling auditor. 1898. 12p.
Handbook of railroad expenses. New York, McGraw-Hill book co. 1913. 559p.
Indirect results of national railway valuation. *Engineering magazine*, Nov. 1913, p. 169-76.
Railroad operations—how to know them from a study of accounts and statistics. New York, Railway age gazette, 1900. 313p.
Studies in freight accounting. Washington, 1898. 13p. *Railway agent and station agent*, June 1898.

EATON, JOSEPH JORDON
Record forms for vocational schools. Yonkers, World book co. 1917. 56p.

EATON, SEYMOUR
Business forms, customs and accounts for schools. New York, American book co. 1895.

EAVES, WILLIAM
Bankruptcy and deeds of arrangement act, 1913. *Incorporated accountants' journal*, Dec. 1913, p. 76-8.
Excess profits duty. *Incorporated accountants' journal*, April 1916, p. 157-8.

EBBELS, F. C.
See Stewart, R. S., joint author.

EBERMAN, W. A.
Records at the Blackstone hotel, Chicago. *Power*, April 18, 1916, p. 551-6.

EBERSOLE, J. F.
Cattle loan banks. *Journal of political economy,* June 1914, p. 577-80.

ECHOLS, F. G.
Account of the methods used and the results obtained by the Greenfield tap and die corporation, Greenfield, Mass., in the application of workmen's representation in the plants of the corporation. *Machinery,* July 1920, p. 1007-12.

ECKEL, EDWIN C.
American iron ore reserves; bases for their valuation. *Engineering magazine,* Oct. 1912, p. 7-15.
Iron ores, their occurrence, valuation and control. New York, McGraw-Hill book co. 1914. 430p.
Portland cement industry from a financial standpoint. New York, Moody's magazine, 1908. 93p.

ECKERSLEY, FREDERICK S.
Form of accounts for local authorities. *Accountant,* Sept. 8, 1906, p. 263-8.
Urban district councils' accounts. London, Gee & co. 1906. 137p. (Accountants' library, v. 45).

ECKLEY, W.
See Oakes, Charles E., joint author.

ECLECTIC key to Complete bookkeeping. Mayhew, Ira.

ECONOMIC aspect of cost accounts and its application to the accounting of industrial companies. Dickinson, A. L.

ECONOMIC aspects of accounting and auditing. Lafrentz, F. W.

ECONOMIC aspects of depreciation. *Railway review,* Aug. 25, 1917, p. 234-5.

ECONOMIC aspects of summer load. *Electrical world,* May 25, 1918, p. 1084-7.

ECONOMIC operation of Smith form-a-truck in public service work. *Engineering and contracting,* Jan. 2, 1918, p. 32.

ECONOMIC status of the public. Warn, C. E.

ECONOMIC study of the four alternate methods considered for the disposal of the garbage rubbish and ashes of Toronto. *Engineering and contracting,* March 27, April 10, 1912.

ECONOMIC value of gas and electric plants. *Gas age,* June 2, 1913, p. 567-8.

ECONOMICAL bank examinations. *Bankers magazine,* Mar. 1912, p. 34.

ECONOMICAL gravel production and haulage for road work. *Concrete,* August 1916, p. 66.

ECONOMICAL interchangeable manufacturing practice. *Machinery,* March 1920, p. 636-41.

ECONOMICAL life of car motors. *Electrical review* (London), Nov. 27, 1908, p. 914.

ECONOMICAL locomotive performance on the Frisco. *Railway age gazette,* May 8, 1914, p. 1018-21.

ECONOMICAL maintenance of storeroom supplies. *Electric railway journal,* April 20, 1912, p. 645.

ECONOMICAL operating methods and the study of economies in waterworks pumping plants. *Engineering and contracting,* April 23, 1913, p. 477-8.

ECONOMICAL post-card monthly bill form. *Electrical world,* Sept. 8, 1917, p. 484-5.

ECONOMICAL voucher record. *Business man's magazine,* Dec. 1910, p. 565-6.

ECONOMICALLY unsound practically unjust. Suffern, E. L.

ECONOMICS
Accountancy and economics. *Journal of accountancy,* June 1908, p. 140.
Accountancy and economics. *Journal of accountancy,* Jan. 1909, p. 237-9.
Aiken, A. Economic position of the Transvaal. *South African accountants' journal,* v.1. p. 50.
Atkinson, H. Economical production and prevention of waste. *Accountant,* May 1, 1920, p. 521-4.
Barnes, G. N. Unemployment, production, high prices and world competition. *Accountant,* Oct. 9, 1920, p. 384-8.
Bastable, C. F. On some economic effects of war. *Accountants' magazine,* 1900, p. 399.
Branford, Victor V. Accounting in its relation to economics. (In Lisle, George. *Encyclopaedia of accounting.* v.1. p. 24-50).
Branford, Victor V. On the correlation of economics and accountancy. *Accountant,* May 25, June 1, 1901, p. 620-8, 642-8.
Brown, William. Notes on value, credit, money. *Accountant,* Sept. 2, 1905, p. 263-9.
Browne, Balfour. Economics of socialism. *Accountant,* Oct. 10, 1908, p. 446-52.
Burton, F. G. Economic aspect of municipal and state ownership. *Incorporated accountants' journal,* 1905-6, p. 222.
Clark, Archibald B. Gold-supply, credit and prices. *Accountants' magazine,* April 1899, p. 238-60.
Clark, Archibald B. Our free trade policy and present day problems. *Accountants' magazine,* June 1899, p. 366-83.
Clark, Archibald B. Trusts in their economic aspects. *Accountants' magazine,* Nov. 1901, p. 482-90.
Cleveland, Frederick A. Dr. Cleveland's response: correspondence. *Journal of accountancy,* Dec. 1906, p. 156-7.
Cleveland, Frederick A. What may accountancy teach economics? *Journal of accountancy,* Oct. 1906, p. 401-19.
Clews, Henry. No danger in great fortunes. *Journal of accountancy,* Feb. 1907, p. 276-84.
Craigie, P. G. Relation of population and food-production. *Accountants' magazine,* May, 1910, 258-75.
Cunningham, W. Back to Adam Smith. *Accountants' magazine,* Jan. 1904, p. 7-22.
Dakin, Edward. Economics and accountancy. *Incorporated accountants' journal,* July 1920, p. 212-4.
Dalton, Hugh. Economics. *Incorporated accountants' journal,* Feb.-March 1920, p. 105-8, 117-20.
Dalton, Hugh. Economics: "Causes of increase and decrease of production. *Incorporated accountants' journal,* Dec. 1919, p. 51-4.
Daniels, W. M. Economic causes as affecting the political history of the United States. *Accountants' magazine,* May, 1907, p. 253-66.
Davenport, Herbert Joseph. Economics of enterprise. New York, The Macmillan co. 1916. 544p.
Economics of business. 1. Production, consumption and value by Joseph French Johnson; 2. Exchange and distribution by Frank L. McVey. New York, Alexander Hamilton institute, c1918. 326p.

ECONOMICS—*(Continued)*

GRAINGER, WILFRED H. Elementary economics. *Accountant,* Sept. 25, 1920, p. 327-31.

HAMILTON, WILLIAM ROBERT. Accountancy in its relation to some economic problems. *Accountant,* May 16, July 25, 1908, p. 716-21; 92-3.

HAMILTON, WILLIAM ROBERT. Some economic considerations bearing on costing. *Accountant,* Feb. 5, 1910, p. 200-6.

HAMILTON, WILLIAM ROBERT. Some economic lessons to be learned from accounts. *Accountant,* March 13, July 24, 1909, p. 372-7, 110-3.

HASKINS, CHARLES WALDO. Economics and pedagogy. *Accountant,* Nov. 3, 1900, p. 983-4.

HASKINS, CHARLES WALDO. Education in accounting. *Accountant,* March 2, 1901, p. 281-3.

HASKINS, CHARLES WALDO. Place of the science of accounts in collegiate commercial education. *Accountant,* July 13, 1901, p. 812-5.

HEATON, J. A. Sweating and legislation. *Accountant,* Oct. 31, 1908, p. 516-20.

JOHNSON, JOSEPH, FRENCH. Relation of economics to higher accounting. *Commerce, accounts and finance,* Feb. 1902, p. 6-9.

JONES, J. H. Social unrest. *Accountants' magazine,* July 1913, p. 393-405.

LEROSSIGNOL, JAMES EDWARD. Relation between accountancy and economics. *American institute of accountants, Yearbook,* 1909, p. 127-41. *Journal of accountancy,* Dec. 1909, p. 81-8.

LIGHTBODY, W. M. Economics and business. *Accountants' magazine,* Dec. 1911, p. 522-9.

MACAN, H. Political economy and local problems. *South African accountants' journal.* v. 2, p. 14.

MACKINDER, H. J. Address at London school of economics, on the opening of the class for the administrative training of army officers. *Accountant,* Nov. 2, 9, 1907, p. 553-8, 569-71.

METHODS of reasoning in economics; a discussion of the article, "What may accountancy teach economics" by F. A. Cleveland in the October number of "The Journal of accountancy". *Journal of accountancy,* Dec. 1906, p. 154-7.

MURPHY, B. E. Some ethical aspects of modern industrialism. *Accounting and commerce,* Sept. 1918, p. 123-5.

MURPHY, B. E. Wealth. *Accounting and commerce,* Jan. 1919, p. 218-21.

NEAL, THEODORE D. Economics and accountancy. *Accountant,* Dec. 15, 1888, p. 815-7.

PRICE, L. L. Recent history of industrial peace. *Accountants' magazine,* Jan. 1905, p. 6.

RICARDO, DAVID. Principles of political economy and taxation. New York, E. P. Dutton & co. 1917. 300p. (Everyman's library).

RICHARDS, W. M. Plain economics and provident institutions. *Accountant,* June 11, 18, July 2, 9, 16, 1898, p. 613, 629, 681, 693, 716.

ROBINSON, MAURICE H. Accounting in its relation to economics. *Journal of accountancy,* Feb. 1909, p. 282-94.

SEAGER, HENRY RODGERS. Principles of economics. Ed.2, revised and enlarged. New York, Henry Holt & co. c1917. 662p.

SHORT, ARTHUR. Introduction to political economy. *Accountant,* March 23, 1901, p. 367-74.

SMITH, ADAM. Inquiry into the nature and cause of the wealth of nations. 2v. New York. E. P. Dutton & co. 1914. (Everyman's library).

SMITH, JAMES C. Sacred income and the sacred property, and the taxable income and the taxable property. *Accountant,* Nov. 11, 1916, p. 433-7.

SUMNER, WILLIAM GRAHAM. Challenge of facts and other essays, edited by Albert Galloway Keller. New Haven, Yale university press, 1914. 450p.

SUMNER, WILLIAM GRAHAM. Earth-hunger and other essays, edited by Albert Galloway Keller. New Haven, Yale university press, 1914. 377p.

SUMNER, WILLIAM GRAHAM. Forgotten man and other essays, edited by Albert Galloway Keller. New Haven, Yale university press, 1918. 559p.

SUMNER, WILLIAM GRAHAM. War and other essays, edited with an introduction by Albert Galloway Keller. New York, Yale university press, 1919. 381p.

TAUSSIG, FRANK WILLIAM. Inventors and money-makers: lectures on some relations between economics and psychology. New York. The Macmillan co. 1915. 138p.

TAUSSIG, FRANK WILLIAM. Principles of economics. 2v. Revised ed. New York, The Macmillan co. 1917.

TODD, J. E. Successive phases of economic evolution. *Accountantants' magazine,* Aug. 1911, p. 412-26.

TOWNSEND, C. Introduction to economics. *Accountant,* Nov. 15, 1919, p. 421-3.

WALMSLEY, FREDERIC. Claims of labour on capital. *Incorporated accountants' journal,* 1890-1, p. 149.

WELD, L. D. H. Methods of reasoning in economics; correspondence. *Journal of accountancy,* Dec. 1906, p. 154-6.

ECONOMICS effected by electric refuse trucks. *Electrical review and western electrician,* June 9, 1917, p. 976. *Municipal journal,* July 12, 1917, p. 32.

ECONOMICS in monthly bills and receipts. *Electrical world,* Nov. 10, 1917, p. 913.

ECONOMICS in the operation of large lighting installations. Law, C. L. and J. E. Buckley. 1917.

ECONOMICS of business. Brisco, N. A. 1913.

ECONOMICS of business; 1. Production, consumption and value by Joseph French Johnson; 2. Exchange and distribution by Frank L. McVey. New York, Alexander Hamilton institute. c1918. 326p.

ECONOMICS of efficiency. Brisco, N. A. 1914.

ECONOMICS of enterprise. Davenport, H. J. 1916.

ECONOMICS of mining. Richard, T. A. 1905.

ECONOMICS of railroad maintenance of way. CUNNINGHAM, W. A. 1910.

ECONOMICS of railway location. *Railway age,* March 20, 1913, p. 610-7.

ECONOMICS of railway operation. Byers, M. L. 1908.

ECONOMICS of retailing. Nystrom, P. H. 1918.

ECONOMICS of rush-hour service. *Electrical railway journal,* March 11, 1916, p. 495-7.

ECONOMIST.. Thomas, S.

ECONOMIZER. Jeschien, O. A. 1917.

ECONOMY and efficiency in the government service. United States. President. 1912.

ECONOMY and efficiency in the government service. *Congressional record,* April 4, 1912, p. 4511-13.

ECONOMY expense book for personal and household use. Woolson, (George B.) and company. 1900.

ECONOMY of concrete over steel. *Concrete*, April 1919, p. 145.

ECONOMY of electric drive for air-compressor service. *Electrical world*, June 28, 1913, p. 1418.

ECONOMY of industrial electric trucks. *Electrical world*, June 23, 1917, p. 1196-9.

ECONOMY of motor trucks. *Engineering record*, Jan. 10, 1914, p. 42.

ECONOMY of motor trucks for haulage. *Building age*, Oct. 1917, p. 580.

ECONOMY of the electric truck for delivering coal-unit costs compared. *Electrical world*, Nov. 6, 1915, p. 1038.

EDDIS, WILTON C.

Auditing. *Accountant*, Feb. 25, 1899, p. 231-7.

Reserve and sinking funds. *Business man's magazine*, Jan. 1905, p. 131-4.

Textbook for the use of manufacturers, merchants, accountants, and bookkeepers. Toronto, 1912. 199p.

——— **AND W. B. TINDALL**

Manufacturers' accounts. Ed.3. enlarged Toronto, Canada, The authors, 1904. 199p.

EDDY, H. C.

Outsider's observations on the Connecticut zone system. *Electric railway journal*, Dec. 27, 1919, p. 1035.

Purchased power in coal mines. *American institute of electrical engineering, Proceedings*, April 1913, p. 858-64. Discussion. Dec. 1913, p. 2206-13.

EDDY, H. P.

Cost comparison of sewage treatment. *Engineering record*, November 4, 1916, p. 557.

EDGAR, A. E.

Question of receipts. *Busines man's magazine*, Sept. 1905, p. 516.

EDGAR, CHARLES

War and rate problems. *Electrical world*. June 22, 1918, p. 1332-3.

EDGAR, W. W.

Loose methods in municipal accounting. *Business man's magazine*, Jan. 1901, p. 32-4.

EDGE ACT

Guaranty trust company of New York. Foreign financing under the Edge act; Guaranty trust company of New York, c1919. 40p.

Mechanics and metals national bank. Edge export finance act as aproved December 24. 1919 and the McLean-Pratt act as approved September 17, 1919. New York, 1920. 18p.

EDGERTON, H. H.

Physical valuation of the railways an account giving graphic chart of construction cost and also detail formation of various valuation corps. *Railway engineering and maintenance of way*, May 1915, p. 143.

Railroad valuation. *Railway engineering and maintenance of way*, Dec. 1914, p. 477.

EDIBLE fats and oils. Simons, W. H. and C. A. Mitchell. 1911.

EDINBURGH chartered accountants students' society, auditor's report in terms of section 23 of the companies act 1900. *Accountant*, June 1, 1901, p. 655-6.

EDMONDS, WILLIAM

Audit of corporation accounts. *Accountant*, Dec. 12, 1896, p. 1025-33.

Building societies' accounts. *Accountant*, Dec. 16, 1893, p. 1055-66.

Corporation accounts. *Accountant*, May 18, 25, June 1, 1889, p. 265-72, 284-8, 298-308.

EDMUNDS, GARNET W.

Brewery accounts. *Accountants' magazine*, Nov. 1907, p. 480-501.

EDSALL, HENRY J.

Handling coal and ashes at Grundy plant, Bristol, Pa. *Power*, Oct. 3, 1916, p. 480-3. Discussion. *Power*, Nov. 14, 1916, Jan. 9, 1917, p. 695, 57.

EDUCATE the educators. Miller, Albert A.

EDUCATING the executive to appreciate costs. Pasley, R. S.

EDUCATING the public. *Journal of accountancy*, May Dec. 1915, Jan. 1916, p. 359-62, 453-4, 52-3.

EDUCATION

Accountancy and the New Zealand expeditionary force. *Accounting and commerce*, Dec. 1918, p. 203-5.

Accountancy and the universities. *Accountant*, Jan. 11, 1913, p. 41-4.

Accountancy education in New Zealand. *Accountant*, Sept. 6, 1913, p. 300-1.

Accountancy in Queen's university. *Journal of accountancy*, Feb. 1911, p. 296.

Accountancy in the University of Minnesota. *Journal of accountancy*, Feb. 1908, p. 319-20.

Accountancy recognized by Columbia university *Journal of accountancy*, May 1914, p. 401.

Accounting at college of the city of New York. *Journal of accountancy*, July 1917, p. 79.

Accounting lectures in London. *Journal of accountancy*, Oct. 1909, p. 471.

Adamson, J. E. Concentration as a quality of mind and a habit of life. *South African accountants' journal*, v. 1, p. 103.

Adults and high school studies. *Journal of accountancy*, April 1909, p. 477-9.

Advantages of mathematical training to an accountant. *Journal of accountancy*, June 1910, p. 137-8.

American association and business education. *Journal of accountancy*, Dec. 1906, p. 139-41.

American association of university instructors in accounting. Papers and proceedings, annual, 1917 to date.

American institute of accountants. Report of committee on education. *American institute of accountants, Yearbook*, 1913 to date.

Barber, Edgar M. Contribution to the history of commercial history; an address delivered at the annual meeting of the Eastern commercial teachers' association held at Brooklyn, N. Y., April 1903. 23p.

Bartholomew, W. E. Fundamental aims in the teaching of bookkeeping. *National educational association, Papers and proceedings*, 1916, p. 362-5.

Beckett, J. Elementary education in relation to local taxation and finance. *Accountant*, July 30, 1904, p. 124-30.

Bennett, Robert Joseph. Educational training of an accountant. *Journal of accountancy*, March 1912, p. 182-93.

Bowden, T. Presidential address: North chartered accountants' students' society. *Accountant*, Feb. 25, 1905, p. 226-9.

EDUCATION—(Continued)

BROAKER, FRANK. Teaching of accounting in commercial schools. *Business man's magazine,* 1906, v. 18, no. 9, p. 166-70. *Journal of accountancy,* Feb. 1906, p. 328-30.

BROWN, ELMER E. Opening address; New York university. Graduate school of business administration, Sept. 28, 1920. 14p.

BROWN, ELMER E. Some educational bearings of accounting; discussion by W. R. Gray; Joseph French Johnson, J. B. Geijsbeek, H. T. Westermann. *American institute of accountants, Yearbook,* 1910, p. 125-39. *Journal of accountancy,* Jan. 1911, p. 165-78.

BRUMMER, LEON. Inception and foundation of the school of commerce, accounts and finance. *Journal of accountancy,* Feb. 1911, p. 252-5.

BUSINESS and the universities. *Accountant,* Feb. 1, 8, 1913, p. 136-9, 169-71.

CARLILL, J. A. Example of Sir Kenneth. *Accountant,* June 29, 1901, p. 754-60.

CARLSON, JOHN C. Accountancy education in Pennsylvania. *Journal of accountancy,* Jan. 1907, p. 195-7.

CATALOGUES of colleges, universities and schools teaching accounting and allied subjects.

CHAPMAN, SYDNEY J. Faculty of commerce, in relation to accounts. *Accountant,* Feb. 24, March 24, 1906, p. 249-54, 365-7.

CHASE, HARVEY S. Teach English, economics, history and law. *Journal of accountancy,* Jan. 1907, p. 191-2.

CHILD, P. Accountant student. *Auditor,* 1890-1, p. 235, 249, 265, 284.

CLARK, J. B. Commercial education in the secondary school. *Accountants' magazine,* Feb. 1920, p. 110-20.

CLEVELAND, FREDERICK A. Suggested curriculum for a professional school of accountancy. *Journal of accountancy,* Jan. 1907, p. 199-202.

CLEWS, HENRY. Business education and commercial and banking methods. *Accountant,* Sept. 16, 1905, p. 305-11.

COLUMBIA alumni news, May 28, 1920. New York, Columbia university. School of business, 1920.

COMMERIAL education. *Accountant,* Jan. 17, 24, 1914, p. 61-4, 100-3.

COMMERCIAL education in Scotland. *Accountant,* Sept. 15, 1917, p. 193-5.

COOPER, JOHN ALEXANDER. Education for the accountant. *Journal of accountancy,* Aug. 1908, p. 261-8.

COPLAND, D. B. University and commercial education. *Federal accountant,* Jan. 1919, p. 38-43.

CORK municipal school of commerce. *Journal of accountancy,* June 1911, p. 133.

DAWSON, SIDNEY S. Post-examination studies of an accountant student. *Accountant,* Nov. 18, 1899, p. 1128-35.

DEGREE of bachelor of commerce. *Accountant,* June 7, 14, 21, 1902, p. 583-6, 605-7, 633-4.

DELPRAT, G. D. Technical education. *Australasian accountant and secretary,* June 1919, p. 24-6.

DRUCKER, A. P. R. Teaching bookkeeping by the historical method. *School science and mathematics,* Jan. 1920, p. 70-7.

DUNCAN, JOHN C. Priority in educational methods; correspondence. *Journal of accountancy,* Feb. 1915, p. 161-2.

DUNCAN, JOHN C. Some scientific and educational problems of the accountancy profession. *American institute of accountants, Yearbook,* 1914, p. 134-52. *Journal of accountancy,* Oct. 1914, p. 260-75.

EDUCATION in accounting. *Journal of political economy,* Jan. 1917, p. 113-4.

EDUCATION of accountant students. *Accountant,* April 30, May 7, 14, 21, 1898, p. 437-40, 463-5, 401-2, 520-2.

EDUCATION of accountant students. *Journal of accountancy,* March 1910, p. 372.

EDUCATION of accountants. *Accountant,* June 1, 1912, p. 824-8.

EDUCATION of English and American accountants. *Accountant,* June 1, 1907, p. 735-6, 764-5. *Journal of accountancy,* April, Sept. 1907, p. 469-73, 378-9.

EDUCATION of municipal accountants. *Accountant,* Jan. 22, 1910, p. 117-9.

EDUCATION of the accountant. *Accountant,* Sept. 19, 1914, p. 307-8.

EDUCATION of the articled clerk. *Accountant,* Aug. 12, 19, Sept. 23, 1911, p. 197-200, 231-4, 369-71.

EDUCATION of the chartered accountant. *Accountant,* May 23, 1908, p. 739-41.

EDWARDS, ALLEN. Higher commercial education and what the Birmingham university is doing. *Accountant,* Sept. 8, 1906, p. 273-9.

ELLIS, C. B. Teaching of bookkeeping. *Journal of education,* April 23, 1914, p. 464.

ELWELL, F. H. Problem of standardizing university courses in accounting. *American association of university instructors, Papers and proceedings,* May 1917, p. 19-41.

ESCUELAS superiores y elementales de comercio de la nacion. Programas para los corsos de peritas mercantiles, tenedores de libros y dependientes idoneos de comercio. Buenos Aires, 1910. 112p.

FISHER, CLAUDE P. Value of study apart from examinations. *Australasian accountant and secretary,* Aug. 1919, p. 28-31.

FISHER, H. A. L. Functions of government in relation to education. *Accountant,* April 26, 1919, p. 341-4.

FITZPATRICK, E. A. Training for public service with special reference to training of accountants. *New York state conference of mayors and other city officials, Proceedings,* 1916, p. 88-94. *Public servant,* Feb. 1917, p. 167-72. *Journal of accountancy,* Jan. 1917, p. 33-8.

FOR the young accountant. *Journal of accountancy,* June 1906, p. 141.

FUTURE training for the accountancy profession. *Incorporated accountants' journal,* Dec. 1914, p. 51-2.

GARRETT, A. A. Professional education. *Incorporated accountants' journal,* April 1912, p. 176-81.

GEIJSBEEK, JOHN B. Teaching of accounting. *Pan American scientific congress, Proceedings,* 1915, p. 532-46.

GEORGIA school of technology. *Journal of accountancy,* June 1912, p. 454.

GILLIES, A. A. Address [on self-culture.] *Accountant,* Oct. 8, 1898, p. 946-50.

GILLIES, A. A. Introductory address; faculty of commerce in the Victoria university of Manchester. *Accountant,* Oct. 31, 1903, p. 1323-31.

GILMAN, STEPHEN W. Accountancy education. *Journal of accountancy,* Dec. 1907, p. 125-6. *American institute of accountants, Yearbook,* 1907, p. 172-3.

GIRDLESTONE, E. D. Comparative value of different studies as an occupation for a professional man's leisure hours. *Accountant,* July 1, 1893, p. 611-5.

GLASGOW CHARTERED ACCOUNTANTS SOCIETY. Memorandum by the committee on the position of apprentices and time expired apprentices now on service with the forces. *Accountant,* March 30, 1918, p. 271-5.

GRASS, DONALD F. Teaching accounting in the collegiate course of study for business. *Pan American scientific congress, Proceedings,* 1915, p. 547-50.

GRAY, JOHN H. Professional accountancy and education. *American institute of accountants, Yearbook,* 1907, p. 169-72. *Journal of accountancy,* Dec. 1907, p. 122-5.

GREELEY, HAROLD DUDLEY. Accountancy training for lawyers. *Journal of accountancy,* July 1908, p. 157-65.

EDUCATION—*(Continued)*

Greeley, Harold Dudley. Legal training for accountants. *Journal of accountancy,* Aug. 1908, p. 234-41.

Green, Arthur E. Technical training of the future incorporated accountant. *Incorporated accountants' journal,* Dec. 1911, p. 65-7.

Hall, J. C. Accuracy. *Incorporated accountants' journal,* 1891-2, p. 61.

Haney, Lewis H. Professional education for accountants. *American institute of accountants, Yearbook,* 1907, p. 179-81. *Journal of accountancy,* Dec. 1907, p. 132-3.

Harvard school of business administration. *Journal of accountancy,* Feb. 1919, p. 157.

Haskins, Charles Waldo. Business education and accountancy. New York, Harper and brothers, c1904. 239p.

Haskins, Charles Waldo. Business training; an address at the fifth annual convention of the Eastern commercial teachers association, March 28, 1902. 20p. *Accountant,* Oct. 4, 1902, p. 993-1000.

Haskins, Charles Waldo. Education in accounting. *Accountant,* March 2, 1901, p. 281-3. *Business world,* Jan. 1902, p. 9-11, 40.

Haskins, Charles Waldo. Higher commercial education. *Commerce, accounts and finance,* Oct. 1901, p. 7-8. New York state university, *Professional education in the United States,* 1903, p. 83-97.

Haskins, Charles Waldo. Place of the science of accounts in collegiate commercial education; a paper read at the thirteenth annual meeting of the American economic association, University of Michigan, December, 28, 1900. 8p. (In his *Business education and accountancy,* c1904, p. 126-37). *Accountant,* July 13, 1901, p. 812-5.

Haskins, Charles Waldo. School of commerce, accounts, and finance of New York University. *Accountant,* Oct. 6, 1900, p. 876-9. *Business,* Sept. 1900, p. 409-13.

Heaton, J. Howard. Accountant student, his course of study and his future. *Accountant,* Oct. 26, Nov. 16, 1907, p. 533-7, 597-9.

Herrick, Myron T. University training for business men. *Journal of accountancy,* Feb. 1911, p. 245-51.

Hotchkiss, Willard Eugene. Higher education and business standards. Boston, Houghton Mifflin company, 1918. 109p.

Humphreys, A. C. Business training for the engineer. *Stevens indicator,* July 1914, p. 241-54. Abstract. *Electric railway journal,* Feb. 14, 1914, p. 366-7. *Journal of the American society of mechanical engineers,* May 1914, p. 199-201.

Humphreys, Alexander C. Should the Stevens curriculum include instruction in bookkeeping and accounting. (In his *Lecture notes on some of the business features of engineering practice.* p. 39-47).

Importance of accounting knowledge. *Journal of accountancy,* Jan. 1917, p. 45.

Institute and student societies. *Accountant,* July 27, 1907, p. 108-10.

International course of lectures on commerce. *Journal of accountancy,* April 1911, p. 461.

Jefferson, H. M. Status of higher education for business. *Business world,* Dec. 1905.

Jenkinson, Mark Webster. Best course of conduct and studies for a chartered accountant's articled clerk in order to render him competent and well-equipped for the pursuit of his profession. *Accountant,* April 28, 1900, p. 395-9.

Johnson, Joseph French. Professional accountancy and education. *American institute of accountants, Yearbook,* 1907, p. 166-9. *Journal of accountancy,* Dec. 1907, p. 119-22.

Johnson, Joseph French. Professional education for business. *Journal of accountancy,* July 1907, p. 191-7. *Incorporated accountants' journal,* 1907-8, p. 89.

Johnson, Joseph French. Training in science of business essential. *Journal of accountancy,* Jan. 1907, p. 208-10.

Johnston, J. G. Accountant's equipment; a practical essay on the functions and education of an accountant. *Accountants' magazine,* June 1902, p. 331-42.

Jones, E. D. Some propositions concerning university instructions in business administrations. *Journal of political economy,* March 1913, p. 185-95.

Joplin, J. Porter. Business college graduate in the business field. *Journal of accountancy,* March 1915, p. 182-90.

Kahn, Joseph and J. J. Klein. Principles in methods in commercial education; a text book for teachers, students and business men. New York. The Macmillan co. 1916. 439p.

Kansas city school of accountancy, law and finance. *Journal of accountancy,* Nov. 1914, p. 405.

Kent, William. College education in accounting; technical experience necessary to the accountant. (In his *Bookkeeping and cost accounting for factories.* 1918. p. 240-1).

Kinley, David. Make a legal graduation of accountants. *Journal of accountancy,* Jan. 1907, p. 197-9.

Kirby, H. Woodburn. Hints on the conduct and training of chartered accountants. *Accountant,* May 27, 1899, p. 596-602.

Latham, Stanley. Bookkeeping; a plea for more scientific and systematic teaching. *Accountant,* Sept. 18, 1897, p. 890-1.

Latham, Stanley. More scientific teaching of book-keeping. *Journal of the society of arts,* v. 45, p. 949.

Lecture on science of accounts. *Journal of accountancy,* April 1908, p. 491.

Liberal education. *Journal of accountancy,* July 1911, p. 201-3.

Luman, John A. Importance of accounting training. *Journal of accountancy,* April 1911, p. 405-13.

Lyon, Leverett. Survey of commercial education in the public high schools of the United States. Chicago, University of Chicago, Sept. 1919. (Supplementary educational monographs, v. 2, no. 5).

McKinsey, J. O. Accounting as an administrative aid. *Journal of political economy,* Nov. 1919, p. 759-81.

MacLean, James A. Commercial education. *Canadian chartered accountant,* April 1914, p. 224-31.

Masters, J. E. Qualifications and responsibilities of public accountants. *Accounting and commerce,* March 1917, p. 274-8. *Journal of accountancy,* Dec. 1916, p. 433-42.

Mather, J. Suggestions and admonitions to chartered accountant students. *Accountant,* March 17, 1900, p. 270-4.

Meade, Edward S. Business education. *Auditor,* 1905, p. 223.

Meade, Edward S. Contribution of the business man to business education. *Accountant,* Sept. 23, 1905, p. 339-42.

Meade, Edward S. Establish preliminary examinations in law and economics. *Journal of accountancy,* Jan. 1907, p. 193-5.

Meats, T. Wheeler. Making of an English accountant. *Commerce, accounts and finance,* Aug. 1902, p. 10-8.

Miller, Albert A. Educate the educators. *Journal of accountancy,* Jan. 1907, p. 202-3.

Mr. Lawrence Dicksee. *Journal of accountancy,* June 1907, p. 141-2.

Modern methods of instruction. *Journal of accountancy,* July 1914, p. 52-3.

Montgomery, Robert H. Accountancy laboratory. *Journal of accountancy,* June 1914, p. 405-11.

EDUCATION—(Continued)

MONTGOMERY, ROBERT H. How teachers can increase the efficiency of accounting and bookkeeping courses. *National educational association, Papers and proceedings,* 1916, p. 387-90.

MONTGOMERY, ROBERT H. Value and recent development of theoretical training for the public accountant. *Business man's magazine,* Aug. 1905, p. 417-9.

NATIONAL ELECTRIC LIGHT ASSOCIATION. Advanced course in electric utility accounting. Committee on accounting education. 17p.

NAU, CARL H. Comparative value of personal reputation and conferred degrees. *American institute of accountants, Yearbook,* 1917, p. 111-7. *Journal of accountancy,* Oct. 1917, p. 247-53.

NEAL, THEODORE D. Commercial faculty; its limitation and possibilities. *Accountant,* April 12, 1902, p. 397-401.

NELSON, CHARLES HEWETSON. Professional education. *Accountant,* Sept. 30, 1911, p. 424-33. *Incorporated accountants' journal,* Oct. 1911, p. 15-20.

NEW accountancy course in Chicago. *Journal of accountancy,* Jan. 1908, p. 252-3.

NEW school of business administration. *Journal of accountancy,* Dec. 1910, p. 145.

NEW schools of accountancy. *Journal of accountancy,* Oct. 1908, p. 441-2.

NEW YORK STATE. UNIVERSITY. Education law as amended to July 1, 1918. Albany, University of the state of New York, 1918. 323p.

NEW YORK STATE. UNIVERSITY. Education law, as amended to July 1, 1920. Albany, The university of the state of New York, 1920. 370p. (Bulletin no. 707).

NEW YORK. UNIVERSITY. Report on higher education. Albany, University of the state of New York.

NICHOLSON, J. SHIELD. Commercial education in the University of Edinburgh. *Accountant,* Jan. 21, 1911, p. 125-7. *Journal of accountancy,* March 1911, p. 377-80.

NORTHRIDGE, H. C. Accountancy education. *Accountant,* Jan. Nov. 22, 1919, p. 33-5, 450-1.

PELOUBET, MAURICE E. Accountancy education. *Journal of accountancy,* Dec. 1914, p. 488.

PERRINE, LEROY L. Advantages of mathematical training to an accountant. *Journal of accountancy,* March 1910, p. 344-51.

POWERS, L. G. Governmental accounting and administration as subjects of university study and research. *National association of comptrollers and accounting officers, Proceedings,* 1917, p. 19-25.

PRELIMINARY requirements. *Journal of accountancy,* April 1916, p. 282-5.

PRICE, H. L. Address to accountant students. *Incorporated accountants' journal,* 1907-8, p. 29.

PROFESSIONAL education. *Incorporated accountants' journal,* Nov., Dec. 1911, April 1912, p. 31-2, 58-60, 170.

PROPOSED degree of commerce in the university of Edinburgh. *Accountants' magazine,* June 1907, p. 244-7.

PURCELL, H. E. One cure for national waste; instruction in simple bookkeeping forms or budget-making. *School and society,* Dec. 9, 1916, p. 899-900.

RAND, WALDRON H. Growth of the profession. *Journal of accountancy,* June 1919, p. 412-9.

REMOLAR, RAMON MARIA. La ensenanza commercial en La Argentina (coleccion de leyes, decretos y reglamentos; concordancias y comentarios). Venezuela, Talleres graficos "optimus" a cantiello, 1917. 589p.

REQUIREMENTS for the C. P. A. *Journal of accountancy,* Sept. 1908, p. 354-6.

ROBINSON, M. H. Accountancy education. *American institute of accountants, Yearbook,* 1907, p. 173-5. *Journal of accountancy,* Dec. 1907, p. 126-8.

ST. PAUL institute of arts and sciences. *Journal of accountancy,* Jan. 1909, p. 241.

SCHOOL of accounts in Milwaukee. *Journal of accountancy,* June 1910, p. 138.

SCHOOL of commerce at Tulane university. *Journal of accountancy,* Sept. 1914, p. 239.

SCHOOL of commerce in Denver. *Journal of accountancy,* April 1908, p. 482.

SCOTLAND'S ideals of accountancy education. *Journal of accountancy,* March 1911, p. 371-4.

SCOTT, J. Training and business of an accountant. *Dominion association of chartered accountants, Yearbook,* 1910.

SELLS, ELIJAH W. Accountancy education should be held to a uniform standard. *Journal of accountancy,* Jan. 1907, p. 189-91.

SMITH, THOMAS SAVAGE. Education of accountants; what they ought to learn, and how they are to learn it. *Accountant,* March 3, 1894, p. 201-4.

SMITH, W. J. Address to accountant students. *Incorporated accountants' journal,* 1896-7, p. 98.

SPENCER, ENOS. Disciplinary value of bookkeeping as a study. *National educational association, Proceedings,* 1903, p. 741-6.

STERRETT, J. E. Education and training of a certified public accountant. *Journal of accountancy,* Nov. 1905, p. 1-15.

STERRETT, J. E. Re-organize the C. P. A. examinations. *Journal of accountancy,* Jan. 1907, p. 204-8.

STONE, W. S. Teaching the fundamentals of accountancy bookkeeping classes or training students to think. *National educational association, Papers and proceedings,* 1915, p. 884-8.

STRACHAN, W. Address to accountant students. *Incorporated accountants' journal,* 1905-6, p. 135.

SYMPOSIUM on accountancy education. *Journal of accountancy,* Jan. 1907, p. 233-5.

TAYLOR, HENRY LEWIS. Professional education in the United States. Albany, University of the state of New York, 1900. (Bulletin 11).

TEACHING of bookkeeping in schools. *Accountant,* Jan. 15, 22, Feb. 5, 1898, p. 57-9, 85-7, 142-4.

TEXAS joins the procession. *Journal of accountancy,* April 1908, p. 483.

TRAINING of Scottish chartered accountants: an article. *Accountants' magazine,* 1909, p. 542-6.

TRELEVEN, JOHN E. Present status of accounting instruction in colleges and universities. *American association of university instructors, Papers and proceedings,* May 1917, p. 5-19.

UNIVERSITY of Illinois. *Journal of accountancy,* Nov. 1917. p. 412.

UNIVERSITY of Michigan. *Journal of accountancy,* Dec. 1908, p. 139.

UNIVERSITY preparation for business. *Journal of accountancy,* Aug. 1907, p. 302-6.

UNIVERSITY training for accountancy in 1908-1909. *Journal of accountancy,* Nov. 1908, p. 52-6.

UNIVERSITY training for accountants. *Journal of accountancy,* April 1910, p. 454.

VAN DE LINDE, GERARD. Articled clerk. *Accountant,* Nov. 23, 30, 1895, p. 946-52, 969-76.

VANDERLIP, FRANK A. Educational ideals of Charles Waldo Haskins. *Journal of accountancy,* Feb. 1911, p. 256-60.

WALTON, SEYMOUR. Accounting education. *Journal of accountancy,* April 1916, p. 292-4.

WALTON, SEYMOUR. Higher education for business men. *Canadian chartered accountant,* July 1915, p. 20-4.

WALTON, SEYMOUR. Higher education for public accountants. *American institute of accountants, Yearbook,* 1907, p. 176-9. *Journal of accountancy,* Dec. 1907, p. 128-32.

EDUCATION— *(Continued)*

WALTON, SEYMOUR. Practical application of theoretical knowledge. *Accountant,* Dec. 1, 1917, p. 433-5. *American institute of accountants, Yearbook,* 1917, p. 118-25. *Journal of accountancy,* Oct. 1917, p. 276-82. *South African accountant,* March 1918, p. 156-8.

WALTON, SEYMOUR. True education. *Journal of accountancy,* Jan. 1914, p. 71-2

WELLS, HERBERT GEORGE. Bookkeeping a la maitre d'Ecole. *Accountant,* Jan. 15, 1898, p. 77-80.

WELTON, T. A. On useful work for students' leisure hours and on statistics generally. *Accountant,* Dec. 5, 1896, p. 999-1001.

WHAT shall be done to put education for accountancy on a professional basis? a symposium. *Journal of accountancy,* Jan. 1907, p. 189-210.

WHITEHEAD, F. E. Hints to articled clerks. *Accountant,* Jan. 8, 1916, p. 50-2.

WHY not Latin *Journal of accountancy,* Oct. 1910, p. 460-3.

WILDE, A. G. Some remarks on the present position of the accountant student as regards education and his prospects in the profession. *Accountant,* Oct. 14, 1905, p. 431-7.

WILDMAN, JOHN R. Relation between secondary schools and universities with regard to the teaching of bookkeeping and accounting; a paper read before the Eastern commercial teachers' association, April 20, 1916. New York university, 1916. 21p.

WILKINSON, GEORGE. Business education from the standpoint of the public accountant. *Accountant,* Sept. 23, 1905, p. 342-3.

WILL, JOHN A. Compulsory apprenticeship: correspondence. *Journal of accountancy,* July 1916, p. 76.

WILLIAMS, O. M. Commercial education in secondary schools. *Commonwealth accountant,* Nov. Dec. 1906, Jan. 1907.

WILLIAMSON, ARTHUR. Education of an accountant. *Incorporated accountants' journal,* April 1913, p. 162-4.

WOOSTER, H. A. University schools of business and a new business ethics. *South African accountant,* June 1919, p. 309-14.

EDUCATION and industrial evolution. Charlton, Frank Tracey. 1913.

EDUCATION and training of a certified public accountant. Sterrett, J. E.

EDUCATION for the accountant. Cooper, J. A.

EDUCATION in accounting. *Journal of political economy,* Jan. 1917, p. 113-4.

EDUCATION law as amended to July 1, 1918. New York state. University.

EDUCATION of accountant students. *Journal of accountancy,* March 1910, p. 372.

EDUCATION of accountant students. *Accountant,* April 30, May 7, 14, 21, 1898, p. 437-40, 463-5, 491-2, 520-2.

EDUCATION of accountants. *Accountant,* June 1, 1912, p. 824-8.

EDUCATION of employees. Galloway, Lee.

EDUCATION of English and American accountants. *Accountant,* June 1, 1907, p. 735-6, 764-5. *Journal of accountancy,* April 1907, p. 469-73.

EDUCATION of municipal accountants. *Accountant,* Jan. 22, 1910, p. 117-9.

EDUCATION of the accountant. *Accountant,* Sept. 19, 1914, p. 307-8.

EDUCATION of the articled clerk. *Accountant,* Aug. 12, 19, Sept. 23, 1911, p. 197-200, 231-4, 369-71.

EDUCATION of the chartered accountant. • *Accountant,* May 23, 1908, p. 739-41.

EDUCATIONAL ideals of Charles Waldo Haskins. Vanderlip, F. A.

EDUCATIONAL training of an accountant. Bennett, R. J.

EDWARDS, ALLEN

Address. 1889. *Accountant,* Nov. 23, 1889. p. 623-5.

Bankruptcy reform. *Accountant,* Feb. 2, 23, March 30, 1907, p. 156-60, 253-8, 417-25.

Bills of exchange. *Accountant,* Dec. 1, 8, 15, 1883.

Card and loose leaf ledger systems and their adaptability to the jewellery trades. *Accountant,* June 6, 1906, p. 756-65.

Higher comercial education and what the Birmingham university is doing. *Accountant,* Sept. 8, 1906, p. 273-9.

Income tax. *Accountant,* 1886, p. 7.

Jewellers', silversmiths' and kindred traders' accounts. London, Gee & co. 1903. 167p. (Accountants' library, v. 23).

Probate accounts. *Accountant,* Nov. 15, 1884.

Some professional views upon bankruptcy and private arrangements. *Accountant,* Dec. 20, 27, 1890, p. 696-9, 705-8.

Suggested reforms in bankruptcy law and administration. *Accountant,* Dec. 7, 14, 1895, p. 987-93, 1010-5.

EDWARDS, AUGUSTUS

Principles of manufacturing on cost or indirect expenses. *Accountant,* April 12, 1919, p. 297-305.

EDWARDS, CHARLES LEWIS

Electric lighting accounts: correspondence. *Incorporated accountants' journal,* April 1912, p. 175.

Railways and the trade of Great Britain. *Incorporated accountants' journal,* 1907-8, p. 176.

EDWARDS, G. W.

Privilege under the bankruptcy acts. *Accountant,* Oct. 15, 1898, p. 969-73.

Question of privilege as between solicitor and cient under the Bankruptcy acts. *Accountant,* Oct. 15, 1898, p. 969-73.

EDWARDS, GEORGE

Accountancy in Canada. *Accountant,* Jan. 1, 1916, p. 25-31. *American institute of accountants, Yearbook,* 1915, p. 122-37. *Journal of accountancy,* Nov. 1915, p. 334-48.

Address to students. *Canadian chartered accountant,* April 1913, p. 261-8.

Books of account. *Accountant,* June 3, 1899, p. 617-21, 672-4.

Organization: its object and their attainment. *Dominion association of chartered accountants, Yearbook,* 1910. *Journal of accountancy,* Aug. 1910, p. 275-85.

EDWARDS, H.

Income tax. *Incorporated accountants' journal,* 1908-9, p. 144.

EDWARDS, H. D.

Preparation for the examination. *Accounting and commerce,* March 1916, p. 285-6.

EDWARDS, H. H.

Careless construction causes early failure of a brick pavement. *Municipal engineering,* Feb. 1918, p. 54-5.

EDWARDS, HENRY MONROE
Accounting for depreciation; read before the National electric light association at its thirty-fourth convention held at New York city, May 29 to June 2, 1911. New York. National electric light association, 1911. 10p. *Electric railway journal,* June 3, 1911, p. 972.
Depreciation accounts; their treatment by Interborough rapid transit co. *Electric railway journal,* June 3, 1911, August 12, 1911, p. 280, 972. Abstract. *Electrical review,* June 10, 1911, p. 1162.
N.E.L.A. accounting section. *Electrical world,* Feb. 20, 1915, p. 498-9.
Regulated electric light accounting. *National electric light association, papers, reports and discussions,* 1912, p. 106. Abstract. *Electric railway journal,* June 15, 1912, p. 1029.

EDWARDS, HENRY MOORE
Electric light accounts and their significance. New York, McGraw-Hill book co. 1914, 172p.

EDWARDS, J.
Cost of producing moving pictures. *Motion picture classic,* July 1917, p. 19-23.

EDWARDS, J.
Bookkeeping; double entry simplified. London, Relfe bros. 1871.
———Same; key. London, Relfe bros., 1871.
Double entry bookkeeping. London, Relfe bros. 1842.
Key to single entry bookkeeping. London, Relfe bros. 1856.
Mercantile accounts. London, Relfe bros., 1842.
Single entry bookkeeping. London, Relfe bros.

EDWARDS, JOHN
Jewellers' account keeping. *Accountant,* April 22, 1905, p. 505-6.

EDWARDS, M. C.
For keeping police records. *System,* Sept. 1903, p. 181-7.

EDWARDS, THOMAS H.
Motor truck lessons cost of maintaining gravel roads in Alabama. *Engineering record,* July 15, 1916, p. 73-4.

EDWARDS, V. E.
Power required for rolling metal. *Iron age,* Dec. 4, 1913, p. 1009-10. *Machinery,* March 1914, p. 572.

EDWARDS, WILLIAM H.
Office accounting methods; in use in the establishment of Roundy, Peckham & Dexter Co. wholesale grocers, Milwaukee, Wisconsin. *Business man's magazine,* Feb. 1910, p. 171-9.

EDWARDS, WILLIAM REA
Debentures. *Accountant,* June 14, 1890, p. 323-7.
Legacy, succession and estate duty. *Accountant,* March 11, 1893, p. 220-8.

EFFECT of an award based on the existence of a trade custom. *Accountant,* Jan. 16, 1909, p. 94-6.

EFFECT of bonus system on quantity and unit cost of basement excavation. *Engineering and contracting,* July 22, 1914, p. 80.

EFFECT of centralization on costs. *Engineering and mining journal,* Aug. 2, 1913, p. 217.

EFFECT of coal prices on central-station rates. *Electrical review and western electrician,* May 26, 1917, p. 899.

EFFECT of fare increase in 61 cases. *Aera,* Dec. 1918, p. 474-5.

EFFECT of fluctuating prices on unit cost systems. *Electrical review,* Oct. 6, 1917, p. 596-7.

EFFECT of increased costs on central station rates. *Electrical review,* Chicago, Nov. 10, 1917, p. 800-3.

EFFECT of machine depreciation upon cost of dye making. *Color trade journal,* April 1920, p. 103-6.

EFFECT of stores department on operating cost. *Railway age gazette,* May 23, 1913, p. 1140-2.

EFFECT of the war on revenue from lighting. *Electrical world,* Nov. 23, 1918, p. 987-8.

EFFECT of the war upon isolated plant costs. *Electrical review,* June 21, 1919, p. 1024-7.

EFFECT of turnover on profits. Gauss, C. A.

EFFECT of war conditions on the operating and maintenance of water works. *Municipal engineering,* Jan. 1919, p. 16-7.

EFFECT of wars and revolutions on government securities. Kerr, Eleanor. 1917.

EFFECT of water rate changes. *Municipal engineering,* Nov. 1916, p. 180.

EFFECT of winding-up on covenants in restraint of competitive bidding. *Accountant,* June 4, 1910, p. 800-1.

EFFECT upon public utilities of depreciation charges on freight rates. *National electric light association, Bulletin,* July 1920, p. 404-8.

EFFECTIVE administration. Fisher, L. O.

EFFECTIVE business letters. Gardner, E. H. 1918.

EFFECTIVE color-tab system for light and power records. *Electrical review and western electrician,* April 15, 1916, p. 673-4.

EFFECTIVE method for handling bad water complaints. *Engineering and contracting,* Nov. 8, 1916, p. 405-6.

EFFECTIVE service voucher. *Electric railway journal,* Oct. 26, 1912, p. 918.

EFFFECTIVE yet simple bonus system for power plants. *Engineering and contracting,* April 9, 1919. p. 369-71.

EFFECTS of self-assertion, a word to younger public accountants. Rand, W. H.

EFFICIENCY, INDUSTRIAL.
See Factory management; Management; Office management.

EFFICIENCY. Duncan, James.

EFFICIENCY. *Journal of accountancy,* Dec. 1919, p. 455.

EFFICIENCY as a basis for operation and wages. Emerson, Harrington. c1914.

EFFICIENCY as practiced by Portland light and power co. *Railway and engineering review,* Nov. 1, 1913, p. 1013.

EFFICIENCY bonuses to executives. *Business digest,* May 29, 1918, p. 705.

EFFICIENCY budg. . of Chicago. *Municipal engineering,* March 1916, p. 111.

EFFICIENCY departments as a new development in trust company organization. *Trust companies,* Aug. 1913, p. 99-100.

EFFICIENCY engineering in the shops of the Milwaukee electric railway. *Electric railway journal,* March 21, 1914, p. 631-7.

EFFICIENCY in city government. *American academy of political and social science.* 1912.

EFFICIENCY in conduct of office business; new methods in a naval bureau. *Railway review,* Oct. 9, 1915, p. 472-4.

EFFICIENCY in handling equipment in Brooklyn. *Electric railway journal,* Dec. 23, 1911, p. 1268-71.

EFFICIENCY in mine management. *Coal age,* January 23, 30, March 20-27, May 29, 1919, p. 200, 246-6, 547-8, 588-9, 1012.

EFFICIENCY in municipal accounting and reporting. Mann, W. D.

EFFICIENCY in public management. Cleveland, F. A.

EFFICIENCY in the office. *Accounting and commerce,* June 1918, p. 50.

EFFICIENCY in water revenue collection. *Annals of the American academy of political and social science,* May 1912, p. 86-92.

EFFICIENCY methods in street cleaning: how New York city lowered costs while extending service and increasing wages. *Municipal engineering,* July 1917, p. 11-3.

EFFICIENCY of mine officials. *Coal age,* Jan 16, March 13-20, April 10, May 8-22, 1919, p. 159-60, 504-5, 548, 678-9, 878-9, 922-3, 967-8.

EFFICIENCY of municipal light plants; comparison of municipal and company plants in Massachusetts. *Municipal journal,* Feb. 24, 1916, p. 266-8.

EFFICIENCY wage scale. *Engineering and contracting,* May 15, 1918, p. 481.

EFFICIENT banking and trust company methods. *Trust companies,* Oct. 1911, p. 244-7.

EFFICIENT book-keeping. Fall, F. A.

EFFICIENT cost keeping. Lewis, E. S. 1915.

EFFICIENT fuel department; a description of the organization, methods of accounting and operation of the fuel department of the Atchison, Topeka & Santa Fe railway, which has shown remarkable results not only in the reduction in the fuel consumption, but also indirectly in improving the condition of the motive power. *American engineer,* 1910, v.84, p. 161-70.

EFFICIENT management of gas plants. *Gas age,* Aug. 15, 1919, p. 139-40.

EFFICIENT personal accounting. Fall, F. A.

EFFICIENT piece work system at the Angus shops. *Railway age* (Mech ed.), May 1914, p. 249-53.

EFFICIENT production of cylindrical work. *Machinery,* Dec. 1912.

EFFICIENT stock keeping; the following method of keeping stock and records was originated by Elliott-Fisher company and is used in the Eliott-Fisher factory. 6p.

EFFICIENT tool-room system. *Iron age,* April 18, 1918, p. 996-7.

EGAN, JAMES W.

Advertising points for retailers. *Business mans magazine,* May 1907, p. 116-22.

EGERMAN, W. V.

Foundry cost accounting. *Foundry,* Dec. 1916, p. 490.

EGGERS, G. C.

Option accounting in the board of trade. *Bookkeeper,* 1902, v.15, no. 6, p. 56-61.

EGGERS, JOHN H.

Pay-roll accounts. *Business,* Jan. 1897, p. 21.

EGGLESTON, D. CARL

Accounting system for a municipal hospital. *Journal of accountancy,* Nov. 1913, p. 366-70.
Brass foundry cost accounting. *Foundry,* March 1907.
Cost accounting. New York, The Ronald press company, 1920. 444p. (Business accounting, v.3)
Cost accounting in the brass foundry. *Iron age,* Nov. 15, 1906.
Distribution of establishment charges. *Business man's magazine,* Sept. 1906, p. 95-8.
Doing away with the ledger. *Business man's magazine,* Dec. 1910, p. 569-72.
Evolution of the machine unit system at the Modern electric co. *Journal of accountancy,* May 1911, p. 44-57.
For model cost system. *Business man's magazine,* Feb. 1907, p. 84-8.
Keeping a city's accounts. *Business man's magazine,* Aug. 1911, p. 138-40.
Manager has opinions of his own. *Business man's magazine,* Jan. 1907, p. 98-100.
Motor manufacturing cost. *Business man's magazine,* Sept. 1907, p. 69-71.
Municipal accounting. New York, The Ronald press co. 1914. 456p. (Ronald accounting series).
Municipal accounts in theory and practice. Chicago, La Salle extension university, 1918. 29p.
Municipal budget accounts. *Journal of accountancy,* Nov. 1911, p. 481-92.
Municipal cemetery accounts. *Journal of accountancy,* March 1913, p. 174-84.
Municipal cost system. *Journal of accountancy,* Dec. 1911, p. 573-87.
Municipal returns. *Journal of accountancy,* July 1911, p. 165-76.
Municipal revenue accounts. *Journal of accountancy,* Oct. 1911, p. 415-21.
Problems in cost accounting. New York, D. Appleton & co. 1918. 349p. (College of the city of New York series in commerce, civics and technology).
Recommendations for a uniform system of school accounts. *Government accountant,* Aug. 1911, p. 158-64.
Schedule order system. *Business man's magazine,* Aug. 1906, p. 79-83.
Series of articles about factory cost accounting. *Business man's magazine,* Dec. 1907, p. 78-100.
Southern wheel company's cost system. *Business man's magazine,* June 1908, p. 419-21.
System in the inspection department. *Business man's magazine,* Oct. 1906, p. 114-18.
System of factory cost accounting. *Journal of accountancy,* Dec. 1906, p. 115-22.
System of stores control. *Business man's magazine,* July 1907, p. 81-9.

EHLE, B.
Ten and three-quarters miles of 36-inch riveted steel pressure line built on Sooke work. *Engineering record,* Nov. 6, 1915, p. 564-5.

EHRHARDT, ALBERT
Alterations in the law of bankruptcy effected by the Bankruptcy act, 1890. *Accountant,* May 30, 1891, p. 417-20.

EHRLICH, M. W.
Meeting gas-engine competition on a basis of motor operating cost. *Electrical world,* Jan. 6, 1917, p. 38-9.

EIGHT cents enough; special masters recomment increased fare for Des Moines city railway. *Electric railway journal.* Dec. 11, 1920. p. 1213.

EIGHT-dollar-a-day accountants. *Journal of accountancy,* Aug. 1915, p. 138.

EIGHT per cent return in New York. *Electrical world,* April 17, 1915, p. 969.

EIGHTEEN months work of the Milwaukee bureau of accounting and efficiency. Commons, J. R. 1912.

EIGHTY-CENT gas decision of the Supreme court. *Engineering record,* Jan. 9, 1909, p. 31.

EINAUDI, LUIGI.
Taxes on property and property increments in Italy. *Quarterly journal of economics,* Nov. 1920, p. 108-38.

EISENBROWN, G. F.
Reading's system of accounting. *League of cities of the third class in Pennsylvania, Proceedings,* 1915, p. 45-52.

EISENMENGER, H. E.
Central station rates in theory and practice. *Electrical review,* July 5-Dec. 27, 1919, p. 19-21, 47-51, 94-7, 138-43, 183-7, 231-6, 266-9, 304-7, 352-5, 388-91, 434-7, 473-6, 513-7, 555-8, 599-602, 643-8, 686-90, 728-32, 771-5, 811-6, 857-60, 898-902, 935-8, 974-8, 1008-11, 1048-53.
Computation of the cost of current. *Electrical review and western electrician,* Aug. 15, 1914, p. 335-9.
Small-customer question. *Electrical review and western electrician,* Oct. 9, 1915, p. 657-62.
Theoretical basis of the multiple rate system. *Electrical world,* May 24, 1913, p. 1085-91.

EKIRCK, A. A.
Ideal teller's cash-sheet—how it worked in a small bank. *Bankers magazine,* Aug. 1909, p. 213-4.

ELBOURNE, E. T.
"All-in" costs. *Engineer* (London), July 30, 1915, p. 101.
Approximation in factory accounting. *Accountant,* March 20, 1915, p. 388-96.
Comprehensive time card. *American machinist,* v. 29, no. 17.
Costing problem. London, Liberty Press. 1919.
Factory administration and accounts; a book of reference with tables and specimen forms, for managers, engineers and accountants; with contributions on the General problems of industrial works designed by Andrew Home-Morton; and Financial accounts by John Maughfling. London, Longman, Green & co. 1918. 638p.
Functions of factory accounts. *Accountant,* May 3, 1919, p. 361-5.
Labour administration. *Engineer,* Nov. 1, 8, 29, 1918, p. 365-7, 388-90, 453-4.

ELDEN, L. L.
Maintenance costs of arc lamps for street lighting. *Electrical world,* December 23, 1916, p. 1229-30.

ELDRIDGE, ARTHUR
Kains commercial bookkeeping: columnar system. London, 1882.

ELDRIDGE, BARNARD HENRY BROOK.
Stock accounts for multiple shops. *Accountant,* Dec. 12, 1903, p. 1532-5.

ELDRIDGE, C.
Increased cost of electric railway operation. *Electric railway journal,* Jan. 3, 1914, p. 7-8.

ELDRIDGE, HERBERT JAMES
Accounting: practical methods and useful statistics. *Associated accountants' journal,* 1908, p. 173.
Cost accounts. *Journal of associated accountants,* 1910, p. 242.
Evolution of bookkeeping from early times to the present day. *Accountant,* Jan. 10, 1920, p. 61-3.
History of bookkeeping and the growth of the accountancy professions. *Associated accountants' journal,* v. 4, p. 177, 283.

ELDRIDGE, W. W.
Piece work or unit system of handling ties and timbers. *Railway age,* Jan. 24, 1913, p. 170-1. *Railway and engineering review,* Feb. 8, 1913, p. 122-3.

ELDRIDGE, WILLIAM J.
On the tapis. *Business man's magazine,* Sept. 1906, p. 79-86.

ELECTION of auditors. *Journal of Accountancy,* Jan. 1918, p. 54-6.

ELECTRIC AND STREET RAILROADS
See also Railroads.
American electric railway transportation and traffic association. Proceedings 1919, containing a complete report of the twelfth annual convention held at Young's million dollar pier, Atlantic City, N. J. October 6, 7, 8 and 9, 1919. New York, American electric railway association, 1919. 238p.
Conway, Thomas. Construction and finances of interurban electric railroads. *Journal of accountancy,* May 1906, p. 1-11.
Conway, Thomas. Traffic problems of interurban electric railroads. *Journal of accountancy,* Sept. Oct. 1908, Jan. 1909, p. 340-50, 426-34, 214-23.
Dalrymple, J. Glasgow corporation tramways. *Accountant,* March 4, April 8, 1905, p. 255-67, 406-10.
Federal commission questionnaire; a list of 168 questions on electric railway topics. *Electric railway Journal,* Sept. 20, 1919, p. 573-5.
London county council tramways report. *Incorporated accountants' journal,* 1907-8, p. 169.
Moxey, Edward Preston. Types of street railway consolidation. *Journal of accountancy,* Oct. 1906, p. 420-9.
Nelson, W. Common good of the city of Glasgow; its origin, history, and present position in relation to the tramway undertaking. *Accountant,* Nov. 4, 1911, p. 610-14.
Note on Mr. Bion J. Arnold's report No. 7 submitted to the public service commission. *Journal of accountancy, April* 1909, p. 482-3.

ELECTRIC AND STREET RAILROADS—*(Continued)*

Peat, W. B. and F. W. Pixley. Report on the London county council tramways. *Accountant,* April 4, 11, 18, 1908, p. 455-8, 486-94, 507-9, 554-7.

Public utilities reports. Rochester, Lawyers cooperative publishing company.

Stoffel, T. H. Handling freight "via electric"—demand for electric line freight service greatly exceeds present equipment and terminal facilities. *Aera,* July 1920, p. 1333-5.

Street railway accounting in the west. *Journel of accountancy,* May 1906, p. 72-3. *Tramway survey,* Oct. 5, 1907, p. 419-23.

Walton, Seymour. Accountants and street railway: correspondence. *Journal of accountancy,* May, 1906, p. 71-2.

Accounting

Accountants' association. Report of standing committee on a "Standard system of street railway accounting." *Street railway review,* 1904, p. 840-1.

Accountants' association proceedings. *Electric railway journal,* Oct. 16, 1920, p. 835-7.

Accounting circular of the Interstate commerce commission. *Electric railway review,* Feb. 29, 1908, p. 266.

Accounting department of the public service railway. *Electric railway journal* (Atlantic City convention section), October 7, 1911, p. 627-35.

Accounting for power in Chicago. *Electric railway journal,* May 16, 23, June 6, 1914.

Accounting methods of Illinois traction system. *Electric railway journal,* July 29, 1911, p. 184-9.

Accounting versus statistics. *Electric railway journal,* May 3, 1913, p. 803.

Accounts prescribed by New York public service commission, second district. *Electric railway journal,* Nov. 14, 1908, p. 1373-5.

Adams, H. E. Report on interstate accounting system. *Electric railway journal,* Aug. 7, 1909, p. 218.

Allen, Albert F. Operating statistics for street railways. *Journal of accountancy,* July 1907, p. 211-15.

American business and accounting encyclopaedia, compiled by E. H. Beach and W. M. Thorne. Detroit, Bookkeeper publishing co. 1901. *Electric railroads,* p. 489-518.

American electric railway accountants' and engineering associations: report of joint committee on engineering accounting. *Electric railway journal,* Oct. 17, 1913, p. 852.

American electric railway accountants' association. Proceedings 1910 to date. American electric railway association, 1910-16.

American electric railway accountants' association; report of the joint committee on engineering accounting. (In its *Proceedings,* 1912, p. 141-89, 160-80. *Bibliography,* p. 471-519).

American electric railway accountants' association annual meeting October 9-12. *Electic railway journal,* Oct. 14, 1916, p. 814-20.

American electric railway accountants' association convention, Atlantic City, Oct. 7-8. *Electric railway journal,* Oct. 11, 1919, sup. 85-6.

American electric railway accountants' association; meeting at Atlantic City, Tuesday, Oct. 14, 1913. *Electric railway journal* Oct. 15, 1913, 761-3.

American electric railway accountants' association: papers at final session of Atlantic City convention. *Electric railway journal,* Oct. 18, 1913, p. 893-9.

American electric railway accountants' association: proceedings at Atlantic City convention, October 17. *Electric railway journal,* Oct. 18, 1913, p. 900-1.

American electric railway accountants' association: report of committee on education. *Electric railway journal,* Oct. 19, 1913, p. 769.

American electric railway association. Maintenance and depreciation; abstracts from commissions' decisions and engineers' reports, including a bibliography. New York, American electric railway association, Dec. 1, 1919. 43p.

American electric railway association; accountants' papers and proceedings. *Electric railway journal,* Oct. 9, 1915, p. 736-44.

Annual meeting of C. E. R. A. accountants. *Electric railway journal,* Dec. 19, 1914, p. 1334-7.

Another device for encouraging power saving. *Electric railway journal,* April 28, 1917, p. 788-9.

Arnold, Bion J. Reply on accounting procedure. *Electric railway journal,* May 23, 1914, p. 1152.

Ayres, M. V. Accounting versus statistics. *Electric railway journal,* May 3, 1913, p. 803-5.

Balfour, H. N. Accounting for betterments and replacements. *Electric railway journal,* April 22, 1916, p. 770-1.

Banner year in accounting progress. *Electric railway journal,* Jan. 2, 1915, p. 9-10.

Barker, Harry. Apportionment of standard account items. (In his *Public utility rates.* 1917. p. 220-2).

Beardsley, H. M. Accounting for four departments. *Street railway review,* Oct. 1905.

Belleville, F. E. What economics can be profitably effected in the accounting department? *Electric railway journal,* March 16, 1912, p. 429.

Bergengren, R. W. Record system of a street railway company. *Business man's magazine,* March 1906.

Bernard, M. Derailments reduced by investigation, classification and study of causes. *Electric railway journal,* June 16, 1917, p. 1101.

Blanchard, A. Convenient inspection record system. *Electric railway journal,* Dec. 30, 1916, p. 1352.

Blank forms—some interesting blank forms of a small interurban railway company. *Electric railway journal,* May 28, 1910, p. 936-7.

Blinn, T. W. Daily work-train report. *Electric railway journal,* Sept. 25, 1915, p. 636.

Boyce, W. H. Complete records help to offset the rising cost of labor and material. *Electric railway journal,* Sept. 16, 1916, p. 478-80.

Brief in accounting scheme submitted to public service commission, second district, on behalf of New York state association. *Electric railway review,* May 16, 1908, p. 591.

Brion, Edward A. Interstate classification of accounts. *Electric railway journal,* May 2, 1914, p. 980-1.

Broad, B. G. Methods of changing the old accounts to the new. *Electric railway journal,* April 24, 1909, p. 779.

Brockway, Walter Belding. Accounting department of interurban railways. *Street railway journal,* October 4, 1902.

Brockway, Walter Belding. Electric railway accounting; the monthly report, the accounting and the accountant. New York, McGraw-Hill publishing co. 1906. 84p.

Brockway, Walker Belding. Small company and the new classification of accounts. *Street railway journal,* March 14, 1908.

Brooks, Henry W. Comparative statements. *Street railway review,* March 20, 1903.

Brooks, Henry W. Province of the street railway accountant. *Street railway review,* Sept. 20, 1903.

ELECTRIC AND STREET RAILROADS— *(Continued)*

BRUSTER, R. R. Relation of accounting officers to other members of official family. *Electric railway journal,* June 17, 1916, p. 1136-9.

BUEHLER, C. E. Reducing the auditor's worries; abstract. *Electric railway journal,* April 21, 1917, p. 737.

BURINGTON, P. V. Electric railway accounting review. *Electric railway journal,* Oct. 9, 1915, p. 720-1.

C. E. R. A. A. meets at Ottawa Beach. *Electric railway journal,* July 24, 1920, p. 168-70.

CALDERWOOD, J. F. Street railway accounting. *Street railway journal,* Jan. 3, 1903.

CALDERWOOD, J. F. Street railway accounting. *Street railway journal,* v.19, p. 536.

CALDICOTT, O. HOLT.. Chartered accountants as experts in commerce and manufactures. *Accountant,* May 22, 1897, p. 524-9.

CAMPBELL, G. E. Card records of Los Angeles track work. *Electric railway journal,* Sept. 4, 1915, p. 407-8.

CENTRAL electric railway accountants' association: proceedings at annual meeting, Dec. 12-13, 1913. *Electric railway journal,* Dec. 20, 1913, p. 1275-80.

CENTRAL electric railway accountants' association 27th meeting. *Electric railway journal,* June 19, 1915, p. 1151-4.

CENTRAL electric railway accountants' association 33rd meeting, Fort Wayne, Ind., Feb. 15. *Electric railway journal,* Feb. 22, 1919, p. 372-3.

CENTRAL electric railway accountants' meeting, Toledo, June 24. *Electric railway journal,* June 27, 1914, p. 1444-6.

CLARK, R. J. Prepayment cars and the accountant. *Electric railway journal,* October 9, 1915, p. 721-2.

CLASSIFICATION of rent items. *Electric railway journal,* Jan. 1, 1916, p. 11-2.

COIN counter at Kansas city. *Electric railway journal,* July 3, 1920, p. 27.

CONFERENCE on standard accounts with the interstate commerce commission. *Street railway journal,* May 23, 1908,, p. 860.

COURSE on electric railway accounting by mail. *Electric railway journal,* May 30, 1914, p. 1214.

CRAM, R. C. Money-saving factors in the maintenance of special work. *Electric railway journal,* July 20, 1918, p. 103-8.

CRITICISM of tentative system of accounts by Central electric railway accountants' association. *Electric railway journal,* March 28, 1914, p. 723-5.

DAILY reports, store room accounting and operating records of the Camden suburban railway. *Street railway journal,* December 19, 1903, p. 1052-61.

DALRYMPLE, JAMES. Glasgow corporation tramways. *Accountant,* March 4, April 8, 1905, p. 255-67, 406-10.

DALRYMPLE, JAMES. Standardisation of tramway accounts. *Accountant,* Oct. 10, 1903, p. 1191-3, 1231-5.

DALRYMPLE, JAMES. Tramway accounts. (In Lisle, George. *Encyclopaedia of accounting.* v.6. p. 225-43).

DANA, E. Reporting and checking car defects in Boston. *Electric railway journal,* Sept. 9, 1911, p. 425-6.

DAVIES, H. J. Cost of service accounting; possible improvements in Cleveland "service at cost" plan pointed out by secretary-treasurer of company. *Aera,* Nov. 1920, p. 363-6.

DAVIES, H. J. Recent legislation affecting electric railway accounting. *Electric railway Journal,* July 1, 1911, p. 26-8.

DAVIES, H. J. Service-at-cost accounting in Cleveland. *Electric railway journal,* Oct. 16, 1920, p. 765-8.

DAVIES, H. J. Some accounting features of the Cleveland railway company's franchise. *Electric railway journal,* Oct. 15 and Dec. 17, 1910. *American street and interurban railway accountants' association, Proceedings,* 1910, p. 125-54.

DAVIES, J. VIPOND. Engineering accounting. *Electric railway journal,* Oct. 17, 1913, p. 864, 840. American electric railway engineering association, *Proceedings,* 1913, p. 488, 415.

DAVIES, O. I. Method of accounting of freight claims. *Electric railway journal,* March 18, 1911, p. 463.

DEDRICK, A. E. Accrued accounts. *Electric railway journal,* Dec. 11, 1915, p. 1169.

DEDRICK, A. E. Light and power accounting. *Electric railway journal,* Dec. 23, 1916, p. 1300, 1281.

DEPARTURE in repair shop accounting. *Street railway journal,* May 20, 1905.

DEVELOPMENT charges. *Electric railway journal,* September 18, 1915, p. 576-7.

DIMMOCK, W. S. Accounting system of the Omaha and Council Bluffs railway and bridge company. *Street railway review,* May 15, 1899.

DOOLITTLE, F. W. Anatomy of the interurban report. *Electric railway journal,* Feb. 10, 1917, p. 242-9.

DOOLITTLE, F. W. Collection of traffic data. *Electric railway journal,* July 17, 1915, p. 94-101.

DUFFY, C. N. Milwaukee electric railway and light company's reply to accounting circular. *Electric railway journal,* April 4, 1908, p. 419.

DUNN, H. A. Accounting inconsistencies and fallacies. *Electric railway journal,* Oct. 14, 1916, p. 775-7. *American electric railway accountants' association, Proceedings,* 1916, p. 76-8.

EFFECTIVE service voucher. *Electric railway journal,* October 26, 1912, p. 918.

ELECTRIC railway appraisals. *Electric railway journal,* Nov. 2, 1907, p. 905.

ELECTRIC tramway accounting and finance. *Electrical review,* London, Nov. 1, 1907, Dec. 13, 1907.

ELKINS, A. F. AND OTHERS. Central electric railway accountants' association. *Electric railway journal,* June 28, 1913, p. 1168.

EMERY, JAMES A. Statistical units used in analysis of electric railway accounts. *American electric railway accountants' association, Proceedings,* 1913, p. 152-66, 403-18. *Electrical railway journal,* Oct. 16, 1913, p. 815-7.

ENGINEERING charges in capital account. *Electrical world,* Nov. 17, 1917, p. 951.

FARE accounting: symposium. *Electric railway journal,* Oct. 4, 1913, p. 582-7.

FORBES, J. F. Importance of accrued accounts. *Electric railway journal,* Oct. 16, 1915, p. 809-10.

FORECASTING and recording track renewals in Brooklyn. *Electric railway journal,* March 6, 1909, p. 432.

FORMS used by the roadway department forces of the Chicago city railway company. *Electric railway journal,* Oct. 5, 1912, p. 534-6.

FORSE, W. H. Accounting inconsistencies and fallacies. *Electric railway journal,* Oct. 28, 1916, p. 937.

FORSE, W. H. Classification of accounts as adapted to coordinate departments. *Electric railway journal,* Dec. 21, 1912, p. 1229-30.

FORSE, W. H. Depreciation and appreciation. *Electric railway journal,* Dec. 11, 1915, p. 1169-70.

FORSE, W. H. Electric railway auditing and accounting. New York, McGraw-Hill publishing co. 1908. 157p.

ELECTRIC AND STREET RAILROADS— *(Continued)*

FORSE, W. H. How to use sinking funds. *Electric railway journal,* Sept. 23, 1916, p. 528-30.

FORSE, WILLIAM F. Sinking funds. *American electric railway accountants' association,* 1913, p. 274. Abstract. *Aera,* Nov. 1913, p. 409.

FULLERTON, IRWIN. Keeping track of the elusive nickel. *Business man's magazine,* Nov. 1911, p. 427-31.

GAULT, E. D. Accounting system for a small electric railway. *Electric railway journal,* Oct. 11, 1911, p. 748-50. *American electric railway association, Proceedings,* 1911, p. 30-68.

GLOVER, M. W. Saving money through accounting. *Electric railway journal,* Oct. 12, 1918, p. 660-1.

GLOVER, M. W. Simple work-order system; the system described is particularly adopted to roads with renewals of less than $100,000 a year. *Electric railway journal,* Sept. 11, 1915, p. 441-2.

GOLDEN, A. J. Method of accounting for a motor railway. *Business man's magazine,* Jan. 1911, p. 101-104.

GOODLOE, J. S. M. Passenger receipts vs. passenger revenue. *Journal of accountancy,* May 1906, p. 27-9.

HAM, W. F. Report of committee on a standard form of report for electric railways. *Street railway journal,* 1902, p. 712-7.

HEMMING, R. H. Accounting and mechanical departments. *Electric railway journal,* June, 19, 1915, p. 1153-4.

HIXON, L. T. Analyzing the balance sheet. *Electric railway journal,* June 12, 1915, p. 1112-3.

HIXON, L. T. Forms for accounts of interurban agents. *Electric railway journal,* April 16, 1910, p. 701-2.

HIXON, L. T. Interline accounting. *Electric railway journal,* March 25, 1911, p. 503-4.

HULETT, FRANK W. Way records on cost per section basis. *Electric railway journal,* April 3, 1915, p. 669-71.

I. C. C. issues accounting answers. *Electric railway journal,* Nov. 18, 1916, p. 1078-9.

INTERLINE accounting. *Electric railway journal.* Oct. 11, 1911, Oct. 18, 1913, p. 745-6. 894-5.

INTERNATIONAL CORRESPONDENCE SCHOOLS. Accounts for electric railways. (In their *I. C. S. reference library,* c1915, 279, section 33, p. 1-13).

INTERSTATE commerce commisison classification of accounts. *Electric railway journal,* June 13, 1914, p. 1321-3.

INTERSTATE system of accounts. *Electric railway journal,* July 4, 1914, p. 14.

INTERURBAN freight service; a classification of operating expense accounts for freight service is suggested. *Electric railway journal,* July 3, 1920, p. 26-7.

JACOBS, B. H. Shop orders. *Electric railway journal,* Dec. 18, 1915, p. 1214.

JOINT hearing on uniform accounts for New York electric roads. *Electric railway journal,* Aug. 8 ,1908, p. 439.

JOINT session of the Engineering and Accountants' association, Oct. 16. 1913. *Electric railway journal,* Oct. 17, 1913, p. 840-2.

KASEMEIER, E. L. Car interchange records. *Electric railway journal,* Dec. 21, 1912, p. 1231-33.

KASEMEIER, E. L. Clearing house for interline traffic accounts. *Electric railway journal,* Dec. 16, 1916, p. 1250.

KEISTER, D. A. Street railway accounting. (In his *Corporation accounting and auditing.* 1909. p. 322-30).

KITTREDGE, A. O. Ideal system of street railway accounts. *Street railway journal,* Jan. 1899, p. 30-2.

KITTREDGE, A. O. Open questions before the committee on a standard system of street railway accounting. *Street railroad journal,* Feb. 1898.

KITTREDGE, A. O. Street railway accounting. *Commerce, accounts and finance,* Dec. 1901, p. 19-22.

KITTREDGE, A. O. Theory of reserve and suspense accounts. *Street railway journal,* December 1898.

KOCHERSPERGER, H. M. Interstate commerce classification. *Street railway journal,* May 2, 1908, p. 729.

LAWTON, WILLARD HUBBARD. New classification of electrical railway expenses. *Journal of accountancy,* June, 1908, p. 114-22.

LINN, A. L. Electric railway accounting. *Electric railway journal,* July 3, 1909, p. 30-3.

LOCAL board and depreciative and renewal funds. *Accounting and commerce,* Aug. 1920, p. 1178-9.

LONDON county council tramways accounts. *Electrician,* London, January 15, 1915.

LONDON county council tramways report. *Incorporated accountants' journal,* 1907-8, p. 169.

MCCOLL, DONALD. Tramway bookkeeping and accounts. London. Gee & co. 1902. 226p. (Accountants' library, v.15).

MCCOLL, DONALD. Tramway bookkeeping and accounts simplified. London, 1907.

MCMAHON, C. R. Car maintenance records facilitate work. *Electric railway journal,* July 19, 1919, p. 119-21.

MCRAE, T. B. Accounting for rents. *Electric railway journal,* Dec. 25, 1915, p. 1260.

MAINTENANCE records that prove invaluable. *Electric railway journal,* April 27, 1918, p. 806-9.

MANGOLD, WILLIAM. System for a street railway. *System,* Sept. 1903, p. 211-2.

MANNING, JAMES. Street railway accounting. *Street railway journal,* 1902, p. 25.

MARSH, S. B. N. Tramways, department. (In Bateson, William. *Pitman's municipal office organisation and management.* p. 407-20).

MARWICK, JAMES. Municipal ownership of street railways; with an analysis of the accounts of the city of Glasgow tramways. *Accountant,* Sept. 9, 1905, p. 281-5.

MAY, IRVILLE AUGUSTUS. Importance of proper accounting in the maintenance way department in general. *Street railway bulletin,* Sept. 1919, p. 329-35.

MAY, IRVILLE AUGUSTUS. Recognize the accounting department. *Electric railway journal,* Jan. 31, 1920, p. 251.

MAY, IRVILLE AUGUSTUS. Street railway accounting; a manual of operating practice for electric railways. New York, The Ronald press co. 1917. 454p.

MAY, W. W. Interstate commerce classification of accounts (letter). *Street railway journal,* April 11, 1908, p. 613.

METHODS of checking tickets and other passenger revenue. *Electric railway journal,* March 5, 1910, p. 411-2.

MICHENNER, A. S. Street railway accounting. *Stone and Webster public service journal,* Aug. 1908, p. 92.

MILLS, J. C. Cutting out needless work. *Business man's magazine,* May 1911, p. 474-80.

MONTAGUE, LLOYD C. Street railway accounting. *Business man's magazine,* Aug. 1905, p. 279-85.

MOXEY, EDWARD P. AND OTHERS. Street railway accounting. (In their *Practical accounting methods.* p. 331-50).

MULHALL, JOHN F. J. Electric railways. (In his *Quasi-public corporation accounting and management.* c1905. p. 142-62).

ELECTRIC AND STREET RAILROADS— ACCOUNTING—*(Continued)*

NATIONAL association of railway commissioners: report of committee on statistics and accounts of electric railways. *Electric railway journal,* Nov. 8, 1913, p. 1013-5.

NAU, CARL. Accounting methods for municipally owned street railways; with discussion. *American electric railway accountants' association, Proceedings,* 1919, p. 112-26.

NAU, CARL. Honest accounting is needed. *Journal of accountancy,* June, 1907, p. 91-2.

NEAL, J. H. Detailed records—their use and value. *Electric railway journal,* October 13, 1910, p. 794-5.

NEW accounting system of the Chicago railways company. *Electric railway journal,* 1908, p. 695-7.

NEW tentative accounting classification for New York adopted by Second district commission from I. C. C. classification. *Electric railway journal,* Feb. 2, 1918, p. 228.

NEW YORK CITY. COMMISSIONERS OF ACCOUNTS. Report of a special examination of Bureau of collection of city revenue to determine correctness of returns of street railways. New York, M. B. Brown, 1901. 277p.

NOT depreciation but retirement; electric railway representatives suggest change of terms. *Electric railway journal,* July 27, 1918, p. 170.

OPINIONS of commission in Third avenue case. *Electric railway journal,* Feb. 10, 1912, p. 237.

PAPERS read at convention of street railway accountants at Cleveland, March 23-24. *Street railway journal,* April 1897.

PARDEE, J. H. Interurban ticket accounting. *Street railway review,* Oct. 1905.

PASSENGER accounts—reports of standing committee, *Central electric railway accountants' association,* June 4, 1913. *Electric railway journal,* July 5, 1913, p. 25-8.

PATTERSON, A. R. Organization of the accounting department of an electric railway and light company. *American street and interurban railway accountants' association, Proceedings,* 1908, p. 35-65.

PEAT, W. B. AND F. W. PIXLEY. Report on the London county tramways. *Accountant,* April 4, 11, 18, 1908. p. 455-8, 486-94, 507-9, 554-7.

PLEA for unification of accounting classifications. *Electric railway journal,* Nov. 4, 1916, p. 979.

POLICY of English municipal tramways respecting renewals. *Electric railway journal,* Oct. 7, 1911, p. 661-3.

PROGRESS profile used by an Iowa interurban. *Electric railway journal,* Oct. 10, 1914, p. 779.

PUBLIC utility reports: annotated. New York, Lawyers co-operative publishing company. See Index under Accounting.

QUESTION box of the Central electric railway accountants' association. *Electric railway journal,* May 4, 1912, p. 742-4.

QUESTIONS and answers under uniform system of accounting. *Electric railway journal,* September 6, 1913, p. 398-9.

QUESTIONS and answers under uniform system of accounts. *Electric railway journal,* May 17, June 7, July 5, Oct. 11, 1913, p. 907, 1036-7; 43-4, 705-6.

RECORD system of the Third avenue railway co., N. Y. *Electric railway journal,* Mar. 27, 1909, p. 546.

RECORDS of electric tramway accounts. *Tramway and railway world* (London), 1904 to date.
See Index for paging.

RENEWALS as defined by the board of supervising engineers, Chicago traction; general rulings, etc. *Electric railway journal,* March 4, 1911, p. 374-7.

REPORT of committee on standardization of accounts. *Street railway journal,* 1898, p. 63-8.

REPORT of joint committee on shop accounting. *American street and interurban railway accountants' association, Proceedings,* 1910, p. 49-99.

REPORT of sub-committee on what constitutes maintenance. *American electric railway engineering association, Proceedings,* 1911, p. 342. Abstract. *Electric railway journal,* Oct. 12, 1911, p. 766.

REPORT of the committee on accounts and statistics of electric railways—National association of railway commissioners. *Electric railway journal,* Nov. 23, 1912, p. 1063-4.

REPORT of the committee on interline accounting. *American electric railway association, Proceedings,* 1909, 1911, 1913, p. 52-8, 69-89, 221-44.

REPORT of the committee on standard classification of accounts. *Street railway journal,* 1905, p. 646-50.

REPORT of the committee on standard classification of accounts and form of report. *American street and interurban railway accountants' association, Proceedings,* 1908, p. 113-22, 1909, v.2, p. 58-72.

REPORT of the joint committee of the American railway mechanical and electrical association and the street railway accountants' association of America on blanks for shop records and accounts. *Street railway journal,* 1904, v. 24, p. 700-1.

REPORT of the joint committee on engineering accounting—American electric railway accountants and engineering associations. *Electric railway journal, Oct.* 12, 1911, p. 778-80.

REPORT of the joint committee on engineering accounting—American electric railway accountants and engineering associations. *Railway age gazette,* Oct. 11, 1912, p. 793-97.

REPORT of the joint committee on engineering accounting. *Electric railway journal,* Oct. 17, 1913, p. 852. *American electric railway accountants' association, Proceedings,* 1913, p. 167-77.

REPORT of the joint comitee on express and freight accounting—American electric railway accountants and transportation and traffic associations. *American electric railway association, Proceedings.* 1911, p. 140-52. *Electric railway journal,* Oct. 12, 1911, p. 785-6.

REPORT of the joint committee on express and freight accounting. *Electric railway journal,* Oct. 10, 1912, p. 767.

REPORT of the joint committee on shop accounting. *American street and interurban railway accounts and engineering associations. Electric railway journal,* Oct. 12, 1910, p. 744-9.

REPORT on accounts of Chicago railways co. *Electric railway journal,* Sept. 4, 1909, p. 354-5.

REPORT on standard system of street railway accounting. *Street railway review,* Sept. 15, 1898.

RESOLUTIONS of New York state association concerning tentative classifications. *Electric railway review,* March 28, 1908, p. 378.

RETAINING a record of transfers. *Electric railway journal,* Jan. 5, 1918, p. 50.

REVISED classification of accounts for electric railways. *Electric railway review,* May 23, 1908, p. 624.

REYNOLDS, JOHN J. Uniformity in claim department records and accounts. *American street and interurban railway claim agents' association, Proceedings,* 1908, p. 63-81.

ROUNDEY, E. P. Way records. *Electric railway journal,* May 15, 1915, p. 945-6.

ELECTRIC AND STREET RAILROADS—
ACCOUNTING—*(Continued)*

ROUTINE of a railway electric and gas lighting company. *Street railway journal,* Nov. 3, 1900.

SALIERS, E. A. Accounting measures to meet business depression in the industry. *Electric railway journal,* Oct. 11, 1919, sup. 722-3, 37-9.

SCHWENKE, A. G. Mechanical aids in accounting. *Electric railway journal,* April 28, 1917, p. 775-9.

SECOND condensation of operating accounts for New York roads. *Electric railway journal,* Jan. 9, 1909, p. 67.

SEGREGATION of power accounts and rents—maintenance repairs, renewals and depreciation. *Electric railway journal,* Nov. 8, 1913, p. 1013-5.

SERVICE order for Milwaukee lines. *Electric railway journal,* Dec. 6, 1913.

SHOP-ACCOUNTING—report of the joint committee of American street and interurban railway accountant and engineering associations. *Electric railway journal,* Oct. 12, 1910, p. 744-9.

SHROYER, W. and others. Report of standing committee on passenger accounts, Central electric railway accountants' association. *Electric railway journal,* July 5, 1913, p. 25-8.

SLICK, E. E. Standardization of claims statistics. *Electric railway journal,* Oct. 16, 1915, p. 813-5.

SMELLIE, H. B. Accounting for electric railroad building. *Bookkeeper,* 1902, v. 14, p. 71-6.

SMELLIE, H. B. Electric railroad accounting. *Bookkeeper,* 1902, v. 15, no. 4, p. 48-55.

SMITH, F. E. Report of committee on standard blanks and accounting for material and supplies. *Street railway journal,* Oct. 12, 1901.

SMITH, F. E. Trip and mileage accounts on the Lynn and Boston. *Street railway review,* Jan. 15, 1899.

STANDARD classification of street railway accounts in New Jersey. *Electric railway review,* Feb. 11, 1911, p. 273.

STANDARD distribution of street railway receipts and expenses. *Street railway journal,* Aug. 1897.

STANDARD form of municipal tramway accounts. *Electrician,* 1904, v. 53, p. 947-50.

STANDARD form of report of the International tramways and light railways association. *Street railway journal,* 1904, v. 24, p. 370-4

STANDARD form of tramway accounts. *Electrical engineer,* 1904, v. 40 (n. s. v. 34), p. 513-6.

STATISTICS and accounts of electric railways: report of committee of the National association of railway commissioners. *Electric railway journal,* Nov. 21, 1914, p. 1142-3.

STEUART, WILLIAM M. Census statistics and the standard form of electric railway accounting. *Street railway review* (Daily ed.) Sept. 4, 1903.

STREET railroads. *International accountants' manual,* 1910, paragraph 98.

STREET RAILWAY ACCOUNTANTS' ASSOCIATION OF AMERICA. Standard system of street railway accounting covering the classification of construction and equipment accounts and classification of operating expense accounts; approved and recommended by the National convention of railroad commisioners; approved by the Board of railroad commissioners of the state of New York. *Street railway accountants' association of America* (1910). 76p.

STREET railway accounting. *Street railway journal,* v. 20, p. 159-60.

STUBBS, N. E. Collection of data concerning pay-rolls and invoices. *Electric railway journal,* Oct. 12, 1910, p. 742-3.

SUIT against classification of additions and betterments of the Interstate commerce commission. *Electric railway journal,* Nov. 18, 1911, p. 1067.

SYSTEM of accounts prescribed by Wisconsin railroad commission. *Electric railway journal,* July 12, 1909, p. 1076-7.

SYSTEM of reports of Denver city tramway. *Street railway journal,* 1903, v. 22, p. 610-6.

TABULATING statistics and accounts by machinery. *Electric railway journal,* May 10, 1913, p. 853-4.

TENTATIVE classification of accounts prepared by New York public service commission. *Electric railway journal,* July 25, 1908, p. 349.

TENTATIVE I. C. C. uniform system of accounts: introductory letter. *Electric railway journal,* March 14, 1914, p. 588.

TENTATIVE system of accounts. *Electric railway journcl,* March 21-28, April 11, 1914, p. 674-5, 720-2, 828-9.

TINGLEY, C. L. S. Interstate commerce commissions proposed classification of accounts. *Street railway journal,* 1908, v. 31, p. 455-9.

TRESILIAN, R. S. Tramway accounts. *Accountant,* Aug. 23, 30, 1890, p. 441-5, 454-8.

TRESILIAN, R. S. Tramways; their working and accounts. *Tramway and railway world,* April 11, 1901.

UNIFORMITY in financial statements. *Electric railway journal,* April 18, 1914, p. 859.

WAY department report forms. *Electric railway journal,* Sept. 4, 1915, p. 296-9.

WEBELACKER, C. F. Street railway repair accounts. *Electrical world,* June 25, 1896.

WHO should keep Way department time? *Electric railway journal,* Sept. 25, 1915, p. 635-6.

WILLCUTT, G. B. Value of railway statistics. *Electric railway journal,* Oct. 9, 1915, p. 705-7.

WILLIAMS, L. R. Tramway accounts. *Accountant,* May 20, 1911, p. 791-801.

WILLIAMS, T. S. Capital accounts from the viewpoint of investors and the public. *Street railway journal,* Oct. 12, 1901.

WILSON, H. L. Accounting co-operation desired. *Electric railway journal,* Nov. 11, 1916, p. 1024.

WILSON, H. L. Accounting versus statistics. *Electric railway journal,* May 10, 1913, p. 859.

WILSON, H. L. Departmental accounts, Boston elevated railway company. *Street railway journal,* 1900, v. 16, p. 1086-8.

WISCONSIN classification of accounts. *Electric railway journal,* Sept. 4, 1909, p. 366.

WRIGHT, W. B. Accounting department. *Electric railway journal,* June 5, 1909.

YAPP, THOMAS. Interstate commerce classification. *Electric railway journal,* June 20, 1908, p. 124.

ZINSMEISTER, W. K. Interurban freight service; a classification of operating expense accounts for freight service is suggested. *Electric railway journal,* July 3, 1920, p. 26-7.

——— **Uniform classifications**

MARYLAND. PUBLIC SERVICE COMMISSION. Regulations governing the appraisal, distribution and apportionment of fixed capital of street and electric railways. Baltimore, 1911. 17p.

MARYLAND. PUBLIC SERVICE COMMISSION. Uniform system of accounts for electric railways, effective July 1, 1915. 112p.

MONTANA. PUBLIC SERVICE COMMISSION. Uniform classification of accounts for street railways: first issue effective July 1, 1913. 53p.

ELECTRIC AND STREET RAILROADS—ACCOUNTING—*(Continued)*

NEW JERSEY. BOARD OF PUBLIC UTILITY COMMISSIONERS. Uniform system of accounts for street or traction railway utilities. First revised issue, effective Jan. 1, 1919. Trenton, 1919. 95p.

NEW YORK STATE. PUBLIC SERVICE COMMISSION. Uniform system of accounts for electric railroad corporations, adopted August 20, 1918. Albany, 1918. 143p.

NEW YORK STATE. PUBLIC SERVICE COMMISSION. Uniform system of accounts for electric railroad corporations (tentative) adopted 1917. Albany, 1917. 109p.

NEW YORK STATE. PUBLIC SERVICE COMMISSION. Uniform system of accounts of street and electric railways for the first district: final order of December 8, 1908 and modifying order of June 18, 1909. (Case 641). New York city, 1917. 88p.

NEW YORK STATE. PUBLIC SERVICE COMMISSION. Uniform system of accounts for street railroad corporations; condensed scheme for corporations having gross operating revenues from street railroad operations amounting to less than $500,000 per annum; adopted November 10, 1908. Albany, 1908. 74p.

NEW YORK STATE. PUBLIC SERVICE COMMISSION. Uniform system of accounts for street railroad corporations, second condensed scheme for corporations having gross operating revenues from street railroad operations amounting to less than $100,000 per annum; adopted December 2, 1908. Albany, 1908. 73p.

UNITED STATES. INTERSTATE COMMERCE COMMISSION. Classification of operating revenues of electric railways; first issue. Washington, Government printing office, 1908. 15p.

UNITED STATES. INTERSTATE COMMERCE COMMISSION. Decision upon questions raised under classifications prescribed for electric railways; effective January 1, 1912. Washington, Government printing office, 1911. 107p. (Accounting bulletin no. 5.)

UNITED STATES. INTERSTATE COMMERCE COMMISSION. Interpretations of accounting classifications for electric railways; effective May 1, 1917 (supersedes accounting bulletin no. 9). Washington, Government printing office, 1917. 143p. (Accounting bulletin no. 14.)

UNITED STATES. INTERSTATE COMMERCE COMMISSION. Regulations to govern the destruction of records of electric railway companies; first issue effective May 1, 1913. Washington, Government printing office, 1913. 16p.

UNITED STATES. INTERSTATE COMMERCE COMMISSION. Selected decisions upon questions raised under accounting clasifications for electric railways. (In Edward P. Moxey and others. *Practical accounting methods.* p. 477-89.)

UNITED STATES. INTERSTATE COMMERCE COMMISSION. Uniform system of accounts for electric railways; effective July 1, 1914 Washington, Government printing office, 1914. 134p.

WISCONSIN. RAILROAD COMMISSION. Uniform classification of accounts for electric railways prescribed January 1909. Madison, 1909. 148p.

Auditing

AUDIT of the accounts of tramway undertakings and tramway finance companies, Great Britain. *Electrical review* (London), Sept. 24. Oct. 1, 1901.

BERGENGREN, E. Auditing department of a great electric railroad company. *Business man's magazine*, Jan. 1905, p. 59-65.

BOYLAN, M. R. Collecting and auditing receipts of prepayment cars. *American street and interurban railway accountants association, Proceedings*, 1910, p. 155-80.

BROCKWAY, W. B. Electric railway auditor, his duties and relation to the organization. *American street and interurban railway accountants association, Proceedings*, 1909, p. 107-20. *Journal of accountancy*, Feb. 1910, p. 253-62.

BROCKWAY, W. B. Reporting a street railway examination. *Journal of accountancy*, May, 1907, p. 16-22.

CARTER, P. H. Tramway audits. *Accountant*, July 26, 1890, p. 401-4.

CASTENHOLZ, WILLIAM B. Electric roads. (In his *Auditing procedure.* 1918. p. 197-203.)

DICKSEE, LAWRENCE R. Electric railways. (In his *Auditing.* Authorized American edition. p. 145-50.)

FORD, GEORGE L. Voucher indexing simplified. *Electric railway journal*, June 28, 1913, p. 1167-8.

FORSE, WILLIAM H. Auditing conductors' collections on interurban railways. *Journal of accountancy*, Aug. 1907, p. 298-301.

MARYLAND notes. *Journal of accountancy*, May, 1906, p. 73.

MAY, IRVILLE AUGUSTUS. Audits. (In his *Street railway accounting.* 1917. p. 358-76.)

MONTGOMERY, ROBERT H. Electric railroad. (In his *Auditing theory and practice.* 1916. p. 656-664.)

SPICER, ERNEST EVAN and ERNEST C. PEGLER. Tramways. (In their *Practical auditing.* 1914. p. 514-15.

WHITE, A. J. Traveling auditor. *Electric railway journal*, March 18, 1911, p. 467-8.

Cost accounting

BRAMBLE, B. E. Accounting for capital expenditures. *Electric railway journal*, June 15, 1912, p. 1023-4.

ELECTRIC tramway costing and statistics. *Electrical review* (London), Dec. 10, 1909, pt. 1.

FULLER, C. H. Estimating cost of track construction on a unit-time basis. *Electric railway journal*, Jan. 8, 1916, p. 80-4.

GAUSMANN, S. Timekeeping and cost records for way department. *Electric railway journal*, Sept. 18, 1915, p. 596-8.

HIXSON, L. T. Departmental expense statements. *Electric railway journal*, June 24, 1916, p. 1176-8.

KALWEIT, GEORGE W. Unit cost work order system. *American electric railway accountants' association, Proceedings*, 1913, p. 38-83. *Electric railway journal*, Oct. 15, 1913.

KASEMEIER, E. L. Compiling operating expenses. *Electric railway journal*, June 27, 1914, p. 1445-6.

MILLER, F. A. Keeping mechanical department costs. *Electric railway journal*, Aug. 19, 1916, p. 312-4.

SPARKS, JOHN B. Electric railway costs. *Electric railway journal*, June 14, 1913, p. 1061-4.

Costs

ALBERGER, W. R. Reduction in power cost affected by the use of coasting recorders. *Electric railway journal*, Sept. 18, 1915, p. 520-1.

AMBERG, E. J. Overhead contact systems, construction and costs. *American institute of electrical engineers, Proceedings*, June 1915, p. 1255-66. Abstract. *Electric railway journal*, July 10, 1915, p. 56.

AYLING, CHARLES L. Purchased power and the street railway. *Electric railway journal*, Jan. 3, 1914, p. 9-10.

BALTIMORE costs mount. *Electric railway journal*, Aug. 3, 1918, p. 210.

ELECTRIC AND STREET RAILROADS—COSTS—(Continued)

BEELER, J. A. Comparative costs of subway and surface lines in Boston; report to the Massachusetts public service commission. *Electric railway journal,* Feb. 16, 1918, p. 313.

BENNETT, S. H. Reducing the operating ratio. *Electric railway journal,* Oct. 10, 1914, p. 764-5.

BERNARD, M. Cost data on special work renewals. *Electric railway journal,* July 21, Aug. 18, Sept. 8, 29, October 27, Nov. 10, 24, Dec. 8, 1917, p. 108, 279, 406, 588, 781, 871, 957, 1043.

CHICAGO electrification report discussed at the New York railroad club. *Electric railway journal,* March 25, 1916, p. 604-5.

COMPARATIVE cost of steam and electric railroad operation. *Chronicle* (Railway section), June 28, 1913, p. 3-4.

COST of electric freight service of Connecticut company discussed at New Haven hearing. *Electric railway journal,* July 28, 1917, p. 142.

COST of electrification of Chicago terminals; summary of the items entering into the expenditure for new equipment. *Railway age,* Dec. 17, 1915, p. 1125-8.

COST of erecting overhead work. *Electric railway journal,* Jan. 20-27, Feb. 10, 24, March 10, 31, April 14, May 12, 26, June 16, 30, 1917, p. 127, 173, 260, 355, 447, 606, 702, 880, 969, 1105, 1195.

COST of supplies in railway units. *Electric railway journal,* Aug. 22, 1914, p. 338.

COX, J. B. Contact system of the Butte, Anaconda & Pacific railway. *American institute of electrical engineers, Proceedings,* Aug. 1915, p. 1447-76. *General electric review,* Aug. 1915, p. 842-59. Abstract. *Electric railway journal,* July 10, 1915, p. 59-60.

COX, J. B. Electrical operation of the Butte, Anaconda & Pacific railway. *American institute of electrical engineers, Proceedings,* Nov. 1914, p. 1729-53. *General electric review,* Nov. 1914, p. 1047-65. Abstract. *Electric railway journal,* Nov. 7, 1914, p. 1050-1.

CRAM, R. C. Analysis of track maintenance costs. *Electric railway journal,* March 17, 1917, p. 479-83.

DAVIES, H. J. Maintenance provisions of Cleveland ordinance. *Electric railway journal,* April 2, 1910, p. 614-15.

DAVIES, JOHN V. Approximate costs of rapid-transit structures. *Engineering record* June 6, 1914, p. 642.

DOOLITTLE, F. W. Operating cost and shifts in service. *Electric railway journal,* Sept. 4, 1915, p. 400.

DOOLITTLE, F. W. Railway operation in Cleveland. *Electric railway journal,* Feb. 19, 1916, p. 359-64.

DOYLE, J. J. Cost of operating the Washington, Baltimore and Annapolis electric railroad. *Engineering and contracting,* Dec. 31, 1913, p. 748-50.

DUER, J. V. B. Third rail and trolley system of the West Jersey and seashore railroads. *American institute of electrical engineers, Proceedings,* June 1915, p. 1237-53. Abstract. *Electric railway journal,* July 10, 1915, p. 58-9.

DUFFY, C. N. Effect of load factor on cost of electric railway passenger service. *Electric railway journal,* Feb. 1, 1913, p. 195-6

ECONOMICS of rush-hour service. *Electric railway journal,* March 11, 1916, p. 495-7.

ELDRIDGE, C. Increased cost of electric railway operation. *Electric railway journal* Jan. 3, 1914, p. 7-8.

EQUIPMENT cost data. *Electric railway journal,* Feb. 27, 1915, p. 427.

ESTIMATED cost of cable railways in Chicago. *Engineering and contracting,* March 20, 1912, p. 338.

ESTIMATED costs of Chicago terminal electrification. *Electrical railway journal.* Dec. 11, 1915, p. 1159-67.

EXPERTS testify to increased costs before New York second district commission. *Electric railway journal,* Aug. 18, 1917, p. 269-70.

FULLER, C. H. Comparative costs of building the Rivoli sub-urban line. *Electric railway journal,* Nov. 21, 1914, p. 1166-7.

GILLETTE, HALBERT P. AND RICHARD T. DANA. Electric railways. (In their *Handbook of mechanical and electrical cost data.* 1918. p. 1517-1644.)

GRUHL, E. Cost of carrying a passenger and proposed work of the Bureau of fare research. *Electric railway journal,* Oct. 18, 1913, p. 893-4.

HAYES, H. W. Unit costs of construction for permanent way. *Electric railway journal,* Jan. 13, 1917, p. 70-1.

HEARING on electric railway mail pay. *Electric railway journal,* Feb. 15, 1913, p. 291.

JACKSON, W. Place of the bus. *Electric railway journal,* April 3, 1920, p. 683-9.

JOHNSON, A. R. Reducing car lighting costs from 36 cents to 8 cents per 1000 car-miles. *Electric railway journal,* March 30, 1918, p. 612.

KATTE, E. B. Maintenance costs on the New York Central. *Electric railway journal* March 20, 1915, p. 580-1.

LAYNG, J. F. Economies in operating small cars. *General electric review,* Aug. 1915, p. 790-5. *Scientific American supplement,* Dec. 11, 1915, p. 378-9.

LEBENBAUM, P. Contact system of the Southern Pacific company, Portland division. *American institute of electrical engineers, Proceedings,* June, 1915, p. 1295-1308. Abstract. *Electric railway journal,* July 10, 1915, p. 57-8.

LEE, I. L. How the costs of operation are steadily mounting. *Electric railway journal,* June 30, 1917, p. 1180-3.

LEONHAUSER, H. A. Maintenance costs—reducing handling of equipment and departmental co-operation. *Electric railway journal,* Feb. 20, 1915, p. 384-6.

MAINTENANCE costs and records with single-phase equipment on the New York, Westchester & Boston railway. *Electric railway journal,* March 21, 1914, p. 643-6.

MAINTENANCE costs on a number of electric railway properties of moderate size; chart. *Electric railway journal,* Feb. 24, 1917, p. 356.

MAINTENANCE costs on Hudson & Manhattan railroad. *Electric railway journal,* July 25, 1914, p. 158-60.

MAINTENANCE on the Pacific electric. *Electric railway journal,* Sept. 6, 1913, p. 387

METHODS and cost of reconstructing the car shops of the Macon railway & light co. Macon, Ga. *Engineering and contracting* May 13, 1914, p. 545-7.

METHODS of handling track work in Kansas city; with cost tables. *Electric railway journal,* Sept. 9, 1916, p. 430-6.

MOUNTING costs of railway operation; Beaver valley traction company. *Electric railway journal,* Aug. 4, 1917, p. 186-7.

MURRAY, W. S. Conditions affecting the success of main line electrification. *American institute of electrical engineers, Proceedings,* Aug. 1915, p. 1873-99; tables, p. 1900-4, 1909-11; discussion, p. 1913-32.

MURRAY, W. S. New Haven operating results. *Eelctric railway journal,* Jan. 30, 1915, p. 229-31.

MURRAY, W. S. New Haven operating results. *Electric railway journal,* Sept. 4, 1915, p. 400.

ELECTRIC AND STREET RAILROADS— COSTS—*(Continued)*

NASH, L. R. Cost of operating in Cleveland. *Electric railway journal,* March 4, 1916, p. 455.

NEW HAVEN operating results. *Electric railway journal,* July 17, 1915, p. 101-2.

NEW ORLEANS higher operating costs more than absorb the gains in revenues for 1917. *Electric railway journal,* Aug. 3, 1918, p. 210.

OPERATION of the Cleveland street railway system by a new company. *Electric railway journal,* Aug. 8, 1908, p. 433.

OVERHEAD charges. *Electric railway journal,* Oct. 18, 1913, p. 895-7.

PATTISON, H. Logical unit for comparing repair costs of electric locomotives and cars. *Electric journal,* Oct. 1920, p. 475-7.

POWER for Massachusetts railways. *Electric railway journal,* Jan. 29, 1916, p. 201.

REDUCING the operating ratio. *Electric railway journal,* Dec. 19, 1914, p. 1340.

REPORT of committee on A. E. R. A. on cost of passenger transportation service. *Electric railway journal,* June 20, 1914, p. 1383-8.

REPORT of committee on overhead charges. *Electric railway journal,* Oct. 15, 1914, p. 865. *American electric railway accountants' association, Proceedings,* 1913, 1914, p. 244, 68.

ROSCOE, A. P. Overhead and time cost to erect elevated railway. *Engineering news,* June 12, 1919, p. 1164-6.

SAFETY car operation. *Electric railway journal,* June 9, 1917, p. 1044.

ST. CLAIR tunnel electrification operating data. *Electric railway journal,* Nov. 27, 1915, p. 1084-5.

SPRINGFIELD company wants 6-cent fare. *Electric railway journal,* June 2, 1917, p. 1000-3.

STATISTICS on the New York railways. *Electric railway journal,* April 25, 1914, p. 915-9.

STILLWELL, L. B. Co-ordination in railway equipment. *General electric review,* Nov. 1914, p. 1016-23.

SUBSTATION operating costs for a New England electric-railway system. *Eectrical world,* April 15, 1916, p. 883-4.

TAYLOR, E. Maintenance cost of old and new motors. *Electric railway journal,* January 24, 1914, p. 175-6.

THIRLWALL, J. C. Maintenance cost of old and new railway motors. *Electric railway journal,* Sept. 27, 1913, p. 495-7.

THIRLWALL, J. C. Operation of frequent service cars in large cities. *Electric railway journal,* Sept. 22, 1917, p. 500-11.

THIRLWALL, J. C. Results of safety car operation. *Electric railway journal,* Oct. 2, 1920, p. 642-6.

UNIT for comparing track upkeep costs. *Electric railway journal,* Sept. 16, 1916, p. 499-500.

UNIT track construction costs for thirty-one jobs. *Electric railway journal,* March 18, 1916, p. 559-62.

WICKERSHAM, L. B. Operation of the Oregon electric railway. *General electric review,* Nov. 1914, p. 1078-82.

ZOGBAUM, F. Construction, maintenance and cost of overhead contact systems: catenary construction. *American institute of electrical engineers, Proceedings,* June, 1915, p. 1267-81.

Depreciation

See Depreciation, depletion and obsolescence—Electric and street railroads.

Fare collecting

AUTOMATIC fare collector and change-making machine. *Electric railway journal,* Nov. 20, 1915, p. 1047-8.

CLARK, R. J. Prepayment cars and the accountant. *Electric railway journal,* Oct. 9, 1915, p. 721-2.

FARE collecting and recording in Buffalo. *Electric railway journal,* Aug. 30, 1913, p. 342.

FORSE, W. H. Improvements in method of accounting for fares. *Electric railway journal,* April 18, 1914, p. 884.

MECHANICAL aids in handling fares. *Electric railway journal;* Aug. 2, 1919, p. 217-20.

TICKET and cash counting fare box. *Electric railway journal,* Aug. 22, 1914, p. 360.

TRANSFER issuing and recording machine. *Electric railway journal,* Nov. 15, 1913, p. 1065.

Fares

ADDITIONS to the list of increased fare cities. *Aera,* Sept. 1918, p. 125.

AMERICAN ELECTRIC RAILWAY ASSOCIATION. Effect of increased rates of fare on operating revenue, on passengers carried and on number of transfers issued. New York, American electric railway association, Jan. 28, 1920, Feb. 16, 1920. 83p.

AMERICAN ELECTRIC RAILWAY ASSOCIATION. Methods of interurban companies in increasing fares. New York, American electric railway association, Jan. 1, 1920. 29p.

AMERICAN ELECTRIC RAILWAY ASSOCIATION. Report of the committe on cost of passenger transportation service. (In its *Proceedings,* 1914, p. 207-12).

AMERICAN ELECTRIC RAILWAY TRANSPORTATION AND TRAFFIC ASSOCIATION. Report of the committee on fares and transfers. *American electric railway transportation and traffic association, Proceedings,* 1914, p. 367-94.

ANOTHER Connecticut fare increase. *Electric railway journal,* Oct. 20, 1917, p. 738.

ANOTHER fare increase for Massachusetts; Milford and Uxbridge street railway. *Electric railway journal,* Aug. 18, 1917, p. 261.

ANOTHER Massachusetts fare increase; 6 cent fare to the Norfolk & Bristol street railway. *Electric railway journal,* Aug. 28, 1915, p. 354-5.

ANOTHER Massachusetts fare increase; the Blue Hill street railway. *Electric railway journal,* Aug. 7, 1915, p. 226-8.

ARE higher fares getting results? *Electric railway journal,* Jan. 25, 1919, p. 186-9.

BARKER, HARRY. Rate problems of street and interurban railway transportation. (In his *Public utility rates.* 1917. p. 208-39).

BASING fares on frequency of use. *Aera,* April 1919, p. 865-6.

BASIS of Portland (Me.) rates. *Electric railway journal,* Aug. 17, 1918, p. 310.

BAUER, JOHN. Control of street railway rates fixed by local franchises in the state of New York. *American economic review,* Sept. 1918, p. 650-3.

BAY state asks 10-cent city fare. *Electric railway journal,* Oct. 19, 1918, p. 707.

BAY state company says last word. *Electric railway journal,* July 29, 1916, p. 189-90.

BAY state loses 6-cent fare case. *Electric railway journal,* Sept. 2, 1916, p. 412.

BAY state opens fare case. *Electric railway journal,* Nov. 13, 1915, p. 1006-7.

BAY state opens mileage rate case. *Electric railway journal,* Nov. 24, 1917, p. 942-3.

BAY state system wants a 10 cent unit. *Aera,* Oct. 1918, p. 242-3.

BAY state zone case closed. Electric railway *journal,* May 11, 1918, p. 937-8.

BENDER, H. C. Results of fare increase in Spokane. *Electric railway journal,* Feb. 28, 1920, p. 433-4.

ELECTRIC AND STREET RAILROADS—
FARES—*(Continued)*

BIBBINS, J. R. Economic limits of passenger haul. *Electric railway journal,* Oct. 3, 1914, p. 619-20.

BIBLIOGRAPHY of copper-zone fare system. *Aera,* June 1917, p. 1279-81.

BLEAKLY, E. G. C. Camden's view of the New Jersey zone plan. *Electric railway journal,* Oct. 11, 1919, sup. 126-7.

BOSTON and Northern half—fare case—special points of interest in connection with the argument of the company as presented to the supreme court of Massachusetts. *Electric railway journal,* July 13, 1912, p. 54-5.

BOTH Washington railways find cost and wage burdens more than present fares will stand. *Electric railway journal,* Sept. 21, 1918, p. 526.

BRADLEE, HENRY G. Profitable limit of five-cent street-railway fare. *Engineering news,* Jan. 30, 1913, p. 214-5.

BRIGHT spot in the industry in Charleston. *Electric railway journal,* Jan. 10, 1920, p. 108-10.

BRUSH, M. C. Favors six-cent fare instead of zone system. *Electric railway journal,* Feb. 2, 1918, p. 229-30.

BRUSH, M. C. Satisfactory service and sound securities. *Aera,* Sept. 1917, p. 86-93.

BRUSH, M. C. To eliminate fare increase delays. *Electric railway journal,* Sept. 8, 1917, p. 400.

BRUSH, M. C. Zone system impracticable in Boston. *Electric railway journal,* Feb. 16, 1918, p. 324.

BUFFALO interurban fares can be raised. *Electric railway journal,* May 24, 1919, p. 1027.

BUFFALO vote on six-cent fare unfavorable. *Electric railway journal,* Aug. 24, 1918, p. 353.

BURKE, W. H. Nickel in 1913 and 1919. *Electric railway journal,* Sept. 13, 1919, p. 512-5.

BUSBY, L. A. Fares in Chicago, Cleveland and Philadelphia compared. *Electric railway journal,* Oct. 25, 1919, p. 795-6.

CAULKINS, W. C. Cincinnati plan explained. *Aera,* Dec. 1918, p. 465-6.

CHANGE in unit fare approved for Massachusetts northeastern street railway. *Electric railway journal,* July 20, 1918, p. 132.

CHARLOTTESVILLE'S fare increase carried unanimously. *Electric railway journal,* May 25, 1918, p. 1030.

CHICAGO asks seven cents. *Electric railway journal,* Sept. 7, 1918, p. 436.

CHICAGO riders are now asking higher fares. *Electric railway journal,* Nov. 30, 1918, p. 951.

CHOATE, J. K. Fare increases. *Aera,* Oct. 1917, p. 197-204.

CHOATE, J. K. Pending applications for New York fare increases. *Electric railway journal,* Oct. 13, 1917, p. 644-7.

CITIES favor six-cent fare for Bay state. *Electric railway journal,* June 30, 1917, p. 1188.

CLAPP, H. Automatic rate system is fair to all; a year's experience with a service-at-cost franchise in Westerville, Ohio. *Electric railway journal,* Aug. 10, 1918, p. 230-1.

CLARK, H. C. Cleveland and its "3-cent" fare: "best service" sacrified in effort to retain low price of riding. *Aera,* 1917, p. 1-13.

CLARK, H. C. Fare increases in New York. *Electric railway journal,* Jan. 3, 1920, p. 32-5.

CLARK, H. C. Fares are seeking higher level: increases made in 1919 indicate readjustment to meet higher operating costs: conditions in all cities having a population of more than 25,000 as they now exist. *Aera,* Feb. 1920, p. 783-814.

CLARK, H. C. Massachusetts cuts loose. *Aera,* June-July 1918, p. 1077-94, 1199-1215.

CLARK, H. C. Public opinion and fare increase. *Aera,* July 1917, p. 1344-51.

CLARK, WILLIAM J. Discussion on rates and fares. *Eelctric railway journal,* Feb. 1, 1913, p. 192-5.

CLEVELAND Ohio city council authorizes higher fare. *Aera,* Aug. 1918, p. 15-6.

CLEVELAND street railway situation. *Municipal engineering,* Oct. 1916, p. 132.

COMMISSION can increase fares without municipal consent. *Electric railway journal,* Feb. 3, 1917, p. 210.

COMMISSIONS without power in New York; Rochester decision of Court of appeals. *Electric railway journal,* April 27, 1918, p. 811-2. *Municipal journal,* May 18, 1918, p. 420-1.

COMPROMISE fare increase approved by Massachusetts commission. *Electric railway journal,* June 22, 1918, p. 1210-11.

CONNECTICUT company goes to zone plan. *Electric railway journal,* Nov. 8, 1919, p. 852-7.

CONNECTICUT fare brief filed. *Electric railway journal,* March 23, 1918, p. 588.

CONNECTICUT six-cent fare is reasonable. *Electric railway journal,* March 30, 1918, p. 620-1.

CONNECTICUT zone system revised. *Electric railway journal,* April 17, 1920, p. 807-11.

CONSTITUTIONAL barrier against fair rates; decision of Public service commission of first district, New York. *Electric railway journal,* Jan. 19, 1918, p. 125-8.

CONWAY, THOMAS. Commission-made rates are paramount. *Electric railway journal,* Jan. 19, 1918, p. 130-3.

CONWAY, THOMAS. Effect of six-cent fares upon the volume of traffic. *Electric railway journal,* Aug. 25, 1917, p. 310-2.

CONWAY, THOMAS. Future of electric railway fares. *Aera,* June 1919, p. 1053-66.

CONWAY, THOMAS. Is the zone system the solution? *Electric railway journal,* Nov. 2, 1918, p. 776-8.

CONWAY, THOMAS. Status of the higher fare in the state of New York. *Electric railway journal,* June 29, 1918, p. 1235-9.

COPPER-ZONE system approved for Boston & Worcester street railway. *Electric railway journal,* Sept. 29, 1917, p. 577-8.

COPPER-ZONE system sustained. *Electric railway journal,* June 10, 1916, p. 1089-90.

COPPER zones for Shore line electric railway. *Electric railway journal,* Sept. 11, 1915, p. 443-5.

COPPER zones in Massachusetts. *Electric railway journal,* Sept. 1, 1917, p. 353-4.

COURT upholds increased fare for Toledo, O. *Municipal journal,* Aug. 31, 1918, p. 176.

CULKINS, W. C. Why do car fares differ? *Electric railway journal,* April 3, 1920, p. 710-11.

DECISION in Indianapolis fare case. *Electric railway journal,* Dec. 15, 1917, p. 1095.

DECISION in Puget Sound electric railway rate case. *Electric railway journal,* May 23, 1914, p. 1174.

DECISION in Rochester fare case. *Electric railway journal,* Feb. 27, 1915, p. 439-40.

DECISION in the Milwaukee fare case. *Electric railway journal,* Aug. 31, 1912, p. 314-23.

DECISION of commission upholding rates of fare in Savannah, Ga. *Electric railway journal,* April 20, 1912, p. 663.

DECISION of Judge Westerhover in the Columbus street railway fare cases. *Minnesota municipalities,* Dec. 1918, p. 192-7.

DECISION of United States district judge Westerhover in street railway fare case. *City bulletin,* Sept. 28, 1918, p. 309-11.

ELECTRIC AND STREET RAILROADS—
FARES—(*Continued*)

DECISION of United States district Judge Westerhover in Columbus, Ohio, street railway fare rate case. *New Jersey municipalities,* October 1918, p. 239-42.

DECREASE in electric-railway traffic resulting from increased fare. *Engineering news,* Aug 13, 1914, p. 353.

DENVER tramway inaugurates 6-cent fare with extensive publicity. *Electric railway journal,* Oct. 5, 1918, p. 613.

DES MOINES value fixed; appraisers for city report that fare of 5¾ cents would yield 7 per cent return. *Electric railway journal,* Nov. 20, 1920, p. 1079.

DETERMININATION of the proper basis for rates and fares. *Electric railway journal,* December 2, 1911, p. 1154-63.

DEVELOPMENT and status of the rate raise case. New Jersey municipalities, May 1918, p. 133-4.

DIAGRAMS showing the need for higher fares. *Electric railway journal,* Jan. 26, 1918, p. 187-8.

DIME fare asked in Jersey; public service railway loses $1,200,000 in year under 7 cent rate. *Electric railway journal,* Dec. 11, 1920, p. 1214.

DISCUSSION by mayor, railroad executive and commissioners follows 6-cent fare appeal in New York city. *Electric railway journal,* March 30, 1918, p. 628.

DISCUSSION of fare systems. *Electric railway journal,* Sept. 27, 1919, p. 610-2.

DISCUSSION on the Milwaukee fare decision. *Electric railway journal,* Jan. 18, 1913, p. 110-1.

DIVISION of five cent fare in New York state. *Electric railway journal,* June 10, 1911, p. 1027.

DOOLITTLE, F. W. Cleveland street railway situation. *Municipal engineering,* Oct. 1916, p. 132.

DOOLITTLE, F. W. Problems of the electric railway industry. *Electric railway journal,* June 3, 1916, p. 1037-8.

DRUMMOND, R. C. S. Six-cent fare problem; past and future. *New York state conference of mayors and other city officials, Proceedings,* 1918, p. 63-77.

DUFFY, C. N. Economics of the Cleveland railway situation as developed in the 1913 arbitration deicsion. *Electric railway journal.* Oct. 15, 1913, p. 770-3.

DUFFY, C. N. Rate of return of electric railways. *Electric railway journal,* May 14, 1910, p. 871-2.

EDDY, H. C. Outsider's observations on the Connecticut zone system. *Electric railway journal.* Dec. 27, 1919, p. 1035.

EFFECT of fare increase in 61 cases. *Aera,* Dec. 1918, p. 474-5.

EIGHT cents enough; special masters recommend increased fare for Des Moines city railway. *Electric railway journal,* Dec. 11, 1920, p. 1213.

ELECTRIC railway must not become anti-social. *Electric railway journal,* June 19, 1920, p. 1269.

ELECTRIC railways in the United States and Canada which have recently been granted permission by regulatory bodies to increase their fares where such consent is unnecessary. *Aera,* Feb. 1918, p. 625-9.

EMERY, J. A. Future fare system for small cities. *Electric railway journal,* Oct. 4, 1919, p. 695.

END eight-year car-fare fight in Cleveland. *Municipal journal,* April 5, 1917, p. 502-3.

ENTER, the transfer-less zone system at last! *Electric railway journal,* Aug. 9, 1919, p. 268.

ERICKSON, H. Indeterminate franchise is most equitable; zone rates for electric railroads. *Electric railway journal,* June 28, 1919. p. 1266-7.

EXISTING fares of Wisconsin road upheld by the commission after a valuation. *Electric railway journal,* July 29, 1911, p. 193-6.

FARE accounting; symposium. *Electric, railway journal,* Oct. 4, 1913, p. 582-7.

FARE case to be reopened; Bay state street railway asks further relief. *Electric railway journal,* June 2, 1917, p. 998-9.

FARE decision in Manchester, N.H.: six per cent return allowed on investment in property. *Electric railway journal,* Nov. 28, 1914, p. 1204-5.

FARE dispute in Toledo. *Electric railway journal,* April 4, 1914, p. 771-6.

FARE includes the tax. *Public service,* June 1919, p. 164-5.

FARE increase allowed in New Jersey. *Electric railway journal,* Nov. 24, 1917, p. 966-7.

FARE increase asked in Milwaukee. *Electric railway journal,* Oct. 23, Nov. 27, 1915, p. 889, 1099.

FARE increase at Atlanta: Georgia state commission raises the local care fare rate to six cents. *Public service,* May 1919, p. 151.

FARE increase on Holyoke street railway. *Electric railway journal,* Dec. 28, 1918, p. 1156.

FARE increases blocked in New York. *Electric railway journal,* April 13, 1918, p. 696-7.

FARE increases granted to sixty-seven companies in U. S. and Canada, since 1914. *Electric railway journal,* July 7, 1917, p. 15-8.

FARE increases in Jersey: seven cents with one cent for transfers awarded to public service. *Aera,* Oct. 1918, p. 247-8.

FARE increases in the larger cities. *Aera,* June 1918, p. 1119-20.

FARE increases in 348 cities. *Aera,* Jan. 1919, p. 539-43.

FARE increases in 348 cities; 176 cities of of more than 25,000 population are paying more. *Public service,* March 1919, p. 84.

FARE situation as it now stands; Press and increased railway fares. *Aera,* Dec. 1918, p. 740-4, 748-80.

FARE situation in 158 cities; increases have already been granted in ninety of them and applications pend in all but seventeen. *Aera,* Nov. 1918, p. 395-8.

FARE situation in United States. *Aera,* Sept. 1918, p. 122-5.

FARE trend is toward 10 cents; with New York omitted; larger number of people now pay dime than nickel for car ride. *Aera,* Dec. 1920, p. 419-31.

FARE zones adjusted in Maine. *Electric railway journal,* July 29, 1916, p. 180-2.

FARES in annexed districts. *Electric railway journal,* Jan. 13, 1917, p. 71.

FARES in Los Angeles, Scranton, Chicago, Syracuse, Worcester. *Electric railway journal,* May 3, 1919, p. 890-3.

FARES increased in Milwaukee. *Electric railway journal,* Nov. 15, 1919, p. 891-5.

FARES up in 388 cities. *Electric railway journal,* June 4, 1919, p. 1193. *Public service,* Aug. 1919, p. 53.

FATE of the five-cent fare. *National municipal review,* Oct. 1919-Feb., June, Sept. 1920, p. 546-50, 606-14, 676-9; 13-6, 78-83, 357-64, 545-53.

FEDERAL authorities intervene in New Orleans; six-cent fare granted only after War finance corporation and National war labor board make vigorous protests against interference. *Aera,* Oct. 1918, p. 233-4.

FINANCIAL relief is blocked; court decision destroys most fare increases in New York. *Electric railway journal,* April 27, 1918, p. 812-3.

ELECTRIC AND STREET RAILROADS—
FARES—*(Continued)*

FIRST two weeks with 7-cent fare in Boston show gain of 30 per cent in gross. *Electric railway journal,* Aug. 24, 1918, p. 347.

FIVE-CENT fare fast disappearing. *Electric railway journal,* July 10, 1920, p. 99-100.

FIVE-CENT fares in Detroit. *Electric railway journal,* Dec. 8, 1917, p. 1053-4.

FIVE cent-seven cent fares for Pittsburgh. *Electric railway journal,* July 6, 1918, p. 15-6.

FLAT fare increase denied by Oregon commission. *Electric railway journal,* Oct. 20, 1917, p. 739.

FORD, FRANK R. Theory of street railway rate regulation as developed by the Coney Island fare case. *Electric railway journal,* October 12, 1910, p. 752-5.

GEORGIA commission lacks jurisdiction over rates; recommends a six-cent fare. *Electric railway journal,* Aug. 31, 1918, p. 391.

GETTING the zone system started at Providence. *Electric railway journal,* July 13, 1918, p. 65-6.

GRUHL, E. Cost of carrying a passenger, and proposed work of the Bureau of fare research. *Electric railway journal,* Oct. 18, 1913, p. 893-4.

GRUHL, E. Shortening present single-fare zones. *Electric railway journal,* Oct. 13, 1917, p. 671-3.

HAMBURG elevated and subway system. *Electric railway journal,* Aug. 2, 1913, p. 177-80.

HEDLEY, F. Why a charge of transfers is justified. *Electric railway journal,* Oct. 13, 1917, p. 667-9.

HENDERSON, S. Z. Burdens on street car patrons. *Aera,* May 1919, p. 959-62.

HIGHER fare publicity; New York companies. *Electric railway journal,* July 28, 1917, p 140-2.

HIGHER fares granted in 238 cities. *Electric railway journal,* Aug. 17, 1918, p. 309.

HIGHER fares granted to New York lines by Public service commission for second district. *Electric railway journal,* Dec. 8, 22, 1917, p. 1029, 1122.

HIGHER rates sought in Kansas city, Mo *Electrical world,* July 5, 1919, p. 33.

HIGHER revenues asked in New York; six-cent fare suggested up-state, and two-cent transfer charge in New York city. *Electric railway journal,* May 19, 1917, p. 916-8.

HILD, F. W. Effect of rate of fare on riding habit. *Electric railway journal,* Jan. 31, 1914, p. 229-33. Discussion. *Electric railway journal,* Jan. 31-Feb. 7, 1914, p. 247-8, 253-6, 315-6.

How can the public be convinced. *Electric railway journal,* March 1, 1919, p. 408-12.

How do fares affect traffic? *Electric railway journal,* Feb. 7, 1920, p. 292.

How New York commissioners differ in basic rate-making views. *Electric railway journal,* Jan. 19, 1918, p. 129.

How the higher fare movement is progressing. *Electric railway journal,* Aug. 11, 1917, p. 226-30.

HYDE, D. W. Fate of the five cent fare. *Canadian municipal journal,* April 1919, p. 118-9. *New Jersey municipalities,* Jan. 1919, p. 13-14, 23.

HYDE, D. W. Some zone fare system considerations. *New Jersey municipalities,* March 1919, p. 83-4.

ILLINOIS traction system rate changes. *Electric railway journal,* Aug. 10, 1918, p. 260.

ILLINOIS two cents a mile law declared in violation of United States constitution. *Aera,* Oct. 1918, p. 259-60.

IN the country's larger cities: fares increased in 186 out of 273 having 25,000 or more inhabitants. *Aera,* April 1919, p. 854-63.

INCREASE in fare ordered by New Jersey commission. *Electric railway journal,* Feb. 22, 1913, p. 324-5.

INCREASED electric railway fares. *Aera,* Feb.-March 1918, p. 601-24, 723-47.

INCREASED fare list is growing. *Aera,* Oct. 1918, p. 235-8.

INCREASES in North Carolina. *Electric railway journal,* Sept. 14, 1918, p. 477.

INDIANAPOLIS fare hearings reviewed. *Electric railway journal,* Sept. 21, 1918, p. 527.

INDUSTRY is facing more serious problems. *Electric railway journal,* July 20, 1918, p. 115-7.

Is the one-cent fare zone the answer to the fare question? *Electric railway journal,* Aug. 10, 1918, p. 223-4.

JACKSON, DUGALD CALEB. Status of the electric railway: zone fares are desirable. *Electric railway journal,* Aug. 23, 1919, p. 391-3.

JACKSON, DUGALD CALEB and DAVID JONES MCGRATH. Street railway fares, their relation to length of haul and cost of service; report of investigation carried on in the research division of the Electrical engineering department of the Massachusetts institute of technology. New York, McGraw-Hill book co. 1917. 169p. (Research division bulletin no. 14).

JACKSON, W. British fare system invades America: an account of the principal departures from the unit fare system; habit, inconvenient coinage system, and the retention of the time-limit, transfer offer unusual difficulties; the failure of the public service railway and the success of others. *Tramway and railway world,* Feb. 12, 1920, p. 77-80.

JACKSON, W. Congestion not due to graded fares. *Electric railway journal,* Feb. 22, 1919, p. 355-9.

JACKSON, W. Possible operating economies and sales methods. *Electric railway journal,* Oct. 11, 1919, sup. 117-21.

JACKSON, W. Side lights in the zone fare—car capacity. *Electric railway journal,* May 3, 1919, p. 875.

JACKSON, W. Side lights on the zone fare-congestion or diffusion? *Electric railway journal,* Aug. 9, 1919, p. 276.

JACKSON, W. Side lights on the zone fare—good service absolutely essential. *Electric railway journal,* June 7, 1919, p 1099.

JACKSON, W. Side lights on the zone fare—the bane of comparative statistics. *Electric railway journal,* May 31, 1919, p. 1052.

JACKSON, W. Sidelights on the zone fare—the problem of currency. *Electric railway journal,* May 10, 1919, p. 921-2.

JACKSON, W. Sidelights on the zone fare—why fare stages should vary in length. *Electric railway journal,* June 21, 1919, p. 1223.

JACKSON, W. Will low fares help to cure high costs. *Modern city,* Oct. 1919, p. 52. *National municipal review,* Oct. 1919, p. 542-6.

JACKSON, W. Zone fare in practice, Aberdeen, Scotland. *Eelctric railway journal,* April 26, 1919, p. 814-22.

JACKSON, W. Zone fare in practice; Belfast. *Electric railway journal,* May 10, 24, 1919, p. 909-14, 1005-11.

JACKSON, W. Zone fare in practice: Dublin. *Electric railway journal,* May 31-June 7, 1919, p. 1038-43, 1087-92.

JACKSON, W. Zone fare in practice, Edinburgh. *Electric railway journal,* May 3, 1919, p. 854-9.

JACKSON, W. Zone fare in practice, Glasgow. *Electric railway journal,* Feb. 22, March 8, 29, 1919, p. 355-9, 446-53, 632-8.

JACKSON, WALTER. Zone fare in practice, Leeds. *Electric railway journal,* July 12, 1919, p. 56-60.

ELECTRIC AND STREET RAILROADS—
FARES—*(Continued)*

JACKSON, W. Zone fare in practice; London county council. *Electric railway journal,* Aug. 2-9, 1919, p. 210-5, 270-5.

JACKSON, W. Zone fare in practice; Reading, England. *Electric railway journal,* June 28, 1919, p. 1258-62.

JACKSON, W. Zone fare in practice; the British electric traction company. *Electric railway journal,* July 26, 1919, p. 154-7.

JACKSON, W. Zone fare in practice; West Ham. *Electric railway journal,* June 14, 1919, p. 1163-9.

JACKSON, WALTER. Zone fares for street railways: their relation to housing congestion and company finances. *National municipal review,* Nov. 1920, p. 705-11.

JERSEY cities win big car fare fight. *Municipal journal,* July 27, 1918, p. 79-80.

JERSEY'S seven-cent fare upheld. *Financial world,* Oct. 28, 1918, p. 6.

JOHNSON, W. F. Proposed street car franchise: its provisions as to rates of fare. *Toledo city journal,* Aug. 9, 1919, p. 421-3.

JOINT meeting of the Accountants' and transportation & traffic associations discusses fares and transfers and express and freight traffic. *Electric railway journal,* Oct. 16, 1913, p. 798-800.

JONES, S. P. Movement for increased street railway fares. *Seattle municipal news,* Oct. 27, 1917, p. 4.

JUDGE HUGHES on rate regulation: argument of former justice of United States supreme court before New York legislative committee. *Aera,* April 1919, p. 847-53.

JUDGE SWAYZE says business judgment is basis of proper rates, in decision upholding seven-cent fare for Public service railway co. *Aera,* Nov. 1918, p. 400-4.

LAW is confiscatory: federal Judge Landis acts on Illinois two-cents-a-mile statute. *Aera,* Feb. 1919, p. 653-4.

LEE, I. L. Crisis in the affairs of the electric railways. *Electric railway journal,* Nov. 23, 1918, p. 917-18.

LEE, I. L. Higher fares benefit the public. *Electric railway journal,* September 15, 1917, p. 441.

LEGISLATIVE action likely in Boston case; public control bill with service-at-cost provision reported for Boston elevated railway. *Electric railway journal,* April 20, 1918, p. 778.

LEWIS, E. G. Future of the electric railway. *Electric railway journal,* July 10, 1920, p. 65-6.

LIABILITIES on which proper return should be allowed. *Electric railway journal,* September 25, 1909, p. 464-66.

LIST of electric railway companies whose fares have recently been increased. *Electric railway journal,* August 10, 1918, p. 258-9.

LOS ANGELES rate case. *Electric railway journal,* May 6, 1916, p. 862.

MCCARTER, T. N. Increased revenue to offset higher wages. *Electric railway journal,* June 29, 1918, p. 1227-8.

MCCARTER, T. N. Rate of return: a 10 per cent dividend fare. *Electric traction weekly,* Feb. 4, 1911, p. 132-3, 135. *Electric railway journal,* Feb. 4, 1911, p. 211-12.

MCCULLOCH, RICHARD. Advocates zone system. *Electric railway journal,* Sept. 28, 1918, p. 593.

MCCULLOCH, RICHARD. Fare should be flexible. *Electric railway journal,* April 27, 1918, p. 822.

MCGRATH, D. J. Long rides for a nickel. *Electric railway journal,* Aug. 5, 1916, p. 222-5.

MACLEOD, FRANK J. Electric railways of Massachusetts. *Aera,* Aug. 1919, p. 102-7.

MAGDEN, WILLIAM L. Some light on British tramway conditions. *Electric railway journal,* Aug. 30, 1919, p. 439-42.

MAINE public utilities commission grants new rate schedule to Lewistown, Augusta and Waterville street railway. *Electric railway journal,* April 6, 1918, p. 654.

MAINE public utilities commission in a recent decision, declares 8.5 per cent to be a reasonable rate of return. *Electric railway journal,* July 29, 1916, p. 180-2.

MANY roads seek increases; statistics show the growing extent of movement to provide sufficient electric railway revenue. *Aera,* Dec. 1917, p. 431-4.

MASSACHUSETTS commission increases on interstate line. *Electric railway journal,* Aug. 31, 1918, p. 392.

MASSACHUSETTS commission prescribes zone system as a means of fare relief for Springfield. *Aera,* April 1918, p. 898-9.

MASSACHUSETTS governor's relief message. *Electric railway journal,* March 9, 1918, p. 472.

MASSACHUSETTS Northeastern fare hearing. *Electric railway journal,* Dec. 25, 1915, p. 1256-7.

MAXIMUM length of profitable ride in Boston. *Electric railway journal,* Aug. 1, 1914, p. 206-7.

MIDDLESEX and Boston fail hearings. *Electric railway journal,* Sept. 19, 1914, p. 543-4.

MIDDLESEX and Boston rate decision. *Electric railway journal,* Nov. 7, 1914, p. 1055-7.

MILEAGE rate for Chicago, North Shore and Milwaukee line. *Electric railway journal,* Nov. 3, 1917, p. 837.

MILEAGE rate system on Boston & Worcester street railway satisfactory. *Electric railway journal,* Dec. 8, 1917, p. 1053.

MILEAGE rate system sought on Boston and Worcester street railway. *Electric railway journal,* Aug. 11, 1917, p. 218-9.

MILFORD, Attleboro and Woonsocket company given choice of seven-cent fare or modified zone system. *Electric railway journal,* Aug. 3, 1918, p. 214.

MILWAUKEE fare case decided. *Electric railway journal,* July 10, 1915, p. 52-3.

MODIFIED Boston plan one solution. *Financial world,* Jan. 13, 1919. p. 6-7.

MOIR, I. H. Zone system advisable for large cities. *Electric railway journal,* Dec. 21, 1918, p. 1107-8.

MORE about Cleveland's low fare. *Aera,* Nov. 1917, p. 300-5.

MORE revenues sought in New York. *Electric railway journal,* May 12, 1917, p. 874.

MORE ten cents cities; statistics compiled by American electric railway association indicate tendency toward basic 10 cent fare. *Electric railway journal,* Nov. 20, 1920, p. 1075.

MORE zone fares for Massachusetts. *Electric railway journal,* May 4, 1918, p. 881-2.

MORTIMER, J. D. Can service costs be collected from the traveling public? *Electric railway journal,* Oct. 11, 1919, sup. 14-7.

MUNICIPAL ownership offer from city results from inability to agree on fares. *Electric railway journal.* Aug. 31, 1918, p. 383.

NASH, L. R. Possibilities in readiness-to-serve fare schedules. *Electric railway journal,* Sept. 27, 1919, p. 647-52.

NASSAU county lines of New York & North Shore traction company secure increase. *Electric railway journal,* July 14, 1917, p. 59.

NAU, CARL H. Experience of Cleveland's street railways with three cent fares. *Journal of accountancy,* April 1907, p. 417-28.

NEED of greater revenue. *Aera,* July 1918, p. 1221-42.

NEW Bay state fares in effect. *Electric railway journal,* Jan. 18, 1919, p. 161-2.

ELECTRIC AND STREET RAILROADS—
FARES—*(Continued)*

NEW BEDFORD & Onset fares hearing. *Electric railway journal,* May 15, 1915, p. 959.

NEW FARE arrangement on Bay state lines. *Municipal journal,* July 13, 1918, p. 37-8.

NEW JERSEY fare decision. *Municipal journal,* Aug. 3, 1918, p. 99.

NEW JERSEY zone fares in doubt. *Electric railway journal,* Oct. 11, 1919, p. 715-7.

NEW JERSEY—rate case; some typical communications received by the League's bureau on the rate case: action of federation of improvement associations of Newark on rate case. *New Jersey municipalities,* Sept. 1918, p. 199-202.

NEW YORK and North Shore traction company presents case. *Electric railway journa,l* July 21, 1917, p. 104.

NEW YORK city lines ask two-cent transfers. *Electric railway journal,* May 26, 1917, p. 957-9.

NEW YORK electric street railways apply for advance in car fares. *Electrical review,* Sept. 1, 1917, p. 372.

NEW YORK fares up again. *Electric railway journal,* June 21, 1919, p. 1249-50.

NEW YORK public service commission grants a seven-cent unit rate. *Aera,* Jan. 1918, p. 558.

NEW YORK transfer cases adjourned. *Electric railway journal,* May 4, 1918, p. 880.

NICKEL reservoir is leaking. *Public service,* Jan. 1919, p. 18.

NINE cent fare in Cincinnati. *Electric railway journal,* Nov. 20, 1920. p. 1080.

NINE-cent fare in Davenport. *Electric railway journal,* Sept. 11, 1920, p. 521.

OBSTACLES encountered in establishing the zone system in New Jersey. *Electric railway journal,* Oct. 18, 1919, p. 744-5.

OPERATING ratio shows increase. *Aera,* Nov. 1918, p. 405-6.

OPERATION of the distance-fare system by Connecticut company: traffic survey made and comprehensive scheme worked out and announced broadcast in advance of installation of system. *Electric traction,* Dec. 1919, p. 829-31.

OPTIMISM prevails at Pennsylvania association meeting. *Electric railway journal,* July 5, 1919, p. 15-7.

OREGON commission had jurisdiction; in Portland six-cent case, State supreme court upholds commission rate change. *Electric railway journal,* Aug. 17, 1918, p. 308.

OREGON takes advanced view; commission permits Portland company to charge a six-cent fare to preserve integrity of property. *Aera,* Feb. 1918, p. 654-8.

OVERHEAD charges in the Bay state case. *Electric railway journal,* Aug. 19, 1916, p. 311.

"OWL car" fares: experience of several companies shows that owl car operation at a 5-cent fare is unprofitable. *Electric railway journal,* July 22, 1916, p. 146.

P. R. T. gaining; receipts increase approximately 20 per cent under 7 cent fare. *Electric railway journal,* Nov. 20, 1920, p. 1076.

PALMER, R. W. Franchise limitations in fare increases. *Electric railway journal,* Oct. 27, 1917, p. 770-1.

PALMER, R. W. Redeemable cash-fare receipts. *Electric railway journal,* March 3, 1917, p. 391-2.

PASSING of the three-cent fare. *Aera,* Dec. 1917, p. 440-1.

PERKINS, R. W. Copper zones in Norwich, Conn. *Electric railway journal,* March 18, 1916, p. 567.

PERKINS, R. W. Zone system in practice; Shore line electric railway, Conn. *Electric railway journal,* Jan. 12, 1918, p. 86.

PHILADELPHIA & Western fare increase. *Electric railway journal,* Oct. 13, 1917, p. 698.

PITTSBURGH railways charging higher fares. *Electric railway journal,* Feb. 9, 1918, p. 278.

PORTLAND company, Oregon, gets partial relief. *Electric railway journal,* Oct. 27, 1917, p. 757-60.

PORTLAND, Ore., case closed. *Electric railway journal,* March 16, 1918, p. 543.

PORTLAND, Ore., six-cent fare in court. *Electric railway journal,* March 9, 1918, p. 479.

POTTER, A. E. Rhode Island company files new tariff after central five-cent zone proves inadequate. *Electric railway journal,* Sept. 7, 1918, p. 434.

PREPARATION of data for street railway rate cases. *Engineering and contracting,* Nov. 19, 1919, p. 576-7.

PREPARING the public for the zone plan. *Electric railway journal,* Dec. 27, 1919, p. 1032-4.

PROCEEDINGS of the 4th annual midyear conference of American electric railway association, 1913. *Electric railway journal,* Feb. 1, 1913, p. 184-96.

PROFIT of 0.267 cent per fare. *Electric railway journal,* Nov. 20, 1920, p. 1075.

PROGRESS of New York fare hearings. *Electric railway journal,* July 28, 1917, p. 145-6.

PROPOSAL for temporary operation at three cents in Toledo. *Electric railway journal,* April 11, 1914, p. 841.

PROPOSED zone system for St. Louis. *Aera,* Oct. 1918, p. 241-2.

PUBLIC operation and receivership result in highest car fare rates. *Public service,* Aug. 1919, p. 38-9.

PUBLIC service railway of New Jersey gets seven-cent fare. *Electric railway journal,* Oct. 5, 1918, p. 636.

PUBLIC service zone report. *Aera,* April 1919, p. 875-82.

PUBLIC utilities reports annotated. Rochester Lawyers co-operative publishing company. See index under Rates.

PUBLIC utility settlements and rates. *Modern city,* Oct. 1918, p. 26-7.

PUGET Sound company upheld in fare case. *Electric railway journal,* Nov. 24, 1917, p. 968.

PUGET Sound electric railway rate case. *Electric railway journal,* May 9, 1914, p. 1059.

PUTNAM, F. Federal action rather than suggestion needed. *Electric railway journal,* Aug. 17, 1918, p. 298-9. Discusison. *Electric railway journal,* Aug. 31, 1918, p. 379-80.

PUTNAM, F. What the rail rate raise means. *Electric railway journal,* June 8, 1918, p. 1103-4.

PUTNAM, F. Zone system does not cause congestion. *Electric railway journal,* July 13, 1918, p. 49-50.

QUACKENBUSH, J. L. Have the New York commissions power to increase fares? *Electric railway journal,* June 23, 1917, p. 1145-7.

RAILWAYS fight for living wages. *Aera,* Aug. 1917, p. 18-27.

RAISE rates to permit higher wages; hearing before War labor board. *Electric railway journal,* June 29, 1918, p. 1223-6.

RAISING the fare from seven to ten cents at the public's request; fair-minded communities served by the Worcester and Warren street railway. *Electric railway journal,* March 9, 1918, p. 457-60.

RANSON, WILLIAM L. Agitation for higher fares. *New Jersey municipalities,* Nov. 1918, p. 263-4, 277-80.

RATE changes in Ohio. *Electric railway journal,* Nov. 3, 1917, p. 837-8.

RATE-making is a sovereign power, Oregon circuit court rules. *Electric railway journal,* March 30, 1918, p. 617-8.

RATE of 25 cents a mile granted by Indiana commission. *Electric railway journal,* Feb. 2, 1918, p. 225-6.

ELECTRIC AND STREET RAILROADS—
FARES—(Continued)
RATES, service and public ownership discussed at National association of railway commissioners convention. *Electric railway journal,* Oct. 27, 1917, p. 765.
RAYMOND, WILLIAM G. Iowa state board of conciliation. *Electric railway journal,* June 28, 1919, p. 1274-6.
RECEIVERSHIPS bring higher fares: street railway companies forced into bankruptcy must reduce service and increase rates to keep in operation. *Public service,* March 1919, p. 91-2.
RECENT street railway fare increases. *Public service,* Feb. 1919, p. 52.
RECORD of increased fares. *Financial world,* Aug. 1919, p. 6.
RELIEF for Los Angeles; fare advance in suburbs. *Electric railway journal,* Sept. 21, 1918, p. 528.
REPORT of committee on A. E. R. A. on cost of passenger transportation service. *Electric railway journal,* June 20, 1914, p. 1383-8.
REPORT of Price, Waterhouse & co. presented in Syracuse fare case. *Electric railway journal,* Aug. 10, 1918, p. 261.
REPORT of the A. E. R. A. committee on fares and transfers. *Electric railway journal,* Oct. 9, 1915, p. 764-5.
REVIEW of six New York fare cases. *Elecrtic railway journal,* March 30, 1918, p. 636.
REVOLUTIONARY change in public service railway fare system. *Electric railway journal,* Aug. 9, 1919, p. 282-4.
REZONING effective on May 9. *Electric railway journal,* April 24, 1920, p. 858-9.
RHODE ISLAND recommendations defended. *Electric railway journal,* March 23, 1918, p. 591.
RIBBINS, J. R. Net result of the 5-cent fare. *Electric railway journal,* Sept. 20, 1919, p. 570-1.
RICHEY, ALBERT S. Zone system proposed for Boston. *Electric railway journal,* Dec. 28, 1918, p. 1141-3.
RIFENBERICK, R. B. Burdens from which we should be relieved. *Electric railway journal,* July 12, 1919, p. 66-7.
ROCHESTER company answers petition of city for order reducing rates. *Electric railway journal,* Jan. 17, 1914, p. 147-8.
ST. LOUIS wants zones. *Electric railway journal,* Sept. 7, 1918, p. 435.
SAN ANTONIO has an inbound-outbound zone. *Electric railway journal,* Jan. 10, 1920, p. 101-2.
SAN FRANCISCO trans-bay rate case. *Electric railway journal,* Dec. 1, 1917, p. 1011.
SCHADDELEE, R. Making casual riders pay. *Electric railway journal,* April 5, 1919, p. 693-4. Discussion. *Electric railway journal,* April 12-19, 1919, p. 747-8, 793-4.
SCHENECTADY asks for higher fare. *Electric railway journal,* Nov. 17, 1917, p. 896-8.
SCHENECTADY fare case decided in favor of company. *Electric railway journal,* May 30, 1914, p. 1232-3.
SEATTLE four-cent tickets go. *Electric railway journal,* Sept. 22, 1917, p. 552.
SELLING the zone fare idea in San Diego. *Electric railway journal,* Aug. 7, 1920, p. 269-70.
SERVICE at cost in Memphis. *Electric railway journal,* April 3, 1920, p. 712-14.
SEVEN cent fare denied by New Jersey commission. *Electric railway journal,* July 13, 1918, p. 79.
SEVEN-cent fare for Boston on Aug. 1. *Electric railway journal,* July 27, 1918, p. 174. *Municipal journal,* Aug. 17, 1918, p. 136.
SEVEN-cent fare for Ithaca. *Electric railway journal,* Nov. 23, 1918, p. 941.
SEVEN-cent fare unit authorized. *Electric railway journal,* Oct. 14, 1916, p. 851.
SEVEN cent fares asked in Birmingham. *Electric railway journal,* Dec. 11, 1920. p. 1215-6.
SEVEN-cent fares in New Jersey. *Municipal journal,* Oct. 26, 1918, p. 335-6.
SEVEN-cent minimum fare allowed to the Middlesex & Boston street railway, Newtonville, Mass. *Electric railway journal,* July 13, 1918, p. 62.
SHONTS, T. P. Good railway service depends on six cent fare. *Record and guide,* June 29, 1918, p. 811.
SIDELIGHTS on some fare situations; Toledo, Cleveland, Buffalo, Rochester, Syracuse and Utica. *Electric railway journal,* March 6, 1920, p. 471-2.
SIX-cent fare asked in New York state by twenty-eight street railways. *Electric railway journal,* June 30, 1917, p. 1187-8.
SIX-cent fare authorized by New Hampshire public service commission. *Electric railway journal,* Nov. 11, 1916, p. 1038-9.
SIX cent fare compromise in New York? *Financial world,* Jan. 27, 1919, p. 6-7.
SIX-cent fare disallowed for Bay state. *Electric railway journal,* Sept. 9, 1916, p. 444-8.
SIX-cent fare for Buffalo. *Electric railway journal,* June 22, 1918, p. 1209.
SIX-cent fare for Kansas City. *Electric railway journal,* July 6, 1918, p. 30-1.
SIX cent fare for Providence. *Electric railway journal,* Oct. 4, 1919, p. 702.
SIX-cent fare for Trenton, N. J. *Electric railway journal,* Oct. 5, 1918, p. 635.
SIX-cent fare granted to Portland, Oregon, line. *Electric railway journal,* Jan. 26, 1918. p. 184-6.
SIX-cent fare granted to the New Bedford & Onset street railway. *Electric railway journal,* Sept. 25, 1915, p. 628-31.
SIX-cent fare in effect in Conecticut. *Electric railway journal,* Oct. 6, 1917, p. 643.
SIX-cent fare needed in Connecticut. *Electric railway journal,* Dec. 15, 1917, p. 1076-7.
SIX-cent fare permitted in St. Louis. *Electric railway journal,* May 25, 1918, p. 1014-5.
SIX-cent fare turned down; Rhode Island House votes in favor of adopting zone system. *Electric railway journal,* April 13, 1918, p. 710.
SIX-cents for Albany. *Electric railway journal,* Aug. 24, 1918, p. 352.
SIX cents for key route of San Francisco-Oakland terminal railways. *Electric railway journal,* August 24, 1918, p. 351.
SIX cents in Baltimore. *Electric railway journal,* October 12, 1918, p. 673.
SIX cents on Chicago elevated. *Electric railway journal,* Nov. 23, 1918, p. 940.
SLIDING scale cost of service plan. *Aera,* Sept. 1918, p. 127-32.
SPRINGFIELD company wants 6-cent fare. *Electric railway journal,* June 2, 1917, p. 1000-3.
SPRINGFIELD, Mass., fare hearing. *Electric railway journal,* Sept. 8, 1917, p. 416.
SPRINGFIELD (Mass.) to have zone fares. *Electric railway journal,* April 6, 1918, p. 663-5.
STANLEY, JOHN J. Fares have essentially been cut in half. *Electric railway journal,* Nov. 2, 1918, p. 770-1.
STATE commission has power to raise rates. *Municipal journal,* Dec. 22, 1917, p. 615-6.
STATE rate-making power upheld. *Electric railway journal,* Nov. 24, 1917, p. 946-7.
STEARNS, R. B. Results with six-cent fares on Bay State railway. *Electric railway journal,* Dec. 8, 1917, p. 1051-2.
STEARNS, R. B. Zone system of fares in practice. *American electric railway association, Proceedings,* 1914, p. 213-48. *Electric railway journal,* Oct. 24, 1914, p. 950-61.
STEARNS, R. B. Zone system of fares in practice, with discussion. *Electric railway journal,* May 1, 1915, p. 836-8.

ELECTRIC AND STREET RAILROADS—
FARES—*(Continued)*

STORER, N. W. Graduated fare system. *Electric railway journal,* Oct. 1919, p. 417-8.

STORRS, L. S. Increased value for fare demanded by and given by patrons and communities. *Aera,* Aug. 1919, p. 83-91.

STREET railroad fares muddle. *Modern city,* Dec. 1918, p. 14-6.

STREET railway fares in Columbus, O. *Minnesota municipalities,* Feb. 1919, p. 19-20.

STREET railway problem still acute; a critical state of affairs in Boston, Memphis and New York city. *Financial world,* Dec. 23, 1918, p. 6-7.

SUBURBAN fare zones on Milwaukee system. *Electric railroad journal,* Jan. 24, 1914, p. 185-6.

SUGGESTED sliding scale of dividends for street railways determined by quality of service. *Engineering and contracting,* Aug. 7, 1912, p. 163-5.

SULLIVAN, P. F. Increases in flat rates for present zones. *Electric railway journal,* Oct. 13, 1917, p. 669-71.

SULLIVAN, P. F. Legislative relief is imperative in Massachusetts. *Electric railway journal,* Sept. 15, 1917, p. 442-3.

SUPREME court decides D. U. R. case; court upholds Chicago 6-cent fare. *Public service,* Feb. 1919, p. 53-5.

SUPREME court decides Detroit United railway case. *Electric railway journal,* Jan. 18, 1919, p. 149-50.

SWARTZ, A. Proper basis for interurban passenger rates. *Electric railway journal,* Nov. 23, 1918, p. 925.

TAFT, WILLIAM H. Higher fares. *Electric railway journal,* June 21, 1919, p. 1248-9.

TEN-cent fare announced for Boston. *Electirc railway journal,* July 5, 1919, p. 45-6.

TEN-cent fare imperative; Connecticut company appeals to state commission for further rate increase—seven-cent rate proves insufficient. *Electric railway journal,* Oct. 9, 1920, p. 739.

TEN-cent fare in Connecticut. *Electric railway Journal,* Oct. 30, 1920, p. 945.

TEN-cent fare refused to Bay state. *Electric railway journal,* Dec. 21, 1918, p. 1102-4.

TEN-cent fare upheld in Pittsburgh. *Electric railway Journal,* March 27, 1920, p. 672.

TEN cents in Pittsburgh. *Electric railway journal,* June 28, 1919, p. 1293.

THIRD avenue opens fare case. *Electric railway journal,* June 23, 1917, p. 1142-4.

THREE cents a mile for interurbans; electric railway war board urges filing of new tariffs. *Electric railway journal,* June 8, 1918, p. 1099-1100.

To zone or not to zone. *Electric railway journal,* April 20, 1918, p. 775.

TRAMWAY adjustment committee reports to Mayor W. F. R. Mills of Denver. *Aera,* July 1919, p. 1199-212.

TRAMWAY and railway world discusses journal's Glasgow articles. *Electric railway journal,* July 5, 1919, p. 34.

TRAFFIC check and what it showed on the Public service railway. *Electric railway journal,* March 29, 1919, p. 644-8.

TREND of regulation for electric railways. *Aera,* July 1920, p. 1326-9.

TRENTON fare increase denied. *Electric railway journal,* Dec. 25, 1915, p. 1258-9.

TRENTON, N. J., fare hearing. *Electric railway journal,* Oct. 30, 1915, p. 931.

TRIAL six-cent fare for Bay state. *Electric railway journal,* July 7, 1917, p. 19-20.

TWENTY-FOUR fare increases since July 1, 1918. *Electric railway journal,* Sept. 28, 1918, p. 593.

TWINING, WILLIAM S. Philadelphia conditions analyzed. *Electric railway journal,* Dec. 20, 1919, 999-1002.

Two interesting experiments. *Aera,* Feb. 1919, p. 667-8.

Two points of view of accountants who inquired into Rochester situation. *Electric railway journal,* Sept. 28, 1918, p. 594.

UNITED STATES. INTERSTATE COMMERCE COMMISSION. Reports. Washington, Government printing office.

UNITED STATES LIBRARY OF CONGRESS. References on street railway rates with special reference to regulation. Special libraries, Feb. 1916, p. 25-6.

UNITED STATES supreme court decision nullifying Minneapolis low fare ordinance. *Electric railway journal,* Jan. 15, 1910, p. 112.

UNITED STATES supreme court reverses lower court in Detroit, United case, and says five-cent fare ordinance may be confiscating. Kansas city six-cent fare upheld by supreme court of Missouri. *Aera,* Jan. 1919, p. 591-5.

UNITED traction co., Albany, N. Y., denied fare increase. *Electric railway journal,* July 8, 1916, p. 62-3.

UNLIMITED ride, transferable weekly pass at Racine, Wis. *Electric railway journal,* Jan. 3, 1920, p. 43-6.

UNLIMITED rides for Racinians. *Electric railway journal,* Sept. 6, 1919, p. 502-3.

USE salesmanship in selling transportation. *Electric railway journal,* Jan. 26, 1918, p. 184-6.

UTAH commission grants partial relief from rising costs by allowing an increase in rates. *Aera,* Jan. 1918, p. 557-8.

VARIOUS values of a nickel. *Electric railway journal,* Aug. 12, 1916, p. 279.

WEATHERWAX, H. B. Higher fares essential. *Electric railway journal,* June 29, 1918, p. 1234-5.

WHAT is wrong with the railways? *Electric railway journal,* Feb. 22, 1919, p. 361-5.

WHEN a reduced rate of fare should not be made. *Electric railway journal,* March 22, 1913, p. 532.

WHERE the increased fare goes. *Public service,* Sept. 1919, p. 63.

WHITTEN, R. H. Zone fares and city planning. *Electric railway journal,* Nov. 1, 1919, p. 831.

WHY Holyoke's zone fares are insufficient. *Electric railway journal,* Sept. 14, 1918, p. 456-8.

WHY present fare regulation system should be changed. *Electric railway journal,* Sept. 15, 1917, p. 438-40.

WHY the street-railways of the country are facing wholesale bankruptcy. *Current opinion,* Nov. 1917, p. 350-1.

WIDESPREAD organized movement for increased fares. *Municipal journal,* May 31, 1917, p. 748-50.

WILCOX, D. F. Effect of fare increases upon street railway traffic and revenues. *National municipal review,* Oct. 1920, p. 633-6.

WILCOX, D. F. Fate of the five-cent fare. *National municipal review,* May 1919, p. 235-43.

WILCOX, D. F. Flexible fare is desirable. *Electric railway journal,* Nov. 17, 1917, p. 900-1.

WILCOX, D. F. Public service railway company vs. 146 New Jersey municipalities; Big issue in rate raise case; Killing the goose. *New Jersey municipalities,* April 1918, p. 101-6.

WILCOX, D. F. Public service rate increase scheme. *New Jersey municipalities,* March 1919, p. 71-3, 88-90.

WISCONSIN supreme court decision in Milwaukee fare case. *Electric railway journal,* June 14, 1913, p. 1081.

WRIGHT, T. A. Higher fares are necessary. *Electric railway journal,* May 19, 1917, p. 921.

ZONE fare in practice, Croyden, England. *Electric railway journal,* Sept. 6, 1919, p. 466-74.

ELECTRIC AND STREET RAILROADS—
FARES—*(Continued)*

ZONE fares are not a primary cause of congestion. *Electric railway journal,* March 2, 1918, p. 401.
ZONE fares finally won in Rhode Island. *Electric railway journal,* April 20, 1918, p. 786.
ZONE fares have been found satisfactory in Milwaukee. *Electric railway journal,* Sept. 27, 1919, p. 613-20.
ZONE fares in Springfield. *Electric railway journal,* Sept. 27, 1919, p. 628-36.
ZONE fares successful in Holyoke. *Electric railway journal,* April 10, 1920, p. 749-54.
ZONE-mile system of the Public service railway. *Electric railway journal,* Sept. 27, 1919, p. 637-44.
ZONE plan in New Jersey. *Electric railway journal,* Jan. 3, 1920, p. 29-32.
ZONE plan on the Shore line. *Electric railway journal,* Oct. 4, 1919, p. 685-7.
ZONE system approved for Holyoke (Mass.) company. *Electric railway journal,* Jan. 12, 1918, p. 77-80.
ZONE system best for Rhode Island; special commisison reports. *Electric railway journal,* March 23, 1918, p. 570-3.
ZONE system for New Jersey. *Electric railway journal,* March 15, Aug. 2, 1919, p. 523-8, 258.
ZONE system in Connecticut modified. *Electric railway journal,* April 10, 1920, p. 777.
ZONE system in Portland; zone fares in Springfield; zone-mile system of the Public service railway. *Electric railway journal,* Sept. 27, 1919, p. 621-44.
ZONE system of fares. *Electric railway journal,* May 1, 1915, p. 826.
ZONE systems. *Electric railway journal,* Oct. 11, 1919, sup. 47-50.
ZONES for San Diego. *Electric railway journal,* May 17, 1919, p. 983.

Finance

AMERICAN street railway investments; published annually by the publishers of the Electric railway journal. New York, McGraw-Hill book co.
ANDERSON, H. D. Handling accident reserves. *Electric railway journal,* May 20, 1916, p. 955-6.
ANOTHER Third avenue chapter. *Electric railway journal,* Feb. 10, 1912, p. 230.
BILLINGSLEY, M. P. Service-at-cost bibliography; selected list of references on a subject of great interest to electric railway men. *Aera,* Nov. 1919, p. 494-501.
BRADLEE, H. G. Actual figures of existing street railways. *Aera,* Dec. 1912, p. 392.
BUCHANAN, R. S. Security-holders should demand independent audits. *Journal of accountancy,* June 1907, p. 92-7.
CITY of Coventry tramways department; report of general manager and professional auditor as to making provision in the accounts for renewals and other questions of financial policy. *Accountant,* Aug. 16, 1913, p. 205-8, 216-20.
CLARKE, H. C. Advantages of service-at-cost for electric railroads. *Electric railway journal,* June 21, 1919, p. 1219-20.
CLARKE, H. C. Service at cost agreements. *Aera,* June, July, Sept. 1919-Feb. 1920, p. 1039-46, 1161-9, 228-36, 417-21, 504-9, 582-93, 723-8.
CLARKE, H. C. Some aspects of service at cost: an examination of seven laws and ordinances adopted to put this system in effect on electric railways. *Aera,* Oct. 1918, p. 203-14.
CONWAY, THOMAS. Construction and finances of interurban electric railroads. *Journal of accountancy,* May 1906, p. 1-11.
COURSE of electric railway earnings in 1919. *Commercial and financial chronicle,* July 3, 1920, p. 16-20.
DOUDS, H. J. Preliminaries to the financing of electric railway projects. *Electric railway journal,* Aug. 1, 1914, p. 208-10.
FISCHER, L. E. Determination of probable operating revenue. *Electric railway journal,* Aug. 23, 1913, p. 301-6, 291.
GRADUATED return to induce economy; proposed service at cost franchise for Akron lines provides return based on fare—monthly accounting provided. *Electric railway journal,* Nov. 20, 1920, p. 1072-3.
HOWARD, EARL DEAN. Types of street railway securities. *Journal of accountancy,* May 1906, p. 12-26.
J. J. STANLEY tells how it is done: reasons why reduction in fares was possible explained by president of Cleveland railways company. *Aera,* March, 1920, p. 920-2.
M'GRATH, D. J. Investment required per passenger. *Electric railway journal,* May 8, 1915, p. 881-3.
MACLEOD, F. J. Service-at-cost plan approved for Massachusetts. *Electric railway journal,* Feb. 2, 1918, p. 226-7.
MAHER, EDWARD A. New service-at-cost bill; analysis. 11p.
MORTIMER, J. D. Reasonable rate of return has advanced; testimony at Milwaukee (Wis.) fare hearing. *Electric railway journal,* Jan. 12, 1918, p. 83-5.
NAU, CARL H. Honest accounting is needed. *Journal of accountancy,* June 1907, p. 91-2.
PROPOSED Minneapolis cost of service franchise, by R. W. Junerson; cost of service in Cincinnati, by C. W. Culkins. *Electric traction,* Sept. 1919, p. 567-72.
PUBLIC officials on service at cost. *Electric railway journal,* Dec. 4, 1920, p. 1141-4.
QUESTION box of the Central electric railway accountants association. *Electric railway journal,* May 4, 1912, p. 742.
RECOMMENDS service at cost for Massachusetts. *Electric railway journal,* Feb. 9, 1918, p. 290.
RODGERS, JAMES H. Tramways finances and policy. *Accountant,* Nov. 9, 1911, p. 615-27.
SERVICE at cost agreements; an analysis of various ordinances which are now in effect in American cities. *Aera,* Dec. 1920, p. 499-504.
SERVICE-at-cost for Chicago; features of new plan now awaiting public approval. *Electric railway journal,* August 24, 1918, p. 344.
SERVICE-at-cost in practice: executives of properties operating under plan tell of its actual workings. *Aera,* Oct. 1919, p. 385-90.
SPOFFORD, CHARLES M. Apportionment of cost of highway bridges between street railways and cities; with discussion. *Journal of the Western society of engineers,* May 1915, p. 405-43.
STOCKWELL, HERBERT G. Street railway bonds as investments; a comparison with steam railroad bonds. *Journal of accountancy,* June 1907, p. 98-111.
STREET railway securities—a symposium. *Journal of accountancy,* June 1907, p. 87-97.
TEICHMANN, MAX. Sound reasons for lower prices of street railway securities. *Journal of accountancy,* June 1907, p. 89-90.
TENNESSEE public utilities commission orders service at cost plan for Memphis; cost-of-service plan established for first time by a state commission. *Electric traction,* April 1920, p. 250-2.
WILCOX, DELOS F. Service at cost in local transportation. *National municipal review,* Dec. 1920, p. 765-72.
WOODWARD, J. T. What constitutes a reasonable return? *Electric railway journal,* May 23, 1914, p. 1153.

ELECTRIC AND STREET RAILROADS— *(Continued)*

Government regulation and control

MARWICK, JAMES. Municipal ownership of street railways; with an analysis of the accounts of the city of Glasgow tramways. *Accountant,* Sept. 9, 1906, p. 281-5.

Management

A. E. R. A. war board submits brief on one-man cars. *Electric railway journal,* Aug. 3, 1918, p. 193-5.

ALBERGER, W. R. Reduction in power cost effected by the use of coasting recorders. *Electric railway journal,* Sept. 18, 1915, p. 520-1.

ANOTHER device for encouraging power saving. *Electric railway journal,* April 28, 1917, p. 788-9.

AUTO-trolley-car shows big saving in operating costs. *Electric railway journal,* Aug. 10, 1918, p. 248.

BARNES, J. P. What economies can be profitably effected in the mechanical department. *Electric railway journal,* March 16, 1912, p. 426.

BAY state way organization. *Electric railway journal,* Aug. 7, 1915, p. 229.

BLANCHARD, A. Convenient inspection record system. *Electric railway journal,* Dec. 30, 1916, p. 1352.

BLINN, THOMAS W. Daily work-train report. *Electric railway journal,* Sept. 25, 1915, p. 636.

BOLON, N. W. Some features of electric railway departmental organization. *Electric railway journal,* Feb. 21, 1914, p. 415-6.

BOYCE, W. M. Complete records help to offset the rising cost of labor and material. *Electric railway journal,* Sept. 16, 1916, p. 479-80.

BRANSON, H. Punches vs. pencils for daily car-shop reports. *Electric railway journal,* Sept. 9, 1916, p. 454.

BUCH, A. M. Graphical solution of electric railway problems. *Electrical railway journal,* Aug. 12, 1916, p. 281.

CAMPBELL, G. E. Card record of Los Angeles track work. *Electric railway journal,* Sept. 4, 1915, p. 407-8.

CAR record and trouble board combined. *Electric railway journal,* Oct. 23, 1915, p. 878.

CHART of organization of the Michigan united railways. *Electric railway journal,* April 29, 1911, p. 738.

CHILD, A. P. How a street railway counts its receipts. *Popular mechanics,* Nov. 1920, p. 676-7.

CLAIM department—public service railway. *Electric railway journal,* Oct. 7, 1911. *Atlantic city convention section,* p. 636-8.

COASTING recorders in New York. *Electric railway journal,* Mar. 20, 1915, p. 572-5.

COASTING records as an aid to faster schedules. *Electric railway journal,* Sept. 1, 1917, p. 355-6.

COASTING records of northern Texas traction company. *Electric railway journal,* June 26, 1915, p. 1198-1200.

COLE, A. B. Electric freight haulage is an economic duty; organization charts. *Electric railway journal,* Jan. 4, 1919, p. 39-48.

COOPER, H. S. Indexing car equipment data. *Electric railway journal,* Nov. 20, 1915, p. 1040-1.

CRAM, R. C. Way department requires particularly complete organization. *Electric railway journal,* Aug. 17, 1918, p. 272-4.

DEAN, J. S. Shop organization. *Electric journal,* Nov. 1919, p. 506.

DEPARTMENTAL organization chart. *Electric railway journal,* Feb. 21, 1914, p. 415.

DISPATCHING work of engineering department; Denver tramway company. *Electric railway journal,* July 28, 1917, p. 134-40.

DOOLITTLE, F. W. Collection of traffic data. *Electric railway journal,* July 17, 1915, p. 94-101.

DOYLE, J. S. Maintenance of coasting recorders. *Electric railway journal,* Jan. 29, 1916, p. 215-6.

EMPLOYEES' pay checks. *Electric railway journal,* Sept. 7, 1918, p. 417.

EQUIPMENT defect records of the San Antonio traction company. *Electric railway journal,* Dec. 6, 1913, p. 1189-90.

EQUIPMENT records on the Binghamton railway. *Electric railway journal,* June 3, 1916, p. 1053-4.

EWING, D. D. Dissecting passenger interchange time graphs. *Electric railway journal,* Oct. 5, 1918, p. 610-2.

FLIGG, H. P. Coasting; Denver tramway gave experience with coasting clocks, showing resulting energy economy. *Electric railway journal,* April 10, 1915, p. 705-6.

FOLLOWING up watt-hour meter records at El Paso. *Electric railway journal,* July 3, 1915, p. 12-13.

GRAPHIC coasting record at Boston. *Electric railway journal,* Jan. 8, 1916, p. 95.

GRAPHICS in maintenance work. *Electric railway journal,* Nov. 6, 1915, p. 947-51.

HIXSON, L. T. and others. Report of the standing freight committee, Central electric railway accountants' association. *Electric railway journal,* July 5, 1913, p. 28-9.

HOW zone fares are collected; resume of European and American practice. *Electric railway journal,* Aug. 31, 1918, p. 373-5.

IMPROVED train order register for interurban railroads. *Electric railway journal,* Feb. 23, 1918, p. 378.

IMPROVEMENTS in the power-saving recorder. *Electric railway journal,* April 20, 1918, p. 770.

INDIANAPOLIS traction and terminal company's method of indexing patterns. *Electric railway journal,* Dec. 27, 1913, p. 1334-5.

INDIVIDUAL hand-made and printed run cards. *Electric railway journal,* Nov. 2, 1918, p. 802.

INDIVIDUAL passenger travel record assists tax collection. *Electric railway journal,* Dec. 8, 1917, p. 1044.

JOHNSON, W. E. Method of recording wear of gears and pinions. *Electric railway journal,* Nov. 8, 1913, p. 1021-2.

KEEPING an accurate record of energy consumption at San Diego. *Electric railway journal,* Sept. 21, 1918, p. 518.

KELLER, C. L. Detroit paint shop work card system. *Electric railway journal,* Nov. 14, 1914, p. 1105-6.

KOEHLER, C. H. Meters and men. *Electric railway journal,* March 27, 1915, p. 633.

LEISENRING, J. and H. W. COE. Substation records increase efficiency on the Illinois traction system. *Electric railway journal,* Aug. 26, 1916, p. 352-6.

LEONHAUSER, H. A. Maintenance costs—reducing handling of equipment and departmental cooperation. *Electric railway journal,* Feb. 20, 1915, p. 384-6.

LITCHFIELD, N. Indexing car equipment data. *Electric railway journal,* Oct. 2, 1915, p. 677-8.

MCCLAY, J. W. Car service inspection in Seattle. *Electric railway journal,* Aug. 14, 1915, p. 272-3.

MCMAHON, C. R. Car maintenance records facilitate work. *Electric railway journal,* July 19, 1919, p. 119-21.

MAINTENANCE records that prove invaluable. *Electric railway journal,* April 27, 1918, p. 806-9.

METER results on Chicago & Milwaukee line. *Electric railway journal,* May 22, 1915, p. 973-6.

ELECTRIC AND STREET RAILROADS— MANAGEMENT—*(Continued)*

MURRIN, W. G. Use of coasting recorders results in economies at Vancouver. *Electric railway journal,* Sept. 18, 1915, p. 573-4.
NEW car-mileage report system. *Electric railway journal,* Oct. 30, 1920, p. 935.
NEW Montreal transfer; the time of leaving terminus is punched and the color change is at 5 p. m. instead of at noon. *Electric railway journal,* Dec. 11, 1920. p. 1200.
NOVEL service record chart. *Electric railway journal,* Feb. 20, 1915, p. 366.
ORGANIZATION chart at Oakland. *Electric railway journal,* Dec. 6, 1913, p. 1190.
ORGANIZATION chart, San Francisco-Oakland terminal railways. *Electric railway journal,* May 16, 1914, p. 1086.
ORGANIZATION of the West Penn railways: chart. *Electric railway journal,* April 28, 1917, p. 784.
PALMER, R. W. Redeemable cash-fare receipts. *Electric railway journal,* Mar. 3, 1917, p. 391-2.
PITTSBURGH railways claim department. *Electric railway journal,* July 24, Sept. 11, 1915, p. 139-45, 436-41.
POWER station organization on Bay state street railway. *Electric railway journal,* Oct. 30, 1915, p. 911.
PROGRESS of the headway recorder. *Electric railway journal,* April 13, 1918, p. 717-8.
PUNCHES vs. pencils for daily car-shop reports. *Electric railway journal,* Sept. 9, 1916, p. 454.
RECORDER for passenger-mile earnings. *Electric railway journal,* May 15, 1915, p. 948-9.
REDUCING maintenance costs on a single phase railway. *Electric railway journal,* Dec. 4, 1915, p. 1108-12.
REYNOLDS, J. J. Card index and what it means. *Electric railway journal,* Oct. 16, 1915, p. 815-8.
ROLLING stock maintenance organization of Mass. electric companies. *Electric railway journal,* June 4, 1910, p. 970-4.
RULING on accident reports. *Electric railway journal,* May 8, 1915, p. 883-4.
RUNNING time terminal clock. *Electric railway journal,* March 7, 1914, p. 547-8.
SCIENTIFIC coasting at Oakland. *Electric railway journal,* Aug. 14, 1915, p. 268-71.
SIMPLIFYING coasting records in Houston. *Electric railway journal,* Dec. 28, 1918, p. 1139-40.
SLICK, E. E. Standardization of claim statistics. *Electric railway journal,* Oct. 16, 1915, p. 813-5.
SMITH, H. L. Testing organization of electric railways. *Electric railways journal,* March 16, 1918, p. 511-7.
SQUIER, C. W. Effect of grades and curves in plotting speed-time graphs. *Electric railway journal, July* 20, 1918, p. 96-8.
SQUIER, C. W. Equipment defects—records of those caught in operation or at inspection. *Electric railway journal,* Feb. 7, 1914, p. 318.
STAFF organization of Winnipeg electric railway. *Electric railway journal,* Nov. 6, 1920, p. 969.
STOTHART, E. C. Graphs, charts and statistics as aids to administration. *Electric railway journal,* Oct. 2, 1915, p. 665-7.
SUGGESTED power-saving test. *Electric railway journal,* Aug. 18, 1917, p. 277-8.
TAX returns simplified. *Electric railway journal,* Dec. 15, 1917, p. 1083.
THIRWALL, J. C. Office end of a maintenance shop—The value of record keeping and of concentrating on the elimination of special defects is clearly set forth by instances from practice. *Electric railway journal,* Nov. 2, 1912, p. 961-3.
UNIT for comparing track upkeep costs. *Electric railway journal,* Sept. 16, 1916, p. 499-500.
VANCOUVER solves information and complaint problem. *Electric railway journal,* Oct. 16, 1920, p. 838.
VAN ZANDT, A. D. B. Handling complaints from patrons. *Electric railway journal,* June 16, 1917, p. 1090-2.
WAY department report forms. *Electric railway journal,* Sept. 4, 1915, p. 396-9.
WILCOXON, K. L. Exacting inspection a good investment. *Electric railway journal,* Dec. 23, 1916, p. 1305-7.

Rates.

See Electric and street railroads—Fares.

Reports

REPORTS of various government departments. and companies.

Statistics

AYRES, M. V. Accounting versus statistics. *Electric railway journal,* May 3, 1913, p. 803-5.
EMERY, J. A. Statistical units used in analysis of electric railway accounts. *Electric railway journal,* Oct. 16, 1913, p. 815-7.
HORTON, R. H. Methods of observing and analyzing passenger traffic. *Electric railway journal,* July 12, 1919, p. 75-8.
JONES, W. E. Work of the statistician. *Electric railway journal,* Oct. 14, 1916, p. 777-9.
LAYING, J. F. Keep graphic records of railway statistics. *Electric railway journal,* Jan. 5, 1918, p. 9-11.
STOTHART, E. C. Graphs, charts and statistics as aids to administration. *Electric railway journal,* Oct. 2, 1915, p. 665-7.
WILSON, H. L. Accounting versus statistics. *Electric railway journal,* May 10, 1913, p. 859.

Stores systems

BATES, H. Maintaining a continuous property inventory. *Electric railway journal,* Jan. 20, 1917, p. 115-6.
BUTLER, H. M. Method of ordering and handling stores including disposition of all scrap material. *Electric railway journal,* March 16, 1912, p. 428.
CENTRALIZING and systematizing the stores department. *Electric railway journal,* Aug. 25, 1917, p. 319-20.
CHICAGO city railway material years; describes the handling of material by this company. *Electric railway journal,* Oct. 5, 1912, p. 537-9.
CLARK, L. M. Cataloguing equipment insures accuracy. *Electric railway journal,* April 15, 1916, p. 739-40.
CRAM, R. C. Cutting costs in storage yards. *Electric railway journal,* Dec. 23, 1916, p. 1284-9.
DAILY reports, store room accounting and operating records of the Camden and suburban railway. *Street railway journal,* Dec. 19, 1903, p. 1052-61.
DIMMOCH, W. S. Materials and supplies accounting. *Street railway review,* 1903, p. 970-4.
ECONOMICAL maintenance of storeroom supplies. *Electric railway journal,* April 20, 1912, p. 645.
EFFICIENCY in handling equipment in Brooklyn. *Electric railway journal,* Dec. 23, 1911, p. 1268-71.
ELLIOTT, C. A. Tool list as aid in economical maintenance of way. *Electric railway journal,* Feb. 8, 1919, p. 271.
GLOVER, M. W. Electric railway storeroom accounting methods. *Electric railway journal,* Sept. 9, 1911, p. 423-5.

ELECTRIC AND STREET RAILROADS— STORES SYSTEMS—(Continued)

HARVEY, A. E. Handling way materials economically. *Electric railway journal,* Jan. 27, 1917, p. 150-2.

INDIANAPOLIS traction and terminal company's method of indexing patterns. *Electric railway journal,* Dec. 27, 1913, p. 1334-5.

INGLEHART, R. S. Keeping the company department store; discussion. *Electric railway journal,* Feb. 28, 1914, p. 459-62.

JOHNSON, A. R. Equipment and stores economies on the Third Avenue railway system. *Electric railway journal,* April 4, 1914, p. 780-1.

KENNEDY, THOMAS. Mechanical department stores accounting. *Electric railway journal,* Oct. 9, 1920, p. 717-20.

LAYOUT and equipment of storage yard for handling large quantities of way materials at Cleveland. *Electric railway journal,* Feb. 24, 1917, p. 336-9.

LEGARE, B. P. How construction materials are stored and handled in San Francisco. *Electric railway journal,* Jan. 27, 1917, p. 155-6.

MILLS, JAMES COOKE. Cutting out needless work. *Business man's magazine,* May 1911, p. 474-80.

MODEL method of supply accounts. *Street railway review,* September 15, 1897.

PIERI, W. D. Simplified system for stockroom storekeeping. *Electric railway journal,* June 23, 1917, p. 1150-1.

PURCHASING and store room accounting on the Brooklyn rapid transit system. *Street railway record,* Oct. 15, 1901.

SAGER, F. A. Further testimony in Buffalo reorganization case. *Electric railway journal,* Feb. 10, 1912, p. 246.

SCHWARZ, A. Storeroom systems. *Electric railway journal,* June 24, 1916, p. 1174-6.

STAUB, W. H. Purchasing and accounting for supplies on electric railway systems. *Street railway review,* Aug. 21, 1903.

STEVENS, F. W. Handling of supplies. *American electric railway association, Proceedings,* Nov. 1916.

STOCK rooms and stock keeping of the Metropolitan street railway company, New York city. *Street railway journal,* Jan. 4, 1902.

TINGLEY, BENJAMIN W. Store room and store room accounts. *Street railway journal,* June 1, 1901.

WESTON, R. A. Stores accounting as a means of stock regulation. *Electric railway journal,* Oct. 16, 1920, p. 779.

YUNGBLUTH, M. J. Distribution of materials and supplies. *Electric railway journal,* March 8, 1919, p. 473-5.

YUNGBLUTH, B. J. How to record materials received. *Electrical railway journal,* Dec. 21, 1918, p. 1095-6.

YUNGBLUTH, B. J. Inventorying materials and supplies. *Electric railway journal,* March 8, 1919, p. 473-5.

YUNGBLUTH, B. J. Regulating materials and supplies. *Electric railway journal,* March 17, 1917, p. 490-2.

Valuation

ABENDROTH, HARRY G. Overhead charges in valuation; a discussion of the elements that must be considered in the appraisal of public utilities; percentages as worked out in the experience of the Milwaukee electric railway and light co. *Aera,* Nov. 1914, p. 354. *Electric railway journal,* June 27, 1914, p. 1434-7.

AMERICAN ELECTRIC RAILWAY ASSOCIATION. Bibliography on valuation of public utilities to December 23, 1915. 61+72p.

AMERICAN ELECTRIC RAILWAY ASSOCIATION. Comparison of the capitalization of electric railways with their valuation as determined by public service commissions or other public authority. New York, American electric railway association, Dec. 3, 1919. 9p.

AMERICAN ELECTRIC RAILWAY ASSOCIATION. Proceedings and abstracts of addresses given at the mid-year meeting at Chicago, Feb. 4, 1916. *Electric railway journal,* Feb. 5, 1916, p. 244-72.

Principles of railway valuation by N. T. Guernsey; Rate of return on railway capital by J. D. Mortimer; Uncertainty of utility valuation by T. S. Williams; Elements of utility valuation, by George Weston; What constitutes utility value by P. J. Kealy.

AMERICAN ELECTRIC RAILWAY ASSOCIATION. Rate of return and valuation of electric railways based on decisions of public utility commissions. New York, American electric railway association, Dec. 1, 1919. 21p.

ANALYSIS of the premises adopted and methods used in determining the cost to reproduce new, together with the depreciation thereon of the physical property of the metropolitan system and the ansas city and Westport belt railway of Kansas city, Mo. *Engineering and contracting,* May 28, 1913, p. 617-20.

APPRAISAL of Memphis street railway. *Electric railway journal,* July 10, 1920, p. 120-1.

APPRAISAL of the city lines of the Detroit united railway. *Electric railway journal,* May 17, 1913, p. 897-8.

APPRAISAL of the New York surface systems. *Electric railway journal,* June 20, 1908, p. 111.

APPRAISAL of the Third avenue street railroad system, New York city. *Engineering and contracting,* June 7, 1911, p. 666.

APPRAISED value of the electric street railways of Detroit, Mich. *Engineering and contracting,* July 6, 1910.

APPROXIMATE value placed on physical property of Brooklyn transit system. *Electric railway journal,* Dec. 25, 1909, Jan. 22, Feb. 5, 1910, p. 1261, 156, 248.

ARBITRATION of operating expense charges in Cleveland. *Electric railway journal,* May 24, 1913, p. 925.

ARNOLD, B. J. Approximate value placed on physical property of Brooklyn transit company. *Electric railway journal,* Dec. 25, 1909, p. 1261.

ARNOLD, B. J. Foundation principles of utility valuation. New York, American electric railway association, 1916.

ARNOLD, B. J. Foundation principles of utility valuation with special application to plans for resettlement. *Aera,* Oct. 1915, p. 189-223. *Electric railway journal,* Oct. 9, 16, 1915, p. 713-9, 803-6. *Engineering news,* Oct. 28, 1915, p. 859.

ARNOLD, B. J. Valuation of the Brooklyn rapid transit system. *Electric railway journal,* July 22, 1910, p. 156.

ARNOLD, B. J. and GEORGE W. WESTON. Valuation of the property of the Chicago consolidated traction co. *Engineering news,* Sept. 1, 1910, p. 241.

BACHELDER, F. J. Procedure in Chicago elevated valuation. *Electric railway journal,* Mar. 3, 1917, p. 386-8.

BADGER, H. R. RALPH. Work of valuation of electric railway property. *Electric traction weekly,* Feb. 19, 1910, p. 197.

BAGG, F. A. Life of railway physical property from the engineering standpoint. *Electric railway journal,* Dec. 9, 1911, p. 1205. Discussion. *Electric railway journal,* Dec. 9, 1911, p. 1210.

BAILEY, A. R. Valuation of track special work. *Electric railway journal,* May 12, 1917, p. 876-7.

BAKER, N. D. Franchises—Inclusion of franchchise values in amount of investment for calculating rate of return for Detroit

ELECTRIC AND STREET RAILROADS— VALUATION—*(Continued)*

united railway. *Electric railway journal,* Jan. 29, 1910, p. 203.

BARCROFT, FREDERICK T. Report and appraisal of the Detroit united railway (city lines), Detroit, Michigan, Oct. 1, 1909. Detroit, 1910. Abstract. Appraisal value of the electric street railways of Detroit. *Engineering and contracting,* July 6, 13, 1910, p. 16, 35. Editorial. Noteworthy article on electric street railway appraisal. *Engineering and contracting,* July 6, 1910, p. 1.

BAY state street railway valuation. *Electric* railway journal, Dec. 4, 1915, p. 1121-3.

BAY state substations. *Electric railway journal,* Jan. 22, 1915, p. 164-5.

BEMIS, E. W. Street railway settlement in Cleveland. *Quarterly journal of economics,* Aug. 1908.

BUREAU OF RAILWAY ECONOMICS. List of references on valuation of railway economics. *Bulletin of the American railway engineering association,* Oct. 1916, 154p.

CHICAGO. DEPARTMENT OF PUBLIC SERVICE. Valuation of the Chicago elevated railways. January 1, 1915. Chicago, Department of public service, 1915.

CHICAGO elevated railway valuation. *Electric railway journal,* June 22, 1912, p. 1087. Abstracts. Reports of appraisal of the physical properties of the elevated railways of Chicago. *Engineering and contracting,* May 15, 1912. Valuation of the elevated railroads of Chicago. *Engineering record,* May 18, 1912, p. 552. Editorial. *Engineering record,* May 18, 1912, p. 534.

CHICAGO elevated railways valuation. *Electric railway journal,* June 1, 1912, p. 919.

CHICAGO traffic, value and finances. *Electric railway journal,* April 14, 1917, p. 686-9.

CHICAGO valuations—agreements to terms by companies. *Electric railway journal,* Dec. 22, 1906, p. 1164.

COMMISSIONERS discuss valuation; National association report shows majority favor investment basis or liberal but not peak reproduction cost. *Electric railway journal,* Nov. 20, 1920, p. 1068-9.

COOK, C. B. Economics and equity in valuation. *Electric railway journal,* Nov. 15-Dec. 13, 1919.

DAVIES, J. VIPOND. Engineering accounting. *American electric railway engineering association, Proceedings,* 1913, p. 488, 495. *Electric railway journal,* Oct. 17, 1913, p. 864,840.

DECISION against original cost theory; Judge Van Valkenburgh considers present fair value correct basis for rate making. *Electric railway journal,* Nov. 27, 1920, p. 1122-3.

DECISION in the Milwaukee fare case. *Electric railway journal,* Aug. 31, 1912, p. 314.

DECISION of arbitrator in Cleveland controversy. *Electric railway journal,* Dec. 25, 1909, p. 1237.

DECISION of commission upholding rates of fare in Savannah, Ga. *Electric railway journal,* April 20, 1912, p. 663.

DECISION of Wisconsin commission: considers the rate of return. *Electric railway journal,* Sept. 10, 1910, p. 404.

DECISION of Wisconsin commission in Superior cases. *Electric railway journal,* Nov. 23, 1912, p. 1067.

DETROIT appraisal. *Electric railway journal,* Aug. 20, 1910, p. 304.

DETROIT united railway files bill of particulars in arbitration, placing reproduction value of property at $24,676,181.75. *Electric railway journal,* April 30, 1910, p. 796.

DIFFICULTY of valuation. *Electric railway journal,* Oct. 17, 1914, p. 924.

DISCUSSION of the Milwaukee fare decision. *Electric railway journal,* Jan. 18, 1913, p. 110.

ELECTRIC railway appraisals. *Electric railway journal,* Nov. 2, 1907, p. 905.

ELECTRIC railway appraisals. *Electric railway journal,* March 21, 1908, p. 446.

ELEMENTS of value in a street railway. *Railroad gazette,* Dec. 28, 1906, p. 567.

ELEVATED values in Chicago. *Electric railway journal,* May 18, 1912, p. 817.

EXISTING fares of Wisconsin road upheld by commission after a valuation. *Electric railway journal,* July 9, 1911, p. 193.

FINAL report on San Francisco. *Electric railway journal,* May 10, 1913, p. 844.

FINDING fair value. *Public service regulation,* Nov. 1912, p. 716.

FORD, F. R. Coney Island and Brooklyn railroad testimony re valuation. *Electric railway journal,* Dec. 25, 1909, p. 1263-9.

FORD, FRANK R. Valuation of intangible street railway property. *Annals of the American academy of political and social science,* Jan. 1911.

GILLETTE, HALBERT P. Uses of an appraisal. *Electric railway journal,* Oct. 28, 1911, p. 948-9.

GRAY, HENRY L. Appraisal of the Spokane and inland empire electric railroad system. *Engineering and contracting,* Dec. 27, 1911, p. 696.

GRAY, HENRY L. Valuation of the Puget Sound electric railway. *Engineering and contracting,* May 25, 1910, p. 482.

HAGENAH, WILLIAM J. Intangible value of electric railways and their determination from accounts. *American electric railway accountants association, Proceedings,* 1912, p. 60. Abstract. *Electric railway journal,* Oct. 9, 1912, p. 698, 715. Editorial. *Stone and Webster public service journal,* Nov. 1912, p. 901.

HEARING in Buffalo on International traction reorganization. *Electric railway journal,* Oct. 21, Nov. 4, 1911, p. 910, 991. Editorial. Values claimed by the Buffalo plan. *Electric railway journal,* Nov. 4, 1911, p. 976.

HEARING on valuation of Coney Island and Brooklyn, R. R. *Electric railway journal,* Sept. 4, 11, 18, 25, Oct. 16, Nov. 27, Dec. 4, 11, 25, 1909, Jan. 15, Mar. 12, 1910, p. 377, 398, 437, 469, 878, 1108, 1148, 1188, 1263, 104, 460.

HEARINGS on Milwaukee fare case by Wisconsin railroad commission. *Electric railway journal,* Aug. 1, 1908, March 6-April 24, May 22, 1909, p. 395; 419, 464, 499, 554, 640, 683, 729, 766, 955. Editorial. *Electric railway journal,* March 13, 27, 1909, p. 452, 536.

INTANGIBLE values in settlement cases. *Electric railway journal,* Jan. 3, 1914, p. 5.

INVENTORY of physical railway property of Toledo company given to city. *Electric railway journal,* Nov. 12, 1910, p. 990.

JACKSON, D. C. Appraisals of electric railway properties. *Electric railway journal,* Oct. 31, 1908, p. 1283.

JACKSONVILLE, Ill. valuation brief. *Electric railway journal,* April 15, 1916, p. 731-2.

KANSAS city appraisals. *Electric railway journal,* March 1, 1913, p. 389-90.

KEALY, P. J. It is time for valuation compromise. *Electric railway journal,* March 15, 1919, p. 511-2.

KEALY, PHILIP J. Kansas city franchise. *Electric railway journal,* Aug. 8, 1914, p. 255.

KEALY, PHILIP J. Methods of conducting the valuation of the physical properties of the Chicago consolidated traction co., with summaries of costs. *Engineering and contracting,* Sept. 28, Oct. 5, 1910, p. 274, 295.

ELECTRIC AND STREET RAILROADS— VALUATION—*(Continued)*

KEALY, P. J. Valuation and accruing depreation. *Journal of the Western society of engineers,* Jan. 5, 1920, p. 11-4. Condensed. *Electric railway journal,* Sept. 13, 1919, p. 530-1. *Public service,* Oct. 1919, p. 112-3.

KEALY, P. J. and others. Principles underlying determination of fair value. *Engineering news,* Aug. 28, 1919, p. 425-8. *Electric railway journal,* Aug. 2, 1919, p. 222-5. Excerpt. *Engineering and contracting,* Sept. 17, 1919, p. 321-2.

LIABILITIES on which proper returns should be allowed. *Electric railway journal,* Sept. 25, 1909, p. 464.

LOS ANGELES. BOARD OF PUBLIC UTILITIES. Report. 1. Inventory and valuation of the Los Angeles railway corporation including city railway. 1914.

MACK, EDWIN S. Some principles established by the Wisconsin railroad commission. *Electric railway journal,* Jan. 28, 1911, p. 164.

MASSACHUSETTS public service commission doubts accuracy of estimating original cost. *Engineering record,* Sept. 16, 1916, p. 342-3.

METROPOLITAN street railway reorganization plan. *Electric railway journal,* April 22,-June 3, Aug. 5, 1911, p. 708, 756, 798, 876, 916, 976.

MILWAUKEE four-cent fare decision. *Street railway journal,* July 1898, p. 397.

MINNEAPOLIS, MINN. CITY COUNCIL. CENTRAL FRANCHISE COM. Report on valuation of property of the Minneapolis street railway company, by majority and minority committees. Public library. Business and municipal branch, 1918. 16p.

MINNEAPOLIS valuation figures presented. *Electric railway journal,* Oct. 21, 1916, p. 902.

NEW YORK railways valuation reported. *Electric railway journal,* May 1, 1920, p. 901-2.

OFFICIAL valuation of the property of the United Railways, St. Louis, Mo. *Electric railway journal,* April 20, 1918, p. 783-4.

ORDER of California commission requiring valuations of electric railways. *Electric railway journal,* Nov. 16, 1912, p. 1207.

OSSOSKI, SIDNEY. Basis of valuation in the case of municipal purchase of street railways. *Electric railway journal,* Nov. 12, 1910, p. 999-1000.

PHYSICAL appraisal of Third Avenue railroad. *Electric railway journal,* Feb. 5, 1910, p. 228.

PITTSBURGH valuation reviewed. *Electric railway journal,* Aug. 30, 1919, p. 436-8.

PLAN for reorganization of Third avenue road disapproved by commission. *Electric railway journal,* Aug. 13, 1910. p. 262.

PROPER recognition for "going value." *Electric railway journal,* March 22, 1913, p. 533.

PROPOSED sale of Toronto utilities to the city. *Electrical world,* Oct. 25, 1913, p. 832-3.

PROUTY, E. N. Valuation of competitive transportation systems in the vicinity of San Francisco. *Western engineering,* April 1918.

PUBLIC utilities reports, annotated. Rochester, Lawyers cooperative publishing company.
See index under Valuation.

REASONS for and methods employed in appraising the value of railway properties with special reference to the Michigan valuation. *Egnineering and contracting,* Dec. 14, 1910, p. 534. Editorial. Method of appraising non-physical railway values. *Engineering and contracting,* Dec. 14, 1910, p. 517.

REPORT of committee of American electric railway association on valuation. *Electric railway journal,* Oct. 14, 1916, p. 806-7.

REPORT of committee on overhead charges. *American electric railway accountants' association, Proceedings,* 1913, 1914, p. 244, 68. Abstract. Report of committee on overhead charges, 1913. *Electric railway journal,* Oct. 18, 1913, p. 895.

REPORT of the committee of fifty. *Electric railway journal,* July 16, 23, 1910, p. 111, 142.

REPORT on street railway system of Kansas city. *Electric railway journal,* April 19, 1913, p. 716.

REPORT on United railways of St. Louis. *Electric railway journal,* Feb. 8, 1913, p. 248.

REPORTS on valuation of Detroit property. *Electric railway journal,* Nov. 20, 1909, p. 1077.

REQUEST for lower fares denied by New Jersey commission. *Electric railway journal,* Nov. 25, 1911, p. 1117.

RESULTS of Detroit investigation. *Electric railway journal,* Dec. 25, 1909, p. 1276.

RIFENBERICK, R. B. Something along the line of physical and intangible valuation as covered by recent legislation. *Electric railway journal,* June 28, 1913, p. 1163-7.

ROSENCRANTZ, CHARLES M. Other elements of value than franchise values. *Electric railway journal,* Oct. 16, 1913, p. 822-4.

SCHREIBER, M. Work of committee on life of railway physical property. *Electric railway journal,* April 25, 1914, p. 932.

STREET railway appraisal methods at Chicago. *Engineering record,* Oct. 29, 1910, p. 501.

STREET railway valuation in Kansas city, Mo. *Engineering news,* May 22, 1913, p. 1053-7.

TAYLOR, A. M. Valuation of electric railway properties. *Electric railway journal,* July 19, 1919, p. 128-9.

TESTIMONY in Cleveland valuation. *Electric railway journal,* Nov. 13, 20, Dec. 4, 1909, p. 1024, 1068, 1159.

$32,083,389 is St. Paul city railway value. *Electric railway journal,* Dec. 11, 1920, p. 1211.

TORONTO valuation report. *Electric railway journal,* Nov. 15, 1913, p. 1047.

TWO estimates of Minneapolis railway values. *Electric railway journal,* Feb. 2, 1918, p. 245.

TWO reports submitted to council committee on values of Chicago elevated railways. *Electric railway journal,* May 11, 1912, p. 797-8.

UNDEPRECIATED valuations urged. *Electric railway journal,* Feb. 28, 1920, p. 440-1.

UNIT prices used in the first appraisal of electric railways in Chicago. *Engineering and contracting,* April 3, 1912, p. 393.

UNITED STATES. INTERSTATE COMMERCE COMMISSION. Reports. Washington, Government printing office.

VALUATION and rates. *Street railway journal,* Aug. 31, 1907, p. 307.

VALUATION of a short term franchise. *Electric railway review,* March 9, 1907, p. 313.

VALUATION of Chicago consolidated traction co. *Electric railway journal,* Sept. 3, Dec. 3, 1910.

VALUATION of electric railway properties. *Public service,* Sept. 1919, p. 75-7.

VALUATION of Glasgow tramways. *Tramway and railway world,* May 5, 1910, p. 353.

VALUATION of Milwaukee properties. *Electric railway journal,* July 22, 1911, p. 160-1, 143.

VALUATION of the Cleveland electric railway. *Electric railway review,* Feb. 1, 1908, p. 149.

VALUATION of the Detroit street railways. *Engineering news,* Aug. 25, 1910, p. 212.

VALUATION of the Kansas city, Mo. traction lines. *Engineering and contracting,* July 2, 1913, p. 16-23.

VALUATION of the street railways at Los Angeles, Cal. *Engineering news,* Feb. 12, 1914, p. 358-60.

ELECTRIC AND STREET RAILROADS — VALUATION—(Continued)

VALUATION of the track of the Detroit street railway system. *Engineering news,* Sept. 8, 1910, p. 249-50.

VALUATION of Toronto electric railways. *Engineering news,* Jan. 1, 1914, p. 55-6.

VALUATION of Toronto public utilities. *Electric railway journal,* Nov. 15, 1913, p. 1053-4.

VALUATION of two street railway power plants. *Engineering and contracting,* Sept. 28, 1910, p. 280.

VALUATION reports on Chicago elevated roads. *Electric traction weekly,* May 11, 1912, p. 556.

VALUATIONS of Chicago elevated railways. *Electric railway journal,* May 18, 1912, p. 829.

VALUATIONS of street railway properties. *Electric railway journal,* June 19, 1909, p. 1122-4.

VALUATIONS of the Detroit united railway. *Electric railway journal,* Aug. 13, 20, 1910, p. 258, 294.

VALUE of property in New York reorganization case. *Electric railway journal,* March 1, 1913, p. 381-2.

VALUE of property of the Chicago consolidated traction company. *Electric railway journal,* Aug. 20, Sept. 3, Dec. 3, 1910, p. 309, 374, 1111.

WASHINGTON, D. C., valuations reviewed. *Electric railway journal,* March 6, 1920, p. 469-70.

WHITRIDGE, FREDERICK W. Official valuation of private property. *Electric railway journal,* Jan. 15, 1910.

WHITTEN, ROBERT H. Bibliography. (In his *Valuation of public service corporations.* 1914, p. 728-32.

WILLIAMS, W. H. Valuation of public service corporations. Abstract. *Electric railway journal,* Jan. 8, 1910, p. 76. *American economic association quarterly,* April 1910, p. 196-238.

YOUNG, C. G. Logical basis for valuations of interurban street railways. *Electric railway journal,* Jan. 21, 1911, p. 115. *Electric traction weekly,* Jan. 21, 28, 1911, p. 67, 99. *Electric review and western electrician,* Jan. 28, 1911, p. 180. *Engineering news,* Feb. 2, 1911, p. 141. Discussion. *Electric railway journal,* Jan. 28, 1911, p. 162.

ELECTRIC BUSES.
See Motor buses.

ELECTRIC calculating machine. *Electrical world,* Nov. 29, 1913, p. 1127.

ELECTRIC commercial vehicle versus the horse. *Electrical review and western electrician,* Aug. 8, 1914, p. 290.

ELECTRIC consumer's ledger sheets. *Electrical world,* Jan. 30, 1915, p. 304.

ELECTRIC CONTRACTORS

CONTRACTOR'S house-wiring estimate sheet. *Electrical world,* Feb. 26, 1916, p. 491-2.

CONVENIENT estimate and proposal sheets. *Electrical world,* Feb. 27, 1915, p. 555-7.

CONVERSE, C. M. Office system and forms for the electrical contractor. *Electrical review and western electrician,* July 24, 1915, p. 150-2.

CO-OPERATIVE electrical contracting. *Electrical world,* Sept. 19, 1914, p. 586-7.

CRAIN, G. D. Business hints for contractor and dealer. *Electrical review and western electrician,* April 10, July 31, Sept. 11, Dec. 11, 25, 1915, Jan. 8-15, Feb. 5, 1916, p. 682, 188-9, 475-6, 1065-6, 1148-9, 81-2, 117-8, 249-50.

CRAIN, G. D. Business hints for dealer and contractor. *Electrical review and western electrician,* Aug. 21, 1915, p. 324-5.

CRAIN, G. D. Business hints for the electrical dealer. *Electrical review and western electrician,* March 11, May 6, June 10, 1916, Aug. 26, 1916, p. 473-4, 816-7, 1084-5, 382-3.

CRAIN, G. D. Cost of stock-room leakage and who shall pay. *Electrical world,* December 25, 1915, 1422-3.

DATA and estimate sheets. *Electrical review and western electrician.* April 4, 1914, p. 673.

DOING business on low overhead expense; W. B. Perry electric company, of Brooklyn. *Electrical world,* Feb. 27, 1915, 544-6.

ESTIMATE sheet for contractors. *Electrical review and western electrician,* Nov. 21, 1914, p. 996-7.

ESTIMATING labor costs. *Electrical review and western electrician,* Aug. 1, 1914, p. 218-9.

GOODWIN, W. L. Putting overhead on a scientific basis. *Electrical review,* Dec. 7, 1918, p. 895-6.

HILL, G. W. Proper handling of accounts payable. *Electrical review and western electrician,* May 13, 1916, p. 861.

HILL, GEORGE W. Overhead: importance to the electrical contractor. *Electrical review and western electrician.* Feb. 10, 1917, p. 246-7.

KEEPING down the contractor's "overhead." *Electrical world,* April 22, 1916, p. 930.

LAVALLE, M. J. Contractor's office forms and systems. *Electrical review and western electrician,* July 10, 1915, p. 62-3.

MORLEY, E. L. Accurate determination of overhead in electrical estimating; with discussion. *Electrical review,* Dec. 14, 1918, p. 943-5.

OFFICE methods for the electrical contractor. *Electrical review and western electrician,* March 20, 1915, p. 550-2.

RAETZ, E. M. Simple price record for electrical contractors. *Electrical review and western electrician,* April 28, 1917, p. 709-10.

RECORD forms for the electrical contractors. *Electrical review and western electrician,* April 17, 1915, p. 724-5.

REORGANIZING the electrical industry; an outline of the Goodwin plan. *Electrical review,* Oct. 6, 1917, p. 579-85.

Accounting

BALL, W. J. Bookkeeping for electrical contractors. *Electrical world,* May 23, 1914, p. 1188 .

DECKER, F. L. System of accounting for electrical contractors. *Electrical review and western electrician,* Nov. 2, 1912.

EVES, ROY W. Accounting system for the small electrical contractor. *Electrical review and western electrician,* April 20, 1912.

HOW do you keep track of your wiring jobs and stock? *Electrical review,* Aug. 28, 1920, p. 321-3.

HOW records for electrical contracting may be kept. *Business man's magazine,* Feb. 1908, p. 206-7.

JONES, A. R. Auditing and accounting for electrical contractors. *Electrical world,* Oct. 17, 1914, p. 783.

KEEPING records for the contracting job. *Journal of electricity,* March 1, 1920, p. 216-7.

LEVY, LOUIS. Bookkeeping for contract work. *Electrical review and western electrician,* April 27, 1912.

MNEMONIC symbols show distribution of construction of expenditures. *Engineering news record,* Nov. 7, 1918, p. 865.

MOXEY, L. W. Bookkeeping and cost-keeping for electrical contractors. *Electrical world,* Nov. 20, 1915, p. 1153-5.

SMITH, FREDERIC A. Cost and accounting system; designed for the use of electrical contractors. *Business man's magazine,* Oct. 1907, p. 46-8.

STANDARDIZED accounting system. *Journal of electricity,* Aug. 15, 1919, p. 168-70.

ELECTRIC CONTRACTORS—*(Continued)*

Cost accounting

BURNS, A. J. How to figure costs in the electrical contracting business. *Electrical review and western electrician*, May 10, 1913.

BURRILL, P. C. Methods of computing overhead expenses of electrical contractors. *Electrical review*, May 18, 1918, p. 849-50.

COGHLIN, J. P. How to estimate cost and keep accounts. *Electrical world*, Oct. 9, 1915, p. 818.

CONTRACTORS' cost-keeping system. *Electrical world*, March 27, 1915, p. 797-9.

CURRAN, M. A. Cost-keeping discussed before contractors. *Electrical world*, March 3, 1917, p. 433.

DOING business in low overhead expense; W. B. Perry electric company of Brooklyn. *Electric world*, Feb. 27, 1915, p. 544-6.

DOLKART, LEE. Cost systems in electrical contracting. *Journal of the western society of engineers*, Dec. 1913, p. 969-83.

EFFECT of fluctuating prices on unit cost systems. *Electrical review*, Oct. 6, 1917, p. 596-7.

HILL, GEORGE W. Direct method job cost for contractors. *Electrical review and western electrician*. Mar. 18, 1916. p. 513-5.

HILL, GEORGE W. Unit time card and payroll system. *Electrical review and western electrician*, April 15, 1916, p. 681-3.

MORLEY, E. L. Accurate determination of overhead in electrical estimating; with discussion. *Electrical review*, Dec. 14, 1918, p. 943-5.

MOXEY, L. W. How the contractor can know where he stands. *Electrical world*, Oct. 16, 1915, p. 870-3.

MOXEY, L. W. Labor costs in interior construction. *Electrical world*, Oct. 23, 1915, p. 924-7.

PACK, O. G. Figuring expenses and profits in contracting. *Electrical world*, June 24, 1916, p. 1466-7.

RAETZ, E. M. Cost methods in electrical contracting. *Electrical review and western electrician*, Aug. 1, 1914, p. 220.

RAETZ, E. M. Keeping costs for the electrical contractor. *Electrical review and western electrician*, April 4, 1914, p. 674.

REPORT on estimating labor costs compiled by the Electrical estimation association of Chicago. *Electrical review*, July 27, 1918, p. 125-31.

SCHMIDT, A. R. Job-cost system for contractors. *Electrical review and western electrician*. April 1, 1916, p. 599.

SMITH, FREDERIC A. Cost accounting system. *Business man's magazine*, Oct. 1907, p. 46-8.

ELECTRIC furnace and central station rates. *Electrical world*, May 15, 1920 p. 1147-8.

ELECTRIC furnace performance for alloys with high zinc content. *Electrical review*, May 17, 1919, p. 814-5.

ELECTRIC heating of domestic hot water supply at Seattle, Washington. *Electrical world*, Aug. 19, 1916, p. 376.

ELECTRIC INDUSTRIES

CENTRAL station merchandising costs. *Electrical world*, April 24, 1920, p. 961.

DEVEREUX, W. System of keeping records of current work in electrical inspection department. *Electrical review and western electrician*, Dec. 18-25, 1915, p. 1122-5, 1156-8.

Accounting

CONTRACTOR-DEALERS adopt standard accounting system. *Electrical review*, April 5, 1919, p. 544-6.

ELECTRIC manufacturing companies' accounts. *Electric review* (London), Dec. 18, 1908.

ELECTRIC manufacturing company. (In *International accountants' manual*, 1910, paragraph 69).

ELECTRICAL manufacturers' accounting and cost system; council makers preliminary issue. *Electrical world*, May 26, 1917, p. 1025.

STAAL, C. P. Some important features of construction accounting. *Journal of electricity*, April 15, 1920, p. 377-9.

STANDARDIZED accounting system. *Journal of electricity*, Aug. 15, 1919, p. 168-70.

SUPPLY jobbers' convention considers accounting. *Electrical world*, Nov. 22, 1913, p. 1037-8.

Cost accounting

EGGLESTON, DEWITT CARL. Evolution of the machine unit system at the Modern electric co. *Journal of accountancy*, May 1911, p. 44-57.

EGGLESTON, DEWITT CARL. For model cost system. *Business man's magazine*, Feb. 1907, p. 84-8.

EGGLESTON, DEWITT CARL. Production center job order cost system. (In his *Cost accounting*, 1920, p. 301-28).

ELECTRICAL manufacturers' accounting and cost system; council makes preliminary issue. *Electrical world*, May 26, 1917, p. 1025.

HALL, H. L. Cost system for an electrical manufacturing concern. *Business man's magazine*, Feb. 1905, p. 312-4.

JESSOP, F. W. Successful cost system for an electrical manufacturing company. *Business man's magazine*, June 1908, p. 493-8.

PIPER, G. D. Cost accounting in the main works of the Westinghouse electric and manufacturing company. *Electric railway journal*, Dec. 19, 1914, p. 1337-40.

PIPER, G. D. Overhead expenses in the main works of the Westinghouse electric and manufacturing company. *Electric railway journal*, Dec. 19, 1914, p. 1339-40.

PLANT of the Bullock electric manufacturing company and its work and cost system. *Iron trade review*, April 3, 1902.

TOWNSEND, R. Costing: some phases of modern cost finding with particular reference to the manufacture of electrical apparatus. *Electrician*, April 30, May 14, 1920, p. 491-5, 540-3.

Stores systems

EGGLESTON, DEWITT CARL. System of stores control. *Business man's magazine*, July 1907, p. 81-9.

STOCK-ACCOUNTING methods for jobbers. *Electrical world*, Sept. 5, 1914, p. 489-90.

ELECTRIC irrigation pumping proves profitable on large scale. *Electrical review*, Nov. 9, 1918, p. 737.

ELECTRIC light accounts and their significance. Edwards, Henry Moore. 1914.

ELECTRIC LIGHT AND POWER COMPANIES

See also Power plants.

Figuring profits and pricing. *Electrical review*, Aug. 11, 1917, p. 242.

LINCOLN, EDMOND EARLE. Results of municipal electric lighting in Massachusetts. Boston, Houghton, Mifflin company, 1918. 484p.

Public utilities reports annotated. Rochester, Lawyers co-operative publishing co.

Accounting

ACCOUNTING. *Electrical review and western electrician*, Oct. 3, 1914, p. 671-2.

ACCOUNTING for replacement of plant retired from service. *National electric light association, Accounting sessions, papers, reports and discussions*. 1913, p. 216.

ACCOUNTING matters. *Electric railway journal*, June 6, 1914, p. 1273-4.

ELECTRIC LIGHT AND POWER COMPANIES —ACCOUNTING—*(Continued)*

ACCOUNTING methods; discussed by N. E. L. A. *Elecetrical world,* June 12, 1915, p. 1531-2.

ACCOUNTING sessions of the N. E. L. A. *Electrical world,* May 29, 1920, p. 1255-6. *Electrical review,* May 22, 1920, p. 873-4.

ACCOUNTING system for small lighting companies. *Electrical world,* Aug. 23, 1913, p. 380-1.

ALLISON, L. W. Accounting at Pasadena plant. *Power,* Sept. 19, 1916, p. 413-4.

ALLISON, L. W. Accounting system for electric companies. *Power,* Nov. 11, 1913, p. 697-700.

AMERICAN business and accounting encyclopaedia, comp. by E. H. Beach and W. W. Thorne. Detroit, Bookkeeper publishing co. 1901. Electric light company accounting. v. 2, p. 481-518.

ANNUAL report of committee on economics of the electric service. *American institute of electrical engineers, Proceedings,* July, 1917, p. 600-1.

BILLING and collecting systems of small companies. *Electrical review and western electrician,* July 31, 1915, p. 184-6.

BILLING and record system of the New York Edison company. *Electrical world,* Sept. 2, 1911, p. 573-4.

BITTING, C. R. Preparation of data in connection with rate cases. *Electric railway journal,* Oct. 11, 1919, sup. 29-30.

BLOMEYER, E. C. Accounts with electric light subscribers. *System,* Jan. 1906.

BOWERS, E. J. Accounting methods as applied to Detroit electric properties. National electric light association, 1911. 16p.

BOWERS, E. J. Collection of bills. New York, National electric light association, 1911. 13p.

BUXTON, T. W. Purchasing department accounting. New York, National electric light association, 1911. 26p.

CAHOON, JAMES BLAKE. Uniform accounting for gas and electric lighting companies. *Engineering news,* June 14, 1900.

CASH statement including bank balances. *Business man's magazine,* June, 1911, p. 581.

CLADER, WILL A. Closing books for fiscal year of electrical and gas corporations. *Journal of accountancy,* April 1910, p. 412-8.

CLADER, WILL A. Electric utilities accounting. *Journal of accountancy,* May 1917, p. 326-37.

CLOUGH, J. L. Model system of bookkeeping for electric lighting companies. *Municipal engineering,* Oct. 1900, p. 251-5.

COGHLIN, J. P. How to estimate cost and keep accounts. *Electrical world,* Oct. 9, 1915, p. 818.

COLLINS, G. A. Small company system for handling accounts. *Electrical world,* July 21, 1917, p. 104-5.

COLUMBUS system of customers' records. *Electrical world,* Aug. 9-16, 1919, p. 307, 365.

COMBINATION gas and electrical billing. *Electrical world,* March 2, 1918, p. 468.

CUTFORTH, A. E. Electric lighting company. (In his *Audits,* 1914. p. 98-100).

DAME, F. L. Criticism of the proposed accounting system for New York electric lighting corporations. *Electrical world,* 1908, v.52, p. 219-22.

DEDRICK, A. E. Light and power accounting. *Electric railway journal,* Dec. 23, 1916, p. 1300, 1281.

DETROIT Edison changes to bi-monthly billing. *Electrical world,* July 14, 1917, p. 68.

DISCUSSION on rule of Ilinois commission covering methods of handling customers' accounts. *Electrical world,* April 6, 1918, p. 729.

ECONOMICAL post-card monthly bill form. *Electrical world,* Sept. 8, 1917. p. 484-5.

EDWARDS, HENRY MOORE. Electric light accounts and their significance. New York, McGraw-Hill book co. 1914. 172p.

EDWARDS, HENRY MOORE. N.E.L.A. accounting section. *Electrical world,* Feb. 20, 1915, p. 498-9.

EDWARDS, HENRY MOORE. Regulated electric light accounting. *National electric light association, Papers, reports and discussions,* 1912, p. 106. Abstract. *Electric railway journal,* June 15, 1912, p. 1029.

EFFICIENCY as practiced by Portland light and power co. *Railway and engineering review,* Nov. 1, 1913, p. 1013.

EISENMENGER, H. E. Small-customer question. *Electrical review and western electrician,* Oct. 9, 1915, p. 657-62.

ELECTRIC consumer's ledger sheets. *Electrical world,* Jan. 30, 1915, p. 304.

ELECTRIC light company. (In *International accountants' manual,* 1910, paragraphs, 62, 144, 143).

ELECTRICITY department. (In Bateson, William ed. *Pitman's municipal office organisation and management,* p. 383-46).

ELECTRICITY supply accounts. *Electrical review,* v.52, p. 277-8.

ELECTRICITY works accounts; weekly articles giving analyses of accounts of various municipal electric supply works in Great Britain. *Electrician,* 1898 to —. See Index for paging.

ENGINE and boiler room records for small plants. *Electrical world,* July 1, 1911, p. 47.

ENGINEERING charges in capital account. *Electrical world,* Nov. 17, 1917, p. 951.

FODEN, WILLIAM EDMUND. Some features of electricity accounts. *Accountant,* Nov. 26, 1910, p. 728-40.

FOWLER, E. J. Value of statistics in central-station operations. *National electric light association, Bulletin,* March 1920, p. 144-7.

FOWLES, R. B. Accounting system for small lighting companies. *Electrical world,* Aug. 23, 1913, p. 380-1.

GAY, E. F. Uniform accounting systems. *American institute of accountants, Yearbook,* 1913, p. 81-101. *Journal of accountancy,* Oct. 1913, p. 268-79.

HART, P. H. Central station accounting from a business standpoint. *Canadian electrical news,* July 1899.

HASKELL, F. E. Uniform system of accounting. *Electrical world,* April 5, 1909, p. 928.

HEYDECKE, F. General office accounting. New York. National electric light association, 1911. 11p.

HILL, G. W. Proper handling of accounts payable. *Electrical review and western electrician,* May 13, 1916, p. 861.

HILL, G. W. Unit time-card and pay-roll system. *Electrical review and western electrician,* April 15, 1916, p. 681-3.

HOBSON, H. C. Construction records and accounts. (In *Pennsylvania electric association, Convention,* Sept. 6-8, 1916).

HOLE, R. J. Collection, billing and meter-reading economy. *Electrical world,* April 5, 1919, p. 691-2.

HUMPHREYS, A. C. Present and growing need for the general adoption of a uniform system of records and accounts. *New England association of gas engineers, Proceedings,* 1907, p. 146.

INTERNATIONAL correspondence schools. Accounts for gas corporations and electric corporations. (In their I. C. S. reference library, c1915. 279, section 30, p. 1-14).

JOHNSON, GEORGE. Electric lighting accounts. London, Gee & co. 1903. 171p. (Accountants' library, v.29).

KEISTER, D. A. Electric light accounting. (In his *Corporation accounting and auditing.* 1909. p. 292-321).

KENNY, G. R. Collecting statistics from customers' accounts. *Electrical world,* April 13, 1918, p. 774-5.

KENTUCKY and West Virginia power company. Financial report of (name of company) for the month of ( ) 1920; comprising manager's monthly letter; statement of as-

ELECTRIC LIGHT AND POWER COMPANIES —ACCOUNTING—*(Continued)*

sets and liabilities; comparative statement of earnings and expenses current month; comparative statement of earnings and expenses for the twelve months ending (date); forms. Kentucky and West Virginia power company.

KENTUCKY and West Virginia power company. General instructions, Jan. 1, 1920. 55 typewritten pages.

KER, H. M. B. Electric lighting accounts. *Incorporated accountants' journal*, 1907-8, p. 83.

KNIGHT, A. S. Modern electric light accounting. *Electrical world and engineer*, Nov. 2, 1901.

LOWERING the cost of handling accounts. *Electrical world*, May 26, 1917, p. 1013.

MACGREGOR, WILLIAM ROBERTS. Books and accounts of an electric lighting company. *Accountant*, May 23, 1908, p. 756-63.

METHOD employed for analyzing of business by Rochester company. *Electrical world*, Feb. 2, 1918, p. 261.

MILLER, HENRY C. Applying efficiency standards in central station accounting. *Journal of accountancy*, Dec. 1913, p. 432-4.

MILLER, HENRY C. Problem of central station accounting. *Journal of accountancy*, Sept. 1916, p. 187-9.

MILWAUKEE electric railway and light company. Classification of accounts. 1910. 163p.

MODIFICATION in New York system of accounts. *Electrical world*, July 15, 1911, p. 150-1.

MOON, CHARLES EDWARD. Electric light accounts. *Accountant*, July 22, 1905, p. 114-7. *Incorporated accountants' journal*, 1904-5, p. 237.

MOORE, S. E. Customers' accounts for electric light companies. *Street railway review*, Oct. 12, 1901.

MULHALL, J. F. S. Electric light works. (In his *Quasi-public corporation accounting and management*. c195. p. 116-24).

N. E. L. A. accounting sessions. *Electric review*, May 24, 1919, p. 843. *Electrical world*, May 12, 1917, p. 915-7.

N. E. L. A. reports and papers on accounting methods. *Electrical world*, June 6, 1914, p. 1322-7.

NATIONAL association of railway and utilities commissioners. Uniform system of accounts for electrical corporations, prepared by committee on statistics and accounts of public utilities. New York, Law reporting company, c1920. 111p.

NATIONAL electric light association. Annual convention; accounting sessions. New York, National electric light association.

NATIONAL electric light association. Conference, Chicago, May 22-27, 1916. *Electrical review and western electrician* for May 27, 1916.

NATIONAL electric light association. Report classification of accounts, June 1914. New York, National electric light association. 115p.

NATIONAL electric light association. Report of committee on a uniform system of accounting for electric lighting companies. N. E. L. A. 1908. 45p.

NATIONAL electric light association. Standard of sub-committee on tentative classification of construction and operating accounts. (In its *Accounting sessions, Papers, reports and discussions*, 1914. p. 46).

NATIONAL electric light association. Suspense accounts. (In its *Accounting session, Papers, reports and discussions*, 1914, p. 223).

NATIONAL electric light association. Thirty-ninth convention; abstracts of papers and reports. *Electrical review and western electrician*, May 27, 1916, p. 981. *Electrical world*, May 27, 1916, p. 1234.

NEW YORK CITY. DEPARTMENT OF WATER SUPPLY, GAS AND ELECTRICITY. [Miscellaneous forms used in the Bureau of gas and electricity]. 1916. 44 forms.

NEW YORK public service commission tentative accounts for electrical and gas corporations. *Electric railway review*, May 2, 1908, p. 532.

NUTTING, H. G. D. Accounting system for small central stations. *Electrical review and western electrician*, Jan. 31, 1914, p. 221-6.

OHIO classification of accounts for electric utilities. *Journal of accountancy*, Dec. 1914, p. 463-4.

ORGANIZATION of municipal department of electricity in Chicago. *Electrical world*, Aug. 25, 1910, p. 438.

PARSONS, GEORGE C. T. Electric lighting accounts. *Accountant*, Jan. 2, 1892, p. 12-22.

PASADENA. MUNICIPAL LIGHTING WORK DEPARTMENT. Classification of accounts. (In *Eighth annual report*, 1914-15. p. 28-30).

PATTERSON, A. R. Organization of the accounting department of an electric railway and light company. *American street and interurban railway accountants' association, Proceedings*, 1908, p. 35-65.

PATTERSON, F. H. Organizing for cost reduction in the consumers' bookkeeping department. *American gas institute, Proceedings*, 1916, pt. 1, p. 316-35. Condensed. Continuous meter reading plan eliminates peaks in Rochester company's bookkeeping department. *American gas engineering journal*, Jan. 1 ,1917, p. 10-11, 14-9. Discussiou. *American gas institute, Proceedings*, 1916, pt. 1, p. 336-54.

PIXLEY, FRANCIS W. Electric lighting undertakings. (In his *Accountancy*, Ed. 2. p. 122).

PIXLEY, FRANCIS W. Form of accounts for electric lighting companies. (In his *Auditors, their duties and responsibilities*. 1910. p. 597-606).

PORTERS, R. J. Electric lighting companies' accounts. (In his *Pitman's dictionary of bookkeeping*. p. 365-75).

PROGRESS toward uniform accounting. *Electrical world*, June 7, 1913, p. 1235-8.

PUBLIC utilities reports, annotated. New York, Lawyers co-operative publishing co.

RECORDS of customers kept in Columbus, Ohio. *Electrical world*, July 12, 1919, p. 81.

RENDERING monthly bills to consumers. *Electrical world*, Dec. 29, 1917, p. 1248.

REPORT of committee on a uniform system of accounting for electric lighting companies. New York, National electric light association, 1908. 45p.

REPORT of committee on accounting service to member companies and the monthly bulletin. *National electric light association bulletin*. Aug. 1920, p. 529-33. Report of committee on customers' records and billing method: billing machine. *National electric light association, Bulletin*, Oct. 1920, p. 726-46.

SCHLEGEL, H. C. Report of committee on customers' records and billing methods; with discussion. *National electric light association, 42d convention, Accounting section sessions*, 1919, p. 115-31.

SCHMIDT, WILLIAM. Central-station accounting in war time. *Electrical world*, July 13, 1918, p.64.

SCHMIDT, W. Extent to which a tabulation machine can be used in accounting work. National electric light association, 1911. 18p.

SEATTLE. LIGHTING DEPARTMENT. Lighting department schedule of accounts, cost data, unit cost of distributing system. (See Annual report, 1912 & 1913).

SHORT-CUT accounting methods for small central stations. *Electrical world*, July 4, 1914, p. 30-1.

SMALL, O. A. Electric light and power accounting. *Electrical railway journal*, June 12, 1915, p. 1113.

ELECTRIC LIGHT AND POWER COMPANIES —ACCOUNTING—*(Continued)*

SPICER, ERBEST EVAN and ERNEST C. PEGLER. Statutory forms of electric lighting companies' accounts. (In their *Bookkeeping and accounts*. 1914. p. 310-6).

STAAL, C. P. Organization and methods of public utilities accounting. *National electric light association, Bulletin,* July 1919, p. 392-7.

STANDARD accounting conference. *Progressive age,* May 1, 1908, p. 267.

STARKWEATHER, W. A. Isolated plant: plea for more thorough systems of record and cost keeping. *Power,* June 9, 1914, p. 818-9.

STEVENS, HENRY MARSHALL. Corporation electricity works accounts. *Accountant,* July 22, 1899, p. 789-93. *Incorporated accountants' journal,* 1898-9, p. 200. *Electrical engineering* (London), July 14, 1899. *Electrician* (London), Aug. 11, 1899.

STEWART, J. H. For small electric light and power companies. *Business man's magazine,* Feb. 1908, p. 179-83.

STONE and Webster management association. Standard classification of construction and operating accounts for electric light and power companies. 1913. 131p.

SUSPENSE accounts. *National electric light association, thirty-seventh convention. Accounting sessions, papers, reports and discussions,* 1914, p. 223.

SYMES, R. W. National electric light association convention address. *National electric light association, Bulletin,* June 1920, p. 361-5.

SYSTEM of accounting for central-station companies. *Electrical review and western electrician,* Aug. 7, 1915, p. 228.

TENTATIVE classification of construction and operating accounts. *National electric light association, Accounting sessions, papers, reports and discussions,* 1913, p. 110.

UNIFORM classification of accounts; with discussion. *Electrical world,* May 24, 1919, p. 1099-1101.

UNITED gas improvement company of Philadelphia. System of accounts for hydraulic power companies. 59p.

UTILITY construction accounting. *Electrical world,* Sept. 18, 1920, p. 574-5.

WALLACE, L. M. N. E. L. A. accounting section. *Electrical world,* March 13, 1915, p. 644.

WARD, A. E. Simplified accounting in the northern Colorado power company's main and branch offices. Dayton, Ohio, National cash register company, 1914. 20p.

WILLIAMS, LEYSHON R. Electricity accounts —points of interest on. *Accountant,* Feb. 25, 1911, p. 308-17. *Incorporated accountants' journal,* 1910-11, p. 95.

WISCONSIN classification of electric accounts, *Electrical world,* Feb. 25, 1909, p. 503.

———— Uniform classifications

CALIFORNIA. RAILROAD COMMISSION. Uniform classification of the accounts for electric corporations adopted Oct. 23, 1912, effective Jan. 1, 1913. San Francisco, California railroad commission, 1912.

COLORADO. PUBLIC UTILITIES COMMISSION. Uniform system of accounts for electric light and power utilities; first issue effective Jan. 1, 1916. Denver, 1915. 71p.

CONNECTICUT. PUBLIC UTILITIES COMMISSION. Order governing the appraisal, apportionment and distribution of fixed capital of electric companies, issued March 6, 1914. 16p.

CONNECTICUT. PUBLIC UTILITIES COMMISSION. Report of the . . . (gas and electric light) company. 20p.

IDAHO. PUBLIC UTILITIES COMMISSION. Uniform system of accounts for electric light and power companies; first edition effective January 1, 1914. Boise, 1913. 98p.

ILLINOIS. PUBLIC UTILITIES COMMISSION. Uniform system of accounts for electric utilities, first issue effective January 1, 1919. Springfield, 1918. 141p.

INDIANA. PUBLIC SERVICE COMMISSION. Classifications and forms for electric utilities. Fort Wayne, 1915. 88p.

INDIANA. PUBLIC SERVICE COMMISSION. Uniform classification of accounts for electric utilities. Indianapolis, 1913. 90p.

MAINE. PUBLIC UTILITIES COMMISSION. Uniform classification of accounts for electrical companies; effective July 1, 1915. Augusta, 1915. 70p.

MARYLAND. PUBLIC SERVICE COMMISSION. Regulations prescribing a uniform system of accounts for electrical corporations, June 12, 1911. Baltimore, 1911. 73p.

MICHIGAN. RAILROAD COMMISSION. Uniform system of accounts for electric light and power utilities; first issue effective January 1, 1915. Lansing, 1914. 76p.

MISSOURI. PUBLIC SERVICE COMMISSION. General order no. 12 in the matter of a uniform system of accounts for electrical corporations and municipalities, effective Jan. 1, 1915. Jefferson city, 1914. 84p.

MONTANA. PUBLIC SERVICE COMMISSION. Uniform classification of accounts for electric utilities; first issue effective July 1, 1913. 48p.

NEVADA. PUBLIC SERVICE COMMISSION. Uniform classification of accounts for electric utilities. Carson city, 1911. 47p.

NEW HAMPSHIRE. PUBLIC SERVICE COMMISSION. Uniform classifications of accounts for electric utilities; effective July 1, 1914. Ed.2. Concord, 1917. 100p.

NEW JERSEY. BOARD OF PUBLIC UTILITY COMMISSIONERS. Annual report of (name of the electric company) to the Board of public utility commissioners of the state of New Jersey for the year ending ( ) forms. 34p.

NEW YORK PUBLIC SERVICE COMMISSION tentative accounts for electrical and gas corporations. *Electric railway review,* May 2, 1908, p. 532.

NEW YORK STATE. PUBLIC SERVICE COMMISSION. Circular no. 45, to electrical corporations and gas corporations. Albany, 1908. 158p.

NEW YORK STATE. PUBLIC SERVICE COMMISSION. Uniform system of accounts for electrical corporations, adopted October 21, 1908. Albany, 1908. 61p.

NEW YORK STATE. PUBLIC SERVICE COMMISSION. Uniform system of accounts for electrical corporations; second condensed scheme, adopted December 16, 1908. Albany, 1908. 60p.

OHIO. PUBLIC UTILITIES COMMISSION. Uniform classification of accounts for electric utilities; effective January 1, 1915. Columbus, 1914. 112p.

OHIO. PUBLIC UTILITIES COMMISSION. Uniform classification of accounts for electric utilities (tentative); effective January 1, 1915. 108p.

PENNSYLVANIA. BUREAU OF ACCOUNTS AND STATISTICS. Memorandum submitted at a public hearing on June 20, 1918 in re: "Statement on behalf of Pennsylvania electric association—with reference to the tentative draft of uniform classification of accounts for electric companies." Harrisburg, 1918. 65p.

PENNSYLVANIA. PUBLIC SERVICE COMMISSION. In the matter of uniform classification of accounts for electric companies; instructions pertaining to forms suggested for the

ELECTRIC LIGHT AND POWER COMPANIES —ACCOUNTING—(Continued) ..

use of class "C" and class "D" companies. Harrisburg, 1919. 17p. + forms.

PENNSYLVANIA. PUBLIC SERVICE COMMISSION. Uniform classification of accounts for electric companies; effective January 1, 1919. Harrisburg, 1918. 178p.

WASHINGTON. BUREAU OF INSPECTION AND SUPERVISION OF PUBLIC OFFICES. Uniform classification of accounts for municipal electric light and power utilities; effective Jan. 1, 1916. Olympia, 1916. 105p.

WISCONSIN. RAILROAD COMMISSION. Uniform classification of accounts for electric utilities, prescribed December 1909. 129p.

Auditing

AUDIT of electric light companies accounts. *Accountant,* June 27, July 4, 1908, p. 919-20; 1-4.

CASTENHOLZ, WILLIAM B. Electric light and power companies. (In his *Auditing procedure.* 1918. p. 206-8).

CUTFORTH, A. E. Electric lighting company. (In his *Audits.* 1914. p. 68).

DICKSEE, LAWRENCE R. Electric lighting companies. (In his *Auditing. Authorized American edition.* p. 141-3).

MACGREGOR, W. R. Books and accounts of an electric lighting company. *Accountant,* May 23, 1908, p. 756-63.

MONTGOMERY, ROBERT H. Electric light and power companies. (In his *Auditing theory and practice.* 1916. p. 672-5.

SPICER, ERNEST EVAN and ERNEST C. PEGLER. Electric lighting companies. (In their *Practical auditing.* 1914. p. 480).

SPICER, ERNEST EVAN and ERNEST C. PEGLER. Electric lighting undertaking. (In their *Audit programmes.* 1919. p. 38-9).

Cost accounting

ACCOUNTING in Philadelphia for power plant and sub-station maintenance and operating costs. *Electric railway journal,* June 11, 1910. p. 1020-1.

BAILEY, H. Chart for determining power costs. *Power,* June 5, 1917, p. 762-3.

CENTRAL-station unit-cost accounting. *Electrical world,* Dec. 20, 1913, p. 1271-2.

DRURY, A. G. Determining labor costs of pole line extensions. *Electrical world,* June 29, 1918, p. 1376.

FAIR overhead charges allowed; Bronx gas and electric company. *Electric railway journal,* Oct. 16, 1915, p. 831.

HOLME, A. L. Advantages of a job cost system. New York, National electric light association, 1911. 8p.

KEMPER, LUDWIG. Cost keeping in the central station contracting department. *Electrical world,* Jan. 28, 1908.

KENT, WILLIAM. Costs in a woodworking shop; bakery; a textile mill; a power plant. (In his *Bookkeeping and cost accounting for factories.* 1918. p. 203-12).

KILDUFF, FREDERIC WILLIAM. Power and service costs. *Journal of accountancy,* June 1919, p. 427-36.

LANDWEHR, G. P. Philadelphia electric company payroll system for cost work on departmental man-hour rate basis. *National electric light association bulletin,* Jan. 1920, p. 47-51.

LEAKE, P. D. Memorandum and criticism on the financial proposals of the London county council report on London electricity supply. (In his *Depreciation and wasting assets.* 1917. p. 178-201).

LINE-construction and cost keeping methods at Milwaukee. *Electrical world,* April 25, 1914, p. 937-8.

MACLANE, H. F. Cost figuring in an electrical plant. *American machinist,* Feb. 8, 1912.

MEYER, H. W. Separation of costs in a combined steam heating and electric plant. *Power,* Sept. 2, 1919, p. 391-2.

MOSES, P. R. Determination of costs in isolated electric plants. *Engineering news-record,* March 1901, p. 1082-8.

NASH, L. R. New light on diversity factors. *Stone and Webster public service journal,* Aug. 1915.

RICE, CALVIN W. Analysis of the cost of the generation and distribution of a unit of electricity. *Electricity,* New York, June 22, 1898.

SYSTEM of cost and time keeping in use at the Columbus, Ohio municipal electric lighting plant. *Engineering news,* Dec. 3, 1908.

THURSTON, THOMAS G. Power plant accounting. *National engineer,* April 1918.

TITTENSON, W. H. Equitable allocation of costs in combined lighting and traction stations. *Electrical engineer* (London) June 28, 1901.

TURNER, M. E. Some suggestions relative to determining the cost of electric supply. *Electrical world,* Aug. 27, 1898. *Western electrician,* Sept. 10, 1898.

WRIGHT, E. H. Small-town distribution and management cost. *Electrical world,* Feb. 6, 1915, p. 338-41.

Costs

ACTUAL construction cost of industrial substation. *Electrical world,* Oct. 19, 1918, p. 747.

ACTUAL construction cost of medium-size station. *Electrical world,* April 20, 1918, p. 830.

ADSIT, CHARLES G and W. P. HAMMOND. Construction elements of the Tallulah Falls development. *American institute electrical engineers, Proceedings,* Oct. 1915, p. 2497-546. Abstract. *Electrical world,* Oct. 23, 1915, p. 915-8.

ANALYSIS of central-station costs. *Electrical world,* Dec. 5, 1908, p. 1239.

ANALYSIS of costs to operate isolated plants; report of sub-committee of the power sales bureau of the N. E. L. A.. with table. *Electrical world,* May 26, 1917, p. 1020-1.

ANALYSIS of incandescent lighting costs for a year. *Electrical world,* Feb. 21, 1920, p. 424.

BAILEY, H. Chart for determining power costs. *Power,* June 5, 1917, p. 762-3.

BAKER, C. A. Load-factor, output and cost; abstract. *Electrical world,* July 3, 1915, p. 20.

BARROWS, H. K. Cost of hydro-electric development; abstracts. *Electrical world,* March 1, 1919, p. 413-7. *Engineering and contracting,* March 12, 1919, p. 271-3. *Power,* April 8, 1919, p. 544-6.

BAY state substations. *Electric railway journal,* Jan. 22, 1916, p. 164-5.

BOWLES, J. D. Cost of electric service for a town of 750. *Electrical world,* July 31, 1915, p. 254.

BURDICK, R. H. Performance of Diesel-engine plants in Texas. *Electrical world,* March 11, 1916, p. 587-92.

CASH, B. K. Comparative costs of gas and electricity for illuminating purposes. *American gas light journal,* March 15, 1915, p. 167.

CENTRAL-station construction—cost data obtained from Tenney central-station companies in Massachusetts. *Electrical world,* Sept. 27, 1913, p. 639-40.

CENTRAL-station costs in Massachusetts. *Electrical review and western electrician,* Feb. 12, 1916, p. 284.

CENTRAL-station costs in Nashville show present rates are equitable. *Electrical review and western electrician,* April 14, 1917, p. 628.

CENTRAL station equipment costs. *Electrical world,* April 28, 1917, p. 800.

ELECTRIC LIGHT AND POWER COMPANIES —COSTS—*(Continued)*

CENTRAL station in Massachusetts reduce manufacturing cost. *Electrical review and western electrician*, June 10, 1916, p. 1072.

CENTRAL station investment to serve electric-range load. *Electrical world*, Sept. 25, 1915, p. 706.

CENTRAL-station labor costs. *Electrical world*, Nov. 16, 1912, p. 1031-2.

CHAMBERS, F. C. Steam-driven auxiliaries versus auxiliary turbine and motor driven units. *Electric railway journal*, April 14, 1917, p. 684-5. Abstract. *Power*, May 8, 1917, p. 644.

CLARK, W. Data showing reduction in cost of lighting. *Electrical review*, March 8, 1919, p. 391-2.

CLEWELL, C. E. Cost tables for the installation of shop- and office-lighting systems. *American machinist*, April 19, 1917, p. 677-80.

CLEWELL, C. E. Initial and operating cost of factory lighting. *Electrical world*, Aug. 18, 1917, p. 292-5.

CONSTRUCTION costs on substation, high-tension line and street lighting. *Electrical review and western electrician*, Jan. 1, 1916, p. 34.

COST figures from Brookings. *Electrical world*, Feb. 21, 1914, p. 434.

COST of a 1,400—K.W. hydro-electric plant. *Engineering and contracting*, June 4, 1913, p. 624-5.

COST of a 2,900-k.w. plant. *Power*, Jan. 4, 1916, p. 18.

COST of arc lighting in Crawfordsville, Indiana. *Electrical world*, Dec. 15, 1917, p. 1154.

COST of electrical equipment. *Electrical world*, Dec. 19, 1914, p. 1204.

COST of magnetite-arc lighting in Worcester. *Electrical world*, June 1, 1911, p. 1451-3.

COST of maintaing four stokers and furnaces for six years. *Electrical world*, Dec. 16, 1916, p. 1197.

COST of operating city lighting plant in Detroit. *Electrical world*, April 29, 1916, p. 997.

COST of operating producer-gas plant. *Electrical world*, May 5, 1917, p. 848.

COST of small central station system. *Electrical world*, Aug. 3, 1912, p. 260.

COST of street lighting in Chicago. *Electrical world*, Aug. 9, 1913, p. 290.

COSTS of electrical equipment. *Electrical world*, Dec. 19, 1914, p. 1204.

CRITICISM of Seattle lighting department cost data. *Journal of electricity, power and gas*, Aug. 8, 1914, p. 131.

DATA on cost per customer served. *Electrical world*, July 31, 1920, p. 247.

DATA useful in estimating the cost of power plants. *Engineering and contracting*, April 23, 1913, p. 460.

DEININGER, A. W. Your lighting bill for 1925. *Scientific American supplement*, Sept. 18, 1915, p. 187.

DESIGN, construction and unit costs of the power house for the new smelter of the Arizona copper co., ltd., Clifton, Arizona. *Engineering and contracting*, Sept. 16, 1914, p. 262-5.

DETROIT production costs at Connors Creek station. *Electrical world*, Sept. 20, 1919, p. 656.

ECONOMIC value of gas and electric plants. *Gas age*, June 2, 1913, p. 567-8.

EFFECT of the war upon isolated plant costs. *Electrical review*, June 21, 1919, p. 1024-7.

EFFICIENCY of municipal light plants; comparison of municipal and company plants in Massachusetts. *Municipal journal*, Feb. 24, 1916, p. 266-8.

EISENMENGER, H. E. Central-station rates in theory and practice. *Electrical review*, July 5-Dec. 27, 1919, p. 19-21, 47-51, 94-7, 138-43, 183-7, 231-6, 266-9, 304-7, 352-5, 388-91, 434-7, 473-6, 513-7, 555-8, 599-602, 643-8, 686-90, 728-32, 771-5, 811-6, 857-60, 898-902, 935-8, 974-8, 1008-11, 1048-53.

ELECTRIC station costs. *Power*, March 6, 1917, p. 310.

ELWELL, D. Use of central-station power by large users; abstracts. *Electrical review and western electrician*, Oct. 21, 1916, p. 720. *Electrical world*, Nov. 11, 1916, p. 958-9.

ESTIMATE of the cost of hydro-electric equipment. *Electrical world*, Feb. 14, 1920, p. 372.

ESTIMATED cost of 2,500-k.w. hydro-electric development. *Electrical world*, March 27, 1920, p. 731.

ESTIMATED costs of hydro-electric plants on Winnipeg river. *Engineering and contracting*, Nov. 8, 1916, p. 412-3.

ESTIMATED total cost of semi-outdoor substation. *Electrical world*, March 23, 1918, p. 621.

FEES, C. A. Determination of operating costs of power installations. *Electrical review and western electrician*, Oct. 18, 1913.

FENNER, T. H. Simple method of determining power costs. *Power house*, Dec. 1918, p. 361-3

GAS and electric street lights; comparison of cost and efficiency. *Municipal engineering*, Sept. 1915, p. 96-8.

GENERATION and distribution expenses of a middle west company. *Electrical world*, Jan. 13, 1917, p. 88.

GILLETTE, HALBERT POWERS and RICHARD T. DANA. First cost and operating expenses of complete electric light and power plants. (In their *Handbok of mechanical and electrical cost data*. 1918. p. 740-77). 1739p.

GOODWIN, HAROLD. Practical economics in distribution with their effect on the commercial policy of a central station company. *National electric light association, Papers reports and discussions*, 1914. p. 655.

GROESBECK, A. Small central station operation. *Power*, July 24, 1917, p. 108-9.

HIGHER costs push up expense of production. *Electrical world*, Nov. 30, 1918, p. 1033.

ITEMIZED cost of 33,000-volt line and sub-station. *Electrical world*, May 1, 1920, p. 1005.

JOBSON, A. Analysis of operating costs. *Electrical world*, April 14, 1917, p. 705.

KENNY, G. R. Analysis of hydro-electric plant costs. *Electrical world*, April 24, 1920, p. 954.

KIEFER, P. J. Central station rate making. *Power*, Aug. 24, 1915, p. 268-70.

KNOWLTON, H. S. Power plant proportional investment costs. *National engineer*, Jan. 1918.

LAW, C. L. and J. E. BUCKLEY. Economics in the operation of large lighting installations. 29 West 39th st., New York city, Illuminating engineering society, 1917. 13p. and tables.

LEONARD, J. A. Construction costs of Rice Rips station. *Electrical world*, Aug. 2, 1919, p. 228-30.

MCKAY, C. W. Public utilities and the war. *Electrical review*, March 30, 1918, p. 548-50.

MCKENZIE, L. J. 3,000 to 5,700-kw. substation at Steubenville, Ohio, built at low cost. *Electrical world*, Aug. 5, 1916, p. 270-1.

METHODS of obtaining cost of electric lighting service to consumers based on decisions of the Wisconsin railroad commission. *Engineering and contracting*, June 10, 1912, p. 48.

MEYER, H. W. Separation of costs in a combined steam-heating and electric plant. *Power*, Sept. 2, 1919, p. 391-2.

MEYERS, F. C. Cost of electric light. *Scientific American*, Dec. 2, 1916, p. 512.

MORRISON, L. H. Steam vs. oil engines for small light plant. *Power*, May 15, 1917, p. 657-9.

NECESSITY for materially increasing off-peak load. *Electrical world*, May 12, 1917, p. 926-7.

ELECTRIC LIGHT AND POWER COMPANIES —COSTS—*(Continued)*

OPERATING costs of an eastern central station. *Electrical world,* Feb. 15, 1919, p. 323.

OPERATING costs, Tamarack mills power plants. *Power,* April 16, 1918, p. 548-9.

OPERATING data of a large railway power plant, Minneapolis, Minn. *Electrical world,* Nov. 22, 1913, p. 1049-54.

OPERATING expenses for Massachusetts steam stations. *Electrical world,* June 17, 1916, p. 1418.

OPERATION of the Pasadena, Calif., municipal plant. *Power,* Dec. 5, 1916, p. 781-2.

OUTDOOR substation of low cost. *Electrical review and western electrician,* Sept. 23, 1916, p. 565.

PALMER, R. Cost of municipal electric lighting at Chicago. *Engineering news,* Oct. 2, 1913, p. 668.

PARSHALL, H. F. Economics of electric power station design. *Electrical world,* Sept. 25, 1915, p. 690.

POLAKOV, W. N. Mastering power production; principle of essential cost and use of standard cost. *Industrial management,* Oct. 1918, p. 321-9.

PRODUCTION cost in a 20,000-k.w. Massachusetts central station. *Electrical world,* Sept. 30, 1916, p. 671.

PRUETT, G. C. Municipal light and power plant; operating costs at Miles city, Montana. *Municipal engineering,* Dec. 1916, p. 217-8.

PUTNAM, H. ST. C. Economical combination of water power and steam plants and a convenient method of solution. *American institute of electrical engineers, Proceedings,* June 1917, p. 531-48. Abstract. *Power,* July 24, 1917, p. 132-4.

RALSTON, J. C. Hydro-electric plant cost considerations. *Journal of electricity, power and gas,* Feb. 21, 1914, p. 155.

REASONABLE charge for off-peak electric current. *Power,* Aug. 20, 1918, p. 275-6.

REDUCTION in cost of electric lighting graphically shown. *Electrical review and western electrician,* June 16, 1917, p. 1014.

REPORT of committee on piping large buildings for gas; economical comparison of gas and electric lighting operating indoors. *American gas institute, Proceedings,* 1914, p. 1431-9.

RESULTS from New York hall of records test. *Power,* March 14, 1916, p. 361-2.

RISING cost of elctrical service. *Electrical world,* Jan. 17, 1920, p. 169.

ROSS, J. D. Hydroelectric cost data. *Journal of electricity, power and gas,* July 18, 1914, p. 55. Letter. Criticisms of Seattle lighting department cost data. *Journal of electricity, power and gas,* Aug. 8, 1914, p. 131.

SORENG, E. M. Cost figures from Brookings. *Electrical world,* Dec. 27, 1913, p. 1321.

SPRINGER, G. B. Cost of conduit and tunnel construction. *Electrical review,* Feb. 22, 1919, p. 315-6.

STARKWEATHER, WILLIAM A. Results in isolated plant for factory. *Power,* April 17, 1917, p. 538-9.

STATION rated at 10,000 kw. produces energy at 6 mills. *Electrical world,* Jan. 8, 1916, p. 99.

STILLWELL, L. B. Water power and transportation. *Electric railway journal,* April 29, 1916, p. 822-3.

TEAGUE, N. N. Installation costs for industrial plant substations. *Electrical world,* June 10, 1916, p. 1358-8.

THUERK, H. C. Energy costs to large consumers of power. *Electrical world,* Feb. 21, 1920, p. 443-4.

TUFTS, B. Cost of serving small customers with lighting. *Electrical world,* Feb. 21, 1920, p. 443.

UNIT costs of the Cleveland electric illuminating company. *Power,* April 9, 1918, p. 513.

UNIT operating expenses of several small Wisconsin utilities. *Electrical world,* March 11, 1916, p. 603.

WAR-time cost of power house coal. *Electric railway journal,* Aug. 11, 1917, p. 222.

WAR time costs of service. *Electrical world,* Sept. 7, 1918, p. 453.

WILCOX, W. D. Street lighting in Chicago—gas v. electricity. *Gas age,* Dec. 1, 1913, p. 547-9.

WILSON, T. Fort Wayne municipal plant. *Power,* April 24, 1917, p. 546-9.

WISCONSIN commission shows Milwaukee that central-station energy is cheapest. *Electrical world,* Sept. 20, 1913, p. 577.

YOUNG, H. .W. Cost of outdoor substations. *Electrical world,* Aug. 12, 1916, p. 324-5.

YOUNG, H. W. Distribution of cost in outdoor substation. *Electrical world,* June 28, 1919, p. 1393.

Finance

DREYFUS, EDWIN D. Reckoning with costs of superseded equipment. *Electrical world,* Aug. 5, 1916, p. 272-4.

Management

BEARDSLEE, F. D. Central-station sales department organiation and work. *Electrical review and western electrician,* Dec. 5, 1914, p. 1073-9.

BONSALL, R. F. Handling of customers' orders. New York, National electric light association, 1911. 11p.

BOOTH, W. H. System in charging. *Power,* April 1, 1913, p. 474-5.

BORDON, S. W. Coupon purchase plan for lamp renewals. *Electrical world,* April 29, 1916, p. 990-2.

BROMLEY, CHARLES H. Operation at Holtwood. *Power,* May 20, 1919, p. 770-6.

CARD index increases efficiency of new business department. *Electrical review and western electrician,* May 15, 1915, p. 899-900.

CARD system for obtaining life record of gas-filled lamps. *Electrical world,* May 15, 1915, p. 1240.

CHART for reducing the cost of billing. *Electrical world,* April 7, 1917, p. 660-1.

CHARTING instructions to get better economies. *Electrical world,* May 11, 1918, p. 982-3.

CHICAGO-reorganization of the department of electricity. *Electrical world,* Aug. 2, 1913, p. 222-3.

CLASSIFICATION of sales department expenses. *Electrical world,* June 22, 1918, p. 1325.

COLLIER, CHARLES A. Handling of customers' orders. *Electrical world,* March 27, 1920, p. 740-1.

CONTRACT routing system of Detroit Edison company. *Electrical world,* Aug. 24, 1912, p. 407-8.

CONVENIENCE of the customer; system of the Commonwealth Edison company, Chicago. *Electrical world,* July 1, 1916, p. 15-20.

CONVENIENT method for filing apparatus costs and station records. *Electrical world,* Oct. 7, 1916, p. 718.

DAVIS, F. H. Notes on the design of central station records and returns. *Electrical engineer* (London), May 8, 1903.

DERR, H. W. Routine necessary for granting service. *Electrical world,* Nov. 10, 1917, p. 914-5.

DISCUSSION on rule of Illinois commission covering methods of handling customers' accounts. *Electrical world,* April 6, 1918, p. 729.

DISTRIBUTION line records. *Electrical world,* Aug. 9, 16, 1913.

DREYFUS, E. D. Graphic analysis of managerial problems. *Electrical world,* Oct. 7, 1916, p. 710-2.

DREYFUS, E. D. Graphic representations of power-plant losses. *Power,* May 11, 1915, p. 638-9.

ELECTRIC LIGHT AND POWER COMPANIES —MANAGEMENT—*(Continued)*

ECONOMIES in monthly bills and receipts. *Electrical world*, Nov. 10, 1917, p. 913.

EFFECTIVE color-tab system for light and power records. *Electrical review and western electrician*, April 15, 1916, p. 673-4.

FELLOWS, W. H. System of serially numbering customers' meters. *Electrical world*, May 13, 1916, p. 1100.

FORMS designed for customer's convenience. *Electrical world*, March 31, 1917, p. 615.

FOSTER, HORATIO ALVAH. Central station management and finance. New York, G. C. Shelley & sons, 1899. 60p.

GENERATING station records. *Electrical review*, London, March 17, 1911.

GILLOOLY, F. Keeping records that aid load dispatching. *Electrical world*, Oct. 25, 1919, p. 864-7.

HAVER, S. Collecting by mail and methods employed. *Electrical world*, Sept. 1, 1917, p. 437-8.

HOW one central station encourages economy. *Electrical world*, Feb. 16, 1918, p. 363-4.

KRAMER, C. W. Forms for keeping record of proportional meters. *Gas industry*, May 1918, p. 1606.

LABOV, M. Maintaining records of underground distribution. *Electrical world*, Oct. 27, 1917, p. 808-9.

counts. *Electrical world*, May 26, 1917, p. 1007.

M'LAUGHLIN, J. C. Office economies for lighting utilities. *Electrical world*, Sept. 8, 1917, p. 483-4.

MANN, H. B. Sales organization of the commercial department. *Electrical world*, May 24, 1913, p. 1093-4.

MARTIN, GEORGE W. Notes on a central station card record system. *Electrical world*, April 6, 1907.

METER-record forms for a small central station. *Electrical world*, July 31, 1915, p. 255-6.

MOTOR-service data at a glance. *Electrical world*, Aug. 14, 1915, p. 370.

NUTTING, H. G. D. New business methods for central stations. *Electrical review and western electrician*, Feb. 14, 1914, p. 325.

OFFICE and stock-room methods. *Electrical world*, April 24, 1915, p. 1036.

OPERATING data for two Kansas plants. *Electrical world*, May 13, 1916, p. 1103-4, 1082.

ORGANIZATION and methods of a central station sales department. *Electrical world*, May 9, 1914, p. 1051-2.

ORGANIZATION of municipal department of electricity in Chicago. *Electrical world*, Aug. 25, 1910, p. 438.

PAINE, R. A. Data forms for underground conduit and cable record—pocketbook. *Electrical world*, July 29, 1916, p. 227.

PAINE, R. A. Identification record for overhead primary circuits. *Electrical world*, Aug. 12, 1916, p. 325.

PECK, E. P. Organizing operating staff to meet emergency. *Electrical world*, Jan. 5, 1918, p. 29-30.

PERCENTAGE of unaccounted for output. *Electrical world*, Oct. 25, 1913, p. 858.

POLAKOV, W. N. Controlling the cost of electricity. *Engineering magazine*, May 1915, p. 235-40.

POLAKOV, W. N. Management of central stations. *Engineering magazine*, Oct. Dec. 1915, p. 367-72.

POLLISTER, E. B. Experiences of small plant operator; economies effected by high efficiency oil engine unit. *Electrical world*, May 8, 1915, p. 1185-6.

POWER station organization chart; Buffalo general electric company, Buffalo, New York. *Power*, July 16, 1918, p. 87.

POWER-station organization chart; Commonwealth Edison co. *Power*, July 30, 1918, p. 164.

POWER-station organization chart; Edison electric illuminating co. of Brooklyn, N. Y. *Power*, July 23, 1918, p. 118.

PRACTICAL operation of central stations. *Electrical world*, March 27, 1915, p. 786-7.

RAITT, C. C. Keeping operating records. *Electrical world*, Nov. 23, 1918, p. 979-82.

RECORD hydraulic data on printed post cards. *Engineering record*, Dec. 9, 1916, p. 715.

RECORDING system for distribution equipment. *Electrical world*, Dec. 28, 1918, p. 1230.

RECORDS for the central-station's new-business department. *Electrical review and western electrician*, May 19, 1917, p. 840-1.

RICHMOND, O. J. Record sheets of a small central station. *Power*, March 20, 1917, p. 388.

STRIKE, J. N. Daily records of plant costs and efficiencies. *Electrical world*, Oct. 25, 1919, p. 870-4.

SYSTEM for recording power installations. *Electrical world*, Sept. 7, 1918, p. 450.

SYSTEM map and card files. *Electrical world*, March 17, 1917, p. 512-3.

TABULATING troubles on transmission line. *Electrical world*, Aug. 31, 1918, p. 401.

TEMPORARY receipts for guarantee deposits. *Electrical world*, March 16, 1918, p. 573.

THURMAN, R. Methods of financing extensions of lines. *Electrical world*, Aug. 31, 1918, p. 404.

TRANSFORMER record card used by western company. *Electrical* world, Dec. 15, 1917, p. 1151.

UNIT analyses of industrial power business. *Electrical world*, Sept. 20, 1919, p. 627-9.

WEBSTER, W. G. Power-plant report sheets. *Power*, Oct. 6, 1914, p. 508-9.

Rates

ABSTRACT of opinion by the Wisconsin Commission upon its investigation into rates, rules and regulations of lighting and power companies in Milwaukee. *Electrical world*, Aug. 31, 1912, p. 439-40.

ACTIVE-room system of rates. *Electrical world*, April 1, 1916, p. 774-5.

ADAMS, WILLIAM. Uniform electric rates based on costs. *Electrical world*, June 26, July 17, 1915, p. 1666-7; 124-5.

ALBERTSON, R. B. Washington utility commission overruled. *American municipalities*, July, 1913, p. 106-8.

ALLISON, L. W. Standard meter rates. *Power*, Feb. 3-17, 1920, p. 183-4, 218-9.

ARMSTRONG, R. D. Connersville sliding scale. *National municipal review*, Oct. 1919, p. 562-6.

ASHLEY, H. W. Public policy and legal regulation of central station charges. *Engineering magazine*, Jan. 1914, p. 545-6.

ASHLEY, H. W. Public service electric rates. *Practical engineer*, Sept. 1, 1914, p. 877-9.

ASHLEY, H. W. Theories of electric-current rate schedules. *Engineering magazine*, Oct. 1914, p. 86-8.

ATTITUDE of central stations on rates. *Electrical world*, Sept. 7, Nov. 2, Dec. 7, 1918, p. 445-6, 832-3, 1075-6.

AVERAGE light and power rates. *Public service regulations*, March 1913, p. 134.

AVERAGE rates for electricity in thirty-six large American cities. *Electrical world*, March 16, 1912, p. 595-6.

BALTIMORE gas and electric rate decision. *Public service regulations*, March 1913, p. 141-7.

BARKER, HARRY. Rate problems of electricity supply works. (In his *Public utilities rates*. 1917. p. 300-17).

BASE electric rates on the cost of coal. *Electrical world*, July 9, 1917, p. 1128.

BAUER, J. Cost versus value of service in rate making. *Electrical world*, Aug. 31-Sept. 7, 1918, p. 388-9, 443-4.

BAUM, F. G. Best control of public utilities. *American institute of electrical engineers, Proceedings*, Jan. 1915, p. 1-23. Abstract.

ELECTRIC LIGHT AND POWER COMPANIES
—RATES—*(Continued)*

Electrical world, Jan. 23, 1915, p. 258-9. Discussion. *American institute of electrical engineers, Proceedings,* Jan. 1916, p. 58-70.

BAUM, F. G. Class rates for light and power systems or territories. *American institute of electrical engineers, Proceedings,* April 1915, p. 485-505. Abstract. *Electrical world,* July 10, 1915, p. 67. Discussion. *American institute of electrical engineers, Proceedings,* Jan.-March, 1916, p. 58-70, 398-400.

BEAUCHAMP, J. W. Tariffs for domestic electricity service. *Electrician,* July 2, 1920, p. 37-9.

BECKFORD, W. C. Rates for electric service. *Electrical review and western electrician,* June 10, 1916, p. 1073-5.

BLACKMAN, A. S. and T. ROLES. Point five tariff. *Electrical world,* July 24, 1915, p. 185-6.

BLAKEBOROUGH, H. A. Light and power rates. *Canadian municipal journal,* Jan. 1917, p. 22-3.

BLUE, F. K. Practical application of the self adjusting standard for rate fixing. *Journal of electricity,* April 26, 1913.

BOOTH, W. H. System in charging. *Power,* April 1, 1913, p. 474-5.

BOUCHEROT, P. Charging for electrical energy according to the consumer's power factor; abstract *Electrical world,* March 9, 1918, p. 523.

BOWDEN, J. H. Standardization of tariffs. *Electrical review and western electrician,* July 18, 1915, p. 117-20

BRIGGS, W. W. Proposed divided—types domestic service rate. *Electrical world,* Oct. 28, 1916, p. 850-3.

CALIFORNIA railroad commission approves rate increase for Pacific electric company. *Electrical world,* Aug. 3, 1918, p. 224.

CALIFORNIA rate increase will further bond issue. *Electrical world,* Feb. 15, 1919, p. 334.

CAMBRIDGE, Mass., Central station practice. *Electrical world,* April 26, 1913, p. 876-7.

CENTRAL power station rates. *Power,* Sept. 9, 1913, p. 371.

CENTRAL-station rate bill opposed at Boston. *Electrical world,* Feb. 13, 1915, p. 441.

CENTRAL-station rate increases during 1917. *Electrical review,* Jan. 5, 1918, p. 18-24.

CENTRAL-station rate making; analysis of and discussion of general theory. *Power,* Aug. 24, 1915, p. 268-70.

CENTRAL-station rates in New York and Brooklyn. *Electrical world,* May 19, 1910, p. 1307-8.

CHANGING from flat rate service to metered basis in Sacremento, California. *Electrical world,* Jan. 27, 1917, p. 187-8.

CHARGING for energy. *Electrical world,* April 3, 1915, p. 859.

CHART used by Canadian company to determine income at known load factor. *Electrical world,* Aug. 17, 1918, p. 309.

CHICAGO, (Illinois) city. Gas, oil and electric light committee. Report of the committees on gas, oil and electric light, on the investigation of the Commonwealth Edison Company. Chicago, May 1913. Chicago, J. F. Higgins, 1913. 113p.

CHRISTIE, A. G. Lethbridge municipal power plant. *Power,* April 4, 1916, p. 466.

CINCINNATI franchise negotiations. *Electrical world,* July 10, 1915, p. 105.

CLEVELAND. MAYOR. Communication relative to a three-cent rate for electric lighting. *Cleveland city record,* Feb. 3, 1915, p. 9.

CLEVELAND, OHIO. Resolution transmitting suggested "application and agreement for the use of "electric current," "explanation of chart showing rate schedule," "conditions," and the rate chart, and providing that rates for electric energy furnished by the department of public utilities, division of light and heat, be fixed in accordance therewith. *Cleveland city record,* May 19, 1915, p. 540-1.

CLEVELAND municipal electricity rates. *Engineering news,* Aug. 20, 1914, p. 411.

CLEVELAND'S new municipal electric plant: selling electricity at a three-cent maximum rate. *Engineering news,* July 30, 1914, p. 258-61.

COAL rates and new business policy. *Electrical world,* Aug. 11, 1917, p. 253-4.

COEUR d'Alene power-rates case. *Engineering and mining journal,* Oct. 11, 1913, p. 679.

COLUMBUS, OHIO. Ordinance to fix rates for sale of current from the municipal light plant for light and power purposes. *Columbus city bulletin,* Nov. 25, 1916.

COMBINATION power rate for limited-hour service. *Electrical world,* Sept. 15, 1917, p. 530.

COMBINED block and room rate for small town. *Electrical world,* June 30, 1917, p. 1265.

COMMISSIONS decision in Indianapolis rate cases. *Electrical world,* Aug. 31, 1918, p. 416.

COMPUTATION of a rate. *Power,* March 23, 1915, p. 419-20.

CONKLIN, L. H. Rates for electric service. *Electrical world,* Dec 6, 1913, p. 1167.

CONTRACTS for purchased power. *Electrical railway journal,* Dec. 6, 1913, p. 1178-81.

COOPER, H. S. Rates for electric service. *Electrical world,* Feb. 7, 1914, p. 326.

CRAVATH, J. R. Rates and by-products. *Electrical world,* April 24, 1915, p. 1029.

CRAVATH, J. R. Street lighting rates. *Electrical world,* Oct. 5, 1912, p. 722-3.

CROWELL, H. H. Report of an investigation of the electric companies of Detroit with special reference to rates and methods of charging. Sept. 28, 1907. 22p.

DARLING, A. G. Justice of the power-factor rate. *Electrical world,* Sept. 13-27, 1919, p. 586-7, 660-1, 708-10.

DATA on electric water-supply pumping for thirty-seven Iowa communities; tabulation. *Electrical world,* Aug. 26, 1916, p. 423.

DAVIES, G. H. Adjustment of American street car fares: growth of cities makes five-cent rate unprofitable; charges based on production cost; advantages of light equipment: origin of five-cent fare; position of New York commission. *Public service,* Aug. 1911, p. 53.

DECISION by Oregon commission, with table of costs for different classes of consumers of the Hood River gas and electric company. *Electrical world,* Aug. 21, 1915, p. 431.

DECISION in Pacific power and light company's rate case. *Electrical world,* Jan. 1, 1916, p. 6-7.

DECISION in rate case in Springfield, Mo. *Electrical world,* July 4, 1914, p. 9-10.

DECISION in the case of Stadtlander et al. vs. The New York Edison company. *Utilities magazine,* July 1915, p. 15-27.

DECISION of California commission in Antioch rate case. *Electrical world,* July 18, 1914, p. 119-20.

DECISION of court of appeals in the Kings county lighting company case. *Electrical review and western electrician,* April 11, 1914, p. 729-31.

DECISION of Massachusetts commission in Worcester street lighting case. *Electrical world,* July 27, 1912, p. 190-1.

DECISION of the Wisconsin railroad commission ordering a revised and reduced schedule of rates for the Beloit water, gas and electric company. *Electrical world,* July 29, 1911, p. 262-3.

DENNISON, E. H. Birmingham (England) increases prices of electricity and gas. *Commerce reports,* no. 81, April 6, 1918, p. 82-3.

ELECTRIC LIGHT AND POWER COMPANIES —RATES—*(Continued)*

DETERMINATION of the "fair rate of return" on the value of the property of the Madison gas and electric co., two theories of rate making. *Engineering and contracting,* June 21, 1911, p. 726.

DETERMINING a proper basis for rates and fares. *Electric railway journal,* Feb. 1, 1913, p. 184.

DE WOLF, R. D. Combination rates for steam heating and electric service. *Electrical world,* July 1, 1911, p. 45.

DE WOLF, R. D. Electric central-station rates. *Engineering magazine,* March 1914, p. 959-61.

DICKERMAN, J. C. Comparison of electric light and power rates. *Power,* July 6, 1915, p. 8-15.

DICKERMAN, J. C. Lower electric rates in Philadelphia. *American city,* April 1916, p. 341-2.

DISCUSSION of Central west rate situation. *Electrical world,* July 27, 1918, p. 165.

DISCUSSION on class rates for light and power systems or territories (Baum), Deer Park, Md. July 2, 1915. *American institute of electrical engineers, Proceedings,* March 1916.

DISCUSSION on "Rates and rate making." New York, October 8, 1915. *American institute of electrical engineers, Proceedings,* Jan. 1916, p. 71-112.

DOANE, S. E. Fixed charges for fixed expenses. *Public service,* Oct. 1909, p. 105-8.

DOANE, S. E. Handling the small consumer in Europe. *Electircal world,* May 23, 1914, p. 1157-74.

DOW, A. Art of rate-making. *Electrical world,* Jan. 2, 1915, p. 17-8.

DREYFUS, E. D. Notes on large power rate. *Electrical review and western electrician,* Feb. 28, 1914, p. 419-23.

DRUAR, JOHN F. Rates and rate making. *Journal of the association of engineering societies,* May 1913, p 221.

DUFFY, C. N Effect of load factor on cost of electric railway passenger service. *Electric railway journal,* Feb. 1, 1913, p. 195.

DUFFY, C. N. Electric utilities rates of fare and return on investment. *Electric railway journal,* Jan. 20, 1912, p. 103.

DUFFY, C. N. Failure of three-cent car fares. *Public service,* Nov. 1913, p. 153.

ECONOMIC aspects of summer load. *Electrical world,* May 25, 1918, p. 1084-7.

EDGAR, CHARLES L. War and rate problems. *Electrical world,* June 22, 1918, p. 1332-3.

EFFECT of coal prices on central-station rates. *Electrical review and western electrician,* May 26, 1917, p. 899.

EFFECT of increased costs on central station rates. *Electrical review,* Chicago, Nov. 10, 1917, p. 800-803.

EFFECT of the war on revenue from lighting. *Electrical world,* Nov. 23, 1918, p. 987-8.

EISENMENGER, H. E. Central-station rates in theory and practice. *Electrical review,* July 5-Dec. 27, 1919, p. 19-21, 47-51, 94-7, 138-43, 183-7, 231-6, 266-9, 304-7, 352-5, 388-91, 434-7, 473-6, 513-7, 555-8, 599-602, 643-8, 686-90, 728-32, 771-5, 811-6, 857-60, 898-902, 935-8, 974-8, 1008-11, 1048-53.

EISENMENGER, H. E. Computation of the cost of current. *Electrical review and western electrician,* Aug. 15, 1914, p. 335-9.

EISENMENGER, H. E. Theoretical basis for the multiple-rate system. *Electrical world,* May 24, 1913, p. 1085-91. Electric furnace and central station rates. *Electrical world,* May 15, 1920, p. 1147-8.

ELECTRIC heating of domestic hot-water supply at Seattle, Washington. *Electrical world,* Aug. 19, 1916, p. 376.

ELECTRIC light and power. *University of Texas bulletin,* 1915, No. 45, Aug. 10, 1915, p. 64-96. (Municipal research service no. 10.)

ELECTRIC light and power rates. *Public service regulation,* Feb. 1913, p. 100.

ELECTRIC lighting rates in some of the principal cities in the United States; comparative electric power rates in some American cities. *California, Board of public utilities, Report,* 1915, p. 21-2.

ELECTRIC public utilities. *Aera,* Nov. 1913, p. 405.

ELECTRIC rate discussion in Chicago. *Electrical world,* July 26, 1913, p. 174-5.

ELECTRIC rate increase movement. *Public service, Chicago,* 1918, p. 154-6.

ELECTRIC rate increases to follow high cost of coal. *Electrical world,* Feb. 2, 1918, p. 240-1.

ELECTRIC rates and classification of customers. *Electrical world,* Feb. 15, 1913, p. 352-4.

ELEMENTS involved in rate investigation; report of committee of Canadian electrical association. *Electrical world,* June 23, 1917, p. 1213-4.

ELLIS, R. L. Rates for electricity. *Engineering magazine,* May, 1912, p. 227-33.

ENGLISH view of central-station rates. *Electrical world,* Sept. 22, 1910, p. 687-8.

ERICKSON, HALFORD. Electric lighting and power rates. *Annals of American academy of political and social science,* Philadelphia, May, 1914, p. 238-50.

ERICKSON, HALFORD. Making rates for electric current charges of many central stations too low. *Public service,* 1911, p. 119-21.

ERICKSON, HALFORD. Making rates for electric plants. *Public service regulation,* Sept. 1912, p. 579.

ERICKSON, HALFORD. Some principles and facts that should be considered in making rates for electrical utilities. Madison, Wis., H. Erickson, 1913.

ESPENSCHIED, F. F. Residence lighting rates and energy consumption. *Electrical world,* Dec. 15, 1917, p. 1153-4.

ESTIMATING the rate of "reasonable return" for a public utility. *Engineering and contracting,* April 30, 1913, p. 482.

EXCESSIVE rates due to holding company. *Electrical world,* April 27, 1911, p. 1017-8.

EXTRACTS from rate research. *American municipalities,* March 1918, p. 168.

FAR ROCKAWAY rate decision. *Progressive age,* Sept. 1, 15, 1911.

FEATURES of the Milwaukee rate schedule. *Electrical world,* Dec. 25, 1915, p. 1431.

FIXING the rate schedule. *Stone and Webster public service journal,* July 1913, p. 35-47.

FLAT rates defended at Cape Cod hearing. *Electrical world,* Jan. 3, 1920, p. 27-8.

FORD, A. H. Flat rates for small consumers. *Electrical world,* July 1, 1911, p. 46-7.

FORD, FRANK R. and others. Determination of the proper basis for rates and fares. *Electric railway journal,* Dec. 2, 1911, p. 1154, p. 1134.

FORD, J. F. Electric light and power rates. *American municipalities,* June 1913, p. 73-6.

FORT WAYNE company offers to take over municipal lighting plant. *Electrical world,* March 4, 1916, p. 531.

FOWLE, F. F. Discrimination in central-station rates. *Engineering magazine,* June 1911, p. 406-15.

GAS rates and electric rates compared. *Gas age,* April 1, 1914, p. 327-8.

GEIGER, C. W. Low electric rates in Los Angeles. *Municipal journal,* Nov. 22, 1917, p. 511-2.

GEIGER, CHARLES W. Power plants get rate increase. *Power plant engineering,* Aug. 15, 1920, p. 799-802.

GESELL, G. A. Minnesota public utility rates. *Minnesota university, Current problems,* Oct, 1914, p, 30-142.

ELECTRIC LIGHT AND POWER COMPANIES —RATES—*(Continued)*

GHILARDI, F. Power-factor as element of rates. *Electrical world,* Aug. 21, 1915, p. 410-1.

GOLDMAN, O. B. Multiplex cost and rate system. *American institute of electrical engineers, Proceedings,* May, 1915, p. 941-57. Discussion. Nov. 1915, p. 2662-5.

HALE, R. S. Demand and load-factor systems. *Electric railway journal,* Oct. 28, 1916, p. 29.

HALE, R. S Explaining the differential. *Electrical world,* March 13, 1920, p. 614-5.

HALE, R. S. Street lighting versus cooking rates: abstracts with discussion. *Electrical review and western electrician,* Sept. 12, 1914, p. 531-2. *Electrical world,* Sept. 26, 1914, p. 621.

HALL, C. I. Factors affecting determination of the maximum demand. *General electric review,* Feb. 1918, p. 148-50. *Electrical review,* Feb. 23, 1918, p. 333-4.

HAMILTON, S. Resume and comparison of rate theories. *Journal of electricity, power and gas,* Oct. 17, 1914.

HARTFORD, CONN. central station developments. *Electrical world,* Sept. 6, 1913, p. 473-6.

HEARING of Massachusetts commission on street lighting rates. *Electric world,* Feb. 9, 1911, p. 358-9.

HIGHER rates favored by Ohio new-business men. *Electric world,* May 19, 1917, p. 979.

HILL, J. B. Principles determining electric rates; extracts from rate research. *American municipalities,* Sept. 1919, p. 172-5, 180-1.

HOAR, F. E. Can central stations offer lower power rates? *Electric world,* May 26, 1917, p. 1014-5.

HOGE, C. H. and E. R. PERRY. Distribution system for domestic power service from commercial and engineering standpoints. *American institute of electrical engineers, Proceedings,* Aug. 1916, p. 1279.

HOLBROOK, A. T. Profitable methods of obtaining old-house lighting business; summary and discussion. *Electrical review and western electrician,* Oct. 3, 1914, p. 674-5.

HOLDING, H. H. Value of the service in rate-making. *Electrical world,* April 24, 1915, p. 1031-2.

HOOD river gas and electric company rate decision. *Electrical review and western electrician,* July 31, 1915, p. 191-2.

HOW increased rates affect gas and electric revenue. *Electrical world,* Sept. 28, 1918, p. 604.

HOW weather conditions affect electric-light bills. *Electrical world,* Feb. 8, 1913, p. 302.

HOXIE, GEORGE L. Features of electric rate making. *Public service,* April 1913, p. 141-2.

HOXIE, GEORGE L. Some features of rate fixing for electric public service properties. Los Angeles, Engineers and architects association of southern California, 1912, 11p.

HYDRO uniform rate association. *Canadian engineer,* April 29, 1920, p. 429.

IMPORTANT rate case. *Journal of electricity, power and gas,* July 31, 1915, p. 85.

IMPORTANT rate decision in Massachusetts. *Electrical world,* July 7, 1910, p. 7.

INCOME per hip-year from various rates and load factors. *Electrical world,* Sept. 21, 1912, p. 611.

INCREASE in electric rates. *Power,* March 12, 1918, p. 385-6.

INCREASE in power rates by the Pittsburg company. *Electrical world,* May 26, 1917, p. 1033.

INCREASE in the rates of the Milwaukee companies. *Electrical world,* Nov. 3, 1917, p. 875.

INCREASED electric rate based on coal cost denied by the Board of public utility commissions of New Jersey. *Electrical review,* Sept. 1, 1917, p. 359.

INDIANAPOLIS electric rate cases. *Electrical review and western electrician,* Aug. 7, 1915, p. 235-7.

INFORMATION concerning commercial lighting and power; tables: *Municipal journal,* Aug. 27, Sept. 24, 1914, p. 274-8, 425-6.

IVES, A. S. Factors in rate-making. *Electrical world,* March 13, 27, April 17, 1915, p. 655-7, 783-6, 987-9.

JACKSON, H. D. Central-station rate making. *Power,* Nov. 2, 1915, p. 626.

JACKSON, H. D. Cost of supplying power for various characters of service. *Practical engineer,* Nov. 15, 1914, p. 1109-1111.

JACKSON, H. D. Discrimination in rates for electricity. *Power,* March 31, 1914, p. 462-3.

JACKSON, H. D. Public versus the public service corporation. *Engineering magazine,* July 1915, p. 402-9.

JACKSON, H. D. Rate discrimination in Massachusetts. *Power,* April 20, 1915, p. 549-50.

JACKSON, H. D. Rates for electricity. *Engineering magazine,* Dec. 1912, p. 326-34.

JACKSON, H. D. Rates for electricity. *Electrical world,* March 21, 1914, p. 659.

JACKSON, H. D. Retail rate-making for energy bought at wholesale. *Electrical world,* Feb. 7, 1920, p. 332-3.

JACKSON, H. D. Theories of electric current rate schedules. *Engineering magazine,* Feb. 1915, p. 728-31.

JACKSON, H. D. Uniform electric rates based on costs. *Electrical world,* July 10, 31, 1915, p. 60, 236-7.

JANSKY, C. M. Rates for electric service. *Electrical world,* April 4, 1914, p. 771-2.

JOYCE, H. B. Power rate for electrically driven ice plants. *Power,* Jan. 22, 1918, p. 137-8.

KENNEDY, S. M. Justification of deviation in rates for electric service. *Public service,* Jan. 13, 1913, 13-14. *Journal of electricity power and gas,* Nov. 30, 1912, p. 479.

KENNEDY, S. M. Rates for electric service. *Electrical world,* Nov. 22, 1913, p. 1066-7.

KENNEDY, T. O. Manager's viewpoint on higher power rates. *Electrical world,* Dec. 13, 1919, p. 1070-1.

KIEFER, P. J. Central-station rate making. *Power,* Jan. 25, 1916, p. 119-20.

KIEFER, P. J. Central-station rate making. *Power,* Aug. 24, 1915, p. 268-70.

KING, ARTHUR C Answer to report of Arthur C. King on electric rates of union gas and electric co., Cincinnati, Ohio. Cincinnati, O., Union Gas and electric co., Dec. 1914, 35p.

KING, ARTHUR C. Central-station rate situation. *Electrical review,* May 17, 1919, p. 806-7.

KING, ARTHUR C. Report on electric rates of the union gas and electric co., Cincinnati, Ohio. Cincinnati, City Clerk, Nov. 1914, 70p.

KING, C. L. Electric rates and their tendencies. *Utilities magazine,* Oct. 1917, p. 7-21.

KINGBRUNNER, C. Rates for electrical energy. *Electric world,* March 23, 1911, p. 739.

KLINGENBERG, G. Electricity supply of large cities; with discussion. *Institute of electrical engineers journal* (London), 1914, p. 123-49.

LAWLER, J. C Schedule of rates involving the investment cost of reaching the consumer. *Electrical world,* June 15, 1911, p. 1562-5.

LEWIS, E. I. Indianapolis rates raised by the Indiana commission. *Electrical world,* Sept. 8, 1917, p. 494.

LIGHTING and power rates of Massachusetts municipal plants. *Municipal journal,* August 27, 1914, p. 279.

LIGHTING vs. power electric rates. *Public service,* Oct. 1913, p. 130-1.

ELECTRIC LIGHT AND POWER COMPANIES —RATES—(Continued)

LINCOLN, P. M. Rates and rate making. *American institute of electrical engineers, Proceedings,* Oct. 1915, p. 2175-214. Abstract. *Electrical review and western electrician,* Oct. 16, 1915, p. 722-3. Discussion. *American institute of electrical engineers, Proceedings.* Jan. 1916, p. 71-112.

LOS ANGELES, CAL. New basis of rates for industrial power: recently adopted schedule places Los Angeles on equal footing with other cities. *Public service,* Jan. 1918, p. 5.

LOUIS D. BRANDEIS on central-station rates. *Power,* Sept. 9, 1913, p. 380-1.

LOWER energy rates are made for small company. *Electrical world,* July 12, 1919, p. 90-1.

LOWER power rates for 135 Illinois towns. *Electrical world,* Aug. 19, 1916, p. 361.

LOWER rates at Fall River, Mass. *Electrical review and western electrician,* Dec. 18, 1915, p. 1101.

McKAY, E. W. Electric utility valuation and rates. *Engineering review,* May 17, June 7, 1919. p. 796-8, 934-6.

McKAY, E. W. Origin of electric rate control. *Electrical review,* May 17, 1919, p. 796-8.

MAKING the rates carry the coal cost. *Electrical world,* July 7, 1917, p. 12-3.

MANY instances of reduction in rates for electricity this fall. *Electrical review and western electrician,* Nov. 11, 1916, p. 849.

MARKS, W. D. Practical rate making and appraisement. South Hadley, Mass., Presidents house, 1914. 269p.

MARLBOROUGH electric company; rate decision. *Electrical review and western electrician,* June 5, 1915, p. 1063-4.

MASSACHUSETTS commission. *Electrical world,* June 14, 1913, p. 1303.

MASSACHUSETTS hearing on rates. *Electrical review and western electrician,* Feb. 20, 1915, p. 347.

MASSACHUSETTS summer rates 35 cents per kilowatt hour. *Electrical world,* June 14, 1919, p. 1287.

MERCHANTS heat and light company, Indianapolis, decision of commission. *Electrical review and western electrician,* Aug. 14, 1915, p. 287-8.

MILES, G. E. Charging for electric current. *Power,* June 10, 1913, p. 831-2.

MILWAUKEE residential electric rates reduced. *Electrical review and western electrician,* Oct. 14, 1916, p. 682.

MINIMUM charges for electricity in cities of 250,000 and over. *Electrical world,* Aug. 12, 1916, p. 343.

MORTIMER, J. D. New conditions affecting rate of return. *Electrical world,* Nov. 3, 1917, p. 859-60.

MOSES, PERCIVAL R. Electric rates; an analysis of elements entering into cost of service. *American municipalities,* May 1915, p. 51-7.

MOSES, PERCIVAL R. Practical co-operation between central station and isolated plant. *Engineering magazine,* Jan. 1913, p. 578-87.

MOSES, PERCIVAL R. Rates for electricity. *Electrical world,* Oct. 25, 1913, p. 853-5.

MOUNTING costs halt rate reductions. *Electrical world,* May 5, 1917, p. 843.

MULTIPLEX cost and rate system. *American institute of electrical engineers, Proceedings,* May 1915, p. 941-57. Discussion at Portland, Ore., Jan. 5, 1915, of Otto B. Goldman's paper, Nov. 1915, p. 2662-5.

MUNICIPAL electric light plants: rates. *Municipal engineering,* Feb. 1915, p. 111-2.

MUNICIPAL lighting plants; figures concerning electric light plants, collected by Mass. state commisison. *Municipal journal,* Jan. 6, 1916, p. 12-3.

N. E. L. A. committee report on rate research. *Electrical world,* June 12, 1915, p. 1527-8.

N. E. L. A. Michigan section annual convention. *Electrical review and western electrician,* June 27, 1914, p. 1275-7.

N. E. L. A. rate research committee report. *Electrical world,* June 6, 1914, p. 1306-10.

NARRAGANSETT electric lighting company rate equalization plan to offset high coal prices. *Electrical world,* Feb. 15, 1919, p. 334.

NEW HAMPSHIRE public service commission asks for jurisdiction over contract and schedule rates. *Electrical world,* Jan. 18, 1919, p. 128.

NEW plan of service-charge schedules for power loads. *Electrical world,* Nov. 9, 1918, p. 893-4.

NEW rate schedule at Sioux City, Iowa. *Electrical review and western electrician,* Aug. 21, 1915, p. 323.

NEW rates of New York Edison company. *Electrical world,* May 8, 1915, p. 1159-60.

NEW rates schedule adopted by New Orleans company. *Electrical review and western electrician,* Dec. 18, 1915, p. 1102.

NEW seasonal rate of Biddeford, Maine, central station. *Electrical world,* Aug. 3, 1918, p. 213.

NEW YORK EDISON COMPANY announces reduced lighting rates. *Electrical review,* July 14, 1917, p. 71-2.

NEW YORK EDISON COMPANY: opinion and order of the first district commission. *Electrical review and western electrician,* Oct. 30, 1915, p. 802-4.

NEW YORK rate reduction accepted. *Electrical world,* March 27, 1915, p. 828.

NEWBURY PORT COMPANY increases its rates. *Electrical world,* Sept. 13, 1919, p. 595.

NICHOLAS, F. Tendencies in central station rate-making. *Electrical world,* Oct. 23, 1915, p. 907-9.

NORTHWEST LIGHT AND WATER COMPANY; decision of commission. *Electrical review and western electrician,* Nov. 27, 1915, p. 976-7.

NORTON, WILLIAM J. Form of electric rates. *Electrical world,* July 4, 1914, p. 20.

NUTTING, H. G. D. Charge for surplus power. *Electrical world,* Dec. 19, 1914, p. 1208.

NUTTING, H. G. D. Public service commissions and demand rates. *Electrical world,* Nov. 28, 1914, p. 1055.

OHIO electric light association. Ohio lighting rates. Greenville, Ohio, Ohio electric light association. 1913. 58p.

OKLAHOMA rates and revenues. *Electrical world,* May 30, 1914, p. 1252-3.

OPINION of the Massachusetts commission in the matter of two complaints of the price of gas sold by the Haverhill Gas Light Company. *Gas age,* March 1, 1913, p. 250-4.

OPINION of the public service commission of Maryland reducing rates charges for gas and electricity by the consolidated gas, electric light and power company of Baltimore. *Gas age,* Feb. 15, 1913, p. 195-200.

OPTIONAL rate on an active-room basis. *Electrical world,* Oct. 6, 1917, p. 676.

PALMER, RAY. Municipal lighting rates. *Annals of the American academy of political and social science,* Jan. 1915, p. 33-44.

PALMER, RAY. Street lighting rates and cost factors. *American city,* Dec. 1914, p. 462-6.

PASADENA municipal lighting plant. *Municipal engineering,* June 1913, p. 505-11.

PASSAVANT, H. Abstract of a paper in the Elek. Zeit. of May 11, on rates. *Electrical world,* July 8, 1911, p. 122.

PECK, B. H. Engineering date necessary for an electric rate determination. *Electrical review,* Dec. 1917, p. 937. *Journal of the western society of engineers,* Jan. 1918, p. 1-20. Excerpt. *Electrical world,* April 20,

ELECTRIC LIGHT AND POWER COMPANIES —RATES—*(Continued)*

1918, p. 825-7. Discussion. *Journal of the western society of engineers,* Jan. 1918, p. 20-7.

PERRY, H. H. Two-rate schedule without time-operated control. *Electrical world,* Dec. 6, 1913, p. 1173-4.

PERRY, H. H. Two-rate tariff system without time operated control. *Journal of the Institute of electrical engineers* (London), 1913, p. 42-5, 150-4.

PETERS, J. W. S. Suggested sliding scale of dividends for street railways, determined by quality of service. *National municipal review,* Jan. 1913, p. 31-8.

PHILADELPHIA electric rate case. *National Municipal review,* Oct. 1916, p. 662-4.

PHILADELPHIA rate case settled. *Electrical world,* April 29, 1916, p. 972-3.

PITTSBURG'S solution of the small customer problem. *Electrical world,* Dec. 13, 1913, p. 1215.

POTOMAC power company rate case. *Electrical world,* Sept. 15, 1917, p. 543.

POWER rates for the Engel copper mining co. *Engineering and mining journal,* Sept. 13, 1919, p. 452.

POWER rates raised by coal cost; action of the Rockford (Ill.) electric company before public utilities commission. *Electrical world,* June 16, 1917, p. 1151-2.

PREFERENTIAL charging for electricity; an English judge's decision. *Electrical review,* Aug. 25, 1917, p. 333-4.

PRICES-British central station; Glasgow. *Electrical world,* Sept. 29, 1910, p. 742.

PROPOSED new rate schedule of New York Edison company and United electric light and power company. *Electrical world and western electrician,* Dec. 16, 1916, p. 1052.

PUBLIC service commission acts in landlord and tenant case. *Power,* Sept. 16, 1913, p. 416-7.

PUBLIC service commission orders Brooklyn Edison electric rates reduced. *Electrical world,* Nov. 4, 1916, p. 893-4.

PUBLIC service rates and depreciation; how these accounts should be kept. *Electrical review,* Jan. 14, 1911, p. 67.

PUNGA, F. Combined flat rate and meter rate; abstract. *Electrical world,* March 27, 1915, p. 788-9.

PURCHASED power in New York state. *Electric railway journal,* June 7, 1913, p. 1016-8.

QUESTIONS involved in New Jersey regualtion. *Electric railway journal,* Sept. 30, 1911, p. 535-7.

QUINN, E. A. Power factor and rates. *Journal of electricity,* April 15, 1920, p. 372-3.

RAILWAY power rates in Chicago. *Electric railway journal,* July 24, 1915, p. 138.

RATE and accounting question at Illinois state electrical association convention. *Electrical world,* Nov. 3, 1910, p. 1036-7.

RATE discrimination by Columbus municipal plant. *Power,* Jan. 20, 1914, p. 110-2.

RATE readjustment in California case. *Electrical world,* July 12, 1919, p. 90.

RATE schedules from the customer's standpoint. *Electrical world,* Jan. 4, 1913, p. 49-50.

RATE tendencies and recommendations thereon; abstract of N. E. L. A. rate research committee report. *Electrical world,* June 9, 1917, p. 1115-6.

RATE that is designed to increase use of energy. *Electrical world,* Sept. 8, 1917, p. 484.

RATES charged by various central stations for steel-mill service; table. *Electrical review and western electrician,* Sept. 23, 1916, p. 553.

RATES cut to meet government sign regulations; Doherty managers adjust schedules. *Electrical review,* Dec. 22, 1917, p. 1060.

RATES for Berkeley, Cal., electric light. *Municipal engineering,* Dec. 1913, p. 538-9.

RATES for light and power tabulation. *Municipal journal,* June 24, 1915, p. 893.

RATES for residence lighting. *Electrical world,* July 29, 1916, p. 243.

RATES of the Queensborough gas and electric co.; the first commodity rate case of the public service commission for the first district of New York; land appraisal; going value, unimpaired investment; fair return development costs. *Engineering news,* Aug. 31, 1911, p. 266.

RATES paid by dry good stores. *Electrical world,* Oct. 7, 1916, p. 732-3.

RATES per kilowatt-hour for lighting of parks in eighteen cities. *Electrical world,* Sept. 29, 1917, p. 624.

RATES should be based on future, not past, cost. *Electrical world,* Dec. 13, 1919, p. 1071-2.

REASONABLE charge for off-peak electric current. *Power,* Aug. 20, 1918, p. 275-6.

REASONS for different rates. *Power,* April 20, May 18, 1915, p. 550-1, 684-5.

RECORD of Pasadena's municipal plant. *Power,* Oct. 28, 1913, p. 626-7.

REDUCED electrical rates in Portland, Ore. ordered by Public service commission. *Electrical world,* June 2, 1917, p. 1076.

REDUCTION of rates ordered in District of Columbia. *Electrical world,* July 21, 1917, p. 126-7.

REID, C. S. Theories of electric current rate schedules. *Engineering magazine,* Dec. 1914, p. 392-5.

REPORT of the rate research committee. New York. *National electric light association,* 1914, p. 801-3.

REPORT on St. Louis rates and valuation. *Electrical world,* March 16, 1911, p. 656-8.

REPORT on Seattle municipal system. *Electrical world,* Oct. 10, 1914, p. 705-6.

RESALE of energy by customer to second central station. *Electrical world,* Sept. 25, 1915, p. 704-5.

RHINELANDER (Wis.) power company. *Electrical review and western electrician,* March 27, 1915, p. 588-9.

ROSE, T. D. Customers demand and what it means. *Electrical review,* March 23, 1918, p. 522-3.

RYAN, W. T. Central station demand and diversity factors. *Electrical age* (Electrical engineering), Feb. 1916.

ST. LOUIS valuation and rates; statement regarding report revaluation of the property of the Union electric light and power co., findings of commission very disappointing to company. *Electrical world,* March 16, p. 329, 656; *Engineering record,* March 11, 1911, p. 261.

SARA, R. A. Municipal electric plant supplying lighting current at 3 cents per kw-hr. at Winnipeg. *Engineering news,* Sept. 24, 1914, p. 655-6.

ergy. *Electrical world,* June 20, 1914, p.

SEABROOK, A. H. Systems of charges for en-

1454.

SEATTLE'S municipal ownership electric light rate is the highest in the land. *Public service,* Sept. 1915, p. 93.

SECURING full-schedule business from breakdown prospects. *Electrical world,* April 19, 1913, p. 832.

SEED, C. R. Reasons for different rates, *Power,* March 16, 1915, p. 383.

SELLING energy along interurban railways. *Electric railway journal,* Oct. 28, 1916, p. 922-5.

SERVICE rates and power-factor. *Electrical world,* Nov. 27, 1915, p. 1209.

SHAAD, GEORGE CARL and C. A. JOHNSON. Measurement of electrical energy, electricity meters, rates for electrical energy University of Kansas, 1916, 93p (Bulletin v. 17, no. 11, Engineering bulletin no, 8.)

ELECTRIC LIGHT AND POWER COMPANIES —RATES—(Continued)

SHELDON, P. H. Controversy over electric rates in Houston, Texas. *Municipal engineering*, Oct. 1914, p. 275-8.

SHELDON, P. H. Houston, Texas, has co-operative lighting franchise. *Municipal engineering*, Jan. 1915, p. 41-3.

SHELDON, P. H. New electric light and power rates in Houston, Texas. *American City*, Jan. 1915, p. 27-8.

SIMPLE rate system. *Electrical review and western electrician*, Nov. 27, 1915, p. 978.

SIMPLIFIED rate schedule of Springfield, Mass., company. *Electrical review and western electrician*, Oct. 23, 1915, p. 753.

SMITH, W. A. Electric-service rates. *Electrical world*, March 21, 1914, p. 658-9.

SOUTHERN CALIFORNIA EDISON is allowed rate increase. *Electrical review*, April 24, 1920, p. 690.

SPECIAL contract for housing of employes. *Electrical world*, May 25, 1918, p. 1092-3.

SPRINGFIELD (Mo.) company asks for rehearing of rate order. *Electrical world*, Aug. 8, 1914, p. 268.

STATEMENT of the rate situation in Illinois. *Electrical world*, June 7, 1919, p. 1221.

STEP meter rate being discouraged in New York. *Electrical world*, Oct. 26, 1918, p. 797. *Electrical review*, Oct. 26, 1918, p. 665.

STREET, A. L. H. Regulation of power rates. *Power*, Aug. 4, 1914, p. 174-5.

STREET-LIGHTING rates for New Brunswick, N. J. *Electrical review and western electrician*, Aug. 12, 1916, p. 283.

SUBSTANTIAL rate increase authorized in California. *Electrical world*, Jan. 18, 1919, p. 146.

SUGGESTED sliding scale for dividends for street railways determined by quality of service. *Engineering and contracting*, Aug. 7, 1912, p. 658.

SUPREME court decision on the Kings county lighting co. rate case, New York. *Engineering and contracting*, April 29, 1914, p. 509-11.

SURCHARGE still needed says New Jersey company. *Electrical world*, June 7, 1919, p. 1234.

SYKES, W. and G. BRIGHT. Mining loads for central stations. *American Institute of electrical engineers, Proceedings*, May 1913, p. 1006-14.

TARR, F. Central station rate making. *Power*, Dec. 7, 1915, p. 798-9.

TESTIMONY before the Maryland public service commission in connection with its investigation into the rates charged for gas and electricity by the consolidated gas, electric light and power company. *Electric world*, Sept. 14, 1912, p. 548-9.

THEORETICAL basis of the multiple-rate system. *Electrical world*, May 24, 1913, p. 1070-1.

TOMLINSON, L. C. Systems of charges for energy. *Electrical world*, April 11, 1914, p. 830-1.

TOONE, C. Rate considerations for light and power service. *Electrical engineering*, May 1914.

UNION gas and electric company, Cincinnati, rates. *Electrical review and western electrician*, Nov. 28, 1914, p. 1043-4.

UNIQUE fare concession in New York. *Electric railway journal*, April 5, 1913, p. 613.

VAN DEN HEUVEK, WILLIAM. Co-operative rate making schedules. *Journal of electricity, power and gas*, Aug. 8, 1914.

VINCENT, W. G. Elements of rate making. *Electrical review*, March 13, 1920, p. 451-2. Excerpts. *Electrical world*, Feb. 28, 1920, p. 502.

WALKER, H. B. Government furnishes cheap electricity in southern Idaho. *Power*, Feb. 16, 1915, p. 228-9.

WAR power problems met by California commission. *Electrical world*, May 11, 1918, p. 998-9.

WAR surcharge in Indianapolis power rates. *Electrical world*, Sept. 15, 1917, p. 525-6.

WAR-TIME electricity rates in Indianapolis. *Electrical review*, Aug. 17, 1918, p. 257-8.

WATERLOO municipal waterworks and electric light plant. *Electrical review and western electrician*, Jan. 9, 1915, p. 77-8.

WATKINS, G. P. Electrical rates in the opinion of the Wisconsin commission. *Quarterly journal of economics*, Feb. 1913, p. 373-8.

WATKINS, G. P. Electrical rates: the load factors and the density factor. *Quarterly journal of economics*, May 1916, p. 519-45.

WATSON, A. P. Original cost as a factor in regulations of gas and electric utilities. *Electrical review and western electrician*, June 27, 1914, p. 1279-80.

WENDALL, C. E. Electric service, energy and charges. *Electrical world*, Jan. 10, 1914, p. 99-100.

WESTCHESTER lighting company cases. *Electrical review and western electrician*, Jan. 2, 1915, p. 35-6.

WHAT commissions are doing in rates. *Electrical world*, June 8, 29, July 27, Aug. 31, 1918, p. 1189-90, 1356-7, 158-9, 397-8.

WHITEHORNE, E. E. Value of the poor man's business. *Electrical world*. Jan. 22, 1916, p. 201-3.

WHITTINGTON, W. P. Electric and steam service for buildings. *Electrcial review and western electrician*, Dec. 23, 1916, p. 1091-3. Abstract. *Electrical world*, Dec. 23, 1916, p. 1240.

WILCOX, NORMAN T. Some reasons for difference in price for different electric services. *Public Service*, June 1911, p. 178-9.

WINSLOW, WILLIAM H. Rate making for central stations. *Electrical world*, Jan. 3, 1914, p. 12-3.

WISCONSIN. RAILROAD COMMISSION. Rates of public utilities in Wisconsin. Madison Railroad commission, 1917. 482p.

WISCONSIN COMMISSION lowers rates. *American municipalities*, March 1919, p. 181-4.

WISCONSIN commission news. *Electrical world*, July 15, 1911, p. 153-4.

WOEHLKE, W. V. Coast cities tame the light trust. *Technical world magazine*, Sept. 1913, p. 28-32.

WOLFORD, R. H. Establishing simple basis for rates. *Electrical world*, Aug. 21, 1920, p. 382-3.

WRIGHTINGTON, E. N. Sliding scale method of regulating public service corporations. *National municipal league*, 1910, p. 103-8.

WYER, S. S. Rate regulation of electric power. *Cassier's magazine*, Jan. 1909, p. 410.

Statistics

CHASE, HARVEY STUART. Holyoke water power company, petitioners v. city of Holyoke, statistics and computations from the annual reports of the Board of gas and electric light commissioners, the returns of certain companies to the commission and the evidence in the case. Boston, George H. Ellis, 1900. 31p.

UNITED STATES. BUREAU OF CENSUS. Census of electrical industries, 1917: central electric light and power stations with summary of the electrical industries. Washington, Government printing office, 1920. 184p.

Stores systems

BRADY, J. T. Tracing storeroom material. New York, National electric light association, 1911. 12p.

MCARDIE, W. P. Store room and tool records. (In *Pennsylvania electric association convention*, Sept. 6-8, 1916).

OFFICE and stock-room methods. *Electrical world*, April 24, 1915, p. 1036.

ELECTRIC LIGHT AND POWER COMPANIES —STORES SYSTEMS—*(Continued)*

REPORT of committee on purchasing and storeroom accounting; with discussion, W. F. Stevens. *National electric light association, 42d convention; Accounting section sessions,* 1919, p. 132-9.

SYMPOSIUM on "inventions and appraisals of properties" by C. L. Cory, W. G. Vincent and W. J. Norton, *American institute of electrical engineers Proceedings,* Sept. 1915, p. 21-49. Discussion, Feb. 1916, p. 236-63. Abstract. *Electrical review and western electrician,* Sept. 25, 1915, p. 568.

Valuation

ABENDROTH, HARRY G. Overhead charges in valuation; a discussion of the elements that must be considered in the appraisal of public utilities; percentages as worked out in the experience of the Milwaukee electric light and railway co. *Milwaukee Aera,* Nov. 1914, p. 354. *Electric railway journal,* June 27, 1914, p. 1434-7.

AMERICAN ELECTRIC RAILWAY ASSOCIATION. Committee on valuation. Bibliography on valuation of public utilities to December 23, 1915. 61+72p.

APPRAISAL of street lighting service. *Engineering record,* July 27, 1912, p. 104.

BRIDGE, J. Rating of electricity supply works. *Accountant,* July 29, Aug. 5, 1905, p. 135-41. 158-62.

BRITTON, JOHN A. Pacific gas rate valuation. *Progressive age,* April 15, 1912, p. 330.

BROOKLYN rate order not accepted. *Electrical world,* Dec. 2, 1916, p. 1093-4.

BRYAN, W. H. Going value as an element in the appraisal of public utility properties. *Journal of the association of engineering societies,* Oct. 1909, p. 147. Abstract. *Engineering and contracting,* Dec. 22, 1909, p. 549-51.

BYLLESBY, H. M. Responsibilities of electrical engineers in making appraisals. *Electric railway journal,* July 1, 1911, p. 16-18.

BYLLESBY, H. M. Responsibilities of electrical engineers in making appraisals. *American institute of electrical engineers, Proceedings,* Sept. 1911, p. 2013-27.

CINCINNATI rate case. *Electrical world,* Aug. 14, 1915, p. 377-8.

CORY, C. L., W. G. VINCENT and WILLIAM J. NORTON. Symposium on "inventories and appraisals of properties." *American institute of electrical engineers, Proceedings,* Sept. 1915, p. 2131-63. Abstract *Electrical review and western electrician,* Sept. 25, 1915, p. 568.

DARLING, B. G. Justice of the power-factor rate. *Electrical world,* Sept. 13-27, 1919, p. 586-7, 660-1, 708-10.

DECISION of court of appeals in the Kings county lighting company case. *Electrical review and western electrician,* April 11, 1914, p. 729-31.

DREYFUS, EDWIN D. Appraisement of small electric properties. *Electric review and western electrician,* March 6, 13, 1915, p. 433-8, 500-5.

DRUAR, JOHN F. Rates and rate making. *Journal of the association of engineering societies,* May 1913, p. 221.

ERICKSON, HALFORD. Making rates for electric plants. *Public service regulation,* Sept. 1912, p. 579.

EXPERTS differ widely on Philadelphia electric plant renewal costs. *Electrical world,* March 11, 1916, p. 584.

FAIR overhead charges allowed; Bronx gas and electric company. *Electric railway journal,* Oct. 16, 1915, p. 831.

FOWLER, CLARENCE P. Some criteria of value in public service industries. *Engineering magazine,* March 1912, p. 873.

GILLETT, HALBERT P. Appraisal of electric properties and the uses to which appraisals may be put. *Engineering and contracting,* Nov. 8, 1911, p. 506. Abstract. *Electric railway journal,* Oct. 28, 1911, p. 948.

GOLSAN, P. Interest charges during construction. *Electrical world,* July 17, 1920, p. 116-7.

HENRIQUES, J. C. Power plant inventory. *Electric railway journal,* March 25, 1916, p. 616-8.

INDIANAPOLIS electric rate cases. *Electrical review and western electrician,* Aug. 7, 1915, p. 235-7.

JACKSON, D. C. Appraisals of electric light and power properties. *National electric light association, Accounting sessions, papers, reports and discussions,* 1914, p. 163.

LOEBENSTEIN, JOHN. Determining first cost of Edison tube system. *Electrical world,* Oct. 7, 1916, p. 713.

McKAY, CHARLES W. Origin of electric rate control. *Electric review,* May 17, 1919, p. 796-8.

McKAY, CHARLES W. Practice in making electric utility appraisals. *Electric review,* Aug. 9, Sept. 13, 1919, p. 226-30, 428-33.

McKAY, CHARLES W. Reproduction cost as applied to the appraisement of electric utilities. *Electric review,* June 28, 1919, p. 1074-7.

McKAY, CHARLES W. Terms used in rate case defined. *Electric review,* June 7, 1919, p. 934-6.

PACIFIC gas and electric company valuation methods. *Electrical world,* Feb. 27, 1915, p. 569-70. *American gas light journal,* March 22, 1915, p. 179.

PECK, B. H. Engineering data necessary for an electric rate determination. *Journal of the western society of engineers,* Jan. 1918, p. 1-20. Excerpts. *Electrical world,* April 20, 1918, p. 825-7. Discussion. *Journal of the western society of engineers,* Jan. 1918, p. 20-7.

PUBLIC service commission news. *Electrical world,* Nov. 30, 1912, p. 1136.

RATE readjustment in California case. *Electrical world,* July 12, 1919, p. 90.

REASONABLE charge for off-peak electric current. *Power,* Aug. 20, 1918, p. 275-6.

REPORT on St. Louis rates and valuations. *Electrical world,* March 16, 1911, p. 656-8.

ROLLINS, R. W., H. H. HOLDING and A. WILLIAMS. Evaluating the isolated plant. *Electrical world,* March 27, 1915, p. 772-3.

SOUTHERN CALIFORNIA Edison case decision. *Electrical world,* Sept. 16, 1916, p. 556-7.

STATUS of Los Angeles power negotiations. *Electrical world,* Nov. 4, 1916, p. 896-7.

STORER, S. B. Relation of load factor to the evaluation of hydro-electric plants. *American institute of electrical engineers, Transactions,* 1906, p. 139.

SUPREME court decision on the King's county lighting co. rate case, New York. *Engineering and contracting,* April 29, 1914, p. 509-11.

TRIBUS, LOUIS L. Unique problem in valuation; inheritance tax appraisal of the Hales Bar hydro-electric plant. *Engineering news,* Feb. 25, 1915, p. 384-5.

VALUATION and rate making principles and precedents; abstract of brief presented to the public service commission of Missouri. *Electric railway journal,* May 2, 1914, p. 989-92.

VALUATION of Cleveland illuminating property. *Electrical world,* Jan. 27, 1917, p. 166.

VALUATION of electric plants. *Engineering record,* Oct. 3, 1908, p. 365.

VALUATION of Los Angeles distributing system. *Electrical world,* Jan. 22, 1916, p. 192-5.

ELECTRIC LIGHT AND POWER COMPANIES
—VALUATION—*(Continued)*

VALUATION of Milford, Mass., utility property. *Electrical review and western electrician,* Oct. 23, 1915, p. 751-2.

VALUATION of the property of the Kansas city electric light company. *Electrical world,* May 22, 1915, p. 1343.

VALUATION of two street railway power plants. *Engineering and contracting,* Sept. 28, 1910, p. 280-1.

VALUE of water rights and going concern in California. *Electrical world,* June 9, 1917, p. 1129.

WASHINGTON water power company's valuation. *Power,* July 30, 1918, p. 179.

WELLS, W. F. Elements affecting the fair valuation of plant and property. *National electric light association, paper, reports and discussions,* 1911, p. 271.

WHAT commissions are doing on rates. *Electrical world,* June 8, 29, July 27, Aug. 31, 1918, p. 1189-90, 1356-7, 158-9, 397-8.

WHITTEN, ROBERT H. Bibliography. (In his *Valuation of public service corporations.* 1914. p. 723-4).

WILLIAMS, W. H. Valuation of public service corporations. New York. *American economic association quarterly,* April 1910, p. 196-238. *Electric railway journal,* Jan. 8, 1910, p. 76-7.

WYER, S. S. Rate regulation of electric power. *Cassier's magazine,* Jan. 1909, p. 410.

ELECTRIC light and power rates. *Public service regulation,* Feb. 1913, p. 100.

ELECTRIC LIGHTING
See Electric light and power companies.

ELECTRIC lighting accounts. Johnson, George. 1903.

ELECTRIC lighting companies and depreciation. *Accountant,* April 11, 1903, p. 490-1.

ELECTRIC lighting rates in some of the principal cities in the United States. Comparative electric power rates in some American cities. *Los Angeles, California, Board of public utilities, Report,* 1915, p. 21-2.

ELECTRIC LINES

Costs

BEARD, J. R. Design of high pressure distributing systems. *Journal of the Institute of electrical engineers,* Jan. 1, 1916, p. 125-41.

COMPARATIVE cost of steel and wooden pole transmission line. *Electrical review,* Jan. 26, 1918, p. 163.

CONCORD, N. H., company shows increased costs from 21 per cent to 285 per cent. *Electrical world,* June 16, 1917, p. 1178.

CONSTRUCTION costs for two 100,000 volt Montana transmission lines. *Electrical world,* Aug. 19, 1916, p. 371.

CONSTRUCTION costs on substation, high tension line and street lighting. *Electrical review and western electrician,* Jan. 1, 1916, p. 34.

COST data on 6,600 volt line. *Electrical world,* July 3, 1915, p. 16.

COST of constructing a short transmission line. *Electrical world,* May 15, 1915, p. 1244.

COST of erecting 110,000 volt transmission lines. *Electrical world,* June 7, 1913, p. 1259.

COST of installing street lighting cables in Boston. *Electrical world,* May 20, 1916, p. 1165.

COST of line materials; data prepared by the Amesbury (Mass.) electric light company *Electrical world,* May 19, 1917, p. 967.

COST of rural lines and revenue therefrom. *Electrical world,* Oct. 7, 1916, p. 708-10.

COST of 66,000 volt transmission line. *Electrical world,* April 10, 1915, p. 904.

COST of transmission lines in New England. *Electrical world,* July 17, 1915, p. 135.

COSTS of extensions. *Electrical world,* May 8, 1915, p. 1191.

COSTS of material for 660 volt line construction. *Electrical world,* May 17, 1913, p. 1047.

CUSHING, A. S. B. Increased cost of line extensions. *Electrical world,* April 20, 1918, p. 832.

DESIGN, construction and unit costs of the power house for the new smelter of the Arizona copper co. ltd., Clifton, Arizona. *Engineering and contracting,* Sept. 16, 1914, p. 262-5.

DETAILED cost of 13,000-volt line. *Electrical world,* Jan. 15, 1916, p. 155.

ESTIMATED cost of overhead inter connection. *Electrical world,* Mar. 22, 1919, p. 583-4.

FENTON, H. H. Inexpensive rural transmission line. *Electrical world,* Sept. 30, 1916, p. 672-3.

GILLETT, HALBERT P. and RICHARD T. DANA. Overhead electrical transmission and distribution. (In their *Handbook of mechanical and electrical cost data.* 1918. p. 878-963).

GILLETT, HALBERT P. and RICHARD T. DANA. Underground electrical transmission and distribution. (In their *Handbook of mechanical and electrical cost data.* 1918. p. 964-1022).

GOODWIN, H. Practical economics in distribution with their effect on the commercial policy of a central station company. *General electric review,* Dec. 1914, p. 1159-74.

HAUSHALTER, F. L. Studies in wood, steel and concrete pole line costs. *Electric review,* April 6-20, 1918, p. 587-9, 625-9, 667-70.

HOOK, E. B. Unit costs for setting transmission line wood poles. *Electrical world,* Feb. 24, 1917, p. 372.

ITEMIZED cost of line construction. *Electrical world,* April 27, 1918, p. 880.

ITEMIZED cost of 33,000 volt transmission line in central Illinois. *Electrical review,* Aug. 2, 1919, p. 207.

LINE construction cost; data presented before Massachusetts public service commission. *Electrical world,* Aug. 18, 1917, p. 301.

MORGAN, JOHN D. Labor data pertaining to installation of cables. *Electrical world,* March 15, 1919, p. 532-3.

MOXEY, L. W. Data on cost of overhead and underground construction. *Electrical world,* Dec. 18, 1915, p. 1378-9.

OAKES, CHARLES E. and W. ECKLEY. Characteristics of iron and steel conductors. *Electrical world,* Oct. 14, 1916, p. 761-2.

POLE lines of C. M. & St. P. electrification; comparative costs of wood pole and steel-tower construction. *Electrical review and western electrician,* Sept. 30, 1916, p. 590-3.

ELECTRIC LOCOMOTIVES.
See Locomotives.

ELECTRIC manufacturing companies' accounts. *Electric review* (London), Dec. 18, 1908.

ELECTRIC motor saves $200 over gasoline-engine costs. *Electrical review and western electrician,* February 12, 1916, p. 289.

ELECTRIC PLANTS.
See Electric, light and power companies; Power plants.

ELECTRIC power cost, a year's record for generating power at the colliery mouth. *Iron age,* July 27, 1911, p. 199.

ELECTRIC power costs at El Tigre. *Engineering and mining journal,* March 8, 1913, p. 523-4.

ELECTRIC public utilities. *Aera,* Nov. 1913, p. 405.

ELECTRIC railway accounting. Brockway, Walter Belding. 1906.

ELECTRIC railway appraisals. *Electric Railway journal,* Nov. 2, 1907, p. 905.

ELECTRIC railway appraisals. *Electric Railway journal,* March 21, 1908, p. 446.

ELECTRIC railway auditing and accounting. Forse, W. H. 1908.

ELECTRIC railway auditor his duties and relations to the organization. Brockway, W. B.

ELECTRIC railway must not become anti-social *Electric railway journal,* June 19, 1920, p. 1269.

ELECTRIC railway securities from the investor's standpoint. *American electric railway association, Proceedings,* 1913, p. 217.

ELECTRIC railway system of Milwaukee and Eastern Wisconsin. *Street railway journal,* June 1899, p. 352.

ELECTRIC railways in the United States and Canada which have recently been granted permission by regulatory bodies to increase their fares where such consent is unnecessary. *Aera,* Feb. 1918, p. 625-9.

ELECTRIC rate discussion in Chicago. *Electrical world,* July 26, 1913, p. 174-5.

ELECTRIC rate increase movement. *Public service,* Chicago, 1918, p. 154-6.

ELECTRIC rate increase to follow high cost of coal. *Electrical world,* Feb. 2, 1918, p. 240-1.

ELECTRIC rates and classification of customers. *Electrical world,* Feb. 15, 1913, p. 352-4.

ELECTRIC recording time clocks for Panama canal shops. *Electric review and western electrician,* Aug. 22, 1914, p. 390-1.

ELECTRIC SHOPS

CRAIN, G. D. Business hints for dealers. *Electrical review and western electrician,* May 1, Oct. 9, 23, Nov. 20, 1915, p. 809-10; 664-5, 755-6, 932-3.

Accounting

FUNKHAUSER, ROBERT D. Bookkeeping system for Delco-light dealers; a descriptive booklet. Dayton, Delco-light company, c1919. 119p.

Cost accounting

BUTZ, R. H. Cost-accounting methods for dealers. *Electrical review,* Sept. 8, 1917, p. 425-6.

STRATTON, GEORGE FREDERIC. Labor-cost distribution at the general electric shop. *Engineering magazine,* March 1908.

ELECTRIC shovel for underground mining. *Scientific American,* May 3, 1919, p. 468.

ELECTRIC SHOVELS

Costs

COMPARATIVE operating costs of steam shovels and electric shovels. *Engineering and contracting,* March 11, 1914, p. 293-4.

COST of electric shovel work at Cleveland. *Electric railway journal,* Dec. 5, 1914, p. 1261-2. *Electrical review and western electrician,* Jan. 23, 1915, p. 172-3.

ELECTRIC shovel for underground mining. *Scientific American,* May 3, 1919, p. 468.

METHODS and cost of electric shovel work; removing slides and side cutting for electric railway. *Engineering and contracting,* Feb. 17, 1915, p. 154-5.

ELECTRIC station costs. Power, March, 6, 1917, p. 310.

ELECTRIC STORES

See Electric shops.

ELECTRIC supply company and depreciation of assets; from the *Statist. Accountant,* Jan. 13, 1900, p. 57-9.

ELECTRIC tramway accounting and finance. *Electrical review* (London), Dec. 13, 1907, p. 959.

ELECTRIC tramway costing and statistics. *Electrical review* (London) Dec. 10, 1909, pt. 1.

ELECTRIC truck reduces cost of coal handling. *Electrical review,* Dec. 28, 1918, p. 1017-8. *Electrical world,* Jan. 11, 1919, p. 86. *Iron trade review,* Jan. 16, 1919, p. 210.

ELECTRIC truck saves $800 a year on horse equipment. *Electrical review and western electrician,* May 26, 1917, p. 897. *Electrical world,* June 2, 1917, p. 1068.

ELECTRIC TRUCKS.

See Automobiles.

ELECTRIC trucks show economy in San Francisco delivery work; daily averages for December 1915. *Electrical review,* Aug. 18, 1917, p. 286.

ELECTRIC utilities accounting. Clader, W. A.

ELECTRIC vehicle department of the Rochester railway and light company—results of experience in the operation of electric vehicles—system of inspection and forms of report. *Electrical world,* April 6, 1912, p. 743-4.

ELECTRIC-vehicle research at the Massachusetts Institute of Technology—special department established to determine comparative costs of operating electric, gasoline, and horse vehicles. *Electrical world,* April 6, 1912, p. 740-3.

ELECTRIC vehicles for meat delivery. *Electrical world,* Aug. 16, 1913, p. 320.

ELECTRICAL ENGINEERING.

See Engineering.

ELECTRICAL engineers and depreciation. *Accountant,* June 25, 1910, p. 891.

ELECTRICAL maintenance methods in a great office building; Equitable building, New York City. *Electrical world,* Jan. 22, 1916, p. 206-8.

ELECTRICAL manufacturers' accounting and cost system; council makers preliminary issue. *Electrical world,* May 26, 1917, p. 1025.

ELECTRICAL refrigeration at 11.7 cents a day. *Electrical world,* May 8, 1915, p. 1202.

ELECTRICAL tabulating machine applied to cost accounting. *American machinist,* July 31, 1902.

ELECTRICALLY driven dragline scrapers dig 45-mile irrigation canal at Sun river project. *Engineering record,* Jan. 29, 1916, p. 148.

ELECTRICITY for irrigation pumping. *Electrical review and western electrician,* June 5, 1915, p. 1022-8.

ELECTRICITY supply accounts. *Electrical review,* v. 52, p. 277-8.

ELECTRICITY works accounts of various municipal electric supply works in Great Britain. *Electrician,* 1898. See index for paging.

ELECTRICS in express service. *Good roads,* Oct. 1, 1919, p. 168.

ELECTRIFYING a water meter factory. *Electrical world,* Oct. 4, 1913, p. 694-5.

ELECTRO PLATING
Accounting
BADGER, ARTHUR. Manufacturer's trading account: its divisions and departments as applied to any one of the following businesses (1) electro plate (2) cutlery including saw, steel, and file trades (3) rolling mills. *Accountant,* June 25, 1892, p. 508-19.

ELECTROPLATING costs by the square foot. *Foundry,* April 1913, p. 158-9.

ELEMENTARY accounting problems. Wildman, J. R. 1914.

ELEMENTARY agriculture and practical arithmetic. Hatch, K. L. and J. A. Haselwood. 1907.

ELEMENTARY bookkeeping. Cropper, L. C. 1910.

ELEMENTARY bookkeeping. Day, W. G. 1901.

ELEMENTARY bookkeeping. Hamilton and Ball. 1896.

ELEMENTARY bookkeeping. Nichols, F. G. 1918.

ELEMENTARY bookkeeping. Shaw, J. W.

ELEMENTARY bookkeeping. Spicer, E. E. and E. C. Pegler.

ELEMENTARY bookkeeping. Tolmie, D. 1885.

ELEMENTARY bookkeeping. Turner, F. W. 1918.

ELEMENTARY bookkeeping. Webster, J. E. and Harry Hughes. 1906.

ELEMENTARY bookkeeping by double entry for evening continuation schools and day schools. Cary, R. H.

ELEMENTARY bookkeeping for day and evening schools and commercial classes. Munro, Andrew. 1910.

ELEMENTARY bookkeeping for schools. Munro, Andrew.

ELEMENTARY bookkeeping in theory and practice, with examples, exercises (and) solutions. Lisle, George. 1894.

ELEMENTARY double-entry bookkeeping. Taylor, J. W. 1898.

ELEMENTARY manual of statistics. Bowlery, Arthur L. 1915.

ELEMENTARY principles of single entry bookkeeping. Hutchinson, C. G. and W. S. Parker. 1884.

ELEMENTARY treatise on bookkeeping by single and double entry. Crittenden, S. W. 1852.

ELEMENTARY treatise on check figure systems. Hay, G. H. 1908.

ELEMENTARY treatise on graphs. Gibson, George A. 1904.

ELEMENTS de comptabilite financiere a l' usage du levant publies par un groupe de professeurs. Novelle edition. Constantinople, Procure des Freres Maristes. (Enclos St Benoit) 343p.

ELEMENTS involved in rate investigation; report of committee of Canadian electrical association. *Electrical world,* June 23, 1917, p. 1213-4.

ELEMENTS of a valid trust. *Trust companies,* Sept. 1913, p. 181.

ELEMENTS of accounting, theory and practice. Klein, J. J. 1916.

ELEMENTS of accounts. Murray, G. S. 1907.

ELEMENTS of accounts for individuals, professional men and institutions. Rittenhouse, C. F. 1918.

ELEMENTS of bookkeeping. Dewhirst, J. M. 1910.

ELEMENTS of bookkeeping. Jenkinson, M. W. 1907.

ELEMENTS of bookkeeping. Kelly, P. 1805.

ELEMENTS of bookkeeping. Palmer, J. H. 1878.

ELEMENTS of bookkeeping, both by single and double entry. Kelly, P.

ELEMENTS of bookkeeping by single and double entry. Isbister, A. K. 1854, 1856, 1897.

ELEMENTS of bookkeeping, by single and double entry. Morrison,, James.

ELEMENTS of bookkeeping, for schools; printed and published by direction of the Commissioners of National Education, Ireland. Dublin, 1850, 1859, 1863, 1870, 1872, 1882.

ELEMENTS of business law. Huffcut, Ernest Wilson, 1917.

ELEMENTS of charge for public utility service. *Municipal engineering,* March 1914, p. 274-5.

ELEMENTS of cost accounting. Belser, F. C.

ELEMENTS of cost in street lighting. *Electrical world,* Nov. 22, 1913, p. 1065-6.

ELEMENTS of practical bookkeeping. Streeter, T. E. 1896.

ELEMENTS of railroad value that might be overlooked. *Engineering record,* April 24, 1915, p. 523-4.

ELEMENTS of railway economics. Acworth, W. M. 1905.

ELEMENTS of record keeping for child helping organization. Ralph, G. G. 1915.

ELEMENTS of state budget making. *Municipal research,* Dec. 1916, 63p.

ELEMENTS of statistical method. King, W. I. 1916.

ELEMENTS of the theory and practice of bookkeeping, based upon the principles of correlative double entry. Walmsley, John. 1906.

ELEMENTS of value in a street railway. *Railroad gazette,* Dec. 28, 1906, p. 567.

ELEMENTS of value of a public utility. *Engineering record,* Oct. 17, 1914, p. 433-4.

ELEMENTS of water works accounting. *Engineering and contracting,* Dec. 30, 1914, p. 600-2.

ELEVATED RAILROADS.
See Electric and street railroads.

ELEVATED values in Chicago. *Electric railway journal,* May 18, 1912, p. 817.

ELEVATORS
See also Grain elevators.

Cost accounting
ARNOLD, HORACE L. Pratt's record scroll. *American machinist,* Sept. 17, 1903.

Costs
BAILEY, JOHN. Operating costs of hydraulic vs. electric elevators. *Power,* May 6, 1913, p. 644.
LIGHTY, W. G. Operating costs in a power plant. *Power,* Aug. 18, 1914, p. 238-40.
NAYLOR, C. W. Operating costs of electric elevators. *Power,* Feb. 5, 1918, p. 188-9.

ELGAR, W. D.
Corporation profits tax. *Incorporated accountants' journal,* Dec. 1920, p. 51-6.

——— **AND W. G. BLAKEMORE**
Theatre accounts. (In Lisle, George. *Encyclopaedia of accounting.* v. 6. p. 210-22).

——— **AND OTHERS**
Private companies and income tax. *Incorporated accountants' journal,* 1908-9, p. 227.
Stating of a balance sheet. *Incorporated accountants' journal,* 1900-1, p. 192.
Surprise visits of auditors. *Incorporated accountants journal,* 1900-1, p. 96.
What is gross profit? *Incorporated accountants journal,* 1898-9, p. 217.

ELIMINATING pencil balances. *Business man's magazine,* April 1911, p. 395.

ELIMINATING the monthly statement. *Business man's magazine,* July 1911, p. 66-7.

ELIMINATING useless trucking from the factory; Ford motor co. *Industrial engineering,* December 1913, p. 506-8.

ELIOT, C. W.
Road to industrial peace. *Nation's business.* Aug. 1917, p. 14-17.

ELKIN, J. J.
Work of the accounting department. *Cincincinnati railway club Proceedings.* Sept. 1916, p. 550-76.

ELKINS, A. F.
Some essentials of public service accounting. *Elertric railway journal,* Dec. 20, 1913, p. 1276.

——— **AND OTHERS**
Central electric railway accountants' association. *Electric railway journal,* June 28, 1913, p. 1168.

ELLERMAN, JOHN REEVES
Companies acts, 1862-80. ***Accountant,* June** 30, 1883.

ELLICK, F. I.
Chart demonstration of the standard uniform cost finding system. *International cost congress of employing printers of America, Proceedings,* 1911, p. 57-73.
Exposition of the standard cost finding system. *International cost congress of employing printers of America, Proceedings,* 1910, p. 76-92.

ELLIOTT, BERTON
System for reducing complaints. *Business man's magazine,* Dec. 1908, p. 480.

ELLIOTT, C. A.
Tool list as aid in economical maintenance of way. *Electric railway journal,* Feb. 8, 1919, p. 271.

ELLIOTT, CHARLES W.
Way to industrial goodwill *Textile world,* April 24, 1920, p. 3012. Discussion, p. 3014.

ELLIOTT, E. CASSLETON
Mining accounts. *Incorporated accountants' journal,* June 1912, p. 247-52.

ELLIOTT, E. M.
Keeping watch on materials. *Factory,* March 1917, p. 332.

ELLIOTT, G.
Mercantile law (principal and agent) *Accountant,* Jan. 14, 21, 1888, p. 27, 38.

ELLIOTT, HOWARD
Hearing before the Interstate commerce commission in the matter of the revenue needs of the railroads; opening statement for the railroads. New York, Association of railway executives. 1920.. 22p.
Problems in connection with federal valuation of the railways. *Trust companies,* 1916, v. 22, p. 264-70.
Transportation needs of the country; abstracts. *Commercial and financial chronicle,* May 29, 1920, p. 2254-5. *Railway age,* May 28, 1920, p. 1517-20. *Railway review,* May 29, 1920, p. 865-9.

ELLIOTT, J. R.
Cost system of Denver combination shop. *Metal work,* Aug. 27, 1915, p. 274-8.

ELLIOTT-FISHER COMPANY, HARRISBURG, PA.
Bookkeeping by machinery; a text book for the guidance of the novice or expert; dedicated to the cause of accounting control. Harrisburg, Elliott-Fisher co. c1918. 121p.

ELLIS, C. B.
Practical bookkeeping. Boston, Allyn & Bacon. 1908.
Reference book for use with Ellis's practical bookkeeping. Boston, Allyn & Bacon, 1908.
Teaching of bookkeeping. *Journal of education,* April 23, 1914, p. 464.

ELLIS, F. W .
Bookkeeping. Infield, 1883.

ELLIS, L. W.
Data on advertising department records. A. W. Shaw, 1917.

ELLIS, N. R.
San Francisco water rate case. Philadelphia utilities bureau. 1917.

ELLIS, R. L.
Cost accounting as applied to selling gas. *Gas age,* Aug. 15, 1919, p. 184, 186.
Rates for electricity. *Engineering magazine,* May 1912, p. 227-33.

ELLIS, WILLIAM
Railway wages, January-July 1919, as reported by the Director general compared with December 1917, and the year 1915 together with the increases in 1919 wages under demands pending April 1920, and the increases in the outlaw strike April 1920. Brooklyn, c1920. 21p.

ELLIS method of home accounting. Wilson, L. A. 1918.

ELLIS PUBLISHING COMPANY
Business directions used in connections with Ellis industrial bookkeeping. Battle Creek, Mich., Ellis publishing co. 1912. 75p.
Cabinet manual. Battle Creek, Mich., Ellis publishing co.
Guide to accompany the Ellis tablet method of teaching bookkeeping; elementary course. Battle Creek, Mich., Ellis publishing co. 1919. 93p.
Guide to Ellis system of actual business training. Battle Creek, Mich., Ellis publishing co.
Students' guide to accompany the Ellis cabinet system of teaching bookkeeping and business practice. Revised ed. Battle Creek, Mich. Ellis publishing co. 1910.
Student's guide to accompany the Ellis tablet method of teaching bookkeeping and business practice: complete course. Battle Creek, Mich., Ellis publishing co. 1910.
Student's tablet of transactions (elementary course); the tablet method of teaching bookkeeping and business training. Battle Creek, Mich., Ellis publishing company, 1919. 109p.
Tablet method of teaching bookkeeping. Battle Creek, Mich., Ellis publishing co.

ELLISON, WILLIAM B.
Pressing financial problems: the inordinate growth of budgets and taxes. *Economic world,* Jan. 27, 1917, p. 125-6.

ELLMS, J. W.
Cost of filter plant operation at Cincinnati. *Engineering and contracting,* Dec. 13, 1916, p. 537-8.

ELLSWORTH, H. W.
Book-keeping and business manual, single and double entry. 2 parts. New York, Taintor bros., Merrill & co.
Book-keeping, single and double entry, and business manual. New York, Author. 1868.
Industrial farm bookkeeping, Mont Vale, N. J. Ellsworth co.
Single and double entry bookkeeping manual. Mont Vale, N. J., Ellsworth co.
Steps of book-keeping single and double entry. New York, Taintor bros. Merril & co.
Steps or shorter course bookkeeping (single and double entry). Mont Vale, Ellsworth co.

ELMES, C. F.
"Normal" value in appraisals. *Engineering and contracting,* Jan. 21, 1920, p. 66-70.
Price levels in relation to value. *Mechanical engineering,* Oct. 1920, p. 553-7.

ELOQUENT advertisement. *Journal of accountancy,* April, June 1916, p. 285-6, 444.

ELOQUENT possibilities of advertising. *Journal of accountancy,* Dec. 1915 p. 455-6.

ELSAS, O.
Piece rate system for wages in cottton mills. *Textile world,* May 1915, p. 213-7.

ELSMAN, R.
Modern utilities organization. *American gas engineering journal,* July 20, Aug. 10, 1918, p. 49-51, 121-3.

ELSON, HENRY WILLIAM
History of the United States of America. New York, The Macmillan co. 1918. 950p.

ELSWWORTH, R. H.
Duplicate receipts for newspaper subscriptions. New form for editors. *Business man's magazine,* Aug. 1908, p. 118.
System for keeping the accounts of a creamery. *Business man's magazine,* May 1908, p. 427-9.

ELSWORTH, THOMAS
Building society accounts and their audit. *Accountant,* Feb. 15, 1913, p. 220-32.

ELWELL, D.
Use of central-station power by large users; abstracts. *Electrical review and western electrician,* Oct. 21, 1916, p. 720. *Electrical world,* Nov. 11, 1916, p. 958-9.

ELWELL, FAYETTE H.
How to find costs by proper distribution of overhead expense. *Paper,* May 26, 1920, p. 13-5.
Laboratory manual; elements of accounting. Madison, Wis., Parker co. 1920.
Problem of standardizing university courses in accounting. *American association of university instructors, Papers and proceedings,* May 1917, p. 19-41.
See also Miner, George Washington, joint author.

ELWORTHY, W. R. AND CLAUDE C. CAMPLING
Book-keeping for traders, manufacturers, and companies. Ed.3. London, Jordon and sons, 1904. 224p.

ELY, O.
Fallacy of the equated revenue cost unit. *Railway age,* July 25, 1913, p. 137.
Inadequacy of present depreciation accounts. *Railway age,* Sept. 20, 1918, p. 553-6. Discussion, D. J. Kerr, *Railway age,* Nov. 1, 1918, p. 764.

EMBEZZLEMENT.
See Defalcation; Fraud.

EMERGENCY irrigation rate for garden farming at Alhambra, Cal. *Engineering and contracting,* May 8, 1918, p. 459.

EMERSON, HARRINGTON
Bases of Emerson incentive; a discussion of the comparison of wage incentive systems. Industrial management, Dec. 1, 1920, p. 413-6.
Efficiency as a basis for operation and wages. Ed 4, revised and enlarged. New York, Engineering magazine co. c1914. 254p. (Works management library).
Efficiency method for determining costs to eliminate all wastes from foundry operations. *Iron trade review,* Jan. 30, 1908, p. 253-6.
Figuring the annual cost of ties. *Railway review,* Aug. 21, 1915, p. 235-6.

EMERSON, HARRINGTON—*(Continued)*
Fundamental truth of scientific management. *Journal of accountancy*, May 1911, p. 17-25.
Location and elimination of wastes. *Engineering magazine*, Jan. 1909, p. 676-83.
Modern theory of cost accounting. *Engineering magazine*, Dec. 1908, p. 336-46.
My objections to the piece rate method of wage payment. *Industrial management*, June-July 1919, p. 470-2; 17-20. Condensed. *Literary digest*, July 12, 1919, p. 106-8.
Percentage method of determining production costs. *Foundry*, Oct. 1904.
Practising efficiency and knowing costs; a letter to a New England manufacturer. New York, Emerson co. 1912. 12p.
Reliable, immediate, adequate, and permanent records. *Engineering magazine*, Jan. 1911, p. 496-506.
Revision of the A. F. A. standard cost system. *Foundry*, Jan. 1915, p. 7-8.
Twelve principles of efficiency. New York, Engineering magazine. 423p.

——— **AND T. T. BOWER**
Annual charge for ties. *Engineering magazine*, March 1915, p. 903-5.
Method of finding the annual charges for ties. *Engineering and contracting*, Feb. 17, 1915, p. 155-6.

——— **AND J. K. MASON**
Revision of American foundrymen's association standard cost system. *American foundrymen's association*, Sept. 1914.

EMERSON, HAVEN
Report of the committee on uniform administrative accounting for health departments. *American journal of public health*, July 1916, p. 746-50.

EMERY, GEORGE FREDERICK
Patent law. *Incorporated accountants journal*, 1898-9, p. 115.

EMERY, HENRY CROSBY
Should speculation be regulated by law? *Journal of accountancy*, April 1908, p. 425-41.

EMERY, JAMES A.
Future fare system for small cities. *Electric railway journal*, Oct. 4, 1919, p. 695.
Statistical units used in analysis of electric railway accounts. *American electric railway accountants' association, Proceedings*, 1913, p. 152-66, 403-18. *Electric railway journal*, Oct. 16, 1913, p. 815-7.

EMIG, W. R.
Stock system of a modern factory. *American machinist*, Dec. 7, 1911, p. 1065-7.

EMMET, BORIS
Extent of profit sharing in the United States; its bearing on industrial unrest. *Journal of political economy*, Dec. 1917, p. 1019-33.
Labor survey of Cleveland cloak industry; from the Monthly labor review (Aug. 1918) of the Bureau of labor statistics. United States department of labor. 24p.
Labor turnover and employment policies of a large motor vehicle manufacturing establishment; from the Monthly review (October, 1918) of the Bureau of labor statistics, United States department of labor, p. 837-54.
Profit sharing in the United States. Washington, Government printing office. 1917. 188p. (United States. Bureau of labor statistics, bulletin no. 208, miscellaneous series no. 13).
Will profit sharing solve labor difficulties? *Monthly review*, Aug. 1917, p. 245-52.

EMMOTT, LORD
Government control and industry. *Accountant*, Jan. 10, 1920, p. 53-8. *Public accountant*, April 30, 1920, p. 307-20.

EMPIRE TRUST CO.
Federal taxes affecting corporations; excess profits tax (Corporations and partnerships); corporation income tax; special excise tax on capital stock; also estate tax as amended. Philadelphia, National bank news, c1917.

EMPLOYEE representation in Illinois utility. *Electrical world*, June 26, 1920, p. 1493.

EMPLOYEE representation indorsed; president's second industrial conference reports. *Iron age*, March 25, 1920, p. 875-9.

EMPLOYEES
FAIRBANKS, C. E. Card record of employees. *Engineering magazine*, Jan. 1915, p. 573-5.
HAMMACK, H. C. Keeping employees' records and benefits therefrom. *Business man's magazine*, March 1906.
KOON, S. G. Card record of employees. *Engineering magazine*, April 1915, p. 88-90.

EMPLOYEES and federal valuation. *Railway age gazette*, Sept. 8, 1916, p. 411-2.

EMPLOYEES' pay checks. *Electric railway journal*, Sept. 7, 1918, p. 417.

EMPLOYEES' pension plan. Midvale steel and ordnance company and subsidiary companies. 1919.

EMPLOYEES' REPRESENTATION.
See Management—Employees representation.

EMPLOYEES' representation plan. Willys-Overland company. 1919.

EMPLOYERS' LIABILITY.
See Workmen's compensation.

EMPLOYES' profit sharing plan; Cities service co. *Gas age*, Aug. 15, 1917, p. 170-1.

EMPLOYES' savings and investment plan. General motors corporation.

EMPLOYMENT AGENCIES
PENNSYLVANIA—Bureau of employment established uniform receipt blanks for private employment agencies. *Pennsylvania department of labor and industry monthly bulletin*, Oct. 1916, p. 48-52.

Accounting
LEEMAN, J. B. Explanation of accounting system. (In *U. S. Department of labor, Employment service, Report of proceedings*, 1918, p. 78-80).

EMPLOYMENT blanks used by the Equitable life assurance company. *Journal of electricity*, March 15, 1919, p. 250.

EMPLOYMENT department and employee relations. Henerschott, F. C. and F. E. Weakly. 1918.

EMPLOYMENT MANAGEMENT
BANCKER, J. W. Records and reports of work. *Annals of the American academy of political and social science*, May 1916, p. 252-72.
BICKLEY, E. H. Records that match the man to the job. *Factory*, July 1918, p. 28-30.
BOWMAN, T. P. Employing a bookkeeper. *Motor age*, Oct. 31, 1918, p. 10-1.

EMPLOYMENT MANAGEMENT—*(Continued)*

BRISSENDEN, P. F. Employment system of the Lake carriers' association. Washington, Government printing office, 1918. 58p. (United States. Bureau of labor statistics).

COOK, CHARLES B. Employment department. *Business man's magazine*, June 1905, p. 1174-8.

DIEMER, HUGO. Employment of labor and labor problems. (In his *Factory organization and administration*. 1914. p. 106-25).

DIEMER, HUGO. Employment problems. (In his *Factory organization and management*, 1917. p. 252-70).

EMPLOYMENT blanks used by the Equitable life assurance company. *Journal of electricity*, March 15, 1919, p. 250.

FOULEY, CHARLES E. Employment department routine of the Curtiss aeroplane and motor corporation. *Industrial management*, Nov. 1918, p. 512-6.

GETTING and recording applications. *Business man's magazine*, March 1912, p. 258.

HALSEY, GEORGE D. Record card for shop employees. *Industrial management*, Oct. 1919, p. 331-3.

HENDERSCHOTT, F. C. and F. E. WEAKLY. Employment department and employee relations. Chicago, LaSalle extension university, c1918. 60p.

HIRE-and-keep employment plans. *Factory*, Nov. 1, 1920, p. 1440-5.

ISING, HAROLD ERNEST. Record of employes. *Business man's magazine*, March 1909, p. 274-5.

JONES, EDWARD D. Employment of labor. (In his *Administration of industrial enterprises*. 1911. p. 188-211).

JONES, M. M. Employment department organization of Thomas A. Edison intersts. *Industrial management*, May 1918, p. 374-9.

KELLY, ROY WILLMARTH. Classification of employment management functions. *Industrial management*, June 1919, p. 476-7.

KELLY, ROY WILLMARTH. Hiring the worker. New York, Engineering magazine co. 1918, 250p. (Industrial management library).

KELLY, ROY WILLMARTH. Labor-saving methods for employment offices. *Industrial management*, Feb. 1918, p. 146-7.

MORGAN, E. B. Visible index for application forms. *Industrial mangement*, Sept. 1919, p. 246-8.

RICHARDSON, J. H. Simple employment plan *Industrial management*, Dec. 1918, p. 511-2.

RUSSELL, FRANKLIN. Recruiting a factory force. *Business man's magazine*, Jan. 1911, p. 30-3.

STANBROUGH, D. G. Packard training schools for employees. *Industrial management*, Nov. 1918, p. 378-82.

SWALLOW, W. C. Employment records at Amoskeag mfg. co. *Textile world*, Jan. 20, 1917, p. 1015.

WALDO, R. Use of charts in the employment department. *American machinist*, Feb. 1919, p. 500.

WELLS, W. S. Visualzing employment records. *Industrial management*, July 1920, p. 67-70.

EMPLOYMENT managers' conference, Boston, Mass, May 10, 1916. *Monthly review*, July 1916, p. 62-70.

EMPLOYMENT system of the Lake carriers' association. Brissenden, P. F. 1918.

EMRICH, WILLIAM H.

Treasury stock. *Auditor*, 1905, p. 209.

ENCYCLOPAEDIA Britannica: a dictionary of arts, science, literature and general information. 1910. Ed. 11. 29v. Cambridge, University press.

ENCYCLOPAEDIA of accounting. Lisle, George. 1903.

ENCYCLOPAEDIAS

ACCOUNTANTS' and solicitors' diary. Edinburgh and London, George Waterston and sons.

ACCOUNTANTS' diary: annual. London, Gee & co.

ENCYCLOPAEDIA Britannica, a dictionary of arts, science, literature and general information. Ed.11. 29v. Cambridge, University press. 1910.

FRENCH, R. DUNCAN and A. L. GEE. Accountants' pocket diary and reference book. London, Gee & co.

END eight-year car-fare fight in Cleveland. *Municipal journal*, April 5, 1917, p. 502-3.

ENDEBROCK, R. A.

Production manager's guide and self-scheduling work. *Machinery*, September 1917, p. 48-50.

ENERGY component in industry *Electrical world*, Sept. 20, 1919, p. 650-2.

ENFORCEMENT of by-laws. Conyngton, Thomas.

ENGBERG R. C.

Annual farm inventory. *Successful farmer*, Jan. 1920, p. 5.

What does the record say? *Successful farmer*, April 1920, p. 10.

ENGER, M. L.

Costs of maintenance of motor driven deep well pumps. *American waterworks association journal*, June 1917, p. 190-1. *Engineering and contracting*, April 11, 1917, p. 344.

Maintenance of motor-driven deepwell pumps. *Municipal engineering*, August 1917, p. 67.

ENGINE and boiler room records for small plants. *Electrical world*, July 1, 1911, p. 47.

ENGINEERING

See also Contractors.

BARWICK, THOMAS. Systems for the engineer and contractor. *Heating and ventilating*, Nov. Dec. 1914, Jan. 1915, p. 27-34, 15-21, 18-22.

BOYNTON, R. H. City engineer's records in Frankfort, Ind. *Municipal engineering*, Aug. 1915, p. 78-9. *Engineering and contracting*, Sept. 1, 1915, p. 165-6.

BURR, HENRY A. Filing engineering clippings. *Engineering record*, Oct. 23, 1915, p. 520.

CARD index record and filing systems for engineers and contractors. New York. *Engineering news*, 1906.

DAVIES, JOHN P. Engineering office systems and methods. New York, McGraw-Hill book co. 1915.

ENGINEERING organization. *Accountant*, Nov. 17, 1917, p. 388-93.

FISH, J. C. L. Construction engineers' field and office diary. *Engineering news*, Jan. 20, 1916, p. 110-2.

FOLLOW-up system for engineering. *Automotive industries*, March 6, 1919, p. 530.

GREGORY, JOHN, H. Indexing and filing engineering computations. *Engineering news*, Jan. 8, 1914, p. 374-5.

HAUER, DANIEL JACOB. Modern management as applied to construction. New York, McGraw-Hill book co. 1918. 194p.

HOPSON, H. C. Accountants and engineers. *Journal of accountancy*, Nov. 1915, p. 397-9.

HORSNAILL, W. O. Organization of small engineering works. *Mechanical world*, Jan. 1, 1909, pt. 1.

HUEY, R. S. Value of records to an engineer. *Iron trade review*, Oct. 5, 1916, p. 689-91.

HUMPHREYS, ALEXANDER CROMBIE. Lecture notes on some of the business features of engineering practice; with lectures and pa-

ENGINEERING—*(Continued)*

pers by other authors. Revised and enlarged. Hoboken, N. J., Stevens institute of technology, 1916. 571p.

KENT, WILLIAM. Mechanical engineers pocket-book; a reference book of rules, tables, data and formulae. Ed. 9, thoroughly revised. New York, John Wiley & sons, 1916. 1526p.

KNOEPPEL, C. E. and HAROLD BUTT. Relation between the accountant and the efficeincy engineer. *Journal of accountancy*, Feb. 1916, p. 101-13.

MCNEAL, JOHN. City engineers' office records. *Municipal journal*, March 23, 1916, p. 397-8.

OSGOOD, MANLEY. System in a city engineer's office. *Municipal engineering*, June 1917, p. 307-9.

PARSONS, J. L. Office record system for civil engineers. *Engineering and contracting*, Nov. 29, 1916, p. 466-9.

PARSONS, W. J. Engineering job diaries. *Electrical review*, March 22, 1913, p. 335-6.

PENDER, HAROLD. Handbook for electrical engineers; a reference book for practicing engineers and students of engineering. Ed. 1, corrected. New York, John Wiley & sons, c1914. 2023p.

RECORDS in a city engineer's office. *Municipal engineering*, Aug. 1913, p. 148-9.

SCHAEFER, C. T. Card system for engineering and drawing room practice. *Business man's magazine*, Dec. 1909, p. 556-9.

SCIENTIFIC methods of management and their application to construction work. *Engineering and contracting*, May 12, 1915, p. 428-32.

SOME of the recording systems of a large engineering corporation. *Engineering record*, Jan. 30, 1909.

TAYLOR, WILLIAM GAVIN. Efficient index system for city engineers' office. *Engineering record*, March 20, 1909.

TRAUTWINE, JOHN C. Civil engineer's pocket-book, revised. 20th ed. Philadelphia, Trautwine company, c1919. 1528p.

TYRRELL, HENRY GRATTAN. Engineering of shops and factories. New York, McGraw-Hill book co. 1912

WELCH, A. W. Practical method for following up construction work. *Engineering magazine*, July 1913, p. 512-7.

WOLF, A. M. Index of details for a structural engineer's office. *Engineering news*, March 22, 1917, p. 482-3.

WULFING, H. E. Schedule board for engineering department. *Electrical world*, June 15, 1918, p. 1274.

ZUR NEDDEN, DIPLING F. Engineering workshop machines and processes. New York, D. Van Nostrand, 1910.

Accounting

ALLEN, LESLIE H. Accounts for material on engineering construction. *Journal of accountancy*, May 1915, p. 352-8.

AMERICAN electric railway accountants and engineering association. Report of joint committees on engineering accounting. *Electric railway journal*, Oct. 17, 1913, p. 852.

BATTERSBY, THOMAS. Perfect double entry bookkeeper (abridged) and the perfect prime cost and profit demonstrator, for iron and brass founders, machinists, engineers, ship-builders, manufacturers, etc. Manchester, 1878.

BENTLEY, HARRY C. Ledger accounts used in bookkeeping for professional and scientific men. (In his *Science of accounts*. 1913. p. 360-6).

BURTON, FRANCIS G. Commercial management of engineering works. Ed. 2. Manchester, Engineering scientific publishing co., 1905, 432p.

BURTON, FRANCIS GEORGE. Engineers' & ship-builders' accounts. London, Gee & co. 1902. 108p. (Accountants' library, v. 14).

COMMERCIAL engineering. *MeMchanical world*, Oct. 2, 1908.

DAVIES, J. VIPOND. Engineering accounting. *American electric railway accountants' association, Proceedings*, 1913, p. 184-204. *Electric railway journal*, Oct. 17, 1913, p. 864-5.

EFFICIENCY as practiced by Portland light & power co. *Railway and engineering review*, Nov. 1, 1913, p. 1013.

ENGINEERING estimates, cost and accounts. London, Ed. 3. Lockwood & son, 1911, 256p.

FERGUSON, J. ERIC. Some notes on the treatment of patterns in engineering accounts. *Accountants' magazine*, July 1917, p. 308-15. *Accounting and commerce*, Jan. 1918, p. 225-8. *Public accountant*, Oct. 1917, p. 98-104.

HARRIS, G. Engineering accounts. *Public accountant*, 1908, p. 22.

JAMESON, JOHN. Diagram accounts for engineering work. *Engineering* (London), Nov. 12, 1897.

KNOEPPEL, F. J. Setting production standards for industrial accounting and engineering. *Journal of accountancy*, Nov. 1918, p. 361-75. *Public accountant*, April 1919, p. 279-92.

LASHER, F. B. and others. The report of the jointly committee on engineering accounting. *Electric railway journal*, Oct. 11, 1912.

LEWIS, J. SLATER. Commercial organization of factories. London, 1896, 540p.

MITCHELL, GEORGE A. Engineering business. London, Gee & co., 1907. (Accountants' library, v. 47)

NARLIAN, C. A. H. Accounts of engineers and contractors. *Journal of accountancy*, Aug. 1920, p. 81-7.

OETERS, GEORGE C. Engineering accounts. *New York accountants' and bookkeepers' journal*, April, May 1904, p. 97-103, 136-40.

PENNELL, W. D. "Present worth" calculations in engineering studies. *Journal of the association of engineering societies*, Sept. 1914, p. 112-45.

PFEIFFER, G. N. Simple accounting system for an engineering office. *Engineering news*, July 22, 1920, p. 154.

QUENNELL, F. T. Survey of the processes and aims of costing more particularly as applied to engineering industries. *Accountant*, May 22, 29, 1920, p. 593-9, 625-40.

SCHOLEFIELD, J. B. Engineering and accounting—their relation with special reference to public utilities. *Journal of the association of engineering societies*, March 1914, p. 153-64. Discussion. L. H. Allen, May 1914, p. 281-8. *Canadian engineer*, May 28, 1914.

SPENCER, HENRY. Commercial organization of engineering factories. London, Spon & Chamberlain, 1907. 221p.

THOMPSON, T. FRAME. Principles and practice of accountancy in relation to engineering design and work. 1912. (Second Frame Thompson lecture before the Institute of civil engineers). *Accountant*, Feb. 7, 1914, p. 181-90.

TURNBULL, GEORGE R. Accounts and accounting. (In Humphreys, A. C. *Lecture notes on some of the business features of engineering practice*. p. 20-8).

VAN VLISSINGEN, ARTHUR. One man business; a complete record for five minutes' work a day. *System*, April 1917, p. 438-40.

Cost accounting

ACCURATE costing in engineering. *Engineering review*, Jan. 15, 1919, p. 187-8.

ALLEN, LESLIE H. Payroll distribution on construction work. *Journal of accountancy*, July 1914, p. 38-46.

ARNOLD, HORACE LUCIEN. Cost finding system of the Link-Belt engineering company, Nicetown, Philadelphia. (In his *Factory manager and accountant*. 1903. p. 24-100).

ENGINEERING—Cost accounting—*(Continued)*

Backenhus, R. E. Card system records cost of engineering. *Engineering record,* Oct. 21, 1916, p. 502-3.

Bakenhus, R. E. Cost records of drafting and engineering. *Engineering and contracting,* Nov. 29, 1916, p. 472-4.

Bardsley, John B. Hints to students on devising systems of engineers' cost accounts. *Accountant,* Oct. 18, 25, 1902, p. 1053-61, 1087-98.

Best, John William. Cost accounts of an engineer and ironfounder. *Accountant,* Feb. 23, March 2, 9, 1901, p. 246-54, 273-80, 304-12.

Best, John William. Cost accounts with special reference to those of an engineer and ironfounder. Ed. 2. London, Gee & co. 1911. 128p.

Bruce, C. R Marine engineering estimates and costs. Glasgow, 1911.

Buel, A. W. Cost system of an engineering works. *Engineering magazine,* v. 28, p. 971.

Burton, Francis G. Engineering estimates and cost accounts Ed. 2. Manchester, Technical publishing co. 1900. 136p.

Cost accounting in the engineering department; explains a system worked out for use on the Northern Pacific. *Railway gazette* (London), Dec. 6, 1912.

Cost keeping and efficiency in engineering. *Canadian engineer,* 1916, v. 30, p. 329-32.

Cost record system used for work done by day labor. *Engineering news,* April 8, 1909.

Cowens, William Edward. Shop and general establishment charges in engineering works and their relation to costs and estimates. *Engineering gazette,* June 1899.

Cowing, John P. Cost keeping in construction and contract work. *Engineering magazine,* Sept. 1905, p. 921-8.

Croissant, V. G. Mechanics of construction cost-keeping. *Government accountant,* March 1908, p. 504-29.

Cunliff, N. Development of a unit cost system. *Journal of the association of engineering societies.* Aug. 1914, p. 74-85. *Engineering and contracting,* Oct. 21, 1914, p. 374-6. Discussion, *Journal of the association of engineering societies,* Aug.-Sept. 1914. p. 85-101, 165-70.

Dana, Richard T. and H. P. Gillette. Cost analysis engineering. In *Cyclopaedia of civil engineering.* Chicago, American technical society. 1913, v.3, p. 313-380)

Dana, Richard T. and H. P. Gillette. Cost analysis engineering. (In *Cyclopedia of commerce, accountancy, business administration.* 1910. v.2. p. 251-318).

Deighton, H. Cost system of an engineering works. *Engineering magazine,* April 1905, p. 40-58.

Discussion of cost accounting on construction work. *Journal of the Boston society of civil engineers,* Oct. 1914.

Engineering and costs. London, Crosby, Lockwood and son, 1896.

Engineering estimates costs and accounts; with examples of estimates and costs and a section on the preparation of costs accounts; by a general manager. Ed.3. London, C. Lockwood & son, 1911. 256p.

Foote, Frederick W. Estimating construction costs. *Engineering and mining journal,* Nov. 11, 1916. p. 857-60.

Gillette, Halbert P. Gathering engineering cost data. School of mines, July 1904.

Gillette, Halbert P. Gathering engineering cost data. (In Humphreys, A. C. *Lecture notes on some of the business features of engineering practice.* p. 473-84).

Gillette, Halbert P. Principles of engineering economics and cost accounting. (In his *Handbook of cost data for contractors and engineers.* 1910. p. 7-118).

Gillette, Halbert P. and Richard T. Dana. Cost keeping system of Fred. T. Ley & co., Springfield, Mass. (In their *Cost keeping and management eningeering.* 1916. p. 256-64).

Godfrey, Stuart C. Cost-keeping and efficiency in engineering construction. *Contractor,* 1916, v.23, p. 29-31. *U. S. Engineering dept. Prof. mem.* Jan.-April 1916.

Godfrey, Stuart C Cost keeping and efficiency in works of the engineer department. *U. S. Engineering dept., Professional mem.,* Washington, Jan.-Feb. 1916, v.18, p. 1-30, 223-39.

Hitchen, G. E. Improved system of engineering costing. *Machinery* (London), March 11, 1920, p. 751-6.

Laughead, Berton M. Cost keeping and its value in relation to estimating on new work. *Journal of the American society of engineering contractors,* April 1911.

Leed, B. R. Simple cost accounting system adaptable to many classes of construction. *Engineering and contracting,* Sept. 19, 1917, p. 226-8.

Lewton, Charles E. Costing as applied to general engineering. *Accountant,* March 22, 1919, p. 231-40. *Engineering and industrial management,* April 17, 1919, p. 310-7.

Livermore, J. E. Suggestions of reform in engineering practice. *Cassier's magazine,* March 1909, p. 626-37.

Moore, De Witt, V. Methods of cost analysis as applied to construction work. *Engineering and contracting,* Feb. 23, 1910.

Nelson, Severin. Common sense cost keeping for engineers. *Mechanical world,* Feb. 23. 1912, pt. 1.

Oeters, George C. Engineering accounts. *New York accountant's and bookkeepers' journal,* April-May, 1904, p. 97-103, 136-40.

Pearn, Sinclair and Frank Pearn. Workshop costs for engineers and manufacturers. Manchester, Technical publishing co. 1904.

Plumpton, Thomas. Manufacturing costs as applied to engineering. *Accountant,* Nov. 19, 26, Dec. 3, 1892, p. 880-8, 899-903, 932-6.

Recsei, Sigm Stephan. Methods of cost calculation in mechanical engineering. *New York accountants' and bookkeepers' journal,* Jan.-April, 1904, p. 1-3, 35-8, 73-6, 108-10.

Ross, G. E. Cost keeping and construction accounting. *Engineering and contracting,* Feb. 20, 1918, p. 197-200.

Ross, George Edward. Cost keeping and construction accounting: adapated to any work consisting of numerous items, departments or divisions on which detailed unit costs are desired; all manner of construction enterprises come under this head, such as irrigation, highway, railroad, shipbuilding and municipal improvement: also adaptable to a large variety of manufacturing enterprises. Ed.2. Salem, Oregon, Ross system co. c1919. 171p. + forms.

Smith, Demster and P. C. N. Pickworth. Engineers' cost and economical workshop production. Manchester, Emmett & co 1914. 148p.

Windett, Victor. Foundation and sewer work costs and comments. *Journal of the Western society of engineers,* Nov. 1911.

Wood, D. M. Cost accounting on construction work. *Stone and Webster public service journal,* Nov. 1914.

Costs

Dana, Richard T. Handbook of construction plant; its cost and efficiency. New York, McGraw-Hill book company, inc. 1914. 702p.

Gillette, Halbert Powers. Handbook of cost data for contractors and engineers; a reference book giving methods of construction and actual costs of materials and labor on numerous engineering works. Ed.2. New York, McGraw-Hill book co. 1910. 1854p.

ENGINEERING—COSTS—*(Continued)*
GILLETTE, HALBERT POWERS and RICHARD T. DANA. Handbook of mechanical and electrical cost data; giving shipping weights, capacities, outputs, and net prices of machines and apparatus, and detailed costs of installation, maintenance, depreciation and operation, together with many principles and data relating to engineering economics. New York, McGraw-Hill publishing co. 1918. 1739p.

Stores
BROWNING, EARL HARRISON. General storeskeeping department of the Browning engineering co. *Engineering magazine,* 1905, v.29, p. 359-80.
McCALL, P. F. How one storekeeper looks at it: recommendation of committee on engineering accounting for a perpetual inventory discussed. *Aera,* March 1916, p. 848-50.

ENGINEERING analysis of a mining share. Pickering, John Clark. 1917.

ENGINEERING and costs. London, Crosby, Lockwood and son, 1896.

ENGINEERING and electric traction pocketbook. Dawson, Philip.

ENGINEERING AND MINING JOURNAL, COMP.
HANDBOOK of mining details; compiled from the Engineering and mining journal by the editorial staff. New York, McGraw-Hill book company, 1912. 372p.

ENGINEERING appraisement of waterworks properties. *Engineering record,* Sept. 27, 1913, p. 358-9.

ENGINEERING business. Mitchell, George A. 1907.

ENGINEERING charges in capital account. *Electrical world,* Nov. 17, 1917, p. 951.

ENGINEERING estimates and cost accounts. Burton, Francis G. 1900.

ENGINEERING estimates, costs and accounts; with examples of estimates and costs and a section on the preparation of costs accounts; by a general manager. London, C. Lockwood & son, 1911. 256p.

ENGINEERING for reproduction estimated in detail. *Engineering record,* Mar. 25, 1916, p. 419-20.

ENGINEERING of shops and factories. Tyrrell, Henry Gratton, 1912.

ENGINEERING organization. *Accountant,* Nov. 17, 1917, p. 388-93.

ENGINEERING valuation of public utilities and factories. *Electrical world,* June 30, 1910, p. 1694.

ENGINEERING valuation of public utilities and factories. Foster, H. A. 1913.

ENGINEERING workshop machines and processes. Zur Nedden, D. F. 1910.

ENGINEERS and shipbuilders' accounts. Burton, Francis George. 1902.

ENGINEERS' cost and economical workshop production. Smith, Demster & P. C. N. Pickworth 1914.

ENGINEERS' cost keeping system, New York state barge canal. *Engineering and contracting,* Sept. 7, 1910.

ENGINEER'S idea of values is usually confused; Prof. John R. Common's views. *Engineering and contracting,* Mar. 31, 1915, p. 284.

ENGINEER'S valuing assistant. Hoskold, H. D. 1905.

ENGINES

Accounting
ZIMMERMAN, A. H. Accounting methods for the motor manufacturing industry. *Business man's magazine,* Sept. Oct. 1908, p. 205-16, 291-4.

Cost accounting
ACCURATE time and material records. *Business man's magazine,* Jan. 1911, p. 100.
ARNOLD, HORACE LUCIEN. C. W. Hunt company, West New Brighton, New York. (In his *Factory manager and accountant,* 1903. p. 317-417).
EGGLESTON, D. E. Motor manufacturing costs *Business man's magazine,* Sept. 1907, p. 69-71.
KENT, WILLIAM. Factory cost of steam engines and of steam turbines. (In his *Bookkeeping and cost accounting for factories.* 1918. p. 115-19).
MALTBY, J. L. Simple method of cost summary. *Business man's magazine,* June 1909, p. 517.
NATIONAL GAS ENGINE ASSOCIATION. Addresses and reports given at the cost accounting session, ninth annual meeting, Chicago, Ill., June 27, 28, 29, 1916. Lakemont, N. Y., National gas engine association, 1916. 64p.
WEBBER, WILLIAM O. Costs of machine-tool operations in steam engine manufacturing. *Engineering magazine,* Aug. 1910, p. 729-36.
WEBBER, WILLIAM O. Reducing the costs of engine building by efficiency methods. *Engineering magazine,* Oct. 1910, p. 86-90.
ZIMMERMAN, A. H. Modern inspection method as foundation for cost system. *Business man's magazine,* Dec. 1907, p. 57-61.

Cost of operation
ESTIMATING direct current machine costs. *Electrical world,* Sept. 15, 1917, p. 533.
GAS engine economy in water works. *Gas age,* June 15, 1914, p. 576-7.
MACCUTCHEON, A. M. Cost versus up keep of mill motors. *Iron trade review,* Dec. 14, 1916, p. 1209-10.
OPERATING costs for oil engine installations. *Electrical world,* Oct. 9, 1915, p. 805-7.
TRACTOR engine cost. *Municipal journal,* Jan. 27, 1916, p. 108.
WANS, OSWALD. Comparison of the working costs of the principal prime movers. *Accountant,* Nov. 24, 1917, p. 413.

ENGLE, G. W.
Labor-saving methods and appliances for loading coal. *Coal age,* Nov. 28, 1918, p. 974-80.

ENGLISH, W. S.
Checking up incoming materials. *System,* October 1913, p. 416-9.
Short cut stock keeping records. *System,* Sept. 1913, p. 304-7.

ENGLISH accountants' examinations. *Accountant,* March 13, 1909, p. 357-60.

ENGLISH and Scottish bankruptcy. *Accountant,* July 4, 11, 25, 1914, p. 6-8, 37-8, 110-1.

ENGLISH and Scottish bankruptcy law. *Accountant,* May 30-June 27, 1914, p. 788-90, 817-20, 850-3, 878-80, 910-3.

ENGLISH and Scottish chartered accountants. *Accountants' magazine,* Jan. 1907, p. 1-9.

ENGLISH bank book-keeping. Easton, H. T.

ENGLISH comment on Mr. Sell's address. *Journal of accountancy,* Feb. 1907, p. 316.

ENGLISH LANGUAGE

C. P. A. language. *Journal of accountancy,* March 1911, p. 404.

CLARITY of diction. *Journal of accountancy,* Sept. 1920, p. 188-9.

PHILBRICK, A. L. Accountants and the use of English. *Journal of accountancy,* Nov. 1914, p. 366-71.

ENGLISH merchants companion. Dafforne, Richard. 1700.

ENGLISH methods of railroad accounting. *Railroad gazette,* Sept. 14, 1888, p. 609.

ENGLISH of commerce. Opdycke, J. B. c1920.

ENGLISH registration bill. *Journal of accountancy,* July 1909, p. 209-10.

ENGLISH synonyms. Crabb, George. 1917.

ENGLISH system of book-keeping. Jones, E. T. 1796.

ENGLISH system of book-keeping for schools. Jones, Theodore.

ENGLISH system of bookkeeping for the million. Jones, T. 1882.

ENGLISH systems of bookkeeping by single and double entry. Jones, E. T.

ENGLISH v. American practice. *Accountant,* May 11, 1907, p. 660-2. *Incorporated accountants' journal,* 1906-7, p. 192. *Journal of accountancy,* March 1907, p. 388-93.

ENGLISH versus American practice again. *Journal of accountancy,* June, 1907, p. 139-40.

ENGLISH versus Scottish degrees. Wright, James.

ENGLISH view of central-station rates. *Electrical world,* Sept. 22, 1910, p. 687-8.

ENGRAVING

Cost accounting

JOHN, ADOLPH. Factory and cost records in engraving. *System,* Jan. 1905.

ENNIS, WILLIAM DUANE

Works management. New York, McGraw-Hill book co. 1911. 174p.

ENSELL, E. H.

Bank service pensions. *Bankers magazine,* Nov. 1912, p. 498-505.

Cost accounting. *Banking law journal,* Dec. 1911, p. 1049-53.

Cost accounting—application of the scientific principles in a large reserve bank—comparative study of the different methods used in analyzing an account. *Banking law journal,* Jan. 1912, p. 70-4.

Outline of cost of an account in a large reserve bank. *Bankers magazine,* March 1911, p. 347-9.

Reconcilement of accounts, system in vogue in large reserve banks. *Bankers magazine,* Jan. 1912, p. 17-9.

ENSIGN desk electric calculating machine. *Electrical review and western electrician,* Nov. 14, 1914, p. 972-3.

ENTER the transfer-less zone system at last! *Electric railway journal,* Aug. 9, 1919, p. 268.

ENTIRE new system of book-keeping by double entry. Brewer, E. C.

ENTIRE new system of book-keeping by single entry. Brewer, E. C.

ENTRY in pass book not an admission. *Banking law journal,* Aug. 1910, p. 710-2.

ENZIAN, CHARLES

Hydraulic mine filing, its use in the Pennsylvania anthracite field; a preliminary report. Washington, Government printing office, 1913. 77p.

EPITOME of naval bookkeeping. Tate, W. 1840.

EPPSTON, HAROLD A.

Process costs. *Journal of accountancy,* April 1920, p. 266-75.

EPSTEIN, M.

See Keltie, John Scott, joint editor.

EQUAL profit sharing with employes; plan of Harvard knitting mills. *Textile world,* Feb. 7, 1920, p. 1156-7.

EQUAL representation in management offered employees of the International harvester co. *Automotive industries,* March 13, 1919, p. 564-8.

EQUALIZATION. New York state. Tax department. 1918.

EQUIPMENT account for each car and locomotive. *Railroad gazette,* Nov. 29, 1907, p. 640-1.

EQUIPMENT cards carry cost history of plant items. *Engineering news,* Sept. 19, 1918, p. 555.

EQUIPMENT cost data. *Electric railway journal,* Feb. 27, 1915, p. 427.

EQUIPMENT defect records of the San Antonio traction company. *Electric railway journal,* Dec. 6, 1913, p. 1189-90.

EQUIPMENT, depreciation and renewal on railways. *Engineering and contracting,* Aug. 31, 1910, p. 193.

EQUIPMENT for the future. *Cassier's magazine,* Sept. 1912, p. 277-8.

EQUIPMENT records on the Binghamton railway. *Electrical railway journal,* June 3, 1916, p. 1053-4.

EQUIPOISE bookkeeping by mechanism. McClure, E. L.

EQUITABLE adjustment of rates for all classes of water service in Freeport, Illinois. *Engineering and contracting,* Dec. 4, 1912, p. 636-8.

EQUITABLE TRUST COMPANY OF NEW YORK

Sacred trust: the succeeding generation: concerning the making of wills and the administration of estates. New York, Equitable trust co. 1918. 14p.

ERB, N.

Supreme court decision generally misunderstood. Moody, July 1913, p. 17-8.

ERBES, A. A.

Cost of brick and bulk ice cream. *Creamery,* July 1919, p. 41-2.

ERICKSON, E. A.

Depreciation and measurement of expired outlay on plant. *Engineering and mining journal,* March 3, 17, 1917, p. 370, 447-9.

ERICKSON, HALFORD

Amortization and other special charges. *Electrical review and western electrician,* Aug. 8, 1914, p. 283.
As to depreciation accounting; discusses methods of providing for depreciation. *Public service regulation,* June 1914, p. 305-7.
Depreciation. Madison, Wisconsin, 1912. 43p.
Depreciation accounting. *American gas light journal,* Aug. 10, 1914, p. 81-5.
Depreciation; address delivered before the convention of central water works association, Detroit, Mich., Sept. 25, 1912. Madison, Democrat printing company, 1912. 43p. *Utilities magazine,* Philadelphia, 1916, v. 1, p. 112-124.
Depreciation problems. *American gas institute, Proceedings,* 1914, p. 1582-1682.
Electric lighting and power rates. *Annals of American academy of political and social science, Philadelphia,* May, 1914, p. 238-50.
Facts relating to depreciation and rate making. *Eelctrical review and western electrician,* Jan. 31, 1914, p. 234-8.
Fair rates of return on utility investment. *Gas age,* Sept. 16, 1918, p. 251-4.
Going value. *Electrical review and western electrician,* Oct. 5, 1914, p. 672.
Importance of costs in valuations and rate making. *Telephony,* July 15, 1916.
Importance of uniform accounts and statistics. Madison, Wis., 1914. 19p. *Gas age,* Aug. 1, 1913, Sept. 1, 1913, p. 112-4, 210-1. *American gas light journal,* July 28, 1913, p. 54, 58, 69.
Indeterminate franchise is most equitable; zone rates for electric railroads. *Electric railway journal,* June 28, 1919. p. 1266-7.
Making rates for electric current charges of many central stations too low. *Public service.* 1911, p. 119-21.
Making rates for electric plants. *Public service regualtion,* Sept. 1912, p. 579.
Methods employed in making water rates under the Wisconsin utility law with a specific example. *Engineering and contracting,* Oct. 1, 1913, p. 377-80.
Methods of determining life of public utilities. *Engineering and contracting,* Oct. 23, 1912, p. 448-50.
Problem of rate making; summary of a paper. *Public service,* June 1909, p. 165-7.
Rates and rate-making under Wisconsin public utility law. *Engineering record,* July 12, 1913, p. 42-3.
Regulation and reasonable returns. *Electrical world,* June 27, 1914, p. 1477-9. Discussion. *Electrical review and western electrician,* June 27, 1914, p. 1296-1300.
Regulation of public utilities in Wisconsin. *Public service,* April 1913, p. 135. *Electrical world,* March 29, 1913, p. 662.
Regulation of public utilities; three discussions. Contents: 1. Rates for electric current. 2. Freight rates. 3. Government regulation of security issues of public corporations. Madison, Wisconsin, Democrat printing company, 1911, 66p.
Some principles and facts that should be considered in making rates for electrical utilities. Madison, Wisconsin, H. Erickson, 1913.
Some problems of public utility accounting. *Electric railway journal,* Feb. 7, 1914, p. 306-7, p. 293-4.
Two views of going value. *Electrical world,* Oct. 3, 1914, p. 651.
Valuation of public utilities. Madison, Wisconsin, 1912. 43p.
What a company should earn. Relation between the valuation and rate of return. *Public service,* Jan. 1915, p. 17-19.
What are fair rates of return? *Electric railway journal,* March 31, 1917, p. 592-4. Excerpts. *Electrical world,* April 7, 1917, p. 646.
Wisconsin method of depreciation accounting. *Gas age,* Aug. 1, 1914, p. 113-7.

——— **AND A. C. HUMPHREYS**

Depreciation, repair and valuations: abstract and papers. *Electric railway journal,* Oct. 31, 1914, p. 999.

ERIE RAILROAD COMPANY

Classification of operating expenses and construction accounts. New York, Erie railroad company, 1902. 124p.

ERION, FRANK L.

Accounting methods for the meat packing house industry. *Business man's magazine,* Sept. 1906, p. 89-90, 124-34.
Accounting methods for the packing house industry. *Business man's magazine,* Dec. 1905, p. 181-5.
System of insurance accounts. *Business man's magazine,* April 1905, p. 737-40.

ERNEST, HENRY

Accountant and book-keeper's manual of commercial calculations reduced to their utmost simplicity. New York, Harper & bros.

ERNEST AND ERNEST

Some accountancy questions and answers. *National retail dry goods association. Accounting department, Bulletin,* New York, 1913, v.2, special, no.2, p. 2-8.

ERRONEOUS data on the lives of buildings. *Engineering and contracting,* April 19, 1916, p. 360-1.

ERROR of treating a bond sinking fund as an element of cost of operating. *Engineering and contracting,* Sept. 24, 1913, p. 388.

ERROR-PROOF method of keeping a bank account. Lewis, Abraham. 1913.

ERRORS

AMERICAN business and accounting encyclopædia, comp. by E. H. Beach and W. W. Thorne. Detroit, Bookkeeper publishing co. 1901. Detection of errors—v.2, p. 461-6.
ASHWORTH, H. M. Some safeguards against fraud and errors. Rochdale, E. Wrigley & sons, 1885.
COX, HENRY C. Errors and their classification; detection of errors by business executives; detection of errors by bookkeeping department; verification of assets and liabilities; correction of errors. In his *Advanced and analytical accounting.* 1920. p. 379-442).
CRUIKSHANK, E. W. Transpositions. *Accounting and commerce,* Dec. 1917, p. 200-2. *Federal accountant,* Oct. 1917, p. 122-6.
ERRORS in accounts. (In his Lisle, George. *Encyclopaedia of accounting.* v. 2, p. 402-8).
FLETCHER, EDWARD H. Observations on errors and frauds. *Accountant,* Oct. 22, 1898, p. 1023-31.
GILMAN, STEPHEN. Treatment of errors. (In his *Principle of accounting.* 1917. p. 242-3).
GOLDMAN, HENRY. Locating errors. *Accountant,* June 5, 1897, p. 572.
How to find a simple transposition. *Business man's magazine,* Nov. 1911, p. 443.
How to recognize transpositions. *Business man's magazine,* June 1911, p. 580.

ERRORS—*(Continued)*
HOWE, GEORGE H. Hints and helps to bookkeepers. *Business man's magazine*, Sept. 1905, p. 500-2.
KESTER, ROY B. Correction of closing errors. (In his *Accounting theory and practice*. 1918, v. 2, p. 476.
KESTER, ROY B. Methods of locating errors. (In his *Accounting theory and practice*. 1918. p. 211-20).
LEISY, R. A. Practical proof system. *Business man's magazine*, Oct. 1905, p. 694-6.
MCNISH, J. H. Prevention of errors. *Business*, Nov. 1895, p. 393-5
ROHRBAUGH, ELMER S. Keystone up-to-date method of detecting and locating errors in bookkeeping and trial balance. York, Pa. E. S. Rohrbaugh, 1914. 12p.
SIME, T. WATSON. Fraud and error in books and accounts. *Accountant*, May 21, 1892, p. 426-31.
SOULÉ, GEORGE. How to detect errors in books of account. (In his *New science and practice of accounts*. 1903. p. 578-96).
SPRAGUE, CHARLES E. Detecting errors in accounts. *Business*, June 1897, p. 176-9.
SPRAGUE, CHARLES E. Precautions against error; detection of error. (In his *Philosophy of accounts*. 1918. p. 110-29).
WALTON, SEYMOUR. Errors in posting and in trial balance. *Journal of accountancy*, Dec. 1919, p. 472.
WALTON, SEYMOUR. Treatment of old errors in books out of balance. *Journal of accountancy*, Nov. 1914. p. 386-8.

ERRORS in balancing. *Accountant*, March 7-April 4, 18, 25, 1896, p. 178-9, 218-20, 247-8, 267-8, 308-9, 332-3.

ERRORS in balancing; a concise hand-book dealing with the more usual causes of differences in trial balances, and the method of their detection; based on articles which have appeared in the Accountant. Ed.3. London, Gee & co. 1912. 31p.

ERSKINE, A. R.
Going cost systems and monthly closings for industrial corporations. *Journal of accountancy*, July 1909, p. 168-72.

ERVIN, J. F.
Cupola operation for continuous pouring. *Iron age*, July 22, 1915, p. 183-5.

ESCHER, FRANKLIN.
Foreign exchange explained; a practical treatment on the subject for the banker, the business man and the student. New York, Macmillan co. 1917. 219p.

ESCUELAS SUPERIORES Y ELEMENTALES DE COMERCIO DE LA NACION.
Programas para los cursos de peritas mercantiles, tenedores de libros y dependientes idoneos de comercio. Buenos Aires. 1910. 112p.

ESHLEMAN, JOHN M.
Reproduction basis of valuation criticised. *Engineering record*, Nov. 20, 1915, p. 625-6.
Reproduction theory. *Utilities magazine*, Jan. 1916.
What determines the fair value of a public utility property. *Case and comment*, 1915, v.21, p. 865-70.

ESPENSCHIED, F. F.
Residence lighting rates and energy consumption. *Electrical world*, Dec. 15, 1917, p. 1153-4.

ESPRIT DE CORPS *Journal of accountancy*, June 1912, p. 433-5.

ESQUERRÉ, PAUL JOSEPH.
Applied theory of accounts. New York, The Ronald press co. 1917. 519p.
Goodwill, patents, trade-marks, copyrights and franchises. *Journal of accountancy*, Jan. 1913, p. 21-34.
New York C. P. A. examinations of June 1912. *Journal of accountancy*, Aug.-Oct. 1912, p. 77-98, 192-210, 310-21.
New York C. P. A. examinations of January 1913. *Journal of acocuntancy*, May, June 1913, p. 377-90, 459-66.
Problems involving the application of the theory of accounts; prepared or selected for use in connection with the applied theory of accounts. New York, The Ronald press co. 1915. 69p.

ESSARY, JESSE FREDERICK
Your war taxes, an interpretation of the new law with complete text. New York, Moffat, Yard & co. 1917. 178p.

ESSAY, on bookkeeping. Webster, William. 1738.

ESSAY on book-keeping according to the true Italian method of debtor and creditor, by double entry, etc. Webster, William.

ESSAY on the elements of book-keeping; by a merchant. 1861.

ESSAY to make a compleat accomptant. Roose, Richard. 1760.

ESSAYS in municipal administration. Fairlie, J. A. 1908.

ESSENTIAL features in a report for credit purposes. Leamy, R. H.

ESSENTIALS dictated by changes in modern conditions. *Municipal journal and engineering*, 1905, v.19, p. 95-8.

ESSENTIALS in paper mill cost accounting. Scovell, Clinton Homer. 1915.

ESSENTIALS of book-keeping for public schools. Childs, C. W.

ESSENTIALS of business law. Burdick, F. M. 1903.

ESTABLISHING the selling price. *Business man's magazine*, Sept. 1911, p. 246-7.

ESTATE ACCOUNTING.
See Executors and trustees—Accounting.

ESTATE accounting. Baugh, F. H. and W. C. Schmeisser.

ESTATE and farm bookkeeping. Jeanette, A. 1878.

ESTATE and record book for use in insolvency cases. Poppleton, G. G. and C. T. Appleby.

ESTATE TAX.
See Taxation—Inheritance.

ESTATES, accounts, precedents and instructions. Wood, S. 1892.

ESTATUTOS del centro de contadores y caligrafos publicos, fundado en el Rosario de Santa Fe el 18 de Diciembre de 1900. 21p.

ESTEP, H. C.
Gray iron foundry operating economies. *Iron trade review*, Feb. 22, 1912, p. 437-45.

ESTES, L. V.
Comparison of wage incentive systems and the 100 per cent time premium. *Industrial management*, Sept. 1920, p. 210-7.
Managing for maximum production. *Industrial management,* July 1919, p. 54-61.

ESTES, P. G.
With a travelling auditor. *Railroad man's magazine,* Dec. 1917, p. 637-42.

ESTEY, J. A.
Indiana tax reforms. *National municipal review,* July 1920.
Unit cost accounting for control; a system for the industrial executive. *Industrial management,* Nov. 1919, p. 359-63.
Work unit in cost analysis units of product per operator per hour. *Engineering and contracting,* April 21, 1920, p. 465.

ESTIMATE of the cost of hydro-electric equipment. *Electrical world,* Feb. 14, 1920, p. 372.

ESTIMATE record blanks in book form. *Metal work,* Jan. 29, 1915, p. 201.

ESTIMATE sheet for contractors. *Electrical review, and western electrician,* Nov. 21, 1914, p. 996-7.

ESTIMATED and actual cost of construction at Panama. *Engineering record,* Jan. 25, 1913, p. 86.

ESTIMATED cost of a 14.5 mile telephone line. *Electrical world,* August 25, 1917, p. 354.

ESTIMATED cost of cable railways in Chicago. *Engineering and contracting,* March 20, 1912, p. 338.

ESTIMATED cost of making gasoline by the Rittman process. *Metallurgical and chemical engineering,* June 15, 1916, p. 678.

ESTIMATED cost of overhead inter connection. *Electrical world,* March 22, 1919, p. 583-4.

ESTIMATED cost of 2,500 kw. hydro-electric development. *Electrical world,* March 27, 1920, p. 731.

ESTIMATED costs of Chicago terminal electrification. *Electrical railway journal,* Dec. 11, 1915, p. 1159-67.

ESTIMATED costs of hydroelectric plants on Winnipeg river. *Engineering and contracting,* Nov. 8, 1916, p. 412-3.

ESTIMATED life and depreciation of water works plants. *Municipal journal and engineer,* May 6, 1908, p. 558.

ESTIMATED total cost of semi-outdoor substation. *Electrical world,* March 23, 1918, p. 621.

ESTIMATES, costs and profits, exterior painting, interior decorating. Vanderwalker, F. N.

ESTIMATES should parallel cost-keeping method. *Automotive industries,* Nov. 6, 1919, p. 930-1.

ESTIMATING and the builder's overhead. *American architect,* Sept. 10, 1919, p. 366.

ESTIMATING building costs. *Concrete,* Nov. 1917, p. 137-9.

ESTIMATING building costs. *Concrete,* Feb. 1918, p. 60-1.

ESTIMATING cost. *American machinist,* 1900, v. 23, p. 1231-3.

ESTIMATING, cost keeping and profit making in the plumbing, heating and sheet metal trades. *Metal worker, plumber and steam fitter.* 1914.

ESTIMATING cost of knit underwear. *Textile world,* Dec. 18, 1915, p. 207.

ESTIMATING direct current machine costs. *Electrical world,* Sept. 15, 1917, p. 533.

ESTIMATING labor costs. *Electrical world & western electrician,* Aug. 1, 1914, p. 218-9.

ESTIMATING on cost of power plants. *Engineering and mining journal,* May 3, 1913, p. 903.

ESTIMATING the cost of an electric plant. *Journal of Franklin institute,* May 1908, p. 397.

ESTIMATING the cost of garbage and refuse collection and haulage in Chicago. *Engineering news-record,* Jan. 16, 1913, p. 106-7.

ESTIMATING the cost of knit underwear. *Textile world,* Dec. 18, 1915, p. 207.

ESTIMATING the cost of woolen goods. *Textile world,* March-April, 1915, p. 576-7, 92-4.

ESTIMATING the cost of woolen goods in English mills. *Textile world,* July, 1915, p. 419-24.

ESTIMATING the cost of work. Ferguson, W. B. 1915.

ESTIMATING the rate of "reasonable return" for a public utility. *Engineering and contracting,* April 30, 1913, p. 482.

ESTIMATING the value of a railway. *Engineering news,* April 12, 1894, p. 308. Editorial. *Engineering news,* April 12, 1894, p. 302.

ESTIMATING the value of railroad property. *Railroad gazette,* Sept. 2, 1904, p. 289.

ETHICAL publicity. *Journal of accountancy,* Oct. 1918, p. 290-2.

ETHICS.
See Professional ethics.

ETHICS. Whitfield, William.

ETHICS of accountancy. Joplin, J. P.

ETHICS of accountancy. McLaren, Norman.

ETHICS of accounting. *Bankers magazine,* v. 62, p. 730.

ETHICS of employing men. Burt, E. R.

ETHOS
L'impot sur le revenu; loi du 29 Octobre 1919 précédée d'un commentaire. Bruxelles, La Journée financiére et economique, 1920. 79p.

ETTELSON, SAMUEL A.
Gas rates and gas service: in the matter of the city's power of regulation. *Chicago city council journal,* Dec. 2, 1918, p. 1221-4.

ETTINGER, RICHARD PRENTICE AND DAVID E. GOLIEB

Credits and collections. Ed. 2. New York, Prentice-Hall, c1917.

EUGENE'S power water and light plants. *Municipal journal,* July 30, 1914, p. 141-2.

EVALUATING depreciation. *Electrical world,* Oct. 7, 1911.

EVANS, E. NESBITT—

See Nesbitt-Evans, E.

EVANS, F. W.

Adding a handshake to the bonus. *System,* June 1920, p. 1161-3.

EVANS, FRANK

Bill of sale. *Accountant,* 1886, p. 475, 485, 500, 511.

EVANS, FRANK S.

Management of traveling salesmen. *Journal of accountancy,* Feb. 1906, p. 310-19.

EVANS, GWILYM ARNOLD

Building clubs: their formation and administration. *Incorporated accountants' journal,* 1907-8, p. 263.

EVANS, H. D.

System the purchasing department. *Iron age,* Feb. 5, 1914, p. 403-6.

EVANS, H. E.

Dividends and profits. *Accounting and commerce,* Jan. 1917, p. 221-7.

Student's auditing. London, Longmans, Green & co., 1914. 204p.

EVANS, H. L.

Purchasing for scattered factories. *Iron age,* Feb. 4, 1915, p. 283-8.

EVANS, HERBERT S.

Appraisal of Boulder exchange plant of the Mountain states telephone and telegraph company. *Journal of engineering.* University of Colorado, 1914-5.

EVANS, HOLDEN A.

Cost keeping and scientific management. New York, McGraw-Hill book co. 1911. 260p.

Distribution of indirect costs. *American machinist,* Dec. 22, 1910, p. 1158-62.

Eliminating unproductive time. *Industrial management,* Oct. 1917, p. 87-93.

Expense accounts and analysis. *American machinist,* Jan. 12, 1911.

Importance of accurate costs. *American machinist,* v. 33, no. 45, pt. 1.

Orders, records and expense accounts. *American machinist,* v. 33, no. 52.

Overhead charges and shop output. *Metal work,* Aug. 29, 1919, p. 257-8.

Purposes of a cost system. *American machinist,* Nov. 24, 1910, p. 955-7.

Various elements of cost. *American machinist,* v. 33, no. 49.

EVANS, I. N.

Combining power, heating and ventilation. *Power,* May 29, 1917, p. 732-7.

EVANS, J. D.

Appraising railroad values. *Moody's magazine,* July 1907, p. 135.

EVANS, J. MEREDYTH

Corporation. London, Shaw & sons, 1897.

Exemplification of a system of accounts for county councils corporations urban and rural district councils and other local authorities. London, Shaw & sons. 145p.

EVANS, J. W.

Value of municipal records of water and sewer systems. *Oklahoma municipalities,* Nov. 1918, p. 36-7.

EVANS, LAWRENCE B.

Judicial control of commission rate making. *Case and comment,* Rochester, N. Y., 1915, v.21, p. 895-93.

EVANS, ROBERT JOHN

Address, 1888. *Accountant,* Nov. 24, 1888, p. 770-2.

Colliery accounts. *Accountant,* 1886, p. 51, 63, 77, 109, 118.

EVANS, W. H.

Getting rid of dead stock in the storeroom. *Electric railway journal,* April 7, 1917, p. 652-3.

EVE, H. TRISTRAM

Simple farm accounts. *Journal Bath and west and southern co. society,* London, 1905, ser. 4, v. 15, p. 77-88.

EVELAND, G. H.

Following up the delivery of raw material. *Factory,* Feb. 1, 1920, p. 273.

EVELEIGH, F. W. ANTON

Income tax guide; an exposition of the income tax (consolidation) act, 1917, including the normal tax, dividend tax, excess profits duty, and the taxation of profits derived from mining, industrial and other sources: including an exact copy of the income tax (consolidation) act, 1917, with side notes, and of the new regulations, and the prescribed forms; a comprehensive and detailed index enabling immediate reference and cross reference to any portion of the law; over one thousand two hundred references, also a number of practical examples and explanations, showing the application of the various taxes. Revised edition. Cape Town, Accountants' book service supply 166p.

Reserves. Johannesburgh, The Transvaal leader, 1915, 16p.

Revenue raising; some observations upon the development of income taxation. *South African accountant,* March 1918, p. 129-32.

Taxation of farmers: some observations and suggestions. *South African accountant,* Sept. 1918, p. 206-111.

EVERARD, W.

Mercantile bookkeeping . London, 1764.

EVEREST, H. A.

Economies in a small coal mine. *American institute mining engineers bulletin,* Jan. 1916, p. 165-7. Discussion, May 1916, p. 982-3.

EVERETT, C. R.

Itemied profits. *Business man's magazine,* May 1905, p. 596-9.

EVERETT, F. C.

Foundry warehouse methods. *Foundry,* July 1908. *Iron age,* Sept. 3, 1908.

EVERETT H. A.

Labor costs. *International marine engineering,* Dec. 1916, p. 555-6.

EVERS, C. C.
Commercial problem in buildings, a discussion of the economic and structural essentials of profitable building and the basis for valuation of improved real estate. New York, Record and guide, 1914.

EVERY man his own accountant. Thornton, 1889.

EVERYBODY'S guide to bookkeeping. Copeland, T. E. 1914

EVERYDAY book-keeping. Bogle, A. M. 1917.

EVERYDAY ethics. Sterrett, J. E.

EVES, ROY B.
Accounting system for the small electrical contractor. *Electrical review and western electrician,* April 20, 1912.

EVIDENCE
ALLOWANCES to prosecutors and witnesses: new rules and orders. *Accountant,* Sept. 17, 1904, p. 281-3.
ASHMAN, WILLIAM N. Preparation of accounts for the courts. *Business,* June 1895, p. 234-9.
BACON, CLEVELAND F. Accountant as an expert witness. *Accountant,* Feb. 3, 1906, p. 155-8. *Journal of accountancy,* Dec. 1905, p. 99-105.
BLACK, A. C. Law of evidence. *Accountants' magazine,* July 1920, p. 428-40.
BOOKS of account as evidence. *Bankers magazine,* 1915, p. 196-8.
BURNS, J. G. Accountant and written evidence. *Accountant,* Jan. 20, 1912, p. 103-9.
CAMPBELL, COLIN B. Loose leaf books and card systems as legal evidence. *Business man's magazine,* March 1905, p. 559-61.
CARTER, C. A. Some criminal offences relating to accounts. *Accountant,* Dec. 17, 1892, p. 970-6.
CRANE, A. C. Books of accountant from a legal standpoint. *Incorporated accountants' journal,* 1901-2, p. 172.
DICKSEE, LAWRENCE R. Accounts for litigation. (In his *Advanced accounting.* 1916. p. 424-33).
EXPERT witnesses and subpoenas. *Accountant,* Aug. 20, 1904, p. 181-3.
GIVING expert evidence. *Accountants' magazine,* June 1910, p. 301-6.
KLEIN, HENRY. Books of account as evidence. *Business man's magazine,* Jan. 1905, p. 58.
McCARDIE, HENRY A. Hints upon the law of evidence. *Accountant,* March 11, 1899, p. 280-4.
MACKAY, DONALD. Business books as evidence *Accountants' magazine,* Nov. 1920, p. 615-8.
MACPHERSON, F. H. Accountant in court. *Business man's magazine,* Sept. 1905, p. 484-98.
MOORE, ALEXANDER. Accountant as an expert witness. *Accountant,* June 29, 1907, p. 879-86.
SAYERS, H. SCHIEFFELIN. Books of account as evidence in commercial litigation. *New York accountants' and bookkeepers' journal,* June July 1904, p. 174-6, 206-9.
SHAWCROSS, WILLIAM H. How to receive and give evidence. *Accountant,* Jan. 15, 1898, p. 67-74.
TOLLETH, W. R. Expert testimony by accountants. *Canadian chartered accountant,* April 1918, p. 294-8. *Accountant,* Aug. 24, 1918, p. 101-3. *Journal of accountancy,* Aug. 1917, p. 88-93. *South African accountant,* Sept. 1918, p. 216-8.

EVIDENT need of a further advance in railroad rates in the United States. *Economic world,* April 19, 1919, p. 553-4. *Railway age,* April 11, 1919.

EVILS of excessive credit expansion. Morawetz, Victor.

EVOLUTION of a machine unit system at the Modern electric co. Eggleston, D. C.

EVOLUTION of double-entry bookkeeping. Henderson, J. A.

EVOLUTION of the New York system. Pleydell, A. C.

EVOLUTION of the trial balance. Thorne, W. W. 1906.

EWEN, JOHN M. AND A. BEMENT
Public and the public service corporation. *Journal of the Western society of engineers,* April 1911.

EWING, D. D.
Dissecting passenger interchange time graphs. *Electric railway journal,* Oct. 5, 1918, p. 610-12.
Economic value of electrically driven pumps for small water works. *Municipal engineering,* Feb. 1919, p. 68-70. Excerpts. *Engineering and contracting,* Feb. 12, 1919, p. 170-1.

EWING, R. O. & COMPANY.
Importance of comments on reports: correspondence. *Journal of accountancy,* May, 1913, p. 391-3.
Incomplete audits; correspondence. *Journal of accountancy,* Sept. 1913, p. 254-5.

EXACT explanation of the theory of double entry bookkeeping. Jenks, Maurice.

EXACT guide to book-keeping by way of debtor and creditor. King, Thomas. 1917.

EXAMINATION faults; from the Accountants' journal. *Canadian chartered accountant,* April 1917, p. 304-9.

EXAMINATION for appointment of field examiners conducted by the State board of accounts of Indiana on May 31, 1910. *Government accountant,* Aug. 1910, p. 173-5.

EXAMINATION, for credit purpose, of a book publishing house. Morse, H. S.

EXAMINATION frauds. *Accountant,* May 27, 1911, p. 805-7.

EXAMINATION hints. *Incorporated accountants' journal,* Feb. 1912, p. 115-6.

EXAMINATION note book for accountant students. Spicer, E. E. and E. C. Pegler. 1914.

EXAMINATION of F. Whinney (and of H. B. Buckley) before the House of Lords select committee. *Accountant,* April 2, 16, May 7, 14, 1898, p. 357, 389, 484, 512.

EXAMINATION of insurance companies. Wolfe, S. H. 1910.

EXAMINATION of prospects. Gunther, Charles Godfrey. c1912.

EXAMINATION of the books of the Bureau of water register, Department of water supply. New York City. Commissioners of accounts. 1901.

EXAMINATION papers. *Canadian chartered accountant,* July 1912, p. 55-61.

EXAMINATION papers for public accountants. *Business,* Jan. 1897, p. 16-8.

EXAMINATION papers in bookkeeping. Medhurst, J. T.

EXAMINATION papers in bookkeeping. Thornton, J.

EXAMINATION papers in book-keeping set at the civil service society of arts, City of London college and other exams. Medhurst, J. T. 1900.

EXAMINATION papers of the chartered accountants of Scotland. London, Effingham Wilson, 1894.

EXAMINATION papers, with answers, Sept. 1907. *Public accountant,* 1908, p. 41, 78, 94.

EXAMINATION questions, August 1908. *Journal of accountancy,* Jan. 1909, p. 257-64.

EXAMINATION questions set at each examinations from November 1899 to November 1907. Pennsylvania. State board of examiners of public accountants.

EXAMINATION system. *Journal of accountancy,* April 1911, p. 455-7.

EXAMINATIONS

See also Accountancy—Law; Accounting—Problems.

ADVICE to examinees. *Canadian chartered accountant,* Jan. 1913, p. 187-90.

ALBAN, FREDERICK J. Preparation for examinations. *Accountant,* March 30, April 6, 13, 1912, p. 510-20, 549-58, 586-9.

ARE examinations worth while. *Accountant,* Nov. 16, 1918, p. 271-2.

BARTLE, A. C. Hints to students and examinees. *Accountant,* Sept. 15, 22, 1917, p. 207-11, 226-32.

BARTLE, CECIL. Hints to students and examinees. *Accountant,* Oct. 30, Nov. 6, 13, 1915, p. 533-9, 564-6, 589-95. *Public accountant,* July, Sept. 1915, p. 12-20, 69-76.

BUTTERFIELD, WILLIAM T. Preparation for examination in bookkeeping, accounts and auditing. *Accountat,* Dec. 22, 1900, p. 1174-9.

CARTER, ROGER N. Hints to accountancy examinees, with special reference to the accountancy subject. (In Feather, J. Stuart, ed. *Joint transaction,* 1911, p. 239-67).

CHILD, PERCY. Examination notes: accountancy. *Accountant,* Feb. 2, 1895, p. 101-8.

CHRISTIAN, G. A. Examinations; preparation and working. *Australasian account ant and secretary,* Nov. 1920, p. 352-5.

CLARIDGE, W. Examinations. *Incorporated accountants' journal,* June 1913, p. 226-9.

COCHRAN, J. TULLIS. Golden rules at an examination. *Accountants' magazine,* Nov 1920, p. 584.

COCHRAN, J. TULLIS. Guide to students; how to answer examination questions. *Accountants' magaine,* May 1920, p. 330-4.

COOPER, D. Hints to examination candidates. *Canadian chartered accountant,* April 1916, April 1918, p. 294-6, 316-18.

CREW, ALBERT. Examinations. *Canadian chartered accountant,* April 1920, p. 273-5.

CROPPER, L. CUTHBERT. Examinations, with special reference to auditing. *Accountant,* Dec. 6, 1902, p. 1270-83.

DAVEY, FREDERICK. Students' catechism on book-keeping, accounting and banking, with exercises and examinaion questions. Ed.2. London, Butterworth & co. 1917. 478p.

DAWSON, SIDNEY S. Minemonic aids. *Accountant,* Nov. 22, 1902, p. 1206.

EDWARDS, H. D. Preparation for the examination. *Accounting and commerce,* March 1916, p. 285-6.

EXAMINATION faults; from the Accountants' journal. *Canadian chartered accountant,* April 1917, p. 304-9.

EXAMINATION frauds. *Accountant,* May 27, 1911, p. 805-7.

EXAMINATION system. *Journal of accountancy,* April 1911, p. 455-7.

EXAMINATIONS. *Journal of accountancy,* Oct. 1909, p. 455.

EXAMINATIONS and their bearing on national efficiency. *Journal of accountancy,* April 1911, p. 459-61.

EXAMINATIONS as a medium for professional efficiency. *Canadian chartered accountant,* April 1914, p. 267-70.

EXAMINATIONS hints. *Incorporated accountants' journal,* Feb. 1912, p. 115-6.

EXAMINERS wanted for the Interstate commerce commission. *Journal of accountancy,* Sept. 1908, p. 358.

FAIR examinations. *Australasian accountant and secretary,* Feb. 1920, p. 42.

HAROLD, J. BLAKE. Pitman's examination notes on bookkeeping and accountancy; including executorship accounts. London, Sir Isaac Pitman and sons, 1911. 58p.

HARTOG, P. J. Examinations. *Canadian chartered accountant,* Oct. 1912, p. 125-7.

HINTS to examinees. *Accountants' magazine,* 1897, p. 653.

LYNCH, H. F. Accountant's preliminary examination course. London, H. Foulks Lynch & co. 1908.

NELSON, C. HEWETSON. Examinations as a medium of professional efficiency. *Incorporated accountants' journal,* Dec. 1914, p. 57-9.

SPICER, ERNEST EVAN and ERNEST C. PEGLER. Examination note book for accountant students. Ed.3. London, H. Foulks Lynch & co. 1914. 183p.

STANGWARD, W. O. On examinations. *Accountant,* Oct. 5, 1912, p. 437-40.

WALBANK, JOHN ARTHUR. Auditing essays and other matters, being hints etc. for examinations and other purposes. Newcastle-upon-Tyne, Northern accountancy coaching classes, 1910. 88p.

WITTY, RICHARD A. How to become a qualified accountant. London, Sir Isaac Pitman and sons. 126p.

WRIGHT, JAMES. English versus Scottish degrees. *Journal of accountancy,* March 1909, p. 407-8.

American institute of accountants

AMERICAN institute of accountants. Examinations. New York, American institute of accountants.

AMERICAN institute of accountants. Examinations, June 1917. *American institute of accountants, Yearbook,* 1917, p. 154-72. *Journal of accountancy,* July 1917, p. 1-20.

AMERICAN institute of accountants. Examinations, November 1917. *Journal of accountancy,* Dec. 1917, p. 413-23.

AMERICAN institute of accountants. Examinations, May 1918. *Journal of accountancy,* June 1918, p. 401-12.

AMERICAN institute of accountants. Examinations, November 1918. *Journal of accountancy,* Dec. 1918, p. 401-11.

AMERICAN institute of accountants. Examinations, May 1919. *Journal of accountancy,* June 1919, p. 401-11.

AMERICAN institute of accountants. Examinations, November 1919. *Journal of accountancy,* Dec. 1919, p. 401-12.

AMERICAN institute of accountants. Examinations, May 1920. *Journal of accountancy,* June 1920, p. 401-15.

AMERICAN institute of accountants. Examinations. Nov. 1920. *Journal of accountancy,* Dec. 1920, p. 401-19.

ANALYSIS of examination results. *Journal of accountancy,* Feb. 1918, p. 121-4.

EXAMINATIONS—American institute of accountants—*(Continued)*

Approaching standardization. *Journal of accontancy,* Aug. 1919, p. 126-9.

Archer, John P. Examiner's impressions. *Journal of accountancy,* Oct. 1918, p. 247-9.

Board of examiners. *Journal of accountancy,* Dec. 1916, p. 451-4.

Fair examination. *Journal of accountancy,* Oct. 1919, p. 286-9.

Finney, H. A. Introduction to acturial science. *Journal of accountancy,* Nov.-Dec. 1919, p. 321-52, 435-50.

Finney, H. A. and Seymour Walton. American institute examinations, May 1920. *Journal of accountancy,* July-Nov. 1920, p. 69-80, 145-60, 214-34, 308-20, 381-5.

First examination of the American institute. *Journal of accountancy,* Sept. 1917, p. 213-4.

Institute examinations. *Journal of accountancy,* Feb. 1917, p. 132-3.

Standardization of examinations. *Journal of accountancy,* Dec. 1917, p. 453-5.

Uniformity of examinations. *Journal of accountancy,* July 1917, p. 52-4.

Vinal, Eugene R. Problems from the examinations of the American institute of accountants. (In his *Mathematics for the accountant.* 1920. p. 143).

Walton, Seymour. Institute examinations. *Journal of accountancy,* April 1917, p. 309-11.

Walton, Seymour. Institute examinations. June 1917. *Journal of accountancy,* Sept.-Dec. 1917, p. 227-37, 307-22, 403-10, 464-81.

Walton, Seymour. Institute examinations. November 1917. *Journal of accountancy,* Jan. Feb. 1918, p. 64-78, 140-54.

Walton, Seymour. Institute examinations. May 1918. *Journal of accountancy,* Aug.-Oct. 1918, p. 143-9, 222-33, 306-18.

Walton, Seymour. Institute examination, November 1918. *Journal of accountancy,* Jan.-June 1919, p. 68-77, 141-54, 227-35, 305-17, 379-94, 466-77.

Walton, Seymour. Institute examination, May 1919. *Journal of accountancy,* July-Sept. 1919, p. 55-68, 143-54, 226-35.

Walton, Seymour. Institute examination, Nov. 1919. *Journal of accountancy,* Jan.-March 1920, p. 67-75, 145-56, 223-34.

Argentine

Sozzi, Francisco. Contabilidad industrial (monagrafia de examen). Rosario, 1916. 52p.

Australia

Cleveland, A. W. Hints to candidates. *Accounting and commerce,* Feb. 1917, p. 262-4.

Examination papers, with answers, Sept. 1907. *Public accountant,* 1908, p. 41, 78, 94.

Final examination papers, Oct. 1904. *Public accountant,* 1904-5, p. 86.

Hemingway, W. H. May examination papers of the Federal institute of accountants. *Australasian accountant and secretary,* July 1919, p. 14-8.

Papers set October, 1909. *Public accountant,* 1910, p. 23, 57, 70, 100, 117.

Questions and answers, October 1906. *Public accountant,* 1906-7, p. 111, 131, 149, 178, 192, 227.

Questions and answers, October, 1907. *Public* accountant, 1908, p. 108, 118, 143, 169.

Questions and answers, October 1908. *Public accountant,* 1909, p. 7, 23, 72, 105, 121.

C. P. A.

Accountancy examinations. *Journal of accountancy,* Jan. 1916, p. 56.

American accountants' examinations. *Accountant,* May 1, 1909, p. 588-90. *Journal of accountancy,* June 1909, p. 132-4.

Bentley, Harry C. C. P. A. examination questions. (In his *Science of accounts.* 1913. p. 295-308).

Bennett, Robert Joseph. C. P. A. questions and answers. *Business man's magazine,* Sept.-Nov. 1909, Jan.-May, July, Aug.-Dec. 1910, Jan.-Dec. 1911, Jan.-June 1912, p. 275-80, 373-6, 481-3, 71-4, 186-9, 278-81, 371-8, 465-72, 93-7, 189-90, 279-82, 384-8, 481-6, 583-7, 93-6, 196-207, 302-6, 397-402, 499-501, 595-7, 74-8, 161-3, 253-6, 353-6, 451-5, 545-9, 93-6, 180-4, 263-9, 346-8, 425-30, 514-16.

Bennett, Robert J. and Frederick W. Morton. C. P. A. questions and answers. Detroit, International accountants' society, 1914. 310p.

Bentley, Harry Clark, comp. C. P. A. auditing questions to January 1, 1914, comprising all the available examination questions in auditing that have been set by C. P. A. examining boards up to and including December 31, 1913. New York, Ronald press company, 1914. 247p.

Broaker, Frank. American accountants manual, v.1: examination questions prepared by the State board of examiners of expert public accountants appointed by the Board of regents of the University of the state of New York; together with answers in concise form, further elucidated by author's comment upon the technique and expression of modern accountancy. New York. Broaker & Chapman, c1897. 210p.

——— Same. New York, Broaker & Chapman, c1915. 210p.

Brownlee, G. C. P. A. problem. *Business man's magazine,* Aug. 1907, p. 116-20.

C. P. A. examination, December 13, 1898. *Journal of accountancy,* Dec. 1906, p. 176-7.

C. P. A. examination questions. *Journal of accountancy,* May 1906, p. 74-8.

C. P. A. examinations. *Business man's magazine,* Feb. 1909, p. 184-9.

C. P. A. examinations; correspondence. *Journal of accountancy,* Nov. 1908, p. 60.

C. P. A. problems. *Business man's magazine,* Jan.-June 1909, p. 57-60, 518-23.

C. P. A. problems and solutions, 1914. 2v. New York, The Ronald press co. 1915. 346+375p. v. 1. Presenting problems, with solutions for the following examinations: Pennsylvania, November 1913; New York, January 1914; Illinois, May 1913; Colorado, December 1913. v. 2. Presenting problems, with solutions for the following examinations: Missouri, December 1913; Ohio, November 1913, New York, June 1914; Massachusetts, October 1914.

C. P. A. problems with solutions, 1915. 2v. New York. The Ronald press co., 1916. 351+361p. v. 1. Presenting problems, with solutions for the following examinations: Wisconsin, April 1914; Ohio, November 1914; New York, January 1915; Pennsylvania, November 1914. v. 2. Presenting problems, with solutions for the following examinations: Missouri, December 1914; Illinois, May 1914; Massachusetts, October 1915; New York, June 1915.

C. P. A. question department: correspondence. *Journal of accountancy,* Nov. 1909, p. 75-80.

Cannon, James G. Address. *Journal of accountancy,* Feb. 1909, p. 330-1.

Chase, William Arthur. C. P. A. examinations and how to pass them. Chicago, LaSalle extension university, 1915. 93p. *Journal of accountancy,* April-June 1910, p. 401-11, 43-50, 113-9.

Chase, William Arthur. How to pass examinations; abstract. *Accountants' magazine,* May 1910, p. 256-8.

Chase, William A. Our critics. *Accountant,* Feb. 12, 1910, p. 257-61, 293-7. *Journal of accountancy,* Oct. 1909, p. 432-9.

Cox, Henry Clay. Classified C. P. A. problems and solutions, 1915; covering the more important questions given in the 1915 examinations of the following states: **Arkansas, Delaware, Florida, Kansas, Louisiana, Maine,**

EXAMINATIONS—C. P. A.—*(Continued)*
Maryland, Massachusetts, Michigan, Minnesota, Missouri, Nebraska, Nevada, New York, Ohio, Oregon Pennsylvania, South Carolina, Washington, Wisconsin. New York, The Ronald press co. 1916. 414p.
DOESN'T want exactly a palace: correspondence. *Journal of accountancy*, March 1909, p. 405.
DUNCAN, JOHN C. Teacher's view of the examiner's attitude. *Journal of accountancy*, Sept. 1909, p. 356-61.
EXAMINERS and examinations. *Journal of accountancy*, April 1910, p. 448-9.
EXAMINERS and publicity. *Journal of accountancy*, March, July 1909, p. 390-2, 216-7.
FOREIGN view of the C. P. A. examinations. *Journal of accountancy*, June 1907, p. 161.
GEIJSBEEK, JOHN B. Critics, not the examiners, are at fault. *Journal of accountancy*, June 1909, p. 97-105.
GREENDLINGER, LEO. Accountancy problems with solutions. 2v. New York, Business book bureau and Key publishing co. 1910-1911. 393+459p.
GREENDLINGER, LEO. C. P. A. question department. *Journal of accountancy*, Sept.-Nov. 1907, Jan.-Nov. 1908, Jan.-Nov. 1909, May-Dec. 1911, p. 399-406, 480-6, 76-80, 257-72, 336-44, 411-24, 494-504, 75-80, 144-56, 220-8, 296-300, 365-80, 448-60, 72-88, 253-64, 340-4, 416-28, 496-504, 60-76, 143-9, 228-36, 312-6, 392-6, 472-6, 65-80, 152-60, 232-40, 312-20, 390-400, 469-80, 72-80, 147-53, 231-40, 311-20, 392-404, 472-6, 74-80, 154-64, 231-44, 315-24, 392-400, 470-84, 79-84, 155-64, 226-40, 313-19, 392-9, 464-80, 550-64, 644.
HUNTER, JOEL. How to pass the C. P. A. examinations. (In his *Thinking in figures*. c1916. p. 110-3). *Journal of accountancy*, July 1915, p. 34-7.
INTERNATIONAL correspondence schools. C. P. A. questions and answers. (In their I. C. S. reference library, c1915, 279, section 42, p. 1-2, section 43, p. 1).
JACOBSON, B. A. Practical accounting problems and theory of accounts, as illustrated in the examinations for the C. P. A. degree at the New York and Illinois universities. *Business man's magazine*, June 1908, p. 503-5.
JACOBSSON, GUSTAVE. Practical accounting—C. P. A. problems. *Business man's magazine*, Oct. 1906, p. 178-80.
JACOBSSON, GUSTAVE. Practical accounting, solution of C. P. A. problems. *Business man's magazine*, April 1909, p. 384-6.
JORDAN, JOHN P. and GOULD L. HARRIS. C. P. A cost accounting problems. (In their *Cost accounting*. p. 481-514).
MOREY, LLOYD and W. B. CASTENHOLZ. C. P. A. problems and solutions. Chicago, LaSalle extension university, 1918. 446p.
PETER, W. F. C. P. A. examinations. *Journal of accountancy*, Nov. 1913, p. 412-4.
PROFESSIONAL examinations in accountancy. *Journal of accountancy*, July 1906, p. 216-8.
REGULATIONS of new C. P. A. board. *Journal of accountancy*, Nov. 1907, p. 68-9.
SECRECY as to examination papers. *Journal of accountancy*, March 1909, p. 402.
STAR chamber vs. public examinations. *Journal of accountancy*, June 1909, p. 128-9.
SUFFERN, ERNEST S. Are C. P. A. examinations always fair? *Journal of accountancy*, March 1909, p. 384-9.
TANNER, JOHN B. C. P. A. examinations and how to prepare for them. Chicago, LaSalle extension university, c1916. 70p.
TANNER-GILMAN SCHOOLS, INC. External auditing: C. P. A. coaching. Chicago, Tanner-Gilman schools, inc. c1918-1919.
THEORY and practice in accounting. *Journal of accountancy*, Oct. 1909, p. 449-52.
TIPSON, FREDERICK S. Practical accounting. *Business*, Jan.-July 1906, p. 18-21, 105-9, 190-5, 278-81, 481-3, 559-61.
Too old for high school studies. *Journal of accountancy*, April 1909, p. 486.
VOLLUM, CHARLES N. C. P. A. examining board. *Journal of accountancy*, Jan. 1909, p. 200-4.
WALTON, SEYMOUR. C. P. A. examinations. *Journal of accountancy*, June 1914, March 1915, p. 459-73, 230-5.
WALTON, SEYMOUR. Incompetent examiners. *Journal of accountancy*, Nov. 1916, p. 406.
WALTON, SEYMOUR. Institute examinations. *Journal of accountancy*, April 1917, p. 309-11.
WALTON, SEYMOUR. Necessity for a national standard. *Journal of accountancy*, Oct. 1916, p. 325.
WALTON, SEYMOUR. Practical hints. *Journal of accountancy*, Jan. 1917, p. 64-71.
WILKINSON, GEORGE. C. P. A. movement and the future of the profession of the public accountant in the United States of America; with discussion. *Federation of societies of public accountants in the United States of America, Official record of the Congress of accountants held at the World's fair*, September 26th, 27th and 28th, 1904, p. 91-119.

———, **California**

CALIFORNIA. STATE BOARD OF ACCOUNTANCY. Examination questions, June 6-8, 1904.
CALIFORNIA. STATE BOARD OF ACCOUNTANCY. Information in regard to examinations for certified public accountants. Sacramento, 1918. 23p.
PLATT, A. G. California examinations for C. P. A. certificates, with questions and answers (In Rahill, J. J. *Corporation accounting and corporation law*. 1906, p. 408-43).
QUESTIONS set at the California state examination of public accountants, June 6, 1904. *New York accountants' and bookkeepers' journal*, Aug.-Sept. 1904, p. 236-9.

———, **Colorado**

COLORADO C. P. A. examination. *Journal of accountancy*, Aug. 1909, p. 295-6.
KINGWILL, J. H. Colorado C. P. A. examination, 1908. *Journal of accountancy*, Aug. 1909, p. 287-94.
REGULATIONS of new C. P. A. boards. *Journal of accountancy*, Nov. 1907, p. 68-9.
WALTON, SEYMOUR. Colorado examination. *Journal of accountancy*, Aug. 1914, p. 134-40.

———, **Connecticut**

CONNECTICUT. STATE BOARD OF ACCOUNTANCY. Circular of information for intending applicants for certificates as certified public accountants, 1913. 8p.
REGULATIONS of new C. P. A. boards. *Journal of accountancy*, Nov. 1907, p. 68.

———, **Florida**

JACOBSSON, GUSTAVE. Treatment of sinking funds; from Florida C. P. A. examination, April 1907. *Business man's magazine*, Feb. 1911, p. 202-4.

———, **Georgia**

GEORGIA. STATE BOARD OF EXAMINERS PUBLIC ACCOUNTANTS. Examination questions, May 21 and 22, 1919. 4 typewritten pages.

———, **Illinois**

ILLINOIS, UNIVERSITY OF. Circular of information in regard to the examinations for certified public accountants. Urbana, 1916. 35p.
ILLINOIS, UNIVERSITY OF. Questions set at the examinations of candidates for the certificate of certified public accountant in Illinois, 1903-12. University of Illinois.
ILLINOIS C. P. A. examinations, May 7-9, 1906. *Journal of accountancy*, June 1906, p. 147-54.
JACOBSSON, GUSTAVE. Practical accounting. University of the state of New York, C. P. A. examination, January 1902, University of

EXAMINATIONS—C. P. A.—*(Continued)*

Illinois—C. P. A. examination, May 1904, University of Illinois—C. P. A. examination, November 1904. *Business man's magazine,* Feb. 1907, p. 132-6.

JACOBSSON, GUSTAVE. Practical questions in accounting; from the Illinois C. P. A. examination, May 1910. *Business man's magazine,* Sept. 1911, p. 257-9.

PROBLEMS from the Illinois examination for May 1914. *Journal of accountancy,* Nov. 1914, p. 388-92.

QUESTIONS and answers for public accountants. *Business world,* Oct. Dec. 1906, p. 816-22, 1099-1104.

QUESTIONS set at the Illinois examination for the degree of certified public accountant. *New York accountants' and bookkeepers' journal,* July 1904, p. 209-13.

QUESTIONS set at the Illinois examination of public accountants. *New York accountants' and bookkeepers' journal,* Jan. 1904, p. 12-7.

UNIVERSITY of Illinois; examination for certificate as certified public accountant May 1908 question 1. *Business man's magazine,* June 1909, p. 525-6.

WALTON, SEYMOUR. Illinois examination of May 1917. *Journal of accountancy,* July 1917, p. 68-71.

WALTON, SEYMOUR. Problems; C. P. A. examination in Illinois, December 1916. *Journal of accountancy,* June 1917, p. 463-8.

———, **Kansas**

ACCOUNTANCY examinations. *Journal of accountancy,* Jan. 1916, p. 56.

KANSAS, UNIVERSITY OF. State law and the university rules for the examination of candidates for the certificate of certified public accountant. Topeka, 1915. 10p.

KANSAS, UNIVERSITY OF. State law and the university rules for the examination of candidates for the certificate of certified public accountants. Topeka, 1919. 8p.

———, **Louisiana**

LOUISIANA. STATE BOARD OF ACCOUNTANCY. Questions and problems set at the examinations held on May 23d to 24th, 1913. 14 typewritten pages.

———, **Maryland**

Questions set at the Maryland examination of public accountants. *New York accountants' and bookkeepers' journal,* Feb. 1904, p. 45-6.

———, **Massachusetts**

MASSACHUSETTS. BANK COMMISSIONER. Registration of pubilc accountants, rules for applicants. 2p.

———, **Michigan**

MICHIGAN. STATE BOARD OF ACCOUNTANCY. Application for examination for C. P. A. certificate, rules governing examination for C. P. A. certificates under the laws of Michigan. 4p.

MICHIGAN. STATE BOARD OF ACCOUNTANCY. Examinations, June 9, 10, 1919. 11p.

MICHIGAN. STATE BOARD OF ACCOUNTANCY. Michigan C. P. A. manual. 1915; comp. by D. W. Springer. Ann Arbor, Michigan state board of accountancy, c1915. 183p.

MICHIGAN. STATE BOARD OF ACCOUNTANCY. Michigan C. P. A. manual, 1920. Ann Arbor, Michigan, State board of accountancy, c1920. 260p.

MICHIGAN C. P. A. examination questions, July 27-28, 1906. *Journal of accountancy,* Oct. Dec. 1906, p. 477, 159-63.

QUESTIONS and answers for public accountants. *Business world,* Oct. Dec. 1906, p. 816-22, 1099-1104.

———, **Missouri**

ACCOUNTANCY EXAMINATIONS. *Journal of accountancy,* Jan. 1916, p. 56.

MISSOURI. STATE BOARD OF ACCOUNTANCY. Statutory requirements and rules of the board relative to qualifications necessary in order to obtain registation as a certified public accountant, 1914. 11p.

———, **Nevada**

NEVADA. BOARD OF ACCOUNTANCY. Rules and regulations. Carson city, 1914. 8p.

———, **New Jersey**

BENTLEY, HARRY C. C. P. A. examination questions, state of New Jersey, 1908. (In his *Science of accounts.* 1913. p. 304).

CERTIFIED public accountants of New Jersey. Examination questions, July 1906, to April, 1909. *Accountant,* Oct. 15, 1910, p. 528-35, 516-8.

NEW JERSEY state board; change of rules. *Journal of accountancy,* Sept. 1910, p. 379-81.

———, **New York**

ACCOUNTANCY in the States. *Accountant,* Nov. 21, 1896, Jan. 9, 1897, p. 951-2, 52-5.

ANOTHER view of New York examinations: correspondence. *Journal of accountancy,* Nov. 1912, p. 421-2.

BENTLEY, HARRY C. C. P. A. questions, state of New York. (In his *Science of accounts.* 1913. p. 297-303).

C. P. A. examination papers, 1902. *Incorporated accountants' journal,* 1901-2, p. 258.

C. P. A. examination questions, Jan. 1906. *Journal of accountancy,* May 1906, p. 74-8.

C. P. A. examinations, 1899. *Business,* July 1899, p. 444-7.

C. P. A. examinations in New York. *Journal of accountancy,* Sept. 1913, p. 230-2.

CERTIFIED public accountants' examination questions, 1900. *Business,* July 1900, p. 346-8.

COLLEY, FREDERICK GEORGE. Appreciation of the New York C. P. A. examinations: correspondence. *Journal of accountancy,* Aug. 1912, p. 148-50.

CONYNGHAM, THOMAS. New York C. P. A. examinations of June 1912. *Journal of accountancy,* Nov. 1912, p. 382-8.

DILLINGHAM, R. H. New York C. P. A. examinations. *Journal of accountancy,* Nov, 1913, p. 410-2.

ESQUERRÉ, PAUL JOSEPH. New York C. P. A. examination of June 1912. *Journal of accountancy,* Aug.-Oct. 1912, p. 77-98, 192-210, 310-21.

ESQUERRÉ, PAUL JOSEPH. New York C. P. A. examinations of January 1913. *Journal of accountancy,* May, June 1913, p. 377-90, 459-66.

EXAMINATION papers for public accountants. *Business,* Jan. 1897, p. 16-8.

GREENDLINGER, LEO. New York C. P. A. problems, June 1898. *Journal of accountancy,* Aug. 1907, p. 319-26.

GREENDLINGER, LEO. New York, C. P. A. problems, June 1907. *Journal of accountancy,* July 1907, p. 239-44.

JACOBSSON, GUSTAVE. Practical accounting problems, University of the state of New York, certified pubic accountants' examination, June 1898—question 6—dissolution of partnership. *Bcsiness man's magazine,* March 1908, p. 289-90.

JACOBSON, GUSTAVE. Practical accounting; problems and theory accounts. University of the state of New York, C. P. A. examination, June, 1903, question 1. *Business man's magazine,* Oct. 1908, p. 330-2.

JACOBSSON, GUSTAVE. Practical accounting problems and theory of accounts; University of the state of New York, C. P. A. examination, June, 1907, questions 1 and 2. *Business man's magazine,* Sept., 1908, p. 238-41.

EXAMINATIONS—C. P. A.—*(Continued)*

JACOBSSON, GUSTAVE. Practical accounting; university of the state of New York, C. P. A. examination, June 1899. *Business man's magazine,* Jan 1907, p. 134-6.

JACOBSSON, GUSTAVE. Practical accounting. University of the state of New York. C. P. A. examination, Jan. 1901. *Business man's magazine,* Nov. 1906, p. 162-70.

JACOBSSON, GUSTAVE Practical accounting; University of the state of New York, C. P. A. examination, January 1902, University of Illinois—C. P. A. examination, May 1904, University of Illinois—C P. A. examination, November 1904. *Business man's magazine,* Feb. 1907, p. 132-6.

JACOBSSON, GUSTAVE. University of the state of New York; C. P. A. examination, for June 1908; question 4. *Business man's magazine,* June 1909, p 526-8.

KINGWILL, J. H. New York problem no. 4: correspondence. *Journal of accountancy,* Sept. 1909, p. 383-4.

LOEWENWARTER, PAUL L. New York C. P. A. examinations: correspondence. *Journal of accountancy,* Jan. 1914, p. 83.

NEW YORK C. P. A. examination, January 29-30, 1907. *Journal of accountancy,* Feb. 1907, p. 326-32.

NEW YORK C. P. A. examination questions, June 1906. *Journal of accountancy,* Aug. 1906, p. 315-320.

NEW YORK C. P. A. examinations. *Journal of accountancy,* March 1903, Feb. 1907, Nov. 1908, p. 446-52, 326-32, 42-8.

NEW YORK C. P. A. examinations, January 1906. *Journal of accountancy,* March 1906, p. 446-52.

NEW YORK C. P. A. examinations, June 1913. *Journal of accountancy,* Sept. 1913, p. 245-52.

NEW YORK C. P. A. examinations, solutions of question. *Journal of accountancy,* March 1914, p. 240-2.

NEW YORK STATE. EDUCATION DEPARTMENT. Certified public accountant syllabus. Albany, New York state education department, 1912. 14p.

NEW YORK STATE. EDUCATION DEPARTMENT. Certified public accountants, law, rules and information, June 1916. 25p. (Handbook 14).

NEW YORK STATE. EDUCATION DEPARTMENT. Examination questions, June 1919. 8 typewritten pages.

NEW YORK STATE. EDUCATION DEPARTMENT. Professional examination papers, 1901. Albany, New York state educational department, 1901. 188p.

NEW YORK state C. P. A. examination questions. *Business world,* March 1902, Feb. July 1905, p. 127-30, 72-4, 354-6.

PETER, W. P. C. P. A. examinations: correspondence. *Journal of accountancy,* Nov. 1913, p. 412-4.

QUESTIONS set at the New York state examination for the degree of C. P. A., June 21-22, 1904. *New York accountants' and bookkeepers' journal,* Oct. 1904, p. 272-6.

QUESTIONS set at the New York state examination of public accountants. *New York accountants' and bookkeepers' journal,* April 1904, p. 113-7.

SCHNACKENBERG, JOHN H. New York C. P. A. examinations of January 1913. *Journal of accountancy,* Aug. 1913, p. 132-44.

SOLUTIONS of practical accounting problems: New York C. P. A. examination, January 29, 1907, problem 1. *Journal of accountancy,* April 1907, p. 493-4.

STEP forward. *Journal of accountancy,* Sept. 1912, p. 219-22.

THORNTON, F. W. Another correspondent attacks New York examinations: correspondence, *Journal of accountancy,* Nov. 1912, p. 427-8.

TIPSON, FREDERICK SIMSON. Theory of accounts. Ed. 2, revised and enlarged, New York, Isaac Mendoza book co. 1913. 216p.

ULMAN, STEPHEN A. New York C. P. A. problem. Jan. 1906. *Journal of accountancy,* April 1906, p. 545-6.

UNIVERSITY of the state of New York; college department, 2nd annual report, 1899: vol. 2, professional education in the United States; prepared by H. L. Taylor. 1900.

UNIVERSITY of the state of New York; C. P. A. examination for June 1908, question 1. *Business man's magazine,* June 1909, p. 524-5.

UNIVERSITY of the State of New York; examination department, 146th examination. *Accountant,* Aug. 7, 1897, p. 781-3.

———, **North Carolina**

NORTH CAROLINA. STATE BOARD OF ACCOUNTANCY. Examinations, Sept. 25, 26, and 27, 1919. 7 typewritten pages.

———, **North Dakota**

NORTH DAKOTA. Examination for certificate of certified public accountant, July 1, 2 and 3, 1919. 15p.

NORTH DAKOTA. STATE BOARD OF ACCOUNTANCY. Law and regulations relating to granting certificates of certified public accountant. 8p.

———, **Ohio**

FINNEY, H. A. Lawyer vs accountant in partnership liquidation: Ohio C. P. A. examination in October 1919. *Journal of accountancy,* May, Oct. 1920, p. 386-96, 315-20.

OHIO STATE BOARD OF ACCOUNTANCY. Examinations for the degree of certified public accountant. Columbus, Ohio, November 12, 13 and 14, 1918. 23p.

WALTON, SEYMOUR. Ohio state board of accountancy; examination in practical accounting, Thursday, November 12, 1914. *Journal of accountancy,* Jan. 1915, p. 65-71.

———, **Oklahoma**

OKLAHOMA. BOARD OF ACCOUNTANCY. Examination, November 12, 13, 14, 15, 1919. 19 typewritten pages.

———, **Oregon**

OREGON. STATE BOARD OF ACCOUNTANCY. Law regulating the practice of public accounting, rules governing examination of candidates, and other information for C. P. A. Portland, 1915. 15p.

———, **Pennsylvania**

BENNETT, ROBERT JOSEPH. Pennsylvania C. P. A. examinations for 1912 with answers and solutions; reprinted from the *Journal of accountancy,* New York, of March, April and May 1913. Philadelphia, R. J. Bennett. 72p.

BENNETT, ROBERT JOSEPH. Pennsylvania C. P. A. examinations of November 1912. *Journal of accountancy,* March, April 1913, p. 198-230, 273-301.

NEW C. P. A. requirements in Pennsylvania. *Journal of accountancy,* Jan. 1907, p. 249-54.

NEW rules for accounting examinations in Pennsylvania. *Journal of accountancy,* July 1906, p. 218-20.

PENNSYLVANIA. STATE BOARD OF EXAMINERS OF CERTIFIED PUBLIC ACCOUNTANTS. Examination questions, 1908-1909. Philadelphia, State board of examiners of public accountants, 1909. 49p.

PENNSYLVANIA. STATE BOARD OF EXAMINERS OF PUBLIC ACCOUNTANTS. Circular of information for intending applicants for certificates of certified public accountants, 1913. 15p.

PENNSYLVANIA. STATE BOARD OF EXAMINERS OF PUBLIC ACCOUNTANTS. Examination in general accounting and commerce, Nov. 5, 7, 8, 9, 1917. 9p.

EXAMINATIONS—C. P. A.—*(Continued)*

PENNSYLVANIA. STATE BOARD OF EXAMINERS OF PUBLIC ACCOUNTANTS. Examination questions set at each examination from November 1899 to November 1907, inclusive, including also copy of the Pennsylvania C. P. A. act and the rules of the board of examiners. Philadelphia, George H. Buchanan co. 1908. 158p.

PENNSYLVANIA. STATE BOARD OF EXAMINERS OF PUBLIC ACCOUNTANTS. General accounting—commercial law, Nov. 4, 6, 7, 8, 1918. 15p.

PENNSYLVANIA C. P. A. examination questions, 1900. *Business world,* Sept. 1902, p. 408-10.

PENNSYLVANIA C. P. A. examination questions, May 1905. *Journal of accountancy,* Dec. 1905, p. 169-80.

PENNSYLVANIA C. P. A. examination questions, Nov. 1907. *Journal of accountancy,* April 1908, p. 494-504.

PENNSYLVANIA C. P. A. examinations. *Journal of accountancy,* Jan. 1907, p. 235-7.

PENNSYLVANIA C. P. A. examinations, May 21-23, 1906. *Journal of accountancy,* July 1906, p. 234-40.

PENNSYLVANIA STATE BOARD OF EXAMINERS OF PUBLIC ACCOUNTANTS. *Journal of accountancy,* Aug. 1913, p. 151-8.

QUESTIONS set at the Pennsylvania examination of public accountants. *New York accountants' and bookkeepers' journal,* March 1904, p. 80-3.

STEWART, WALTER D. Pennsylvania C. P. A. examinations of November 1912; commercial law. *Journal of accountancy,* May 1913, p. 370-6.

———, **Rhode Island**

STATE of Rhode Island examination questions, Dec. 1907. *Journal of accountancy,* Jan. 1909, p. 253-7.

———, **South Carolina**

SOUTH CAROLINA. BOARD OF EXAMINERS OF PUBLIC ACCOUNTANTS. Examination questions, 1919. 9 typewritten pages.

———, **South Dakota**

SOUTH DAKOTA. BOARD OF ACCOUNTANCY. Rules for the examination of applicants for certificate as certified public accountants, effective from July 1, 1917. 7p.

———, **Texas**

TEXAS. STATE BOARD OF PUBLIC ACCOUNTANCY. Application for certificates as certified public accountant. 4p.

———, **Virginia**

VIRGINIA. STATE BOARD OF ACCOUNTANCY. Examinations, Nov. 1918. 14p.

VIRGINIA. STATE BOARD OF ACCOUNTANCY. Laws and rules. Richmond, 1910. 12p.

VIRGINIA C. P. A. examination; complete list of questions set at the first examination held by the Virginia state board of accountancy, Nov. 17 to 19, 1910. *Business mans' magazine,* Feb. 1911, p. 205-10.

VIRGINIA C. P. A. examination; complete set of questions used by the Virginia state board of accountancy, October 18-20, 1911. *Business man's magazine,* Dec. 1911, p. 549-54.

———, **Washington**

BENTLEY, HARRY C. C. P. A. examination questions, State of Washington, 1905. (In his *Science of accounts.* 1913.)

EXAMINATION questions, August 1908. *Journal of accountancy,* Jan. 1909, p. 257-64.

WASHINGTON. STATE BOARD OF ACCOUNTANCY. Circular of information for intending applicants as certified public accountants. Tacoma, 1910. 8p.

———, **West Virginia**

WEST VIRGINIA. BOARD OF EXAMINERS FOR THE EXAMINATION OF PUBLIC ACCOUNTANTS. Questions, May 26 and 27, 1919. 13p.

———, **Wisconsin**

WISCONSIN. STATE BOARD OF ACCOUNTANCY. C. P. A. examination questions, Madison, Wisconsin, May 14, 15, 17 and 18, 1916. 45p.

WISCONSIN. STATE BOARD OF ACCOUNTANCY. C. P. A. examination questions. Madison, Wisconsin, April 9, 10, 11 and 12, 1918. 35p.

WISCONSIN. STATE BOARD OF ACCOUNTANCY. C. P. A. examination questions, April 29, 30, May 1 and 2, 1919. Madison, Wisconsin state board of accountancy, 1919. 31p.

WISCONSIN. STATE BOARD OF ACCOUNTANCY. Governmental accounting questions and answers, 1914, 1915, 1916, 1917, 1918. Madison, Wisconsin, state board of accountancy. 50p.

———, **Wyoming**

WYOMING. STATE BOARD OF ACCOUNTANCY. By-laws and rules, 1912. 6p.

Canada

COOPER, D. Problem department. *Canadian chartered accountant,* Oct. 1911, Jan. April July, Oct. 1912, April, July 1913, Jan. 1914, p. 78-82, 149-54, 223-9, 48-54, 137-41, 288-97, 54-62, 203-6.

EXAMINATION papers. *Canadian chartered accountant,* July 1912, p. 55-61.

EXAMINATIONS of the Institute of chartered accountants of Ontario. *Canadian chartered accountant,* Jan. 1913, p. 182-6.

INSTITUTE of chartered accountants of Ontario. Information for intending candidates, 1919. 16p.

INSTITUTE of chartered accountants of Ontario. Questions set at final examination, May 19th, 20th, 21st, 1897. *Accountant,* May 29, 1897, p. 548-52.

PROBLEM department. *Canadian chartered accountant,* April 1915, p. 348-50.

England

See also Examination—Institute of charatered accountants of England and Wales; Examinations—Society of incorporated accountants and auditors.

ADVANCED examination papers in book-keeping with notes by J. Thornton. London, Macmillan, 1898. 32p.

BEDFORD, EDWARD H. Intermediate [solicitors'] examination guide to book-keeping; the examination questions with answers. Ed. 2. London, Stevens & sons, 1875.

BELL, JOHN. Bookkeeping examination questions. Edinburgh, W. & R. Chambers, 1867.

BELL, JOHN. Chamber's examination bookkeeping, with civil service and other papers fully solved. London and Edinburgh, W. & R. Chambers, 1908.

BLAKE, HAROLD T. Examinations, notes on book-keeping and accountancy. London, Sir Isaac Pitman & sons.

BOOK-KEEPING examination papers for 1910, with fully worked answers compiled by H. W. Porrit and W. Nicklin. London, Sir Isaac Pitman & sons, 1910. 39p.

CARY, R. H. Society of arts' book-keeping: 16 papers set at the society's examinations, during 1886-99; notes and glossary of commercial terms. London, Simpkin, Marshall Hamilton, Kent & co. 1899. 108p.

CENTRAL ASSOCIATION OF ACCOUNTANTS. Final examination questions, December 1919. Central association of accountants. 15p.

CENTRAL ASSOCIATION OF ACCOUNTANTS. Intermediate examination questions, December 1919. Central association of accountants. 10p.

EXAMINATIONS—ENGLAND—*(Continued)*

CENTRAL ASSOCIATION OF ACCOUNTANTS. Licentiate examination, December 1909. *Accountant,* April 9, 1910, p. 512-3.

CHARTERED ACCOUNTANT STUDENTS' SOCIETY OF LONDON. Debate on examination questions. *Accountant,* March 7, 1914, p. 338-41.

CHARTERED ACCOUNTANT STUDENTS' SOCIETY OF LONDON. Discussion of examination questions. *Accountant,* July 27, 1901, p. 849-54.

CHARTERED ACCOUNTANT STUDENTS' SOCIETY OF LONDON. Discussion of the questions set at the December (1903) examination. *Accountant,* March 26, 1904, p. 399-404.

CHARTERED ACCOUNTANT STUDENTS' SOCIETY OF LONDON. Discussion on examination questions. *Accountant,* Oct. 26, 1901, p. 1169-73.

CHARTERED ACCOUNTANT STUDENTS' SOCIETY OF LONDON. Discussion on examination questions. *Accountant,* June 27, 1903, p. 839-43.

CHARTERED ACCOUNTANT STUDENTS' SOCIETY OF LONDON Discussion on the May examination questions, 1912. *Accountant,* Oct. 19, 1912, p. 491-6.

CHARTERED ACCOUNTANT STUDENTS' SOCIETY OF LONDON. June examination questions discussed. *Accountant,* Nov. 7, 1903, p. 1367-73.

DAVEY, FREDERICK. Student's catechism on book-keeping, accounting and banking; with exercises and examinations questions. Ed. 2. London, Butterworth & co. 1917. 478p.

DICKSEE, LAWRENCE ROBERT. Institute of secretaries. (In his *Bookkeeping for company secretaries.* 1908. p. 110-80).

DOWLER, FRANK and E. M. HARRIS. Examination papers set by the Royal society of arts (In their *Auditing, accounting and banking.* p. 311-6).

HARLOW, EDWARD. Examinations questions in book-keeping, with answers. London, Blades, 1894.

HARROLD, J. BLAKE. Key to Practical papers in book-keeping and accountancy. London, Meiklejohn & sons, 1906. 80p.

HARROLD, J. BLAKE. Pitman's examination notes on book-keeping and accountancy: including executorship accounts. London, Sir Isaac Pitman & sons, 1911. 58p.

HARROLD, J. BLAKE. Practical papers in book-keeping and accountancy; including papers set by principal examining bodies with the Society of arts advanced examination paper 1905 and full solution. London, Meiklejohn & Holden, 1905. 96p.

HUNTER, JOHN. Examination questions in book-keeping by double entry, with answers. London, Longmans, Green & co. 1863.

KEEFE, JOHN. Civil service book-keeping: New ed. London, Murray, 1904.

MACLEAN, JOHN DALZIEL. Appendix to book-keeping; examination papers. London, Simpkin, Marshall, Hamilton, Kent & co. 1895.

MACLEAN, JOHN DALZIEL. Introduction to counting-house and examination book-keeping, with examination papers and an appendix on government book-keeping. London, 1892.

MANCHESTER CHARTERED ACCOUNTANTS STUDENTS' SOCIETY. Discussion on examination questions, June 1889. *Accountant,* June 21, 1890, p. 335-6.

MANCHESTER CHARTERED ACCOUNTANTS STUDENTS' SOCIETY. Institute's auditing questions, June final 1902. *Accountant,* Jan. 31, 1903, p. 161-6.

MAUJI, DINSHAW E. and K. N. BISNI. Questions and answers in book-keeping and accountancy of the London chamber of commerce. London, Simpkin, Marshall, Hamilton, Kent & co. 1908.

MEDHURST, JOHN T. Book-keeping by double entry, theoretical, practical; society of arts examination paper fully worked out. London, G. Bell & co. 1898. 130p.

MEDHURST, JOHN T. Examination papers in bookkeeping. London, Bell & sons, 1888.

——— Same. Ed. 8. London, 1903.

MEDHURST, JOHN T. Examination papers in book-keeping set at the civil service, Society of arts, city of London, college and other exams. London, Bell, 1900. 222p.

MURRAY, P. Graduated exercises and examination papers in book-keeping for national, intermediate and private schools, business colleges and civil service academies. London, G. Bell & sons, 1900. 232p.

NICHOLSON, LESLIE C. Notes on local authority finance and accounts and local government law in the form of answers to the questions, set at examinations of the Institute of municipal treasurers and accountants. Southampton, 1908.

NIXON, ALFRED and J. H. STAGG. Examination papers. (In their *Accounting and banking.* 1912. p. 445-89).

PORRITT, H. W. and WILLIAM NICKLIN. Pitman's book-keeping annual; papers set by the principal examining authorities during 1909, fully worked. London, Sir Isaac Pitman & sons.

SHEPHERD, J. M. Practical accounting problems. (In *Cyclopaedia of commerce, accountancy, business administration.* 1910. v.7, p. 283).

SHERRY, G. E. and E. JONAS. Practical papers in civil service book-keeping. London, 1886.

SOCIETY of arts examinations, 1890—book-keeping. *Accountant,* May 24, 1890, p.
SOCIETY of arts examinations, 1890—book-
278-9.
keeping. *Accountant,* April 25, 1891, p. 319-20.

THORNTON, J. Advanced examination papers in book-keeping, with notes. London, Macmillan & co.

THORNTON, J. and F. OLIVER THORNTON. Junior bookkeeeping examiner, consisting of recent examination papers in bookkeeping with notes. London, Macmillan & co.

THORNTON, J. and F. O. THORNTON. Key to Thornton's senior bookkeeping examiner. London, Macmillan & co.

THORNTON, J. and F. O. THORNTON. Senior book-keeping examiner. London, Macmillan & co.

UNIVERSITY of London. *Accountant,* Nov. 12, 1904, p. 608-10.

WHYTE, W. Law examination manual for students. Edinburgh, 1889.

WILSON, EDWIN. Master key to the examination papers in bookkeeping for 1911. E. Wilson, London, 1912.

WITTY, RICHARD A. How to become a qualified accountant. London, Sir Isaac Pitman and sons. 126p.

Holland

EXAMEN der Nederlandsche Accountants-Vereeniging, 1917.

EXAMENS ter verkrijging van het mercurius-diploma, uitgereikt door de Federatie van Handels en-Kantoorbedienden-Vereenigingen in Nederland, 1917. 35p.

Institute of chartered accountants of England and Wales

ACCOUNTANTS' manual; being the questions set at the Institute of chartered accountants' examinations, 1884-1902 to date. London, Gee & co. 1884 to date.

CARLILL, JOHN ALBERT. How to prepare for chartered accountant examinations. London, Gee & co. 1908. 23p. *Accountant,* March 31, 1900, p 311-8.

EXAMINATIONS—INSTITUTE OF CHARTERED ACCOUNTANTS OF ENGLAND AND WALES—*(Continued)*

CARTER, ROGER N. Hints to accountancy examinees, with special reference to the accountancy subjects. *Accountant,* Nov. 25, 1911, p. 727-36. *Incorporated accountants' journal,* Dec. 1911, p. 71-8.
CARTER, ROGER N. Institute examinations. *Accountant,* March 4, 11, 1911, p. 346-50, 395-403.
CARTER, ROGER N. Institute examinations: some hints to students. *Accountant,* Nov. 23, 30, Dec. 7, 14, 1907, p. 645-56, 673-4, 697-8, 731-2.
CUTFORTH, ARTHUR EDWIN. Can the institute examination be improved upon? *Accountant,* June 8, 1912, p. 868-72.
CUTFORTH, ARTHUR EDWIN. Early stages of preparations for the accountancy papers of the intermediate examinations. London Gee & co. 1906. 100p.
CUTFORTH, ARTHUR EDWIN. Month before the examinations. London, 1908.
DAWSON, SIDNEY S. Law papers of the institute examinations and how to prepare for them. *Accountant,* Nov. 1, 1902, p. 1116-23.
DICKINSON, WALTER SIGISMUND. Preparation and study for the institute examinations. *Accountant,* April 30, 1910, p. 606-12.
DICKSEE, LAWRENCE R. Students' guide to accountancy. Ed. 2. London, Gee & co. 1907. 48p.
ENGLISH accountants' examinations. *Accountant,* March 13, 1909, p. 357-60.
INSTITUTE examinations. *Accountant,* Feb. 9, 1889, p. 65-6.
INSTITUTE'S examinations: some hints to students. *Accountant,* Jan. 18, 1908, p. 73-6.
LYNCH, H. FOULKS. Revise work for accountant students: a digest of all the questions in the examination law papers from July 1882, to June 1891. London, H. Foulks Lynch & co. 1891.
NIXON, JOHN GEORGE. Guide to the final examination of the Institute of chartered accountants; questions set from December 1893, to June 1903. London, 1904.
NIXON, JOHN GEORGE. Guide to the intermediate examination of the Institute of chartered accountants; questions set from December 1893, to June 1903. London, 1904.
NORTON, GEORGE P. and H. F. LYNCH. Chartered accountants' examination guide and students' help to self-preparation for the intermediate and final examinations. Huddersfield, 1887.
POWNALL, ALFRED H. Address. *Accountant,* April 18, 1891, p. 300-4.
PREPARATION for the institute's examinations. *Accountant,* July 20, 1907, p. 75-8.
SHAW, W. H. Examinations of the institute. *Accountant,* May 13, 1911, p. 757-8.
SHUTTLEWORTH, T. E. Accountancy papers in the institute examinations. *Accountant,* March 2, 1912, p. 356-60.
STUDENTS' telephone papers of English institute of chartered accountants, with answers, 1887 to date. London.
VAN DE LINDE, GERARD. Articled clerk. *Accountant,* Nov. 23, 30, 1895, p. 946-52, 969-76.
VICKERY, B. G. Preparation for the examinations of the institute. *Accountant,* Dec. 25, 1920, p. 691-6.
WELCH, ALLAN. Mnemonics, and other aids to preparation for the institute examinations. (In Feather, J. Stuart, ed. Transactions, 1911. p. 158-76). *Accountant,* June 17, 1911, p. 922-8.

New Zealand

EXAMINATION for B. com. and professional examinations in accountancy, Nov. 1919. *Accounting and commerce,* Feb. March, April 1920, p. 261-3, 285-6, 14-15.
NEW ZEALAND SOCIETY OF ACCOUNTANTS. Answers to bookkeeping and accounting. 1918, answers by H. L. Halliday. *Accounting and commerce,* April-June 1919, p. 18-23, 42-6, 66-7.
NEW ZEALAND SOCIETY OF ACCOUNTANTS. Examination for B. com. and professional examinations in accountancy, November 1916. *Accounting and commerce,* Feb. 1917, p. 251-4, 255, 258.
NEW ZEALAND SOCIETY OF ACCOUNTANTS. Examination for B. com. and professional examinations in accountancy, November 1915. *Accounting and commerce,* Jan. Aug. 1916, Jan. 1917, p. 230-1, 248-55, 273-9, 17-20, 33-4, 55-63, 79-82, 107-11, 232-40.
NEW ZEALAND SOCIETY OF ACCOUNTANTS. 1914 November examination. *Accounting and commerce,* April, May, Sept. 1915, p. 13-4, 40-1, 135-7.
NEW ZEALAND SOCIETY OF ACCOUNTANTS' preliminary examination. *Accounting and commerce,* Oct. 1915, p. 165-6.

Scotland

EXAMINATION papers of the Chartered accountants of Scotland. London, Effingham Wilson, 1894.
GLASGOW CHARTERED ACCOUNTANTS STUDENTS' SOCIETY. Papers set at the test examination on Thursday, 24th April, 1913. *Accountants' magazine,* June, July, 1913, p. 364-9, 409-17.
GLASGOW CHARTERED ACCOUNTANTS STUDENTS' SOCIETY. Papers set at the test examination held 31st March 1915 and 1st April 1915. *Accountants' magazine,* June, July 1915, p. 325-9, 370-5.
GLASGOW CHARTERED ACCOUNTANTS STUDENTS' SOCIETY. Papers set at the test examination held Thursday, 23rd October 1913. *Accountant's magazine,* Dec. 1913, Jan. 1914, p. 669-73; 23-7.
GLASGOW CHARTERED ACCOUNTANTS STUDENTS' SOCIETY. Papers set at the test examination held 23rd April 1914. *Accountants' magazine,* May, June 1914, p. 285-9, 344-52.
GLASGOW CHARTERED ACCOUNTANTS STUDENTS' SOCIETY. Papers set at the test examination held 21st October, 1914. *Accountants' magazine,* Dec. 1914, Jan. 1915, p. 605-9, 28-33.
JACOBSSON, GUSTAVE. Chartered accountants' examinations in Scotland. *Business man's magazine,* Sept. 1909, p. 280-1.
LISLE, G. Papers of Scottish C. A. general examining board for December 1893, with answers. Edinburgh, 1894.
SCOTTISH chartered accountants' examinations. *Journal of accountancy,* July 1910, p. 220-1.
SCOTTISH CHARTERED ACCOUNTANTS' GENERAL EXAMINING BOARD. Papers, December, 1896. *Accountants magazine,* Jan. Feb. April, 1897, p. 44-80, 130-44, 263-88.
SCOTTISH CHARTERED ACCOUNTANTS' GENERAL EXAMINING BOARD. Papers, June 1897. *Accountants' magazine,* July, Nov. 1897, p. 449-88, 573-91.
SCOTTISH CHARTERED ACCOUNTANTS' GENERAL EXAMINING BOARD. Papers, December, 1897. *Acccountants' magazine,* Jan. Feb. 1898, p. 50-86, 117-36.
SCOTTISH CHARTERED ACCOUNTANTS' GENERAL EXAMINING BOARD. Papers, June 1898. *Accountants' magazine,* July, Aug. Nov. 1898, p. 400-34, 456-69 515-29.
SCOTTISH CHARTERED ACCOUNTANTS' GENERAL EXAMINING BOARD. Papers December, 1898. *Accountants' magazine,* Jan., Feb. March, April 1899, p. 43-77, 123-33, 198-205, 268-86.
SCOTTISH CHARTERED ACCOUNTANTS' GENERAL EXAMINING BOARD. Papers, June 1899. *Accountants' magazine,* July, Aug., Nov., Dec. 1899, p. 443-80, 501-9, 567-82, 631-40.
SCOTTISH CHARTERED ACCOUNTANTS' GENERAL EXAMINING BOARD. Papers, December 1899.

EXAMINATIONS—SCOTLAND—*(Continued)*
Accountants' magazine, Jan. Feb. March, May 1900, p. 42-80, 92-3, 155-60, 311-3.
SCOTTISH CHARTERED ACCOUNTANTS' GENERAL EXAMINING BOARD. Papers, June 1900. *Accountants' magazine*, July, Aug. 1900, p. 428-68, 497-500.
SCOTTISH CHARTERED ACCOUNTANTS' GENERAL EXAMINING BOARD. Papers, December, 1900. *Accountants' magazine*, Jan. Feb. 1901, p. 50-90, 114-9.
SCOTTISH CHARTERED ACCOUNTANTS' GENERAL EXAMINING BOARD. Papers, June 1901. *Accountants' magazine*, July, Aug. 1901, p. 388-426, 451-60.
SCOTTISH CHARTERED ACCOUNTANTS' GENERAL EXAMINING BOARD. Papers, December 1901. *Accountants' magazine*, Jan., Feb. 1902, p. 51-90, 120-7.
SCOTTISH CHARTERED ACCOUNTANTS' GENERAL EXAMINING BOARD. Papers, June 1902. *Accountants' magazine*, July, Aug. 1902, p. 403-36, 463-6.
SCOTTISH CHARTERED ACCOUNTANTS' GENERAL EXAMINING BOARD. Papers, December 1902. *Accountants' magazine*, Jan., Feb. 1903, p. 47-82, 117-20.
SCOTTISH CHARTERED ACCOUNTANTS' GENERAL EXAMINING BOARD. Papers, June 1903. *Accountants' magazine*, July, Aug. 1903, p. 415-48, 481-6.
SCOTTISH CHARTERED ACCOUNTANTS' GENERAL EXAMINING BOARD. Papers, December 1903. *Accountants' magazine*, Jan. Feb. 1904, p. 47-80, 106-11.
SCOTTISH CHARTERED ACCOUNTANTS' GENERAL EXAMINING BOARD. Papers, June 1904. *Accountants' magazine*, July, Aug. 1904, p. 384-416, 443-8.
SCOTTISH CHARTERED ACCOUNTANTS' GENERAL EXAMINING BOARD. Papers, December 1904. *Accountants' magazine*, Jan. Feb. 1905, p. 50-84, 109-14.
SCOTTISH CHARTERED ACCOUNTANTS' GENERAL EXAMINING BOARD. Papers, June 1905. *Accountants' magazine*, July, Aug. 1905, p. 382-416, 447-51.
SCOTTISH CHARTERED ACCOUNTANTS' GENERAL EXAMINING BOARD. Papers, December 1905. *Accountants' magazine*, Jan. Feb. 1906, p. 48-80, 116-20.
SCOTTISH CHARTERED ACCOUNTANTS' GENERAL EXAMINING BOARD. Papers, June 1906. *Accountants' magazine*, July, Aug. 1906, p. 389-422, 453-6.
SCOTTISH CHARTERED ACCOUNTANTS' GENERAL EXAMINING BOARD. Papers, Dec. 1906. *Accountants' magazine*, Jan. Feb. 1907, p. 52-84, 123-5.
SCOTTISH CHARTERED ACCOUNTANTS' GENERAL EXAMINING BOARD. Papers, June 1907. *Accountants' magazine*, July, Aug. 1907, p. 393-426, 454-60.
SCOTTISH CHARTERED ACCOUNTANTS' GENERAL EXAMINING BOARD. Papers, December 1907. *Accountants' magazine*, Jan. Feb. 1908, p. 46-80, 114-23.
SCOTTISH CHARTERED ACCOUNTANTS' GENERAL EXAMINING BOARD. Papers, June 1908. *Accountants' magazine*, July, Aug. 1908, p. 396-432, 456-66.
SCOTTISH CHARTERED ACCOUNTANTS' GENERAL EXAMINING BOARD. Papers, December 1908. *Accountants' magazine*, Jan. Feb. 1909, p. 50-84, 100-14.
SCOTTISH CHARTERED ACCOUNTANTS' GENERAL EXAMINING BOARD. Papers, June 1909. *Accountants' magazine*, July, Aug. 1909, p. 382-420, 455-65.
SCOTTISH CHARTERED ACCOUNTANTS' GENERAL EXAMINING BOARD. Papers, December 1909. *Accountants' magazine*, Jan. Feb. March 1910, p. 52-86, 125-31, 171-6.
SCOTTISH CHARTERED ACCOUNTANTS' GENERAL EXAMINING BOARD. Paper, June 1910. *Accountants' magazine*, July, Aug. 1910, p. 373-408, 428-41.
SCOTTISH CHARTERED ACCOUNTANTS' GENERAL EXAMINING BOARD. Papers, December 1910. *Accountants' magazine*, Jan.-March, 1911, p. 42-68, 86-95, 153-9.
SCOTTISH CHARTERED ACCOUNTANTS' GENERAL EXAMINING BOARD. Papers, June 1911. *Accountants' magazine*, July, Aug. 1911, p. 375-404, 437-45.
SCOTTISH CHARTERED ACCOUNTANTS' GENERAL EXAMINING BOARD. Papers, December 1911. *Accountants' magazine*, Jan.-May 1912, p. 45-76, 104-7, 147-55, 204-12, 248-54.
SCOTTISH CHARTERED ACCOUNTANTS' GENERAL EXAMINING BOARD. Papers June 1912. *Accountants' magazine*, July, Aug. Nov. 1912, p. 370-400, 423-33, 468-82.
SCOTTISH CHARTERED ACCOUNTANTS' GENERAL EXAMINING BOARD. Papers, December 1912. *Accountants' magazine*, Jan.-March, May 1913, p. 52-80, 108-11, 161-8, 290-306.
SCOTTISH CHARTERED ACCOUNTANTS' GENERAL EXAMINING BOARD. Papers, June 1913. *Accountants' magazine*, July, Aug. Nov. 1913, p. 434-68, 529-44, 582-95, 664.
SCOTTISH CHARTERED ACCOUNTANTS' GENERAL EXAMINING BOARD. Papers, December 1913. *Accountants' magazine*, Jan.-April 1914, p. 47-80, 107-15, 155-65, 218-28.
SCOTTISH CHARTERED ACCOUNTANTS' GENERAL EXAMINING BOARD. Papers, June 1914. *Accountants' magazine*, July, Aug. Nov. 1914, p. 410-40, 485-500, 543-54.
SCOTTISH CHARTERED ACCOUNTANTS' GENERAL EXAMINING BOARD. Papers, December 1914. *Accountants' magazine*, Jan.-March 1915, p. 51-84, 119-32, 176-88.
SCOTTISH CHARTERED ACCOUNTANTS' GENERAL EXAMINING BOARD. Papers, June 1915. *Accountants' magazine*, July, Aug. Nov. 1915, p. 387-420, 448-76, 521-9.
SCOTTISH CHARTERED ACCOUNTANTS' GENERAL EXAMINING BOARD. Paper, December 1915. *Accountants' magazine*, Jan.-March 1916, p. 40-72, 99-115, 150-63.
SCOTTISH CHARTERED ACCOUNTANTS' GENERAL EXAMINING BOARD. Papers, June 1916. *Accountants' magazine*, July, Aug. Nov. 1916, p. 340-72, 389-405, 437-54.
SCOTTISH CHARTERED ACCOUNTANTS' GENERAL EXAMINING BOARD. Papers, June 1917. *Accountants' magazine*, July, Aug. Nov. 1917, p. 332-60, 378-95, 430-47.
SCOTTISH CHARTERED ACCOUNTANTS' GENERAL EXAMINING BOARD. Papers, June 1918, July, Aug. Nov. Dec. 1918, p. 314-44, 365-81, 423-34, 473-81.
SCOTTISH CHARTERED ACCOUNTANTS' GENERAL EXAMINING BOARD. Papers, December 1918. *Accountants' magazine*, Jan.-March, May 1919, p. 39-72, 95-102, 148-55, 235-54.
SCOTTISH CHARTERED ACCOUNTANTS' GENERAL EXAMINING BOARD. Papers, June 1919. *Accountants' magazine*, July, Aug., Nov. 1919, p. 363-92, 424-37, 479-503.
SCOTTISH CHARTERED ACCOUNTANTS' GENERAL EXAMINING BOARD. Papers, December 1919. *Accountants' magazine*, Jan. 1920, p. 51-60.
SCOTTISH CHARTERED ACCOUNTANTS' GENERAL EXAMINING BOARD. Examination papers, June 1920. *Accountants' magazine*, July 1920, p. 468-500.
SCOTTISH CHARTERED ACCOUNTANTS' GENERAL EXAMINING BOARD. Solutions to papers, Dec. 1919. *Accountants' magazine*, March-May 1920, p. 213-20, 273-84, 349-56.
SCOTTISH CHARTERED ACCOUNTANTS' GENERAL EXAMINING BOARD. Solutions to papers, June 1920. *Accountants' magazine*, Aug. Nov. 1920, p. 559-72, 630-52.

Society of incorporated accountants and auditors
FINAL examination. June 1890: questions with answers. *Incorporated accountants' journal*, 1890-1, p. 115.

EXAMINATIONS—SOCIETY OF INCORPORATED ACCOUNTANTS AND AUDITORS—*(Continued)*

FINAL examination, June 1891; selection of questions with answers. *Incorporated accountants' journal,* 1891-2, p. 48.

INCORPORATED accountants, questions and answers, intermediate and final examinations. December 1900 and June 1901. 2v. London, 1901.

INCORPORATED students' telephone; questions and swers to the intermediate and final examinations of the Society of incorporated accountants and auditors, 1910 to date; answers by D. F. de l'Hoste Ranking and Spicer & Pegler. London, H. Foulks Lynch & co.

MEATS, THOMAS W. Preparation of a student for the accountancy portion of the society's final examination. *Incorporated accountants' journal,* 1901-2, p. 105.

NELSON, C. H. Critical guide to the incorporated accountants' examinations. London.

SELECTIONS of questions, with answers, final and intermediate examinations, June, 1889. *Incorporated accountants' journal,* 1889-90, p. 28, 34, 47.

TEST questions on legal points in accountancy, with answers. *Incorporated accountants' journal,* 1896-7, p. 52, 72, 83, 110, 126, 143, 159, 179, 190; 1897-8, p. 14, 29, 46, 61, 77, 97, 116, 137, 157, 176 192, 209; 1898-9, p. 14, 31, 66, 84, 104, 121, 145, 163, 185, 206, 221, 237, 1899-1900, p. 15, 42, 64, 80, 99, 120, 135, 151, 168.

Union of South Africa

ASSOCIATION OF CHAMBER OF COMMERCE OF SOUTH AFRICA. Paper in bookkeeping and accountancy, 1916. *South African accountant and auditor,* Dec. 1916, p. 228-33, 235-6.

FINAL and intermediate examination papers, 1906. Transvaal society of accountants. *South African accountants' journal,* v. 1, p. 36, 74.

UNIVERSITY OF SOUTH AFRICA. South African school of mines and technology. Examination papers, 1918. *South African accountant,* Dec. 1918, p. 251-68.

United States

See also Examinations—American institute of accountants; Examinations —C. P. A.

ADAMS, WILLIAM JAMES. Up-to-date regents questions in bookkeeping. Syracuse, C. W. Bardeen. 1919. 49p.

EXAMINATION for appointment of field examiners, conducted by the State board of accounts of Indiana on May 31, 1910 *Government accountant,* Aug. 1910, p. 173-5.

NEW YORK STATE. Department of public instruction. Questions and answers in the first-grade subjects; algebra, bookkeeping, physics, given at the uniform examinations, Syracuse, C. W. Bardeen, 1896.

NEW YORK STATE. Questions in bookkeeping, with answers. Syracuse, New York, C. W. Bardeen.

WOLFF, MARK. Bookkeeper and accountant civil service examination instruction; 250 questions and answers, including problems and solutions and 500 specimen questions; Board of education questions for license to teach bookkeeping in high schools and evening schools, N. Y. city; digest of uniform accounting systems prescribed by the Public service commission, First district, New York; certified public accountant, answers to New York state examination questions: practice questions and answers on bookkeeping; commercial practice and terms. New York, Civil service chronicle, 1918. 108p.

EXAMINATIONS *Journal of accountancy,* Oct. 1909, p. 455.

EXAMINATIONS and their bearing on national efficiency. *Journal of accountancy,* April 1911, p. 459-61.

EXAMINATIONS as a medium for professional efficiency. *Canadian chartered accountant,* April 1914, p. 267-70.

EXAMINATIONS for B. com. and professional examinations in accountancy, Nov. 1919. *Accounting and commerce,* Feb-April 1920, p. 261-3, 285-6; 14-5.

EXAMINATIONS hints. *Incorporated accountants' journal,* Feb. 1912, p. 115-6.

EXAMINATIONS notes on book-keeping and accountancy. Blake, H. T.

EXAMINATIONS of the institute of chartered accountants of Ontario. *Canadian chartered accountant,* Jan. 1913, p. 182-6.

EXAMINATIONS questions in book-keeping. Harlow, Edward. 1894.

EXAMINATIONS questions in book-keeping by double entry, with answers. Hunter, John.

EXAMINERS and examinations. *Journal of accountancy,* April 1910, p. 448-9.

EXAMINERS and publicity. *Journal of accountancy,* March, July, 1909, p. 390-2, 216-7.

EXAMINERS wanted for the Interstate Commerce commission. *Journal of accountancy,* Sept. 1908, p. 358.

EXAMINING and sizing up mine prospects. *Mining world,* April 23, 1910.

EXAMPLE of depreciation charges. *Journal of accountancy,* Jan. 1908, p. 201-4. *Accountant,* March 7, 1908, p. 343-4.

EXAMPLE of inadequacy depreciation. *Public service regulation,* Jan. 1913, p. 2.

EXCAVATION

DAILY report form for steam shovel and dray line excavation work. *Engineering and contracting,* Sept. 20, 1916, p. 265.

GILLETTE, HALBERT P. Handbook of rock excavation; methods and costs. New York, McGraw-Hill book company, inc. 1916. 825p.

Costs

ANDERSON, J. M. Openpit steam-shovel costs. *Engineering and mining journal,* Jan. 27, 1917, p. 183-4.

BECHTEL, A. E. Cost of earth work of the second unit of the Dodson North canal, Milk river project. Malta, Montana. *Engineering and contracting,* Sept. 20, 1916, p. 266-7.

BRUSH, W. W. Trenching machine work. *Journal of the American water works association,* Dec. 1917. p. 521-31.

BURKHOLDER, J. L. Drainage works of the Rio Grande irrigation project. *Engineering news-record,* Sept. 18, 1919, p. 543-9.

CAISSON excavation cost reduced. *Concrete,* July 1917, p. 17.

CANAL excavation with electric drag-line scrapers. *Electrical world,* Jan. 29, 1916, p. 255-6.

COST of drag line excavator operation on drainage construction. *Engineering and contracting,* Feb. 20, 1918, p. 200.

COST of excavating drainage ditches with steam and electric machines. *Engineering record,* Dec. 26, 1914, p. 704-5.

EXCAVATION—Costs—*(Continued)*
Cost of excavating pavement, trenching and steam pipe laying. *Engineering and contracting,* July 19, 1916, p. 62.
Costs of electric shovel work at Cleveland. *Electric railway journal,* Dec. 5, 1914, p. 1261-2. *Electrical review and western electrician,* Jan. 23, 1915, p. 172-3.
Costs on excavation and concrete for Mayfair pumping station, Chicago, Ill. *Engineering and contracting,* Oct. 25, 1916, p. 364.
Dana, R. T. Analysis of trenching methods and costs: comparative data on sandy soil excavations by hand and by steam shovel. *Engineering record,* May 23, Oct. 10, 17, 1914, p. 581-4, 409-10, 432-3.
Dana, R. T. Excavators. (In his *Handbook of construction plant.* 1914, p. 302-16.
Ditch dug with dynamite at 15 cents per cubic yard. *Engineering record,* Nov. 27, 1915, p. 673.
Dragline excavation costs. *Engineering and mining journal,* May 27, 1916, p. 940-1.
Earth excavated for less than six cents per yard in district no. 9, Mississippi county, Arkansas. *Engineering record,* Feb. 6, 1915, p. 176.
Effect of bonus system on quantity and unit cost of basement excavation. *Engineering and contracting,* July 22, 1914, p. 80.
Electrically driven dragline scrapers dig 45-mile irrigation canal at Sun river poject. *Engineering record,* Jan. 29, 1916, p. 148.
Excavation of Cleveland railway company. *Railway review,* Jan. 9, 1915, p. 67-8.
Ferriss, H. R. Cost of excavating abutments and wing-walls for a street bridge. *Engineering and contracting,* July 7, 1915, p. 14.
Fitzgerald, P. S. Profit or loss with the steam shovel. *Engineering record,* March 14, 1914, p. 307-8.
Ford, C. W. Electrically operated ditcher effects big saving. *Electric railway journal,* Nov. 30, 1918 p. 960-1.
Gardner, E. D. Cost of initial mining excavations. *Journal of the association of engineering societies,* May 1915, p. 210-9.
Gillette, Halbert P. Excavation. (In his *Handbook of cost data for contractors and engineers.* 1910. p. 119-257).
Hay, William W. Unit costs and organization for building site excavation. *Engineering and contracting,* May 19, 1915, p. 453-4.
Hicks, H. L. Compressed air in street excavating and tamping. *Municipal journal,* Aug. 2, 1917, p. 108-10.
Humphreys, E. W. Cost of machine trenching under difficult conditions for water mains and services at Erie, Pa. *Municipal and county engineering,* May 1918, p. 189-90.
Inexpensive excavation by Cleveland railway company. *Engineering and contracting,* July 19, 1916, p. 56.
Labor cost of excavating in stiff white clay. *Engineering and contracting,* May 15, 1918, p. 477.
Landon, H. C. Construction of the Watauga and Yadkin valley railroad with details of methods and costs of earth and rock excavation. *Engineering and contracting,* April 1, 1914, p. 391-5.
McDaniel, A. B. Methods of excavation for building. Engineering record, Jan. 16, 1915, p. 68-71.
McDaniel, A. B. Operation analysis of new machines which cheapen the moving of earth on road work. *Engineering record,* July 31, 1915, p. 126-8.
Methods and costs of electric shovel work removing slides and side cutting for electric railway. *Engineering and contracting,* Feb. 17, 1915, p. 154-5.
Nash, P. C. Clamshell digs first cut on subway in Boston. *Engineering news,* June 7, 1917, p. 508-9.
Nickel, L. W. Cost data on drag-line operation for coal mine. *Electrical review,* Jan. 19, 1918, p. 101-2. *Coal age,* Feb. 16, 1918, 323-4. Abstract. *Engineering news,* April 11, 1918, p. 742.
Owen, R. S. Cost of excavating drainage ditch with a drag line excavator. *Engineering and contracting,* March 11, 1914, p. 303.
Parsons excavating equipment—comparison of cost of machine and hand work. *American gas engineering journal,* May 26, 1917, p. 515.
Rapid trench excavation at Canadian camp follows war's call. *Engineering record,* Feb. 6, 1915, p. 182.
Reducing the cost of drainage excavation. *Engineering record,* Dec. 26, 1914, p. 693-4.
Rogers, H. W. Dredges and excavating machinery. *American institute of electrical engineers, Proceedings,* Dec. 1915, p. 3035-9.
Roscoe, A. P. Overhead and time cost of pit and trench excavation. *Engineering news-record,* July 10, 1919, p. 89-90.
Shallow excavation by steam shovels. *Municipal engineering,* Jan. 1916, p. 39-41.
Steam shovel work in road construction. *Engineering and contracting,* Nov. 6, 1918, p. 446.
Tile drainage by day labor and by the rod. *Engineering news,* March 9, 1916, p. 450-2.
Trench excavator cuts cost of duct line between tracks. *Engineering news-record,* July 25, 1918, p. 195.
Trench spoil moved cheaply by tractor-trailor trains. *Engineering news,* Oct. 28, 1915, p. 842-3.
Unit cost of excavation for Panama canal. *Engineering and contracting,* Feb. 21, 1917, p. 190-1.
Williams, A. D. Conditions determining maximum grades and methods and cost of road grading in West Virginia. *Engineering and contracting,* Jan. 6, 1915, p. 16-17. Excerpt. Cost of grading and excavating. *Concrete-cement age,* Dec. 1914, p. 267-8.
Yarnell, D. L. Excavating machinery used in land drainage. *Engineering and contracting,* Jan. 26-Feb. 9, 1916, p. 89-90, 116-7, 120-2, 128.

EXCAVATION of Cleveland railway company. *Railway review,* Jan. 9, 1915, p. 67-8.

EXCERPTS from by-laws. Western foundrymen's association. 1895.

EXCESS profits and income tax frauds. *Incorporated accountants' journal,* Jan. 1918, p. 68-71.

EXCESS profits duty. *Accountant,* Nov. 20, 1920, p. 560.

EXCESS profits duty. *Incorporated accountants' journal,* Aug. 1917, p. 231-3.

EXCESS profits duty and manager's commission. *Incorporated accountants' journal,* April 1919, p. 126-8.

EXCESS profits duty and profits of controlled establishments. Spicer, E. E. and E. C. Pegler, 1918.

EXCESS profits duty, government amendment to finance bill. *Incorporated accountants' journal,* July 1920, p. 207-11.

EXCESS profits duty: official statement. *Accountant,* July 21, 1917, p. 50-3. *Incorporated accountants' journal,* Aug. 1917, p. 231-3.

EXCESS profits (including excess mineral rights) duty and levies under the munitions of war acts. Snelling, W. E. 1917,

EXCESS PROFITS TAX.
See Taxation.

EXCESS profits tax in Great Britain. Wright, James.

EXCESS profits tax primer. United States. Treasury Department.

EXCESS profits tax procedure. Montgomery, R. H. 1920.

EXCESSIVE rates due to holding company. *Electrical world*, April 27, 1911, p. 1017-8.

EXCHANGE.
See Foreign exchange; Stock exchanges.

EXCHANGE and distribution. McVey, F. L. c1918.

EXCHANGE tables for converting dollars into francs and francs into dollars at all rates from 5.00 to 5.79, thus covering wartime and normal requirements. Levy, Ernest, comp.

"**EXCHANGE** value" and "fair value for rate making purposes". *Stone and Webster public service journal*, Nov. 1914, p. 327.

EXCHANGES and speculation. Atwood, A. W. c1918.

EXCHANGES, WOMEN.
See Women's exchanges.

EXECUTION of trusts (war facilities) amendment act. *Incorporated accountants' journal* Aug. 1915, p. 252-3.

EXECUTIVE budget in relation to governmental accounting. Chase, H. S. c1917.

EXECUTIVE officer for the American association of public accountants. *Journal of accountancy*, Oct. 1910, p. 458-9.

EXECUTOR'S account book. London, Bell.

EXECUTOR'S account book. Kuhn, R. K.

EXECUTOR'S account book. Matthews, R. 1839.

EXECUTORS' accounts. Widdifield, C. H. 1919.

EXECUTORS and administrators. Gosset, Thoald.

EXECUTORS and no next-of-kin. *Accountant*, March 14, 1908, p. 345-7.

EXECUTORS AND TRUSTEES
See also Bankruptcy; Life tenant and remainderman; Liquidations and receiverships.

ACCOUNTANTS as receivers and trustees. *Journal of accountancy*, Dec. 1910, p. 153.
SUFFERN, EDWARD L. Relative advantages of trust companies and accountants as trustees and executors. *Journal of accountancy*, Aug. 1906, p. 241-7.

Accounting

ABBOTT, CHARLES E. E. Taking of accounts in chambers. *Accountant*, April 18, 1908, p. 575-8.
ACCOUNTS of the distribution of the estates of deceased persons (1) liability of the real and personal estates for the payment of debts, legacies &c. (2) interstates' estates act of 1890. *Accountant*, June 11, 18, July 2, 16, 1910, p. 819-23, 853-7; 7-9, 75-8.
ADJUSTMENT of trust accounts. *Accountant*, Dec. 13, 1913, p. 859-60.
AMERICAN business and accounting encyclopaedia; comp. by E. H. Beach and W. W. Thorne. Detroit, Bookkeeper publishing co. 1901. Executorship accounts, p. 525-9.
ANNAN, WILLIAM. Trust accounts. (In Lisle, George. *Encyclopaedia of accounting*. v.6. p. 308-37).
APPORTIONMENT of dividends on death. *Accountant*, July 19, 1902, p. 735-6.
APPORTIONMENT of income in trust accounts. *Accountant*, 1887, p. 186, 201, 215, 229.
BARTLE, A. C. Executorship accounts. *Accountant*, Oct. 21, 28, Nov. 4, 1916, p. 361-7, 384-90, 411-6.
BAUGH, FREDERICK H. and W. C. SCHMEISSER. Estate accounting. *Trust companies*, Sept. 1912, p. 245-7.
BAUGH, FREDERICK H. and W. C. SCHMEISSER. Theory and practice of estate accounting for accountants, lawyers, executors, administrators and trustees. Baltimore, M. Curlander, 1910.
——— Same. Baltimore, M. Curlander, 1917. 321p.
BEALTY, CHARLES. Practical guide to the death duties and to the preparation of death—duty accounts. London, 1911.
BELL, E. D. Executorship accounts in relation to rural properties. *Accounting and commerce*, Nov. Dec. 1916, p. 180-8, 201-10.
BENNETT, GEORGE E. Estate accounting. (In his *Constructive accounting*. 1920. p. 404-14).
BIRKS, W. J. Trust accounts. (In Feather, J. Stuart, ed. *Joint transactions*. 1911. p. 314-22). *Accountant*, Jan. 6, 1912, p. 15-8.
BLEASE, WALTER. Executorship accounts. *Accountant*, 1883, p. 593.
BLEASE, WALTER. Executorship accounts. *Accountant*, Sept. 15, 22, 1888, p. 593-5, 598-9.
BONSON settlement trust; specimen of form of account employed by the public trustees in rendering a statement of trust to beneficiaries.
BOWLES, B. Executors and executorship accounts. *Associated accountants' journal*, 1912, p. 257.
BREWIS, ARTHUR STEPHEN. Duties and accounts of trustees. *Accountant*, 1886, p. 320.
BREWIS, ARTHUR STEPHEN. Executorship accounts. *Accountant*, April 4, 1885.
BUCK, WILLIAM. Some points in executorship accounts. *Federal accountant*, April, July 1916, p. 57-64, 82-4.
BURGESS, HENRY J. Executorship accounts. *Incorporated accountants' journal*, 1896-7, p. 18.
CALDICOTT, OSWALD H. Executors' and trustees' accounts. *Accountant*, April 28, 1883.
CALDICOTT, OSWALD H. Executorship accounts. *Accountant*, May 30, 1885.
CALDICOTT, OSWALD H. Executorship accounts. Ed.3. London, Gee & co. 1906. 82p. *Accountant*, Nov. 9, 16, 23, 30, Dec. 7, 1889, p. 594-6, 604-12, 630-6, 644-51 663-8.
CARTER, PHILIP H. Some points in connection with estate accounts. *Accountant*, Jan. 20, 1900, p. 75-80, 345.
CARTER, ROGER N. Bankruptcy statement of affairs, deficiency account. (In his *Advanced accounts*. p. 760-83).
CARTER, ROGER N. Executorship accounts. *Incorporated accountants' journal*, 1908-9, p. 172.
CARTER, ROGER N. Some hints to students, with special reference to executorship accounts. *Accountant*, Jan. 16, 1909, p. 82-5.
CARTER, ROGER N. Some notes on executorship accounts. *Accountant*, Feb. 24, 1900, p. 209-12.

EXECUTORS AND TRUSTEES—ACCOUNTING—*(Continued)*

CARTER, ROGER N. Students' guide to executorship accounts. Ed.2. London, Gee & co. 1912. 240p.

CHANDLER, PRETOR W. Accounts of executors and trustees. *Accountant,* Nov. 7, 1908, p. 566-9, 541-4.

CHANDLER, PRETOR W. Accounts of executors and trustees, with specimen register, ledger, and accounts for the residuary legatees, next of kin and others. 2v. London, Butterworth & co. 1906.

CHANDLER, PRETOR W. Guide to trust accounts. London, Buterworth & co. 1907.

——— Same. Ed.2. 1910. 303p.

——— Same as Trust accounts, including the history, preparation, investigation and audit thereof.

CHANDLER, PRETOR W. Trust accounts, including the history, preparation, investigation and audit thereof. London, Butterworth & co. 1910.

CHARLESWORTH, A. Trust companies and their audit. London, Gee & co. 1894.

CHILD, PERCY. Accounts of executors and trustees. *Accountant,* Nov. 6, 1897, p. 1038-42.

CHILD, PERCY. Paper on some of the bookkeeping questions set at the June examinations. *Accountant,* Dec. 31, 1898, p. 1264-71.

COLE, WILLIAM MORSE. Some general principles illustrated in trust accounting. (In his *Accounts their construction and interpretation.* c1915. p. 255-62).

COLE, WILLIAM MORSE. Trusteeship. (In his *Bookkeeping, accounting and auditing.* c1914. p. 384-6).

COLLINGE, BRAMWELL. Executors and their accounts. *Accountant,* Jan. 4, 1913, p. 27-37.

CONGER, WILLIAM H. Approved and new system for trust estate accounting. *Trust companies,* June and July 1914, p. 500-11; 23-31.

CORY, Z. F. Executorship. London, William Pickering, 1839.

COSTS of litigation in trust accounts. *Accountant,* Aug. 17, 1918, p. 81-2.

CRAKE, JAMES. Executorship accounts. *Accountant,* Jan. 24, 1903, p. 122-5.

CUTFORTH, A. E. Executors' accounts. (In his *Audits.* 1914. p. 101-2).

DAWSON, SIDNEY STANLEY and H. R. GRAVES. Accounts of trustees, liquidators, and receivers. London, Gee & co. 1905. 125p. (Accountants' library, v. 41).

DENNEHY, JOHN G. Executorship accounts. *Accountant,* May 3, 1902, p. 473-80.

DICKINSON, WALTER S. Executorship accounts. *Accountant,* March 22, April 12, 1902, p. 313-8, 374-6.

DICKINSON, WALTER S. Executorship accounts. *Accountant,* May 23, 1903, p. 696-702.

DICKSEE, LAWRENCE R. Executorship and trust accounts. (In his *Advanced accounting.* 1916. p. 113-56).

EDWARDS, ALLEN. Probate accounts. *Accountant,* Nov. 15, 1884.

ESQUERRE, PAUL JOSEPH. Accounts of fiduciaries. (In his *Applied theory on accounts.* 1917. p. 491-501).

ESTATE account, estate bookkeeping. (In Lisle, George. *Encyclopaedia of accounting.* v.2. p. 410-1).

EXECUTOR'S account book. London, Bell.

EXECUTORS' trading accounts. *Accountant,* Sept. 1, 1900, p. 777-9.

EXECUTORSHIP accounts. *Accountant.* April 7, 1888, Sept. 4, 11, 18, 25, Oct. 2, 9, 1897, p. 206-207, 836-7, 856-7, 880-1, 904-6, 924-5, 937-8.

EXECUTORSHIP accounts. *Accountant,* Jan. 31, 1920, p. 134. *Australasian accountant and secretary,* May-Aug. 1920, p. 142, 179-81, 206-7, 249-55.

FEES chargeable in trust accounts. *Accountants' magazine,* Feb. 1911, p. 78-84.

FOSTER, A. J. Some points arising in Allhusen v. Whittell and other executorship cases. *Accountant,* March 15, 1913, p. 405-7.

GERRISH, F. W. Executorship accounts. *Accountants journal,* 1908-9, p. 406.

GOTTSBERGER, FRANCIS. Accountant's guide for executors, administrators, assignees, receivers and trustees. New York, George G. Peck, c1902. 196p.

GREEN, ARTHUR E. Trust accounts. *Incorporated accountants' journal,* 1908-9, p. 188.

GRIFFIN, J. L. Accounts of executors, administrators and trustees; abstract. *Accounting and commerce,* Sept. 1920, p. 137.

GRIFFITH, JAMES B. Trustees' and executors' accounts. Chicago, American school of correspondence, 1909. (In *Cyclopedia of commerce, accountancy, business administration.* 1910. v.6. p. 163-92).

GUNDRY, WILLIAM HICLEY. Municipalities and trust accounts. *Accountant,* Oct. 21, 1905, p. 453-4.

HARDCASTLE, JOSEPH. Accounts of executors and testamentary trustees. New York, University school of commerce, accounts and finance. 1903. 75p.

HARDCASTLE, JOSEPH. Problem in executor's accounts. *Journal of accountancy,* Aug. 1906, p. 311-4.

HARDIE, W. Manual of bookkeeping for law agents, with forms for trust accounts. Edinburgh, W. Green, 1893.

HARRIS, WILLIAM. Probate accounts. *Accountant,* Oct. 20, Nov. 3, 10, 1888, Jan. 12, 1889, p. 670-9, 719-33, 731-40; 20-3.

HARROLD, J. BLAKE. Pitman's examination notes on bookkeeping and accountancy; including executorship accounts. London, Sir Isaac Pitman & sons, 1911. 58p.

HAWKINS, LESLIE WHITTEN. Bookkeeping for executors and trustees. London, Gee & co. 1906. 51p.

HAWSON, WILLIAM G. Executors' and trustees' accounts. *Accountant,* Jan. 5, 12, 1884.

HEWITT, ELKANAH. Executors and their accounts. *Accountant,* July 28, 1888, p. 483-6.

HODSOLL, SYDNEY. Practical accounts for executors and trustees. London, 1914. 175p.

JAUDON, WILLIAM BAINBRIDGE. Administrators' and executors' accounts. *The office,* July 1889, p. 125-6.

JENKINS, F. PERCY. Some notes on trust accounts. *Accountant,* Oct. 19, 1912, p. 496-9.

JENKINS, FREDERICK A. Executors' and trustees' accounts. *Accountant,* March 8, 1884.

JORDON, F. C. Executorship accounts. *Public accountant,* 1910, p. 41.

KEISTER, D. A. Estate accounting. (In his *Corporation accounting and auditing.* 1909. p. 331-45).

KESTER, R. B. Accounts and reports of receivers and trustees. (In his *Accounting theory and practice.* 1918. v.2. p. 620-54).

KING, GEORGE C. Some points in executorship accounts. *Accountant,* Aug. 26, 1911, p. 271-7.

KUHN, R. K. Administrator's account book. Philadelphia, David McKay.

KUHN, R. K. Executor's account book. Philadelphia, David McKay.

KUHN, R. K. Guardian's account book. Philadelphia, David McKay.

LAIRD, THOMAS P. Trust accounts and apportionment of dividends. *Accountants' magaine,* Nov. 1912, p. 452-67.

LAIRD, THOMAS P. Trust and executry accounts and apportionment of dividends. Edinburgh, William Blackwood & sons, 1919.

LAIRD, THOMAS P. Trust and executry, their preparation and audit. Edinburgh, Macniven and Wallace, 1892.

EXECUTORS AND TRUSTEES—ACCOUNTING—*(Continued)*

LAW society and trust accounts. *Accountant*, July 29, Aug. 12, 1911, p. 133-6, 147-9, 200-1.

LISLE, GEORGE. Trust and executry accounts. (In his *Accounting in theory and practice*. 1900. p. 175-93).

LOOMIS, JOHN R. Contents and mode of stating executors' accounts; and discussion thereon at the December monthly meeting of the New York state society of certified public accountants, December 10, 1907. 24p. *Journal of accountancy*, Jan. 1907, p. 219-32.

MADDEN, JOHN THOMAS. Fiduciary accounting. (In his *Accounting practice and procedure*. c1917. p. 137-54).

MADDOCK, J. C. Executor's schedules in final accounting. *New York accountants' and bookkeepers' journal*, Aug.Sept. 1904, p. 225-9).

MATTHEWS, R. Executor's account book. London, Crofts, 1839.

MAYBURY, C. W. Trust accounts. *Incorporated accountants' journal*, 1891-2, p. 79.

MERCHANT, F. R. Hints on the study of executorship accounts. Bombay, 1915.

MILLAR, THOMAS J. Methods of stating ac-accounts, with particular reference to trust accounts. London, Gee & co., 1908. *Accountant*, May 16, July 25, 1908, p. 725-32, 89-92.

MOXEY, EDWARD P. and others. Executor's work: Estate bookkeeping system. (In their *Practical accounting methods*. p. 374-90).

NELSON, WALTER. Trusts; an outline of the course to be followed in their administration. *Accountant*, Feb. 23, March 2, 1907, p. 259-64, 289-98.

NEWMAN, JARED TREMAN. Account book for executors and administrators. Rochester, Williamson law book company, 1904. 152p.

NEWMAN'S executors' and administrators' account book. Rochester, Williamson law book company. 1915. 125p.

NIXON, ALFRED and J. H. STAGG. Executorship accounts. (In their *Accounting and banking*. 1912. p. 413-26).

NIXON, ALFRED and J. H. STAGG. ' Trust accounts. (In their *Accounting and banking*. 1912. p. 427-44).

OLLIFFE, W. G. Preparation of an estate duty account, corrective affidavit and residuary account. *Incorporated accountants' journal*, May 1915, p. 182-5.

PHILLIPS, W. B. Accounts of executors, administrators and trustees; with summary of the law in so far as it relates to accounts. London, Sir Isaac Pitman and sons, 1913. 150p.

PORTERS, R. J. Executor, residuary account. (In his *Pitman's dictionary of bookkeeping*. p. 380-411, 636-41).

PRICE, HARRY L. Executorship accounts. *Incorporated accountants' journal*, 1904-5, p. 106.

PROBLEMS in executor's accounts. *Journal of accountancy*, Aug. 1906, p. 311-14.

RANKING, D. FEARON DE L'HOSTE. Handbook of executorship law and accounts. Ed.4. London, H. Foulks Lynch & co. 1915. 312p.

RANKING, D. FEARON DE L'HOSTE, E. E. SPICER and E. C. PEGLER. Handbook of executorship law, with the mode of keeping executorship accounts. Ed. 3. London, H. Foulks Lynch & co. 1911.

ROBERTSON, JOHN B. Principal and income. *Journal of accountancy*, Sept. 1914, p. 235-8.

ROSEBERRY, L. H. Standardization of trust forms and indentures; set of trust instruments. *Trust companies*, July 1919, p. 13-6.

SAUNDERS, A. F. Notes on executorship accounts. *Accountant*, Oct. 31, 1914, p. 503-7.

SHAW, WILLIAM H. Notes on executorship accounts. *Accountant*, June 5, 1909, p. 798-808.

SHORT, T. Executors account-book. London, Longman, 1846.

SPICER, ERNEST EVAN. Accounts of an executor. Ed. 4. London, . H. Foulks Lynch & co. 55p.

SPICER, ERNEST EVAN. Accounts of an executor. *Accountant*, Nov. 28, 1908, p. 651-60.

STEWART, C. J. Accountants' work under the public trustee act. *Accountant*, April 29, 1911, p. 673-8.

STRACHAN, WALTER. Digest of the law of trust accounts chiefly in relation to life owner and remainderman. London, Effingham Wilson, 1911. 224p.

STRACHAN, WALTER. Some difficulties in trust accounts, with special reference to adjustments between life owner and remainderman where property is realisable. *Accountant*, Jan. 5, 1907, p. 19-23.

TRUST accounts. *Accountant*, May 30, June 13, 1885.

TRUST accounts—apportionment. *Accountant*, Dec. 30, 1911, Jan. 27, 1912, p. 893-6, 118-9.

TRUSTEES' accounts. *Accountant*, May 22, 1909, p. 724-6.

VAN NECK, ARTHUR P. Executorship accounts. *Accountant*, March 16, 1901, p. 346-51.

VIERLING, FREDERICK. Fiduciary accounting. Chicago, La Salle extension university, 1918. 47p.

WALTON, SEYMOUR. Commuting a life interest. *Journal of accountancy*, Oct. 1916, p. 315-6.

WEBSTER, GEORGE COLIN. Concise forms of procedure (a) on undertaking the audit of a manufacturing concern (b) on the appointment of a trustee under an assignment deed (c) on preparing administration accounts for the executors of a deceased person's estate. *Accountant*, May 18, 25, 1901, p. 590-6, 614-8.

WEISS, W. F. Principal and income. *Journal of accountancy*, May 1914, p. 395-8.

WHINNEY, ARTHUR F. Executorship accounts. (In Lisle, George. *Encyclopaedia of accounting*. v.2. p. 450-62).

WHINNEY, FREDERICK. Executorship accounts. *Accountant*, April 12, 19, 1884.

WHINNEY, FREDERICK. Executorship accounts; a lecture delivered to the chartered accountants students' society of London, on the 10th, 17th and 24th April, and 1st May 1888 and an appendix containing an epitome of a will and a set of executorship accounts by Arthur F. Whinney. London, Gee & co. 197p.

——— Same. Reissued and brought up to date by the lecturer, assisted by Arthur F. Whinney. London, Gee & co., 1901. 267p.

WHITAKER, LAWRENCE A. Principles involved in the preparation of trust accounts. *Accountant*, March 27, 1909, p. 440-3.

WIDDIFIELD, CHARLES HOWARD. Executors' accounts. Toronto, Carswell company, 1919. 585p.

WOOD, FREDERICK. Estates, accounts, precedents and instruction. London, Sweet and Maxwell, 1892.

WOOD, FREDERICK. Solicitors' reports on, and accountants' balance sheets in administrations and executorships; their objects and advantages. London, 1888.

WOOD, F. Special estate accounts in administrations and executorships, etc.; with instructions for the preparation and completion thereof. 1887.

Auditing

AUDIT of trust accounts. *Accountant*, Nov. 14, 1914, p. 555-7.

CASTENHOLZ, WILLIAM B. Trustees' and executors' accounts. (In his *Auditing procedure*. 1918. p. 289-93).

CHARLESWORTH, A. Trust companies and their audit. London, Gee & co. 1894.

EXECUTORS AND TRUSTEES — AUDITING — *(Continued)*

CUTFORTH, ARTHUR EDWIN. Executor's accounts. (In his *Audits*. 1914. p. 70-1, 101-2).

DE PAULA, FREDERICK R. M. Audit and investigation of the accounts of executors and trustees. *Accountant*, April 9, 1910, p. 503-7.

DICKSEE, LAWRENCE R. Executors' and trustees' accounts. (In his *Auditing*. Authorized American edition. p. 155-7).

JENKINSON, MARK WEBSTER. Audit of various businesses. *Accountant*, April 4, 1914, p. 499-502.

KEISTER, D. A. Expert examination of the accounts and financial affairs of executors, administrators, guardians, trustees, assignees and receivers. (In his *Corporation accounting and auditing*. 1909. p. 443-67).

MACINTYRE, WILLIAM A. D. Legal notes on trust audits. *Accountants' magazine*, June 1913, p. 327-43.

MONTGOMERY, ROBERT H. Executors and trustees. (In his *Auditing theory and practice*. 1916. p. 713-18).

PEGLER, ERNEST C. Audit of trust accounts under the Public trustee act, 1906. London, H. Foulks Lynch & co. 1911. 35p.

PEGLER, ERNEST C. Audit of trust accounts under the public trustee act, 1906. (In Feather, J. Stuart. ed. *Joint transactions*, 1911. p. 196-222). *Accountant*, Sept. 23, 1911, p. 376-85.

PIERSON, E. L. Auditor's duties in relation to accounts of executors. *Accountant*, March 16, 1912, p. 446-8.

PIXLEY, FRANCIS W. Executors and trustees. (In his *Auditors, their duities and responsibilities*. 1910. p. 504-9).

PIXLEY, FRANCIS W. Judicial trustees. (In his *Auditor's their duties and responsibilities*. 1910. p. 497-8).

RANKING, D. FEARON DE L'HOSTE. Investigation and audit of executors' and trustees' accounts. (In his *Handbook of executorship law and accounts*. 1915. p. 270-8).

SPICER, ERNEST EVAN and ERNEST C. PEGLER. Estate agent. (In their *Audit programmes*. 1919. p. 40-1).

SPICER, ERNEST EVAN and ERNEST C. PEGLER. Executors and trustees' accounts. (In their *Audit programmes*. 1919. p. 42-4).

SPICER, ERNEST EVAN and ERNEST C. PEGLER. Executors and trustees' accounts. (In their *Practical auditing*. 1914. p. 482-3).

THOMAS, J. E. Partial survey of the duties of an accountant in relation to the examination of trust accounts. *Public accountant*, 1908, p. 149.

TRUSTEES' accounts bill (as amended on report). *Accountant*, Oct. 9, 1909, p. 456-7.

WATSON, JOHN. Law relating to executors and administrators. *Accountant*, June 7, 1913, p. 876-83.

Australia

JORDON, F. C. Duties of executors. *Public accountant*, 1906-7, p. 126.

LINGEN, J. T. Executors and trustees; summary of two lectures. *Public accountant*, 1910, p. 74, 85.

England

ACCOUNTANTS; their duties and responsibilities; executors and administrators. *Accountant*, July 28, Aug. 4, 11, 18, Sept. 1, 22, 29, 1883.

ADMINISTRATION of insolvent estates. *Accountant*, June 22, 29, July 6, 13, 20, 27, Aug. 10, 24, Sept. 14, 21, 1878.

ATKINSON, GEORGE J. Duties of trustees. *Incorporated accountants' journal*, 1905-6, p. 139.

BAKER, G. A. Legal personal representatives; their duties and liabilities. *Accountant*, Dec. 6, 1913, p. 832-41.

BINNIE, ANDREW. Some legal decisions and legislative enactment from a chartered accountant's point of view. *Accountant*, April 29, 1916, p. 487.

BOWSTEAD, W. Trust and trustee (England). (In Lisle, George. *Encyclopaedia of accounting*. v.6. p. 262-92).

BROWN, WILLIAM HENRY TROTTER. Trusts and trustees. *Incorporated accountants' journal*, 1903-4, p. 165.

CARMONT, JOHN. Responsibility of trustees. *Accountants' magazine*, June 1910, p. 307-14.

CARPENTER, JAMES S. Contracts by trustees. *Incorporated accountants' journal*, 1907-8, p. 244.

CHARLESWORTH, G. H. Trustees' investments. *Accountant*, June 9, 1888, p. 369-72.

COMMITTEE on the organisation of the office of the public trustees. Final report. *Accountant*, Jan. 10, 1920, p. 41-53.

CONCHAR, JOHN. Some points in executorship law. *Accountant*, Aug. 15, 22, 1914, p. 192-4, 210-6.

COOK, JOHN J. Personal liability of trustees and judicial factors. *Accountants' magazine*, June 1900, p. 333-53.

COOPER, E. B. Administration of estates of deceased persons. *Incorporated accountants' journal*, 1892-3, p. 67-72.

COSTELLO, LEONARD W. J. Some points on executorship law. *Incorporated accountants' journal*, 1910-11, p. 278.

DEFECTS in procedure: special managers and trustees. *Accountant*, Aug. 31, Sept. 7-21, Nov. 9-23, 1901, p. 940-2, 961-4, 979-81, 1008-9, 1203-5, 1231-2, 1264-6.

DEZOUCHE, R. C. Miscellaneous points regarding trust estates. *Accountant*, June 21, 1913, p. 939-46.

DOUGLAS, THOMAS. Powers, duties and liabilities of executors. *Incorporated accountants' journal*, 1897-8, p. 55.

DUNDERDALE, CHARLES. Responsibilities of trustees. *Accountant*, Sept. 13, 27, 1890, p. 492-3, 510-3.

EXECUTION of trusts (war facilities) amendment act. *Incorporated accountants' journal*, Aug. 1915, p. 252-3.

EXECUTORS and no next-of-kin. *Accountant*, March 14, 1908, p. 345-7.

EXECUTORS as registered shareholders. *Accountant*, Aug. 26, 1899, p. 885-8.

EXECUTORS' retainer and insolvent estates. *Accountant*, Feb. 24, 1912, p. 307-8.

EXECUTOR'S right of retainer. *Incorporated accountants' journal*, 1901-2, p. 101.

FOSTER, NORRIS T. Duties and liabilities of executors and administrators. *Accountant*, Sept. 9, 1893, p. 771-6.

GATLEY, CLEMENT C. Points relating to executors and administrators. *Incorporated accountants' journal*, Jan. 1914, p. 116-9.

GIBSON, J. GRANT. Present system of administering the estates of insolvent persons. *Accountant*, Sept. 18, 25, Oct. 9, 1897, p. 884-9, 908-12, 935-7.

GOSSET, THORALD. Executors and administrators. (In Lisle, George. *Encyclopaedia of accounting*. v.2. p. 429-50).

HOPKINSON, A. Administration of assets of deceased persons; with discusison. *Accountant*, 1886, p. 706-722.

JONES, EDWARD FURNIVAL. Rights and duties of executors and administrators. *Accountant*, Jan. 30, 1909, p. 168-72.

KELLAND, HENRY PHILIP C. Some notes on executorship matters. *Accountant*, Jan. 6, 1906, p. 18-28.

LATHAM, ALEXANDER M. Duties and liabilities of trustees other than those in bankruptcy. *Incorporated accountants' journal*, 1893-4, p. 92.

LIVERSIDGE, HOWARD W. Law of negligence

EXECUTORS AND TRUSTEES — ENGLAND — *(Continued)*
with regard to trustees and executors. *Incorporated accountants' journal,* 1906-7, p. 74.
MEAD, CHARLES W. Duties of an executor. *Accountant,* Feb. 20, 1897, p. 214-8.
NEW orders &c., the public trustees rules, 1907. *Accountant,* Dec. 21, 1907, p. 775-82.
NORDEN, A. E. Duties and liabilities of an executor. *Federal accountant,* Oct. 1916, Jan., April, July 1917, p. 121-4, 20-8, 57-64, 82-8.
OFFICIALS as custodians of trust funds. *Accountant,* Sept. 30, Oct. 7, 1899, p. 977-80, 1004-5.
PATRICK, NEIL K. COCHRAN. Some distinctions in English and Scottish trust administration. *Accountants' magazine,* June 1898, p. 349-56.
PEARSON, F. S. Administration of debtor's estates. *Accountant,* Oct. 31, 1896, p. 904-8.
PEARSON, FRANK. Powers and duties of executors. *Accountant,* April 2, 1898, p. 361-6.
PERSONAL responsibilities of trustees. *Incorporated accountants' journal,* 1901-2, p. 77.
PICTON, GEORGE WILSON. Law of executors and administrators. *Accountant,* Feb. 4, 1899, p. 146-51.
POWERS of the public trustee. *Accountant,* June 1, 1912, p. 823-4.
PRESTON, FRANCIS M. Executorships. *Accountant,* June 27, July 4, 11, 1891, p. 499-500, 513-6, 527-31.
PUBLIC trustee act, 1906. *Accountant,* Feb. 16, 1907, p. 223-8.
PUBLIC trustee (fees) order, 1909. *Accountant,* March 27, 1909, p. 443-6.
PUBLIC trustee rules. *Accountant,* March 9, 1912, p. 401-6.
RANKING, D. F. DE L'HOSTE. Some points in executorship law. *Incorporated accountants' journal,* 1905-6, p. 192.
RANKING, D. FEARON DE L'HOSTE, E. E. SPICER and ERNEST C. PEGLER. Handbook of executorship law, with the mode of keeping executorship accounts. Ed.3. London, H. Foulks Lynch & co. 1911.
REID, JAMES W. Officialism and the proposed public trustee. *Acocuntant,* Dec. 2, 1905, p. 655-7.
RELATION of the Board of trade to trustees. *Accountant,* June 13, July 11, 1885.
SMITH, M. GILBART. Law relating to receivers of mortgaged estates. *Incorporated accountants' journal,* 1896-7, p. 168.
SOLICITORS and trust funds. *Accountant,* May 12, 19, June 2, 30, July 7, 1900, p. 447-8, 463-4, 483-4, 511-13, 589-92, 614-17, 623-5.
STATHAM, A. Legal duties of accountants in the administration of assets. *Incorporated accountants' journal,* 1889-90, p. 48.
STEVENS, T. M. Administration of partners' estates in bankruptcy. *Accountant,* July 8, 1899, p. 721-6.
STEWART, C. J. Public trustee. *Accountant,* Sept. 14, 18, 1912, p. 345-51, 393-8.
STEWART, C. J. Public trustee act, 1906. *Accountant,* Jan. 2, 1909, p. 20-7.
STOCKDALE, R. H. H. Administration of the estates of deceased persons. *Accountant,* Dec. 29, 1906, p. 793-8.
STUART, WILLIAM J. Legal position of an executor, a trustee or a receiver, carrying on business. *Accountant,* Feb. 12, 1910, p. 245-52.
TALLENT-BATEMAN, CHARLES TALLENT. Law and practice of executorships and administrations. *Accountant,* Sept. 13, 20, 1884.
TRUSTEE and guarantee premiums. *Accountant,* Nov. 4, 11, 1899, p. 1079-81, 1093-5.
TRUSTEES for debenture-holders. *Accountant,* March 22, 1902, p. 305-6.
TRUSTEES' liability for costs. *Accountant,* June 27, 1885.
TRUSTEES under deeds of arrangement and debtor's leasholds. *Accountant,* April 27, May 4, 11, 1912, p. 642-5, 673-4, 714-6.
WADE, JOHN MERRETT. Estate management. *Accountant,* Nov. 21, 1891, p. 815-20.
WADE, JOHN MERRITT. Trustees: their duties and liabilities. *Accountant,* Dec. 8, 1888, p. 801-5.
WAR loan (trustees) act, 1915. *Incorporated accountants' journal,* Aug. 1915, p. 253.
WARREN, ARTHUR O. Public trustee act, 1906. *Accountant,* March 6, 1909, p. 337-42.
WATSON, WILLIAM I. Law of trusts. *Accountant,* Dec. 9, 1905, p. 685-90.
WELSBY, THOMAS. Duties and liabilities of trustees. *Accountant,* July 5, 1902, p. 684-8.
WILKINS, E. T. Rights and duties of a trustee under a deed of arrangement. *Accountant,* Dec. 2, 1905, p. 644-6.
WILSON, ERNEST. Rights and duties of executors, trustees and administrators. *Accountant,* May 14, 1910, p. 681-4.
WILSON, HORACE. Executorship law. *Accountant,* April 22, 1916, p. 461-9.
YOUNG, PALLISTER. Outlines of the war of devastavit. *Incorporated accountants' journal,* 1907-8, p. 60.
YOUNG, T. M. Work of the public trustee office in the north. *Accountant,* Feb. 27, 1915, p. 292-8.

New Zealand
MAZENGARB, C. R. Precautions for trustees investing in mortgage of freehold. *Accounting and commerce,* Sept. 1916, p. 135-6.

Scotland
BURNS, JOHN. "Average rate" of income. *Accountants' magazine,* May 1918, p. 187-91.
EXECUTORS (Scotland) act, 1900. *Accountants' magazine,* Nov. 1900, p. 527-8.
EXECUTORS (Scotland) amendment bill, 1899. *Accountants' magazine,* June 1899, p. 361-6.
HOWDEN, C. R. A. Investment of trust funds and the personal liability of trustees. *Accountants' magazine,* Dec. 1906, p. 538-44.
HOWDEN, C. R. A. Trust and trustee (Scotland). (In Lisle, George. *Encyclopaedia of accounting.* v.6. p. 292-308).
LIABILITY of trustees of judicial factor for expenses of litigation. *Accountants' magazine,* Jan. 1899, p. 9-12.
PATRICK, NEIL K. COCHRAN. Some distinctions in English and Scottish trust administration. *Accountants' magazine,* June 1898, p. 349-56.
SANDERSON, KENNETH. Bonds of caution in executries, curatories, etc. *Accountants magazine,* 1901, p. 163.
WARDHAUGH, JOHN B. States for settlement with beneficiaries in cases of testacy and intestacy, *Accountants' magazine,* June, July 1914, p. 315-35, 374-90.

United States
BRADY, JOHN E. Bank management of estates under the New York statutes. *Banking law journal,* Aug.-Sept., Nov. 1919, p. 599-608, 685-90, 847-54.
CORPUS juris; being a complete and systematic statement of the whole body of the law as embodied in and developed by all reported decisions; ed. by William Mack and W. J. Hale. New York, American law book co.
EQUITABLE TRUST COMPANY OF NEW YORK. Sacred trust: the succeeding generation: concerning the making of wills and the administration of estates. New York, Equitable trust co. 1918. 14p.
HILL, FREDERICK TREVOR. Care of estates. New York, Baker, Voorhis & co. 1901. 176p.
INVESTMENTS by trustees when sinking fund should not be provided. *Trust companies,* March 1915, p. 263.
LIVERMORE, RUFUS P. Livermore's trustees' handbook. Ed.2. revised. New York, L. K. Strouse & co. 1885. 102p.
LORING, AUGUSTUS PEABODY. Trustee's handbook. Ed.3. Boston, Little, Brown & co. 1907. 224p.

EXECUTORS AND TRUSTEES—UNITED STATES —*(Continued)*

SEARS, JOHN HAROLD. Trust estates as business companies. Detroit, Counselors publishing co. c1912. 387p.

THULIN, F. Formal creation of a trust inter vivos; an outline of the requirements in drawing up various forms of trust indentures. *Trust companies,* March, April, May 1915.

TRUSTEES and premiums. *Journal of accountancy,* May 1907, p. 48-9.

WEISS, WILLIAM F. Principal and income and some court decisions thereon of interest to the accountancy profession and discussion thereon at the January monthly meeting of the New York state society of certified public accountants, January 17, 1907. 47p. *Journal of accountancy,* July, Aug., Sept. 1907, p. 167-84, 247-60, 350-62.

EXECUTORS as registered shareholders. *Accountant,* Aug. 26, 1899, p. 885-8.

EXECUTORS' retainer and insolvent estates. *Accountant,* Feb. 24, 1912, p. 307-8.

EXECUTORS right of retainer. *Incorporated accountants' journal,* 1901-2, p. 101.

EXECUTORS (Scotland) act, 1900. *Accountants' magazine,* Nov. 1900, p. 527-8.

EXECUTORS (Scotland) amendment bill, 1899. *Accountants' magazine,* June 1899, p. 361-6.

EXECUTORS' trading accounts. *Accountant,* Sept. 1, 1900, p. 777-9.

EXECUTORSHIP. Cory, Z. F. 1839.

EXECUTORSHIP accounts. *Accountant,* April 7, 1888, p. 206-7.

EXECUTORSHIP accounts. *Accountant,* Sept. 4, 11, 18, 25, Oct. 2, 9, 1897, p. 836-7, 856-7, 880-1, 904-6, 924-5, 937-8.

EXECUTORSHIP accounts. *Accountant,* Jan. 31, 1920, p. 134. *Australasian accountant and secretary,* May-Aug. 1920, p. 142, 179-81, 206-7, 249-55.

EXECUTORSHIP accounts. Caldicottt, O. H. 1906.

EXECUTORSHIP accounts. Whinney, Frederick.

EXECUTORSHIP law and accounts. Ranking, D. F. de l'Hoste and E. F. Wiseman. 1901.

EXEMPLIFICATION and guide to the keeping of the accounts of school boards. Gibson, George. 1876.

EXEMPLIFICATION of a system of accounts for county councils, corporations, etc. Evans, J. M. 1897.

EXEMPLIFICATION of the accounts of urban and rural sanitary authorities. Gibson ,G. 1876.

EXEMPLIFICATION of the general order for accounts. Gibson, G.

EXEMPLIFICATION of the general order for accounts issued. Fry, D. P. 1867.

EXEMPLIFICATION of the general order for accounts issued by the local government board. Lloyd-Roberts, H. 1880.

EXEMPLIFICATION of the general order for accounts issued by the Poor law board. Fry, D. P. 1867.

EXEMPLIFICATION of the system of accounts for county council corporations, urban and rural district councils and other local authorities. Evans, J. M.

EXEMPTION for accountants. *Journal of accountancy,* Sept. 1918, p. 212-5.

EXERCISES in accounting, Rittenhouse, C. F. and P. F. Clapp. 1917.

EX-GOVERNOR Charles E. Hughes favors Carson-Martin bill: sustains constitutionality of measure to vest power to increase public utility rates in public service commissions. *Real estate record and builders guide,* March 15, 1919, p. 334.

EXHIBITIONS

Accounting

CRAIG, J. HAMILTON. Accounting in connection with exhibition. *Accountants' magazine,* June 1911, p. 291.

MACLEOD, JOHN M. Exhibition accounts and finance, and the system of checking income and expenditure. *Accountant,* May 9, 16, 1903, p. 637-43, 661-73. *Accountants' magazine,* Jan. 1903, p. 6-26.

EXISTING fares of Wisconsin road upheld by the commission after a valuation. *Electric railway journal,* July 29, 1911, p. 193-6.

EXPENDITURES for permanent and perishable features of roads. *Engineering record,* Dec. 12, 1914, p. 635.

EXPENSE books for solicitors, auctioneers, accountants, etc. Tuffs, E. J.

EXPENSE classification. Cincinnati. Auditor.

EXPENSE classification. William, F. M.

EXPENSE of freight car and locomotive repairs, renewals and depreciation for year ending June 30, 1912, with cost per mile run for five years. *Railway and engineering review,* Jan. 4, 1913, p. 10-1.

EXPENSE of fuel for locomotives; ten years record. *Railway and engineering review,* June 7, 1913, p. 532-3.

EXPENSE of operating heating and ventilating plants. *Power,* Sept. 23, 1913, p. 437-8.

EXPENSES

See also specific heading, e. g. Organization expenses.

WALTON, SEYMOUR. Capitaling extraordinary expenses. *Journal of accountancy,* Aug. 1915, p. 151-2.

WILLIAMS, F. M. Expense classification; a classification and a sugestion: correspondence. *Journal of accountancy,* June 1911, p. 137-9.

EXPENSES for operation renewals and depreciation of Milwaukee city system. *Electric railway journal,* May 22, 1909, p. 955.

EXPENSES in operating retail grocery stores. Harvard university. Graduate school of business administration. Bureau of business research. 1915.

EXPERIENCE in industrial democracy. Macpherson, F. H.

EXPERIENCE of Cleveland's street railways with three cent fares. Nau, C. H.

EXPERIENCE requirements depreciated: correspondence. *Journal of accountancy,* June 1918, p. 478.

EXPERIENCE tested plans for machine shop manager. *Factory,* June September 1918, 1, 46, 170, 270, 546.

EXPERIENCES in efficiency. Franklin, B. A. 1918.

EXPERT accountants no longer needed: correspondence. *Journal of accountancy,* Dec. 1912, p. 501-3.

EXPERT and stock companies accounting and auditing. Keister, D. A. 1894.

"EXPERT-COMPATABLE" in France. *Accountant,* Jan. 7, 1911, p. 7-9.

EXPERT King's double entry book-keeping manual. King, Thomas. 1906.

EXPERT TESTIMONY.

See Evidence.

EXPERT testimony by accountants. Tolleth, W. R.

EXPERT valuation of railway and other corporate property in Michigan. *Engineering news,* Dec. 20, 1900, p. 430.

EXPERT witnesses and subpoenas. *Accountant,* Aug. 20, 1904, p. 181-3.

EXPERTS differ widely on Philadelphia electric plant renewal costs. *Electrical world,* March 11, 1916, p. 584.

EXPERTS testify to increased costs before New York second district commission. *Electric railway journal,* Aug. 18, 1917, p. 269-70.

EXPIRATION register. New York, Spectator company.

EXPLANATION of Grieg's accounting. Greig, W. M. 1913.

EXPLANATION of the numerical system of the American bankers' association. American bankers' association. 1911.

EXPLANATIONS for the guidance of railroad companies in making reports to the board of commissioners. New York. Board of railroad commissioners. 1884.

EXPLICIT directions for public uitlity accounting. *Electric railway journal,* Feb. 7, 1914, p. 293.

EXPLORATION COMPANIES

Accounting

DONALD, T. Accounts of gold mining and exploration companies. London, 1901.

EXPLOSIVES

Costs

COST of explosives. *Engineering and mining journal,* Jan. 4, 1919, p. 12.
COST of explosives and production of gold. *Engineering and mining journal,* Dec. 14, 1918, p. 1039-40.

EXPORT TRADE

See also Commerce; Ships and shipping.

GUARANTY TRUST COMPANY OF NEW YORK. How business with foreign countries is financed. New York, Guaranty trust company of New York, 1919. 55p.
HOUGH, B. O. Practical exporting; a handbook for manufacturers and merchants. Ed. 3, revised. New York, Johnston export publishing co. 1919. 529p.
IRVING NATIONAL BANK. Foreign trade thought of 1918; excerpts from addresses delivered at the fifth national foreign trade convention, Cincinnati, Ohio, April 18-20, 1918. New York, Irving national bank, 1918. 75p.
MOSKOWITZ, WILLIAM. Records for the exporter. *System,* Nov. 1916, p. 534-6.
ROSE, STANLEY HERBERT. Common-sense management of an export department. Chicago, La Salle extension university, c1916. 38p.
RUSSELL, H. A. Export price records. *Iron age,* Nov. 11, 1915, p. 1114-5.
RUSSELL, H. A. Recording export shipments; how the detail instructions of different foreign buyers are preserved. *Iron age,* Oct. 21, 1915, p. 930.
UNITED STATES. BUREAU OF FOREIGN AND DOMESTIC COMMERCE. Foreign commerce and navigation of the United States for the year ending June 30, 1918. Washington, Government printing office, 1919. 1031p.
UNITED STATES. BUREAU OF FOREIGN AND DOMESTIC COMMERCE. Statistical classification of domestic commodities exported from the United States and regulations governing statistical returns of exports of domestic commodities, approved September 28, 1920. Washington, Government printing office, 1920. 35p.
WALLACE, JARDINE. Export agency business. *Business man's magazine,* Nov. 1906, p. 80-1.
WALTON, SEYMOUR. Inter-branch accounts. *Journal of accountancy,* June 1916, p. 470-3.
WILLIAMSON, J. G. Export trade. (In his *Counting house and factory organization.* 1909. p. 125-31).
ZIMMERMAN, ERICK W. and W. C. CLARK. Foreign trade and shipping. New York, Alexander Hamilton institute, c1918. 356p. (Modern business, v.15).

Accounting

CALVERT, ALFRED. Shipping office organization, management and accounts; a comprehensive guide to the innumerable details connected with the shipping trade; with numerous forms and facsimiles of shipping documents. London, Sir Isaac Pitman & sons. 203p.
FITTON, ARTHUR. Shipping house accounts. *Incorporated accountants' journal,* Oct. 1912, p. 21-5.
FOLLOWING up export trade. *Business man's magazine,* Nov. 1911, p. 439-40.
HORNEMANN, G. A. Overseas consignments. *Accountant,* Jan. 6, 1917, p. 17-22. *Accounting and commerce,* Nov. Dec. 1916, p. 176-80, 197-9.
RUBBER consignment. *Accountant,* March 1, 1913, p. 299-300.
SHMERLER, MAXWELL. Accounting for an export house. *Journal of accountancy,* Aug. 1920, p. 106-17.
WALTON, SEYMOUR. Foreign shipments. *Journal of accountancy,* June 1915, p. 483-6.

EXPORTATION of British capital. Spicer, Ernest Evan. 1912.

EXPRESS

Accounting

INTERNATIONAL CORRESPONDENCE SCHOOL. Accounts for express companies. (In their *I.C.S. reference library,* c1915, 279, Section 32, p. 1-14).
WELLS FARGO AND COMPANY. Instructions for use of agents cash book. Oct. 1, 1911. 4p
WELLS FARGO AND COMPANY EXPRESS—rules for accounting, October 1, 1911. Issued from office of general auditor. Oct. 1, 1911. 27p.

——— **Uniform classifications**

UNITED STATES. INTERSTATE COMMERCE COMMISSION. Decisions upon questions raised

EXPRESS—Accounting—*(Continued)*
under classifications prescribed for express companies; effective on July 1 ,1910. Washington, Government printing office, 1910. 14p.

United States. Interstate commerce commission. Form of general balance sheet statement for express companies; effective July 1, 1911. Washington, Government printing office, 1911. 32p.

United States. Interstate commerce commission. Interpretation of accounting classifications embodied in the uniform system of accounts for express companies; effective on January 1, 1917. 27p. (Accounting bulletin no. 13).

United States. Interstate commerce commission. Regulations to govern the destruction of records of express companies; effective on July 1, 1915. 43p.

United States. Interstate commerce commission. Selected decisions upon questions raised under accounting classifications prescribed for express companies. (In Edward P. Moxey and others. *Practical accounting methods.* p. 489-93).

United States. Interstate commerce commission. Uniform system of accounts for express companies; effective on July 1, 1914. Washington, Government printing office, 1914. 113p.

Rates

Another $23,500,000 added to express service cost: Director genral McAdoo disregards suggestion made by Interstate commerce commission for keeping rates down and orders advance company asked. *Greater New York,* Nov. 25, 1918, p. 7-8.

Barker, Harry. Problems of express transportation rates. (In his *Public utility rates.* 1917. p. 201-7).

Bradley, V. L. Railway revenue and the parcel post. *Engineering magazine,* Jan. 1915, p. 593-6.

Caldwell, B. D. Meeting the problems of the express companies. *Railway age,* February 26, 1915, p. 367-9.

Chandler, William Henry. Express service and rates. Chicago, La Salle extension university, 1914-16. 340p.

Decision in the express rate cases. *Railway age gazette,* Aug. 8, 1913, p. 233-5

Express companies granted higher rates. *Railway age,* July 30, 1915, p. 214-5.

Express rate increase of 12½ per cent authoried. *Railway review,* Aug. 21, 1920, p. 280-1.

Express rates increased. *Railway age gazette,* June 28, 1918, p. 1565-7.

Express rates to come down. *Literary digest,* Aug. 16, 1913, p. 234-5.

Field, A. S. Express charges prescribed by the Interstate commerce commission. *American economic review,* Dec. 1913, p. 831-62.

Field, A. S. Rates and practices of express companies. *American economic review,* June 1913, p. 314-40.

I.C.C. decision on express rates. *Current affairs* (Boston), Nov. 18, 1918, p. 23.

Increased express rates and the reasons for them *Railway review,* July 31, 1920, p. 161-2.

Increased express rates are authoried. *Railway age,* Aug 20, 1920, p. 317-20.

Interstate commerce commission grants express companies 12½ per cent increase in rates. *Commercial and financial chronicle,* Aug. 21, 1920, p. 754-5.

Interstate commerce commission orders reduction in express rates. *Railway and engineering review,* Aug. 9, 1913, p 751-3.

Interstate commerce commission's decision in the express rate cases. *Railway age gazette,* Aug. 8, 1913, p. 233-5.

Interstate commerce commission's revision of express rates. *Engineering news,* Oct. 9, 1913, p. 719-20.

New express rates. *Literary digest,* Jan. 31, 1914, p. 231.

Order for increased express rates beginning Jan. 1, 1919, issued by director general. *Official bulletin,* Nov. 22, 1918, p. 3.

Relief for the express companies. *Literary digest,* Aug. 7, 1915, p. 272.

Relief granted the express companies. *Review of reviews,* Sept. 1915, p. 282.

Statistics of express companies for 1914. *Railway age,* May 21, 1915, p. 1053.

Supplemental increase in express rates. *Railway age,* Oct. 1, 1920, p. 574.

Tucker, R. H. Application of cost accounting in ratemaking. *Journal of political economy,* June 1915, p. 585-98.

Tucker, Robert H. Minnesota express rate case; statement and analysis. *Journal of accountancy,* Feb. 1915, p. 107-17.

United States. Interstate commerce commission. In re-increase in express rates (exparte no. 64), 1918. 72p.

United States. Interstate commerce commission. In the matter of express rates, practices, accounts and revenues. Washington, Government printing office, 1913. 1098p.

United States. Interstate commerce commission. Opinion and order on express rates, practices, accounts and revenues. Washington, Government printing office, 1912. 540p.

Statistics

United States. Interstate commerce commission. Annual report on the statistics of express companies in the United States for the year ended December 31, 1918. Washington, Government printing office, 1920. 25p.

United States. Interstate commerce commission. Statistics of express companies in the United States for the year ending June 30, 1916 and 1915, Dec. 31, 1917 and 1916. Washington, Government printing office.

EXPRESS companies granted higher rates. *Railway age,* July 30, 1915, p. 214-15.

EXPRESS rate increase of 12½ per cent authorized. *Railway review,* Aug. 21, 1920, p. 280-1.

EXPRESS rates increased. *Railway age,* June 28, 1918, p. 1565-7.

EXPRESS rates to come down. *Literary digest,* August 16, 1913, p. 234-5.

EXTENDED bond tables. Sprague, Charles Ezra. 1915.

EXTENDED logarithms. Little, A. S.

EXTENDING the inquisition. *Journal of accountancy,* Jan. 1915, p. 50-2.

EXTENDING the uses of interpolation. Little, A. S.

EXTENSIVE work thru income tax. *Cornell countryman,* June 1918, p. 521-2.

EXTENT to which a tabulation machine can be used in accounting work. Schmidt, W. 1911.

EXTERNAL auditing. Tanner-Gilman schools, inc. c1908-19.

EXTRA compensation and stock ownership plan. International harvester company. 1920.

EXTRACTION and recovery of radium, uranium and vanadium from carnotite. Parsons, C. L. and others. 1916.

EXTRACTS from letters from attorneys, bankers, merchants, manufacturers etc. of the State of Ohio, endorsing proposed bill for the regulation of the practice of public accountants. Columbus, Ohio, 1906.

EXTRACTS from papers on various municipal services. International municipal congress and exposition, Chicago.

EXTRACTS from rate research. *American municipalities*, March 1918, p. 168.

EXTRACTS from rate research. *American municipalities*, Jan. 1919, p. 116-18.

EXTRACTS from report of the secretary of the Ohio state board of accountancy. *Journal of accountancy*, March 1910, p. 375-7.

EXTRAORDINARY, but is it unreasonable. *Journal of accountancy*, Feb. 1914, p. 123-4.

EYE, C. M.

Mine cost keeping. *Mining and scientific press*, Aug. 16, 1913, p. 261-2.

EYES opened by systematic cost keeping. *Rock products and building materials*, 1916, v. 18, p. 14-5.